As an owner of a computer consulting firm and a past professor of computer sciences at the college level, my experience has taught me that Mark Minasi is one of the premier experts on Microsoft operating systems and problems. My first experience with one of his books was after actually trying to do roaming user profiles in Microsoft Windows NT and finding that **out of the five books I consulted only Mark Minasi's was accurate and complete.**

This book should be on the bookshelf of any administrator who is working in a Windows 2000 Server environment or anyone who wants to understand the system.

Harold McFarland
Courtesy of Amazon.com

As, I'm sure you know, **your books are the best on the market.** They're the first place I look and, 99 times out of a 100, the best. If you weren't in the industry, my job would be a HELL of a lot harder.

Scott Sonbuchner
Systems Administrator
Sovereign Specialty Chemicals

Mark is simply the godfather of NT. I have browsed so many NT books and they are so annoying, including Microsoft's at times. The sheer command with which Mark expresses the knowledge is amazing. I'm glad I read his books and it has helped me a lot in my career.

Samuel Offor
Design, Implement, and Support Engineer
NUI Corporation

Just three years ago, I was a fast-food deliverer who couldn't tell the difference between DOS 6.22 and NT. Just look at me now: I am in charge of a company with 300 PCs and 18 servers, and I am on top of the game. I learned everything from only your book and practice. **Because of the book, I've finally found a job and a career that I really love and enjoy.** Thanks, Minasi, you are the Guru.

Michael Song
IT System Admin
Instructor of NT 4 Server

I have read all your books and have learned more just from you than I learned attending four years of college in electrical engineering. ...**People like yourself make it fun to learn new things and be part of this industry.**

Harvey Lee Hayes, BSEE, BSCS
Systems/Network Engineer
VISN 7 Exchange Administrator
Information Technology Department

After years of research and going through hundreds of reference books over time, I have run across a book that is a fixture on my bookshelf at work as well as my home office (having purchased two copies).

To anyone who is searching through the mounds of material out there, I offer three words: GET THIS BOOK.

It is a pleasure to read from an author that deals in real-world experience. Mark's book is well written. It is so much of a relief compared to the usual "dry" material offered by others.

Mark is now one of those authors I search out whenever I'm looking for clear and correct information, as well as real solutions.

Robert M. De Witte
Analyst of Database/Languages/Emergency Services
Unisys

If you only have one Win2000 book on your shelf, make sure this is it! **This book has been an invaluable to me during a large Win2000 migration at a Fortune 50 company.** Mark's writing style is unique, making it easy to retain and understand important concepts. He leaves no technical stones unturned and even has a companion Web site and newsletter to update the book and correct/clarify any technical issues.

Bernhard Klinder
Editor, LabMice.net
Courtesy of Amazon.com

Mark, I've enjoyed reading your books and the knowledge contained in them. I never feel there is a loss of investment with your name on it. You're a credit to your work and an invaluable source to the IT field.

J.C. Cullum
Senior Network Technologist
Raytheon

Mark, this book is awesome! I went through Microsoft training on NT 5/Windows 2000 for more than one year, and I can honestly say **I have learned more from this book than that training.** Well done, and thanks!

Mike Steinberg
Windows NT/2000 Support Engineer
Microsoft Corp.

Mastering Windows 2000 Server is phenomenal! **It is my new reference for everything Windows 2000.** Thanks.

Jonathan Ferrara
Network Administrator
Revere Public Schools

TELL US WHAT YOU THINK!

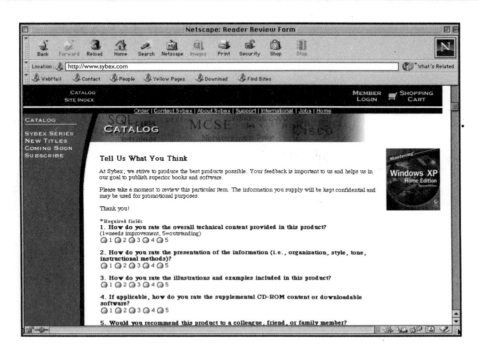

Your feedback is critical to our efforts to provide you with the best books and software on the market. Tell us what you think about the products you've purchased. It's simple:

1. Go to the Sybex website.
2. Find your book by typing the ISBN or title into the Search field.
3. Click on the book title when it appears.
4. Click **Submit a Review.**
5. Fill out the questionnaire and comments.
6. Click **Submit.**

With your feedback, we can continue to publish the highest quality computer books and software products that today's busy IT professionals deserve.

www.sybex.com

SYBEX Inc. • 1151 Marina Village Parkway, Alameda, CA 94501 • 510-523-8233

I'm currently an MCSE/MCT and am using the Microsoft Self Study guides to prepare to pass the Win2K exams. But **when I want to get a clear, precise explanation of a topic, and go even deeper than just what is needed to know to answer a test question, I crack open Mr. Minasi's book.**

Not only is this book well written, but Mark also has an excellent newsletter and answers his readers' e-mail questions faster than anyone I have ever dealt with. Kudos to Mr. Minasi on a job well done.

Kerry Keller, MCSE, MCT
Courtesy of Amazon.com

There's a reason why your books have sold so many copies. **Your book has saved my ass more than once. It's simply the best as far as information and** *readability.* You have a gift for *great* writing. Keep up the good work.

Alan Lloyd
NT Administrator
J.D. Edwards

I've been attending course 1579 this week and have been able to furnish answers from the book numerous times. I've made a believer out of the other class members. Most will be placing orders this week. I'm glad it arrived last week!

Warren Bierley
Technology Consultant
Compaq Computer Corporation

As a Windows 2000 trainer since the early beta days, I can honestly say that this is by far the best book on the market for general Windows 2000 Server information. **Minasi has always been considered one of the best Windows technical writers, and this book is no exception.** Well written, highly informative, and even entertaining, this book will teach you things that Microsoft never will.

Robert Bush, MCT
Courtesy of Amazon.com

This is the book that made me wonder how come all those other technical books make learning Windows 2000 such a difficult and confusing task.

With absolutely no experience,...I had to learn Windows 2000 Server....I literally read the whole thing over a weekend and went ahead the following week to single-handedly set up a Windows 2000–based LAN for a small company and was able to easily cope with all their demands. The network was soon up and running with the Active Directory, DNS, WINS, DHCP, and TCP/IP in perfect working order. **It is no exaggeration to say I owe the project's success to this book alone.**

Mark Minasi has deep insider's knowledge of the product, and you can sense his enthusiasm as he shares his knowledge with you, leaving nothing out, and all with a light touch of humor and very well organized.

Steven Nicolaou, MCP
Courtesy of Amazon.com

Mastering
Windows Server 2003

Mastering™
Windows® Server 2003

Mark Minasi

Christa Anderson

Michele Beveridge

C.A. Callahan

Lisa Justice

SYBEX®

San Francisco   London

APR 1 9 2004

005.713769
M626 m

Associate Publisher: Neil Edde

Acquisitions and Developmental Editor: Chris Denny

Production Editor: Kylie Johnston

Technical Editor: Jim Kelly

Copyeditor: Sally Engelfried

Compositor: Interactive Composition Corporation—Rozi Harris

Graphic Illustrator: Interactive Composition Corporation—Rozi Harris

CD Coordinator: Dan Mummert

CD Technician: Kevin Ly

Proofreaders: Laurie O'Connell, Yariv Rabinovitch, Nancy Riddiough, Monique van den Berg

Indexer: Ted Laux

Book Designer: Maureen Forys, Happenstance Type-O-Rama

Cover Designer: Design Site

Cover Illustrator/Photographer: Tania Kac, Design Site

Copyright © 2003 SYBEX Inc., 1151 Marina Village Parkway, Alameda, CA 94501. World rights reserved. No part of this publication may be stored in a retrieval system, transmitted, or reproduced in any way, including but not limited to photocopy, photograph, magnetic, or other record, without the prior agreement and written permission of the publisher.

An earlier version of this book was published under the title *Mastering Windows 2000 Server*, Fourth Edition © 2002 Sybex Inc.

Library of Congress Card Number: 2002115479

ISBN: 0-7821-4130-7

SYBEX and the SYBEX logo are either registered trademarks or trademarks of SYBEX Inc. in the United States and/or other countries. Mastering is a trademark of SYBEX Inc.

Screen reproductions produced with FullShot 99. FullShot 99 © 1991–1999 Inbit Incorporated. All rights reserved. FullShot is a trademark of Inbit Incorporated.

The CD interface was created using Macromedia Director, COPYRIGHT 1994, 1997–1999 Macromedia Inc. For more information on Macromedia and Macromedia Director, visit www.macromedia.com.

Internet screen shots using Microsoft Internet Explorer 5 reprinted by permission from Microsoft Corporation.

TRADEMARKS: SYBEX has attempted throughout this book to distinguish proprietary trademarks from descriptive terms by following the capitalization style used by the manufacturer.

The author and publisher have made their best efforts to prepare this book, and the content is based upon final release software whenever possible. Portions of the manuscript may be based upon pre-release versions supplied by software manufacturer(s). The author and the publisher make no representation or warranties of any kind with regard to the completeness or accuracy of the contents herein and accept no liability of any kind including but not limited to performance, merchantability, fitness for any particular purpose, or any losses or damages of any kind caused or alleged to be caused directly or indirectly from this book.

Manufactured in the United States of America

10 9 8 7 6 5

Software License Agreement: Terms and Conditions

The media and/or any online materials accompanying this book that are available now or in the future contain programs and/or text files (the "Software") to be used in connection with the book. SYBEX hereby grants to you a license to use the Software, subject to the terms that follow. Your purchase, acceptance, or use of the Software will constitute your acceptance of such terms.

The Software compilation is the property of SYBEX unless otherwise indicated and is protected by copyright to SYBEX or other copyright owner(s) as indicated in the media files (the "Owner(s)"). You are hereby granted a single-user license to use the Software for your personal, noncommercial use only. You may not reproduce, sell, distribute, publish, circulate, or commercially exploit the Software, or any portion thereof, without the written consent of SYBEX and the specific copyright owner(s) of any component software included on this media.

In the event that the Software or components include specific license requirements or end-user agreements, statements of condition, disclaimers, limitations or warranties ("End-User License"), those End-User Licenses supersede the terms and conditions herein as to that particular Software component. Your purchase, acceptance, or use of the Software will constitute your acceptance of such End-User Licenses.

By purchase, use, or acceptance of the Software you further agree to comply with all export laws and regulations of the United States as such laws and regulations may exist from time to time.

Reusable Code in This Book

The author(s) created reusable code in this publication expressly for reuse by readers. Sybex grants readers limited permission to reuse the code found in this publication, its accompanying CD-ROM or available for download from our Web site so long as the author(s) are attributed in any application containing the reusable code and the code itself is never distributed, posted online by electronic transmission, sold, or commercially exploited as a stand-alone product.

Software Support

Components of the supplemental Software and any offers associated with them may be supported by the specific Owner(s) of that material, but they are not supported by SYBEX. Information regarding any available support may be obtained from the Owner(s) using the information provided in the appropriate read.me files or listed elsewhere on the media.

Should the manufacturer(s) or other Owner(s) cease to offer support or decline to honor any offer, SYBEX bears no responsibility. This notice concerning support for the Software is provided for your information only. SYBEX is not the agent or principal of the Owner(s), and SYBEX is in no way responsible for providing any support for the Software, nor is it liable or responsible for any support provided, or not provided, by the Owner(s).

Warranty

SYBEX warrants the enclosed media to be free of physical defects for a period of ninety (90) days after purchase. The Software is not available from SYBEX in any other form or media than that enclosed herein or posted to www.sybex.com. If you discover a defect in the media during this warranty period, you may obtain a replacement of identical format at no charge by sending the defective media, postage prepaid, with proof of purchase to:

SYBEX Inc.
Product Support Department
1151 Marina Village Parkway
Alameda, CA 94501
Web: www.sybex.com

After the 90-day period, you can obtain replacement media of identical format by sending us the defective disk, proof of purchase, and a check or money order for $10, payable to SYBEX.

Disclaimer

SYBEX makes no warranty or representation, either expressed or implied, with respect to the Software or its contents, quality, performance, merchantability, or fitness for a particular purpose. In no event will SYBEX, its distributors, or dealers be liable to you or any other party for direct, indirect, special, incidental, consequential, or other damages arising out of the use of or inability to use the Software or its contents even if advised of the possibility of such damage. In the event that the Software includes an online update feature, SYBEX further disclaims any obligation to provide this feature for any specific duration other than the initial posting.

The exclusion of implied warranties is not permitted by some states. Therefore, the above exclusion may not apply to you. This warranty provides you with specific legal rights; there may be other rights that you may have that vary from state to state. The pricing of the book with the Software by SYBEX reflects the allocation of risk and limitations on liability contained in this agreement of Terms and Conditions.

Shareware Distribution

This Software may contain various programs that are distributed as shareware. Copyright laws apply to both shareware and ordinary commercial software, and the copyright Owner(s) retains all rights. If you try a shareware program and continue using it, you are expected to register it. Individual programs differ on details of trial periods, registration, and payment. Please observe the requirements stated in appropriate files.

Copy Protection

The Software in whole or in part may or may not be copy-protected or encrypted. However, in all cases, reselling or redistributing these files without authorization is expressly forbidden except as specifically provided for by the Owner(s) therein.

Dedicated to the memory of Scott Anderson (1964–2002). Christa's husband was, for lack of better words, a great guy. I (Mark) met him in 1992 and thus was fortunate enough to enjoy his company for a decade. He was a smart, funny, capable-at-nearly-everything person who told good stories, played games masterfully, and brewed good beer. It has to be one of life's great ironies that a man with so much heart was betrayed by that very organ, and far too soon.

As a computer type, I'm used to a world of reversible catastrophes; there are always backups. It is daunting to be reminded that some things *can't* be restored.

Even precious things.

Acknowledgments

THIS BOOK WAS A *lot* of work, so I'm sure glad I didn't have to do most of it!

This is essentially the twelfth edition of the *Mastering NT Server* book that debuted in 1994. In every other edition, we always had contributors who only worked on a chapter or a less, and so did not get co-author credit. This time, I wanted everyone who worked on it to get their name on the cover, and turned to two old tried-and-true contributors. Christa Anderson has contributed in a major way to every version of this book, and this one is no exception. Lisa Justice's work also appeared in the past six editions and she is a welcome addition to this one as well.

This book also introduces two newcomers to book writing, but not to networking. Michele Beveridge, the University of Georgia's Active Directory architect, and veteran tech teacher C.A. Callahan come from solid backgrounds in both working with technology and communicating it, and I think you'll agree that their first outing as geek book co-authors is a successful one. They dug into every chapter, forsaking family and friends in order to get this done. I owe all four co-authors quite a bit, and am quite thankful for their efforts. (Additionally, Michele tells me that a techie friend of hers, Martijn Middleplaats, helped her with some of the heavy lifting by researching some of her chapter material. She thanks him and so do I.)

While this *should* have been an easy book to write, it wasn't, as I'll explain in the Introduction—that's my fault. That made life horrendous for the Sybexers involved, and I can't thank them enough for their help in getting this volume out.

Chris Denny and Neil Edde got the ball rolling, and Sally Engelfried edited the chapters. Many thanks also to technical editor Jim Kelly for his painstaking checking and verifying.

There is, of course, the whole production crew to thank as well. Without them, all we'd have is a collection of electronic files. Kylie Johnston steered the project smoothly through the production channels, as she did with previous editions; Rozi Harris at Interactive Composition Corporation transformed the manuscripts into the handsome book before you; and the proofreaders—Laurie O'Connell, Yariv Rabinovitch, Nancy Riddiough, and Monique van den Berg—scrutinized the many pages to ensure that no stone was left unturned. Thanks also to Ted Laux, the indexer, and Dan Mummert and Kevin Ly of the CD team.

Finally, we could not have done this without the assistance of Microsoft, who not only created the product but also allowed us to see it before it was finished.

Contents at a Glance

Contents

Chapter 17 • TCP/IP Server Services (IIS, NNTP, Telnet, SMTP, POP3, and FTP) 1303

Introduction

I SAID IT IN the Acknowledgments, and I'll say it again: *man*, was this book a lot of work! But trust me, I don't say that to complain; rather, it lets me explain—to explain what is probably the question in most prospective readers' minds:

"Is this a book only for people who use Windows Server 2003?"

The answer is, *definitely not*. Yes, it's a Server 2003 book—but it's *also* basically *Mastering Windows 2000 Server*, FIFTH *edition*. Here's what I mean.

When planning this book, I decided early on that it had to have *two* major goals. First, it had to cover the new features in Server 2003, or the title would be downright wrong. But the differences between 2000 and 2003 are, while not insignificant, not huge either. And that led me to the second goal. I'm guessing that almost no one reading this will have thrown away all of their "old" Windows 2000 Server systems when adopting Server 2003; as a matter of fact, many of you tell me that you're still running Windows NT 4 Servers! Nor is that a bad thing—NT 4 and Win2K are both *really* good tools, in my opinion. Yes, in some ways Server 2003 is better—and you'll learn those ways in this book—but not so much better that many can justify tossing out the Win2K systems to make room for Server 2003. No, I'm guessing that Server 2003 will move into your network gradually, and so you'll be living in a server environment that includes *both* Windows 2000 Server and Windows Server 2003 for quite a while. That's why I asked my co-authors to "think of this as the Fifth!"

Instead of taking the *Mastering Windows 2000 Server* book and looking for things that we'd have to change to make it a Server 2003 book, we started with the topics that previous editions of the Windows 2000 Server book explored and took them further, to build on the book series' growth. For example, previous editions didn't consider a lot of Active Directory maintenance issues, like checking database integrity or compacting the database, so this one did, even though it wasn't a new-to-2003 topic. A look at the Macintosh chapter will reveal that what *was* a chapter consisting of only a handful of pages in previous editions is now 50 or so pages long, with completely new information on Mac OS/X clients.

We tried, then, to make this essentially two books in one; I hope you think we succeeded.

What's Inside

In Chapter 1, I briefly list and explain what's new in Windows Server 2003. As you'll see, Server 2003 is basically 2000 Server, version 1.1. But when you consider what a big product Windows 2000 Server is, and what a major change it was from NT 4, then you'll understand that even just a 1.1 version of 2000 would involve a lot of changes—this chapter outlines them. In Chapter 2, I offer a basic answer to the question, "Why do we network?" for those who are just joining us. Folks who have no idea what a domain is, or why they'd want one, should take a look at Chapter 2 and in no time you'll sound like a grizzled network veteran.

Lisa Justice then shows you in Chapter 3 how to navigate the Server 2003 user interface. Thank God it wasn't as large a change as the NT-to-2000 shift, and that it doesn't come out of the box configured in the XP "Playskool" user interface. But you'll find a few things have changed, and Lisa will guide you through the new stuff. She also walks you through the process of creating your *own* user interface with taskpads, a great way to build customized tools for administrators.

The user interface is *one* way to control Server 2003, and that's why Lisa covers it in Chapter 3. But the *other* way is via the Registry, 2000's place to store system settings and home to hundreds of undocumented or poorly documented switches, dials, knobs, and levers. No NT, 2000, XP, or 2003 techie can last long without a bit of Registry work, and so in Chapter 4 I introduce it.

By now, you'll be itching to load it up and try it out, so in Chapter 5 I not only show you how to shove a CD into a drive and answer questions, but I also cover scripting 2003 installs, using the Remote Installation Server, and finally, how Sysprep can make setting up systems and cloning them easier. Microsoft has made automated rollouts—scripts, RIS, and Sysprep—quite a bit easier and more powerful. Study Chapter 5 and you'll see how to deploy 2003 with style and grace…but mostly with a minimum of effort on your part!

Chapters 6 and 7 permit me to explain how TCP/IP works, both in a general sense and in the specific sense of configuring Server 2003 to use it. In Server 2003, Microsoft has taken another baby step toward making the NT platform an IP-only platform, as NetBEUI is no longer even an *option* for protocols. Chapter 6 explains the basics: how to get on an internet; how IP addresses, subnet masks, and routing work; and how to use a Server 2003 as a router. Chapter 7 then explains the three basic TCP/IP services that every Microsoft network needs: DHCP, WINS, and DNS. Server 2003 doesn't really do much that's new in DHCP and WINS, but DNS now offers several new features, all of which the chapter covers. The biggest changes in the chapter, however, are in the structure of the DNS section, which now spans almost 200 pages. It's not only a primer on DNS; in this edition I completely reoriented the discussion and the examples around building not just any DNS infrastructure, but a more secure infrastructure, using split-brain DNS techniques—and if you don't know what that means, don't worry, the chapter covers it all. You'll also see in Chapters 6 and 7 that I've worked hard to unify the step-by-step examples so that they all fit together, allowing you to follow along and build a small network that is then completely ready for Active Directory…which is the next chapter's topic.

Chapter 8 is basically a medium-sized book in itself, at 81,000 words and 110-plus figures. It takes you from the basics of "What is an Active Directory and why would you want one?" to designing an AD, implementing one, managing it, optimizing it, rearranging its structure when necessary, and fixing it when it breaks. Server 2003's changes permeate this topic, as you'll see. The migration section is much larger than in the 2000 Server book, and it and the rest of the chapter offers many step-by-step examples that allow you to build a small working AD.

Lisa returns in Chapter 9 to explain the ins and outs of creating and managing user accounts. That's a *big* topic, as it includes user profiles and group policies, which Lisa explains in detail. She also showcases and shows you how to use 2003's new Resultant Set of Policies troubleshooting tool for group policies. GP fans will love it.

Windows 2000 handles storage differently than NT did, and 2003 changes things a bit more, as you'll learn in Chapter 10. In that chapter, Michele Beveridge shows you how to connect, partition, and format drives, and she also covers Windows 2000's RAID functions. I was very fortunate to get Michele's help on this book, as she's responsible for the University of Georgia's Active Directory, both its design and implementation. Her years of real-world, in-the-trenches experience with NT in its various forms show through in her coverage of both this and the companion Chapter 11. That chapter covers shared folders, including how to secure those shares with both share and NTFS permissions, as well as coverage of Windows 2000 and Server 2003's Distributed File System and the File Replication Service. In that chapter, you'll also learn about the Encrypted File System—which has changed in some subtle but important ways since Windows 2000—and offline folders, a modification of the network redirector that offers greater network response, laptop synchronization support, and network fault tolerance.

C.A. Callahan joins us in Chapter 12 to describe one of 2000, XP, and 2003's nicest features for desktop support folks: central software distribution. Callahan has been in the technical teaching business for many years and has a well-honed talent for digging into a topic, getting excited about it, and explaining to you so that *you'll* be excited about it as well. (She's also a Mac geek, which is why she rewrote the Mac chapter [Chapter 16] completely and made it about ten times larger than it was before.) Christa returns in Chapter 13 to describe how to network printers under Server 2003. Lisa then explains, in Chapter 14, how to connect client PCs to a Server 2003 network, whether those PCs are running DOS, Windows, or whatever. And you may be surprised to hear that it's now *impossible* to connect a DOS or Windows 9*x* system to a 2003-based Active Directory...unless you know the trick. (Of course, Lisa lets you in on the secret.)

Christa then warms to a favorite topic of hers in Chapter 15, where she covers the built-in Terminal Services feature of Server 2003 and remote server administration in general. And if you have no idea what Terminal Services does, check out that chapter: Terminal Services makes your Server 2003 system a multiuser computer, in many ways combining the best of the PC and the mainframe! Then, in Chapter 16, Callahan "cracks the Mac," as I've already mentioned.

Once your organization is connected to the Internet, you'll probably want to get a Web server up and running. Server 2003 includes a Web server, as did NT 4 and Windows 2000, but 2003's IIS 6 is built to be both more secure and more reliable, so you won't want to miss Lisa's coverage of it, including not only the Web piece but also the FTP server piece, the SMTP mail server, *and* 2003's new POP server. Yes, that's right, Server 2003 now comes with a complete e-mail server service built in, and you can read about it in Chapter 17.

Then, in Chapter 18, Christa offers some advice and instruction on tuning and monitoring a Server 2003–based network, and in Chapter 19, she looks at disaster recovery—never a happy topic, but a necessary one.

Michele returns for a lengthy and quite complete look at dial-up, ISDN, and frame relay support in Routing and Remote Access Service (RRAS) in Chapter 20. Callahan then finishes the book with coverage of NetWare coexistence in Chapter 21.

Conventions Used in This Book

As you know, when discussing any network technology, things can get quite complex quite quickly, so I've followed some conventions to make them clearer and easier to understand.

Referring to Windows NT, 2000, XP, and 2003

Throughout this book, you'll see me refer to *Server 2003*, *Windows 2000*, *NT 4*, and just plain *NT*. I don't want to confuse, so let me clarify what I mean when I use those terms.

When I say "Server 2003," "Windows 2000" or "NT 4," then of course I mean those particular products. But when I say "NT," I'm referring to the various versions of the NT operating system that have come out, including NT 4, Windows 2000, Windows XP, and Windows Server 2003. Despite the name change from NT-version-something to Windows-model-year, under the hood, NT 4, 2000, XP, and 2003 are quite similar. The underlying kernel, the piece of the operating system that manages memory, handles multitasking, and loads and unloads drivers, changes with every revision, but not in any earthshaking way. For example, from NT 4 to 2000 the *look* of NT changed, but under the hood the main *kernel* difference we saw as administrator types was Plug and Play. Basically, you can think of it this way:

- Windows 2000 = NT 5.0, in both Workstation and Server flavors.
- Windows XP Professional = NT 5.1 Workstation. (XP Home is also NT 5.1 Workstation, but crippled. Don't use it.)
- Windows Server 2002 = NT 5.2 Server, no Workstation version. (The next version of Workstation probably won't appear until 2005, code-named "Longhorn.")

I wish they'd just kept calling things "NT version *something*," because then simply saying "NT" would obviously refer generically to all versions of the OS. In this book, therefore, I'm going to use the phrase "NT networks" to mean "anything running NT 4, 2000, XP and/or 2003." When I'm talking about NT *4*–based things, I'll include the "4."

Call It "Server 2003"

And speaking of names...Microsoft is working so hard to "brand" the name Windows that now they've attached the name to three totally different operating systems. The first of the "original" Windows—versions 1.0, 2.0, 2.1, 3.0, 3.1, 3.11, Windows for Workgroups 3.1 and 3.11, Windows 95 and 98—is an ever-evolving operating system built to extend the life of Microsoft's cash cow, MS-DOS. The second was NT, a project intended originally to extend an older operating system named OS/2. And the third is Windows CE, an OS designed for smaller, diskless computers, including the of-dubious-value "AutoPC," a computer designed for your car's dashboard. (Oh great, now I get to worry that the bozo in front of me in traffic will be distracted playing Warcraft; good call, Bill.)

Now, of course, what should have been called "NT Server 5.2" has the much-longer name "Windows Server 2003, Standard Edition." If I stopped to write that every time I needed to identify the product, I wouldn't get the book done until about 2009, so permit me to just shorten it to "Server 2003."

I can't wait until Microsoft sends Pella and Andersen cease and desist letters enjoining them from using the word "Windows" in their corporate name and product-line descriptions.

Directory Names: \windows, system32

In a change from previous versions of Server, Windows Server 2003 installs by default into a directory named \windows on some drive. Upgrades from previous versions stay in whatever directory you installed the previous version in—probably \winnt. You can decide at installation time to put the operating system somewhere else, but almost no one does.

As a result, I have a bit of a problem: I often need to refer to the directory that Server 2003 is installed into, and I need a phrase less cumbersome than "whatever directory you installed your server into" or the brief and technically accurate but nonintuitive %systemroot%. So you'll see references to the \windows directory, which you should read as "whatever directory you've installed Windows Server 2003 into."

Similarly, both Server 2003 and every other version of NT includes a directory inside \winnt or \windows or whatever called system32—\winnt\system32 on older OSes and upgrades, \windows\system32 on fresh installs. I'll refer to that directory as system32. But let me stress this: *If you see a reference in this book to* \windows *or* \windows\system32 *and you do not have a* \windows *or* \windows\system32, *don't panic—just substitute* \winnt *and it'll work.*

Stay Up-to-Date with Our Free Newsletter

With the first version of this book, I tried out a way to keep you folks informed about book errata, changes to the NT family, or just plain new stuff that I've learned. No matter how long 2003 stays around, we'll *never* know everything about it—there will always be new things to learn. And certainly I'll include the things that I learn into new editions of the book—but why wait for the next edition? I'd rather get you at least *some* of that new information immediately!

So I'm extending the following offer to my readers. Visit my Web site at www.minasi.com and register to receive my free Windows Networking newsletter. It covers everything from NT 4 to 2000 to XP to 2003 and even a little Linux. Every month that I can, I send you a short update on tips and things that I've learned, as well as any significant errata that appear in the book (which I'm praying don't appear). It won't be spam—as the saying goes, "Spammers must die!"—just a short heads-up on whatever I've come across that's new (to me) and interesting about NT, 2000, XP, or 2003. Past newsletters have also included lengthy articles on DNS troubleshooting, Indexing Service, and IPSec, so I think you'll find it a worthwhile newsletter for the price.

Well, okay, about the spam part: there will be *one* bit of naked marketing—when the next edition of the book comes out, I'll announce it in the newsletter.

For Help and Suggestions: Check the Newsletter and *www.minasi.com/gethelp*

As always, if I can help, I'm available on e-mail. Got a question the book didn't answer? Visit my FAQ page at www.minasi.com/gethelp and, if that doesn't help, there are instructions on how to e-mail me. I can't promise that I'll have the answer, but I'll sure try! I'm often traveling, sometimes for weeks at a time, and I don't pick up e-mail when I'm on the road, so if I take a week or few to respond, don't worry, I'll get back to you as soon as I can. It's easiest to help with questions which are specific but brief—please understand that I sometimes open my e-mail to find more than a hundred questions waiting for me!

In addition to offering help, I'd appreciate *your* help and feedback. Sybex and I have been able to get a new edition of this book out roughly annually since NT Server first appeared in 1993. I don't know everything about Microsoft networking—I'm not certain *anyone* does—and through the years, reader suggestions and "book bug reports" have been a tremendous source of assistance in making the NT books better and better. ("Gasp! An *error*? In *my* book? No, say it isn't so!") Got a tip, something you want to share with the world? Pass it along to me, and I'll include it in the next edition and acknowledge your contribution.

And by the way, to all of you reading this book: thank you so much, and I hope you enjoy our coverage of Microsoft's flagship networking platform!

Chapter 1

Windows Server 2003 Overview

IF YOU LIVED THROUGH the change from NT 4 Server to Windows 2000 Server, then you might be a bit gun-shy about Windows Server 2003; how much more will you have to learn, and how hard will it be? If so, then I have good news: while Server 2003 offers a lot of new stuff, there's not nearly as *much* new stuff—if 2000 was a tsunami, 2003 is just a heavy storm. (If, however, you're an NT 4 guy getting ready to move to 2003, then yes, there's a whole *lot* of new stuff to learn. But don't worry, this is the right book, and I'll make it as easy as is possible!)

Clearly explaining what Server 2003 does is the job of the entire book, but in this chapter I'll give you a quick overview of what's new. I'm mainly writing this chapter for those who already know Windows 2000 Server and are looking for a quick overview of what's new in 2003, so if you're just joining the Microsoft networking family then don't worry if some of this doesn't make sense. I promise, in the rest of the book I'll make it all clear.

Four Types of Server

Once, there was just one kind of NT Server. Under 3.1 it was called NT Advanced Server 3.1, which confused people—was there a cheaper "basic" server available?—and so Microsoft just renamed it NT Server 3.5 for its second outing, and it stayed that way through NT Server 3.51. But with NT 4 came a slightly more powerful (and expensive) version called Enterprise Edition, which offered a different memory model and clustering but not much else, so not many chose it.

Pre-Server 2003 Varieties

Under Windows 2000, the basic server was just called Windows 2000 Server, and Enterprise became Windows 2000 Advanced Server. It offered a bit more incentive to buy it than Enterprise had, but not much; its most enticing feature was a new tool called Network Load Balancing Module, something that Microsoft had purchased and decided to deny to the buyers of basic Server. (But it's now shipped in the basic Server, thankfully.)

Microsoft also started releasing a third version of Server called Datacenter Server, but you couldn't just go to the store and buy it—they only "OEMed" it, which means that they allowed vendors to buy Datacenter and tune it very specifically for their particular hardware. The only way that you're going to get a copy of Datacenter is if you spend a whole lot of money on a high-end server computer, and then you get Datacenter with it.

Should you feel left out because you can't buy a copy of Datacenter 2000 and slap it on your TurboClone3000 no-name Web server? Probably not. Yes, there are a few things that Datacenter 2000 can do that the others can't: eight-computer clusters is the main one, but for most of us the loss isn't great. Unfortunately, that changes with Windows Server 2003.

Windows Server 2003 Flavors: Web Edition Makes Four

As you'd expect, Microsoft introduced a number of new features with Windows Server 2003 but didn't make them available in all of the versions. It also added a new low-cost version, Web Edition, and reshuffled the features among the four versions. There are actually a whole pile of different versions of Server 2003 if you include the 64-bit versions, the embedded versions, and so on, but the main product grouping is the four "product editions":

◆ Windows Server 2003, Standard Edition

◆ Windows Server 2003, Enterprise Edition

◆ Windows Server 2003, Datacenter Edition

◆ Windows Server 2003, Web Edition

I'm going to focus on Standard Edition in this book, but let's take a very quick look at each edition.

"REGULAR OLD SERVER" GETS A NAME

For the first time since 1983, the basic variety of server has a name; it is now Windows Server 2003, Standard Edition. (I suspect I may have to sue Microsoft for the extra carpal tunnel damage that I'm getting writing this book—where I could once just say "NT 4," now I'm typing half a sentence just to identify the product.) In general, it has just about all of the features that it did back when it didn't have a name.

Standard Edition comes with a bunch of new features that are new to all of 2003's editions, as you'd expect, but it also comes with a bit of quite welcome news: Standard Edition includes Network Load Balancing (NLB). NLB's not new, as it was included in Windows 2000 Advanced Server, the more expensive version of Windows 2000 Server. But where Microsoft once required you to buy the pricier version of 2000 Server to get this very useful feature, it's now included in all four editions of Windows Server 2003. (You'll learn how to set it up in Chapter 6.) But that's not all that's new in Standard Edition—for instance, how does, "You finally get a complete e-mail server free in the box" sound? But I'm getting ahead of myself.

WEB EDITION DEBUTS

The newest and fourth option for Server is Web Edition. The idea is that Microsoft really wants their Web server, IIS, to completely crush, overtake, and overwhelm the competition: Apache and Sun Web servers. So they ripped a bunch of things out of Server and offered it to hardware vendors as an

OEM-only copy of Windows Server 2003. It can only address 2GB of RAM (NT has always been able to access 4 or more GB) and cannot

- Be a domain controller, although it can join a domain
- Support Macintosh clients, save as a Web server
- Be accessed remotely via Terminal Services, although it has Remote Desktop, like XP
- Provide Internet Connection Sharing or Net Bridging
- Be a DHCP or fax server

So it's unlikely that you'll actually see a copy of Web Edition, but if you do, then don't imagine that you'll be able to build a whole network around it. As its name suggests, it's pretty much intended as a platform for cheap Web servers.

WHAT YOU'RE MISSING: ENTERPRISE AND DATACENTER FEATURES

Back in the NT 4 days, Microsoft introduced a more expensive version of Server called NT 4 Server, Enterprise Edition. It supported clusters and a larger memory model. When Windows 2000 Server came around, Microsoft renamed it Windows 2000 Advanced Server. With Server 2003, Microsoft still offers this higher-end version of Server, but with yet another name change. Now it's called Windows Server 2003, Enterprise Edition. Yes, you read that right: once it was Enterprise Edition, then it became Advanced Server, and now it's back to Enterprise Edition. (Don't shoot me, I just report this stuff.)

Enterprise Edition still does clusters—four-PC clusters now. It also lets you boot a server from a Storage Area Network (SAN), hot-install memory like Datacenter can, and run with four processors.

With Windows Server 2003, Microsoft has finally made me covetous of Datacenter. It has this incredibly cool tool called Windows Resource Manager that basically lets you do the kind of system management that you could do on the mainframe years and years ago. How'd you like to say to your system, "Don't let SQL Server ever use more than 50 percent of the CPU power or 70 percent of the RAM?" WRM lets you do that, and it only ships with Datacenter. Datacenter also now supports eight-PC clusters as well as hot-installing RAM—yup, that's right, you just open the top of the server *while it is running* and insert a new memory module, wait a second or two and poof! the system now recognizes the new RAM, no reboot required.

XP Support Comes to Server

For the first time in a long time, Microsoft shipped NT in two parts, delivering NT Workstation version 5.1—that is, Windows XP Professional and its sadly eviscerated sibling, XP Home—over a year earlier than its NT Server counterpart, Windows Server 2003. I don't think that Microsoft originally intended for there to be a year and a half interregnum, but that unintended extra time let Microsoft make Windows Server 2003 much more than "XP Server"—it's NT Server version 5.2.

XP was a nice upgrade from 2000 Professional but not a great one, not a must-upgrade for current Windows 2000 Professional systems, but a very attractive step up for those running NT 4 or Windows 9x/Me on their desktops. Okay, I might have understated things a bit there—let's go back and italicize that "very." And for people running—auggh—Wintendo (9x and Me) put that "very" in double-sized bold text. (This assumes, of course, that you have the minimum reasonable hardware to run XP—128MB RAM and a 600MHz processor.) But, again, if you're already running 2000 Pro and you want some you-are-a-fool-if-your-company-doesn't-upgrade-to-XP reasons, then I can't help.

But that doesn't mean that XP didn't introduce some neat features, and now with the introduction of Windows Server 2003, the server side of the NT house has them as well.

XP Integration

Windows 2000 Server came with a file named `adminpak.msi`, which would let you install all of the administrative tools for a 2000 network on a 2000 Pro desktop. I *loved* that, as NT Workstation never really did a great job as an administrator's desktop and I always ended up running Server as my desktop OS. But 2000 Pro was a different story; get `adminpak.msi` on the Win2K Pro box and you could do all the server administration that you wanted.

But then XP arrived.

I was perfectly happy with my Win2K desktop, but it's kind of my job to use the latest version of NT, so I upgraded to XP, only to immediately find that none of the server administration tools worked anymore—the only way to control my DNS server, AD domain controllers, DHCP server, and the like was by either keeping a Win2K machine around somewhere, walking over to the server to work on it, or just using Terminal Services to remotely control the server. It was irritating. Microsoft soon shipped a beta version of administrative tools that worked on XP, but I'm kind of leery of running my actual commercial network with beta tools, if you know what I mean.

So it's good news that Server 2003 brings a welcome addition: a new set of administrative tools that run fine on XP.

Server Understands XP Group Policies

To my mind, XP's two absolute best features from an administrator's point of view were its remote control/support and software restriction capabilities. Both of those capabilities either absolutely require or considerably benefit from group policies, but Server 2000 knew nothing about them, and so required some tweaking to support XP-specific policies on a Windows 2000–based Active Directory. That's all taken care of now.

New Free Servers: An E-Mail Server and SQL Server "Lite"

Thank you, Microsoft.

Not too many people remember this, but back when Server first came out, it wasn't all that impressive in terms of performance. But over time, it took market share away from network OSes that were, in many ways, faster, more flexible, or more reliable. How'd they do it? Many reasons, but I've always thought that there were two biggies. First, NT used the Windows interface, which meant that once you'd mastered Solitaire you were well on the way to administering an NT Server.

The second reason was that NT came with a lot of stuff free in the box. From the very beginning, NT contained software that most vendors charged for. At one time, most server OS vendors charged for the TCP/IP protocol, but NT always had it. Ditto remote access tools, or Macintosh support, or a Web server, FTP, and a dozen other things. In terms of features, Microsoft made NT an attractive proposition.

So I could never understand why they didn't include an e-mail server. Well, okay, I understood it—they wanted to sell you MS-Mail (you in the back there, stop laughing) or Exchange, and didn't want to offer a free alternative. But I've never understood that. Exchange is a mail server that, while powerful, is complex, difficult to set up, and expensive. Why not offer an e-mail server that is nothing more than an SMTP and POP3-based system? It would serve that five-person office well, and they're probably not about to buy Exchange. Nor would it keep the 100-person (or 100,000-person) enterprise from buying Exchange, as they're probably large enough that they want support of shared calendars, IMAP, mailbox forwarding, antivirus add-ons, and so on, and a super-basic POP3 service wouldn't do it.

I got my wish. Windows Server 2003 in all flavors includes a POP3 service. The other part, SMTP, has always existed, so between the two of them, you've got a complete low-end mail server. Again, there are no hooks for antivirus software, no way to set a mailbox to automatically forward somewhere else, and no way to create an autoresponse message for a mailbox a la, "Jack doesn't work here anymore, please don't send anymore mail here to his address," but it may still do the job for you.

The next goodie wasn't on my wish list, but I'll bet it was on a lot of other peoples': a free database engine. Even better, it's a free database engine that is a copy of SQL Server 2000, although with a "governor" and no administrative tools.

For years, Microsoft has offered a thing called Microsoft Database Engine or MSDE. It was never generally available to NT users, but it was available to various groups of developers. The idea with MSDE was that Microsoft took SQL Server 2000—a fairly expensive piece of software—and crippled it in three ways:

- First, they limited the database size to 2GB. That may not sound like much, but a "real" application of any size could grow beyond that in not too much time. But it's a great size for testing and developing database-driven apps, or for managing a database that will never get very big.

- Second, they put a "throttle" (Microsoft's word) on it so that if more than five people access it, it slows down. Again, it's a barrier to using this for member registration on a thousand-member Web site, but fine for testing and small networks.

- Finally, they do not ship any administrative tools for MSDE. If you want to do something as simple as changing the password on the default "sa" account, you'll have to do some scripting.

None of that is intended to sound negative, even though it's true the MSDE is a severely cut-down version of SQL Server 2000. The price is right and once you get past the basic lack of admin interface—the hard part—then you'll find that it's a pretty nice add-on.

General Networking Pluses

XP's new networking features made it to Windows Server 2003, with some extras as well.

NAT Traversal

First, XP introduced NAT Traversal. For those who don't know what that is, NAT Traversal tries to solve the problem of "how do I communicate from inside one NAT network to another?"

More specifically: suppose you've got a cable modem or DSL connection with a connection sharing device of some kind, like a DSL router. The DSL router has two IP addresses. First, there's the honest-to-God, fully routable IP address that it got from your Internet provider, connected to the DSL or cable modem connection. Then there's the connection to a switch that you've got all of your internal machines connected to—the old Windows 9x boxes, NT machines, 2000 systems, Macintoshes, or whatever. The DSL router's job is to share the one "legal" Internet address among several devices. But every device needs a unique IP address. Lots of devices, but just one IP address—what to do?

As you may know, DSL routers solve this problem by giving all of the internal systems—those Windows, NT, 2000, and Mac machines—IP addresses from a block of addresses set aside to be nonroutable. Anyone can use them.

NOTE   *By the way, if you've never worked with IP, don't worry too much about this—read Chapter 6 on the basics of TCP/IP on Server 2003.*

There are several of these nonroutable blocks, but most DSL routers seem to use the 192.168.1.x or 192.168.0.x subnets. The DSL routers then use something called network address translation or, more correctly, port address translation (again, see Chapter 6 if this isn't familiar) to share the one routable address with all of the internal systems. How it does it is pretty simple: whenever an internal system wants to access the Internet, perhaps to browse some Web site, then that system just says to the DSL router, "Please forward this request to Internet address so-and-so," as routers normally do. But the DSL router knows perfectly well that it *can't* do that: if it says to the Internet, "Hey, someone at 192.168.1.3 has a request," then the first Internet router to see the message will simply refuse to route it, as the address is in a range of addresses that are, by definition, NONroutable. So the DSL router *doesn't* say "192.168.1.3 wants something"; instead, the DSL router substitutes *its* routable address. Then, when the answer to 192.168.1.3's question comes back, the DSL router remembers which machine asked the question in the first place and routes the answer to 192.168.1.3. The result is that to the general Internet, that DSL router sure seems like a demanding system, when in fact it is simply busy because it is impersonating a bunch of systems.

In any case, notice that it's possible for an internal system (one with one of those 192.168.x.x addresses) to initiate a communication with a device on the public, routable Internet, but it's NOT possible for a device on the public, routable Internet to initiate a conversation with an internal 192.168.x.x system.

Here, then, is the problem. Suppose I'm sitting at a Windows 2000 Pro box in my home that has a 192.168.x.x address, accessing the Internet via my DSL router or cable modem sharing device. You're sitting in *your* house, also using some kind of DSL router or cable modem sharing device to access the Internet. We meet on-line and decide to play some networkable game and start to set up our connection. One of us acts as the server and one as the client. The client then initiates communication with the server. That's where the problem appears. I could initiate a communication to a routable address, or YOU could initiate a communication to a routable address, but neither of us has a routable address… and so we can't communicate.

(Note that some of you might be scratching your heads saying, "Mark, I don't have that problem." In that case, I'm guessing that you use your Windows 98 SE, Windows Me, or 2000-based system as the DSL or cable modem–sharing device. As you know if you read Chapter 6 of *Mastering Windows 2000 Server*, you can easily activate something called Internet Connection Sharing to make your 98 SE/Me/2000 device into a simple NAT router. But if you do your gaming while sitting at that box, then NAT isn't a problem, as that particular computer has a legal IP address, recall, as *it's* the device connected to the Internet.)

How, then, to create a meeting of the minds in PC-land? With NAT Traversal. The idea is that if your DSL router (or other sharing device), your opponent's sharing device, and your game software understand NAT Traversal, then the two sharing devices work out the details to allow 192.168.x.x-to-192.168.x.x communications with no muss, fuss, or greasy aftertaste. And XP Pro's version of Internet Connection Sharing supports NAT Traversal, so if you replaced your DSL router with an XP Pro (or Home) box, you'd have all the more online gaming options. (And of course it's good for more than just gaming; you could use this for any peer-to-peer communications that must go through a NAT-type router, like Webcam-type videoconferencing—once there's videoconferencing software that understands NAT Traversal.)

NAT Traversal's migration to Windows Server 2003 is, then, pretty good news.

IPSec NAT Traversal

I discussed NAT Traversal as if it were mainly of interest to gamers, and I suppose that at first it was. But you could just as easily imagine 192-to-192 type network communications in business as well. Consider a business with two offices in different cities and about 50 employees in each location. They'd like to connect the offices but don't want to have to buy a dedicated leased line or frame relay between the offices, so they get DSL in each location.

In each location they end up with network addresses that look like 192.168.0. something, but they'd like to communicate from location to location. Their problem is, as you can see, exactly the same problem that the gamers in my earlier example face. So they could just put in NAT Traversal hardware and software and be done with it.

But then they'd be transmitting office-to-office data in cleartext over the Internet. An OK thing in 1993, I suppose, but a definite no-no in these modern times. Running sensitive data over the Internet is exactly what IPSec (Internet Protocol Security) was built for. IPSec (also covered in Chapter 6) converts an IP connection into an *encrypted* IP communication.

The only trouble is that IPSec and NAT don't mix. Or didn't, until Windows Server 2003.

Windows Server 2003 includes a new kind of IPSec that is NAT Traversal–aware. So you can have as many 192 networks as you like, and they can all talk to one another, and securely. Of course, this isn't free—you need firewalls and routers that are NAT Traversal–aware—which is probably one reason Microsoft has started selling network hardware, including some interesting wireless devices.

RRAS's NBT Proxy Eliminates Network Neighborhood Problems

Routing and Remote Access Service (RRAS) has always been a source of troubles, largely due to the fact that one of its main jobs is to allow networking over dial-up lines, and dial-up lines are noise-ridden, unreliable things. Another RRAS problem stems from the fact that you normally use it to connect some remote computer, like a home PC, to a distant larger network, such as your company's network, meaning that your home PC is now a network segment all by itself, and in effect the RRAS server has to act as router, authentication server, and a host of other things.

A side effect of your home system being a network segment all its own is that Network Neighborhood or My Network Places doesn't have much to show, as it normally displays the systems on the local segment. (I'm simplifying but that's basically right.) That doesn't mean that users cannot access servers on the corporate network; unless configured otherwise, a remote user can connect to any server at the office. But people aren't comfortable using Find Computer or some other way to connect to a server, and unfortunately Network Neighborhood is the tool of choice for many when looking for a server—so an empty NetHood is disconcerting to many users.

Seeing tons of computers in NetHood while in the office a none while at home troubles some users, but Windows Server 2003 can fix that. Server 2003's RﻰAS server includes a feature called the NetBIOS over TCP/IP proxy or NBT proxy. This basically takes the Network Neighborhood that any system inside the office sees and ships it over to the dial-in system.

Of course, in the long run users are going to have to get used to finding servers and resources by searching the Active Directory rather than browsing NetHood, but this provides a useful interim tool.

DNS Conditional Forwarding Supports Multidomain AD-Integrated DNS

As you learned when creating your Windows 2000–based AD, or as you'll learn when you create your Windows Server 2003–based AD, AD needs a sturdy and secure DNS infrastructure. A big part of the "secure" aspect of DNS comes from a DNS design called split-brain DNS where you essentially keep two sets of books, DNS-wise—a DNS server that the outside Internet sees, which holds the address information for your Web, mail, and FTP servers, and a separate DNS server (or a set of DNS servers) inside your intranet that serves AD's needs.

Split-brain DNS works by bypassing the normal process whereby a DNS server converts DNS names like www.bigfirm.biz to an IP address. And it works fine, except when joined with a very useful feature of Windows called Active Directory–integrated zones. You'll learn more about this in Chapter 7, but basically AD-integrated zones let you secure a zone for a DNS domain (like bigfirm.biz) with one limitation: the DNS servers for bigfirm.biz must be domain controllers (DCs) for an Active Directory domain whose name is *also* bigfirm.biz.

Where that presents a problem is the case wherein you want to run more than one Active Directory domain in your intranet. Each AD requires a DNS zone to back it up (and, again, if you're not sure about what these things are, don't worry, I'll cover them in detail in Chapter 7, starting from th basics). If you want to use AD-integrated zones, however, then you'll have to have a separate set of DNS servers for each domain… and that's where the problem lies. It's easy to keep a separate set of books on just one DNS domain, as you divide the world up into two areas: folks on the outside of your network, who only see your external DNS server's information, and folks on your intranet, who see your internal server's DNS information and incidentally can also see DNS information on the outside world—so even though the folks inside your intranet are being deceived, so to speak, about the contents of your internal Active Directory's associated DNS data (bigfirm.biz in my example), they get the unfiltered DNS information about other DNS, like microsoft.com, whitehouse.gov, and the like.

Now add that second internal domain; let's call it acme.com. To make the bigfirm.biz folks see the correct separate set of books, you point all of their servers and workstations to the internal DNS servers that contain the internal-only version of the bigfirm.biz information. Recall that these servers must be Active Directory domain controllers for the bigfirm.biz AD domain. To support the people in acme.com, you'd set up a different set of DNS servers for your internal-only information for acme.com and point all of acme.com's servers and workstations to those acme.com DNS servers.

People in bigfirm.biz can, then, get the internal-only DNS information about bigfirm.biz, as well as the public DNS information for any other domain. People in acme.com can get the internal-only DNS information about acme.com, as well as the public DNS information for any other domain.

Here's the problem: if a bigfirm.biz member wants to log onto some resource on acme.com, then that bigfirm.biz-ite will have to find a domain controller for acme.com, as DCs handle logons. But you find DCs in Active Directory via DNS. A bigfirm.biz user, however, uses DNS servers that know the internal-only information about bigfirm.biz, not acme.com. So if someone in bigfirm.biz tries to look up a DC in his local DNS server, that local DNS server will end up asking the public DNS server for acme.com, "Where are your DCs?" The answer will be a puzzled look from the public DNS server for acme.com, as it has no clue what a DC is.

There are workarounds for this, but Windows Server 2003 offers a terrific one: conditional DNS forwarding. It lets me set up the bigfirm.biz DNS servers by saying, "OK, you already know the internal-only information about bigfirm.biz. And you know that if you have to find out DNS information for someone else, like www.google.com or www.cnn.com, or the like, then you go search the public Internet. But here's a new bit of information: on the off-chance that you ever need to find out information about a zone called acme.com, then go straight over to that server over there (pointing to the internal-only acme.com DNS servers) and it'll have the answer." A great new feature for folks rolling out Active Directory forests with more than one domain. You'll see it at work in Chapters 7 and 8.

Active Directory Improvements

For a first try, Windows 2000's Active Directory was pretty good... not bad for a 1.0, Microsoft. (Of course, they *did* have Banyan and Novell's directory services to learn from, but let's ignore that for this discussion.) In Windows Server 2003, Microsoft dishes up a 1.1 version of AD that solves several irritating problems, makes running branch offices easier, and expands AD's flexibility.

While I don't want this to sound negative, it's a fact that Active Directory still suffers from most of its inflexibility—there is no simple way to rearrange the structure of an existing forest, to merge forests into one forest, or to break off a piece of a forest and make it a forest of its own. Don't think that those scenarios are marginal or unusual ones—they're not. The reorganizations that most organizations undergo every year or so will often require rearranging a forest. Two firms merging need to be able to merge their forests as well. And a firm divesting itself of a subsidiary would want to be able to detach one or more domains or trees from a forest. But perhaps that will appear in a future version of Server; let's hope so.

Meanwhile, the 2003 edition of AD has, again, some very good news. Here's a look at its high points.

Forest-to-Forest Trusts

Combining a bunch of AD domains into a forest offers two main benefits: first, those domains all automatically trust each other, and, second, the domains share a set of "super" domain controllers called global catalog (GC) servers, which are domain controllers that contain a subset of information not just about their own domains but about every single domain in the forest. Doing away with the unreliability of NT 4 trusts for the convenience and dependability of AD's automatic trusts is a big win for AD users.

But, as I suggested a few paragraphs back, AD forests were and are still pretty inflexible. So suppose you're an organization that finds itself with more than one forest, and you need to get those forests to share things? Well, there's always been the hard way—get a migration tool and copy all of the user accounts, machine accounts, and other objects from Forest 1 to Forest 2, then just plain delete Forest 1. The problem with that answer is that while migration tools are pretty nice, they don't do the whole job and they're a lot of work to get working.

With a Windows Server 2003–based forest, however, you have a new answer: forest root trusts. With these, you just build one new trust relationship between Forest 1 and Forest 2 and instantly every domain in Forest 1 trusts every domain in Forest 2 and vice versa. Cool; thank you, Redmond.

But I said that forests had two main features—complete trust and a centralized database of forest information called the global catalog. A forest-to-forest trust gives us back the first benefits of a single forest; what about the second? Unfortunately, two forests that trust each other do not share a global catalog. That means that forest trusts will not let applications that are GC-dependent see the trusting forests as one single overall directory. What apps are GC-dependent? Well, the most prominent one is Exchange 2000: it really wants to see your organization as one big forest. Forest trusts don't solve that problem.

I was surprised to learn of another limitation to forest trusts: they're not transitive. Interestingly enough, if Forest 1 trusts Forest 2 and Forest 2 trusts Forest 3, then Forest 1 does not trust Forest 3. Bummer. And *none* of this forest trust stuff works at all until you've upgraded every single DC in every single domain of both forests. So, overall the forest trusts are a good step forward… but not the whole story.

Group Replication Problem Solved

It's always been ironic that while Active Directory can support a far larger user list than could NT 4 domains, AD couldn't support *groups* as large as NT 4. You can create literally millions of users in an AD, but because of a quirk in AD's method of keeping domain controllers' information consistent ("AD replication") in combination with the way that group membership is stored in AD, you can't put more than about 5,000 users into a group.

In 2003's AD, Microsoft restructured the way they store group membership, and now the sky's the limit. It also solves another problem wherein it is possible in 2000's AD that you and I work in the same world-wide company and you change a group's membership while sitting in the Edenton office while I change that same group's membership while sitting in the Port Angeles office, and one of our changes overwrites the other person's changes. With 2003, that's fixed.

To get this benefit, you must upgrade all of the DCs in all of the domains in your forest.

Good News for Branch Offices

Branch offices have always presented a problem for IT folks. Many firms have one or two large centralized locations and dozens (or hundreds!) of small offices housing a dozen or two employees. These small branch offices are important but expensive to run, as a firm typically has to install some kind of persistent connectivity—frame relay, DSL, T1, cable modem, or the like—to the branch office so that the employees there have access to the corporate intranet and potentially the Internet.

As branch offices are typically served by only one WAN link and WAN links aren't always so reliable, companies have to make some tough choices: do we put a domain controller on every site? Does each site need a DNS, WINS, DHCP, etc. server? If we put servers on a branch office site, will they do so much chattering over the WAN link with the servers in the central office that they'll chew up a significant proportion of that link's bandwidth? And most importantly, when the WAN link is down, how do we ensure that the employees in the branch office can still get logged in and remain productive?

Server 2003 can't solve all of those problems because, well, unreliable WAN connections aren't Microsoft's fault. But 2003 offers some changes that will make setting up and maintaining branch offices easier.

SIMPLIFIED BRANCH OFFICE DC INSTALLATION

I've helped a number of firms get AD up and running. Sometimes, however, they call me back to help out with a particularly difficult part. In one case, it was the Case of the Dial-Up Office.

This company had a branch office that did not have a persistent connection either to the Internet or to the head office; instead, they dialed up when necessary. And they were having trouble getting a domain controller set up in that branch office. Now, you see, to create a domain controller, you start from a regular old vanilla Windows Server, either vintage 2000 or 2003, and run a program called DCPROMO, a wizard that will convert a member server into a domain controller or will decommission a DC back to a member server. In order to create a new DC, you must have a live connection back to the main office, so before trying to set up the DC I dialed out to the Internet and from there established a connection to the "mothership" back at HQ.

DCPROMO started out fine, accepting my credentials and okaying the idea of promoting this member server. But a new DC needs a copy of the Active Directory, so DCPROMO's last act is to hook up with another DC and download the latest version of AD. This firm had a few thousand employees, so their AD was actually not too large—under 10MB.

Did I mention that their phone line was a bit noisy? That it only connected at about 26 kilobits? And that it tended to disconnect at inconvenient times?

Anyway, DCPROMO would try to start replicating and get partway through... and then the line would hang up. Sometimes a reboot and another DCPROMO would get us back to member server, where we could start all over again; in a couple of cases, I had to reinstall Win2K Server from scratch. After only about a day of trying, though, I found that the phone lines were quiet and clean enough around midnight to allow the initial replication to complete. Grrrr.

I really would have welcomed Windows Server 2003 in that case. With Server 2003 you can take a backup of your AD domain database with you to the remote site, and DCPROMO then lets you start a new DC out from the backup of the AD, rather than forcing a complete initial replication over the WAN. From there, you connect the new DC up to that unreliable phone line, and all the DC must do is to replicate whatever's changed in AD between when the backup occurred and now, which usually isn't much.

This feature does *not* require you to upgrade every DC in creation; in fact, this works fine if the very first Server 2003–based DC in your network is the one that you're installing in that branch office.

BRANCH OFFICE REPLICATION CONTROL

Should you put a DC in a branch office or not? It's not an easy question. On the one hand, having a local DC in a branch office means that when the WAN link is down the local users can still log on. On the other hand, having a local DC means that DC must keep a complete copy of the entire domain's Active Directory database. So if there are 15 users in the branch office and 50,000 members of the domain, every time those 50,000 people change their passwords those changes must be replicated across the WAN link to your branch office's DC. (That's an example of what I meant when I said earlier that server communications can seriously burden the WAN links to branch offices.)

AD has always tried to limit its effect on branch offices in a couple of ways. First, it uses a routing algorithm that is designed to enable it to get data from a DC in one office to a DC in another office in the least-cost way. Second, it compresses the data before moving it between DCs. Those both sound like good features, but Server 2003 improves upon them.

First, there is a large body of literature about optimal routing algorithms... but the Microsoft programmers working on AD in Windows 2000 didn't employ them. Instead, they made up an algorithm all their own. (Why? I don't know. But I do know that many firms, Microsoft included, are sometimes struck by what's called the "NIH syndrome"—short for Not Invented Here. It refers to the fact that it's more fun to sit down and reinvent your own wheel than it is to merely reimplement someone else's wheel.) Microsoft found that AD bogs down when faced with more than a few hundred sites; implementing industry-standard algorithms shot that up into the multithousand-site range.

Second, odd as it sounds, apparently some branch offices found that the CPU power required to compress and uncompress data outweighed any benefits gained from bandwidth recovery. So in Server 2003, Microsoft lets you choose to shut off intersite compression.

Both of these features require that you upgrade every DC in every domain in your forest.

BRANCH OFFICE LOGON INFO CACHEABLE

When the WAN goes down, does everyone get a day off? Well, that's essentially true if they need the WAN to do a logon. Windows 2000 and later systems require several ingredients in order to log on. First, of course, a workstation must be able to find a domain controller; that's always been true. Second, Active Directory member machines need to be able to find a global catalog server in order to log a user on.

It is, then, possible that you might have a local DC but not a local GC. In that case, a WAN failure means that you'd only be halfway to logon, so you're logged on with "cached credentials." One answer is to put a GC on every site, but that can be very expensive in terms of WAN bandwidth: GCs not only replicate from other DCs in their same domain, GCs also replicate from every other domain in the forest!

AD 2003 offers a nice workaround: Server 2003–based DCs will locally cache the information that they need from a GC. So if you logged on yesterday from your branch office, your local DC collected enough information over the WAN from your GC that it was satisfied to let you log on. If the WAN's down today then your local DC remembers that it logged you on yesterday, and logs you on today.

The best part of this news is that it requires no other upgrades—the DC in your branch office can be the first Windows Server 2003 introduced into your enterprise and this will still work fine.

Domains Can Be Renamed

One of 2000's most annoying AD limitations was that it prevented you from renaming a domain; if Bell Atlantic had had an AD forest when it merged with GTE and was renamed Verizon, there would have been no way to rename an AD domain named bellatlantic.com to verizon.com. Now you can rename a domain, but it's not a simple matter, even now.

First, you will have to be completely Server 2003ed in the domain: every DC in the domain to be renamed (not all DCs in the forest, just the ones in the domain) must be running Windows Server 2003. And second, there are... well, I was going to write "... a few steps to perform in order to complete the domain renaming," but the truth is that Microsoft has a white paper online explaining how to do it.

The paper is *60 pages long*. So it's *possible*, just not easy, at least not yet.

AD Can Selectively Replicate

Active Directory is a database, and domain controllers are database servers, just like systems running Access, Oracle, MySQL, or SQL Server and holding some other kind of database. (Well, not *just* like...

DCs do not respond to SQL queries. Instead, their query language is LDAP.) While the AD database was originally designed for storing user accounts, machine accounts, and the like, there's no reason application designers can't take advantage of AD's built-in database engine to store other information.

Microsoft's own programmers did just that when designing 2000's DNS server. As you may know, 2000 introduced you to the option to create a DNS zone that was an Active Directory–integrated zone. A zone of that type stores the DNS info for your systems in the AD itself and replicates it along with the normal domain information from DC to DC. But *only* DCs get copies of the database, so if you choose AD-integrated DNS, all of your DNS servers must be DCs.

But now consider: what if you had a lot of DCs, but only a few of them were DNS servers? Wouldn't that be a bit wasteful? You'd use precious bandwidth to replicate DNS info to every DC, whether it used it or not. Server 2003 solves that problem with the notion of an *application partition*. Partitions are subsets of the AD that only replicate to a subset of DCs. Microsoft then applied that notion to their DNS servers, so in a network using AD-integrated zones only the DCs running DNS will get the DNS info. This feature doesn't require any preparation; you get its benefit on any DC running Windows Server 2003.

Remote Administration Upgrades

For years, remote administration and control of Microsoft operating systems drove me nuts. It seemed only Microsoft OSes required you to be physically sitting down at a computer in order to control the software running on it. Sure, there were third-party alternative tools like PCAnywhere or VNC, but remote control/admin always seemed like something that really needed to be "in the box," integrated into the OS.

Windows 2000, then, was a great advance, incorporating remote Telnet sessions and a remote control tool called Terminal Services that was a cut-down version of a program from a company named Citrix. Terminal Services only ran on Server, though, so remote control of 2000 Pro boxes was dicey. But then came XP and now Windows Server 2003.

First, the workstation/desktop version of Windows Server 2003, Windows XP Professional, includes Microsoft's adaptation of Citrix's remote control product. It and the server version of Terminal Services are built around a tool called the Remote Desktop Protocol (RDP). Microsoft has improved RDP to make it run on slower connections, and I'm not exaggerating when I say that remote control over a 40-kilobit dial-up connection works very well, almost as well as sitting at the computer.

RDP also matures in that it automatically gives your remote control session access to your local printers and drives, something that Terminal Services for Windows 2000 couldn't do. It supports colors beyond the simple 8-bit, 256-color of Windows 2000's RDP, and transports sound as well.

Perhaps even better, Windows Server 2003 and XP repackage RDP in two forms: *remote desktop support* and *remote assistance*. These are ways to provide remote control or offer remote assistance but are nothing more than new user interfaces placed atop Terminal Services. If you've not used them yet for XP, I think you're really going to like them on Windows Server 2003.

Finally, Windows Server 2003 offers a completely new set of remote control tools in the form of Web pages. You can install a bunch of modules on your server that will let someone do approximately 80 percent of the administrative functions you'll ever need, all through a secure Web connection. The bottom line is that we don't have to put up with those Unix guys kicking sand in our faces telling us that their OS is more manageable!

Command-Line Heaven

Okay, I admit it, the command line is harder than the GUI. GUI-based administrative tools walk you through a process and offer tons of online help and wizards while they're at it. The command line is definitely an acquired taste. But may I offer a very heartfelt bit of advice?

Acquire the taste. You'll be glad you did.

Take a common problem that I hear about a lot: a private DNS root. Through a process that I'll cover in Chapter 7, it's possible to set up a DNS server that lives in its "own private Idaho," and is unable to resolve names on the rest of the Internet. It happens through a common bit of misconfiguration. And it can be fixed from the GUI, with about two paragraphs of explanation. Or you can just open up a command line and type

```
dnscmd /zonedelete /f .
```

Then press Enter and it's done. (Most of the time, but I'm keeping this simple.) Command lines let you type a few dozen characters and accomplish amazing things. Just a few keystrokes can often accomplish quite a lot.

But how's that different from saying, "Use the GUI, and in a few dozen mouse clicks you can get a lot done?" Well, that's true, you can. But the command line offers two more things:

◆ First, simply opening a Telnet session lets you run one of those powerful command-line commands on a remote computer, so it's a great way to do remote administration. "Wait a minute, Mark," you say, "didn't you just tell me a page or two back how well Terminal Services runs in low bandwidth?" Sure, but command-line sessions run in even *lower* bandwidth. Imagine administering your computer remotely with nothing more than your cell phone and either a wireless keyboard or a bit of patience and the phone dialing keyboard. It's possible with command lines.

◆ Second, suppose you have some repetitive administrative job, something that needs doing pretty regularly or, worse, regularly at some inconvenient time, like 3 A.M. daily. It's a task so simple that you could train a monkey to do it... if they'd only let you hire monkeys and give them administrator accounts. Instead, you can create an "e-monkey." Figure out how to do the task from the command line. Then type those commands into an ASCII text file with Notepad. Give the file the extension .CMD. And whammo: you've just written a batch file that you can schedule to run at 3 A.M. Try writing a batch file that stores *mouse clicks* and you'll see how neat the command line can be!

Windows 2000 made some great strides in offering better command-line tools, but didn't go all the way. With Windows Server 2003, it's actually possible to do about 98 percent of your administration from the command line.

Desktop Support Improvements

Most of you don't use Server as a Desktop operating system, so you wouldn't expect much in the way of improvements to Desktop control, but recall that Windows Server 2003 incorporates all of the new things that came to XP. If keeping Desktops up and running is part of your job, then you'll like what Windows Server 2003 brings, although in most cases you need XP on the Desktop to see Server 2003's improvements.

Profiles and Policies

When they first arrived, roaming profiles seemed like a great idea... but then we tried them. Slow, prone to breaking... auugh. But Windows 2000 made them more palatable, and so has Windows Server 2003.

First of all, there's a new group policy that you can apply to a machine (or machines) that says, "Ignore all roaming profiles." This is terrific—now I can ensure that just my laptop and desktop get my roaming profile, by setting up all of the public access/shared systems and the servers to "ignore roamers."

Another group policy makes roaming profiles better for laptop users. Sometimes I'll check into a hotel and find that it offers Ethernet connections to the Internet (yippee! I will sleep on a *stone floor* if it means I get high-speed Internet access), so I plug my laptop into the Ethernet and boot it up, only to realize that my stupid laptop is trying to suck my roaming profile over the Internet. A half-hour later, it gives up.

Or at least that's what *used* to happen. Now I just set the group policy on my laptop that stops and asks, "Do you want to download your roaming profile?" I say no and log on in seconds. (Of course, the laptop must be running XP.)

Those are just two examples of the new things you can do to control profiles; there is a ton more, as a look at the Group Policy Editor (which you'll meet in several places in the book) shows.

Software Restriction Group Policies

Every help and support desk person has a little list of things she'd like to see. One is almost always, "I'd really like to keep users from running particular programs on the system." (If you're having trouble thinking of examples, then see if the names Morpheus or Kazaa ring any bells.) With XP desktops, you can do that.

XP and Windows Server 2003 include a whole new set of group policies called software restriction policies. With them, you can tell a Desktop, "Nothing runs except Word, Internet Explorer, Outlook, and the Palm Desktop." It's pretty neat and pretty powerful, and you can learn more about it in Chapter 9.

The Group Policy Management Console (GPMC)

After reading the last page, you may be shaking your head saying, "Yeah, that's nice and all, but you're talking about group policies? Those guys are a nightmare." Yes, they can be, particularly when a group policy refuses to run—"Let's see, I just created this policy that keeps Access from running on Ronnie's desk and he can *still* run Access!" Several things might keep your new policy from running—Ronnie's Desktop might not have refreshed policies, or it might have refreshed policies but your policy might have been overridden by another policy. You look and see that there are only 24 other policies that apply to Ronnie and his Desktop, so time to start sifting through policies... or not.

Microsoft has been working on a really terrific group policy troubleshooting tool called Group Policy Management Console. It *didn't* ship with Windows Server 2003, but as of this writing Microsoft expects to give it away free on their Web site by March/April 2003. You'll learn more about it in Chapter 9.

Tightened Security

Sometime in late 2001, two things occurred to Bill Gates: first, network security is important and, second, Microsoft software is buggy as heck when it comes to security (among other things), so a lot of Microsoft security is lacking a bit. So he derailed virtually all of Microsoft's coding efforts for two months as Microsoft trained nearly everyone about security.

In the end, this was a good thing. NT has always had a reputation of being an insecure operating system, but it's an inaccurate reputation. NT (3.1–4, and Windows 2000) is an extremely secure OS in that it provides the option to lock many things; a properly tweaked NT server is a secure server indeed. NT's reputation comes, however, from the fact that a default installation leaves the vast majority of those locks unlocked. For Windows Server 2003, that changes.

For example, NT 4 and Windows 2000 installed an unsecured Web server by default on every server you ever installed. Not a good idea, as we learned in June 2001 when a worm called Code Red infected millions of servers—*though the Web server*. (As I write this in late 2002, there are still thousands of servers out there infected with the Nimda virus, a year after Nimda's arrival.) With Windows Server 2003, in contrast, you don't get IIS unless you ask for it. And even then, it's a pretty locked-down version of IIS. (You'll learn how to set up IIS in Chapter 17.)

To see another example, look at the NTFS permissions on the C: drive of any Windows Server 2003. Where the default permission for every previous version of NT was Everyone/Full Control—"C'mon in, y'all, we're all friends here!"—Windows Server 2003 gives Everyone only Read and Execute permission on the root of C:. The Users group has more power, as it can read files and create folders on C:, but it cannot create new files on the root of C:. You can change all of this, of course, but by default Windows Server 2003 is a bit tighter security-wise than its predecessors.

That's a good thing. But it won't be an unmixed blessing. I'm sure that at least once in your Windows Server 2003 career you will be sitting at the server trying to get something done but getting nowhere. You've got Help open, or a book at your side—this one, I hope!—clicking where the book says to click and dragging where the book says to drag, but it's not working. In that case, you may be doing the right thing but lack the permissions to do it. So Windows Server 2003 offers you one more impediment to getting our jobs done: you'll have to wend a maze of security to do some things.

But don't take that as a negative comment. It is simply a fact of life in the twenty-first century that there are tons of dirt bags out there and the Internet has now given them the chance to come knock at your door so we have no choice but to install locks on our doors. Yes, it was nice back in the days when we didn't have to lock our doors or carry keys, but those days are gone forever. NT 5.2 changed, yes, but it was just changing with the times.

Reliability

Continuing from the last section's topic, what makes an OS secure? In addition to the traditional security topics, like the ones that I just discussed, there's a more visceral sort of security—do you trust the thing not to crash on you?

In general I have always found NT to be sturdier than its compatriots; I think that no one would argue with me when I say that it's always been more reliable than Windows 3.x, 9x, and Me. I'd argue further that it was more reliable than the Mac, at least through OS 9.x. (OS/X is a completely different story; I think Apple did a great thing with OS/X—the result will be eventually be, I think, both Apple and Microsoft sometime in the future both offering OSes so reliable that we'll actually trust those OSes implicitly. Unfortunately we're not there yet. But I think it's possible.)

Windows 2000's System File Protection and Driver Verifier made great strides in making Windows 2000 far sturdier than its NT 4 predecessor; XP took that further with System Restore, Application Verifier, and Driver Rollback. As with some other Windows Server 2003 features, they're not exactly new, as they first appeared in XP, but they're new to Server. Unfortunately, one of the three,

System Restore, apparently doesn't come with Server, and that's puzzling: it's an XP tool that lets you roll back the entire state of a system to some time in the past, undoing the effects of installing some new unreliable program that's made your previously reliable system wobbly. I don't know why they left it out of Server; perhaps we'll see it return with a future version of Server.

Driver Verifier was—and is—a useful tool for checking up on new device drivers and other system-level programs. It was a great addition to 2000 and still is, with Windows Server 2003; smoking out problems with kernel-mode programs is far easier with its help. Application Verifier performs a similar service, but for user-mode programs.

Have a program that ran fine under NT 4 or Windows 9x but won't run under Windows Server 2003? Then run it under Application Verifier. When it fails, Application Verifier will tell you what caused it to fail and, even better, it can add information to the application that lets it run under Windows Server 2003.

Another source of operating system instability can be new drivers. You've got the system running fine, but the vendor of one of your pieces of hardware comes out with a new driver. As it looks like you're running smoothly, you're leery about chancing it with a new driver... there must be some subtle bug that someone found that this updated driver fixes, but this new driver could make your system unstable ... what to do? Well, Driver Verifier is a great way to check out a new driver, as it was in Windows 2000. But now it's got a simple partner in Driver Rollback. You load a driver and decide that it's no good... now, where did you put the old driver? Just go to Device Manager, find the device with the new driver, right-click it and choose Properties ... you'll see a new button, Rollback Driver. Like XP, Windows Server 2003 keeps the previous version of all drivers.

Storage News

XP and Windows Server 2003 brought some much-needed fixes to NTFS and one great new feature: volume shadowing.

In brief, volume shadowing lets you take snapshots of a file share. At predetermined times of the day, Windows Server 2003 will record the status of whatever it's shadowing and let you roll back to that quickly and easily. For example, suppose you keep your important documents in a share \\serv01\documents. You could tell Server 2003 to take snapshots—*shadow copies* is the Microsoft term—of the files in that share at 7 A.M., 10:30 A.M., noon, and 6 P.M.

A few days later, at 10:15 A.M., you realize that you've accidentally deleted an important document. But all's not lost; just fire up the shadow copy client software (included with Server 2003) and restore the 7 A.M. version of the document. A few hours' work lost, but that's all. And no need to go find the tape librarian and beg to get a tape with last night's backup mounted.

Volume shadowing lets you create a kind of imaginary copy of a file, with the state of that file frozen in time. That means that you can take shadow copies of open files and then back up the shadow copy! For example, suppose you have a SQL database that you need to back up every day, but there's never a good time to stop the database server. No problem: take a shadow copy at 3 A.M. That copy does not change on a second-by-second basis, unlike your real SQL database file, so you can back it up at your leisure.

I told you that NTFS got some other improvements; they include

- NTFS clusters can be any size, unlike Windows 2000, where their cluster size could not exceed 4KB or the volume could not be defragmented.

- A server can now host as many Dfs (Distributed File System) roots as you like; Windows 2000 only allowed each server to host just one root.
- Offline files can now cache encrypted files.
- You can set up encrypted files so that more than one person can view an encrypted file.
- You can now both compress and encrypt a file.
- EIDE drives can now run independently, meaning that you can run a small database server with two EIDE drives rather than SCSI drives—one drive for the database, the other for the transaction log. This was always possible in NT, but never made sense, as EIDE drives were limited to only run one at a time—if your SQL software said to the hardware, "Save these bytes to the database file and those bytes to the transaction log," then in actuality the OS would make the EIDE drives take turns. It might first write the bytes to the drive holding the database file while the drive holding the transaction log cooled its heels, and then write to the transaction log while keeping the database idle. The techie term for this would be that EIDE drives are now *asynchronous*, at least when they are on different channels—for example, this works if one hard disk is on the primary EIDE channel and the other is on the secondary EIDE channel.

None of those are truly earth-shaking, but they're all quite welcome improvements. Which brings me to my last point in this chapter...

Windows Server 2003: Not Yet or Good Bet?

Should you upgrade? Is it worthwhile to move up to Windows Server 2003, Standard Edition? That's a really tough question.

On the one hand, it's hard to point to any one feature that grabs you by the throat and says, "You gotta have me." For some people it'll be the new Active Directory stuff, either forest roots, domain renames, or the new branch office–friendly features. Or it might simply be that they've been waiting to go to a full-blown LDAP-based directory service like Active Directory for a while but were leery of the version 1 feel of Windows 2000's AD. But are these reasons to toss out an already-existing infrastructure built on Windows 2000 Servers? Buying all of those server licenses might be a hard sell in a place with a lot of servers. For those with just a handful, then the upgrade might be simple, not too expensive, and the fact that you needn't buy new client access licenses when upgrading to Windows Server 2003 has to make Server 2003 go down easier. But again 2003 seems to lack that one killer feature.

Furthermore, as I wrote this book I found time and time again that some section of Windows Server 2003 didn't do anything that Windows 2000 Server didn't do but that Microsoft had changed the user interface, wizards, syntax or the like. As a result, much of the time that I spent researching the book was time spent trying to figure out how to do something that I'd already figured out in 2000!

On the other hand, Server 2003 has a real preponderance of attractive features. Even the much-maligned (by *me*, to tell the truth) XP user interface has been toned down in Windows Server 2003 and is pretty nice—it's convenient in the Active Directory tools to select a group of users and do one operation on them, or to just drag and drop them between organization units. The more I work with Windows Server 2003, the more I like it. This is always true, of course—features that you first think are kinda okay soon become "man, do I miss them" when running an earlier version of the operating system. Some people will find particular small aspects compelling, as in the case of conditional DNS forwarding.

I first met Windows Server 2003 in its beta 2 form in 2001, and I can't say that I was impressed. But from beta 3 onward it's grown on me and as I write this, just before its final release, I can say honestly that I will replace all of my Windows 2000 Servers with Windows Server 2003s, as soon as I can. That's not to say that I think that all of you should do that—read the rest of the book and decide for yourself.

As you can see, there's a lot of fun new stuff to play with and learn about in Windows Server 2003. But Windows Server 2003 is sort of the second chapter in the second book in a series—NT 3.1, 3.5, 3.51, and 4 were basically chapters in the first book, and Windows 2000 was the first chapter in the second book. Some of you have been following along with the Server story and you're ready for the new Server 2003 stuff; but for those of you just joining us, we've got the next chapter, which brings up to speed those who are new to Microsoft networking. So if you're already NT-savvy, skip ahead to Chapter 3. If you're new to the Microsoft networking game, or just want a short refresher, then turn the page and let's review The Story So Far.

Chapter 2

The Basics: Networking Software, Servers, and Security

IN A LOT OF ways, Windows Server 2003, Standard Edition (which I'll call "Server 2003" or "2003" in this chapter) should be named "NT 2.1." Anyone coming into the Microsoft networking story without any previous experience with some version of NT, Windows 2000, or Server 2003 probably feels just as lost as someone who gets dragged into a movie theater to see *The Empire Strikes Back* while knowing nothing of the original *Star Wars*. They end up asking things like, "Who *is* the tall guy with the black shiny mask and the bad attitude; and speaking of attitude, what is *with* that woman whose hairdo looks like she strapped a couple of Danishes on her head?"

In this chapter, I'll give you a bit of history on Server 2003 and then take a very high-altitude look at why we're using Microsoft's networking software in the first place. This is *not* intended to prepare you for a test on networking essentials, nor is it a complete book on NTs past and present. (When I say "NT," remember that Windows Server 2003, Standard Edition is really just NT Server 5.2.) What I'm trying to accomplish in this chapter is to answer the questions:

◆ Why should I care about all of this networking stuff, anyway?

◆ Why does Microsoft's networking software approach networking the way that it does? Here, I'm referring to the fact that much of why Server 2003 works the way that it does is simply *because NT always did it that way*—so knowing more about NT's history makes 2003 make more sense.

What's the Point of Networks and Networking?

In a way, this chapter is penance for my youthful misdeeds.

When I was in the seventh grade, I had a math teacher named Mr. Schtazle. Seventh-grade math was a kind of potpourri of mathematical topics—I recall one chapter that took pains to drill into our heads the difference between precision and accuracy—and I'd plague the poor man at the beginning of every chapter by asking him, "How will we use this?"—a slightly more-polite version of "why do we care?" Well, nowadays I find that when I'm teaching a room full of people about Windows 2000, *I've* got to be careful to answer that question, "Why do you care?" even if it isn't asked. Because if I don't answer that, then many people in the room will leave the class with a pretty good notion of *how* to accomplish a bunch of tasks but not a really good feel for *why* they'd do the tasks in the first place. And you know what? Answering the "Why do I care?" question can be pretty rough some times.

So, Mr. Schtazle, if you're out there…my apologies.

Let's consider the two questions that I asked a paragraph or two back:

◆ Why network in the first place, and

◆ If we agree that networking is a good thing, why do we do it this way?

The answer to the first question will turn out to be pretty straightforward: Networking solves a set of problems for us. The answer to the question, "Why do we do it this way?" is a bit longer.

First and foremost, you're doing this to try to solve some problem that networking can help you with. Your company might want, for example, a great Web site, or to be able to send and receive e-mail, or a simple file and print server for a small office. These are the goals; a network is the means or tool to reach them. In short: *The ultimate goal of any networking project is to provide some kind of service.* Everything else is just a necessary evil—but there are a *lot* of those necessary evils!

Second, there are many kinds of services that networks can provide, and every kind of service needs different software to make it work. For example, suppose you wanted to set up a Web site on the Internet. Network services, including Web sites, need two main pieces: a *server* piece and a *client* piece. To put up that great Web site, you'll create the site itself with HTML and drop that HTML onto a Web server. One way to get a Web server is by taking one of your computers and putting a piece of software on that computer to make it function as a Web server. But that's only half the story—in order for your customers to enjoy that Web server's content, they will need a piece of client software called a *Web browser*. That's our first networking piece: *Every network service needs server software and client software.*

Third, you need to ensure that there's a way for your information to get from your server to your clients, a physical system that the service can travel over. If the clients and servers are in the same building, then you only need a local area network (LAN), and setting that up only requires pulling wires through the building. If, however, you want to offer your service to the world, as in the case of a Web server, then you'll need some kind of WAN (wide area network) connection to the Internet. In other cases, you'll need a WAN connection, but not to the Internet: many organizations with more than one location connect those locations via private communications links with names like *leased line, T1,* or *frame relay*. That's our next networking piece: *Networks need connection hardware (switches, hubs, routers, modems) and links (phone lines, network cables, frame relay, DSL, cable modem, ISDN, etc.) or the clients can't connect to the servers.*

Fourth, to provide a service over a network, your server and your clients must agree on how to transmit information over that network. That agreement is called a *network protocol,* and the one that you'll most probably use in the Windows 2003 world is called the Transmission Control Protocol/Internet Protocol (TCP/IP). You may have heard of it before, as it's the network protocol that the Internet uses, but you needn't be on the Internet to use it. In short: *Clients and servers must speak the same network protocols.*

Fifth, once you've got the channels open, and before information starts flowing in both directions, you'll almost certainly need to worry about security. When you use the tool that is networking, you want to be sure it doesn't increase your risk, and in fact you can shape the tool so it reduces hazards. Briefly: *Networks need security.*

Sixth and finally, once you've set up that terrific network service, you need a way for people to *find* that great service. You do that with a "naming" system. Windows 2003 has two of them—one that appeared years ago before the first version of NT, and a newer (to NT, anyway) method that the Internet's been using for years. The last network piece, then is that: *Networks must provide a way for users to find their services.*

Let's examine these pieces in order, take a closer look at why they work the way that they do, and get some insight into how Windows 2003 in particular handles them.

Network Client and Server Software

The reason that we network computers in the first place is so that computers acting as clients can benefit from the services of computers acting as servers. For example, suppose you want to visit my Web site, www.minasi.com. Two of the ingredients that you'll need to make that possible are software:

- ◆ You'll need a computer running a program that knows how to request Web information and then how to receive it—in other words, a *client application.*

- ◆ I'll need a computer running a program that knows how to listen for requests for Web information and then how to deliver that information—in other words, a *server application.*

As sometimes occurs *too* often in the computer business, you've got choices about both the client and the server.

THE CLIENT PIECE: A WEB BROWSER

I've said that first you'll need a computer, of course, one that's running a Web browser program like Netscape Navigator or Internet Explorer. But let me rephrase that in basic network client-server terms.

There is technically no such thing as "the World Wide Web." Instead, there is an agreement about how to transfer text, pictures, and the like, and that agreement is called the HyperText Transfer Protocol—which is normally shortened to HTTP. The phrase World Wide Web just refers collectively to all of the HTTP servers on the Internet. When you think you're surfing a Web page, what really happens is this:

1. Your client computer asks the Web server (oops, I meant *the HTTP server*) something like, "Do you have any documents?"

2. The Web server responds by saying, "Here's my default document," a simple text file that is the so-called home page for that Web server. The Web server sends that file to your client using the HTTP protocol.

3. Once your client receives the text file, it notices that the page is full of references to *other* files. For example, if the home page that you requested has pictures on it, your Web browser (HTTP client) didn't originally know to ask for them, so the Web server (HTTP server) didn't send them. Your client notices the lack of the images and requests that the server send them, which it does—again using the HTTP protocol.

Here, "HTTP client" just means a program that knows how to speak a language that transfers a particular kind of data—Web data. Your computer is deaf to the Web unless it knows how to request and receive data via HTTP.

Notice what *client* means here. It doesn't refer to you, or even to your computer. Instead, it just means a program that your computer runs.

THE SERVER PIECE: A WEB SERVER

Next, let's consider what's sitting on my side of the conversation.

I'll need a computer running a special piece of software that is designed to listen for your computer (or anyone else's, for that matter) requesting to see my Web pages via the HTTP protocol, and that can respond to those requests by transferring those pages to the requesting client software. You *might* call such a piece of software an "HTTP server" program, although almost no one calls it by that name. You'd more *commonly* call it "Web server" software. There is a variety of Web server software that I might run on my Windows Server 2003 computer, but I'm most likely to run the one that comes free with Server 2003, a program called Internet Information Services (IIS) 6. Alternatively, I might find, download (probably using HTTP!), and install a popular piece of free Web server software called Apache.

Once again, notice carefully what "server" means here. It does not really refer to the particular computer hardware that I've got stashed in my network room connected to the Internet. Instead, "server" means "the program running on Mark's computer that listens for HTTP requests and knows how to fulfill them."

Now that I've gone through all of that, consider again the question that I asked at the beginning of the chapter—why are you bothering with a network? The answer is probably "because you want to offer a Web site, either internally or on the public Internet, and you that think that IIS is the best (highest-performance, cheapest, or some combination of the two) Web server software around"— which means that you must use Server 2003, as it's the only operating system that supports IIS 6. (Or you could use an earlier version of Server and an earlier version of IIS, but why not go with the latest and greatest?)

OTHER TYPES OF SERVERS

I'll tend to use the Web client-server example for this discussion. But I don't want to lose sight of the fact that there are quite a few client-server systems, besides Web servers, that are in common use and that you may want to use 2003 to create. Returning to the theme of this chapter, then— "Why do I care or why do I need this stuff?"—networks offer several valuable services, and you may want to set up a computer to act as a server and offer some of those services. Here are a few besides the Web server example.

File Servers   File servers act as central places to store data files. Why put them on a server rather than just keep them on your local computer? Well, in some cases someone else created the file, and placing a file on a central server is a simple way to make the files available to others. The other good thing about storing files in a central location is that they're more easily backed up that way. 2003 comes with file server software built in.

Print Servers   Print servers let you share printers. Not everyone wants to put a printer on their desk, and besides, if you share the printers, you can afford more expensive (and presumably better) models. 2003 comes with print server software built in.

E-Mail Servers   Mail servers are essential if you're going to do e-mail. Some computer (or computers) must act as the post office, collecting e-mail from the local users and sending it to other mail servers across the Internet and acting as a receiving point for other mail servers to send mail destined for your organization. You *can* outsource this function by letting your ISP act as your mail server, but running your own mail server gives you more flexibility. (However, it *does* require a persistent connection to the Internet.) 2003's new features include a basic e-mail server. Yes, it's "basic" because Microsoft *really* wants to sell you Exchange as your mail server. But it's not a bad server for many people's needs.

Group Scheduling Servers   The centralized nature of servers means that they're a great place to keep track of scarce resources like meeting rooms or your time. 2003 does not come with a scheduling server, as Microsoft wants to sell you Exchange to do that sort of thing. But there are alternatives to Exchange; there are some terrific Web-based scheduling tools that work great on 2003—for one example, take a look at `www.mattkruse.com/scripts/calendar/` or other tools, like Lotus Notes.

E-Commerce Online Stores   If you've got something great to sell, then the Web's one place to do it. There are thousands of online stores on the Web, and a good number of them run on 2003. While 2003 includes a Web server, it doesn't include the other software that you'd need to create a complete online store. But there are a lot of consulting and programming firms that would be happy to help you create an online store atop 2003!

Networks Need Connection Hardware and Links

If I want to offer a server service and ensure that you can enjoy that service, then we'll both need to be physically attached to the same network—the same series of cables, satellite links, or whatever—or your computer's requests will never get to my computer in the first place. That probably means that we're both on that huge network-of-networks called the Internet, but we could just be working for the same company in a single wired building, or a multilocation firm connected by a private intranet.

Now, notice that if I'm going to run a Web server, I'll need to be connected to our common network (Internet or otherwise) persistently: I couldn't decide to run a Web server out of my house and just dial in to the Internet now and then. Of course, if I'm only serving some private network that we share, then an Internet connection is unnecessary, as we already have connection to a common network.

People who worry about the physical connection part of networking concern themselves with getting cables run through walls, calling the phone company to arrange for persistently connected data links of various kinds—links with names like DSL, cable modem, frame relay, leased lines, T1 or T3 lines—and then work with a family of hardware that helps get the bits going off in the right direction—devices with names like switches, hubs, and routers.

Does 2003 help you with this part of the job? In some parts, it can. Switches and hubs are very basic, simple devices, and 2003 has nothing to do with them—although clearly 2003 depends on their presence in order to network! Routers are, however, more complex devices. You probably know that the market leader in the router world is a firm named Cisco Systems, but you may not know that a router is really just a small, single-purpose computer. If you wanted to, you could use a computer running Server 2003 to replace a Cisco router. Additionally, if you wanted to allow people outside your network to dial in to your network, you could use a Windows Server 2003 to make that possible. (It's not the best answer, as you'll see in Chapter 6, but it *is* possible.)

Clients and Servers Must Speak the Same Protocols

But simply being connected to the same wire isn't enough—we need a common communications language. If I were to pick up a phone and dial some number in Beijing, I'd have a physical connection with whatever poor soul picked the phone on the other end—but that would be the extent of our interaction. In the same way, computer networks need to agree on things like, "What's the biggest block of data that I can ever send you?" and, "How shall I acknowledge that I actually *got* that block of data?" or, "Should I bother acknowledging receipt of data at all?" and hundreds of other questions.

The answers to all of those questions are contained in the "network language" or, in network techie terms, the *network transport protocol*. It probably won't surprise you that more than one network transport protocol exists, and over the years NT has generally supported three of them:

- NetBEUI (Network Basic Input/Output System Extended User Interface), an old Microsoft/IBM/Sytek protocol designed to support small networks
- IPX/SPX (Internet Packet Exchange/Sequenced Packet Exchange), the protocol that Novell NetWare predominantly used for years
- TCP/IP (Transmission Control Protocol/Internet Protocol), the protocol of the Internet and intranets

Although you have three choices, it's a good bet that your Microsoft software-based network uses TCP/IP. Why TCP/IP? Well, there have been some really great protocols over the years, but as the Internet uses TCP/IP and as the Internet is so popular, TCP/IP has sort of trumped the other protocols. In fact, it's impossible to do a fair number of things that 2003 and its predecessors Windows 2000 and, to a lesser extent, Windows NT 4 are capable of *without* TCP/IP. So I'm going to assume for our discussion and indeed for most of this book that your network will use TCP/IP.

Oh, and one more thing—once you've decided that TCP/IP is your network protocol of choice, then you'll need to install several *more* servers to support TCP/IP's infrastructure. And here again, when I say "more servers," I'm not suggesting that you have to buy more PCs, although you might. What I mean is that you'll have to install software on some computer or group of computers to perform three basic pieces of plumbing or infrastructure jobs:

- A Domain Naming System (DNS) server keeps track of the names of the computers in your network (an important task, believe it or not).
- A Dynamic Host Configuration Protocol (DHCP) server configures the specifics of TCP/IP on each computer in your network, both great and small.
- A Windows Internet Name Server (WINS) does something like what DNS does—keeps track of names—but isn't really necessary on a "pure" Windows 2003 network—its main job is to support older Microsoft operating systems like Windows 9x, Me, and NT 3.x and 4.

You'll learn more about the specifics of DNS, DHCP, and WINS in Chapter 7. I should point out that if you're a one-person shop, then you might not need all of that, as your ISP might be handling it for you—but I'm assuming throughout this book that you are probably a network administrator/manager for a network of at *least* a few computers, and possibly for a tremendous number of computers.

Keeping the Bad Guys Away: Security

Once you've gotten the first four things done, then your job's finished, in a sense—people can now read and write files on that file server, view pages on that Web server, print to that shared printer, set up meetings with you over your scheduling server, and so on. I mean, hey, networking's all about sharing, so just open the doors and let 'em in!

As you've probably realized, there's a missing piece here: security. While there's a lot to security, it basically boils down to two things: *authentication* and *permissions*.

- First, you want to be able to identify who's entering your network. That's authentication.

- Second, once you know for sure who you're talking to—once you've authenticated—then you must be able to look up somewhere what that person is allowed to do, his *permissions*. For example, a network logon could figuratively go something like, "Okay, now I know you're Jack…but I've been told to deny Jack access to everything." Merely being authenticated doesn't mean that you get access!

AUTHENTICATION

The first part of security is called *authentication*, and you usually accomplish it through usernames and passwords, although as time goes on you'll eventually use the more science-fiction means of authentication: One day, the computer may recognize you by your fingerprint, face, voice, retina blood vessel pattern, or some other item that's distinctly you. The geek term for those authentication approaches is *biometric*.

For now, however, it's user accounts and passwords that identify users. I realize that nearly everyone who's reading this book has undergone an authentication at some point—you've logged in to a network some time. It all sounds simple, doesn't it? And yet user accounts and passwords present special problems.

Storing Authentication Information

First, you'll need some kind of program that lets administrators create user accounts and store them in a file. In their simplest form, user accounts consist of a database of usernames and passwords. That's no big deal—it's a very simply structured database, and there are tons of database programs out there—but don't forget that you need to *encrypt* that information. Otherwise, there's the possibility that someone could come along and steal the database file, take it home, and perhaps crack it for your user's passwords.

Just such a thing happened to NT 4. NT stored user information in a file named SAM. If you leave me in the same room as your server, then I can copy that SAM onto a floppy and take it off-site to analyze it. Wasn't it encrypted? Well, yes, but sometimes encryption isn't enough—a group of hackers figured out how to crack SAM's encryption. With just a bit of work, anyone could extract passwords from an NT SAM. (Which is a good reason to keep your servers behind lock and key, so that it's harder for someone to steal your account files.) Windows 2000- and 2003-based domains (a term I'll define soon) use a more sophisticated encryption scheme on its user account/password file (which is named `NTDS.DIT`, not SAM), but unfortunately even that file can be cracked with some determination. Again, let me stress that this is only a danger if you let someone physically sit down at the servers that do logons, a set of servers called domain controllers, so don't worry that 2003 isn't secure. Any security person can tell you that you should *never* give the bad guys physical access to your important servers—lock 'em up!

The tool that lets administrators create, modify, or delete user accounts is called Active Directory Users and Computers. *Active Directory* refers to Windows 2000 and 2003's system for storing usernames and passwords. It's called a directory because *directory* is the current network lingo for "database of user accounts." Personally, I think it's kind of confusing—in my mind, directory conjures up visions of drive letters, like C:\DOS—but it's the current argot, so it's worth knowing. And, in case you're wondering, the "Active" part is just Microsoft marketing; don't look for any deep meaning there. (It's not like Novell makes a product called Comatose Directory or Lethargic Directory.)

Authenticating without Compromising Security

So you've got a server somewhere that contains the list of usernames and passwords. Those are only good if someone can use her username and password to be authenticated and get access to things on the network. So you need some way for a user sitting at her workstation computer to be recognized by that server. You're already familiar with this recognition process: we call it logging on.

Suppose I'm sitting at my Windows XP workstation and I want to get to some files on a file server named files-r-us.bigfirm.biz. Before files-r-us will give me access, I've got to submit myself for authentication—I've got to log on. One of the many programs that comes with every version of NT since version 3.1 is called `winlogon.exe`, and it's the program that pops up when you first turn your workstation on, asking you to punch in your username, password, and domain. (Again, I'll explain what a domain is in a minute.)

So imagine that I'm trying to access some data on files-r-us. Files-r-us responds by asking my workstation, "What's his name and password?" *Now* I've got a problem.

You see, what I'd *like* to do is to just say over the network line, "This is Mark and his password is 'swordfish.'" Then files-r-us can just look in its directory file of usernames and passwords and see if it has a user named Mark with a password of "swordfish." If so, then it lets me in. If not, it doesn't. Simple, eh?

Well, there's one flaw here—the part where my workstation passes "swordfish" over the network. A class of programs called "sniffers" can record and display any data that passes over a network wire. So passing passwords around on an unencrypted Ethernet cable isn't a great idea. That means you've got another challenge: how to prove to a server across the network from you that you've got Mark's password without actually showing that password to the server.

Over time, networks have come up with different answers, but Active Directories, whether based on Windows 2000 or 2003, use an old authentication method called Kerberos which some folks at MIT first invented in the mid '80s. It replaces an older method employed by NT 3.*x* and 4 called NTLM, which was short for NT LAN Manager, a reference to one of NT's predecessors. What follows is an extremely simplified version of how Kerberos works. (It's actually a wildly simplified description, but it'll help you understand the more complete explanation that you'll see in the next section.)

Let's return to files-r-us. I try to access its data, so files-r-us needs to first log me in. It does that by saying, "I'll tell you how to access my data," and sends me some instructions on how to get to its data. But the data is *encrypted*—with my password! In other words, *anyone* could claim to be me, and files-r-us would happily send these vital instructions-for-connection. But only I can decrypt those instructions, so only I can benefit from them. So files-r-us ensured that only someone with my password could gain access, without sending my password over the wire.

Centralizing and Sharing User Account Information: Domains

But my simple example about trying to access one file server is, well, a bit *too* simple. Most companies will end up with more than one server, and in fact it's not unusual to end up with dozens or hundreds of servers. And that leads to the following problem. Recall that I said a page or so back that if you're going to employ user accounts, then you'll need a file to store them in. But what if you have more than one server? What if in addition to the server named files-r-us.bigfirm.biz, I've also got a mail server named postoffice.bigfirm.biz and a Web server named www.bigfirm.biz? I might want to log in to any one of those three, so they *all* have to be able to accomplish logons. But now let's examine what that actually means in terms of keeping track of user accounts. Should each server contain a complete copy of `NTDS.DIT`, the file containing the names and passwords for users?

That might work, but it'd be a pain, for several reasons. First, `NTDS.DIT` can get pretty big, and I'd end up burning up a lot of disk space copying it to every server in my enterprise. Second, if servers are connected by low-speed WAN links, the process of copying the changes to `NTDS.DIT` to all of the servers on my network (a process called *directory replication*) would take up a lot of time and network bandwidth. Third, do I *really* want to have to create a network "storm" of file copying amongst the servers every time someone just changes his password? And finally, what about the issue of securing the `NTDS.DIT` file in the first place? If I copy `NTDS.DIT` to every single server in the enterprise, there are bound to be a few that are out in the open, not physically secured. It'd be easy for an intruder to copy the `NTDS.DIT` from a poorly secured computer and spirit it off-site, to crack it at leisure.

The better idea that we've used in networks for years is to put the user directory, the `NTDS.DIT`, not on every single server, but instead on a relatively small subset of the servers. Those `NTDS.DIT`-holding servers then serve in the role of *logon server*, doing the job of authenticating for the other servers. In Microsoft parlance, a logon server is more commonly called a *domain controller*. So, to return to the example of accessing data on files-r-us, imagine that files-r-us is *not* a domain controller and doesn't contain a copy of `NTDS.DIT`, and that another computer, vault.bigfirm.biz, *is* a domain controller and contains a copy of `NTDS.DIT`. In this newer arrangement, I don't directly log into files-r-us but instead enlist the aid of vault.bigfirm.biz in order to authenticate with files-r-us.

In a purely Active Directory network (which can only include Windows 2000, XP, and 2003 systems), vault.bigfirm.biz would help me log in to files-r-us with Kerberos. In order to understand how Kerberos works, you first need to understand that under Kerberos, not only do the users have passwords, the server programs do also. Thus, the file server program running on files-r-us has its own password. So both the user and the server each have passwords—remember that.

When I tell my workstation to try to get some data from files-r-us, my workstation sees that it'll need to get me logged in to files-r-us. It does that by asking the domain controller, vault, to give me something called a "ticket" to the file server service on files-r-us. The domain controller responds by handing my workstation an encrypted piece of data, which is the Kerberos ticket.

The ticket can be decrypted with my password, making its contents a mystery to anyone but me (or my workstation, which obviously knows my password). My workstation decrypts the ticket, which contains two things. First, it contains a message saying "your special one-time-only password for accessing the file server at files-r-us is 'opensesame.'" Second, it contains *another* encrypted message—but this one's not encrypted with my password, so I can't decrypt it! But my workstation knows to send it to the file server, which decrypts it successfully, as the file server has its own passwords. Once the file server receives and decrypts the part of the Kerberos ticket that I sent it, the file server sees that that ticket piece says something like, "The special one-time-only password for communicating with Mark is 'opensesame.' And by the way, you should have gotten this message from Mark sometime between 10:45 A.M. and 10:50 A.M. from his IP address, which should be 117.39.82.3."

Once the file server gets its half of the Kerberos ticket, it knows a few things:

◆ The user claiming to be Mark who wants access to the file server is indeed Mark.

◆ Any messages from that now-authenticated person named Mark should have originated from IP address 117.39.82.3.

◆ If Mark and the file server really want to maintain a secure connection, they could even encrypt their communications using this shared—but secret—password, opensesame.

Security Roles and Definitions: Domains, Domain Controllers, and Member Servers

Armed with this information, I can define a few Microsoft networking terms.

Domain   You just saw an example where one machine (vault) let me log in to another machine (files-r-us). I haven't mentioned this yet, but before I could get *anywhere* I needed to log in to the computer at my desk, my workstation—and when I first tried to log in to my workstation, it was once again vault.bigfirm.biz that authenticated me. Clearly, then, my workstation and files-r-us "trust" vault.bigfirm.biz in some fashion.

The collection of machines that share the same list of user accounts, the same `NTDS.DIT`, is a *domain*. Or, to put it a bit more specifically: several computers hold a copy of `NTDS.DIT` and are willing to act as "logon servers" (domain controllers) with that `NTDS.DIT`. The collection of machines that are willing to accept logons from those domain controllers (in Microsoft terms, who "trust" those domain controllers) and the domain controllers themselves are collectively called a domain. So my workstation, vault, and files-r-us are all part of the same domain.

Domain Controller   A server, such as vault.bigfirm.biz, that contains a copy of the user account/password data, and that therefore can let users log in to servers, is a *domain controller*. Domain controllers exist to centralize the user account/password information so that you needn't put the `NTDS.DIT` on every server.

Member Server   A machine that is running NT 3.*x*, 4.0, 2000, or Server 2003 but *not* acting as a domain controller will not contain a copy of `NTDS.DIT` and therefore can't authenticate domain members. Such a machine is called a *member server*.

PERMISSIONS AND ACCESS CONTROL LISTS (ACLS)

Once a server has determined that I am indeed me, does that mean that I'll get access to the server's information? Not necessarily. Authentication just identifies me. The next step in security is access control, also known as (depending on what network operating system you are using) *rights*, *permissions*, or *privileges*.

Ever since its earliest versions, NT (which includes Windows Server 2003) has had a very flexible system of file and directory permissions. As you'll see later in this book, you can exert very fine-grained control, such as specifying that Mary can read or write to a given file, that Bill can only read it, and that June cannot access the file at all. Don't get the idea, however, that permissions refer only to files. There are permissions to do things like create, modify, and destroy user accounts, and even permissions to create domains in the first place. The flexibility of these permissions is one of Microsoft networking's great strengths.

Just about everything in the Microsoft networking world has security on it. Want to read a file? You need the permissions to read it. Want to shut down the program that provides the Web server? You need the permissions to shut it down. Want to create a new user account on your network? You need the permissions to create a new user.

These permissions are stored as a list. In the case of the file, the operating system sets aside a little space for every file that it creates, and keeps the permissions in that space. A set of permissions for a file, then, might look like

- ◆ A user named June can do anything that she wants to the file.
- ◆ Another user, Joe, can only read it.
- ◆ Any user in a group named Cube-dwellers can read or modify the file, but not delete it.
- ◆ The operating system can do anything that it wants to the file.

In Microsoft networking-speak, that list is called an access control list or, inevitably, *ACL*. Each of the four entries are called access control *entries* or ACEs. You will learn in this book that *lots* of things have ACLs, and adjusting those ACLs is how you configure security in your network.

ACCESS TO EARLIER SECURITY SYSTEMS

The last challenge that Windows 2000 and 2003's security designers faced was the so-called "legacy" support—ensuring that they could interact with the security systems built into Windows for Workgroups, Windows 9*x*, NT 3.*x*, and 4. I've described in very broad strokes how Kerberos works, but Windows and NT didn't use anything like that and in fact *couldn't* do Kerberos logons; Kerberos first appeared in the Microsoft networking world in February 2000, with the introduction of Windows 2000. Microsoft knew that you wouldn't be very happy if they required you to throw away all of your old Windows 9*x* and NT systems before you could implement Active Directory, so Windows 2000, XP, and Server 2003 know a variety of logon methods—NTLM 1.2 for Windows 9*x* and NTLM 2.0 for NT 3.*x* and 4—in addition to Kerberos.

It's hard to overstate the importance of security. For example, in the past, one of Novell's *main* advantages over NT was in the way that it stored user accounts and handled logins—Novell's security was faster and more flexible. Sure, one could argue that Novell moved data around file servers more quickly, but not so much more quickly that anyone would really modify a buying decision. Basically, people were buying Novell for Novell's security system, something called NetWare Directory Services (NDS). NDS was essentially a big-time user database, something with a more enterprise feel to it than NT's older SAM-based system. In short, security is *important*.

Names: Finding Servers and Resources

When PC-based networking first appeared, we didn't do much Web work—the earliest common LAN functions were file and print services. So from the very beginning (all of 15 years ago) of PC-based networking, we've done file and print services; they're the most basic network services. But now suppose that you've got a network with more than one server on it, and you want to find out which server has a printer available for sharing, or you can't remember which server holds that share called `hrdocuments`; how do you search for network functions?

That's one of the oldest problems in networking, and not just in Microsoft networking. Microsoft's most current answer to the "how can I find resource X on the network?" question is to store that information in the Active Directory database. But they're not there by any means yet and, even if you have an all-Windows 2003 and XP network (which is unlikely), you'll find that by default the Active Directory isn't all that much help in finding file and printer shares. I'm sure that's going to change as new versions of NT appear, but for now, we Microsoft operating systems users are pretty much stuck with an old technology known colloquially as the Network Neighborhood or, in Windows 2000 and later, My Network Places. Here's where it came from and how it works.

How would you set up a system that provided a centralized directory of services on a network, a kind of "yellow pages" that lets a user quickly find a file share or shared printer? Microsoft networking uses a name server system called the *computer browser* or *browse services*—it has nothing at all to do with the Web, it's had that name since before the Web existed—where you, the network administrator, don't have to do *anything*; the name servers set themselves up automatically. Sounds good? Well, it *is* for small networks, but it gets troublesome for larger ones—which is why Microsoft is trying to phase it out.

The servers in a Microsoft network that contain information about network services are called *browse masters* or *master browsers*. What's different about the concept of Microsoft browse servers is that no one computer is fixed as the browse master. Instead, when your computer logs in to your network, it finds a browse master by broadcasting a request for one, saying, "Are there any browse masters out there?" The first browse master to hear the workstation (there can be multiple browse masters, as you'll see) responds to the workstation by saying, "Just direct all your name service requests to me."

When a server starts up, it does the same thing. It broadcasts, "Are there any browse masters out there?" and when it finds one, it says to it, "I am a server with the following shares. Please add me to your list of servers." The list of servers that a browse master maintains is called the *browse list*, not surprisingly.

TIP *This is the really irritating thing about the browse list: it's broadcast-based. That means that if your network isn't 100 percent broadcast-friendly, then you'll sometimes end up with an incomplete list of servers on your network. So if you have a network built in more than one segment (and who doesn't?), or you use some kinds of Ethernet switches rather than hubs, then you may experience missing servers in the browse list. That's part of why Microsoft is trying to phase out the browse list. But for now, understand that the browse list is a largely lame and unreliable technology. You'll see later on, in Chapter 7, that you can install a service called the Windows Internet Name Service (WINS) to reduce the chance that the browser breaks, but trust me—you'll eventually come to a point where you've done everything that you can do, but the browser still doesn't work. When that happens, don't feel bad—we've all been there. I'll suggest some ways to make it work better and reduce your dependence on the browser a bit later in this section.*

By now, you may be wondering, "How come I've never seen one of these browse lists?" You have. If you ever worked with earlier versions of NT or with Windows for Workgroups, then you saw Figure 2.1 when you opened the File Manager and clicked Disk/Connect Network Drive.

FIGURE 2.1

FIGURE 2.1

Sample browse list from Windows for Workgroups or Windows NT version 3.*x*

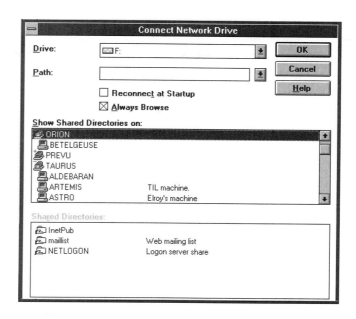

From Windows 9*x* or Windows NT 4, you can see a browse list by opening the Network Neighborhood folder, as in Figure 2.2.

FIGURE 2.2

Sample browse list from Windows NT 4 or Windows 9*x*

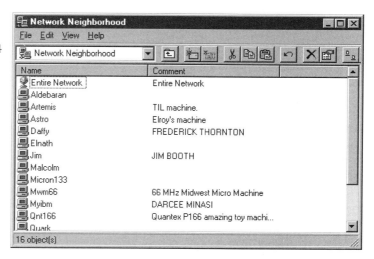

From DOS or indeed any command line, you can see a browse list by typing **net view** or **net view** ***machinename***. You see a screen like the one in Figure 2.3.

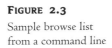

FIGURE 2.3

Sample browse list
from a command line

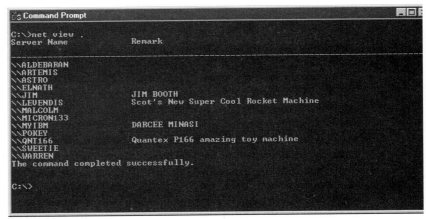

NOTE   *What's with that* \\ *thing? Microsoft's network software has, since 1985, used a way of writing the names of servers and of shares on servers called a Universal Naming Convention or UNC. It looks like* \\servername\ *sharename. So, for example, if I had a server named bigserver that contained a file share called mydata, I'd refer to that share as* \\bigserver\mydata—*that would be the UNC for that share. You'll learn more about this in Chapter 11, on file shares, but I wanted to explain the mystifying* \\ *briefly here. And by the way, you pronounce "**" as "whack-whack" in the Microsoft world. Now, to my way of thinking, that'd mean that a regular forward slash—* / —*would be pronounced "backwhack" in Microsoftese, but I've never gotten confirmation on that.*

Each figure shows you the list of servers available: Aldebaran, Artemis, and Astro, just to list a few. Other servers—Daffy and MWM66—appear only in some of the browse lists because a few minutes passed between taking the screen shots, and a few "test" servers went up or down in those few minutes. In all three cases, the workstations that these screens were taken from got their browse lists from a local browse master.

You can drill down further into these browse lists, as well. In Windows 9*x*/Me, Windows NT 4, 2000, XP, or Server 2003 (in 2000, XP, or Server 2003, open My Network Places), you can double-click any one of those servers and see the list of shares that the servers offer; that too, is information from the browse list. In Windows for Workgroups or Windows NT 3.*x*, you'd just click a server once, and the list of its shares would appear in the bottom pane of the dialog box. From DOS or any other command line, you'd get the list of servers by typing **net view**, as you've already seen, and then you get the list of shares for any given server by typing **net view *servername***, where *servername* is the name of the server whose shares you want to see.

WHEN BROWSE LISTS GET TOO LARGE: WORKGROUPS TO THE RESCUE

As I've described them so far, browse lists seem pretty convenient. But in the little test network that I used for the previous screen shots, you saw only a few servers. Hell, *everything* works fine on *small* networks.

Now let's talk about *your* network. Sit down at a corporate network of any size and you see dozens, hundreds, or *thousands* of servers. Scrolling down through a 500-server browse list would be a bit time-consuming—to say nothing of how much work the browse master would have to do to keep it up-to-date! The problem to solve is, then, managing the size of the browse list. There are two ways to do that:

- Reduce the number of servers in your enterprise.
- Divide the enterprise-wide browse list into several smaller browse lists called *workgroups.*

Disable Peer-to-Peer Sharing on Workstations

The first answer is actually a bit off the main topic, but let me digress for a moment and talk about it before returning to the main item: workgroups. When I say, "Reduce the number of servers," I'm talking about an unfortunate side effect of running Windows for Workgroups, Windows 9x/ME, Windows NT, 2000, or XP workstations—they all have the capability to become peer-to-peer servers. The browse masters don't distinguish between industrial-strength servers running NT Server and low-octane peer-to-peer servers, so you could end up with a browse list that's *supposed* to only list your servers, but *actually* lists all of your servers and workstations. In general, I think peer-to-peer networking is a bad idea. If a piece of data is important enough to be used by two employees, then it's a company asset that should be backed up regularly and so should go on a managed file server, not a desktop machine that's probably backed up once a decade. My recommendation is this: Disable the peer-to-peer sharing option on your Windows for Workgroups, Windows 9x/ME, Windows NT, 2000, and XP workstations. How you do this depends on the operating system of the workstations in question. In NT 3.x and 4, open the Control Panel and then the Services applet; locate the service called Server and stop it, as well as disabling it for future reboots. In Windows 9x, go to Control Panel/Network/File and Print Sharing and make sure both options, to share files and printers, are unchecked. In Windows for Workgroups, make sure the sharing control in Network Setup is set *not* to enable file or printer sharing. In Windows 2000 and later, right-click My Computer and choose Manage, then find the Services folder and stop the Server service. (You'll see more about doing this later in the book.)

Not only will your network have less traffic—workstations will no longer have delusions of serverdom, so they won't be chattering at the browse master all of the time—but not loading the server part of the workstation's operating system saves RAM on the workstation.

Divide the Browse List into Workgroups

The other approach to keeping a browse list to a manageable size is to subdivide it in some way. That's a reasonable thing to suggest if you realize that, no matter how large an organization *seems* to be, it's usually composed of lots of smaller groups, such as Manufacturing, Sales, Marketing, Accounting, Finance, Personnel, Senior Management, and so on. Each of those groups can be called *workgroups*, and you can pretty much chop up your enterprise into workgroups in any way you like (but a rule of thumb says that a workgroup should be a group of people for whom 95 percent of the data generated by that group stays within that group).

From a more network-technical point of view, the minimum definition of a workgroup is just *a group of workstations that share a browse list.* (That's my definition, not Microsoft's.) The idea is that when someone in Accounting opens up her browse list, you want her to see just the Accounting servers, not the Manufacturing servers, as she has no use for the Manufacturing servers. (Besides, there's a good chance that she doesn't have permission to access the Manufacturing servers anyway—but I'll get to workgroups and security in a little bit.) How do you join a workgroup? See the sidebar "How Do I Join a Workgroup?"

HOW DO I JOIN A WORKGROUP?

Generally, all you need to do is to tell the networking software on your workstations and servers that they're members of a given workgroup. There isn't any "security" in being part of a workgroup—you pretty much just declare yourself a member and you are a member. (As a matter of fact, if you misspell the name of the workgroup, you end up accidentally founding a whole new workgroup all by yourself, which I'm sure was not your intention!)

Specifically, you designate which workgroup you're a member of in one of the following ways:

From a DOS or Windows for Workgroups workstation   In the [network] section of the SYSTEM.INI file you'll find a WORKGROUP=parameter. (You'll have a SYSTEM.INI even if you're just running DOS, because the network client software creates one.) You can also set the workgroup from the MS-DOS Network Client Setup program, or in the Windows for Workgroups' Network applet of the Control Panel.

From Windows 9*x*   Open the Control Panel and double-click the Network icon. In the property sheet that you see, click the Identification tab. You see the place to fill in the workgroup name.

On Windows NT 3.*x*   Open the Control Panel and double-click the Network applet. You'll see a button labeled Domain or Workgroup. (NT has a kind of confusing way of blurring workgroups and domains, which I'll make clearer later in this chapter.) Click that button, and you can change the workgroup you're a member of. Again, NT complicates choosing a workgroup somewhat, so read the rest of this chapter if you want to change an NT workgroup.

On Windows NT 4   Open the Control Panel and double-click the Network applet. Like Windows 9*x*, Windows NT 4 has a property sheet with an Identification tab. Click Change to change the workgroup. Again, with NT you may see no references to workgroups at all; instead you see references to domains. Read on to understand the differences.

On Windows 2000   If you're a member of a domain, then *do not* join a workgroup—I'll explain that in a minute. Otherwise, right-click My Computer and choose Properties. Click the Network Identification tab and then the button labeled Properties. Fill in a new workgroup in the field named Workgroup; then close the dialog box and reboot.

On Windows XP and Server 2003   Right-click My Computer and choose Properties. (You may have to click the Start button to find My Computer.) Click the tab labeled Computer Name, then the button labeled Change. In the resulting dialog box, you'll see the choice to become a "Member of:" either a domain or a workgroup. Click the radio button next to Workgroup and fill in the workgroup name, then close the dialog box and reboot.

NOTE   *Workgroup names are like Windows 9x and NT 3.x/4.x machine names and can be up to 15 characters long.*

So, to review what you've seen so far:

♦   Network browse lists allow a user at a workstation to see all of the servers on the network, and from there to see all of the shares on a given server.

◆ Browse lists can get fairly long, so you can partition your entire network into *workgroups*, which are just groups of people that share a browse list.

◆ When you request a browse list, you don't get the entire list of servers in your enterprise network, you only get the list of servers within your workgroup.

◆ Each workgroup has one or more servers that act as gatherers of browse information. They're called browse masters or master browsers, and they're picked automatically.

◆ Machines that are only workstations and don't act as servers even in a peer-to-peer capacity do not appear on browse lists.

As the question of what machines go on a browse list and what machines don't is important to the length of a browse list, let me list the kinds of machines that can act as servers in a Microsoft enterprise network:

◆ Windows 3.*x* (with the Workgroup Add-On for MS-DOS clients)

◆ DOS (with Workgroup Add-On for MS-DOS clients)

◆ Windows for Workgroups

◆ Windows 9*x*/Me

◆ NT Workstation

◆ NT Server

◆ Windows 2000 Professional

◆ Windows Server 2003

HOW DO I VIEW A BROWSE LIST?

Microsoft has built different browse programs into its various network client software.

From a DOS or NT/2000/XP/2003 Command Line Type **net view**. That shows you the list of servers. You can view the shares on a given server by typing **net view *servername***. To see the browse list for a workgroup other than your own, type **net view /workgroup:workgroupname**.

From NT, 2000, XP or Server 2003, don't use **/workgroup:** in the command; instead, use **/domain:**.

From Windows for Workgroups or Windows NT 3.*x* Open the File Manager, click Drive, and then click Connect Network Drive. You'll see a window with two panes. The browse list for your workgroup and a list of the other workgroups on the network appears as the list of possible servers in the top pane and, when you click a server, that server's shares appear in the bottom pane. To see the browse list for a workgroup other than your own, double-click the name of the workgroup in the top pane.

From Windows 9*x* or Windows NT 4 Open the Network Neighborhood folder. You'll see the servers in your workgroup represented as PC icons in a folder. Double-click one of the servers, and a folder will open up showing you the shares. To see the browse list for a workgroup other than your own, double-click the Entire Network icon and you'll see a list of workgroups. On Windows NT 4, click Entire Network and then Microsoft Network, and you'll get a list of the other workgroups.

Continued on next page

HOW DO I VIEW A BROWSE LIST? *(continued)*

From Windows 2000   If your system is in a workgroup, open My Network Places and then the icon labeled Computers Near Me. If your system is part of a domain, then that icon isn't available. Instead, open My Network Places and the icon labeled Entire Network, then the icon named Microsoft Windows Network. You'll see one or more icons representing the workgroups on your network—open the one representing your workgroup and you'll see your workgroup's browse list.

From Windows XP or Server 2003   Open My Network Places. It might be on your desktop, or it might be on the Start menu, or you might have to right-click the Desktop and choose Properties, then click the Desktop tab, followed by the Customize Desktop button, then check the box next to My Network Places and click OK twice. My Network Places will be on your desktop. Once you have My Network Places open, then you'll either see a Network Task on the left of the folder labeled View Workgroup Computers or you might have an icon labeled Entire Network, in which case you should double-click that, then double-click Microsoft Windows Network. You'll then see an icon of three PCs representing your workgroup—click that and you'll get your workgroup's browse list.

As it's an unusual product, let me just explain that the Workgroup Add-On for MS-DOS is a separate Microsoft product that lets you use a DOS machine as a peer-to-peer server. (Also, it's pretty old, so I have no idea where you'd get a copy these days.) Again, I recommend that you disable file and print sharing on all of these machines except, of course, for the machines dedicated to the task of being servers, all of which are probably running NT Server.

And once you're in a workgroup, you'll no doubt want to see your browse list; the sidebar "How Do I View a Browse List?" tells you the specifics.

Now, if you *tried* that on a working network, then you might have gotten one of NT and family's less helpful responses, like "System error 1230 has occurred." That gives me the chance to offer another important bit of advice for anyone using a modern Microsoft operating system: how to convert a numeric error code into a bit of explanatory English text—see the sidebar for more information.

HOW TO CONVERT A NUMERIC ERROR CODE TO ENGLISH TEXT

Just type **net helpmsg** *number*, where *number* is the error code. For example, you'll probably stumble across error 5 now and then: "access is denied." It means that you didn't have the right to do something that you tried to do. Another common one is error 53, "the network path was not found." It means that you tried to access some server that the system can't find or, as is usually the case for me, you misspelled the server's name.

Before leaving the topic of the browser, let me offer one more piece of advice: try to avoid it, as it's unreliable. If your users need access to particular file shares, then you can deliver access to those shares in a few ways. First, you can map file shares, which means that you can create imaginary drive letters on your user's workstations. In other words, if the user often uses \\server1\compdata, then you could set up her workstation so that she'd see a new drive V: which isn't a local hard disk—although it *looks* like a local hard disk—but is instead a network drive. Or you could simply create a shortcut to the UNC on her desktop. You'll learn how to do both of those things in Chapter 11.

Summary: The Necessary Evils

I hope in this section that I've provided a bit of an answer to the question, "Why do we have to worry about all of this stuff just to get a mail server up and running?"

- First, you need a piece of server software that can accomplish whatever it is that you're trying to do—Web server, mail server, or whatever.

- Next, you need to be compatible with and connected to a physical network that connects to your clients—either the public Internet or a private network of some kind.

- Then your server must move its data around in the same way that your clients' machines do, using the same network language or protocol, probably TCP/IP. TCP/IP itself will require some server functions as well, to maintain it.

- It wouldn't be necessary in a perfect world, but in our imperfect world your network needs to protect its data with a security system, and in today's world that unfortunately means an *elaborate* security system.

- Finally, you'll need some way of finding what you put in that network, once you've got it working. Active Directory will become that way in the future, but for now it's a kludgy thing called the Computer Browser that you see in My Network Places.

So presumably you now see why your network needs so many moving parts. Why buy them from Microsoft?

So Why Use NT/2000/Server 2003?

I hope that by now I've convinced you that networking seems like a good thing. But you could build your network atop any number of operating systems, including Unix, Linux, Novell NetWare, IBM's OS/400 or MVS, or Compaq's VMS, just to name a few. Why NT or its most recent incarnation, Windows Server 2003?

Well, understand when I answer that question that (1) I'm not from Microsoft, (2) I'm not here to sell NT/2000/2003 to you, I'm just here to tell you how to make it work, and (3) the reality of the matter is that every one of the OSes that I just named are good products that have not only their adherents and detractors, but that also have many solid positive features. After decades of business computer use, the market has filtered out both the truly terrible products and some perfectly good but inadequately marketed products, leaving only products that are at least competent (and always well-marketed). So if you want to read that Server 2003 is not only your best choice, but also that you're a total fool to try to use anything else, then I'm afraid you've come to the wrong place. Yes, I like NT, including its latest incarnation (Server 2003), but it's not the only answer.

But it *is* a very good answer. Here's why.

It's the Market Leader

Most stats that I see say that the Microsoft family of operating systems has the largest market share—43 percent of servers according to the last set of numbers that I saw. Being part of the biggest market share means that it's easier to find consultants, support, and third-party tools. Oh, and it *also* means that there's plenty of demand for your services once you become an expert!

Its Familiar GUI Makes It Easier to Get Started

The fact that Windows Server 2003 uses a GUI that is basically the same as Wintendo—oops, I meant Windows 9x/Me—means that hundreds of millions of people already know how to navigate the 2003 Desktop. Yes, some things have been moved around, but in general once you know Windows, you know how to get around on 2003.

In contrast, I have recently done a lot of work with Linux and, while it's a quite powerful operating system, the user interface is *not* for novices; even its multitude of GUIs are still clumsy, although that'll probably change with time. (That's not to say that you shouldn't use Linux—just that I think the Microsoft OSes have an easier-to-use GUI.) With 2003, you can often figure out how to solve a problem by noodling around in the GUI—it lends itself more to exploration than would an operating system that relies mainly upon command-line commands to control it.

Many Tools Come "in the Box"

When NT 3.1 first came out, it was pretty amazing that it came with a dial-in module and a host of other goodies that you had to buy separately in order to run its competition at the time, Novell NetWare. NT had a free TCP/IP stack when many other OSes were charging big bucks for it, a free Web server, and so on. Since then, other server operating systems have continued to include more and more things with the basic operating system—for example, the variety of tools that comes with Linux is nothing short of stunning—but Microsoft has kept the heat on the competition by including a variety of new tools with every release. At this point, the basic version of Server 2003 includes (in addition to its basic functionality of a file and print server) a Web server, an FTP server, a sophisticated Internet router, automated workstation rollout tools (Remote Installation Services), centralized software distribution tools (Group Policies), a two-level disk storage system (Remote Storage Manager), encryption (Encrypted File System), an e-mail server, a SQL-based database server and lots of other tools.

Not all of the tools are stellar; for example, the disk quota system, which allows you to keep any given user from stealing all of the disk space on the shared file servers, is pretty lame. But because Server 2003 provides at least a basic quota functionality, the many shops that are trying to minimize the number of vendors they deal with can get an awful lot of their networking needs met in just one package: Server 2003.

When you view Microsoft products, bear in mind that you usually won't encounter really cutting-edge tools; in my judgment, that's not Microsoft's market niche. Instead, they seem to focus on incrementally improving existing products, as well as adding new tools by imitating competitors. Not being the first on the block can sometimes be a pretty good thing, as you get to watch the competition's mistakes. Very little in Windows Server 2003 is truly never-seen-before-in-the-world new. Instead, it's a distillation of a lot of other people's good ideas. Yes, some may see that as *stealing* other people's good ideas, and there's some merit to that view. And Microsoft has what some might call an unfair advantage in that they've got enough money to keep trying and trying and trying; for example, their first two networking products, MS-NET and LAN Manager, were pretty weak compared to the competition's, but they had the money and tenacity to keep slugging away it, finally releasing the far-better NT product. Another example of this strategy occurred in 2001, with Microsoft's release of the Pocket PC 2002 operating system. They're trying to crush the PalmOS guys in the palmtop market, and they've made two weak attempts with Windows CE 1.0 and 2.0, but they're learning. I don't know if Pocket PC will beat PalmOS—as a long-time Palm user, I tend to think not—but they'll *definitely* steal more of PalmOS's market share with Pocket PC than they ever did with Windows CE.

And while Microsoft's detractors like to paint Microsoft as nothing but a bunch of rip-off artists, it's actually hard to find who *originated* these ideas. Some say that Microsoft stole Novell and Apple's best ideas; well, Novell certainly didn't invent networking, and their IPX/SPX protocol is blatant "theft" of a Xerox protocol. Apple didn't invent the GUI that Microsoft supposedly stole—Xerox did. (Hmmm, maybe there's a pattern here.) Nor is Active Directory a rip-off of an original Novell product, Netware Directory Services—NDS is based on a directory standard called X.500 and terms that many people think that Novell invented, like "organizational unit," are X.500 terms. In any case, it *is* something of a comfort for people to be able to buy a single product that is a decent fit for just about all of their networking needs, instead of looking for the best of breed in each area. Why? Anyone who's ever tried to troubleshoot a multivendor network problem knows why: Both vendors just point the finger at the other vendor and say, "That's him—he's the guy causing your problem." (They're hoping you'll get tired and go away. Most of us do, sadly.)

In contrast, the same people are developing all of 2003's pieces; so you have to believe that at some point *someone* would have noticed if they didn't fit together. Or that if someone didn't notice it *before* they shipped, they'll get around to fixing it afterward.

In sum, why use 2003? It's fairly reliable, it does most of what you want a network operating system to do, it's reasonably priced, and enough other people use it that you're probably not going to go terribly wrong.

A Brief History of NT

Let's finish this chapter with a look at how NT has grown and changed since its early days.

Even in the early 1980s, Bill Gates knew that networking was a key to owning the computer business. So, on April 15, 1985, Microsoft released its first networking product, a tool called MS-NET, and its companion operating system, DOS 3.10. Most people knew about the new DOS and were puzzled at its apparent lack of new features. What it contained, however, were architectural changes to DOS that made it a bit friendlier to the idea of networks.

Now, Microsoft wasn't big enough at that time to create much hoopla about a new network operating system, so they let others sell it—no matter how high or low you looked, you couldn't buy a product called MS-NET. Instead, it sold mainly as an IBM product under the name of the IBM PC Network Support Program; IBM viewed it as little more than some software to go along with their PC Network LAN boards and, later, their Token Ring cards. The server software was DOS-based, offered minimal security, and, to be honest, performed terribly. (Believe me, I *know*; I used to install them for people.) But the software had two main effects on the market.

First, the fact that IBM sold a LAN product legitimized the whole industry. IBM made it possible for others to make a living selling network products. And that led to the second effect: the growth of Novell. Once IBM legitimized the idea of a LAN, most companies responded by going out and getting the LAN operating system that offered the best bang for the buck. That was an easy decision: NetWare. In the early days of networking, Novell established itself as the performance leader. You could effectively serve about twice as many workstations with Novell NetWare as you could with any of the MS-NET products. So Novell prospered.

As time went on, however, Microsoft got better at building network products. 3Com, wanting to offer a product that was compatible with the IBM PC Network software, licensed MS-NET and resold it as their 3+ software. 3Com knew quite a bit about networking, however, and recognized the limitations of MS-NET. So 3Com reworked MS-NET to improve its performance, a fact that didn't escape Microsoft's attention.

From 1985 to 1988, Microsoft worked on their second generation of networking software. The software was based on their OS/2 version 1 operating system. (Remember, Microsoft was the main driving force behind OS/2 from 1985 through early 1990. Steve Ballmer, Microsoft's number two guy, promised publicly in 1988 that Microsoft would "go the distance with OS/2." Hey, the world changes and you've got to change with it, right?) Seeing the good work that 3Com did with MS-NET, Microsoft worked as a partner with 3Com to build the next generation of LAN software. Called Microsoft LAN Manager, this network server software was built atop the more powerful OS/2 operating system. As with the earlier MS-NET, Microsoft's intention was never to directly market LAN Manager. Instead, they envisioned IBM, 3Com, Compaq, and others selling it.

IBM did indeed sell LAN Manager (they still do in the guise of OS/2 LAN Server). 3Com sold LAN Manager for years as 3+Open but found little profit in it and got out of the software business. In late 1990, Compaq announced that they would not sell LAN Manager because it was too complex a product for their dealers to explain, sell, and support. Microsoft decided then that if LAN Manager was to be sold, they'd have to do the selling, so on the very same day as the Compaq withdrawal, they announced that they would begin selling LAN Manager directly.

NOTE   *Interesting side note: Ten years after Compaq decided that their sales force couldn't sell network software, they reversed direction and said that they'd sell a special version of Windows 2000 called Datacenter Server. It's special because you cannot buy it from Microsoft—you must buy it preinstalled on specially certified vendor hardware. In other words, the hardware vendors (Compaq's not the only one selling Datacenter) now believe that they can sell complex network operating systems. I wish them the best of luck, but stay tuned to see the outcome of this particular marketing maneuver!*

LAN Manager in its first incarnation still wasn't half the product that Novell NetWare was, but it was getting there. LAN Manager 2 greatly closed the gap, and in fact, on some benchmarks LAN Manager outpaced Novell NetWare. Additionally, LAN Manager included administrative and security features that brought it even closer to Novell NetWare in the minds of many network managers. Slowly, LAN Manager gained about a 20 percent share of the network market.

When Microsoft designed LAN Manager, however, they designed it for the 286 chip (more accurately, I should say again that LAN Manager was built atop OS/2 1.*x*, and OS/2 1.*x* was built for the 286 chip). LAN Manager's 286 foundation hampered its performance and sales. In contrast, Novell designed their premier products (NetWare 3 and 4) to use the full capabilities of the 386 and later processors. Microsoft's breakup with IBM delayed the release of a 386-based product and, in a sense, Microsoft never released the 386-based product.

Instead of continuing to climb the ladder of Intel processor capabilities, Microsoft decided to build a processor-independent operating system that would sit in roughly the same market position as Unix. It could then be implemented for the 386 and later chips, and it also could run well on other processors, such as the PowerPC, Alpha, and MIPS chips. Microsoft called this new operating system NT, for new technology. Not only would NT serve as a workstation operating system, it would also arrive in a network server version to be called LAN Manager NT. No products ever shipped with that name, but the wallpaper that NT Server displays when no one is logged in is called LANMANNT.BMP to this day.

In August 1993, Microsoft released LAN Manager NT with the name NT Advanced Server. In a shameless marketing move, they labeled it version 3.1 in order to match the version numbers of the Windows desktop products. This first version of NT Advanced Server performed quite well. However, it was memory-hungry, lacked Novell connectivity, and had only the most basic TCP/IP connectivity.

September 1994 brought a new version and a new name: Microsoft Windows NT Server version 3.5. Version 3.5 was mainly a "polish" of 3.1; it was less memory-hungry, it included Novell and TCP/IP connectivity right in the box, and it included Windows for Workgroups versions of the administrative tools so network administrators could work from a Workgroup machine rather than an NT machine. Where many vendors would spend 13 months adding silly bells and whistles, NT 3.5 showed that the Microsoft folks had spent most of their time fine-tuning the operating system, trimming its memory requirements, and speeding it up.

In October 1995 came NT version 3.51, which mainly brought support for PCMCIA cards (a real boon for us traveling instructor types), file compression, and a raft of bug fixes.

NT version 4, 1996's edition of NT, got a newer Windows 95–like face and a bunch of new features, but no really radical networking changes. Under the hood, NT 4 wasn't much different from NT 3.51.

From mid 1996 to early 2000, no new versions of NT appeared, an "upgrade drought" such as we'd not seen in quite some time from Microsoft. Then, in February 2000, Windows 2000 ("NT 5.0") shipped. 2000 included a whole lot of new stuff, but perhaps the most significant was a new way of storing and organizing user accounts and related information: Active Directory domains. Closely following AD in importance was the then-new notion of group policies, something that you'll see has become quite important to anyone wanting to run a network based on XP and Server 2003.

The next version of NT shipped in pieces for the first time since 1993. First NT Workstation 5.1 or, as it's better known, XP Professional and its lesser sibling, XP Home. Microsoft intended to follow up with the server version of NT 5.1, but events conspired to compel them to wait a bit longer, and produce NT Server 5.2—that is, Windows Server 2003. As you read in the last chapter, it's a "1.1" version of Windows 2000, a welcome improvement to 2000's fit and finish.

That's not the end of the story for NT. Sometime in 2004 or 2005, we will see a re-unified NT (5.3? 6.0? Time will tell) code-named Longhorn. *That* in turn will pave the way for yet another version of NT, code-named Blackcomb, but let's wait for another edition or two of this book to cover *that* product.

Well, I hope this chapter wasn't boring for those already expert in NT—I *did* warn you!—and helped bring the newbies up to speed. No matter what version of NT you're running, however, you'll need to configure it. And there are, as there always have been, two main ways to do it. The preferred way is through the GUI with windowed programs that offer help and a bit of error-checking, or its somewhat more complex relatives, the command-line tools. The less-preferred, but often necessary, way is to directly tweak some setting in its lair … a place called the Registry. The next two chapters introduce these two configuration approaches.

Chapter 3

Configuring Windows Server: The Microsoft Management Console

IN WINDOWS 2000 WE saw a significant departure from the NT 4 user interface. Windows Server, however, simply builds on the Windows 2000 interface, with a few enhancements here and there. If you've been working with Windows 2000 for a while now, Server 2003 looks a little different from 2000 at first glance, but don't let the empty Desktop and the new Start menu fool you. Most of your tools are where they were in Windows 2000, and the Microsoft Management Console (MMC) still reigns supreme, with a full array of administrative tools and build-your-own administrator tool capabilities. After a brief detour to make your Desktop more administrator-friendly, we'll take a look at the MMC framework and the prepackaged admin tools. Then you'll learn how to customize a MMC console to fit your needs.

Fixing the Server 2003 GUI

Although the Windows Server GUI isn't all that different from Windows 2000, there are a few annoyances (I mean inconveniences) for those of us who are used to the Windows 2000 UI. For one thing, the Desktop is now empty of My Computer and My Network Places and the ever-present Internet Explorer. Only the Recycle Bin remains. If it weren't for the Start menu and Taskbar, you could be sitting at a Mac. Also, the Start menu has been redesigned, which isn't a bad thing, except for a couple of nuisances. For one, the Run link has been moved from its former home right above the Shut Down and Log Off options to the adjacent column. If, like me, you are accustomed to rapidly launching programs from Start/Run by entering the program file name (for example, Start/Run/CMD or Start/Run/COMPMGMT.MSC), this change can be a little disorienting. Another little nerve plucker is the new Start menu's way of putting links to your most recently used programs right above the place where the Run link used to be. Even worse, the list keeps changing as you work.

Overall, the changes to the UI are for the better. Several NT 4 applets that were missing from Control Panel in Windows 2000 have reappeared, though sometimes with different names. The Start menu has been redesigned to make it easy to access your most commonly used programs. The empty Desktop acknowledges that users want to customize their Desktops to fit their own requirements and work style. However, this user wants My Computer and My Network Places and Internet Explorer on the Desktop so I can right-click and get to my destination with as little navigation as possible. This user has decided to stick with the new Start menu, but many admins would rather have the classic Start menu back, at least in the beginning. So the first thing you may want to do is restore those icons to your Desktop and change back to the classic Start menu.

Restoring your Desktop Icons and Start Menu

To restore the My Computer and My Network Places icons to your Desktop, right-click the Desktop and choose Properties, or click the Start menu, slide over to the Control Panel, and click Display when Control Panel expands. Go to the Desktop tab (take a moment to check out the lovely new background pictures), and click Customize Desktop at the bottom left (see Figure 3.1).

FIGURE 3.1

The Desktop tab in the Display applet

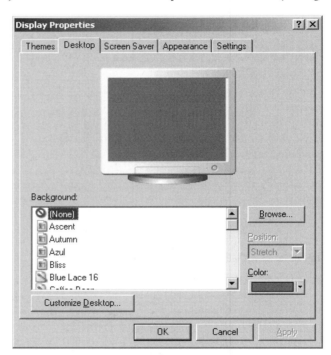

To show My Computer and My Network Places on your Desktop, check the boxes next to those items in the Desktop Items window (shown in Figure 3.2) and click OK. You can also choose to display My Documents and Internet Explorer on your Desktop.

To change the Start menu back to the Windows 2000 style, right-click the Start menu and choose Properties. Alternately, you can right-click the Taskbar and choose Properties, then go to the Start Menu tab. Choose the radio button for the Classic Start Menu (see Figure 3.3) and click OK.

NOTE If you configure your Display applet to show My Computer on the Desktop, you can still right-click it and choose Manage, which launches the Computer Management Tool, or choose Properties to access System Properties. Likewise, after putting it back on the Desktop, right-click My Network Places and choose Properties to launch the Network Connections applet.

FIGURE 3.2

Customize your
Desktop items.

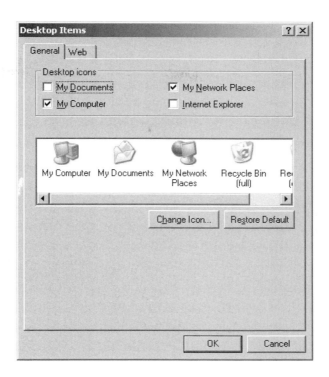

FIGURE 3.3

The Start Menu
Properties tab

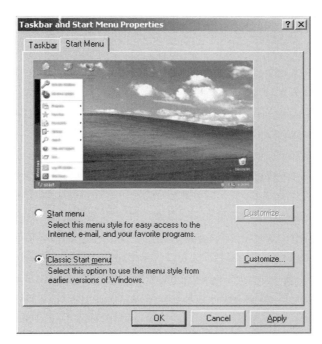

Finally, if you like the new Start menu in general, but don't like every little thing about it, you may be able fix it to suit you. Just click the corresponding Customize button in the Taskbar and Start Menu Properties applet to see your options. For instance, many items on the new Start menu can be configured to act either as menus (they expand when you hover your mouse over them) or links (they open in a new window when you click them) or to not display at all.

Setting Administrator-Friendly Folder Options

For administrators, the default folder options for Explorer can also be annoying. The context-sensitive task links that appear on the left side of every window may be helpful to newbies, but they are just a waste of space to me. Additionally, whenever I want to go do some maintenance in the Program Files or System directories, I've got to click past patronizing user-proofing screens that essentially say, "Hey, look, buddy, you're probably too stupid to mess with these files, are you *sure* you want to see this directory?" I need to see the hidden and system files, and in general, Details view is best for maintenance operations. Additionally, I've never found the address bar or standard buttons of much value in administrative tasks; they just rob me of screen space.

The first thing that I must do, then, when faced with a new system is to get Explorer into "administrator-friendly" mode. To save you time, here are the steps:

1. Open My Computer.
2. From its menu bar, choose Tools/Folder Options.
3. In the General tab, under Tasks, choose Use Windows Classic Folders.
4. Click the View tab.
5. Check the box labeled Display the Full Path in the Title Bar.
6. Click the radio button labeled Show Hidden Files and Folders.
7. Uncheck the box labeled Hide File Extensions for Known File Types.
8. Uncheck the box labeled Hide Protected Operating System Files (Recommended) and click Yes when it asks you to confirm your choice.
9. Click OK.
10. Back in the main My Computer folder, click View/Details.
11. Right-click any blank space to the right of the menu bar and uncheck Standard Buttons.
12. Right-click any blank space to the right of the menu bar and uncheck Address Bar.
13. Click the close icon on the My Computer window—the icon in the upper right corner that looks like an X.

Now reopen My Computer and apply those settings to all folders:

1. Click Tools/Folder Options.
2. Click the View tab.
3. Click the button toward the top of the page labeled Apply to All Folders.
4. Click Yes to confirm the message.

5. Click OK to close Folder Options.

6. Close My Computer.

Without all those empty calories, Explorer is now a lean, mean administrator's machine. To make it even leaner, you can navigate to individual folders and select Choose Details from the View menu to add or remove the details you want to see for that folder. For example, you might want to see the file system types for each logical drive in My Computer, or you might not want to see the lengthy service descriptions in the Control Panel.

A Microsoft Management Console Primer

To master Windows Server administration, you must master the Microsoft Management Console. In this section, I'll discuss the key MMC terms you should know, briefly look at the Computer Management console to illustrate these terms, and, finally, introduce you to creating your own MMC-based administrative tools.

What Is This MMC Thing?

Before Windows 2000 came onto the scene, NT administrators had to master multiple administration tools plus independent third-party tools. With all the different menus, buttons, toolbars, wizards, tabs, HTML, Java (you get the picture), mastering a new tool's concepts took second place to learning how to navigate the software. NT Administrative software also lacked granularity. There was no simplified version of User Manager for Domains for Account Operators to use, and no way to hide sensitive menu items for those without full administrator rights. Administrative folks would typically install the full set of NT administrator tools on their workstations, whether they needed them all or not; if administrators failed to guard access to their desktops, or if regular users were permitted to log on to these administrative workstations, then anyone with the ability and knowledge could gain access to the entire range of management tools—not smart.

The Microsoft Management Console (MMC) was designed to overcome these limitations and accommodate the requirements of today's increasingly complex networks.

MMC is a framework for management applications, offering a unified administrative interface for Microsoft and third-party management tools. MMC doesn't replace management applications; it integrates them into one single interface. There are no inherent management functions in MMC at all. It uses component tools called *snap-ins*, which do all the work. MMC provides a user interface; it doesn't change how the snap-ins function.

MMC KEY BENEFITS

MMC offers the following benefits:

- ◆ You only have to learn one interface to drive a whole mess of tools.

- ◆ Third-party (ISV) tools are now using MMC snap-ins. IBM, HP, Seagate, and Symantec are all using the MMC framework to build admin tools for their products.

- ◆ You can build your own consoles, which is practical and fun. Admins can even create shortcuts on the console to non-MMC tools like executables, URLs, wizards, and scripts.

◆ By customizing MMC consoles, admins can delegate tasks to underlings without giving them access to all functions and without confusing them with a big scary tool.

◆ Help in MMC is context sensitive; it displays help subjects for only the appropriate components.

WHAT'S NEW WITH MMC?

If you've been using MMC-based tools for a while now, you'll notice a few minor changes in the new version (MMC 2 version 5.2). Many of these are enhancements to the Active Directory management tools:

◆ In all of the console tools, the Console menu is now renamed the File menu, which makes good sense and is consistent with other Microsoft tools.

◆ MMC snap-ins now have "drag-and-drop" capabilities. You'll notice this most in the Active Directory tools if you need to move user, group or system accounts from one organizational unit to another.

◆ You can now select multiple objects and perform the same operation on them or edit the properties for them all. This enhancement is long overdue, in my opinion.

◆ In the Active Directory Users and Computers snap-in, the ability to save and re-use queries simplifies documentation and reporting as well as preparations for complex operations like upgrades or restructuring the Active Directory.

◆ In addition to editing multiple objects, you can now reset access control list (ACL) permissions to the default, show the effective permissions for an object, and show the parent of an inherited permission.

WHAT *CAN'T* YOU DO WITH MMC (NON-MMC TOOLS)?

When I said that MMC offers a unified interface for administration, I didn't mean that all administrative tools in Server 2003 are MMC-based. Many system-level functions are accessed using wizards, hypertext applications like Manage Your Server, or plain old executables. In general, you will use a wizard or hypertext app to add or remove new software and services or to set system-level options locally. Then, once a new service (DNS, Remote Access, DHCP, Active Directory) is installed, you can use an MMC tool to remotely configure it and monitor its activity. Let's also not forget all the new command-line tools that Microsoft has written for Server 2003. On the other hand, because MMC tools can be created and customized, you can integrate non-MMC apps into the MMC interface by creating links to them in your custom tools. In "Building Your Own MMC Tools," you'll do just that.

MMC Terms to Know

This section defines important terms you'll need to know when working with MMC.

A *console*, in MMC-speak, is made up of one or more administrative tools in an MMC framework. The admin tools that are included with Server 2003, like Active Directory Users and Computers, are console files. You can configure your own console files without any programming tools—you needn't be a C or Visual Basic programmer, as I'll discuss a bit later. The saved console file is a *Microsoft saved console (MSC)* file and it carries the .MSC extension.

It's important to distinguish between the Microsoft Management Console and console tools. The terms *console* and *tool* are sometimes used interchangeably when discussing MMC. Strictly speaking though, a console is not a tool, and as I pointed out in the previous section, not all tools are consoles. MMC.EXE is a program that presents administrators (and others creating console tools) with a blank console to work with. When you create a Microsoft Word document, you first load the program (WINWORD.EXE), then create or modify documents within that context. Similarly, you create MMC tools by first loading a blank console (MMC.EXE) and then creating a customized "document" based on the available options and add-ins. In this way, MMC provides a framework for your tool, and the new console you create is the finished product.

Snap-ins (also called *plug-ins*) are the administrative tools that can be added to the console. For example, the DHCP admin tool is a snap-in, and so is the Disk Defragmenter. Snap-ins can be created by Microsoft or by other software vendors. (You *do* need programming skills to make these, in other words.) A snap-in can contain subcomponents called *nodes*, or *containers*, or even *leaves*, in some cases. Although you can load multiple snap-ins in a single console, most of the prepackaged administrative tools contain only a single snap-in (including the Computer Management tool, COMPMGMT.MSC).

An *extension* is basically a snap-in that can't live by itself on the console but depends on a stand-alone snap-in. It adds some type of functionality to a snap-in. Sometimes the same code is implemented as both a snap-in and an extension. For example, the Event Viewer is a stand-alone snap-in, but it's also implemented as an extension to the Computer Management snap-in. The key point is that extensions are optional. You can choose not to load them. For example, Local Users and Groups is an extension to the Computer Management snap-in. If you remove the extension from the COMPMGMT.MSC file used by your support folk, or simply don't include it in a custom console that uses the snap-in, those who use the tool won't have the option to create or manage users and groups with the tool. They won't even see it. (Please note that this will not prevent them from creating users and groups by other means, if they have the correct administrative privileges.)

To create a new MSC file, customize an existing MSC file or create one from a blank console. The MMC.EXE plus the defined snap-ins, views and custom tasks create the tool interface. Although it's possible to open multiple tools simultaneously, each one runs in a single instance of the MMC.EXE process. To see what I mean, open an MSC file and check out the Task Manager while it's running— you only see the MMC.EXE process running, not the MSC file, just as you see WINWORD.EXE running in Task Manager, but not the Word document's name. However, you can open separate *nodes* in separate windows within the tool. You could have separate windows open to the Event Viewer and the Device Manager within the same tool, for instance.

By default, prepackaged console tools open in *User mode*. Changes cannot be made to the console design. You can't add or remove snap-ins, for example. To create or customize a console, use *Author mode*. When a user is running a tool and not configuring it, it should be running in one of the User modes. When a tool is running in Author mode, additional items will appear on the File and Action menus. Also, the Favorites menu doesn't appear in User mode consoles. Favorites can only be configured in Author mode.

Figure 3.4 shows a sample console tool, with the parts of the interface labeled. This console is running in Author mode to show all the parts of the MMC interface. This is a custom console, but to open any existing tool in Author mode, invoke it from the Start/Run dialog box with the **/a** switch. Alternately, right-click the tool's icon and choose Author to open it in Author mode. This does work with the links to tools in the Administrative Tools group, but remember not to overwrite the original file!

FIGURE 3.4

Anatomy of a console tool

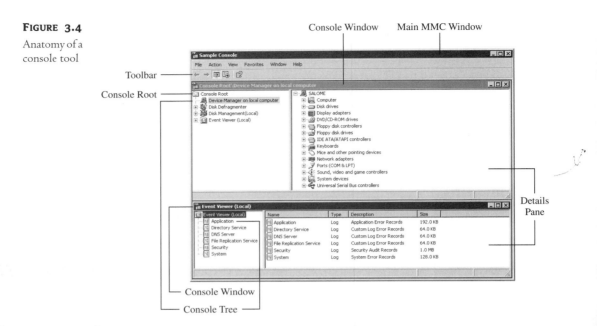

In addition to its traditional functions (New, Open, Save, Save As) the File menu in the Main window is used to add and remove snap-ins and set console options. The Action menu and the Toolbar are context sensitive and will reflect the options of the selected snap-in tool or component. The Favorites menu functions like the Favorites menu in Explorer; however it stores only links to locations in the console tree.

The hierarchical list of items shown by default in the left pane is called the *console tree*, and at the top is the *console root*. The right pane is called the *details pane*. Snap-ins appear as nodes on the console tree. The contents of the details pane change with the item selected on the console tree.

The Computer Management Console

Now it's time to practice the new MMC terms you've learned as we take a look at the Computer Management console. COMPMGMT.MSC is *the* main tool for administering a single server, local or remote. If you only have one or two Server 2003 servers on your network (and are not implementing Active Directory), the Computer Management console contains most of the tools you'll need. You'll find Computer Management in the Administrative Tools program group, or right-click My Computer on the Start menu and choose Manage.

USING COMPUTER MANAGEMENT REMOTELY

There are several ways to use COMPMGMT.MSC to manage remote servers on your network:

◆ Run COMPMGMT.MSC with the switch /COMPUTER=*COMPUTERNAME*.

◆ If you are working in an Active Directory context, within Active Directory Users and Computers, right-click the machine's icon and choose Manage.

Continued on next page

USING COMPUTER MANAGEMENT REMOTELY *(continued)*

◆ Open Computer Manager and highlight Computer Management (local) at the root of the console, then right-click and choose Connect to Another Computer.

◆ If you are creating a custom console that includes the Computer Management snap-in, specify the remote server the tool will point to when you add the snap-in, or check the box that allows you to specify the remote computer at the command line, as described in the first option.

There are three nodes in the Computer Management console tree: System Tools, Storage, and Services and Applications (see Figure 3.5). Notice that the tool manages the local machine by default; to connect to other computers on the network, highlight the Computer Management icon at the root of the tree, right-click, and choose Connect to Another Computer. You can also choose Connect to Another Computer from the Action menu, but right-clicking an object in the console tree reveals both the Action and View menu options, so it's more efficient.

FIGURE 3.5

The Computer Management console tree

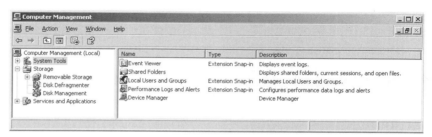

Expand the nodes in the Computer Management console tree to reveal the configuration tools and objects, as shown in Figure 3.6. Most of the core functions are under System Tools.

FIGURE 3.6

The expanded Computer Management console tree

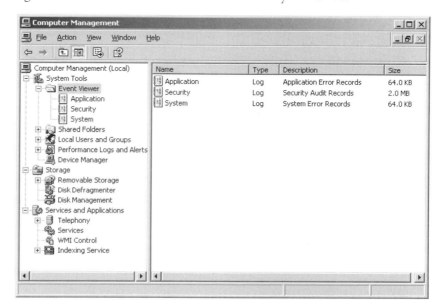

NOTE   To manage NT 4 or Windows 98 boxes remotely with COMPMGMT.MSC, *install the Windows Management Instrumentation (WMI) Version 1.5 Core Components on the legacy system. This is available as a download (*WMICORE.EXE*) from Microsoft's Web site. The WMI add-on component is available for Windows 9x and NT 4. Windows Me, 2000, and XP include WMI.*

In the System Tools node, you can perform the following tasks:

◆ View events and manage the event logs. The Event Viewer is available as a snap-in, an extension to the Computer Management tool (as shown here), or as a stand-alone prepackaged tool (EVENTVWR.MSC). Some services, such as DNS and Active Directory, have their own logs and these will appear in the details pane if the service is installed on the system.

◆ Manage shared folders. View, create, and manage shares; view sessions and open files; and disconnect sessions.

◆ Create and manage local users and groups (Chapter 9 is all about creating and managing users and groups). If the system is a domain controller running Active Directory, however, the local users and groups extension will not load.

◆ Set up performance logs and alerts (see Chapter 18 for specifics on configuring performance alerts).

◆ Manage devices. This version of Device Manager functions in read-only mode when it's looking at remote systems, but it's still a good resource if you want an overview of the remote system's hardware or are troubleshooting a resource conflict.

TIP   For a better (but still read-only) look at a remote system's hardware and software configuration information, run MSINFO32.EXE. *This little tool is powerful and includes options to run a search, view a history of changes, print out system information, or export the data to a file.*

The Storage node includes options for managing removable storage (CD-ROMs and CD Jukeboxes, for example), along with the Disk Defragmenter tool and the Disk Management tool for managing disks, partitions, and volumes. The Logical Drives extension that was present in the Windows 2000 version of this tool is gone now.

The Services and Applications node includes, at a minimum, telephony settings, services configuration, and an indexing extension. As new services are installed on the system, the components available in the Services and Applications node will change. For instance, if the server is a DHCP server or is running DNS, the appropriate management tools will appear under Services and Applications—otherwise, you won't see them. I'm quite fond of this feature; when I'm checking out a server for the first time, I can determine what key services are installed on the system and look at the configuration for those services using the same tool.

Other MMC Tools

If you're like me, you don't want to get carpal tunnel syndrome just trying to open something from the Administrative Tools group. If you want to have quick and easy access to your tools, and you prefer to use Start/Run as much as possible to open programs, it's nice to know their filenames. To save your hands and your sanity, Table 3.1 lists most of the core MSC filenames. Keep in mind that some tools, like DNS and DHCP, may not be available on the system until the corresponding service is installed. Also, remember to include the program extension in the Start/Run box. For example, entering just **DSA** to open Active Directory Users & Computers doesn't work. You'll need to enter **DSA.MSC**.

TABLE 3.1: CORE MSC FILES

MSC FILENAME	COMMON NAME
AZMAN.MSC	Authorization Manager
CERTMGR.MSC	Certificates snap-in
CERTSRV.MSC	Certificate Services
CERTTMPL.MSC	Certificate Templates
CIADV.MSC	Indexing Service
COMPMGMT.MSC	Computer Management
DCPOL.MSC	Domain Controller Security Policy
DEVMGMT.MSC	Device Manager
DFRG.MSC	Disk Defragmenter
DFSGUI.MSC	Distributed File System
DHCPMGMT.MSC	DHCP Manager
DISKMGMT.MSC	Disk Management
DNSMGMT.MSC	DNS Manager
DOMAIN.MSC	Active Directory Domains & Trusts
DOMPOL.MSC	Domain Security Policy
DSA.MSC	Active Directory Users & Computers
DSSITE.MSC	Active Directory Sites & Services
EVENTVWR.MSC	Event Viewer
FXSADMIN.MSC	Fax Service Manager
FILESVR.MSC	File Server Management
FSMGMT.MSC	Shared Folders
GPEDIT.MSC	Group Policy Editor
IAS.MSC	Internet Authentication Service
IIS.MSC	Internet Information Services

Continued on next page

TABLE 3.1: CORE MSC FILES *(continued)*

MSC FILENAME	COMMON NAME
LUSRMGR.MSC	Local Users and Groups
NTMSMGR.MSC	Removable Storage Manager
NTMSOPRQ.MSC	Removable Storage Operator Requests
PERFMON.MSC	Performance Monitor
RRASMGMT.MSC	Routing and Remote Access
RSOP.MSC	Resultant Set of Policy
SECPOL.MSC	Local Security Policy
SERVICES.MSC	Services Configuration
TAPIMGMT.MSC	Telephony
TSCC.MSC	Terminal Services
TSMMC.MSC	Remote Desktops
WMIMGMT.MSC	Windows Management Instrumentation

Most of the tools listed in Table 3.1 are found in the \Windows\system32 directory and are therefore in the default search path; you'll have no problem running them from a command line or using Start/Run. A couple, however, are found in other directories that are not included in the default search path. The tool to manage Internet Information Services (IIS.MSC) is a good example; it's found in \Windows\system32\inetsrv. If you need to run any of these tools on a regular basis, and they aren't in your search path and you still don't want to use the Start menu (we admins can be stubborn), you have several options to make these tools more readily accessible. You can copy the tool(s) to the \Windows\system32 directory; or if you don't mind a cluttered Desktop, just create Desktop shortcuts to the tools. Another approach is to change the search path to include the directories that contain your tools. This is a bit more of a pain; you'll need to open the System applet and go to the Advanced tab, then choose the Environmental Variables button to edit the system variable called Path. Oh, yes, and then reboot. Is it worth it? Many don't think so. In the past, I used this strategy: I copied all the tools I needed to a separate directory, and then added *that* directory to the search path. That way I didn't have to edit the path variable multiple times.

You may think this is a lot of trouble just to use a couple of tools, but after you install a bunch of third-party tools on your server you may change your mind. They'll probably all use their own installation directories.

Building Your Own MMC Tools

If the existing MMC tools don't fit your needs exactly, you can create a customized tool with your most frequently used components. Creating your own admin tool is easy using the MMC framework and snap-ins provided by Microsoft and third-party software vendors.

Although it's quite simple to create a customized MMC tool, there are so many options for customizing that I can't tell the full story here. Nevertheless, no discussion of MMC would be complete without an example or two of authoring administration tools.

Building a Simple Microsoft Saved Console

To configure your own custom admin tool, open a blank MMC in Author mode by opening Start/Run and typing **mmc.exe**. This will open up an untitled console (Console1) and display a generic console root, shown in Figure 3.7. You can now open existing MSC files (just as you open DOC files in Word or XLS files in Excel) by choosing Open from the File menu. These files will automatically open in Author mode if you open them in a blank console. If you wish to open and fiddle with existing MSC files, most (but not all) of them are in the \Windows\system32 directory. Just be sure to leave the original MSC files intact; you might need them again. In the example that follows, you'll be creating a tool from scratch, starting with a blank console and loading snap-ins.

FIGURE 3.7

A generic
console root

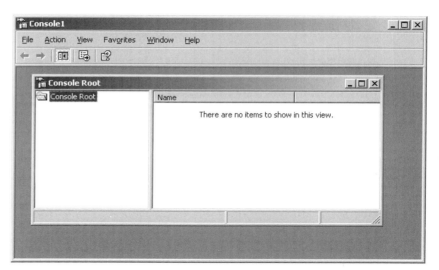

Suppose you need a tool for hardware management and troubleshooting. To create it, follow these steps:

1. Start by renaming the console root Hardware Tools; right-click the console root and choose Rename (you can perform this step later if you prefer).

2. Now you're ready to add snap-ins. Choose Add/Remove Snap-in from the File menu in the Main window. As you can see in Figure 3.8, you must choose where to add the snap-in. Right now, it's only possible to add snap-ins to the console root (now called Hardware Tools), but you can group related tools by first adding folders to the console root. Folders are implemented as snap-ins, permitting you to organize tools into groups on the console tree.

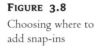

Choosing where to
add snap-ins

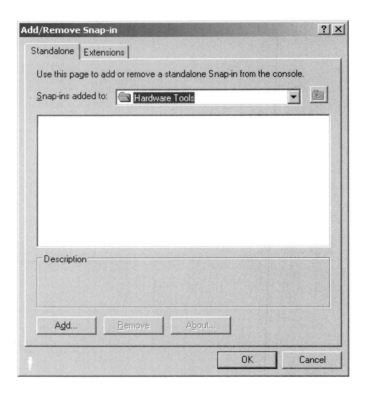

3. To add folders to the console root, choose the Add button to open the Add Standalone Snap-In dialog box (see Figure 3.9). You'll now see both dialog boxes, sort of cascaded. Items chosen from the list in the Add Standalone Snap-In dialog box will appear in the list of snap-ins in the parent dialog box. Scroll through the list until you see the Folder snap-in. Choose Add, and the folder appears in your list of snap-ins in the Add/Remove Snap-In dialog box. Choose Add again and you'll see two. Now close the Add Standalone Snap-In dialog box to return to Add/Remove Snap-In, and click OK to close it.

4. Back at the console in progress, right-click the folders to rename them. Figure 3.10 shows a Hardware Tools console with three folders, renamed to Disk Tools, Other Tools, and Web Sites.

5. The Web Sites folder will contain snap-ins that are hyperlinks to hardware vendor and support sites. To add links to the Web Sites container, open the Add/Remove Snap-In dialog again (choose Add/Remove Snap-In from the File menu), select the Web Sites folder as the container, choose Add, then scroll through the list until you find Link to Web Address. Click the Add button, and follow the wizard prompts to create a new Internet shortcut; simply fill in the URL and give the shortcut a friendly name. Choose Close and then OK to close the Add/Remove Snap-In page and return to the console. Now when you select the link in the console tree, the Web page will appear within the details pane. You can surf

the Web from within the console, although technically you'll need links to leave that particular site.

FIGURE 3.9

The Add Standalone
Snap-In dialog box

FIGURE 3.10

Customizing
the console

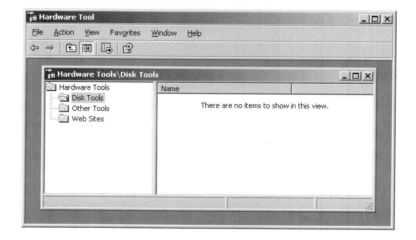

To add tools to the other folders, follow the same process and choose the appropriate tools from the list of snap-ins available. Some third-party software vendors are now implementing their tools as snap-ins, so this list will expand and vary with the system configuration and software installed. Some tools will prompt you to select a computer to manage. Others, such as the Event Viewer snap-in, also present the option to choose the machine when you start the tool from the command line, as shown in Figure 3.11. To specify a remote system to manage when you open the tool, enter ***FILENAME*.MSC** **/computer=*computername*** in the Start/Run box or at a command prompt.

FIGURE 3.11

Selecting a computer for the snap-in to manage

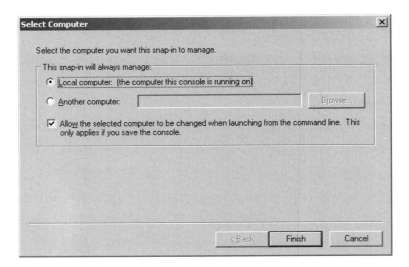

While adding the stand-alone snap-ins, be sure to check out the available extensions for them. It's interesting to note that the Computer Management snap-in components are all implemented as extensions (see Figure 3.12), although most of these also exist as stand-alone snap-ins. When loading the Computer Management snap-in, you have the option to deselect the extensions that aren't needed for your custom tool. All available extensions are added by default.

FIGURE 3.12

Select or deselect extensions

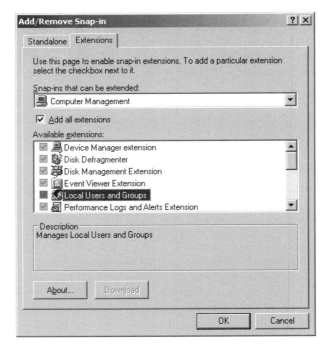

In Figure 3.13, you can see what your final tool could look like: a customized Hardware Tools console. This one consists of a `Disk Tools` folder (with Defragmenter and Disk Management), a folder called `Other Tools` that includes the Device Manager and the Event Viewer, and a `Web Sites` folder that can be filled with helpful hardware support links.

To save the custom console, choose Save from the File menu, name the file and click Save. Now the MSC file is ready to use.

FIGURE 3.13

A custom Hardware Tools console

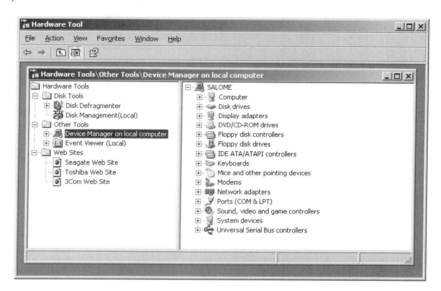

Designing Tools with Taskpad Views

It's possible to design simple views of an MMC tool for junior administrators, foregoing their need to learn the different tools and navigate the console tree nodes. You might also wish to present a limited set of tasks and hide others that are normally available in a regular MMC tool view. Taskpad views fill this need and allow you to create a tool that looks like the one shown in Figure 3.14. This tool presents a limited set of tasks instead of the entire console tree structure. Now novice administrators can perform delegated tasks without drilling down through the tree, expanding and collapsing, hoping to find the right tool. Instead, they can click the icon and go right to the task.

Taskpad views are HTML-based pages that can include links to console menu commands, wizards, scripts, simple executables, even URLs. At least one snap-in is required to create a taskpad view, although you can create links to tasks that are unrelated to the snap-in, such as scripts. To include menu command and property page tasks, however, the corresponding snap-in must be loaded beforehand.

Before designing a console with taskpad views, or any type of console for that matter, put your thinking cap on and visualize the tool you need. What tasks will the tool include? Which snap-ins will be required? You'll need to be somewhat familiar with the available snap-ins and their functions. Will your tool include only one taskpad view with a bunch of tasks in a single window? Or do you need a tool with several tabs, each containing a set of related tasks? Figure 3.14 shows a tool with only one taskpad view; tasks are all together in one window, and the console tree is hidden from the user. Figure 3.15 illustrates a multiple taskpad tool with several different tabs, perhaps for a more experienced support person who needs to perform several different types of tasks.

FIGURE 3.14

A simple taskpad tool

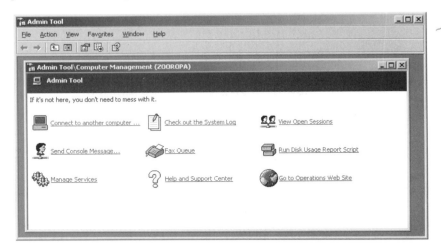

FIGURE 3.15

A multiple taskpad tool

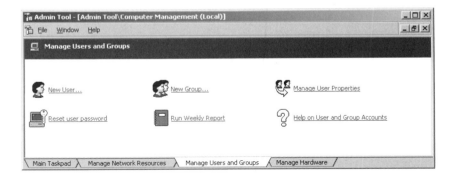

There are a couple of possible strategies for creating taskpad views. One is to assemble a specific set of tasks into one or more taskpad views. For example, when the tool is opened, you might see a single taskpad view called Routine Admin Tasks with links labeled Create New User or Create New Share. If you click the link called Create New User, the dialog box or wizard to create new users appears. In a tool like this, you might want to prevent users from navigating around, so you hide the console tree and present only the taskpad view.

Another technique is to create taskpad views for particular items in the tree; for example, a taskpad for Users and Groups, another for Shared Folders, and a third for the Event Viewer. Again, you might choose to hide the actual console tree and normal views for this tool. In that case, you should create a main taskpad with links to other taskpads located at different branches of the tree. Imagine a taskpad view called Main Taskpad, which contains links called Open Services and Manage IIS. Click the former and another taskpad appears, with a list of services and links to stop, start, or restart a service. You can use the Forward and Back buttons on the toolbar (as you do in Explorer) to return to the Main Taskpad view.

Alternately, you might choose to present these taskpad views in addition to the normal views without hiding the console tree. In this case, the taskpad will enhance the functionality of the console tool by presenting a set of simple task options (for people who don't like playing Marco Polo in admin tools) without imposing any limitations on what the user can see or access.

Whichever approach you choose, keep in mind that taskpad views are meant to simplify and facilitate the use of a console. They can even limit, to some extent, the administrative options that are presented. However, you should not consider them a foolproof way to prevent admin types from performing certain tasks. Even if they can't get around the limitations of the custom console, which is by no means certain, they may have access to other tools that are not restricted. The best way to restrict another admin's power is to use all of the other built-in security options that are available in appropriate combinations: security group memberships, rights, group policies, and delegation are some of the more reliable tools for this purpose. Don't rely on a customized, locked-down console tool instead.

In this section, you will create a Main Taskpad view for the Computer Management snap-in and then create links to tasks. Then you will set up taskpad views for particular items in the console tree, with links from the Main Taskpad. Finally, you will customize the tool's interface to hide the console tree and present a simplified set of options to the user.

CREATING TASKPAD VIEWS

Once you've decided which tasks your user or admin person will perform with this tool and identified the necessary snap-ins, you are ready to create the console. To keep things simple in this example, use the Computer Management snap-in to create a view and a select set of tasks.

Open a blank console as described earlier (Start/Run and enter `mmc.exe`) and load the Computer Management snap-in. You can also use an existing console that contains the necessary snap-in as long as you open it in Author mode. Although many of the Computer Management extensions, such as the Event Viewer and Device Manager, can be added as standalone snap-ins, the Computer Management snap-in has a special capability that will facilitate remote management, as you'll see in a moment. As you load the snap-in you may want to point it to your file server and select the option to specify a server to manage when starting the tool from the command link (this option was shown back in Figure 3.11). If you choose not to do this, you can still connect to remote systems, but the tool will always point to the local computer when it initiates.

To create a taskpad view at the top of the Computer Management node, follow these steps:

1. Select the Computer Management node in the console tree, right-click it to see a context menu (or pull down the Action menu), and choose New Taskpad View. You will always add, delete or modify taskpad views by first navigating to the node in the console tree where the taskpad is anchored. For instance, if you have a taskpad view created for the Event Viewer, select the Event Viewer node on the tree (the taskpad will display when the node is selected) and then select your option from the context menu or the Action menu.

2. The New Taskpad View Wizard appears. Click Next to continue.

3. Select the style of the taskpad view (see Figure 3.16). Do you want the Taskpad View to also display the actual items that would normally appear in the details pane (such as a list of

users or a list of services)? If so, choose to display either a vertical list (to accommodate lots of columns) or a horizontal list (for longer lists). In this case, you want to create a view of links and don't want to see the details pane information, so choose No List. If you were to choose a list type, however, you would use the List Size drop-down menu to determine how much of the window can be taken up by the list. By default, the "normal" details pane will not be accessible to the viewer once the Taskpad View is created. However, if you want to make the normal details pane available, deselect the option Hide Standard Tab. The standard details pane will then be viewable by clicking the Standard tab. Now, select the style you want for your task descriptions. If you need a longer explanation to appear alongside the link, choose Text. However, for this example you want more room for task links and a description that pops up when you hover over the link, so choose InfoTip. Choose Next to continue.

FIGURE 3.16

Configuring taskpad display

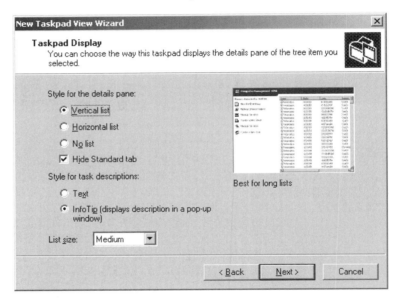

4. In the next screen (Figure 3.17), you must decide whether to apply the view to the selected tree item only or to any other tree item of the same type. If you choose the latter, you have the option to change the default details pane display for those items to the taskpad view (although the normal view will still be accessible through the Standard tab if it's not hidden). Choose to apply the view only to the selected tree item. This taskpad view will only display when the Computer Management root node is selected. Choose Next.

5. The final step is to supply a name for your taskpad (I called mine Main Taskpad) and an optional description. The description you supply will appear under the title in the details pane. That's it! In the final screen of the wizard, you have the option to kick off the New Task Wizard and start creating tasks (uncheck the box beside Start New Task Wizard to avoid creating a new task for now). Click Finish to close the wizard and create the new taskpad view.

FIGURE 3.17

Selecting a taskpad target

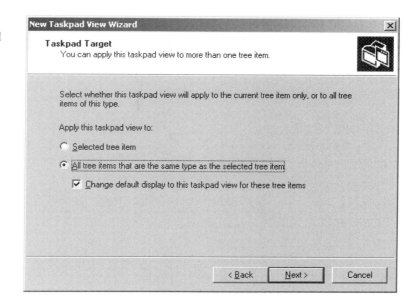

Figure 3.18 shows your new taskpad before any tasks are created. Notice the tabs at the bottom of the details pane that allow you to move between the taskpad view and the standard view of the details pane. In a moment, I'll show you how to hide the console tree on the left and remove the Standard view tab to achieve the look and feel of the console shown back in Figure 3.14.

FIGURE 3.18

A console with a taskpad view

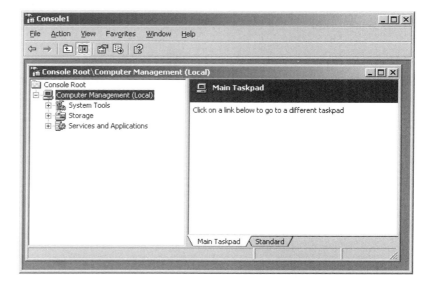

If you want to create multiple taskpad views, as shown in Figure 3.15, follow steps 1–5 again. You can create additional taskpad views at the same place on the console tree or at other points on the tree. To create a taskpad view for Event Viewer, for example, just navigate down to that node and create the taskpad from there.

To remove a taskpad view, select it and choose Delete Taskpad View from the context menu or from the Action menu. Be aware that wherever you have multiple taskpads anchored at the same place on the console tree, you must select the target taskpad's tab before you can delete or edit it. To make changes to an existing taskpad, select Edit Taskpad View from the context menu or from the Action menu. In the taskpad view property page (Figure 3.19), you can change the style of the view and add, remove, or modify tasks.

FIGURE 3.19

The taskpad property page

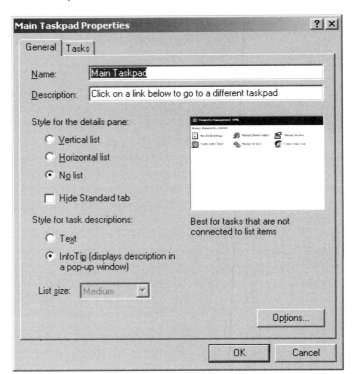

CREATING TASKS

The New Taskpad View Wizard will automatically kick off the Start New Task Wizard if you don't uncheck the box in the last screen of the wizard. Another way to create tasks is by choosing Edit Taskpad View from the Action menu. From the taskpad properties page (shown in Figure 3.19), move to the Tasks tab and click New to start the New Task Wizard. The following steps illustrate how to create a task link for the Connect to Another Computer command:

1. In the New Task Wizard, click Next to begin creating a new task. Click a radio button to choose whether the task will be a menu command (from the context or Action menu in the

console), a shell command, or a navigation command, which points to a link in the Favorites tab (see Figure 3.20). Although menu commands are limited to the functions of a loaded snap-in, a shell command could be an executable (like a wizard), a script, or even a URL. In any of these cases, the shell command task kicks off the command called. So think of it as a shortcut or a link to something outside of the tool. For example, you can create a shell command task to open a related Help (CHM) file or to run a disk usage report script. You'll create a menu command in this example, but if you choose to create a shell command at another time, you'll need to specify the path to the command and any command-line parameters (also called *switches* or *arguments*), the "start in" directory, and whether the command should run in a normal window, minimized, or maximized. Figure 3.21 shows the command-line task dialog box.

FIGURE 3.20

Creating a new task

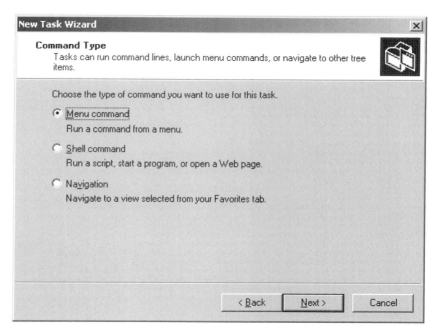

TIP One really neat feature of the shell command task is that little right arrow you see beside the parameters option in Figure 3.21. Some snap-ins and extensions support passing variable values to scripts. To see the variables you can use in that context, click the right arrow. Highlight one of the variables to add it to the list of command-line parameters.

NOTE In contrast to shell command tasks, which refer to commands outside the tool, navigation command tasks are shortcuts to places within the console. For instance, if you want a shortcut to the Disk Defragmenter, find and select it on the console tree, then add it to the tool's favorites (just choose Add to Favorites from the Favorites menu). Then, when you create your navigation task, choose the Disk Defragmenter from the list of existing favorites. Once the shortcut is created, clicking the task icon opens the Disk Defragmenter tool.

FIGURE 3.21

Creating a shell
command task

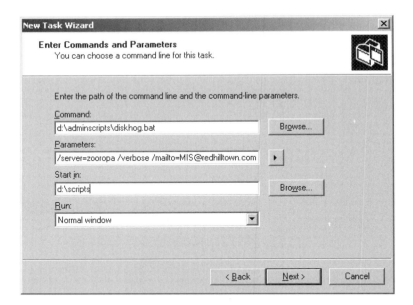

2. After choosing to create a menu command, select a source for the command in the next screen
(see Figure 3.22) and choose a command from those available on the right. You can choose
whether the source of the command will be an item in the details pane or a specific item in
the console tree. In this case, you are creating the latter, a tree item task. Now you'll see the
Computer Management node in the left pane, and Connect to Another Computer is among
the available commands on the right. Highlight Connect to Another Computer and click Next.

FIGURE 3.22

Selecting a menu
command

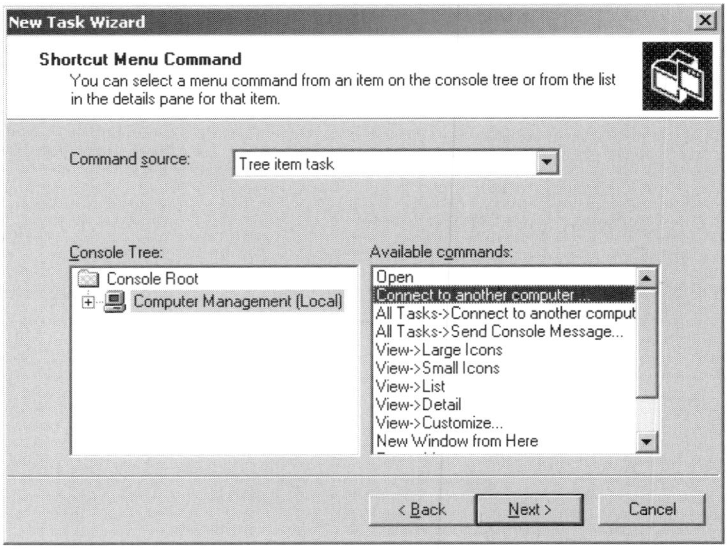

3. Give the task a name and a description. The description you supply will either appear alongside the task icon or pop up when you hover over it, depending on the style choice you made for the taskpad. Click Next.

4. In the next screen (shown in Figure 3.23), choose a task symbol. Unfortunately, the selection of symbols is pretty limited. Some tasks have recommended symbols; highlight a symbol to see its common meanings. Or you might find a custom icon you like better by browsing to \Windows\system32\shell32.dll. Select a symbol and click Next.

FIGURE 3.23

Choosing an icon for the task

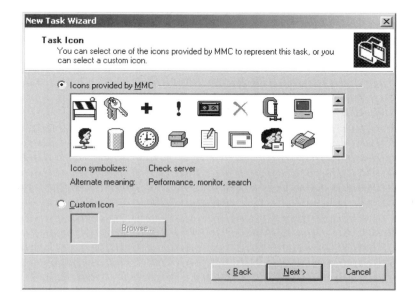

5. The wizard confirms your task creation (see Figure 3.24), displaying a list of created tasks and giving you the option to run the wizard again to create another task. Click Finish, then click OK to close the taskpad property page. The new task will appear in the taskpad as a link. Click the link once to run it.

6. For practice, run the New Task Wizard again, creating a new menu command based on another tree item. In the New Task Wizard, scroll through the Computer Management tree and locate Shares under System Tools/Shared Folders. The task you're looking for is New Share. Running this command will kick off the Share a Folder Wizard. Now your taskpad should look something like the one shown in Figure 3.25. Using the tasks you've created, you can connect to a remote machine and create a shared folder on it. For the sake of completeness, the taskpad shown in Figure 3.25 also includes a shell command task (Run Disk Usage Report) and a Navigation task (Open Disk Defragmenter).

FIGURE 3.24

Completing the New
Task Wizard

FIGURE 3.25

A taskpad with tasks

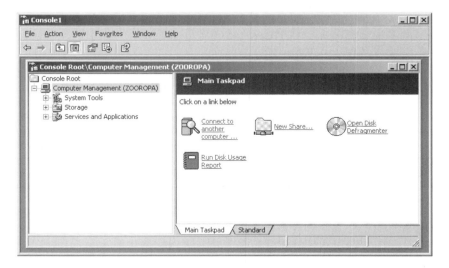

Steps 1 through 5 illustrate how to create a task to connect to another computer, which is important
if the tool is to function remotely. This is why the Computer Management snap-in was used instead
of the individual component snap-ins. When adding individual component snap-ins like the Event
Viewer and Services, the Connect to Another Computer function is also available, but each snap-in has
to be pointed to a remote computer separately. If you use the Computer Management snap-in, you
can easily change the focus for the entire tree of tools at once. Otherwise, you might find yourself
looking at your local Event Viewer while stopping and starting services on a remote machine.

NOTES ON TASKPAD VIEWS AND MENU COMMANDS

In the example of creating a taskpad, you had the choice in step 4 to apply the view to the selected tree item only or to any other tree item of the same type. When a taskpad view is applied to the selected tree item, it will only be visible when you navigate to that node in the console tree or use a link such as a Favorite to get there. When a taskpad view applies to other tree items of the same type, different event logs, for instance, it will display the same taskpad view and tasks no matter what log is selected for viewing in the details pane. A taskpad view created for the Application log, configured to display for all items of the same type, will also be accessible when you look at the Security log or the System log.

Also, when you're choosing a menu command source in the New Task Wizard, tree item tasks can point to any item on the tree, but detail pane choices are limited to operations you could perform by right-clicking an item in the details pane at that particular place on the tree. The command applies to the selected item. It also follows that detail pane commands don't work unless you actually choose to display the details pane list when you create the taskpad. So why would you want to create task links that are limited to the command options in the details pane at all? Isn't it quicker to right-click? Isn't right-clicking a universal skill at this point? Well, this capability could be useful if you need to frequently perform the same tasks on different items in the list.

As an example of the preceding points (selected tree versus same type views, and tree item menu commands versus detail pane commands), you'll create a taskpad view for an event log and create the following tasks: view the details of a particular log entry, refresh the log view, archive the log, clear the log, and open an archived log file. I would use the Services tool as an example (start service, pause service, etc.) but Microsoft beat me to it: there's already an extended view of Services that covers those functions.

1. First, open the Event Viewer and select one of the event logs. Choose New Taskpad View from the Action menu. The wizard will open. Click Next to continue.

2. Select your display options for the taskpad. There will be a long list of log entries, so a vertical list is appropriate, although selecting a horizontal list will allocate more room to display the columns. I recommend leaving the task description style on InfoTip, as this will allow more room for task links. Click Next.

3. Choose to apply the taskpad view to all tree items of the same type, and to change the default display to this taskpad view. These are the default settings for new taskpad views. Choose Next.

4. Give the taskpad a name (I called mine Log Options) and a description, which will appear under the name in the details pane. Click Finish to create the taskpad and start the New Task Wizard (if you leave the box checked, it's selected by default).

5. To create a task, click Next in the New Task Wizard. Choose to create a menu command and click Next.

6. This time, in the Shortcut Menu Command page, you'll choose your command from the list in the details pane for the log you selected. As you can see in Figure 3.26, the log entry context-menu commands are also available. Select Properties (it doesn't matter what entry is selected on the source side at this point) and click Next.

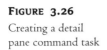

FIGURE 3.26

Creating a detail pane command task

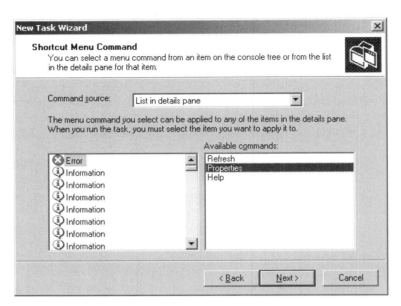

7. Name the task View This Entry. Click Next. Now choose an icon from the list, click Next, click Finish in the confirmation page, and you're done.

8. Run the New Task Wizard again to create each of the remaining tasks, but change your selection in the Shortcut Menu Command page to select a tree item task (shown in Figure 3.27). The menu commands to use are Refresh, Save Log File As, Clear All Events, and Open Log File. Name these Refresh Log View, Archive this Log, Clear this Log, and Open Archived Log File, in that order.

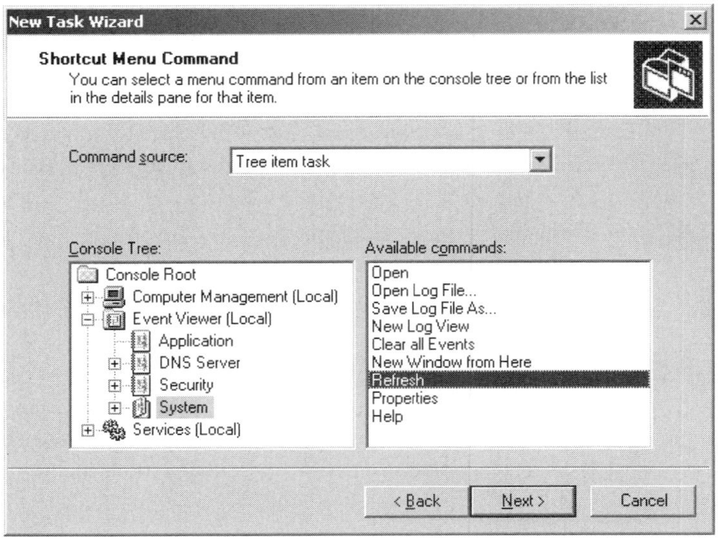

FIGURE 3.27

Creating a tree item task

Figure 3.28 shows the final taskpad with tasks. Now when you navigate to any of the event logs in the Event Viewer, the taskpad displays the list of log entries, and the tasks you've created appear to the left (or under) the entries. This effectively illustrates the difference between tree item tasks and detail pane command tasks; to view a particular log entry (a detail pane command), you must first select it from the list and choose View This Entry. To archive the log or refresh the log view, however, just click the link; the context for the command has already been established.

FIGURE 3.28

The final Event Log taskpad

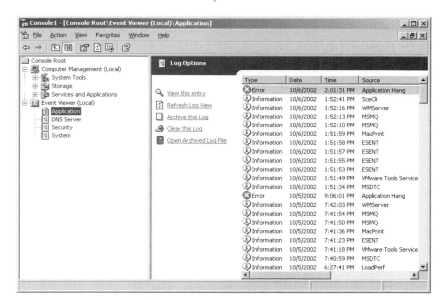

CUSTOMIZING THE CONSOLE INTERFACE

Now that you've loaded snap-ins and created customized taskpad views and task links, you can give your customized tool a simplified look and feel by hiding the console tree and the navigation tabs that allow end users to move between the standard and the taskpad view of the detail pane.

You know, that reminds me, if you hide the console tree and the navigation tabs, lock the tool down, and prevent the user of the tool from navigating the console tree, they have no way of getting down to the Log Options taskpad you created in the earlier example. They'll be stuck at the Main Taskpad. So, before you customize the console interface, you need a task in the Main Taskpad that acts as a link to the Log Options taskpad. There are two ways to accomplish this, and both seem to work equally well.

The first way to create a link to another taskpad is to navigate down to the log while the console tree is visible in Author mode and add that location to the list of Favorites. Then, create a navigation task in the Main Taskpad and select the Favorite as the destination. The Favorites link must exist, however, before you can create a navigation task for it. Remember, though, if you are hiding the console tree altogether, you'll need to create a Favorite and a corresponding link for each log you want the user to access.

If you don't want to use the Favorites method, create a menu command task in the Main Taskpad and select as the source a tree item task. Navigate to the log and select the command Open (shown in Figure 3.29). Or choose New Window from Here to open the log in a new window. Name the task Open Application Log, for example. If the taskpad is configured to be the default display, that's all you need to do. From the Main Taskpad, the user needs only to click the link Open Application Log to go to the Log Options taskpad. Just as with the Favorites method, you'll need to create a link for each log. Of course, you can create a link to the Event Viewer instead of the individual log, and users can then select the log they are interested in viewing, but you won't have the same fine-grained control. It's also possible to create a taskpad consisting entirely of links to other taskpads, which in turn link to other taskpads on the console tree, if you feel up to it. As I said in the beginning of this section, the options are too numerous to cover them completely in this book.

FIGURE 3.29

Creating a task to open a console taskpad view

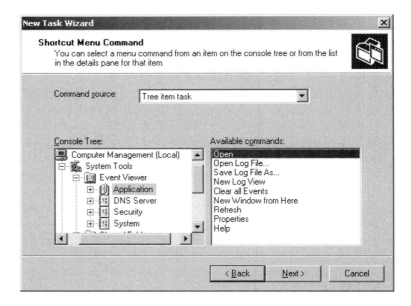

A final word before you lock down the console: just as you would create a home link on a Web site to prevent a user from getting stuck on a particular page, it's a good idea to create links back to the main taskpad on second- or third-tier taskpads. This is especially true if you intend to hide the console tree and the toolbar because the forward and back buttons will not be available.

To customize the console interface, choose Customize from the View menu. Figure 3.30 shows the view options, with default values. Items are shown when the boxes are checked and hidden when they are cleared. As you uncheck selections, you can see the changes being updated in the console.

Hide the Console tree to achieve that single window appearance. Clear the Standard Menus check box to hide the Action, View, and Favorites menus. Removing the Action menu prevents the user from selecting an item and pulling down the Action menu to see a complete set of task options, but they can still access the context menu by right-clicking an item. If you clear the check box labeled

Standard Toolbar, the toolbar with the forward and back buttons disappears (along with the Show/Hide Console Tree, Export List, and Help buttons). Remember that you need those buttons if the tool has to navigate the tree. Consider our earlier example of the Main Taskpad with a link to the Application log taskpad. If the Standard toolbar is removed, you cannot return to the Main Taskpad from the Application Log taskpad without a link. If the console tool is only running wizards or scripts, however, removing the navigation buttons won't be a problem. To really simplify the window, clear both the Status Bar and the Description Bar check boxes (the status bar is displayed by default, but the description bar is not). Clear the Taskpad Navigation Tabs check box to remove the tabs from the bottom of the details pane; without access to the Standard view, users will only be able to view the taskpads you've created.

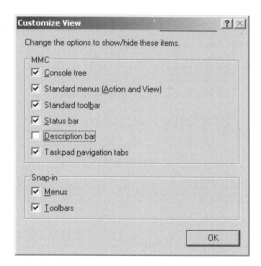

FIGURE 3.30

Customizing the console view

Each snap-in can have its own menu items and toolbar buttons. To hide these for all snap-ins in the tool, clear the two check boxes in the Snap-In section of the dialog box. You can't pick and choose which toolbars and buttons to hide; you either hide them for all snap-ins or reveal them for all snap-ins.

Packaging Up the Tool for Users

When the tool is ready to be published, choose Options from the Console menu of the Main window and change the tool's name (from `Console1` to something descriptive), as shown in Figure 3.31. The new name will now appear in the title bar. You might also want to assign a different icon than the generic MMC icon. Finally, assign a default mode to the MSC file. Use one of the three User modes to prevent changes to the tool, such as adding and removing snap-ins or editing taskpads. The three different User modes represent varying degrees of restrictions, including whether the user can open multiple windows. Limited Access Single Window is the most restrictive.

Notice the two configuration check boxes at the bottom of Figure 3.31. Check Do Not Save Changes to This Console to prevent users from saving any changes they make to the console. Users can customize views by default. To prevent this, uncheck the box that says Allow the User to Customize Views. You haven't locked down anything at all until you do this. Otherwise, the user can open up Customize View by clicking the Console icon at the top left of the window and undo all your modifications. Choose OK to close the Options dialog box, then save the console as an MSC file if you haven't already.

FIGURE 3.31

The Console Options dialog box

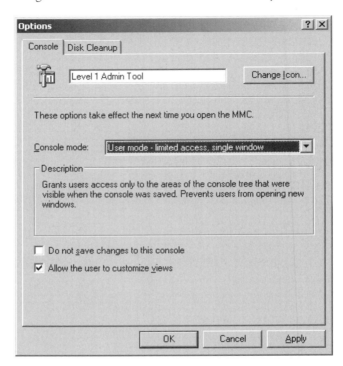

Figure 3.32 shows a basic admin tool running in User mode with limited access and a single window. The console tree and taskpad navigation tabs, as well as the Action and View menus, are hidden. This tool does reveal the Standard toolbar, however, since it's necessary to be able to go forward and back in the tool. Too bad you can't hide some buttons and not others.

FIGURE 3.32

The final product

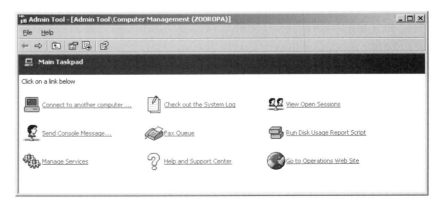

WARNING *A locked down MMC tool is not to be relied on as a security or control measure. Control a user's actions using appropriate group memberships, rights and object permissions, and with delegation.*

Distributing the Tool

When the tool is finished, distribute it as you would a normal file; e-mail it to someone, put it on the network file server in a shared folder, or use Active Directory services to publish it. Appropriate administrative permissions for the tasks and access to the snap-ins, either on the local machine or on the network, are required to use the tool.

Unfortunately, the version of MMC distributed with Windows 2000 and prior versions of Windows client systems will not run tools created using MMC 2 Version 5.2. They will run only on other Server 2003 systems and Windows XP. Windows Server and XP can run consoles created on Windows 2000 systems, however.

Editing a Custom Console Tool

Making changes to the console is easy, even when the tool opens in User mode by default. The tool can be opened in Author mode using one of several methods:

- Open the tool using Start/Run and enter the filename with the **/a** switch.
- Right-click the file's icon and choose Author.
- Open a blank console using Start/Run and enter **mmc.exe**, then choose Open from the Console menu to pull up any MSC file in Author mode.

How can you keep others from making changes to the tool using these tricks? Chapter 9 explains how to restrict access to Author mode, and even particular snap-ins, using group policies.

In this chapter, you learned how to gracefully weather the minor user interface changes introduced with Windows Server 2003. We also explored the Microsoft Management Console and learned a few of its inner secrets. Now you are ready to unleash the real power of MMC by using its authoring features to create consoles that fit the needs of your MIS/IT department.

Chapter 4

Configuring Windows Server: The Windows Server 2003 Registry

ANY EXPLANATION OF HOW to solve problems and get things done in Server 2003 (or indeed any version of NT) will soon turn to a bit of software fiddling called "modifying the Registry" or "hacking the Registry." This chapter explains exactly what the Registry is, why you care about it, and how to work with it. If you've already worked with Windows 9x, Me, or, again, any previous version of NT, then this will be old stuff. But the newcomers should read carefully!

Anyone who works with Server 2003, whether as a user or as an administrator, makes a fair number of adjustments to it—from the small ones, such as changing a background color, to larger ones, like changing a network IP address. Similarly, when you use an application, you inevitably end up configuring it as well, directing it where to save files, how the application should start up, whether to automatically run macros, and the like. And, of course, when you reboot a computer or whenever you start up an application, you expect your configurations to still be in effect—the things that you tell an operating system or application to do should survive a reboot. But where are these customizations stored?

Over the years, different operating systems have answered that question in different ways. Windows 2 and 2.1 actually stored a lot of their configuration information inside their own program files, which unbelievably meant that every time you made a change like installing a new video card, the Windows Setup program would build an entirely new copy of Windows with that driver's information embedded in the Windows program itself! Not every configuration change in Windows 2.x required a rebuild of the operating system, thankfully, as Windows 2.x and then 3.x used ASCII text files with names like WIN.INI, SYSTEM.INI, CONTROL.INI, and so on to store configuration information. INI files weren't a bad thing overall—their ASCII nature made changing them simple, a task for Notepad or an easy-to-write BASIC program—but the growing complexity of Windows in both its 9x and Windows NT incarnations created a need to be able to store more complex configuration information.

Microsoft's answer to that increased need arrived with the first version of NT, Windows NT 3.1, in the summer of 1993. The answer was a group of files with the collective name of the *Registry*.

(Microsoft always capitalizes it—the Registry—so I will, too, but it always seems a bit overdone, don't you think?) The Registry is terrific in that it's one big database that contains all of the Server 2003 configuration information. Everything's there, from color settings to local user account's passwords. (Not domain users—those are in the separate files that store the Active Directory database. And by the way, you can't just look in the Registry to see local passwords—they're encrypted.) Even better, the Registry uses a fault-tolerant approach to writing data to ensure that the Registry remains intact even if there's a power failure in the middle of a Registry update.

So you've just *got* to like the Registry. Except, of course, for the *annoying* parts about it, including its cryptic organization and excessively complex structure. But read on and see what you think.

What Is the Registry?

The Registry is a hierarchical (that is, tree-structured) database of settings that describe your user account, the hardware of the server machine, and your applications. Any time you make some change with the Control Panel or some MMC snap-in, the effect of that change is usually stored in the Registry. (I say "usually" because some information is stored in the Active Directory, which is separate from the Registry.)

The Registry Stores Most of a Computer's "State"

If you can make changes to your system and they're then stored in the Registry, you might ask, "Who cares? What's the value of the Registry?" Well, consider how much time you spend configuring a new workstation or server. If that machine died for some reason, you'd want to set up another machine to replace the now-dead one—do you really want to spend all that time reconfiguring the replacement machine to look like the original? No, of course not. You would much prefer to be able to just put Server 2003 on the new machine and then restore all of the preferences and settings in one fell swoop, and you can do that, *if* you've got a backup of the old machine's Registry. Then all you need do is to put Server 2003 on the replacement machine and restore the old machine's Registry to the new machine. That, then, is the Registry's first value: when backed up, it preserves much of a machine's "state."

The Registry Stores Dynamic Hardware Information

Preserving user settings is nice, but it's not the Registry's sole value. In addition to storing the settings that *you've* made in the Registry, Server 2003 saves many settings that you never see, such as dynamic settings that Server makes to itself every time it boots—for example, whenever Server 2003 boots, it creates a census of the hardware attached to it and stores that census in the Registry. The Registry also contains internal adjustments that Server's designers preset with the intention that you would never touch them—and *that's* where the fun begins, at least for us noodlers.

The Registry Is the Only Way to Make Some System Adjustments

Ninety-nine point nine percent of 2003's settings are of no interest whatsoever. But a few are quite powerful and largely undocumented or documented solely by obscure Knowledge Base articles. The occult nature of these Registry settings has predictably become the source of countless "tips and tricks" about how to tune up NT's, 2000's, XP's and now Windows Server 2003's performance or how to solve some knotty problem. Perhaps the most remarkable of these appeared a few years ago when NT internals expert Mark Russinovich discovered that the only real difference between

NT Workstation 3.51 and NT Server 3.51 was *a few Registry settings!* Twiddling the Registry, then, is often of value to Windows troubleshooters.

The tough part about working with the Registry is in grasping the programs and terminology used in editing the Registry. You're just supposed to *understand* sentences like these:

> *If you are trying to determine why your user profile did not download properly, then you should activate USERENV.DLL's logging feature and examine the log that it creates in \Windows\Debug\UserMode\ Userenv.log.*

> *To enable USERENV.DLL logging, go to the subkey HKEY_LOCAL_MACHINE\SOFTWARE\ Microsoft\Windows NT\CurrentVersion\Winlogon and add a new entry called UserenvDebugLevel of type REG_DWORD. Set its value to 30002 hex and reboot the system.*

Sentences like these are a major reason for this chapter. You will come across phrases like that in Microsoft literature, magazine articles, and even parts of this book. Much of that information contains useful advice that will make you a better network administrator if you understand how to carry it out—in fact, these snippets are incredibly useful if you've got a busy network and people are having trouble logging in. My goal for this chapter, then, is to give you a feel for the Registry, how to edit it, and when to leave it alone.

Registry Terminology

What did that stuff with all the backslashes mean? To get an insight, let's look at the Registry. You can see it by running the program REGEDIT.EXE (it's in the \Windows directory); just click Start/Run and fill in **REGEDIT.EXE** or simply **REGEDIT**.

Run Regedit and click the HKEY_LOCAL_MACHINE window. You'll see a screen like the one in Figure 4.1.

FIGURE 4.1

Registry Editor screen

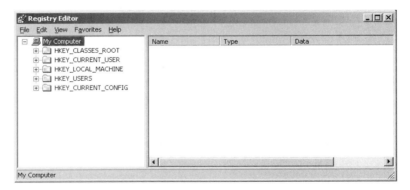

The terms to know in order to understand the Registry are *subtree, key, value, data type,* and *hive.*

WARNING   *While looking around in the Registry, please do* not *make any changes unless you truly want them! Because Regedit is an "editor," you might think that it's like Notepad or Word in that none of your changes actually take effect until you choose to Save them—but that is* not *the case at all. Make a change in Regedit and Regedit changes the Registry immediately. And, worse yet, there is no "undo" key for Regedit changes. So please. . . until you know what you're doing, look—but don't touch! (Unless you like re-installing from scratch, that is.)*

Subtrees

A first look at Regedit can be a bit misleading, as it looks an awful lot like a directory/folder structure on a hard disk—so you may think that you're seeing some hidden directories somewhere. But you're not. Regedit's view of the Registry represents the *logical* structure of the Registry far better than it represents the *physical* locations. (If you just can't wait to find out where the Registry physically resides, then here's the quick overview: some of the Registry lives in files called *hives*; the rest of it doesn't exist anywhere on disk at all, as it's dynamic data that gets recreated whenever you reboot the server.)

Notice that under the My Computer icon, Regedit shows five folder icons; those icons represent logical groupings of Registry information called *subtrees*. Table 4.1 has an overview of what's in those subtrees.

TABLE 4.2: THE FIVE SUBTREES OF THE REGISTRY

SUBTREE	DESCRIPTION
HKEY_LOCAL_MACHINE	Contains information about the hardware currently installed in the machine and the settings for systems running on the machine. This key, and HKEY_CURRENT_USER, contain most of the important Registry configuration information. *This* key contains the information specific to your computer; the next one contains information specific to you, your user account. This subtree is used so often that it has a common abbreviation, HKLM.
HKEY_CURRENT_USER	Contains the user settings and preferences for the person currently logged on to the computer. These settings include things like how you like your desktop arranged as well as settings for particular applications, like Word or Visio. This key's common use leads to it having the abbreviation HKCU.
HKEY_USERS	Contains a pointer to the HKEY_CURRENT_USER subtree and also to a profile called the DEFAULT profile. The DEFAULT profile describes how the machine behaves when no one's logged on. For example, if instead of a blue background you wanted a machine to display a green background when no one was logged on, or if you wanted to display a particular wallpaper when no one was logged on (which I've found quite useful for keeping clear in my mind which machine was which when using a keyboard switch or just a table full of identical-looking machines), then you'd modify that DEFAULT profile.
HKEY_CLASSES_ROOT	Holds the file associations, information that tells the system, "Whenever the user double-clicks a file with the extension .BMP in Windows Explorer, start up PBRUSH.EXE to view the file." It also contains the OLE registration database, the old REG.DAT from Windows 3.x. This is actually a redundant subtree, as all its information is found in the HKEY_LOCAL_MACHINE subtree. It also gets placed in the HKEY_CURRENT_USER\SOFTWARE\CLASSES key.
HKEY_CURRENT_CONFIG	Contains configuration information for the particular *hardware* configuration you booted up with.

In general, you'll do most of your work in the first two subtrees. Some Registry entries are specific to a machine (HKEY_LOCAL_MACHINE, HKEY_CLASSES_ROOT, HKEY_CURRENT_CONFIG), and some are specific to a user (`HKEY_USERS`, `HKEY_CURRENT_USER`, as well as other Registry files that are in the `\Documents and Settings\USER ID` directories, which you'll meet later—but for now, just understand that the `\Documents and Settings` folder is where Windows 2000 and later machines store user preference information). That's important, and it's a great strength of the Registry's structure. The entries relevant to a particular machine should, of course, physically reside on that machine. But what about the settings relevant to a user: the background colors you like, the programs you want to see in your Start menu, the sounds you want on the system? These shouldn't be tied to any one computer; they should be able to move around the network with that user. Indeed, they can. As with NT 4, Windows 2000, and XP, Windows Server 2003 supports the idea that "roving users" can have their personal settings follow them around the network via *roaming profiles*, which you will learn more about in Chapter 9.

Registry Keys

In Figure 4.1, you saw the Registry Editor display the Registry's sections as folders under a top-level PC icon. The whole window looks like Windows Explorer. In Explorer, those folders represented subdirectories, as I suggested before. In Regedit, however, they separate information into sections. (If you ever worked on the old Windows 3.*x* systems, then this is kind of similar to the way old Windows INI files had sections whose names were surrounded by square brackets, names like `[386enh]`, `[network]`, `[boot]`, and the like.) Even though their icons look like folders, most people don't speak of "Registry folders"—the folders are called Registry *keys*.

You'll see more folder icons inside other folder icons and so, so it's logical that you'll sometimes hear the word "subkey." In most cases the terms "subkey" and "key" can be used interchangeably.

To examine one example key, open up the `SYSTEM` key under `HKLM`; simply click the plus sign to the left of `HKEY_LOCAL_MACHINE`, then click the plus sign next to the System key. It contains subkeys named `ControlSet001`, `ControlSet002`, `CurrentControlSet`, `Select`, and `Setup`, and `CurrentControlSet` is further subkeyed into `Control` and `Services`.

Notice, by the way, the key called `CurrentControlSet`. It's very important. Almost every time you modify your system's configuration, you do it with a subkey within the `CurrentControlSet` subkey.

Key-Naming Conventions

The tree of keys gets pretty big as you drill down through the many layers. `CurrentControlSet`, for example, has dozens of keys, each of which can have keys/subkeys. (Remember, the two terms are basically interchangeable.) Identifying a given subkey is important, so Microsoft has adopted a naming convention that looks just like the one used for directory trees. `CurrentControlSet`'s fully specified name would be, then, `HKEY_LOCAL_MACHINE\SYSTEM\CurrentControlSet`. In this book, however, I'll just call it `CurrentControlSet` to keep key names from getting too long to fit on a single line.

Value Entries, Names, Values, and Data Types

If I drill down through `CurrentControlSet`, I find the subkey `Services`, and within `Services`, there are many subkeys. In Figure 4.2, I have opened and highlighted one of those subkeys—the key `HKEY_LOCAL_MACHINE\SYSTEM\CurrentControlSet\Services\Browser\Parameters`.

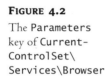

FIGURE 4.2

The `Parameters` key of `Current-ControlSet\ Services\Browser`

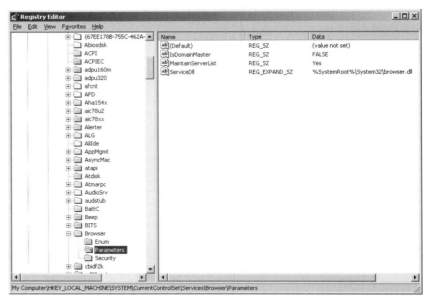

In the right pane of Regedit, you can see several lines broken into three parts; two of them look like

```
IsDomainMaster          REG_SZ      FALSE
MaintainServerList      REG_SZ      Yes
```

These are examples of two system settings; on this particular computer, a setting called `IsDomainMaster` is set to FALSE and `MaintainServerList` is set to Yes.

NOTE *As to what exactly those things mean, look to Chapter 18's discussion of the browser. It would be really great if you could right-click every line like the two above in the Registry and get a little Help message about what that line does and what modifying it would do, but nothing like that exists. That's why there are so many books on the Registry!*

Each line like `IsDomainMaster REG_SZ FALSE` is called a *value entry*. The three parts are called *name*, *data type*, and *value*, respectively. In this example, `IsDomainMaster` is the *name*, `REG_SZ` is the *data type*, and `FALSE` is the *value*.

Microsoft notes that each value entry cannot exceed about 1MB in size. It's hard to imagine one that size, but it's worth mentioning.

What is that `REG_SZ` stuff? It's an identifier to the Registry of what *kind* of data to expect: numbers, messages, yes/no values, and the like. Microsoft defines five data types in the Registry Editor (although others could be defined later), shown in Table 4.2.

Those who first met the Registry with Windows 95 will notice a few differences here. Windows 95 has six subtrees, but only three data types—*string*, which encompasses `REG_SZ`, `REG_MULTI_SZ`, and `REG_EXPAND_SZ`; *dword*, which is the same as `REG_DWORD`; and *binary*, which is identical to `REG_BINARY`.

And if you're wondering how on earth you'll figure out what data type to assign to a new Registry value, don't worry about it; if you read somewhere to use a particular new value entry, you'll be told what data type to use. Failing that, I usually just guess `REG_SZ` if it's textual in nature, `REG_DWORD` if it's numeric.

TABLE 4.3: DATA TYPES AS DEFINED BY THE REGISTRY EDITOR

DATA TYPE	DESCRIPTION
REG_BINARY	Raw binary data. Data of this type usually doesn't make sense when you look at it with the Registry Editor. Binary data shows up in hardware setup information. If there is an alternative way to enter this data other than via the Registry Editor—and I'll discuss that in a page or two—then do it that way. Editing binary data can get you in trouble if you don't know what you're doing. The data is usually represented in hex for simplicity's sake.
REG_DWORD	Another binary data type, but it is 4 bytes long.
REG_EXPAND_SZ	A character string of variable size, it's often information understandable by humans, like path statements or messages. It is "expandable" in that it may contain information that will change at runtime, like *%username%*—a system batch variable that will be of different sizes for different people's names.
REG_MULTI_SZ	Another string type, but it allows you to enter a number of parameters in this one value entry. The parameters are separated by binary zeroes (nulls).
REG_SZ	A simple string.

Working with the Registry: An Example

Now, I know you want to get in there and try it out despite the warnings, so here's an innocuous example. Remember, it's only innocuous if you *follow* the example to the letter; otherwise, it will soon be time to get out your installation disks.

That's not just boilerplate. Don't get mad at *me* if you blow up your server because you didn't pay attention. Actually, you *may* be able to avoid a reinstallation if the thing that you modified was in the CurrentControlSet key; Server 2003 knows that you often mess around in there, and so it keeps a spare. In that case, you can reboot the server and, when the boot menu prompts "Please select the operating system to start:," press F8 for the Windows Advanced Options menu. (If you don't have a boot menu—as would be the case if Server 2003 is the only OS on your disk—then it's a bit of a video game, I'm afraid; try to press F8 just as the initial power-on screen for your computer appears. With a little practice it becomes easier.) One of the options you'll get will be Last Known Good Configuration (Your Most Recent Settings That Worked). That *doesn't* restore the entire Registry; it just restores the control set. Fortunately, the current control set is a *lot* of the Registry. It doesn't include user-specific settings, however, like, "What color should the screen be?" Thus, if you were to set all of your screen colors to black, rendering the screen black on black (and therefore less than readable), rebooting and choosing Last Known Good Configuration wouldn't help you.

In any case, let's try something out, something relatively harmless. Let's change the name of the company that you gave Server 2003 when you installed it. Suppose I decided to change my company's name from MR&D to Bigfirm, the example that I use in much of this book. Suppose I'd already installed a bunch of Server 2003 machines and filled in MR&D when prompted for an organization. Suppose also that I want to change that so the Help/About dialog boxes say that I'm Mark Minasi of Bigfirm, but I don't feel like reinstalling. Fortunately, the Registry Editor lets me change company names without reinstalling:

1. Open the Registry Editor. From the Start menu, choose Run.

2. In the command line, type **regedit** and press Enter.

3. Open the HKEY_LOCAL_MACHINE folder. Inside that you'll find a folder called SOFTWARE; open that. Inside that you'll find a folder named Microsoft; open that. Inside the Microsoft folder you'll find a folder named Windows NT; open that and you will see a folder named CurrentVersion. Click it and you'll see something like Figure 4.3.

FIGURE 4.3

HKEY_LOCAL_
MACHINE\SOFTWARE\
Microsoft\
Windows NT\
CurrentVersion

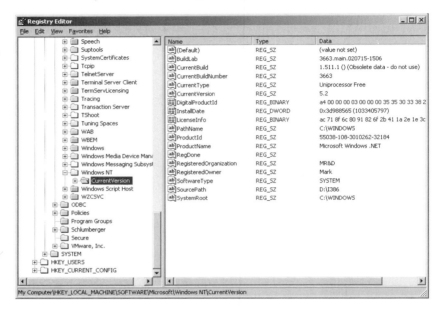

4. In HKEY_LOCAL_MACHINE\Software\Microsoft\Windows NT\CurrentVersion you can see, among other things, value entries named RegisteredOrganization and RegisteredOwner. Mine say MR&D and Mark, but yours will say different things.

5. Double-click RegisteredOrganization, and a String Editor screen appears. You'll see something like Figure 4.4.

FIGURE 4.4

Registry string editor

6. Highlight the old value and replace it with **Bigfirm**. Click OK, and close up the Registry Editor. Do the same thing with Mark in RegisteredOwner, changing it to **Mark Minasi**.

Now click Help/About for any program—even the Registry Editor will do—and you'll see that your organization is now MR&D.

WARNING *I remind you again: click all you like; you will not find a Save button or an Undo button. When you edit the Registry, it's immediate and it's forever. So, once again, be careful when you mess with the Registry.*

How Do You Find Registry Keys?

How did I know to go to `HKEY_LOCAL_MACHINE\Software\Microsoft\Windows NT\CurrentVersion` in order to change my organization name? I found it by poking around the Registry. Regedit let me do it with its neat Find feature.

I figured that the word "Name" would appear a lot in the Registry, so looking for a field with my name called "Name" didn't sound promising. But "Organization" isn't as common, so I figured I'd try it. Here's how you can, too:

1. Start Regedit if you haven't already.
2. Click the My Computer icon in Regedit.
3. Click Edit/Find and a Find dialog box will appear that looks like Figure 4.5.

FIGURE 4.5

Regedit's Find dialog box

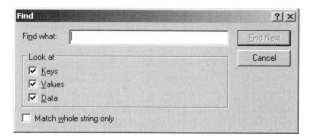

4. In the Find What text field, type in **organization**. Note that Regedit will search key names, value entry names, and the actual data in value entries. There is a lot more data in the Registry than there are key and value entry names, so skip searching data whenever possible; uncheck the Data check box and click Find Next.

On my system the first hit I got was for a key called `MSExtOrganization`, which was clearly not what I wanted, so I pressed F3 to tell Regedit to find the next match.

Several false hits later, I found `RegisteredOrganization`.

But how else can I find Registry keys? Microsoft's Knowledge Base and white papers are great sources of useful Registry keys. Random Web searches can sometimes turn up some pretty neat stuff—or, as is usually the case with random Web searches, neat-sounding stuff that doesn't work.

Even More Cautions about Editing the Registry

If you're just learning about the Registry, you're probably eager to wade right in and modify a value entry. Before you do, however, let me just talk a bit about using caution when you manipulate the Registry. (I know I've mentioned it before, but it's important, so I'm mentioning it again.)

The vast majority of Registry items correspond to some setting in the Control Panel, Active Directory Users and Computers, or some MMC snap-in. For example, you just saw how you can change the `RegisteredOrganization` directly via the Registry Editor. I only picked that example, however, because it was fairly illustrative and simple to understand. In general, *don't use the Registry Editor to modify a value that can be modified in some other way.*

For example, suppose I choose to set a background color on my screen to medium gray. That color is represented as a triplet of numbers: 128 128 128. How did I know what those color values meant? Because they're the same as Windows 3.*x* color values. Color values in Windows are expressed as number triplets. Each number is an integer from 0 to 255. If I input a value greater than 255, the Registry Editor would neither know nor care that I was punching in an illegal color value. Now, in the case of colors, that probably wouldn't crash the system. In the case of other items, however, the system could easily be rendered unusable. For example, I'm running Server 2003 on a system with just a single Pentium III processor, so the Registry reflects that, noting in one of the HARDWARE keys that 2003 is running in a "uniprocessor" mode. Altering that to a multiprocessor mode wouldn't be a very good idea.

Why, then, am I bothering to tell you about the Registry Editor? Three reasons.

First, there are settings—important ones—that can only be altered via the Registry Editor, so there's no getting around the fact that a Server 2003 expert has to be proficient in the Editor.

Second, you can use the Registry Editor to change system value entries on remote computers. To use a very simple example: I'm at location A and I want to change the background color on the server at location B. To do that I have to physically travel to location B in order to run the Control Panel on the computer at that location. Instead of doing that, however, I can just start up the Registry Editor, choose Registry/Select Computer, and edit the Registry of the remote computer. (This is a lot less true than it once was with earlier versions of Server, as 2000 Server and Server 2003 have some very good remote control tools; but I'm sure that there will be instances where this is still useful advice.) This assumes that you have the security access to change the Registry of the remote computer—that is, you're a member of the Administrators group on that computer.

Third, Server 2003 comes with a couple of programs named `regini.exe` and `reg.exe` that let you write scripts to modify Registries. Such a tool is quite powerful; in theory, you could write a REGINI script to completely reconfigure a Server setup. Again, however, before you start messing with that program, please be sure that you have become proficient with the Registry. I've explained the various kinds of mischief that you can cause working by hand with the Registry Editor. Imagine what kinds of automated disasters you could start at 2.5GHz with a bad REGINI script!

And while I've mentioned REG, I should mention that it does a whole *bunch* of things—it will search your Registry, do automated search-and-replace (think how quickly you could destroy a Registry with *that!*), automate creating and deleting keys and value entries, and import and export Registry data. Do a `reg /?` for more info.

By the way, there's another way to automate Registry changes through REGEDIT. You can create an ASCII text file with the desired Registry changes, then use an undocumented `/s` (for "silent") switch to introduce the changes.

The file has a particular format. The first line must be `Windows Registry Editor Version 5.00`, followed by a blank line. Then you enter a line with the full name of the Registry key that contains the value that you want to modify, surrounded by square brackets. Then type a line for each value that you want to modify, with the name of the value, an equal sign, and the desired value. Strings should be surrounded by quotes, and numbers—as in the DWORD type—should be prefixed by

`DWORD:`; for example, consider the following file:

```
Windows Registry Editor Version 5.00

[HKEY_LOCAL_MACHINE\SOFTWARE\Microsoft\Windows NT\CurrentVersion]
"RegisteredOrganization"="MR&D"
"NumberOfLicenses"=dword:00000003\
```

The first line identifies the file as a set of Registry changes. That first line is probably to keep someone from accidentally feeding some random file to REGEDIT, causing untold havoc from just an ill-thought-out mouse click. Then there's a blank line and then the description in square brackets. The line afterward sets the `RegisteredOrganization`, as described earlier, and the final entry is just an imaginary setting that I created just to show how to do a number. If I put those five lines—it's *five*, remember the blank line—into a file and called it `mystuff.reg`, I could make REGEDIT modify the Registry with it like so:

```
Regedit /s mystuff.reg
```

And by the way, here's a useful tip: if you use REGEDIT's export function (Registry/Export Registry File), the resulting exported file is ASCII and is in the proper format for using `/s` to apply the values to another computer.

Where the Registry Lives: Hives

The Registry is mostly contained in a set of files called the *hives*. ("Mostly" because some of it is built automatically every time you boot up your system. For example, Server doesn't know what devices are on a SCSI chain until you boot.) Hives are binary files, so there's no way to look at them without a special editor of some kind, like the Registry Editor. Hives are, however, an easy way to load or back up a sizable part of the Registry.

Most, although not all, of the Registry is stored in hive files. They're not hidden, system, or read-only, but they are always open, so you're kind of limited in what you can do with them.

A Look at the Hive Files

The machine-specific hive files are in the `\WINDOWS\system32\config` directory. The user-specific hive files are in the `\Documents` and `Settings\`*username* directories. (Actually, that's where *local* user settings go; people with "roaming profiles"—discussed in Chapter 9—also store copies of their `NTUSER.DAT` on a network share.) You can see the hive files that correspond to parts of the subtree listed in Table 4.3.

TABLE 4.4: HIVE FILES

SUBTREE/KEY	FILENAME
HKEY_LOCAL_MACHINE\SAM	SAM (primary) and SAM.LOG (backup)
HKEY_LOCAL_MACHINE\SECURITY	SECURITY (primary) and SECURITY.LOG (backup)

Continued on next page

TABLE 4.4: HIVE FILES *(continued)*

SUBTREE/KEY	FILENAME
HKEY_LOCAL_MACHINE\SOFTWARE	SOFTWARE (primary) and SOFTWARE.LOG (backup)
HKEY_LOCAL_MACHINE\SYSTEM	SYSTEM (primary) and SYSTEM.ALT (backup)
HKEY_USERS\DEFAULT	DEFAULT (primary) and DEFAULT.LOG (backup)
HKEY_USERS\Security ID	NTUSER.DAT
HKEY_CURRENT_USER	NTUSER.DAT
HKEY_CLASSES_ROOT	(Created from current control set at boot time)

Table 4.3 needs a few notes to clarify it. First, about the HKEY_CLASSES_ROOT subtree: It is copied from HKEY_KEY_LOCAL_MACHINE\SOFTWARE\Classes at boot time. The file exists for use by 16-bit Windows applications. While you're logged on to Server 2003, however, the two keys are linked; if you make a change to one, the change is reflected in the other.

The local user profiles live in \Documents and Settings*username*, where each user gets a directory named *username*. For example, I've got a user account named mark, so there's a directory named \Documents and Settings\mark on my computer. If I look in it, I find the files ntuser.dat and ntuser.dat.log.

To summarize, then, the core of the Registry is the four *S*s and DEFAULT:

- SAM
- SECURITY
- SYSTEM
- SOFTWARE

SAM contains the user database; SECURITY complements SAM by containing information such as whether a server is a member server or a domain controller, what the name of its domain is, and the like. Domain controllers do not have SAM files, but workstations (XP, 2000 Professional, etc.) and member servers all have SAMs. SYSTEM contains configuration information like what drivers and system programs the computer uses, which should be loaded on boot-up, and how their parameters are set. SOFTWARE tends to contain more overall configuration information about the larger software modules in the system, configuration information that does *not* vary from user to user. And then every user has an NTUSER.DAT with their specific application preferences in it.

One question remains about the hive files, however. Why do all the files have a paired file with the extension .LOG? Read on.

Fault Tolerance in the Registry

Notice that every hive file has another file with the same name but the extension .LOG. That's really useful because Server 2003 (and in fact every version of NT) uses it to protect the Registry during updates.

Whenever a hive file is to be changed, the change is first written into its LOG file. The LOG file isn't actually a backup file; it's more a journal of changes to the primary file. Once the description of the change to the hive file is complete, the journal file is written to disk. When I say "written to disk," I *mean* written to disk. Often, a disk write ends up hanging around in the disk cache for a while, but this write is "flushed" to disk. Then the system makes the changes to the hive file based on the information in the journal file. If the system crashes during the hive write operation, there is enough information in the journal file to "roll back" the hive to its previous position.

The exception to this procedure comes with the SYSTEM hive. The SYSTEM hive is really important because it contains the CurrentControlSet. For that reason, the backup file for SYSTEM, SYSTEM.ALT, is a complete backup of SYSTEM. If one file is damaged, the system can use the other to boot.

Notice that HKEY_LOCAL_MACHINE\HARDWARE does not have a hive. That's because the key is rebuilt each time you boot so Server 2003 can adapt itself to changes in computer hardware. The Plug and Play Manager, which runs at boot time, gathers the information that Server needs to create HKEY_LOCAL_MACHINE\HARDWARE.

Confused about where all the keys come from? You'll find a recap in Table 4.4. It's similar to Table 4.3, but it's more specific about how the keys are built at boot time.

TABLE 4.5: CONSTRUCTION OF KEYS AT BOOT TIME

KEY	HOW IT'S CONSTRUCTED AT BOOT TIME
HKEY_LOCAL_MACHINE:	
HARDWARE	Plug and Play Manager
SAM	SAM hive file
SECURITY	SECURITY hive file
SOFTWARE	SOFTWARE hive file
SYSTEM	SYSTEM hive file
HKEY_CLASSES_ROOT	SYSTEM hive file, Classes subkey
HKEY_USERS_DEFAULT	DEFAULT hive file
HKEY_USERS\Sxxx	Particular user's NTUSER.DAT file
HKEY_CURRENT_USER	Particular user's NTUSER.DAT file

Registry Permissions

Clearly you wouldn't want just anybody messing with your Registry. So how is it secured? With permissions. Recall in Chapter 2 that you read that things in Server 2003—and let me get technical and stop saying "things," and instead say "objects"—can have *access control lists* or *ACLs* associated with them. You can view and change these ACLs—assuming you have the proper permissions!—in Regedit by right-clicking any folder and choosing Permissions.

As time goes on, Microsoft learns more about how to properly secure Server from outside attacks. Many Microsoft security patches are nothing more than just adjustments to the ACLs on some Registry key.

Remote Registry Modification

You can modify another computer's Registry, perhaps to repair it or to do some simple kind of remote maintenance, by loading that computer's Registry. Regedit lets you do that simply; just click File/Connect Network Registry, and Regedit then asks for the name of the remote computer. You fill in the name, click OK and, if necessary, Regedit will ask for a username and password with permissions to access the remote computer's Registry. Once Regedit is satisfied that you're Da Man permission-wise, you get a new icon under your My Computer icon and the HKEY_LOCAL_MACHINE and HKEY_USERS subtrees of that remote computer. (The others don't show up, as they're all either dynamic or are simply mappings to subsets of the other subtrees.)

You can then edit the remote computer's Registry as if you were there. When done, just click File/Disconnect Network Registry and Regedit breaks the connection.

You can also load a particular hive with the Load Hive or Unload Hive commands. More specifically, you can load or unload the hives only for HKEY_USERS and HKEY_LOCAL_MACHINE. Here's how:

1. Start Regedit.
2. Under My Computer, click either the HKEY_LOCAL_MACHINE folder or the HKEY_USERS folder.
3. Click File/Load Hive.
4. In the resulting dialog box, point to the exact hive file itself—a particular NTUSER.DAT on a share somewhere.

The hive shows up as another key. You can then edit it and use File/Unload Hive to disconnect from it.

WARNING   *And I know you're getting tired of me reminding you, but I* have *to point out that Unload is not the same as Save. Those changes you made happened* immediately.

Again, the Load Hive option appears only if you've selected one of those two subtrees. Unload Hive is available only if you've selected a subkey of one of those two subtrees.

Why, specifically, would you load a hive or a remote Registry? In my experience, you typically load a hive in order to get to a user's profile. Suppose a user has set up all of the colors as black on black and made understanding the screen impossible. You could load the hive that corresponds to that user, modify it, and then unload it.

You could load and save hive files to a floppy disk, walk the floppy over to a malfunctioning machine, and load the hive onto the machine's hard disk, potentially repairing a system problem. This wasn't possible if you used NTFS on the boot disk of an NT 4 system unless you had multiple copies of NT 4—there wasn't an easy way to get to a system with an NTFS boot drive. Under Windows 2000, XP, and Server 2003, however, you can go to the advanced boot options and boot to a command prompt even if the system's damaged.

There is yet another way to control Registries remotely, through something called system policies, which are covered in Chapter 9.

Backing Up and Restoring a Registry

By now, it should be pretty clear that the Registry is an important piece of information and that it should be protected. It protects itself pretty well with its LOG files, but how can you back it up?

Unfortunately, the fact that Registry hive files are always open makes it tough to back up the Registry since most backup utilities are stymied by open files. The NTBackup program that comes with Server 2003 works well, and, while it's a bit primitive, it *can* back up the Registry hive files. So if you use NTBackup—and it's pretty good, when you consider its price—then you should tell it to back up your Registry every night.

NT 4 had a terrific tool named RDISK that would back up your entire Registry with just a few keystrokes, but that's nowhere to be found in Windows 2000 or later, including Server 2003. The replacement for RDISK can be found in the Backup program, which offers to create a System Repair Disk, just as RDISK did, through these steps:

1. Launch Backup (Start/Programs/Accessories/System Tools/Backup).
2. Click the Backup tab.
3. Make sure all directories and files are unchecked.
4. Look under My Computer's list of drives; the last option will be System State; check that.
5. Next to the list box labeled Backup Media or File Name, fill in a filename or click Browse and choose a filename; this is where the Registry backup will go.
6. Click the Start Backup button.
7. In the next dialog box, click the Advanced button.
8. Uncheck Automatically Backup System Protected Files with the System State.
9. Click OK to dismiss the dialog box.
10. Click Start Backup. Backup will then save the Registry. You can restore the Registry with Backup as well.

What if you want to back up only a portion of the Registry? As you've already read, Server 2003 includes a program called REG.EXE. It will, among other things, let you back up the Registry from the command line and while the system is running—but only *one subtree at a time*. It looks like REG SAVE HKLM\subtreename destination, where *destination* is the place that you want the backup to go, and the subtree names are, of course, SECURITY, SAM, SYSTEM, and SOFTWARE in the case of HKEY_LOCAL_MACHINE. Note also the abbreviation: REG accepts HKLM in place of HKEY_LOCAL_MACHINE, HKCU in place of HKEY_CURRENT_USER, HKCR in place of HKEY_CLASSES_ROOT, and HKCC in place of HKEY_CURRENT_CONFIGURATION.

A complete Registry backup to a directory named C:\RB would, then, require several lines:

```
Reg save HKCR c:\rb\hkcr
Reg save HKCC\Software c:\rb\hkccsoft
Reg save hkcc\system c:\rb\hkccsys
```

And so on. You'd restore the Registry with REG as well.

No one *wants* to play around in the Registry, but in real life, most network administrators will find a bit of Registry spelunking to be the only answer to many problems. Knowing how the Registry is organized and what tools are available to modify it will prove valuable to all Server repair folks.

Chapter 5

Setting Up and Rolling Out Windows Server 2003

EVERY NEW VERSION OF Windows or its big brother, NT, is a mixed blessing. We usually get more capabilities, but also more complexity. Now, you'd think that a more complex operating system would be more complex to set up, but here's a case where Microsoft has done a pretty decent job, as their setup routines get better and better with each OS version.

If you've ever set up an NT 4 system, then you're probably used to struggling with Setup to get it to accept third-party hardware drivers, but Plug and Play—which first appeared in Windows 2000 in the NT family and Server 2003 still has—largely solves that problem. Older NT required us to decide whether a computer would be a domain controller at setup time, but as with Windows 2000, all servers are born equal—you don't have to decide which will be domain controllers until after the servers are deployed.

Even better, Server 2003 comes with a variety of tools to assist you in rolling out servers unattended. You can script an install, as before, but scripts are easier. If you choose to use a disk-cloning routine like Ghost or Drive Image, Server 2003 includes an updated version of Sysprep, the utility that solves the duplicate SID problem that made many people chary of using cloners. And Server 2003 also includes my personal favorite rollout routine, the Remote Installation Service. Even if you're not interested in scripting, cloning, or RIS, you'll still like Server 2003's Setup routine for its simplicity.

The hard part comes when you want not only a stable, reliable installation, but also a *repeatable process*. This repeatable process will allow one-stop shopping for all of your installation needs and give you that clean and efficient install every time. However, to produce those perfect results time and time again, the planning and preparation phase of the install becomes even more important. Failure to properly plan out an install will most certainly result in a reinstall.

Throughout this chapter, I'll cover key fundamental planning steps, help you prepare your system for Server 2003, run through an install, and, finally, troubleshoot the mess we got ourselves into.

Planning and Preparation

As it's gotten on in years, NT has become more complex; putting an NT 3.1 system side by side with a Windows Server 2003 reveals that the OS's complexity has probably grown by more than a factor of ten. Complexity means options and options require planning.

Well, I guess that's not right—options don't really require planning. So long as, that is, you don't mind frequently reinstalling the operating system...

Server 2003's Setup is indeed better designed than earlier Setups, but it'll still go far more smoothly with a bit of planning. So stay with me in this section and I promise you'll end up saving time overall.

System Hardware Requirements

Once again, Microsoft has upped the ante on system requirements. Let's see what you'll need, minimum, to build a system with decent performance.

CPU NEEDS

While you *can* get Server 2003 running on something as slow as a 266MHz system, I strongly recommend at least a 1GHz system. Of course, 2GHz would be better, as would multiple processors. But one gig will do, provided you have lots of RAM. Which brings me to...

RAM REQUIREMENTS

We tend to think of CPUs as determining a system's speed, but as has always been the case for the NT family, having enough RAM to give the OS a lot of elbow room is every bit as important in ensuring snappy performance in a server.

But how much memory should you have? That's a tough question because it depends on what you want to *do* with the server: a simple file and print server might run just fine with 256MB of RAM, where a system running SQL Server, Exchange, IIS, and the like probably needs at least a couple of gigabytes of RAM to run well. But even though it's impossible for me to tell you *a priori* how much RAM you'll need, let me offer this advice: put at least a gigabyte of RAM on *any* Windows Server 2003 that you build, more if you can. If you turn your server on and the lights don't dim, then you haven't put enough RAM in the system! (Just kidding...)

More memory means more places for the memory hardware to fail, however, and that's why you need error-correcting code or ECC memory. You may recall something called *parity*, a set of circuits attached to memory systems of PCs in the '80s whose job was to monitor the memory and detect data loss in a PC's RAM. Such data loss could be caused by a bad memory chip, and you can find bad chips by testing your RAM with a good RAM tester program like CheckIt or QAPlus before deploying the server. But even perfect RAM chips can fall prey to random events that cause data loss; static electricity, power surges, and, believe it or not, infrequent extremely low-level radioactivity from the memory chips *themselves* can damage memory data. (Don't worry, you won't get cancer or mutations from your memory chips. Many, many everyday things in our world are mildly radioactive: the bricks cladding your house and, indeed, most kinds of ceramic produce an extremely small amount of radioactivity. Memory chips produce a radioactive particle once in a great while, and when they do, that particle may happen to cross paths with a location in memory—and when *that* happens, the memory bit may be flipped from a 0 to a 1 or vice versa.)

In any case, parity was kind of frustrating in that it could detect that *something* was wrong, but it didn't know *what* was wrong. PCs with parity memory were usually designed to simply shut down the PC when a memory error was detected using the parity method (which the error message would usually incorrectly call "a parity error" rather than a "memory error"—after all, if parity detected the memory error, then parity was working fine!), and shutting down an entire system just because parity discovered one damaged bit is a trifle extreme.

In contrast, most modern Pentium II-and-later–based systems (which, again, include the Xeon, Celeron, and of course the Pentium III and 4) can go a step further and implement ECC. ECC is cool because it not only *detects* memory errors, it *corrects* them automatically. So when that stray alpha particle or (more likely) power glitch scrambles a bit, ECC finds that problem and fixes it without ever bothering you.

Now you may be wondering, "How much would such a wonderful feature cost?" Well, back in the old days, I worked on minicomputer systems with ECC that cost thousands of dollars. But most Pentium II–based systems can do it for about $20 per 128MB of RAM. Here's the trick: most PC memories these days are implemented as synchronous dynamic random access memory, or SDRAM, packages. SDRAMs come in a 64-bit version or a 72-bit version. The difference in price between ECC and non-ECC RAM is small—about $25 on a gigabyte of RAM, when last I checked. That's a pretty good price for a "data insurance policy."

TIP Recently I've noticed that people selling RAM don't label it as "64-bit" or "72-bit"; rather, they've taken to calling all memory modules "64-bit" and then adding the phrase "w/ECC" or the like. If you're in doubt about what you're buying, insist that a phrase like "with enabled ECC memory" or something similar be in the invoice. And yes, you have to insist on that. I flatly cannot understand why anyone sells any PC system nowadays without ECC, but the majority of systems are still without the benefit of ECC.

You may have to go into your system's setup BIOS in order to turn on the ECC feature. Not all systems activate ECC by default.

STORAGE REQUIREMENTS

A basic bare-bones installation of Windows Server 2003, Standard Edition chews up about 1.5GB of space on a hard disk. Of course, you'll want to put things on the disk other than the OS, so you'll need more than that—how much more is up to you based on what you want to do with the server. But if you're just planning on building a system to play around with to get to know the OS better, I found a 4GB C: drive to be about the right size.

Server 2003 brings some terrific news about inexpensive EIDE drives in that they are now treated *asynchronously*. Here's what that means in English: throughout computing history, it's often made better sense to buy a bunch of smaller drives instead of one large drive. That's because each hard disk has its own independent set of read/write heads. More than one drive means more than one set of read/write heads, which means that it's easier for the computer software to do more than one thing at a time. For example, you could often speed up an NT server by spreading its paging file across several separate physical hard disks.

Unfortunately, that advice only worked with SCSI drives. The driver for EIDE drives, atapi.sys, couldn't "juggle"—if you told it to simultaneously work with two or more EIDE drives, it would instead just alternate between the drives. Whatever software you were running would *work* fine; it would just run more slowly than it would if the EIDE driver *could* juggle.

With Server 2003, that changes, and the atapi.sys driver is more facile. EIDE drives *can* run simultaneously, so long as they are on different EIDE channels. That's not to say that I don't recommend SCSI drives for servers—they're almost always a better answer than EIDE—but for those on a severe budget, EIDE drives now look like an okay idea, where in earlier versions of Server, EIDE drives were a terrible idea.

A bootable CD-ROM drive, although not required, is always highly recommended. A time always comes when your server crashes and you need a reinstall fast. Rather than scrambling for boot disks to get you connected to your installation source on the network, you simply pop the CD in and off you go.

A network-bootable system—one that supports the Preboot Execution Environment (PXE) standard, version 0.99C or later—would be a real plus. This lets you set up a computer to boot from the network. You'll like having this feature because it makes installing Server (or XP, for that matter) from a central RIS server *much* easier.

All of your hardware requirements can be further summed up by referencing the *Hardware Compatibility List (HCL)*. Every piece of hardware in your system should be on the list. Anything not on the list could generate problems from application failures to system crashes and probably won't even install at all. Why? Most likely, if your hardware is not on the list, you will have a hard time locating a driver. Should you happen to have an OEM driver that came with the hardware, you are risking system insta- bility because Microsoft hasn't tested or guaranteed it to work. Why do you care? Because if you get on the phone to Microsoft and give them the requisite $245 in order to get them to help you with a problem, and *then* you tell them that you've got hardware that's not on the HCL, the Microsoft support person gets to say, "Golly, I'm sorry, your stuff isn't on the HCL, that's the problem," and hang up. Result: a free quarter kilobuck for Bill and no solution for you. If you trust the manufacturer of the hardware who provided the driver to have fully tested it with all aspects of Server 2003, fine. Be cautious, though. The best recommendation is that if you are buying new hardware, consult the list first. You can find the HCL on your Server CD (\Support\HCL.txt) or on the Web at ftp://ftp.microsoft.com/services/whql/HCL/.

Preparing the Hardware

Once you have your hardware, I strongly recommend that you get it working and compatible first. Throughout the process, Setup will examine, activate, reexamine, configure, poke, and prod at every piece of hardware in your system that it can find. This is where the Plug-and-Play intricacies come in. If everything in your system is true Plug and Play, this process should go off without a hitch. Mix in a few older devices that don't fit this bill and you could get some serious problems, including complete setup failure.

In this section, we'll do whatever we can to avoid these problems before we even launch Setup.

Preparing the BIOS

Most machines have highly configurable BIOSes, which can really play an important role in how Server 2003 operates. For the pre-Setup phase, you can look for obvious settings that may interfere with your installation. Your boot device order may need customizing to allow you to boot to the CD. This, I find, is one of the most convenient ways to do an install. But then again, if you weren't expect- ing the CD to be bootable, you could inadvertently keep rebooting into the initial install phase from the CD over and over again, thinking you were getting the hard drive. Nothing major, but it has happened to the best of us.

The most important parts of the BIOS you'll prepare are Plug-and-Play configuration and inter- rupt reservations. Because most systems capable of running Server 2003 are fairly modern by default, this step is a little bit easier. The problem comes when you try to add older, non-Plug-and-Play components into your Plug-and-Play system. For example, you may have a non-Plug-and-Play device that is an old ISA network adapter, hard-coded for interrupt 10. When your Plug-and-Play devices come online, let's say that you may have one that prefers to initialize on interrupt 10, not knowing that your ISA card will soon request the same. As soon as the driver initializes the ISA card, there's conflict.

The best thing to do is to configure interrupt 10 under your Plug-and-Play BIOS settings to be reserved for a non-Plug-and-Play card. This tells any Plug-and-Play device to leave that interrupt alone. But now you have the problem of determining *what* those interrupts are *before* you start the install. Your non-Plug-and-Play device may have a configuration disk that programs it for specific settings. There may be jumpers on the hardware. Most troublesome, there may be no obvious clue as to what it is set for. In this case, a DOS-level hardware analyzer may be required to identify those resources being used.

TIP   *Actually, let me rephrase that last topic sentence. The best thing to do is to only buy Plug-and-Play—compatible hardware for your server.* Period.

Once you have identified and recorded all required hardware information, return to your BIOS configuration. You may have a Plug-and-Play configuration screen that lets you define whether certain interrupts are available for general use—including being allocated by Plug-and-Play boards—or whether they should be reserved for ISA boards. Since non-Plug-and-Play boards are generally not BIOS-aware, they will continue to use the interrupt that has been reserved, but note that when your Plug-and-Play boards initialize, they will be denied the resource usage as defined by the BIOS.

In most cases, the procedure of reserving resources through the BIOS will allow all hardware to work in harmony. If not, you may find it necessary to remove all nonessential, non-Plug-and-Play devices from your system before you begin. Then, once you have a successful install, add your hardware. Again, though, let me stress: if all of your hardware is Plug-and-Play, then you will probably have no trouble at all—so avoid that old non-PnP stuff as much as possible!

Partitioning

In my opinion, planning the partitioning scheme seems to be one of the most overlooked portions of the installation process. Although Server 2003 gives you some more advanced features for managing your partitions after the install, what you decide on prior to the install will most likely stick with you throughout the life of your server.

Knowing what type of server you are building plays a tremendously big part in the planning process. Let's go back to our simple member server that serves out several shared directories and a few print queues. You may find it more convenient in the long run to keep your data on one partition and the system on another. In that case, you only need enough space for the OS, with a little breathing room—my suggestion is a 4GB partition minimum for the OS.

If you are intending to use the Remote Installation Services, then be sure to set aside a *big* partition solely for its use. RIS cannot store system images on either the system partition (the partition that the system boots from, usually C:) *or* the boot partition (the one containing \windows). (And yes, the definition of "boot" and "system" partitions *is* completely backward, but then remember that this is an operating system where you click Start to stop it.)

At this point, as both drive space *and* drives are cheap, I tend to buy more than one disk drive even for the smallest systems. Even my low-end EIDE-using servers have at least two hard disks—a 20GB drive that I make C: and put programs on, and a much larger other drive (120GB minimum) for data. And please note that I wrote that sentence in late 2002, so if you're reading this in 2004, when the smallest hard disk you can buy will be 300GB, keep the time context in mind!

Filesystems

How to format your drives—NTFS, FAT, or FAT32? Nowadays, it's a slam-dunk: NTFS. It's secure, resilient, and fast. Yes, people tell me now and then that FAT32 is faster for large sequential reads and writes as proven by some benchmark, but I suspect that benchmark was done a long time ago in the days of slow drives, slow processors, and little RAM; I simply cannot create a scenario where FAT32 mops the floor with NTFS. In the absence of a strong performance difference, I can't imagine why anyone would use anything but NTFS on a Server 2003 server.

The most compelling argument in favor of a FAT C: drive on NT 4 for me was recovery. If I made C: a FAT drive and something went wrong, then I could boot a DOS/Windows 9*x* bootable floppy and fix things—DOS can't read NTFS drives. But versions of NT from Windows 2000 on include something called the Recovery Console, which is basically a DOS for NTFS repair tool—you'll learn more about it in Chapter 19.

NOTE *Speaking of that, you'll sometimes hear people say that NTFS-formatted drives are the way to go (which I agree with) because they're entirely secure (which I don't agree with). The reasoning is that an NTFS drive supposedly can't be read by booting up a DOS diskette, so someone sitting down at your server can't just boot a DOS floppy and see your files. As nice as it sounds, this is a bogus argument because there are several approaches to reading NTFS drives when booted from a floppy running either DOS or Linux. The point is that if you let someone physically sit down at your server and boot a floppy, then you've got a serious security problem. No operating system can protect a server from a physical attack. I mean, it doesn't matter how good your passwords are: if I want to damage your network and can get to your server, then I don't need passwords to drop the server out of an eighth-story window.*

One final point about file systems: if you *do* create a server on a FAT drive, you always have the option to convert the file system to NTFS later; just open up a command line and type **convert /fs:ntfs**. There is *not*, by the way, an option to convert back to FAT, so don't make the change to NTFS unless you're sure that it's the way that you want to go!

Server Name

This seems like a no-brainer, but it's a good idea to plan your naming convention. There are two ways that most people make living with server names difficult. The first is underestimating the importance of server names. The second is overdoing it when it comes to a standard convention.

By underestimating naming conventions, you end up with server names like GEORGE, ELROY, JUDY, and ASTRO on your network. This is fine for a small office LAN that will never grow too far beyond your ability to remember these names. When you start getting more than those few servers, it gets difficult to remember who is what.

Sometimes people overdo standard conventions by defining so many formats, items, and indexes into the name that it becomes just as confusing. Some of the things people put in a name is the server's geographic location, building location, room number, role, and an index. For example, a server in Annapolis residing in the Commerce Center building that is an Exchange server might be named ANNCCBEXC01. This information is fine, but keep it to useful information that resembles the important features in your network. Does your network and its users really care what building the server is in? What about the city? What if you add another Exchange server in the courthouse? That would be named ANNCRTEXC01. Perhaps a better method here would be to put the EXC first. Simplicity is key. You may want to define your network into systems and that's it. If you had two

Exchange systems, one for the Commerce Department and one for the Treasury Department, you may want COMMAIL01 and TREMAIL01. This may allow a better grouping of servers.

The bottom line here is to really think about it. Get the customers and the people who will manage the network involved. Get a consensus on what is important and what is not important. Although you can easily change the name of the server later, you can't easily change the hundreds or thousands of users' workstations that connect to it.

NOTE *Here's an interesting improvement: in earlier versions of NT it was a fairly bad idea to name workstations and user accounts the same—putting Joe on a machine named Joe led to the domain containing two accounts named JOE, both a user account and a machine account. That gave NT a bit of heartburn. But ever since Windows 2000, NT solves that problem by assigning machines account names ending in $, so Joe's workstation's account wouldn't be JOE, it'd be JOE$. You do not see this $ in most domain tools, but it's there.*

Network Connection and Options

Not knowing your network configuration ahead of time isn't usually going to be a showstopper. Knowing it can save you time though.

PROTOCOLS

Ever since NT 3.5, Microsoft has been trying to chivvy us into abandoning NetBEUI and making our networks 100 percent TCP/IP. Don't get me wrong, I think it's a great idea, but they've had to move slowly because lots of networks used NetBEUI, *and* because Windows 95 clients never ran very well with *just* TCP/IP—a few things like Network Neighborhood ran better with NetBEUI than with TCP/IP on 95.

With Server 2003, Microsoft takes things a step or two further.

First, as with Windows 2000, the only protocol that Server 2003 installs by default is TCP/IP. But Server 2003 is new in that it doesn't even offer NetBEUI as a protocol option, offering only IPX and AppleTalk as TCP/IP alternatives. NetBEUI *is* available on the Server 2003 CD in the \VALUEADD\MSFT\ NET\NETBEUI folder, but you've got to do a bit of looking to find it! So if your network still has a bit of residual NetBEUI, now's the time to do a little spring cleaning and go TCP/IP all the way.

Setting up TCP/IP requires knowing a few things about your system—what its IP address, subnet mask, default gateway, and preferred DNS server will be, for starters, or will you instead use DHCP? (If you're not clear on what those things are, take a look at Chapters 6 and 7.) Find out this protocol info ahead of time—those network gurus are never around when you need them in mid-install.

DOMAIN MEMBERSHIP

Almost every server will be a member of a domain rather than a workgroup, and in early versions of Windows NT you had to make some serious you'd-better-get-this-right-the-first-time-there's-no-going-back decisions at Setup time. Ever since Windows 2000, however, there's a bit less pressure. In the pre-2000 days, you had to decide at Setup time whether a system was a domain controller or just a member server. With 2000 and later versions of Server, you needn't answer that question now; instead, all systems come out of Setup as member servers and you can decide to change any of them to domain controllers later with a program called DCPROMO, which you'll meet in Chapter 8.

You can, however, join an existing domain from Setup. If you want to do that, you will need to have a computer account created in the domain. A computer account is almost identical to a user account, and like a user account, it resides in the accounts database held with the domain controllers.

If the server is a member of a domain, it can assign rights and permissions to users belonging to its member domain or any of its trusted domains. This is important to your users. They should log in once to the network and never have to be asked for a password again. If the server resides in a workgroup, then the ability to give rights to domain users is out of the question, causing multiple login points.

UPGRADING DOMAIN CONTROLLERS

Speaking of domain membership, here's an important note about domain *controllers*. If you are thinking of upgrading an NT 4 box that is acting as a domain controller, then I urge you to think once and twice before upgrading. You can cavalierly upgrade just about any other computer, but the domain controllers need some planning, or you'll be very, very sorry!

You see, upgrading an NT 4 domain controller has an important side effect: it upgrades your NT 4 domain to an Active Directory—the Windows 2000 Server and Server 2003 name for a domain. Server 2003's Setup doesn't allow you to upgrade any of your backup domain controllers until you've upgraded the *primary* domain controller. So you might want to think twice before simply upgrading your existing DCs. Personally, I prefer a domain upgrade technique called "clean and pristine," and I'll discuss it in Chapter 8, the Active Directory chapter. You might want to read up to that chapter before doing any NT-to-Server 2003 surgery on your domain controllers. Basically, however, I advocate building a brand-new, empty Active Directory domain built atop either Windows 2000 Server or Server 2003 systems, then moving the user accounts over to that domain, leaving your old NT 4 domains in place "just in case" as you migrate. For small domains, however—say, 500 users or fewer—you may not have to do that much work, and an in-place upgrade to Active Directory may be an acceptable option. More on that in Chapter 8.

NETWORKING COMPONENTS

These are the additional services to be installed, like Internet Information Services and DNS Server. This is where I like to say things like "Ooh… Quality of Service Admission Control Protocol… sounds neat, gimme that." That's exactly what we shouldn't say. Don't overdo it here. Every option selected installs another service or utility that will consume more resources on your server, and more software in your system means more places where bugs could lurk—and *that* means more potential places for viruses to attack. Keep those servers as lean and mean as you can by minimizing the amount of software running on them!

Also be aware of the effect certain services may have on the rest of your network. Some services will require clients to be connected explicitly to a given server. On the other hand, some, like DHCP Server, act on a broadcast level and can affect clients just by being present. In addition, most services, also just by being present, have an adverse effect on available system resources. Hard-disk space is consumed for additional files, memory is taken up by loading more programs, and processor cycles are consumed by running excessive services that really don't have anything to do with what your server is intended to do. Unless you will specifically be using the service on this particular server, don't install these additional components.

SERVER LICENSING

Licensing options remain pretty much the same as they have since NT 3.51. You are given per-seat or per-server licensing modes:

◆ Per-seat licensing requires that every client on the network that accesses your server has its own license. This is the easiest method of adding up your licensing, because you only account for how many clients you have; you don't need to worry about either concurrent connections from those clients into a single server or to how many servers each client holds a connection.

◆ Per-server licensing differs in that each client-to-server connection requires a license. If a client connects to 25 different servers, that client will take up 1 license on each server, totaling 25 licenses. You may know this as a "concurrent use license." It's simpler because it's easy to track—once that 26th person tries to attach, he's just denied the connection—but it's usually more expensive because you then have to buy a bunch of licenses for *each* server.

Which way to go? Well, the short answer is: Per-seat is almost always the right technique. But if you want more details...

WARNING   *Let me stress that licensing is not so much a technological issue as it is a legal issue. I'm not a lawyer and therefore not qualified to be your sole advisor about software licensing. The following is just my layman's understanding of a legal issue. Do not make all of your licensing decisions based on information in this book. Microsoft's licensing is so complex that you can ask the same licensing question of four people and get five answers. So the best you can do is to equip yourself with the facts and then go buy the licenses from some firm that sells Microsoft stuff.*

Per-seat is usually the cheapest licensing method if you have more than one server. Under per-seat licensing, you buy a client access license, or CAL, for every *computer* that will attach to your enterprise's servers. Again, that's *computer*, not person. So if Joe Manager reads his Exchange mail from the computer on his desktop sometimes, reads it on the road with his laptop sometimes, and once in a while comes in through the firewall from home, then you need to buy *three licenses for Joe Manager*. Surprised? Most people are. On the one hand, it means that if three people share a computer, then those folks only need one CAL. On the other hand, nowadays everyone has one *or more* computers, so CALs start to add up. By the way, CALs list for around $40, although you can buy them in bulk more cheaply and large organizations usually have some kind of an unlimited-client deal. But you don't want to run afoul of the software watchdogs, so if you go with per-seat licensing, then be darn sure that you've got every computer covered! (And, sadly, that may mean that you have to disallow employees from checking their e-mail or using other corporate resources from their home, unless they're using a company-issued laptop.)

Per-server licensing is simpler. You tell a server that you've purchased some number of CALs. The server's Licensing Service (a built-in part of Windows Server 2003) then keeps track of how many people are connected to the server at any moment. If you have X licenses and the $X+1$st person tries to attach to the server, that person is denied access.

This sounds simple, but the problem is that you've got to buy a CAL for each connection for each server. For example, suppose you have 4 servers, 25 employees, and 40 workstation PCs—there are more PCs than employees because of laptops and "general access" PCs. Suppose your goal is that all 25 employees can access any and all servers at any time.

Under per-server licensing, you'd have to buy 25 CALs for *each* server, or 100 CALs total.

Under per-seat licensing, you'd license each of the machines—all 40 of them—with a CAL. That one CAL would enable someone sitting at a machine to access any and all of the servers, no matter how many domains your system contains. Thus, in this case, 40 CALs would do the trick. In general, you'll find that per-seat is the cheaper way to go, but again, be careful about remembering to license all of the laptops and (possibly) home PCs.

Most likely, especially in larger environments, the licensing has already been worked out ahead of time. Prior to starting your first install, make sure that your licensing is best suited not just for your network, but also for the way your clients use the network.

UPGRADE OR FRESH INSTALL?

Finally, you need to decide whether you will be upgrading an existing operating system or performing a clean install.

This can be a real toughie. On the one hand, if you've got a server that's already running a bunch of services, and each one took quite some time to get just so, then running Setup as an upgrade is pretty attractive. On the other hand, if you're upgrading a system that will be working for some time to come, then it's awfully appealing to use the fact that you're changing the operating system as an excuse to also clean house, starting from ground zero and building a nice new system uncluttered by who-knows-what old data or programs that are just hanging around.

Personally, I do a clean install whenever possible. But the key words there are "whenever *possible*." If I really have about two hours to get an install done before the server's got to be up and ready in a production environment, then an upgrade's the way to go. But if I have a bit more time, I go with a clean install. Cleanly installed systems take time to tweak to whatever standards you're using in your organization.

Furthermore, I've had, well, spotty results from upgrades. In my experience upgrading from NT 3.1 to 3.5 (I lost my printer shares), 3.5 to 3.51 (some domain controllers simply refused to work), and 3.51 to 4 (several miscellaneous problems), I've run into problems. Having said that, I should in all honesty say that pretty much all of my NT 4-to-2000 upgrades were pretty smooth, so perhaps Microsoft has gotten the hang of upgrades. If you *do* upgrade, however, be sure to defragment your disk when you get done, and use the free `pagedfrg.exe` utility from `www.sysinternals.com`—it defrags your pagefile, a large and important file on your system.

If you've decided on a clean install, there isn't much more you need to do. If you're running an upgrade, there are still a few considerations. The last thing you want to do is upgrade a cluttered system and carry over any issues that belong to the clutter. Many people sit in front of the server so much that they install their mail client, office suite, and other programs and utilities that are not related to what the server is supposed to be doing. These should all be uninstalled before running an upgrade. Look at your services on the server. Any third-party services, such as antivirus, Web publishing, disk defragmenting, or other types of software, should also be removed prior to beginning an upgrade. By doing so, there is much less to get in the way of your upgrade.

Setting Up and Installing

Now that we have analyzed the life out of planning for an install, let's get to it. Setup runs in three stages. First, the Preinstall Setup Wizard runs; you'll only see this if you're installing Server 2003 from inside NT 4 or Windows 2000 Server—that is, if you've popped the Server 2003 install CD into a system already running NT 4 or Win2K. This process defines those options that configure *how* to do the install. The second stage is the text-based setup, which simply defines where to install. Finally, the graphical-based setup stage, also called a setup wizard, customizes everything from installed protocols and services to computer name and domain membership to the system time and date. After this final stage is complete, your server should be ready for final cleanup.

Preinstallation: Phase 1

You install Windows Server 2003 from a set of files on your installation CD, the files in the I386 directory. As with all installations, though, there's the very important question, "How do I make my computer able to see, copy, and execute these files?" The size of I386 means that you can't put the whole operating system on a floppy. (Those days are *waaaay* gone forever.) Instead, you'll have to deliver the files to your computer in one of several ways:

◆ Put I386 on a bootable CD-ROM disc. This is how it ships from Microsoft. It's easy to just boot the CD and follow the prompts, *but* this method won't work for every system because some systems lack CDs, and some older systems *have* CD drives but cannot boot from them. Thankfully, this is not a very common problem, but it *does* pop up now and then.

◆ Put I386 on a shared volume on the network. This works, but you then have to somehow get the computer booted up enough to access network shares. We'll talk more about this later.

◆ Set up a Remote Installation Services (RIS) server and set up your computer to boot to the RIS server with a Preboot eXEcution (PXE) client. I'll cover that in the later section on RIS.

◆ Set up a simpler operating system (DOS or Windows 98 without the GUI, for example) on the computer, copy I386 to the computer's local hard disk, and start Setup from inside the simpler operating system. You'll see how to do this when we discuss the `winnt.exe` and `winnt32.exe` commands.

NT and 2000 veterans may be waiting for me to list the last option: start from boot floppies. For systems that had CD-ROM drives but could not boot from them, NT and 2000 could generate four floppies that could "wake the computer up" enough to read the CD-ROM drive and commence Setup. That's no longer available under Server 2003.

From MS-DOS, Windows 3.1, or Windows for Workgroups 3.11, you will need to start your setup in the DOS-based mode found with `winnt.exe`. Or, from Windows 9*x*, you can start in Safe Mode Command Prompt and run `winnt.exe` after issuing the LOCK command.

From a Windows 9*x* system, or earlier versions of NT, you'll launch the installation from the `winnt32.exe`. This GUI version of the setup executable gives you that user-friendly, yes-or-no click method of initiating the install. For this example, I'm using the drive letter F: as the CD source on an Intel-based system. To follow along, select Start/Run and enter the following:

```
F:\I386\winnt32.exe
```

WHEN UPGRADING

If you have a system that can be upgraded to Server 2003, you will immediately reach the prompt to decide whether to run a clean install or an upgrade. If you do not have an upgrade-capable machine, you will be informed that an upgrade is not available, and the upgrade option will be grayed out.

NOTE   *Only Windows NT 4 and Windows 2000 servers can be upgraded to Windows Server 2003.*

If running an upgrade, you'll see an overall list of things that Setup will do, as well as a Welcome to Windows Setup opening wizard screen where you first choose whether to do an upgrade or not. You'll then see the License Agreement screen, where you click I Accept This Agreement. But *do* take a minute to read it—most people don't realize that in agreeing you assent to becoming an organ donor if Bill Gates needs a transplant. Okay, I'm kidding, but seriously you really *should* read this End User License Agreement or EULA (pronounced "yoola") and every other one that you agree to…some of them are pretty scary!

Following the license agreement, Setup will ask for the 25-character product key, presuming that you have a version of Server 2003 that requires that. Larger organizations will have CD-ROMS with the niftier corporate version of Setup, which does not require a product key.

Next you'll see something new to Server's Setup program: Get Updated Setup Files. (New to Server, but XP's done it since 2001.) The idea here—which is an great one, in my opinion—is that Microsoft realizes that over time bugs and security holes appear; in fact, it's downright scary to install Windows 2000 on a system that's attached to the Internet, as some IIS worms will actually find it and infect it before you're even finished installing the silly thing! The updated Setup files (or Dynamic Update, as it's called) let you pull down installation files that are newer than the ones on your CD, files that would be prepatched against the worm du jour. Now, of course, those files can be pretty large; as I write this there aren't really any downloadable Setup files to speak of, but I'm sure in time you'll need to download a few hundred megabytes of updated files. That's why you'll like that you can collect the dynamic update files to a share on your network and then tell Setup to use those files from a local share, rather than making you do a day-long download every time you install Server 2003. I'll cover more on dynamic updates later in this chapter.

Once you've told Setup whether or not to use dynamic updates, it goes out and checks for any particular items that might cause trouble with the installation. That'll look something like Figure 5.1.

FIGURE 5.1

Setup troubles

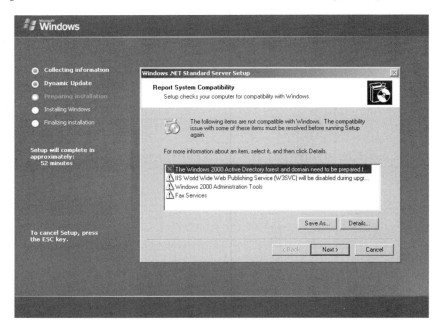

You'll likely get at least a few warnings; *read them*, and if they're no problem just click past them to continue Setup. If you have a real showstopper, as in my figure, then Setup will just stop.

Let me say again: read those warnings and errors! Microsoft does a pretty good job of explaining what they mean and how to address them. For example, note the IIS one—believe it or not, Setup *disables* IIS unless you've run their IIS Lockdown Tool, something that I personally don't care for, or unless you make a Registry change. While an automatic Next is often the answer for wizards, it's not in this case. Imagine running what seems to be a simple upgrade on your Web server, only to find that the Web server doesn't work anymore!

Once you've gotten past the warnings, assuming that you have any, then the system doesn't ask you much else—upgrades don't require a lot of interaction.

WHEN INSTALLING FRESH

If, on the other hand, you started Setup from inside NT 4 or Win2K Server, then you will initially see the same things just described in "When Upgrading." But in a fresh install, unlike an upgrade, Setup will then need a bunch of answers from you.

Following the Product Key page, you get the Windows Setup page. This lets you set the desired language and accessibility settings.

Copy Installation Files from This Folder   Refers to the place from which you will be installing Windows Server 2003. This is useful if you're installing from a folder where you've precopied all of the I386 files. If you're installing from the CD, then you typically needn't worry about this.

Copy to This Folder on My Hard Drive   Tells Setup what directory to install Server 2003 to. This defaults to \Windows (note the new directory—no more winnt!) but it can be changed to another directory if you want. If you intend to install multiple copies of Server on a system, then use a different directory name. This field won't take the drive letter. Note that if you're upgrading from 2000 or NT, you'll end up with two OSes—one in \winnt and one in \windows. That can pose some problems, so either tell it to put the OS in \winnt so it'll overwrite the old one, or skip starting Setup from inside the old OS and just boot from the CD and wipe the hard disk clean before installing Windows Server 2003.

Copy All Installation Files from the Setup CD   Creates a complete setup source on one of your local hard drives under the directory \win_nt.~1s. Under this directory, you will find the I386 source you are so familiar with.

NOTE   Most systems won't need the Copy All Installation Files option selected. Server 2003 will do a pretty good job of loading the right drivers to reconnect you to your source after the reboot. However, if you fail to find your source for the text-based setup, this option will get you back on track.

I Want to Choose the Install Drive Letter and Partition During Setup   Allows you to define which partition you will be installing Server 2003 in. Select it and you will get a prompt following the reboot to choose your partition.

Accessibility Options   Those available for Setup include the Narrator and Magnifier. By selecting these options now, the tools will be available during the next installation phase.

After this page in the wizard, Setup asks about dynamic updates, and then copies the installation files to your hard disk. Setup's now ready for the text-based portion of Setup, and it'll prompt you for a reboot.

ANATOMY OF A MACHINE READY FOR SETUP, PHASE 2

Ever wonder what makes a system continue along its setup path after a reboot? Or have you ever started into the second phase of the setup, had all sorts of problems, and wanted to start from scratch? It will help to know exactly what causes the second phase to start upon reboot so you can easily remove it later. These components are going to be present on your system after completion of the preinstallation phase of the setup:

◆ On the boot partition, a directory named win_nt.~bt has been created.

◆ All critical Server 2003 boot files, including enough drivers to access the network or CD source, have been copied to the win_nt.~bt directory.

◆ In the win_nt.~bt directory, a file named winnt.sif contains the information you provided from the first phase of the setup.

◆ The Server 2003 boot files have been copied to the boot partition (unless you've overridden them with a winnt or winnt32 option) if not already present. The system is now Server 2003–bootable. (Note that when I say "boot" I mean it in the standard this-is-the-drive-that-the-computer-boots-from meaning, rather than Microsoft's "official" definition—for some reason, they define the partition that contains the bulk of the operating system files as the "boot" partition, and the partition that you boot from as the "system" partition. Don't ask me why.)

◆ The boot.ini is configured to default to the win_nt.~bt\bootsect.dat after 5 seconds.

Text-Based Setup: Phase 2

The text-based portion of Server 2003 Setup is very similar to Windows 2000's text Setup. You get your welcome screen, make a few selections on where you want to do your install, and then you sit back and watch the Setup program copy a whole bunch of files. It's a really simple click-Next-to-continue process, but there are some gotchas hiding in there, so I'll go through it a bit at a time.

NOTE   *This is the first phase you'll see if you're installing by booting from the CD-ROM.*

As soon as your machine boots into the text-based portion of Setup, you may notice a prompt at the bottom of the screen that tells you to press F6 if you need to install additional SCSI or RAID drivers. If you don't want these additional drivers, just wait a few seconds and it will go away. But if your system has a SCSI or RAID controller that you know isn't going to initialize without an OEM-provided driver, you'll need to watch this part of Setup closely and hit F6.

The install starts off with a Welcome to Setup screen. You have the choice to set up Server 2003, repair an existing Server 2003 installation, or quit. The Press F3 to Quit option will live with you throughout this phase of the setup. If at any time during this phase you decide that you want to abort your setup attempt, this will be your escape route. Upon this exit, your system will be rebooted, but be aware that your boot.ini file will not have been changed. Subsequent reboots will still by default cause your machine to restart the setup after 5 seconds at the boot menu. To get rid of this permanently, edit your `boot.ini` to reflect the default equal to your other operating system boot path of choice. My machine looked like the following:

```
[Boot Loader]
Timeout=5
Default=C:\$win_nt$.~bt\bootsect.dat
[Operating Systems]
multi(0)disk(0)rdisk(0)partition(2)\winnt="Microsoft
↳Windows 2000 Server"/fastdetect
C:\="Microsoft Windows 98"
C:\$win_nt$.~bt\bootsect.dat="Microsoft Windows Server 2003 Setup"
```

To restore my machine to its original boot preferences, I changed the Default line back to my Windows 2000 Server boot selection and deleted the entire Windows Server 2003 Setup option. Consequently, my `boot.ini` looked like this:

```
[Boot Loader]
Timeout=5
Default=multi(0)disk(0)rdisk(0)partition(2)\winnt
[Operating Systems]
multi(0)disk(0)rdisk(0)partition(2)\winnt="Microsoft
↳Windows 2000 Server"/fastdetect
C:\="Microsoft Windows 98"
```

Press Enter, and if you already have some NT-family operating system running on this computer then Setup will ask if you want to repair it. As we're installing fresh, press ESC to continue. That'll take you to the Disk Partitioning and Installation Location Selection screen. Be careful here. There are two things to do. The most obvious is the selection of the partition in which you want Server 2003 installed. Highlight the partition where you would like Server 2003 installed, and press Enter.

Let's take this a step further. Beneath this screen is a very handy disk-partitioning utility. From here, you can completely redo your partitioning scheme. You can delete existing partitions, create new partitions out of unpartitioned space, and format partitions in either the NTFS or FAT format file systems.

NOTE *You can find more information on disk partitioning in Chapter 10.*

Before we begin partitioning our drives, let's go back to the planning session we had earlier. Suppose for the sake of example that we want a 1GB Windows 98 C: partition, a 2GB system partition on drive D:, and a 4GB data partition on drive E:. Just to give us all the necessary scenarios to describe how the setup phase partitions drives, we'll assume we have a current partition scheme of a 1GB C: with Windows 98, a 1GB D:, a 2GB E:, and a 3GB F: partition. To go from a 1-1-2-3 gigabyte partition scheme to a 1-2-4 gigabyte partition scheme, we are forced to delete almost all partitions, since we cannot reorder partitions. In other words, we cannot massage our existing second partition of 1GB into a 2GB partition without giving it more room first.

Let's start by deleting the 1GB D: partition. Use the arrows to highlight the D: partition, and press D to delete. A confirmation screen will appear asking you to now either press L to continue the partition deletion or Escape to abort.

WARNING *Always take this opportunity to second-guess yourself. Once you press L to confirm the deletion of the partition, your partition and everything that was on it is gone. Ask yourself what data is on the D: drive. Make sure you can afford to lose it all. Do you have a backup of the data? If it contains a previous Server installation, do you have a backup of the security and accounts databases? If rebuilding a domain controller, have you promoted someone else to PDC? Do you have a recent Emergency Repair Disk available? If you are 100-percent confident that you don't need anything on the partition, press L.*

When you come back to the main Disk Partitioning screen, you'll see that the second partition of 1GB is now marked as unpartitioned space. Of course, it does no good to repartition this space now because the most you'll get is 1GB again. That would defeat the purpose of the exercise. You need 2GB. So move on down the list to what was the 2GB E: partition and delete it in the same fashion. When you return to the main screen again, after confirming the deletion of the 2GB partition, you'll find that the adjacent, unpartitioned spaces have turned into a single block of unpartitioned space equaling 3GB. Just to keep it simple, we now have our 1GB C:, a 3GB unpartitioned space from our combined, deleted 1GB and 2GB partitions, and a remaining 3GB partition.

At this point, we'll go ahead and create our new 2GB D: partition. Highlight the 3GB free space and press C for create. You'll move into a new screen where you're shown the total available space within which you can create a partition and are asked how large a partition you want to make. By default, the maximum available space is filled in: 3GB. We want to drop that down to 2GB. Press Enter and presto! We have a 2GB new (unformatted) partition, followed by our remaining 1GB that we left out and the 3GB data partition.

After we delete our 3GB partition, it will melt into the adjacent 1GB partition, forming a 4GB unpartitioned space. We can create the new 4GB space and we're set with partitioning anyway.

Now we still have to format our partition before we can use it. To format a partition, highlight the space listed as New (Unformatted) and press Enter to select the partition as your Server 2003 installation directory. Really, you're not selecting a partition to format; you're just selecting a partition in which to install Server 2003. If Setup finds that your chosen installation partition is not formatted, you'll get an additional screen to do just that. You are shown options to format FAT or NTFS, and now Server 2003 includes the options to do "quick formats" in each case. Once again, return to our planning phase of the setup. We should already know what format we want. Once the format is complete, we continue onward with the installation.

TIP *If you want only to partition and format drives without continuing to do an installation, you can always choose to go backward after the format and select another partition to format or install to, or you can simply exit the installation program.*

Setup will now examine your disks. This examination is not an intensive look into the reliability of your disk. It merely runs a CHKDSK-like utility to verify a clean file and directory structure. After the examination, Setup will copy all Server 2003 installation files to your chosen install location. Finally, the system will ready itself for the graphical setup phase and reboot.

CHANGES FROM NT 4'S TEXT-BASED SETUP

If you're used to NT 4 servers and haven't previously done a setup of either 2000 or Server 2003, then you'll notice some things missing from this phase of the Windows 2000 setup compared to the setup for previous versions of Windows NT. You no longer get the options to define the following:

◆ Basic PC type

Continued on next page

CHANGES FROM NT 4'S TEXT-BASED SETUP *(continued)*

◆ Video system

◆ Keyboard

◆ Country layout for keyboard (defined in phase 1)

◆ Mouse

They're not necessary anymore because Server 2003 (and 2000, for that matter) supports Plug and Play.

Graphical-Based Setup: Phase 3

As soon as you boot into the graphical-based setup phase of the install, Server 2003 will run a Plug-and-Play detection phase to configure all your hardware. This can take quite a while, and because disk formatting and file copying (both in Phase 2) take some time and Setup reboots itself and moves directly to the PnP detection phase, I just walk away for a half-hour when the system starts formatting. By the time I come back, the format, copy, and PnP detection's done, and I can start answering the wizard's questions.

PLUG AND PLAY, REGIONAL AND LANGUAGE, AND NAME AND ORGANIZATION SCREENS

Something you'll really like about Server 2003 and, for that matter, XP and 2000, is that their PnP engine isn't as annoying as Windows 98's—if it can't find a matching driver, Server 2003 doesn't stop in its tracks and say, "Find me a driver or I won't do anything else." Instead, you just see a question mark in Device Manager, and you can go find a driver and give it to Server 2003 at your leisure. As always, though, it's a good idea to check the Hardware Compatibility List (HCL) at `www.microsoft.com/hcl/default.asp` for the most up-to-date list.

TIP   If you have a device that isn't supported on the HCL or doesn't have a prepackaged device driver on the CD, you can use the `/copysource` or `/copydir` switch to copy an additional directory to be used during the setup. This can make your device drivers available for detection. Look for more details in "Performing Unattended Installs" later in this chapter.

Did you take my advice and go do something else while Setup formats the disk, copies the files, and runs the PnP detection? (Try something like computing the first prime number with more than a million digits or designing a working faster-than-light starship. You'll have ample time.) Then, when you return, you'll first see the Regional and Language Options screen. Set it as you like and click Next. (What's that you say? "No Setup war stories about this page, Mark?" Okay, I have to sheepishly admit that as an American I live in the land of Defaultia—that is, all of the default language and regional (currency, date format, keyboard configuration) settings are American. So as a Defaultian I don't honestly have much in the way of advice here, sorry.)

Next is the Name and Organization dialog. The name and organization listed here show who the product is registered to; it isn't used for anything related to the computer name or other means of defining the server on the network.

PRODUCT KEYS AND WINDOWS PRODUCT ACTIVATION

Click Next and you'll get the Product Key screen, where you'll type in the 25-character product key that came with your system. As I noted in my discussion of upgrades, your copy of Windows

Server 2003 may not require this if you're one of the lucky dogs who work for a big company and get the no-product-key CDs.

If you *do* have to enter a product key, though, then get ready for a *new* Setup irritation, a brand-new Server feature called Windows Product Activation. You may know it from XP, but this is the first time that it's appeared in Server. It's a Microsoft copy protection scheme, and here's how it works.

When you get a copy of Server 2003, you also get a 25-character product key. Server 2003 tells you when you first run it that you must "activate" it. If you don't activate it within some number of days—14 days on the copy that I'm working with, but I've seen different numbers on different copies of XP, so I presume that Server 2003's got different activation limits as well—then it stops running. Activating Server is pretty easy, just a few mouse clicks and you needn't even tell Microsoft anything about yourself. Your server first inventories the hardware on your server and boils that down to a 50-digit number. Your server then goes out over the Internet to a Microsoft database somewhere and says, "Hi, I'm a copy of Server with a product key of [whatever your 25-character product key is]. Have you seen me before?"

If no one has ever activated a copy of Server with this particular product key, then the database server just says, "No, you're fine, I'll remember your hardware configuration," and you're activated.

But what if the database server *does* have a record that says that someone activated a copy of Server with that product key before? Then one of two things are happening, at least in Microsoft's eyes: either you've reinstalled Server 2003 onto the same hardware, and you just need to be reactivated, or someone's trying to put the same copy of Server on two different machines. So the database server looks at the 50-digit hardware description value that it already has for that particular product key. If the hardware description matches or is very close to the one stored in the database, then the database server tells your copy of Server to go ahead and activate (reactivate, actually) itself. But if the hardware description value already in the database is sufficiently different from the one that the wants-to-be-activated server sent to the database server, then the database server sends a "do not activate" message to your computer. And, by the way, every time your computer boots, it computes that hardware description value and compares it to your system's state upon the last boot. Again, if your system's hardware is too different, then it'll force you to reactivate, or at least to try to reactivate.

How different is "different?" Suppose you have to change the hardware in your system—how much can you change it before it refuses to run? The answer is, no one knows but Microsoft, and they're not talking. As XP's been out for a while, people have come up with some heuristics, but here's one hard fact that Microsoft let out: your base hardware value resets every 120 days. Therefore, if you only make one major change every 120 days, then your system will never come to believe that it should be deactivated.

And in case you're wondering, yes, this *is* incredibly annoying. But there are a few workarounds.

First, if you're going to rebuild your system, back up \windows\system32\wpa.db1. It's the file that your system uses when it boots to assure itself that you're properly activated, and it also contains the hardware information. It's encrypted with the RC4 algorithm, so apparently it's not anything that you can look at. But if you back up wpa.db1, reinstall your operating system, and restore wpa.db1 to sytem32 and reboot, then in my experience it doesn't annoy you about having to reactivate.

Second, if you *did* change a lot of hardware and your system requires you to reactivate, then go ahead and try. If it fails—it probably will—then the activation program gives you a toll-free number to call Microsoft where Allen Neiman, the Microsoft guy who is the mad scientist behind all this, assured me, "We'll trust you," and reset the database so that you can activate. Now, I've never had to actually do this (thank God), but from what I'm told, you have to read the 25-character product key as well as the 50-digit hardware description value (the activation program will furnish it) over the phone to a Microsoft employee, who then reads you back a 42-digit number that you will then type into the activation program. Sounds like real fun; I can't wait until I have to do it.

LICENSING, NAMES, AND PASSWORDS

Once you've punched in the product key and clicked Next, the next dialog configures your licensing options, which are the same as previous versions of NT. There is per-seat licensing and per-server licensing. Per-seat usually makes more sense than per-server, but we've discussed licensing earlier—enter whatever makes sense for your network.

After you click Next comes the computer name and administrator password definition. Setup offers a bizarre combination of letters and numbers based on your organization name, which you may want to change, unless of course you really want your servers called CX-7352RR35. You've also got to set a password to the local administrator's account. Between the worms, viruses, and legions of disgruntled unemployed IT people who've decided to take up a career hacking, you've kind of got no choice these days but to put good passwords on your accounts, and the local administrator is no exception. Server 2003 helps you do that by suggesting that you use a "complex" password—six or more characters and a combination of at least three of the following: uppercase, lowercase, numbers, and punctuation. You don't *have* to use a complex password, but if you don't, Setup asks if you're sure.

WARNING   *And if you're thinking of being* really *lazy and setting a blank password, you might not want to—one of Server 2003's new features is that accounts with blank passwords will not work over the network!*

No matter what password you give the administrator, though, make sure you can remember it. I get tons of letters from people who say that they (1) did not create any other administrative accounts and (2) forgot the administrator's password. They then hope that I can help them. I can't. Winternals (www.winternals.com) has a neat program named ERD Commander that can reset the administrator's password, but when last I checked it cost just under $400.

I really want to stress how important this is. On a clean install, the administrator account is the only way to log in. Don't forget this. But *do* pick good passwords. If a hacker's going to try to crack into your system by guessing a password, then make his work harder by using a complex password. Then be sure to write that Administrator password on a sticky note and put it on the side of your monitor so you won't forget it. (Just kidding.)

KEEPING TIME—TIME ZONES ARE IMPORTANT!

Next you'll see the date and time settings. By default, Microsoft figures that everything is in Pacific time, which is, I guess, in keeping with their Redmond-centric way of thinking—perhaps they want to free us from the tyranny of the Green Witch or whatever the name of those GMT guys are. What I've always found odd, though, is that Microsoft sometimes uses a city to represent every time zone, and for Pacific, it's Tijuana. Now, I've got nothing against Tijuana, but I could name a few more important cities in the Pacific time zone. Like Fresno.

Seriously, this dialog is important because of Active Directory, assuming that you will be or are using it. In order for AD logons to succeed, workstations and member servers (which have to log on) must have their internal system clocks pretty well synchronized with the system clocks on domain controllers (which do the logging on of people and machines)—in fact if a DC's time is more than five minutes out of sync with another computer's time, then that DC can't log that computer on.

What gets some folks in trouble, then, is that they say, "The heck with the time zone," and just set the clock to the local time. But Active Directory doesn't care about time zones; it does all of its internal work in universal time—all time is in Greenwich (there's that Green Witch again) Mean Time or Zulu time. So suppose a domain controller (call it DC) and a workstation (call it WS) are in New York. It's 9 A.M. The DC's clock is set to 9 A.M., and its time zone is set to Eastern. Meanwhile, the workstation's clock is set to 9 A.M., but its time zone is set to Pacific. Both clocks look like they're at the same time, but they're not. Even though their clocks both show 9 A.M., the DC thinks it's 2 P.M. GMT (Eastern time is five hours behind GMT for most of the year) and the WS thinks it's 5 P.M. GMT. That's three hours' difference between their internal clocks, so the workstation can never successfully authenticate with the DC. So set your time zones properly!

NETWORKING SETTINGS

After adjusting the time settings, Setup rattles the disk drives for a couple of minutes, announcing that it is "installing the network." The network settings give you two choices: typical and custom. The typical settings assume that you will want the Client for Microsoft Networks, TCP/IP using DHCP addressing, and File and Print Sharing.

By choosing custom settings, you can add, remove, or customize protocols, clients, and services. If you want to assign static IP information, highlight TCP/IP and click Configure. By clicking the Add button, you will be given a choice of Client, Protocol, or Service. You can add more clients, like Client for Novell Networks; more protocols, like AppleTalk, IPV6; or more services.

At the Workgroup or Computer Domain selection page, you can join either a workgroup or domain by selecting the appropriate radio button and typing the workgroup or domain name in the corresponding box. If you join a domain, you must have an account created for your machine name. You can do this two ways.

The first way is to select the Create Computer Account button. After clicking OK to join the domain, you will be asked to enter an administrative account name and password. This account must be one with either Administrator or Account Operator rights. If you're using an account from the domain you are joining, enter the account name and password. If you're using an account from a trusted domain of the one you are joining, type the full domain and account name in the *DOMAIN\ USERNAME* format. This will inform the validating domain controller of the location of your account. The account creation will be initiated from the server you are installing.

The second method is to not select Create Computer Account but have one created ahead of time. You may want to employ this method if the person running the install doesn't have the appropriate rights and doesn't want to have to hunt down an administrator when this step comes up. In this scenario, go to Server Manager for the NT 4 domain on which you want to add the server and select Computer/Add to Domain, or go to Active Directory Users and Computers and select New/Computer. Select NT Workstation or Server and type the name of the computer. During the installation of the server, leave the Create Computer Account option unselected, enter the correct domain name, and you should be set.

Because of security concerns, though, the computer account you create will change its password immediately upon a successful joining of the domain. This means that if, for some reason, you redo a clean install of a machine that already has a computer account, you can't have your new install assume that account. You must either delete and re-create the account with the same name, or build the new server with a different name.

COMPUTER ACCOUNTS

Computer accounts are just like user accounts, and you can see them in the Active Directory Users and Computers tool (which we'll discuss in Chapter 8) or in Server Manager on NT 3.x and 4. If you have enabled auditing of successful account management on the domain, you will see an Account Manager security event #624 logged in the PDC of an NT 4 domain or a similar event on any DC of an AD domain. A 624 event is a "create user account" event. Let's say you create a computer account for a new server named CADDY in the LAB domain. Under the details of the security event, the account name that was created will show as CADDY$. This CADDY$ account will be used for all communication between the server and the domain, such as validating user passwords. Once the new server and the PDC "shake hands," the server will initiate a password change for the CADDY$ account. Every 7 days thereafter, the server will again initiate a password change. The same procedure of account and password maintenance is used between domains for trust relationships.

So why is changing a password such a big deal? Well, the server is going to assign permissions to its resources based on domain user accounts. The server isn't going to blindly trust that anyone who claims to be from the LAB domain is a valid user; it wants to make certain that they are in fact a LAB user from the real LAB domain. By having this unique account with a highly secured password, the server can do just that. If the server asks the LAB domain to validate a user but the LAB domain doesn't recognize the correct CADDY$ account and password, authentication fails. This makes it nearly impossible to transport a server out of its domain and gain access to its data.

Once you've clicked Next, Setup starts actually, well, setting up. The system will reboot and you've got a working server. The `boot.ini` will now be changed to reflect the new Server 2003 install as the default boot option. There is, however, one more step that can optionally be done here. If you need to run another program, perhaps a setup program for some utility or application, then you can tell Setup to run it automatically, using the `winnt32.exe` command-line parameter /cmd:*command*. (Of course, using this command-line parameter means that you needed to add that /cmd option when you *started* running Setup, so if you've been doing Setup while following along, this advice is a bit late.) This could be used to run a batch file or utility to perform such tasks as transferring user data, installing programs, or other means of further automating your installs. (This is covered in more detail later in this chapter in the section on unattended installs.) The system will now reboot into a full-fledged Server 2003 operating system.

TIP But if it doesn't, then try running WINNT32 with its debug switches, WINNT32 /debug2, /debug3, or /debug4, which offer more information. Debug3 gives more information than debug2 and, in case you're wondering, debug1 is just the default. The log file is in `\windows\winnt32.log`, *or you can add a colon and the name of a log file, as in* `winnt32 /debug4:whathappenedanyway.log`.

Postinstallation Procedures

After the installation is complete, there are still a few more steps to perform to finalize the server and prep it for production:

♦ On the first reboot, the Manage Your Server page will pop up automatically. It will identify the last few steps that must be completed to configure your server based on the additional network components you installed. It will also ask you some questions about your existing network to help you determine whether you want to install an Active Directory. I personally find the Manage Your Server page unhelpful and tend to just close it, but that's just my opinion—try it if you like. I'll show you how to manage *your* server with as few of those dumb wizards as possible!

NOTE *See Chapter 8 for more information about Active Directory and when and how to launch the Active Directory Installation Wizard, DCPROMO.*

♦ Check your device manager for undetected or nonfunctioning hardware components. If you removed any hardware prior to the install due to conflicts, add them back in now. Before you are truly done with the install, every piece of hardware should work properly.

♦ You'll want to finalize your disk partitions. In many clean install scenarios, you may have unpartitioned space left on your hard drive. Refer to Chapter 10 and take care of these partitions now.

♦ For most new installations using TCP/IP, a DHCP address will be in effect. This may not be a standard practice for production servers. If necessary, acquire and configure the appropriate static TCP/IP information. See Chapters 6 and 7 about TCP/IP and related services.

♦ In many larger network environments, certain services, utilities, tools, or other programs are loaded on all servers. For example, some sites may utilize enterprise management tools that require the usage of an agent that runs on the server to collect and pass information up to a management console. Most likely, some sort of backup software will need to be installed also. Find out what additional software is needed and install it now.

TIP *You always want to completely configure a server and install all of its additional components before it goes into production. By production, I mean the point at which the first user connects to the server. Since many additional services, configurations, and software components will require a reboot, you'll want this out of the way up front to avoid further disruptions of your users' work.*

♦ Run through the Control Panel applets to set all server configurations the way they should be for the long haul. Especially noteworthy are the System Control Panel settings for the pagefile and maximum Registry size.

♦ At this point, you may get the urge to walk away. Well, hold on just a minute. Too many times, people make some last-minute changes, like the Control Panel settings, and leave it at that. Even though you were never told to reboot the system—your changes were instantly accepted—there may be some unexpected side effects the next time you reboot. Just in case, give it another reboot now, before your users begin counting on the server being available.

◆ If the system is a dual-boot machine, which is usually not the case on a server, boot into all operating systems to make sure the system integrity is intact and all data is available from all required operating systems.

◆ Once the system itself is complete, create an automated recovery disk. And as an extra safeguard, you may also want to run a full backup.

◆ Finally, a step we rarely perform is documenting the server. Ask yourself if anyone else could take care of the server should you decide to take a week off for a golf vacation. If there are any special things you have to do, like restart a service every day, it should be documented. This is a step you *must* take before you can consider your operating system "installed." See Chapter 19, which covers preparing for and recovering from server failures, for more details.

At this point, you should have a production-ready server and a method for creating this same server time and time again. It seems like a lot of extra work is required in addition to actually installing Server 2003, but it is well worth the trouble.

Troubleshooting an Installation

Server 2003 produces a relatively smooth installation. Plug and Play helps in many ways by eliminating the need to know and preconfigure all of your hardware prior to launching an install. There will be a few instances where you will have problems, though.

We discussed failed hardware components earlier. If your system locks up during the hardware detection and configuration phase, you have something that does not play nicely in the sandbox. Sometimes it will be obvious which component is the culprit. Sometimes it won't be so easy. Start with the obvious methods of troubleshooting—the /debug setup parameter discussed in the "Command-Line Automation" section later in this chapter. This will definitely help identify where the install goes wrong. The next step is to either resolve or work around the problem.

If you have hardware conflicts causing problems with your install, you have a couple of options. First, you could configure the hardware and BIOS, as was discussed earlier in "Preparing the Hardware," to get along with the other hardware. Maybe the troublesome hardware is a sound card that refuses to accept the detection phase. Rather than spend x amount of time trying to get it to work, pull it out of the system. Get the Server software running first. Then add the component later.

Let's say you completely blow an install at some point. You want to start over from scratch, but you don't want to format your partition and lose potential data. There are three things on your hard drive related to the install that you will want to clean up before starting over:

◆ The `$win_nt$.~ls` directory if you copied all files to the system

◆ The `$win_nt$.~bt` directory

◆ A line in your `boot.ini` pointing to `$win_nt$.~bt\bootsect.dat`

Removing these entries will make your system completely forget that an install was ever happening, allowing you to start over at square one. Be careful when modifying the `boot.ini`. If you're reverting to an old operating system, make sure your `boot.ini` default is put back to the way it was. Leaving an entry pointing simply to C:\ will let your DOS or Windows 9*x* operating system's files boot the system. Here's a sample `boot.ini` file for a dual-boot Server 2003 and Windows 98 machine:

```
[boot loader]
timeout=30
```

```
default=C:\
[operating systems]
multi(0)disk(0)rdisk(0)partition(2)\windows="Microsoft Windows Server 2003"
C:\="Microsoft Windows 98"
```

The [boot loader] section defines how your boot menu will act. This example shows a time-out of 30 seconds, at which point the default operating system on C:\ will be booted. Once the boot process continues to the C:\, it will require the standard boot files of that operating system. In Windows 98's case, that is the MSDOS.sys and IO.sys. The [operating systems] section defines the selection menu and where the operating system corresponding to each choice resides. Here, Windows 98 resides in C:\, and Server 2003 resides on multi(0)disk(0)rdisk(0)partition(2)\windows. This translates into the \winnt directory of the disk and partition defined by the address of multi(0)disk(0)-rdisk(0)partition(2). (And in case you're wondering, no, I wouldn't put 98 on a disk with Server—this is just an easy-to-follow example.

NOTE   *See Chapter 10, "Managing Windows Server Storage," for complete details on how logical drives are defined in Server 2003.*

NOTE   *In the unlikely event that you have put both 98 and Server on the same system (perhaps for testing) and you want to get rid of the Server 2003 boot menu altogether and return to your single bootup in Windows 9x, you must delete the* boot.ini, NTDetect, *and* NTLDR *from your boot partition. After they are gone, you will need to re-SYS your boot partition to make it fully DOS- or Windows 9x–bootable again. The best way to make sure this will work is to first boot into your DOS or Windows 9x operating system, format a bootable floppy, and copy* sys.com *to the floppy. Delete the Server 2003 boot files just listed, reboot your system to the floppy, and run a* SYS C: *command.*

The Recovery Console

Server 2003 has a nifty new Recovery Console that can go miles farther than the old methods of fixing broken installations. Take this scenario—one that I've dealt with numerous times. An important system file gets corrupted...umm, deleted. You know how it goes, "Let's see, NTFS.SYS, I never use NTFS.SYS, let's just delete it to make more space." The next time you reboot, the system won't come up. Go figure. Now you need to copy a new NTFS.SYS to your hard disk. You make a bootable floppy, put NTFS.SYS on it, reboot to the floppy, and find out that your system partition is NTFS. We all know that you can't boot to a DOS floppy and access an NTFS partition. Enter the Recovery Console.

What is the Recovery Console? It is a scaled-down cross between a DOS command-line environment, certain Server 2003 Setup functions, and partition-correcting utilities, all with the capability to access NTFS partitions.

The first thing you need to do is get into the Recovery Console. There are two ways to do this. First, you can launch the WINNT32 Setup program with the /cmdcons parameter. A brief setup routine and file-copying session will take place to create your console. Once completed, your boot.ini will reflect a new operating system selection, Microsoft Windows Server 2003 Command Console. Simply boot your machine and then select that menu item. Of course, this method would only work if you had the foresight to install the console before the system broke down. If you haven't created it ahead of time, don't worry, you can get there from the normal setup routine.

Launch Setup as you normally would—from the CD, the boot floppies, whatever you prefer. At the Welcome to Setup screen, select the Repair option. From there, you will get the option to repair your installation using either the emergency repair process or the Recovery Console, and off you go.

Once you enter the console, you get a selection of all Server 2003 installations on the system. Enter the number of the installation you want to work on and press Enter.

NOTE *When entering the console from Setup, you go straight into the console. When entering the console from your boot menu, you'll need to press F6 at the Press F6 prompt to install SCSI drivers. This will let you access your SCSI hard drives or CD-ROMs that require a driver.*

The next step is validation. One of the major differences between the FAT and NTFS filesystems is security. Even though you can see the NTFS partitions now, you still need to have access to the filesystem. The console will ask you to enter the Administrator password. After you enter the password, you are dropped at a command prompt in the `systemroot` directory of the installation you chose. Simple!

Well, now what? You're at this command prompt. What do you do with a command-prompt-only version of Server 2003? Start off with a HELP command, which shows you a list of all available commands. You can do things like copy files, change directories, format drives, and other typical DOS-like file operations. To resolve the current problem, you just copy your `NTFS.SYS` from your floppy to your Windows Server 2003 installation folder and you should be back in business. In addition, there are some other commands that can help you get your server back up and running:

DISKPART This command will launch a disk partitioning utility almost identical to the utility we used during the text-based phase of setup.

FIXBOOT This command will make a new boot sector on your drive of choice and make that partition your new boot partition. If you happened to destroy your boot sector information and can't boot at all, this may be your best bet.

FIXMBR This command will repair the master boot record on the selected drive.

DISABLE If you are having problems with a device that is not letting Server boot completely—let's say you accidentally changed a device's startup parameter or installed a new service that keeps killing your system—the DISABLE command will let you prevent that service or device from starting.

ENABLE This is just the opposite of DISABLE. Let's say you disabled an important boot device; reenabling it may be the easiest solution.

LISTSVC Both the DISABLE and ENABLE commands require that you tell it *which* service or device to alter. This command will give you a list of all devices and services.

SYSTEMROOT This command gives you a quick return path back to your `systemroot` directory without having to fight those long, pesky CD commands. It also helps you when you forget which drive and directory your chosen Server 2003 installation resides in.

LOGON The logon command takes you back to your first prompt of the Recovery Console so you can choose another installation to repair.

HELP In case you can't remember the command, this is a nice little reminder.

Now that you know what the Recovery Console does, let's run through a couple of examples. We'll take the first example from our earlier scenario, a known missing or corrupt `NTFS.SYS`. Once we've logged in to the Recovery Console for our Server installation and copied a fresh `NTFS.SYS` to our A: drive, we need to copy it to our `systemroot` directory. We should already be in the `systemroot` directory, but just to be sure, we type **systemroot**. Now, we type **copy A:\NTFS.SYS**. Easy, huh?

Here's another problem. We have recently installed a new service named RudysNeatVirusScanner. It is set to start automatically during boot up, but as soon as it does, blue screen! Into our Recovery Console we go. At the prompt, type **listsvc**. We should see, among our many devices and services, RudysNeatVirusScanner service set to automatic. Now, we type **disable RudysNeatVirusScanner**. Next time we reboot into Server, we should get in just fine and should probably uninstall the problem software.

The Recovery Console is a handy utility that can get you out of a lot of trouble. Once you have installed Server 2003, it might not be a bad idea to run the `winnt32.exe` with the /cmdcons parameter. This won't actually launch Setup, just configure the console. You will always have the console available in your boot menu, although it won't be set as default.

Performing Unattended Installs: An Overview

Got 50 servers to install? Getting a little tired of shoving CD-ROMs into drives and baby-sitting the setup process, answering the same dumb questions over and over again? Then you need to learn about unattended installs!

An unattended install is simply a method of providing the answers for the setup questions before they are asked in order to automate the installation process. There is no other difference in the install itself. But why do you need to automate? Usually, automation is most beneficial in large networks where Server 2003 machines will frequently be built. By automating these installs, numerous hours can be spared that would otherwise be spent sitting at the console. Another benefit of unattended installs is that they can be run by non-experts and produce the same wonderful results every time. This could help in those environments where the only on-site server operator is not an experienced administrator. Rather than spend hours walking them through an install to your specifications, you can merely give them a single command line and be done with it.

Microsoft provides three different tools to make it possible for you to do unattended installations, and I'll explain them to you in the remainder of this chapter. Before getting into the details of these tools, however, I want to provide some perspective on how you'd use these tools. I'll cover three major areas:

◆ Scripting installations
◆ Using Remote Installation Services
◆ Using Sysprep

Scripting

In its simplest form, a script is just a file that preanswers all of those questions that Setup asks—what shall we call the computer, what is your name, what's the product ID value, that sort of thing. So what's to learn? Well, first of all, you have to learn the language of scripts; like most computer things, scripts have a specific syntax that you must follow or they won't work. It's not a *hard* syntax—I don't want to scare you away—but there's a syntax nonetheless. Microsoft has made your script-writing job pretty easy, in that they've included with Server 2003 a program that asks you some questions and then spits out a script. It's only a basic one, and you'll have to add a few lines to make it useful, but it's a good start.

Once you've done a little scripting, however, you'll soon want more flexibility and power out of the scripting language—and you can get it. There's a whole next level of scripting power via what are called the OEMPreinstall options, and you'll learn them next.

Delivery: CD-ROM or RIS

All a great script does is to save you having to answer questions while running Setup—but first you've got to get Setup running in the first place. The next set of tools simplifies the process of delivering all of the setup files to the new PC to begin with.

The simplest way to start up a setup is to shove a CD into the computer's CD-ROM drive and then boot from the CD. But how to supply the script? With a trick, as you'll see—put the script on a floppy disk and call the script `winnt.sif`. But who wants to walk around with a CD-ROM, and, besides, what if you want to deploy more than just the operating system? Well, under NT 4, you'd have to create a network share that contained all of the NT installation files, then you'd have to figure out how to get a computer with nothing on its hard disk connected to the network in the first place.

Windows Server 2003 (and 2000, for that matter) again simplifies matters with a tool called Remote Installation Services (RIS). With RIS, you can store prebuilt Windows 2000, XP, and Server 2003 installation files and scripts on a server—a RIS server. Then RIS eliminates the need to wonder how you're going to get your new computer attached to the network in the first place by supporting a network boot standard that many new computers support called PXE, the Preboot Execution Environment. And if you don't have a PXE-compliant computer, that's not a problem; RIS can generate a generic floppy disk that will allow most desktops and some laptops (laptops are the weak point here, as you'll see) to connect to a RIS server, with no built-in PXE support needed.

And if you're a current Windows 2000 RIS expert, then you might be thinking, "Wait a minute, Mark—RIS only distributes 2000 *Professional*. You can't use it to deliver *Server*." But you *can*, actually; that's one of Server 2003's new features.

Sysprep

For some folks, the two things that I've just described—scripting and delivering setups—is the slow way to do things. Many firms prefer to first create a computer that looks just exactly as they'd like all of their computers to look. Then they create hundreds of exact duplicates of that prototype computer, "cloning" the prototype's hard disk, and in the process quickly roll out hundreds of ready-to-work desktop or server computers.

The only problem with this method is that until the advent of 2000, Microsoft didn't support people who do that, as cloning results in computers that lack unique SIDs, security identifiers. But, as of 2000, Microsoft has a tool that makes a prototype computer "clonable," called Sysprep. And, as you'd imagine, it's gotten better with Server 2003.

Now we're almost ready to get into the details of scripting—but before we do, let's take a quick look at the program that starts off a Server 2003 Setup in the first place or, rather, the *two* programs that start a Windows Server 2003 Setup: `winnt.exe` and `winnt32.exe`.

Command-Line Automation: Controlling WINNT[32]

When you simply boot a system from the CD-ROM, then you're not aware of the name of the program that starts off the setup process. But you can also initiate a Windows Server 2003 setup from the command line with one of two commands: `winnt32.exe` if you're starting the setup from a computer that's already running Windows NT or later, or `winnt.exe` for a system running DOS or Windows 3.x or 9x.

NOTE   *Someone always e-mails me to correct me, saying that you use* `winnt32.exe` *for Windows 9x. Not me. I boot 9x systems to Safe Mode Command Prompt, use the LOCK command to lock the C: drive, and install.* There *you need* `winnt.exe`.

The command-line parameters of these programs tell the Setup program where your source installation files are, where you want to install Server, where your answer file is located, and other information needed to prepare for the setup. A command-line parameter can also be used to copy an additional folder to your setup source so that those files will be available during the installation. This is handy when you have OEM drivers for the hardware you want to install during the setup rather than waiting until afterward.

Before you start using command-line parameters, it is important to *really* understand them. They can have a very profound impact on the installation process, so let's go over the WINNT32 options:

/checkupgradeonly   Whenever Setup begins, it checks to see if an upgrade is possible. Setup will not attempt to actually run the install.

/cmd:*command*   This option will launch the given command line before the setup process has completed, which will allow you to perform some additional customization or launch other programs.

/cmdcons   If you have a failed installation on your system, this option will add a Recovery Console item to your `boot.ini` operating system selection menu.

/copydir:*folder*   When you're doing automated installs for a large number of machines, this may be one of the most useful options in your arsenal. How many times have you been stopped in the middle of an installation because your network card drivers are, well, on the network? You resort to copying files to a floppy, spend 10 minutes trying to find one, format it, copy files, and hike them back to your server. What a bother. The /copydir option can really help you out here. It will copy the specified folder to your installation directory during setup—while you're still connected to your network.

/copysource:*folder*   Similar to the /copydir option, the /copysource option copies a specified folder to your installation directory. The major difference between the two is that the /copysource directory is deleted after setup is complete.

/debug[*level***][:***filename***]**   You can tell Setup to log debugging information to a given file based on the following criteria. Level 0 logs severe errors only, 1 adds regular errors, 2 includes warnings, 3 adds all informational messages, and 4 incorporates detailed information about the setup for complete debugging purposes. For example, you could use `/debug3:setuplog.txt`.

/dudisable   This option lets you skip the dynamic update part of Setup.

/duprepare:*path containing CAB files with updates* This is not a command that you'd run at Setup. Instead, you use this to prepare a directory that contains updates so that when you *do* run Setup on a system, you can use the /dushare option to point Setup to these updates. This is a pretty new process in the Microsoft OS world and the instructions on how to do this change regularly, but the most current details are at www.download.windowsupdate.com/msdownload/update/v3/static/DUProcedure/Dynamic%20Update.htm. You don't go to the regular windowsupdate .microsoft.com location to download fixes en masse; instead, you go to windowsupdate.microsoft .com/catalog.

/dushare:*path to share created by duprepare* Once WINNT32 /duprepare has reconfigured the patch and update files that you downloaded from Windows Update, you can set up a new computer and simultaneously apply the latest patches with the /dushare: option.

/m:*folder* This option can be dangerous. When the setup process begins to copy files, the /m option tells it to look in the specified folder first. If that folder contains files to be used in setup, those files be will used. If the files are not present, they will be retrieved from the regular installation source. This can be helpful if a hotfix or alternative version of a file that you choose to use for every install (rather than the default version on the CD) is available. Instead of running your install and then running an update or replacing files, you can use /m and perform these tasks in one swift step.

/makelocalsource Have you ever had problems reconnecting to your installation source after you've rebooted and started the setup? This could be due to things like Setup not recognizing your CD-ROM or network card. This option tells Setup to copy the entire source to your hard drive so that you can guarantee it will be available later.

/noreboot There may be times when you want to launch the first stage of Setup, get your machine ready for the installation, but not reboot quite yet. This option will bypass the screen at the end of the first setup wizard and return you to your existing operating system without a reboot. When you do reboot, though, Setup will continue.

/s:*sourcepath* This seems like a redundant switch. You've already found your source path if you've gotten as far as launching the setup. Setup even knows where it's coming from. This parameter does help identify where your source is—the I386 directory—but it also does something better. You can specify multiple source paths and have Setup copy files from each simultaneously. This can really save you time if you have a slow CD and a slow network. Be careful, though; the first source path identified must be available or Setup will fail.

/syspart:*drive* Another very powerful option here when you're considering mass deployments is the /syspart parameter. This will start your setup to the specified drive and mark that drive as active. Once Setup is complete, you can physically take that hard drive out of the system, place it in a new system, and boot right into Setup. You must use the /tempdrive parameter with /syspart.

/tempdrive:*drive* Setup will use the specified tempdrive to place temporary setup files. If you have space concerns with drives or merely a preference on where you want temporary files to go, use this parameter.

/unattend The /unattend option will do an automated, no-input-required upgrade of your previous operating system. All configurations and settings of the old operating system will be used for the upgrade.

/unattend[*num*]:*answer_file* This launches one of the most powerful features of unattended installations: the answer file. The answer file is a text file containing any or all answers to be used throughout the entire setup process. I'll talk about building the answer file in the next section. If your current operating system is Windows 2000, you can also specify a time delay for the reboot, determined by [num].

/udf:*id*[,*udf_file*] One of the problems with automated installations is that you can't fully automate an install unless you provide a name for the server, and all servers—all machines for that matter—on your network *must* have a unique name. This requires that you either enter the name during the setup or use an answer file on all machines, giving them the same name. Neither of those are viable options. The /udf parameter allows you to specify unique information about each installation based on the file specified in the UDF file—uniqueness database file. Here's how it works. In the UDF file, there is a listing of names and a section matching each name with computer-specific information. Usually the computer-specific information will be just the computer name, but anything you put in this file will override the same entry in the answer file. Take a look at a sample UDF file named `unattend.udf`:

```
;SetupMgrTag
[UniqueIds]
    BS01=UserData
    BS02=UserData
    BS03=UserData
    BS04=UserData
    BS05=UserData
[BS01:UserData]
    ComputerName=BS01
[BS02:UserData]
    ComputerName=BS02
[BS03:UserData]
    ComputerName=BS03
[BS04:UserData]
    ComputerName=BS04
[BS05:UserData]
    ComputerName=BS05
```

I have five specified, unique computers defined—BS01 through BS05. If I'm sitting down to install a machine for BS03, I would send the /udf:BS03,unattend.udf parameter. The Setup program will look in the UDF file and have any entries under the BS03 section override those in the standard answer file. So if the ComputerName entry in the answer file is BSxx, Setup will substitute BS03 in its place for my installation.

Those are all of the possible command-line parameters that you can feed the WINNT32 program. To better see how they work, let's try a few samples of running WINNT32 from the CD located in F:.

We are installing to a server that is very specific about using OEM drivers for the network card. If we start the setup and reboot, the default drivers with Windows Server 2003 won't get us back online. We'll use the /copysource option to copy down our drivers from the network folder of Z:\NIC\OEM. Just to be on the safe side, we also want to use a /makelocalsource option so we have all files available for use. We'll launch the following command:

```
F:\I386\winnt32 /copysource:z:\nic\oem /makelocalsource
```

During the first phase of Setup, the entire z:\nic\oem directory will be copied to the hard drive to be used during the installation. Once completed, the directory will be removed to free up our space again. We will also get a complete copy of the I386 directory copied to our local installation source. Between the two, we should have no problems with the installation not being able to find files.

Now, we want to launch a setup using an answer file named C:\w2k\setup\unattend.txt and a uniqueness database file named C:\w2k\setup\unattend.udf. To keep parity with the earlier scenario, we'll install this machine with the BS03 ID. In this case, we run this command:

```
F:\I386\winnt32
↳/unattend:c:\w2k\setup\unattend.txt
↳/udf:BS03,c:\w2k\setup\unattend.udf
```

WINNT supports a subset of those options—/s, /t, /u, and /udf—as well as these

/e:	Specifies a command to execute after Setup finishes
/a	Enables accessibility options
/r:	Tells Setup to copy a folder to the target machine, leaving it in place after Setup finishes
/rx:	Like /r:, but deletes the folder after Setup finishes

Scripts, Part I: Basic Answer Files with Setup Manager

The easiest way to get started with scripts is to let a program called Setup Manager build one for you.

INSTALLING SETUP MANAGER

Setup Manager isn't installed by default—here's how to get it.

1. Insert the Server 2003 CD into your computer's CD drive.
2. Open the folder named Support and, inside that, another folder named Tools.
3. In Support\Tools, you'll see a file named deploy.cab. Double-click it to open it.
4. Select all of the files in deploy.cab, right-click, and choose Copy.
5. Create a directory named DepTools on your computer's hard disk. Right-click the DepTools folder and choose Paste.
6. Open the DepTools folder and double-click the Setupmgr.exe icon.

RUNNING SETUP MANAGER

That starts up Setup Manager, which is a wizard and therefore starts off with a Welcome screen. Click Next to get past it and you'll see a screen like Figure 5.2.

FIGURE 5.2
New file or modify
an old one?

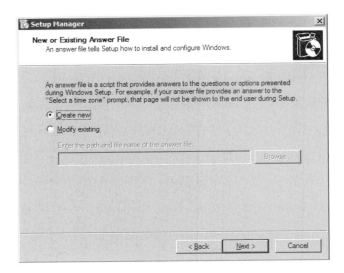

As you can see, Setup Manager will either create a new script file or edit an existing one.

WARNING *In general, I recommend that you never use Setup Manager to edit an existing script, because when starting up Setup Manager to change just one thing in a script, I find that it sometimes gets a bit rambunctious and decides what-thehey, while I'm here why don't I fix all of these other bad ideas that I see in this script?*

Tell it that you're creating a new script and choose Next. You'll see a screen like Figure 5.3.

FIGURE 5.3
What kind of script?

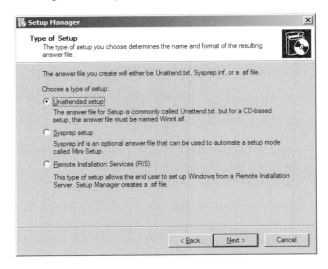

Setup Manager can build scripts that you can use either for a simple unattended install, for RIS, or for Sysprep. We're doing just a simple install, so choose that and click Next. You'll then see a screen like Figure 5.4.

FIGURE 5.4

What flavor?

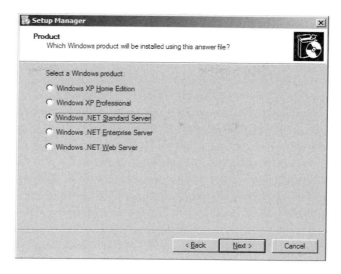

Setup Manager will create scripts to install either Professional or Server in any of their incarnations (except Datacenter); choose Windows .NET Standard Server and click Next to see Figure 5.5.

FIGURE 5.5

Just how hands-off?

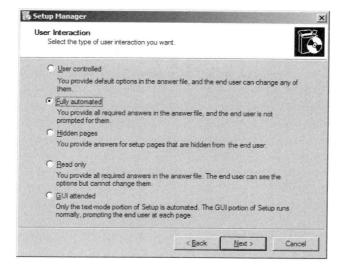

This screen advises Setup Manager how thorough it should be in creating the script. In theory, choosing Fully Automated will cause Setup Manager to fill in enough information that you can just start an install using WINNT or WINNT32, walk away for 45 minutes, return, and be done. In actual fact, you'll have to include a few other things, as you'll see. Choose Fully Automated and click Next to see a screen like Figure 5.6.

FIGURE 5.6

Configuring a
distribution share

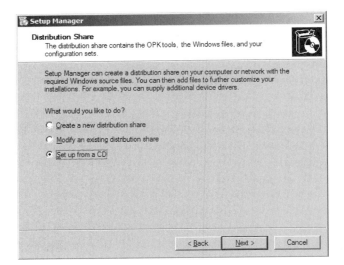

One approach to automated rollouts involves copying all of the installation files to a share on the network; Microsoft calls this the *distribution share*, and Setup Manager will help you create one if you like. We're just looking to create an answer file here, though, so choose Set Up from a CD and click Next to see Figure 5.7.

FIGURE 5.7

Agreeing to the
EULA

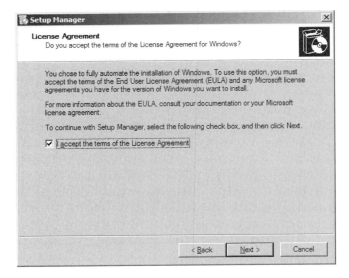

From this point on, the Setup Wizard mainly asks the same kinds of questions that Setup has already asked, so I'll go through them quickly. First, there's the end-user license agreement (EULA). As with every other piece of software nowadays—both Microsoft and non-Microsoft—Server 2003 comes with a sign-it-or-else "contract" called a software license. The point of the software license is to give the software vendor more ability to restrict what you do with the software than they'd normally get from copyright laws. By agreeing to it here, you avoid having the Setup program stop and ask you to agree to the EULA in mid-install. Check the box and click Next to fill in your name and organization, and then Next to configure the display settings, Next for time zone, Next for product key, Next to fill in the client licensing option, per-seat or per-server. Click Next to see Figure 5.8 and set the computer name.

FIGURE 5.8

Machine names and automatic UDFs

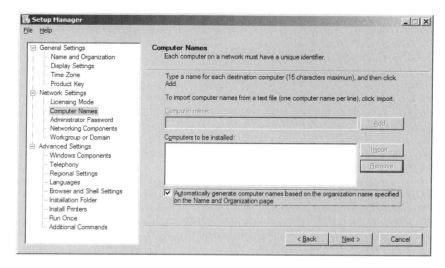

You can enter a name and click Add, or you can, as I have, check the Automatically Generate Computer Names… check box. Computer names aren't very interesting, but what *is* interesting is that you can use the Setup Manager to create a UDF, like the one you saw earlier in this chapter; if you enter more than one name, that's how to make this answer file useful. Click Next to see Figure 5.9.

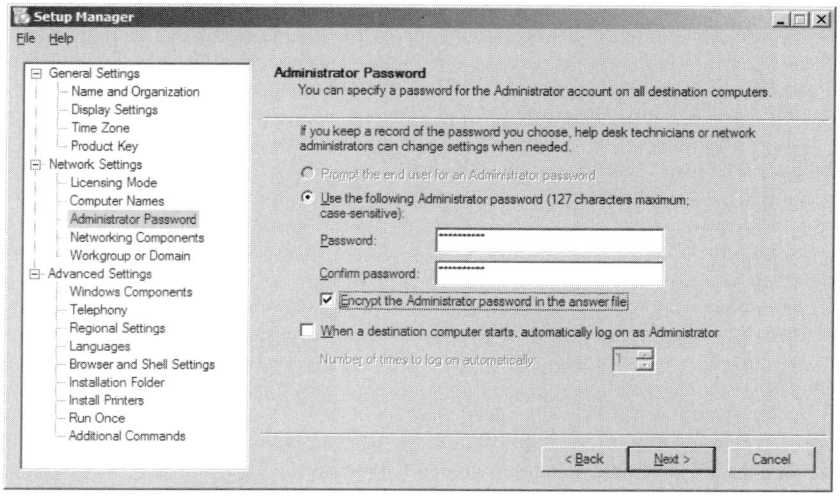

FIGURE 5.9

Setting the admin password

This is really good news for anyone who's built an answer file in the past. Most of it's self-explanatory, but notice the new check box that says Encrypt the Administrator Password in the Answer File. Very cool—now we don't have to worry about people looking in the scripts and seeing the admin's password! Click Next to see Figure 5.10.

FIGURE 5.10

Typical or custom network settings?

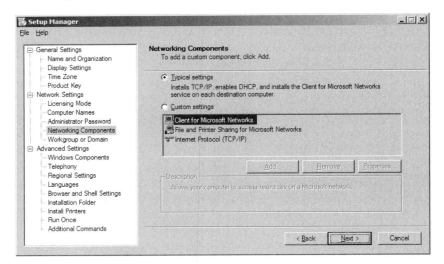

You'll usually choose Typical Settings, but let me take a moment and point out one of Setup Manager's strengths. If you decide to take Server 2003's default networking settings, then you'll get a pretty basic setup script—you'll use DHCP to get your IP address (and if you don't know what DHCP is, don't worry, I'll be explaining it in the next few chapters—for now, just understand that it makes the process of setting up the TCP/IP software on a computer far easier). But what if you *didn't* want to use DHCP for configuration—what if you wanted to script an install with a specific set of TCP/IP configuration parameters, like a specific IP address? Here's where Setup Manager shines. Perhaps it's the fact that I seem to be afflicted with AFS (After-Forty Syndrome), but I can never remember the combination of script commands needed to specify an IP address. So I cheat by just running Setup Manager and telling it to set up a simple script for a system with a prespecified IP address. I can then look at the resulting script and cut and paste to create my desired script. That's not to say that Setup Manager knows how to create *every* possible kind of script, but it's pretty smart, making it a kind of automated cheat sheet.

Anyway, after deciding to do typical network settings and clicking Next, you'll get a panel that lets you specify whether you're going to join a domain or a workgroup. Click Next to see a new screen for Server 2003's Setup Manager, as in Figure 5.11.

With this very useful screen, Setup Manager lets you choose what does and doesn't get installed on your system, a real, *real* plus! Instead of just automatically installing (for example) the Index Service on every system when only two or three systems in your whole enterprise need it, this lets you just say no to every component but the ones that you need. This is an improvement over Windows 2000's Setup Manager, which made you do this answer file-tweaking by hand. Go through it, make your changes, and click Next.

FIGURE 5.11

Choosing
components

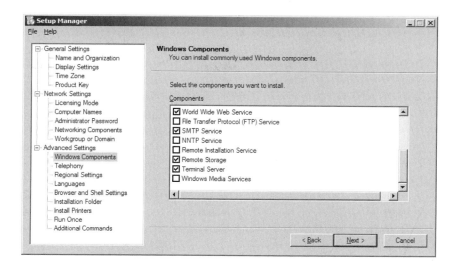

If you've got a modem, you'll be asked about Telephony settings; fill them in and click Next. You can then adjust Regional Settings—keyboard, currency, that kind of thing and, in the next panel, language support. (Things we Defaultians must shamefully admit that we don't know jack about.) Then you get to set up the Browser.

It really irritates me that every time I set up a new computer and start Internet Explorer for the first time, it jumps out to MSN; I've always wanted to say to NT, 2000, and now Server 2003's Setup programs, "Look, I swear, I will *never ever use MSN in my entire life*—so stop making me either wait for MSN to load or have to click the Stop button!" When I start up a browser, I want it to start *immediately*, so my home page is "about:blank." I can make that happen in an answer file with the following commands:

```
[Branding]
BrandIEUsingUnattended = Yes
[URL]
Home_Page = about:blank
```

But I don't have to mess with the answer file to do this, as Setup Manager gives me those options. The next page lets you specify an installation folder—whether to put the files in \windows, \winnt, or whatever you want. Administrators will love the next screen, as you can see in Figure 5.12.

Set this up, and your users will log in already set to use a networked printer. The next two screens are a bit out of order, in my opinion. The first one specifies things that go in the Run Once Registry key. This lets you enter commands that you want run the first time that the computer has rebooted after completing Setup. You'd use this to tell your new copy of Server 2003 to do something like run DCPROMO to create a domain controller automatically, or perhaps to kick off a SQL Server installation. The screen after that lets you specify additional commands, which are commands to execute at the end of Setup. This can be useful if you want to do something like automatically install the Recovery Console; the command would be

```
e:\i386\winnt32 /cmdcons
```

FIGURE 5.12

Preconfiguring
network printers

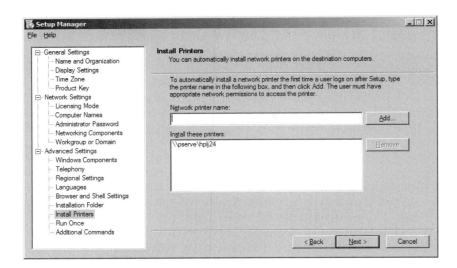

The only problem with this is the e:—I typed that for example, but what actual drive letter will your CD-ROM end up being at the end of Setup? On a complex system, this might not be obvious. In any case, this seems out of place to me because *these* commands execute *before* the Run Once commands—wouldn't you think the panels would appear in something resembling the order in which they occur?

Finally, Setup Manager will ask you where to put the answer file, and what to call it. Click OK and you'll then be able to exit the Setup Manager.

EXAMINING SETUP MANAGER'S SCRIPT

The script that Setup Manager created for me looks like this:

```
;SetupMgrTag
[Data]
    AutoPartition=1
    MsDosInitiated="0"
    UnattendedInstall="Yes"

[Unattended]
    UnattendMode=FullUnattended
    OemSkipEula=Yes
    OemPreinstall=No
    TargetPath=\WINDOWS

[GuiUnattended]
    AdminPassword=43e140893084ea91cd85ddec2cd0905daf4d42d86df9ebd57b0641c94aa4c438
    EncryptedAdminPassword=Yes
    OEMSkipRegional=1
    TimeZone=35
    OemSkipWelcome=1
```

```
[UserData]
    ProductKey=11111-22222-33333-44444-55555
    FullName="Mark Minasi"
    OrgName="MR&D"
    ComputerName=*

[Display]
    BitsPerPel=16
    Xresolution=1280
    YResolution=1024

[LicenseFilePrintData]
    AutoMode=PerSeat

[Components]
    accessopt=Off
    calc=On
    charmap=On
    clipbook=On
    deskpaper=On
    templates=On
    mousepoint=On
    paint=On
    freecell=Off
    hearts=Off
    zonegames=Off
    minesweeper=Off
    solitaire=Off
    spider=Off
    indexsrv_system=On
    msnexplr=Off
    certsrv=Off
    certsrv_client=Off
    certsrv_server=Off
    iis_www=On
    iis_ftp=Off
    iis_smtp=On
    iis_smtp_docs=On
    iis_nntp=Off
    iis_nntp_docs=Off
    reminst=Off
    rstorage=On
    TerminalServer=On
    wms=Off
    wms_admin_asp=Off
    wms_admin_mmc=Off
    wms_server=Off
    chat=On
```

```
        dialer=On
        hypertrm=On
        cdplayer=On
        mplay=On
        media_clips=On
        media_utopia=On
        rec=On
        vol=On

[GuiRunOnce]
    Command0="rundll32 printui.dll,PrintUIEntry /in /n \\pserve\hplj24"

 [Networking]
    InstallDefaultComponents=Yes

[Identification]
    JoinDomain=bigfirm.biz
    DomainAdmin=admindude
    DomainAdminPassword=hihihihi
```

This is a pretty basic script. Notice that an answer file is like a typical INI file, around since the early days of Windows; it's a simple ASCII file that you could, if you wanted to, create with Notepad. There are sections of the file that are broken up into groups; they're identified by their headers and surrounded by square brackets, like [*HEADER1*]. Within each section are different settings and the corresponding values to be used during the setup, formatted as *ITEM=VALUE*.

The first section is called [Data] and it's pretty much boilerplate, simple you-gotta-have-them instructions. MSDOSInitiated should equal 0 if you're doing an install from the CD-ROM, or 1 if you're doing an RIS install. AutoPartition must be equal to 1, or Setup will stop and ask you which partition to install Server 2003 into. UnattendedInstall should be, um, obvious.

The [Unattended] section tells Setup what level of user interaction to expect, and you see FullUnattended, which is the script-syntax equivalent of the Fully Automated option we chose from Setup Manager. OEMSkipEula just says "don't make him accept the license agreement." OEMPreinstall is a *very* powerful command that you'll meet later. Turning on the OEMPreinstall features will, as you'll see, unlock a whole bunch of extra automated setup capabilities—but for now, let's stick with the basics; "no" leaves those features off.

[GUIUnattended] controls the second, graphical part of Setup, answering many of the questions that section asks. Without OEMSkipWelcome=1, Setup would stop at the beginning of Setup and ask if you want to continue. (Now, what part of FullUnattended did you not understand, Setup Manager?) Note AdminPassword= and that big long string—that's my password, encrypted. Set it to just *— that is, asterisk—to make it blank, although I don't know why you'd do that nowadays.

[UserData] lets you brand the PC with your name and organization, and the name of a PC. "ComputerName=*" tells Setup to cook up a name for this machine. Windows 2000 vets may recall that the command for the product key used to be ProductID; now it's ProductKey, as you see. (And no, that ProductKey doesn't work!)

[Display] sets up the video display. [LicenseFilePrintData] just specifies how you're going to license the clients. [Components] is a simple, if lengthy, list of all of the things that you can choose to install or not install on a Server 2003 system. As you'd guess, you tell Setup to install or not to install with "On" or "Off," which would lead you (incorrectly) to believe that everything gets installed but is turned off.

[GuiRunOnce] contains our printer setup command.

[Networking] is simple in this example; it just says to take the defaults.

Look at the [Identification] section, and let's consider what that does. You want to join this computer to a domain, and of course you'll need at least *some* level of administrative control to do that. That's what that administrative name and password are for—to give Setup the authorization to create a computer account. But obviously you might not be too happy about the idea of putting the account name and password of a domain administrator into an unencrypted ASCII file. Fortunately, you can create a lower-power administrator that can only create and destroy *machine* accounts—it can't mess with user accounts or anything else on the domain—and you'll learn how to do that at the end of the chapter.

Improving Setup Manager's Script

We didn't ask Setup Manager to do anything fancy, which is why we got a pretty short script—I just wanted to create a basic script. But you might want to add one command: Repartition. You might want to add the command Repartition=Yes, which goes in [Unattended]. This command tells Setup to delete all partitions on the first physical drive and create one big NTFS drive. If you *don't* use the Repartition command, then you have to either prebuild the partitions on the computer somehow (there are third-party tools that can do that) or accept that Setup will stop partway through the text portion and prompt you to ask which partition to place Server 2003 on.

Getting the Script Ready to Try

Want to try this out? Add the Repartition command that I just mentioned and, of course, make whatever changes will work in your system. If this is just a simple tryout then you might not want to join a domain; in that case, change the [Identification] section so that it looks like this:

```
[Identification]
    JoinWorkgroup=(your workgroup name--anything will do)
```

Then you'll need just a few ingredients:

- First, of course, you'll need a computer. Note that as I've included the Repartition=Yes command, this will blow away any partitions on its first physical hard disk.

- Next, you'll need to copy your script file to a floppy. The floppy needn't be bootable. Rename the script file name to `winnt.sif`. That's a "magic" name—if you name it something else, then this won't work. Put the floppy in the A: drive.

NOTE   *Please note that if you have told Explorer on your system to hide file extensions, the filename looks like* `unattend` *rather than* `unattend.txt`. *Now and then someone will not realize that the filename is actually* `unattend.txt` *rather than* `unattend`, *and when they try to rename the file to* `winnt.sif`, *Explorer renames it instead to* `winnt.sif.txt`. *Now, it still looks like* `winnt.sif` *in Explorer, but its real name is* `winnt.sif.txt`. *So be sure to tell Explorer to show you file extensions before renaming* `unattend.txt` *to* `winnt.sif`.

◆ After that, insert the Server 2003 installation CD in the CD-ROM drive.

◆ Finally, in your computer's BIOS, you need to rearrange the boot order.

Ideally, you'd like a system that lets you tell it to first boot from the CD-ROM and then, if that wasn't bootable, to try the C: drive, and only if *those* two weren't available, to boot from A:. Now, with the CD-ROM in its drive and the floppy in the A: drive, boot the system. It'll ask you to press a key to boot from the CD-ROM and, if you don't, then it boots from the hard disk.

Then you just walk away.

What's going on? A trick built into Windows 2000 and later versions of NT. If it boots from its setup CD, it then looks on the A: drive for a file named `winnt.sif`. If it finds one then it presumes that the `winnt.sif` file is the script that it should use to do an unattended install. Pretty neat, eh? Hey, stay tuned, it gets even better.

Improving the Script More

Once you've got a basic script like that working, you can take it considerably further, as the script language is pretty extensive. Look back in the directory where you copied the files from `deploy.cab` and you'll see a large WordPad document named `unattend.doc`—a roughly 180-page document— that documents all of the scripting parameters. Here are a couple suggestions.

MOVE DOCUMENTS AND SETTINGS

Windows 2000 and later OSes store the user profiles by default in a directory `C:\Documents and Settings`; if you want to move that, then add the line ProfilesDir=*path* to put the profiles some-where else.

PRECONFIGURE INTERNET EXPLORER

As I mentioned a few pages back, you can configure Internet Explorer in the script as well. For example, here's a piece from a script that I use:

```
[FavoritesEx]
    Title1="Mark Minasi Home Page.url"
    URL1="http://www.minasi.com"
[Branding]
    BrandIEUsingUnattended=Yes
[URL]
    Home_Page=about:blank
```

The first section preloads my home page into my Favorites. The second just warns Setup that we'll be configuring IE via a script, and the third section defines my home page as about:blank.

Now, for those of you who are IEAK (Internet Explorer Administration Kit) wizards, then your hard work isn't wasted—there's a script setting that tells Setup to find the file containing your IEAK settings and then to apply them. (Run Setup Manager and you'll see the option.)

POSTINSTALL POLISHING: ADDING SUPPORT AND BRANDING INFO

Now that you've got your system set up, let's add a bit of branding and support info. (Truthfully, the branding info is a bit silly—though fun—but the support info isn't silly, it's useful.)

Try this: log in to your Server 2003 system as Administrator (that's probably the only account you've got built yet anyway), and find the icon on the Desktop labeled My Computer in the upper-left corner. Right-click it and choose Properties. You'll see a multitabbed properties page like the one you've seen elsewhere in Windows. You can add a picture (or any bitmap) to it in the empty space on the left side, like so:

◆ Take any bitmap that's roughly 175 × 175 pixels.

◆ Name it oemlogo.bmp.

◆ Place it in \windows\system32 or \winnt\system32, whichever you've got the OS in.

Next, let's add some support information. You can "brand" a computer to describe its model, and also add an arbitrary set of lines of text for support information by including a file in \winnt\system32 named oeminfo.ini. This is an ASCII text file with two sections, [General] and [Support Information]. It looks like this:

```
[General]
Manufacturer=<descriptive vendor name>
Model=<particular model>
[Support Information]
Line1=<first line of text>
Line2=<second line of text>
Line3=<and so on >
```

For example, you might have an oeminfo.ini file that looks like the following:

```
[General]
Manufacturer=Clonetronics
Model=DeskWidget 820 (60GB disk, 733 Processor)
[Support Information]
Line1=For Tech Support call:
Line2=(555) 555-1212
Line3=After hours, call Bill
Line4=(If you can find him)
```

Try it and you'll see that it works quite well and can be a useful way to "brand" a system.

Scripts, Part II: Distribution Shares and OEM

You've seen that one way to start an unattended install is to shove a floppy and a CD into a system, boot, and walk away. But that's really only of value if you just want to install the operating system with the basics. Next, let's see how to load a whole *bunch* of new software, and also do some other great stuff, including installing applications on top of the OS.

STARTING A SETUP WITH WINNT/WINNT32

Like previous versions of NT, Server 2003 ships on a CD and includes a large directory called I386. Inside I386 are a pair of programs that you've already met, winnt.exe and winnt32.exe. As you've already read, one way to start Windows Server 2003's Setup program is to just type **winnt** or **winnt32** with a sequence of options. You *could*, then, install Server on a system this way (I don't recommend it, although there's a good reason why I'm explaining it):

1. Clean up about 2GB of space on a drive on a computer's hard disk.
2. Copy the I386 directory on the CD and its subdirectories to the drive with 2GB or more space.
3. Change directories over to the copied I386 directory that is now on the computer's local hard disk.
4. Open a command line and type either **winnt** or **winnt32** with whatever options are appropriate at the time, depending on what kind of install you want to do. (And, again, use WINNT if you're currently running DOS or Windows 9*x*, WINNT32 to start a Server 2003 Setup from inside NT, 2000, XP, or Server 2003.)

WINNT[32] AND DISTRIBUTION SHARES

Now, why did I explain this to you if I recommend that you not use it? Because many people *do* use a variation on this theme. Over the years, many of us have done WINNT/WINNT32 installs not by copying I386 to the target machine, but instead by putting I386 on a shared folder (called a *distribution share* or *distribution folder*) on a file server. *Then* you walk over to the machine that you want to put Server 2003 on, connect to the file share, and type **winnt** or **winnt32**. Summarized, then, the idea with a distribution share is that you first copy the I386 files over to some share on the network; then to put Server 2003 on a new machine, you just walk over to the machine, log in to the network, connect to the distribution share, run the WINNT program in the share, and Setup starts. You can, of course, script an installation this way as well, and so the whole process can become basically unattended.

THE CHICKEN AND THE EGG

The only problem with this whole approach has always been that part about taking a brand-new machine and logging in to the network with it—namely, how the blazes do you *do* it? Computers with empty hard disks don't know jack about networks (at least, not usually—stay tuned for the RIS section to see the alternative), so simply stuffing an Ethernet card into a new PC and hooking it up to the company network accomplishes nothing besides making another LED on the Ethernet switches light up. You need a network stack—protocols, a network file client, all that kind of stuff. It's always sort of been true that "you need to be on the network to be able to connect to the software that you'll need to install in order to get onto the network." Kind of a chicken-and-egg thing.

Microsoft used to offer a two-floppy set of code called the MS-DOS Client for Microsoft Networks that helped a bit. You'd first stick DOS on the new machine, then load the MS-DOS Client for Microsoft Networks, then reboot the system. That would let you log in to a domain and from there attach to a distribution share—but it was an awful lot of installing just to start off the Setup programs for NT 4 or later OSes. Worse yet, the Client didn't include drivers for any NICs built after the Punic Wars, so you always had to hunt around for a set of DOS-compatible drivers for the modern network card in your computer.

With a bit of luck and determination, I was sometimes able to fit the whole mess onto a floppy, and that wasn't so bad—just boot the new computer from the A: drive and I'd be connected to the network. Of course, I had to reengineer the floppy for every different model of NIC, which partially explains why I (a) only bought 3Com Ethernet cards for years and (b) resisted going to 100-megabit Ethernet a year or two longer than I should have—I was reluctant to have to create a new network boot floppy.

Where does that leave you nowadays? Well, to my knowledge, Microsoft doesn't distribute the Client anymore. You can solve the how-do-I-get-to-the-distribution-share in the first place problem in one of three ways:

- Find an old copy of the MS-DOS Client for Microsoft Networks and cook up network boot floppies. (And please don't e-mail me, I can't distribute them—they're copyrighted.) There are some useful bootable disk images at www.bootdisk.com; it's worth a moment or two to see if they've got one you can use.

- Given that many new systems ship with Wintendo (Win 9x) on them anyway, you already have a network-aware operating system sitting on your new computer's hard disk. Use that to connect to the distribution share.

- A lot of new computers have the ability to do a PXE or "network boot." Windows 2000 and Server 2003's Remote Installation Services (RIS) is built to support PXE boots, and so can let a computer with even an empty hard disk get to an RIS server and then install Server 2003 from a server. Fortunately, Server 2003's RIS can roll out not only Professional but Server images as well—an upgrade from Windows 2000!

EXTENDING *I386*: PREINSTALLING SERVICE PACKS

Let's presume, then, that you've figured a way to get your workstations attached to a network distribution share. Now we can start reaping the benefits of doing installs from a share on a hard disk rather than a CD-ROM: we can *add* to the data on the CD.

The first terrific thing that we can do is to preinstall service packs. You can typically download a service pack as one big EXE. As I write this, there aren't any service packs for Windows Server 2003—it's just been released!—but assuming that Server 2003's service packs continue to work as 2000 and XP's do, this should work. First, download the service pack; let's call it sp20031.exe, although I have no idea what Microsoft will call Server 2003's service packs. You can attach a service pack to Server 2003's I386, "assimilating" it so that when you do an installation from that I386, you instantly have a copy of Server 2003 with some service pack installed, rather than having to first install Server 2003 and *then* apply the service pack. Here's how.

1. Create a directory on a server's hard disk and copy the I386 folder to it. Let's say, for example, that you put it in C:\I386.

2. Put the sp20031.exe file on that computer's disk (it doesn't matter where and please remember, that's a hypothetical filename), open a command line, and type **sp20031 -x** to extract all of the service pack files. It'll ask you where to put them, so specify a directory wherever it makes sense for you. Let's just say you tell it to put the files in C:\SP.

3. Once sp20031 has extracted itself, look in the directory that sp20031 created, C:\SP, to find a directory named C:\SP\I386\update. In there you'll find a program named update.exe.

4. Run update.exe with the -s option and point it at the drive containing I386, *not* the I386 directory itself. For example, if you put I386 on C:, then type **c:\sp\i386 update -s:c:** to put the service pack files into C:\I386.

Microsoft says that the -s stands for "slipstream," but I tend to think that it stands for "aSsimilate," as that's what the service pack does—assimilates itself into the I386. Notice that, because the service pack will only take the name of the directory *above* I386 as an input, you really *must* store the data from the CD's I386 folder in a folder also named I386. This isn't a great hardship—most distribution shares I've ever seen are named I386—but now there's a reason that you really *have* to call the directory I386.

TIP   *Now that you've seen how to automatically install a service pack, you're probably wondering how to automatically add the latest hotfixes. I'll show you how to do that in the upcoming section "Tell Setup to Run Commands with* cmdlines.txt.*"*

OEM: MORE *I386* POWER

Look back at my example script and you'll see, in the [Unattended] section, a command OEM-Preinstall=No. Let's change that No to Yes and unlock a bunch of convenient unattended setup features:

◆ You can tell Setup to create directories and files on the newly installed machine.

◆ You can tell Setup to run any number of commands at the end of setup—for example, commands to tell Setup to install other applications.

◆ You can supply Setup with newer device drivers than the ones that ship with Server 2003, or device drivers for hardware that didn't even exist when Server 2003 shipped.

◆ You can specify that you want to install a particular Hardware Abstraction Layer (HAL). You wouldn't do this very often (so I'm not going to cover the topic any further), but once in a while you'll try to build a setup script for a system that needs a custom HAL, and this is the only way to tell Setup to use it while unattended.

Here's how to use the power of OEM. Inside an I386 directory, create a directory named OEM. For example, suppose you'd copied the I386 directory to the E: drive and then perhaps slipstreamed a service pack onto it. Before starting to do installs from that E:\I386 directory, create a directory named E:\I386\OEM. We'll do our work in the following sections in that directory.

Setup Bitmaps and Logos

While the Setup program runs on a user's machine, you might want to include instructions or information on the screen. You can do that with the [OEM_Ads] section. Create a section in your script with a logo= and a background= command, like so:

```
[OEM_Ads]
logo=ourlogo.bmp
background=backgrnd.bmp
```

Place the files ourlogo.bmp and backgrnd.bmp in the \I386\OEM directory. They must be simple Windows-type bitmap files—you can't use GIF or JPEG files. The background file will display as the background, centered on the Setup screen. Don't use a bitmap larger than 640×480, as that's the resolution that Setup runs in.

And by the way, here's an important tip: Try out the bitmap and logo before using it for a user's system install. Setup puts a couple of big dialog boxes up that obscure most of the background, so if you actually want to pass along some information, then you'll have to be careful about where you place the info on the bitmap or logo; otherwise, the information won't be readable.

Create Directories and Copy Files

If you create a directory inside OEM with a one-letter name, like I386\$OEM$\E or I386\$OEM$\D, then Setup will copy any file (or directory) in that directory to the drive letter of the same name on the newly installed computer. For example, suppose I want my computers to all have a directory on C: called Data, which will contain a file named basic.txt. Let's assume that I've got the I386 distribution share on a server, on its D: drive, so I've got the setup files in D:\I386. To ensure that every new system created from this share has a directory named C:\Data and containing the basic.txt file, all I need do is this:

◆ Create a directory named D:\I386\OEM\C.

◆ Create a directory inside *that* directory named Data -D:\I386\OEM\C\Data.

◆ Place the basic.txt file inside the D:\I386\OEM\C\Data directory.

OEM also has a few "magic" directory names that you can exploit to place files into the system folders. First, there's the $$ directory. Anything in I386\$OEM$\$$ goes to winnt. What's the value of that? Well, when you're writing an installation script, you might not know beforehand which drive winnt will go on. Rather than having to create a directory named I386\$OEM$\C\winnt and then accidentally try to use that to put files in winnt on a system that puts its operating system on the D: drive, putting files in I386\$OEM$\$$ will ensure that those files will end up in winnt on the drive that contains the operating system.

So, for example, if you liked the idea of including support information on your system, then recall that you store the support and branding information in a file named oeminfo.ini, which must sit in \winnt\system32. You could create an oeminfo.ini file and then place it in a distribution share at I386\$OEM$\$$\system32, and the file would then automatically get copied to the system32 directory of any newly installed systems. You'd be ensuring that every new system gets the support information without requiring any extra work on your part.

Including Updated Drivers

Every version of Server includes a pretty large collection of drivers in its initial offering. But from the minute they ship a version of server, boatloads of new hardware appear, so as a version of Server gets older, it'll be more and more likely that either you have a piece of hardware that didn't exist at the time of that version's birth (and therefore that version lacks a driver for it), or the hardware's manufacturer has created a newer and better driver—and Server 2003 is no exception. You can automate the process of telling Server 2003 to use a new or updated driver, using the OEMPnPDrivers command.

Create the directories for new or updated drivers in OEM\$1\, then specify them in OEMPnP-DriversPath. For example, suppose I've got some new video and audio drivers, and I place the new video drivers into a directory named I386\$OEM$\$1\newvid. Then I put the new audio drivers in I386\$OEM$\$1\newaud. I can then tell Setup to look for them by adding this line to the [Unattended] section of my setup script:

```
OEMPnPDriversPath="newvid; newaud"
```

Notice that we describe directories by their path below OEM\$1. Don't include I386\$OEM$\$1 in the path.

WARNING   *Note that you should keep the list of directories to 40 or fewer characters. This is a limitation of OEMPnP-DriversPath. But don't make them single-character directory names, or Setup will try to create files on drive C:, D:, E:, etc., on the target machine!*

Tell Setup to Run Commands with cmdlines.txt

Once your system is set up, you might want to install some applications beyond the basic operating system, or you might want to delete some little-used files that Setup leaves behind, or you might want to accomplish any number of other small tasks. You can do that with a file named `cmdlines.txt`, which must be located in the `$OEM$` directory.

`cmdlines.txt` is just a list of command-line commands that you want Setup to execute. That may sound to you as if I'm suggesting that `cmdlines.txt` is an old DOS-style batch file, but it isn't. For some reason, it needs a specific format. The first line must be [Commands] on a line all by itself. Then, you list the commands that you want Setup to run—but you must surround the commands with double quotes. For example, consider this example `cmdlines.txt` file:

```
[Commands]
"msiexec /i \\server\share\somefile.msi"
"regedit /s myhacks.reg"
```

As you see, the first line is just [Commands]. Then, the second line is the first command that you want Setup to run. If you've never heard of MSIEXEC, then let me introduce you—it's a command that you'll use a lot when building `cmdlines.txt` files. You see, under Windows 2000, XP, and Server 2003, you install an application using a service called the Windows Installer service. Instead of installing programs with a traditional **setup.exe** program, you install programs by handing a "package" to the Installer. This package is the collection of files that you need to run the program, as well as a set of instructions about how to install the program—"this file goes here, this icon goes on the Start menu, create these Registry entries"—and the Installer looks at the instruction file (which, by convention, has the extension `.msi`) and carries out its instructions. (You'll learn more about this in the chapter on software deployment; I'm just giving you the barest of sketches about how it works here.)

Normally you deploy an MSI-type package using Active Directory, as you'll learn a bit later in this book. But if you want to install an application from the command line, then you'll use a program called `msiexec.exe`. The /i option says to install the program from its MSI, silently. Again, you'll learn more about where you get MSI files from a bit later in the book—I just thought that an `msiexec /i` example would be useful.

TIP   *In order to make this work,* `msiexec.exe` *must be in the* `$OEM$` *directory; copy it from a functioning Windows 2000 or later OS.*

The second command may be familiar to experts in any NT version from 4 on. Sometimes the easiest way to set up NT, 2000, or Server 2003 to work *exactly* the way you want is to apply a bunch of Registry hacks. The REGEDIT command offers a pretty neat command-line way to modify the Registry.

For example, I find the AutoRun feature of CD-ROMs *really* annoying. I don't want Server 2003 offering to install every time I pop the Server 2003 CD into a drive just to get a file or two. Now, I *could* shut off AutoRun by opening up a Registry Editor, navigating down to HKEY_LOCAL_MACHINE\SYSTEM\ CurrentControlSet\Services\Cdrom, and then editing the entry labeled AutoRun, setting its value to 0. But I don't want to hand-edit the Registry—and that's where REGEDIT comes to the rescue. Just create a four-line ASCII file (call it CDFix.reg) with these contents:

```
REGEDIT4

[HKEY_LOCAL_MACHINE\SYSTEM\CurrentControlSet\Services\Cdrom]
"AutoRun"=dword:00000000
```

Note the blank line between REGEDIT4 and [HKEY; you need that. Now open up a command line and tell REGEDIT to apply this change by typing **regedit /s cdfix.reg**; the /s means, "Shut up and do it!" so you won't get a message. But reboot your NT or later machine and you'll find that AutoRun is now disabled. Notice how what I could call the REGEDIT "command language" works: the first line is REGEDIT4, then a blank line, then you indicate what key you want to work with, in brackets, and then the value entry. And that line starting with [HKEY_LOCAL_MACHINE is just one line when typed, no matter how long. You can put a whole bunch of changes into a single file, or create different .reg files and apply them sequentially.

As with msiexec.exe, be sure to put regedit.exe in the OEM folder, or this won't work. And you may be wondering, how did I figure out how to create a file in "REGEDIT format?" Simple. I just highlighted a key that I wanted to apply and then exported it. The exported file turned out to be a simple ASCII format—and an import showed that REGEDIT imports files in the same format as it exports.

Using CMDLINES.TXT to Install the Latest Hotfixes

Here's an even more valuable use for cmdlines.txt: preinstalling hotfixes. Hotfixes are files that fix some critical problem in NT 4 or later, things that will eventually make their way into the next service pack but that Microsoft felt were important enough that they couldn't wait for the next service pack. You can find them by going to www.microsoft.com/security and then clicking the Security Bulletins link. Now, that works as of the time that I am writing this, but Microsoft is fond of rearranging their Web site, so if that doesn't work, then just do a search for "security bulletins" on their site and you'll find them. For step 1, download them and collect them into the OEM directory. They'll have names like q329834_WXP_SP2_ENU.exe, which tells you

◆ that you can find out about what this fixes in Knowledge Base article 329834,

◆ that you apply this to Windows XP Pro (WXP),

◆ that it is post-Service Pack 2, and

◆ that it works on the version of the operating system that is localized for English.

If you've ever applied a hotfix, then you know that you just run it as a program, which is nice and simple. But what's *not* so simple is that every time you install a hotfix, the stupid hotfix insists that you reboot the computer. Let's see, 16 hotfixes in the post-SP2 world (to use XP as an example)... figure a minute a reboot... I've only got 1000 computers to do this on. Naaah. But there's good news. Fortunately, most hotfixes written since mid-2002 have two options, -q and -z, that tell the hotfixes to install quietly and not to force a reboot.

Now, if you ever did this with Windows 2000, then you may be expecting me to next talk about a utility called `qchain.exe`, which arranges hotfixes on your system. But I've got some good news for you... QCHAIN is no longer necessary on Windows XP or Server 2003. So just apply the hotfixes and you'll be up to date.

Make sure that all of the hotfixes are in the `$OEM$` directory. Then modify `cmdlines.txt` to invoke each of the hotfixes with the -q -z options, and finally run -q -z options. A simplified `cmdlines.txt` with four imaginary hotfixes—I'll spare you the 16-liner that I actually use— might look like this:

```
[Commands]
"msiexec /i \\server\share\somefile.msi"
"regedit /s myhacks.reg"
"q302755_w2k_sp3_x86_en.exe -q —z"
"q303984_w2k_sp3_x86_en.exe -q —z"
"q301625_w2k_sp3_x86_en.exe -q —z"
```

Notice, as I've said before, that you must surround the commands in quotes.

Pretty nifty, eh? I used to roll out test machines without hotfixes mostly because I felt that it took too much time, but too many of those machines fell prey to the Worm of the Week. Now I'm (relatively) secure from the first power-up.

I hope I've convinced you that `$OEM$` holds some pretty powerful capabilities. If you use it and the OEMPreinstall=Yes command, then you can extend the power of an unattended installation pretty far.

GUIRunOnce

I haven't included this section in my example scripts yet, but I should mention that you can include a section, [GUIRunOnce], in a setup script. It tells Server 2003 to finish installing and then to reboot. Once Server 2003 reboots, it then lets you log in. Once you've logged in, Setup runs the commands in GUIRunOnce—typically these are setup commands for applications. They run under whatever user account you logged in as, so if you're installing something that requires Administrator-level privileges, then be sure to log in with a powerful-enough account.

Items in the [GUIRunOnce] section must be surrounded by quotes. One example that I've seen of GUIRunOnce's power is the automatic starting and running of DCPROMO, the program that creates domain controllers. You'll learn more about DCPROMO in Chapter 8.

So you can see that you can do pretty neat things with scripts and the OEMPreinstall features. But don't let me oversell this; let's remember that there's still that chicken-and-egg problem of "how do I get on the network to get to the network share in the first place?" We'll solve that problem next, with Remote Installation Services, or RIS.

Installing Server 2003 with Remote Installation Services

Well, by now, you've probably tried shoving the CD-ROM into some computer's drive and installing Server 2003. You may well have had some luck at it and found that after a bit of twiddling, you could make it work quite well. "Cool," you might have thought, "Installing Server 2003 will be a snap."

But then, you probably realized that you'd have to do it for *several hundred machines*. Let's see now, doing the exact same set of twiddling several hundred times would take...well, more patience and time than many of us have. It would be nice to be able to spend a fair amount of time on just one computer, getting it just right, and then to "photocopy" that configuration onto dozens or hundreds of other computers.

And for years, many of us did just that. Back when I worked in training labs teaching Windows 3 running atop DOS 5, it was a simple matter to just boot up a workstation with a floppy containing the Novell client software, format the workstation's C: drive, and then XCOPY an entire drive image from a Novell shared volume onto the workstation. The whole process was completely automated once I got it started, and took no more than about 20 minutes.

Later on, with the advent of bigger operating systems like Windows 95, drive copier programs like Ghost and Drive Image Pro came out. These drive copiers didn't care what files were on a computer; they'd just copy a physical hard disk or partitions from that hard disk to a network folder for you. Then you could set up a new computer to look just like the prototypic computer by booting the new computer from a floppy and then pulling down the Ghost or Ghost-like (would that be "Ghostly"?) image.

That worked fine for Windows, but not for NT, as NT is secure, and so each computer with NT installed on it has long and machine-specific strings of numbers embedded in it, numbers called security IDs, or SIDs. Cloning one machine's NT image onto thousands of machines would lead to thousands of machines with identical SIDs. While that might not *sound* terrible, it could have some very bizarre side effects.

For example, suppose you start up a new PC with a cloned copy of NT Workstation or Windows 2000 Professional on it, logging in the first time as the default administrator. The first order of business is then to create a local user account for yourself. But inside NT, that account would get an SID. As this is the first account created besides the built-in Administrator and Guest accounts, that account's SID will be the first available in the range of SIDs on this machine.

Now imagine that Janice down the hall, who has a machine containing the exact same cloned image on her system, also logs in to her new machine as its default administrator and creates herself an account. It'll have a different name than your account—but that won't matter. NT doesn't really care what your name is; it cares what your SID is. And what value SID does Janice have? Well, as it's the first created account, you guessed it—her account now has the same SID as yours.

What does that mean? Well, suppose you made your local account an Administrator account. That means that when she's logged in to her own machine with her own account, she can use Windows 2000's remote control tools to do administrator-like things to your system over the network. That's not a good thing, unless you and Janice are really good buddies.

As a result, disk-cloning vendors have come up with "SID scrambler" programs. You copy the cloned image onto a new machine and then run the SID scrambler. It creates a unique set of SIDs on the newly cloned machine and all should be well. Microsoft, however, says that the SID scramblers from the two big players, Symantec's Ghost and PowerQuest's Drive Image Pro, won't do the whole job. I honestly don't know if this true or if it's just Microsoft... well, being Microsoft. In any case, now Microsoft has a method for rolling out a single workstation image to dozens, hundreds, or thousands of machines while simultaneously ensuring that each machine has a unique SID. It's a tool called the Remote Installation Services (RIS). In this section, you'll learn how to set it up and how to get those images out to all of those PCs hungering for an operating system.

RIS solves the other big rollout problem, as well: the "how do I get a computer with nothing on its hard disk connected to the network so that I can do a network-based install?" problem. You'll see how to do that in this section, but before I go further, let me offer this warning:

WARNING   *I've included RIS in this chapter because it's a rollout and deployment tool, but RIS won't work unless you have an Active Directory infrastructure in place and some knowledge of another infrastructure tool called the Dynamic Host Configuration Protocol (DHCP) and are also comfortable with file and directory permissions on NTFS disk drives. If any of that sounds a bit scary, then just skip this RIS section and go on to the Sysprep section. Then, once you've gotten through the TCP/IP and Active Directory chapters, come revisit this section.*

RIS Overview

RIS lets you designate a server or a set of servers as *RIS servers*. A RIS server contains the files necessary to install Windows 2000, XP, or Server 2003 onto a computer from across the network. RIS can deliver an operating system to a waiting PC in one of three formats:

Simple I386-based Installation   In this simplest form, RIS is just a place to store the installation files for various versions of NT from Win2K on. How is it different from just putting I386 onto a directory on any old file server and then sharing that directory? Not very much, except in one important way: it solves the "how do I get to the network in the first place?" problem. You can go to the PC that you intend to put 2000, XP, or Server 2003 on and boot it with just one floppy, and you'll be off and running, no messing around with the DOS Client for Networks or the like. Of course, once this installation starts up, you must sit at the computer and answer all of Setup's questions, baby-sitting the computer while Setup runs.

Scripted I386 Install   This installation is like the preceding situation, with the added benefit of unattended installation. You just go out to the target PC, boot the floppy, and away it goes. These first two options are called *flat image format* images. (If you've been using this since Windows 2000 then you'll recall that they were called "CD images" in 2000.)

Complete System Image with Minimal Setup Interaction   This option is really the more interesting option for many people. You build an entire prototypical machine running Windows 2000 Pro or Server, XP, or Server 2003, complete with applications. Then you use RIS to create an image of that machine on a RIS server. You then boot the target PC with a RIS-built floppy again, and RIS transfers the entire disk image, complete with operating system and applications, to the target PC. It's not entirely hands-off, however, as it needs a bit of machine-specific customization: you need to punch in a unique machine name, for example. This kind of image is called a *RIPrep image format* image.

New-to-Server 2003 RIS Goodies

RIS was neat under Windows 2000, but Windows Server 2003 offers several bits of good news. First, as I've mentioned already, 2000 only deployed Windows 2000 Professional images. Server 2003's RIS will roll out Windows 2000 Server, Windows 2000 Professional, Windows XP Professional, Windows XP Home, or Windows Server 2003 images. Great news (and it's about time)!

Second, as you've already learned, RIS is a neat way to roll out operating systems to computers. But getting those computers to talk to a RIS server requires that the computers (call them "RIS clients") be built in a particular way. Without this RIS client support, also called PXE support, you can't use RIS to put an OS on a computer. But RIS has always had a workaround in that it will create a floppy disk that will support network cards for client systems that aren't set up to get the benefits of RIS. That floppy has been revised for Server 2003 to support a wider range of systems.

Finally, RIS under Windows 2000 always had the annoying feature of sending your password *in cleartext* over the network cable when you first logged on. It only happened once, but it was still a bad idea security-wise. RIS for Server 2003 and its revised clients now encrypt passwords before putting them on the wire.

RIS Limitations

Before getting too excited about RIS—it's nice, but the Ghost guys needn't worry about being put out of business—let's look at what it *can't* do.

RIS CLIENTS MUST HAVE PARTICULAR PCI NETWORK CARDS; SOME LAPTOPS WON'T WORK

I'll cover this later, but you can only get a RIS system image onto a computer that knows how to ask for one, and the only way that system knows how to ask is if the system supports something called the Preboot Execution Environment (PXE) protocol, version 0.99C or later. If you've seen computers that can be "network managed," then there's a good chance that the computer has PXE support in its BIOS. In addition to PXE support, you'll need a NIC that works with PXE. No ISA NIC that I know of supports PXE, and I've only heard rumor of PCMCIA/PC Card/CardBus laptop NICs that support PXE. Most PXE-compatible NICs are PCI cards. Laptops aren't completely shut out, as some laptops now ship with an integrated NIC built to the "mini PCI" specification— I've seen some IBM ThinkPads that fit in this category. Such a laptop might be RIS-compatible. (And believe me, RIS's convenience is sufficiently great that PXE/mini-PCI compliance will be a "must-have" characteristic of all of my future laptops!)

In Server 2003 and later, you'll find that many laptops come with an integrated Ethernet card; again, take a moment and ask the vendor two questions: first, is it mini-PCI (rather than PCMCIA) and, second, does it support "network boot?" If so, the chances are good that such a machine will work with RIS.

What if your computer doesn't support PXE? RIS comes with a program called `RBFG.exe`, the Remote Disk Boot Generator (RDBG). (It *was* Remote Boot Floppy Generator in 2000 but Microsoft renamed the program without renaming its file, so the program's abbreviation is RDBG but its file name is rbfg.exe.). It's a program that lets your computer support PXE, so long as your computer has one of the particular 32 NICs that `RBFG.exe` supports. It's annoying that RIS doesn't really support pre–year 2000 laptops and most pre-1998 desktops, but truthfully that's often the case with Windows technologies: the coolest features of any version of Windows often require some new technology. I often find myself telling audiences that "the latest version of NT will solve many of your existing problems; all you have to do to get those benefits is to replace all of your hardware and software!"

CERTAIN SERVICES KEEP RIS FROM WORKING

It's great that Server 2003 lets us use RIS on both servers and workstations—2000's RIS didn't—but you can't use RIS on *every* kind of server. You can't, as far as I can see, use RIS on a server that is acting as a DHCP or RIS server, or on a server that acts as a domain controller.

RIS CAN ONLY IMAGE THE C: DRIVE

When you build a prototype computer whose image you will then propagate all over the enterprise, you'd better build a computer with just one hard-disk partition C:. RIS will merely copy the C: drive and whatever's on it.

RIS HAS A FAIRLY SPARSE ADMINISTRATIVE UI

While RIS doesn't require a *lot* of administration, there are few tasks that you'll do frequently, and RIS doesn't provide a very good way to do them. For example, if you had a RIS server that contained many system images, but you didn't want every user to see every possible image (which is very likely— odds are that you'd have one image for the accounting folks, another for the programmers, and so on), then the only way to restrict the choice of images that a user sees is through NTFS permissions rather than via some simple administrative interface.

RIS SEEMS NOT TO WORK ON MULTIHOMED SYSTEMS

I've been using RIS on Windows 2000 for years and Server 2003 for a while and in both cases I have found that putting RIS on a system with more than one NIC is simply asking for trouble. I have no idea why this is, but I've run into far too may situations where I've got an up-and-running (in theory) RIS server that simply cannot see any clients. Other things work fine on the server, but RIS is just plain deaf on multihomed systems. I may simply be doing something wrong, but in my experience multihomed RIS servers are not reliable, so I don't recommend them.

Steps to Making RIS Work

The first time you set up a RIS server, it can seem a bit complicated if you're not ready for it, as RIS is a bit different from other Server 2003 services. What I'm referring to is that to install most Server 2003 network services, like IIS or WINS, you just install them on a server, reboot the server (and many times you needn't even reboot), and you're done. Setting up RIS on a server, however, requires fiddling a bit with Active Directory.

TIP   *Before you can use RIS, you must have Active Directory running. It seems to work fine with either a 2000-based or Server 2003–based AD, but you need AD. As you'll learn later or you might already know, you can't have AD without a functioning DNS server that supports RFC 2782 SRV records and RFC 2136 dynamic updates, as described in Chapter 8.*

WARNING   *In order to explain how to set up RIS, I'll need to assume that you already know what a DHCP server is. If, however, you have not worked with previous versions of NT and so probably don't know DHCP, then don't worry about it—just skip this section until you've learned about TCP/IP, DHCP, and Active Directory in the next few chapters, then return to this section. (And in that case, please accept my apologies for making you jump around the book.)*

To get a RIS server working, follow these steps:

1. Set up a Server 2003 system and make it a member of an Active Directory domain. The server must have a fairly large NTFS drive available, and that drive can't be the boot drive or the drive containing the operating system. (When I say "drive" here I mean "partition." You needn't have two physical hard disks for a RIS server, but you *do* need to have at least two logical drives.)

2. Authorize the soon-to-be-RIS server in the Active Directory as a Dynamic Host Configuration Protocol (DHCP) server, even though it's *not* a DHCP server.

3. Add the Remote Installation Services service to the server and reboot it.

4. Run RISetup, the Remote Installation Setup Wizard, to prepare the large drive for receiving RIS images and to put an initial image on the drive—it's just a simple copy of I386.

5. At that point, the RIS server is ready. You can add new images to it with a wizard called RIPrep.

We'll examine each of these steps in the following pages.

Getting Ready for RIS

RIS's job is to let you take a PC with an empty hard disk, attach the PC to your enterprise network, put a RIS-created floppy disk into the PC's A: drive, and boot the PC. The small program on the floppy disk is just smart enough to get an IP address for the PC, then locate an Active Directory domain controller and ask the Active Directory domain controller where to find a RIS server. Once the PC finds the RIS server, it can then start the process of pulling down a particular system image so that the PC becomes useful.

Necessary Infrastructure

But RIS needs some infrastructure to make all of this work right. The PC gets an IP address from a DHCP server, so you'll need at least one DHCP server running in your enterprise to make RIS work. (In case you've never worked with an IP-based NT network before, DHCP's job is to automatically assign unique network addresses to each server and workstation on the network. TCP/IP *requires* that every machine have a unique IP address, or the network software just doesn't work.) Once it has an IP address, the PC finds an Active Directory server by looking it up in DNS—so you'll need a DNS server. And the PC can't query an Active Directory domain controller for the location of a RIS server unless you've got an Active Directory domain controller—so you'll need an Active Directory–based domain (as opposed to a bunch of Server 2003s in a domain built out of NT 4 domain controllers). Of course, if you're running an Active Directory–based domain, then you've *got* to have DNS running, so the simplified list of things you'll need before RIS will work is an Active Directory–based domain and at least one DHCP server.

A Drive for SIS

Furthermore, the RIS server needs a partition to store the RIS images. For some reason, RIS will not store images on the boot partition—which is usually drive C:—or the system partition, which is the drive that contains \windows and the other NT system files.

NOTE   Please, *don't write me letters explaining to me that Microsoft's definition of "boot drive" is the one that contains* \winnt *or* \windows, *and their definition of "system drive" is the drive that you boot from. I know that's what they call it, but it makes no sense, so I'm going to tend to say "system drive" for the one with the operating system, and "boot drive" for the drive that you boot from. I know, that's not what Microsoft told you, but to quote John Candy from the movie* Planes, Trains, and Automobiles, *"If they told you that wolverines made great pets, would you believe that too?"*

I found this you-need-a-drive-that-is-neither-system-nor-boot thing kind of frustrating the first time I went to set up RIS, as the server that I intended to put RIS on had only two drive letters and Windows 2000 (this was back when I first tried RIS, under Win2K) installed on the D: drive. C: was the boot, D: the system, and so RIS wouldn't install. I reinstalled Windows 2000 on the C: drive, freeing up D:, and RIS worked fine. You can have other things on RIS's drive, like files of other types; you just can't have the system files on the drive. Remember that while RIS will make an image of whatever filesystem is on the original workstation, it must be placed onto an NTFS partition on the server.

While it's not entirely clear to me why RIS is allergic to system files, there's a very good reason why it wants a drive pretty much to itself. Imagine a RIS server that contained 20 system images—how much space would that need? Well, Windows 2000 Professional (to use the example of one OS that RIS supports) takes up about 450MB on a hard disk, so let's be generous and say that the applications added to the image only total 50MB, leading to a 500MB image; it's just easier to calculate this way. Ten half-gigabyte images totals 5 gigabytes. But now let's look more closely at those 10 images. The vast majority of the files in the images are identical: For example, each image contains a file named `Drivers.cab` that's nearly 50MB in size, and the file is exactly the same for each of the 10 images. That's a terrible waste of space—500MB to store 10 identical copies of a 50MB file!

RIS solves that problem with a service called the Single Instance Store, or SIS. SIS is a service called the SIS Space Groveler (is that a great service name, or what?) that runs in the background and searches the directory that RIS uses to store system images looking for duplicate files. It then frees up space by deleting the duplicate files, putting in their place a directory entry that makes it appear as if the duplicate is still in place. In actuality, however, the duplicate is no more than a sort of pointer to the complete copy of the file. Clearly a trick like this will require a bit of magic, and that magic comes from a combination of the NTFS of SIS and Windows 2000 and later—that dedicated-to-RIS drive must be an NTFS volume.

EXTENDING SIS: SIDE NOTES

It's a shame that SIS only loads as part of RIS; I could easily imagine many cases wherein recovering space from duplicate files could be beneficial, such as in the case of a server containing hundreds of users' home directories—there's likely to be *plenty* of duplication there.

Actually, if you're feeling a bit brave, then you actually *can* get SIS to run on other drives, according to Knowledge Base article 226545. It says that SIS identifies which drives to do its magic on by looking for three things:

◆ First, the drive must be an NTFS drive.

◆ Second, the drive must contain a hidden folder in its root named `SIS Common Store`.

◆ Finally, that `SIS Common Store` folder must contain a file named `MaxIndex`.

I honestly have not tried this myself, but I pass along the information in case it's of help. So, for example, to apply SIS to any given file server, just install the RIS service on that system (even if you do not intend to make the server a RIS server), place a hidden folder named `SIS Common Store` in the root of whatever drive you want SIS to work on, and don't forget `MaxIndex`.

While I'm on the subject of advanced SIS maintenance, here's another tidbit from the Knowledge Base, article 272149. You can, if you want to, tell SIS to ignore a particular directory in this way:

1. Start up a Registry-editing tool.
2. Navigate to the key named `HKEY_LOCAL_MACHINE\SOFTWARE\Microsoft\Windows NT\CurrentVersion\Groveler\ExcludedPaths`.
3. Create a new value entry with any name that you like, of type REG_SZ.
4. In the data for that value entry, include the name of the directory without the drive letter.

For example, suppose I wanted SIS to ignore a directory named `mystuff` on a SIS volume. I'd just go to the key named above and create a new value entry. I could call that value entry NoMyStuff. I'd make it of type REG_SZ, and in the entry I would place the string "\mystuff." Then either I'd have to reboot to see the changes take effect, or I'd have to stop and start the SIS Space Groveler service.

WARNING *Be aware, however, that I'm told that unless you back up this drive with a backup program that is SIS-aware, then SIS drives aren't backed up properly. Sometimes the backup program* thinks *that it's backing up a file, but it actually just backs up SIS's pointer to a drive. Restoring that pointer without the file is usually not helpful.*

Authorizing RIS in Active Directory

Microsoft figured—probably rightly—that you wouldn't want just *anybody* putting a RIS server on the network. So before you can get the RIS service working on a server, that server must be authorized in the Active Directory. For some reason, however, you don't authorize it as a RIS server; you authorize it as a DHCP server.

To do that, find a DHCP server and log in to it with an account that is a member of the Enterprise Administrators domain group. Click Start/Programs/Administrative Tools/DHCP. Click Action on the menu bar, and you'll see the option Manage Authorized Servers; click that and you'll see an option.

Manage Authorized Servers. You then see the list of currently authorized DHCP servers like the one in Figure 5.13.

FIGURE 5.13

List of current authorized servers

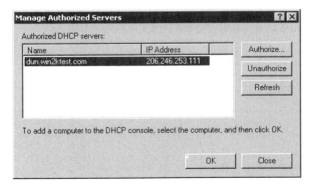

Here, you see that I've already got a server authorized named dun.win2ktest.com. Click Authorize and you'll get a dialog box like the one in Figure 5.14, letting you punch in the IP address of the server that you're going to make into a RIS server.

FIGURE 5.14

Entering IP address of RIS server

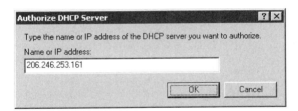

Click OK, and it'll confirm your choice, as Figure 5.15 shows.

FIGURE 5.15

Confirming the
new server

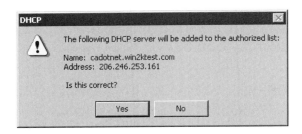

NOTE   If you don't know the IP address of the soon-to-be RIS server, go over to that server and log in to it. Then open a command prompt (Start/Programs/Command Prompt), type **ipconfig**, *and press Enter. It will report the IP address; if you have several IP addresses, take the one in the section labeled Ethernet Adapter Local Area Connection rather than PPP Adapter.*

Now that Active Directory is ready for RIS, let's get RIS ready.

Installing RIS

Next, you'll put the RIS service on the server:

1. Log in to the server that you want to add RIS to, using an Administrator account, and open the Control Panel (Start/Settings/Control Panel).

2. Start the Add/Remove Programs applet.

3. Choose the Add/Remove Windows Components icon.

4. A wizard screen labeled Welcome to the Windows Components Wizard will appear; click Next and it will show you the optional server components, as you see in Figure 5.16.

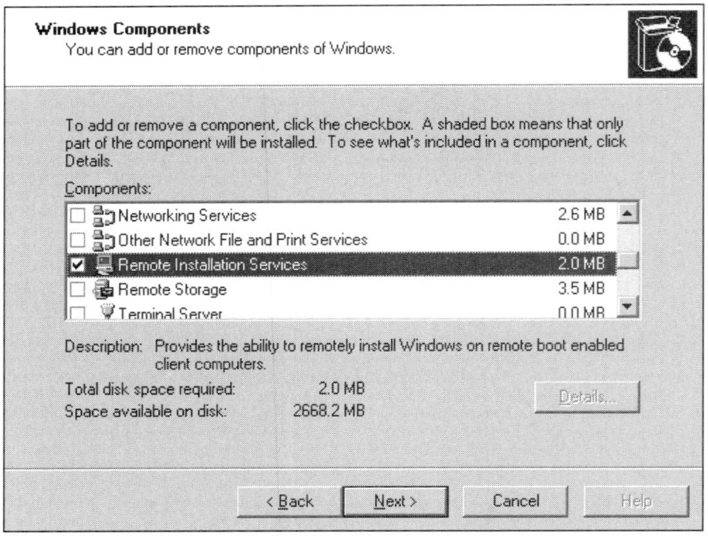

FIGURE 5.16

Windows
Components
screen

Windows Components
You can add or remove components of Windows.

To add or remove a component, click the checkbox. A shaded box means that only
part of the component will be installed. To see what's included in a component, click
Details.

Components:

☐ 🖧 Networking Services	2.6 MB	▲
☐ 🖧 Other Network File and Print Services	0.0 MB	
☑ 🖳 Remote Installation Services	2.0 MB	
☐ 🖳 Remote Storage	3.5 MB	
☐ 🖳 Terminal Server	0.0 MB	▼

Description: Provides the ability to remotely install Windows on remote boot enabled
client computers.

Total disk space required: 2.0 MB
Space available on disk: 2668.2 MB   Details...

< Back   Next >   Cancel   Help

5. Scroll down and check the box labeled Remote Installation Services. Then click Next and Finish.

6. You'll be prompted to reboot, so reboot the server.

Running RISETUP

When installing most Server 2003 services, you just choose the option in Windows Components, wait for the Control Panel to pull the new service off I386, reboot the computer, and it's up and running. RIS is a bit more work than that, however, as RIS must claim its drive and set up SIS. For good measure, RIS also creates a first image. That first image is the simplest one possible—it's just a copy of the I386 directory from the Windows Server 2003 CD-ROM, Standard Edition. (You could alternatively offer it XP Pro, XP Home, 2000 Server, or Professional. For that matter, you could offer it any version of Server 2003 as well.)

Log in to the would-be RIS server with an administrative account and run RISETUP (either from a command prompt or click Start/Run, fill in **risetup**, and press Enter) and the Remote Installation Services Setup Wizard starts. The initial screen is shown in Figure 5.17.

FIGURE 5.17
RISetup initial
screen

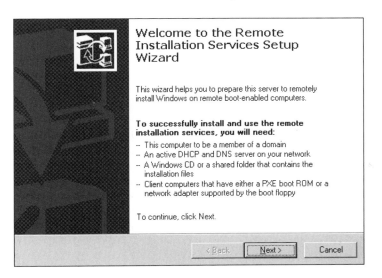

Click Next and the wizard will quickly scan your drives looking for a likely place to keep RIS's files. In my case, it found drive F:. It wants to create a directory named RemoteInstall, as you can see in Figure 5.18.

After you click Next, RISetup will ask you if you want the server to respond to requests from PCs for operating systems, as shown in Figure 5.19. Inasmuch as you don't have any useful images on the RIS server at the moment, tell the server not to respond to those requests.

FIGURE 5.18

Suggested location
for RIS images

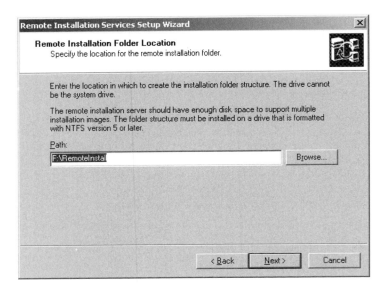

FIGURE 5.19

Telling RIS to ignore
requests until we're
done configuring it

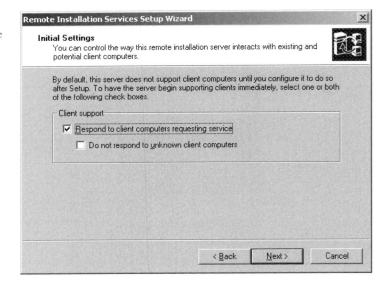

Click Next and, as you can see in Figure 5.20, RIS will ask where to find an I386 of
some type.

Now's a good time to pop the Windows 2000 Professional, Server 2003, XP Pro, or whatever
kind of disc you like into your CD-ROM drive. Alternatively, if you have some operating system's
I386 directory on one of your hard disks, you can point RISetup there. (Think how useful this

is—you can pre-load a service pack onto an I386 on a hard disk and RIS then rolls your pre-SPed images!) Click Next and you'll get the screen you see in Figure 5.21.

FIGURE 5.20

Looking for a set of installation files

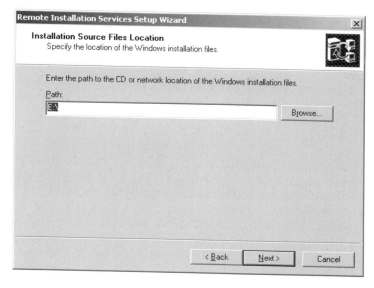

FIGURE 5.21

Folder name for the simple I386 option

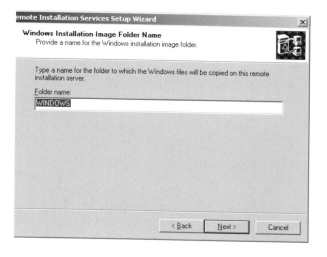

Recall that a RIS server can have many images on it. Each image gets a folder within the RemoteInstall folder. This first, simple I386 image needs a name too, and RISetup suggests just Windows, which is probably fine for our needs. Click Next to continue and you'll see a screen in which you can describe the image, as shown in Figure 5.22.

FIGURE 5.22

Describing the simple image

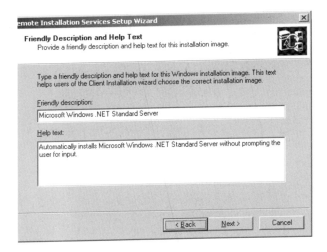

When someone plugs a new machine into the network and boots from the RIS-prepared boot floppy, he may be offered several choices of OS images to download. (After all, one of the things that RIS is supposed to offer is the ability to keep a bunch of images around for different uses.) This screen lets you add some descriptive text. Click Next and you'll get a summary "this-is-your-last-chance" screen like the one in Figure 5.23.

FIGURE 5.23

Checking on the settings

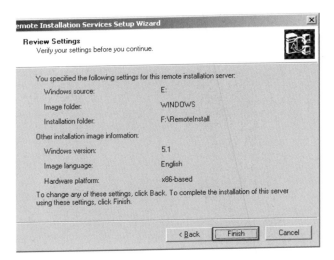

Click Finish and go away for a while. A screen like Figure 5.24 will appear.

As you see from the screen, RISetup has a lot to do. It copies the I386 files over to its local folder, starts SIS, and does other housekeeping. Expect it to take 10 minutes or so at least.

FIGURE 5.24

Progress indication
screen

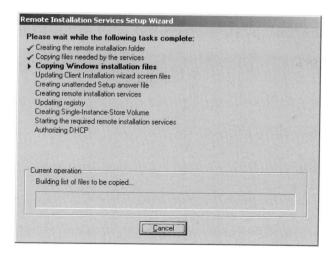

Checking That RIS Is Running

RIS is a mite sparse on administrative interfaces, as you'll see, so it can be hard to be 100 percent sure whether it's up or not. The best way to see if RIS is running is to go to the Services snap-in (Start/Run and type **services.msc** or look under Services in Computer Management) and look to see that these services are running:

- ◆ Remote Installation
- ◆ Single Instance Storage Groveler
- ◆ Trivial FTP Daemon

You'll also see a number of events in the Event Viewer's Application log:

- ◆ An Information event ID 4096 from Groveler
- ◆ An Information event ID 100 from ESENT
- ◆ An Information event ID 1003 from BINLSVC
- ◆ An Information event ID 1024 from BINLSVC
- ◆ Finally, an Information event ID 4097 from Groveler

Now, to look at these events, you'd think that everything is hunky-dory with RIS, and perhaps indeed it is. But remember that you have to approve RIS in Active Directory as if it were a DHCP server. If you don't do that, you still get all of those comforting-looking events in the Application log. To see if RIS is actually *not* running because it's not approved as a DHCP server in AD, flip over to the System log, where you'll see an event ID 1046 from DhcpServer like this:

```
The DHCP/BINL service on the local machine, belonging
  to the WindowsAdministrative domain win2ktest.com,
  has determined that it is not authorized to start.
```

```
⸾It has stopped servicing clients.  The following
⸾are some possible reasons for this...
```

And it then goes on to enumerate some possible reasons, but basically it's time to ensure that your RIS server can contact the AD and that it's approved as a DHCP server. After authorizing a RIS server in DHCP, then in theory all you need do is to restart the Remote Installation Service on the RIS server, but in my experience it's best to reboot the RIS server.

Enabling RIS for Clients

Amazingly, after RISetup does its work, the RIS server does not reboot! But it's time to put the RIS server to work, or at least to respond to requests for I386 installs. Make sure you are logged in as a domain administrator at the RIS server, then click Start/Run, fill in DSA.MSC, and press Enter. If the RIS server happens to be a domain controller, then it's even easier—just click Start/Programs/ Administrative Tools/Active Directory Users and Computers. (Notice that you've got to start the DSA from Start/Run because for some reason Setup *installs* the Active Directory tools on all servers, but only puts entries for those tools on the Start/Programs menus of domain controllers.)

In the left pane of the window, you'll see an icon depicting several computers, intended to represent your domain. Open it (double-click or click the plus sign) and it'll open to some folders, including one named **Computers**. It's likely that your RIS server is there. Right-click the RIS computer's icon and choose Properties. You'll then see a properties page.

On the property page, you'll see several tabs, with one labeled Remote Install. Click that and you'll see a page like the one in Figure 5.25. There's not much in the way of an administrative and management interface for RIS, just this page and a few tabs on the Advanced screen, which you'll see a bit later.

FIGURE 5.25

Remote Install tab of the properties page for RIS server

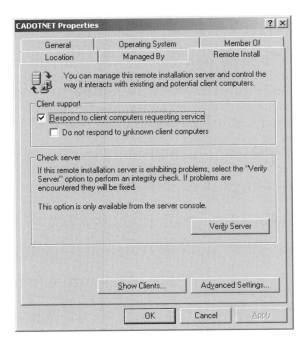

On this screen, there's not all that much to do except to turn it on. Check Respond to Client Computers Requesting Service, and it's ready to go!

Installing an OS on a Workstation from the RIS Server

It's working; let's give it a try. The RIS server is up on the network and the Active Directory knows about it. Suppose I have a computer that I want to put some RIS-compatible OS on (call it the target computer); these are the steps.

The target computer gets the attention of the RIS server through something called the Preboot Execution Environment protocol, abbreviated PXE and pronounced "pixie." Some computer vendors sell PCs with PXE in the BIOS. To connect a PXE-equipped PC to a RIS server, you don't even need a floppy disk; you just plug it into the network, turn it on, and you'll eventually get a prompt like "boot from the network y/n?" If you let it boot from the network, it'll first seek out a DHCP server, then find an Active Directory server with DNS, and kick off RIS—all the code for doing that is in the PC's BIOS ROM.

NOTE *You may have to adjust your system's CMOS settings in order to tell it to try to boot from PXE rather than the hard disk, floppy, or CD-ROM. Exactly how you do that depends on your system. On my IBM T21 ThinkPad, I press F12 when I turn on the computer to tell it to choose to boot from the Intel Boot Agent. I've seen Dells where you tell it to boot "fromMBA." Basically, though, here's the approach: start up your system's BIOS setup routine. You'll usually (sorry for the weasel words, but this does vary from system to system, and not every system even allows you to do a PXE boot) see an option to arrange the boot order. On my T21, I get the five options for devices to boot from: the floppy, the hard disk, the CD-ROM, the Intel Boot Agent, and Network Boot, which I haven't found a use for yet. I can then rearrange the boot order, so as to tell my system, "First try to boot from the Intel Boot Agent, and if that's not available then try the CD-ROM, and if that doesn't work then boot from the hard disk, and if that doesn't work then boot from the floppy, and never try to boot from Network Boot."*

What's that you say, your system isn't PXE compliant? Well, you're not barred from the RIS fun; you've got two ways to make your system a possible RIS client.

First, you could buy a PCI NIC that has a ROM on it that contains a PXE client. Believe it or not, I've got a bunch of five-year-old test machines that run 400MHz Pentiums and they're all PXE-bootable. How do I accomplish this? I just bought the "managed" versions of the Intel and 3Com Ethernet cards and replaced my old NICs with the new "managed" NICs. "Managed" usually means there's a PXE-compatible boot ROM on the board, so I'm instantly PXE-friendly.

But if you don't feel like buying a new NIC, all's not lost. Microsoft includes a utility with RIS that will generate bootable floppy disks that replace the PXE BIOS for the PXE-deaf among us. It's called RBFG.exe, and you'll find it on any RIS server in the \RemoteInstall\Admin\I386 directory. Run it and you'll see a screen like Figure 5.26.

Running it is pretty simple—just put a floppy into A: and click the Create Disk button. A great improvement over its older cousin, the Network Client Administrator, the Remote Boot Disk Generator (RBDG) doesn't require that you provide it with blank floppies. That's the good news.

The *bad* news is that this will only work if your computer has PCI expansion slots and one of the 32 supported PCI network cards. (The good news is that under 2000 it was only 25 network cards.) Fifteen years' experience with network software has made me conservative enough that almost all of my NICs are made by 3Com—not because I think 3Com makes a better card, but because I don't want to have to search after drivers—and so RBDG supports all of my machines. But that might not be the case for all of your systems.

FIGURE 5.26

Remote Boot Disk
Generator dialog box

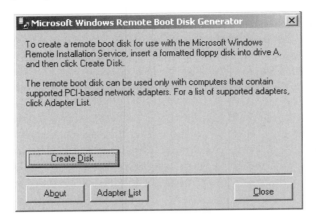

Actually, let me take that back. Not *all* of my systems will work with an RBDG floppy—my older laptops won't. As I mentioned earlier, only systems with mini-PCI type integrated network cards have a prayer of being supported. The Server 2003 flavor of RBDG has, however, a mini-PCI driver for 3Com NICs, which is good if your laptop has that kind of NIC. My newer laptops, however, have either the Intel mini-PCI or the Realtek mini-PCI. Does that leave me out? No, because fortunately my laptops not only have mini-PCI cards in them, they also have PXE clients in their ROMs, so, again, all's not lost if your system doesn't have one of the Magic 32 NICs in it.

There's some more bad news about RBDG. What about the fact that new network cards appear all of the time? It's not unreasonable at all to suggest that a year after Server 2003's release you might find yourself trying to install an OS on a system with a brand-spanking-new network card that RBDG simply doesn't know how to handle. How do you introduce RBDG to a new set of drivers?

Unfortunately, you can't. Microsoft promised back in the Windows 2000 days that they would "periodically" update `RBDG.exe`, but the fact is that they never did. So let me say again that you may never need a PXE boot disk if you're buying new computers. Any computer with a PXE BIOS and an integrated NIC can use RIS without any floppies at all—these computers have been *designed* to support RIS, so to speak, and so won't need a floppy. As time goes on, it's reasonable to hope that more and more computers will be "net-bootable."

In any case, if you generate a PXE boot disk, stick it into the target machine and boot the machine. You'll see a screen with something like the following text:

```
Microsoft Windows Remote Installation Boot Floppy
   Copyright 2001 Lanworks Technologies Co. a subsidiary of 3Com Corporation
All rights reserved.
3Com 3C90XB / 3C90XC EtherLink PC
Node: 00105AE2859F
DHCP...
TFTP...............
Press F12 for network service boot
```

Press F12, and a text screen appears that says:

```
Welcome to the Client Installation wizard. This wizard helps
↳you quickly and easily set up a new operating system
↳on your computer. You can also use this wizard to keep
↳your computer up-to-date and to troubleshoot computer
↳hardware problems.
In the wizard, you are asked to use a valid user name, password,
↳and domain name to log in to the network. If you do not
↳have this information, contact your network administrator
↳before continuing.
Press Enter to continue
```

You are looking here at some client software downloaded from the RIS server called the Client Install Wizard. Look back to the first screen and notice the TFTP with all the periods after it—that was the Trivial File Transfer Protocol transferring a very simple text-based operating system to your computer.

TIP   But what if you don't get a response from PXE? If your system just searches and searches for DHCP but gets no response, then check your network switches. I once worked at a site where we couldn't get a PXE boot to work to save our lives. Then someone noticed that the Ethernet switches had a feature called "minimal spanning tree" enabled. Apparently it filtered or slowed down the DHCPDISCOVER broadcasts that the workstation did to find a DHCP server, and so the workstation never got an IP address from DHCP. So check your network infrastructure before you assume that a RIS client has bad hardware. And if it still doesn't work, then think about putting a network packet analyzer on the network segment so that you can watch the DHCP/TFTP process. Also check the NIC. I had one RIS server that worked perfectly for 90 percent of my workstations, but 10 percent just plain couldn't see it. The problem? It had a 10-megabit NIC and they had a 100-megabit NIC. Why that should trouble some 100Mb NICs and not others is a mystery to me, but you might want to be careful about matching 100Mb client NICs with 100Mb NICs on RIS servers. As I've said earlier, avoid multi-NIC systems for RIS servers.

What's kind of interesting about this initial RIS setup screen is that the introductory screen, and all of the other text screens that you'll see from the Client Install Wizard, are built on a slightly modified version of HTML. You can see the "source code" for that first screen by looking on the RIS server in \RemoteInstall\OSChooser\English directory and examining the file named welcome.osc. It looks like the following:

```
<OSCML>
<META KEY=ENTER HREF="LOGIN">
<META KEY=F3 ACTION="REBOOT">
<META KEY=ESC HREF="LOGIN">
<META KEY=F1 HREF="LOGIN">
<TITLE>  Client Installation Wizard
    Welcome</TITLE>
<FOOTER>  [ENTER] continue </FOOTER>
<BODY left=5 right=75>
<BR>
<BR>
<BR>
```

```
Welcome to the Client Installation wizard. This wizard helps
↳you quickly and easily set up a new operating system
↳on your computer. You can also use this wizard to keep
↳your computer up-to-date and to troubleshoot computer
↳hardware problems.
<BR>
<BR>
In the wizard, you are asked to use a valid user name, password,
↳and domain name to log in to the network. If you do not
↳have this information, contact your network administrator
↳before continuing.
</BODY>
</OSCML>
```

If you've got any familiarity with HTML, then understanding this is simple—things surrounded by angle brackets <> are *tags*, commands to the computer. They're often in pairs like right and left parentheses—<oscml> starts the "program," </oscml> ends it. That forward slash (/) indicates that it's the end of a command—for example, <TITLE> Client Installation Wizard</TITLE> indicates that there's a command, <TITLE> (which, as you can guess, puts a title in the screen), then there's the text that's supposed to go into the title, and then </TITLE>, which says, "That's the end of the title text." Again, they're like left and right parentheses. The <META KEY> commands tell the wizard what to do when you press particular keys. <META KEY=ENTER HREF="LOGIN"> means, "When the user presses the Enter key, run the program login.osc." <META KEY=F3 ACTION="REBOOT"> means that if the user presses the F3 key, then just reboot the system.

My intent here isn't to document the entire programming language—Microsoft hasn't completely documented it yet, to my knowledge—but to point out that you could *easily* change the generic welcome text to something customized to your particular company.

Anyway, once you press Enter, you're prompted for a username, password, and domain. The account that you log in with must have the ability to create new computer accounts. You'll next be advised that the process will delete any data on the existing hard disk:

```
The following settings will be applied to this computer installation.
Verify these settings before continuing.
Computer account: ADMINMARK1
Global Unique ID: 00000000000000000000000105AE2859F
Server supporting this computer: CADOTNET
To begin Setup, press Enter. If you are using the Remote
↳Installation Services boot floppy, remove the floppy
↳diskette from the drive and press Enter to continue.
```

Here, the RIS client software has chosen a name for the computer, ADMINMARK1, that it constructed by taking my login name—ADMINMARK was the account I used at the time—and adding a number to it. The Global Unique ID, or GUID (pronounced "gwid"), is just an ID number that RIS assigned to that computer. PXE-capable machines all have a GUID built right into them, but machines using RIS boot floppies get a GUID constructed for them consisting of 20 hex zeros followed by their NIC's MAC address. Finally, the Client Install Wizard tells you the name of the RIS server that it's getting its image from. Once you press Enter to confirm, pop the floppy out of the A: drive and walk away for a half hour or so. When you return, whatever OS you chose will be installed completely hands-off on the machine.

RIS sets the system up like so:

◆ The new machine joins the RIS server's domain.

◆ RIS repartitions the machine's hard disk into just one large partition and formats that partition as NTFS, no matter how the drive was previously partitioned.

◆ The new system has all of the settings you'd find in a typical install.

Want to change any of that? Then you'll need to create some system images.

Creating a System Image with RIPrep

Even doing a no-frills installation on a new system with RIS is pretty nice. But it would be nicer to provide not only a vanilla operating system but perhaps a few settings and certainly an application or two—now, *that* would make the Ghost guys sweat! (But not sweat all *that* much, as you'll see. Ghost is still better than RIS. But Ghost costs money, and RIS comes free with Server from the 2000 edition onward.) You can do such a thing, creating what's called a *RIPrep image format* image. Here's how you do it:

1. Set up a prototypical Win2K, XP, or Server 2003 system as you'd like it. Make sure that all of the code and data are on drive C:—no other drives will be copied by RIS.

2. Run the Remote Installation Preparation Wizard (RIPrep), which strips the SIDs off the prototypical machine.

3. Once the image is on the RIS server, it's available to new systems for installation.

For my example, I've installed Office 2000 onto an XP Professional workstation. To create the RIPrep image, I log in to that prototypical machine with a domain administrator account. I then open up My Network Places and navigate over to my RIS server, the machine named CADOTNET. RIS creates a share called REMINST on every RIS server. I open REMINST, then I open up the folder inside labeled Admin, and then I open the folder inside that labeled I386. Inside is a file named riprep.exe. I double-click it and see the opening screen, as shown in Figure 5.27. Click Next to see the screen shown in Figure 5.28.

FIGURE 5.27

Opening screen of RIPrep

Welcome to the Remote Installation Preparation Wizard

This wizard helps you convert this Windows installation, including its programs and configuration settings, to a remote installation image. The image is then replicated to a remote installation server, where it can be installed by remote boot computers.

The hardware of the computer that installs the image does not need to exactly match the hardware on this computer. See the documentation for any restrictions.

To continue, click Next.

< Back   Next >   Cancel

FIGURE 5.28

Choosing the destination RIS server

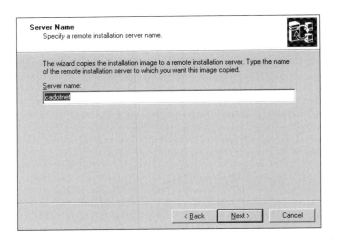

You can send the resulting image to any RIS server; I'll choose the one I've been working with, the server named cadotnet, and click Next, which leads to the screen in Figure 5.29.

FIGURE 5.29

Naming the new folder

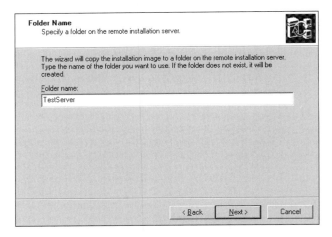

As with the CD image that RISetup insisted upon, this new image will need a folder name. Once I name the folder and click Next, a screen in which I add a description appears, as shown in Figure 5.30.

Now, for RIS 2000 veterans, the next screen or two might be a surprise. RIPRep checks over the system looking for any showstoppers or warnings. For example, you can't use RIS on a server acting as a domain controller, RIS server, or DHCP server. Because RIS will remove all existing local security information, you probably won't be able to do much with local profiles, as you'll see in Figure 5.31.

Then RIPrep spends a few screens telling you that it's going to shut down a few services and suggesting that you shut down any programs that you're running, and finally, it confirms your choices, as you see in Figure 5.32.

FIGURE 5.30
Describing the new folder

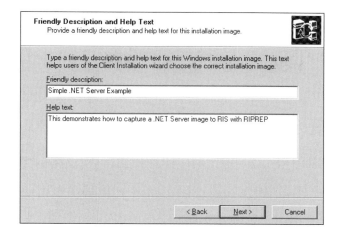

FIGURE 5.31
Profiles might not work warning

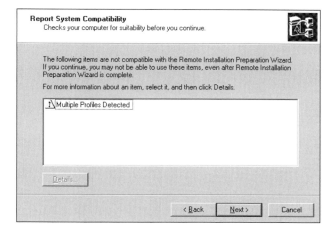

FIGURE 5.32
Final Riprep confirmation

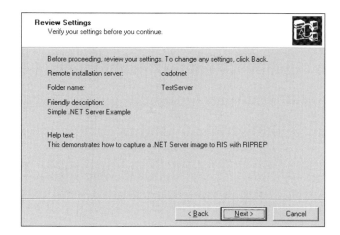

Reconfiguring the Prototype

After transferring the system image to the RIS server, you're directed to reboot the prototype. You'll then see something odd—it looks as if the prototype is running Setup all over again! In order to make the prototype's image usable to RIS, RIPrep scrubs all of the user-specific settings and SIDs off the machine. Once you reboot, your system runs a kind of "mini-setup" to restore that information. Once the system reboots, you'll be prompted to do the following:

◆ Agree to the license agreement.

◆ In a move designed to irritate even the calmest administrator, you must re-enter the 25-digit product key (on those versions of Server that require a product key); you will also have to re-activate your copy of Server.

◆ Choose a keyboard and localization.

◆ Fill in a username and organization.

◆ Specify a computer name and password for the default Administrator account.

◆ Pick a time zone.

◆ Decide whether to do typical or custom network settings.

◆ Join either a workgroup or domain.

The mini-setup doesn't take nearly as long as Setup did, however, as it's not necessary to run Plug and Play. Nevertheless, it *is* a real time-waster.

Creating a "Flat" or "CD-ROM" Image

Using RIS's Ghost-like way of putting a complete system image on ice is useful, but I'm kind of partial to doing simple scripted installs, and RIS can do it my way as well. All I need do is to place an I386 for whatever OS I want to deploy on the RIS server, and then any RIS client will see an option to install from that I386.

This is useful for two reasons. First, as I've said, it's a nice way to be able to kick off installs from a central server (the RIS server), allowing me to store all of my installation files and scripts on one box. Second, being able to store I386es on my RIS server lets me store I386es that have already had a service pack slipstreamed onto them, as I've suggested before.

Let's see how to put an I386 from XP Professional onto my RIS server. I'll slipstream Service Pack 1 onto it.

First, let's get the slipstreamed copy of XP's I386 onto the RIS server's hard disk. I've already talked about how to do this in this chapter, but here's a reminder. First, copy the I386 from an XP Pro installation CD onto the RIS server's hard disk; call it C:\XPPro\I386. Then expand XP's Service Pack 1 and use the update.exe program to slipstream the service pack onto that I386:

```
update -s:c:\xppro\
```

Next, get the I386 image in C:\XPPro\ into the RIS server:

1. Start up Active Directory Users and Computers (it's either on your Start menu as Start/Programs/Administrative Tools/Active Directory Users and Computers, or click Start, then Run, type **DSA.MSC**, and press Enter).

2. Open the folder labeled `Computers` and find the RIS server. Right-click its icon and choose Properties, then click the tab labeled Remote Install.

3. At the bottom of that tab, you'll see a button labeled Advanced Settings; click it. You'll see another properties page with three tabs labeled New Clients, Images, and Tools. Click the Images tab and you'll see something like Figure 5.33.

FIGURE 5.33

Listing of images on your RIS server

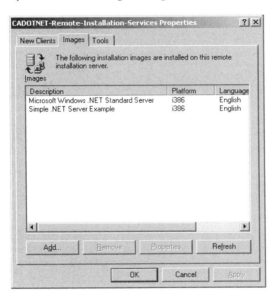

4. You'll see a listing of the images that your RIS server has. If you've just installed it, then you'll probably only have one image, with a name like Windows .NET Standard Server. Click the Add button at the bottom of the page and you'll see a screen like Figure 5.34.

FIGURE 5.34

Adding a new image

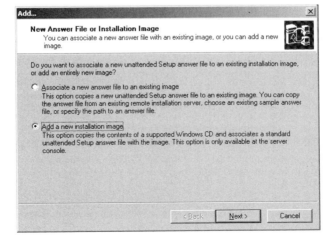

5. Notice that RIS lets you create an "image" simply by writing a script and associating that with an existing I386 directory, or it'll let you introduce a whole new I386 directory, as I've checked. Choose Add a New Installation Image and click Next.

6. This starts off a wizard that basically just asks you where to find the image (C:\Xppro\I386, in this example); click Next and it'll ask you what to call the new folder, as you see in Figure 5.35.

FIGURE 5.35

What to call the new folder

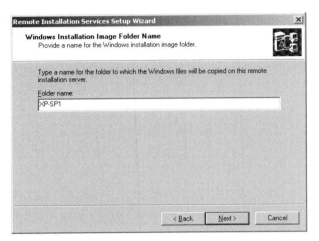

7. Here, I've called it XP-SP1. That means that the I386 files will go on my RIS server's SIS drive into a folder named \RemoteInstall\Setup\English\Images\XP-SP1. Click Next and RIS will want a "friendly name" for this image, as you saw when you created other RIS images. Click Next from that and you'll see a question about the "client installation screens," as you see in Figure 5.36.

FIGURE 5.36

What to do with the client installation screens

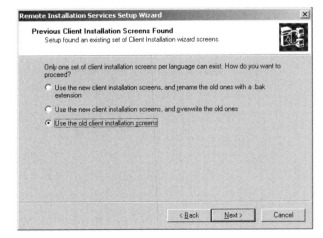

8. The client installation screens are the HTML-like files that control what the user sees when first connecting to the RIS server. I'd just leave them as is, as you see on the screen. Click Next a couple more times and RIS will copy the I386 into the \RemoteInstall\Setup\English\ Images\XP-SP1 directory (or whatever you named it) and add that image to its list of images.

Creating a Scripted Image

One subtype of "flat" images is a scripted image. By default when you install an I386 image like the one you just did, then RIS installs it hands-off, with no user intervention. How, you might wonder, does it do that? Well, it turns out that RIS has a prebuilt answer file like the winnt.sif that we built earlier in this chapter. That basic script installs the defaults and joins a system to the domain.

But where *is* that script? I just told you that XP-SP1 got its own folder on the RIS server in \Remote-Install\Setup\English\Images\XP-SP1 folder. Inside *that* folder is a folder named \RemoteInstall\ Setup\English\Images\XP-SP1\I386\Templates, which contains a file named RISTNDRD.SIF. It's a script like the ones that you've seen so far, although not exactly the same; you may recall that Setup Manager offered as one of its options the ability to create a RIS script.

But you may not want to go with the no-frills RISTNDRD.SIF script. You may make your own customized one; but how to introduce it to RIS? Very simply; RIS sees a script as an image all itself. Just start up the wizard to add a new image, as you just read how to do. But instead of choosing Add a New Installation Image, choose Associate a New Answer File to an Existing Image when in the wizard panel shown back in Figure 5.34.

Delivering a RIPrep Image to a Target PC

Now that you know how to create a system image, a flat image consisting of a new I386, or a flat image consisting of a new script, how do you deliver that image to a target PC? In exactly the same way that you got the first one onto a target PC. Either press F12 when the PXE ROM tells you to or boot from an RBDG-generated floppy.

NOTE   You do not need to build a separate RBDG-generated floppy for each system. You can build just one and carry it with you, using it to start as many different RIS image transfers as you'd like. Or, as you've already read, your newer systems may already have PXE boot abilities in their BIOS, and you therefore don't need a floppy to get a RIS install started.

Now that you've got more than one image on your server, the Client Installation Wizard will offer you one more screen. After you log in, it'll list the available images and their descriptions, allowing you to choose one. Then, as before, it'll remind you that it's about to destroy any data on the hard disk and, from there, all you need do is to pop that RBDG floppy out of the floppy drive, walk away, and come back in a half-hour—the entire install is hands-off.

WARNING   Once again, don't take the "this will zap the hard disk" warning lightly. If (for example) your RIPrep image is based on a system with a 1500MB C: drive formatted as FAT32, then RIS will repartition and reformat the C: drive of the target PC to 1500MB and FAT32 no matter how the drive was partitioned on the target PC before. RIS will leave any remaining space unpartitioned.

Authorizing Users to Let RIS Create New Computer Accounts

The idea, then, with RIS is this: Joe comes into your office and tells you that his computer's hosed, and would you reinstall his operating systems and applications when you get a chance? You reply that you've got an even better idea and hand him an RBDG floppy. You tell him to boot it, press F12 when prompted, then log in to the Client Installation Wizard and choose the Standard Productivity Desktop option, an image that you've built with all of the company's standard desktop software—Office, Palm's HotSync software, and Lotus Organizer.

Now, if Joe goes back and tries this, he'll see an error message like this:

```
The user Joe currently logged in to this computer does not
↳have the permissions needed to create a computer account
↳or modify the computer account NEWPC (NEWPC$) within
↳the domain apex.com.
This error may also indicate that the server CADOTNET supporting
↳this client cannot contact the directory service to perform
↳the operation.
Restart this computer and try again. If the problem persists,
↳contact your network administrator for assistance.
```

What's going on here is that, in the process of installing the RIS image on Joe's machine, RIS must also create a *machine account*—remember, in domains, machines have accounts just as people do—and not just any old user can create machine accounts. By the way, he also has to be able to delete machine accounts, as there's probably already a machine account floating around that has the same name as the one he's about to create, as well as a few other machine permissions.

But what permissions does he need? Joining a machine to a domain is actually sort of complicated. Here's what's going on:

◆ First, not just anyone can tell a given workstation that it's going to join a domain. Only someone with a local administrator account can tell a machine to join a domain. Therefore, if you've got a machine that's already installed and you want to join it to a domain, you should first log on as someone who's a member of the machine's local Administrators group. And remember that just because you're an administrator on one machine, you may not be one on another.

◆ Second, it's one thing for a machine to want to join a domain; it's quite another for a domain to be willing to accept that machine as a member. Joining a machine to a domain, then, requires help from someone with a certain amount of administrative power not on the machine, but on the domain. That's why when you're joining a machine to a domain the machine will pop up a dialog box asking you to log in. What it's saying here is, "Okay, I [the machine] accept that you have the authority to tell me to join this domain, but this isn't going to work unless you have the authority to tell the domain to accept me; can you give me the name and password of a *domain* account that can do that?"

Those are the basics. But in many cases we're not just installing, we're *reinstalling*. That adds a subtle but important wrinkle.

Suppose you have a workstation named MYPC. It's gone south and you decide that just blowing up the system and reinstalling it is the way to go. You've got a RIS-bootable system, and so you kick off a RIS boot. Now, by default RIS comes up with some goofy machine name for you automatically, but you don't like that, and so you modify RIS's scripts (I'll show you how in a bit) to let you specify a particular machine name. Of course, you choose MYPC. The RIS install goes all right for a while, but then it stops and says that it can't join you to the domain. To make things even stranger, it occurs to you that you first installed this system with RIS and gave your system the name MYPC at the time, and RIS took that without a complaint.

What's different?

What's different is that the first time, RIS only had to create a brand new machine account named "MYPC$." (Remember that machines get account names equal to the machine name with a $ tacked on the end.) That only required the power to create a new machine account. And, as it turns out, regular old nonadministrative users have the ability to create 10 machine accounts in their lifetime. (Don't ask me why Microsoft set it up that way, I have no idea.)

But they *don't* have the power to *delete* machine accounts. Or change the passwords on machine accounts. When you tried to reinstall an OS on MYPC and tried to join a domain as MYPC, then the domain looked around and said to itself, "Hmmm, that's not right… there's already a MYPC account. I don't want to overwrite some poor machine's account," and denied the request. What you were really asking the domain to do was to first delete the MYPC account (or simply change its password, depending on what OS you're using), and your regular old user account didn't have the power to do either of those things.

But you can change that. If you like, you can create a whole new group called Installers. Then we'll give the group the power to change machine passwords and delete machine accounts. Then, when Joe wants to reinstall his computer, all you have to do is to just put him in the Installers group for the day. When his system is reinstalled, just take him out of the Installers group.

Now, creating the Installers group will be a bit of a lengthy procedure, but you'll only have to do it once.

NOTE *This is a neat example of something that you're going to learn in an upcoming chapter about Active Directory. Active Directory lets you create groups of administrators with sets of powers that you can control very finely. It's part of a process called* delegation, *and we'll take it up in detail in the Active Directory chapter.*

Creating the Installers Group

You'll find creating the Installers group easiest while sitting at a domain controller:

1. Log in using an account with domain administrator rights and then start the Directory Service Administrator DSA.MSC by clicking Start/Administrative Tools/Active Directory Users and Computers. In the left pane, you'll see an icon representing your domain with a plus sign next to it; click the plus sign to expand the domain.

2. Next, create the Installers group. Right-click the Users folder and choose New/Group.

3. That raises a dialog box called Create New Object–(Group). In the field Name of New Group, type in **Installers**. This will create a global group named Installers, which is what you want, so click OK and the dialog will close.

4. Back in the DSA's menu, click View/Advanced Features. That will show the Security tab on the properties page, which will be essential to give Installers the permissions that it needs.

5. Next, you're going to give the Installers group the ability to create new computer accounts and by default computer accounts go in a folder labeled Computers, so right-click the folder, icon labeled Computers and choose Properties. You'll get a dialog box named Computers Properties.

6. Click the Security tab in the properties page. Installers doesn't currently have any permissions, so you'll need to add a record for them. Click the Add button and you'll now see a dialog named Select Users, Computers, or Groups.

7. Type in **Installers** and then, just for good measure, click Check Names. It'll think about it for a second. Once it's checked that there is indeed a group called Installers, Installers will be underlined. Click OK.

8. Back in the Computer properties page, find Installers in the Name list box and click it, then click the Advanced button.

9. You'll see a dialog box labeled Advanced Security Settings for Computers. Again, locate Installers—this part of the operating system isn't intended for regular old users, so the UI's a bit convoluted here—to indicate the Installers record that you created. It'll currently have some very basic permission like Read or the like. Click the Edit button.

10. Now you'll see a dialog named Permission Entry for Computers. Scroll down in the list box labeled Permissions to find the Create Computer Objects permission. You'll see two columns of check boxes, one labeled Allow and the other Deny. Check the Allow box. Click OK to clear the Permission Entry for Computer Objects dialog box.

11. That permission made the folders accept the new machine objects. But once created, Installers have very limited control over the machine accounts themselves. They can delete or modify machine accounts, but only the ones that they created. Now, if you only want users to have the power to reset machine accounts that they created, you can stop here and skip down to step 14. But if you want Installers to be able to reset even machine accounts that they did *not* install, then let's keep going. From the Access Control Settings for Computers dialog box, click Add, choose Installers again, and click OK. The Permission Entry for Computers dialog box then appears.

12. Click the Apply Onto drop-down list box and choose Computer Objects. Check the Allow box next to the Write All Properties, Change Password, and Reset Password permissions. In the lower left corner of the page, check the box that says Apply These Permissions to Objects and/or Containers within This Container Only. Click OK and you'll return to the Advanced Security Settings for Computers dialog box.

13. Scroll down in the Permission Entries list box and you'll see that there are now two or five new entries for Installers, depending on how much power you decided to give Installers.

14. Click OK to dismiss the Advanced Security Settings dialog box.

15. Click OK to dismiss the Computers properties page.

Now that that's done, you can put Joe into the Installers group:

1. Open the Users folder and locate the Installers group.

2. Right-click Installers and choose Properties.

3. Click the Members tab.

4. Click the Add button.

5. Find Joe's account, click Joe, click OK, and then click OK again.

Finally done. Yes, that was a bit of work, but worth it in the end, I think.

Restricting RIS Image Choices

Once you turn Joe loose with that floppy, you might not want him accidentally loading the wrong image. He might just decide that he'd *love* to download the Programmer's Workstation image, complete with the C++ and Java compilers, interactive debuggers, and the like—none of which he has any use for. You can, as it turns out, keep him from seeing all of the images on the RIS server. But you'd never guess how you do it.

The RIS server has a set of directories that exist in \RemoteInstall\Setup\English\Images. If you've got a simple I386 installation called Windows, then its image is in \RemoteInstall\Setup\English\ Images\Windows. Each RIS image, then, has a directory inside \RemoteInstall\Setup\English\Images; remember that.

Each image contains a folder named I386, which contains yet *another* folder named Templates. *That* folder contains a file named with the extension .sif. It's an answer file that RIS uses to be able to do the installation without any user intervention. So, for example, if you have an image called Programmers, there's an SIF file in \RemoteInstall\Setup\English\Images\I386\Templates.

The way that you keep Joe out of the Programmers image is to set the NTFS permissions on the SIF file so that he's denied Read access. Once RIS sees that he's not supposed to see the file, the Programmers image won't even be offered to him.

Advanced RIS

Those are the basics about Remote Installation Services. But before you go running off to take advantage of them, you should know about some fine points.

ADVANCED RIS I: USING *OEM*

Once you start getting a bit fancy with your RIS-based installs, you'll soon pine for the power of the OEM folder. So you might tunnel down into your \RemoteInstall\Setup\English\Images\ *whateveryoucalledit*\I386 folder and place an OEM folder inside that I386 folder, hoping to see some of OEM's power transferred to RIS.

But it won't work.

The problem? For some bizarre reason, RIS installs need the OEM folder *at the same directory level* as I386, not inside it. So, for example, if I created an image folder just called serverinst, then I'd place the OEM folder at \RemoteInstall\Setup\English\Images\serverinst\$OEM$, not \RemoteInstall\ Setup\English\Images\serverinst\I386\$OEM$.

ADVANCED RIS II: BUILDING RIS SCRIPTS

If you've built a few RIS flat images, then you know that by default RIS will wipe the first physical hard disk on a target computer, make that first drive one big NTFS volume, and do a mainly unattended installation of your OS—"mainly" because it'll prompt you for a product key.

Unattended is good; *mainly* unattended isn't. So let's see how to script a RIS install. As with the winnt.sif-style scripts, you can use the Setup Manager to create RIS scripts. But I find that the Setup Manager isn't much help here. I pretty much use Setup Manager to create a basic script, then I hand-adjust it, as you saw earlier in this chapter.

But there's no need to have Setup Manager create a basic script for RIS—you see, every RIS install gets its own basic script, called `ristndrd.sif`. Look in the I386 directory of any RIS image directory and you'll see a directory named `Templates`. Inside *that* is a file named `ristndrd.sif`. Mine looks like the following.

```
[data]
floppyless = "1"
msdosinitiated = "1"
OriSrc = "\\%SERVERNAME%\RemInst\%INSTALLPATH%\%MACHINETYPE%"
OriTyp = "4"
LocalSourceOnCD = 1
DisableAdminAccountOnDomainJoin = 1

[SetupData]
OsLoadOptions = "/noguiboot /fastdetect"
SetupSourceDevice = "\Device\LanmanRedirector\%SERVERNAME%\RemInst\%INSTALLPATH%"

[Unattended]
OemPreinstall = no
FileSystem = LeaveAlone
ExtendOEMPartition = 0
TargetPath = \WINDOWS
OemSkipEula = yes
InstallFilesPath = "\\%SERVERNAME%\RemInst\%INSTALLPATH%\%MACHINETYPE%"
LegacyNIC = 1

[UserData]
FullName = "%USERFIRSTNAME% %USERLASTNAME%"
OrgName = "%ORGNAME%"
ComputerName = %MACHINENAME%

[GuiUnattended]
OemSkipWelcome = 1
OemSkipRegional = 1
TimeZone = %TIMEZONE%
AdminPassword = "*"

[LicenseFilePrintData]
AutoMode = PerSeat

[Display]
BitsPerPel = 16
XResolution = 800
YResolution = 600
VRefresh = 60

[Networking]
```

```
[NetServices]
MS_Server=params.MS_PSched

[Identification]
JoinDomain = %MACHINEDOMAIN%
DoOldStyleDomainJoin = Yes

[RemoteInstall]
Repartition = Yes
UseWholeDisk = Yes
[OSChooser]
Description ="Microsoft Windows .NET Standard Server"
Help ="Automatically installs Microsoft Windows .NET Standard Server
↳without prompting the user for input."
LaunchFile = "%INSTALLPATH%\%MACHINETYPE%\templates\startrom.com"
ImageType =Flat
Version="5.1 (0)"
```

This won't need all that much in the way of changes because, after all, it's already able to direct an almost-unattended installation. But here are a few changes that I made to make my Server-installing RIS image more useful for me.

First, I added a ProductKey= line to the [UserData] section. That kept it from stopping to prompt me for a product key.

Next, I changed OEMPreinstall=No to OEMPreinstall=Yes, so I could then set up an OEM directory (at the same directory level as I386, recall, not *inside* I386) and get the benefits of OEM— cmdlines.txt, preloaded files and directories, extra driver directories, and so on. That also let me include an [OEM_Ads] section to specify background and logo bitmaps for the install—not necessary items, but I like them and clients like when I set them up, as it makes an install look like a "company brand" install rather than a Microsoft commercial.

Then I changed the [Identification] section. RIS normally uses some command that refers to an "oldstyledomainjoin" that seems to work fine if you let RIS pick the machine name, but if you want to pick your own, then it seems not to work unless you do it by specifying a user account and password that can create and destroy machine accounts. Again, it needn't be an actual domain administrator—just someone from the Installers group will do fine.

Then I changed the [Display] section so that the systems come up on 1024×768 resolution rather than the unwieldy 640×480. I used [Components], as before, to remove the games and to enable Terminal Services, and [FavoritesEx] to preconfigure defaults for Internet Explorer. I ended up with a script that looks like this; I have highlighted the lines that I added or modified:

```
[data]
floppyless = "1"
msdosinitiated = "1"
OriSrc = "\\%SERVERNAME%\RemInst\%INSTALLPATH%\%MACHINETYPE%"
OriTyp = "4"
LocalSourceOnCD = 1
DisableAdminAccountOnDomainJoin = 1
```

```
[OEM_Ads]
background=backg.bmp
logo=logo.bmp

[SetupData]
OsLoadOptions = "/noguiboot /fastdetect"
SetupSourceDevice = "\Device\LanmanRedirector\%SERVERNAME%\RemInst\%INSTALLPATH%"

[Unattended]
OemPreinstall = yes
FileSystem = LeaveAlone
ExtendOEMPartition = 0
TargetPath = \WINDOWS
OemSkipEula = yes
InstallFilesPath = "\\%SERVERNAME%\RemInst\%INSTALLPATH%\%MACHINETYPE%"
LegacyNIC = 1

[UserData]
FullName = "%USERFIRSTNAME% %USERLASTNAME%"
OrgName = "%ORGNAME%"
ComputerName = %MACHINENAME%
ProductKey="11111-22222-33333-44444-55555"

[GuiUnattended]
OemSkipWelcome = 1
OemSkipRegional = 1
TimeZone = %TIMEZONE%
AdminPassword = "*"

[LicenseFilePrintData]
AutoMode = PerSeat

[Display]
ConfigureAtLogon = 0
BitsPerPel = 16
XResolution = 1024
YResolution = 768
VRefresh = 72
AutoConfirm = 1

[Networking]

[NetServices]
MS_Server=params.MS_PSched

[Identification]
JoinDomain=%MACHINEDOMAIN%
DomainAdmin=machineguy
DomainAdminPassword=swordfish
```

```
[RemoteInstall]
[data]
floppyless = "1"
msdosinitiated = "1"
OriSrc = "\\%SERVERNAME%\RemInst\%INSTALLPATH%\%MACHINETYPE%"
OriTyp = "4"
LocalSourceOnCD = 1

[SetupData]
OsLoadOptions = "/noguiboot /fastdetect"
SetupSourceDevice =    "\Device\LanmanRedirector\%SERVERNAME%
↳\RemInst\%INSTALLPATH%"
[Components]
Solitaire=Off
Minesweeper=Off
Pinball=Off

 [FavoritesEx]
Title1="Mark Minasi Home Page.url"
URL1="http://www.minasi.com"
[Branding]
BrandIEUsingUnattended=Yes
[URL]
Home_Page=about:blank
```

Now, how did I make that change take effect? Simple—I made the changes to the `ristndrd.sif` file and just resaved `ristndrd.sif` to its original location. Alternatively, I could have written another script and then gone to the Advanced button of the RIS page on Active Directory Users and Computers, as you saw me do a few pages back. If I wanted to, I could have any number of scripts all doing unattended installs from the same Server I386 directory.

ADVANCED RIS III: MODIFYING THE CLIENT WIZARD

If you implemented something like the preceding script, then you might have noticed a sort of annoying thing about RIS: machine names. By default—and it takes a bit of doing to defeat the default, so to speak—RIS names the first machine that you install *yourusername*1, the second *yourusername*2, and so on. For example, I just started a RIS install of a server and, when the Client Installation Wizard asked me to log in, I logged in as ADMINMARK so RIS named the server ADMINMARK1. I'd much prefer it if the Client Installation Wizard would just *ask* me what to call the server. Look back to the line in the `ristndrd.sif` script that names the server:

```
ComputerName = %MACHINENAME%
```

So, clearly some kind of environment variable is set by RIS, and the value in the environment variable is then used to name the machine. As a matter of fact, a close look at `ristndrd.sif` shows *several* of these environment variables—%MACHINEDOMAIN%, %TIMEZONE%, %ORGNAME% and the like—that RIS somehow constructs and then passes to the Setup routine on a computer that RIS installs.

Is there a way for us to *directly* control those variables, and therefore to have greater control over how RIS installs the server? Yes. As a matter of fact, you can even create new environment variables—but to see how that works, let's go back and reexamine all of those .osc files. On your RIS server, there's a directory named \RemoteInstall\Oschooser\English. In that directory, you'll find (on my system, anyway) 45 text files with the extension .osc. I don't pretend to understand entirely how they work, but here's what I've pieced together from a variety of sources.

When you first connect to a RIS server, you get a screen driven by the file welcome.osc. Let's revisit that file:

```
<OSCML>
<META KEY=ENTER HREF="LOGIN">
<META KEY=F3 ACTION="REBOOT">
<META KEY=ESC HREF="LOGIN">
<META KEY=F1 HREF="LOGIN">
<TITLE>  Client Installation Wizard                    Welcome</TITLE>
<FOOTER>  [ENTER] continue </FOOTER>
<BODY left=5 right=75>
<BR>
<BR>
<BR>
Welcome to the Client Installation wizard. This wizard helps
↳you quickly and easily set up a new operating system
↳on your computer. You can also use this wizard to
↳keep your computer
up-to-date and to troubleshoot computer hardware problems.
<BR>
<BR>
In the wizard, you are asked to use a valid user name,
↳password, and domain name to log on to the network.
↳If you do not have this information, contact your
↳network administrator before continuing.
</BODY>
</OSCML>
```

First, notice the <META> commands. They define what happens when you press one key or another. I've seen two variations on the <META> command—the HREF and the ACTION variations. For example,

```
<META KEY=ENTER HREF="LOGIN">
```

This tells the Client Installation Wizard that if the user presses the Enter key, then the wizard should next find and load the file login.osc. Like an HTML "<A>" tag, it provides a link to another OSC file. But now consider this <META> command:

```
<META KEY=F3 ACTION="REBOOT">
```

This time, pressing F3 doesn't take you to a file reboot.osc. Instead, "REBOOT" means just what it sounds like—it tells the wizard to reboot the computer. Other ACTION= values that I've seen include

LOGIN   Takes the information on the screen (this shows up in the wizard panel that asks you to log in) and tries to log in to an Active Directory domain.

ENUM IMAGES   This seems to tell RIS to take all of the operating system images available on this server and only show users the options that they have access to—remember that you can keep users from seeing images by adjusting the file and directory permissions on that image.

Clearly, then, the job of `welcome.osc` is to get you to press Enter so that you'll next go to `login.osc`. That looks like this:

```
<OSCML>
<TITLE>  Client Installation Wizard                              Logon</TITLE>
<FOOTER>  [ENTER] continue     [ESC] clear      [F1] help
↳[F3] restart computer</FOOTER>
<META KEY=F3 ACTION="REBOOT">
<META KEY=F1 HREF="LOGINHLP">
<META KEY=ESC HREF="LOGIN">
<META ACTION="LOGIN">
<BODY left=5 right=75>
<BR>
<BR>
Type a valid user name, password, and domain name.
↳You may use the Internet-style logon
format (for example: Username@Company.com).
<BR>
<BR>
<BR>
<FORM ACTION="CHOICE">
  User name: <INPUT NAME="USERNAME" MAXLENGTH=255>
   Password: <INPUT NAME="*PASSWORD" TYPE=PASSWORD MAXLENGTH=20><BR>
Domain name: <INPUT NAME="USERDOMAIN" VALUE=%SERVERDOMAIN% MAXLENGTH=255>
<INPUT NAME="NTLMV2Enabled" VALUE=%NTLMV2Enabled% MAXLENGTH=255 type=VARIABLE>
<INPUT NAME="ServerUTCFileTime" VALUE=%ServerUTCFileTime%
↳MAXLENGTH=255 type=VARIABLE>
</FORM>
<BR>
<BR>
<BR>
Press the TAB key to move between the User name, Password, and Domain name fields.
<BR>
<BR>
You are connected to %SERVERNAME%
</BODY>
</OSCML>
```

Looking at the <META>s up top shows that they either reboot you, get help, or—<META ACTION="LOGIN">—commence the Active Directory logon. But where do we go next? To see that, look at the <FORM ACTION="CHOICE"> command as well as the next four lines. This defines a simple "form" on the screen. The form gathers three pieces of information—your username, your password, and the name of the domain that your account is a member of. Here, then, is what this

<FORM> command is doing: first, it collects values for USERNAME, PASSWORD, and USER-DOMAIN. Then, once you press Enter to indicate that you're done entering those values, the form moves you along to "CHOICE." But what is CHOICE? Well, apparently the "ACTION=" parameter means something a little different in a <FORM> than it does in a <META>, as it just takes you to the screen defined by choice.osc.

But here's where things get a bit weird. Here's what's in choice.osc:

```
<OSCML>
<META KEY=F3 ACTION="REBOOT">
<META KEY=F1 HREF="CHOICHLP">
<META SERVER ACTION="DNRESET">
<META SERVER ACTION="FILTER CHOICE">
<TITLE>Client Installation Wizard
    Main Menu</TITLE>
<FOOTER>[ENTER] continue     [F1] help     [F3] restart computer</FOOTER>
<BODY left=5 right=75>
<BR>
<BR>
Use the arrow keys to select one of the following options:<BR>
<P left=8>
<FORM>
<SELECT SIZE=10>
<OPTION VALUE="OSAUTO" TIP="This is the easiest way to install
↳an operating system on your computer. Most installation
↳options are already configured by your network administrator.">
Automatic Setup
<OPTION VALUE="CUSTOM" TIP="With this option, you can define a
↳unique name for this computer and specify where the computer
↳account will be created within the directory service. Select
↳this option if you are setting up this computer for someone
↳else within your company.">
Custom Setup
<OPTION VALUE="RESTART" TIP="A previous remote installation attempt
↳has been detected on this computer. Select this option to
↳restart a previously started installation.">
Restart a Previous Setup Attempt
<OPTION VALUE="TOOLS" TIP="This option gives you access to tools
↳for keeping your computer up-to-date and for troubleshooting
↳problems.">
Maintenance and Troubleshooting
</SELECT>
</FORM>
</P>
<BR>
<BOLD>Description:</BOLD>  
<TIPAREA>
</BODY>
</OSCML>
```

Here's the weird part: *I've never seen this screen appear, no matter how I set up RIS.* But I *did* notice that a screen flashes by very quickly with the words Main Menu in its upper-right corner (one of the benefits of working with slow machines is, I suppose, that you can see a little more of what they're up to—with a 2GHz box, I might not have seen the Main Menu) before moving to a screen that is clearly created by a different file, `oschoice.osc`.

I theorized that the two <META SERVER> commands were the things causing me to skip ahead to `oschoice.osc`, so I tried removing them, and my Client Installation Wizard did indeed stop at a screen labeled Main Menu. Even better, one of the options in the Main Menu was to specify my machine's name! Why, then, did Microsoft write `choice.osc` so that it always zips past any user input? I haven't a clue. But if you remove the two lines, as I did, and choose the Main Menu option Automatic Setup, then the script seems to say that next the wizard panel `osauto.osc` should load. It's just one line:

```
<META SERVER ACTION="CHECKGUID OSCHOICE DUPAUTO">
```

Which *seems* to tell the system to run the `oschoice.osc` panel, so let's look at that next:

```
<OSCML>
<META KEY=F3 ACTION="REBOOT">
<META KEY=ESC HREF="CHOICE">
<META SERVER ACTION="ENUM IMAGES">
<TITLE>  Client Installation Wizard                    OS Choices</TITLE>
<FOOTER>  [ENTER] continue           [ESC] go back
↳             [F3] restart computer</FOOTER>
<BODY left=5 right=75>
<BR>
<BR>
Use the arrow keys to select one of the following operating systems:
<P left=8>
<FORM ACTION="WARNING">
<SELECT NAME="SIF" SIZE=12>
%OPTIONS%
</SELECT>
</FORM>
</P>
<BOLD>Description:</BOLD>  
<TIPAREA>
</BODY>
</OSCML>
```

This seems to figure out which images you're eligible to install. It appears the server passes the list of images to a form (<FORM ACTION="WARNING">) through a variable called %OPTIONS%. Whichever you choose goes into an environmental variable called SIF, and it appears to next take you to `warning.osc`—which basically just puts up a "warning, you're about to blow away anything on the hard disk, are you sure?" kind of message; when you press Enter, it takes you to `install.osc`, which looks like this:

```
<OSCML>
<META KEY=ESC ACTION="REBOOT">
```

```
<META KEY=ENTER ACTION="REBOOT">
<TITLE>  Client Installation Wizard          Installation Information</TITLE>
<FOOTER>  [ENTER] continue</FOOTER>
<BODY left=5 right=75>
<BR>
<BR>
The following settings will be applied to this computer installation.
↳Verify these settings before continuing.
<BR>
<BR>
Computer account:                %MACHINENAME%
<BR>
<BR>
Global Unique ID:                %GUID%
<BR>
<BR>
Server supporting this computer:  %SERVERNAME%
<BR>
<BR>
<BR>
To begin Setup, press ENTER. If you are using the Remote
↳Installation Services boot floppy, remove the floppy
↳diskette from the drive and press ENTER to continue.
</BODY>
</OSCML>
```

This panel also basically just displays some information. But notice something odd about the <META> commands—they say that no matter whether you press ESC or Enter, you'll reboot. But you'd *think* that "reboot" would, well, reboot the computer—which would sort of abort the whole RIS process. But no—on this particular panel, "reboot" means "full speed ahead!" for the RIS install. So, we've seen that a standard RIS install progresses from welcome.osc to login.osc to choice.osc (in "stealth" mode) to osauto.osc (also "stealthed") to oschoice.osc to warning.osc and then finally to install.osc. Here's where I'm going to make use of this to control the machine name: I'll add an extra panel between oschoice.osc and warning.osc and include a form that gives the user the ability to enter a machine name.

Looking back at oschoice.osc, you recall that we *got* from oschoice.osc to warning.osc by way of the form in oschoice.osc: the <FORM ACTION="WARNING"> command. *That's* where I'll break the chain from oschoice.osc to warning.osc, by modifying that one item in oschoice.osc from <FORM ACTION="WARNING"> to <FORM ACTION="PICKNAME">. Using the other .osc files as a model, I then come up with this file, which I name pickname.osc:

```
<OSCML>
<META KEY=ESC ACTION="REBOOT">
<META KEY=F3 HREF="OSCHOICE">
<TITLE>Client Installation Wizard
    Choosing Names</TITLE>
<FOOTER>[ENTER] continue      [ESC] Reboot F3 Pick Install</FOOTER>
<BODY>
```

```
<FORM ACTION="WARNING">
Machine Name: <input NAME="MACHINENAME" VALUE=%MACHINENAME% maxlength=20><br>
%OPTIONS%
</SELECT>
</FORM>
</BODY>
</OSCML>
```

This file starts off by defining ESC as "reboot" and F3 as "return to oschoice.osc." Then it defines title and footer text for the screen. Then it defines a form that will progress to the warning.osc panel, once you press Enter for this form. Inside the form is just one field—an input field that lets you type a machine name of up to 30 characters. The NAME="MACHINENAME" means that whatever you type will go into the environmental variable named MACHINENAME. The VALUE=%MACHINENAME% tells the Client Installation Wizard to offer as default text the name that RIS *wants* to use, like ADMINMARK1.

Still not sure this would be useful? Then consider this: Suppose you had to roll out hundreds of servers, each with static IP addresses—as a large international Web-hosting ISP had to recently. They built themselves some RIS Client Installation Wizard panels that let them type in IP addresses and subnet masks, then pass that information to the ristndrd.sif file. Now, in my example, I used the built-in environment variable named MACHINENAME, but there's nothing keeping you from making up your own environment variable. For example, what if I'd added these two <input> commands to my pickname.osc file:

```
IP address:<input name="IPADR"><br>
Subnet mask:<input name="SUBMSK">
```

Then, inside ristndrd.sif, I just adjust the script so that it doesn't get IP addresses from DHCP, but instead assigns static IP addresses. Part of the revised ristndrd.sif, then, would include these lines:

```
IPAddress=%IPADR%
SubnetMast=%SUBMSK%
```

You can create as many new environmental variables you like—IP address is just one example. RIS offers a lot of flexibility—so much so that it's changed my PC hardware buying habits. From now on, it's all PXE machines for me.

ADVANCED RIS IV: NEW NIC DRIVERS

Now, all of this will work fine, *unless* your computer requires a NIC driver that's not on the I386 for the OS that you're installing. For example, suppose you wanted to use Server 2003's RIS to roll out Windows 2000 Professional installs but your computers had a NIC that made its market debut after February 2000, when 2000 Pro shipped. Supposing that this new computer can PXE boot, then it'll boot to the RIS server all right and Setup will start. But just a few minutes into the text mode Setup, you may see this message:

```
The network server does not support booting Windows 2000.
↳Setup cannot continue. Press any key to exit.
```

You see, once Setup kicks in, it does a quick check to see if it can fire up your network card; for some reason, it won't use the TFTP transfer ability built into PXE to copy the Setup files. As the NIC is newer than the drivers that Setup knows about, Setup can't initialize the card, and stops.

But wait—what about that OEMPnPDrivers command? If you put the drivers for the new NIC into `$OEM$` and pointed to them with OEMPnPDrivers, then Setup ought to be able to use those drivers, right? Well, not exactly. Windows 2000, XP, and Server 2003 like their drivers digitally signed, and many sets of drivers don't come with digital signatures. You can work around that by adding this line to the `ristndrd.sif` script:

```
DriverSigningPolicy = Ignore
```

Put that in the [Unattended] section. Then put the NIC drivers on the RIS server in `$OEM$` as before, but Microsoft recommends a more specific procedure. Create a directory `\$OEM$\$1\Drivers\NIC` and put the NIC drivers there. Create an OEMPnpDrivers command that looks like OemPnp-DriversPath=`\Drivers\Nic` in the `ristndrd.sif` file, and then you ought to be able to get RIS started on a system with a new NIC. (And yes, I *did* recommend that you keep the names of driver directories short due to the 40-character limit on the OemPnpDriversPath command, but I wanted this text to be clear, so I used a longer name. You'd do fine with a directory named `\$OEM$\$1\DR\NIC` instead of `\$OEM$\$1\Drivers\NIC`.)

Apparently a driver has to be in the `I386` directory for the text mode portion of Setup to see it, so Microsoft says in Knowledge Base article 246184 that you've got to put the INF and SYS files from the network driver into the `I386` directory on the RIS server. You may have to do a bit of experimenting to find out exactly which SYS and INF files you actually need in the `I386` directory, because you don't want to *have* to put `oeminfo.inf` in `I386`—after all, it seems like every board comes with an `oeminfo.inf`.

Microsoft *also* advised in the KB article that you restart the BINL service in the Services applet of Manage Computer. (Right-click My Computer, choose Manage Computer, open Services and Applications, and then click Services. In the right pane you'll see a service named Remote Installation. Right-click it and choose Restart.) Using this process, I have successfully set up RIS for several computers with very recent—post-2000—NICs.

Ghost's Little Helper: Sysprep

RIS and scripting are cool, but the fastest way to blast an image onto a new system continues to be Ghost or something like it. The idea is to first create a server or workstation just the way you like it, as you would before RIPrepping a system. Then use a disk-copying tool like Symantec's Ghost or PowerQuest's Drive Image Pro to essentially "photocopy" the drive—these tools don't look at files, they just copy an entire partition from one drive right atop another. (Or, for about $1000, you can forgo buying Ghost or Drive Image and buy a drive-to-drive copier. These are pretty neat—you plug the source hard disk into one side, pop some empty drives into the "receiver" receptacles, push the Start button, and walk away. I'm told that some of these can copy a gigabyte a minute!)

This drive-copying method works great for Windows 9*x*, but it's a terrible idea for NT and 2000, as each NT or 2000 system has a unique set of numbers embedded into it called its security identifiers or SIDs. Copying a drive copies the SIDs, making the network unable to tell the difference between the two drives. Unfortunately, the consequences of having systems with identical SIDs wasn't severe enough to warn people off from cloning drives, so many firms do drive cloning. In response to the need to handle the duplicate SID problem, the Ghost and Drive Image folks have written "SID scramblers," which create a unique set of SIDs on every computer. And while that ought to solve the duplicate SID problem, Microsoft won't support a computer that's been cloned, even with an SID scrambler.

I once asked a Microsoft techie why they wouldn't support a cloned system, even if it had its SIDs scrambled. Does it actually cause a repeatable problem, I asked, or was Microsoft refusing to support cloned systems just to play it safe? The Microsoft support person said, "Well, we can't prove any problems with cloning—but we've seen cloned systems that had problems that went away when we wiped their hard disks and did a fresh install." I looked at him with one eyebrow raised and said, "You do realize that wiping and reinstalling is a technique that we use all of the time, on systems both cloned and noncloned, don't you?" He had nothing to say.

Using Sysprep: Overview

In any case, Microsoft knows that many people use cloning products and that they'd do well to help their customers use those cloning products. So Server 2003 comes with a "SID scrubber" called System Preparation Tool (`Sysprep.exe`). Sysprep's simple to use—here are the basic steps.

1. Put `Sysprep.exe` and `setupcl.exe` on a directory named `\Sysprep` on whatever drive the operating system is on. You can then script it, and if you do, put the script in `\Sysprep`, calling the script `sysprep.inf`.

2. While you were acting as the administrator and setting the system up, you probably created some default software settings that would be convenient for others to have. Copy the local Administrator's profile to the Default Users profile so that anyone who gets a clone of this system gets those software settings.

3. Run Sysprep. It strips the SIDs off your computer and shuts down your machine.

4. *Do not boot your computer from the hard disk.* Instead, boot from a floppy (probably to DOS) and run your disk-cloning program—Ghost, Drive Image Pro, or whatever. You do not want to let the computer boot up because when it does, it will realize that it is SID-less and will generate a new set of SIDs—which is what you ran Sysprep to get rid of in the first place.

Let's look at this in more detail. Before we do, one more quick point: Sysprep won't prepare a server that's acting as a domain controller, a certificate server, or a cluster member. Other than that, it'll prepare just about any system running Windows 2000 or later.

Set Up the Computer

Start off by creating a computer—whether a server or a workstation—and get it just the way that you want it. Don't bother joining a domain—Sysprep will just unjoin you. As Sysprep removes all existing security-related information, any domain membership info will just be redundant.

Add whatever applications you'll need, configuring the software settings as you think they should be. For example, I hate all that Web content in the Explorer folders and turn it off immediately. But it'd be nice to *always* have it turned off, and I can do that. The idea is this: while I've been logged in as an administrator, I've been making changes to the OS, and the OS remembers those changes—but only while I'm logged in as administrator! If I create a second user account and log in as that person, then I won't keep any of my settings, and have to reteach the computer how I like it to work.

Create a New Administrative User

Once you've got the computer the way you want it, you'll want to copy the administrator's profile to `Default User`, so you need another user account to do that, because an administrator can copy any profile in the system *except* his/her own. You need a second admin account in order to be able to copy the first admin account. Here's how to create an admin account.

1. Click Start\Run, and fill in **compmgmt.msc**, then press Enter to start the Computer Management snap-in.
2. In the left pane, you'll see an icon labeled Local Users and Groups with a plus sign next to it. Click the plus sign to expand it to two folders named, not surprisingly, `Users` and `Groups`. Right-click the `Users` folder and choose New User.
3. That'll give you a dialog box that will let you create a user account that is only recognized by this computer. Let's call it ADMIN2. Fill in the rest of the dialog box and the password, however you like. Click Create, then Close.
4. Click the `Users` folder to show the users in the right pane. Right-click ADMIN2 and choose Properties.
5. In the resulting properties page, click the tab labeled Member Of (which shows the groups that ADMIN2 is a member of) and then the Add button.
6. That will display the list of local groups on this computer. Choose Administrators, then Add, then OK, then OK again.
7. Close the Computer Management snap-in.

Log In as the New User

Now log out of the default Administrator account and log back in as ADMIN2.

Locate the folder named `Documents and Settings`—it's probably on the same drive as the operating system—and open it. You'll see a folder or two in there—these folders store the user profiles (i.e., the settings and preferences) for the people who've used this computer. You'll probably see one for the Administrator. You want to copy this to a profile called Default User—but there are two things standing in your way. First, Default User's profile folder is hidden by default, so unless you've told Server 2003 to show you hidden folders, then you won't see the folder. Second, you can't copy one profile to another just by copying the folder contents—you have to use a Control Panel tool.

First, let's see that `Default User` folder. If you haven't done it yet, open the `Documents and Settings` folder. Click Tools, then Folder Options, and then, on the resulting properties page, click View. Click the radio button labeled Show Hidden Files and Folders, then OK, and `Default User` should pop into view. Next, let's copy the Administrator profile to the Default User profile.

Open the Control Panel (Start/Settings/Control Panel) and then the System applet. The System applet will show five tabs: General, Network Identification, Hardware, User Profiles, and Advanced. Click User Profiles and you'll see a list of profiles stored on this computer. Locate the one named *machinename*\Administrator of Type "Local," and click the Copy To button; you'll see something like Figure 5.37.

FIGURE 5.37

Copying the Administrator's profile

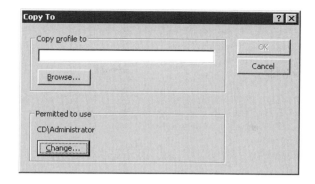

That's a Windows 2000 screen shot, and it's what you'd see if you were Sysprepping a 2K box. XP and Server 2003's dialogs are similar. First, click the button labeled Change in the group labeled Permitted to Use. Right now, only the Administrator account can use this profile—let's change that so that anyone can use it. You'll get a list of possible groups and users, one of which is called, appropriately, Everyone. Choose Everyone and click OK.

Next, copy the profile to \Documents and Settings\Default User. Either type in the whole path name (including whichever drive letter you have Documents and Settings on), or use the Browse button and navigate to the folder. Once you've got \Documents and Settings\Default User in your sights, click OK and the deed is done!

Copy Sysprep to *C:\Sysprep*

Now your system's ready for Sysprepping. Just open a command line and type

```
cd \sysprep
sysprep -reseal -quiet -mini -pnp
```

Or, alternatively,

```
sysprep -reseal -quiet
```

The difference is whether or not you want the Plug-and-Play information reset. With the -mini -pnp options, you create a Sysprep image that you can take from a computer with one set of hardware and get it to work on a system with very different hardware. But there's a price: the -mini -pnp settings slow down a cloned system's first startup, as the Plug-and-Play hardware detection can take another 10 or 15 minutes.

With either option, Sysprep will then strip the SIDs off of your system and shut the computer down. Now copy its hard disk in whatever way you prefer—with a hardware copier or by booting from a floppy or CD-ROM and running Ghost, Drive Image Pro, or something like that.

Now, whenever you copy that disk image to a new hard disk and boot a computer from that hard disk, then the copy of whatever OS you Sysprepped will recognize that it lacks SIDs, and so it'll generate some. In the process, it has to rejoin the domain, ask for a product ID, and so on. Don't want to have to babysit the cloned systems every time they're first Ghosted? No problem. You can make a Sysprep setup script, which is actually just a minor variation on the scripts we've been doing all chapter. Even better, Setup Manager will make a basic Sysprep script for you, and then you can tweak it for your particular needs. Here's the only thing you've got to do in order to make the Sysprep script work. First, you must name the script sysprep.inf. Second, you must include the sysprep.inf file in the C:\Sysprep directory before

Sysprepping your model machine. As before, you've got to add the ProductID entry if your copy of Windows 2000 requires product IDs, and you can use "computername=*" as you've already seen to have the computer create its own unique, random name. If it's XP or Server 2003, don't use ProductID, use ProductKey—Microsoft changed the command for some reason. Here's an example `sysprep.inf`:

```
;SetupMgrTag
[Unattended]
    OemSkipEula=Yes
    InstallFilesPath=C:\sysprep\i386

[GuiUnattended]
    AdminPassword=43e140893084ea91cd85ddec2cd0905daf4d42d86df9ebd57b0641c94aa4c438
    EncryptedAdminPassword=Yes
    OEMSkipRegional=1
    OEMDuplicatorstring="Test Sysprep image"
    TimeZone=35
    OemSkipWelcome=1

[UserData]
    ProductKey=11111-22222-33333-44444-55555
    FullName="Mark Minasi"
    OrgName=""
    ComputerName=CCXP

[Display]
    BitsPerPel=16
    Xresolution=1024
    YResolution=768
    Vrefresh=70

[SetupMgr]
    DistFolder=C:\sysprep\i386
    DistShare=windist

[Identification]
    JoinDomain=bigfirm.biz
    DomainAdmin=administrator
    DomainAdminPassword=swordfish

[Networking]
    InstallDefaultComponents=Yes
```

That's all there is to it—and it's well worth looking into Sysprep, as many people are finding that the absolutely fastest way to get a 2000 or later image on a system is to take a Sysprepped and Ghosted image that's been burned onto a CD, boot the new computer from that CD, and then Ghost the image to the computer's hard disk.

If you've made it with me this far, then you've probably seen that Windows Server 2003 offers us a considerably improved set of rollout tools than the ones we had with NT 4. Start playing around with scripting, RIS, OEM, and Sysprep, and you may find that deployment's not so bad after all!

Chapter 6

Understanding and Using TCP/IP in Server 2003

WHEN NT FIRST APPEARED, TCP/IP was the mildly scary, obscure, complex protocol used by just a few—those "oddballs" in research, education, and government who were attached to that large but still-private club called "the Internet." Most of us chose either NetBEUI in small networks for its simplicity or IPX for its partial interoperability with Novell NetWare.

Since the early '90s, however, IPX has been dethroned as the corporate protocol of choice and TCP/IP has replaced it. Where NetBEUI was once Microsoft's "home protocol," so to speak, the one protocol that you could be sure that *everything* worked on, Server 2003 doesn't even offer it as an option by default—you can find it on the CD, but when you tell 2003 that you want to add a protocol, the only major protocols that you'll see are IP and IPX. Ever since Windows 2000, the Microsoft networking world has required TCP/IP to get the most out of Redmond OSes. For example, to use Active Directory and Group Policies—two of the big pluses of Windows 2000, XP, and Server 2003—you must use TCP/IP. In a very large sense, TCP/IP is *the* mandatory protocol for Server 2003.

TCP/IP is a big subject, so the book takes three chapters to cover it. In this, the first of those, I'll explain what TCP/IP is and how its networks—both the worldwide Internet and your firm's intranet—work. In this first TCP/IP chapter, you'll see how to build a basic intranet and you'll understand some of the vexing-but-necessary parts of putting one together—in particular, you'll learn about IP addresses, subnet masks, and IP routing. I'd like to be able to tell you, "You needn't worry about any of that—just run the Intranet Creation Wizard" or some other mythical tool, but sadly such tools are just that—mythical. However, things like subnet masks sound scarier than they actually are, which is why I'm going to take you through the ugly details.

In the next chapter, we'll look at three very basic and essential TCP-related technologies that allow you to create an infrastructure for your network: the Dynamic Host Configuration Protocol (DHCP), the Domain Name System (DNS), and the Windows Internet Name Service (WINS).

Then, in Chapter 17, you'll see how to set up the server service that is perhaps the most popular type of server on TCP/IP-based networks—a Web server, with the built-in Internet Information Server (IIS) shipped with Server 2003.

A Brief History of TCP/IP

Let's start off by asking, "What *is* TCP/IP?" TCP/IP is a collection of software created over the years, much of it with the help of large infusions of government research money. Originally, TCP/IP was intended for the Department of Defense (DoD). You see, the DoD tends to buy a *lot* of equipment, and much of that equipment is incompatible with other equipment. For example, back in the late '70s when the work that led to TCP/IP was first begun, it was nearly impossible to get an IBM mainframe to talk to a Burroughs mainframe. That was because the two computers were designed with entirely different *protocols*—something like Figure 6.1.

FIGURE 6.1

Compatible hardware, incompatible protocols

To get some idea of what the DoD was facing, imagine picking up the phone in the U.S. and calling someone in Spain. You have a perfectly good hardware connection, as the Spanish phone system is compatible with the American phone system. But despite the *hardware* compatibility, you face a *software* incompatibility. The person on the other end of the phone is expecting a different protocol, a different language. It's not that one language is better or worse than the other, but the English speaker cannot understand the Spanish speaker and vice versa. Rather than force the Spanish speaker to learn English or the English speaker to learn Spanish, we can teach them both a universal language such as Esperanto, the universal language designed in 1888. If Esperanto were used in my telephone example, neither speaker would use it at home, but they would use it to communicate with each other. With time, however, Esperanto might become so flexible and expressive that more and more people might find themselves using it both at home and in public, and English and Spanish might fall into disuse. That's what happened with TCP/IP.

TCP/IP began as a simple *alternative* communications language, an Esperanto for networks. But in time, however, TCP/IP evolved into a mature, well-understood, robust set of protocols, and more and more of the networking world has tossed aside their home-grown, "native" network language in favor of TCP/IP. Let's first look at a little bit of the history of how that happened before we get into the specifics of TCP/IP on Server.

Origins of TCP/IP: From the ARPANET to the Internet

The original DoD network wouldn't just hook up military sites, although that was an important goal of the first defense internetwork, a network called the ARPANET. Much of the basic research in the U.S. was funded by an arm of the Defense Department called the Advanced Research Projects

Agency, or ARPA. ARPA gave, and still gives, a lot of money to university researchers to study all kinds of things. ARPA thought it would be useful for these researchers to be able to communicate with one another, as well as with the Pentagon. Figures 6.2 and 6.3 demonstrate networking both before and after ARPANET implementation.

FIGURE 6.2

Researchers before
ARPANET

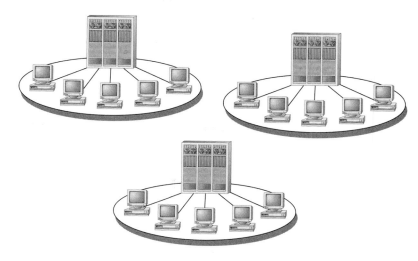

FIGURE 6.3

Researchers after
ARPANET

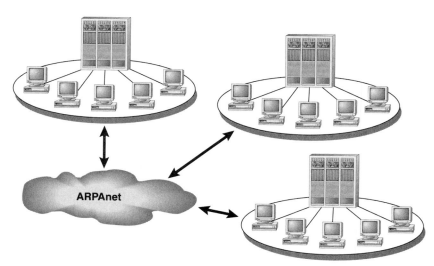

The new network, dubbed ARPANET, was designed and put in place by a private contractor called Bolt, Beranek, and Newman. (They're still around at www.bbn.com.) For the first time, it linked university professors both to each other and to their military and civilian project leaders around the country. Because ARPANET was a network that linked separate private university networks and the separate military networks, it was a "network of networks."

ARPANET ran atop a protocol called the Network Control Protocol (NCP). NCP was later refined into two components, the Internet Protocol (IP) and the Transmission Control Protocol (TCP). The change from NCP to TCP/IP is the technical difference between ARPANET and the Internet. On January 1, 1983, ARPANET packet-switching devices stopped accepting NCP packets and only passed TCP/IP packets, so in a sense, January 1, 1983 is the "official" birthday of the Internet.

ARPANET became the Internet after a few evolutions. (Well, that's a "few evolutions" unless you happen to believe that Al Gore invented it in his spare time while a senator.) Probably the first major development step occurred in 1974, when Vinton Cerf and Robert Kahn proposed the protocols that would become TCP and IP. (I say *probably* because the Internet didn't grow through a centralized effort, but rather through the largely disconnected efforts of several researchers, university professors, and graduate students, most of whom are still alive—and almost *all* of whom have a different perspective on what the "defining" aspects of Internet development were. And all of whom have a Web site on Internet history...) Over its more than 20-year history, the Internet and its predecessors have gone through several stages of growth and adjustment. In 1987, the Internet could only claim a few thousand users. By 1993 it had grown to about 20 million. In 2002, there were nearly 600 million users, according to a study at `www.nua.ie/surveys/how_many_online/index.html`. *All* of those numbers should be taken with a pound of salt, but no matter what numbers you believe, it's clear that the Internet's still growing pretty quickly.

Internet growth is fueled not by an esoteric interest in seeing how large a network the world can build, but rather by just a few applications that require the Internet to run. Perhaps most important is Internet e-mail, followed closely by the World Wide Web, and then the File Transfer Protocol (FTP), but more on those later in Chapter 17. (And okay, let's tell the truth—if we took the pornography and the stolen MP3 files off the Net, then the Internet's free bandwidth would probably grow by a factor of 20.)

Originally, the Internet protocols were intended to support connections between mainframe-based networks, which were basically the only ones that existed through most of the 1970s. But the 1980s saw the growth of Unix workstations, microcomputers, and minicomputers. The Berkeley version of Unix was built largely with government money, and the government said, "Put the TCP/IP protocol in that thing." Adding IP as a built-in part of Berkeley Unix has helped both Unix and the Internet grow. The IP protocol was used on many of the Unix-based Ethernet networks that appeared in the '80s and still exist to this day—I know very few Linux boxes that run anything but TCP/IP, for example. In fact, you'll find that most ISPs mainly run Unix—something you'll discover when you try to connect your Microsoft-based network to the Internet and hear the derision in the voice of the (Unix-oriented) tech support guy at the ISP. (For example, my ISP recently needed me to reconfigure my router to reflect a change in their system software. When the tech support guy on the phone asked me what I did for a living, I told him that I wrote books about Windows networking. "You have my sympathies," he said.)

In the mid-1980s, the National Science Foundation created five supercomputing centers and put them on the Internet. This served two purposes: It made supercomputers available to NSF grantees around the country, and it provided a major "backbone" for the Internet. The National Science Foundation portion of the network, called NSFnet, was for a long time the largest part of the Internet. It is now being superseded by the National Research and Education Network (NREN). For many years, commercial users were pretty much kept off the Internet, as most of the funding was governmental;

you had to be invited to join the Net. But those restrictions have vanished, and now the vast majority of Internet traffic is routed over commercial lines rather than government-run lines. In fact, commercial and private users dominate the Internet these days, so much so that the government and educational institutions are now working on a faster "Internet 2."

It's customary to refer to the Internet as the information superhighway. I can understand why people say that; after all, it's a long-haul trucking service for data. But I think of it more as "Information Main Street." The Internet is growing because businesses are using it to get things done and to sell their wares. All of this book was shipped back and forth on the Internet as it was being written. Heck, that sounds more like Main Street than a highway.

The network protocol wars are over. We're not running NetBEUI, or IPX, or X.25, or HDLC, or DDCMP—the TCP/IP based Internet is *it*, and has been at least since 1995. It seems like there can't be more than one person left on the *planet* without an e-mail address…and I'm still working on my mother.

Let me not leave this section without defining a few terms: internet, Internet, and intranet.

- An *internet* is any network that uses TCP/IP.

- *The* Internet—capital *I*—is the informal term that I'll use to describe the public Internet, the one that connects networks the world over.

- An *intranet* is a term that popped up in the mid '90s because people found it confusing to have to say "THE Internet" when speaking of the world-wide public Internet rather than "AN internet" when referring to a private network that uses TCP/IP. *Intranet*, then, usually means basically the same thing as *internet*—little *i*—perhaps refined to mean "your internal network that not only uses TCP/IP but is also separated from the public Internet in some fashion, perhaps by a firewall."

Goals of TCP/IP's Design

But let's delve into some of the techie aspects of the Internet's main protocols. When the DoD started building this set of network protocols, they had a few design goals. Understanding those design goals helps in understanding why it was worth making the effort to use TCP/IP in the first place. Its intended characteristics include:

- Good failure recovery

- Ability to plug in new networks without disrupting services

- Ability to handle high error rates

- Independence from a particular vendor or type of network

- Very little data overhead

I'm sure no one had any idea how central those design goals would be to the amazing success of TCP/IP both in private intranets and in *the* Internet. Let's take a look at those design goals in more detail.

GOOD FAILURE RECOVERY

Remember, this was to be a *defense* network, so it had to work even if portions of the network hardware suddenly and without warning went offline. That's kind of a nice way of saying the network had to work even if big pieces got nuked.

Can Plug in New Subnetworks "On-the-Fly"

This second goal is related to the first one. It says that it should be possible to bring entire new networks into an intranet—and here, again, *intranet* can mean your company's private intranet or *the* Internet—without interrupting existing network service.

This seems kind of basic nowadays, doesn't it? But a lot of the old network protocols were *really* fragile. Trust me, if we'd all stayed with some of the early PC networking protocols, then I'm only exaggerating a little bit when I say that we'd all have to reboot the Internet every time someone connected.

Can Handle High Error Rates

The next goal was that an intranet should be able to tolerate high or unpredictable error rates and yet still provide a 100-percent reliable end-to-end service. If you're transferring data from Washington, D.C., to Portland, Oregon, and the links that you're currently using through Oklahoma get destroyed by a tornado, then any data lost in the storm will be resent and rerouted via some other lines.

Host Independence

As I mentioned before, the new network architecture should work with any kind of network and not be dedicated or tied to any one vendor.

This is essential in the twenty-first century. The days of "We're just an IBM shop" or "We only buy Novell stuff" are gone for many and going fast for others. (Let's hope that it doesn't give way to "We only buy Microsoft software.") Companies must be able to live in a multivendor world.

In fact, the Internet has achieved this wonderfully. When you connect to CNN, IBM, the White House, or my Web site, do you have any idea whether those Web servers are running some Microsoft Server OS, Unix, Linux, VMS, MVS, or something else? Of course not. My Web server runs atop a Microsoft OS and my e-mail server runs on Linux, and they get along just fine.

Very Little Data Overhead

The last goal was for the network protocols to have as little overhead as possible. To understand this, let's compare TCP/IP to other protocols. While no one knows what protocol will end up being *the* world protocol 20 years from now—if any protocol *ever* gets that much acceptance—one of TCP/IP's rivals is a set of protocols built by the International Organization for Standardization (ISO). ISO has some standards that are very similar to the kinds of things that TCP/IP does, standards named X.25 and TP4. But every protocol packages its data with an extra set of bytes, kind of like an envelope. The vast majority of data packets using the IP protocol (and I promise, I *will* explain soon how it is that TCP and IP are actually two very different protocols) have a simple, fixed-size 20-byte header. The maximum size that the header can be is 60 bytes if all possible options are enabled. The fixed 20 bytes always appear as the first 20 bytes of the packet. In contrast, X.25 uses dozens of possible headers, with no appreciable fixed portion to it. But why should *you* be concerned about overhead bytes? Really for one reason only: performance. Simpler protocols mean faster transmission and packet switching. We'll take up packet switching a little later.

But enough about the Internet for now. Let's stop and define something that I've been talking about—namely, just what *are* TCP and IP?

Originally, TCP/IP was just a set of protocols that could hook up dissimilar computers and transfer information between them. But it grew into a large number of protocols that have become collectively known as the *TCP/IP suite*.

Getting There: The Internet Protocol (IP)

The most basic part of the Internet is the Internet Protocol, or IP. If you want to send data over an intranet, then that data must be packaged in an IP packet. That packet is then *routed* from one part of the intranet to another.

A Simple Internet

IP is supposed to allow messages to travel from one part of a network to another. How does it do this?

An intranet is made of at least two *subnets*. The notion of a subnet is built upon the fact that most popular LAN architectures (Ethernet, Token Ring, and ARCNet) are based on something very much like a radio broadcast. Everyone on the same Ethernet segment hears all of the traffic on their segment, just as each device on a given ring in a Token Ring network must examine every message that goes through the network. The trick that makes an Ethernet or a Token Ring work is that, while each station *hears* everything, each station knows how to ignore all messages except the ones intended for it.

You may have never realized it, but that means that in a single Ethernet segment or a single Token Ring ring, there is *no routing*. If you've ever sat through one of those seemingly unending explanations of the ISO seven-layer network model, then you know that in network discussions, much is made of the *network layer*, which in ISO terms is merely the routing layer. And yet a simple Ethernet or Token Ring never has to route. There are no routing decisions to make; everything is heard by everybody. (Your network adapter filters out any traffic not destined for you, in case you're wondering.)

But now suppose you have *two* separate Ethernets connected to each other, as you see in Figure 6.4.

FIGURE 6.4

Multisegment
internet

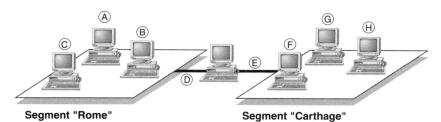

Segment "Rome"   Segment "Carthage"

In Figure 6.4, you see two Ethernet segments, named Rome and Carthage. (I was getting tired of the "shipping" and "finance" examples that everyone uses.) There are three computers that reside solely in Rome. Each one has an Ethernet card built into it, and I've labeled those Ethernet cards A, B, and C. Three more computers reside in Carthage; I've labeled their Ethernet cards F, G, and H. One PC has *two* Ethernet cards—one labeled D that's connected to Rome, and one labeled E that's connected to Carthage.

Subnets and Routers: "Should I Shout, or Should I Route?"

Much of intranet architecture is built around the observation that the PCs with Ethernet cards A, B, and C can communicate directly with each other, and the PCs with Ethernet cards F, G, and H can communicate directly with each other, but A, B, and C *cannot* communicate with F, G, and H without some help from the machine containing Ethernet cards D and E. That D/E machine will function as a *router*, a machine that allows communication between different network segments. A, B, C, and D could be described as being in each other's "broadcast range," as could E, F, G, and H. What I've just called a broadcast range is called more correctly in intranet terminology a *subnet*, which is a collection of machines that can communicate with each other without the need for routing.

For example, F and H can communicate directly without having to ask the router (E, in their case) to forward the message, and so they're on the same subnet. A and C can communicate directly without having to ask the router (D, in their case) to forward the message, and so they're on the same subnet. But if B wanted to talk to G, it would have to first send the message to D, asking, "D, please get this to G," so they're not on the same subnet.

Now, this whole trick of somehow knowing that F and H are on the same subnet and so do not need to enlist the aid of a router—F can just "shout" the message and H will hear it—or knowing that A and F are on different subnets—so A would need the help of D to get to F and F would require E's assistance to get to A—is IP's main job. Essentially, IP's job is to figure out "should I shout, or should I route?" and then, if routing's the way to go, IP has to figure out which router to use, assuming there's a choice of routers.

IP Addresses and Ethernet/MAC Addresses

Before continuing, let's briefly discuss the labels A, B, C, and so on and how those labels actually are manifested in an intranet. Each computer on this net is attached to the net via an Ethernet board, and each Ethernet board on an intranet has two addresses: an *IP address* and an *Ethernet or MAC address*. (There are, of course, other ways to get onto an intranet than via Ethernet, but let's stay with the Ethernet example as it's the most common one on TCP/IP intranets.)

ETHERNET/MAC ADDRESSES

Each Ethernet board's Ethernet address is a unique 48-bit identification code. If it sounds unlikely that every Ethernet board in the world has its own unique address, then consider that 48 bits offers 280,000,000,000,000 possibilities. Ethernet itself only uses about one quarter of those possibilities (2 bits are set aside for administrative functions), but that's still a lot of possible addresses. In any case, the important thing to get here is that a board's Ethernet address is predetermined and hard-coded into the board. Ethernet addresses, which are also called Media Access Control (MAC) addresses (it's got nothing to do with Macintoshes), are expressed in 12 hex digits. (*MAC address* is synonymous with *Token Ring address* or *Ethernet address*.) For example, the Ethernet card on the computer I'm working at now has MAC (Ethernet) address 0020AFF8E771, or as it's sometimes written, 00-20-AF-F8-E7-71. The addresses are centrally administered, and Ethernet chip vendors must purchase blocks of addresses. In the example of my workstation, you know that it's got a 3Com Ethernet card because the Ethernet (MAC) address is 00-20-AF; that prefix is owned by 3Com.

NOTE *To see a Server 2003 system's MAC address—or addresses, if it has more than one NIC—just open a command line and type* **getmac**, *then press Enter. The string of numbers and letters under the column Physical Address is the MAC address of your NIC.*

IP ADDRESSES AND QUAD FORMAT

In contrast to the 48 bits in a MAC address, an IP address is a 32-bit value. IP addresses are numbers set at a workstation (or server) by a network administrator—they're not a hard-coded hardware kind of address like the Ethernet address. That means that there are four billion distinct Internet addresses.

It's nice that there's room for lots of machines, but having to remember—or having to tell someone else—a 32-bit address is no fun. Imagine having to say to a network support person, "Just set up the machines on the subnet to use a default router address of 10101110100-101010010101100010111." Hmmm, doesn't sound like much fun—we need a more human-friendly way to express 32-bit numbers. That's where *dotted quad* notation comes from.

For simplicity's sake, IP addresses are usually represented as *w.x.y.z*, where *w*, *x*, *y*, and *z* are all decimal values from 0 to 255. For example, the IP address of the machine that I'm currently writing this at is 199.34.57.53. Each of the four numbers is called a *quad*; as they're connected by dots, it's called *dotted quad* notation.

Each of the numbers in the dotted quad corresponds to 8 bits of an Internet address. (*IP address* and *Internet address* are synonymous.) As the value for 8 bits can range from 0 to 255, each value in a dotted quad can be from 0 to 255. For example, to convert an IP address of 11001010000011111010101000000001 into dotted quad format, it would first be broken up into 8-bit groups:

   11001010   00001111   10101010   00000001

And each of those 8-bit numbers would be converted to its decimal equivalent. (If you're not comfortable with binary-to-decimal conversion, don't worry about it: Just load the Server 2003 Calculator, click View, then Scientific, and then press the F8 key to put the Calculator in binary mode. Enter the binary number, press F6, and the number will be converted to decimal for you.) Our number converts as follows:

   11001010   00001111   10101010   00000001
      202   15   170   1

which results in a dotted quad address of 202.15.170.1.

So, to recap: Each of these computers has at least one Ethernet card in it, and that Ethernet card has a predefined MAC address. The network administrator of this network has gone around and installed IP software on these PCs and, in the process, has assigned IP addresses to each of them. (Note, by the way, that the phrase "has assigned IP addresses to each of them" may not be true if you are using the Dynamic Host Configuration Protocol, or DHCP, which I'll describe in detail in the next chapter. For most of this chapter, however, I'm going to assume that you're not using DHCP and that someone must hand-assign an IP address to each Ethernet card.)

Let me redraw our intranet, adding totally arbitrary IP addresses and Ethernet addresses, as shown in Figure 6.5.

FIGURE 6.5

Two-subnet intranet with Ethernet and IP addresses

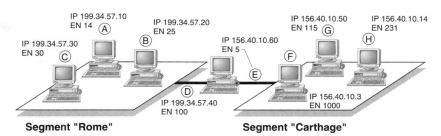

NOTE   *Remember, MAC addresses are burned into a network card; they come "out of the box," so to speak. IP addresses, in contrast, are assigned by a network administrator or software configured by a network administrator. There isn't any mathematical relationship between the two numbers; don't try to see if there's some connection between, say, the bottom 32 bits of a MAC address and the IP address—there won't be one.*

IP Routers

Now let's return to the computer in the middle. It is part of *both* segments, both subnets. How do I get one computer to be part of two networks? By putting two Ethernet cards in the computer in the middle. (A computer with more than one network card in it is called a *multihomed* computer. Don't ask me why, the term has never made sense to me; I suppose it flows better than "multiNICced.") One of the Ethernet cards is on the Rome subnet, and the other is on the Carthage subnet. (By the way, each computer on an intranet is called a *host* in TCP-ese.)

Now, each Ethernet card must get a separate IP address, so as a result, the computer in the middle has *two* IP addresses, D and E. If a message is transmitted in Rome, adapter D hears it and E doesn't. Then, if a message is transmitted in Carthage, adapter E hears it but D doesn't.

How would we build an intranet from these two subnets? How could the computer with Ethernet card A, for example, send a message to the computer with Ethernet card G? Obviously, the only way that message will get from A to G is if the message is received on the Ethernet adapter with address D and then re-sent out over the Ethernet adapter with address E. Once E resends the message, G will hear it, as it is on the same network as E.

In order for this to work, the machine containing boards D and E must be smart enough to perform this function whereby it resends data between D and E when necessary. Such a machine is, by definition, an *IP router*. A Server 2003 computer can act as an IP router, as you'll learn later.

Under IP, the sending station (the one with Ethernet card A, in this case) examines the address of the destination (the PC with Ethernet card G, in this case) and realizes that it does not know how to get to G. (I'll explain exactly *how* it comes to that realization in a minute.) Now, if A has to send something to an address that it doesn't understand, then it uses a kind of "catchall" address called the *default router* or, for historical reasons, the *default gateway* address. A's network administrator has already configured A's default router as D, so A sends the message to D. Once D gets the message, it then sees that the message is not destined for itself, but rather for G, and so it resends the message from board E.

Routing in More Detail

Now let's look a little closer at how that message gets from A to G. Each computer, as you've already seen, has one *or more* IP addresses. It's important to understand that there is no relation whatsoever between an Ethernet card's address and the IP address associated with it: The Ethernet MAC address is hardwired into the card by the card's manufacturer, and the IP addresses are assigned by a network administrator.

But now examine the IP addresses and you'll see a pattern to them. Rome's addresses all look like 199.34.57.*z*, where *z* is some number, and Carthage's addresses all look like 156.40.10.*z*, where, again, *z* can be any number. The Ethernet addresses follow no rhyme or reason and are grouped by the board's manufacturer. That similarity of IP addresses within Rome and Carthage will be important in understanding routing.

Now, let's reexamine how the message gets from A's computer to G's (for simplicity's sake, I'll say "A" instead of "the computer with the Ethernet card labeled A," and the same for G's computer and so on):

1. The IP software in A first says, "How do I get this message to G—can I just broadcast it, or must it be routed?" The way that it makes that decision is by finding out whether or not G is on the same *subnet* as A is. A subnet is simply a broadcast area. The host with Ethernet card A then, is asking, "Is G part of Rome, like me?"

2. A determines that it is on a different subnet from G by examining their addresses. A knows that it has address 199.34.57.10 and that it must send its message to 156.40.10.50. A's computer has a simple rule for this: If the destination address looks like 199.34.57.z, where, again, z can be any value, then the destination is in the same subnet and so requires no routing. On the other hand, 156.40.10.50 is clearly *not* in the same subnet.

   If, alternatively, G *had* been on the same subnet, then A would have "shouted" the IP packet straight to G, referring specifically to its IP and Ethernet address.

3. So A can't directly send its IP packets to G. A then looks for another way. When A's network administrator set up A's IP software, she told A the IP address of A's *default router*. The default router is basically the address that says, "If you don't know where to send something, send it to me and I'll try to get it there." A's default router is D. So now A has a sort of sub-goal of getting a message to nearby D, with IP address 199.34.57.40. We're almost ready to hand this over to the Ethernet card—*except* that Ethernet cards don't understand IP addresses; they understand MAC addresses.

   TCP/IP's got an answer for this: Address Resolution Protocol (ARP). A just sends a broadcast to the local segment, saying, "If there's a machine out there that goes by the IP address 199.34.57.40, please send me back your MAC address." D hears the request and responds that its MAC address is 100.

   A then sends an Ethernet frame from itself to D. The Ethernet frame contains this information:

   ◆ Source Ethernet address: 14
   ◆ Destination Ethernet address: 100
   ◆ Source IP address: 199.34.57.10
   ◆ Destination IP address: 156.40.10.50

4. Ethernet card D receives the frame and hands it to the IP software running in its PC. The PC sees that the IP destination address is not *its* IP address, so the PC knows that it must route this IP packet. Examining the subnet, the PC sees that the destination lies on the subnet that Ethernet adapter E is on, so it ARPs to get G's MAC address; G responds, "My MAC address is 115," and then E sends out a frame, with this information:

   ◆ Source Ethernet address: 5
   ◆ Destination Ethernet address: 115
   ◆ Source IP address: 199.34.57.10 (note this is A's address, not E's)
   ◆ Destination IP address: 156.40.10.50

5. G then gets the packet. By looking at the Ethernet and IP addresses, G can see that it got this frame from E, but the original message really came from another machine, the 199.34.57.10 machine.

That's a simple example of how IP routes, but its algorithms are powerful enough to serve as the backbone for a network as large as the Internet.

TIP *There are different kinds of routing algorithms in TCP/IP. Server 2003 supports the Routing Information Protocol (RIP) version 2, Open Shortest Path First (OSPF), and IGMP version 2. For other routing approaches, or for very high-capacity routing needs, you need either third-party software or a dedicated hardware router to build large, complex intranets with Server 2003. But Server 2003 can handle a considerably larger set of routing tasks than did its predecessors.*

Class A, B, and C Networks, CIDR Blocks, Routable and Nonroutable Addresses, and Subnetting

Before leaving IP routing, let's take a more specific look at networks, subnets, and IP addresses.

The whole idea behind the 32-bit IP addresses is to make it relatively simple to segment the task of managing the Internet or, for that matter, *any* intranet.

To become part of the Internet, you'll need a block of IP addresses and a name (like acme.com) or a set of names. Find a local Internet service provider (ISP) for the block of addresses. ISPs may also handle registering names for you, but it's just as easy to register a name yourself with Network Solutions or another name registrar; surf over to www.networksolutions.net to find out how.

But how do the *ISPs* get their IP addresses? Originally, an organization named the Internet Assigned Numbers Authority (IANA) handed out addresses. In 1993, however, an Internet document RFC 1466 (the rules describing how things work in the Internet are called Requests for Comment, or RFCs) explained that it made more sense to distribute the job as the Internet became bigger. The IANA, which is now in the process of becoming the Internet Corporation for Assigned Names and Numbers (ICANN), divides its number-assigning authority among three Regional Internet Registries (RIRs, inevitably): RIPE (Reseaux IP Europeens, or European IP Networks) handles Europe, the Middle East, Africa, and the better part of Asia; APNIC (Asia Pacific Network Information Center) handles the rest of Asia and the South Pacific; and ARIN (American Registry for Internet Numbers) handles the Americas. Rather than say "The IANA/ICANN, RIPE, ARIN, APNIC, or one of their suborganizations," however, I hope you won't mind if I just say "IANA" when referring to the IP-allocating groups.

A, B, and C Class Networks

The IANA or an ISP assigns a company a block of IP addresses according to the company's size. That block of addresses is called a *network*. (As you'll soon see, a subnet is just a subdivision of that set of assigned addresses, hence *subnet*.) Big companies get class A networks (there are none left; they've all been given out), medium-sized companies get class B networks (they're still around but pretty scarce), and others get class C networks (they're still available). Although there are three network classes, there are five kinds of IP addresses, as you'll see in Figure 6.6.

FIGURE 6.6

Internet network classes and reserved addresses

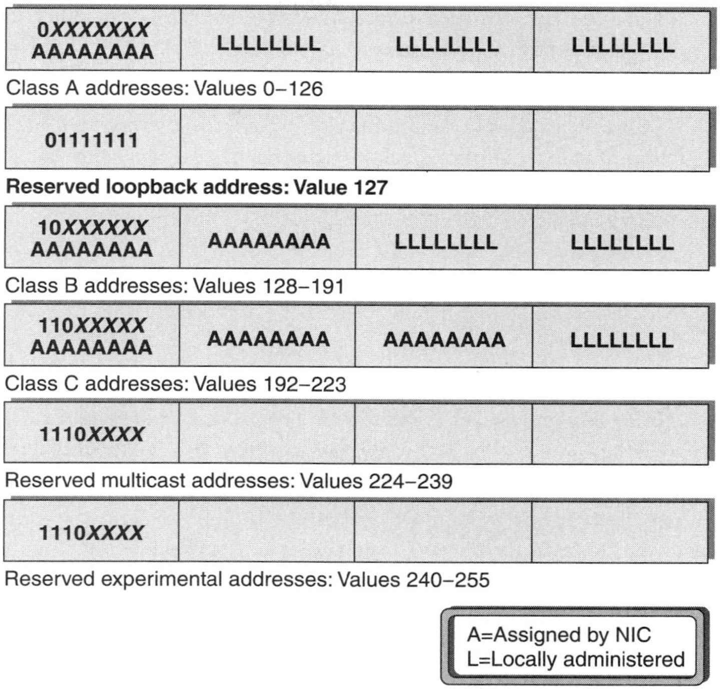

0*XXXXXXX* AAAAAAAA	LLLLLLLL	LLLLLLLL	LLLLLLLL

Class A addresses: Values 0–126

01111111			

Reserved loopback address: Value 127

10*XXXXXX* AAAAAAAA	AAAAAAAA	LLLLLLLL	LLLLLLLL

Class B addresses: Values 128–191

110*XXXXX* AAAAAAAA	AAAAAAAA	AAAAAAAA	LLLLLLLL

Class C addresses: Values 192–223

1110*XXXX*			

Reserved multicast addresses: Values 224–239

1110*XXXX*			

Reserved experimental addresses: Values 240–255

> A=Assigned by NIC
> L=Locally administered

Because it seemed, in the early days of the Internet, that four billion addresses left plenty of space for growth, the original designers were a bit sloppy. They defined three classes of networks of the Internet: Large networks, medium-sized networks, and small networks. The creators of the Internet used 8-bit sections of the 32-bit addresses to delineate the difference between different classes of networks:

Class A Networks   A large network would have its first 8 bits set by the NIC, and the network's internal administrators could set the remaining 24 bits. The leftmost 8 bits could have values from 0 to 126, allowing for 127 class A networks. Companies like IBM get these, and there are only 127 of these addresses. As only 8 bits have been taken, 24 remain; that means that class A networks can contain up to 2 to the 24th power, or about 16 million, hosts. Examples of class A nets include General Electric (3.*x.y.z*), BBN (4), IBM (9), Xerox (13), Hewlett-Packard (15), DEC (16), Apple (17), MIT (18), Ford (19), Eli Lilly (40), DuPont (52), Merck (54), Boeing (55), the U.S. Postal Service (56), various defense groups—remember who built this—and some unexpected ones: Networld+Interop, which has the 45.*x.y.z* network set aside for its use (not bad, an A network for two week-long conferences a year!), the U.K. Department of Social Security (51), and Norsk Informasjonsteknologi (32).

Class B Networks   Medium-sized networks have the leftmost 16 bits preassigned to them, leaving 16 bits for local use. Class B addresses always have the values 128 through 191 in their first quad, then a value from 0 to 255 in their second quad. There are then 16,384 possible class B networks. Each of them can have up to 65,536 hosts. Microsoft and Exxon are examples of companies with class B networks. (So Apple and IBM have class A networks and Microsoft only has a class B. What do you want to bet that this kind of thing keeps Bill up late nights?)

Class C Networks   Small networks have the leftmost 24 bits preassigned to them, leaving only 8 bits for local administration (which is bad, as it means that class C networks can't have more than 254 hosts), but as the NIC has 24 bits to work with, it can easily give out class C network addresses (which is good). Class C addresses start off with a value from 192 to 223. As the second and third quads can be any value from 0 to 255, that means that there can potentially be 2,097,152 class C networks. (That's what my network, minasi.com, is.) The last C network, when it's assigned, will be $223.255.255.z$; remember that the owner of that network will be able to control only z.

Reserved Addresses   Some addresses are reserved for multicast purposes and for experimental purposes, so they can't be assigned for networks. In particular, address 224.0.0.0 is set aside for *multicasts*, network transmissions to groups of computers.

Routable and Nonroutable Addresses

Once upon a time, getting hold of a bunch of IP addresses was easy. But nowadays, they're scarcer and scarcer. Four billion possible addresses sounds like a lot, but the A/B/C class approach tends to waste addresses on large companies and those who just got in line at the right time: With all due respect to the organizations involved, it's hard to believe that certain universities, Apple, and the Network+Interop conference each really need 16 million unique IP addresses. Don't misunderstand me, I'm not suggesting that we change their address allocation—first come, first served in the IP land rush is a reasonable first approach to allocation. But big and small firms alike need IP addresses, and they're not as plentiful as they once were.

RFC 1918's Nonroutable Addresses

We've heard for years that the Giant Brains of the IP world are working on promoting a replacement for IP called IPV6, a 128-bit–based addressing scheme that would allow more IP addresses than there are electrons in the universe (okay, I rechecked, it's only about the size of the square root of the number of electrons in the universe, but it's still a big number), but then I've been hearing about the "imminent" nature of IPV6 since about 1993. Until it's more widely accepted, we need some way to stretch our IP addresses. And there *is* a way that's been widely adopted.

In RFC 1918, the Internet folks defined three nonroutable ranges of IP addresses. They are

- 10.0.0.0–10.255.255.255
- 172.16.0.0–172.31.255.255
- 192.168.0.0–192.168.255.255

The original idea with the ranges of nonroutable addresses was to set aside some addresses that people could use to build "test" intranets without having to go to the IANA for a range of numbers—anyone can build an IP-based network using these addresses. Furthermore, even if networks based on the above addresses *were* attached to the Internet, then they couldn't cause any mischief, because Internet routers are programmed to *ignore* them! As messages sent from these ranges won't be routed on the public Internet, they are logically called the *nonroutable* ranges.

This means that literally millions of networks in the (for example) 192.168.1.0–192.168.1.255 range could exist, all at the same time, because they cannot communicate with the public Internet, and therefore can't cause any trouble. And that offers a kind of side benefit to companies choosing to use the nonroutable addresses: security. Clearly if my system has address 10.10.10.10, then I'm protected from outside hackers, because if they can't connect to me, then they can't cause trouble, right?

Because of this, most companies use at least two sets of IP addresses: Addresses used in their company's *internal* Internet (or "intranet," as we say nowadays) and a range of "official" Internet addresses obtained from an ISP or directly from a part of the IANA.

ROUTING THE NONROUTABLE, PART I: NETWORK ADDRESS TRANSLATION

Now, from what I've said so far, it sounds like the folks whose machines have nonroutable addresses are sort of left out in the cold; they can route *inside* their company's network, but they're shut out of access to the public, *routable* Internet. But not any more. In fact, a little technological trick has made it possible for companies to offer public Internet access to their nonroutable addresses. You see, there is a class of routers called network address translation (NAT) routers that can perform a small bit of magic and let you use private, non-IANA–assigned IP addresses on your company's intranet and still be able to communicate with the Internet.

So, for example, suppose your firm had obtained a class C address range from the IANA or an ISP: 256 addresses. Although you have thousands of computers, the fact that there are only 256 addresses is no problem as the NAT router can handle communications with the Internet. NAT is kind of interesting in that it lets machines with nonroutable addresses *initiate* conversations with machines on the routable public Internet, but doesn't allow machines out on the Internet to initiate conversations in the other direction. For example, if I were sitting at a machine with IP address 192.168.1.17 behind a NAT router and tried to surf `www.microsoft.com`, then I'd get in, no problem. But if someone in the public Internet tried to connect to my system at 192.168.1.17, they'd be rebuffed, as *their* local router would know better than to pass a request to a nonroutable address.

You'll see a bit more about NAT (and an important partner, PAT, *port* address translation) later in the chapter. And in case you wondered, NAT and PAT have a *down*side: under the wrong circumstances, NAT and PAT *can* let the bad guys in.

You Can't Use *All* of the Numbers

There are some special rules to IP addresses, however. There's a whole bunch of numbers that you can never give to any machine. They're the default route address, the loopback address, the network number, the broadcast address, and the default router address.

THE DEFAULT ROUTE ADDRESS

As you'll see later, the address 0.0.0.0 is another way of saying "the entire Internet." But as 0.*x.y.z* is in the class A range of addresses, all of 0.*x.y.z* must be set aside—all 16 million addresses.

THE LOOPBACK ADDRESS

The address 127.0.0.1 is reserved as a loopback. If you send a message to 127.0.0.1, then it should be returned to you unless there's something wrong on the IP software itself; messages to the loopback don't go out on the network, but instead stay within a particular machine's IP software. And so no network has an address 127.xxxxxxxx.xxxxxxxx.xxxxxxxx, an unfortunate waste of 16 million addresses.

THE NETWORK NUMBER

Sometimes you need to refer to an entire subnet with a single number. Thus far, I've said things like "My C network is 199.34.57.z, and I can make z range from 0 to 255." I was being a bit lazy; I didn't want to write "199.34.57.0 through 199.34.57.255," so I said "199.34.57.z."

It's not proper IP-ese to refer to a range of network addresses that way. And it's necessary to have an official way to refer to a range of addresses.

For example, to tell a router, "To get this message to the subnet that ranges from 100.100.100.0 through 100.100.100.255, first route to the router at 99.98.97.103," you've got to have some way to designate the range of addresses 100.100.100.0–100.100.100.255. We could have just used two addresses with a dash between them, but that's a bit cumbersome. Instead, the address that ends in all binary 0s is reserved as the *network number*, the TCP/IP name for the range of addresses in a subnet. In my 100.100.100.z example, the shorthand way to refer to 100.100.100.0 through 100.100.100.255 is 100.100.100.0.

Notice that this means you would never use the address 100.100.100.0—you never give that IP address to a machine under TCP/IP.

For example, to tell that router, "To get this message to the subnet that ranges from 100.100.100.0 through 100.100.100.255, first route to the router at 99.98.97.103," you would type something like **route add 100.100.100.0 99.98.97.103**. (Actually, you'd type a bit more information, and I'll get to that in the upcoming section on using your machine as a router, but this example gives you the idea.)

IP BROADCAST ADDRESS

There's another reserved address, as well—the TCP/IP broadcast address. It looks like the address of one machine, but it isn't; it's the address you'd use to broadcast to each machine on a subnet. That address is all binary 1s.

For example, on a simple class C subnet, the broadcast address would be $w.x.y.255$. When would you need to know this? Some IP software needs this when you configure it; most routers require the broadcast address (as well as the network number). So if I just use my class C network 199.34.57.0 (see how convenient that .0 thing is?) as a single subnet, then the broadcast address for my network would be 199.34.57.255.

DEFAULT ROUTER ADDRESS

Every subnet has at least one router; after all, if it didn't have a router, then the subnet couldn't talk to any other networks, and it wouldn't be an intranet.

By convention, the first address after the network number is the default gateway (router) address. For example, on a simple class C network, the address of the router should be $w.x.y.1$. This is not, by the way, a hard-and-fast rule like the network number and the IP broadcast address—it is, instead, a convention.

Suppose you have just been made the proud owner of a class C net, 222.210.34.0. You can put 253 computers on your network, as you must not use 222.210.34.0, which describes the entire network; 222.210.34.255, which will be your broadcast address; and 222.210.34.1, which will be used either by you or your Internet Service Provider for a router address between your network and the rest of the Internet.

Subnet Masks

If you had a trivially small intranet, one with just one segment where everyone can just "shout" to one another, then no routing is required. But that wouldn't be the case for most—routing is a great way to isolate parts of your network and is absolutely essential whenever connecting a wide area network to a local area network. Or you might simply have too large a number of IP addresses to fit on one segment even if you wanted to. Consider IBM's situation, with a class A network that can theoretically support 16 million hosts. Managing *that* network cries out for routers. For this reason, it may be necessary for your IP software on your PC to route data over a router even if it's staying within your company. Let's ask again, and in more detail this time, "How does a machine know whether to route or not?"

That's where subnets are important. Subnets make it possible, as you've seen, for a host (that is, a PC with an IP address) to determine whether it can just lob a message straight over to another host or if it must go through routers. You can tell a host's IP software how to distinguish whether or not another host is in the same subnet through the *subnet mask*.

Recall that all of the IP addresses in Rome looked like 199.34.57.z, where z was a number between 1 and 255. You could then say that all co-members of the Rome subnet are defined as the hosts whose first three quads match. Now, on some subnets, it might be possible that the only requirement for membership in the same subnet would be that the first *two* quads be the same—a company that decided for some reason to make its entire class B network a single subnet would be one example of that. (Yes, they *do* exist: I've seen firms that make a single subnet out of a Class B network, with the help of some bizarre smart bridges. Imagine it—65,534 machines all able to broadcast to one another; yikes. And no, I don't recommend it.)

When a computer is trying to figure out whether the IP address that it owns is on the same subnet as the place that it's trying to communicate with, then a subnet mask answers the question, "Which bits must match for us to be on the same subnet?"

IP does that with a *mask*, a combination of 1s and 0s like so:

```
11111111 11111111 11111111 00000000
```

Here's how a host would use this mask. The host with IP address 199.34.57.10 (station A in Figure 6.5) wants to know if it is on the same subnet as the host with IP address 199.34.57.20 (station B in Figure 6.5). 199.34.57.10, expressed in binary, is 11000111 00100010 00111001 00001010. The IP address for B is, in binary, 11000111 00100010 00111001 00010100. The IP software in A then compares its own IP address to B's IP address. Look at them right next to each other:

```
11000111 00100010 00111001 00001010 A's address
11000111 00100010 00111001 00010100 B's address
```

The leftmost 27 bits match, as does the rightmost bit. Does that mean they're in the same subnet? Again, for the two addresses to be in the same subnet, certain bits must match—the ones with 1s in the subnet mask. Let's stack up the subnet mask, A's address, and B's address to make this clearer:

```
11111111 11111111 11111111 00000000 the subnet mask
11000111 00100010 00111001 00001010 A's address
11000111 00100010 00111001 00010100 B's address
```

Look down from each of the 1s on the subnet mask, and you see that A and B match at each of those positions. Under the 0s in the subnet mask, A and B match up sometimes but not all the time. In fact, it doesn't matter whether or not A and B match in the positions under the 0s in the subnet mask—the fact that there are 0s there means that whether they match is irrelevant.

Another way to think of the subnet mask is this. The IANA and friends give you a range of addresses, and you allocate them as you see fit. Of the 32 bits in your IP addresses, some are under your control and some are under the IANA & Co.'s control. In general, however, the bits that the IANA controls are to the left, and the ones that *you* control are to the right. For example, the IANA controls the leftmost 8 bits for a class A network, the 16 leftmost bits for a class B network, and the leftmost 24 bits for a class C network.

How do you know what value to use for a subnet mask? Well, if you have a class C number and all of your workstations are on a single subnet, then you have a case like the one we just saw: A subnet mask of 11111111 11111111 11111111 00000000, which, in dotted-quad terminology, is 255.255.255.0. Remember that, by definition, the fact that I have a C network means that the IANA has "nailed down" the leftmost or top three quads (24 bits), leaving me only the rightmost quad (8 bits). Since all of my addresses must match in the leftmost 24 bits and I can do anything I like with the bottom 8 bits, my subnet mask must be 11111111 11111111 11111111 00000000, or 255.255.255.0. Again, with subnet masks, the 1s are always on the left and the 0s on the right—you'll never see a subnet mask like "11111111 11110000 00001111 11111000" or "00000000 11111111 11111111 11111111."

Getting back to my C network, however, that 11111111 11111111 11111111 00000000 mask assumes that I'll use my entire C network as one big subnet. Instead, I might decide to break one class C network into two subnets. I could decide that all the numbers from 1 to 127—00000001 to 01111111—are subnet 1 and the numbers from 128 to 255—10000000 to 11111111—are subnet 2. In that case, the values inside my subnets will only vary in the last 7 bits rather than (as in the previous example) varying in the last 8 bits. The subnet mask would be, then, 11111111 11111111 11111111 10000000, or 255.255.255.128.

The first subnet is a range of addresses from *w.x.y*.0 through *w.x.y*.127, where *w.x.y* are the quads that the NIC assigned me. The second subnet is the range from *w.x.y*.128 through *w.x.y*.255.

Now let's find the network number, default router address, and broadcast address. The network number is the first number in each range, so the first subnet's network number is *w.x.y*.0 and the second's is *w.x.y*.128. The default router address is just the second address in the range, which is *w.x.y*.1 and *w.x.y*.129 for the two subnets. The broadcast address is then the *last* address in both cases, *w.x.y*.127 and *w.x.y*.255 respectively.

Subnetting a Class C Network

If you're going to break down your subnets smaller than class C, then having to figure out the subnet mask, network number, broadcast address, and router address can get kind of confusing. Table 6.1 summarizes how you can break a class C network down into one, two, four, or eight smaller subnets with the attendant subnet masks, network numbers, broadcast addresses, and router addresses. I've assumed that you are starting from a class C address, so you'll only be working with the fourth quad. The first three quads I have simply designated *w.x.y*.

TABLE 6.1: BREAKING A C CLASS NETWORK INTO SUBNETS

NUMBER OF DESIRED SUBNETS	SUBNET MASK	NETWORK NUMBER	ROUTER ADDRESS	BROADCAST ADDRESS	REMAINING NUMBER OF IP ADDRESSES
1	255.255.255.0	w.x.y.0	w.x.y.1	w.x.y.255	253
2	255.255.255.128	w.x.y.0	w.x.y.1	w.x.y.127	125
	255.255.255.	w.x.y.128	w.x.y.129	w.x.y.255	125
4	255.255.255.192	w.x.y.0	w.x.y.1	w.x.y.63	61
	255.255.255.	w.x.y.64	w.x.y.65	w.x.y.127	61
	255.255.255.	w.x.y.128	w.x.y.129	w.x.y.191	61
	255.255.255.	w.x.y.192	w.x.y.193	w.x.y.255	61
8	255.255.255.224	w.x.y.0	w.x.y.1	w.x.y.31	29
	255.255.255.	w.x.y.32	w.x.y.33	w.x.y.63	29
	255.255.255.	w.x.y.64	w.x.y.65	w.x.y.95	29
	255.255.255.	w.x.y.96	w.x.y.97	w.x.y.127	29
	255.255.255.	w.x.y.128	w.x.y.129	w.x.y.159	29
	255.255.255.	w.x.y.160	w.x.y.161	w.x.y.191	29
	255.255.255.	w.x.y.192	w.x.y.193	w.x.y.223	29
	255.255.255.	w.x.y.224	w.x.y.225	w.x.y.255	29

For example, suppose you want to chop up a class C network, 200.211.192.*z*, into two subnets. As you see in the table, you'd use a subnet mask of 255.255.255.128 for each subnet. The first subnet would have network number 200.211.192.0, router address 200.211.192.1, and broadcast address 200.211.192.127. You could assign IP addresses 200.211.192.2 through 200.211.192.126, 125 different IP addresses. (Notice that heavily subnetting a network results in the loss of a greater and greater percentage of addresses to the network number, broadcast address, and router address.) The second subnet would have network number 200.211.192.128, router address 200.211.192.129, and broadcast address 200.211.192.255.

In case you're wondering, it is entirely possible to subnet further, into 16 subnets of 13 hosts apiece (remember that you always lose three numbers for the network number, router address, and broadcast address) or 32 subnets of 5 hosts apiece, but at that point, you're losing an awful lot of addresses to IP overhead.

Subnetting a Class C Network the RFC/CCNA Way

Now, I *guarantee* that the previous page or so got the readers with a CCNA (Cisco Certified Network Administrator) certification all cranked up. I just told you that you could chop a C network into two subnets of 126 addresses, or four subnets of 62 addresses, or eight of 30 addresses. That's a fact that will actually work in the real world. But if you do your routing by the book or, rather, by the RFC, then you'll get a different answer. The RFC point of view would say that you *cannot* chop a C network into 126-address subnets at all. The RFC would also say that you can indeed chop a C network into 62-address subnets, but that you only get two of them, or only six 30-address subnets. Here's why.

The RFC on subnetting is RFC 950; it says

> In certain contexts, it is useful to have fixed addresses with functional significance rather than as identifiers of specific hosts. When such usage is called for, the address zero is to be interpreted as meaning "this," as in "this network." The address of all ones are to be interpreted as meaning "all," as in "all hosts." For example, the address 128.9.255.255 could be interpreted as meaning "all hosts on the network 128.9." Or the address 0.0.0.37 could be interpreted as meaning "host 37 on this network." It is useful to preserve and extend the interpretation of these special addresses in subnetted networks. This means the values of all zeros and all ones in the subnet field should not be assigned to actual (physical) subnets. In the example above, the 6-bit wide subnet field may have any value except 0 and 63.

What this means in English is this: RFC 950 says to use neither the first subnet nor the last subnet. Thus, if you're going to be completely RFC-compliant (which is never a bad idea), you would *not* be able to use subnets 199.34.57.0 and 199.34.57.192. And my earlier example of dividing 199.34.57.0 into two subnets by using subnet mask 255.255.255.128 would not work at all.

Should you care? If you're using modern routers or NT machines for routers, you won't run into trouble using all possible subnets. But if you've got some routers that are sticklers for the rules, you might cause trouble by using those other subnets. It's kind of a shame, as the 255.255.255.192 subnet for a C network yields four 62-address subnets, and staying strictly RFC compliant means you only get *two* 62-address subnets.

Oh, and one more reason to understand RFC 950's restrictions: If you take any exams, such as the Microsoft or Cisco certification exams about TCP/IP, the RFC 950 answer will be right—the practical answer will be "wrong," even if it *would* work in the real world.

Classless Inter-Domain Routing (CIDR)

Now that we've gotten past some of the fine points of subnet masks, let me elaborate on what you see if you ever go to the IANA or an ISP looking for a domain of your own.

The shortage of IP addresses has led the IANA to curtail giving out class A, B, or C addresses. Many small companies need an Internet domain, but giving them a C network is overkill, as a C network contains 256 addresses and many small firms only have a dozen or so computers that they want on the Internet. Large companies may also want a similarly small presence on the Internet: For reasons of security, they may not want to put all of the PCs (or other computers) on the Internet but rather on an internal network not attached to the Internet. These companies *do* need a presence on the Internet, however—for their e-mail servers, FTP servers, Web servers, and the like—so they need a dozen or so addresses. But, again, giving them an entire 256-address C network is awfully wasteful. However, until 1994, it was the smallest block that an ISP could hand out.

Similarly, some companies need a few hundred addresses—more than 256, but not very many more. Such a firm is too big for a C network but a bit small for the 65,536 addresses of a B network. More flexibility here would be useful.

For that reason, the IANA now gives out addresses without the old A, B, or C class restrictions. This newer method that the IANA uses is called Classless Inter-Domain Routing, or CIDR, pronounced "cider." CIDR networks are described as "slash x" networks, where the x is a number representing the number of bits in the IP address range that IANA controls.

If you had a class A network, then the IANA controlled the top 8 bits and you controlled the bottom 24. If you decided somehow to take your class A network and make it one big subnet, then what would be your subnet mask? Since all of your A network would be one subnet, you'd only have to look at the top quad to see if the source and destination addresses were on the same subnet. For example, if you had network 4.0.0.0, then addresses 4.55.22.81 and 4.99.63.88 would be on the same subnet. (Please note that I can't actually imagine anyone doing this with a class A net; I'm just trying to make CIDR clearer.) Your subnet mask would be, then, 11111111 00000000 00000000 00000000, or 255.0.0.0. Reading from the left, you have eight 1s in the subnet mask before the 0s start. In CIDR terminology, you wouldn't have a class A network; rather, you would have a *slash 8* network. It would be written "4.0.0.0/8" instead of "4.0.0.0 subnet mask 255.0.0.0."

With a class B, the IANA controlled the top 16 bits, and you controlled the bottom 16. If you decided to take that class B network and make it a one-subnet network, then your subnet mask would be 11111111 11111111 00000000 00000000, or 255.255.0.0. Reading from the left, the subnet mask would have 16 1s. In CIDR terms, a B network is a *slash 16* network. So if your firm had a B network like 164.109.0.0 subnet mask 255.255.0.0, in slash format that would be 164.109.0.0/16.

With a C class, the IANA controlled the top 24 bits, and you controlled the bottom 8. By now, you've seen that the subnet mask for a C network if you treated it as one subnet is 11111111 11111111 11111111 00000000. Reading from the left, the subnet mask would have 24 1s. In CIDR terms, a C network is a *slash 24* network. Thus, one of my C networks (206.246.253.0, mask 255.255.255.0) can be written "206.246.253/24." Grasping this /24 nomenclature is important because you'll see it on some routers. My Ascend router never asks for subnet masks—just slashes.

Where the new flexibility of CIDR comes in is that the IANA can in theory now not only define the A-, B-, and C-type networks, it can offer networks with subnet masks in between the A, B, and C networks. For example, suppose I wanted a network for 50 PCs. Before, IANA would have to give me a C network, with 256 addresses. But now they can offer me a network with subnet mask 11111111 11111111 11111111 11000000 (255.255.255.192), giving me only 6 bits to play with. Two to the sixth power is 64, so I'd have 64 addresses to do with as I liked. This would be a *slash 26* (/26) network.

In summary, Table 6.2 shows how large each possible network type would be.

TABLE 6.2: CIDR NETWORK TYPES

IANA NETWORK TYPE	"SUBNET MASK" FOR ENTIRE NETWORK	APPROXIMATE NUMBER OF IP ADDRESSES
slash 0	0.0.0.0	4 billion
slash 1	128.0.0.0	2 billion
slash 2	192.0.0.0	1 billion
slash 3	224.0.0.0	500 million
slash 4	240.0.0.0	250 million

Continued on next page

TABLE 6.2: CIDR NETWORK TYPES *(continued)*

IANA NETWORK TYPE	"SUBNET MASK" FOR ENTIRE NETWORK	APPROXIMATE NUMBER OF IP ADDRESSES
slash 5	248.0.0.0	128 million
slash 6	252.0.0.0	64 million
slash 7	254.0.0.0	32 million
slash 8	255.0.0.0	16 million
slash 9	255.128.0.0	8 million
slash 10	255.192.0.0	4 million
slash 11	255.224.0.0	2 million
slash 12	255.240.0.0	1 million
slash 13	255.248.0.0	524,288
slash 14	255.252.0.0	262,144
slash 15	255.254.0.0	131,072
slash 16	255.255.0.0	65,536
slash 17	255.255.128.0	32,768
slash 18	255.255.192.0	16,384
slash 19	255.255.224.0	8192
slash 20	255.255.240.0	4096
slash 21	255.255.248.0	2048
slash 22	255.255.252.0	1024
slash 23	255.255.254.0	512
slash 24	255.255.255.0	256
slash 25	255.255.255.128	128
slash 26	255.255.255.192	64
slash 27	255.255.255.224	32
slash 28	255.255.255.240	16
slash 29	255.255.255.248	8
slash 30	255.255.255.252	4
slash 31	255.255.255.254	2
slash 32	255.255.255.255	1

I hope it's obvious that I included all of those networks just for the sake of completeness, as some of them simply aren't available, like the slash 0, and some just don't make sense, like the slash 31—it only gives you two addresses, which would be immediately required for network number and broadcast address, leaving none behind for you to actually use. The smallest network that the American subgroup of the IANA, ARIN, will allocate to a network is a slash 20, a 4,094-address network.

CIDR is a fact of life if you're trying to get a network nowadays. With the information in this section, you'll more easily be able to understand what an ISP is talking about when it says it can get you a slash 26 network.

What IP *Doesn't* Do: Error Checking

Whether you're on *an* intranet or *the* Internet, it looks like your data gets bounced around quite a bit. How can you prevent it from becoming damaged? Let's look briefly at that, and that'll segue to a short talk on TCP.

An IP packet contains a bit of data called a *checksum header*, which checks whether the header information was damaged on the way from sender to receiver.

Many data communications protocols use checksums that operate like this: I send you some data. You use the checksum to make sure the data wasn't damaged in transit, perhaps by line noise. Once you're satisfied that the data was not damaged, you send me a message that says, "Okay—I got it." If the checksum indicates that it did *not* get to you undamaged, then you send me a message that says, "That data was damaged—please resend it," and I resend it. Such messages are called ACKs and NAKs—positive or negative acknowledgments of data. Protocols that use this check-and-acknowledge approach are said to provide *reliable* service.

But IP does not provide reliable service. If an IP receiver gets a damaged packet, it just discards the packet and says nothing to the receiver. Surprised? I won't keep you in suspense: It's TCP that provides the reliability. The IP header checksum is used to see if a header is valid; if it isn't, then the datagram is discarded.

This underscores IP's job. IP is not built to provide end-to-end guaranteed transmission of data. IP exists mainly for one reason: routing. We'll revisit routing a bit later, when I describe the specifics of how to accomplish IP routing on a Microsoft OS-based machine.

But whose job *is* end-to-end integrity, if not IP's? The answer: its buddy's, TCP.

TCP (Transmission Control Protocol)

I said earlier that IP handled routing and really didn't concern itself that much with whether the message got to its final destination or not. If there are seven IP hops from one point to the next, then each hop is an independent action—there's no coordination, no notion of whether a particular hop is hop number three out of seven. Each IP hop is totally unaware of the others. How, then, could we use IP to provide reliable service?

IP packets are like messages in a bottle. Drop the bottle in the ocean, and you have no guarantee that the message got to whomever you want to receive it. But suppose you hired a "message-in-the-bottle end-to-end manager." Such a person (let's call her Gloria) would take your message, put it in a bottle, and toss it in the ocean. That person would also have a partner on the other side of the ocean (let's call him Gaston), and when Gaston received a message in a bottle from Gloria, Gaston would then pen a short message saying "Gloria, I got your message," put *that* message in a bottle, and drop that bottle into the ocean.

If Gloria didn't get an acknowledgment from Gaston within, say, three months, then she'd drop *another* bottle into the ocean with the original message in it. In data communications terms, we'd say that Gloria "timed out" on the transmission path and was *resending*.

Yeah, I know, this is a somewhat goofy analogy, but understand the main point: We hired Gloria and Gaston to ensure that our inherently unreliable message-in-a-bottle network became reliable. Gloria will keep sending and resending until she gets a response from Gaston. Notice that she doesn't create a whole new transmission medium, like radio or telephone; she merely adds a layer of her own watchfulness to the existing transmission protocol.

Now think of IP as the message in the bottle. TCP, the Transmission Control Protocol, is just the Gloria/Gaston team. TCP provides reliable end-to-end service.

By the way, TCP provides some other services, most noticeably something called *sockets*, which I will discuss in a moment. As TCP has value besides its reliability feature, TCP also has a "cousin" protocol that acts very much like it but does *not* guarantee end-to-end integrity. That protocol is called UDP (User Datagram Protocol).

That's basically the idea behind TCP. Its main job is the orderly transmission of data from one intranet host to another. Its main features include

◆ Handshake
◆ Packet sequencing
◆ Flow control
◆ Error handling

Where IP has no manners—it just shoves data at a computer whether that computer is ready for it or not—TCP makes sure that each side is properly introduced before attempting to transfer. TCP sets up the connection.

Sequencing

As IP does not use a virtual circuit, different data packets may end up arriving at different times and, in fact, in a different order. Imagine a simple intranet transferring four segments of data across a network with multiple possible pathways. The first segment takes the high road, so to speak, and is delayed. The second, third, and fourth do not and so get to the destination more quickly. TCP's job on the receiving side is to then reassemble things in order.

Flow Control

Along with sequencing is flow control. What if 50 segments of data had been sent and they all arrived out of order? The receiver would have to hold them all in memory before sorting them out and writing them to disk. Part of what TCP worries about is *pacing* the data—not sending it to the receiver until the receiver is ready for it.

Error Detection/Correction

And finally, TCP handles error detection and correction, as I've already said. Beyond that, TCP is very efficient in the way that it does error handling. Some protocols acknowledge each and every block, generating a large overhead of blocks. TCP, in contrast, does not do that. It tells the other side, "I am capable of accepting and buffering some number of blocks. Don't expect an acknowledgment until I've gotten that number of blocks. And if a block is received incorrectly, I will not acknowledge it, so if I don't acknowledge as quickly as you expect me to, then just go ahead and resend the block."

Sockets, Ports, and the Winsock Interface

Just about anything that you want to do with the Internet or your company's intranet involves two programs talking to each other. When you browse someone's Web site, you have a program (your Web browser, a *client* program) communicating with their Web server (obviously, a *server* program). Using the File Transfer Protocol (FTP), which I'll discuss later in this chapter, requires that one machine be running a program called an *FTP server* and that another computer be running an *FTP client*. Internet mail requires that a mail client program talk to a mail server program—and those are just a few examples.

Connecting a program in one machine to another program in another machine is kind of like placing a telephone call. The sender must know the phone number of the receiver, and the receiver must be around his or her phone, waiting to pick it up. In the TCP world, a phone number is called a *socket*. A socket is composed of three parts: the IP address of the receiver, which we've already discussed, the receiving program's *port number*, which we *haven't* yet discussed, and whether it's a TCP port or a UDP port—each protocol has its own set.

Suppose the PC on your desk running XP wants to get a file from the FTP site, which is really the PC on *my* desk running Server 2003. Obviously, for this to happen, we have to know each other's IP addresses. But that's not all; after all, in my PC I have a whole bunch of programs running (my network connection, my word processor, my operating system, my personal organizer, the FTP server, and so on). So if TCP says, "Hey, Mark's machine, I want to talk to you," then my machine would reply, "Which *one* of us—the word processor, the e-mail program, or what?" So the TCP/IP world assigns a 16-bit number to each program that wants to send or receive TCP information, a number called the *port* of that program.

The most popular Internet applications have had particular port numbers assigned to them, and those port numbers are known as *well-known ports*. You can see some well-known ports in Table 6.3.

TABLE 6.3: INTERNET PROTOCOLS AND PORT NUMBERS

INTERNET PROTOCOL	PORT NUMBER
FTP	TCP 20/21
Telnet	TCP 23
Simple Mail Transport Protocol	TCP 25
DNS	UDP and TCP 53
Trivial FTP (TFTP)	UDP 69
Hypertext Transfer Protocol (Web)	TCP 80
Kerberos logons	UDP and TCP 88

Continued on next page

TABLE 6.3: INTERNET PROTOCOLS AND PORT NUMBERS *(continued)*

INTERNET PROTOCOL	PORT NUMBER
Post Office Protocol v3 (POP3)	TCP 110
Network News Transfer Protocol (NNTP)	TCP 119
Simple Network Time Protocol (SNTP)	UDP 123
NetBIOS	UDP and TCP 137, UDP 138, TCP 139
IMAP4	TCP 143
SNMP	UDP 161/162
LDAP	TCP 389
Secure HTTP (SSL)	TCP and UDP 443
SMB over sockets (CIFS)	TCP/UDP 445
ISAKMP (key exchange for IPSec)	UDP 500
SQL Server	UDP/TCP 1433

Specific programs may use their own particular ports, as in the case of Active Directory's global catalog server, which uses port 3268. Someone in the Navy has put up a nice page collecting many more ports at www.nswc.navy.mil/ISSEC/Docs/Ref/Networking/new_ports.html.

How Ports and Sockets Work

So, for instance, suppose I've pointed my HTTP client (which you know as a Web browser, like Internet Explorer) to an HTTP server (which you know as a Web server, like a copy of Internet Information Server). Let's also assume that I'm going to visit www.acme.com, that acme.com's Web server is at 123.124.55.67, and that my computer has IP address 200.200.200.10.

My Web browser tries to contact the machine at 123.124.55.67. But just knowing a machine's IP address isn't sufficient; we need also to know the port address of the program that we want to talk to because, for example, this computer might also be a mail server, and I want to surf its Web pages, not send or receive e-mail. My Web browser knows that by convention the Web server lives at port 80. So my Web browser essentially "places a call"—that is, sets up a TCP/IP session—with port 80 at address 123.124.55.67, sometimes written 123.124.55.67:80, with a colon between the IP address and the port number. That combination of an IP address and a port is called a *socket address*.

In order for the Web server computer to chat with my computer, the Web server computer must be *ready* to chat—there's got to be someone at the Web browser "listening" when I "call." That's a lot of what a Web browser program does—it just sits and waits, "listening" on port 80. When the Web browser first starts up, it says, "If anyone calls on port 80, wake me up—I'm willing to take calls on that port." That's called a *passive open* on TCP.

So my Web browser talks to the Web server at the Web server's port 80. But how does the Web server talk back—what port does it use on *my* computer, what port on my computer is now listening for the server's response? Well, port 80 might seem the logical answer, at first—but it can't be. Here's why: suppose I'm sitting at a computer that's *running* a Web server and I fire up Internet Explorer to surf a different Web site. Could that Web site talk back to my computer at port 80? No, because port 80 on my computer is *already* busy, as *my* Web server would be running there.

Instead, the Web server negotiates with my Web browser to pick a port that my system's not using. So the conversation might look like

1. (From my computer to the Web server): "Hi there, anyone home at port 80 on 123.124.55.67?"
2. (From the Web server to my computer): "Sure; how should we talk?"
3. (From my computer to the Web server): "Ummm, how about port 40000?"
4. (From the Web server to my computer): "Great, then, let's set up a connection to 40000."

So my questions to the Web server go to 123.124.55.67:80, and the answers come back on 200.200.200.10:40000. (And yes, I've left a few steps out, like "how did the Web server ask which port to use in the first place," but I'm trying not to turn this into a whole *book* on TCP/IP!) Here's the point that I want to make: Communications to a server employ a well-known port, like 80 on HTTP. In contrast, however, communications back to a client don't use any particular predefined port—the server and client just agree on one on-the-fly.

NOTE *And in case you're wondering, servers can carry on more than one conversation over a given port. If 500 people are all surfing a Web server, then the Web server can keep those conversations separate.*

Routing the Nonroutable, Part II: PAT and NAT

Now that you know about ports, I can tell you how a bit of magic that you'll see a little later works. Server 2003 includes a couple of tools called Internet Connection Sharing (ICS) and port address translation (PAT) that let you share a single routable IP address with any number of computers, even though those computers all bear *non*routable addresses. Let's look at how the simpler one, ICS, works.

INTERNET CONNECTION SHARING OVERVIEW

Suppose you have a bunch of computers in your home, all connected via an Ethernet network. Suppose also that you've got a high-speed Internet connection like a DSL or a cable modem connection. Those kinds of connections usually come with one—and one only—routable IP address, which you give to one of your computers.

But what about the other ones? How can you get all of your Windows 9*x*, NT 4, and Server 2003 boxes in the house *all* on the Internet at the same time? After all, only one computer can use a given IP address, so trying to put that one routable IP address on every computer in the house not only won't help, it'll hurt—the Internet connection will work fine as long as only one computer's using the DSL or cable modem vendor-supplied address, but put it on a second system and *neither* system will be able to get to the Internet. Instead, here's how to put everyone in the house on the Internet.

First, connect all of the computers to your home Ethernet. Do not give those computers an IP address; instead, tell their TCP/IP software to obtain IP addresses "automatically" (and I promise, we'll do that soon; I'm just explaining the outline of the method right now). Next, give the routable IP address (let's make it 200.200.200.10 for the sake of example) to a Server 2003 computer. Finally, turn on a Server 2003 feature called Internet Connection Sharing—there are specifics on this at the end of this chapter. Then reboot all of the computers except for the one with the routable IP address. Result: once rebooted, all of those computers will be able to access Internet resources.

HOW ICS SHARES A ROUTABLE ADDRESS WITH NONROUTABLE MACHINES

What happened? Well, first of all, the routing computer—the one running ICS—distributes unique IP addresses to all of your other computers. But *what* IP addresses? Well, it's not kosher to start making up routable IP addresses and handing them out unless you actually *own* those addresses, so the routing computer hands out "safe" IP addresses from one of the nonroutable ranges specified in RFC 1918, the range from 192.168.0.2 through 192.168.0.254, and gives itself an extra IP address, 192.168.0.1. So far, so good—the computers in your home network can all "see" each other, even the routing computer.

Here's where the magic happens. Suppose one of your nonroutable computers (let's give it address 192.168.0.10) wants to surf my Web site at 206.246.253.200. That nonroutable computer says to the routing computer, the only one with a routable, acceptable-on-the-Internet address, "Please connect me to the Web server at 206.246.253.200." Now, clearly, the 192.168.0.10 system can't directly talk to my Web server, as 192.168.0.10 is a nonroutable address and no router will pass any 192.168.*y.z* traffic over the Internet. But the routable computer can employ its 200.200.200.10 address to establish that connection to the Web server at 206.246.253.200. The routable computer at 200.200.200.10 acts as a kind of "relay" to forward the nonroutable computer's request to my Web server, passing messages back and forth. My Web server hasn't a clue that the *real* client is sitting on a nonroutable address; as far as my Web server's concerned, it's talking to 200.200.200.10.

But the 200.200.200.10 computer running ICS can go further than that, as it can simultaneously relay requests for every single computer in your nonroutable network. So could you have 15 machines in your nonroutable network all talking to my Web site at the same time? Sure. But my Web site would think that the machine at 200.200.200.10 was holding 15 simultaneous conversations with it—peculiar, perhaps, but not unallowable. But what if each of the 15 people sitting at the 15 computers were surfing *different* pages on my Web site—how would the routing computer on your network keep it all straight? With ports. It could be that the session between the first nonroutable computer and my Web site took place on 200.200.200.10:40000, the second on 200.200.200.10:40001, and so on. The routing computer is then using the incoming port number to figure out which of its local, nonroutable computers made a particular request, so that it can *translate* that incoming port into a nonroutable address, so to speak. That's why the process is called *port address translation* or PAT. ICS is a piece of PAT routing software built into Server 2003.

PAT IS ALMOST A FIREWALL, BUT ONLY *ALMOST*

PAT is, then, a pretty neat bit of routing magic. Say your ISP only gives you one routable IP address—here's a way to stretch it across dozens of machines. Even better, PAT offers a simple, basic kind of anti-hacker security. Consider that your nonroutable computers can access e-mail, Web, and other services on the public Internet, but still remain basically invisible in the sense that your internal computers can *initiate* a conversation with a server on the Internet, but no computer on the public Internet can initiate a conversation with one of your nonroutable computers. It's harder, then, for jerks—oops, I mean hackers—to attack your internal machines.

Harder, yes, but not impossible, I should point out. Once one of your internal, nonroutable systems establishes contact with a computer on the public Internet through your PAT routing computer, then there's obviously a channel now open from that computer on the public Internet and your nonroutable computer. While I'm not a security expert by any means, I'm told by people that I trust that this "open port," as they call it, can be a method for "e-bottom feeders" to potentially attack your system. And no matter what sort of security you use, remember that once you've downloaded a program to one of your internal computers and run that program, then the program can have malicious intent. Remember also that many kinds of files can contain programs nowadays: Web pages can contain VBScript macros, Word files can contain programs, and you might end up downloading and installing a kind of program called an ActiveX object simply by viewing a Web page. (That's why I keep my security settings fairly paranoid in Word, Outlook, and Internet Explorer, and I recommend that you do also—look in Tools/Macro/Security in Word and Outlook, or Tools/Internet Options/Security in Internet Explorer.)

And by the way, I've cast my PAT example as a home-based one, but don't think that only homes and small businesses can use it. Most large organizations only assign their routable addresses to a small number of systems, and put nonroutable addresses on the vast majority of their machines. Then they use PAT or PAT-like routers to let their employees access the Internet.

NAT VERSUS PAT

PAT's a nice piece of routing software built into Server 2003 (and in fact every Microsoft OS shipped since 1998), but not the only one. ICS is nice, but it's pretty inflexible. It's supplemented by a more powerful bit of routing software called network address translation (NAT). In fact, it's far more likely that you've heard of NAT than PAT, because many PAT routers are mistakenly called NAT routers. (And understand that while a purist might quibble about whether a router is a PAT or NAT router, the fact is that the definitions have blurred so much in popular usage that in actual fact you'll probably *only* hear the phrase "NAT" rather than "PAT." As you'll see later in this chapter, Server 2003 contains software that will do both NAT and PAT, but it calls the capability "NAT routing." So after this section, I'll surrender and just refer to NAT rather than PAT.)

A simple NAT router lets you connect a particular routable IP address with a particular nonroutable IP address. Thus, for example, if you had a Web server on a machine with the nonroutable address 10.10.10.50, then the outside world couldn't see or access that Web server. But suppose you had a few dozen routable addresses, including (for example) 100.50.40.10? You could put those addresses on a NAT router and tell the NAT router for example, "connect the routable 100.50.40.10 address with the nonroutable 10.10.10.50 address." When someone on the public Internet tried to surf the Web site at 100.50.40.7, then, the NAT router would transparently redirect all of that traffic to the system at the nonroutable address 10.10.10.50.

There's yet another permutation of port address translation that you'll see, built into Server 2003's NAT routing software. In NAT, as you saw, the router completely assigned an entire routable IP address to a machine with a nonroutable IP address. But Server 2003 also lets you assign a particular port on one system to a particular port on another system. So, for example, I could tell a Server 2003 system acting as a router, "Whenever traffic comes in for 100.50.40.7 on port 80, send it to the nonroutable 10.10.10.50 system, on port 5000." (I'm not saying you would *want* to do it, I'm just explaining that it's possible.) So, in that case, you would set up the Web server on the 10.10.10.50 system and reconfigure the Web server so that it didn't use the standard port 80, but rather port 5000—and yes, IIS lets you do that, as you'll see in Chapter 17.

Winsock Sockets

Before moving on to the issue of Internet names (rather than all this IP address stuff that we've been working with), let me define a term that you'll hear in the Microsoft TCP/IP networking business: *winsock* or "windows sockets." The value of sockets is that they provide a uniform way to write programs that exploit the underlying Internet communications structure. If, for example, I want to write a networked version of the game Battleship, then I might want to be able to quickly turn out versions for Windows, OS/2, the Mac, and Unix machines. But maybe I don't know much about communications, and don't *want* to know much. (I'm probably supposed to note here that Battleship is a registered trademark of Milton Bradley or someone like that; consider it done.) I could just sit down with my C compiler and bang out a Battleship that runs on Unix machines. Just a few code changes, and *presto!* I have my PC version.

But the PC market requires some customization, and so a particular version of the sockets interface, called Winsock, was born. It's essentially the sockets interface but modified a bit to work better in a PC environment.

The benefit of Winsock is that all vendors of TCP/IP software support an identical Winsock programming interface (well, identical in theory, anyway) and so TCP/IP-based programs should run as well atop FTP software's TCP/IP stack as they would atop the TCP/IP stack that ships with NT and 2000, as well as Windows for Workgroups, Windows 9*x*, and Windows Me. That's why you can plop your Netscape Web browser on just about any PC with TCP/IP and it should work without any trouble.

Telling Software to Use TCP/IP Over Other Protocols: Network Binding

This discussion has covered a particular set of network protocols—TCP/IP—so far, and TCP/IP is a pretty flexible protocol. You can use it for just about anything that you'd need a network protocol for, and in fact many networks use only TCP/IP. But your network might include other protocols running alongside TCP/IP on your Ethernet cables; in particular, it's not unusual to see Microsoft networks running IPX/SPX or NetBEUI in addition to TCP/IP. You might be running IPX/SPX because you've also got some Novell servers around, or you might be running NetBEUI because you still have some older Microsoft operating systems, either on clients or workstations. (Although you *really* have to work to get NetBEUI on a modern Microsoft operating system.) If either of those things are true, then you might have to run NetBEUI and/or IPX/SPX on your Windows Server 2003 systems as well. And that leads me to discuss network binding.

Suppose I have a workstation running TCP/IP, IPX/SPX, and NetBEUI protocols, trying to talk to a file server that runs only TCP/IP. The workstation and server employ several pieces of software to set up the workstation-to-file-server file sharing connection:

◆ There's a piece of software on the workstation that knows how to ask the file server for data; technically, we could call it the *file-server-client software*, the client part of the file sharing client-server software. Microsoft calls it the Client for Microsoft Networks.

◆ The client software gets to the network by choosing a protocol to use to communicate over the wire to the server. If the workstation runs TCP/IP, IPX/SPX, and NetBEUI, then the Client for Microsoft Networks doesn't know which to choose, so it uses them all, duplicating its request to the file server over all three.

◆ The protocols run over the network cables to the server. As we've seen, the server doesn't respond to all of them, as it's not running software to make it aware of IPX/SPX or NetBEUI. But it *does* understand TCP/IP.

◆ The server-side piece of the file sharing software connects to the one protocol running on the server, TCP/IP.

What's wrong with this? Nothing really, except that it's a bit inefficient. The workstation essentially makes the "server, please talk to me" request over one protocol, then another, and then, if there's no response, finally the third protocol. So the order in which a piece of software tries different protocols can speed up or slow down a computer's performance. You could probably pretty easily imagine some not-so-great scenarios here; for instance, suppose this three-protocol-using workstation lived in an environment with 20 file servers, and 19 of the 20 file servers used TCP/IP exclusively. Suppose also that this workstation always first tried IPX/SPX, then NetBEUI, and then TCP/IP whenever it wanted to contact a file server. Clearly that'd run terribly.

The word for the order in which a given piece of network client or server software—like the Client for Microsoft Networks—taps a protocol is called the *network binding order*. You can control that from a Windows Server 2003 system like this.

1. Right-click My Network Places.

2. Choose Properties.

3. You'll see a Network Connections window that contains icons that represent your different ways of connecting to a network, whether a network adapter or a dial-up connection.

4. Do *not* right-click Local Area Connection—surprised you, eh? Instead, look at the Network and Dial-Up Connections window, and notice that it's got an unusual item on its window menu—Advanced. Click Advanced and then Advanced Settings; *that* will raise another window, labeled Advanced Settings, with Adapters and Settings and Provider Order tabs. Click Adapters and Settings.

5. The resulting property page has an upper and lower part. The upper lets you choose which adapter you want to arrange bindings for; click it and you will see the applications that communicate through that adapter.

In the lower part of the dialog box, you'll see the various network applications running on your computer. For example, most systems run Client for Microsoft Networks (the file sharing client software) and File and Printer Sharing for Microsoft Networks (the server piece of the file sharing software). Under each application, you'll see the protocols that use it. Up- and down-arrow buttons then let you choose the order of the protocols to try—the *binding order* for that application. In my example where you've got a client computer in a network that incorporates 20 file servers, 19 of which use only TCP/IP, then, it'd make sense to adjust the bindings for the Client for Microsoft Networks to use TCP/IP before IPX/SPX or NetBEUI.

Internet Host Names

Thus far, I've referred to a lot of numbers; hooking up to my Web server, then, seems to require that you point your Web browser to IP address 206.246.253.200, TCP port number 80, which is written "206.246.253.200:80" in socket terminology.

Of course, you don't actually do that. When you send e-mail to your friends, you don't send it to 199.45.23.17; you send it to something like robbie@somefirm.com. What's IP got to do with it?

IP addresses are useful because they're precise and because they're easy to subnet. But they're tough to remember, and people generally prefer more English-sounding names. So TCP/IP allows us to group one or more TCP/IP networks into groups called *domains*, groups that will share a common name like microsoft.com, senate.gov, army.mil, or mit.edu.

NOTE   *Internet naming, and in particular the Domain Name System (DNS), is a big topic—in fact, it'll take up the majority of the next chapter; this section is just a brief summary. Stay tuned to Chapter 7 for the truly ugly (but necessary) details.*

Machines within a domain will have names that include the domain name; for example, within my mmco.com domain I have machines named earth.mmco.com, narn.mmco.com, minbar.mmco.com, zhahadum.mmco.com, and vorlon.mmco.com. Those specific machine names are called *host names*.

How does TCP/IP connect the English names—the *host* names—to the IP addresses? And how can I sit at my PC in mmco.com and get the information I need to be able to find another host called archie.au when archie's all the way on the other side of the world in Australia?

Simple—with HOSTS, DNS, and (if you have a network that does not yet use Active Directory) WINS, which is covered in the next chapter. The process of converting a name to its corresponding IP address is called *name resolution*. Again, how does it work? Read on.

Simple Naming Systems (HOSTS)

When you set up your subnet, you don't want to explicitly use IP addresses every time you want to run some TCP/IP utility and hook up with another computer in your subnet. So, instead, you create a file called HOSTS that looks like this:

```
199.34.57.50   keydata.mmco.com
199.34.57.129  serverted.mmco.com
```

This is just a simple ASCII text file. Each host goes on one line, and the line starts off with the host's IP address. Enter at least one space and the host's English name. Do this for each host. You can even give multiple names in the HOSTS file:

```
199.34.57.50   keydata.mmco.com markspc
199.34.57.129  serverted.mmco.com serverpc bigsv
```

You can even add comments, with the octothorp (#):

```
199.34.57.50   keydata.mmco.com markspc #The Big Dog's machine
199.34.57.129  serverted.mmco.com serverpc bigsv
```

Ah, but now comes the really rotten part.

You have to put one of these HOSTS files on *every single workstation*. That means that every single time you change anyone's HOSTS file, you have to go around and change *everybody's* HOSTS file. Every workstation must contain a copy of this file, which is basically a telephone directory of every machine in your subnet. It's a pain, yes, but it's simple. If you're thinking, "Why can't I just put a central HOSTS file on a server and do all my administration with *that* file?"—what you're really asking for is a *name server*, and I'll show you two of them, the Domain Name System (DNS) and the Windows Internet Name Service (WINS), in this chapter.

You must place the HOSTS file in `\WINDOWS\SYSTEM32\DRIVERS\ETC` on an NT or Server 2003 system, in the `Windows` directory on a Windows for Workgroups or Windows 9*x* machine, and wherever the network software is installed on other kinds of machines (DOS or OS/2).

HOSTS is reread every time your system does a name resolution; you needn't reboot to see a change in HOSTS take effect.

Domain Name System (DNS)

HOSTS is a pain, but it's a necessary pain if you want to communicate within your subnet. How does IP find a name outside of your subnet or outside of your domain?

Suppose someone at exxon.com wanted to send a file to a machine at minasi.com. Surely the exxon.com HOSTS files don't contain the IP address of my company, and vice versa?

Well, back when the Internet was small, HOSTS was sufficient—the exxon.com and minasi.com machines *would* have found each other in HOSTS back in 1980. The few dozen people on the early Internet just all used the same small HOSTS file. With the Internet's machine population in the hundreds of millions, however, that's just not practical; we needed something better.

The Internet community came up with an answer in 1984: Distribute the responsibility for names. That's done by the Domain Name System (DNS). There is a central naming clearinghouse for *the* Internet, the Internet Corporation for Assigned Names and Numbers (ICANN), which you met earlier in this chapter. (Obviously, if you're only running a private intranet that's not connected to the public Internet, then *you* perform the function of name manager.) ICANN is the overall boss of DNS naming, but it delegates particular domains to particular *name registrars*, as for example when it delegates keeping track of all of the .com domains to VeriSign's Network Solutions subsidiary.

Instead of trying to keep track of the name and IP address of every single machine in the Internet, ICANN and its delegated registrars require that every Internet domain have at least two machines (although some now only require one) running that contain a database of that domain's machines. These machines are called *DNS servers*.

ICANN then needs only to know the IP address of the domain's DNS servers, and when a request for a name resolution comes to ICANN's servers, ICANN's servers just refer the questioner to the domain in question's local DNS machines. (We'll see how this works in greater detail in the next chapter.)

Thus, if you wanted to visit my Web site at www.minasi.com, you'd start up your Web browser and point it at `www.minasi.com`. Before your browser could show you anything, however, it would need to *find* the machine named www.minasi.com. So it would fire off a DNS query, "What's the IP address of www.minasi.com?" to its local DNS server. The local DNS server probably wouldn't know, and so it would ask ICANN's DNS servers. ICANN's servers would know that the IP address for minasi.com's DNS server is 206.246.253.111 and would tell your local DNS server that it could find www.minasi.com's IP address by asking the question of the 206.246.253.111 machine. So your local DNS server would then re-ask the question, this time of my local DNS server, and would then get the answer "206.246.253.200." And most DNS servers remember past queries for a few hours or perhaps a day, so if you revisited my Web site the same day, when your Web browser asked your local DNS server for the IP address of www.minasi.com, your local DNS server would respond, "206.246.253.200," without hesitation.

You've no doubt noticed that many Internet domains end with `.com`, but there are other endings as well. Back in the pre-ICANN days, the InterNIC (ICANN's predecessor) started off with six initial naming domains: EDU was for educational institutions, NET was for network providers, COM for commercial users, MIL was for military users (remember who built this?), ORG was for organizations, and GOV was for civilian government. For example, there is a domain on the Internet called whitehouse.gov; you can send Internet e-mail to the President that way, at `president@whitehouse.gov`. There are more root domains these days, such as `.int`, `.museum`, `.name`, and a long list of two-letter codes for countries such as `.fi` for sites in Finland, `.uk` for sites in the United Kingdom, and so on.

What kind of computer do you need to run a DNS server? Just about any kind—there's DNS server software for IBM mainframes, DEC Vaxes, Unix and Linux, and of course, Server 2003—in fact, a DNS server module not only ships with Server 2003, you can't even run an Active Directory without a DNS server. You'll see how to set up a DNS server in the next chapter.

E-Mail Names: A Note

If you've previously messed around with e-mail under TCP/IP, then you may be wondering something about these addresses. After all, you don't send mail to minasi.com, you'd send it to a name like `help@minasi.com`. `help@minasi.com` is an e-mail address. The way it works is this: A group of users in a TCP/IP domain decide to implement mail.

In order to receive mail, a machine must be up and running, ready to accept mail from the outside world (that is, some other subnet or domain). Now, mail can arrive at any time of day, so this machine must be up and running all of the time. That seems to indicate that it would be a dumb idea to get mail delivered straight to your desktop. So, instead, TCP mail dedicates a machine to the mail router task of receiving mail from the outside world, holding that mail until you want to read it, taking mail that you want to send somewhere else, and routing that mail to some other mail router. The name of the most common TCP/IP mail router program is *sendmail*. The name of the protocol used most commonly for routing e-mail on the Internet, by the way, is the Simple Mail Transfer Protocol (SMTP). Once e-mail is sitting on your local mail server, you then retrieve it via another mail protocol, the Post Office Protocol (POP3).

Windows Server 2003 can act as both POP3 and SMTP server, so if you're connected to the Internet 24/7, then your Server 2003 machine could be your e-mail server. Or you might be running Microsoft's Exchange Server, that is also a POP3/SMTP server. Or you might run any of dozens of different programs that could make a Linux, Unix, Novell, or NT/2000/Server 2003 into a POP3/SMTP server. You can see how mail works in Figure 6.7.

FIGURE 6.7

The interrelation of host names, e-mail names, and the Internet

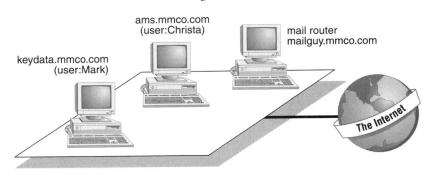

In this small domain, we've got two users: Mark and Christa. Mark works on keydata.mmco.com, and Christa works on ams.mmco.com. Now, suppose Christa wants to send some mail to her friend Corky, executive director for Surfers of America; Corky's address is `corky@surferdudes.org`. She fires up a program on her workstation, which is called a *mail client*. The mail client allows her to create and send new messages as well as receive incoming messages. She sends the message and closes her mail client. Notice that her mail client software doesn't do routing—it just lets her create, send, and receive messages.

The mail client has been configured to send messages to an SMTP server, which is running in this subnet on mailguy.mmco.com. mailguy is kind of the post office (in Internet lingo, a *mail router*) for this group of users. The SMTP server on mailguy.mmco.com stores the message, and it then sends the message off to the machine with the DNS name surferdudes.org, trusting IP to route the message correctly to surferdudes. Hmmm…there's no one machine named surferdudes.org; where should the mail go? As you'll learn in the next chapter, a DNS administrator can advertise that e-mail should go to a particular machine. Thus, surferdudes.org might have a machine named po.surferdudes.org; when mailguy.mmco.com tries to send the mail to corky, mailguy first asks DNS, "What machine is supposed to get mail for surferdudes?" and DNS replies, "po.surferdudes.org."

Additionally, the SMTP server knows the names Christa and Mark. It is the workstation that is the interface to the outside world vis-à-vis mail. Note, by the way, that *DNS* has no idea who Mark or Christa is; DNS is concerned with *host* names, not *e-mail* names. It's DNS that worries about how to find mailguy.mmco.com.

A bit later, Corky gets the message and sends a reply to Christa. The reply does *not* go to Christa's machine ams.mmco.com; instead, it goes to mailguy.mmco.com because Corky sent mail to `christa@mmco.com`. The mail system sends the messages to mmco.com, but what machine has the address mmco.com? Simple: DNS directs it to send mail for mmco.com to mailguy.mmco.com.

Eventually, Christa starts up the mail client program once again. The mail program uses POP3 to send a query to the local mail router mailguy.mmco.com, saying, "Any new mail for Christa?" There *is* mail, and Christa reads it.

Attaching to an Internet

So far, I've talked quite a bit about how an internet works and what kinds of things there are that you can do with an internet. But I haven't told you enough yet to actually get *on* an internet, whether it's your company's private intranet or *the* Internet.

- ◆ You can connect to a multiuser system and appear to the Internet as a dumb terminal. This doesn't happen much any more, so it's unlikely that you'll do this.

- ◆ You can connect to an Internet provider via a serial port and a protocol called Point-to-Point Protocol (PPP) and appear to the Internet as a host. This is what you're doing when you dial up with a modem to an Internet service provider (ISP) such as AOL.

- ◆ You can connect to an Internet provider via either a modified cable television network ("cable modem") or via modified phone lines ("digital subscriber line" or DSL).

- ◆ You can be part of a local area network that is an Internet subnet and then load TCP/IP software on your system and appear to the Internet as a host. This is probably how most people get on the Internet—either when the computer on your desk connects to the Internet via your company's network, or if you connect at home via a cable modem or DSL.

Each of these options has pros and cons, as you'll see. The general rule is that in order to access the Internet, all you basically have to do is to connect up to a computer that is already on the Internet.

The essence of any internet is in *packet switching*, a kind of network game of hot potato whereby computers act communally to transfer each other's data around. Packet switching is what makes it possible to add subnetworks on-the-fly.

Dumb Terminal Connection

This was once a common way to attach to the Internet. You'd dial up to a multiuser system of some kind—usually a Unix box of some stripe—and do simple terminal emulation. You'd then have a character-based session with typed commands only—no mouse, no graphics. Very macho, but not as much fun as surfing with a graphical Web browser. On the other hand, the distant multiuser machine did all the heavy lifting, computing-wise.

Unfortunately, this terminal access approach was kind of limited. Suppose, for example, that I live in Virginia (which is true) and I connect to the Internet via a host in Maine (which is not true). From the Internet's point of view, I'm not in an office in Virginia; instead, I'm wherever the host that I'm connected to is. I work in Virginia, but if I were dialing a host in Maine, then from the Internet's point of view I'd be in Maine. Any requests that I make for file transfers, for example, wouldn't go to Virginia—they'd go to my host in Maine.

Now, that can be a bit of a hassle. Say I'm at my Virginia location logged on to the Internet via the Maine host. I get onto Microsoft's FTP site—I'll cover FTP in Chapter 17, but basically FTP is just a means to provide a library of files to the outside world—and I grab a few files, perhaps an updated video driver. The FTP program says, "I got the file," but the file is now on the host in Maine. That means that I'm only half done, as I now have to run some other kind of file transfer program to move the file from the host in Maine to my computer in Virginia.

PPP Serial Connection

If you've got one of those $10/month or $20/month dial-up Internet accounts, then you fit in this category. Instead of connecting to the Internet with an Ethernet card, you connect with a serial port connected to a modem, which in turn is connected to the ISP with phone lines.

To do this you will need software to support a protocol called the Point to Point Protocol or PPP. (Once upon a time PPP had a sibling protocol named the Serial Line Interface Protocol, or SLIP, but I've not seen anyone use it since 1997.) But you needn't look very far for PPP software—it's built into every version of Windows and NT since 1995. When setting up 2003 systems to dial up to an ISP, you're using PPP by default.

Nor is PPP only for use in dialing up to ISPs. Server 2003's Routing and Remote Access Server (RRAS) supports PPP, so if you dial into your company's servers, you do that with PPP.

Cable Modem and DSL Connections

Cable modem and DSL are a sort of halfway step between the previous connection type, simple dial-up, and the next type, direct network connection. Where dial-up is pure WAN connection and networks are pure LAN connection, cable modem and DSL are half and half in that they employ devices called "cable modems" and "DSL modems" that communicate on one side to a wide area network—the cable company's television signal network or the phone network in the case of DSL—and on the other side to your local area network.

Cable modems connect to cable networks using the same kind of "F" type connector that you'd use to connect your TV to a cable antenna. Then they connect to your computer or your local area network with an RJ-45 connector using Ethernet signals. To connect just one PC to a cable modem, then, you would put an Ethernet card in the computer and plug a standard Cat5-type patch cable between the cable modem and the Ethernet card. To connect an entire home or small office network, you'd hook the cable modem's RJ-45 port to an Internet sharing device like the roughly $200 devices you can find from DLink, Linksys and others, or you could put a second NIC in your PC and then use the PC as an Internet sharing device—you'll see how at the end of the chapter. Many cable modems also offer USB connections, although I strongly recommend against using them because of driver problems. If you connect to your cable modem using an Ethernet card then the only drivers that your computer needs are the drivers for the Ethernet card, and those are usually pretty reliable. But connecting to the Internet via the USB connector on the cable modem requires a USB driver for the cable modem, and I've seen a number of cases where cable modem drivers were flaky.

DSL "modems"—I hate the term because they are by no means modems, but are instead something called a control service unit/data service unit (CSU/DSU)—typically have a standard familiar telephone-type RJ-13 connector that you use to connect them to a phone line in your house—one that's been specially tuned by the DSL provider—and then an RJ-45 jack that you use to make an Ethernet connection to a computer or a group of computers, in much the same way as you would with a cable modem. Some DSL modems have USB connections as well—my advice about cable modem USB connections also applies here.

LAN Connection

The most common way to connect to an internet is simply by being a LAN workstation on a TCP/IP-using network. Again, this needn't be *the* Internet—almost any LAN can use the TCP/IP protocol suite. This is the connection that most Server 2003 servers will use to provide TCP/IP services.

Terminal Connections versus Other Connections

Before moving on to the next topic, I'd like to return to the difference between a terminal connection and a PPP or LAN connection. In Figure 6.8, you see three PCs on an Ethernet attached to two minicomputers, which in turn serve four dumb terminals.

The minicomputer-to-minicomputer link might be SLIP or PPP, or then again they might be LANed together. Notice that only the *computers* in this scenario have Internet Protocol (IP) addresses. Whenever you send mail to one of the people on the PCs at the top of the picture, it goes to that person's PC. If you were to scrutinize the IP addresses—and most of the time, you will not—you'd see that everyone had the same IP address. In contrast, the people at the *bottom* of the picture get their mail sent to one of the minicomputers, and so in this example, each pair of terminals shares an IP address. If Shelly and George in your office access your company's intranet through terminals connected to the same computer, then a close look at mail from them would show that they have the same IP address. But, if you think about it, you already knew that; if you send mail to `george@mailbox.acme.com` and to `shelly@mailbox.acme.com`, then the machine name to which the mail goes is the same; it's just the usernames that vary.

FIGURE 6.8

When Internet connections involve IP numbers and when they don't

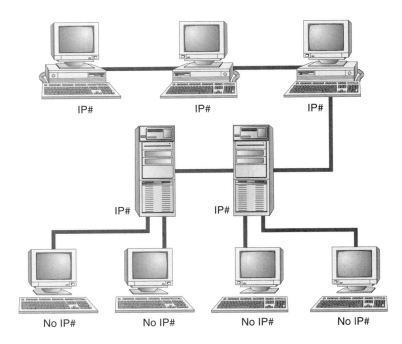

So, in summary: If you want to get onto *the* Internet from a remote location, then your best bet is to sign up with a service that will bill you monthly for connect charges, like Delphi. To attach to a private intranet, you need to dial up to a multiuser computer on that intranet, or you need a SLIP or PPP connection, or you have to be on a workstation on a LAN that's part of that intranet. You then need to talk to your local network guru about getting the software installed on your system that will allow your computer to speak TCP/IP so that it can be part of your intranet.

NOTE   *There is one case where Figure 6.8 isn't complete. If one of the terminals pictured is not simply a dumb ASCII terminal attached to a minicomputer but is instead a Windows Terminal—still a dumb terminal, but one built to work specifically with Server 2003 Terminal Services, Windows Terminal Server 4, or Citrix Metaframe—then that terminal will have its own IP address.*

So Where Do I Get My IP Addresses?

You can't get anywhere in the next section without some IP addresses. How does what you've read so far in this chapter relate to where you should go to get IP addresses?

◆   If you're part of a large corporation, there is almost certainly a group who manages (or doles out, in other words) the IP addresses; if so, go to them for the IP addresses you'll need.

◆   If you're just playing around with this, then you can use any addresses you like, provided you're not connected to the Internet. But it's a good idea to use one of the RFC 1918 ranges in any case—it's a good habit.

◆ If you're with a small firm and it's your job to get the firm on the Internet, then you have two tasks. First, you've got to figure out how you'll be connected. Do you need constant, 24/7 connection to the Internet? You will if you intend to run your own Web or mail servers on your site, and in that case, you'll probably need to get a frame relay connection to your ISP. On the other hand, does your firm just need periodic access to the Internet? Then you may be perfectly happy with the cheaper alternative of some kind of shared dial-on-demand system, either using analog modems or ISDN. Second, how many IP addresses do you need? If you put in a NAT router, by purchasing one from Cisco or some other router vendor, or if you use a Server 2003 machine as a NAT router (you'll read later how to do that), then you'll only need one dedicated IP address from your ISP. On the other hand, if you want all of your firm's computers to have their own routable IP addresses, then you should expect to have to pay your ISP a bit more for them than you would for just one IP address—but having all routable IP addresses keeps things simpler, in my experience.

◆ If you're a home user with an existing Internet connection, such as a dial-up modem, an ISDN dial connection, cable modem, or DSL, and you want to share that connection with other machines on a home network, then just use Internet Connection Sharing, which you'll read about later in this chapter.

The Basics of Setting Up TCP/IP on Server 2003 with Static IP Addresses

Enough talking about TCP/IP internetworking; let's do it, and do it with Server 2003.

Traditionally, one of the burdens of IP administrators has been that they must assign separate IP numbers to each machine, a bit of a bookkeeping hassle. You can adopt this "static" IP address approach, and in fact you will *have* to assign static IP addresses to at least a few of your systems. In actual fact, however, you'll find that assigning a static IP address to every single IP-using computer in your enterprise soon palls, and you'll assign IP addresses to most systems automatically with the Dynamic Host Configuration Protocol, covered in the next chapter.

No network can completely avoid static IP addresses, however, so we'll start out with this older method of putting an IP address on a Server 2003 computer. In the next chapter, we'll take up dynamic IP addressing with DHCP.

Here's the most basic set of TCP/IP configuration tasks, and the first ones we'll tackle:

1. Set the IP address and subnet, default gateway, and DNS server.
2. Prepare the HOSTS file, if you're going to use one.
3. Test the connection with Ping.

Let's take a look at those steps, one by one.

Configuring TCP/IP with a Static IP Address

First, let's apply an IP address to the network interface card on this system. Do that by getting to its property page: click Start/Control Panel/Network Connections and then, when your mouse is on Network Connections, *right*-click the mouse and choose Open. You'll see something like Figure 6.9.

FIGURE 6.9
Network and Dial-
Up Connections

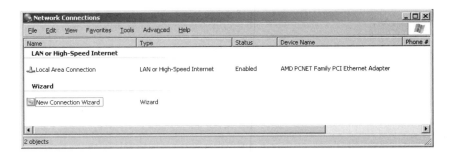

This window describes each NIC in your system and also lists every item in your `Dial-Up` directory—so if you've got your system set up to be able to dial an ISP or perhaps a distant Windows 2000 network, then you'll see a line for each of those DUN directory entries—as well as an icon that can start a wizard to add new Dial-Up entries. This computer hasn't got a modem and therefore has never dialed up anywhere. If this machine had two NICs, then you'd see two Local Area Connection entries.

Bring up the properties for the NIC by right-clicking the NIC (Local Area Connection is the name of the NIC in Figure 6.9) and choosing Properties. That will give you something like Figure 6.10.

FIGURE 6.10
LAN Connection
properties page

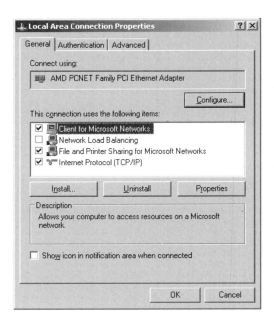

Click Internet Protocol (TCP/IP) and then the Properties button. You'll see a dialog box that looks like Figure 6.11, or anyway it will once we're through with it.

FIGURE 6.11

IP properties page
after modification

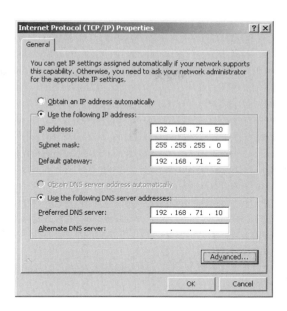

When you first see this dialog box, the Obtain an IP Address Automatically and Obtain DNS Server Address Automatically radio buttons will be selected. You should click the Use the Following IP Address and Use the Following DNS Server Addresses radio buttons. As mentioned earlier, you'll need to know four things to configure this screen: your IP address, the subnet mask, the IP address of your default gateway, and the IP addresses of one or more DNS server. In the case of the computer I'm configuring here, the IP address is 192.168.71.50, the subnet mask is 255.255.255.0, the default gateway is 192.168.71.2, and I've got a DNS server at 192.168.71.10.

TIP   *Do you recognize those IP addresses? They're in one of the RFC 1918 "nonroutable" ranges. It's safe to assume, then, that the router referred to at address 192.168.71.2 is a NAT router. (Notice that it's not the .1 address that you'd expect; that's a side effect of a particular network product that I'm using—remember that I told you that using .1 for the default gateway was a custom, not a rule!) But **please** do not—and I repeat, do **not**—simply type in numbers to make your dialog box match mine. You'll have to plan the layout of your IP-based network. Just making up IP addresses will, I can pretty much guarantee, not work.*

Click OK to clear the IP and LAN properties pages, and you'll have your IP address configured. But does it work? Read on.

Testing Your IP Configuration

There are three basic tools you'll use to verify that TCP/IP's working on your system: IPConfig, Ping, and netsh.

IPCONFIG

First, check your IP configuration by opening a command prompt and typing **ipconfig /all**; you'll then see a screen like Figure 6.12.

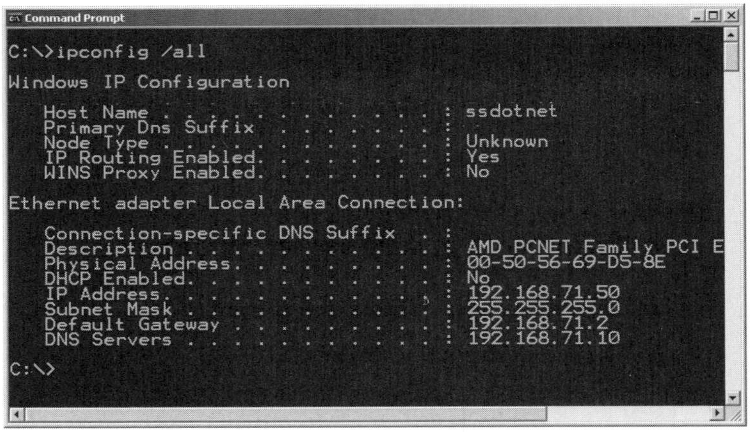

FIGURE 6.12

Output of `ipconfig /all`

```
Command Prompt                                                          _|□|×

C:\>ipconfig /all
Windows IP Configuration

    Host Name . . . . . . . . . . . . : ssdotnet
    Primary Dns Suffix  . . . . . . . :
    Node Type . . . . . . . . . . . . : Unknown
    IP Routing Enabled. . . . . . . . : Yes
    WINS Proxy Enabled. . . . . . . . : No

Ethernet adapter Local Area Connection:

    Connection-specific DNS Suffix  . :
    Description . . . . . . . . . . . : AMD PCNET Family PCI E
    Physical Address. . . . . . . . . : 00-50-56-69-D5-8E
    DHCP Enabled. . . . . . . . . . . : No
    IP Address. . . . . . . . . . . . : 192.168.71.50
    Subnet Mask . . . . . . . . . . . : 255.255.255.0
    Default Gateway . . . . . . . . . : 192.168.71.2
    DNS Servers . . . . . . . . . . . : 192.168.71.10

C:\>
```

`ipconfig /all` should be your first step when checking a TCP/IP installation or when trouble-shooting one. This particular IPConfig output starts out with some general information about this machine and then displays specific information about the Ethernet adapter. It's laid out like this because, in some cases, you may have two or more NICs in a system, and each NIC will have an IP address. Additionally, you may have a modem on your system and may be connected to the Internet via a dial-up connection. In that case, you'd again have more than one IP address—your Ethernet card would have an IP address (the one you just assigned it if you were following along with the previous text), and your modem would have an IP address that your ISP gave it when you dialed up.

In the IPConfig output, ssdotnet is the machine's name.

WARNING *In general, you should avoid underscores in your computer names. Microsoft's old-style NetBIOS-based networking doesn't mind it, but the Internet document on legal Internet names, RFC 1123, doesn't permit underscores. According to RFC 1123 in its "assumptions" section, each piece of an Internet name can be no more than 24 characters long—that is, each piece between the periods—and the only legal characters are a–z, 0–9, and the hyphen/minus sign. In fact, the earliest 32-bit Microsoft TCP/IP software, the code that shipped with Windows for Workgroups 3.11, would simply refuse to work on a machine with an underscore in its name. That's not true anymore, and in fact, the Active Directory uses a fair number of underscored names, but that's acceptable, as AD communications will mainly just go on amongst computers running Microsoft software. But avoid underscores in workstation names as it may potentially cause trouble when trying to use resources on the Internet, which may be running on computers that aren't running Microsoft software.*

Primary DNS Suffix is the end of the DNS name; if this computer had a full DNS name like ssdotnet.bigfirm.biz, then the primary DNS suffix would be "bigfirm.biz." (It *doesn't* have one because I've not told you how to configure one yet.) Node Type answers the question, "How does the system convert an old-style NetBIOS name like \\SNOOPY into an IP address?" That's a long and complicated story, and we'll take it up in the next chapter. IP Routing Enabled asks whether this computer is acting as an IP router. As you saw in the example in the beginning of the chapter with machines A through H, you've got to have two IP connections to do that, so this clearly isn't a potential router—I have no idea why 2003 decided to enable IP routing. I will show you before the end of the chapter, however, how to make a Server 2003 machine into an IP router. I'll explain WINS Proxy Enabled in the next chapter.

Looking at the specific information under Ethernet Adapter Local Area Connection, the first entry is Connection-Specific DNS Suffix. This refers not to a Server 2003 domain but to an Internet domain name, such as minasi.com, microsoft.com, or whitehouse.gov. Back in the NT 4 and earlier days, NT's TCP/IP software would only let you put a machine in just one Internet domain. That wasn't a big deal for most of us, but some people wanted their systems to be able to seem to be members of several domains, to have a sort of multiple citizenship in two or more domains. Such a machine might have a NIC in it that was connected to bigfirm.biz's network, and it might have another NIC in it connected to minasi.com's network. If the machine's name were tadpole, then it might want to be able to be recognized both as tadpole.acme.com and tadpole.apex.com. Now, when configuring tadpole under NT 4, you would have had to choose whether tadpole was in acme.com or apex.com—you couldn't choose both as you had to choose domain membership for the whole machine. Under Server 2003, however, you can say that one NIC is a member of acme.com, and that the other is a member of apex.com. In my particular case, I really have no need to do that, which is why Connection-Specific DNS Suffix is empty. In fact, I haven't set the Internet domain name for the adapter *or* the entire machine as I'm going to get to that a bit later in this chapter.

Next are an English-like description of the NIC's brand and type and the MAC address of the NIC. DHCP Enabled indicates whether I punched in the IP address directly or let DHCP set the IP address for me. As I set the IP address myself, the value is No. If it were Yes, then—as you'll see in the next chapter—IPConfig would furnish more DHCP-specific information. IPConfig then reports the IP address, subnet mask, and default gateway. Finally, it displays the IP address of the DNS server that I configured.

PING

So all of the settings are correct—but can you reach out to the outside world? TCP/IP has a very handy little tool for finding out whether your TCP/IP software is up and running and whether you have a connection to another point: Ping.

Ping is a program that lets you send a short message to another TCP/IP node, asking, "Are you there?" If it is there, then it says "yes" to the ping, and Ping relays this information back to you. You can see an example of Ping in Figure 6.13; the first line of the screen shows you the syntax, `ping` *ipaddress.*

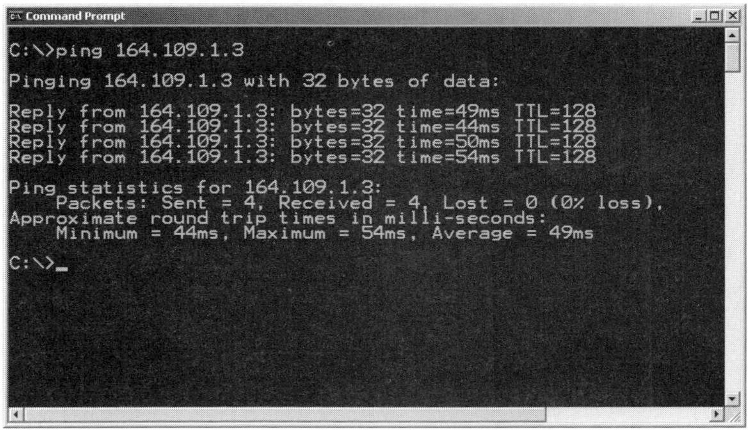

FIGURE 6.13

A sample Ping output

```
Command Prompt                                                    _|□|×|

C:\>ping 164.109.1.3

Pinging 164.109.1.3 with 32 bytes of data:

Reply from 164.109.1.3: bytes=32 time=49ms TTL=128
Reply from 164.109.1.3: bytes=32 time=44ms TTL=128
Reply from 164.109.1.3: bytes=32 time=50ms TTL=128
Reply from 164.109.1.3: bytes=32 time=54ms TTL=128

Ping statistics for 164.109.1.3:
    Packets: Sent = 4, Received = 4, Lost = 0 (0% loss),
Approximate round trip times in milli-seconds:
    Minimum = 44ms, Maximum = 54ms, Average = 49ms

C:\>_
```

In the figure, I pinged the IP address of a server I know of on the Internet. The ping was successful, which is all that matters, and it's a very telling test as the address that I pinged is across the Internet from my system—the fact that I got a response from 164.109.1.3 means that not only is my TCP/IP software working across my segment and across my enterprise, but across the Internet as well.

But when *you're* testing your Internet software, don't use that IP address as there's no sense in flooding the Digital Express guys, the folks who own that machine. Instead, go ahead and ping my router—206.246.253.1 or 68.15.149.65. (I used to use `www.microsoft.com` as my Ping example, but now they've got their system rigged so that it won't respond to pings. I guess they couldn't figure out a way to charge for them.)

Use the approach outlined in the sidebar "How Do I Make Sure That TCP/IP Is Set Up Properly?" to get the most out of Ping.

NETSH DIAG GUI

Windows XP introduced a new diagnostic tool for NICs that 2003 includes; to see it, open up a command prompt and type **netsh diag gui**. You'll see a Help and Support Center screen containing a hyperlink labeled Scan Your System; click it and you'll see a short scanning process, followed by an HTML-like screen reporting on your system. You'll see a Modems and Network Adapters section and under that section a line, Network Adapters, with a plus sign next to it and, if all is well, the word PASSED; click the plus sign and you'll see something like Figure 6.14.

FIGURE 6.14

Sample `netsh gui diag` output

There wasn't room for the whole report, but it's a pretty nice summary of how your NIC and protocol are configured, as well as a few very simple ping tests.

Configuration Continued: Setting Domain Names

Thus far, my computer's name is just plain ssdotnet, which is a mite shorter than most Internet names; one might expect a name more like ssdotnet.bigfirm.biz or the like, a name that looks like *specific machine name.organization name.root,* where *root* is a suffix like *com, gov,* or some country identifier.

I intend for my computer ssdotnet to be part of an Internet domain named bigfirm.biz, so its complete Internet name will be ssdotnet.bigfirm.biz. What that really means, in essence, is that if someone pings ssdotnet.bigfirm.biz, I want the machine to respond. If I decide to run Web server software on it later, then I want people to be able to see whatever content is on it by pointing their Web browsers to `http://ssdotnet.bigfirm.biz` rather than having to use `http://192.168.71.50`. (I know this probably seems obvious to many of you, but stay with me, there's a point coming.)

HOW DO I MAKE SURE THAT TCP/IP IS SET UP PROPERLY?

With these ping tests, you're demonstrating two things: First, that your IP software can get a packet from your computer to the outside world (in other words, that your IP connectivity is functioning), and second, that your connection to a DNS server for name resolution is working.

First, test IP connectivity by pinging specific IP addresses.

In most cases, your connection will work the first time. Start out with an overall "does it work?" test by pinging some distant location on the Internet. As mentioned in the text, you're welcome to ping my router, 206.246.253.1, or 68.15.149.65. If that responds correctly, then you've demonstrated that your IP software can get out to the Internet and back.

If it doesn't work, then try pinging something not so far—your default gateway. (Actually, the next thing to do is to look around back and make sure the network cable is still in place. There's nothing more embarrassing than calling in outside network support only to find that your LAN cable fell out of the back of your computer.) If you can successfully ping the default gateway but not my router, then either your firm's external Internet routers have failed or perhaps your default gateway is configured incorrectly. (Or perhaps my friends at my local telephone company and cable companies have had failures in their systems again—a far-too-often occurrence.) Another tool you might try is tracert, a souped-up Ping that shows you each of the hops that the IP packet had to use to get from your machine to the destination. It's a command-line command: Just type **tracert** followed by an IP address or DNS name. You can see a sample output in the following figure.

Continued on next page

HOW DO I MAKE SURE THAT TCP/IP IS SET UP PROPERLY? *(continued)*

If you can't get to the default gateway, then try pinging another computer on your subnet. If you can get to another machine on your subnet but not the gateway, then perhaps you've got the wrong IP address for the gateway or perhaps the gateway is malfunctioning.

If you can't get to another system on your subnet—and I'm assuming that you've already walked over and checked that the other machine is up and running—then it may be that the IP software on your computer isn't running. Verify that by typing `ping 127.0.0.1`.

127.0.0.1 is the "loopback" address. IP software is designed to *always* report success on a ping to 127.0.0.1, if the IP software is functioning. Recheck that you've installed the TCP/IP software and rebooted after installing.

Once you're certain that IP works, try out DNS. Try pinging a distant location, but this time, don't do it by IP address, do it by name—try pinging `www.whitehouse.gov`, `www.internic.net`, or `www.minasi.com`. If the ping works, great; if not, check that you've got the right address punched in for your DNS server and then check the DNS server.

I would have guessed that unless I found some way to tell ssdotnet that its full name was actually ssdotnet.bigfirm.biz, it wouldn't know to respond when someone pinged it by its full name. But, as it turns out, that's wrong.

If you're sitting at your computer and you type `ping ssdotnet.bigfirm.biz`, then your computer asks your local DNS server what ssdotnet.bigfirm.biz's IP address is. *Then* your computer just pings that IP address, and ssdotnet.bigfirm.biz never even knows *what* name your computer originally called it by. If one of the people running IBM's DNS servers were to decide on a whim to insert an entry into IBM's DNS database that said "iguana.ibm.com has IP address 206.246.253.1," then anyone anywhere pinging iguana.ibm.com would end up pinging my router at that address.

The point is, then, that in order to have my computer named ssdotnet recognized as ssdotnet.bigfirm.biz, I've got to be concerned more with informing bigfirm.biz's DNS server of ssdotnet's IP address than I should be concerned about telling ssdotnet that it's in bigfirm.biz. So how do I ensure that bigfirm.biz's DNS server finds out about ssdotnet? As it turns out, there are three ways to do this. (And even though handling DNS servers is a topic I won't get into until next chapter, it's worth covering this here.)

ADD A STATIC DNS ENTRY

The first way to make the DNS server for the Internet domain bigfirm.biz know that there's a machine named ssdotnet.bigfirm.biz whose IP address is 192.168.71.50 is for an administrator to simply sit down at the DNS server and *tell* it. Depending on what kind of machine the DNS server is running on, the admin will either edit a file or run some kind of management tool. (Again, you'll see how to do that with Server 2003's DNS server in the next chapter.)

JOIN THE ACTIVE DIRECTORY DOMAIN OF THE SAME NAME

The second way to tell the DNS server for the Internet domain bigfirm.biz to include ssdotnet.bigfirm.biz in its list of known hosts is for ssdotnet to join the Active Directory domain *named* bigfirm.biz, assuming that there is one. This is a positive side effect of Active Directory's unifying of AD domain names and Internet (DNS) domain names. If the server named ssdotnet joins an Active Directory domain named bigfirm.biz, then by default the DNS server for the *Internet* domain named bigfirm.biz adds a record in that Internet domain for ssdotnet.bigfirm.biz. (I should point out that this isn't always true when you use a DNS approach called "split-brain DNS" but I'll cover that in the next two chapters.) Joining a domain is fairly easy as long as you have a domain administrator account on bigfirm.biz.

NOTE *I know I've not covered Active Directory yet, but don't sweat these references to AD. For now, all you need to know is that an Active Directory domain is a group of computers that trust each other, and you have to join a domain to be part of that trust. You'll see lots more on the topic in Chapter 8 but, again, that's all you need to know for now.*

While logged onto ssdotnet with an account with local administrative powers, click Start/Control Panel/System. You'll see a properties page with several tabs, one of which is labeled Computer Name. Click that tab and you'll see a screen something like Figure 6.15.

FIGURE 6.15

Computer Name tab

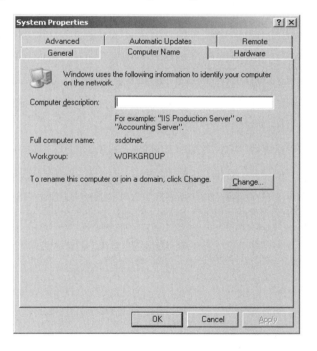

Notice the text that says Workgroup:—that means that this computer is not currently a member of a domain. (If it were a member of a domain, then you'd see Domain: bigfirm.biz or something like that.) Note also that the full computer name is simply ssdotnet, not ssdotnet with anything after it. I'll join ssdotnet to the bigfirm.biz domain, and you'll see that change. I click Change and see something like Figure 6.16.

FIGURE 6.16

The change-domain dialog box

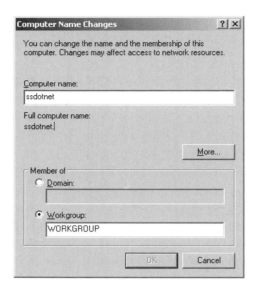

I click the radio button next to Domain and fill in the text field next to Domain with the name of the Active Directory domain, **bigfirm.biz.**

Fill this in, changing the Workgroup radio button to the Domain radio button and filling in the domain name bigfirm.biz. When I click OK, though, the dialog box stops and asks me to demonstrate that I'm an administrator with the ability to create new domain accounts in the bigfirm.biz domain, as you see in Figure 6.17.

FIGURE 6.17

Checking domain administration credentials

I fill in an administrator name and password and click OK. The system runs the hard disk for a while and finally I get the message "Welcome to the bigfirm.biz domain." And—no surprise—I've got to reboot to make it take effect. (Interestingly, the screen in Figure 6.15, when it returns, reflects the name change I've just done, with a yellow "caution" triangle indicating that the changes don't take effect until after I reboot.)

After the reboot, two things happen: First, another look at the Network Identification tab shows that the machine's full computer name is now ssdotnet.bigfirm.biz. Second, a peek in the DNS database for bigfirm.biz shows that there's now an entry for ssdotnet.bigfirm.biz with IP address 192.168.71.50. But how does the DNS server know? Because all Active Directory domains are partially built around a DNS server, and in particular a DNS server that accepts RFC 2136–compliant dynamic updates—that's Geekish for "a DNS server that lets computers register themselves with the DNS server, so administrators don't have to add DNS records by hand for those servers.) When ssdotnet booted up, it saw that it had a DNS suffix of bigfirm.biz, so it located the primary DNS server for bigfirm.biz and added its name to the bigfirm.biz names database. (And I promise, I'll describe the whole DNS registration process in detail in the next chapter—those last few sentences were just a teaser.)

DIRECTLY ENTER THE DOMAIN NAME INTO NETWORK IDENTIFICATION

But wait—this last scenario may not always make sense. Phillip Morris owns Kraft Foods and Miller Brewing Company. From an internal corporate point of view, it may be (I don't know, as I've never worked for any of the three entities) that everyone working for any of the three thinks of themselves as "Phillip Morris employees," and Phillip Morris could be headquartered in one large complex in Richmond, Virginia. So from an internal management and IT point of view, they're one organization.

But to the outside world, the three entities seem to behave like separate firms, particularly on the Internet: A visit to `www.kraft.com` or `www.millerbrewing.com` gives no clue that Phillip Morris owns them. It just might be, then, that Phillip Morris doesn't want to be forced to make its DNS names jive with its Active Directory domain names. And they aren't, with Server 2003. You just have to do a little fiddling in the Computer Name tab.

Now that ssdotnet is a member of the bigfirm.biz Server 2003 domain, let's say for the sake of example that we wanted it to be part of the minasi.com Internet (DNS) domain.

I start renaming ssdotnet DNS-wise by returning to Computer Name: Start/Control Panel/System, then click the Computer Name tab. In that tab, click the Change button. This time, though, then click the More button to see a dialog box like in Figure 6.18.

FIGURE 6.18

DNS Suffix and NetBIOS Computer Name dialog

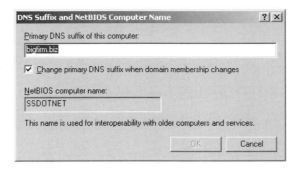

Notice the check box that says Change Primary DNS Suffix When Domain Membership Changes— *that's* the only thing connecting Internet domain names with Active Directory domain names! To let this computer be part of the minasi.com Internet DNS domain but still be part of the bigfirm.biz Active Directory domain, I would just uncheck the box, and in Primary DNS Suffix of This Computer, I just fill in minasi.com. Of course, after such a momentous change, a reboot is required!

Before leaving this topic, I should point out that there is one more side effect to associating a machine with a domain: the domain search order. Bring up TCP/IP properties—again, click Start/ Control Panel/Network Connections and then the object for your network card, probably a name like Local Area Connection. In the resulting dialog box, click the General tab and then the Properties button. That will raise a property page about your NIC's properties. Click the General tab and then click the object labeled Internet Protocol (TCP/IP) and then the Properties button. That will bring up the Internet Protocol (TCP/IP) properties page, as you saw back in Figure 6.11. Now click the Advanced button in the lower-right part of the page, which will bring up yet another properties page, the Advanced TCP/IP Settings page. It will have four tabs:

IP Settings   Lets you add more IP addresses or modify some routing properties to a NIC, as you'll see later.

DNS   Controls how your TCP/IP connection uses DNS, and that's the tab that we'll be looking at next.

WINS   Controls how your TCP/IP connection identifies and communicates with computers that can't use Active Directory—Windows 9x and NT 4, for example.

Options   Lets you restrict which ports your TCP/IP connection can use to communicate.

For now, click the DNS tab and you'll see something like Figure 6.19.

FIGURE 6.19
DNS advanced properties page

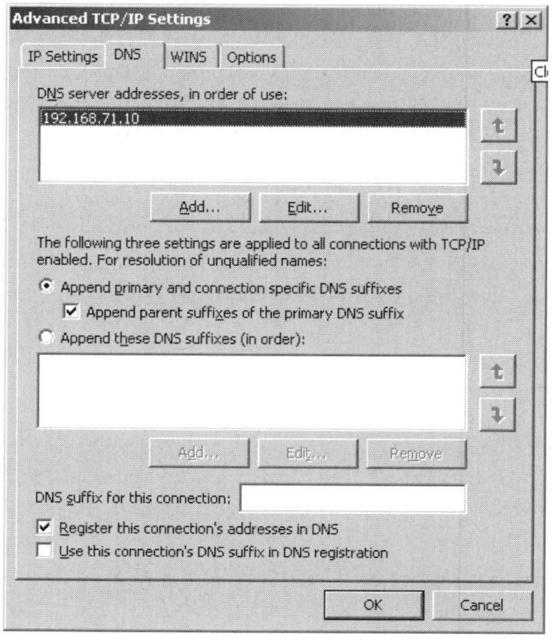

The top field in the screen, DNS Server Addresses in Order of Use, is a bit mislabeled; it really means "these are the DNS servers that IP will use to resolve DNS names." The section in the middle of the dialog box is the part that I'm mainly interested in here, the part that starts at the radio button labeled Append primary and connection specific DNS suffixes through the radio button labeled Append these DNS suffixes (in order).

To understand domain search order, consider the following question. Suppose you're part of the research division of American Rocketry, Ltd., working in its Tidewater regional offices in southeast Virginia. American Rocketry might have divided up their DNS domain, americanrocket.com, into three divisions: research, management, and manufacturing, each with its own child domains: research.americanrocket.com, mgmt.americanrocket.com, and manufacturing.americanrocket.com. Furthermore, the folks running the research.americanrocket.com DNS server might have decided to divide up the DNS management job further with two child domains as there are two research facilities—one in the Tidewater area and one at the Bonneville Salt Flats in Utah—so they've created child domains tidewater.research.americanrocket.com and bonneville.research.americanrocket.com. If you work in Tidewater as a researcher and your computer's name is surveyor, then the complete DNS name of your computer is surveyor.tidewater.research.americanrocket.com. If there's a Web server down the hall that holds all of the content that you use in your intranet named memoryalpha, then to get to it you've got to start up your Web browser and point it at `http://memoryalpha .tidewater.research.americanrocket.com`, which could get a bit tedious.

The value of domain search order is this: Your system will be configured with a computer name of surveyor and a domain name of tidewater.research.americanrocket.com. Now that Server 2003 knows your domain name, you can refer to another system in tidewater.research.americanrocket.com by its computer name rather than having to type in the FQDN; you could point the Web browser to `http://memoryalpha` and the browser would find the Web server without any trouble. Just type in a computer name without any periods in it, and your system will know to add your domain name to the end before querying DNS.

By default, Server 2003 does just that—it adds your domain name to the end before querying DNS, and that's how NT 4 operated as well. But as Server 2003 offers you the ability to put different NICs in different Internet domains, you may have a system with multiple-domain citizenship; that's what Append Primary and Connection Specific DNS Suffixes refers to.

But what if you're working for a firm like my mythical Phillip Morris/Kraft/Miller example, where a workstation might be in tacobell.com, pizzahut.com, pepsi.com, or kfc.com? Then you might want to have your system try a whole *bunch* of DNS queries before giving up. That's why you have the option later in the dialog box to enter domain names to search.

Before leaving this dialog box, note Register This Connection's Addresses in DNS. Remember that the DNS servers associated with an Active Directory enterprise can accept dynamic, RFC 2136 DNS updates so that a workstation or server can insert itself into the DNS name database rather than requiring an administrator to sit down and enter that machine's IP address and name by hand. Server 2003 machines automatically seek out their local DNS server and try to add themselves to that DNS server's list of names and IP addresses. If, for some reason, you do *not* want your workstation to do that, then you can just uncheck the box.

Handling Old Names: Configuring Your Workstation for WINS

While in that advanced properties page for TCP/IP, click the WINS tab and you'll see something like Figure 6.20.

FIGURE 6.20

WINS client
configuration tab

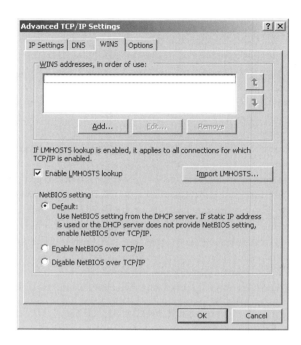

Now, if you're *really* lucky, then you'll never have to look at this screen. But I doubt that you're that lucky.

I'll cover WINS in detail in the next chapter, but for now all you need to understand is that you have one or two Server 2003 (or possibly NT) servers acting as name resolvers or WINS servers. This dialog box lets you fill in the names of a primary and secondary WINS server.

In brief, here's what WINS is all about. As you've read, most of the Internet in general as well as Server 2003 uses something called DNS to convert network names to network addresses (or, in network lingo, to "resolve network names"), but now I'm saying that we'll *also* use something else, called WINS, to do what sounds like the same thing. What's going on? In truth, you shouldn't really have to set up WINS at all; NT and Microsoft enterprise networking in general should use DNS for all of its name resolution, but it didn't in Windows for Workgroups, Windows 9*x*, NT 3.*x*, and NT 4. It wasn't until Server 2003 shipped that Microsoft networking started relying on Winsock and DNS.

The reason is that Microsoft wanted NT's networking modules to work like the already-existing LAN Manager system, and LAN Manager used a naming system based on its NetBIOS application program interface. A computer's NetBIOS name is the computer name that you gave it when you installed it. When you type **net view \\ajax**, something must resolve \\ajax into an IP address—a NetBIOS-to-IP resolution. WINS does that. In contrast, the rest of the Internet would see a machine called ajax as having a longer name, like ajax.acme.com. If there were a Web server on ajax, then someone outside the company would have to point her Web browser to http://ajax.acme.com, and some piece of software would have to resolve ajax.acme.com into an IP address. That piece of software is the socket or Winsock interface, and in either case, it will rely upon not WINS but DNS to resolve the name. In a few words, then, programs written to employ NetBIOS will use WINS for name resolution, and programs written to employ Winsock use DNS for name resolution.

I can probably guess what you're thinking now, and, yes, DNS and WINS should be integrated, but they can't really ever be completely integrated, because, as you'll see in the next chapter, DNS and WINS serve different masters—DNS serves standard Internet-type applications like Web browsers and newer Microsoft tools like Active Directory, and WINS serves older Microsoft-centric tools like network workgroups or NT 4 domains.

The bigger question at this point is *why am I even talking about this*? After all, it's 2003. That bad old NetBIOS and NT 4 stuff is dead, right? Nope, not in most networks. It's pretty likely that you've still got some Windows 98, Windows Me, and NT 4 systems still attached to your network and who knows, you might even have a few Windows for Workgroups and Windows 95 systems. Back when Active Directory first appeared in Windows 2000, Microsoft kept promising us that WINS would no longer be necessary once 2000 Server—yes, that's 2000 Server, not Server 2003—had been out for a while, but there was some fine print, namely "so long as you throw away all of your old machines or put Windows 2000, XP, or Server 2003 on them." Most of us can't afford to do that, so we'll be living with WINS servers for the time being—which means that your Server 2003 systems must know where those WINS servers are; hence this dialog box. (Remember that in our simple example we've not configured a WINS server yet, which is why that last figure had a blank WINS Addresses, in Order of Use field.)

I could tell this computer to use a WINS server at 192.168.71.10 by clicking Add, filling in the IP address, and clicking OK. You could only tell pre–2000 Server systems about two WINS servers, but for some reason 2000, XP, and Server 2003 allow you to list as many WINS servers as you like in this dialog box.

Even at its best, WINS can't do the whole name resolution job. Some tough name resolution problems can only be solved with a HOSTS-like file called LMHOSTS. The Enable LMHOSTS Lookup check box lets you use an LMHOSTS file if you've got one installed on your system. I'll explain LMHOSTS in detail in the next chapter.

Below all that is a group of controls labeled NetBIOS Setting offering three options:

◆ Default

◆ Enable NetBIOS over TCP/IP

◆ Disable NetBIOS over TCP/IP

If you're an old Windows 2000 hand, then you'll notice that these options changed a little bit—what is now Default used to be Use DHCP Setting.

The Enable NetBIOS over TCP/IP versus Disable NetBIOS over TCP/IP radio buttons embody a deceptively momentous choice, so it's odd that the choice is tucked away in this obscure properties page. Another way of phrasing the WINS-versus-DNS dichotomy is to say that all of the Microsoft operating systems prior to 2000 Server built all of their networking tools atop a programming interface called NetBIOS, and Windows 2000, XP, and Server 2003 break with that tradition by instead using another programming interface called Winsock. An all–Windows-2000-or-later network would be perfectly happy running only network programs—Web servers, e-mail, file servers, even domain controllers for authentication—that used Winsock. But if those servers want to communicate with older Windows and NT systems, then they must use older networking programs that are compatible with these old systems, and those older networking programs are built atop NetBIOS.

That means that if your Server 2003 system is acting as a file or print server for any older machines, it needs to keep NetBIOS around. If it's running any applications built for pre–2000 Server versions of NT, it'll probably need NetBIOS. Put simply, you can't shut off NetBIOS until you're free of both old client machines and old network applications. But one day you'll be able to axe NetBIOS, and when you can, you should, as it'll reduce network chatter and free up server memory and CPU power.

Adding IP Addresses to a Single NIC

If you're still in the Advanced TCP/IP Settings page, click the IP Settings tab, and you'll see something like Figure 6.21.

FIGURE 6.21

IP Settings advanced properties tab

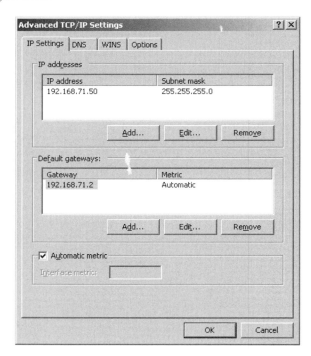

This NIC already has the 192.168.71.50 IP address that I gave it earlier. But notice the Add button. This lets you attach different IP addresses to the NIC to assign more than one IP address to a single NIC.

Why would you want to do that? Normally, you wouldn't. But there *is* one case where it would be very useful: when you're hosting multiple Web sites on a single Web server.

For example, suppose I've got two Internet domains, minasi.com and win2kexperts.com. I intend to put up a Web site for minasi.com (`www.minasi.com`) and another for win2kexperts.com (`www.win2kexperts.com`). But I want them to be very different Web sites; perhaps the minasi.com site is a personal site and the win2kexperts site is a business site. Even though `www.minasi.com` and `www.win2kexperts.com` are both hosted on a machine at 206.246.253.100, I don't ever want anyone visiting the business site to see pictures of my last vacation, and I don't think my friends care much about my professional résumé.

I separate the two by creating two *virtual sites*. There are two basic ways to give a single Web server "multiple personalities." You'll read more about how to do that with Internet Information Server in Chapter 17, and in that chapter you'll learn *one* way to create multiple virtual sites. That method doesn't work with old browsers—Netscape 1.*x*, Internet Explorer 1.*x* and 2.*x*, Spyglass—but only with *really* old browsers, so what you'll read in Chapter 17 may well be all you need. But if you ever need the slightly more expensive (and when I say *expensive* here, I mean that you'll have to use an IP address for each virtual site) method that works with *any* browser, then here's briefly how to do it—and it's a great example of why you'd put multiple IP addresses on a single NIC:

1. I assign an extra IP address to the Web server so that it now has two addresses—let's say they're 206.246.253.100 and 206.246.253.101.

2. I then set up DNS so that `www.minasi.com` points to the first address, 206.246.253.100, and `www.win2kexperts.com` points to the second address, 206.246.253.101.

3. I've already got the minasi.com Web site running, so I'll need a place to put the win2kexperts.com content. I just create a folder on the Web server called `w2kx` and put the HTML, images, and so on for win2kexperts.com there.

4. I next tell the Web server to create a "new site." It then basically needs to know two things: where to find the content (`C:\w2kx`) and which IP address to associate with the site. I've got to tell it to "start" the site, and I'm in business.

The important thing here is to understand that every one of these sites, each of these "personalities" of your Web server, burns up an IP address, and as you see, you use the IP Settings property tab to add those extra IP addresses to your Web server's NIC.

Whew! Getting IP running on that system was a bit of work. Good thing we can do most of our machines automatically with DHCP—but even that requires configuring, which is why we went through all of this detail. Now that I've got IP on a system, I can return to some of the more techie infrastructure issues—like IP routing.

Setting Up Routing on Server 2003, NT, and 9x Machines

Up to now, I've assumed that all of your TCP/IP-using machines had a single default gateway that acted as "router to the world" for your machines. That's not always true, as real-life intranets often have multiple routers that lead a machine to different networks. I've also assumed that your Server 2003 network is connected to the Internet, or to your enterprise intranet, via some third-party (Compatible Systems, Bay Networks, Cisco Systems, or whomever) router. That's also not always true, as NT machines can act as IP routers.

Routing problems aren't just *server* problems; they're often workstation problems, as well. So, in this section, I'll take on two topics:

◆ How to set up routing tables on your workstations and servers

◆ How to use your Server 2003 servers as IP routers

An Example Multirouter Internet

Suppose you had a workstation on a network with two gateways, as shown in Figure 6.22.

FIGURE 6.22

A workstation on a network with two gateways

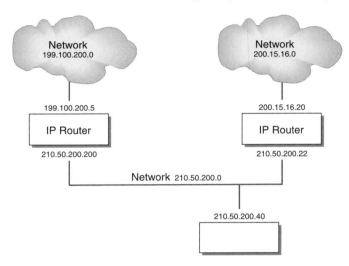

As is the case for most of these diagrams, a multinetwork picture can be cryptic, so here's an explanation of what you are looking at.

First, there are three separate Ethernet segments, three separate subnets. They are all class C networks, just to keep things clean. Two of the networks are only represented by clouds; thus, the cloud on the left containing 199.100.200.0 is just shorthand for an Ethernet with up to 254 computers hanging off it, with addresses ranging from 199.100.200.1 through 199.100.200.254. Notice that I said 254, not 253, because *there is no default gateway for these subnets.* As there are only three subnets, this is an intranet, not part of the Internet. One side effect of not being on the Net is that you can use the .1 address for regular old machines. I left the Internet out of this first example because I found that it confused me when I was first trying to get this routing stuff down. I'll add it later, I promise.

There is also another cloud, to the right, representing a network whose addresses range from 200.15.16.1 through 200.15.16.254—network number 200.15.16.0.

In between is a third subnet with address 210.50.200.0. You see a rectangle representing a PC in the middle that has only one Ethernet card in it, and its IP address is 210.50.200.40. The rectangles on the right and left sides of the picture are routers, computers with two Ethernet cards in them and thus two IP addresses apiece. Each has an address on the 210.50.200.0 network, and each has an address either on the 200.15.16.0 network or on the 199.100.200.0 network.

Adding Entries to Routing Tables: *route add*

Having said that, let's now figure out how to tell the machine at 210.50.200.40 how to route anywhere on this network. These are some of the facts it needs to know:

◆ To get a message to the 199.100.200.0 network, send it to the machine at 210.50.200.200.

◆ To get a message to the 200.15.16.0 network, send it to the machine at 210.50.200.22.

◆ To get a message to the 210.50.200.0 network, just use your own Ethernet card; send it out on the segment, and it'll be heard.

You tell a workstation how to send packets with the `route add` command. Simplified, it looks like this:

```
route add destination mask netmask gatewayaddress
```

Here, *destination* is the address or set of addresses that you want to be able to get to. *Netmask* defines how *many* addresses are there—is it a C network with 250+ addresses, something subnetted smaller, or perhaps a "supernet" of several C networks? *Gatewayaddress* is just the IP address of the machine that will route your packets to their destination.

The `route add` command for the 199.100.200.0 network would look like this:

```
route add 199.100.200.0 mask 255.255.255.0 210.50.200.200
```

This means, "Send a message anywhere on the 199.100.200.0 network, send it to the machine at 210.50.200.200, and it'll take care of it."

TIP   *If you just type the* `route add` *statement as you see it in the previous text, then your system will forget the routing command when next you boot. You can tell it to remember that route next time with the* `-p` *("permanent") switch, as in* `route -p add 199.100.200.0 mask 255.255.255.0 210.50.200.200`. *This only works on NT and 2000; you can't make routes permanent under Windows 9x.*

Just a reminder on subnetting, for clarity's sake: Suppose the network on the upper left wasn't a full C network, but rather a subnetted part of it. Suppose it was just the range of addresses from 199.100.200.64 through 199.100.200.127. The network number would be, as always, the first address (199.100.200.64), and the subnet mask would be 255.255.255.192. The `route add` command would then look like this:

```
route add 199.100.200.64 mask 255.255.255.192 210.50.200.200
```

Anyway, back to the example in the picture. Add a command for the right-side network; it looks like this:

```
route add 200.15.16.0 mask 255.255.255.0 210.50.200.22
```

That much will get a Server 2003, NT, XP, 9x, Me, or even DOS-based TCP/IP system up and running.

Understanding the Prebuilt Routes

Even if you don't ever type a `route add` command at a Windows workstation, you'll find that there are prebuilt routing statements that are automatically generated. Let's look at them. First, we'd need an explicit routing command to tell the 210.50.200.40 machine to get to its own subnet:

```
route add 210.50.200.0 mask 255.255.255.0 210.50.200.40
```

Or, in other words, "To get to your local subnet, route to yourself."

NOTE   *Remember, you need not run this or any other* route add *command in this section—they're default routes, therefore they're always around.*

Then, recall that the entire 127.*x.y.z* range of network addresses is the loopback. Implement that like so:

```
route add 127.0.0.0 mask 255.0.0.0 127.0.0.1
```

This says, "Take any address from 127.0.0.0 through 127.255.255.255 and route it to 127.0.0.1." The IP software has already had 127.0.0.1 defined for it, so it knows what to do with that. Notice the mask, 255.0.0.0, is a simple class A network mask.

Some Internet software uses intranet multicast groups, so the multicast address must be defined. It is 224.0.0.0. It looks like the loopback route command:

```
route add 224.0.0.0 mask 255.0.0.0 210.50.200.40
```

The system knows to multicast by *shouting*, which means communicating over its local subnet.

Viewing the Routing Table

Let's find out exactly what routing information this computer has. How? Well, on Server 2003, Windows NT, Workgroups, and 9*x* workstations, there are two commands that will show you what the workstation knows about how to route IP packets. Type either **netstat -rn** or **route print** at a command line—the output is identical, so use either command—and you see something like Figure 6.23.

FIGURE 6.23

Sample route print output

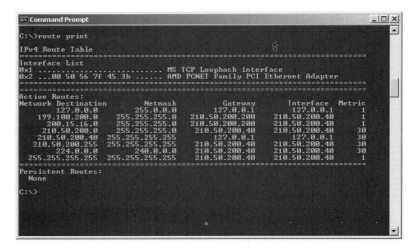

Notice that the output of route print is similar to the way you format data in route add. Each line shows a network address, which is the desired destination; the netmask, which indicates how many addresses exist at the desired destination; and the gateway, which is the IP address that the workstation should send its packets to in order to reach the destination. But note two more columns: Interface and Metric.

THE INTERFACE COLUMN

Interface asks itself, "Which of my local IP addresses—the ones physically located inside me, like my loopback and all the IP addresses attached to all of my network cards—should I use to get to that gateway?" On this computer, it's a moot point because it only has one network card in it.

What might this look like on a multihomed machine, like the router on the left side? It has two IP addresses, 199.100.200.5 and 210.50.200.200. A fragment of its `route print` output might then look like this:

```
Network Destination  Netmask        Gateway         Interface      Metric
199.100.200.0  255.255.255.0  199.100.200.5  199.100.200.5        1
210.50.200.0   255.255.255.0  210.50.200.200 210.50.200.200       1
```

There are two networks that the router machine can get to (obviously, or it wouldn't be much use as a router), and each one has a gateway address, which happens to be the local IP address that the router maintains on each network. But now notice the Interface column: Rather than staying at the same IP address all the way through, this tells the computer, "I've already told you which gateway to direct this traffic to; now I'll tell you which of your local IP addresses to employ in order to get to that gateway in the first place."

THE METRIC COLUMN, PART I: WHAT *METRIC* DOES

The Metric column (what, no English option?) helps IP figure out which route to take when it has more than one option. It was once a simple-to-explain concept, but from Windows XP onward, Microsoft has muddied it a bit. Still, it's an important concept to understand, so hold onto something solid, the ride's about to get a bit bumpy.

"Metric" is a value that you can set with the `route add` command, like so:

```
route add 200.15.16.0 mask 255.255.255.0 210.50.200.22 metric 2
```

In that command, adding `metric 2` to the end says, "This route will effectively get you to some destination on the 200.15.16.0 subnet, but you've got to go through one router to get there." The metric number is 2 because you always add 1 to the number of routers to pass through—one router, add one, get a metric of 2.

IP software takes no notice of metrics unless it has to choose between more than one possible route. For instance, suppose your computer is trying to get to some IP address—call it A. Suppose also that your computer is connected to two routers—call them X and Y—and *both* routers can find their way to the destination address A. Your IP software must, then, make a choice: get to A through X or through Y?

I make a similar choice all the time when choosing airlines. I always start from the same place—Norfolk Airport in southern Virginia. But suppose I want to get to, say, Philadelphia, and that I've got two choices: United will fly me to Dulles, outside Washington, DC, and I'll change planes and then fly from Dulles to Philly. Alternatively, USAir will fly me direct from Norfolk to Philadelphia. Which do I choose?

Well, in real life there might be plenty of reasons to choose one over the other, but I think for most of us the answer would be "whichever involves the least number of stops, minimizing the amount of chances that the airline has to lose my bags or screw up my connection." We'd say that the number of stops is the major *metric* in determining which *route* to take. And IP packets feel the same way, apparently: whenever given the choice between one or more routes, they take the one with the fewer number of hops. So if router X's route involved three hops (and thus had a metric of 3+1 or 4) and router Y's route involved one hop (and thus had a metric of 1+1 or 2) then system A would choose to route its packet through Y rather than X.

To review, then, `metric` *used* to refer to the number of routers that an IP packet would have to pass through in order to get to its destination. A metric value of 1 originally meant "your destination is on the same subnet." A `metric` value of 2 originally meant "you have to go through one router to get to your destination," and so on. So a route's `metric` value equalled the number of routers your IP packet would have to travel through, plus 1.

THE METRIC COLUMN, PART 2: HOW WINDOWS USES IT

Or at least, that's the way it *used* to be. As of XP and Server 2003, Microsoft seems to have redefined metric. At startup, Server 2003 tries to communicate through each network interface, and based on the speed of their responses, it sets a default metric for each interface, based on the perceived speed of the link:

Link speed	Metric assigned
200 Mbps>	10
20–200 Mbps	20
4–20 Mbps	30
500 Kbps–4Mbps	40
<500 Kbps	50

In other words, Microsoft has taken what used to mean "the number of hops in a route" and redefined it as "roughly how fast this link is." I imagine their idea was that the whole point of metrics was to find the fastest from amongst a set of possible routes, and that by doing this on-the-fly speed test of a link that they came up with a better approach. I suppose it's not a bad answer, but it's one that runs counter to the way that everyone else uses metrics in IP routing. And let me stress that as far as I can see there's no harm in it, so long as you don't intend to do much in the way of static routing and truthfully you probably won't want to do much static routing on a workstation.

HOW TO DISABLE AUTOMATIC METRICS

Again, you can probably run a network where all (or almost all) of your systems have automatic metrics, but if you want to follow along in this discussion of IP routing then you'll want to disable them.

Recall that every network card in your system has an IP stack and that there is a properties page for that IP stack, as you saw in Figure 6.11. That includes an Advanced button, which leads to an Advanced TCP/IP Properties page, which contains a tab labeled IP Settings, as you saw in Figure 6.21. Go to that page and you'll note a field at the bottom of the IP Settings page with a check box labeled Automatic Metric. Un-check that box and in the field below it labeled Interface Metric, enter **1** and then click OK, then close any other TCP/IP-related dialog boxes. Do this for each NIC in your system. If I do that, then my `route print` output changes, as you can see in Figure 6.24.

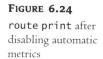

FIGURE 6.24

route print after disabling automatic metrics

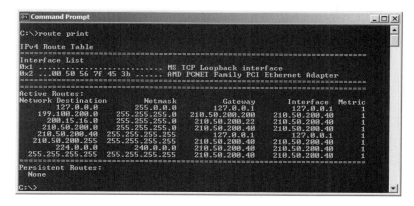

BACK TO THE METRIC FIELD

Now that we've got Server handling metrics in the standard way, let's return to the output in Figure 6.24. As I've already said, the correct value for the metric column should be the number of routers that you've got to hop over in order to get to the subnet in the routing table entry. Since the .40 workstation must go through a router to get to either the 199.100.200.0 or the 200.15.16.0 network, both of those networks should get a metric of 2.

But the screen show shows a metric of 1, not 2, for both the 199.100.200.0 and 200.15.16.0 route—why? Because the computer's not smart enough to figure out how many hops a new **route add** command involves. But *you* can, by adding the metric parameter and the desired value. A more complete set of **route add** commands would be

```
route add 200.15.16.0 mask 255.255.255.0 210.50.200.22 metric 2
route add 199.100.200.0 mask 255.255.255.0 210.50.200.200 metric 2
```

Had I done that, then you'd have seen the metric value of 2. You'll learn a bit later that a protocol called RIP will make this process automatic, but for now I want to stick to this manually constructed set of routing tables. (Using hand-constructed routing tables is called *static routing*; the automatic methods like RIP are called *dynamic routing*, and I'll get to them later.)

ROUTE PRINT OUTPUT EXPLAINED

Now that you can decipher each column in the **route print** output, I'll finish up explaining the output.

The first line is the loopback information, as you've seen before. It's automatically generated on every 2003/2000/XP/NT/Workgroups/9x machine running the Microsoft TCP/IP stack. The second and third lines are the manually entered routes that tell your machine how to address the 200.15.16.0 and 199.100.200.0 networks. The fourth line is another automatically generated line, and it explains how to address the 210.50.200.0 subnet, which is the local one. The fifth line refers to 210.50.200.40 itself. The mask, 255.255.255.255, means that these aren't routing instructions to get to an entire network, but rather routing instructions to get to a particular computer. It basically says, "If you need to get data to 210.50.200.40, send it to the loopback address." The result: If you ping 210.50.200.40, then no actual communication happens over the network. The sixth line defines how to do a local subnet broadcast. Again, it doesn't point to an entire network, but rather to the particular subnet broadcast address. The seventh line serves Internet multicasting, as you saw before. And the final address is for something called the *limited broadcast address*, a kind of generic subnet broadcast address.

Adding the Default Gateway

Suppose you wanted to set up my 210.50.200.40 machine. How would you do it? More specifically, you'd ask me, "Which is the default gateway?"

Well, in the TCP/IP configuration screen that you've seen before, you'd obviously be able to supply the information that the IP address should be 210.50.200.40 and the subnet mask should be 255.255.255.0. But what should you use to fill in the Default Gateway field? I mean, there are *two* gateways, 210.50.100.22 and 210.50.100.200. Which should you use?

The answer? Neither. A *default gateway* is just another entry in the routing table, but it's not specific like the ones you've met so far; it's a catchall entry. This network doesn't get to the Internet, and it can only see two other subnets, each with their own routers (gateways), so I left the Default Gateway field blank. And there's an advantage to that.

"DESTINATION HOST UNREACHABLE"

If I were to try to ping some address not on the three subnets, such as 25.44.92.4, then I wouldn't get the message that the ping had timed out, or experienced an error, or anything of the sort; rather, I'd get a "destination host unreachable" message. That's important: "Destination host unreachable" doesn't necessarily mean that you can't get to the destination host, but it *does* mean that your workstation doesn't know *how* to get to that host—it lacks any routing information about how to get there at all. Do a `route print` and you'll probably be able to see what's keeping you from getting to your destination.

BUILDING A DEFAULT GATEWAY BY HAND

When *would* a default gateway make sense in our network? Well, let's add an Internet connection to the network, as shown in Figure 6.25.

FIGURE 6.25

Network with an
Internet connection

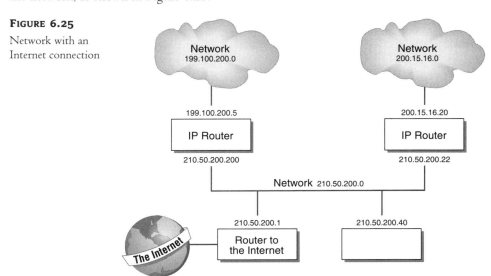

Now we need another **route add** command—but what should it look like? I mean, what's the generic IP address of the whole Internet?

Believe it or not, there *is* such an address: 0.0.0.0. Think of it as "the network number to end all network numbers." Remember, any given network's number is just the first address of the network. And what's the first address of the Internet? 0.0.0.0. And the network mask? Well, since it doesn't matter *what* address bits match which other address bits—after all, no matter what your address is, you're still on the particular "subnet" that is the entire Internet—the subnet mask is also 0.0.0.0. But you've got to hop across a router to get to this 0.0.0.0 "subnet," so let the metric reflect that with this command:

```
route add 0.0.0.0 mask 0.0.0.0 210.50.200.1 metric 2
```

HANDLING CONFLICTS IN ROUTING INFORMATION

Let's take a minute and look once more at that metric parameter. You see, we've now made IP's job a bit more complicated, as I promised that we would back when we started talking about metrics. Look at some of the instructions that you've given the IP software about how to route:

- There's a rule about handling the specific address 210.50.200.40: Just keep the message local at 127.0.0.1, no routing.

- There's a rule about how to handle the range from 210.50.200.0 through 210.50.200.255: Shout it out on the subnet, no routing.

- There's a rule about how to handle the range from 199.100.200.0 through 199.100.200.255: Send it to 210.50.200.200.

- There's a rule about how to handle the range from 200.15.16.0 through 200.15.16.255: Send it to 210.50.200.22.

- There's a rule about how to handle *all* Internet addresses: Send the messages to 210.50.200.1.

Here's what I mean about a conflict: Suppose you want to send an IP packet to 200.15.16.33. You have one rule that says, "Send it to 210.50.200.22" (the local specific router for that subnet) and another that says, "Send it to 210.50.200.1," (the router to the Internet). Which rule does the software on your computer follow?

Answer: When in doubt, *first* look for the route with the smallest metric. If there is more than one candidate, then take the *most specific* one—in other words, choose the one with the most specific subnet mask.

In this case, there are two entries in the routing table that point to the destination, 200.15.16.33. I haven't shown you their metrics, but both of them require hopping over one router, so each route has metric 2. As their metrics are tied, you look next to the subnet mask. As the 210.50.200.1 route has a very generic subnet mask (0.0.0.0), your machine would ignore it in comparison to the more specific 210.50.200.22's subnet mask of 255.255.255.0.

Suppose workstation 210.50.200.40 wanted to get a message to another machine on the subnet; let's say that its address is 210.50.200.162. Again, there's a routing conflict, as one route entry just says to send it to 210.50.200.40—in other words, don't route, shout! There's another routing entry—the 0.0.0.0 one again—that says it can also get the IP packet to 210.50.200.162, as it claims it can get any packet *anywhere*. Which to choose? Well, if constructed correctly, an excerpt of the routing table will look something like this:

Destination	Netmask	Gateway	Interface	Metric
0.0.0.0	0.0.0.0	210.50.200.1	210.50.200.40	2
210.50.200.0	255.255.255.0	210.50.200.40	210.50.200.40	1

The first entry is the default gateway. It's got metric 2 because you've got to hop over at least one router to get to the Internet. (In actual fact, it's probably not a bad idea to set this value a bit higher, just to be sure internal IP packets *never* try to get sent over the Internet.) The second entry basically says, "To send data to your local subnet, just say it out loud on your Ethernet card"—again, don't route, shout. As the Internet metric is higher, your machine will know not to try to send a local message by sending it to the default gateway.

One more thing: You wouldn't, of course, want to have to type in those `route add` commands every time you start up your computer. So you'd use a variation on the `route add` command. Just type **route -p add**. Recall that when you add the **-p**, that entry becomes permanent in your system's routing table.

All Routers Must Know All Subnets

I've talked about how I'd set up my sample network from the point of view of a workstation. It would work, but you can see that it's a real pain to punch in all of those `route add` statements for each workstation. The answer is to make the routers smarter; *then* you can just pick one router to be the default gateway for the .40 workstation, and the workstation needn't worry about anything. So let's take a minute and see how each of the three routers in this system would be set up.

The first router is the one on the left, which routes between 199.100.200.0 and 210.50.200.0. It must know three things:

- ◆ It can get to 199.100.200.0 through its 199.100.200.5 interface.
- ◆ It can get to 210.50.200.0 through its 210.50.200.200 interface.
- ◆ It can get to the Internet through 210.50.200.1, which it gets to through its 210.50.200.200 interface.

In fact, you would not have to type in routing commands telling it how to get to 199.100.200.0 or 210.50.200.0; assuming it's an NT machine, the NT routing software figures that out automatically. But you can tell it to get to the Internet by setting a default gateway:

```
route add 0.0.0.0 mask 0.0.0.0 210.50.200.1 metric 2
```

The routing software is then smart enough to realize that it should get to 210.50.200.1 via its 210.50.200.200 interface.

The second router, the one on the right, routes between 200.15.16.0 and 210.50.200.0. It can get to both of those networks directly, and, as with the first router, we don't have to tell it about them. But to get to the Internet, it must route packets to 210.50.200.1, and so, like the first router, it should have a default gateway of 210.50.200.1.

Now let's tackle the third router, the machine at 210.50.200.1, which is the Internet gateway. It must know that it should use the Internet as its default gateway. For example, on my Compatible Systems routers, there is a magical address WAN that just means the modem connection to the Internet. I essentially tell it, "Route add 0.0.0.0 mask 0.0.0.0 WAN," and packets travel to and from the Internet over the modem. The router must then be told of each of the three subnets, like so:

```
route add 210.50.200.0 mask 255.255.255.0 210.50.200.1 metric 1
route add 199.100.200.0 mask 255.255.255.0 210.50.200.200 metric 2
route add 200.15.16.0 mask 255.255.255.0 210.50.200.22 metric 2
```

Using RIP to Simplify Workstation Management

Thus far, I've shown you how to tell your workstations how to exploit routers on the network. In most cases, you won't need to build such large, complex routing tables by hand, and in almost no case will you *want* to build those tables.

Ideally, you shouldn't have to type in static tables; instead, your workstations could just suck up routing information automatically from the nearby routers, using some kind of browser-type protocol. You *can* do such a thing with the Routing Information Protocol (RIP).

RIP is an incredibly simple protocol. Routers running RIP broadcast their routing tables about twice a minute. Any workstation running RIP software hears the routing tables and incorporates them into its *own* routing tables. Result: You put a new router on the system, and you needn't punch in any static routes.

RIP version 2 ships as part of Server 2003. The Microsoft implementation supports both IP and IPX. Routes detected by RIP show up in `route print` statements just as if they were static routes.

An Alternative Dynamic Routing Protocol: OSPF

Although RIP has been around for some time, it's an awfully chatty protocol. Twice a minute, each RIP router broadcasts its entire routing table for all to hear. A more intelligent and bandwidth-parsimonious but more complex to set up dynamic routing protocol is available in the form of the Open Shortest Path First (OSPF) protocol. You have to feed the routers a bit more information about the layout of your sites, but once you do, OSPF quickly generates the shortest routes for your packets.

Using an NT Machine as a LAN/LAN Router

In the process of expanding your company's intranet, you need routers. For a network of any size, the best bet is probably to buy dedicated routers, boxes from companies such as Cisco Systems, Bay Networks, or Compatible Systems.

Dedicated routers are fast and come with some impressive management tools: neat GUI programs that let you control and monitor your network from your workstation. But routers have one disadvantage: They're expensive. I haven't seen an Ethernet-to-Ethernet IP router available for less than $3,000. Again, don't misunderstand me: These routers are probably worth what they cost in terms of the ease that they bring to network management and the speed with which they route data. But you might have more than one subnet on a given site, and you might *not* have the three grand, so you're looking for an alternative.

How about a software alternative? Any NT server, from 3.51 through Server 2003, can act as a simple IP router—all you need is a multihomed PC (one with two or more network cards installed in it) and Windows NT 4.

Just open the Control Panel, open the Network applet, then the Protocols tab, and the TCP/IP protocol. Click the Routing tab, and you see an option called Enable IP Routing. That's how you turn on NT's routing capability.

Making a Server 2003 system a router is a bit more complex. Let's see how to set up this router. Let's return to that cross-Mediterranean rivalry and set up a LAN-to-LAN router for Carthage and Rome. Imagine you have an intranet that looks like Figure 6.26.

FIGURE 6.26

A sample intranet

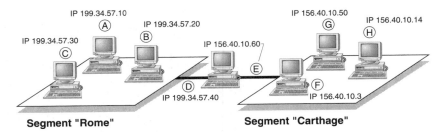

We're going to use the machine that's on both Rome and Carthage as the router. Actually, there's no choice here, as it's the *only* machine in both TCP/IP subnets, and any router between two subnets must be a member of both subnets. First I'll look at how to set up the machine with adapters D and E as a router, and then I'll take a slightly more complex example:

1. The machine between Rome and Carthage—let's call it MEDITERRANEAN—needs two Ethernet cards. Install two network cards (let's use Ethernet for this example) in a Server 2003 system machine. Microsoft *intended* for you to only be able to use 2003 Server for IP routing, but you can use XP as well with a Registry hack, so long as you're only doing static routing— I haven't been able to figure out how to make Professional do RIP or OSPF routing.

2. Configure the Ethernet card on the Rome subnet with IP address 199.34.57.40 and the Ethernet card on the Carthage subnet with IP address 156.40.10.60. Here's how: Once you've got a second NIC installed in the MEDITERRANEAN system, open up Network and Dial-Up Connections and it'll look like Figure 6.27.

FIGURE 6.27

Network and Dial-Up Connections with two NICs

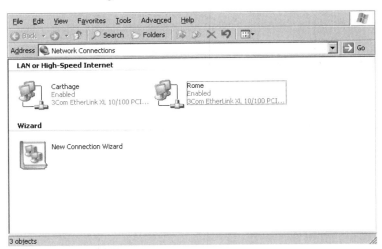

3. Right-click either of the two connection objects and choose Properties, and you'll then see the screen that lets you modify the TCP/IP properties for that NIC, including its static IP address. (Notice you can also rename the NICs; I've renamed them from Local Area Connection to more descriptive names.) Once I've set the IP addresses properly, an `ipconfig /all` looks like Figure 6.28.

FIGURE 6.28

`ipconfig /all` before enabling routing

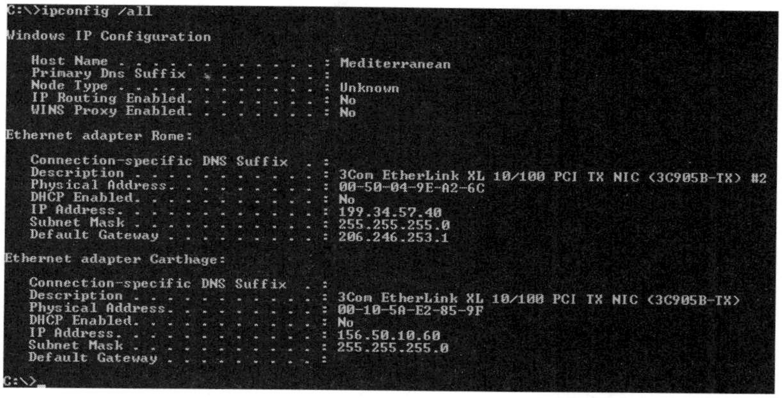

```
C:\>ipconfig /all

Windows IP Configuration

   Host Name . . . . . . . . . . . . : Mediterranean
   Primary Dns Suffix  . . . . . . . :
   Node Type . . . . . . . . . . . . : Unknown
   IP Routing Enabled. . . . . . . . : No
   WINS Proxy Enabled. . . . . . . . : No

Ethernet adapter Rome:

   Connection-specific DNS Suffix  . :
   Description . . . . . . . . . . . : 3Com EtherLink XL 10/100 PCI TX NIC (3C905B-TX) #2
   Physical Address. . . . . . . . . : 00-50-04-9E-A2-6C
   DHCP Enabled. . . . . . . . . . . : No
   IP Address. . . . . . . . . . . . : 199.34.57.40
   Subnet Mask . . . . . . . . . . . : 255.255.255.0
   Default Gateway . . . . . . . . . : 206.246.253.1

Ethernet adapter Carthage:

   Connection-specific DNS Suffix  . :
   Description . . . . . . . . . . . : 3Com EtherLink XL 10/100 PCI TX NIC (3C905B-TX)
   Physical Address. . . . . . . . . : 00-10-5A-E2-85-9F
   DHCP Enabled. . . . . . . . . . . : No
   IP Address. . . . . . . . . . . . : 156.50.10.60
   Subnet Mask . . . . . . . . . . . : 255.255.255.0
   Default Gateway . . . . . . . . . :

C:\>
```

Note that this IPConfig output is larger than the previous ones, mainly because it's got to report on two NICs. There's no DNS server specified and no domain name specified because (1) it simplified the IPConfig output and (2) routers usually needn't have DNS names for their interfaces. Note also that IP Routing Enabled is No. That's important— just because a Server 2003 system has NICs attached to different subnets doesn't automatically mean that the system will act as a router.

4. Next, turn on routing. You can turn on simple static routing for either a Server 2003 or Professional machine by looking in the key `HKEY_LOCAL_MACHINE\System\CurrentControlSet\Services\Tcpip\Parameters` for the value named `IPEnableRouter`, which will be set to 0. Change the value to 1, reboot the system, and it'll do static routing between the subnets that it's directly connected to.

I suggested the Registry hack because it's the only way that I've found to make an XP or 2000 Professional machine an IP router—which is odd, because under NT 4 Workstation there was a check box in the Control Panel to enable IP routing. Maybe it was an oversight, or perhaps Microsoft wants to sell you a copy of Server if you want to do even the simplest IP routing?

In any case, if the routing machine is running 2003 Server, then no Registry fooling around is needed. Instead, click Start/Administrative Tools/Routing and Remote Access, which will show you an MMC console like Figure 6.29.

Note the red arrow next to MEDITERRANEAN. That indicates that routing hasn't been turned on yet. To turn routing on, right-click MEDITERRANEAN in the left pane and choose Configure and Enable Routing and Remote Access. That, not surprisingly, starts off a wizard, the Routing and Remote Access Server Setup Wizard. Click Next and you'll then see a screen like Figure 6.30.

FIGURE 6.29

Opening RRAS
administrator screen

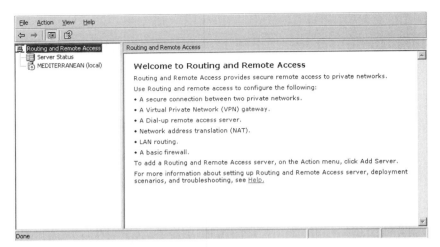

FIGURE 6.30

Initial RRAS setup
wizard screen

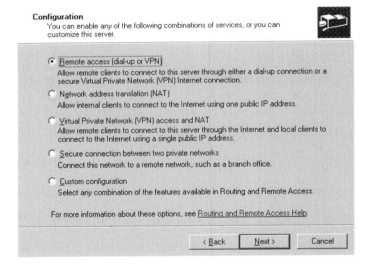

Setting up a router can be a bit challenging, so Microsoft built four "precooked" router setups and offers them in combination with a fifth option that allows you to build the router as you like. Take that fifth option, Custom Configuration, and click Next to go to the Custom Configuration screen, as you see in Figure 6.31.

Check LAN Routing and Next and Finish to complete the wizard. Server 2003 will beep and ask you if you want to start the Routing and Remote Access Service; click Yes. You'll then see a screen like Figure 6.32.

You have now successfully built your first router! As MEDITERRANEAN's routing is turned on and because it's directly connected to both the 199 and 156 networks, it will automatically route packets between the networks. Try it out if you like—put one computer on the same segment as

MEDITERRANEAN's 156.40.10.60 NIC, give the machine an address in that subnet, like 156.40.10.17, and set its default gateway (okay, we're being a bit lazy, but this is just a test) to 156.40.10.60. On the segment connected to MEDITERRANEAN's other NIC, attach a machine with an IP address of 199.34.57.21 and set its default gateway to 199.34.57.40. You will find that the two "outer" machines, 199.34.57.21 and 156.40.10.17, can ping each other.

FIGURE 6.31

Choose what the router will do

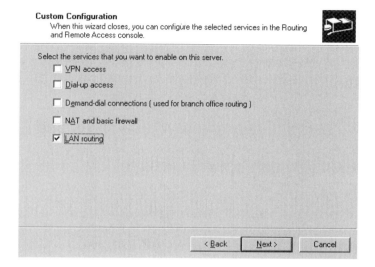

FIGURE 6.32

RRAS management console with routing enabled

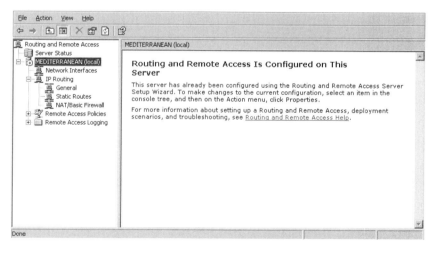

One more point before moving on. You've already learned how to use **route add** from the command line to add a static route. RRAS lets you do that from the GUI as well. In the left panel, you see an object labeled IP Routing. Open it and you'll see three other objects, one labeled General, one labeled Static Routes and one labeled NAT/Basic Firewall. Right-click Static Routes and choose New Static Route, and you'll see a dialog box like Figure 6.33.

FIGURE 6.33

Dialog box for adding a new static route

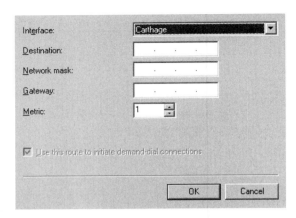

Okay, so it's not a very useful dialog box—I could probably type the `route add` command more quickly than I could open this dialog box and punch in its values—but at least it's not another three-screen wizard that only asks one question, right?

More Complex Static Routing

By now, you've set up an IP router to move traffic from one subnet to another. It will *not*, however, route traffic among three or more subnets. Why not? Well, the default router software isn't very smart. Look at Figure 6.34, and you'll see what I mean.

FIGURE 6.34

An intranet with three subnets

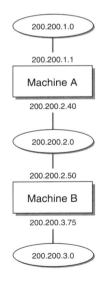

Here, you see an intranet with just three subnets: 200.200.1.0, 200.200.2.0, and 200.200.3.0. For ease of discussion, let's call network 200.200.1.0 "network 1," 200.200.2.0 "network 2," and 200.200.3.0 "network 3." The network 1 to network 2 router, machine A, has addresses 200.200.1.1 and 200.200.2.40, and the network 2 to network 3 router, machine B, has addresses 200.200.3.75 and 200.200.2.50.

Once you turn on IP routing in machine A, it's smart enough to be able to route packets from network 1 to network 2 and packets from network 2 to network 1. But if it receives a packet from network 1 intended for network 3, it has no idea what to do about it.

Machine B has the same problem, basically. It knows how to go from network 2 to network 3 and from network 3 to network 2, but it has no idea how to find network 1.

How do you solve this problem? Either with static routes or with RIP. The best answer is probably to put the RIP router on both machine A and machine B, and they will end up discovering each other's routes through the RIP broadcasts. But how would you tell machine A how to find network 3 and how would you tell machine B to find network 1? With static `route add` commands.

On machine A, tell it about network 3 like so:

```
route add 200.200.3.0 mask 255.255.255.0 200.200.2.50
```

(Or, if you're feeling GUI, use RRAS.) You're saying to this machine, "In order to find network 200.200.3.0, use the IP address 200.200.2.50; it's attached to a machine that can get the packets to that network." For the sake of completeness, you might add the "metric 2" parameter to the end.

On machine B, tell it about network 1 in a similar way:

```
route add 200.200.1.0 mask 255.255.255.0 200.200.2.40
```

Remember that in both cases the "mask" information says, "I'm giving you information about a subnet, but the mask says how useful the information is." And if you want the router to *remember* these routes through reboots, don't forget the -p option to make the route permanent.

Using Server 2003 as an Internet Gateway/Router

Thus far, we've talked about networks that talk to one another and that are somehow connected to the Internet. Now let's see *how* to get your network connected to the Internet, and where Server 2003 can fit in. There are a few ways to do this:

- You could dial in to the Internet with a standard modem from a Server 2003 and then use a built-in service called Internet Connection Sharing to share Internet access to all of the systems in your network.

- You could connect to the Internet via a persistent, high-speed connection like cable modem or DSL and share that connection with Internet Connection Sharing.

- You could do either of the above and instead of Internet Connection Sharing you might use Network Address Translation, another routing option on Server 2003.

You'll see how to do these in the next few sections. But before we get too heavily into this, let me offer a bit of advice: you may not truly *want* to use your server as a LAN/WAN router. If possible, this is a job for a dedicated device. (You know—one without a rotating hard disk that could develop problems with its bearings or a snazzy graphics card that could fail.)

I first figured out how to make a computer with an Ethernet card and a modem into a LAN/WAN Internet router back in 1992, when everything with the name "router" cost thousands of dollars and inexpensive persistent Internet connections like DSL and cable modem were just a fantasy of a techno-future. But that's all changed tremendously by now. My PC-based routers—which first ran OS/2, then ran NT 3.5 and 3.51—were prone to all of the unreliability that *anything* PC-based suffers from, from varying degrees of software reliability to, again, problems with hard disks and video cards. But they were still cheaper than shelling out the price of a small car to buy a Cisco router at the time.

But that's slowly changed. By the mid-'90s, we were able to replace our NT router box with the Compatible Systems mr900i, a terrific box that I picked up for $850. It was easy to manage, came with a nice Windows-based router management program, did RIP, was much cheaper than buying a Pentium and a copy of Server 2003, and was as fast as the wind. It only connected via modem, but that worked fine for our needs at the time. On later networks, I've used the Lucent Pipeline router, another quite good product in the $550 to $2000 range, which includes an optional security package to turn the router into a firewall-like device. In another network, I've used the Cisco 1602, at a cost of about $1500, if I recall rightly.

But nowadays, there is no need at all to even think about spending more than $200 to share a single IP address, whether acquired with dial-up or via cable modem or DSL. Firms like Dlink, Linksys, and Lucent make some terrific devices that act as LAN/WAN router, offer network address translation, firewall protection, and even sport an easy-to-use Web-based control interface. Some even do wireless. Now, understand that these will only work if you're sharing *one* IP address—devices for sharing more IP addresses are more expensive—but even the expensive multi-address devices (like the Cisco 1602 that I mentioned) are still faster, cheaper, and more reliable than a Windows-based router.

Why, then, do I include the following section, where I show you how to do all of these routing tasks with Windows Server 2003? Because sometimes you just have a system lying around and it doesn't cost you anything, because you've already paid for it; in that case, you might want to use it as a router. Or because you have some very specialized routing task that you want to handle, and 2003 systems are naturally more flexible than a dedicated special-purpose device. Or you might want to sit down and simply "do it yourself," as I initially did—it was a great way to learn IP routing.

WAN Connection Options

Take a look at Figure 6.35 to see how we'll get your internal network connected to the Internet using Server 2003.

FIGURE 6.35
LAN/WAN router
overview diagram

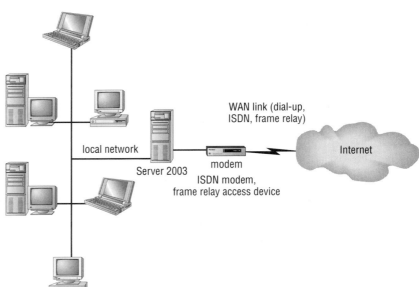

To the left in Figure 6.35, you see your company's local area network connected to the Server 2003 machine that will act as the gateway server. Your computer has two network connections, as do all routers: an Ethernet card that connects it to your internal network, and then some kind of WAN connection to your Internet provider.

The most common kinds of WAN connections are

- A dial-up modem, offering a connection speed of up to 56Kbps
- An ISDN modem, offering a connection speed of up to 144Kbps
- A cable modem, with speeds in the megabit per second range
- A DSL modem, with cable-like speeds
- Your "WAN" connection to the Internet might actually be a LAN connection, as you might be a small group inside some larger company—for example, you might be setting up a training room inside your firm and want to separate your training room's network from the corporate network.

NOTE   *In every case, I'm going to assume that you get just one routable IP address from your ISP and that you'll use some kind of NAT/PAT-like system to share it by giving the PCs in your intranet nonroutable addresses. If you're getting more than one address from your ISP then you'll probably get a dedicated router of some kind from them to do the job; it normally doesn't make sense to use Windows servers in that event.*

People tend to freeze up at the WAN connection part, expecting some insurmountable complexity. But it's not too bad.

Modem and ISDN connections are dial-up connections, not continuous connections. If you intend to host any Internet servers on your local network, such as if you want to run your own DNS, Web, FTP, or e-mail servers, then your network needs a *persistent* connection; it must be connected to the Internet 24 hours a day, 365.24219878 days a year (to be *nearly* exact, that is).

NOTE   *That's an important point: if you're planning on running a server that offers information to the Internet, then your Internet connection must be persistent, and you need to ensure that you have the same IP address from your ISP constantly. Servers are no good unless people can find you, and unless you have the same IP address all the time and are connected to the Internet all the time, they won't be able to find you.*

Dial-up is a pain for building consistent connections because it's hard to keep up and connected. Years ago, when I had my company connected to the Internet on a shoestring budget, I connected our network to our ISP with a 14.4Kbps modem. I used a "flat-rate" phone account, one that cost $25 a month with no charges for local calls. The call to the ISP was local, so I figured I'd just dial up and not hang up. Essentially, I figured, $25 a month bought me a moderately noisy 14.4K dedicated line to the Internet—good deal, right?

It was a constant pain, and let me try to convince you not to try it for your routed Internet connection. First of all, the phone company computers go around and periodically disconnect any dial-up connection that's been up and running too long. Second, most ISPs think *fault-tolerant* refers to their belief that customers will tolerate the ISP's faulty infrastructure, so many ISPs end up reboot-ing their systems periodically, which kicks anyone off the modems and drops the dial-up connection.

Back in 1992, when I had the 14.4 connection running, I had to establish the dial-up connection myself, and when the connection would drop periodically, I'd have to reestablish it with a few commands at the router. You'll see that RRAS has a feature called *on-demand dialing*, which is supposed to sense whenever anyone on the local network needs to get to the Internet, and when the Server 2003 router senses that need, it dials up the Internet. It *sounds* as if this might be the way to ensure that a dial-up connection dials up and stays up: Why not just run a simple batch file that does a ping to somewhere out on the Internet and use the Scheduler service to automatically run the batch file every 20 minutes or so? Seems like a great idea, but in my experience the demand dialer has trouble figuring out whether the modem is currently connected. I've had RRAS tell me that a demand-dial connection was up and running when I could clearly see that the "carrier detect" light on the modem was off.

ISDN offers some of the same problems with the extra fact that you usually get charged by the minute for ISDN connections, which can run up the meter fairly quickly.

The answer for many may be a dedicated connection called a *frame relay* connection. You're charged a flat monthly rate for it, depending on things like how far away you are from the ISP and how fast the connection is. In my experience, a fairly low-speed, 56Kbps frame relay runs around $150–$200 per month. That's just the telco charges for the frame, however; the ISP will levy additional charges to rent you the IP addresses, route your packets, and whatever other services they offer. But you probably will not connect your frame relay directly into your Server box directly; you'll probably only be using frame relay if you've leased a group of IP addresses from your ISP and, as I've suggested, in that case the ISP will probably strongly recommend that you let them install a dedicated router device on your site.

Both cable modem and DSL are very easy to set up in that they connect to your gateway PC using a simple Ethernet connection—nothing new to learn there.

Collect the Pieces and Get Started

If you're connecting with cable modem or DSL then have this information beforehand:

- If you've arranged for a static IP address, have the IP address, subnet mask, and address of the default gateway, and
- The address of any DNS and e-mail servers on the ISP's network.

If you're dialing in, then get those pieces of information, but also get the number to dial into the ISP. If you're dialing in with ISDN, then be sure to talk to the ISP beforehand and get the SPIDs... no two ISPs seem to do ISDN the same way. Once you've collected that information, get started by doing the following:

- Get network cards in all of the local machines and in the server.
- Install the TCP/IP protocol on them. Set their TCP/IP stacks to get IP addresses from DHCP; you'll see more about that later.
- Attach the WAN connection device—modem, ISDN, DSL modem, cable modem, or whatever—on the gateway.

From this point, you've got a few different options to connect your intranet to an ISP; we'll take them one at a time.

Lower-Cost LAN-to-WAN Routing with Internet Connection Sharing

As I've already said, the main aspects of this LAN/WAN connectivity are that:

◆ The only machine on the network with a "regulation," IANA- or ISP-issued IP address is the gateway.

◆ The other machines have nonroutable addresses.

◆ All of the "heavy lifting," routing-wise, is being done by the gateway computer. In fact, the ISP has no idea whatsoever that all of those other computers are accessing the Internet via the gateway.

Recall from our earlier "routing the nonroutable" discussion that this functionality is generically called network address translation (NAT) routing and was until recently fairly expensive to implement, requiring special routers. But ever since Windows 98 Second Edition, Microsoft Windows OSes have included the ability to act as a NAT router. (Even XP or 2000 Pro can do it.) Called Internet Connection Sharing, this will work on any kind of Internet connection, whether it's a modem, ISDN, cable modem, DSL, or whatever.

NOTE *Just to be on the safe side, check your "use agreement" with your ISP. Some ISPs specifically forbid any kind of sharing.*

Basically, there are just four steps to make this work:

1. Attach all of your internal computers together in a network.

2. Connect one of the computers (the one running ICS) to the Internet either via a modem or another Ethernet card. And yes, that's *another* Ethernet card—you can't put the Internet connection on the same segment as the connection to the internal, nonroutable machines. So if you wanted to share a cable modem or DSL connection with your Server system, then you'd have two Ethernet cards in your Server: one connected to your DSL/cable modem, and the other connected to your internal network.

3. You'll now have two connections on the ICS computer—one to the local Ethernet connecting the internal nonroutable machines, and one to the Internet. On the Internet connection, turn on ICS.

4. Tell all of the internal, nonroutable computers to automatically get their IP addresses (which they'll end up getting from the ICS machine), then reboot them.

Once you do all that, the internal systems will have nonroutable IP addresses in the range 192.168.0.2–192.168.0.254—but they'll be able to access the Internet because of ICS's abilities.

WARNING *Before starting, ensure that Routing and Remote Access Services are* not *running on this computer. ICS will refuse to run on a system with RRAS enabled.*

Step One: Connect the Internal Network—and Meet APIPA

This is easy. Just put an Ethernet card in every computer in your home, small business, or whatever set of machines you need ICS for. (I'm kind of hoping you've already done this, or it's reasonable to wonder why you're reading this book!) When configuring the TCP/IP settings as you saw back in Figure 6.11, don't bother punching in any values; instead, just click the radio button labeled Obtain an IP Address Automatically.

Now boot the systems and do an `ipconfig /all`. You'll find that they all have IP addresses in the range between 169.254.0.1 through 169.254.255.254. Where did *those* addresses come from? They're a feature of Microsoft networking since Windows 2000 called Automatic Private IP Addressing (APIPA).

The idea in most IP-based networks, as you'll see in the next chapter, is to set up a kind of server called a Dynamic Host Configuration Protocol (DHCP) server somewhere on the network. That DHCP server then automatically supplies IP addresses to all systems on the network, freeing you from having to walk around to every system and punch in a different IP address. But what happens if you have a system that (1) expects to find a DHCP server and therefore doesn't *have* a static IP address, but that (2) finds itself on a network without a DHCP server? Well, under NT 4, that system would basically just disable its TCP/IP software, and running IPCONFIG would just show your NIC with an IP address of 0.0.0.0. Under Windows 2000 and later OSes, however, it randomly assigns itself an address in the range of 169.254.0.1 through 169.254.255.254, checking to make sure that no one else has this address. Granted, it's not a terribly useful way to get IP addresses on important systems like Web servers, but for a small network that's not intending to talk to any other network, it's not a bad answer. But it's only a temporary answer, as we'll see, because ICS actually includes a basic, no-configuration-necessary DHCP server inside it, and so when we get ICS running, then its DHCP server will hand out more useful addresses to the machines on your internal network— your "intranet."

Step Two: Get Connected to Your ISP

The next step is just to get connected to your ISP. How you do that depends on whether you're dialing up or connecting via some high-speed connection like cable/DSL modem or directly via a corporate network. We'll look at how to get connected via dial-up first.

GET CONNECTED TO YOUR ISP (DIAL-UP)

NOTE   If you connect via DSL or cable modem, then skip this section and go to the next, "Get Connected to Your ISP (Cable Modem/DSL)."

As has been the case with Microsoft OSes since Windows 95, you tell your system to dial up to an ISP by creating a Dial-Up Connection object or, to use Microsoft's phrase, you will create a *connectoid.* (Where they come up with their "wordoids" is beyond me, although I *do* find the tech world's willingness to coin new phrases at a hatdrop—see, I can do it too—interesting.)

Click Start/Control Panel/Network Connections/New Connection Wizard and Server will start a new wizard; click Next to get past the inevitable initial screen and you'll see something like Figure 6.36.

Click Connect to the Internet and Next, and you'll see a screen like Figure 6.37.

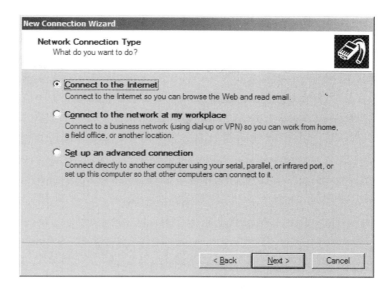

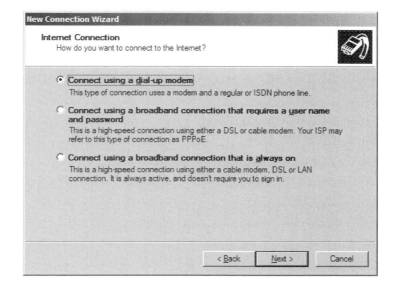

FIGURE 6.36

Creating a new connection

FIGURE 6.37

How to connect?

Tell the wizard that this is just a modem dial-up to the Internet by clicking the radio button labeled Connect Using a Dial-up Modem and click Next. You'll then see a screen like Figure 6.38.

This asks for your ISP name, but don't think that Server will then go out to the Internet (as if it could at this point!) and download info on this ISP; this is really just a label for this connectoid. Fill in a descriptive name and click Next to see something like Figure 6.39.

FIGURE 6.38

Name that
connectoid

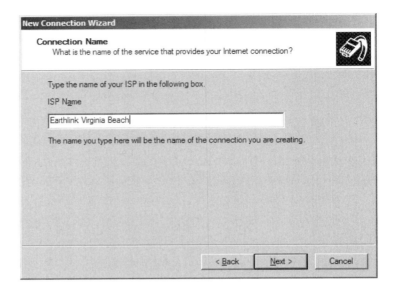

FIGURE 6.39

Number to dial

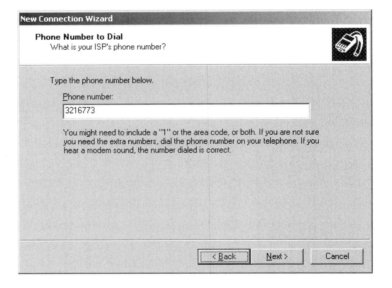

Fill in the number to dial for your ISP and click Next to see Figure 6.40.

Server 2003 wants to know which profiles should use this. As we're just building a router, and routers don't much care *who's* routing through them, set this to Anyone's Use and click Next. You'll see Figure 6.41.

FIGURE 6.40

Who gets to
use this?

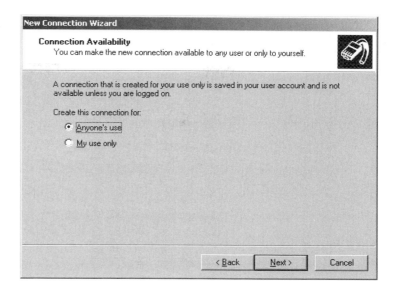

FIGURE 6.41

Login information

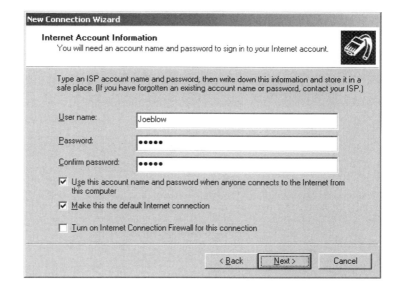

Finally, you need to tell the system what user name and password to employ to get onto the ISP. Fill that in, click Next and Finish and you've got your connectoid, which will open automatically, looking something like Figure 6.42.

FIGURE 6.42

Initial connectoid

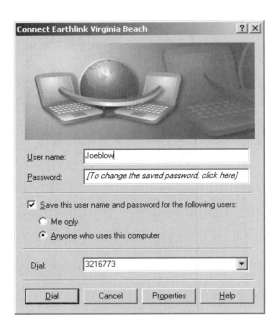

Click the Dial button to check your connectoid. Make sure that you can ping places on the Internet both by IP address and by name. Remember, *first* ping with IP addresses to ensure that routing is working. *Then* ping by DNS names, like www.minasi.com. If pinging by IP address works but pinging by DNS names does not, then the routing is working fine—the problem's with DNS. Then also check that you can ping inside your internal network, your intranet. Again, we're just worried about routing here, so just ping the internal systems by their IP addresses.

Hooked up and pinging okay? Great—then skip down to "Step Three: Turn ICS On."

GET CONNECTED TO YOUR ISP (CABLE MODEM/DSL)

If you connect to the Internet via DSL or cable modem, then you won't be creating one of those connectoids. Instead, as I said earlier in the chapter, you usually connect to a DSL/cable modem with a regular old Ethernet card. Typically, then, all you have to do is install an Ethernet card in your system—remember that it will be a separate Ethernet card from the one that connects to your other computers—and then run a standard Ethernet cable from your DSL/cable modem to the Ethernet card.

I said "usually" because you might choose instead to connect your DSL/cable modem to your PC with a USB connection. I recommend against this for reasons that I mentioned earlier. And once in a great while, you might have to load an extra bit of software on your computer to be able to communicate with your cable modem provider. I've never seen this myself but I'm told that some DSL modem companies make you install some extra piece of software that looks a bit like a modem dialer program so that you can log onto their cable modem network. (I'm *hoping* you don't have to use that kind of connection because honestly I can't advise you about how to share it, as there's no guarantee that such a nonstandard LAN/WAN connection would work with ICS.)

In most cases, though, it's simple: put the Ethernet card in your PC, connect it to the DSL/cable modem, and turn the computer on. A DHCP system at the DSL/cable provider will give your PC a routable IP address. Note that this will probably be an IP address that changes from time to time, so you may have to approach your provider about a static—that is, unchanging—address if you want to host Internet-visible services like Web or mail.

Now try it before going any further. Make sure that the Server 2003 machine attached to the DSL/cable modem connection can surf the Net without any trouble. And check that its other NIC also has a 169.254.x.x address, as there's no DHCP server on your intranet segment. An `ipconfig /all` should show one NIC with a routable address and another with a 169.254.x.x address. You should also be able to ping the computers inside your intranet.

At this point, you might be tempted to put a hub on that cable modem or DSL connection and then just hang your other internal PCs off that hub. *Don't.* At least, not if you want ICS to work.

Step Three: Turn ICS On

If you haven't already done it, go to Network Connections (Start/Control Panel, then right-click Network Connections and choose Open), and you'll see a dialog box like the one that you saw back in Figure 6.9, Network and Dial-Up Connections. You'll see at least one Ethernet connection, probably labeled Local Area Connection, which represents the NIC attached to the internal network. You'll also see an object representing your connection to the Internet—if you dial up with a modem then it'll be a Dial-Up connectoid, or if you're using DSL or cable modem it'll be another Local Area Connection object.

Right-click that object and choose Properties, then in the resulting property page click Advanced. The Advanced page for a connectoid contains different information than the Advanced page of a connectoid for a network card, so you'll either see something like Figure 6.43 or 6.44.

FIGURE 6.43

Advanced properties for a dial-up connection

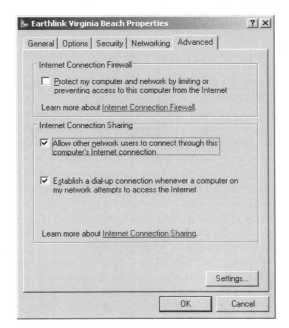

FIGURE 6.44

Advanced properties
for a network card

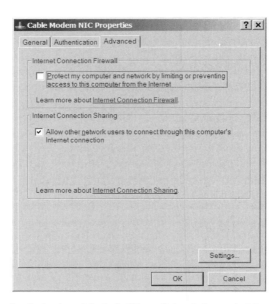

In those figures, check the box labeled Allow Other Network Users to Connect through This Computer's Internet Connection, and click OK. When you click OK to clear the properties page, you may get a confirmation message saying something like this:

```
When Internet Connection Sharing is enabled, your LAN adapter will be set to use
    IP address 192.168.0.1. Your computer may lose connectivity with other computers
    on your network. If these other computers have static IP addresses, you should
    set them to obtain their IP addresses automatically. Are you sure you want to
    enable Internet Connection Sharing?
```

I say "may" because sometimes it pops up and sometimes it doesn't; I've not figured out what makes it appear or not.

Click OK and you'll return to Network Connections, where you'll see that your connectoid or NIC now have the status "shared" in addition to "enabled," "connected," or the like. For example, the shared cable modem connection produces a Network Connection window that looks like Figure 6.45.

FIGURE 6.45

Network
Connections with
ICS enabled

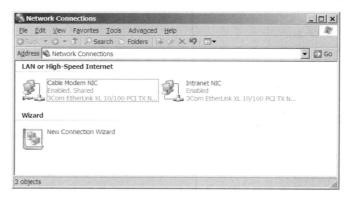

Step Four: Configure the Intranet Machines

You're now ready to share the wealth, Internet connection-wise. You have already configured your systems in your internal network, your intranet, to get their IP addresses automatically. "Automatically" means that they look for a DHCP server and if there is one then they get their IP addresses from that DHCP server. If there's no DHCP server—which has been the case until recently on your intranet—then they just give themselves APIPA addresses in the 169.254.x.x range.

Now that ICS is running, your network now has a DHCP server, as ICS includes a simple DHCP server. You need to go tell your systems on your intranet to try to find a DHCP server again and, while there are several ways to do that, the simplest is to just reboot. But before you do, check the machines—it appears that XP systems are smart enough to detect that there's now a DHCP server in residence, and so you'll probably find that they've *already* got an address. The client systems will all have addresses in the 192.168.0.x range.

What About the Firewall?

You probably noticed back in Figures 6.43 and 6.44 the check box referencing something called the Internet Connection Firewall (ICF). It's a very simple firewall, but better than nothing. It basically rejects any data originating out in the public Internet... *unless* that data from the public Internet is a response to a request from your computer.

Suppose, for example, that my computer tried to ping your computer. A ping is just a packet of data that asks your computer to respond, as you've seen. Your computer would not respond to the ping, as the firewall would see the incoming ping packet ("ICMP packet" is the more accurate phrase) and ask, "Does this answer some question that we asked someone on the Internet?" Of course, it wouldn't, as I initiated the conversation, not you.

In contrast, suppose you pinged *me* from behind your firewall. (Assume I don't have a firewall, and have a routable address on the public Internet.) Your ICMP request comes to me and my computer responds with an acknowledgment packet. That acknowledgment goes to your computer and is examined by ICF, which says, "Hmmm...why is this guy sending me data? IS HE TRYING TO HACK ME???" As ICF has been keeping track of all of the outgoing traffic, however, it says, "Ah, now I see...this is just an answer to our ping," and so it lets it past. Such a firewall type is called a "stateful" firewall, as it keeps track of the "state" of conversations on the Internet.

If you decide to use ICF, then you should be aware of a few things. First, don't ever turn ICF on *inside* your network, particularly on servers. Remember, ICF rejects any incoming data that isn't a response to some request; but servers don't *make* requests, they *answer* requests. (Well, basically.) So if you had your Web server behind ICF then everyone who tried to connect to your Web server would be rebuffed. You'd have a *secure* server, all right, just not a very useful one. Additionally, servers in a domain do a lot of back-and-forth communication for authentication, and ICF would block a lot of that communication, which would render any ICFed system unable to participate in the domain. ICFing a workstation would make it impossible to offer its user remote control, use backup agents, and the like. So if you are going to use ICF, only use it on a machine that stands between your intranet and the Internet—what firewall types call your "edge" machine.

I just suggested that ICF would make a Web server useless, but that's not 100 percent true. If you had a Web server directly connected to the public Internet and you wanted some basic firewall protection for it—a quite good idea—then ICF's not a bad idea. But how do you keep it from turning your Web visitors away? Back on that Advanced tab, click the Settings button and you'll see check boxes that tell ICF to pass traffic for particular kinds of servers—Web, FTP, e-mail, etc. You can even open particular ports if you know their numbers.

Beyond ICS: Setting Up Network Address Translation (NAT) on Server 2003

ICS is great, but what if you want more? On the one hand, ICS lets you easily connect a bunch of internal machines to the Internet via one routable address—it's quite literally a matter of a click or two and you're done. But you can't change the range of addresses that ICS's mini-DHCP server gives out. Nor can you facilitate *incoming* traffic—ICS is basically a simple port address translation router. Any system inside your network can initiate an outbound conversation, but outside systems on the public Internet can't initiate an incoming conversation. Furthermore, ICS really only makes sense if you only have one routable IP address. That won't always be true—and so you'll sometimes want to configure network address translation rather than ICS.

For simplicity's sake, let me assume that your Internet connection is via a NIC of some kind— DSL, cable modem, or perhaps you've built an isolated network within your Internet-connected business—rather than a dial-up connection. For example, consider a training lab: Most medium- to large-sized companies have a room or two filled with a bunch of networked computers used for teaching classes. Those computers typically get nonroutable addresses but sometimes need outside Internet access, and so corporate IT departments usually need to set aside a routable address or two for the training lab and then need to somehow share those routable addresses with the training lab's non-routable addresses. Most places use a Cisco router to accomplish that sharing, but there's no reason why a Server 2003 server that's already in the training lab can't do that job and save the training department the cost of the Cisco router.

And, before we go any further, let me clarify that the machine sitting between the private non-routable network and the public Internet is a Server 2003 machine. It *can't* be an XP Professional machine, as Pro only offers ICS—no NAT. For the sake of this explanation, let's call that in-between box Between. As you've already read, looking in Network Connections will show two Local Area Network connection objects.

As you've also already read, enabling ICS in this scenario is simple. Just open Network Connections, find the NIC that's connected to the Internet and choose Properties. In the properties page that results, click the Advanced tab, check the box labeled Allow Other Network Users to Connect through This Computer's Internet Connection, click OK, and then click Yes to the resulting dialog box. No news here—you just read how to do that. After a brief delay, ICS will start working. The NIC attached to the private network now has the static IP address 192.168.0.1. Your Internet-attached computer now runs a simple kind of DHCP server that hands out IP addresses in the private network range of 192.168.0.0 through 192.168.0.255. Set the computers on the internal network to look to DHCP for their IP addresses and reboot them, and they will get addresses on the 192.168.0.0 network and will look to the 192.168.0.1 system as their default gateway. Try a ping from any system on the internal network and you'll see that network now has Internet connectivity.

ICS LIMITATIONS

But ICS is limited in several ways. First of all, you cannot configure anything about the DHCP server built into ICS. Second, while any system on the internal network can access systems on the Internet, it's not possible for systems on the Internet to access the systems on the private network—if I were to ping your system at (for example) 192.168.0.100 from a computer on the Internet, I would not get a response from your system. That could be good from a security point of view, and so many people might not see this as a disadvantage at all.

But suppose you had a Web server on an internal machine hosting a terrific site that you wanted to offer to the public Internet. And suppose a *different* machine, also on the internal network, ran a mail server that, of course, won't be much good unless it can both send mail and receive mail. You could, of course, also just install the mail server and Web server software on Between, but you might not want one box acting as router, mail, and Web server—to make that work you'll have to abandon ICS and instead use NAT and its support of "inbound" connections. But NAT's a bit more complex to set up, so let's start out by duplicating ICS's functions, then we'll add inbound connections.

RRAS/NAT SETUP TO DUPLICATE ICS

Start off by disabling Internet Connection Sharing on Between; let me start this explanation by first using NAT to simply reproduce what ICS does. *Then* we can add on it.

For ease of explanation, name the NIC attached to the public Internet Cable modem NIC. Name the NIC attached to your intranet Intranet NIC.

Assign the address 192.168.0.1 to the Intranet NIC. (You needn't use *that* IP address in general— I'm just duplicating ICS's functionality as closely as I can.) Next, 2003 requires that we enable our old friend Routing and Remote Access. I've walked you through RRAS a few times now, so I'll be brief:

1. Click Start/Administrative Tools/Routing and Remote Access.

2. You will see an icon representing your Server 2003 server system in the left panel of the MMC screen. Right-click it and choose Configure Routing and Remote Access, which starts the RRAS Setup Wizard.

3. Click Next to get to the first screen, labeled Configuration, as you see in Figure 6.46.

FIGURE 6.46

RRAS Configuration page

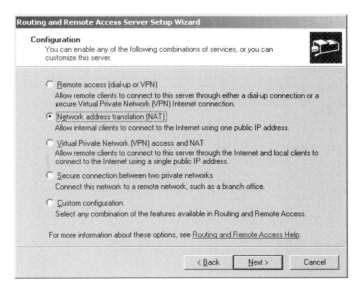

4. Choose Network Address Translation (NAT) and click Next to get to the NAT configuration screen in Figure 6.47.

FIGURE 6.47

NAT connection

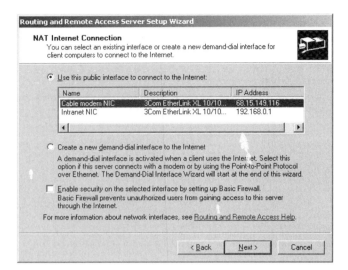

5. There's a lot going on in this panel. First, up top, the wizard wants you to tell it which NIC is attached to the Internet. It has guessed that the Cable modem NIC is, as it's got a routable address. If it guesses wrong in your case, then just click the NIC that *is* attached to the public Internet. Second, notice the Create a New Demand-Dial Interface to the Internet option. You'd use this if you wanted to use a modem to attach to the Internet. I'm not going to walk you through that step-by-step because if you click that radio button then the process looks pretty much identical to what you saw in the earlier ICS discussion. Finally, at the bottom, there's a check box to turn on a simple ICF-like firewall. Again, turn it on if you like—but only on systems that truly face the public Internet directly. If you were just creating an internal training network inside your company and the "public" NIC were in fact just a NIC on your corporate intranet, then you probably wouldn't want a firewall enabled. Once you've got this as you'd like it, click Next to see something like Figure 6.48.

FIGURE 6.48

How to handle DNS and DHCP

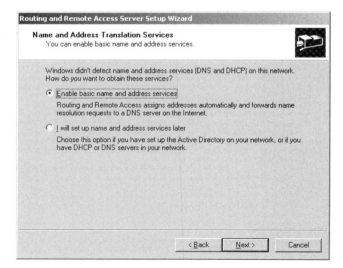

6. NAT under 2003 works a bit differently than it did under 2000—for the better, in my opinion. The basic firewall is a nice touch, but the ease of configuring NAT is just as welcome. Click Enable Basic Name and Address Services, and click Next to tell NAT what addresses to use, as you see in Figure 6.49.

FIGURE 6.49

NAT sets up an address range

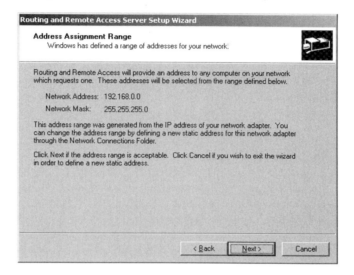

7. Another nice touch—NAT just looks at the address that you set for the Intranet NIC and says, "Well, I guess he wants me to use the subnet that address fits in."

8. With that, click Next and Finish and your NAT router is working. RRAS will look something like Figure 6.50.

FIGURE 6.50

RRAS after NAT setup

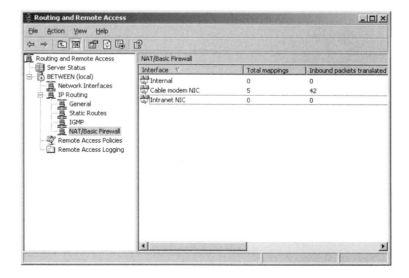

BEYOND ICS I: PORT MAPPING

Now we've duplicated ICS's functionality in NAT. Let's take it further.

Discussions of sharing a single routable address, or a small number of routable addresses, with a larger number of machines on a *non*routable network usually have DSL or cable modem connections in mind. But that's not the only potential "target market," so to speak, for NAT. As you've read elsewhere in this chapter, sharing a routable address via ICS only allows the internal (nonroutable) computers to initiate conversations to the outside Internet, not the reverse. For example, an internal computer could surf an external Web site; but if you were to set up one of the internal 192.168.0.0 computers as a Web server, then it would be impossible for a computer on the routable public Internet to surf that Web server. Is there a way around this? Well, if your internal-network-to-Internet connection is just a machine running ICS, then you're stuck—but with NAT, you can easily arrange matters so that external computers can connect to resources on your internal network.

How you'd let the Internet access an internal Web server (or mail server, FTP server, or whatever else; I'll stick to Web servers here for simplicity, but making any type of server available works the same) depends crucially on one question: How many routable IP addresses do you have available? Let's first consider the case wherein you only have one routable IP address available. In case it's not obvious, you have no choice about what to do with that address: You've got to assign it to the computer acting as the router (which, for simplicity, I'll just call the router).

One way to offer a public Web server in this one-address case would be, of course, to set up IIS on the router. But you might not want to do that, either because NT (and therefore 2003) has never been all that good at doing a lot of different things on one machine, or perhaps because you need a system with more horsepower to run a complex site.

Just to make this explanation concrete, let's arbitrarily assign a few IP addresses. Let's say that the router has a routable IP address of 68.15.149.116, and that its internal nonroutable address is 192.168.0.1. Let's suppose the computer on the internal network that's running the Web server is on the internal nonroutable address 192.168.0.51. That Web server needs a routable address to be visible to the public Internet, but you've already used your only routable address on the router—what to do?

NAT allows you to redirect a particular port from the router to a particular port on a particular computer on the internal network. Web connections usually come into a Web server on port 80, so you just tell the router to refer any incoming communications on the router's port 80 to port 80 on 192.168.0.51. And as I promised, I'll show you how to set up that Web server on 192.168.0.51…but I need to take an intermediate step first.

To tell NAT that you're going to map a particular port to a particular internal address, open RRAS and open the NAT/Basic Firewall object in the left pane. In the right pane you'll see three objects: your intranet NIC, the NIC connected to the Internet (Cable modem NIC, in our example), and something called Internal. Right-click the NIC connected to the Internet and choose Properties, and then click the tab labeled Services and Ports. You'll see a screen like Figure 6.51.

This page lists the most common servers that you'd probably want to build for your network—mail servers, remote control, VPNs, just about anything you'd want.

Notice I said "*just* about." For some reason, a regular old Web server isn't there. We've got to build it as a custom port map, which is why I'm leaving it for a bit later. Right now, let's say that the machine at .51 is a POP mail server. Check the box labeled Post-Office Protocol Version 3 (POP3). That raises a dialog box called Edit Service, as you see in Figure 6.52.

FIGURE 6.51

Mapping ports to
particular systems
in NAT

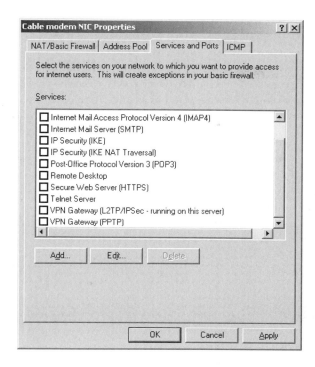

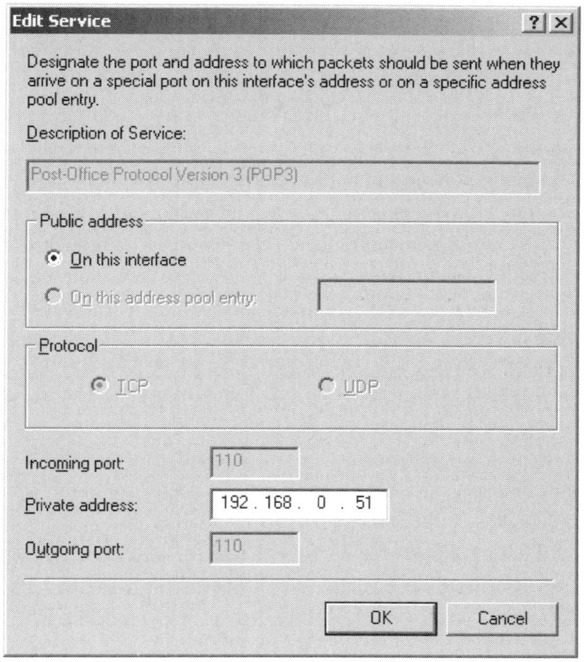

FIGURE 6.52

Assigning an internal
address for the port

All you need do is to punch in the server's IP address in the "private address" field, and click OK. In a nice touch, this causes the basic firewall to open that port, if you've got the basic firewall enabled.

Now let's punch a "custom" hole in the NAT router for our Web server. Back at that Cable modem NIC properties page (which will have a different name, recall, if you didn't name the NIC attached to the public Internet Cable modem NIC) and the Services and Ports tab that you saw in Figure 6.51, click Edit to see a dialog box like Figure 6.53.

FIGURE 6.53

Defining a
Web server

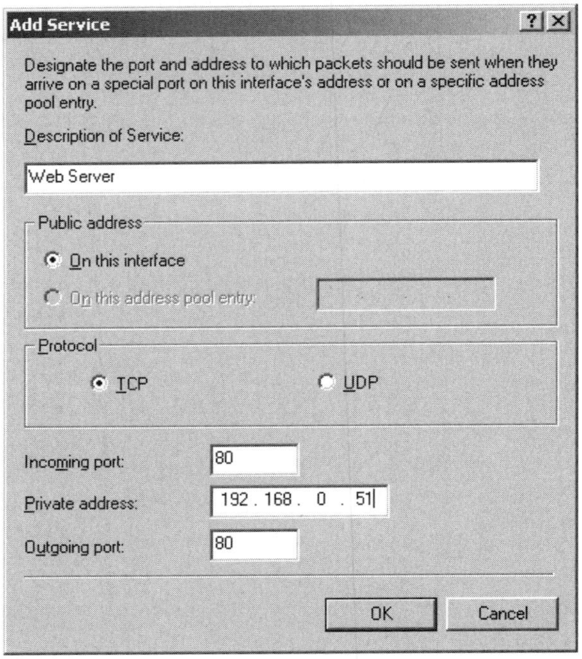

It's very similar to the dialog that you saw in Figure 6.52, but you have to add a name (Web Server), specify an incoming and outgoing port (80 in both cases, as you see in the figure) and finish up by telling NAT which internal address to map the port 80 traffic to.

To review what I'm trying to accomplish here: A request comes in to the Web server at 68.15.149.116 or, in other words, a request comes in to 68.15.149.116:80, as 80 is the HTTP port. What I want NAT to do is move the request over to the machine addressed as 192.168.0.51, and address it to port 80 on that machine. When might I have set the incoming and outgoing ports to different values? In my experience, you *wouldn't* do it all that often, but if for some reason you wanted to set up the Web server at 192.168.0.51 on port 10000, then you'd fill in **10000** on Outgoing Port so that traffic from the Internet—which expects to do Web business on port 80—would get to the Web server.

BEYOND ICS II: ADJUSTING ADDRESS RANGES AND FIREWALL OPTIONS

But recall that one of my complaints with ICS was that it forced me to use the 192.168.0.x range. Can NAT do better? Sure. In RRAS, right-click the object labeled NAT/Basic Firewall and choose Properties, then click the tab labeled Address Assignment and you'll see something like Figure 6.54.

FIGURE 6.54

Changing the internal address range

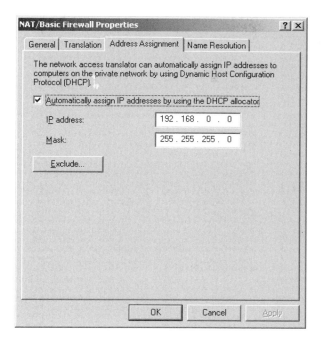

From this page you could change your range of internal addresses to anything you want. But if you do, then be sure that the static address that you give the intranet-attached NIC is on the same subnet as your address range! Also, if you have systems inside your intranet with static IP addresses, you can just click the Exclude button and specify them. Then the mini-DHCP server in NAT doesn't accidentally give those addresses to some other system on your intranet.

Finally, what if you initially turned off the firewall but then decide that you'd like it enabled? Open the NAT/Basic Firewall object in the left pane of the MMC and in the right pane you'll see an object representing the NIC attached to the Internet—Cable modem NIC, in my example. Right-click that and choose Properties, then click the NAT/Basic Firewall tab. It will look like Figure 6.55.

Just click Enable a Basic Firewall on This Interface, and you've got at least *some* protection from the bad guys.

TROUBLESHOOTING ICS AND NAT

Sometimes you'll try to set up ICS or NAT and it doesn't work. Don't give up—fixing routers can be easy. Just be methodical. Consider that there are three components to any intranet-to-Internet routing system—the Internet, the gateway (the box running ICS, NAT, or whatever—the thing acting as a router), and the intranet (the machines inside your network that want to get to the Internet).

FIGURE 6.55

Turning the firewall
on/off

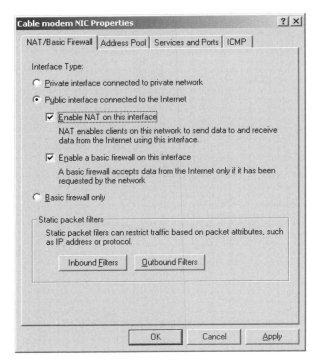

First, check that the gateway PC can communicate with the Internet. Check this with a ping to an IP address, *not* a DNS address—check IP connectivity without confusing things vis-à-vis name resolution; for example, ping 206.246.253.1. *Then* do a ping to some location by its DNS address; for example, ping www.minasi.com. If these don't work, then either your connection to the outside world (cable, DSL, or whatever) has failed, or you've got something strange going on in your routing table that makes it try to route to the Internet via the internal network. If IP pings work but DNS pings don't, then check DNS.

Next, check that the gateway can communicate with the intranet. Ping systems inside your network, again by IP address and then DNS. Same approach here—check routing if it's an IP problem, DNS/WINS if it's a name problem.

Then check that the intranet systems can ping the gateway. As before, ping the IP address (the intranet side, 192.168.0.1, or whatever you set it to), then the name.

Finally, check that the intranet systems can ping the outside world through the gateway, by IP and by name. Using this simple methodology breaks down the problem into something tractable.

Understanding IPSec

Basic garden-variety IP lacks security, and that's fine in most cases—if you're just visiting my Web page, then you really don't care much if anyone were to snoop on you, unless of course your boss had issued an edict against visiting my site. And it's possible but very unlikely that someone on the Internet, sitting on a computer between you and me, would take the time to somehow intercept the data that my Web site were sending your browser, modifying it before sending it to you so as to produce a falsified page.

But many communications *do* need security. If you were to visit my Web site to buy something online, then you'd want *that* communication secured. SSL solves that problem, but it's pretty much restricted to a Web-only protocol. If a company had two offices across the country from one another but used the Internet to connect a server in one site to a server in the other site, then the company would probably want to ensure that any communications between those two servers both couldn't be snooped upon and couldn't be modified along the way by evildoers. SSL wouldn't really be the answer for that.

Instead, another set of protocols called IP Security (IPSec) seek to provide a generic answer for securing IP-based networks. IPSec operates at the same layer as IP, rather than SSL, which, again, is an application-layer protocol. IPSec is also a necessary part of using the Virtual Private Network (VPN) protocol L2TP—you can't run L2TP without IPSec.

IPSec's Four Security Options

IPSec lets you choose how secure a communication between two computers will be. Basically, it offers four levels of security:

- ◆ Block transmissions
- ◆ Encrypt transmissions
- ◆ Sign transmissions
- ◆ Permit transmissions to travel unchanged, without signing or encrypting them

Let's examine those in a bit more detail.

Block Transmission

This does just what it sounds like: It blocks transmissions. When you tell IPSec to "block" traffic from machine X to machine Y, then the IPSec code on machine Y just simply discards any traffic coming in from machine X.

Although this might seem at first blush to be kind of useless, if you think about it then you'll see that it isn't at all. In some senses, blocking traffic is the most extreme option for security, right? For example, my firm might have a competitor whose systems run on subnet 200.200.100.0, and I don't want them to be able to send me mail, visit my Web site, or communicate with my network in any way. (These could clearly be mortal-enemy types of competitors.) I could set up IPSec on my systems to block that subnet, just discarding any packets that arrive.

Encrypt Transmission

Here, I *want* to allow traffic to pass from machine X to machine Y, but I'm worried that someone will eavesdrop on the network connection between X and Y. So I tell IPSec to use a protocol called the Encapsulating Security Payload—and I'll bet you didn't need to be precognitive to guess that its acronym is ESP—to encrypt the traffic before putting it on the network. Snoopers will only see an unreadable, random-looking stream of bytes.

Notice how convenient it is that IPSec works way down at the network protocol layer—it can encrypt *anything*. Do you like the convenience of Telnet but hate that it sends its information in cleartext? Just tell IPSec that whenever machine X and machine Y are using Telnet to communicate that IPSec should use ESP to encrypt the communication. No modification required at all to the Telnet server or client.

When would encryption be useful? Perhaps you have a few machines inside your intranet that handle very sensitive information—payroll info or perhaps customer credit cards. The data might be kept on a machine named SQL1, and it might be entered and edited only from workstations WS1, WS2, and WS3. You might fear that an insider might set up a sniffer on the network to trap this traffic as it goes by, collecting privileged information. You can keep people from accessing SQL1's database in the first place with permissions, as you already know. But you can keep people from listening on the wire by creating IPSec policies on SQL1 that force it to encrypt any communications to and from WS1, WS2, or WS3, and you can create similar policies on those workstations.

Or, in another instance, suppose you had a server in Chicago and offices all around the country, containing workstations that need to access data on that server. Suppose also that the only way that the offices connect to Chicago is over the public Internet, and you're (rightly) concerned that running company data over the public Internet might not be the best idea, security-wise. You could create an IPSec policy on the Chicago server so that it will only accept encrypted traffic—it never accepts cleartext communications. You would then create IPSec policies on the workstations so that they only communicate with the Chicago server via ESP.

NOTE   *And in case you're thinking, "What if that company had firewalls at every location—would IPSec work through a firewall?" The answer is yes. You must open UDP port 500 and permit protocols number 50 and 51.*

Sign Transmission

In certain kinds of network attacks, the bad guys fool your computer into thinking that transmissions from them are transmissions from someone that you trust. Or other attacks involve grabbing transmission packets somewhere between you and the trusted person, modifying the packets and sending them along to you—a so-called "man-in-the-middle" attack. IPSec lets you guard against this with a protocol called Authentication Header (AH). AH is a method for digitally *signing* communications. If your computer and mine are performing signed communications, then we're *not* encrypting our data—anyone listening on the wire could overhear our communications. Instead, digital signing adds a bit of data to the end of our network packets that we can use to verify that the data wasn't changed in transit.

Permit Transmission

Permit is IPSec's phrase for "no security at all." It just tells IPSec to let the traffic pass without any changes to it and no checks on its integrity. This is basically what happens in a TCP/IP-based network that doesn't include any IPSec. Why, then, have a "permit" action at all? So that you can create rules that restrict some things but not others, such as a rule (which you'll see us build later) that says, "Block all incoming traffic *except* for traffic on ports 80 and 443—permit that traffic."

IPSEC FILTERS

Now that you know what IPSec can do, let's examine an important flexibility about IPSec—its filters. In my examples so far, I've said that you can direct IPSec to encrypt traffic between two particular systems. In another example, I said that you could tell IPSec not only to encrypt transmissions between two particular systems, but that you could further refine IPSec's mission by saying that it should encrypt transmissions between those two systems *only when running Telnet*. In the section on blocking traffic altogether, I suggested that you might want to tell your Web server to block any traffic at all from subnet 200.200.100.0.

More specifically, you can use filters to restrict IPSec to securing communications:

◆ By the source computer's IP address, IP subnet, or DNS name

◆ By the destination computer's IP address, IP subnet, or DNS name

◆ By the port and port type (TCP, UDP, ICMP, and so on)

All of this makes for a very nice amount of flexibility in IPSec-ing.

IPSEC RULES = IPSEC ACTIONS + IPSEC FILTERS

Blocking, encrypting, signing, or permitting traffic is said to be an IPSec *action*. You've just met IPSec filters. But to use IPSec, you combine a filter and an action to produce a *rule*. For example, suppose you want to tell the IPSec system on a given computer, "Encrypt all Telnet traffic from the computer at 10.10.11.3." *That's* a rule. It has a filter part and an action part:

◆ The *filter* part says, "Only activate this rule if there is traffic that is (1) from IP address 10.10.11.3, and (2) uses TCP port 23." (In case you didn't know, Telnet uses port 23.)

◆ The *action* part says, "Encrypt the traffic."

We'll build some IPSec rules, filters, and actions in a bit, once I've gotten a few more concepts out of the way.

SIGNING AND ENCRYPTING NEED ONE MORE PIECE: AUTHENTICATION

To make either digital signatures or encryption work, you need a set of agreed-upon *keys*—passwords, basically. So whenever you create an IPSec rule, then you'll have to tell IPSec how to authenticate.

Microsoft's IPSec supports three methods of authenticating: Kerberos, certificates, or an agreed-upon key. The Kerberos option only works between computers that are either in an Active Directory domain, or in AD domains that trust one another. Simply having two computers that have Kerberos clients won't be sufficient and, insofar as I can see, even two Windows systems that are members of the same Unix-based Kerberos version 5 realm (the Kerberos version of what we call a domain in the Microsoft world) can't use IPSec to communicate while authenticating with Kerberos. Perhaps Microsoft should have called this option "Active Directory" rather than "Kerberos."

The *certificates* option allows you to use Public Key Infrastructure (PKI) certificates to identify a machine. The *preshared key* option lets you use a regular cleartext string as the key. Not very secure, but as Microsoft is always very careful to say, "Hey, it was in the RFC, so we had to include it." *I* love the preshared key option, myself, as it's great for experimentation. No need to set up a certificate or an AD domain—just tell both machines to use a preshared key and they type in some text, like "this is a secret" on both machines. I wouldn't use it in a production environment, but for teaching and testing purposes, it's great.

WARNING   *Microsoft's IPSec implementation of authentication has a sort of annoying habit: It demands an authentication method whether IPSec needs it or not. You see, simply permitting traffic through without changing it, or blocking it altogether, does not require any agreed-upon keys, so in theory any rule that only includes permitting and blocking should not require choosing an authentication method—it'd be like the Department of Motor Vehicles asking you whether you put regular or high-test gas in your electric car when you registered it. But, again, Microsoft's IPSec asks you for an authentication method anyway, even though it'll never use it. So if you're building an IPSec rule that only permits and/or blocks, then go ahead and choose any authentication method; it doesn't matter.*

HOW IPSEC WORKS IN WINDOWS

That was the theory. Let's see how to actually do IPSec in Win2K and later OSes. There isn't really an "IPSec manager" program built into Windows; instead, Microsoft set things up so that you do IPSec entirely through policies, whether local policies or domain-based policies.

NOTE   I know we haven't covered domain-based group policies yet, but don't worry—I'll show you how to do this with a local policy. Then, as you'll learn later when we cover domain-based group policies in Chapter 9, the only real difference between local policies and domain policies is that you can centrally create a domain policy on an Active Directory domain controller and it then gets distributed to machines around the network. That's convenient because it means that you needn't travel around to each machine on your network to configure IPSec—or any of the hundreds of other things that domain policies can do.

To make IPSec do our bidding, we'll first open the Local Security Policy snap-in: Click Start/ Programs/Administrative Tools/Local Security Policy, or Start/Run and type **secpol.msc** and press Enter. It's a standard MMC snap-in, and in the left "command" pane, you'll see icons for Account Policies, Local Policies, Public Key Policies, and one called IP Security Policies on Local Machine— click on that. You'll see a screen like Figure 6.56.

FIGURE 6.56

Initial IPSec policies

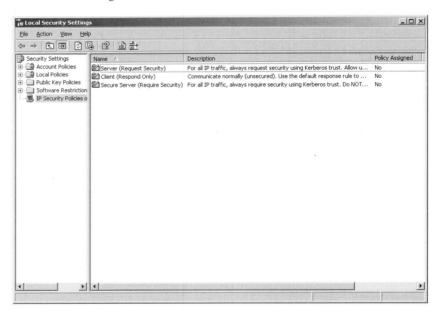

In the right pane, you see three policies—Client (Respond Only), Secure Server (Require Security), and Server (Request Security). Those are three prebuilt policies that Microsoft ships with the OS. In the extreme right column, you see No next to each one; that means none of them are activated or *assigned* in Windows lingo. You can activate any policy by right-clicking it and choosing Assign. But you can only have one policy assigned at a time, that's important—if you want to add some functionality to a current IPSec policy, then you can't just create a new policy and assign it, as that will *un*assign whatever policy is currently in force.

So, for example, suppose I were configuring IPSec on a server and I wanted to instruct that server to always encrypt communications when talking to server SV1 and to always digitally sign communications when talking to server SV2. I could create a policy that forces my system to encrypt when talking to SV1 and a second policy that forces my system to sign when talking to SV2. But if I did, then I'd see that I can only have one policy in force at a time. The *correct* way to see to handling SV1 and SV2 correctly would be to create *one* policy that contained *two* rules—one for SV1 and one for SV2. And note that you do not have to have *any* IPSec policies assigned at a given time—in fact, in Figure 6.66, no policies were assigned.

Let's review what we've seen so far about IPSec:

◆ You control and enable IPSec on Microsoft operating systems through policies. You can only have one IPSec policy active on any given machine.

◆ Policies contain rules, which tell IPSec what to do, and authentication methods, which tell IPSec how the receiver (or receivers) and the transmitter (or transmitters) will exchange a password. They will then use that password in order to sign or encrypt the traffic. Even though permit and block rules don't use authentication, Windows requires that you specify an authentication method.

◆ IPSec lets you authenticate via the Active Directory, PKI certificates, or a preshared key.

◆ Rules contain a filter or filters that tell the rule when to kick in, and rules contain actions that tell the rule what to do.

◆ There are four possible actions: block, encrypt, sign, or permit.

If that sounds like perhaps more work than you bargained for just to get a bit of secure traffic, then wait, don't run away—Microsoft has prebuilt three nice, generic policies that might just fill the bill for you. So you might not have to write any policies at all—just find the one that works for your needs and turn it on.

Default IPSec Policies

The three policies that come with IPSec are called Client (Respond Only), Server (Request Security), and Secure Server (Require Security).

The Client (Respond Only) policy tells a computer not to use IPSec unless requested. So, for example, suppose you set this policy on your workstation and try to access a Web site on a system that doesn't support IPSec. In that case, the server (the Web server) won't try to initiate IPSec with your computer, so your computer won't insist on IPSec-ing the transaction, so all is well. But if your computer tries to connect to a server that *does* do IPSec, then the server will say to your workstation, "let's do IPSec," and your workstation will be able to oblige.

The Server (Request Security) policy should cause your computer to attempt to initiate IPSec whenever possible. But if the client computer either can't or won't use IPSec, then your computer should talk to it anyway.

As you'd expect, the Secure Server (Require Security) policy is designed to disallow any communications that don't use IPSec.

Creating a Custom IPSec Policy

Let's walk through a simple example of setting up an IPSec policy that will ensure an encrypted connection between two machines. Suppose you work at home and have a persistent connection to the Internet—DSL, cable modem, or the like—with a static IP address of 199.10.10.3. Your job involves updating a database on a machine across the Internet from you, a machine at 206.20.20.10. You want that connection to be encrypted and, just for simplicity's sake, we'll use a preshared key. In this simple example, I'll assume that the only system that 199.10.10.3 wants to IPSec with is the 206.20.20.10 machine, and vice versa.

We'll need two policies—one for the 199.10.10.3 machine and one for the 206.20.20.10 machine. Each has two rules in addition to the default rule. The first rule for 199.10.10.3 will consist of this:

Filter   Trigger the rule whenever there is traffic to 206.20.20.10, over any port.

Action   Encrypt the data.

Authentication   Preshared key, key "secret."

The second rule is the reverse—trigger the rule whenever there is traffic *from* 206.20.20.10; the rest of the rule is the same as the first.

The easiest way to create a rule is to first define filters and actions, and *then* create the rule out of the new filter and action.

To define a filter, in Local Security Policy, right-click the object labeled IP Security Policies on Local Machine and choose Manage IP Filter Lists and Filter Actions. You'll see a dialog box like the one in Figure 6.57.

FIGURE 6.57

Dialog box to manage filters and actions

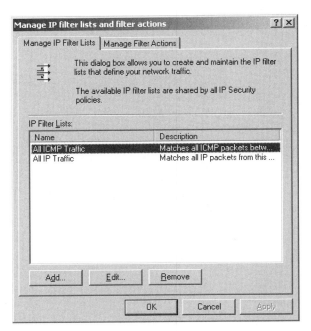

Notice that there are already two filters—All ICMP Traffic and All IP Traffic. They are there because Microsoft needed them to define the three prebuilt policies. I'll create the "traffic to 206.20.20.10" rule by clicking Add to open the dialog box in Figure 6.58.

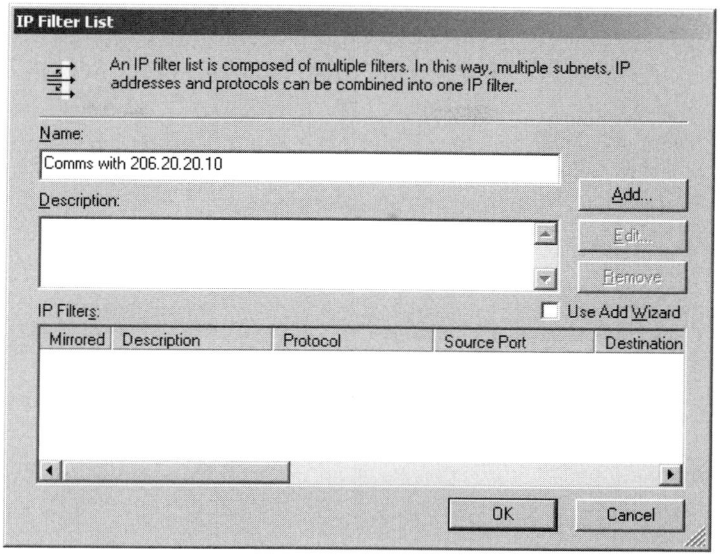

FIGURE 6.58

Creating a new filter, part 1

This dialog box doesn't actually let you create a new filter; it's sort of a staging area for new filters. (Don't ask me why they built it this way.) Give the filter a name, such as Comms with 206.20.20.10. Then, to define the filter, uncheck Use Add Wizard and click Add to raise the dialog box you see in Figure 6.59.

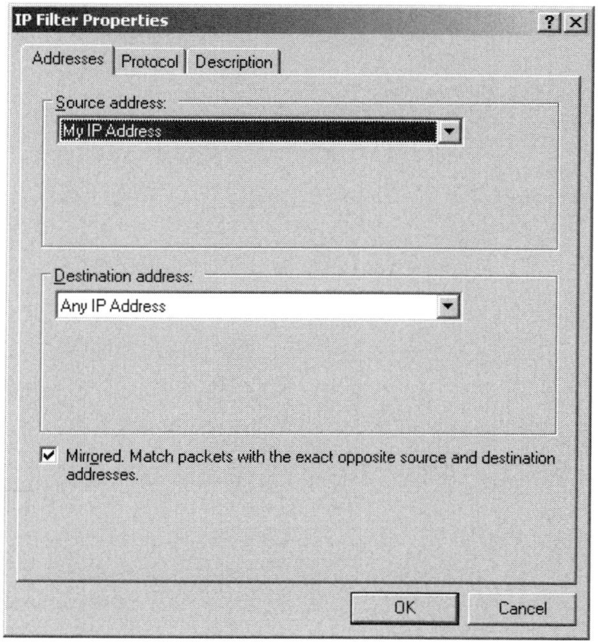

FIGURE 6.59

Filter Properties dialog box

For Source Address, leave it as is. For Destination Address, click the drop-down arrow and you'll see nine options: My IP Address, Any IP Address, A Specific DNS Name, A Specific IP Address, four options (DNS, DHCP, WINS and Default Gateway) that dynamically refer to those four types of servers, and A Specific IP Subnet. Choose A Specific IP Address, and punch in **206.20.20.10**. If you like, click the Description tab and describe the filter. If you were going to specify only traffic on a particular port, then you'd click the Protocol tab—it lets you specify the protocol type (UDP, TCP, ICMP, and others) and a port number.

One more thing before you click OK—the Mirrored check box. Leave it checked. *Mirror* means to use the rule in both directions—don't just activate it from "my address" to 206.20.20.10; also activate it from 206.20.20.10 to "my address." This saves us the trouble of creating that second rule—quite convenient. Now you're ready to click OK until you're back to the Manage IP Filter Lists and Filter Actions dialog box.

Defining an Action   Next, to define an action, click the tab labeled Manage Filter Actions. You'll see something like Figure 6.60.

FIGURE 6.60

Default filter actions

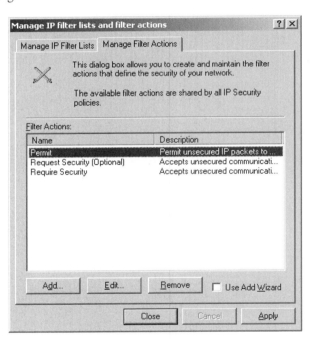

As before, skip the wizard—it's of no help. Uncheck Use Add Wizard, and click Add to show a dialog box like Figure 6.61.

Thus far, I've said that IPSec offers four possible actions, but you see only three here—Permit, Block, and Negotiate Security. That's because Negotiate Security includes signing and encryption. You can see the check box that tells your system to accept nonsecured information, but leave it unchecked: We want to be sure that this communication is secured, or we don't want to do it at all. To specify the encryption, ensure that the radio button Negotiate Security is chosen, and then click Add to see a dialog box like the one in Figure 6.62.

FIGURE 6.61

Defining the action

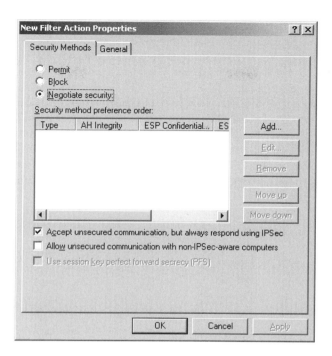

FIGURE 6.62

Choosing signing
or encryption

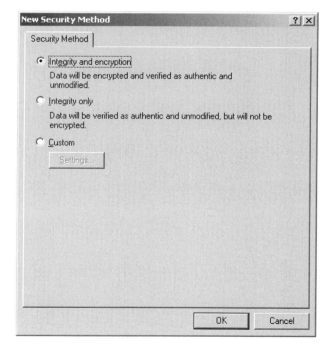

Click Integrity and Encryption and OK to choose encryption. As you can see, you could choose signing-only by clicking Integrity Only. Click OK to clear the dialog box and return to New Filter Action Properties. Click the General tab and give the filter a name, such as Require Encryption. Click OK to return to the Manage IP Filter Lists and Filter Actions dialog box, and then click Close to close that dialog box.

Building an IPSec Rule Now let's assemble the filter and action into a rule. In Local Security Policy, again right-click the object labeled IP Security Policies on Local Machine and choose Create IP Security Policy. That will start a wizard; click Next and it will prompt you for a name and description of the rule. Name it Secure comms to 206.20.20.10 and click Next.

Next, the IPSec Policy Wizard will ask if you want to include the "default response rule." Uncheck the check box—skip the default response rule—and click Next, then Finish. You'll see a dialog box like Figure 6.63.

FIGURE 6.63

Showing rules in the policy

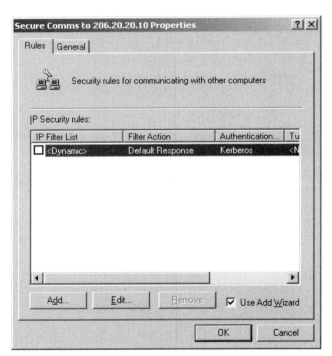

Make sure that the Use Add Wizard check box is unchecked, and click Add to show a dialog box like you see in Figure 6.64.

You've done most of the hard work; now just stitch a filter to an action, choose an authentication method, name the rule, and you'll be done. Choose the filter by clicking its radio button—Comms with 206.20.20.10 in my example—and click the Filter Action tab to reveal the possible actions. Click the radio button next to your desired action—I called mine Require Encryption—and click the tab labeled Authentication Methods. You'll see a dialog box like the one in Figure 6.65.

FIGURE 6.64

Defining a rule

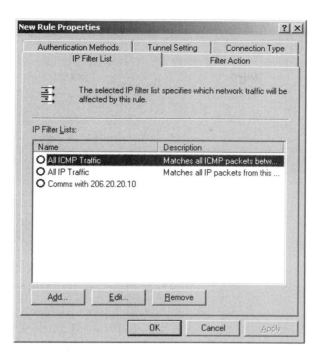

FIGURE 6.65

Authentication
methods

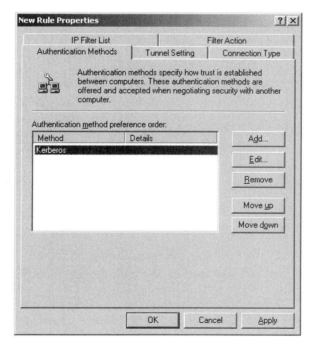

Click Add to choose the authentication method, and you'll see the dialog box in Figure 6.66.

FIGURE 6.66

Choosing an authentication method

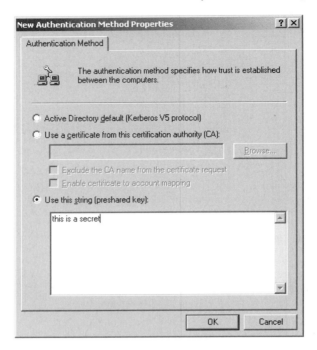

Here you can see the three options for authentication—Kerberos, certificate, or a preshared key. If both machines were in the same Active Directory domain, then the easiest thing to do would be the default—Kerberos, which I've suggested should be labeled "Active Directory" instead. But for simplicity's sake, I'll use a preshared key. So I click the Use This String option and type in a phrase. I used the extremely-hard-to-guess phrase, "this is a secret." Then I click OK three times, and I'm back in Local Security Settings. In the right pane, I see the possible IPSec policies, and the one that I just created will be there. I right-click that policy and choose Assign.

Now I'm done on the 199.10.10.3 side. Next, I'd go to the 206.20.20.10 machine and create an identical policy, *except* that I'd replace the references to 206.20.20.10 with 199.10.10.3. But how could you check that you've actually got encryption working between the two systems? With a program called Ipsecmon—just click Start/Run and type **ipsecmon** and click OK. Ipsecmon isn't very pretty, but it *will* identify systems that you are communicating with via IPSec and what level of security you are using.

USING IPSEC TO PROTECT SYSTEMS THROUGH PACKET FILTERING

Here's another neat thing that you can do with IPSec—filter packets. It's not a common use of IPSec, but it works pretty well.

One way to at least partially secure a system is to shut down unused ports, to tell your system, "Don't accept any traffic except on the following ports." For example, suppose you've got a Server 2003 system that is solely a Web server; that's all that it does. You *could* decide to tell that system, "only accept incoming traffic on TCP ports 80 and 443," as TCP port 80 is the port that, by default, Web browsers will use to access a Web site. Point your browser to www.acme.com and your browser will ask the machine at www.acme.com, "Please accept this request at your port 80." Your Web server uses port 443 for *secured* communications—SSL. In this section, I want to show you how to use IPSec to disable every port on your system except 80 and 443. But before I do, two notes on this process.

First, you probably know that you can do this far more simply via the built-in filtering ability of TCP/IP. If not, take a look at the Advanced properties of your IP stack—right-click My Network Places, choose Properties, and you'll see an icon for your network adapter. Right-click *that*, and choose Properties, and you'll see a properties sheet that includes objects for, among other things, an object called Internet Protocol (TCP/IP). Left-click that object, then click the Properties button, and you'll get a properties page on your TCP/IP stack. In that page, click Advanced and then Options. The Options page will probably offer two items—IP Security and TCP/IP Filtering. Click TCP/IP Filtering and then the Properties button.

You'll see a dialog box that allows you to tell your system, "Only accept the following ports." So, with a few clicks, you could tell your system to only accept traffic on TCP ports 80 and 443—believe me, far fewer clicks than will be required with IPSec. So why do it this way? For three reasons: First because it's a nice, easy example of working with IPSec. And second, and more importantly, you wouldn't want to have to walk around to every system and do all of that clicking; you issue IPSec commands to your system via group policies, either local policies or domain-based policies. It's *very* convenient to be able to describe a port filter once in the form of an IPSec policy, then use group policies to apply that filter to dozens of machines with just a few clicks in the Active Directory. And, finally, although the built-in TCP/IP filtering is nice, it only lets you shut down every port *except* a small list of ports. What if you wanted to do the reverse—allow every port *except* a few? You can't do that from TCP/IP filtering. You *can* easily do it from IPSec. When might this be useful? Consider that you'd also like to secure machines that *don't* run a Web server. As you know, Microsoft seems obsessed with installing IIS on just about every machine, so you may have a lot of Web servers running that you never knew about. But so many viruses attack Web servers, so you *really* want to protect these "accidental" Web servers. One way might be to create a policy that is the reverse of what I'm doing here—create an IPSec policy that passes everything *except* ports 80 and 443. Then apply that policy to every machine *except* the Web servers.

My second caveat is to note that simply filtering ports 80 and 443 on a Web server is a very simple approach to security, and probably *too* simple. The built-in SMTP server that runs on every IIS box by default wouldn't work, as SMTP needs port 25. And, worse, any remote access tool, such as Telnet or Terminal Services, wouldn't work either, as they employ ports other than 80 and 443. You would then have to do all of you Web server administration by sitting down at the Web server and logging in locally. If you were *really* going to secure your system, you'd want to do a bit more research to discover which ports your particular installation uses.

The Rules

As before, we'll first create the filter and the action, and then assemble it into a rule. (I'll spare you the dialog box screen shots; the process is the same as in the earlier example. I'll just focus on what you'll need to know to make this work.) This time, we'll need more than one rule—four, actually. If they don't make sense upon an initial reading, don't worry—I'm about to explain them. In IPSec-ese, then, you'd state the objective "block all traffic except the traffic coming in on TCP ports 80 and 443" with four rules:

◆ If network traffic of any kind or any port *enters* this computer from any other computer, block it.

◆ If network traffic of any kind or any port *originates* at this computer and is addressed to go to any computer on the Internet, let it pass.

◆ If TCP traffic on port 80 enters this computer from any other computer, let it pass.

◆ If TCP traffic on port 443 enters this computer from any other computer, let it pass.

Upon first reading those four bullet points, you're likely to say, "Wait...the first rule says to block *all* traffic of any kind, and the third one says to allow TCP port 80 traffic. Doesn't that conflict?" It looks that way, but it's the only way that we can give IPSec an even mildly complicated filtering rule. When IPSec comes across a conflict in rules, it takes the more specific of the conflicting rules. Let's stress that.

The rule about conflicting IPSec rules is this: The specific rule beats the more generic rule.

So, for example, suppose traffic comes in on TCP port 80. Rule One says, "It's incoming data; ignore it." Rule Three says, "It's incoming data *on port 80*; keep it." Rule Three is more specific, so it wins. Let's see how to build the policy's four rules.

Building Rule One

Rule One says, "Block all incoming traffic." Let's break that down into its filter and its action. As you've seen, you create a filter by specifying this:

◆ Source address: the address that the potentially filtered data comes from

◆ Destination address: the address that the potentially filtered data is going to

◆ Port and protocol: the protocol and port that the data travels to or from

◆ Mirroring: Whether or not to automatically mirror the filter

A filter that wants to describe "all incoming traffic" would have these values:

◆ Source address: any IP address

◆ Destination address: my IP address

◆ Port and protocol: any

◆ Mirroring: no

Notice that you do *not* want mirroring. That's because I want to block all incoming traffic and permit all outgoing traffic. If I wanted to do that same thing to both incoming and outgoing traffic, then I'd mirror the rule. As all four rules are *asymmetric*, we won't mirror any of them.

Rule One's action is to block traffic, so create a block action. Stitch the "all incoming traffic" filter with the "block" action, and you've got Rule One.

But what about authentication? Recall that blocking and permitting don't modify the data, they just pass it through or discard it, so they don't need any password. But IPSec wants to see authentication, so pick any type that you like—it won't matter. (Although if you pick Kerberos on a system that is not a member of an Active Directory domain, then the GUI will offer a dire-sounding dialog box that basically says, "Are you sure?" Just tell it that yes, you're sure.)

Building Rule Two

The second rule permits all outgoing traffic. The filter is very much like the last one, although source and destination are reversed:

- ◆ Source: my IP address
- ◆ Destination: any IP address
- ◆ Ports and protocols: any
- ◆ Mirroring: no

For an action, choose the already-built Permit one. Assemble the rule and, again, choose any authentication method that you like.

Building Rules Three and Four

Next, we'll build the rules that pass traffic on ports 80 and 443. The filter is a trifle more complicated; here's the criteria for the port 80 one:

- ◆ Source address: any IP address
- ◆ Destination address: my IP address
- ◆ Ports and protocol: port 80 on TCP
- ◆ Mirrored: no

When building the filter, first set the source and destination addresses, and then uncheck the Mirror check box. Then click the Protocol tab to see something like Figure 6.67.

FIGURE 6.67

Configuring a protocol filter

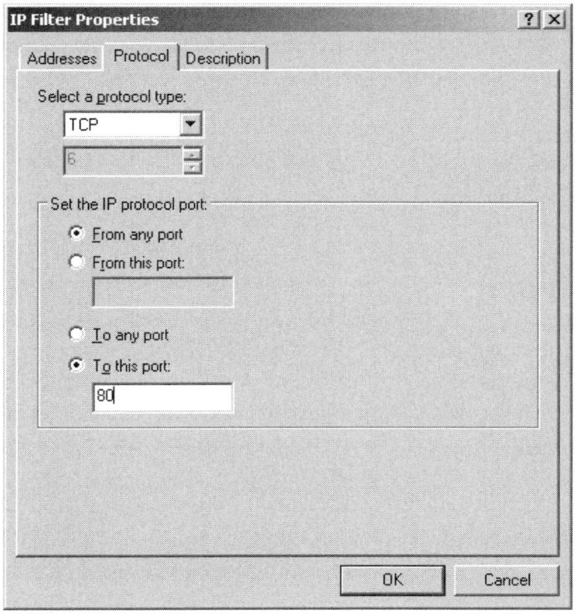

In the Protocol tab, first choose TCP under Select a Protocol Type, and then click the radio button To This Port and fill in **80**.

For the action, choose the Permit action. Again, do anything that you like for Authentication, as it does not matter. Do the same thing for Rule Four, except specify port **443** instead of port 80.

Once you've got your policy assembled, assign it and then try it out. You won't be able to ping your Web server, nor will you be able to access its SMTP server, nor an FTP server if you have one running on that system. But you *will* be able to access its Web pages, both secured and unsecured.

A FEW FINAL THOUGHTS ABOUT IPSEC

I haven't covered all of IPSec here, as IPSec could probably fill a book—I've just tried to hit the high points. But I don't want to leave without mentioning a few things.

First, IPSec will *not* work in conjunction with Network Address Translation unless both sides of your communication run a relatively new (late 2001 and later) modification of IPSec called IPSec NAT Traversal. If your workstation sat behind a NAT router, at, say, 192.168.23.3, and you wanted to create a secure IPSec connection with a server on the public Internet, then you would not be able to use IPSec unless the NAT router were a Server 2003 or later system. Basically you need pretty recent and IPSec NAT traversal-aware routers on both sides to make it work.

Second, I've been talking about IPSec as a one-to-one way for systems to communicate. But IPSec also has a feature called *tunneling* whereby most of your systems needn't be IPSec aware at all. Instead, they'd funnel all of their communications through a single IPSec-aware computer that is prepared to "relay" their communications to another IPSec-aware computer on a remote site. Thus, if you had 100 machines at one location and 100 machines at another location, and you wanted machines at each location to be able to talk to all of the machines on the other location, but you wanted security while the data traveled from one location to another, then you could just designate one machine at each location as a sort of "firewall" box. Those boxes would tunnel IP traffic from one site to another.

Third, IPSec is a standard, not just a Microsoft functionality. So in theory you should be able to use Microsoft's IPSec to communicate with other vendor's tools. But test that before you start to rely upon it—I've heard that many non-Microsoft implementations can run into trouble trying to talk with IPSec-enabled Windows boxes.

Fourth, IPSec first appeared with 2000 Server. Earlier versions of the operating system—and lamer ones, like Windows Me—cannot do IPSec communications.

Network Load Balancing Clusters (NLBC)

Sometimes you'll put a server on your network and it gets *popular*. Whether it's a Web server, FTP, or firewall server, you sometimes get to the point where you either need to get a bigger and faster server, or fewer customers. Most of us will opt for the former rather than the latter option, but it's a shame to take a server that's doing the whole job and then just replace it with another—sure, it's nice to have the greater power of the faster server, but wouldn't it be neat if that new server could *add* to the old server's power, instead of replacing it?

NLB Overview

You can achieve this with Network Load Balancing Clusters (NLBC). It's a feature that first appeared in Windows 2000 Server in the more-expensive Advanced Server offering, but now Microsoft offers it on all editions of Server 2003. NLBC lets you take two or more computers and make them look like one computer to the outside world. Incoming requests are divided up between the two or more members of the NLBC "cluster," letting you slowly add more and more computers to create a pretty powerful Web site. That means that you could gang together a bunch—32 maximum—of cheap computers to create a seemingly powerful Web presence ... although of course having to buy a whole bunch of Server 2003 *licenses* might eat up your hardware savings!

It's important that you understand that this is *not* "clustering" in the high-powered sense that Enterprise/Advanced offers. Basically, two or more computers each have their own static IP address, as usual. But they also take on an extra IP address—and every one of the NLB cluster members take on the same value for their extra IP address. Anyone in the outside world can connect to that IP address, as they would to any other IP address. But what's different here is that, again, two or more systems *share* that IP address. That normally wouldn't work, as giving two systems the same IP address usually means that at least one of them can't communicate; but NLB fixes that. As systems ask to be connected to the shared IP address, NLB invisibly assigns each visitor to a particular cluster member. So, for example, if I had two servers running IIS with the same content, I could make them an NLB cluster and give them a new cluster IP address. When the first person asks to attach to that cluster address, then one of the servers will get the request. When the second person asks to attach to the cluster address, she gets connected to the second server. The third person gets connected to the first server, and so on.

This clearly only works if you've got two or more servers that offer the precisely same data. It also presents some problems if these servers accept data from a customer and then store it somewhere. For example, if we were clustering two Web servers that took orders for, say, books, then each of those servers has to be able to store those orders. If they store them on local databases then at the end of the day you'll have two separate databases, each containing about one half of the day's orders, so you'll have to merge those databases somehow. Or you could have both Web servers store their transactions on a separate shared database server, or something like that. What I'm trying to point out here is that some things will require more planning in order to make them work as an NLB clustered application than others. (And as this isn't a Web application building book, I'm going to duck those issues...) But remember that some kinds of server applications, like file servers, are really not a good match with NLB. But Web servers, Terminal Servers, and Microsoft's Internet Acceleration and Security (ISA) firewall can benefit from NLB.

Getting Ready

Here's the very simplified list of what you'll need in order to build a two-system NLB cluster:

- ◆ Every system needs a static IP address: each of the two servers needs a static IP address, so get that ready.
- ◆ You'll need *another* static IP address for the shared cluster address.
- ◆ You'll need a DNS name for the cluster, like cluster.bigfirm.biz, and the DNS entry should correspond to the shared static IP address from the cluster. (I know, I've not done DNS or, for that matter, Web servers yet, forgive me—this topic doesn't exactly fit in anywhere. If you like, just skim this now and return to it after learning about DNS and Web. I'll wait!)
- ◆ You'll need whatever kind of server software that you want to cluster on both systems. In my example, that means installing Internet Information Service on each server.

I'm going to show you how to do an NLB cluster with in its simplest form—two Web servers. I worked out this example on two systems with the following characteristics:

- One of the servers is named CADOTNET and has a static IP address of 206.246.253.151. Remember, every member of an NLB cluster must have a static IP address.
- The other server is named 5000SC and has a static address of 206.246.253.150.
- The NLB cluster's shared IP address will be 206.246.253.152.

Step One: Install Static IP Addresses and Server Software

Let me warn you that NLB is a neat tool when it works, but that it has very exacting requirements and can produce some very disconcerting-looking errors while you set it up. So I'm a strong believer that you need to get each of the two servers running on their own in tip-top shape before you start tilting with NLB.

In my example system, I configured 5000SC with a static address of 206.246.253.150, a subnet mask of 255.255.255.0, and a default gateway of 206.246.253.1. Those numbers make sense for me because they're in my C network range, but use whatever range works for you. Remember, though: at minimum you must supply an IP address, subnet mask, default gateway, and IP address for a DNS server. Do that for both systems. (You can copy my IP address range to try it out, but make sure that you set all of your test systems it use the IP address range or, again, adapt the example for your IP address range.)

WARNING   *All cluster members must have static IP addresses in the* same *subnet!*

Then make sure that the Web server software is running on each server. In pre-2003 versions of Server, you pretty much always got a Web server installed on every server, but that's not the case any more, thank goodness. But do get IIS on both CADOTNET and 5000SC. Put simple home pages on them—I just create a file in Inetpub\wwwroot named `default.htm` that just contains the text, "Hello, you're visiting [the computer's name]." It works fine for testing purposes. Remember that in an actual implementation you would put identical Web content on each server.

Go to some other computer, start up Internet Explorer and try to view those Web server pages. For simplicity's sake I just punch the actual IP addresses into IE's Address bar so that I needn't even create DNS entries for the cluster members CADOTNET and 5000SC. Make sure the home pages come up as expected; if not, fix them—NLB just makes problems like this worse!

Step Two: Create a DNS Entry for the Cluster

The cluster's not built yet, but let's get DNS ready for it. (Again, sorry I'm referring to things later in the book.) Assign the cluster a name and, as you've already read, a static IP address. In my example I've decided to call my cluster cluster.bigfirm.biz and give it an IP address of 206.246.253.152. I just go to the DNS server for bigfirm.biz and create a static host entry—an "A record"—matching cluster.bigfirm.biz with the IP address 206.246.253.152.

As you'll read in the next chapter, you can test that your new host entry is installed right with the `nslookup` tool—just type `nslookup cluster.bigfirm.biz` and the command should return the IP address that you assigned to cluster.bigfirm.biz.

Step Three: Set Up NLB for CADOTNET

It actually doesn't matter which of the two systems you set up first; I arbitrarily set up CADOTNET first. Open the properties for CADOTNET's NIC as you've seen before: Start/Control Panel/Network

Connections/Local Area Connection or whatever name CADOTNET's NIC has. In the resulting Local Area Network Status page, click the Properties button. It'll look something like Figure 6.68.

FIGURE 6.68

NIC properties page

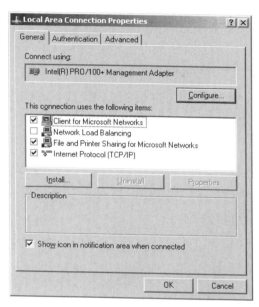

You may have noticed before that the service named Network Load Balancing was unchecked; time to put it to work. Check the box next to it and then click the Properties button. You'll see something like Figure 6.69—well, only *like* it; I've already filled it in in that screen shot.

FIGURE 6.69

Identifying the cluster

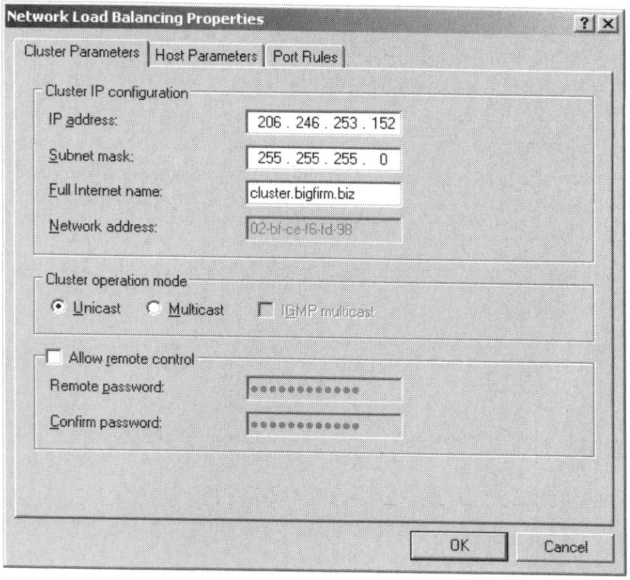

This is where we breathe life into the cluster. Remember that we needed an extra static IP address that all of the cluster members would share? This is where you enter it, along with its subnet mask and cluster name. For Cluster Operation Mode, I've not found much use for Multicast and it can give some routers fits, so I tend to stay with Unicast. Make the cluster remote-controllable if you like; I avoid it and use other remote control tools. You will have to configure a screen like this for every cluster member—*fill in the same information on the Cluster Parameters* tab for every member! Then click the Host Parameters tab to see Figure 6.70.

FIGURE 6.70

Member-specific information

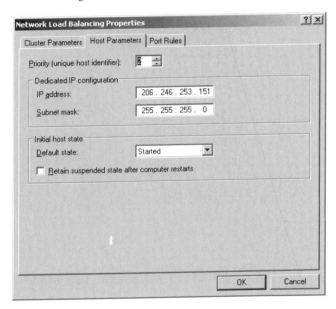

I just said that you configure the Cluster Parameters identically for each member; *this* tab is where you configure the particular member. In Dedicated IP Configuration, just repeat the static IP address and subnet mask of this particular system—note that I have not filled in the cluster's IP address, just the static IP address that *this* computer has. You'll also need to set a value for Priority, as each computer in the cluster must have a different value. Even though it's called Priority, in the particular application that we'll have—Web servers, again—it doesn't really do much in the way of prioritizing. I've set CADOTNET to a priority of 2.

At this point, just click OK to close Network Load Balancing Properties and return to Local Area Connection Properties.

Step Four: Add the Cluster IP Address to CADOTNET's IP Software

CADOTNET's almost done…but not quite yet. Next, click the Internet Protocol (TCP/IP) object and the Properties button, then the Advanced button and the IP Settings tab to get the Advanced TCP/IP Settings page and the IP Settings tab in that page. We're going to add a second IP address here—the shared IP address that identifies the cluster.

Under IP Addresses, click the button labeled Add and fill in the IP address of the shared cluster IP address. In my example, that's 206.246.253.152. You are not *replacing* the server's current

IP address; you're just adding another IP address to the server's NIC. Click Add when you've filled in the cluster's shared IP address and subnet, and the Advanced TCP/IP Settings page will look like Figure 6.71.

FIGURE 6.71

CADOTNET with cluster IP added

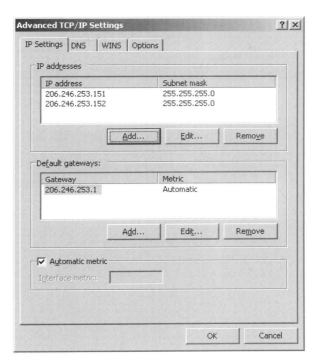

Click OK to clear the Advanced TCP/IP page, OK to clear the Internet Protocol (TCP/IP) properties page, and Close to close the NIC's property page. Try an `ipconfig /all` to make sure that it worked, and it'll look something like Figure 6.72.

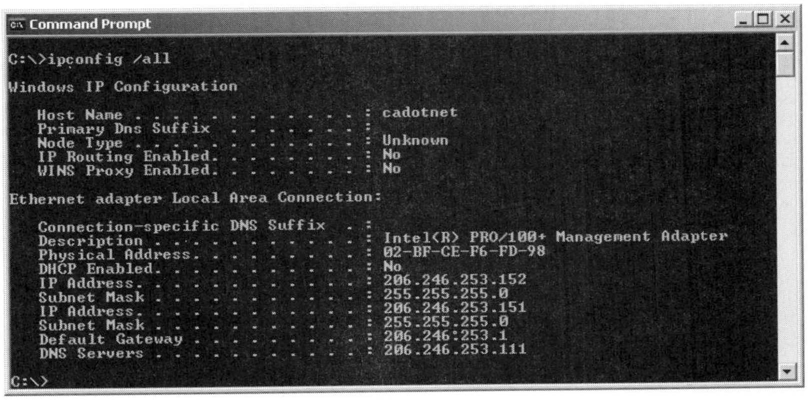

FIGURE 6.72

`ipconfig /all` after adding second IP address

If you just see addresses like 0.0.0.0, then don't panic—NLB can sometimes take up to five or so minutes to get things settled. If Server raises any panicky messages about things not being configured right, click the messages away and give it five minutes, *then* try the `ipconfig /all` again. If the IP addresses are still wrong, then go back and check the things that you punched into the dialogs.

At this point, CADOTNET is done.

Step Five: Configure 5000SC

Next, go back and do the same thing for 5000SC. Check the box for Network Load Balancing and fill in the Cluster Parameters tab exactly as you did for CADOTNET. On the Host Parameters page, use 5000SC's IP address of 206.246.253.150 rather than 206.246.253.151, and set the Priority to 1. Again, go to Advanced TCP/IP Properties and add a second IP address, 206.246.253.152.

When you close all of the NIC's property pages and dialog boxes, just relax—the cluster will *definitely* take several minutes to get set up, and the second system that you set up (5000SC in this case) will emit all kinds of scary "TCP/IP is not configured properly..." messages. Relax. Go get a snack. Don't watch—it's better for your blood pressure. Microsoft *really* needs to remove the trauma from this process. But after a few minutes, all will be well.

Go to a machine on your subnet (or any other machine that can route to your cluster's IP addresses, actually), start up Internet Explorer and try typing in the static IP addresses of each server, as well as the cluster's IP address. You should see the home pages from each server, and then one of the two server's home pages when you use the shared cluster IP address. Now go to other machines, run IE and again point to the shared cluster IP address—you'll see that different machines get different home pages. Your cluster is working! (Again, in the real world you'd have the same content on both Web servers, so no one could easily figure out which cluster member he was on...which is just what you want.)

One more note before I leave this: do not try to ping one cluster member from another cluster member. A side-effect of NLB is that while all of the cluster members can all connect as easily to client machines as each other, the cluster members cannot communicate with each other!

Well, by now, you're on an intranet in the traditional way. Microsoft adds two possible options to this setup: the Dynamic Host Configuration Protocol (DHCP) and the Windows Internet Name Service (WINS). You'll meet these two, as well as the essential third (Domain Name System, DNS) and a few other services, in the next chapter.

Chapter 7

TCP/IP Infrastructure: DHCP, WINS, and DNS

WHETHER YOU'RE HOOKING UP a two-computer intranet in your house to share an Internet connection or weaving a world-spanning Internet, you've got to solve two basic problems. First, every system on the network needs a unique IP address and requires configuration—it needs to know the address of its default router, what its domain name is, where the nearest DNS server is, and the like. And second, it needs help finding its way around the network: How do I send mail to Jane over at Acme Industries? How do I connect to the server that will let me buy books or shoes online? Or, more mundanely, how do I find a server that will log me in?

Microsoft OS-based networks that are TCP/IP-based need three technologies to accomplish IP configuration and name management: the Dynamic Host Configuration Protocol (DHCP), the Domain Name System (DNS), and the Windows Internet Name Service (WINS). Of the three, WINS is something of a relic, a technology that in *theory* you can forgo altogether, but in practice you can only do it if your network includes nothing but computers running Windows 2000 or later, and if your network-aware applications are built for post-NT 4 rather than NT 4 or earlier operating systems. Furthermore, this chapter is *essential* because if you don't do a great job designing your DNS architecture, then Active Directory will run terribly; in many ways, DNS is the foundation of Active Directory.

DHCP: Automatic TCP/IP Configuration

In Chapter 6, you learned how to set up IP on a Server 2003 system. Ah, but now ask yourself, "Do I really want to walk around to 3000 workstations and do this by hand?" Auuugghhhh! Oops, sorry, what I really meant was, "Of course not." Who wants to have to remember which IP address you gave to *that* machine so you don't put the address on *this* machine? Or how'd you like to get a phone call every time some visiting dignitary needs an IP address for his laptop? No thanks. DHCP will greatly simplify the task, so let's see how to set it up.

By the way, this discussion assumes you've already read Chapter 6; don't think if you decided from the start to go with DHCP that you could jump in here without reading the preceding chapter.

Simplifying TCP/IP Administration: BOOTP

"I have a little list / it never can be missed." Well, OK, that's not exactly what Pooh-Bah sings in *The Mikado*, but it fits here. You see, back when I first put TCP/IP on my company's computers, in 1993, I had to keep this list of PCs and IP addresses in a notebook. It was basically a kind of master directory of which IP addresses had been used so far.

Obviously, I had to consult it whenever I put TCP/IP on each new computer. Obvious, sure, but what's unfortunate is that I never seemed to have the notebook with me when I needed it. So I started keeping this list of computers and IP addresses on one of my servers, in a kind of common HOSTS file. It served two purposes: First, it told me what IP addresses were already used, and second, it gave me a HOSTS file to copy to the local computer's hard disk.

But, I recall thinking, this is silly. Keeping track of IP addresses and the machines using them is a rote, mechanical job—you know, the kind of job computers are good at.

Unknown to me, the Internet world apparently had a similar feeling and so invented a TCP/IP protocol called "the bootstrap protocol," usually abbreviated "BOOTP," which was first described in RFC 951. With BOOTP, a network administrator would first collect a list of MAC addresses for each LAN card. I've already mentioned the 48-bit identifiers on each network card, which are good examples of MAC addresses.

Next, the administrator would assign an IP address to each MAC address. A server on the company's intranet would then hold this table of MAC address/IP address pairs. Then, when a BOOTP-enabled workstation would start up for the day, it would broadcast a request for an IP address. The BOOTP server would recognize the MAC address from the broadcaster and would supply the IP address to the workstation. So BOOTP was (and is) a neat way to configure TCP/IP on a computer without having to travel to it.

But BOOTP doesn't stop there. Once a BOOTP server delivers an IP address to a computer, it also delivers a small startup operating system, a "bootstrap loader." (That's where the phrase "boot disk" comes from; in the old days, we'd have to hand-enter a small program into a computer to make the computer smart enough to be able to read its own disk drive or to start communicating on the network. That small program let a computer "lift itself by its own bootstraps," in the old phrase, and became known as a bootstrap loader and eventually just became "the boot loader," "boot disk" and similar phrases.) The idea with BOOTP was that you could have a computer that ran entirely off the network, with no local hard or floppy disks at all. As such a computer couldn't boot from its (nonexistent) floppy or hard disks, then it needed to get its startup programs from *somewhere*. A BOOTP server solved that by first handing the computer an IP address and then downloading a startup boot program.

This was a great improvement over the static IP addressing system that I've described so far. Administrators didn't have to physically travel to each workstation to give it its own IP address; they needed only to modify a file on the BOOTP server when a new machine arrived or if it was necessary to change IP addresses for a particular set of machines.

Another great benefit of BOOTP is that it provides protection from the "helpful user." Suppose you have user Tom, who sits next to user Dick. Dick's machine isn't accessing the network correctly, so helpful user Tom says, "Well, *I'm* getting on the Net fine, so let's just copy all of this confusing network stuff from my machine to yours." The result is that both machines end up with identical configurations—including identical IP addresses, so now neither Tom *nor* Dick can access the network without errors! In contrast, if Tom's machine is only set up to go get its IP address from its local BOOTP server, then setting up Dick's machine identically will cause no harm, as it will just tell Dick's machine to get *its* address from the BOOTP server. Dick will get a different address (provided that the network administrator has typed in an IP address for Dick's MAC address), and all will be well.

DHCP: BOOTP Plus

BOOTP's ability to hand out IP addresses from a central location is terrific, but it's not dynamic, and in the PC world we typically don't care about getting bootstrap code from a central server; as you probably know, we tend to boot our computers from a local read-only memory chip called the BIOS and then from code on a local hard disk. Additionally, BOOTP requires the network administrator to find out beforehand all the MAC addresses of the Ethernet cards on the network. This isn't *impossible* information to obtain, but it's a bit of a pain (usually typing `ipconfig /all` from a command line yields the data). Furthermore, there's no provision for handing out temporary IP addresses, such as an IP address for a laptop used by a visiting executive. (I suppose you could keep a store of PCMCIA Ethernet cards whose MAC addresses had been preinstalled into the BOOTP database, but even so, it's getting to be some real work.) So someone came up with a somewhat simplified tool that is BOOTP-like but that doesn't focus on delivering boot code: DHCP.

DHCP improves upon BOOTP in that you just give it a range of IP addresses that it's allowed to hand out, and it gives them out first come, first served to whatever computers request them. If, on the other hand, you want DHCP to maintain full BOOTP-like behavior, then you can; it's possible with DHCP to preassign IP addresses to particular MAC addresses (it's called *DHCP reservation*), as with BOOTP.

With DHCP, you only have to hardwire the IP addresses of a few machines, such as your BOOTP/DHCP server and your default gateway.

Both DHCP and BOOTP use UDP ports 67 and 68, so you won't be able to install both a BOOTP server and a DHCP server on the same computer. Now, Microsoft does not supply a BOOTP server; this note would mostly be relevant only if you tried to install a third-party BOOTP server. But Windows NT 4 Server and its newer siblings also allow you to make a computer a *BOOTP forwarding agent*. If you enable that software on a DHCP server, the server stops giving out IP addresses.

Let's see how to get a DHCP server up on your network so the IP addresses will start getting handed out, and then we'll take a look at how DHCP works.

AVOID STATIC IP: USE DHCP EVERYWHERE!

In a minute, I'll get into the nitty-gritty of setting up DHCP servers and handing out IP addresses. But before I do, let's address a big, overall network configuration question: Which machines should have static IP addresses, and which machines should get their addresses from DHCP servers?

In general, the answer is that the only machines that should have static IP addresses should be your WINS servers, DNS servers, and DHCP servers. In actual fact, you'll probably put the WINS, DNS, and DHCP server functions on the same machines.

"But wait!" I hear you cry, "Are you suggesting that I let my domain controllers, mail servers, Web servers, and the like all have floating, random IP addresses assigned by DHCP willy-nilly?" No, not at all. Recall that you can assign a particular IP address to a particular MAC address using a DHCP reservation. My suggestion, then, is that you sit down and figure out which machines need fixed

IP addresses, get the MAC addresses of the NICs in those machines, and then create reservations in DHCP for those machines. (You'll see how a bit later.)

Installing and Configuring DHCP Servers

DHCP servers are the machines that provide IP addresses to machines that request access to the LAN. DHCP only works if the TCP/IP software on the workstations is *built* to work with DHCP. If the TCP/IP software includes a *DHCP client*. Nowadays, just about every network-aware OS includes DHCP clients—Macs, Linux, and every Microsoft desktop and server OS since 1994 have included them.

INSTALLING THE DHCP SERVICE

To get ready for DHCP configuration:

♦ Have an IP address ready for your DHCP server—this is one computer on your network that *must* have a hardwired ("static") IP address.

♦ Know which IP addresses are free to assign. You use these available IP addresses to create a pool of IP addresses.

You install the software to make your server a DHCP server in the same way that you install most other network services, from the Add/Remove Windows Components applet of the Control Panel. Step-by-step, it looks like this:

1. Open the Control Panel's Add or Remove Programs applet (Start/Control Panel/Add or Remove Programs).
2. Click Add/Remove Windows Components and wait a bit while the Windows Components Wizard starts up.
3. Click Networking Services and then the Details button.
4. Click the check box next to Dynamic Host Configuration Protocol (DHCP).
5. Click OK to return to Windows Components.
6. Click Next to install the service. The system will say that it is "Configuring Components" for a while, probably a few minutes. Make sure you have the Server CD around; it'll want you to insert it. A couple of rounds of FreeCell, and the Completing the Windows Components Wizard screen appears.
7. Click Finish to end the wizard.
8. Click Close to close Add/Remove Windows Components.

And best of all, you needn't reboot afterward. You control DHCP with the DHCP snap-in, which you'll find in Administrative Tools: Start/Administrative Tools/DHCP. Start it up, and the opening screen looks like most MMC snap-ins, with the left and right panes. This particular one lists your server, with a plus sign next to it. Click the plus sign and you'll see a screen like Figure 7.1.

Notice that this snap-in lists the server in the left pane. That's because you can control as many DHCP servers as you like from this program. All you need do to add a DHCP server to the list of servers that you control is to just select Action/Add Server.

FIGURE 7.1

DHCP manager
opening screen

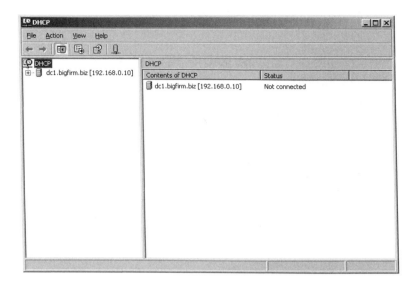

AUTHORIZING DHCP SERVERS (FOR ACTIVE DIRECTORY USERS)

Now, before we go any further, I have to add a note here about DHCP and Active Directory because if you're running AD, then you won't be able to make your DHCP server work without a little adjustment—hence the note *now* rather than in the next chapter. If you're not running AD, then feel free to skip this section, but just remember that you saw this—or it'll come bite you *later*, when you've gotten your AD up and running.

Click the plus sign next to the small icon that looks like a tower computer in Figure 7.1. There's a small circular blob next to it. It's sort of small, so you may not be able to see it in the screen shot, but to the left of "dc1.bigfirm.biz [192.168.0.10]" is a small arrow that points downward—in color, it's red. That arrow represents a nice touch on Microsoft's part.

You see, under NT 4, 3.51, and 3.5, anyone with an NT Server installation CD could set up NT Server on a computer and make herself an administrator of that server. With administrative powers, she could then set up a DHCP server. Now, the job of a DHCP server, recall, is to hand out IP addresses to computers who want to be part of the network. The problem arises when the administrator of this new server decides just for fun to offer a bunch of meaningless IP addresses, a range of addresses that your firm doesn't actually own. The result? Well, the next time a machine in the company needs an IP address, it asks any server within earshot for an IP address. The server with the meaningless addresses responds, as do the valid servers—but the server with the bogus addresses is likely to respond more quickly than the valid servers (it doesn't have anything else to do) and so many client PCs will end up with IP addresses from the server with the bogus addresses. Those addresses won't route and so those people won't be able to get anything done on the network.

Why would someone set up a server with bogus addresses? Usually it's not for a malicious reason. Rather, it's more common that someone's just trying to learn DHCP and sets up a server to play around with, not realizing "test" DHCP servers are indistinguishable from "real" DHCP servers to the client machines. Such a DHCP server is called a *rogue* DHCP server.

Windows 2000 and later versions of Server solve the problem of rogue DHCP servers by disabling new DHCP servers until a member of AD's most powerful forest-wide group, the Enterprise Admins (you'll meet them in the next chapter), "authorizes" them in the Active Directory. With those versions of Server, anyone can set up a DHCP server, but the server won't start handing out addresses until authorized. This isn't foolproof, as only machines that are members of Active Directory–based domains seek to be authorized. Someone who wanted to maliciously set up a rogue DHCP server could simply install a copy of Server 2003 and not join it to the domain, *then* set up a DHCP server—but, again, that's not the most common problem.

You authorize a server with the DHCP snap-in by starting up the DHCP snap-in while logged in as an Enterprise Admin. From the DHCP snap-in, click the server and then select Action/Manage Authorized Servers, and you'll see a dialog box like the one in Figure 7.2.

FIGURE 7.2

List of authorized DHCP servers

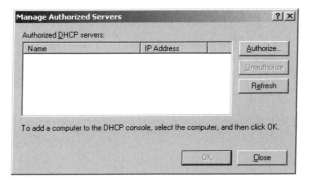

You can see that there are no servers authorized yet, so let's authorize this one. Click Authorize and you'll see the dialog box in Figure 7.3.

FIGURE 7.3

Authorizing a new DHCP server

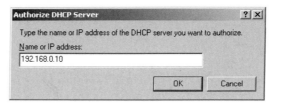

I've filled in the IP address of this server. Click OK, and you'll be asked to confirm that you do indeed want to add this server. Click the Yes button, and you'll return to the list of authorized servers. Click Close to close that dialog box and you'll see the DHCP snap-in looking as in Figure 7.1, save that the red down-pointing arrow is now a green up-pointing arrow.

You should be able to click the server and then press F5 to refresh the display to see the green arrow. In my experience, however, you usually have to close the DHCP manager and then reopen it to see the green arrow appear. (Once I not only had to close and reopen it, I also had to press F5. Clearly the DHCP manager isn't one of those chatty kinds of entities that constantly yammer on about their current condition—no, this app is downright reticent about its mood.)

Now you can offer IP addresses with this server.

If you *don't* have an Active Directory running, then you needn't authorize the server, as clearly there wouldn't be anything to authorize it *with*. But here's an interesting side effect of how 2000 or 2003 servers authorize DHCP servers. (Again, I know that some of you don't even *have* an Active Directory yet, but pay attention to this, or it'll bite you when you first set up your AD.)

If you are running a DHCP server on a network without an Active Directory, and all of a sudden bring up an AD, then the DHCP server will sense that, *even if it's not part of the AD domain*. It will then shut itself down. This *always* trips me up when I'm doing a class and I'm demonstrating Active Directory—first I get the DHCP and DNS servers up and running, then I create the AD, but then forget to authorize the already-running DHCP server that conveniently sniffs out the Active Directory and consequently disables itself. Anyway, just thought I'd mention it—now let's get back to the whys and wherefores of DHCP setup.

CREATING A RANGE OF ADDRESSES: DHCP "SCOPES"

That DHCP snap-in isn't really much to look at, is it? Well, it won't be, as there are no scopes set up yet. Scopes? What's a scope?

CREATING THE SCOPE

For DHCP to give out IP addresses, it must know the range of IP addresses that it can give out. Microsoft calls a range of IP addresses, and the descriptive information associated with them, a *scope*. To create a scope, right-click the server's icon and choose New Scope, which starts the New Scope Wizard. Click Next from its opening screen and you'll see a screen like the one in Figure 7.4.

FIGURE 7.4

Naming the scope

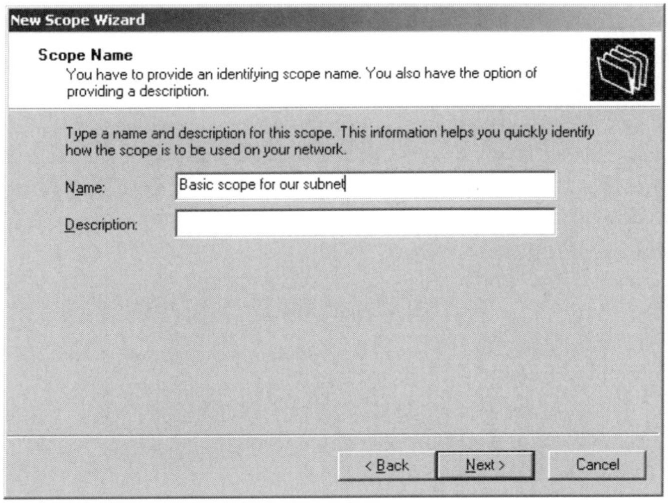

In this screen, you simply identify the scope, giving it a name and a comment. In my experience, I've never really figured out why there's a name *and* a comment, as the name has no real use; it could well *be* a comment, in effect. Fill in appropriate values for your network, and click Next to see a screen like Figure 7.5.

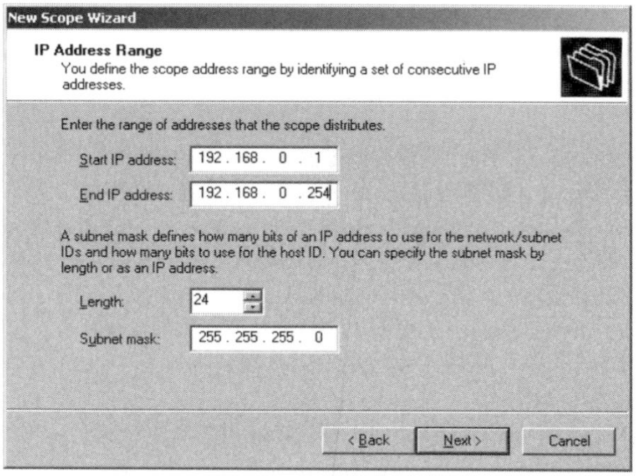

FIGURE 7.5

Defining the IP address range

SPECIFYING IP ADDRESS RANGE

A scope is simply a range of IP addresses—a pool from which they can be drawn. In the example in Figure 7.5, I've created a scope that ranges from 192.168.0.1 through 192.168.0.254—in other words, I'm going to use DHCP to help me create and manage a class C intranet of nonroutable addresses.

I don't want to get too sidetracked on the issue of scopes just now (I'll cover multiscope considerations later), but let me mention why you'd have more than one scope on a DHCP server. You can assign a scope to each subnet serviced by your DHCP servers—and, yes, it is possible for one DHCP server to handle multiple subnets. In contrast, however, a DHCP server won't let you create more than one scope *in the same subnet*. I will, however, show you how to get more than one server to act as a DHCP server (for the sake of fault tolerance) in a minute.

I put DHCP in charge of giving out *all* of my Internet addresses, but clearly that makes no sense, as I must have at least *one* static IP address around—the one on my DHCP server. So I need to tell the DHCP server not to give *that* one away, but how to do it? Click Next twice—the wizard seems to need two clicks on the Next button here—to see the next screen, where I'll tell the server what addresses to avoid, as in Figure 7.6.

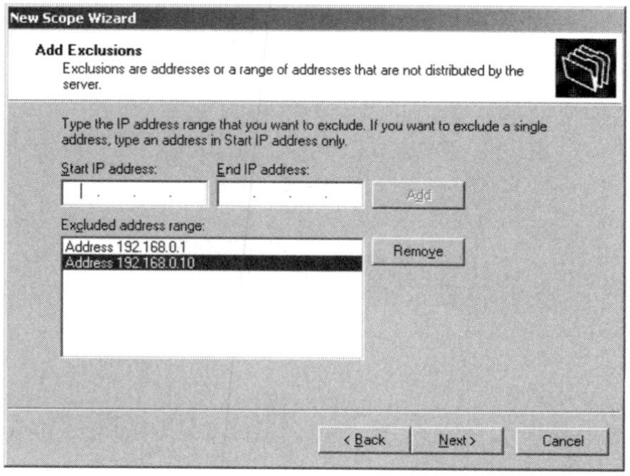

FIGURE 7.6

Excluding address ranges

As you see, I've excluded several addresses: The .1 address is the default gateway, a NAT router, and the .10 address is this server itself. Notice that you can specify one address by itself; you don't *have* to specify starting and ending addresses in a one-address range.

SPECIFYING MORE RANGES: SUPERSCOPES

As you read in Chapter 6, in general there's a one-to-one relationship between physical network segments and subnets. IP was designed to let systems that could directly "shout" at each other do that, communicating directly rather than burdening routers.

Sometimes, however, you'll see two separate subnets on a single segment. That's often because a single network can't accommodate all of the segment's machines. For example, if you started your enterprise with 180 hosts and acquired a slash 24 network, you'd have enough addresses for 254 devices, presuming that you didn't subnet. But what about when your firm grows to need 300 machines? You might go out to your ISP and get another slash 24, another 254 addresses.

Now you've got two networks. You *could* break your network up into two segments and apply one set of network addresses to each segment. But you might not want to: Suppose your one segment can support all of your machines and you can't see the point in messing around with more routers—what then?

You create a *superscope*. The idea with a superscope is that it contains more than one range of IP addresses—more than one scope—but applies them to a single segment. You can do it simply—just define two separate scopes on a DHCP server, then right-click the server, choose New Superscope, and you'll have the superscope. You can then add scopes to the superscope as you like; don't forget that you might have to change the subnet mask to reflect the larger range of addresses.

But what about the mechanics of a superscope? When you put a new machine on this subnet and it broadcasts to find a DHCP server and get an IP address, will it get an IP address from the first scope or the second? The answer is that it doesn't matter. If you're just shoehorning two IP subnets onto the same physical segment simply because you're out of IP addresses on an existing subnet, then it doesn't matter whether a workstation gets an IP address from the first range of IP addresses or the second range of IP addresses, as all of the enterprise's routers know how to find either range.

Once in a while, however, you have two ranges of IP addresses on the same physical network for a reason—perhaps one range is composed of IANA- or ISP-assigned IP addresses and the other is composed of nonroutable addresses. You probably have good reasons, then, to put some computers on the routable addresses and some on the nonroutable addresses. But how to get DHCP to help there? After all, both the routable and nonroutable ranges are in the same shouting radius, so to speak. When a workstation asks DHCP for an address, how would DHCP know whether to give that workstation a routable or nonroutable address?

The answer is that DHCP can't—there's no magic here. There would have to be some kind of setting on the client that the client could use to give DHCP a clue about what network it wanted to be a member of, the routable or nonroutable. What you must do in a situation like that is decide which machines go in the routable network and which go in the nonroutable network and then enter their MAC addresses by hand into DHCP with *reservations* (which I'll cover later), much as network administrators must when using BOOTP instead of DHCP.

SETTING LEASE DURATION

Returning to the wizard, click Next and you see a screen like Figure 7.7.

FIGURE 7.7

Set lease duration.

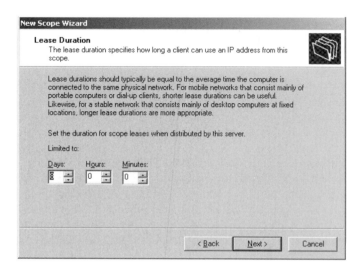

As you'll read in a few pages, when I explain the internals of DHCP, the DHCP server doesn't give the client PC an IP address to use forever. The client PC only gets the IP address for a specific period of time called a *lease*, and by the time the lease period's up, the client must either lease it or another address from a DHCP server, or the client must stop using IP altogether, immediately. But how long should that lease be? Although that was something of an issue when DHCP first appeared in NT 3.5, it doesn't matter all that much what you set it for now, so long as you set it for longer than a few days; the default of eight days is probably good.

Actually, what I just wrote is true unless, that is, you're creating a subnet that will serve computers connecting with wireless 802.1x network cards. Those connections tend to be more short-term, so in that case you might want to set the lease time shorter. What do you do if your subnet supports both wired and wireless connections? Then you have to make the call—short, long, or somewhere in between?

We'll talk more about lease durations when we discuss DHCP internals later. Click Next to move to Figure 7.8.

SETTING CLIENT OPTIONS

Remember all of those options in the Advanced tab for TCP/IP Properties when you configured static IP addresses in the preceding chapter? Well, you needn't travel around to the workstations and set them, as DHCP lets you configure those things right from the server. DHCP can provide default values for a whole host of TCP/IP parameters, including these basic items:

◆ Default gateway
◆ Domain name
◆ DNS server
◆ WINS server

FIGURE 7.8

FIGURE 7.8

Configure DHCP
Options screen.

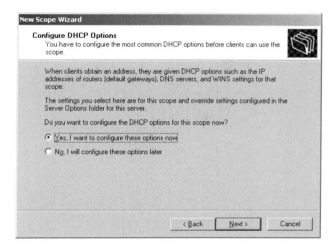

Notice I said *default*. You can override any of these options at the workstation. For example, if you said that by default everyone's DNS server was 10.0.100.1 but wanted one particular PC to instead use the DNS server at 10.200.200.10, then you could just walk over to the PC and use the Advanced button in the TCP/IP properties page (see Chapter 6 if you don't recall how to find that) to enter a DNS name. Even though the DHCP server would offer a DNS server address of 10.0.100.1 to the PC, the PC's DHCP client software would see that the PC had been configured to use 10.200.200.10 instead and would use that address rather than 10.0.100.1. Any other DHCP-supplied options, however, wouldn't be ignored. The general rule is, then:

> *Any TCP/IP characteristic specifically configured on the client, such as a DNS server or WINS server, overrides any value that DHCP provides.*

Click Next to tell DHCP that you want to configure these options, and to see the first client option, shown in Figure 7.9.

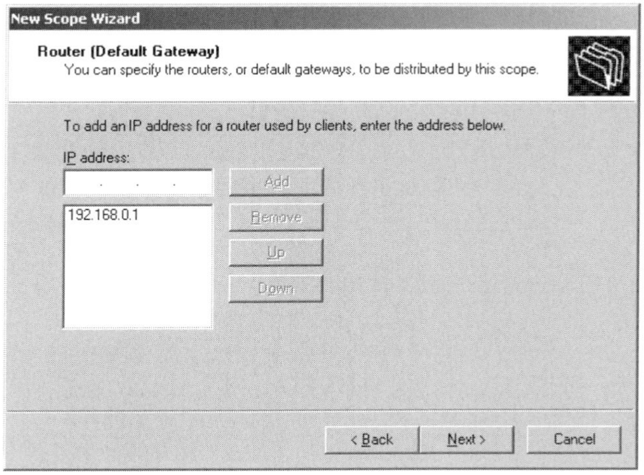

FIGURE 7.9

Set default gateway.

You may recall that in the last chapter I said that when configuring TCP/IP on a Windows system, the "big four" characteristics, so to speak, are IP address, subnet mask, IP address of the default gateway, and address or addresses of local DNS server(s). By its nature, any DHCP lease gives the first two; this is the third.

Although you *can* enter any number of gateways, there's no point in entering more than one, as I've never found a situation wherein Microsoft's IP could use a second, third, or fourth possible gateway upon discovering that the first gateway is down. In fact, Microsoft specifically recommends that you only specify *one* default gateway on a system, even if it's got multiple NICs with independent Internet connections!

Following that advice, I've only specified one gateway, as you see in Figure 7.9. Click Next to see the next option screen, as in Figure 7.10.

FIGURE 7.10

Set domain name.

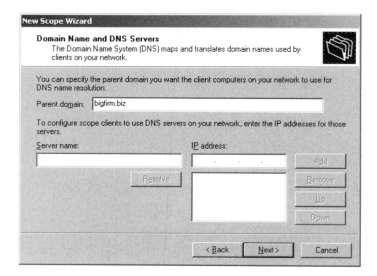

In this wizard screen, you tell the DHCP server that whenever it leases a client PC an IP address from this scope, it should also set that client PC's DNS domain name to some value—win2ktest.com, in this case—and to tell the client PC that it can find DNS servers at some address. I've chosen *not* to specify DNS servers, however, because *all* of the scopes in my enterprise share two DNS servers, and I don't want to have to reenter these DNS servers for every scope. As you'll see in a few pages, I can instead just tell this server, "Give this particular DNS server to *all* scopes." I have, however, specified a DNS suffix of bigfirm.biz for all systems. That way, every system's DNS name ends with bigfirm.biz and that means, as you'll see later in the DNS section, that the system registers itself with the DNS server for bigfirm.biz. Click Next to see the next screen, as in Figure 7.11.

Most of us will still have the necessary evil of WINS servers; here's where you tell the client where to find your enterprise's WINS servers.

FIGURE 7.11

Set WINS server(s).

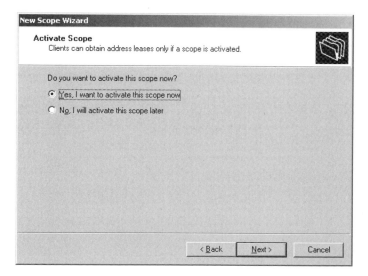

FIGURE 7.12

Activate the scope.

ACTIVATING THE SCOPE

Click Next and you can get the scope started, as you see in Figure 7.12.

That's all for the basic scope options, so the wizard's done. On the way out, it asks if you're ready for this server to start handing out leases on IP addresses. Click Yes and Next, and the wizard will finish, starting the scope in the process. The DHCP snap-in then looks like Figure 7.13.

Taking a minute and looking at the hierarchy in Figure 7.13 underscores a few things about how DHCP works. The snap-in enables you to control any number of DHCP servers from a central location, although you see only one in this example screen, the machine at 192.168.0.10. Each server can have several subnets that it serves, with one range of IP addresses for each subnet. The ranges are called scopes, and again this example machine only shows one scope, but could host many—I've seen one large corporate DHCP server that hosts 1200 scopes! Within the scope there are several pieces of information: the range of addresses (`Address Pool`), the list of addresses that this server has given out (`Address Leases`), addresses that we've preassigned to particular systems (`Reservations`, which I'll cover a bit later), and particular TCP/IP settings that the DHCP server should give to any clients (`Scope Options`). If you were to click Scope Options, then you'd notice that the options include something we didn't set—WINS/NBT Node Type. That's DHCP-ese for the fact that the client PC will be set up to use a WINS server—in other words—that the client will be set up as something called a *hybrid node*, which I'll cover later in this chapter in the WINS section.

FIGURE 7.13

DHCP snap-in with activated scope

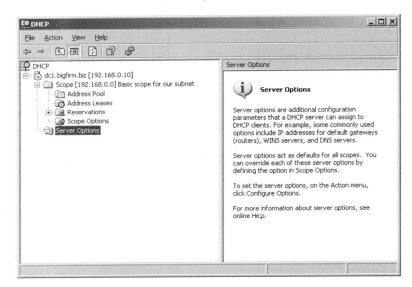

SETTING OPTIONS FOR ALL SCOPES

Notice the folder lower in the interface labeled `Server Options`. The server options are useful when you're putting more than one scope on a server. It could be that if you have three different subnets and a couple hundred machines, you've only got two DNS servers, and those machines serve your entire enterprise. When configuring those scopes, it would be a pain to have to retype in those DNS servers—the same two DNS servers—for all three scopes. `Server Options` solves that problem by allowing you to set options for *all* of a given server's scopes in one operation. Just right-click the `Server Options` folder and choose Configure Options to see a dialog box like the one in Figure 7.14.

Here I've clicked DNS Servers, and you can see that it allows me to enter DNS server addresses, as the wizard did. A bit of scrolling down shows that there are a *lot* of potential DHCP options. But, despite the fact that there seem to be bushels of sadly unused parameters mutely begging to be used, *don't*. Even though they exist, the Microsoft DHCP *client*—the part of Windows, DOS,

Windows 9*x*, NT, Windows 2000, XP, and 2003 that knows how to get IP addresses from a DHCP server—does not know how to use any options save the ones I just mentioned. Microsoft included the other things just to remain compatible with BOOTP.

FIGURE 7.14

Server Options dialog box

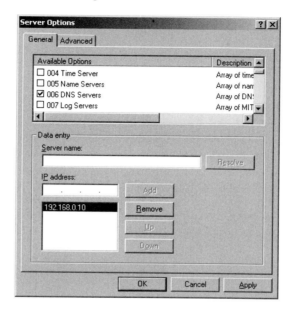

FORCING A PARTICULAR IP ADDRESS ON A CLIENT: DHCP RESERVATIONS

Sometimes, BOOTP doesn't seem like a bad idea. There are times that you'd like to be able to say, *this* computer gets *that* IP address. Fortunately, it's easy to accomplish that with DHCP reservations.

Look at the DHCP snap-in and you'll see a folder labeled `Reservations`. Right-click that folder and choose New Reservation. You'll see a dialog box like the one in Figure 7.15.

FIGURE 7.15

Reserving an IP address

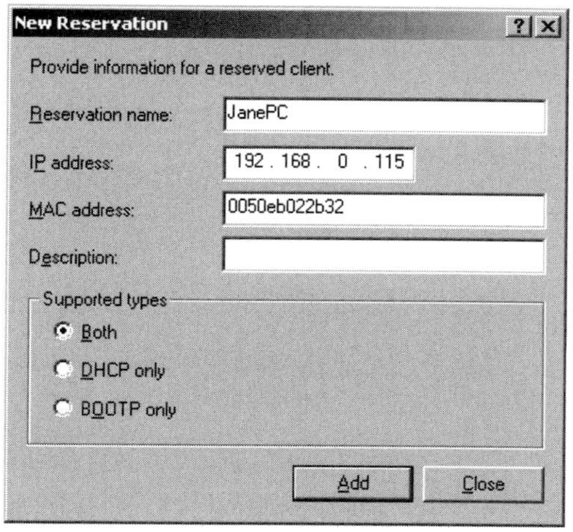

Here, you see that I'm assigning the .115 address to a machine with a particular MAC address.

So far, it sounds like DHCP pretty much hasn't changed since NT 4, and in large measure that's true. But it has added superscopes and support for dynamic DNS even on systems that don't understand dynamic DNS. And there's one more interesting difference. Once you've created a reservation, open the `Reservations` folder and you'll see an object representing that reservation. Right-click it and you'll see Configure Options; click that and you'll see that you can set things like DNS server, domain name, WINS server, and the like for one specific reservation! Now, that's a pretty neat new feature.

ADVANCED OPTIONS: USING AND UNDERSTANDING USER AND VENDOR CLASSES

As you've seen, you can assign different DHCP options either to all scopes (the `Server Options` folder) or to a particular scope. You've even seen that you can assign DHCP options to a particular machine's reservation! But there's another way to assign options, through *user classes* and *vendor classes*. Here's how you use them.

You can make a machine a member of a user class by just telling the computer that it's a member of that class. You could have classes such as laptop or test-computers.

Machines are also potentially members of vendor classes, but you can't control that—it's hard-wired into their operating systems. For example, all Windows 2000 machines are automatically members of a vendor class called Microsoft and one called Microsoft Windows 2000; Windows 98 and Me computers are automatically members of vendor classes Microsoft and Microsoft Windows 98. Vendor classes determine what options are available for you to give to your DHCP client.

You can use DHCP to apply a particular option to a particular system. The vendor class determines which options are available to the system—"default" includes the basic by-the-RFC stuff you've always seen, for example, Microsoft vendor options would offer nonstandard new options that would only be relevant to a system running a Microsoft operating system—and the user class determines whether to apply that option. Thus, you could use user and vendor options to say, "If this system is a member of the IBM-laptops class (a user class), then set the Router option (which is in the DHCP Standard Options vendor)."

You can see the user and vendor class controls like so:

1. Open the DHCP snap-in (Start/Administrative Tools/DHCP).

2. Open either a scope's options or the server options by right-clicking the `Scope Options` or `Server Options` folders and choosing Configure Options.

3. Click the Advanced tab. You'll see something like Figure 7.16.

Prebuilt Vendor Classes

Click the Vendor Class drop-down list and you'll see four options: DHCP Standard Options, Microsoft Options, Microsoft Windows 2000 Options, and Microsoft Windows 98 Options. (Interesting that there are Win2K options, but no XP or 2003 options, hmmm?) While DHCP Standard Options is enabled, notice that you get all of the usual options—router, domain name, time server, name server, and so on. But click Microsoft Options, and you'll see a few non-RFC options that Microsoft added.

FIGURE 7.16

Advanced tab
showing vendor
and user class
drop-down lists

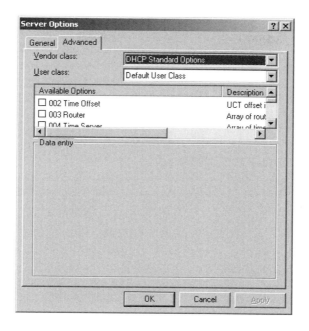

The Microsoft Disable NetBIOS Option tells the computer to shut down the NetBIOS-over-TCP (NetBT) interface. If you don't know what NetBT is, then don't worry—I'll cover it right after I finish DHCP. But briefly, it's a piece of software that pretty much all NT-aware software built before Windows 2000 depends upon. If you've got an NT 4 workstation logging onto an Active Directory–based domain, then you need NetBT. Most modern networks still have enough pre-2000 stuff around that they still need NetBT, but in time—2004 or 2005, I'd guess—most of us will be able to shut NetBT off. The result, once you can do it, is a noticeably faster network. To enable this—that is, to shut off NetBT—check the box next to Microsoft Disable NetBIOS Option, which will enable the Data Entry/Long field; enter **0x2**.

Check the Microsoft Release DHCP Lease on Shutdown Option and fill the Data Entry/Long field with **0x1** to enable. This tells a Windows 2000 system and later to release its DHCP lease upon shutdown, as the name indicates. Why is this useful? Consider this scenario: An employee works at her laptop in the office during the day, with her laptop connected to the company network via an Ethernet connection. The user shuts down the machine and takes it home. At home, she wants to check her mail, so connects her laptop to a phone line to dial in. She turns on the computer, which sees that it has an Ethernet card that has a DHCP lease. It tries to re-contact the DHCP server but fails, but that's no problem—it's got time on the lease and merrily sets up a TCP/IP stack atop an Ethernet card that's not attached to anything. The user dials up and now the computer has *two* IP stacks—one that actually goes somewhere, via the modem, and one that doesn't do anything. Some services bind to the useless Ethernet card and the user experiences either failures or slow service. One answer: Tell the user to disable the Ethernet card. Another answer: Tell the user to type **ipconfig /release** before shutting down the laptop at work. But the easier answer is to enable this feature—shutdowns lead to DHCP lease releases. (This would also bedevil users with Ethernet connections at home, so it's a good practice in that case also.)

The third option lets you modify the default metric of DHCP-supplied gateways. I'm honestly not sure where this would be useful.

Click Microsoft Windows 2000 Options, and you'll get the same three options. Click Microsoft Windows 98 Options, and you won't see any options—apparently Microsoft has hard-coded the vendor class into 98 but didn't do much with it. Again, you cannot create new vendor classes of your own.

Prebuilt User Classes

Next, click the User Class drop-down list, and you'll see three prebuilt user classes: Default BOOTP Class, Default User Class, and Default Routing and Remote Access Class. Here's where you'll see each of the classes:

Default BOOTP Class All of your Windows 2000, XP, and 2003 systems will be members of this class.

Default User Class The class that a system reports if it lacks class (finds belching in public funny, blue screens just for the heck of it, that kind of thing) or, more likely, has a DHCP client that simply doesn't understand what a user class is in the first place—DHCP user classes weren't even a fully accepted RFC standard when Microsoft released Windows 2000. An NT 4 system, then, would end up with Default User Class.

Default Routing and Remote Access Class If you're connected via RRAS, then you're in this class. This is potentially a pretty useful class; for example, the DHCP Help for Windows 2000 shows you how to set the lease times for dial-in users—members of the Default Routing and Remote Access Class—to smaller values than for other users; that way, folks who typically only visit a site for a day end up with a day-long rather than a week-long lease.

You can see which user classes a system belongs to (there is no way to view the vendor classes for a system) by typing **ipconfig /showclassid** *; a sample run might look like the following:

```
C:\>ipconfig /showclassid *

Windows IP Configuration

DHCP Class ID for Adapter "Local Area Connection":
     DHCP ClassID Name . . . . . . . . : Default
     ⮡Routing and Remote Access Class
     DHCP ClassID Description  . . . . : User
     ⮡class for remote access Clients
     DHCP ClassID Name . . . . . . . . : Default BOOTP Class
     DHCP ClassID Description  . . . . : User class for BOOTP Clients
     DHCP ClassID Name . . . . . . . . : Laptop
     DHCP ClassID Description  . . . . : Identifies laptops
```

Here, this computer is a member of three user classes—Default BOOTP Class (it's a Windows 2000 computer), Default Routing and Remote Access Class, and a class called Laptop (which I created).

Note, however, that you may get different results from an `ipconfig /showclassid *` if you try it on different OSes; for some reason I sometimes get different class IDs when running this on 2000 machines than I do on XP or 2003 machines.

User-Defined User Classes

How did I define my own user class? In two steps. First, I told the DHCP server about the new user class and, second, I told some of my workstations that they were members of the class.

You create a new user class in the DHCP snap-in. Right-click the server's icon and choose Define User Classes, and you'll get a dialog box like the one in Figure 7.17.

FIGURE 7.17

DHCP user classes

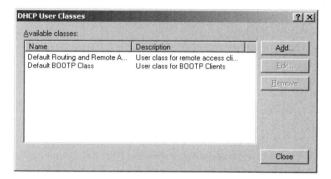

This dialog box doesn't show the Default User Class; however, your DHCP server—*every* 2000-based and later DHCP server, in fact—has it. Let's create a new user class and use it. Suppose I want all of the people in building 12 to have the domain suffix b12.bigfirm.biz. To create the new user class, I click Add. Then in Display Name I fill in **Building12**, and in Description I fill in **Machines in Building 12**, as you see in Figure 7.18.

FIGURE 7.18

New user class for Building 12

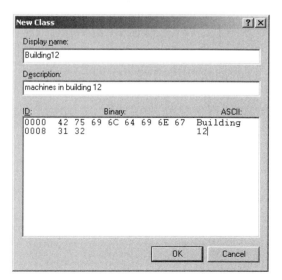

The only non-straightforward part of filling out the dialog box was the ID part; it's not obvious, but you've got to click the mouse in the empty area below the word *ASCII* to be able to type in the class identifier. You can't have blanks in the identifier. Click OK and Close to return to the DHCP snap-in. Now right-click Server Options again and choose Configure Options, click Advanced, and notice that under User Class, there is now a class called Building12. (Case matters—as you'll see in a minute, this won't work unless you add the client machines to a class spelled "Building12" exactly—case and all.) Choose Building12 under User Class. Now you want to assign a particular DNS suffix to the Building12ers, and that's in the default options, so for Vendor Class just choose DHCP Standard Options. Look for the line 015 DNS Domain Name, choose it, and in the Date Entry/String Value field, enter **b12.bigfirm.biz.** and click OK. You're ready on the server side. Don't worry about the hex on the left side; it's just an alternative way of entering the data.

Next, find a machine and make it a member of the Building12 user class. Open a command line and type this:

```
ipconfig /setclassid "Local Area Connection" Building12
```

Then type **ipconfig /renew** and you should get an output something like this:

```
Windows 2000 IP Configuration
Ethernet adapter LAN:

        Connection-specific DNS Suffix  . : b12.bigfirm.biz.
        IP Address. . . . . . . . . . . : 192.168.0.2
        Subnet Mask . . . . . . . . . . : 255.255.255.0
        Default Gateway . . . . . . . . : 192.168.0.1
        DHCP Class ID . . . . . . . . . : Building12
```

Two notes on this:

First, notice in the ipconfig /setclassid line where I have "Local Area Connection" in quotes. That is the *name* of your network adapter. Didn't know that it *had* a name? Recall that you saw that in Chapter 6. To see it, right-click My Network Places and choose Properties. The page that results will have an icon for a LAN connection and the name next to it. The default name is *Local Area Connection*, but you can rename it. If you have more than one NIC, then you'll have a different name.

If this doesn't work the first time that you do it, don't be surprised—this often behaves a bit flakily the first time you use it—I have no idea why. Try an ipconfig /release after you do the /setclassid command before the ipconfig /renew.

The DHCP user class will survive reboots; to clear the user class info, type this:

```
ipconfig /setclassid "Local Area Connection"
```

And if your NIC has a different name than Local Area Connection, then substitute that, of course.

If you script your installs, then you can also set an adapter's class ID by adding this parameter to its [MS_TCPIP parameters] section:

```
DHCPClassId = name
```

ADVANCED SERVER CONFIGURATION

Before leaving configuration, let's take a look at some overall server configuration items—in particular, logging and DNS client registration. In the DHCP snap-in, right-click the server and choose Properties. You'll see a page with three tabs. The first is named General, as you see in Figure 7.19.

FIGURE 7.19

General server
configuration page

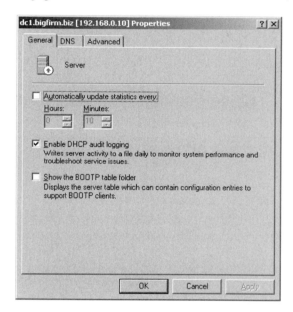

The main thing to notice here is the logging option. It's a default option, so don't worry about having to check it. But where is the log kept? Well, for one thing, there are seven logs, one for each day of the week—that makes finding a record for an action on a particular day easier. The logs are in simple ASCII format, so you can examine them with Notepad, although it would be nicer if the DHCP snap-in would go get them *for* you. They're in \winnt\system32\dhcp in files whose names include the day of the week. Part of one log looks like the following:

```
63,07/03/99,00:44:30,Restarting rogue detection,,,
51,07/03/99,00:45:30,Authorization succeeded,,win2ktest.com,
11,07/03/99,00:47:09,Renew,206.246.253.135,
PC400.win2ktest.com,00105A27D97A
10,07/03/99,00:48:00,Assign,206.246.253.2,
PC400.win2ktest.com,5241532000105A27D97A000000000000
10,07/03/99,00:48:00,Assign,206.246.253.3,
PC400.win2ktest.com,5241532000105A27D97A000001000000
63,07/03/99,01:51:51,Restarting rogue detection,,,
51,07/03/99,01:52:52,Authorization succeeded,,win2ktest.com,
```

Rogue detection is a process whereby the DHCP server seeks to find unauthorized DHCP servers. To entrap these dastards, the DHCP server craftily pretends it is just a PC looking for an IP address. It gets offers from other DHCP servers, and the DHCP server then checks their IP addresses against the list of authorized DHCP servers in the Active Directory. If it finds a scoundrel, then it reports that in the Event Viewer.

On the third line, you see that the machine at 206.246.253.135 has "renewed" its IP address—that is to say, it has said to the DHCP server, "You once gave me this IP address and the lease is running out. May I extend the lease?" The two "assign" statements give the .2 and .3 addresses to PC400 to then hand out—you see, PC400 is a RAS server and needs IP addresses to give away to dial-in clients. RAS has given those two addresses for PC400 to use.

The properties page has another interesting tab, the DNS tab. Click it, and you'll see a screen like the one in Figure 7.20.

FIGURE 7.20

Configuring the dynamic DNS client from DHCP

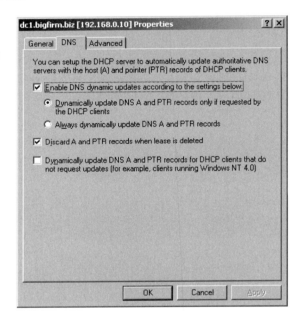

Although DNS is a topic for later in this chapter, let me jump ahead a bit and explain briefly how it works. DNS is a database of machines and names: My local DNS server is the machine that knows there's a machine named dc1.bigfirm.biz with an IP address of 192.168.0.10. But how does it *know* that? With DNS under NT 4, I'd have to start a program called the DNS Manager and hand-enter the information. But with the DNS client built into Windows 2000 and later OSes, dc1.bigfirm.biz is smart enough to talk to its local DNS server and say, "Listen, I don't know if you knew this, but I'm a machine on the network, my name's dc1.bigfirm.biz, and my IP address is 192.168.0.10." Additionally, the DNS server—which is running Server 2003, although any DNS server on Windows 2000 Server or later will work—is smart enough to *hear* this information; older DNS servers wouldn't be expecting machines to register themselves with their local DNS server, and the local DNS server wouldn't have a clue about what to do with the information anyway. But post-1998 DNS servers have a feature called *dynamic* DNS, which enables them to accept this name/address (*name registration*) information from other machines rather than having to have a human type the information in.

There are two important points to notice in the preceding paragraph. First, the DNS server's got to be smart enough to listen to and act upon the name registrations when they come from the clients. Second, the clients have to be smart enough to *issue* name registration information! If my workstation's running NT 4 rather than Windows 2000 or later, then it hasn't been programmed to offer name/address information to its DNS server because the whole dynamic DNS technology didn't even exist in 1996 when Microsoft wrote NT 4! From the point of view of the state-of-the-art DNS server running on the Windows 2000 or Server 2003, then, the old Windows 9*x*, Windows for Workgroups, and NT clients are just plain dumb. Or, more exactly, from the point of view of the DNS server, those clients *don't even exist*. There's no way that the DNS server could figure out they are there.

That's what the dialog box in Figure 7.20 accomplishes. This DHCP server will notice when it's handing out an IP address to a machine that doesn't know about dynamic DNS; although the DHCP server cannot modify the code running on the older client, it can fill in for the older client's lack of knowledge, and register the client's name/address with DNS for it. Notice the option labeled Dynamically update DNS A and PTR records for DHCP clients that do not request updates; that's the feature I've been discussing here. Make sure that box is checked, and DHCP will handle the DNS registrations for the older systems.

Monitoring DHCP

Once you've got a DHCP server set up and running, you may want to find out how many leases remain, who's got those leases, and the like. Open the `Address Leases` folder and you'll see something like Figure 7.21.

FIGURE 7.21

Assigned leases

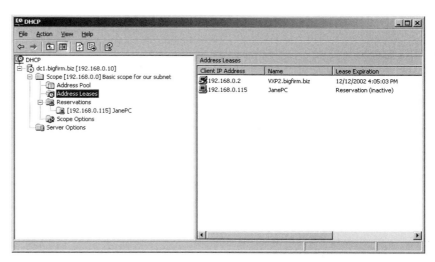

This folder displays all of the leases that DHCP has currently outstanding, which machine (by name) has them, as well as the machine's MAC address.

But how many addresses are left? Right-click any scope and choose Display Statistics, and you'll see a message box like Figure 7.22.

FIGURE 7.22

Lease statistics

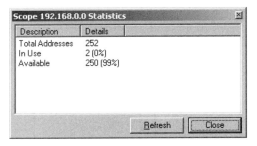

With just a few clicks, you can bring up this message box and find out whether your network's hunger for IP addresses is being met.

Rebuilding a Damaged DHCP Server

Once in a while, something goes wrong and you lose a DHCP server. The scopes, reservations, classes…all go poof! and you're in for an hour or two of configuration, assuming that you kept good documentation. If you didn't, well, then it'll take longer…

You can avoid that with just one command. Server 2003 lets you get your DHCP server just so, just as you like it, and then lets you back up the DHCP server's configuration with just one command:

```
netsh dhcp server dump
```

Or, if you're not sitting at the server,

```
netsh dhcp server ipaddress dump
```

That spews line after line of configuration information to your screen. Save it by redirecting it to an ASCII file:

```
netsh dhcp server dump > dhcpbackup.txt
```

Then, if the DHCP server falls apart, all you have to do is to put the DHCP server service on some other machine, copy over your backup file, and use `netsh exec`, like so:

```
netsh exec dhcpbackup.txt
```

You won't get back the lease information, but you'll get everything else—classes, options, scopes, reservations, etc.

DHCP on the Client Side

Now that you've set up DHCP on a server, how do you tell clients to use that DHCP? Simple. Any Microsoft operating system from Windows for Workgroups to Windows 9*x* to NT 3.*x* to NT 4.*x* to Windows 2000 all have DHCP configuration as an installation option, although some of those clients refer to it as "automatic" configuration rather than DHCP configuration. (By the way, the Microsoft Client software for DOS and Windows supports DHCP as well.)

Once a system has gotten an IP address, you can find out what that address is by going to that system, opening a command line, and typing **ipconfig /all**. On a Windows 95 workstation, click Start/Run, and then type **winipcfg** and press Enter. Windows 98 supports both IPConfig *and* WINIPCFG. Windows NT only supports IPConfig. IPConfig's useful for other DHCP client– fiddling, as well. You can force a DHCP client to abandon its DHCP-supplied IP address and look for a different one by typing first **ipconfig /release** and then **ipconfig /renew**.

Windows XP, Server 2003, and later Windows versions support an all-in-one command to rebuild an IP connection:

```
netsh int ip reset filename
```

where *filename* is a file that reports the command's progress. I highly recommend learning this command if you've got XP or 2003 (and if you didn't have 2003 then I'm not sure why you'd be reading this book); it's more reliable than the pair of `ipconfigs`.

DHCP in Detail: How DHCP Works

That's setting up DHCP. But how does it work, and unfortunately, how does it sometimes *not* work?

DHCP supplies IP addresses based on the idea of *client leases*. When a machine (a DHCP client) needs an IP address, it asks a DHCP server for that address. (*How* it does that is important, and I'll get to it in a minute.) A DHCP server then gives an IP address to the client, *but only for a temporary period of time*—hence the term *IP lease*. You might have noticed you can set the term of an IP lease from DHCP; just right-click any scope and choose Properties, and it's one of the settings in the resultant window.

The client then knows how long it's got the lease. Even if you reboot or reset your computer, it'll remember what lease is active for it and how much longer it's got to go on the lease.

FINDING THE CLIENT LEASE INFORMATION

On a Windows 3.*x* machine, lease information is kept in `DHCP.BIN` in the `Windows` directory. On a Windows 95 machine, it's in `HKEY_LOCAL_MACHINE\System\CurrentControlSet\Services\VxD\DHCP\ Dhcp-infoxx`, where xx is two digits. And if you want to enable or disable the error messages from the DHCP client on a Windows 95 machine, it's the value PopupFlag in the key `HKEY_LOCAL_MACHINE\ System\CurrentControlSet\Services\VxD\DHCP`; use "00 00 00 00" for false, or "01 00 00 00" for true. Alternatively, opening a command line and typing **ipconfig /release** will erase this infor- mation. To find the place in the Registry holding DHCP lease information on an NT machine, run REGEDIT and search for DHCPIPAddress in `HKEY_LOCAL_MACHINE\System\CurrentControlSet`. The key or keys that turn up are the location of the DHCP lease info. On a Windows 2000 system, it's probably `hkey_local_machine\system\currentcontrolset\services\TCPIP\parameters\Interfaces`; within there you'll find GUIDs (Global Unique IDs, the things that look like {CE52A8C0-B126-11D2- A5D2-BFFEA72FC}) for each adapter and potential RAS connection. There's a DHCPIPAddress value in each adapter that gets its addresses from DHCP. On Windows XP systems, it's just `HKEY_LOCAL_ MACHINE\SYSTEM\CurrentControlSet\Services`, and you'll notice those keys with GUID names right up top; each of those keys has a Parameters\TCPIP key within it. Delete the GUID's key and you eliminate any settings for that adapter. As to figuring out which GUID goes with which adapter, ummm, well, that's a matter of trial and error.

So, if your PC had a four-day lease on some address and you rebooted two days into its lease, then the PC wouldn't just blindly ask for an IP address; instead, it would go back to the DHCP server that it got its IP address from and request the particular IP address that it had before. If the DHCP server were still up, then it would acknowledge the request, letting the workstation use the IP address. If, on the other hand, the DHCP server has had its lease information wiped out through some disaster, then either it will give the IP address to the machine (if no one else is using the address), or it will send a *negative acknowledgment* (NACK) to the machine, and the DHCP server will make a note of that NACK in the Event Log. Your workstation should then be smart enough to start searching around for a new DHCP server. In my experience, sometimes it isn't.

Like BOOTP, DHCP remembers which IP addresses go with what machine by matching up an IP address with a MAC (Media Access Control—that is, Ethernet) address.

Normally a DHCP server can send new lease information to a client only at lease renewal intervals. But DHCP clients also "check in" at reboot, so rebooting a workstation will allow DHCP to reset any lease changes such as subnet masks and DNS services.

GETTING AN IP ADDRESS FROM DHCP: THE NUTS AND BOLTS

A DHCP client gets an IP address from a DHCP server in four steps:

1. A *DHCPDISCOVER* broadcasts a request to all DHCP servers in earshot, requesting an IP address.

2. The servers respond with *DHCPOFFER* of IP addresses and lease times.

3. The client chooses the offer that sounds most appealing and broadcasts back a *DHCPREQUEST* to confirm the IP address.

4. The server handing out the IP address finishes the procedure by returning with a *DHCPACK*, an acknowledgment of the request.

Initial DHCP Request: DHCPDISCOVER

First, a DHCP client sends out a message called a DHCPDISCOVER saying, in effect, "Are there any DHCP servers out there? If so, I want an IP address." Figure 7.23 shows this message.

FIGURE 7.23
DHCP step 1:
DHCPDISCOVER

DHCP
client

Enet addr: 00CC00000000
IP addr: 0.0.0.0

"Is there a DHCP server around?"

IP address used: 255.255.255.255 (broadcast)
Ethernet address used: FFFFFFFFFFFF (broadcast)
Transaction ID: 14321

DHCP
server

Enet addr: 00BB00000000
IP addr: 210.22.31.100

You might ask, "How can a machine communicate if it doesn't have an address?" Through a different protocol than TCP—UDP, or the *User Datagram Protocol*. It's not a NetBIOS or NetBEUI creature; it's all TCP/IP-suite stuff.

Now, to follow all of these DHCP messages, there are a couple of things to watch. First of all, I'm showing you both the MAC addresses (the 48-bit unique Ethernet addresses) and the IP addresses because, as you'll see, they tell somewhat different stories. Also, there is a *transaction ID* attached to each DHCP packet that's quite useful. The transaction ID makes it possible for a client to know when it receives a response from a server exactly *what* the response is responding to.

In this case, notice that the IP address the message is sent to is 255.255.255.255. That's the generic address for "anybody on this subnet." Now, 210.22.31.255 would also work, assuming that this is a class C network that hasn't been subnetted, but 255.255.255.255 pretty much always means "anyone who can hear me." If you set up your routers to forward broadcasts, then 255.255.255.255 will be propagated all over the network; 210.22.31.255 would not. Notice also the destination Ethernet address, FFFFFFFFFFFF. That's the Ethernet way of saying, "Everybody— a broadcast."

DHCP Offers Addresses from Near and Far

Any DHCP servers within earshot—that is, any that receive the UDP datagram—respond to the client with an offer, a proposed IP address, like the one shown in Figure 7.24. Again, this is an offer, not the final IP address.

FIGURE 7.24

DHCP step 2: DHCPOFFER

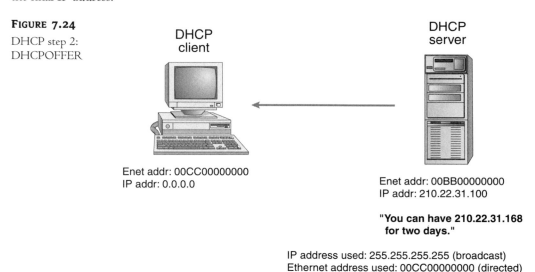

DHCP client

DHCP server

Enet addr: 00CC00000000
IP addr: 0.0.0.0

Enet addr: 00BB00000000
IP addr: 210.22.31.100

"You can have 210.22.31.168 for two days."

IP address used: 255.255.255.255 (broadcast)
Ethernet address used: 00CC00000000 (directed)
Transaction ID: 14321

This offering part of the DHCP process is essential because, as I just hinted, it's possible for more than one DHCP server to hear the original client request. If every DHCP server just thrust an IP address at the hapless client, then it would end up with multiple IP addresses, addresses wasted in the sense that the DHCP servers would consider them all taken, and so they couldn't give those addresses out to other machines.

Side Note: Leapfrogging Routers

Before going further, let's consider a side issue that may be nagging at the back of your mind. As a DHCP client uses *broadcasts* to find a DHCP server, where do routers fit into this? The original UDP message, "Are there any DHCP servers out there?" is a broadcast, recall. Most routers, as you know, do not forward broadcasts—which reduces network traffic congestion and is a positive side effect of routers. But if DHCP requests don't go over routers, then that would imply that you have to have a DHCP server on every subnet—a rather expensive proposition.

The BOOTP standard got around this by defining an RFC 1542, a specification whereby routers following RFC 1542 would recognize BOOTP broadcasts and would forward them to other subnets. The feature must be implemented in your routers' software, and it's commonly known as *BOOTP forwarding*. Even if you live in a one-subnet world, by the way, that's worth remembering, as it's invariably a question on the Microsoft certification exams: "What do you need for client A to communicate with DHCP server B on a different subnet?" Answer: The router between A and B must either "be RFC 1542–compliant" or "support BOOTP forwarding."

Okay, so where do you *get* an RFC 1542–compliant router? Well, most of the IP router manufacturers, such as Compatible Systems, Cisco, and Bay Networks, support 1542. New routers probably already support it; older routers may require a software upgrade. Another approach is to use a Windows 2000 or NT system as a router, as Windows 2000 and NT routing software includes 1542 compliance. But what if you've got dumb routers, or router administrators who refuse to turn on BOOTP forwarding? Then you can designate an NT, Windows 2000, or Server 2003 machine as a *DHCP relay agent*.

A DHCP relay agent is just a computer that spends a bit of its CPU power listening for DHCP client broadcasts. The DHCP relay agent knows there's no DHCP server on the subnet (because you told it), but the relay agent knows where there *is* a DHCP server on another subnet (because you told it). The DHCP relay agent then takes the DHCP client broadcast and converts it into a directed, point-to-point communication straight to the DHCP server. Directed IP communications can cross routers, of course, and so the message gets to the DHCP server.

What do you need to make a DHCP relay agent? Well, with NT 4, you could use any NT machine—workstation or server. For some annoying reason, Windows 2000 and Server 2003 only include software to make a DHCP relay agent with Server.

To make an NT machine into a DHCP relay agent, just open the Control Panel, then the Network applet. Click the Protocols tab and double-click the TCP/IP protocol. In the resulting dialog box, you'll see a tab labeled DHCP Relay. Click it, and you'll see a dialog box like the one shown in Figure 7.25.

To make this work, just click the Add button and fill in the IP address of a DHCP server or servers. The dialog box is simple, but there are two things that confuse people about making a computer into a DHCP relay agent, so let me note them in the following tip and warning.

TIP   *The NT DHCP relay agent can run on any NT system; the system needn't be a router.*

Under no circumstances should you make a DHCP server into a DHCP relay agent. The net effect will be for the DHCP server to essentially "forget" that it's a DHCP server and instead just forward every request that it hears to some other DHCP server. This prompts me to wonder why the silly DHCP relay agent function isn't grayed out altogether on a DHCP server—certainly the Obtain an IP Address from a DHCP Server option is.

FIGURE 7.25

Configuring an
NT 4 computer
to be a DHCP
relay agent

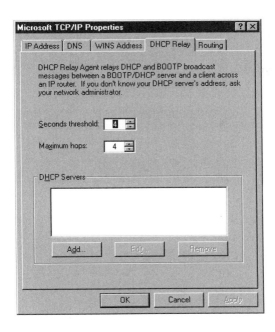

To make a Windows 2000 Server or Server 2003 system—remember, Server only—into a DHCP relay agent, you've got to use Routing and Remote Access Service. Basically any RRAS configuration will do; you needn't enable WAN routing or dial-in. Look back to Chapter 6 to see how to configure an RRAS system—again, click Start/Administrative Tools/Routing and Remote Access, then right-click the server's name and choose Configure and Enable Routing and Remote Access to start the wizard, then choose Custom Configuration, click Next, check the box next to LAN Routing, and finish the wizard. You'll see a screen like the one in Figure 7.26.

FIGURE 7.26

RRAS main screen

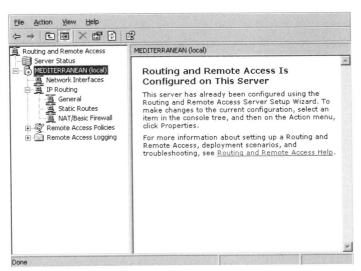

Open the IP Routing object (click the plus sign) and one of the objects you'll see inside it will be a folder labeled General. Right-click the General folder and choose New Routing Protocol to see another dialog box. One of the options offered will be DHCP Relay Agent; choose it and click OK. Back in the RRAS snap-in, you'll now have an object under IP Routing named DHCP Relay Agent, as you see in Figure 7.27.

FIGURE 7.27

RRAS console with DHCP Relay Agent highlighted

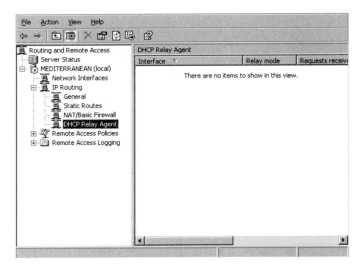

Right-click the DHCP Relay Agent object and choose Properties and you'll see a dialog box like the one in Figure 7.28.

FIGURE 7.28

Relay agent config-uration screen

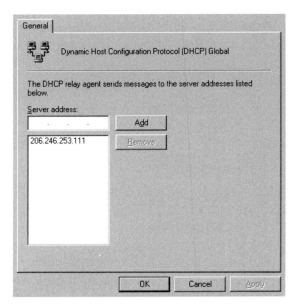

You configure the agent by telling it where to find DHCP servers. Enter the IP address of the DHCP server and click Add to add a server to the list. Finally, you've got to enable the agent to listen on the local network for DHCP requests to forward. Right-click DHCP Relay Agent and choose New Interface. Choose Local Area Connection and the agent will then be active on the network.

Discussion of relay agents and 1542-compliant routers leads me to yet another question. What if a DHCP server from another subnet gave an IP address to our client? Wouldn't that put the client in the wrong subnet? If a DHCP server serves a bunch of different subnets, how does it know which subnet an incoming request came from? DHCP solves that problem with BOOTP forwarding.

Assuming that your routers implement BOOTP forwarding, then a client's original DHCP request gets out to all of them. But how do you keep a DHCP server in an imaginary subnet 200.1.2.z from giving an address in 200.1.2.z to a PC sitting in another imaginary subnet, 200.1.1.z? Simple. When the router forwards the BOOTP request, it attaches a little note to it that says, "This came from 200.1.1.z." The DHCP server then sees that information, and so it only responds if it has a scope within 200.1.1.z.

Notice that although to the higher-layer protocol (UDP) this is a broadcast, the lower-layer Ethernet protocol behaves as though it is not, and the Ethernet address embedded in the message is the address of the client, not the FFFFFFFFFFFF broadcast address. Notice also that the transaction ID on the response matches the transaction ID on the original request. End of side trip, let's return to watching that client get its address from DHCP.

Picking from the Offers

The DHCP client then looks through the offers it has and picks the one that's "best" for it, or so the Microsoft documentation says. In my experience—and I've done a bunch of experiments—"best" means "first." It seems that the first server that responds is the one whose offer it accepts. Then it sends another UDP datagram, another broadcast, shown in Figure 7.29.

FIGURE 7.29

DHCP step 3:
DHCPREQUEST

**DHCP
client**

**DHCP
server**

Enet addr: 00CC00000000
IP addr: 0.0.0.0

Enet addr: 00BB00000000
IP addr: 210.22.31.100

**"Can I have the 210.22.31.168 IP address,
  and thanks for the other offers, but no thanks."**

IP address used: 255.255.255.255 (broadcast)
Ethernet address used: FFFFFFFFFFFF (broadcast)
Transaction ID: 18923

It's a broadcast because this message serves two purposes. First, the broadcast *will* get back to the original offering server if the first broadcast got to that server, which it obviously did. Second, this broadcast is a way of saying to any *other* DHCP servers who made offers, "Sorry, folks, but I'm taking this other offer."

Notice that both the Ethernet and the IP addresses are broadcasts, and there is a new transaction ID.

The Lease Is Signed

Finally, the DHCP server responds with the shiny brand-new IP address, which will look something like Figure 7.30.

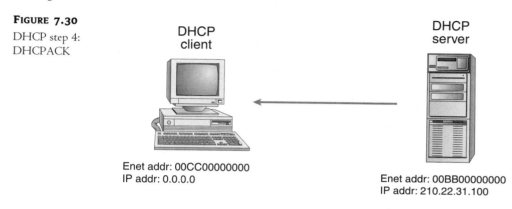

FIGURE 7.30
DHCP step 4: DHCPACK

DHCP client

DHCP server

Enet addr: 00CC00000000
IP addr: 0.0.0.0

Enet addr: 00BB00000000
IP addr: 210.22.31.100

"Sure; also take this subnet mask, DNS server address, WINS server, node type, and domain name."

IP address used: 255.255.255.255 (broadcast)
Ethernet address used: 00CC00000000 (directed)
Transaction ID: 18923

It also tells the client its new subnet mask, lease period, and whatever else you specified (gateway, WINS server, DNS server, and the like). Again, notice it's a UDP broadcast, but the Ethernet address is directed, and the transaction ID matches the previous request's ID.

You can find out what your IP configuration looks like after DHCP by typing `ipconfig /all`. It may run off the screen, so you may need to add `|more` to the line. This works on DOS, Windows for Workgroups, and NT machines. You can see a sample run of `ipconfig /all` in Figure 7.31. Windows 95 machines have a graphical version of IPConfig called WINIPCFG.

Lost Our Lease! Must Sell!

What happens when the lease runs out? Well, when that happens, you're supposed to stop using the IP address. But you're not likely to lose that lease—Windows DHCP client software is pretty vigilant about keeping its DHCP leases as long-lived as is possible.

When the lease is half over, the DHCP client begins renegotiating the IP lease by sending a DHCP request to the server that originally gave it its IP address. The IP and Ethernet addresses are both specific to the server.

FIGURE 7.31

Run of IPConfig

The DHCP server then responds with a DHCPACK. The benefit of this is that the DHCPACK contains all of the information that the original DHCPACK had—domain name, DNS server, and so on. That means you can change the DNS server, WINS server, subnet mask, and the like, and the new information will be updated at the clients periodically, but no more than 50 percent of the lease time.

Now, if the DHCPACK doesn't appear, then the DHCP client keeps resending the DHCP request out every two minutes until the IP lease is 87.5 percent expired. (Don't you wonder where they get these numbers from?) At that point, the client just goes back to the drawing board, broadcasting DHCPDISCOVER messages until someone responds. If the lease expires without a new one, the client will stop using the IP address, effectively disabling the TCP/IP protocol on that workstation.

But if you've messed with the DHCP servers, then the renewal process seems to get bogged down a bit. It's a good idea in that case to force a workstation to restart the whole DHCP process by typing **ipconfig /renew** or, better, **ipconfig /release** followed by **ipconfig /renew**; that will often clear up a DHCP problem.

Even with an infinite lease, however, a DHCP client checks back with its server whenever it boots. Therefore, you can often change from infinite to fixed leases by just changing the lease value at the server. Then stop and restart the DHCP service.

Designing Multi-DHCP Networks

Clearly the function of the DHCP server is one that shouldn't rest solely on the shoulders of one server (well, okay, servers don't have shoulders, but you know what I mean). So, how can you put two or more DHCP servers online to accomplish some fault tolerance?

Microsoft seems a bit confused about how to go about providing multiple DHCP servers for a given subnet and has offered different advice at different times.

In one document, *Windows NT 3.5 Family Upgrade Course*, it said several things. First, "There is *no* mechanism in DHCP that allows two or more DHCP servers to coordinate the assignment of IP addresses from overlapping IP address pools."

No argument there. If you had two different DHCP servers on the same subnet, and they both thought that they could give out addresses 202.11.39.10 through 202.11.39.40, then there would be nothing keeping the first server from giving address 202.11.39.29 to one machine while simultaneously the other server was giving out that same 202.11.39.29 address to another machine. (It's almost as if helpful Tom has returned!)

Then, it goes on (pages 147 and 148) to demonstrate two different machines running DHCP server and each machine having a different scope. Both scopes are, however, taken from a single subnet.

In contrast, the NT Resource Kit (version 3.5, but 3.51 has no updates on the matter) takes issue with the idea of more than one scope referring to a subnet like so: "Each subnet can have only one scope with a single continuous range of IP addresses."

What this boils down to is this: I don't know what the official Microsoft approach to DHCP fault tolerance *is*. I *do*, however, know what works and what has worked for me. Like many people, I came up with an approach such as the one in the NT training guide. I just run DHCP on multiple machines and create multiple scopes that refer to the same subnet. I make absolutely sure that the ranges of addresses in the scopes do not overlap at all, and everything seems to work fine.

I guess I should note for the sake of completeness that you can provide fault tolerance for DHCP servers by putting your DHCP server on a cluster of two or more machines. A perfectly valid answer, but not a very cheap one.

Name Resolution in Perspective: Introduction to WINS, NetBIOS, DNS, and Winsock

Consider the following two commands, both issued to the same server:

```
ping server01.bigfirm.com
```

and

```
net use * \\server01\mainshr
```

In the ping command, the server is referred to as server01.bigfirm.com. In the **net use** command, that same server is called server01. The difference is important for these reasons.

Ping relies upon a traditionally Internet-oriented programming interface called *Winsock*, and any program running Ping generally needs access to something called a *DNS server* in order to execute the ping command.

net use relies upon a traditionally Microsoft networking–oriented programming interface called *NetBIOS*, and any program running **net use** generally needs access to something called a *WINS server* to execute the **net use** command.

Let's do a bit of background work in order to understand Winsock, DNS, NetBIOS, and WINS.

Two Different Lineages, Two Different Names

The ping command is clearly a TCP/IP/Internet kind of command. You can't run it unless you're running TCP/IP, and as a matter of fact, it's a valid command on a Unix, VMS, Macintosh, or MVS machine so long as that machine is running a TCP/IP protocol stack.

In contrast, net use is a Microsoft networking command. You can do a net use on an NT network no matter what protocol you're running, but the command usually wouldn't be valid on a Unix, VMS, Macintosh, or whatever kind of machine; in general, Microsoft networking is pretty much built to work on PCs. (Yes, I know, NT is in theory architecture-independent, so you could find an Alpha machine using net use commands, but on the whole, NT is an Intel *x*86 operating system at this writing—and I haven't seen announcements of an NT/390 for the IBM mainframe world, NT VAX for the Digital world, or NT SPARC for the Sun world.)

Application Program Interface = Modularity

The difference is in the network application programming interface (API) that the application is built atop. API? What's that?

Well, years ago, most PC software had no understanding of networks at all. But that's not true anymore; there are many "network-aware" programs around. For example, the software that lets a Server 2003 system be a file server is network aware; what good would a file server be without a network? Other network-aware server software includes Web servers such as Internet Information Server or e-mail servers such as Exchange.

Desktop machines—*clients*—use network-aware software as well. The program that lets you browse file servers with My Network Places on Windows 2000 and later systems, browse Network Neighborhood on Windows 9*x* and NT 4 systems, or do command-line commands such as net view (which lets you view the servers in a workgroup or the shares on a server) or net use is generically called a "client for Microsoft networking" and is network aware. So also is a Web browser (the client software for a Web server, like Internet Explorer) or an e-mail client.

But the programmers who build network-aware applications such as file server clients or Web browsers aren't generally the programmers who write the rest of the networking software—the NIC drivers, the protocols, and so on. Different pieces of network software are usually designed to fit together in a modular fashion. But the only way that the folks who write the Web browsers can remain compatible with the folks who write the TCP/IP code is if the application developers and the protocol developers agree on an interface, a kind of "software connector" between the two pieces of software. More and more, designers build software to be modular specifically so that the Web browser people don't have to coordinate closely with the TCP/IP protocol–writing people.

The interface between a protocol and the applications that rely on it is called the *application programming interface* (API). Think of an API as being something like the controls you use when driving a car. Your car's steering wheel, accelerator, and other controls form the interface that you see, and you learn to use them to operate the car. You might have no idea while you're driving what's under your car's hood—you just push down the accelerator and the car goes faster. If someone snuck into my garage tonight and replaced the internal combustion engine in my Honda with a magic engine that didn't use gas, I would have no idea, nor would I care until I eventually noticed that the gas gauge seemed to be broken. As a driver, I really don't have to know anything at all about engines—all I've got to know is that the pedal on the right makes the car go faster. So long as the magic engine makes the car go vroom-vroom when I push down the right pedal, I'm happy.

The "automobile API" consists of a few "primitive" commands: Brake the car, accelerate the car, shift the car's transmission, and so on. There is no command "back the car out of the driveway," and yet I can still back a car out of a driveway by just assembling several of the primitive commands into the actual action of backing a car out of a driveway. The best part about this generic automobile

API is that once you learn how to drive one car, you can instantly use another. In other words, you are an "application designed for the car driver controls API."

In contrast, consider how private pilots learn to fly. They have two pedals on the floor of their plane, but the left pedal turns them left and the right pedal turns them right. Someone trained as a private pilot would be an "application designed for the private plane API." Taking someone who can fly a plane and plunking him down in a car without any other training wouldn't work too well. In the same way, if an application is built for *one* network API, then it won't work on another. But if you built a car whose controls acted like an airplane's, airplane pilots could drive the car without any trouble.

NetBIOS and Winsock

I'm stretching a point a bit here, but I could say that cars and planes are just different ways of solving the same problem: transportation. In the same way, various network vendors over the years have tackled the same problem and come up with different solutions. In particular, Microsoft has, since 1985, built its network applications atop a network API called the Network Basic Input-Output System (NetBIOS) that first appeared on a product from a company called Sytek and that was later promoted and expanded by IBM and Microsoft. The Internet world, on the other hand, has used a different network API called *sockets*. In the Microsoft world, we call our special version of sockets *Winsock*.

Recall that the value of an API is that it separates your network applications from your network vendor—you needn't buy your network operating system from the same people you bought your network fax software from. For example, if you buy a network fax application designed for a network API named NetBIOS, you should be able to run that network fax application on any network at all, so long as the network supports the NetBIOS API. Over time, we've seen a number of seemingly dissimilar networks that all sported NetBIOS as their API, including Lantastic, OS/2 LAN Server, LAN Manager, HP's LM/UX, Digital's PathWorks, Windows for Workgroups, and the NT family. Code written for one of these networks could run with little or no changes on any of the others.

Similarly, at one time there were several vendors selling a version of TCP/IP for Windows for Workgroups back in 1992–1994. If the Winsock implementations on each of those TCP/IP versions were built right, then you should have been able to run the exact same copy of Eudora Light (a free Internet e-mail program) or Netscape Navigator on any of them.

Can your network live with just Winsock or NetBIOS programming interfaces? Probably not. You want to run the NetBIOS-based programs because anything written for Microsoft networks prior to Windows 2000 was written to run on NetBIOS. And you want to run Winsock-based programs because so many Internet-type applications exist—the Web and e-mail stand out, but there are many more—and they're built to work with Winsock.

In fact, one of the major changes in NT wrought by Windows 2000 (and later OSes) was that almost all of Windows 2000's networking will work fine on Winsock and doesn't need NetBIOS at all. (Not everything; for example, some Exchange 2000 configurations need NetBIOS, and server clusters need NetBIOS, as does the ability to restrict users to only logging onto specific workstations.) But any Windows 9x, Workgroups, or NT system needing to access data on Windows 2000 or Server 2003 servers will do so via NetBIOS. Similarly, any pre–Windows 2000 applications running on a Windows 2000 system can only run atop NetBIOS, even if all of the systems in the network are Windows 2000 systems. The result is that virtually all Windows 2000 systems need a complete NetBIOS infrastructure.

Name Resolution Defined

Something that both NetBIOS and Winsock have in common is that they both want to support easy-to-work-with machine names. Yes, every machine on the Internet and on virtually all Server 2003 networks has a unique IP address, but no one wants to use that to identify servers: Opening My Network Places should show servers with names such as \\PERSONNEL rather than 220.10.99.32, and Amazon wants to be able to tell you to shop for books at www.amazon.com rather than 208.216.182.15. So we need some kind of database server around that can translate www.amazon.com to 208.216.182.15 and \\PERSONNEL to 220.10.99.32. This problem of converting a name into an IP address is called *name resolution*. For NetBIOS and Winsock, it's the same problem but with two different solutions. NetBIOS looks for its name resolution from a Windows Internet Name Service (WINS) server; Winsock looks for its name resolution from a Domain Name System (DNS) server.

NetBIOS versus Winsock still not clear? Then consider one more analogy. Think of the APIs as communications devices. Telephones and the mail service are communications devices, also, so I'll use them in an analogy. Ping's job is to communicate with some other PC, and **net use** also wants to communicate with some PC. But Ping uses Winsock (the telephone) and **net use** uses NetBIOS (the mail). If you use the telephone to call a friend, then that friend's "name" as far as the phone is concerned may be something like (707) 555-2121. As far as the mail is concerned, however, the friend's "name" might be Paul Jones, 124 Main Street, Anytown, VA, 32102. Both are perfectly valid "names" for your friend Paul, but they're different because different communications systems need different name types. In the same way, server01.bigfirm.com and \\server01 are both perfectly valid but different names for the same server.

Handling Legacy and NetBIOS Names: The Windows Internet Name Service

Anyway, for those of you NT 4 vets hoping that WINS would bite the dust in Windows 2000 or *certainly* by Server 2003, I've got to report that sorry, looks like we've still got to support it. So let's see how to support this "legacy name resolving system." (*Legacy* is computer industry-ese for "crappy old stuff that we hate and that's why we upgraded in the first place, but we can't seem to get rid of all of it and so now we have to support both the new incomprehensible stuff *and* the crappy old stuff." But *legacy* sure makes it sound better, at least to me.)

NetBIOS atop TCP/IP (NBT)

The NetBIOS API is implemented on the NetBEUI, IPX/SPX, and TCP/IP protocols that Microsoft distributes. That makes Microsoft's TCP/IP a bit different from the TCP/IP you find on Unix (for example), because the Unix TCP/IP almost certainly won't have a NetBIOS API on it; it'll probably only have the TCP/IP sockets API on it. (Recall that as with all PC implementations of TCP/IP, Microsoft's TCP/IP form of sockets is called the Winsock API.)

NetBIOS on the Microsoft implementation of TCP/IP is essential, again to make older operating systems and applications happy. And NetBIOS over TCP (which is usually abbreviated NBT or NetBT) needs a name resolver.

Now, basic old NetBIOS converted names to network addresses by just broadcasting—"Hey, I'm looking for \\AJAX; if you're out there, \\AJAX, tell me your IP address!"—but clearly that's not going to be the answer in a routed environment; all of those "name resolution shouts" will stop dead at the routers. If \\AJAX is across a router from us, our software will never find \\AJAX.

NetBIOS name resolution over TCP/IP is, then, not a simple nut to crack. Many people realized this, and so there are two Internet RFCs (Requests for Comment) on this topic, RFC 1001 and 1002, published in 1986.

B NODES, P NODES, AND M NODES

The RFCs attacked the problem by offering options.

The first option was sort of simplistic: Just do broadcasts. A computer that used broadcasts to resolve NetBIOS names to IP addresses is referred to in the RFCs as a *B node*. To find out who server01 is, then, a PC running B node software would just shout out, "Hey! Anybody here named server01?"

Simple, yes, but fatally flawed: Remember what happens to broadcasts when they hit routers? As routers don't rebroadcast the messages to other subnets, this kind of name resolution would only be satisfactory on single-subnet networks.

The second option was to create a name server of some kind and to use that. Then, when a computer needed to resolve a name of another computer, all it needed to do was send a point-to-point message to the computer running the name server software. As point-to-point messages *do* get retransmitted over routers, this second approach would work fine even on networks with routers. A computer using a name server to resolve NetBIOS names into IP addresses is said to be a *P node.*

Again, a good idea, but it runs afoul of all of the problems that DNS had. *What* name server should be used? Will it be dynamic? The name server for NetBIOS name resolution is, by the way, referred to as a NetBIOS name server, or NBNS.

The most complex approach to NetBIOS name resolution over TCP/IP as described in the RFCs is the *M node*, or *mixed* node. It uses a combination of broadcasts and point-to-point communications to an NBNS.

MICROSOFT FOLLOWS THE RFCs, ALMOST

When Microsoft started out with TCP/IP, it implemented a kind of M node software. It was "point-to-point" in that you could look up addresses in the HOSTS file, or a file called LMHOSTS, and if you had a DNS server, then you could always reference that; other than those options, Microsoft TCP/IP was mainly B node-ish, which limited you to single-subnet networks. (Or required that you repeat broadcasts over the network, clogging up your network.) Clearly, some kind of NBNS was needed, and the simpler it was to work with, the better. As the RFCs were silent on the particulars of an NBNS, vendors had license to go out and invent something proprietary and so they did—several of them, in fact, with the result that you'd expect: None of them talk to each other.

That's where WINS comes in.

WINS is simply Microsoft's proprietary NBNS service. What makes it stand out from the rest of the pack is Microsoft's importance in the industry. They have the clout to create a proprietary system and make it accepted widely enough so that it becomes a de facto standard.

Microsoft's NetBIOS-over-TCP client software not only implements B, P, and M nodes, it also includes a fourth, non-RFC node type. Microsoft calls it an H, or Hybrid, node.

But wait a minute; isn't *M node* a hybrid? Yes. Both M nodes and H nodes (and note well that at this writing, M nodes are RFCed and H nodes aren't) use both B node and P node, but the implementation is different:

- In M node, do a name resolution by first broadcasting (B node) and then, if that fails, communicate directly with the NBNS (P node).
- In H node, try the NBNS first. If it can't help you, then try a broadcast.

M NODE VERSUS H NODE

"Hmmm," you may be saying, "Why would anyone want to first broadcast, *then* look up the answer in the name server? Why clutter up the network cable with useless broadcasts when we could instead go right to the source and reduce network chatter?"

The answer is that it's a matter of economics. Recall that the RFCs on NetBIOS over TCP were written back in the mid-1980s, when a typical PC had perhaps an 8MHz clock rate and a 5MHz internal bus. An Ethernet full of XTs would have had a lot of trouble loading the network enough for anyone to even notice. The bottleneck in networks in those days was the CPU or disk speed of the network server. But if the network includes routers—and if it doesn't, then broadcasting is all you need—then consider what the routers are connected to: wide area network links, probably expensive 9600, 14,400, or 19,200bps leased lines. In a network like this, the LAN was a seemingly infinite resource, and wasting it with tons of broadcasts was of no consequence. In contrast, creating more traffic over the WAN by having every machine ask for NetBIOS names (presuming the NetBIOS Name Server was across the WAN link) could greatly reduce the effectiveness of that expensive WAN. Besides, the reasoning went, the vast majority of the time a PC only wanted to talk to another PC on the same LAN, so broadcasts would suffice for name resolution most of the time. The result? M nodes.

The economic picture in 1994, when Microsoft was inventing WINS, was another story entirely: LANs were clogged and WAN links were far cheaper—so H nodes made more sense.

You can force any DHCP client to be a B, P, M, or H node. One of the options that you can configure via DHCP is the WINS/NBNS Node Type. You give it a numeric value to set the client's NetBIOS name resolution technique. A value of 1 creates a B node, 2 is used for a P node, 4 for an M node, and 8 for an H node, the recommended node type.

UNDERSTANDING THE NBT NAMES ON YOUR SYSTEM

A major part of the NetBIOS architecture is its lavish use of names. A workstation attaches up to 16 names to itself. Names in NetBIOS are either group names, which can be shared—workgroups and domains are two examples—or normal names, which can't be shared, like a machine name. As you'll soon see that WINS keeps track of all of these names, you may be curious about what all of them *are*—so let's take a minute and look more closely into your system's NetBIOS names.

You can see the names attached to your workstation by opening a command line from a Windows for Workgroups, Windows 95, NT, Windows 2000, or XP machine and typing **nbtstat -n**. You get an output like this:

```
Node IpAddress: [192.168.0.41] Scope Id: []

            NetBIOS Local Name Table

       Name            Type       Status
    ---------------------------------------------
    GX240          <00>  UNIQUE   Registered
    WIN2KTEST      <00>  GROUP    Registered
    GX240          <03>  UNIQUE   Registered
    GX240          <20>  UNIQUE   Registered
    WIN2KTEST      <1E>  GROUP    Registered
    MM100          <03>  UNIQUE   Registered
```

In this example, the WIN2KTEST group names are my workgroup and domain. GX240 is my machine's name, and MM100 is my name—notice that NetBIOS registers not only the machine name, but the person's name as well. You can see the list of registered names on any computer in your network by typing **nbtstat -A <ip address>**, where the -A *must* be a capital letter.

But why is there more than one GX240? Because each different part of the Microsoft network client software requires names of its own, so they take your machine name and append a pair of hex digits to it. That's what the <00>, <20>, and the like are—suffixes controlled by particular programs. For example, if some other user on the network wanted to connect to a share named STUFF on this computer, she could type **net use * \\gx240\stuff**, and the redirector software on her computer would then do a NetBIOS name resolution on the name GX240<00>, as the <00> suffix is used by the redirector. Table 7.1 summarizes suffixes and the programs that use them.

TABLE 7.1: EXAMPLES OF MACHINE NAMES

UNIQUE NAMES	WHERE USED
<computername>[00h]	Workstation service. This is the "basic" name that every player in a Microsoft network would have, no matter how little power it has in the network.
<computername>[03h]	Messenger service. Used for administrative alerts or pop-up messages; NET SEND messages use this name. Without this, you can't get NET SEND messages. (Or the irritating online spam that some people do with this service.)
<computername>[06h]	RAS Server service.
<computername>[1Fh]	NetDDE service; will only appear if NetDDE is active or if you're running a NetDDE application. (You can see this by starting up Network Hearts, for example.)
<computername>[20h]	Server service; name will only appear on machines with file/printer sharing enabled.
<computername>[21h]	RAS Client service.
<computername>[BEh]	Network Monitor agent.
<computername>[BFh]	Network Monitor utility.
<username>[03h]	Messenger service; any computer running the Messenger service (which is just about any MS networking client) would have this so that NET SEND commands to a user could be received.
<domain name>[1Bh]	This system is the primary domain controller (or PDC emulator, if the domain is Active Directory). There is only one of these per domain.
<domain name>[1Ch]	This says that this machine is a domain controller on this domain. In NT 4 domains it means that it could be either a BDC or the PDC. This is, therefore, not a unique name; more than one DC can exist, so more than one system can have this name.

Continued on next page

TABLE 7.1: EXAMPLES OF MACHINE NAMES *(continued)*

UNIQUE NAMES	WHERE USED
<domain name>[1Dh]	Master browser.
<domain name>[00h] or *<workgroup name>*[00]	Domain name; indicates that the computer is a member of the domain and/or workgroup. If a client is a member of a workgroup whose name is different from a domain, then no domain name will be registered on the client.
<domain name>[1Eh] or *<workgroup name>*[1Eh]	Used in browser elections, indicates that this computer would agree to be a browser. Will only show up on servers. (Potential browser.)
MSBrowse	Domain master browser.

No matter what kind of computer you have on a Microsoft enterprise network, it will have at least one name registered—the *<computer name>*[00] name. Most computers also register *<workgroup>*[00], which proclaims them as a member of a workgroup. Those are the only two names you would see if you had a DOS workstation running the old LAN Manager network client without the Messenger service or a Windows for Workgroups 3.1 (not 3.11) workstation that had file and printer sharing disabled.

Most modern client software would also have the Messenger service enabled and so would have the *<computer name>*[03] and *<username>*[03] names registered, as well.

Adding file and/or printer sharing capabilities to a computer would add the *<computer name>*[20] name. Servers all agree to be candidates for browse master by default, so unless you configure a machine to *not* be a candidate for browse mastering, then the *<workgroup name>*[1E] name will appear on any machine offering file or printer sharing. If the machine happens to be the browse master, it'll have *<workgroup name>*[1D] as well. Workstations use the [1D] name to initially get a list of browse servers when they first start up: They broadcast a message looking to see if the [1D] machine exists, and if it does, then the [1D] machine presents the workstation with a list of potential browsers.

Browse masters get the network name [01][02]__MSBROWSE__[02][01] as well—it's a group name, and only the *master* browsers are members. Master browsers use that name to discover that each other exists.

Name Resolution before WINS: LMHOSTS

Clients written prior to WINS, or clients without a specified WINS server, try to resolve a NetBIOS name to an IP address with several methods. The tools they'll use, if they exist, are:

◆ A HOSTS file, if present

◆ Broadcasts

◆ An LMHOSTS file, if present

◆ A DNS server, if present

You met HOSTS before—it's just a simple ASCII file. Each line contains an IP address, at least one space, and a name. LMHOSTS works in a similar way to HOSTS. And yes, you'd do well to understand LMHOSTS, as it solves many name resolution problems with pre–Windows 2000 servers and perhaps even Windows 2000 Servers or Server 2003 machines in an enterprise with both Windows 2000– and NT 4–based domains.

Let me stress that: Don't skip this section. It's not a history lesson; it can sometimes be the only way to fix a networking problem even with Server 2003, believe it or not.

Introducing LMHOSTS

Recall that HOSTS is an ASCII file that lists IP addresses and Internet names, such as the following:

```
100.100.210.13 ducky.mallard.com
211.39.82.15 jabberwock.carroll.com
```

Microsoft reasoned that if a simple ASCII file could supplement or replace DNS to resolve Winsock names, why not create an ASCII file to hold NetBIOS names? The result is the LMHOSTS file. LMHOSTS consists of pairs of IP addresses and names, like HOSTS, but the names are 15-character *NetBIOS* names, not Internet-type names:

```
100.100.210.13 ducky
211.39.82.15 jabberwock
```

I assumed in the previous example that the NetBIOS name is identical to the leftmost part of the Internet name, although that's not necessary, as you may recall from the earlier discussion in the previous chapter about setting up TCP/IP on a system.

REPRESENTING HEX SUFFIXES IN LMHOSTS

But how to handle the nonprinting characters in a NetBIOS name, the <1B> used by the primary domain controller, the <1C> used by all domain controllers? Recall that the hex suffixes are always the 16th character in a NetBIOS name, so write out a suffixed NetBIOS name like so:

- ◆ Enclose the name in quotes.
- ◆ Add enough spaces to the end of the name so that you've got 15 characters in the name.
- ◆ After the spaces, add \0x followed by the hex code.

For example, suppose I had a domain named CLOUDS and a domain controller named \\CUMULONIMBUS at address 210.10.20.3. I'm creating an LMHOSTS file that I can put on systems around the network so that they can find \\CUMULONIMBUS and recognize it as the primary domain controller for CLOUDS. The LMHOSTS file would look like this:

```
210.10.20.3 cumulonimbus
210.10.20.3 "clouds        \0x1B"
```

This indicates that the machine at IP address 210.10.20.3 has two names (or at *least* two names). As CLOUDS is a six-letter word, I added nine spaces to the end of it.

USING HEX SUFFIXES TO SOLVE AUTHENTICATION PROBLEMS

Suppose you have a system that absolutely cannot find a domain controller; no matter what you do, you get "no domain controller found." Or suppose you have an Active Directory domain and an NT 4 domain that you are trying to build a trust relationship between, but the AD seems unable to find the NT 4 domain or vice versa.

In this case, you need desperate measures. You need LMHOSTS.

I'm going to show you a trick whereby you can take a particular system and "nail" it to a particular DC. Do this trick on a balky workstation and you do a couple of things. First, you force the workstation to use a particular DC when logging in—no ifs, ands, or buts. Second, you remove all of the workstation's normal methods of finding DCs…so the DC that you designate in LMHOSTS had better be up and running!

Systems connecting to NT 4–type networks or, for that matter, Active Directories in mixed mode (again, apologies, we'll explain all of the ins and outs of domains in the next chapter) query NetBIOS for a machine with a name equal to the domain's name, suffixed with a "1C." As you just learned, you can create a LMHOSTS entry that does this very thing by adding enough spaces so that there are 15 characters between the open double quote and where the \0x part starts. So let's suppose that I had a difficult system that seemed unable to see I had a DC named SATURNV in a domain named BOOSTERS. Let's also say that SATURNV is the PDC of that domain, and its IP address is 10.10.100.2. I'd create the following LMHOSTS entries:

```
10.10.100.2 saturnv
10.10.100.2 "boosters        \0x1C" #PRE
10.10.100.2 "boosters        \0x1B" #PRE
```

All three entries refer to the same computer. The first says that its name is saturnv, the second says that it is a domain controller of a domain named boosters, and the last says that it is not only *a* domain controller of boosters, it is *the* primary domain controller of that domain. I'll explain the #PRE in a few paragraphs.

A SPECIAL SUFFIX FOR DOMAIN CONTROLLERS: #DOM

In most cases, the only hex suffix you'll care about is <1C>, the suffix indicating a domain controller. You can create an entry for it as previously, with a \0x1C suffix, or you can use a special meta-command that Microsoft included in LMHOSTS: #DOM.

To indicate that a given entry is a domain controller, enter a normal LMHOSTS entry for it, but add to the end of the line #DOM: and the name of the domain controller. In the CUMULONIMBUS example, you could register CUMULONIMBUS's name and the fact that it is a domain controller for CLOUDS like so:

```
210.10.20.3 cumulonimbus #DOM:clouds
```

But \x01C and #DOM behave a bit differently, in my experience. If you enter a \x01C entry in an LMHOSTS, then NT will use it and only it, ignoring WINS or any other information—so if you're going to use an \0x1C entry, make sure it's right! Furthermore, if you try to tell NT about more than one domain controller in a given domain using the \0x1C suffix, it will only pay attention to the *last* one mentioned in the LMHOSTS file.

"LISTEN TO ME!": THE #PRE COMMAND

This is a bit out of order, as I haven't taken up WINS in detail yet, but as long as I'm discussing LMHOSTS, it kind of fits. As you'll learn later, a normal H node type of client will first send a name resolution question to a WINS server before consulting its local LMHOSTS file, if one exists. Only if the WINS server returns a failure, saying, "I'm sorry, I can't resolve that name," does the client look in its LMHOSTS file. But sometimes you want to tell a PC, "I have a particular entry here in LMHOSTS that is more important than anything that WINS tells you. If you need to look up this particular NetBIOS name, use the LMHOSTS entry rather than looking at WINS." For those entries, you can use the #PRE metacommand. In the case of CUMULONIMBUS, the previous line would look like:

```
cumulonimbus  #DOM:clouds #PRE
```

#PRE's job is this: If WINS and LMHOSTS offer conflicting answers to the question, "What's the IP address of CUMULONIMBUS?" then in general the client listens to WINS rather than LMHOSTS—in other words, by default WINS, uh, wins. But #PRE gives an LMHOSTS entry precedence over anything that WINS has to say.

CENTRALIZED LMHOSTS: #INCLUDE, #ALTERNATE

LMHOSTS is powerful but can require a fair amount of running around because for a user's PC to benefit from LMHOSTS, *the LMHOSTS file must be on the user's PC.* Yuck. That means you'd have to go out Amongst The Users, a happy time for some but a—ummm—mixed blessing for others. Every time you changed LMHOSTS, you'd have to walk around replacing the old LMHOSTS file with a new one on every single machine—ugh, double yuck. Is there a better way?

Sure. You can put a small LMHOSTS file on a user's machine with just one simple command: "Go to this server to read the 'main' LMHOSTS file." Even better, you can specify as many backups for this server as you like. You do it with the #INCLUDE and #ALTERNATE metacommands. Here's a sample LMHOSTS:

```
#BEGIN_ALTERNATE
#INCLUDE \\shadows\stuff\lmhosts
#INCLUDE \\vorlons\stuff\lmhosts
#INCLUDE \\centauri\stuff2\lmhosts
#END_ALTERNATE
```

You can use #INCLUDE without the #ALTERNATEs, but it seems to me that if you're going to go to all the trouble of having a central LMHOSTS, you might as well add some fault tolerance, right? And I would hope that it would go without saying that either \\SHADOWS, \\VORLONS, and \\CENTAURI would have to be on the same subnet as the client PC, or you should add a few lines above the #BEGIN ALTERNATE to tell the PC where to find those three servers.

```
#INCLUDE also takes local filenames:
#INCLUDE D:\MORENAME
```

LMHOSTS is a pretty powerful tool, and it still makes sense in today's NetBIOS-using networks because, as you'll see, WINS is not without its flaws.

WINS: A NetBIOS Name Service for Windows

You've seen that the world before WINS was a rather grim place, where everyone shouts and many questions (well, resolution requests) go unanswered. Now let's look at what happens with WINS.

WINS Needs NT or Later Server

To make WINS work, you must set up an NT 4 or later Server (it won't run on anything else, including NT Workstation) to act as the WINS server. The WINS server then acts as the NBNS server, keeping track of who's on the network and handing out name resolution information as needed.

WINS Holds Name Registrations

Basically, when a WINS client (the shorthand term for "any PC running some kind of Microsoft enterprise TCP/IP network client software designed to use WINS for NBT name resolution") first boots up, it goes to the WINS server and introduces itself, or in WINS-speak, it does a name registration. (In fact, as you recall, most machines have several NetBIOS names, so clients register each of those names with WINS.) The client knows the IP address of the WINS server either because you hard-coded it right into the TCP/IP settings for the workstation or because the workstation got a WINS address from DHCP when it obtained an IP lease.

You may recall that the client actually gets *two* IP addresses, one for a "primary" and one for a "secondary" WINS server. The client tries to get the attention of the primary and register itself on that machine. But if the machine designated as a primary WINS server doesn't respond within a certain amount of time, the client next tries to register with the secondary WINS server. If the secondary will talk to the client and the primary won't, the client registers with the secondary. You can tell that this has happened by doing an `ipconfig /all` at the client. Among other things, this reports the address of the primary WINS server. If that address is the *secondary's* address, then you know that the primary was too busy to talk—and that turns out to be an important diagnostic clue, as you'll see later when I discuss how to design multiserver WINS systems.

In the process of registering its name with a WINS server, the workstation gets the benefit of ensuring that it has a unique name. If the WINS server sees that there's another computer out there with the same name, it will tell the workstation, "You can't use that name." The name registration request and the acknowledgment are both directed IP messages, so they'll cross routers. And when a workstation shuts down, it sends a "name release" request to the WINS server telling it that the workstation will no longer need the NetBIOS name, enabling the WINS server to register it for some other machine.

WINS Client Failure Modes

But what if something goes wrong? What if you try to register a name that some other workstation already has, or what if a workstation finds that the WINS server is unavailable?

Duplicate names are simple—instead of sending a "success" response to the workstation, the WINS server sends a "fail" message in response to the workstation's name request. In response, the workstation does not consider the name registered and doesn't include it in its NetBIOS name table; an `nbstat -n` will not show the name.

But if a workstation can't find the WINS server when it boots up, then the workstation simply stops acting as a hybrid NBT node and reverts to its old ways as a Microsoft modified B node, meaning that it depends largely on broadcasts but will also consult LMHOSTS (and perhaps HOSTS, if configured to do so) if they're present.

It's My Name, but for How Long?

Like DHCP, WINS only registers names for a fixed period of time called the *renewal interval*. By default, it's 6 days (144 hours), and there will probably never be a reason for you to change that. Forty minutes seems to be the shortest time that WINS will accept.

In much the same way that DHCP clients attempt to renew their leases early, WINS clients send "name *refresh* requests" to the WINS server before their names expire—*long* before. According to Microsoft documentation, a WINS client attempts a name refresh very early after it gets its names registered—after one-eighth of the renewal interval. (My tests show that it's actually *three*-eighths, but that's not terribly important.) The WINS server will usually reset the length of time left before the name must be renewed again (this time is sometimes called the *time to live*, or TTL). Once the client has renewed its name *once*, however, it doesn't renew it again and again every one-eighth of its TTL; instead, it only renews its names every one-half of the TTL. (My tests agree with that.)

Installing WINS

Installing WINS is much like installing all the other software that we've installed elsewhere in this chapter and in the book.

When you're planning how many WINS servers you need and where to put them, bear in mind that you need not put a WINS server on each subnet (which is one of the great features of WINS). It *is* a good idea to have a second machine running as a secondary WINS server, however, just for fault tolerance's sake. Remember that if a workstation comes up and can't find a WINS server, it reverts to broadcasting, which will limit its name resolution capabilities to just its local subnet and will cause it to do a lot of shouting, which adds traffic to the subnet. Why would a WINS client not find a WINS server if there's a working WINS server?

Well, normally the client would find the server just fine. but in some small percentage of the cases, the WINS server might be too busy to respond to the client in a timely fashion, causing the client to just give up on the server. That will probably only happen rarely, unless you're overloading the WINS server. Unfortunately, a very common way to overload a WINS server is to put the WINS server function on the same machine that's also acting as a domain controller. Think about it: When is a WINS server busiest? First thing in the morning, when everyone's booting up and registering names. When's a domain controller busiest? First thing in the morning, when everyone's logging in. That leads to a warning.

If possible, don't put the WINS server function on a domain controller. Or a system with more than one NIC.

That's where a secondary is useful. If you have a backup domain controller, then put a WINS server on that machine as well. The WINS software actually does not use a lot of CPU time, so it probably won't affect your server's performance unless you have thousands of users all hammering on one WINS server. If *that's* the case, I'd dedicate a computer solely to WINS-ing.

To get a WINS server set up, follow these steps:

1. Open the Control Panel (Start/Control Panel/Add or Remove Programs).
2. Click Add/Remove Windows Components and wait a bit while the Windows Components Wizard dialog appears.
3. Click Networking Services and then the Details button.

4. Click the check box next to Windows Internet Name Service.

5. Click OK to return to Windows Components.

6. Click Next to install the service. The system will say that it is "Configuring Components" for a while, probably a few minutes. A bit later, the screen labeled Completing the Windows Components Wizard appears.

7. Click Finish to end the wizard.

8. Click Close to close Add or Remove Windows Components.

No reboots needed anymore—thanks, Microsoft—and you'll see in Start/Administrative Tools that you've got a new snap-in to control WINS. Start it up, click the plus sign next to the server, and it will look like Figure 7.32.

FIGURE 7.32

The initial WINS manager screen

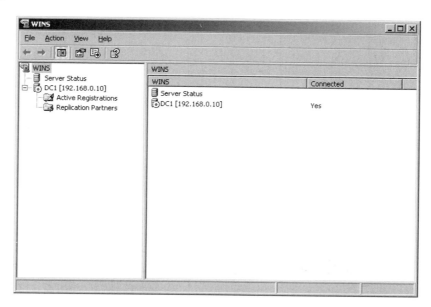

No need to authorize WINS servers, in case you're wondering. The first thing you should do on your WINS server is inform it of the machines on your subnet that are not WINS clients but use NetBIOS on TCP/IP. There won't be many of them, but they may exist; for example, you may have some old pre-1995 Microsoft Windows machines around. Machines with hard-coded IP addresses don't need to be entered, so long as they use WINS: If they know the address of a primary or secondary WINS server, they will register their names with that server. If you *do* have an old system requiring a static mapping, right-click Active Registrations and choose New Static Mapping. You then see a dialog box like the one shown in Figure 7.33.

Alternatively, if you have an existing LMHOSTS file, you can click Action at the top menu, then Import Hosts, and the program will take that information to build a static-mapping database.

FIGURE 7.33

The Static
Mapping table

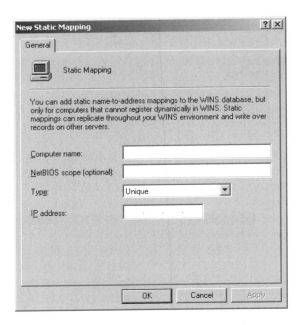

Configuring a WINS Server

Right-click the server in the left pane of the WINS snap-in, and choose Properties. You'll see a properties page like the one in Figure 7.34.

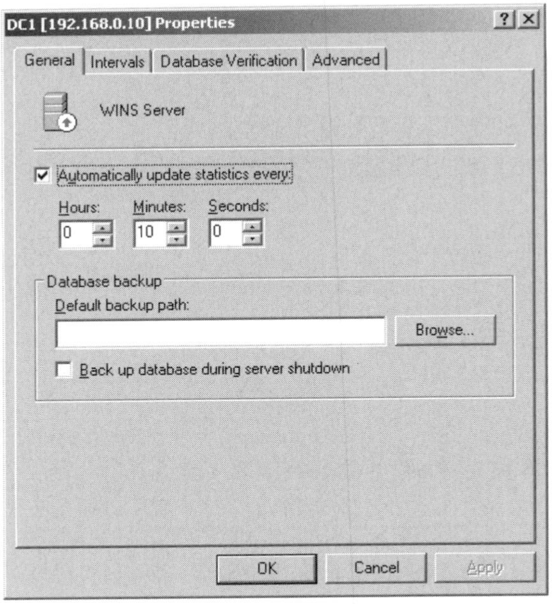

FIGURE 7.34

Server configuration
properties page

WINS will regularly back up its database—a good disaster recovery step—if you fill in a directory name in Default Backup Path. You can even use a UNC, such as \\ajax\central\wins or the like. A check box allows you to tell WINS to also do a backup specifically when the server is shut down.

Click the Database Verification tab, and you'll see a page like Figure 7.35.

FIGURE 7.35

Configuring WINS verification

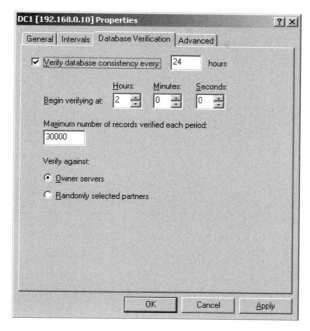

This is a real improvement in WINS over NT 4's WINS service. WINS has always had trouble as a distributed database: Name records get transmitted around the network and databases get corrupted. The corruption spreads and before you know it, you're erasing your WINS databases and starting all over. The option at the top of the screen tells your WINS server to periodically check its records against those of any other server in your enterprise. It's a good idea. If you enable it, I'd let it check every 24 hours, as is the default, and to check against the *owner* rather than a random server. *Owner* in WINS terminology means "the WINS server that generated the original name record." Thus, it could be in a multi-WINS server world that I registered my PC's name with WINS Server 1, which then told WINS Server 2 about me. (This happens automatically, recall—you needn't do anything to get your system registered with WINS except to specify a WINS server in your TCP/IP settings.) WINS Server 2 might run into some kind of trouble and corrupt the record about my machine. But checking with WINS Server 1 would point out the problem, and WINS Server 2 would be set straight.

Click the Advanced tab and you'll see a page like the one in Figure 7.36.

The first interesting thing here is logging. You can leave logging enabled, but think twice about logging detailed events. Basically, if you enable this, then WINS adds a lot of chatter to the Event Viewer, and WINS gets *really* slow. It's not a bad idea if you're trying to get some insight into what WINS does on a small network, but I've had it freeze a WINS server right up on me.

FIGURE 7.36

Advanced WINS
server configuration

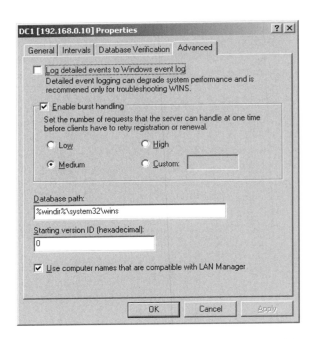

Enable Burst Handling is a work-around to handle an old WINS problem. WINS is busiest first thing in the morning, when everyone's logging on and trying to register their system names. Before registering a name, however, WINS must check its database to ensure that there's no duplication, that no one's trying to register a computer name that already exists. But that takes time, so WINS cheats.

The chances are good that early morning (the busy time) registrations are simply reregistrations, so WINS goes into burst mode, meaning it pretty much agrees to every registration request. It then says, "Come back and reregister in a few minutes," which gives it a chance to *really* check a registration when things are slower. It only shifts into burst mode when it has a lot of outstanding registration requests in its queue. How many? That's what the radio buttons are for—to set how soon WINS goes into burst mode. The default is probably fine, but if you're getting a lot of refused registrations— where WINS simply doesn't respond—then set the threshold to Low.

Designing a Multi-WINS Network

Thus far, I've discussed a situation where you have one WINS server and a bunch of clients. I've *also* mentioned the notion of a secondary WINS server, suggesting that at least one additional WINS server would be in order. How should you set up this second WINS server? And how about the third, fourth, and so on? And while we're at it, how many WINS servers should you have?

FROM MANY SERVERS, ONE DATABASE

The theory with multiple WINS servers is that you might have one in Europe, one in Africa, and one in North America. Europeans do their registrations with the European server, Africans with the African server, and Americans with the North American server. Then, on a regular basis, the three WINS servers get together and create a master worldwide list of WINS records, a kind of sort/merge amalgamating three different databases. But how to do it? We certainly don't want to have to transmit—*replicate* is the WINS term—the entire African name serving database over WAN links to Europe and America, particularly because the database probably hasn't changed all that much since yesterday.

As a result, WINS time-stamps and sequence-numbers name records so that it can take up less WAN bandwidth. That's great in theory, but in practice it means that WINS servers that are being asked to *do* all that sorting and merging will be pretty occupied CPU-wise, which will of course mean that they're falling down on the job as name resolvers. It also means that it might be a good idea to designate a relatively small number of servers—say, perhaps *one*—to essentially do nothing but the sort/merges.

Minimizing the Number of WINS Servers

People assume that as with domain controllers, it's a great idea to have a local WINS server, and lots of them. But it's not, and in fact you should strive to keep the WINS servers to an absolute minimum.

A local WINS server would be great because it could quickly perform NetBIOS name resolutions for nearby machines. And in fact it would be great if you could install a WINS server in every location that only did name resolutions—but remember that every WINS server does *two* things: name resolutions and name registrations. This, in my opinion, is the crux of why multiple WINS networks can be a pain. If you could simply say, "Go to local machine X for name resolutions, but for those infrequent occasions when you need to do a name *registration*, go across the WAN to the central WINS server named Y," then WINS would be more trouble free. Sure, a morning logon would get a bit slower, as the registration would happen over the WAN, but you'd not get the corrupted WINS databases that are sadly so common in big WINS installations.

Why this happens is easy to understand. Merging two WINS databases and "boiling them down" to one database is simple. Merging three is harder, and merging 100 could be, well, a lot of work, perhaps more than WINS's database engine is capable of. That's why for years, Microsoft has maintained that no enterprise on the entire planet needs more than 14 WINS servers. More than that, and database corruption becomes far more likely.

People want a local WINS server for name resolution, but actually they're not getting much for it. If your WINS server were across the WAN from you, how much time would a name resolution take? Well, an entire name resolution request and response is only 214 bytes. Let's see, at 56Kbps that would be, hmmm, three-hundredths of a second. Here's a case where the wide area network will *not* be the bottleneck! WINS may have its drawbacks, but one thing that it was designed to do, and designed well, is to respond to name resolution requests quickly. Even a 66MHz 486 running NT 4's WINS server can handle 750 resolution requests per minute—so when it comes to WINS servers, remember: Less is more.

Adding the Second WINS Server

Of course, having said that, a *second* WINS server isn't a bad idea.

When setting up a Microsoft TCP/IP client, you're prompted for both a primary and a secondary WINS server address. When your PC boots up, the PC goes to the primary WINS server and tries to register the PC's NetBIOS name with that WINS server. If it's successful, it never even tries to contact the secondary WINS server unless a subsequent name resolution attempt fails.

What that implies is important: Suppose you've been a good network administrator and created a backup WINS server, and then you've pointed all of your workstation's Secondary WINS Server fields to that backup. The primary goes down. Where are you?

Nowhere very interesting, actually. You see, that secondary WINS server doesn't know much, as no one has ever registered with it. If a WINS client successfully registers with its primary server, it does not try to register with the secondary server.

If the primary goes down and everyone starts asking the secondary to resolve names, the secondary will end up just saying, "Sorry, I can't answer that question." So you've got to convince the primary to replicate to the secondary. Fortunately, there's an easy way: *push/pull partners*.

Keeping the Second Server Up-to-Date

In general, you've got to configure two WINS servers to be push/pull partners, but it's possible to have them discover each other with a setting in the WINS snap-in. Right-click the Replication Partners folder, choose Properties and click the Advanced tab, and you'll see a screen like Figure 7.37.

FIGURE 7.37

Choosing automatic discovery of replication partners

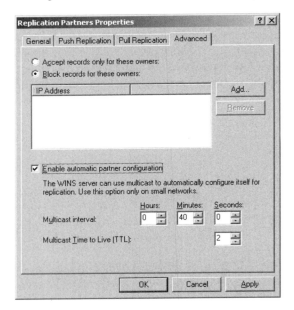

Here, I've checked the box Enable Automatic Partner Configuration, which will cause the WINS server to periodically broadcast (well, actually it will *multicast*) to find other WINS servers and from there automatically replicate. This will, however, only work for WINS servers on the same subnet, as most routers don't pass IP multicasts. On a big network, this is a bad idea, but for a small network it'll save the administrator a bit of time and trouble.

Alternatively, you've got to introduce the replication partners. WINS database replications transfer data from a push partner to a pull partner. Those terms *push* and *pull* aren't *bad* terms description-wise, but they need a bit of illumination. Suppose for the purposes of the example that you have two machines named Primary and Secondary. Suppose also that Primary is the machine that gets the latest information, as it is the *primary* WINS server, and that all you really want to do with Secondary (the name of the machine that is the secondary WINS server) is have it act as a kind of backup to Primary's information. Thus, Secondary never really has any information to offer Primary. In that case, you'd have to set up Primary to *push* its database changes to Secondary.

You can tell a WINS server to create a push, pull, or push/pull relationship with another WINS server by right-clicking the folder labeled Replication Partners and choosing New Replication Partner. You're prompted for the IP address of the WINS server with which you want to establish a replication relationship.

In a push/pull relationship, data gets from Primary to Secondary in one of two ways. First, Secondary (the pull partner) can request that Primary (the push partner) update Secondary, telling Secondary only what has changed in the database. Alternatively, Primary can say to Secondary, "There's been a fair amount of changes since the last time I updated you. *You really should request an update.*" I italicized the last sentence to emphasize that it's really the pull partner that does most of the work in initiating the database replication updates. All the push partner really "pushes" is a suggestion that the pull partner get to work and start requesting updates.

Having said that, could I just tell Secondary to be a pull partner with Primary, without telling Primary to be a push partner for Secondary? Wouldn't it be sufficient to just tell Secondary, "Initiate a replication conversation with Primary every eight hours"? It would seem so, as there wouldn't any longer be a need for Primary to do any pushing—but there's a catch. If Secondary starts pulling from Primary, Primary will refuse to respond to Secondary's pull request unless Primary has been configured as a push partner with Secondary, because WINS servers are configured by default to refuse replication requests from all machines but partners, remember?

WINS services are totally independent of Active Directory domain security, as is DHCP. A WINS server can serve workstations throughout your network. In fact, if your network is connected to the Internet and doesn't have a firewall, you could actually publish your WINS server address, and other networks across the Internet could share browsing capabilities! (Whether you'd want to do that is another issue.)

CONTROLLING REPLICATION

So now you see that the right thing to do is to make Secondary a pull partner with Primary and make Primary a push partner with Secondary. What triggers the replication? What kicks off the process of WINS database replication? To see, right-click any server listed in the `Replication Partners` folder, choose Properties, and click the Advanced tab. You'll see a screen like the one in Figure 7.38.

FIGURE 7.38

Configuring WINS replication

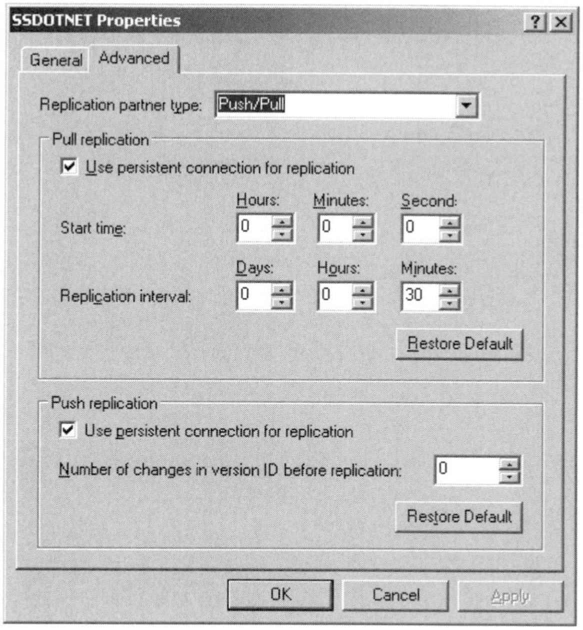

Well, recall that either the push partner or the pull partner can start the conversation. In the case of the former, you configure a push partner to tap its partner on the shoulder and suggest a replication session based on the number of database changes. You can tell Primary, "Notify Secondary whenever 50 changes have occurred to the WINS database on Primary," or whatever number you like, so long as you like numbers above 19; 20 is the minimum number of changes that NT will allow you to use to trigger replication. (You can alternatively trigger replication from the WINS snap-in.) The default, zero, essentially turns off push triggers.

A pull partner, in contrast, can't possibly know how many changes have occurred and so needs another way to know when to request updates. So pull partners request updates based on time—you configure a pull partner to contact its partner every so many minutes, hours, or days.

The bottom line, however, is that most of us will just set up our WINS replication relationships to the defaults, particularly if we set up our WINS enterprise as a hub-and-spoke design, as you're about to read. You *might* want to set your partners to replicate less often in a large enterprise.

WINS REPLICATION DESIGN

Now that Microsoft has had years of experience supporting big clients using WINS, some Microsofties have recommended a push/pull partner architecture to me, something like a hub-and-spoke design. You see it pictured in Figure 7.39.

FIGURE 7.39

Suggested primary/ secondary WINS server configuration

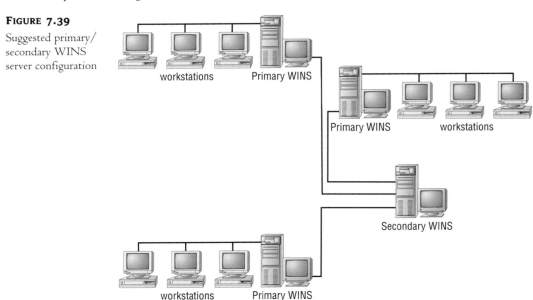

The goal of this design is to keep WINS servers responsive while still handling replication. In the picture, you see three different networks, each served by a WINS server labeled Primary WINS. In each network, each workstation points to the local WINS server as its primary server and the central machine labeled Secondary WINS as its secondary. In other words, then, every machine in the enterprise designates that one central machine as their secondary WINS server and a closer machine as their primary WINS server. This works because every WINS server hears about a particular machine from only one WINS server, instead of from several replication partners. Result? No confusion.

The main job of the central WINS server is to gather the three primary servers' databases, aggregate them into one enterprise-wide WINS database, and replicate that database out to the local primaries. Each primary WINS server, then, designates the central WINS server as its sole push/pull partner.

Many firms implement a mesh-type structure, where every WINS server designates every other WINS server as a push/pull partner. The result is a nightmare of corrupted WINS databases and lost records. To add another WINS server, just make sure that it has some kind of connectivity to the central WINS server and make it a push/pull partner of that machine. If you end up with too many WINS servers for one central machine, just put hubs and spokes on the ends of the hubs and spokes, building a hierarchy.

No matter what kind of WINS replication architecture you create, ensure that there are no loops in your replication. For example, if WINS server A replicated to B, which replicated to C, which replicated to A, then records can be replicated and re-replicated, causing WINS problems.

Avoiding WINS Problems

Sources inside Microsoft tell me that WINS generates more support calls than any other of NT's "core" network technologies. That won't be surprising to anyone who's ever tried to track down a WINS problem. Here are a few tips to save you some time and help you avoid having to pay Microsoft more money to keep the product that you bought from them working.

WINS Servers Should Point to Themselves as a Primary WINS Server Only

When you're configuring the TCP/IP stack on a WINS server, do not fill in a value for a secondary WINS server, and in the Primary field, fill in the server's own value. This avoids a situation wherein the WINS server is busy but needs to reregister its own address. As it is busy, however, it cannot— believe it or not—respond quickly enough to *itself*. As a result, the WINS client software on the WINS server seeks out another WINS server, and so WINS server A's name registrations end up on WINS server B. The result is WINS instability, as the WINS server software is built assuming that each WINS server's name is registered on its own database.

Be Careful Replicating to "Test" WINS Servers

Don't set up a "test" WINS server, register a few names on it, have a "production" WINS server pull the names from the test server, and then shut off the test WINS server for good. WINS will refuse to delete names that it got from another server, no matter how old and expired they are, until it can do a final double-check with the WINS server that it got the names from originally; if you shut off the test and never turn it back on, those records will never go away without a bit of operator intervention!

To remove all of the records created by a defunct WINS server, go to one of its replication partners and start the WINS snap-in. Right-click the `Active Registrations` folder, then choose All Tasks/Delete Owner. That allows WINS to finally purge the old owner's records.

Don't Make a Multihomed PC a WINS Server

A PC with more than one NIC can hear communications from several subnets. That's gotten WINS in trouble when a WINS server is multihomed, as WINS sometimes gets confused about where a name registration came in from. Several service packs have claimed to fix it, but each service pack brings more trouble reports. My suggestion: Don't make a multihomed machine a WINS server.

By the way, the same advice goes for PDCs. Multihomed PCs shouldn't be PDCs. The reason is that the PDC ends up being the master browser in a domain, and again, having workgroup announcements coming in from several different network segments causes problems for the browser software.

DON'T MAKE A DC A WINS SERVER

As explained earlier, both the domain controller and WINS functions are at their busiest at the same time. Mixing DC and WINS responsibilities on a single machine will make a mediocre DC and a mediocre WINS server. (Of course, on a small network this isn't the case; if you have 25 users, feel free to make one machine your domain controller, WINS, DHCP, DNS, and file server—but be sure you know how to do disaster recovery on it!)

Deleting, Tombstoning, and Purging WINS Records

You'll eventually look at your WINS name database and realize that there are a bunch of old, useless records that you'd like to get rid of. Some of those records may be, as mentioned earlier, garbage left over from an old, now-defunct WINS server. Those are easy to get rid of—just choose the Delete Owner function, as described earlier.

For other records, though, the approach is a bit different.

Consider how a record gets created and propagated around an enterprise. A machine named TRAY (what server doesn't have a tray?) registers itself with WINS Server 1. That generates a record in WINS Server 1's database. WINS Server 1 is said to be the "owner" of that record.

Now suppose WINS Server 1 replicates TRAY's name record (or more likely, records) to WINS Server 2. WINS Server 2 now contains copies of those records, but it also knows that WINS Server 1, not itself, originated—"owns"—those records. Even if WINS Server 2 were to replicate this record to yet another WINS server, then WINS Server 2 wouldn't "take credit for" this record; it would say to this new WINS Server, "Hey, just in case you don't know about this, here's a record for the TRAY computer—but I didn't discover TRAY, WINS Server 1 did. *It* owns TRAY's name record."

Now let's suppose we decommission the TRAY server. Working at WINS Server 2, you (an administrator) notice that the TRAY record is still in the WINS database, and so you delete the TRAY record. (In `Active Registrations`, right-click a record and choose Delete.) That causes the WINS snap-in to raise a dialog box asking whether you want to do one of two things:

- Delete the record only from this server, or
- Replicate deletion of the record to other servers (tombstone).

If you were to choose the first option, then TRAY would disappear from WINS Server 2's WINS snap-in...for a while. The next time that WINS Server 1 and WINS Server 2 replicated, then WINS Server 1 would say to WINS Server 2, "My goodness, why don't you have a TRAY record?" and quick as a wink, TRAY is *baaaaack*.

How, then, to stomp TRAY for good? With the alternative to deleting—tombstoning. When you tombstone a record, you don't remove it from the database; rather, it marks it as being in a *tombstone state*.

The purpose of the tombstone is this: WINS Server 2 has already written TRAY off, but it knows that the rest of the enterprise doesn't know that TRAY is history, because WINS Server 1 owns the

TRAY record. So the next time WINS Server 1 replicates a TRAY record to WINS Server 2, WINS Server 2 may be tempted to insert a new record in its database for a machine named TRAY— but then it sees the tombstone record with TRAY's name and so can say, "Ah, I should just ignore that record; I have more up-to-date information than WINS Server 1 does." When WINS Server 2 next replicates to WINS Server 1, it'll tell WINS Server 1 that TRAY is tombstoned, and so WINS Server 1 will tombstone TRAY in its database as well. Eventually TRAY will be marked as tombstoned in the entire WINS enterprise.

By the way, tombstoned entries don't get purged from a WINS database until WINS runs a *scavenging operation*. That happens every three days by default, or you can initiate a scavenging operation from the WINS Manager by right-clicking a server, then choosing Scavenge Database.

If for some reason you stop the WINS service more often than every three days, your WINS database will never be scavenged. If that's the case, manually initiate scavenging from the WINS Manager.

A badly designed WINS replication structure may need a bit of tombstoning help, and here Server 2003's graphical WINS Manager is of assistance. When you click Delete Mapping, you get an option—delete or tombstone? You use tombstone *always* if you want to delete a record on server X but you're working from server Y. You typically delete rather than tombstone if you're sitting right at the server that owns the record that you're about to delete. And if you find that you've been trying to get rid of a record but it keeps coming back, you tombstone it.

WINS Proxy Agents

Using an NBNS (NetBIOS naming server) such as WINS can greatly cut down on the broadcasts on your network, reducing traffic and improving throughput. But, as you've seen, this requires that the clients understand WINS; the older network client software just shouts away as a B node.

WINS can help those older non-WINS-aware clients with a *WINS proxy agent*. A WINS proxy agent is a regular old network workstation that listens for older B node systems helplessly broadcasting, trying to reach NetBIOS names that (unknown to the B node computers) are on another subnet.

To see how this would work, let's take a look at a simple two-subnet intranet, as shown in Figure 7.40.

FIGURE 7.40

An example of a two-subnet intranet

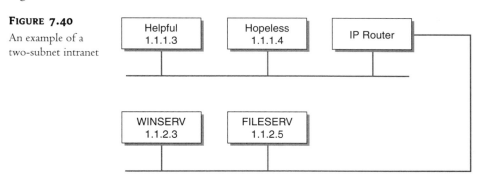

Here, you see two class C subnets, 1.1.1.0 and 1.1.2.0. There's a router between them. On 1.1.1.0, there are two workstations. One is a WINS-aware client named HELPFUL, which is also running a WINS proxy agent. The other is an old B node client named HOPELESS, which is not WINS-aware. On 1.1.2.0, there are a couple of servers, a machine acting as a WINS server and a regular old file server.

When HOPELESS first comes up, it'll do a broadcast of its names to ensure that no one else has them. The machine that it really should be talking to, of course, is WINSERV, but WINSERV can't hear it. HELPFUL, however, hears the B node broadcasts coming from HOPELESS and sends a directed message to WINSERV, telling it that there's a workstation named HOPELESS trying to register some names.

WINSERV looks up those names to ensure that they don't already exist. If they *do* exist, then WINSERV sends a message back to HELPFUL, saying, "Don't let that guy register those names!" HELPFUL then sends a message to HOPELESS, saying, "I'm sorry, but *I* already use the name HOPELESS." That keeps HOPELESS from registering a name that exists on another subnet.

Assuming that HOPELESS names do *not* currently exist in the WINSERV database, however, WINSERV does *not* register the names; putting a WINS proxy agent on 1.1.1.0 doesn't mean that the non-WINS clients will have their names registered with WINS. That means that it's okay to have the same NetBIOS name on two different computers, so long as they are both B node clients and are on different subnets.

Suppose then that HOPELESS does a `net use d: \\fileserv\files`—in that case, the name \\fileserv must be resolved. Assuming that HOPELESS does not have a HOSTS or LMHOSTS file, HOPELESS will start broadcasting, saying, "Is there anyone here named FILESERV? And if so, what's your IP address?" HELPFUL will intercede by sending a directed IP message to WINSERV, saying, "Is there a name registered as FILESERV, and what is its IP address?"

WINSERV will respond with the IP address of FILESERV, and HELPFUL will then send a directed message back to HOPELESS, saying, "Sure, I'm FILESERV, and you can find me at 1.1.2.5." Now HOPELESS can complete its request.

Make sure there is only one WINS proxy agent per subnet! Otherwise, two PCs will respond to HOPELESS, causing—how do the manuals put it? Ah yes—"unpredictable results."

Name Resolution in More Detail

Now that you know how to configure DHCP and WINS, you may be faced with a troubleshooting problem in reference to name resolution. Perhaps you try to FTP to a site inside your organization, but you can't hook up. Even though you know that `ftp.goodstuff.acme.com` is at one IP address, your FTP client keeps trying to attach somewhere else. You've checked your DNS server, of course, and its information is right. Where else to look?

Review: Winsock versus NBT

Remember first that there are two kinds of name resolution in Microsoft TCP/IP networking, Winsock name resolution and NetBIOS name resolution. A `net view \\`*somename* needs NetBIOS-over-TCP name resolution, or NBT name resolution. In contrast, because FTP is, like Ping, an Internet application, it uses Winsock name resolution. So, to troubleshoot a name resolution problem, you have to follow what your client software does, step by step.

DNS/Winsock Name Resolution

I type `ping lemon`, and get the response "unknown host lemon." But I suspect there's a lemon out there, and I'm not talking about a computer from a certain Texas computer company. How did Server 2003 decide that it couldn't find lemon? It certainly takes long enough to decide that it can't find lemon, after all—usually on the order of 20 to 30 seconds on a 400MHz system. *Something* must be going on.

When faced with a question such as this, I turned to the Microsoft documentation for help, but there wasn't much detail. So I ran a network monitor and issued ping commands to computers that didn't exist, to see the sequence of actions that the network client software tried in order to resolve a name. The HOSTS and LMHOSTS files do not, of course, show up in a network trace, so I inserted information into those files that didn't exist on the DNS or WINS servers and then tried pinging again, to demonstrate where the HOSTS and LMHOSTS files sit in the name resolution hierarchy. (And if you think about it, LMHOSTS and WINS should have nothing at all to do with a Winsock resolution. Perhaps in a non-Microsoft world, but not in any version of Windows created after 1995.) Pinging for a nonexistent apple, I found that the name resolution order proceeds as shown in Figure 7.41.

Before I get into the details here, let me warn you that Microsoft has changed how their OSes resolve DNS names; in particular, Windows 2000 and later (XP, 2003) are a bit different, and I'll explain that as we go along. Step by step, it looks like this:

First, consult the HOSTS file, if it exists. If you find the name you're looking for, stop.

Next, look in the DNS cache. This only applies to Windows 2000 and later systems, and I'll cover this later, but basically all Win2K and later systems remember previously successful DNS name resolutions. So if I successfully looked up apple in DNS a moment or two ago, then my system would pull that successful resolution out of cache, and it'd be done. Note that this happens *after* the HOSTS lookup, contrary to some sources. You can, if you like, clear the DNS cache by typing `ipconfig /flushdns`. You can see the current contents of the DNS cache by typing `ipconfig /displaydns`.

Next, if there's a specified DNS server or servers, then query them. Most Microsoft OSes recognize that a name like apple clearly isn't a complete DNS name, as DNS names usually have parts to them like apple.bigfirm.biz or the like. In a case like that, the system adds its DNS suffix to the query. For example, if I were sitting at a workstation named mypc.bigfirm.biz and typed `ping apple`, then my workstation wouldn't query DNS for apple, it would query for "apple.bigfirm.biz." You can, if you like, add even more DNS suffixes for your system to try when presented with a too-short DNS name; look in TCP/IP Advanced Properties, the DNS tab, and you'll see where you can add them. By the way, Windows 95 systems seem to not add the DNS suffix; a Win95 system would actually ask DNS to resolve apple in my theoretical case. If DNS finds the name, then stop.

You would think that would be it for DNS name resolution, and indeed for most OSes it is— look in HOSTS, look in DNS and if there's no luck, then just stop looking. That's also how a Windows 2000 or later system works, if you have disabled NetBIOS over TCP/IP. (Almost no one does nowadays. But one day, when we're free of WINS...) Assuming that you're running NBT, though, Microsoft takes it further and involves its *NetBIOS* lookup engine as well. So if your system still hasn't gotten an answer to a name query...

If there's a specified WINS server or servers, then query the WINS server(s). The name WINS looks for is apple <00>, the name that *would* be registered by the Workstation service, if the apple machine existed.

If that fails, then do three broadcasts looking for a machine with NetBIOS name apple <00>, requesting that it identify itself and send back its IP address. Again, this would succeed with a workstation running some NetBIOS-over-TCP/IP client, even a relatively old one, as it would have registered the apple <00> name already, if only on its own name table. Unfortunately, this only works if the machine is on the same subnet.

FIGURE 7.41

The name resolution order

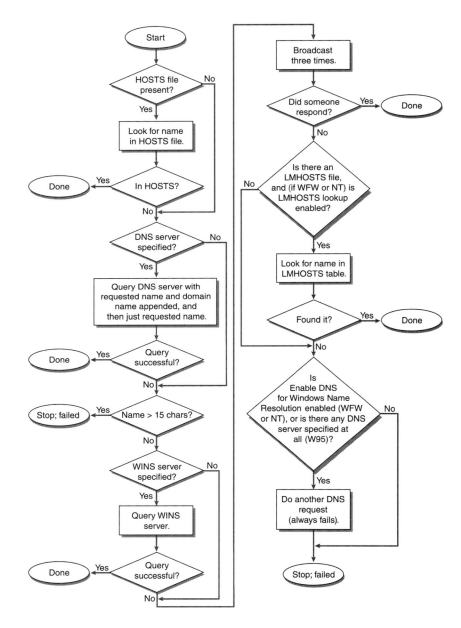

If the name still hasn't been resolved, then NT 4 and earlier systems next read the LMHOSTS file, unless configured to ignore LMHOSTS. Windows 2000 and later systems do *not* use LMHOSTS to assist in DNS/Winsock name resolution, whether configured to use LMHOSTS or not.

If the system still hasn't succeeded, then under some circumstances a pre-Win2K system will do yet another DNS lookup which will, of course, fail.

Summarizing, then, a Windows 2000 or later system first looks in its DNS cache, then its HOSTS file, then asks a DNS server, then a WINS server, and finally broadcasts. If you disable NetBIOS over TCP/IP then Win2K and later systems just look in the DNS cache, then HOSTS, and then ask the DNS server.

Why the broadcasts and the WINS lookup? I'm not sure, but I guess Microsoft just threw them in for good measure. The broadcasts are a pain because they waste network bandwidth, but they *would* be of benefit when you tried to execute a TCP/IP command on a computer in your network but wanted to use the shorter NetBIOS name rather than the longer DNS name, such as apple instead of apple.mmco.com.

Getting back to an earlier question, what happened on that workstation that could not access the FTP site? There was an old HOSTS file sitting in the `Windows` directory that pointed to a different IP address, an older IP address for the FTP server. HOSTS is read before anything else, so the accurate information on the DNS or WINS servers never got a chance to be read. So be very careful about putting things in HOSTS if they could soon become out-of-date!

There is an explicit Enable DNS for Windows Name Resolution check box in Windows for Workgroups and NT 3.51 clients, but how do you control whether DNS gets into the act on a Windows 95 client? You can't, at least not entirely; where Workgroups and NT 3.51 separate the options about whether to specify a DNS server and whether or not to use that DNS server as a helper when resolving NetBIOS names (that's what Enable DNS for Windows Name Resolution means), Windows 95 seems not to do that.

Controlling WINS versus DNS Order in Winsock

Now, what I just showed you is the order of events by default in NT, Windows 9x, or later clients. But if you feel like messing around with the way that Winsock resolves names, you can. As usual, let me take this moment to remind you that it's not a great idea to mess with the Registry unless you know what you're doing.

Look in the Registry under `HKEY_LOCAL_MACHINE\System\CurrentControlSet\Services\Tcpip\ServiceProvider` and you see `HostsPriority`, `DnsPriority`, and `NetbtPriority` value entries. They are followed by hexadecimal values. The lower the value, the earlier that HOSTS, DNS (and LMHOSTS), and WINS (and broadcasts) get done. For example, by default DNS's priority is 7D0 and WINS's is 7D1, so DNS goes before WINS. But change DNS's priority to 7D2, and WINS does its lookup and broadcast *before* the client interrogates the DNS server.

Again, I'm not sure *why* you'd want to do this, but I include it for the sake of completeness and for the enjoyment of those who delight in undocumented features.

NetBIOS Name Resolution Sequence

Readers send me many questions about networking Microsoft OSes, but unfortunately I usually can't help much, usually because the problem boils down to either some hardware or software that I'm not familiar with, so all I can do is to make a few suggestions to help them try to smoke the problem out on their own. Of all of the troubleshooting suggestions that I make, however, here's the most common one.

Many problems sound like "I can't get X machine to connect to and communicate with Y machine," as in "I have a file server named ABEL that workstation BAKER can't access." Most people don't realize the very important fact there are *two* problems to troubleshoot here:

◆ First, you must have IP connectivity.

◆ Second, you must have proper name resolution—and "proper" means DNS/HOSTS if the application is Winsock-based, or WINS/LMHOSTS if the application is NetBIOS-based.

I know I've touched on this elsewhere, but I really want to hit home with this point. First, make sure that the two systems can ping each other. Do a ping from each side to the other. Without the ability to transfer IP packets back and forth, your network can go no further—"don't mean a thing if you ain't got that ping," y'know.

Once you're sure that you have IP connectivity, check that your systems can resolve each other's names. Here's where I find that readers sometimes go wrong. Someone will tell me that workstation \\ABEL can't contact server \\BAKER, "even though I pinged BAKER from ABEL." In other words, the reader typed ping baker or something similar while sitting at ABEL. But Ping doesn't use NetBIOS to resolve the name "baker," of course—it uses DNS. That's no help, although it *does* demonstrate that there's IP connectivity. We need to test that ABEL can resolve the name \\BAKER via *NetBIOS*, not DNS. I'm not sure why, but Microsoft doesn't include a NetBIOS-based ping in any versions of NT and later OSes, and I wish it did. It'd make life a lot easier. About the closest thing that you can get to a NetBIOS-based ping is probably a net view command, as in net view \\baker. That command will list the shares on the BAKER server, but it's not a great test, as other irrelevant factors can cause it to fail.

To really chase down a NetBIOS name resolution problem, you've got to understand what's going on under the hood, exactly how the "WINS client"—the word for the piece of software that runs on your workstation and resolves NetBIOS names—operates.

I'll assume for this discussion that you haven't modified the way that the WINS client resolves NetBIOS names—that is, that you haven't told the client to disable the LMHOSTS file—and that you are using WINS. (Come to think of it, that's an important troubleshooting step: Make sure that all of the communicating parties are connected either to the same WINS server, or to WINS servers that replicate to each other.)

Summarized, the name resolution sequence appears in Figure 7.42.

The NBT name resolver uses the following steps; if any succeed, then it stops looking:

◆ The resolver caches the result of NetBIOS-name-to-IP-address resolutions that have succeeded in the past 30 seconds, and looks first in that cache. You can see the current state of your NetBIOS name cache by typing **nbtstat -c**. You can clear and reload the cache by typing **nbtstat -R**.

◆ If the client is a Windows 98, Me, NT 4, Windows 2000, or later system, then the first thing to check is whether the name to the right of the \\ is either an IP address or a recognizable DNS name—that is, that it has a period in its name. If the name is just an IP address, as in a command like net use * \\199.33.29.15\Stuff, then forget the name resolution and just go to that IP address. If it's a DNS name, like net use * \\myserver.region8.acme.com\files, then resolve the name using the *DNS* client, not the WINS client (and you'll read about how DNS resolves names in the remainder of the chapter).

NAME RESOLUTION IN MORE DETAIL

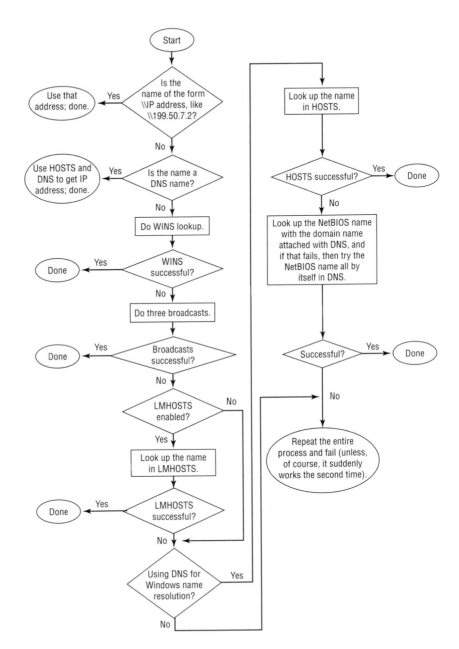

FIGURE 7.42

Name resolution
sequence under
NetBIOS

◆ If the name wasn't IP or DNS—or the client was too old to be able to respond to that—then
the next part is the WINS client, if the client software is WINS aware. If WINS is disabled
under Windows 95, or if there is no WINS server specified in Workgroups or NT 3.51,
then the client skips this step.

◆ If WINS isn't being used, then the client does three broadcasts. For example, `net view \\apple` causes three broadcasts looking for a workstation with the name apple registered rather than apple.mmco.com or the like.

◆ Next, if LMHOSTS is enabled—and it appears that LMHOSTS is *always* enabled on Windows 95/98/Me/2000/XP clients but must be enabled with the Enable LMHOSTS check box for NT 3.51 and Workgroups—then the client looks up the name in LMHOSTS. Surprised? When doing NBT name resolutions, LMHOSTS gets consulted *before* HOSTS, a reversal over Winsock name resolutions. Recall that LMHOSTS only contains 15-character NetBIOS names, not longer DNS-like names.

◆ If you've checked Enable DNS for Windows Name Resolution in Workgroups or NT 3.51, or if you have specified a DNS server in Windows 95/98/Me/2000/XP, then the workstation's client software will look at HOSTS, and if HOSTS can't help, it will interrogate the DNS server (or servers, as you can specify up to four DNS servers).

The NT/Workgroups clients and the 9*x* clients use DNS differently. The NT/Workgroups clients do a DNS query for the name with the domain name appended to it and then a DNS query of just the name. For example, if your domain is acme.com and you're doing a `net view \\myserver`, then an NT workstation will ask DNS first to resolve the name myserver.acme.com—it automatically adds the domain name for the first resolution. Then, if the DNS server can't resolve the name with the domain name attached, the client will request that the DNS server just resolve myserver.

In contrast, the Windows 9*x* client software only asks the DNS server to resolve the name with the domain name appended; in my example, a Windows 9*x* workstation would ask DNS to resolve myserver.acme.com but would not ask about myserver.

Then there's a final step in NetBIOS name resolution—it's an odd one. If the client software is the NT client (not the Workgroups or Win9*x* clients), and if it has been unsuccessful so far, then it goes back and does it all over again, I suppose in the hope that it'll work the second time.

DNS: Name Central in Active Directories

Windows 2000 or, more precisely, Active Directory turned names in Microsoft networking on its head, and it's stayed that way in XP and 2003. From 1985's MS-Net through the versions of LAN Manager through Windows for Workgroups, Windows 9*x*, and NT 3.*x* and 4.*x*, NetBIOS reigned supreme and anyone running a TCP/IP–based network needed WINS or, before WINS's appearance, LMHOSTS files to support NetBIOS names, as you've just read. DNS, where it existed, was something of an afterthought.

With Active Directory–based networks, all of that changes. The heart of naming in AD is DNS. As you've already read, in a network of *only* Windows 2000 and later systems and applications united through an Active Directory domain, WINS would be completely unnecessary. And no matter what kind of domain you've got, DNS is important, as you need it to find things on the Internet.

DNS is, for those just joining us, a name resolution system invented in 1984 for the Internet. It enables you to point your Web browser to a "friendly name" such as www.continental.com when you want to look up Continental Airlines' flight schedule rather than having to know that Continental's

Web server is at IP address 208.229 .128.54. It makes e-mail work smoother through its MX records (which you'll read about later) and has proven itself to be an easily expanded way of maintaining names in the largest network in the world. DNS's ability to grow—its *scalability*—is a real plus for the Active Directory, as Microsoft hopes that the AD will be the basis of some very large networks.

Why DNS Matters to Active Directory

Why is DNS a big deal all of sudden? After all, in truth NT 4 experts could get away with knowing basically nothing *about* DNS, and in fact you could probably even have passed the NT 4 TCP/IP elective exam without answering any of the DNS questions. So why did it become so important with the advent of Windows 2000 and later implementations of NT?

DNS is significant for several reasons, but here's the main one: DNS is now the central name repository for Active Directory, replacing WINS's role in NT 4. Yes, WINS will be around for a good time longer—so long as you have pre-2000 operating systems and application software running anywhere on your network—but WINS is in its twilight years. Or so we hope, anyway. It sometimes seems that the two truths about WINS are

◆ #1: WINS, your days are numbered!

◆ #2: Unfortunately for the rest of us, that number is *really* big.

WINS is on its way out because although basic NT 4 services accessed the network via NetBIOS, which relies upon WINS for name resolution, Windows 2000 and later instead accesses the network via Winsock, which uses DNS for its name resolution.

To see how the importance of names has shifted from WINS to DNS, consider this example: Both NT 4–based domains and Active Directory domains use a set of machines called *domain controllers* to act as the keepers of the enterprise's user accounts. When one domain controller learns something new about a user, such as a new password, that machine must pass that information on to the other domain controllers. But how does it *find* those domain controllers? Well, an NT 4 DC would find another DC via WINS. But an AD DC would find another DC via DNS. Similarly, before your workstation can log you in first thing in the morning, that workstation must find a DC—which it needs in order to log you in—with DNS. So where DNS access was a kind of "nice to have" feature of NT 4 domains, in Active Directory DNS is really a "need to have" feature—no DNS, no logon.

DNS, then, is now a basic service, no less important than electricity, at least as far as your network is concerned.

Anatomy of a DNS Name

DNS has rules for naming computers, rules that are in some senses actually more restrictive than the ones that we lived with under NetBIOS.

DNS NAMES ARE SEGMENTED

DNS names are arranged in pieces separated by periods so that, for example, a PC name such as mypc.test.minasi.com has four pieces to it. Each piece can't exceed 63 characters in length, and the entire name can't exceed 255 characters total. The only acceptable characters in a DNS name (according to RFC 1123—as you'll see, Microsoft bends this rule in its Active Directory names) are A–Z, a–z, 0–9, and a "-" (that is, a hyphen or a dash—no underscores allowed under RFC 1123.

That's worth keeping an eye on if you're upgrading systems from pre–Windows 2000 operating systems. NetBIOS lets you use considerably more characters than DNS does.

THE COMPUTER NAME IS THE LEFTMOST PART

When picking apart a DNS name, the leftmost piece is the computer name, and the remaining pieces to the right are the computer's DNS domain or DNS suffix. (Some sources call it a *DNS domain*, others a *DNS suffix*. I think the Microsoft literature favors *DNS suffix* because it's easy to get confused between *DNS* domains and *Active Directory* domains.) So, for example, in the machine mypc.test. bigfirm.biz, visualize two pieces:

> mypc + test.bigfirm.biz, or
>
> machine name + DNS domain name/suffix

Now that I've pointed out that the leftmost part is the machine name, let me answer a question that might be in the minds of those who've used NT. I said a couple of paragraphs back that each piece of a DNS name can be up to 63 characters long. Is that *really* true when it comes to the leftmost piece—can I *really* assign a machine name that is that long?

Well, it depends. Windows 2000, XP, and 2003's NetBIOS software is only really aware of the leftmost part of the name, so from NetBIOS's point of view, mypc.test.bigfirm.biz would simply be named \\mypc. But NetBIOS doesn't like computer names longer than 15 characters, so any Windows 2000 or later system with a machine name longer than 15 characters but shorter than 64 characters (and remember, we're talking about just the leftmost piece here—mypc, not mypc.test.bigfirm.biz) would be able to communicate from a Windows 2000 PC to a Windows 2000 or later PC, but pre-2000 systems would not be able to see a computer with a 16+ character name, so Windows 2000, XP, and 2003 keep a *truncated* NetBIOS name in that case. That might not be a problem—but if two systems with long computer names both truncated to the same name, as would be the case with a system named marksfavoritepc0001 and marksfavoritepc0002—then the NetBIOS software on one of those systems would simply shut itself down, as duplicate names are a no-no for NetBIOS, and thus pre-2000 systems would not be able to access that second system.

The DNS Namespace: The Key to DNS

The huge size of networks that DNS can handle naming for is downright amazing. Given the name of any computer on the Internet, it can give you the IP address of that computer, and usually in just a few seconds. How many computers *are* there on the Internet—how big is the database that DNS is searching for you when it resolves a name? Honestly, I don't know the exact number of machines on the Internet, but I'm sure that "hundreds of millions or more" is a reasonable guess. The database of machine names for the entire Internet is a *big* database, and it changes all the time—but it works. From any computer on the Internet, you can find the address of any other computer on the Internet, using the worldwide DNS hierarchy or "namespace." Furthermore, you can get that information relatively quickly, usually in a few seconds.

How does a DNS hierarchy or namespace work? You need to know this for a couple of reasons. First, even if you create a DNS hierarchy that *isn't* connected to the public DNS hierarchy, you still need to create a hierarchy, and the tiniest DNS namespace works exactly the same as the public DNS namespace, it's just smaller. Second, if you *do* decide to build your DNS so that it's a part of the public DNS hierarchy, then you'll need to know how that hierarchy works. (And, I suppose, the third reason would be that it's just interesting to understand how this essential part of the Internet works. Interesting to me, at least, but then I don't get out much.)

You'll see people use the term *namespace* and *hierarchy* when referring to DNS. I'll tend to use *hierarchy* here, but if you read something that refers to a *DNS namespace*, then just substitute *DNS hierarchy* and you'll be correct.

INTRODUCING THE HIERARCHY: BACK TO LEFT-TO-RIGHT

As I suggested in the first paragraph of the last section, you read DNS names left to right, whether they're names in the worldwide DNS hierarchy or in your own private four-computer private DNS hierarchy. But what are you reading? Let me explain this in some detail and use it as my vehicle to introduce how the DNS hierarchy works.

To rephrase a question I posed a couple of paragraphs ago, "How on Earth could a database as large, widespread, and ever-changing as the DNS machine-name-to-IP-address database be managed and maintained and yet still offer reasonable query times?" Well, as you'll see later in this chapter, the *only* reason that it's possible is because no one person or organization must keep track of those names. Instead, the responsibility for keeping track of the name-to-IP-address relationship is maintained locally—if you point your browser to www.minasi.com and your local DNS server then tries to figure out the IP address of www.minasi.com, then your local DNS server is soon going to be talking to *my* local DNS server to resolve that name. That means that it's *my* job to make sure that you can find the www machine in the minasi.com domain because minasi.com is my domain. If by contrast you go looking for www.acme.com and *Acme* drops the ball on keeping track of *their* domain, then it only affects the people trying to get to the Acme systems—you wouldn't be hampered at all in trying to find a computer in the minasi.com domain.

Let's consider a PC whose full name is mypc.test.minasi.com in order to start examining how the hierarchy works. What do the placements of the periods in the name—the parts of the name—tell us?

First, we know that its machine name is mypc. Second, we know that its domain is test.minasi.com.

But what *is* test.minasi.com? Well, reading left to right, you see that *test* is a subdomain or child domain (RFCs use both terms, so I don't think one is the "official" name) of another domain named minasi.com. That means that whoever created the test.minasi.com domain needed the permission of whoever's in charge of the minasi.com domain in order to create the test.minasi.com domain.

Next, let's move to the right, and consider *minasi.com*. What is this domain? It is a child domain of a domain named, simply, com. (Yes, there is such a domain.) To create the minasi.com domain, someone (well, *me*, actually) needed to contact the people in charge of the com domain and get permission to create a subdomain of com named "minasi" or, in other words, "minasi.com." That's what you do when you visit www.networksolutions.com to try to register a new "dot-com" domain.

But where did the com domain come from? Is it a child of some other domain? Well, if it weren't for a very common bit of sloppiness, then it'd be more obvious. You see, mypc.test.minasi.com isn't, strictly speaking, a complete DNS name—instead, mypc.test.minasi.com. *is*. What's the difference? Look again—the correct one ends with a period. The com. domain is actually a child domain of a domain named just "." that is, by the way, pronounced "dot" and is called the *root* of the DNS hierarchy. And as long as I'm introducing terminology, the phrase *complete DNS name* isn't really correct—the Internet-speak phrase is *fully qualified domain name* (FQDN).

Now you know why I've been calling the way that DNS stores names a "hierarchy"—DNS distributes responsibility. To create the com domain only required the permission—granted *once*—of whomever owned the root (.) domain. (Originally it was the U.S. government, but that responsibility has moved to a nonprofit group called the Internet Corporation for Assigned Names and Numbers, or ICANN. They're doing a terrible job, apparently, and the Feds are threatening to take the root back.) I got to register minasi.com because I provided some information and a credit card number to the people who run the com domain, Network Solutions. (They're a division of a for-profit firm named VeriSign.) Now, if someone were to come to me and ask to create a domain named thisistheplace.minasi.com, she wouldn't have to talk to ICANN or VeriSign—she'd only have to talk to me.

Let me underscore that. To create minasi.com, I only needed the permission of the people who run the .com domain. I didn't have to get permission from other .com companies, such as microsoft.com, ibm.com, or saralee.com—I just needed the OK from the .com parent domain, which is controlled by Network Solutions. Nor did Network Solutions have to ask the ICANN guys—once ICANN (the root people) delegated control of the com. directory to the Network Solutions folks, then ICANN doesn't care who Network Solutions delegates to. In the same way, if I wanted to create a subdomain of minasi.com, such as hq.minasi.com, then I not only needn't tell microsoft.com, ibm.com, or saralee.com, I also needn't tell Network Solutions.

WHY BUILD THE DNS HIERARCHY THIS WAY?

Let's back up for a bit and see what led to DNS looking as it does today. In the TCP/IP world, anything with an IP address is called a *host*. Back in the early '80s, when the Internet (which wasn't yet *called* the Internet—it was the ARPAnet then) consisted only of a few hundred computers, a server on MIT's campus held a file that listed the names and IP addresses of those few computers. That file was named HOSTS because it listed all of the hosts on the Internet. When someone at some distant site added a computer to their local network and attached that computer to the ARPAnet, then he or she would just contact someone at MIT, who'd update the HOSTS file, and once a day everyone would attach to that MIT server and download the latest HOSTS file.

As you know, the HOSTS file still exists, although in a much less important role. But why not keep running things the old way, with one big central HOSTS file? Well, let's see: Assume 200 million computers on the Internet, and about 40 characters per HOSTS line; that'd be about 8 gigabytes. So every day you'd have to connect to some location and download 8 gigs—yuck. Even worse, every single time you put a computer on your network, adding pc0012 to acme.com, you'd have to tell someone at the one worldwide central repository of the HOSTS file and hope that they'd update the file in a timely fashion. And when you add a new system to your network, or perhaps assign a name to a different IP address—such as when you move www.acme.com from one machine to another, changing an IP address in the process—then you better hope that everyone out there in Internetland who you'd *like* to be able to find your Web server is working from the latest HOSTS file—ugh, double and triple yuck.

THE ROOT, TOP-LEVEL, SECOND-LEVEL, AND CHILD DOMAINS

Having explained how the hierarchy *doesn't* work, let's look at how it *does* work. Take a look at Figure 7.43.

FIGURE 7.43

The public DNS
hierarchy

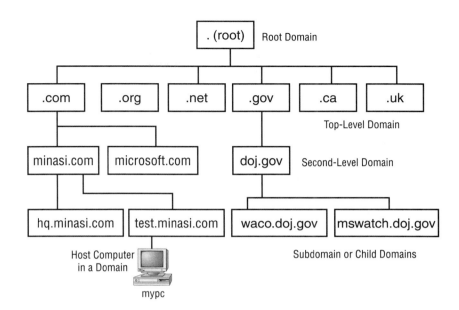

Top-Level Domains

Below the root are hundreds—yes, hundreds—of *top-level* domains. Most of the ones we tend to think of around the world are .com, .net, and .org, as they've become sort of the worldwide "catch-all" domains. Then, each country has its own top-level domain—the United States has .us, Canada .ca, the United Kingdom .uk, and so on. Some countries have decided to offer their top-level domain for registrations, as in the case of the Cocos Keeling Island, the owners of the .cc top-level domain that many are using as an alternative to .com, .org, or .net. The island has a total population of 604 and in 1995—the last year I could find data for—their main export was copra. Who knows, perhaps nowadays they're all sharing the wealth from being the "kings of dot-cc." In another example, the somewhat-larger (population 10,000) island nation of Tuvalu ended up with the top-level domain with the salable name of .tv. Top-level domains .gov, .mil, and .edu tend to point to U.S. government, military, and educational institutions—remember who invented the Internet—although I guess in theory, groups of those types in other countries might register names under those top-level domains as well.

In November 2000, ICANN created several new top-level domains. I don't exactly get why they did some of them, but they are presented in Table 7.2.

TABLE 7.2: NEW TOP-LEVEL INTERNET DOMAINS

DOMAIN	PURPOSE	CONTROLLING ORGANIZATION
.aero	Aerospace-oriented firms, including airlines	Societe Internationale de Telecommunications Aeronautiques (Belgium)
.biz	Basically an "expansion area" for .com	JVTeam, LLC

Continued on next page

TABLE 7.2: NEW TOP-LEVEL INTERNET DOMAINS *(continued)*

DOMAIN	PURPOSE	CONTROLLING ORGANIZATION
.coop	Business cooperatives	National Cooperative Business Association
.info	Information sources	Afilias, LLC
.museum	Museums, clearly	Museum Domain Management Association
.name	People's names (see text)	Global Name Registry (the U.K.)
.pro	Various professional groups—doctors, lawyers, accountants, that sort of thing	RegistryPro (Ireland)

The top-level domains .biz and .info are both wide-open domains that anyone can register names in. If you're Acme Termite Inspection service and acmetermite.com, acmetermite.net, and acmetermite.org are taken, then you might still be able to get acmetermite.biz or acmetermite.info. The domain .pro is *not* wide open; there are people running various subdomains there. For example, you couldn't (as far as I can see) just register engineer.pro; rather; someone would administer engineer.pro and you'd get a name below that, like janesconstruction.engineer.pro. (As I write this, there's already a cpa.pro, medical.pro, and legal.pro.) The idea behind the .name domain is that someone would create an overall registry of people whose last name was Minasi and therefore control the minasi.name domain. I'd then get a subdomain under that called mark.minasi.name.

Different organizations control different top-level domains. For example, clearly Ottawa designates who hands out registrations under .ca, and the .tv sellers couldn't be doing those sales without the permission of the Tuvalans. The top-level domains that are biggest by far, however, are of course .com, .net, and .org, all administered by a company called Network Solutions, based in northern Virginia—but you may hear this company referred to by several names. Before the late '90s, a consortium of U.S. government agencies called the InterNIC controlled the entire DNS naming hierarchy, and they contracted with Network Solutions, a private firm, to handle the nuts and bolts of keeping the .com, .org, and .net top-level domains working. As a result, people have a tendency to use the terms *Network Solutions* and *the InterNIC* interchangeably, although they're not the same thing, and the InterNIC has become pretty irrelevant now that the U.S. has ceded control of the public DNS hierarchy to ICANN. Network Solutions is also not the same as ICANN—ICANN worries about *all* of the top-level domains. You might even see people refer to Network Solutions as VeriSign, the e-commerce security folks; that's because VeriSign bought Network Solutions in 1999.

Roll-Your-Own Top-Level Domains: For Internal Use Only!

Before I move to second-level domains, I want to toss in something that I'll be covering in detail later. Although the public Internet only uses a handful of top-level domains (TLDs in geek-speak), that doesn't mean you can't create others of your own sometimes. As you'll see, I strongly recommend that the DNS servers that support your Active Directory *not* be visible on the public Internet, if you can avoid it. You can, as you'll learn, create a DNS server that is perfectly capable of resolving names on the public Internet, but that also hosts a domain that is "invisible" to the public Internet. (You'd do this for security's sake.) You can accomplish this in several ways, but one simple way is just to use a domain name with a nonstandard TLD. For example, suppose your company's publicly visible Internet domain name were acme.com; you might choose to create an Active Directory domain name of acme.local. Never heard of a domain called something-dot-local? No wonder—there's no such TLD on the Internet. But you can do anything you like on your *intra*net, creating domains with any TLD that you like. So I guess I *could* have an e-mail name of mark@minasi—but only people inside my company could use it! Again, we'll cover more on this later, but I wanted to plant that idea in your head now so I can expand on it later.

There was a proposed standard working its way through the RFC process that would have suggested a reserved internal-only top-level domain of ".pri" for "private" but it appears to have gone nowhere.

Second-Level Domains: Searching the Hierarchy

Sadly, ICANN's not about to give me my own .minasi top-level domain, so I guess I won't be able to change my e-mail address to mark@minasi any time soon. So the second-level domains are the more interesting ones for most of us.

As you just read, you can create a second-level domain with the permission of the owner of the parent domain. To create your second-level domain, the parent domain only has to do one thing: "delegate" name responsibility for your second-level domain to some machine. That's an important concept, and I'll get to it in a minute. But first, let's see how DNS uses its hierarchical nature with an example.

Suppose you point your browser to www.minasi.com. Your browser needs to know the IP address of the www.minasi.com machine, so it asks your local DNS server to resolve www.minasi.com into an IP address. (This is a simplified example—we'll consider a more complete one later.) Where should your local DNS server go to ask the IP address of the www machine in the domain minasi.com? Simple—it should go to the DNS server for minasi.com. That's a perfectly correct answer but not a very helpful one. How is your DNS server supposed to find the DNS server for minasi.com? Well, in general, you can find the address of a domain's DNS server by asking the domain's *parent's* DNS server—in other words, the DNS servers in the com domain can tell you the addresses of the DNS servers in the minasi.com domain.

But we're still not done, because *now* the question is, "What is the IP address of the DNS server (or servers) for the com domain?" Well, as you just learned, you get a domain's DNS server addresses from the DNS servers in that domain's parent's DNS server, so you'd get com's DNS server address from the DNS servers for com's parent, "."—the root.

Hmmm…if you've been patient enough to follow this so far, then you've probably realized that we've run into a bit of a brick wall. You find the DNS servers for minasi.com by asking the DNS servers for com, and you find the DNS servers for com by asking the root, but who do you ask to find out the DNS servers for the root, as the root has no parent? (Hey, that'd be a great computer trivia question: Which is the only "orphan" DNS domain?)

The answer is, "you cheat." Every piece of DNS server software that I've ever seen comes with a kind of a cheat sheet called the *root hints file,* which contains the name and IP addresses of the 13 root DNS servers. On a Microsoft OS-based DNS server, you'll find a file named `cache.dns`—an ASCII file that you can examine with Notepad—in `\winnt\system32\dns` (or perhaps `\windows\system32\dns`) on any server that you've installed the DNS server service on. Anyway, once your DNS server has located a root DNS server's address in its root hints file, it asks that root DNS server for the addresses of the DNS servers for the com domain, then asks one of the com DNS servers for the address of the minasi.com DNS server, *then* asks the minasi.com DNS server for the address of the machine named www in the minasi.com domain and finally resolves the name for you. To summarize what happened when your local DNS server tried to resolve www.minasi.com:

1. First, your DNS server decided to find the minasi.com DNS server.

2. To find the minasi.com DNS server, your DNS server decided to look for the addresses of the com domain's DNS servers, as com is minasi.com's parent domain.

3. To find the com domain's DNS server, your DNS server decided to look for the root DNS servers.

4. It knew the IP addresses of the root DNS servers through its local root hints file.

5. Using the IP address of a root DNS server, it asked that root DNS server for the address of a DNS server for the com domain.

6. The root DNS server told your DNS server the addresses of the com domain's DNS servers.

7. Your DNS server then took one of those addresses and asked that com DNS server for the addresses of the minasi.com DNS servers.

8. That DNS server for the com domain told your DNS server the addresses of minasi.com's two DNS servers.

9. Your DNS server then asked one of minasi.com's DNS servers to resolve the name www.minasi.com.

10. The minasi.com DNS server resolved the address, returning the IP address of www.minasi.com.

Third Level, Child, or Subdomains: More on Delegation

Now suppose I choose to divide my domain into subdomains or child domains. Suppose I create a subdomain named hq.minasi.com. What's involved? Delegation.

You saw from the previous example about resolving www.minasi.com that a DNS server resolves a name by working its way up the DNS hierarchy until it gets to the root, then works its way back down until it finally finds the DNS server that can answer its question. But, in some senses, *shouldn't* the root servers be able to resolve www.minasi.com? After all, www.minasi.com *is* in their domain, sort of. Or I could argue that the DNS servers for the com domain should be able to resolve www.minasi.com, as that address is inside the com domain, *sort* of "once removed," so to speak.

The answer is no, the root and com domains should *not* be able to resolve www in the minasi.com domain because they have *delegated* name resolution responsibility for minasi.com to a set of DNS servers, the minasi.com DNS servers. More specifically, the root domain contains records called NS (name server) records that delegate the responsibility for the com domain to the com DNS servers, and the com domain's DNS servers contain NS records that delegate name server responsibility for the minasi.com domain to the minasi.com servers. In fact, the people who maintain the database for the com zone *could* keep the name resolution record for www.minasi.com in the com database, but that would defeat the whole purpose of the hierarchy, and it would be a pain for me—if I ever moved the Web function from one of my computers to another, I'd have to bother the Network Solutions people and ask them to change the name resolution record for www.minasi.com.

So why would I create a subdomain of minasi.com? Perhaps I've got the same kind of problem that Network Solutions does—that is to say, perhaps I want to enable a group to use DNS names within my domain, but I don't want to have to do the maintenance on the DNS records. Suppose, for example, that I buy a company in Singapore, 12 time zones away from me. Now suppose they put a new machine online and need a name resolution record for that machine installed in the minasi.com DNS database. They can't call me when they need that, as it's not only a long way away, but also because I'm usually asleep while they're working. That gets kind of annoying and after a while they say, "Can't you just give us control of the name resolution for our own machines?" Well, I'm not particularly keen about giving them control of the whole minasi.com domain, but I'd like to grant their request for local control of their machine names. So I create a subdomain and call it test.minasi.com. Making their subdomain a reality requires two things:

◆ First, they'll need to make one of their computers into a DNS server for the test.minasi.com subdomain. That machine will, of course, need to be on the Internet persistently.

◆ Second, I'll need to tell the rest of the world to look at their server when resolving names in the test.minasi.com domain. I do that by delegating name server responsibility, by placing an NS record in my minasi.com DNS database that says, "There's a subdomain named test in the minasi.com domain, and if you want to look up any names in that, then don't ask me, ask this other DNS server, the one in Singapore."

You'll learn more about NS records a bit later, when I get more specific about building DNS zones, but in a nutshell that's all there is to delegation—it's a one-line command in a parent DNS server's database that says, "Hey, don't ask *me*—go talk to this other DNS server."

DNS DEFINITION: "AUTHORITATIVE"

Before moving on to my next DNS topic, let me define a term: *authoritative*. I've been telling you that to look up names in minasi.com you need to find minasi.com's DNS servers, and that you find minasi.com's DNS servers by asking the DNS servers in minasi.com's parent domain, com. The names of the minasi.com DNS servers that the com servers report to you are called the authoritative servers for minasi.com.

In other words, I could, in theory, have 50 DNS servers set up for minasi.com running on my network. (Don't ask me why I'd do that; I can't think of a reason offhand.) But if the com domain's DNS servers only know about three of those minasi.com DNS servers, then when people ask the com domain's servers for the names of the minasi.com servers, the com domain servers will only contain three NS records for minasi.com, so they will only report the three minasi.com DNS servers that they know about. In the same way, if my imaginary Singapore office ran 47 DNS servers but I had only entered one NS record in the minasi.com DNS database for test.minasi.com, then only the one DNS server named in that NS record would be authoritative for test.minasi.com.

Exercise: Set Up a DNS Server and Work with *nslookup*

Time to leave the theory for a moment; let's set up a simple DNS server and do some name resolution. We will build upon this server as the rest of this chapter goes on, and then I'll use this server as the foundation of an example Active Directory that we'll build in the next chapter. I've integrated these examples for one reason: Active Directory will not work without the proper underlying DNS infrastructure. I get tons of letters from readers who say that they've got a small AD set up and it isn't working. In my experience nine out of ten times, it's DNS that gets in the way. Without correct DNS setup, your systems cannot find each other to authenticate, and if one machine in a domain wants to talk to another machine in a domain then they must authenticate, or nothing happens. So I'll walk you through an example, step by step.

In this step, we'll just get the DNS server up and running.

INTRODUCING BIGFIRM.BIZ

We're going to create a DNS domain and eventually an Active Directory for a mythical company called bigfirm.biz. To that end, we'll end up with two things. First, we'll have a DNS domain named bigfirm.biz, and this computer will be the authoritative DNS server for that domain. Second, we'll have an Active Directory named bigfirm.biz. And just to keep the number of machines that we'll need to a minimum, we'll also make this machine a domain controller for Bigfirm.

All I want right now, though, is the most basic DNS server possible, one that only knows how to go out on the Internet and answer queries. Let me stress that you do not need a Server 2003–based DNS server to run Active Directory; a Windows 2000 Server–based DNS server or for that matter many other vendors' DNS servers will do fine for AD. But this gives me an excuse to show you how to set up a Server 2003–based DNS server.

WHAT YOU'LL NEED

I know that some of you will just read along and not actually try this out, but let me counsel you *not* to do that. People often ask me how to learn a product—what books, seminars, videos, Web sites, or the like should they use? My answer is always the same: get a good basic text or other starting point, get a computer whose hard disk you don't mind wiping clean and rebuilding, and then just install the software and play with it. (I'm hoping that you've decided that you've got that "good basic text" in your hands, but use whatever works.)

In any case, you do not need a big beefy machine just to play around with Server 2003; as I write this, my test machine is a 450MHz laptop with an 8GB drive and 196MB of RAM. I wouldn't use it to create the main DNS server for Earthlink, but it's fine for testing. Just make sure that the system is

◆ Running Windows Server 2003

◆ Has a connection to the Internet, and

◆ Keeps the same IP address throughout this exercise

In general, real honest-to-God DNS servers that enterprises rely upon will have either static IP addresses, or unchanging IP addresses delivered via a DHCP reservation. Ultimately I'll have you set this machine to some IP address, but for now it doesn't matter. But let me stress that (1) any machine that you intend to be a DNS server for your network must have a constant IP address, and (2) if you want that DNS server to be able to resolve addresses on the public Internet, then that DNS server must have an IP address that connects to the Internet. Note that it is perfectly fine for the machine's address to be in one of the nonroutable ranges of addresses—your machine could have a 192.168.x.x, 10.x.x.x, or 172.x.x.x address. As long as it can ping IP addresses to the public Internet, then it'll do just fine as a simple DNS server for this example.

No matter how you plan to do this, however, make sure you know your system's IP address: open a command line and type `ipconfig` and press Enter to find out. Keep that address handy.

Then I'll add a couple of nice, but not essential, characteristics to this server:

◆ Any domain controller for an Active Directory has to have a DNS suffix whose name matches the AD. Again, in the next chapter we'll create a domain named bigfirm.biz, so let's get ready and make sure that this DNS server—which will ultimately be a DNS server for bigfirm.biz— already has its DNS suffix set to bigfirm.biz. This isn't essential for these early examples, but let's get it out of the way now; besides, if DNS servers don't have any DNS suffix set at all, then you get some annoying warning messages in the DNS Server event log.

◆ Finally, let's agree on a machine name for this computer. Again, not essential, but it's nice if my screen shots look somewhat the same as yours. This machine will ultimately do a lot for bigfirm.biz, so let's call it bigdog.

In case you're not 100 percent sure how to name the system bigdog and give it a DNS suffix of bigfirm.biz, let's walk through that now.

CHANGING A SYSTEM'S NAME AND DNS SERVER SUFFIX

You change a system's name and DNS name in the Computer Name tab. More specifically:

1. Click Start, then right-click My Computer and choose Properties.
2. Click the Computer Name tab.
3. Click the Change button to raise a dialog box labeled Computer Name Changes.
4. In the Computer Name field, enter **bigdog**.
5. Click the More button.
6. In the DNS Suffix and NetBIOS Computer Name dialog box, fill the field labeled Primary DNS Suffix of This Computer with **bigfirm.biz**.
7. Click OK to return to the Computer Name Changes dialog.
8. Click OK to close the Computer Name Changes dialog.
9. That will raise a dialog box that warns that you've got to reboot to see these changes take effect. Click OK to clear the dialog.
10. Click OK to close the System Properties page.
11. Click Yes to reboot your computer.

Once the system has rebooted, try an `ipconfig /all` command. You should see that the Host Name is bigdog and the Primary DNS Suffix is bigfirm.biz.

CHECK IP ADDRESS AND CONNECTIVITY

While you've got the `ipconfig` output in front of you, make a note of the IP address. Then check that your system can ping the outside world. Open a command prompt and try typing `ping 164.109.1.3`, the address of a DNS server on a large ISP, or 152.163.159.232, one of AOL's DNS servers. If you're not sure what I just said to do, *do not go any further*; please go back and review the previous chapter. (I promise, we won't go anywhere until you get back.)

INSTALL THE DNS SERVER SOFTWARE

Now we're ready to get the DNS server running. The steps to installing DNS are exactly the same as for installing any of the other network services, like DHCP or WINS. Make sure you've got the Server CD around, or are connected to whatever set of I386 files you installed this system from, as it'll need to go out to the CD to find the DNS server software. Then do this to install the DNS server software:

1. Open Add/Remove Programs (Start/Control Panel/Add or Remove Programs).

2. Click Add/Remove Windows Components and wait a bit while the Windows Components Wizard starts up.

3. Click Networking Services and then the Details button.

4. Click the check box next to Domain Name System (DNS).

5. Click OK to return to Windows Components.

6. Click Next to install the service. The system will say that it is "Configuring Components" for a while, probably a few minutes, and may need the original Server installation CD. A bit later, the Completing the Windows Components Wizard screen appears. If you currently have an IP address from DHCP, then the wizard will stop and suggest that while it's not going to *make* you give this server a static IP address, it's a *really* good idea to set one. It then brings up the TCP/IP properties screen. In a real DNS production server you would always use either a static IP address or a DHCP reservation. But if you're just playing with a DNS server, then you can work with whatever random IP address your ISP's DHCP server (or for that matter the built-in DHCP server in your DSL/cable router, if that's how you connect) gives you. Just click OK three times and the wizard will leave you alone.

7. Click Finish to end the wizard.

8. Click the Close box in the Add/Remove Windows Components window.

POINT THE DNS SERVER TO ITSELF

You're going to be sitting at the server while doing the sample DNS queries, so when the server wants to resolve a DNS query you want the server to ask *itself* (that is, the DNS server software running on it) to resolve names. Do that through the GUI as you saw in the last chapter—in Network Connections, right-click Local Area Connection or whatever your NIC's name is, choose Properties, click the General tab, then click Internet Protocol (TCP/IP) and the Properties button, and then click the radio button labeled Use the Following DNS Server Addresses and fill in the DNS server's IP address. So, for example, let's say that you've got your test machine, the one that you just put the DNS server software on. Suppose its IP address is 192.168.0.12. You must now go into TCP/IP Properties for that test machine and fill in the Preferred DNS Server field with its own IP address, 192.168.0.12.

You can alternatively set the preferred DNS server from the command line:

```
netsh int ip set dns name static ipaddress primary
```

where you replace *ipaddress* with the server's actual IP address and *name* with the first word from the NIC's name. So if your system had an IP address of 192.168.0.12 and a NIC named Local Area Connection, then you could set its preferred DNS server this way:

```
netsh int ip set dns local static 192.168.0.12 primary
```

If, on the other hand, the server's NIC were named Wireless Network Connection, then you'd replace "local" with "wireless," as in

```
netsh int ip set dns wireless static 192.168.0.12 primary
```

Why "wireless" and "local?" Because if you have more than one NIC, then netsh needs to know which NIC you're referring to. Each NIC has a name like "Local Area Connection," "Local Area Connection 2," "Wireless Network Connection," or the like. You can either write out the whole name, or just use the minimum number of letters necessary to make clear which you mean. Thus, if you had two network connections named "Local Area Connection" and "Wireless Network Connection" then you could just type "l" or "w" to tell netsh which you meant. You need quotes in the name when the name has spaces, as in "Local Area Connection."

Here's another example. If you had a system with a NIC named Local Area Connection and another NIC named Local Area Connection 2, then you'd have to specify the whole name in quotes, as in

```
netsh int ip set dns "Local Area Connection 2" static 192.168.0.12 primary
```

TIP   *That's a general rule—you should usually set up DNS servers to point to themselves for name resolution; specify the server's IP address in the Preferred DNS Server field. If you configure the server via a DHCP reservation, then you can specify the server's preferred DNS server address in the reservation as well.*

Double-check that you've got this set up right by typing **ipconfig /all** at the command prompt. You should see the same IP address next to both "IP Address" and "DNS Servers" in that output. If they don't match, go back and reassign the preferred DNS server either in the GUI or with the netsh commands above.

START THE DNS SNAP-IN

As with DHCP and WINS, you needn't reboot when you install the server software. Click Start/Administrative Tools/DNS and you'll see the DNS snap-in. You'll see an icon representing your server in the left pane; click the server and you'll see a screen like Figure 7.44.

FIGURE 7.44

Initial DNS
snap-in screen

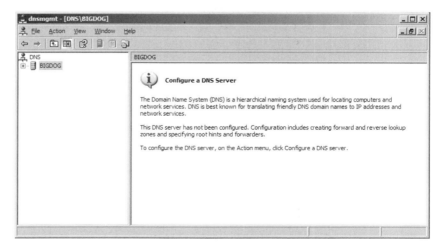

Notice the seemingly helpful message in the right pane offering to configure your DNS server. Take my advice:

WARNING *Never let Configure a DNS Server configure your DNS server.*

If you right-click the server's icon and choose Configure a DNS Server, then you start a wizard that has a tendency to make some bad assumptions about how you want your server set up. It's particularly good at mistakenly making your DNS server something called a "private root." (This is less of an issue in 2003 than it was in 2000, but I still advise against it.) It's not hard to fix private roots, but they're scary-looking when you've never seen one before. Trust me, I'll show you how to get it "configured" with no trouble (and no help from the Configure a DNS Server Wizard) in this chapter.

Before we leave the snap-in, let me direct your attention to a place that I hope to habituate you to looking at: the Event Viewer logs. Click the plus sign next to the server's icon and you'll see a folder labeled Event Viewer; inside that is a folder labeled DNS Events. Click that and you'll see entries in the right pane that offer information about how your DNS server is running. If you've followed my steps here, then you'll only have two events in your log. The first will be a lengthy Event ID 708, which basically just says, "Hmmm, it looks like this DNS server isn't holding onto any DNS information, so you must only want it to go resolve names from elsewhere—that is, to be a 'caching-only' server." It's just an information-only message and is nothing to worry about. The second will be an Event ID 2, which just says that the DNS Server service has started. So we had two information-only messages; was looking in the Event Viewer a waste of time? Not at all. It pays to take a look at it periodically...even if some of the messages that you'll come across *are* a bit cryptic!

TRY A NAME RESOLUTION

Now that we've got a DNS server running and a computer relying on that DNS server (that is, the server itself), let's do the simplest thing in the world—just resolve a name. We'll resolve www.minasi.com.

Then open a command prompt (unless you've still got one open) and type **nslookup** and press Enter. You'll probably see something like this:

```
C:\>nslookup
DNS request timed out.
    timeout was 2 seconds.
*** Can't find server name for address 206.246.253.12: Timed out
Default Server: UnKnown
Address: 206.246.253.12
>
```

Your IP address will be different, but otherwise you'll probably see something like this. Or you might see a somewhat less-scary set of output, like this:

```
C:\>nslookup
Default Server: ip68-106-120.hr.hr.cox.net
Address: 68.106.183.120
>
```

The only difference is in how some other DNS servers are set up. If you keep getting the "*** can't find server name for..." error, then ignore it. You'll see how to get rid of it later. Now, nslookup is a bit impatient and complains about timeout messages if a DNS server doesn't respond to it in *two seconds*. Let's relax it a bit. Type

```
set timeout=10
```

Ten seconds seems a bit more reasonable.
Next, type

```
www.minasi.com
```

and again press Enter. You should see something like

```
Default Server: UnKnown
Address: 206.246.253.12

Non-authoritative answer:
Name:    cablenic.minasi.com
Address:  68.15.149.117
Aliases:  www.minasi.com


>
```

Again, the exact text may vary because your DNS server uses a different IP address than mine does, and I might well have reconfigured the IP address on my Web server by the time you try this out. Here's the important thing: *it resolved a name on the Internet*. Not impressed, you say? Well, consider this: how much configuration did you do to the DNS server in order to "teach" it to resolve names on the public Internet? Answer: none.

That's *really* important. We're going to talk later about something called *forwarders*. Many people somehow get an idea that they need to configure forwarders for DNS servers in order for the DNS servers to be able to resolve addresses on the Internet. It's not true; all a DNS server needs is a connection to the Internet and the list of ICANN's 13 root servers. Again, the server's IP address needn't even be routable as long as there's a NAT/PAT router around. Try it—set up Internet Connection Sharing as we discussed in the last chapter and put a system on your internal network, the network that gets the 192.168.0.x addresses. Make the system a DNS server and try what we just did, and it'll still work fine, at least so long as my connection to my ISP is intact. (Try a name like www.ibm.com if mine doesn't work.)

So when you set up a DNS server, make it a habit to do a simple little troubleshooting step as soon as you've got DNS on the system—point a system to that DNS server, start `nslookup`, and try to resolve a name out on the public Internet.

TROUBLESHOOTING THE SIMPLE DNS SERVER

If it doesn't work, what to do? Check the following things.

- Double-check that the DNS service is actually running. While sitting at the server that's running the DNS service, open the DNS snap-in and right-click the icon representing the DNS server and choose All Tasks, then look at the options offered. Toward the bottom of the options, you should see Stop, Pause, and Restart, rather than Start. If you see Start, that means that the DNS server service isn't running; choose Start and it *should* start up. If it doesn't, or if it starts and then stops, look in the folder named `Event Viewer` in the DNS snap-in; there may be an error or warning message that can shed some light on the problem.

◆ Check that the DNS server points to itself: do an `ipconfig /all` and ensure that the IP address and the address of the DNS server are the same.

◆ Check that the server can route to the Internet. Try a ping to a few fairly reliable IP addresses like the ones that I mentioned a page or two back. If you can't ping to an IP address, then it's not a DNS problem, it's a router problem.

◆ Check that your network guys haven't installed some insanely paranoid firewall that's blocking your attempts to do DNS lookups. Type **nslookup**, press Enter, and then type **server 164.109.1.3** to point your system to that large ISP's DNS server. You should now be able to resolve www.ibm.com and the like. If not, then either you've got a really damaged copy of `nslookup` (something I've never seen) or your ability to communicate with the public Internet is being severely hampered by a firewall.

◆ Again, look in the `Event Viewer` folder. There are often *very* useful hints there.

With hope, by now you've successfully set up a DNS server and gotten a bit of hands-on with it. So it's time to return to some concepts and theory...

Zones versus Domains (and More on Delegation)

I've been talking about how DNS servers maintain a database for a "DNS domain," but strictly speaking, DNS servers don't hold name information for domains, they hold them for *zones*. What, then, is a zone? It's a DNS-specific term that basically means "the range of Internet addresses that this DNS server will be concerned about." To see how this works, let's consider Acme Industries (acme.com), a firm familiar to any Warner Bros. cartoon fan. And, in the process, we'll also consider another example of delegation.

When Acme got its Internet connection, it set up a primary DNS server at its corporate headquarters in Chicago and gave DNS names to its machines. There are machines with names such as jills-pc.acme.com, bigserver.acme.com, www.acme.com, and so on.

As time went on, however, Acme began to feel the bite of competition from its hated and long-time rival, Apex Limited (apex.com). So it moved its Gadgets group—the guys who brought us Acme Instant Hole, Acme Rocket Sled, or Acme Spring-Powered Shoes—to Mexico in the hopes of lower prices. Meanwhile, Acme bought a munitions firm in Belgium and decided to close its other big domestic division, the Explosives group, and sell the Belgian explosives instead.

At this point, Acme has three loci of operation: the suits in Chicago, the gadgeteers in Mexico, and the demolitions folks in Belgium. The question for Acme's network engineers is, "How do we arrange our DNS?" They decide to create two child domains, explosives.acme.com and gadgets.acme.com. Although some machines will stay in the top acme.com domain—the Web server, www.acme.com, is an obvious choice—many machines will be either *machinename*.explosives.acme.com or *machinename*.gadgets.acme.com. Why split up the domain into child domains? Any of several reasons, but one obvious one might be just simplicity—you can look at a machine's name and immediately figure out to which department it belongs.

NOTE *Please note that I'm talking about DNS domains, not Active Directory domains. If I have an AD domain named acme.com then it'd be a really good idea to also give the DNS suffix acme.com to all of the machines in that domain; if my PC were named mypc then its full DNS name would be mypc.acme.com. But Microsoft says that you don't have to match DNS domain names with AD domain names, so in theory if my computer were named mypc in an AD domain named acme.com, then I could choose to give it a completely different DNS name, like mypc.xyz.org. I am told, however, that this leads to Kerberos problems (Kerberos is the protocol that accomplishes Active Directory authentications). I've tried to nail down exactly what the problem is but I haven't had much luck. Nevertheless, I've heard this enough that I'd think twice about giving a system a DNS suffix that didn't match its Active Directory domain.*

Acme has two basic options for setting up its DNS, shown in Figures 7.45 and 7.46.

FIGURE 7.45

Acme with one
DNS zone

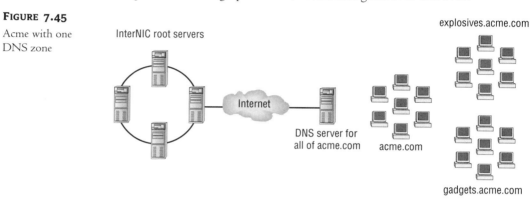

FIGURE 7.46

Acme with three
DNS zones

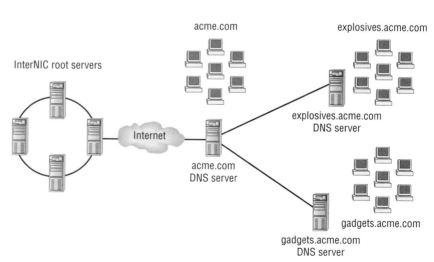

In Figure 7.45, Acme keeps things as they've been: There is one server that is the primary authority for all of Acme's machines. It's a perfectly fine answer, but not everyone may like it, as you'll probably guess if you recall my earlier example of my mythical Singapore office.

This is not, understand, a *wrong* answer; it's just one of several possible answers, and some may not like it. The folks in Belgium must rely on some network operators in Chicago to keep their machines properly listed in the DNS database, and it may be that every time Belgium needs some new machines and IP addresses stuffed into the database, it's morning in Belgium and the middle of the night in Chicago, so the Belgians get to wait. And, as they're the explosives guys, that might weigh heavily on the minds of the suits in Chicago when the Belgians ask for their own DNS server. Mexico could experience the same kinds of long-distance administration problems as the ones that Belgium faces. That could lead to the setup shown in Figure 7.46.

In Figure 7.46, Explosives has its own DNS server, and Gadgets has one of its own as well. The acme.com DNS server in Chicago has a pretty sparse database—basically, it just names a few machines in Chicago and then contains a few records that say, "While I *am* the acme.com DNS server, don't ask me about anything with a name like something-dot-explosives.acme.com or something-dot-gadgets.com; rather, go ask these other machines." Recall that in DNS terms, we'd say that the acme.com server has *delegated* name resolution for gadgets.acme.com to some DNS server in Mexico and delegated name resolution for explosives.acme.com to some other DNS server in Belgium.

Now, acme.com is still just one domain, but its DNS responsibilities—techies would say "DNS *namespace* duties"—have been spread out. What, then, to call these subsets of domains for which Acme's new DNS servers are authoritative? The term is *DNS zone* or *zone*. In Figure 7.45, Acme implemented its DNS as one zone. In Figure 7.46, Acme has three zones: its top-level acme.com zone, the explosives.acme.com zone, and the gadgets.acme.com zone.

How is this relevant to Active Directory? Well, if your network uses AD domains—and it will—then each domain requires a DNS zone of its own. So, for example, from the point of view of DNS in a no-AD world, Acme could implement acme.com, explosives.acme.com, and gadgets.acme.com as either one big zone, two zones, or three zones. Acme won't retain that flexibility if it creates Active Directory *domains* named acme.com, explosives.acme.com, and gadgets.acme.com; Active Directory would, in that case, require three separate zones.

FORWARD AND REVERSE LOOKUP ZONES

Thus far, I've described DNS's main task as converting host names such as kiwi.fruit.com to IP addresses such as 205.22.42.19. But DNS can do the reverse as well; you can ask a DNS server, "What host name is associated with IP address 205.22.42.19?"

The process of converting a host name to an IP address is called a *forward name resolution*. The process of converting an IP address to a corresponding host name is called *reverse name resolution*.

DNS maintains information about a given domain such as fruit.com in files called *zone files*. Fruit.com, then, has a zone file that DNS can use to look up kiwi.fruit.com's IP address. But where does DNS go to look up the host name associated with IP address 205.22.42.19?

Well, recall that the Internet authorities hand out blocks of addresses. There's a DNS zone called a *reverse lookup zone* for each Internet network. So, assuming that fruit.com's working with a class C network 205.22.42.0, it's someone's job to keep a reverse lookup zone for 205.22.42.0.

The *name* of the reverse lookup zone is odd, though. To construct it, take the dotted quads that the Internet authorities gave you—drop the ones that you control—and reverse them, then add .in-addr.arpa to the end of the name. Thus, whoever is responsible for 205.22.42.0 would create a reverse lookup zone 42.22.205.in-addr.arpa. A few other examples:

◆ 164.109.0.0/16, a class B network, would drop the two zeroed quads and reverse the remaining two to yield a reverse zone name of 109.164.in-addr.arpa. Notice there were only two dotted numbers, as it's a B network and the owner controls the bottom two quads.

- 4.0.0.0/8, a class A network, would have reverse zone 4.in-addr.arpa. In the case of an A network, only the top quad is set, so there's only one number in the reverse zone.
- 200.120.50.0/24, a class C network, would drop the zeroed quad and reverse the numbers to get a reverse zone name of 50.120.200.in-addr.arpa.

EXERCISE: CREATING THE BIGFIRM.BIZ ZONE

Let's see what's involved with setting up new DNS domain, or, to adopt the techier talk that you'll hear most DNS experts use, a DNS zone. Let's make a zone for bigfirm.biz. As it's going to be a zone where you hand the DNS server a computer's name, like mypc.bigfirm.biz, and get back an IP address, this will be a forward lookup zone. Here's how to create the bigfirm.biz zone.

1. Open up the DNS snap-in, if it's not already open: Start/Administrative Tools/DNS.
2. Next to the icon representing the server itself—the icon named bigdog—click the plus sign to open up the server object. (If there's a minus sign then you needn't do anything.)
3. Under bigdog, you'll see three folders: Forward Lookup Zones, Reverse Lookup Zones, and Event Viewer. Right-click the Forward Lookup Zones folder and choose New Zone, which starts up the New Zone Wizard. Click Next to see a figure like 7.47.

FIGURE 7.47

New zone options

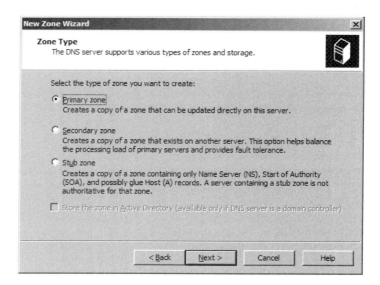

4. Notice that you have three options for a zone—Primary, Secondary, and Stub. We'll use a primary zone, so select that—actually it's probably already selected—and click Next to see a screen like Figure 7.48.
5. As the page suggests, fill in the zone name, which is bigfirm.biz in this case. Click Next to see a screen like Figure 7.49.

FIGURE 7.48

Name the zone

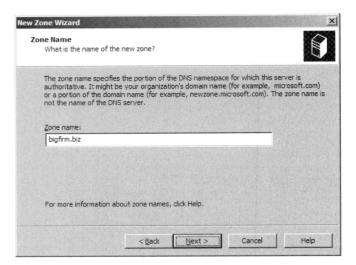

FIGURE 7.49

What to name the zone file

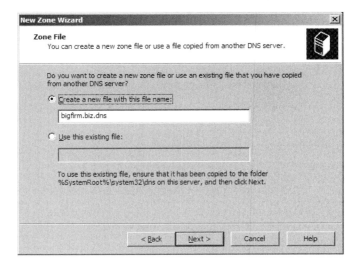

6. Most varieties of DNS servers store their zone information in an ASCII text file and by default Server 2003's DNS server is no exception. ("By default" because, as you'll see later, you can choose to store the DNS information in Active Directory's database.) Unless you tell it otherwise, the DNS server creates a file named *zonename*.dns. The DNS server stores these files in \windows\system32\dns. This is actually pretty convenient, as it makes disaster recovery on DNS a snap. If bigdog croaked, then you could cook up a replacement in a twinkling, assuming that you've got a backup of bigfirm.biz.dns. Just set up another 2000 or 2003 server as a DNS server, then take the bigfirm.biz.dns file from the old server and copy it to \windows\system32\dns on the new server. Run the wizard as we're doing here, but at this page in the wizard choose Use This Existing File and point the wizard at bigfirm.biz.dns.

7. To continue creating the bigfirm.biz zone, click Next to see a screen like Figure 7.50.

FIGURE 7.50

Dynamic update settings

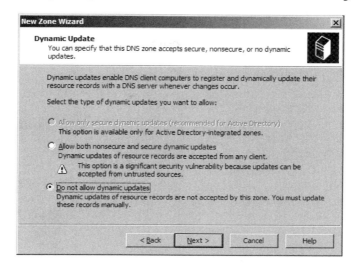

8. You'll learn about dynamic DNS a bit later, but briefly, it lets systems register information about themselves in DNS automatically, as they can with WINS servers. DNS only got this ability a few years ago, so the wizard has it disabled by default. But we're going to find it useful, so click Allow Both Nonsecure and Secure Dynamic Updates—don't worry about the dire-sounding warning—and click Next and Finish to create the zone.

9. Open the Forward Lookup Zones folder and you'll see a bigfirm.biz folder; click that in the left pane and you'll see something like Figure 7.51.

FIGURE 7.51

The bigfirm.biz zone, version 1

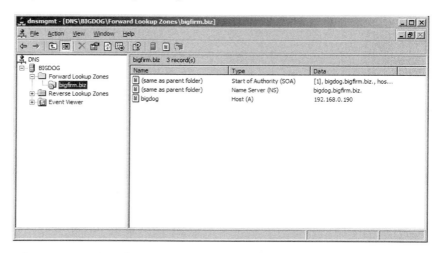

Notice that it's got three items in the right pane. They're called DNS records—"records" because it's a database—and notice that they're of three different "types"—something called an SOA, another called an NS, and a third called an A record. What's that all about? Read on.

BIGFIRM.BIZ OVERVIEW

I'd like to start introducing different types of DNS records and offer hands-on examples of them where possible in my mythical bigfirm.biz domain. So let's imagine that Bigfirm has a set of servers as depicted in Figure 7.52.

FIGURE 7.52

bigfirm.biz servers

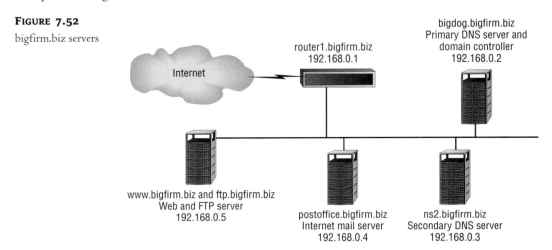

Now I'm going to get a bit more serious about structuring this example, so I've got to specify IP addresses. I'm going to build bigfirm.biz assuming that it uses a nonroutable class C network at 192.168.0.1.

There are just a few machines important enough that they must have entries in DNS:

◆ As I've mentioned before, it's convenient to name the router at 192.168.0.1.

◆ The mail server for bigfirm.biz is a machine named postoffice.bigfirm.biz, at 192.168.0.4.

◆ The Web server for bigfirm.biz is a machine named www.bigfirm.biz, at 192.168.0.5.

◆ That same 192.168.0.5 machine is also the FTP server, and we want it to respond to the name ftp.bigfirm.biz.

◆ The bigdog.bigfirm.biz machine that we've built already will, again, act both as a domain controller (once we set up AD in the next chapter) and as the primary DNS server. Please give it a static IP address of 192.168.0.2.

◆ There's another DNS server that also acts as a file server at ns2.bigfirm.biz with address 192.168.0.3.

SOME IMPORTANT NOTES ABOUT THIS EXAMPLE

As I've said, I've assigned addresses for these machines in the 192.168.0.0 range, which is a range of nonroutable addresses. (Recall that you learned about nonroutable addresses and Network/Port Address Translation in the previous chapter.) This implies a few things:

◆ If you set up this example with a few machines of your own, then these machines will be unable to access the public Internet, *unless* your router is a NAT/PAT router. Just set up the machine or machines with one of the IP addresses in the example and set the subnet mask to 255.255.255.0 and the default gateway to 192.168.0.1.

♦ You may recall from the previous chapter that Windows 2000 and later operating systems can act as NAT routers and that there's a kind of simplified NAT router called ICS that you can set up with just a click or two. ICS is set up to use addresses 192.168.0.1–192.168.0.254, which is one reason I designed this example with those addresses. Where I've got a hardware router pictured in Figure 7.52, you could be running a Windows 2000 or later system acting as the ICS router. In that case, you needn't set its IP address to 192.168.0.1 because, as you learned in the last chapter, enabling ICS automatically sets the IP address on the Ethernet card on the intranet side of the router to 192.168.0.1. Or, alternatively, your NAT/PAT router might simply be an existing corporate router or a DSL/cable modem dedicated router.

♦ Recall that systems with nonroutable addresses accessing the Internet via a NAT/PAT router such as ICS have the ability to *initiate* communications to the public Internet and systems on the public Internet can respond to queries from the systems with the nonroutable addresses, but systems on the public Internet cannot *initiate* conversations with nonroutable addresses. That means that these servers can only serve computers in their 192.168.0.*x* network. Systems on the public Internet could not access the Web or DNS servers, for example, unless you configured the NAT/PAT router to map ports on the publicly visible router to particular ports on servers in the 192.168.0.*x* network, or if you had extra routable IP addresses that you could then use the NAT/PAT router to assign to particular systems in the 192.168.0.*x* network. You saw in the previous chapter how to do that.

CHANGING BIGDOG'S IP ADDRESS

Previously, I said that you could give bigdog.bigfirm.biz any IP address that you wanted but, again, now I need to ask you to change its IP address to a static 192.168.0.2. You can do that from the GUI, as you learned in the last chapter, or from the command line with a `netsh` command:

```
netsh int ip set address name static 192.168.0.2 255.255.255.0 192.168.0.1 2
```

That command's all one line, even though it broke on the page. Either replace *name* with the full name of your NIC surrounded by quotes, as in

```
netsh int ip set address "Local Area Connection" static
    192.168.0.2 255.255.255.0 192.168.0.1 2
```

Or you can just specify the first part of the NIC's name without quotes, as in

```
netsh int ip set address local static 192.168.0.2 255.255.255.0 192.168.0.1 2
```

Then change its preferred DNS server, again as you've seen how to do it. If your NIC's name is Local Area Connection and there are no others, then this command would do it:

```
netsh int ip set dns local static 192.168.0.2 primary
```

As before, do an `ipconfig /all` and ensure that the value next to IP Address and DNS Servers is 192.168.0.2. Then restart the DNS server:

```
net stop dns & net start dns
```

If you've got the DNS snap-in running, close it and open it to ensure that it refreshes properly. You should see the bigdog A record report an IP address of 192.168.0.2.

Basic DNS Record Types

I've been referring vaguely to "DNS databases." Now let's consider in more detail exactly what these databases look like and what's in them. DNS databases contain several kinds of database records—there's more there than just names and IP addresses. Take a look at Figure 7.53, and you'll see a listing of some DNS records at the minasi.com domain. You've seen the DNS snap-in earlier; this is what it looks like with a real-live zone or two running on it.

FIGURE 7.53

Sample DNS records for a domain

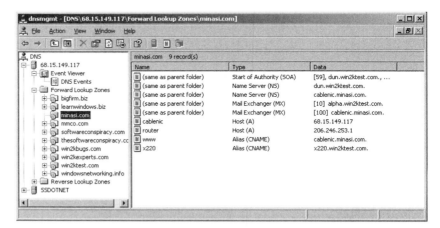

This is like the bigfirm.biz screen that you saw in Figure 7.51, but with a greater range of record types.

A RECORDS (HOSTS)

The simple record that says that cablenic.minasi.com is at IP address 68.15.149.117, the record that relates names to IP addresses, is called an *A record* or *host record*. (It's called an A record because DNS's internal database, a set of ASCII files called *zone files*, uses an *A* to indicate that a record is a host record.) Host records are usually the most numerous, although in this zone there are just two—the one for cablenic and the one for router. The router entry, by the way, does indeed point to the network's router. Giving the router a name isn't necessary; it just makes pinging it easier.

NOTE   I know I'm calling them A records *even though the graphical UI doesn't call them that. But I'm doing it because, again, zone files use the A designation—cablenic's record in a zone file might look like* `cablenic A 68.15.149.117`*—and I believe that you'll agree by the end of the chapter that you can get a lot done with zone files, from both an administration and troubleshooting standpoint. So throughout this section, I'll be presenting the records both as Server 2003's DNS refers to them and as zone files refer to them.*

Back in our simple bigfirm.biz example, notice that you have an A record—bigdog.bigfirm.biz. And because I've introduced information from an actual Internet domain (minasi.com), let me add the following important warning.

WARNING *This is very important. Please note that minasi.com and win2ktest.com are domains that I host. I use sample screen shots from them, but* please do not use the domain name win2ktest.com or minasi.com in your network. *If you're live on the Internet, that will make your system attempt to log in to my domain controllers and register records in my win2ktest.com or minasi.com zones (and that's just not polite, if you know what I mean!). That goes for other names that you'll see in this chapter as well, such as the acme.com references that you'll see around the book in examples. Someone owns that domain and would view attempts to log in to his domain or add records to his DNS servers as hostile acts, and take action accordingly. (After all, what would you do if you found some stranger taking up residence in your front room?) I've specifically driven many of my examples around a domain named bigfirm.biz because I own that domain, and honestly only bought it so that I'd have a nice example domain that I knew wouldn't cause anyone any heartburn. I strongly suggest when you're playing around with DNS zones that you ensure that you're not connected to the Internet, that you register a DNS domain name with the proper DNS name authorities such as www.network-solutions.com, or that you set up "split-brain DNS," which I'll describe later. That will ensure that you're a "good Internet citizen." Thanks!*

EXERCISE: ENTERING A OR HOST RECORDS

If you're following along in the bigfirm.biz example, then it's time to punch in records for each our servers:

◆ router.bigfirm.biz for 192.168.0.1

◆ ns2.bigfirm.biz for 192.168.0.3

◆ postoffice.bigfirm.biz for 192.168.0.4

◆ www.bigfirm.biz for 192.168.0.5

To create the first A record for router, right-click the `bigfirm.biz` folder and choose New Host (A) to see a dialog like the one in Figure 7.54.

FIGURE 7.54

Creating a host (A) record

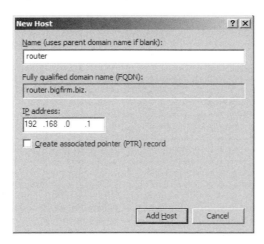

I've typed in router and entered the IP address 192.168.0.1; all I've got to do now is click Add Host, and I've got the record. Notice the Create Associated Pointer (PTR) Record check box; I would use this if I wanted to add not only my A record, which says, "If you ask me router.bigfirm.biz's address, I will tell you that it's 192.168.0.1," but also a *reverse* record, which says, "If you ask me what 192.168.0.1's name is, I will tell you that it's router.bigfirm.biz." A "reverse A record" is called a PTR record, and you put them in *reverse* lookup zones, which we discussed earlier. I haven't checked the box because I don't have a reverse zone set up, so there would be nowhere to put the PTR record.

Click Done, and DNS stores the record and confirms that it created the record. DNS then leaves the dialog up, making it simple to punch in more Host records. Enter the ns2, postoffice, and www records in the same way. When you've got them all in, click Done and the New Host dialog goes away.

CHEAP "CLUSTERS": BUILDING FAULT TOLERANCE WITH MULTIPLE A RECORDS AND ROUND-ROBIN DNS

This isn't a record type, but as long as I'm talking about A records, let me explain a great (and free!) way to handle a lot of Web traffic.

How Round Robin Works

Suppose I've got a Web server at IP address 206.246.253.100. I've named it www.minasi.com because, well, that's what people expect the Web server at minasi.com to be named. But now let's suppose that several thousand people all decide at the same time to hit my Web site to find out how to hire me to speak at their next engagement. (Hey, it could happen.) At that point, my poor Web server's overloaded, lots of people get some kind of "server is too busy to respond to you" message, and I lose lots of potential business. That would be bad. Really bad.

Alternatively, I could set up three more machines with IIS on them, at IP addresses 206.246.253.101 through 206.246.253.103. *Then*—and here's the clever part—I just enter host name records, A records, for each of them and name *all* of them www.minasi.com.

Now that I've got all four machines, each named www.minasi.com, suppose someone points her browser to www.minasi.com. My DNS server is then asked by *her* DNS server to resolve the name www.minasi.com. So my DNS server looks at the four addresses that have www.minasi.com and responds with the four IP addresses, saying, "You can find www.minasi.com at 206.246.253.100, .101, .102, and .103." Then, seconds later, someone else's DNS server asks my DNS server what IP address goes with www.minasi.com. My DNS server then responds with the same information, but in a different order, offering first 206.246.253.101, then .102, .103, and finally .100. The DNS client will usually take the first address offered first, so the first visitor will tend to go to .100, and the second to .101. The third person to ask about www.minasi .com gets the four addresses in the order of .102/.103/.100/.101, the fourth as .103/.100/.101/.102, and then for the fifth, DNS cycles back to .100/.101/.102/.103.

This process, called *round-robin DNS*, spreads out the load on a machine. If I had these four Web servers set up, they each would get roughly one-fourth of the incoming Web requests. In that way, I could build a "scalable" Web site. Now, understand that this *isn't* a replacement for Enterprise Edition and multisystem clusters. DNS has no idea what's going on with the various Web servers, and if one of them goes down, DNS knows nothing of the problem and just keeps giving out the bad server's IP address to every fourth inquirer. But it's a free way of doing load balancing and worth a try before spending tens of thousands of dollars on cluster systems.

NOTE   *Note that although I used an example of four consecutive IP addresses, you need not use consecutive addresses for your round-robin groups. Also, another great way to load-balance on Web servers is with Network Load Balancing Clusters, which you read about in the previous chapter.*

Exercise: Configuring Round Robin

If you'd like, you can try it out with bigfirm.biz. First, check that the round-robin feature is enabled on your DNS server. It's enabled by default, but you can control it from your server's Advanced Properties page. To see that, right-click the server's icon (bigdog in our example) and choose Properties, then Advanced to see something like Figure 7.55.

FIGURE 7.55

A DNS server's Advanced Properties page

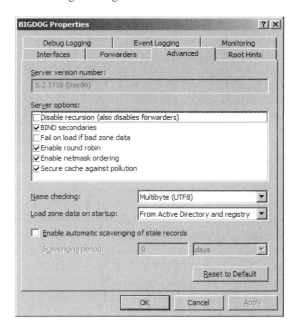

Note that one of the options is Enable Round Robin, and it's checked. As far as I know, you can only configure round robin at the server level, not the zone level—a DNS server that contained a lot of zones could not do round robin on one zone and not another. Click Cancel to remove the dialog box.

To see this in action, we'll add two more A records for the www host name for bigfirm.biz, giving them IP addresses 192.168.0.10 and 192.168.0.25. Remember that we already have a www.bigfirm.biz record at 192.68.0.5, so we'll end up with three possible answers for www.

Enter the A records for www at 192.168.0.10 and 192.168.0.25; when done, you should see all three www records in the bigfirm.biz folder in the DNS snap-in. Now try it out. Type **nslookup** and press Enter. Now type **www.bigfirm.biz** and press Enter. I get three addresses as an answer— 192.168.0.25, then 192.168.0.10, and then 192.168.0.5. (You may get a different order; if so, don't worry about it.) Now try it again; type **www.bigfirm.biz** and press Enter. I then get the three addresses again, but in a different order this time—.5, then .25, and then .10. Do it once more and I get yet another order—.10, then .5, and finally .25. (Again, you may see a different order; that's not important. What's important is that if you repeatedly query for www.bigfirm.biz, then you keep getting the three results, but in a different order.) Figure 7.56 shows a sample run that I got from my bigfirm.biz DNS server.

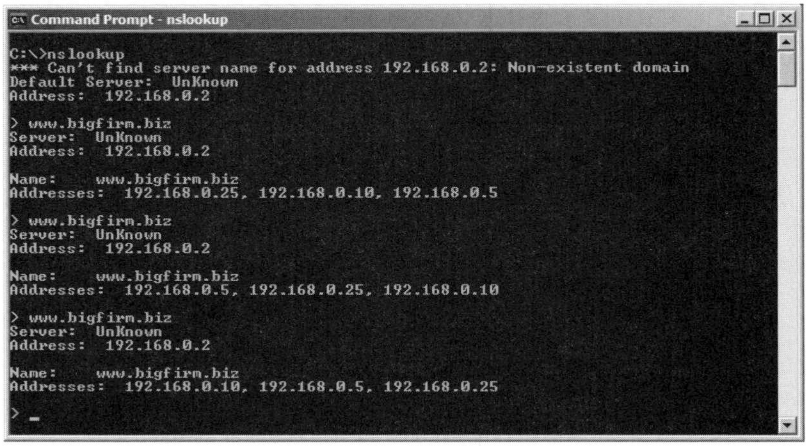

FIGURE 7.56

Round robin
in action

SIMPLE ROUTE OPTIMIZATION: SUBNET MASK ORDERING

If you've set up round-robin DNS, where you have several systems that have the same name but different IP addresses, then Server 2003–based DNS servers not only can do round robin for you, they can also ensure that clients get directed to the nearest server that matches their request.

Suppose I have 10 machines all named server1.minasi.com and 10 subnets on my network. Then suppose I have one of these machines on each subnet. Think about what happens when a computer on a particular subnet asks DNS to resolve server1.minasi.com. Simple round robin would just offer the 10 IP addresses in some random order. But clearly it'd make life easier on the routers if I could somehow tell DNS, "Listen—when someone asks for the IP address of server1.minasi.com, *and* if one of the server1.minasi.com systems is on the same subnet as that someone, then always offer the IP address of the *local* server1.minasi.com first." Server 2003's DNS server will do that—it's called *subnet mask ordering*. It is enabled by default. (You can turn it off in the Advanced tab of the DNS server's properties page, as you'll see if you look back to Figure 7.55.)

If you feel like seeing this in action, go to bigfirm.biz and delete the .10 and .25 entries for www.bigfirm.biz. Then create a www.bigfirm.biz entry in a different subnet, like 10.0.0.1. Then try the nslookup for www.bigfirm.biz. You'll still get two answers in return, but the 192.168.0.5 entry will always be the first one, because it's on the same subnet as the computer that you're sitting at— it's subnet mask ordering that makes that happen.

Go ahead and delete the .10 and .25 www records at this point, just to keep the zone simple.

SOA RECORDS (START OF AUTHORITY)

Every domain has a *start of authority* record, abbreviated in zone files as an *SOA* record. It's the record that names the primary DNS server for the domain, provides an e-mail address for an administrator for the domain, and specifies how long it's okay to cache its data. (I'll explain what a "primary" and a "secondary" DNS server are a bit later, but here's the short version: The primary DNS server for a zone contains the only read/write copy of the zone. Secondary servers—there can be as many as you like—contain read-only copies of the zone, so they can help.) It also alerts the outside world when any of the domain's records have changed through a serial number. In Figure 7.53, the [59] in the SOA record is the domain's serial number and indicates that since the domain was set up, there have been 52 changes—new records, deleted records, modified records. Secondary DNS servers can use this to see whether data on the primary server has changed, requiring them to go get updates from the primary DNS server.

Exercise: Examining an SOA Record

You can see (and modify) an SOA record for bigfirm.biz by just double-clicking the record in the folder that says "(same as parent folder) Start of Authority (SOA) [1]..." to see a dialog box like Figure 7.57.

FIGURE 7.57

SOA record for bigfirm.biz

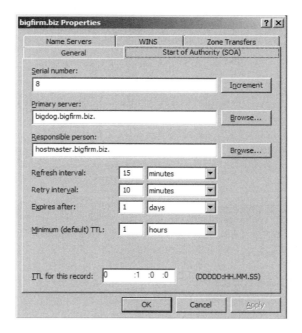

There's a whole *ton* of stuff in an SOA record, but it's not bad when taken one piece at a time.

First, there's the serial number. Note that in this case it's 8, which reflects the number of changes that I've made to the zone. If you want to increase it for some reason, then click the Increment button; just changing the number doesn't do anything.

Next, the primary DNS server is this machine, bigdog.bigfirm.biz. After that comes the Responsible Person, hostmaster.bigfirm.biz. What's that all about? I mentioned previously that the SOA record includes the e-mail address of the domain's administrator. And while hostmaster.bigfirm.biz doesn't look like any e-mail address that you've ever met, it's DNS's way of writing the more familiar-looking hostmaster@bigfirm.biz. For some historical reason you write the admin's e-mail address this way.

So if I wanted the SOA record to reflect my e-mail address, help@minasi.com, then I'd modify this to say help.minasi.com.

Notice something about the Primary Server field and the Responsible Person field—they're both written as fully qualified domain names. See the period at the end of the name? That's because all DNS records that aren't fully qualified get the domain's name added to them. Thus, if I specified the primary as bigdog.bigfirm.biz rather than bigdog.bigfirm.biz.—remember, that final period is the only difference—then the DNS server would think that I meant that the primary DNS server for bigfirm.biz should be called bigdog.bigfirm.biz.bigfirm.biz!

The remaining fields all describe important time intervals. The first two, Refresh Interval and Retry Interval, basically control how often secondary DNS servers return to this, the primary DNS server, for up-to-date information. As I've not covered secondaries yet, though, I'll return to these later.

Remember that when a DNS server gets information from another DNS server, the first one caches the information for some amount of time; if your DNS server looks up www.bigfirm.biz at 2 P.M. one day and you ask it for www.bigfirm.biz ten minutes later, then the DNS server's not about to go ask Bigfirm again where to find its Web site. But how long should your DNS server cache Bigfirm's information? However long Bigfirm tells it to. And here's where Bigfirm does that.

Minimum (Default) TTL advises other DNS servers how long to cache information received from this server. It's 60 minutes by default, so any DNS server that does a name resolution on bigfirm.biz and then needs the same name resolved 59 minutes later need not re-query one of the bigfirm.biz DNS servers. Sixty minutes is the Microsoft default, and personally I think it's a bit short—I'd set it somewhere between four hours and a day. The field is called Minimum TTL because every single record in a DNS zone file can have its own separate TTL. The vast majority of the time, however, you won't assign a specific TTL to a specific DNS record, so this "Minimum" TTL is probably more properly called a "Default" TTL. You can override that on any given record, and that's what the field at the bottom of the dialog does—you can use it to say "I don't care what the default TTL for this zone is, I want to set a different one *for just this SOA record.*"

NAME SERVER/NS RECORDS (DNS SERVERS)

Name server records (called *NS* records in a zone file) define the name servers in the domain. The two NS records in the minasi.com zone name the two DNS servers currently supporting the minasi.com DNS domain.

NOTE   *By the way, a single machine running DNS server software can act as a DNS server for as many zones as you like, within the limits of CPU power and memory space. You need not dedicate one server to one zone. Actually, you saw that in Figure 7.53; notice that this DNS server acts as a name server for several domains.*

Notice that both records look like "(same as parent folder) Name Server *servername.*" Notice that one of the servers' IP addresses (dun.win2ktest.com) isn't listed anywhere here. That's because it's a server on another domain. To find its IP address, you'd search DNS for its A records in the win2ktest.com zone.

NS Records and Delegation

Second, notice the "(same as parent folder)"; what that means is that these are name servers for this domain. But you can also use the NS records to delegate authority to a subdomain, a zone. An NS record for an imaginary zone westcoast.minasi.com might look like (in zone file terms):

```
westcoast   NS   surfers.earthlink.net.
```

That record would say, "To resolve names for *somename*.westcoast.minasi.com, go to surfers .earthlink.net."—notice again that the surfers address ends with a period and is an FQDN. Knowing how to create NS records that point to DNS servers for subdomain zones will come in handy later when you're seeing how to cope with non–2000/2003-based DNS servers.

Exercise: Working with and Creating NS Records

A look at bigfirm.biz will—or should, anyway, if you've been following along—show that record that says

```
(same as parent folder) Name Server (NS) bigdog.bigfirm.biz.
```

But I've suggested that we'll have two DNS servers for bigfirm.biz. In addition to bigdog, we'll also have a system ns2.bigfirm.biz. You've already entered ns2.bigfirm.biz's A record. Here's how to add it to the list of name servers—another name for DNS servers, in this case—for bigfirm.biz.

You'd expect, or at least *I* expected, that you could just right-click the bigfirm.biz folder and choose New Name Server (NS) Record or something like that, but for some reason you can't. Instead, right-click the `bigfirm.biz` folder and choose Properties and then click the Name Servers tab on the resulting property page to see something like Figure 7.58.

FIGURE 7.58

Name Servers tab for bigfirm.biz

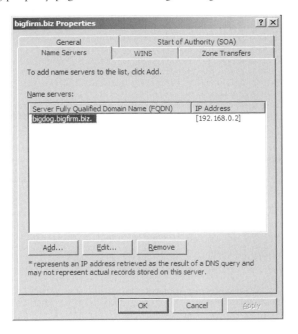

NS records are pretty simple, much simpler than an SOA record—you just tell the record what DNS server to add an NS record for. We can add ns2.bigfirm.biz's record by clicking Add to see a screen like Figure 7.59.

This dialog wants to know both the name and IP address of the new DNS server, but all you have to do is type the name into the Server Fully Qualified Domain Name (FQDN) field and click

Resolve, and the DNS server will go out and get its IP address for you. Note that this dialog box is smart enough that if you don't put a period on the end of the name—you type ns2.bigfirm.biz instead of ns2.bigfirm.biz.—it will add the period for you.

FIGURE 7.59

Adding
ns2.bigfirm.biz's
NS record

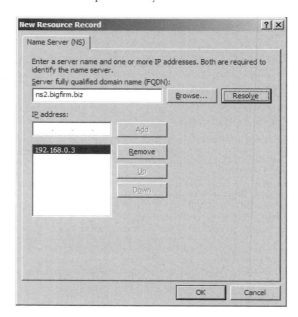

Click OK twice and you'll be back at the bigfirm.biz folder in the DNS snap-in. You should then see the new NS record.

CNAME RECORDS (ALIASES)

Many times, you'll need a host to respond to more than one name. For example, my Web server has two NICs in it and each has an IP address. One NIC is connected to my intranet and has the name dun.win2ktest.com; the other is connected to the public Internet and is called cablenic.minasi.com.

Using CNAME/Alias Records

When folks from the outside world want to visit my Web site, I want them to address my Web server through the cablenic.minasi.com interface. (By the way, please don't look at that configuration and try to make a lot of sense out of it—there are no deep insights on How to Design the Optimal Web Server, trust me. It's just a matter of "I need to get some time to straighten this thing out." Shoemaker's kids and all that.) So when someone punches www.minasi.com into a Web browser, I want that person to go to cablenic.minasi.com.

But how to make that happen?

Well, I could surrender and just rename cablenic.minasi.com. But now suppose this were also my ftp server that I wanted to name ftp.minasi.com? Basically here I'm saying that I want to take a particular IP address and give it multiple names. I do that with an Alias or CNAME record. A

CNAME record says something like, "If you need a machine to respond to www in this domain, then point to the machine at webpc.minasi.com." Notice how a CNAME record looks:

```
www  Alias(CNAME) cablenic.minasi.com.
```

Notice that the left portion only says *www*, not *www.minasi.com*. This is another example of how DNS handles fully qualified or non-fully qualified names. If you create a CNAME within a given domain, the CNAME must be for a name that ends with the domain's name, hence www rather than www.minasi.com. In contrast, the machine that it's being equated to, cablenic.minasi.com, need not be in the domain, and so its full name is entered in the DNS record, *including* the trailing period—leave off the period and it'll just add the zone's name and it'll think that you mean to equate www.minasi.com to cablenic.minasi.com.minasi.com!

CNAME, by the way, stands for *canonical name*. I don't know why they didn't use Alias from the very beginning—it's got the same number of letters—but for whatever reason, we call these CNAME records in the DNS business.

Only One CNAME to a Name, Please

For some reason, you're not allowed to have more than one of a given CNAME. For example, suppose I wanted to give the name www.minasi.com to both NICs on the server, that is, to both dun.win2ktest.com and cablenic.minasi.com. Can I create two CNAME www records in minasi.com?

You *can*, but it's not a good idea, or at least so I'm told. I've never found the particular RFC that says not to have multiple CNAMEs with the same alias name, but several threads on the message boards for BIND, the most popular DNS server, suggest that a BIND server might not handle multiple www CNAMEs in the same zone. So, while you can force your 2003-based DNS server to accept multiple CNAMEs with the same name by directly editing the zone files, you could run into trouble if the person trying to visit your Web site was resolving your DNS names with a BIND-based DNS server. So to be safe, don't do multiple CNAMEs with the same name.

Just to make this very clear:

◆ You *cannot* use CNAMEs to give more than one IP address the name www.

◆ You *can* use CNAMEs to give more then one name to a given IP address—I could use a CNAME to give the www.minasi.com *and* the ftp.minasi.com names to cablenic.minasi.com.

◆ There is no problem at all with multiple A records with the same name, as you saw when we did the www.bigfirm.biz round-robin exercise—there we created three different A records, all for www.bigfirm.biz. Adding three CNAMEs for www in bigfirm.biz would, again, not be kosher.

Exercise: Adding the ftp Name to Bigfirm's Web Server

I mentioned in my early description of Bigfirm that they've got a Web server with the host name www.bigfirm.biz, as you may recall. That system is also their ftp server. Now, they *could* tell the world to access their ftp server at www.bigfirm.biz, but they'd like to be able to tell people to go to ftp.bigfirm.biz and have that work. The answer here is to give www.bigfirm.biz a second name, ftp.bigfirm.biz, and a CNAME is just the answer.

Right-click the bigfirm.biz folder and choose New Alias (CNAME) to see a dialog box like Figure 7.60.

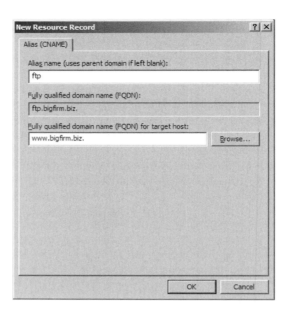

FIGURE 7.60

Adding a new
CNAME

You can see that I've filled in the new alias, ftp, as well as the host name that it'll be associated with. Note that I only filled in ftp, not ftp.bigfirm.biz. Click OK and you've got an alias. An `nslookup` of ftp.bigfirm.biz will look like

```
Name:       www.bigfirm.biz
Address:    192.168.0.5
Aliases:    ftp.bigfirm.biz
```

MX RECORDS (MAIL EXCHANGE)

If I send mail to `bill@acme.com`, then I've told my e-mail program that I want the mail to go to someone named Bill and that Bill has an account on some server in the acme.com domain.

MX Records: Enabling Flexible Mail Addresses

What I *haven't* told my e-mail program is where exactly to send the e-mail for Bill, what his mail server's name is. If it's not immediately obvious why this is important, consider: If you know that my domain is named minasi.com, how do you know where to find my Web or FTP server? There's an *informal* convention in the world that I'd call my Web server www.minasi.com and my FTP server ftp.minasi.com, but nothing *requiring* that. You can't simply tell your Web server, "Go check out the minasi.com Web site." But you *can* tell an e-mail program, "Send this mail to minasi.com." That's because DNS includes something called a *mail exchange* or *MX* record, which answers the question, "Which machine is the mail server for minasi.com?"

Look back to Figure 7.53 and you'll see that my domain has two MX records; these answer the "which server to send the e-mail to?" question. A mail server would read that information and understand that mail for `someone@minasi.com` should go to the machine named alpha.win2ktest.com—a machine in a completely different DNS domain.

MX and Mail Fault Tolerance

Why wouldn't the distant mail server send mail to the server named in the other MX record, dun.win2ktest .com? Because of the number in square brackets—notice that the MX record for alpha.win2ktest.com is [10] and the number on the second NS record, the one for cablenic.minasi.com, is [100].

My main e-mail server, alpha, is a Linux box that runs an e-mail server called sendmail. It's pretty reliable, but its NIC is connected to the less-reliable of my two ISPs. (Actually, it's not the ISP's fault. The problem is that the frame relay between them and me is run by Verizon, and they can't seem to keep it up. That's why the www CNAME was connected to the cablenic [the NIC connected to the cable company's Internet connection] rather than dun [the NIC connected to Verizon].)

When alpha's disconnected from the Internet, then I need a place for my incoming mail to go. My Web server has the simple SMTP service that comes with IIS, and of course that's not a full mail server. But it *is* enough to receive incoming mail and to hold onto it until the main mail server, alpha, comes back online. So I run the SMTP service on the Web server and add its name as my "use in the event that alpha's not working" e-mail server. But again, how do I tell outside mail servers to prefer alpha over cablenic?

Notice that the MX record for alpha.win2ktest.com has a "priority" number in brackets, [10]. In contrast, cablenic.minasi.com's MX record has a priority number of [100]. With the priority number, you indicate to DNS which mail server you prefer—lower numbers are preferred over higher numbers. Giving cablenic a priority of 100 means that no one ever tries to deliver to it unless alpha's not responding. Then, when alpha's back up, cablenic hands it the mail.

I am told that if you specify two MX records of the same priority, then DNS will end up load-balancing the two mail servers, but I've never tried this.

Exercise: Adding an MX Record

Bigfirm's only got one mail server, postoffice.bigfirm.biz. Let's tell the world to send any mail to *anyname*@bigfirm.biz to postoffice.bigfirm.biz.

Right-click the bigfirm.biz folder and choose New Mail Exchanger (MX) and you'll see a dialog like Figure 7.61.

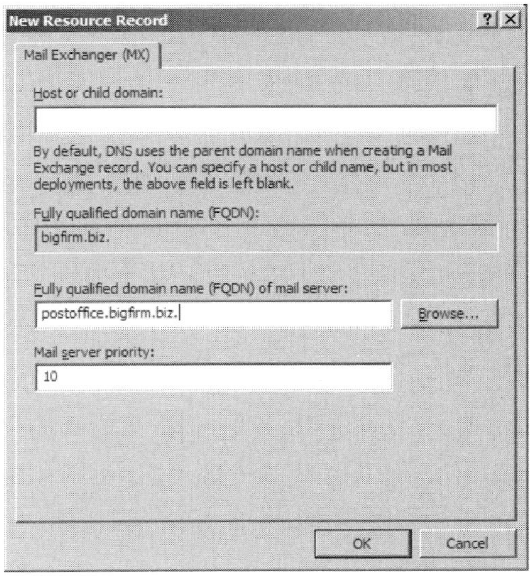

FIGURE 7.61

Adding an MX record to bigfirm.biz

Notice that I didn't put anything in the Host or Child Domain field. That's because for many DNS records, "blank" means "fill in the name of this domain automatically." As this will be an MX record for bigfirm.biz and this is bigfirm.biz's zone file, just leave that field blank. In the Fully Qualified Domain Name (FQDN) of Mail Server field, I fill in postoffice's FQDN. The dialog box offers a priority of 10, which works just fine. Click OK to accept the new record.

SRV RECORDS

The record types you've read about so far have been around for quite some time. But SRV records are new—they first appeared in RFC 2052 (a 1995 document) and were later revised in RFC 2782. They are, however, essential to the Active Directory. You simply cannot run an Active Directory without DNS servers that understand SRV records.

SRV records are fairly long; here's an example:

```
_kerberos._tcp.marksite._sites.dc._msdcs 600 SRV 0 100 88 dc1.win2kbugs.com.
```

SRV records let DNS become a sort of "directory of services" for a domain. For example, if I tell you that my domain's name is minasi.com, how would you know the name of the Web server for that domain? By convention, you'd guess—it's just a guess—that the name of the Web server for minasi.com is www.minasi.com. But what if I wanted to call my Web server something other than "www" and still have you able to find it? I can't, as our common convention for naming Web servers is inflexible. Similarly, how would you find my FTP server, if I had one? You'd guess that its name would be ftp.minasi.com. Fine, so long as I only have one FTP server and want to call that computer ftp.minasi.com, but troublesome otherwise.

If it's still not clear why this might be a problem, consider this real-world example: Suppose I go to Bigfirm's headquarters to apply for a job. How would I find the HR office in the Bigfirm building, presuming that's where I go to apply for a job? Well, if we assigned rooms in corporate buildings the way that we assign names for Web and FTP servers, then we'd have some kind of convention such as, "The HR office is always in room 120, no matter what company we're talking about—*every* company's HR office must be in room 120." Sound like it might cramp your style? It probably would, which is why we have a building directory on the first floor of most buildings.

Anatomy of an SRV Record

Put simply, an SRV record lets you say, "If you're looking for *this* kind of server, it's over *there*." More specifically, SRV records let you identify a server or servers who

- ◆ Run a particular service.
- ◆ Run on either the TCP or UDP protocol.
- ◆ Live in a particular DNS domain.

Once retrieved, the SRV record tells you the name of the server or servers who meet those criteria, as well as telling you what TCP or UDP port to address them on to access that service. Additionally, because you can specify more than one server, you can also give different servers different priorities, as we could the MX record priorities.

Service, Protocol, and Domain Information

Let's start examining SRV records with a really simplified SRV record:

```
_kerberos._tcp.bigfirm.biz. SRV dc1.bigfirm.biz.
```

This isn't a complete SRV record and wouldn't work, but it's a perfectly good starting point.

The left part has three pieces to it: a service, a protocol, and a domain. In this case, _kerberos is the service, _tcp is the protocol, and bigfirm.biz is the domain. This oversimplified SRV record, then, says, "If you're looking for a Kerberos server that you access via TCP (rather than UDP) that serves the bigfirm.biz DNS domain, then go to dc1.bigfirm.biz." Kerberos is a service that does authentication for Active Directory and other OSes as well. As you've already learned in Chapter 6, TCP is the connection-oriented way to establish communications over IP, and of course bigfirm.biz is just the name of our example domain. I guess they add the underscore to the front of the name to avoid accidental collisions with existing servers; calling the record kerberos.tcp.bigfirm.biz instead of _kerberos._tcp.bigfirm.biz is a bit more readable, but there's the small probability that some other system already has that name (really small).

What other services are there? There's a list of common services in the ASCII text file `\windows\system32\drivers\etc\services`, but you can use any service name that you like. Suppose I came up with a completely new kind of service called engspa, a service to which you could give a block of English text and that would return the equivalent translated Spanish text. As it's a simple question-and-answer system, I might implement it over UDP. I could then develop and offer engspa server software and people could put it on servers on the Internet. Then I'd develop engspa client software, maybe an add-in for Internet Explorer. You'd just grab some English text and paste it into the engspa window in IE. IE would then look around for an engspa server to translate the text for it...but how to find such a server? With an SRV record. Perhaps Bigfirm runs an engspa server on a computer called polyglot.bigfirm.biz. It might then advertise this with this (oversimplified) SRV record:

```
_engspa._udp.bigfirm.biz. SRV polyglot.bigfirm.biz.
```

Don't get the idea that there's any magic here; whoever writes the engspa client program has to write code into that program to teach the engspa client software to go ask for an SRV record named _engspa._udp in whatever domain it's working in. And *somebody* has to insert the SRV records for the engspa servers. But it's a nice standard way to announce services. Or here's another example. Remember, I pointed out that in order for people to find your Web servers you pretty much have to name them www? Well, if our Web browsers were smart enough to understand SRV records, then we could tell the world that Bigfirm's Web server was named spider.bigfirm.biz with an imaginary record looking something like

```
_http._tcp.bigfirm.biz. SRV spider.bigfirm.biz.
```

HTTP is the technical name of the Web service, and as far as I know all Web transfers are TCP, hence the _http._tcp. Again, this will not currently work, as Web client software—browsers—isn't programmed to look for SRV records. In an Active Directory you will only see four services:

♦ _kerberos is the authentication service.

♦ _kpasswd is a secure service for changing passwords.

◆ _ldap is the Lightweight Directory Access Protocol, the language that programs use to talk to the Active Directory.

◆ _gc is just LDAP, but Microsoft gives it another name because "gc" is the service that talks to a subset of domain controllers called Global Catalog servers. (You'll meet GCs in the next chapter.)

You actually wouldn't write even my oversimplified SRV records as I've been writing them—do you see why? I've been including the FQDNs of the names just to make them easier to read. But in the DNS world, we tend not to use FQDNs on the left side of DNS records. My Kerberos, engspa, and Web server examples would probably look more like these:

```
_kerberos._tcp SRV dc1.bigfirm.biz.
_engspa._udp SRV polyglot.bigfirm.biz.
_http._tcp SRV spider.bigfirm.biz.
```

The difference makes for shorter records, but they're not as clear; nevertheless, that's the standard.

Ports, Priorities, and TTLs

I have been referring to my example SRV records as "oversimplified" because they don't match actual in-the-real-world SRV records like this one:

```
_kerberos._tcp.marksite._sites.dc._msdcs 600 SRV 0 100 88 dc1.win2kbugs.com.
```

Let's take it apart and see what we *do* know about it. First, what does _kerberos._tcp.marksite._sites.dc._msdcs tell us? Well, we see from _kerberos that it's a Kerberos server—that is, a domain controller—and runs Kerberos over TCP. What's the rest of the left part, marksite._sites.dc._msdcs? It's a subdomain. This is a record in a DNS domain called win2kbugs.com, but an Active Directory domain named win2kbugs.com doesn't register domain controllers as simply _kerberos._tcp .win2kbugs.com; instead, Microsoft designed AD to take your domain and make subdomains in it, and subdomains in that, and subdomains in that, and so on. marksite._sites.dc._msdcs means that when AD created win2kbugs.com, it also created a subdomain of win2kbugs.com called _msdcs .win2kbugs.com, and a subdomain inside that called dc._msdcs.win2kbugs.com, and a subdomain inside *that* called _sites.dc._mscds.win2kbugs.com, and finally, a subdomain inside that called marksite._sites.dc._msdcs.win2kbugs.com. (Microsoft had their reasons, trust me. And don't worry, these subdomains get built automatically when you create an AD, as you'll see in the next chapter.)

So far, then, we know that there's an SRV record for a Kerberos server using TCP in a subdomain of win2kbugs.com.

Next, there's 600 SRV. The SRV part you know. The 600 is a record-specific TTL. Remember TTLs (time to live)? This says that if you look this record up, then you can cache it, but only for 600 seconds. In other words, once you know that this is a domain controller for win2kbugs.com, don't count on it still being one in ten minutes—go back and check before you try to authenticate to it in the future.

Then there are two more numbers, 100 and 88. 88 is the port that the service runs on. A computer in an Active Directory asks, "Are there any Kerberos-over-TCP servers in win2kbugs.com? I'd like to log on." DNS responds, saying, "Sure, we've got a server named dc1.win2kbugs.com that does that—it does it on port 88." Sort of like walking into a shopping mall and asking the information booth, "Are there any bookstores in this mall?" and getting the answer, "Sure, there's one at store location 233."

Finally, the 100 is a priority number and it works just like the MX record's priority numbers. If I had a bunch of _kerberos._tcp SRV records for a given Active Directory domain, then that would be the domain's way of saying that it has more than one Kerberos server, or, put differently, more than one server that can provide authentication or logon services—put one final way, more than one domain controller. (These phrases honestly do mean the same thing.) But which to use? Pretty much any one that you want, *so long as they have the same priority level.* Suppose DNS told you about five different domain controllers, three with priority 50 and two with priority 100. You would attempt to contact each of the priority 50 DCs before you even considered the priority 100 systems. By default, AD gives all DCs the same priority, 100. But you might want to monkey with the priorities to bias your systems towards or against a particular DC; this is how you'd do it. More on this next chapter.

To summarize, then, this SRV record:

```
_kerberos._tcp.marksite._sites.dc._msdcs 600 SRV 0 100 88 dc1.win2kbugs.com.
```

says, "There is a Kerberos server using TCP (that is, a domain controller) in the marksite._sites.dc_ msdcs subdomain of win2kbugs.com at dc1.win2kbugs.com. It will respond to Kerberos requests when addressed via TCP port 88. You should use a priority weighting of 100 for this, which is to say that if you see similar records for other Kerberos servers with smaller priority numbers, then use them first, before this one. If you're caching this record, please don't cache it for more than 600 seconds."

Don't let SRV records scare you. There's a lot of information there, but much of it is specific to the program using it. In the Active Directory world, we can completely ignore SRV records most of the time, as they're handled automatically. But when we're troubleshooting AD problems, then knowing SRVs will come in handy—you'll see more on that in the next chapter.

INTRODUCTION TO PTRs: REVERSE LOOKUP ZONES REVISITED

Those are the common record types you'll find in a forward lookup zone. Now let's consider reverse lookup zones. In general, they have a smaller variety of records: they have SOAs and NS records, as do all zones, and PTR or "pointer" records.

A *pointer record* works just like a host record—an A record—except that where you use an A record to look up the IP address associated with a given host name, a pointer record lets you look up a host name associated with a particular IP address. But before we worry too much about PTR records, let's revisit the home of PTR records—that is, reverse lookup zones; that'll provide me an excuse to cover PTR records.

Do You Need a Reverse Lookup Zone at All?

In the perfect world, every computer would have at least two records about it in DNS: an A record to identify it by name, and a PTR record to identify it by IP address. In the real world, many systems do not have PTR records, and in fact you can probably run a network for years without either reverse lookup zones or PTR records with no worse side effects than those irritating "unable to find server" messages when you start nslookup.

Before you start worrying too much about this, I should explain that in some cases you not only needn't set up a reverse lookup zone, you may actually be *unable* to. If you own the bigfirm.biz domain, then you clearly get to set up and manage the corresponding zone file because, again, you own it.

But reverse lookup zones aren't oriented toward DNS names; they're oriented toward ranges of IP addresses. Who owns those IP addresses? Well, that sorta depends. If you're like me, and have a small range of addresses, either a C network or a CIDR block, then it's not like you got that block straight from the IANA guys; the Big Internet Authorities don't handle IP allocations under a few tens of thousands at a clip. That means that as far as the Big Internet Authorities are concerned, *your ISP* owns your IP addresses, at least reverse DNS-wise.

Some ISPs insist on managing the reverse zones, so your ISP might say, "You've got DNS responsibility for bigfirm.biz, and you've got the addresses in such-and-such range of IP addresses, but we'll keep track of its reverse lookup zone for those IP addresses." You can ask yours if you can be authoritative for your network, but if they won't let you, it's not the end of the world.

As far as I can see, there are no mandatory reasons for running or controlling the reverse lookup zones for your IP addresses. I've seen four reasons to control a reverse lookup zone:

◆ Having a reverse lookup zone avoids the annoying "UnKnown" complaints from `nslookup`.

◆ If your internal network connects to the Internet by dialing up, then having a reverse lookup zone avoids a lot of unnecessary connections, perhaps saving you on phone charges.

◆ Some Internet servers will not communicate with you unless your forward and reverse lookups match.

◆ If it appears that one of your systems is attacking another system on the Internet, then it's polite to allow the attackee to look up your domain name and thereby find contact information so as to call or e-mail you and say, "Knock it off!"

Let's consider this separately.

A Reverse Lookup for nslookup

Depending on how your network is set up, starting `nslookup` on bigdog.bigfirm.biz results in one of two kinds of responses. `nslookup`'s first output probably looks something like this if you've set it up as I've suggested:

```
C:\>nslookup
*** Can't find server name for address 192.168.0.2: Timed out
Default Server: UnKnown
Address: 192.168.0.2
>
```

That may even be preceded by some complaining about the server timing out. What's causing this annoying message? A quirk of `nslookup`. Remember that you're sitting at Bigdog and that Bigdog not only runs DNS *server* software, it also runs DNS *client* software. In fact, virtually every system that you run nowadays runs the DNS *client* software—without it, that system wouldn't know how to query DNS, and if you can't query DNS you can't get very far in an TCP/IP-based network, whether it's connected to the public Internet or not.

When you start `nslookup` on Bigdog, it asks the DNS client software on Bigdog, "Who's your preferred DNS server?" We've configured Bigdog to prefer itself for DNS queries and Bigdog's IP address is 192.168.0.2, so the DNS client software responds, "192.168.0.2." For reasons known only to `nslookup`'s designer, `nslookup` then says, "Well, let's go see what DNS name this server has," and of course the only way to do that is to do a reverse lookup on the zone named 0.168.192.in-addr.arpa. So `nslookup` asks the DNS server—that is, the one running on Bigdog—to look up the specific 2 PTR entry in the 0.168.192.in-addr-arpa zone—"2" because Bigdog's IP address is 192.168.0.2.

This leads to a problem. There isn't a server with a 0.168.192.in-addr.arpa zone. Remember, 192.168.x.x is a range of addresses set aside for private networking. There are, then, thousands, hundreds of thousands, maybe millions of small networks using 192.168.x.x addresses. You might have a system at 192.168.0.2 and I might have one with the same IP address, and we don't conflict with each other because (1) we're not on the same physical network, and (2) we're using addresses that everyone agrees should not be routed over the Internet.

So when `nslookup` asks your DNS server who does reverse lookups for the 192.168.0.x range of IP addresses, then of course there's no server to do that. But we can fix that—let's create a reverse lookup zone for 192.168.0.x. It'll only be visible from inside our network; outsiders won't be able to use it to reverse-resolve entries in our reverse lookup zone, but who cares? They're nonroutable addresses anyway so there wouldn't be any point in them even trying to reverse-resolve our internal systems.

1. Open the DNS snap-in.
2. Right-click the `Reverse Lookup Zones` folder and choose `New Zone`.
3. That opens the New Zone Wizard; click Next, and, as before, choose Primary Zone and Next. You'll see a wizard page like Figure 7.62.

FIGURE 7.62

Naming a reverse lookup zone

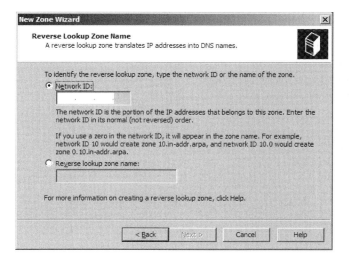

4. In the Network ID field, enter the network number for your subnet—**192.168.0**. Then click Next and again click Next.
5. In the Dynamic Update page, choose Allow Both Nonsecure and Secure Dynamic Updates, then Next and Finish.

Creating a PTR Record

Here's a perfect opportunity to see how to create a PTR record. Let's create one for Bigdog. You'll now have a folder inside `Reverse Lookup Zones` labeled `192.168.0.x Subnet`; right-click it and choose New Pointer (PTR) to see a dialog like Figure 7.63.

FIGURE 7.63

Creating a new PTR record

Fill in the last quad of the IP address—**2**—and the fully qualified domain name of the host; just "bigdog" won't do it here.

Now try `nslookup`; you'll see a response of

```
Default Server: bigdog.bigfirm.biz
Address:  192.168.0.2
>
```

We now have the Bigdog heeling properly, so to speak. Before I leave this, though, let me make one point that we'll return to a bit later. As I've suggested already, this DNS server now satisfies the need for a reverse zone, but it will only do that for systems that use this DNS server as their preferred DNS server. Tell a client to prefer some other DNS server and start up `nslookup`, and you'll be back to the old complaints.

Reducing the Mysterious Dial-Ups

Many people run a small network that only connects to the Internet via some kind of dial-up connection, either a simple modem or ISDN. If you're in that company, then you have my sympathy; in the game of networking, modems are the dice. They're unreliable and hard to troubleshoot, as I'm reminded every time I travel. In any case, if you connect your internal network to the Internet via some kind of dial-up, then you may find that your connect charges go through the roof when you first install Windows 2000 or later systems, either workstations or servers, on your network.

Here's what's going on: Windows 2000 Professional, 2000 Server, XP Pro, XP Home, and Server 2003 all include a dynamic DNS client. While we haven't talked about dynamic DNS much yet, I've mentioned the basic purpose of it: with DDNS, a system can insert its own records into DNS. For example, a mail server might insert its own MX records into DNS, or a domain controller might insert its own SRV records into DNS, or, more commonly, any system might insert its own A and PTR records into DNS.

That's where the problem comes in. You're running your network with some set of nonroutable addresses, like 192.168.x.x. A workstation or server wakes up, gets a set of IP addresses from DHCP or perhaps has a static address, and wants to register a PTR record. But where does it go? Who's the official receiver of dynamic PTR registrations for the 192.168.x.x IP range?

Well, as you read in the last section, there isn't one, as it's a private range. But the dynamic client on DNS tries to find the DNS server for PTR records in 192.168.x.x and register with it. And where does that search take it? Out to the Internet root servers. That's what's causing those mysterious dial-ups. A system starts up and wants to register, or perhaps a system renews a DHCP lease, which also triggers a reregistration. The system asks its DNS server who to go to with registrations for 192.168.x.x, and so the DNS server looks for that server.

The IANA has created a catch-all server for reverse registrations on the three ranges of nonroutable addresses. It doesn't accept dynamic registrations, but at least it's there, so DNS servers don't waste their time trying and retrying to find that authoritative DNS server for the reverse lookup zones of the nonroutable ranges. The IANA servers have an interesting set of names: blackhole-1.iana.org and blackhole-2.iana.org. An SOA record reveals that the *primary* DNS server is named prisoner.iana.org.

This freaks network administrators out who are trying to troubleshoot some network problem; they start looking at network logs and see references to prisoner.iana.org or blackhole-something-or-other.iana.org—sure sounds like a hacker site, doesn't it? Well, it isn't. Messages like that mean that your system's just trying to register their PTR records.

How can you kill off these pointless searches and stop the unwanted dial-ups? The same way that we made `nslookup` happy—just create that reverse zone and make it dynamic. It'll happily take your registrations, and your systems will stop looking for the prisoner in his black hole.

Pleasing Servers That Match Forward and Reverse Lookups

This is less of an issue than it once was, but back in the old days I was unable to access some news group (NNTP) servers or FTP servers unless my workstation's forward resolution matched its reverse resolution. When I'd try to access some FTP site, then unknown to me, it would see my incoming IP address, and it would do a reverse lookup on that address. The reverse lookup would tell the FTP server my computer's FQDN. The FTP server would then look up that FQDN in DNS to get an IP address. That IP address had to match my IP address, or the server assumed that I was an evildoer.

It wasn't a bad way to ensure that someone's actually who they say they are, but it doesn't work in today's world. If an ISP gives you a block of addresses, then the ISP either doesn't bother populating its reverse lookup zones, or fills them with generic names. For example, if I had IP address 200.100.100.5 and my ISP ran the reverse lookup zone for 200.100.100.x, then it might insert a PTR record for 5 called Host5.subnet200100100.myisp.net. Thus, if someone asks the Internet's DNS servers what the name of 200.100.100.5 is, it'll be told host5.subnet200100100.myisp.net. Now, that's not anything *like* what I named my system, so as far as I'm concerned the PC probably has a name like markspc.bigfirm.biz. The mismatch would cause the FTP, news, or whatever server to reject me unless the ISP took the time to actually create forward lookup zones that match the FQDNs in the reverse lookup zones. Or alternatively, I suppose I could call my ISP up every time I rename a system and ask them to update my PTR record...yuck. Thankfully, this authentication approach is not very common anymore. Note that setting up a local in-addr.arpa zone would *not* solve this problem because the outside world would not know to ask your local DNS server about that reverse lookup zone, as your DNS server's not authoritative for that zone.

Helping Outsiders Find You

In the late fall of 2001, the Nimda worm made its way around IIS-based Web servers around the world. The worm causes your IIS server to try to find and infect other IIS servers. You can patch your system against Nimda, and one would hope as you're reading this that *everyone* with an infected system would have found and fixed it.

A vain hope, sadly.

I can set up a new IIS server, wait a few days, and look in its logs. Believe it or not, in that time I'll see some idiot or, more likely, several idiots have tried to infect my Web server. What causes this? Someone sets up an NT 4 or 2000 server and both of those OSes install a Web server, whether you asked for it or not. The server gets infected, but the guy using it doesn't notice, because he never uses the Web function. Okay, my Web server's patched against Nimda and friends, but it's still irritating.

My Web log tells me only the IP address of the Web server, not its name or owner. How do I find the unwitting Webmaster, smack him upside the head, and say, "Willya *please* shut that thing off?" With a reverse lookup.

Unfortunately for reasons we've already seen, not everyone can or does set up reverse lookup zones. If you can, however, then it's a good way to help the outside world warn you that one of your systems is Doing Something Bad.

Fault Tolerance: Primary and Secondary DNS Servers

Now that we've got *one* DNS server running, let's next consider how to make this DNS database highly available and fault-tolerant.

If a ton of people all decide at the same time to come surf www.bigfirm.biz, then that means that a ton of *DNS servers* will all be trying at the same time to resolve the address www.bigfirm.biz. But what if I only have one DNS server? That's asking for trouble. It'd be nice if I had more than one DNS server containing a copy of the bigfirm.biz zone file; then those servers could share some of the burden of name resolution. (Of course, those extra DNS servers had better be listed in the DNS servers for the biz domain—if a DNS server isn't recognized as authoritative by being listed in its parent's DNS servers, then no one will ever know to even *try* to query the DNS server.)

But that might be a bit chaotic. Suppose I've got five DNS servers that all hold a copy of the bigfirm.biz zone file. When I want to make a change to the zone file, perhaps to add or delete an A record, how do I do that? Must I make the identical change to each of the five copies of the zone file by hand? That doesn't sound like much fun.

Fortunately, I needn't do that. DNS has a built-in system for managing updates to a zone's file. Here's how it works. Each domain has one and only one "primary" DNS server. That's the one that you make changes and updates to the zone file on. And when you set up a DNS server for a particular domain, you must tell the DNS server whether it is the primary DNS server for that domain. As I suggested a few pages back, you designate which DNS server is authoritative for a given zone by naming that DNS server in the SOA record for the zone. You can have only one primary DNS server for a given zone.

NOTE   *A zone's primary DNS server is the only one that can accept additions, deletions, or changes to DNS records for that zone.*

SECONDARY DNS SERVERS HOLD READ-ONLY ZONE COPIES

You can have as many *secondary* DNS servers for a zone as you like, however. When you set up a zone on a DNS server, you tell the DNS server whether it should act as the primary DNS server or secondary DNS server for the zone. If it's to be a secondary DNS server, then you must tell the DNS server that is the primary DNS server for that zone, so that the secondary knows where to go to get the "official" copy of the zone files.

NOTE   *Note that any DNS server can act as the primary server for more than one zone. In fact, a DNS server can simultaneously act as the primary server for several zones while at the same time also acting as a secondary server for several zones. DNS servers can hold any number of zones. So it's never meaningful to talk simply of a "primary DNS server"; rather, a DNS server can only be primary or secondary for a particular DNS domain or zone.*

HOW PRIMARY AND SECONDARY DNS SERVERS SYNCHRONIZE

As the zone files change, you need some kind of mechanism to update the zone files on the secondaries on a regular basis or, to use another popular phrase, to *replicate* the zone files. Here are the mechanics of how DNS servers stay in sync.

Recall that you make any changes to a zone on the primary DNS server for that zone; if you were to make a change to a zone on a secondary server for that zone, then the change would be lost. So how do those changes on the primary get synchronized to the secondaries?

When the primary learns something new, it does *not* contact the secondaries; rather, it's normally the job of the secondaries to periodically ask the primary if there are any changes. Five things cause a replication:

When you start up a secondary server for a zone   If you restart the DNS service on a DNS server that happens to be a secondary for a given zone, then the DNS server contacts the primary for that zone to get the latest zone data.

When you force a zone transfer   If your DNS server is secondary for a zone, you can force it to get a new copy of the zone from the primary by right-clicking the folder for the zone and choosing Transfer from Master to simply update the changes, or Reload from Master to completely wipe the local copy of the zone clean and reload it from the primary DNS server for that zone.

When the zone data expires   Remember when I showed you an SOA record and told you that I'd explain three of the numbers (refresh interval, retry interval, and expires after) when we got to secondaries? Here's the time. The refresh interval tells a zone's secondary DNS servers to ask the primary every 15 minutes, "May I see your SOA record?" The secondary asks about the primary's SOA record because it will then use the *serial number* on the primary to determine whether something has changed—see, that serial number came in handy! Every time the primary stores a new change, it increments the serial number. If that number hasn't changed since the last time the secondary talked to the primary, the secondary doesn't have any replicating to worry about.

So for example, let's say that the secondary has updated its zone from the primary at 10:00 A.M., learning among other things that the latest serial number for the zone is 237. At 10:01 A.M., you add a new host A record at the primary. The primary stores that new A record and increments the serial number to 238. The secondary, of course, knows nothing of this.

But 15 minutes after the last synchronization, the secondary asks the primary for the SOA record. When the primary responds, the secondary notices that the serial number is now larger than it was the last time it asked, so something must have changed. The secondary requests an update on the zone records, and now it's in sync. Fifteen minutes later, it requests the SOA record again and, if the serial number hasn't changed, does not request an update. The secondary thus polls the primary every 15 minutes, whether things have changed or not.

But what if the primary doesn't respond? In that case, the Retry Interval option in the SOA record instructs the secondaries how often to try to communicate with the primary. It's every 10 minutes by default. If the primary's unavailable for a long time, then the Expires After value in the SOA record tells the secondaries that if they are unable to communicate with the primary DNS server for some time—one day by default—then they should assume the information that they have is too far out-of-date and discard it. In other words, when a secondary cannot access the primary for more than one day, then the secondary basically stops answering name resolution queries.

When the primary tells the secondary, "Come get my zone data"   It's called *notifying*, and you'll see a bit later how to tell the primary DNS server to tell any or all of the secondaries to come get the latest zone data. It's relatively new in the DNS world, having only appeared in RFC 1996.

Secondary DNS servers are just machines that hold a backup copy of the primary DNS server's database. They can also satisfy DNS name resolution queries when asked. They cannot accept changes to the zone files. When the primary DNS server will be down for some time, you can promote any secondary to be the primary DNS server for a domain. In general, however, that's something that an administrator's got to initiate—secondary DNS servers will not promote themselves.

EXERCISE: SETTING UP A SECONDARY DNS SERVER FOR BIGFIRM.BIZ
This seems like a perfect time to create our second DNS server, ns2.bigfirm.biz. If you want to follow along, you'll need a second computer running Server 2003. Install the DNS server on it as you did on Bigdog. Point ns2.bigfirm.biz at itself for a preferred DNS server. Be sure to give ns2 the IP address 192.168.0.3, the computer name ns2, and DNS suffix bigfirm.biz. Once you've got DNS running on ns2, open the DNS snap-in, right-click the Forward Lookup Zones, and choose New Zone, which as before, starts up the New Zone Wizard. Click Next to arrive at the first page, where you specify that you want a primary, secondary, or stub zone. Choose a Secondary and click Next. You'll then see a page like Figure 7.64.

Here, I've filled in bigfirm.biz. Notice that this dialog is different from the one shown when creating a primary, as the server doesn't ask you what to call the zone file. A DNS secondary just uses zone files with the same name as the ones that the primary uses. Click Next to see where to tell the server where to find the primary DNS server for this zone, as you see in Figure 7.65.

FIGURE 7.64

Enter domain name for secondary DNS server

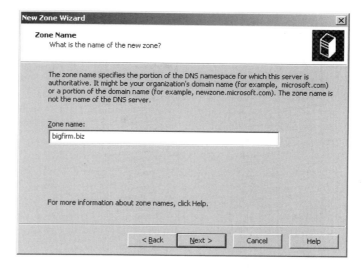

FIGURE 7.65

Specify the zone's primary ("master")

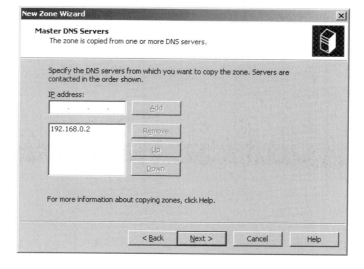

As you've already read, DNS uses a single primary server for a zone. The secondaries then copy the zone and treat the zone as read-only—you should make any changes to the zone on the primary, not any of the secondaries. Fill in the primary's IP address, add it, and click Next, then Finish to create the zone.

At this point, I usually find that the DNS snap-in complains that the zone didn't transfer correctly, and all the pressing of F5 that I can do doesn't change that error message. Just close the DNS snap-in and then reopen it at ns2.bigfirm.biz, and you'll find the zone completely copied at ns2.

While you're there, try right-clicking the bigfirm.biz zone folder and you'll see Transfer from Master, a command to force a secondary to synchronize its zone information with the primary. This synchronization happens automatically every 15 minutes by default, but the Transfer from Master command is the way to force a replication whenever needed.

REPLICATING ZONES: FULL VERSUS INCREMENTAL TRANSFERS

Until recently, DNS servers replicated data to their secondaries in a fairly primitive way.

The secondary servers in a domain periodically contacted the primary DNS server and copied its database to theirs. The *whole* database. So if a zone file contained 4000 lines of information and only one line changed, the secondary servers got the whole file when they requested an update.

RFC 1995 changed that, allowing for "incremental zone transfers." Put simply, RFC 1995–compliant DNS servers would know how to transfer just the few records that have changed, rather than resending the whole zone file. Server 2003's DNS server is RFC 1995–compliant, and will do incremental zone transfers whenever communicating between Windows 2000 or 2003–based DNS servers. If a Windows 2000 or 2003 DNS server detects that it's talking to a DNS server running on something other than a 2K or 2003–based DNS server, however, then it will do complete zone transfers rather than incremental zone transfers.

You cannot to my knowledge configure 2000 or 2003–based DNS servers to always do full zone transfers to other 2000/2003 systems. But you can configure a 2000 or 2003–based DNS server to do incremental zone transfers to non-2000/2003 DNS servers.

1. Open the DNS snap-in (Start/Administrative Tools/DNS).
2. Right-click the icon representing the server and click Properties.
3. Click the Advanced tab on the resulting properties page.
4. On the Advanced tab, uncheck the box labeled BIND Secondaries. Nonintuitive as this sounds, you must uncheck the box to have 2003's DNS do incremental zone transfers.
5. Click OK or Apply, and the server will do incremental zone transfers to all other DNS servers. Close the snap-in.

If you like, try making ns2 a secondary DNS server for the reverse lookup zone 0.168.192.in-addr.arpa as well.

If you read about full transfers versus incremental transfers, you may stumble across an odd bit of terminology. When taking Microsoft's Windows 2000 certification exams, I ran across several DNS questions that referred to AXFR versus IXFR operations. I had no idea what they were talking about at first, but it quickly dawned on me that this idea of full versus incremental transfers was *another opportunity for an obscure acronym!* As you've probably guessed by now, AXFR just means "do a full zone transfer when updating a secondary," and IXFR means "do an incremental zone transfer when updating a secondary." The two phrases are apparently the internal commands that DNS servers use. In any case, don't blame Microsoft entirely for this—AXFR and IXFR are liberally used terms in DNS-related RFCs.

CONFIGURING ZONE TRANSFERS AND NOTIFICATION

For a secondary DNS server to operate, it has to copy the information in the primary DNS server's zone files to its own zone files—to ensure that its database of names and IP addresses is up-to-date. Copying zone information from one server to another is called *zone transfers*, as you've already read. Why control this? Security. You might not want just *anyone* being able to make themselves into secondary DNS servers on one of your zones. You tell a DNS server whether or not to allow zone transfers, and if so to whom, from the Zone Transfers tab. You can get to that in the DNS snap-in by right-clicking the zone's folder and choosing Properties, then click the Zone Transfers tab to see something like Figure 7.66.

By default, this DNS server will transfer the contents of its zone files to any server that asks. But knowing the names of your system's machines can help bad guys compromise security on your network, so Server 2003's DNS gives you the option to disallow transfers altogether, to name a set of acceptable DNS servers to limit transfers to, or to just transfer to the other name servers listed on the Name Servers page—a quite logical option. If you've got a group of people in your organization who set network security policy, then check with them before leaving zone transfers open to just anyone.

FIGURE 7.66

Controlling zone transfers

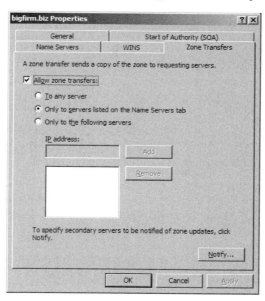

Recall that secondaries get updated by the primary in one of four ways: when the secondary DNS server gets restarted, when the operator forces the secondary to do it, when the secondary checks the latest serial number every 15 minutes (by default), or when the primary taps the secondary on the shoulder and says, "I've got zone changes, you should come get them." That last idea is called "notification" and it's configured from the Zone Transfers page by clicking the Notify button. You then see a dialog like the one in Figure 7.67.

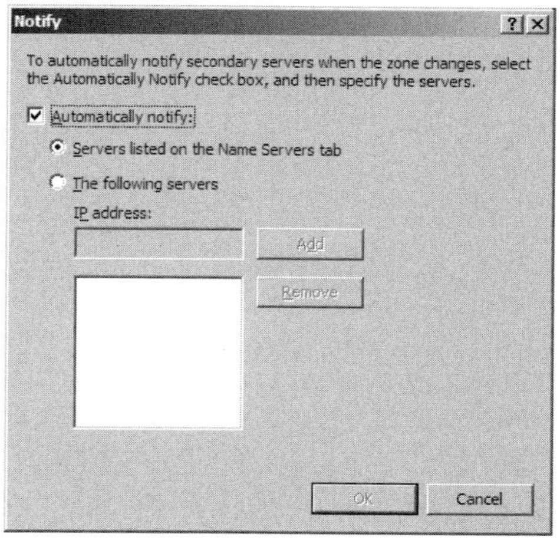

FIGURE 7.67

Setting up the primary to "push" zone changes to secondaries

You'll see that these settings—which are the defaults for Server 2003—tell the primary to notify the secondaries whenever there's a change. These notifications, which are just UDP datagrams, aren't mandatory commands to do an update; they're just suggestions.

AN ALTERNATIVE ZONE REPLICATION METHOD: ACTIVE DIRECTORY–INTEGRATED ZONES

Microsoft's DNS server can do all of the things that I've described so far; it follows the RFCs, the rules of the road for the Internet. But it can do more as well, offering a non-RFC mode that lets you create a zone that is neither a standard primary nor secondary zone, but instead an *Active Directory–integrated zone*. Active Directory–integrated zones offer two features:

◆ They eliminate the notion of primary and secondary DNS servers, making all DNS servers into primary DNS servers.

◆ They secure dynamic DNS by keeping unwanted outsiders from registering dynamic DNS records. Only machines that are members of an associated Active Directory domain can dynamically register records with an AD-integrated zone.

Why is the first notion—doing away with primary versus secondary DNS servers—interesting? Because of dynamic DNS. You've already read several times in this book that AD really relies upon DNS; I've said that AD relies upon DNS in that machines in an AD find domain controllers with DNS. That's important because DCs are the subset of servers that perform the essential function of authenticating machines and users to an Active Directory domain. But that's only one of the things that AD needs from DNS; AD not only needs to find out information about a DC's whereabouts, it also needs to be able to *store* information about where domain controllers exist. The technology that lets a DC register its whereabouts with DNS is dynamic DNS—the ability for a system to store SRV, A, or other records on a DNS server.

Microsoft's DNS server supports dynamic DNS for this very reason, as Microsoft's thinking was that if you want to set up an AD and your current DNS server doesn't support dynamic DNS, then you'd at least have the option to replace that DNS server with one that could do dynamic DNS—Microsoft's. But now imagine that you have 10,000 machines in a domain served by one primary DNS server and 30 secondary DNS servers. Every morning people turn their computers on and those computers want to go reregister their A records with a DNS server…but which one? Well, in a standard primary/secondary system, there's only one DNS server in a zone that can accept changes, remember? The primary. That would suggest that the primary might be pretty busy, so it'd be nice to share its load. Standard by-the-RFC dynamic DNS doesn't support that; AD-integrated zones do.

If your zone is supported by Server 2003–based DNS servers and you have an Active Directory working, then you can choose to store your zone data not in ASCII files but instead in the Active Directory itself. Once you do that, there are no primaries and secondaries; instead, any DNS server can accept dynamic registrations.

There's just one catch: in an AD-integrated zone, your DNS servers must also be domain controllers. Yes, you can still have DNS servers for a zone that are *not* DCs, but they can only be old-style secondary DNS servers, and so cannot take registrations.

To tell your DNS server to store the zone information in the AD—that is, to create an AD-integrated zone—open the DNS snap-in and find the folder for the zone that you want to make an AD-integrated zone. Right-click the folder, choose Properties, and click the General tab. You'll see a page like the one in Figure 7.68.

FIGURE 7.68

Properties for the bigfirm.biz zone

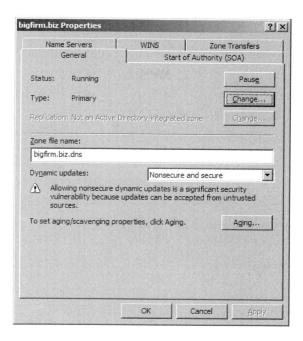

Notice the label Type: Primary and the nearby Change button. Click the Change button to see the dialog in Figure 7.69.

FIGURE 7.69

Zone type options

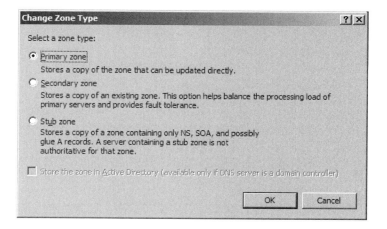

You could use this dialog to promote a secondary DNS server to the primary, if you had a standard single-primary, many-secondaries zone and the primary died. Or you could choose to store your zone information in the Active Directory with the grayed option, Store the Zone in Active Directory (Available Only if DNS Server Is a Domain Controller). It's grayed in Figure 7.69 because we haven't created an AD yet.

Summarizing, then, making a zone AD-integrated means that any DNS server in the zone can accept registrations, and you can restrict registrations to domain members. But AD-integrated also means that only domain controllers can be DNS servers. (Although other systems can act as secondaries still—they just can't accept registrations.) I find that I like AD-integrated zones for Active Directory work, but we'll take this up again when we look at dynamic updates in greater detail.

Delegating: Creating Subdomains in DNS

Now bigfirm.biz is running well. But suppose we wanted to delegate control of some of Bigfirm to another group within the organization, as you see in Figure 7.70?

FIGURE 7.70

Expanded bigfirm.biz DNS structure

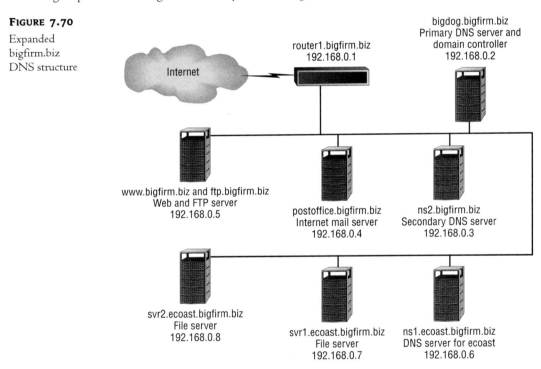

In that figure, I've added three systems: ns1.ecoast.bigfirm.biz (192.168.0.6); svr1.ecoast.bigfirm.biz (192.168.0.7), a file server of some kind; and svr2.ecoast.bigfirm.biz (192.168.0.8). Notice that all of the names have gotten longer—they're all *something*.ecoast.bigfirm.biz—and that means that we'll need another DNS server. For whatever reason, the bigfirm.biz IT management decided to let the ecoast.bigfirm.biz folks administer their own DNS, and so wants to give them a new subdomain, ecoast.bigfirm.biz. There are three parts to setting up a new subdomain that someone else's DNS server keeps track of:

◆ Tell the upper-level domain that there will be a lower-level domain under another system's control.

◆ Tell the upper-level domain's DNS server where to find a DNS server for the new lower-level domain.

◆ Set up the new lower-level domain's DNS server.

In DNS-ese, we'd call this *delegating control of a zone*. (And if you find yourself nodding off, then let me plead with you to pay attention here—many of you will use this to make the Active Directory fit into an existing Microsoft-hostile DNS infrastructure!) Briefly, do it this way:

1. Right-click the upper-level domain (bigfirm.biz) in the DNS snap-in and choose New Delegation.

2. That starts a wizard that basically wants to know just three things: what the subdomain will be called and what are the name and IP address of its first authoritative DNS server. Tell it that the new delegated domain is named ecoast (it adds the bigfirm.biz all by itself), that the name server for ecoast.bigfirm.biz is called ns1.ecoast.bigfirm.biz, and that its IP address is 192.168.0.6.

3. Go to the new DNS server for the new ecoast.bigfirm.biz subdomain (that server is ns1.ecoast.bigfirm.biz, recall) and set up the new ecoast.bigfirm.biz subdomain in the exact same way that you've already created other DNS domains.

Here's a look at a step-by-step example of how to do it in bigfirm.biz.

TELL BIGFIRM.BIZ TO DELEGATE ECOAST.BIGFIRM.BIZ

There are actually a few steps under the hood to telling bigfirm.biz that it needn't worry about name resolution for anything whose name ends with ecoast.bigfirm.biz. In the days before the DNS snap-in you'd have had to do those steps one at a time. The DNS Delegation Wizard, however, handles them all for you. I right-click the `bigfirm.biz` folder and choose New Delegation, which starts up a wizard. Click Next past its title screen and you'll see a screen like Figure 7.71.

FIGURE 7.71

Naming the subdomain to delegate to

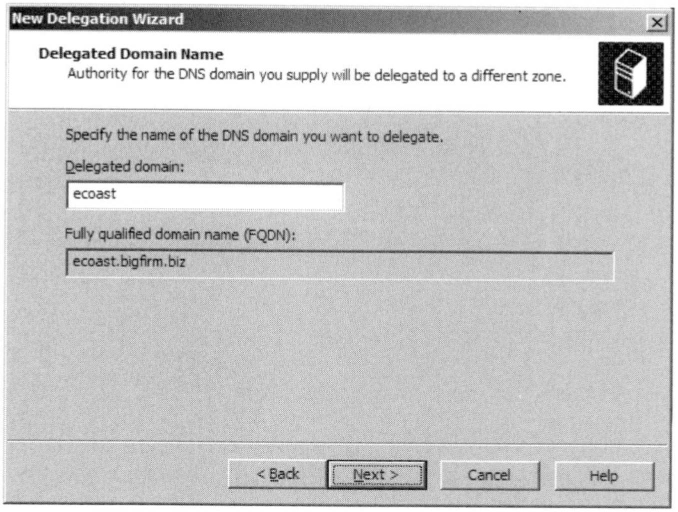

Here, I fill in the name of the subdomain ecoast, not the whole ecoast.bigfirm.biz domain. Again, it's just the new part of the domain name, ecoast rather than ecoast.bigfirm.biz. I then click Next and see something like Figure 7.72.

FIGURE 7.72

What DNS server to delegate to

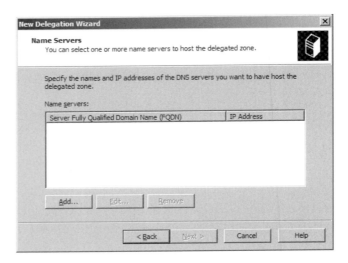

This panel wants to know the name and IP address of the DNS server (or servers) for the new sub-domain. I can enter a name and IP address by clicking Add, which shows the dialog box in Figure 7.73.

FIGURE 7.73

Specifying the DNS server

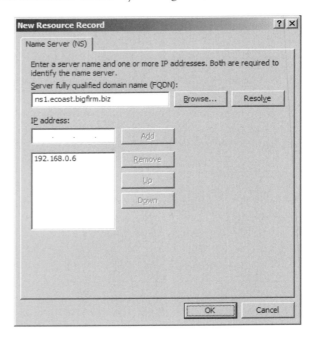

You've got to fill in *both* IP address and name to satisfy this dialog box, because clicking the Resolve button will fail—it can't look up ns1.ecoast.bigfirm.biz until there's an ecoast.bigfirm.biz zone to look it up in! Click OK and Next, and the final screen is a confirmation. Click Finish, and the delegation is done. The snap-in now looks like Figure 7.74.

FIGURE 7.74

DNS snap-in with delegated domain

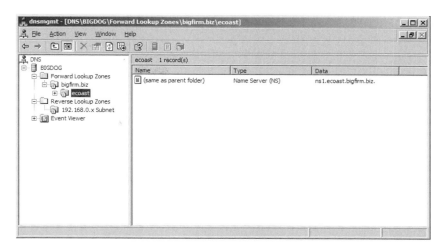

It doesn't look very different on a black and white page, but instead of the usual light yellow that most folders show, the **ecoast** folder is gray, indicating it's a delegated domain. At this point, the work's done on this server; time to go work at ns1.ecoast.bigfirm.biz.

CREATING THE LOWER-LEVEL DOMAIN, ECOAST.BIGFIRM.BIZ

Working from ns1.ecoast.bigfirm.biz, run its DNS snap-in, right-click its **Forward Lookup Zones** folder and choose New Zone. From this point on, it ought to look familiar. You create a subdomain with exactly the same wizard you used to create the domain.

In fact, if you think about it, it makes perfect sense. If you get a domain name from Network Solutions with a name such as bigfirm.biz, then Network Solutions has already gone to *its* domain named simply com and delegated control of a subdomain of com—that is, bigfirm.biz. We don't think about that much because it's not anything we worry about normally. But the second part of the process, creating the zone, we *do* think about, as that's usually our job as network engineer types.

STUB ZONES

You may have noticed that Server 2003 lets you create three kinds of zones—primary, secondary, and stub zones. But what's a stub zone, and what good is it? Now's the time to explain it.

A stub zone is something like a reduced-size secondary zone. Like a secondary, it's just a copy of the primary's information, and you can't make changes to a zone at a stub zone. But it's unlike a secondary in that it only contains name server information for its zone.

For example, suppose I were to put a DNS server on a server and then create a new stub zone for bigfirm.biz. A look in the zone file would show just three kinds of records:

◆ The SOA record for bigfirm.biz

◆ The NS records naming the DNS servers for bigfirm.biz

◆ The A records identifying the IP addresses of the DNS servers listed for bigfirm.biz (these are called *glue records*, as you'll learn later)

That's it, no other bigfirm.biz records would be there. What good are these zones? It often makes sense to create something called a "split-brain DNS" design on your network. With split-brain DNS, you'll create a set of zones that are only visible inside your network. To make it easy for the DNS servers in your network to find these invisible-to-all-but-your-insiders zones, you put stub zones for each of the zones on each of your internal DNS servers. I'll take this up later in greater detail, when we consider split-brain DNS.

Peeking at the Zone Files

Before I leave our simple zone, let's take a look beyond the GUI and see how the DNS data is stored for a delegation. So long as you do not choose to create an Active Directory–integrated zone, then Server 2003's DNS server stores your DNS records in the same format as a BIND DNS server would—in a simple ASCII file called a *zone file*. The Server 2003 DNS server stores these zone files in the \windows\system32\dns folder; look there, and you'll see a file named bigfirm.biz.dns.

Why would you bother doing this? Troubleshooting or recovery. Sometimes it's just easier to stop the DNS service and then directly examine the zone files. (You must stop the DNS service, because if you modify a zone file without first stopping the DNS service, then your changes will be lost.) We'll see a bit more about recovery a bit later in the chapter.

Returning to the bigfirm.biz.dns file, after a bit of editing to rearrange the records (which doesn't affect DNS's behavior at all) and remove some comments, mine looks like this:

```
@ IN  SOA bigdog.bigfirm.biz.  mark.bigfirm.biz. (
     25           ; serial number
     900          ; refresh
     600          ; retry
     86400        ; expire
     3600       ) ; default TTL

@           NS      bigdog.bigfirm.biz.
@           NS      ns2.bigfirm.biz.
@           MX      10 postoffice.bigfirm.biz.
ftp         CNAME   www.bigfirm.biz.
bigdog      A       192.168.0.2
ns2         A       192.168.0.3
postoffice  A       192.168.0.4
router      A       192.168.0.1
www         A       192.168.0.5
ecoast      NS      ns1.ecoast.bigfirm.biz.
ns1.ecoast  A       192.168.0.6
```

This zone file contains SOA, NS, A, CNAME, and MX records. Let's see what they say. As you've seen so far:

- ◆ The A records relate host names to IP addresses.
- ◆ The NS records identify name servers for particular zones.
- ◆ The MX records identify mail servers for particular machines or zones.
- ◆ The SOA record describes the characteristics of the zone and who to contact if there's a problem with the zone.
- ◆ The CNAME record lets you add an extra recognized name to an IP address.

Most records have three pieces of information on them: the object being described, the record type, and the descriptive information. For example, consider a record like this:

```
postoffice  A     192.168.0.4
```

This would mean, "The host named postoffice in this domain has IP address 192.168.0.4." Notice that the leftmost part of the text says postoffice rather than postoffice.bigfirm.biz. Within zone files, descriptive labels in general are assumed to be only host names, and zone names are appended automatically. If you *don't* want that to happen, put a period at the end of the name, as in:

```
postoffice.  A     192.168.0.4
```

Notice the period after postoffice. That would assign the IP address to a host whose fully qualified domain name was simply postoffice, with no .com or the like after it. (You probably wouldn't ever want this.)

I've mentioned TTL, or time to live, information. None of the previous records have TTL information, but if you want to put a TTL on a record, then just put the number of seconds that it's good for. So, for example, to tell the world that postoffice.bigfirm.biz has the IP address 192.168.0.4, but to check back with us on that information every day, we might have this A record:

```
postoffice  86400  A  192.168.0.4
```

SOA RECORD IN ZONE FILE FORMAT

The first record is the SOA record:

```
@ IN  SOA bigdog.bigfirm.biz.  mark.bigfirm.biz. (
```

It's basically saying, "This the start of authority record for bigfirm.biz."

Wait a minute—I don't see "bigfirm.biz" anywhere in that line. Where'd I get that this is the SOA for bigfirm.biz? The answer is the @ sign. It's got a magic meaning inside zone files completely *different* from the magic meaning that it has in e-mail addresses. Instead of separating an e-mail name from a user's domain, the @ here is shorthand for "this zone." So, because this is the bigfirm.biz zone, @ is just a shorthand way of saying bigfirm.biz. If you wanted to, you could write the SOA record as this:

```
bigfirm.biz. IN SOA bigdog.bigfirm.biz. ...
```

This is why you can't type the e-mail address of the responsible person for the zone with an @. If you did, DNS would just expand the @ to bigfirm.biz, leading to a pretty funny-looking e-mail address.

The `IN` is a holdover from the early days of DNS—it stands for *Internet* and refers to the fact that at one point it appeared that there would be other namespaces that DNS would worry about. Strictly speaking, every one of these records needs the `IN` part—I've worked with older DNS servers that wouldn't function without it—but it appears that the Server 2003 DNS server doesn't need it. You might have to edit zone records to insert an `IN` before the record type—for example, all of the As might have to become `IN As`—if you wanted to put a Server 2003 DNS zone file on an older DNS server.

Following the `@ IN SOA` is `bigdog.bigfirm.biz.`—that's the DNS name of the primary DNS server for this zone.

NOTE   Notice—that's the primary *DNS server, which is not necessarily the* authoritative *DNS server. How can you tell by looking at this zone file which server is authoritative? You can't. You find out which DNS server is authoritative, recall, by looking in the zone files of the parent domain to find out how the parent delegates name resolution responsibility for the child.*

Following that is the e-mail address of the technical contact for the domain, the e-mail address of the person to mail to if there's a problem with the domain. Then there are the five numbers that the SOA record uses to describe the domain data, as explained earlier.

A RECORDS IN ZONE FILE FORMAT

As with most zones, the bulk of the records are A records:

```
bigdog        A    192.168.0.2
ns2           A    192.168.0.3
postoffice    A    192.168.0.4
router1       A    192.168.0.1
www           A    192.168.0.5
ns1.ecoast    A    192.168.0.6
```

There are just two points to make about these records. First, notice that all of the names do not end in periods, so they're relative to the zone name. In other words, www is short for www.bigfirm.biz. Second, notice that you *can* have periods in the middle of a name. Even though ns1.ecoast.bigfirm.biz is not, strictly speaking, in the bigfirm.biz zone—it should be in the separate ecoast.bigfirm.biz zone—you can still include its A record by labeling that record ns1.ecoast and, as DNS just tacks on the domain name by default, it ends up being clear (to the DNS server, anyway) that this is an A record for ns1.ecoast.bigfirm.biz. (Remember that record—I'll have more to say about it in a minute.)

NS RECORDS IN ZONE FILE FORMAT AND "GLUE" RECORDS

Next are two NS records, as follows:

```
@ NS bigdog.bigfirm.biz.
@ NS ns2.bigfirm.biz.
```

These records say that the name servers for this zone, bigfirm.biz, are bigdog.bigfirm.biz and ns2.bigfirm.biz. Again, this works because @ gets automatically translated by the DNS server to "this zone" or, in this case, bigfirm.biz. They could have just as well been written like so:

```
bigfirm.biz  NS  bigdog.bigfirm.biz.
bigfirm.biz  NS  ns2.bigfirm.biz.
```

There's another NS record farther down:

```
ecoast       NS      ns1.ecoast.bigfirm.biz.
```

Now, *this* one has a different job than identifying the DNS servers for bigfirm.biz. Can you figure out what it does? It's an NS record, so its job is to identify a DNS server for a zone. But it doesn't refer to @ or bigfirm.biz., it refers to ecoast, and notice that there's no period at the end of it. That means that we're supposed to add the zone name, bigfirm.biz, to get its full name. Expanded, then, the DNS server reads this record like so:

```
ecoast.bigfirm.biz.  NS  ns1.ecoast.bigfirm.biz.
```

This is the delegation record for the ecoast subdomain. *This* is the record that essentially "creates" the ecoast.bigfirm.biz zone. If you were to look in the (huge) zone file that serves the com domain, then you'd see a similar record for your "dot-com" domain (assuming you have one). This is half of what the wizard that performed the domain delegation did. The *other* half of what the New Delegation Wizard did was to add an A record for ns1.ecoast.bigfirm.biz that could be written in one of two ways:

```
ns1.ecoast.bigfirm.biz.   A  192.168.0.6
```

or

```
ns1.ecoast   A  192.168.0.6
```

Notice that the first example includes a fully qualified name, as it ends with a period. That A record (however you enter it) for NS1 is called a "glue" record. Let's see why.

Suppose you want to resolve a name in the subdomain ecoast.bigfirm.biz. How does your DNS server do it? Well, it wants to find the DNS server for ecoast.bigfirm.biz so that it can query that DNS server about whatever name it's trying to resolve. As you've seen, you find the DNS server for ecoast.bigfirm.biz in the DNS server for bigfirm.biz. Specifically, your DNS server asks the bigfirm.biz DNS server for any NS records that are relevant to ecoast.bigfirm.biz. And, as you can see, the DNS server would return the answer, "You can find a DNS server for ecoast.bigfirm.biz at the machine named ns1.ecoast.bigfirm.biz."

If that were *all* that the bigfirm.biz DNS server said, then it wouldn't be very useful. So to look up a name on ecoast.bigfirm.biz, I ask a machine named ns1.ecoast.bigfirm.biz? Okay, then I guess I need to find the IP address of that machine named ns1.ecoast.bigfirm.biz; I wonder who I'd ask about that? Well, let's see, ns1.ecoast.bigfirm.biz is part of the ecoast.bigfirm.biz domain, so the DNS server I'll query to find the IP address of ns1.ecoast.bigfirm.biz would be...umm...ns1.ecoast.bigfirm.biz. So, in other words, the only way to get the phone number for Mel's Grocery is to call Information, but before I can call Information I must know the phone number for Information, and the place to call to find all numbers (including Information's) is Information.

To avoid this chicken-and-egg situation, DNS zones often contain A records for hosts that aren't part of that zone. In some senses, you might say that they're out of place—but without them, we'd never be able to find the IP address of ns1.ecoast.bigfirm.biz. So adding this seemingly out-of-place A record solves the problem. Such an A record is called a *glue record*.

CNAME RECORDS IN ZONE FILE FORMAT

Next, you see a CNAME record:

```
ftp        CNAME  www.bigfirm.biz.
```

This CNAME equates ftp.bigfirm.biz to a machine named www.bigfirm.biz. The result is that anyone seeking to resolve ftp.bigfirm.biz gets returned the IP address of www.bigfirm.biz.

MX RECORDS IN ZONE FILE FORMAT

Lastly, let's consider the MX record, which looks like

```
@          MX 10  postoffice.bigfirm.biz.
```

Notice how it's laid out: again, starting with an @ to indicate it refers to the entire domain, then the record type MX, then the preference value, and finally the name of the mail server. I could have more than one, but this zone only has one.

DIRECTLY MANIPULATING ZONES FILES: AN EXAMPLE

I'll return to looking at the ASCII files that drive a standard DNS server (and a Server 2003 DNS server, provided that you don't make your zones AD-integrated) a bit later, but before leaving the topic for now, let me offer some step-by-step advice on working directly in a zone file.

Suppose you wanted to add a host name entry—an A record—for a machine named test.bigfirm.biz, at address 192.168.0.10. You could do it via the GUI, but here's how to add the entry to the zone files directly. Basically, you stop the DNS service, modify the zone file, then start it up again:

1. In the DNS snap-in, right-click the icon representing the DNS server and choose All Tasks/Stop. This stops the DNS service on that server.

2. Look in \winnt\system32\dns to find the zone file named `bigfirm.biz.dns`. Edit it with Notepad.

3. Add **test A 192.168.0.10** to the end of `bigfirm.biz.dns`, and as you type it, you need only remember to start the line with **test**, then leave at least one space, then the capital A, then at least one space, then the IP address.

4. Increase the numeric value in the Serial Number entry of the SOA record by one so that the other servers (such as ns2, if you built it, or for that matter any other DNS server out there looking to this one to resolve bigfirm.biz) know there's new data in the zone.

5. Save the file.

6. Return to the DNS snap-in, right-click the server, and choose All Tasks/Start.

Once the DNS server has started again, take a look in the bigfirm.biz zone. You'll see that test's entry is visible. Once again, why would you modify the ASCII file instead of just clicking? Well, you might not—but you *might* decide to make large-scale changes to the zone via some program or macro that you wrote, a program that reads and massages the ASCII zone file. You'd follow basically the same approach in that case—stop the DNS service, run the program that modifies the zone file, then start the DNS service.

Dynamic DNS (DDNS)

Well, I've been dropping hints about it for the past 40 pages or so—so let's talk about *dynamic DNS*, or DDNS to the acronym-oriented.

For years, WINS has been a pain in the rear for many reasons. But it was better than DNS in one important way: Its database was automatic and dynamic. What I mean is that you almost never had to tell a WINS server about a machine out on the network. Instead, the machines would tell WINS about themselves automatically; whenever they booted up or renewed their DHCP leases, they'd go back and reregister themselves with WINS. The result? WINS automatically kept a database of machines on the network.

Now DNS, in contrast, wasn't automatic. You had to punch in A records for every one of your machines by hand, either by editing a zone file or by clicking in a GUI. It would have been pretty nice if DNS servers could collect information about the names and addresses of the machines on the network in a similar way to WINS.

Well, now DNS can, with DDNS. RFC 2136 describes a process whereby DNS clients—the workstations and servers that rely upon DNS for name resolution—can register themselves with DNS automatically, telling DNS to create an A (or any other type) record for them, without requiring any work on an administrator's part.

SEEING DDNS WORK

Want to see it in action? You can, if you've been following along and built the bigdog.bigfirm.biz machine. Just put Windows 2000 Pro, Server, XP, or Server 2003 on a computer. Call that computer MYPC. Give it a static IP address of 192.168.0.20, subnet mask 255.255.255.0, don't fill in the default gateway, and set the DNS server to 192.168.0.2—that is, bigdog. Finally, set the DNS suffix to bigfirm.biz and reboot the computer.

Once MYPC has rebooted, go over to bigdog, start the DNS snap-in, and open the bigfirm.biz forward lookup zone. You will see an A record for MYPC with an IP address of 192.168.0.20—an automatically created A record.

Next, stop the DNS service so that the zone data gets flushed out to the zone files, and take a look at \windows\system32\dns\bigfirm.biz.dns. You'll see an A record for MYPC that looks like this:

```
mypc 1200 A 192.168.0.20
```

Notice the 1200—remember what that is? It's a time to live value for the A record. 1200 seconds is 20 minutes. So when MYPC registered with the DNS server, it basically said, "I'm mypc.bigfirm.biz and I'm at 192.168.0.20, but if anyone asks about me, tell them that I might be a different address in 20 minutes—so don't cache the data for any longer than that."

NOTE *You can change that value if you care to by creating a REG_DWORD value entry called DefaultRegistrationTTL in* HKEY_LOCAL_MACHINE\SYSTEM\CurrentControlSet\Services\Tcpip\Parameters. *Fill the value entry with the length in seconds that you'd like the TTL set to. I can't think of a reason why you'd mess with it, but I include this for the curious. Please note that this is* not *how often your system reregisters with DDNS—there really isn't a Registry entry to affect that, as you'll see later in this chapter.*

If you look at the reverse lookup zone for 0.168.192.in-addr.arpa, then you may see a PTR record for 192.168.0.20, as the computer normally automatically registers both the forward and reverse entries. (I say "may" because XP and Server 2003 seem not to automatically register PTRs if their IP addresses are in a nonroutable range. That's not anything that I've been able to get verified, but it makes some sense, as it'd cut down on those unnecessary dial-ups to talk to prisoner.iana.org.)

The registrations might not have worked if you didn't set up 0.168.192.in-addr.arpa or the bigfirm.biz zone willing to accept dynamic entries—remember that zones aren't dynamic by default. You can easily check that both zones accept dynamic updates. In the DNS snap-in, right-click the folder representing your bigfirm.biz zone, then choose Properties and click the General tab. Then choose Nonsecure and Secure under Allow Dynamic Updates.

WHAT TRIGGERS DDNS REGISTRATIONS?

If you forgot to make the zones dynamic until after MYPC booted, how can you force MYPC to re-try registering? Well, clearly you could turn MYPC on and off, but who wants to do that? Instead, open a command line at MYPC and type this:

```
ipconfig /registerdns
```

Then check the zones—you should now see the updates.

How do the registrations work? Well, remember that DDNS registrations are *initiated by the client*. The DNS server does not ask the client to register; instead, the client requests the registration of the server. Five events cause a client to register or, more likely, to *re*register:

- The computer has been rebooted and the TCP/IP software has just started.
- You've changed the IP address on a system with a static IP address.
- Your computer gets its IP address from DHCP and the computer has just renewed its DHCP lease.
- You type `ipconfig /registerdns`.
- 24 hours has passed since the last time the system registered with DDNS.

You can change that 24-hour period to another one with a Registry change to `HKEY_LOCAL_MACHINE\SYSTEM\CurrentControlSet\Services\Tcpip\Parameters`: add a new value entry DefaultRegistrationRefreshInterval of type REG_DWORD. You can then specify how often to reregister in seconds. The default is 86,400, the number of seconds in a day.

DDNS REGISTRATIONS IN MORE DETAIL

My simple example with one workstation—MYPC—and just one DNS server—bigdog—obscured some of the complexity of a DDNS registration. Here is more specifically how a registration happens.

On a System with a Static IP Address

1. First, the client computer asks its local DNS server to retrieve the SOA record for the client computer's DNS suffix. So, for example, because MYPC sees that its DNS suffix is bigfirm.biz, it asks its local DNS server (which happens to be bigdog) to go find the SOA record for bigfirm.biz.

2. The local DNS server queries its DNS hierarchy for the answer to the client's question. In the case of bigdog, it already *knew* the answer, as bigdog contained the zone files. But if MYPC had been hooked up to a different DNS server, that DNS server could still have queried other DNS servers to get the SOA record for bigfirm.biz, and returned that information to MYPC.

3. Inside the SOA is, you may recall, the name of the DNS server that is primary for the bigfirm.biz zone. That's why MYPC wanted the SOA record: It has to register (or reregister) with the DNS server that acts as the primary DNS server for the bigfirm.biz zone, because recall that only the primary DNS server can change a zone. Even if a secondary DNS server for bigfirm.biz chose to accept MYPC's registration, it wouldn't be any good because that secondary DNS server wouldn't replicate MYPC's A record to other DNS servers, and they wouldn't listen if it tried anyway. The registration must be done at the primary (unless you build an Active Directory–integrated zone).

4. Now that MYPC knows the name of the primary DNS server for bigfirm.biz, it contacts that DNS server and sends its registration requests: "Please create an A record for mypc.bigfirm.biz at 192.168.0.20."

5. But it's not done yet—now it needs to register a PTR record with the reverse zone. So it asks for the SOA record for the reverse zone and then uses that SOA record to identify the primary server for the reverse zone. Once it knows the primary server for the reverse zone, it asks the reverse zone's primary server to register it.

On a System That Uses DHCP

That's how MYPC worked, as it has a static IP address. But if MYPC had gotten its IP address from DHCP, then things would work just a bit differently.

When a system gets its address from DHCP, then the system only registers its *forward* record—the A record—rather than the PTR record. The DHCP server handles registering the reverse zone's PTR record. Furthermore, you may, if you like, tell the DHCP server to handle *all* registrations, both forward and reverse. Look back to Figure 7.20 in the section on DHCP and you see the DNS tab on a DHCP scope's properties. It's not the default, but you can choose a radio button labeled Always Update DNS and, if you do, then the clients don't do registrations, the DHCP server does.

Remember that I said that DDNS registrations are initiated by the client. But what about if the client *isn't* running Windows 2000? A Windows 98, Windows Me, or NT 4 system wouldn't know how to register itself in DNS, nor would it know that it even had to. Recall that also back near Figure 7.20, I explained—and it seems a good time to say again—that the Server 2003 DHCP server is smart enough to detect systems that don't know to register themselves with DNS. In that case, the DHCP server will register both the forward and reverse entries for those systems. (Unless you tell it not to; that's an option.)

MUST MY SYSTEM REREGISTER?

Anyone with a good knowledge of how WINS works will probably assume, as I did, that you *must* reregister with DDNS on a regular basis, or the DDNS server will simply "forget" your system's dynamically registered records.

By Default, 2003's DNS Server Does Not Clean Out Old Records

Actually, though, that's not true. At least, not by default.

In fact, if you leave the DNS server defaults in place, your workstation really need only register once. Once it has told the DNS server to create an A record and a PTR record (and whatever other records it may need created), then those records stay in the zone file indefinitely.

Scavenging: Cleaning Out the Old

That may sound a tad inelegant. I mean, dynamic DNS is supposed to be *dynamic*, right? So if one day I shut down the machine named pc152.bigfirm.biz and never start it up again, then I really shouldn't have to go root around in the bigfirm.biz zone file and delete its records. Can't the system do this kind of housekeeping itself?

Yes, it can. The process is called *scavenging*. Scavenging is a process whereby a DNS server periodically (you can configure how often, as you'll see) checks its dynamically created records to see how long it's been since they were registered (or reregistered). Then, if the scavenger finds records that haven't been registered or reregistered in a long time (and you can configure how long "a long time" is), it deletes them from the zone file.

Controlling Scavenging: Just Three Numbers

To see how to set up scavenging, right-click the DNS server's icon in the DNS snap-in and choose Set Aging/Scavenging for All Zones and you'll get a dialog box like Figure 7.75.

Check the box labeled Scavenge Stale Resource Records and click OK twice (you'll see another dialog box asking about AD-integrated zones; again, just click OK to go with the defaults) to enable scavenging. But what about those two time values, the No-Refresh Interval and the Refresh Interval? Well, there are three numbers relevant to how scavenging works; here, you see two of them—and I'll explain them in a minute, but if you're in a real rush, then here's the short version: just use the defaults, they're fine.

FIGURE 7.75

Setting scavenging parameters

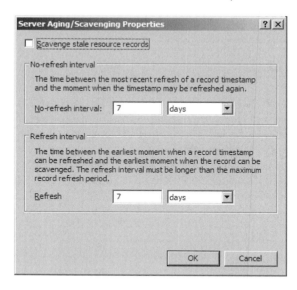

But you're not done setting up scavenging. Right-click the server again, choose Properties, and click the Advanced tab. You'll see something like Figure 7.76. Check Enable Automatic Scavenging of Stale Records to kick off the scavenger on a regular basis.

FIGURE 7.76

How often to scavenge?

The No-Refresh Interval   Now let's consider those three numbers.

Look back to Figure 7.75 and you'll see the first value, something called the No-Refresh Interval. It creates a period of time wherein your computer *cannot* reregister itself in DNS. So, for example, if the no-refresh interval were one day and your computer had reregistered at 9:00 A.M. on Tuesday morning, then any attempts to reregister itself before 9:00 A.M. Wednesday morning would simply be ignored by the DDNS server.

Why'd Microsoft bother with something like this? Mostly because you have the option, as I've mentioned (and will discuss later in some detail) to store your zones not in a traditional zone file, but instead in the Active Directory, a so-called "Active Directory–integrated zone." Any time that your system reregisters, that creates a change in the AD, and any change in the AD must be replicated to every other AD controller in the enterprise. Replication traffic can clog your WAN links and slow down the DCs, so I guess the idea with the no-refresh interval is to reduce the burden imposed on the AD by overzealously reregistering systems.

If you're experimenting and want to force an immediate reregistration within the no-refresh interval, just open the zone in the DNS snap-in and use the GUI to delete the A record for the system that you want to register. Then go to the system that you want to reregister and type `ipconfig /registerdns` at a command line.

The Refresh and Scavenging Intervals   Figure 7.75 also includes a field called the Refresh Interval. But that's not a very descriptive name. A better name would be The Remainder of the Immunity from Scavenging Period. It's an interval that says to the scavenging routine, "If this record's age is less than the sum of its no-refresh and refresh intervals, then don't even *think* of scavenging it."

For example, suppose I've got a no-refresh interval of one day and a refresh interval of two days. And let's suppose that the scavenging routine runs every day. (You set the scavenging interval shown in Figure 7.76.) Your system registers at 9:00 A.M. Tuesday morning. As you read before, that means that the DDNS server would be deaf to any attempts by your system to reregister. Let's say that the scavenging routine runs every evening. It sees that the no-refresh plus the refresh intervals equals three days. The scavenger then sees that your workstation's A record is less than a day old. That age is less than three days, so the scavenger leaves the record alone.

Let's suppose that you're on vacation for the week. So 9:00 A.M. Wednesday morning is when your DDNS server would accept a reregistration for your system, but your system's not on, so it doesn't try to reregister. Wednesday evening, the scavenger sees that your workstation's A record is about a day and a half old—still too young to scavenge. The same thing happens Thursday night, when the scavenger sees a two-and-a-half-day-old record. But on Friday night, your workstation's A record is three-and-a-half days old, so the scavenger munches it.

Simplified, think of it this way. Add the No-refresh and the Refresh intervals together. That's how long you want a record to stay in a dynamic DNS zone.

Choosing a Good No-Refresh and Refresh Interval   There really isn't any relationship between the scavenging interval and the no-refresh/refresh intervals. But you should take a minute to ensure that you don't set the no-refresh/refresh intervals too small. The sum of those two should be larger than the frequency of reregistration.

Here's an exaggerated (and impossible) example of what I mean. Suppose your system reregisters with DDNS only once every 30 days. But then suppose you set a no-refresh interval of six days and a refresh interval of seven days, and a scavenging interval of one day. Let's follow the process through from Jan. 1:

1. On Jan. 1, your system registers with DDNS.

2. The DDNS server will not accept another registration from your system until Jan. 7, but that's no problem—your system doesn't intend to reregister until Jan. 31.

3. Every day until Jan. 14, the scavenger runs and sees that your system's A record is less than 13 days (6 plus 7) old, and so leaves it alone.

4. Around Jan. 14, however, the scavenger runs, finds the record older than 13 days, and deletes it.

Remember that this is a client-driven registration system, so there's no method for the DDNS server to give the client a heads-up that it's time to reregister.

So, clearly you should set the sum of your no-refresh and refresh intervals so that they always exceed the maximum possible interval between subsequent reregistrations. But what's the maximum possible interval between reregistrations? Recall the things that trigger a reregistration: They happen every 24 hours (if the system stays up), upon a DHCP lease renewal, or when you turn your computer on. So the longest you'd probably ever go between reregistrations would be as long as you ever have your computer off—seven days, perhaps, unless you're in the habit of taking two-week vacations.

Setting Scavenging for One Zone

Figure 7.75 showed you how to set the scavenging values for all zones. To set a different set of refresh and no-refresh intervals for just one zone, then you'll need to right-click the zone and then choose Properties. Click the General tab and you'll see an Aging button; click it and you'll get a dialog box that looks like Figure 7.77.

FIGURE 7.77

Scavenging settings for a particular zone

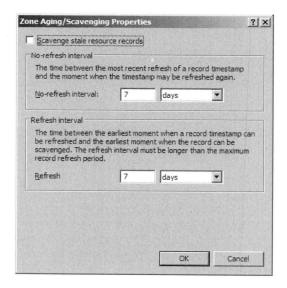

Notice that it's identical to Figure 7.75. The defaults of seven days apiece are probably just fine. Notice the information field at the bottom of the dialog box—that says when scavenging could next occur. If you look in the zone file at a dynamic record after you've turned on scavenging, you might see an entry like this:

```
ca  [AGE:3505395]  96  A  192.168.0.21
```

You should recognize the `ca 96 A 192.168.0.21` part—that's just an A record for a host named ca.bigfirm.biz at address 192.168.0.21 with a TTL of 96 seconds. The `[AGE:3505395]` is the "birthday" of this record, the hour in which it was created. As near as I can tell, this is a value measured in hours since January 1, 1600, or thereabouts, and don't bother with decimals—it seems that scavenging works in units of hours or larger.

WARNING *Note something about that* `[AGE:]` *entry—it's not a standard part of a DNS record. Therefore, if you turn on scavenging, you'll still have zone files, but they won't be portable to non-Microsoft-based DNS servers anymore, at least not without some work—you'd have to edit the zone files to remove the* `[AGE:]` *items before trying to transplant a 2000 or 2003 zone file onto another kind of DNS server.*

In sum, then, to enable scavenging you must remember to:

◆ Set the no-refresh and refresh intervals for the server as a whole, as in Figure 7.75.

◆ Turn on scavenging, as in Figure 7.76.

◆ If you want to set different intervals for each zone, then adjust their specific refresh properties.

Viewing When a Record Will "Go Stale"

If you want, you can find out when a particular record will go stale, although not directly. Start up the DNS snap-in and choose View/Advanced. Then right-click any record and choose Properties; you'll then see something like Figure 7.78.

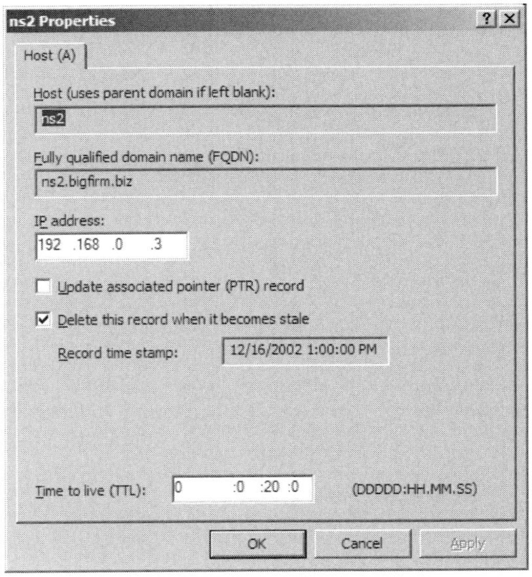

FIGURE 7.78

Viewing a record's properties with View/Advanced enabled

Here, I took the ns2 system and deleted its record in the zone on bigdog, after turning on scavenging on bigfirm.biz. Then I went over to the ns2 system and typed **ipconfig /registerdns** to make ns2 reregister itself dynamically with bigdog. The date that you see of 12/16/2002 at 1:00 P.M. isn't telling me that this record goes stale at that time; instead, it's telling me that this record *was created*—registered—at that date. To find out when it'll go stale, I'd have to first add the no-refresh plus the refresh intervals. Suppose the no-refresh interval is two days, and the refresh interval is three days. That'd tell me that the earliest time that this record can go stale is five days later at 1 P.M. on Dec. 21, 2002. But, of course, that's not the *only* information that I need. Recall that stale records only get deleted when the scavenging routine runs, so I'd need to know when the scavenging routine runs to determine exactly when this record will disappear.

Viewing Scavenging Logs

Windows 2000 Server and Server 2003–based DNS servers report what happened in every scavenging cycle in the Event Viewer in the System log. Just look for a DNS event with event ID 2501.

WINS REGISTRATION VERSUS DDNS REGISTRATION

Now that you've seen how DDNS registration works, you might have committed a bit of mental shorthand (I know *I* did when I first learned this) along the lines of "DDNS for Winsock is equivalent to WINS for NetBIOS—and so many of the same issues apply." That's *partially* right; but there's one significant difference between WINS and dynamic DNS, and that difference will affect how you decide how many DNS servers you need, and where to place them.

As you've seen, every TCP/IP-enabled computer gets a "primary WINS server" and a "preferred DNS server." At first blush, it looks like a system's primary WINS server and its preferred DNS server do basically the same thing, and in some senses they do: Your preferred DNS server is the DNS server that resolves DNS names for you, and your primary WINS server is the WINS server that resolves NetBIOS names for you. But here's the difference: Your system needs to register with both the WINS and DNS databases. Your system registers its NetBIOS name with its primary WINS server, but it *doesn't* register its DNS name with its *preferred* DNS server; instead, it registers its DNS name with the *primary* DNS server for its zone.

As you've previously read, every WINS server has two very different tasks. First, it resolves NetBIOS names from its database. Second, it collects names to populate that database. Clearly a WINS server that serves one-fifth of the organization would only receive registrations from one-fifth of the organization, and therefore would be ignorant of the other four-fifths—and so any time that one of the WINS clients asked that WINS server to resolve a machine name in the organization, there'd be an 80-percent chance that the WINS server wouldn't know the name. That's silly, so, as you've read, any enterprise that uses more than one WINS server must set that WINS server up to share its database with the other WINS servers and to accept databases from other WINS servers and to merge those other databases with its own so that it (and every other WINS server) has a consistent, enterprise-wide database of machine names, hence the Microsoft "14 WINS servers worldwide" rule of thumb. That's a shame from the name resolution side—it'd be really great to be able to somehow scatter dozens of WINS servers all over the place to resolve names. But that'd be a nightmare if all of those dozens or hundreds of WINS servers each contained a little database that needed to be merged with all of the other databases—that's just asking for database corruption. Wouldn't it be cool if you could just create a kind of "low-octane WINS server" incapable of accepting registrations, a kind of "resolving-only" WINS server? You'd give it a copy of the WINS database somehow and it could focus only on resolving names. With tons of them around, each one could serve just a small number of clients, with the result that all of those clients would receive very snappy response on their name resolution requests.

Well, sadly, you can't do that with WINS, which brings me to the major point about how WINS and DDNS are different.

Should you limit yourself to 14 servers total with DNS? Absolutely not. In WINS, the machine that you register with *must* be the one that you use to resolve names. With DNS, the machine that resolves names is your preferred DNS server. You register with a different computer—the primary DNS server for your zone. The result is terrific—you can place any number of DNS servers in your organization whose only job is to resolve names and therefore help your network respond to clients more swiftly.

DDNS SECURITY IS WEAK, IF YOU CARE

One thing that troubles some people about vanilla, by-the-RFC DDNS servers is that they will accept a registration from anyone. So, for example, if bigfirm.biz's DNS server were "live" on the Internet, then anyone anywhere could just set their Windows 2000, XP, or Server 2003 computer's domain suffix to bigfirm.biz and type `ipconfig /registerdns`. This would work even if that machine's local DNS server didn't do DDNS. Remember, all that your preferred DNS server must do is be able to retrieve the SOA record for bigfirm.biz—and any DNS server can do that.

Should the bigfirm.biz people care that people are registering on their domain? So what if the machine at 62.11.99.3 registers itself as poindexter.bigfirm.biz? A Microsoft person told me that it might matter. For example, he explained, consider the 128-bit downloadable versions of Internet Explorer. In the past, you weren't supposed to be able to download them if you weren't in the United States or Canada. Microsoft's Web site determined whether you were in the United States or Canada by looking at your domain. If bigfirm.biz's record in the Network Solutions database showed a U.S. address, then the download was okayed, so someone from outside the United States or Canada could sneak in that way.

Presumably, a hacker could first register with bigfirm.biz, then try to hack some system. If the system administrator of the attacked system noticed that he was being hacked by someone at bigfirm.biz, that might make for a bit of a hassle for the bigfirm.biz administrator. Particularly if the hacker was trying to crack an NSA or CIA site.

Not every brand of DDNS server software is wide open. There are now RFCs on secure dynamic DNS registration, although when last I checked, Microsoft's dynamic DNS software can't interoperate with it. You can, as I've suggested, secure a Microsoft DNS zone by making it AD-integrated; I'll cover that soon.

Making Windows 2000/XP Computers Not *Do Dynamic Registration*

Windows 2000 and later Microsoft operating systems automatically attempt to register their host names and IP addresses with the primary DNS server of the DNS domain that they belong to, as you've seen. But that can cause some problems in places that haven't adopted the Active Directory or that use static DNS servers for some reason.

I had a client that used Unix-based BIND servers and that hadn't made their DNS zone dynamic. (There wasn't any reason to, as they hadn't rolled out an AD yet.) The PC guys rolled out a few hundred Windows 2000 Professional systems.

The BIND guys—a different group—noticed.

All of a sudden, the DNS server logs were chock-full of warnings and errors about all of these computers trying to register with their static DNS zones. That worried the BIND guys, so they tracked it down to all of these new PCs. What to do? Well, the BIND folks could have just ignored the messages. But that *does* seem a bit inelegant. So rather than lowering the river, why not just raise the bridge? In other words, how could they get the 2000 or, for that matter, XP or Server 2003 boxes to stop bugging the DNS servers?

You can tell a Windows 2000/XP/Server 2003 computer to forgo registering altogether either from the GUI or with a Registry hack. The Registry hack is in `HKEY_LOCAL_MACHINE\SYSTEM\CurrentControlSet\Services\Tcpip\Parameters`. Add a new value entry, DisableDynamicUpdate— it's a REG_DWORD entry—and set it to 1 and reboot the computer. That'll keep the computer from attempting a dynamic update whenever the computer has a static address or got it from DHCP. Or here's a (long) command line to do it:

```
reg add hklm\system\currentcontrolset\services\tcpip\parameters /v
 DisableDynamicUpdate /t REG_DWORD /d 1 /f
```

That's all one line. You can even do it on a remote system by prefixing the Registry key's name with the system's name. For example, to reach across the network and make this change to Bigdog, you'd type

```
reg add \\bigdog\hklm\system\currentcontrolset\services\tcpip\parameters /v
 DisableDynamicUpdate /t REG_DWORD /d 1 /f
```

You can tell the computer not to try to update DNS in the GUI, as well; it's in the Advanced TCP/IP Settings property page, on the DNS tab. Uncheck the Register This Connection's Addresses in DNS box.

But what if you want to distribute this setting to bazillions of machines? The best solution is probably a custom policy; either a system policy would work (if you've got Windows 2000/XP workstations on an NT 4 domain) or a group policy (if you're running the AD). Custom policies are a big topic, though, so I won't go through the step by steps here—see Chapter 9 on how to create a custom system policy. Microsoft has a Knowledge Base article that explains how to build a group policy to tell a workstation to stop trying to register with their DNS servers at 294832.

Active Directory–Integrated Zones

You've read that DNS zones come in three flavors: primary, secondary, and stub zones. But 2000 and 2003's DNS offer you a third type of zone called an *Active Directory–integrated* zone. As I see it, AD-integrated zones offer two main benefits: multimaster zone replication and a DDNS registration process that is both load-balanced and secured. But they've got a drawback as well: They stray from the RFCs for DNS a bit—but *just* a bit—and you've got to make your domain controllers into DNS servers. Let's see how to make a zone an AD-integrated zone, then look into the pluses and minuses in some detail.

CREATING AN AD-INTEGRATED ZONE

Go to any primary zone on a Microsoft DNS server and right-click it, then choose Properties. The resulting properties page looks like the one back on Figure 7.59. To convert between a primary and an AD-integrated zone, click the Change button and you'll see a dialog box like the one back in Figure 7.69.

As I noted earlier, if you've been following along in the bigfirm.biz example, your Store the Zone in Active Directory (Available Only if DNS Server Is a Domain Controller) option will be grayed out. That's because you can only host an AD-integrated zone on an Active Directory domain controller, and the DNS server that we created for bigfirm.biz— bigdog —isn't a DC. (Recall that in fact we haven't created any domains at all yet.)

It may not be immediately obvious from Figure 7.69, but you've got a lot of flexibility if you want to experiment with an AD-integrated zone versus a standard primary zone. Just a mouse click or two converts a zone from primary to AD-integrated or vice versa—going AD-integrated isn't a one-way trip.

Once you make a zone an AD-integrated zone, then a visit back to the General tab of the properties page for that zone (right-click the zone in the DNS snap-in and choose Properties) will look like Figure 7.79.

FIGURE 7.79

Properties of an
AD-integrated zone

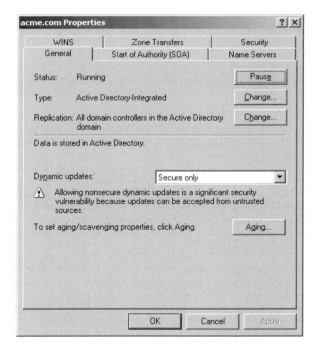

Notice that the Dynamic Updates drop-down no longer says Secure and Nonsecure but instead shows Secure Only, an option that only appears once you're AD-integrated. (Notice also that this is not a property page for bigfirm.biz, as again we've not created its AD domains yet—that's in the next chapter.)

MULTIMASTER ZONE REPLICATION

You've already read that under standard DDNS, only one computer can accept registrations in a given zone—the computer that happens to be the primary DNS server for that zone. That means that a worldwide company might think twice about using DDNS (and therefore the Active Directory), because no matter where a 2000/XP-based workstation or server was situated, it would have to find and communicate with that *one* computer in the world every time that it wanted to reregister. And recall that Windows 2000 and later–based computers want to reregister whenever they renew their DHCP lease, reboot, every 24 hours, or when you type `ipconfig /registerdns`. So if your worldwide enterprise has an office in Khartoum with 200 machines and a primary DNS server in New York, then every single time the computers in Khartoum want to reregister, they've got to do it live-on-the-WAN to New York. That might be impractical.

With an AD-integrated zone, you can have as many primary DDNS servers as you like. Any one of these DDNS servers can accept DDNS registrations. They then replicate this information among themselves. So you could have a domain controller in Khartoum that not only handles logons for the users, but also handles machine registrations. Then, instead of requiring every system to talk to New York one at a time, the Khartoum DC just chatters with the closest DC now and then, perhaps a machine in Cairo, and tells the Cairo DC about the new DDNS registrations. Cairo's DC might forward that to the Paris DC, which sends it to the New York DC, and so eventually every DNS server knows about the Khartoum DDNS registrations.

Is it a lot of work to tell Khartoum how to find Cairo and then telling Cairo how to find Paris and so on? Not really, but here's the important point: As you'll see in the next chapter, you have to set this up to have a worldwide Active Directory domain anyway. The DCs share this information as part of their normal DC-to-DC chatter. So once you've set up the DCs to be able to send normal domain information back and forth, then you don't have to do anything at all to enable them to send DDNS registration information back and forth.

Once you've converted a zone to an Active Directory–integrated zone, you can install the DNS server service on any other DC for that domain. You enable that DNS server to assist in name resolution and registration for the domain by just creating a new forward zone, as you've seen, just as if you were creating a secondary zone for an existing domain—but instead of choosing Secondary Zone, you choose Active Directory–Integrated Zone. From that point on, everything's automatic. The AD-integrated DNS servers will then automatically tell some machines to register with one DDNS server, others with a different DDNS server, and so on.

NEW TO 2003: CONTROLLING DNS SERVER REPLICATION

As you've read, AD-integrated zones store the zone information—the DNS records—not in an ASCII file but as data in the Active Directory. In general, the kind of data in AD is account information: if you have a user account on the domain then your account information is part of the AD. When domain controllers talk to domain controllers, they are mainly updating each other on account information—"We have a new user account for someone named darla82, it's got a password of 'swordfish,'" that sort of thing. Domain controllers are basically database servers that hold onto the database of domain information.

But keeping more than one or two database servers up to date on a database, whether it's user account information or a stamp collection, is a nontrivial issue. So when Microsoft designed the programs to allow a server to be a domain controller, they had to do a lot of work on the programs that DCs use to keep each other up to date—the "replication engine," so to speak, of Windows 2000 and Server 2003, and they did a pretty decent job at it. What's interesting about that is that there are plenty of uses for a piece of software that allows a bunch of distributed database servers to remain in sync automatically without needing a lot of management by network administrators. Uses that have nothing to do with keeping track of accounts and passwords. (Microsoft even offers a version of the Active Directory database engine that *doesn't* keep track of accounts, passwords and the like—it's just a distributed database engine that developers can put any kind of data on without the need of an Active Directory. It's called ADAM, Active Directory Application Mode.)

It was this flexibility that led Microsoft to offer AD-integrated zones. The idea was, as you've already read, to add the DNS zone information to the other account information being passed around among DCs. But only DCs get the AD database information, which is what leads to what is (as you'll read in a page or two), in my opinion, AD-integrated zones' biggest weakness—to wit, AD-integrated zones force you to put DNS only on your domain controllers.

But to some people, putting the DNS info on the AD database presented another problem. All DCs in a domain get the same database information, as you've seen, so all DCs get the DNS info. But what if you have a DC that is *not* a DNS server? As it's a DC, it gets the DNS info, even though it's not going to use that info. Some people felt that this was a waste of network resources and wanted to fine-tune AD's replication of DNS zones. They got their wish in Server 2003, as Figure 7.80 shows.

FIGURE 7.80

Controlling how AD replicates DNS info

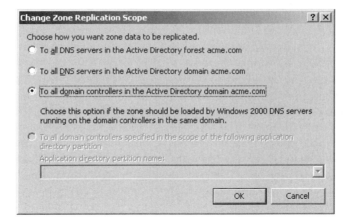

In a Windows 2000–based Active Directory, an AD-integrated zone's DNS info was only replicated to DCs in that zone's domain—in other words, the bigfirm.biz DNS info would only get copied to the domain controllers in the bigfirm.biz AD domain. As you'll learn in the next chapter, organizations can create groups of domains and cause them to automatically trust one another with security information, and those groups of domains are called *forests*. But under Windows 2000, only bigfirm.biz's DCs got the DNS information—not the other domains in whatever forest bigfirm.biz was a member of. (This screen shot refers to acme.com rather than bigfirm because we haven't created a bigfirm domain yet and I didn't want you to wonder how to duplicate that screen shot with the machine that we've been doing exercises on—you can't. It's not possible to make a zone AD-integrated until you have an Active Directory, and we don't yet.)

With a Server 2003–based DNS server, you can control how primary DNS servers keep their secondaries up to date. As you see in Figure 7.80, you have three replication options.

The third and default option, "To all domain controllers in the Active Directory domain acme.com," works identically to 2000's DNS server, replicating DNS information to all DCs in acme.com, whether those DCs are DNS servers or not—that's the selected option. This option does *not*, however, replicate the DNS information to other DNS servers in acme.com's forest; that made AD-integrated zones a bit harder to work with in Windows 2000.

That's why Server 2003's DNS server includes the first option, To All DNS Servers in the Active Directory Forest acme.com. Any Server 2003–based DNS server that is a member of any domain in the same forest as acme.com will automatically get acme.com's zone.

The third option, To All Domain Controllers in the Active Directory Domain acme.com, is the interesting one if you want to cut down the Active Directory chatter about DNS, as it only replicates the acme.com zone info to machines that are both DCs and DNS servers in acme.com.

Of the three options, the one that shares the DNS info with the most systems in your forest is the first one, To All DNS Servers in the Active Directory Forest *domainname*, so if you find that DCs for different domains can't find each other once you start building domains, then try that setting. Alternatively, you can solve that problem with something called *conditional forwarding* or *stub zones*. We've discussed these a bit, but we'll cover this in detail in just a few pages when I explain something called *split-brain DNS*.

SECURE DDNS REGISTRATION

I've got several domains running in my network, but I have one main Active Directory domain in my network, named win2ktest.com. It needs, as you know by now, a dynamic DNS zone to support the Active Directory, and besides I liked the whole idea of DDNS, so I set up win2ktest.com as a DDNS zone early on, back in the Windows 2000 Beta 3 days. I made it a standard primary zone rather than an AD-integrated zone.

Then the first edition of my earlier book *Mastering Windows 2000 Server* came out.

Because I sometimes take screen shots from an actual running network—mine—my examples tend to show dialog boxes from the DDNS server that hosts win2ktest.com. Unfortunately, some readers don't understand that win2ktest.com is only an example domain name, rather than the one that they should use, so they create domains named win2ktest.com on their test networks. Unfortunately, if those readers are sitting at machines with routable IP addresses attached to the public Internet, then their Windows 2000 machines will attempt to find the primary DDNS server for win2ktest.com and then try to register themselves with that machine's zone files.

In other words, with *my* DNS server's.

I didn't imagine that this would be a big problem when 2000 Server book's first edition came out. But I happened to look in the win2ktest.com zone files about four weeks after the book came out and found that *1000* machines had registered with win2ktest.com from around the world—yikes! Clearly I needed to do *something* to keep the *rest* of the world from registering with my domain, but what? The simplest answer was to convert my zone from a simple primary zone to an AD-integrated zone and then to enable Only Secure Updates on that zone. (That's two steps—just converting the zone to an AD-integrated zone doesn't set dynamic updates to Secure Only. You have to go to Properties for that zone and drop down the Dynamic Updates list box to select Secure Only.)

The value of doing that was this: Machines can only register DNS records with an AD-integrated zone on a DDNS server by first *logging in to the AD domain*. So any random Windows 2000, XP, or 2003 machine on the other side of the world that happens to have a DNS suffix of win2ktest.com can't register itself with my DDNS server unless it has a machine account on the win2ktest.com domain.

And for those new to Microsoft networking, there is indeed such a thing as a machine account, nonintuitive as it might seem! When you first attach a machine to an NT or an AD domain, you must have at least some administrative powers, as you're asking the domain to create an account much like a user logon account. Unlikely as it seems, every time that you turn your Server 2003, XP, Windows 2000, or NT–based computer on, it goes out to its domain and *logs in*. That's how AD-integrated zones keep my zone from growing beyond the size of my computer's hard disk!

As time has gone on, it has become clear that converting the zone to an AD-integrated one was a good idea. Once I briefly converted the win2ktest.com zone back to a standard primary zone to get a screen shot *just for 30 seconds* and, when I changed it back, I noticed that *two* machines had registered on the temporarily opened win2ktest.com zone! So if you see a message like this in your Event Viewer, then you'll know that your system tried to register with my DDNS server and was rebuffed:

```
The system failed to register network adapter with settings:

    Adapter Name: {994A8620-8987-4D4A-ABA9-507122C08F28}
    Host Name: dodo
    Adapter-specific Domain Suffix: win2ktest.com
    DNS server list:
      206.246.253.111
    Sent update to server: 206.246.253.111
    IP Address(es):
      210.20.10.4

The reason it could not register was because the DNS server refused the dynamic
    update request. This could happen for the following reasons: (a) current
    DNS update policies do not allow this computer to update the DNS domain name
    configured for this adapter, or (b) the authoritative DNS server for this DNS
    domain name does not support the DNS dynamic update protocol.

To register a DNS host (A) resource record using the specific DNS domain name for
    this adapter, contact your DNS server or network systems administrator.
```

POTENTIAL AD-INTEGRATED PROBLEMS

So is Active Directory integration the answer for you? Probably. The whole idea of basing my DNS infrastructure on a nonstandard Microsoft implementation troubled me at first, but the more I think about it, the less troublesome it seems. Let's consider the issues.

First of all, does using AD-integrated zones force you to use only Microsoft DNS servers? Not at all. You can use other DNS servers as secondary servers on an AD-integrated zone. Those secondary servers receive zone transfers from the AD-integrated servers, as before. Yes, it *is* true that the AD-integrated servers must all be Microsoft Windows 2000 or Server 2003 DDNS servers, but what's the harm in that? If we were to stay with a standard BIND-type DNS implementation, then we'd be restricted to just one primary DNS server. In effect, all AD integration does is to expand the number of possible "primary" DNS servers. I have tested a Linux box running BIND as a secondary DNS server on an Active Directory–integrated zone and experienced no trouble whatsoever.

Second, once you "go Microsoft," is there no going back? Not at all. A few mouse clicks converts an AD-integrated zone back to a standard primary zone. Once you convert a zone back to standard primary and shut down the DDNS server, then you'll have a standard ASCII zone file that you can place on a non-Microsoft DNS server, instantly "migrating" your DNS hosting from a Windows 2000 or Server 2003 box to some other DNS system.

No, if I have a complaint with AD-integrated zones, it's this one: The only machines that can be AD-integrated servers are Active Directory domain controllers. That worries me because I've always thought it a bad idea to put the name registration services on the same computer that does the logons. Remember that whenever you reboot your computer, it tries to reregister with DDNS. When do most people boot their computers? First thing in the morning. But what else do people do first thing in the morning? Log in to the domain. Early in the day, then, is when the domain controllers are busiest, logging people in. It seems to me that the busiest time of the day for a DDNS server is *also* first thing in the morning. Why take two functions that are both busiest at the same time and put them on the same machine? It seems somewhat unwise. But consider the alternative: If you use only a single primary DDNS server, then you've set up your enterprise so that if that one machine goes down, DDNS registrations don't happen. (But, on the other hand, don't forget that if you haven't turned on scavenging, then it's not going to be a big deal.)

What's the right answer, then? I can't say that I have the 100-percent best answer, but on balance I'd say that using AD-integrated zones makes the most sense in a predominantly 2000, XP, and/or 2003–based shop.

DNS Resolution in Detail

Now that you've seen how to set up a Server 2003–based DDNS server, let's look at how DNS works from the *client's* point of view. And in the process, I'll get a chance to discuss several important concepts I haven't covered yet.

Let's say you're sitting at a Windows 2000, XP, or Server 2003 machine attached to the Internet. You start up Internet Explorer or Netscape and point it to my Web site, www.minasi.com. Your browser hasn't a clue that www.minasi.com is the DNS name of the machine with IP address 68.15.149.117, so it needs something to do that name resolution for you—a local DNS server. I'll assume you're sitting at work while doing this, and that your firm has at least one local DNS server, which needn't be a Microsoft-based DNS server; any type of DNS server will do the trick here. Here are the specific steps that your workstation and the local DNS server perform to turn www.minasi.com into 68.15.149.117.

We're going to do a few exercises along the way, so if you like, get ready for them. Make sure that you're (1) sitting at bigdog.bigfirm.biz and (2) that system is connected to the public Internet—that you can ping some IP address out on the Internet. You don't *have* to do these exercises, so don't worry if you don't have a computer handy.

STEP 1: CHECK HOSTS

As has been the case with Microsoft DNS clients from the beginning, your workstation will first look in \windows\system32\drivers\etc for an ASCII file named hosts. If the DNS name that it's looking for is there, then your workstation will use that IP address and not look any further. The hosts file only stores A records, but the "what IP address does www.minasi.com have?" question is an A record lookup, so that'd be relevant here.

Exercise: Messing with hosts

Just to prove that hosts always beats anything else, try this.

1. Open up the hosts file: click Start/Run and fill in **notepad %systemroot%\system32\drivers \etc\hosts**, then press Enter.

2. Add a line to the bottom of the hosts file that looks like this:

   `136.1.240.21 www.minasi.com`

   Be sure to press Enter at the end of that line. Save the file, but don't close Notepad.

3. Now start up Internet Explorer and point your browser to `www.minasi.com`.

Where did you end up? As I wrote this, 136.1.240.21 was the IP address of one of Ford Motor Company's Web servers. They might have changed it by the time you read this, but if not, pointing IE to my Web site sends you instead to Ford's. The power of hosts!

Before we leave, please go *delete that line from hosts and save hosts*! (Thanks; I'd miss you guys if you couldn't visit my Web site.)

STEP 2: CHECK THE DNS CLIENT CACHE

On a Windows 9*x* or NT 3.*x* or 4 computer, the next thing that your workstation would do to resolve www.minasi.com would be to ask the local DNS server, "What's the IP address for www.minasi.com?" But the DNS client software on Windows 2000 and later Microsoft OSes—that is, the built-in software that knows how to ask DNS servers to resolve names—has an extra new feature: It caches the results of name resolution requests.

Viewing the DNS Client Cache

Here's how DNS caching works. Suppose you pointed your browser to www.minasi.com first thing in the morning; that causes your workstation to go ask the local DNS server to search the public DNS namespace for the IP address of www.minasi.com. But then suppose you returned to www.minasi.com 20 minutes later; in *that* case, your workstation wouldn't *have* to ask a DNS server for the IP address of www.minasi.com because the Windows 2000/XP/2003 DNS client software remembers the answers to old name resolution requests. Want to see what DNS names your workstation currently knows? Open up a command line and type this:

`ipconfig /displaydns`

You'll see a list of names and addresses, as well as the TTL in seconds. Like a DNS server, the Windows 2000/XP/2003 DNS client will only cache information for as long as the TTL specifies. Thus, if your system asks my DNS server to resolve www.minasi.com, then my system says, "Its IP address is 68.15.149.117 and its TTL is 3600 seconds," so for the next hour your system wouldn't bother to try to re-resolve www.minasi.com, choosing instead to assume that the address hadn't changed.

Adding caching on the DNS client was a good move on Microsoft's part precisely because, as you may recall, Active Directory uses DNS the way NT used WINS, as the basic workhorse naming system. There are probably servers in your network that your workstation communicates with all the time; relieving the local DNS servers of having to resolve and re-resolve the names lightens the burden on those servers and reduces network chatter.

Remembering Resolution Failures: "Negative" Caching

Once in a while, however, you'll want the DNS client to *forget* what it's learned. For example, suppose you'd built the simple bigfirm.biz DNS system, but misspelled bigdog as the machine, accidentally miskeying it as bgidog or something like that. You then sit down at some other machine and type **ping bigdog.bigfirm.biz**, and your system tells you that there's no machine by that name. You realize the error and go over to BGIDOG, rename it to bigdog and reboot it. You go over to your workstation and try another **ping bigdog.bigfirm.biz**, but it *still* tells you that there's no such system. Huh? You *fixed* the silly thing—*now* what's wrong? What's wrong is called *negative caching*. The DNS client not only caches the *successes*, it also caches the *failures*, remembering any failed name resolution attempts for five minutes. So if you wait a few minutes more, **ping bigdog.bigfirm.biz** will work. But who wants to wait? You can alternatively tell your system to forget all of its cached entries with this command:

```
ipconfig /flushdns
```

So remember: When you're doing network troubleshooting, flush your DNS cache regularly so you don't get errors arising out of previously failed DNS resolutions that *shouldn't* fail anymore but that do anyway for some mysterious reason. Negative caching is the reason, so flush that cache after re-trying any failed command! And if you decide that five minutes is too long or too short a period to remember failed name resolutions, you can change that. Just look in the Registry in HKEY_LOCAL_MACHINE\SYSTEM\CurrentControlSet\Services\Dnscache\Parameters to find the value entry named NegativeCacheTime. It's a value in seconds.

But if you've never tried to resolve www.minasi.com before from this workstation, then clearly the IP address for my Web site won't be in your cache. So in that case it would be time to check with the local DNS server.

Exercise: Working with the DNS Cache

Let's try out the DNS cache. Make sure if you added the bogus entry in the hosts file for www.minasi.com that you took it out. While sitting at a Windows 2000, XP, or Server 2003 system, start Internet Explorer and view www.minasi.com. Close IE and open a command prompt. Type **ipconfig /displaydns** and you'll see something like this:

```
C:\>ipconfig /displaydns

Windows IP Configuration

        www.minasi.com
        ----------------------------------------
        Record Name . . . . . : www.minasi.com
        Record Type . . . . . : 5
        Time To Live  . . . . : 375
        Data Length . . . . . : 4
        Section . . . . . . . : Answer
        CNAME Record  . . . . : cablenic.minasi.com
...[more output follows]
```

Note the Time To Live—just 375 more seconds, and I'll have to look it up again!

Next, try flushing the cache with **ipconfig /flushdns**. Then try another **ipconfig /displaydns**; you'll see that your cache only contains entries for the loopback, 127.0.0.1.

STEP 3: THE PREFERRED DNS SERVER LOOKS IN *ITS* CACHE

If the local DNS cache didn't have the answer, then your workstation must ask for the help of a DNS server. When configured, every computer running TCP/IP gets the IP address for a *preferred DNS server*. That's the server that the workstation should first go to when it needs a name resolved. You can include a second choice DNS server, which the TCP/IP software will query to resolve a name *only* if the preferred DNS server doesn't respond at all. (You can also offer a third, fourth, fifth, sixth, seventh, and eighth choice server.)

DNS Queries Go to Port 53

The client—your workstation—queries the DNS server on port 53. (In the network traces that I've done, the queries seem to all run on *UDP* port 53, but there might be a TCP-based implementation.) The workstation also supplies a port number for the DNS server to respond on; as is usually the case with TCP or UDP communications, the port for server-to-client responses isn't a "well-known" port; it's basically just a random value—in effect, the client says, "Well, I've *got* to address DNS queries on port 53. What port should the DNS server use to talk back to me? How about 1066? Yeah, that sounds good, 1066—Battle of Hastings and all that. Hey, listen, DNS server, can you resolve www.minasi.com for me and send me back the answer on port 1066 here at my IP address, 210.10.20.11? Thanks."

DNS Servers Also Have Cache

Like the Windows 2000-and-later DNS client, the Server 2003 DNS server caches entries for places that it's already visited. In fact, that's been true for as long as I can remember for DNS servers of *all* kinds, Microsoft and otherwise. So if someone has asked your DNS server to look up www.minasi.com in the past hour—the TTL that I set on my www.minasi.com record—then that DNS server need not query any other servers to resolve www.minasi.com. Instead, it just looks into its cache and finds the answer.

You can see what your DNS server has in its cache by enabling the Advanced View (in the DNS snap-in, click View and look at Advanced; if it's not checked, then click Advanced) and you'll see a folder in the snap-in labeled Cached Lookups. Open it and you'll see all of the places that DNS has cached. You can clear the cache, should you want to—perhaps for troubleshooting purposes—by right-clicking the Cached Lookups folder and choosing Clear Cache. Typing `ipconfig /flushdns` while sitting at the DNS server will not clear the cache; instead, it would only clear the *DNS client cache* on that particular computer.

Definition: A Caching-Only DNS Server

Before leaving this section, it's worth briefly defining a term: *caching-only* DNS server. I've just explained that a DNS server that contained a zone for some domain would look in that zone first, rather than searching the Internet. But I haven't explicitly pointed out yet that you might well be running DNS servers *that contain no zones at all*—in fact, the majority of DNS servers are zoneless. What's the point of a zoneless DNS server? Simple: It focuses solely on searching other DNS servers to resolve name resolution questions. The fact that the server caches the answers to DNS queries that it has received previously leads to the name of this kind of DNS server—a "caching-only" server.

If it's not clear why a caching-only DNS server can be useful, consider Figure 7.81.

FIGURE 7.81

Simple SOHO
Internet connection

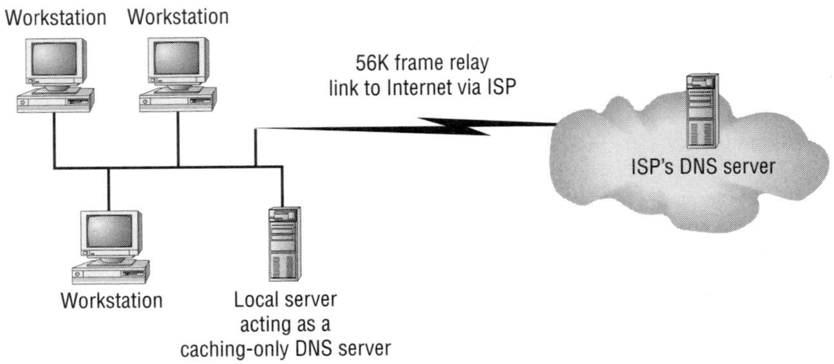

In Figure 7.81, you see a typical small office/home office (SOHO) connection between a small LAN and the Internet. The SOHO setup has a persistent 56K frame relay connection between it and the Internet. Does 56K sound unreasonably slow? It's not—first of all, if you want more than one IP address, then your ISP typically doesn't connect to you via cable modem or DSL, and, second, the vast majority of the world doesn't have the option for DSL or cable modem.

So here's the question: What DNS server should we use as the preferred DNS server for the workstations in the small office? The ISP runs a DNS server and is perfectly happy for us to point all of our workstations to that DNS server as their preferred DNS server. The ISP then worries about keeping the thing up and running, and we needn't buy a DNS server.

Alternatively, however, we could set up a DNS server locally. It wouldn't have to be a dedicated machine, and as you've seen we could just add the DNS server function to an existing Server 2003 (or Linux or Novell or you-name-it) server. That server would know how to search the other DNS servers on the Internet, and we'd configure all of the workstations to use that local DNS server as their preferred DNS server. Which is the better answer?

I think most network architects would go with the latter approach—set up a local DNS server. To see why, ask this: What's the bottleneck in this network? It's a common one for many networks, namely, the connection to the Internet. The fact that a DNS server caches the responses to name queries keeps us from burning up that WAN link. For example, suppose four people in the company decide to visit Microsoft's Web site. In the case where we use the ISP's DNS server, that's four DNS queries that go over the WAN link. But with a local DNS server, then the local DNS server queries other DNS servers on the Internet once to find the IP address of Microsoft's Web site. The local DNS server can resolve the subsequent three queries from its own cache, meaning that those three queries stay on the fast local network. So it can make good sense to set up a local DNS server on your site, even if it *doesn't* hold any zones.

Let's return to following our system in resolving www.minasi.com...

STEP 4: THE PREFERRED DNS SERVER LOOKS IN ITS ZONES

But what if the DNS server *hasn't* been asked to resolve www.minasi.com recently? Is it time to go out to other DNS servers on the Internet? Maybe, but maybe not. It depends on whether this DNS server contains any zones...and if it does, then there's the possibility of *split-brain DNS*—possibly one of the two or three most important concepts in this chapter. (So if you were nodding off or starting to skim, then KNOCK IT OFF—some important stuff's coming! Or at least *I* think so, anyway, so I ask that you humor me.

Local Zones Take Priority

If you were sitting on a workstation computer in my local network, then it's likely that the preferred DNS server for that computer would be the same DNS server that acts as the primary DNS server for minasi.com. In that case, the workstation's primary DNS server would be the perfect machine to ask the question, "What's the IP address for www.minasi.com?"

When queried, DNS servers look in their local zones—whether primary or secondary—before querying other servers on the Internet (or, if your DNS hierarchy isn't connected to the public DNS system, other servers in your private DNS hierarchy).

IMPORTANT DIGRESSION: INTRODUCING SPLIT-BRAIN DNS

You're going to learn a bit later in this chapter that sometimes you quite deliberately want to present one set of DNS names to your private internal intranet and quite a different set of names to the external Internet—I think of it as "keeping two sets of books" DNS-wise. Some people call it "split-brain DNS." I don't want to hit you with all of those details right now, but I *do* want to get you ready by highlighting the basic reason split-brain is possible: when a DNS server attempts to resolve an address, it first looks in its local zone files. If it finds a zone file whose name matches the zone that it's looking for, then the server will look no further than that zone file, even if there's a zone by the same name out on the public Internet. In short, local zone files take precedence over anything on the Internet.

At first glance, it makes perfect sense to say that if your local DNS server also happens to be the authoritative DNS server for minasi.com, then when you ask that server to resolve www.minasi.com, the DNS server gets the answer from its local zones rather than querying other servers on the Internet. After all, if your local DNS server is the only authoritative DNS server for minasi.com, there wouldn't be much point to looking elsewhere on some other DNS server to resolve a minasi.com name...there aren't any others.

Virtually All Active Directories Need Split-Brain

But what happens if your local DNS server has a minasi.com zone, but isn't the *authoritative* DNS server for minasi.com? Is your DNS server smart enough to say, "Hmmm, I'm not the authoritative server for minasi.com...this zone must be bogus, I'll ignore it?" Nope. But that's good, as it lets us fool a DNS server into thinking that it's authoritative for any zone that we like. *That* is absolutely essential and, as I said a few paragraphs back, is the way that split-brain DNS is going to work. But this isn't some obscure trick; no, it's a major tool in a DNS admin's tool belt. I'm not exaggerating when I say that *over 90 percent of the Active Directories out there use or will use split-brain DNS*; if anything, that's an underestimate. So this is a must-understand skill.

People use split-brain DNS for Active Directory security. To see why, let's review what you've seen so far about DNS and Active Directory.

- ◆ Machines in a domain must find domain controllers, so there has to be a list of DCs installed on every machine (which is impractical) or a group of servers standing by to answer the question, "Which machines are DCs for this domain?"

◆ Microsoft designed Active Directory to use DNS as its DC locator service, matching DNS zone names to AD domain names. Thus, an AD named bigfirm.biz needs a corresponding DNS zone named bigfirm.biz.

◆ More specifically, machines in a domain look for Kerberos (authentication) and LDAP (query) services by asking DNS for SRV records.

That's another way of saying that anyone who can look in the DNS zone that corresponds to your Active Directory domain can see the names and addresses of your domain controllers—which is something of a security breach. I mean, it's not a *terrible* breach of security, as it's not like you store the passwords in your DNS zone or anything like that. But DCs are pretty powerful servers, and there's no sense in announcing their location to all and making life easier for the weasels. But there's one more thing to consider about AD/DNS security:

◆ For all this to work, someone or something has to insert a bunch of SRV records into that DNS zone. Microsoft decided to use dynamic DNS to allow DCs to insert—"register"—their own SRV records.

In this context, dynamic presents *another* potential security risk in addition to the ones that I enumerated a few pages back. Suppose someone figures out how to build a piece of software that mimics a domain controller. Once installed in a network, this bogus DC fools machines into trying to log onto it by giving the faux DC the account names and passwords of the machine and its user. (Such a piece of software does not exist, as far as I know, nor would it be very easy to write, so don't lose too much sleep over it.) In order for this imaginary DC to do damage, machines on the domain would have to somehow find the bogus DC, and how do machines find DCs in Active Directory? Through DNS records. So one way to secure an AD domain would be to set up its DNS servers so that the outside world cannot see them, and thus would have no chance to register false SRV records for malicious would-be DCs.

For many organizations, then, the right way to set up DNS for Active Directory is to have a non-dynamic DNS zone that the outside world sees that contains only the names of the Web and mail servers for that firm, and a separate, internal dynamic DNS zone that serves your AD clients.

Let's try it out with our working bigfirm.biz DNS server. If you don't have one working, don't worry, you can read along.

An Example Exercise: Faking dell.com

Suppose you wanted to visit Dell and buy a computer from them over the Web. You'd start out by pointing your browser to www.dell.com, and your preferred DNS server would search the Internet's other DNS servers to get the IP address of Dell's Web site. So far, so good—nothing that I said in the preceding sentence should run counter to your real-life experience.

Try this experiment.

1. While sitting at Bigdog, start nslookup. Type **www.dell.com** and press Enter. nslookup will respond with an IP address, or probably several IP addresses. Type **exit** to exit nslookup.

2. Next, open up the DNS snap-in at Bigdog and create a new forward lookup zone named dell.com. Add an A record for www and give it the IP address 68.15.149.117.

3. Now return to the command prompt. Type **ipconfig /flushdns** and press Enter. Then start up nslookup. Again, try to resolve www.dell.com and you'll get just one IP address—68.15.149.117.

4. Start up Internet Explorer and surf to www.dell.com. You won't end up at Dell, you'll end up at my Web site.

5. Now that you've seen that it works, do yourself a favor; open up the DNS snap-in and delete the dell.com folder now, while you still remember to do it. It could be awfully frustrating to try to visit Dell for tech support sometime in the next day or two, only to find yourself trapped in my site!

Let's review what you did. By putting a new primary zone called dell.com on one of your local DNS servers, you caused anyone who uses that particular DNS server as their preferred DNS server to be unable to get to the real Dell. You didn't crash Dell's worldwide empire—*everyone else on the Internet can still find Dell without a problem.* Sure, you've got a bogus dell.com zone, but it doesn't affect anyone else, because there would be no reason for anyone to visit your DNS server to resolve www.dell.com. The only people who *would* use that DNS server to resolve www.dell.com would be those people who happen to use that DNS server as their preferred DNS server.

Another Example: Internal versus External bigfirm.biz Zones

As you sat at the Bigdog server to do the Dell example, something might have occurred to some of you. Bigdog is the primary DNS server for bigfirm.biz, as you know. But did you ever try sitting at another computer, opening up Internet Explorer and surfing to www.bigfirm.biz, just to see what would happen? If you did, then you know that "www.bigfirm.biz" takes you to www.minasi.com, my Web site. But it wasn't marketing that led me to do that. You see, in earlier books I used examples like acme.com and bowsers.com for my DNS zones. As I said earlier, it dawned on me one day that people misconfiguring my examples could cause hundreds or thousands of systems to try to register with the acme.com or bowsers.com DNS servers. Not nice. So I registered bigfirm.biz so that any resulting problems would be mine.

But here's the important point: there is currently an Internet domain that is properly registered with the naming authorities called bigfirm.biz. But our examples have, by working with a local zone named bigfirm.biz, completely bypassed that properly registered DNS domain.

In other words, *we've been doing split-brain DNS from the very beginning!*

Here's another use for split-brain. You could run a dynamic DNS service in a company that perhaps doesn't want to put a DDNS server on the public Internet. For example, imagine that Bigfirm already *has* an externally hosted zone called bigfirm.biz, and you want to create an Active Directory internally called bigfirm.biz. The external bigfirm.biz zone is probably run by some ISP on a static DNS server—*they're* not about to make their zone dynamic just to make you happy. Sure, you *could* take charge of—that is, become authoritative for—your zone, but it's not necessary.

Suppose you set up a DNS server—a dynamic one—of your own, with a bigfirm.biz zone on your intranet. As long as all of your workstations used that DNS server as their preferred DNS server, then any time that a workstation or server asks that DNS server to resolve a bigfirm.biz name, the DNS server will notice that it *holds* a zone file for bigfirm.biz. It will then say to itself, "Heck, I don't have to go out on the Internet to resolve this name—I'm 'the guy' for this zone! *I* have the answers!" Systems could then register names for bigfirm.biz with this DNS server and your AD would work like a charm. *That's* the basics of how I recommend that you set up your DNS server. But we'll cover this in more detail later in this chapter; for now, let's get back to seeing how resolution occurs.

STEP 5: THE PREFERRED DNS SERVER FINDS AND QUERIES MY DNS SERVER

Well, presuming that the local DNS server can't resolve the query from its local cache or zone files, what next? As you read earlier in this chapter, your local DNS server will next try to locate a DNS server that is authoritative for minasi.com and then go query *that* server. But how to find that authoritative server? Recall from the discussion earlier in this chapter that

- your local DNS server wants to find the zone for the com domain because that will contain the record pointing to the DNS server for minasi.com,
- but before your DNS server can query the com server, it needs to know the DNS server for com,
- and the way it gets *that* is by querying the root servers,
- and the way it knows how to find the root servers is that your DNS server comes prepackaged knowing the names and addresses of the 13 root servers.

Once your DNS server obtains the IP address of the minasi.com domain's DNS servers, then your DNS server will go ask one of the minasi.com DNS servers to resolve www.minasi.com, and report the value back to your computer.

At least, that's what I told you a few sections back—that's basically right, but I left out some details. Now I'll fill them in.

Talking to the Root

Let's back up a minute and consider what the client asked of the server. The DNS client software running on your workstation said to your local DNS server, "Please resolve the name www.minasi.com." But it said more than that: More completely, it said, "Please search for the answer, even if you have to talk to a bunch of DNS servers." And your local DNS server will do that, doggedly following the trail of other DNS servers until it gets the answer or discovers that no answer is possible.

In contrast, let's consider what happens when your local DNS server queries a root server. I've been saying up to now that your local DNS server asks the root for the address of the com DNS server so that it can ask the com server the address of the minasi.com DNS server, but that's not exactly true. Actually, your DNS server asks the root server, "What's the IP address of www.minasi.com?"

Now, the root server *could* choose to go root around (no pun intended) and get that answer for my DNS server. But it doesn't want to do any more work than is necessary—hey, it's pretty busy, just 13 root servers for the entire DNS hierarchy of Planet Earth means 13 pretty overworked computers—so instead of answering the question, the root server says, in effect, "I could find that answer for you, but I'm not going to. But here's what I'll do instead—I'll give you the name and address of the *next* DNS server that you should ask the question of." Your DNS server then re-asks the question, "What's the IP address for www.minasi.com?" of the DNS server that the root server referred it to. That subsequent server might be designed to go get the complete answer for your DNS server, or it might just be set up to work like the root servers, saying, "I won't give you the answer, but here's the next guy to try." For example, here's what the conversation might look like when your DNS server tries to find www.minasi.com:

1. Your DNS server asks a root server, "What's the IP address of www.minasi.com?"
2. The root server probably answers, "Don't ask me, ask one of these servers," and lists the names and addresses of the DNS servers for the com domain.

3. Your DNS server picks one of those names and says to the DNS server for the com domain, "What's the IP address of www.minasi.com?"

4. The com DNS server answers, "Don't ask me, ask either the DNS server at 206.246.253.111 or the one at 206.246.253.112." (Those are the IP addresses of my two DNS servers and, yes, one of them is the same computer as the Web server.)

5. Your DNS server asks my DNS server, "What's the IP address for www.minasi.com?"

6. My DNS server responds, "www.minasi.com is at 206.246.253.111."

Definition: Recursive *versus* Iterative *Queries*

So you've seen that your DNS server will go to great lengths to answer a query. Mine works that way, too, and so will most DNS servers with which you'll ever work. But those root servers and the DNS servers for the com domain and other top-level domains don't do that. That's because DNS recognizes two kinds of queries: recursive and iterative.

A *recursive* query is the kind that you make against your local DNS server. You tell it to keep asking the questions until it gets an answer.

An *iterative* query is what the root servers do. When asked to resolve a name, they'll only resolve the name if they have the information right there in their zone files. If not, they just pass along the name of the next DNS server—or servers, usually—in the chain.

Down at the programming level, it's possible for a DNS server to specify when querying whether it wants a recursive or iterative answer. But that won't matter if the server has been configured to only answer recursively.

Controlling Recursive and Iterative Behavior

By default, the Server 2003 DNS server answers queries recursively, searching as long as is necessary. But you can modify that behavior. In the DNS snap-in, right-click the icon representing the DNS server, click Properties and then the Advanced tab, and you'll see a page like you did back in Figure 7.55, Advanced DNS Properties.

By checking the box labeled Disable Recursion, you cause the DNS server to respond in an iterative ("*I* don't have that answer, but if you ask *this* guy he could probably help you") rather than a recursive ("I looked all over and here's your answer") manner.

Summarizing, then, these are the major steps that happen when your Windows 2000, XP, or Server 2003 system—let's generically call it the *client*—needs a DNS name resolved:

1. First, the system looks as well as steps 4–7 in the local file named `hosts`.

2. If that doesn't help, it looks in the DNS client's local cache.

3. If the local cache can't help, it then contacts the client's preferred DNS server, asking it to resolve the name.

4. The preferred DNS server looks in its cache and then its zones to answer the query.

5. If it can't answer, then the preferred DNS server looks for the DNS server that *can* answer the query, the DNS server (or, usually, servers) that is authoritative for the domain in question. It does that by asking the root servers, which direct it to the next level of DNS servers, finally getting the IP addresses of the authoritative DNS servers.

6. The preferred DNS server then directly queries the authoritative DNS server, getting the IP address of the target system.

7. Finally, the preferred DNS server returns the answer to the client.

DNS Forwarding

We've got one more basic DNS concept to cover, and it's an important one: forwarding. DNS forwarding includes three topics:

- ◆ Centralized caching of DNS records
- ◆ Securing internal DNS servers from exposure to outside attack
- ◆ Knitting together a system of DNS servers doing split-brain DNS

Centralizing DNS Caches with Forwarding

As time goes on, the percentage of computers in your network that can be full-fledged Active Directory clients and servers and the share of applications in your network that are Active Directory–compliant will grow. That's important because once your network consists entirely of AD-compliant pieces, then DNS becomes the main name resolver, and WINS fades away. When that happens, you'll want fast-responding DNS servers.

Now, thankfully, Microsoft put a DNS cache on every workstation, so you might hope that most of those name resolutions will be resolved by the workstation itself, out of its DNS cache. Despite that, though, there will be an awful lot of name resolutions in your network that can't be handled by the 2000, XP, or 2003 DNS client's cache, and so network designers will constantly face this inescapable truth: Networks that resolve names slowly will be perceived as slow networks.

Fast name resolution isn't the only thing that you'll need for a fast network, but you can't have a fast network without it. So how do you plan to provide fast name resolution?

On the face of it, the answer would seem to be DNS servers, and lots of them. If you have lots of DNS servers sprinkled around your network and a low DNS client-to-server ratio, then client machines will see fast response, won't they? Well, yes, except for one consideration: caching on the DNS servers.

THE "MANY DNS SERVERS" SCENARIO

Imagine that we're designing the DNS architecture for Megabucks Corporation, a firm with 2000 employees on a single large campus. Megabucks is attached to the Internet via a few T1 lines that are always busy transmitting and receiving e-mail, Web traffic, and streaming multimedia. Every unnecessary access to the Internet creates congestion on those lines.

We figure that one DNS server for every 100 employees seems like a good ratio (I just made that up, please don't take it as an actual rule of thumb—I don't think it'd be possible to come up with a rule of thumb for DNS servers that would be simple and useful, sadly), so we set up 20 DNS servers that we'll call ns01.megabucks.com through ns20.megabucks.com. Let's watch them work.

First thing in the morning, people show up and start working. One employee, Mary, sits at a workstation whose preferred DNS server is NS01. She points her browser to www.cnn.com to get the headlines, and so her workstation asks NS01 to resolve www.cnn.com. NS01 hasn't been asked for www.cnn.com yet today, so it's got to go out on the Internet to get the answer. When other people whose workstations subsequently go to www.cnn.com, NS01 has the name already resolved and so can respond to their name resolution requests instantly.

But now Bill sits at his workstation, starting off his day with the headlines at www.cnn.com. *His* workstation, however, uses ns02.megabucks.com as its DNS server. NS02 hasn't been asked for www.cnn.com's IP address yet, so it has to go out to the Internet to answer that query. Similarly, NS03, NS04, and so on—each of the 20 DNS servers—each have to separately learn the IP address of www.cnn.com. (That's presuming that they have to learn it at all—for example, NS17 might only serve a bunch of people who might only use their computers to do work rather than the high-tech equivalent of reading the paper in the office.) In other words, if our servers could somehow get together on what they know in their caches, then we could reduce by up to 20-fold the amount of WAN bandwidth that the DNS servers suck up.

THE "ONE BIG DNS SERVER" SCENARIO

Or we could take a different tack. Instead of installing DNS on a bunch of machines, some of which might also be serving in other roles, we go spend some of the company's money for a monster eight-CPU system with several gigabytes of RAM. Then we point *every* workstation in the plant to this system. The benefit? One server means one cache. After Mary causes the server to resolve www.cnn.com, then Bill's subsequent resolution request can be answered instantaneously.

If *this* scenario makes you a bit queasy, then it should. Although one big cache would be nice, putting all of my eggs in one basket has always made me wish for a titanium basket. Is there a way to both unify the cache and get the benefits of scattering DNS servers all over the place?

DNS FORWARDERS: THE BEST OF BOTH WORLDS

We *can* centralize the cache and yet keep our 20 DNS servers. The trick is called *forwarding*. Figure 7.82 shows how it works.

FIGURE 7.82

A DNS forwarder

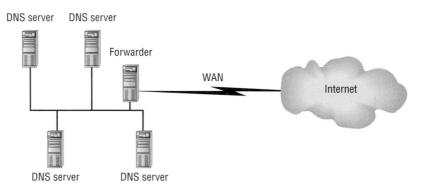

You've read how a DNS server normally resolves a name—it looks in its cache and its zones, and then starts looking out on the Internet for the authoritative DNS server. With forwarding, you add an intermediate step. At Megabucks, you'd set up a 21st machine as a DNS server and then tell the 20 other DNS servers to use that 21st machine as a *forwarder*. Then they'd resolve a name in this way:

1. As before, look in the local cache and zones.
2. If the local cache and zones don't have the answer, then don't go out on the Internet. Instead, query the forwarder.

3. If the forwarder has the answer in its local cache or zones, then it can answer the question. If not, then the forwarder searches the DNS servers on the Internet, as you've already learned.

4. Once the forwarder has the answer, it sends that back to the querying DNS server.

5. *But* if the forwarder doesn't respond in a reasonable amount of time, then the querying DNS server just gives up on the forwarder and searches the DNS servers on the Internet itself.

Now, at first blush, it might look like we've just made things slower by adding a new step in the resolution process—querying and then waiting for the forwarder. But consider how the forwarder communicates with the local DNS servers—through the company LAN. That LAN's likely to be 100 megabits per second or faster—almost certainly in any case faster than the WAN link to the Internet. The value of the forwarder at Megabucks is this: Mary and Bill still have separate DNS servers, but their DNS servers don't ever have to communicate on the Internet. Because Mary first looked up www.cnn.com, that caused her DNS server (NS01) to try to resolve the name. It asked the forwarder, who also didn't know the IP address for www.cnn.com. So the forwarder went out over the WAN link to the Internet to find out www.cnn.com's IP address, and told Mary's DNS server. Minutes later, when Bill's DNS server (NS02) needed to resolve www.cnn.com, it asked the forwarder to go look it up—and the forwarder responded instantly over the company's LAN because the forwarder already had the answer in its cache. The result? Now www.cnn.com is in the caches of NS01, NS02, and the forwarder—but it only went out on the Internet once.

Telling a Server 2003 DNS server to use a forwarder is simple. Just open the DNS snap-in and right-click the icon representing the DNS server, choose Properties, then click the Forwarders tab on the properties page. You'll see a screen like Figure 7.83.

FIGURE 7.83

Configuring a DNS forwarder

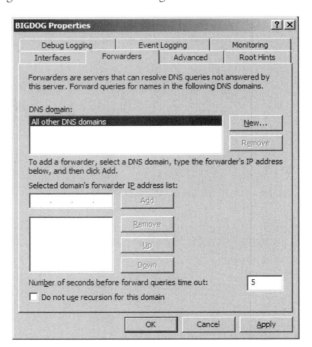

If you're a Windows 2000 DNS veteran, then you'll immediately notice that 2003's DNS does forwarding a lot differently than 2000's DNS did—and the UI's not immediately obvious. To tell a 2003 DNS server to forward any queries that it can't resolve out of its own zones to another DNS server, click All Other DNS Domains under DNS Domain. Then look below that to the field labeled Selected Domain's Forwarder IP Address List, where you can punch in an IP address— the DNS server will now forward to the DNS server at that IP address.

Note the field in the lower right part of the Forwarders tab labeled Number of Seconds before Forward Queries Time Out and its default value, five seconds. This is the "reasonable amount of time" that I referred to when describing how a forwarder works a page or two back.

Does the forwarder need to be a particularly powerful machine? Not really; answering a query out of the cache isn't that stressful for a system. But you'd do well to give the forwarder a *lot* of RAM. The more RAM, the more items it can cache without having to page them out to disk.

DO FORWARDERS PRESENT A SINGLE POINT OF FAILURE?

A bit earlier I suggested that the "one big DNS server" scenario might make you a bit nervous, as it was a case of putting all of your eggs in one basket. But isn't having a bunch of intranet DNS servers relying on a single forwarder just the same thing—isn't that one forwarder a new single point of failure? Not necessarily.

First, remember that when you specify a forwarder for a DNS server you also specify a timeout value. If the forwarder doesn't respond within that time, the DNS server simply bypasses the forwarder and resolves the name on the public DNS hierarchy all by itself.

Second, take another look at Figure 7.83 and you'll see that you can specify more than one forwarder. Having more than one forwarder has a down-side in that you no longer have one system that all queries funnel through, and so you don't have the one big master cache; instead, you'd have a group of forwarders, and each forwarder would have a pretty wide variety of things in its cache, but not as large a cache as if there were just one forwarder.

Adding more than one forwarder does mean that you'll end up having to repeat some DNS queries over the public Internet, and so name resolution will be a trifle slower than it would be with one forwarder. But on balance, I'd be willing to accept that in return for the benefit of fault tolerance on forwarding—if one forwarder fails, we're not without any forwarders. That will become even more important as we *slave* our internal DNS servers to external forwarders to secure those internal DNS servers, as we'll do in a few pages.

EXERCISE: SETTING UP A FORWARDER

We'll try out forwarding with this exercise. If you've been following along with the exercises in this chapter, then you'll have two systems set up as DNS servers:

- bigdog.bigfirm.biz, a Server 2003 DNS server with IP address 192.168.0.2 as well as the ability to route to the public Internet and a local bigfirm.biz zone.
- ns2.bigfirm.biz, a Server 2003 DNS server with IP address 192.168.0.3 and, again, the ability to route to the public Internet. No zones necessary on this server for this exercise.

In this exercise, we'll try telling Bigdog to forward all of its DNS queries out over ns2 and also see what happens when we adjust the timeout values. Ensure that Bigdog's IP address is 192.168.02 and ns2's IP address is 192.168.0.3. (If they're *not* those values, then the exercise will work fine—just substitute your system's IP addresses as appropriate.) And ensure that both systems can ping the public Internet. Tell Bigdog to forward through ns2 like so:

1. At Bigdog, open the DNS snap-in.
2. Right-click the icon representing the server—forwarding is a characteristic of a server, not a zone. Choose Properties.
3. In the Bigdog DNS properties, click the Forwarders tab.
4. Under Selected Domain's Forwarder IP Address List, enter **192.168.0.3** and click Add.
5. In the field labeled Number of Seconds before Forward Queries Time Out, fill in 60.
6. Click Apply.

Don't close the DNS snap-in; we'll be adjusting it again. Now open a command prompt at Bigdog. Clear the DNS cache with an `ipconfig /flushdns` command, then start `nslookup`. As Bigdog will end up asking its questions to ns2, which will in turn have to go search the Internet, then make sure `nslookup` is a bit more patient: type **set timeout=30** and press Enter to tell it to wait at least a half minute before emitting its irritating "DNS request timed out" error. Then try resolving an address on the public Internet, like www.nasa.gov. You should get the normal response, as a forwarded query looks no different from a direct one. Exit `nslookup` with the `exit` command.

How do you know that the forwarding actually worked, other than taking my word for it? Let's use a little split-brain to prove the point.

1. At Bigdog, clear the DNS client cache with `ipconfig /flushdns`. As Bigdog also runs a DNS server, clear the DNS server's cache by opening the DNS snap-in. Right-click the server icon for Bigdog and choose Clear Cache.
2. Over at ns2, create a forward primary zone, nasa.gov. It doesn't matter how you set its dynamic DNS properties. In the zone, add a new host record, www, and give it the IP address 10.10.10.10.
3. Clear the cache on Ns2.
4. Back at Bigdog, open a command prompt, start `nslookup`, and set the timeout to 30 seconds again. Then try the www.nasa.gov query. You should get the answer "10.10.10.10" rather than the actual value.

Clearly the NASA Web server isn't at IP address 10.10.10.10, so we've demonstrated that Bigdog does indeed get its DNS info from ns2.

Let's do one more thing just to be sure that forwarding works as I've described it. We've made Bigdog dependent on ns2 for DNS queries; what happens if ns2 fails? We'll stop the DNS service on Ns2 and try that NASA query again.

1. Go to ns2 and open the DNS snap-in. Stop ns2's DNS service by right-clicking its server icon, then choose All Tasks/Stop.
2. Go to Bigdog and open its DNS snap-in. Clear Bigdog's server cache—right-click the server icon and choose Clear Cache.
3. We don't want to have to wait a long time for Bigdog to figure out that ns2 isn't going to answer it, so let's drop the timeout value. Right-click the Bigdog server icon, choose Properties and the Forwarders tab. Change 60 back to the default of 5 and click Apply.

4. Open a command prompt and clear the DNS client cache with `ipconfig /flushdns`. Then start `nslookup` and this time, set the timeout to 30 seconds as you did before.

5. Tell `nslookup` to look up www.nasa.gov. You'll get the actual IP address of NASA's Web server this time.

In this case, Bigdog is still forwarding through ns2, but ns2 didn't respond, so after a timeout, we saw that Bigdog will bypass its forwarder.

Uprooting a DNS Server: When Forwarders Are Grayed Out

Before moving on to security and caching, it's time for a short digression. If you've just set up your DNS server and are following along with the book, then you might have seen something disconcerting—the controls on the Forwarders tab are grayed out. Click the Root Hints tab, and you see the same thing. What happened? You've got a false root. (Let me note that I've only seen this on Windows 2000–based DNS servers, where it showed up often; I've only *heard* of them on 2003 DNS servers, but I'm including this for the sake of completeness.)

What's happening here is that your DNS server thinks that it is *the* only DNS server in the world, that it is the root of the public DNS hierarchy. How'd it happen? In most cases, the Configure a DNS Server Wizard mistakenly decided that your DNS server was on an intranet completely disconnected from the public Internet. In that case, the 13 root servers aren't available. But a DNS hierarchy needs a root...so your server's elected to be a "private" root. Root servers can't use forwarders (although they can use conditional forwarding), and—here's the really annoying part—they can't search DNS servers on the public Internet, because they don't even know that public Internet *exists*.

Installing a private root on a DNS server tells it that there *isn't* any other DNS server around to which to refer questions. So if your DNS server doesn't have a zone that it can look something up in, then it just assumes that no one knows the answer.

Anyway, that's what went wrong. How to undo it? Here are three ways to reintroduce your DNS server to the rest of the world. All three share the same basic approach: they delete the root domain from your DNS server. I'm explaining all three approaches so that I can also offer some insight into how to do a bit of under-the-hood work on DNS.

First, there's the command-line approach. This needs a command called DNSCMD.EXE, which doesn't automatically install with Server 2003 but *is* included in the Server Tools add-on, which you can find on the Server 2003 CD in the `\SUPPORT\TOOLS` folder. Once DNSCMD is installed, you can de-root your DNS server with one command:

```
dnscmd /ZoneDelete .
```

Note the spacing—first `dnscmd`, then a space, then the option `/ZoneDelete`, then another space, then ".", the name of the zone to delete. I notice in dnscmd's Help that there's an option `/dsdel` that you must run to delete the zone if it's Active Directory–integrated, but I'm not quite sure how you'd end up with an AD-integrated root domain, at least not without a lot of work! Uppercase and lowercase seem not to matter. Once you execute the command, I recommend restarting the DNS service. Then open up the DNS snap-in and try to examine the Forwarders or Root Hints tabs on the server's properties page—you'll see that they're no longer grayed out.

You can also de-root a DNS server from the DNS snap-in. Open up the `Forward Lookup Zones` folder and you'll see a folder whose name is simply "."; as you now know, that's the root domain. Right-click that folder and choose Properties. In the properties page, check that the zone type is

Primary rather than Active Directory–integrated; if it *is* AD-integrated, just click the Change button next to the type and convert it to a standard primary zone. Close the properties page.

In the Forward Lookup Zones folder, right-click the root zone and click Delete. Close the DNS snap-in, restart the DNS Server service, and re-open the DNS snap-in. You'll see that Forwarders and Root Hints tabs are no longer grayed out.

Finally, for those who enjoy a bit of Registry tweaking, here's a third uprooting procedure. As far as I know, this only works on a standard primary zone. First, stop the DNS Server service, either from the GUI or from the command line with this:

```
net stop "DNS Server"
```

Then edit the Registry to altogether remove the key at HKEY_LOCAL_MACHINE\SYSTEM\CurrentControlSet\Services\DNS\Zones\. and, again, notice that final period—that was part of the key, not the end of the sentence. Restart the DNS service, and you're back in the public DNS hierarchy.

Of course, now and then you might actually *want* a DNS server with a private root; I'll tell you how to set one up a bit later in this chapter.

Securing Internal DNS Servers with Forwarding/Slaving

While forwarders are useful as a way to centralize cache, as I've just described, I think most people do forwarding less to speed up name resolutions than to secure DNS servers that are inside their firewalls. They do that by adjusting their internal DNS servers so that they don't *forward* to another DNS server, they *slave* to it. Slaving is a slight modification of the forwarding algorithm that forces the internal DNS server to depend *entirely* on the forwarder.

So how's it useful?

Well, imagine this scenario. You have a bunch of DNS servers inside your network. You're concerned about them being attacked if they make their presence known to the outside world but you don't want to have go through the time and expense of "hardening" them all against attack. So you create *one* hardened DNS server and put it outside the firewall. Then you set up the internal DNS servers to forward through the one external DNS server.

This makes your internal systems safer because of a characteristic of most firewalls—the "stateful inspection" characteristic that we discussed in the previous chapter. Systems outside the firewall cannot communicate with the DNS servers inside the firewall, *unless* the systems outside the firewall are answering queries made by the internal DNS servers. That's the value of the one hardened server outside the firewall: the internal systems ask it to do their queries, and it passes back the answers. The external system *is* outside the firewall but can still communicate with the systems inside the firewall because the external system is answering their questions. As the external system is the only one that queries other DNS servers on the Internet, the internal guys are safe, right?

Almost, but not quite. Remember how a DNS server uses a forwarder? It passes queries along to the forwarder and waits for the forwarder to search the Internet's DNS servers to resolve those queries. But remember that it only waits *so* long; if the forwarder doesn't respond in a particular period of time (a configurable period, but it's five seconds by default on Server 2003 DNS servers), then the internal DNS server just takes the bull by the horns and searches the Internet itself.

That's the troublesome part. If a server from behind a firewall initiates a conversation with a DNS server on the public Internet, then that server is essentially asking a question and waiting for an answer. To allow the server on the public Internet to answer the query of the system behind the firewall, address translating routers must temporarily leave a link in place, an open port on the firewall leading back to the internal DNS server. Why exactly is that bad? Over the years the bad guys have sometimes found weaknesses in DNS server software, and they then write virus software to exploit it. That virus software masquerades as a DNS server, and when a server running buggy DNS server software asks the fake DNS server a question, the fake DNS server infects the unsuspecting DNS server. That's why you've got that one hardened system outside the firewall; you're careful to put all of the latest patches and antivirus software on it, so the bad guys' attacks just bounce off it.

So here's the problem: you have that external hardened system that you want to do all of your queries. You tell all of your internal DNS servers to forward through that external server. *But* if the external DNS server doesn't respond quickly enough, then the internal servers start querying DNS servers on the public Internet on their own. What to do?

The fix is simple. Just modify your internal DNS servers' behavior when they send queries to the forwarder. Tell your internal DNS servers, "If the external forwarder doesn't respond to your query, too bad—just consider the attempt failed." This is called *slaving* the internal DNS server to the forwarder. To see how to do that, look at the tab on a DNS server's properties page that controls forwarding (look back to Figure 7.83). Just check the box labeled Do Not Use Recursion for This Domain, and you've slaved the server. Slaving a DNS server to another DNS server is, then, nothing more than a restricted form of forwarding a DNS server to another DNS server.

If you *do* slave internal DNS servers to external forwarders, then make sure that it's external forwarders, plural. If all of your internal DNS servers were slaved to one external DNS server and that external DNS server went down, then you wouldn't be able to resolve any names on the public Internet.

EXERCISE: SLAVING BIGDOG TO NS2

This is a quick exercise. We've already got Bigdog forwarding through ns2, and in the last exercise we stopped the DNS server service on ns2. You saw that if we ask Bigdog to resolve www.nasa.gov, Bigdog would wait a while for ns2 to respond and finally, when it didn't, Bigdog could just resolve the name itself by querying DNS servers on the public Internet.

Now let's configure Bigdog to be slaved to Ns2.

1. On Bigdog, open the DNS snap-in.
2. Right-click the Bigdog server icon, choose Properties and the Forwarders tab.
3. In the Forwarders tab, check the box that says Do Not Use Recursion for This Domain.
4. Click OK to close the properties page.
5. Right-click the server icon and choose Clear Cache.
6. Close the DNS snap-in.
7. Now clear the client DNS cache and try to resolve www.nasa.gov. Open a command prompt, type **ipconfig /flushdns**, and then **nslookup.**
8. Once the **nslookup** ">" prompt appears, type **www.nasa.gov** and press Enter.

You should get a message from **nslookup** saying that the request timed out, demonstrating that Bigdog is slaved to ns2.

Conditional Forwarding: Another Split-Brain Tool

We've already talked a bit about split-brain DNS, a method for fooling clients of a particular DNS server into thinking that the server is authoritative for a given zone. Remember how that worked: first, you put a zone on a DNS server for a given DNS domain—one that DNS server is *not* authoritative for. Any machines who look to that DNS server for name resolution then get false information whenever they query that domain.

So let's suppose that for some odd reason I decided that I wanted all of the 50 systems in my intranet to have the DNS suffix microsoft.com. I might accomplish that by pointing all of my 50 systems to a DNS server that I've set up at 10.1.1.5, and putting a microsoft.com zone on that DNS server. I'd also set up my local DHCP server to give systems the DNS suffix microsoft.com by default, and if I enabled dynamic updates on that DNS server at 10.1.1.5 *and* set up all 50 systems so that they used 10.1.1.5 as their preferred DNS server, then I'd have accomplished the dubiously useful goal of having my own little micro-Redmond on my site. (Remember, there would be a cost here—any attempt to access a Web server in Microsoft's site would fail, as my one DNS server would think that it was authoritative for the microsoft.com domain and therefore would never look to see if there was an actual site by that name.)

So far, this looks like the split-brain DNS examples that I've offered in the past. But now consider this. A friend down the road runs a small company of his own, with about 60 systems and, again, one DNS server. He decides to go with Active Directory and for some reason thinks it would be just a hoot to call his Active Directory novell.com, so he needs a dynamic DNS zone by that name. As the domain name is already taken, he too adopts a split-brain approach, putting a dynamic novell.com zone on his one DNS server. His users can, like mine, use DNS to find their internal domain controllers in their Active Directory named novell.com, and they can surf the public Internet, except if they want to see something on the actual Novell Web site, send someone at Novell a piece of e-mail, or whatever. (Again, I have no idea why you'd do that, I'm just providing a simple example here.)

Time goes on and my friend and I decided to embark on some joint ventures. We're not going to merge the companies or anything like that, but we *do* need to access some of each other's resources. I might give his folks some limited access to our intranet Web server's content, share an e-mail server or something like that. That's where the problem arises.

His Web server is named www.novell.com. Whenever my folks punch that into IE's address field, then they go to the real Novell Web site. His split-brain system fools the machines who depend on his DNS server, but only them. Hmmm…so what if I just point all of my systems to his DNS server? Well, that would let my systems find his Web server, but then they'd lose the ability to find *my* servers, as asking any microsoft.com question of my friend's DNS server would get an answer about the *real* microsoft.com! It seems that I'm in trouble either way. Or I could convince my DNS server to do split-brain for my friend's novell.com zone by making my DNS server a secondary server for novell.com and point to his DNS server as the "master" for novell.com…but we might not be *that* good friends, and he might be leery about shipping his internal zone to one of my servers.

There's another answer: conditional DNS forwarding. Here, I tell my DNS server, "If you ever need to resolve a name in the novell.com zone, then don't go looking all over the Internet—ask *that* server," pointing to my friend's DNS server. I could, if I wanted, have conditional forwarding commands for as many other DNS zones as I liked.

Server 2003's DNS server software lets you set up conditional forwarding for as many zones as you like. Just open the server's properties page and click Forwarders as you've done before, to see a screen like the one back in Figure 7.83. Then set up conditional forwarding this way:

1. Click the New button in the upper right part of the page. You'll then see a dialog box like Figure 7.84.

FIGURE 7.84

Adding a conditional
forwarding setting

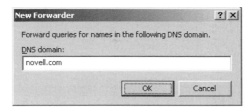

2. There, I've filled in novell.com by way of example. Click OK, and your Forwarders page will look like Figure 7.85.

FIGURE 7.85

Forwarders showing
a conditional
forwarding

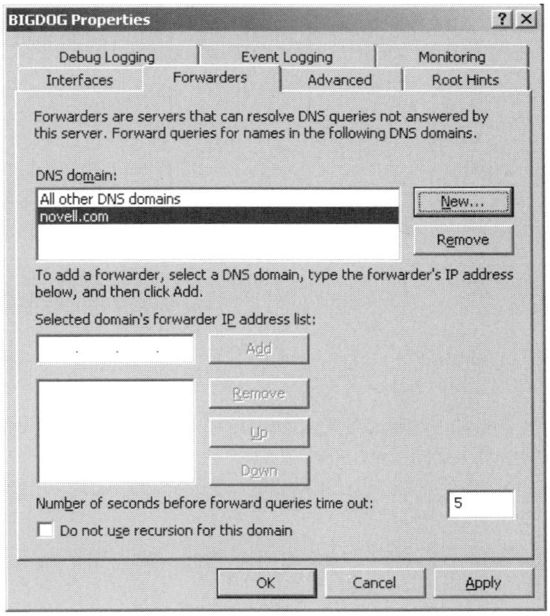

3. To specify the IP address of the server to ask whenever looking for novell.com information, fill the server's IP address into the Selected Domain's Forwarder IP Address List field and click Add.

Although it's not obvious, this page keeps separate lists of forwarders. So, for example, if this DNS server normally forwards to a server at 10.0.0.2, but forwards novell.com questions to a different server at 10.20.1.10, then you would only see the 10.20.1.10 IP address if you clicked novell.com; clicking All other DNS domains would then show a server address of 10.0.0.2.

EXERCISE: WORKING WITH CONDITIONAL FORWARDING

In this exercise, we'll tell Bigdog to forward to ns2, but *only* when looking for records in nasa.gov. We'll prove that Bigdog only forwards to ns2 when looking for nasa.gov information by creating two zones on ns2—a nasa.gov and an ibm.com zone. You'll see that resolving nasa.gov information reflects the zone on Bigdog, but resolving ibm.com information does *not* reflect the ibm.com zone on ns2.

1. First, remove any forwarding that we've set up on Bigdog. At Bigdog, open the DNS snap-in and right-click Bigdog's server icon, then choose Properties and click the Forwarders tab. Click any IP addresses under Selected Domain's Forwarder IP Address List and then click the Remove button so that when you're done, the only entry under DNS Domain is All Other DNS Servers and there are no IP addresses under that.

2. Now tell Bigdog to forward to ns2, but only for nasa.gov questions. Working still in the Forwarders tab, click New.

3. In the New Forwarder dialog that appears, fill in **nasa.gov** and click OK.

4. Back in the Forwarders page, ensure that the nasa.gov line in the DNS Domain list is highlighted. In Selected Domain's Forwarder IP Address List, fill in **192.168.0.3** and click Add.

5. Increase the Number of Seconds before Forward Queries Time Out to 15. Leave Do Not Use Recursion for This Domain unchecked.

6. Click OK. Clear Bigdog's cache.

7. Now go to ns2. Open its DNS snap-in.

8. Create a primary forward zone called nasa.gov and another called ibm.com.

9. In the nasa.gov zone, create a host (A) record for www with IP address 10.0.0.1.

10. In the ibm.com zone, create a host (A) record for www with IP address 10.200.10.1.

11. Clear ns2's server cache.

12. Return to Bigdog and open a command line, then type `ipconfig /flushdns` to remove any client cache information. Then start `nslookup`.

13. Type **www.nasa.gov** to query DNS for NASA's Web server. You should get "10.0.0.1" as an answer.

14. Type **www.ibm.com** to query for IBM's Web server. You should get a number of IP addresses in answer—and none of them will be 10.200.10.1.

COMPARING CONDITIONAL FORWARDING, STUB ZONES, AND SECONDARY ZONES

In my simple microsoft.com/novell.com example where two intranets have split-brain DNS but need to be able to resolve each other's names, I touched on the fact that conditional forwarding is not the only answer; let's take minute here and explore that in a bit more detail.

As I've said, split-brain DNS is not unusual at all and is in fact the norm for name services in most intranets. That gives rise to a problem: assuming that you've done split-brain on your intranet, how do people *outside* the intranet—clients, corporate partners, or even employees telecommuting—resolve names of systems inside your intranet? The whole point of split-brain DNS is in disconnecting your zone from the public DNS hierarchy; how do you make an exception for a few?

Let's imagine that one company has an internal split-brain zone called abc.com and another firm has an internal split-brain zone called xyz.com. We could set them up so that abc.com can resolve xyz.com's names in three ways:

Secondary zones   We could create a secondary zone for xyz.com on each of the abc.com DNS servers. Every time that someone at abc.com tries to resolve a name, then their local DNS server would have an xyz.com zone right on it, and thus wouldn't go out on the public Internet to resolve the name. This makes for fast xyz.com name resolution. The down-sides are that xyz.com's administrators would have to set up their DNS servers to allow the abc.com DNS servers to suck the xyz.com zone information off their servers, a security issue for some. Additionally, if xyz.com's zone is large—which is often the case with internal zones—then the bandwidth required to constantly retransfer the xyz.com zones over the Internet to the abc.com servers might be undesirable.

Stub zones   In the secondary case above, I said that the bandwidth required to transfer the xyz.com zones might be unacceptable. In that case, use a stub zone. An xyz.com stub zone on an abc.com DNS server would work like a secondary zone in that it causes the abc.com DNS server to get xyz.com zone information from the xyz.com DNS servers, but it only transfers the NS and SOA records—a fairly small amount of data. (You would never make a DNS server holding a stub zone for a given domain authoritative for that domain, as it can't answer most questions about the zone.) When someone queries an abc.com DNS server for xyz.com information, the abc.com DNS server sees that it has a local zone for xyz.com and would therefore normally look no further. But as the abc.com DNS server sees that it's a *stub* zone, then the abc.com server knows the name of the DNS servers for xyz.com and queries them. A server with a stub zone for xyz.com, then, always knows the names and IP addresses of the DNS servers that are authoritative for xyz.com. If the xyz.com folks change their DNS servers, then you don't have to do anything to keep your stub zones up to date—normal zone transfers will accomplish that.

Conditional forwarding   Conditional forwarding is very similar-looking to stub zones. With a stub zone, a DNS server looks at a stub zone to find out who to query for information on xyz.com; with conditional forwarding, the DNS server is directly configured to treat an xyz.com DNS server as a forwarder. Note that if the list of DNS servers for xyz.com changed, then you'd have to go reconfigure each of the abc.com DNS servers by hand—something you wouldn't have to do with stub zones. But that can be a *benefit* in many split-brain cases, as conditional forwarding is quick and easy to set up. And additionally conditional forwarding requires no permission from xyz.com DNS servers. For example, you could decide to set up your DNS servers to conditionally forward any names in minasi.com to the server at 68.15.149.117, because that's one of my DNS servers. You wouldn't need my permission. In contrast, if you tried to create a stub server for minasi.com, that would fail, as my DNS server will not do zone transfers except to approved DNS servers. Conditional forwarding *does* have a potential cost, though. If you put a long list of conditional forwarding rules on a DNS server, then the server would have to check that list every time it resolves a name. That could burn up a lot of CPU time and make the DNS server respond more slowly than you'd like.

Summarizing, then, the difference between stub zones and conditional forwarding is that stub zones ensure that abc.com's DNS servers are always up-to-date on xyz.com's DNS servers but require permission to transfer zones from xyz.com; conditional forwarding does not require permission to transfer zones and doesn't automatically keep up-to-date on zones but offers a certain amount of control in that you can say, "I want to know exactly what *that* server knows about xyz.com."

Designing Your DNS Architecture

By now, you know a lot about DNS. Let's put that knowledge all together to see how to design a system of DNS servers that will serve your organization's needs.

A DNS architecture typically needs to solve several problems:

◆ You want performance—fast name resolution through multiple DNS servers and centralized cache through forwarders.

◆ But you want to secure your network, so you'll probably slave the internal DNS servers to forwarders that are a small number of hardened systems outside of a firewall.

◆ To secure your network further, you will probably want to present one set of DNS names internally and a different one externally so that the outside world only sees a small subset of that firm's computers. You will, then, need to know how to maintain a separate namespace internally and externally. This is the split-brain DNS that we've been talking about.

◆ You may have outside entities that you want to be able to see your internal namespace—business partners, clients, telecommuting employees, and others—so you'll need to consider how to accomplish that.

We've covered a lot of this so far, but let's step back and focus on normal and split-brain approaches.

Earlier, we figured out how Megabucks Corporation should place the DNS servers that will resolve names for their internal folks. But now they've got another problem: How should they set up the DNS servers that will hold the megabucks.com zone files? For most firms, it's not as easy as just running the Create New Zone Wizard. Let's look at the kinds of decisions that Megabucks has to make when configuring their IP subnets and DNS names, given that they are both running their own intranet and are connected to the Internet.

One Scenario: Completely Open on the Internet

We know that Megabucks has about 2000 employees, so let's suppose it has about 2500 computers and therefore needs about 2500 IP addresses. That'd be about 10 class C–sized subnets. In the simplest network layout we could imagine, Megabucks goes out and gets 10 class C networks from an ISP. Every one of those 2540 IP addresses are fully routable on the public Internet. They put one IP address on each one of their computers, and so each computer can ping anywhere on the Internet. (And anyone on the Internet can ping any one of those computers.) They then register the domain megabucks.com with Network Solutions. When Network Solutions asks for the IP addresses of two DNS servers that will act as the authoritative servers for the megabucks.com domain, the Megabucks folks just give them the addresses of two Server 2003 machines, and then run the DNS service on those machines—let's call those two machines primary.megabucks.com and secondary.megabucks.com. Then they create a primary megabucks.com forward lookup zone on one of the two DNS servers (primary.megabucks.com, as you've no doubt guessed), and a secondary megabucks.com forward lookup zone on the other DNS server, secondary.megabucks.com. They enable dynamic DNS updates on the megabucks.com zone, and so the megabucks.com zone is soon filled with about 2500 A records naming every Win2K, XP, or 2003 system on the Megabucks network.

Notice that for an internal Megabucks system to resolve the name of another internal Megabucks system, then that system (or its DNS server) ends up asking either primary.megabucks.com or secondary.megabucks.com. Notice also that whenever someone in the public Internet tries to resolve a megabucks.com name, such as when she tries to visit www.megabucks.com or sends mail to somebody@megabucks.com, her DNS server also gets its name resolution query answered by the same two servers, primary.megabucks.com and secondary.megabucks.com, using the very same megabucks.com zone.

In short, in this scenario, Megabucks' internal DNS and external DNS are the same.

What's wrong with this? Well, technically there's nothing illegal about it, but this scenario would trouble most security experts. Using the same DNS server for your internal network as you use to allow external people to resolve names in your domain exposes your entire domain to the Internet. What concerns the security folks—and please understand that I do not by any means consider myself a security expert—is that there's a general principle of security that goes something like, "The less that you tell the weasels, the harder it is for the weasels to attack you." (Others call it "security through obscurity.")

For example, suppose a potential slimeball looked at all of those A records. That's a complete listing of the names and IP addresses of all of the workstations on your network. Everybody knows that many users are pretty lax about things like passwords and security on their own workstations, so they'd be a good starting point—probably an easier cracking job than the servers. If you're running Active Directory, then you get even more information from DNS than usual; for example, DNS will tell you the names of the system's domain controllers. That's not a bug—DNS under Windows 2000 and later is *supposed* to do that, remember? The bottom line is that most firms would prefer for the DNS server that the public Internet sees to only know a few records—the obligatory SOA record and NS records, as well as an MX record or two so that the company can receive Internet e-mail, as well as A or CNAME records for its Web and perhaps FTP servers.

A Better Scenario: Split-Brain DNS

Now let's see if we can do a better job for Megabucks with split-brain. As you've read a number of times by now, I recommend this setup for most people.

Megabucks likes those 2500+ routable IP addresses, so it decides to stay with them. But it'd like the public to see just a small subset of the megabucks.com DNS information, while allowing its internal users to see everything—and that not only means everything in the internal megabucks.com network, but the rest of the Internet as well.

A SPLIT-BRAIN DESIGN

Take a look at Figure 7.86 to see how Megabucks can change its network to make things work a bit more to its liking.

To keep the diagram simple, I reduced the number of internal name-resolving DNS servers from 20 to just 2—instead of NS01 through NS20, we've only got NS01 and NS02. There are several concepts in that diagram, but the single most important is that now we have *two* primary DNS servers for megabucks.com and two sets of secondary DNS servers for megabucks.com.

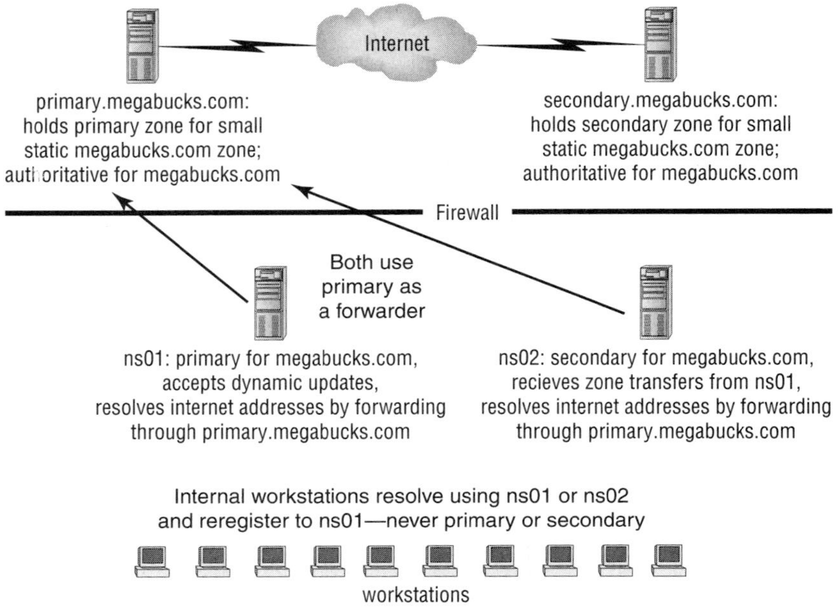

FIGURE 7.86

Using *two* sets of primary/secondary DNS servers for megabucks.com zone

primary.megabucks.com:
holds primary zone for small static megabucks.com zone; authoritative for megabucks.com

Internet

secondary.megabucks.com:
holds secondary zone for small static megabucks.com zone; authoritative for megabucks.com

Firewall

Both use primary as a forwarder

ns01: primary for megabucks.com, accepts dynamic updates, resolves internet addresses by forwarding through primary.megabucks.com

ns02: secondary for megabucks.com, recieves zone transfers from ns01, resolves internet addresses by forwarding through primary.megabucks.com

Internal workstations resolve using ns01 or ns02 and reregister to ns01—never primary or secondary

workstations

The servers primary.megabucks.com and secondary.megabucks.com are still primary and secondary servers for the megabucks.com domain, and they are still the two authoritative DNS servers for the domain, as far as Network Solutions is concerned. But now those zones are static, not dynamic, and they contain just a handful of records, as I suggested at the end of the last section. There's an SOA record, two NS records (one for primary and one for secondary), MX records to point to the publicly available mail servers, and A or CNAME records to point to the Web servers, FTP servers, and any other servers that Megabucks wants the outside world to see. These two DNS servers are *not*, however, the primary and secondary DNS servers as far as the internal Megabucks systems are concerned.

TIP *Let me underscore this. I'm asked often, "We have a registered Internet domain, and we're going to do Active Directory. Right now our ISP hosts our zone—do we have to take that back? Must we become authoritative for our zone?" The answer is, "Absolutely not." Go ahead and leave the public zone on an ISP, where it's (hopefully) safe, sound, and secure. (And someone else's problem.) It'll handle the external requests, and as you'll see, you'll run some servers of your own for the internal ones.*

Instead, the DNS servers that previously only did name resolution—the ones that were caching-only servers—now contain a zone: the megabucks.com zone. We told ns01.megabucks.com that it was the primary DNS server for megabucks.com, and authorized dynamic updates for the zone. We told NS01 that the megabucks.com zone had a secondary DNS server as well, ns02.megabucks.com. We did *not* tell it that primary.megabucks.com and secondary.megabucks.com (the external DNS servers) held megabucks.com zones; as far as NS01's concerned, it and NS02 are the only DNS servers for megabucks.com. ns02.megabucks.com has been set up as a secondary server on megabucks.com and told to pull its zone file from NS01.

Additionally, the workstations inside megabucks.com only know about NS01 and NS02 vis-à-vis DNS servers. Some machines are configured with NS01 as their preferred DNS server, and some are configured instead with NS02 as their preferred DNS server. No workstations are configured with primary.megabucks.com or secondary.megabucks.com as their preferred DNS server. Whether they query NS01 or NS02 for an SOA record for megabucks.com, they'll be told the same thing— that NS01.megabucks.com is the primary DNS server for megabucks.com and therefore is the place to go to reregister with dynamic DNS. (This works just as well if NS01 and NS02 are Active Directory domain controllers and their megabucks.com domain is set up as an Active Directory–integrated domain, in case you're wondering.)

SPLIT-BRAIN AS A TWO-WAY MIRROR

Let's follow a few name resolutions through to see how this meets Megabucks' needs.

First, what happens if someone in the public Internet tries to resolve www.megabucks.com? That person's local DNS server will ask the root servers where it can find the DNS servers for megabucks.com, and the root servers will reply, "Either primary.megabucks.com or secondary.megabucks.com can answer your name queries about megabucks.com." The person's local DNS server will then ask primary or secondary and will get back the address of the Web server that Megabucks wants the outside world to see.

Well, how about if that person on the outside Internet tries to resolve ns01.megabucks.com? Again, their local DNS server will be directed to primary or secondary. The megabucks.com zone sitting on primary and secondary doesn't include a record for NS01, and there's no way for that person out on the public Internet to know that there are other DNS servers on megabucks.com that could answer the question. As a result, the attempted name resolution for NS01 will fail. That includes any attempts to find domain controllers for the megabucks.com Active Directory, whenever it gets the domain running. So, summarized, outsiders can't see into the megabucks.com intranet's naming service.

Let's look at it from the reverse point of view. What would a person on an internal system be able to do?

Well, first, suppose someone inside Megabucks tried to resolve www.microsoft.com, and presume that information wasn't in their system's local DNS cache. In that case, their workstation would contact one of the internal DNS servers (NS01 or NS02). If the internal DNS server had been asked the question recently, then it'd have the answer in cache. If not, the internal DNS server would forward the request out to secondary.megabucks.com, which would be able to get the answer and reply back to the internal DNS server.

Next, consider the case where someone inside Megabucks tries to resolve the name of another machine inside Megabucks. No problem there—NS01 contains a megabucks.com zone that knows the names of every internal machine, as they all register with NS01, and NS02 has a copy of that zone, as it's a secondary.

Basically, then, split-brain DNS on megabucks.com lets us create a kind of "two-way mirror": People outside the domain can't see in, but people inside the domain can see out.

There *is* one case where things get a little tricky. What about if someone at one of the internal megabucks.com systems tries to resolve www.megabucks.com or one of the other publicly visible

Megabucks systems? From what you've seen so far, that resolution attempt would fail. The internal system would address its query to NS01 or NS02, and both DNS servers contain a zone for megabucks.com. But would there be a www record in that zone? Not by default, as the Web server wouldn't register itself with the dynamic DNS servers—it's supposed to be visible on the public Internet, so its preferred DNS server would likely be either primary.megabucks.com or secondary.megabucks.com.

That leads to the unusual side effect that the only people on the planet who can't get to www.megabucks.com are the people who work for Megabucks. Which might not be so bad, if Megabucks were planning to announce the layoffs on the Web.... Seriously, though, the fix here is easy: Just add a static entry into NS01's megabucks.com zone for www, as well as records for the mail, FTP, and any other servers.

SECURING SPLIT-BRAIN

Let's take this a bit further and see how Megabucks could secure their internal systems further. First, clearly they should have some kind of firewall that hinders external systems from talking to their internal systems without invitation; at minimum some kind of stateful tool like a NAT router. But that's not all; recall that if an internal DNS server doesn't get a response from a forwarder, then that internal server will initiate a search on the public Internet.

Should that happen, it's possible that an external DNS server on the public Internet infected with a virus could pass that virus to the internal DNS server. You may recall that we can ward that off with slaving. Megabucks should do two things:

- First, they should install more than one forwarder for fault tolerance, as I've covered before.
- Second, they should harden the forwarder systems, as you would on any system directly connected to the Internet.
- Finally, they should slave all of the internal DNS servers to the external forwarders. Each internal DNS server should have the IP addresses of *all* of the external forwarders on its list of forwarders. (Mix their order up a bit to load balance.)

SPLIT-BRAIN IN A SINGLE-DOMAIN ENVIRONMENT STEP-BY-STEP

Here's a review of the essential steps and concepts to making split-brain DNS work in a hypothetical bigfirm.biz domain.

If someone else hosts your domain, leave it that way.   This is a concept that many people stumble on. Assuming that you already have an externally visible DNS server for your zone, that's great; don't do anything with it. Leave it nondynamic. Heck, let an ISP host it. If your company's DNS domain name is bigfirm.biz and huge-isp.com hosts a DNS zone for bigfirm.biz, then go ahead and build your own bigfirm.biz zone on an internal DNS server. That's the way that split-brain is *supposed* to work. That way, external visitors' queries are handled by the zone on the huge-isp.com's DNS servers, which know nothing of your internal network. Remember, as the security experts say, "Security...through obscurity."

Plan and document your servers.   Decide how many DNS servers you'll have on your intranet, including what their names and IP addresses will be. Keep that information documented and up to date on a text file, spreadsheet, database, whatever works for you.

Install the software on the servers.   As you've seen in this chapter, install the DNS service on each one.

Point *every* DNS server to itself.   Configure every DNS server to point to itself as a preferred DNS server. No alternate DNS servers, just itself.

Every server must be either primary or secondary for bigfirm.biz.   Make one of your DNS servers the primary DNS server for bigfirm.biz. Make all of the other internal DNS servers secondary DNS servers for bigfirm.biz. If you leave any internal DNS servers without a local copy of the bigfirm.biz zone, then any systems querying that server for bigfirm.biz information will cause the DNS server to search the public Internet's DNS hierarchy, and the system will end up getting an answer from the externally hosted DNS server—which will almost certainly produce the wrong info. This is an important step—every internal DNS server *must* be primary or secondary for bigfirm.biz.

Once you build your Active Directory then you have the option to make the zone AD-integrated. When you've done that, then any of the DNS servers that are also domain controllers for bigfirm.biz can become primaries even if they were secondaries before, as AD-integrated allows for multiple primary DNS servers on a zone. If you go AD-integrated but have DNS servers that are *not* domain controllers then that's no problem, but they can only act as secondary DNS servers.

Copy any external records to the internal zone.   There are probably things in the external bigfirm.biz zone—the one that huge-isp.com runs—that you need people inside the network to see to the internal. For example, the www and MX records. People ask me how to automate this and, while I'm sure there's a way—one could probably do some scripting to do this—there isn't an automatic method that I know of. Remember that this split-brain stuff is a trifle underhanded as far as DNS is concerned, so we can't expect too much help if we decide to swim against the current.

Set up two or more external forwarders.   These are the servers outside of the firewall that all of your internal DNS servers will forward through. You really want these systems to be simple and easily hardened. These do not have to be NT-based systems at all, and I can think of at least one fairly good argument against it: license costs. If you just want a DNS server "appliance," something that only queries the public Internet's DNS servers and holds no zones of its own, then it's kind of expensive to buy a whole Windows Server 2003 license just for that. I've set up Linux boxes with BIND, and they offer three benefits. First, there's the obvious cost factor. Second, you can do it with cast-off hardware. For example, I recently decommissioned a 300MHz server that had 128MB of RAM and had worked fine as a backup domain controller and print server. That's not really enough hardware for Server 2003, but it's a fine platform for RedHat, provided I don't install the GUI. Third, you can, with a little work, strip a Linux box pretty clean, basically removing everything but the BIND DNS software.

Slave the internal DNS servers to the external forwarders.   This way, the internal DNS servers never show their faces to the public Internet. Be sure to increase the timeout value from its default of five seconds to a more reasonable minute or so—experiment to find what's best.

Configure every single machine inside the intranet to use only internal DNS servers.   Every machine inside the intranet must point to one or more of the internal DNS servers. Configure every workstation and server to point to one of your internal DNS servers as its preferred DNS server and another as the alternate DNS server. *Never* point a machine to an external DNS server, even as an alternate DNS server. If you do, then any queries to the external DNS server for bigfirm.biz information would end up at the DNS server at huge-isp.com, and that's not what you want to see happen.

Follow these steps and you'll have a perfectly running DNS system.

SPLIT-BRAIN CHANGES FOR MULTIPLE DOMAINS

If your only domain is bigfirm.biz, then you'll be able to accomplish split-brain with the instructions above. But if you have more than one domain, or if you're going to be participating in another organization's domain, then you'll need to add one wrinkle: conditional forwarding or secondary/stub zones. We've gone through them in some detail, so I won't recapitulate that here in great detail. But I do want to remind you that you'll have to use at least *one* of these techniques, or multiple-domain split-brain just won't be possible. In simple terms, here's your goal: all of those internal DNS servers must be able to properly resolve names for all of your split-brain domains.

Yet Another Scenario: Different Names

I just explained how to create one set of DNS names internally and another externally, but that's not the way that everyone handles their inside/outside name dichotomy. Some firms just register two different DNS domains and use one on their internal network and the other on their external network. For example, before Compaq and then HP bought them, Digital Equipment Corporation used to use digital.com for their externally visible network and dec.com for their internal network.

Other firms register both the .net and .com versions of their company name, so Megabucks might use the megabucks.com DNS domain for their externally visible systems and megabucks.net for their internal systems.

Still others create child domains. Megabucks might decide to create a child domain named internal.megabucks.com. All of the internal systems would have names like *machinename*.internal .megabucks.com, and we'd place an internal.megabucks.com zone on all of the DNS servers on the internal network. The DNS servers for the parent level, megabucks.com, would all live out on the external network, but there would be no delegation records on that external DNS server to indicate that there is a child domain of megabucks.com called internal.megabucks.com.

Whatever names you decide to use internally, make sure they're registered with the worldwide DNS hierarchy. Otherwise, someone *else* could unwittingly register a domain with that name, and as a result your internal users couldn't resolve any names in that domain. If that's not clear, think back to my example about what would happen if you created a dell.com zone on your internal network: Whenever one of your users tried to surf to www.dell.com, they'd be directed to one of your Web servers, not the actual Dell ones.

DNS Recovery

Once you've gone to all of the trouble to set up your DNS server, what happens if it fails? How hard is it to get another DNS server up and running to take the place of a dead one? It's quite easy, actually.

DNS Backup

Once you have your DNS server up and running, back up your server's configuration like so:

1. Stop the DNS service.
2. Start Regedit and navigate to HKEY_LOCAL_MACHINE\System\CurrentControlSet\Services\DNS.
3. Right-click the DNS folder and choose Export. Give the file the name dns1 and press Enter.
4. Now navigate to HKEY_LOCAL_MACHINE\SOFTWARE\Microsoft\Windows NT\CurrentVersion\ DNS Server.
5. Right-click the DNS Server folder and choose Export. Name the file dns2 and press Enter.

You've just created two Registry files called dns1.reg and dns2.reg. Put them on a floppy or some other storage location that's not on the server.

Look in your \Windows\System32\DNS directory and copy all of the files with the extension .dns to wherever you stored the .reg files. Now you're backed up; restart the DNS service.

DNS Restoration

If your DNS server has failed, you can get another one in its place quickly:

1. Set up a Server 2003 system. Give it the same machine name, DNS suffix, and IP address as the old DNS server.
2. Install the DNS service on the system.
3. Copy all of the files with the .dns extension to \windows\system32\dns.
4. Stop the DNS service.
5. Locate the two files with the .reg extension. Double-click them, one at a time, and confirm that you want them installed in the Registry.
6. Restart the DNS service.

You should now have a replacement for your DNS server. Remember that if all you want to do is move the primary role for a zone from one computer to another, you can just copy the *.dns file over to the target computer and run the New Zone Wizard, telling it that you already have a zone file.

Application: Grafting an Active Directory Domain into an Enterprise with Old DNS Servers

Suppose you bring Server 2003 into your firm, acme.com. At a meeting of the IT planning staff, you sell the CIO on the whole idea of the Active Directory as a directory service. Everyone loves the idea (or at least no one has attacked you with a sharp object) until you enthusiastically say something like, "And Microsoft was even smart enough to use DNS as its naming infrastructure!"

All of a sudden, the Unix guys, who have been scowling in the corner, say in unison, "Whaaaaaat????" They're not dumb. They know what this means. You see, if your firm is like many, your internal DNS servers are probably running on Unix boxes rather than something else. The program that the Unix box is running, BIND, is well understood and fairly stable. The Unix folks know that if the Active Directory uses DNS as its naming system, then that almost certainly means that Server 2003 comes with a DNS server—and while they were able for years to safely shoot down any ideas about using NT 4's DNS server, Server 2003's DNS server is not only a pretty good product, it's pretty well integrated with the Active Directory. No, you don't *have* to use 2003's DNS server to make the Active Directory work, but the Unix guys see the writing on the wall. No way they're polluting their BIND system with some less-reliable DNS server from Redmond, they say. The Active Directory? "I say it's spinach," they say, "and I say I don't like it."

You've got several answers to this objection. First of all, you may be able to make them happy and keep using BIND. Any DNS server that supports RFC 2136 dynamic updates and RFC 2782 SRV records and that allows you to put underscores—which are not exactly kosher, RFC-wise—into host names will support Active Directory. You needn't use Microsoft's DNS server. As you've read, the latest version of BIND meets those criteria, and in fact I've set up the Active Directories using only BIND-based DNS servers.

But perhaps your enterprise is on an earlier version of BIND or some other DNS server and doesn't want to upgrade. What to do? Simple: Get them to delegate a subdomain to your DNS servers. That way, if acme.com doesn't want to have all of its DNS servers assimilated into the Microsoft DNS Collective, then they needn't be. The Unix servers can continue to handle the acme.com top-level domain. You just ask for a subdomain such as win2k.acme.com (some people are proposing ds.*domainname*, as in ds.acme.com—the *ds* stands for *directory service*) or some such, and you then put all of the Windows 2000, XP, and 2003 machines in the subdomain. The DNS server that keeps track of them can then be a Server 2003 server without affecting the rest of acme.com.

Why is this an application of understanding zone files? Because someone may decide to make it *your* job to add the records to the BIND servers that delegate the win2k.acme.com zone to your Server 2003 server. And this way, you'll be able to just sit right down and make the necessary modifications. (Although, now that I mention it, there's this vi editor thing you should know about...)

I know that this was a big chapter, but believe me, it was the shortest that I could make it without skipping important details. WINS, DHCP, and DNS are as essential to a functioning network as electricity. I promise you that if you take the time to design and implement a good WINS/DHCP/DNS infrastructure, you'll avoid many troubleshooting sessions.

But what did we set all of that infrastructure up for? One reason was to enable us to build a sturdy Active Directory. In the next chapter, you'll learn how AD works and how to *make* it work.

Chapter 8

Active Directory

ONE OF THE MOST important concepts in Microsoft networking is the notion of a *domain*. Put as simply as possible, a domain is just a group of servers and workstations that agree to centralize user and machine account names and passwords in a shared database. That's useful—essentially, really, in a network of any size—because it allows a user to have just one account name and password and use that name and password on the dozens, hundreds, or thousands of machines in an organization's domain. When your company hires a new employee, you as an administrator can just sit down and create a single account for that new employee that she can immediately (well, nearly immediately—we'll learn about "replication" in this chapter and you'll see what I mean) get access to any system in your network that you've allowed her access to. And when it's time to change her password, she does it just once, and the whole domain recognizes that new password.

But centralized user and machine accounts and passwords are just the start. As NT has evolved over the years, NT domains have become a way to centralize other things as well. First, in NT 3.51, came user profiles, a tool that lets you take your desktop and settings with you wherever you log in. They've always been troublesome, but they're getting better and you'll read more about them in the next chapter. Then, in NT 4, domains became a place to centralize "system policies," a set of instructions that machines use to build and control user environments. Windows 2000's domains could centralize DNS information, as in the Active Directory–integrated zones that you read about in the previous chapter, and offered an improved successor to system policies called "group policies," which you'll read about in this chapter and the next. Ever since their appearance in 2000, it's seemed to me that group policies are *the* way that Microsoft is making it possible to control not just user environments—desktops, applications, and the like—but also servers and server software. Group policies are becoming sort of the Control Panel for your entire network...and group policies are stored in a domain's database.

Let me stress that you do not *need* a domain to network a bunch of computers running some flavor or flavors of Windows, but it's *far* easier to do virtually everything in Microsoft networking with a domain, so it's really worth your time to learn about domains. In this chapter, we'll start from the basics of what domains are and what they do for you, and then move from there to concepts and planning and yes, I *did* say "planning"—this is *not* a pop-the-CD-in-and-guess-the-right-answers-to-the-wizard's-questions sort of thing. Then we'll get into the nuts and bolts of building a domain, and play with a small domain. From there we'll take on some troubleshooting and advanced (but necessary) topics and some migration advice, and then finally we'll talk about a useful security feature that you really can't even consider using without a working AD: public key infrastructure.

What Active Directory Domains Do for Us

I know that some of you already know what domains are for and, if you fit in that category, then feel free to skip this section. If you're wondering what's new in Active Directory in Windows Server 2003, then of course I'll cover that here, but for a quick overview of what's new in AD, please flip back to Chapter 1 for a short summary of 2003's AD-oriented improvements. For those looking for a bit of "why we're here in the first place," here's a look at what domains do for us.

Domains do several things for us. I've suggested a few, but here's a more complete list. They:

◆ Keep a central list of users and passwords.

◆ Provide a set of servers to act as "authentication servers" or "logon servers" known as *domain controllers.*

◆ Maintain a searchable index of the things in the domain, making it easier for people to find resources—"which share do we keep the Sales figures on, anyway?"

◆ Let you create users with different levels of powers, from nearly powerless guest accounts to regular user accounts to all-powerful domain-wide administrators. But they also let you create subadministrators, user accounts with *some* of the power of domain-wide admins but not all of their power.

◆ Allow you to subdivide your domains into subdomains called organization units or OUs. You can then assign varying amounts of control and power over these OUs to particular individuals. This lets you create what might be called "departmental administrators"—users with lots of power but only over a small group of machines and users.

In the next few sections, we'll take a look at these in greater detail.

Security: Keeping Track of Who's Allowed to Use the Network and Who Isn't

A network's first job is to provide service—central places to store simple things like files or more complex things like databases, shared printing, or fax services. To make it possible for people to communicate in ways like e-mail, videoconferencing, or whatever technology comes up in the future. And, more recently, to make it easier for people to buy things.

Fast on the heels of that first job, however, is the second job of every network: security. Once, most computer networks were unsecured or lightly secured, but human nature has forced a change and there's no going back. Just as businesses have locks on their doors, file cabinets, and cash registers to protect their physical assets, so also do most modern firms protect their information assets. And no matter what vendor's network software you're using, computer security typically boils down to two parts: authentication and authorization. To see why, consider the following example.

We met Bigfirm in the last chapter. Bigfirm competes with Acme, a well-known firm specializing in devices for removing birds from the desert. Bigfirm is not as well-known but is trying to wrest market share from Acme by selling innovative products to solve a wide range of needs, tools like perpetual motion machines, skyhooks, X-Ray glasses, and the like. They have a sales manager named Ivana Cellalot; Ivana wants to see how the sales of a new product, Instant Hole, is doing. Bigfirm has it set up so that Ivana can review sales information through her Web browser—she just surfs over to a particular location on one of the company's internal Web servers and the report appears on her screen.

Of course, Bigfirm management wouldn't be happy about just *anybody* getting to these sales report pages, so the pages are secured. Between the time that Ivana asks for the pages and the time that she gets them, two things happen:

Authentication   The Web server containing the sales reports asks her workstation, "Who's asking for this data?" The workstation replies, "Ivana." The server then says, "Prove it." So the workstation pops up a dialog box on Ivana's screen asking for her username and password. She types in her name and password, and assuming that she types them correctly, the server then checks that name and password against a list of known users and passwords and finds that she is indeed Ivana.

Authorization   The mere fact that she has proven that she's Ivana may not be sufficient reason for the Web server to give her access to the sales pages. The Web server then looks at another list sometimes known as the *access control list*, a list of people and access levels—"Joe can look at this page but can't change it," "Sue can look at this page and can change it," "Larry can't look at this page at all." Presuming Ivana's on the "can look" list, the server sends the requested pages to her browser.

Now, the foregoing example may not seem to contain any deep insights—after all, everyone's logged into a system, tried to access something, and either been successful or rejected—but understanding how Active Directory works requires examining these everyday things a bit. Here's a closer look at some of the administrative mechanics of logins. First, you need a list of known users, then you need some kind of service that will look someone up upon request and say, "Yes, this is someone that I know." Next, you've got to answer the question, "Hmmm...that service says that the woman that says she's Ivana is indeed Ivana...but why do I believe the service?" And finally, once you've got this service working and you trust its abilities, how can you extend it to authenticating for software other than Microsoft code?

Maintain a "Directory" of Users and Other Network Objects

Every operating system with even the most minimum security has a file or files that make up a database of known user accounts. Early versions of NT, from 3.1 through 4, only used a single file named SAM, short for the less-than-illuminating Security Accounts Manager. It contained a user's username (the logon name), the user's full name, password, allowed logon hours, account expiration date, description, primary group name, and profile information. Of course, the file was encrypted; copy a SAM from an existing NT 4 system and pull it up in Notepad, and you'll see only garbage. To this day, NT-family systems still use SAMs on workstations, including Windows 2000 Professional and XP. By default, Windows Server 2003 servers also contain and use a SAM. But a small number of systems will hold Active Directory's centralized database. Those servers are called *domain controllers,* and they do not have a SAM. In the old NT 4 and earlier days, domain controllers used a SAM, but ever since Windows 2000 Server arrived they've used something different—an "Active Directory."

Active Directory is SAM's successor—I suppose we could call AD the Son of SAM—and it stores most of its user information in a file called `NTDS.DIT`. But `NTDS.DIT` is different from SAM in a few ways. First, `NTDS.DIT` is a modified database built using basically the same technology as Microsoft's Access database, and Active Directory domain controllers actually contain a variant of Access's database engine in its machinery. (Microsoft used to call the Access database engine JET, which stood for Joint Engine Technology—no, the meaning isn't obvious to me either, I think they just liked the acronym—but now it's called ESE, pronounced "easy," which stands for the equally useful name Extensible Storage Engine. But I'm kidding a bit when I say that it's an Access database. Microsoft needed Exchange to have a pretty good database engine while shuffling around both information about Exchange user accounts as well as the mail itself. That's probably why they renamed it.) Second, as you'll see demonstrated over and over again, `NTDS.DIT` stores a much wider variety of information about users than SAM ever did.

The information in `NTDS.DIT` and the program that manages `NTDS.DIT` are together called *the directory service*. (As a matter of fact, most folks will never say "`NTDS.DIT`"; they'll say "directory service.") Which leads to a question: What exactly is a "directory"?

It would seem (to me, anyway) that what we've got here is a database of users and user information. So why not call it a *database*? No compelling reasons; mostly convention, but there *is* one interesting insight. According to some, databases of users tend to get *read* far more often than they get *written*. That allows a certain amount of database engine "tweaking" for higher performance. This subset of the class of databases gets a name—*directories*. I guess it makes sense, as we're used to using lists of people called *office directories* or *phone directories*. I just wish the folks in power had come up with some other name; ask most PC users what a directory is, and they start thinking of hard disk structures. "`C:\WINDOWS`—isn't that a directory?"

Before I leave this topic, I should add a side note about a difference between ADs and the old NT 4–based domains: ADs can be *way* bigger. You can fit about 5000 user accounts comfortably in an NT 4 domain, forcing large enterprises to create multiple domains in order to accommodate all of their user accounts; such a domain design was called a *multimaster* model. In contrast, an AD domain can fit 1.5 million users (or more, depending on whom you talk to) into its Active Directory database—which ought to be a sufficient number of user accounts for even the largest companies. AD lets many large companies that were forced back in the NT 4 days to use multiple domains because of the sheer size of their workforce to consolidate all of their older domains into a single AD domain. That *doesn't*, however, imply in any way that only large enterprises benefit from AD, not at all—AD supports many tools that even the smallest organization can benefit from.

OFFER AN "AUTHENTICATION SERVICE:" DOMAIN CONTROLLERS

Consider for a moment when your workstation will use that user information located in the Active Directory. When you try to access a file share or print share, the Active Directory will validate you. More specifically, if you're sitting at machine A and try to access a file in a file share on member server B, then B asks A who the heck you are so that B can then determine whether or not to let you get to the file. A and B then end up going over to a domain controller to get you validated. So, again, AD provides a central database of user accounts that Microsoft-based file servers can rely upon for authentication. But let's take a closer look at why that's useful, and how it can be even *more* useful.

Suppose I have 10,000 users, 10,000 workstations (one of which is machine A) and 500 servers (one of which is machine B). Any one of my 10,000 users should be able to get to any one of my servers and potentially access those servers' files or printers, unless I've specifically denied them access to something. And any one of my 10,000 users should be able to sit down at any one of my 10,000 workstations, log in and do some work. But how would I accomplish this without a domain? I'd have to re-enter every one of my 10,000 user accounts into each one of my workstations' SAM file, and each one of my servers' SAM file. Arrgh.

The beauty of a domain is that we anoint a small number of servers to hold onto a database of users and passwords—the `NTDS.DIT`—and then provide a service to the rest of the network whereby a system can say, "Hey, I'm server B, and there's a guy at workstation A claiming to be Mark, is he really Mark?" It's a central service, just like a file service or a print service or a database service or a Web service.

We could call it a "logon service" or an "authentication service" and then call the small number of servers that provide it "logon servers" or "authentication servers." But for whatever reason we don't call them that; rather, Microsoft calls them "domain controllers," usually abbreviated DCs. And note that I keep using the plural—you really want at least two DCs, *minimum*, in any domain, so that if one fails then you haven't lost your domain database.

Domain controllers are, then, computers that

◆ Run some version of NT Server—to get the latest features of Active Directory, then you'll probably want your DCs running Windows Server 2003. But you can sometimes get away with having a mix of DCs running 2003, Windows 2000, and even NT 4.

◆ Maintain the database of domain information.

◆ Ensure that their copies of the domain information are consistent: if you have five DCs in your network, then part of what keeps those DCs busy is a process called *replication* whereby the DCs keep each other up to date on database changes, such as when you create a new user account, change a password, or the like.

◆ Provide an authentication service that other computers can rely upon to log on users. (And machines, for that matter, as you'll see.)

DEFINING THE DOMAIN: "TRUST"

So now we've got a server that can authenticate a user, a DC. But for whom will it do this authenticating? Not just any system. A PC (whether workstation or server) can only use a domain's DCs to authenticate if that PC "joins" a domain to become a "domain member." Systems that are not members of any domain can only authenticate using the user accounts in their local SAM file; systems that are domain members can either authenticate a user with those local SAM accounts or ask one of their domain's DCs to authenticate the user. In the world of Microsoft networking, we say that systems not in any domain *trust* only their local SAM, but that systems in a domain *trust* their SAM and their domain's DCs. Joining a domain creates a "trust relationship" between the PC and the DCs. Before a workstation will trust a domain controller to provide it with logon services and before a domain controller will trust a workstation enough to *provide* those logon services, Microsoft software requires the agreement both of a domain-level administrator and a workstation-level administrator. When you join a machine to a domain, you are typically logged in using an account that workstation recognizes as a local administrator, but when you try to join the machine to a domain, you'll see that the domain then comes back and says, "Now I need to see an administrative account that the *domain* recognizes." Just as a treaty between two countries requires signatures from leaders of *both* countries, so also does trust between machines and domains require authorization from both local and domain-level admins.

But trusts can go further than that. As you'll see later in this chapter, you can create trust relationships not only between machines and domains, but between domains and domains. Thus, if my PC is a member of the bigfirm.biz domain and if the bigfirm.biz domain trusts the minasi.com domain, then my local DCs can authenticate information about not only user accounts in bigfirm.biz but also about user accounts in minasi.com. What you've seen here, then, is that

- ◆ A domain is a group of machines that trust a given domain's DCs, and
- ◆ Domains can be configured to trust one another.

That brings up another benefit of Active Directory: automatic trust relationships. Under NT 4, trusts tended to be fragile and would sometimes break for no reason. Active Directory enables you to build larger networks by making the process of building and maintaining multidomain networks easier. Where once an administrator of a multidomain network had to build and maintain a complex system of trust relationships, Active Directory lets you build a system of domains called a *forest*. A forest's main strength is that once a group of domains has been built into a forest, the trusts are *automatically* created and maintained. There are additionally smaller multidomain structures called *trees* that also feature automatic trusts; you'll read more about trees and forests later in this chapter.

AUTHENTICATING FOR MANY VENDORS

"Please, can't we set things up so I only need to remember *one* password?"

AD domains let us set up a bunch of Microsoft OS–based file and print servers to centralize authentication. But AD can do more. When fully implemented, the Active Directory can save you a fair amount of administrative work in other network functions as well.

For example, suppose your network requires SQL database services. You'll then run a database product such as SQL Server or Oracle on the network. But adding another server-based program to your network can introduce more administrative headaches because, like the file and print servers, a database server needs authentication and authorization support. That's because you usually don't want to just plunk some valuable database on the network and then let the world in general at it— you want to control who gets access.

So the database program needs a method for authentication and authorization. And *here's* where it gets ugly: In the past, many database programs have required their administrators to keep and maintain a list of users and passwords. The database programs required you to duplicate all that work of typing in names and passwords—to redo the work you'd already done to get your Novell, Linux, NT, or whatever type LAN up and running. Yuk. But it gets worse. Consider what you'd have to do if you ran both some version of NT as a network operating system *and* Novell NetWare as a network operating system: Yup, you're typing in names and passwords yet again. Now add Lotus Notes for your e-mail and groupware stuff, another list of users, and hey, how about a mainframe or an AS/400? More accounts.

Let's see—with a network incorporating NT, Oracle, NetWare, and Notes, each user owns *four* different user accounts. Which means each user has *four* different passwords to remember. And, every few months, four different passwords to remember to change.

This seems dumb; why can't we just type those names and passwords once into our Active Directory domain controller and then tell Oracle, NetWare, and Notes to just ask the local domain controller—we'll have more than one DC—to check that I am indeed who I say I am rather than making Oracle, NetWare, and Notes duplicate all of that security stuff? Put another way, we have a centralized computer that acts as a database server, another that acts as a centralized e-mail server, another as a print server—why not have a centralized "logon" server, a centralized "authentication" server? Then our users would only have to remember (and change) one password and account name rather than four.

Centralized logons would be a great benefit, but there's a problem with it: How would Notes actually *ask* a server acting as an AD domain controller to authenticate? What programming commands would an Oracle database server use to ask a Microsoft "logon server" (the actual term is *domain controller*, as you've already learned) whether a particular user should be able to access a particular piece of data?

Well, if that domain controller were running NT 4, the programming interface wouldn't have been a particularly well-documented one. And third parties such as Oracle, Lotus, and Novell would have been reluctant to write programs depending on that barely documented security interface because they'd be justifiably concerned that when the *next* version of NT appeared (Windows 2000 Server—recall that it was the first version of NT to support Active Directory domains), then Microsoft would have changed the programming interface, leaving Lotus, Novell, and Oracle scrambling to learn and implement this new interface. And some of the more cynical among us would even suggest that Lotus and Oracle might fear that Microsoft's Exchange and SQL Server would be able to come out in Windows 2000 Server–friendly versions nearly immediately after Windows 2000 Server's release.

Instead, Microsoft opted to put an industry-standard interface on its Active Directory, an interface called the Lightweight Directory Access Protocol (LDAP). Now, LDAP may initially sound like just another geeky acronym, but it's more than that—what Microsoft has done by putting an LDAP interface on the Active Directory is to open a doorway for outside developers. And here's how important it is: Yes, LDAP will make Oracle's or Lotus's job easier should they decide to integrate their products' security with NT's built-in security. (They haven't yet, to my knowledge. I guess Microsoft's got to support more than just LDAP to win Larry Ellison's trust.) But LDAP also means that it's (theoretically, at least) possible to build tools that create Active Directory structures—domains, trees, forests, organizational units, user accounts, all of the components. It means that if we like AD but hate Microsoft's AD administration tools, then some clever third party can just swoop in and offer a complete replacement, built atop LDAP commands.

This, after you spend a bit of time with the Microsoft Management Console, may not seem like a bad idea—but I'll leave you to make your own judgment about that once you meet the MMC.

Searching: Finding Things on the Network

Thus far, I've been talking about the directory service as if it only contains user accounts. But that's not true—the DS not only includes directory entries for people, it also contains directory entries describing servers and workstations. And that turns out to be essential, for a few reasons.

FINDING SERVERS: CLIENT-SERVER RENDEZVOUS

Client-server computing is how work gets done nowadays. You check your e-mail with Outlook (the client), which gets that mail from the Exchange machine down the hall (the server). You're at your PC (the client) accessing files on a file server (the server). You buy a shirt at L.L. Bean's Web server (the server) from your PC using Internet Explorer (the client).

In those three cases, the copy of Outlook on your desktop had to somehow know where to find your local Exchange server, you couldn't get files from your file server until you knew which file server to look in, and you couldn't order that shirt until you'd found the address of the L.L. Bean Web server, www.llbean.com.

In every case, client-server doesn't work unless you can help the client find the server, hence the phrase *client-server rendezvous*. In the Outlook case, your mail client knows where your mail server is probably because someone (perhaps you) in your networking group set it up, feeding the name of the Exchange server into some setup screen in Outlook. You may have found the correct file server for the desired files by poking around in Network Neighborhood in Windows 9*x*, or in the My Network Places if your workstation is running Windows 2000 Professional or XP Pro, or perhaps someone told you where to find the files. You might have guessed L.L. Bean's address, saw it in a magazine ad, or used a search engine like Google.

Those are three examples of client-server rendezvous; many more happen in the process of daily network use. When your workstation seeks to log you in, the workstation must find a domain controller, or to put it differently, your "logon client" seeks a "logon server." Want to print something in color and you wonder which networked color printers are nearby? More client-server rendezvous.

In every case, the Active Directory can simplify the process. Your workstation can ask the Active Directory for the names of nearby domain controllers. You can search the Active Directory for keywords relevant to particular file shares and printers. And, to use an example of how applications built for AD can exploit AD's built-in tools, Exchange 2000 stores its user information in the Active Directory, so Exchange can use AD's search tools to look up e-mail names, so the Exchange programmers didn't have to reinvent any wheels.

NAME RESOLUTION AND DNS

But merely getting the name of a particular mail, Web, print, or file server (or domain controller) isn't the whole story. From the network software's point of view, www.llbean.com isn't much help. To get you connected to the Bean Web server, the network software needs to know the *IP address* of that server, a four-number combination looking something such as 208.7.129.82. That's the second part of client-server rendezvous.

In the case of a public Web site such as Bean's, your computer can look up a Web server by querying a huge network of publicly available Internet servers called the Domain Name System, or DNS. The public DNS contains the names of many machines you'll need to access, but chances are good that your company's internal network doesn't advertise many of its machines' names on the Internet; rather, your internal network probably runs a set of private DNS servers.

After its inception in 1984, DNS didn't change much. But 1996 and 1998 brought two big changes referred to as RFC 2782 and RFC 2136 (you read about them in Chapter 7), transforming DNS into a naming system that's good not only for the worldwide Internet but also for internal intranets. Many of the pieces of DNS software out in the corporate world don't yet support 2782 and 2136, so it's a great convenience that Server 2003's DNS server supports those features.

Creating New Types of Subadministrators

The next network challenge becomes apparent after a network has grown a bit. When a network is small or new, a small group of people do everything, from running the cables and installing the LAN adapter boards to creating the user accounts and running the backups. As time goes on and the network gets larger—and more important to the organization—two things happen. First, the organization hires more people—*has* to hire more people because there are more servers to tend and user accounts to look after—to handle all the different parts of keeping a network running. And second, networks get political: All of a sudden, some of the higher-ups get clued to the fact that *what those network geeks do affects their ability to retain their power in the organization.*

Both of those things mean that your firm will soon start hiring more network helpers. In some organizations, these newly created positions get to do much of the scut work of network administration, stuff that is (a) pretty simple to train people to do and (b) of no interest to the old-timer network types. Examples of the I-don't-want-it-you-can-have-it jobs in a network include:

Resetting passwords   For security's sake, we usually require users to change their passwords every couple months or so. We also inveigh against the evils of writing those passwords down, so it's pretty common for users to forget what their most recently set passwords are. Resetting passwords to some innocuous value is something that really needs to be done quickly—the natives get restless when you take a week to let them back on the network—and it's a relatively simple task, so it's perfect for the newly hired, minimum-wage network assistant.

Tending the backups   For tediousness, nothing matches the sheer irritation of backups. Most of us are forced to use tape drives for backups and, well, some days it seems like tape drives were invented by someone who was abused by network administrators as a small child. They're balky, prone to taking vacations at random times, and you never can predict exactly how much data you can get on 'em—eight gigs one day, three the next, and as a result, *someone* has to be around ready to feed in another blank tape. And somebody's got to label them and keep track of them; ask most network admin types what job they'd most like to give someone else to worry about, and backups are likely to be at the top of their wish list.

Hiring a few low-wage backup watchers and password fixers also gives a firm a sort of a "farm team," a place to try out folks to see if they're capable enough to learn to eventually become network analysts with more responsibilities (and, they hope, more salary).

But regular old users can't do things like resetting passwords and running backups—you need at least some administrative powers to do those things. Recall that you'd like to hire this "network scut-work" person or persons at a pretty low hourly rate, and that's troublesome from a security point of view. If he can leave this job and go off to one with the same pay level but whose main challenge is in remembering to say, "Would you like fries with that?" then it might not be the brightest idea to give him full administrative control over the network. Is there a way to create a sort of partial administrator?

NT 4 domains gave us *some* of that, as there was a prebuilt group called Backup Operators, but there wasn't a Reset Password Operators group, and besides, all NT 4 offered was a small set of prebuilt groups of types of administrators—the groups were called Server Operators, Account Operators, and Backup Operators—with different levels. There wasn't a way to create a new type of group with a tailor-made set of powers. Active Directory domains change that, offering a sometimes bewildering array of security options.

Delegation: Subdividing Control over a Domain

In the last section, I offered two examples of things that might motivate a change in how the network works—a growing set of network duties that require some division of labor (which I covered in that section) and growing attention from upper management as it becomes increasingly aware of the importance of the network in the organization. That second force in network evolution is perhaps better known as *politics*. Despite the fact that it's something of a bad word, we can't ignore politics (it's the eighth layer of the OSI model, after all), so how does Active Directory address an organization's political needs?

To see how, consider the following scenario: Some fictitious part of the U.S. Navy is spread across naval facilities across the world, but perhaps (to keep the example simple) its biggest offices are in San Diego, California, and Norfolk, Virginia. There are servers in San Diego and Norfolk, all tended by different groups. For all of the usual reasons, the officers in charge of the Norfolk facility don't want administrators from San Diego messing with the Norfolk servers, and the San Diego folks don't want the Norfolk guys anywhere near *their* servers, with the result that the Navy technology brass wants to be able to say, "Here's a group of servers we'll call Norfolk and a group of users we'll call Norfolk Admins. We want to be able to say that only the users in Norfolk Admins can control the servers in Norfolk." They want to the same thing for San Diego. How to do this?

Well, under NT 4, they could do it only by creating two separate security entities called *domains*. Creating two different domains would solve the problem because separate domains are like separate *universes*—they're not aware of each other at all. With a Norfolk domain and a San Diego domain, they could separate their admins into two groups who couldn't meddle with one another. It's a perfectly acceptable answer and indeed many organizations around the world still use NT 4 in that manner—but it's a solution with a few problems.

For one thing, enterprises usually want *some* level of communication between domains, and to accomplish that, the enterprises must put in place connections between domains. We've briefly discussed these connections between domains before—they're called *trust relationships*. Without a trust relationship, it's flatly impossible for a user in one domain to access something—a printer, a file share, a mail server or the like—in another domain. The simple process of having a user in one domain access a resource in another requires a logon; the domain that contains the resource (printer, file share, mail, and so on) must recognize and log in the user. But there's no way for the resource-owning domain to even *try* to log in a user from the user's domain unless the two domains have been "introduced"—that is, unless administrators from each of the two domains have agreed to allow their domains to trust one another.

Specifically, here's how the Navy would solve its problem with NT 4 domains:

◆ First, they'd create two different NT 4 domains. NT 4 domains had names of up to 15 characters, so they might call the two domains NORFOLK and SANDIEGO.

◆ When created, every NT 4 domain automatically creates a user group called Domain Admins. Anyone in that group has complete and total control over the domain. So they'd just put the people that they wanted to be Norfolk administrators into the Domain Admins group of the NORFOLK domain, and put the people that they wanted to make San Diego admins into the Domain Admins group in the SANDIEGO domain.

◆ Once those domains were created, they'd next create a user account for each person at the Norfolk facility in the NORFOLK domain and create a user account for each person at the San Diego facility in the SANDIEGO domain. Similarly, any member servers and workstations in Norfolk would join the NORFOLK domain and member servers and workstations at San Diego would join the SANDIEGO domain.

◆ Finally, they'd create a trust relationship between NORFOLK and SANDIEGO or, actually, they'd create *two* trusts, as NT 4–style trusts are one-way only. Two domains can only trust one another if the domain administrators on both sides agree, so both the NORFOLK and SANDIEGO Domain Admins groups would have to cooperate to create the "NORFOLK trusts SANDIEGO" trust and the "SANDIEGO trusts NORFOLK" trust.

This would work, but it might not be the most convenient thing to keep running. For one thing, I've already explained that NT 4 trust relationships can be quirky and unreliable, and this model relies upon two of those trusts. With AD domains, in contrast, the Navy need only create *one* domain and then divide it up using a notion that first appeared in the Microsoft world with Active Directory— a concept called *organizational units*, usually abbreviated *OUs*.

More specifically, the Navy would solve their problem using Active Directory this way:

◆ They'd create one domain named (for example) navy.mil. (Recall that AD domains have DNS-like names.)

◆ Inside navy.mil, they'd create an organizational unit named Norfolk and another San Diego. They would set up their servers and then place each server into the proper OU.

◆ Also inside navy.mil, they'd create a user group named Norfolk Admins, and another named San Diego Admins. They'd create accounts for their users and place any administrators into their proper group, depending on whether they were based in San Diego or Norfolk.

◆ Finally, they'd give the San Diego Admins group complete control over the San Diego OU and give the Norfolk Admins group complete control over the Norfolk OU.

Let me clarify two things at this point. First, understand that the San Diego Admins (kinda sounds like a baseball team, doesn't it?) didn't have any power until someone explicitly gave them control of the San Diego OU. There's no magic in Active Directory that says, "Well, there's an OU named San Diego and a group named San Diego Admins, I guess that must mean I should let these Admin guys have total control over the servers in the San Diego OU." You have to create that link by *delegating control* of the San Diego OU to the user group San Diego Admins. (There's a wizard that assists in doing this, as you'll see when we walk through a delegation example later in this chapter.) You'll see that OUs are a useful tool for building large and useful domains.

Second, the fact that AD domains have DNS-like names and OUs are subunits of domains leads people to think that OUs also get DNS-like names. For example, many people presume that the Norfolk OU of navy.mil would be named norfolk.navy.mil or something like that. But that's not true—while you name *domains* using DNS, you name just about everything else in Active Directory using LDAP naming conventions. You can safely avoid a lot of LDAP, but just for completeness' sake, here's the LDAP name of Norfolk: "ou=Norfolk,dc=navy,dc=mil." You'll meet more LDAP later.

Satisfying Political Needs

"That's *my* data, so I want it on *my* servers!" As information has become the most important asset of many firms—for example, I once heard someone comment that the majority of Microsoft's assets resided in the crania of their employees—some firms have been reluctant to yield control of that information to a central IT group. Nor is that an irrational perspective: if you were in charge of maintaining a five-million-person mailing list, and if that list generated one half of your firm's sales leads, then you might well want to see that data housed on a machine or machines run by people who report directly to you.

Of course, on the other side of the story there is the IT director who wants Total Control of all servers in the building, and her reasoning is just as valid. You see, if a badly run server goes down and that failure affects the rest of the network, it's *her* head on the chopping block.

So on the one hand, the department head or VP wants to control the iron and silicon that happens to be where his data lives, and on the other hand, the IT director who's concerned with making sure that all data is safe and that everything on the network plays well with others wants to control said data and network pieces. Who wins? It depends—and that's the "politics" part.

What does Active Directory do to ameliorate the political problems? Well, not as much as would be nice—there is no "make the vice presidents get along well" wizard—but AD's variety of options for domain design gives the network designers the flexibility to build whatever kind of network structure they want. Got a relatively small organization that would fit nicely into a single domain, but one VP with server ownership lust? No problem, give her an OU of her own within the domain. Got a firm with two moderately large offices separated by a few hundred miles? Under NT 4, two domains and a trust relationship would be the answer, and you could choose to do that under AD, but that's not the only answer. As AD domain controllers are extremely parsimonious with WAN bandwidth in comparison with NT 4 DCs, you might find that a single domain makes sense as it's easier to administer than two domains, but it's not impossible from a network bandwidth point of view. And bandwidth utilization is our next topic.

Connectivity and Replication Issues

More and more companies don't just live in one place. They've purchased another firm across the country, and what once were two separate *local* area networks is now one firm with a wide area network need. If that WAN link is fast, then there's no network design headache at all: Hook the two offices up with a T1 link and you can essentially treat them as one office.

That's beneficial because each site will usually contain a domain controller—one of those servers that hosts the Active Directory database and which acts as a machine to accomplish logins. But those domain controllers must communicate with each other whenever something changes, as when a user's password changes or when an administrator creates a new user account. This is called *Active Directory replication*. The same thing happened with NT 4, as NT 4 also allowed you to put multiple domain controllers in an enterprise.

In NT 4, suppose you had two offices connected by a slow WAN link. Suppose further that you had a domain controller in each of these offices. They needed to replicate their SAM database between domain controllers. NT 4's domain controller updates happened every five minutes. That means that a domain controller might try to replicate changes to another domain controller every five minutes, even if they're only connected with a very slow link. All that chatter could well choke a WAN link and keep other, more important traffic from getting through.

AD improves upon that by allowing you to tell Windows 2000 and Server 2003 domain controllers about how well they're connected. The idea is that you describe your enterprise in terms of *sites*, which are basically just groups of servers with fast connections—groups of servers living on the same local area network, basically. You can then define how fast (or probably, slow) the connections *between* those sites are, and AD will then be a bit smarter about using those connections.

In particular, Windows 2000 Active Directory servers compress data before sending it over slow WAN links. Taking the time to compress data requires a certain amount of CPU power, but it's well worth it, as AD is capable of a 10:1 compression ratio! You'd think that would make everyone happy, but some folks would prefer that AD *not* spend CPU power doing the compression and decompression, as they've got bandwidth to burn. For them, Server 2003–based ADs offer an improvement over Win2K-based ADs: you can now choose to shut off compression.

Not only do we often face slow links, we often must live with *unreliable* links, ones that are up and down or perhaps only up for a short period of time every day. Active Directory lets you define not only a WAN link's speed but also the times that it is up. All in all, site control makes life considerably easier for those managing multi-location networks.

Simplifying Computer Names or "Unifying the Namespace"

We discussed this in the previous chapter, but it's worthwhile revisiting the topic of names, particularly if you're new to Microsoft networking.

Devices on a network mainly identify themselves by some long and unique identification number. On an intranet or the Internet, it's a unique 32-bit address called an *IP address*. Networks also commonly exploit a 48-bit address burned into each network interface card called a *MAC address*. Any Ethernet, Token Ring, ATM, or other network interface has one of these addresses, and conventions that network manufacturers have agreed upon ensure that no matter from whom you buy a NIC, it will have a 48-bit address that no other NIC has. Some parts of Windows NT, 2000, or Server 2003 identify PCs by their IP address (or addresses—a machine with multiple NICs will have an IP address and MAC address for each NIC), others by the PC's MAC address or addresses.

But people don't relate well to long strings of numbers—telling you that you can send me mail to `mark@11001110111101101111110111001000` is technically accurate (presuming that you can find a mail client that will accept network addresses in binary) but not very helpful. It's far more preferable to be able to instead tell your mail program to send mail to `help@minasi.com`, which you can do. Somehow, however, your mail client must be able to look up minasi.com and from there find out where to send mail for minasi.com. In the same way, pointing your Web browser to `www.microsoft.com` forces the browser to convert `www.microsoft.com` into the particular IP address or addresses that constitute Microsoft's Web site. This process of converting from human-friendly names such as minasi.com to computer-friendly addresses such as 11001110111101101111110111001000 is called *name resolution*. It's something every network must do.

So why is name resolution a problem with NT? Because most of the networking world uses *one* approach to name resolution, and up through version 4, NT used a different one.

Most every firm is either on the Internet or has an internal intranet, or both. Intranets and the Internet use a form of name resolution called the Domain Name System, or DNS. DNS names are the familiar Internet names such as `www.microsoft.com`. In contrast, Microsoft networking has for years used a different and incompatible naming system called NetBIOS names, which are simpler—no more than 15 characters long, no periods.

PCs resolve DNS names by consulting a group of servers around the world called, not surprisingly, *DNS servers*. Your company or Internet Service Provider operates one or more DNS servers and your Internet software uses these nearby DNS servers to resolve (for example) `www.minasi.com` to the Internet address 206.246.253.200.

NT-based networks using Internet software don't use DNS for much of their work. Instead, Microsoft invented its own name servers somewhat like DNS but using NetBIOS names; they called these name servers Windows Internet Name Service, or WINS, servers.

That leads to this problem: Nearly every firm is on the Internet—*has* to be on the Internet—and so every firm must give DNS names to their computers. But if they're also using NT, then they need to give their systems NetBIOS names. That in and of itself is not a great burden; what *is* a burden is that these names are important to the programs that use them, and programs can typically need one of the two names and can't use the other of the two.

Let's take an example. Suppose someone wants to log in to an NT 4 domain at Bigfirm. To accomplish that, her workstation must find a domain controller for that domain. Her workstation does that by searching for a machine with a particular NetBIOS name. Let's say that Bigfirm does indeed have a domain controller around named LOGMEIN (its NetBIOS name) that *also* acts as a Web server with the DNS name reptiles.pictures.animalworld.com, as it hosts pages of local reptile pictures. Let's also suppose that for some reason Bigfirm has no WINS servers but has a great network of DNS servers.

DNS names are of no value to the workstation looking for a logon to an NT 4-type domain. You could have the finest set of DNS servers in the world, but it would make no difference—without a functioning WINS server, that workstation would probably be unable to locate a domain controller to log you in. On the other hand, if someone sitting at that same workstation sought to view the reptile pictures on `http://reptiles.pictures.animalworld.com`, she'd just fire up Internet Explorer and point it at that URL. Internet Explorer is, of course, uninterested in NetBIOS names, relying mainly on DNS names. The workstation would quickly locate the Web server and browse its pages, even as that same workstation was unable to detect that the very same server could perform logins.

With the advent of Windows 2000's Active Directory it seemed that NetBIOS would soon go away, taking WINS with it, as AD uses DNS. But there's so much old stuff out there—Windows 9*x* systems, NT 4 systems and the like—that it appears that even most Server 2003–based networks will still use NetBIOS and WINS to talk to at least some of their clients and software. Eventually, however, WINS will be just a bad memory. But not yet!

Enabling Centralized Support Tools

Put simply, there just plain aren't enough support people around but there's no shortage of users to support. In 1987, many firms retained one support person for every 100 users; in many companies nowadays, that ratio is more like one support person for every 2,000 users.

That means that where it was once possible for a support person to physically visit every user's PC to perform support tasks, it's just not reasonable to expect any more. Support people need tools that allow them to get their support work done from a central location as much as is possible. And, although not every user is all that happy about it, one way to simplify a support person's job is to standardize each PC's desktop. In some cases, support staffs need software tools to allow them to *enforce* that standard desktop. (As you can imagine, it's a political issue for many firms.)

In NT 4, Microsoft started helping support staffs centralize their desktop control with something called *system policies*. But system policies were lacking in a few ways. The Active Directory improves upon system policies with a kind of "system policies version 2" called *group policies*. AD becomes a great support tool because basically, AD is a database, as you've already read. But in addition to being a database of users and machines, it's also the place that Windows 2000 and later store much of their administrative information. In the following sections, I'll give you some examples.

AD Stores Zero Administration Info

Ever had to rebuild a user's workstation from scratch? How long did it take—would you measure it in minutes, hours, days, or weeks? There are commercial tools such as Symantec's Ghost that can assist in that task, but Windows 2000 and Server 2003 has a Ghost-like tool built right in called the Remote Installation Services, as you read in Chapter 5. RIS lets you take a new computer right out the box, plug it into the network, and boot a floppy. The floppy gets the computer onto the network and locates an Active Directory server. From there, AD takes over and directs the process of getting a working disk image onto the workstation in 30 to 45 minutes, unattended. The information about where to keep those disk images and who gets which ones is stored in AD.

Anyone who's ever struggled with system policies under NT 4 knows that they're no picnic: You've got to generate a `NTCONFIG.POL` file, put it on a domain controller, and set up replication for `NTCONFIG.POL` among domain controllers. With Windows 2000, however, all of the system policy stuff—which is now called *group policies*—is stored and automatically replicated by AD.

Ever tried to "push" out an application with SMS or a similar tool? Again, no fun. But one of AD's functions is to store and decide who gets what applications.

AD Supports Directory-Enabled Networking

Windows 2000, XP, and Server 2003 allow you to control bandwidth within your intranet using QoS (Quality of Service) control in TCP/IP. You can, then, say that a particular person should get more bandwidth on Tuesday afternoons when she needs it for videoconferencing. And where is that information stored? In the Active Directory.

AD Will Eventually Replace the Browser

Over the years, Microsoft has gamely tried to support a simple way of browsing the servers on your local network. First called the Browser, then Network Neighborhood, the whole idea was that you could just open up a window and see what was available on your company's network. You'd first see the servers, and then you could drill down into a particular server to see its file and print shares.

The problem with the Browser has always been that Microsoft's networking model grew out of a peer-to-peer paradigm rather than a client-server model. Rather than letting a central server maintain a list of available servers, Microsoft's Browser depended on servers finding each other and electing one of their numbers to act temporarily as the keeper of the server list. It was a good try, but it never really worked that well and over the years, the cry, "Why can't I see [my computer, some server, anything at all] in Network Neighborhood?" has wasted person-millennia of support time.

The Browser still exists in Server 2003, but it's slowly being supplemented by a central list of servers and shared resources maintained on the Active Directory—this is another aspect of the slow passing of NetBIOS that I've referred to before. That list includes the names of servers, the shares available on the system, and the printers available on the system. As more and more AD-aware applications appear, we'll see AD act more and more as the place to go to find network services. But enough overview, let's get down to some details.

Understanding and Using Active Directory's Features

With the overview out of the way, let's next dig into some details. And AD has a *lot* of details!

NT 4 domain designers had just a few tools: domains, user accounts, machine accounts, groups, and trust relationships. AD designers, in contrast, have all of those things and also the extra tools of organizational units, trees, forests, and sites.

In this section, I'll give you an overview of AD's main enterprise-building tools:

◆ Domains
◆ User and machine groups
◆ Organization units
◆ Sites
◆ Trees of domains
◆ Forests of trees of domains
◆ Group policies

Domains

The typical way to explain an AD domain is to say that it is "a security boundary" and that it uses "multimaster replication." That's true, but it's not very illuminating, so let's see what it means.

As you've read earlier in this chapter, every network with any kind of security at all needs to keep a list of information about users—the names, passwords, and other information about people authorized to use the system. You also read that once you've got more than one machine, you run into a problem—how to share that list with all of the machines in our company? Recall that you do that by setting up a small number of servers called domain controllers with a database of your users, a database named NTDS.DIT. The member servers and workstations still have their lists of *local* user accounts, a list maintained in a file named SAM, but in most cases you won't make much use of these local accounts—rather, you configure your workstations and members servers to *trust* the list of users on the domain controllers. When someone tries to sit down at a workstation and claims to be a member of your domain, then the workstation takes the name and password offered by the user and hands it to the DC, saying, "Is this a valid username and password on your domain database?" And, again, if the DC says that the name/password combination is OK, then the workstation *trusts* that the DC is telling the truth.

Where the "security boundary" stuff comes in is if you have more than one domain. If Bigfirm had two AD domains, one named bigfirm.biz and the other named coolstuff.com, then as an employee of Bigfirm I would have a user account—but the user account would have to live in *either* bigfirm.biz or coolstuff.com. There's no such thing as dual citizenship. (I could, of course, have more than one user account, but again each one exists in one and only one domain.) Similarly, a workstation, member server, and DC are members of one and only one domain.

As I've said before, the heart of any domain is a database of some kind. But a database of what? I've used the example of user accounts so far—each user account is just another record in the domain database. But what *other* kinds of things do we keep in that database? Lots, in fact. Every machine that's a member of the domain has a machine account. OUs are described by records in the AD; so are sites. Group policies, the linchpin of central AD support, which we'll be talking about a lot for the remainder of the book, are all stored in things called group policy objects or GPOs—and GPOs are just records in the AD database. AD stores records that describe file shares, printer shares, groups of users, DNS information, something called a "contact" that we'll take up later, and more.

In fact, a programmer can tell an AD to store just about anything that he wants in its database. Which leads me to an interesting thing about the particular engine that drives the Active Directory: it's a database engine that uses *multimaster replication*. The second part, "replication," refers to the process that ensures that every copy of the domain database matches every other one. In other words, if I'm sitting in the Topeka office and I create a user account, then that new record—the user account—exists only on the Active Directory DC in Topeka at that moment. Part of the job of AD's database engine is to get that new information out to the other DCs as quickly as is reasonably possible—that's replication. The "multimaster" part comes from the fact that you can insert a change into the AD database from any DC. That's a change from many replicated database approaches, including the one for NT 4—with NT 4, you could have lots of DCs, but only one of them accepted database changes. Whether creating a new user account, changing a password, or joining a machine to a domain, the resulting modification to the domain's SAM had to happen on the one machine with the ability to change the SAM database—the machine called the *primary* domain controller. AD mainly does away with the idea of a primary domain controller, and all DCs are basically equal. (That's only "basically" because of something called *operations masters* that I'll cover later in this chapter.)

Take the facts that (1) DCs are just database servers, (2) they do multimaster replication, and (3) that programmers can add whatever kind of data that they want to the domain database, and you now have a kind of interesting result: DCs are collectively the basis of a fairly flexible distributed database system, whether it contains user and machine accounts or not. That's why with Server 2003 Microsoft now offers you the ability to set up a bunch of what are essentially DCs that do multimaster replication amongst themselves...but that do not have a domain. The idea is that some folks might find AD's database engine useful but might not want a domain. For those people, Microsoft offers Active Directory in Application Mode or ADAM.

So when understanding what AD can do and what it requires in mind, remember that it is, at its base, a database maintained by a bunch of database servers. If you have database experience, you'll see some of the ramifications of this:

- Databases can be more or less flexible—SAM was pretty inflexible and didn't let you add things. AD, in contrast, is very flexible.

- Databases with more than one database server must solve the problem of maintaining database consistency between the servers. AD's multimaster replication system is nice, but you will, as you'll see in this chapter, sometimes run into problems when one DC just plain can't get up-to-date with the other DCs. That's not a problem that I ever ran into with NT 4's simpler "one master, many slaves" replication model—more power usually means more complexity and more things that can break.

- Databases use query languages that anyone wanting to write programs or scripts relevant to domain work must know. Active Directory offers several, but the two most common are LDAP and something called the Active Directory Scripting Interface or ADSI.

- Databases often have size limitations. As you've read, NT 4 domains started falling down around 5,000 accounts. In contrast, Microsoft says that AD can handle a few million objects. That's not a hard limit, however. A former Compaq techie put 100 million records in an Active Directory and not only did it work, it worked *fast!* AD could respond to queries on that directory in a second or two.

- Databases need defragmentation and garbage collection periodically. Active Directory does some of that automatically, or you can take it offline now and then and give it a thorough cleaning with a tool called NTDSUTIL. (You'll meet that tool in this chapter a few times.)

◆ Databases need disaster recovery scenarios. You can back up and restore an AD using the built-in Backup utility that comes with Server 2003.

◆ Databases need security, controls on who can modify what, when and where. Active Directory lets you set security down to the record level—if you really wanted to, you could say, "The only person who can modify Joe's account is Sue."

That's basically how domains are structured; now let's look at a great time saver for managing access to things in a domain: groups.

User (and Now Machine) Groups

Much of a network engineer's job involves using the built-in security features of a network OS to enforce company policy. For example, there might be files on the network that only the managers of the Manufacturing division should see. If people were all trustworthy, then you could just mark a file "Manufacturing managers only, please" and leave it at that. But sadly, they aren't, so NT in all of its forms has always included the notion of file *permissions*, meaning that you can attach a list to any file or group of files, a list that describes who may access those files and what level of access they should enjoy. This way you can protect that Manufacturing-only file by applying permissions to it that restrict its access to Manufacturing managers only.

But how to apply those permissions to just the Manufacturing managers? Well, of course you *could* figure out which of the user accounts belong to those managers, then you could grant access to each of those accounts one at a time. That'd be a lot of work, however, and furthermore, it would *remain* a lot of work, as you'd have to shuffle permissions around every time someone joined or left the ranks of the Manufacturing managers.

A far better answer, and one that Active Directory enables, is to create a special kind of account, which is neither a user account nor a machine account, called a *group*. You'd create a group named Manufacturing Managers—any name will do, actually. Then you can choose particular user accounts to add to that group. Finally, you'd modify the file permissions by granting access rights not to a particular user account or accounts, but instead to the group. Anyone in the group would essentially inherit file access by virtue of being a member of the group.

In other words, if Jane, Sue, and Tom are all promoted to Manufacturing Manager and you were then directed to give them access to the 10 shares that Manufacturing managers have exclusive access to, then without groups, you'd have to visit each one of those shares, adding the three names to each one. In contrast, with groups, you would have already visited those shares a long time ago and just told the shares that anyone in the group Manufacturing Managers had access to those shares. Having done that in the past, *now* all you have to do is to just add Jane, Sue, and Tom to the Manufacturing Managers group, and they instantly get access to the 10 shares.

NOTE *Both local machine SAMs and Active Directory support groups. As you'll see, though, SAMs support a smaller range of types of groups.*

BOTH USERS AND MACHINES CAN EXIST IN GROUPS

NT 4 didn't let you put machine accounts into a group, and that was unfortunate, as it would have often been convenient to create groups of machines upon which to apply system policies. AD under Windows 2000 and later fixes this, and you can now have groups that contain machines, users, or a combination of those two. You cannot, however, apply group policies to groups, oddly enough— you apply them to organizational units, covered a bit later, and yes, you can put machines into OUs.

GROUPS CAN EXIST INSIDE GROUPS INSIDE GROUPS INSIDE GROUPS

Sometimes it's convenient to put a group inside a group. For example, every server has a group built into it called Administrators. Anyone in the group is, as you'd guess, treated by that server as an administrator, someone with the power to perform any task on that server. But what if I had a group in the enterprise that I wanted to be able to act as administrators on *every* machine? Well, I *could* walk over to every single machine in the company and add each of those enterprise-wide administrators' names to the local Administrators group of each machine. Yuk. No fun.

It's a bit easier to create a group on some computer somewhere called BigDogs or something like that and make all of the enterprise-wide administrators' user accounts a member of BigDogs. Then I can visit each machine in the company and just add the BigDogs group to each of those machines' Administrators group. Sure, it's still a lot of work, but this way I only have to add *one* thing—the BigDogs group—to each Administrators group, instead of having to add a whole bunch of user accounts to each Administrators group. And if someone gets fired or hired, I need only delete/add a user account to BigDogs, and it'll automatically be recognized as a former or present BigDog.

So putting groups inside groups was something of a convenience for administrators. But Microsoft didn't want to have to worry about what might happen if you put group A inside group B, then put group B inside group C, and then accidentally put group C inside group A; that could be confusing for NT to decode. As a result, Microsoft simplified the groups-inside-groups abilities of NT. In general, it figured that there would be groups like Administrators, which really only describes a specific machine; being a member of Administrators for machine X doesn't mean that you have any power at all on machine Y—you'd have to be a member of machine Y's Administrators group for that. As these groups were really only relevant to their local machines, they were called *local* groups.

In contrast, groups such as BigDogs get created on some machine, but they're not really connected to that machine closely. BigDogs was interesting because it could be placed into the local Administrators group of some other machine. Such groups could, one supposes, be called traveling or export groups, but Microsoft called them *global* groups.

To ensure that you couldn't put a group inside a group, which was inside another group, and so on—the more exact way to say that would be "to ensure that you couldn't *nest* groups in more than one level"—Microsoft designed NT to allow you to put global groups into local groups. As a global could not go into a global, and as a local couldn't go into anything, you could not nest groups beyond one group inside another group. The net effect was one level of nesting—a global goes into a local and that's that.

Active Directory extends the notion of groups by increasing the number of group types from two to four and allowing more nesting levels. What used to be called simply a "local group," which lived on a local SAM, is now called a *machine local* group. There is a new type of group that you can create on the domain level called a *domain local* group. Global groups work largely as they did before, although they're a bit more flexible. And an entirely new type of group, a *universal* group, lets you do just about anything that you want with it, albeit at a price in performance and compatibility with NT 4. Let's take a more detailed look, then, at Active Directory's four kinds of groups:

- ◆ Machine local groups
- ◆ Domain local groups
- ◆ Domain global groups
- ◆ Universal groups

Machine Local Groups

Machine local groups do pretty much what they did before. Every machine has a SAM that contains a bunch of prebuilt groups like Administrators, Power Users, Users, Backup Operators, and the like. If you're a member of the Users group, you can log in to that machine and perform basic functions. If you're a member of the Administrators group, you can do anything. There are other groups as well; you can see a machine's machine local groups by right-clicking My Computer, then choosing Manage. An MMC window will appear. In its left panel, open System Tools. Within that, open Local Users and Groups. Within *that*, open Groups. You'll see something like Figure 8.1.

FIGURE 8.1

Machine local groups for Windows Server 2003 machine

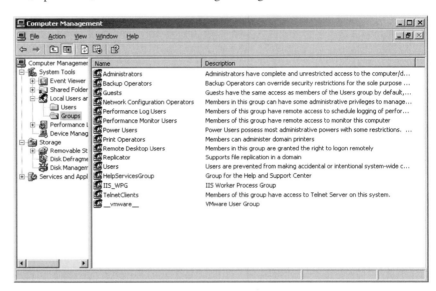

Machine local groups can include global groups, as they've been able to since NT 3.1. They can also include

- Domain local groups from their home domain
- Universal or global groups from their home domain or any other domain that they trust, whether Active Directory or NT 4 domain

Domain Local Groups

Active Directory brought two new kinds of groups: domain local groups and universal groups. Universal groups are very powerful, an answer to a prayer. Domain local groups, on the other hand, are, well, enigmatic...I've never found a use for them.

    Domain local groups are, like global and universal groups, a type of group that you can only create on a domain controller—it's impossible for a workstation or member server to host a domain local group. You can put a domain local group into any of the local groups on a machine, provided that the machine is in the same domain as the domain local group. In other words, suppose bigfirm.biz has a domain local group called People. Any machine that belongs to bigfirm.biz could put the People group in any of the machine's local groups—for example, a system could put People into its local Users group. In contrast, a machine from any other domain could *not* include People in any of its local groups.

Domain local groups can contain global groups from any trusted domain. Thus, while People can only be included in local groups in its domain, it can contain global groups from any trusted domain. Domain local groups can also contain other domain local groups, but, as you'd guess, they've got to be from the same domain.

What perplexes me about domain local groups is this: they are basically capable of only a subset of what global groups—which have existed since NT 3.1—can do. So my question is always "why bother—why not use global groups?"

Global Groups

Global groups are the original "traveling group." Every since NT 3.1 you've only been able to create global groups on a domain controller, and that's still true. You can put global groups in any local group of any machine living in a group that trusts the global group's domain. You can also now put global groups inside global groups, but only so long as they're from the same domain. When you want to create domain-wide groups of users so that you can easily drop those groups into local groups on a domain, global groups are the most common way to do it.

Universal Groups

If the artificial division between groups that mainly receive other groups and user accounts (local groups) and groups that mainly exist to be placed in other groups (global groups) seems a bit contrived, well, perhaps it is. Why not just have a type of group that can contain other groups (as with a local group) and that can also "travel" to other groups (as with a global)? Historical reasons, mostly—NT 4 and earlier only supported locals and globals. Active Directory, in contrast, supports a "does it all" group, called a *universal* group. A universal group can contain *any* global or universal group from *any* domain in the forest.

I've thrown a lot of "this kind of group goes into this kind of group" stuff at you; let me summarize it with two graphics. First, Figure 8.2 summarizes a simplified version of the "what kind of group goes into what other kind of group?" relationships. In that figure, I've left out the stuff that I don't think you'll ever make use of. For the sake of completeness, however, I include Figure 8.3, which is more complete.

FIGURE 8.2

Group nesting relationships simplified

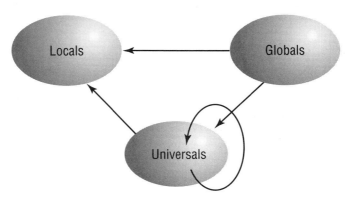

FIGURE 8.3

More complete
group nesting
relationships

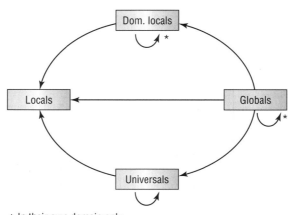

* In their own domain only

The next logical question, then, is, "Okay, why don't we use universal groups whenever we need groups?" Two reasons: First, you can't create a universal group until all of your domain controllers are Windows 2000 or later machines (NT 4 machines can be backup domain controllers in an Active Directory domain, so long as it's in Windows 2000 mixed functional level), and second, universal groups have a significant effect on the size—and therefore the responsiveness—of something called the *global catalog*.

"BDCs" IN ACTIVE DIRECTORY

One reader objected to that last paragraph in the *Mastering Windows 2000 Server* book, saying that an NT 4 machine *couldn't* be a backup domain controller (BDC) in an Active Directory for the simple reason that there *is* no such thing as a BDC under the Active Directory. The issue apparently troubled him mightily as he went on to question my competence and parentage. So in case you too are troubled, here's why the paragraph's right. First of all, the NT 4 domain controllers in an Active Directory domain don't even *know* that they're in an AD and, in fact, haven't a clue about what an Active Directory is. They think they're BDCs in a Windows NT 4 domain, and one—that's right, just one—AD domain controller is, to the NT 4 BDCs, the primary domain controller. They will accept account updates from no other computer. Second of all, although Microsoft likes to say that all DCs are equal under Active Directory and later, it's plainly not true. Some domain controllers assume a particular role called Flexible Single Master of Operations (FSMO)—something you'll read about elsewhere in this chapter—and one of those roles is called the Primary Domain Controller FSMO. If you shut the PDC FSMO down without first anointing another DC as the PDC FSMO, then some pretty bad things will happen to your network. Yes, Microsoft has *largely* decentralized the role of domain controller with Active Directory when compared to NT 4's domain controllers, but not *completely* decentralized those roles. It seems reasonable, then, to refer to the system running the PDC FSMO role as "the PDC" and the other domain controllers as "backup domain controllers," even if it *isn't* regulation Microsoft terminology. (And third, as to that parentage thing, my folks were married a good five years before I was born—I have records to prove it.)

Mixed versus Native Mode and Universal Groups

For compatibility's sake, Active Directory domains can include NT 4 domain controllers as backup domain controllers. But because NT 4 domain controllers don't have the same abilities as Win2K or

Server 2003 machines, an AD domain that includes NT 4 domain controllers must forgo some of its capabilities. One of those capabilities is the notion of heavily nested groups. As universal groups are the most "nestable" of AD group types, an AD domain can't support universal groups until all of its domain controllers are Windows 2000 or later machines; the last NT 4 domain controller must be shut off.

When first installed, Active Directory domains assume that there's at least one NT 4 domain controller around. For safety's sake, then, all new AD domains start up in Mixed mode and will not create universal groups.

Once all of your domain controllers are Windows 2000 or later machines, you can shift your domain to Native mode, which will allow universal groups. And while we're on this subject, let me mention something new to Server 2003–based ADs: yet another Native mode. Just as you had to tell 2000-based ADs when the last NT 4 DC was gone in order to get the full power out of your 2000-based AD, so also must you sweep either your domain or perhaps your entire forest clean of Windows 2000–based DCs in order to get the full power that 2003-based ADs offer. There's a sort of 2003 Native mode, although it's not called that. Instead, if you have a domain and all of its DCs run in 2003, then you can shift that domain into Windows Server 2003 functional level. If you have a forest and all of the domain controllers in all of the domains of that forest run 2003, then you can shift the forest from its default functional level—Windows 2000 functional level—into Windows Server 2003 functional level. You'll see as this chapter goes on that you'll need Windows Server 2003 functional level forests before you can use many of 2003's new AD goodies. (I'll cover functional levels a bit later.)

The Global Catalog and Universal Groups

One reason that you sometimes wouldn't use universal groups is because of their effect on something called the *global catalog*. But what's a global catalog?

As I've hinted so far and as you'll read a bit later, Active Directory helps you build big multidomain networks by allowing you to create a multidomain structure called a *tree* or a larger structure called a *forest*. Without stealing the later tree-and-forest section's thunder, let me motivate the global catalog discussion by saying that one of the benefits of having a tree/forest of domains is that anyone from any domain can log in to any workstation from any other domain in the tree/forest. This is great in theory but in practice constitutes a major performance hassle. Suppose you had a forest with 50 domains: Every time you wanted to log in to a workstation, that workstation would have no idea which of the 50 domains to query to authenticate your logon. So it would have to search one domain after the other ("Hey, do you know a guy named Ralph023?"), and the result could be *extremely* slow logons.

The global catalog (GC) solves that problem. It's an abbreviated version of *every domain in the forest*. Clearly this could get to be pretty big, but the GC remains manageable in size because it only contains a small subset of information from the Active Directory: What users each domain includes and what domain they're from is one of those pieces of information. (There's another value here as well, but I'll cover it later when I discuss forests and trees.)

Another piece of information stored in the GC is the name of each global group in each domain in the forest. That wouldn't constitute too much space and wouldn't make the GC grow too much, but universal groups make it a completely different story: The GC not only knows all of their names, it also knows what users are members of each universal group! As a result, heavy use of universal groups could considerably slow down network logons—so it's a good idea to use universals sparingly.

In case you're wondering, there is not, as far as I know, any tool that lets you directly browse or examine the global catalog—although some search operations use it. (And I *will* cover the GC in greater detail later—this is just a brief look at it.)

GROUP SIZE IS LIMITED TO 5000 MEMBERS IF NOT IN WINDOWS SERVER 2003 FOREST FUNCTIONAL LEVEL

Groups can also contain groups, as you'll see later in this chapter, and that turns out to be useful. For some reason, groups cannot contain more than 5000 members, meaning that if you need a group with more than 5000 members, you'll have to create several groups, each with under 5000 members, and then place *those* groups into a single "super" group, then apply whatever permissions you want to that super group. Yes, it's a pain, but you can fix it…provided you upgrade every single DC in all of your forest's domains. Server 2003–based ADs solve the problem, but, again, you've got to upgrade all of the DCs to get that benefit.

NOTE *If the max size on a group is 5000, then what happens with the automatically created group named "Domain Users" that automatically includes every user account in the domain? Every user is a member of that group, and if you build an AD larger than 5000 users, then Domain Users doesn't crash. What's going on? The answer is that Domain Users isn't really a group—it just looks like one. It can be any size you like.*

There are a few more details about groups, but I'll leave them for now and cover them in more detail in Chapter 9. Thus far, you've seen domains, which are a way of defining a collection of users and machines that share the same security rules, and groups, which make managing access to servers easier. Next, you'll see how to subdivide a domain with organizational units.

Organizational Units (OUs): Subdomains

Sometimes a domain is too large an area to cede control of. For example, suppose you've got to hire some people to act as backup operators, so you put them in the Backup Operators group. But suppose that your domain is spread out geographically, and you really only want to hire people to do backups in the St. Louis office—you don't want someone to be able to just waltz into the San Francisco office and log in to one of those machines. You'd like such people to have backup operator power, but not over the entire network—just over a subset of the network.

Or perhaps you need a staff of people who can reset passwords or manage printers or adjust permissions on a set of servers. But you don't want those folks to have those powers over the entire domain. That could be true for either geographic reasons (St. Louis and San Francisco) or organizational reasons (for example, the Marketing department might want their own password-changer person). The answer in each case is to subdivide the domain into organizational units, or OUs.

ORGANIZATIONAL UNITS ARE FOLDERS

OUs look like folders when viewed with AD's administrative tools. When you create a user account in an AD domain, you can choose to either create the account right in the domain or create it inside one of the folder-like things that you'll see in that domain. When you first create an Active Directory domain, you'll automatically get a folder named Users and another named Computers. Although it may *seem* that user accounts should go into the Users folder and machine accounts should go in the Computers folder, that's not the case at all. (That'd be too obvious.) Instead, the only real reason for the Users and Computers folders, which are somewhat like OUs but lack an important aspect of OUs (you cannot assign group policies to Users or Computers) is so that Active Directory has a place to put any user accounts and machine accounts from an upgraded NT 4 domain. The folders are also useful because, if you use some third-party tool to create user accounts and the tool was built in the pre-AD world, then Active Directory will sense that and put any user accounts the tool creates into the Users folder.

WHAT YOU CAN DO WITH OUS

OUs have two main uses. You can

- Give control of a set of user and/or machine accounts to a set of users, allowing you to, for example, define a set of people who can reset passwords in a particular department without having to make them administrators of greater power than might be desirable and furthermore restrict the range of people whose passwords they can change to a small set of users.

- Control and lock down user desktops through the use of group policy objects, control tools like NT 4's system policies; despite their name, however, group policies aren't applied to user groups—they apply to organizational units, domains, or sites.

Using OUs to Create Subadministrators

Or suppose the Graphics department has a bunch of expensive printers shared on the network. They don't want the regular IS people controlling the printers for some reason; they want their local techies to serve as the printer admins. In that case, you could create an OU called Graphics Printers or the like and put the fancy printers into that OU. Then you can give control of that OU and, in the process, of the printers in the OU to a particular user account or perhaps a group containing the names of the admins that Graphics likes.

NOTE   The process of giving a user or group of users control of an OU is called delegating control *of that OU. Right-click the OU and you can run the Delegation Wizard to make that adjustment. You'll see some examples of that later.*

If the International Trade and Arbitrage department's VP insists on a separate set of administrators for her servers, OUs can meet her needs. Again, just create a separate OU for her servers, a group for her admins, and delegate control of the OU to the group.

You'll see plenty more on the topic of delegation later in this chapter.

Using OUs to Apply Policies

NT 4 introduced the idea of a *system policy*. Policies let you control user desktops through those users' Registries. You'd place in a centrally accessible location a file called NTConfig.pol that contained instructions about what you wanted changed on the user's Registries. NT 4 workstations would then automatically read that file and make changes to their Registries according to the file's orders. In this way, you could control Desktops from a central location.

TIP   That sentence seems to imply that system policies only work on NT 4 systems, but that's not true. System policies still work on Windows 2000, XP, and 2003 systems, but only if the domains that those systems live in do not offer any group policies. If a 2K, XP, or 2003 system sees any domain-based group policies then it will ignore any domain-based system policies.

But what if you wanted to control just a subset of a domain, a collection of machines or users? You couldn't apply a system policy to a collection of machines. You could apply a system policy to a group of users, or at least in theory you could. In practice, groups and policies didn't work so well.

As I've mentioned before, Active Directory domains can offer has a much farther-reaching kind of policy called a *group policy*. (Group policies only work on 2000, XP, and 2003 systems—NT 4, Wintendo, and earlier systems don't pay attention to or use them.) You can apply group policies to subsets of a domain. The subset? Not a group, as the name suggests, but an OU.

The OU Policy Exception: Account Policies

There is one case where you cannot apply policies to an OU: account policies. That means passwords (how long they can be, how often to change them) and account lockout settings. You can also, you will learn, apply policies to *sites*. Here again, policies that change any password or account lockout settings are ignored. That's the really irritating thing about this exception—no warnings. AD lets you create all the site-based or OU-based policies that you like, but if these policies try to do anything with account policies, then they're ignored without a single "are you sure?" Such policies *only* work when applied to an entire domain.

MULTIPLE DOMAINS VERSUS OUs: WHEN EACH MAKES SENSE

Notice in each case cited here that you could *also* accomplish those same ends with multiple domains. International Trade could be its own domain with its own administrators and trust relationships to the rest of the firm. Ditto Graphics. In the first case, all of the administrators could be lumped into a domain off by themselves, and indeed that's been done many times with NT 4—and can still be done for Active Directory.

When, then, should you use one domain divided into OUs, and when should you have different domains? Well, in general, my rule of thumb would be, "Don't use multiple domains unless you must." So the real question, then, is, "When do multiple domains make sense?" In a few cases:

Replication problems due to poor bandwidth   Probably the best reason. All domain controllers in a domain really need to be online and available to each other all of the time. If one office is in Timbuktu and the other is in McMurdo Base and they don't really share much save very limited WAN support, make them separate domains. Think of it this way: Suppose you had one office in Chicago and another in Sydney (Australia) with an expensive, low-bandwidth link between the two. Suppose also that you had 20,000 people in the Chicago office and 150 in the Sydney office. Every time the Chicago people changed their passwords, you'd have to replicate all of that traffic over the expensive-and-slow WAN link to the domain controllers in Sydney. Not a great use of WAN links. It'd be better to just build two domains.

Different account policies   With NT 4, you could set account policies—things such as how often users must change their passwords, whether to lock out users who've entered too many incorrect passwords, and how many is "too many"—but you could only set them on a domain-wide basis. As you read a bit earlier, AD has the same constraint, as policies that include account policies will only work if applied to a domain—they're ignored if applied to an OU or a site.

You don't trust the branch office   Suppose you're a one-domain company with a large corporate headquarters and a bunch of small branch offices. You've got a branch office somewhere with 15 employees. So you put a server—just one—in that building. It serves as the local domain controller, Exchange server, file server, and print server. (And when you're not around, they use it as the receptionist's workstation.)

This server is left out in the open. Yes, there's a lock on the main front door of the office suite, but it's only locked at night. As the server isn't physically secured, someone could steal it or, with just a screwdriver and a few minutes, could steal its hard disk. That hard disk holds a copy of the Active Directory for the entire company, as you work for a one-domain firm.

If this happened under NT 4, you might end up compromising the passwords of all of your users company-wide, as there are programs around that can read a SAM and crack its passwords, producing cleartext. But no one will ever write an AD password cracker, right? Unfortunately, they already have. I'm told the latest version of l0phtcrack (`www.atstake.com`) will extract Active Directory passwords, although the Web site says nothing about that (and I didn't feel like spending $250 to download it and find out). But whether an AD password cracker is currently available is irrelevant to what I'm saying. There will eventually be one, rest assured. So physical security is a top priority—these cracker programs in general will only work if you're physically sitting at the DC.

As a result, you can see that by putting one or more of your domain controllers in a location that's not physically secure, you potentially threaten every password in your enterprise. In that case, you might consider separate domains. That way, if the bad guys compromise a single domain's passwords then at least they haven't compromised *all* of the enterprise's passwords.

Politics   Eighth-layer OSI stuff. Same as it ever was.

We just found it this way, honest!   Your firm buys another firm, and you have to blend the two organizations. There are third-party tools around that will help assimilate the new domain into your existing domain, but that'll be a big undertaking and maybe you don't have the time to do that just at the moment. In that case, you're living in a multidomain world for a while. Multi*forest*, most likely. If you can, however, I recommend you consider merging the two domains with a tool like Active Directory Migration Tool, which I'll cover later in this chapter.

I know I've said it already, but let me weigh in again with my opinion about multiple domains, or rather, why I'd avoid them. First of all, NT 4 multiple domain enterprises were a major pain, as trusts tended to break. Supposedly this won't happen under Active Directory and thus far I haven't seen it, but in general, the fewer "moving parts" in my enterprise, the better. Additionally, NT has had its growing pains over the years about security. What if the next NT security hole appears in AD trusts? (Again, that is a *thoroughly* fictitious example. No problems of that kind have arisen in trusts since AD appeared in 2000.)

And then there's the issue of bugs in general: I'd prefer to work with the parts of Server 2003 that have been tested most thoroughly. For example, my personal experience with multiple-processor machines running various versions of NT is that they're more fragile and a bit more crash prone. I can't prove it, but my guess is that, if Microsoft has 200 people on campus testing some version of Server, the majority of them have a single-processor machine on their desks. Isn't it logical to assume then that 2003 has been better tested on single-processor machines than multiprocessor machines? For the same reason, ask yourself: Of all of the people beta-testing Server 2003 (or Service Pack 1 or Service Pack 2 or whatever), do you think most of them tested it in a single-domain or multi-domain environment? My guess is the former, which would imply that it's the better way to go for reliability. Understand, however, that these are just guesses on my part.

OUs VERSUS GROUPS

So far, I've described two kinds of things that hold other things—that is, I've described something called a *group*, which can contain users and/or machines, and I've described something *else* called an organizational unit, which *also* can contain users and/or machines.

So what's the difference? Well, in an oversimplified sense, you put the things that you want to control into an OU. Then you grant that control to a group. If you wanted to, for example, create a subgroup of an enterprise like a department and then designate a group of people who could act as administrators to that department, then the department would be an OU and the desired administrators would be a group. You'd then delegate authority for the OU to the group. But here's some more detail.

A user account can only be in one OU, but it can be a *member* of as many groups as you like. A user account or machine account exists in only one domain in a general sense, but the account may also live in an OU *inside* that domain, much as you or I can live inside some city in a state, but we each live in only one city. In contrast, no matter which city you live in, you can be a member of as many associations—groups—that you like. Put another way.

◆ OUs are *containers* that can contain objects in the AD, like user or machine accounts or even other OUs. That's why your user account can exist in only one OU. (Well, it can exist in more than one OU, but only if the OUs are nested—for example, if I modeled my OU pattern on U.S. cities and states, then my user account might live in the Dallas OU, which is contained in the Texas OU.)

◆ Groups are, in contrast, just attributes of an object.

You can use groups to assign permissions—you can, for example, deny access to a file to anyone in a given group. AD won't let you do any permission work with OUs; you can't deny access to a printer or a file share to an entire OU.

OUs let you define *logical* divisions in a domain. But knowing about the *physical* subdivisions is important as well: I might not want to transfer that half-gigabyte file to server DISTRIBUTE01 if I know that it's only connected to the rest of the domain with a 56K link. That's where sites come in handy.

Sites

As you read earlier in this chapter, one of NT 4's weaknesses was the fact that domain controllers replicate data among themselves in a very "chatty," bandwidth-intensive way. That's not a problem for domain controllers on the same LAN, as there's typically bandwidth to burn on a LAN, but WAN links are nothing to toss away lightly.

AD improves upon that with the notion of *sites*. In addition to knowing about machines and users in an enterprise, the AD also keeps track of the geographic aspects of an enterprise. Each LAN-connected area is called a *site*. Active Directory domain controllers, as well as Windows 2000, XP, and 2003 systems, use the insights that you give it about your physical layout to figure out where the WAN links—the slower and more expensive part of your network—are. It then does two very helpful things: First, it compresses the replication traffic (again, by a factor of as much as *10*, quite impressive!), and second, it uses route costing information that you supply to figure out how best to route the replication traffic at lowest cost.

The Active Directory also uses sites in a feature called Distributed File System or Dfs. With Dfs, you can create a file share that contains some important information and then create a "replica" version of that file share on each of your sites. A tool called the File Replication Service ensures that all of those file shares contained the identical information. If you had four sites, for example, then you'd have four replicas. But the four of them all look like just one share to users. When a user attaches to a Dfs share with replicas on multiple sites, then, Dfs uses the AD's site information to ensure the user gets connected with the *local* replica, if possible.

By the way, if you've got experience with Exchange, then all of this will sound somewhat familiar, and it should—Exchange first pioneered the idea of sites several years ago. In fact, I once heard a Microsoft speaker say, "You may have participated in the five-year beta process for Active Directory; you may have known it as Exchange 4.0, 5.0, and 5.5." (He was, in case you're wondering, clearly speaking with his tongue in his cheek.)

At this point, you've met domains, groups, organizational units, and sites. Next, let's meet two ways of organizing *collections* of domains: trees and forests.

Building Multidomain Structures I: Trees

Real-world experience with NT from version 3.1 through 4 showed that people needing multiple-domain enterprises tended to build *hierarchies* of domains, what computer people call *tree structures* despite the fact that computer trees tend to have their roots up top in the air and their "leaves" at bottom. Microsoft designed AD to use DNS as a naming system, and DNS is hierarchical in nature anyway, so Active Directory exploits this happy coincidence and encourages you to build multi-domain enterprises as hierarchies.

NOTE *As you read in the DNS chapter, hierarchies of names are sometimes alternatively called* namespaces. *Thus, if Bigfirm is divided into bigfirm.biz, westcoast.bigfirm.biz, and eastcoast.bigfirm.biz, then you might hear the Bigfirm managers refer to the Bigfirm namespace or perhaps Bigfirm's Active Directory namespace. All* namespace *means here is "the system that we use to choose names that make some kind of sense."*

The first AD domain that you create is called the *root* of the tree. Suppose, following the earlier example, that the root's name is bigfirm.biz. Domains below it are referred to as *child domains*, as you've read. You can decide to divide your organization geographically—for example, eastcoast.bigfirm.biz and westcoast.bigfirm.biz—or organizationally, as perhaps manufacturing.bigfirm.biz, finance .bigfirm.biz, and sales.bigfirm.biz. In case it's not clear, here's the rule for naming child domains: A child domain must have a name like *name.parentdomainname*. So, for example, a child domain of bigfirm.biz must have a name like *name*.bigfirm.biz—so eastcoast.bigfirm.biz or westcoast.bigfirm.biz would be fine, and apex.com would *not* be fine, as it doesn't include bigfirm.biz in it.

You can then create another level if you choose—perhaps sales.eastcoast.bigfirm.biz, manufacturing.eastcoast.bigfirm.biz, finance.eastcoast.bigfirm.biz, and sales.westcoast.bigfirm .biz, manufacturing.westcoast.bigfirm.biz, and finance.westcoast.bigfirm.biz (six domains!)—and another and another, to create as complex a system as you want. Active Directory helps you by automatically creating trust relationships between each domain and its child domains. For example, merely creating westcoast.bigfirm.biz automatically creates a two-way trust relationship between westcoast.bigfirm.biz and bigfirm.biz. This two-way trust means that bigfirm.biz administrators may choose to extend file and print permissions to finance.bigfirm.biz users and vice versa.

And as I mentioned earlier, AD trust relationships are *transitive*. Creating finance.westcoast.bigfirm.biz creates a two-way trust relationship between finance.westcoast.bigfirm.biz and westcoast.bigfirm.biz, but it doesn't stop there: Because westcoast.bigfirm.biz and bigfirm.biz *also* have a two-way trust, finance .westcoast.bigfirm.biz ends up with an automatic trust relationship with bigfirm.biz. (If that doesn't sound interesting, then you didn't work with NT 4 and earlier versions, which required you to hand-build every single trust relationship.) Thus, because eastcoast.bigfirm.biz trusts bigfirm.biz and bigfirm.biz trusts westcoast.bigfirm.biz, then eastcoast.bigfirm.biz trusts westcoast.bigfirm.biz.

Building Multidomain Structures II: Forests

Domain trees, then, offer the benefits of automatic trust relationships, a very good thing. But there's just one minor problem with that—all of the domain names must fit into a nice hierarchy. The child domains must contain the names of the parent domains.

FOREST BASICS

Suppose in contrast that your enterprise divides into bigfirm.biz and apex.com, two former rivals that have merged. Suppose further you've decided to go with a multiple-domain enterprise and want to keep some of your firm as bigfirm.biz and some as apex.com.

It looks like two things are true, then: First, you're probably going to have two domains, and second, those two domains won't fit into a tree.

You can choose to build these two Active Directory domains into a unified structure, but it can't be a tree because of their dissimilar names. Instead, you can choose to create a *forest*. A forest is just a group of trees, as you see in Figure 8.4.

FIGURE 8.4

Example Active Directory forest

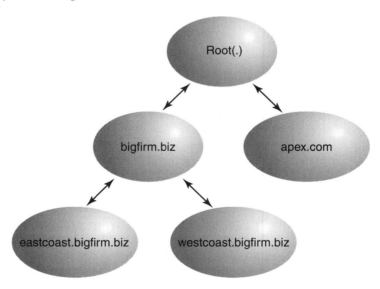

Here, you see a forest built from the bigfirm.biz and apex.com trees.

Other than different naming hierarchies, the trees in the forest act like one tree in terms of their trust relationships—Active Directory builds transitive trusts automatically. So, for example, as eastcoast.bigfirm.biz trusts bigfirm.biz, bigfirm.biz trusts apex.com, and eastcoast.bigfirm.biz trusts apex.com—all automatically.

YOU MUST BUILD TREES AND FORESTS TOGETHER

This sounds great, and of course it's a terrific improvement over NT 4. But hidden in this potentially rich notion of many domains joined into a tree and many trees joined into a forest is a dirty little secret. Here it is: you cannot join already-existing domains into a tree. Nor can you join already-existing trees into a forest. The only way to add a domain to a tree, or a tree to a forest, is to build it from scratch onto an existing tree or forest.

Hard to believe? Well, it's true. Once you place domains in a forest, you cannot move them to another forest. You also can't delete them if they have any child domains. AD's forest structure it, then, painfully inflexible and that's true even if you're completely upgraded to Server 2003.

You Can't Glue Domains Together

So suppose I were to create an AD domain named bigfirm.biz on one network. Then, on a completely separate network totally unconnected to bigfirm.biz's network, I create an AD domain named eastcoast.bigfirm.biz. I cannot then attach the two networks and effect a tearful reunion of parent and child domain. Nor could I build apex.com and bigfirm.biz AD trees in isolation and then connect them, after the fact, to create a forest.

Attaching existing domains to existing trees or forests is called *pruning and grafting* and it can't be done, at least not with the tools supplied by Windows Server 2003. Thus, for example, if Exxon buys Mobil, and Exxon already has a domain named exxon.com and Mobil's got a domain named mobil.com, it's not possible to join them together in a tree with the supplied 2000 and 2003 Active Directory tools.

"...But Only the AD Wizard Can Make a Tree"

(My apologies to Sergeant Joyce Kilmer.) Let's review what I'm saying here. If I've created an AD domain named bigfirm.biz and want to create a child domain in its tree named eastcoast.bigfirm.biz, then I sit down at the machine that I want to be the first DC in eastcoast.bigfirm.biz and create the eastcoast.bigfirm.biz domain, explaining to the Active Directory Installation Wizard, a program named DCPROMO (which you'll meet a bit later) that I want it to be part of an existing tree, bigfirm.biz. Before the wizard will go any further, it demands the name and password of an administrator for the bigfirm.biz domain. DCPROMO will refuse to create a child domain unless it can contact the parent domain right at that moment and get permission. In the same way, if you want to create a second tree in a forest, then the wizard will require that you tell it the name and password of an administrator for the first tree. (What about the third tree or fourth tree—what account do *they* need to provide? From the second to the millionth tree in a forest, you've got to provide an admin account from the first tree in the forest. As you're about to read in the next section, that first tree is "magic.")

TIP   You're probably wondering exactly what *administrative account you need to create new domains in a forest. The answer is, any account that is a member of a group called Enterprise Admins. You will only find that group in the very first domain that you create in a forest.*

Combining Domains, Trees, and Forests: Server 2003 to the Rescue, Kind Of

So suppose you *do* have separate domains, trees, or forests that you want to attach to existing domains, trees, or forests—what do you do? Well, the *best* answer would be if you could link those objects with one of those nifty AD two-way transitive trust relationships. In some senses, that's all there *is* to a tree or forest; it's just a bunch of domains strung together with two-way transitive trusts. So if you could build two-way transitive trusts between any arbitrary set of domains, trees, or forests, then you could essentially build whatever kind of AD structure that you liked.

But you can't do that at all under an AD that contains any Windows 2000 Servers as domain controllers. You can *sort* of do it in an Active Directory composed of all Windows Server 2003–based DCs with something called a *transitive forest root trust*. In fact, it's probably the single most significant Active Directory improvement between Windows 2000 Server and Windows Server 2003.

As you've already learned, the neat thing about a forest is that all of its domains trust each other because of transitive trusts—even if domain A doesn't trust domain B directly, it might be that A trusts D, D trusts C, and C trusts B. As these trusts "flow through," there's a kind of "six degrees of Kevin Bacon" way that everyone trusts everyone. But hooking up that transitive trust rela-tionship between forests wasn't possible until 2003. With 2003, you can create one trust relationship between Forest 1 and Forest 2, and from that point on every domain in Forest 1 trusts every domain in Forest 2 and vice versa. Thus, suppose Bigfirm buys Apex, both of which have an existing forest. Bigfirm wants its forest to work well with Apex's, so they create a single forest-to-forest root trust and trust is universal.

This is good news, but there are a few reasons why this may not be all that Bigfirm and Apex wanted. Here's why.

- First, this is only possible if both bigfirm.biz and apex.com are upgraded to Windows Server 2003 forest functional level. In other words, they must upgrade every domain controller from Windows 2000 Server to Windows Server 2003. Not *one* DC can be running 2K. That might be expensive.

- Second, two trusting forests do not exactly equal a single forest as far as some AD-aware soft-ware is concerned. That's because, as you'll soon learn, there is another very important bit of "glue" binding forests together in addition to their transitive trusts: the global catalog. Each domain in a forest has its own database of users, machine accounts, and the like, but there is a sort of "database of databases" that contains a centralized summary of most of the important stuff for all of the domains in a forest called the global catalog. Exchange, for example, sees your enterprise as one big firm no matter how many domains it has because Exchange thinks "all domains sharing a global catalog equal one enterprise." So here's the problem: two separate trusting forests *still have two separate global catalogs.*

- Third, and this is probably a smaller issue, forest-to-forest trusts are, believe it or not, not transitive *across forests*. By that I mean this: if Forest 1 trusts Forest 2, then as you've seen, all of Forest 1's domains trust all of Forest 2's domains and vice versa. But now let's say that you set up a transitive trust between Forest 2 and Forest 3. Now all of Forest 2's domains trust all of Forest 3's domains (and vice versa). But what about Forest 1 and Forest 3—what rela-tionship do they have? None, as it turns out. Forest-to-forest trusts do not "flow through." You'd have to build a whole separate trust between Forest 1 and Forest 3 in order to have every forest around trust every other one.

You'll see the nuts and bolts of setting up trusts towards the end of the chapter in the "Migration Strategies" section.

But You Can Rearrange the Tree

Windows Server 2003 improves upon things in one way—you can *rearrange* domains in a forest. By renaming a domain, you could move it from one tree in a forest to another. There's a price, though—every DC in the forest must be running Windows Server 2003. Still, it's a nice plus for 2003.

Using Migration Tools to Combine Domains, Trees, and Forests

If transitive forest trusts aren't right for you, and you just simply *must* either merge two domains into one, or perhaps you want to take two domains from different forests and join them together into a single forest, then you'll have to go a bit more complex route: domain migration. You'll start out by either buying a so-called "migration" tool, such as the ones offered by Fastlane, NetIQ, Aelita, and Entevo, or you'll use the free one that ships with 2003 Server—Microsoft's Active Directory Migration Tool (ADMT). ADMT is free but a bit limited, and I'll show you how to use it in the "Migration Strategies" section later.

Migration tools copy user and machine accounts and permission information between one domain and another. You would, then, merge two domains by creating an empty domain in the same tree/forest as one of the domains, then copying the objects from the other domain.

For example, suppose I had two distinct AD domains, bigfirm.biz and apex.com, and wanted to merge them into a forest. Using a migration tool, I'd work something like this:

1. Create a new empty domain named apex2.com (or something like that—you'll run into trouble if you try to work with two domains both named apex.com) in bigfirm.biz's forest, using the Active Directory Installation Wizard.

2. Build an old-style NT 4 trust relationship between the apex.com domain and the apex2.com domain. (Even though they're called "NT 4–style" trusts, they work between Active Directory domains in different forests.) *Or*, if the domains are both in Active Directory forests that use only Windows Server 2003–based DCs and are at Windows Server 2003 forest functional level, then I could build a transitive forest-to-forest trust. Again, that's only possible in a pure 2003-to-2003 situation.

3. If I built an NT 4-style trust between apex.com and apex2.com, then I'd also have to build an old-style NT 4 trust relationship in the other direction, between the apex2.com domain and the apex.com domain. If I'd built a transitive forest trust, then I'd be done building trusts, as forest trusts are two-way.

4. Use the migration tool to copy the user and machine accounts from apex.com to apex2.com.

5. Now tell the users in apex.com to no longer log in to apex.com, but instead to log in to their accounts on apex2.com.

The process isn't trouble-free, but it works. I'll cover it more in the "Migration Strategies" section later.

The Case for an Empty Root

Look back to Figure 8.4. In that figure, I drew an extra root domain in addition to apex.com, bigfirm.biz, and bigfirm.biz's two child domains. I did that to make the diagram "look" right—we're used to seeing hierarchies end up at a single point.

In a tree, it's simple to see which domain is the root or top-level domain—it's simple to see that apex.com is the top of the apex.com tree and that bigfirm.biz is the top of the bigfirm.biz tree. But when you build two trees (apex.com and bigfirm.biz) into one forest, then which domain is the "top" or "root" domain? Or isn't there a root; perhaps all trees are equal?

In an Active Directory forest built of several trees, there *is* a single forest domain root. It's just not obvious which one it is.

NOTE   *The root domain of a forest of Active Directory domains is the first domain that you installed in the forest.*

So suppose you came across an AD forest that contained just three domains—bigfirm.biz, apex.com, and consolidated.com. Which domain is the forest root? The answer isn't obvious because the three domains seem to sit at the same level. I don't know of a quick way to find out which domain is the forest root, but here's a slightly slower one. Remember that only the forest root domain contains a group named Enterprise Admins; that's how you'll find the root.

Start Active Directory Users and Computers (Start/Programs/Administrative Tools/Active Directory Users and Computers). In the left pane of the MMC snap-in, you'll see an icon representing a domain; it looks like three tower PCs clustered together. Right-click that icon and choose Find. In the resulting dialog box, there's a drop-down list box labeled In, which lets you tell the program which domain to search in; click it and you'll see that you have the ability to search any one of your forest's domains. Choose one of your top-level domains. Then notice the field labeled Name; enter **enterprise*** and press Enter. If the search found a group called Enterprise Admins, then you've found the root. If not, drop down the In list box and try another domain until you locate the one with Enterprise Admins.

Suppose bigfirm.biz turned out to be the root domain in my Bigfirm/Apex/Consolidated example. There are probably three domains because there are or were at some time three different business entities that for some reason are one firm now. Who *cares* if the Bigfirm guys happen to be the forest root?

Well, the Apex and Consolidated guys, that's who—whether they know it or not. You see, members of the Enterprise Admins group, which happens to live in the Bigfirm domain, have powers in *every domain in the forest*. They're not members of the Domain Admins group in those domains, but they might as well be, as Enterprise Admins have Domain Admin–like powers everywhere.

That means that although in *theory* Bigfirm, Apex, and Consolidated have separate domains, with those nice, convenient security boundaries, in *practice* the Apex and Consolidated folks have to just kind of hope that the Bigfirm guys don't get the lust for power one day and decide to do something scary in the Apex or Consolidated domains. So you can see why Apex and Consolidated might be a bit nervous.

The answer? Don't create three domains, create four. The first domain—the root domain—should be some domain that you're never going to use, e-gobbledygook.com or something like that. Create one administrative account in that domain, including it in the Enterprise Admins. Let the CIO create it and then have her write down that account name and password, and then stuff the paper on which she's written them into her safe and use the Sopranos personnel-termination procedure on anyone who knows the password besides you and her. (Just kidding. But this *is* a powerful account—you don't want any nonessential people getting access to it.) At the same time, create the other three domains—you'll need the CIO for a while, she'll have to type in the username and password for that Enterprise Admin account in order to create those three domains. Then you can put away the Enterprise Admin account and you'll only need it now and then.

This idea of creating a first domain and then populating it with only an account or two, then doing nothing else with it, is called an *empty root* AD design.

Some firms create an empty root domain even if it's just a one-domain enterprise in case it acquires other companies at some time in the future. It's not a bad bit of bet-hedging, and I'd recommend it to some. Of course, the downside of it is that you've got to have a DC or, better yet, two DCs, sitting around running, doing nothing to support the root domain, and each of them will need a copy of Server 2003. But, again, it may not be a bad investment——an empty root is one case where I'd break my single-domain-preferred preference.

Finding Domain Controllers for Logins Under AD

All of the machinery that the Active Directory includes enables Active Directory domain members—2000, XP, and 2003 systems—to be a bit smarter about logons than NT 4 domain clients were. Here's a brief look at how AD uses sites and DNS to log in machines and users.

When you start up your Windows 2000 or later desktop machine, it must log in to your Active Directory domain—machines log in as well as people. "Machines" here refers to systems running some version of NT (NT 3.1–4, Windows 2000, XP Pro—Home cannot participate in domains—or Server 2003). They log in, Windows 9*x* and XP Home systems do not.

The hard part about logons is in finding a domain controller—that is to say, a computer that offers Kerberos logon services. Once your system has found a DC, then transacting all of the Kerberos back-and-forth stuff about checking your password and user ID (or your machine's password and user ID) is very simple. The problem is finding a machine to *present* these credentials to.

In its most basic form, a machine finds a domain controller by asking DNS, "I'm a member of the bigfirm.biz domain. Do you know of any machines in that domain that offer the Kerberos protocol?" As to *how* it queries DNS, remember last chapter's discussion of SRV records? That's how a workstation finds a DC. The DNS server then responds, "Sure, the following systems here do Kerberos, and they use port 88 to do it." Armed with that information, the workstation can begin logging onto bigfirm.biz—but there's more to it than that. You don't want to be logged in by just *any* DC, you want to be logged in by a *local* DC, so you're not waiting around for a lot of traffic to go over the WAN.

But actually Active Directory organizes its DNS SRV records pretty carefully. AD domain controllers register their SRV records with a domain's DNS dynamic zone, as you saw in the last chapter. But the DCs don't just dump all of the SRV records into the zone willy-nilly; instead, AD creates subdomains (and here "domain" means "DNS domain," not "AD domain") in the DNS zone that it uses to store its SRV records. More specifically, recall the AD notion of sites. Suppose Bigfirm has two offices—one in Edenton and one in Bath. Where NT 4 domains have no idea where DCs are physically located, ADs keep track of that information via those subdomains in their DNS zones. When you create a bigfirm.biz AD domain and then define two sites named Edenton and Bath, AD responds by creating a subdomain in the bigfirm.biz DNS zone called "Edenton" and another named "Bath." DCs that are located in Bath then store some of their SRV records in the Bath subdomain. Not *all* the SRV records because AD wants to maintain two places to find out about DC's availability—first the site-specific subdomain, and then a global subdomain. So every DC writes an SRV record to its site subdomain in DNS and then writes a copy of that the global subdomain. (If *that* sounds complicated, believe me, it *isn't*, at least compared to the reality—I gave you a simplified version of the truth! And yes, I'm tempted to quote Jack Nicholson's character from *A Few Good Men* at this point, but I'll refrain. I mean, you *could* handle the truth, you just don't need to know most of it in this case.)

The value of all of this work lies in making it possible for a workstation to find a local DC. By creating site-specific DNS subdomains, your workstation can do more than just ask, "Are there any DCs for bigfirm.biz?" Instead, your workstation can ask, "Are there any DCs for bigfirm.biz in the Bath office?" Every 2000 or later machine knows where it logged in last time, as that information lives in the Registry in the entry DynamicSiteName in `HKEY_LOCAL_MACHINE\System\CurrentControlSet\Services\Netlogon\parameters`. You can see that on your system, assuming that it's a member of an Active Directory domain, by typing this command:

```
reg query hklm\System\CurrentControlSet\Services\Netlogon\parameters
  /v dynamicsitename
```

You'll get a result that looks like

```
! REG.EXE VERSION 3.0
HKEY_LOCAL_MACHINE\System\CurrentControlSet\Services\Netlogon\parameters
    dynamicsitename      REG_SZ   Headquarters
D:\>
```

In that example, my workstation is in a site named "Headquarters." But how does a workstation know what site it's in? The last DC to log it in tells it. This is most easily explained using the example of a laptop, as they potentially move around from site to site.

Suppose that I was in Bath yesterday, but today I'm in Edenton. I plug my laptop into the Edenton network and turn it on, so that I can log onto the domain. The laptop looks in its Registry and sees that it's in Bath. (It's wrong, that that's what it thinks.) It then contacts DNS and says, "Please tell me the names of the Kerberos servers in Bath," and DNS complies. The laptop then contacts each of the Bath DCs, saying, "Will you please log me on?" The first Bath DC to respond notices from the laptop's IP address that my laptop is in Edenton, not Bath, and replies, "Well, I'd be happy to log you on, but you're not in Bath, you're in Edenton." The laptop says, "Oops," and queries DNS to find the Edenton DCs. It asks the Edenton DCs to log it on and updates its Registry to remember that it's in Edenton for next time.

Now, if all of the Edenton DCs are dead or too busy to respond—the laptop waits 100 milliseconds for each to respond before going on to the next one—then it goes back to DNS and queries not the Edenton DNS subdomain, but the global subdomain. In effect, the laptop says, "Okay, I give up, clearly no one in Edenton's responding to me—I'll take *any* DC for bigfirm.biz." DNS returns the global list of every DC in bigfirm.biz, and the laptop starts working its way through that list to eventually find a machine that will log it onto the domain.

Summarized, then, Windows 2000, XP, and 2003 systems that are members of ADs find domain controllers by first using their knowledge of their site locations and domain names to query DNS for the names of nearby domain controllers. The machines then contact the nearby domain controllers and ask them to log them in. The DC that agrees to log them in first checks that it is the closest DC available, and if it is *not*, then it redirects the machine to a closer DC.

You can find out which server logged you in by opening a command prompt and typing **set**. One of the pieces of information that you'll get is a line starting with `LOGONSERVER=`; to the right of the equals sign is the name of the DC that logged you in.

Building an Active Directory: Some Hands-On Experience

Let's take a break from the concepts for a while and do a little hands-on work. Let's build a small tree of domains to get a feel for what the Active Directory process looks like. In this tree, I'll create two domains: one called bigfirm.biz and another, a child domain called ecoast.bigfirm.biz. As I'll want an account that can act as an administrator across the whole tree, I'll also create a user named bigguy with those powers.

NOTE *If you created bigdog.bigfirm.biz in the examples of the last chapter, then you'll use that machine as bigfirm.biz's first domain controller.*

If you want to do something like this, you'll need two machines because every machine can only be a domain controller for one domain; two domains, therefore, would require two machines—more, in fact, if you wanted to start adding extra DCs or member servers.

Building the First Domain

One of the really nice things about Windows 2000 and later versions of Server is that Microsoft separated the process of installing Server from the process of creating a domain controller. You can do a fairly vanilla installation of Windows 2000 Server or Server 2003 (or have an equipment supplier preinstall it, as companies such as Dell, HP, or IBM do) without having to worry about two of NT 4's biggest pains—that you needed to designate a machine as a domain controller during Setup, and that you couldn't install a backup domain controller unless your computer was connected live on the LAN to the domain's PDC. So you can start this process from pretty much any machine running Windows 2000 Server or Server 2003. (I'll stick to Server 2003 in this example.) But before you do, consider four caveats: memory, DNS, NTFS, and disks. Let's take a minute and consider those.

HARDWARE: MEMORY, DISKS, AND NTFS

The memory part is easy. As far as I can see, Server 2003–based DCs use *at least* 136MB of memory. You don't *need* to have 136MB of actual RAM in a machine before using it as an AD domain controller, but if you *don't* have at least that much, be prepared for nearly constant disk activity as Server pages pieces of itself on and off disk. It's a matter of taste, but I found all of that disk chattering extremely annoying and so I originally upgraded my machines to 256MB of RAM—thank heavens memory's finally dropped in price—and now buy all systems with at least 1GB of RAM. You'll hear a lot of people talking about how you need gigahertz-plus systems to run 2003, but in my experience it's RAM that's important—I have a workgroup DC that runs on a 400MHz Pentium II with 512MB of RAM and I'm pretty satisfied with its performance. (And don't forget to use ECC RAM!)

Next, you'll get better performance out of your Active Directory servers if you can put two separate physical SCSI, EIDE, or FireWire hard disks in your system. SCSI has always been the performance leader, but nowadays I'd say that small servers could work well with two EIDE or FireWire hard disks. If you go with two EIDE hard disks, make sure that they are on different EIDE channels; two EIDE drives on the same channel cannot operate simultaneously. It's not that they won't work in that case, just that they won't work *as quickly.*

The third consideration is relatively easy. Active Directory servers *need* an NTFS partition, so before trying to make a server a domain controller, be sure that it's got at least one NTFS partition.

DNS: AD's FOUNDATION

The final, and most important, caveat is about DNS. The Active Directory stores its list of domain controllers and global catalog servers in DNS, as you've already read, and it uses dynamic DNS to do it. Recall that a computer registers itself with the dynamic DNS zone by first requesting the SOA record for that zone and then reading the SOA record to determine the name of the primary DNS server for that zone. Then the computer contacts the primary DNS server and registers itself. That means that for you to even *think* about setting up a domain called bigfirm.biz your would-be new domain controller must do the following:

- Ask its preferred DNS server to get the SOA record for bigfirm.biz. Thus, before you try to convert a system to an Active Directory domain controller, you should really reexamine the DNS server or servers that this system will use to make DNS requests. You're almost certainly doing split-brain DNS of some kind, so double-check that when your soon-to-be domain controller asks DNS for the name of the primary DNS server for bigfirm.biz that it gets the right answer.

- Your soon-to-be DC will then try to send dynamic updates to the DNS server pointed to by that SOA record. That DNS server had better be willing to accept those updates, or you are not going to be able to make this computer a domain controller.

As I've said, my example will create an AD domain called bigfirm.biz. That's a domain that I've registered, and I run a zone by that name *that is not dynamic*. I registered the domain and set up a simple non-dynamic zone on it for some specific reasons. First, I didn't want to use a domain example that someone was using, as I was concerned that they might not like having lots of people trying to register with their no-doubt-nondynamic DNS server. Second, I wanted to *ensure* that the primary DNS server associated with bigfirm.biz wasn't dynamic so as to be 100-percent sure that you'd have to master split-brain DNS before you could get the AD to work.

If you followed along with my example in the previous chapter, then you have a system running with IP address 192.168.0.2 (or perhaps .1) called BIGDOG running a DNS server that contains a local zone for bigfirm.biz. That machine points to itself for a preferred DNS server, and so when it asks, "Who's the primary DNS server for bigfirm.biz?" then the answer will be, "You are." If you've followed previous chapter's instructions, then you also have that zone set up to be dynamic, and so you'll be able to make this an Active Directory domain controller.

As a matter of fact, inasmuch as you've set up split-brain DNS, you *could* call your AD anything. You could create a microsoft.com AD. But if you *did*, then recall that your DNS server would never be able to find the *real* microsoft.com!

Before going any further, you might want to just take a moment to find out which DNS server your computer will try to send the updates to. Sit down at the machine that you intend to make the first domain controller of bigfirm.biz—I recommend the BIGDOG system we created in the last chapter—and log in, then open up a command prompt. Now use `nslookup` to do a preflight DNS check.

```
E:\>nslookup
Default Server:  bigdog.bigfirm.biz
Address:  192.168.0.2

> set type=soa
> bigfirm.biz
```

```
Server:  bigdog.bigfirm.biz
Address:  192.168.0.2

bigfirm.biz
        primary name server = bigdog.bigfirm.biz
        responsible mail addr = admin.bigfirm.pri
        serial  = 48
        refresh = 900 (15 mins)
        retry   = 600 (10 mins)
        expire  = 86400 (1 day)
        default TTL = 3600 (1 hour)
bigdog.bigfirm.biz       internet address = 192.168.0.2
>exit
```

As you saw in the previous chapter, nslookup starts out by telling you which server it's getting its answers from and, as I want BIGDOG to point to the DNS service on itself, then the results you see above are initially encouraging. Then I type **set type=soa** because I want to retrieve the SOA record. Then I enter **bigfirm.biz** and nslookup retrieves and displays the info in the SOA record, which includes the *primary name server*. That is the machine at 192.168.0.2, so I'm in business, as I'm *sitting* at 192.168.0.2 and that's the machine that I intend to make a DC.

Remember that this does not mean that you *must* put DNS on the machine that will be your DC, this is just one answer. Refer back to the discussion in the previous chapter about the steps to making split-brain DNS work properly for AD. And you may have modified your AD setup and, if so, then use nslookup to ensure that your computer returns the results that you wanted. For example, if you've decided to call your AD mydomain.com, then you'd ask nslookup for SOA information on mydomain.com. And, again, recall that I'm setting things up so that the primary DNS server and the DC for bigfirm.biz are the same systems; there's no particular reason why you'd have to do that, unless you wanted to create an Active Directory–integrated zone (remember that AD-integrated zones are great, but they only allow you to put DNS on domain controllers). If you've got enough machines, then go ahead and set up this DC on a machine at 192.168.0.10 or something. Just make sure that the system's preferred DNS server points at whatever machine is the primary for bigfirm.biz or at a DNS server that acts as a secondary for bigfirm.biz. For example, if you've got three machines and wanted to build an example that mimicked big networks more closely, then you might do this:

◆ Put Windows Server 2003 on all three systems.

◆ On a computer at IP address 192.168.0.2, set up DNS and create the primary zone for bigfirm.biz, as we've already done. Call the system BIGDOG.

◆ On a computer at IP address 192.168.0.6, set up DNS and make it a secondary DNS server for bigfirm.biz. It's kind of like what we did in the previous chapter with the machine named ns1.ecoast.bigfirm.biz, but without the delegated subzone. Call the system ns2.bigfirm.biz.

◆ On yet another computer give it IP address 192.168.0.20 (these are all arbitrary addresses that I'm using, of course). Don't put DNS on it. But set its "preferred DNS server" to the address of either DNS server.

You needn't build your example with this much complexity, of course; I just didn't want you to get the idea that in the real world there's only one DNS server in an enterprise, or that every DC must be built on the same machine as the primary DNS server for a zone.

Of course, none of this is a problem if all you're going to do is just read the text and follow along with the screen shots.

RUNNING DCPROMO

To convert a Server 2003 system to a domain controller—it must be a server, you can't make a Professional machine a DC—click Start/Run and then type in **dcpromo**. That starts the Active Directory Installation Wizard, as you see in Figure 8.5.

FIGURE 8.5

Starting
DCPROMO

You use this not only to convert member servers into domain controllers, but the reverse as well, to "demote" a domain controller to a member server.

TIP   At this point, let me note a convenient improvement of Server 2003–based DCs over 2000-based DCs. You can rename a 2003-based domain controller. Yay!

The wizard asks a series of questions and then, based on the answers to those questions, sets up a new tree, forest, or domain or creates another domain controller in an existing domain. Click Next and you'll see a screen like Figure 8.6.

This page warns you that if you create a domain based on Windows Server 2003 systems, then you'll have to bid your Windows 95 systems adieu because of something called SMB signing. The idea with SMB signing is that Microsoft wants to be very certain that it's not going to be easy for anyone to hack an AD system. So they require that any communications between a client and a domain controller must be 100 percent sure that no one's intercepting and changing those communications. In the past, some networks have been prey to a class of attacks called "man in the middle" attacks whereby I would sit on the network between you and a server and intercept your communications, modify them, and pass them along, thus enabling me to both listen in and change the communication. One way to be pretty sure that a communication has not been tampered with is to digitally sign that communication, and NT first started supporting that in Service Pack 3 for NT 4. SMB signing's been around a while, but it's never been mandatory. 2003-based ADs *make* it mandatory. And there's the rub.

FIGURE 8.6

Warning: DOS and
Windows 95 are
outta here!

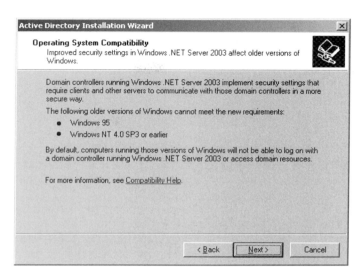

You see, Windows 95 does not support SMB signing and Microsoft doesn't offer any software to *make* it support SMB signing, so Windows 95 and DOS clients are simply out of luck—"take a walk," it says to the old guys. Windows 98 can add the functionality with a piece of client software that comes on the Server CD, the Active Directory Client for Windows 98, so you'd have to add that before any Windows 98 systems could talk to a 2003-based AD domain. NT 4 has the ability, but again you've got to upgrade to at least SP4 to make that happen. I can't see that being a problem, however, as anyone still using NT 4 has already gone to SP 6A, or at least I pray that they have…you'd be open to too many attacks otherwise.

Now that you know the risks to old systems inherent in running a 2003-based AD, click Next to see Figure 8.7.

FIGURE 8.7

Are you creating
a new domain?

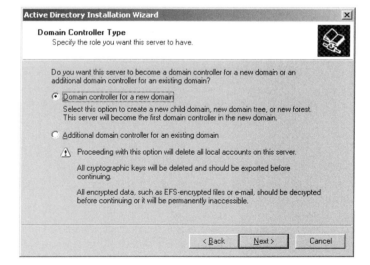

The way that you create a new domain is simple: Set up a machine as the first domain controller for that domain. Building a domain's first domain controller and creating a new domain are exactly the same thing. But you wouldn't have just one domain controller for most domains. For one thing, each site within a multisite domain will usually have at least one DC, to enable logons. Another reason you'd have multiple DCs on a single domain—whether single- or multiple-site—is to handle many logon requests. As you know, login requests don't space themselves out nicely throughout the day. Instead, most login requests happen all around the same time, first thing in the morning. The more DCs, the more logons your domain can handle. The second, third, fourth, and further domain controllers in a domain were called *backup* domain controllers under NT prior to Windows 2000, but Active Directory doesn't give them any special name because they're all supposed to be equal. As you'll see in the later discussion on FSMOs/operations masters, however, that's not true.

TIP   So would it be a good idea to make all of your Server 2003 machines into domain controllers, to speed logons? No. Making a server a DC takes up memory and CPU power. Additionally, too many DCs means extra LAN chatter as they keep each other updated on changes to the Active Directory. The warning at the bottom of the screen is trying to say that non-DCs have a SAM with local accounts, and DCs instead have an NTDS.DIT. *DCPROMO deletes a computer's SAM contents when the computer becomes a DC. There's a kind of optimal number of DCs that you should have in a network and that number varies from network to network. Personally, I monitor the* lsass.exe *process to get a feel for when to add a DC.*

The first question that DCPROMO asks, then, is whether to create a whole new domain or just another DC in an existing domain. We're creating a new domain, so I select that and click Next. That leads to the screen in Figure 8.8.

FIGURE 8.8

Choosing to create an altogether new tree, a child domain in an existing tree, or new forest

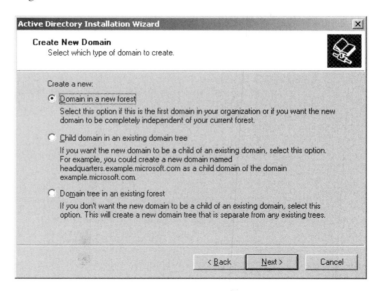

Recall that Active Directory lets you build domains into trees and trees into forests, so logically the Active Directory Installation Wizard must know where to put this new tree—in an altogether

new forest or in an existing forest, right? This is the first domain in a new tree, and the first tree in a new forest, so I choose that and click Next to see the screen in Figure 8.9.

FIGURE 8.9

The domain's full DNS name

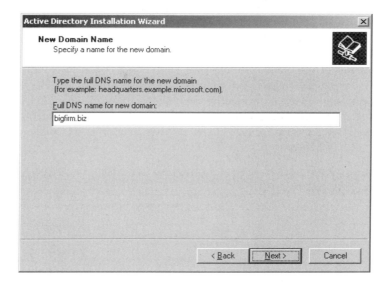

Just type in the name of the new domain, which in this case is bigfirm.biz. Clicking Next leads to the screen in Figure 8.10.

FIGURE 8.10

The domain's NetBIOS/legacy name

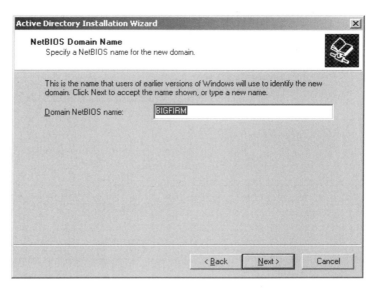

Unless your network is 100-percent Windows 2000 and later, both servers and workstations, then your network contains machines running network software written in the NT 3.*x* and 4.*x* days, when domain names could be no more than 15 characters long and could not have a hierarchy of any kind. Those older systems—and you know, I tend to want to call them *legacy* systems, as that's been the *chic* term for old software for about 10 years now, but it seems that the current Microsoft term is *downlevel* systems—wouldn't understand a domain named bigfirm.biz, and so they need a more familiar name. For that reason, Active Directory domains have two names: their DNS-like name (for example, bigfirm.biz) and an old-style domain name (which can be anything that you want, but bigfirm seems like a good choice; but whatever you do, *do not* include periods in downlevel domain names— it'll give you headaches later). As network names under NT 3.*x* and 4.*x* were chosen to accommodate an old network programming interface called NetBIOS, this old-style domain name is also called a *NetBIOS name*. The wizard will by default offer the text to the left of the leftmost period, so it here offers the NetBIOS name BIGFIRM, which is fine. I click Next and the screen in Figure 8.11 appears.

FIGURE 8.11

Placing system files

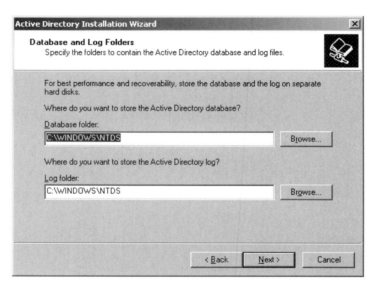

Active Directory stores the Active Directory database in two parts, as is often the case for databases: the database itself and a transaction log. Two things to bear in mind here are that the actual Active Directory database file should be on an NTFS volume for better performance and that it's a good idea to put the transaction log in a different physical hard disk than the Active Directory database. (You see them on the same drive in the screen shot because the machine I was doing this on had only one physical hard disk.) Putting the transaction log in a different physical drive means that the system can update both the AD database and the log simultaneously, and believe me, in a production environment, you'll see a significant difference in performance by using a two-drive system rather than a one-drive system. As I mentioned earlier, you can do this with SCSI, FireWire, or EIDE drives, but if you use EIDE drives, make sure they are on different EIDE channels so that they can run simultaneously without a significant performance hit. But we're not finished with drives yet; click Next and you'll see why, in Figure 8.12.

FIGURE 8.12

Placing the
SYSVOL volume

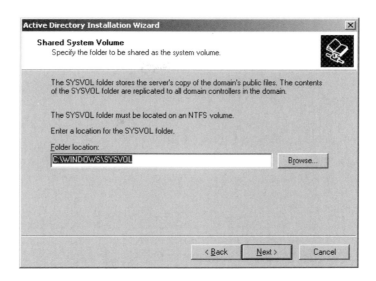

Remember the caution earlier on that you need at least one NTFS drive on an Active Directory server? This is where you'll use it. Anyone who's ever set up an NT 4 domain controller will soon realize how cool this is. You see, NT 4 stored a lot of important user configuration and control information in a directory named `NETLOGON` on the primary domain controller—system policy files, default profiles, and login scripts. But *backup* domain controllers needed the `NETLOGON` information as well, so network administrators had to somehow ensure that all of the files from the PDC's `NETLOGON` would somehow get copied to the BDC's `NETLOGON`s. With Active Directory, however, that's not a problem: All of that data goes into a directory called the `Sysvol` directory, which is *automatically* replicated to other domain controllers. It's an excellent labor saver and a hidden plus for Active Directory, at least over NT 4 domains. I click Next, and it's time to start worrying about DNS, or at least I'll have to if I get a screen like Figure 8.13.

FIGURE 8.13

DCPROMO's not
happy about DNS

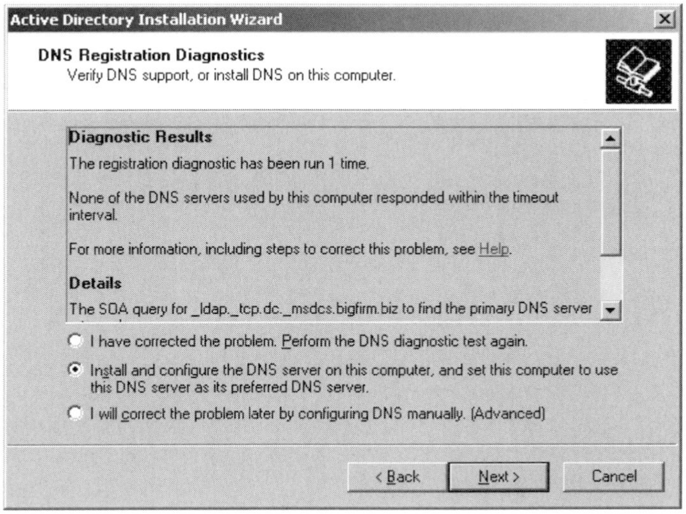

This is a really nice improvement in 2003 over 2000—when 2000's DCPROMO failed, it wasn't very helpful. Here, DCPROMO is saying, "This computer can't seem to contact any of its DNS servers." What happens here is that DCPROMO tries to find and contact the DNS server for bigfirm.biz. (See, I *told* you that DNS was important!) Some trouble occurred along the way, leading to this warning message. Basically one of two things can go wrong with DNS here:

DCPROMO didn't get a response from any of the DNS servers for bigfirm.biz.   That's what happened here, nearly—it was Bigdog's local DNS servers that didn't respond to *it*. Check connectivity and re-try the `nslookup`.

DCPROMO *got* **a response from the DNS servers for bigfirm.biz but found that they didn't accept dynamic updates.**   Suppose I'd already set up a machine as the DNS server, but the machine was an NT 4 server. The DNS service that shipped with NT 4 didn't include support for RFC 2136, probably because NT 4 shipped before RFC 2136 was released. RFC 2136 supports the idea of dynamic updates, which are very important to the way that AD maintains information about sites and domain controllers. I tend to get this error a lot because when I set up my DNS zones beforehand, I sometimes forget to make the zones accept dynamic updates.

If you get this error message then it means you don't have DNS set up right. I strongly recommend you cancel DCPROMO and fix DNS before going any further. DCPROMO *does*, you will note, offer you the option to just set up a DNS server on this system, *but never take the option*. *Always* take the time to get DNS right before running DCPROMO, or you'll run into trouble with attaching extra domain controllers to a domain, as well as problems joining workstations and member servers. Once you've got it working, you won't see a screen like the last figure; instead, you'll see Figure 8.14.

FIGURE 8.14
DCPROMO is
happy about DNS

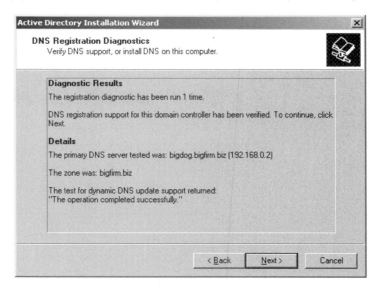

TIP   *If you're still having trouble with DNS, then hang on a bit and we'll revisit it in the upcoming section "AD-Related DNS Design and Troubleshooting."*

Now that all's well, click Next and one more warning appears, as you see in Figure 8.15.

FIGURE 8.15

Choose whether
NT 4 RAS servers
will be in the network.

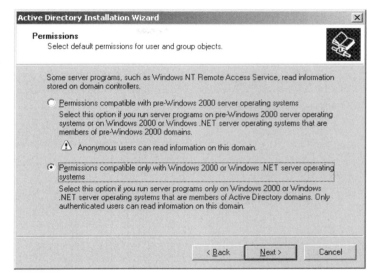

This isn't the clearest screen in all of Active Directory. NT has, since its inception, supported what is called "the anonymous login." The idea is that you don't have to be authenticated to do a few things—not big things, but a few things. One of those things is NT 4's RAS. In order to authenticate a dial-in client to an NT 4 domain the RAS software would ask the NT 4 domain controller a few things about the account, basically just looking at a few attributes of the user's account. Here's the problem: suppose the RAS server is a member server, and not a domain controller. It wants to authenticate the user, but really lacks the credentials to just go up to a DC and ask about the user, so the RAs server has to be kind of sneaky in getting the information that it needs to figure out if the dial-in person is valid or not. It's not just the username and password; you have to be approved to dial-in in order to dial-in. Merely having a domain account isn't enough. So the RAS server has to ask the DC if this account is valid for dial-in. The RAS server doesn't have any rights to ask the DC that kind of thing, so it just uses this long-standing "back door" in NT, the anonymous login. Once anonymously logged in, a RAS server can ask if a user is on the "OK for dial-up" list. Where this presents a problem is that the anonymous login is clearly a dumb idea, as you've probably figured out. Microsoft clearly agreed, as they offer you the option when building ADs to disable anonymous logins.

The problem with that should be clear: NT 4 RAS servers won't work in a domain without anonymous logins. So while slamming the anonymous door's a good idea, it might irritate your dial-in users, presuming that you haven't upgraded your RAS servers to 2000- or 2003-based servers. So DCPROMO offers you the option to leave the door open.

This isn't a "forever" choice. Once you have your AD up and running, open up the tool Active Directory Users and Computers; inside it you'll see a folder called `Builtin`. Inside that is a group named Pre-Windows 2000 Compatible Access. To become NT 4 RAS-compatible, just add the Everyone group. Once you've zapped your last NT 4 RAS server, just take Everyone out.

Choose which makes sense for you right now and click Next, and you'll get a screen like Figure 8.16.

FIGURE 8.16
Directory Services Restore Mode password

Active Directory Installation Wizard
Directory Services Restore Mode Administrator Password
This password is used when you start the computer in Directory Services Restore Mode.
Type and confirm the password you want to assign to the Administrator account used when this server is started in Directory Services Restore Mode.
The restore mode Administrator account is different from the domain Administrator account. The passwords for the accounts might be different, so be sure to remember both.
Restore Mode Password:
Confirm password:
For more information about Directory Services Restore Mode, see Active Directory Help.
< Back
Next >
Cancel

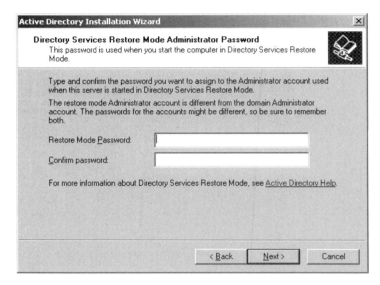

One of Win2K and Server 2003's at-boot-time options is to rebuild a damaged Active Directory database to restore it to an earlier version that is internally consistent, but which has probably lost a lot of information. You don't want just anyone doing that—a malicious individual telling a DC to rebuild its database is basically telling it to *destroy* its database—so Windows 2000 or Server 2003 asks for a password that it'll use to challenge anyone trying to rebuild the AD database. Fill that in and click Next, and you'll see the screen in Figure 8.17.

FIGURE 8.17
Confirming your choices

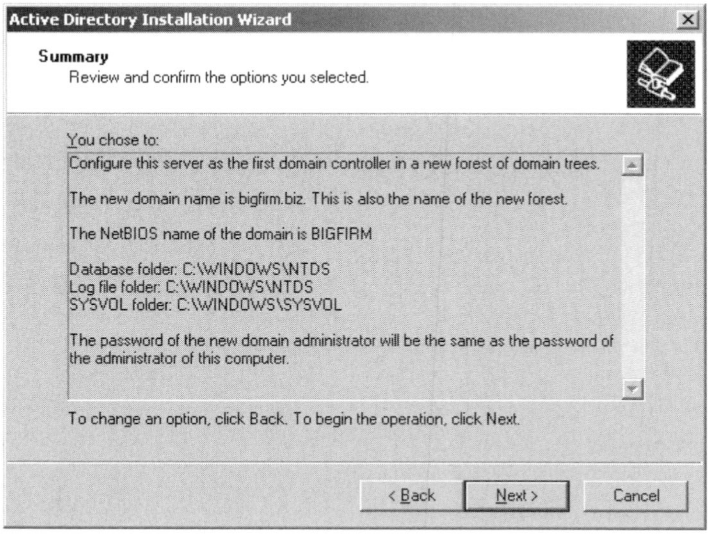

Active Directory Installation Wizard
Summary
Review and confirm the options you selected.
You chose to:
Configure this server as the first domain controller in a new forest of domain trees.
The new domain name is bigfirm.biz. This is also the name of the new forest.
The NetBIOS name of the domain is BIGFIRM
Database folder: C:\WINDOWS\NTDS
Log file folder: C:\WINDOWS\NTDS
SYSVOL folder: C:\WINDOWS\SYSVOL
The password of the new domain administrator will be the same as the password of the administrator of this computer.
To change an option, click Back. To begin the operation, click Next.
< Back
Next >
Cancel

Read this last screen carefully, and if you did anything you didn't like, back up and make the changes before clicking Finish! The reason is simple: Once the Active Directory setup process starts, you'll see a screen like Figure 8.18.

FIGURE 8.18

Starting up the AD creation process

You'll be seeing *that* screen for a goodly time, at least 20–30 minutes in my experience. You can speed that up a bit with two hard disks, as mentioned before, but it takes a while. The reason to be double-sure before clicking Finish is that, if you realize after the AD creation process is underway that you want to go back and redo something, then you have to *first* sit through the entire AD creation process, *then* you get to reboot the server—never a quick process with Server—and *then* you get to run the Active Directory Installation Wizard again to break down the domain, *then* you get to reboot again, and finally you run the Active Directory Installation Wizard a *third* time, getting all the settings right this time, and of course, once that's done, it's another 20–30 minutes waiting and a reboot. Total elapsed time between "Oops, I clicked Finish and didn't mean it" and "Ah, now it's finally fixed" can be on the order of an hour and a half—plenty of time to kick yourself. Anyway, once the directory's ready, the wizard ends with a screen like the one in Figure 8.19.

FIGURE 8.19

Final DCPROMO report

Once it's done, you'll have to reboot this new domain controller. Note, by the way, what this message says—that you now have a site named Default-First-Site-Name. Remember sites? AD needs at least *one* site to function, and Microsoft figured that a lot of us wouldn't give a hoot enough about sites to bother naming one, so you start out with Default-First-Site-Name. We'll see how to do some site preparation later in this chapter.

Preparing the DC for the Second Domain

Next, you'll set up the first DC in another domain—ecoast.bigfirm.biz. But, as always, you need to get DNS ready, so, go to the DNS server at bigdog.bigfirm.biz and create a new zone: ecoast.bigfirm.biz. (I know that's not exactly what we did in the last chapter, but I'm trying to minimize the number of machines you'll need to follow along.)

You've already seen how to do this, but here's a summary and reminder:

1. Open the DNS snap-in at Bigdog.
2. In the Forward Lookup Zones folder, right-click and choose New Zone, then run the resulting wizard to create a new primary zone for ecoast.bigfirm.biz. Be sure to allow dynamic updates.

If you like, you can then right-click the bigfirm.biz zone and choose New Delegation to introduce parent (bigfirm.biz) and child (ecoast.bigfirm.biz), but it's not really necessary. Surprised? Think about it—you're doing split-brain DNS, which means you're creating zones that are pretty much disconnected from the whole DNS hierarchy. This will work either way because, recall, you will make sure that every single DNS server in your intranet has a local copy of the ecoast.bigfirm.biz zone, whether because that DNS server is a primary server for ecoast.bigfirm.biz or a secondary.

Next, set up a machine that'll be the domain controller for ecoast.bigfirm.biz. Call it svr1.ecoast .bigfirm.biz—remember to set its domain suffix to ecoast.bigfirm.biz—and give it an IP address of 192.168.0.7. Also, ensure that it uses 192.168.0.2 for its preferred DNS server.

Once you've booted your fully outfitted srv1.ecoast.bigfirm.biz, look in the ecoast.bigfirm.biz zone on the DNS server at bigdog.bigfirm.biz; SRV1 should have registered itself. If not, recheck that you made the zone dynamic, that the DNS suffix is ecoast.bigfirm.biz, and that SRV1 points to .2 for its DNS server. Also, try an `ipconfig /registerdns` command to force a dynamic registration. Finally, when you're looking at the DNS zone for ecoast.bigfirm.biz, don't forget to refresh (F5) before you look to see if SRV1 made it to the zone.

Once again, you'll make life easier if you're 100 percent sure that DNS is working before you start adding new domains or domain controllers with DCPROMO, or even just adding member servers and workstations. In the next section, I'll show you how to do that, and also how to check a number of potential DNS problems.

Using DNS to Troubleshoot DCPROMO and Logon Problems

After all that hard work you still might run into a DNS-related AD problem. It might show up in one of three cases:

◆ You're trying to add a second (or third or fourth or *whatever*th) domain controller to an existing domain, or

◆ You're trying to create a new domain in an existing forest, or

◆ You're trying to log on to a domain and you get an error message along the lines of "no domain controller found."

Furthermore, you wouldn't *see* an error message necessarily, but if a member server couldn't find a DC to log it on for more than a week then that member server would probably not find itself a member of the domain any more, as workstations and member servers are expected to change their passwords once a week.

Now, if the problem crops up when you're running DCPROMO on the *first* domain controller on the first domain in the forest, then I've already covered what to do about it—check the SOA record and ensure that your would-be domain controller is contacting the correct DC. But if you see any of these other symptoms, then the probable cause is this: The machine contacted DNS to look up the SRV records for a domain controller and was unsuccessful. But you have a terrific troubleshooting tool at your fingertips—nslookup.

In the particular case of SRV1, you need to know that it can do two things. First, it must be able to log onto bigfirm.biz, because you'll have to prove that you're a pretty important person—an enterprise administrator—before DCPROMO will let you add a new ecoast.bigfirm.biz domain to the forest. Thus, you'll give DCPROMO a name and password from a bigfirm.biz account, and DCPROMO must then use that name and password to log you on. But DCPROMO can't do that if it can't find a DC for bigfirm.biz—and finding a DC is DNS's job. Second, once DCPROMO is satisfied that you have the credentials to proceed, then it'll need to start creating the subdomains and SRV records that will naturally get created when it creates the new domain ecoast.bigfirm.biz for you. Again, DNS enters the picture, as DCPROMO will need to find the primary DNS server for ecoast.bigfirm.biz before it can start writing those records.

AD stores the SRV records for domain controllers and global catalog servers under the following names:

- Global catalog servers (and I'll cover GCs in more detail later) are stored on a site-by-site basis under the name _ldap in domains named _tcp.*sitename*._sites.gc._msdcs.*domainname*, and all of the domain's global catalog servers are stored under the name _ldap in the domain named _tcp.*sitename*.gc._msdcs.*domainname*. In both cases, the SRV records for GCs will use port 3268.

- Domain controllers' SRV records are stored also on a site-by-site basis under the name _kerberos in domains named _tcp.*sitename*._sites.dc._msdcs.*domainname*. An all-in-one collection of all domain controllers in all sites is stored under the names _kerberos in a domain named tcp.dc._msdcs .*domainname*. Remember when I said a while back that AD creates subdomains to provide places to store SRV records for DCs so as to reveal their site location? This is what I was talking about.

So, for example, suppose you're sitting at srv1.ecoast.bigfirm.biz. You want to use nslookup to check that the would-be DC for ecoast.bigfirm.biz can find a DC for bigfirm.biz. At this point you have only one site, default-first-site-name. To find a domain controller, srv1.ecoast.bigfirm.biz would ask DNS if there was an SRV record named _kerberos._tcp.default-first-site-name._sites.dc._msdcs.bigfirm.biz. An nslookup run would look like this:

```
C:\>nslookup
Default Server:  bigdog.bigfirm.biz
Address:  192.168.0.2

> set type=srv
> _kerberos._tcp.default-first-site-name._sites.dc._msdcs.bigfirm.biz
Server:  bigdog.bigfirm.biz
Address:  192.168.0.2
```

```
        _kerberos._tcp.default-first-site-name._sites.dc._msdcs.bigfirm.biz↵
           SRV service location:
                   priority       = 0
                   weight         = 100
                   port           = 88
                   svr hostname   = bigdog.bigfirm.biz
        bigdog.bigfirm.biz       internet address = 192.168.0.2
        >
```

If you're doing this for a different domain, then remember to replace "bigfirm.biz with the AD domain's name and replace default-first-site-name with whatever your site is named.

Recall that if your system can't find a DC in its site, or if no DCs in the site respond, then it simply asks for the complete list of all DCs in all sites. This is clearly a short list in this simple one-DC network, but the SRV lookup is, again, for _tcp.dc._msdcs.*domainname* or, in this case, bigfirm.biz:

```
        > _kerberos._tcp.dc._msdcs.bigfirm.biz
        Server:  bigdog.bigfirm.biz
        Address:  192.168.0.2

        _kerberos._tcp.dc._msdcs.bigfirm.biz      SRV service location:
                   priority       = 0
                   weight         = 100
                   port           = 88
                   svr hostname   = bigdog.bigfirm.biz
        bigdog.bigfirm.biz       internet address = 192.168.0.2
        >
```

You can do the same searches for global catalogs by just replacing the .dc. with .gc. and _kerberos with _ldap—you can see an example here, where I search for all global catalog servers across all sites:

```
        > _ldap._tcp.gc._msdcs.bigfirm.biz
        Server:  bigdog.bigfirm.biz
        Address:  192.168.0.2

        _ldap._tcp.gc._msdcs.bigfirm.biz          SRV service location:
                   priority       = 0
                   weight         = 100
                   port           = 3268
                   svr hostname   = bigdog.bigfirm.biz
        bigdog.bigfirm.biz       internet address = 192.168.0.2
        >
```

Notice the port, 3268; you will see other records returned in some cases that have the _ldap name but that only run on port 389—those are not global catalog servers.

I cannot stress how powerful these nslookups are. They are the *key* to troubleshooting logon failures—and, as logon failures make creating new DCs or simply logging on fail, they're pretty useful.

But that just shows that you'd be able to log on to bigfirm.biz when running DCPROMO. How to ensure that srv1.ecoast.bigfirm.biz can find the zone for ecoast.bigfirm.biz? Recall that we did something like that before—just run nslookup, set type=any, and query on ecoast.bigfirm.biz. nslookup should return a primary name server of bigdog.bigfirm.biz.

Build an Enterprise Administrator

You're not quite ready yet to create ecoast.bigfirm.biz. As you've learned, you'll need an enterprise administrator. You *could* use the built-in administrator account at bigfirm.biz, but this is a great time for some more useful hands-on examples: creating an account in bigfirm.biz and making it all-powerful.

CREATING A FORESTWIDE ADMINISTRATOR

Before creating ecoast.bigfirm.biz, you'll need to create an administrative account that will be recognized as an administrator throughout this domain forest that you're creating. Creating user accounts is covered later in Chapter 9, but here's a quick cheat sheet on creating a forestwide admin.

Once that first domain controller for bigfirm.biz is up and running, log in as its local administrator as that's the only extant account at the moment. Because bigfirm.biz was the first domain created in the tree, it's a little bit special and, you may recall, is called the *forest root*. It's special because any other trees or domains that you create after this first domain sit below that first domain.

Running Active Directory Users and Computers

Anyway, once you're logged into the bigfirm.biz domain controller Bigdog, click Start/Administrative Tools. The first time you do this, you'll notice that you've got three new tools: Active Directory Sites and Services, Active Directory Domains and Trusts, and Active Directory Users and Computers. As you can guess, you create user accounts with Active Directory Users and Computers, ADUC to its friends. This application is also the tool you use to modify user accounts. When started, its first screen looks like Figure 8.20.

FIGURE 8.20

Opening ADUC screen

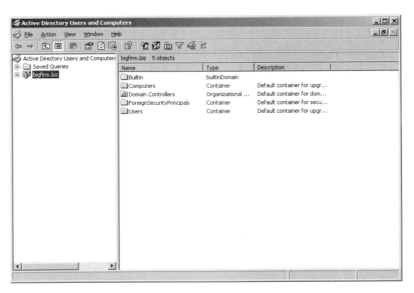

This is showing you the current domain, bigfirm.biz. In the right pane, you see five things that look like folders—Builtin, Computers, Domain Controllers, ForeignSecurityPrincipals, and Users. Although it'll be no surprise when I tell you that the folder labeled Users contains user accounts, I want to stress that it's not *necessary* to use that folder—DCPROMO creates that folder to provide a default place to keep user accounts. If for some reason you wanted to create all new user accounts in the folder labeled Computers, nothing would stop you and you could make everything work just fine. If you knew at this point that your domain would be subdivided into an OU called Hatfields and another called MccCoys, then you could create those OUs right now and create each new user account in either the Hatfields OU or the McCoys OU.

Creating a New User Account

I'm going to be unoriginal here, however, and have you create a user account in the Users folder. To do that, just right-click the Users folder. The context menu will offer a submenu labeled New, and one of the options will be User; choose that and get a screen like Figure 8.21.

FIGURE 8.21

Creating the new
user account

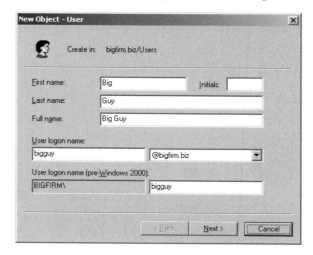

Much of this is self-explanatory, but let's go through this screen. First you fill in a first and last name as well as a full name. These three characteristics are largely just labels of very little use save for displays and searching. The fifth field, User Logon Name, is the "magic" name, the one that this user will use to log in. Note that you can add an @ suffix to the name and a domain name, giving you a logon name that looks like an e-mail name. Now, there's some complexity in that name that's not immediately apparent, so let me digress a bit about logon names.

User Principal Names (UPNs) or Logon Names

As I've explained and as you already know if you worked with NT 4, it was possible to have an enterprise built of many different domains that trusted each other, where *trusted* in this context meant "allowed each other to share security information and logins." Thus, if I had a user account named Mark that was built in a domain named ORION but wanted to log in to a machine that was a member of a different domain named AQUILA, then the AQUILA machine would in general refuse to log me in unless the AQUILA domain *trusted* the ORION domain. I'd then log in to the machine from AQUILA by telling it three things: my username, password, and domain. If I'd merely tried to log in as Mark from AQUILA, the login would have been refused, as no AQUILA domain controller would have a Mark account—only the ORION ones would. By saying that I was "Mark from ORION," I told the AQUILA machine how to find a domain controller that could vouch for me—I was telling it, "Go find one of the ORION domain controllers, they can verify that I'm me." (This also had another benefit—it was possible to have both a Mark account in ORION and a Mark account in AQUILA, and they'd be completely separate. They could have different passwords and in fact different people could use them.)

In a multidomain AD world, you can still do that. If I already had ecoast.bigfirm.biz built and I wanted to log in to a ecoast.bigfirm.biz machine with a Mark account from bigfirm.biz rather than ecoast.bigfirm.biz—two different domains, recall—then I could sit down at a ecoast.bigfirm.biz machine and, as before, say, "I'm Mark from bigfirm.biz," by typing **mark** into the username field, selecting Bigfirm from the Domain drop-down list, and filling in my password. The ecoast.bigfirm.biz machine would then know to go find a bigfirm.biz domain controller to verify my login.

The point is this: simply saying, "My username is Mark, log me in" doesn't provide enough information, any more than my telling you, "Hi, my name is Bill" would lead you to believe that I was a former president of the U.S.—there are *lots* of Bills around. I could be a lot more specific by adding a last name in my attempted deception ("Hi, my name is Bill Clinton"). So also anyone wanting to log into a domain has always needed to provide what might be called a first and last name—that is, a username and the name of the domain that the username resides in. In NT 4 terms, my "full name" looks like *domainname\username*, so that Mark from ORION would be ORION\Mark. As a matter of fact, you'll still find this useful in an AD world, so long as you use the NetBIOS name of the domain for *domainname*. For example, Mark from bigfirm.biz could be shortened BIGFIRM\Mark.

That *domainname\username* structure is a little lame, though, for reasons I'll make clear in a page or two, so AD introduced a new kind of full name. When logging on to an AD, instead of logging on by specifying a domain and a username, you can enter just one name that identifies (through a somewhat indirect method) your username and domain. Microsoft calls that newer kind of logon name a User Principal Name or UPN. (I'd have called it a universal login name, but who knows, maybe Microsoft liked UPN as an acronym better than ULN.)

What I think you'll find interesting about UPNs, though, is what they look like; here's an example: **mark@acme.com**.

Waitaminute, I hear you cry—*that's an e-mail address!*

Nope, it's not. It just *looks* like one and, as it turns out, for a fairly good reason. Stay tuned a few pages and I'll make it make more sense. For now, though, just understand that the "modern" way to log onto an AD forest is with a UPN, a UPN looks like an e-mail name, and a UPN does double-duty of providing your username *and* domain.

You can see that a UPN stands in for name *and* domain simply. Just sit down at a Windows 2000 Pro or XP Pro desktop that is a domain member and try to log in. (You may have to click the Options button to make the username, password, and domain fields visible.) In the Username field, type a name followed by an **@**, and you'll see the Domain field gray out. Once Winlogon, the program that puts up the Log on to Windows dialog up, sees an @ symbol, then it knows that it's getting a UPN, not a *username/domainname* pair, and so it grays out the domain field.

Getting back to this account that we're creating, you see that by default Active Directory Users and Computers suggests that BigGuy's UPN should be `bigguy@bigfirm.biz`. Presuming that you agree and create his account with that UPN, he can then sit down at any machine in the forest and log in with just `bigguy@bigfirm.biz`, and a password, without having to fill in a domain name.

UPN Suffixes and the Global Catalog

At this point, you may be thinking, "Big deal—how does that save any typing?" Whether you type into one field of the Winlogon screen that you're *someone@somedomain* and a password, or whether you alternatively type into the Name field that you're *someone* and type into the Domain field that you're from *somedomain* with a given password, what's the difference? What's the big deal?

Well, now, *that's* the interesting part.

You see, you can basically specify any domain name that you like after the name. When I first played with ADUC and saw that AD suggested that I give Bigguy the UPN bigguy@bigfirm.biz, I assumed that there was an iron-clad relationship:

UPN = user account name + "@" + AD domain name

I mean, it certainly seemed a reasonable assumption given this example. But my assumption was wrong. If I wanted to, I could give BigGuy's UPN the suffix @microsoft.com, even though I clearly don't own the microsoft.com domain name. The latter part of a user's UPN need not have *anything to do with the user's domain*. You could have domains bigfirm.biz, apex.com, and greatstuff.com, with user accounts scattered throughout the three domains, but you could then give everyone UPNs like *somename*@bigfirm.biz. You can see the specifics on how to add more possible UPN suffixes to your AD in the "How Do I Add a UPN Suffix?" sidebar.

HOW DO I ADD A UPN SUFFIX?

In the example about UPN suffixes and the global catalog, I suggested that I could give Bigguy a UPN of bigguy@microsoft.com. But a bit of clicking around ADUC doesn't yield any obvious ways to give myself the microsoft.com suffix. How do I get the DSA to let me use another suffix? Follow these steps:

1. Click Start/Administrative Tools/Active Directory Domains and Trusts.

2. In the left pane, there's a list of the domains in your enterprise. Above that list is a line Active Directory Domains and Trusts; right-click that and choose Properties. You'll see a dialog box like the one shown here.

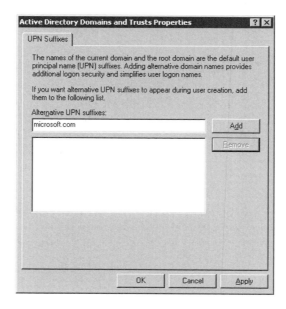

Continued on next page

3. Fill in the suffix that you'd like, such as microsoft.com or whatever. Click Add.

4. Click OK.

5. Close Active Directory Domains and Trusts.

So What's the Point of Using E-mail Like Logon Names?

This raises two questions. First, why would you do this, and second, how does it work? The answer to the first question is that obviously Microsoft intended the name to be your e-mail name, such as joe.blow@bigfirm.biz.

At this point, I must confess that I figured Microsoft did this merely to give me yet another reason to buy Exchange. But I wronged them. Here, instead, was Microsoft's reasoning.

In large corporations, you might have hundreds of domains, and those domains don't have nice names such as THIRDFLOOR or MARKETING; instead, they're the CORP0123X domain. So when teaching a user how to log on, techies had to tell the user, "You are johnax12 from domain CORP0123X with password YiKeSiWiLlNeVeRrEmEmBeRtHiS72." Folks had trouble remembering all of that. So Microsoft wanted to simplify it. It wanted to give every user a unique name. So Microsoft asked: Do users currently have a name that is relatively unique? And the answer was yes, their e-mail name. So if johnax12 has the email name johnax@bigfirm.biz, or perhaps j9391@aol.com, then we can let him use that as his logon name. And note that I offered an AOL e-mail name. There's no reason you can't give a user an e-mail name from another domain because it's *not really an e-mail name.* The system never *uses* it as an e-mail name.

Basically, Microsoft let us have users log onto forests using names that *look* like e-mail names for one and only one reason: It makes user training easier.

That leads to the second question: How do we make this work? Sure, it's lovely that I can log on to my very complex corporate network as mark@microsoft.com, but how does my workstation find out that my *real* logon name is mmina in a domain named bigfirm.biz? By adding a new step to logons. I log in as mark@microsoft.com, and then my workstation has to say to itself, "Well, 'mark'...*if* that's your real name! Let's find out who you *really* are," and then proceeds to "crack" my logon name. But how does it do that? With the help of an Active Directory service mentioned a few times before in this chapter called the *global catalog* (GC). The GC service runs on one or more domain controllers, and among other things, it keeps an index relating people's UPNs—their logon names—to the names of their actual domains. Thus, if I created an account for myself with UPN mark@microsoft.com and tried to log in to a bigfirm.biz machine, that machine would quickly pop over to a local GC server (which, by the way, the machine finds by looking it up in DNS—that's one of the many examples of Active Directory services that systems use DNS to find) and ask the GC server, "Where does mark@microsoft.com *really* live?" The GC server would reply, "In bigfirm.biz," and so my workstation would then contact a domain controller in bigfirm.biz (finding a DC for bigfirm.biz in DNS) and log me in. So the GC is a pretty positive thing, as it speeds up logons. But it *does* have one disadvantage: It can keep you from being able to log in— where your workstation once only needed to find a DC to log in, it now needs to first find a GC, and then a DC.

Handling Branch Offices and Global Catalogs

If your workstation cannot find a global catalog server in a multidomain Active Directory forest, then you cannot log in. So it's a good idea to have more than one around. (As far as my experiments show, you don't need a GC to log in to a single-domain forest.) But there are workarounds for this.

First, you can tell your local DC to accept logons even when it can't find a GC with a Registry entry, according to Microsoft Knowledge Base article 241789. Just create an entry in `HKEY_LOCAL_MACHINE\System\CurrentControlSet\Control\Lsa` called IgnoreGCFailures of type REG_DWORD and set it to 1. It's not a really great idea, however, as it means that your workstation will skip a security step while logging you on—it bypasses checking your universal group membership. That's important because you may be a member of a universal group that has been denied access to the workstation, and normally that'd be a reason to deny you the logon. But I mention it for those cases when a successful logon that ignores a universal group denial is more important than denying a logon because a workstation can't find a global catalog.

Second, you can use Windows Server 2003–based DCs. 2003-based DCs cache information that they've gotten from GCs, if you tell them to. You turn on GC caching at the site level rather than on a DC-by-DC basis. Here's how.

1. Open Active Directory Sites and Services—Start/Administrative Tools/Active Directory Sites and Services.

2. In the left pane, you'll see a folder labeled `Sites`; open it and you will see an object that looks like a skinny three-story pale yellow building; this represents a site. If you have only one site, then you'll have only one building; if you have more than one, then you'll have a building for each site. In the case of my simple example, you'll probably only have one site named Default-First-Site-Name. Click the site's object.

3. In the right pane, you'll see three objects: a folder-like icon labeled Servers, an object with an icon that looks something like a certificate labeled Licensing Site Settings, and an object with an icon that looks like a building with a cyan-colored gear growing out of it. (It looks like it's either a flying saucer hovering next to the building or a frame of stop-action footage just before an unpleasant industrial accident.) That object is labeled NTDS Site Settings. NTDS means NT Directory Service, an old name for Active Directory. Right-click it and choose Properties, and you'll see a dialog like Figure 8.22.

4. Note the Enable Universal Group Membership Caching check box; if you check this, then you'll tell AD to have all of the DCs in that site cache GC info.

That's *how* to do it, but *should* you do it? That's a tougher question. You might change a user's status and want that change in status quickly propagated throughout the network, but if the branch office's WAN link is offline then of course you wouldn't see the effects of those changes at that branch office. If that branch office is caching, then the user will get logged on, although with the old status, and that might be bad. On the other hand, if you'd left caching off, then *no one* from that office could log on if the branch office's WAN connection was down. It's basically convenience versus security, and you'll have to make that call yourself.

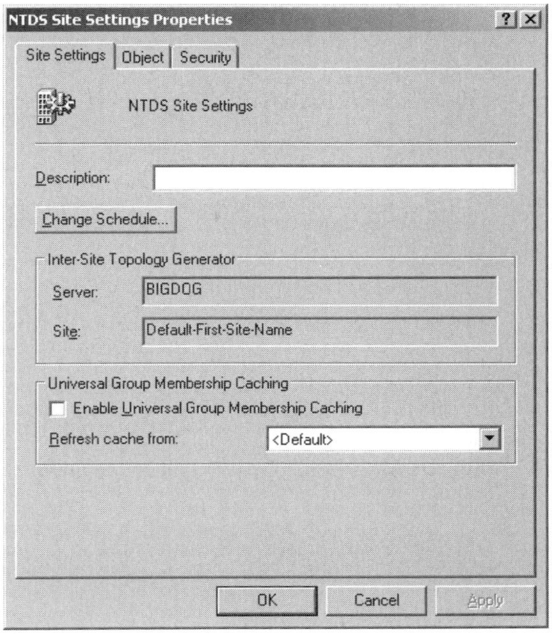

FIGURE 8.22

NTDS settings
for a site

NTDS Site Settings Properties

Site Settings | Object | Security

NTDS Site Settings

Description:

Change Schedule...

Inter-Site Topology Generator

Server: BIGDOG

Site: Default-First-Site-Name

Universal Group Membership Caching

☐ Enable Universal Group Membership Caching

Refresh cache from: <Default>

OK | Cancel | Apply

Creating Global Catalog Servers

Before leaving GCs to return to the nuts and bolts of creating a user account, let's see how to create more global catalog servers. Only domain controllers can be global catalog servers. You can make any DC a GC by opening Active Directory Sites and Services which is, again, in Administrative Tools. Recall that in the left pane you'll see an icon—or icons—representing different geographic sites on your network, and if you've only created a basic AD and haven't done any work on your sites yet, then AD will have automatically created one site called Default-First-Site-Name. Inside each site's folder you'll find a folder named "Servers." Open a site's Servers folder and you'll see icons representing every domain controller. Open any domain controller's icon and you'll see a folder named NTDS Settings, as you see in Figure 8.23.

Note that this is *not* the same NTDS Settings folder as the one that we looked at when setting up a site to do GC caching. *That* NTDS Settings folder referred to settings for an entire site; *this* one refers to settings for just a domain controller. (Notice also that calling the folder Servers is misleading—it contains objects for domain controllers only, not servers in general.)

Right-click the NTDS Settings folder and choose Properties, and you'll see a properties page like the one in Figure 8.24.

To make a DC act as a GC, just check the box labeled Global Catalog, click OK, and then close AD Sites and Services. As a rule of thumb, you'd like to see two GCs on every site. And if you're a one-domain enterprise, then you should, at least according to a Microsoft AD expert, make every *one* of your DCs into global catalog servers.

FIGURE 8.23

Active Directory
Sites and Services

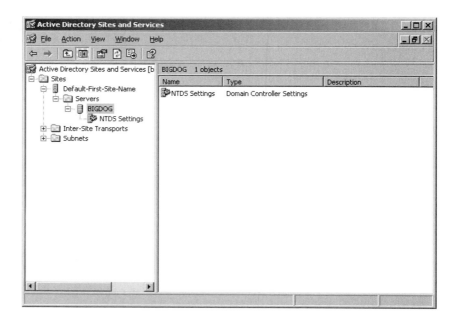

FIGURE 8.24

NTDS folder
settings

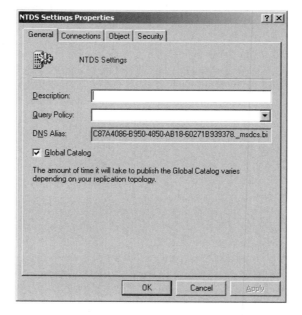

Finishing Up the User Account

Anyway, let's return to Active Directory Users and Computers, where we were in the middle of creating the bigguy account. Notice that ADUC automatically creates a downlevel username. This is the name that bigguy would be recognized as if he tried to log in to an NT 4 or earlier server. Simply sticking with bigguy for a downlevel name seems fine, so I click Next and the screen changes to Figure 8.25.

FIGURE 8.25

Setting a password

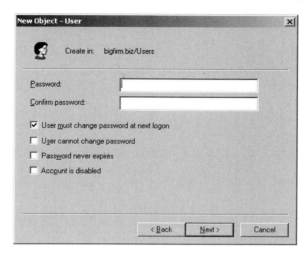

A straightforward screen; un-check "user must change password at next logon" then click Next and I'm asked to confirm the account information and click Finish. Opening the Users folder, I can see that bigguy is now created, as you see in Figure 8.26.

FIGURE 8.26

Contents of the Users folder after creating bigguy

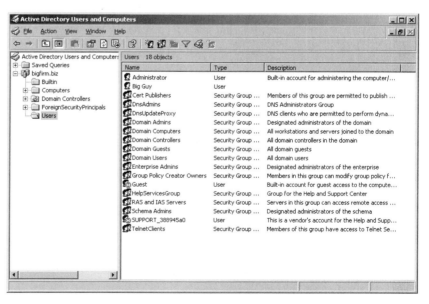

Notice the groups that DCPROMO automatically created when you build a domain controller. The one we're interested in is the group named Enterprise Admins; as you read earlier, anyone in that group is recognized as an administrator all around the forest. Adding bigguy to that group is simple.

First, open the Enterprise Admins group by either double-clicking it or by right-clicking it and choosing Properties, and you see something like Figure 8.27.

FIGURE 8.27

Enterprise Admins folder properties

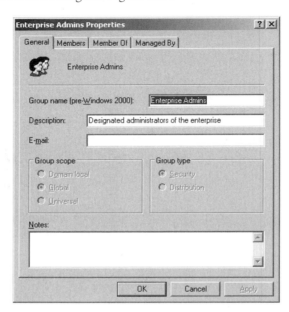

Clicking the properties page Members tab shows the list of members of Enterprise Admins, as you see in Figure 8.28.

FIGURE 8.28

Members of Enterprise Admins

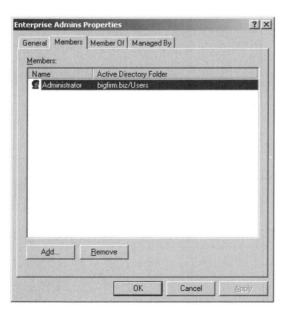

Notice that the local administrator account for the bigfirm.biz domain controller is an Enterprise Admin. DCPROMO sets that up automatically. Recall that bigfirm.biz is the root domain, and there's got to be at least one forestwide administrator. By clicking the Add button, you get a dialog box like Figure 8.29.

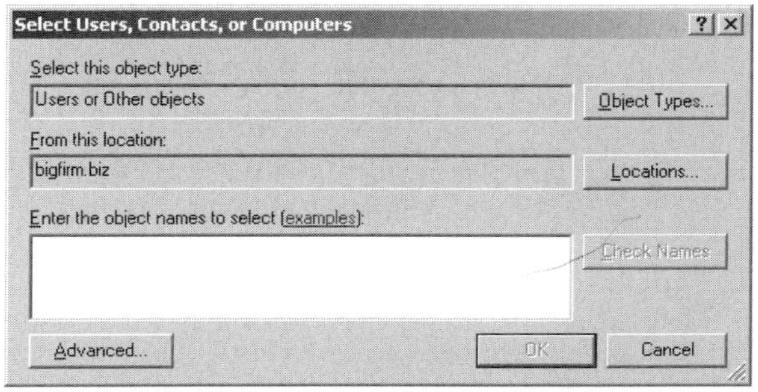

FIGURE 8.29

Adding bigguy to Enterprise Admins

Now, veterans of Windows 2000 will recognize this dialog for what it is: a lame cop-out. Under Windows 2000, you'd get a dialog box that showed you all of the users in the domain (or actually the first 20,000 of them, and you could adjust that), and you'd just pick the user that you wanted to add to the group. But that dialog's gone. Instead, now you've got to type in Bigguy's name and click Check Names. The dialog then checks the AD for a name that matches what you typed in. Microsoft did this, I'm told, because it could take *hours* for the Windows 2000–vintage Select Users, Contacts or Computers dialog box to populate itself on a large domain, and they got some flack over that. Their answer seems to have been, "Hey, if you don't like our nice helpful list of users, then the heck with you—go type in the names yourself."

This isn't a totally unforgiving dialog box, though. If you type **b** and press Check Names, then it'll see that you only have one user whose name starts with *b* and will fill in Bigguy. If there is more than one user starting with *b*, then it'll show you them and you can choose the one you want. Or you can click the Advanced button and be offered a Find Now option where you can use wildcards and become pretty specific about what you want it to find. All in all you can easily get used to this new dialog box...I just wish the old one were available as an option.

For now, just select the bigguy account, click OK, and bigguy's a forestwide administrator.

TIP By the way, even now bigguy isn't a complete Superman in this domain. There is a group that the Enterprise Administrators aren't a part of—the Schema Administrators. This group can, as its name suggests, make changes to the forest's schema, which includes changing what the global catalog stores. By default, the only member of the Schema Administrators group is the default Administrator account on the PDC of the domain that is the forest root (or, for the purists, "the default administrator on the machine that happens to serve in the role as PDC FSMO for the domain that is the forest root"). Also, machines in the domain would not allow bigguy to sit down and administer them—they would not recognize him as an administrator. To fix that, put bigguy in another group, Domain Admins. So to make bigguy truly a Big Guy, add him to Schema Administrators and Domain Admins. Or put Enterprise Administrators inside Schema Administrators.

BUILDING SUBDOMAIN CONTROL WITH AN ORGANIZATIONAL UNIT

You read earlier that one of AD's strengths is that it can let you grant partial or complete administrative powers to a group of users, meaning that it would be possible for a one-domain network to subdivide itself into Uptown and Downtown, Marketing and Engineering and Management, or whatever. Let's look at a simple example of how to do that.

Let's suppose that there are five people in Marketing: Adam, Betty, Chip, Debbie, and Elaine. They want to designate one of their own, Elaine, to be able to reset passwords. They need this because "I forgot my password, can you reset it for me?" is probably the number one thing that Marketing calls the central IS support folks for. The central IS folks are happy to have someone local to Marketing take the problem off their hands, freeing them up to fight other fires.

Here's the process:

1. Create an organizational unit called Marketing. (You can call it anything that you like, of course, but Marketing is easier to remember later.)
2. Move Adam's, Betty's, Chip's, Debbie's, and Elaine's already-existing user accounts into the Marketing OU.
3. Create a group called MktPswAdm, which will be the people who can reset passwords for people in the Marketing OU. (Again, you can actually give it any name that you like.)
4. Make Elaine a member of the MktPswAdm group.
5. Delegate password reset control for the Marketing OU to the MktPswAdm group.

If you want to follow this along as an exercise, get ready by creating accounts for Adam, Betty, Chip, Debbie, and Elaine as you did for BigGuy, except don't make them administrators. Or do it from the command line: type **net user *username* /add** and you'll get a basic user account built in the Users folder. For example, create Adam like so:

```
net user adam /add
```

You've got to be sitting at the domain to do this. You can create domain users from any other system at the command line, but you must then add the option "/domain" as in

```
net user adam /add /domain
```

Creating a New Organizational Unit

Creating a new OU is simple. Just open up Active Directory Users and Computers, right-click the domain's icon in the left pane, and choose New/Organizational Unit. A dialog box will prompt you for a name of the new organizational unit. Fill in **Marketing** and click OK and you're done.

Moving User Accounts into an OU

Next, to move Adam, Betty, Chip, Debbie, and Elaine to the Marketing OU, open ADUC, open your domain (mine's bigfirm.biz, yours might have another name), and then open the Users folder. (If you created the five accounts somewhere other than Users, then look there.)

You can move all five users over by clicking Adam, then holding down the Control key and left-clicking the other four accounts. Then right-click one of the five accounts and you'll get a context menu that includes a Move option; select Move and you'll get a dialog box asking you where to move the "object." It'll originally show you your domain name with a plus sign next to it; just click the plus sign and the domain will open to show the OUs in your domain. Choose Marketing and click OK, and all five accounts will move to the Marketing OU. In ADUC, you can open the Marketing OU and you will see that all five accounts are now in that OU.

Or...if you want to use a new ability in Server 2003, try out drag-and-drop. In ADUC, click the Users folder in the left pane. You will be able to see the contents of Users in the right pane. In the left pane you'll not only be able to see Users, you should be able to see the Marketing OU as well. Select the users and then drag them from the right pane to the Marketing OU, and release the mouse button. Instant OU movement! (What's that you say, you're not impressed? Well, believe me, when you do a lot of user management, you'll find it a nice bit of lagniappe. Trust me on this.)

Creating a MktPswAdm Group

Next, to create a group for the folks who can reset Marketing passwords. Again, work in ADUC. Click Action/New/Group. (You can also right-click the Marketing OU and choose New/Group.) You'll see a dialog box like Figure 8.30.

FIGURE 8.30

Creating a new group

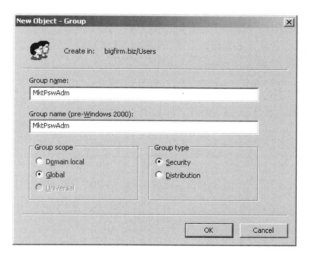

You see that the dialog box gives you the option to create any one of the three types of groups in an Active Directory. A global group will serve our purposes well, although in this particular case—the case of a group in a given domain getting control of an OU in that same domain—then either a domain local, global, or universal group would suffice. I've called the group MktPswAdm. Click OK and it's done.

Next, put Elaine in the MktPswAdm group. Right-click the icon for MtkPswAdm and choose Properties, as you did earlier when creating bigguy. Click the Members tab, then the Add button, then Elaine's account, then Add, then OK, and you'll see that Elaine is now a member of MktPswAdm. Click OK to clear the dialog box.

Delegating the Marketing OU's Password Reset Control to MktPswAdm

Now let's put them together. In ADUC again, locate the Marketing OU and right-click it. Choose Delegation and the first screen of the Delegation of Control Wizard will appear, as you see in Figure 8.31.

FIGURE 8.31

Opening screen
of the Delegation of
Control Wizard

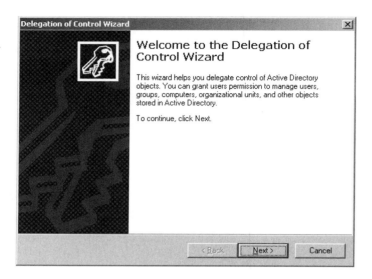

The wizard is a simplified way to delegate, and it'll work fine for our first example. Click Next and you'll see Figure 8.32.

FIGURE 8.32

Before selecting
a group

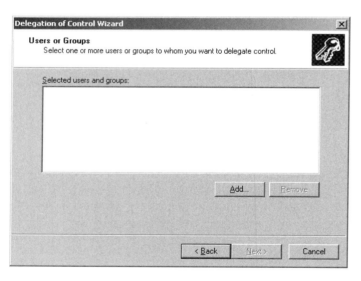

Next, you've got to tell it that you're about to delegate some power to a particular group, so you've got to identify the group. Click Add and choose the MktPswAdm group. After choosing MktPswAdm and clicking OK to dismiss the Add dialog box, the screen looks like Figure 8.33.

FIGURE 8.33

MtkPswAdm
selected

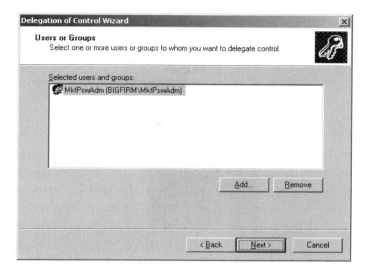

Now click Next, and you'll get a menu of possible tasks to delegate, as you see in Figure 8.34.

FIGURE 8.34

Options for
delegation

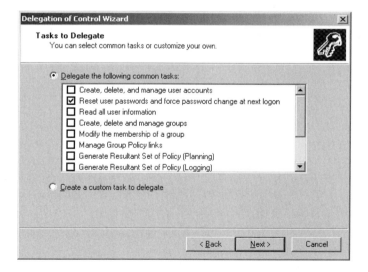

Once you do a bit of exploring here, you'll see that there are many, many functions that can be delegated. Rather than force you to wade through a long list of things that you'll never care about, however, Microsoft picked the top dozen or so things that you'd be most likely to want to delegate, one of which is the ability to reset passwords. I've checked that in the figure; press Next and the final screen in the wizard appears, as you see in Figure 8.35.

FIGURE 8.35

Confirming your
choices

Click Finish, and it's done.

Remember, delegation lets you designate a set of users who have some kind of control over
a set of users and/or computers. You accomplish that by putting the controlling users into a
group, the things that you want them to control into an OU, and then delegate control of the OU
to the group.

TIP   Or, to put it in a bit more eccentric fashion, think of it this way: The victims go into an OU, the oppressors into a group.

ADVANCED DELEGATION

Although that's a nice—and useful—example, it only hints at the power of delegation. You actually
needn't use the wizard to delegate, it just makes things simpler for a range of common applications.
Here's how to more directly manipulate delegation.

*TIP   Even if you're not terribly interested in delegation, stay with this example. It shows how to navigate the three levels
of progressive complexity in Server 2003 Security dialogs, which is something you'll be doing a lot of as an admin in a
2000, XP, and 2003 world.*

First, open up ADUC and click View/Advanced Features. New things will pop up on the screen,
as in Figure 8.36.

Right-click Marketing and choose Properties. You'll get a properties sheet with a tab labeled
Security. Click it, and you'll see something like Figure 8.37.

Here, I've scrolled down a bit to show what the dialog box tells you about the MktPswAdm group.
It appears that the group has powers that can only be described as "special," which isn't all that
helpful. This is the top level of a 2003 Security dialog. Think of it as the overview level of security
information. But I quite frankly find this top level view pretty limited. About all it really tells me
is that there are ten entries in this dialog—you can't see that because they don't all fit in here—and
you may recall that each of these entries are called Access Control Entries or ACEs. The list in total
is called the Access Control List or ACL, pronounced "ackull," rhyming with "shackle."

FIGURE 8.36

ADUC with View Advanced Features enabled

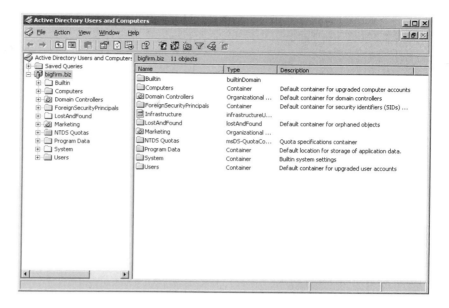

FIGURE 8.37

Security tab on Marketing OU

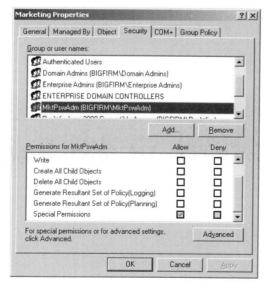

In theory you should be able to click any of the ACEs in the top part of the dialog box and in the bottom part you see what powers that ACE gives the thing named in the ACE. For example, you see in the figure that MrkPswAdm has "special" powers. That's one reason that I don't like this dialog all that much, as "special" doesn't tell me much. The other reason is that this dialog box only shows a really simplified list of possible powers, and so what you see will be sometimes misleading. That's why it's nice that you can zoom in one level by clicking the Advanced button. If you do that in ADUC, you'll see a screen like Figure 8.38.

FIGURE 8.38

Advanced security
settings for
Marketing OU

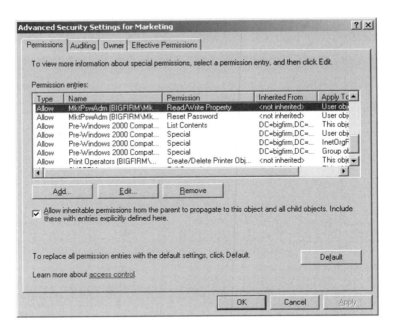

Scroll down to highlight MktPswAdm and you see two entries for it. One gives the power to read and write some kind of property, and the other gives the power to reset passwords. The "reset password" makes sense…but what's the "read and write property?" Click it and choose Edit and you'll see something like Figure 8.39.

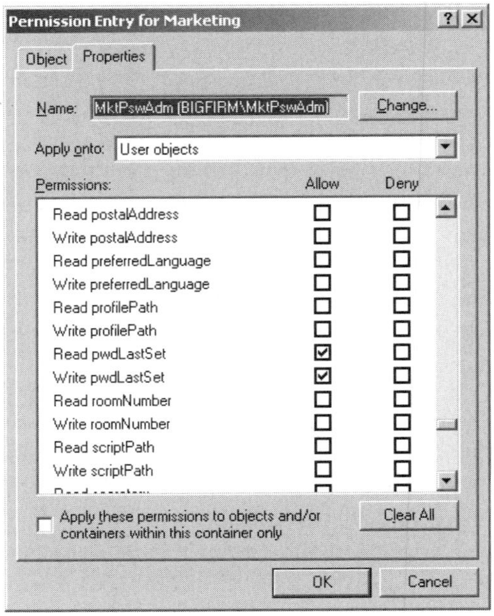

FIGURE 8.39

Specific
MktPswAdm
abilities

Here you see that we've given MktPswAdm the ability to read and write a user's properties, but *only* the pwdLastSet property—AD-ese for "current password." Go back and look at the other record for MkwPswAdm and Edit it and you'll see Figure 8.40.

FIGURE 8.40

Giving the power to reset passwords

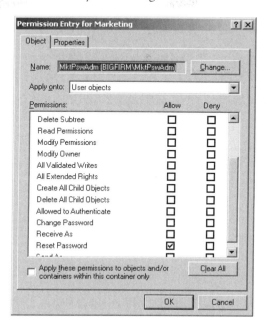

As you can see from the figure, there are a *lot* of powers that you can grant to a particular group in controlling a particular OU!

Where might you make use of this? Well, you gave MktPswAdm the ability to change passwords, but you didn't take it away from the groups who originally had it—the domain admins, enterprise admins, and the like can still reset passwords. That's not a bad idea, but if you really ever *do* come across a "feuding departments" scenario, wherein Marketing wants to be sure that they're the *only* people who can administer accounts, then you'd first delegate the Marketing OU to some group, and then you'd go in with the Security tab and rip out all of the other administrators.

TIP   *And to see a step-by-step example of a more advanced delegation, look back to the end of Chapter 5, where we created a new kind of group called Installers.*

HOW DO I FIND OUT WHAT DELEGATIONS HAVE HAPPENED, OR UNDELEGATE?

Time for some bad news.

Suppose you're not the administrator who set up the Active Directory. Suppose, instead, you're the *second* administrator, the person hired to clean up a mess that some guy—who's now gone—made. You know these kind of administrators, the "mad scientist" variety: the guys who just click things in the administrative tools until they solve the problem…they think. And *document*? Heck, real administrators don't document. After all, this network was hard to design, it should be hard to understand!

So you're wondering what this guy did. How did he change the company's AD from the default AD that you get when you run DCPROMO? That's a hard question to answer. First, of course, the OUs that he created are obvious—just look in Active Directory Users and Computers and you'll see the new folders. But what delegations did he do?

Sad to say, there is no program you can run that will compare the standard AD structure and delegations to the current AD structure and delegations and spit out a "this is what changed" report. About the best you can do is to right-click all of the containers—the domain itself, `Users`, `Computers`, and any OUs—and choose Properties and look in the Security tab. (Don't forget to do View/ Advanced before doing that, or the Security tab won't appear.) So let me offer a really heartfelt piece of advice: Always document delegations. *Always.* Try to control who can do delegations and make clear that delegations are only authorized sparingly.

While I'm here, I should also mention that although the Delegation of Control Wizard is a nice little tool, it's only a *delegation* wizard, not an *un*delegation wizard. If you want to remove MktPswAdm's ability to change Marketing passwords, you've got to go into the Security tab, find the references to MktPswAdm, and rip them out.

CREATING A SECOND DOMAIN

But suppose you're not happy with just one domain; that OU stuff just wasn't enough for the boss. Resigned to politics, you're ready now to create the second domain, ecoast.bigfirm.biz. Recall that one machine can only be a domain controller in one domain, so you need a second machine to act as DC for ecoast.bigfirm.biz before you can create that domain. Starting from srv1.ecoast.bigfirm.biz, start DCPROMO.

DCPROMO starts out as before. Tell it that you're creating a new domain but not a new tree, choosing the option Child Domain in an Existing Domain Tree. Before you go any further, DCPROMO asks you to log in, as you see in Figure 8.41.

FIGURE 8.41

Establishing credentials for creating a child domain

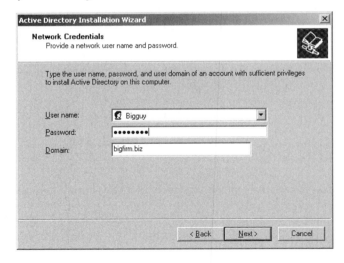

Notice that for some reason you've got to specify account and domain—the UPN doesn't work here. Here, I've filled in bigguy's login information. DCPROMO pauses a bit to authenticate the bigguy account. Once I've filled that in, I click Next and the screen in Figure 8.42 appears.

FIGURE 8.42

Naming the child domain

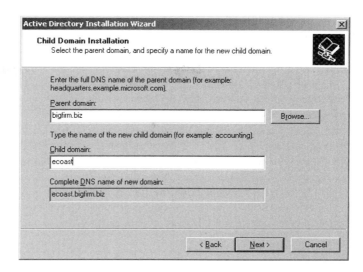

DCPROMO now needs to know which domain to add a child to and what to call the child. You can fill in that the parent's name is bigfirm.biz, or just press the Browse button and chosen from the domains in the forest. The child domain will be named ecoast.bigfirm.biz, but DCPROMO just wants you to type in **ecoast** for the child name, and it then assembles it and the parent domain into the complete name ecoast.bigfirm.biz for the child domain.

You'll then progress through DCPROMO much as with the first domain, so I'll spare you the screens—but notice Figure 8.43.

FIGURE 8.43

NetBIOS name for child domain

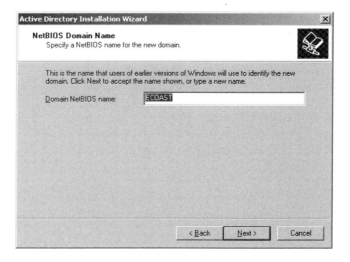

The bigfirm.biz domain got the downlevel name (or NT 4 or NetBIOS name, take your pick, they all mean the same thing) of bigfirm. But how to name the child domains with the more complex names? Just take out the periods and take the leftmost 15 characters? Do some kind of truncated name with tildes on the end, in the same way that long filenames get converted to 8.3 names? Well, you can actually give your domains any downlevel name that you like, but the default ones are just the leftmost portion of the domain name, as you see in the figure. As *ecoast* is the leftmost portion of the domain name, the domain gets the downlevel name ecoast by default.

From this point on, you'll just answer DCPROMO's questions as you did for the first domain, so I'll spare you those screens. Another 20 to 30 minutes of Active Directory setup and the second domain is done.

Before leaving here, let me make a few points about using DCPROMO to build domains. First, as you've already read, get DNS ready before starting. Second, DCPROMO's kind of rigid about the order in which you create domains. The first domain that you create in a forest is the forest root domain, and there's no changing that. Third, you've got to add domains by creating them; you can't create a domain green.com and another yellow.com separately and then decide later to merge them into a forest. Instead, you must first create green.com as the first domain in a forest and then create yellow.com as the first domain in a new tree but in an existing forest.

Other Active Directory Objects: Contacts, Shared Folders, Printers and More

You might have noticed when you right-clicked the domain in the Active Directory and chose New, there were three other things that you can create:

◆ Contact
◆ Shared Folder
◆ Printer
◆ MSMQ Queue Alias
◆ InetOrgPerson

None of them are quite what they appear to be, so let's take a minute and see what they're good for.

INETORGPERSON AND MSMQ QUEUE ALIAS

These two objects are new to Server 2003 and are of kind of limited value to the general AD-using public, but here's the short version of what they're good for. InetOrgPerson object is an entry describing a person, but in a way compatible with Sun's iPlanet directory service. MSMQ Queue Alias supports a Microsoft service called Microsoft Message Queue. I haven't found a use for this yet, but I imagine that MSMQ-using tools like Exchange and Microsoft Operations Manager will create objects of this type automatically.

CONTACTS

Another object that you can create is called a "contact." It's something that acts very much like a user account...but *isn't* a user account. It doesn't have a password and cannot log on to the network.

So what good is it?

Open up a real-live user account, and you'll see that it's got bunches of tabs. There are places for information such as street address, e-mail address, manager's name, phone numbers, home page, and other items. You can, therefore, use your Active Directory as a kind of low-octane Human Resources database. This won't be news to Exchange users, as Exchange has kept a database like this for years.

So, for example, if you created a bunch of users and took the time to type in all of their managers' names in the Manager fields, then you could do queries such as, "Show me all of the users whose manager is Evelyn Wilson."

If that sounds interesting, then you might want to be able to include information on people who *aren't* users on your network—friends, family, business associates, and so on. Contacts let you do that. Once you create a contact, you'll see that it has fields for that same kind of information as user accounts do: phones, addresses, managers, and the like. From a Windows 2000, XP, or 2003 system, then, you could click Start/Search/For People and, in the Look In drop-down box, specify the Active Directory. The Search for People dialog box then lets you search by names, e-mail addresses, and the like. Once you find a person, you right-click his record and choose Send Mail and it starts up your mail client, with the e-mail address all filled in. AD, then, becomes a kind of simple contacts database.

The whole notion of first looking up a name in AD and then right-clicking to send that person mail is a bit cumbersome. I think, however, that this wasn't Microsoft's main idea; I believe, instead, that you can make this more useful if you're running Exchange 2000 or Exchange Server 2003. I don't use Exchange, however, so I can't say. Additionally, as you *can* query the Active Directory with LDAP, you could in theory build or use any of a number of tools to query your AD-based contacts database. I say *in theory* because also in theory you should be able to look up names in Outlook 2000 from an LDAP-compatible server. As I said, I don't use Exchange. But I *do* use Outlook as a mail client, and I've tried telling it to look up people's names in the AD. So I should be able to type into the To field a name in the database, such as Mike Smith and then Outlook should automatically fill in Mike's e-mail address. I've not been able to make that work and the folks that I've asked at Microsoft about it just kind of look bewildered and say, "Well, I guess it *should* work, but we all use Exchange, so I've never tried it…." People tell me that Office XP's brand of Outlook can use an AD to look up names. Anyway, the bottom line is that contacts are apparently of quite limited value unless you're running Exchange 2000 or 2003.

SHARED FOLDERS

You'd think that creating something called a *shared folder* in the Active Directory would, well, *share* a folder. But that's not what happens. Instead, creating a shared folder in the Active Directory just puts a notice in the AD saying, "Someone shared a folder at the following location, and it's got the following stuff in it." This is known as *publishing* a share in the AD.

For example, suppose we create a directory on C:\ on BIGDOG called JUNK and share it as JUNK. (Just create the directory JUNK in C:\, then right-click its folder and choose Sharing. Click the radio button Share This Folder, and then OK.) Then copy a few files to the folder, so that there's something in there.

Now go to Active Directory Users and Computers and right-click some folder—the domain icon, the Users folder, or whatever—and choose New, then Shared Folder. You'll see a dialog box like the one in Figure 8.44.

Create a name for it—I've used Company Documents—and fill in the address of the share as *servername**sharename* and click OK. You'll then see an icon that looks like a hard disk on a network cable in Active Directory Users and Computers. Double-click it and you'll see something like Figure 8.45.

FIGURE 8.44

Creating a shared
folder in AD

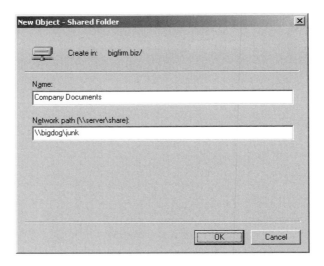

FIGURE 8.45

Modifying the
shared folder object's
properties

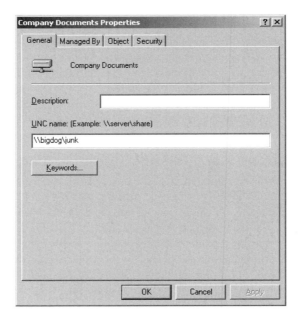

Take a look here and you can see where this would be useful. You can fill in the Description field,
or, even better, you can click Keywords and fill in words that describe the share.

Now how's that useful? Just as with the contacts, you can search for shared folders. Open up Active
Directory Users and Computers, right-click the domain and choose Find, and you'll see that one of
the things that you can search for are shared folders—just type in keywords and you'll get the folders
that match those keywords. Click the folders and they'll take you straight to the shared data.

This has several advantages over the standard Network Neighborhood operation that you're probably familiar with:

Keywords   First, obviously, you can search for the content that you're seeking, rather than wandering around Network Neighborhood hoping that someone has named a share in a meaningful way.

No broadcasts   All of that data in Network Neighborhood/My Network Places gets there because every single server and, usually, every single workstation broadcasts its presence every 12 minutes. You'd be amazed how much network bandwidth is wasted with those broadcasts. Once you shut them off by disabling NetBIOS over TCP/IP—which you can't do in a practical sense now, but it will make sense for many networks by 2007 or so—then you'll get a bunch of bandwidth back, up to 15 percent on some networks.

You disconnect the users from the UNCs   To find this company data in a standard non-AD system, I've got to just somehow know that the data is sitting on BIGDOG in a share called Junk. In such a network, you refer to the share by its UNC (Universal Naming Convention), \\bigdog\ junk. But what if I moved the data to \\server1\data? Then I'd have to tell everyone to stop looking on BIGDOG and instead look on SERVER1. *But* if everyone is instead searching the Active Directory, or if they know that the folder published in the AD as Company Data is the place to go, then they are completely unaware of the data's UNC. When I move the data from \\bigdog\junk to \\server1\data, then, all I need do is to modify the published item in the Active Directory.

All in all, this notion of publishing shares is a big step forward. It *does* require teaching users to find and exploit shared folders a bit differently, though.

You may have one question: Why do you have to go through the extra step of publishing a share? When you shared \\bigdog\junk in the first place, why wasn't there a little check box on the Sharing dialog box saying something such as, Publish to the Active Directory? I have no idea. And do you want to hear something totally bizarre? Back when this first appeared, in the Windows *2000* beta, *the check box was there*.

Even stranger: printers. A *printer* isn't really a printer, it is, like a shared folder, just a published entry in the AD to the effect that there's a printer shared somewhere, complete with descriptive information on it. But here's the odd part: When you share a printer, *it publishes itself*. You need do nothing. Strange, no?

AD-Related DNS Design and Troubleshooting

We covered DNS in the previous chapter, but mostly from the point of view of DNS in a generic setting—the things that you need to make DNS work with or without the Active Directory.

Choosing Your Top-Level Domain: .com, .local, or Something Else?

DNS is connected to names, so part of your AD planning involves coming up with an AD name, and of course the first part's easy—if you're Acme or Bigfirm, then that'll be your AD name. But is it bigfirm.biz? Or something like bigfirm.local? What's .local all about?

Well, if you're going to run your own DNS system and don't care if it's visible to the outside Internet, then you needn't use a standard .com, .org, .biz (and so on) top-level domain (TLD). Many folks use .local, as in bigfirm.local. Or there was an Internet standard working its way through the committees that suggested using .pri—for private. It's a good idea, but I haven't heard much about it. Still, I can't imagine that ICANN will ever create an official .local or .pri TLD. So if you want to be "with it" name-wise, then go with *something*.pri.

Does it matter what TLD you use? Possibly, but not likely. Here's the scenario that we're concerned about: You call your AD bigfirm.local. Then, a few years down the road, ICANN approves a new TLD, .local. Someone else registers the now-publicly-available bigfirm.local domain and sets up a Web server, mail server, and so on. Someone inside your network tries to access their stuff but can't get to those servers, as the local domain has that name.

Again, in my opinion we won't see a .local TLD anytime soon, so I'm not sure that it matters whether you use .local, .pri, or, as some are doing, .ds for *directory service*.

Building an AD-Friendly DNS Infrastructure

In my example Active Directory, I made life a bit easier for you by starting out with a guaranteed AD-compatible DNS infrastructure, one built atop a dynamic DNS zone running on a Windows 2K or later server. But you may not have the luxury of a network whose DNS options are wide open, and you don't *need* that luxury—AD works well with non-Microsoft DNS servers, and I've built a couple of forests without any Microsoft-based DNS servers at all. In this section, you'll first understand what AD needs of DNS and then you'll see the various ways to make different DNS configurations work with AD.

WHAT AD NEEDS FROM A DNS SERVER

The Active Directory absolutely needs two things of its DNS server:

Support of underscores in DNS names Yes, I know I told you not to use underscores in your machine names, but no one told Microsoft apparently—some important subdomains of your AD need underscores in their names. Every DNS server that I know of will tolerate underscores, but not all do by default, so you might have to turn this feature on with yours. Microsoft's DNS servers from NT 4 onward tolerate underscores by default. (I'm not even sure that it's *possible* to make a Microsoft DNS server reject names with underscores.)

Support of SRV records Recall that SRV records are a generic way to store information about a server's abilities in DNS. Simplified, SRV records store two pieces of information about a server's abilities—the protocol that it supports and the port that it runs that protocol on. For example, you could in theory use SRV records to ask a domain, "What is your Web server's address?" by making an SRV record request for a server running the HTTP protocol (the Web protocol, as you may know). Similarly, Windows 2000, XP, and Server 2003 systems locate Active Directory domain controllers via SRV records, asking the domain's DNS servers, "Do you have any SRV records for a server running the Kerberos protocol in the Kempsville site?" They also locate global catalog servers—which, recall, are essential for logons—by requesting SRV records for servers running the LDAP protocol on port 3268. Without those records, machines cannot find a domain controller…and not much happens in AD if you can't find a DC.

Furthermore, AD is light-years easier to run if it supports:

Dynamic DNS   You've already seen that 2K, XP, and Server 2003 systems register their host records via dynamic DNS. But AD domain controllers rely upon dynamic DNS for more than that—DCs create subdomains and register SRV records via dynamic DNS. Now, DDNS isn't 100-percent essential, as you could simply punch in all of the SRV records by hand—sounds like fun, doesn't it?—but I strongly recommend that you make your DNS zone dynamic.

YOU DO *NOT* NEED TO USE A MICROSOFT DNS SERVER

I said this before, but I want to stress it. Most people use a Unix or Unix-derivative machine running a program called BIND to act as their DNS server. Active Directory can work perfectly well in an environment where a Unix-based BIND server acts as its DNS server, so long as it's a version of BIND that supports SRV records (RFC 2782) and dynamic updates (RFC 2136) and permits machine names with underscores. (I know—I've done it. I successfully created a three-domain AD forest using a single DNS server running BIND on Linux. Worked like a charm, dynamic zones and all.) Or you might be using Lucent's QIP DNS/DHCP replacement, a good alternative to either BIND or Microsoft's DNS.

In that case, you need not configure a Windows 2000 or Server 2003 system as a DNS server.

WHAT TO DO IF YOUR CURRENT DNS SERVER ISN'T AD FRIENDLY

But, as the song goes, we can't always get what we want. What do you do if you don't have a DNS infrastructure doesn't want to do things Microsoft's way? You do have a few alternatives.

Generally the issue is that DNS admins are concerned about enabling dynamic DNS. They think—rightly—that it creates one more potential security problem. But all's not lost in that case. Let's examine the possibilities.

If Your DNS Supports SRV and Underscores but Not Dynamic DNS

If you can't convince your DNS folks to adopt any of the suggestions that follow this one, then let me get the worst case DNS scenario out of the way. In this scenario, we'll leave dynamic DNS shut off.

I hope that none of you ever have to *do* this, but it's a chance to highlight an interesting feature of AD that you may find useful for troubleshooting. It's a last-ditch way to stitch together a DNS zone that will make an AD happy.

Let's say that you're working with a modern DNS server that supports SRV records and underscores, but no dynamic updates. How to make it AD friendly? With the help of a file named `netlogon.dns`.

Back when Microsoft was first putting AD together, they talked to a lot of their big customers about what AD would require and some of those customers balked. They had a big BIND infrastructure that, well, *worked*—Unix-based systems often have the interesting characteristic of being complex to get working, but once they're working, you can pretty much leave them alone and they require almost no care and feeding—and so they didn't want to change those servers one whit.

"Not changing them one whit" included dynamic DNS—it has to be admitted that dynamic DNS offers some potential security issues, and so flipping the switch to turn their BIND servers into *dynamic* BIND servers met some opposition. SRV records were no problem; underscores were no problem. But DDNS was a sticking point.

So Microsoft engineered the AD to offer a compromise.

Every DDNS-aware computer writes its own A (host name) records into DDNS by itself. But the AD *really* relies upon all of those SRV records, and *they* are written to the zone files by the Netlogon service. Whenever you reboot a domain controller, or restart its Netlogon service, or if some time has gone by without an update, then the Netlogon service contacts the primary DNS server and registers its SRV records.

But it also does something else: It writes those records to an ASCII text file called `NETLOGON.DNS`, stored in `\WINDOWS\SYSTEM32\CONFIG`. Try it—go to any AD domain controller and use Notepad to look at `\WINDOWS\SYSTEM32\CONFIG\NETLOGON.DNS`. It's a bunch of SRV records.

Those companies that are *completely* anti-dynamic DNS, then, *could* set up their DNS to support AD like so without dynamic DNS. Here's how our fictitious bigfirm.biz domain might do it, using an NT 4 DNS server (I use NT 4 to stress how much latitude you've got in your choice of DNS servers here)—you'd do the same thing with a nondynamic BIND server:

1. First, set up a bigfirm.biz zone as a primary zone on a DNS server. Call the zone file bigfirm.biz.dns.

2. Enter A records for each domain controller.

3. Go to each AD domain controller and restart its Netlogon service.

4. Copy the `\WINDOWS\SYSTEM32\CONFIG\NETLOGON.DNS` file from that DC to a floppy or a file on the network.

5. Once you've got all of the `netlogon.dns` files, merge them into one big ASCII file on the primary DNS server for bigfirm.biz.

6. At the bigfirm.biz DNS server, stop the DNS service.

7. In `\WINNT\SYSTEM32\DNS`, open the file `bigfirm.biz.dns` with Notepad.

8. Add in the extra lines with the SRV records that you collected when you merged all of the `netlogon.dns` entries into a single file into `bigfirm.biz.dns`.

9. Save the `bigfirm.biz.dns file`.

10. Restart the DNS service (or, if it's a Unix box, the daemon).

That DNS server—and any of its secondaries—can now support an Active Directory. So why wouldn't everyone do this? Well, first of all, it's a lot of work collecting all of those `netlogon.dns` files. And, second, it's not very, well, *dynamic*. If you ever take one of these DCs offline, you'd have to delete its zone records. And every time you put a new one on your network, you'd have to collect and merge *its* SRV records. Not much fun...but definitely possible. If all else fails DNS-wise, you can always do this dynamic-DNS-by-hand approach to DNS.

Using NT 4 DNS Servers in an AD

Can you use NT 4 DNS servers for an AD? Sure, with some work. My first guess was that NT 4's DNS didn't do SRV records, as their RFC appeared not terribly long before NT 4's release. And in general I was right. But if you install Service Pack 6a on an NT 4 system a funny thing happens...the DNS server now supports SRV records! So, if you wanted, you really *could* do the hand-built zone file routine that I outlined previously, even on a DNS server running atop NT 4.

Sound like too much work? It probably is. But there's a completely useful potential function for an NT 4 DNS server in an AD.

Use it as a *secondary* DNS server. Recall that a simple standard DNS setup for a given zone has just one primary DNS server and any number of secondary DNS servers. And recall that the only DNS server that accepts changes to a zone is the primary. The secondaries just accept their zone copies from the primary using a standard zone transfer—in other words, secondary DNS servers really don't ever need to support dynamic DNS.

You could, then, have a single Win2K Server– or Server 2003–based DNS server as the primary server in a zone. That would accept all of the dynamic updates from the various servers and workstations and boil them down to a standard DNS zone file. Then it would copy that zone file to the secondaries, which could be running NT 4 with Service Pack 6a. Then, whenever a workstation needed to look up an SRV record so that it could find a global catalog server or a DC, the NT 4 systems could easily answer the request.

Upgrade to DDNS/SRV Compliance or Replace It

If you have DNS servers that don't support underscores and SRV records, then you must change your DNS infrastructure to make the AD work. Either upgrade your existing non-Microsoft DNS servers to newer versions of their software that support DNS or replace them with Windows 2000 or later servers. Heck, those Unix guys are *always* eager to replace their well-known BIND systems on the Sun boxes with Microsoft stuff—they're all closet Microsoft junkies, really! (Joking, joking...)

Create and Delegate Your Domain to an AD Child Domain

If bigfirm.biz has an existing set of DNS servers that do not and never will support SRV, DDNS, and the like, then one answer is to create a child portion of your current DNS names and delegate the control of those names to a Windows 2000 system. For example, if you've already got several hundred Unix, Windows, and NT machines in an Internet domain named bigfirm.biz and the DNS server for bigfirm.biz is an ancient BIND implementation, then you can always tell the old BIND server that there's a new subdomain (a *zone* in DNS-ese) called win2k.bigfirm.biz (which would contain machines with names such as bluebell.win2k.bigfirm.biz, rover.win2k.bigfirm.biz, or metrion.bigfirm.biz) that will have its own name server. Of course, that name server will be one of your new Windows 2000 or Server 2003 servers. The Active Directory doesn't insist upon having RFC 2782, 2136, and underscore support for *all* of the company's machines—just the AD DCs.

Delegate the AD-Specific Subdomains

The previous solution is a good one, but it troubles many people, as they want their systems to have names such as *something*.bigfirm.biz instead of *something*. act-dir.bigfirm.biz. So they'd like the AD situated at the firm's "top level," so to speak, but they don't want the top-level DNS to be AD friendly. There *is* a work-around in this case. But it's a bit trickier.

Create an Active Directory and look in the DNS zone and you'll see that the AD has created a bunch of folders in your DNS zone, as you see in Figure 8.46.

FIGURE 8.46

DNS subfolder
structure in an
AD domain

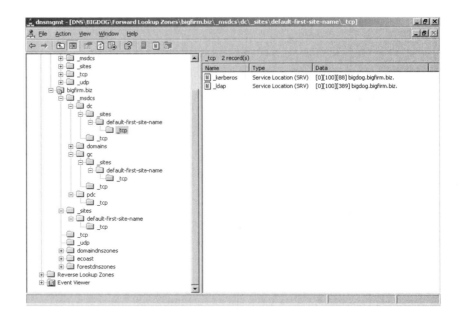

Notice that bigfirm.biz has four folders:

- _msdcs
- _sites
- _tcp
- _udp

Thus, just as there's a DNS domain named bigfirm.biz, there are also now subdomains named _msdcs.bigfirm.biz, _sites.bigfirm.biz, _tcp.bigfirm.biz, and _udp.bigfirm.biz; DCPROMO created them. (I'm sure you've noted the underscores in the subdomain names—what *were* those Microsoft folks thinking, anyway?) Those are subdomains just like one named AD.bigfirm.biz would be. DCPROMO created them as simple folders in the same zone file as bigfirm.biz, but there's no reason why you couldn't have created them as four separate domains, four separate zone files potentially on four different servers. (You've probably noticed that bigfirm.biz has other subdomains as well—that's because it's a forest root domain.) It gets the extra subdomains named domains.bigfirm.biz, domaindnszones .bigfirm.biz, and forestdnszones.bigfirm.biz for forest root info rather than domain info, so ignore those extra domains. Any nonforest root domain only gets _msdcs, _sites, _tcp, and _udp.

Recall that the really important DNS records aren't so much the A (host) records for the DCs, it's the SRV records. So if you leave the top bigfirm.biz zone static and just punch in the host records by hand and then create the subdomains by hand *on a DNS server that supports DDNS*, then everyone's happy—the DCs can write their SRV records and the workstations.

So if bigfirm.biz's zone were hosted on a static DNS server, then all you'd have to do would be to first set up a DNS server that supports dynamic DNS (and SRVs and underscores, of course). Then, on the new DNS server, set up the four subdomains. Then go to the static DNS server with the bigfirm.biz zone and delegate the four zones to the new DNS server—just as I showed you how to create the ecoast.bigfirm.biz zone in the previous chapter. Set the four new zones to dynamic. Finally, hand-enter A records for the domain controllers in the static bigfirm.biz zone— and you're done.

Create a Parallel "Split-Brain" Windows-Based DNS for Your Microsoft Systems

You saw in the previous chapter how to do this. If you want to run an AD named bigfirm.biz, then one way to do it is to set up a Server 2003 system as a dynamic DNS server. Then create a bigfirm.biz zone and make it dynamic. Do *not* register this server as an authoritative server with Network Solutions or whoever the parent domain is—you do *not* want visitors from the public Internet. Then set up the Microsoft boxes so that they all look to this one DNS server as their DNS server. As that server has a zone named bigfirm.biz, then any queries about bigfirm.biz will end up being answered out of that zone. The DNS server will also accept dynamic DNS registrations. You can take it a step further and set up more DNS servers so as to spread out the name resolution load in your intranet, and use DHCP to tell different Microsoft systems to use different DNS servers. But make sure that these DNS servers are secondary DNS servers for the internal bigfirm.biz zone. Forward the DNS servers to a server outside your firewall—actually, *slave* the internal DNS servers for security's sake.

And don't forget to copy any externally visible records for bigfirm.biz, such as www.bigfirm.biz to the internal bigfirm.biz's zone. Again, I've discussed this in greater detail in the previous chapter, so look that over before adopting this approach.

Operations Masters/FSMOs

Thus far, you've seen how to set up AD domains, the DNS that it requires to run, and a bit of user and group management. Those are the basics of AD setup.

But there's more to AD planning than that. Making an AD run also requires knowing about

Operations masters a particular function that some DCs must assume.

Time synchronization believe it or not, AD simply will not run unless all of the AD members and DCs all agree on what time it is, to within five minutes.

Domain database synchronization DCs in a domain all have a copy of the Active Directory database, and all of the DCs should have the same data in their database copies.

Sites AD gives YOU the ability to divide up Your network into sites so that AD can best use (or *not* use) Your WAN bandwidth. You *could* create an AD and just tell it that the 200 offices across the world that comprise your company are just one big site and the AD would work, kind of ... but it's silly not to use the tools that Microsoft gives you to define and exploit sites.

In the next few sections, we'll take on this kind of intermediate-level AD planning and operation. First, we'll take up operations masters.

Multimaster versus Single-Master Replication

As I've mentioned before, one of the things that differentiates AD domains, and DCs, from NT 4 and earlier domains, is *multimaster* replication rather than *single master* replication. Under NT 4 and earlier products, you had one DC called the primary domain controller, which held a copy of the SAM, the file that contained the user accounts. That SAM on the PDC was the only one that you could modify. All other DCs in an NT 4-and-earlier domain were *backup* DCs. They could authenticate people, but not accept changes to their accounts. If, for example, you work out of your firm's Tulsa, Oklahoma, office, which has a BDC, then that local BDC can log you in sometime in the morning without having to communicate with the PDC, which I'll place for the sake of argument in Columbus, Ohio. But if a local Tulsa administrator wants to change your password, then she starts up the NT tool named the User Manager for Domains. It's not obvious, but at that point User Manager for Domains locates and connects with the DC in Columbus over a WAN link. At that point, the administrator can do things like create new accounts or perhaps reset your password, and the DC in Columbus would eventually replicate that new information to the BDC in Tulsa (and other BDCs as well, of course). But if the WAN link is down, then User Manager for Domains will refuse to let her do any account maintenance. Because only one DC holds the "master" or writeable copy of the SAM, this approach to maintaining a database of users is called a *single-master* replication system.

AD improves upon that with multimaster replication. Under multimaster, *any* DC can accept changes to the user account, so in the Tulsa example, a local Tulsa admin could start up an administration tool such as User Manager's successor, Active Directory Users and Computers, and make a change to a user's account, even if the link between Tulsa and Columbus was down. As any DC can accept changes, any DC is then a "master," hence the phrase *multimaster*.

WARNING *You only get multimaster replication once your AD domain is in Native mode ("Windows 2000 domain native functional level" in 2003-speak) or Server 2003 domain functional level. Mixed-mode domains and Server 2003 interim-mode-domains use a single-master replication scheme because of the continued presence of old NT 4 BDCs, which can't handle the needs of multimaster replication.*

But Not Everything Is Multimaster

In general, the Active Directory tries to carry this notion of decentralized control throughout its structure. In general, all DCs are equal, but, to paraphrase George Orwell, some DCs are more equal than others. Those DCs are the ones that serve in any of five roles called either *operations master* or Flexible Single Master of Operator roles. By the way, no one says *flexible single master of operator*; it gets acronym-ized to FSMO and is pronounced "fizz-moe." Strictly speaking, FSMO was the phrase that Microsoft used through most of Windows 2000's development process, but they renamed FSMOs to *operations masters* late in the beta process. As a result, you'll hear some people say *operations master*, but the FSMO name has stuck with many, even now in the days of Server 2003, probably because it's quicker to say "fizz-moe." (*And* more fun.) So, for example, the phrases *domain-naming operations master* and *domain-naming FSMO* refer to the exact same thing.

Certain jobs in the AD just need to be centralized, and so we end up with FSMOs. For example, take the job of creating new domains. Suppose I've got a domain bigfirm.biz and someone decides to set up a new domain controller and thereby create a child domain, hq.bigfirm.biz. Creating a domain causes AD to build a lot of data structures—a domain for hq.bigfirm.biz, more work for the global catalog, changes to the overall forest AD database, and so on. Now imagine that two people both try to create a new domain named hq.bigfirm.biz at roughly the same time. That could be a nightmare—the parent domain would be receiving conflicting requests to modify the AD database, there might be potential security issues, and it might keep the whole forest from functioning.

Domain Naming: A FSMO Example

What's that you say? The chances of trying to create two identical domains "at roughly the same time" are unlikely? Not necessarily. If you have two offices in your enterprise, and you only connect the two offices to synchronize their domain controllers once every few days—and you can do that; AD only *requires* that you sync DCs every 60 days at the maximum—then you could easily have two different people try to create a domain with the same name, in each office, within a span of a few days. You don't want that happening, so AD chooses one DC to act as a sort of central clearinghouse for new domain creation and whenever you run DCPROMO to create a DC in a previously nonexistent domain (and therefore to create a new domain), DCPROMO stops and locates the one DC in the entire forest that is the "keeper of the domain names." That DC is said to be the *domain-naming FSMO* or *domain-naming operations master*. If DCPROMO on the new would-be DC cannot establish contact with the domain-naming FSMO, then it flatly refuses to go any further.

Let me repeat that: If you have a worldwide enterprise with dozens of domains, hundreds of offices all around the world, thousands of domain controllers and hundreds of thousands of workstations, there is one and only one computer that serves as the domain-naming FSMO. If it were, for example, in the Okinawa office and you were in the New York office sitting at a server trying to create a new domain in the forest, then your computer would be unable to proceed until it contacted the Okinawa computer and got its OK on building the new domain. Putting subsequent systems on that domain would not require contacting Okinawa.

Why Administrators Must Know about FSMOs

Lest you get the idea that I'm saying that this is a terrible failing on AD's part, understand that I'm *not* saying that. You don't create domains all that often, one hopes, so this isn't much of a hardship, in my opinion. In general, you won't think about the DCs that act as FSMOs in your forest much at all. But you *do* need to do a little planning about which DCs will be FSMOs, and you need to know how to assign a particular FSMO role to a particular DC.

Which reminds me: you *do* have to manage the FSMO roles by hand. The AD automatically picks a particular DC to act in each FSMO role—the first DC that you install—but it's not bright enough to move those roles around. So, for example, consider this scenario. Your company decides to play around with AD and sets up its first DC on a "junk" machine in a test lab—say, the old 200MHz system with 128MB of RAM. They see that AD works pretty well, and so start buying some "big guns" to be the production DCs—Pentium 4s, Itaniums, or whatever. They roll out these big DCs and things seem to work pretty well.

Until one Monday, folks come to work and the AD apparently still thinks it's the weekend because AD's not working. Administrators find that they can't create new user accounts or join machines to a domain. Someone has tried to install Exchange 2000, but it complains about not having the authorization to change something called the *schema*. The Cleveland office was scheduled to create a new child domain, but that's refused, too. The remaining NT 4 domain controllers—perhaps the firm has decided to run in Mixed mode for a while—complain that they can't find the PDC, and account changes like password resets are clearly not getting to those NT 4 backup domain controllers.

What happened? Well, someone was playing around in the lab that weekend and needed an extra machine with which to do some experimenting. The 200MHz system was just sitting there, still running Server 2003 and acting as an AD domain controller. But it wasn't really relevant anymore, the weekend noodler reasoned, as the firm now has several dozen big DCs running. So our experimenter wiped the hard disk on the 200MHz system and put Linux on it.

You see, by default, AD assigns the FSMO roles to the first DC that you install. Which means that 200MHz system has been quietly serving in a very important role. But now it can't. And AD isn't smart enough to figure that out and then to nominate a new computer in that role. You might say that our "sparkling" forest has lost its "fizz moe." It's now your job to transfer the FSMO roles to other DCs.

That's why you care about FSMOs.

> **NOTE**   *Actually, there is one case where AD automatically moves the FSMO role: when you use DCPROMO to demote a domain controller that holds one or more FSMO roles into a member server. DCPROMO finds another appropriate domain controller and moves the FSMO roles to that DC. In that case, decommissioning the Pentium 200 would have resulted in no problems. So perhaps the best advice here is, "When you want to get rid of a domain controller, always use DCPROMO to decommission it before FDISKing it."*

FSMO Roles

There are five FSMO roles in AD:

- Schema
- Domain naming
- RID
- PDC
- Infrastructure

There is only one schema FSMO in the entire forest, and similarly only one domain-naming FSMO. Each domain in the forest, however, has its own RID, PDC, and infrastructure FSMO.

SCHEMA

Schema is the word for the structure of the AD database—the fields. It's the list of things in the database, like username, password, and so on. In some senses, it's the directory to your Active Directory.

Examining the Schema with the Schema Snap-In

You can look at the schema with the Active Directory Schema snap-in. It's not sitting in Administrative Tools, however; follow these steps to run it.

1. Open a command prompt and type **regsvr32 schmgmt.dll**. You should get a message box that says DllRegisterServer in schmmgmt.dll succeeded. Click OK to clear it.
2. Click Start/Run and enter **mmc /a**, then press Enter to start the Microsoft Management Console in Author mode.
3. Click Console, then Add/Remove Snap-in.
4. In the resulting dialog box, click the button labeled Add, which will raise yet another dialog box, Add Standalone Snap-in.
5. In the Add Standalone Snap-in dialog box, locate and click the object labeled Active Directory Schema, then click the Add and Close buttons.
6. Back in the Add/Remove Snap-in dialog box, click OK to close.

You'll then see a screen like Figure 8.47.

FIGURE 8.47

Schema Manager
snap-in

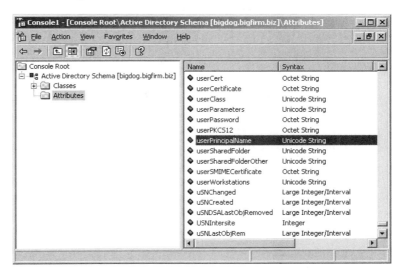

Here, I've highlighted the part of the schema that tells us that there's an attribute called user-PrincipalName, which, you know by now, is the login name. Double-click it and you'll see a dialog box describing its properties, but they'll probably be grayed out, even if you're an Enterprise Admin. Recall that even Enterprise Admins can't modify the schema—you must be a member of the Schema Admins group to do that. But if you're a Schema Admin, then you'll see the properties page with everything enabled, as in Figure 8.48.

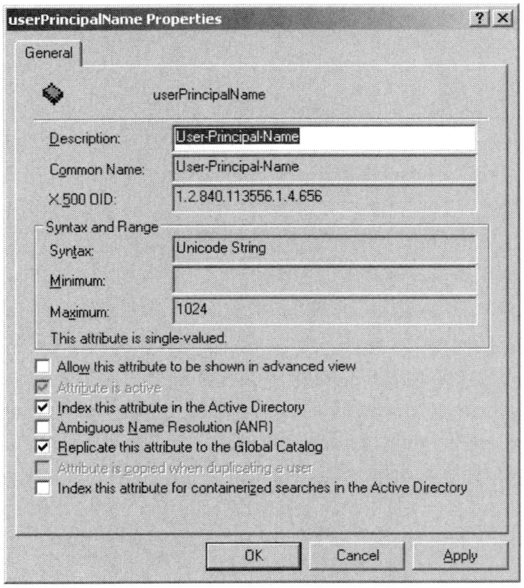

FIGURE 8.48

Properties page for
User Principal Name

Notice the check box labeled Replicate This Attribute to the Global Catalog. You can, using the Schema Manager, control what does and doesn't replicate in the GC.

The Schema and Your AD

Will you change the schema very much or very often? Probably not. But there are few things that you should bear in mind.

First, remember that there is only one schema for the entire forest; it's not meaningful to talk of changing the schema for a particular domain, as any changes to the schema are changes to the schema of an entire forest. So a bit of innocent schema-dabbling will affect every domain controller in every domain in the forest, as all of those DCs will have to be notified of the changes and thus will have to make room for the new schema items in their copy of the schema, which burns up some CPU and disk time.

Second, when will you change the schema? Usually the only thing that you'll do that will cause the schema to change will be adding new server-based applications such as Exchange 2000, server-based apps that were designed with the Active Directory in mind.

Keeping Schema Changes Orderly

Inasmuch as schema changes affect the whole forest, it's reasonable to say that the schema *does* change—we want it to change in an orderly fashion—it'd be really bad if two people both modified the schema at the same time.

For that reason, and because there's only one schema for the entire forest, there's only one computer that can approve schema changes in the entire forest. That computer is said to have the *schema FSMO* role. By default, the AD places the schema FSMO role on the first domain controller that you install in the first domain of the forest. So the first DC that you set up should be a well-protected one!

You can see which computer is the schema FSMO computer, or move that role to another computer, like so:

1. Right-click the object labeled Active Directory Schema and choose Change Domain Controller.

2. In the resulting dialog box, click Specify Name and type in the name of the domain controller to which you want to transfer the schema FSMO role. If you're not going to transfer the FSMO role, then any DC will do.

3. The snap-in will think for a minute and refresh its screen. Then right-click the Active Directory Schema object and choose Operations Master to see a dialog box like Figure 8.49.

4. Click the Change button and the system will ask you if you really want to make the change; confirm that you do.

5. Oddly enough, the dialog box for changing the FSMO remains up on the screen, but doesn't offer an OK button (it's disabled)—it only offers a Cancel button, which you'd *think* would un-do moving the FSMO. But it doesn't; the FSMO's already moved. Click Cancel to clear the dialog box, and you've successfully moved the schema operations master.

FIGURE 8.49

Changing the
schema FSMO

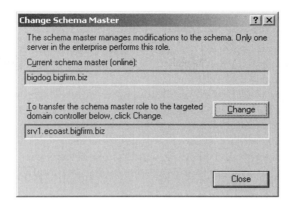

You must be a Schema Admin to move the schema FSMO role.

Planning for Schema Changes...and Conflicts

Before leaving the subject of the schema, let me offer a thought about how it will affect your organization. As I write this in early 2003, there are truthfully very few AD-aware applications. But now let's consider what happens in the near future, when there are many of them.

Let's imagine that we work at a big university with a lot of independent departments. The university's forest has many domains—Chemistry, English, Microbiology, Astronomy, Music, Geology, and others—that all live in a single forest and therefore have only one schema. Now imagine that Astronomy just got a cool new application that will aid its professors in researching something, and so they put it on the AD. It adds a few dozen things to the schema, including a Magnitude field, which stores a star's brightness. Then suppose Geology buys some neat new application that will help them in seismology research, which also adds a few things to the schema—such as a Magnitude field, where they'd store information on earthquake power. What happens when Geology tries to install an application that wants to create a schema field whose name already exists? Well, to make a long story short, it depends...and not all possible outcomes are good.

My point is this: Geology should have *known* when it first installed its app that the app would conflict with an existing one. But how could they have known? Well—and here's the part you won't like—every forest should consider keeping a testing lab up and running all the time, with a DC or two that run a working but independent version of your forest. Prior to rolling out any server-based apps, you should test them out on the test lab to see if they create schema changes that will make AD bellyache.

What's that you say? Astronomy and Geology are used to running things independently, not having to ask each other's permission to run applications? Yes, I can believe that—research and educational institutions have that tradition. But once you make the decision to stitch your organization together into a single forest, then your organizational components must communicate a bit more to keep things working. And *somebody's* going to have to keep that test lab up and running all the time. Which means staffing it and finding space, machines, and software for it. Golly, that argument about how Windows lowers total cost of ownership (TCO) doesn't seem quite as compelling now....

In case it's not clear, I think this is a bit of a weakness in the Active Directory. Basically, in this case, the AD is just another piece of software that says, "If you want to use me, you'll have to modify the way that you do business," and that seems awfully backward to me—sort of like a mouse manufacturer saying, "Gosh, we're sorry that our revolutionary mouse design doesn't fit your hand...have you perhaps considered surgery?"

There's some good news on this front, however, as you incorporate Server 2003 into your network. Once all of your domain controllers in all of your domains in your forest have been upgraded to Server 2003 and you shift your forest to Server 2003 functional level, then your schema becomes less fragile. When collisions are about to occur, a 2003 functional-level forest will automatically keep them from happening, and apparently transparently. I say "apparently" because I can't really test this—there are, as I've said, very few AD-aware apps as I write this, and none that conflict.

Global Catalog Changes and the Schema in Windows 2000

While I'm here discussing the schema, there's one more side effect of schema changes that you ought to know: what happens when you change the global catalog's structure.

Recall that every schema item has a check box telling AD whether to include it in the global catalog. Check the box, and you tell the GCs, "Listen, there're about 1000 items in the AD, but I only need you to extract a few dozen of them for the GC. I just added a new item." That leads to a nonintuitive result. (At least, nonintuitive from my point of view.)

Suppose the GC used to keep track of, say, 25 items in the Active Directory. You check a box and so now the GC must build a slightly larger GC. How does it do it? Now, *I* would guess that it would just say to itself, "Well, I've got 25 of the 26 already...so I'll just contact my DC partners in the other domains and go get that 26th item."

But it doesn't.

Instead, it says, "Hmm...things have changed. The only way to be absolutely sure that I'm not missing something important is to just *dump the whole global catalog and start over.*" Yikes! This means that any change to the list of items in the GC kicks off a message to every global catalog server in the forest to just flush its copy of the GC and to start contacting other DCs to rebuild the GC from scratch. In other words, get ready for some network activity and a set of global catalog servers that will be fairly unresponsive for a while.

What can you do about this? Two things: Install the server-based apps early on, when there is only a small number of global catalog servers, or wait a bit and make sure that all of your domain controllers are running a version of NT that is later than Windows 2000.

In the first approach, you start out creating your Active Directory by creating your first DC, and you immediately install the server-based applications to that DC. Then, any future DCs will have your augmented schema and global catalog structure from the very beginning, and you'll never see the global catalog servers decide to quit working and have a midday party just because someone installed an application on a server. Some apps make that easier to do; for example, Exchange 2000's Setup program has an option that allows you to only modify the schema. It doesn't install any files—it just makes room for Exchange's schema needs, should you ever decide to install an Exchange server later. If you're even thinking about running Exchange, I suppose it's not a bad idea to pump up the schema in anticipation of a possible Exchange future. (Although I should point out that installing Exchange on a virgin AD roughly triples the number of fields in the schema.)

GC Changes and the Schema in Windows Server 2003

The second approach just says something like, "Don't do the Active Directory until you get your hands on Server 2003." Server 2003 helps out by changing the global catalog's behavior. Under a forest populated by post-Windows 2000 global catalog servers, changes to the GC only cause the global catalog servers to contact other DCs for just the changes—adding a 26th item to the GC would only cause GC servers to go get the 26th item and add it to the GC, rather than dumping the whole thing and starting over. The neat thing about this is that it works in *any* functional level. Thus, if you have some GCs built on 2000 and some on 2003, a change in the GC will still cause panic amongst the 2000-based GCs but not the 2003-based GCs.

DOMAIN-NAMING FSMO

You've already met this one—I used this FSMO as my example earlier of why you'd need an operations master in the first place. There is only one of these for the entire forest. As with the schema operations master, the AD places the domain-naming operations master role on the first domain controller that you install on the first domain that you install.

You change the domain-naming operations master role with the Active Directory Domains and Trusts tool, which you've already met. First, change AD Domains and Trusts's focus to the machine that you want to shift the domain-naming FSMO role to. Just open AD Domains and Trusts and right-click the object in that MMC snap-in labeled Active Directory Domains and Trusts, then choose Connect to Domain Controller, and you'll see a dialog box like Figure 8.50.

FIGURE 8.50

Changing the focus DC

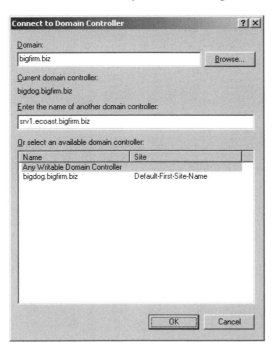

In this dialog box, you'll point AD Domains and Trusts (ADDT) to the DC that you want to serve as domain-naming FSMO. Fill in its name in the Enter the Name of Another Domain

Controller field and click OK, and ADDT's screen will then appear unchanged. But you will have shifted ADDT's focus to the other DC—I used srv1.ecoast.bigfirm.biz in my example—and you can now change the domain-naming FSMO. Again right-click the Active Directory Domains and Trusts object and choose Operations Master and you'll see a dialog box that looks just like the one in Figure 8.49, except it changes the domain-naming FSMO instead of the schema FSMO. Click Change and you'll modify your forest's domain-naming FSMO.

WARNING *The domain-naming FSMO role should only be placed on a DC that is also a global catalog server. Apparently the AD developers got a little lazy and decided that, inasmuch as the global catalog knows about things from all over the forest, the domain-naming FSMO could exploit the GC's knowledge.*

You must be an Enterprise Admin to change the domain-naming FSMO.

RID POOL FSMO

One of the things that any Native-mode AD domain controller can do is to create new accounts (user and machine) without having to go find some "central" or "primary" DC. In the NT/2000 world, everything has a unique identifier called its *security ID* or SID. SIDs look like this:

S-1-5-21-D1-D2-D3-RID

The 1-5-21 applies to all SIDs. What I've called *D1, D2,* and *D3* are actually three randomly generated 32-bit numbers. When AD first creates a domain, it generates these three unique 32-bit numbers, and they remain constant for any SID generated in that domain. And it's not just a matter of a separate D1/D2/D3 for a domain—the local SAM on a workstation or member server also has its own set of three unique 32-bit numbers.

NOTE *I know, you're wondering, "How does AD ensure that your computer's D1/D2/D3 is different from one built randomly in, say Pocatello?" My answer is: I don't know. I'd guess that they partially build the D1/D2/D3 from something unique, like the MAC address on the domain controller. But that's just a guess.*

So, for example, if I created a domain named bigfirm.biz and it happened to come up with D1=55, D2=1044, and D3=7, then every SID in bigfirm.biz would look like S-1-5-21-55-1044-7-*something*, where *something* is a 32-bit number. In other words, all SIDs in a domain are identical, save for the last 32 bits. That last 32 bits is the only *relative* difference between SIDs and is therefore called the *relative ID* or RID. Some RIDs are fixed; for example, the SID for the default Administrator account on a computer.

Anyway, if a DC needs to generate a new SID, then it *knows* what the first part of the SID will be. It just needs a unique RID. So there's one DC in every domain that hands out pools of 500 RIDs at a clip. Each DC can, then, create up to 500 accounts before it has to go back to this one central DC, which then doles out 500 more RIDs. (Actually, DCs don't wait until they're "on empty;" they refill their pool once they've used only 100 or 250 of them—100 if they're Windows 2000 Servers running SP3 or 250 if running 2000 and SP4 or Server 2003.) The computer that hands out the 500-RID bunches is called the RID operations master or the RID FSMO. By default, it is the first DC installed *in a domain*. Note that there is a RID FSMO for each domain, not just one per forest.

You move the RID FSMO function from one DC to another with Active Directory Users and Computers. Open up ADUC, right-click the object representing the domain, and choose Connect to

Domain Controller, then choose a DC as you did for the domain-naming FSMO. Then return to the icon representing the domain, right-click it again and choose Operations Masters to see a dialog box like the one in Figure 8.51.

FIGURE 8.51

Transferring RID, PDC, or infrastructure operations masters

Notice that there are three tabs on that dialog—RID, PDC, and Infrastructure. Those three FSMO roles are domain specific, not forest specific, and you use this dialog box to transfer any of those roles to another DC. By default, AD assigns those roles to the first DC created in a domain.

As you saw in transferring the domain name FSMO role, just click Change and confirm the change, and ADUC will transfer the FSMO role to the DC that you've indicated.

You must be a Domain Admin for a given domain to transfer the RID FSMO role for that domain.

INFRASTRUCTURE AND PDC FSMOS

In a multidomain network, it is, according to the Microsoft folks, difficult to quickly reflect changes to group and user accounts across domains. So you might rename a user, or put a user in a group in the domain that you administer, but that change might not show up in other domains for a while. Something called the *infrastructure operations master* speeds this process up. You change its role in the same way that you'd change the RID FSMO. There is one infrastructure FSMO per domain.

WARNING   *There's one oddity about the infrastructure operations master role: Don't make a DC that is a global catalog server into an infrastructure FSMO, unless every DC in your domain happens to be a global catalog server. The very first DC that you set up assumes all five operations master roles, which means that initially your infrastructure master is on a global catalog server. That's OK so long as all of your DCs are GCs, and of course that's true if you only have one DC.*

You must be a Domain Admin for a given domain in order to transfer the infrastructure FSMO role for that domain. You also use the infrastructure FSMO to prepare to shift an existing Windows 2000–based AD to a 2003-based AD, as you'll learn in the "Migration Strategies" section later.

Finally, there's the PDC emulator FSMO. It's a very important one.

In many cases, computers running a pre–Windows 2000 operating system need to find the PDC of the domain that they're a member of. Some of those cases will be obvious: For example, clearly an NT 4 BDC will look for its PDC when the BDC needs to update the information in its SAM. But there are many other cases where only the PDC will do; here are a few significant ones:

- The Network Neighborhood/My Network Places is populated by a computer acting as the "master browser" that collects the names of local computers. By default, the PDC acts in that role.

- When Windows 95 systems log in, they look for a file of system policies called `config.pol`— but they'll only look to the PDC for that file; BDCs are no good, as far as they're concerned.

- If an NT 4 domain is trying to establish a trust relationship with an AD domain, then the NT 4 domain will need to contact the PDC for that AD domain. That's because NT 4 doesn't understand multimaster replication and therefore thinks that it *must* do its negotiation with the one writeable version of the domain—the PDC.

Arbitrarily dubbing one of an AD domain's DCs as the "primary" DC, then, makes sense. And while an AD domain is in Mixed mode, the PDC emulator FSMO is more than just an emulator; it's the only DC that can accept account changes.

But does that mean that a PDC emulator becomes irrelevant once you're in Native mode and have no pre-2000 boxes around? Not at all. The PDC emulator still serves in two extremely important functions. Although we haven't covered replication yet, you probably know that replicating AD changes can take time—sometimes a significant amount of time. So suppose the following happens: I'm working in St. Louis and need my password changed. So I call the company help desk, which is, unknown to me, in Ottawa. The help-desk person changes my password, and it seems that all will be well.

But consider: What DC did the help-desk person change my password on? Well, she probably did it on a DC that was physically close to her, a DC in Ottawa. So an Ottawa DC knows my new password. But how long will it be before my local St. Louis DCs know my new password? Well, it could be hours. So does that mean that I'll have to just twiddle my thumbs for a few hours waiting for my new password to find its way to Missouri? Well, if we were talking about any other attribute besides a password, then the answer would be yes—but passwords are special.

When an admin changes a password on some DC somewhere, that DC immediately contacts the system acting as the PDC emulator FSMO for that domain. So the PDC FSMO almost always knows the most up-to-date passwords. When I try to log in to the domain, it is a local DC that tries to log me in. As I tell that DC my new password, the local DC is inclined at first to decline my logon, as the password that I offer doesn't match what the DC has. But before declining my logon, the DC connects to the PDC emulator FSMO for its domain and double-checks—and if the password that I gave my local DC matches the new one that the PDC has, then I'm logged in. This "high-priority replication" also occurs for one other user attribute—account unlocks. Thus, when a user forgets his password and retries to log on with the wrong password over and over, then not only does he need a new password, he probably also locked himself out of his account. So when the administrator resets the user's password, the admin probably also has to unlock the account. Immediately replicating the new password without replicating the account unlock wouldn't be very helpful.

That's one important job for the PDC FSMO—what's the other one? We'll cover that in an upcoming section, "Forestwide Time Synchronization."

You can change the PDC FSMO from Active Directory Users and Computers, as you did with the infrastructure or RID FSMOs. You must be a Domain Admin for a given domain in order to transfer the PDC FSMO role for that domain.

Transferring FSMO Roles the Hard Way

Transferring FSMO roles is very simple via the GUI, as I've shown you. But there's a catch: You can only use the GUI to transfer a FSMO role *if the present FSMO is up and running*. If you FDISK-ed the computer that was acting as your PDC FSMO, then there's no one around to "approve" transferring the PDC FSMO role to another computer. In that case, you don't just *transfer* the operations master role—you "seize the master."

If your PDC FSMO or infrastructure FSMO will be temporarily offline, then it's perfectly safe to transfer those FSMO/operations master roles to another computer, and you can actually do it through the GUI. It'll tell you that the operations master is offline and that you can't transfer the role, but ignore it and click Change anyway. You'll get the usual confirmation request and then *another* dialog box, like this:

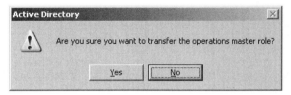

After a bit more thought, you'll get a *final* confirmation dialog box:

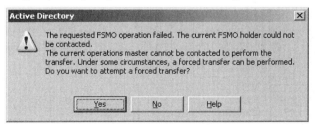

And notice the "FSMO" reference—see, even Microsoft doesn't want to get rid of the term! But to transfer the RID, domain naming, or schema FSMO, you'll need to use a command-line tool, NTDSUTIL. You start it from the command line by typing **ntdsutil**. Then do this:

1. Type **roles**; NTDSUTIL will respond by changing the prompt to `fsmo maintenance:`.
2. Type **connections** to point to the computer that you are going to transfer the FSMO role to. NTDSUTIL will respond by changing the prompt to `server connections:`.

3. Type **connect to server** *servername*, where *servername* is the server that you want to transfer the FSMO role to.

4. Type **quit** to return to FSMO maintenance.

5. Type **transfer** *fsmotype* **master**. You'll get a request for confirmation if NTDSUTIL finds that it cannot contact the current FSMO to get its approval. Confirm that you want to force a transfer.

6. If that works—if there are no error messages—then you're done. But if the transfer fails, then type **seize** *fsmotype* **master**. A bit more drastic, but it always works.

7. Type **quit** twice and you should be done.

For example, here is a session where I seized the RID master role from a computer called dc2 .bigfirm.biz to a computer named bigdog.bigfirm.biz (what I typed is in bold; the computer's responses are not bold):

```
C:\>ntdsutil
ntdsutil: roles
fsmo maintenance: connections
server connections: connect to server bigdog.bigfirm.biz
Binding to bigdog.bigfirm.biz ...
Connected to bigdog.bigfirm.biz using credentials of locally logged on user.
server connections: quit
fsmo maintenance: transfer rid master
ldap_modify_sW error 0x34(52 (Unavailable).
Ldap extended error message is 000020AF: SvcErr: DSID-032108D3, problem 5002
    (UNAVAILABLE), data 1722

Win32 error returned is 0x20af(The requested FSMO operation failed. The current
    FSMO holder could not be contacted.)
Depending on the error code this may indicate a connection, ldap, or role transfer
    error. Server "bigdog.bigfirm.biz" knows about 5 roles
Schema - CN=NTDS Settings,CN=BIGDOG,CN=Servers,CN=Default-First-Site-Name,
    CN=Sites,CN=Configuration,DC=bigfirm,DC=biz
Domain - CN=NTDS Settings,CN=BIGDOG,CN=Servers,CN=Default-First-Site-Name,
    CN=Sites,CN=Configuration,DC=bigfirm,DC=biz
PDC - CN=NTDS Settings,CN=BIGDOG,CN=Servers,CN=Default-First-Site-Name,
    CN=Sites,CN=Configuration,DC=bigfirm,DC=biz
RID - CN=NTDS Settings,CN=DC2,CN=Servers,CN=Default-First-Site-Name,
    CN=Sites,CN=Configuration,DC=bigfirm,DC=biz
Infrastructure - CN=NTDS Settings,CN=BIGDOG,CN=Servers,CN=Default-First-Site-Name,
    CN=Sites,CN=Configuration,DC=bigfirm,DC=biz
fsmo maintenance:
```

Hmmm—transfer didn't work. Let's seize:

```
fsmo maintenance: seize rid master
Attempting safe transfer of RID FSMO before seizure.
ldap_modify_sW error 0x34(52 (Unavailable).
```

```
Ldap extended error message is 000020AF: SvcErr: DSID-032108D3, problem 5002
    (UNAVAILABLE), data 1722

Win32 error returned is 0x20af(The requested FSMO operation failed. The current
    FSMO holder could not be contacted.)
Depending on the error code this may indicate a connection, ldap, or role transfer
    error.
Transfer of RID FSMO failed, proceeding with seizure ...
Searching for highest rid pool in domain
Server "bigdog.bigfirm.biz" knows about 5 roles
Schema - CN=NTDS Settings,CN=BIGDOG,CN=Servers,CN=Default-First-Site-Name,
    CN=Sites,CN=Configuration,DC=bigfirm,DC=biz
Domain - CN=NTDS Settings,CN=BIGDOG,CN=Servers,CN=Default-First-Site-Name,
    CN=Sites,CN=Configuration,DC=bigfirm,DC=biz
PDC - CN=NTDS Settings,CN=BIGDOG,CN=Servers,CN=Default-First-Site-Name,
    CN=Sites,CN=Configuration,DC=bigfirm,DC=biz
RID - CN=NTDS Settings,CN=BIGDOG,CN=Servers,CN=Default-First-Site-Name,
    CN=Sites,CN=Configuration,DC=bigfirm,DC=biz
Infrastructure - CN=NTDS Settings,CN=BIGDOG,CN=Servers,CN=Default-First-Site-Name,
    CN=Sites,CN=Configuration,DC=bigfirm,DC=biz
fsmo maintenance:
```

To transfer or seize the RID FSMO, type **transfer rid master**, or **seize rid master** as you see above. For domain-naming operations master, use **domain naming master**; for the schema operations master, use **schema master**.

WARNING   *If you seize a RID, domain-naming, or schema master, make sure that the old master never comes online again, or AD havoc will result! If need be, boot it from a DOS/Win 9x floppy and FDISK it.*

Forestwide Time Synchronization

As you'll read in the upcoming sections on replication, the AD needs all of its domain controllers to pretty much agree about the current time and date. They don't have to be *exactly* the same, but they need to be close—Kerberos fails if a domain controller and the system trying to use that DC to authenticate it disagree about what time it is by more than five minutes. Under NT 4 and earlier, establishing time synchronization across a domain was difficult to accomplish. But Windows 2000, XP, and 2003 include a service called the Windows Time service that keeps all of your Windows 2000, XP, and 2003 workstations and servers in good time sync.

Machines in an AD stay in sync this way. The PDC emulator FSMO of the forest root—the first created domain's first domain controller, recall—is the Master Time Server Dude. All other servers automatically create a hierarchy, sort of like a "telephone tree," to distribute time synchronization information. Everyone below that top dog automatically gets time synced from someone above it in the hierarchy. Specifically,

◆ Member servers and workstations synchronize to the DC that logged them in.

◆ DCs in a domain all look to the DC in their domain that holds the PDC emulator operations master role.

◆ If there is more than one domain in the forest, then there will be more than one PDC emulator, as each domain has a PDC emulator. The PDC emulators must agree on the time, so they choose one of their number to be "the source"—the PDC emulator for the *first* domain in the forest, the forest root. So, again, it's the PDC emulator FSMO for the forest root domain that is the ultimate time authority.

But who syncs that top dog, the forest root domain's PDC FSMO?

First of all, odd as this sounds, you *needn't* sync the FSMO. All that matters in AD is that all of the servers think it's the same time. Sure, it'd be nice if it was the *actual* time, but that's not necessary. If your whole enterprise was ten minutes early, that would constitute no problem for AD, as long as *all* of the servers are ten minutes early.

WARNING   *But it's very important that you set the time zones correctly on all of your systems! AD stores and syncs time in "universal time," so in its heart of hearts AD is always working on London, England time. 2K, XP, and 2003 use the time zones to understand the system clock's time and to display time that you'll understand. So if you were to leave everyone's time zone to Pacific and then just set the system clocks to whatever the local time was, each of those systems would think that the time in universal time was hours different. . .and synchronization would fail. Such a situation will drive you crazy, as you'll be looking at a DC and a workstation whose time looks identical—but unknown to you, their time zones are set differently—so it's a mystery why they won't talk to one another. It wouldn't be if you could see their beliefs about what the universal time was! You can quickly check a system's time zone by opening a command prompt and typing* `w32tm /tz`.

But as long as we've got this hierarchy, let's do it right and sync that root domain PDC somewhere reliable. You could use an atomic clock, one of those roughly $100 things that read the official time off some A.M. signals out of Colorado or other places. Or you could save a buck or two and just let the Internet set your time.

The suite of Internet standards includes a way of sharing time information called the Simple Network Time Protocol (SNTP), RFC 1769. Many, many machines on the Internet serve as SNTP servers and will provide up-to-date time information to any machine running an SNTP client. Fortunately, Windows 2000 and later systems include an SNTP client—in fact, it is *the* protocol that AD uses to synchronize its member systems. You can tell a Windows 2000 or later machine to synchronize its clock from a given Internet time server with this command:

```
net time /setsntp:DNSNAME
```

For example, if a machine named clock.atomictime.org were an SNTP server, you could tell your system to use it to synchronize with this command:

```
net time /setsntp:clock.atomictime.org
```

You can specify multiple time servers by separating them with spaces and surrounding them with double quotes, like so:

```
net time /setsntp:"clock1.bigfirm.biz clock2.bigfirm.biz clock3.bigfirm.biz"
```

If you forget what server you told the clock to sync with, you can find out by typing this:

```
net time /querysntp
```

By default, the forest root's PDC FSMO will try to synchronize with its time source once every 45 minutes until it successfully connects with the time source. Then it does it again in 45 minutes, and again 45 minutes later. It keeps resynchronizing every 45 minutes until it has successfully synchronized three times in a row. Then it reduces its frequency to once every eight hours. You can change this with a Registry entry, although I'm not sure why you'd need to. (All Time Service parameters are in HKLM\System\CurrentControlSet\Services\W32Time\Parameters.)

But where to find an SNTP server? Oddly enough, there are many around. Most ISPs' big DNS servers seem to act as SNTP servers. You can find out if a particular machine is an SNTP server with a neat little free tool called ntpquery.exe from http://www.bytefusion.com/ntpquery.html. You just point it at a DNS name or IP address and if that machine is a time server, you get a screen full of incomprehensible long numbers.

There doesn't seem to be a way to enable success/failure logging to the Event Log. But there is a diagnostic program that you can use to figure out if you're connected to a useful time server. Shipped on all 2000, XP and 200s machines, the program is called w32tm. Although it's not as pretty as ntpquery.exe, it's free and integrates with the time service.

To find out if a system's time server is working, open a command prompt and type **w32tm /resync**. It'd look like

```
c:\>w32tm /resync
Sending resync command to local computer...
The command completed successfully.
```

Or, if it *didn't* work, you'll see

```
The computer did not resync because no time data was available.
```

This service requires that port 123 be open to the outside world, so set your firewalls appropriately.

TIP   You can even use this if you don't have an Active Directory running. If, for example, your home machine were a Windows 2000 Professional or XP machine, then you could use net time /setsntp *to give your workstation the name of a time server, and the workstation would periodically resynchronize with that server. But only do this if you're connected to the Internet via cable modem or DSL...it might be quite unsettling to have your workstation dial up Earthlink at 3:30 in the morning just to get the time! And if you're running XP or 2003 then you can set the time server from the GUI—just double-click the time in the system notification area (most of us call it the "system tray") and you'll see a tab Internet Time where you can set a server. You won't see it on an AD member system, as AD selects time servers in an AD.*

Local AD Replication

You've already read that AD uses a multimaster replication scheme, which means that any change to an AD object—a new machine account, a modification to a machine account, a new user account, and so on—can happen on any domain controller. As replication takes time, that means that at any given second it could be possible that every single DC in a domain might have a slightly different copy of the AD database for that domain. But if left alone for long enough (that is, if no one changed anything about the AD), then every copy of the AD database sitting on all of the DCs would eventually be identical.

> **WARNING**   *Note that this is only true if your Active Directory is in Native mode or Windows Server 2003 functional level. Mixed-mode ADs or Windows Server 2003 Interim-mode domains will employ single-master replication.*

How does this work—how can we have many different sources of changes to a database and not end up with a hopelessly garbled database? Let's start off by understanding local AD replication, the way that AD replicates at a single site. (Recall that a site is a collection of networks connected at high speed—say, for example, a bunch of Ethernets. Any device in a site should be able to communicate with any other device in a site at millions of bits per second.) We'll add WAN considerations later.

AD Local Replication Starts as a Loop

If you set up a site containing more than one domain controller, then those domain controllers will discover each other (not a terribly hard thing to do, as they're all publicized via DNS and the AD) and then they'll automatically work out a replication sequence. So as to avoid chaos, every DC doesn't replicate to every other DC. As to how it does that, here's a simplified version.

Suppose the bigfirm.biz domain exists in a single site that contains four DCs named BIGDOG, DC2, DC3 and (unoriginally) DC4. AD replication sort of works like this: BIGDOG replicates it info to DC2, which takes BIGDOG's news, adds it to DC2's news, and passes all of that news to DC3. DC3 then takes the things that it learned from DC2 (which included BIGDOG's changes), adds them to its (DC3's) changes and then sends all of *that* to DC4. DC4 then takes everything that it's learned from DC3, as well as any changes that DC4 knows of, and sends them to BIGDOG, closing the loop.

I said that was the *simplified* version. Now let's fill in a few details and complicate things a bit.

WELL, ACTUALLY, IT'S *TWO* LOOPS

First of all, there isn't just one loop, there are two—you might say that AD replicates in both a clockwise and counterclockwise direction. bigfirm.biz's DCs might replicate as you see in Figure 8.52.

FIGURE 8.52

AD replication loops on a small site

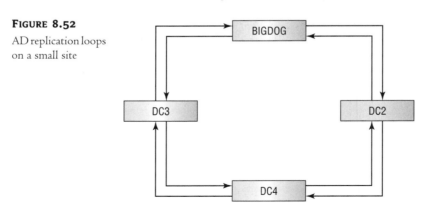

In that picture, notice that every domain controller replicates with *two* other DCs. BIGDOG replicates any changes that it receives to both DC4 and DC2. And notice that this points out one way in which my simple text example above was inaccurate: If replication actually worked as I suggested, then when BIGDOG received a bit of news, it would pass that news to DC2, who'd pass it on to DC3, who'd pass it on to DC4, who'd end up telling it again to BIGDOG. But that *won't* happen. Suppose we modify the user account for a user named Tom to reflect the fact that he has a new manager. Instead, BIGDOG will tell its news ("Tom has a new manager!") to both DC2 and DC3. DC2 will soon tell DC4 about Tom's new manager, and at about the same time, *DC3* will also tell DC4 about Tom's new boss. There's no way to know beforehand who'll get to DC4 first, but no matter which one it is, when the other DC tries to tell DC4 something that it already knows, then DC4 just says, "Thanks, but I already knew that." Result? The news has made its way around the AD fairly quickly.

And by the way, I've been writing things like "BIGDOG tells its news to DC2," and that's a little incomplete. More specifically, AD replication is always "pull" replication. More correctly, I should say, "BIGDOG notifies DC2 that it's got some news and eventually DC2 asks BIGDOG to communicate any changes that BIGDOG has seen" but that's a bit cumbersome to write. (The techie phrase that the AD uses is "pull replication with notification"—BIGDOG notifies, DC2 pulls.)

LOCAL REPLICATION HAPPENS EVERY FIVE MINUTES

Domain controllers within a site replicate to their two replication partners—what you might call their "clockwise" and "counterclockwise" partners—every five minutes. As far as I know, that's a hard-wired value; you can't change it. If there's nothing to say, then a DC says nothing at those five-minute intervals. But if a DC doesn't hear from either of its replication partners for an hour, it nudges that partner anyway, saying, "Are you *sure* you don't have anything new to tell me—that is, are you still alive?"

THE KCC MAKES THE LOOPS

Who forms this loop? Who decides which DC will be the two replication partners for a given DC? A program that runs on every DC called the Knowledge Consistency Checker (KCC). It pops up every 15 minutes, looks around, and asks, "Have we lost any DCs or gotten any new ones since the last time I looked?" If the DC population has changed since the last time, then the KCC—or rather KCCs, as there's one running on every DC—adjusts the loops.

You can't see the KCC in Task Manager because it's part of LSASS.EXE. But watching LSASS.EXE can be a great way to figure out whether you need another DC. Using Performance Monitor, log the Process object and look at LSASS.EXE's percentage of CPU use over time. If it grows considerably—or if you find that when LSASS.EXE is busy then the total CPU utilization is usually 100 percent—then you know that it's time for an extra domain controller.

By the way, you may see DCs with more than two partners, even in a small network. That happens for several reasons. First, if you've just brought a DC up, then the KCC may not have had time to re-adjust the replication to an optimal loop configuration. Second, I'm talking here about replication within a domain, but there is other replication going on as well—I'll get to that in the upcoming "There Is More Than One Replication Topology" section—and so a DC might have other partners because it's part of replicating things other than just the domain's data. Finally, as you'll see in the next section, a KCC will assign more than two partners if there are a lot of DCs.

How can you find out the names of the replication partners for a given DC? With Active Directory Sites and Services. Open it (it's in Administrative Tools, recall) and you'll see icons that look a bit like a tall building with windows in it. You may have more than one of those icons, as you get one for each site. Open one of the site icons and you'll see a folder named Servers and, inside that, icons representing each DC. If I first actually create enough DCs for bigfirm.biz so that we've got DC2, DC3 and DC4 in addition to BIGDOG, then I can start AD Sites and Services to see the four DCs. If I open any server icon I'll see a folder named NTDS Settings; I open *that* and I get Figure 8.53.

FIGURE 8.53

Viewing DC4's replication partners

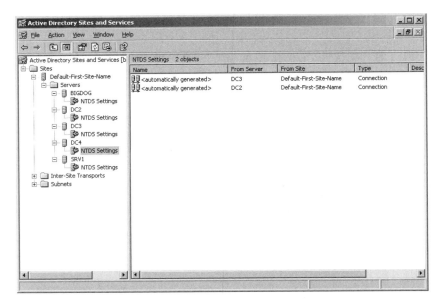

Here, I've created extra DCs for bigfirm.biz—BIGDOG, DC2, DC3, and the unoriginally-named DC4—as well as SRV1, the DC from the ecoast.bigfirm.biz domain. You can see that DC4 replicates with both DC2 and DC3—two separate rings. Notice that you are seeing the *pull* partners here. DC4 pulls data from DC2 and from DC3.

If you *really* want to, you can lay out the entire replication scheme in an AD. Just right-click in the right pane and choose New/Connection, and you can specify which DCs replicate to what DCs. I recommend against it, *but* you might do it when in a troubleshooting situation.

You can force the KCC to run by installing a program called repadmin.exe and then typing **repadmin /kcc**. REPADMIN is one of the Resource Kit tools that you get free with Server—look in the \Support\Tools folder and install the tools by double-clicking the file named SUPPTOOLS.MSI.

BUT SOMETIMES IT'S NOT A LOOP, IT'S A MESH

This sounds pretty good, until you start thinking about what might happen in a company with *lots* of domain controllers. Suppose you had 200 DCs. That'd mean that if one DC started replicating some change to the Active Directory, the change could take up to 100 replications to get to all other DCs. Let's see: 100 replications, each of which happens at roughly five-minute intervals—500 minutes— that's *more than eight hours*. Would you call *that* an acceptable interval for replication within a site? Well, no, of course you wouldn't, and Microsoft didn't think so, either. So the KCC looks around and asks,

"Are any DCs more than three hops apart?" If so, the KCC just adds more links, converting the loop into a mesh. I've seen ADs with several dozen DCs—unusually large domains, to be sure—where some DCs had eight replication partners apiece.

I've been calling the process of moving an AD change though a set of domain controllers a "loop," but as you see, it might not *be* a loop; it might be a mesh. That's why Microsoft has a different term to describe the path that an AD change might take through a set of DCs: the *replication topology*.

THERE IS MORE THAN ONE REPLICATION TOPOLOGY

Even a simple network, however, is a bit more complex than I've described. I've described a single loop—oops, I mean replication topology—but every forest will have more than that. Every forest has at least three replication topologies.

To see why, recall that a forest is a collection of domains. Each domain has its own "private" information that it (mostly) only replicates among the DCs for that domain. (For example, the information in your user account, such as your name and password, stays in your domain's replication topology. If you were to create a new user account in one domain, then the other domains would know nothing of that, so it wouldn't generate replication in the *other* domains, save for a bit of activity on the global catalog servers.) That domain-specific data is one replication topology: the pathway for updates from one DC to another within a domain. But recall that there is some data that is specific to the *forest*, not the domain; that data needs to be seen by *every* DC, no matter what domain that DC is a member of. The forestwide data is called the *schema and configuration naming contexts*, and it replicates among all DCs in the enterprise, not just the DCs in one domain, so the KCC creates a replication topology for that data that is distinct from the replication topology that any single domain uses.

NOTE *Just a word on that phrase* naming context. *It's an LDAP term that Microsoft adopted, unfortunately in my opinion. It just means "a database that must be replicated amongst a bunch of computers." So when you read a high falutin'-sounding phrase such as, "The KCC creates a replication topology for the bigfirm.biz domain-naming context," you can translate it to this: "The KCC figures out which DCs replicate to which DCs so that they can replicate bigfirm.biz's domain info, such as usernames, attributes, passwords, and the like."*

There is also, recall, a database that consists of a subset of data from all of the domains: the global catalog. The KCC creates a replication topology that global catalog servers use to replicate the GC as well.

This all means that you could have *quite a few* replication topologies running. For example, a four-domain forest would have one replication topology for each domain, then one for the forestwide data, and then finally one for the global catalog—six, in all. You can see a simpler example—replication in an imaginary two-domain forest—in Figure 8.54.

In this example, you see the two triangles labeled Domain1 and Domain2—recall that Active Directory diagrams always use triangles to represent AD domains. Domain1 has three DCs that have formed a two-way loop to replicate their domain information amongst themselves, and Domain2 has four DCs that have created a similar loop. There is also a third loop that incorporates all of the DCs, which replicates the schema and configuration naming contexts. (For simplicity's sake, I left out one replication path, the global catalogs.)

FIGURE 8.54

Two domains, three replication topologies

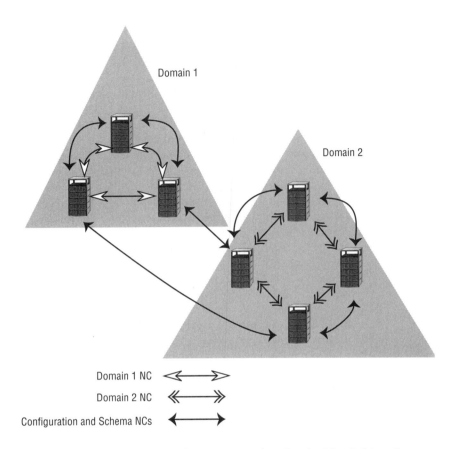

Domain 1 NC ⟨⟨———⟩⟩

Domain 2 NC ⟨⟨———⟩⟩

Configuration and Schema NCs ⟨———⟩

You can figure out what kind of replication each connection does by double-clicking the connection object between any two DCs. For example, I just looked into the NTDS Settings folder for my BIGDOG domain controller in my bigfirm.biz domain, and I see that it replicates with three DCs—DC2, DC3, and SRV1. SRV1 is, you may recall, the sole DC for ecoast.bigfirm.biz. Why do BIGDOG and SRV1 replicate if they're not in the same domain? Two reasons. First, BIGDOG is a global catalog server and therefore needs to gather information from every domain, and, second, because all they share the forest-wide naming contexts Configuration and Schema, and they have to be replicated. If I double-click the BIGDOG-SRV1 connection object, it has a properties page like Figure 8.55.

Notice the fields Replicated Naming Context(s) and Partially Replicated Naming Context(s)—these tell the tale. <Enterprise Configuration> says that this connection replicates the Configuration and Schema naming contexts. Then, ecoast.bigfirm.biz tells that SRV1 tells BIGDOG about the ecoast.bigfirm.biz domain, but not *everything* about the domain. Why would one DC give only partial information about its domain to another DC? Again, because BIGDOG is a global catalog server. In contrast, click most of the other connection objects in a domain like this and you will see nothing in the Partially Replicated Naming Context(s) field and the domain's name in the Replicated Naming Context(s) field.

FIGURE 8.55

Properties for a connection object between domains

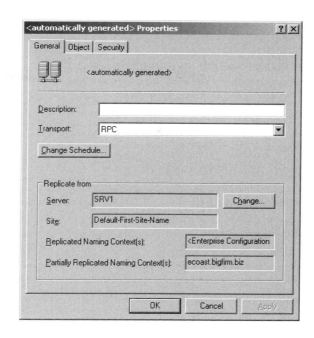

BUT WHAT ABOUT "REPLICATION CRASHES"?

Recall that back in my picture with the four bigfirm.biz domain controllers, I said that if we changed Tom's manager then the information would replicate its way both clockwise and counterclockwise until the news hit DC4 roughly simultaneously from both sides. But we don't want DC4 recording the fact of Tom's manager change over and over again, so I said that AD has a way of making DC4 smart enough to say, "Thanks, but I already know about it" the second time that it hears of Tom's new manager. I'll show you exactly *how* in a few pages, but for now I'll ask you to trust me that AD knows how to keep a piece of news from going 'round and 'round and 'round the network forever. But there's another kind of potential replication problem: collisions. Suppose an administrator connected to BIGDOG changes Tom's manager to one value. At about the same time, an administrator connected to DC4 changes Tom's manager also but to a different name.

Who wins?

To see, let's look a bit under the hood at replication. Back when we created Tom's user record, someone probably filled the Manager field with the name of Tom's manager—as in the song on Paul Simon's old *Graceland* album, let's call him Al. Let's suppose that our bigfirm.biz domain initially contained information looking something like this:

Object	Tom's user account
Attribute	Manager
Value	Al Jones
Version number	1
Modified	1 December 2000 1:01 P.M.

A couple of months later, the admin attached to BIGDOG updates Tom's user record to reflect the fact that his new manager is named Beth Meadows. BIGDOG then stores (and replicates) this database information:

Object	Tom's user account
Attribute	Manager
Value	Beth Meadows
Version number	2
Modified	5 February 2001 4:22 P.M.

Notice that in addition to the new value, there's a new timestamp and a new version number. Version numbers are simple: a DC is just supposed to increment them when it changes an attribute. As the previous value had version number 1, the change gets version number 2. If we changed it again, it'd be version number 3, and so on.

Now, over at DC4, another administrator thinks that he's supposed to update Tom's record with Beth's name, but he figures that Beth must *really* be Elizabeth, so he enters that, resulting in DC4 storing and replicating this data:

Object	Tom's user account
Attribute	Manager
Value	Elizabeth Meadows
Version number	2
Modified	5 February 2001 4:25 P.M.

Notice that the version number here is 2, not 3. That's because from the point of view of the domain controller DC4, this *is* the second version. It doesn't yet know that BIGDOG has changed the record.

BIGDOG then tells DC2 about Beth, and DC4 tells DC3 about Elizabeth. Soon thereafter, either DC2 tries to replicate to DC3 or vice versa—it's just a matter of chance. It's then clear that there's a conflict: two different items are trying to update the same attribute of the same record. Time for conflict resolution. How does AD do that? Fairly simply:

If one candidate has a later version number, then it wins. If they have the same version number, then the later modification wins.

See why time synchronization is so important? In both cases, the version number is 2, so that's irrelevant. But Elizabeth appeared three minutes after Beth, so she wins.

It's just a might sleazy, but I should mention that there is, therefore, a way that the admin at BIGDOG could have improved the chances that his changes would be more collision-proof. If he'd changed the manager to Beth, then Elizabeth, then back to Beth, then his replicated record would have had a version number of *4*, because by AD's lights, the attribute had changed three times in just a few moments. The Beth record would have had a higher version number than the Elizabeth record, and it would have won, even if it were an older record.

AD REPLICATION NUTS AND BOLTS

I hope you will never have to worry about how the AD gets its data from one DC to another. But just in case you need to troubleshoot replication, here's how it works under the hood.

A note on this explanation, though: Recall that Active Directory is a database. It stores a lot of information about the objects in its database. Recall also that some examples of those objects are user and machine accounts, but there are many other kinds of things stored in AD. For the purposes of explaining AD replication, however, I'm going to simplify just a bit and use only user account creations and modifications in my examples.

AD in a One-Domain Controller World

Let's consider what happens when you connect to a DC and create a user account. Again for purposes of readability, I'll simplify the structure of a user account record and say that user accounts only keep track of these things:

- The user's name
- The user's UPN (logon name)
- The user's password
- The name of the user's manager

Suppose I create a user named Dawn, with a UPN of dawn@bigfirm.biz. Let's say that her password is "swordfish" and her manager's name is Wally. Suppose when I create Dawn's account, Bigfirm has only one DC—BIGDOG—and so that's the DC that creates the account.

Now, you'd think that all that AD would store would be something like "created a user account; name=Dawn, UPN=dawn@bigfirm.biz, password=swordfish, manager=Wally, time and date of creation=10:00 A.M. 28 February 2001." But it's a bit more complex than that. I only mentioned this in passing, but AD does not replicate entire *records*; instead, it replicates *single attributes*. So if I change Dawn's manager to Jane in a few months, then AD won't replicate "name=Dawn, UPN=dawn@bigfirm.biz, password=swordfish, manager=Jane;" instead, it'll only say something like "for Dawn's record, manager now equals Jane." That's important because it implies that we must keep track of updates to each attribute, not each record.

Introducing Update Sequence Numbers (USNs)

The AD keeps a running total of changes that it has seen in its history called an *update sequence number* or USN. Every DC has its own set of USNs, as you'll see, but for now let's just stick with the one DC that I'm creating Dawn on. (Recall that for the moment we're assuming a one-DC world. And let me add here that this is a really bad idea in the real world—always have at least two DCs for each domain!) BIGDOG might have seen 5000 changes since I first created its Active Directory, so it would associate Dawn's name with USN=5001. You may recall also that AD keeps version numbers on each attribute, so it'd store a version=1 for that attribute. Creating Dawn's user record, then, would cause the DC to think the following:

- "Got a new object in the database. It's a user account that I'll give a SID of 1-5-21-43-534-83-1188."
- "Got a new username for 1-5-21-43-534-83-1188, Dawn. It's the 5001st thing that I (the DC) have learned, so I'll associate her name with USN=5001. Version number is 1."

- "Got a UPN for 1-5-21-43-534-83-1188, value=dawn@bigfirm.biz. It's the 5002nd thing I have learned, so I'll give it USN=5002. Version number is 1."
- "Got a password for 1-5-21-43-534-83-1188, value=swordfish. It's the 5003rd thing I have learned, so I'll give it USN=5003. Version number is 1."
- "Got a manager for 1-5-21-43-534-83-1188, value=Wally, USN=5004, version number is 1."

So now we've created a user account for Dawn. She logs in the first time, and her workstation asks her to change her password, so she changes it to "secret." AD stores that new password like so:

- First, it computes a USN for the new password. We've probably created other user accounts and done maintenance on other accounts between the time that we first created Dawn's account and now, so it's likely that the latest USN is higher than 5004. Let's just say that this DC's USNs are up to 5716.
- Next look at the previous version number for the password attribute for Dawn. It was version=1, so the new password will have version=2.
- AD then stores something like "got a password for 1-5-21-43-534-83-1188, value=secret, USN=5716, version number is 2."

The following table summarizes what BIGDOG knows about Dawn.

Attribute	Value	USN	Version
Name	Dawn	5001	1
UPN	dawn@bigfirm.biz	5002	1
Password	secret	5716	2
Manager	Wally	5004	1

But if an AD increments its USN number every single time there's a change, won't it run out of USNs? Then what happens? Well, the USN is a 64-bit number, so you could have 18,446,744,073,709,551,616—that's more than 18 quintillion—changes before it becomes a problem. Remember that I said earlier that someone at Compaq had created an AD with 100 million members? Well, if you created an AD that large, then you could apply on average more than 18 billion changes apiece to each of those accounts before you maxed the USNs out. Or, in other words, if you made 1000 changes a second, then it would take about 18 quadrillion seconds to cause the USNs to roll over. Eighteen quadrillion seconds is (if I've done the calculation right) more than 500 million years.

And you just *know* that Microsoft will come out with a radically different update to the Active Directory by then...so we'll have to reset our USNs at that time anyway, and the count will start all over again!

Adding a Second Domain Controller
Well, thus far, we haven't done anything with replication, inasmuch as there's only been one DC. Let's add one named (you guessed it) DC2. It's got a brand-new, basically empty AD database file. It connects to BIGDOG and gets the current state of the domain's AD. Let's suppose that the very

first account that it gets from BIGDOG is Dawn's account. Dawn's name, UPN, password, and manager will then get USNs 0–3, as you see in the following table:

Attribute	Value	USN	Version
Name	Dawn	0	1
UPN	dawn@bigfirm.biz	1	1
Password	secret	2	2
Manager	Wally	3	1

Notice something *very* important here. USNs from one domain controller do not have to match USNs from another domain controller. If we had a third domain controller that also held a copy of Dawn's user account information, then that DC's Dawn records would almost certainly have a different set of USNs.

Limiting Replication: Using USNs and Introducing "High-Water Marks"

What, then, does a USN do? Basically this: It helps replication partners know how much replication they have to do. BIGDOG replicated everything that it knew to DC2, item by item, and there were plenty more records than just Dawn's to pass along. As BIGDOG told things to DC2, it also told DC2 the USNs—that's BIGDOG's USNs—for each piece of data. Let's suppose that the highest USN in BIGDOG's AD database at the time was 6729. In general, DC2 doesn't care all that much about BIGDOG's USNs. But as BIGDOG finished replicating to DC2, then DC2 made a note to itself, saying, "The last time that I replicated from BIGDOG, BIGDOG's highest USN was 6729." That is DC2's *high-water mark* value for BIGDOG.

Five minutes later, DC2 wants to replicate again from BIGDOG. But how much of BIGDOG's database does DC2 need in order to be up to date? We certainly don't want to replicate all of BIGDOG's AD database to DC2 every five minutes! To avoid that, DC2 starts out the replication process by asking BIGDOG, "What's your currently highest USN?" The replication conversation could, then, go something like this:

DC2: What's your currently highest USN?

BIGDOG: It's 6729.

DC2: Hmmm, let's see—my high-water mark value for you is also 6729. As that was the last USN that you replicated to me, I already *have* that change, so I guess I'm up to date. Thanks, I guess we're done!

Alternatively, if BIGDOG had said, "My currently highest USN is 6800," then DC2 would know that it had missed 71 changes to AD and so could ask BIGDOG to send along the changes associated with BIGDOG's USNs 6730 through 6800. That would lead to these events:

- DC2 would record BIGDOG's changes in its copy of the Active Directory.
- Those changes would have USNs *on DC2*, and so DC2's highest USN is now higher.
- DC2 would now know that its high-water mark value for BIGDOG is no longer 6729, but instead now 6800.

A Problem: Infinite Loops

Reviewing, then:

◆ Each DC maintains a separate copy of the Active Directory on its domain.

◆ That AD contains USNs for each item in the AD.

◆ USNs in one domain controller's copy of a given AD record will generally not match the USNs in another DC's copy of the AD for the same record—if Mary Smith's password has USN 10030 on one DC, that same password for Mary will be stored on a different DC, but with a different USN.

◆ Each DC remembers the highest USN that it has heard from each of its partners. Those highest-USNs-so-far are called the *high-water mark* values for each replication partner.

◆ DCs use the high-water marks to be able to tell their replication partners, "Only tell me what's new since the last time we spoke."

So far, so good. But so far, there's no way to avoid an infinite loop. To see that, let's suppose that we start off with our two domain controllers, BIGDOG and DC2. Let's say that BIGDOG's highest USN is 5000, and DC2's highest USN is 1000. The system is quiescent, so BIGDOG's high-water mark for DC2 is 1000, and DC2's high-water mark for BIGDOG is 5000.

Now suppose an administrator makes a change on BIGDOG—we change the value for Tom's Manager field, as in the earlier example. BIGDOG gives that AD change—that "update" in AD-ese— a USN of 5001.

DC2 says to BIGDOG, "What's your highest USN?" BIGDOG responds, "5001."

DC2 now knows that it's hopelessly behind and so seeks to get back "in sync" with its buddy BIGDOG. So it says, "Send me all of your updates with USNs higher than 5000." BIGDOG responds with the new information. DC2 records this new manager for Tom dutifully, and that change gets USN 1001 on DC2. DC2 also records that BIGDOG's high-water mark is now 5001.

Eventually BIGDOG says to DC2, "What's new?" Or, in AD-ese, "Do you have any updates after that last one that I got from one, any greater than 1000?"

DC2 says, "Sure, I've got a 1001." (Which is true.) So BIGDOG realizes that now *it* is hopelessly behind the times (which is not true) and asks DC2 for this new information. DC2 responds by telling BIGDOG about Tom's "new" manager. BIGDOG records this information, bumping its highest USN up to 5002 and recording that DC2's latest high-water mark value is 1001.

But now what happens the next time that DC2 says to BIGDOG, "What's your highest USN?" Well, of course BIGDOG replies, "5002," and the whole mess starts all over again. Although this would make for very busy-looking domain controllers, it wouldn't be of much use...so Microsoft included a "propagation dampening" feature to stop the loops. It's got two parts: the originating USN and something called the up-to-date vector.

Originating USNs: Credit Where Credit Is Due

I've told you so far that whenever a DC stores an update (update=change, recall) to the Active Directory, then it identifies the update by a USN, and that USN is local to that DC—all other DCs in the domain will eventually know the information included in that update, but those DCs will all end up assigning a different USN to the information.

But what I *didn't* tell you was that DCs also store some more information: the name of the *originating DC* and the USN on that DC. So the table that I showed you a few pages back of how part of DC2's AD might look after replicating from BIGDOG might be more completely represented like so:

Attribute	Value	USN	Version	Originating DC	Originating USN
Name	Dawn	0	1	BIGDOG	5001
UPN	dawn@bigfirm.biz	1	1	BIGDOG	5002
Password	secret	2	2	BIGDOG	5716
Manager	Wally	3	1	BIGDOG	5004

As before, this table shows four attributes and values for a user named Dawn. Each attribute has a USN that is a *local* USN, the USN that DC2 created when copying the records from BIGDOG, and a version number. But now we've got the originating DC, which identifies the DC that *first* made the change, and that DC's USN. Thus, even if we had 100 DCs here, they'd all have their own different USNs on their local copies of Dawn's information—but every one of them would remember that the first DC with this information was BIGDOG and would remember BIGDOG's corresponding USNs.

Up-to-Date Vectors: Breaking the Loop

What good are those originating USNs? They're the key to stopping the infinite loops. You've already heard that each DC remembers the highest USN that it's ever heard from each of its partners. Those numbers are, again, called the *high-water mark* table for that DC. Now let me add a bit more information that's kept by each DC: the highest *originating* USN that it's ever heard, *from all DCs*—not just the replication partners. This table of highest originating USNs is called the *up-to-date vector*.

Thus far, I've told you this (incomplete) story about how DCs update each other: One DC remembers the high-water mark that it's seen so far from its partner, and so it asks the partner, "What records do you have in your AD with a higher USN than this high-water mark that I have for you?" In actuality, the more complete request goes, "What records do you have in your AD with a higher USN than this high-water mark that I have for you, *but that do not include any originating USNs less than or equal to my table of up-to-date vectors?*"

A Replication Example Using High-Water Marks and Up-to-Date Vectors

Let's revisit my earlier BIGDOG/DC2 replication example. Suppose our story starts as follows:

DC	Highest USN	High-Water Mark for Partner	UTD Vectors BIGDOG	DC2
BIGDOG	5000	1000	4817	388
DC2	1000	5000	4817	388

I'm making this example easier by starting from a quiescent, "everybody knows exactly the same things" state. Things work as well otherwise, but this is clearer. BIGDOG knows DC2's highest USN accurately, DC2 knows BIGDOG's accurately, and they each have the same UTD vector. (Note that every DC's table includes its *own* highest originating USN as well!)

Now, suppose an administrator is connected to BIGDOG and makes a change—again, Tom's manager works fine. In storing this new item, BIGDOG gives it USN 5001, identifies the originating DC as BIGDOG, and the originating DC's USN as 5001. BIGDOG also updates its UTD vector to reflect that the latest originating USN that it knows of from BIGDOG—itself—is 5001.

Now DC2 asks BIGDOG, "What items do you have in your AD that have a USN greater than 5000 (DC2's current high-water mark for BIGDOG) *and* whose originating USNs are greater than the ones that I have in this up-to-date vector: BIGDOG=4817, DC2=388?"

BIGDOG now examines everything with a USN higher than 5000. It finds one record, the one that describes Beth's new manager. BIGDOG examines its originating DC/USN and finds that it originated on BIGDOG with a USN of 5001. BIGDOG then looks at the up-to-date vector that DC2 sent it and sees that as far as DC2's concerned, any item that originated at BIGDOG after USN 4817 is news...so BIGDOG sends the info about Beth's manager along to DC2.

DC2 then stores this information as local USN 1001, originating DC=BIGDOG and originating DC's USN=5001. It also notes that the highest originating USN from BIGDOG is 5001, and a high-water mark for BIGDOG of 5001. The current state of replication then looks like this:

DC	Highest USN	High-Water Mark for Partner	UTD Vectors	
			BIGDOG	DC2
BIGDOG	5001	1000	5001	338
DC2	1001	5001	5001	338

Next, BIGDOG seeks to replicate with DC2. BIGDOG last knew of USN 1000, so it asks DC2 for any updates after 1000, provided that their originating USNs exceed the ones in BIGDOG's up-to-date vector; BIGDOG includes the contents of its current up-to-date vector.

DC2 notes that it has a USN 1001 and considers sending it to BIGDOG. But then it makes a second check of the originating DC and USN and notes that the record came from BIGDOG. So it then asks, "What is the latest originating USN from BIGDOG that BIGDOG knows about?" and the answer is 5001. DC2 then says to itself, "Well, this record was new to me...but clearly BIGDOG already knows about it, as it knows all of the BIGDOG-originated records up to the one with a BIGDOG USN of 5001."

DC2 then replies, "No, I don't have anything that you don't know. But my highest USN is now 1001." BIGDOG makes a note of that, and the replication is done—we're back to quiescence.

Adding More Domain Controllers

Let me wrap up this discussion of replication nuts and bolts with a somewhat more complex example. To demonstrate how all of that works, let's see how my four bigfirm.biz DCs—BIGDOG, DC2, DC3, and DC4—would replicate. BIGDOG holds all of the FSMO roles, but other than that is indistinguishable from the others. After giving them 15 minutes to run the KCC and settle down into a replication structure, I opened four copies of AD Sites and Services to show the NTDS Settings folders for all four, as you see in Figure 8.56.

FIGURE 8.56

Replication
partner settings for
BIGDOG, DC2,
DC3, and DC4

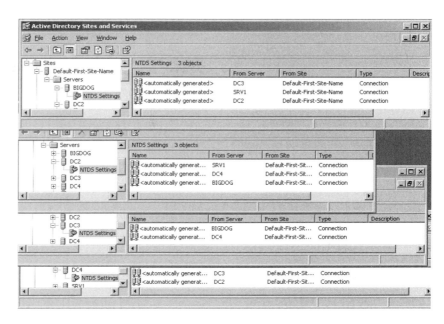

By the way, you can use the NTDS Settings folder to force replication. Just right-click any replication partner and you'll see an option to Replicate Now; that will force the DC to replicate with
that replication partner immediately. Sketched out, the bigfirm.biz replication structure looks like
Figure 8.52 a few pages back.

Recall that each domain controller has an up-to-date value for every other DC—not just its
replication partners. You can see the entire up-to-date vector for any domain controller with a
command-line tool called REPADMIN. REPADMIN is part of the mini-Resource Kit that comes
with Server that I mentioned earlier. Recall that you can install it by looking in the \Support\Tools
folder of the Server CD for a file called SUPPTOOLS.MSI; double-click it and answer the prompts and
you'll get several useful and interesting tools.

REPADMIN runs from the command line, and it's as cryptic as most command-line Resource Kit
tools. To see the up-to-date vector for a domain controller, make sure that you're sitting at the
domain controller and open up a command prompt, then type this:

```
repadmin /showutdvec dcname naming-context
```

where *dcname* is the name of your domain controller and *naming-context* is just the name of your
domain, but written strangely. Take each part of the AD DNS-like domain name and write it as
DC=*firstpart,***DC=***secondpart,***DC=***thirdpart* and so on for as many parts as the domain name includes.
For example:

acme.com becomes DC=acme,DC=com

hq.bigfirm.biz becomes DC=hq,DC=bigfirm,DC=com

And so bigfirm.biz is just dc=bigfirm,dc=com. Why REPADMIN wants it this way has to
do with the internal representation and storage of the Active Directory. AD is built to use a

database-access language called the Lightweight Directory Access Protocol (LDAP), and that's how LDAP refers to domain names. There's far more to know about LDAP, but I've been trying my hardest to spare you its cryptic nature, so you won't hear any more LDAP stuff than is absolutely necessary. Here's a sample run of repadmin /showutdvec:, although not on our imaginary network:

```
C:\>repadmin /showutdvec bigdog dc=bigfirm,dc=biz
Caching GUIDs.
..
Default-First-Site-Name\DC3      @ USN      4747 @ Time 2003-01-18 14:45:18
Default-First-Site-Name\DC4      @ USN      4968 @ Time 2003-01-18 13:59:00
Default-First-Site-Name\BIGDOG   @ USN      6454 @ Time 2003-01-18 14:49:34
Default-First-Site-Name\DC2      @ USN     39469 @ Time 2003-01-18 14:45:18
```

You can see that BIGDOG's up-to-date vector even includes an entry for itself. Now, if you try this out on *your* network, then you might come across a confusing but common sight—more lines than you've got DCs! Suppose your domain had five DCs, and you ran a repadmin /showutdvec on one of your DCs. You'd expect five UTD entries, and perhaps that's what you'd get. But you'll often see entries in the UTD vector that don't have a name, but instead have a long string of letters and numbers. That string of letters and numbers is called a *globally unique ID*, or GUID. What you're seeing (if you see something like that) is the remnants of old DCs. If, in the five-DC example, you perhaps *used* to have a couple of DCs in your domain that you have demoted (that is, you ran DCPROMO on them to convert them back to member servers), then those now-gone DCs will have entries left in the other DC's up-to-date vector tables. The GUID is the only information left about that old DC—the AD recognizes that it no longer exists, but the process of demoting a DC does not direct the other DCs to scrub its up-to-date value from their up-to-date vectors. (Old DCs never really die apparently; they just fade away.)

Now, let's suppose that I change the AD, again by modifying Tom's manager while attached to DC2. Clearly DC2 is going to replicate that account to its partners, BIGDOG and DC4; that part's easy to understand. But it's just as clear that BIGDOG will want to replicate the new account to DC3—*and* that DC4 will want to replicate the account to DC3. Clearly we don't want DC3 getting any more replication traffic than is necessary, so how does AD keep DC3 from getting the same report twice?

Step One: Create the New User on DC2
First, let's change Tom's manager at DC2 and review what happens to DC3. When things start out, suppose DC3 has the following up-to-date vector:

DC3	4747
BIGDOG	6454
DC2	39469
DC4	4968

Let's assume that the AD is quiescent when I change Tom's manager, so those are also the current high-water values for those domain controllers. I make the change to Beth's account on DC2 and, as you saw earlier, DC2's highest USN increments. Let's say that the update on DC2 has a USN of 39473. I'll simplify this example and focus mainly on the up-to-date vector, as I hope that the highest-USN and high-water mark's use is clear by now. (Also, explaining a complete four-DC replication with all the bells and whistles takes pages and pages and pages.) DC2 bumps up its up-to-date vector for itself to 39473.

Step Two: DC2 Replicates the New User to BIGDOG

After a little while, DC2 says to its two replication partners BIGDOG and DC4, "I've got a new USN; you might want to come replicate with me." Let's say that BIGDOG responds a bit more quickly than DC4, saying, "Send me all the new entries whose originating USNs exceed 4747 if it came from DC3, 6454 if it came from BIGDOG, 39469 if from DC2 or 4968 if from DC4." DC2 sees that the record's originating DC is DC2 but that the originating USN is 39473—which is larger than 39469. So it sends along Tom's new manager. BIGDOG increments its USNs and stores away the information about Tom's new manager, including the fact that the information originated at DC2 with USN of 39473. BIGDOG also changes the value in its up-to-date vector entry for DC2 up to 39473.

Step Three: BIGDOG Replicates to DC3 and DC2

Armed with this new information, BIGDOG taps both DC3 an DC2 on the shoulder and says, "Hey, check out my new USN." Perhaps DC2 responds first, saying, "Tell me any new stuff as long as it originated with DC3 after 4797, BIGDOG after 6454, DC2 after 39473, or DC4 after 4968." BIGDOG says, "Hmmm, I guess this info about Tom's manager isn't all *that* new...it's from DC2 and has a USN of 39473. Never mind, DC2."

DC3 responds similarly but not identically: "Tell me any new stuff as long as it originated with DC3 after 4797, BIGDOG after 6454, DC2 after 39469, or DC4 after 4968." Notice that DC3's got an older up-to-date vector entry for DC2. BIGDOG sees that the info on Tom's manager is originally from DC2 but has a USN larger than 39469 and replicates the information to DC3. DC3 stores it, noting again that the information originated with DC2—not BIGDOG, even though he's the one that passed the info along—and that DC2's USN for the information was 39473. DC3 updates its value in the up-to-date vector table for DC2 to 39473.

Step Four: DC2 Updates DC4

While BIGDOG is updating DC3, the chances are good that DC4 finally responded to DC2, saying, "What's new since the last time we talked, DC2? But only tell me things if they originated with DC3 after 4797, BIGDOG after 6454, DC2 after 39469, or DC4 after 4968." (As you can see, DC4 has the same up-to-date vector that DC3 had a moment ago.) DC2 sees that the only new record that it has originated at DC2 and has a USN of 39473, so replicates it to DC4. DC4 stores that information, including the fact that the information originated with DC2 and updates its up-to-date vector table entry for DC2 to 39473.

Note that as of now, all four DCs have the latest information. Additionally, all four DCs have an up-to-date vector table entry for DC2 of 39473. Thus, when any DCs consider sending the information on Tom's new manager to any other DC, they stop, as they see the other DC's up-to-date vector and realize that the other DC already knows!

Peeking at AD Replication

How can you monitor AD replication? You've already seen how to use REPADMIN to find up-to-date vectors. It'll do other stuff, too.

Finding Replication Partners REPADMIN will also tell you what systems are replication partners with a given DC Just type **repadmin /showrepl *DCname naming-context*** where DCname is just the DNS name of a domain controller and naming-context is the LDAP name of the naming context. Here's an excerpt of the output from `repadmin /showrepl bigdog dc=bigfirm,dc=biz`:

```
C:\>repadmin /showrepl bigdog dc=bigfirm,dc=biz
Default-First-Site-Name\BIGDOG
DC Options: IS_GC
Site Options: (none)
DC object GUID: 8ab4d1e6-c1e9-4d4a-ac31-deae028ac046
DC invocationID: 8ab4d1e6-c1e9-4d4a-ac31-deae028ac046

==== INBOUND NEIGHBORS =======================================

dc=bigfirm,dc=biz
    Default-First-Site-Name\DC3 via RPC
        DC object GUID: 17311f00-9de0-4484-a7cf-2115a4c9a184
        Last attempt @ 2003-01-18 16:13:06 was successful.
    Default-First-Site-Name\DC2 via RPC
        DC object GUID: 2cebe5be-f5e8-4f08-85ef-b4c6123d1600
        Last attempt @ 2003-01-18 16:13:24 was successful.
```

Here's what this is telling you: First, notice the `DSA Options: IS_GC`; that tells you that this server is a global catalog server. Second, you see that this replicates with DC3, which is in the site named Default-First-Site-Name. (I'll cover sites in a moment.) It also replicates to DC2 in the same site. Finally, you see when it last replicated.

Seeing High-Water Marks You can see a DC's high-water marks by adding `/verbose` to the `/showrepl` command.

So, for example, to see the high-watermark table for DC2 as seen from BIGDOG's perspective, use REPADMIN like so:

```
C:\>repadmin /showrepl bigdog dc=bigfirm,dc=biz /verbose
... (skipping output) ...

==== INBOUND NEIGHBORS =======================================

dc=bigfirm,dc=biz
    Default-First-Site-Name\DC2 via RPC ...
        USNs: 34330/OU, 34330/PU
        Last attempt @ 2003-01-18 16:45:18 was successful.
```

You'll see a line for each replication partner; I've skipped some output to keep the size manageable, as the `/verbose` option tends to be, well, verbose. The high-watermark value is the number followed by the `/OU`—34330, in the case of that example. That's the highest USN from DC2 that BIGDOG has seen.

Forcing Replication You can force any two replication partners to replicate a particular naming context with the `/replicate` option:

```
repadmin /replicate destination-DC source-DC namingcontext
```

For example, to force DC2 to pull information from BIGDOG:

```
c:\>repadmin /replicate dc2 bigdog dc=bigfirm,dc=biz
Sync from bigdog to dc2 completed successfully.
```

It would be convenient sometimes to tell AD to get off its butt and replicate every DC with every DC *now*, and it'd be really great if there were one command to do that. Unfortunately there isn't, but you *can* tell a given DC to replicate with all of its partners with REPADMIN via the `repadmin /syncall` *destinationDCname namingcontext* command. So, for example, to tell BIGDOG to replicate with all of its replication partners in win2ktest.com, I'd type this:

```
repadmin /syncall bigdog.win2ktest.com dc=win2ktest,dc=com
```

Logging Replication Info to the Event Log   Those are the basics of how the AD shuffles information around its various sites and domain controllers without duplicating efforts. Would you like to watch the replication process for yourself? Then look in `HKEY_LOCAL_MACHINE\SYSTEM\CurrentControlSet\Services\NTDS\Diagnostics`. There are about a dozen value entries in there, and they can all accept numeric values between 0 and 5. 0 means "don't tell me anything"; 5 means "fill up the Event log with lots of replication details!" And I *do* mean fill it up. It's interesting stuff, but there's a *lot* there.

Sites Revisited

Once you've built your TCP/IP infrastructure, you've got to tell the Active Directory about it. There are several reasons for that, but the most important is that the Active Directory is smarter than the old SAM-based NT 4 domain system in the way that it uses bandwidth. When replicating from domain controller to domain controller, it needs to know whether it's communicating via a high-speed link, and thus can be voluble without worrying about choking the link, or if perhaps it's talking to its domain controller sibling over a 56K link and then will take the time to compress the data a bit, becoming a trifle more terse and bandwidth friendly.

But the domain controller can't know the answer to that question unless you help it. A DC knows that it can communicate at high speed with another DC if they're both in the same *site*. But how does it know that?

How Sites Work

The answer is this: They look to find themselves in the `Servers` container of one of the `Sites` containers of the Active Directory. There is a separate container for each *site*, where a site is defined as "a collection of subnets that communicate with each other at very high data rates." You define sites and then place domain controllers in sites.

Workstations and servers, however, don't get that help. They've got to choose domain controllers to log them and their users in, and clearly they want to be logged in by a nearby domain controller. They determine who's nearby by examining what subnet *they're* in, then the subnet that each domain controller's in to figure out which DC is nearest. They need to know which subnets are close to one another—in other words, which subnets are in the same sites.

"But," you might wonder, "how did the Active Directory figure out what sites it had, what subnets it had, and which subnets go into what sites?" *That's* the part that requires a little administrative elbow grease, so let's see how to apply that elbow grease. Our tool of choice will be a snap-in called Active Directory Sites and Services, located in Administrative Tools. Open it and you'll see a screen like Figure 8.57.

FIGURE 8.57

Initial Active Directory Sites and Services screen

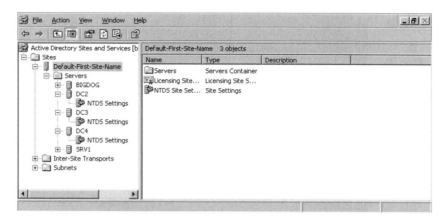

Notice that there's only one site, one called Default-First-Site-Name. When you create an Active Directory forest, the AD just creates a site by that name and assumes that everything's in it. Open up Default-First-Site-Name, and you'll see that your domain controllers are in there. The idea with setting up AD's site topology is that you must:

◆ Define each site.
◆ Define each subnet.
◆ Assign each subnet to a site.

From there, the domain controllers figure out by themselves to which site they belong.

Renaming Default-First-Site-Name

Let's first rename our first site from that goofy Default-First-Site-Name to something simple like HQ.

1. Open Active Directory Sites and Services.
2. Open the Sites folder to reveal the folder labeled `Default-First-Site-Name`.
3. Right-click the `Default-First-Site-Name` folder.
4. Choose Rename.
5. The name Default-First-Site-Name will be highlighted. Just overtype it with **HQ** and click anywhere else on the screen.

This works best if you do it *early* in your AD creation. In fact, it's really best to rename `Default-First-Site-Name` when you create your first DC. You *may* have to reboot your DCs to make this take effect, although restarting the Netlogon service on them may do the trick.

Defining a Site

Suppose I set up another site, across town from my first site. The Active Directory needs to know about that site. Right-click the Sites folder and choose New Site, and you see a screen like Figure 8.58.

FIGURE 8.58

Creating a new site

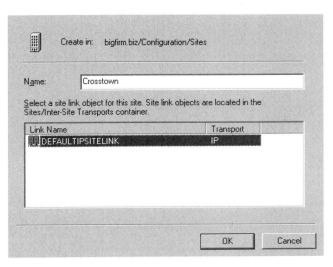

I just fill in a name for the new site (Crosstown), and then click the DEFAULTIPSITELINK object and click OK. When I do, I get a message box like Figure 8.59.

FIGURE 8.59

Checklist for hooking up the new site

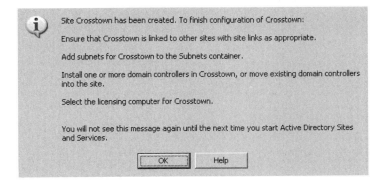

Defining a Subnet and Placing It in a Site

Next, I'll describe the subnets in my enterprise. Suppose the original site is at 206.246.253.0 and the Crosstown site is at 200.200.200.0. I need to tell Site Manager about these subnets. Right-click the Subnets folder and choose New Folder and you'll see a dialog like Figure 8.60, where I define the 206 subnet and associate it with HQ.

FIGURE 8.60

Creating a new subnet

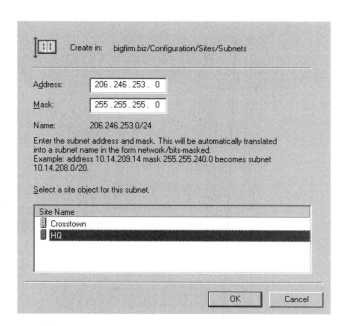

Notice that AD then asks me to associate the subnet with a particular site. I'll define another subnet for the Crosstown site, 200.200.200.0, as well, and now Active Directory Sites and Services will look like Figure 8.61.

FIGURE 8.61

Sites and Services after defining sites and subnet

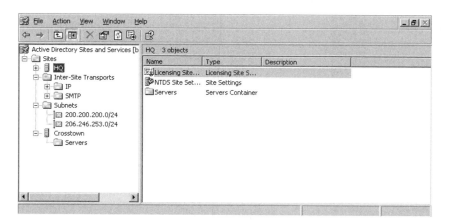

Placing a Server in a Site

Right now all four of bigfirm.biz's DCs are in HQ. Suppose DC3 belongs in Crosstown. I could tell AD that by finding DC3 in the HQ\Servers folder in Sites, right-clicking it, and choosing Move to see a dialog box like Figure 8.62.

FIGURE 8.62

Moving a server

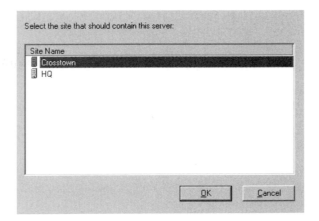

It's a little bit of work, but arranging your servers in Sites and Services Manager pays off if your enterprise spans WAN links.

Inter-Site Replication

Now that you've seen how to create subnets and a site, let's see how to get them to communicate with one another.

You already know that within a site, AD replicates by building a replication topology that is either a two-way loop (in a site with seven or fewer DCs) or a mesh. But a loop or mesh topology across WAN links would be inefficient, so AD instead creates a minimal spanning tree, meaning that it creates a set of site-to-site replication paths that minimizes the load on your WAN bandwidth. Take a look at the AD Sites and Services snap-in shown in Figure 8.63.

FIGURE 8.63

AD Sites and Services for a two-subnet, two-site enterprise

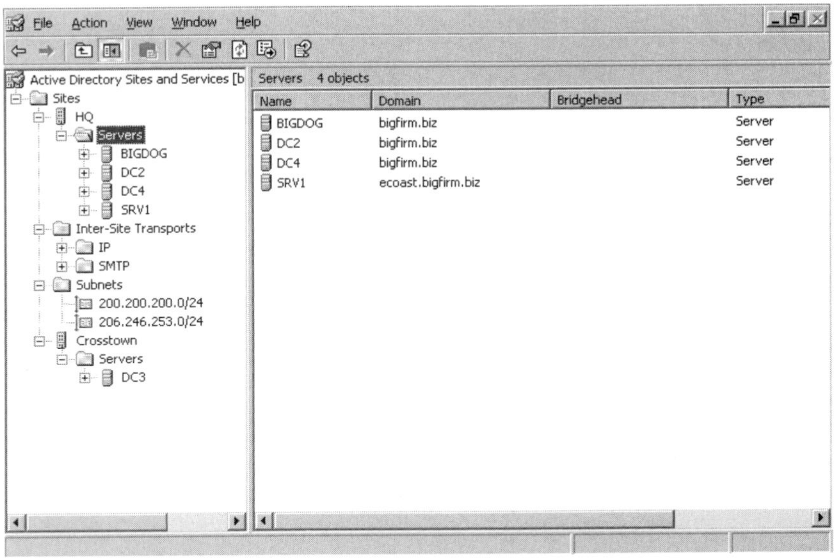

This is obviously a very simple "enterprise." But it'll serve fine to let me explain what you've got to worry about in a multisite world. You see, once you set up your sites, then they figure out how to replicate all by themselves, *within the site*. But across sites, they need a little help. You need to define how bits get from (in the example pictured) HQ to Crosstown.

Huh? The AD needs you to tell it how to get from point A to point B? Hasn't it ever heard of IP? I mean, Ping can figure out how to get from HQ to Crosstown—why can't the AD?

The AD can easily figure out how to get from one place to another, but it doesn't know three things:

♦ If you have more than one connection from point A to point B, as you might in an intranet or the Internet, is there a connection that you'd prefer that the AD uses over another one?

♦ Is the connection available all the time, or only part of the time?

♦ Would you like to use real-time RPC connections to replicate, or e-mail-based SMTP connections?

You tell AD about connections between sites by creating *site links*. Right-click either the IP or SMTP folders, choose New/Site Link, and you'll see a dialog box like the one in Figure 8.64.

FIGURE 8.64

Creating a new site link

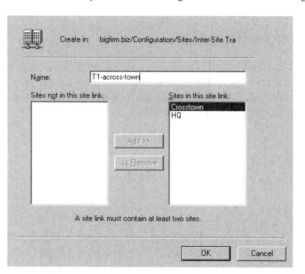

In this dialog box, I tell AD which sites this link will join, name the link, and click OK. An icon will then appear in Active Directory Sites and Services in the IP folder (or the SMTP folder if you created it in there, but the chances are that you'll almost always create site links with IP, as you'll see). Double-click the site link object and you'll see a dialog box (Figure 8.65) that looks just a little different from the one that let you create the site link.

This dialog box is *very* important for three reasons. First of all, notice the spinner box labeled Cost; you'll use that to nudge the AD to use a link more or less. The AD will choose lower-cost links over higher-cost links. Second, you can control how often the AD tries to replicate over this link. Notice that site-to-site linking is quite different from intrasite links; replicating across a WAN link every five minutes might not be a low-cost approach for a wide-area based directory service, unless you put up all of those WAN links solely for AD's convenience! The minimum interval that you can specify for a replication across a WAN link is 15 minutes—the maximum intrasite time for replication. Click the Change Schedule button, and you'll see a dialog box like Figure 8.66.

FIGURE 8.65

Site link properties

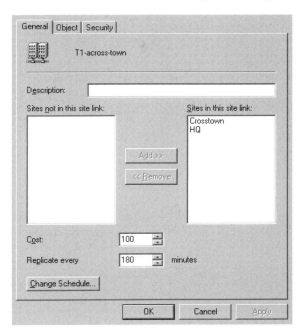

FIGURE 8.66

Setting the replication schedule

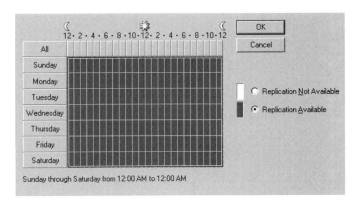

It could be that the HQ-to-Crosstown link is a dial-up link that's only up from 2 P.M. to 3 P.M. on Tuesdays. In that case, you can tell AD not to bother trying to replicate before then.

WARNING   *AD sites* must *replicate at least once every 60 days or less. AD throws away objects that have been inactive for 60 days, so if one site and another didn't talk for a few months, then they'd start deleting objects from their copies of the AD that they weren't using but that other DCs in other sites were still using. Do not reconnect a DC that hasn't replicated to the AD for more than 60 days back to the network.*

Finally, you create a site link either in the IP or SMTP folder to indicate how to replicate. SMTP *sounds* like a great answer: It doesn't need to be running all of the time, the link needn't be up that often—heck—we might even be able to send replication updates via Hotmail!

Unfortunately, it's not that useful. First of all, you can only replicate the forestwide schema and configuration naming contexts, so you could not use only SMTP to, for example, update one domain controller in domain X from another domain controller in domain X that was on a different site. They must replicate with RPC, a real-time connection. And, second, you can't use just any old mail server. You need a public key certificate on that server to ensure secure mail before security-conscious AD will let you use it to replicate. (Oddly enough, you *could* do domain replication in the betas that appeared mid-way through Windows 2000's gestation. But nothing much has changed in Server 2003 on that score, unfortunately.)

Once you tell AD all of these things about sites, a souped-up version of the Knowledge Consistency Checker called the Inter-Site Topology Generator or ISTG (there's one ISTG DC at each site, and they choose themselves, so there's no FSMO seizing to worry about here, it's automatic) talks to the other ISTGs and figures out which links to use so as minimize cost.

Understanding Functional Levels

Too bad previous versions of NT weren't a flop.

If they *had* been flops, then we wouldn't have to worry about mixing versions of NT. If Microsoft knew that you greeted every new version of NT by throwing out the old stuff and upgrading every single server and workstation—"You! All of the 2000 stuff! Out *now*! And that goes for the NT 4 stuff as well, it's not even supported any more!"—then it'd be easy to add new features. But that doesn't happen, nor should it—the old stuff runs pretty well, in general.

Mixed and Native Modes in Windows 2000

But that introduces some problems as to what ADs can and can't do—and so we have functional levels. When Microsoft came out with Windows 2000, then they might have said, "You can't use 2000-based AD domains until you FDISK all of your NT 4 DCs," but that would have been a marketing disaster and would have annoyed all of us. (That's what I meant when I said that it was too bad that earlier versions of NT weren't flops; when NT came out, in theory it followed a Microsoft networking OS called LAN Manager, but it had a tiny market share and so very few people worried about "How will I convert my LAN Manager domains to NT 3.1 domains?" That's not the story for Server 2003, however, as NT 4 and Windows 2000 are collectively the most popular server OS.)

So Microsoft said that sure, you could continue to use your NT 4–based BDCs in an Active Directory. You upgraded the primary domain controller to Windows 2000 and that 2000 box created an AD, but it also continued to work with the old NT 4–based BDCs, Clearly the NT 4 boxes don't understand (for example) OUs, and so the NT 4–based BDCs couldn't really be full members of the

DC family if the 2000-based DCs exercised a lot of their new-to-Windows-2000 powers. The result was Mixed mode.

A Mixed-mode AD was one that had a Windows 2000 system acting as a domain controller and holding the PDC role or, rather, the PDC emulator role, and any number of BDCs running NT 4. Windows 2000–based ADs would not exercise a few powers—universal groups and multimaster replication are the most important—until the last NT 4 BDC was shut off. Once all of a 2000-based AD's DCs were running Windows 2000, though, an administrator could click a button in Active Directory Users and Computers that would shift the domain into Native mode, and at that point a 2000-based AD could strut its stuff.

Let me stress that all that you have to upgrade to go to Native mode is the DCs. All other systems could be NT 4 systems for all that a 2000-based AD cares. Native versus Mixed mode is only a matter of the OSes on the DCs. As you'll see, that's the case with 2003's "modes" as well.

Domain Functional Levels in Server 2003

In Windows 2000–based ADs, there were only two possible conditions: either a population of DCs that were all 2000-based or a population of DCs that included both 2000 and NT 4—that's why there were only two modes. But ADs that include Server 2003 can have several possible combinations of DCs, each with their own mode or, in 2003's preferred term, *functional level* or, as I sometimes write it "domain functional level" to distinguish it from *forest* functional levels that you'll meet soon.

You change a domain's functional level by opening Active Directory Users and Computers and right-clicking the icon representing the domain. Choose Raise Domain Functional Level and you'll see a dialog box like Figure 8.67.

FIGURE 8.67

Raising a domain's functional level

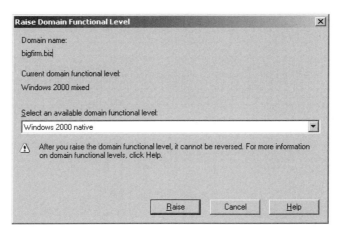

In this case, the domain is at something called Windows 2000 mixed functional level, and you've got the option to change to two other possibilities. Here's what you get from each functional level:

◆ **Windows 2000 mixed domain functional level**: a domain that can have some DCs running Windows Server 2003, others Windows 2000 Server, and still others NT 4 Server. This still works if you're running only 2003 and 2000 or just 2003, but in those cases you'll want to raise the functional level to enable your AD to use as many features as is possible. This is basically just Windows 2000's Mixed mode, but with 2003 servers added. Newly built AD domains, domains upgraded from 2000-based mixed mode ADs, and domains directly upgraded from NT 4 domains start in this functional level. Even if your network consists of a forest composed of one domain which is in turn contains just one DC and that DC is running Server 2003, it'll be in Windows 2000 mixed domain functional level. Like 2000's Mixed mode domains, these domains lack multimaster replication and universal groups. They also cannot use something called "SID histories," which we'll cover in the later "Migration Strategies" section, and they cannot convert distribution groups (e-mail lists) to security groups (that is, regular old groups) and vice versa.

♦ **Windows 2000 native domain functional level**: a domain with only 2000-based or 2003-based DCs. Like 2000's Native mode, but with Windows Server 2003 DCs added. When you upgrade a 2000-based AD then you get this functional level, or you get it if you raise the functional level yourself. You can't use 2000 native functional level if you have any NT 4-based DCs. Systems in 2000 native domain functional level can use universal groups, multimaster replication, SID histories, and they can convert between distribution and security groups. They really only miss out on one thing: they cannot rename domains, or at least they can't use the new-to-2003 simplified domain renaming feature.

♦ **Windows Server 2003 interim domain functional level**: I honestly don't know much about this because I've not found much of a use for it. You can raise your domain to this level only if none of your domain's DCs are running Windows 2000. NT 4 BDCs are OK and of course Windows Server 2003–based DCs are fine. You can only get to this functional level with a separate tool from Microsoft and as far as I can see you get nothing out of an interim functional level that you don't get from a regular old 2000 mixed domain functional level. (Well, there are a few small things, but nothing of any significance.)

♦ **Windows Server 2003 domain functional level**: the Big Enchilada. To get here you've got to have all of your DCs in the domain running Windows Server 2003. And once you've reached that lofty level, are you ready for what new functionality you get? Well, here it comes: you can easily rename domains.

"Whaaaaat?" you say? Okay, there's another important reason to get to 2003 functional level. You see, you can't upgrade your *forest* functional level until all of the domains in the forest are at 2003 domain functional level. Which brings us to...

Forest Functional Levels in Server 2003

2000 only had different kinds of domains because that's all that NT 4 had—domains. But both Windows 2000–based ADs and 2003-based ADs have forests, leading inevitably to different functional levels for forests.

When you upgrade DCs or domains in an existing forest, or if you create a new forest, then 2003 assumes for safety's sake that not all DCs and domains are entirely 2003-based, and so it will not stretch its wings to use all of the new capabilities that 2003 offers. To get all of those abilities, you must shift the forest from its default level, which is called Windows 2000 forest functional level, to the all-2003 setting, Windows Server 2003 forest functional level.

You raise a forest's functional level with Active Directory Domains and Trusts—Start/Administrative Tools/Active Directory Domains and Trusts. Right-click the icon in the left pane labeled Active Directory Domains and Trusts and you'll see Figure 8.68.

FIGURE 8.68

Raising a forest's functional level

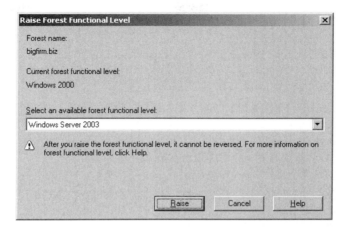

You can't go to Windows Server 2003 forest functional level unless every single DC in every single domain in the forest is running Windows 2003. But think about that—doesn't that mean that all of your domains must be in 2003 domain functional level before Domains and Trusts lets you raise the forest functional level? No, it doesn't, as it turns out. When you open the dialog in Figure 8.68, then you'll either get the screen that you see in that figure, or you'll get a message that says, "You can't go to 2003 level," and tells you (or, rather, offers to generate a text file telling you) exactly which DCs must be upgraded before you can go to 2003 forest functional level. When you right-click AD Domains and Trusts, then, the forest does a quick census of its list of DCs. If they're all 2003-based DCs, then you get the option to raise the forest functional level, and, if not, you get the option to see which ones must be upgraded. That leads to what seemed, to me anyway, an odd thing: you can raise your forest's functional level even *if* the domains are all set at Windows 2000 native domain functional level—they needn't be at Windows Server 2003 domain functional level. As it turns out, this is something of a convenience. Provided that all of your DCs are running 2003 and you raise your forest's functional level, then AD Domains and Trusts also automatically raises the functional level of all of your domains to 2003 domain functional level.

So what do you get from this improved functional level? Several items that I've discussed elsewhere, but that I'll summarize here:

◆ **Transitive forest trusts**. One trust makes every domain in each of two forests trust each other... but only if both forests are at 2003 forest functional level.

◆ **More flexible group membership replication**. 2000's old problem about "if you change a group's membership and I change that same group membership at about the same time, then one of our changes will be lost" goes away in a 2003-level forest.

◆ **Better inter-site routing**. 2003 saw a completely massive rewrite of the code that handles site-to-site replication, with the result that where 2000-based forests would fall apart at about 200 sites, 2003-based forests can handle up to 5000 sites.

- ◆ **GC fixes.** Any change to the structure of the global catalog, such as the type that usually happens when you install an AD-aware application, causes GCs on a 2000-level forest to completely panic; they dump their entire databases and rebuild them from scratch, causing massive replication loads over the network. 2003-level forests are much smarter, as their GCs focus only on the changes to the database, rather than restarting from square one.

- ◆ **Schema redefines.** AD's somewhat inflexible schema structure loosens up a bit on a 2003-level forest. You still can't delete or undo schema changes, but the schema manages itself to ensure that you'll never have one AD-aware app accidentally step on another AD-aware app's schema changes.

As anyone who lived through an initial AD rollout under 2000 knows, the road to native mode was sometimes long, and I'm sure that'll be the case when moving a forest to Windows Server 2003 forest functional level. But once there, it's worth it. As I've observed elsewhere, you *paid* for this stuff…you may as well get what you paid for.

AD's Long Arm: Group Policy Overview

I've talked so far in mildly vague terms about how you can accomplish different kinds of control in an Active Directory. The specific tool for exerting much of that control is group policies, something that first appeared in Windows 2000 but that many people don't know much about even today because it seems too complex—but it isn't, once you understand a few things. Here's an overview of what they do and how they work but, again, it's just an overview—I'll cover it in more detail in the next chapter.

Differences in System Policy and Group Policy Implementation

With Windows 9*x*, Me, and NT 4's system policies, you could control a wide variety of things—you could give a user a particular Start/Programs menu, give him a particular look to a desktop, restrict the user from running many programs, and the like. All of these restrictions would be collected into a single file called NTCONFIG.POL (for NT 4, 2000, XP, or Server 2003) or CONFIG.POL (for Windows 9*x* and Me), which you'd then place on each of the domain controller's NETLOGON shares. When a Windows 9*x*, Me, NT 4, Windows 2000, XP, or Server 2003 system starts up and logs onto an NT 4 or AD domain, then that system downloads CONFIG.POL or NTCONFIG.POL and performs whatever instructions are in encoded in the POL file—again, to modify the Start Programs menu, change the desktop, or whatever. That's an important point—system policies work because the client operating systems request the policy files and follow their orders, not because the DC that logs them on forces the files and settings upon the client (and remember here "client" can mean *any* machine logging onto a domain, whether it's a workstation, member server, or DC—DCs must log on also).

You can have only one NTCONFIG.POL or CONFIG.POL policy file. And you did read that right in the previous paragraph—you can use NTCONFIG.POL/CONFIG.POL–type system policies on *either* NT 4–based domains or AD domains. Why can you still use system policies on ADs when ADs have the more powerful *group* policies available to them? Because systems prior to Windows 2000 are completely deaf to group policies. Recall that I said that policies work because the client knows to download and execute them; Windows 9*x*, Me, and NT 4 systems don't know to go get group policies, and so system policies make sense on AD domains that have these older systems connected to them. Again, Windows 2000 and later systems will *also* look for, download, and execute system policies—but *only* if there are no group policies present on the domain and, of course, NT 4–type domains will never contain any group policies.

So system policies are contained in a file, stored on the NETLOGON share of DCs in an NT 4 or AD domain, and work because many Microsoft OSes know to download and use them. How are group policies different?

- ◆ First, group policies can only exist on an Active Directory domain—you can't put them on an NT 4 domain.

- ◆ Second, group policies do a lot more than system policies do. For example, you can use group policies to deploy software to a desktop automatically.

- ◆ Third, group policies clean up after themselves when removed, unlike system policies.

- ◆ Fourth, group policies get applied more often than do system policies. System policies only get applied when you log on. Group policies get applied when you turn the computer on, when you log on, and automatically at random times throughout the day.

- ◆ Fifth, you have a lot finer control over who gets—or *doesn't* get—a policy.

- ◆ Sixth, group policies are neat, but they only apply to Windows 2000, XP, and Server 2003 systems.

That's the overview; here are few more details.

Group Policies Apply to Sites, Domains, and OUs—Not Groups (Mostly)

System policies applied to domains only. But as you've seen, AD has the notions of sites and OUs. Group policies are OU-aware and site-aware; you can create a GPO—group policy object, recall, a record on the AD that contains one or more group policy instructions—and apply it to domains, OUs, or sites.

But what about groups? Why did I mention OUs rather than groups? Because oddly enough, "group" policy objects don't apply to groups—only sites, domains, or OUs. You can't directly say, "Everyone in the ACCOUNTANTS group gets QuickBooks Pro 2002 deployed to their desktop." Now, if ACCOUNTANTS were an OU rather than a group, then you *could* deploy QuickBooks Pro 2005 to all of the accountants. (As I write this, there isn't a QuickBooks Pro 2005, but I'm guessing that there will be.)

Is it *completely* impossible to apply a policy to a group, then? Well, not exactly.

Policy Filtering and Group Policies

What I said in the preceding section wasn't completely true—you *can* deploy an application to a group. But how you do it is a bit sneaky.

As you've read, AD lets you apply group policies to sites, domains, and/or organizational units. Microsoft even has an acronym for those three—SDOU. But you can use someone's group membership to influence whether or not he gets the effect of a particular policy.

I've already said that GPOs are not files, but they share one thing with files: they have permissions associated with them. And you can apply permissions to groups. One of the permissions associated with GPOs is Apply Group Policy; if this permission isn't granted, then the policy doesn't apply.

To apply a policy to just the ACCOUNTANTS group, then, you'd apply a policy to the entire domain, but then you'd set permissions for the Domain Users group so that Apply Group Policy was not allowed, and then you'd add a separate permission for just the Accountants group, allowing them to apply the group policy.

Policy filtering is a bit troublesome for two reasons. First, it can greatly complicate trying to figure out what someone else did when setting up policies: If you were to walk into an already-configured enterprise without any documentation and try to figure out what policies are supposed to do for that enterprise, you'd have your work cut out for you. As a matter of fact, there's an acronym relevant to that: RSOP, which stands for Resultant Set of Policy. To see what it means, consider the following question. I've got a new user, Bob, in a given organizational unit, which is in a particular domain, and Bob's machine is in a particular site. That means that the site may have policies that apply to Bob, the domain may have policies that apply to Bob, and the OU may have policies that apply to Bob. And don't forget that OUs can live inside OUs, so there might be an entire hierarchy of OUs that Bob lives in—each of *those* OUs could have policies attached to them. And on top of it all, policy filtering may affect whether or not all of those policies apply to Bob. The question is, which policies apply to Bob? It's not an easy question—you have to thread through which policies apply, the order in which they apply—a later policy generally overrides an earlier policy, although it can be configured differently—and then policy filtering must be taken into account. Determining the set of policies that actually affect Bob—his RSOP— is a difficult computational task, and you'll see a class of applications called *RSOP modelers* whose job is to do that very thing.

The second concern about policy filtering is that it slows down the process of applying GPOs to a user when logging in, which slows down the login process.

Group Policies Undo Themselves When Removed

One of the troublesome things about NT 4's system policies is that once a system policy is applied to a user account or a machine, the policy remains in place even if it is removed from the domain controllers. So, for example, if for some reason you create a system policy to set everyone's background color to green, then the Registry of every computer that logs in from that point on will be changed to set the background to green. If enough users scream about this and you remove the policy, their screens will remain green. They could certainly *change* the color themselves, but it'd be nice if the policy had undone itself on the way out. With Windows 2000, XP, or Server 2003 clients, that happens: Remove a policy and its effects are reversed. This can be quite powerful: For example, if you used a group policy to deploy an application and then remove the policy, the application uninstalls itself!

You Needn't Log In to Get a Group Policy

NT 4 only applied system policies at startup (for machine policies) and logon (for user policies). In contrast, Windows 2000, XP, and Server 2003 systems apply group policies every 90 minutes or so for workstations and member servers and every five minutes for domain controllers.

What You Can Do with Group Policies

You can do basically anything with group policies that you could do with system policies, and lots more. Here are a few examples:

Deploy software   You can gather all of the files necessary to install a piece of software into a *package*, put that package on a server somewhere, and then use group policies to point a user's desktop at that package. The user sees that the application is available, and again, you accomplish all that from a central location rather than having to visit every desktop. The first time the user tries to start the application, it installs without any intervention from the user.

Set user rights   You may know from NT 3.*x* and 4.*x* that NT had the notion of "rights," the ability to do a particular function. One such example is the one I've already used about a standard user not being able to change his workstation's time and date. Under NT 4, you had to visit a machine to modify user rights; now it's controllable via a GPO, meaning again that you needn't wear out any shoe leather to change a distant machine's rights.

Restrict the applications that users can run   You can control a user's desktop to the point where that user could only run a few applications—perhaps Outlook, Word, and Internet Explorer, for example.

Control system settings   The easiest way to control disk space quotas is with group policies. Many Windows 2000 systems are most easily controlled with policies; with some systems, policies are the *only* method to enable and control those systems.

Set logon, logoff, startup, and shutdown scripts   Where NT 4 only supported logon scripts, Windows 2000 allows any or all of these four events to trigger a script, and you use GPOs to control which scripts run.

Simplify and restrict programs   You can use GPOs to remove many of the features from Internet Explorer, Windows Explorer, and other programs using GPOs.

General desktop restriction   You can remove most or all of the items on a user's Start button, keep her from adding printers, or disallow her from logging out or modifying her desktop configuration at all. With all of the policies turned on, you can really lock down a user's desktop. (Too much locking down may lead to unlocking the automatic rifles, however, so be careful.)

There's lots more to work with in policies, but that was a basic introduction to get you started. (You can read more in the next chapter, and you'll see references to group policies throughout the rest of the book.) Let's return now to the larger issues of AD—namely, how best to get it on your system.

Watching the Network: Auditing with the Active Directory

You *know* they're out there, don't you?

You know—the bad guys. The ones who are trying to Take Down Your Network.

Okay, that's a big exaggeration. There really aren't all that many people attacking networks, and, truthfully, most networks face more threats from *inside* people than outsiders. So my pathetic scare tactic in the first three sentences wasn't all that effective. Hmmm, let's see if I *can* find a scenario sufficiently frightening to the average administrator to get your attention. Ah, got it! How about this one: Something goes wrong, or it seems that something went wrong, and so the boss asks: "What kind of network activity have we had recently? Are there any clues to who's logged on recently, or tried to?"

And you have look at her and say, "Ummm, I really don't know."

Now, *that's* scary. So let's see how to answer that question with verve and aplomb, or at least some of how to answer that question with verve and aplomb—through audits.

What You Can Audit

AD will optionally track a number of activities and save what it finds about those activities in event log entries, in the Security log. (And let me warn you, some of those entries are somewhat less than totally useful—but this is still worth doing.) Windows 2000 and every subsequent version of NT support several kinds of audits:

- Audit account logon events
- Audit logon events
- Audit account management
- Audit directory service access
- Audit policy change
- Audit system events
- Audit process tracking
- Audit object access
- Audit privilege

LOGON EVENTS

Audit logon events and audit account logon events are two slightly different items that are both quite valuable in tracking who did what where to whom. As you know, domain-based networks rely on a small number of computers to validate—log on—users. So a user Ray might try to access a member server \\SV1, and \\SV1 might try to authenticate that user at a domain controller \\DC2. Here's what these two settings would track:

- Audit account logon events would tell \\DC2 to log the fact that it was asked to validate Ray and did. That would appear in \\DC2's log.
- Audit logon events would tell \\SV1 to log the fact that it needed to check to see that Ray was a recognized user prior to letting him access something on that machine. The log entry would appear on \\SV1's log.

Did you notice the point about where the entries live? That's important: *There is no central domain repository of logs.* Part of your job as an administrator is to collect and manage the logs of all of your systems. Fortunately, the only logs you typically need are the ones for the domain controllers and members servers…although workstation logs can be sometimes useful as well.

OBJECT ACCESS

Audit object access is possibly the most important, or at least shares the most important spot, in my opinion, with the logon events audits. Why? Because you can ask your systems to keep track of who reads, writes, deletes, or creates any file or any group of files on themselves. Wondering if the user deleted his e-mail PST file or it disappeared all by itself? With object access auditing, you're able to look at the user's workstation's logs and tell exactly when the file met its maker.

Tracking files and directories on a given machine—or tracking any other object, for that matter, as printers count as objects as well—requires *two* steps: First, enable object access auditing on the computer that stores the object and, second, tell the computer to audit that particular object. You see, by default simply turning object access on at a particular computer won't result in a single entry in the Security event log. You've got to then say, "Watch this directory" or, "Watch this file" or even, "Watch this file, but only when Joe is working with it." You'll see more about how to do that in Chapter 11.

ACCOUNT MANAGEMENT

As its name implies, this is also a good item to audit. Any changes to user or group accounts get logged here. Create a user, create a group, modify a group's membership, change a password, and you're logged.

POLICY CHANGE

Think of this as an audit of the auditors: Turn off logging to do something sneaky, and you will have left behind an entry that tells when you turned logging off. It also logs changes in user rights—why exactly did that administrator let that user log on locally to the domain controller between 9:50 and 10:10, anyway—and changes in trust policies.

PRIVILEGE USE

This is a potentially useful tool but, boy, does it generate output. Every single time that you exercise a right—not a permission—then it's logged here. You'd be surprised how often you exercise rights— logging on, shutting down a system, changing the system time, taking ownership, and so on—so be prepared for larger logs if you turn this on. It'd be great if you could just turn on one or two particular privileges, but I've not found a way to do that.

SYSTEM EVENTS

System events doesn't generate all that many entries and is probably worth running. It logs whenever you restart the computer or shut down the computer and also logs whenever you do something that "affects the system security or Security log," in the documentation's words. My experience is that it tracks the Security log—when you cleared it, resized it, and so on.

DIRECTORY SERVICE ACCESS

This is a kind of catch-all that logs any activity that trips a permission on the Active Directory. Think of the Active Directory as a container and users, machines, policies, organization units, and the like as just objects in that container, such as files in a directory. Just as NTFS permissions on a directory tell you when someone's been creating or deleting files, this setting tells you who's been doing things that modify the AD. I have not found much use for this. It *seems* as if anything that causes an Account Management logging entry also causes a Directory Service Access entry.

PROCESS TRACKING

It's a programmer thing…we admins wouldn't understand. This tracks activity between a program and the operating system—creating handles, starting execution, calling other programs, and the like. You probably won't find this useful…

...Or *would* you? I've used this now and then to find out why something didn't work. A well locked-down system is a good thing, but it can be frustrating sometimes. When I first tried to learn Indexing Services, I played with Indexing Services on my Web server for a week but got nothing to work. Nada, niente, zip. Very frustrating. Then I set up an out-of-the-box system and tried Indexing Services...and it worked. The problem? My Web server was—doh!—locked down, like all good Web servers. Unfortunately, I'd locked it down so tightly that I locked Indexing Services out of being able to access anything. So it was working, all right; it was just coming up snake eyes whenever I asked it a question.

At times like this, I'd love a "Security Monitor"—a little window on my desktop that says, "Yup, you just tried to run XYZ program and you used all the right commands, but nothing happened, because you lack the permissions to do what XYZ was trying to do. You need to be a Domain Admin to do *that* kind of thing, dodo." The next best thing can be process tracking—just flip it on and try to do whatever's not working. (Do not leave it running unnecessarily; it will fill up your Security log in no time flat.) When the app fails, go back and shut off process tracking, then look in the log to see what right you needed but didn't have. I don't want to oversell this—you run a *lot* of processes, and the output's not necessarily crystal-clear—but you can often get just the clue you need to make something work.

How to Audit

You audit network activity by enabling one or more kinds of auditing on the computer in question. Let me stress that: If you've got 1000 machines in your network, then you may need all 1000 machines to have auditing turned on, depending on what you want to audit. For example, tracking file and directory changes requires having object auditing enabled, so if you wanted to track files on every workstation, then you'd need auditing enabled on every workstation. Which, in the worst-case scenario, would mean visiting every one of those machines. But that's only the worst case; if you have a domain, then it's easier.

You turn auditing on for a particular machine via a policy, either a local policy or a domain-based group policy. I'll discuss local versus domain policies in the next chapter, but here's the short version of the differences: You've already read about the kinds of things that you can do with domain-based group policies, and you can probably see that domain-based group policies are pretty powerful. Ideally in a network with an Active Directory domain then, you'd use the power of domain-based group policies to centralize the process of enabling auditing, and I'll show you how in a minute.

You don't always *have* an Active Directory domain, however, and in case you've not yet built yours but want to start auditing immediately, then here's how to enable auditing: with a tool called the Local Security Policy snap-in. Start it up by clicking Start/Administrative Tools, then Local Security Policy. (You may recognize it from our work with IPSec in Chapter 6.) You'll see an icon in the left pane called Security Settings and, underneath it, folders labeled `Account Policies`, `Local Policies`, `Public Key Policies`, and `IP Security Policies`. Open up the `Local Policies` folder, and you'll see three folders inside: `Audit Policy`, `User Rights Assignment`, and `Security Options`. (Aren't they *all* security options? And aren't the `Account Policies` referred to in the top-level folder by that name referring to the *local* system? The names for this tool perplex me.) Open up `Audit Policy` and you'll see something like Figure 8.69 in the right window.

FIGURE 8.69

Auditing Options

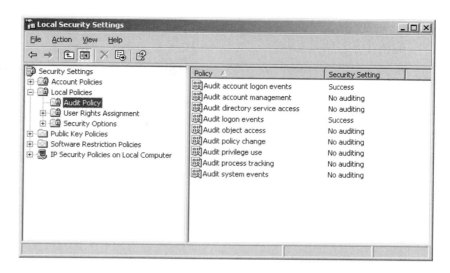

But you probably don't want to have to go visit every single computer to turn this stuff on. That's where a group policy can make life easier. To enable auditing using domain-based group policies, then create a group policy object and look in the Computer Configure/Windows Settings/Local Policies/ Audit Policy. Apply that object to the particular machines for which you want to enable auditing. So, for example, if it's something generic that you want to apply to every machine, then create the group policy object on the domain. But if it only applies to the domain controllers, then apply the policy to their OU. Or, if there's a different group, then use policy filtering—it's covered in the next chapter. (And to see what you actually *see* when you look at a log in the Event Viewer, look to Chapter 18.)

MANAGING LOGS

What, then, should you audit? I can't tell you what's right for you—there's no good answer because you must trade off log management versus coverage level. Look at it this way: If you turn on all logging on every single machine, then in theory you'd have a wealth of knowledge...but you'd need terabytes of storage space to store it all, and in practical terms you'd never get a chance to review it.

At minimum, I'd log logon failures. Logging all logons is potentially interesting, but so many successful logons occur in a day that you end up filling the log with the information. Policy change and system events aren't too numerous—they won't cost much in terms of numbers of events. Privilege use can be valuable but creates more log clutter.

You should also consider how to manage log size with the log settings. Open up any event log in Manage Computer, right-click the log's icon, and choose Properties, and you'll see a dialog box like the one in Figure 8.70.

Notice how the system manages the amount of space that a log takes: You set an amount of disk space for the system to set aside for that log file. The log can't exceed that space. This is actually a security measure; otherwise, an attacker could bring your system down by doing things that the system would log, such as a failed logon attempt. Merely by deliberately trying and failing to log on, the attacker could make the log grow if it weren't set to a maximum size to actually fill your hard disk— crashing your system.

FIGURE 8.70

Configuring the
Security log

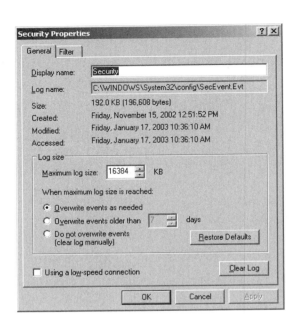

So fixed log sizes protecting you from fill-the-hard-disk attacks are the *good* news; the bad news is that a fixed-size log can be filled up. So you're faced with some more tough choices: What to do to keep that from happening? The system will, at your request, do one of three things when the log fills:

Just overwrite the oldest events. Not a terrible low-maintenance answer, particularly if you provide enough space for the logs. (I recommend that you set the size of each log to 10MB—it's fairly hard to fill up that much space for logging.) But it leaves you open to an attacker doing something bad and then deliberately causing some series of innocuous events to happen over and over again so as to fill up the log with those innocuous events. So let's say that I'm a bad-guy administrator who's just created an administrative account that I will then use for fell purposes. I don't want you to know that I created the account, so I write a little batch file that does something like open a file over and over and over again…"Oops, I guess there was a bug in my batch file," I'll just say. As I know that you're auditing object access to the opened file, then every time that the batch file opens the file, an event gets added to the log. If I let the batch file run long enough, then soon there will be nothing in the log but reports that a batch file opened a file over and over again.

Overwrite events after *x* days. The default behavior; the system erases events after seven days. For complete coverage, you'd have to back up the logs, although with hope you'd know about intrusions within seven days. Old logs are mainly useful for assessment of how long the bad guy's been around.

Clear logs manually. This never erases anything. It's the most secure approach, but again requires you to "touch" every system periodically to back up, archive, and clear the logs. There's also the issue of, "What happens if the log fills?"

By the way, what happens if the log *does* fill up, as in the case that you've told it to keep all events for *x* days or you've told it to never delete events? That's up to you. In that case the system would by default just stop logging new events but keep running. There is a policy that you can set with group policies, however, that causes the server to stop altogether. I don't generally recommend this setting, as it could be clearly used to crash a server—fill the log and the system freezes. And, again, I'd set the logs to 10MB in size. You have to work *really* hard to fill up 10MB in an evening, so it'd be tough for an attacker to use a full log to cover his tracks.

That leads me to another point: What we've talked about so far is not, by far, the hardest part of auditing. The hardest part is managing the darn logs. Ten thousand machines means 10,000 logs. They get larger every day, they fill up, and they've got to be regularly stored somewhere and cleared to make space for more logs. I have not come across an automated way to do that, so we're talking about creating a nontrivial amount of administrative work. Given the size of modern hard disks you certainly could let the event log grow to gigabytes in size, so you wouldn't have to back it up and clear it very often, but then what happens when the bad guy clears the log? All you've got—as you've not backed it up often—is a record of the seemingly suspicious activity that someone cleared the log. Sure, you can look 'em in the eye and ask why they did it, but they can always say it was a mistake.

Logs are only useful if they're respected. Harsh as it sounds, to make them useful you must protect them. There should be a specific procedure for clearing logs, perhaps something that requires two administrators' sign-off. Anyone clearing a log otherwise should face disciplinary review and if security is important enough then you might make clearing a log without authorization an "instant termination" offense. Sound harsh? I don't know—what would you do to a bookkeeper who'd deliberately thrown out a few week's receipt and disbursement records?

Managing Logs: EventComb

Let me leave the issue of auditing and logs with a splash of cold water:

It may well make good sense for you not to bother with auditing and managing event logs.

In the perfect world, you turn logging on for every server and workstation. You also collect the logs on all of those machines to some central place regularly—certainly every day or two—and archive them. You additionally peruse those logs before archiving them, looking for traces of wrongdoing or just incipient system failures.

You've got time for that, right?

Unfortunately, most admins don't. There are third-party tools—NetIQ's got one called Operations Manager that it sold to Microsoft, who's now renamed it Microsoft Operations Manager—but they are expensive, costing you per-user (all users, not just administrators) fees that mount quickly. So here's my final advice on logs: Do the math. Figure out how much in terms of personnel time, equipment, media, and the like that a decent auditing process will cost. And try to assess your downside—what *would* it cost you not to be able to answer the kinds of questions that logs can answer? Present these numbers to the boss and if she still wants you to audit, then tell her how many more people and servers you're going to need.

I live about three quarters of a mile from the Atlantic Ocean in a hurricane-prone area. In the perfect world, I'd have a cool 100-foot-high seawall buried in the ground with a set of huge motors that would spring that seawall up into a deployed position at a few minutes' notice. Gargantuan pumps would stand ready to pump floodwaters away from my house. Massive generators would, at my command, spring to life and power the whole process while driving motors that shutter my house's windows. But in the real world that stuff costs money, and so I've just got insurance, some good water-proof containers for my important documents, and I back up my servers daily. I had to accept a practical level of disaster preparedness…and so does your firm. But *make* the boss examine this trade-off, and do it now—she won't want to hear about this on the morning that you discover that you've been hacked, while you're trying to explain why the logs have been cleared. In practice, you'll come up with some compromise between fully backed up and monitored logs and no logging at all—but get everyone's agreement on it.

Having said all that, you really need a way to look at your logs that doesn't break the bank, and thankfully Microsoft's got a free tool to do that called EventComb.

EventComb is part of a Microsoft document called "Security Operations Guide for Windows 2000 Server." You can download it at www.microsoft.com/downloads/release.asp?releaseid=36834. (And if it's not there when you read this, please don't e-mail me asking where it is. Microsoft likes to rearrange their Web site hourly and I'll just tell you to do the same thing that I'd do—just search the Microsoft Web site for "eventcomb.") That link downloads a program called secops.exe which, when run, uncompresses to create a folder called SecurityOps that then contains a folder named EventComb, which contains a compiled HTML help file and the program itself. Start EventComb by just executing eventcomb.exe.

When it starts, you'll see why EventComb is free; the user interface, well, kind of leaves something to be desired, as you see in Figure 8.71.

FIGURE 8.71

Typical EventComb opening screen

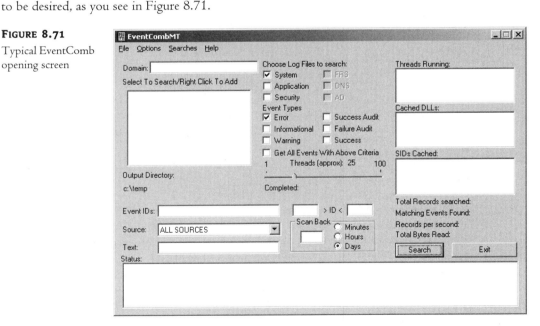

But don't let that scare you away; this comes with a pretty good Help file and once you get over the "interface overload," it starts to make sense. Here's a walk-through of a simple event log search. You'll look for an event on your computer that you almost certainly have—540. That indicates successful logons or logoffs. Again, you'll just be looking on the computer that you happen to be sitting at, but you can tell EventComb to simultaneously search the logs of as many computers as you like.

1. In Select to Search/Right-Click to Add, right-click inside the empty area.
2. In the options that appear, click Add Server.
3. In the resulting server name, fill in **localhost** and then click Add Server and Close.
4. In Event IDs, fill in **540**.
5. Under Choose Log Files to Search, check Security.
6. Under Event Types, check Success Audit and Failure Audit.
7. Back under Select to Search/Right-Click to Add, you'll see that localhost is in the list but is not highlighted—click it once to highlight it.
8. Click the Search button.
9. When finished, EventComb will open a window showing `C:\TEMP`—inside it will be a file named `localhost-Security_LOG.txt`. Open it.

Inside you'll see the events that met your search criteria.

As you can see from a look at EventComb, you can create and prestore searches as well as construct far more complex searches than the one you created here. Again, let me stress—this is not the greatest tool in the world, but the price is right.

Migration Strategies

I've been talking as if you were creating a brand-new network where there was none before, but that's not likely these days. Instead, it's more likely that you've already got an NT 4 domain or a Windows 2000–based Active Directory domain and you want to move to a Server 2003–based Active Directory domain. Or you might have two ADs that you want to make into just one AD. Either way, that kind of work falls under the topic heading of "migration."

Before I start talking about migration, however, let me offer a bit of advice that quite frankly you would be crazy not to take. If you're migrating, then that means that you probably already have a domain that currently works. You intend to convert this domain to a Server 2003–based AD domain that works. The scary part is in getting from the "before" to the "after." You'll really make people unhappy if you mess up partway, as an NT 4 domain is better than no domain at all...and messing up partway leaves you with no domain at all. So here's the advice: don't even think about starting your migration until you've tried the process out on a test network. No book, video, magazine article, or instructor can give you the level of understanding that a little hands-on can. So *please* set up a few systems and try this out before doing surgery on your company's network!

There are two basic philosophies about migrating to an AD domain: "in-place" upgrades versus "clean and pristine" migration.

In-Place Upgrade

In the in-place upgrade approach, you let Server 2003's Setup program convert your domain's from its current SAM file (if it's NT 4) or Active Directory (if it's Windows 2000) to a Server 2003–based Active Directory.

GETTING READY FOR THE UPGRADE

Before you do this, make absolutely sure you've got your DNS infrastructure in place—do all of those `nslookup` checks that I covered earlier in this chapter. And just to be certain that you've got something of a fallback position, go to one of your NT 4 backup domain controllers or Windows 2000 AD domain controllers and synchronize it, and then take it offline. Then, if worst comes to worst, you can always just shut down the new AD domain controller, turn the BDC back on, promote it to PDC, and then walk around to the other BDCs and force them to synchronize with the newly anointed PDC. If you've gone from 2000-based AD to 2003-based AD then you can do something similar: shut down the new 2003-based DC, start up an old 2000-based DC and, if necessary, seize any FSMO roles to that system. (But let's hope it doesn't come to that.)

HOW TO DO AN IN-PLACE UPGRADE FROM NT

You must do this at the primary domain controller; if you try to upgrade a backup domain controller then Server 2003's Setup program will simply stop and refuse to go any further.

But before you do it, you need to make a change to your PDC's Registry (and the Registry of *any* NT 4 domain controller that you intend to upgrade in place to Server 2003). Navigate to `HKEY_Local_Machine\System\CurrentControlSet\Services\Netlogon\Parameters` and add a new value entry called NT4Emulator of type REG_DWORD. Set its value to 1. (I'll talk about what it does later.)

TIP   I've gotten a fair amount of mail asking me something like, "I want to do an in-place upgrade, but I want my new Pentium 4 system to be the PDC. How do I do this?" Simple. First, install NT 4 on the Pentium 4, and tell it that you want the new computer to be a backup domain controller on the existing NT domain. Then, once it's installed, use the NT 4 Server Manager to promote that new BDC to the PDC. Then put the Windows Server 2003 Server CD into the new PDC's CD-ROM drive and do an in-place upgrade.

When you do an in-place upgrade on an NT 4 domain controller, then the normal Server 2003 Setup runs as usual. But the first time that you boot the machine after Setup, it immediately starts up DCPROMO and goes directly to the screen asking whether you want to create a new tree or a child domain in an existing tree. DCPROMO runs as you've seen it run before, with one important difference: You don't get to choose the NetBIOS name for the domain. The new AD domain will have the old NetBIOS name of the old NT 4 domain, whether you like it or not. You can, however, give the new AD domain any *AD* name that you like. So, for example, if you're upgrading the PDC on an NT 4 domain named AUTOSERVICE, then your new AD domain—which you can make part of an existing tree or forest, or create your own new forest—could be named bigfirm.biz. But its NetBIOS name would continue to be AUTOSERVICE, so that the old NT and Windows systems would still be able to find it, as they know it by the AUTOSERVICE name.

NOTE   Let me stress that, as I get a lot of letters on it—the "downlevel" NetBIOS name needn't be connected at all to the Active Directory domain name. If your domain was called ABC under NT 4 and you upgrade it, then its NetBIOS name is still ABC. You can give it any AD domain name that you like—mycoolnewdomain.org, for example. Then the DC responds to old-style NT 4 (or any NetBIOS) request to the domain ABC, and any AD requests for mycoolnewdomain.org.

You'll also see one other new thing when upgrading an NT 4 domain, as you see in Figure 8.72.

FIGURE 8.72

2003 interim functional level?

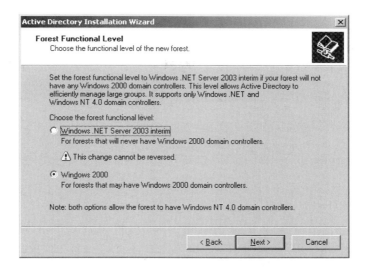

I haven't found a lot of use for this, but you can choose to move your new AD domain (and forest) to Windows Server 2003 Interim Functional Level. You should only choose it if there won't be any 2000-based DCs. Then finish running DCPROMO as always.

Old DCs Still Work

At this point, you've now got an Active Directory with only one of your DCs actually running Server 2003, and the others are still running NT 4. As I've said before, this is why there's a Mixed mode or, as 2003 calls it, Windows 2000 mixed functional level—the lone AD DC knows that it *could* do a lot of cool things, but that then its domain data would be incomprehensible to the NT 4 BDCs. So it denies itself a few features—multimaster replication and universal groups are the most important ones—and continues to work fine with the NT 4 BDCs.

As soon as you can, you'll want to get those BDCs upgraded. Once the last one's done, then you can move up to either Windows 2000 native functional level or all the way to Windows Server 2003 functional level, and then you'll finally get all of the features for which you paid. That's worth stressing.

And remember—it's only the state of your DCs that determines what domain functional level you can shift to:

- All of a domain's DCs must be running Windows 2000 or Server 2003 for the domain to shift to Windows 2000 native functional level.
- All of a domain's DCs must be running Server 2003 for the domain to shift to Windows Server 2003 functional level.

It does not matter at *all* about the other systems—they could all be NT 4 workstations and member servers and you could still be at 2003 functional level, so long as all of the DCs run 2003.

Avoiding Trouble with the Windows 2000 Machines

There is one quirk about in-place upgrades that you should be aware of.

Suppose, as is the case for many people, that you've introduced a bunch of Windows 2000 member servers and workstations into your NT 4 domain, and then you upgrade a single DC to AD. You'll see a curious effect. Once you have a single AD domain controller in a Mixed mode environment, all of the 2000 Professional machines will only go to *that* machine to log in. (I do not know of a similar problem for XP Pro, but I've never heard otherwise, either.) When those 2000 Pro machines saw only NT 4 domain controllers, then they'd log in to any one of them. But if there is at least one 2000- or 2003-based DC in the domain, then the 2000 Pro boxes will only log in with that one (and any other AD DCs in the domain).

So if you have an NT 4 domain with a lot of 2000 Professional systems in it, then you'll probably want to upgrade those BDCs quickly. Or you can make the Registry change that I suggested at the beginning the section. That keeps the 2000 boxes from becoming fixated on one DC. But you *must* make that Registry change before upgrading. If you make the Registry fix *after* you upgrade, then any 2000 boxes who have logged onto the domain since the upgrade will remain fixed on that one DC. The only fix is to run around to all of those 2000 boxes and unjoin them from the domain, then rejoin them. Not pleasant.

HOW TO DO AN IN-PLACE UPGRADE FROM 2000-BASED ADs

As you'd guess, an in-place upgrade from a Windows 2000–based AD to a Server 2003–based AD isn't as drastic as is an upgrade from an NT 4 domain. But it does require a few things: you must expand your forest's schema to make room for 2003's new AD items, and you've got to rearrange your existing domain's AD database likewise. You do this with a tool on the Server 2003 CD called adprep.exe. It's in I386.

Prep the Forest/Schema and Domain

Even if you're only going to upgrade one domain in your 2000-based forest to Server 2003, you've got to change your domain's schema before 2003 can install its AD machinery. But, as you know, there isn't any such thing as a *domain* schema—all domains in a forest share the same schema. So you've got to change your entire forest's schema. You'll do that on the forest's schema operations master/FSMO. Pop the Server 2003 Setup CD into the computer's CD drive, open a command prompt and navigate to the I386 directory on whatever drive holds the CD. So, for example, if your CD drive were drive D:, you'd open a command prompt, type **D:** and press Enter, and then type **cd \I386** and then press Enter.

Now run adprep by typing **adprep /forestprep** and press Enter. You'll see something like this:

```
D:\I386>adprep /forestprep

ADPREP WARNING:

Before running adprep, all Windows 2000 domain controllers in the forest should be
    upgraded to Windows 2000 Service Pack 1 (SP1) with QFE 265089, or to
    Windows 2000 SP2 (or later).

QFE 265089 (included in Windows 2000 SP2 and later) is required to prevent
    potential domain controller corruption.

For more information about preparing your forest and domain see KB article Q331161
    at http://support.microsoft.com.
```

```
[User Action]
If ALL your existing Windows 2000 domain controllers meet this requirement, type C
    and then press ENTER to continue. Otherwise, type any other key and press
    ENTER to quit.
```

Now, adprep is not screwing around here—make sure your DC is up to SP2 or SP3 before going further. If you're at that level, then just type **c** and press Enter to see the adprep in action:

```
Opened Connection to W2KSV
SSPI Bind succeeded
Current Schema Version is 13
Upgrading schema to version 30
Connecting to "W2KSV"
Logging in as current user using SSPI
Importing directory from file "C:\WINNT\System32\sch14.ldf"
Loading entries.............................................................
111 entries modified successfully...
```

This goes on for a while, as AD imports and installs a bunch of schema changes. Finally, it says

```
Adprep successfully updated the forest-wide information.
D:\I386>
```

Now you're ready to prep your domain—yes, that's right, you've got to run adprep at least twice to upgrade a 2000-based AD domain. Go to the infrastructure operations master/FSMO, insert the CD and get ready as before to run adprep. Type **adprep /domainprep** and it'll look like

```
D:\I386>adprep /domainprep

Adprep successfully updated the domain-wide information.
D:\I386>
```

Much less chatty, and quicker, too. Reviewing, then, before you can upgrade a Windows 2000–based AD domain to a Server 2003-based AD domain, you must

1. Upgrade the forest by running adprep /forestprep on the schema FSMO computer for your forest, even if that machine is not in the domain that you're going to upgrade.

2. Upgrade the domain structure by running adprep /domainprep on the infrastructure FSMO for the domain that you are going to upgrade.

Run Setup

Now you're ready to run Setup. Just do an in-place Setup as described in Chapter 5—put the CD in, double-click it in My Computer if it doesn't auto-start and select the Upgrade option. It will ask you for a product key, and then warn you about anything that will change in this upgrade. It will also check that you've forestprepped and domainprepped properly. (A nice touch—Microsoft makes you type in that irritating product key, only to immediately say, "Oh, golly, Setup can't run, you haven't prepped right." Grumble grumble grumble…) From there, Setup runs hands-off and there's nothing to do until it's done and you log onto your newly upgraded Server 2003 DC for the first time. If your domain was previously in Mixed mode, it'll now be in Windows 2000 mixed domain functional level, and if it was in Native mode before, it'll be in Windows 2000 native domain functional level. If this is the first domain in the forest that you've upgraded, then DCPROMO will set the forest's functional level to Windows 2000 forest functional level. At this point, you're upgraded!

IN-PLACE UPGRADES: PRO

To summarize, then, the things in favor of in-place upgrades are the following:

◆ They don't require new machines.

◆ Your users keep their old SIDs and the domain keeps its old trust relationships, so any servers in other domains—resource domains containing perhaps file and print servers or e-mail servers, for example—will still recognize those users without trouble.

◆ The users keep their old passwords.

◆ It's simple, just a quick upgrade.

◆ If you're going from 2000-based ADs to 2003-based ADs then the upgrade seems pretty trouble-free.

IN-PLACE UPGRADES: CON

Although in-place upgrades have a lot going for them, I recommend that many people *not* do them; here's why:

◆ You cannot make your former NT 4 PDC into a domain controller on an existing AD domain; upgrading a PDC will always result in the creation of a new AD domain.

◆ You cannot set the new domain's NetBIOS name, as it's automatically set equal to the old NT 4 domain's name.

◆ You cannot merge your old NT 4 domain into an existing AD domain.

◆ You upgrade *all* of the accounts, and it's a one-way trip—there's no AD Rollback Wizard. (Although you can, as I've suggested, keep an old DC "on ice" as an emergency measure.) I prefer more gradual approaches.

◆ Any leftover junk in your old NT 4 domain SAM remains in your new Active Directory database.

Clean and Pristine Migration

The other approach is called *clean and pristine* (C&P). In this approach, you leave your existing domains (NT 4, 2000-based AD, or even 2003-based AD domains) alone and create a new, empty AD domain. Then you use a program called a *migration tool* to copy user and machine accounts from the old domain (or domains) into the new AD domain.

C&P IS GRADUAL

In many cases, I prefer the C&P approach. For one thing, it's gradual. With an in-place upgrade, you walk your domain through a one-way door. If you find later that Server 2003–based ADs just aren't the thing for you, then too bad; you're stuck. But if you have a new domain and you copy some subset of your users over to that domain, then you just tell those users to log in to this new domain. If they start using the new domain and you find after a week or two that the AD's just not the tool for you, then you can always just tell the users to go back to their old domain accounts.

Another thing that troubles me about an in-place upgrade is born of a bit of caution. Most operating system Setup programs offer two modes: a clean wipe-and-build-from-scratch mode, and an upgrade-without-disturbing-existing-settings-and-programs mode. Clearly the upgrade option sounds like less work, but stop and think about it—which mode is more likely to be buggy? My guess is that the upgrade would be much harder to write than the wipe-and-install, and more complex means greater chances for error.

On the other hand, that could just be paranoia growing out of spending 30 years in the computer business. I've never seen a 2000 upgrade "blow up" an NT 4 domain, and all of the 2000-to-2003 upgrades I've seen haven't showed any troubles. No, the main thing that I really like about a clean and pristine upgrade is that it lets me migrate small groups of users rather than all of them at once.

HANDLING PERMISSIONS WITH THE NEW DOMAIN

Suppose you decide to go that C&P route. It might look like this will cause you a bunch of extra work. Suppose your premigration environment includes a bunch of NT 4 domains that trust each other, perhaps the standard admin domain/resource domain model. A user named Joe in the NT 4 admin domain has permissions to access some server in another NT 4 domain, the resource domain. Can he still? After all, the permissions allow Joe-at-the-old-domain to access the server; Joe-at-the-new-domain is a completely different user account. How can you get that server to let Joe's *new* account access that server? There are two approaches: re-ACLing and SID histories.

Re-ACL the Server

One approach is the obvious (and somewhat laborious) way: Just walk over to all of those old servers and add Joe's new account to the permissions lists on those servers. This is called *re-ACLing* because the other name for a list of permissions on a network service is the access control list. It can be a real pain, but some migration tools will do that for you automatically.

Use SID Histories

You know that every user has a SID; that's been true since NT 3.1. But under Windows 2000 native and Windows Server 2003 domain functional levels, Active Directory lets users keep more than one SID. As migration tools create the new AD user accounts, those accounts of course get new SIDs. But the migration tools can tack the user's old SIDs onto the new user account as well, exploiting a feature called *SID history*.

What SID Histories Do   Then, when a user tries to access some resource that he had access to under his old account, his workstation tries to log him in to that resource, using his new Active Directory account. As with all domain logons, AD builds a *token* for the user which contains both his user SID as well as the SIDs of any global and universal groups that he belongs to. Here's the trick to SID histories: AD says, "He's a member of a group with *this* SID"—and sends along his old SID from the old domain! Even though it's a user account's SID, the AD domain controller passes the SID along as if it were a global group SID, and apparently this is acceptable. The resource says, "Hmmm...do I know any of these guys? Well, there's this user SID...nope, I don't know that guy...but wait, look, he's a member of the 'Joe from the old domain' group. Dang, I always thought that Joe was a *user*, not a group. Well, in any case, I've got an ACL for that 'group,' so I guess he's in." Thus, even though Joe is logged in as a person from the new group with a new SID, he's dragging the old SID around, and it gets him access to his old stuff.

What You Need to Create SID Histories Several notes about SID histories are important:

- You need a migration tool that knows how to create SID histories. Microsoft's free Active Directory Migration Tool, which I'll cover a bit later in this chapter, can do that.

- Migration tools create SID histories as they copy user accounts from older NT or AD-based domains to your new 2000 native/2003 functional level domain. Before a migration tool can work, you must create a trust relationship between the old and new domains. But no matter which migration tool you've got, your migration tool cannot create SID histories unless you have created that trust relationship with NETDOM or with ADMT's Trust Wizard. I'll cover how to do this in a few pages in the "Trust Relationships in More Detail" section.

- You can only create SID histories in a domain whose functional level is either Windows 2000 native or Windows 2003. So when you create that new clean-and-pristine AD domain, then make sure that it's already shifted into Windows Server 2003 functional level—after all, you're building a fresh new domain, you may as well get the most out of it—before creating the trust relationship and running the migration tool.

Getting Rid of Old SID Histories You can keep SID histories for quite a while—systems running Windows 2000 Service Pack 3 or Windows Server 2003 can store up to 120 old SIDs. But SID histories are really just temporary measures, as you really only need your old SIDs as long as your old domains are around. That probably won't be for long. Once you've moved all of your servers and workstations out of the old domain, then the old SID is of no value. So it'd be convenient to be able to trim those old SID histories off of your user accounts. You can do that with a short VBScript that Microsoft describes in their Knowledge Base article 295758.

DISADVANTAGES OF CLEAN AND PRISTINE

Although I've said that C&P has the advantage of reversibility, thus helping you to manage your risk, it's not without costs.

- First of all, you need more machines than you would if you were just upgrading. You'll need machines to act as domain controllers in the new domain.

- Most migration tools cannot copy passwords. The users will then have to create new passwords the first time that they log in to the new AD domain. This isn't terrible, but it's annoying to some.

- You've got to buy a migration tool. There *is* ADMT, but it's really intended for small-scale migrations of a thousand users at best. These tools aren't cheap, costing somewhere in the neighborhood of $10 per user. That's *per user*, not per administrator, so those pictures of Alexander Hamilton start adding up.

- You cannot create an Active Directory domain with the same NetBIOS name as the old NT 4 domain, because that would require you being able to create two domains with the same NetBIOS name (since you don't decommission the old NT 4 domains when you do a clean and pristine migration).

- It's more work. You've got to worry about when to move any given set of users, you may have to re-ACL, and so on.

CLEAN AND PRISTINE ADVANTAGES

To summarize its advantages:

◆ C&P lets you do gradual upgrades.

◆ C&P *copies* user accounts, it doesn't *move* them. The old accounts are still there if something goes wrong.

◆ C&P lets you create your DCs from clean installs, avoiding the extra complexity and potential bugs of an in-place upgrade.

◆ C&P lets you consolidate domains, collapsing a morass of many domains into just one, or just a few.

Trust Relationships in More Detail

If you want to connect an old and a new domain to do a clean and pristine migration, or if you want domains in one forest to trust domains in another forest, or even if you want a workstation or a server to accept authentications from your domain—that is, if you want to join that workstation or server to the domain—then in every case you must create a trust relationship. As you've read before, to "trust" is to accept authentications from a domain's DCs. When a workstation joins a domain, that workstation is essentially saying to the DCs, "Before, I was only willing to accept authentications that *I* did, from the data in my local SAM. But now I'm willing to believe that if you tell me that such-and-such person is indeed who she says she is, then I'll accept that as reliable information"—again, the workstation now *trusts* the DCs. When a domain trusts another domain, then the first domain is saying that it once was only willing to accept authentications from its own DCs, but now it'll accept authentications from the second domain's DCs as well.

But how to build one of those trusts? In the case of domain-to-domain trusts (which is what people usually mean when they speak of trust relationships—most people don't understand that joining a domain means to establish a trust), I know of three ways: through the GUI, with a command-line tool named NETDOM, and with ADMT.

TRUSTS HAVE DIRECTION

To understand trusts in depth, the first thing to grasp is that trusts have direction. That shows up particularly clearly in trusts with NT 4 domains, as NT 4 trusts are all one-way only. AD trusts are all two-way, and of course you can simulate a two-way trust with NT 4 by building two trusts—one in each direction. But let's take a moment to discuss trust directions.

Any trust between two domains has a trusting and a trusted domain. The trusting domain is willing to accept login information and authentications from the trusted domain. For example, suppose I have two domains—an NT 4 domain named FACTORY and an AD domain named bigfirm.biz. Suppose also that FACTORY is a domain that contains very few user accounts; instead, it contains the machine accounts for several hundred servers. People with user accounts in bigfirm.biz need to get access to data in FACTORY's servers.

This is an example of a fairly common NT 3.*x* and 4 domain model called a *master/resource model* or *administrative/resource model*. The idea was to build at least two domains, a "master" domain and then one or more "resource" domains. You'd put all of the company's user accounts into the master domain (bigfirm.biz, in this case) and then put the servers into a resource domain or, in most cases, you'd have several resource domains, and each server would have an account in the resource domain that made the most sense.

So in the master/resource scenario, you'd have servers in the resource domain and users in the master domain. The users would want to access data on the servers, so the servers needed to be able to recognize and accept login data not from their own (resource domain) domain controllers, but rather from the DCs in the user's (master) domain. So I need FACTORY's servers to accept logins from bigfirm.biz's domain controllers.

Or, in other words, I need the FACTORY domain to *trust* the bigfirm.biz domain.

If you've not messed around with trust relationships in the past, then go back and read that again so you're clear on it. The primary goal is to allow bigfirm.biz people access to FACTORY's data. But FACTORY's servers will not, of course, let any users get to that data unless they can authenticate those users. But FACTORY can't authenticate the users, only their home domain's DCs can. Therefore, FACTORY must begin accepting authentication from bigfirm.biz. That's the definition of "to trust" here: to accept authentications, to trust another domain's DCs when they provide authentication. So bigfirm.biz folks get to use FACTORY's data because bigfirm.biz is *trusted*, and FACTORY lets them because it is *trusting*.

This notion of one-way trusts is largely irrelevant in networks that have no NT 4 DCs, but not entirely. There are actually *many* one-way trusts in an Active Directory…*between the DCs and the domain member machines*. The workstations and member servers accept authentications from the DCs, but no DC would accept an authentication from a workstation—you'd be completely out of luck if you tried to log on to a domain using a local account.

TRUSTS DO NOT REMOVE ALL SECURITY

People sometimes fear creating trusts between two domains, thinking that if domain A and domain B trust one another than anyone with a user account in A can make mischief in B and vice versa. That's not true at all. Establishing trusts between two domains just means that a system in the A domain can recognize a user in B and B in A. To see why this isn't the end of the world, consider: can a user in domain A do anything that he wants on any system in domain A? Of course not—group policies, user rights, and permissions control all of those things.

I think people get that idea because they're used to working in networks running older versions of NT that have been configured with default permissions and rights. As earlier versions of NT's permissions were something like "everyone in the world is welcome here," hooking up domain A and domain B meant that yes, anyone from A could do anything to any machine in B (and the other way around as well). But modern networks are tighter for two reasons. First, the default permissions and rights that a user has in a network running XP Professional and Windows Server 2003–based domains are a lot more restrictive than the ones for a network running NT 4 workstations and domain controllers, and second, administrators are just plain more aware of security, and so more likely to take a close look at how they secure their servers. Once a server in domain A is well-protected from the users in domain A, then it'll be pretty much automatically protected from users in any other trusting domain.

TRUSTS INVOLVE ADMINISTRATORS FROM BOTH SIDES

The decision to let domain A accept authentications from domain B (to use a one-way trust example) isn't one that A can make unilaterally, nor is it one that B can foist onto A. Creating a trust relationship is sort of like creating a treaty between countries—you need signatures from both sides to make it legal. Now, I realize that in many cases one person—probably you—will be the domain admin on both sides, but you will nevertheless have to establish credentials on both domains before you'll be able to create that domain.

FOUR KINDS OF TRUSTS

In a Windows Server 2003 world, there are four kinds of trusts: external, shortcut, forest, and realm. You will probably only work with the external and, on rare occasions, forest trusts, but let's take a quick look at what they are.

- **External** trusts are basically the kinds of trusts that I've been mostly talking about when I talk about domain-to-domain trusts. If you want a domain in a forest to trust a domain *outside* the forest or, in Microsoft terms, an *external* domain, then you build an *external* trust. You'll use these for migration. For example, if you're migrating from an NT 4 domain to a new empty Windows Server 2003–based AD domain, then you must first create an external trust between the two domains so that you can copy the user accounts and other things to the new domain.

- **Shortcut** trusts help speed up authentication in large forests. As you know, every domain in a forest trusts every other domain in the forest, and so any DC in any domain in a forest can authenticate a user from any other domain in the forest. But this can take time, particularly if a DC has to ask one domain to authenticate the user in question, and *that* domain needs to ask another domain, and so on. Shortcut trusts allow you to essentially "introduce" two different domains in the forest, saying "if domain A ever needs to authenticate someone from domain B quickly, then don't search around the forest to find a DC for domain B—just come right over and ask." I have never seen a forest so large that it needs this…but I'm sure that the few forests that *are* large enough to need this spend enough with Microsoft to have made it worth Redmond's time to add this kind of trust!

- **Forest** trusts are the neat new-to-2003 trust that lets you build one trust relationship between two forests. Once done, every domain in the first forest trusts every domain in the second forest.

- **Realm** trusts allow trust relationships with Unix systems that use Kerberos for authentication. (What we call domains, Unix Kerberos users call realms.)

We'll mostly use external trusts, but I'll show you how to build a forest trust also.

THE SWISS ARMY KNIFE OF TRUST TOOLS: NETDOM

As I've said, the true under-the-hood meaning of "trust relationship" extends beyond domain-to-domain trusts; it includes the connection between domain members and their DCs, meaning that even someone operating a one-domain enterprise deals with trusts. But there's a tendency for administrative tools to either handle domain-to-domain trusts or domain membership trusts; there's only one tool that I know of that envisages trusts in their entirety. It's called NETDOM. First introduced in the NT 4 days, NETDOM has become more powerful and useful with every version—and 2003's version is no exception. To get NETDOM on your system, pop your Server CD into your CD-ROM drive and take a look in `support.cab`, a file that you'll find in the `\Support\Tools` folder. Among other things, you'll see a program called `netdom.exe`. (Or double-click the MSI file and install all of the support tools—there are many useful ones.)

NETDOM and Domain Members: Add, Join, Move

Most of NETDOM's options affect domain membership trusts. I don't want to devote too much space to this, as I'm mainly interested in discussing domain-to-domain trusts, but it's worth listing some of the NETDOM options.

`netdom add` adds a machine account to a domain. It doesn't join the machine to the domain, it only creates the machine account on the target domain and, if the domain is an AD domain, you can even tell NETDOM what OU to put the machine account in. This is useful because a machine's local administrator can join that machine to a domain, *if* a domain administrator has already created a machine account for that machine on the domain. Here's what its syntax looks like:

```
netdom add machine /domain:domainname /userd:destination-domain-admin-account
    /passwordd:destination-domain-admin-password /server:dcname /ou:destination-OU /DC
```

That looks like a mouthful; let's pick it apart to make it easier to understand. If I wanted to create a machine account in a domain, then I'd need to know:

◆ The name of the machine that I wanted to create a domain account for. That's what the *machine* parameter supplies.

◆ Next, I'd need to know what domain I was joining that machine to. That's what the /domain:*domainname* parameter supplies. If I don't specify this, then the machine account gets created in my current domain.

◆ That domain's only going to let me add a machine account if I'm someone with the permissions to do that on the domain. That's what the /userd and /passwordd parameters supply. Of course, if I'm already logged on as someone with those permissions, then I needn't resupply them.

◆ I might want to force this operation to occur on a particular DC. The /server option lets me do that.

◆ I might want to place this new machine account in a particular OU; the /ou option accomplishes that. Unfortunately, you've got to specify the OU in LDAP terminology.

◆ Finally, machine accounts for domain controllers are a bit different than the rest of the machine accounts, so NETDOM includes the /DC option for that eventuality.

So if I wanted to create a machine account named Matterhorn in a domain named apex.com and place its account in an OU named Workstations, I'd type

```
netdom add Matterhorn /domain:apex.com /ou:"ou=Workstations,dc=apex,dc=com"
```

Again, that does *not* join Matterhorn—there needn't even *be* a system named Matterhorn for this to work. But now it'd be possible for a local administrator at Matterhorn to join apex.com, and she would not have to fill in a domain account/password to satisfy her workstation OS. But what if you wanted to both create the machine account *and* join the machine to the domain? For that, there's `netdom join`. It looks like

```
netdom join machine /domain:domainname /userd:destination-domain-admin-account
    /passwordd:destination-domain-admin-password /ou:ou /usero:local-machine-admin-
    account /passwordo:/local-machine-admin-password /reboot
```

Most of those options will seem pretty familiar. As before, I need to tell NETDOM what machine to join, what domain to join it to, and perhaps what OU in that domain to place the machine account in. As this creates a machine account on the domain, I'll need to present domain-level administrative credentials. But now because I'm also joining the machine to the domain, I'll need the *machine's* permission as well, so I'll need to show that I've got an account that the machine recognizes as a local administrator account—that's what passwordo and usero do. Think of the "o" at the end as "object," as in "we're joining this object to the domain." The same for userd and passwordd—they're the user account with admin privileges on the *destination* domain. Finally the "/reboot" tells the workstation or member server to reboot to make the changes take effect. Interestingly enough, you needn't be anywhere near the target machine to do this—it'll work remotely without a problem! So, for example, suppose I wanted to move a system named Saturn into a domain named planets.com. The administrator account on the Saturn machine is named satadmin with password "hi," and planets.com has a domain administrator named planadmin with password "so." The command would look like

```
netdom join Saturn /domain:planets.com /reboot /usero:satadmin /passwordo:hi
    /userd:planadmin /passwordd:so
```

I told you that NETDOM could help with migration by letting you move a machine from one domain to another—that's the NETDOM move command. It'll need *three* sets of account names and passwords, because to move a machine from domain A to domain B, then you'll need to demonstrate administrator credentials on domain A, domain B, and on the machine that you're moving. As before, you specify userd, passwordd, usero, and passwordo. But now you'll need to specify userf and passwordf—an account name and password on the *former* domain. By now, all of the options should be familiar:

```
netdom move machine /domain:destination-domainname /ou:ou /reboot /userd:destination-
    domain-admin-account /passwordd:destination-domain-admin-password
    /usero:local-machine-admin-account /passwordo:/local-machine-admin-password
    /userf:former-domain-admin-account /passwordf:former-domainadmin-password
```

So suppose I wanted to move a machine named saturn.planets.com from a domain named planets.com to one named cars.org. Say that I've got an admin account on Saturn named satadmin, a domain admin account on planets.com called planadmin, and a domain account on cars.org called caradmin. Finally, let's suppose that each of those admin accounts have the password "hi." The command would look like

```
netdom move saturn.planets.com /domain:cars.org /usero:satadmin /passwordo:hi
    /userf:planadmin /passwordf:hi /userd:caradmin /passwordd:hi /reboot
```

Before moving to Netdom's domain-to-domain trust abilities, let me mention that it can help out in other ways in maintaining domain member trusts:

◆ netdom reset resets a machine's account. Sometimes you'll sit down at a system and be unable to log onto the domain because the machine has lost its domain account, or so it says. Sometimes just resetting it does the job.

◆ netdom resetpwd resets a machine's domain password. You must be sitting at the machine for this to run. Sometimes if a machine has not connected to the domain for several weeks then its account password expires; this can fix that.

◆ netdom remove removes a system from a domain.

◆ netdom renamecomputer renames a computer and its machine account. Be careful about doing this with Certificate servers; they are installed to be name-dependent.

Building Domain Trusts with NETDOM

Now let's see how to build a trust with NETDOM. Recall that we'll work with two kinds of trusts: external (domain-to-domain nontransitive) and forest (forest-to-forest transitive) trusts. Let's first take up external trusts. By now, it'll be easy to guess how NETDOM does it. You need to specify who will trust whom and present domain admin credentials for each domain.

Here's the syntax:

```
netdom trust trustingdomainname /uo:trusting-admin /po:trusting-admin-password
    /d:trusteddomainname /ud:trusted-admin /pd:trusted-admin-password /add /twoway
    /enablesidhistory
```

Remember that in the most basic trusts, there is a *trusting* and a *trusted* domain. The trusting domain accepts authentications from the trusted domain. You can choose to make it two-way, but even if you do, NETDOM insists that you call one domain the trusting and one the trusted. (Of course, if you're building a two-way trust, then it doesn't matter which you make the trusted and which you make the trusting.) As before, you present credentials, but this time you use the /uo and /po parameters to specify the username and password for a domain admin from the trusting domain, and /ud and /pd to specify the username and password for a domain admin from the trusted domain. The /add parameter says to create the trust, the /twoway parameter says to build it in both directions. That's optional—if you *do* want a one-way trust, then don't include /twoway. As you can guess, /enablesidhistory makes a trust that can support migration tools that create SID histories.

So, for example, to make apex.com and bigfirm.biz trust each other, let's suppose that apex.com has a domain admin named apeadmin with password "ook" and bigfirm.biz has a domain admin named bigadmin with password "hithere"; we could make them trust one another with this command:

```
netdom trust apex.com /uo:apeadmin /up:ook /d:bigfirm.biz /ud:bigadmin /pd:hithere
    /add /twoway /enablesidhistory
```

Trust relationships can fall apart for a variety of reasons, so if you create a trust and leave it for a few months, and then try to use it to migrate then you might find that it doesn't work. NETDOM can "refresh" a trust with the /reset option:

```
netdom trust trustingdomainname /uo:trusting-admin /po:trusting-admin-password
    /d:trusteddomainname /ud:trusted-admin /pd:trusted-admin-password /reset
```

It's the same as the command that creates the trust, but instead of ending with /add /twoway /enablesidhistory, you just type /reset. Or, instead of /reset, use /verify to just check that the trust is working; if not, then try /reset. I *strongly* recommend that you verify a trust before trying a migration tool! You can also verify *all* of the domains that a domain trusts like this:

```
netdom query /d:domainname /ud:adminacct /pd:password trust /verify
```

Then, once the trust isn't needed any more, you can break it with this syntax:

```
netdom trust trustingdomainname /uo:trusting-admin /po:trusting-admin-password
    /d:trusteddomainname /ud:trusted-admin /pd:trusted-admin-password /remove /twoway
```

Once you've got that trust in place, you're ready to start migrating. But before you do, let's look at one more kind of trust...

When It Doesn't Work: LMHOSTS to the Rescue

Once in a while, I can't make NETDOM or, for that matter, any trust-making tool, work. No matter what I do, NT's User Manager for Domains (often) or AD Domains and Trusts (less frequently) complains that it cannot contact a domain controller for the other domain.

That could be because of something very simple. If one system can't ping the other system, then you can't establish a trust. Trust also could fail if one system cannot resolve the other system's name—the NetBIOS names, if it's an NT-4-to-AD trust, or DNS names, if it's an AD-to-AD trust. So check basic connectivity, WINS, and DNS if you can't get one domain to acknowledge another's existence.

But once in a while, there's simply nothing that you can do to make an NT 4 system see an AD domain controller. So in that case, you need to employ the "emergency measures"—a file called LMHOSTS. As you read in the previous chapter, LMHOSTS is an ASCII file that you place in `system32\drivers\etc`. You can use it to help one domain find another domain's primary domain controller—which NT needs to find if it's to create a trust. In each domain controller, create an LMHOSTS entry that points to the other domain controller by entering a line like this in LMHOSTS:

```
IPaddress-of-other-DC  "name-of-other-domain <spaces to fill to 15 chars> \0x1B"
```

That should be typed as just one line, even if it broke on the printed page. The idea here is that you're creating an LMHOSTS entry that points to a DC whose ID is "1B" hex, which designates the primary domain controller. For example, if the domain controller for bigfirm.biz that is acting as the PDC FSMO had the IP address 25.7.4.11, then you'd enter this line into the LMHOSTS on the primary DC on APEX:

```
25.7.4.11  "BIGFIRM       \0x1B"
```

Notice that the name in the entry is the *domain's* name, not the PDCs. As BIGFIRM is seven characters long, you add eight spaces after its name, before the `\0x1B`. And you must use the double quotes. That entry goes into the LMHOSTS file on the PDC for APEX so that it can find the PDC for bigfirm.biz. In all likelihood, that'll work; but if the bigfirm.biz system still claims to be unable to find the PDC for APEX, then find out the IP address for APEX's PDC—let's say that it's 25.10.10.19—and put *this* entry in the LMHOSTS file on bigfirm.biz's PDC FSMO:

```
25.10.10.19 "APEX          \0x1B"
```

This time, pad the name with eleven spaces because APEX is four characters long. Those entries identify the PDC of a domain, but there's another designation that you may need—a simple declaration that the PDC also happens to be a regular old domain controller. You do that with a 1C entry—it looks identical to the 1B except for the "C":

```
25.7.4.11  "BIGFIRM       \0x1C"
```

Again, you name the *domain*, not the domain controller, with this trick.

BUILDING TRANSITIVE FOREST TRUSTS

Before I move along to ADMT from forests, let's cover forest trusts. As far as I can see, you can't get NETDOM to create the really cool new-to-Server-2003 transitive trusts between forests. For that, you'll need a GUI tool—Active Directory Domains and Trusts.

Before starting ADDT, however, let's make sure that you've got a few things ready. First, as always, check DNS with a few `nslookups` to see that the folks in each forest will be able to find domain controllers in the other forest. Then, make sure that both of the forests are at Windows Server 2003 forest functional level. Finally, make sure that you have the name and password of an account that is either in Enterprise Admins or in Domain Admins for the forest root domain—and you'll need one of those accounts from each forest.

Start up Active Directory Domains and Trusts (Start/Administrative Tools/Active Directory Domains and Trusts) and right-click the icon representing the forest root domain (you can't create a forest trust from any other domain), choose Properties, and in the resulting page click the Trusts tab. It'll look like Figure 8.73.

FIGURE 8.73

Viewing a domain's trusts

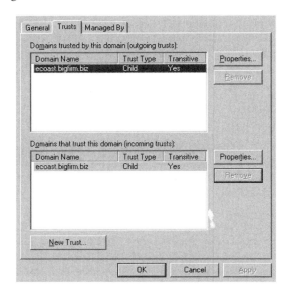

My screen shots show how to create a forest trust between bigfirm.biz (which is, recall, a forest root domain) and apex.com, the forest root of another forest. Notice that the screen shows that I've already got a trust from bigfirm.biz to ecoast.bigfirm.biz. That shouldn't be a big surprise, as ecoast is a child domain. You cannot use ADDT to delete a trust between domains in a forest, but you can use ADDT to build just about any other kind of trust. Click New Trust… and a Welcome to the New Trust Wizard screen appears; click Next and you'll see something like Figure 8.74.

FIGURE 8.74

Who will you trust?

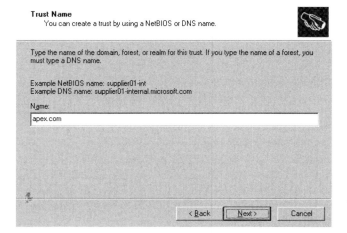

I've filled in apex.com. Click Next to see the *important* question, as you see in Figure 8.75.

FIGURE 8.75

What kind of trust?

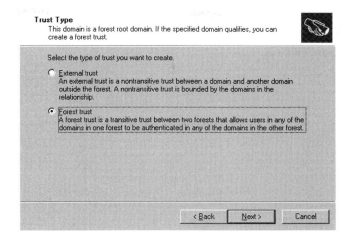

Recall that an external trust is a simple domain-to-domain trust, and a forest trust is the transitive trust that we want. Choose Forest Trust and click Next to see Figure 8.76.

FIGURE 8.76

Which way should the trust go?

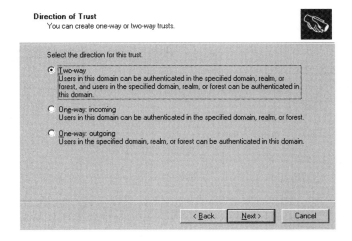

As you've seen, at its heart a trust has two sides—the domain that trusts and the one that is trusted. This page lets you choose who trusts whom, and whether or not trusts should just run bidirectionally. Choose Two-way and click Next to see Figure 8.77.

This is a real time-saver. As I said before, one administrator can't create a trust for two domains; it takes admins from both sides. That used to mean that you'd first set up one side of the trust on one domain, then run over to a DC for the other domain and finish setting up the trust at the other domain. This, however, saves you the trouble. If you click Both This Domain and the Specified Domain, and Next, then the wizard will ask you for an administrator account and password on the other domain. Fill in the administrative account and password, click Next, and you'll see Figure 8.78.

FIGURE 8.77

Set up both sides or just this one?

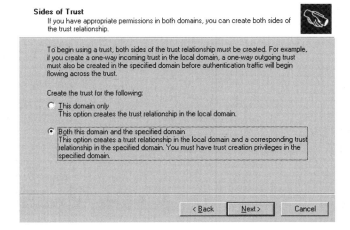

FIGURE 8.78

How friendly are we?

Here's another example of Server 2003's better attention to security detail. In most cases, you create a forest trust because you want all of the domains in one forest to trust all of the domains in the other forest. If that's the case, then choose Forest-wide Authentication. If, on the other hand, you want to more finely tune the kind of authentication info that passes between the forests, then choose Selective Authentication. But if you do, you'll have a lot more work ahead of you! Then click Next and the wizard will ask you the same question from the point of view of the other forest; select whatever you prefer and click Next again. You'll get two more information panels confirming what you've selected; click Next to get past them. Then you'll be asked if you want to confirm the link between forests. This sounds like a good idea, but it's not—it'll only work if you built the two halves of the trust by hand. Click No to get past those pages and you'll end up at a final "this is what you did" page. Click Finish and it's done—Apex and Bigfirm are working as one.

Microsoft's Free Migration Tool: ADMT

If you're thinking about a clean and pristine migration, then you need a migration tool…and if you've priced migration tools, then you might be reconsidering a C&P. But you needn't, as Server 2003 includes a migration tool called the Active Directory Migration Tool or ADMT. Originally written for Microsoft by NetIQ, ADMT 2 maintains the ease of use of the first version and adds some nice features as well.

AN EXAMPLE MIGRATION SETUP

To show how ADMT works, I'll demonstrate how to do a simple but fairly complete migration from an NT 4 domain named NT4HOLDOUT to our Active Directory bigfirm.biz. (Let me stress that the process is the same to go from an Active Directory domain—it just seems that more people migrate from NT 4, and simply upgrade in-place from 2000-based ADs, so I chose NT 4 for my example.) I'll explain this step-by-step so that you can duplicate this if you like. (But you needn't do that—you'll understand basically what ADMT does whether you try it or just read along. Additionally, I refer here to file shares and NTFS ACLs, which we've not covered yet but we will in three chapters—skip ahead to the file shares chapter if you don't know that stuff yet. I'm using them in a very basic way in any case.) You'll see:

- How to migrate a user account to an AD domain from an NT 4 domain with ADMT
- How SID histories allow the migrated user to access resources on the old domain whose ACLs have not been changed
- How ADMT can re-ACL a member server in the old resource domain
- How ADMT can migrate member servers from the old domain to the new AD domain

To make this work, I'll set up four systems—two in NT4DOMAIN, two in bigfirm.biz. The two in NT4DOMAIN are:

- A PDC for NT4DOMAIN, an NT 4 system named NT4HOLDOUT. On NT4HOLDOUT, I create:
  - A domain user account named Jane, password "jane."
  - A global group named Accountants and make Jane a member.
- A member server for NT4DOMAIN named NT4MEM. On NT4MEM, I create:
  - A share named \\nt4mem\janepersonal, with both share and NTFS permissions allowing only Jane access; I then put a few files in \nt4mem\janepersonal.
  - A share named \\nt4mem\taxes that only the Accountants group can access, and put a few files in that.

The Active Directory domain contains two machines as well:

- A DC for bigfirm.biz, our old friend bigdog.bigfirm.biz set up as we've done it in this chapter and the previous one.
- An XP Pro workstation named vxp2.bigfirm.biz. It could as easily be a 2000 Pro workstation or an NT 4 workstation. Whatever the OS, it should be a member of the bigfirm.biz AD.

WARNING   *The target domain* must *be a Windows 2000 native or Windows Server 2003 functional level domain for ADMT to work.*

My goals here are to:

◆ Get Jane an account in bigfirm.biz without interrupting her ability to access the shares on NT4MEM while NT4MEM is still part of the NT4DOMAIN domain.

◆ Eventually migrate NT4MEM to bigfirm.biz so that I can shut down the NT4DOMAIN domain altogether.

Before we go any further, check that we won't have any name resolution problems—either point all of the systems to the same WINS and DNS servers or ensure that each system's DNS servers and WINS servers talk to one another. And yes, WINS is important here because we've got NT 4 systems still running.

ESTABLISH THE TRUST

Next, establish the trust between the two domains. As you've already read, I'd recommend using NETDOM to do this. And always be sure to use the latest NETDOM (which in this case is the one on the Server 2003 CD). As we'll want a two-way trust, it doesn't matter which we call the trusting and which the trusted. Assuming that NT4DOMAIN has an admin account nt4admin with password "swordfish" and bigfirm.biz has an admin account bigadmin with password "bigguy", then the following NETDOM command would do the trick:

```
netdom trust nt4domain /uo:nt4admin /po:swordfish /d:bigfirm.biz /ud:bigadmin
    /pd:bigguy /add /twoway /enablesidhistory
```

I like to stop and test things at this point—is the trust working, are the permissions correct on NT4MEM? To try that, I'd log onto VXP2, the XP box that is a member of bigfirm.biz, and try to log on as Jane. (You know, sort of to get in touch with my feminine side—some people cross-dress, I cross-logon.) First of all, if Jane can log on, then the two domains do indeed trust one another. And, of course, Jane should be able to access both the \\nt4mem\janestuff and \\nt4mem\taxes shares. So in a sense a trust relationship is kind of a mini-migration tool of its own, as Jane can now log onto a bigfirm.biz member machine and access her stuff.

But that's not what we *really* want. We want to get rid of NT4DOMAIN and all of its members eventually. Eventually Jane will have a bigfirm.biz account, and NT4MEM will be a member of bigfirm.biz, and NT4HOLDOUT (the PDC of the NT 4 domain) will be shut off and given to charity or reformatted as a member of bigfirm.biz. But, again, we want to do all of this gradually, and that's where ADMT comes in. So it's time to...

GET BOTH SIDES ADMT-FRIENDLY

ADMT can be an absolutely frustrating nightmare of a program because of its needs. It's a program that takes information that is fairly private and internal to a domain—user accounts and passwords—and reveals them to a completely different domain. Before ADMT can do that, we'll have to open up a number of locked doors. Here's what we've got to do.

Put Domain Admins in Each Other's Administrators Groups

We'll work from a machine in the NT4DOMAIN domain—the PDC, named NT4HOLDOUT—and a machine in the bigfirm.biz domain, bigdog.bigfirm.biz. Each system's local Administrators group must contain the Domain Admins global group from the *other* domain. To do this, go to NT4HOLDOUT and open User Manager For Domains. Then double-click the Administrators group and add the Domain Admins group from bigfirm.biz. Of course, User Manager won't call the domain bigfirm.biz but rather its old NetBIOS name, BIGFIRM, as you're working on an NT 4 system that doesn't understand AD. Make sure that you're adding the Domain Admins group from BIGFIRM, not NT4DOMAIN.

Over at bigdog.bigfirm.biz, open up Active Directory Users and Computers as we've done before and look in the `Builtin` folder to find the Administrators group. Open it up and add the Domain Admins group from the NT4DOMAIN; again, make sure that it's the NT4DOMAIN's Domain Admins that you're adding, not the bigfirm.biz Domain Admins—they're already there.

Turn On Auditing

ADMT has some specific auditing needs, presumably so that it can monitor how it's doing. The source domain—the one the users are being copied from NT4DOMAIN—needs both success and failure audit enabled for user and group management. Turn that on in User Manager for Domains, clicking Policies/Audit and checking the boxes for Success and Failure next to User and Group Management.

On the target machine (bigdog.bigfirm.biz) on the target domain (bigfirm.biz), enable auditing by modifying a group policy called Default Domain Controller Policies in Active Directory Users and Computers. Right-click the Domain Controllers OU and choose Properties, then the Group Policy tab; the Default Domain Controllers Policy; double-click it and the group policy editor appears. To get to the policy you're looking for, open Computer Configuration, then Windows Settings, then Security Settings, then Local Policies, and finally inside Local Policies you see Audit Policy. Inside Audit Policy, double-click Audit Account Management and make sure that Define These Policy Settings is checked, as is Success and Failure. Then click Close…but don't close the GP editor; your work's not nearly done yet.

Enable Anonymous Access

While in the GP Editor for the Default Domain Controllers Policy at bigdog.bigfirm.biz, go next from the `Audit Policy` folder to another just two folders down on the same level, `Security Options`. We've got to loosen up an item in here. Set Network Access: Let Everyone Permissions Apply to Anonymous Users to Define This Policy Setting and Enabled.

That's all you need from that policy, so you can close up the Group Policy Editor, the properties page for the Domain Controllers OU, and ADUC.

Put Everyone in the "Pre-Windows 2000 Compatible Access"

Remember when DCPROMO asked about loosening up permissions to make NT 4 RAS servers happy? Well, you've got to do that loosening-up to make ADMT happy. No, you needn't run DCPROMO to do this; instead, you can just open a command prompt (still at bigdog.bigfirm.biz) and type this:

```
net localgroup "Pre-Windows 2000 Compatible Access" Everyone /Add
```

You should get the response "The command completed successfully."

Install ADMT on bigdog.bigfirm.biz

Put the 2003 Server CD into bigdog's CD drive and navigate to `I386\ADMT`. Double-click the file named `ADMIGRATION.MSI`. That starts a Setup wizard which asks the usual things—agree to the license, where do I put the files, etc. Tell it to put ADMT in `C:\ADMT`.

Create a Password Key on the Target

Now, we want Jane's password to move over with Jane's account, and ADMT 2 can do that—ADMT 1 couldn't—but it's going to take a little work. Before it'll migrate passwords, ADMT requires that you create a password encryption file on bigdog and then copy that over to NT4HOLDOUT, and NT4HOLDOUT will use that to be able to send passwords over the wire—but encrypted.

To do this, you've got to run ADMT from the command line. Open a command line and change directory to wherever you put ADMT (`C:\ADMT` in my example), and type

```
admt key NT4DOMAIN c:\
```

This says to prepare a key that NT4DOMAIN can use to transfer passwords to bigfirm.biz. (Bigfirm's not explicitly mentioned because you're working on a bigfirm.biz DC.) The C:\ just says where to put the file. If your server has a floppy drive, then A:\ works fine too. It doesn't matter where you put it—just understand that you'll have to transport that file to the NT4DOMAIN DC, NT4HOLDOUT, somehow. When it runs properly, ADMT will return a message looking something like

```
The password export server encryption key for domain 'NT4DOMAIN' was successfully
    created and saved to 'C:\MDLKDOV.pes.'
```

You're done on bigdog.bigfirm.biz for the moment. But before you leave bigdog, reboot it. That's *very* important! Time to move to NT4HOLDOUT.

Move Over the PES File

Once logged in at NT4HOLDOUT, you need to get that PES file from bigdog to a local drive; I usually just create a share and copy it over across the network; you can alternatively put it on a floppy, a CD-ROM disc, or whatever you want—but it's got to get over to NT4HOLDOUT one way or another.

Install the Password Migration DLL on NT4HOLDOUT

You need just a couple of files from the Server 2003 CD on NT4HOLDOUT, so put the CD in its drive. In `\I386\ADMT\PWDMIG`, you'll see `PWMIG.EXE`; double-click it to start the ADMT Password Migration DLL Installation Wizard, perhaps the world record-holder for wizard name length. After clicking Next, you'll see something like Figure 8.79.

Here, it thinks that the file is on a floppy, and that's a perfectly good way to transport it from bigdog.bigfirm.biz to NT4HOLDOUT. In my case, I've copied it over the network to C:\, so I'd click Browse to direct the program to the file's location. Two Nexts and a Finish and the DLL is installed, and you're prompted to reboot the system. But don't do that just yet, as you need to do a little Registry fiddling...

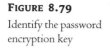

FIGURE 8.79

Identify the password encryption key

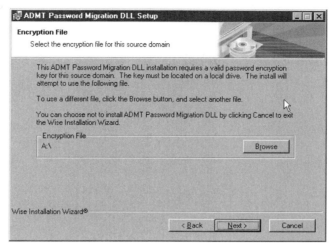

Modify Registry Entries for Local Security Authority on NT4HOLDOUT

Open up Regedit and navigate to `HKEY_LOCAL_MACHINE\SYSTEM\CurrentControlSet\Control\LSA`. There you will see an entry called AllowPasswordExport, with a value of 0. Change that to 1 and create a new REG_DWORD value entry named TcpipClientSupport, which you also set to 1.

If you're starting to think that maybe it'd be easier to just retype all of the usernames than it would be to get ADMT set up, take heart—you're almost done. *Now* reboot NT4HOLDOUT.

START UP ADMT AND MIGRATE THE ACCOUNTANTS GROUP

When migrating users from one domain to another, the basic sequence of events is:

1. Set up the trusts, registry entries, etc.

2. Migrate the global groups from the old domain to the new domain. The new global groups get SID histories from the old ones, so anyone in the new BIGFIRM\Accountants group will have access to anything that people in the NT4DOMAIN\Accountants group had access to. This means that as you migrate users from NT4DOMAIN to bigfirm.biz that they can be automatically placed in the Accountants group in bigfirm.biz and they will have immediate access to all of their old stuff.

3. Migrate the users. Once you've got the global groups migrated, you can migrate the users at whatever pace works for you. Users migrated to the new domain will be able to access file shares, shared printers, and other resources from the old domain, because the migrated user accounts have SID histories from the old domain.

4. Migrate the servers to bigfirm.biz. Change the domain membership of the member servers and workstations from NT4DOMAIN to bigfirm.biz. This will require another ACL fix-up, as you want the server to no longer have ACLs that refer to groups in NT4DOMAIN, and instead to replace those ACLs with references to groups in bigfirm.biz.

5. Once all of the member servers are moved over to bigfirm.biz and you've checked that all of the permissions have been correctly changed from NT4DOMAIN references to bigfirm.biz references, you can decommission NT4DOMAIN—break the trust relationship, shut off the NT4DOMAIN DCs, and trim the SID histories from our migrated user accounts.

Time to migrate the global groups, so let's do it. Move over to bigdog.bigfirm.biz and start up ADMT (Start/Administrative Tools/Active Directory Migration Tool). It's a kind of sparse-looking UI, but if you right-click the Active Directory Migration Tool icon then you'll see that it can do a lot of things, as in Figure 8.80.

FIGURE 8.80

ADMT functions

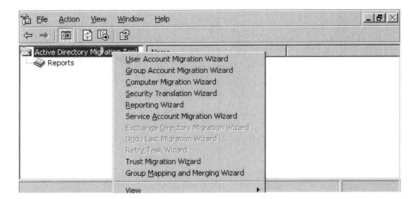

ADMT does a *lot* of things, more than I can cover in a short time—I'll just cover the basics here. I *strongly* recommend that you read the Help that comes with it, as ADMT is a powerful and useful tool that can migrate users, groups, machines, and even Exchange setups! On the ADMT menu, choose Group Account Migration Wizard and click Next to see the first panel, as you see in Figure 8.81.

FIGURE 8.81

Is this real or a drill?

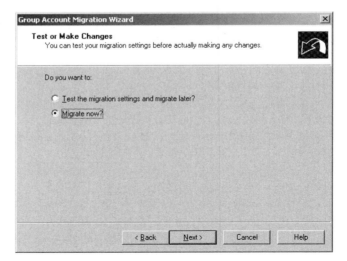

I'm running this "for keeps" here because I've done it enough to know how to get it right the first time, but I strongly recommend that you run it in test mode until you've gotten some experience with ADMT. As you've seen, ADMT is *very* demanding in the things that it needs before it'll run correctly, and you really don't want to leave your network half-migrated. Run it in test mode until you're comfortable that you've got all the pieces in place to do the real thing. Click Next and you'll see Figure 8.82.

FIGURE 8.82

Choose source and destination domains

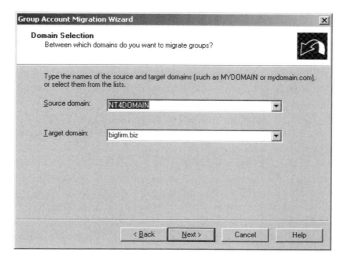

This panel is straightforward; you pick the domain that you're moving from and the one that you're moving to. But it's actually quite useful as well, as it serves as a test of connectivity. If NT4HOLDOUT weren't up, your only options on both "from" and "to" would be bigfirm.biz...which wouldn't be a very interesting migration. Once you choose the domains, click Next and you'll notice a pause as the DCs connect and show Figure 8.83.

FIGURE 8.83

What group or groups to migrate?

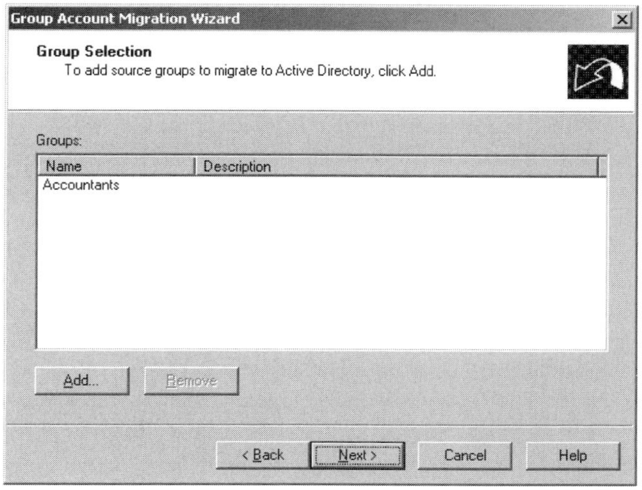

In this panel, you tell ADMT which group or groups to move over. Before I took this shot, I clicked Add and chose Accountants, although I could have chosen any number of groups. Click Next and you're led to Figure 8.84.

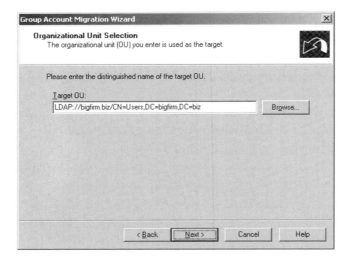

FIGURE 8.84

Where to put the group?

Like all good AD-aware tools, ADMT lets you choose what OU to place the migrated group into. But don't worry that you have to master that cumbersome LDAPish—you can click the Browse button and ADMT then lets you navigate though the AD structure. Click Next to see Figure 8.85.

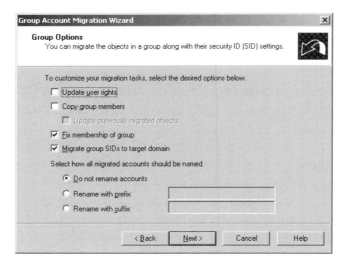

FIGURE 8.85

Choosing group options

The defaults on most of these panels are fine, but in this one you get an important option—to create a SID history on the group. Check the box labeled Migrate Group SIDs to Target Domain, which is ADMT's way of saying "create a SID history item in bigfirm.biz for the Accountants group." Clicking Next to this panel is something of a useful diagnostic—if something isn't in place to allow the SID history mechanism to work, ADMT emits an error message. Or it issues the warning in Figure 8.86, which is actually a *good* sign.

FIGURE 8.86

Creating a "helper group" for SID histories

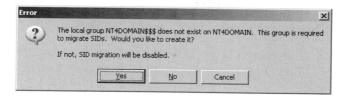

Whenever you use a SID history, the authenticating system checks with the old domain, NT4DOMAIN in this case. This group has something to do with how ADMT ensures that the SID histories will work right, but the wizard checks anyway to ensure that it's okay to create the group. Click Yes and you'll see a login screen, as if you haven't already presented your credentials frequently enough; Next takes you to Figure 8.87.

FIGURE 8.87

Handling conflicts

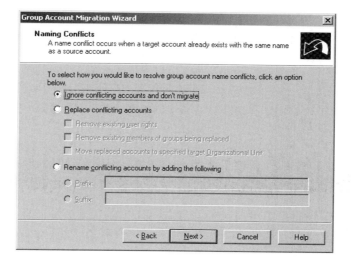

You're migrating a group named Accountants, but what if there already *is* a group named Accountants? This panel answers the question—skip the migration, zap the existing Accountants group, or add a prefix to the name. Once you make these choices—the defaults are usually fine—just a few more Nexts and it's done.

TEST THE NEW ACCOUNTANTS GROUP

As the Accountants group in bigfirm.biz has a SID matching the one on the Accountants group in NT4DOMAIN and *that* group has access to \\nt4mem\taxes, then anyone in the new Accountants group should be able to get to \\nt4mem\taxes. Let's try it out.

1. In the bigfirm.biz domain, create a user named Tom.

2. Put Tom in the Accountants group.

3. At the workstation that is a member of bigdog.biz. log on as Tom.

4. Open a command prompt.

5. Type `dir \\nt4mem\taxes` and press Enter. You should see the files in \\nt4mem\taxes. Then try looking in those files—you (as Tom) should be able to do it. SID histories work!

MIGRATE JANE TO BIGFIRM.BIZ

Now let's see how to migrate a user account. On the ADMT menu, choose User Account Migration Wizard. It starts out looking just like the Group Account Migration Wizard, asking about the source and destination domains, whom to migrate, and where to place her new account. But then you see a panel different from the Group panels, as you see in Figure 8.88.

FIGURE 8.88

What to do with the passwords?

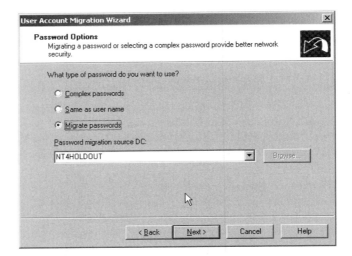

This panel will bring joy to the hearts of ADMT 1 veterans. Under ADMT 1, your newly migrated user accounts could either all have the same password, or they could have passwords equal to their usernames, or you could feed ADMT a cleartext ASCII file of names and passwords—all clumsy answers. But now that you're running ADMT 2 and have done the work of creating a password encryption key and moving it over to NT4HOLDOUT, ADMT 2 offers a new option—to move the passwords over. That's what I picked. Then click Next to see Figure 8.89. . . *if* the password encryption worked. You *don't* see 8.89 if you didn't dot all the i's and cross all the t's (you get an error message), so that Next is a useful diagnostic tool in its own right.

Migrating a user means that you copy her old account to a new domain. But it's a *copy*, not a *move*, so she's still got the old account. That means that she could start the day by logging on to either account—but you probably don't want that. You'll usually either want her to immediately start logging on with the new account, or to stay with the old account for a little longer, as you get the final arrangements for the new domain in place. That's where this panel is useful. It'll automatically disable the old account, or keep the new one disabled until you enable it, or keep the new account disabled for some number of days.

FIGURE 8.89

Enable or disable the old and new accounts?

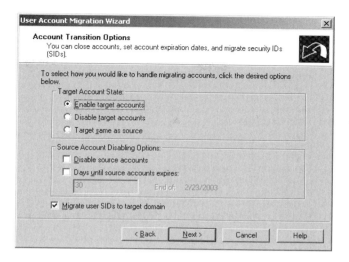

But this panel does something else that's important—it tells ADMT whether or not to create SID histories for the user. Click Next, and you'll get a login screen; fill in your credentials and click Next and you'll see a screen like Figure 8.90.

FIGURE 8.90

Making the new user feel at home

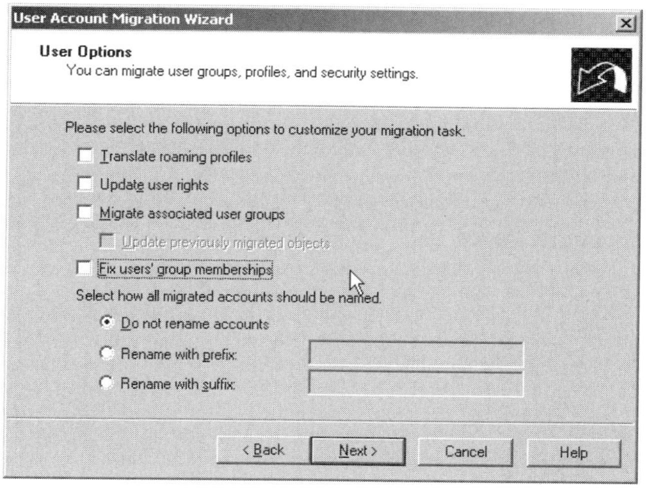

This is another powerful panel. In it, you can make ADMT give the new user the same rights as she had before, which isn't a simple matter when moving from NT 4 to AD in any flavor. It'll make sure that whatever groups Jane was a member of follow her over to the new domain. You can also, if you like, "brand" all users with a particular prefix or suffix. This would be useful if you were combining a number of different domains and wanted to avoid name collisions, as more than one domain might have a "Jane" account. You might, for example, say that all accounts from the old MANAGERS domain keep their names, but with "MGR" suffixed to the end of the name, so Jane would become JaneMGR. And speaking of name conflicts, click Next to see how to handle them in Figure 8.91.

FIGURE 8.91

Handling name
collisions

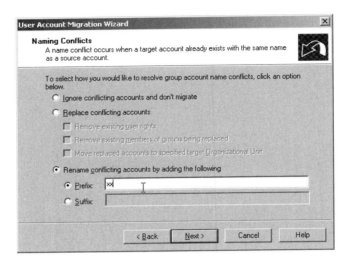

Assuming that you don't tack a prefix or suffix onto every name in a given domain when assimilating that domain's names, it would again be possible to have two Janes—the new one and one that's been around for a while. This page says that in a case like that, just prefix the new Jane's user account name with "xx." From here, you just click Next to confirm your choices, and the migration happens.

How did it end up? Jane was automatically joined to the Accountants group at bigfirm.biz. I logged Jane onto VXP2, the XP box that is a member of bigfirm.biz. It liked her old password, so the password came across correctly. Then I tried to access her personal shares that only the original Jane could access. She got to them with no trouble, demonstrating that the SID history works. My simple migration was a complete success, and all of your migrations will be, also...so long as you do your homework.

RE-ACLING WITH ADMT

You've now moved the global group Accountants and a domain user named Jane over to the new bigfirm.biz domain. There's just one holdout... your faithful member server, NT4MEM. (What about the PDC of that domain, NT4HOLDOUT? You can't migrate PDCs over. But when you don't need it any more, you can always wipe it and rebuild it, and then make it a DC in the new domain.) What's involved with moving NT4MEM over? Well, clearly you've got to change NT4MEM's allegiance to NT4DOMAIN, but that's not hard—recall the earlier discussion of NETDOM move and you'll know that you could do this with just one command.

But that wouldn't make the NT4DOMAIN émigrés very happy. For example, consider what happens when someone in the bigfirm.biz Accountants group tries to access \\NT4MEM\taxes. NT4MEM looks at the SID for the bigfirm.biz Accountants group and initially says to itself, "Nope, I don't have any ACLs that give *those* guys access, I'll just tell 'im to take a walk and oh...hey...there's this *other* ACL, for the Accountants group right here in NT4DOMAIN. Well, heck, they've got backstage access here at \\NT4MEM\taxes, come on in!"

Thus, if I used NETDOM to move NT4MEM to bigfirm.biz, then everyone who could get to \\NT4MEM\taxes could still get to it. But it'd seem sort of a roundabout way—here both NT4MEM and Accountants would be both part of the bigfirm.biz domain at that point, but the only way that the bigfirm.biz version of Accountants could get to the taxes share would be through an old—and now basically obsolete—connection. That seems inefficient. But it gets worse; you see, whenever NT4MEM wants to use a SID history, NT4MEM must go back to the original domain to authenticate it. Thus, if we shut down NT4HOLDOUT (the PDC of NT4DOMAIN), then the SID histories would stop working and the Accountants group in bigfirm.biz couldn't access shares on NT4MEM—which is also in bigfirm.biz.

What we need is a tool that will not only move NT4MEM over to bigfirm.biz, but also examine all of the shares on NT4MEM and change any of the old ACLs that refer to NT4DOMAIN things to corresponding bigfirm.biz things. This is sometimes called "re-ACLing" and, not surprisingly, ADMT can handle re-ACLing and moving a server. You'll see Computer Account Migration Wizard on the ADMT menu, and it works very much as the Group and User Migration Wizards do, so I'll spare you the screen shots. But there is *one* trick to making ADMT's Computer Account Migration Wizard work: run it from the PDC emulator of the *target* domain (bigfirm.biz, in our example), but log in as the domain administrator for the *source* domain (NT4DOMAIN in my example). Do that, and it'll work. Try it any other way and you'll just receive frustration.

There is a lot more that ADMT can do; all I've done here is to get you started. Again, I strongly recommend that you study the Help files before doing anything drastic with ADMT. But I think you'll like what the tool can do for you.

AD Maintenance

AD is, as I've said before, a database and, as I've also said, AD's DCs are database servers. So once you have your AD up and running you will almost certainly run into the same kinds of problems that any database administrator runs into. The three most common in the AD world are probably

- ◆ Defragmenting the database: it does it itself, but you can do a better job by taking the DC offline and doing it.

- ◆ Cleaning out improperly deleted objects: what happens if you simply FDISK a domain controller instead of DCPROMOing it to decommission it? (Or, worse, what happens if you FDISK *all* of the DCs in a child domain?) You leave junk in the database. I'll show you how to take that junk out.

- ◆ Renaming a domain: so you say your company used to be called Bigfirm and now it's called Megabucks? Great, congratulations. I'll show you how to rename its AD domain.

Offline Defragging a DC's Copy of the AD

Defragmenting your hard disk doesn't defrag one of the most important files—the AD database. AD defrags itself online, but it can't do a thorough defragging and compacting while acting as a domain controller. You can clean up your AD and potentially speed up a DC's performance by doing an offline defragmentation; here's how.

GET THE DC INTO DIRECTORY SERVICE MODE

Restart your domain controller and, as it's restarting, press F8 to bring up the Recovery menu. One of the many options will be Directory Services Restore Mode; choose that. The system will start up in a kind "safe mode" and may confuse you a bit when you try to log in. You log in as Administrator, but you do *not* use the normal password of your local Administrator account; rather, you use the Directory Services Restore password. What's that, you ask? Well, if you think back to DCPROMO-ing, you were asked to choose a Directory Services Restore password—well, here's where it gets used.

RUN NTDSUTIL

Now open a command prompt and start NTDSUTIL. It will compact and defrag the `NTDS.DIT`, the database file, to an alternative location. You'll then copy that file to its normal spot `\windows\ntds` or `\winnt\ntds`, reboot, and you'll be back in business. Here's what to do in NTDSUTIL:

1. Type **file** and press Enter. You'll get a prompt `file maintenance:`.
2. Type **compact to** followed by some target location like `compact to c:\`. This creates a compressed copy rather than working directly on the actual AD. The output will look like this:

```
Initiating DEFRAGMENTATION mode...
          Database: C:\WINDOWS\NTDS\ntds.dit
     Temp. Database: c:\ntds.dit


              Defragmentation Status (% complete)

     0    10   20   30   40   50   60   70   80   90   100
     |----|----|----|----|----|----|----|----|----|----|
     ..................................................


Note:
  It is recommended that you immediately perform a full backup
  of this database. If you restore a backup made before the
  defragmentation, the database will be rolled back to the state
  it was in at the time of that backup.

Operation completed successfully in 7.510 seconds.


Spawned Process Exit code 0x0(0)

If compaction was successful you need to:
    copy "c:\ntds.dit" "C:\WINDOWS\NTDS\ntds.dit"
and delete the old log files:
    del C:\WINDOWS\NTDS\*.log
```

3. Type **quit** and press Enter twice to exit NTDSUTIL.

COPY THE NEW AD TO %SYSTEMROOT%\NTDS

If all went well, then copy the `NTDS.DIT` file that you just created to either `\windows\ntds` or `\winnt\ntds`, depending on how your OS is set up. In that same directory, delete any files with the extension *.log. Restart the DC and you'll be done!

Note that this only defrags the `NTDS.DIT` file on that DC...if you have other DCs then you'll need to take them offline and defrag them as well. (Not all at once, of course!)

Cleaning Out Objects with NTDSUTIL

Active Directory likes orderliness, neatness in all things. When you remove something from the AD database, you're supposed to do it in an orderly manner. For example, suppose you get rid of a DC or, as is most common, you decided to wipe and rebuild the DC...without first DCPROMO-ing. Whenever you decommission a DC, you should first DCPROMO it.

Unfortunately, you can't always have the amount of order that you might like in our domains; DCs may crash and never boot again, making a DCPROMO pretty unlikely. The database objects representing the directory remain, even though there's no corresponding physical objects. Is that terrible, or can you just live with leftover junk in the AD database?

Leftover AD junk is probably undesirable for several reasons. First, it's, well, extra junk. We've all faced software problems that arise in *well-maintained* systems; who knows what kinds of bugs pop up when a database is in an unknown state? Second, as long as AD thinks a DC exists, it'll keep trying to talk to it. That leads to errors in the log files, which can be distracting and irritating. Third, you cannot decommission a *domain* until the last DC is gone. This has tripped me up a couple of times. In one case, I'd created a child domain with just one DC just to play around with it, and then FDISKed the DC. I later needed to decommission the forest's root domain, but found that DCPROMO would not let me do it, as it can't decommission the forest when there are still child domains around! Clearly, I was stuck until I could "get rid of the kids," removing first the DC's object from the database and then the child domain itself.

You can do all those things, with NTDSUTIL. It has a function called "metadata cleanup" that will zap just about anything. The only trouble is that NTDSUTIL's user interface is, well, a bit obtuse. The idea is this: you use a bunch of NTDSUTIL commands to identify some object, like a DC or a domain; that's the cumbersome part. Then, once they're identified, you tell NTDSUTIL to delete them.

I'll walk you through the process by using NTDSUTIL to get rid of ecoast.bigfirm.biz. Recall that ecoast.bigfirm.biz is a child domain of bigfirm.biz and has only one DC. The DC's name is srv1.ecoast.bigfirm.biz. Suppose that system had been destroyed by fire, effectively destroying the domain as well. (That's why you always want at least *two* DCs!) Here's how I'd do an ecoast-ectomy on bigfirm.biz: first, I'd start up NTDSUTIL and tell it to select the last ecoast.bigfirm.biz DC, srv1.ecoast.bigfirm.biz. Then I'd tell NTDSUTIL to delete the DC's object from the AD database. Once that's done, I could then just say to delete the ecoast.bigfirm.biz object as well. I'd do this while sitting at a domain controller, logged in as a domain admin (if the DC is a root domain DC) or an enterprise admin.

1. First, open a command prompt and type **ntdsutil**.

2. Type **metadata cleanup** and press Enter. It's the section that deletes objects, but before it can do that, you've got to log onto a DC (yes, it's dumb, you're *sitting* at a DC, but that's software for you), then you've got to tell NTDSUTIL what you want to delete, and only *then* can you delete the DC and then the domain.

3. At the resulting metadata cleanup prompt, type **connections** and press Enter.

4. That changes the prompt to server connections; type **connect to server localhost** and press Enter.

5. Back up to metadata cleanup by typing **quit** and pressing Enter; the prompt will return to metadata cleanup.

6. Now it's time to select a victim. Type **select operation target** and press Enter.

7. You choose domains, sites, and servers by first asking NTDSUTIL to list them. It lists them, giving them all numbers. So, for example, as you have two domains, select ecoast.bigfirm.biz by asking NTDSUTIL to list the domains, and it will list that and bigfirm.biz, numbering them 1 and 0, respectively. Select domain 1 rather than domain ecoast.bigfirm.biz. Then do the same thing for sites and servers. First, type **list domains** and press Enter. You'll see a list of domains, and ecoast.bigfirm.biz is probably number 1.

8. Type **select domain 1** and press Enter to choose ecoast.bigfirm.biz (unless it comes up as a different number on your system).

9. Next, choose the site that your soon-to-be-deleted DC lives in. But you need to know what number site is HQ, where SRV1 lives. You find out what sites exist and what their numbers are by typing **list sites** and pressing Enter.

10. HQ shows up on my system as site 0. Typing **select site 0** and pressing Enter chooses it.

11. Now that we've got a domain and a site, you're closing in on the server. Find its number by typing **list servers for domain in site** and pressing Enter.

12. As there's only one DC, it's no surprise that SRV1's number is 0. Select it by typing **select server 0** and pressing Enter.

13. You've now got your sights on the target, time to pull the trigger. Type **quit** and press Enter to return to metadata cleanup.

14. Now type **remove selected server** and press Enter. You'll get two "are you sure?" dialogs; tell them yes and the server's gone.

15. Finally, type **remove selected domain** and press Enter, then confirm the resulting dialog box and the domain's gone also.

16. Type **quit** and press Enter twice, and you're out of NTDSUTIL.

As your AD gets more and more real use, you'll find yourself using metadata cleanup a few times a year. It's quite useful; I just wish it had a better UI.

Renaming a Domain

So you say you want to rename your domain from acme.com to apex.com? Well, I've got just one question for you, pardner…*are you sure?*

Server 2003 makes it possible to rename domains, so you could indeed rename an AD named acme.com to one named apex.com. But there's more to it than just renaming, as renames also let you *rearrange* a forest. For example, suppose I have a forest containing three domains:

◆ bigfirm.biz
◆ ecoast.bigfirm.biz
◆ apex.com

This forest contains two trees, bigfirm.biz and apex.com, and one of the trees—bigfirm.biz—has a child domain. Suppose I rename ecoast.bigfirm.biz to acme.com? Then I've got these three domains in the forest:

◆ bigfirm.biz

- acme.com
- apex.com

See the difference? Still three domains, but now I've got three trees as well, and no child domains. So renaming is more than just cosmetic—it's a forest rearranger. Renaming cannot, unfortunately, merge domains; for example renaming ecoast.bigfirm.biz to apex.com will not result in all of ecoast.bigfirm.biz being melded into the existing apex.com—the outcome of a rename operation must always leave as many domains in the forest as there once were. And you can't use renaming to change which domain is the forest root, although you can rename the forest root domain.

It all sounds good, doesn't it? Well, get ready for the bad news…it's a fairly lengthy process. You will need to perform, at minimum, 14 steps to do this. As Microsoft says in their documents on domain renames, they intended for it to be a *possible* but not *frequent* operation. And, having spent a couple of weeks experimenting with domain renames, I'd say that they're right. Domain renaming is sufficiently complex that I can't even cover it in detail here without adding at least another 60 pages to the book; Microsoft has about 100 pages of documentation on it online and trust me, there's not a lot of fluff there. So just take this as an overview of what you'll have to do when renaming a domain, and please get the Microsoft papers and read them through—the object of this section is to give you a feel what a domain rename will entail.

THE BASICS

You've already read some of the basics—domains can either be renamed without moving them in the forest, or renames can cause forest moves. Here are a few other top-level considerations.

- This takes your domain out of service for a while. The domain renaming tool, `random.exe`, attempts to convert all of the DCs over at about the same time. That'll keep all of those DCs busy and, to ensure that people don't change things in the domain while the rename is happening, the DCs basically become deaf to normal requests that clients would make of DCs. So plan for a time when it's okay to bring the network down for a few hours.

- Rendom tries to do all of the DC conversion by remote control, but in case that doesn't work you might want some way of remotely controlling any DCs in a different site, either with Server 2003's new "headless server" feature, terminal services, or a human onsite. DCs that for some reason can't handle renaming must be removed from the domain. It's worth stressing that the domain rename doesn't propagate via normal AD replication; it's a separate bit of remote control on Rendom's part to get all the DCs converted.

- If you have a group policy in one domain that is linked to a different domain and either of those domains is the domain that will be renamed, then you'll have to break the link and rebuild it by hand after the rename is finished.

- You cannot rename a domain unless your forest is at Server 2003 forest functional level.

GET THE TOOLS

You can find two programs you need to do the rename on your Server CD in `\VALUEADD\MSFT\MGMT\DOMREN`, `random.exe` and `gpfixup.exe`. There's also a document in that directory that briefly discusses domain renaming and includes a URL to a Microsoft site where you'll find the documents on domain renaming. *Please* download and read them before trying to rename one of your domains.

DOING THE RENAME

In this example, I'll describe how to rename ecoast.bigfirm.biz to acme.com.

1. First, you set up DNS so that there's a dynamic zone ready to receive new SRV records for the new domain name. Create a DNS zone named acme.com and make it dynamic.

2. Next, double-check that your forest is at 2003 functional level. Open Active Directory Domains and Trusts and right-click the Active Directory Domains and Trusts icon, then choose Properties and ensure that the forest functional level is Windows Server 2003 instead of Windows 2000. If it's not 2003-level, then look back in this chapter to see how to raise the functional level.

3. Then build a "shortcut trust" from the domain that you're going to rename to its future parent, if it's going to move in the forest. The idea is that as the move is happening, there's a brief time when the old automatically built trust will be broken and the new one won't yet be in place. So create a two-way shortcut trust between the domain that's being renamed and its parent because the renamed domain will have to communicate with the parent *during* the rename process. For example, suppose you were renaming bld2.se.acme.com to just bld2.com. The old parent domain was se.acme.com, and now the new parent domain will be whatever is the root domain. So you'd create a shortcut trust to that root domain. But what about ecoast.bigfirm.biz? As you're moving from a child domain to a tree of its own, does its parent change? No, not in this case, because ecoast.bigfirm.biz's parent is bigfirm.biz...which happens to be the forest root. Both ecoast.bigfirm.biz and acme.com end up with the same parent. Now, if you're not 100 percent sure whether you need to create a trust or not, go ahead and build one—it doesn't hurt. Use Active Directory Domains and Trusts to create the trust as you saw earlier in our discussion of forest trusts. The wizard's smart enough to keep you from creating unnecessary trusts.

4. After that, look at any Dfs references. We haven't talked about the Distributed File System yet, but you'll learn in three chapters that it's an improvement over the standard file sharing system that lets you create file system connections not to something like \\servername\sharename, but instead to \\domainname\sharename, so your users don't have to know what server a share's on. It's a neat system...but it won't work after a rename. So go to any systems that use drive mappings, shortcuts, etc. that refer to Dfs shares by domain names and rebuild them to refer to server names.

5. Now it's time to get busy, but to do that you'll need to locate a member server in the domain that you're going to rename; you'll run Rendom from there. Yes, you read that right—you can't rename a domain while sitting at a DC. This will be annoying to people in small domains with just two servers, both of which are DCs. (I suppose you could demote one DC, run Rendom and repromote the server back to a DC.)

6. Log on to the member server as an enterprise admin and put Rendom and Gpfixup on the member server. Open a command line and type **rendom /list**. You'll get a response "The operation completed successfully."

7. Rendom created a file called `domainlist.xml` in whatever directory you ran Rendom in. Open up `domainlist.xml` with Notepad. Mine looks like this:

```
<?xml version ="1.0"?>
<Forest>
```

```
<Domain>
    <Guid>de18a3e1-225c-4756-962a-944963e30290</Guid>
    <DNSname>ecoast.bigfirm.biz</DNSname>
    <NetBiosName>ECOAST</NetBiosName>
    <DcName></DcName>
</Domain>
<Domain>
    <!-- PartitionType:Application -->
    <Guid>eea9bbe2-de49-4d32-a234-1e605c901e63</Guid>
    <DNSname>DomainDnsZones.bigfirm.biz</DNSname>
    <NetBiosName></NetBiosName>
    <DcName></DcName>
</Domain>
<Domain>
    <!-- PartitionType:Application -->
    <Guid>d6af0d02-b21c-44b2-a409-88de08dc5f59</Guid>
    <DNSname>ForestDnsZones.bigfirm.biz</DNSname>
    <NetBiosName></NetBiosName>
    <DcName></DcName>
</Domain>
<Domain>
    <!-- ForestRoot -->
    <Guid>ca18330e-f33a-48f1-a11c-8878536cf06c</Guid>
    <DNSname>bigfirm.biz</DNSname>
    <NetBiosName>BIGFIRM</NetBiosName>
    <DcName></DcName>
</Domain>
</Forest>
```

In case you've never seen an XML file before, it's a way of storing data in what is intended to be a self-describing way. The things in the angle brackets are called *tags*—<Domain>, <DNSname>, <NetBiosName>, and the like are tags. Notice that every tag has a partner tag with a / in the front of its name, like </Domain>, </DNSname>, and </NetBiosName>. Think of these <tag> and </tag> pairs as being sort of like left and right parentheses that also describe the data between them. For example,

```
<NetBiosName>ECOAST</NetBiosName>
```

Means "this particular object has a NetBIOSName of "ECOAST." Armed with this info, you can see a few things. First, the whole file describes a forest, as you can see from the fact that the very first line is <Forest> and the last is </Forest>. Within that are several <Domain>-and-</Domain> sets. Each domain contains a Guid, a DNSname, a NetBiosName, and a DcName—we'll need to use the DNSname and NetBiosName sections. Notice that the first domain's DNS name is ecoast.bigfirm.biz and its NetBiosName is ECOAST—that's the domain whose name you want to change. Believe it or not, the way that you tell Rendom to rename the domain is to directly edit this file—so change ecoast.bigfirm.biz to acme.com and "ECOAST" to "ACME," and save the file.

8. Next, check your work by typing **random /showforest** to make sure that you didn't mess up the XML file. The output will look something like this:

```
acme.com [FlatName:ACME]
bigfirm.biz [ForestRoot Domain, FlatName:BIGFIRM]
   DomainDnsZones.bigfirm.biz [PartitionType:Application]
   ForestDnsZones.bigfirm.biz [PartitionType:Application]

The operation completed successfully.
```

That looks correct—ecoast.bigfirm.biz is gone, and acme.com is visible.

9. Now run random /upload. That creates another XML file, dclist.xml, that lists the DCs that the domain rename routine will have to find and modify.

10. Then run random /prepare, which reads the dclist.xml file and uses it to find DCs and get them ready for the domain rename. You'll see output something like this:

```
C:\domren>random /prepare
Waiting for DCs to reply.
Waiting for DCs to reply.
memsv1.ecoast.bigfirm.biz was prepared successfully
srv1.ecoast.bigfirm.biz was prepared successfully
bigdog.bigfirm.biz was prepared successfully
3 servers contacted, 0 servers returned Errors


The operation completed successfully.
```

11. Now you're ready for the big step—random /execute. My output looks like this:

```
C:\domren>random /execute
Waiting for DCs to reply.
Waiting for DCs to reply.
The script was executed successfully on memsv1.ecoast.bigfirm.biz
The script was executed successfully on srv1.ecoast.bigfirm.biz
The script was executed successfully on bigdog.bigfirm.biz
3 servers contacted, 0 servers returned Errors


The operation completed successfully.
```

12. The domain's mostly renamed, but there are a few items left. First, reboot all member servers and workstations in the renamed domain, *twice*. You need both reboots to confirm the membership and change the domain suffix.

13. Unfortunately Rendom can't make the DCs change their domain suffixes automatically, as it did with the member servers and workstations. So you've got to do it by hand—go to each DC and change its DNS suffix from the old domain name to the new one. If you're a Windows 2000 veteran and are looking at me strangely when I tell you to go rename your DC, that's a nice new feature of Server 2003—you can now rename DCs just as you rename all

other systems. (Right-click My Computer and choose Properties, then click Computer Name, in case you've forgotten how.)

14. Then the group policies need adjustment. Do that with `gpfixup.exe`, whose syntax looks like

```
gpfixup /olddns:oldname /newdns:newname /oldnb:oldNetBIOSname
    /newdb:newNetBIOSname /dc:name-of-PDC-emulator
```

Where olddns and newdns refer to the old and new DNS-like AD names, and oldnb and newnb refer to the old and new NetBIOS names. *name-of-PDC-emulator* is, as you'd imagine, the DNS name of the DC in the renamed domain that acts as the PDC FSMO. In this example, you'd type

```
gpfixup /olddns:ecoast.bigfirm.biz /newdns:acme.com /oldnb:ecoast /newnb:acme
    /dc:srv1.acme.com
```

And that's it. Congratulations, you're renamed a domain! Again, let me stress that this was an *easy* rename, as we had only a tiny number of DCs and all in a single site. Be sure to read the two Microsoft documents before trying it on a real domain.

Active Directory Oddities

We're almost done with the Active Directory but, before I forget, I want to alert you to a few "gotchas" in AD. I'll list them briefly.

If Two Admins Both Modify a Group, One's Changes Get Lost

One of AD's strengths in comparison to NT is its replication model. Instead of a single read-write domain controller backed up by a bunch of read-only domain controllers, every DC is read-write and a complex multimaster replication structure makes sure that each DC knows about the changes that each other DC receives. Replications over slow WAN links compress data 10 to 1 before transmitting, and administrators can schedule when those replications happen. When you changed a single attribute about a user account under NT 4, NT replicated the user's entire record; AD only replicates the changed attribute.

So where's the problem? AD stores a group's membership as one attribute. Group membership as an attribute in combination with multimaster replication creates another potential problem: membership change collisions. The demise of the single-master model makes the following scenario possible: Suppose there's a DC in St. Louis and another in Ottawa, both part of the same domain. A group called FaxServerOperators contains, not surprisingly, the names of the users allowed to administer some mythical fax server software. Now suppose that Julie, a domain administrator in Ottawa, adds herself to the FaxServerOperators group, and at roughly the same time Steve, an admin in St. Louis, adds himself to that group.

They've each changed the members attribute that is part of the record that describes the FaxServerOperators object. Ottawa starts replicating Julie's change locally and across the WAN, St. Louis starts replicating Steve's change, and eventually they collide. Who wins? There's a long algorithm that AD uses to figure that out, but basically it's whoever's change happened last.

What to do about this? There are three possible answers.

First, it might be that you don't modify group memberships all that often, and so there's nothing to worry about. But if you want to ensure that changes to group memberships don't collide, then you could return to the days of NT 4, so to speak, by choosing one of your domain's domain controllers as a kind of "administrative clearinghouse," telling all of your administrators around the globe that before they change a group's membership, they should first focus Active Directory Users and Computers on that "clearinghouse" domain controller. You can do that, by the way, by right-clicking the icon representing your domain. Then choose Connect to Domain Controller and fill in the name of the DC that you want to work with.

Second, you could always use the sneaky "version number" trick that I showed you a few pages back (heh, heh).

Third and best, this is fixed in forests at Windows Server 2003 forest functional level. So get to 2003 forest functional level as soon as possible!

Make Changes on DCs Near the Target Client

The group collision discussion leads to some general advice for administrators in geographically scattered domains: Don't assume that AD's replication structure will respond quickly enough to serve your clients' needs. Let's return to St. Louis and Ottawa, but this time let's make Steve in St. Louis a regular user without any administrative powers, and Julie an admin in a centralized, company-wide help desk. Steve needs something changed in his AD account, perhaps because he's in a different department or his phone extension has changed. He contacts Julie and asks her to update his AD record, and she does.

But how long will it be before Steve sees the changes?

Both St. Louis and Ottawa contain DCs. When Steve queries AD about his account, he's probably talking to a DC in St. Louis. When Julie makes an AD change, however, she's likely to be communicating with a DC in Ottawa. If she and Steve worked on the same site, then all of the domain controllers on the site would know of the change that Julie made within a fairly short time—DCs replicate any changes to the other DCs in their site in 15 minutes. But what about replication across WAN links—how fast is that and how quickly would Steve's local DCs know about Julie's changes? That's up to whoever designed your AD replication structure. Frequent updates across WAN links mean that news of account changes travels quickly, but it also sucks up WAN bandwidth, so if Julie and Steve's company is parsimonious in its use of WAN bandwidth for replication then it might be a while before Steve's local DCs see Julie's changes. But Julie can change that by focusing Active Directory Users and Computers on a DC near to Steve. By initiating the AD change in St. Louis rather than Ottawa, Julie ensures that Steve's local DCs will see the account changes more quickly. The cost is that Julie must do account changes through a DC that's communicating with her at WAN speeds rather than LAN speeds—but what price customer service?

You're probably thinking, "What about changes to passwords? Will they suffer from slow replication?" What if Steve asks Julie to give him a new password, as he's forgotten his old one, and so she does—but while she's connected to an Ottawa DC, not a St. Louis DC. Will Steve have to wait for however long it takes for Ottawa to replicate the new password to St. Louis? No: AD treats passwords a bit differently. Suppose Steve tries to log in immediately in St. Louis, before any of the St. Louis DCs know of his new password. His attempted logon fails, but before the St. Louis DC reports that failure, the St. Louis DC communicates with the single DC in the domain, which acts as something called the PDC Flexible Single Master of Operations, even if that PDC FSMO is across a WAN link. That machine always has the most up-to-date password, and can authenticate Steve for St. Louis.

Choose Your Domain Names Well

Some things never change. Once you've created a domain, you can't change its name. Of course, there are two work-arounds to that.

First, you could always create a new domain with the newly desired name, then use some directory migration tool to copy user and machine accounts over to that new domain, but that's a nontrivial process, no matter how easy our friends at NetIQ, Fastlane, Entevo, and Aelita are trying to make it.

Second, you can use the Domain Rename Wizard... but it only works if your forest is at 2003 functional level.

Planning Your Active Directory Structure

The idea of this chapter is to give you an overall idea of how AD's pieces work. I strongly suggest that you peruse the rest of this book before starting in on building your AD structure, as the AD *permeates* Windows 2000 and Server 2003. But here are few hints on how to get started on designing your AD structure.

Examine Your WAN Topology

Domain controllers in a domain must replicate among themselves in order to keep domain information consistent across the domain. DCs need not be connected exactly 24/7—you *could* just dial connections between branch offices and the home office every day or so and then try to force replication to occur, although it's not simple and may lead to problems down the road—but on the whole you'll find that domains work best if they have constant end-to-end connection. If you have an area that's poorly or sporadically served by your WAN connections, perhaps it's best to make it a separate domain.

Lay Out Your Sites

Once you know where the WAN connections are, list the sites that you'll have, name them, and figure out which machines go in what sites. Also document the nature of their connections—speed and cost—to assist Active Directory in using the inter-site bandwidth wisely.

Figure Out Which Existing Domains to Merge and Merge Them

You'll probably want to reduce the number of domains in your enterprise. One way to do that would be to merge old resource domains into an old master domain. The idea here would be that you first upgrade the master domain to Server 2003, then merge the old NT 4 resource domains into that master domain as organizational units, using NETDOM, ADMT, or whatever other migration tools you might buy.

What Needs an OU and What Needs a Domain?

As you read earlier, you can divide up enterprises either by breaking them up into multiple domains or by creating a single domain and using organizational units to parcel out administrative control, or you can do any combination of those.

This is partially a political question, but you can get a head start by looking at the perceived needs of the organization. Is administration centralized or decentralized? Do the company's divisions work together closely, or is there not very much collaboration? And be sure to get corporate sign-off on these matters from the executive suite or be prepared to deal with the bruised egos later.

From a technical point of view, there are really only a few reasons to use more than one domain, as you've read. The biggest reason is replication traffic. If you have two large domains connected only by a slow WAN link, then you may find that it makes sense to keep them as separate domains. But think carefully about it—Active Directory is very efficient at using WAN links for domain replication traffic. There's also the "we don't trust the branch office" reason, as well as the far less likely reason that you need to grant different account policies to some group.

Choose an OU Structure for Delegation, Then for Group Policies

I haven't discussed group policies all that much in this chapter—they'll get more coverage later in Chapters 9 and 12 and other places—but one thing worth noting about group policies is that they're a tool for controlling users and computers.

As you read earlier, group policies don't really apply to groups; they apply to OUs. That would seem to mean that you should organize groups of people that you want to control into OUs so that it's easy to create and apply group policies to them.

On the other hand, recall that the great strength of organizational units under Active Directory is that you can create groups of users, which you can give varying degrees of control (*delegate*) over those OUs. In the end, you'll find that delegation can affect system performance more than group policies, so when you're chopping up your domains into OUs, choose OUs that make sense from a delegation point of view. Does Manufacturing want their own local administrators? Put the Manufacturing users into an OU. Does Publicity want to control their own printers? Then put their printers into an OU. In any case, you probably won't find much conflict between an OU structure that's group policy–centric over an OU structure that's delegation-centric: after all, any group that wants to share an administrator probably also wants that administrator to have control over it through group policies.

Use Just One Domain if Possible

Sorry for the repetition, but let me say one more time: minimize the number of domains. In fact, minimize them to just *one* domain, if possible. Active Directory domains can be truly huge, able to contain millions of objects, large enough for almost any enterprise. And AD's site-awareness allows it to make good use of your low-speed, expensive wide area network bandwidth.

Develop Names for Your Domains/Trees

Active Directory allows a wider variety of domain names than NT 4 allowed, but sometimes you can have too much of a good thing, too *many* options. If you're going multidomain, how will the domains fit together? Do you divide geographically, by division, by function? Where are the lines of control in the organization now?

Get the DNS Infrastructure Ready

I hope I've beaten this one to death enough so far, so I'll keep this short. Remember:

◆ Create a DNS zone whose name matches your AD domain's and don't be afraid to use an imaginary top-level domain.

◆ Make sure it's dynamic or do the jiggery-pokery with delegating the subzones.

◆ You needn't use a Microsoft DNS server, but it's not a bad idea, particularly with AD-integrated zones.

◆ Split-brain DNS is a not only a good idea, it's the *right* idea to protect your zones from external prying eyes for 99 percent of the ADs.

◆ If you're having trouble creating extra domain controllers, joining machines to the domain, or just plain logging in, use the `nslookup` tool to check the SRV records for global catalog and domain controllers.

Use the Power of Inheritance

The notion of things existing inside things runs throughout: organizational units can exist inside other OUs, and of course all OUs ultimately exist inside domains, domains exist inside trees, and trees exist inside forests.

When you set a permission or some other security policy on an object (*object* here meaning an OU, domain, forest, or tree), then anything created thereafter inside that object takes on that security policy. This is called *inheritance*. So, for example, if you wanted every user account in a forest to have to change its password every 10 days, it's far easier to set that rule up at the top of the forest before creating other domains, trees, OUs, and the like, because in general, from that point on, any new trees, domains, or OUs created in the forest will have the 10-day-password-change rule. (I said "in general" because it's possible to block inheritance; it's possible for an administrator to configure an object to ignore effects from higher-level objects.)

Overall AD Design Advice

There's lots to consider in building your AD and only you know what your organization needs and wants—I can't pass along a standard one-size-fits-all design for an AD. But overall, remember these things:

◆ Use sites to control bandwidth and replication.

◆ Use organizational units to create islands of users and/or computers, which you can then delegate administrative control over.

◆ Use domains to solve replication problems and possible political problems.

◆ Use forests to create completely separate network systems. If, for example, your enterprise had a subsidiary that wasn't completely trusted (in the human sense, not the NT sense) and you were worried that the automatic trust relationships (in the NT sense) created by common membership in a forest might lead to unwanted security links, then make them separate forests. The value of separate forests is that there is no security relationship at all between two forests unless you explicitly create the relationship using NT trust relationships.

Understanding and Using Certificates

Before leaving the Active Directory, let's cover a tool that enhances some of the AD's abilities. You've probably heard the terms *digital certificate* or, more likely, simply *certificate* and perhaps *public key* or *public key infrastructure*, or its inevitable TLA, "PKI." You've probably also heard that Microsoft has included

PKI infrastructure components into its NT-based OSes since Windows 2000. So what can it do for you, and how can you make Windows Server 2003 do it?

PKI is a topic so large that I'd need a fair-sized book to do it real justice, so this section is just an overview of Microsoft's implementation of PKI. The two most significant points that you should get out of it, however, are the following:

- PKI is a standards-based and OS-independent way to authenticate you—to prove who you are.
- Although it's got a lot of promise, PKI's not yet heavily used in Windows server operating systems, save in a few applications.

So to answer the "what does this do for you" question broadly: A certificate is a kind of ID card, a passport that proves with a high degree of reliability that you are indeed you. But they're not only good for identifying people—they work for servers as well or, for that matter, just about anything that needs to prove its identity.

But there's more to it than just that. Certificates aren't a Microsoft invention; they're based on standards and vendors other than Microsoft support them, and in fact some of Microsoft's competitors have been heavy users of PKI for years before Microsoft noticed the field. Of course, that may not be a bad thing; after all, that means that Microsoft's PKI tools are based on the latest versions of well-understood technologies. One standard that you'll hear of a lot is X.509, a certificate format that Microsoft adopted for their certificate services.

That was the good news. The bad news is that PKI on 2003 Server is still something of a work in progress. If you were to, for example, "get religion" about PKI and decide that you'd like to rip out the standard underlying Microsoft security systems and replace them with just PKI, then you can't. You can't, for example, tell domain controllers to stop authenticating each other with Kerberos and start using PKI. You *could* set your users up to log on using certificates, but it'd be a bit expensive (see the following comments about smart cards). Here's what you can do with PKI under Windows Server 2003:

- **Create and use certificates to allow two systems from different domains use IPSec.** As you read in Chapter 6, IPSec is a very nice way to authenticate and/or encrypt IP communications between two (or, actually, more than two) systems across the Internet. But those systems need to be able to authenticate and Microsoft (and the RFCs) only offer three options: Both sides share a simple phrase as the password (yuck), both sides authenticate via Kerberos (not bad, but only works if their systems are in the same forest), or via certificates. Certificates are really the only way that two systems that are not members of the same forest can accomplish IPSec.
- **Securing Web access.** One of the many ways that you can control who accesses your Web sites is via certificates.
- **Create and use certificates to secure e-mail inside an organization.** You can create user-specific e-mail certificates that users can use either to authenticate or encrypt their e-mail communications. The only problem is that all parties involved must accept as valid certificates that *your* server creates. Clearly that's a doable thing if we're talking about one company or a couple of companies in partnership, but it wouldn't work so well to secure mail to the great wide world. For that, you need to go to a generally trusted certificate source such as Thawte, which I'll cover later.

- **Smart card logons.** Certificates are a neat tool…but can you use them for logons? After all, that's the authentication that I'm most interested in most mornings. Sure, you can use them…but there is the small problem of entering the certificate to begin with. In a normal logon with a normal user account and password, you type in your logon name, such as jane@acme.com, and a password. But typing in a certificate would be pretty difficult, as they can be thousands of bytes long. So you *can* log onto a domain or server with a certificate, but only if you've got that certificate stored on a credit-card-sized device called a *smart card*. You also need a smart card *reader* on your system to do this. I found that add-on USB smart card readers cost about $40 apiece— not a deal-breaker, but, if you need a lot of them, probably a bit much to spend for a technology that's just getting started in the Microsoft world. In any case, smart cards relate to certificates in this way: If you want to do smart cards, then you *must* use certificates.
- **EFS recovery agents.** The Encrypted File System lets you set up people who can decrypt your files in the event that you don't remember your password. You designate new *recovery agents*— the emergency decrypter guys—with certificates.
- **Signing programs.** As you probably know, Windows 2000 and later operating systems support the idea of "signing" a given program, software installation package or driver, ensuring either the software's provenance or that it's been tested by Microsoft's hardware lab. That signing is done with certificates.

All of this is a good thing, but as I say it's just an interim step. In the future, it'll be possible (as a matter of fact, this is possible now, but it's unusual) to carry around one smart card that holds your personal certificate. Now suppose you have an account that you use on a Novell network, one on an Active Directory forest, a One-Click account at Amazon.com, and so on. Here's how public keys will make your life easier: You give a copy of your certificate to the Novell network's administrator, the AD forest's admin, Amazon, and the other folks who have an account of yours. They then make an association between your certificate and the local account that they keep for you, a process called "mapping the certificate to the account." From that point on, your smart card gets you access to all of those accounts. Just one password to worry about, and finally that Holy Grail of account management—single logons. Log on once at your PC and you're connected everywhere.

Of course, that's not the only way that PKI could work. You could keep a certificate encrypted on your workstation and then use a standard login to decrypt it; it would then get you logged onto your Novell, Amazon, and other accounts. Or why not just put the certificate on a floppy? That'd work too…but in every case security is the issue, and as floppies are easy to copy and hard to secure I suppose that's why you don't see this answer. It's a shame, though, because although smart cards are a neat idea, it's going to be years (if ever) before smart card readers are standard on PCs. (And then we get to fight over which vendor's smart card technology we adopt, and, well, you've seen that movie before.) So personally I wish that we could use floppies as a sort of interim smart card, but I don't imagine it's going to happen soon.

Let's look a bit at how PKI works under the hood, then look at some of the specifics of PKI in Windows Server 2003.

Public Key Pieces I: Public Keys, Private Keys, and Authentication

Certificates and PKI terminology includes a lot of references to *public* and *private* keys. Let's see what they are and how they let people identify themselves to others. For example, suppose I want to negotiate a contract with you electronically, over e-mail. It's easy enough to send proposed documents back and forth, but the last part—the legally binding signature indicating agreement—that's been tough to do over e-mail. But what if I could send you an e-mail saying "I agree" that you could be 100-percent sure came from me? That'd do the trick.

All I'm looking to do here is prove that I sent it. There's nothing secret in the e-mail, so I have no need to encrypt it; I just want to *authenticate* it, or, in public key terminology, to "sign" it.

KEY FACTS ABOUT KEYS

To do this, I ask my computer to generate two numbers called a *private* key and a *public* key. They're called *keys* because I can use them to lock (that is, encrypt) some bunch of data, or to unlock (that is, decrypt) that data. (I know I just said that I don't want to encrypt the e-mail, but we *will* need to encrypt a bit of data, as you'll see.) PKI can be easy to understand, but you'll find it puzzling unless you're clear on a couple of things:

- Again, there are two different "keys" generated.
- They are quite long numbers, hundreds of digits long. That's so that it'd be nearly impossible for someone to just try every combination with a computer program—some keys are so long that the fastest computer in the world would take trillions of years to try every combination! (And by then, I probably wouldn't worry about the attacker cracking my data.)
- PKI uses the keys for encryption and decryption of data.
- We arbitrarily choose one of the two keys to be the private key and keep it hidden—no one should ever see this. The other key is the public key, and we can hand out it to anyone. For a long time, cryptographic algorithms used "symmetric" encryption, meaning that you used the same key to *encrypt* as to *decrypt*. But in 1970 or 1976—depending on whose story you believe—mathematicians came up with an interesting new kind of cryptographic method that uses *one* key to encrypt and a *different* key to decrypt. This is called *asymmetric* encryption. PKI uses asymmetric encryptions.

NOTE   *I say "depending on whose story you believe" because for a long time the researchers credited with first describing and making practical an asymmetric encryption technique were two American mathematicians named Whitfield Diffie and Martin Hellman, who first presented their technique in 1976. In 1997, however, a British cryptologist named James Ellis claimed he'd created the idea for British intelligence back in 1970.*

- If you encrypt something with the public key, only the private key can decrypt it. If you encrypt something with the private key, only the public key can decrypt it. Things encrypted with the public key *cannot* be decrypted with the public key, and things encrypted with the private key cannot be decrypted with the private key.

PREPARING AND SIGNING A MESSAGE

So let's see how I can use public and private keys to send some secured e-mail.

First, I run a program to generate a public/private key pair. I hide the private key somewhere safe on my hard disk. I make my public key easily available to anyone who wants it—hand it out on floppies, put it on my Web site, whatever. (We're going to refine this process soon, I promise, but for now let's just hand out public keys this way.)

Next, I prepare my message for you, something like "I agree to the following contract," followed by the text of the contract. That's our message body. I give it to my e-mail client and tell the client to "sign" the message.

The e-mail client then runs the message text through a program called a *hash function* that boils down the message to just a few bytes, a *digest.* Hash functions are also called *one-way functions* because you stuff in some data (your message, in this case) and get out a digest, *but you can't necessarily reverse the process.* That's not necessary. For example, suppose I wanted to hash the message "Meet me at the bridge." I want to boil that down to just a single number. I could do that by noticing that text files are all ASCII and that ASCII codes are numeric—"m" is 109, "e" is 101, a space is 32, and so on. My message then becomes this:

```
m e e t <space> m e <space> a t <space> t h e <space> b r i d g e
109+101+101+116+32+109+101+32+97+116+32+116+104+101+32+98+114+105+100+103+101 = 1,920.
```

Thus, I've boiled down the message into a single number, a digest. We're going to use that in a minute to prove that the message did indeed come from me. But before I do, let's notice why this is a one-way function. There would be no way to deduce from 1920 that the original message was "meet-me-at-the-bridge" short of generating all possible messages, computing their digests and then looking at the messages whose digests were 1920—and there'd be a lot of them—and guessing which one was my original message. (And, by the way, I just showed you the simplest hash function possible—crypto systems actually use more complex ones.)

So let me stress—digests aren't for *transmitting* data; they're for *authenticating* a data stream's author, or at least that's what we're about to try to do.

Now we've got a message body and a digest created from that message body—now it's time to do some encrypting. Using my private key, my e-mail program encrypts the digest. It then sends you an e-mail containing two things: the message text and the encrypted digest of the message text.

RECEIVING AND VERIFYING THE MESSAGE

Now let's see what you do on your end. Your e-mail client receives the message and notices that it is signed. Time to check the signature! So the e-mail program takes the message and, using the same hashing function as my e-mail client, computes a digest for the message.

Now, if the digest that I sent you (based on the message text that I sent) is the same as the one that you compute (based on the message that you received), then we can be pretty sure that you received the message accurately. But how do you know that the message came from *me*? That's where the encrypted digest comes in. You compute that the digest of the received message equals 1920. You want to check that against the digest that I sent you—but it's encrypted. Remember that I encrypted it using my private key. The only key that can decrypt it, then, is my public key—which you've already gotten. So your e-mail program decrypts the digest and sees that the decrypted value is 1920.

You could only have gotten a decrypted value of 1920 from my public key if the original value that encrypted the digest was my private key. You got a matching value—1920—so the message digest must have been sent by me. If anyone had tampered with the message en route, then you'd have a message that would lead to a different message digest value.

In this way, we can use public keys to verify that a message did indeed come from a particular sender.

WHY THIS IS IMPORTANT: NO "SHARED SECRETS"

Notice something about that communication—I sent something to you that I was able to guarantee came from me using encryption; I was able to perform the equivalent of physically signing a contract, but at a distance. We didn't *need* public and private keys to do that, however. Alternatively, I could have just called you up at the beginning of our negotiation process and said, "Let's do this over e-mail, but to make sure that we authenticate each communication, we'll send along encrypted digests of the mails." So far, this is no different from what we did. But if we didn't have public key technology, then you'd say to me, "Okay, how do I decrypt these digests?" I'd then have to say, "Hmmm...for this negotiation, I'll encrypt the digests with the password u8Kj$3NsF. Use that password to decrypt the digest." In other words, we'd do the same thing as we did before, but instead of using an asymmetric encryption method, we'd use a symmetric encryption method. That involves no great brain power, as people have been doing symmetric encryption for centuries. This password, which is known to us both, is called a *shared secret*, and all symmetric encryption methods require shared secrets.

But do you see the weaknesses in this method?

I'd have to get on the phone with you and read you a password—quite a pain. You might mistranscribe it, as uppercase and lowercase matter. You'll probably write it down somewhere, certainly as you're taking the message from me. And what if it's just plain difficult to find a time when we both can get on the phone, such as if you're on the other side of the Earth? (That may be the reason we're creating a business agreement electronically to begin with.) Or I guess I could just send it to you in an e-mail, but then I'm sending a password over the Internet—the not-so-secure Internet—and then I'd have to worry that someone intercepted that password.

Additionally, I'd have to come up with a different password every time I negotiated something via e-mail, as I wouldn't want to use the same password with more than one person—if word got out that I always used "rutabaga" as my password, then anyone could digitally impersonate me.

That's the neat part about public/private key pairs. I didn't have to tell you anything except my public key, and I don't care *who* has that.

Public Key Pieces II: Encrypted Communications (SSL)

You've seen that one of the keys—no pun intended—to PKI is encryption. We just used it to verify a message's sender, but we didn't really encrypt much of anything—just a few bytes of a message digest. But sometimes we want to carry on an entire conversation in secret, to encrypt the entire transmission.

For example, let's consider an encrypted transmission method that you've probably used quite a bit over time—a Secure Sockets Layer, or SSL, communication. You do one every time you buy something on the Internet and that little lock icon appears in your Internet Explorer status bar. That communication depends upon public and private keys, as you'll see.

Suppose you're going to buy something from Bigfirm on its Web site. You click the Buy Now link next to some piece of merchandise, and your Web browser sees that the destination of that link wants security—the URL of the page is https://something rather than http://something. (The extra *s* means *secure*.)

Your browser and Bigfirm's Web server will communicate via symmetric encryption. They'll agree on some key and then they'll use that key to encrypt transmitted data and also use that same key to decrypt received data. (Why not asymmetric encryption, you ask? Well, for one thing, it takes a *lot* more CPU time than symmetric encryption.)

So your Web browser and Bigfirm's Web server say, "Okay, just for today we'll agree that we'll use the key KD39z82fRnx+H to encrypt and decrypt. If we ever talk again, we'll pick another random key for *that* session—but use this one for this particular session."

Simple, eh? Sure, except for one problem: *How do they agree on the key?* The whole idea is that you don't want someone to be able to just listen in on the communication and decrypt the traffic as it goes by, particularly if that traffic includes the information "Joe Smith lives at this address and his credit card number is such-and-such." So we encrypt the communication, and so no one can listen in. Sounds good, except for one little thing.

How does Bigfirm's Web server tell your Web browser, "Let's use the key KD39z82fRnx+H?" Clearly it shouldn't communicate that information in cleartext (that is, unencrypted text), or the bad guys will just make use of the very same key to listen in on (and perhaps even modify) the conversation. So symmetric encryption will help us...if only we can get the whole thing started with a secure exchange of keys.

That's where *asymmetric* encryption comes in. Let's see how.

To begin with, Bigfirm's Web server has a public and a private key. Your Web browser, on the other hand, does not. (Why not? Well, do you remember telling it to create one? No? Then it hasn't got one. And even if it did, it wouldn't use it in this context, trust me.) So how could we use encryption to exchange keys? Well, the Bigfirm Web server *could* generate a session key—that's the phrase for these use-'em-one-and-throw-them-away keys, like that KD39z82fRnx+H key I've been talking about—and encrypt it before sending it to your Web browser.

But consider this: If Bigfirm encrypts the key with its private key, then the public key will decrypt it...but *everyone* has Bigfirm's public key. Well, then, what if Bigfirm encrypts the key with its public key? Well, then, you'll need Bigfirm's private key to decrypt it, and the bad guys don't have Bigfirm's private key, so they won't be able to steal the session key.

Unfortunately, *you* won't be able to use it either, as you also lack the private key. What to do?

Let's look at the other way around: What if *your Web browser* were to suggest the session key? Here's how it works:

◆ Your Web browser knows Bigfirm's public key and uses it to encrypt the session key.

◆ Your Web browser then sends the encrypted session key to Bigfirm's Web server, which uses its private key to decrypt.

◆ *Now* you've got an agreement on a key that you can use for encrypting traffic between your Web browse and Bigfirm's Web server!

You will hear the phrase *key exchange* a lot in PKI. It usually means the same thing: We intend to establish some communication that we want to encrypt using a symmetric encryption algorithm. But to agree on a key in the first place, one side encrypts a suggested session key with the *other* side's public key. The other side can then decrypt it, and no one can snatch the session key as it goes by on the wire but the intended recipient.

Public Key Pieces III: Certificates and Certificate Authorities

Thus far, you've seen that we can "sign" or "authenticate" a communication, leaving the communication in cleartext but allowing the receiver to verify that I'm the message's sender and that the message wasn't modified along the way. You've also seen that we can use public and private keys to exchange session keys that we can then use to encrypt an entire transmission, both authenticating it and ensuring that no one snoops on it.

But there's something I've kind of swept under the rug so far—how those public keys get disseminated. How would your Web browser get a copy of Bigfirm's public key? How would your e-mail client get my public key to use in verifying my message in the first place? I kind of waved my hands and said that I could give you my public key on a floppy or put it on my Web site, and that's only partly true. Yes, I could put my public key on a floppy, but then how would I get it to you? If you lived down the street, then I could hand it to you. If you lived far away, I could FedEx it to you, but that would get kind of expensive, and takes time. Sure, I could put my public key on my Web site, but then we're faced with a chicken-and-egg question: How do you know that you're actually looking at my Web site when you grab that public key and not a clever copy that some bad guy creates while somehow diverting your DNS lookups of www.minasi.com? You can't, so we need another method of handing out public keys. That method is called *certificates*.

WHAT'S IN A CERTIFICATE

A digital certificate isn't a physical certificate with an attractive border and your name in big fancy letters; instead, it's just a bunch of bytes that contain, at minimum:

- The name of the thing that the certificate describes—it might be a person (the e-mail example), a server (the SSL example), or anything else. Certificate documents call this the *entity*, as it's a nice generic name for "person, server, or whatever."
- The public key of the entity. (Notice how quickly we slip into that cert-speak—entity.)
- When the certificate expires. Certificates have an expiration date. For example, the SSL certificate on my Web server expires every two years.
- What kind of certificate this is. There are certs for securing e-mail, certs for identifying servers for IPSec, certs for securing Web servers via SSL, and so on.
- Who issued the certificate. I'll explain this in a minute.
- Other identifying information, which varies with the type of the certificate.

GETTING A CERTIFICATE

That's what's *in* a certificate—but what *is* a certificate? Put simply, it is a public key and some identifying information about you, as you saw in the previous bullets, all collected and then digitally signed by someone else. The idea is that when I need to give you my public key then, as I said before, I can't just hand it to you unadorned, as you have no real way to know that it came from me. So instead I hand it to you...but the bytes that I hand you have been digitally signed by some third party that both you and I trust.

If that's not clear, let's see what happens a bit more specifically. First of all, I need a certificate before I can give one to you. Here are the steps to getting one.

First, I generate a public/private key pair. But why would anyone believe that it was actually me that generated the pair or, actually, the public key, as I'll never show you the private key? That's where the next step comes in.

Next, I contact a company that issues certificates, a *certificate authority*, or CA. Examples of such companies would be VeriSign, Thawte, or Baltimore. I give them my public key and ask them to create a certificate. Only *they* can create a certificate signed by them, as only they have their private key, and they generally charge for the service. (Or, in some cases, I might instead create my *own* CA and start minting my own certificates. I'll show you how to do that later.)

After that, the CA wants to make sure that I'm actually me, so they usually want to see something that validates my claim. For example, if I want a certificate for www.minasi.com, then I've got to prove that I actually own minasi.com and am doing business under that name. Verifying *some* certificate types is easy; to validate an e-mail certificate, you've just got to send the certificate to that e-mail address.

Once the CA is satisfied that I'm me, they build the certificate, including my name, public key, expiration date, and who they—the issuing CA—are. Then they run it through their hashing function, and the digest for the certificate pops out. They then pull out their private key and encrypt the digest. Put it all together and it's a certificate. They e-mail it to me and I install it on the appropriate software—it might be Outlook if it's a "Hey, I'm really Mark Minasi" certificate for e-mail, or IIS if it's a Web server certificate.

USING A CERTIFICATE

Once I've installed the certificate on my system, here's how it gets used. Suppose again that I send you a piece of e-mail that I want to digitally sign. I'll take you through the steps on it, but first let's cover certificate types.

Types of Certificates

I'm about to explain how I could use a certificate to prove that a piece of e-mail that I send you actually came from me. But I want to note that while I've been just saying "certificate" as if they were all the same, they are *not*, not by any means. Certificates associate some identity and usually some attribute to a computer, user, or service. For example:

E-mail   I've already mentioned e-mail signing certificates and encrypting certs without actually saying that they are two different kinds of certs. You can get a certificate that does both, but you sometimes won't. Inside that certificate would be a bit of information that says, "This certificate can be used for e-mail signing," or, "This certificate can be used for e-mail encryption," or both. *Why* would you have two different certificates for signing and encryption? Because you use them in different ways. You need the encryption key to decrypt encrypted mail that people send you. You need the signing key to prove that you are you over e-mail. You'd have two keys because you want to back up the encryption key, *and you never want to back up the signing key*. If you lost the encryption key, then you would not be able to read any old or new encrypted mail, so you'd want to restore that key. But if you lost your *signing* key, then there's no problem—you just get another one. But you would never want to back up your signing key because if someone got hold of the backup and installed it on her system then she could impersonate you! E-mail certificates are typically associated with a user.

Web browser   Suppose you want to access a restricted Web site. How do you prove who you are? One way is to create a Web browser certificate and associate it with your user account. This is different from an e-mail certificate because it is typically associated with a particular user account *on the Web server*.

Server   If you wanted to use IPSec to secure communications between two computers and wanted to use certificates, then each of those computers would have to have server certificates— a certificate associated with a computer rather than a person.

CAs   CAs have certificates that identify them as certificate-issuing authorities.

EFS recovery agents   You can designate extra people who can recover encrypted files, *EFS recovery agents*, only by issuing certificates identifying those people.

Software   Microsoft signs drivers with certificates that are not user or computer-oriented, but instead certify that someone has tested a piece of software.

Using a Certificate to Sign an E-mail

First, I create the message. As before, Outlook runs the message through a hashing function and gets a digest. It then uses *my* private key to encrypt the digest. Outlook then assembles the e-mail message by combining the message and the encrypted digest as before, but then adds *a copy of my certificate*, sending them all as one digitally signed e-mail message.

After a bit, your computer receives it. It sees that there's a certificate attached to the message and looks in the certificate for the issuing CA. (Let's just say that it was Thawte. They'll give you an e-mail certificate just for the asking at / www.thawte.com/html/COMMUNITY/personal/index.html.)

Next task: to validate this certificate. Remember that your system isn't validating my message; that'll come in time. Instead, this is your e-mail client—let's say you run Outlook also—saying, "I'm going to use Mark's public key to validate his message, but I only know that it's his public key because Thawte says that it is. But how do I *know* that Thawte actually generated this certificate? Ah, the certificate contains an encrypted digest *of the certificate*. I can check that..." and so it hashes the certificate to get a digest *of the certificate*, not the message. It then wants to compare to the digest attached to the certificate to the one that it just computed. But how does your computer decrypt this digest so that it can compare it to the one that it just computed? Well, Thawte created the e-mail certificate with its private key, so your computer needs Thawte's public key. But where does your computer get Thawte's public key?

You may be surprised to learn that it's already on your hard disk. So let's make a slight digression and talk about certificate stores and how to see the ones on your system.

Certificate Stores: User, Computer, and Service

Your computer has a place in its Registry called its *certificate store*. And not only does your *computer* have a certificate store, your user account also has one. It's also in the Registry. Services running on a system even have certificates. (I'm not going to cover certificates for services much here, so I won't mention this again, but whenever I refer to computer and user certificate storage, remember that there's a certificate storage for each service as well.)

That's an extremely important point, so let me say it again: There is more than one certificate store on a computer. Sometimes you'll want a certificate in your user store rather than your computer store or vice versa. For example, you will find that your copy of Windows in just about any version comes with copies of certificates containing the public keys of Thawte, VeriSign, Baltimore, and dozens of other CAs. Those sit in the computer's certificate store, not yours.

To underscore how that might affect you, consider what might happen if a brand-new certificate authority appeared, Joe's Discount Certificates. Where VeriSign wants hundreds of dollars to issue a certificate to your Web server so that you can do SSL transactions, Joe will issue one for five bucks. So a favorite vendor of yours, Acme Closeout Center (ac-close.com), buys and installs some Joe's Discount SSL certificates, saving themselves a few bucks.

You notice this the next time that you try to visit ac-close.com. Your computer wants to set up a secure SSL session with ac-close.com and when it examines ac-close.com's certificate, then your computer wants to validate that certificate. It sees that Joes' Discount Certificates signed the certificate, and so it wants to validate Joe's Discount Certificates...but your computer can't, as it doesn't already have a copy of Joe's public key in a certificate. So IE pops up a scary-looking message informing you that it can't validate the SSL transaction.

The Acme guys know this and have placed a note on their Web page explaining that you need to first download and install Joe's certificate containing his public key. So you download the certificate. But here's the question: Do you download it to your machine's certificate store or your user account's certificate store? It depends. If your user account roams then you might want to have Joe's public key in your user store, as it'd roam with you. No matter what computer you were sitting at, the copy of IE on that computer could set up secure SSL sessions with Acme Closeouts, as it'd find a certificate for Joe's, the issuing CA for Acme's SSL certificate. On the other hand, if you wanted anyone who sat at a particular computer to be able to connect to Acme without any complaints, then you'd put the certificate into the machine's certificate store.

NOTE   *I should mention here that if you're using the Active Directory then a lot of this stuff becomes automatic. I'm showing you the simpler non-AD setup so that you can understand what's going on under the hood.*

WARNING   *If you're using Netscape Navigator, then things work a bit differently—for some reason, the PC version of Netscape doesn't use the certificate store built into the operating system. So assume that when I'm referring to some behavior in a Web browser I'm referring to Internet Explorer.*

Installing the MMC Certificates Snap-In

But how do you acquire, view, and remove certificates? You manage certificates with an MMC snap-in. You're going to create a custom MMC that will let you manage certificates for both your accounts *and* your computer's account:

1. Start up a blank MMC: Click Start/Run, then fill in **mmc**, and press Enter.

2. In the MMC, choose Console, then Add/Remove Snap-in, then Add and choose Certificates, and click Add again.

3. As you can manage certificates for your user account, your computer's account, or a service's account, the MMC needs to know which you intend, and offers you all three choices. Tell it that you will manage certificates for Computer Account rather than My User Account or Service Account, then click Next and Finish.

4. Now you'll add a *second* Certificates snap-in, but this second one will manage your user account's certificate store. In Add Standalone Snap-In, Certificates will already be highlighted. Click Add again to add it to your MMC the second time. This time, when it asks whether you'll manage a computer, user, or service account, just click Finish.

5. Now click Close to clear the Add Standalone Snap-In dialog box and OK.

6. You're going to save this snap-in, so do a bit more cleanup. Click File, then Options.

7. Where you see Console Mode, choose User Mode—Limited Access, Single Window.

8. Next to the icon at the top of the dialog box, click the Change Icon button so you can find a better icon than that lame old hammer.

9. In the Change Icon dialog box, click the Browse button. It'll take you to winnt\system32. Navigate to C:\WINNT\system32\certmgr.dll and double-click it to display its icons.

10. Pick an icon and click OK.

11. Click OK to clear the Options dialog box.

12. Save the tool so you don't have to build it again. Click File/Save As and in the File Name field, fill in a name, such as **Certificate Manager** and then click the Save button. Now, when you open Certificate Manager.msc, if you expand all of its folder, then you'll see something like Figure 8.92.

FIGURE 8.92

Certificate Manager for user and computer certificate stores

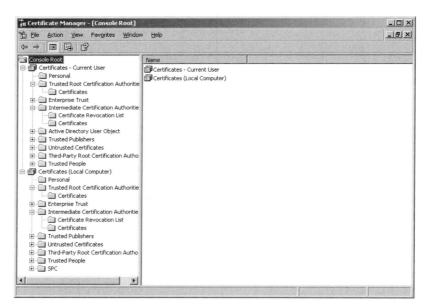

TIP   You may well have other folders in your Certificate Manager, particularly if you're on a system that's a member of an AD. Don't worry about it; all of what I'm describing will still work.

Look in the folders named Trusted Root Certification Authorities\Certificates under both the computer and the user store, and you'll see the certificates that I mentioned—VeriSign, Baltimore, Thawte, and dozens of others.

But even though it *looks* as if all of those CAs have certificates in your user store, they don't really. Instead, when you log onto a system, you temporarily "inherit" all of the certificates that the machine's store holds. You can see this with a little more clicking.

Click Certificates (Local Computer) and then choose View/Options. You'll see a Physical Certificate Stores check box; check it and click OK. Then click Certificates—Current User and, again, choose View/Options and check Physical Certificate Stores. When you open the folders under Trusted Root Certification Authorities, then your MMC will look something like Figure 8.93.

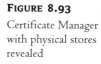

FIGURE 8.93

Certificate Manager with physical stores revealed

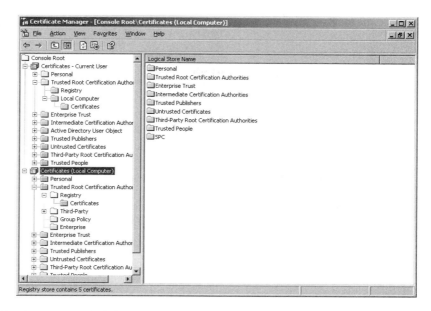

Notice that under the computer's folder, there are four folders—`Registry`, `Third-Party`, `Group Policy`, and `Enterprise`. This reflects the four places that together make up the machine's certificate store. Click `Registry/Certificates` and you'll see all of the CAs that you saw before. But now look under the Current User's icon for Trusted Root Certification Authorities—there is a `Registry` folder again (which you'll probably find is empty), and a folder called `Local Computer` with a folder inside it called `Certificates`.

That `Local Computer` folder is nothing more than a kind of "shortcut" to the Third-Party section of the *machine's* certificate store! Click there and you'll see all of the same CAs that you just saw.

And in case you're wondering, the `SPC` folder (which also has subfolders for `Registry`, `Group Policy`, and `Enterprise`) holds certificates of software publishers that you have agreed to trust— or at least Help says that it's supposed to be. Mine's empty even though I've trusted Microsoft and Macromedia software signing certs in the past.

Outlook Verifies the E-mail Key

Now that I'm done with the side-trip about certificate stores, let's finish up the signed e-mail example. Recall that your computer had just gotten the e-mail and needed to verify the certificate. Your system has a copy of Thawte's public key and uses it to decrypt the digest on the certificate. It checks out— the digest created by Outlook from the certificate's contents matches the decrypted digest attached to the certificate—and so Outlook knows that it can trust the information on the certificate.

Now that Outlook knows that it can trust the information on the certificate, it reads *my* public key from the cert. It can then use that public key to verify the message that I sent, by again computing a digest, this time on the entire message, and then decrypting the enclosed digest and comparing them.

Trusting Certificate Authorities

Thus far, you've seen that:

◆ Public/private key pairs provide a way to authenticate or sign communications and to encrypt communications without having to use shared secrets.

◆ I need your public key for us to communicate, and you must enclose it in a certificate when providing it to me.

◆ I want to know that this is indeed *your* public key and so you ask a certificate authority to digitally sign the certificate.

◆ To validate that CA's digital signature I need the CA's public key, also provided in the form of a certificate.

◆ This could lead to the question "who validates the CA's certificate" *ad infinitum*, so Microsoft makes life easier on us by prestoring the certificates of major CAs on my computer in a certificate store.

◆ Computers and user accounts (and services as well) each have their own certificate stores.

The fact that Microsoft preloads Thawte's certificate on my computer relieves me of having to worry about how to get an honest-to-God copy of that certificate. But what if I want to use a CA other than the ones preinstalled? And that's not an unlikely circumstance, as two very common events would require me to answer that question:

◆ My company will probably set up its own CA for issuing certs that it will use internally.

◆ My firm might also have business partners, and we might have agreed to trust each other's certificates. Thus, if Bigfirm and Acme agree to give each other some amount of access to each other's servers, then they need to authenticate each other. Certificates can be quite a useful way to do this. If Bigfirm agrees to accept Acme's certificates, then Bigfirm will need to install a certificate containing Acme's CA's public key on its systems, and Acme will need to do the same things for Bigfirm's CA's public key.

TRUST AND SELF-SIGNED CERTIFICATES

Consider that *trust* word I've been using. What does it mean in a certificate sense? Consider a real-world thing that is sort of like a certificate: my driver's license. Suppose I want to get on an airplane. The ticket agent needs to see my ID or I don't get a boarding pass; let's see why.

The airline's desire is to verify that the ticket issued to Mark Minasi is indeed in the hands of Mark Minasi. It tries to do that by reasoning in this way: First, match the written name on the ticket to the written name on the driver's license. Then, verify that the name Mark Minasi goes with the person holding the driver's license by looking at the picture on the driver's license and then comparing it to the face of the person holding the license. Finally, they know that the license, which associates the name Mark Minasi with the face in the picture, is trustworthy because it was issued by the state of Virginia.

That's the key to understanding trust here—they don't really trust the driver's license, they trust that the state of Virginia has done some work to validate my identity. If a driver's license is a certificate, then, Virginia is the certificate authority.

But why should they trust Virginia? I mean, they don't have an army, issue currency, or have treaties with foreign countries; they don't have a seat on the UN, so why trust them? The answer is, "Because we just do." Even if I'm in a state other than Virginia, the driver's license is still accepted—Florida residents, for example, trust Virginia. As a matter of custom and convenience, at some point you choose to trust some authority for identification.

But that doesn't always work. Most places outside of the United States don't accept driver's licenses issued by U.S. states as proof of identification. Instead, they want a passport. But let's imagine that some country, say, Turkey, didn't require a passport, and instead accepted U.S. driver's licenses as proof of ID. Why would Turkey "recognize" Virginia? It probably wouldn't. Instead, Turkey might reason in this way: "We have treaties with the U.S.; we believe that they are a viable and relatively reliable political entity. Now we look at this certificate—driver's license—for this guy Mark Minasi. We don't know him, but he's got this ID issued by some 'state' called Virginia. We don't know *them*, either, but they're vouched for by the U.S. government—and *them*, we know! So we accept that this guy is indeed Mark Minasi."

This is an example of a "hierarchy of trust." Let's apply it to the e-mail example. To review:

◆   You wanted to validate my certificate, which was signed by Thawte.

◆   So you needed Thawte's public key to check my digest.

◆   You found it in Thawte's certificate, which was sitting in your certificate store.

But now let's take it a step further: How do you validate Thawte's certificate, the one that Microsoft put in your certificate store when you installed Windows on your system? Well, if you take a look at Thawte's certificate, then you will see that it, too, is digitally signed and therefore can be validated.

But who signed it?

Thawte, that's who. The certificate containing Thawte's public key is signed, all right—using Thawte's public key. It's a "self-signing" certificate.

Well, what the heck good is *that*? Well, it's a *little* useful. After all, it's at least *internally* consistent; if the certificate's digest didn't match an actually computed digest, that'd be bad. But in the end analysis, you are simply trusting—in the colloquial sense of the word—that Thawte is a well enough run company that they won't give out bogus certificates (it'd be bad if Thawte gave some hackers a certificate for a Web server that said, "Yes, this is the dell.com Web server") and that Microsoft didn't put the wrong certificate for Thawte into your copy of Windows.

In the PKI sense, "trusting" a CA means that you have installed their certificate in your certificate store.

TRUST MODELS

So you've seen that PKI can't work without trust and that a given machine trusts certificates issued by a given CA by placing that CA's root CA certificate in the machine's certificate store. You might call this the *Web trust* model—just as Microsoft has placed 98 root CA certificates in your Windows Server 2003 certificate store, you can add root CA certs for other CAs as well.

But there's one more piece to trusting that's worth mentioning here—delegation of trust. It's possible for your organization to have a *hierarchy* of CAs. Instead of just one machine issuing all of the firm's certificates, a number do. Why divide up the job? Three basic reasons: to spread out the work, to let subdivisions of the organization control their own machines acting as CAs, and to *truly* secure the root CA machine.

The first reason should be obvious. I haven't mentioned this yet, but if you integrate your PKI with the Active Directory then every user and machine account *automatically* requests a certificate. With a large organization of tens of thousands of people, it'd be just impossible to get fast enough turnaround from one machine. So perhaps the Chicago office gets its own CA, Minneapolis gets one, and so on. But instead of having to run around and tell every machine to trust certs from Chicago, Minneapolis, and the other cities, you just tell them all to trust your root CA. What happens, then, when a machine gets a certificate created by a subdivision's CA? Well, recall the sequence of trust—you used my e-mail cert's signature to trust it because it was signed by some CA and you trusted that CA because it had a certificate which was signed...by the CA itself. With a lower-level or "subordinate" CA, you just add a layer: A machine in Minneapolis has a cert signed by the Minneapolis CA, which has a cert signed by the root CA, which has a cert signed by itself. No more administration, but a good way to balance out the load. Nice—very scalable.

The second reason may happen if your firm's divisions tend to run their own IT infrastructure. Maybe Engineering wants their own CA. Or perhaps you view different kinds of certs as more or less important—maybe you want to secure the system that hands out SSL certificates more than the one that hands out e-mail certificates. In any case, it's the same approach. The subordinate CA has a certificate signed by the root CA.

The final reason is kind of interesting. I did some work for a large public certificate authority and at one point, they said, "Would you like to go see the Root CA?" (I could just hear the capital letters in their voices.) "Sure," I said. They took me through this vault into a room with layers and layers of security, which led to a room that contained...a computer. Just a computer, no network connections. Just a stand-alone machine. The idea is this: Companies such as VeriSign, Thawte, Baltimore, and the like don't have just one CA, they have many machines. But it's a hierarchy and *something*'s got to be at the top. So they build a bunch of subordinate machines that generate certificates. Once that's done, there's really not much for the root CA to do but to generate certificates for the subordinate CAs. Once that's done, it probably makes good sense to keep the top dog off the network, as the hierarchy of trust ends with it. If someone were to hack that system and steal its private key, then they could issue bogus certificates in the CA's name...and they'd be instantly out of business. This way, the worst thing that happens is that a subordinate CA gets hacked. Then *it* could be impersonated, but not the entire CA.

Running Your Own Certificate Authority with Windows Server 2003

Let's sit down and try it. You'll build a simple CA with Windows Server 2003 and create a few certificates.

CREATING A CERTIFICATE AUTHORITY

All you need to make a Windows Server a CA is to install Certificate Services...and convince some systems to trust your certificates! I'll establish a CA called Avian Secure CA on a system called SPARROW, a system with an Active Directory.

TIP *If you plan to set up Web enrollment support to allow people to get certificates, set up IIS before installing Certificate Services, and be sure to explicitly enable ASP pages. (They're normally disabled in Windows Server 2003.) If you install Certificate Services first and then install IIS, you'll need to create the required virtual roots by hand by typing* `certutil` `-vroot` *at the command prompt.*

To install the Services, open Control Panel, choose Add or Remove Programs, and then choose Windows Components. Click Certificate Services and Details and you'll see a dialog box like Figure 8.94.

FIGURE 8.94

Details view of
Certificate Services

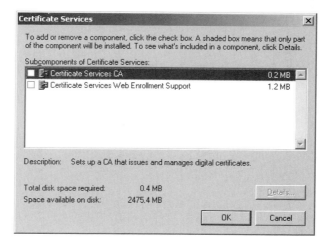

Check both boxes if they're not already checked. When you choose to install Certificate Services CA, Control Panel will check that you really mean it, warning you that you can't rename the computer or change its domain membership after installing Certificate Services, as this would invalidate the certificate, and asking if you want to continue. Choose Yes and OK so that Control Panel reconfigures your server. You'll get a few screens that ask about how to configure this certificate server; the first looks like Figure 8.95.

FIGURE 8.95

Which kind of
certificate server?

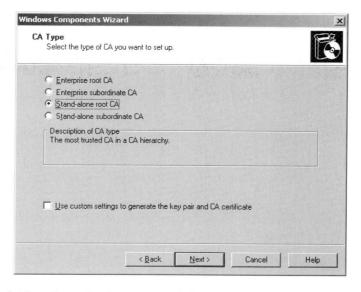

I've chosen Stand-Alone Root CA for my example here. Click Next, and you'll see a screen like Figure 8.96.

FIGURE 8.96

Describing the CA

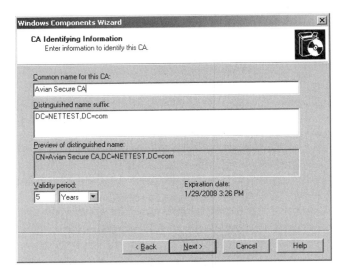

This box will list the information needed to find the server in the Active Directory. Fill it in and click Next. Windows Setup will generate the cryptographic key, and you'll see something like Figure 8.97.

FIGURE 8.97

Where to store the certificate information

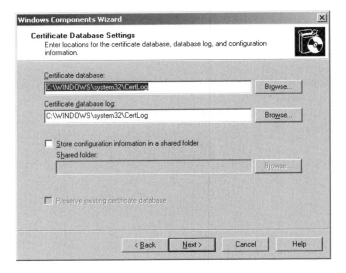

If you choose to store the certificate database on a network share, you'll need to provide the folder for it. Click Next and Finish and the software's installed.

CREATING AND INSTALLING CERTIFICATES

Now that the Avian's CA is up and running, let's issue a certificate. Let's suppose that I've got a system named PERMADC that wants a server certificate, so it asks SPARROW for one.

There are three steps to getting a certificate: You first request that the CA issue you one, then the CA decides to actually give you the certificate, and then you download and install it.

Requesting the Certificate

NOTE   *I request the certificate from the new CA by pointing my Web browser to the enrollment pages, prebuilt forms that I can get to by typing in the CA's DNS address and adding the phrase /certsrv to make a URL. As PERMADC is requesting a certificate from SPARROW, another computer on its same intranet, I just log onto PERMADC as an administrator, start up IE and type* **http://sparrow/certsrv** *to see a screen like Figure 8.98. If you get a 404 error and you installed Certificate Services before installing IIS, make sure that you've created the virtual root folder.*

FIGURE 8.98

Opening a
certificates
Web page

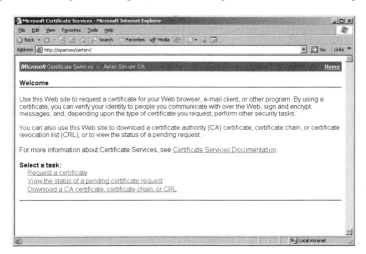

You see that there are three options here, but the one that will get me a cert is clearly Request a Certificate, so I click that if it's not already clicked and then the Next button to see a screen like Figure 8.99.

FIGURE 8.99

What kind of
certificate?

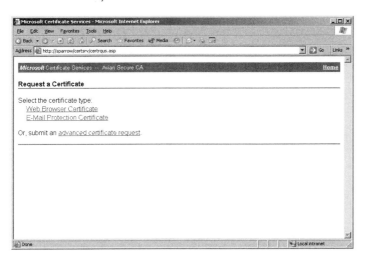

I guess the most commonly requested certificates are e-mail certs and Web browser certs, hence their presence here. But I'm just looking for a basic server certificate, so I need to click Advanced Certificate Request and choose Create and submit a request to this CA. That shows Figure 8.100.

FIGURE 8.100

More details on certificate type

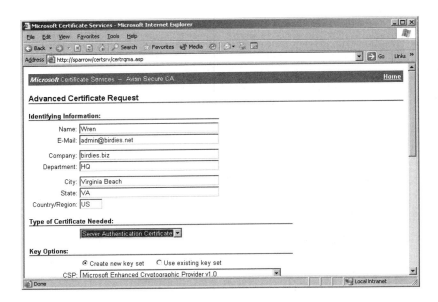

I have to fill in two items, the name of the server and a contact e-mail. Then I choose the type of certificate that I'm looking for under Type of Certificate Needed:— Server Authentication Certificate. But there's more to see here also, so I scroll down in the browser to see something like Figure 8.101.

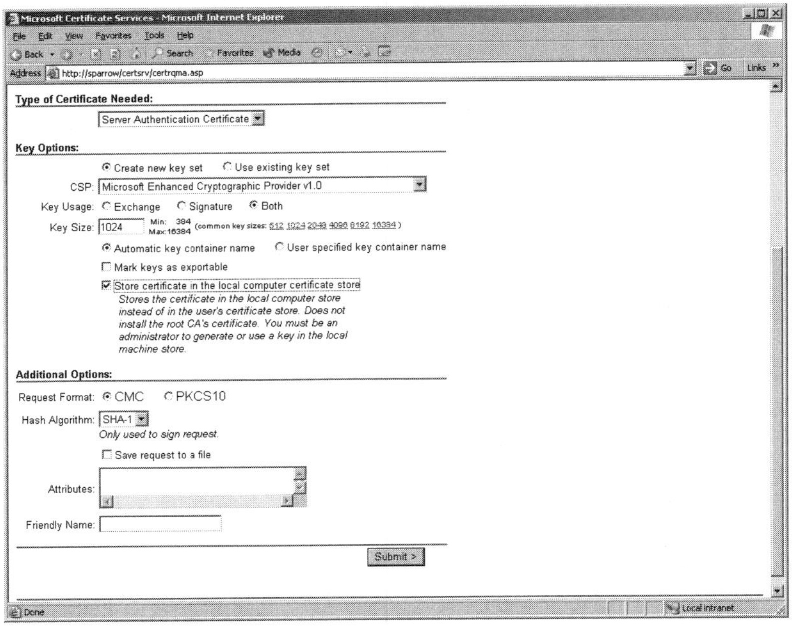

FIGURE 8.101

Putting the certificate in the machine store

Notice a few things in this option screen. First, recall that I talked earlier about the fact that you might sometimes want a separate key for signing and encryption; you see that here in the Key Usage options—Exchange means "use for encryption." You can set the key length—longer keys are more secure but require more CPU power to encrypt and decrypt. I tend to use the default. The only thing that I change here is checking Store Certificate in the Local Computer Certificate Store. I do this because it's me running IE, and so any actions that I do—including creating certificates—will by default be associated with me rather than the computer. But this is a *server* authentication cert, and so it goes in the *machine's* store of certificates, not mine. This check box ensures that the key goes to the right place.

I click Submit to start the process. PERMADC creates a private and public key pair, encrypts the private key, stores it and the public key somewhere in the Registry, and sends the public key to the CA so that the CA can bind it into the certificate. I then get a message that the request was submitted, and to return later to retrieve the certificate.

The CA Issues the Certificate

Now the certificate request sits at the CA, waiting to be approved by an administrator. (That "administrator" would be me in this case.) So I log onto the CA computer, SPARROW, to approve the certificate.

There's a tool on SPARROW that arrived with the Certificate Services—an MMC called Certificate Authority. I start it and click the Pending Requests folder to see Figure 8.102.

FIGURE 8.102

Certificate Authority snap-in

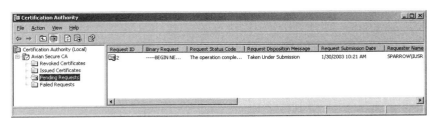

You see the certificate request in the figure; I need only right-click it and choose All Tasks /Issue and the certificate is issued. (If someone requested a certificate that I did not want to issue, I could choose Deny from the same context menu.)

NOTE *You can, if you want, tell your CA to automatically generate any CA requested. Just open up the Certification Authority snap-in and right-click the icon for the server. Choose Properties (no surprise there, eh?) and the Policy Module tab. In that tab, click the Properties button and choose the Default Action tab in the resulting policy page. On that tab you'll see two radio buttons telling the CA what to do when it receives a certificate request. By default, the first option, which sets requests to Pending until the administrator explicitly issues them, is selected, but there's also a second option to automatically issue newly requested certificates. However, I can't see why you'd do that. Handing out certificates to any random person who requests one doesn't sound very secure.*

Retrieving the Certificate

Moving back to PERMADC, I return to `http://sparrow/certsrv` and this time I choose the radio button for the task Check on a Pending Certificate and click Next to show me a page like Figure 8.103.

FIGURE 8.103

Choose a pending
certificate request

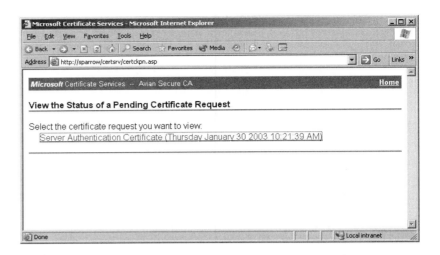

There's only one pending request so I just click it and get the news that it's been issued, as you see in Figure 8.104.

FIGURE 8.104

The certificate is
ready for installation

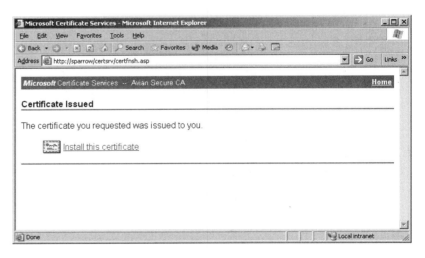

I click the Install This Certificate link, confirm that I trust the Web site issuing it, and get a final Web page telling me that it installed without a hitch.

WARNING   *Remember, I'm assuming that you're using Internet Explorer. You've got to do more work to make this work with Netscape.*

Remember that I checked that box telling the system to create the key pair in the local machine store? I can check that now by opening up the Certificate Manager snap-in on PERMADC. The new cert is *either* in the `Personal` folder on the Local Computer store or in the user store, as you see in Figure 8.105.

FIGURE 8.105

The new certificate is installed

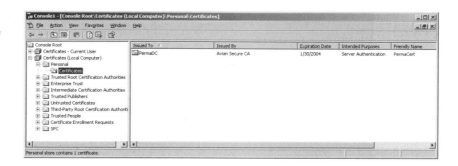

Notice that the certificate turns out to be in the Local Computer store, as I wanted. If I were to do everything else the same—but hadn't asked to put the certificate in the local computer store—then the certificate would end up in the user store. That's not to say that I couldn't *move* it from the user's `Personal` folder to the computer's `Personal` folder by just cutting and pasting in the Certificate Manager snap-in—but specifying where to put it from the beginning saves a bit of work and keeps me from forgetting to do that and wondering why the cert isn't where I expect it to be.

NOTE   *In an Active Directory–integrated CA, your machine could* automatically *request the certificate, the CA could automatically issue the cert, and the machine would* automatically *install it.*

TRUSTING THE NEW CERTIFICATE AUTHORITY

So PERMADC now has a certificate created by a certificate authority called Avian CA—but isn't something missing here? *PERMADC doesn't trust Avian CA!* We never introduced them! So what happens when a system holds a certificate created by a CA that it doesn't trust? Well, you can see that by double-clicking the certificate and then the Certification Path tab, as in Figure 8.106.

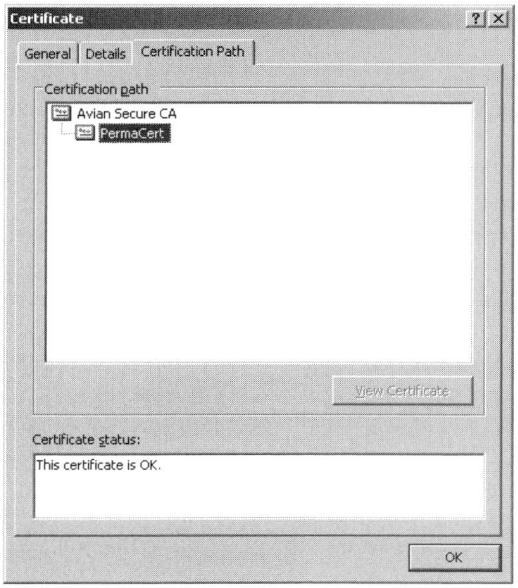

FIGURE 8.106

Certification path for new certificate

Hmmm...now, is *that* odd—it seems that PERMADC likes this certificate and the whole idea of the Avian CA altogether. What's going on here? A look in the Trusted folder shows that *there's an Avian certificate in there.* Windows Server 2003 got a little sneaky and stayed one jump ahead of us—when it installed the new certificate for PERMADC, it also installed the root CA certificate for the CA that created the certificate. Well, that saves us some work.

But sometimes you'll want a system to trust a CA even if that system *doesn't* hold any certificates issued by that CA. In that case, you need to download and install the root CA certificate for that CA.

There's an easy way to do it, via the /certsrv URL that you've already met. You might have noticed that one of the options on the first page was to Download a CA Certificate, Certificate Chain, or CRL. Click that and you'll see a screen like Figure 8.107.

FIGURE 8.107

Fetching the root CA's certificate

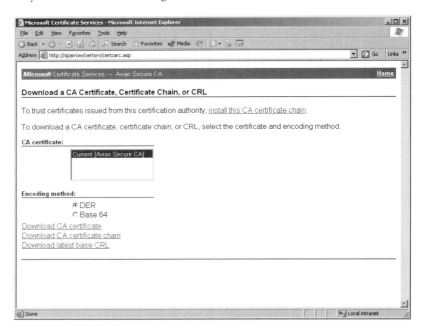

Click Install This CA Certificate Chain, and you'll get the CA's root certificate. IE will put the new certificate into the Trusted Root Certification Authorities for both Local Computer and Current User.

Windows 2000–based CAs also maintain a URL for direct download of their root CA: http:// *servername*/certenroll/*servername_CAname*.crt, where *servername* is the DNS name of the server and *CAname* is the certificate authority's name. So, for example, if the certificate server's DNS name were swallow.bigfirm.biz and the CA's name were Avian, then the URL would be http://swallow.bigfirm.biz/certenroll/swallow.bigfirm.biz_Avian.crt. You can represent blanks in a URL with %20—for example, as our CA's full name is Avian secure CA on a server simply named swallow, its URL would be http://swallow/certenroll/swallow_avian%20secure%20ca.crt.

Using PKI in Windows Server 2003

Now that you've seen how to get a simple certificate, let's look at the specifics of getting some of Windows Server 2003's PKI-aware components to work.

IPSEC

You read in Chapter 6 that IPSec is a pretty powerful and flexible way to sign and/or encrypt communications between two machines or amongst a greater number of machines. But IPSec needs authentication and only supports three kinds—Kerberos (which is simple but only works between machines from the same domain), a shared secret (which is all too easily compromised, as all sides must agree upon the secret), and certificates. If you want to use IPSec to secure communications between two systems in different domains, or for that matter any set of systems that might be in any number of domains or workgroups, then certificates are the way to go.

Using certificates for IPSec is simple, once you know what *kind* of certificate to use. First of all, you're looking for a certificate that goes on the Local Computer certificate store, so use the Advanced Certificate Request and check the Use Local Machine Store when filling out the form. Under Intended Purpose, choose either Client Authentication Certificate or IPSec Certificate. (For some reason, a *server* authentication certificate won't let two servers communicate via IPSec. Go figure.) Make sure that all systems that want to use IPSec to talk to each other have a certificate from the same CA.

Finally, when you select the authentication method for your IPSec rule, then choose Use a Certificate from This Certificate Authority and click Browse; you'll see a list of the CAs that the system recognizes. Choose the one CA that lists all of your IPSec-ing systems, and IPSec will work like a charm.

But before you try this the first time, do yourself a favor: Get the IPSec working, and *then* add the certs. If you're unfamiliar with both IPSec and certificates then you're bound to miss a step somewhere and not know where to go. Start out with a simple shared secret for authentication—it's just a configuration step. Once IPSec's working, get the certificates from the CA onto the machines and check their Local Computer stores to ensure that the certs are there and are the right type. *Then* change the IPSec rule to use certificates.

E-MAIL

As I've already said, a Windows Server 2003 PKI can generate certificates for signing and/or encrypting e-mail. It's even fairly simple to create the certs because, as you may recall, e-mail certs are one of the two "one-click" certificates in the Web-based request page. But there are few specific wrinkles about e-mail certificates that you should know.

First, recall that when you request a certificate you must fill in a small form. Two of those items are Name, which you can use to name the certificate, and e-mail address, which was pretty irrelevant in the server certificates that we've talked about so far. (In fact, I've often left the field blank, and it works fine.) But for e-mail, that's not the case: Whatever e-mail account you fill in there is the only e-mail account that can use this certificate. If you regularly use several e-mail addresses, then you'll need at least one certificate for each one.

Second, when you *do* request the certificate, either through the simplified or Advanced Request interface, the type of certificate that you want is called an E-mail Protection Certificate. You *can* use the simplified interface, but you might choose to use the Advanced Request interface for two reasons.

◆ First, you can mark the private key as exportable in Advanced; you can't do that in Basic. Why would you want to? Because you can export the keys to a floppy and lock them away somewhere. Then, if your system crashes and you must rebuild it, you can reinstall (*import* is certificate-ese) the keys to the new system.

◆ Advanced lets you create separate certificates for signing and encryption. (Recall that for some reason Advanced calls encryption certificates *Exchange* certificates.) *That's* important because you *would* export and store your *encryption* keys, you'd never export and store your signing keys. If you lose a signing key, just revoke its certificate (more on that later) and request a new one.

TIP   *If you start requesting an e-mail certificate from the simple interface and want to use the advanced options such as marking a private key for export, you can click a link in the simple interface to fill out the advanced form.*

Third, both the sender and receiver of a piece of e-mail may need certificates. If all I want to do is send you a piece of signed e-mail, then all I need is an e-mail certificate issued by an authority that you recognize. You need not have any certs. But if I want to send you *encrypted* e-mail, well, that's a bit tougher.

Recall how SSL encryption worked: The server has a certificate and the client (your Web browser) usually doesn't. So they need to agree on a password for symmetrical encryption in their session. But how to agree on that key without sending it in plaintext? Simple—the client offers a password (*session key* is the better phrase, actually) to the server by encrypting it *with the server's public key*. No one can decrypt this but the server, so the secret's safe.

Now suppose I want to encrypt some e-mail to you. As with SSL, I'll use *your* public key to encrypt the mail that I want to send to you. But e-mail's not a real-time communication process, so you might not even be online when I try to mail you. Therefore, I would have no way to *get* your public key unless you send it to me beforehand! To send you encrypted mail, then, I'd *first* have to ask you to send me a piece of mail with your public key on it. *Then* I could use that from this point on to encrypt mail to you.

Finally, you must tell your e-mail client software to use your certificates and when to use them. As there are a ton of popular e-mail clients, I can't explain how to do it on all of them—but most clients have an Options/Security or the like. You can usually tell your system whether to sign and/or encrypt everything (which seems a mite extreme to me), or just pick which items to sign or encrypt.

Remember also that the e-mail certs that you issue with your CA won't be much good on the public Internet. But Thawte is generous enough to hand out Internet-friendly e-mail certs for free, so if you'd like to start signing your e-mails then visit `www.thawte.com/html/COMMUNITY/personal/index.html`.

WEB BROWSER

Browser certificates are popular in so-called "extranet" situations, where you want to secure a Web site—that is, you don't want just anyone to be able to access it—but you want some people outside your firm to be able to get to the pages. So how do you limit access to a Web page or pages?

One simple way is to secure the pages with NTFS permissions. You can say that only Joe, Jane, and Sue can read `blahblah.htm` on your Web site; so if anyone tries to access `http://yourwebservername/blahblah.htm`, then a logon dialog box will pop up in Internet Explorer asking for a name, password, and domain. NTFS permissions on Web pages are simple to set up and secure for logons—that dialog box does a challenge-response authentication, so no passwords are flying around in cleartext.

But that means that you've got to create user accounts for Joe, Jane, and Sue and, worse, that means that you've got to maintain them. Even worse yet, it's really only going to work if Joe, Jane, and Sue sitting on-site at that other company are using Windows and Internet Explorer! A better answer is a client authentication system that works across platforms; X.509 certificates are good ones. An in-depth discussion of this would require more details about IIS than I've got space for here, but here's the overview.

Setting Up Certificate-Based Access Control

Basically you can limit who gets access to a Web site server in a few steps.

WARNING   *Notice that this will only apply at the Web site level—you cannot use certificates to control access to particular Web pages.*

1. First create and install a Server Authentication Certificate from your internal CA. Don't forget to tell the enrollment page to place the certificate in the local computer's certificate store. Now the certificate is on the server and IIS sees it, but IIS doesn't know which, if any, Web sites to associate the certificate to.

2. Then attach it to this particular Web site in IIS. In the Internet Information Services Manager, right-click the icon for the Web site that you want to secure, choose Properties and click the Directory Security tab. Then click the Server Certificate button to start a wizard. Choose to assign an existing certificate, pick the available certificate from the list, choose a port for SSL to use (the default of 443 is fine), and then click Next again to install the certificate with those options. Click Finish to finish the wizard.

3. Next, require people to use certificate-secured communications; in the same Secured Communications area as the Server Certificate button that you just pushed. Click Edit and, in the resulting dialog box, check the Require Secure Channel (SSL) box and Require Client Certificates. Click OK twice to clear the dialog boxes.

4. That Web site can only be accessed with URLs starting with `https://` rather than `http://`, so set up all of your hyperlinks accordingly on pages that refer to your newly secured site.

5. Clients will also need certificates. Just run the Web enrollment page as you've seen before, and this time choose a Web Browser Certificate.

Now when a client tries to connect to the Web site they will be refused unless they've got a certificate from a CA trusted by the IIS machine.

Tightening Up Certificate and IIS Security: The Certificate Trust List

Notice that—all you need is a certificate from *any* trusted CA. Unfortunately, that's probably not what you wanted.

To see what I mean, suppose ABC company wants to set up a Web site that a few of XYZ company's employees can access. So ABC does what I just described—sets up the Web site, creates a CA, puts a server authentication certificate on the Web server, tells IIS to use that certificate for directory security, requires secure channel, and hands out Web browser certificates to the small number of XYZ employees who they want mucking around on their Web site. This will work fine, and those XYZ employees will be able to access the ABC Web site.

Unfortunately, so will other people.

All IIS requires in this case is a Web browser certificate from *any* CA that the IIS server's operating system trusts. Therefore, any Joe Blow coming to ABC's restricted Web site will get access even *without* a Web browser certificate from ABC's CA; a Web browser certificate from Thawte, VeriSign, Baltimore, or any of the dozens of other in-the-box, "pretrusted" CAs will do.

Fortunately, IIS has a mechanism to restrict the CAs that it should accept certificates from to authenticate to a particular Web site. It's called a *certificate trust list*. When you create and activate one, you modify IIS's behavior in this way: Where it previously would take certs from any trusted CA, now it only takes certs from the specific CAs that you list. To create one:

1. Open up Internet Information Services Manager (Start/Programs/Administrative Tools/ Internet Services Manager).

2. Right-click the site that you've secured with certificates and choose Properties.

3. Click the Directory Security tab.

4. In the Secure Communications section, click Edit.

5. In the resulting dialog box, check Enable Certificate Trust List.

6. You'll need to create a CTL now. Click the New button to start a wizard. Click Next to get to the first page.

7. In the Certificates in the CTL page, click Add from Store and choose the CAs whose certificates you want IIS to accept for access to your Web site. (Ctrl-click to choose more than one at a time.) Once you've done that, choose Next.

8. In the following panel, fill in the fields to describe the CTL. Click Next, Next again, and Finish. You should see a message telling you that the Certificate Trust List Wizard succeeded. Just click OK, and OK again, and you'll be set.

Other Certificate Uses In IIS

You can take this further if you like, with *one-to-one* or *one-to-many* mapping. The idea here is that you could create a set of local or domain user accounts and associate particular certificates with particular user accounts. So if the Web browser certificate Lara Wilson is associated with—*is mapped to*—a user account lwilson then you can use IIS's normal security features to control Lara's access. But Lara can get to the Web site using, again, non-Windows desktops. In a *many-to-one* situation, you do something similar but instead of mapping certs to users one by one, you write some rules that the system uses to do that mapping on the fly.

If you use auditing, then you should be aware of a somewhat annoying side effect of certificates: Anyone accessing a secure Web site with certificates always generates a "logon failure" item in the Security event log. It's kind of annoying, as it gives the false impression that you're under a major hack attack.

You'll read more about IIS in Chapter 17.

EFS CERTIFICATES

You'll read more about the Encrypting File System in Chapter 10, but the basics are that it lets you encrypt and thereby protect files. But if you forget your password to your user account, then you can't decrypt your files. That's why EFS requires that you create at least one account that has the ability to decrypt files, an *EFS recovery agent*. The Administrator account is a recovery agent, but if you want to delegate that job to someone else, you'll need to create a new EFS recovery agent. To do this, you'll need to get a file recovery certificate. You can download a recovery agent certificate from the CA using the Web interface you've already seen. Just move to the Advanced page and choose that option from the list. If you don't see the option in the list, you can still get the certificate by choosing Other and filling in the proper OID. The object ID (OID) for the file recovery certificate is 1.3.6.1.4.1.311.10.3.4.1. Fill out the remainder of the form as you've already seen.

TIP   You can find out the OID for any certificate by looking at its properties. For example, to find out the OID for a recovery cert, I looked at the extant one for the Administrator that's located in Public Key Policies/Encrypting File System. Turn to the Details tab and look for the Enhanced Key Usage entry. Select it, and you'll see the OID in the pane.

Once you've got the certificate, you can install it on the target machine, using the Local Security Policy snap-in under the Public Key Policies/Encrypting File System folder. Right-click it, choose Add Data Recovery Agent, and a wizard lets you assign the new Recovery Agent. The only catch is, as usual, that the system where you're installing the file recovery cert must accept certificates from the CA. For more about EFS and recovery agents, see Chapter 10.

Revoking Certificates

This whole PKI/certificate thing is pretty neat, but there are a few wrinkles to be aware of. For one, what happens when you've got to get rid of a certificate? For example, suppose my laptop has a certificate on it and someone steals the laptop. I sure don't want them sending e-mail with my digital signature on it! There is an answer—certificate revocation. In this section, you'll see how that works.

Revoking a certificate is straightforward. Just start up the Certification Authority snap-in and look in the Issued Certificates folder. Find the certificate that you want to revoke and right-click it and choose All Tasks/Revoke Certificate. It'll offer you the chance to record one of seven reasons (including Unspecified), and the certificate then goes into the Revoked Certificates folder.

WARNING   Although there is an Unrevoke Certificate option for revoked certificates, it only works if you choose Certificate Hold as the reason for revoking the cert. Choosing any other option, including Unspecified, permanently revokes the cert.

So the certificate is now officially *persona non grata* around the network? Well, not exactly, not just yet. Remember that one of the great strengths of certificates is the fact that they rely on a hierarchy of trust—that is, if your system holds a cert that's signed by a server whose cert your system also holds, then the system won't stop every time that it examines the cert to locate and contact the root CA or even the issuing CA. So it takes a little time for a client (or a server) to realize that a certificate is no longer any good.

In the PKI world there is an important acronym, CRL. It stands for Certificate Revocation List. CAs issue CRLs on a regular basis, weekly by default, but you can make it more or less often. (In Certificate Authority, right-click the `Revoked Certificates` folder and choose Properties and you'll see a Publication Interval, which you can change.) Or you can force a CA to generate—*publish* is PKI-ese—a new CRL—by right-clicking the `Revoked Certificates` folder and choosing All Tasks/Publish.

Different client systems check CRLs at different intervals and upon different events. But most will automatically get a new CRL when the old one expires, so you might want to set the expiration time to be more frequent than the weekly default value. Of course, that means more network traffic.

If you need to find out the age of the CRLs on an IIS server, look in `\system32\certsrv\certenroll` for files with the `.crl` extension. (They are probably in folders *inside* that folder, and when you open one it will be copied to your profile directory.) Double-click the CRL files, and you'll see when they were published and when the next update will be.

Need to have an IIS server immediately recognize a revoked certificate? Then do this: First, force the CA that issued the certificate to publish a new CRL. Second, go to the IIS server and find and delete the CRL file for the CA that issued the certificate. Finally, restart IIS—not just the one site, but the entire IIS service. (Again, just the service—you needn't reboot the entire server.) Clients trying to access the Web site will see an "HTTP 403.13—Forbidden: Client certificate revoked" message.

By now, we've covered a lot of theory and a smaller amount of concepts. Let's move to more nuts and bolts, starting with a discussion of user accounts—in the next chapter.

Chapter 9

Managing and Creating User Accounts

BY NOW YOU'VE LEARNED the basics of Active Directory, how to install and configure major components of Windows Server 2003, and the ins and outs of the MMC, as well as the care and feeding of the Registry. Now let's tackle something at the heart of an administrator's job: creating and managing users and groups. In this chapter, you'll first learn how to create user accounts, both in a workgroup and domain-based environment. You'll then see how to use groups—there are four types—to simplify your administration tasks. After that, you'll understand how to use policies to simplify user management, extend user rights, and lock down desktops. Then you'll learn how to use and manage profiles.

Creating Local and Domain User Accounts

While most of you will be using Active Directory, a few of you might still be using NT 4 domain controllers, and so, of course, you'd create any of those user accounts the old way, with User Manager for Domains. But if you need to create a *local* account on a Windows Server 2003 system, then you can still do that, using the Computer Management tool instead of Active Directory Users and Computers. In the next two sections, I'll show you how to create user accounts both locally and on an Active Directory domain.

Use Computer Management for Local Accounts

The bulk of the chapter assumes an Active Directory context. By this point, you have already read about domains, forests, and trees and know the benefits of using Active Directory on your network. In many cases, particularly if you have NT 4 workstations, Windows 2000 Professional, or XP Professional systems as clients, it's desirable to create a domain (even if you only have one server) in order to take advantage of the additional features of Active Directory. However, it's possible that a small organization might want to keep life very simple or even (brace yourself here) that the company's primary network OS is not Windows 2000 or Server 2003. For example, in a network that is Unix- or NetWare-based, there may be a need to set up a special-purpose NT server without all that AD stuff. In that case, if your server is not a domain controller (DC) and you aren't using

Active Directory, create your user accounts using the Computer Management tool (`COMPMGMT.MSC`). Users and groups created with `COMPMGMT.MSC` are local accounts, which is to say they exist and are valid on that local machine only. However, `COMPMGMT.MSC` is a remote enabled tool, so you can use it to create and manage local users and groups on remote member servers in a domain or on remote stand-alone servers. Just choose Connect to Another Computer from the Action menu to do this.

TIP *The Action menu is the menu that you see (instead of an Edit menu) to the right of the File menu in the Microsoft Management Console tools. See Chapter 3 for an overview of MMC and console anatomy.*

To create user accounts on a non–Active Directory server, use the Computer Management tool. If the machine you are working on is a domain controller, use Active Directory Users and Computers (`DSA.MSC`) to create accounts. On a domain controller, the Local Users and Groups node is not available in the Computer Management tool.

In `COMPMGMT.MSC`, open System Tools and then Local Users and Groups, as shown in Figure 9.1. Notice the users and groups that are created by default when you installed the Server OS. (In Figure 9.1 the Groups container has been opened in a separate window for your viewing convenience) On a stand-alone server, with no particular network services such as IIS, Terminal Services, DHCP, or DNS installed, the only built-in accounts are Administrator and Guest. The Guest account is disabled by default as a security precaution. The Administrator account, of course, has powers and abilities well beyond those of mortal users. It cannot be deleted or disabled, even if you set stringent account-lockout policies (which lock the account after a certain number of bad logon attempts). The Administrator account is not ordinarily subject to this policy and therefore cannot be locked out, even after a million bad logon attempts, which could be more than enough to crack a weak password. However, you *could* deny the Administrator account access to the computer from over the network. Then the would-be hacker would have to physically sit at your computer to try those million passwords. You'll see how to deny the Administrator network access later, when we talk about user rights and policies.

FIGURE 9.1

Computer Management/Local Users and Groups

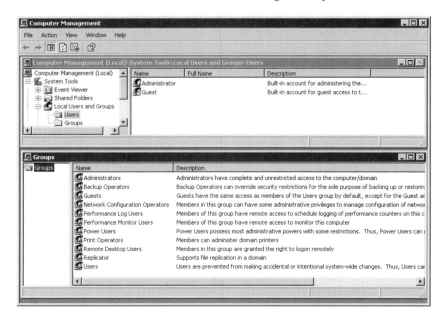

The Guest account is disabled by default as a security precaution. The Guest account, on a stand-alone server or in an AD context, creates a huge hole in the security of a system by allowing unauthenticated access. That's right, unauthenticated access. No password is required for the Guest account. You can use it without any knowledge of a username or password, which is why it's disabled by default. So it's a good thing that Guest is a very poor account as far as powers and abilities are concerned.

NOTE *One common security practice is to rename both the Guest and Administrator accounts. This prevents a would-be intruder from taking advantage of the well-known usernames when attempting to log in.*

A non-DC Windows Server 2003 has a few more built-in local groups than its Windows 2000 counterpart; in addition to the Administrators, Backup Operators, Guests, Power Users, Replicator, and Users groups, Windows Server creates Network Configuration Operators, Performance Log Users, Performance Monitor Users, Print Operators, and Remote Desktop Users. Additional built-in groups are created on a domain controller system, as you'll see in a moment. All of these built-in groups have a predefined set of rights and permissions. To empower users with those rights and permissions, just make those users members of the appropriate group. We'll discuss the built-in groups and their rights a bit later in this chapter.

To create a new user account on a non-DC server, open the Users folder under Local Users and Groups. Then choose New User from the Action menu, or right-click Users in Local Users and Groups and choose New User. Fill in the fields for Username, Password, and Confirm Password (the other fields are optional) as shown in Figure 9.2, and click Create. To change account properties, or to assign group memberships, a logon script, and a home folder, or to grant dial-in permission to the user, right-click the user account and choose Properties. To set a user's password, highlight the account and right-click, then choose Set Password. All of these options and more will be discussed a bit later when we're creating AD accounts.

FIGURE 9.2

Creating a local user

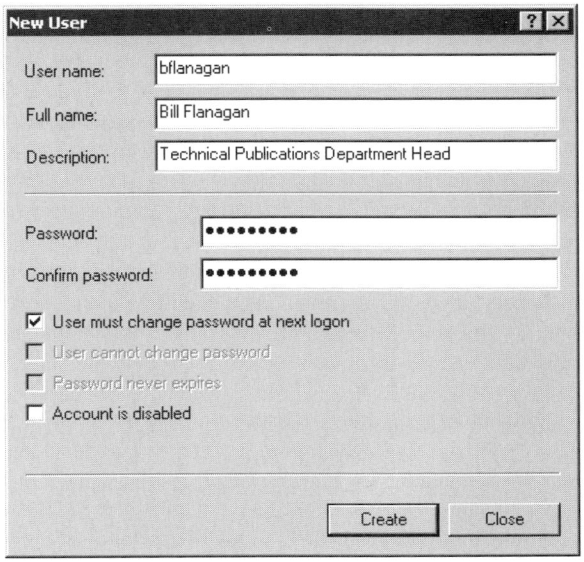

New User	? X
User name:	bflanagan
Full name:	Bill Flanagan
Description:	Technical Publications Department Head
Password:	••••••••
Confirm password:	••••••••

☑ User must change password at next logon
☐ User cannot change password
☐ Password never expires
☐ Account is disabled

[Create] [Close]

NOTE   *The local accounts you create on a stand-alone server, member server, or workstation are stored in the SAM (Security Accounts Manager) database, just as they were in NT 4. The SAM is located in* `\Windows\system32\config`.

That's it! To set account policies, such as lockout restrictions or auditing, use the Local Security Policy tool (`SECPOL.MSC`) or the Group Policy snap-in (`GPEDIT.MSC`). The process is very similar to configuring Group Policy with the Active Directory tools except that, since the machine is not a domain controller, changes will apply to the local policy for the machine. (I'll show you how to use the Group Policy snap-in to set account lockout and password policy for the domain later in the chapter.) The policies created will be local policies, which will live in the local machine's Registry database. Not surprisingly, the scope of policy settings is more limited for local polices than for group policies in an Active Directory environment. I'll also discuss group policies and how they differ from local policies later in this chapter.

Use Active Directory Users and Computers for Domain Accounts

Since the release of Windows 2000, Active Directory Users and Computers (`DSA.MSC`) has been the primary administrative tool for managing user accounts, security groups, organizational units, and policies in a single domain or in multiple domains. The Windows Server 2003 version of the tool only runs on Windows XP or another Server 2003. By default, `DSA.MSC` is only installed on Server 2003, and it only appears in the Start menu programs on domain controllers. To run `DSA.MSC` on a Windows XP Professional system, install the Admin Pack found in `\Windows\system32\ADMINPAK.MSI` on the server. The Admin Pack installs the three Active Directory tools on a workstation, and like other Windows Installer–based programs, it can be published using Group Policy and the Active Directory for installation on XP Professional desktops. See Chapter 12 for more information on publishing software in the Active Directory. `DSA.MSC` is also useful for managing computer accounts, organizational units, resources like printers and shared folders, and even domain controllers. However, the focus in this chapter is on creating and managing users and groups, including the management of users' environments and group policies.

NOTE   *What about the Admin Pack that came with Windows 2000 Server? Can you still use that version of* `DSA.MSC` *to administer Active Directory from your Windows 2000 Professional workstation? Well, yes, you can. The tool will still function. However, some of the options and object properties have changed. You won't be able to manage the new properties using the old tool. Besides, the absence of drag-and-drop in the old tool is really annoying. Instead of trying to use the previous version of* `DSA.MSC` *to administer AD, use a Remote Desktop Connection to connect to Server 2003 or domain controller and you'll have access to all of the most recent versions of the admin tools.*

WHERE DO USER AND GROUP ACCOUNTS LIVE?

Local user accounts on a stand-alone server, member server, or XP Professional workstation are stored in a Security Accounts Manager (SAM) database, usually located in `\Windows\system32\config`, depending on where you created your system root directory.

For Active Directory, the file is called `NTDS.DIT`, and it's found in `Windows\NTDS` by default, but you can specify a different path in the DCPROMO routine. As you learned in Chapter 8, the `NTDS.DIT` database stores a lot more information than the SAM does. It also stores information about servers and workstations, resources, published applications, and security policies. `NTDS.DIT` and the software that runs it are generally referred to together as the *directory service* or the Active Directory. This data structure is replicated throughout the domain to all domain controllers in a given domain for fault tolerance and load balancing. It's actually a database that uses an engine similar to the one used by Access, but one that programs control via the Lightweight Directory Access Protocol (LDAP) specified in RFC 1777. Although Windows 2000 Server was somewhat lacking in robust AD management tools, the Server 2003 distribution includes a number of graphical and command-line programs for working with Active Directory, and the Support Tools package on the CD offers a few more.

SECURITY IDENTIFIERS

User accounts, when first created, are automatically assigned a *security identifier (SID)*. A SID is a unique number that identifies an account. SIDs have been used since NT began; the system doesn't really know you by your name, but rather by your SID. User IDs are just there for the human interface. SIDs are never reused; when an account is deleted, its SID is deleted with it. A typical SID may look like this:

S-1-5-21-1659004503-193565697-854245398-1002

SIDs can be broken up into segments like this:

S-1-5-21-D1-D2-D3-RID

S-1-5 is just a standard prefix (actually, the 1 is a version number, which hasn't changed since NT 3.1, and the 5 means that the SID was assigned by NT); 21 is also an NT prefix; and D1, D2, and D3 are just 32-bit numbers that are specific to a domain. Once you create a domain, D1 through D3 are set, and all SIDs in that domain henceforth have the same three values. The *RID* stands for relative identifier. The RID is the unique part of any given SID. Each new account always has a unique RID number, even if the username and other information is the same as an old account. This way, the new account will not have any of the rights and permissions of the old account and security is preserved.

QUICK TOUR OF USER- AND GROUP-RELATED FUNCTIONS IN *DSA.MSC*

Active Directory Users and Computers provides the network administrator with the means to perform the following tasks:

◆ Create, modify, and delete user accounts

◆ Assign logon scripts to user accounts

◆ Manage groups and group memberships

◆ Create and manage group policies

Open Active Directory Users and Computers from the Administrative Tools group on the Start menu, or choose Start/Run and type in the filename (DSA.MSC). The tool needs to connect to a domain controller to obtain information and transmit your changes. In DSA.MSC, you will see the name of the contacted DC at the top of the console tree (zooropa) and your domain name right under the console root, as shown in Figure 9.3. To manually connect to another domain or domain controller, click the console root to highlight it, and then choose Connect to Domain or Connect to Domain Controller from the Action menu.

FIGURE 9.3

AD Users and
Computers
console

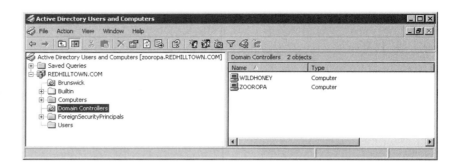

NOTE DSA.MSC *seeks out any nearby domain controller if you're running in Windows 2000 native or Windows Server mode; if you're in Windows 2000 mixed mode, then of course it must contact the PDC operations master, as mixed mode means that you've still got a single-master model.*

You can also specify the domain controller or a different domain to connect to when starting DSA.MSC from a command line or the Start/Run dialog box. To specify a particular domain controller, type **DSA.MSC /SERVER=servername**. To specify another domain, type **DSA.MSC /DOMAIN=domainname**.

In the left pane, you see listed a set of containers and organizational units (OUs) that were created automatically with the domain: Builtin, Computers, Domain Controllers, ForeignSecurityPrincipals, and Users (Brunswick is an organizational unit that I created). As with all the console applications, click an object in the console tree (on the left) to see its contents and information in the details pane (on the right). Notice also that the description bar for the details pane tells you how many objects there are in the container. The description bar, like the status bar and the toolbars, can be hidden if you want a more simplified view. Just choose Customize from the View menu and uncheck the Description Bar check box.

The Users and Computers containers are the default places to put user, group, and computer accounts when a machine is upgraded from NT 4. They gotta go somewhere. But you don't have to put new ones there, and you can move them to OUs as needed. As you'll quickly discover, you can put a user account in any OU, even directly in the "domain" container. Builtin is the container for those special built-in local groups—such as Administrators, Account Operators, Guests, and Users—that exist on every server machine, including domain controllers. More on this in a bit.

Domain Controllers is the default OU for new domain controllers. This is where the accounts are located when you first create a DC. Like the accounts in the Computers container, DC accounts can be moved to other OUs.

ForeignSecurityPrincipals is a default container for objects from external, trusted domains. In this chapter, we'll be working only with users and groups from this domain.

To create something new, select the container object where you want to locate it, then select New from the Action menu or right-click to select New from the context menu. As shown in Figure 9.4, you can choose to create a shared folder, a user account, a printer, an OU, a group account, a contact, or a computer account. There are also two new choices with Server 2003: InetOrg Person and MSMQ Queue Alias. An InetOrg Person is a type of user account that exists for compatibility with and migration of user accounts from non-Microsoft LDAP and X.500 directories. The MSMQ Queue Alias exists for use with Message Queuing 3 (commonly known as MSMQ). MSMQ is a distributed or store-and-forward messaging application. An MSMQ alias creates a reference in the Active Directory to a queue (another word for a distribution list) that does not exist in the directory.

FIGURE 9.4

Creating a new object

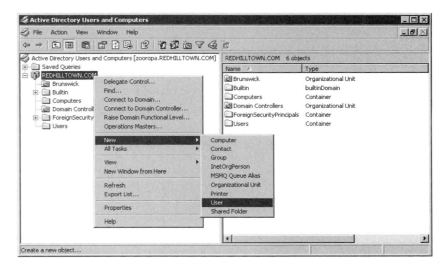

Any of these choices kicks off a corresponding wizard to create the object. In each case, to fill in all the details, go back and edit the properties of the object after creating it (right-click the object and choose Properties).

Because they aren't really OUs, but instead mere containers, you can't create an OU inside the Users or Computers containers, and you can only create users, computers, and groups inside the Builtin container.

DSA.MSC, like other MMC tools, is context-sensitive. Right-click an object to see its context menu. Notice that context menu choices change with the selected object. Right-click a user account and you have the option to disable it or reset the password, for example; right-clicking a computer account reveals options like Move and Manage (Manage opens up COMPMGMT.MSC connected to the selected computer).

This chapter is really not about managing machine accounts or printers or shared folders, so I'll leave those discussions for another chapter. However, contacts and OUs do relate to user and group management, so we'll take a look at those items in a moment.

PREBUILT ACCOUNTS: ADMINISTRATOR AND GUEST

If you have just created a new domain, you'll notice that several accounts were created automatically during the process: Administrator, Guest, and SUPPORT_388945a0. If you've been working with NT and Windows 2000 for a while now, you'll already be familiar with the Administrator and Guest accounts. The SUPPORT account, however, is a new account in Server 2003; it exists to provide Help and Support Service interoperability with non-Microsoft systems.

690 CHAPTER 9   MANAGING AND CREATING USER ACCOUNTS

The Administrator account is, as you've guessed, an account with complete power over a machine or a domain, depending on the context. You can't delete the Administrator account but you can rename it. You assigned a password for the Administrator account when you installed the server software and then again when you ran DCPROMO.EXE to create a new domain. The first was a local Administrator account and password, but when you created a domain, a new Administrator account and password for the domain replaced it. Don't lose that password, as there's no way to get it back! (Well, you can always rebuild from scratch, but that's no fun.)

The Guest account is for users who don't have their own account on the domain. *Guest* means "anyone that the domain controller doesn't recognize." By default, this account is disabled, and it should *stay* that way. If you've ever worked with a different network, like a Unix or NetWare network, you're probably familiar with the idea of a guest account—*but Server 2003 works differently, so pay attention!* You can get access to most other operating systems by logging in with the username Guest and a blank password. That Guest account is usually pretty restricted in the things it can do. That's true with Server 2003 as well, although the Everyone group also includes guests.

Here's the part that *isn't* like other operating systems. Suppose someone tries to access a shared printer or folder on a server or domain that has the Guest account enabled. She logs on to her local machine as melanie_wilson with the password happy. Even without an account on the server or domain, Melanie can still work on her local machine. Windows 9*x* machines don't care who you are, having no local accounts at all. On an NT 4, Win2K, or XP Professional workstation, she would have to log in to an account on the local machine. However, none of these operating systems requires authentication by a server or domain controller in order to access the local workstation. Suppose that this domain or server doesn't even *have* a melanie_wilson account? Now she's working at a computer and tries to access a domain resource. Guess what? She gets in. Why? The Guest account does not actually require a password at all.

WARNING   *Even though an explicit domain login requires that you use a username of Guest, you needn't explicitly log in to a domain to use guest privileges. If your network is attached to my network and your Guest account is enabled, I can browse through your network and attach to any resources that the Guest account can access. I needn't log in as Guest; the mere fact that there is an enabled Guest account pretty much says to leave the back door open. So be careful when enabling the Guest account.*

CREATING A NEW USER ACCOUNT

Before I discuss the ins and outs of account properties, UPN names, profile information, and all the other user settings, let's just go through the steps to create a new user account with the wizard. Then I'll go back and discuss all the settings for the newly created account.

To create a user account, in DSA.MSC select the Users container (or any other container/OU where you want the account to be located), then pull down the Action Menu or right-click and select New/ User (shown in Figure 9.4 a few pages back). A wizard appears with a dialog box shown in Figure 9.5. Fill in the First Name, Initials, Last Name, and Full Name fields as shown in the figure. (You don't actually have to fill in all the name fields, but you must supply information for at least one of the name fields to continue.) Next, fill in the user logon name (devans) and choose the Universal Principal Name (UPN) suffix to be appended to the username at logon time; recall that we discussed UPNs in Chapter 8. For logging in to an NT 4 or Windows 9*x* machine, there is also a downlevel logon name, which uses the old-style *DOMAINNAME\username* syntax.

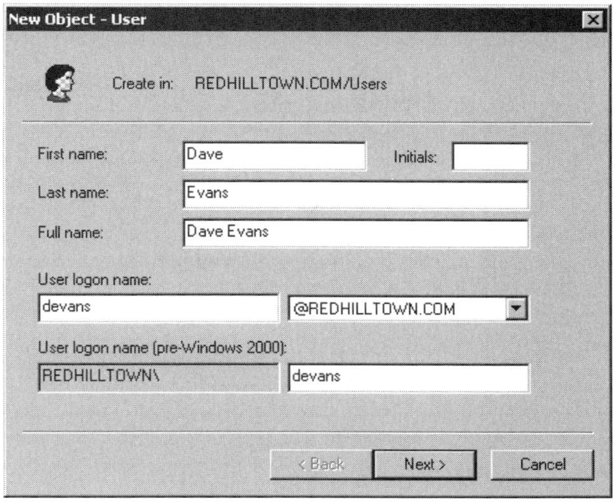

FIGURE 9.5

Creating a new user

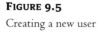

Windows Server 2003 usernames must follow these rules:

◆ The name must be unique to the machine for local accounts (or unique to the domain in the case of domain accounts). However, a domain user account name may be the same as a local account name on a non-DC that is a member of the domain, a fact that causes much confusion because they are completely separate entities.

◆ The username cannot be the same as a group name on the local machine for a local account (or the same as a group name on the domain in the case of domain accounts).

◆ The username may be up to 20 characters, upper- or lowercase or a combination.

◆ To avoid confusion with special syntax characters, usernames may not include any of the following:
  " / \ [ ] : ; | = , + * ? < >

◆ The name may include spaces and periods, but may not consist entirely of spaces or periods. Avoid spaces, however, since these names would have to be enclosed in quotes for any scripting or command-line situations.

Before going on, I want to point out that there are *three* significant usernames in Figure 9.5. First, the Full Name is Dave Evans. That was nothing but decoration in NT 4, but it's significant in Active Directory, as it is part of your LDAP name. Dave's LDAP name would look like this:

```
cn="Dave Evans",cn="Users",dc="REDHILLTOWN",dc="com"
```

You should know what Dave's LDAP name is if you want to use some of the command-line tools that "speak" in LDAP, (such as DSMOD.EXE or DSADD.EXE) or if you wish to do some WSH scripting using the AD Services Interface (ADSI). In LDAP-ese, cn is container, and yes, user accounts are containers. So there's a container Dave Evans inside a container named Users (the Users folder), and that folder is in a domain named REDHILLTOWN.com. You describe domain names in LDAP in terms of their components, the pieces separated by a period—in the case of REDHILLTOWN.com, it'd be REDHILLTOWN and com. You separate those with dc, which means domain component. If Dave's account were not in the Users folder, but instead were in an OU called, say, Brunswick, then you'd replace the cn (container) with ou:

```
cn="Dave Evans",ou="Brunswick",dc="REDHILLTOWN",dc="com"
```

The second name, devans@REDHILLTOWN.com, is the Active Directory logon name or UPN (user principal name). You read in Chapter 8 that while this *looks* like an e-mail address, it's not—it's just a convenient, easy-to-remember name to give a user instead of making the user remember a domain name and username.

The third name, REDHILLTOWN\devans, is the older-style NT 4–type logon name. You can use this name when logging on from a Windows 9*x* workstation or an NT 4 workstation. Or you might find yourself using it on older programs that run fine on Windows 2000/XP/Server systems, but that don't understand UPNs. I find, for example, that some Windows 2000 Resource Kit tools require you to identify yourself, but don't understand a logon name like lnjustice@REDHILLTOWN.com; they need to see something like REDHILLTOWN\lnjustice.

Once you've filled in all the username information, choose Next. In the following screen, shown in Figure 9.6, set a password for the user account and confirm it. Set the password and account options summarized in Table 9.1, then choose Next. User Must Change Password at Next Logon is the only option selected by default.

FIGURE 9.6

Setting password and account options

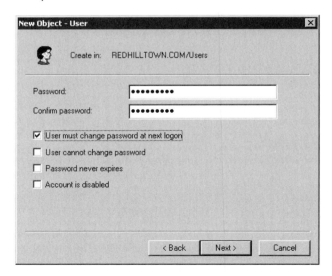

The final screen of this Create New Object Wizard, shown in Figure 9.7, simply confirms all the information you've supplied, including the container/OU where the account will live, the full name, the logon name, and the password or account options selected. Choose Finish and your user account is created.

TABLE 9.1: PASSWORD AND ACCOUNT OPTIONS FOR CREATING A NEW USER ACCOUNT

OPTION	DESCRIPTION
User Must Change Password at Next Logon	Forces a user to change their password the next time they log in; afterward the box will be unchecked.
User Cannot Change Password	If checked, prevents the user from changing the account's password. This is useful for shared accounts and accounts that run services like Exchange.
Password Never Expires	If checked, the user account ignores the password expiration policy, and the password for the account never expires. This is useful for accounts that run services and accounts for which you want a permanent password (such as the Guest account).
Account Is Disabled	If checked, the account is disabled and no one can log in to it until it is enabled (it is not, however, removed from the database). This is useful for accounts that are used as templates and for new user accounts that you create well in advance, such as new hires that will not begin work for several weeks.

FIGURE 9.7

Confirming new user information

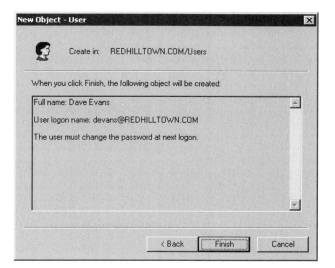

USER ACCOUNT PROPERTIES

Now let's go back and look at the properties of the account you just created. Right-click the user account object and you'll see several options in the context menu, shown in Figure 9.8. From here you can quickly copy the account, manage the user's group memberships, disable or enable the account, reset the user's password, move the account to a different container or OU, open the user's home page, or send him mail (these last two require that the home page URL and e-mail address be specified in the account information). You can also choose to delete or rename the user account from this menu.

WARNING   Each user and group account is assigned a unique identifier, called a SID, when it is created. Deleting a user or group account deletes the unique identifier. Even if you re-create an account with the same name, the new account will not automatically have the rights or permissions of the old account.

FIGURE 9.8

The context menu for a user account

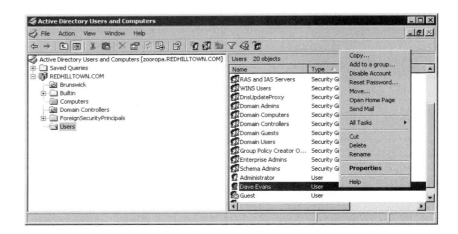

Choose Properties from the context menu to bring up the full user account information. Figure 9.9 shows 13 different properties tabs for this user account. In the General tab shown in Figure 9.9, you can add a description of the user account, supply the name of the office where the user works, and add telephone numbers, an e-mail address, even Web page addresses. The Address tab in Figure 9.10 shows fields for a user's mailing address. The Telephones tab (Figure 9.11) offers a place for home, pager, mobile phone, fax, and IP phone numbers, as well as a place to enter notes.

FIGURE 9.9

User properties General tab

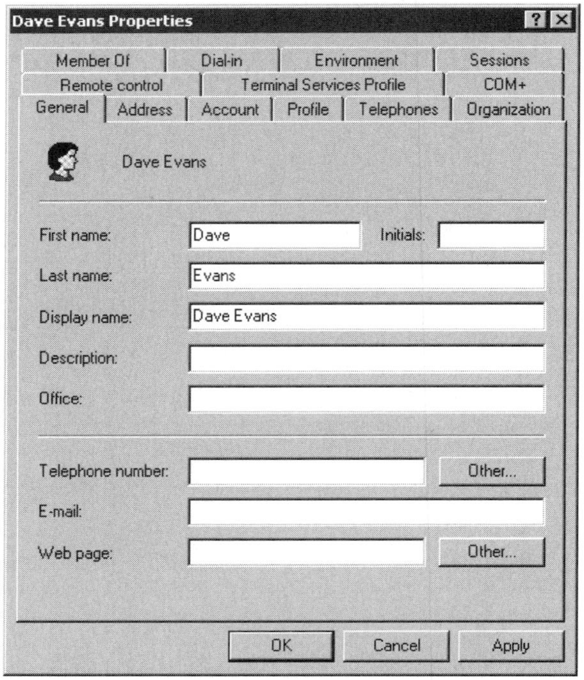

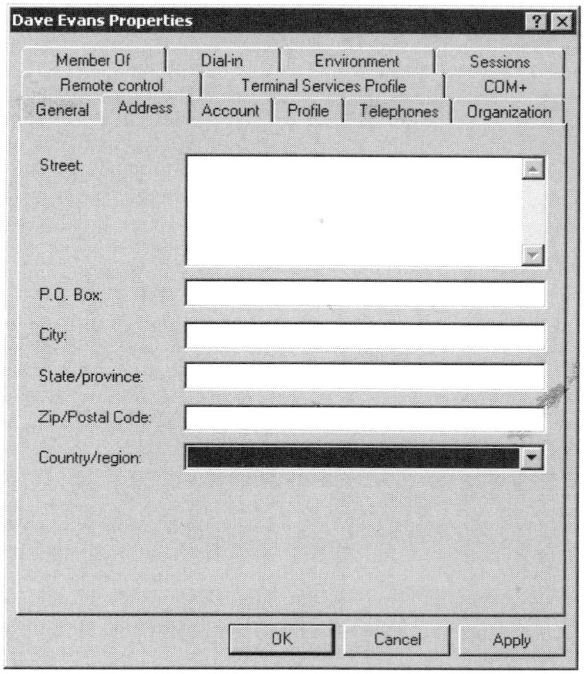

FIGURE 9.10

User properties
Address tab

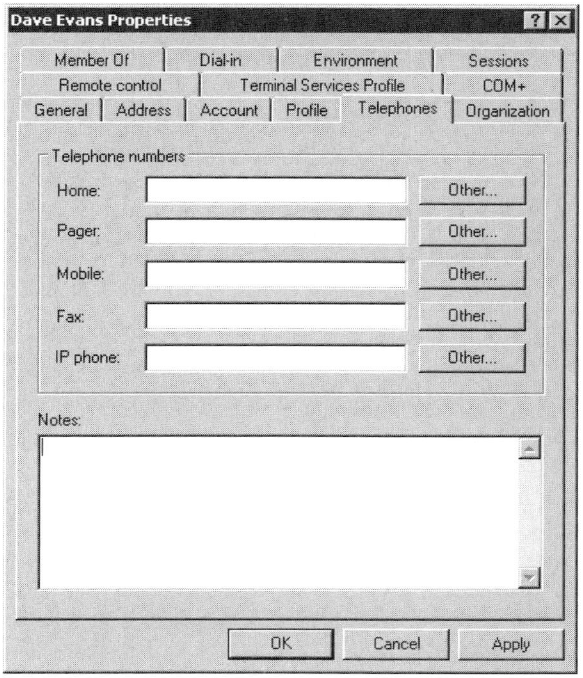

FIGURE 9.11

User properties
Telephones tab

In Figure 9.12 you see the Organization tab, where you can enter information about someone's actual job title, manager, and direct reports.

FIGURE 9.12

User properties Organization tab

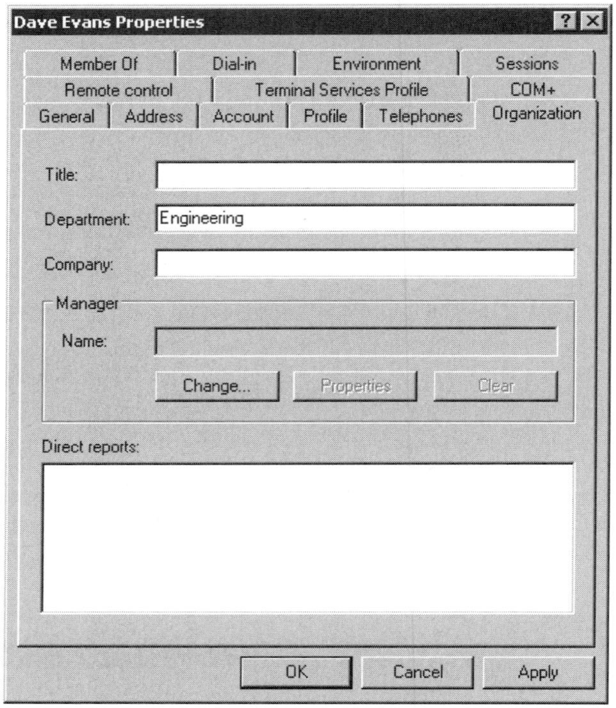

So 4 of the 13 tabs displayed in the user account properties are just about contact information, not what we old-time NT admins would call account properties. You begin to understand why they call it directory services.

NOTE *So why does the Active Directory need to hold all this contact information for users? If you have used Exchange on your network, you know that you can enter almost all of this stuff in the Exchange mailbox properties. Exchange 2000, however, has no separate method for creating user accounts; it uses the information that AD has about the user.*

Of the remaining properties tabs, four (Remote Control, Terminal Services Profile, Sessions, and Environment) pertain to Terminal Services, covered in Chapter 16. In Chapter 12, you'll learn about using the COM+ property tab to assign users to applications on COM+ partitions configured on application servers. We'll also leave the Dial-In tab to Chapter 20, which covers the Routing and Remote Access Service. That leaves us with four "core" property tabs: General, Account, Profile, and Member Of. In the next few sections we will tackle account settings, profile information, and group memberships.

Account Settings

If you need to modify the user's logon name or UPN suffix, go to the Account tab (Figure 9.13). This is also the place to specify permissible logon hours, account options, and all that stuff. By default, users are allowed to log in any day of the week at any time of the day (24/7), but you can choose the Logon Hours button to designate particular permitted hours and days (see Figure 9.14).

FIGURE 9.13

User account properties

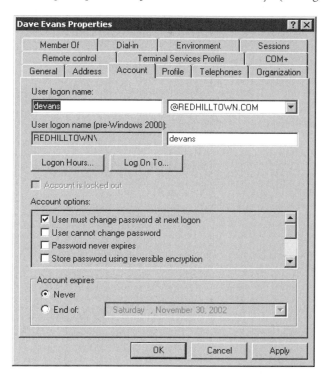

FIGURE 9.14

Setting logon hours

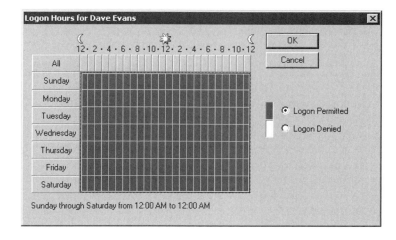

NOTE *By default, a user will not be logged off automatically when logon hours expire, but there is a setting to accomplish this. The setting is called Automatically Log Off Users When Logon Hours Expire, and it's found in the Group Policy snap-in, under* `Computer Configuration\Windows Settings\Security Settings\Local Policies\Security Options`. *This parameter can also be set using the Domain Security Policy tool or the Local Security Policy tool (depending on the context). In either case, look for the setting under* `Local Policies\Security Options`. *(We'll look at Local Security Policy and group policies a bit later in this chapter.)*

By default, users can log in to the domain from any workstation, but logon workstations may still be specified by NetBIOS names (see Figure 9.15). However, you must still be using NetBIOS on your network in order for this to be enforced.

FIGURE 9.15

Permitted logon workstations

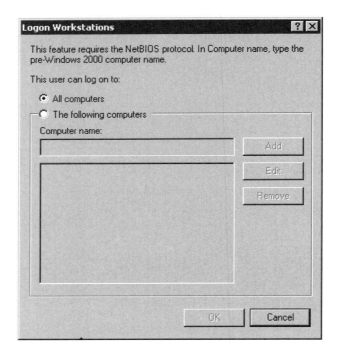

Looking back at the Account tab (Figure 9.13), you'll see that the Account Is Locked Out check box is grayed out. If the account is locked as a result of bad logon attempts (configurable using one of the various Policy tools, as I'll explain later), the box will show up as checked and available. If you wish to manually unlock the account, just uncheck the box. At the bottom of the Account tab you see the account expiration setting. By default, an account never expires, but if you enable the option, the default interval is 30 days. Notice also that a number of account options are available (scroll down in the Account Options box to see all the options). Several of these, like User Must Change Password at Next Logon, are familiar to Windows administrators and fairly self-explanatory to others. Table 9.2 summarizes the available account options.

You may have noticed that the user's password cannot be reset from the Account tab. To reset a user's password, close the account properties sheet and right-click the username in the details pane of `DSA.MSC`. Choose the option to reset the password, and you will be able to type in and confirm a new password, as shown in Figure 9.16. You should also select the check box to force the user to change their password at the next logon.

TABLE 9.2: ACCOUNT OPTIONS FOR USER ACCOUNTS

OPTION	DESCRIPTION
User Must Change Password at Next Logon	Forces a user to change their password the next time they log in; afterward the box will be unchecked.
User Cannot Change Password	If checked, prevents the user from changing the account's password. This is useful for the Guest account, other shared accounts, and accounts that run services like Exchange.
Password Never Expires	If checked, the password for the account never expires. This is useful for the Guest account and accounts that run services.
Store Password Using Reversible Encryption	Enable this option only for users logging on from Apple computers.
Account Is Disabled	If checked, the account is disabled and no one can use it until it is enabled. Use this option to protect accounts that are used only as templates.
Smart Card Is Required for Interactive Login	This user has a smart card reader attached to their computer. The user must swipe the card into the reader and supply a PIN number instead of their username and password.
Account Is Trusted for Delegation	Enable this option only for service accounts that need to gain access to resources on behalf of other user accounts.
Account Is Sensitive and Cannot Be Delegated	Use this option on a guest or temporary account to ensure that the account will not delegated by another account.
Use DES Encryption Types for This Account	Enable to support Data Encryption Standard (DES). DES supports multiple levels of encryption, including MPPE Standard (40-bit), MPPE Standard (56-bit), MPPE Strong (128-bit), IPSec DES (40-bit), IPSec 56-bit DES, and IPSec Triple DES (3DES).
Do Not Require Kerberos Preauthentication	Enable to permit an account to use an alternate implementation of the Kerberos protocol.

FIGURE 9.16

Resetting a user's password

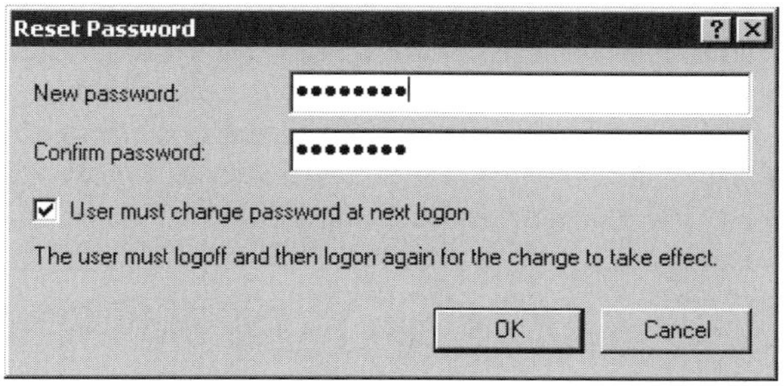

Profile Information

Use the Profile tab, shown in Figure 9.17, to specify a user's profile path, a logon script, and a home folder. These options exist to support pre-Windows 2000 clients; these settings and many more can be specified using Group Policy. However, Group Policy only works on Windows 2000 and XP systems. It may be a while before companies abandon Windows NT and 9x workstations completely. Until then, you'll want to use the options in the Profile tab. I'll discuss user profiles and logon scripts in more detail in the sections to come, but the following paragraphs give you the basics about these features.

FIGURE 9.17

User profile properties

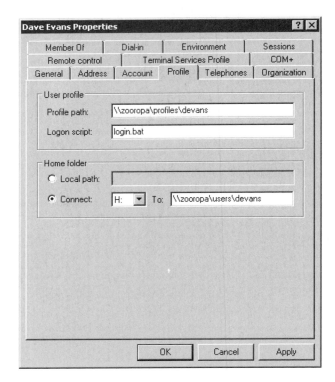

A user's Desktop settings, from Start menu content right down to a color scheme and mouse orientation, can be stored in a network location so that the user can log in from any system on the network and see the same Desktop. You can specify a shared network location for that purpose. This is also useful if you want to force a user (or group of users) to keep the same settings all the time. Such an arrangement is called a *roaming profile* if it's not forced on a user and if they can make changes. If the user is compelled to load that profile and can't log in without it, it's called a *mandatory profile* (or a *shared mandatory profile,* if more than one user is shackled to it). This feature is most useful for NT 4 clients because Windows 2000 and XP clients support folder redirection and Desktop configuration using group policies. For many more details, refer to "Working with Roaming User Profiles."

A *logon* or *login script* is one that runs at logon time to configure a user's environment and assign network resources, such as mapped drives and printers. Though the art of the logon script is well known in other network operating systems, including NetWare, logon scripts in Microsoft networks have not always been emphasized. Many Microsoft networks were small in the beginning, and users could browse for network resources. Login scripts are, however, filling a more important role for Windows environments; today's networks are larger, and administration of resources and users is becoming increasingly more complex. See "Zen and the Art of Login Scripts" later in this chapter for details, but for now, you should know that the server provides a default path where the logon script will be stored (in the SYSVOL share, which is by default the \Windows\SYSVOL\sysvol directory, but it's configurable). That's why you only need to specify the script's name in the dialog box. However, it is possible that the logon script could be stored in a subdirectory of SYSVOL, for example in SYSVOL\Sales\saleslogin.bat. In that case, you would need to specify the relative path from the SYSVOL root, such as Sales\saleslogin.bat.

A *home folder*, also known as a *home directory*, is a folder assigned to the user for their private use. Although applications may have their own default folder for saving and opening files, the home folder will be the default working folder for a user at the command prompt. You can specify a local path for a user's home folder, but it's only useful if the user will be logging in locally to the machine. For users logging in from the network, you need to choose the Connect option and specify a network path following the UNC convention *machinename**servername**directoryname*. You can also use a variable as a folder name, *%username%*, to indicate that the home folder name is the same as the user ID.

When you specify a home folder path for the user, if the network share already exists and you have permission to write to it, the server will create the user's home folder automatically. This saves admins a lot of time. If you need a step-by-step procedure to create and assign home folders, see Chapter 11, which covers creating and managing shared folders.

In any discussion about home folders, questions about how to limit disk space consumption are bound to arise. Windows NT 4 had no built-in mechanism to set or enforce disk quotas at all. One strategy was to set up a separate partition for user directories, confining the problem to that partition (kind of like growing horseradish). The hapless admin sometimes ran routine "diskhog" scripts and asked, begged, or publicly humiliated users into cleaning up their home folders. Others threatened to start deleting files at random if users didn't comply. But the best option was to purchase a third-party disk quota tool. However, Windows 2000, and now Windows Server 2003, comes with a simple quota management system for NTFS volumes. You simply enable it for a volume and then set thresholds for warnings and so forth. Read about it in Chapter 10.

Group Memberships

To specify group memberships for a user account, open the Member Of tab in the account properties sheet. As you see in Figure 9.18, by default a new user is a member of the group Domain Users. The Active Directory Folder column on the right indicates the container or OU path for the group. To add a user to another group, choose Add to open the Select Groups dialog box (Figure 9.19). Now you see something interesting. Instead of finding and displaying a list of all available groups, as you did in Windows 2000, now you can specify the object type (groups or built-in security principals) and the location of the object (REDHILLTOWN.COM domain, in this case) and either type in the group name or perform a search for groups within the given context.

FIGURE 9.18

Setting group
memberships

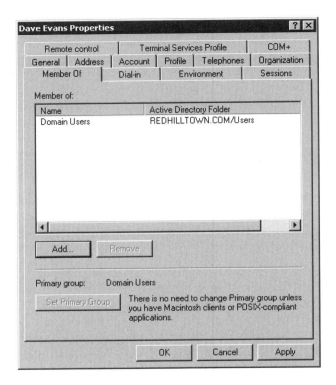

FIGURE 9.19

The Select Groups
dialog box

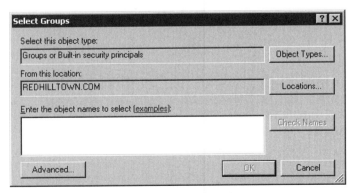

The purpose of this change is not to make your life miserable. Your network could conceivably contain hundreds or thousands of groups in dozens of organizational units; the new Select Groups function prevents you from having to wait while DSA searches for all those groups. It also prevents you from having to scroll through a long list of groups to find the one you are looking for.

If you know the name of the group or groups, just type in the group names, separated by semicolons. Then click the Check Names button to confirm that the names you typed are valid group names. If you don't remember the exact name of the group but want to select it from a list, click the Advanced button to expand the dialog box and permit searches (shown in Figure 9.20). Use the Locations button to narrow your search within the domain to selected containers or organizational units. Use the Common Queries options to find the group, or simply choose Find Now to pull up a list of all groups within the location context you specified. Figure 9.20 shows the results of a search for all groups in the REDHILLTOWN.COM domain. Select the group name from the list, and click OK. The group name will appear in the Select Groups dialog box. Click OK to add your user to the group and return to the Member Of property tab. The groups you selected should now display in the list. Click OK or Apply to save your changes. Now that wasn't too difficult, was it?

To remove users from groups, use the Remove button in the Member Of tab. See the section "Working with Security Groups" for the skinny on group memberships.

FIGURE 9.20

Using the Advanced Options in Select Groups

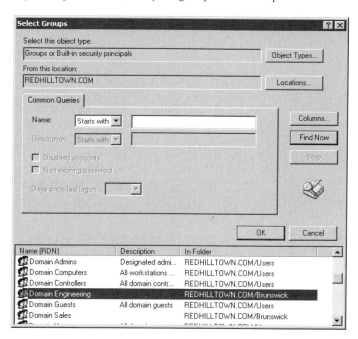

MANAGING ACCOUNTS

In the preceding sections, I discussed how to make changes to a single user account. Now let's talk about how to make changes to several (or many) accounts at once. While we're on the subject, I'll cover a couple of other multiple-account issues, including how to create a bunch of users at a time.

In DSA.MSC you can select multiple accounts in the details pane by holding down the Shift key while you work the down arrow key, or you can hit the Ctrl key as you click each of the accounts and then right-click to see the context menu while those accounts are selected. As you see in Figure 9.21, you can choose to move them all to another container or OU; add them to a group (to remove members of a group, you'll need to go to the properties sheet of the group itself); or disable, enable, or delete accounts. You can also send them all mail, assuming you have specified e-mail addresses for the accounts.

TIP   Remember, changes to a user's account, such as group memberships, will not take effect until the next time the user logs in.

FIGURE 9.21

Selecting multiple users in DSA.MSC

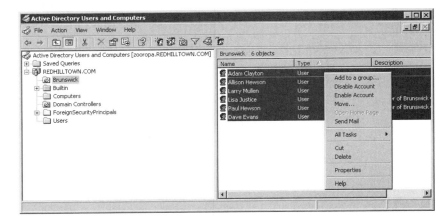

Choose Properties from the context menu while several accounts are selected to open the properties screen for Multiple Objects (see Figure 9.22). This presents a subset of the properties configurable for each individual account. There is no Member Of tab, for example, but you can use this function to have all selected users change their passwords at next logon.

FIGURE 9.22

Account tab for multiple selected objects Account tab

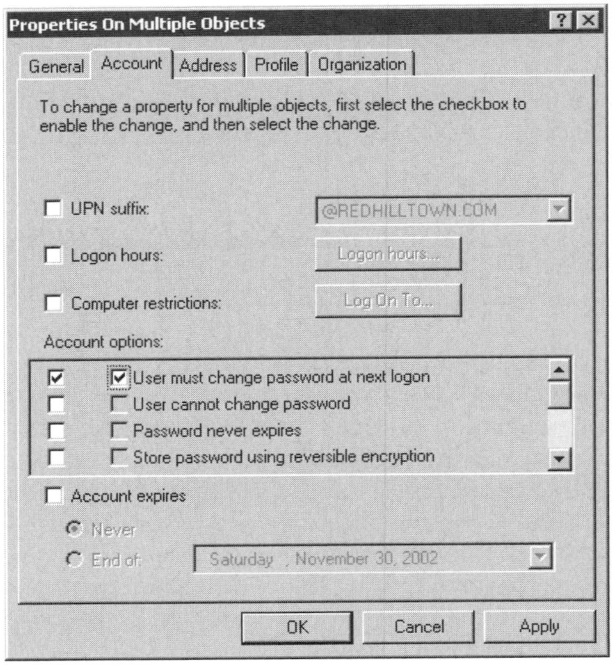

Notice in Figure 9.22 that the Account tab for Multiple Objects looks a little different from the Account tab for an individual account. The first check box beside each option tells `DSA.MSC` that you want to configure that option for all of the accounts. Once checked, the button, drop-down list, or second set of check boxes becomes enabled so you can specify what you want the value to be for each property configured. For example, to expire all selected accounts' passwords, first select the leftmost check box beside User Must Change Password at Next Logon. Then you can select the second check box to expire all of the users' passwords labeled. If you checked the leftmost box and not the one closest to the option, you would be choosing to have none of these user's passwords expire.

To create multiple users with like settings, create an account template and copy it. Properties that are copied include account settings (such as Password Never Expires), group memberships, account expiration date (if supplied), and the UPN suffix. The profile information (home directory, user profile path, and logon script) is also copied, and if you used the *%username%* variable to set up the template user's home folder, it will be created automatically for new users when the account is copied.

What if you need to make changes to lots of users at once? You can't select all the users if they don't all display in the details pane of `DSA.MSC`. Members of a particular group may exist in different domains or organizational units, so it's not feasible to try to select all the members of a group at once to make changes. And how can you create, say, 50 or 500 users at a time? You could use the good old net user command that's been around since NT 3.51, but it's somewhat limited in its options. The addusers utility, which is available in the Windows 2000 Resource Kit, is much more flexible because it can accepts input from a comma-delimited text file and assign global and local group memberships. However, addusers is not AD-aware; for example, you can't use it to put users into OUs as you create them. Windows Server now offers some robust command-line tools that can be used in batch files or scripts to add user accounts, modify properties, and import or export objects from the Active Directory. `DSADD.EXE` and `DSMOD.EXE`, invoked with the user argument, add and modify (respectively) users in the Directory. `CSVDE.EXE` is used to import or export data using CSV (comma-separated value) formatted files.

RESETTING PASSWORDS

The most commonly changed part of a user's account is the password. You can reset a password from the GUI by right-clicking the user's account in Active Directory Users and Computers, but how about changing it from the command line?

Well, if it's a local user account, then simply type **net user** *username newpassword*; so, for example, to change the local admin's password to bigsecret, you'd type the following:

```
net user administrator bigsecret
```

But that only works for local accounts. To change a password on a domain account, add the /domain option. So to change the default administrator password on the domain to reallybigsecret, type this:

```
net user administrator reallybigsecret /domain
```

To reset the password to a random value, use the /random switch:

```
net user administrator /domain /random
```

The randomly created password will display on the screen after the command completes, so that you can write it down. Why would you want to set a password to a random value? Personally, I don't want people using the default Administrator account, but it's so hard to break them of the habit. So I randomize the password, make people use their own Domain Admin account, turn on auditing, and threaten Severe Punishment to anyone caught setting the Administrator password back to something else—unless there's a good reason.

Another way to change passwords, but only from a Windows XP workstation or Server 2003, is to use dsmod. It's not quite as simple as the net user command, however, because you have to use the Distinguished Name (DN) for the account. To reset Dave's password and force him to change it at next logon, you would type this:

```
dsmod user "CN=Dave Evans, CN=users, DC=REDHILLTOWN, DC=com"
   -pwd H@wkMO@n269 -mustchpwd yes
```

Understanding Groups

Assigning users to groups makes it easier to grant them rights to perform tasks and permissions to access resources such as printers and network folders. Assisting you in this endeavor are several built-in groups with built-in rights. You'll also want to create your own user groups and assign them certain rights and permissions. The members of the groups you create can, in turn, be granted the ability to administer other groups and objects, even whole organizational units. Groups can contain computers and contacts as well as users and other groups. They can also be used as e-mail distribution lists. So it's important to understand the different types of groups that exist and how to work with them to delegate control, grant access to necessary resources, and configure rights. That is the subject of the next few sections.

Creating Groups

To create a new group in Active Directory Users and Computers, navigate to the container where you want the group to live. Groups can be created at the root of the domain, in a built-in container such as Users, or in an OU. While you have the container highlighted, right-click or pull down the Action menu and choose New/Group (Figure 9.23). Supply the name of the group (Domain Engineering) and the pre–Windows 2000 name if it will be different; then choose the group scope and group type, as shown in Figure 9.24. By default, the group scope is Global and the type is Security. For an explanation of group types and group scope, see the upcoming sections. Click OK to create the group in the selected container.

Now let's fill in the rest of the group information and add users to the new group. Find and double-click the group you just created to open the group's properties sheet. In the General tab shown in Figure 9.25, fill in a description if you wish and an e-mail address if a distribution list exists for the group.

FIGURE 9.23

Creating a new group

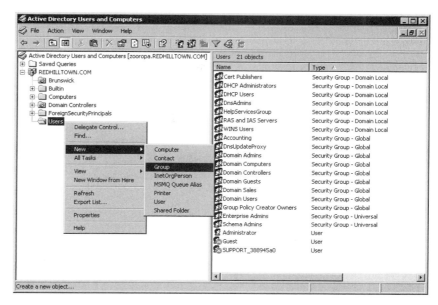

FIGURE 9.24

Information for a
new group

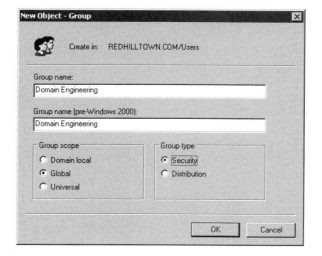

To populate the group, go to the Members tab and click Add. Except for the different object types selected, this is the same dialog box you saw back in Figure 9.19. In this context you may select users, other groups, contacts, and even computers to join the group. Group members can also come from different OUs. Type in the names of the users or groups you want to add, or use the Advanced button to find them. Click OK to finalize your additions and return to the properties pages. To view or modify the local and universal groups to which the group (Domain Engineering, in our example) belongs, open the Member Of tab (Figure 9.26). The Managed By tab is for optional contact information and does not necessarily reflect any direct delegation of control.

FIGURE 9.25

A group's properties on the General tab

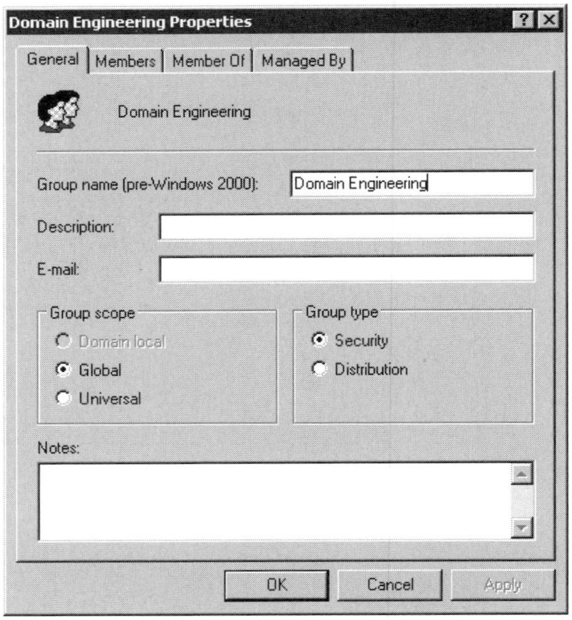

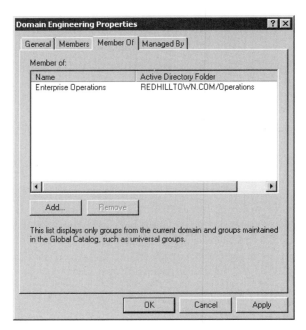

FIGURE 9.26

The Member Of tab in group properties

Another way to add members to a group is to right-click the user account and choose Add to a Group from the context menu. If you want to add several selected users to the same group at once, hold down the Ctrl key as you select the users, then right-click and choose Add to a Group. There's also a button on the toolbar to add one or more selected objects to a group.

One final how-to note: it will probably be necessary to move a group from one container or OU to another at some point. To do this, right-click the group icon in the details pane of the console and choose Move. Navigate to the container that will be the new home for the group (Figure 9.27), select it, and click OK. Alternately, just select your groups and use the new drag-and-drop feature to move them from one OU to another.

FIGURE 9.27

Moving a group to another container

TIP   *You cannot use Active Directory Users and Computers to move directory objects between domains. If you need to move users, groups, or organizational units between domains in a single forest, use the* MOVETREE *command-line tool included in the Windows Support Tools.*

Group Types: Security Groups versus Distribution Groups

When creating group accounts, you have the option to classify a group as a *security group* or as a *distribution group*. Security groups are not really new; they are equivalent to user groups as we knew them in all versions of Windows NT. Their new name serves only to distinguish them from distribution groups, which are sort of "non-security groups."

SECURITY GROUPS OVERVIEW

Security groups are groups used to assign rights and permissions. Like user accounts, security groups are assigned SIDs. When you view or edit an object's access control list (ACL), for example, the group names that appear on the list are security groups (sometimes they show up as SIDs if the friendly names are slow to resolve). These user and group SID entries on the ACL are matched up with a user's credentials to permit or deny access to the object.

There are three major types of security groups: local, global, and universal—although you might prefer to think of them as four different groups: local, domain local, global, and universal.

Local groups are the kind of groups you find on a stand-alone server, a server that is a member of a domain, a Windows 2000 or XP Professional workstation. Local groups are local to the machine. That is, they exist and are valid only on that workstation or that non-DC server.

Domain local group is the special name for a local group that happens to be on a domain controller. Domain controllers have a common active directory that is replicated between them, so a domain local group on one DC will also exist on its sibling DC. As you'll see when we get into the details, domain local groups are different from other local groups.

Global, universal, and, of course, domain locals live on the DCs in the Active Directory. Global groups are still pretty much like they were in NT 4; they are used to grant access rights and permissions across machine (and domain) boundaries.

Universal groups have been with us since Windows 2000 and can also serve the function of global groups, granting rights and object permissions throughout domains and between domains. Universals are more useful than globals or locals because they are infinitely more flexible with regard to nesting, but you can really use them only when your domain has gone "Windows 2000 native," which requires that all domain controllers be running either Windows Server 2003 or Windows 2000.

DISTRIBUTION GROUPS AND CONTACTS

Until Windows 2000 appeared, all NT groups were security groups. They were assigned security IDs; they could be granted rights and permissions. A distribution group is simply a non-security group. Distribution groups don't have SIDs and don't appear on ACLs. So what are they for? If you've worked with Exchange or a similar product, you are familiar with distribution *lists*. These are groups of recipient addresses. It's easier to send mail to ACME Managers, for example, than to individually select each manager's name from a list.

Assuming that you have entered mail addresses for your users, your security groups in the Active Directory are also unofficial distribution lists. Just right-click a group name in DSA.MSC and you'll see the option to send mail to the group members, just as you see the option to send mail to a user account when you right-click it. This kicks off your default mail-handling program, and the system will try to send mail using the e-mail address supplied in the account information. So, if you have a set of people working in the finance department and you place all those people in a security group called Finance, you can not only assign permissions for resources to the Finance group, but you can also send mail to the members of the Finance security group, assuming you have filled in e-mail information for each member.

Sometimes organizations need distribution lists that are unrelated to their security groups. For instance, say your company is a communications provider and has a distribution list called Outage Alert. This distribution list is used to notify certain people in the case of a major outage that will affect service to your customers. The members of this list might include people from operations, customer relations, even the chief executive officer. Plus, the distribution list could include external e-mail addresses of key business partners (also known as *contacts*). These people will not have a security group in common, and it's silly to have to create a separate security group just because you need a distribution list. So you can classify a group in the Active Directory as a distribution group, a group with no security privileges. No security identifiers are created for a distribution group, and the membership is not included in a user's credentials at logon time. You can't grant printer permissions to a distribution list because it doesn't appear in the ACL. This group is strictly for e-mail.

In other words, distribution groups are basically only useful if you've adopted Exchange 2000. I can't resist saying it: "Resistance is futile. You will purchase our technology..."

It's part of Exchange 2000's raison d'être: it merges the list of e-mail users (the "directory") that Exchange 5.5 and earlier versions had to maintain separately with the list of domain users kept on domain controllers. Exchange 2000 basically doesn't *have* a directory anymore. Instead, it just exploits AD's directory parasitically. You can change a security group to a distribution group and back again, but not if you're still running in Mixed mode. As with everything else that's truly useful, this action requires that you be running in Windows 2000 Native mode or Windows Server mode.

NOTE   *Contacts are to user accounts what distribution groups are to security groups. Contacts are objects that store information about people, including e-mail, telephone, and related information. Contacts can be members of security or distribution groups, but they are not accounts, so contacts have no security identifier (SID) and cannot be assigned user rights or permissions.*

Group Scope: Locals, Domain Locals, Globals, and Universals

Where are they recognized and what can they contain? These are the main issues surrounding local, domain local, global, and universal groups. Since they are used to grant rights and permissions, you need to know where that group membership means something, where it is accepted (kind of like American Express). Since you want to nest groups to simplify rights and permissions assignment, you need to know the rules and recommendations for nesting as well.

LOCAL OR MACHINE LOCAL GROUPS

The basic local group, also called a "machine" local group, is the only type of group that exists on stand-alone servers and Windows 2000 or XP Professional workstations. A stand-alone server or Professional workstation that is not a member of a domain is like an island nation with no knowledge of the outside world. It only recognizes its own local groups and users. Local groups are the only ones that can be granted permission to access resources, and membership is limited to local users. When the machine joins the domain, however, that island nation becomes a member of a greater governing body, like a federation of island nations. It can have local user accounts, as you saw earlier in this chapter, but it can also accept user accounts built on a domain controller—the domain controller's Active Directory is a centralized database of user accounts, saving you the trouble of re-creating them on every single machine.

A machine uses its local groups to simplify administration. For example, suppose I've got a server with a printer on it and I want to control who can use the printer. I create a local group called PrinterUsers and give the PrinterUsers group permission to print to the printer. But there's no one in PrinterUsers initially, so I'd better populate the group. Perhaps I want to let people from the domain print on the printer. I *could* insert user accounts from the domain into PrinterUsers one by one, but that's too much work, so it's more convenient to just grab a group that already *contains* those domain users and stuff the domain-based group into the local group. Just a few clicks and I'm done.

But I got a bit sneaky when I just said "domain-based group"—I left out a bit of important information. You can't insert local groups in local groups. You'd *think* that you ought to be able to just drop Group A into Group B indiscriminately, but you can't. That's why local groups are called *local* groups, to differentiate them from the other kinds of groups. The other kinds of groups—there are three types—can only be built on domain controllers. A local group can contain any of the three domain-based groups—they're called global, domain local, and universal.

GLOBAL GROUPS

The first domain-based group type is the *global group*. (It resembles NT 4 global groups, if you're familiar with them.) They can only contain user accounts from the domain, as with NT 4 global groups. But Active Directory gives them a bit more power—global groups can exist inside other global groups, so long as the global groups are in the same domain.

You can put a global group inside a local group of any domain that trusts the global group's domain. So you could stuff a global group into a local group for a member server in the same domain as the global group or into a local group for any other domain in the forest. Think of global groups as "traveling groups." They're a convenient collecting point for domain user accounts.

DOMAIN LOCAL GROUPS

The second kind of domain-based group is called a domain local group. There are actually two factions of domain local groups: built-in domain locals and other domain locals. You see, when a server becomes a domain controller, its machine local groups become domain local groups and go live in the `Builtin` container in the Active Directory. They have familiar names, like Administrators, Backup Operators, and Print Operators. There are also some new groups that were created with the domain, like Server Operators and Account Operators. Now here's the tricky part. These groups are just like machine local groups, except for the fact that all of the domain controllers in a domain share the same security database. So each and every domain controller will have the same local groups and group members as all of the other domain controllers. If you are a member of Server Operators on one DC, you are a member of Server Operators on all DCs (they are all of one mind...). These "built-in" domain local groups cannot be moved or deleted, and they cannot become members of other local groups at all. Furthermore, other local groups cannot be members of built-in domain local groups. Just think of the built-in domain local groups as machine local groups on domain controllers.

As if things weren't already complicated, there are also domain local groups that are not subject to the limitations of the built-in domain local groups. Unlike the domain local groups in the `Builtin` container, these domain local groups start off life in the `Users` container, but they can be moved and deleted. Any new domain local groups you create will have these properties. I'll warn you right up front that I'm still not quite sure why they exist or what good they do. They're basically domain-restricted versions of global groups.

NOTE   In the following paragraphs, assume that I am referring to "non-built-in" domain local groups, unless they are specifically called built-in local groups.

You just read that global groups are groups built on a domain controller, can contain user accounts from the local domain, and can be placed in any local group in any machine in any domain within the forest (or in any other domain that trusts the global group's domain). So if you have a global group built in domain A and domain B trusts domain A, then you can put that global group in any local group on any machine in domains A or B. A domain local group acts like a global group, except that it cannot be used outside of the domain. You can only put a domain local group into the local groups of machines within the same domain. In this example, then, a domain local group created in domain A could only be placed in a local group on a machine on domain A. Even if domain B trusts domain A, you still can't put any of domain A's domain local groups into domain B's local groups.

So why do these domain local groups exist at all? To tell you the truth, I'm just not sure. I can think of one benefit only: domain local groups do not increase the GC's workload; globals do. The global catalog includes, among other things, names and members of all global groups in all domains in the forest. In contrast, the global catalog does not contain any information about the domain local groups. So I guess a domain local group has a smaller impact on a global catalog. If a large organization wanted to use a single domain model instead of multiple domains, domain local groups could be used instead of global groups to lower the GC replication overhead. But, in any case, it's not much of a difference.

One reason you *do* want to know about domain local groups is if you intend to take the Microsoft certification exams. Now, *they* like domain local groups. You'll get a question or two that will try to trip you up by offering you a solution that involves putting a domain local group into a local group of a different domain. You always know *that* answer's wrong.

UNIVERSAL GROUPS

The third, and coolest, type of domain-based group is a universal group. Summarized, a universal group can do *anything*, just about. You can only create them on a domain controller, as with domain local and global groups. But you can do the following:

- Put a global group from any domain in the forest into a universal group
- Put a universal group into any kind of local group (machine local, domain local, or built-in domain local)
- Put a universal group inside a universal group (this is the cool part)

Finally, the group that we've always wanted. Just like the Russian *matryoshka* dolls (those dolls that open to contain a doll, which can be opened to contain a doll and so on), you can have universal groups in universal groups inside universal groups....

So the logical question is why don't we just use universal groups for everything and not even worry about domain local or global groups anymore? There are two reasons. First, universal groups can only be used in Windows 2000 Native mode or Windows Server mode. This is only possible after you have upgraded all NT 4 domain controllers to Windows 2000 or Server; the NT 4 DCs can't handle this universal group thing. Second, if you use only universal groups, your global catalog will become bloated and replication issues could occur. You see, universal group names and membership are both replicated to the other global catalog servers (typically, one for each site); global group names, in contrast, appear in the global catalog, but their members don't. With multiple domains, the global catalog contains replicated information for every domain in the forest, and the size (and replication time) will increase exponentially if universal groups contain a large number of objects. A close examination of universal groups, then, leads me to echo Microsoft's general advice about them: they're pretty neat, but use them sparingly.

OTHER FACTS ABOUT GROUPS

You should know two other things about groups.

First, you can put machine accounts in groups. You couldn't do that in NT 4; you could only put user accounts in groups prior to Windows 2000. Why would you *want* to create groups of machines?

Well, when you start messing around with group policies, then you'll want to create policies that apply only to *some* people or machines. Groups with machines in them are an essential part of accomplishing that.

Second, there's a limitation in Windows 2000's Active Directory that limits a group's size to about 5000 members. That's fixed in Windows .NET Server, but you should keep it in mind if you're using Windows 2000 Domain Controllers. So if you want to have a group with 15,000 members, you have to break it up into, say, three smaller groups and then put those smaller groups into a group together.

If you're still unsure about which kind of groups can go into which other kinds of groups, I've summarized it in Figure 9.28.

FIGURE 9.28

Group relationships

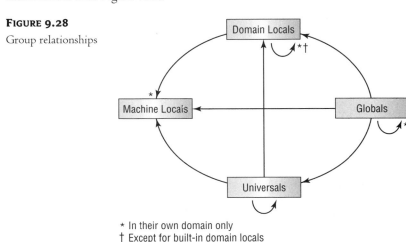

* In their own domain only
† Except for built-in domain locals

Working with Security Groups

All right, enough talk about global, local, domain local, and universal groups. You need some examples of how this works. However, let me first emphasize how important it is to think about your group structures ahead of time. Once you've "prenested" your larger membership groups (including the local and universal groups) and granted access to the local groups when you set up your resources, you'll only have to fiddle with global and universal group memberships from then on. This will save time and simplify the task of granting object permissions.

Some good, basic nesting examples can be drawn from the nesting patterns that are set up automatically within a domain. One is the nesting of administrator groups. The Administrator account on a local system draws its powers from membership in the local Administrators group. Take Administrator out of the Administrators group, and the account has no special powers or abilities (but I don't recommend it). The Active Directory automatically creates the Domain Admins global group, although it doesn't assign broad admin rights to the group as you might think. When a server joins a domain (or becomes a DC), the global group Domain Admins and the universal group Enterprise Admins are automatically placed in the membership of the local Administrators group. Figure 9.29 shows the membership of the domain local group Administrators for the REDHILLTOWN.com domain.

FIGURE 9.29

Members of the Administrators domain local group

The net effect of this nesting is that a member of the Domain Admins or Enterprise Admins group is a local administrator on every member machine in the domain. You can override this default behavior by removing Domain Admins or Enterprise Admins from a machine's local Administrators group, but again, I don't recommend this unless you have a special reason to do so. You can replace the Domain Admins or Enterprise Admins group membership in the local Administrators groups with more specific Admin-type global groups, such as F&A Admins or CS Admins. However, having no global or universal groups at all in the local Administrators group limits control to local Administrator accounts and unnecessarily complicates remote administration tasks.

Another example of group nesting is the membership of the local Users group. On a domain member or domain controller, Users automatically includes Domain Users. When you create a new user account in a domain, the new user is automatically assigned to the Domain Users group. It's sort of an All Users in the Domain group. The net effect is that a user account in a domain is automatically granted local user privileges on every domain member machine by default. The user account goes into the global group Domain Users, and the global group Domain Users goes into the local group Users, which is granted local rights and permissions on a system.

You should also know, just for the record, about a couple of other nestings: Domain Guests is automatically a member of the local group Guests on all domain member machines, and Enterprise Admins (a universal group) is a member of the local Administrators group.

Now let's look at the fictional case of Green Onion Resources (GOR), a national IT consulting and integration firm. Green Onion uses Active Directory with Windows Server, Windows 2000, and NT 4 domain controllers. The company has grouped its IT resources into domains by regional offices—for example, GOR South domain, GOR West domain, and GOR East domain. Finance and Accounting (F&A) people are similarly grouped into global groups by region, as are other functional units of GOR. So there are global groups called F&A South, F&A West, and F&A East. Keeping the Finance people in different global groups within different domains allows finer control of region-specific resources and administration. Some central resources, however, must be accessible to all F&A people at GOR. Those resources are located in the Central Finance share on the server called GOR_ALPHA1. Now, administrators (or their delegates) have set up a local group called F&A Central on GOR_ALPHA1 and have put each global group (F&A South, F&A West, and F&A East) into the local group called F&A Central. The local group F&A Central has access to the shared resource Central Finance. The following diagram illustrates the GOR strategy for F&A Central access:

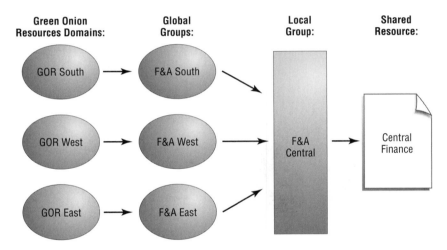

This will work and is definitely the way to go in Windows 2000 Mixed mode. When someone leaves or is hired for one of the F&A departments, admins have only to add or remove the user account from the global group to grant or deny access. This will also grant access to the region-specific resources already accessible by the global groups. But when Green Onion Resources upgrades all existing domain controllers to Windows 2000 and Windows Server 2003, they can raise the domain functional level to Windows 2000 Native mode (or Windows Server mode, if all DCs are running Windows Server) and the fun begins. Now they can keep the granularity of having global groups by functional unit and region and can also group these F&A regional groups into a new universal group called GOR F&A. The GOR enterprise admins put the three groups, F&A South, F&A West, and F&A East, into the universal group GOR F&A. They can now use the universal group to directly permit access to F&A organization-wide resources, such as the Central Finance folder, instead of using the three global groups—although it's still considered good form to put the universal group into a local group and grant access to the local group. The following diagram illustrates the adjustment once GOR switches to Native or .NET mode.

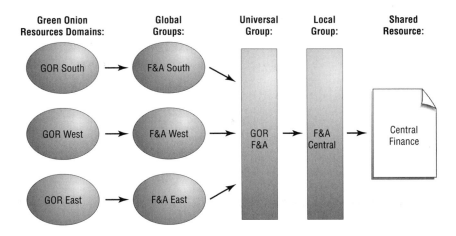

NOTE *Windows 2000 Native mode and Windows Server mode are identical in their support of universal groups and full group nesting.*

Why should you keep nesting global and universal groups into local groups even after switching to Windows 2000 or Windows Server mode? Certainly, you can instead just put a bunch of accounts into the GOR F&A universal group. If you have a single domain for your organization and never plan to add more, this strategy is perfectly acceptable. With multiple domains, however, remember that the global catalog must replicate the names and members of all universal groups throughout the forest. Domain local groups and global groups are listed in the global catalog, but each individual member is not. Having all 600 or so bean-counter accounts from the various domains in one universal group therefore becomes a replication (read "performance") issue between designated global catalog servers.

You can also grant access to the shared resource directly to the universal group and bypass the local group nesting altogether. Current thinking holds that it's easier to just set up access on the resource once, then modify it by manipulating the membership of the group that has access. This was especially true under NT 4, when managing permissions on remote shares was a bit cumbersome, but Active Directory management is changing all that. Granting access directly to the universal group seems to be in keeping with that principle, though, if you plan to keep universal group membership down and limit it to other groups. The drawback is that domains and their global groups might come and go—especially now that an entire domain can be wiped out without reinstalling the operating system. If ACL entries refer to global or universal groups that are no longer recognized, due to a defunct domain or a broken trust relationship, the ACL will report an entry as "Account Unknown" and the Forces of Darkness will increase and multiply and chaos will reign…Well, maybe not. But it's messy. If you *always* grant access to a local group, the machine will *always* recognize it. Then you can simply grant or deny access to a resource by manipulating the membership of that local group.

BUILT-IN DOMAIN LOCAL GROUPS

You might have noticed in our earlier tour of DSA.MSC that all the built-in user accounts, like Guest and Administrator, are placed by default in the Users container (shown in Figure 9.30). The Users container also contains predefined universal, domain local, and global groups. But some domain local groups were created in the Builtin container (shown in Figure 9.31) when you created the domain. There's a very important difference between groups that are created in the Builtin container and other domain local groups. Domain local groups that are homed in the Builtin container function like machine local groups, but on domain controllers. Like machine local groups, they can contain global or universal groups and accounts, but they cannot be members of local groups on other servers or domains. Unlike the domain local groups in the Users container, you cannot move the Builtin container's domain local groups to other OUs.

FIGURE 9.30
DSA.MSC Users container

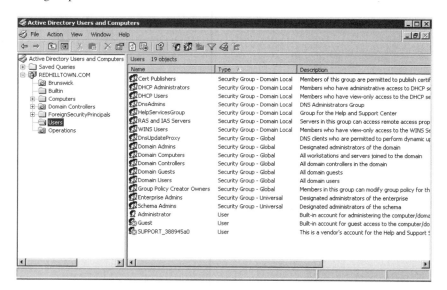

FIGURE 9.31
DSA.MSC Builtin container

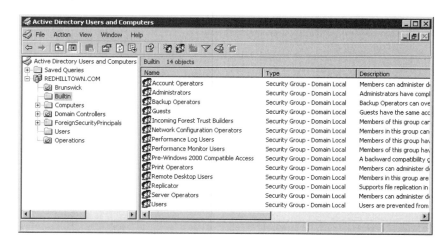

Built-in domain local groups have predetermined rights and permissions for the purposes of administration. Membership in these (or any) groups grants the user all the powers and abilities granted to the group. This is a way to quickly assign well-defined administrative roles rather than having to create them from scratch. For example, Server Operators have the rights needed for creating and managing shared folders. Backup Operators have the right to back up files and directories, even if they don't have permission to read or modify them.

The following paragraphs list the built-in domain local groups and their special abilities. Here are a few points to keep in mind about these groups:

◆ Unless otherwise noted, these groups also exist as local groups on non-DC servers. If they are local groups, their rights are limited in scope to the local machine. If they are domain local groups, their rights apply to all of the domain controllers in the domain.

◆ Some default group nesting patterns (sounds like we're describing migratory birds, doesn't it?) appear to extend built-in domain local group rights to all systems in the domain; however, this is an illusion. Global, and sometimes universal, groups are used to accomplish this. Take note of any automatic global group nestings that grant domain-wide administrative rights.

◆ Be aware that you can't delete the `Builtin` container domain local groups. You can, however, create other users and groups within the `Builtin` container, although they won't have any special rights unless you assign them.

◆ There should be no need to say this, but I will anyway. Exercise caution when adding accounts to these groups, or to any groups with administrative rights and special permissions.

TIP *In general, rights grant the ability to do something, often something admin related or otherwise restricted. Permissions, on the other hand, give you the ability to access resources such as files and printers as well as Active Directory objects such as group policies.*

Administrators Administrators have almost every built-in right, so members are basically all-powerful with regard to administration of the system. Domain Admins and Enterprise Admins are by default members of the Administrators group, so members of the Administrators domain local group have full control of all domain controllers and full power in the domain.

Account Operators Members of the Account Operators group can create user, computer, and group accounts for the domain and modify or delete most of the domain's user accounts and groups. They cannot, however, delete or modify groups in the `Builtin` folder or the Domain Controllers OU, Administrator accounts, the Domain Admins global group, or the domain local groups Administrators, Server Operators, Account Operators, Print Operators, and Backup Operators. Account Operators cannot administer security policies, but they can log on locally to domain controllers and shut them down. This group only exists on domain controllers and has no default members. Members of the domain local Account Operators group cannot modify user or group accounts on member servers.

Backup Operators Members of Backup Operators have the right to back up and restore files, whether or not they have permission to access those files otherwise. They can also log on locally to servers and shut them down. There are no default members of the Backup Operators group. Members of the domain local Backup Operators group only have these rights on domain controllers.

Guests   Members of the domain local Guests group have no special user rights. The Guest account (which is disabled by default) and the global group Domain Guests is a member of this group by default. Members of the local Guests group on non-DC systems can log in and run applications. They can also shut down the system, but otherwise their abilities are even more limited than Users. For instance, Guests cannot keep a local profile.

Print Operators   Members of this domain local group can create, manage, and delete Active Directory printer shares and printers that are attached to domain controllers. Additionally, they can log in at and shut down domain controllers. There are no default members of this group and no default group nesting occurs with local Print Operators groups on non-DC servers.

Server Operators   On domain controllers, members of the Server Operators group can create, manage, and delete printer shares and network shares; back up and restore files; start and stop services; format the server's fixed disk; lock and unlock servers; unlock files; and change the system time. Server Operators can also log on locally and shut down the system. This group exists only on domain controllers and has no default members. Members of the Server Operators group only have these rights on domain controllers.

Users   Because the Domain Users group is a member of this group by default, all accounts created in the domain are also members of the domain local Users group. Members of the domain local Users group have no special rights on domain controllers, and they cannot log on locally to the servers. However, members of the local Users group on workstations can run applications (but not install them). They also can shut down and lock the workstation. If a user has the right to log in locally to a workstation, they also have the right to create local groups and manage those groups they have created.

Replicator   This group is strictly for directory replication. The group has no default members. A user account is used to run the Replicator service, and that user should be the only member of the group.

Incoming Forest Trust Builders   Members of this group can create incoming, one-way trusts to the forest. This group has no default members and only exists on domain controllers.

Network Configuration Operators   Members can modify TCP/IP settings on domain controllers in the domain. Non-DC servers have an equivalent machine local group. This group has no default members.

Pre–Windows 2000 Compatible Access   This group has read access to all users and groups in the domain and has the right to access domain controllers from the network and to bypass traverse checking. The only members of this group should be using workstations running Windows NT 4 or earlier. The special identity Everyone is a member of this group by default.

Remote Desktop Users   Members of this group can log on remotely to domain controllers in the domain. There are no default members of this group.

Performance Log Users   Members have remote access to logged performance counters on domain controllers. There are no default members of this group.

Performance Monitor Users   Members have the ability to remotely monitor domain controllers. There are no default members of this group.

Power Users This group only exists as a machine local group on 2000 and XP Workstations, and on nondomain controller servers. Members have a subset of the Administrator's rights. Power users can create user accounts and local groups and can manage the membership of Users, Power Users, and Guests, as well as administer other users and groups that they have created.

OTHER BUILT-IN GROUPS

In the Users container, other predefined domain local groups and global groups may be created as part of the configuration of a certain service. These groups might serve to allow users access to certain services (DHCP Users and WINS Users, for instance) or to provide a group container for administrators of the service, as in the case of DHCP Administrators and DNS Admins. These and other predefined global groups may also have special rights and/or permissions for particular actions, but not the broad rights and permissions of Administrators, Server Operators, or another built-in local group.

NOTE   Some predefined groups, including Domain Computers and Domain Controllers, are designated for machine accounts, although you can add a user account to Domain Computers if it gives you a thrill.

A Windows Server 2003 domain controller has several built-in global and universal groups, among them Domain Admins, Domain Users, and Domain Guests. These groups will only appear on domain controllers. In fact, it's impossible to create global and universal groups anywhere *other* than on domain controllers. Although you might use an administration tool like DSA.MSC while sitting at a non-DC to create the global groups, the groups will exist only on domain controllers. Table 9.3 describes the most important built-in global and universal groups.

TABLE 9.3: BUILT-IN GLOBAL GROUPS

GROUP	WHAT IT DOES
Domain Admins	By placing a user account into this global group, you provide administrative-level abilities to that user. Members of Domain Admins can administer the home domain, the workstations of the domain, and any other trusted domains that have added this domain's Domain Admins global group to their own Administrators local group. By default, the built-in Domain Admins global group is a member of both the domain's Administrators local group and the Administrators local groups for every NT, Windows 2000, or XP Professional workstation in the domain. The built-in Administrator user account for the domain is automatically a member of the Domain Admins global group.
Domain Users	Members of the Domain Users global group have normal user access to, and abilities for, both the domain itself and any NT/Windows 2000/XP Professional workstation in the domain. This group contains all domain user accounts and is by default a member of every local Users group on every NT/Win2K/XP workstation in the domain.
Group Policy Creator Owners	Members of this group can modify domain Group Policy. Administrator is a member of this group by default.

Continued on next page

TABLE 9.3: BUILT-IN GLOBAL GROUPS *(continued)*

GROUP	WHAT IT DOES
Enterprise Admins	Members of this universal group have full power over all domains in the forest. You'll only see it in the forest root domain. Enterprise Admins is a member of all Administrators groups on all DCs in the forest. Administrator is a member of this group by default.
Schema Admins	This universal group only appears in the forest root domain. Members have the ability to modify the AD schema, which is very scary indeed. Administrator is a member of Schema Admins by default.

SPECIAL BUILT-IN GROUPS

In addition to the built-in local, global, and universal groups, several special "identities" that are not listed in DSA.MSC (or Computer Management Users and Groups for that matter) will appear on Access Control Lists for resources and objects, including the following:

INTERACTIVE   Anyone using the computer locally.

NETWORK   All users connected over the network to a computer.

EVERYONE   All current users, including guests and users from other domains.

NOTE   *Incidentally, the INTERACTIVE and NETWORK groups together form the Everyone local group.*

SYSTEM   The operating system.

CREATOR OWNER   The creator and/or owner of subdirectories, files, and print jobs.

AUTHENTICATED USERS   Any user who has been authenticated to the system. Used as a more-secure alternative to Everyone.

ANONYMOUS LOGON   A user who has logged in anonymously, such as an anonymous FTP user.

BATCH   An account that has logged in as a batch job.

SERVICE   An account that has logged in as a service.

DIALUP   Users who are accessing the system via Dial-Up Networking.

How Do Organizational Units Fit In?

Organizational units (OUs) are logical containers in a domain. They can contain users, groups, computers, and other OUs, but only from their home domain. You can't put global groups or computers from another domain into your domain's OU, for example.

The usefulness of OUs is strictly for administration. Administrators can create and apply group policies to an OU and can delegate control of OUs, as well. The idea is to have a subdivision of a domain but still share common security information and resources. Grouping users, groups, and resources into organizational units allows you to apply policies in a more granular fashion and also to decide specifically who manages what and to what extent. So when you're advised about how to group your OUs, keep in mind that the tool must fit your hand; your organization may be unique, so your approach to OUs may be as well.

Rather than creating OUs for locations (that's what sites are for), departments, and so on, think about how your organization will be administered. Design your OUs with delegation in mind. Keep it simple for your own sake. Thousands of nested OUs just make more work for you. Also, OUs are unrelated to the process of locating resources on your network, so you needn't group them with a browse list in mind, either.

What's the difference between an OU and a container? An OU is a container, but not just a container like the Users container in DSA.MSC. You can delegate control of a container (you can delegate control of anything), but you can't apply Group Policy to one.

How are OUs different from groups? A user can be a member of many groups but can only be in one OU at a time. Like groups, OUs can contain other OUs. Group names appear on ACLs, so you can grant or deny access to groups. OUs do not appear on ACLs, so you can't give everyone in the Finance OU access to a printer, for example. On the other hand, you can't assign a designated set of Desktop applications to everyone in a security group, but you can publish or assign the company accounting package to the entire Accounting OU.

Zen and the Art of Login Scripts

Login scripts are an ancient revered method for configuring a user's working environment and assigning network resources. Before we had Network Neighborhood, in a time before Microsoft networks came into prominence, network clients were relatively unenlightened about the network around them. Login scripts were written in the common language of the client and ran from the server on the client at the time of logon. These scripts would create local drive mappings to the servers, redirect local ports to assign printers, synchronize the system clock with a central designated timeserver, and perform other honorable related tasks. One could say, Grasshopper, that logon scripts reached their peak in the Age of NetWare, when the color red blanketed the networking world. In the Age of NT 4, networking clients become more aware of the network around them. In small isolated networks, the Art was all but abandoned, but logon scripts still flourished in large complex environments, prized for their eternal usefulness. During this time, the Art became more sophisticated. While logon scripts are now used to perform increasingly complex tasks, the essential Art, the True Art of Login Scripts, has remained unchanged.

Since Windows 2000 came onto the scene, we've had the ability to use not only logon scripts, but also logoff scripts, startup scripts, and shutdown scripts. We're no longer confined to a limited set of shell commands, either. Organizations now use a myriad of scripting and even programming languages to accomplish eye-popping configuration feats compared with those of 10 years ago. There is no way to do justice to everything that's out there in the few pages allotted here, but I will discuss your choices of scripting language, take a look at an example logon script, and tell you how to assign a logon script to users.

SCRIPTING LANGUAGES

A wide variety of scripting environments and languages are available today, including the native Windows shell commands, Windows Scripting Host (WSH), KiXtart, XLNT, Perl, VBScript, JScript, even Python. You can use literally any language that is useful to you and is understood by your client machine. Login scripts are only limited by a couple of things: developers and clients. A script developer (that includes you) must know how to use the chosen tool. It's no good to try writing a logon script in C if you can't even figure out how to make it say "Good morning." The vast majority of us aren't programmers, so we must use simpler tools, such as shell scripts or special logon script languages like KiXtart or XLNT. The client, as well, must understand the language of the script, so if you want to use Perl, for example, you need a Perl interpreter installed on each client system.

If all of your clients are Windows 98 or later, you might want to look into Microsoft Windows Script 5.6, a package that seems to include all of the current Windows scripting technologies, including Windows Scripting Host (WSH), an environment for running Visual Basic Scripting Edition (VBScript) and JavaScript natively on Windows platforms. The Scripting Host and a Script Debugger are included with Windows Server 2003 and Windows 2000. WSH is an installation option for Windows 98, but if you need WSH for 95 or NT you'll need to download it from Microsoft (go to http://msdn.microsoft.com/scripting). The site is an excellent source of information on Windows scripting with links to newsgroups and other fun stuff.

Why not use Windows shell commands for logon scripts? Well, it's definitely an option. No special client software is required, although the command set for pre-NT clients is rather limited. Since NT 4, command-line language has become fairly robust in comparison to earlier Windows operating systems, and there is a great deal of backward compatibility built into the NT, Windows 2000, and XP shell language. However, Windows shell scripting is still less flexible or intuitive, in my humble opinion, than any of the various Unix shell languages. Remember that Windows software (even Win2K and XP) was not designed primarily for command-line geeks, but for people with mice (the electronic kind). However, Microsoft is showing some major improvements in the command-line arena, so let's encourage them.

Perl (Practical Extraction and Reporting Language) was initially developed for system administrators as a tool to run reports. It has become much, much more. Platform independent like Java, but without the memory overhead of the Java virtual machine, Perl has proven its usefulness to Unix administrators and developers and has become one of the more popular scripting languages in the Windows world as well. You will have to install a Perl interpreter and modules on your clients, although this process is relatively painless. Alternately, there is a utility called Perl2Exe that converts Perl scripts to executables. If you don't mind the overhead of running a program that's around 700K (script, interpreter, and any modules) across the network whenever users log in, download it from http://www.indigostar.com. The latest version of Perl for Windows, ActivePerl, is available as a Windows Installer (MSI) package from www.activestate.com/Products/ActivePerl/. ActivePerl includes Perlscript, an ActiveX scripting engine like VBScript or JScript. There is also a wealth of information on Perl in bookstores and at www.perl.com.

There are numerous other scripting environments, including C shell, PythonWin, XLNT, and the MKS Toolkit by Mortice Kern Systems, Inc. (MKS is a toolkit for Unix-heads; it includes Korn shell, Vi editor, AWK, and more). However, the login script processor of choice for many Windows-based network administrators is KiXtart. KiXtart was designed by Ruud van Velsen at Microsoft Netherlands. For a long time it was available as freeware, but today it is distributed as CareWare (Ruud asks that you make a charitable donation to support the people of Nepal). KiXtart is extremely flexible and easy to use. The latest version, KiXtart 2001 (Version 4.11) is available from http://www.scriptlogic.com/kixtart. An HTML help file and many other resources are also available at this site. One big advantage of KiXtart is that a wide range of Windows clients can use the exact same command set. The bad news is that you do have to either install the KIX32.EXE executable locally, or run it from a location on the network. Windows 9x clients also require a couple of DLLs to be installed locally.

ASSIGNING THE LOGIN SCRIPT

Specify a logon script in the user account profile information in DSA.MSC, or assign scripts using Group Policy. Either way, the scripts and any other necessary files must be in the SYSVOL share, found in \Windows\SYSVOL\sysvol on the domain controller. Pre–Windows 2000 clients look for a share called NETLOGON to get to the script. Windows 2000 Servers and Server 2003 create a NETLOGON share in \Windows\SYSVOL\sysvol\domainname\scripts for backward compatibility. Make sure that users have Read and Execute permissions on the script file.

If you have Win2K or XP Professional machines as clients, Group Policy can be used to assign a logon script. Scripts assigned to Win2K/XP machines using Group Policy run asynchronously in hidden windows, so the user shell may actually start before logon script processing is complete. Scripts assigned in account properties run synchronously in visible windows by default. In that case, the user shell does not start until the script is done.

EXAMPLE LOGIN SCRIPTS

Login scripts can perform a wide variety of functions; the most frequent tasks are mapping network drives, connecting users to printers, gathering inventory information, and updating software or virus definitions. The login script can also be used to synchronize client systems with a timeserver on the network. The sample scripts in this section illustrate how to accomplish some of these common tasks in a logon script.

In my first and most basic example, I'll use the Windows shell language. The server's name is SERVER1.

Example 9.1: Login.bat *(Simple Shell Script)*

```
@echo off
REM Login.bat Version 1.0
REM Exit if user has logged on to the server
IF %COMPUTERNAME%.==SERVER1. GOTO END
REM Delete pre-existing drive mappings
NET USE H: /DELETE >nul
NET USE J: /DELETE >nul
REM Map H: to Users Share
NET USE H: \\SERVER1\USERS /YES >nul
REM Map J: to Apps Share
NET USE J: \\SERVER1\APPS /YES >nul
REM Synchronize time with server
NET TIME \\SERVER1 /SET /YES
:END
```

As you can see from the comment statements, the script first checks to see if the local computer name matches the server name and exits if it does. This is to prevent unnecessary mappings if an admin logs on locally to the server. After deleting any pre-existing drive mappings, the script maps drives to the Users and Apps shares on the server. The final command tells the workstation to synchronize with the server without prompting the user for confirmation.

The script shown in Example 9.1 works great (for Windows 9*x* clients and XP systems) if you have only one server, if all users will have the same drive mappings, and if all users will use the same login script. It doesn't map any printer connections, though. And it's very likely that your network is more complex than this. You'll need to map drives based on group memberships; unfortunately there is no super-simple way to do this with the Windows shell.

My second example uses KiXtart to obtain group membership information, map drives, connect to printers, and call an update script to upload any new virus definitions or software patches. The software update script is not included here, but I show the `call` command in the main routine as an example of using logon scripts to perform other configuration tasks.

In this configuration, `kixlogin.bat`, the designated logon script, calls the main script (`kixlogin.scr`). This is to accommodate Windows 9*x* clients; if you have only Windows NT/2000/XP clients, the executable `KIX32.EXE` can be specified as the login script in the User's account properties with a script name as an argument (for example, `Kix32.exe kixlogin.scr`).

The KiXtart script (`kixlogin.scr`) uses semicolons for comments, which I have supplied to explain what the script commands are doing. `Kixlogin.bat` uses native shell scripting, so comment lines are preceded by the command `REM`. Since this is a sample logon script and not a textbook example of shell scripting or KiXtart scripting, I've included numerous comments instead of a line-by-line explanation or the usual commented-out statements in the script to let you know what's going on.

All of the executables used in the scripts are kept in `NETLOGON` for simplicity's sake (we have Windows 2000, XP, NT 4 workstations, and a few straggling Windows 98 clients).

Example 9.2: Kixlogin.bat *(Shell Script that Calls Kixlogin.scr)*

First, turn off the command echo:

```
@echo off
```

Since NT/2000/XP and 9*x* call logon scripts differently, check the `%OS%` variable to see if it's set to Windows_NT. If it isn't, skip to the subroutine for Windows 9*x* clients:

```
@if not "%OS%"=="Windows_NT" GOTO 9XOS
```

NT-based machines can run the script with a UNC path. The `kix32` executable takes as its argument the name of the script:

```
:NTOS
\\SERVER1\NETLOGON\kix32.exe \\SERVER1\netlogon\KIXLOGIN.scr
GOTO EOF
```

Windows 9*x* machines temporarily map the Z: drive to `NETLOGON` during the logon sequence. They cannot run the script using a UNC path. The path statement is not for `KIX32.EXE`, but rather for other executables called later:

```
:9XOS
path=z:\
z:\kix32.exe z:\kixlogin.scr
```

```
GOTO EOF
:EOF
EXIT
```

Example 9.3: Kixlogin.scr *(KiXtart Login Script Called by Kixlogin.bat)*

```
:STAGE1
```

Statements preceded by a question mark (?) cause the text that follows on the same line to be displayed on the console screen, much as ECHO does in the native shell language:

```
? "Login script now processing..."
? "Querying your System Information..."
```

I need to check again for 9*x* versus NT/2000/XP machines, because variables are set differently for each. @INWIN is a KiXtart variable used for this purpose. Again, the script processing skips to the appropriate subroutine, SETVARNT or SETVAR95, depending on the OS. Win2K and XP boxes will process like NT machines and Windows 98 systems will process like Windows 95 machines:

```
IF @INWIN = 1
    GOTO SETVARNT
ELSE
    GOTO SETVAR95
ENDIF
```

These commands set variables on Windows 9*x* clients using SHELL and WINSET.EXE. SHELL is a KiXtart routine to call a native shell command, and WINSET.EXE is an executable from the Windows 95 CD that sets environmental variables. @USERID and the other words preceded by @ are variables that KiXtart understands. Thus, I am using KiXtart variable values to set actual system environmental variables:

```
:SETVAR95
SHELL "winset.exe USERNAME=@USERID"
SHELL "winset.exe ADDRESS=@ADDRESS"
SHELL "winset.exe COMPUTER=@WKSTA"
SHELL "winset.exe DOMAIN=@DOMAIN"
SHELL "winset.exe COMMENT=@COMMENT"
SHELL "winset.exe FULLNAME=@FULLNAME"
SHELL "winset.exe HOMEDIR=@HOMEDIR"
SHELL "winset.exe HOMESHR=@HOMESHR"
SHELL "winset.exe LSERVER=@LSERVER"
SHELL "winset.exe PRIV=@PRIV"
GOTO STAGE2
```

On NT, Win2K, and XP boxes, the following commands set variables without "shelling out" to the native command environment. The SET command sets user variables, and SETM defines system variables:

```
:SETVARNT
;set variables on NT clients using set command
```

```
SET USERNAME="@USERID"
SETM ADDRESS="@ADDRESS"
SETM COMPUTER="@WKSTA"
SETM DOMAIN="@DOMAIN"
SET COMMENT="@COMMENT"
SET FULLNAME="@FULLNAME"
SET HOMEDIR="@HOMEDIR"
SET HOMESHR="@HOMESHR"
SET LSERVER="@LSERVER"
SET PRIV="@PRIV"
```

Time synchronization is an important function in many logon scripts. The SERVER1 listed here is a designated timeserver that synchronizes regularly with a reliable external time source:

```
:STAGE2
? "Synchronizing your system's clock"
;synchronize with timeserver
SETTIME \\server1
```

Next, I check to see if the time synchronization was successful. If it wasn't, a message box pops up to get the user's attention.

```
IF @error = 0
    ? "System clock synchronized"
ELSE
    MESSAGEBOX ("Cannot synchronize the system clock.
    Please inform your administrator.","XYZ Login Script", 0)
ENDIF
?
```

The most recent version of KiXtart automatically enumerates group memberships from the user's security token and stores them in the Registry. This makes it very simple to query group membership information when mapping network drives. Just in case, I'll first delete any preexisting drive mappings. Again, if there are errors while deleting previous drive mappings, a message box will get the user's attention.

```
? "Now mapping network drives..."
?
;delete any previous drive mappings and check for errors
USE "*" /DELETE
IF @error = 0
    ?"Previous mappings deleted..."
ELSE
    MESSAGEBOX ("Cannot delete previous drive mappings.
    Please inform your administrator.",
    "XYZ Login Script", 0)
ENDIF
;MAP Drives by Group Membership
```

```
;Map Domain F & A to M: drive
IF INGROUP ("Domain F & A") = 1
    use M: "\\server1\F&A Control"
    ? "F & A Drive Mapped"
ENDIF
;Map Domain Sales to S: drive
IF INGROUP ("Domain Sales") = 1
    use S: \\server1\Sales
    ? "Sales Drive Mapped"
ENDIF
;Map Domain Tech Services to T: drive
IF INGROUP ("Domain Tech Services") = 1
    use T: \\server1\TechSvcs
    ? "Tech Services Drive Mapped"
ENDIF
;Map common drives for Domain Users
IF INGROUP ("Domain Users") = 1
    use G: \\server1\apps
    use P: \\server1\public
    use N: \\server1\infosys
    use H: @HOMESHR
    ? "Global Drives and Home Directories Mapped"
ENDIF
```

Finally, the script will call the `update.bat` script, which checks to make sure the system has all the current virus definitions and software patches installed.

```
    shell update.bat
? "Login Script Complete"
EXIT
```

Understanding User Permissions and Rights

Much of what we've got to do as administrators is to both provide our users with access to *some* network resources and keep the users *from* other network resources. Ever since NT 3.1, Microsoft operating systems have let you control access with two tools: permissions and rights.

Object Permissions, ACLs, and ACEs

You've seen some references to permissions so far, and you'll see a lot more of them in the next chapter, which is on file and directory shares. Basically, a *permission* is just a setting that controls your level of access to some object on the network. For example, I could create a file called MYSECRETS.TXT and set its file permissions so that only I can read, write, and delete it and so that some other user— perhaps a father-confessor figure?—can read it, but nobody else can access it at all. Permissions let me do that; they control access to an object.

You probably think of permissions mainly in terms of files and directories, but there are many more things in the NT family of Microsoft operating systems that have permissions. A few include the ability to control things like the following:

◆ Registry keys, which determine who can read or modify a given key or value entry

◆ Contents of domains and organization units, which determines who can add things (for example, users or machine accounts) to a domain or an OU

◆ System services, so you can control who can start or stop a given service

◆ Directories and files, both of which have permissions

As you'll learn throughout the rest of the book, many things have permissions. You can usually find an object's permissions by right-clicking the object and choosing Properties. In the resulting property page, there is usually a tab labeled Security. That's not always true, and in some cases, the UI doesn't reveal the underlying security items. In other cases, you may have to take some extra steps to see the permissions. For example, you will not see the Security tab on a domain or organizational unit in Active Directory until you choose View/Advanced in Active Directory Users and Computers, as you may recall from the "Advanced Delegation" section in Chapter 8.

Here's a simple example of permissions. I've right-clicked a file named TESTIT.TXT on my hard disk, chosen Properties and then the Security tab. It shows me Figure 9.32.

FIGURE 9.32

Security tab for a file

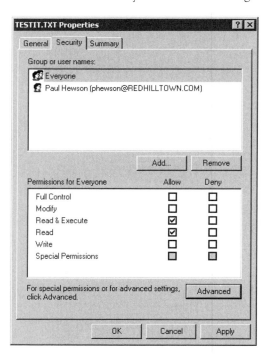

You see from it that the Everyone group has read permission. To see the permissions for the other account shown in the figure (phewson@REDHILLTOWN.COM), you have to highlight

the account name in the permissions dialog box. Also notice that the object has six possible permissions: Full Control, Modify, Read and Execute, Read, Write, and Special Permissions. The Special Permissions are accessible using the Advanced button; they include permissions like Change Ownership and Write Attributes. Collectively, this set of permissions is called an access control list or ACL (pronounced *ackel*). Each entry in the ACL—the phewson@REDHILLTOWN.com and Everyone entries, I mean—are called access control entries (ACEs). But there's a lot more detail possible; click the Advanced button to see more, and you'll see a dialog box like the one in Figure 9.33.

FIGURE 9.33

Advanced Security Settings dialog box

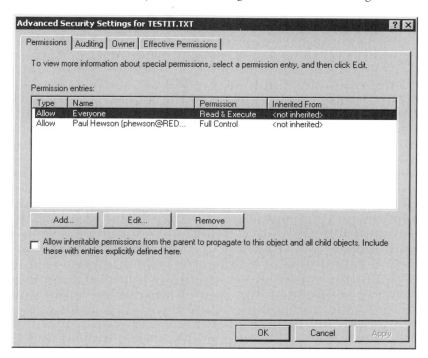

You can get to this dialog box from *any* Security dialog box, as far as I can see, by clicking the Advanced button. It makes more or less sense, depending on the object type. In the case of this file, you can see that it really doesn't show you much that you didn't already know. But the other two tabs are useful; Auditing lets you tell the system whether or not to audit access to this file and what level of detail to log, and Owner lets you find out who owns the file and lets you change the owner. (In Microsoft terms, an object's "owner" is a person who has an unstoppable right to change permissions on that object. We'll discuss that in greater detail in the next chapter.)

To find out the most nitty-gritty details that you can about the ACE for Everyone, click it and then Edit. That shows you a dialog box like the one in Figure 9.34.

Again, you'll see a dialog box *like* this for any object that has ACLs, but the exact contents of the dialog box vary from object to object. In this particular case, you see 13 very specific permissions, the lowest-level permissions possible on a file. The list of permissions that you saw in the first dialog box (Full Control, Modify, Read and Execute, Read, and Write) aren't really permissions at all—they're *groups* of these 13 lowest-level permissions.

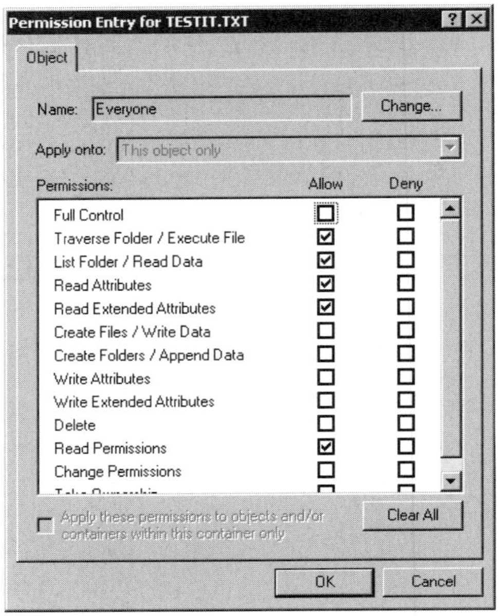

FIGURE 9.34

Lowest-level
permissions
for a file

User Rights

While permissions grant different access to different objects, rights give you the ability to do particular things. And yes, the line between permissions and rights *is* a little fuzzy. For example, is the ability to create user objects a permission or a right? Well, under the hood, a user is just an object in a particular "container" called the domain. So creating a user in a domain is very similar to creating a file in a directory, and it is permissions that control that. But what about the ability to physically sit down at a server and log on? That's not a permission; that's a right.

In general, rights tend to apply to a particular system (for example, the right to log on to the system, the right to change its time, and the right to shut it down). So I guess, in a sense, Microsoft could simply have considered any given system to be a "container" and then made those powers (local logon, time change, shutdown) into ACLs on the system. But they didn't, and so we have rights.

Additionally, some rights are basically system-specific powers that override ACLs. For example, one right is the right to back up files. Clearly, you'd think that you can't back up files if you can't read them, but anyone with the back-up right *can* back up any file on a system, including the ones that he or she is denied access to—rights trump permissions. But don't worry about your privacy, because the Backup Operators group's rights are only valid in conjunction with a backup routine. Backup Operators can't just open files on the server and read the contents, for example.

Windows Server 2003's built-in groups have certain rights already assigned to them. You can also create new groups and assign a custom set of user rights to those groups. As I've said before, security management is much easier when all user rights are assigned through groups instead of to individual users.

To view or modify the local rights assignment for a user or group, open the Local Security Policy tool from the Administrative Tools group on a non-DC or use the Domain Controller Security Policy tool for a DC. Open `Local Policies\User Rights Assignment`. A listing of rights and the users or groups to which those rights have been granted will be displayed in the details pane on the right, as shown in Figure 9.35.

FIGURE 9.35

Local user rights policy

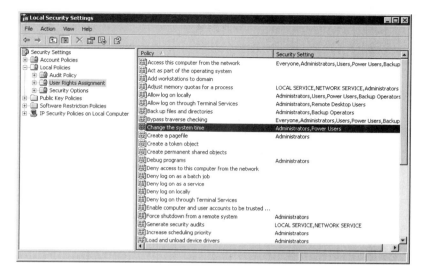

To add or remove a right to or from a user or group, double-click the right as displayed in the details pane or right-click the selected right and choose Properties. In Figure 9.36 you see the property information for the right to change the system time. To remove this right from a group, highlight the name of the group and choose Remove. To add a group or user to the list, choose Add User or Group and in the Select Users, Computers, or Groups dialog box, type in a name or use the Advanced button to search for the name. Table 9.4 lists the most commonly modified user rights with descriptions.

FIGURE 9.36

Local security policy setting for a user right

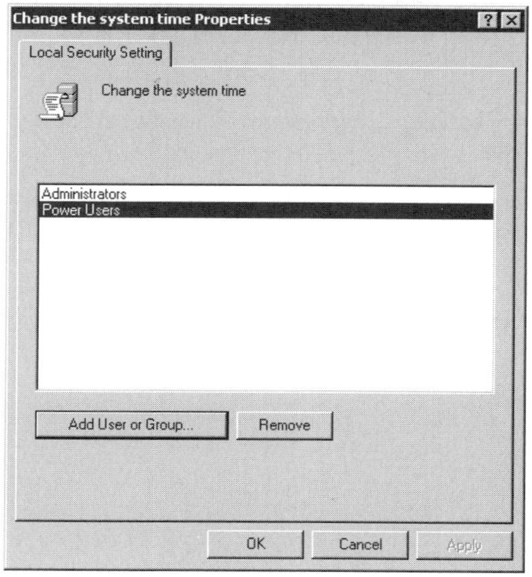

TABLE 9.4: LOCAL USER RIGHTS

USER RIGHT	DESCRIPTION
Access this computer from the network	Connect over the network to a computer.
Act as part of the operating system	Act as a trusted part of the operating system; some subsystems have this privilege granted to them.
Add workstations to domain	Make machines domain members.
Back up files and directories	Back up files and directories. As mentioned earlier, this right supersedes file and directory permissions.
Bypass traverse checking	Traverse a directory tree even if the user has no other rights to access that directory. For example, if I have no access to C:\Files but *do* have access to C:\Files\Department\Sales, then I can't access C:\Files\Department\Sales *unless* I can bypass traverse checking.
Change the system time	Set the time for the internal clock of a computer.
Create a pagefile	Create a pagefile.
Create a token object	Create access tokens. Only the Local Security Authority should have this privilege.
Create permanent shared objects	Create special permanent objects.
Debug programs	Debug applications.
Deny access to this computer from the network	Opposite of the "Access this computer from the network" right; specifically revokes the right to users/groups that would normally have it.
Deny logon as a batch job	Revokes the right to log in as a batch job.
Deny logon as a service	Revokes the right to log in as a service.
Deny logon locally	Revokes the right to log in locally.
Enable computer and user accounts to be trusted for delegation	Designate accounts that can be delegated.
Force shutdown from a remote system	Allows a computer to be shut down from a remote system.
Generate security audits	Generate audit log entries.
Increase quotas	Increase object quotas (each object has a quota assigned to it).
Increase scheduling priority	Boost the scheduling priority of a process.
Load and unload device drivers	Add or remove drivers from the system.

Continued on next page

TABLE 9.4: LOCAL USER RIGHTS *(continued)*

USER RIGHT	DESCRIPTION
Lock pages in memory	Lock pages in memory to prevent them from being paged out into backing store (such as PAGEFILE.SYS).
Log on as a batch job	Log on to the system as a batch queue facility.
Log on as a service	Perform security services (the user who performs replication logs in as a service).
Log on locally	Log on locally at the server computer itself.
Manage auditing and security log	Specify what types of events and resource access are to be audited. Also allows viewing and clearing the security log.
Modify firmware environment values	Modify system environment variables (not user environment variables).
Profile single process	Use profiling capabilities to observe a process.
Profile system performance	Use profiling capabilities to observe the system.
Remove computer from docking station	Remove a laptop computer from its docking station.
Replace a process level token	Modify a process's access token.
Restore files and directories	Restore files and directories. This right supersedes file and directory permissions.
Shut down the system	Shut down Windows Server 2003.
Synchronize directory service data	Update Active Directory information.
Take ownership of files or other objects	Take ownership of files, directories, and other objects that are owned by other users.

Many rights, such as the right to debug programs and the one to profile a single process, are useful only to programmers writing applications and are seldom granted to a group or user. When would you mess with these? Some third-party applications require you to extend some set of rights to a user before you can run the application.

You can set user rights on a machine-by-machine basis with Local Security Policy or, as you'll learn soon, SECEDIT.EXE; you can also set rights wholesale over a number of machines with Group Policies.

Local and Domain-Based Group Policies

An administrator's work is never done. Users are constantly fiddling with their settings. It's hard to maintain "standard builds," and rolling out new applications is a big headache in large networks or small. It's a pain to package up applications, remote management systems like SMS are unnecessarily complex, and Admin privileges are needed to install many applications on NT, Win2K, and XP machines. What a marketing opportunity!

When it comes to configuration management, there are a lot of buzzwords flying around these days: system policies, Group Policy, Change and Configuration Management (CCM), Intellimirror. What do these words mean to an everyday admin who just wants to maintain some continuity in Desktop configurations?

CCM and Intellimirror are marketing monikers for a group of Win2K, XP, and 2003 Desktop management features, including roaming profiles and folder redirection, offline folders, software distribution, and Desktop configuration control (I mean management). Despite the fancy terms, many of these features (including folder redirection, software distribution, and remote Desktop configuration) are easily implemented with group policies.

Group Policy Benefits

The term for the most broad-reaching control and support technology, however, is *group policies*. It's a confusing term because it doesn't really refer to groups. There are two kinds of group policies, the kind *with* a domain to back them up and the kind *without* a domain. (In case you're wondering, *domain* here means Active Directory domain.) Without a domain you use a tool called Local Security Policies and a command-line tool called SECEDIT; *with* a domain you use domain-based group policies (where the Active Directory does much of your work).

But what exactly can you *do* with group policies? Here's a brief list:

◆ Publish or assign software packages to users or machines.

◆ Assign startup, shutdown, logon, and logoff scripts.

◆ Define password, lockout, and audit policy for the domain.

◆ Standardize a whole bunch of other security settings for remote machines—settings previously configurable only by editing the Registry or using a third-party security configuration tool. Some features, like the ability to enforce group memberships and services configuration, were made available with the release of Windows 2000 Server.

◆ Define and enforce settings for Internet Explorer.

◆ Define and enforce restrictions on users' Desktops.

◆ Redirect certain folders in users' profiles (such as `Start Menu` and `Desktop`) to be stored in a central location.

◆ Configure and standardize settings for features like offline folders, disk quotas, and even Group Policy itself.

Many of these features are discussed in sections of their own throughout this book. Software distribution is covered in Chapter 12, "Software Deployment." Chapter 11, "Creating and Managing Shared Folders," touches on offline folders. User profiles are discussed later in this chapter. Folder redirection is really a lightweight approach to user profiles ("Profiles Lite"), allowing you to use a subset of the full, roaming profile features, so we'll talk about that, too, later in this chapter. The key point here is that Group Policy provides a single point of administration, allowing administrators to easily install software and apply standardized settings to multiple users and computers throughout an organization.

Group Policies Compared to System Policies

Group policies have been around since Windows 2000. Before that, a much smaller subset of these things, mostly just Desktop restriction and a few security settings, were accomplished using system policies. Group policies have improved on system policies in a couple of major ways.

THE ACTIVE DIRECTORY HANDLES REPLICATION

With NT system policies, you had to see to it that a file named NTCONFIG.POL was properly replicated to every domain controller's NETLOGON share. You did that by setting up the NT directory replication service, which was a nice try but tended to be a bit flaky. In contrast, domain-based group policies live partially in the Active Directory and partly in Sysvol, the Window 2000-and-later replacement for NETLOGON. Both Active Directory and Sysvol replicate themselves automatically, with no work required on your part.

DOMAIN-BASED GROUP POLICIES UNDO THEMSELVES WHEN REMOVED

NT 4–type system policies write permanent changes to the Registry when they are applied. This phenomenon is commonly called *tattooing*. Remove the policy and the settings remain. You actually have to "reverse the policy" (by applying a policy with opposite settings) or change the settings manually. Group policies, on the other hand, write their information only to certain parts of the Registry and so are able to clean up after themselves when the policy is removed.

For example, suppose you'd created an NT 4–type system policy that set everyone's background color to some nauseating hue and also set up a policy that kept them from changing the color back. Those changes got written into the system's Registries. So if you deleted the policy, then they'd still have those items in their Registries, and therefore the ugly background as well. You'd actually have to write a *second* policy to undo the Registry effects. With domain-based group policies, that's not necessary. Just removing the policy will undo its effects.

YOU NEEDN'T LOG ON TO GET DOMAIN-BASED GROUP POLICIES

System policies are applied only once: at logon for user settings and at startup for computer settings. Group policies are applied this way, too, but they are reapplied at specific intervals. Furthermore, Windows NT always had the peculiar characteristic of taking its policies from the user's domain. Why was that a problem? Well, suppose your workstation was a member of a domain called MACHINES and your user account was a member of a domain called USERS. Presumably, you'd want the machine policies that affect your machine to come from the machine's domain, MACHINES. But under NT 4, that never happened. Instead, when the user logged on, the machine would go grab a NTCONFIG.POL file from the user's domain, USERS. It would then hand any machine policies to itself and any user policies to the user. Under Windows 2000 and later with Active Directory, machines get their policies from their domain when they power up (recall that machines log on also) and users get policies from *their* domain when they log on.

Additionally, workstations check with Active Directory every 60 to 120 minutes to see if there are any new policies. If there are, then the workstations apply them—both user and machine policies. Further, group policies do a lot more than just modify Registry settings.

GROUP POLICIES ONLY WORK ON WINDOWS 2000 AND LATER MACHINES

The bad news about group policies, both locally and domain-based, is that they only work on Windows 2000, XP, and Server 2003 machines, and they require Active Directory, although it is possible to apply a more limited set of "local policies" without AD.

You can only use group policies to control Windows 2000 Server, Windows 2000 Professional, XP Professional, and Windows Server 2003 systems. If your users run Windows 9*x* or Windows NT Workstation 4 on their Desktops, you'll have to use the same old tools as before—Windows 9*x* profiles and system policies and Windows NT 4 profiles and group policies. Yes, you read that right—you may have to worry about one set of policies for the Windows machines, another for the NT 4 machines, and a third set of group policies for the 2000 and XP machines. Similarly, you might have a set of profiles for Windows 9*x* users, another for the NT 4 users, and a third set for the Win2K/XP users. If it's any consolation, you can store *all* of these things on Windows Server 2003—you don't have to keep an old NT 4 server around to hold the NT profiles.

In the sections that follow, you will learn how group policies work and how to create and modify them. You will become familiar with the different nodes and settings in the Group Policy snap-in and look at a few examples of deploying group policies in your organization. Finally, we'll discuss some of the dos and don'ts of group policy.

Local Group Policies: Security Templates

You'll see in a minute that having a domain around to hang domain-based group policies on is a pretty attractive thing. But if your domain is still an NT 4–based domain (or perhaps if you have Windows 2000 and XP systems around in a network based on Unix, Novell, or some other network OS), then you will still want to be able to accomplish what policies can do, and you can, in the main, albeit with a bit more work. That's where local group policies come in.

You've already met the Local Security Policy snap-in; it's the simple, GUI way to control a particular right on a particular machine. But domain-based group policies let you do considerably more than the Local Security Policy snap-in does, so you need something a trifle more powerful, and Windows 2000 and its descendants have that: a very useful tool called security templates. Let me suggest that if you've been overlooking them, then you've *got* to start using them. In this section, you'll see why.

Worms, viruses, disgruntled employees, and our ever-growing reliance on computers all add up to one thing: a need for security. Clearly there are more and more reasons to secure our computers and, for most of us, there are more and more computers around to secure! But who wants to make security a full-time job? Not me. That's why you should know about a set of tools that can simplify your job of locking down 2000 (and later) boxes.

Let's say that you've decided that you want to ensure that the Power Users groups on your workstations should be empty—you don't want anyone in those groups. You also are awfully tired of stomping out Code Red on all of those computers that installed IIS by default, so you're going around and disabling Web Publishing Service on all servers that don't need it.

But, man, that's a lot of work. So you adopt Plan B: The Security Requirements Document. In this document, you outline exactly what must be done for any workstations or servers approved here at Acme Corporation. You distribute the document. And no one has time to read it. Nor is there any easy way to check up on systems to see if they meet the requirements. Or so it seems.

Wouldn't it be great to just push a button and make those changes on every system? You can, with a few tools: `secedit.exe`, an MMC snap-in named Security Configuration and Analysis, and Security Templates.

WHAT TEMPLATES CAN DO

Basically, a security template is an ASCII file that you feed into a program named `SECEDIT.EXE`. That template is a set of instructions—basically a script—that tells `SECEDIT` to make various kinds of changes in your system.

Templates don't let you modify anything that you couldn't modify otherwise; they just provide a nice, scripted, reproducible way to make modifications and then easily audit systems to ensure that they meet the template's requirements. You could make any of these changes by hand with the GUI, but it'd be time-consuming. With templates, you can change the following:

NTFS permissions   If you want the directory `C:\STUFF` to have NTFS permissions of System/ Full Control, Administrators/Full Control, and to deny access to everyone else, then a template can make that happen. And as you can apply templates not only to one machine but also to many (provided you're using group policies), you could enforce that set of NTFS permissions on the whole domain.

Local group membership   Perhaps you have a policy that workstations are set up so that the only accounts in the local Administrators group should be the local Administrator account and the Domain Admins group from the domain. But now and then, some support person "temporarily" elevates a user account to the Administrators group, with the innocent intention of undoing the action "as soon as the need is over." And, as that support person is as busy as all support folks are, that undoing never gets done. By applying a security template that says that "only Adminis- trator and Domain Admins can be in the local Administrators," reapplying the template kicks everybody out who's not supposed to be there.

WARNING   *Templates automate the process of setting some security information, just as if you'd sat down and done it from the GUI. There's no magic guardian angel that constantly monitors a system to ensure that your desired template settings are always enforced. The only way to ensure that your settings remain in force is to either reapply the template on some regular basis or create a group policy to apply the template, as group policies reapply themselves to a system roughly every 90 minutes.*

Disable IIS and control over who can start and stop services   Want to shut off IIS on all machines but a few? That can be a pain, as Windows 2000 (unlike Windows Server 2003) installs IIS on every server by default. With a security template, you can turn off or even disable services. Templates also let you control who has the permissions to *change* that—you can restrict who can turn a service on or off, or you can grant that power to some user who you want to be able to do that, but who you don't want to make into an administrator.

Registry key permissions   The Registry contains a lot of information that users can read, but can't change. For example, you may have noticed that there are a number of Desktop applications that worked fine under NT 4 and that allowed someone with just user privileges to run them, but those same applications won't let a user run them under Windows 2000 or XP Professional—

only an administrator can run them. What's the difference? There are a few keys in the Registry that users could both read and write under NT 4, but that they can only read under Windows 2000/XP. Thus, if you have one of those applications—AutoCAD is one example—and you want users to be able to run those apps on their Windows 2000 or XP Desktops, then you can either make all of your users local administrators (which may not sound like a great idea) or just loosen up the permissions on the Registry keys to dial them back to their NT 4 settings. You could do that painstakingly from REGEDT32.EXE, but it's so much easier to just apply a template to accomplish the same thing.

Local security policy settings   Every machine has dozens of local security settings, things like, "Should I show the name of the last person who logged in?," "How often should passwords on locally stored accounts be changed?," and "Who should be allowed to change the time on this system?" to name a few. The Local Security Policy snap-in, or secpol.msc, helps you define these policy settings.

Working with Templates

It's easiest to show you how to work with templates with an example, so let's build a template to do three things:

- We'll ensure that no one is in the local Power Users group.
- We'll set NTFS permissions so that a directory C:\SECRET will only be accessible to the local Administrators group.
- Finally, we'll shut down Internet Information Service, that pesky Web server that seems to install itself on every operating system that Microsoft makes.

First, we'll need some tools. Let's build an all-in-one tool using the MMC. We'll need two snap-ins: Security Templates and Security Configuration And Analysis. Set it up like so:

1. Click Start, then Run, and type **mmc /a** in the Open field, then press Enter to bring up the empty MMC.
2. In the empty MMC, choose Add/Remove Snap-in from the File menu.
3. In the Add/Remove Snap-In dialog box, click the Add button. That raises the Add dialog box.
4. In the Add dialog box, click Security Configuration And Analysis and then the Add button. Then click the Security Templates object and Add.
5. Click Close and then OK.
6. Save your new custom tool for future use.

Your tool should look like the one in Figure 9.37.

Expand the Security Templates node and you'll see a container named C:\Windows\Security\Templates. Expand that and you'll see a list of eight prebuilt templates in that directory with descriptions of each template. These correspond to .INF files in the Templates directory. If you want to point the Security Templates node to another directory with other templates, right-click it and choose New Template Search Path. If you are going to modify the existing templates, it's a good idea to go ahead and create another directory for your modified templates, copy the existing ones from `C:\Windows\Security\Templates` into the new directory, and then add that directory to the search path in your tool. This way, you can make changes to the copies of the templates without worrying about messing up the originals. Figure 9.38 shows my Security Console tool with a second search path added (`C:\Windows\Security\REDHILLTOWN templates`). The eight templates you see in that directory are just copies of the default templates.

FIGURE 9.37

MMC with Security Templates and Security Configuration and Analysis Snap-ins

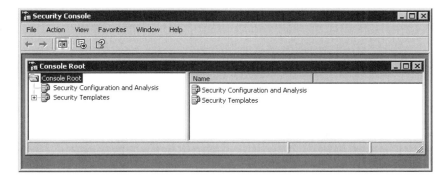

FIGURE 9.38

Security Console tool with custom template directory

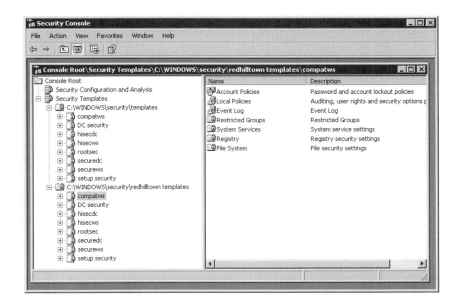

Expand any of the prebuilt security templates, and you'll see, in the right pane, folders corresponding to everything that you can control—Account Policies (sets password, account lockout, and Kerberos policies), Local Policies (controls audit settings, user rights, and security options), Event Log settings, Restricted Groups (controls what goes into and stays out of various local groups), System Services (turns services on and off and controls who has the rights to change any of that), Registry security (sets permissions to change or view any given Registry key and which keys will have changes audited), and File System (controls NTFS permissions on folders and files). The eight security templates in `C:\Windows\Security\Templates` are described next.

Compatible (*compatws.inf*)   This template increases the default permissions of the Users group, enabling members to run applications that are not certified by the Windows Logo Program. This is an alternative to making local users members of the Power Users group.

Domain Controller Default Security (DC *security.inf*)   These are the default security settings for a domain controller. Applying the template resets file and Registry and system security settings to the default values set during the promotion to domain controller. It may also overwrite permissions on new files and Registry keys created since `DCPROMO.EXE` was run.

Secure Domain Controller (*securedc.inf*) **and Secure Workstation or Server** (*securews.inf*) `securedc.inf` defines enhanced security settings for domain controllers, but with an eye on application compatibility. `securews.inf` elevates selected security settings for workstations and servers that are not domain controllers. Both templates include stronger password, lockout, and audit policy settings; limit the use of older, less secure authentication protocols; and enable server-side SMB packet signing.

Highly Secure Domain Controller (*hisecdc.inf*) **and Highly Secure Workstation** (*hisecws.inf*) These templates apply super-secure settings to domain controllers and workstations or non-DC servers, respectively. You'll want to read the documentation on this template carefully before applying it to your systems; it makes several changes to client-server authentication and encryption requirements. It also removes all members of the Power Users group and removes all members from the local Administrators group except Domain Admins and the local Administrator account.

System Root Security (*rootsec.inf*)   This file contains, and can be used to reapply, the root permissions for the system drive.

Setup Security (*setup.inf*)   `setup.inf` contains a record of the settings that were applied during the upgrade or clean installation of the OS. It's a really big file, in comparison to the other INF files, and you probably can't view it using your MMC console tool. This file can't be used on domain controllers; use the DC `security.inf` file instead. Microsoft warns you never to apply the `setup.inf` template using Group Policy because it contains such a large amount of data. It can be applied in parts, though, for disaster recovery purposes, using `SECEDIT.EXE`.

WARNING   *Before applying any of the predefined templates to your systems, do your homework. Test the templates in a nonproduction environment before deployment. The templates do not roll your system back to default security settings before applying their own changes, so you might get unexpected results.*

But we're interested in building a new template from scratch. To do that, right-click the template path and choose New Template from the context menu. Type in a name for the template, and a description if you wish. The new template will appear as a folder in the left pane, along with the prebuilt templates. I've named mine Simple. First, let's clean out the Power Users group:

1. Open Simple.
2. Inside Simple, you'll see a folder named Restricted Groups. Click it so that it appears in the left pane.
3. Right-click Restricted Groups and choose Add Group. Type in Power Users in the Add Group dialog box, or use the Browse function to select the Power Users group. Note that if you are working from a domain controller, then you won't, of course, have a Power Users group.

By default, including a group in a security template tells the template to remove everyone from the group, so we're done. If you wanted to use the security template to put someone in the group, then just right-click the group and choose Properties, which lets you specify members of the group.

Next, let's set up the security template so that any system with a folder named C:\SECRET will only be accessible to the local administrators.

1. Back in the left pane, right-click File System and choose Add File.
2. In the dialog box that appears, you can either browse to a particular directory or simply type the directory name in. Yes, the menu item was Add File, but you can choose directories as well. Type **C:\SECRET** and click OK.
3. Now you'll see the standard Windows NTFS permissions dialog box. Delete permissions for all users and groups except for Administrators. Grant Full Control Permission to Administrators.
4. The program will ask if you want these permissions to apply only to this folder or to all child folders. Set it as you like.
5. Click OK.

Finally, let's shut down IIS.

1. Click System Services.
2. In the right pane, right-click World Wide Web Publishing Services and choose Properties.
3. Check the Define This Policy Setting in the Template check box, and click the Disabled radio button.
4. Click OK.

Now save the template—right-click Simple or whatever you called the template and choose Save. Unless you set up a separate folder for your templates as I described earlier, you now have a file named simple.inf in your \Windows\Security\Templates folder.

CREATE A SECURITY DATABASE

Now, you'd think that all you need do to apply this template would be to just, well, apply it. But you can't. Instead, you have to essentially compile it from its simple ASCII form to a binary form called a "database." You do that from the other snap-in, Security Configuration and Analysis.

1. Right-click Security Configuration and Analysis and choose Open Database to open the Open Database dialog box, which asks what database you want to load.

2. Within the Open Database dialog box, you want to create a new database, but there's no option for that; instead, just type the name of the new database. Using my example, type **Simple** and press Enter. Typing in a name of a new database causes the snap-in to realize that you want to *create* a new database, so it then asks which template to build it out of. (Yup, it's nonintuitive.) By default, a dialog shows you the files with `.INF` extensions in the `Windows\Security\Templates` folder.

3. If you're following my example, choose `simple.inf`. Before you click, though, notice the Clear This Database Before Importing check box. That's useful. Otherwise, when you're experimenting with a template, the snap-in makes your changes cumulative (which might well be your intention, but it's not usually mine) rather than wiping the slate clean and starting from scratch.

4. Choose the template and click Open. Nothing obvious has happened, but the snap-in has now "compiled" (which is my word, not Microsoft's, but it seems a good shorthand for the process of converting your ASCII template into a binary security database) the template into a security template named `simple.sdb` in `My Documents\Security\Database`. In the details pane, you'll see an HTML message that "the page cannot be displayed."

Next, right-click Security Configuration and Analysis and you'll see two options: Analyze Computer Now and Configure Computer Now. Analyze doesn't change the computer. Instead, it compares the computer's state to the one that you want to create with the template. It then shows you—and saves a log file that explains—how your system varies from what the template instructs. The log file is written to `\My Documents\Security\Logs`.

But who wants to just find out how a system varies from our (administrative) desires? It'd be far more interesting to just tell the system, "Do this." And you can. Instead of choosing Analyze Computer Now, pick Configure Computer Now to modify the system's settings to fall into line with the template.

That's all very nice, you may be thinking, but how do I apply it to dozens of computers? Do I have to visit each one? No; you can use a command-line tool for that. A command-line program called `SECEDIT.EXE` will both convert templates into databases and apply databases. To read a template, apply, and then create a database in the process, use the following syntax:

```
Secedit /configure /cfg templatefilename /db databasefilename/overwrite
   /log logfilename
```

To apply an existing database without first reading the template, just leave off the `/cfg` switch and argument. To apply the template to your workstations, you could include the `secedit` command in a logon script (be sure and specify full path names for the template, database, and log files) that will reapply it with every logon. You could also use the Task Scheduler service to run a batch file and reapply the template at specific intervals. Or you could enable the telnet server on your Windows 2000 and XP machines and just apply the template whenever you like.

By the way, there's another way to create a template, although you can't build a complete template—Restricted Groups and other functions of this snap-in aren't included here—by opening Local Security Policies and right-clicking Security Settings. Then choose Reload and Export Policy to create a template based on the existing local security settings.

USING DOMAIN-BASED GROUP POLICIES TO APPLY TEMPLATES

Secedit is nice, but it has to be invoked manually or from a batch file, which means a lot of messy editing of logon batch files or fiddling with the Scheduled Tasks on all your systems. If you use a login script, the security template only gets applied at logon time. How do you enforce security settings more often? With group policies.

Domain-based group policies have a few benefits. First of all, it's easy to control whom they apply to, much easier than having to figure out which batch files go where. Second, they reapply themselves not only at logon time, but also throughout the day—the workstation seeks them out every 60 to 120 minutes. So, if domain-based group policies sound neat, then read on—we're just about to get started with them!

Group Policy Concepts

Let's start with some important concepts, terms, and rules you need to know to master Group Policy. In the process of explaining the functionality of Group Policy, I will mention several settings without actually showing you how to turn them on in the Group Policy snap-in. Just focus on the concepts for now. Later on in this section, we'll take a full tour of the Group Policy console, and I'll point out all of the settings (such as No Override and Block Inheritance) that are discussed in this section.

Administrators configure and deploy Group Policy by building *group policy objects (GPOs)*. GPOs are containers for groups of settings (*policies*) that can be applied to users and machines throughout a network. Policy objects are created using the Group Policy Object Editor, which is usually invoked with the Group Policy tab in DSA.MSC or DSSITE.MSC. The same GPO could specify a set of applications to be installed on all users' Desktops, implement a fascist policy of disk quotas and restrictions on the Explorer shell, and define domain-wide password and account lockout policies. It is possible to create one all-encompassing GPO or several different GPOs, one for each type of function.

There are two major nodes in the Group Policy Object Editor, Computer Configuration and User Configuration. The computer configuration policies manage machine-specific settings such as disk quotas, auditing, and Event Log management. User configuration policies apply to user-specific settings such as application configuration or folder redirection. However, there is a good bit of overlap between the two. It's not unusual to find the same policy available in both the User Configuration and Computer Configuration nodes. Be prepared for a certain amount of head scratching as you search for the policy you want to activate and decide whether to employ the user-based policy or the computer policy. Keep in mind that you may create a policy that uses both types of settings or you may create separate User and Computer Configuration policy objects.

Contrary to their name, group policies aren't group oriented at all. Maybe they are called group policies because a bunch of different configuration management tools are *grouped* together in one snap-in (maybe "assorted policies" just didn't have the same ring to it). Regardless, you cannot apply them directly to groups or users, but only to sites, domains, and OUs (Microsoft abbreviates these collectively with the term *SDOU*) within a given forest. This act of assigning GPOs to a site, domain, or OU is called *linking*. GPOs can also be linked to local policy on a particular Windows 2000, XP, or Server 2003 machine, as you'll see in a moment. The GPO-to-SDOU relationship can be many-to-one (many policies applied to one OU, for example) or one-to-many (one policy linked to several different OUs). Once linked to an SDOU, user policies are applied at logon time, and computer policies are applied at system startup. Both policies also refresh periodically, with a few important exceptions.

When I said GPOs were stored in the AD, that wasn't exactly accurate. Group policy objects are stored in two parts, a Group Policy Container (GPC), and a policy folder structure in the SYSVOL. The container part is stored in the Active Directory and contains property information, version info, status, and a list of components. The folder structure path is `WindowsINNT\SYSVOL\sysvol\Domainname\Policies\GUID\` where *GUID* is a Global Unique Identifier for the GPO. This folder contains administrative templates (ADM files), security settings, info on available applications, and script filenames with command lines.

Group policy objects are rooted in the Active Directory of a domain. You can't copy them to other domains, but you can link them across domain boundaries (although it's not recommended). Windows Server 2003 now supports some cross-forest functionality that wasn't available in Windows 2000. For example, a user in Forest A can log on to a computer in Forest B and still have group policies apply from Forest A. Also, group policy settings can contain references to servers in other forests now.

NOTE *Group policies aren't just Registry changes. Several policies are applied with Client Side Extension (CSE) DLLs. Examples are disk quota policy, folder redirection, and software installation. In fact, there is a CSE DLL that processes the Registry changes,* USERENV.DLL.

POLICIES ARE "ALL OR NOTHING"

Each GPO contains many possible settings for many functions; usually you'll configure only a few of them. The others will be left "inactive," sort of like putting REM in front of a command in a script or using a semicolon at the beginning of a line in an INF file. The workstation or server still has to read the whole policy, but it only acts on the options you've enabled. However, once you've configured a set of policies and told AD that "this GPO is linked to the REDHILLTOWN.com domain," for example, the individual settings or types of settings cannot be selectively applied. All User Configuration settings will be applied to all users on Windows 2000, XP, and 2003 systems in the linked domain. All Computer Configuration settings will be applied to all Windows 2000, XP, and 2003 machines in the domain. Remember that neither will be applied to NT 4 or 9x clients.

Now, let's say you've created a GPO that deploys a set of standard Desktop applications like Word, Excel, and Outlook, and you threw in a bunch of shell restrictions to prevent users from changing their configurations. If you don't want your IT support group users to be subject to those ridiculously stringent shell restrictions (although those users may need them most of all!), you can do a couple of things. You can create a separate GPO for those policies and link it to a lower-level container, such as an OU that contains all the regular users. But that OU will be the only one that gets the Office applications. You can alternately set permissions on the GPO that prevent the policy from being applied to the IT support group (this is called filtering). However, if you use filtering to solve this problem, none of the settings in the GPO will apply to the IT support group at all.

Group policy application is all or nothing, so sometimes you really need separate policies for separate functions. The best way to approach this might be to create a GPO for standard software deployment, and a GPO for shell restrictions. Both could be applied at the domain level, but shell restrictions can be filtered for the IT support group. The point is, it's not possible to create one monolithic policy and then specify who gets what settings, and you wouldn't want to do that anyway. At least, you wouldn't want to troubleshoot it.

POLICIES ARE INHERITED AND CUMULATIVE

Group Policy settings are cumulative and inherited from parent Active Directory containers. For example, REDHILLTOWN.com domain has several different GPOs. There is a domain-level policy that sets password restrictions, account lockout, and standard security settings. Each OU also has a policy to deploy and maintain standard applications as well as folder redirection settings and Desktop restrictions. Users and computers that are in both the domain and the OU receive settings both from the domain-level policy and from the OU-level policy. So some blanket policies can be applied to the entire domain, while others can be hashed out according to OUs.

REFRESH INTERVALS FOR GROUP POLICY

Policies are reapplied every 90 minutes, with a 30-minute "randomization" to keep the domain controller from getting hit by dozens or even hundreds of computers at once. Policies on DCs are refreshed every 5 minutes. There is, however, a policy to configure all of this, as you'll see in the section coming up, "Group Policy Policies." (So, if I set a policy for the refresh interval on Blanket Vanilla Policy Policy, would that be referred to as a Blanket Vanilla Policy Policy policy?) Exceptions to the refresh interval include folder redirection and software installation. These are only applied at logon or system startup time; otherwise, you might end up uninstalling an application while someone is trying to use it. Or a user might be working in a folder as it is being redirected to a new network location. That would be bad.

Local Policies and Group Policy Objects

When you use Active Directory Users and Computers or Active Directory Sites and Services to create and link group policies, you are working with group policy *objects* to specify a collection of settings to be applied at user logon or machine boot time. The information in the GPO says things like "change this, change that, install this, disable that." But administrators also need to be able to view the actual settings for these policies sometimes.

In NT 4, it was possible to use the System Policy Editor to view and edit those Registry entries for the local machine (rather than creating or editing a policy, you chose to open the Registry). As such, the System Policy Editor served as a more user-friendly Registry editing tool than either REGEDIT.EXE or REGEDT32.EXE. Similarly, the Group Policy snap-in provides the ability to view local policy settings on a machine.

When you open the Group Policy tool (GPEDIT.MSC), it automatically focuses on the local machine, as shown in Figure 9.39. Administrators can use the tool as they would use the Local Security Policy tool to configure account settings (such as minimum password length and number of bad logon attempts before locking the account) and to set up auditing. However, the domain-based policy editor includes a number of settings (including software installation and folder redirection) that are not available for local policies.

NOTE   *The local Group Policy folder structure is equivalent to that of other GPOs and is found in* \Windows\ system32\GroupPolicy.

FIGURE 9.39

The Group Policy Object Editor— local machine

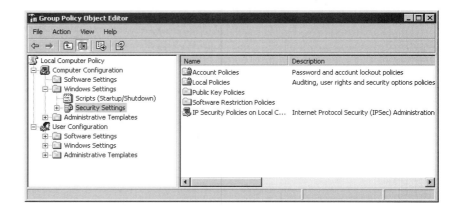

To focus on another computer's local policy, you must have Administrator rights on that machine. You can select a computer while adding the Group Policy snap-in to a custom management console, as shown in Figure 9.40. If you know the name of the computer, just fill it in or click the Browse button. The snap-in can focus on a local machine or on a group policy object; the Browse button allows you to locate and find group policy objects linked to sites, domains, OUs, or computers (Figure 9.41). Additionally, if you select the Allow the Focus of the Group Policy Snap-in to Be Changed option when opening the snap-in from the command line, it's possible to select the policy object as an argument when you start the console. GPEDIT.MSC, the Group Policy console that ships with Windows 2000 and Server 2003, has this option turned on.

FIGURE 9.40

Adding the Group Policy snap-in

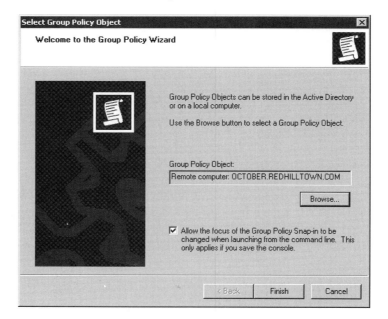

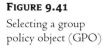
FIGURE 9.41

Selecting a group policy object (GPO)

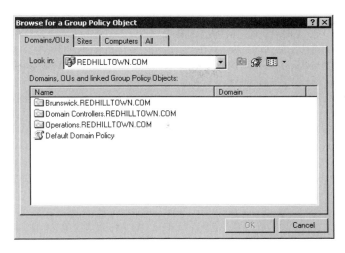

The syntax to open GPEDIT.MSC and look at the local policy on a remote machine is as follows:

    GPEDIT.MSC /gpcomputer: *machinename*

So you could type, for example:

    GPEDIT.MSC /gpcomputer: salome

Or you could type:

    GPEDIT.MSC /gpcomputer: salome.REDHILLTOWN.com

Be sure to include a space between **/gpcomputer:** and the machine name, though.

There is one important limitation when using GPEDIT.MSC to modify policy on a remote machine. The security settings extension to the Group Policy snap-in will not work when the tool is focused on a remote machine. That's worth saying again. You cannot open GPEDIT.MSC with the switch **/gpcomputer:** *computername* and modify the security settings on a remote machine. Apparently, Microsoft considers it a security vulnerability to allow it. Another example of software telling us what's best for us?

NOTE *If you are using group policies, local policy is always processed before site, domain, or OU group policies.*

Creating Group Policies

Now that you understand the major concepts involved in group policies and know the difference between local policies and group policy objects, let's go through the steps of creating and editing a group policy object. In this section, I'll show you all the settings we discussed in the preceding "theory" section.

To open the Group Policy snap-in in DSA.MSC, right-click your domain name at the root of the console and choose Properties from the context menu. Move to the Group Policy tab, shown in Figure 9.42, to see what GPOs have been linked at the domain level. If you haven't already created other policies, you'll see only the default domain policy listed. Notice the Block Policy Inheritance check box at the bottom left of the Group Policy tab. It prevents any group policy settings at a higher level from trickling down to this one. Remember the order in which policies are applied: first is the site level, then the domain level, then policies for OUs.

FIGURE 9.42

A domain's Group Policy properties

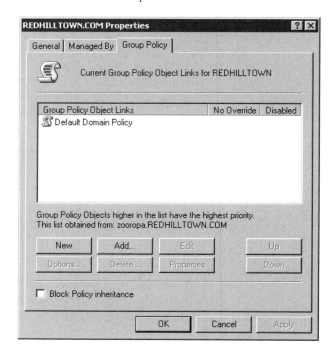

> **NOTE** *To view the GPOs that are linked to a container (site, domain, or OU), right-click the object in the console (`DSA.MSC` for domains and OUs and `DSSITE.MSC` for sites) and choose Properties from the context menu. Then navigate to the Group Policy tab. From that point, the interface to configure policies is the same regardless of the container it's linked with.*

To turn on No Override, highlight the policy and choose Options, then select the No Override check box (see Figure 9.43). When this setting is on, other policies applied down the line are prevented from defeating the settings of this policy, even with Block Inheritance enabled. Note that Block Policy Inheritance is turned on at the link level (site, domain, or OU), whereas No Override is enabled per policy. Check the Disabled box to turn off the policy so that it won't be processed or applied at this level. Disabling the policy doesn't disable the object itself. For example, the same policy, disabled at the domain level, could theoretically be applied at the site or OU level. If either option (No Override or Disabled) is turned on, there will be a check in the corresponding column of the Group Policy tab. You can activate both options using the context menu for the policy. Just right-click a selected policy to view the context menu.

FIGURE 9.43

Group Policy
options

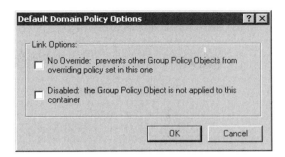

Back in the REDHILLTOWN.com properties sheet, choose New to create a new GPO. This will create a policy called New Group Policy Object and then allow you to rename it. If you miss that opportunity and end up with a policy called New Group Policy Object, just highlight the policy, right-click, and choose Rename from the context menu.

Choose Properties to view and modify your new group policy object's properties. The General tab shown in Figure 9.44 shows creation and revision information as well as options to disable the User or Computer Configuration portion of the policy. Depending on how you subdivide your domain into OUs, you may choose to create some policies with only computer settings and others with only user-specific settings. In that case, if the unused portion of the GPO is disabled altogether, policy application and updates are faster. If, however, your cold medicine has caused a momentary lapse of reason and there are important settings in the node you disable, those settings will be removed from the client machine. So the GPO Editor will ask you to confirm that move, just to be sure.

FIGURE 9.44

Group Policy
General properties

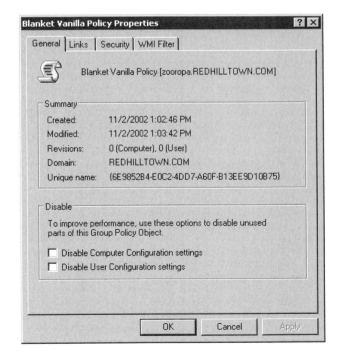

The Links tab gives you the opportunity to search for sites, domains, or OUs that use this GPO, if there are any. Because searching for other links takes a few moments and some resources, no linked containers will be displayed until you perform the search. Click the Find Now button to start the search.

The Security tab in the properties sheet reveals the GPO's default permissions (see Figure 9.45). Highlight a name at the top to view the permissions in the lower section. Notice that Domain Admins and Enterprise Admins have Read and Write permissions as well as Delete and Create All Child Objects, whereas the Authenticated Users group only has Read and Apply Group Policy. Read and Write are required to change a policy; Read and Apply are required to be a recipient of the policy.

FIGURE 9.45

Group Policy permissions list

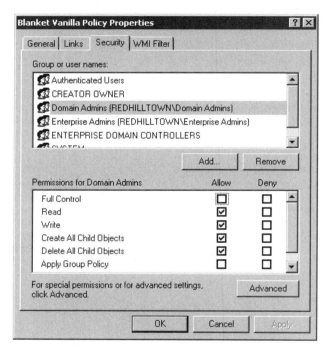

NOTE *Don't think that Domain Admins and Enterprise Admins are not subject to a group policy's settings just because they are not granted Apply Group Policy permission by default. Users will have all the permissions of all their groups; therefore, as members of Authenticated Users, the members of Domain Admins and Enterprise Admins will also be granted Apply Group Policy permissions.*

The WMI Filter tab reveals a capability that's new in Windows Server 2003. You can choose to apply your GPO according to certain computer criteria, based on information gathered by Windows Management Instrumentation (WMI). We'll discuss this new feature in more detail shortly.

Back in the Group Policy tab of our REDHILLTOWN.com domain properties page, if you highlight the new GPO that you have just created and click either the Up or Down button, you can move the policy up or down in the window. This is an important tidbit to know: When multiple GPOs are linked to one container, as is the case in Figure 9.46, they will be applied from the bottom up, so the one at the top is applied last. Therefore, GPOs higher in the list have a higher priority. If there are conflicting settings, the higher policy wins.

FIGURE 9.46

Increasing the priority of group policy objects

To delete a GPO, or to just remove it from the list, highlight the policy and click Delete. The GP Editor will ask you whether you want to delete it altogether (Figure 9.47) or to remove it from the list while preserving the policy to be linked to another container at another time.

FIGURE 9.47

Removing a group policy object

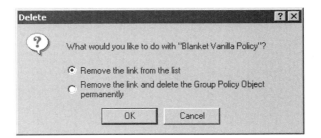

Click the Add button on the Group Policy tab to link an existing group policy object to the desired container. As you see in Figure 9.48, you can look for GPOs that are linked to other domains/OUs or to other sites, or you can just ask for a list of all GPOs. It took me a minute to grasp this simple operation: double-click the container name (the OU for Brunswick.REDHILLTOWN.com, for example) to view the policies linked to it. Then highlight the policy and click OK to add it to the list back on the Group Policy tab.

FIGURE 9.48

Adding a group policy link

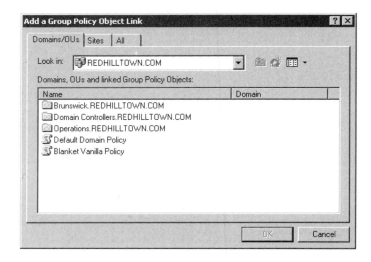

Now let's view and modify our new policy. Back in the Group Policy tab, highlight the policy and click Edit. This will open the Group Policy snap-in in a separate window, and you'll see the policy object name at the root of the namespace, in this case Blanket Vanilla Policy [zooropa .REDHILLTOWN.COM] Policy. This indicates to us what policy is being viewed and edited. Figure 9.49 shows the policy expanded in the console tree to show the major nodes of the group policy object.

FIGURE 9.49

Group Policy namespace

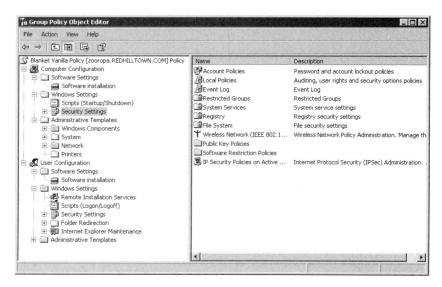

There are two major types of settings, as I mentioned earlier. Computer Configuration settings are applied to machines at startup and at designated refresh intervals. User Configuration settings are applied to the users' working environments at logon and at designated refresh intervals.

We'll explore the various policies according to subject matter later, but prepare yourself for the fact that policies are not all configured in a uniform way as far as the interface is concerned. You'll need a few examples to see what I mean:

◆ To specify software packages under `Software Settings\Software Installation`, open the folder and choose New/Package from the Action menu. An Open dialog box asks for the location of the package. Once it's been located and selected, you configure the package properties.

◆ To set the interval that users can wait before changing passwords, go to `Computer Configuration\Windows Settings\Security Settings\Account Policies\Password Policy`. Double-click Maximum Password Age in the details pane on the right, enable the setting by clicking the box that says Define This Policy Setting, and supply a time interval value.

◆ To set a policy that restricts group memberships, go to `Restricted Groups` under `Security Settings` in `Computer Configuration\Windows Settings` and choose Add Group from the Action menu. A dialog box asks you to enter a group or browse for it. Once the group is added to the list in the details pane on the right, double-click the group name to open a dialog box and supply the names of the users who must be or are allowed to be in the group. You can also define group memberships for the group itself.

◆ To set up folder redirection, go to `User Configuration\Windows Settings\Folder Redirection` and choose a folder (for example, `Start Menu`). The details pane on the right will be blank. Right-click white space in the details pane (or pull down the Action menu) and choose Properties. The properties page appears and you can now specify a location for the Start menu and configure redirection settings.

The point of this wild ride through the Group Policy Editor is not to disorient you, but rather to illustrate the fact that the Group Policy Editor has several nodes to accomplish various tasks, and procedures to specify settings will vary with the node and the task. There is no one way to configure a setting, although many do follow the pattern of the second example. So, when in doubt, right-click or look at the Action menu. It's a strategy to live by.

Once you've configured your Group Policy settings, simply close the Group Policy window. There is no Save or Save Changes option. Changes are written to the GPO when you choose OK or Apply on a particular setting, although the user or computer will not actually see the change until the policy is refreshed.

Group Policy Troubleshooting: GP Application Order

Now that you've got a GPO or two running, you'll soon find the troublesome part of group policies: figuring out what they're doing. Imagine, for example, that a user calls up and says, "Why is my background purple?" You then realize that there are a *lot* of places that your system gets policies from, and they might disagree on things like, for example, background color. So which one *won*?

POLICIES EXECUTE FROM THE BOTTOM UP, IN THE GUI

Let's start out by just considering a simple situation: just policies on a domain. Suppose I look at my domain in Active Directory Users and Computers. I right-click the domain, then choose Properties and click the Group Policies tab to see something like Figure 9.50.

FIGURE 9.50

Multiple policies in
a domain

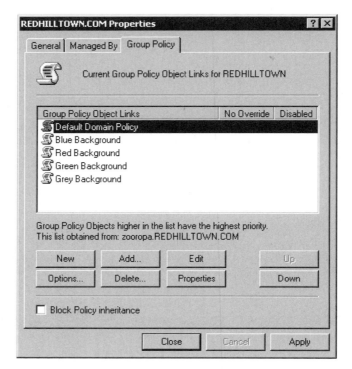

In this (admittedly fanciful) situation, the domain has five group policies, four of which attempt to set a workstation's background color to gray, green, red, or blue. (The other is the Default Domain Policy, which has nothing to say on the issue.) Who wins? Gray, red, green, or blue? The answer lies in two basic conflict resolution rules for group policies:

Rule 1   Listen to the last policy that you heard from.

Rule 2   Execute policies from the bottom up, as they appear in the GUI.

Reading from the bottom of the dialog box up, you see that the system will first see the policy that sets the background gray, then the one that sets it green, then the one that sets it red, and finally the one that sets it blue. As blue is the last one heard from, it wins, and the effects of the previous three are obviated.

But what if you *want* the red background policy to win? Notice the Up and Down buttons in the figure? You can shuffle them around to your heart's content.

GROUP POLICY APPLICATION ORDER

That example only considered domain policies. But you can apply policies to different levels:

◆   Sites can have policies, and no matter what domain's machines and users are in that site, those policies apply. (That's why you've got to be an Enterprise Administrator to create site policies.)

- ◆ OUs can have policies. And OUs can contain OUs, and OUs can contain OUs that contain OUs, and so on.

- ◆ There are also *local* policies, don't forget.

So, again, who wins? Policies are applied in the following order: local policy, sites, domains, organizational units, then OUs inside of OUs. If the domain policy says, "You must be logged in before you can shut down the machine," and the OU policy says, "Allow shutdown before logon," the OU policy takes precedence because it is applied last. If one policy says, "Lock it down," and the next one says, "Not configured," the setting remains locked down. If one policy says, "Not configured," and the next one says, "Lock it down," then it's locked down in this case, as well. If one policy says, "Leave it on," and the next one says, "Turn it off," it's turned off. If one policy says, "Turn it off," and another, closer one says, "Turn it on," then a third one says, "Turn it off," guess what? It ends up turned off. However, for the preservation of your sanity, it is desirable to avoid these little disagreements between policies.

FILTERING GROUP POLICY WITH ACCESS CONTROL LISTS

But we're not *nearly* finished here. It *could* be that while it looks as if many policies apply to your system, in fact, only a small number do. The reason: group policies have ACLs.

Right-click the container linked to any given GPO (in our example, the domain) and choose Properties. Select the Group Policy tab and highlight the policy you wish to filter. Click the Properties button and go to the Security tab (shown back in Figure 9.45). Now you see the access control list (ACL) for the policy object.

As I pointed out before, Domain Admins and Enterprise Admins have Read and Modify permissions, and Authenticated Users have Read and Apply Group Policy. It may happen that you create a policy to restrict Desktops and you don't wish to apply it to a certain group of people. The group Authenticated Users includes everyone but guests, so by default, the policy will apply to everyone but guests; that means even Domain Admins and Enterprise Admins will receive the policy settings. To prevent Domain Admins and Enterprise Admins from receiving this policy, you must check the box in the Deny column next to Apply Group Policy (Figure 9.51). A member of both groups will only need the Deny setting for one of the two groups, but you'll need to check the Deny box for both groups if the members of Domain Admins and Enterprise Admins are not the same people. To "excuse" others from receiving the policy, put them all in a security group and add that group to the list. It is not enough to "not check" the granted box for Read and Apply Group Policy; the users in your special security group are also members of Authenticated Users, so you actually need to choose the Deny option for them as well. Deny takes precedence over Allow.

If you wish to filter policy for a certain machine (or group of machines), follow the same strategy. Add the computer accounts to a security group, add that group to the ACL for the policy object, then deny the group Read and Apply Group Policy permissions.

There is an alternative to adding a security group to the ACL and denying them Read and Apply permissions. You could also remove Authenticated Users from the ACL altogether, preventing anyone from receiving the group policy. Then you would simply add entries to the ACL for any security groups you *do* want to receive the policy. Be sure, though, to allow them *both* Read and Apply Group Policy. Figure 9.52 shows the permissions list for Blanket Vanilla Policy in which Authenticated Users has been removed and the Domain Engineering group has been added. This is a useful strategy if you don't want the policy to apply to all users and computers in the linked container by default.

FIGURE 9.51

Denying the Apply Group Policy permission

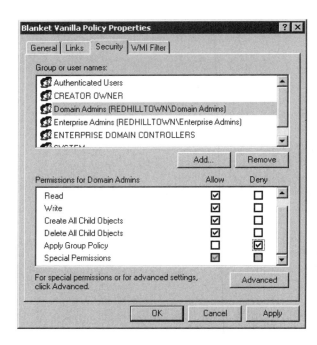

FIGURE 9.52

Group Policy ACL without Authenticated Users

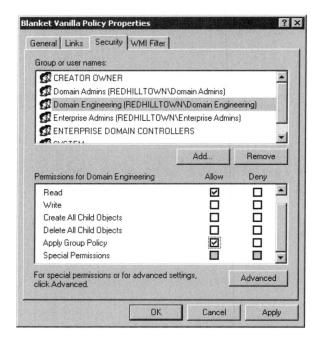

By the way, there is nothing to prevent you from adding individual users to the permissions list for a group policy object. Let me stress, then, that policy filtering is incredibly powerful—you might say that it's the tool that lets you oppress individuals or groups. In the real world, however, adding ACLs to a policy can be a nightmare for the poor fool trying to figure out two years later why a policy is attached to a domain but *isn't bloody applying to most of the people in the domain!*

USING WMI FILTERS WITH GROUP POLICY

Windows Server offers a WMI filtering option for group policies, which it didn't offer in Windows 2000. WMI filters run queries created in WMI Query Language (WQL) to determine whether or not to apply the entire policy. You can't pick and choose among the policy settings. To use WMI filtering, open the properties tab of a GPO and go to the WMI Filter tab (it's adjacent to the Security tab) shown in Figure 9.53. Use the Browse/Manage button to add, edit, or delete WMI filters.

FIGURE 9.53

Enabling the WMI Filter option for group policy objects

There are literally thousands of WMI-based variables for you to choose from. For instance, you might wish to have a policy apply only to laptops. First, you'd need to determine the make and model of laptops used, and then you could create a query that looks something like this:

```
Root\CimV2; Select * from Win32_ComputerSystem where manufacturer = "Toshiba" and
    Model = "Portege 2000" OR Model = "Portege 4010"
```

Other WMI criteria you could use to filter policies are disk space thresholds, version of the operating system, absence or presence of an existing software package, or even network information. Figure 9.54 shows a WMI filter for systems with DHCP enabled.

FIGURE 9.54

Managing WMI filters for group policy objects

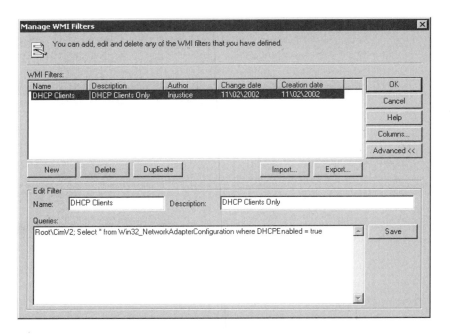

This WMI filter thing sounds great, right? Well, here's the down side: you can only have one WMI filter per GPO. If you use WMI filters, you'll probably end up creating more GPOs than you normally would. First you would create one or more "generic" GPOs, the ones that apply to the entire site, domain, or OU without any of the hardware or software-dependent settings. Then you would create a bunch of "mini-GPOs" that each use a WMI filter to determine whether or not to deploy.

TIP   *Another disadvantage of using WMI filters is that you have to learn the WMI scripting variables. Or you can cheat and download the unsupported Scriptomatic tool from* `http://www.microsoft.com/technet/scriptcenter/wmimatic.asp`. *This little hypertext application reveals all the WMI classes, properties, and methods you need to use the WMI filtering capability.*

NO OVERRIDE AND BLOCK INHERITANCE

Just as filtering can be used to counter the blanket application of policies, Block Inheritance is a special setting on a policy to prevent higher-level policies from trickling down. When Block Inheritance is turned on, the settings of higher policies will not be applied to lower containers at all. For example, if you create a GPO for a specific OU, say Brunswick, and set up all the necessary settings for the Brunswick OU, and then you want to prevent the REDHILLTOWN domain GPOs from affecting the Brunswick OU, you'd turn on Block Inheritance. The only policies applied will be the Brunswick OU policies.

There is also a counter to the Block Inheritance counter. (Isn't this becoming like a *Batman* episode? "Robin, they've blocked our transmission. It's time for the block-anti-block Bat-transmitter!") When No Override is turned on for a policy, settings in subsequent policies are prevented from reversing the ones in the No Override–enabled policy. For example, if domain admins have a set of highly disputed settings turned on at the domain level and those renegade Brunswick admins set up their own OU with its own policies and turn on Block Inheritance, the Brunswick OU effectively escapes the disputed settings, but only until the domain admins get wise and turn on No Override. Then the domain admins win, and the Brunswick OU people have to live with the same restrictions as everyone else. No Override beats Block Inheritance (just like paper covers rock).

Like all secret weapons, No Override and Block Inheritance are best used sparingly. Otherwise, in a troubleshooting situation it becomes rather complicated to determine what policies are applied where. This could be detrimental to the mental health of a network administrator.

Whew! To summarize the factors that can decide which group policy object wins:

◆ Examine policies in this order: local policies, then site policies, then domain policies, OU policies, and any OUs inside the OUs, and so on.

◆ Within any unit—site, domain, or OU—examine the policies as they appear in the GUI, from the bottom up.

◆ If policies conflict, only pay attention to the last one that you examined, *unless* you already saw a policy that said No Override—that means that no matter what policies come afterward, you should ignore them if they conflict with the No Override policy.

◆ Before you actually apply a policy, check its ACLs—if you don't have the Read and Apply Group Policy ACLs, then the policy doesn't apply.

GROUP POLICY EXAMPLE: FORCING COMPLEX PASSWORDS

Before leaving this, let's look at a conflict resolution example that will also offer an example of a useful policy. You may recall that an early NT 4 service pack (either 2 or 3, I forget) included a file called `passfilt.dll` which, if installed on your domain controllers, would force users to select "strong" passwords, where Microsoft's definition of "strong" ("complex" seems more appropriate to me) is that a password must fit the following criteria:

◆ Be at least six characters long

◆ Contain three of the four types of characters: uppercase letters, lowercase letters, numbers, or "special" (punctuation, etc.) characters

◆ Not contain your username

Under NT 4, you just installed `passfilt.dll` on all of your DCs. To make your Active Directory domain require complex passwords, however, you use a different process.

First of all, you needn't install `passfilt.dll` and, in fact, you won't find it anywhere on the 2000 or Server 2003 CD; its functionality is built into Windows 2000 and Windows Server 2003. You need only turn that functionality on with a group policy. The short version of how to do that is to enable the Passwords Must Meet Complexity Requirements policy. Here are some more step-by-step details:

1. Open up Active Directory Users and Computers.

2. In the left pane (the "command pane") you'll see a three-computer icon representing your directory. Right-click it and choose Properties, then click the Group Policies tab in the resulting property page. Create a new policy object, called Complex Password Policy and click the Edit button to open the GPO Editor.

3. This policy is a machine policy, not a user policy. (This surprised me, as it seemed as if it should be a user policy—after all, we're controlling how users set policies, no? But I guess this is a policy that affects any action on this particular machine—i.e., the domain controller.) Therefore, open up the Computer Configuration node.

4. Within that, open Windows Settings and then Security Settings. There may be a bit of a pause here, but don't worry, just give it a few seconds. Then open Account Policies and finally the Password Policy folder.

5. Inside the Password Policy folder, you'll see an entry labeled Passwords Must Meet Complexity Requirements. Double-click it.

6. Check the Define This Policy Setting check box.

7. Click the Enable radio button.

8. Close the GP Editor.

But you're not done yet—don't expect this to take effect immediately. Domain controllers reapply policies every five minutes, but they can only apply a policy that they know about, so you've also got to wait for the policy information to replicate to other domain controllers. (Obviously, if you have only one DC, then replication isn't a problem.)

Now, I *did* all that, and then created a user account and tried to give it a short one-character password, expecting to get an error message. But I didn't; the system accepted the short password despite the new policy. I even opened a command line and typed **secedit /refreshpolicy machine_ policy**, hoping that would push the system into seeing the policy. But it still didn't work.

Here's what I forgot. Domains automatically get a policy called Default Domain Policy. When I created my new policy, Complex Password Policy, then the Group Policies user interface placed it below the Default Domain Policy, as the UI does by default—reading top to bottom, you can see the order in which policies were created and/or linked to the domain. I hadn't realized it before, but the Default Domain Policy object *disables* strong passwords!

So there's a conflict in policies here. My Complex Password Policy said to use complex passwords, and the Default Domain Policy said not to. Who wins? Well, by default, a system pays attention to the *last* command that it heard, and the system executes policies from the one at the bottom of the list in the user interface to the top. (It's true, believe it or not.) So the system first got the command to force strong passwords, and then as it worked its way up the UI it came across the Default Domain Policy, which said *not* to force strong passwords. So no strong passwords.

The answer? I could have simply set my Complex Password Policy object to No Override. Instead, I just moved it above Default Domain Policy in the UI. Result: strong passwords.

And one more note, embarrassing as it may be: I thought originally to just try this strong password policy out on an organizational unit, but the policy didn't work. Then I remembered—duh—that account policies don't apply to OUs; you've got to make account policies on domains or they'll be ignored.

Delegating Group Policy Administration

The ability to delegate creation and configuration of group policies to Administrative personnel (or to others, for that matter) is extremely useful, especially in a large organization. In this section I'll explain how to allow persons who are not members of Domain Admins or Enterprise Admins to create and manage policies for designated sites, domains, or organizational units.

Group policy objects, by default, can be created by a member of the Administrators group for the domain or by members of the global group called Group Policy Creator Owners. However, while members of Administrators have full control of all GPOs, members of Group Policy Creator Owners can only modify policies they themselves have created, unless they have been specifically granted permission to modify a policy. So, if you put a designated group policy administrator into the security group Group Policy Creator Owners (that's almost as awkward as Active Directory Users and Computers), that person can create new policy objects and modify them.

It's one thing to create a group policy; linking that GPO to a site, domain, or OU is another matter. Administrators have this power by default, but a special permission called Manage Policy Links must be granted on the ACL of the site, domain, or OU before anyone else can create policy links to it. Also, there doesn't seem to be a way to create a group policy without linking it to something, at least initially. So if you want to use the Group Policy Creator Owners security group, you need to go ahead and set permissions on a container object to allow them to manage policy links. You'll need to use the Delegation of Control Wizard to accomplish this.

To allow members of Group Policy Creator Owners to create links to a particular OU (I've created a special OU with no users or groups in it, called GPO Holding Pen), right-click the OU in DSA.MSC. Choose the option Delegate Control from the context menu. Choose Next in the initial wizard screen to go to the part where you add the users and groups to whom you will delegate control. Choose Add and type **Group Policy Creator Owners** in the space provided. Click OK and then Next to return to the Users or Groups window, as shown in Figure 9.55. The Group Policy Creator Owners will appear in the Selected Users and Groups box. Choose Next to proceed to Tasks to Delegate window. Select Manage Group Policy Links from the predefined common tasks to delegate (see Figure 9.56). You should also enable both of the RSOP links, but we'll talk about RSOP in a bit. Now click Next and confirm your choices in the last screen by clicking the Finish button.

FIGURE 9.55

Delegation of Control Wizard's Users or Groups window

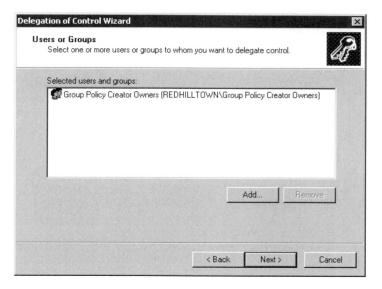

Members of Group Policy Creator Owners can now create new GPOs linked to the GPO Holding Pen OU. After they've created the policy objects, you or another trusted admin can actually do the task of linking the GPO to an actual site, domain or OU. They can also modify policies that they have created, but if there are other policies on the OU, members of Group Policy Creator Owners can't edit them by default. You'll have to grant the group Read and Write permission on the policy object's ACL.

FIGURE 9.56

Delegating
management of
Group Policy links

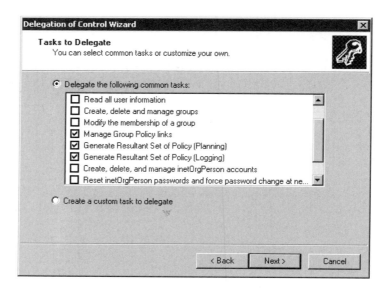

TIP *To test GP objects before deploying them, put one or more test environment computer, user, and security group accounts into the holding pen OU you created. This way, you can see the effect the policy will have before linking the GPO to a production site, domain, or OU.*

Designating a regular user or junior admin as a member of Group Policy Creator Owners and giving them the ability to manage group policy links, even if it's just at the OU level, is a real exercise in faith and quite taxing for us control freaks (I mean, letting-go-challenged people). If you want finer control when delegating group policy administration tasks, set up a custom MMC console. You may even elect to limit administration to your special GPO Holding Pen by loading the Group Policy snap-in focused on that GPO. Enable only the extensions you want your delegate to use. It's further possible to configure a policy to permit the use of certain Group Policy snap-in extensions and prevent the use of others, just in case the delegate stumbles on to Author mode by accident. See the section "Group Policy Policies" later in this chapter for specifics.

TIP *See Chapter 3 for a discussion on customizing Microsoft Management Consoles.*

That was a lot of information, so let's review the primary requirements for creating and editing GPOs:

♦ To create a GPO, you must be a member of either the Administrators group (and this includes nested groups, so membership in Domain Admins is acceptable, for example) or of Group Policy Creator Owners. If you insist on the McGyver approach, however, you at least need access to a domain controller, Read/Write permissions on SYSVOL, and Modify permission on the directory container. When creating an "OU God," then, make sure the would-be OU God is a member of the domain's GP Creator Owner group.

♦ To edit a policy, a user must (a) have full Administrator privileges, or (b) be creator owner of the GPO, or (c) have Read and Write on the ACL of the GPO.

User and Computer Configuration Settings

Now that you've learned all about creating and linking and delegating administration of Group Policy, we'll explore some of the policy settings themselves in the next few sections. Since you can use various types of policies to configure a range of settings, we won't try to cover every single setting in the pages allotted to this chapter (otherwise it could be a book all by itself!). Rather, think of this section as an overview of what group policies can accomplish to make your life easier as an administrator. To follow along, open the Group Policy snap-in for a GPO by navigating to the Group Policy tab in the container's properties pages, highlight an existing policy, and click the Edit button.

As you see in Figure 9.57, there are two main nodes to the Group Policy snap-in: User Configuration and Computer Configuration. Both nodes have the following subnodes: Software Settings, Windows Settings, and Administrative Templates. The difference between the two is this: Policies set for User Configuration will apply to the user's settings, and those set for Computer Configuration will apply to the machine configuration. For example, if Registry settings are involved, as is the case with `Administrative Templates`, the changes will be written to `HKEY_CURRENT_USER` (HKCU) for User Configuration stuff and to `HKEY_LOCAL_MACHINE` (HKLM) for Computer Configuration settings. Otherwise, the differences aren't so obvious and there is some overlap in the settings, just as HKCU contains some of the same entries as HKLM. You may wish to create separate policies for machines and users, to keep things straight, but be on the lookout for any conflicts. If a value set in the computer settings is also specified in the user policy settings, the User Configuration settings will take precedence by default.

FIGURE 9.57

Group Policy nodes and subnodes

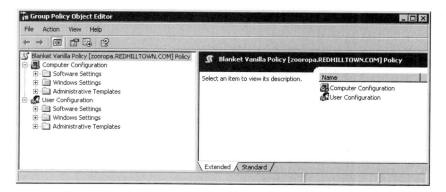

For both User Configuration and Computer Configuration, the `Software Settings\Software Installation` subgroup can be used to publish, assign, update, and even remove applications from a user's Desktop. See Chapter 12 for the full story on using group policies to set up application packages.

SPECIFY SCRIPTS WITH GROUP POLICY

You can specify logon and logoff scripts, as well as scripts to run at system startup and shutdown, using `Windows Settings` in either the User Configuration node or the Computer Configuration node. Expand `Windows Settings` to reveal `Scripts`, then select the script type (Startup, Shutdown, Logon, or Logoff) in the details pane on the right; Figure 9.58 shows the scripts available in User

Configuration. From here, double-click the script type (such as Logon) or highlight it and choose Properties from the Action menu. Add scripts to the list using the Add button (see Figure 9.59). Supply a script name and parameters when prompted. To edit the script name and parameters (not the script itself), choose Edit. If more than one script is specified, use the Up and Down buttons to indicate the order in which the scripts should run.

FIGURE 9.58

Group Policy startup scripts

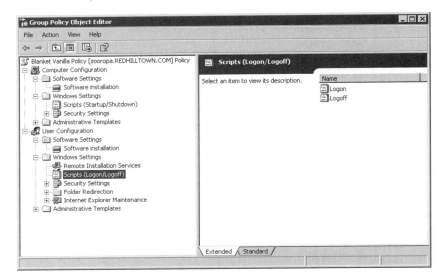

FIGURE 9.59

Adding a script to Group Policy

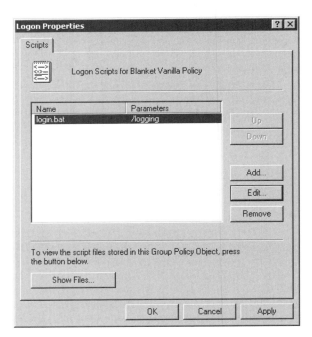

The scripts you create and assign should be copied to the following path in the SYSVOL directory: \Windows\SYSVOL\SysVol*domainname*\Policies\{GUID}\Machine\Scripts\Startup or Shutdown (or User\Scripts\Logon or Logoff, depending on whether you are assigning scripts to the Computer Configuration or to the User Configuration node). The Global Unique Identifier (GUID) for the group policy object is a long string that looks like {FA08AF41-38AB-11D3-BD1FC9B6902FA00B}. If you wish to see the scripts stored in the GPO and possibly open them for editing, use the Show Files button at the bottom of the properties page. This will open the folder in Explorer.

As you may know, you may also specify a logon script in the properties page of the user account in DSA.MSC. Microsoft calls these *legacy logon scripts* and encourages you to assign scripts with Group Policy for Windows 2000 and XP clients. Of course, Windows 9*x*/NT clients don't use group policies, so you'll still assign their logon scripts in the account properties. Other than that, the only real advantage to using the Group Policy scripts is that they run asynchronously in a hidden window. So if several scripts are assigned, or if the scripts are complex, the user doesn't have to wait for them to end. Legacy logon scripts run in a window on the Desktop. On the other hand, you might not want the scripts to run hidden (some scripts stop and supply information or wait for user input). In that case, there are several policy settings available to help you define the behavior of Group Policy scripts. These settings are located in the Administrative Templates node under System\Scripts. There you'll find settings to specify whether to run a script synchronously or asynchronously and whether it should be visible or invisible. Legacy logon scripts can be run hidden, like Group Policy scripts, by using the setting shown in Figure 9.60. The Computer Configuration settings also include a maximum wait time for Group Policy scripts, which is 600 seconds by default. This changes the time-out period, which is the maximum allotted time allowed for the script to complete.

FIGURE 9.60

Policy to run legacy scripts hidden

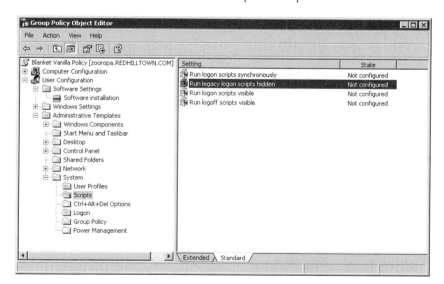

FOLDER REDIRECTION

One of the more useful things you can do with User Configuration settings in Group Policy is to arrange for a user's Application Data, Desktop, Start Menu, or My Documents folder to follow her around from computer to computer. These folders are important elements in a user's working environment. `Application Data` stores application-specific user information (Internet Explorer uses it, for example), and `Desktop` may contain important folders and shortcuts that need to be just one click away for the user. The `Start Menu` folder contains program groups and shortcuts to programs; `My Documents` is the default place to save and retrieve files, sort of like a local home directory. With user profiles in NT 4 and now 2000/XP, you can preconfigure these folders' contents and assign network locations. With the System Policy Editor for 9*x* or NT, it was also possible to specify a location for these folders. But, unlike the Default User profiles behavior, redirected folders live in one designated place all the time. They are not copied to each machine the user logs in to, causing "profile build-up." Instead of using the folder in the user's local profile, she will be *redirected* to the location specified in the group policy. Group policy folder redirection replaces and enhances those functions offered previously in system policies, with additional options to manage the redirected folder behavior.

There are several good reasons to use folder redirection. For one thing, it's convenient for users who log in from several different machines. Also, if you specify a network location for some or all of these folders, they can be backed up regularly and protected by the IT department. If roaming profiles are still in use, setting up folder redirection speeds up synchronization of the server profile with the local profile at logon and logoff, since the redirected folders need not be updated. Redirecting the `Desktop` and `Start Menu` folders to a centralized, shared location facilitates standardization of users' working environments and helps with remote support issues, because help desk personnel will know that all machines are configured in the same way. Best of all, you can mix and match. It's possible to specify a shared location for the `Desktop` and `Start Menu` folders while allowing each user to have his own `My Documents` and `Application Data` folders. Let's take a look.

To set a network location for the `My Documents` folder in Group Policy, go to `User Configuration\Windows Settings\Folder Redirection\My Documents`, right-click the highlighted `My Documents` folder, and choose Properties from the context menu. The properties page reveals that this setting is not configured by default. Choose Basic from the drop-down list to specify a single location for the `My Documents` folder, to be shared by all the users; or choose Advanced to set locations based on security group membership. If you want a single location for a shared `My Documents` folder, just fill in the target location with a network path or browse for it. To designate different locations, first choose a security group and then specify a network path. Figure 9.61 demonstrates redirecting the `My Documents` folder for all members of Domain Engineering to the CentralEng share on the server Zooropa. Whether you choose the Basic or Advanced redirection option, the policy permits you to choose from four different options:

- ◆ Redirect the folder to the user's home directory
- ◆ Create a folder for each user under the root path
- ◆ Redirect to the following location (which you specify)
- ◆ Redirect to the local user profile location

For our example, choose the second option; all of Engineering will use the same root path, but they will have individual `My Documents` folders. When you use this option, the system creates a subfolder named after the user in the path you specify.

FIGURE 9.61

Policy to redirect the user's My Documents folder

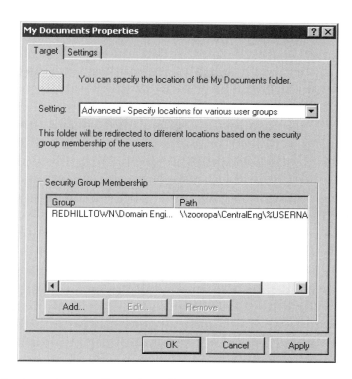

Now click the Settings tab to configure the redirection settings. For the sake of completeness, the redirection settings for My Documents are shown in Figure 9.62. The redirection settings for all the other folders are the same except that My Documents has the My Pictures subfolder, so there are a couple of extra items to configure.

The options you see in Figure 9.62 show default selections for the My Documents folder. Notice that the user will have exclusive access to the folder by default. The contents of the corresponding folder will be copied to the new location by default. Even after the policy is removed, the folder will remain redirected unless you say to "un-redirect" it. One notable exception is the Start Menu folder. You can pretty much assume that a redirected Start Menu folder is a shared Start Menu folder (otherwise, why bother?), and making it private or copying over it would generally be a bad thing. Therefore, both the option to grant exclusive rights and the option to move the contents of a user's Start Menu folder to the new location are grayed out in the Settings tab.

SECURITY SETTINGS

Security settings, along with administrative templates, make up a large part of Group Policy. The default security settings are purposely open, to keep down administrative headaches and to ensure that users and applications work as intended. As security increases, users and applications have more restrictions and support time goes up. In other words, security is inversely proportional to convenience. As you start locking down systems, something is bound to stop working. Hey, regular users can't even install applications on a Windows 2000 or XP system by default. When you start enforcing passwords that are 8 characters or more, contain both letters and numbers, can't use any part of a user's name, and cannot be reused until 15 other passwords have been used, things get complicated for the everyday Joe. As important as security is, Microsoft judged (wisely, I believe) that functionality had to come first. For organizations that want to increase security, there are tools and guidelines. But there is one problem with this approach. A big problem.

FIGURE 9.62

Redirection Settings for My Documents

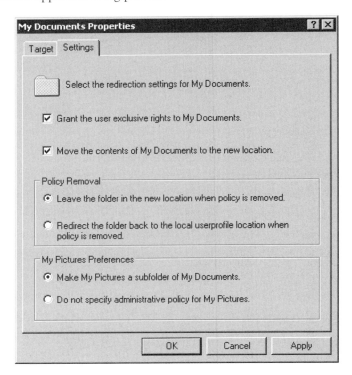

If you've ever "hardened" an NT 4 server according to established military or other high-security guidelines, you know that you have to set particular permissions on particular folders, that you must change the default permissions on certain Registry keys, and change or create other Registry entries as well. All in all, it takes a few hours of work on a single server, even for an efficient admin. What if you have 50 servers and 500 Professional workstations? Some things can be scripted, but others can't. Try as they might, there is no Microsoft or third-party tool that does everything automatically for all machines.

Here's where Group Policy comes to the rescue. Assuming you are going to standardize throughout the organization somewhat, you only have to change those sticky Registry permissions and settings once, using Group Policy. You only have to set the NTFS permissions once. They can even be set up in one policy and copied to another. Whether you need a lot of security or just a little more than the default, chances are you'll want to make at least some standardized changes, and the Security Settings node will certainly make your life easier. The bulk of security settings are found under Computer Configuration\Windows Settings\Security Settings, although public-key policies and software restriction policies are also found in the User Configuration node in the same path. The following summarizes the major categories of settings under Security Settings:

Account Policies   Specify password restrictions, lockout policies, and Kerberos policy.

Local Policies   Configure auditing and assign user rights and miscellaneous security settings.

Event Log   Centralizes configuration options for the Event Log.

Restricted Groups   Enforce and control group memberships for certain groups, such as the Administrators group.

System Services   Standardize services configurations and protect against changes.

Registry   Creates security templates for Registry key permissions, to control who can change what keys and to control Read access to parts of the Registry.

File System   Creates security templates for permissions on files and folders to ensure that files and directories have and keep the permissions you want them to have.

Public Key Policies   Manage settings for organizations using a public key infrastructure.

Software Restrictions Policies   Place restrictions on what software runs on a system. This new feature is designed to prevent viruses and untrusted software from running on a system. It only works on Windows XP or Server machines, though.

IMPORTING SECURITY TEMPLATES

A full discussion of all these security settings is certainly beyond the scope of this chapter, but you should be aware that several security settings templates are available and installed with the Server to ease the burden of wading through and researching all the settings. It's also safer to configure settings offline and then apply them than it is to play with a live working group policy.

As you read in the earlier section on *local* group policies, the Security Settings templates take the form of INF files and are found in \Windows\security\templates. When applied directly or via Group Policy, the templates incrementally modify the default settings. You can view and modify the templates using the Security Templates snap-in, shown in Figure 9.63. As you see in the figure, these settings are the same as those found in Group Policy Security Settings, with the exception of Public Key Policies and IP Security Policies, which cannot be configured with templates. The values for the settings in each template are configured to meet the necessary level of security. These templates, or new ones you create, can then be applied directly to a Windows 2000, XP, or Server machine's local policy by using a command-line program called SECEDIT.EXE, or they can be imported into Group Policy.

Every fresh installation of Windows 2000, XP, or 2003 gets a standard set of local computer policies with default security settings. For this reason it's a good idea to export your existing settings to a file by using the Group Policy Editor focused on the local machine (GPEDIT.MSC will open that way by default) before making any drastic changes. Security settings for upgraded systems do not have their local policy changed in case the configuration has been customized.

Remember that I promised you when I discussed templates how to apply them with domain-based group policies? This is how: To import a security template into Group Policy, go to

`Computer Configuration\Windows Settings\Security Settings` and right-click Security Settings. Choose Import Policy from the context menu, and select your policy from the list of templates. Group Policy automatically looks for the template in `\Windows\security\templates`, but you can tell it to look someplace else if you wish. The INF file will be imported to modify the settings in the selected group policy object.

FIGURE 9.63

Security Templates snap-in

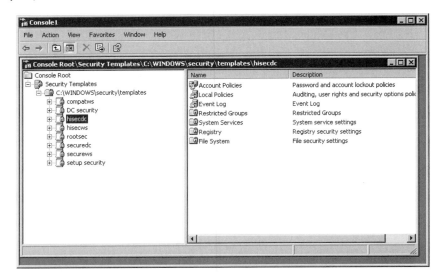

In the spirit of this template idea, the various subcomponents of Security Settings (like Account Policies or Local Policies) also support a copy-and-paste function, which appears in the context and Action menus when the subcomponent is selected. An admin person can actually copy that part of the template information to the Clipboard and apply it to another policy.

ADMINISTRATIVE TEMPLATES

Administrative Templates is the part of Group Policy that is most like System Policies in NT. The settings available here are based on template files (ADM files, like those used in NT and Windows 9x System Policies). These settings specify Registry entry changes to adjust various aspects of a user's environment or a machine configuration, including those famous options to restrict a user's Desktop to the point where they can only run a limited set of programs and nothing else.

The user changes specified in `Administrative Templates` are written to `HKEY_ CURRENT_USER\Software\Policies`, and computer changes are written to `HKEY_LOCAL_ MACHINE\Software\Policies`. Like the NT 4 System Policy Editor, Group Policy Administrative Templates loads ADM files to disclose collections of configurable settings. These ADM files are in `\Windows\inf`. Capabilities of Administrative Templates can also be extended with custom ADM files. Right-click the Administrative Templates node and choose Add/Remove Templates to see a list of loaded ADM files (shown in Figure 9.64).

FIGURE 9.64

ADM files loaded in Administrative Templates node

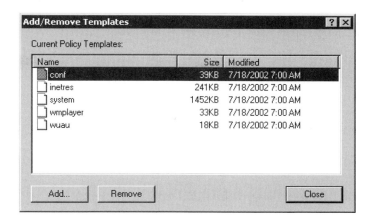

Of the five templates you see in Figure 9.64, the most important are system, which exposes system settings and inetres, which contains settings for Internet Explorer. conf controls settings for NetMeeting, wmplayer has the Windows Media Player settings, and wuau contains configuration options for Windows Update and Automatic Update.

NOTE *When you load an Administrative Template, the ADM files are copied to* \SYSVOL\Domainname\Policies\ GUID\Adm.

What's the difference between User Configuration and Computer Configuration with regard to Administrative Templates? Good question. Depending on the nature of the configuration settings, some live in the user part of the Registry (HKCU), while others live in the machine part (HKLM). Other settings exist in both places, which makes things really confusing. Settings for Task Scheduler, for example, are exactly the same in both places. So, other than asking yourself, "Which node has the setting I want?" the difference is whether the policy should apply to the machine, regardless of who logs in, or whether the policy should apply to the users and follow them from machine to machine.

One really useful feature about Administrative Templates is that most of the settings include a lengthy description and minimum software or system requirements that display automatically if you are using the Extended View in the tool (see Figure 9.65). If you prefer the Standard View, open the individual item and you'll see the Supported On information at the bottom of the Setting tab. Click the Explain tab to see the description information (shown in Figure 9.66). That beats the heck out of having to stop and look something up in Help every time you have a question.

What can you do with Administrative Templates settings? Among the primary functions is "Keep users from changing *X*" or "Disable or hide option *Y*." But mostly it's just a large collection of configuration options loosely organized together to ease our administrative burden and help us achieve the power and control of our networks and users that we crave and feel we truly deserve. An attempt to catalog each subnode and all of its policy settings would be a boring and futile exercise in the Microsoft style of documentation and is best left to those who write the Resource Kits. Besides, many of these policies should not be discussed in a vacuum and are best approached in the context of the particular application or service they configure.

FIGURE 9.65

Extended View
Information in
Administrative
Templates

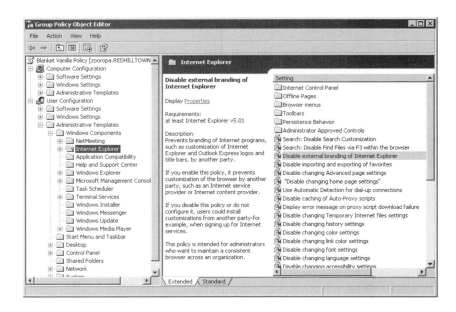

FIGURE 9.66

Descriptions of
settings in the
Explain tab

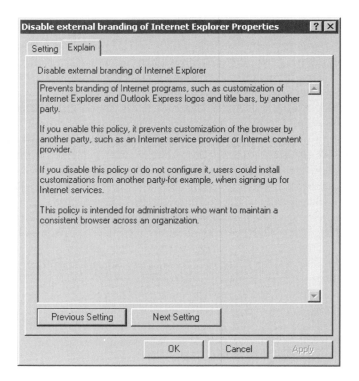

Nonetheless, this section would be lacking if it did not include at least a few pointers on individual policies. So the following sections offer a few highly opinionated comments on some of the settings you'll find in Administrative Templates.

Restricting Internet Explorer

For every setting in Internet Explorer, there seems to be policy to disable it. Considering that a good deal of time at work is spent surfing the Web, it's a particularly cruel and clever thing to impose such control over IE settings (unfortunately, many companies use Netscape Navigator instead of Internet Explorer). Here are a couple of settings that I find useful: If you want to prevent users from messing with the security zones you set up, or if you want Internet Explorer to use the same security zones and proxy settings for all users on the computer, then enable the Security Zones and proxy settings under `Computer Configuration/Administrative Templates/Windows Components/Internet Explorer`. To prevent users from downloading offline content to their workstations, enable the policy named Disable Adding Schedules for Offline Pages under `User Configuration/Administrative Templates/Windows Components/Internet Explorer/Offline Pages`. To prevent users from making any changes to IE's Security, Connections, or Advanced Properties pages, disable access to these and other IE Control Panel pages in the User Configuration node under `Internet Explorer/Internet Control Panel`. If you want to keep users from downloading any software from the Web, however, that's a little more difficult. There is a policy under `User Configuration/.../Internet Explorer/Browser Menus` that disables the Save This Program to Disk option. However, this won't prevent users from installing the software without saving it, and there are probably a couple of other ways around the restriction for a determined power user.

Prevent Users from Installing or Running Unauthorized Software

While I'm on the subject of preventing users from installing software, enable the policy found under `User Configuration/.../Windows Components/Windows Installer` named Prevent Removable Media Source for Any Install to keep users from running installations from a CD-ROM or a floppy drive (remember those?). And if you are going to do that, you should also enable the policy to Hide the "Add a Program from CD-ROM or floppy disk" Option in `User Configuration/.../Control Panel/Add or Remove Programs`. The Control Panel node includes several options to disable or remove all or part of the Add/Remove Programs applet. Disabling Add/Remove Programs will not prevent users from running setup routines in other ways, however. Anyone who can use a command line can circumvent these restrictions, so you'd need to open the System node of the User Configuration policies and enable the policy to Prevent Access to the Command Prompt. If you are looking for that infamous policy to Run Only Allowed Windows Applications, it's found in the System node of the User Configuration templates (shown in Figure 9.67). Be careful with this one, though; you have to make a list of all applications that can be launched from Explorer. There is also a setting in the same location called Don't Run Specified Windows Applications. For this one, you'd need to make a list of disallowed programs.

TIP *Figure 9.67 also shows the location of a policy to Prevent Access to Registry Editing Tools. Enabling this policy prevents users from running* `REGEDT32.EXE` *and* `REGEDIT.EXE`*, although regular users only have Read access to the vast majority of the Registry anyway.*

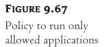

FIGURE 9.67

Policy to run only allowed applications

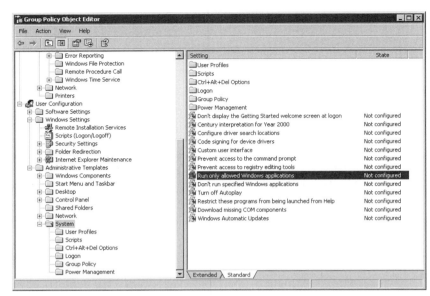

The same principle applies to the Start Menu and Taskbar option to remove Run from the Start menu. Experienced users will not be prevented from running unblessed programs just because Run is removed from the Start menu, so you have to seek out all the other ways of launching programs and disable them as well (users can also launch programs from the Task Manager unless you disable it in the Ctrl+Alt+Delete options).

TIP *If you want to achieve a simplified and consistent Desktop and Start menu for your organization or department, you'll probably need to combine folder redirection with the restrictions that are available in the Administrative Templates. You should also look at the last section in this chapter to explore your options for preconfiguring user profiles or the Default User profile.*

Configure Time Servers and Clients Using Administrative Templates

Synchronizing time across a big network can be a bit of a headache. Admins often use login scripts to execute the `net time` command, or install a third-party service on NT or 2000 systems. For Windows XP and Server 2003 only, you can use the Computer Configuration Administrative Templates to enable and configure NTP clients and servers and to specify global parameters for time sources. These settings are found in the System node under Windows Time Service.

USING GROUP POLICY TO SET PASSWORD AND ACCOUNT LOCKOUT POLICY

In NT 4, any account policies set in User Manager for Domains applied to domain account and password functions; the audited events, such as restarts, failed logon attempts, and security policy changes, were those occurring on domain controllers. Group policies are much more powerful. If you choose to create a policy at the domain level, the settings will apply to all domain member machines—servers, workstations, and domain controllers included. Domain controllers receive their settings from domain-level account policies and will ignore the settings in policies linked to OUs. In fact, you'll see an error in the Event Log if an OU-level policy contains these settings. So unfortunately, you still can't make administrator types change their passwords more often than everyone else does (not without a big stick, anyway). Differing Local Policy settings can be applied to OUs, however, so the audit policy can be stricter on "high security" OUs and more lax on others.

NOTE *Password and account policies should always be set at the domain level; if they are set at the OU level they are ignored. However it is possible for OU policies to override local policy settings such as auditing and user rights.*

Password and account lockout policy settings are located under `Computer Configuration/Windows Settings/Security Settings`. Password policy includes the following options:

Enforce Password History   Enable this option to specify the required number of consecutive unique passwords before a given password can be used again.

Maximum Password Age   This option sets the amount of time for which a password can be used before the system requires the user to pick a new one. Organizations usually set this interval somewhere between 30 and 90 days.

Minimum Password Age   The value set here is the amount of time for which a password must be used before the user is allowed to change it again.

Minimum Password Length   This option defines the smallest number of characters that a user's password can contain. Seven or eight characters is a good minimum length for passwords. Setting this policy also disallows blank passwords.

Passwords Must Meet Complexity Requirements   In case you are wondering "what requirements?," this setting used to be called Passwords Must Meet Complexity Requirements of Installed Password Filter. A password filter DLL was available as an option for NT 4, but it's built in to Windows 2000 and Server 2003. Password filters define requirements such as the number of characters allowed, whether letters and numbers must be used, whether any part of the username is permitted, and so forth. If you enable this policy, all new passwords and changed passwords must meet the following requirements:

- They must be at least six characters long.
- They cannot contain the username or part of the username.
- They must use three of the four following types of characters: uppercase letters (A–Z), lowercase letters (a–z), numbers (0–9), and special characters (e.g., @, %, &, #).

Store Passwords Using Reversible Encryption   Yes, this policy is definitely a security downgrade, telling the domain controller that it's OK to store passwords in a reversible encryption. This is one step away from clear text; passwords are normally stored in a one-way hash encryption. If you only need this for individual user accounts (like Apple users) enable the option in the user account properties instead. Reversible encryption is required, however, if you are using CHAP authentication with Remote Access or Internet Authentication Services.

Account Lockout Policy, once enabled, prevents anyone from logging in to the account after a certain number of failed attempts. The options are as follows:

Account Lockout Duration This setting determines the interval for which the account will be locked out. After this time period expires, the user account will no longer be locked out and the user can try to log in again. If you enable the option but leave the minutes field blank, the account will stay locked out until an administrator unlocks it.

Account Lockout Threshold This value defines how many times the user can unsuccessfully attempt to log in before the account will be locked out. If you define this setting, be sure to specify the number of permitted attempts, or the account will never lock out.

Reset Account Lockout Counter After This setting defines the time interval after which the count of bad logon attempts will start over. For example, suppose you have a reset count of two minutes and three logon attempts. If you mistype twice, you can wait two minutes after the second attempt and you'll have three tries again.

USING GROUP POLICY TO MANAGE MMC

Delegation is a great feature of Active Directory under 2000 and 2003, and the Microsoft Management Console is a big part of that. Many administrators will want to create consoles to accomplish particular tasks and distribute them to the responsible parties. Group Policy offers options to control MMC so that others can't make changes to existing MMC tools or access snap-ins and extensions that are off-limits, not the least of which are the Group Policy snap-ins and extensions.

You see, in NT 4, users could either run the Server Manager tool or they couldn't. If they could run the tool, they might only be able to create machine accounts (if they were members of Account Operators) but not to promote domain controllers. That didn't keep users from seeing the option in the menu or from attempting operations that were not permitted in their security context. Now, not only can you design a tool that includes just the snap-ins and extensions that you want your admins to use, but you can also explicitly forbid any changing of the tool by preventing Author mode. What's more, you can completely forbid access to a particular snap-in, regardless of the tool employed by the user. Please note that this does not actually set a user's security level (that's what security groups and rights are for), but it can effectively limit access to certain administrative tools. Cool, eh?

The Microsoft Management Console policies are found under `Administrative Templates\Windows Components\Microsoft Management Console` in the User Configuration node (see Figure 9.68). The main policies shown in this figure are to restrict Author mode (which prevents the user from creating console files and from adding or removing snap-ins) and to restrict users to an explicit list of permitted snap-ins. These two policies are not exactly mutually exclusive, as you might think; nor does enabling the first policy eliminate the need for the second.

A user who is not permitted to enter Author mode is unable to do any of the following:

◆ Run `MMC.EXE` from the Start menu or a command prompt; it opens, by definition, in Author mode with a blank console window.

◆ Open any console with the `/a` (Author mode) switch.

◆ Open any console that is configured to always open in Author mode.

FIGURE 9.68

MMC group policies

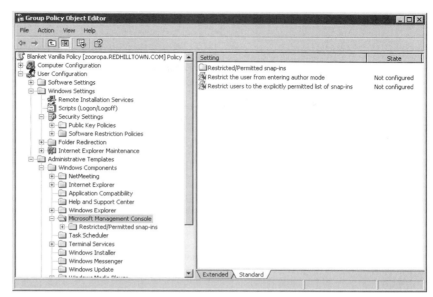

All of the prebuilt administrative consoles that are included in Administrative Tools are User mode tools, so they can be used when the restriction is activated. However, if you create a console and distribute it but forget to set it to open in User mode, the user will not be able to access the tool with this policy in effect.

If the policy to restrict users to only the expressly permitted list of snap-ins is enabled, users will not be able to add or remove restricted snap-ins or extensions to console files when in Author mode (they will not even appear in the list of available snap-ins). More importantly, if a console file already contains a restricted snap-in or extension, when a user who is subject to this policy runs the tool, the restricted snap-in or extension will not appear in the console. For example, if you don't have access to the Group Policy tab for Active Directory tools (set this policy in the Group Policy node under `Restricted/Permitted Snap-Ins`), you won't even see the tab in Active Directory Users and Computers (or AD Sites and Services) when you open the properties of the site, domain, or OU.

If you do choose to restrict users to only the expressly permitted list of snap-ins, be sure to filter the policy for exempt admin types. Also, you need to go to the `Restricted/Permitted Snap-Ins` folder and enable those snap-ins that you want to be available. Otherwise, *no snap-ins will be available* to nonexempt users regardless of their power and status on the network. This could be very bad, so think carefully before you disable access to the Group Policy snap-in, or you might not be able to reverse the damage.

Even if you don't enable the policy to restrict snap-in and extension use, you can still deny access to certain snap-ins. You see, if the policy Restrict Users to the Explicitly Permitted List of Snap-Ins is configured, enabling a certain snap-in means that it *can* be used. But if you leave this policy turned off, enabling a certain snap-in means that it *cannot* be used.

Figure 9.69 shows a partial list of snap-ins that can be permitted or restricted. There is a separate list of extension snap-ins that can be restricted/permitted (Figure 9.70). Extensions are implemented as dependent modules of snap-ins, but sometimes they do the same things as full-blown snap-ins. For example, the Event Viewer is a snap-in and can exist by itself in a console, as it does in the Event Viewer administrative tool, but it is also implemented as an extension in the Computer Management tool. So you'll need to know whether the thing you want to restrict is a full snap-in or an extension. See Chapter 3 for additional information on MMC consoles and snap-ins.

FIGURE 9.69

Permitted or restricted MMC snap-ins

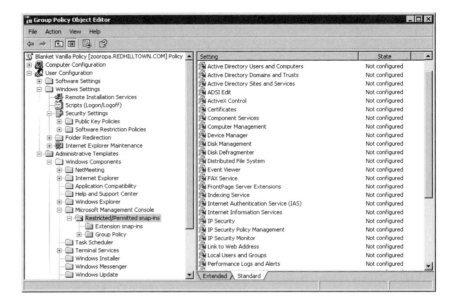

FIGURE 9.70

Permitted or restricted MMC extensions

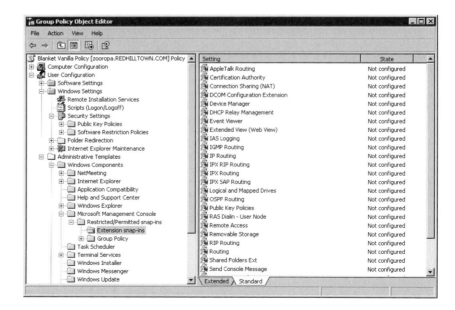

There is a separate folder for the Group Policy snap-in and related extensions (Figure 9.71). These allow you to restrict or permit access to the Group Policy tab in DSA.MSC and the GPO Editor) as well as to different extensions within the tool. This could be configured, for example, to permit delegated admin types to assign software for installation without granting access to the Security Settings node. *Be careful when restricting access to the GP snap-ins*. This policy should be filtered for trusted, responsible (and polite) administrators.

FIGURE 9.71

Setting up Group Policy snap-in restrictions

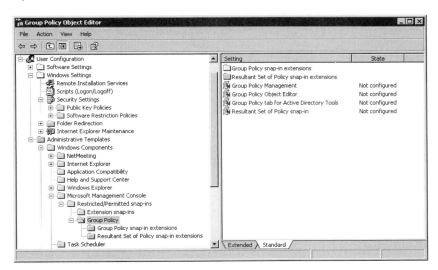

A final note about MMC policies: If the user doesn't have all the necessary components installed on her machine, the MSC file won't work properly and may not even run. There is a very useful policy called Download Missing COM Components, which directs the system to search for those missing components in the Active Directory and download them if they are found. For some reason, this policy is found in User Configuration\Administrative Templates\System and in the corresponding path of Computer Configuration.

Managing Group Policies

In the preceding section, we touched on using Group Policy settings to restrict access to certain MMC snap-ins and extensions, including the Group Policy snap-ins. Let's finish up our discussion of group policies with an exploration of the other Group Policy configuration options that are actually included as group policies (Group Policy policies). Then I'll close with a few select observations and suggestions for configuring and managing group policies in your organization.

GROUP POLICY POLICIES

Policies to control Group Policy are found in Administrative Templates of both the User Configuration and Computer Configuration nodes (Administrative Templates\System\Group Policy). The Computer Configuration node contains most of the policies we'll be discussing. Figures 9.72 and 9.73 show the User Configuration and Computer Configuration options for Group Policy. The following paragraphs summarize the most important configuration options.

FIGURE 9.72

User Configuration settings for Group Policy

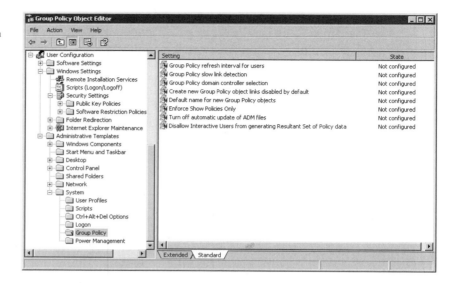

FIGURE 9.73

Computer Configuration settings for Group Policy

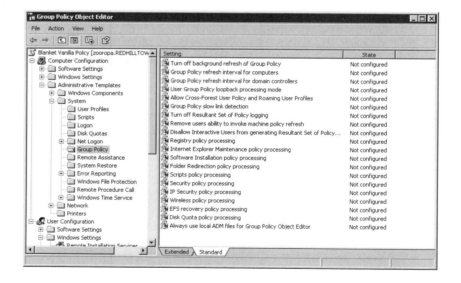

Group Policy Refresh Intervals for Users/Computers/Domain Controllers   These separate policies determine how often GPOs are refreshed in the background while users and computers are working. These parameters permit changes to the default background refresh intervals and tweaking of the offset time.

Turn Off Background Refresh of Group Policy   If you enable this setting, policies will only be refreshed at system startup and user logon. This might be useful for performance reasons, since having 1500 computers refreshing policies every 90 minutes could cause congestion on an Ethernet.

Policy Processing Options   These policies, with names such as Registry Policy Processing and Folder Redirection Policy Processing, are available to customize the behavior of the different GPO components. Each policy (see Figure 9.74 for an example) presents at least two of the following three options:

> **Allow Processing Across a Slow Network Connection**   For slow connections, some policies can be turned off to enhance performance (you can define what a "slow link" is by using the Group Policy Slow Link Detection setting). Security settings and Registry policy processing will always apply, however, and cannot be turned off.
>
> **Do Not Apply During Periodic Background Processing**   Specify which components will be refreshed periodically. Software installation and folder redirection policies will never be refreshed while a user is logged in, so the option is not available for them.
>
> **Process Even If the Group Policy Objects Have Not Changed**   To conserve network and system resources, GPOs are, by default, not refreshed if there have been no changes. To increase security, however, and guard against a user's changing a policy setting, enable the policy to ensure that all settings are reapplied at each refresh interval. Please note that enabling this policy may cause noticeable performance degradation.

FIGURE 9.74

Scripts policy processing options

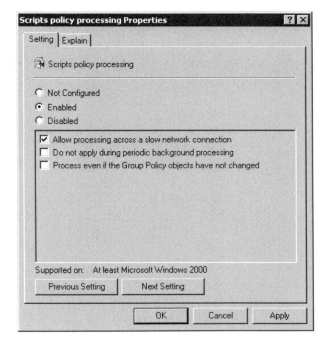

When you want *user* **settings on a particular** *machine***: loopback processing mode**   By default, user policies are processed after Computer Configuration policies, and user policies will take precedence if there are conflicts. Also by default, users receive their policy regardless of the machine they use to log in. Sometimes this is not appropriate and policies need to be applied according to the computer's policy objects instead ("loopback processing"). For example, if I log in to a server to do administration, it's not appropriate for my office productivity applications to start installing themselves. Another example of when you would want computer policies to override user policies is if you want to apply more stringent policies for machines that are exposed to the anonymous public (machines in libraries, university computer labs, or kiosks in shopping malls and tourist attractions, for instance). Two modes are used to control this behavior (see Figure 9.75): Merge mode and Replace mode.

Merge mode   Processes user policies first, then computer policies. Computer policies will therefore override conflicting user policies.

Replace mode   Disregards user policies and processes only computer policies.

FIGURE 9.75

User Group Policy loopback processing mode policy

GROUP POLICY OVER SLOW LINKS

Group Policy still works over slow links such as dial-up connections. Even better, it's applied whether users log in using Dial-Up Networking or whether they log in with cached credentials and then initiate a connection. However, application of Group Policy over slow links can pose performance issues, so there are also policy settings to define a slow link and to define how policies are applied over a detected slow link.

The default definition of a slow link, as far as group policies are concerned, is anything under 500 kilobits per second. The system performs a test using the Ping utility to determine the speed of the connection. If the Ping response time is under 2000 milliseconds, the connection is fast. You can change the definition of a slow link, however. This policy setting, called Group Policy Slow Link Detection, is available in both the User Configuration and Computer Configuration, under `Administrative Templates\System\Group Policy` (see Figure 9.76 for the properties page of the policy). To change the default parameter, enter a number in Kbps or enter 0 to disable slow-link detection altogether. If you disable slow-link detection, all policies will be applied regardless of the connection speed.

FIGURE 9.76

Group Policy's slow-link detection properties

As I mentioned in the preceding section, policy processing settings for individual policy components (these have names such as Folder Redirection Policy Processing and are found in the same path as the Slow Link Detection setting, under `Computer Configuration\Administrative Templates\ System\Group Policy`) allow you to specify whether a portion of the policy object will be processed over a slow-link connection. Again, this is not an option for Registry-based policies or for security settings; these will always be processed, even over slow links. The other modules will not be applied over slow links by default.

To have logon scripts run over slow links, for example, open the policy called Scripts Policy Processing. Enable the policy and check the box beside Allow Processing Across a Slow Network Connection (shown back in Figure 9.74). Click OK and the policy is set. Repeat as necessary for the other policy processing entries.

Troubleshooting Group Policies

In case it's not clear by now, group policies are powerful...and also complex. And they can be kind of opaque—sometimes you create a bunch of policies on a domain controller that you intend to control some Desktop, then restart the Desktop, log in, and wait to see the effects of the new policies...but nothing happens.

Windows Server 2003 now includes a couple of decent tools to assist you in troubleshooting group policy issues. The Resultant Set of Policy (RSOP) snap-in and console tool provides a graphical interface, and GPRESULT.EXE performs equivalent functions from the command line. GPOTOOL.EXE is a Windows 2000 Resource Kit tool, and it looks for inconsistencies between GPOs that are stored on domain controllers. This little utility can help you identify replication issues are causing a problem with group policy application.

THE RESULTANT SET OF POLICY (RSOP) TOOL

Troubleshooting group policies has been, for administrators, a major obstacle to complete control and domination of the network environment. The problem was our inability to view the cumulative policy settings that were in effect for a user or computer. This little capability to display actual policy settings, referred to as the Resultant Set of Policy (RSOP), is built into Windows Server and XP Professional systems. Although RSOP is not supported on Windows 2000 systems, even if you can't see the actual RSOP data, you can run a "what if" scenario using RSOP on a server, and make an educated guess about the problem. Without RSOP, you have to look at the properties of each site, domain, and OU to see which policies and containers are linked. Then you must view the ACLs and WMI info to see if there's any filtering, and check out the disabled, Block Policy Inheritance, and No Override options. Finally, you need to view the settings of the policies in question before you can get to the bottom of things. You'll need to take notes. Personally, I prefer the RSOP tool.

RSOP is a query tool that can retrieve information from individual XP and Server 2003 systems about which policies were applied in what order and with what precedence. When RSOP is retrieving actual information from a system about applied policies, it's running in *logging mode*. RSOP logging mode works by using WMI to create a database called the Common Information Management Object Model (or CIMOM) database, which contains the group policy logging information. When a computer logs on to a network and group policies are applied, the settings and changes are writing to the CIMOM database. It can also run in *planning mode*, where you create a "what if" scenario and manipulate different factors in the group policy application results.

RSOP logging and planning queries can be run for individual users and computers. For sites, domains, and OUs, you can only run planning queries. Apparently Server 2003 doesn't have a place or capability to store a CIMOM database for sites, domains, and OUs. You cannot run RSOP queries for members of a security group. Remember, policies don't apply to security groups.

You can create and run RSOP queries directly from Active Directory Users and Computers, Active Directory Sites and Services (for site-level RSOP queries), or by loading the RSOP snap-in. In my example, I'll use DSA.MSC as my starting point. I have three different policies in effect in my REDHILLTOWN.COM domain. The Default Domain Policy applies at the domain level, the Default Domain Controllers Policy applies to domain controllers (unless you remove them from the Domain Controllers container!), and my Blanket Vanilla Policy applies only to the Brunswick OU.

My users are not receiving the Desktop restrictions I specified for them, and I'd like to know why. Let's run RSOP in logging mode to see what policies are applying to user Paul Hewson (phewson) when he logs on to his XP computer named ANGEL. From within DSA.MSC I find the icon for user Paul Hewson and right-click it to open the context menu. I select All Tasks\Resultant Set of Policy (Logging), as shown in Figure 9.77. The RSOP Wizard starts and asks what computer and user I want to use for the RSOP query. I tell it to use REDHILLTOWN\Angel as the computer, but it's already selected phewson as the user for me. If you haven't already figured this out, you can only run a logging mode query against a user who has actually logged on at that machine. To run a query involving a new user who has never logged on, I have to use planning mode. If you are only interested in seeing user RSOP settings, you can check a box to not display the computer policy settings (or vice versa, depending on the context). Once I've made my user and computer selections, the wizard displays my choices (see Figure 9.78), and I click Next to start the query. When the wizard is done gathering information, I click Finish to close it. An RSOP console opens in a new MMC window (shown in Figure 9.79). It looks very much like a Group Policy Editor window, except that the root of the console displays the name of the query instead of the name of a policy.

FIGURE 9.77

Start the RSOP Wizard from DSA.MSC

FIGURE 9.78

RSOP Wizard selections

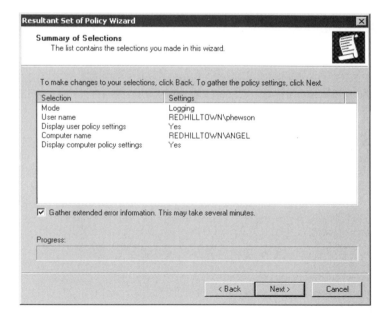

FIGURE 9.79

The RSOP
results console

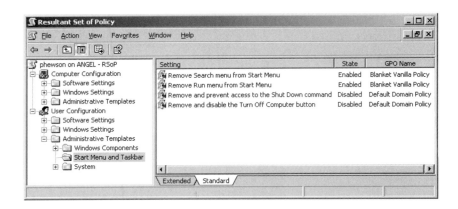

If RSOP encountered any warnings or errors while running the query, a yellow flag or a red X will appear over the User or Computer Configuration nodes. To see details of warnings and errors generated while running the RSOP query, right-click the User or Computer Configuration node, choose Properties, and then go to the Error Information tab. The General tab (see Figure 9.80) shows the GPOs that were applied to the computer (or user, as the case may be). The GPOs will display in order, with the last policy applied at the top of the list. In Figure 9.80, you can see that the local policy applied, then the Default Domain policy, and then the Blanket Vanilla Policy had its turn. By enabling the option to display all GPOs and filtering status, you can also see whether any filtering affected the application of these group policy objects. It's a little counter-intuitive, but "applied" means that a filter did not cause the policy to be excused. If it looks like a security filter is the problem, use the handy Security button to view the ACLs on a selected GPO. The Edit button will open the GPO Editor for the policy selected from the list.

Back in the console window, I scroll down to find the problem settings. A nice thing about the RSOP console is that you don't have to look through a trillion undefined settings to see the applied policies. Although you do have to drill down through the tree structure, you should only see the specific settings that were applied by one of the policies in the details pane. Now glance back at Figure 9.79 for a moment. Notice the Start Menu and Taskbar settings in the User Configuration node. Two of the settings were defined by the Blanket Vanilla Policy and two were defined by the default domain policy. My user Paul was complaining that Run and Search were missing from his Start menu, even though the default domain policy explicitly enabled these options. But if the Blanket Vanilla policy removes Run and Search, then it wins, because OU GPOs take precedence over domain-level GPOs. Just to confirm this, I click the Remove Run Menu setting and go to the Precedence tab (Figure 9.81). Just as I suspected, the Default Domain Policy specifically enabled Run on the Start menu, but then the Blanket Vanilla Policy came along and disabled it.

Now that I think I've found the problem, I'll make the appropriate changes and refresh the query to see if the results are different. First I put Paul into a security group with deny permission for Apply Group Policy, thus excusing him completely from the draconian Blanket Vanilla Policy. Then I right-click the query name at the root of the console tree and choose Refresh Query from the context menu. But nothing's changed. Doh! Remember, the query is taking actual logging information from the computer! I either have to log Paul off the workstation and back on again, or wait for the group policy refresh interval, which means Paul will know if it worked before I will. What good is that? Alternately, I can run a query from DSA.MSC in planning mode to see if the policy is reversed.

FIGURE 9.80

The General tab

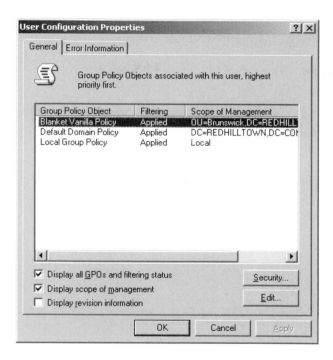

FIGURE 9.81

The RSOP Precedence tab for a GPO setting

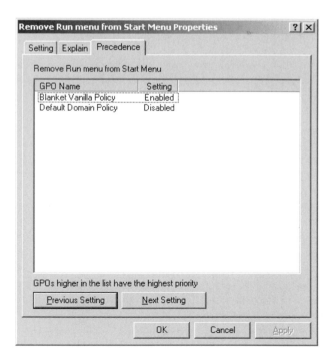

Because it simulates settings and circumstances for group policy results, the planning mode version of the wizard has a lot more options than the logging mode version. You can simulate the effects of loopback processing, a slow network connection, different security group memberships, or WMI filters. Or, if you only want to run a query against a selected user and computer, just choose the option to skip to the final page of the wizard (see Figure 9.82).

FIGURE 9.82

The RSOP Wizard in planning mode

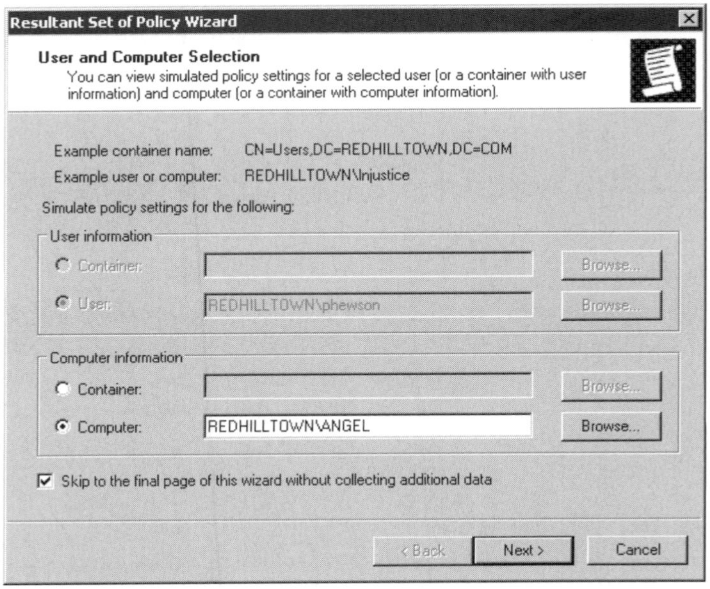

Using the RSOP.MSC tool is not much different from invoking it from DSA.MSC, except that when you open it, it automatically runs a query using the current username and local machine. If that's what you want, fine. If not, you'll need to right-click the query name at the root of the console tree or pull down the Action menu and choose Change Query. This invokes the Logging Mode Wizard, and you can specify a computer and username to use. Apparently, you cannot invoke the Planning Mode Wizard from the RSOP.MSC tool. You can run RSOP in planning mode if you use the snap-in, though.

To use the RSOP snap-in, open an instance of MMC.EXE in author mode and choose Add/Remove Snap-in from the File menu. Add the Resultant Set of Policy to the console. Pull down the Action Menu or right-click the RSOP node in the console root and choose Generate RSOP Data. The RSOP Wizard offers you a choice of logging mode or planning mode before asking you for all of the other usual information. Once a query is created, it can be changed or refreshed, but you can't change it over to the other mode. If you want to create a console for running queries, load more than one instance of the RSOP snap-in into the MMC. For one node, choose to generate a query in logging mode. Choose planning mode for the other one. Save your console, and now you have a placeholder for a logging mode query and a planning mode query. You can change the queries as often as you like. Alternately, you can create several queries and save them all. When you make changes, just refresh the queries to evaluate the ripple effects.

As you can see, the RSOP tool will soon be a valuable asset in the Group Policy administrator's toolkit. The ability to see what policies are in effect, where they came from, and how they are being filtered makes all the difference in the world. Now administrators can actually start using group policies, instead of just admiring them from a safe distance.

GPRESULT

GPRESULT.EXE is an RSOP tool that complements the RSOP snap-in by adding command-line and batch file capabilities to the RSOP arsenal. Run without arguments or options, GPRESULT will generate the following RSOP information for the current user at the local machine:

- The DC that the workstation got the policies from
- When the policies applied
- Which policies applied
- Which policies were not applied due to filtering
- Group memberships
- User rights information (if used in verbose mode)

To generate RSOP information for a remote user on a remote machine, use the /S *systemname* and /USER *username* arguments. For instance, to get RSOP information on the remote workstation OCTOBER for the user phewson, type: gpresult /S OCTOBER /USER phewson. The targeted remote system must be running Windows XP or Server 2003, though. GPRESULT doesn't work remotely on Windows 2000 systems.

You can get more detailed information with options:

- /V says to give more verbose information: gpresult /V.
- /Z says to give even *more* information; it is the "Zuper-verbose" option: gpresult /Z.
- If you know that you're zeroing in on just a machine policy, add /SCOPE MACHINE; if you're only interested in user policies, add /SCOPE USER. So, for example, to get the maximum information about the user policies applied to this system, add gpresult /Z /SCOPE USER. It's also a simple matter to generate a report by redirecting the output of the command to a text file:

```
gpresult /S OCTOBER /USER phewson /Z >gpinfo.txt
```

GPOTOOL

Sounds like the Windows 2000 Resource Kit's only Irish program, doesn't it? GPOTOOL.EXE checks all of your group policies to ensure that they are "whole." Group Policies exist in two parts: First, there is a text file in Sysvol for each policy, which is called the Group Policy Template (GPT), and second, each policy shows up as a record in the Active Directory called the Group Policy Container (GPC). If one replicates and the other one does not, then the policy won't work.

GPOTOOL checks each policy and ensures that it has replicated both in the GPC and GPT. But GPOTOOL has one annoying feature, in fact, a feature shared by many GP tools: it doesn't refer to policies by their English name or "friendly name," as Microsoft calls it. Instead, it reports on policies by their globally unique ID (GUID), a scary-looking hexadecimal string. You can look up a GUID's friendly name with some techniques outlined in a Knowledge Base article (Q216359) or with this script:

```
set RootDSE = GetObject("LDAP://RootDSE")
Domain = RootDSE.get("DefaultNamingContext")
```

```
wscript.echo "The domain name is: " & domain & vbCrLf
Set GPCContainer = GetObject("LDAP://cn=Policies,cn=System," & domain)
For Each object in GPCContainer
   wscript.echo "Friendly name: " & object.displayname
   wscript.echo "Container GUID: " & object.guid
   wscript.echo vbCrLf
Next
```

(That's from the book *Windows 2000: Group Policy, Profiles, and IntelliMirror*, ISBN 0-7821-2881-5, by Jeremy Moskowitz, from Sybex.) You make the script work by opening Notepad and typing those lines into Notepad. Save the file as c:\seepols.vbs, ensuring that Notepad doesn't tack on an extra .txt. Then open a command prompt and type **cscript c:\seepols.vbs** and you'll get a list of all policies and their GUIDs and friendly names.

REGISTRY KEYS TO REVEAL POLICIES

Thankfully, the RSOP tool makes it much simpler to find and resolve issues with group policy application. However, if you want to take the geekiest approach possible to troubleshooting, the Registry can also reveal policies. It actually keeps a record of what policies applied to your computer and your account in HKEY_LOCAL_MACHINE\Software\Microsoft\Windows\CurrentVersion\Group Policy\History for the machine settings and HKEY_CURRENT_USER\Software\Microsoft\Windows\CurrentVersion\Group Policy\History for user settings. You can also enlist the Registry's aid in logging GP information with a couple of keys.

In HKEY_LOCAL_MACHINE\Software\Microsoft\Windows NT\CurrentVersion, create a completely new key—not a value entry, a key—named Diagnostics. In that new key, create a value entry Run-DiagnosticLoggingGroupPolicy of type REG_DWORD and set it to 1. Reboot the computer. You'll get a tremendous amount of information about what group policies applied to this computer. (Turn it off when you no longer need it, or you'll gain new skills, like learning how to make the Event Log larger and how to clear it. Those policies can be a bit voluble!)

USERENV.DLL is a DLL that drives much of group policies as well as handles your roaming profiles. It reveals some of what it's doing with a Registry change: Go to HKEY_LOCAL_MACHINE\SOFTWARE\Microsoft\Windows NT\CurrentVersion\Winlogon and create a new entry UserenvDebugLevel and set it to 1. You'll get an ASCII log file in WINNT\Debug\UserMode\userenv.log. It's a log file, so it doesn't reset itself with every reboot; if you're about to do some troubleshooting, then go delete or rename any existing userenv.logs, or you'll make the job of picking through its cryptic output even harder.

TROUBLESHOOTING 101: KEEP IT SIMPLE

I predict that, even with the RSOP tool, working with group policies will not be a walk in the park for most. Here are a few suggestions to help minimize troubleshooting time:

◆ Keep your policy strategy simple. Group users and computers together in OUs if possible, and apply policy at the highest level possible. Avoid having multiple GPOs with conflicting policies that apply to the same recipients. Minimize the use of No Override and Block Policy Inheritance.

◆ Document your group policies strategy. You may want to visually depict your policy structure and put it on the wall, like your network topology diagrams. That way, when a problem arises, you can consult the diagram to see what's going on before you go fishing.

♦ Test those group policies before deployment! This is absolutely essential to conserve your help desk resources and ensure that applications and system services continue to run properly.

Coming Attractions: The Group Policy Management Console

You probably noticed that it takes several different tools to manage group policies. Microsoft is planning the release of a tool, called the Group Policy Management Console (GPMC) that will simplify management of group policies by providing a single interface to all of its functions. It should be available as a free download shortly after Windows Server 2003 hits the shelves. GPMC can be used to manage Windows 2000 and Server Active Directory domains, plus it adds some much needed management features:

♦ Backup and restore of GPOs

♦ Import/export and copy/paste of GPOs and WMI filters

♦ HTML reporting

♦ RSOP information

The tool itself is an MMC snap-in which can only run on a Windows Server 2003 system or Windows XP Professional Service Pack 1 with an additional post-SP1 hotfix (QFE Q326469). Once you install the GPMC snap-in, it replaces the Group Policy tab in the properties of the site, domain, and OU (in DSA.MSC and DSSITE.MSC). Well, actually the Group Policy tab is replaced by a tab with a button to open GPMC (see Figure 9.83).

FIGURE 9.83

GPMC replaces the Group Policy tab in DSA.MSC

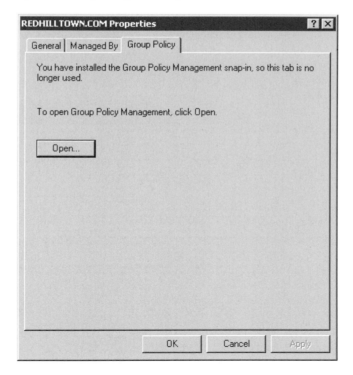

Figure 9.84 shows the GPMC for the REDHILLTOWN.COM forest. The site, domain, and OU hierarchy is shown in the left pane, with separate nodes for Group Policy objects and WMI filters. Group Policy Modeling is what they are calling RSOP planning mode, and Group Policy Results is another name for RSOP logging mode. Select a policy object in the console tree to view its properties in the details pane on the right. The Scope tab has most of the useful information, as you can see in Figure 9.84; it contains information on links, security filters, and WMI filters. The Details tab includes timestamp and version information, and the option to disable either the user or computer configuration settings. The Settings tab is not yet functional, but the final version is supposed to display an HTML-based read-only view of the GPO policy settings. The Delegation tab is the entire ACL for the GPO.

FIGURE 9.84

The Group Policy Management console

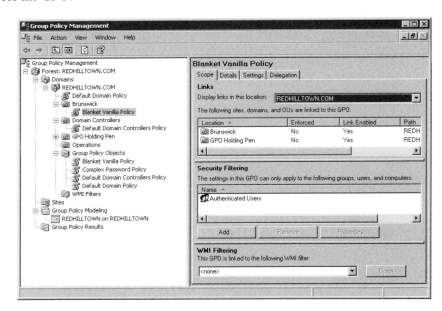

GPMC is still missing a few features, like reporting, and you have to actually open the GPO Editor (using a link) to see the policy object's individual settings, but it does provide a sort of one-stop shopping experience in a busy little MMC console.

A Closing Thought or Two on Group Policy

In the last few sections, I have discussed the concepts of group policies, including local policies. We have created a sample group policy and seen how to turn on the various settings, like No Override and Block Policy Inheritance. We have looked at filtering policies for security groups and delegating policy administration to others. We have explored many of the actual policy settings, including administrative templates for Desktop control, security settings, folder redirection, MMC management, even Group Policy policies. But before you close this chapter and begin to configure group policies on your network, you want to be very aware that group policies affect network and system performance.

The more group policies there are to apply, the longer the logon time. Each time a user logs in (or a computer is restarted), each of the GPOs associated with the user's or computer's containers (SDOUs) is read and applied. This can slow down logons considerably, and users may start calling the help desk to ask, "What's wrong with the network?" Therefore, you should keep the number of policies to a minimum. Another thing that can bog down a machine or a network is the background refresh rate. Refresh your policies too often and you'll see a hit because the machine is always busy asking for policy changes. Think about disabling the background refreshes altogether unless you're worried about users changing their settings to escape policies. With the background refresh disabled, user and computer policies are only reapplied at logon and startup, respectively. The worst thing you could do for performance is have a bunch of different policies in effect and tell Group Policy to reapply at each refresh interval even if there are no changes. Another way to streamline GPO processing is to avoid assigning GPOs from different domains. Just because you can do it doesn't mean it's a good idea.

Working with Roaming User Profiles

As you use Windows—any version of Windows—and applications, you end up customizing your Desktop and the applications on your Desktop to your particular preferences. Things like your choice of Desktop fonts and color, how an application should start up (e.g., minimized or windowed), and how you want the application to work are all part of something called your *user profile*. You've got one, whether you want it or not, stored on your computer's local hard disk.

But as you move from computer to computer in an organization, it'd be nice to have those settings follow you around. Or, even if you don't use more than one workstation, it'd be nice to be able to wipe that workstation's hard disk clean, reinstall the OS and applications from scratch, and not lose your Desktop and applications settings. You can accomplish that with a variation on a user profile: a *roaming* profile. Not every version of Windows supports roaming user profiles, but NT 3.x and later do. (Although, truthfully, they weren't of much value until NT 4.) In this section, you'll see how they work and what you can do with them.

NOTE *Let me stress that NT 4, Windows 2000, XP, and Server 2003 all handle profiles almost identically. Even though this discussion uses XP Professional clients for examples, everything will work the same way if you're supporting Windows 2000 or NT 4 workstations. The main difference is the name of the profile directory. As you'll learn in a page or two, for some incomprehensible reason, Microsoft moved profiles from* \WINNT\PROFILES *in NT 4 to* Documents and Settings *in Windows 2000 and XP. Just make that substitution in your head and you'll be able to apply all of this to NT workstations.*

I said that these settings may be configured by a user who wishes to personalize her Desktop, but they can also be set by a system administrator responsible for configuring Desktops, or by a combination of the two. In other words, a user may create shortcuts and select a screen saver, while an administrator may configure special program groups for the user's Desktop. However, the two are not mutually exclusive. By default, every user on an NT, Windows 2000, or XP machine (except members of the Guests group) keeps a local profile directory that the system names after the user ID. Guests are not allowed to keep local profiles.

User profiles can be implemented in several different ways, according to the needs of your organization. In situations where a network-based solution is not feasible or not desirable, there are still several options to keep in mind:

Local profiles Users keep only local profiles and create and configure these profiles themselves. User settings don't follow a user around in this case, and a wiped-and-rebuilt workstation won't keep its settings.

Preconfigured default user profile Users keep only local profiles, but an administrator pre-configures a "magic," locally stored user profile called the "default" user profile. Anyone who logs onto this system gets that default user profile as a jumping-off point for his or her personal user profile.

Preconfigured local profiles Users keep only local profiles, but an administrator preconfigures all or part of the local user profiles. (This can be labor intensive.)

Enabling roaming user profiles, which are of course networked, can exploit the centralizing power of networks and opens up four more possibilities:

Roaming profiles Add a profile path to the user's account information to automatically create and maintain a copy of the user profile in a network location (the user can configure her own profile).

Preconfigured roaming profiles Add a user profile path to the user's account information and copy a preconfigured profile to the network location specified (the user can make changes to her profile, but the administrator creates the initial state of her profile).

Network default user profiles Create a default user profile and copy it to the NETLOGON share of the authenticating domain controller(s). This will hand out default profiles to all new users (users can make changes to their profiles). This option can be used in conjunction with roaming or local profiles.

Mandatory profiles Add a user profile path to the user account, copy a preconfigured profile to that path, and use special filename and directory name extensions to specify that this is a mandatory profile. The user must use the profile and cannot make any changes. A mandatory profile can be shared by a group of users.

Anatomy of a User Profile

A local user profile is created automatically by the system the first time a user logs in to a NT, Windows 2000, or XP machine. This profile directory is located in %SYSTEMROOT%\PROFILES on an NT 4 machine or a Windows 2000 machine that was upgraded in-place from NT 4. On a cleanly installed Windows 2000, XP, or Server 2003 system, the profiles are stored in a directory called Documents and Settings on the same drive as the operating system. (You can change that location if you like, but you've got to do it at setup time by scripting the install.) Figure 9.85 shows the contents of the Documents and Settings directory on an XP Professional system.

The Documents and Settings directory contains a profile for every user who logs in to the machine (in this case, user lnjustice and the user Administrator), as well as a directory called All Users and one called Default User. The All Users directory stores common program groups (programs available to all users on a specific machine) and shortcuts that will appear on every user's Desktop on that machine. For example, the Administrative Tools program group is stored in the All Users folder (under Start Menu/Programs), so the programs listed in this group will be made available to anyone logging in to the machine. The Default User folder, which is hidden by default, exists because the operating system uses it as a template for creating individual profiles for new users. Figure 9.86 shows the contents of an individual user profile directory, C:\Documents and Settings\larry.

FIGURE 9.85

Documents and Settings directory

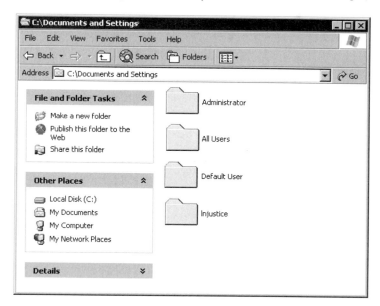

FIGURE 9.86

An individual profile directory

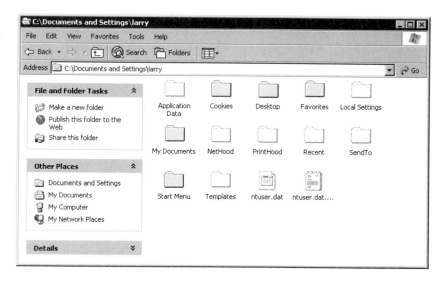

Each user's profile contains several folders with links to various Desktop items plus the `NTUSER.DAT` file, which contains Registry configuration settings for that user. `NTUSER.DAT.LOG` is a transaction log file that exists to protect `NTUSER.DAT` while changes are being flushed to disk (you won't find an `NTUSER.DAT.LOG` for the `Default User` profile directory because it is a template). The other folders store information on the contents of the user's Desktop and Start menu items, including shortcuts and program groups. Remember that a user's profile also includes the common program groups and shortcuts indicated in the `All Users` folder. Table 9.5 describes the various folders in a user profile on a Windows XP Professional system.

TABLE 9.5: FOLDERS IN A USER PROFILE

FOLDER	EXPLANATION
Application Data*	A place for applications to store user-specific information.
Desktop	Any file, folder, or shortcut in this folder will appear directly on the user's Desktop.
Cookies	Internet Explorer cookies.
Favorites	Shortcuts to favorite Web sites and bookmarks can be stored here.
Local Settings*	A part of a profile that does *not* roam, even if you make the profile roam. A place for things like temporary files, which can be large and disk-hungry but don't have a reason to network.
NetHood*	Shortcuts placed here will appear in Network Neighborhood.
My Documents or Personal	You'll see a Personal folder on NT 4 systems, My Documents on later systems. It's the place where Microsoft recommends that applications save user data, so that your documents are all in one place. You can change the location of My Documents through policies, so don't be alarmed if you have a profile that doesn't have a My Documents.
PrintHood*	Shortcuts placed here will appear in the Printers folder.
Recent*	Shortcuts to recently used files are stored here. Linked to Documents in the Start menu. Windows XP calls this folder My Recent Documents on the Start menu.
SendTo*	The Send To menu is a list of options that appears on the context menu of items on your Desktop and in Explorer. Place additional shortcuts to apps, printers, and folders here to quickly copy an item to a predefined place, to open a file within a specific application (such as Notepad), or even to print a file.
Start Menu	Contains personal program groups and shortcuts to program items.
Templates*	Contains shortcuts to templates created by applications such as PowerPoint and Word.

*These folders are hidden by default in Windows 2000 and XP. NT also hides the NetHood, PrintHood, Recent, and Templates folders.

In addition to the folders, a user profile includes numerous user-definable settings for Windows Explorer (View All Files and Display Full Path in the Title Bar); the Taskbar (Auto Hide and Show Clock); Control Panel (command prompt, mouse, and display preferences); and Accessories (Calculator, Clock, and the Address Book). Network printers, drive connections, and Help topic Favorites are also saved in the user profile. Virtually any application written for Windows NT–based systems can remember user-specific settings. These settings, which are not directly linked to Desktop items, are contained in the NTUSER.DAT file.

NTUSER.DAT is the Registry part of a user profile. It corresponds to the HKEY_ CURRENT_USER subtree in the Registry Editor (REGEDT32.EXE).

Configuring Your Own User Profile

Before you configure user profiles on your network, you will need to master techniques for configuring your own profile. You can then use these skills to configure profiles for other users.

The NTUSER.DAT file for the user currently logged in may be edited using a Registry editing tool such as REGEDT32.EXE or REGEDIT.EXE, although these tools are not particularly intuitive (an understatement if I have ever heard one). The System Policy Editor (POLEDIT.EXE), a tool that originated in Windows 95 for creating system policies (which are covered in an appendix on the CD, in case you've got Windows 9x or NT 4 Desktops to worry about), is more user-friendly and can be used to directly edit several selected settings in the local Registry. The System Policy Editor comes with NT Server and all flavors of Windows 2000, but for some reason it's not installed with XP or Windows Server by default. It's not necessary, though, just convenient.

The System Policy Editor is a "selective" Registry editor and is easier to use, as it does not require any knowledge of Registry syntax or structure. While this application offers several options that are not available in the graphical interface, very little would be of interest to normal users setting up their own profiles, even if they have access to the application. Even though the System Policy Editor can be used to edit the machine's local Registry, as shown in Figure 9.87, most of the Local User options focus on restricting a user's Desktop. Joe User probably would not do that to himself. However, this little piece of information will come in handy when *you* want to restrict other users' Desktops.

FIGURE 9.87

Using the Windows 2000 System Policy Editor to change the local Registry

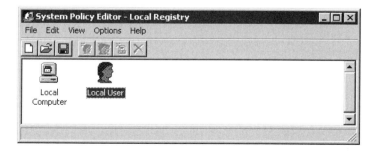

Actually, the best way to configure the NTUSER.DAT part of your profile is simply to configure your Desktop. By using the applets in the graphical interface to change your color scheme, map network drives, and connect to printers, you are making changes to NTUSER.DAT. Use a Registry editor only when you want to make a change that is not offered in the Control Panel. For example, under NT 3.51, the only way to change the icon title font, size, and style was in the Registry, under

HKEY_CURRENT_USER\CONTROL PANEL\DESKTOP. In NT 4, 2000, and XP, however, these and other formerly unavailable options can be adjusted using the Appearance tab in Control Panel/Display.

WARNING *As I've warned you before, you're just asking for trouble if you start playing with your machine's Registry for no good reason. Don't edit the Registry if you can make the changes using the Control Panel.*

To configure the Taskbar and customize your Start menu, right-click the Taskbar and choose Properties. The Taskbar and Start Menu Properties dialog box (shown in Figure 9.88) allows you to customize the appearance of these items.

FIGURE 9.88

Specifying Taskbar options in the Taskbar and Start Menu Properties dialog box

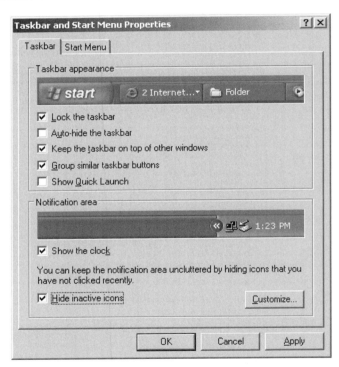

Toggle the check boxes to see how your display will change. Use the options in the Start Menu tab (Figure 9.89) to select a menu style and customize folders. (An NT 4 or Windows 2000 version of this will look a little different.)

If you choose the Classic Start menu and then click Customize, you can add and remove items from the Start menu using the Add and Remove buttons, or click the Advanced button to be taken directly to your Start Menu folder in Explorer. From there, you can add a folder to create a program group and add a program to add a program item. Folders and shortcuts may be added in Explorer or by double-clicking My Computer on your Desktop. Either way, changes to the folders in your profile directory show up right away on your Desktop. You can also create shortcuts and drag them right over your Start menu button to create a shortcut on the Start menu. For XP Professional systems, you can't use the Customize option to add and remove program groups or items from the new XP Start menu, because you don't have to. Just add folders and shortcuts directly to the Start Menu folders or subfolders in Explorer, or right-click an executable and choose Pin to Start Menu.

FIGURE 9.89

Customizing the Start menu in the Taskbar and Start Menu Prop erties dialog box

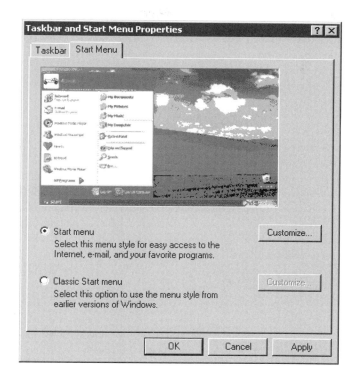

TIP   *Add a few shortcuts to the* SendTo *folder in your profile. If* SendTo *contains shortcuts to your home directory, word processing or spreadsheet applications, and printers, you'll be able to right-click a file to copy it to your home directory, open it in Word, or even print it!*

Birth of a Local Profile

The next step in mastering user profiles is to understand how Windows XP Professional (or Windows 2000 or NT) creates a user profile and how a user obtains one. In short, when a user (we're calling him Larry) logs in for the first time, there is no profile for him yet. So the system creates a new profile folder for him. The Default User profile information is copied to that new directory. This information, along with the shortcuts and program items found in the All Users folder, is then loaded to create Larry's working profile. The new profile now exists in a folder named after the user in the same path as the Default User profile directory, \Documents and Settings\Larry. (Again, if this were an NT 4 workstation, the local profile would instead be located in \Winnt\PROFILES\Larry. After the system creates the local profile, any user-specific changes made by Larry, to elements such as Desktop color schemes, shortcuts, persistent network connections, or personal program groups, will be saved to Larry's profile.

NOTE *Contents of the* All Users *folder are not copied to a user's profile directory; the system checks the contents when the user logs on and combines the information in the user's profile directory with the information in the* All Users *folder.*

By the way, if that profile is created on an NTFS partition, Larry will be the *owner* of the profile because he created it. Permissions will be set to allow him to modify his own profile. SYSTEM and Administrators will also have full access to the profile. The system sets the permissions like so:

- SYSTEM gets Full Control.
- The local Administrators group gets Full Control.
- The user's account gets Full Control.
- Other users will be denied access to Larry's profile folder.

Even if an individual profile is created on a FAT partition, the system sets Registry key permissions on the NTUSER.DAT file to prevent other users from using or modifying the Registry hive file. (For more information about ownership and permissions, see Chapter 11.)

If the All Users folder is created on an NTFS partition when the system is installed, only users who are members of the local Administrators group may make changes to the folder.

So, to summarize: If you log onto a workstation either with a local or domain account and you don't have a roaming profile, then the workstation needs to find one for you *somewhere*. First, the workstation looks in its profile directory and, if it finds one for your account, then it uses that one. If there *isn't* one for your account, then the workstation needs to create one and uses the "template" profile stored in Default User.

That's how *local* profiles work. Now let's see how things change when we network the profiles, as "roaming" profiles.

Roaming Profile Basics

A network administrator might choose to specify a path on the network to store a user profile. A profile is a *roaming profile* (rather than a local profile) when the user's account information indicates a profile path, even if that path is local. In the simplest of scenarios, the administrator has simply created a share on the server, set appropriate permissions on the share (and directories), and indicated in Computer Management/System Tools/Local Users and Groups or Active Directory Users and Computers that a copy of the user's profile should be stored there.

Thus far, we haven't given Larry a roaming profile; so far, he's just created a local profile on the workstation that he uses all the time and that workstation keeps the one and only copy of that profile locally, in C:\Documents and Settings\Larry. (Notice that this applies whether Larry has a local account or a domain account; merely having a domain account doesn't confer a roaming profile. But let's say for the sake of the example that Larry's account is on an Active Directory domain.)

Suppose now that Larry is downstairs in Paul's office and wants to get to the domain. Paul logs off, and Larry logs on. Larry doesn't yet have a roaming profile, and so Paul's computer doesn't have a clue about how Larry likes his system set up, so it creates a new profile for Larry by making a copy of the Default Users directory. That means more work for Larry. We'd like his Desktop settings to follow him around. So we'll give him a roaming profile. Here's how to specify a roaming profile path for a user in two easy steps:

1. Create a shared directory. I like to create a share and name it profiles or PROFILES$ (to hide it from the browse list). Set share-level permissions to Change or Full Control to allow all users

storing profiles to alter their profiles. You do not have to create profile directories for the users. The workstation operating system will create the profile directory for the user and set appropriate permissions.

2. Open Active Directory Users and Computers, navigate to the user account in question, open its properties page, go to the Profile tab, and fill in the path for the user profile directory as shown in Figure 9.90. The figure shows the user's roaming profile located in `\\ZOOROPA\profiles\larry`. `profiles` is the name of the share, not the directory name, so if you created a hidden share for the profiles, as mentioned in step 1, you'll need to use `PROFILES$` instead. Use `%USERNAME%` in place of the username if you are specifying roaming profiles for more than one user account. You may also specify the user profile path as the user's home directory, as shown in Figure 9.91.

FIGURE 9.90

The profile path field on the Profile tab of the user account's properties page

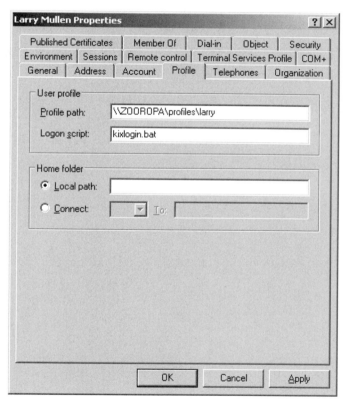

So Larry has logged onto his local system in the past, and his local system has a profile for him. Now that we've specified a profile path, the Active Directory has set aside a place for a roaming profile. But how does AD fill that place—how does it create the user's profile? As it turns out, that can be a bit complex. Let's first consider the case where Larry has been granted a roaming profile, but already has one on his workstation.

FIGURE 9.91

The profile path set to the same location as the user's home directory

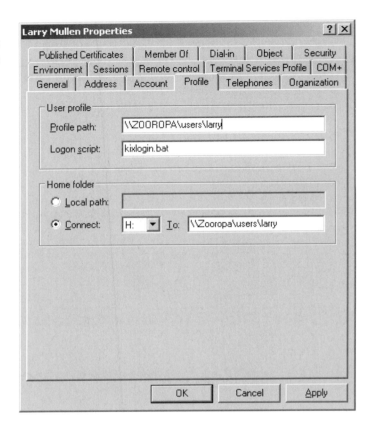

CREATING A ROAMING PROFILE WHEN A LOCAL ONE EXISTS

The next time Larry logs in, the workstation will see that there is a network path specified for the profile. Recall that Larry already has a local profile in his workstation. This appears to pose a problem, however—there is no profile on the server yet, but one does exist on the local machine. So, the workstation simply loads the local profile and creates a directory on the server to store the roaming profile. When Larry logs out, the workstation operating system (NT, 2000, or XP) will copy the local profile directory to the network path. In other words, the OS used the preexisting local profile to create the roaming profile directory on the server. From now on, whenever Larry logs in, the workstation operating system will check to make sure that the profiles still match (using a time stamp) and will load the most recent version. The workstation operating system will save any changes Larry makes to both profiles: the local copy and, when Larry logs out, Larry's profile directory on the server.

Okay, why all this rigamarole about saving the user profile to the local path and to the server? The server is the first option, but by default, the workstation operating system will always keep a local profile folder to ensure that the user can access his profile if the network profile is unavailable. This is also useful with slow network connections.

If the profile directory on the server is unavailable for some reason when Larry logs in (perhaps because the server is down), the workstation operating system will simply let him know this and load the local copy. In that case, the workstation operating system will not attempt to copy changes to the server when Larry logs out. The next time he logs in, the workstation will display another dialog box saying, "Your local profile is more recent than your server profile." Larry can then choose which profile to load. (In case you are wondering, this scenario for Win2K and XP Desktops can be managed with group policies.)

CREATING A ROAMING PROFILE WHEN THERE IS NO LOCAL PROFILE

Next, let's consider what happens if a user logs onto a workstation and a domain for the first time. What if newcomer Adam also has a roaming profile path specified in the Active Directory and he logs in to his workstation for the first time? Like Larry, Adam doesn't have a profile directory on the server at all. Unlike Larry, he has no local profile on the workstation. In this case, the workstation operating system will use the information in `Default User` on the local machine to create a local profile and will also create a profile directory in the network path. Just as with Larry, when Adam logs out, the workstation will copy his local profile, including any changes, into the newly created directory.

Table 9.6 illustrates the order for loading a user profile, given the two scenarios we've discussed.

TABLE 9.6: LOADING A USER PROFILE WHEN THE ROAMING PROFILE IS NOT YET CREATED

SITUATION	WHAT THE WORKSTATION OS DOES
A local profile exists.	The workstation OS loads the local profile and creates a roaming profile directory on the server. Changes to the local profile are updated automatically. When the user logs out, the contents of the local profile directory are copied to the server profile directory.
No local profile exists.	The workstation OS uses the Default User profile to create a local profile. The local profile is updated dynamically. A roaming profile directory is created on the server. When the user logs out, the OS copies the contents of the local profile directory to the server.

NOTE   Although it is possible to specify a roaming profile for a local account on a workstation using the Computer Management tool, it's not really useful unless you are setting up mandatory profiles for the local machine. And it's not really a roaming profile at all in this case, because it cannot be loaded when the user logs in elsewhere. Also, do not expect consistent roaming profile behavior if the user is logging in locally and has a roaming profile path specified on the local machine.

Note that if you log onto more than one kind of Desktop—that is, if you sometimes log on to workstations running NT 4, sometimes ones running XP, and sometimes ones running 2000, and if you log on with a roaming profile, then you'll see some odd behavior. For example, if you have a profile first created on a 2000 workstation and you log onto an NT 4 workstation, then the icons look odd and you'll get a few error messages. It's not the end of the world, but it can be unsettling to the nontechnical user. Or it can just be annoying; for example, when I first set up an XP system on my Active Directory domain, I logged on as my normal domain account, which dragged my profile over to the XP system. XP then set my colors to all of the goofy bright XP colors, giving my Desktop a kind of Playskool look.

For performance reasons, some folders in a user profile are configured never to roam, even if roaming profiles are enabled. These include Local Settings, Temporary Internet Files, History, and the user's Temp Directory by default, but you can configure additional non-roaming folders using REGEDT32.EXE or Group Policies (for Windows 2000, XP, and Server systems). In fact, you can use a combination of roaming profiles with non-roaming folders and folder redirection.

Preconfiguring User Profiles

This idea that people start out from some Default User profile is all well and good, but you'd probably like to gussy that thing up a bit, perhaps customize it to look like a corporate standard or perhaps to simplify the Desktop a bit for your less-techie users or the like. So one way to make things easier for users would be to preconfigure the Default User profile. (It'd be even better to preconfigure one profile that would affect the whole domain, but we'll get there in a minute. For now, let's just see how to make the Default User profile do our bidding on a given workstation.)

To preconfigure the Default User profile, just create a bogus user account, log on as the bogus user, and set up the Desktop and other profile settings just as you want Default User to be. Then log off the bogus user account and log back on as a local administrator. Now you can copy the contents of the newly created profile over the existing contents of the Default User profile on the local machine, using the System applet in Control Panel. On a 2000 or XP system, remember that you must first unhide the Default User folder or set the Explorer folder options to show hidden files and folders.

You can also copy that profile folder to a server location, to implement a preconfigured roaming profile. You can even change the name of the folder and assign appropriate permissions during the process if you use the System applet to perform the copy rather than Explorer or another file management tool. Although a copy from Explorer would work in some scenarios, you would still have to set the directory permissions separately. Also, in certain other procedures regarding user profiles, the operating system needs to know that you are dealing with *profiles* here, not just files and directories. So get into the habit of using the System applet when dealing with user profiles.

Figure 9.92 shows the User Profiles applet on an XP system. To get there, open the System applet, go to the Advanced tab, and click the User Profile Settings button. For Windows 2000 or NT, open the System Applet and select the User Profiles tab to see the same information. Select the profile you have configured (Larry, in my case) and choose Copy To. Specify the path for the copy as shown in Figure 9.93—remember to change the Permitted to Use information, or only the bogus user will be able to load the profile. Give Everyone, Authenticated Users, or some other appropriate group on your network permission to use the profile.

This procedure can be used for several functions, depending on the Copy To path you specify. On the local level, you can copy the customized profile to C:\Documents and Settings\DEFAULT USER to preconfigure profiles for all new users on the workstation who do not already have a roaming profile stored on a server. It's also possible to copy the customized profile to other workstations if you have administrative rights on them. Take advantage of the fact that the system root directory on all of the workstations is shared as ADMIN$. Use the path \\*MACHINENAME*\ADMIN$\Documents and Settings\DEFAULT USER to preconfigure the Default User profile on other workstations.

You can easily overwrite existing user profiles (although it's a good way to make enemies) by typing in **Documents and Settings***username*, or the appropriate UNC path; but again, don't forget to set permissions. You also need permission to overwrite the user's existing profile, so you should be logged on as an administrator for this.

FIGURE 9.92

The User Profiles tab in the System applet

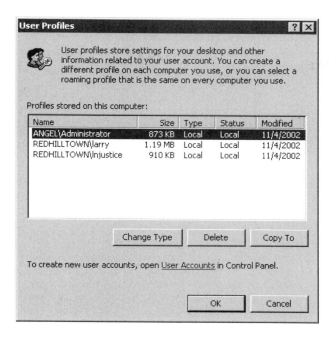

FIGURE 9.93

Copy the profile over Default User

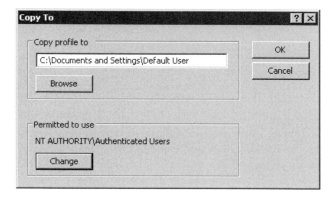

HOW DO I CREATE AND COPY A PRECONFIGURED DEFAULT USER PROFILE?

1. On a Windows XP Professional workstation, create a new user account using Manage Computer\ System Tools\Local Users and Groups, as you learned earlier in this chapter. For this example, I'll call the new user account Dave. Dave doesn't need any particular user rights or group memberships. While you are logged on as an administrator, either unhide the Default User folder in Documents and Settings or tell Explorer to show hidden files.

Continued on next page

HOW DO I CREATE AND COPY A PRECONFIGURED DEFAULT USER PROFILE? *(continued)*

2. Log off and log back in to the workstation as Dave. Windows will create a user profile for Dave using the default.

3. Customize Dave's Desktop. Create any Desktop shortcuts and put those shortcuts into the Start menu. Set up persistent network connections. Using Explorer or by right-clicking the Taskbar and choosing Properties, you can add new program groups or shortcuts to the Start menu folders.

4. When the profile is exactly the way you want it, log out. The system will save the changes in the user's profile directory (\Documents and Settings\Dave). Actually, they are flushed to disk as you make changes to the profile.

5. Log back on to the workstation as a local administrator. Right-click My Computer and choose Properties to get the System applet (also accessed through Control Panel/System). Choose the User Profiles tab. You should see at least a user profile for your administrator account and for Dave. If no one else has ever logged in to the workstation, that's all you will see.

6. Select the template profile from the list, and then choose Copy To. Browse to the location of the target Default User directory, or type in the path. This may be a local path or a network path. The system will create the profile directory where you specify as long as you have permissions to write to that path. Be sure to give Authenticated Users or the Everyone group (or other appropriate users or groups) permission to use the profile; Dave is the only user who has access right now. Click OK to start the copy process. Figures 9.92 and 9.93 show the dialog boxes you will be using in this step.

7. Log off. You're done! When a new user logs on and the system makes a copy of the Default User profile to create a new one for the user, they'll also get all those nice customizations you did for them. Keep in mind, though, that users can still make changes to their own profiles by default.

PRECREATING ROAMING PROFILES

You can set up preconfigured roaming profiles by copying a customized profile to the UNC path you specified in the user account properties. In other words, if Adam has never logged onto a workstation before, then you could precreate a profile for him, copy the profile to the path *MACHINENAME*\ PROFILES\Adam, and specify that path as the user profile path for Adam's domain account.

Preconfigured local profiles may also be set up this way, but you must specify a path in the user's local account information. Do not try to just put the directory into the Documents and Settings directory: NT, 2000, or XP have no way of linking that profile with the new user, so the machine will just create a new directory (for example, Adam001).

PRECREATING A *DEFAULT* ROAMING PROFILE

If you want to precreate roaming profiles for a lot of users, then you don't want to have to put a precreated profile into each user's directory. And you needn't. You can copy the profile to the NETLOGON share on a domain controller to set up a domainwide Default User profile. You see, if a user is logging in to a domain, the machine first looks for a Default User directory in the NETLOGON share of the authenticating domain controller (recall that XP and Win2K provide a NETLOGON share in \WINNT\SYSVOL\sysvol*domainname*\SCRIPTS to support Windows 9*x* and NT clients). Only if no Default User directory is found in the NETLOGON directory does the machine use the local Default User information. If a Default User directory exists in this network path (where logon scripts and system policies are also stored), all new domain users with NT, 2000, or XP workstations will use this directory as the domain-wide Default User template, instead of using the local `Default User` directory. Copy the folders to `\\MACHINENAME\SYSVOL\domainname\Scripts\Default User`. Alternatively, you can save the profile directly to the `NETLOGON` share (`\\MACHINENAME\NETLOGON\Default User`) if you are in the Administrators group (by default, the Everyone group has Read permission only to the share, while the Administrators group has Full Control permission). Be sure to name the directory Default User and grant permissions to Everyone (or another appropriate group) to use the profile. Users will need Read, Execute, and Read List of Folders permissions in order to access the profile.

In any of the scenarios described above, users can still modify their own profiles once they are created. A variation of this procedure is used to set up mandatory profiles; it will be discussed later.

EDITING THE *NTUSER.DAT* HIVE FILE

You can change many user profile settings by editing the contents of the folders or by configuring the Desktop. However, if you want to place restrictions on the preconfigured Default User or roaming profile to protect the system from inexperienced users, you will need to edit the hive file (`NTUSER.DAT`) of the template profile. To do this, you will need a Registry-editing tool.

WARNING   *As always,* do not edit the Registry unless you really know what you're doing. *Editing the Registry can have disastrous consequences: you could ruin your system configuration and have to reinstall your whole operating system. Be careful!*

USING *REGEDT32.EXE*

To edit user profiles using `REGEDT32.EXE`, open `HKEY_USERS`, as shown in Figure 9.94. The hive file for the active profile (the one for the currently logged on user) is the one with the long SID number. The key .DEFAULT is not the Default User hive file, as you might think. That is located in `\Documents and Settings\PROFILES\DEFAULT USER\NTUSER.DAT`. The .DEFAULT hive file is loaded from `C:\WINNT\SYSTEM32\CONFIG\.DEFAULT` and is known as the *system default profile*. Microsoft describes it as the profile in effect when nobody is logged in. This seems to be a dangling chromosome from NT 3.51 profiles, when profiles were nothing more than individual hive files.

FIGURE 9.94

HKEY_USERS subkey

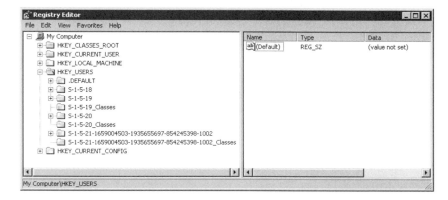

The system default and Default User profiles are independent of each other. That is, changing the color scheme in the Registry for the .DEFAULT hive will not affect the Default User profile hive in Documents and Settings. Otherwise, when I set the system default (.DEFAULT) profile to use some neat (I mean practical and informative) bitmap wallpaper, any user who logged in without an already established profile would also get stuck with my wallpaper.

NOTE *Have you ever wanted to change that default Windows bitmap you see on the screen when nobody is logged in? Well, that bitmap is the wallpaper for the SYSTEM profile (also known as the system default profile). Since SYSTEM is a user (or at least an entity), it makes sense that SYSTEM should have a profile, right? The SYSTEM default profile is the profile in effect when no one is logged in (you see the Ctrl+Alt+Del login dialog box). Simply use a Registry editor such as REGEDT32.EXE or REGEDIT.EXE to specify different wallpaper. The entry is found in HKEY_USERS\ .DEFAULT\CONTROL PANEL\DESKTOP. Edit the value entry for Wallpaper, specifying the full path of the bitmap that tickles your fancy as the value of the string. You will be editing the hive file %SYSTEMROOT%\SYSTEM32\CONFIG\ DEFAULT. Screensavers in effect when no one is logged in can be specified in the same way. This works for NT, Win2K, and XP systems as well.*

You can use REGEDT32 to edit a user profile other than the system default and the profile that is actively loaded. If you aren't doing this on an XP machine, be sure to use REGEDT32—REGEDIT can't do this job! On Windows XP, REGEDT32.EXE and REGEDIT.EXE point to the same program. This upcoming example is from XP, but it works the same in 2000 or NT. And one more point: You don't *have* to do the following Registry hacks to control how a profile gets loaded. System and group policies can handle all of that stuff; look back to the group policies section for more info or read the section on NT 4's system policies on the CD if you're using NT 4 Desktops.

Load the hive file using the Load Hive option from the Registry menu (Figure 9.95). This may be the NTUSER.DAT file from the Default User profile directory or any NTUSER.DAT file; you can browse for it (Figure 9.96). NT will prompt you for a temporary key name (Figure 9.97) and will then load the hive into the Registry Editor, as shown in Figure 9.98. Now make your changes to the Registry settings of the Default User profile. To finish up, select the loaded hive and choose Unload Hive from the Registry menu to save changes and clear the hive from the Registry Editor.

FIGURE 9.95

Loading the hive in REGEDIT.EXE

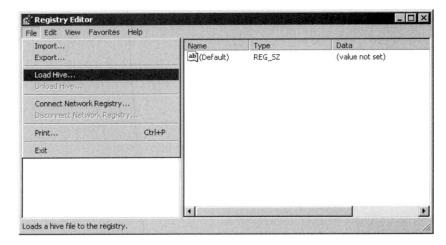

FIGURE 9.96

Browsing to find
the hive file

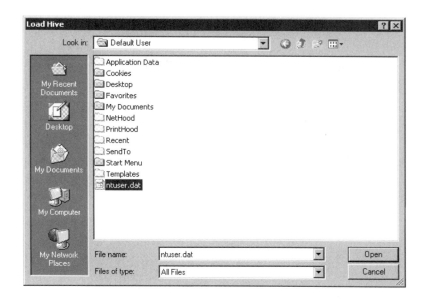

FIGURE 9.97

Assigning a tempo-
rary key name

FIGURE 9.98

The hive is loaded.

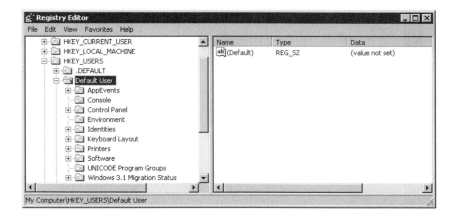

So which changes do you make once the hive is loaded? Ah, that is the real question. You might configure all profiles to wait for logon scripts to execute before starting the user's shell. That way, any drive mappings or environmental variables specified in the logon script will take precedence over those in the user's profile. This entry is called `RunLogonScriptSync` (run logon scripts synchronously)

and is found in HKEY_USERS*KEYNAME*\SOFTWARE\MICROSOFT\WINDOWS NT\CURRENTVERSION\WINLOGON (Figure 9.99). Although I could suggest a couple of other Registry entries to modify, the fact is that REGEDT32.EXE and REGEDIT.EXE are not all that user-friendly. Without spending copious amounts of your time reading Registry documentation (which is not always helpful) and experimenting, you do not know what is possible. You need a GUI Registry Editor. At this point, the System Policy Editor steps back onto the scene.

FIGURE 9.99

The RunLogon-
ScriptSync entry

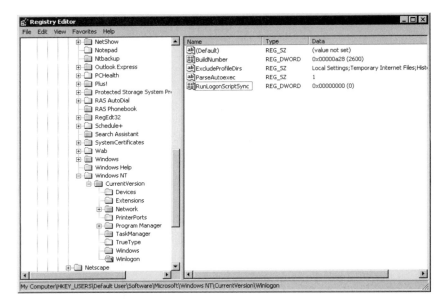

SYSTEM POLICY EDITOR TO THE RESCUE

Instead of trying to hack everything out in REGEDT32.EXE, use group policies Administrative Templates settings to make changes on a Windows 2000, XP, or Server 2003 system. If you are still supporting NT 4 machines, the System Policy Editor (POLEDIT.EXE) can be used to make changes to the current profile.

Run POLEDIT.EXE while logged in as your template user (Larry, in my case). Choose File/Open Registry/Local User, as shown in Figures 9.100 and 9.101. Now you can actually read about your options in English (Figure 9.102). Apply your restrictions. You'll notice that you can take away the Run, Find, and Settings in the Start menu, as well as many other built-in options on the Desktop. You'd better be careful, though: changes will apply immediately to the open profile you are configuring, so you might want to make that the last thing you do when configuring the profile. Also, don't touch Local Computer or you will be making changes to your other local hive files (like the System hive). These restrictions are written to the Registry, in HKEY_CURRENT_USER\SOFTWARE\ MICROSOFT\WINDOWS\CURRENTVERSION\POLICIES\EXPLORER.

NOTE *The examples in this section are based on Version 5 of the System Policy Editor, which comes with Windows 2000 Service Pack 3. NT 4 Service Pack 6 includes Version 4, so some of the options may vary from Version 5.*

FIGURE 9.100

Open local Registry

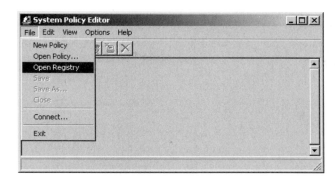

FIGURE 9.101

Local User/Local
Registry

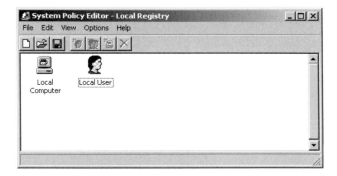

FIGURE 9.102

Local User
properties in
POLEDIT.EXE

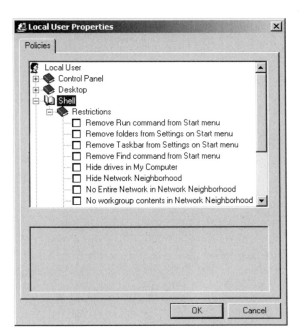

NOTE   *Windows XP and Server 2003 do not include* POLEDIT.EXE. *However, profiles that are modified on a Windows 2000 system using POLEDIT can then be distributed to XP users, as long as the modified Registry entries are common to Windows XP systems. So you can build a profile and set restrictions on a 2000 Professional system, then deploy that profile with reasonable success to XP users and 2000 users alike.*

When you finish, close POLEDIT.EXE, log out, log back in as an administrator, and follow the steps outlined earlier to copy the profile, restrictions and all, to the Default User folder or roaming profile path.

If you are configuring a domain-wide default profile, test your work by logging in to the domain as a new user; you should get the preconfigured default profile and any restrictions you built in. This will be a good opportunity to look for any loopholes or problems. And remember to create your own profile or an administrator profile before doing this stuff, or it will apply to you as well!

THE BAD NEWS ABOUT PRECONFIGURED DEFAULT PROFILES

The problem with a "powerless, preconfigured" Default User profile becomes apparent when a new administrator or some such person logs in for the first time. Your new administrator's profile will be created from this template, and she will be the irritated but unintentional recipient of a highly restricted Desktop (oops). In this case, you would need to keep a stash of unrestricted profiles in reserve somewhere (make a copy of an untouched Default User profile, for instance). Users who should not get these powerless, preconfigured profiles must have unrestricted profiles specifically assigned to them. Furthermore, these profiles will have to exist in the profile path specified in the user account options before the user ever logs in. If she has already logged in and received the altered Default User profile, you have to delete her profile from the local machine and from the server to remedy the situation. In other words, the user will need to start over with a new profile and will lose any changes made to customize her Desktop. (That's why people tend not to use profiles to restrict user behavior—these days they use group policies instead.)

PROBLEMS WITH PRECONFIGURED AND ROAMING PROFILES

As you create profiles for users or simply allow users to have roaming profiles, keep in mind that a user profile includes settings on screen placement, window sizes, and color schemes. The display adapters and monitors on the workstations should be taken into consideration. If Larry has a 21-inch monitor with the latest and greatest AGP card and sets up his Desktop accordingly, he may get an unpleasant surprise when he logs in to Adam's machine equipped with lesser video capabilities. When preconfiguring a profile for a user, sit at a computer that has the same video capabilities as the user's primary workstation. If you are configuring a Default User profile or one that will be used by multiple users, those workstations must have the same video capabilities. Alternately, you can use the lowest common denominators to ensure that the settings will work on all platforms.

A Special Note about Shortcuts and Link Tracking

Video problems are not the only issue. If you are installing applications on the Desktop, always use default installation directories so that shortcuts created will resolve more smoothly. Also, keep in mind that shortcuts will first attempt to resolve using the link tracking method, which is the absolute path for the shortcut. Failing that, the shortcut will try to resolve with the search method, which means it will search the local drive. In other words, if you created a shortcut to Notepad on \\OCTOBER, saved the profile as a roaming profile, then sat down and logged in at \\SALOME, the shortcut would first try to resolve to \\OCTOBER\WINDOWS\SYSTEM32\NOTEPAD.EXE. If the user cannot connect to \\OCTOBER, the system will supposedly search for the program in %Systemroot%\SYSTEM32\NOTEPAD.EXE. But if \\OCTOBER exists, the user is prompted for a username and password to access \\OCTOBER\C$, the hidden drive share that's reserved for remote administration. This leaves users scratching their heads, saying, "What did I do?"—or worse, calling the help desk to ask, "What did you do?" To prevent this problem, when creating shortcuts, use expandable variables (such as %WINDIR%, %SYSTEMROOT%) whenever possible. Luckily, shortcuts work just fine when they point to a shared directory on the server, as long as they are created properly and permissions are appropriate.

Another consideration to keep in mind is that when users on your network regularly move from one profile-creating workstation to another, every machine they use will store a copy of their local profile. These will eventually add up and consume a chunk of disk space. An administrator can delete local profiles periodically, using the Delete option in the User Profiles tab of the System applet. You may also use System Policy Editor or Group Policies to compel the workstations to delete cached copies of roaming profiles when the user logs out. This is a machine-specific setting that is implemented in the Registry in HKEY_LOCAL_MACHINE\SOFTWARE\MICROSOFT\WINDOWS NT\CURRENTVERSION\WINLOGON. If you are doing a direct Registry edit, the name of the value entry should be DeleteRoamingCache, with a data type REG_DWORD and a value of 1; it should read

```
DeleteRoamingCache:REG _DWORD:1
```

NOTE *For Windows 2000 and XP/Server systems, use Active Directory's group policies settings instead of the System Policy Editor to remove copies of roaming profiles. In the Group Policy Editor, look in* Computer Configuration\ Administrative Templates\System\Logon, *and there's a policy named Delete Cached Copies of Roaming Profiles.*

Finally, using roaming profiles across a WAN link is not recommended. Whenever possible, load profiles from a server locally. Besides eating up network bandwidth (when the profile is sucked off the server at logon and copied back to the server at logoff), time-out intervals for slow connections will cause numerous problems in synchronizing the local and server copies of the profiles.

"CACHED" PROFILES: A TIP

Talking of mandatory profiles reminded me of a peculiar behavior, one that may bedevil you if you're extremely security conscious.

Suppose I've given you a workstation (again, NT, 2000, or XP will all work the same way) named \\ANGEL, but I've not created a local account for you. Instead, I've given you a domain account on the SONGBIRDS domain and told you to log in from that. Thus, every morning you sit down at your workstation and tell your machine that you want to log in from a SONGBIRDS account, not an ANGEL account. That is, you want your workstation's Local Security Authority *not* to look in your workstation's SAM but rather to use NETLOGON to communicate with one of the DCs in SONGBIRDS, and then to ask one of those controllers to look up your user account in the domain SAM.

Sounds good—but what about those times when you get that dratted "No domain controller found" error message? If your workstation's NETLOGON can't find a DC, it seems that there's no way for your local LSA to establish your credentials. That seems to mean also that if there's no DC around, you can't get on your workstation, doesn't it? Or does it?

Continued on next page

"CACHED" PROFILES: A TIP *(continued)*

The first time this happened to me, I was somewhat taken aback to see that my workstation logged me in *anyway*, using "cached credentials." The idea is that, if you got in all right *yesterday*, we'll give you the benefit of the doubt *today*, even if the local LSA *can't* find a DC. Cool, eh? Well, yes, it might be cool for many—but the more security-conscious among us might be quite unhappy about the idea that if a network administrator modifies or deletes your account on Tuesday, by Wednesday your workstation might not know about it.

Fortunately, there's a Registry setting that you can use to make a workstation require a domain logon before providing access to the local machine. Just go to HKEY_LOCAL_MACHINE\Software\Microsoft\Windows NT\ CurrentVersion\Winlogon and create a value entry called CachedLogonsCount, of type REG_DWORD, and set its value to 0. Make this change on every NT workstation on which you want to require strict logons. Use group policies to limit cached logons for Windows 2000, XP Professional, and Windows Server systems.

NOTE   DELPROF.EXE *a command-line utility included in the NT Workstation and NT Server Resource Kits, allows administrators to delete user profiles on a local or remote computer running any version of Windows NT through 4, but not Windows 9x. Of particular interest is the utility's ability to delete profiles that have been inactive for x number of days.*

Mandatory Profiles

So far in this discussion, all types of user profiles allowed users to make changes to customize their own profile (assuming you did not set up System Policy Editor to discard changed settings at logoff). Another option for controlling user profiles is to assign a *mandatory profile* to the user or to a group of users.

NOTE   *I don't really recommend using mandatory profiles. Their goal is to lock down a user's Desktop and, as I've indicated before, the better tool for that is policies, not profiles. But I include information about them for the sake of completeness.*

A mandatory profile is a read-only profile that the user must use. Mandatory profiles are a tad more work than roaming profiles. The profile must exist ahead of time and it must exist in the path you point to, or else the user cannot log in. Remember, with roaming profiles, we could just let the workstation copy the profile to the network path unless we wanted Larry to use a profile we created for him.

The mandatory profile is a type of roaming profile, in that you must specify a profile path in the user's account information. To create a mandatory profile directory, name it with the extension .MAN (for example, \\ZOOROPA\PROFILES\LARRY.MAN). This tells the operating system that the profile is mandatory and that the user will not be able to log in if the profile is unavailable. In that case, the user will see a dialog box that says, "Unable to log you in because your mandatory profile is not available. Please contact your administrator."

Also, rename the NTUSER.DAT file to NTUSER.MAN so that the user cannot save changes to the profile. Once the local profile is created on the workstation, the locally created copy of the profile will also be read-only. This does not set permissions on the profile per se, so it works on both FAT and NTFS. Nor does changing the name to NTUSER.MAN set the read-only attribute on the file. It's just a special extension for the profile that tells NT not to save changes at logoff (changes will apply while the user is logged in but will be lost when the user logs out). This feature is useful if you want to assign one profile to a group of users and you do not want these users to be able to save changes. In other words, everybody shares a copy of the same profile, and it is protected against users' "personal touches."

The following are your options for setting up mandatory profiles:

Use a read-only profile   Simply rename the file NTUSER.DAT to NTUSER.MAN before you assign the profile to the user or users. Keep in mind that when a user first logs in, the workstation does not know that this user's profile is a mandatory profile (because the directory name is *USERNAME*, not *USERNAME*.MAN). If the profile is unavailable, the system will load a local or default profile. However, once the system loads the mandatory profile from the profile path, the System applet on the workstation shows the profile as mandatory. The user or users will not be able to save changes to the Desktop. At this point, if the network profile becomes unavailable, the system will load the local profile, but because the system now considers it a mandatory profile, changes will not be saved.

Incidentally, renaming the NTUSER.DAT file to NTUSER.MAN can be done as an afterthought, as well. In other words, if a user formally has a local and configurable profile, you can go to the \Documents and Settings*Username* directory and rename the hive file. It will be read-only from that point on.

Force the user to load a particular profile   If you specify the directory path on the domain controller or server as DIRECTORYNAME.MAN but you do not rename the hive file to NTUSER.MAN, the operating system will not see it as a mandatory profile. If the hive file is not named NTUSER.MAN, the workstation will classify it merely as a roaming profile. In this scenario, users can make changes to their Desktops. At logon, however, the user will not be able to log in if the profile directory does not exist in the specified path.

Create a read-only profile that must be used   Specify the directory name as DIRECTORYNAME.MAN and rename the NTUSER.DAT file to NTUSER.MAN. This is ideal if you want to force users to load a profile off the network and you want to prevent them from making any changes to it.

HOW DO I CONFIGURE A MANDATORY PROFILE?

Mandatory profiles are created in much the same way preconfigured profiles are created. Mandatory profiles can be assigned to individual users or to groups. Here is how to create a shared mandatory profile and assign it to everyone in a particular group (Engineering):

1. Create a user, log in as that user, and set up the Desktop, network and printer connections, and so forth.

2. Apply any restrictions you want, as described earlier. Log off.

3. Log back on to the machine as an administrator.

4. Use the System applet (under Control Panel/System/User Profiles) to select the profile and copy it to a shared directory on the network, naming it *SOMETHING*.MAN. Remember to set permissions to allow your user (or a group) at least Read and Execute access to the profile and its contents. I named the directory Engineering.man and assigned permissions to the group Domain Engineering.

5. Rename the copied NTUSER.DAT file to NTUSER.MAN.

6. In the properties sheet for the user account, fill in the profile directory path, pointing to your mandatory profile directory. DSA.MSC now allows you to select multiple accounts and change the profile path field to the same value for all of them, so it's easy to select a number of user accounts and assign them all to use the same mandatory profile.

7. You are now ready to have users log in and receive their mandatory profiles.

Continued on next page

HOW DO I CONFIGURE A MANDATORY PROFILE? *(continued)*

You can see what profiles are saved on a local machine, and what type they are, in the System applet—the same place you go to copy profiles. The following properties sheet shows all three types on a machine:

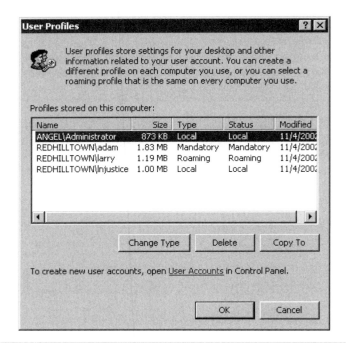

Setting Up a Group Template Profile

As you can see, it's relatively easy to assign "shared" profiles to users and groups. However, any time two or more users are pulling their profiles from the same profile directory, they should be pulling a mandatory (and read-only) profile. Otherwise, changes made by each user to the group profile directory on the server will be saved. Larry and Adam will have to deal with Paul's Eggplant color scheme or Ninja Turtles icons.

What we really need is to provide profiles with elements in common, like network connections and any corporate-wide security settings, but also allow users to make customizations. Group Policy is the real answer to this dilemma, but for your NT workstations (or just for the sake of argument), how much more trouble is it to preconfigure and assign profiles based on, say, group membership, which will then be under the control of the individual user? This would not be a mandatory profile but just a point of departure for the user. Actually, it's a lot more trouble. Sure, you can make profile templates for groups, but how do you assign them and still let users customize the Desktop according to their own preferences or needs? Let's see how to do this.

ASSIGNING USER-CONFIGURABLE PROFILES TO GROUPS

If you use the standard preconfigured user profile procedure, follow these steps.

First, make group template profiles by creating three security groups (CLEAVERS, ADAMSES, and CLAMPETTS). Then create three template group member accounts, naming them, for instance, Wally, Tuesday, and Granny (you were getting pretty tired of Larry and Adam, weren't you?). Log on as each template user in turn, and configure a group profile for each one. When you are finished, log off and log back on to the system as an administrator.

When you are creating user accounts, before adding Ward or June user to the CLEAVERS group, open the System applet and copy the CLEAVERS group template profile to a shared profile directory, renaming it after the new user you are about to create. Don't forget to give the new user permission to use the profile. Then create the user, specifying his or her profile path as *MACHINENAME*\ *SHARENAME**USERNAME*, indicating the directory where you copied the profile.

This process is not complicated overall, but you do have to remember to copy a new profile to the shared directory and assign the profile to that specific user each time you create a new account. This permits the users to start off on the right foot with all the settings you want them to have, but also to make changes as needed to their own profiles.

How Does a Client Choose between Local, Roaming, and Mandatory Profiles?

In all of this discussion about locally cached profiles, roaming profiles stored on a server, and mandatory profiles, it's important to understand the order in which NT, 2000, or XP looks for a profile and how the system chooses among the three. Plus, there are a couple of considerations that I haven't yet explained. To make this simple, let's view the scenarios from two perspectives: that of a user who has never before logged in to that workstation (Morticia), and that of a user who has logged in to the machine already (Gomez).

Morticia logs in to her newly assigned Windows 2000 workstation. Assume that there is no profile path specified for Morticia in her account information. She only has a local profile. The workstation must create a profile for her from a `Default User` directory. If Morticia is logging in to an Active Directory domain (Windows 2000 or Server), the operating system will first look in the `NETLOGON` share of the authenticating domain controller for a Default User profile (it has to look there anyway for the logon script; why not just kill two birds with one stone?). There's no `Default User` directory in the `NETLOGON` share? Oh well, the system will just have to use the Default User info from the local machine.

If there *is* a profile path specified for her account, however, the system looks in that path for the profile directory. If the profile exists, the Desktop loads it and uses it to make a local copy. This may be a roaming or a mandatory profile. If there is no profile in the specified path and a roaming profile is specified (\\SERVERNAME\SHARENAME*USERNAME*), the workstation will make one using a copy of the Default User folder. Again, for a Win2K/Server domain logon, the system first checks in `NETLOGON`. If no `Default User` directory is found there, the system creates Morticia's profile from the local `Default User` directory. If no profile exists in the path and the path was indicated as mandatory, the user will not be allowed to log in at all!

So far, so good. Now let's tackle Gomez, who has been using his workstation for a few weeks already. If no profile is specified in his account information, nothing changes for Gomez. He continues to use his locally stored profile.

On the other hand, if by chance you decide to implement roaming profiles one evening or weekend and Gomez comes in the next morning and logs in, his workstation has to check a few things. First, if a profile path exists in the account info, his workstation must first check to see if Gomez has changed his roaming profile type back to local. Aha! You see, Gomez might have grown tired of waiting for his roaming profile to load off the server and decided to tell his workstation not to bother, to just use the local copy all the time. He can do this by opening the System applet and the User Profiles tab, selecting his own profile, and choosing Change Type. Gomez then sees the dialog box shown in Figure 9.103. Gomez could not do this if the profile was mandatory, and of course, you cannot change a local profile to a roaming profile unless you are changing it *back* to a roaming profile.

FIGURE 9.103

Changing a user
profile from
roaming to local

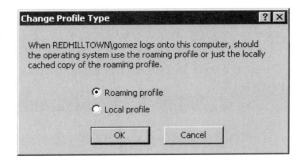

Any user may change an unrestricted roaming profile back to a local profile. On NT 4 systems, the user may also choose the option to automatically Use Cached Profile on Slow Connections. If Gomez checks that box, he's saying to his operating system, "If there is a slow network connection, just go ahead and load my local copy and don't bother me." What qualifies as a slow connection? That depends on an interval set in the Registry, called `SlowLinkTimeout`. The default interval is two seconds. Generally, if the two-second interval is exceeded, Gomez will see a dialog box stating that a slow network connection has been detected and asking whether to load the local or the roaming profile. By default, Gomez has 30 seconds to choose (that value is determined by a Registry entry called `ProfileDlgTimeout`), after which time the system will load the local profile. But if Gomez enables the Use Cached Profile on Slow Connections option, the workstation will automatically load the local profile without asking Gomez. Hmmm.

The Registry entries affecting detection of slow network connections are found in `HKEY_LOCAL_ MACHINE\SOFTWARE\MICROSOFT\WINDOWS NT\CURRENTVERSION\WINLOGON`. All of the following values can be set using the System Policy Editor and Group Policy Administrative Templates:

SlowLinkDetectEnabled   Has a data type of `REG_DWORD` and possible values of 0 (disabled) or 1 (enabled). Slow-link detection is enabled by default, and the system is told to be aware of slow network connections.

SlowLinkTimeOut   Has a data type of REG_DWORD and a default value of 2000 (2 seconds expressed in milliseconds). Possible values are 0–120,000 (up to 2 minutes). When this threshold is exceeded and SlowLinkDetectEnabled is set to 1, users can log in by using a local profile instead of the roaming profile.

ProfileDlgTimeOut   Has a data type of REG_DWORD and a default value of 30 (expressed in seconds). This value determines how many seconds a user has to choose between a local or server-based profile when the value of SlowLinkTimeOut is exceeded.

Assuming that there is no slow network connection and assuming Gomez has not changed his roaming profile back to a local profile (he hasn't had a chance yet, right?), the system will check to see whether (1) the profile is mandatory or (2) the profile on the server is more current.

If either (1) or (2) is true, the system will load the server copy. If neither is true, then Gomez gets a pesky dialog box. You see, if (2) is not true, then the profile on the server is not more current than the local copy. This implies that there was a problem in synchronizing the profiles the last time Gomez logged out. So the operating system will announce that the local profile is more recent than the network profile and will ask if Gomez wants to load the local instead.

Whew! That was a bit complex, so maybe the following flow charts will help. Figures 9.104 and 9.105 describe Morticia (new user to the workstation, with local profile and roaming profile), and Figure 9.106 follows Gomez (an existing user with locally stored profile). Finally, I've thrown in Figure 9.107 to show how a user's profile is saved at logoff.

FIGURE 9.104

How a new user gets a local profile

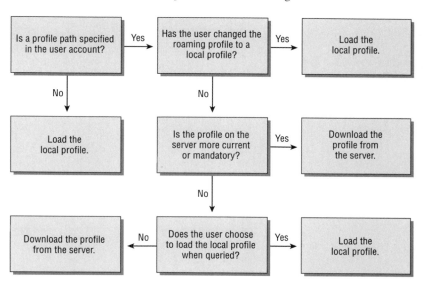

FIGURE 9.105

How a new user gets a roaming profile

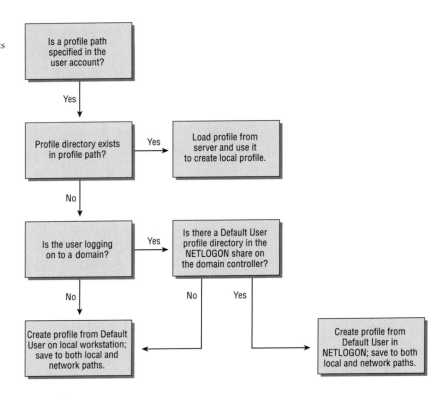

FIGURE 9.106

How a user with a local profile gets a roaming profile

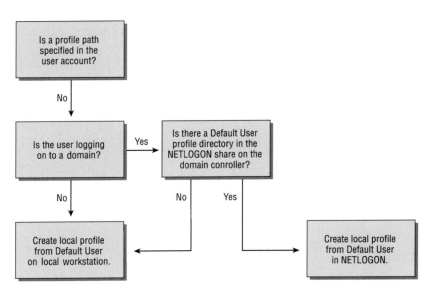

FIGURE 9.107

How user profiles are saved at logoff

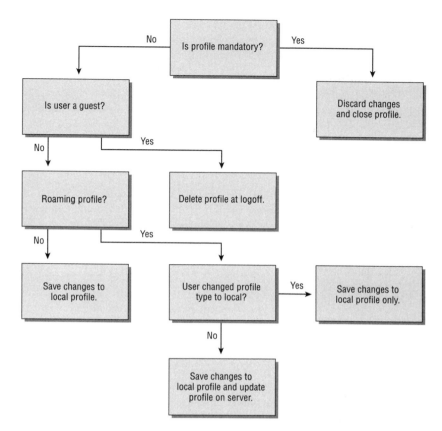

Which Type of Profile Is Right for My Network?

Now that you are a Microsoft user profile guru, you'll need to decide what kind of profiles to implement on your network. Even if you do nothing, you are still making a choice to let users just keep local profiles. To help you decide, the following paragraphs summarize the pros and cons of the different types of profiles:

Local profiles only Local profiles may be the best choice in a mixed client environment or where users don't need to roam. Windows 9x profiles are not interchangeable with NT/2000/ XP Workstation profiles, though the Desktop is similar, so users moving from one client OS to another need *either* local profiles only *or* two roaming profiles. (Do you feel a migraine coming on?) This option has the lowest administrative overhead and offers the fewest options for preconfiguring profiles and controlling Desktops. However, you can still use System Policy Editor and group policies (for 2000 and XP systems) to configure Desktops and impose restrictive policies without implementing roaming profiles.

Roaming profiles A roaming profile has two major benefits: mobility and fault tolerance. Not only can users move from Desktop to Desktop and have their preferred settings follow them, they also have a "backup" of their profile stored on the server. If you have to reinstall the workstation, the user doesn't necessarily have to reconfigure the Desktop. Plus, you can let the workstation create the profile for you as long as there are no special settings to hand out to users.

This is also the option to use if you want profiles to be centrally located and controlled. The downside is that roaming profiles may follow you to another machine but may not work flawlessly once they are downloaded. Shortcuts to applications that exist only on the user's "home workstation" and different display capabilities are only two of the possible problems users may encounter. Also, roaming profiles shooting across your Ethernet every time a user logs in or out will generate more traffic and slow down user logons. If it's a consideration at 10 and even 100Mbps, think of the problems if you have an ISDN connection at 64Kbps.

Finally, remember that NT, 2000, or XP will store a local copy of the profile for every user that logs in to a given machine. If users roam and roam and roam, they leave copies behind, taking up hard drive space as well as presenting a security issue (my Desktop may have a few items on it I don't want to leave behind). To address this problem, set up the machines to delete cached copies of roaming profiles.

Mandatory profiles   Mandatory profiles, because they are also roaming profiles, have the benefit of being mobile and fault tolerant. They can also be centrally located and controlled, like roaming profiles. Plus, mandatory profiles are the only way you can force a user to load a particular profile. Because it is read-only, users can share a profile; you keep fewer profiles stored on the server instead of one for every single user. While mandatory profiles offer more control than roaming profiles, they also require more setup on your part. You must manually create a mandatory profile and place it in a network path; the operating system can't create a mandatory profile for you. Finally, if a user attempts to log in and the mandatory profile is unavailable, NT, 2000, and XP systems will not allow the user to log in. This prevents a malicious user from logging in with the Default User profile and running amok, but it can also be a drawback if a legitimate user cannot log in and perform their job.

Network default user profile   One of the best things about a domain-wide Default User profile is that it can be implemented in conjunction with roaming profiles. This offers a great way to preconfigure all new user profiles, and although it does not help you hand out special program groups to, say, the accounting department, it can be used as a point of departure. You can use the NT or Windows 2000 System Policy Editor and group policies to hand out custom Start menu items to group members. However, if you place heinous restrictions on the Default User profile in the NETLOGON share, you'll have to create a special roaming profile and assign it to folks who shouldn't get the restrictions (such as new MIS employees).

IMPLEMENTING USER PROFILES: AN EXAMPLE

Let's see what you've learned by looking at a sample situation and determining the best way to use profiles.

Suppose you manage several computer labs at a university, and each lab has 35–100 NT 4, 2000, or XP workstations. Up to 10,000 students at the university, who all have accounts on the university-wide system, visit various labs using various machines. A few students cause problems in the network. Some of these students are malicious, while some are just inexperienced. If you stand by and do nothing, users will leave profiles behind when they log out. You'll have to periodically delete profiles. If you allow users to have access to all possible tools on the Desktop, administrative overhead increases as you troubleshoot problems and reinstall the OS on the workstations.

Solution #1: Preconfigure a Domainwide Default User Profile

With this solution, you may have to create more than one Default User profile if user accounts are in multiple domains. Restrict profiles as necessary, assign roaming profiles, and configure systems to delete cached copies of roaming profiles using System Policy Editor, the Resource Kit utility DELPROF.EXE, or Group Policies.

TIP   Actually, there is a very simple solution to the local profile detritus problem. Rather than going to the trouble of setting up a policy to delete cached copies of roaming profiles, editing the Registry of every machine, or running DELPROF.EXE at regular intervals, you can make every user a guest at the local machines in the lab. Although this approach has several other implications that might make it unfeasible for your situation, it would take care of profile buildup. Members of the Guests group are not allowed to keep local profiles unless they are also members of the Users group.

This solution poses one very big problem. Even if users have restrictions placed on the profile, with roaming profiles for every user, the network servers will hold thousands of copies of the very same profile. Not only that, but savvy users may be able to change their own Registry settings and break free of restrictions.

Solution #2: Create a Shared Mandatory Profile

A better solution is to create a restricted profile directory, name it USERS.MAN, rename the hive file to NTUSER.MAN, and assign this as a shared mandatory profile to all users. You'll still need to delete cached copies of roaming profiles, but this way, even if a user manages to edit the Registry settings to remove the restrictions, changes will be discarded at logoff. You also save space on the network servers.

WARNING   There is one possible problem with this solution, if you're still using NT 4: If many students try to download the mandatory profile at exactly the same time, they may experience sharing violations (NT 4 Service Pack 2 fixed this problem, though).

DISTRIBUTING USER PROFILES

You may also want to keep several copies of the mandatory profile (for example, one on each domain controller) for load balancing. There is a way to distribute user profiles across domain controllers using the environment variable %LOGONSERVER%: create a share of the same name on each DC, copy the mandatory profiles into each of the shared directories, and then indicate the profile path in account properties as something like \\%LOGONSERVER%\PROFILES\USERS.MAN. To prevent major profile synchronization problems, don't use this approach with regular roaming profiles; use it only with mandatory profiles.

If you don't want to store profiles on the DCs, you can tell the workstation where to look for the mandatory profile by creating a new environmental variable on each of the workstations. The new environmental variable will be %PROFILESERVER% and will point to the local lab server keeping the mandatory profile.

HOW DO I MAKE USERS LOAD PROFILES FROM LOCAL SERVERS?

Use the System applet's Environment tab to set a system variable pointing to the local server, as shown in the following System properties sheet. Fill in the information as shown. In this case, the local lab server will be LAB01UMDCP. (Do not include % signs or \\ as part of the variable.) Choose the Set button and click OK. The new variable will be set, but you will need to restart the computer before these settings take effect (since the operating system reads the system variables at startup).

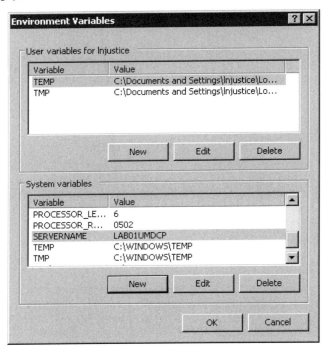

Once you have defined the %SERVERNAME% variable on each of the workstations (REGINI.EXE, a command-line Resource Kit utility, can be pretty handy for that type of thing), created a share of the same name on each profile server, and copied the mandatory profiles to those shared directories, you can then indicate the profile path in the user's account properties as \\%PROFILESERVER%\PROFILES\ USERS.MAN.

Comparing Windows NT 3.51, NT 4, and 9x Profiles

As described in the preceding sections, there's a lot that can be done with NT 4, Windows 2000, and XP user profiles in an NT/Win2K/Server 2003 environment. However, in case you are still managing legacy client systems, let's round out our discussion with a quick rundown of the differences between NT 3.51, NT 4, and Windows 9x user profiles. The important thing to keep in mind is that Windows 9x, NT 3.51, and NT 4 profiles are not cross-platform profiles. In other words, a user who requires a roaming profile and customarily sits at several types of legacy workstations would need a separate profile for each type of client.

NT 3.51 PROFILES

In NT 3.51, each user profile is a single hive file (found in %SYSTEMROOT%\SYSTEM32\CONFIG), and profiles are stored with the rest of the systems' Registry hive files. Instead of a bunch of folders and a hive file, everything is included in the one file. NT 3.51 supports per-user profiles (equivalent to roaming profiles) and mandatory profiles. The profile path for an NT 3.51 personal profile would be specified as \\SERVERNAME\SHARENAME\USERNAME.USR in the user account properties, and for a mandatory profile it would be \\SERVERNAME\SHARENAME\FILENAME.MAN.

Because there was no System Policy Editor under NT 3.51, options for restricting profiles were very limited. NT 3.51 did provide a tool called User Profile Editor (UPEDIT.EXE), which allowed you to log in as your bogus user, configure the Desktop, and save a configured profile with a skimpy set of restrictions to the current user or system default. This was also the tool used to save the profile to a specified path when implementing per-user or mandatory profiles.

NT 4 profiles are entire directories, like the Windows 9x profile structure. NT 3.51 per-user profiles were simply files. NT 3.51 profiles will be converted to NT 4 profiles when upgrading from 3.51 to NT 4. NT 3.51 profiles formerly named USERNAME.USR, for example, will be converted to a directory called USERNAME.PDS. Likewise, mandatory profiles named USER.MAN will be converted to a directory called USER.PDM. New profile directories created on upgraded machines will not carry this special extension. If a user is working in a mixed environment, however, she will have a separate profile for each OS, and they will not be synchronized (changes made to one won't show up in the other) if changes are made after the initial migration.

Windows 9x Profiles

In Windows 9x, individual profiles are not created by default but must be enabled in Control Panel/Passwords. If roaming profiles are enabled on the Windows 9x machine, they will be stored automatically in the user's home directory. You need not specify a profile path for the user in Active Directory Users and Computers. Otherwise, Windows 9x profiles operate in the same way as NT/2000/XP profiles.

Individual mandatory profiles can be used in Windows 9x, but shared mandatory profiles cannot. For this reason, the administrator must create a profile for each user and copy it to that user's home directory.

The structure of a Windows 9x user profile contains differences from an NT, 2000, or XP user profile. Instead of an NTUSER.DAT file, Windows 9x has a USER.DAT file. Instead of NTUSER.DAT.LOG (the log file that stores changes to the NTUSER.DAT file), Windows 9x uses a file called USER.DA0. These two files are not exact equivalents. Windows 9x uses USER.DA0 as a "backup," writing a copy of USER.DAT to USER.DA0 every time the user logs out. NT 4 (and 2000 and XP) uses NTUSER.DAT.LOG as a transaction log file to protect the hive file while it is being updated. To create a read-only mandatory profile, rename the 9x USER.DAT file to USER.MAN. NT 4 and Windows 9x use basically the same folder structure, except that the Application Data folder does not exist in Windows 9x.

Additional differences in Windows 9x profiles include the following:

- Not all Desktop items will roam; only LNK (shortcuts) and PIF (program information) files will.
- Common program groups aren't supported in Windows 9x.
- Windows 9x can't use a centrally stored Default User profile.

NOTE *If you're still supporting NT 4 and Windows 9x clients, then don't skip the chapter on the CD about system policies for NT and 9x clients!*

Chapter 10

Managing Windows Server Storage

WHAT IS "STORAGE," YOU ask? Well, if terms like *pagefile*, *master file table*, *partition table*, and *clusters* make you shudder because they remind you of how much you *don't* know about what goes on beneath the operating system, stick with me through this complex but incredibly important chapter. Here, I hope to make the concept of storage one more piece of the puzzle that you *do* know.

Basically, when someone refers to storage in a computer environment, they are talking about hard drives, the file systems on those drives, and what you can do with those file systems to organize your data so that it is easier to manage. In this chapter, I'll cover everything you need to know about how Server 2003 views and uses the physical hard drives that you put into your servers, and what you can do to help manage the files that you store on those drives.

Remember that whether your Server 2003 is a print server, an e-mail server, a Web server, or any kind of server you can think of, it's still in many ways a file server. No matter what kind of resources a server is providing to the network, the server has to store a lot of files to support those resources.

Having lots of files means a lot of storage, and a lot of storage means maintaining it. In this chapter, I'll talk about the tools Server 2003 includes to help you manage and maintain your disks and other storage media. With NT 4, this mostly meant the Disk Administrator. I'm going to start with The Tool Formerly Known As The Disk Administrator (which became the Disk Management tool in Win2K), but there's a lot more to it than that. Encryption, new disk formats, disk quotas, and Remote Storage were introduced in Win2K, and some of these features have even been improved upon in Server 2003. There are also some useful new features that Server 2003 gives us to make our lives even easier.

One of these new features, Volume Shadow Copy Service, which was introduced in XP and is available in Server 2003, could make the sysadmin's task of restoring users' lost files a thing of the past. You can now extend basic disks in Server 2003, and Microsoft has made the job of recovering from a failed mirrored system disk much easier. No more editing the boot.ini! Server 2003 now offers support for Storage Area Networks (SAN) and has added open file backups to complete the package. You can also now defrag the master file table in Server 2003, and there is a really cool new command-line utility that will allow you to manage your disks as well as—in some ways, even better than—the GUI will allow, including the ability to script disk management for your unattended installs. If your eyes are glassing over and you are thinking that this might be the chapter to skip, stay tuned as I make all these terms part of your sysadmin vocabulary. My hope is that you'll be a storage expert by the time you get to Chapter 11.

The Basics of Disk Management

Let's start off with the some of the basics of disk management and a little history. I'll begin by defining some of those terms you may not be familiar with, like partitions and logical drives, and once you have the vocabulary, I'll begin to show you how you can manage your storage issues with Server 2003.

Disk Management Terminology

Before we get into the discussion of how you can use the Disk Management tool to arrange and protect your data, you need to know some of the terms that I'll be tossing around. These terms will be explained further in due course, along with how to use the tools in Server 2003 that relate to them, but this section will give you a basic level of understanding until then.

PHYSICAL DISKS VERSUS LOGICAL PARTITIONS

To understand disk management, you must understand the difference between physical disks and logical drives or partitions. A *physical disk* is that contraption of plastic and metal that you inserted in your server's case or have stacked up next to it. The Disk Management tool identifies physical drives by numbers (Disk 0, 1, 2; CD 0, 1, 2) that you cannot change.

NOTE *If you have multiple disks in your computer, they're numbered by their status on the drive controller. For example, in a SCSI chain, the disk with SCSI ID 0 will be Disk 0, the drive with the next SCSI ID will be Disk 1, and so on. The SCSI ID and the disk number are not directly related and will not necessarily match—the only correspondence lies in the disk's priority in the system.*

You cannot change the size of a physical disk. The size given to it when it was low-level formatted (something you almost certainly don't have to worry about if you're installing Server 2003 on the disk— you can't low-level format an EIDE drive and don't need to low-level format a SCSI drive—it's done before you buy it) is the size the drive will remain. So, in short, a physical disk is a solid piece of hardware with a fixed size and, once physically installed, the Disk Management tool will recognize it and allow you to assign it a drive letter or mount it to a path on an NTFS volume. Wondering what it means to mount a drive to a path? I'll cover that in a moment.

In contrast to a physical disk, a *partition* or *volume* or *logical drive* is a method of organizing the available space on the physical disk (or disks) that the Disk Management tool has identified in your system. Once you have created these partitions using the Disk Management tool, they will act as if they are separate physical disks. Even if you want the physical disk to be one big partition, you still have to create *one* partition on the disk in order for it to be utilized by the operating system. You can change drive-letter assignments and adjust the size of these logical partitions (since they have no physical presence) with the Disk Management tool. A logical partition can be part or all of a physical disk or even, in the case of volume sets, mirror sets, and stripe sets, can extend across more than one physical disk. I'll talk more about these sets when I talk about RAID. For now, let's look at how you actually create these logical partitions.

WHAT IS AN EXTENDED PARTITION, ANYWAY?

When I talk about *partitions* or *volumes* or *logical drives*, I am really talking about the same thing from about a thousand feet in the air. When you zoom in and look more closely though, there are differences in how you can divide up your disks. There is a file that resides on the physical disk called a disk partition table, which is where the OS keeps track of how the physical disks are logically divided. For now, we'll stick with the basics and say that the partition table can only describe four partitions, because each description is 16 bytes and the partition table file is 64 bytes. Since you only have four partitions, there are a limited number of ways in which you can divide up this logical structure. Only one of these four can be designated as "active" at any time. This is the partition to which the OS will boot. You can have up to four primary partitions or three primary partitions and an extended partition, which itself can have multiple logical drives; this helps to overcome the four-partition limit. Now that you have an idea of how you can logically divide disks, let's talk about the way you look at the available space on the disk.

FREE SPACE VERSUS UNALLOCATED SPACE

The definition of *free space* seems obvious: "Free space on a disk is just space that's free, right?" It's not. Free space does not refer to unused areas within established drives. Rather, *free space* means an extended partition that doesn't yet have any logical drives in it, or that the space within that partition is not yet divided into a logical drive.

This definition of free space is different from the one used in NT 4 and previous versions, where free space was space on a disk that was not part of a volume. Disk space formerly called free space is now called *unallocated space*. It's not committed to be part of any volume or partition. Both basic and dynamic disks may have unallocated space. I'll talk more about basic and dynamic disks, a new way to look at storage that was introduced in Win2K, once we get through the basics.

MASTER BOOT RECORD

Each disk needs to share a "starting point," a place where critical information about the disk can be found. Information such as the number of and type of logical divisions that exist on the disk needs to be relayed to the system when it boots. And, of course, there must be a place in which the BIOS can store the initial boot program that actually begins the process of loading the OS. This is called the *master boot record* (*MBR*).

PARTITION TABLE

Located within the MBR, this file describes the logical divisions on the disk. It has enough room to account for four partitions, only one of which can be *active*, which means that the OS can boot from that partition.

MOUNTED DRIVES

The Disk Administrator you used with previous versions of NT identified each logical disk volume by a drive letter. This method is simple and has the advantage of making a really short way of leaping to that partition: you type the letter representing it. The disadvantage, of course, is that so long as Server 2003 insists on using the Roman alphabet, you're limited to a total of 26 letters for all local drives and mapped network connections. It also means that it is not possible to add more space to an existing logical drive. To get around these limitations, Server 2003 supports mounting volumes to empty folders on NTFS volumes. Mounted volumes work *only* with NTFS, because they depend on some attributes not found in FAT or FAT32. However, they work with both basic and dynamic disks.

The basic idea of mounting a partition to a folder is that you're redirecting to the partition all read and write requests sent to that folder. Mount a new partition to X:\\`Mounted Folder` and every file I/O request you send to X:\Mounted Folder will be rerouted to the new partition, even if the original drive X: is on a different physical disk entirely. You can mount a volume to as many paths as you like. The only restrictions are that the folders must be empty at the time of mounting, not mapped to any other volumes, and on NTFS volumes on the local computer. NTFS 3.1 is the only filesystem format that Server 2003 supports that can use the reparse points that redirect path information.

The mounted volumes show up as drives in the path you mounted them from, instead of folders, as you can see in Figure 10.1. The User Data folder you see here is actually mounted to a different drive. The user doesn't know where the data is actually being written once he saves his files to User Data.

FIGURE 10.1

Mounted volumes within a folder

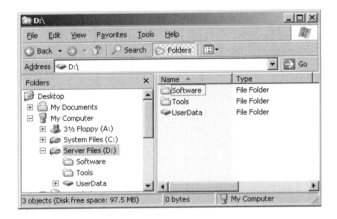

Why bother with mounting volumes to NTFS folders? There used to be three reasons, but improvements in Server 2003 leave us with two. First, it means that you're in no danger of running out of drive letters for local and network partitions. Mounted drives render the 26-letter limitation irrelevant.

Second, you can use this technique to create a fault-tolerant area on a non-fault-tolerant volume. That 2GB volume you created can be a stripe set with parity or a mirror set, even if the disk containing drive X: is a basic disk and therefore does not support fault-tolerant volumes. For example, you could create a new folder on drive X: called Home Directories, then mount a RAID volume to that folder. Whenever someone saves a file to any subfolder of X:\Home Directories, it'll go to the RAID volume even if the rest of drive X: is *not* fault tolerant. Don't worry if you are unclear about the definition of fault tolerance—I'll cover that concept in a minute.

NOTE *Until recently, mounting a volume to an NTFS folder was the only way that you could effectively enlarge a volume on a basic disk by creating a little breathing room elsewhere, since a limitation in Win2K meant that there was no way to actually enlarge a basic disk. Until the release of XP (and now with Server 2003), you could only do that with dynamic disks. For example, say that drive X: was running short of room on a basic disk using Win2K. You couldn't make drive X: any bigger. Instead, you could add a new disk, create a 2GB volume on that disk, then map the new 2GB volume to an empty folder on drive X:. Drive X: would now be, in a circuitous kind of way, 2GB larger. It was okay for a workaround, but life is much improved with the advent of the cool and slightly dangerous command-line tool called DiskPart. I'll go into more detail on it once I fill you in on the concepts of using basic disks in Server 2003.*

Incidentally, volume mappings are transparent to the user. The user doesn't have to care whether drive X: is on the computer where he's working or on a file server in a different physical location or whether the folder he's saving to is located on the same physical disk as the rest of drive X: or on another disk altogether. You can also mount a drive to multiple paths or both mount it and assign it a drive letter.

Experiment with mounting drives to NTFS paths. Although this feature was introduced in Win2K, I am amazed at the number of people who haven't started using them. They are a really cool addition to Windows storage capabilities.

FAULT TOLERANCE

I read recently that on the space shuttle there exist two pairs of identical computer systems. As long as the first pair is communicating and performing according to programmed expectations, the other pair is never used. If, however, some stray cosmic ray affects the performance of the first pair, the other pair automatically chimes in and takes over the job of the original, faulty pair. And, just in case, there is a fifth computer on board which is programmed to the exact specifications of the first two pairs but by different programmers who work for a different company, using different code. That fifth computer doesn't failover automatically though. It has to be done manually by the astronauts. Now, *that* would have to be a tense moment! Knowing this, I have to say I will no longer feel quite the same tension when undergoing what I, until now, had classified as a *dangerous operation* in the machine rooms that I have worked in. This is a great example though, of what I'll be referring to as *fault tolerance* in this chapter. What fault tolerance really means is the ability for either software or hardware to withstand some amount of failure and still persist in doing its job, like flying our astronauts home safely.

Now that you have the basic idea of what fault tolerance is all about, I'll get a bit more specific. In this chapter, I'll be going over the details of software fault tolerance available in Server 2003. Server 2003, like its parents, and even its grandparents in the Windows Server family, has the ability to provide a certain level of software fault tolerance. Of course, software fault tolerance has its limitations, which I'll discuss soon.

SLED

An acronym for *single large expensive drive*, SLED is a way of arranging your data on one very large, very (I hope) reliable drive. SLED was, as history has it, a popular method of arranging data for two reasons:

- ◆ It's simple. You only have to buy one disk and store your data on it.
- ◆ Dedicated RAID hardware was expensive in the past. And even though it's not nearly as expensive as it used to be, it still reflects an added cost.

Trouble is, if that one very large and very reliable drive fails, then your data goes with it. That's where RAID comes in.

RAID

"Apply a shot of RAID, and all those nasty data problems will be gone!" No, it's not really a household product. RAID (Redundant Array of Independent Disks) is a method of protecting your data by combining or copying the space on hard disks to improve disk fault tolerance and/or data throughput.

As I said before, fault tolerance can be provided through both hardware and software solutions. Here I'll concentrate on the software side, but the RAID definitions are the same either way.

There are many levels of RAID implementation, each of which works in a different way and has different applications and benefits. Most of the discussion of RAID in this chapter will focus on its fault-tolerance attributes. Server 2003 supports levels 0, 1, and 5, also known as striping without parity, disk mirroring, and striping with parity, respectively. I'll talk about exactly what these *mean* in the next section.

NOTE   *RAID isn't always redundant (another word for fault tolerant). RAID level 0 (disk striping without parity) isn't fault tolerant because it contains no redundant data to help you re-create lost data, as you'll see in a minute.*

Understanding RAID in Server 2003

Server disks must be faster, more reliable, and larger than their workstation-based cousins. How do you achieve those goals of speed, reliability, and size? Well, there's always the simple answer: Spend more money for a drive with more of those three characteristics. But there is another solution: a group of drives can band together and, acting in concert, provide speed, capacity, and fault tolerance. This solution is called *Redundant Array of Independent Disks (RAID)*. Until relatively recently, putting RAID on your server required buying an expensive hardware-based RAID system. However, this changed with Windows NT, was improved in Win2K, and the improvements continue in Server 2003. With the Disk Management tool in Server 2003, you can take a bunch of hard disks and "roll your own" RAID system. This doesn't make hardware-based RAID obsolete by any means, since hardware RAID is still both more flexible and reliable than its software cousin. (And it's a heck of a lot easier on your computer—some software RAID can be ruinous to computer performance.) Software RAID just offers a less expensive option for those who want this kind of data protection but can't afford hardware RAID solutions. Let's talk a bit more about the differences between software and hardware RAID.

HARDWARE OR SOFTWARE RAID?

Software RAID is simple to set up and, if you own an operating system that supports it, you can experiment with RAID at no additional cost other than for the drives needed to support your chosen RAID model. However, for serious applications it's wanting. Here's why:

Accessibility   Server 2003 RAID volumes are invisible to any operating system other than itself. Even NT can't read these RAID volumes, since they require the use of dynamic disks, which Windows NT has never heard about.

Recovery time   You've got a mission-critical system up and running, and one of the four drives in a stripe set with parity goes to The Land Where Hard Drives Are Eternally Blessed. Your next move is to bring the server down, replace the bad drive with a new good one, and then reintegrate the new disk into the stripe set in order to keep the data fault tolerant. You must do this as quickly as possible, because the data is no longer fault tolerant and, according to Mark's Law of Disk Injustice, the more you are dependent on those disks, the greater the likelihood that one of them will fail. To do this, however, you must bring down this mission-critical server while you take out the old drive, install a new drive, and put the stripe set back together. We're not talking about a two-minute fix here. Imagine this happening on the space shuttle *Atlantis!*

In contrast, you could buy a *hardware* RAID system: a box containing several drives that are coordinated by a separate controller to act as one, which looks to the Server 2003 system like just one drive. An external RAID box costs a bit more, but a hardware-based RAID system can rebuild itself faster than software RAID. And best of all, most hardware-based RAID systems allow you to hot-swap the bad drive—that is, you can replace the bad drive without bringing down the server.

Management   Software RAID volumes use individual disk partitions grouped to create a single RAID partition, which can complicate management—with software RAID and three disks, you can set up three parallel RAID 5 partitions, each requiring its own parity calculations that stress the server. Hardware RAID generally treats disks as single-partition entities and the separate controller does the calculations, which takes the stress off of the main processor.

Most people who use Server 2003's built-in RAID use its mirroring capability, since the processing required to support RAID 5 seriously degrades server performance. However, if you're serious about data protection for Server 2003, you'll probably consider using hardware RAID, preferably one of the more advanced sorts, which offers its own processor and the ability to hot-swap failed disks.

Basic Disks versus Dynamic Disks

Server 2003 supports two kinds of disk storage: dynamic and basic. Aside from the structural differences in the way that information about the disks is stored on the disk itself, there are some pretty large differences with regard to software support and the amount of disk flexibility that each has to offer. In terms of support, any OS can detect a basic disk, even if it can't read the logical volumes on that disk. Only Win2K and Server 2003 can detect dynamic disks, however, and although there are strict limitations on how you can install the OS on a dynamic disk, you must use the new disk structure if you want to use multidisk volumes like RAID.

For logical volumes, Microsoft uses the term *partition* when you are using basic disks and *volume* when you are using dynamic disks, but if I say "partition" or "volume" or "logical drive" throughout this chapter, I'm speaking of generally the same thing: a way of making some logical sense out of physical disk space.

BASIC DISKS

When you install Server 2003 and create the first partition on which you will install the operating system, the disk defaults to a basic disk. Basic storage is the kind of storage that has been around since the DOS days, allowing for primary and extended disk partitions and logical drives. Basic disks use a partition style called master boot record (MBR). The MBR lies in the first sector of a basic disk, as does the partition table. These files hold critical information relating to the disk structures on that disk, including the starting and ending sectors, total number of sectors, and partition and RAID information. This is the kind of storage that I have been talking about throughout this chapter. Server 2003 still supports this kind of storage, although some of the functionality of Server 2003 can only be garnered if you are using dynamic disks, which I'll talk about in the next section.

If you're upgrading from NT 4 to Server 2003, then the basic disks which currently reside on your NT 4 system may include the mirror sets, volume sets, and stripe sets that you created using NT 4 Disk Administrator, using a basic disk type of storage available in the former OS. Unfortunately, there is no support for these outdated structures in Server 2003, so any mirrored, volume, or stripe sets that exist on an NT 4 server must be wiped out before you upgrade to Server 2003. If you don't do this, Server 2003 will render them unreadable during the upgrade and you will lose your data. The only way you can utilize mirror sets, volume sets, or stripe sets in Server 2003 is by using dynamic disks, and they have to be created after the install. Yes, there *was* limited support for upgrading these structures from NT 4 to Win2K, but that ability has been removed in Server 2003.

TIP   *Of course, if for some reason you end up having to come face to face with an angry ex-NT 4 system which has been upgraded to Server 2003 before the old disk structures were removed, there is a handy tool that will at least allow you to recover the data from those drives. It is a command-line tool called* `ftonline`*, and it's available in the Support/ Tools folder on the Server 2003 CD.*

Basic disks have their limitations. For compatibility reasons, they conform to the four-partition limit imposed by the structure of the disk partition table. Remember? It has a 64-byte file in the first sector of any disk that lists the physical locations of any logical partitions on the disk, but it can only describe four partitions because each description takes up 16 bytes. Of course, this type of storage will probably remain the most commonly used storage because, since an installation or boot of the OS requires the old-fashioned partition table entries in the MBR disk style, it is not always the best decision to upgrade to dynamic disks, nor is it always possible.

DYNAMIC DISKS

Dynamic disks were first introduced in Windows 2000 and are not supported by any Windows operating system prior to Win2K. They are still present in Server 2003, so if you want to use any kind of fault-tolerant or multidisk volumes, then you'll need to use dynamic disks.

Dynamic disks work together in Server 2003 in logical units called *disk groups*. You'll learn more about disk groups later, when we start really playing with dynamic disks in the section called "Using Dynamic Disks." For now, let's talk about what *dynamic disk* really means. Remember the partition table and the master boot record? When you make a disk dynamic, you are replacing the contents of the partition table (you know, all that critical disk information about the disk and the partitions) with a single entry which basically means, "Go read the dynamic disk database to get my partition information because *I* am a dynamic disk."

When you create a dynamic disk, you're writing a 1MB database of information at the end of that disk volume. This database contains all the partition information for each of the dynamic disks in the server. One of the nicer features of dynamic disks is that the information in that 1MB file is replicated to all the other dynamic disks in the system. The contents of the database on each disk are identical. (The changes are time-stamped, so that if a disk happens to be missing for a while, the newer changes will be automatically replicated to the disk when it returns, without any intervention on your part.) This is a big advantage over basic disks, which have a real single point of failure when it comes to all that critical information needed to maintain the integrity of the disk. If anything happens to the first sector of a basic disk, you will be hard pressed to recover from it. "Ah, *now* I know what they mean when they talk about a corrupted boot record," you'll say! If you import a "foreign" disk (a disk belonging to another dynamic disk array on another computer) to the mix, then the database entries in the existing array are copied to that new (foreign) disk, and any entries on the foreign disk are copied to the database of the disk array you're importing the disk into. In other words, importing the foreign disk merges the two databases because, if the task of importing a disk simply overwrote that foreign disk's database, it'd lose any existing volumes, and that wouldn't be very effective.

When you upgrade a basic disk that already has partitions on it (as the system disk will) to a dynamic disk, you'll have the original partition table to deal with. The contents of that table are copied to the database. The rest of the disk is then reserved for new volumes that will be recorded *only* in the database, not in the partition table. What that means is that there is a difference in the way volumes on a dynamic disk are viewed, depending on whether they were created *before* or *after* the conversion to dynamic.

When you boot a computer with dynamic disks in it, the BIOS reads the partition table, looks for the active partition, and reports the boot partition to work from. Finding the operating system, it goes through the boot process described in Chapter 19, "Preparing for and Recovering from Server Failures." The drivers for supporting dynamic volumes—DMLoad, DMAdmin, and (if the volume is a boot volume) DMBoot—are loaded early in the process of loading all Server 2003 drivers.

Remember how I said that you will need to use dynamic disks in order to use multidisk volumes with Server 2003? Does that mean that you should *always* upgrade disks to dynamic? The answer is no— not even Microsoft thinks dynamic disk are the right answer all of the time. In multidisk systems, dynamic disks can be very useful, but think hard about upgrading a disk before doing it. Dynamic disks are visible only to Windows 2000 and later versions of Windows. They're incomprehensible— in fact, invisible—to any locally installed operating system other than Win2K, XP Professional and Server 2003. Additionally, although you can revert a dynamic disk to a basic disk, you can only do this if the dynamic disk doesn't have any volumes on it. If you upgrade a basic disk that already has data on it to a dynamic disk, you'll have to delete the volumes on which that data is stored (and thus delete the data) before you can revert the disk to basic.

In short, to create new fault-tolerant volumes or multidisk volumes, you'll need to upgrade your disks to dynamic. If you need local compatibility with other operating systems, then stick with basic disks. If you've only got one disk in the server and don't plan to add more, you might as well leave it basic and save yourself the 1 MB of space that the dynamic metadata would use, because dynamic disks have no benefits in single-disk computers.

NOTE *Dynamic disks are not supported on laptops. See the later section "Not All Disks Are Upgradable" for the details.*

DIVIDING BASIC DISKS

The ways in which you can arrange the space on a physical disk are dependent on whether the disk is basic or dynamic. Basic disks support three kinds of organizational divisions: primary partitions, extended partitions, and logical drives.

Primary and Extended Partitions

Earlier in this chapter, I gave you a general idea of what partitions, logical drives, and volumes are— now I'll go into a little more detail about partitions and logical drives. I'll discuss volumes when we get to the topic of dynamic disks.

A *partition* is a portion of a hard disk set up to act like a separate physical hard disk, rather like splitting a single physical hard disk into several logical drives. There are two kinds of partitions: primary and extended.

A *primary partition* is a portion of a physical hard disk that the operating system (such as Server 2003) marks as bootable. Under DOS, you can only have one primary partition. Under Server 2003, Win2K, NT, XP, or Windows 9x, you can have multiple partitions on a drive, but only one partition at a time is marked active, which means you can boot from it. You can't break primary partitions into subpartitions, and you can create only up to four partitions per disk because that's all there's room for in the partition table. You might partition your hard disk so one primary partition is running Win2K and another is running Linux, but only one disk is marked Active at a time.

Four logical divisions on the disk aren't enough? You can create an *extended partition* from unallocated space on a physical disk. Once you do, you'll see a new area of free space on the drive, with a dark green border. The dark green border identifies the extended partition's area (the brilliant, neon green inside is the free space within that extended partition until you carve it up). You can only have one extended partition on a physical disk, but you can supplement it with up to three primary partitions, for a total of four blocks, which is all the partition table can manage.

You can't put any data into an extended partition or assign it a drive letter until you create one or more logical drives in that extended partition. Until then, it's just free space.

Logical Drive

A *logical drive* is a logical division of an extended partition that behaves like an entity unto itself. You can divide an extended partition into as many logical drives as you like if you make each partition the minimum size required (this minimum size will be shown in the wizard that helps you create the partition).

Logical drives are indicated in the Disk Management tool display with a royal blue stripe. Because they're part of an extended partition, they'll have a dark green border that encompasses all drives in the partition and any neon green free space left in it after you create the drives.

DIVIDING DYNAMIC DISKS

I hate to keep hammering this home, but it's important and, I've found, not intuitive: You'll use dynamic disks any time you want to use any kind of logical divisions of disk space that use multiple disks. Forget RAID, forget fault tolerance… the key point to dynamic disks is their support for storage areas that may extend over more than one disk. Of those areas, remember that dynamic disks support volume sets, mirror sets (RAID 1), stripe sets without parity (RAID 0), and stripe sets with parity (RAID 5).

Volume Sets

Although historically, the word volume has been used to generically refer to any logical disk division, for Server 2003's purposes, a *volume* is a logical division of the unallocated space on a dynamic disk. Since the advent of dynamic disks in Win2K, Microsoft has used this term to differentiate a dynamic disk from a basic disk. A volume in Server 2003 works like a logical drive or primary partition except for one major difference: Whereas logical drives and primary partitions in Server 2003 must be confined to a single disk, volumes using NTFS may either exist on a single disk or on more than one. This makes volumes much more flexible—and potentially more space efficient—than partitions or drives. As you can see in Figure 10.2, it's much easier to figure out how to fit 30MB of data into a 35MB volume set than it is to fit it into one 20MB logical drive and one 15MB logical drive. Especially if that 30MB is a single database.

Win2K supports two kinds of volume sets: simple volumes, which take up space on one disk, and spanned volumes, which take up space on multiple disks. You can extend either kind of volume; if you extend a simple volume onto another physical disk, it becomes a spanned volume. You cannot make the volume set smaller unless you delete it and create a new one.

FIGURE 10.2

How a volume
set works

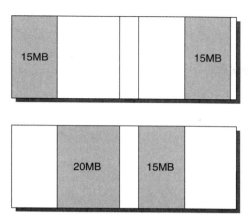

In this figure, 65MB of free space is available, but no more than 20MB of this space is contiguous. To get the most efficient use of this space, you could combine it in a volume set so all of the data is considered in one large chunk. Once this free space has been made into a volume set, you could store a 65MB chunk of data in it, even though the largest contiguous space is only 20MB in size.

NOTE *At one time, you could only extend NTFS-formatted volumes created on a dynamic disk. Volumes made from converted logical drives or partitions could not be extended. This is no longer true, with the help of the command-line tool called DiskPart. I'll go into more detail in the "Extending a Basic Partition: DiskPart" section.*

Volume sets do not protect your data; they are not fault tolerant. They only let you use available drive space more efficiently. If something happens to one of the hard disks used in a volume set, that volume set is dead, even if the other hard disks are fine. The more hard disks you have, the more likely it is that one will fail at any given time, so be sure to back up volume sets regularly.

Mirror Sets: RAID 1

Mirror sets are the simplest form of Server 2003 fault tolerance. They write two copies of all data onto volumes on two separate disks so that if one disk fails, the data is still available on the other. If anything happens to the disk storing your original data, you still have an identical copy on the disk which stores the other half of the mirror set.

Collectively, the two volumes are called a *mirror set*, or RAID 1. They have a couple of advantages:

◆ You can mirror an existing simple volume set, making it fault tolerant.

◆ You only need two physical disks to create a mirror set, instead of the minimum of three that RAID 5 volumes require.

Disk mirroring is simpler to use in Server 2003 than it was in NT 4. You can create mirrored volumes without rebooting, and you don't have to regenerate data to recover it if one of the disks supporting the mirror crashes. The data will remain available—it just won't be fault tolerant until you mirror it again.

If you've ever heard of disk mirroring, you've probably also heard the term *disk duplexing*. As shown in Figure 10.3, disk duplexing is much the same as disk mirroring, except that duplexing generally refers to mirroring information on two separate disks—each with its own disk controller—so that the data is not vulnerable to controller failures. When Server 2003 talks about disk mirroring, it is referring to both duplexing and mirroring. Server 2003 can't tell whether you have multiple controllers or not.

FIGURE 10.3
Disk mirroring
versus disk
duplexing

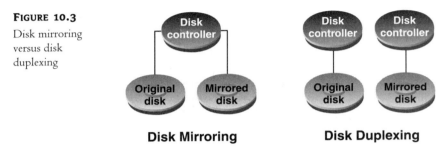

When compared to RAID 5, this level of RAID has relatively good performance, especially with two controllers, but they're not very space efficient because every piece of data that you record has an identical twin on the other half of the mirror set—so you need exactly twice as much storage space as you have data. Remember that the two halves must be of equal size.

Stripe Sets: RAID 0

Volume sets are useful because they allow you to combine many differently sized areas of unused disk space into a single volume. However, they don't offer any performance benefits. To use space on multiple disks and decrease read and write times, consider using disk striping without parity, also known as RAID 0.

When you create a stripe set from free space on your disks, each member of the stripe set is divided into stripes of equal size. Then, when you write data to the stripe set, the data is distributed over the stripes. A file could have its beginning recorded onto stripe 1 of member 1, more data recorded onto stripe 2 of member 2, and the rest on stripe 3 of member 3, for example. If you're saving data to a stripe set, a file is never stored on only one member disk, even if there is room on that disk for the entire file. Conceptually, striping looks something like Figure 10.4.

If you take free space on your disks and combine it into one stripe set with its own drive letter, the disk access time for that drive will be improved since the system can read and write to more than one disk at a time. To do striping without parity information included, you need at least 2, but not more than 32, disks.

Disk striping has a speed advantage over volume sets, but consider this:

♦ You cannot extend a stripe set as you can a volume or extend it over more disks once it's created. The size that you make the stripe set is the size it will stay.

♦ You cannot mirror a stripe set with software, although you *can* mirror a simple volume. There is simply no way to make a stripe set fault tolerant other than backing it up.

FIGURE 10.4

Stripe set without parity

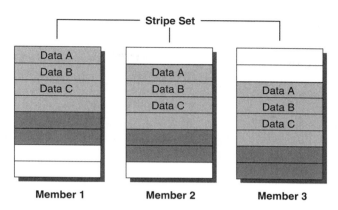

Different data files are represented here with different shades of gray. As you can see, an entire data file is never all put onto one member of the striped set. This improves read time since, if Data A is called for, the disk controllers on all three members of the set can read the data. With a SLED data arrangement, only one of the members could read the data.

If you're looking for performance, use stripe sets without parity. If you're looking for flexibility and expandability, use simple or spanned volume sets. If its fault tolerance that you're after, use mirror sets or stripe sets with parity.

Stripe Sets with Parity: RAID 5

For data protection, or to decrease your disks' read time, you can select areas of unallocated space on your disks and combine them into a *RAID 5 volume*, also known as a *stripe set with parity*. RAID 5 volumes are the most cost-effective form of RAID that Server 2003 supports because they require less space for redundant data than mirroring does. The catch is that they're also very processor intensive.

How does disk striping with parity work? Every time you write data to a RAID 5 volume, the data is written across all the striped disks in the array, just as it is with regular disk striping, RAID 0. Parity information for your data is also written to disk, always on a separate disk from the one where the data it corresponds to is written. That is, there isn't a separate "parity" disk, although RAID 4, which is not supported in Server 2003, organizes data that way. Rather, each disk supporting the RAID 5 volume may contain a piece of original data or the parity information needed to reconstruct that original data, but not both the original and its parity information. That way, if anything happens to one of the disks in the array, the data on that disk can be reconstructed from the parity information on the other disks. This is shown in Figure 10.5.

If you think about it, writing parity information every time you save a document could turn into a big waste of space and time. Take, for example, the document I'm creating for this book. If I've protected my data with level-5 RAID and parity information is stored to disk every time this file is saved, does that mean that there is parity information for every incarnation of this document from the time I began writing? If so, how can all the parity information and data fit on the disks?

The answer is, of course, that it doesn't, and this is what produces the performance degradation that's unavoidable in striped disk writes. Every time a document is saved to disk, its parity information must be updated to reflect its current status. Otherwise, you would have to keep backup parity information for every version of the document that you ever saved.

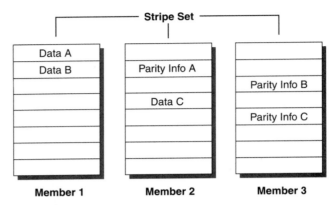

FIGURE 10.5

Disk striping with parity information

As you can see, no single member of the stripe set keeps all the original data or all the parity information. Instead, the data and parity information are distributed throughout the stripe set so, if one member disk fails, the information can be reconstructed from the other members of the stripe set.

There are two ways to update the parity information. First, since the parity information is the XOR of the data, the system could recalculate the XOR each time data is written to disk. What is an *XOR?* On a *very* simplistic level, the XOR, or *exclusive OR arithmetic,* is a function that takes two 1-bit inputs and produces a single-bit output. The result is 1 if the two inputs are different or 0 if the two inputs are the same. More specifically:

0 XOR 0 = 0

1 XOR 0 = 1

0 XOR 1 = 1

1 XOR 1 = 0

When you're XORing two numbers with more than one bit, you match the bits up and XOR each pair individually. For example, 1101010 XOR 0101000 equals 1000010. The result you get from this function is the parity information, from which the original data can be recalculated.

Having to recalculate all the data stored in the volume each time you write to disk would take quite a while. A more efficient way of recalculating the parity information, and the one that Server 2003 uses is to read the old data to be overwritten and XOR it with the new data to determine the differences. This process produces a *bit mask* that has a 1 in the position of every bit that has been changed. This bit mask can then be XORed with the old parity information to see where *its* differences lie, and from this the new parity information can be calculated. This seems convoluted, but this second process only requires two reads and two XOR computations rather than one of each for every drive in the array.

RAID 5 volumes are great in theory, but in Server 2003's implementation they don't work so well. First, needing to generate parity information for every write to disk slows down the write process. Second and more important, RAID 5 represents a serious drain on processor time. In high-end hardware RAID, the system is configured with a separate processor that handles all the calculations necessary. Software RAID, such as what we're discussing in this chapter, relies on the server's processor to do all that calculating. You almost certainly won't use software RAID 5 much on a production server because of the performance toll it extracts, especially on processor-intensive applications.

Using the Disk Management Tool

The Disk Management tool made its debut in Win2K and offered significant improvement over the Disk Administrator offered in NT 4. Whereas the Disk Administrator required you to reboot after any change to the partition system, or possibly if you breathed too hard on the hard disk, Win2K's version allowed you to create and delete volumes without rebooting. You could mount partitions to paths on other NTFS volumes instead of just assigning drive letters to new volumes. You could format volumes while creating them rather than having to format them from the command prompt or from Explorer as was necessary in the past. All in all, it was a good tool and a great improvement over previous iterations of the Disk Administrator. With Server 2003's new and improved version of the Disk Management tool, you can do even more. You can make changes to disks on-the-fly with no shutdown required, you can expand volumes, configure software RAID, add and remove disks and, generally, do just about anything you need to manage the physical and logical storage on your system. More specifically, with the Disk Management tool, you can do the following:

- Create and delete partitions on a hard disk and make logical drives
- Get status information concerning these items:
  - Disk partition sizes
  - Free space left on a disk for making partitions
  - Volume labels, their drive-letter assignment, filesystem type, and size
  - Disk health
- Alter drive letter and volume mounting assignments
- Enlarge disk volumes
- Create, delete, and repair mirror sets
- Format any volume
- Extend volumes
- Create and delete stripe sets and regenerate missing or failed members of stripe sets with parity
- Create volume shadow copies

The Disk Management tool is the GUI way of managing your storage and is a very effective tool for seeing the logical disk layout on your disks, complete with shiny colors that help identify the kind of disk and the various flavors of logical volumes or sets contained on those disks. But, if the puke green color of the volumes on your dynamic disk doesn't turn you on, you can use the cool new command-line utility DiskPart, which can do everything that the Disk Management tool is capable of and more, and is installed by default when you install the OS. In fact, if you want to extend a basic disk, this tool is your *only* option. I'll cover this tool in more detail in the section "Extending a Basic Partition: DiskPart." Let's move on to another basic, but important, disk management topic, installing physical disks.

Installing a New Physical Disk

When you first add a new hard disk to your computer, Server 2003 will not recognize the new disk even if it shows up at boot time (SCSI or IDE). You must add support for the new drive, either manually or by following the Initialize and Convert Disk Wizard, which was known as the Write Signature and Upgrade Disk Wizard in Win2K. The wizard will start up automatically when you open the Disk Management tool in the Computer Management interface and have new physical disks attached to the system.

There are two steps to setting up a new hard disk: writing a disk signature and choosing whether the disk should be basic or dynamic. Server 2003 writes disk signatures as part of the Initialize and Convert Disk Wizard.

To add a new disk, follow the wizard. The disks you just added are already selected for initialization, although you have the option of unselecting one or more. The next screen allows you to choose whether you would like to convert your disk or disks to dynamic disks, something you should think through before doing because, as you'll see, you can't always undo it very easily. This is unchecked by default. Server 2003 will write a signature to the disks so that they are ready for you to begin logically dividing them.

Using Basic Disk Features

Basic disks, recall, are the default in Win2K and Server 2003. A basic disk is a normal disk, available from any operating system, and uses primary and extended partitions to divide up physical disk space into logical units. You'll need to stick with basic disks if you want to make disks available to operating systems other than Win2K or Server 2003. This will keep you from using RAID, but then again, even before Win2K introduced dynamic disks you couldn't access mirrored or other RAID volumes from any operating system other than NT anyway. On basic disks, you can create primary partitions, extended partitions, and logical drives.

USING PRIMARY PARTITIONS TO STORE OPERATING SYSTEMS

Although you'll set up at least the initial disk partitioning for your system/boot partition when you install Server 2003, you can use the Disk Management tool in the Computer Management section of the MMC (Computer Management is in the Administrative Tools program group) to edit the logical divisions of your disk after you've installed Server 2003.

Forgetting dynamic disks, you normally boot a computer from a primary partition. When you install Server 2003, the Setup program will automatically create a primary partition to put the OS on. Once Server 2003 is installed, you can create more bootable partitions or partitions to store data that's separate from your system partition. Right-click any area of unallocated space on the hard disk and choose New Partition to start the New Partition Wizard. Click through the welcome screen, then choose the type of partition you want to create (see Figure 10.6).

In the next screen of the wizard, specify the size of the primary partition. It can be anywhere from the minimum specified in the wizard to the full size of the unallocated space.

FIGURE 10.6

You can create primary partitions from unallocated space.

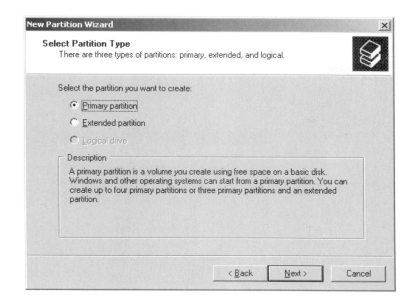

NOTE   *In Win2K, you had to make sure that you made the partition as big as it would ever need to be, because you did not have the ability to extend primary partitions. With the new DiskPart command-line tool, you can now extend basic partitions. I'll show you how in the section "Extending a Basic Partition: DiskPart."*

In the next wizard screen (see Figure 10.7), you have three options: choose a drive letter for the new primary partition, mount it to an empty folder on an NTFS volume, or do neither.

FIGURE 10.7

Pick an identifier for the partition.

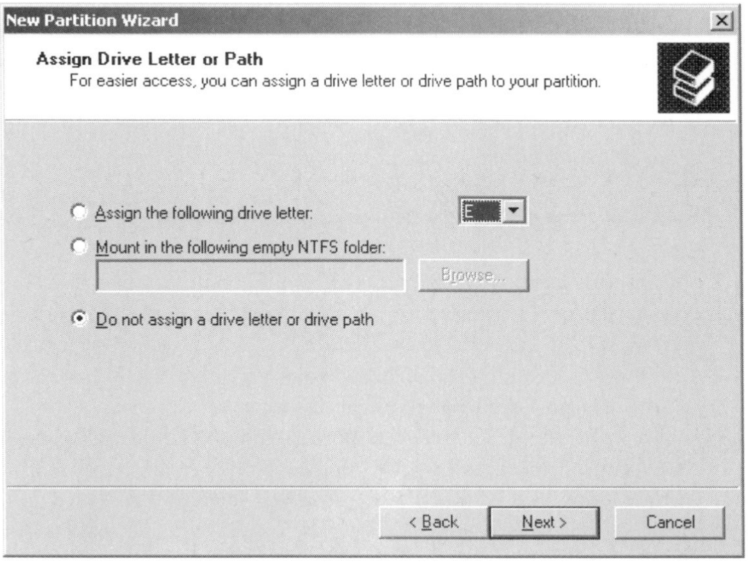

NOTE *At some point, you'll have to assign the partition a drive letter or path if you want to use it. You can't save data to an area of the disk that isn't named and you can't format it—there's no way to get its attention, so to speak.*

Next, you'll be prompted to choose a format for the disk (see Figure 10.8). Server 2003 supports NTFS (the default file format), FAT, and FAT32. You'll only have the option to compress the volume if you format with NTFS. Quick formats, which just wipe the disk without checking it for errors, are available with any format type.

FIGURE 10.8

Choose a disk format.

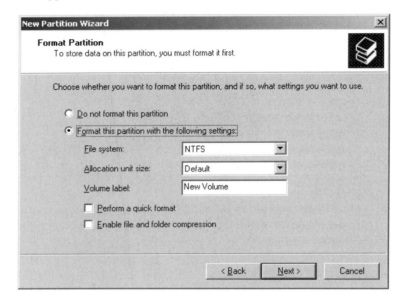

You don't actually have to format the partition now—you can format a volume at any time by right-clicking it and choosing Format from the shortcut menu—but you'll have to format it before you use it.

When you've finished, you'll see a finish screen like the one in Figure 10.9. Review your choices to make sure the new partition is set up the way you want it, and click Finish.

USING LOGICAL DRIVES TO ORGANIZE INFORMATION

Even if you rely on the SLED model for your data storage, you may want to divide that single large physical drive into smaller logical ones. You could, for example, keep all the accounting information on logical drive C:, the engineering information on logical drive D:, the personnel information on logical drive E:, and so on. As discussed earlier, you can also mount logical drives to NTFS folders on other local disks. Although you can also do all this with primary partitions, logical drives have an advantage: no four-division limit per physical disk.

To create a logical drive, you must first take unallocated space and convert it to an extended partition. Creating an extended partition is much like creating a primary partition, except for the different partition type that you'll choose in the first page of the wizard and the fact that you won't be asked to format or label the new partition. The new extended partition will be labeled Free Space.

FIGURE 10.9

Review your choices before finishing the logical drive.

WHAT FILESYSTEMS ARE AVAILABLE?

I'll talk about the benefits and drawbacks of the filesystems Server 2003 supports shortly, but when experimenting with creating partitions, you might wonder why some filesystems are available for some partitions but not for others.

The filesystems available will depend on the size of the partition you're formatting and the tool you're using to do it. If you format with the Disk Management tool as described here, you can format a partition smaller than 4GB (4096MB) with any filesystem that Win2K and Server 2003 support: FAT, FAT32, or NTFS. For volumes larger than 4GB, the Disk Management tool will only offer the formats of FAT32 or NTFS. For partitions larger than 2GB but smaller than 4GB, FAT will be an option, but when you choose that filesystem you'll see a message warning you that the partition you're formatting will not be compatible with previous versions of Windows, since the filesystem will use clusters bigger than 32KB.

In Win2K, if you were formatting partitions with Explorer, then all three filesystems appeared in the list of available file formats regardless of the size of the partition. If you formatted a partition 4GB or larger, then FAT would still appear in the list of available file formats; when you clicked the OK button to begin the format, Win2K would chug away as though formatting the volume. However, when it finished you'd see an error message saying that the format couldn't be completed. The partition you tried to format would be unformatted, in its original condition, and any data on the volume before the intended format would still be there. This is fixed in Server 2003. The option to format with FAT is no longer there if the partition is larger than 4GB.

Once you've created the extended partition, you're ready to create a logical drive so that you can store data. To do so, right-click free space in the extended partition and choose New Logical Drive from the shortcut menu. This will start the New Partition Wizard that you've seen before. Click through the first screen, and you'll see the one shown in Figure 10.10.

FIGURE 10.10

Choose to create a logical drive.

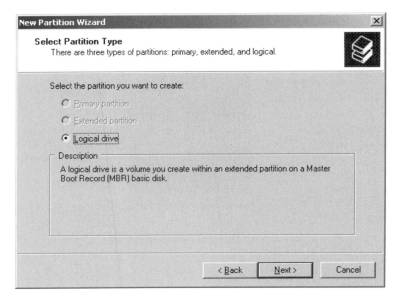

Notice that you only have one option here; you can't create partitions within an extended partition. Click Next to open the next page of the wizard and choose the size of the drive you want to create (see Figure 10.11).

FIGURE 10.11

Specify the size of the new logical drive.

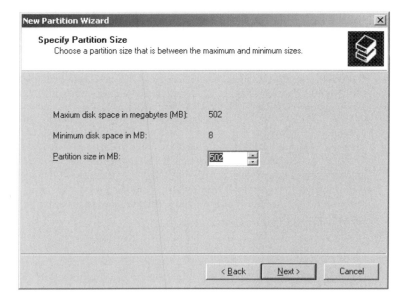

In the next screen of the wizard, you can once again choose to either mount the drive or assign it a drive letter. Format the drive with the filesystem you want, and you'll arrive at the finish screen showing you the options you picked. Click Finish, and the logical drive will appear in the extended partition.

DELETING A BASIC DISK PARTITION OR DRIVE

To delete any basic disk partition, right-click it and choose the Delete Partition or Delete Logical Drive option (whichever applies). A dialog box will pop up and warn you that any information in the volume that you're deleting will be lost and ask if you're sure you want to continue. Click Yes to delete the volume.

The deleted basic disk volume will revert to whatever it was before you created the volume. Primary partitions and extended partitions revert to unallocated space on the drive; logical drives revert to free space.

EXTENDING A BASIC PARTITION: DISKPART

I mentioned before the inability in Win2K to extend basic partitions and the new command-line tool called DiskPart that now makes that possible. What's more, DiskPart has all of the functionality of the Disk Management tool in a command-line utility, which means that—you guessed it!—you can now script your disk management chores. Imagine how useful this will be when you are rolling out machines by the dozens, or hundreds, or even thousands using an unattended setup or Sysprep, which offers support for only one boot volume. Be careful though: DiskPart is a *very* powerful tool. Compare it with the Registry editor with which, without careful attention to detail, you can completely destroy your OS. If you are lucky you'll have your data stored on a separate disk and will still be able to recover it. With DiskPart, you can destroy the logical organization of those disks and delete disks, volumes, partitions, and volumes sets with the same ease as editing the Registry. Imagine trying to recover from a mistake like that. Of course, you can also do a great deal of good with this tool Right now, I'll show you how to use this tool to expand your basic disks which, as I said before, you cannot do with the Disk Management GUI.

From the DOS prompt, type the command **diskpart**. DiskPart is a command-line interpreter, which means that once DiskPart is called with the command you just typed, it will be ready to accept additional commands at the *DISKPART>* command prompt. To perform any action on a specific disk, volume, or partition in your system, you must first select it, which shifts the focus of the DiskPart tool to that specific structure. Of course, in order to select a disk, volume, or partition, you'll want to list those structures so you can ensure you are making the correct selection. To do this, you use DiskPart's **list** command. Type **list** and then follow it with either **disk** or **volume** in order to view those structures. For example, in the following you can see the effects of listing the disks contained in the system.

```
C:\Documents and Settings\Administrator>diskpart

Microsoft DiskPart version 5.2.3663
Copyright (C) 1999-2001 Microsoft Corporation.
On computer: STORAGE

DISKPART> list disk
```

```
Disk ###  Status       Size     Free     Dyn  Gpt
--------  ----------   -------  -------   ---  ---
Disk 0    Online       6142 MB  8033 KB    *
Disk 1    Online       6142 MB  8033 KB    *
Disk 2    Online       6142 MB  6142 MB
```

Listing the disks shows you the basic details about the disks, including the size, whether it is dynamic or basic, and any free space not allocated to volumes or partitions on the disk. The GPT detail is used for the Itanium platform, as the partition style of the Itanium differs from both the MBR style and the dynamic disk style; I won't cover that here.

When you use the `list volume` command, DiskPart shows you a list of *all* of the volumes on every disk in the system. To get a list of the partitions, though, you have to first `select` a single disk onto which DiskPart will shift its focus. Then use the **list partition** command for each disk separately by first selecting a specific disk and then running the command for that particular disk, as shown here:

```
DISKPART> list disk

Disk ###  Status       Size     Free     Dyn  Gpt
--------  ----------   -------  -------   ---  ---
Disk 0    Online       6142 MB  8033 KB    *
Disk 1    Online       6142 MB  8033 KB    *
Disk 2    Online       6142 MB  1137 MB

DISKPART> select disk 2

Disk 2 is now the selected disk.

DISKPART> list partition

Partition ###  Type              Size     Offset
-------------  ----------------  -------  -------
Partition 1    Primary           1004 MB   32 KB
```

Now that you know how to view the structures on the disks using DiskPart, let's pick a basic disk and try to extend it. You can tell that Disk 2 is a basic disk as it does not have a checkmark in the Dyn column. Since Disk 2 has already been selected (you just viewed the partitions on it, remember?) all you need to do to extend the disk is use the **extend** command. The syntax for the command is as follows:

```
extend [size=N] [disk=N] [noerr]
```

The *size=N* parameter allows you to select the amount of unallocated space (in MB) that you want to add to the partition. If you don't specify a size, the disk is automatically extended using all of the room in the next contiguous unallocated space.

You can use the *disk=N* option to pick a disk that you want to extend. (If you have already selected a disk, you don't need to use this option.) It will extend the disk you currently have selected, so make sure you know which disk you have selected before you use the **extend** command.

If you are using DiskPart to script the disk management for your unattended installs, you can use the *noerr* parameter to ignore errors and continue executing commands. Without this option selected, when DiskPart encounters an error, it will cease to run and will exit with an error code.

EXTENDING THE BASIC DISK

Before actually extending the basic disk, you'll need to remember a few things:

You cannot extend the system or boot partition on a basic disk.

If the partition is already formatted with NTFS, when you expand the disk the new space is automatically formatted with NTFS. Without NTFS, the command will fail.

The unallocated space you want to use must be on the same disk as the partition on which you have focused DiskPart.

For basic disks, the unallocated space has to be located immediately after the partition you want to extend on the disk. It can't jump a partition and use the unallocated space available at the end of the disk.

Okay, remember that you first selected Disk 2 and then selected Partition 1, and thus you are ready to execute the *extend* command. Here's what it looks like:

```
DISKPART> extend

DiskPart successfully extended the volume.
```

That's it. Quick as a flash, what was once an impossible task has been completed in seconds with little effort. Remember, extending basic volumes can only be done using the DiskPart tool—it can't be done with the GUI (not yet, anyway).

I have to admit to really liking this new tool, especially its scripting capabilities, although at the time of this writing, I was getting some kind of flaky results using the *size=N* parameter. Any time I tried to expand a basic disk using that option, the command would fail with an error, but it seemed to expand the disk using my size specifications anyway. And any time I received an error, DiskPart seemed to forget whatever disk, volume, or partition I was working on and I'd have to go through the process of reselecting all of those structures to refocus DiskPart on the job at hand. It would be okay if I knew the command really worked, but this isn't the kind of tool where a "maybe" is okay. Of course, I am working with a Beta version of Server 2003 as I write this, so maybe it will be fixed before the final release. Other than my difficulties with the *size=N* parameter, I find DiskPart to be a very handy tool.

I recommend learning this tool whether you are planning to use it for its scripting functionality or not, as it has fixed issues for me that could not be fixed using the Disk Management tool. But, as I said before, if you fear editing the Registry (and you should), you should fear using DiskPart even more—it's the dragon's breath in terms of potential for damage, so beware.

I'll go into some more detail about DiskPart in the "DiskPart For Disk Management" section. But first, you need to learn more about the basics of managing disks using Server 2003's Disk Management tool.

CONVERTING A BASIC DISK TO A DYNAMIC DISK

Even after you partition part of the disk, you can convert a basic disk to a dynamic disk so that any new volumes you create in the remaining space can span multiple physical disks. Before you start converting, however, here are a few things you should consider.

You Can't Easily Undo This!

If you don't read another word in this section before skipping to the instructions, read this. If you upgrade a disk to dynamic, then you cannot make that disk a basic disk again without deleting every volume on it. There is no way to preserve a dynamic disk's organizational structure when making it a basic disk.

Not All Disks Are Upgradable

These instructions will not work on every disk. If you don't see an option to upgrade a basic disk, there may be a reason:

◆ Only fixed-disk drives may be dynamic disks. Removable disk drives such as Jaz drives can only be basic disks. The reasoning is simple: A dynamic disk volume may extend over more than one physical disk. A removable disk might not always be present.

◆ If the disk has a sector size larger than 512 bytes, then you won't be able to upgrade it. Notice that that's the *sector* size, not the *cluster* size. I'll get into the difference more in the later section on formatting, but for the moment just understand that (a) this is a problem you're unlikely to encounter, and (b) you can't change the sector size of your disks with a Server 2003 format. Cluster size, yes; sector size, no.

◆ You can't make disks on a laptop computer dynamic—Server 2003 doesn't support this. The logic is that laptops normally only have a single physical disk. First, this means that they can't reap any of the benefits of dynamic disks, since those benefits are all tied into RAID. Second, if a laptop has a second hard disk that's available when the laptop is in a docking station, then the database containing information about the dynamic disks in the computer would easily become out of date if the two dynamic disks only sometimes worked together.

◆ For those using Windows Server 2003, Enterprise Edition or Windows Server 2003, Datacenter Edition, you can't make the shared storage system in a cluster dynamic.

What's Happening to My System and Boot Partitions?

Before upgrading a basic disk, consider what effects the change will have on existing system data—both for Server 2003 and for any other operating systems on the computer:

◆ You will *not* be able to install Server 2003 onto a volume on a dynamic disk unless the volume was upgraded from a basic disk. That is, the volume must have existed on the physical disk before you upgraded it to dynamic. Although Windows Setup can "see" a native dynamic volume—i.e., it will appear in the list of available partitions for installation—if you select it, Setup will not be able to recognize the partition and will ask you to pick another one, as the original partition table must be there to be able to boot from it.

◆ You can (usually) upgrade the disk with the system partition on it, but the upgrade will not take effect until you restart the computer. (Actually, this is true for any disk that has files open during the upgrade, not just the system partition.) This is one of the few times that you'll need to restart the computer for a change in the Disk Management tool to take effect.

◆ You will not be able to access the dynamic disks from any locally installed operating system other than Win2K or Server 2003. That is, you'll be able to get to them from across the network, but in a dual-boot computer, the other operating systems will not be able to see the dynamic disks. That, by the way, includes *booting* from those dynamic disks, so don't convert a disk with other operating systems on it.

◆ You can't use dynamic disk or volume sets on clustered storage devices, although there are some third-party products that allow for dynamic disks to be clustered.

Keep in Mind What You Have

You may not *want* to upgrade a basic disk to dynamic. Seriously. You'll need to do it to get the full benefits of Server 2003's multidisk volumes and software RAID support, but upgrading can be hard to reverse and a pain to resolve if you can't. Keep the following in mind:

◆ You cannot extend the volumes on the converted disk if the volumes were originally created on a basic disk. Only volumes originally created on a dynamic disk may be extended to other disks or made larger with unallocated space on the same disk.

◆ Although you always have the option of converting dynamic disks back to basic disks, you must delete any volumes on the disk first.

Upgrading the Basic Disk

Now that you're thoroughly intimidated, let's go through the process of doing the conversion:

1. In the Disk Management tool, right-click the gray area on the left side of the physical disk you want to convert (see Figure 10.12).

FIGURE 10.12

You must start from the physical disk, not from one of the logical volumes on the disk.

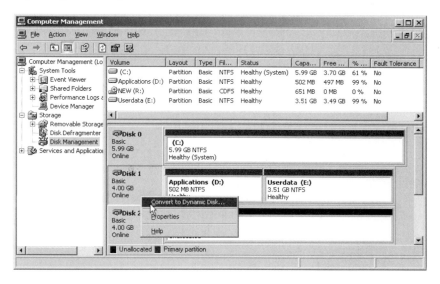

2. From the context menu that appears, choose Convert to Dynamic Disk to open the dialog box in Figure 10.13. All basic disks on the computer that are available to be converted (recall, this includes only fixed-disk drives) will be listed and identified by number.

FIGURE 10.13

Choose the basic disk(s) you want to convert.

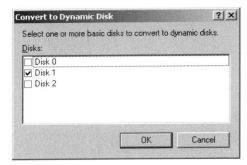

3. Click OK, and the Disk Management tool will then display a list of the disks it's going to convert. This dialog box is much like the preceding one except for a Details button. Click this button, and you'll see a list of the logical drives on the physical disks (see Figure 10.14).

FIGURE 10.14

The Disk Management tool will show you what logical drives are on the disk to be converted.

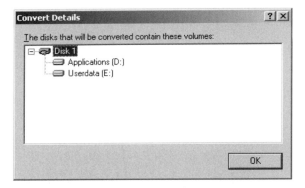

4. Exit the Details box and return to the Disks to Convert box by clicking OK. If you're still sure you want to upgrade, click the Convert button. You'll see a message like the one in Figure 10.15, warning you that other versions of Windows will no longer be able to boot from this disk. Click Yes, and you'll get *another* message warning you that all mounted file paths will be dismounted. (If you regret upgrading a disk to dynamic, it's not going to be Microsoft's fault.) Click Yes to get through this message box.

FIGURE 10.15

Be sure not to convert any basic disks that other versions of Windows will need to access.

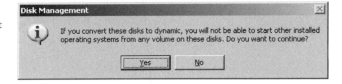

Once you've clicked Yes, the hard disk will grind away for a couple of minutes. When the operation is completed, any partitions or logical drives that had previously been on the disk will now be simple volumes. If the disk had open files—as with the system disk—then you'll need to reboot.

Why Didn't the Upgrade Work?

That's how it's supposed to work. If you're attempting to upgrade disks that should work (see "Not All Disks Are Upgradable") and the upgrade doesn't take, then something may be wrong with the disks or with a volume on the disk.

When Disk Management attempts to convert a basic disk to dynamic, it first performs a system check to make sure that the conversion will take. The disks must be working (you can't write a 1MB database of disk information to a disk that's having I/O errors), and the volumes on the disks have to be working and visible to the Server 2003 Volume Manager. For instance, if you create a partition with something other than the Disk Management tool, then until you restart the system the Volume Manager may not be able to "see" it. If the Volume Manager is unaware of that volume, it will stop the disk conversion process.

Using Dynamic Disks

You'll need to use dynamic disks if you want to use Server 2003's software RAID protection. Read on for more information about how to create and delete RAID volumes and use them to improve fault tolerance and/or disk performance.

CREATING A DYNAMIC DISK VOLUME

Creating a dynamic disk volume is much like creating a volume on a basic disk, but you'll have some more options depending on the number of dynamic disks you have available and the kind of volume you're creating. The basic process goes like this:

1. In the Disk Management tool, right-click unallocated space on any dynamic disk to open the shortcut menu. Choose New Volume.

2. You'll open the New Volume Wizard. Click past the opening screen to the one shown in Figure 10.16. Pick a type of volume to create.

FIGURE 10.16

Choose a type of dynamic volume to create.

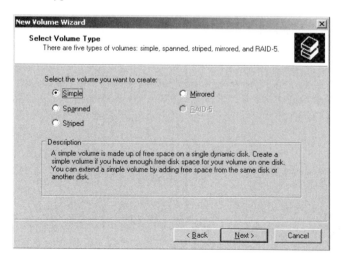

NOTE *Not all volume types will always be available. If you have available only a single dynamic disk with unallocated space, you'll only be able to create a simple volume. Two dynamic disks with unallocated space available will permit you to create a stripe set, spanned volume, or mirror set. To create a stripe set with parity, at least three dynamic disks with unallocated space must be present.*

3. In the next screen, choose the disk or disks that you want the volume to reside on. The currently selected disk will be in the list on the right side (see Figure 10.17) and the available disks will be on the left side. Select a disk and click the Add or Remove buttons to pick the disks you want the volume set to be on.

FIGURE 10.17

Choose the disks that should support the volume.

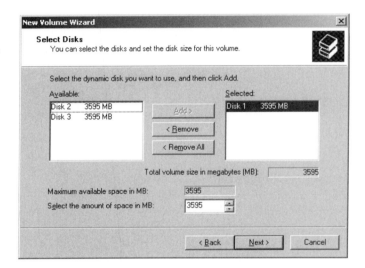

4. In the same screen of the wizard, pick the size you want the volume to be. By default, the new volume will be as large as possible, based on the amount of unallocated space available on the disks you've chosen. You can make it smaller than this size, down to 1MB, but you obviously can't make the volume bigger.

5. In the next screen of the wizard (see Figure 10.18), choose a drive letter or map the new volume to a path on an NTFS volume. Although you don't have to do either at this time, you will need to call the new volume *something* before you can use it.

6. Click to open the next screen of the wizard and choose a disk format for the new volume: NTFS, FAT32, or FAT. Again, as you can see in Figure 10.19, you don't have to format the volume while creating it, but you will need to format it before you can use it.

NOTE *You can always perform a quick format on any volume (just wiping the volume and not checking for bad clusters), but file and folder compression—and other features such as disk quotas and file encryption—are only available for NTFS volumes.*

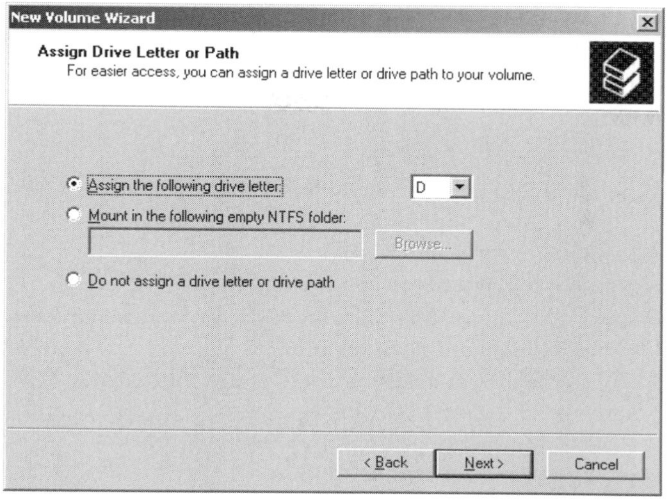

FIGURE 10.18

Choose a drive letter or mount the volume to a drive path.

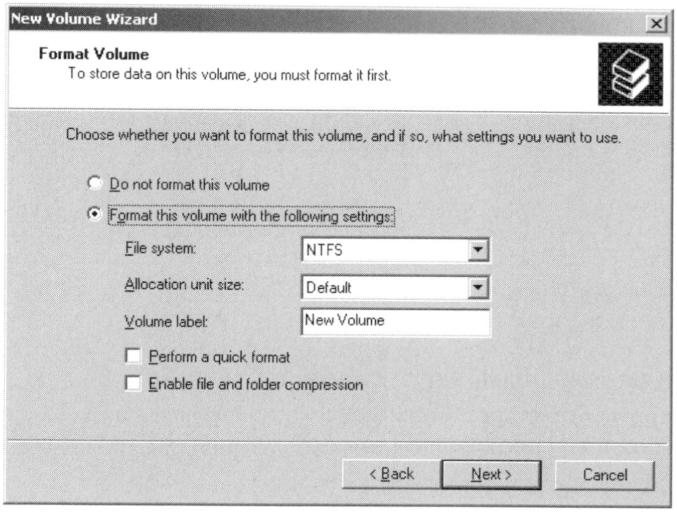

FIGURE 10.19

Format the new volume.

The final screen of the wizard displays the choices you've made so that you can go back and change them if need be. Otherwise, click Finish, and the new volume will be accessible as soon as it's formatted—no rebooting required.

DELETING A DYNAMIC DISK VOLUME

Deleting a dynamic disk volume is straightforward: right-click the volume to delete and pick Delete Volume from the shortcut menu. You'll see a message like the one in Figure 10.20, warning you that you're about to delete any data on that volume. Click Yes to continue deleting the volume and it's instantly gone—no rebooting or further warnings required.

FIGURE 10.20

Deleting a volume
permanently deletes
the data stored
on that volume.

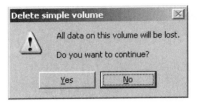

CONVERTING A DYNAMIC DISK TO A BASIC DISK

If you mistakenly upgrade a basic disk to dynamic, all is not lost. You can reverse the process. The only catch is that you can't convert volumes on a dynamic disk to basic disk volumes, because they don't exist in the disk's partition table—just in the dynamic disk database. If you have volumes on the disk, then the Convert to Basic Disk option in the disk's shortcut menu will be grayed out. You'll need to delete all volumes before this option becomes available.

Assuming that the disk is empty, however, the process is simple for a data disk. Right-click the gray area of the physical disk (all the way to the left in the Disk Management tool's display) and choose Convert to Basic Disk. That's it. No reboot required.

Creating a Volume Set

I explained how to build a dynamic disk volume in the earlier section, "Creating a Dynamic Disk Volume." The only volume set–specific parts to remember are these:

◆ Simple volume sets will only use space on one dynamic physical disk.

◆ Spanned volume sets may use space on from 2 to 32 dynamic physical disks.

Other than that, the process of creating a simple or spanned volume is now blessedly simple: pick the disks to place the volume on, pick a size for the volume, assign the volume a drive letter or mount it to a path, format it, and you're done.

ENLARGING A VOLUME SET

If it turns out that your NTFS-formatted volume set is smaller than you need it to be, it's not necessary to delete it and re-create it from scratch. Instead, you can *extend* it by adding areas of free space to its volume.

NOTE *You cannot make a volume set smaller. To do that, you must delete the volume set and create it again.*

To extend an existing simple or spanned volume set, follow these steps:

1. Right-click the simple or spanned volume set you want to expand and choose Extend Volume from the shortcut menu. You'll start up the Extend Volume Wizard.

2. Click through the initial page of the wizard to display the screen shown in Figure 10.21. From here, choose the disk or disks onto which you want to extend the volume set. Only dynamic disks with unallocated space will be available.

FIGURE 10.21

Pick the disks to add to the volume set and specify how much space you want to add.

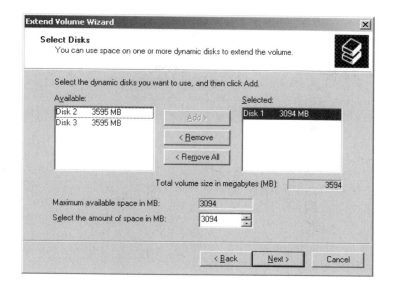

3. In this same screen, choose the amount of unallocated disk space you want to add from the new disk. The Disk Management tool will display both the amount of space that you're adding and the total size of the newly extended volume.

4. The final screen of the wizard will show the choices you've made. Review them and click either Back to make changes or Finish to extend the volume set.

The volume set is now the larger size that you specified, and all of the area in it will have the same drive letter. The unallocated space that you added is automatically formatted to the same filesystem as the rest of the volume set—NTFS.

There are a few catches to extending volume sets:

♦ You can only extend NTFS volumes, so you'll need to reformat or convert FAT or FAT32 volumes to NTFS before you can extend them.

♦ When you convert a basic disk to dynamic, it makes any partitions that exist on the basic disk become simple volumes. With Win2K, you could not extend *those* simple volumes. Only volumes originally created on a dynamic disk were extensible. That is still partially true in Server 2003, at least for volumes originally created on a basic disk in Win2K. Consider the following example. If you have upgraded a basic disk to dynamic in Win2K, which includes the volumes originally created on that basic disk, and then you upgrade to Server 2003, you will be unable to extend those volumes. If, however, you upgrade a basic disk to dynamic in Server 2003, which includes volumes originally created on those Server 2003 basic disks, you will be able to extend them. It's an improvement in Server 2003, but not one that can reach back and fix the existing problem in Win2K.

♦ Again, you cannot use this procedure to make a volume set smaller. To do that, you need to delete the volume set and create a new one.

♦ You cannot combine two volume sets, nor can you add a logical drive to a volume set.

Creating a Stripe Set

Creating a stripe set without parity is just like creating any other dynamic disk volume: make sure that you've got at least two dynamic disks with unallocated space available, right-click an area of unallocated space, and choose New Volume to start the wizard. In the first screen that includes any data, make sure that you've selected the Striped Volume type as shown in Figure 10.22.

FIGURE 10.22

Choose striped volumes to reduce disk access times.

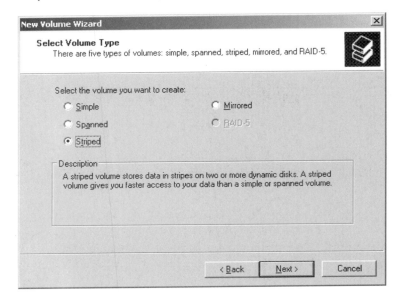

From here, the volume creation process is the same for all dynamic volumes, as described in the earlier section, "Creating a Dynamic Disk Volume." Just keep in mind the following:

◆ Stripe sets must include at least 2 and no more than 32 physical disks.

◆ Each stripe will be the same size. That is, if the largest area of unallocated space on Disk 0 is 50MB, then the largest stripe set you can create on three disks is 150MB, even if Disk 1 and Disk 2 each have, say, 200MB of unallocated space.

◆ Stripe sets do not include any parity information, so the volume size the wizard lists is an actual reflection of the amount of data you can store on the striped volume.

If anything happens to any member disk of your non-parity stripe set, all the data in the set is lost. It doesn't hurt the other disks in the stripe set, but it means that the data in the stripe set itself is unavailable.

DELETING A STRIPE SET

If you make a stripe set too small or too big, there's no way to resize it. You'll need to delete the stripe set and start over. Just right-click it and choose Delete Volume from the shortcut menu. As always, you'll be prompted to confirm that you want to delete the volume, and when you do, the stripe set—and all the data stored on it—will disappear.

Establishing a Mirror Set

To create a mirror set, you can either start from unallocated space on a dynamic disk or mirror an existing simple volume.

NOTE You cannot mirror a volume on a basic disk. Although Win2K supports mirrors on basic disks left over from upgrading NT to Win2K, Server 2003 has no support for this.

To create a mirror set from unallocated space, right-click an area and choose New Volume from the shortcut menu. Go through the wizard as described in the earlier section, "Creating a Dynamic Disk Volume," noting the following:

◆ You'll need two dynamic disks with unallocated space on them.

◆ Both halves of the mirror set will be the same size. You cannot mirror a large volume with a smaller one.

◆ A mirror set can use any disk format: NTFS, FAT32, or FAT.

To mirror an existing simple volume, right-click the volume and choose Add Mirror from the shortcut menu. You'll open a dialog box like the one in Figure 10.23, asking you to select the disk that you want to create the mirror on. Click the disk so that it's highlighted—this won't work otherwise.

FIGURE 10.23

Choose a dynamic disk to hold the mirrored data.

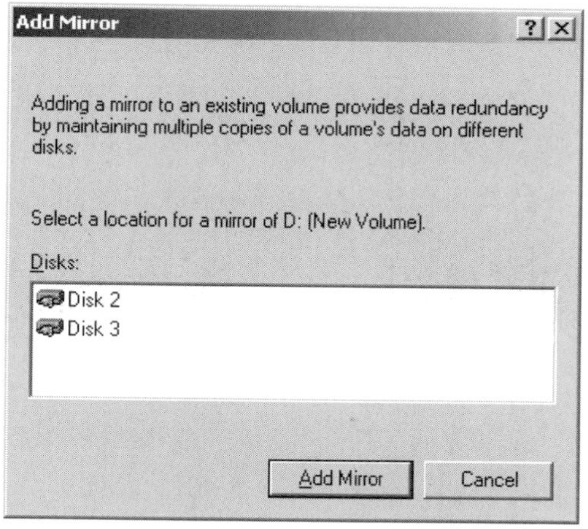

NOTE Only dynamic disks with areas of unallocated space big enough to mirror the selected volume will be listed. If no area of unallocated space is big enough, then you won't have the option of mirroring the volume.

Click the Add Mirror button, and the Disk Management tool will create in the unallocated space a partition that's the same size as the simple volume being mirrored. The partition will be formatted to match the filesystem on the original volume, and the redundant data will be regenerated. (Depending on the size of the volume you're mirroring, this may take a while. It's not a fast process on large volumes.)

The new partition will have the same drive letter or mounted path as the one you mirrored and will be available immediately—no reboot required.

GETTING RID OF AND RECOVERING DATA FROM A MIRROR SET

If you don't want to maintain redundant information anymore, then you can delete the mirror set. *How* you get rid of it depends heavily on what you're trying to do:

◆ If you don't want any of the information in the mirror set anymore, then *delete* the mirror set.

◆ If you only want to keep half the data in the mirror set (either the original volume or the redundant half), then *remove* the mirror set.

◆ If you want to keep all the data—original and redundant—but don't want to mirror it anymore, then *break* the mirror set.

You don't have to delete, remove, *or* break a mirror set to keep using its data if half of it fails—it just won't be fault tolerant until you replace the failed disk and establish a mirror again.

Deleting a Mirror Set

To destroy all data in a mirror set, right-click the mirrored volume and choose Delete Volume from the shortcut menu. The Disk Management tool will ask you if you're sure; click Yes to continue deleting the mirror.

This will delete both halves of the mirror set—and destroy the partition—so only do this if you don't need the data or you've backed it up. (Strictly speaking, you shouldn't mess around with your data unless you've backed it up anyway, but this time you'll *definitely* delete it.)

Removing a Mirror Set

If one of the disks dies, the data on the still-functioning disk will still be accessible, but it won't be protected anymore (see Figure 10.24).

FIGURE 10.24

If one of the disks supporting a mirrored volume dies, then the mirror set is displayed as failed.

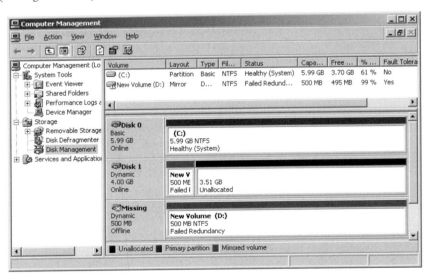

To protect it again, you'll need to remirror the volume. However, you can't *re*mirror a mirrored volume, and even if half of it's dead, the mirror itself is still valid. To start protecting the data again, you'll need to get rid of the original mirror.

To delete one half of the redundant data and stop mirroring, remove the mirror set. Right-click the mirror set and choose Remove Mirror from the context menu. You'll see a dialog box like the one in Figure 10.25.

FIGURE 10.25

Pick a half of
the mirror set
to remove.

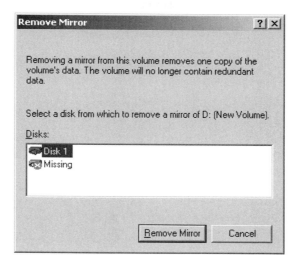

Be sure to pick the half that you *don't* want to keep. When you click Remove Mirror, the Disk Management tool will ask if you're sure. Click Yes to continue. The partition you selected will be deleted. The mirrored partition that you *didn't* select will become a simple volume. Its data will not be affected.

Breaking a Mirror Set

If both halves of the disk are still working, but you don't want to mirror the data anymore, then you can break the mirror set and thus make the two volumes act again like simple volumes. Both volumes will begin their new lives with all the data they had as their half of the mirror set; breaking the set does not affect the data.

To break the mirror set, right-click a mirror set that's still functioning (if the mirrored volume has failed, then you'll have to remove the mirror, not break it) and choose Break Mirror from the shortcut menu. You'll see a message asking if you're sure and warning you that your data will no longer be fault tolerant. Click Yes to continue.

NOTE *If an application is referencing data stored in the mirror set—even if its contents are just displayed in Explorer—you'll see an error message telling you that the volume is in use. Stop using the mirror set before breaking it if you want to copy the data currently being viewed to both halves of the mirrored volume.*

The two halves of the mirrored volume will now become simple volumes. One half will retain the drive letter that had belonged to the mirrored volume, and the other will have the next available drive letter.

MIRRORING CONSIDERATIONS

As you're deciding whether or not to protect your data by mirroring it, keep these things in mind:

◆ Mirroring to drives run from the same drive controller does not protect your data from drive controller failure. If any kind of controller failure occurs, you won't be able to get to the backup copy of your data unless you are mirroring to a disk run from a separate controller.

◆ For higher disk-read performance and greater fault tolerance, use a separate disk controller for each half of a mirror set.

◆ Disk mirroring effectively cuts your available disk space in half. Don't forget that as you figure out how much drive space you've got on the server.

◆ Disk mirroring has a low initial cost, since you must purchase only one extra drive to achieve fault tolerance, but a higher long-term cost due to the amount of room your redundant information takes up.

◆ Disk mirroring will slow down writes, as the data must be written in two places every time, but will speed up reads, as the I/O controller has two places to read information from. It gets the best performance of the two fault-tolerant RAID levels.

◆ You cannot extend a mirrored volume. The size it is when mirrored is the size it will stay. (Of course, you can always break the mirror, extend the simple volume that you are left with and then create a new mirror with that bigger volume.)

Establishing RAID 5 Volumes

To create a RAID 5 volume on a computer, follow these steps:

1. Right-click any area of unallocated space on any dynamic physical disk. From the shortcut menu that appears, choose New Volume.

2. Click through the opening screen of the wizard. On the first real screen, select RAID 5 Volume, as shown in Figure 10.26.

3. In the next screen (see Figure 10.27), choose at least three disks that you want to be involved in the stripe set. The disk you started with (the one with the area of unallocated space) will be in the right column of disks to use; the other dynamic disks with unallocated space will be on the left side. In the figure, I've selected three disks to use. To add a disk to the stripe set, select it in the list of all available dynamic disks and click the Add button. To remove a disk from the stripe set, select it in the list of selected dynamic disks and click the Remove button.

4. In this same dialog box, pick the size of the stripe set. In the Size box, the Disk Management tool will display the maximum size of the stripes based on the unallocated space on the chosen drives. You can go smaller than this amount, but not bigger. The value in Total Volume Size will reflect the total amount of room available for *data*, not the total space in the stripe set. Since $1/n$ of the space in a RAID 5 volume (where n is the number of disks in the set) is used for parity information, the more disks you have, the larger percentage of room for data you'll get.

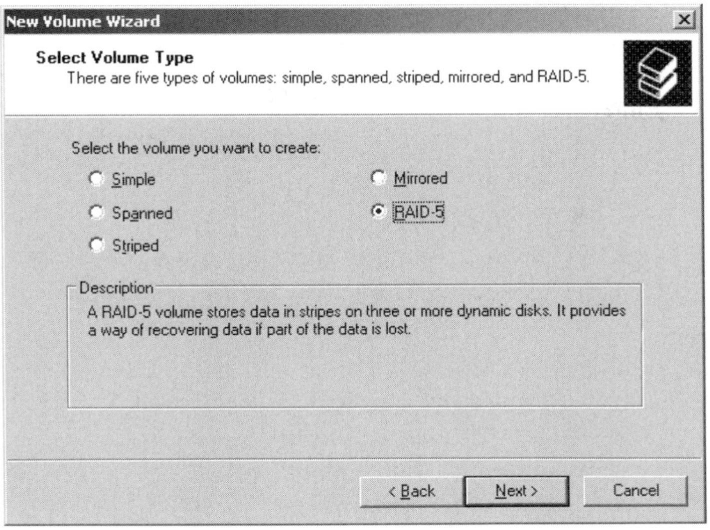

FIGURE 10.26

Choose RAID 5 to establish a stripe set with parity.

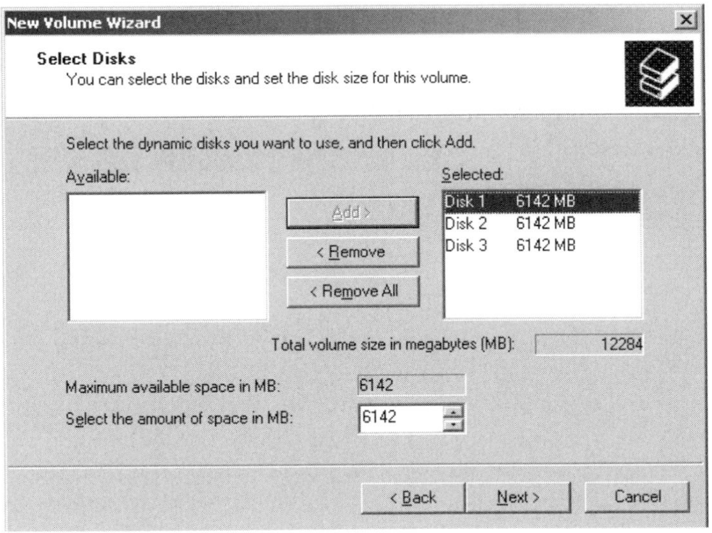

FIGURE 10.27

Select the disks to be in the stripe set and the size of the set.

NOTE   The amount of unallocated space on each physical disk will determine the size of the stripe set. Each section of the stripe set must be the same size, so if one disk has only 50MB unallocated space on it, then the entire stripe set spread across three disks can be no more than 150MB, even if the other two disks have 500MB of unallocated space each. That said, not all the unallocated space must be contiguous. If a single disk has one chunk of unallocated space that's 50MB and another that's 100MB, then the disk can contribute 150MB to the RAID 5 volume.

5. Choose to assign a drive letter or mount the volume to an NTFS path (see Figure 10.28).

FIGURE 10.28

Assign the volume a drive letter or path.

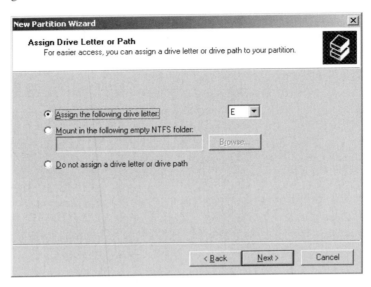

6. Choose whether or not to format the new volume right away and choose the disk format you want to use (see Figure 10.29).

FIGURE 10.29

Pick a format for the volume.

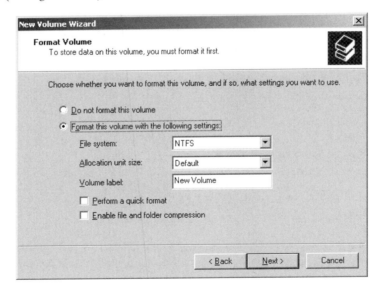

7. Review your choices, backing up to change any of them or clicking Finish to create the RAID 5 volume.

Server 2003 will grind away for a few minutes, setting up the new stripe set. When it's done, the RAID 5 volume will be immediately ready to use.

RETRIEVING DATA FROM A FAILED STRIPE SET

If an unrecoverable error to part of a stripe set with parity occurs, you'll still be able to read and write to the volume, but the volume will be marked Failed in the Disk Management tool (see Figure 10.30). This is a warning: lose one more disk, and the data will be inaccessible and unrecoverable.

FIGURE 10.30

You can still read and write to failed RAID 5 volumes, but they're no longer fault tolerant.

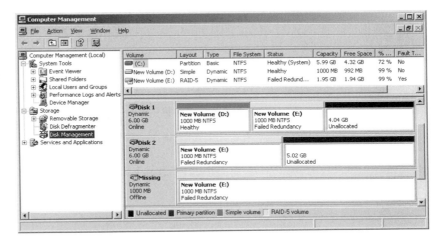

To make the volume fault tolerant again, replace the failed disk, rescan the disks, and reactivate the disk. If this doesn't make the volume healthy again, then right-click the stripe set and choose Reactivate Volume. The computer will chug away for a couple of minutes, rebuilding the missing data with the parity information on the remaining disks, and the stripe set will be back in one piece. You don't have to reboot. If you don't have the choice to Reactivate the volume, then choose Repair Volume from the options. You will be asked to choose the disk you would like to use to regenerate the stripe set.

DELETING A STRIPE SET

Deleting a stripe set is quite simple. Right-click the volume and choose Delete Volume from the shortcut menu. You'll see the usual warning message telling you that you're about to delete the volume and lose data; click through it, and the stripe set will again be unallocated space. Don't forget that deleting a stripe set destroys the data in it—even the parity information.

THINGS TO REMEMBER ABOUT DISK STRIPING WITH PARITY

Keep these things in mind when it comes to disk striping with parity:

◆ Striping with parity has a greater initial hardware cost than disk mirroring does (it requires a minimum of three disks rather than two and can contain no more than 32 disks). Nevertheless, it allows you to get more use out of your disk space.

◆ You cannot make a stripe set bigger (even if more unallocated space becomes available) or extend it to another physical disk.

◆ Although you can access the information in a stripe set even after one of the members has failed, you should regenerate the set as quickly as possible. Server 2003 striping cannot cope with more than one error in the set, so you're sunk if anything happens to the unregenerated stripe set.

◆ Striping with parity places greater demands on your system than disk mirroring, so add more memory and processor power to the server if you plan to use disk striping.

◆ If you have fewer than three dynamic disks on your server with unallocated space, you cannot make stripe sets with parity.

Performing Disk Maintenance

The job doesn't end with setting up disk volumes on the physical disks. To keep those volumes working well, you'll need to perform some routine maintenance on them. There are several tools which can help you do that which we'll talk about here.

Background: Disk Geometry and File Formats

Before getting into some of these routine maintenance chores like disk formats, disk defragmenting, and evaluating the health of your disks, let's take a quick look at the relationship between Server 2003 and hard disks and how this relationship makes all these tasks necessary.

A hard drive is not one but several disks called *platters*. Each platter is divided two ways: pie-shaped wedges and concentric circles. The pieces defined by the intersection of these divisions are called *sectors* and are the physical units of storage on a hard disk. Each sector on a disk is normally 512 bytes in size.

Server 2003 doesn't know a sector from a hole in the ground. To let its file storage component store and retrieve data on the disk, Server 2003 must impose some kind of logical structure over the physical structure of the disk. That logical structure is called a *disk format*, and it groups sectors together in logical units called *clusters*. The number of sectors in a cluster varies, depending on the size of the disk partition (all other things being equal, larger disks typically have more sectors per cluster) and the disk format you're talking about. All clusters have at least one sector in any filesystem that Server 2003 supports.

A cluster is the smallest organizational unit that the filesystem can recognize, which means that you can only store one file per cluster. If a file is too big to fit into a single cluster, then it will be spread over multiple clusters, as close together as possible. If a file is smaller than the cluster size, it will still fit into a single cluster, and any unused space in that cluster goes to waste. Larger clusters reduce the likelihood that files will get fragmented, but smaller clusters generally use file space more efficiently.

Sound irrelevant? Trust me: you'll need this background on clusters and sectors when it comes to performing basic disk maintenance.

Formatting Disks

Server 2003 is the first generation of NT sensible enough to let you format volumes while creating them with the Disk Management tool. However, you can still format volumes from Explorer or from the command prompt, as you needed to do in earlier versions of Windows.

DISK FORMATS SUPPORTED IN SERVER 2003

Server 2003 supports three disk formats: the old FAT format that includes long-filename support, the FAT32 file format introduced with Windows 95 OSR 2, and an updated version of the NTFS format that's been around since NT 3.1.

FAT and FAT32

FAT is the granddaddy of Microsoft filesystems, the one that all Microsoft operating systems support. It uses a simple catalog called the *file allocation table* to note which cluster or clusters a file is stored in. If a file's stored in more than one cluster, then the cluster includes a pointer to the next cluster used for that file until the final cluster includes an End of File marker.

FAT and FAT32 have a great deal in common: a simple set of attributes that note creation and access dates and the settings of the hidden, archive, system, and read-only bits. The main difference between FAT and FAT32 lies in their relative cluster sizes. FAT is actually FAT16, which means that it uses a 16-bit addressing scheme that allows it to address up to 2^{16} (that is, 65,536) clusters. To address very large volumes that include a lot of sectors, therefore, FAT must organize those sectors into very large clusters and can't format a volume larger than 4GB.

FAT32, in contrast, has 32-bit addresses, which means that it can name up to 2^{32} (that is, 4,294,967,296) clusters. Because of this, FAT32 can use much smaller clusters even on large volumes; on volumes up to 8GB, it uses 4KB clusters. Other than this difference, however, it's the same as FAT.

The main reasons FAT and FAT32 are included with Server 2003 is for downward compatibility with other operating systems. Most often, the advanced features of NTFS will make it your first choice for a server filesystem.

NTFS

NTFS is the filing system especially designed for use with Server 2003, Win2K, and NT Server:

- NTFS is designed for system security (that is, setting file permissions); FAT and FAT32 are not. (You can, however, restrict access to *shared* directories even when using FAT.) To learn how file permissions work, see Chapter 11, "Creating and Managing Shared Folders."

- Only NTFS volumes support Server 2003 file encryption, disk quotas, volume mounting, and data compression. Only volumes formatted with NTFS may be extended.

- NTFS keeps a log of activities in order to be able to restore the disk after a power failure or other interruption. It won't replace *data* on the NTFS drives, but if it's interrupted in the middle of a write procedure, it will restore the volume structure. This prevents the disk's volume from becoming corrupted.

Server 2003 uses a later version of NTFS than either Win2K or NT 4 does. Not only that, if you install Server 2003 onto a machine with Win2K or NT 4 already installed, Server 2003 will automatically upgrade the NTFS volumes to NTFS 5.1, rendering those volumes unreadable by NT 4. The good news is that NT 4 can read and write to the latter version of NTFS if you install Service Pack 4 or later. To set up a dual-boot system, install NT 4, install SP4 or later, then install Server 2003. That way, when NTFS volumes exist, you'll never have a time when you can't read the NTFS volumes from NT 4.

One of the other things that NTFS can do is find its own shortcuts when you move the file that the shortcut points to—even if the shortcut is on a different computer from the one where the file is located. For example, say that there's a file called `myfile.txt` on `\\serpent\workingfiles`, a shared directory. You refer to `myfile.txt` often, so you create a shortcut to that file (using its UNC `\\serpent\workingfiles\myfile.txt`) on the Desktop of your workstation so you don't have to drill down to find the file. Even if the file gets moved on SERPENT, the shortcut on your computer will still work because the properties of the shortcut will note the new location. This feature is called Distributed Link Tracking and was introduced in Win2K.

NAMING CONVENTIONS FOR LONG FILENAMES

All disk formats in Server 2003 support long filenames. Even FAT uses the extensions that make this possible. Filenames in Server 2003 can be up to 256 characters long with the extension, including spaces and separating periods. You can use any upper- or lowercase character in a long or short filename except the following, which have special significance to Server 2003:

> ?   "   /   \   <   >   * | :

Even though NTFS supports long filenames, it maintains its compatibility with DOS by automatically generating a conventional FAT filename for every file. The process doesn't work in reverse, however, so don't save a file with a long filename when working with an application that doesn't support long filenames, or else you'll only have the abbreviated name to work with. If you do, the application that doesn't like long names will save the file to the short name and erase all memory of the long filename. The data won't be erased, however; only the descriptive filename is affected.

When converting a long filename to the short format, Server 2003 does the following:

◆ Removes spaces.

◆ Removes periods, except the last one that is followed by a character—this period is assumed to herald the beginning of the file extension.

◆ Removes any characters not allowed in DOS names and converts them to underscores.

◆ Converts the name to six characters, with a tilde (~) and a number attached to the end.

◆ Truncates the extension to three characters.

You may want to keep these points in mind when using long filenames so your filenames will make sense in both versions. For example, you could name a file `PRSNLLET-Personal letters file.DOC`, so that the shortened name would be `PRSNLL~1.DOC`.

You can't format a floppy to NTFS format. There's a good reason for this: the NTFS file structure is complex, so finding data on large disks is fast and easy, but it takes up more room than a floppy disk can supply. Floppy disks don't need NTFS.

However, you can create files with long names on a floppy, since the Server 2003 version of FAT supports 256-character filenames. Server 2003 keeps two names for floppy files, the long name that you originally assigned and a truncated 8.3 name. DOS sees the shorter 8.3 name, making it possible for you to work with files that have long names under Server 2003 but short names under DOS.

Which Filesystem?

Which filesystem should you use? Table 10.1 gives you an at-a-glance comparison of NTFS and the FAT filesystems.

TABLE 10.1: COMPARING NTFS AND FAT IN SERVER 2003

FEATURE	NTFS	FAT32	FAT
Filename length	256 characters	256 characters	256 characters under Windows 9x, NT, Win2K; 8.3 under DOS
File attributes	Extended	Limited	Limited
Associated operating system	Server 2003, Win2K, and Windows NT	Server 2003, Win2K, Windows 9x, OSR2	DOS
Organization	Tree structure	Centrally located menu	Centrally located menu
Software RAID support?	Yes	Yes	Yes
Accessible when you boot the computer from a DOS floppy?	No	No	Yes
Maximum volume size supported	2TB minus 4KB (basic), 256TB minus 64KB (dynamic)	32GB (and will not format volumes smaller than 512MB)	4GB
Cluster size on a 1GB volume	2KB	4KB	32KB
Supports extensible volumes?	Yes	No	No

NTFS supports file compression, file encryption, transaction logging that can keep your disks from becoming corrupted due to aborted writes, and granular local security. It's more efficient than FAT in the way it uses disk space, particularly on the large disks that are so common these days. You need to use it to support drive mounting and extended volumes, discussed earlier in this chapter. It builds strong bodies 12 ways. (Okay, maybe that was Wonder Bread.) So, when *shouldn't* you use NTFS?

The only times NTFS won't work for you is when you need to support other operating systems which reside *on the same computer* as Server 2003. (When it comes to network access, the filesystem does not matter—a Windows 98 computer can read an NTFS volume across the network.) FAT is widely supported by other operating systems, so you should use it on any volume that you'll need to have accessible to other OSes on the same computer. (You'll also need to put those volumes on a basic disk, recall.) The exception to this is Windows 95 OSR 2 or Windows 98. FAT32 is more space efficient than FAT, so you should use FAT32 on any volumes that need to be locally accessible to both Server 2003 and Windows 9x. FAT32 volumes are *not* readable by NT 4 without the FAT32 support available for purchase from www.winternals.com, so if you need to keep data for NT 4, Windows 9x, Win2K, and Server 2003 and don't have this tool, you should use FAT.

SHOULD I USE FAT ON THE SYSTEM PARTITION?

Mastering Windows NT Server 4 recommended that you format the system partition with FAT. If you did this, then you could copy the installation files from the CD to the system partition.

The only trouble with keeping all system files and said installation files on a FAT-formatted partition is that doing so is enormously wasteful of disk space. Like many of us, Server 2003/Win2K/NT has gotten fatter as it's gotten older. To be pretty sure I wouldn't run out of room, I'd need a system partition at least 2GB in size. You can format a 2GB partition with FAT—barely. That's the largest amount of disk space that FAT can "see" under Server 2003. But doing so is horribly wasteful. As discussed earlier in this chapter, the FAT filesystem is wasteful of space on large partitions because it organizes the disk into very large clusters. 2GB might not be enough to store all the system files.

Thankfully, a new tool first introduced in Win2K called the Recovery Console makes formatting the system drive with FAT no longer necessary. I'll go into the Recovery Console in detail in Chapter 19, but the short version is that it's an NTFS-compatible command-line recovery tool that you can use to get at your system directory and make repairs. You can install support for the Recovery Console while you still have a working OS; you can also get to this tool from the Server 2003 Setup program. As long as you have the original CD or the Setup boot floppies, you can get to the Recovery Console and fix things, which means that it's fine to use NTFS on the system partition.

FAT system partition or no, it's still a good idea to copy the installation files to the hard disk. That way, you've always got an easily accessible copy of them when you need them to install a new driver or service.

USING THE FORMATTING TOOLS

If you chose not to format a volume that you created in the Disk Management tool, you can format it whenever you are ready to use it. Or you may also want to reformat an already formatted volume to quickly delete all data. You can accomplish this task either in Explorer or from the Disk Management tool, and, yes, my fellow command-line junkies, you can still do this with the command-line tool.

Of course, if you skipped Win2K altogether and are upgrading from NT4, you'll find that formatting in Server 2003 is a little different from formatting in NT and perhaps a little more confusing in terms of the GUI. First, fault-tolerant volumes can use any format that Server 2003 supports, not just NTFS. Second, you can use the Quick Format option to format any new volume, even fault-tolerant volumes, which you could not do with NT 4.

Using the Gooey (GUI)

Something that drives me a little insane when using the GUI tools to format in Server 2003 is that every dialog box seems to be different depending on how I access the volume (or do I mean disk?). Stick with me in this section and you may find yourself wanting to switch to the command-line version to format your volumes.

If you try to access an unformatted volume from Explorer, one that you have initialized but have not yet formatted, you'll see a message telling you that the disk (volume, really, but it says "disk") isn't formatted and asking if you want to format the volume now. Click Yes to format the disk, and you'll open the Format Local Disk dialog box in Figure 10.31.

FIGURE 10.31

Choose a filesystem for the new volume.

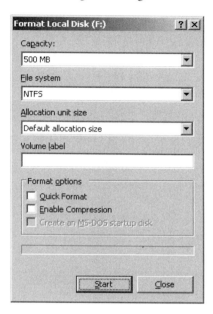

In the Format Local Disk dialog box, choose the filesystem that you want to use on the partition: NTFS (the default), FAT32, or FAT. If you format with NTFS, you can even change the cluster size—but that's a trick reserved only for the true filesystem junkies out there. (And for you junkies, note that file compression is only supported on NTFS volumes that have cluster sizes of 4KB or less.)

When you format a volume that has been previously formatted (either to change the existing filesystem to a different filesystem or simply to delete all the data on that volume) using either the Disk Management tool or Explorer, right-click the volume and choose Format from the shortcut menu. When you do this from Explorer, you'll see almost the same dialog box you just saw in Figure 10.31, but instead the dialog is titled Format New Volume (or whatever you titled the new volume when you initially formatted it), as shown in Figure 10.32.

If, however, you choose to perform this task from the Disk Management tool, you'll see a completely different dialog box altogether, as you can see in Figure 10.33. The only real difference (besides the obvious shape of the box) is that it doesn't show you the Capacity of the volume, as it does from Explorer. Type in any name you like and then choose the disk format you want to use: NTFS, FAT32, or FAT. Click OK, and Server 2003 will format the selected volume. Of course, any data already on the disk will be irrevocably deleted in the course of the format, so if you're reformatting, be sure that you've already saved any data on the volume that you want to keep.

FIGURE 10.32

Format and label the previously formatted partition or drive from Explorer.

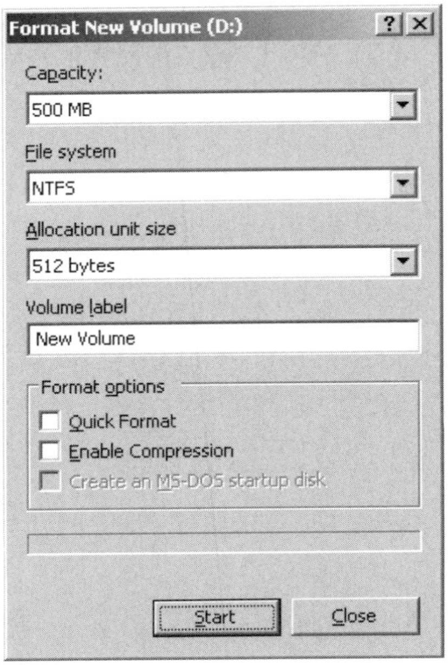

FIGURE 10.33

Format and label the new partition or drive from the Disk Management tool.

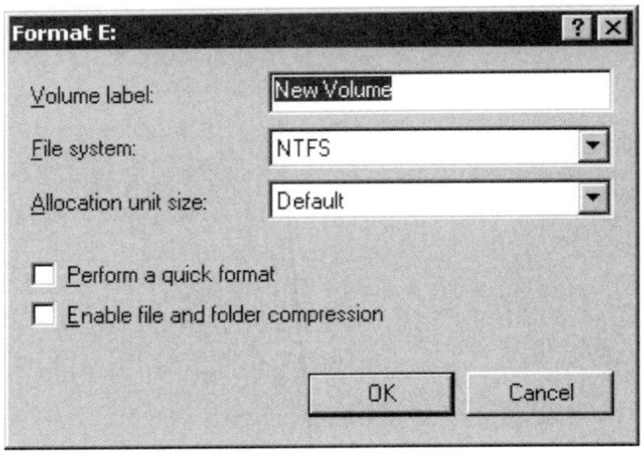

If you are trying to format a dynamic volume using the Disk Management tool, you will find that only the NTFS file system will be available, although you can format dynamic volumes with any filesystem you like by using either the command-line tool or Explorer. Whew! I hope this wasn't too confusing. As you can see, there are lots of ways to format a disk in Server 2003 using the GUI.

The Command Line

If you're addicted to the command prompt, you can still use it to format disks. To do so, open the command prompt from the Start menu and type the following:

```
format driveletter: /fs:filesystem
```

driveletter is, of course, the drive letter of the logical drive, and *filesystem* is FAT, FAT32, or NTFS. For example, to format a newly created E: drive as NTFS, you would type **format e: /fs:ntfs**. You must specify a file format—there's no default.

When you are ready to start formatting, keep in mind that you cannot format either the system or the boot volume. Also, if you choose to do a quick format, the files are deleted, but the disk itself is not checked for bad sectors. You should only perform a quick format if the disk was previously formatted completely and you are sure the disk is healthy.

And remember, for the best security, make all of your partitions NTFS, which is locally accessible to Server 2003, Win2K, and NT (with Service Pack 4 or later installed) and, of course, to any operating system across the network. With the addition of the Recovery Console (discussed in Chapter 19), it is no longer necessary to format the system partition with FAT for recovery purposes.

CONVERTING FAT OR FAT32 TO NTFS

If you have FAT or FAT32 volumes on your disk that you'd like to be NTFS, you don't have to back up their data, reformat the disks, and start over. Instead, you can use the CONVERT command-prompt utility. Its format is simple:

```
convert driveletter: /fs:ntfs
```

So, for example, to convert the P: drive to NTFS, you'd type **convert p: /fs:ntfs**. You'd see output like the following:

```
The type of the file system is FAT32.
Volume Serial Number is B447-D3E5
Windows is verifying files and folders...
File and folder verification is complete.
Windows has checked the file system and found no problems.

  523,247,616 bytes total disk space.
        4,096 bytes in 1 files.
  523,239,424 bytes available on disk.

        4,096 bytes in each allocation unit.
      127,746 total allocation units on disk.
      127,744 allocation units available on disk.

Determining disk space required for file system conversion...
Total disk space:               512000 KB
Free space on volume:           510976 KB
Space required for conversion:    5329 KB
Converting file system
Conversion complete
```

Notice that you must have a certain amount of free space (in this case, *free space* means unused space in the partition) on the volume to convert it. That's a place to store data while the clusters are being reorganized. If you don't have enough free space, then you can't convert the volume. Thus, it's a good idea to convert volumes before they get too full.

You cannot convert to any filesystem other than NTFS, and you cannot reverse the process. You also can't convert the current drive, which means that you cannot convert the system drive to NTFS without rebooting. The conversion will happen during the reboot process.

Defragmenting Disks

One of the simpler ways you can improve disk performance is to regularly defragment disks that need it, thus putting all the parts of each file into the same place on the disk for easier retrieval.

Defragmenting? What's that? Well, recall that each cluster can hold only one file at most, even if the data file is 1KB and the cluster is 8KB. If a file is too big to fit into a single cluster, then the remaining file data will go in the next available cluster, and the next, and the next, until the file is completely stored. Each cluster that the file's stored in contains a pointer to the next cluster where that file's data is contained, until you get to the last cluster containing data for that file and the pointer says, "That's all, folks." When you open a file stored on disk, the filesystem driver looks in the file catalog—remember the master file table?—at the top of the disk and finds the clusters that the file is stored in. It then pulls the data from those clusters and reads it into memory.

HOW DISKS GET FRAGMENTED AND WHY YOU CARE

When a disk is new, the available clusters are all next to each other, so it doesn't matter much if a file is distributed among several clusters. As you use a disk, however, this is likely to change. Create and delete files, and clusters get freed up unevenly. And the filesystem driver doesn't look for a run of clusters big enough to store all a file's data in one place; it just stores data in the first clusters available. If clusters 1–3, 10, and 15–100 are available, file A (which needs six clusters) will go into clusters 1–3, 10, 15, and 16 and not into contiguous clusters 15–20. When a file is spread among several noncontiguous clusters, it's said to be *fragmented*.

NOTE *Because large FAT volumes use much bigger clusters than large NTFS volumes, files on NTFS volumes are more likely to be fragmented. This isn't an argument in favor of using FAT—those larger clusters also imply more wasted disk space, and you don't get the other benefits of NTFS—but it is an observation about how clusters work. You can increase the cluster size on NTFS volumes if you'd like to reduce file fragmentation.*

Data is stored in the cluster it's originally put in—if a more convenient cluster becomes available, then the data isn't moved. Even if clusters 4–9 become free when a file is deleted, file A will keep using the same clusters it started with.

This isn't terrible. You'll still get all the data from the file, even if the file is fragmented. However, it will take a little longer to open fragmented files, and in case of serious disk errors, it's harder to recover badly fragmented files than ones stored in contiguous clusters. A *very* fragmented system disk can actually cause Server 2003 to crash if it takes too long to find a file that it needs. Therefore, it's a good idea to keep your disks defragmented.

WHAT'S NEW IN SERVER 2003'S DEFRAG TOOL?

Server 2003 comes with a defragmenter tool which has seen some much needed improvements over the version that was previously released with Win2K. Until now, you were not able to defragment volumes that were formatted with greater than a 4K cluster. In addition, Disk Defragmenter (the new defragmentation tool) can now defrag the master file table (MFT)—Win2K couldn't do this, which was certainly one reason why so many chose a third-party defragmentation utility over the free one. Essentially, the MFT keeps track of all of the files on a volume—it's similar to the file allocation table in FAT partitions—and if that gets fragmented, it can cause serious performance issues, since it increases the number of reads required to find a file. Microsoft says that Server 2003's defragmenter tool has also been seriously improved in terms of speed. These are good improvements, but they may not be enough to convince administrators not to look elsewhere for a defrag tool, since most of the better third-party tools include the ability to defrag across the network along with other useful tools.

USING THE DISK DEFRAGMENTER

To use Disk Defragmenter to defragment a volume or see whether it needs to be defragmented, right-click the volume in Explorer or in the Disk Management tool and open the volume's property sheet. Click the Tools tab that's shown in Figure 10.34.

FIGURE 10.34

The Tools tab contains all disk maintenance tools.

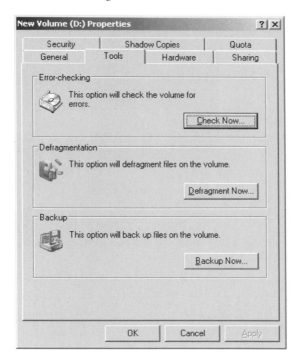

Click the Defragment Now button to open the screen shown in Figure 10.35. Notice that only local volumes are listed. You can't defragment volumes across the network.

First, see whether the disk needs to be defragmented at all. Highlight the volume in the list and click the Analyze button. The Disk Defragmenter will chug away for a minute (it's pretty fast—a 2GB volume took only a few seconds to analyze) and then display its recommendation (see Figure 10.36). If the analysis says the volume is "dirty" which indicates possible corruption, you should run CHKDSK to assess the health of the volume. You'll learn all about CHKDSK in the next section if you are not already familiar with the tool. You can find out if a volume is dirty by typing **fsutil dirty query at the** command prompt.

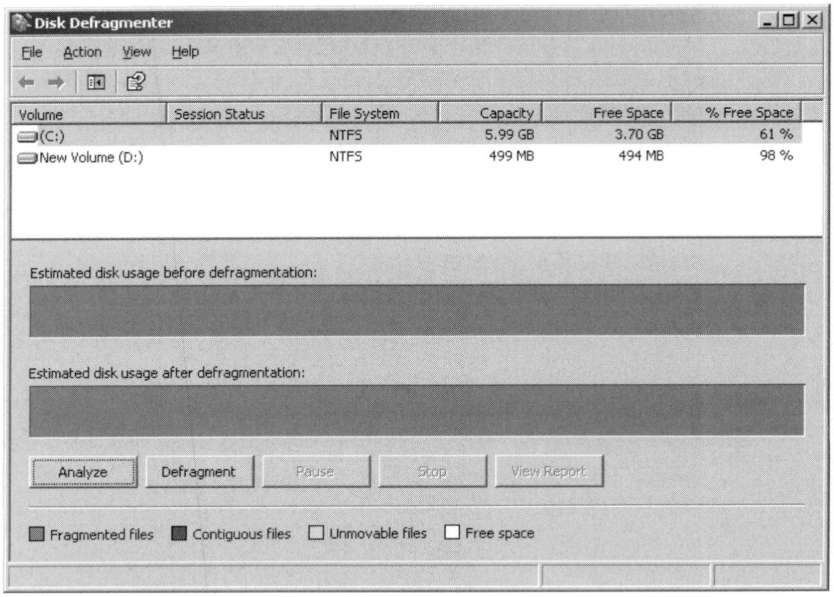

FIGURE 10.35
The Disk Defrag-
menter shows all
logical volumes on
the computer.

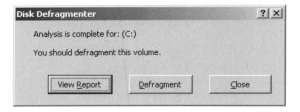

FIGURE 10.36
Analyze disks before
defragmenting them.

If you want to see more information about how fragmented your disk is, click the View Report button to open the dialog box shown in Figure 10.37.

WHAT DOES ALL THIS MEAN?

What are you looking at here? The top part of this dialog box displays six types of information:

- ◆ Basic volume statistics
- ◆ Volume fragmentation
- ◆ File fragmentation
- ◆ Pagefile fragmentation
- ◆ Folder fragmentation
- ◆ Master file table fragmentation

FIGURE 10.37

View the report
to see how badly
the disk is
fragmented.

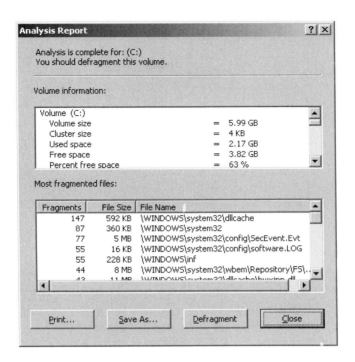

Most of the information about the volume should be pretty simple to figure out: the volume size is the size of the partition, the cluster size is the size of each logical storage unit on the drive (in this case, 4KB, or 8 sectors), and the rest of the section describes how much space on the disk is currently used, how much is free, and what the percentage of free space is. Although you can't see all of the details of the report in Figure 10.37, if you will run a report of your own, you can follow along while I discuss the rest of the information which is visible by using the scroll bar in the upper window of the Analysis Report dialog box.

The Volume Fragmentation section below the Volume Information section is a little more relevant to the question of how much file reads are delayed, describing the status of the files themselves. The total fragmentation describes how fragmented the entire disk is; the file fragmentation tells how fragmented the used parts of the disk are (that is, the proportion of files that are fragmented), and the free space fragmentation describes how fragmented the unused space on the disk is. Free space fragmentation matters when it comes to creating new files—the more fragmented the unused space, the more likely it is that new files will be fragmented too.

File fragmentation gives you file-level fragmentation information. This area lists the total number of files on disk, the average size of a file, the total fragments, and the average number of fragments per file. Ideally, the value for fragments per file should be as close to 1.00 as possible, as that number indicates that all files are contiguous. In this particular analysis, the ratio is 1.25, which indicates that about 25 percent of files are fragmented into two or more clusters. As you can see in Figure 10.37, the recommendation was that running defrag was necessary in this case. The Most Fragmented Files window at the bottom of this dialog box gives you more specifics about which files are most fragmented, but you don't need to worry about this unless you're interested in comparing the "before" and "after" results.

TIP   *If you are interested in comparing the before and after readings, click the Save As button to save the entire fragmentation report as a text file or click the Print button to print out a report.*

The rest of the information shows fragmentation for specific parts of the disk volume structure so you can see just how fragmented the pagefile and master file table are in your system.

That's the current status of your volume. To fix it, close any files (including application files) currently using the fragmented volume, then click the Defragment button. The tool will start reorganizing the files on the disk to put them into contiguous clusters. Defragmenting the disk will *not* free up space on the disk, but it will group all free space together to allow it to be used more efficiently, which can greatly improve the performance of your system.

NOTE   *You can defragment a volume with open files, but this makes it difficult to defragment the system volume. It will take much less time if you close all files first.*

GIVE DEFRAG SOME SPACE!

When's the last time you cleaned out your desk? It usually works best to take everything out and lay it on top of the desk or on the floor beside you before you start putting everything back into the desk, carefully setting things back in a more orderly fashion than they were before. After all, why would you bother cleaning it out if you weren't going to make it more organized? That is what the defrag tool is all about, and it needs some room to do the job. So make sure that you defragment your disks before they get too full. The Disk Defragmenter requires 15 percent of free volume space to store data that it's rearranging. If the volume is too full, you'll need to remove files or (if possible) extend the volume before you can defragment it.

FOR REAL ADMINISTRATORS: THE COMMAND LINE

For those of you who thrive on never using the mouse unless Microsoft forces you to, Server 2003 also ships with a command-line tool that will both analyze and defragment your disks. It isn't nearly as pretty as the GUI version, so if you analyze your disks just to see the bright colors that represent your files as a quick pick-me-up on an otherwise dreary day, this isn't the tool for you. Here's what the output looks like for a quick volume analysis and report.

```
C:\>defrag c: /a /v
Windows Disk Defragmenter
Copyright (c) 2001 Microsoft Corp. and Executive Software International, Inc.

Analysis Report

        Volume size             = 5.99 GB
        Cluster size            = 4 KB
        Used space              = 1.93 GB
        Free space              = 4.06 GB
        Percent free space      = 67 %
```

```
Volume fragmentation
    Total fragmentation                 = 10 %
    File fragmentation                  = 21 %
    Free space fragmentation            = 0 %

File fragmentation
    Total files                         = 12,033
    Average file size                   = 190 KB
    Total fragmented files              = 1,503
    Total excess fragments              = 3,063
    Average fragments per file          = 1.25

Pagefile fragmentation
    Pagefile size                       = 768 MB
    Total fragments                     = 1

Folder fragmentation
    Total folders                       = 807
    Fragmented folders                  = 37
    Excess folder fragments             = 545

Master File Table (MFT) fragmentation
    Total MFT size                      = 13 MB
    MFT record count                    = 12,856
    Percent MFT in use                  = 99
    Total MFT fragments                 = 2

  You do not need to defragment this volume.
```

I just showed you the command to do just the analysis and report. Here are some of the other available commands you can use with the defrag tool.

To perform an analysis on a single drive, you should type:

```
defrag <drive>: /a
```

To both perform an analysis and see results of the analysis, type:

```
defrag <drive>: /a /v
```

To defragment a drive, type:

```
defrag <drive>:
```

If you want to both defragment a drive and see the defrag report, type:

```
defrag <drive>: /v
```

While the volume is being defragmented, you will see a blinking cursor. When the defrag tool is finished, it will display the analysis and/or the defrag statistics—depending on what you asked for— and then exit to the command prompt. Note that you can only run one version of the defrag tool (you have to choose either the GUI or the command-line version) at one time, even on two different volumes. If you try to run both the Disk Defragmenter and the defrag command-line tool at the same time, you will get an error that looks like this.

```
C:\>defrag c: /a /v

Another command line or GUI defragmenter is already running.
Only one instance of Windows Disk Defragmenter can run at a time.
```

As with the GUI version of this tool, you can send output to a file. It might also be handy to know that you can now defragment at the same time you are performing a backup on the volume; this is new in Server 2003.

Using CHKDSK

File data is stored in clusters. If a file is stored in more than one cluster, then each cluster the file's stored in contains a pointer to the next cluster holding file data. If those pointers are lost, you can't pull up the entire file from disk.

NTFS's transaction logging prevents this from happening. Each NTFS volume maintains a *transaction log* of all proposed changes to the volume structure, checking off—*committing*—each change as it's completed and only then. When you restart the system, NTFS inspects the transaction log and rolls the state of the disk back to the last committed change. Basically, it's similar to the Last Known Good option that you can choose on startup to restore your server to its status at the last successful boot, except that transaction logging and rollback is automatic. Notice that transaction logging works only for *system* data, not for user data. If the disk failed in the middle of a write action, then the data that was supposed to be written to disk is lost. However, the volume structure of the disk will be all right. Any data already written to disk will be recoverable.

FAT and FAT32, however, do not have transaction logging. If the disk fails—perhaps due to a kicked power cord or a good hard knock by the infamous janitorial staff's vacuum cleaner—before a write action is completed and you restart the disk, there's no record of the last valid disk structure. You may need to run CHKDSK to check the pointers used in the file allocation table.

NOTE *This isn't to say that there's never any need to run CHKDSK on an NTFS volume—NTFS protects the integrity of filesystem data, or* metadata, *not user data.*

You can use the command-line version of the tool to edit the size of the transaction log or to check the disk for bad sectors (sectors to which the filesystem shouldn't write because they're damaged and might not read properly). Read on to learn more about what CHKDSK is doing and how to use both the graphical and command-line versions.

WHAT IS CHKDSK DOING?

Let's take a look at how CHKDSK works on an NTFS volume. When you run CHKDSK, you're telling the tool to make three passes over the specified drive to examine the structure of the metadata on the disk—again, that's the data describing how user data is organized on the disk. Metadata tells the filesystem what files are stored in which clusters, how many clusters are free and where they are, and what clusters contain bad sectors. In addition, it provides pointers to files.

During CHKDSK's first pass over the selected drive, it scans each file's record in the master file table (MFT). It examines each file's record for consistency and lists all the file records in use and which clusters those file records are stored in. It then compares this record with the drive bitmap stored in the MFT. Any discrepancies between the two are noted in CHKDSK's output.

During the second pass, CHKDSK checks the drive's directory structure. It makes sure that each index record in the MFT corresponds to an actual directory on the drive and that each file's record in the MFT corresponds to a file stored somewhere in the volume. CHKDSK also makes sure that all time and date stamps for all files and directories are up to date. Finally, it makes sure there aren't any files that have an MFT entry but don't actually exist in any directory. If the MFT entry is complete, the file can usually be restored to the directory where it should be kept.

The third pass of CHKDSK is for checking the integrity of the security descriptors for each file and directory object on the NTFS volume. During this pass, CHKDSK makes sure that all security settings are consistent. It does not check the security settings to make sure that they're appropriate to a particular folder or even to make sure that the group or user account named exists. Rather, the security pass of CHKDSK simply makes sure that, assuming all security information is correct, the security settings for the files and directory objects in the volume will work.

The final and optional pass of CHKDSK (performed only if you use the /R switch) tests the sectors in the volume reserved for user data (the metadata sectors are always checked) to see whether all of them can be read from and written to correctly. If CHKDSK finds a bad sector, then it marks the placement of this sector in the volume report. If the sector was part of a cluster that was being used, CHKDSK will regenerate and move the data to a new cluster that contains only good sectors if the volume is fault tolerant, or fill the bad sector with a string that means "no data should be stored here." The data in the bad sector won't be recovered unless there's some redundant data to copy it from, but at least the filesystem won't store more data in the cluster containing the bad sector.

How long does this process take? Depends on the size of the volume, the depth of the check, and what else the computer is doing during the check. CHKDSK is extremely CPU and disk intensive, and if it must contend with other processes for CPU time, the check will necessarily take longer. The best rule of thumb is that, if you can avoid it, you shouldn't run CHKDSK on a computer that is actively trying to do something else. In any case, you can't run CHKDSK on a volume that currently has files open. If you attempt to do so, CHKDSK will tell you that it can't get exclusive control of the volume and ask if you want to schedule the check for the next time the computer restarts.

There are two forms of CHKDSK in Server 2003: the graphical tool and the command-line utility. The graphical tool is simpler to use, but the command-line utility has many more options and is more flexible.

NOTE   *The version of CHKDSK changes as the file systems change. In other words, the version that came with NT 4 is not compatible with the newer versions of NTFS because the NTFS file structure is different. So make sure you use the version of CHKDSK that comes with the OS that you are working on.*

RUNNING CHKDSK FROM EXPLORER

The simplest way to run CHKDSK is from Explorer, as this tool doesn't demand that you know the command syntax and just uses the default options. To use the tool, select a drive in Explorer and open its property sheet. Turn to the Tools tab, then click the Check Now button to open the dialog box in Figure 10.38.

FIGURE 10.38

The graphical disk checker

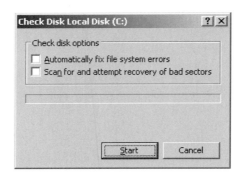

There are two options available from the graphical version of CHKDSK. If you tell CHKDSK to attempt to fix file system errors, then it will try to resolve any orphaned files—files that have entries in the file system catalog but don't appear in a directory on the volume. If you check the box that tells CHKDSK to scan for and attempt recovery of bad sectors, you're telling it to make the optional fourth pass of checking each sector on the disk instead of just those containing metadata. As you'll recall from the description of what CHKDSK does, data in bad sectors will not always be recoverable—only if the volume is fault tolerant and CHKDSK can get the data's redundancy information elsewhere is the data recoverable.

To begin checking the selected volume, click the Start button. The computer will begin grinding away using the options you supplied. (If you don't check either box, CHKDSK runs in read-only mode. Since the graphical tool doesn't display a report, read-only mode doesn't help you much.) The dialog box will display each phase of the disk check and display a status bar showing how far along each pass is until it's completed.

When the disk check is done, a message will appear telling you that the disk has been checked. No report of bad sectors or other information will appear. You can check another disk by exiting the current drive's property sheet and selecting another drive from Explorer.

RUNNING CHKDSK FROM THE COMMAND PROMPT

You have little control over how CHKDSK works when you run it from Explorer. If you'd like more control, you'll need to use the command prompt. The command-line options can be a little tricky to use, but they're faster and more flexible than the GUI once you get accustomed to them.

Without any arguments, CHKDSK runs in read-only mode on the current drive. You'll see command-line output showing the progress of each pass over the volume, and then you'll get a report like the following, showing you how the total disk space is used:

```
2096450 KB total disk space.
1011256 KB in 9214 files.
   2248 KB in 539 indexes.
      0 KB in bad sectors.
  31116 KB in use by the system.
   4096 KB occupied by the log file.
1051830 KB available on disk.

   2048 bytes in each allocation unit.
```

```
1048225 total allocation units on disk.
 525915 allocation units available on disk.
```

You should recognize the terminology used from the previous discussions of how NTFS organizes files on disk. The indexes are in fact directories on the disk. The log file is the transaction log used to record changes to the volume metadata so that any incomplete changes can be rolled back. The allocation units are clusters.

So—you've got a disk report, but that report doesn't allow you to do anything. To control the process, you'll need to plug in one or more of the switches explained in Table 10.2.

TABLE 10.2: COMMAND-LINE SWITCHES FOR CHKDSK

SWITCH	WHAT IT DOES
/f	Tells CHKDSK to attempt to fix file system errors, such as orphaned files. The help file for this switch says that it fixes errors on the disk, but that's not really accurate. It fixes inconsistencies in the file system catalog.
/v	Has different results depending on whether you use the switch on FAT volumes or on NTFS. On FAT volumes, this switch lists the full path of every file on the volume. On NTFS volumes, it runs CHKDSK in verbose mode, reporting any cleanup messages relevant to fixing filesystem errors or missing security descriptors.
/r	Checks every sector on the disk to make sure it can be written to and read from. Any bad sectors are marked as bad.
/x	Forces the volume to dismount first if dismounting is necessary to run CHKDSK (that is, if there are open handles to the chosen volume). Choosing this option will dismount the volume being checked.
/i	Tells CHKDSK not to check the indices on NTFS volumes. In other words, CHKDSK will skip the second pass of the disk checking operation. Although selecting this option can save you quite a bit of time on volumes with a lot of directories, it's not a good idea to use this switch unless you must; using it causes any inconsistencies in the directory structure to go unnoticed.
/c	Tells CHKDSK not to check for cycles on the NTFS volume. Cycles are a rare kind of disk error wherein a subdirectory becomes a subdirectory of itself, creating an infinite loop. You can probably turn this switch on safely since cycles are rare, but it won't save you much time.
/l[:size]	On NTFS volumes, specifies a new size for the transaction log. The default size is 4096KB, and for most purposes that's just fine.
volume	Specifies the mount point, volume name, or (if followed by a colon) the drive letter of the logical volume to be checked.
filename	On FAT volumes, tells CHKDSK to evaluate the specified filename to report on how fragmented it is. This option does not work on NTFS volumes.

The order of the switches is as follows:

```
chkdsk [volume[[path]filename]]] [/f] [/v] [/r] [/x] [/i][/c] [/l[:size]]
```

Advanced Disk Management Topics

The earlier sections in this chapter covered the basics, introducing the grammar of disk management in Server 2003 and showing you how to set up the various kinds of logical divisions available on the physical disks. I also discussed how to maintain your disks and the data that resides on them. So, as long as all you're ever planning on doing is setting up volumes once, you're fine.

Things rarely remain that simple, however. What if you want to install a second copy of Server 2003 on the same computer—what kind of volume can it reside on? Dynamic disks on the same computer, as you've learned, share information. If you move a physical disk from one computer to another, then what happens to that shared information? For that matter, how do you recover from a boot disk failure if you mirrored it? That's what we're going to talk about here.

Windows Server 2003 Setup and Dynamic Disks

Say that you've installed Server 2003 on a computer, fudged around with the Disk Management tool a bit, and now want to create a parallel installation of the OS. If you have dynamic and basic disks and a variety of the divisions of those disks available, where can you install Server 2003?

If you're attempting to install to a basic disk, it's easy. You can install Server 2003 on a primary partition or on a logical drive within an extended partition. (It's okay to install on an extended partition. Server 2003 will make it a boot partition.) Or, if the basic disk has enough unallocated space, you can use Setup to create a new partition. If you've ever installed Win2K or Server 2003, you know all about installing to basic disks, since that is the default.

Dynamic disks make life more complicated. Setup (and the Recovery Console described in Chapter 19) only recognizes dynamic disk partitions that are *hard-linked*, or created when you upgrade a basic disk (with preexisting primary partitions or logical drives configured) to dynamic. Each of the preexisting partitions retains a legacy-style partition table entry (type 42 for primary and type 05 for extended), even after upgrading the disk to dynamic. These special hard-linked entries allow Setup to recognize them as valid partitions for installation. In other words, you cannot install Server 2003 to a volume that you created *after* upgrading the disk to dynamic. The disk may appear in the list of available options in Setup when you're picking the partition to install to; Setup will display a drive letter for the dynamic volume, so if your dynamic disk had only one volume, you might be fooled into thinking everything is okay. However, if you select the native dynamic volume, Setup will tell you that it can't recognize it and ask you to pick another option. This means that you cannot install Server 2003 onto a simple volume, spanned volume, stripe set without parity, or stripe set with parity created on a dynamic disk, since by definition all those volume types are created from unallocated space on a dynamic disk. You can install Server 2003 onto a dynamic disk only if you pick a partition that existed before you upgraded the disk and is now a simple volume. Remember though, the partition had to exist while the disk was a basic disk, so that Setup can find the disk location in the disk boot record.

Good so far? Here's where things get strange. If you decide not to believe a word that I have said about not being able to install Server 2003 on a native dynamic partition and you insist on trying it yourself, you'll find some very strange behavior. Say you're creating a parallel installation of Server 2003 and attempt to install it onto a dynamic disk. You might see what looks like your dynamic disk—it will have the volume name and even the drive letter you assigned it—but the disk space estimates will probably be way out of synch with what you know the volume to be. And if you try to delete an existing dynamic partition and attempt to create a new partition, you'll just end up deleting ALL the volumes on that disk and in the end you will find yourself with a basic disk. In other words, creating new volumes on a dynamic disk during Setup will destroy any data currently on the disk and convert it to basic without warning.

WARNING   *Don't create partitions on dynamic disks during Setup.*

In short, keep the following in mind when choosing a location for a secondary Server 2003 installation:

- Any partitioned or unpartitioned space on a basic disk: good
- Any hard-linked volume on a dynamic disk: good
- Any soft-linked volume on a dynamic disk: impossible
- Creating new partitions on a dynamic disk: very bad

Frankly, if you want to make the system partition fault tolerant, then the easiest way is—as was the case for Win2K—still to install Server 2003 onto a basic disk and then upgrade that disk to dynamic. The primary partition that you installed Server 2003 into will become a simple volume, and you can mirror that volume onto another dynamic disk. Which leads us nicely to our next topic: making the system disk dynamic.

Upgrading a System Disk to Dynamic

When you upgrade disks in Windows Server 2003 from basic to dynamic, all partition information is moved into a private database at the end of the disk. Only one partition table entry of type 0x42 is entered in the master boot record (MBR) at sector 0.

The process of becoming dynamic is different for disks containing the system or boot partition. The process with system/boot disks is called *rooting*. When Server 2003 roots a disk, the system partition remains intact, but the Filesystem ID fields are changed to 0x42 to show that they are dynamic volumes recorded in the database at the end of the volume. The system partition remains intact so that the BIOS knows how to communicate with the disk and can boot Server 2003. This is done so that the BIOS can load the kernel and other files necessary to start the Disk Management driver files to read the dynamic volumes. If there is any unallocated space on the volume, an entry is added similar to those of other dynamic volumes (not rooted) that encompasses the rest of the space.

If you want to revert the system disk, you're a bit stuck. As noted earlier, the option to revert volumes from dynamic to basic only exists if the disk is empty and unpartitioned. You can't delete the system partition when you're using it. Backing up the system configuration, reformatting the disk, and reinstalling is really your only option.

Moving a Dynamic Disk

You might want to move a dynamic disk to a new computer, say, if you're moving half a mirror set to re-create duplicate data on a different computer. Recall that Server 2003 organizes dynamic disks into disk groups. When you move a dynamic disk from one computer to another, you're moving it to a new group, because even if those disk groups have the same name (as they will, since Windows Server 2003, Standard Edition only supports one disk group per computer and they're numbered starting with 0), they're not the same group. Therefore, to make this work, you'll need to introduce the disk you're moving to its new disk group—*without* deleting the volume information on the disk you're moving.

NOTE   *In case it's not obvious, when you move the last dynamic disk from a computer, the disk group no longer exists, since dynamic disk information is stored only on dynamic disks.*

PREP WORK

Before you start swapping disks around, take a look at what you've got. First, if any multidisk volumes don't show up as Healthy in the Disk Management tool, then fix them before moving the disk. Second, if you're planning to move more than one dynamic disk from the same disk group that contains parts of the same multidisk volume, it is a *very* good idea to move all those disks at once. Spanned volumes won't work unless all their disks are present—you will lose their data if you only move one of the disks supporting a stripe set or spanned volume—and fault-tolerant volumes may get out of sync. For instance, say that you have a mirror set on server ALPHA. If you *break* that mirror set and move half of it to server BETA, then you don't have a problem. But if you keep the mirror set intact, move half of it to server BETA, and keep using the disks on both systems (you can keep writing to a failed mirror set in Server 2003; it'll just show up as Failed Redundancy in the Disk Management tool), then try to move the other half from ALPHA to BETA, the data on the two mirror halves will be inconsistent. In such a case, Server 2003 will re-create the mirror set with the data from the physical disk moved first to BETA.

In this discussion, I'm going to call the computer you removed the disk from the *source* computer and the computer you moved it into the *destination* computer. When you remove a dynamic disk from a computer, information about it and its volumes is retained by the remaining online dynamic disks. The removed disk is displayed in the Disk Management tool on the source computer as a Dynamic/Offline disk with the name Missing. You can remove this Missing disk entry by removing all volumes or mirrors on that disk, and then use the Remove Disk menu item associated with that disk.

INTRODUCING THE NEW DISK

After you physically connect the disks to the destination computer, open the Action menu and choose Rescan Disks. The new disk will show up as Dynamic/Foreign. By default, Dynamic/Foreign disks should be brought online automatically, but if it's not, then right-click the disk and choose Online.

To use Dynamic/Foreign disks, you'll need to *import* them. Right-click one of the moved disks and choose the Import Foreign Disks option. The importing procedure works slightly differently depending on whether there's already a disk group on the new computer. If there are no preexisting online dynamic disks, then the disk group is brought online directly as it is, except that you'll lose any nonredundant information partially contained on disks you didn't move (e.g., if you moved only one disk supporting a stripe set). The disk group remains the same as it was; the database doesn't change. If a disk group was already present on the destination computer, then Server 2003's Volume Manager will merge the old disk group information with the new disk group information, so that all the dynamic disks can work together. The imported disks will become members of the local disk group.

CAN I USE THE DATA ON THE MOVED DISKS?

So what happens to the volumes on the dynamic disks you moved? Well, that depends on whether you moved enough data for the volume to work. Either the data or the redundancy data to re-create the data must be on the destination computer.

Simple volumes, which are contained on a single disk, should be fine if they were fine before you moved the disk.

If you moved only part of a multidisk but non-fault-tolerant volume, such as a volume set or stripe set, that volume is disabled on both the source and destination computers until and unless you move the disks containing the rest of it. So long as you don't delete the volume on either the source or destination computer, you should be able to move the rest of the volume to the destination computer and re-enable it, but you will need to move all the disks supporting that multidisk volume. If you delete and overwrite part of the volume, you can't rebuild the volume.

If you move a disk containing part of a RAID 5 volume, then the data may be available even if you didn't move the entire volume to the destination computer; this depends on whether you moved enough parity data to regenerate what's missing. If the parity information is valid, one disk of the RAID 5 volume can be missing and the volume should still work, just as it would if one of the disks in the volume failed.

If you move a mirror set that's up to date, then you can use the data on the new computer or even (if you broke the mirror set on the source computer) re-create the mirror set using unallocated space on a dynamic disk on the destination computer. If you move the two halves of the mirror set at different times, then reaffixing the mirror set on the source computer will cause the first mirror half to overwrite any data on the second mirror half. So, if you made changes to the second mirror half and then moved that disk to join its ex-twin on the new machine, those changes will be lost, not merged when the two halves come together again.

WARNING *All these comments apply to* data *disks. If you move the system disk to a new computer, the computer will not boot unless the right Plug-and-Play ID information for the mass storage controller is already in the Registry. Otherwise, Server 2003 will not be able to load the right drivers. The simplest way to avoid this situation is to only move system disks to computers that are identical to the source computer.*

Changing a System Drive Letter

Under a couple of circumstances, you might need to change the system drive letter. If you mirrored the boot disk and the main disk fails, then when you break the mirror, the second—working—partition will automatically be assigned the next available drive letter. Which means that if Server 2003 still thinks that, say, C: is the boot drive, you're going to have a hard time booting if the only working system drive is now called J:. Or, as one reader wrote:

> *I made the mistake of leaving an alternate drive in my laptop when I installed [DOS followed by] W2K on the primary drive. Now the boot disk (which ought—in the natural order of things—to be "D", as I have the DOS partition) is H:. And of course, the W2K tools won't let me reassign the drive letter at all. (In NT, you could reassign the drive letter—but you had to reboot when you left Disk Manager.) Know of any way that I can get that H: to D:?*

Although this question was written during the days of Win2K, this dilemma still exists in Server 2003 and, since it's still a common question, I'll include it. Trouble is, if you right-click the system volume in Disk Management and choose Change Drive Letter and Paths from the shortcut menu, then, although you'll be able to open the dialog box you'd normally use for this purpose, when you click the Change button to do the actual editing you'll see an error message telling you that you can't modify the drive letter of your system or boot volume. What to do?

To change or swap drive letters on volumes that cannot otherwise be changed using the Disk Management snap-in, you'll need to edit the Registry. For example, say that you want to swap H: and D:. Open REGEDIT or REGEDT32 and go to the `HKLM\SYSTEM\MountedDevices` key. Within that key are values for each of the lettered drives on your computer. In the list, find `\DosDevices\D:`. Right-click it and choose Rename to edit it to `\DosDevices\Y:` (or some drive letter not currently being used).

TIP   To make this change, you'll need Full Control over the HKLM\SYSTEM\MountedDevices *key. In Win2K, you would have had to edit the security settings for the key in REGEDT32 and then use REGEDIT to actually rename the key. Finally (!), Microsoft has merged those two tools, combining the best features from both. REGEDIT had some good features and REGEDT32 had some* different *good features. Now you can use either tool to both edit the security settings and rename the key. In fact, the interface for both tools is identical. Way to go Microsoft!*

Next, right-click \DosDevices\H: and change it to \DosDevices\D:. Finally, right-click \DosDevices\Y: and rename it to \DosDevices\H:. (If you're only changing one drive letter, then you don't need to do the swapping—just change the drive letter to the unused letter.) You'll then need to restart the computer.

Recovering a Failed Data Disk

Recovering from simple disk failure isn't too bad, if the disk that died is not the disk with the operating system files on it. If you accidentally switch off an externally mounted drive, or if the drive comes loose in the box, any volume sets or nonparity stripe sets that depended on that disk will be temporarily dead—reasonable, because for all practical purposes, one of its disks has failed. The missing disk either will not show up in the Disk Management tool at all (if you rebooted with the disk off) or will show up with a Missing label on it (see Figure 10.39).

FIGURE 10.39

A dead drive in the Disk Management tool

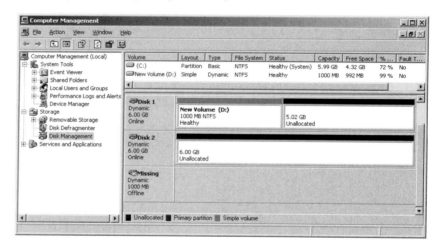

If it's a simple matter of a loose cable or an accidentally flipped power switch, just reconnect the cable or switch the drive back on. After you've done so, right-click the Disk Management tool's icon in the left pane with the rest of the Computer Management tools and choose Rescan Disks. You'll see an informational dialog box telling you that the Disk Management tool is rescanning. When it's done, right-click the failed volume and choose Reactivate. Server 2003 will caution you to run CHKDSK on the volume. Click OK, and your disk will appear as it was before, and the volume set will again have a drive letter and be operational.

Or, if you're just recovering from a single failed data disk in a fault-tolerant disk volume (mirror set or RAID 5 volume), you can use the procedures I just described to regenerate the missing data and make the volume fault tolerant again. Even before you do so, the data will still be available.

TIP   If you are using disk duplexing—where each disk has its own controller—prior to installing a new disk to replace a failed disk in a mirror set, make sure you break the mirror and look in the system logs to make sure the disk is really the problem. It could be the controller. If the controller is failing, installing a new disk will not solve the problem, you'll have to replace the controller.

Creating and Using a Fault-Tolerant Dynamic Disk for System Recovery

A lot of people ask whether they can use a dynamic disk for their boot disk and thus make it fault tolerant. The answer is yes... to a point. Since you can't install Windows Server 2003 onto a native dynamic disk partition (Setup and the Recovery Console rely on the partition table, not the disk group's database, to find disk partitions) you can only use mirroring to protect a system disk. A RAID 5 volume is, by definition, a native dynamic disk volume, but a mirror may be built from a partition on a basic disk later upgraded to dynamic.

NOTE   Just a reminder: you will need at least two physical hard disks in the server to mirror its system partition.

To mirror the system files, install them onto a basic disk as you would normally; we'll call this Disk 0. Having made sure that there is an area of unallocated space of equal size to the system partition, on another disk—Disk 1—upgrade Disk 0 to dynamic. Upgrade Disk 1 to dynamic as well. Now, right-click the system partition on Disk 0 and choose Add Mirror. As described earlier in this chapter, select the dynamic disk with the empty space that you want to copy the original system data to, and create the mirror. The data on the newly mirrored system partition will be copied—*resynched*, in Disk Management tool lingo—to the blank half of the mirror set, as shown in Figure 10.40.

FIGURE 10.40

Building a mirrored boot partition

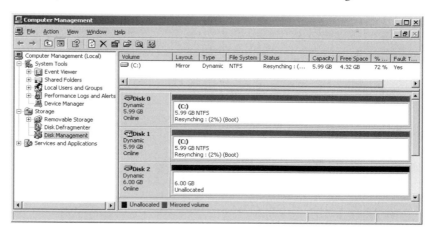

The system disk is now fault tolerant. Good thing, because the next time you boot the computer, you see a message like this:

```
Windows 2000 could not start because of a computer disk hardware configuration problem.
Could not read from the selected boot disk. Check boot path and disk hardware.
Please check the Windows documentation about hardware disk configuration and your
hardware reference manuals for additional information.
```

This message does not inspire happy thoughts. What we've got here is a failed primary partition.

Microsoft has made yet another huge improvement with the release of Server 2003. In the old days of Windows 2000, if the primary partition failed, Win2K wasn't smart enough to say, "Hey—the partition I normally boot from isn't working. I guess I'll boot from this mirrored partition that was so cleverly built for me and then tell the sysadmin that the primary boot partition failed so they can fix the mirror." When that happened, you had to create a Windows 2000 boot disk, edit the `boot.ini` file to let Win2K know where to boot from, then reboot the machine using the floppy to get into Win2K. It wasn't clever enough to realize that since the system partition was mirrored, it could simply boot from the remaining half of the mirror. In Server 2003, however, the system recognizes the mirror as soon as you create it and edits the `boot.ini` file for you, allowing you to boot from the mirrored partition any time you boot the machine.

The Rest of the Story

There were lots of new features introduced in Win2K that related to storage, among them encrypted file system, dynamic disks, disk quotas and mounted volumes. Server 2003 has added even more features and functionality to the OS, both improving some services that debuted in Win2K and giving us a few new tools, such as the Volume Shadow Copy Service, which will enable users—yes, *users!*—to be able to restore lost versions of files without calling the overworked and (admit it) sometimes testy sysadmins. Some other examples of cool new features in Server 2003 are open file backups, support for SANs, and the ability to extend basic disks using the new and powerful command-line disk management utility DiskPart. (I introduced DiskPart, which is installed by default, in my discussion of basic disks.)

Now that you are (I hope) more comfortable with the types of storage that Server 2003 offers and know how to manage the disks in your system, I'll go over a few of the more useful features that can give you even more control over the way you manage the files on those disks.

Using Encrypted NTFS

Native public key encryption, allows you to secure your documents and folders so that only you—or the people you give the key to—can view the documents. It's a handy way of keeping even shared documents private or of protecting files on a machine that can be easily stolen, such as a laptop.

Encryption doesn't conceal the fact that the documents exist. Rather, when you attempt to open an encrypted file, Server 2003 checks to see whether you have a key to that file. If you don't, then you're forbidden access to the file. This denial is not application dependent—for example, a Word document won't be accessible in Word *or* WordPad. The user without the public key can't open the file object at all.

TIP   *The process of checking for an encryption key is processor intensive, so it's probably best not to encrypt files stored on a terminal server or other CPU-bound server.*

Since encryption is an attribute, like compression or the archive bit, it's only supported on NTFS volumes in Win2K and Server 2003, as far as servers go.

HOW SERVER 2003 ENCRYPTION WORKS

When you encrypt data, you're generating a request for a new security certificate identifying you to Server 2003 as who you say you are. A *cryptographic service provider (CSP)* generates two 56-bit keys: a public key, used for encrypting data for you, and a private key, used for decrypting that data. The two keys are unrelated—knowing a public key does not give you the ability to guess the private key.

The CSP passes the public key to the certificate authority, which uses it to create a public key for you. The certificate and public key are stored in the `Personal/Certificates` folder located in the Certificates add-in to the MMC (see Figure 10.41).

FIGURE 10.41

Personal encryption certificate

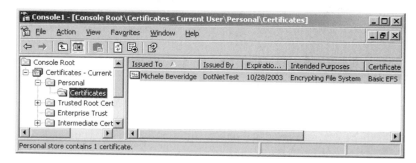

Users can encrypt data across the network, but the data is only encrypted when written to a disk, not while traveling across the network—you'll need network encryption for that. Only Server 2003, XP and Win2K users will be able to encrypt and decrypt data. Even though NT and Windows 9x users can read and open files on the newer NTFS volumes and, even though encryption standards apply to them too, the NT and Windows 9x users don't have the tools they'd need to encrypt the data unless they're running a Server 2003, XP or Win2K session.

This information isn't required when it comes to encrypting or decrypting your own data, but it could come in handy when it comes to recovering someone else's encrypted data or in protecting laptop encryptions. We'll do the simple part first, and then return to the question of why you need to protect certificates and how you can do it.

Encrypting Files

To encrypt a file or folder from Explorer, right-click the file or folder (you cannot encrypt entire volumes) and open its property sheet. On the General tab, click the Advanced button to open the Advanced Attributes dialog box shown in Figure 10.42.

TIP   If there isn't an Advanced button visible, make sure that you're looking at an NTFS volume, not a FAT or FAT32 one.

FIGURE 10.42

Encryption is an advanced NTFS attribute

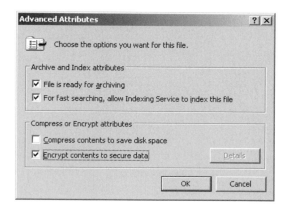

You can either compress or encrypt file data, not both. Check the option you want and click OK. If the folder containing the file is not encrypted, you'll be warned of this and prompted to encrypt both the folder and the file. Normally, it's a good idea to let Server 2003 encrypt the folder as well. If you leave the folder unencrypted and then save an encrypted file within that folder using the Save As feature, the file will be left unencrypted since it is effectively now a new file. All new files created within a folder inherit the folder's encryption attributes.

TIP   *If using encryption, encrypt the* My Documents *folder for all users (*%userprofile%\My Documents*) to ensure that the personal folder, where most Office documents are stored, will be encrypted by default.*

The encryption attribute is now set. If anyone but you, even someone with administrator privileges, attempts to open the file or run the encrypted executable, they'll be denied access. Encrypted files will appear in an alternate color in Explorer if your folder options are set to the default.

COPYING, MOVING, AND BACKING UP ENCRYPTED FILES

New files in a directory inherit the encryption attributes of that directory: if the directory is encrypted, the file will be encrypted as well. If the directory is not encrypted, the file won't be encrypted. What about files *copied* to a directory? This is where it can get a little tricky:

◆   If you copy or move an unencrypted file to an encrypted NTFS directory, that file will become encrypted.

◆   If you copy or move an encrypted file to an unencrypted NTFS directory, the file will remain encrypted.

◆   If you copy or move an encrypted file to a FAT or FAT32 directory, that file will no longer be encrypted (since encryption is an NTFS attribute).

◆   Backups of encrypted documents are stored and restored in their encrypted state even if the backup media is a FAT-formatted drive.

You can also encrypt files from the command prompt with the CIPHER command. To encrypt a single folder in the current directory, type **cipher /e** *foldername*, where *foldername* is the name of the folder you want to encrypt. To decrypt the same folder, replace the /e switch with /d, like this: **cipher /d** *foldername*. The command will report back to you whether the operation succeeded or not.

NOTE   *Again, you can't encrypt compressed data or vice versa. If you attempt to encrypt a compressed file with CIPHER, it won't work. If you try to encrypt a compressed folder with CIPHER, it won't encrypt the contents of the folder, but it will add the encryption attribute to the folder so that any new files added to that folder will be encrypted (but not compressed—remember, you can only have one of these attributes for any file or folder at a time). Uncompress the folder and try again to encrypt it, and the operation should be successful.*

Normally, CIPHER will only encrypt the files in the immediate folder you specify, not the subfolders. It will also only encrypt parent folders if told to, leaving the files' parent directories unencrypted. To keep from accidentally decrypting a file (by "Saving As" a new file in a decrypted folder), encrypt the folder as well by typing **cipher /e /s:***foldername* **/a**. This will encrypt all files within the specified folder and all subfolders within the folder.

Enforcing Encryption

The contents of an encrypted folder are displayed like any other shared or locally available data, except that they are displayed in a lovely spring green color to identify them as encrypted. (Compressed files and folders are blue.) Sadly, the error messages you get when attempting to access files that someone else has encrypted represent a help-desk call waiting to happen. Whether accessing the encrypted file locally or from the network, from Server 2003 or from an earlier operating system, you'll see an error message like the one in Figure 10.43.

FIGURE 10.43

Windows 9x and NT 4 users may not be sure why they can't open an encrypted file.

> Microsoft Word
>
> Word cannot open the document: user does not have access privileges
> (\\DOTNETTEST\Shared\Encrypted letter.doc)
>
> OK

What about administrators? If someone with administrator privileges opens the file's property sheet and edits the encryption attribute, they'll be unable to apply the change—they'll be denied access. What happens if an administrator takes ownership of the file? File ownership doesn't actually matter to encryption. Even if you (as the administrator) take ownership of an encrypted file, you won't be able to read it unless you are a designated recovery agent, which is a user who has been designated as someone who can decrypt a particular file or set of files.

Sometimes, you may just want to know who encrypted a file. If you create an unencrypted file and are that file's owner, and you allow me read and write permissions on the file, then I can encrypt it, and you won't be able to see its contents anymore because you're not the one who encrypted it. Still with me? Anyone with read and write permissions on an unencrypted file has the ability to encrypt it, rendering it unavailable to everyone else with rights to that file. To find out who encrypted the file, you can click the Details button in the Advanced Attributes sheet. This will reveal the list of users who have the ability to encrypt the file and any recovery agents who are defined. As a recovery agent, you can fix things by decrypting the files, as you'll see in the next section, "Recovering Encrypted Files."

Another way of finding out who can encrypt a file is by using a command-line Resource Kit utility named EFSINFO. You can run EFSINFO with the /u option (to show user information), the /r option (to show Recovery Agent information), and the /s option (to show directory and subdirectory information) like this:

```
efsinfo /u /r /s:c:\userdata
```

It'll tell you whether the folder and its files are encrypted, who encrypted the folder and files, and who can decrypt them. Here's the output from that command:

```
c:\userdata
.: Encrypted
  Users who can decrypt:
    DOTNETTEST\Michele (Michele Beveridge(michele@dotnettest.local))
  Recovery Agents:
    DOTNETTEST\Administrator (Administrator)

Encrypted letter.doc: Encrypted
```

```
Users who can decrypt:
  DOTNETTEST\Michele (Michele Beveridge(michele@dotnettest.local))
Recovery Agents:
  DOTNETTEST\Administrator (Administrator)

Recipes.doc: Not Encrypted

C:\>
```

Protecting Encryption Keys

Microsoft positioned these encryption services especially for laptop users who wanted to keep their data secure even if their laptop was stolen. However, there's one major hole in this security plan. If someone *does* steal a laptop and can log in with administrator rights, they can edit the certificate settings in a way that allows them to decrypt the data.

NOTE   *Of course, if you don't password-protect your laptop, then decrypting your files is as easy as logging in as you.*

To avoid this problem, Microsoft recommends exporting each user's certificate and saving it to disk, then deleting the certificate on the computer. To do so, follow these steps:

1. In the MMC, add the Certificates snap-in.
2. In the `Personal` folder, open the `Certificates` folder. The per-user certificates on the computer will be displayed in the right pane.
3. Right-click the certificate that you want to export as a file and choose Export from the All Tasks menu. This will start the Certificate Export Wizard, which asks whether you'd like to export the private key along with the certificate. You'll need the private key to decrypt data.
4. In the next screen, choose the export options, including the file type, the strength of encryption you want to use, and what you want to do with the local key if the export works.
5. If you chose to export the private key, you'll need to supply a password to import the key again. Choose this password carefully, as it's protecting your encryption.
6. Choose a filename for the key by either typing a path or browsing for it. You can save the file on any volume, not just NTFS.
7. The final screen of the wizard will display your choices. Review them carefully and click Finish to export the keys. If the export operation worked, Server 2003 will pop up a quick message box to tell you it was successful.

Save the certificate on a floppy disk or, better yet, a safe network location where it can get backed up, then delete it from the computer. You'll be able to open encrypted files, but the certificate will no longer be on the machine.

To import the certificate to another computer or replace it on the same one, open the same `Personal` folder, right-click the `Certificates` folder, and choose Import from the All Tasks menu. This will start the Import Certificate Wizard:

1. Browse for the file you saved.

2. If the certificate you're importing includes the private key, you'll need to supply the password assigned when the key was exported. Type it in and choose the degree of control you want over the private key.

3. Specify where the new key should go. For user keys, the `Personal` folder should be fine.

4. Review the importing options and click Finish to import the key. Server 2003 will tell you if the importing action succeeded.

NOTE   *For more about certificates, see Chapter 8.*

Recovering Encrypted Files

If I encrypt a file, how do I recover the file? This is where the recovery agent comes in. By default, workstations and member servers' recovery agents are just the default Administrator account—not members of the Administrators group, but the Administrator *account*. The default recovery agent for a domain is the default administrator for the computer that was the first domain controller installed for that domain.

To recover a file for someone, you must log in as the recovery agent and decrypt the file, either through the GUI by removing its encryption attribute in the Advanced section of the file or folder properties, or with the CIPHER command that we discussed earlier:

```
cipher /u/a filename
```

In other words, EFS doesn't see any difference between you (the person who originally encrypted a file) and the recovery agent; if you had an encrypted Word file and the recovery agent tried to open it, she'd see your file. If you've denied the recovery agent access to your Word file, then she won't be able to open it. Of course, if the recovery agent doesn't have access to your file, then she also can't decrypt it for you—but that's easily remedied by an administrator who can take ownership of the file and then grant read and write access for the file to the recovery agent. Again, if you haven't changed the defaults, then the recovery agent is the default Administrator. That account can do just about anything anyway, so getting control of a file is no trouble.

Let's look a bit further into the recovery agent account. First, do you really want to have to use the default Administrator account for anything? Probably not—that's a lot of power to give to the person in charge of making sure users can read their files—so how do you change which account can handle emergency decryptions? It's harder than you might expect. EFS encrypts and decrypts your files using a simple symmetrical algorithm; the same "password" (not a user password that you can change, but a "password" that you give to EFS to permit it to encrypt and decrypt) encrypts and decrypts your files. But it *stores* that password using an asymmetric, public key–type of encryption method. When you encrypt a file, EFS encrypts the password using your public key and stores the now-encrypted password in NTFS. When EFS needs to decrypt a file, it asks NTFS for that encrypted password. NTFS passes the request to an independent module of the EFS driver that handles all reads, writes, and opens on encrypted files and directories, as well as operations to encrypt, decrypt, and recover file data when it is written to or read from disk, and which passes the information back to NTFS. NTFS then gives the password to the EFS driver, which uses your private key to decrypt the password. Now that it has the password, it can decrypt the file. (You've probably guessed by now that encrypting files slows things down a trifle.) How does EFS, then, allow more than one person to decrypt a file? By again exploiting NTFS: Not only can it store the file's password encrypted with your public key, EFS will also include that same password encrypted with the public key or keys of as many recovery agents as you like.

Where things get sticky is in the process of introducing EFS to a prospective recovery agent's public key/private key pair: you need a hierarchy of certificate authorities recognized by your computer. Without a certificate hierarchy, there are no certificates, and without certificates, you can't introduce new recovery agents to EFS. (With an exception—stay tuned.) So you'll need at least a certificate server or two running before you can monkey with the list of recovery agents. In an Active Directory environment, that's not too hard to accomplish, although it does require some work: AD doesn't install a certificate hierarchy by default. And in a stand-alone server environment, you could, if you wanted, install a certificate server to act as a one-server hierarchy and issue certificates with that.

But wait—at least one account has a certificate without having to go through all of the certificate-authority stuff. Where did the first recovery agent, the default Administrator, get its certificate? Here's the exception. Apparently EFS generates a self-signing certificate for the default Administrator. I've not been able to find a way to get it to build certificates like that for other accounts; it'd be a nice, low-overhead way to add some flexibility to EFS administration.

In Win2K, the absence of a recovery agent meant that you could not encrypt files, and EFS was basically disabled (a backward way of allowing you to turn encryption on or off). That was the only way that you could disable encryption on a system. With Server 2003, the EFS policy actually gives you the ability to turn EFS on or off, allowing you to decide on which systems you enable the service. Because it is a machine policy, you can apply it wherever you want in the domain. This is a significant improvement, since if you removed the recovery agent, it was basically a one-way street. Without installing a certificate authority, you couldn't reverse the decision not to run EFS. Now you can turn it on, off, and back on again with just a flip of the venerable Group Policy switch.

Decrypting Files

Decrypting encrypted files is a simple matter if you're the person who encrypted the file in the first place. When you open it, the file is automatically decrypted—the action is completely transparent to the user.

That decryption is temporary, however—as soon as you close the file, it's encrypted again. If you want other people to be able to use the file, then you'll love the newest encryption (or rather decryption) feature included in Server 2003. You now have the ability to assign other users the right to access (or decrypt, basically) your encrypted files. Here's how it works. First, you need to make sure the users that you want to access your encrypted documents have the right to access them in the first place. By that, I mean that the users must have the proper NTFS permissions to access those files. Next, right-click the document that you want to "share" and choose Properties. Clicking the Advanced button will expose the Advanced Attributes dialog box, as shown back in Figure 10.42, except in this case the Details button will no longer be unavailable.

Click the Details button and you will see the Encryption Details sheet, as seen in Figure 10.44, which will display users who have the right to decrypt the file and any recovery agents defined. Click Add to configure new users to be able to decrypt the file. You can add users from either the local account or the domain.

To permanently decrypt a file or folder from Explorer, open its property sheet and click the Advanced button on the General tab. Uncheck the box next to Encrypt Contents to Secure Data. The file is now open to anyone who has the right to access it.

FIGURE 10.44

Encryption Details
property sheet

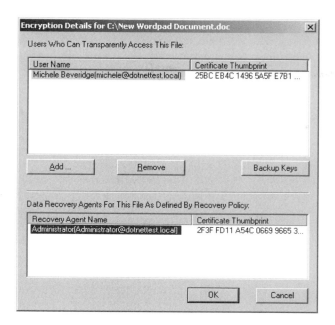

Dealing out Disk Space...Managing Disk Quotas

Many administrators found NT 4 incomplete in one way or another, and one of the perennial complaints was its lack of quota management tools. Without quota management, it's hard to control the amount of disk space people on the network use; even in these days of cheap and plentiful storage, there comes a limit to the amount of time and money you want to put into storing every single JPEG John Doe receives.

Several NT-compatible quota management applications exist, but adding quota management to NT has historically not been cheap. To help those who need a basic form of quota management, Win2K was released with a set of simple quota management tools, and those have been continued but not improved in Server 2003. Server 2003's quota management tools don't include all the functionality some third-party products do—one big shortcoming is that you must assign disk quotas on a per-user basis—but they're a start and have the usual advantage: you've already paid for them.

BACKGROUND: HOW QUOTA MANAGEMENT WORKS

The process of quota management is straightforward: The quota manager keeps an eye on writes to the disk of protected lettered volumes based on criteria set by the network administrator. If the protected volume reaches or exceeds a certain level, then a message is sent to the person writing to the volume warning them that the volume is near quota, or the quota manager prevents the user from writing to the volume altogether, or both. The mechanics of how all this works varies from product to product, but the basic effect is the same: users can't write to volumes that are at or exceed their preset quota.

Server 2003's quota management is based on both the user's identity and the attributes regarding quotas that are set for the volume on which that particular user is storing information, so you can control how much space a person uses on any particular volume.

SETTING UP USER QUOTAS

By default, Server 2003 quotas are turned off. To start working with quota management, open Explorer, right-click the volume you want to protect, and choose Properties. This can be any NTFS volume with a drive letter, be it a local drive or a drive letter mapped to another server that was created with Win2K, Server 2003, or upgraded from NT 4. Click the Quota tab shown in Figure 10.45.

FIGURE 10.45

Disk quotas are disabled by default.

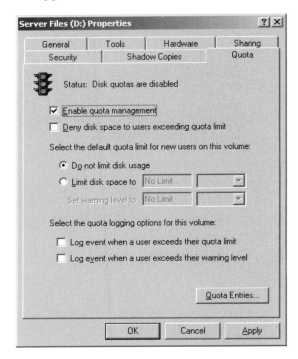

NOTE   *You cannot enable quotas on a folder within a volume; you can only set them on the entire volume.*

The first order of business is to enable quotas. To turn on disk quotas and make the management options available, check that box. You can set up all the options before clicking OK or Apply to enable quotas. Choose Apply to keep the property sheet open.

Next, choose whether to enforce quotas by denying disk space to anyone violating a quota. If you don't check this box (it's not checked by default), then people violating their disk space quotas will still be able to write to the volume.

WARNING   *Never enforce a quota on a system partition and deny disk space to those exceeding it. When booting, Server 2003 writes data to the disk. If you enforce quotas, then the system may not be able to boot. Actually, there's really no reason to put quotas on the system partition if it's separate from the data partition.*

Third, set a default quota limit. Notice that the default value is 1KB, which means that unless you're in a particularly draconian mood, you're going to want to change the default to something a bit more reasonable. You might, for example, limit each user's quota on the volume containing home directories to 10MB.

Finally, set the logging options, sending events to the System log in the Event Viewer tool when users exceed their quotas or reach the warning level. Users will be identified by name in the System event log, so you know who is running out of assigned disk space.

You've now done the basic job of setting up quota management on the volume. Next, you'll need to create quotas for each person who'll be using that volume. To do so, click the Quota Entries button to open the screen in Figure 10.46.

FIGURE 10.46

Add quota entries to the list.

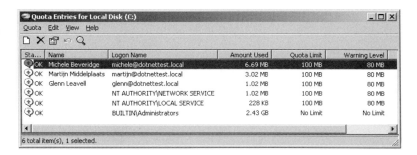

When you start, the only entries will be the default entry for the local server's administrator and any users that already have data that resides on the disk. To add a new entry, choose New Quota Entry from the Quota menu. You'll see the dialog box in Figure 10.47.

FIGURE 10.47

The Select Users dialog box

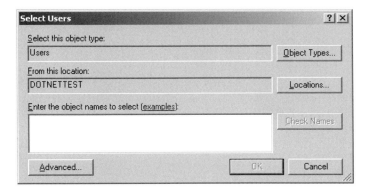

You can enter accounts from either the local user account database or the domain. Specify the location from which you want to add the names, either the local machine or the directory, by clicking the Locations button. When you are ready to add users, you can either type in each account name you want to add, or you can choose the Advanced button, which will expose the advanced Select Users dialog box as shown in Figure 10.48. You can search for accounts using queries or by clicking the Find Now button to enumerate a list of users from the location you specified in the first Select Users dialog box. You can also select a new location from which to search for user accounts here by clicking the Locations button.

FIGURE 10.48

The advanced Select Users dialog box.

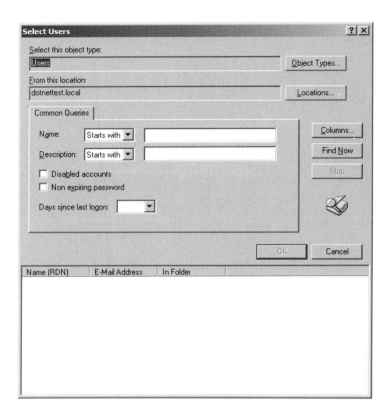

Because quotas are enforced on a per-user basis, you can't create quota entries on a per-group basis. This is unfortunate, and more than a bit ungainly. However, you can create quota entries for multiple users by holding down the Ctrl key while selecting the users you want to add. All users will start with the same settings. When you have the users you want, click OK to return to the first Select Users dialog box and then click OK again. This will bring you to the Add New Quota Entry dialog box, as shown in Figure 10.49.

FIGURE 10.49

Specify the amount of disk space allocated to the new quota entry.

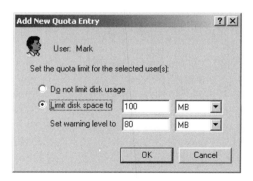

Here you can choose whether to enforce quotas for the new entries, and (if so) how much disk space in the volume they get. The amounts shown in this window will be the default you set on the Quota tab.

In this same box, specify the level at which the users will be warned that they're about to run out of disk space. The warning level, obviously, should be less than the quota limit. Server 2003 will fuss at you if the warning level is more than the quota and make you edit the value so that the warning level is less than or equal to the quota.

Click OK, and you'll return to the list of quota entries. The new entries will be listed and take effect immediately. If you elected to deny your users disk space when they exceed their quota and a user attempts to write to the volume once she has exceeded that limit, she will get a write error. The exact nature of the error message will depend on what application users are working with when they attempt to write to the volume, but the basic idea will be the same: they're denied access to the volume because it's now write-protected. To write to the volume, they'll need to delete some of their files to get below quota or have someone else take ownership of their files. The files in the Recycle Bin are also considered part of a user's quota on the local volume. In addition, compressed files, although smaller than their original value, are calculated using the uncompressed value for the purpose of calculating quota limits.

NOTE *Some quota management software allows users a "grace write" when they're over quota, permitting them to save the file they're working on before locking them out. Server 2003's quota management does not.*

If you want to use the same quota limits on more than one NTFS volume, you can export the quotas and import them on the new volume. To export a quota, select it in the list in the Quota Entries management tool and choose Export from the Quota menu. The extension for the export files is not displayed. Choose a name for the file and save it. To import the quota settings, open the Quota Entries management tool for a volume and choose Import. Browse for the file, and you can import the quotas.

Quotas may not work as expected on volumes that you originally formatted with FAT or FAT32 and then converted to NTFS. Any files that users created on the FAT volumes will appear to the quota manager to belong to the Administrator, not to the person who created them, since the FAT filesystems don't distinguish file ownership like NTFS volumes do. Therefore, the files that people created on the FAT volume before it was converted to NTFS won't be charged to their quotas, but to the Administrator.

MANAGING QUOTA ENTRIES

Some time after you implement quotas in your network, people will start running up against them. If you open the Quota Entries folder, you'll see three possible statuses for quotas. Quotas may be within acceptable limits, at warning levels, or over quota (if you haven't prevented users from writing to volumes for which they're over quota).

Server 2003 doesn't include any messaging application that is tied to quota limits, so you'll need to keep an eye on this yourself. You can sort the entries in the list by clicking the columns, so if you need to find all the people (for example) who have crossed the warning threshold for quotas, you'd click the Status column. Sadly, there's no mechanism from here to send people messages; you'll need to rely on e-mail or some other messaging technique.

TIP   *Of course, you can always use the command-line tool called EVENTTRIGGERS to alert you to certain events that you specify, including those for quotas.*

Volume Shadow Copy Service

You are sitting at your desk, desperately trying to figure out how you will ever get enough done so you can spend just a little time at home tonight playing Death Match instead of working into the wee hours of the morning…again. Suddenly the phone rings. It's a (groan) user. "Um, I can't seem to find the spreadsheet that Mr. Dickle needs to present at the World conference in Hawaii tomorrow. I think, somehow, it may have been deleted. Can you help me get it back?" This is an all-too-common scene in many a sysadmin's daily life and, usually, a huge waste of time. "Okay, what was the name of the file, and when did you last have a working copy of it? Where is it stored?"

Wouldn't it be great if you could, with just a little bit of user training, let your users help restore their own files simply by accessing the properties sheet of the file? "A pipe dream?" you ask. "Are you trying to tease us, Mark?" No, my friends, it's true, and it's brand new in Server 2003.

The Volume Shadow Copy Service (VSS for short) debuts in Server 2003 and it offers two services that I think you'll like. First, it will allow users to access and/or restore previous versions of saved files using a client feature called Previous Versions. The server feature is known as Shadow Copy to us administrators. Secondly, VSS enables applications that take advantage of the volume shadow copy API to access locked files or files that are in use by other services or applications. We'll look at this first.

Applications Can Use the API

"What does that mean," you ask? Well, let me give you an example. Since Server 2003's backup software has been built to take advantage of this API, it is now able to offer the new and improved functionality of backing up open or locked files. Here's what happens. If, during a backup, a file is locked by another application, the backup application can't access the file to copy it. In the old days, that might have meant that the backup couldn't complete and, of course, you wouldn't know about it until you came in the next morning. More often, nowadays, it means that those files will be skipped during the process and won't be backed up, unless you have a really expensive backup software. What the VSS does is to take a snapshot of these open or locked files when applications, like Server 2003's Backup Utility, come face to face with the lock. This allows the application that needs access to those files to use the shadow copy as its source for those files. Of course, if the file was open and being edited at the time of the backup (and subsequent shadow copy), the backup will reflect the file as it existed when the snapshot was taken. This API is available to vendors, and I am sure that other applications will take advantage of it. Microsoft has announced that the newest versions of Exchange and SQL will feature great improvements based on the use of this API. The VSS is available by default to applications that use the API, regardless of whether you enable shadow copies (for the user, this means Previous Versions) on your volumes, which is a manual process.

Volume Shadow Copy and Previous Versions

When an administrator enables volume shadow copies for a volume, it gives the users the ability to restore previous versions of the files that they access through a share on that volume. In fact, it *only* works through shares. The previous versions of the files won't be accessible to the user if they access the file locally. You *can* map a drive through Explorer if you want to access a file on that volume from the console though. Shadow copies can only be enabled on a per-volume or per-partition basis. For a network share, you will need to configure shadow copies on the volume where the share resides. Once enabled, VSS immediately takes a snapshot of the volume. You can also create a manual snapshot of the volume any time, or you can create a schedule for the VSS snapshots. The scheduler offers a very granular way to schedule this routinely.

When you initially enable VSS on a volume, you will find that a new hidden folder called System Volume Information appears in the root of the volume. This is where the snapshots are stored by default, along with the log files. This folder is created for each volume on which you enable VSS. The minimum amount of disk space you'll need for a snapshot is 100MB. You can configure a maximum allowable space for this folder, but you need to have a good idea of how much space you'll need for these snapshots, because going over the maximum means the deletion of the older Previous Versions files. I don't know exactly how to estimate the space needed for this other than to experiment, at this point. The default storage space allocated is 10 percent of the size of the volume that is being copied. It is recommended that you store the shadow copy on a different volume from the one you are copying from. I'll show you where you can configure this, but first, let's look at how to enable VSS on a volume.

How to Enable VSS

Right-click the volume on which you would like to enable volume shadow copies and choose Properties. Select the Shadow Copies tab to open the Shadow Copies property sheet, as shown in Figure 10.50.

FIGURE 10.50

Highlight the volume and click Settings to configure the Volume Shadow Copy Service.

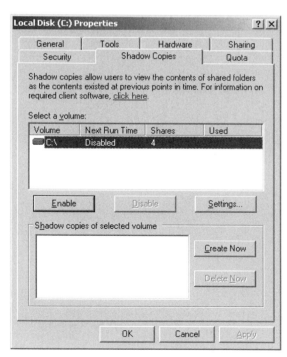

Highlight the volume you wish to enable and click the Settings button to determine where you want to store the shadow copy data, configure the space allocated to the shadow copies, and set up a schedule for the service. Click OK to apply your settings and return to the Shadow Copies properties sheet. Shadow copies are now enabled on the volume. As you can see in Figure 10.50, you can elect to manually take a snapshot of your volume by clicking Create Now. You can also delete snapshots here. Once a volume has been enabled, when a user accesses the properties sheet of a file, they will notice a new tab has appeared, called Previous Versions. This tab can only be seen when volume shadow copying has been enabled on the volume that a file resides on, and only if the user accesses the file through a share.

How It Works

Here's how it works. When the administrator enables volume shadow copies on a volume, a snapshot is taken of the entire volume and all of its files. When I say snapshot, I don't mean a backup or a copy, just that the VSS records the "state" of the volume and all of the files that reside on it. Are you with me? Keep this in mind. The VSS now has a "memory" of the volume and all the files on it at the moment that snapshot was taken. Let's say I, the user, have a Word document that resides on a volume where VSS is enabled (which I access through a share) and that a snapshot was taken this morning at 7:30 A.M. before I arrived at work. When I arrive at 8:00 A.M., I edit the document and make some changes. As soon as I commit those changes to memory (i.e., save the file), the VSS goes to work.

VSS says, "Hey, I've got a file that has changed here. Do I have anything about this file in my snapshot?" The file existed on the volume when the snapshot was taken this morning, and it was in a different state than it is now that I am trying to commit changes to it. So, the VSS says, "Yup, that Word doc that is being saved is different from what I see in the snapshot." The VSS then creates and saves an exact copy of the Word doc as it existed at 7:30 A.M. this morning when the snapshot was taken, and it stuffs it in the System Volume Information folder. VSS then makes that file available to me, the user, by placing a link to that 7:30 A.M. version of the Word file in the Previous Versions tab of the property sheet of the Word document that I just saved. Now, if I access the file by double-clicking it or opening it from Word, I am editing the version that I saved at 8 A.M. However, if I access the properties of that doc and view the Previous Versions tab, I will have available to me the version of the file as it existed at 7:30 this morning (VSS saved that for me when I saved the file at 8:00 A.M.).

Okay, stick with me here. Keep in mind that the VSS is scheduled to take a snapshot of the volume every morning at 7:30 A.M. Here's what that means to me, the user. Since the time that I edited that Word document at 8:00 A.M. this morning, I have made several more changes. It is now 10:00 A.M. and I decide to save the file again. When I last checked, I had one previous version available to me (the one from the 7:30 A.M. snapshot that was given to me because I changed the file at 8:00 A.M.). Since I am saving the file again, I should have two now, right? Actually, no.

Remember how I said that when I commit a change to a file, the VSS goes out and looks at the last snapshot it has of the volume to see if the file is different from the snapshot? And how, if the VSS finds that the snapshot is indeed different, it creates and then saves an exact copy of that file, as it existed at 7:30 A.M. during the last snapshot? Well, I did this once already this morning at 8 A.M., and that file was indeed copied and made available to me in the properties sheet of the file. Since the only information the VSS has to work from is the 7:30 A.M. snapshot, its job is done. The file, as it existed the last time the VSS recorded a snapshot was made available to me at 8 A.M. and it can't be done again, not until two things happen. First, another snapshot has to be taken (tomorrow morning at 7:30, according to the schedule) and second, once that snapshot is taken, I have to make changes (and save those changes) to the file. Once those two things happen (and not before then), I'll have yet another previous version available to me when I access the properties sheet of that file. I could make 10 more changes to that Word document today, and if I completely destroy the formatting and want to roll it back to a previous version, my only option is the copy of the file as it existed at 7:30 A.M.

The same rules apply to the deletion of the file, with one exception. Let's say that Word file was called `BigMeeting.doc`, and let's say that at 11:00 A.M. I accidentally deleted it. I took a snapshot of the volume that morning at 7:30 A.M. "No problem!" you say. "Just go to the property sheet of the file…and, um…" Okay, I'll bet you're with me here, aren't you? How can I access a previous version of a file, if I can't access the Previous Version tab on the properties sheet on the file because the file has been deleted? Well, it's easy and it's not. What I have found is that you can simply recreate a file with the exact same name. When you access the properties of that file, the previous version will be available to you. It will be an exact copy of the file as it existed the last time a shadow copy was taken. So what's not easy about that? Well, what if I can't remember what the file was called? "I've had a lot on my mind and my kids are sick and I was late and…" Sound like your average user? Sure. The best way to think about it is this: if you don't know the name of the file, there is no way you can recreate it to see the previous versions of the file. If you were restoring this file from tape, you'd be in the same boat. You just can't get around needing to know the name of the deleted file to restore it.

When a user accesses the Previous Versions tab of a file's properties sheet, as seen in Figure 10.51, they can view the list of the previous versions of that file and will have three choices, in terms of what they can do with that file. They can view the file, they can copy the file to another location, or they can restore the file, which will overwrite the current version of the file. A couple of interesting things to note here:

◆ When you view a previous version of a file, the resulting action will depend on what kind of file it is. If the file is viewable, it will be opened for you to see. If it is an executable, it will attempt to run it. One of the first files that I tested the VSS on happened to be an `autoexec.bat` file that I had recently edited. VSS wasn't able to run it, but it tried. Perhaps "view" is not the best choice of words for this feature.

◆ If you copy a file to a different folder, it will inherit the permissions of the new folder, much like the file copies that you know now.

◆ If you rename the file, you will lose the previous versions that you have collected to date. You won't have any previous versions available to you until, a) the next snapshot is taken for the volume and, b) you commit changes to the newly named file.

Of course, since this feature is new to Server 2003, that is the only version of Windows that has the full features of the VSS built-in. Once you have installed Server 2003, the Previous Version client for XP can be found in the `Windows\system32\clients\twclient\x86` folder. It is an MSI file (`twcli32.msi`) and thus can be distributed through a network share or applied using Group Policy or SMS.

FIGURE 10.51

The client's view of the Previous Versions property sheet

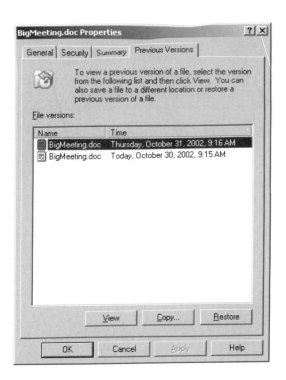

Remote Storage

One nice feature that was initiated in Win2K and continues in Server 2003 is Remote Storage. What the Remote Storage feature does is allow you to mix tape-drive space and hard-drive space as if they were one unit.

The idea of Remote Storage is this. Suppose you have a 24GB hard disk on your server; perhaps it's a nice amount of storage, but not quite enough for your users' needs. Suppose also that you've got a tape backup device, a carousel device that can automatically mount any one of 16 tapes into the tape drive without the need for human intervention. Perhaps it's a DLT loader and each tape can store 20GB of data; that works out to about 320GB of tape storage and, again, 24GB of hard-disk storage. Here's what Remote Storage lets you do:

It lets you lie about the amount of hard disk space you have.

You essentially advertise that you've got a volume containing 320 plus 24, or 344GB of online storage space. As people save data to that volume, Remote Storage first saves the data to the hard disk. But eventually, of course, all of that user data fills up the hard disk; at that point, Remote Storage shows off its value. Remote Storage searches the hard disk and finds which files have lain untouched for the longest time. A file could have, for example, been saved eight months ago by some user but not modified since. Remote Storage takes those infrequently accessed files and moves them from the hard disk onto the tape drives, freeing up hard-disk space.

Ah, but Remote Storage has been claiming the file that was untouched for eight months is ready and available at any time. What happens if someone decides to go looking for that file and it's on the tape? Remote Storage just finds the file on tape and puts it back on the hard disk, where the user can get to it. Yes, it's slow, but the fact is that many files are created and never reexamined, which means there is a good chance that putting the file on tape and off the hard disk will never inconvenience anyone.

I worked with mainframe systems that did things like this years ago, and it was quite convenient—files untouched for six months or so would be said to be "migrated" to tape. I could "unmigrate" the tapes, and that would take a while, but it wasn't that much of a nuisance and it helped keep the mainframe's disks free.

DiskPart for Disk Management

Earlier I discussed how to use DiskPart to expand basic disks, a feat that the Disk Management tool in Server 2003 is simply not capable of doing. I have also used DiskPart to accomplish other tasks that the GUI couldn't seem to handle, like deleting a boot partition that should never have been there in the first place. Here's what happened. During an upgrade from Win2K to Server 2003, a system with two physical disks gave me a little trouble. The first disk contained the OS and it faired well during the upgrade process (this is what I was actually trying to test). The second disk had a bit of a history and had been through several different conversions from one filesystem to another, converted from basic to dynamic and back again—basically a misfit disk without any real duties at the time of the upgrade. I believe, in the end, that it was a dynamic disk with a single volume on it just before the upgrade, but the important part about this disk was what happened during the upgrade. When I looked at the Disk Management tool, intending to use this lost disk for some data I wanted to house, the disk was marked as Dynamic Missing, and the lone volume that Server 2003 was calling a boot volume was still there. Nothing I did in the Disk Management tool fixed the fact that Server 2003 couldn't seem to recognize this misfit disk, nor would it allow me to delete the volume. However, DiskPart had no trouble recognizing or deleting that volume, and I was able to restore the disk in no time at all. DiskPart's commands are pretty intuitive and it has proved to be a great tool for me. It is installed by default in Server 2003, and I suggest that you add it to your bag of sysadmin disk tricks.

SCRIPTING WITH DISKPART

If you are deploying your systems using Unattended Installs or Sysprep and want to create more than just the sole partition those tools are capable of creating, you might look at DiskPart's scripting features. There are 42 commands that you can use with DiskPart's command-line interface that will allow you to create, delete, expand, and manipulate the disks in a system in any way that you can (and more!) by using the GUI. For example, you can use a single script to delete all those crazy partitions that come installed on so many OEM machines (I once received a box with *six* 2GB partitions on it!). Then you can create the logical disk division so that it is standardized across all of those similar machines that are sitting in boxes just waiting to be deployed on your users' desktops.

Here's how it works. Create a simple text file with the commands that you need to create your logical disk environment and include that file when you call the script. To run a DiskPart script, you'll type the following at the command prompt:

```
diskpart /s Myscript.txt
```

Myscript.txt, of course, is the name of the text file you'll create that contains your DiskPart commands.

You can type the following if you want to redirect DiskPart's output from the script to a file:

```
diskpart /s Myscript.txt > MyLogFile.txt
```

LogFile.txt is the name of the text file to which you want DiskPart to write the output.

*TIP   By default, DiskPart will not continue the script if it encounters an error. You can avoid this and force DiskPart to continue processing the script by using the **noerr** parameter. You have to make sure your syntax is correct though, because the **noerr** option will not help you there. DiskPart can't process a command with syntax errors; it will return an error.*

The Evolution of Storage

When Win2K was released early in 2000, its storage management toolkit included quite a few new features to support the storage environment, some for which NT administrators had been clamoring for years. With the release of Server 2003, Microsoft has managed to add even more functionality to their storage management and has improved upon several of the features that debuted in Win2K. All told, Server 2003 is starting to look a lot more like an enterprise solution than NT 4 ever hoped to be. It's becoming a far more "grownup" solution than many ever expected and that some Microsoft adversaries prayed it would never become.

In this chapter, you saw how the Disk Management tool works to protect data and system disks and learned about the available options for choosing a disk format and the ways to logically divide those disks. You also learned about some of the advanced features of NTFS, like disk quotas, encryption, Remote Storage, and the Volume Shadow Copy Service. I hope by now you feel pretty comfortable with the concepts of storage and how to better manage your systems. Using these tools, you should now be better able than ever to protect and manage your data files.

Chapter 11

Creating and Managing Shared Folders

MICROSOFT THREW ALL SORTS of new services, features, and functions into Windows 2000 Server, but at the heart of it all was still the requirement to be a good file server. Windows 2000 took the solid file sharing capabilities of Windows NT, extended them with the Distributed File System (Dfs), and made permissions and shares easier to manage—not to mention that this was all on top of a more stable and powerful operating system. The release of Server 2003 brought a few enhancements, the most important being that the new default permission sets are far more secure than they were in Windows 2000. In this chapter, I will talk about what file sharing really is, how those permissions work, and how to set it all up. Next, we'll dig into the Dfs. You'll find out what it is, how it works, and how to make it work for you. Finally, you'll take the basic file sharing capabilities and push them right out to your users' Web browsers. I'll also show you how to make your users files available for offline use.

Basics of File Sharing

The core component of any server is its ability to share files. In fact, the Server service in all of the Windows NT family, including Server 2003, handles the server's ability to share file and print resources. But what exactly does that mean, and why is it so important? By default, just because you have a server running doesn't mean it has anything available for your users. Before they can actually get to resources on the server, you must share out your resources. Let's say you have a folder on your local I: drive named APPS with three applications in subfolders, as shown in Figure 11.1.

When you share this folder out to the network under the name of APPS, you allow your clients to *map* a new drive letter on their machines to your I:\APPS folder. By mapping a drive, you are placing a virtual pointer directly to where you connected. If you map your client's M: drive to the APPS share of the server, their M: drive will look identical to the server's I:\APPS, as shown in Figure 11.2.

FIGURE 11.1

Subfolders in
I:\APPS

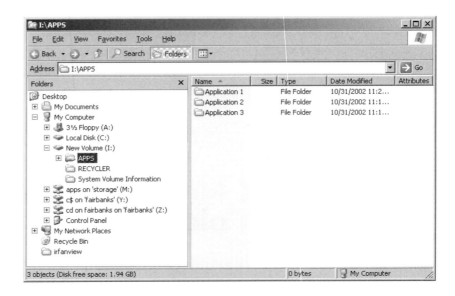

FIGURE 11.2

M:\ mapped to
I:\APPS

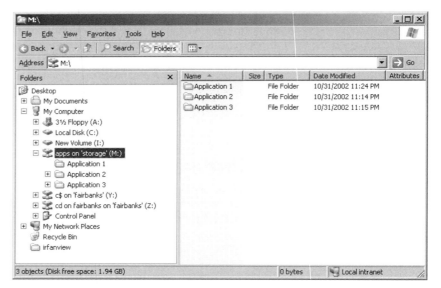

NOTE *Don't worry, I'll slow down and explain how to create this share later—and I'll explain how to connect to it in Chapter 14.*

That's really all there is to it. Sharing resources means that you allow your users to access those resources from the network. No real processing goes into it as far as the server is concerned; it just hands out files and folders as they are.

Creating Shared Folders

Before you can create a shared folder, you must have appropriate rights to do so. This requires that you are either an Administrator or a Power User. You can create shares in a few ways: You can use the Explorer interface when sitting at the server or use the Computer Management Console to create shares either at the server or remotely.

Creating Shares from Explorer

If you're sitting at the server, the Explorer interface provides a simple and direct means for creating and managing all properties of a share. Let's go back to the I:\APPS folder that you want to make available to the network under the name of APPS.

NOTE   *Don't forget that not all clients can handle names longer than eight characters. This applies to shares as well. If you have old DOS LAN Manager clients, they won't be able to interpret share names longer than eight characters, for example, if you named the share* Applications *instead of* APPS. *For this chapter, I am assuming at least a Windows 98 user base, so long filenames and share names won't be a problem.*

In Explorer, right-click the APPS folder and select the Sharing and Security menu option. This will bring up the properties page for the folder APPS, already set to the Sharing tab. To share the folder, click the Share This Folder radio button, as shown in Figure 11.3.

FIGURE 11.3

Properties for the APPS share

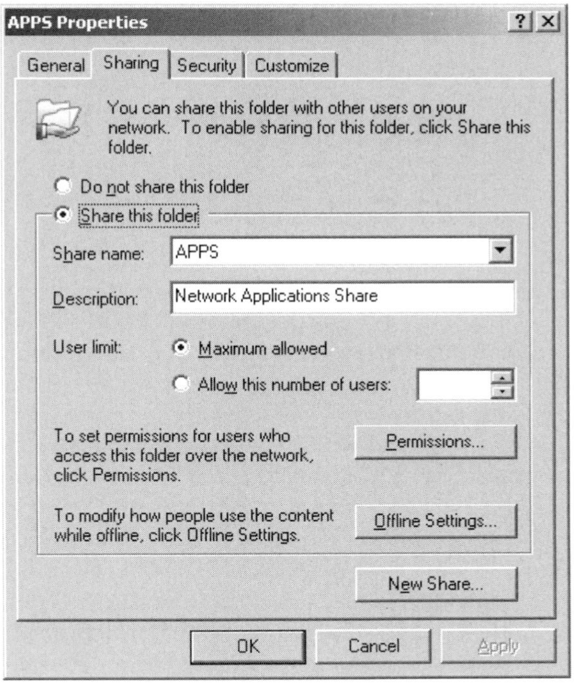

NOTE *If you want to stop sharing this folder later through the Explorer interface, go back into the properties as you just did and select the Do Not Share This Folder button.*

The Share Name option on this page is the most critical entry. This is how your users will reference this share. For our purposes, share this folder as APPS. The Description field is used to provide more descriptive information about this share. Technically, the description has no real bearing on the server or client; it just makes browsing a little less cryptic—I'll comment this share as Network Applications Share. This information will be visible to the users in the Comments field when they browse My Network Places for available shares, as shown in the Explorer window in Figure 11.4. Click OK, and your share is enabled and ready for immediate use by your users.

FIGURE 11.4

Browsing network shares

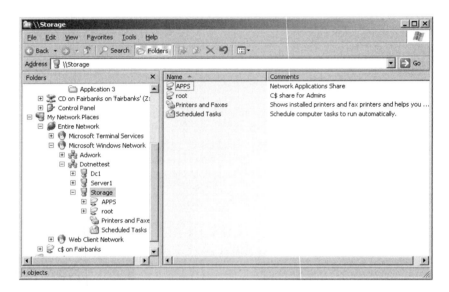

Once you share the folder, you can revisit the properties sheet by right-clicking the shared folder and choosing the Sharing and Security option. This looks like the same properties page as before, but there is now an additional option available, the New Share button, as you can see in Figure 11.5.

If you click the New Share button, you'll see the dialog box shown in Figure 11.6. Here you can share the folder using a different name and different permissions.

Of course, once you set up a share, you need to worry about securing it. You can define your share permissions by choosing the Permissions button. I'll discuss this in more detail later in the section titled "Managing Permissions."

You can enable another feature from the Sharing properties page with the Offline Settings (formerly known as Cacheing) button. You've probably heard of *cacheing* or *offline files* and that is exactly what we are talking about here. Offline Settings is a handy tool that gives your users offline file and folder access so they can get to their resources when they are away from the office. This will be covered in more detail in the "Using Offline Files/Client-Side Cacheing" section.

FIGURE 11.5

The New Share button is only available once you have shared a folder.

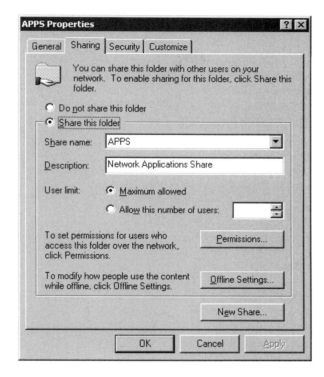

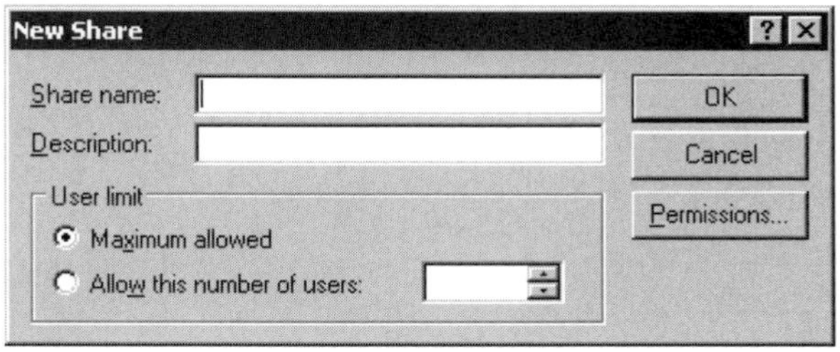

FIGURE 11.6

Share the folder using a different name with different permissions.

SETTING USER LIMITS

You can also configure how many users can connect to a share simultaneously in the User Limit area of the Sharing properties page. If the applications under your share are each licensed for 100 concurrent users you can configure your server share to maintain a that limit, even though you may have 200 users on your network. Just check the Allow This Number of Users radio button and fill in the appropriate number (it defaults to 10). As users connect to the share, they build up to the user limit. As users log off, or disconnect from the share, the number drops. This type of licensing enforcement can be handy in reducing your licensing costs.

Continued on next page

SETTING USER LIMITS *(continued)*

Be careful with your licensing, however. Not all applications have a concurrent license mode, although they might have a client license mode. (Unfortunately, as Microsoft has abandoned concurrent licensing, more and more other firms have stopped offering this useful licensing option.) With client license mode, the manufacturer doesn't care how many users are accessing the application at any given time, they just care about how many people have installed the application altogether. This user-limit option will not protect you in these cases.

Another thing to keep in mind is that this user-connection concurrency limit is based on the entire share. It cannot be defined further to each folder within a share. If Application 1 has a concurrency limit of 100, and Application 2 and Application 3 are unlimited, you don't want to inadvertently limit those other applications.

Finally, you need to consider how your users connect to the share to use these applications before you limit them based on concurrency. If your users all connect to the share upon logging in, but don't disconnect until logging off, your concurrency limit may be used up based on who shows up for work first, and you'll have 100 people using up your concurrency limit even if only a small percentage of them are actually using the application. If connections are made only when actually using the application, the user limit will work quite nicely.

Remotely Creating Shares with the Computer Management Console

Within your Administrative Tools program group is the Computer Management Console. With this tool you can, among other things, create and manage shares locally or remotely. In contrast, within the Explorer interface, if you right-click a folder that is not local to your machine, you won't see the Sharing menu option. If you are going to create a share using the Computer Management Console from your local machine, you're set. If you want to manage a share on a remote server, you have to first connect to that server. Right-click the Computer Management (Local) icon, and select Connect to Another Computer. From there, you can type in the name of the server you want to manage or browse the network for the computer you want.

To begin with the share management, you need to select `Computer Management\System Tools\Shared Folders\Shares`, as shown in Figure 11.7.

FIGURE 11.7

Computer Management, Shares

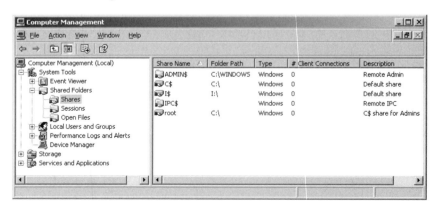

You can now either select the Action menu or right-click in the Shares window and select New Share. Click Next in the initial screen of the Share a Folder Wizard, and you will see the screen shown in

Figure 11.8. Make sure that the Computer Name field is correct so that you are creating the share on the right computer. To create the share, you can browse through the given drives and folders, or you can create a new folder on-the-fly by simply typing out the full drive and folder name in the box labeled Folder path. For this example, share the I:\APPS folder. Once you have completed the path, click Next.

FIGURE 11.8

Specifying a folder location in the Share a Folder Wizard

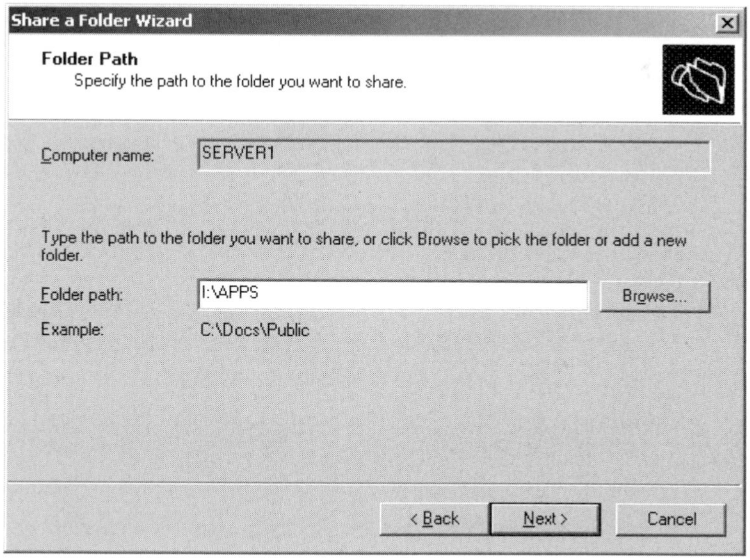

You'll then see the screen shown in Figure 11.9. Here you enter the name you want this share to be given, along with a brief description; select Next to continue through the wizard.

FIGURE 11.9

Assign a share name and description.

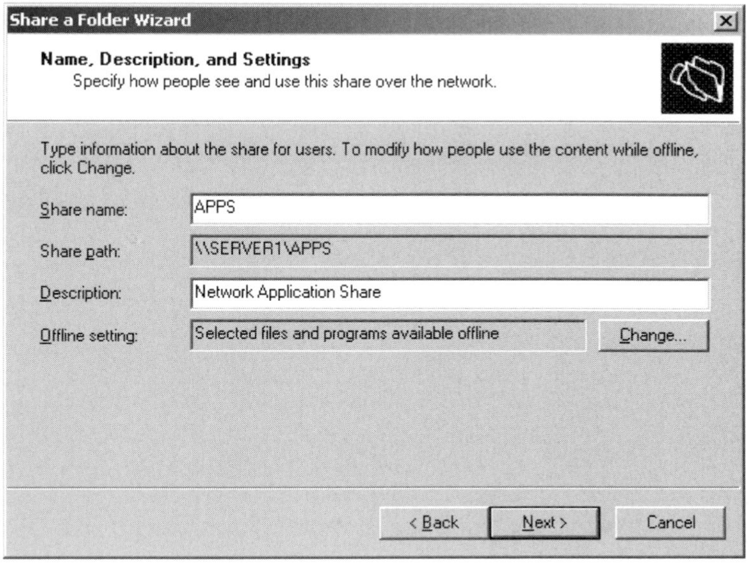

NOTE   *Remember that share permissions apply only to users who connect via the network. They don't apply to users who log in locally, either by sitting directly at the server or in the case of terminal server users, whose access is also considered local. Keep in mind though, that share permissions are the only way to secure network resources on FAT or FAT32 volumes.*

From here, you jump straight to defining your share permissions. In the next screen (Figure 11.10), you are given four options for defining permissions:

All Users Have Read-Only Access   This option allows the Everyone group (which, in Server 2003, no longer contains Anonymous User) to have read-only access to the contents of the folder. This is the default setting in Server 2003 and is a great new feature that brings home the extra focus that Microsoft has given to security in the last year. Until now, the default, Everyone—Full Control, included anonymous users coming in across the network! Now, when creating a share, you don't have to start with a wide-open door. You start off with a closed door and open it up per your specifications at your leisure.

Administrators Have Full Access; Other Users Have Read-Only Access   This option ensures that your users can view data and run programs, but they can't modify or delete anything within the share. This still gives administrators the appropriate rights to manage the data.

Administrators Have Full Access; Other Users Have Read and Write Access   This option allows the users to do anything they want except delete files or folders, change permissions, or take ownership of the files.

Use Custom Share and Folder Permissions   This option lets you define permissions based on specific users or groups.

FIGURE 11.10

Controlling computer access in the Share a Folder Wizard

NOTE   In Windows 2000, there existed an option where administrators had full control and other users had no access. This was a handy option to choose when you knew that you wanted to customize the permissions but weren't sure how you wanted to set them up. You could choose this option and feel secure about the share until you opened it up at your leisure. That option doesn't exist anymore, but there are still two ways to get almost the same thing. Either use the second option, which still allows users read access, or customize the share by choosing the fourth option. Then add the Administrator account with full control and remove the read attribute from the Everyone group.

Once you set up the permissions on your share, click Next to see the final screen of the Share a Folder Wizard, which lists the results and gives you the option to run the wizard again, as shown in Figure 11.11.

FIGURE 11.11

The final dialog box shows a summary of the share you created.

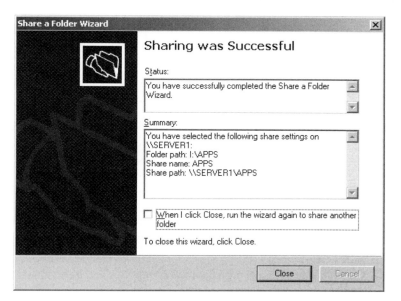

Publishing Shares in the Active Directory

One of the great things about the Active Directory is that it can unify all resources in an enterprise into a single directory, whether it's printers, groups, users, organizational units, or just about anything you can dream up—or more appropriately, serve up. This counts for shares too. To publish a share, you need to be in your Active Directory Users and Computers Management Console. Right-click the organizational unit of choice and select New/Shared Folder. From there, you'll be asked to provide a name for this publication of the share and, of course, the share name. That's all there is to it—your share is now published in the Active Directory. However, it is published under the name you provided, and not as its original share name. If you publish the share \\BS1\APPS as Network Applications, that is all the users will see.

Also keep in mind that you will need to perform this function with the appropriate rights. You'll need to be a domain administrator or an enterprise administrator, or to have been delegated the proper authority to publish shares. Remember to consider using the RunAs feature, which allows you to masquerade as a powerful admin just long enough to do the job.

Managing Permissions

Now that you've shared out your resources to the world, it's time to protect them *from* the world. Of course, there are numerous ways to secure your server and its resources from the outside—using routers and firewalls, for instance—but by setting permissions on your files and shares, you are more likely to stop an intruder who *does* manage to make it all the way past your other barriers. And, of course, this also ensures that even the folks on the inside are only allowed access to what they need. The two kinds of permissions that I'll talk about here are *share permissions* and *file and directory (NTFS) permissions*. These permissions let you control who accesses your data and what they can do with it.

NOTE *NTFS (NT File System) is the most common and the most secure file system used for Windows Server. For more information about NTFS, see Chapter 10.*

Share permissions are applied any time a user accesses a file or folder across the network, but they are not taken into consideration when a user accesses those resources locally, as they would by sitting directly at the computer or by using resources on a terminal server. NTFS permissions, in contrast, are applied no matter how a user accesses those same resources, whether they are connecting remotely or logging in at the console. So, when accessing files locally, only NTFS permissions are applied. When accessing those same files remotely, the sum of both share and NTFS permissions are applied by calculating the most restrictive permissions of the two types.

Share Permissions

Share permissions are possibly the easiest forms of access control you will deal with in Windows Server. Remember that share permissions only take effect whenever you try to access a computer over the network. Consider share permissions to be a kind of access pass to a secure building. When you walk up to the front door and show your identification, the guard looks up your name and gives you a pass that shows your access level for everything else on the inside. If your pass says "Level One access," then your pass will get you into every door on Level One—and nowhere else. Once inside, try to get into a room with Level Two access requirements, and it won't work. By defining share permissions, you can safely control the access level for each person at the front door.

Keep in mind, though, that this front door—or share-level permission—isn't the entire picture. The share-level permission only represents the *maximum* level of access you will get on the inside. If you get read permissions at the share, the best you can do once you've connected remotely to the share is read. Likewise, change permissions will grant change at best. If you want full control to *anything* inside the share, you need full control *at* the share. But understand that when I say the share permission is the *maximum* level of access you will get inside the share, it is entirely possible to restrict access more once you're inside, using file-level (or NTFS) permissions. You can have full control at the share, but an object inside can still have NTFS permissions that say you can only read it.

NOTE   There are cases every once in a while where you will choose one of the FAT file systems for your logical drives. FAT has no file and directory permission capabilities, which leaves your data very insecure. However, you can alleviate some of these pains through share permissions. Even on FAT partitions, you can share out folders and assign whatever level of share permissions you like. In this scenario, the share permissions are it—they won't be overridden by file or directory permissions because there aren't any. If you get to change the share, you get to change everything within the share. Unfortunately, this still doesn't prevent an intruder from accessing data directly at the console. Physical security of the server is your only surefire protection.

DEFINING SHARE PERMISSIONS

To define share permissions, we will work through the Computer Management Console. Select the share you want to secure by right-clicking the share name and selecting Properties, then selecting the Share Permissions tab. You can get to the same place from Explorer by right-clicking the locally shared folder, selecting Sharing and Security, and then clicking the Permissions button; both methods will bring you to essentially the same dialog box which is shown in Figure 11.12.

FIGURE 11.12
The Share
Permissions tab

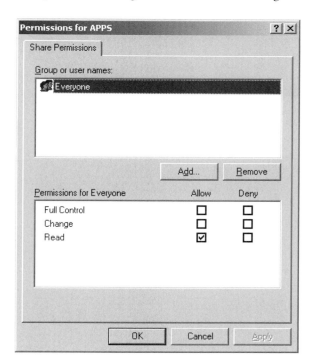

NOTE   Note that the Everyone group, by default, has Read access permissions, which is a great step forward in the Windows world in terms of security. Until, Server 2003, the Everyone group was given Full Control access by default. Another new feature in Server 2003 is that the Everyone group no longer contains the Anonymous User account, which will help keep your resources more secure.

In this dialog, you are shown a Group or User Names box that lists users and groups assigned to the share; when a user or group is selected, the permissions for that user or group to access the share are revealed. You can assign different levels of permission for different users and groups. At the share level, you have the following types of permission:

Permission	Level of Access
Full Control	The assigned group can perform any and all functions on all files and folders through the share.
Change	The assigned group can read and execute, as well as change and delete, files and folders through the share.
Read	The assigned group can read and execute files and folders, but has no ability to modify or delete anything through the share.

The example in Figure 11.12 shows read access for Everyone. Although you won't see the administrator's account listed with any specific rights, note that local administrators always have full control of the shares on the computer. If you want to change share permissions to give all your network administrators full control, you will need to add the group and assign them rights. Select the Add button to see the dialog box shown in Figure 11.13.

FIGURE 11.13

Select Users, Computers, or Groups dialog box

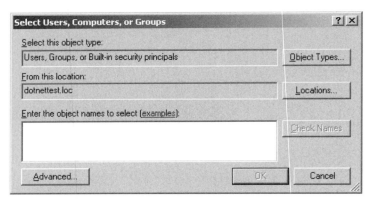

You can either type in the name of the account or group that you want to add, or click the Advanced button, which will bring you to the second Select Users, Computers, or Groups dialog box, shown in Figure 11.14. This dialog box enables you to search the directory.

You can either use the Active Directory search functions on the Common Queries tab to narrow down your choices or select the Find Now button, which will enumerate all of the users in the directory. From here you locate the group that you want to add—the Domain Administrators group in the example—and click OK and then OK again. This brings you back to the Share Permissions tab with the Domain Administrators group added to the display and highlighted. Select the Full Control check box, and as you can see in Figure 11.15, everything else is checked automatically.

FIGURE 11.14

Enumerate users and groups by clicking the Find Now button in the Users, Computers, and Groups dialog box.

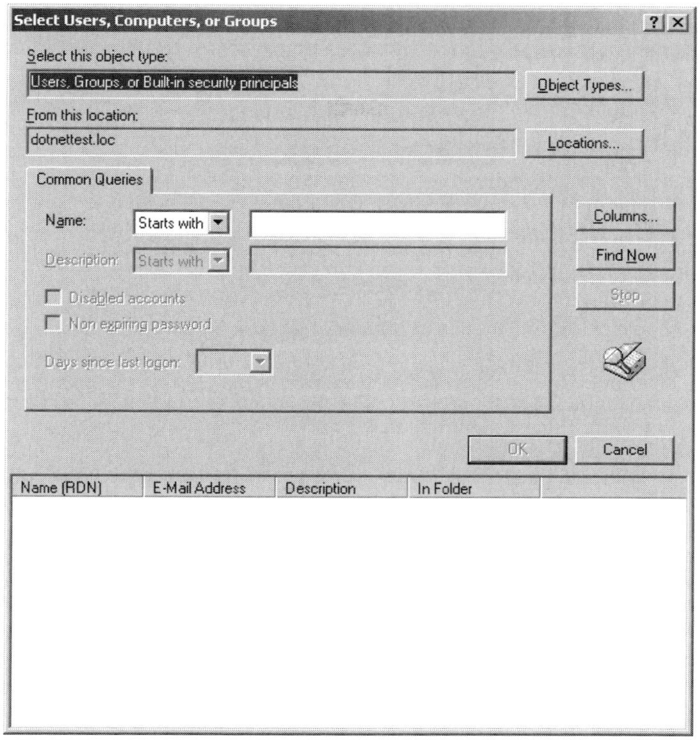

FIGURE 11.15

Share permissions, Full Control for Domain Administrators

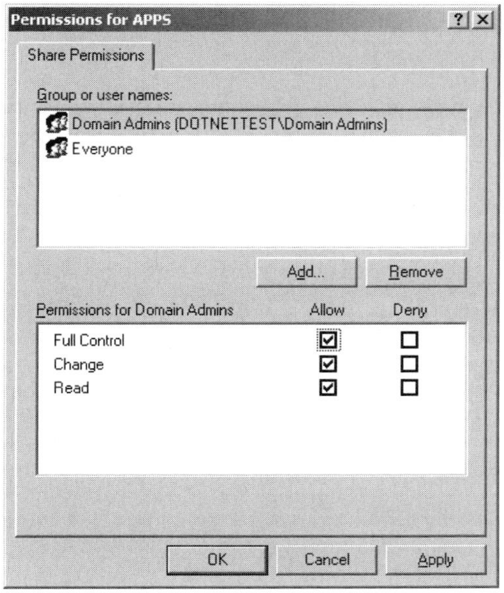

Again, keep in mind that share-level permissions are just your first filter for users accessing files over the network. Whatever level of permissions you get at the share level will be the highest level of permissions you can get for files and directories (the most restrictive apply, remember?). If you get read-only rights to the share, but full-control rights to the file, the share will not let you do anything other than read.

UNDERSTANDING ALLOW AND DENY

You probably noticed when you checked the Allow check box on the Full Control permission for the Domain Administrators group in the previous example that there also exists a Deny check box for each permission listed. Share permissions are just about the simplest set of permissions that we'll deal with, so they're a great place to explain this "allow" and "deny" notion. Here's how they work:

- An administrator of a share, file, user account, or whatever can change permissions on that object. (That's almost a complete definition of an administrator, actually.) There are several kinds of permissions—Full Control, Change, or Read in the case of shares. Anyone can be allowed or denied by the administrator, or the administrator can choose to clear *both* Allow and Deny, leaving a user with neither allow nor deny on that permission.

- If the user has no permissions, no allow or deny, then the user does not have access to the object.

- If the permission is checked Allow, the user can exercise the permission; if Deny is checked, the user can't. I know that's obvious, but let's see how it affects more complex situations.

Objects may have more than one permission on them. Figure 11.12 showed just one permission— Everyone/Read—but you'll see some Security dialog boxes with many entries giving different permissions to different individuals or groups. (Recall that these individual entries are called access control entries or ACEs, and the entire list is called an access control list or ACL, pronounced "ackel.") There may be conflicts in that case. For example, suppose I want to access some share, and there's an ACE for the group Domain Users that has neither the Allow nor Deny box checked. (I'm a member of that group.) Suppose there's also an ACE naming a group called Managers (which I'm a member of) where the Allow box is checked. Finally, suppose there's an ACE that names me specifically and checks the Deny box. Which permission wins?

The operating system looks at all of the ACEs relevant to me and computes this way: First, it ignores any "no checked" entries. No allow or deny from Domain Users. Next, it looks for any Allow checks. If I have none, then I don't get in. But I *do* have an Allow check, as I'm in Managers. So far, I've got one Allow check and no Deny checks. Finally, it looks for any Deny checks. If it finds even one of them, then I'm denied. And there is one, in the third ACE. Rephrased, then: I get permission if I have at least one Allow checked and no Deny checks. I am denied permission if I have no Allow checks at all, or if I have at least one Deny check.

For example, to deny just one person access to something, just add an ACE with their name on it and check Deny. To allow only one person access to something, remove all ACEs from the object and add that one person with an Allow check. Do *not* add that one person with an Allow check and then add Everyone with a Deny check—that one person is a member of Everyone, and so would have a Deny check...and would be denied access.

Here is where it gets dangerous. What if you have a share to which you allow read permissions for the Domain Users group, then you explicitly deny read permissions for another group called

Employees? I log in as a user who just so happens to be both a Domain User and Employees member. Now what? When I connect to that share, every group that I belong to, as well as my username, is checked against the permissions list for that share. If any one of those groups or my username comes up in the Deny column, I'm denied—end of story. Likewise, if through one group I'm allowed full control, but another group I belong to has the Deny box checked for the change permission, I can read but not change. So be careful when using Deny permissions on a share. In practical uses, you might find it extremely helpful to Deny specific individuals. You might want to create a group for Offenders that you want to specifically block. Denying general groups, though, could get you into more of an administrative nightmare than you bargained for.

File and Directory Permissions

The old days of Microsoft networking (before the arrival of the NTFS file system) utilized share-level permissions only. Once connected to a share with a given set of permissions, you had those permissions for everything under the share. If you had 1000 users who all wanted private access to their data, you would have to create 1000 shares with specific permissions on each share. Then, with the introduction of Windows NT to the Microsoft networking platform, you could create one share for all users, and customize access via file and directory permissions—permissions that could be assigned directly to the files and folders. With this new feature came an unending ability to customize the security of your data.

You may hear a lot about how NTFS, in conjunction with file and directory permissions, can help you protect the server itself from an intruder. Theoretically, this is true. Assuming that you do not know an administrator username and password, if you sit down at the server, you cannot gain access to the server's data. The idea is that NTFS will not let you boot to anything less than the NT operating system and view files. This feature lets you relax a bit about the physical security of the server. You know that no one can log in to the server, and that your partitions are using the NTFS file system. Pop a DOS boot disk in, reboot the server, and you can't see a thing on the hard drive.

Well, it was only a matter of time. Someone *did* come up with a utility that allows you to gain access to NTFS partitions via a simple boot disk. Microsoft's Recovery Console, released with Windows 2000, lets you boot from the Windows 2000 Server or Professional CD. But actually, there was a similar package that existed long before Microsoft gave it to us. Mark Russinovich and Bryce Cogswell wrote a utility called NTFSDOS way back in 1996 that let you mount an NTFS volume from a boot disk. Mark is the same smart guy who discovered that the only difference between NT Workstation and NT Server code was just *one* Registry entry. You can still find this tool—and many others—through Mark and Bryce's freeware company, Sysinternals, or its sister company Winternals. (You can find out more at www.sysinternals.com.) What all this means is that, to be secure, go back to square one: Lock your server up so no one can sit at its keyboard.

PERMISSION TYPES

Before you assign permissions to your files and folders, you need to have a good understanding of what those permissions mean and how they work. There are two different levels of permissions.

To see the higher level, go to any NTFS folder, right-click it and choose Properties, and then the Security tab. You'll see a permissions dialog box like the one in Figure 11.16.

FIGURE 11.16

Top-level NTFS permissions dialog box

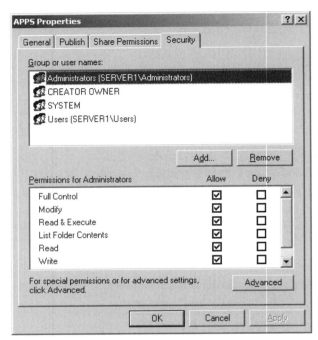

Compare Figure 11.16 to Figure 11.15, a standard share-level permissions dialog box. Notice that share-level permissions only offered three permission types—Full Control, Change, and Read. Very simple, and note that there was no Advanced button in the dialog box, unlike Figure 11.16. You've already seen in Chapters 8 and 9 that most permissions dialog boxes have an Advanced button that lets you drill down to a lower, more-specific level of permissions. The permissions you see in Figure 11.16 are actually built up out of the lower-level permissions. For example, the high-level permission List Folder Contents comprises five lower-level permissions—Traverse Folder/Execute File, List Folder/Read Data, Read Attributes, Read Extended Attributes, and Read Permissions. I think of them as "molecular" and "atomic" permissions. There are 13 atomic permissions for NTFS. You'll see that other object types have more or less atomic permissions; for example, any Active Directory object (a user account, a machine account, an organizational unit, a group policy object, and so on) has more than 35 atomic permissions. (Which leads to some odd things: What would a child object be for a group policy? The answer is of course that there *is* no such thing. But other sorts of Active Directory objects, such as organizational units, *can* have child objects because you can create users and other OUs inside OUs.) All AD object types share the same set of atomic permissions, even the ones that are irrelevant—go ahead and grant someone the ability to create child objects for a group policy object; it'll be about as useful as granting someone at a brick factory the ability to set the sex of the bricks.

Look at Table 11.1 to see how groups of atomic permissions in the left column make up molecular permissions.

TABLE 11.1: ATOMIC AND MOLECULAR PERMISSIONS

ATOMIC	WRITE	READ	LIST FOLDER CONTENTS	READ AND EXECUTE	MODIFY	FULL CONTROL
Traverse Folder/ Execute File			X	X	X	X
List Folder/Read Data		X	X	X	X	X
Read Attributes		X	X	X	X	X
Read Extended Attributes		X	X	X	X	X
Create Files/Write Data	X				X	X
Create Folders/ Append Data	X				X	X
Write Attributes	X				X	X
Write Extended Attributes	X				X	X
Delete Subfolders and Files						X
Delete					X	X
Read Permissions	X	X	X	X	X	X
Change Permissions						X
Take Ownership						X

SOME PERMISSIONS DO DOUBLE DUTY: FILES VERSUS DIRECTORIES/FOLDERS

Notice in the table that some permissions have two names, such as Traverse Folder/Execute File or Create Folders/Append Data. What in the blazes does that mean? It's just one more little hurdle to get past when understanding permissions.

You see, NTFS permissions apply both to directories (or *folders*—the terms are interchangeable) and files. And Microsoft only allocated so much space on a file or folder for describing permissions—13 bits, to be exact. They use that same 13 bits whether describing a person's access level to a file or a folder.

But the kinds of things that you can do with files and folders are not exactly the same. Sure, they're similar—you change permissions on a file or folder, you read attributes of a file or folder—but some things are a bit different and in a few cases you end up with a file operation that has no corresponding action on folders and vice versa. For example, there's the "execute file" permission. You use this when you've got a file that is actually an executable file, such as winword.exe. If I deny you the Execute File permission, then you can't run Word, plain and simple. It's a useful permission, so it's good that Microsoft included it.

But there is *nothing* even remotely similar to it for folders. You don't execute folders.

So Microsoft looked around for a permission that was useful and that applied to folders, but that lacked a file analog. That permission is Traverse Folder. The idea is this: Suppose there's a folder you'd like to get to that is several levels deep, say a folder named C:\toplevel\level2\level3\level4. You have been denied access to C:\toplevel, C:\toplevel\level2, and C:\toplevel\level2\level3... but you have Full Control of C:\toplevel\level2\level3\level4. So you have godlike powers inside level4... if you can just *get* there.

The Traverse Folder permission lets you bypass all of the locks on the upper levels and essentially "beam yourself" right into level4. Like Execute File, it's a useful permission, but it has nothing to do with files. What's happening is this: When NTFS is examining a permission, it pulls up the 13 bits. When looking at the first one, it asks itself the question, "Is this a file or a folder?" If it's a file, then it interprets that first bit as Execute File permission. If a folder, then it's Traverse Folder permission. You'll see this in a somewhat less extreme manner on some of the other permissions as well.

Let's look at the other atomic permissions in some detail.

ATOMIC PERMISSIONS

We'll start at the atomic level. These permissions are the building blocks of the permissions that we normally speak of, like Read, Modify, and Full Control. You will probably never see these permissions, much less refer to them on their own.

Traverse Folder/Execute File   We just covered these in the previous section.

List Folder/Read Data   List Folder permissions allow you to view file and folder names within a folder. Read Data permissions allow you to view the contents of a file. This atomic right is the core component of Read.

Think of the separation between these two atomic permissions. Is there really much of a difference? Yes, but probably not for long. Remember the days when we called everything files and directories? Now the file and *folder* terminology has become mainstream. Just when we start really getting used to it, another term is coming into play: *objects*. Everything on your machine is an object—both files and folders. This atomic permission could almost be rephrased to *read object*. Regardless of whether this permission applies to a file or folder, this right lets you examine the contents of an object.

Read Attributes   Basic attributes are file properties such as Read-Only, Hidden, System, and Archive. This atomic-level permission allows you to see these attributes.

Read Extended Attributes   Certain programs include other attributes for their file types. For example, if you have Microsoft Word installed on your system, and you view the file attributes of a DOC file, all sorts of attributes will show up, such as Author, Subject, Title, and so on. These are called *extended attributes*, and they vary from program to program. This atomic permission lets you view these attributes.

Create Files/Write Data   The Create Files atomic permission allows you to put new files within a folder. Write Data allows you to overwrite existing data within a file. This atomic permission will not allow you to add data to an existing file.

Create Folders/Append Data   Create Folders allows you to create folders within folders. Append Data allows you to add data to the end of an existing file, but not change data within the file.

Write Attributes   This permission allows you to change the basic attributes of a file.

Write Extended Attributes   This permission allows you to change the extended attributes of a file.

Delete Subfolders and Files   This atomic permission is strange. Listen to this: With this permission, you can delete subfolders and files, even if *you don't have Delete permissions on that subfolder or file*. Now how could this possibly be? If you were to read ahead to the next atomic permission—Delete—you would see that that permission lets you delete a file or folder. What's the difference? Think of it this way: If you are sitting at a file or folder, Delete lets you delete it. But let's say you're sitting at a folder and want to delete its *contents*. This atomic permission gives you that right. There is a very vague difference between the two. One lets you delete a specific object, the other lets you delete the *contents* of an object. If I am given the right to delete the contents of a folder, I don't want to lose that right just because one object within that folder does not want to give me permissions. Hey, it's my folder, I can do with it what I want.

Delete   Plain and simple this time, Delete lets you delete an object. Or is it plain and simple? If you have only the atomic permission to delete a folder but not its big-brother atomic permission to delete subfolders and files, and one file within that folder has no access, can you delete the folder? No. You can't delete the folder until it is empty, which means that you need to delete that file. You can't delete that file without having either Delete rights to that file, or Delete Subfolders and Files rights to the file's parent folder.

Read Permissions   The Read Permissions atomic permission lets you view all NTFS permissions associated with a file or folder, but you can't change anything.

Change Permissions   This atomic permission lets you change the permissions assigned to a file or folder.

Take Ownership   We'll talk about what ownership is and what it does in more detail later, but this atomic permission allows you take ownership of a file. Once you are the owner, you have an inherent right to change permissions. By default, administrators can always take ownership of a file or folder.

MOLECULAR PERMISSIONS

A full understanding of what atomic permissions do and of Table 11.1, which shows the atomic makeup of molecular permissions, provides exceptional insight into what these molecular permissions are and how they work. This section will try and put the atomic makeup of permissions in better perspective, but you should flip back and forth to the table while you read about these permissions. This information will form a solid foundation to help you manage permissions later.

Read   Read permissions are your most basic rights. They allow you to view the contents, permissions, and attributes associated with an object. If that object is a file, you can view the file, which happens to include the ability to launch the file, should it be an executable program file. If the object in question is a folder, Read permissions let you view the contents of the folder.

Now, here is a tricky part of folder read. Let's say that you have a folder to which you have been assigned Read permissions. That folder contains a subfolder, to which you have been denied all access, including read access. Logic would say that you could not even see that subfolder at all. Well, the subfolder, before you even get into its own attributes, is *part of* the original folder. Because you can read the contents of the first folder, you can see that the subfolder exists. If you try to change to that subfolder, then—and only then—will you get an Access Denied.

Write   Write permissions, as simple as they sound, have a catch. For starters, Write permissions on a folder let you create a new file or subfolder within that folder. What about Write permissions on a file? Does this mean you can change a file? Think about what happens when you *change* a file. To change a file, you must usually be able to open the file, or read the file. To change a file, Read permissions must accompany your Write permissions. There is a loophole though: If you can simply append data to a file, without needing to open the file, Write permissions will work.

Read and Execute   Read and Execute permissions are identical to Read, but give you the added atomic privilege of traversing a folder.

Modify   Simply put, Modify permissions are the combination of Read and Execute and Write, but give you the added luxury of Delete. Even when you could change a file, you never really could delete the file. You'll notice that, when you select permissions for files and folders, if you select Modify only, then Read, Read and Execute, and Write are automatically checked for you.

Full Control   Full Control is a combination of all previously mentioned permissions, with the abilities to change permissions and take ownership of objects thrown in. Full Control also allows you to delete subfolders and files, even when the subfolders and files don't specifically allow you to delete them.

List Folder Contents   List Folder Contents permissions apply similar permissions as Read and Execute, but they only apply to folders. List Folder Contents allows you to view the contents of folders. More important, List Folder Contents is only *inherited* by folders, and is only shown when looking into the security properties of a folder. The permission allows you to see that files exist in a folder—similar to Read—but will not apply Read permissions to those files. In comparison, if you applied Read and Execute permissions to a folder, you would be given the same capabilities to view folders and their contents, but would also propagate Read and Execute rights to files within those folders.

Special Permissions   Special Permissions is simply a customized grouping of atomic rights you can create when one of the standard molecular permissions just covered isn't suited to your specific situation. Although it might appear that the Special Permissions feature is new to Server 2003, it did, in fact, exist in Windows 2000. It just wasn't visible as a molecular permission. In fact, in Win2K, there wasn't any way to tell whether or not a folder had customized atomic permissions unless you looked in the Advanced tab of the Securities properties sheet. In Server 2003, you can tell just by looking at the Allow/Deny check boxes used for Special Permissions whether the ACEs have been modified. If the check boxes appear shaded, then, by clicking the Advanced tab, you can view and edit those modifications.

INHERITED PERMISSIONS

A tool that was released with Windows 2000 is the *inherited permissions* feature. By now, you are probably already accustomed to using this great feature, but for those of you who might not know about it yet, or who are upgrading from NT4, I'll explain. In Windows NT, if you wanted to set permissions for all files and directories for an entire directory tree, you had to check a box to apply permissions down from the root. When that happened, the server literally went through every single file and set the permissions as defined—what a tedious process. Now, there is inheritance. If a file or folder is set to inherit permissions, it really has no permissions of its own; it just uses its parent folder's permissions. If the parent is also inheriting permissions, you simply keep moving up the chain of directories until you get one that actually has some cold, hard permissions assigned. That being said, the root directory cannot inherit permissions.

For example, I have a folder named APPS, with three subfolders and files. All of the subfolders and files allow inheritable permissions. If I set my permissions on APPS to allow read and execute permissions for Users, all subfolders and files automatically mirror those new permissions. What if I want to customize the permissions on Application 1 so that users can also write? I right-click Application 1, select Properties, and then click the Security tab to view the permissions on the folder. If the check boxes for anything other than Special Permissions are grayed out, I can tell that the folder is inheriting permissions from its parent. From here, I need to select the Advanced tab in order to see the Allow Inheritable Permissions from Parent to Propagate to This Object and All Child Objects option (now there's a mouthful for you). This option shows me whether the object is inheriting permissions and lets me choose whether to allow inheritance or not. To get rid of those inherited permissions, I clear the check box and am immediately presented with the dialog box shown in Figure 11.17.

FIGURE 11.17

You're warned when you remove inheritance.

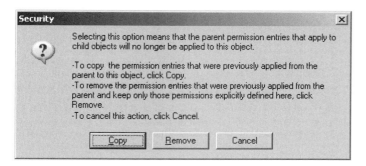

What is happening now is that this object is no longer going to be using inherited permissions; it will be using its own permissions. The problem is that it really doesn't have permissions of its own yet. This dialog box asks you how to start. Do you want to use the original parent permissions as a guide or baseline, or do you want to start from scratch with no permissions for anyone? If you already had highly customized permissions, you'd probably want to choose to copy those permissions and tweak them down a little further. In this case, I'll choose to copy the original permissions, and then I can just add the required write permissions on top of those. Of course, if you already have a combination of inherited permissions and permissions that you have applied directly to the folder, you could select the second option, which would remove the inherited permissions but keep the permissions that you have explicitly defined for the folder intact.

I've covered removing the inherited permissions, but what about down the road, when I want to reset everything back to the standard top-level permissions at APPS? Just as easy. Simply reselect the check box, Allow Inheritable Permissions from Parent to Propagate to This Object and All Child Objects option. This will keep any custom, explicitly defined permissions of those objects and add the inherited permissions from the parent folder.

In Windows 2000, the effect of this action would have removed all permissions and replaced them with only the inherited permissions. A new feature in Server 2003 will allow you to see where the specific permissions come from. In Figure 11.18, you can see that specific permissions, or ACEs, have an entry in the Inherited From column, which shows you this valuable information.

FIGURE 11.18

The Inherited From column allows you to see whether the permissions are inherited or not and, if inherited, from which folder the permissions are inherited.

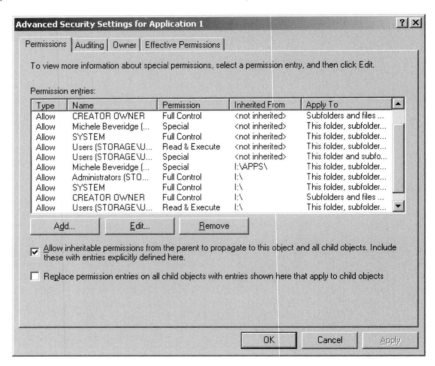

In addition, by viewing the information in the Apply To column, you can determine where the ACEs will be applied further down the folder tree. You can highlight an entry and choose Edit to specify where those permissions should be applied in the tree, as shown in Figure 11.19.

Active Directory Objects and Inheritance

Although I said that you can specify which child objects will inherit permissions by using the Apply Onto feature, something different happens when you use this in an Active Directory environment. Although the permissions you created will only be applied to the subset of files, folders, and subfolders that you chose when you used the Apply Onto functionality, a copy of the ACE will be given to every child object, regardless of whether you specified that it should receive it, but only the ones you specified actually implement it.

FIGURE 11.19

You can apply permissions downward in a variety of ways.

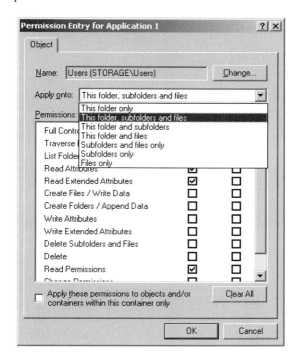

Deny or Allow with Inheritance

When you add permission inheritance to the mix, things can get a little strange. Do you remember when I said that Deny always wins, that if you have a Deny entry you cannot access the object, whether you have an explicit Allow or not? That isn't exactly true for objects that have inherited permissions from a parent. If an object has an explicit Allow set on the object itself, then even if a Deny permission is inherited from a parent, the Allow will win out. Simple enough?

There is one other interesting note with respect to inheritance. Keep in mind that these ACEs can get pretty complex, with lots of different permissions having to battle it out. When an object is receiving inherited permission from more than one parent, the permission inherited from the closest parent will prevail. What, you say? This is starting to get complicated? Well, Microsoft has made it a little bit easier to determine what the end results of the various permission sets will be with a tool called Effective Permissions, which I'll tell you about next.

ASSIGNING FILE AND DIRECTORY PERMISSIONS

Once you understand what the different permissions mean, assigning them to files and folders is a piece of cake. Start off in Explorer. Find the file or folder you want to assign rights to, right-click it, select Properties, and then select the Security tab. Take a look at Figure 11.20.

FIGURE 11.20

The Security properties tab

The top window shows the different groups or users to whom permissions are assigned, and the bottom window shows the permissions assigned to the selected user or group. I'm starting off in my APPS folder. Ideally, because this is for applications, I want all users to have Read and Execute permissions and not have the ability to change, add, or delete anything. I also want to keep administrators in full control so they can still maintain the data, and there is also a group of database managers that I want to give Modify rights. Since the Users and Administrators groups already have an entry by default, I'll start off by adding the Database Managers group and giving that group Modify rights. Click the Add button, and the Select Users, Computers, or Groups dialog box appears, as shown in Figure 11.21.

FIGURE 11.21

Select Users, Computers, or Groups

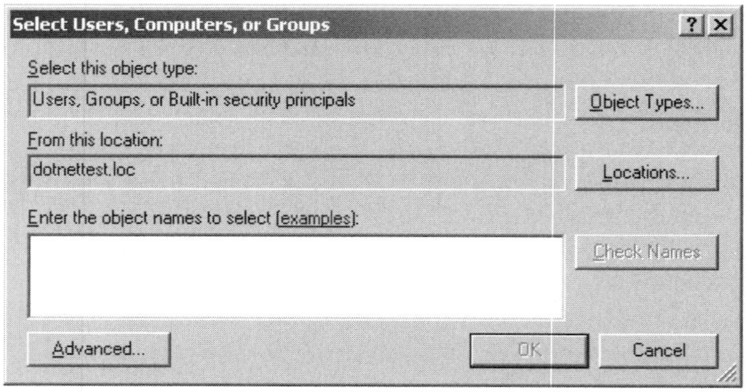

You can type in the name of the user or group, select the Advanced button, and click the Find Now button, or set up your query manually to enumerate a list of domain accounts. Since I know the name of the group I want to add (Database Managers), I'll just type it in here and then select the Check Names box. This will cross-check my manually typed entry with the list of names to find a match. Once the name is underscored, click OK to return to the Security tab of the properties page of APPS. Now that I have added the Database Managers group, the dialog box should look like the one shown in Figure 11.22.

FIGURE 11.22

The Database Managers group is added.

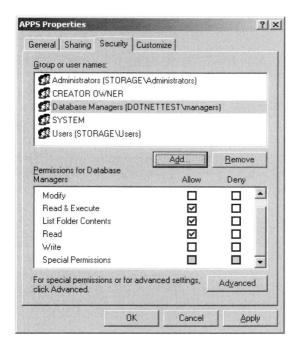

NOTE *You can add multiple users and groups at one time using either interface in the previous example. When you type the names in manually, just type the first name then click the Check Names box and start typing the next name. If you don't type a complete name before clicking Check Names, it will give you the closest match to your typed entry. If you choose to use the Active Directory Search interface, you can select multiple accounts by clicking on the first entry and then holding the Ctrl key down while you click additional entries.*

Now that I have added the Database Managers group, all I have to do is assign the correct permissions, which are Modify rights. Highlight the Database Managers group and check the Modify box in the Allow column. The Security tab should now look like Figure 11.23. Since the Users and Administrators groups were added by default when I created the share, let's look at the default permissions that were applied and see if I need to make any adjustments. Click the Users ACE, and you will see the dialog box in Figure 11.24.

FIGURE 11.23

New permissions

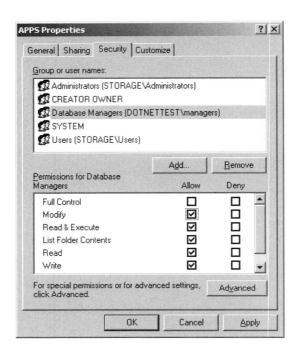

FIGURE 11.24

Default permissions
for the Users group

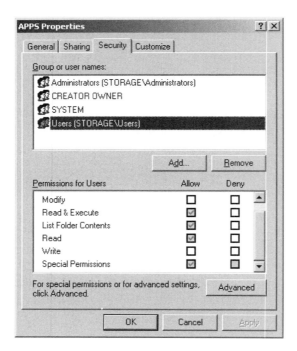

NOTE *You need to be careful when selecting some permission levels. Selecting Read and Execute includes all of the rights of Read, so Read is automatically checked. If, on the other hand, you want to clear Read and Execute, unchecking the Read and Execute box won't automatically uncheck Read.*

You can see, in Figure 11.24, that the Users group already has some default permissions, including Read and Execute, List Folder Contents, and Read. You can also tell that these are inherited because of the gray shading in the Allow boxes. However, as you may remember, the shading in the Special Permissions box doesn't mean that these permissions are inherited (although they might be). The shading here just represents the fact that there are more permission entries than you can see in this particular dialog box; click the Advanced tab to find out more. If you look at Figure 11.25, you will see a much more complex version of the permission entries you saw in Figure 11.24. I'm not quite sure why the good folks at Microsoft provide us with a sort of table of contents for the permissions story, when they could simply provide us with the whole story all at once. After all, we're not talking *War and Peace*, here. Just remember that you can get a basic idea of what is going on in the first screen, but you'll need to drill down to get to the details.

FIGURE 11.25

Advanced Security
Settings for APPS

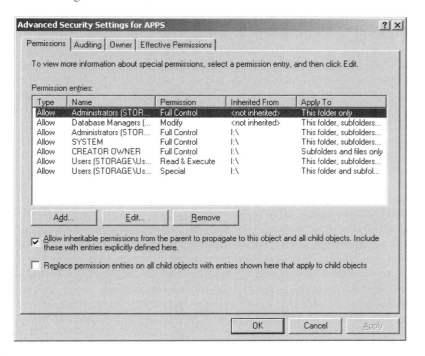

The Permission Entries box shows your selected groups and users, with a description of their rights. The Allow Inheritable Permissions from Parent to Propagate to This Object check box is the same, and you can still add and remove entries from this box. So, what is different here? In this window, you get to see a few more details. First, you can see that what might have been one entry (ACE) in the previous screen can become two or more detailed entries, allowing you to see exactly which rights are inherited and from where, or whether the entries were specifically created for this resource by hand. For example, notice that the Users group has two entries, both of which are inherited by the volume. You can also see exactly where the permissions flow downward by looking at the Apply To column. Of course, having all these details is great for troubleshooting because you finally have all the information in one place (well, almost).

You have the ability to tailor your extended permissions to the atomic level by choosing an entry and clicking the Edit button. Be careful, though. With so many permissions coming from so many different places (and we aren't even considering share permissions here!), this process can easily become messy to troubleshoot. Try to simplify your resources and users as much as possible, by volume, by group, or by machine, and your life will be a lot simpler when dealing with permissions.

To see what rights the Users group has so you can make sure they have the correct access to the APPS folder, select the Users entry with Read and Execute permissions, then click the Edit button. You'll get the options shown in Figure 11.26.

FIGURE 11.26

Viewing and editing the atomic permissions gives you the most information.

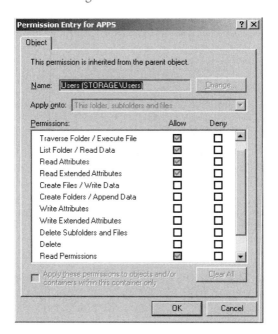

TIP   Notice that when you click the Users entry with Read and Execute permissions, the Remove button becomes unavailable. Why? Well, you can see that this ACE is inherited from I:\, and you would have to disable inheritance if you wanted to remove this entry.

These permissions break down Read and Execute into smaller parts. If you want your users to have all the benefits of Read and Execute but don't want to allow them to view permissions, you can simply clear the Read Permissions box. Of course, there are still 13 atomic permissions available here. It seems odd, since there are, have always been—and who knows—may always be, 13 atomic permissions in NTFS, that they did not build the window size so that you can view them all at one time. However, for our purposes, the permissions you see checked in Figure 11.26 are all of the applicable atomic permissions for Read and Execute that apply to the Users group.

TIP   You might have noticed that the Apply Onto drop-down list is also unavailable for the Users group entry. Remember, you couldn't remove it because of inheritance, and this is yet another result of inheritance. You can consider inheritance as an order from on high. These permissions will be applied to this folder, subfolder, and files unless and until you remove the inheritance check box and create your own custom permissions. Or you could go straight to the source, since, as the administrator, you are the ruler when it comes to inheritance. If you open up the properties for the volume itself and edit the entries for the Users group, you can remove or modify the permissions; you can then specify exactly where you want them applied throughout the volume by using the Apply Onto button from there.

These permissions are Read and Execute, by the book. No more and no less, these five atomic permissions make up Read and Execute. Consider it law.

But wait, there were two entries for the Users group, remember? Server 2003's default permissions are sure a lot more interesting (and safer) than those given to us in Win2K. (Remember, in Win2K, Everyone had Full Control on *everything!*) Let's examine the atomic permissions for the other Users group entry. If you are still looking at the dialog box in Figure 11.26, click Cancel—you don't need to modify the Read and Execute entry because that is exactly what you want for the APPS directory. Back at the Advanced Security Settings for APPS window, click the other entry for the User group and then click Edit. You'll see the dialog box in Figure 11.27.

FIGURE 11.27

Editing the Special Permissions for the Users group

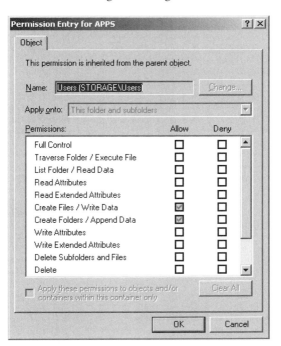

The default permissions for the Users group include the ability to create files and folders on the volume as well as the ability to write data and append data to the files contained within that volume—unless, of course, you specifically deny that ability to any particular resources on the volume. So, what you have here is a set of permissions that is in between two of the molecular groups we discussed previously. The first set of atomic permissions we looked at for the Users group made up the Read and Execute molecular permission. If you add these two atomic permissions, the molecular set falls somewhere between Read and Execute and Modify. In full, the Modify permission also includes the right to Write Attributes, Write Extended Attributes, and Delete files and folders.

If you know that you do not want to allow the Users group to have these extra two atomic permissions anywhere on the volume, you can simply edit the properties sheet for the volume and remove this particular entry for the Users group. If, however, this volume will also house directories where the users might need those permissions, you can edit these properties on the specific folders you want to restrict. Since this folder is used exclusively for applications and you know we don't want the Users to create anything, you can do one of two things. You can disable inheritance for this folder and modify the permissions, or you can simply deny the Users groups these two permissions on this folder.

For a couple of reasons, the easier of the two solutions is to use the Deny function. First, you don't have to worry about the rest of your inherited permissions from the volume, some of which you will need to keep—when you remove inheritance, you are given the right to copy the existing inherited permissions and can edit them as you like. Second, by removing inheritance, you take away your ability to push out permissions from the volume on a global scale, which is a pretty handy feature. As I said before, if you can simplify the permissions by doing things on a global scale, you can save yourself a lot of time and energy. To disable the ability for the Users group to create files or folders or to write or append data with the APPS folder, simply click the Deny check box (see Figure 11.28) for both of the atomic permission entries and click OK.

FIGURE 11.28

There isn't enough information to determine the *whole* permissions story from the initial property sheet.

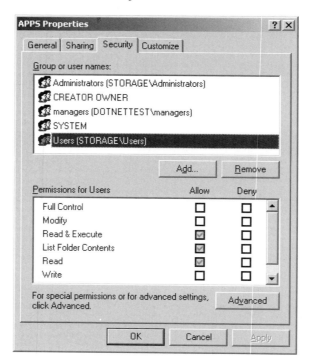

Removing a Group or User

To remove a group or user entry, just click the Remove button from either of the two property sheet interfaces that you just saw. If a user or group is there because of inheritance, the Remove option will be unavailable and you will have to disable inheritance by clicking the Allow Inheritable Permissions from Parent to Propagate to This Object and All Child Objects option.

Use the Detailed Interface to Get the Whole Story

Look at Figure 11.28. Remember this dialog box? Let me remind you of something I said before about the interfaces used for managing NTFS permissions: This window just doesn't give enough information and it's kludgey. If you decided to disable inheritance to get rid of the Users group's Write permissions and clicked the Remove button in this interface to accomplish that, you'd remove *both* of the Users entries that you saw back in Figure 11.25. Also, if you used this window to add a user or group account, you'd only be able to check the molecular permissions boxes you see here—you wouldn't be able to specify exactly where you wanted those permissions applied using inheritance. You'd have to drill down to the interface in Figure 11.25 to do that. It's best to just bypass this unnecessary dialog box and go straight to the detailed view. That way, you have the full story to start with.

CONFLICTING PERMISSIONS

You can assign permissions to files, and you can assign permissions to directories. Just as share permissions can conflict with file and directory permissions, file permissions can conflict with directory permissions. In share-level conflicts, the share wins; in file and directory permission conflicts, the file wins. If you assign read-only rights to a directory, but you assign change rights to a file within that directory, you will still be able to change the file.

Here is an interesting permissions riddle that I came across recently. Let's say you have read and execute permissions on a file and on the directory it resides in. You open the file and modify it. Sounds simple, right? Well, I've found that some applications actually *delete* the original file when they save a file with modifications, even if you don't change the filename. You are allowed to open the file, read it, and make your changes, but the minute you try to save it you will get an access denied message. Weird, isn't it? If you want to try this yourself, use Microsoft Word. I know that particular application behaves in this way, and perhaps others do as well.

MULTIPLE PERMISSIONS

Now for another problem. You have given your Administrators group full control over the APPS folder, and everyone else has read and execute permissions only. Here is where permissions once again come into conflict. Everyone is a user, right? Even administrators are users. Hmmm. How does this work? Well, in the case of multiple permissions, the *least restrictive* permissions will prevail, as long as share permissions aren't involved. Let's say you have an administrator named Bob. Bob is part of the Users group, which has read-only rights on a file. Bob is also part of the Administrators group, which has full control. In this case, Bob will get full control because it is least restrictive.

DENY PERMISSIONS

We talked about Deny permissions with respect to shares earlier and then briefly talked about the effects of inheriting permissions as it relates to Allow and Deny. The same thing applies in file and directory permissions, but in a way that's just a tad bit more complex because of the increased number of security options. Think of a corporate bonus-award spreadsheet file that you are trying to protect. You want everyone to see the file, but you only want the managers to be able to actually change the file. It makes sense: Grant Employees the right to read and Managers full control. Imagine that, somewhere along the line, some low-level supervisor falls into both groups. They need to be part of Managers for some things, but are more like Employees in others. If you leave the permissions as I just described, this supervisor is going to get the best of both worlds with this spreadsheet—full control. For this reason, you decide that you explicitly don't want anyone in Employees to have full control. Now what?

Easy enough: simply deny those excess permissions. What you need to do is find out which permissions you specifically do *not* want Employees to have and check them in the Deny column; this way you can make sure that Employees are given Read rights only. To do this, from the Advanced interface (see Figure 11.29), right-click the file and choose Properties. Now click the Security tab and then click Advanced. Remember this interface from Figure 11.25? From here, highlight the entry for the Employees group and click Edit, which will allow you to modify the atomic permissions for the spreadsheet. Check the Deny column for the entries that you see in Figure 11.29.

FIGURE 11.29

Deny permissions

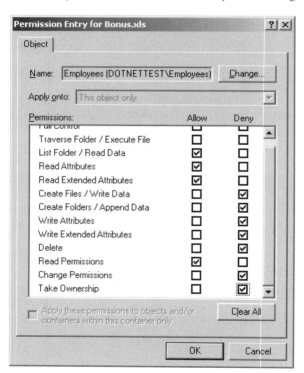

You'll need to individually check the Deny boxes for each attribute. If you check the Deny box for Full Control, however, everything else below that will automatically be selected in the Deny column because Full Control *includes* all permissions.

For this example, you want to allow Read and deny Write. When you click OK to have these new permissions take effect, you'll get a warning that tells you that Deny permissions override Allow permissions. Now, in the case of the multiple-permissions scenario, the Deny takes precedence, and even if the supervisor in question has both Managers and Employees memberships, he'll get cut off with the Deny.

EFFECTIVE PERMISSIONS

What is the end result of all of these permissions if some are inherited, some are not, some apply to users, and some apply to groups? Who will get to do what and with which files? By now you have seen that permissions can conflict with each other and sometimes have to battle it out to determine the winner. How can you tell what the result of all of these permissions will be for any group, user, or object? Well, Microsoft has included a new tool in Server 2003 that allows you to calculate the effective permissions for any particular user or group on a particular object. Take a look at the dialog box in Figure 11.30. Once again, it's the advanced property sheet for your APPS folder that, by now, you should know well. Remember that Administrators have Full Control, Database Managers can Modify and Users have Read and Execute permissions?

FIGURE 11.30

Advanced permissions for the APPS folder

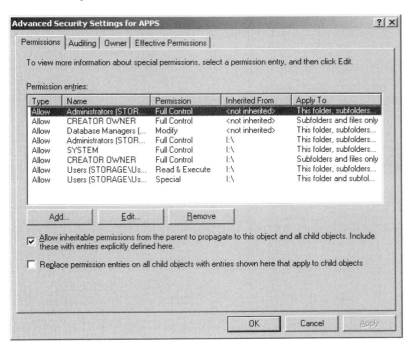

To see how exactly all these permissions work, click the Effective Permissions tab, and you will see the dialog box shown in Figure 11.31. It's simple. Just select a user or group name to view the permissions based on Global and Local group permissions, local permissions, and local privileges.

Figure 11.31

Effective
Permissions

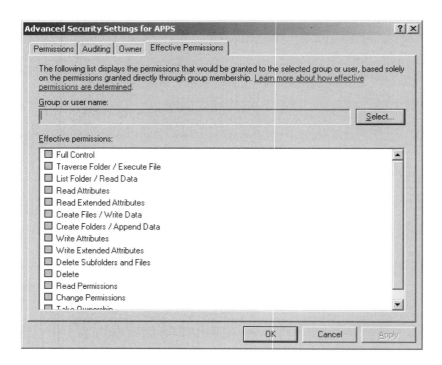

Of course, you have to have the appropriate rights to view the permissions on whatever resource you are checking, and there *are* some limitations in terms of the factors that are used to determine the effective permissions. For instance, you may not be able to view permissions for every user or group. Consider the local users group on the server called Storage, where your APPS share is located. Because this server is a member of an Active Directory domain, the global group called Domain Users is automatically nested within the local Users group. You can view the effective permissions on the local users group by selecting the local location called Storage (instead of the directory) after clicking the Select button from the screen in Figure 11.31. You get the results shown in Figure 11.32, which were obtained by calculating the permissions for the two entries that exist for the Users group in Figure 11.30.

Because the Domain Users group is nested in the local users group, domain users have the same rights to the folder, barring the existence of any other set of permissions that would conflict with these. But when you try to get the effective permissions for the Domain Users group using this tool, it comes up empty because this tool cannot calculate the effective permissions for domain groups that are nested in local groups.

Here are some other limitations:

◆ This tool does not take into account any share permissions.

◆ It does not take into account many of the SIDs that users have, based on how they are logged in. For instance the Network SID, Terminal Service SID, and many others are not taken into account by this utility.

This certainly limits the effectiveness of the tool, but you can still use it to calculate multiple ACEs for a user or group, as you saw in the previous example.

FIGURE 11.32

Effective Permissions for the Users group

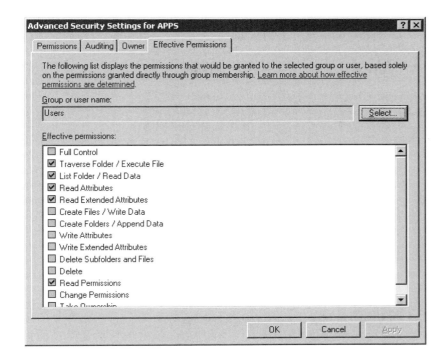

OWNERSHIP

Through the course of assigning and revoking permissions, you are bound to run into the problem where no one, including the administrators, can access a file. And you can't change the file's permissions because you need certain permissions in order to assign permissions. This could be a really sticky situation. Fortunately, ownership can help you out.

There is an attribute of every object called an *owner*. The owner is completely separate from permissions. There will always be *some* owner for *every* object. Yeah, that's great, but how does that help me? Well, the owner of an object has a special privilege—the ability to assign permissions. So if I'm the owner of a file, but don't have access to the file, I can take advantage of my ownership to reassign permissions to myself. Neat-o.

Well, how do I get to be the owner anyway? For starters, whoever creates an object is the default owner. Should that person be a regular user, that's the owner. If there is no apparent creator of the object, which is the case for many system files and folders, ownership is set to the domain's Administrators group.

Here is another problem: The file you are trying to get to but have no permissions for was created by a user and therefore is owned by that user. So you don't have permissions, and you're not the owner, which means that you can't reassign the permissions. Aha. There is a right that is assigned to Administrators that allows them to take ownership of objects. With this right, you can go into that restricted object, seize ownership, and then use that new ownership to reassign permissions.

Let's walk through this whole scenario: I have a share called USERS. Under USERS is a folder named `Brian`, to which I have installed Full Control permissions for Brian only. While logged in as Administrator, I try to access the `Brian` folder and receive an Access Denied message. The time has come for me to check out what Brian has been up to. I right-click the `Brian` folder and select Properties, then select the Security tab. I receive the dialog box shown in Figure 11.33.

FIGURE 11.33

Permissions for the `Brian` folder

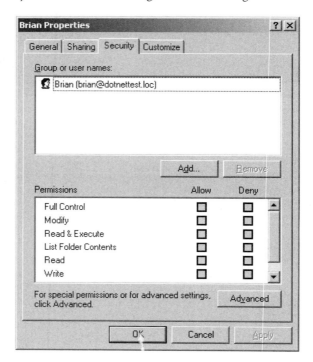

Well, I can see that Brian has some set of permissions on this folder, but the check boxes are all shaded, indicating that I have no right to edit these permissions. Let's look at the Advanced permissions dialog box to get more detail. I click the Advanced button and see the dialog box shown in Figure 11.34.

I can see that Brian has full control, but no one else is in the access list at all. But wait a minute, if I'm not in the access list, how am I even seeing these permissions? I select the Owner tab and a dialog box like Figure 11.35 appears, showing my ownership.

That's right, I was the one who originally created the folder `Brian`, so I'm the owner. As the owner, I can reassign permissions. That does it, I'm adding Administrators to the access list with full control. I click the Permissions tab to return to the Advanced permissions screen. I select Add, find the Administrators group, and then grant them full control. My permissions now look like Figure 11.36.

NOTE   *If I had initially created Brian's permissions for this folder using the Add button (see Figure 11.33), the Brian entry would have had check marks in all the Allow boxes and I could have edited them from there. But because I created these permissions using the Advanced Security Settings dialog box, all I could see was that there were additional viewable permissions that I'd have to edit in the Advanced dialog box. As I've said, I prefer to manage all my ACEs from the Advanced tab because this initial screen doesn't give you the whole picture, but don't let it confuse you: you can edit these permissions because you are the owner of the file—you just can't do it in the initial screen.*

FIGURE 11.34

Advanced permissions for the Brian folder

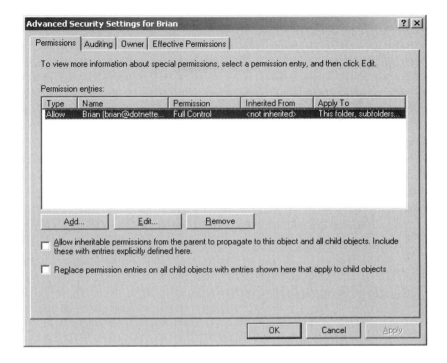

FIGURE 11.35

Advanced security settings, showing current owner

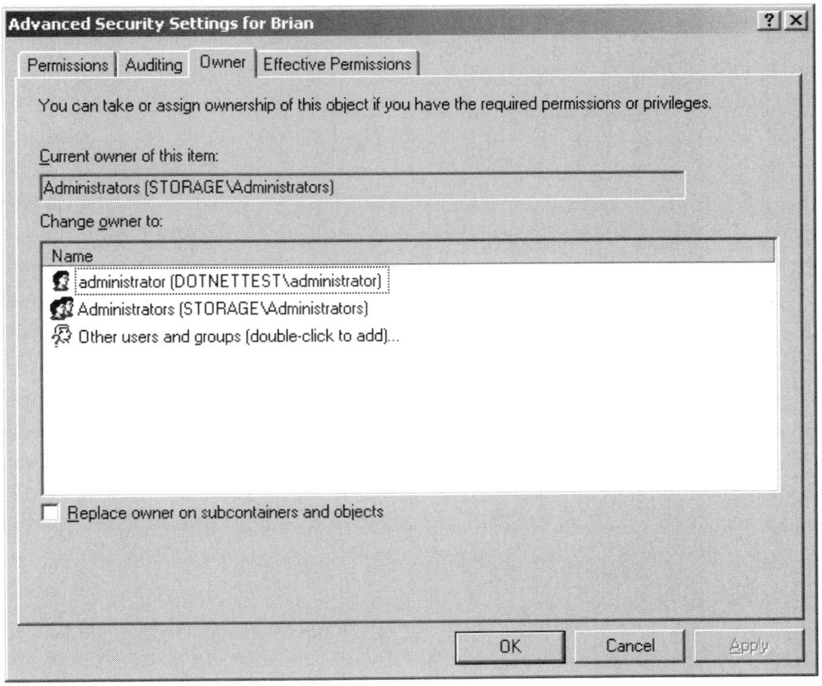

FIGURE 11.36

New permissions

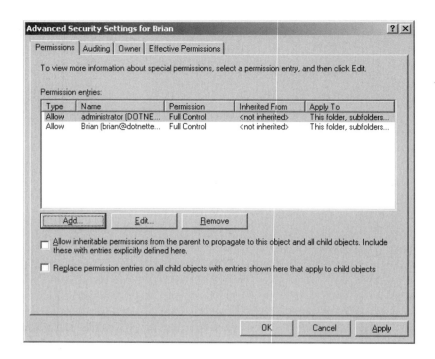

Now, back to Explorer, I click the Brian folder and I'm in, only to find a folder that Brian created named Secret. I click that folder—Access Denied. Easy enough, I'll just go in and do the same thing. I right-click Secret, select Properties, and then select Security. This time, I get a different message, as shown in Figure 11.37.

FIGURE 11.37

I have no permissions for this folder.

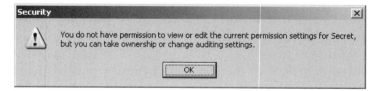

I don't have permissions, but I can take ownership. Why is it different this time? Well, last time I had created the folder named Brian, so I was the owner; therefore I could still view and change permissions. This time Brian created the folder, which means that Brian is the owner, so I—Administrator— have no inherent rights to even see the permissions. This becomes obvious when I see the Security properties tab, shown in Figure 11.38.

I am looking at the Security properties tab, but I can't see who has what permissions. I also can't add or change permissions. In fact, everything in this dialog box is grayed out, except for the Advanced button. Well, let's hit it. Under the advanced properties, I see a similar sight—the advanced Permissions tab options are grayed out entirely. So I select the Owner tab (see Figure 11.39).

FIGURE 11.38

Permissions as viewed when not the owner

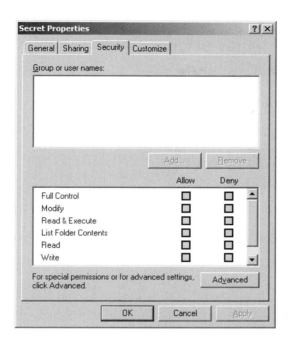

FIGURE 11.39

Unknown owner

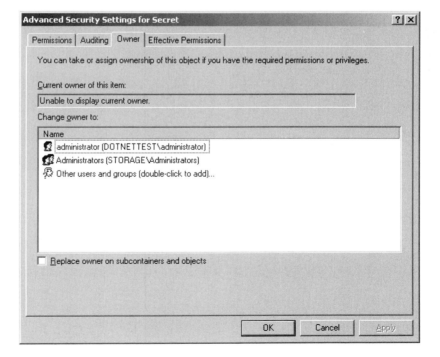

I can't tell who the owner is, but it is safe to say that it isn't me. From here, I want to take ownership. Under the Change Owner To box, you will see the different users or groups that I belong to who have rights to take ownership. As you can see, I can select either Administrator or Administrators. Do I want to use the individual Administrator account or the Administrators group? In this case, I won't want every administrator on the network to be able to view Brian's secret folder, so I'll select Administrator. If I simply select Administrator and hit OK, I'll be given rights to the folder, but I will probably run into the same roadblock with subfolders and files. To get it all over with in one shot, I click the check box next to Replace Owner on Subcontainers and Objects. A translation of this into old Windows NT terms would be Replace Owner on Subdirectories and Files. I hit OK and see the dialog box shown in Figure 11.40.

FIGURE 11.40

Taking Full Control of the folder can be automatic.

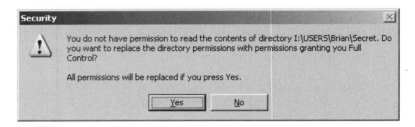

What this is telling me is that, even though I am making the move of becoming an owner, I will still have no access to the folder until I give myself some rights. If I click No, then I will have to manually go in and give myself Full Control permissions on the folder. Here, Server 2003 is saying that it will do it for me. This is an improvement over Windows 2000, where it was a two-step process. I click Yes and return to the less helpful dialog box from Figure 11.38, but now I'm the owner and I have full control over the folder. Now when I click OK to finish out the task and try to access the folder, presto, I'm in!

This will also pass my new permissions down throughout the entire Secret directory structure, so I shouldn't have to worry about anything Brian might create in the future.

Auditing File and Directory Access

Security's no good unless you use it. Who deleted that file out of the common share? Who modified that file? You can use NTFS's permissions to track that stuff to the event log.

There are two steps to logging file and directory access: First, you've got to tell your computer to enable auditing, and, second, you've got to tell your system which files and directories to audit.

Enabling Auditing

I don't know why you can't simply say to an NT/2000/XP/Server 2003 system, "Log any accesses to this to file," but you can't, at least not without first enabling the whole idea of auditing. I'm guessing it's a performance issue—auditing must be driven by some kind of "watchdog" routine that peeks at file accesses and logs those accesses it's been told to log. But I guess the watchdog must suck up some CPU time, hence disabling auditing by default.

You turn on auditing as you read in Chapter 8, but here's a review. You can enable auditing on a system-by-system basis with the Local Security Policy snap-in, or you can flip it on for groups of machines via group policies. To turn it on for a particular system, click Start/Programs/Administrative Tools, then Local Security Policy. Then open up Local Policies and then Audit Policy. You'll see something like Figure 11.41.

FIGURE 11.41

Auditing options

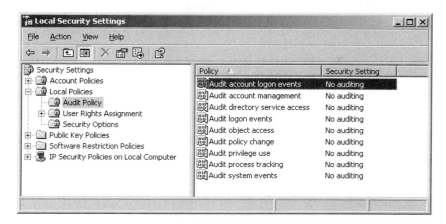

To track file and directory access, double-click the Audit Object Access item, and you'll see a dialog box like Figure 11.42.

FIGURE 11.42

Enabling object auditing

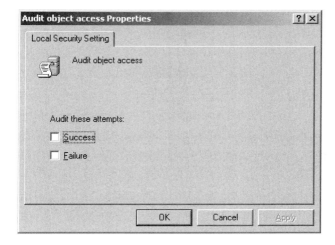

Notice that, as you learned in Chapters 8 and 9, any domain-based group policies will override local group policies—but of course if you don't have an Active Directory, there won't *be* any domain-based group policies.

To enable auditing using domain-based group policies, create a group policy object and look in the Computer Configuration/Windows Settings/Security Settings/Local Policies/Audit Policy. Apply that object to the particular domain or OU for which you want to enable auditing.

All you've done at this point is make auditing *possible*. Now tell the system which files you want to audit. Do that by getting to the Security tab of any file or folder (right-click the file or folder and choose Properties, then the Security tab) and then the Advanced button to raise the Advanced Security Settings for *objectname* property page. That will have four tabs: Permissions, Auditing, Owner, and Effective Permissions. Remember this box? We've already looked at three of those four, so let's look at Auditing. Click Auditing and you'll see something like Figure 11.43.

FIGURE 11.43

Auditing property page

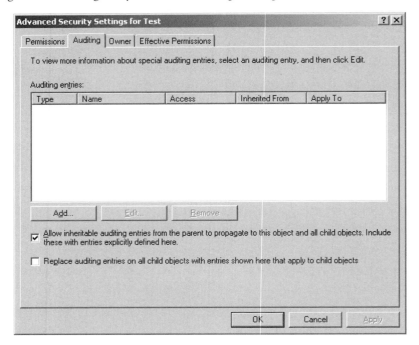

Note that inheritance applies to Auditing as well as permissions. The two check boxes are the same ones you saw earlier in this chapter, and they work the same way here.

Click Add and you'll be prompted for the users to audit—you've seen this dialog box before, so I'll spare you the figure—and you can say that you only want to watch a particular user (you've always had your eye on that Peter character, haven't you?) or a group, including local and domain groups. You *then* see the atomic permissions dialog box, which, again, you've also seen before. But where the previous atomic screen shot gave you an Allow or Deny check box for each type of permission, this one gives you a Successful and Failed check box.

Thus, you could decide that you only want to know when someone transfers ownership of a file and don't care if someone tries and fails to modify ownership. The atomic permission is Take Ownership. You'd check the Successful check box because you only care if someone actually *changed* ownership—if he failed in his attempt, then you don't care. (Understand that I'm not *recommending* you only audit ownership changes; this is just an example.)

Once you've set up auditing on a directory (or a file), you can see who's been working with it by looking in the security log. For example, an event type 560—a file write—shows the following information:

```
Object Open:
    Object Server: Security
```

```
Object Type:    File
Object Name:    D:\test\test.txt
New Handle ID: 208
Operation ID:   {0,5892625}
Process ID: 1208
Primary User Name:    panderso
Primary Domain:    BIGFIRM
Primary Logon ID: (0x0,0xE90B)
Client User Name: -
Client Domain: -
Client Logon ID:  -
Accesses     READ_CONTROL
        SYNCHRONIZE
        ReadData (or ListDirectory)
        WriteData (or AddFile)
        AppendData (or AddSubdirectory or CreatePipeInstance)
        ReadEA
        WriteEA
        ReadAttributes
        WriteAttributes
```

You see from this that you're opening a file named D:\test\test.txt and the person doing it is named panderso in a domain called BIGFIRM. You can then see the various atomic permissions that panderso exercises (whether he knows it or not) when he closes a file in Notepad that's changed.

Everything that you read in Chapter 8 about auditing applies here: Be sure to do something about managing the logs. They can get large quickly. And remember that logging is of no value if you don't check the logs now and then!

Hidden Shares

As you've seen before, once you share a folder out to the network, it becomes visible to the user community. But what if you don't necessarily want everyone to see the share? For example, I have created an installation source share on my server so that whenever I go to a user's workstation, I can install whatever applications I need to without having to bring CDs. It's really just a convenience for me, but at the same time, I don't want the users clicking away through the shares, installing every program they can get their hands on. Sure, I could limit the share to allow permissions only to me, but that is kind of a pain, too. I don't want to log off the user and log in as myself every time I do an install, especially if user profiles are being used. This is where creating hidden shares can help. I want the share to be there and available, but just not as easily visible. Although not a completely secure solution, it is a deterrent to the overly browse-active.

To create a hidden share, proceed as normal in sharing a folder, but place a dollar sign at the end of the name. That's it. Now, whenever the server registers its information to the browse list with its available resources, it simply will not register that hidden share.

The share that I am creating will be called INSTALL$, which will be shared from D:\Install. I create the share as normal, making sure to call it INSTALL$ instead of INSTALL (see Figure 11.44).

FIGURE 11.44

Creating a
hidden share

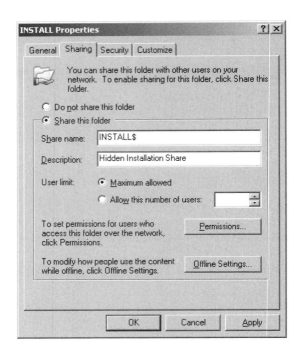

Now, from my client workstations, I will not see the INSTALL$ share listed in the browse
list, but I can still map a drive to the INSTALL$ drive connection if I manually type the share name,
as I've done in Figure 11.45.

FIGURE 11.45

Mapping to a
hidden share

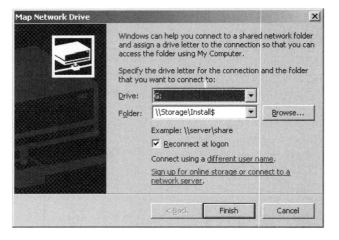

Although the hidden share will not show from your Explorer browse list, the share is visible
through the Computer Management Console. This helps keep you from forgetting which hidden
shares you have created.

Common Shares

In Windows Server, you may find that several common shares have already been created for you. Most of these shares, you will find, are hidden shares (see Figure 11.46).

FIGURE 11.46

Common hidden shares

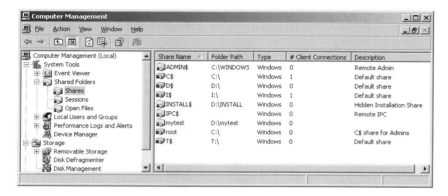

C$, D$, and So On

All drives, including CD-ROM drives, are given a hidden share to the root of the drive. This share is what is called an *administrative share*. You cannot change the permissions or properties of these shares, other than to configure them for Offline Files (we'll talk about Offline Files at the end of this chapter) and if you try to stop sharing these administrative shares, you will see the message shown in Figure 11.47. As soon as you reboot the computer or restart the server service, they will automatically be shared again. These shares come in handy for server administrators who do a lot of remote management of the server. Mapping a drive to the C$ share will be the equivalent of being at C:\ on the server.

FIGURE 11.47

You can only stop sharing administrative shares temporarily.

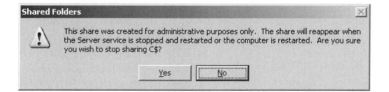

NOTE *Only administrators or backup operators can connect to administrative shares.*

ADMIN$

ADMIN$, like its C$, D$, and other drive share counterparts, is an administrative share. This share maps directly to your system root, or where your Server 2003 operating system resides. I installed my Server 2003 operating system to D:\Windows, so that's where my ADMIN$ maps to.

Why is this necessary? Let's say I manage 50 servers, and I want to copy an updated INI file to all servers to have them configured differently. (Of course, I have already tested the configuration change thoroughly. The last thing you want to do remotely is change the configuration of an operating system without knowing exactly what is going to happen when you reboot or otherwise initiate the change.)

The problem is that about half of my servers are new Server 2003s with the system installed into C:\Windows. The other half are a mixed bag of old upgraded servers and random installs performed by different admins, so my system root can be anything from D:\Winnt to C:\Windows2k to who knows what. Thus the ADMIN$ share. I have one common connection point that I can connect to across the board, with no guesswork required.

PRINT$

Whenever you create a shared printer, the system places the drivers in this share. See the chapter on printing services (Chapter 13) for more information.

IPC$

The IPC$ share is probably one of the most widely used shares in interserver communications. You know how you can map a drive letter to a share on a server and use that drive to access files and folders. What about other resources? How do you read the event logs of another computer? You don't actually map a drive, you use *named pipes*. A named pipe is a piece of memory that handles a communication channel between two processes, whether local or remote.

REPL$

Whenever the replication service is used, a REPL$ share is created on the export server. The export server sends a replication pulse to import servers. The individual import servers connect back to the export server to get a replicated set of the data. This REPL$ share is where your import computers will connect. This share is a critical element of replication, so it's best to leave it alone.

NETLOGON

The NETLOGON share is used in conjunction with processing logon requests from users. Once users successfully log in, they are given any profile and script information that they are required to run. This script is usually going to be a batch file. For example, I have a common batch file that I want all of my users to run every time they log in. This allows me to have all clients run a standard set of commands, like copying updated network information, mapping standard network drives, and so on. These batch files, scripts, and profiles go in the NETLOGON share. The NETLOGON share is required on all domain controllers.

Connecting to Shares via the Command Line

Now that you have these shares, how do people use them? Assuming that I've got a share called APPS on a server called STORAGE1, how would someone attached to the network get to that share? There are several ways to use the GUI to get to shares:

◆ Right-click My Network Places or My Computer and choose Map Network Drive, then follow the wizard that starts.

- Browse the network from My Network Places.
- Look for a share in the Active Directory.

All of those techniques are convenient, but they require a fair amount of network "superstructure"—they only work well if the network's working well. But sometimes you need to attach to a share when things aren't working so well—in fact, sometimes you need to attach to a share specifically *because* things aren't working so well, and the share contains some tools to help you get it working right. That's where the command line comes in handy.

Introducing *net use*

The command I'm talking about is net use. In its basic form, it looks like this:

```
net use driveletter \\servername\sharename
```

For example, to attach to the share APPS on the server named STORAGE1, and then to be able to refer to that share as drive V: on my system, I'd open a command prompt and type this:

```
net use v: \\storage1\apps
```

If I didn't want to worry about figuring out which drive letters are free, I'd just use an asterisk instead of a drive letter, as in the following:

```
net use * \\storage1\apps
```

net use will then just choose the first available letter.

Using a Different Account with *net use*

Sometimes you're logged in to one account and need to connect to a share, but you only have permissions to access that share from another account. In such a case, you can tell net use to try to connect you with the share while using that different account with the /user: option. With this option, net use looks like this:

```
net use driveletter \\servername\sharename password
↳/user:domainname\username
```

So, for example, if I were logged onto a domain named CANISMAJOR (note we're talking older NetBIOS-type domain names here; although net use has been improved to understand the newer DNS-type names in Server 2003) under an account named Joe, and I wanted to access a share named DATA on a server named RUCHBAH on a domain named CASSIOPEIA, then I might have a problem, particularly if the CASSIOPEIA domain doesn't have a trust relationship with CANISMAJOR. But perhaps I have an account named Mark on the CASSIOPEIA domain, with password "halibut." I could then type this:

```
net use * \\ruchbah\data halibut /user:Cassiopeia\mark
```

You needn't type the password, in case you're concerned that someone might be watching. Leave it off, and net use will prompt you for it. Also, since net use now understands the new DNS-type names, you could substitute either */user:dotteddomainname\username* or */user: username@dotteddomainname* in the above example.

"A Set of Credentials Conflicts"

Sometimes when you're trying to attach to a share, you'll get an error message that says something like, "A set of credentials conflicts with an existing set of credentials on that share." What's happening there is this: You've already tried to access this share and failed for some reason—perhaps you mistyped a password. The server that the share is on has, then, constructed some security information about you that says that you're a deadbeat, and it doesn't want to hear anything else about you. So you need to get the server to forget about you so that you can start all over. You can do that with the /d option. Suppose you've already tried to access the \\STORAGE1\APPS share and apparently failed. It might be that you *are* actually connected to the share, but with no permissions. (I know it doesn't make sense, but it happens.) You can find out what shares you're connected to by typing just **net use** all by itself. Chances are, you'll see that \\STORAGE\APPS is on the list. You have to disconnect from that STORAGE1 server so that you can start over. To do that, type this:

```
net use \\storage1\apps /d
```

But then do another **net use** to make sure that you've got all of those connections cleaned up; you may find that you have *multiple* attachments to a particular server. *Then* your **net use** will work. Or... in a few cases, you may have to disconnect *all* of your file shares:

```
net use * /d
```

net use-ing over a WAN

Now we are into one of our most difficult networking areas: connecting to your resources across long distances and great unknowns. If you've ever had to rely on remote computing, you know well not to rely on it. We have a new little function set in our **net use** arsenal that takes a lot of the "unknown" out of the picture. Instead of relying on getting to the appropriate name resolution server, getting through to that server, and getting accurate reliable resolution over an inaccurate and unreliable network link, you can now just map a drive straight to your server via its IP address. Granted, you now need to know that IP address, but it is a good failsafe. In my case, I work from several different locations connected with frame relay WAN links. My Network Places isn't always so good about being able to convert server names into IP addresses, so net use \\storage1 usually tells me that my machine couldn't *find* \\STORAGE1. Even if it *does* work, name resolution—converting a name such as STORAGE1 to a network address—takes time.

If you know the IP address of the server that you're trying to contact, then you can use the IP address in lieu of the server's name. I know that STORAGE1's IP address is 134.81.12.4, so I can simply type this:

```
net use \\134.81.12.4\apps
```

And, as you're probably connecting from a different network, you might have to add the /user: information. And it's never a bad idea to add /persistent:no so that your system doesn't spend five minutes trying to reconnect to it the next time that you start up. So, for example, if STORAGE1 is a member of a domain named dotenettest.loc and I have an account on dotenettest.loc named "boss," I could ensure that STORAGE1 will know who I am and log me on like so:

```
net use \\134.81.12.4\apps /user:dotenettest.loc\boss /persistent:no
```

Know the **net use** command; you'll find it useful.

The Distributed File System

If you haven't started playing around with Distributed File System (Dfs), you should. Although Windows NT4 with SP3 can host a stand-alone Dfs root, the tool really became useful with the release of Windows 2000 and Active Directory. And in Server 2003, there are even more enhancements that we will explore in more detail in this section. What is Dfs, you ask? Well, with Dfs, you can create a single share that encompasses every file share–based resource on your network. Think of it as a home for all the file shares on your network with a "links" page that points the clients to the particular server or servers that actually house those shares. Under this one root share, you create links that point to all of your other shares across numerous servers, one link per share. Now, using this Dfs share, your users only need to remember one place to connect.

Let's say you had the following set of shared resources across the network:

UNC Path	Users' Mapping	Resource Description
\\DC1\APPS	G:	All generic applications
\\RESOURCE1\APPS	G:	The same applications as \\DC1\APPS
\\STORAGE\SALES	S:	The corporate sales data
\\STORAGE2\USERS	H:	All user directories
\\STORAGE\FINANCE	Q:	The corporate financing data
\\RESOURCE2\APP2	P:	Miscellaneous applications

This could become a real pain for users (not to mention administrators!), who have to remember where to go to connect to their various resources. Here, there are five different servers housing resources. This also means that if a client needed to access APPS, SALES, USERS, and FINANCE all at the same time, they would be required to make three different connections. Well, three doesn't sound too bad, but I have been in large networks where there were literally no more available drive letters left on clients to map another share; every single letter from A: to Z: was mapped to something. You also have to remember which clients connect to \\DC1\APPS and which connect to \\RESOURCE1\APPS, which are identical shares housed on two different servers. Again, it's not a big deal in this particular example, but if you had 50 servers containing the same set of APPS, this could become a nightmare to keep track of.

NOTE *As you can probably see, Dfs is most beneficial in large enterprises and probably not worth the effort in small office networks.*

Now, let's put this same scenario into a Dfs instead. You would have one Dfs Root—we'll call it CORP—with all of your corporate shares listed within. I'll show you how to do all of this later, but your end result will look like Figure 11.48.

Now, isn't that pretty? All those resources, no matter where they reside physically, show up under the domain's Dfs root volume named CORP. The links to the shares show up to the users as sub-directories under CORP. Users don't know, see, or ever care what server each of those subdirectories point to, nor will they ever even need to know that there *are* other servers involved at all. To them, it is one big share with everything they need.

FIGURE 11.48

Dfs root view

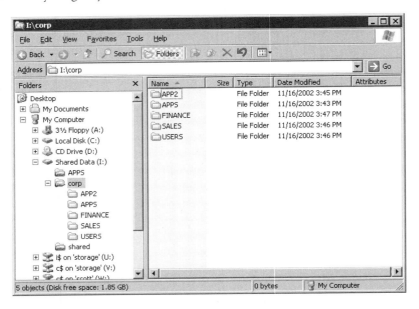

Understand, though, that Dfs isn't a new kind of file server. In a sense, it's not a file server at all—it is, instead, a way of putting a kind of "table of contents" on a bunch of existing file shares and pointing the clients to that source of information when they need to connect to a share that is referenced in that table. Dfs does *not* create file shares; you must create all of the file shares on the various servers first, *then* use Dfs to impose some order. To underscore that point, here's another fact about Dfs: the file shares needn't be NT or 2000 or Server 2003 file shares. If you had Unix NFS, Banyan VINES, and Novell NetWare client software on your computer, then you could actually create a Dfs "share" that only points to NFS, VINES, and NetWare volumes!

But does that mean that this new Dfs root—this "table of contents"—constitutes a new single point of failure? If that one server that houses the root—the place where all of our users go to find their resources—goes dead in the water, so do our users, right? Not necessarily. Combined with the Active Directory, Dfs roots can be made to be fault tolerant. Instead of the actual, physical root being housed on one server, it can be stored in the Active Directory, which is maintained across all domain controllers. Now, if one of those servers housing the root—in the Active Directory—goes down, our users are automatically directed to another location to retrieve root information without even a hiccup.

Again, let's stress the function of Dfs. "Fault-tolerant Dfs" doesn't mean that you're backing up the data in the file shares. It only means that the "table of contents" that is a Dfs root gets backed up, so that if the computer hosting the Dfs root goes down—and sorry to be stressing this point, but again there's a good chance that the machine hosting the Dfs root *does not contain one single byte of shared files*, just the pointers to the servers that contain those files—then there's another computer standing by to assume the role of "table of contents server" or, in Server 2003-ese, the Dfs root.

But *can* you somehow protect those file shares and their data with some kind of fault tolerance? Yes, with *link fault tolerance.* You saw earlier that you had two different servers with an APPS share. Assuming that those servers contain identical sets of APPS data, there is no need for them both to be listed in your Dfs. Remember, under the Dfs root, you create one Dfs link per share? Well, if you want to house identical information for both of these shares called APPS, then there is no need to create two links.

You can have one APPS link listed, which is pointed to two targets, which point to the actual file shares. Then the users are referred to either one of the targets or replica sets when they are looking for the APPS share. I say replica sets, because if you have two identical shares, then you can set up your Dfs, in conjunction with the File Replication System (FRS), to actually replicate the data within those shares, ensuring their consistency. It's a great way of streamlining your network, and you can even choose or customize your replication topology, which was impossible in Win2K. You can also use Sites in Active Directory to ensure that your clients are not directed to a share over a slow line if a faster one is available.

Using the File Replication Service, Dfs can keep all copies of replicated targets in sync with each other. With your two APPS shares, you make a change on one share, and Dfs takes care of getting those changes out to the other targets. Again, this has shortcomings—this time in principle, not in the technical details. If you have dynamic data within a link at all—and by dynamic I mean anything that changes as the users access it, such as Word documents, spreadsheets, databases, or anything else that requires users to change data on the server—you probably shouldn't replicate it. Let's say Jane and Bob are both editing the same document, but both are editing different replicated copies on two different shares. Jane makes her changes and closes the document, then Bob makes different changes and saves his version. Who wins? Bob will win because he saved it last. Once saved, the document is replicated to the other share, overwriting Jane's changes. So, remember, if a user is editing a document and they are accessing that document on a link that is a replica, their changes will get overwritten next time the replication occurs. Use caution when using link replicas and replication.

Dfs Terminology

Before we go much further, you need to understand the terminology of Dfs. Just like learning to understand Active Directory, a whole new set of concepts and terms comes into play.

You start with a *root.* This translates roughly into the share that will be visible to the network. In the example, CORP was the root. You can have many roots in your site, and with Server 2003 one server can now hold more than one root, which was a limitation in Win2K. A root is shared out to the network, and actually operates like any other share. You can have additional files and folders within the shared folder.

Under a root, you add *Dfs links.* The link is another share somewhere on the network that is placed under the root. I guess the term *link* is part of our never-ending terminology shift. In this case, it seems to be shifting to more of an Internet nomenclature. Picture the Dfs root as a Web home page with nothing on it but the name of the page and a bunch of links to other Web pages. The links within the Dfs hierarchy are like hyperlinks on a Web page that automatically direct you to a new location. You, the user, don't need to know where that link will take you, as long as you get the Web page you were looking for. Once you find your home page (the Dfs root), you will be directed by those hyperlinks (your Dfs links) to any other Web site you want (your shares).

A *target or replica* can refer to either a root or a link. If you have two identical shares on the network, usually on separate servers, you can group them together within the same link, as *Dfs targets*. You can also replicate an entire root—you know, the table of contents—as a *root replica member*. Once the targets are configured for replication, the File Replication Service manages keeping the contents of roots in sync.

Stand-Alone versus Fault-Tolerant Dfs

Before you begin making a Dfs, you need to decide which kind of Dfs you want. This will be primarily decided based on whether you have an Active Directory. The big difference is going to be on the root of the Dfs. In an Active Directory–based Dfs, or fault-tolerant Dfs, the root itself can have replicas. In other words, that one single point of failure—the root—has been spread out into the Active Directory. Using root replicas, if you have 27 servers housing the Active Directory, you have 27 places where the Dfs information lives. Well, not all Dfs information, just enough information to point clients to one of the Dfs root replicas. With that, as long as the Active Directory is alive and available, the Dfs is too. Also, when integrated into the Active Directory, link replicas can be configured to use automatic replication. With automatic replication, the File Replication Service takes over the synchronization of the contents of replicated folders to ensure that all replicas contain the same information. It might be safe to say that if you have an Active Directory–based domain, you should choose the fault-tolerant Dfs.

But here's the really cool part of an Active Directory–based Dfs. If I host my Dfs in the Active Directory of the dotnettest.loc domain, not only do my users not need to know which server a particular share is on, but now they don't even need to know which server the Dfs itself is on. Instead of having to map a drive to \\servername\dfsname, my users could map a drive to \\dotnettest .loc\dfsname. Now, using the same logic a client uses to find an available domain controller for the Active Directory, it can search for a host of the Dfs. If one fails, the client just calls on another.

A domain-based Dfs automatically publishes its topology in the Active Directory. What this means is that the actual Dfs hierarchy—the root(s), links, targets—is published into the Active Directory so that all domain controllers will know where the Dfs lives, what it looks like, and how to get to it. It *doesn't* mean that every domain controller is a Dfs root replica server.

If you've gotten this far, you probably don't have an Active Directory to publish to. What about the non-AD-based networks? Some companies have migrated to Active Directory (and most others are at least in the planning stages, since support for NT4 is ending). Some have at least put up a few member servers here and there. For those who have not gone through the process of migration, the Dfs provides an enhancement to the basic file server that lets an enterprise step out of its physically bound shackles into a more user-friendly and manageable state. A stand-alone Dfs is a solid step forward into the world of Windows 2000 or Server 2003, without requiring a major Active Directory initiative. With a stand-alone Dfs, you don't get the nice fault tolerance of the root itself, you don't get the automatic replication, and you don't get the Dfs published in the Active Directory. But you still get all the other goodies, like combining all of your network shares into a single namespace and finally killing the dependency on physical server names and locations when it comes to getting your users to their resources. In just a little bit, I'll talk about how these new benefits brought to you by the Dfs can be put to use in a practical environment—with or without an Active Directory—but first, let's jump into learning how to actually build these things.

Creating a Dfs Root

To get to the Dfs management console, select Start/Administrative Tools/Distributed File System. Now, the first thing you need to do is create the root. Right-click the Distributed File System in the left pane and select New Root. Of course, a wizard greets you. Select Next at the welcome screen, and you are then asked which kind of root you want to create (see Figure 11.49).

FIGURE 11.49

Select the Dfs root type.

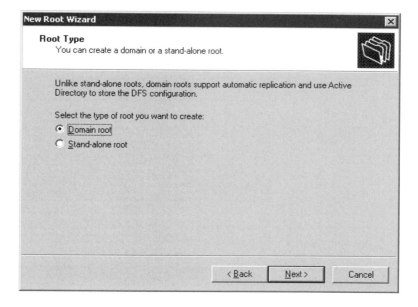

Your choices for the Dfs root type are domain root and stand-alone root. A domain root will publish itself in the Active Directory, while a stand-alone root will not. This fundamental difference is the deciding factor on how much functionality you will receive. Keep in mind that a domain Dfs root must be hosted on a domain controller, so that there is an Active Directory to post to. One of the most important benefits of being published in the Active Directory is that domain roots can have replica roots. Again, a root replica lets you have any domain controller host the root, which greatly improves fault tolerance. Because the roots require the Active Directory to be replicas at this level, stand-alone roots cannot be nor have replicas. Because my test server, DC1, is already a domain controller, I'll choose a domain root.

The next step is choosing a domain that will host the Dfs, as shown in Figure 11.50. If you were to select a stand-alone Dfs, you would not get this option.

The purpose behind selecting a domain to host the root is to publish the Dfs into the Active Directory. This clues you into yet another *big* advantage of using fault-tolerant roots. Jump forward in your mind, if you will, to what this may look like to the clients later on. If you publish this root called CORP into the Active Directory on the domain dotnettest.loc, you will later see this shared out to the world under the name of `dotnettest.loc\corp`, as well as `dc1.dotnettest.loc\corp`. If you were using a stand-alone root, you would only be able to see this as `dc1.dotnettest.loc\corp`. How does this help? This is one less thing you have to configure at the workstation level. Simply point all of your clients to dotnettest.loc, and they never need to worry about which server houses which resources.

FIGURE 11.50

Select a domain to host Dfs.

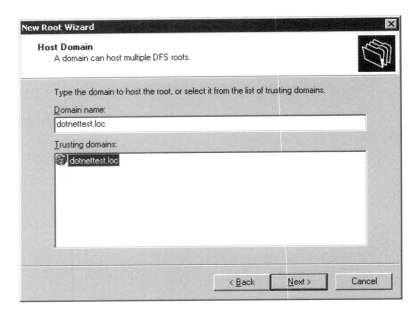

After you select which domain will host the root, click Next so you can select the server that will host the root, as shown in Figure 11.51. This is where the actual resource will reside.

FIGURE 11.51

Select a server to host Dfs.

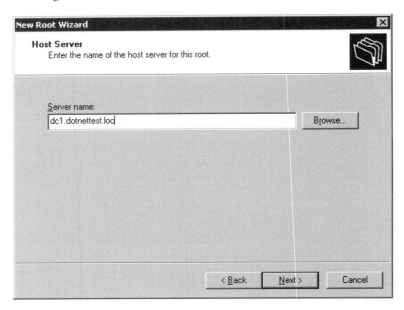

Click Next to provide a Dfs root name and a description as shown in Figure 11.52. The name for each root must be unique for the domain. Unlike shares, whose names can be the same as long as they are on different servers, there can only be one CORP Dfs root per domain. This is a side effect of having the Dfs root accessible from the domain instead of the server, and I would say that this is a very acceptable side effect.

FIGURE 11.52

Select a root name.

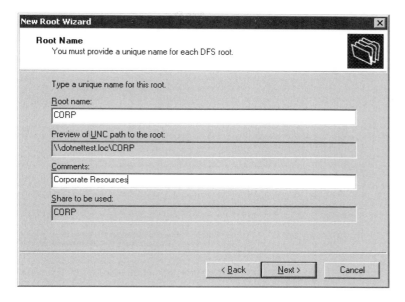

The next screen in the wizard allows you to define the actual share for the root. Remember, this can be a regular share. You can select an existing share on your host server to be the root of your Dfs, or you can create a new one on-the-fly (see Figure 11.53).

FIGURE 11.53

Select a share for the Dfs root.

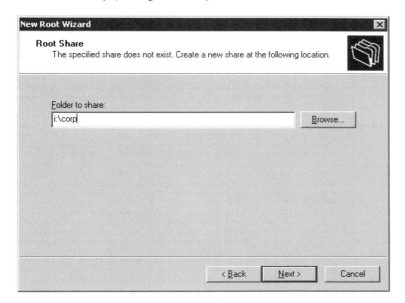

I've decided to make a new share called corp. This is going to be my corporate resource Dfs root. I don't already have one, so I've chosen to create a new share. Since the path for the share I entered does not exist, I am confronted with the dialog box in Figure 11.54.

FIGURE 11.54

Dfs will create the share for you.

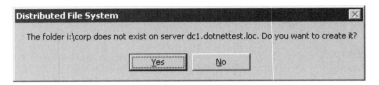

Once I select Yes, the share will be created automatically so don't worry about Alt+Tabbing back and forth just to get your folder set up ahead of time.

Finally, I am shown a confirmation dialog box with all of my selections, and the root is created. When I return to the Dfs Management Console, I see the new root listed as \\dotnettest .loc\corp, as shown in Figure 11.55. Notice how the path appears as \\dotnettest.loc\corp, instead of \\dc1.dotnettest.loc\corp or even \\dc1\corp.

FIGURE 11.55

The new root

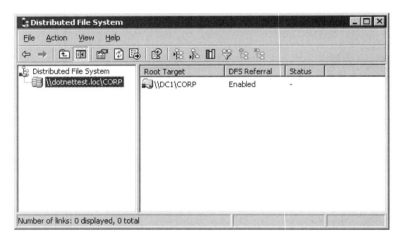

Adding Links to a Dfs Root

Once you have your root, you need to add your Dfs links. Let's start with APPS. First, you want to select your new root in the left pane of the console. You will notice that in the left pane, the root is \\dotnettest.loc\CORP, indicative of its membership with the domain, whereas the right pane shows that the share, or the physical location of the resource, is \\DC1\CORP. Right-click the root—that would be \\dotnettest.loc\corp—and select New Link. This is where you add another network resource to your Dfs. Start with the \\DC1\APPS share (see Figure 11.56).

The first field, Link Name, will be used to reference the netware share you are about to add to the Dfs root. We'll call ours APPS. Simply type it in. The second field, Path to Target (Shared Folder), is the name of an existing share on the network. You can enter the UNC for the share, or browse your network for the share that you want to point users to. Sorry, but you can't create a share on-the-fly here; it must already exist.

FIGURE 11.56

Add the Dfs link.

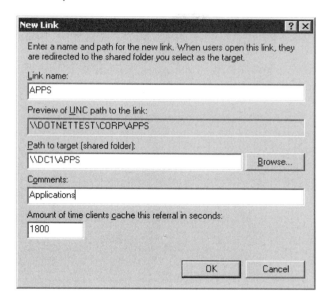

The Amount of Time Clients Cache This Referral in Seconds value tells the client how long to wait before they check back with the hosting server to update share information. When a client connects to \\DOTNETTEST\CORP\APPS, they are told by the hosting server, which happens to be \\DC1, to connect to \\DC1\APPS, *but* check back with me in 1800 seconds. At that time, the client will call back the Dfs host to see if everything is okay. If you take a link offline—applicable when you have replica links, or if you simply redirect a link to a different share, the client will be told this information at that time and will be directed back to the appropriate share accordingly. Think about this value carefully. The shorter the interval, the more network traffic you will create. The longer the interval, the longer it takes a client to check back for an update. Let's say you have defined an interval of 3600 seconds, or one hour. A client connects to \\DOTNETTEST\ CORP\APPS at 10:00 exactly, and is redirected to \\RESOURCE1\APPS. They won't check back until 11:00. At 10:10, you find out that you need to take the server down. You want to take RESOURCE1 offline and redirect all clients to a replica member of APPS on DC1. (I'll cover replicas in a minute.) So you configure your replica set to have RESOURCE1 offline. If you take RESOURCE1 down now, your client who connected at 10:00 could lose data. The best thing to do is wait until all clients have reported back so they can see that RESOURCE1 is offline, and redirect to DC1. This means that you may have to wait the longest possible interval before shutting down your server—an hour. If your interval was 10 minutes, then you could be fairly comfortable that within 10 minutes, RESOURCE1 would be free from any client connections to APPS.

Going back to the network resources given earlier, repeat the above process to create all child nodes—except for \\RESOURCE1\APPS—using the information below:

When a User References	Send the User To
\\DOTENETTEST\CORP\APPS	\\DC1\APPS
\\DOTNETTEST\CORP\APPS	\\RESOURCE1\APPS
\\DOTENETTEST\CORP\SALES	\\STORAGE\SALES
\\DOTENETTEST\CORP\USERS	\\STORAGE2\USERS
\\DOTENETTEST\CORP\FINANCE	\\STORAGE\FINANCE
\\DOTENETTEST\CORP\APP2	\\RESOURCE2\APP2

When you're done, the Dfs Console will look like Figure 11.57.

FIGURE 11.57
The new child nodes in the Dfs console

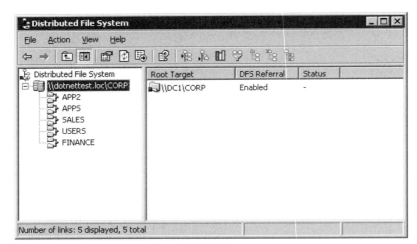

Configuring Dfs Replicas

Now you want to make a replica link of APPS. Remember how you had \\DC1\APPS and \\RESOURCE1\APPS? You want to combine those into one logical resource: \\DOTNETTEST\CORP\APPS. Right-click the APPS link and select New Target. What you get is a condensed version of the dialog box that created the Dfs link in the first place (see Figure 11.58).

Enter the path for the next share that is to be available as part of this resource, and check whether you want to add the target to the replication set. The File Replication System (FRS) in Server 2003 works with the Distributed File System to synchronize files on the included shares within the link. If you choose to include the new target in your replication topology, when you click OK you'll see the dialog box shown in Figure 11.59. Some Server 2003 improvements to the FRS include compression of the replication traffic and the ability to differentiate between necessary and unnecessary replication traffic.

FIGURE 11.58
Add a new Dfs
replica member.

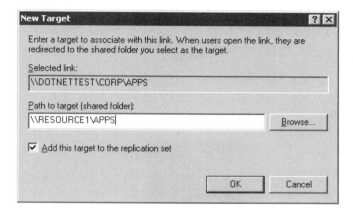

FIGURE 11.59
You are given the
option to configure
replication when you
create a replica.

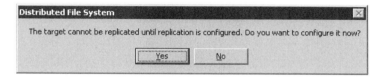

You can configure replication now or go back and do it later. If you select Yes now, you will start
the Configure Replication Wizard. Click Next to move through the initial screen and you will arrive
at the window shown in Figure 11.60.

FIGURE 11.60
Choosing a master
share for replication

One of the shares that you have configured in the replica will need to be initialized as the Master in order for the replication process to start. Once the Master is chosen, replication will become a multi-master process, so this is just a temporary assignment of duty.

Replication for the Dfs has improved in .NET: you can now choose from the various topologies available, including the ability to create a custom topology design for replication. You can view the options in Figure 11.61.

FIGURE 11.61

Choosing a replication topology

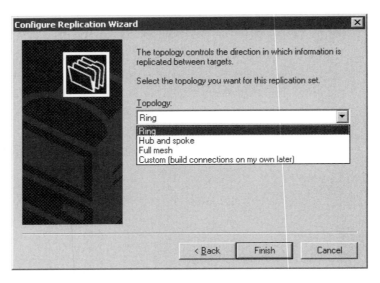

Choose a basic ring topology and then click the Finish button, which ends the Configure Replication Wizard and returns you to the Dfs Management Console. You have just added another target to your APPS link and thus have two shares available for users to seamlessly connect to through the Dfs. You can see this by looking at Figure 11.62.

FIGURE 11.62

Viewing multiple shares in the APPS link

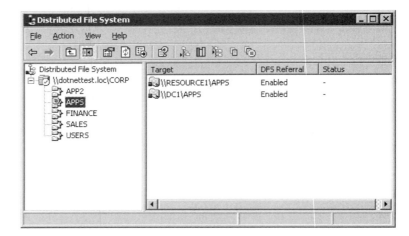

You have also configured replication between the shares, so that new applications should only have to be added to one share, automatically replicating to the other. Note that there is now a Replication tab available when you right-click the APPS link and choose Properties (see Figure 11.63). From here, you can reconfigure your replication topology or the replication schedule at any time. You can even decide which specific files or subfolders in the share are replicated, including wildcards like *.doc, which would include all files with an extension of .doc in the replication arrangement.

FIGURE 11.63

Viewing replication properties for the APPS link

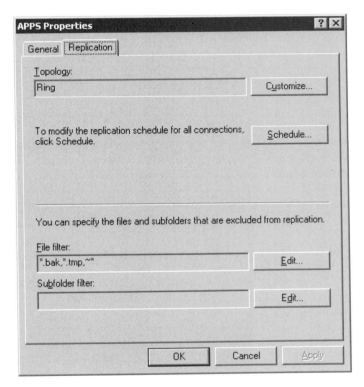

From now on, when your clients connect to \\DOTNETTEST\CORP\APPS, they will be directed to either \\DC1\APPS or \\RESOURCE1\APPS.

To remove a replica member from a Dfs link, right-click the member and select Remove Target. If you want to take \\RESOURCE1\APPS out of the replica set, leaving only \\DC1\APPS, you could remove it from the Dfs, just like that. When removing a replica member, however, nothing on the replica member's server is altered in any way. \\RESOURCE1\APPS will still be shared, and all data will still be available within that share. The only thing that is affected is the Dfs topology.

Understanding Dfs Replication

Replication itself is simple. In a stand-alone Dfs, the replication is manual, and one link replica is the master. In other words, changes from that particular master server propagate to all other replica servers. If the physical share you want to keep synchronized resides on an NTFS volume on a Windows 2000 Server, replication is automatic and uses multi-master replication. With multi-master replication, you can modify files on any one of the link replicas, and the changes will be automatically copied to the other members. Really, with automatic replication, there is no such thing as a Master after the initial replication. The first replication will need a Master to ensure that all shares have the same starting point. It is advised, though, that you do not mix automatic and manual replication within a single replica set.

To manage replication within the Dfs Management Console, you'll need to change the way you view the console. Highlight the links for which you have enabled replication—you'll see a blue circular icon over the links in the left pane if you have configured replication—then click the Action button from the Console menu. Choose Show Replication Information. This will add a column in the Target window called File Replication, as shown in Figure 11.64. You can also view the status of the targets in your link by highlighting the link and clicking Check Status from the Action menu, but you can only do one of these at a time. You can view either status information or replication information at any one time, but not both.

FIGURE 11.64

Viewing replication information from the console

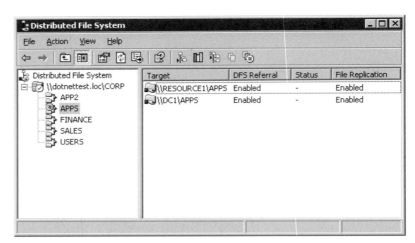

Each member within the replication set is shown in the Management Console, along with information as to whether replication is enabled. All the members of the replication set will now have their data synchronized, based on the schedule you chose.

Managing Dfs

After you have configured your Dfs, there are a few steps you must go through to properly manage the roots, links, and the clients that are connected to them.

TAKING REPLICA MEMBERS OFFLINE/ONLINE

When you have multiple members belonging to a replica set, you may find occasions to take one offline. Say, for instance, you need to perform maintenance on a server. You don't want to just take a server down and have users lose their connections. You also don't want to go through the process of dropping a member from the replica set and adding it again later once your maintenance is done. Instead, right-click the member share and select Enable/Disable Referral. This will toggle a member's status. You can see that a member is disabled in Figure 11.65, although the machine itself, and therefore its shares, are still online.

FIGURE 11.65

An offline member

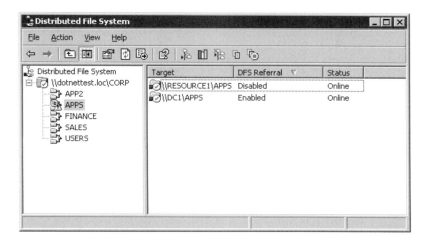

CHECKING NODE STATUS

Periodically, you should verify the status of each link within the Dfs topology. To check the status of a link, right-click the share in question and select Check Status or click the Action menu item and choose Check Status. Actually, there is even an icon in the Management Console toolbar for this. It looks like a bar graph. A green check mark indicates that the node is working properly. A red icon with an X through it indicates a problem (see Figure 11.66).

FIGURE 11.66

A failed node

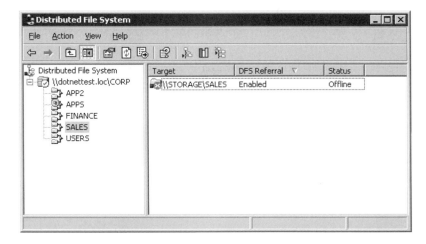

A failed node indicates that there is a problem accessing the shared folder to which the child node refers. Try checking out the share directly to make sure it is still available to the network. More severely, the entire server that hosts the child node could be down.

DELETING CHILD NODES

In Figure 11.66, the SALES node has failed. (It really failed because I took down the server that the share resides on so I could show you what it looks like.) Now I want to completely remove SALES from my Dfs. Right-click the link in the left pane and select Delete Link. This will remove the SALES folder from the CORP hierarchy, but will not touch the actual SALES share or any of its data on the remote server. Users will still be able to connect to \\STORAGE\SALES directly. If I wanted to remove the share from the network altogether, I would need to stop sharing and delete the SALES folder from STORAGE.

CONNECTING AND DISCONNECTING FROM ROOTS

Within the Dfs Management Console, you can connect to any Dfs root on your network to manage. Right-click the Distributed File System line in the top of the left pane, and select Show Root. From there, you can browse your network for roots or type in the location of the root. For my CORP root hosted on DC1, I could type in **dotnettest****corp** or just expand the domain and then the Domain Dfs roots folder, as shown in Figure 11.67. Note that I have two Dfs roots available for management, the one we created called CORP and another root called IT. Click Cancel to return to the Management Console. To remove a Dfs root with the Management Console, you can right-click the root and select Delete Root.

FIGURE 11.67

Viewing available
Dfs roots

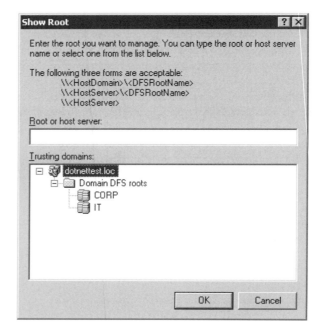

THE PHYSICAL ROOT

One of the problems with understanding this whole concept of a logical root with no physical bounds is trying to figure out what—physically—this Dfs really is. For starters, let's go back to the Dfs we've been creating throughout this chapter. Originally, I put my Dfs root on DC1 in the folder I:\corp. From there, I've created links of APPS, USERS, SALES, FINANCE, and APP2. If you look at I:\corp, you see a folder structure like that of Figure 11.68.

FIGURE 11.68

The physical root

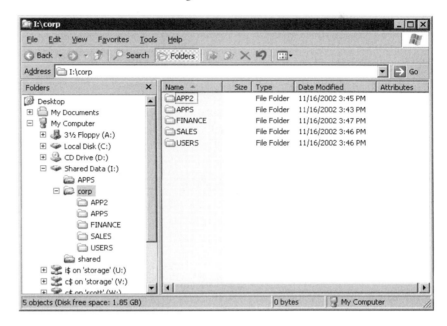

Notice anything? Those folders were all created automatically under I:\corp as I created the links. If I try to look into one of those folders under I:\corp, I get an Access Denied because the system has those areas protected in order to handle the Dfs referrals—the process of passing users to a respective link member, rather than the physical subdirectory.

Speaking of referrals, when a client goes to hit the APPS folder within the Dfs CORP, what exactly happens? Using the Network Monitor, you can trace out the referral process. There are two important transactions between the client and the server. The client initially tries to access APPS just as it would any other directory within a share, except the server returns a message that tells the client to get a referral link. Why can't the server just direct the client there in the first place? Well, if you had the root server act as a middleman to the entire process—for every share, folder, and file access—your bandwidth would go through the root to and from that server. You have to force the client to make the connection to the actual link member. By getting this "error" message, the client has to go to Plan B, which in this case is to find out who—if not the root—has the data in question. Now the client sends a Get Dfs Referral message to the root server, requesting a filename of \DOTNETTEST.LOC\CORP\APPS. The root server responds to the referral with the actual share name that the client needs to contact. In this case, the server has chosen RESOURCE1, so it responds with

\RESOURCE1\APPS. It also includes a Dfs TimeToLive value equal to the parameter configured for the client cacheing interval so the client will know how often it has to check back with the Dfs root for updating information about where to access the file, folder, or application.

PRACTICAL USES

Before you start setting up your root, throwing in some links, and reorganizing the way your users access their resources, let's take a quick look at some good ways that Dfs can actually add value to your network. Remember, it's not about playing with cool new features; it's about making life easier.

Consolidated Enterprise Resources

The example Dfs we've worked through in this chapter would be a good way to consolidate enterprise resources. You can take all of your shared resources across the network and put them under one logical share. Then, instead of having to know which logical drive a resource resides on, you only need to know the subdirectory. The neat thing is that actually configuring the Dfs has absolutely no impact on the configuration of your network. You can build and experiment with Dfs configurations all day long in a production environment without anyone even knowing that it exists. All of the old shares on your network remain in place, data is untouched, and users don't see anything different. Once you're ready with your new Dfs, the hard part comes in—changing your users' drive mappings from one drive per \\server\share to one drive for all shares. Don't underestimate this task. It's more than just mapping a new drive letter to the Dfs root. All applications need to know that they will no longer be on drive X:, but rather drive Y:.

Life-Cycle Management

The good news is that with Dfs, this is the last time you'll ever deal with changing drive mappings. If you need to move data from one server to another for purposes of life-cycling a new server in and an old one out, you don't need to play the game of backing up data, wiping the server, rebuilding it new with the same name, and restoring data to make it look like it is the same physical machine. With Dfs, you can set up a brand new server and configure it as an offline link replica for the share you want "moved." After you verify that all data has been ported over successfully, bring it online and take the old one off. The users don't know that they are hitting a new server. The Dfs handles it all in stride.

Web Sharing

Web sharing is a feature that debuted in Windows 2000. It allows you to share folders directly for use via HTTP requests coming from Web browsers.

NOTE   You must be running Internet Information Services for this option to be available. If your server doesn't support Web access at the server level, it won't matter whether your shares are Web enabled. Your users won't be able to get to those shares through their Web browsers anyway.

Configuring Web sharing is extremely simple. Within your Windows Explorer, right-click the folder you want to share out to the Web and select Sharing. At the top of the folder properties page that appears, you'll notice a Web Sharing tab (see Figure 11.69). Selecting that tab allows you to configure how this folder will be shared out to the Web. I'm going to enable Web sharing for my `Marketing` folder.

FIGURE 11.69

Web Sharing folder properties

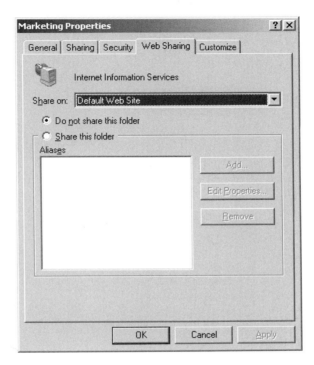

At the top of the Web Sharing tab is a Share On drop-down list. In that list are the different Web sites that have been created via the Internet Services Manager. Select the Web site that you want to add this folder into. For our purposes, I'm just going to use the default Web site, and this is where I will place my `Marketing` folder.

The next step is to select the radio button for Share This Folder. Once selected, a dialog box will pop up to configure the Web alias for this folder, as shown in Figure 11.70.

The alias is what Web clients will refer to in order to access this resource. Choose which permissions you would like Web clients to have for the data in this share. You can select any combination of Read, Write, Script Source Access (which allows clients to execute scripts through this share), and Directory Browsing (which allows clients to see folder lists without being required to enter a valid filename to view). Choose the application permissions level from None, Scripts, and Execute. Once completed, you will be returned to your Web Sharing tab and will have the new alias shown as a configured alias (see Figure 11.71).

You can add more aliases for this folder by selecting the Add button, or remove unwanted aliases by selecting the alias and clicking the Remove button. You can also revisit alias properties by selecting the alias and clicking Edit Properties.

FIGURE 11.70

The Edit Alias
dialog box

FIGURE 11.71

The configured
Web alias

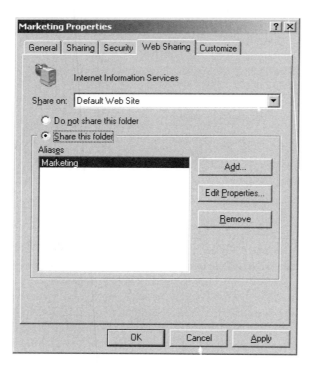

Once you click OK, the alias will be registered to your selected server's Web site and ready for browsing. Go to your Web browser and enter the URL for this alias. On my machine, that would be `http://resource1.dotnettest.loc/marketing/`. Because I enabled directory browsing for my alias, I can see the files and folders within that folder, and I see the Web page shown in Figure 11.72.

WARNING *I tried to combine a few of these features into one step by enabling my CORP share—which is my Dfs root—as a Web folder. When I look at* \\DOTNETTEST\CORP *within the regular Explorer, I can see the full Dfs. If I try to look at my own* I:\CORP *folder, however, I can see all the directories corresponding to my child nodes, but since they are not* real *resources on my machine—rather redirections to other shares somewhere else—the server gives me an Access Denied message. When I enable Web sharing for the CORP share on my server, and try to access* http:// resource1.dotnettest.loc/corp, *access is denied again. When navigating through the Web browser function, the client never gets a chance to ask for a link referral.*

FIGURE 11.72

Browsing the Web folder

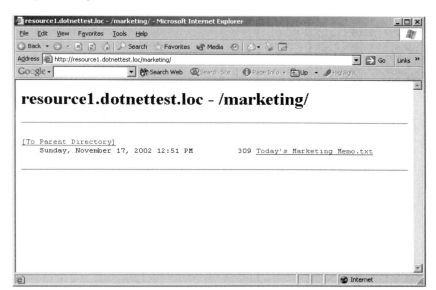

Using Offline Files/Client-Side Cacheing

As you've seen, the Windows family of OSes file server functionality has grown to include Dfs as well as Web folders, while retaining the old NT file server capabilities. But it doesn't stop there: Not only do some of these features improve the *server* side of file servers, they also jazz up the *client* side. Released in Windows 2000, Offline Files is one of those tools about which I find myself saying, "I could have used this feature a long time ago!"

Introducing Offline Files

If you have laptop users in your network environment, you'll love the Offline Files, or Client-Side Cacheing (Microsoft uses both names interchangeably), feature. In fact, it will appeal to almost anyone who uses a network. Offline Files provides three main advantages: It makes the network appear faster to its users, smoothes out network "hiccups," and makes the now-difficult task of keeping laptop files and server files in sync simple and transparent.

How Offline Files Works

Offline Files acts by automatically cacheing often-accessed network files, storing the cached copies in a folder on a local hard drive, a folder not surprisingly called `Offline Files`. Offline Files then uses those cached copies to speed up network access (or apparent network access), as subsequent accessing of a file can be handled out of the local hard disk's cached copy rather than over the network. Offline Files can also use the cached copies of the files to act as a stand-in for the network when the network has failed or isn't present—such as when you're on the road.

Offline Files is a write-through cacheing mechanism; when you write a file out, it always goes to the network, and it is also cached to your local hard disk. And when you want to access a file that Offline Files has cached, then as you've already read, Offline Files would *prefer* to give you the cached (and faster) copy, but first Offline Files checks that the file hasn't changed at the server by examining the file date, time, and size both on the server and in the cache; if they're the same, then Offline Files can give you the file out of the cache without any worries; otherwise, Offline Files fetches the network copy, so you've got the most up-to-date copy.

As a network file could easily be modified by someone else when you're not using it, there's a pretty good chance that the network copy of a file would often be different from the cached copy. But if *that*'s the case, then what good is Offline Files? After all, if the file changes on the network a lot, then you'll just end up having to retrieve it from the network instead of enjoying the speed of getting it from cache. Offline Files increases the chances that it has the most up-to-date copies of your cached files by doing background synchronizations in several user-definable ways. This synchronization is largely invisible to the user, who simply utilizes My Network Places or a UNC to access network files, as has been the case with earlier versions of NT and NT client software.

NOTE *Offline Files only works on Windows 2000 and later machines; you can't get this benefit if you've got Windows 9x or NT 3.x or 4.x on your Desktop. If you are using a Win2K or XP Desktop, however, Offline Files will be useful even if you're accessing a server running pre–Windows 2000 software, such as NT 3.x or 4.x.*

You'll like Offline Files for several reasons. As these oft-used cached files will reside on the local hard disk in the `Offline Files` folder, you'll immediately see what seems to be an increase in network response speed: Opening a file that appears to be on the network but that is really in a local disk folder will yield apparently stunning improvements in response time, as little or no actual network activity is required. It also produces the side effect of reducing network traffic, as cached files needn't be retransmitted over the LAN. Having frequently used files in a local cache folder also solves the problem of "What do I do when the network's down, and I need a file from a server?" If you try to access a file on a server that's not responding (or if you're not physically connected to the network), Offline Files shifts to "offline" mode. When in offline mode, Offline Files looks in your local Offline Files network cache and, if it finds a copy of that file in the cache, it delivers the file to you just as if the server were up, running, and attached to the user's workstation. And anyone who's ever had to get ready for a business trip knows two of the worst things about traveling with a laptop: the agony of getting on the plane, only to realize that you've forgotten one or two essential files, and the irritation of having to remember when you return to make sure that whatever files you changed while traveling get copied back to the network servers. Offline Files greatly reduces the chance of the first of those problems because, again, often-used files tend to automatically end up in the local network cache folder. It greatly reduces the work of the second task by automating the laptop-to-server file synchronization process.

Enabling Offline Files on Your Desktop: The Basics

When you first install Windows 2000 or XP on your desktop, Offline Files does not work by default. You must turn it on in one of two ways: either by telling Offline Files to keep track of a particular file, or by going to Folder Options—it's available in the Control Panel, or in the Tools menu of any folder window. Then just check the box labeled Enable Offline Files.

Once activated, Offline Files will often *automatically* cache a file just as a side effect of you using the file. (I'll get to why it *often* rather than *always* does this in a bit.) You can, however, tell Offline Files to *ensure* that a particular file or an entire folder on the network is always in the `Offline Files` folder (recall, the name for the Offline Files cache) in just two steps: First, find the desired file (or folder) in My Network Places. Second, right-click the file. My Network Places will then display the file's context menu with the usual items—Open, Rename, Delete, and the like—but some files' context menus will include the option Make Available Offline, as you can see in Figure 11.73.

FIGURE 11.73

"Pinning" a file so that it is always in the `Offline Files` folder

Forcing Offline Files to keep a copy of a particular file in the `Offline Files` folder (that is, forcing Offline Files to keep a copy of a file on the PC's local hard disk) is called *pinning* that file or folder. The first time that you pin a file, Offline Files will start up a configuration wizard, called the Offline Files Wizard, that asks a few questions, then sets up Offline Files to run based on your answers. And although it *sounds* like a great idea, be careful about making entire folders available offline, as that has the effect of copying the entire folder and all of its contents to your local hard disk. That can take some time when it's first set up, and of course it can be a bit irritating when it fills up your hard disk. (Subsequent synchronizations may be quite quick though, as you'll read later.)

Now that you have enabled Offline Files, if you choose Tools/Folder Options from Explorer or My Network Places, you'll see the property page shown in Figure 11.74.

FIGURE 11.74

Options for
Offline Files

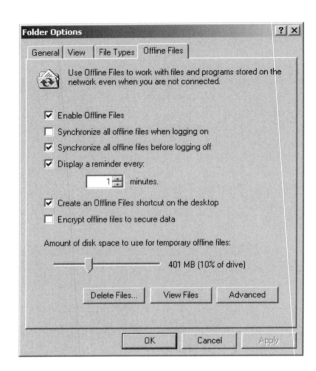

In the Offline Files page, the first check box tells a Windows 2000 or XP machine to enable its Offline Files capability. The next two tell Offline Files to compare every file in the Offline Files folder with the file's "actual" values out on the network servers, forcing Offline Files to synchronize its local file copies with the file originals every time you log on or off. (That's only one of *several* options you have for controlling offline file synchronization, and you'll read more about those options later.) The next check box controls how Offline Files tells the user that one or more servers are not currently available, leading Offline Files to place that server or servers into offline mode. If you'd like, you can tell Offline Files to remind you every so often that one or more servers are in offline mode, with a ToolTip-like balloon such as you see in Figure 11.75. You can also decide whether you want to place a shortcut to your Offline Files folder on your Desktop and whether you want to encrypt the files that you cache.

FIGURE 11.75

Offline Files
reminding you that
you're offline

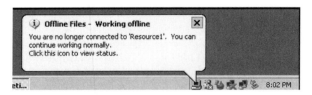

If you know that one of your servers is about to go offline, or if you're a mobile user about to go on a trip, then you will often need to know whether a particular file is already in your PC's cache, its `Offline Files` folder. You can see which files are in the local `Offline Files` folder, as well as their status, in a few ways: In the Offline Files Settings page, click the View Files button. Alternatively, in a check box on the same page, as you saw before, you can direct Win2K or XP to place a shortcut to your `Offline Files` folder right on your Desktop.

While the whole idea of network file cacheing is attractive, there's a built-in limitation to how many files can be cached on a user's local hard drive. There are often tens of gigabytes worth of files out on the network, and usually much less than that available on most workstations. It is entirely possible that you could, in a short period of time, examine more files on the network than would fit on your hard disk. Clearly, if left to itself, Offline Files could use up all of your free disk space. You can control how much free space Offline Files is allowed to fill up, though, in the Offline Files Settings page. However, you can only control how much space Offline Files allocates to the automatically cached files, and when that space is exhausted—by default, it's 10 percent of your disk's space— then Offline Files just drops the file that hasn't been used in the longest time to make room for more automatically cached files. In contrast, you can pin as many files as you like, forcing Offline Files to cache *them*—but you of course could run out of disk space doing that, too. If that happens, Offline Files just pops up a dialog box directing you to either unpin some files or to free up some disk space.

Getting and Keeping Things in the Offline Files Folder

Once you've turned Windows 2000 or Windows XP's Offline Files feature on, how do you use it? In a given day, you may access many files on a network—which ones get copied into the `Offline Files` folder?

It's easier to conceptualize how Offline Files caches files if you understand that files get into the `Offline Files` folder in one of two ways: either you *direct* Offline Files to cache a file by pinning it (recall that you do that by choosing Make Available Offline from a file's context menu) or Offline Files decides by itself to cache some files without you having to ask it to. Offline Files calls these automatically cached files *temporary offline files*.

SITUATIONS IN WHICH FILES WON'T CACHE

You can't always cache network files, however. Sometimes you'll look at a network file's context menu and the Make Available Offline option doesn't appear; when that happens, Offline Files won't cache the file either by pinning or by making it a temporary offline file. One of three things causes this cacheing prohibition: First, if the file is on a non-SMB server, such as a NetWare server, then you don't get the option to cache the file. Offline Files can only cache files on SMB servers, which means that it can cache files from NT 3.x, 4, and Windows 2000 servers and workstations as well as Windows XP. Files on Windows 9x machines running File and Printer Sharing services can also be cached. (Of course, it can also cache files from Windows Server 2003s.) Second, if you have disabled Offline Files by unchecking Enable Offline Files in Folder Options, the option won't appear. Third, you will not get the option to pin a file if the shared folder that the file resides in has been declared noncacheable by a network administrator. A network admin may declare a share noncacheable in the share's property page at that share's server. They just right-click the shared folder and choose Sharing and Security, then click the Offline Settings button. A dialog box like the one shown in Figure 11.76 will appear.

FIGURE 11.76

Adjusting cache
settings for a
shared folder

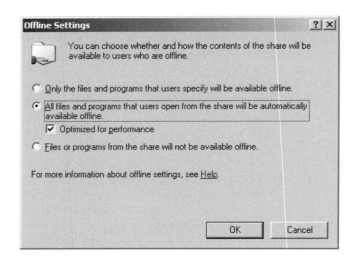

If the network administrator checks the Files or Programs From The Share Will Not Be Available Offline option, then no one will be able to cache files in that folder.

MANUAL AND AUTOMATIC CACHEING

Assuming you're working at your workstation and trying to access a network file that *can* be cached, pinning that file will prompt Offline Files to immediately copy the network copy of the file to your local Offline Files folder; a dialog box appears showing you the progress of that copy.

Other files get cached in the Offline Files folder if the files are in a network share on a Windows 2000, XP, or Server 2003 machine and if that share has been designated for *automatic* cacheing. Using the Offline Settings dialog box, an administrator can designate a share so that Only the Files and Programs That Users Specify Will Be Available Offline, which is the default setting. Or you can choose the check box for All Files and Programs That Users Open From the Share Will Be Automatically Available Offline. Selecting the first option will allow the users to choose which files they want to cache. The second option causes automatic cacheing to occur. That means that, when you open any file from a share configured for automatic cacheing, that share's server tells your workstation, "While you're at it, cache this file or program." Your workstation then makes a local copy in the Offline Files folder, noting that the copy is a temporary offline file. The only difference between cacheing for documents or for programs is that Offline Files will run an EXE in a cached-for-programs folder without checking to see whether it's up to date—without synchronizing that file first. It's a bit quicker that way, though of course it could cause trouble if you modified that EXE frequently.

HOW OFFLINE FILES MANAGES CACHE SPACE

Offline Files allocates space for pinned files a bit differently than it does for temporary offline files. Recall that the Offline Files Settings page includes a slider that you can use to control how much of your hard disk space to allow Offline Files to use. A second look shows that this amount only applies to the *temporary* offline files. The space taken by the files that you *pin* into the cache does not count against the space allocated in the Offline Files Settings page. As I said earlier, if the `Offline Files` folder is full and Offline Files automatically caches a new temporary offline file, it must drop one or more older files from the `Offline Files` folder to keep the size of the temporary offline files below the maximum allowed amount given in Offline Files Settings.

And don't bother looking on your hard disk for the `Offline Files` folder—it's actually a series of folders inside `\Winnt\Csc` hidden not with the Hidden attribute, but the System attribute. You can find it, but first you've got to go to the `Winnt` folder, then choose Tools/Folder Options, then go to the View tab and uncheck Hide Protected Operating System Files (Recommended) and confirm the choice. You'll then be able to browse through `\Winnt\Csc`. What you *won't* find there are useful filenames—all cached files are tagged with long numerical names rather than their actual names. I still haven't found the files in XP, but since they aren't really useful to me, why bother?

Offline Files in Action: Before the Trip

Now that you've got Offline Files set up, let's put it to work. It's useful to both mobile and fixed-location users, but its benefits are most dramatic for those mobile users, so here's a step-by-step look at how someone might use Offline Files to make life on the road easier.

PUTTING THE FILES IN THE CACHE

A user named Jim is about to go on a trip. He connects his laptop into his company's corporate network and opens a share named Marketing on a server named Resource1. Jim's network administrator has set up the Marketing share with automatic cacheing. Marketing contains two files that Jim needs, `file1.txt` and `file2.txt`. Jim right-clicks those files and chooses Make Available Offline. Over the course of the day, he also accesses `file3.txt` and `file4.txt`, although he does not pin them.

ENSURING THEY'RE IN THE CACHE

Before shutting down the laptop prior to getting on the road, Jim wants to double-check that copies of `file1.txt` and `file2.txt` are on his laptop's hard disk. He opens his `Offline Files` folder and sees a screen something like the one in Figure 11.77.

FIGURE 11.77

Jim's `Offline Files` folder contents after accessing the Resource1 server

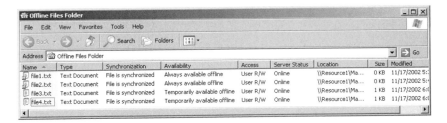

Note that under the Availability column, `file1.txt` and `file2.txt` are designated as Always Available Offline, meaning that they've been pinned; the little (blue) modification to the files' icons indicates that they are pinned. Note also that `file3.txt` and `file4.txt` are in the `Offline Files` folder, even though Jim didn't pin them—Offline Files automatically cached them. You can tell this because under the Availability column head, these files are noted as being Temporarily Available Offline. They could end up pushed out of the Offline Files cache without warning if Jim were to exceed the amount of space he originally allocated to his offline files cache by re-attaching to his corporate network and accessing enough other cacheable files.

Note also that the server status of Online means that Jim's still attached to the corporate network and that Resource1 is online. Actually, his laptop will consider Resource1 online until the laptop notices that Resource1 is not responding to attempted communication. Jim can view his `Offline Files` folder via a shortcut on the Desktop (assuming he has configured his system to show one), or he can navigate to the Offline Files Settings page and click the View Files button.

GETTING THE MOST RECENT VERSION OF THE FILE

If Jim has even more files to synchronize, perhaps entire folders, then he can employ Mobile Sync, available by choosing Start/Programs/Accessories/Synchronize. When started, its screen looks like Figure 11.78.

FIGURE 11.78

Choosing shares to synchronize with Offline Files

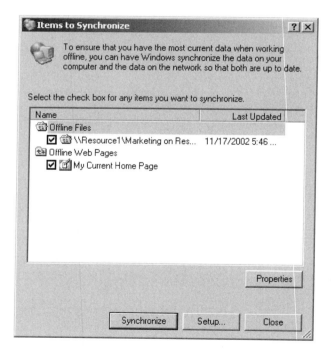

Mobile Sync lists all of the folders that contain pinned files that Offline Files knows about. Jim can then check the folders he's interested in synchronizing and click the Synchronize button. Clicking Properties just displays the contents of the `Offline Files` folder, and the Setup button allows Jim to configure synchronization when he's *not* traveling (see the later section "Controlling Synchronization for Nonmobile Users").

Working and Making Changes on the Road

On the plane to a client site, Jim starts up his laptop and opens My Network Places. His Desktop looks the same as it did back at the office, except now his system tray contains a small icon depicting a PC. Moving a mouse over the PC icon gets the message "Offline Files—the network is not available." Right-clicking that icon offers a context menu that includes Status, which will simply report again that the network is not available; Synchronize, which obviously won't accomplish much until he's reconnected to the network; View Files, which opens up the `Offline Files` folder; and Settings, which brings up the Offline Files Settings page.

ACCESSING "NETWORK" FILES ON THE ROAD

Despite the fact that Jim is not attached to any network, My Network Places shows a "networked folder" icon for Marketing on Resource1. If he opens up that folder, he'll see `file1.txt`, `file2.txt`, `file3.txt`, and `file4.txt`, just as if he were connected to the corporate network. He could open a command window and type **net view \\Resource1** to get a list of shares available on Resource1, including Marketing. Or he could find `file1.txt` in the `Offline Files` folder.

Jim sees a problem with `file1.txt` and edits the file and saves it, and Offline Files allows Windows 2000 Professional (or Windows XP) to make it seem as if he's attached live on the corporate network. He also makes a few changes to `file2.txt`. After a meeting, he creates a completely new file, `file5.txt`, and saves it in the Marketing volume, again as if he were connected to the company network.

WARNING: SOMETIMES OFFLINE FILES DON'T WORK

Oh, by the way, this all sounds good, but sometimes it has gone haywire on me. In the typical traveling scenario, I've got a laptop and a file server, and I pin some files or perhaps a complete share or folder on the file server. Whenever you pin an entire folder, you have to wait a minute or two while Offline Files goes out and copies all of the files from the pinned folder to your local hard drive. In the case where my laptop is a member of a different domain than the file server, I've seen Offline Files *look* like everything syncs up fine when I pin the folder. But when I disconnect from the network and try to *access* the files, I've gotten error messages like "The network name is not available." I've also had situations where I originally logged in under a particular username and then had to enter a different username to access some share. When I then pinned that share, again Offline Files looked as if it were copying every single file. When on the road, however, Offline Files refused to let me view or work with the file, claiming that it didn't exist at all. My advice follows in the warning.

WARNING   *If you are going to depend on Offline Files, make sure that your laptop, file server, and user account are all in the same domain. If that's not the case, be absolutely sure while you're still in the office to disconnect the network cable after synchronizing your pinned files and double-check that you can access those files. Offline Files is great, but don't trust it until you can be really sure of it!*

Back in the Office: Syncing Up

After Jim returns from his trip, he plugs his laptop into his company's network and powers up the computer. He has updated `file1.txt` and `file2.txt` and created a completely new file, `file5.txt`, and he wants all three of these new or modified files written to the network servers.

As his laptop's operating system loads, it senses that it's back on the corporate network and tries to update the three files on Resource1's share. The first two we'll look at, `file1.txt` and the new `file5.txt` are no problem—the version of `file1.txt` is the same as it was before Jim left. The file called `file5.txt` didn't exist before, so there's no conflict and Offline Files writes it to the server share. But unknown to Jim, someone *else* modified `file2.txt` and updated the server copy while he was on the road. This presents a conflict to Offline Files, a conflict that it can't resolve by itself, so it prompts Jim for guidance (see Figure 11.79).

FIGURE 11.79

Resolving a file version conflict

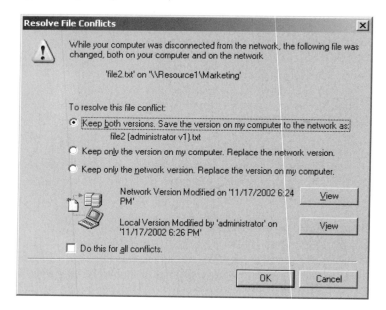

Jim uses the View buttons to examine both versions and decides that his update has more recent information, so he clicks the Keep Only the Version on My Computer button and then clicks OK. At this point, the files on his laptop and the ones on the network servers are synchronized.

Applying Offline Files to the Office: When Servers Fail

But suppose you're not a traveling user. What does Offline Files offer you? Greater network reliability and speed would be the primary advantage. By cacheing commonly used documents, Offline Files offers you a productivity safety net in the event that the network fails.

BULLETPROOFING WORD WITH OFFLINE FILES

Suppose you're working on a Word document. You keep the DOC file on a server rather than your local hard disk so that you can work on it from any workstation and because it'll be automatically backed up every night. But Word's frequent background saves and AutoRecover writes mean that your workstation must often communicate with the server where the document resides. A network failure or even a short hiccup in network or server response can cause problems that can lead to

Word losing your document. With Offline Files, Word has a much softer landing. Once the server becomes unresponsive, Offline Files automatically shifts all of that server's folders to offline mode. Your first clue that there's a network problem, other than the initial delay from an unresponsive network, is that the Offline Files PC icon has appeared in your system tray, and a balloon message tells you that the server you were working with is now offline. You can continue to work with and save the file, but of course it'll really save to the `Offline Files` folder, at least until you reconnect to the server and synchronize. Additionally, you'll see this kind of network fault-tolerant behavior on *any* cached file, whether a pinned file or a temporary offline file. As you saw before, Offline Files will cache any file that you access on an automatically cached share, or any file that you pin in a manually cached share. This suggests that you should consider either pinning all of the Word files that you use from a server or setting the server shares' cacheing settings to Automatic Cacheing for Documents.

RESUMING NORMAL OPERATION

When the server is available again, Offline Files will sense that and modify its icon to the one shown in Figure 11.80. Click the Offline Files icon, and you'll see a dialog box (Figure 11.81) offering to reestablish connection to the server.

FIGURE 11.80

Ready for
reconnection

FIGURE 11.81

Reestablishing
network connection
with Offline Files

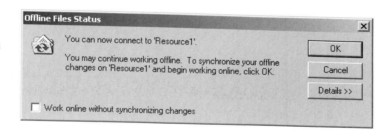

Click OK and you'll get a warning to close whatever files you are working on, as Windows 2000 and XP will have to close any open files before they can synchronize them.

Controlling Synchronization for Nonmobile Users

In addition to its fault-tolerant-like benefits, Offline Files's other great strength for nonmobile users is that it can improve a user's network experience by reducing the time between when a user requests a file on the network and when the user gets that file. There's no magic in that quick response, of course: Offline Files gets those files to the user so quickly because the files are already sitting on the user's hard disk in the `Offline Files` folder. But that's really only half the story. Sure, it's nice to get your files quickly—but are they the *right* files? The answer is yes, but there's a lot of underlying machinery ensuring that.

Before offering the locally cached file copy as correct, Offline Files does a quick synchronization with the original network file. That synchronization need not be an entire copy; instead, it is a simple consistency check. For example, try pinning a 100+MB file to your `Offline Files` folder. The initial synchronization will be a simple file copy, and it'll take a good long time. But then right-click the large file and do a synchronization, and you'll see that synchronization finish in seconds. This is true even for large files; for example, in one test, a 4MB JPEG file on a network server was pinned to a workstation's `Offline Files` folder, then the JPEG file was modified by another workstation, reducing its size by 30 percent. Synchronizing the first workstation to the JPEG file's new size took less than 5 seconds.

So you might find when accessing a file via the `Offline Files` folder that there is a short delay while your workstation synchronizes with the offline file's original copy. That might be acceptable, but Offline Files improves further upon that performance by periodically resynchronizing its offline files *before* you need them.

In addition to the synchronizations that occur when you reconnect after being offline, when actually accessing the file, or after choosing Synchronize on a pinned file's context menu, you can also configure your Windows 2000 or XP workstation to synchronize at logon, at logoff, when the workstation is idle, or at particular times of day. You configure these synchronizations either by starting Mobile Sync via Start/Programs/Accessories/Synchronize and then clicking the Setup button, or by opening a folder and choosing Tools/Synchronize and then clicking the Setup button on the resulting page. You get a properties page like the one shown in Figure 11.82.

FIGURE 11.82

Initial synchronization configuration screen

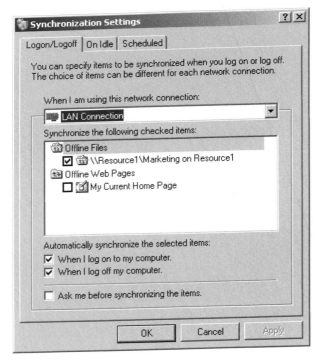

There are three tabs on this properties page: Logon/Logoff, On Idle, and Scheduled. The first two have a single-selection drop-down list box, When I Am Using This Network Connection, that allows you to specify whether you want this synchronization done over a LAN or WAN connection.

In the first tab, you can instruct Offline Files to synchronize at logon or logoff or both. And if you think that synchronizing might be a lengthy process and would like to be able to skip it, you can select the Ask Me Before Synchronizing the Items option, and Offline Files will display the Mobile Sync screen, letting you choose which—if any—folders to synchronize.

The second tab allows Offline Files to essentially synchronize in the background, waiting until your computer sits idle (see Figure 11.83).

FIGURE 11.83

Controlling foreground/ background synchronization

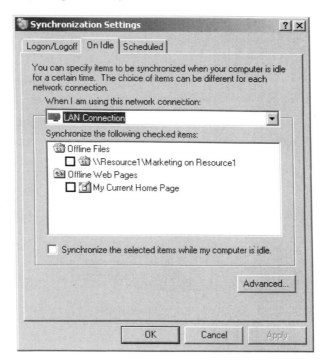

As with the Logon/Logoff tab, you can specify which folders to synchronize. The Advanced button lets you control how long your workstation should be idle before synchronizing, and how often to synchronize if the computer is idle for long periods of time. You can also indicate that you don't want synchronization to occur when the computer is running on battery power.

The final tab, Scheduled, lets you set up synchronization activity for particular times of day. You can tell it to synchronize every *n* days, every day, or every weekday.

Cleaning Out Offline Files

Sometimes Offline Files won't go away, however. Say you once connected to a server named MANGO and pinned a couple of files. You'll never see MANGO again and the files aren't important any longer, but the system wants to synchronize with MANGO and you get an error message every time you log in or log off. What to do?

Simple. Go to the `Offline Files` folder and unpin all of the files (or perhaps folders) in MANGO. Alternatively, you should be able to do that in My Network Places. Unpin everything related to MANGO, reboot, and you *should* hear no more about MANGO. Sometimes, however, it just stays around forever. In that case, zap *all* of the cached files. (Be sure to synchronize the folders that are still relevant first!)

You might want to flush out all offline files for several reasons. You might be about to give a laptop or desktop to someone and don't want them poking around inside your `Offline Files` folder or `\Winnt\Csc`. Or maybe you've just gone a bit pin-crazy and have so much stuff cached that you don't have any hard disk space left. In that case, unpin what you can first. But finish the job by choosing Start/Programs/Accessories/System Tools/Disk Cleanup. You'll notice that one of the things that Disk Cleanup will do is to wipe out your offline files.

WARNING *Again, make sure there's nothing cached that you want to synchronize with the file server before doing this; if you've made changes and haven't synchronized, cleaning out the* `Offline Files` *folder will lose your changes!*

You'll probably first notice Offline Files when you see how much easier it makes keeping laptop files and network files in lockstep. But you may soon notice that your in-house network is a bit snappier, and that the occasional network failure doesn't keep you from getting work done. And if *that* isn't a killer app, what is?

Chapter 12

Software Deployment

IN A PREVIOUS CHAPTER the wonders of RIS were covered in glorious detail. No doubt you already have plans for all the free time you'll now have. Finally, you too can do what previously only people who had the budget to buy third-party products could do. Not only can you do unattended installs, but you can build Windows Workstation (or Server) images, each with applications installed to perfection.

Can I get an alleluia?

Not to burst your bubble, because RIS is great, but what if:

♦ The mixed bag of workstations in your network don't all have PXE-capable network cards?

♦ Those machines don't even have network cards that are included in the RIS boot disk utility?

And, even if you have RIS-compatible network cards, what if the users actually save data to their machines (even only temporarily)? If you image their systems over the weekend, come Monday the users are going to be mighty upset when they find out their data's gone.

Hmmmm, that *is* a bummer.

Now, what I'm going to talk about is not interested in hardware. It'll get the software where it needs to go, without wiping the machines' hard drives, and without stopping to inspect your network card. And it's all managed through the Active Directory.

I'm talking about software deployment, baby.

Say you manage to get an operating system on the user workstations. But now your manager wants you to make sure everyone has Office XP so they can use the new Word templates from corporate. No hurry, tomorrow would be good.

RIS isn't going to cut it. So it looks like you're going to have a long night ahead of you.

Nope. Maybe an hour or so of your time, a few test runs, and voila, it's all good.

I'm not saying it doesn't take some forethought. I'm not saying it doesn't take some planning. But I am saying it may not be as bad as you think it will be. Realize something up front: not only are you going to be expected by said manager to install the software immediately, but you are probably also going to have to uninstall it when he changes his mind. And if management doesn't change its mind, what about updates and patches later on; are they going to be managed from Active Directory too?

You betcha.

Isn't that what it's all about? Working the system, rather than it working you? So sit back, turn some pages, and learn how to make your life just a little bit easier....

Windows Installer and Group Policies

Basically software deployment depends on three components: the installation file itself, Windows Installer (currently at version 2.0 with Server 2003), and group policies.

The Windows Installer Package

Let's start at the beginning. It doesn't start with group policies, it doesn't start with any special service, it starts with the installation file. In order to install any software you need to have the setup file for it. In the good old days (okay, maybe not so good) it'd be called `setup.exe` or perhaps `install.exe`. It was basically up to the programmer as to what the file would be called. It was also up to him as to how it worked. In other words, not a lot of standards were followed. It was something of a free-for-all.

Now, imagine if you wanted to customize the install a little. For example, ensuring that an application saves its user preferences to a particular network path rather than locally. Well, with the old-fashioned setup files, you'd be out of luck because they were all one nonstandard object.

That also meant, if you hadn't noticed, that uninstalls were problematic, because the software setup made some assumptions and installed files, and then the operating system made some assumptions and wrote over those files, then other installed software packages made assumptions and wrote over those files again. Pretty soon things got confused and the uninstall program would fail to delete everything. Or worse yet, it would delete something that another program assumes will be there and then that program wouldn't work. Happens all the time.

That's why Microsoft is focusing on an install file standard. One where the install files are packaged in such a way that all the components are independent. You can check them out, tweak them, choose to load them locally, or not at all. This standard is known as Windows Installer or the Microsoft Software Installer (MSI) package. The MSI package is a database of all of the changes that are made during the install, including files copied and folders created. These installs can then be undone with more success than most uninstalls I've ever seen.

An MSI file is called a *package* because the actual executable information (the code and data that *is* Office) is packaged with its install database into one object. This does not mean the MSI package is the only file needed for the install, like setup files of old; it can still refer to additional files around it. You'll see that when you set up some administrative installs later in this chapter.

Windows Installer can only really recognize a few file types:

MSI The Microsoft Software Installer file extension and one of only two main file types that Windows Installer can deploy.

MSP The Microsoft Software Patch file.

MST The Microsoft Software Transform file, which allows you to modify the install data of an MSI file.

AAS The AAS file, an install script that gets stored with the Group Policy object.

ZAP The extension recognized for a text-based file you create to get legacy `setup.exe`-based installs onto user machines. You cannot uninstall them or have them install in the background, however. And they're not self repairing. More on that later.

Products like Microsoft Office XP are packaged as MSIs, ready for easy install. In this chapter, we are going to be using Office extensively, so that's convenient. The PDF reader we will be using

(Adobe Acrobat), on the other hand, will not be packaged as an MSI, seeing as it is not yet a Microsoft product. (By the way, why did I choose to use Office as my primary example? Most businesses I know use it. So I figured it might be useful for you too....)

Windows Installer, How It Really Works

Now let's talk about how Windows Installer really works. Every user and every computer can have an account in Active Directory. These accounts can have group policies applied to them. In the same way, you can create a group policy that applies software installation packages to the account. There are two ways that a software package can be applied using Windows Installer. It can be assigned or published.

Publishing, the more optimistic of the two, is when the software is made available to the user through Add/Remove Programs. These published software packages can then be installed at will. The users might think of it as a lottery approach to software installation—it can keep them looking in Add/Remove Programs hoping for a prize. Another nice feature is auto-install. An application can be the default program to open a particular file extension (such as .doc or .pdf). When the user double-clicks on a file with that extension, the system will install the required software package automatically, just as if the user had gone into Add/Remove Programs themselves.

Assigning, on the other hand, is when software gets installed automatically without any user intervention. Instead, the software is pushed onto the local system during login, when an associated file is accessed, or when the application icon is first clicked.

Both types of installation use the MSI file extension and come with some nice advantages. These advantages include giving the software packages the ability to link to their install source for reinstalling, uninstalling, or repairing themselves should the software become corrupt.

In general, I assign most of my software packages. Why? Well, convenience, really. Say a user accidentally uninstalls a package that had been published to them. The next day, they go to use the software, and it's not there. All the user knows is that the software is not there, and all they remember is that it's your job to put it there. So they call your boss, who calls you, wondering where the software is that the user needs for their big presentation. If that package had been assigned, then on login the user would have had the package reinstalled. No phone call would have been made, at least, not that day for that reason.

Published packages are not considered *resilient* in that way. (I love the way Microsoft interprets the word "resilient." Software that can repair itself when it's broken or even reinstall itself when it's uninstalled is *resilient*. I wish I were that resilient.)

NOTE *Keep in mind, computers have accounts just like users, and as such, they too can have group policies that run Software Install packages. Logically, they cannot have software published to them (no computer I know can go check out Add/Remove Programs and decide what software it wants to install that day), so packages can only be assigned to computer accounts. Again, you can only assign software to a computer, but you can either publish or assign software to a user account.*

ZAP-installed files are even less resilient than a published MSI file. At least published packages are still MSI packages. They still link to their source and can repair themselves (or be repaired from Add/Remove Programs). A ZAP file is a text file that just points to a common everyday setup.exe. Because a ZAP file installs in the foreground, it requires user participation. It therefore must be published and not assigned. And since a ZAP file doesn't have a nice organized database of Registry changes and added files, it cannot be repaired or easily uninstalled. If it breaks, however, you can just reinstall it.

If you assign a piece of software to an account, and that user or computer does not have that software the next time the applicable group policy gets checked (at login/start up), it will get reinstalled, period. No questions asked. No phone calls made.

I don't like the phone. I don't publish packages unless I have no choice.

But that's just me.

Using Group Policy to Do Deployment

Now that you know what a Microsoft Software Installer (or Windows Installer) package is, and you realize you can apply it to either users or computers, it's time to think about how and to whom to deploy the package. This does take some forethought, because unexpected things can happen if you lose track of what is getting installed to whom and where. It's always a good idea to think before you click. Just like any group policy, there is an order of application (local, site, domain, OU), and the last one done is the one that is applied. If you install Office XP at the domain level and you uninstall it at the OU level, somebody might not get Office, depending on inheritance and overrides. (Not sure about that sort of thing? Check out Chapter 9 for more details)

Generally, users are organized by what they do. Therefore, users in one OU tend to all need the same software. That's convenient. You also may want to organize the computers themselves by location or type of use, for the same reason. Once you know how the user and computer accounts are organized, deploying software is much easier. There are some caveats though. What if you need to deploy a service pack for Windows XP Professional domain wide? You may expect to keep it simple and apply it to all of the computer accounts. But what if some of those computers are *not* running Windows XP? What if they are running Windows 2000 because their hardware doesn't support the newer OS? What do you suppose will happen to those Windows 2000 machines when you apply a service pack for the wrong operating system? Pandemonium perhaps? It's hard to say....

And, since computer accounts tend to be organized by where they are located or who uses them for what, you may find Windows XP Pro workstations all over the place in Users and Computers. So what can you do, other than pick and choose machines individually? The answer is to put them in groups. Computers have accounts, accounts can be added to groups, and groups aren't affected by the boundaries of something as simple as an OU. I know, I know, group policies aren't applied to groups, they are applied to containers like OUs. Apply the policy to the domain, then go to the Security tab and uncheck the Apply Group Policy check box for all groups but the computer group of your choice. Ta-da, all done, time for a latte.

DEPLOYING TO USER ACCOUNTS

Microsoft had to make a decision about how software was actually going to be deployed to the users. If it's published, that's easy. The software doesn't get put on the user's system until they ask for it from Add/Remove Programs. Even if you choose to have it auto-install when someone opens a file that has an extension associated with it, Windows Installer will just look in Active Directory for it and install from the path there.

Assigning software, now that's tricky. Microsoft could have made the assign feature force Windows Installer to deploy the product whole hog onto the user's machine, but that would take a long time when the user first logs in and possibly take up too much space. Or Microsoft could have made an educated guess as to what parts of Office users utilize the most and only install those features, something like a "standard install." But what if they were wrong?

Instead, Microsoft chose to do something similar to publishing and install only enough of the package to invoke a full install when the shortcut to the application is double-clicked. That way, the software gets "installed" onto a user's system really quickly when they log in. And that way, no one yells at anybody.

Okay, so this means that the first time someone really uses the product is when the package spends the time to install. And, of course, that's when the user is always in the biggest hurry. But at least this way, if a user never uses Access it never has to get installed. No wasted space, no wasted time, and no wasted network bandwidth while installing it. That is why, even when assigned, the software isn't really installed on the computer until it is invoked by the user. Ahhh, that's why those shortcuts on the Start menu, or Desktop don't actually point to any software. Ever check out the properties of a shortcut that hasn't had the software installed for it? It's not pointing to a target that's on the system. No siree. As a matter of fact, when I checked online to see if I could find a way to sneak a peek at the source for the shortcut, all I found was an article about how to write a short C++ program that would find the source.

Cool. I guess.

(Maybe I'll just double-click the thing and find the source that way…)

Because software is not installed locally from the start by default but only when the user "asks" for it, it is considered "advertised." You know, the user account knows where to get it if it needs it, as if it heard it on TV.

DEPLOYING TO COMPUTER ACCOUNTS

Notice in the last paragraph I said user account. Unlike software assigned to a user account, when a computer gets software assigned to it, the package is really installed. Also, since it is assigned to the computer account (and essentially belongs to the computer), the user can't uninstall it unless they have the appropriate privileges. Something to think about if you are in a situation where avoiding uninstalls is important.

Because you can apply an application to both a computer and a user, it may be tempting to sort of "overapply" software to guarantee that it gets installed. Don't do it. What do I mean by that? I mean that you should *not* do either of the following:

◆ Create a single group policy that assigns the same software packages to both computers and user.

◆ Create a group policy that assigns software to a user, and create another group policy to assign the same software package to a computer the user is likely to use.

Among other things, either of these actions can cause the system to remove and then reinstall the software *every time* the user logs in to that computer, potentially just repeatedly uninstalling and reinstalling so that the processor can't be bothered to let the user get to the Desktop for more than a few seconds at a time. I've experienced that one in my travels, and it is pretty unmistakable. If you have a user (or user group) in need of a software package and they always use the same computer (or group of computers), do not have Windows Installer deploy the package anew each time a person logs in—that's not nice. If they need the package, deploy it once to the computer account(s) and be done with it.

A Quick Look at What Everything Does before You Start Clicking

I don't know about you, but I really can't just do things by rote. If I open a dialog box, I want to know what all the check boxes mean and what all the buttons do (or what dialog box they open up) before I blindly commit to anything.

Before you start clicking, let me show you what software deployment looks like and what everything can do. Then, once you've seen all the buttons, you'll actually do it.

I am taking it for granted that you either have already used group policies or have read Chapter 9 of this book. Even so, you may not have really gone into software installation, so I'll cover that. If you are confident you know the SI (software installation) portions of the Group Policy, feel free to skip this part and move on to the deployment scenarios.

Let's start by looking at an important item, the Options button. It is located under the Group Policy tab of the container (such as an OU) properties in Active Directory Users and Computers (see Figure 12.1).

FIGURE 12.1

OU properties,
Group Policy tab
dialog box

You know how easy it is to create a new Group Policy Object (GPO), look at its properties, edit it, and delete it, but what is often overlooked when it comes to setting up a GPO is the Options button. Within the Options button's dialog box (see Figure 12.2), you can choose to have no other GPO override the one you have selected, or you can disable the selected one.

Why would you want to disable a GPO? Three reasons:

◆ First, if you are having problems with an account in the container and you think that a GPO might be causing it, as a last resort you can disable it and see what happens.

◆ Secondly you could leave an old, no longer relevant, GPO linked to the container so you know where it is if you need to recycle it later.

FIGURE 12.2

The GPO Options
dialog box

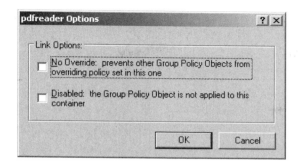

- ◆ Finally, and most importantly for software installation, disabling lets you pre-create your software-installing GPOs in an afternoon of setting up network shares, writing ZAP files, and performing administrative installations before deploying any of them. It also lets you make sure you clicked the correct check box or radio button before it's too late and the software is pushed to the entire network. I don't like to enable the GPOs until I'm good and ready and not a moment sooner.

The next interface you need to be familiar with is the Group Policy Management Console (see Figure 12.3). This console is covered in great detail elsewhere, but I want to focus on the software installation here. The Software Installation icon is located right beneath the Software Settings folder in the list on the right side of the window. It looks like a blue box with a CD coming out of it (or going into it…you never know). Because you can assign software to a user or computer, there are configuration options for both. As in much of Windows Server, the context menu is where to go to do anything. If you right-click the Software Installation icon (not the Software Settings folder), you can add any crucial new package that you'd like to deploy. The Software Installation object itself has properties that can be used to set the default deployment options for any package that gets linked to it (see Figure 12.4). Let's look at that dialog box before moving on.

On the General tab, there are a few items of interest. The Default Package Location can be useful if you have (or plan to have) all of your MSI files stored in one place.

Surprisingly, the Browse button on this dialog box is network aware. When you click it, it immediately looks across the network. If you go to the folder where you store your packages, it will in fact realize that it requires a network path. This is not that common. Most of the location fields in the dialog boxes you will come across may need a network path, but generally default to looking for files on the local drive.

Also under the General tab you can set default information about deployment, such as the options for the Deploy Software dialog box. The Deploy Software dialog box pops up after you've added a new package to a GPO and allows you to choose whether to publish, assign, or do more advanced deployment. You can choose not to display the Deploy Software dialog box and instead have one of the two deploy choices (Publish or Assign) apply immediately. Or, you can choose Advanced. Advanced deployment will allow you to set each package's deployment options in more detail before deployment occurs. I actually prefer the advanced setting, since I have grown comfortable with all of the options, and tend to tweak as I go. For this chapter, though, assume that I have left it in its default, Display the Deploy Software Dialog Box.

At the bottom of the General tab are the Installation User Interface options. You can choose Basic, which means that the users will see as little as possible of the install process, or Maximum, which means that the users will see as much as possible of the install process (some might say too much). For some reason, Maximum is selected by default. I always go Basic. Remember though, that this choice doesn't affect ZAP files. They go through their setup as they normally would.

FIGURE 12.3

Group Policy Management Console

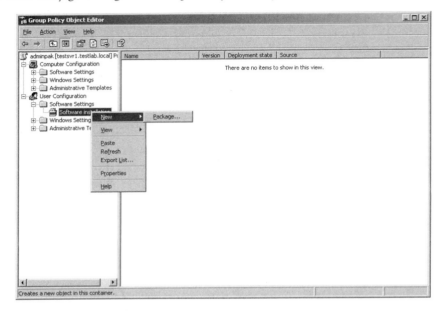

FIGURE 12.4

Software Installation default properties

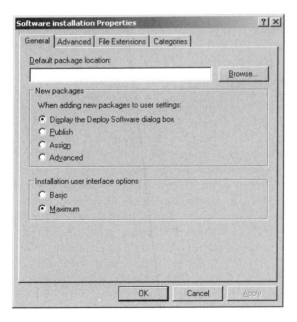

Under the Advanced tab (see Figure 12.5), there are several check boxes. The first allows you to uninstall applications (note the plural) when they fall out of scope of management. That means if the GPO client user or computer were to be removed from the container or group that this GPO applies to, the installed package would be removed from the machine and would no longer be advertised to their account. This is a great feature and I always have it on by default.

FIGURE 12.5

Software Installation properties Advanced tab

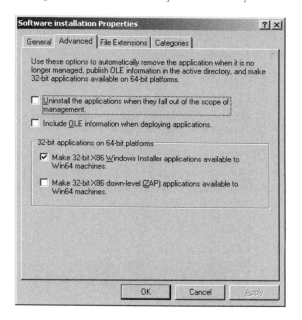

NOTE *To ensure that software is removed properly after it has been deployed, make certain that the Uninstall the Applications When They Fall Out of the Scope of Management option is checked before the package is first assigned or published. If that option is checked, Windows Installer will write the package uninstall information to the account profile. That way, if the account loses access to its source MSI package for any reason, it will still be able to uninstall itself using the account profile information.*

The second check box allows you to include OLE information if the application being deployed has special COM components it needs to access from Active Directory. And the last two check boxes allow you to have 32-bit applications work if you are installing them (as either MSIs or ZAPs) onto 64-bit machines running 64-bit enabled Windows.

The next tab is File Extensions (see Figure 12.6). Here you can view the list of file extensions that will be associated with all the packages added to the GPO. There is nowhere within the individual package properties dialog box to specify extensions—the MSI file lists its associations in its database, and you manually specify associated extensions in the text of a ZAP file. Therefore, this tab is here to help you avoid conflicts if two added packages activate on the same extension. This is particularly important if the extension is contested, such as MP3 or MPG. You can move the packages listed up or down to enforce precedence, with the item closest to the top getting first dibs.

The last tab, Categories, (see Figure 12.7) is used to organize the view of installed packages in Add/Remove Programs. If you would like to associate categories with your packages, you must create them in this tab of the Software Installation properties before they can be listed in the packages' own properties.

FIGURE 12.6

File Extensions tab

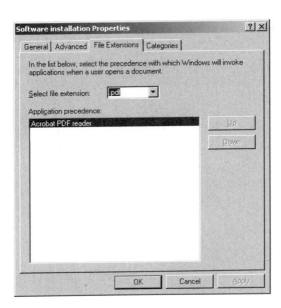

FIGURE 12.7

Categories tab

That's it for the Software Installation properties. Now, on to the package properties.

You can get to the package properties page in two ways: by right-clicking a pre-existing package and selecting Properties, or clicking Advanced during the deployment of a newly added package. Either way, you'll end up in the same place.

In the General tab (see Figure 12.8) is the Name field for the package. This field is self-explanatory, but it's useful if you have multiple deployments of the same software with different configurations.

Also under this tab is product information and a support URL field. This field is usually filled in with the package maker's URL (usually Microsoft, whatta surprise), but it is editable. This URL field also shows up under support information in the clients' Add/Remove Programs, so it might be useful to enter the URL to your intranet support page.

FIGURE 12.8

Software Installation
package properties

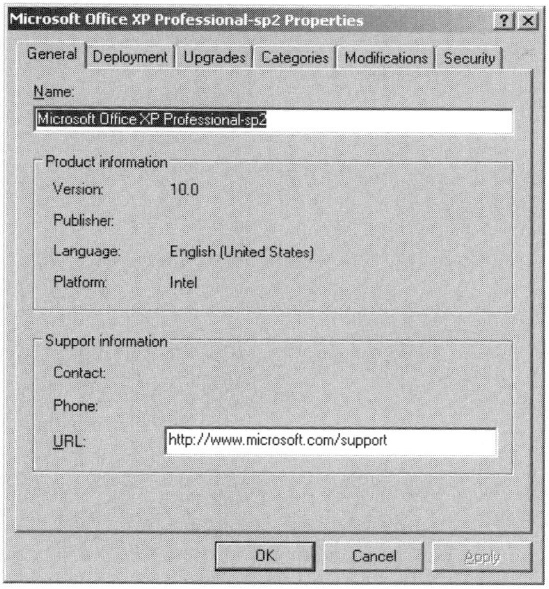

The second tab is Deployment (see Figure 12.9), which looks similar to the Software Installation properties dialog box. Which options are available under this tab depends on whether you are assigning or publishing and if the package is a ZAP file.

In the Deployment Type section, you can choose Assigned or Published. Only those two options are listed because this *is* advanced deployment. Under Deployment Options you'll see the default settings made in Software Installation properties (you can of course change them, they are only defaults). The first option is Auto-install This Application by File Extension Activation. If this option is checked but grayed out, chances are the package has added its associated extensions to the software installation list. If you were to go back and check the Software Installation's File Extensions tab after you finish with your package, you'll probably find it listed with at least one file extension associated with it. Also the Uninstall This Application When It Falls Out of the Scope of Management option is here (instead of under Advanced as it is in software installation). Notice it is singular, but the Software Installation reference to uninstalling is plural.

The Do Not Display in Add/Remove Programs option makes it a little more difficult for the users to uninstall their software and prevents them from repairing the package if it isn't working properly.

And finally, the brand new and much-needed Install This Application at Logon option. This makes certain that the package is not advertised to install on first use but actually goes ahead and installs the whole package when the client logs on. Of course, this means that it will take quite a while to log on when the package deploys. But no more waiting for clip art to install when the user tries to use it for the first time. Of course, you can't choose this option if you publish the package rather than assign it.

FIGURE 12.9

Deployment tab

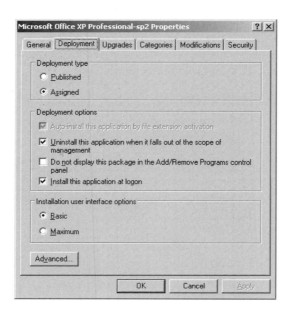

Now for an option most people don't even know is available. If you click the Advanced button, you'll bring up the Advanced Deployment Options dialog box (see Figure 12.10). From here, you can choose to ignore language and make a 32-bit application available on a 64-bit machine. (If it wasn't set as a default, you can turn it on here.) My favorite part of this dialog, however, is the Deployment Count. By keeping an eye on this, you can keep track of how many times you have had to redeploy a package. In some circumstances, this can come in handy.

FIGURE 12.10

The Advanced Deployment Options dialog box

The next tab is Upgrades (see Figure 12.11). If the package you are deploying is supposed to upgrade or replace a previous version, use this tab to make sure it happens. The first section is the list of packages to be upgraded. If you would like the package to sense and remove previous versions of its software that may not have be installed by deployment, select the Required Upgrade for Existing Packages check box. At the bottom of the page is the list of packages within that GPO that are set to upgrade this package. Obviously, the packages that are going to be upgraded are expected to have been previously deployed, so if you click Add to bring up the Add Upgrade Package dialog box (see Figure 12.12), expect to have to browse through GPOs to find the package that is going to be upgraded. Once you have selected it, you can choose to have your new package upgrade over that older version, or have the older version removed and replaced by the new install.

FIGURE 12.11

Upgrades tab

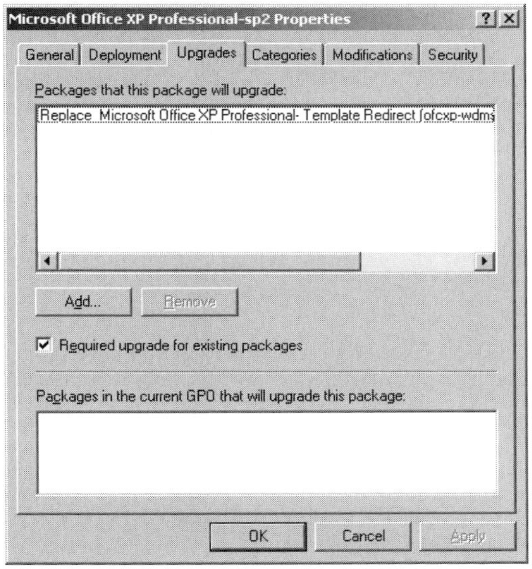

FIGURE 12.12

Add Upgrade
Package dialog box

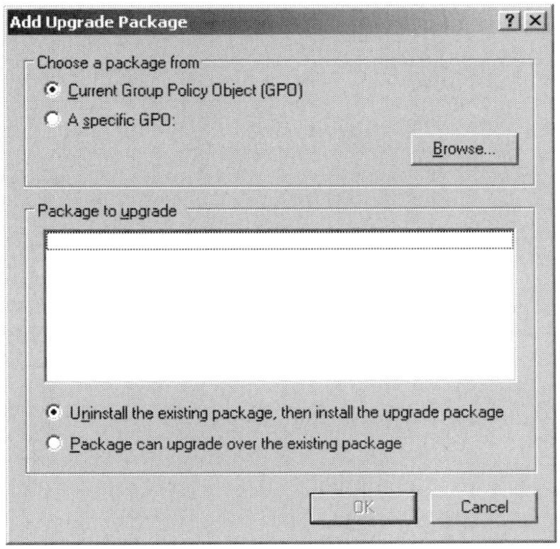

The next tab is Categories (see Figure 12.13). It has two columns: Available Categories on the left, lists the categories that were created in the Software Installation properties page, and Selected Categories on the right, lists the categories that the package has been assigned to. And there are the obligatory Select/Remove buttons that move items from the available categories to the selected categories (or just get rid of categories you may have assigned the package to by mistake).

FIGURE 12.13

Categories tab

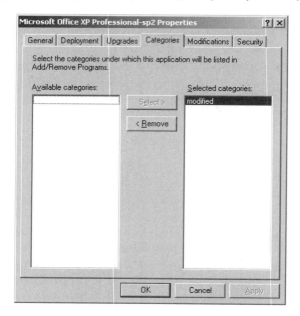

On to the Modifications tab (see Figure 12.14). This tab is where you go if you have created a file that customizes an MSI install. The MST file is used during installation to tell the MSI package the particulars about how to install components, modify application settings, and such. Because it is only used at installation, it stands to reason that you can only add an MST (or several of them if you'd like) to a deployment before it runs. If you click OK before you finish adding your transform files, you're out of luck—it's all or nothing. This is definitely not something to come back to later.

TIP   *In my experience, the special voodoo that gets software installation to really work is to do everything you intend to do before you deploy the package. If the client gets the deployment and it works fine, they may not check back with the server to see if there have been any changes, so it's better not to make any after deployment. This is another reason to use the Advanced Deployment option as a default. It'll give you a chance to double-check your settings before clicking OK.*

And finally we come to the Security tab (see Figure 12.15), where you can choose permissions that are appropriate for the package file itself. Remember, if you want to check out the permissions to whom this GPO will apply, you will have to go to the GPO's properties.

FIGURE 12.14

Modifications tab

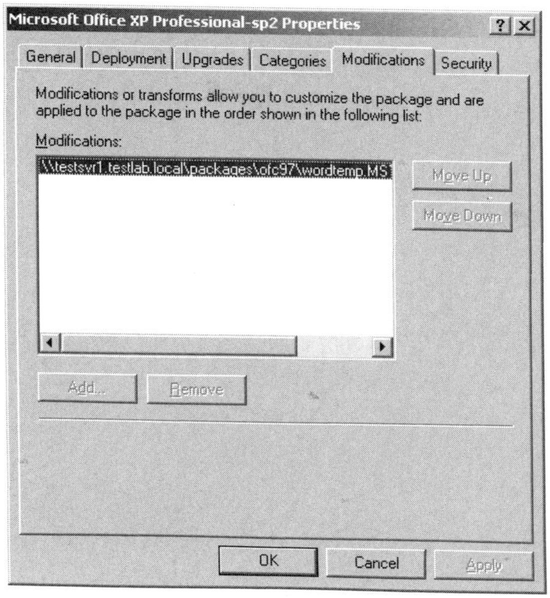

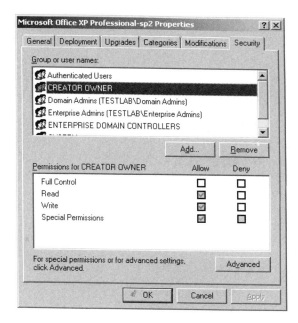

FIGURE 12.15

The Security tab

Phew. I'm glad we got that out of the way. I just can't leave a button unclicked....

The Scenario: What You Can Do with Software Deployment

Now let's look at a scenario that might lend itself to the kind ministrations of software deployment:

- An IT staffer has complained once too often, and you decided to publish administrative tools to all IT personnel so they can have them no matter where they log in from. That should make them happy.

- Well, it should have made them happy, but they are too lazy to go to Add/Remove Packages, so you end up assigning it and redeploying it instead.

- Then the IT staffer who first made the suggestion is found abusing the administrative tools. He gets moved to sales. Obviously he shouldn't have admin tools anymore.

- The CEO hears about the IT staffer's indiscretions and decides administrative tools cannot be deployed to any workstation other than those in the secure network room. You will need to remove the tools and assign them only to the secure network room computers.

- Then your boss wants you to upgrade Office 2000 to Office XP, Service Pack 2, on every machine in the building. He also wants you to change the default location of the Microsoft Word Workgroup Templates to a shared folder on the server. No hurry, tomorrow would be fine.

- The corporate office sends out a memo demanding that all Windows XP Professional workstations have Service Pack 1 installed before the end of the week.

- The sales staff needs to be able to read PDF documents, but the PDF reader your company bought has an EXE install file.

- Oh, and all users need to be able to create self-extracting ZIP files for non–Windows XP clients. But that program doesn't use an MSI, and not all users can use Add/Remove Programs.

Alrighty then, I think we've covered the basics. Now that you know where I'm going with this, let's get down to it.

PUBLISHING AN MSI PACKAGE

In the preceding scenario, the first thing you need to do is publish the administrative tools to all of the IT staff accounts. To start, you need to find the MSI file for the software. It just happens to be called adminpak.msi, and it is located on the Windows Server CD, in the I386 folder (x:\I386\adminpak.msi). This MSI package is considered "flat" because it can be deployed as is. That is, it stands alone, unmodified, with no administrative intervention needed before applying it. That being said, you can just put it in a shared location, link it to a GPO, publish it, and it's done.

Seriously. I'll show you:

1. Copy the file adminpak.msi to a shared folder on the server. On my server I organize all of my MSI packages in their own folders under a folder called, creatively enough, packages. On the server it would be C:\packages\adminpak\adminpak.msi, as shown in Figure 12.16.

FIGURE 12.16

Saving the
`adminpak.msi`
file to a shared
folder on the
server

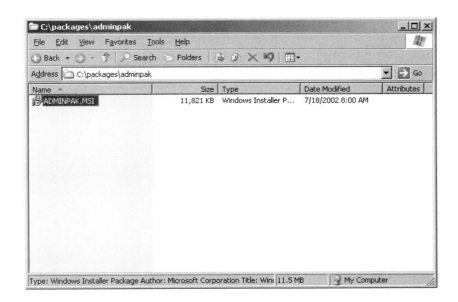

2. Open the Active Directory Users and Computers MMC. As you can see in Figure 12.17, there are a few organizational units, and one of them is called IT Staff. Not surprisingly, that is the organizational unit that the `adminpak.msi` is going to be published to. To get to the properties and add a group policy, right-click the IT Staff OU.

FIGURE 12.17

Right-click the
OU in Users and
Computers to create
a new group policy.

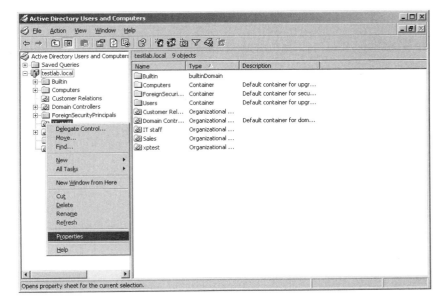

3. Take a look at Figure 12.18. On the properties page, click the Group Policy tab. Click the New button. It will put a new, unnamed Group Policy object in the list area. Name it adminpak. Click the Edit button.

FIGURE 12.18

Edit the new Group Policy

4. At this point, I always check to see what groups of users this GPO actually applies to. It's always good to pay attention to who has the Apply Group Policy permission. Right-click the adminpak group policy icon at the top of the list. Select Properties. In the properties page (see Figure 12.19), go to the Security tab. Click Domain Admins and notice that Apply Group Policy is not checked in the list of permissions. They can read it, but they don't have to obey it. To make sure the group policy applies only to them, check the Apply Group Policy box, and make sure it is unchecked for your general authenticated user. That way, if someone accidentally gets moved to the IT Staff OU, they won't have administrative tools.

5. In the Group Policy Management Console, you can see that there are two basic configurations to choose from on the left: User Configuration or Computer Configuration. Since the adminpak.msi is going to be applied to the IT staff user accounts, it stands to reason that you should go for the User Configuration. Before you add a new package though, make sure that it will uninstall if a user leaves the IT staff. Beneath User Configuration, click the plus sign next to Software Settings, and right-click Software Installation. In the pop-up menu, click Properties. Click the Advanced tab (see Figure 12.20) and make sure the Uninstall the Applications When They Fall Out of the Scope of Management option is selected. Click OK. Now any package added to this software installation configuration will bear this option.

FIGURE 12.19

Verifying that the Domain Admins have Apply Group Policy permission

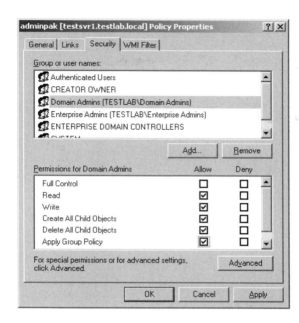

FIGURE 12.20

Ensuring that the package will uninstall if a user leaves the IT staff

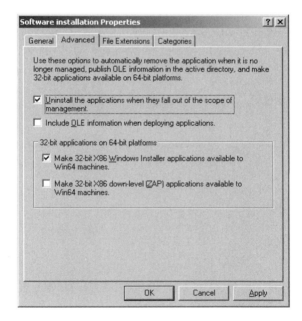

6. Now it's is time to create the package. Right-click Software Installation and go to New\Package (see Figure 12.21).

FIGURE 12.21

Create a new software installation package

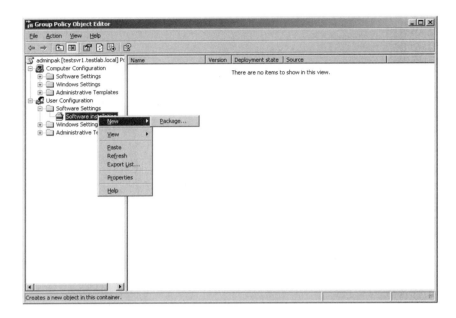

7. The dialog box obviously means for you to click the location where the file is currently located. *Do not do that.* The temptation is there, but you must remember that you are setting up the path to the MSI file that will be accessed across the network. Be sure to type in the full path to the package. (As you can see in Figure 12.22, in my case it is `\\tstsvr1.testlab.local\packages\adminpak\adminpak.msi`.) Then click Open.

FIGURE 12.22

Type in the full path to the MSI package

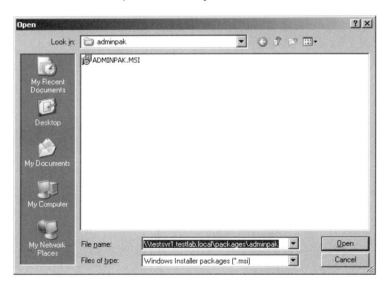

8. That's it, the package is linked to the GPO. Now you have to decide how to deploy it. In this example, you are going to publish. In the Deploy Software dialog box that pops up (see Figure 12.23), make sure that Published is selected and click OK.

FIGURE 12.23

Deploying a package by publishing it

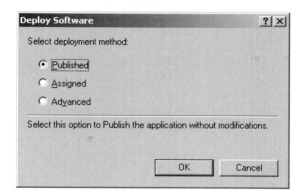

9. Voila. The package is there. Take a look at Figure 12.24 and check out the new administrative tools package on the right side of the window. Notice that under Deployment State it says Published. Also, check your path and make sure it is correct.

FIGURE 12.24

New package to publish

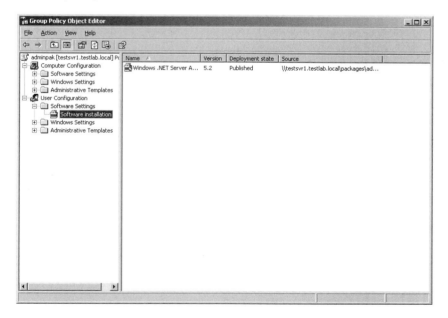

10. That's it. Now when an IT staffer logs in, they can go to Add/Remove Programs and add administrative tools from there (see Figure 12.25).

FIGURE 12.25

New administrative tools are now available for installing in Add/Remove Programs

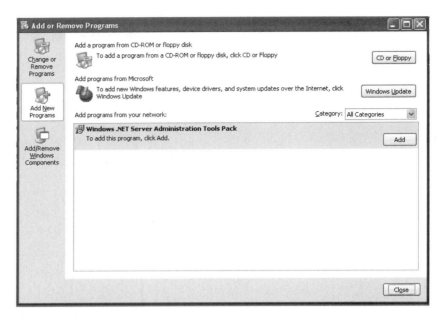

NOTE *It is in Add/Remove Programs that all installed software is listed (unless you set it to not display under Deployment Options in the package properties). It's also where a user can go to manually try to repair an installed software program if it is not working properly. By clicking the Click Here for Support Information option, the user can then click Repair, and the corrupted or missing files will be replaced by the source MSI file.*

Again, the basic steps to publishing an MSI package are as follows:

1. Copy the MSI file to network share.
2. Make the group policy. Make sure it applies to the users you want it to.
3. Link the MSI to the group policy.
4. Choose to publish it and make sure it uninstalls if it goes out of the scope of management.
5. At the next login, the user will have the option of installing the program from Add/Remove Programs or whenever they activate an associated extension.

REDEPLOY (IF AT FIRST YOU DON'T SUCCEED...)

Within days of publishing the `adminpak.msi` to the IT Staff, you realize something important: People are generally lazy. You have gotten three e-mail messages asking if you could just assign the MSI rather than making them perform the extra steps to install it. You decide you might as well, because you'd rather the tool kit be used than neglected.

There are several good reasons to redeploy software. One is that you should assign software to people's machines rather than publishing it. And, although you might think changing the deployment state from Publish to Assign is enough, I think that it's a better idea to redeploy the package to apply the change. Why? Because it ensures that the installed copy on the user machine changes its deployment status as soon as possible, rather than waiting to get around to it when it needs to repair itself.

NOTE *Remember: If you are going to make any changes to the deployment state or options of a package, make sure that the accounts that are to be affected have logged off and on (or shut down and restarted) at least once after you make any changes. If they don't do this, the clients may not be aware of the change and will remain unaffected.*

Another reason to redeploy is if the MSI file has been updated or modified in some way that requires that a changed version be installed on the users' systems. The problem with redeploying is that it does force a reinstall of the software all over again. This can take up network bandwidth and may frustrate the users temporarily, but if it makes work better they will eventually forget about it.

1. To redeploy the `adminpak.msi` file to be assigned rather than published, go to the appropriate GPO, and edit it (by right-clicking the container, going to Properties, going to the Group Policy tab, selecting the adminpak GPO, and clicking the Edit button). Then right-click the MSI package and choose Assign (see Figure 12.26).

FIGURE 12.26

Assigning adminpak

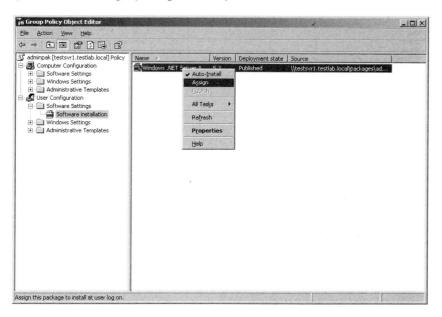

2. The Deployment State of the package will go from Published to Assigned. Right-click the package again, go to All Tasks (you'll see that Publish and Assign are listed here too for your convenience. Assign, of course, is now grayed out.), and select Redeploy Application (as shown in Figure 12.27).

3. After you redeploy, there will be a warning dialog box (see Figure 12.28), and it is serious. Redeploying software can take up bandwidth on a busy network. Click Yes if that's not an issue. That will redeploy the `adminpak.msi` file as assigned. No more manually installing administrative tools.

FIGURE 12.27

Redeploying
adminpak

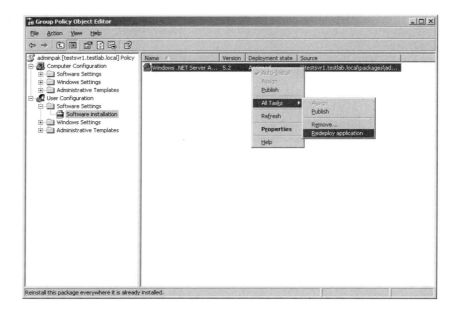

FIGURE 12.28

Redeployment
warning

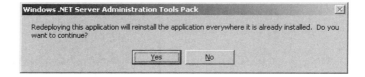

SCOPE OF MANAGEMENT

Now, there was a reason I wanted you to make sure the Uninstall This Application When It Falls Out of the Scope of Management check box was checked when you first set up the adminpak for deployment. As I mentioned earlier, when a software package is added to a GPO and deployed to an OU, its scope of management is limited to that OU. When a user is moved out of that OU, they fall out of that GPO's ability to manage that software. Because the Uninstall This Application option was checked before the package deployed, the software will be uninstalled from the user's machine if they move out of the OU, and will no longer be available to that user for as long as they are no longer in the OU. Remember the scenario? The very person who wanted administrative tools wherever they log in has been caught being naughty (they abused the admin tools). So (instead of being fired) they have been transferred from the IT department to the Sales department.

You already set the software to be uninstalled if someone moves out of the OU; so when the staffer is moved from the IT Staff OU to the Sales OU, they will no longer have administrative tools.

REMOVE A MANAGED MSI PACKAGE

Of course, because one bad apple spoiled the barrel, you now have to essentially do a recall on the very administrative tools you recently deployed. As you may remember, the CEO now wants to be sure that no one outside of the secure network room has those tools. So step one is just removing the software from everyone's systems. We'll worry about getting the admin tools back later....

1. Go to the properties dialog box of the IT Staff OU and click the Group Policy tab. Select the adminpak GPO. Edit it. Right-click the administrative tools package. Select All Tasks from the popup menu (see Figure 12.29) and choose Remove.

FIGURE 12.29

Removing a package

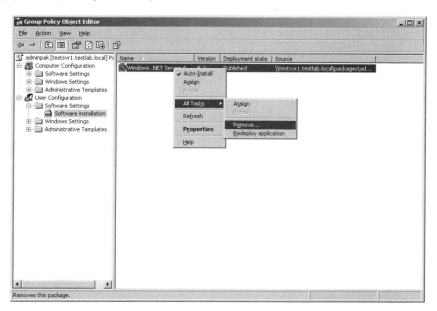

2. The Remove Software dialog box, which comes up as soon as you choose to remove a package (see Figure 12.30), gives two options: to uninstall the software immediately, or allow the copy to remain on the user's machine, but prevent new installations. Choose the option to immediately uninstall (no time like the present, I always say). Click OK and the package disappears. If an IT staffer logs on now, their admin tools will be gone and there'll be no possibility of reinstalling.

FIGURE 12.30

Removing the package immediately

WARNING *To ensure that software is removed properly after it has been deployed, make certain that the Uninstall This Application When it Falls Out of the Scope of Management option is checked before the package is first assigned or published. If that option is checked, Windows Installer will write the package uninstall information to the account profile. That way, if the account loses access to its source MSI package for any reason, it will still be able to uninstall itself using the account profile information. How can software lose access to the source MSI? If a package has been recently deployed and you remove it before the affected accounts have had a chance to log on and log off, the clients may not have had a chance to check the server and notice the change so they may not update their own information to reflect the change. If the software later realizes that it should be uninstalled, but it can't find its source installation information, then it also can't find its source uninstall information. At that point, it is considered orphaned. It remains on the system, must be uninstalled manually, and, of course, can't self-repair. Despite the fact that the point of uninstalling applications when they fall out of the scope of management was to ease the administrative burden of managing the software of users that are promoted, demoted, or transferred, it also, inadvertently, helps manage any piece of software that might someday be removed.*

ASSIGN AN MSI PACKAGE TO A COMPUTER

Well, the CEO did say that the IT staff *could* have administrative tools in the network room, so let's assign an MSI package to some computer accounts.

The beauty of computers, as opposed to users, is they (usually) don't roam and if they start acting strange, they aren't considered to be eccentric, they are broken. And they can't leave voice mail. I love assigning packages to computers. Software that is assigned to a computer is installed, period, on that system at startup. No one is going to be idly uninstalling the software because the software is not assigned to its user account. It belongs to the computer's account.

The adminpak GPO still exists but it's not deploying software anymore. Let's use it to deploy the administrative tools to the computers in the IT Staff OU. Waste not, want not.

1. Go to the properties page of the IT Staff OU. Select the adminpak GPO. Edit it. Right-click Software Installation under Computer Configuration (see Figure 12.31) and from the context menu, choose New\Package.

FIGURE 12.31

Computer software installation

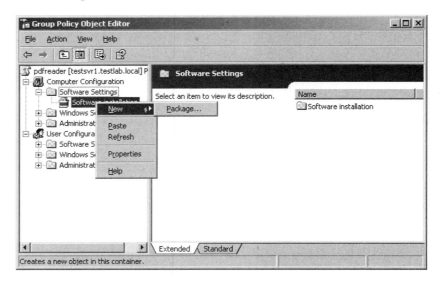

2. Add the `adminpak.msi` file as a new package. You must choose Assign as the deployment method.

That's it. The package is now assigned to install at startup for all computers in the IT Staff OU.

COMPLEX DEPLOYMENT AND CUSTOMIZATION

The next thing to take care of in our scenario is that Office XP needs to be installed and available to every user on the network. In addition, it needs to be patched, and the install needs to be modified to point to a shared `Template` folder. This process obviously has several steps. First, the software needs to be made available to the users. Second, the software itself needs to have the necessary service packs applied to it (currently up to SP2). Third, the software install needs to be modified. We'll start with making the software available.

Administrative Install

Before you create the Software Installer GPO, the Office XP MSI package must be prepared to be an administrative install.

"What?" I hear you ask? "Why do I need to do that? I didn't have to do that with the adminpak." I know. That's why admin tools is so easy to use as an example. Unfortunately, Office is one of the more popular MSI package that gets deployed and managed.

The Office MSI is not a flat MSI. It refers to files outside of itself, it's filled with components both independent and shared, and it can be customized like crazy. It's not an "as-is" item. Because of this, Office XP requires more explanation than just share and go.

Back when Office 97 came out, it had a special network install you could perform so you could accept the EULA, type in the product key, and enter the company information so the users didn't have to. This made it possible to install Office 97 on every user machine without having to type in anything. Heck, just not having to hand out the product key was more than enough reason to use the administrative install version rather than just sharing out a folder that had the contents of the Office 97 CD in it.

Microsoft, like most of us, tends to keep a good thing. So Office XP has an administrative install that does basically the same thing the Office 97 version did.

The files that actually get installed on the user workstation are system file–sensitive. This means the installer has different files (such as DLLs) for different operating systems. To get the installation to work reliably on a workstation, it needs to be administratively installed from that workstation (or a spitting image of it).

Doing the administrative install is really easy:

1. Make sure there is a shared folder on the server to use as a network sharepoint (as you can see in Figure 12.32, mine is under the shared `packages` folder, in a folder I named `OfficeXP`) for the new MSI and its accompanying files.

2. Go to a workstation that has the same operating system on it as the machines you will be deploying to. Make certain the workstation has network connectivity and can see the sharepoint. Oh, and have the Office XP CD handy.

3. Make sure you are logged in with at least enough administrative rights to run software on that machine and to write to the sharepoint.

FIGURE 12.32

Administrative
install sharepoint

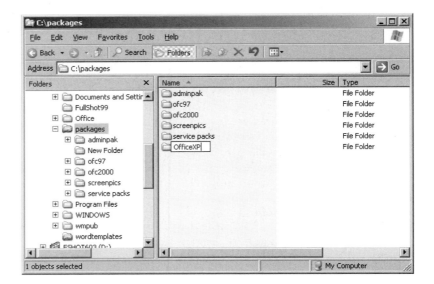

4. Put the CD in the CD-ROM drive, go to Start\Run, type **x:\setup /a** (where "x:\" is the CD-ROM drive letter), and click OK (as shown in Figure 12.33).

FIGURE 12.33

Running
administrative
install

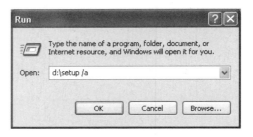

The administrative install will begin. It has a few wizard steps to go through, most notably when it asks you where to put the administrative files (remember that you should choose the shared folder on the server—mine is in the `OfficeXP` folder under `Packages`—and be sure to use the full network path). It also asks for company name, product key, and prompts you to accept the EULA by proxy for anyone who uses the product from your install (see Figure 12.34).

There are quite a few files in the sharepoint (see Figure 12.35), but `proplus.msi` is the important one. This is the administrative-install type of MSI file that looks for the information you gave during setup. Because an administrative install is aware that it will be a standard copy used by multiple clients, it was designed with convenient, centralized customization and updates in mind.

Updating and customizing is what you'll do next. Remember, always do everything you can with the file before you deploy it.

So let's do the service packs and modifications first. We'll finish with the easy part, the deployment.

FIGURE 12.34
Administrative
installation in
progress

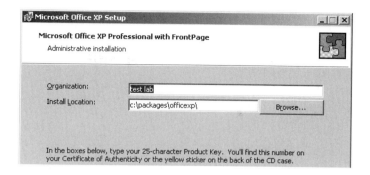

FIGURE 12.35
Administrative
install sharepoint
contents

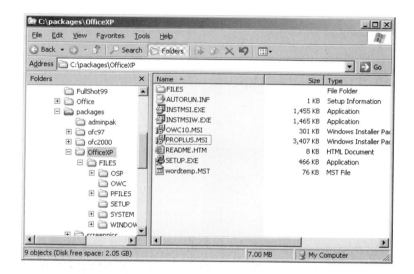

Updating an Administrative Install

Because the boss wants you to install Office XP with Service Pack 2, you should probably apply SP2 before you deploy the software. Updating the administrative install is a convenient way of updating the software on the client computers. After the update, just redeploy the package, and it should reinstall the updated version of the software when a user logs in.

To apply a service pack to an administrative install, you need to download it (unless you have it on CD) and be sure you get the *administrative* version. It is the version that was designed specifically to be applied to an administrative install. The service pack I am using, SP2a, is called oxpsp2a.exe.

1. When the service pack is on your system, double-click it to allow it to self-extract. Choose a location to extract it to (see Figure 12.36). This can be a local path because it does not need

to be accessed across the network (notice that it says "location," not "path," in the dialog box). For simplicity's sake, I used `c:\adminupdates`.

FIGURE 12.36

Service Pack self-extraction

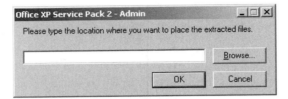

2. Go to the `adminupdates` (or whatever name you gave your location) folder and you'll see that it has two MSP files. The one I am going to use is `mainsp2ff.msp`.

3. To apply the patch to the administrative install, you will need to run the MSIEXEC command to specify which MSP you would like to apply to what MSI. In the Run box (see Figure 12.37), type the following:

```
MSIEXEC /a c:\packages\officexp\proplus.msi /p
c:\adminupdates\mainsp2ff.msp shortfilenames=1
```

Click OK.

FIGURE 12.37

Applying Service Pack 2 to the administrative install

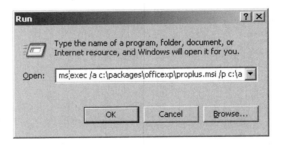

NOTE *MSIEXEC is a command-line tool for working with MSI files locally. It cannot do network deployment, but it is powerful to say the least. An entire chapter alone can be dedicated to using MSIEXEC.*

4. What looks like a software installation will start. It will ask you to confirm your organization name, product key for the product it is updating, and EULA confirmation. Then it will install.

5. When the administrative install is updated, just go to the Group Policy Management Console for Office XP's GPO and redeploy the Office XP package. If all goes well, when the users log on they will be redeployed the updated version of Office XP. To confirm that the update worked, open any Office XP feature, such as PowerPoint, and go to the About box under the Help menu. The service pack will be listed (as shown in Figure 12.38).

FIGURE 12.38

An updated Office XP application

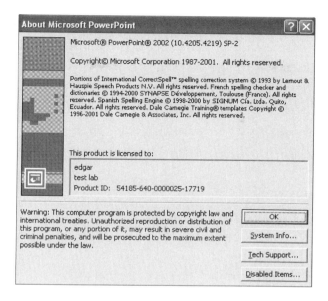

AN ALTERNATIVE METHOD OF UPDATING IF CLIENT SYNCHRONIZATION IS AN ISSUE

There are several reasons a client may fall out of sync with its source MSI—one of the biggest is if the version of that MSI changes. Applying service packs to an administrative install would do just that.

On a fast, smooth-running network, if all of the computers run well, and the users log in and off on schedule, and the machines are restarted regularly, then there are no problems with lack of synchronicity.

If your network is not a fast, smooth-running machine with orderly shutdowns and logoffs, then when you change the administrative install of a package and do a redeploy, some users may log in and see a dialog box asking to install Office from a CD. Heck, that may happen even on the smoothest, fastest running network.

If this happens, do not despair. First, try having the user log off and log back in again. Sometimes there is simply a delay between the redeployment and the client realizing that the software has changed. If logging off and on a few times does not work, however, you have two options to fix it: a short one and a long one.

The short option is to create a logon script that has the client accounts recache and reinstall the software to apply changes. By using MSIEXEC, you can rerun the install by pointing to the path of the administrative install MSI file and tell it to REINSTALL whatever features (such as Word or Excel) you'd like, or just do ALL to reinstall all the features (which is what I do). Then specify the switches you'd like to apply to the REINSTALL. The switches I suggest are vomus—I know that looks like a Latin word for a gross bodily function, but it actually stands for a list (or "stack") of switches (notice that there are no forward slashes for these switches):

◆   v = Run from source and recache the local package

◆   o = Reinstall if file is missing or if an older version is installed

Continued on next page

AN ALTERNATIVE METHOD OF UPDATING IF CLIENT SYNCHRONIZATION IS AN ISSUE *(continued)*

◆ m = Rewrite all required machine-specific Registry entries

◆ u = Rewrite all required user-specific Registry entries

◆ s = Overwrite all existing shortcuts

Using all of those switches might seem like overkill, but it's better to be safe.

The syntax for this MSIEXEC command line is as follows:

```
MSIEXEC /I "path for the admin install MSI" REINSTALL= "featurelist or ALL"
    REINSTALL= vomus
```

You only need to run the MSIEXEC once, at the logon following your modification of the source MSI. After you are sure that all users have been reached and won't be orphaned, remove the script. Otherwise, it will recache and reinstall every time the user logs in.

If you think MSIEXEC won't work in your circumstance, there is a longer method that is also effective. This option also helps ensure that no client ends up trying to refer to the wrong version of the MSI source. It is a bit clunky, but it gets the job done.

Before any updates are applied, make a copy of the administrative install folder. Make your changes to the copy (such as hot fixes or service packs). Create a new GPO that has the exact same settings as the current GPO—that is, add the changed MSI, MSTs, categories, and whatever else is necessary to get it to match the current Office XP deployment.

If your environment allows it, you can also check the Install This Application at Logon box in the package properties. It will cause slow logins (especially if everyone logs in at the same time). However, it may be worth the wait to ensure that no lingering component of the prechanged MSI is left behind on the client to cause problems later, especially if being out-of-sync is a consistent problem in your environment.

Then make sure (before you click OK) that the new, changed package upgrades the current Office XP GPO package and that the current package is removed by the upgrade.

Disable the current GPO and move the new GPO up the list until it is above the current Office XP GPO (remember order counts, from the top down).

Then wait and see if any users have problems. Notice that the current GPO wasn't removed, but it won't advertise its version of the MSI to any new users. Leave it that way for a while, and make sure every user has logged in several times. Give every account every chance to upgrade of its own free will. That's the trick: making sure no one has missed the upgrade train. Then delete the no-longer-current GPO for Office XP and delete the old administrative install. No one should be pointing to it anymore.

This method might seem a little extreme, but it is only one extra GPO to ensure peace and harmony throughout your kingdom. It may be worth it. And, if someone who was out on leave logs in and can't get Office XP to work because it keeps asking for the install disk, you can just restore the old administrative install so the client can point to it. It may take a few logins for an account to realize it has a new GPO (usually two), but it will get upgraded. Then you can delete the original administrative install again.

Customizing an MSI

Your boss has decreed that Word XP needs to point to the `Template` folder on the server. How can you change that in the administrative install to apply the customization to every users' install? It's easy.

To customize Office XP, you need the Custom Installation Wizard. It is located in the Office XP Resource Kit, which can be found either on the Office XP CD or on Microsoft's Web site in the Downloads section. The Office XP Resource Kit file on the CD is called `ORK.msi`.

The Custom Installation Wizard creates a modifier file, like an INI, that the MSI refers to during install to customize Office. The customization file is called a Transform file and its extension is `.mst` (one of the few files that Windows Installer recognizes, as you may recall).

The Resource Kit is a collection of really cool Office tools that are beyond the scope of this chapter (books have been written about them). We only need the CIW to change the default template path, so none of that other stuff is for us.

Download and install the `ORK.msi` file. It does not need to be run from a workstation, the server is fine, because it doesn't need to check the system files. It'll add several nifty Office management tools, but the only one you need is Custom Installation Tools. Select that from the Start menu to get started.

1. The wizard introduces itself with a standard welcome screen; click Next. On the Open the MSI File screen (see Figure 12.39), type in the network path of the MSI package for which you are going to make a transform file. Note that no MSIs are harmed in the making of this MST. Click Next.

FIGURE 12.39

Specifying the MSI
to customize

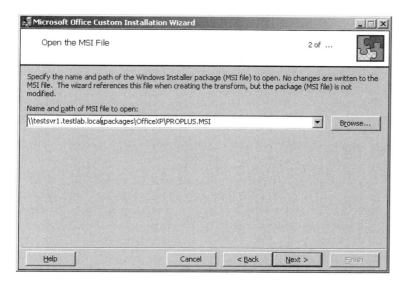

2. The Open the MST File screen (see Figure 12.40) lets you specify whether you are creating a new MST file or editing an existing one. (This is a nice option to know about if you forget something. Remember though, if it is already linked to an MSI package that has been deployed and you make a change, you must redeploy it.) Select Create a New MST File and click Next.

FIGURE 12.40

Create a new MST.

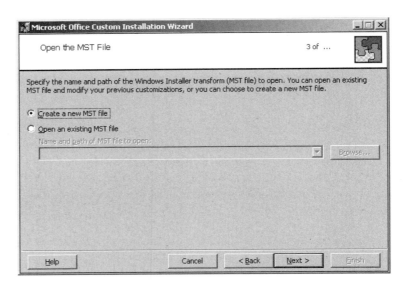

3. The Select the MST File to Save screen (see Figure 12.41) will name the MST and specify the path for it. Whenever a dialog box or wizard says "path," it never hurts to assume they mean full network path. It's also a good idea to keep MSI files and their MSTs in the same folder. Because this MST will specify an alternate network path for Word templates, I've named it wordtemp.mst. Click Next.

FIGURE 12.41

Supply a name and location for the new MST.

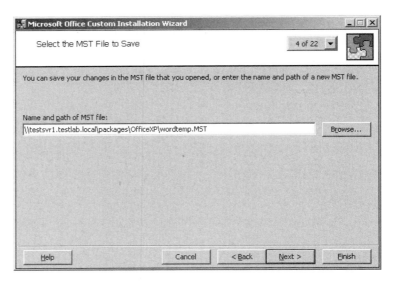

4. In the Specify Default Path and Organization screen, you can change the default folder location for the client installation, but for this exercise, the default install location is fine. While you're at this screen, however, notice the page number drop-down button at the top

right. If you click its down arrow, you'll see a list of the upcoming steps of the wizard (see Figure 12.42); move to the screen that is relevant to you. This is a time saver, since there are 22 screens and you only need to change the location of one folder. Click Next.

FIGURE 12.42

Drop-down list of wizard screens

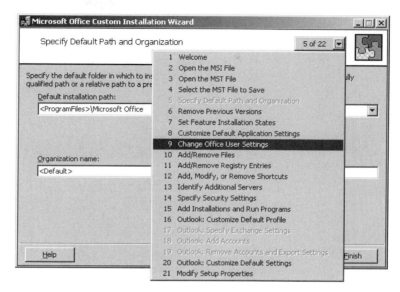

5. The Remove Previous Versions screen gives you a chance to remove previous versions of the software (see Figure 12.43). It is a good idea to avoid version conflicts, so removing the previous version (but keeping user preferences and such) is always a wise choice. However, for this example, let's have Windows Installer handle it during deployment. Click Next.

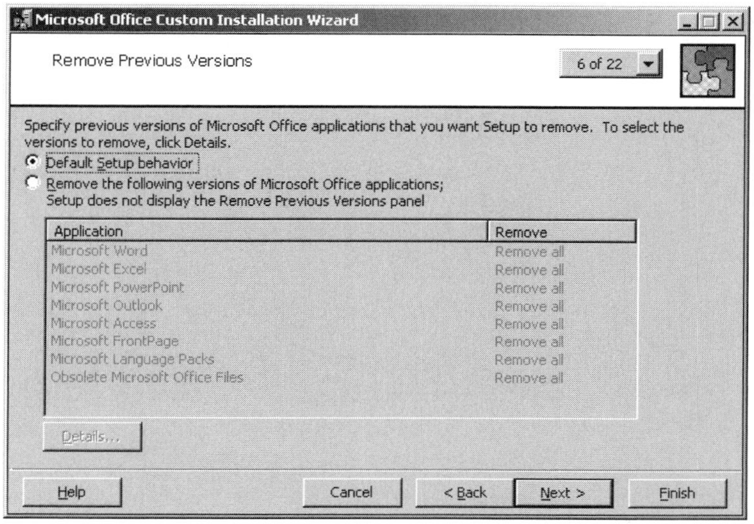

FIGURE 12.43

Remove Previous Versions screen

One reason not to manage upgrades with an MST is that you can also manage them as part of software deployment. If you use both methods, you may find yourself being redundant, telling the MST to upgrade any older version of Office, and adding packages to upgrade in the package properties. Try to choose one or the other—that way, if something goes wrong, it's easier to troubleshoot.

6. In the Set Feature Installation States screen (see Figure 12.44), you can choose which applications and their components get installed and how they install. The items that are gray have additional components under them; white items are single components with no subordinates. You aren't going to do anything here, but it's a nice option to be aware of. At this point, use the page number drop-down button to skip to screen 9, the Change Office User Settings screen.

FIGURE 12.44

Setting feature install states

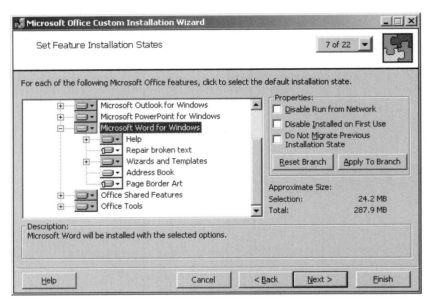

7. Here's the screen you've been waiting for (see Figure 12.45). Here's where you can set up the workgroup (shared by everyone) `Template` folder on the server so Word users have only one place to go to get new corporate forms.

   There are many things you can customize from this screen, but you only need to set the workgroup `Template` folder. Because templates are shared by several Office applications, it's located under `Microsoft OfficeXP (User)`. Choose `Shared Paths\Workgroup Templates Path`. Double-click it to bring up a dialog box in which you can type the path to the shared folder that is to be its new home. I chose `\\testsvr1.testlab.local\wordtemplates` (as shown in Figure 12.46). I know that applications other than Word use the `Templates` folder, but it needs a name that will remind administrators why it's there.

FIGURE 12.45

Changing office user settings

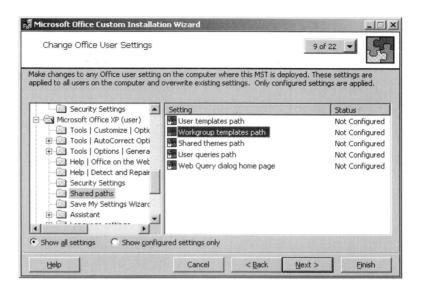

FIGURE 12.46

Setting the workgroup template location

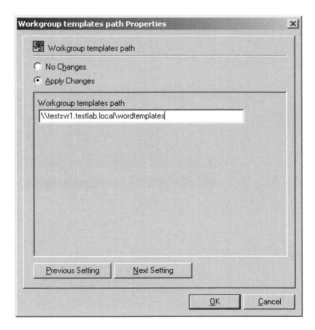

8. That's all you need to do with this MST, so click Finish. The wizard displays a screen about how to apply your transform file if you are not using group policies (see Figure 12.47), but you are, so you're finished.

NOTE *You can change many things in an MST. You can even go back and edit it later. That means you can create one big MST file that includes many different modifications and deploy it, or you can make many smaller MSTs with a single change and add them all at the time of deployment. It's up to you. A single MST for an MSI package is easier to handle, but if you forget what you clicked while making the MST, you'll have to search through all of those components to find every one of them. Just a thought.*

Deploying Office XP with Its New MST and Service Pack

This deployment is going to be more particular than any of the others because of the MST. While you are configuring the options of the new package, do not click OK before you add the MST file to the modifications list. I'm serious: *do not* click OK. Clicking OK before you add your MST to the modification list will render the package deployed without it. As far as Windows Installer is concerned, a modified MSI is a fundamentally different beast than an unmodified MSI. Because of that, once you deploy a package, you can't go into its properties and add the MST file. If you try, the Add button on the Modifications tab will be grayed out. If you do click OK on the properties page before you add the MST, the only way to modify the package will be to either remove the package and start over, or create a different GPO with the modified package to "upgrade" the one you just messed up. This is one *big* reason I like to disable my GPO before I add a modified package (an MSI that has an MST), so that I don't deploy anything to anyone until I am positive that the package is configured correctly.

That being said, go ahead and create a new GPO on the domain container called ofcxp-wdmst. You can disable the GPO by right-clicking on it and selecting Disabled from the pop-up menu, or by clicking the Options button and checking the Disabled box. It will be marked Disabled in the dialog box, as shown in Figure 12.47.

FIGURE 12.47

Disabling the new GPO

1. Edit the GPO, which opens the Group Policy Management Console. Since the package is going to be assigned to users, right-click Software Installation under User Configuration.

2. Before you make a new package, you might want to check the default options, if only to add any categories you might want to assign the package to. Go to the properties page and make sure that the package will uninstall when it falls out of the scope of management, will install with a basic interface, and the category you want it to be listed under in Add/Remove Programs is there (This is very helpful for modified installs, as they will be organized by category, so you can clump them together for easier identification. The category name I've chosen to add for this example is Modified.) Never hurts to check your defaults.

FIGURE 12.48

Adding a category to default Software Installation properties

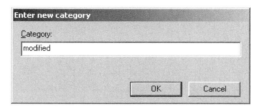

3. Now it's time to add the new package. Right-click Software Installation and, from the context menu, choose New\Package. Type in the network path for the MSI file and click OK.

4. In the Deploy Software dialog box, you must select Advanced (see Figure 12.49). If you do not, the package will deploy without its MST.

FIGURE 12.49

Advanced deployment

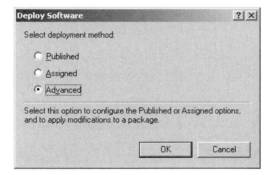

5. On the General tab (see Figure 12.50), which is often overlooked, edit the display name of the package, which will show up in Add/Remove Programs. Specifying the modification is a good idea, as in my example, Microsoft Office XP Professional—Template Redirect. Not catchy, but it does the job.

6. On the Deployment tab (see Figure 12.51), make sure that Assigned is selected. Under Deployment Options, make certain that Uninstall This Application When It Falls Out of the Scope of Management is selected and, under Installation User Interface Options, that Basic is chosen.

FIGURE 12.50

Changing the
display name

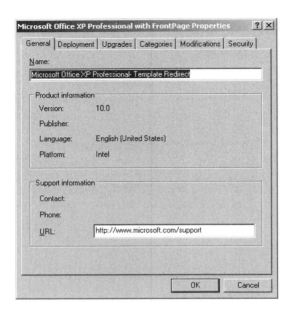

FIGURE 12.51

Deployment settings
for modified
Office XP

7. On the Upgrades tab, you can upgrade a previously deployed version of Office. In this example, it will be Office 2000. Click Add to specify what packages this MSI will upgrade (see Figure 12.52). You can choose to either have the package upgrade or remove and replace the previously deployed versions. I prefer to remove and replace to ensure that no stray bits of the previous version will remain. If the previous versions were not installed by Windows Installer, you can require an upgrade (which basically removes and replaces) by checking the Required Upgrade for Existing Packages check box under the Add button back on the Upgrades tab.

FIGURE 12.52

Adding the upgrade package

8. Assign the modified category to the package, as shown in Figure 12.53. The category that you created in the Software Installation properties page should appear in the left column. After you select the category, add it to the right column to make sure that it has been applied.

FIGURE 12.53

Adding a category

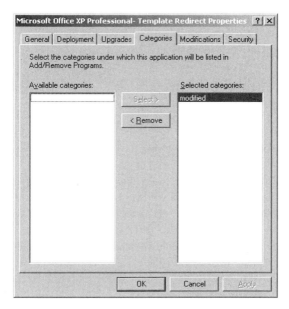

9. Okay, this is the important part of the operation modification. Notice the warning at the bottom of the Modifications tab that says not to press OK until you're sure you've made all the appropriate modifications. Heed this warning. Click Add to get the MST. Make sure to type in the full network path. Click Open. As shown in Figure 12.54, the MST will be listed in the Modifications list box.

FIGURE 12.54

Adding the MST modification file

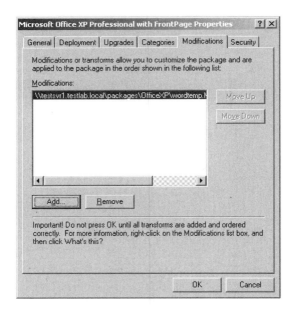

10. Take a deep breath; you're done. Click OK. The package is ready to deploy. Close the Group Policy Management Console and go back to the domain properties page. You can check the Security tab to make sure everyone who should be getting the install is listed with the Apply Group Policy box checked. Then go to the Group Policy tab, and uncheck the Disable This GPO check box. If you are superstitious, click Apply, otherwise just click OK.

It's enabled. Now, when domain users log on, they will be getting the service-packed, modified Office XP.

DEPLOYING OPERATING SYSTEM UPDATES

Next on the list is installing Service Pack 1 for Windows XP.

No problem.

You can force users to be unable to do automatic updates on their computers with a group policy. Although it is a good idea to control which version of what the users have on their systems (especially since patches can be great little carriers of viruses), it does mean that you will have to patch their systems for them. To this end, Microsoft has made life easy. A little quirky perhaps, but easy.

Remember, service packs affect computers, so do not deploy them to users. Also, do not apply a service pack for one operating system to a computer that is running a different operating system. In

Active Directory, I created a group for XP Professional computers and a group for 2000 Professional (the two OSes I have on my network). To apply a group policy, I only need to add the Windows XP group to the security list in the GPO properties, and make sure that no other group is checked to apply group policy.

1. Download the network installation version of the service pack and extract its contents to a folder. For convenience, download it onto the machine that you are going to extract the contents to. You'll see why in a moment. For Service Pack 1 in this example, the filename is `xpsp1_en_x86.exe`, and I downloaded it onto `testsvr1`.

2. In the Run box, type **xpsp1-en-x86.exe /u**. No matter what path you give the service pack to extract to, it will create a randomly named folder on the C: drive and extract to that (see Figure 12.55). Maybe later service packs won't behave this way, but this one does.

FIGURE 12.55

Service pack extraction to a random folder

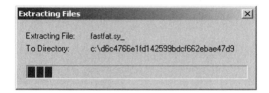

While it's extracting, make note of this random folder name. When it's done, go to the folder and check to make sure that the extraction worked (see Figure 12.56). An example of a problem would be if the folder were empty.

FIGURE 12.56

Random folder on the C: drive

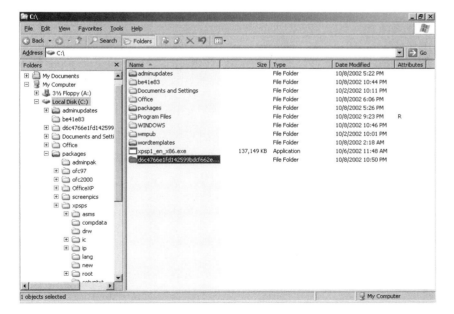

3. Copy the contents of the random folder (in it will be many files and folders; don't leave any behind) to the folder from which you want to share the service pack (in my case, it is in the 1-sp folder within the `service packs` folder, under the `packages` folder).

4. From here, it is just a matter of creating a GPO for the domain, going to the GPO's properties, and making sure that under the Security tab no one but the XP computer users are going to have this group policy apply to them. I do this by adding my domain local group XP Machines and ensuring that no one but that group has the Apply Group Policy permission checked (as shown in Figure 12.57).

FIGURE 12.57

Filtering the GPO to apply only to XP machines

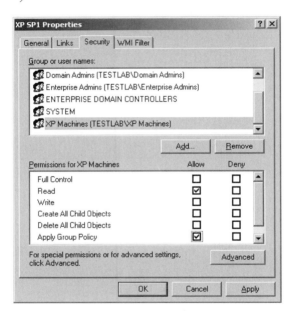

5. Edit the GPO and right-click Software Installation under Computer Configuration. Add the `update.msi` package. In this example, it's stored in the `Update` folder among the extracted files, which are located in `\\testsvr1.testlab.local\packages\service packs\1-sp\update\update.msi`.

6. You have to assign the package—no publishing to computers is allowed. Click OK.

You're done. Now you just have to wait for the Windows XP Professional computers to restart a few times to ensure that the GPO has been applied.

CREATING AND DEPLOYING A ZAP

The next thing on the boss's list is deploying the PDF reader. Funny, the easiest thing to deploy is the most limited. To support legacy installation files, Windows Installer recognizes the ZAP file. A ZAP file is a simple text file, like an INI or `unattend.txt`, that points to an executable file and runs it. It's that simple.

ZAP files, as you may recall, cannot be assigned, upgraded, reliably uninstalled, or anything else that requires extensive rollback information. It can only be published. That's it. But you can publish service packs that you want users to install. You can publish any setup file that you can get in its entirety. I have even published self-extracting zipped files containing anything from templates to backgrounds. The point of a ZAP is to get an application to the users. Nothing fancy, but it works.

To create a ZAP file, open Notepad. The file must be a simple text file, no Word documents here, no formatting. Just words.

This sort of file is broken into sections. The section names are in square brackets ([ ]), such as [application]. The syntax is simply *command = thing that applies to the command*. The command itself must be one word and cannot contain spaces. If it's a two-word command, the command becomes a compound word, for example, **setupcommand**. And, like any good batch or INI file, comment lines are always preceded by a semicolon (;). An underscore (_) is used as a continuation symbol if you need a path to be read as if it were all one line, but it's too long to fit.

Another interesting syntax point is the extensions section. To indicate an extension that is associated with the program you're installing, type the three-letter extension and an equal sign, for example, **zip =**. That's it—there's nothing after the equal sign. (I always end up wondering, "Equal to what?") If you type something after the equal sign, it will be ignored.

NOTE *The ZAP file points to the actual setup file in order to run it. Make sure the setup command line truly equals the setup's location in relation to the ZAP file. Don't move it after the ZAP file is made and expect the ZAP to work. I, being lazy, always make sure the setup file and its ZAP are in the same folder. That way, I don't have to type in any long paths to show the setup command location.*

Here's an example of how easy it is to make a ZAP file:

1. Open Notepad and type in the following, which is two sections, four command lines and some comments (see Figure 12.58).

```
;Zap file for Adobe Acrobat Reader 5.0.5

;the application section is required

[application]
;friendlyname and setupcommand are required, displayversion is just for
;my convenience.  It shows the version in add/remove programs

friendlyname = "Acrobat 5.0.5"
setupcommand = ar505enu.exe
displayversion = 5.0.5

[ext]
;this section is optional
PDF =
```

Remember that the extensions you add to the [ext] section will be the auto-install file associations.

FIGURE 12.58

Acrobat ZAP file

```
;Zap file for Adobe Acrobat Reader 5.0.5

;the application section is required

[application]
;friendlyname and setupcommand are required, displayversion is just for
;my convenience.  It shows the version in add/remove programs

friendlyname = "Acrobat 5.0.5"
setupcommand = ar505enu.exe
displayversion = 5.0.5

[ext]
;this section is optional
PDF =
```

2. Save the file with a `.zap` extension; for example, `Acrobat.zap`. Make sure that the file does not end up being saved with the `.txt` extension tacked on to the end, such as `Acrobat.zap.txt`. The file must have a `.zap` extension at the end of the filename.

3. To deploy it, just add the ZAP to a GPO for the Sales OU, as if it were an MSI. Then publish it.

Pretty easy, huh? It works really well when the EXE file must get out to the clients as quickly as possible—as long as it can be published, that is.

But what if you need to *assign* an EXE to the clients? Or maybe you need to deploy the software by computer account? What then, are you doomed to manual installs?

No, you'll just have to make your own MSIs. That's right, make your own. For free too. It's a little time consuming and a little detail oriented, but it can be done.

HOW TO TURN AN ORDINARY INSTALLATION FILE INTO AN MSI

The last item in the boss's scenario is to give the users the ability to create self-extracting ZIP files for their clients. Sounds like a job for ZAP, doesn't it? Except for one small thing: the users cannot be depended on to (or should not) go to Add/Remove Programs and install their own software, so the software should not be published.

You could just have the users invoke the software by opening a previously zipped file, but they are not using the software to open ZIP files, they are using it to create them, and there's a chance they will have to create the self-extracting ZIP before they end up opening one. So, publishing the software and hoping that the users invoke it properly can't be guaranteed to work either. This looks like a job for (drum roll, please) an MSI assigned to the user accounts. Thus, the need to make your own.

The point of making an EXE file into an MSI is to be able to handle the installation as if it were a native Windows Installer package. It sounds almost too good to be true, and yes, there are some wrinkles in the system, but all in all it works pretty well.

Also, you can't publish to a computer account, so if a standard installation absolutely, positively must be on every machine in your company, you have to use a MSI, because a ZAP must be published. That's why Microsoft and a company called OnDemand Software got together to bundle a free MSI package creator with every copy of Server 2003. Now, be aware, as of this writing, OnDemand Software has not released the current version of their product, so it may not be on the Server 2003 CD. Instead, you will have to download it (check the Server CD for details). It'll be free either way, though.

What is this nifty free MSI packager called, you ask? It's called WinINSTALL LE (Lite Edition) of the full-blown WinINSTALL 8. Despite its "lite" designation, WinINSTALL LE is a surprisingly useful piece of software.

The concept is pretty straightforward. For an MSI to function, it has to have a table of information (and access to the files themselves) about what files get added to a system upon installation, what files get deleted, and what Registry changes get made. But with standard installation files such as `setup.exe`, there is no list of what those changes were or copies of what files were added for recovering from corruption.

Hmmm, EXEs change things upon execution, and MSIs change things *and* keep a database of those changes. The only difference, really, is that there is a record of what was changed along with the actual executable itself.

What if I took a snapshot of a workstation before I run an installation file like `setup.exe`, and took a snapshot after I ran it, then compared the two and created a big, detailed table of all the things that were changed? That would include all the added files, all the deleted files, and any other changes, like shortcuts and Registry alterations. I wonder if that would work?

Yes, it would. As a matter of fact, that is what WinINSTALL LE does. Of course, it's not absolutely perfect. Because there are so many different kinds of programs out there, especially ones with copy protections and other security features, no one can be ready for everything. Some products frequently alter what WinINSTALL LE would consider static (like time-sensitive security information that might change every time the computer reboots). This makes the package keep reinstalling itself because it thinks that the changes mean something has gotten corrupted. For that reason, products with these kinds of features are not candidates for packaging into an MSI (or as Microsoft calls it, "repackaging").

To make sure it won't miss anything, WinINSTALL LE tends to be *too* thorough and records hardware changes or system information that is not necessarily something it needs to worry about. That's why you need to be familiar with what gets excluded and included in any MSI that WinINSTALL LE builds. It's a pretty easy fix and a really convenient way to make do-it-yourself MSIs without having to be a programmer.

The Server 2003 version of WinINSTALL LE has not been released as of the writing of this chapter, but OnDemand Software assures us that there will not be that many interface changes, so ignore the fact that my version has Veritas written all over it (not to mention subtle references to Seagate Software, from which Veritas was spawned), and that yours will probably say OnDemand Software. (That's because Veritas bought it from OnDemand Software, and then OnDemand Software bought it back. Such is business.)

WARNING *WinINSTALL LE isn't without its quirks. The most significant is its tendency to not save the changes it has made to the Registry. This means that, at login, the software might query its MSI to update the Registry for each user every time they log in. On occasion, it may even do a query when the software is opened for the day. This may be irritating and is therefore worth mentioning. To avoid this problem, you might want to have Windows Installer install software with elevated privileges (to allow programs installed at the user level to write to the Registry). Elevated privileges can be abused by knowledgeable users, so it may not be the most secure thing you could do, but it is a workaround.*

I happen to know that WinINSTALL LE works well on those little things that everyone needs, like WinZip and Acrobat Reader. I have also used it to deploy things like MP3 players (other than Media Player, of course), screenshot packages, and such. But, because WinINSTALL LE essentially records and then plays back *anything* that was changed between snapshots, you can do more than just make MSIs of installs. You can change the toolbars of the product being installed, add shortcuts to the quick launch area of the Taskbar, remove shortcuts from the Desktop, change preferences and options within the product, and do anything else you could think of that you would like to have set up before deploying the package to the user. It is a lot like working with an MST.

But there's more. What if you want to add a folder with a handbook, forms, phone directory, and other things in it, to the Desktop of all new employees? If you don't want to write a login script for these users, you can create an MSI using WinINSTALL LE. Just make a snapshot of a workstation, create the folder with the files in it on the Desktop, then do the After snapshot. Then, after making sure it does work fine (sometimes you have to make sure that it isn't trying to handle extraneous information, like computer names), deploy it to the users of your choice. Even if the users delete it, it will come back at their next logon. WinINSTALL LE is a pretty flexible and very useful tool, despite its simplicity.

Let's create an MSI package for WinZip. Remember, everyone in the company must be able to create self-extracting ZIP files, so this is it. To create an MSI, you need four things:

- The installation file upon which you are basing the MSI.
- The network sharepoint where the MSI will be stored.
- A "clean and quiet" workstation to create the snapshots on. This workstation needs to have the same OS (including service packs) as your user workstations and network access to the sharepoint.
- WinINSTALL LE itself, with its discovery program accessible from the clean workstation.

The frustrating thing about using WinINSTALL LE is that the workstation that the snapshot will be taken on *must* be perfectly clean. What that means is it needs to be stripped to the bare operating system with whatever service packs the user machines will have. No fancy wallpaper, no mapped drives, nothing. This is the snapshot you will be making a record of the complete state of the system. To be sure that no DLL file or system tray doodad is picked up that may conflict with something that could be installed on the target computers when the new MSI gets deployed, there must be no extraneous fluff on the snapshot workstation.

Now, that may sound easy, but it means that every time you create a new MSI and you install software on the clean workstation, the software needs to be removed completely. You'll have to wipe and reinstall the workstation every time you do a new snapshot, because it has been tainted with files that might distract WinINSTALL LE from its job. This is why it is a *really* good idea to create an image (using something like RIPrep, for example) for the clean workstation you will be working with. It makes it much easier and faster to make several MSIs in a day without spending hours wiping and reinstalling. Other than that, the rest of the process is rather easy.

Before you can use WinINSTALL LE, it has to be installed, of course. Chances are you will need to use the link provided either in the help files on Server 2003 or on the CD to download the necessary installation file. Be sure to install it on any other network accessible machine *except* the clean workstation. Quite logically, WinINSTALL LE is not going to be on the users' workstations, so it should not be part of an MSI snapshot. For this example, I downloaded it to and installed it on my Server 2003.

WinINSTALL LE comes in two parts: the discovery executable (called DiscoZ, interestingly enough), and the Software Console. The discovery program is what takes the snapshots and must be accessible from the clean workstation, so it should be located in a sharepoint. The Software Console is the program that makes it possible for you to view and edit the MSI's contents. It does not need to be accessed from the clean workstation, although it may be convenient to be able to do so.

TIP   *I tend to share out only the folder with the discovery program in it. If rights to that share were to fall into the wrong hands, those hands would still not be able to access the MSI editor.*

Once everything is in place—WinINSTALL LE is installed, your shares are set up, and the clean workstation is ready and imaged—you can get started.

Creating the MSI

The first half, the actual MSI creation, happens at the clean workstation. Make certain you are logged in with an account that has the right to write to the sharepoint where the MSI will be saved, access and execute the DiscoZ discovery file, and install software on the clean workstation. Generally, this is an Administrative account.

After you log in, you can either go to Start\Run and type in the network path to the discovery program (mine is `\\testsvr1.testlab.local\winstall\discoz.exe`), or browse to the share containing DiscoZ. The icon is a magnifying glass (see Figure 12.59). Double-click it.

FIGURE 12.59

The DiscoZ discovery executable

WinINSTALL LE's Discover Wizard will open. Close any windows you may have been browsing through before moving on—you want your Before snapshot to be as clean as possible (and notice in Figure 12.60 that the wizard basically says the same thing). To begin the discovery process, click Next.

FIGURE 12.60

Discover Wizard

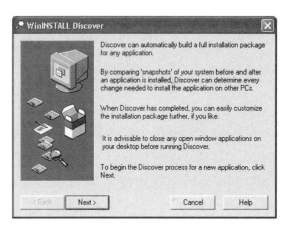

At this screen (see Figure 12.61), you will need to specify the installation file you are building the MSI for, the filename and location where the MSI (and its associated files) will be saved, and what language the installer dialog boxes should be in. My installation name is WinZip and the location of the MSI is \\testsvr1\packages\winzip.MSI, and, not surprisingly, the language I need for my dialog boxes is English. Click Next.

FIGURE 12.61

Specifying the MSI name and path

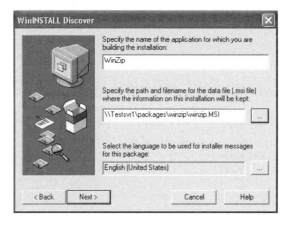

WARNING   *Do not neglect this part of the MSI building process. Because the MSI will be referred to by the client installs, it will explicitly record its location in its own database. Changing your mind and moving the MSI after it has been created is a bad idea. Although you can move the MSI and edit it later to point to its new location, it's better to keep it simple and do it right the first time.*

At this point (see Figure 12.62), you'll need to select the drive where Discover will store its temporary files. When the discovery process is over, these files will be removed. Unless you are really short on space, I suggest keeping the default C: drive selected. Click Next.

FIGURE 12.62

Choosing where to put Discover's temporary files

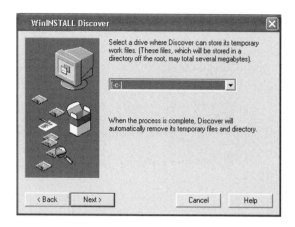

At this screen (see Figure 12.63), you choose which drives WinINSTALL LE will scan for changes. Select the drive(s) of your choice on the left and click the Add button to move it to the list on the right. Be sure to choose only the drives that are necessary. Unnecessary drives will slow down the process and will probably cause WinINSTALL LE to erroneously record changes that aren't really relevant to the install. Click Next.

FIGURE 12.63

Choosing drives to scan

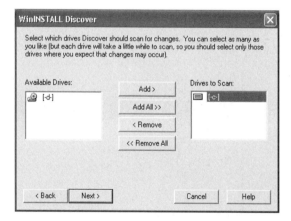

The next screen lets you specify what files and folders to exclude from the Discover scan. Here you can ensure that the My Documents folder will be ignored (should WinZip really care if you delete a file from the My Documents folder?), in addition to the Recycle Bin, temp folders, and swap files. If there are folders or files that you definitely want ignored during the scan, this is where to add them. The defaults are generally more than adequate, so if you are not sure what to exclude, stick with what's already there.

As shown in Figure 12.64, at the top left of the screen is a drop-down box. This is where the drives that you chose to be scanned are listed, one drive at a time. Each drive can have files and folders that need to be excluded. Beneath the drive drop-down box is the list of all the directories available for the selected drive. Faithfully following the theme so far in this wizard, on the right is the list of items actually selected to be excluded. Below that list of exclusions is a check box for Enhanced Registry Scan. Because the Registry can be complex, it's difficult to be sure that every single piece of data is caught in the scan. If you feel that you need to be extra thorough, check this box, although it will increase the time that it takes to do the snapshots. However, I find that this option simply creates more entries to go through during the edit phase, so I generally do not check it.

FIGURE 12.64

Deciding what to exclude from the Discover scan

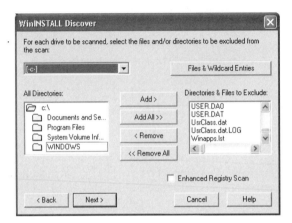

Above the exclude list is the Files and Wildcard Entries button. Click this to add a file or group of files (not just folders) to be excluded. Clicking it will bring you to a dialog box, shown in Figure 12.65, that will give you ample opportunity to browse through and select the files and folders you'd like to exclude from the Discover scan. If you do not wish to exclude any wildcard entries, click Cancel to return to the exclusion dialog.

FIGURE 12.65

Directories and Files to Exclude dialog box

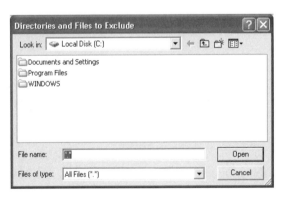

If you have nothing else to exclude that isn't already listed by default, click Next.

Immediately, the scan will start (see Figure 12.66). You can watch and see what files and Registry keys are read. A dialog box will come up, announcing that the Before snapshot is complete and asking for the setup program before completely closing out. Click OK and it will give you an opportunity to browse to the setup file and open it. In the example, my copy of the install file for WinZip is on the Server 2003, so I just browse to it and double-click.

FIGURE 12.66

The scan before software is installed

Again, immediately, the normal install process for WinZip begins.

The install finishes and WinZip opens. If you have to reboot after the install, be sure to do it, log back in with the same account (so you will have all of the rights you will need to finish the process), and open the newly installed program.

NOTE *By the way, although the evaluation version of WinZip is free, the registered version is not, and registration is required to make self-extracting files for distribution. Not only is it really cheap considering how darn useful it is, but you can also purchase a WinZip site license, to make it even cheaper per machine.*

Now is the time to modify the install to suit your users. I removed the shortcut from the Desktop, added the Make Exe button to the toolbar, and got rid of the Tip of the Day. This is also the time to run the program through its paces and make sure it works. If it doesn't work now, it won't work when you deploy it. Remember, if it's a product that keeps track of recently opened files and you opened some during this process, clear that list before going any further. Especially if you cannot guarantee that those files will be on the client workstations at the time of deployment.

A TRICK WITH SHORTCUTS

It is at this point in the MSI building process that I like to do one more thing. You see, WinINSTALL LE sees things in terms of packages, features, and components. Office XP has features like Word, Excel, or PowerPoint, which are separate executables but part of the same package. Each of these features has many components, such as clip art, a spell checker, templates, wizards, etc. Each feature of Office XP has its own shortcut. Well, the same thing is true of WinZip and most other products.

Now, strangely enough, any shortcut that WinINSTALL LE records for any feature does not actually point directly at the executable (as many shortcuts do), but at the feature, which then tells the shortcut where to go. Due to a shortcoming in WinINSTALL LE itself, the actual path to the feature and its executable may not work quite as one would hope. In an unusually complicated way, MSIs indicate location by creating folder properties, so each step in a path to an MSI is a property and doesn't resemble a path in any way that Windows would recognize. Because of this, it's possible that every time you double-click on the shortcut to the program, it will get a bit disoriented and reinstall itself. To prevent this from happening, I make note of every shortcut that WinZip creates; then, when I am in the Software Console, I redirect the shortcuts that I want to keep to point directly at the WinZip executable, *not* at a feature, and delete the ones I don't want. I find this really helps cut down on the times I have to tweak the MSI, reinstall, tweak, reinstall.

Once you've made all the changes that you feel are necessary, it is time to do the scan of what has changed, otherwise known as the After snapshot. Once again, either run DiscoZ or browse to it and give it a double-click. Remember to close all windows before you actually run the After scan.

The WinINSTALL LE Discover screen returns (see Figure 12.67). This time, sensing that a Before snapshot has been taken, it confirms the installation filename, MSI name, and path. If this is the correct information, make sure that Perform the "After" Snapshot Now is selected; otherwise, the Before snapshot will be abandoned and the After snapshot won't be taken. Then click Next.

FIGURE 12.67

Starting the After snapshot

TIP *If you just realized that you are not done configuring your installation, that's okay. Click Cancel, make your changes, and run DiscoZ again. Canceling does not abandon the process.*

The scanning begins (see Figure 12.68). Let it run through its paces. This may take a while, especially if you have chosen to do an enhanced Registry scan.

FIGURE 12.68

The scan after software is installed

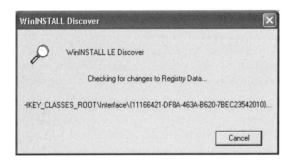

When the After snapshot is complete, you will get to experience a dialog box in conflict with itself (see Figure 12.69). The box will say Conversion Successful in the title bar, but will probably have several warnings listed within. As long as there are no explicit error messages displayed, it's all right. Generally, the warnings are about paths and URLs that WinINSTALL LE is worried will not work (a bit of CYA, I believe) or that should be installed once on a system and made available to all users (that is, assigned to a computer account). Remember that WinINSTALL LE has problems with paths and URLs, and because the MSI itself needs to be saved to a network sharepoint, there is nothing you can do to avoid having at least one URL warning. Windows accesses resources using paths, period. Make note of the warnings in case you can use the information when checking out the MSI itself, and click OK. You will then get a dialog box announcing that the After snapshot is complete. Congratulations.

FIGURE 12.69

Conversion Successful dialog box

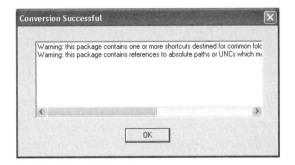

NOTE *The reason the conversion was successful was because WinINSTALL LE creates a NAI (OnDemand's own kind of installer package) and REG file and then converts them at the last minute into an MSI. Copies of the NAI and REG are kept in the same folder as any MSI that is created by WinINSTALL LE. The NAI refers to the REG (not surprisingly, it has the Registry edits in it) and can be used to recover an MSI that has gone bad. Just close the currently open MSI in the Software Console, go to File, and choose Convert NAI to MSI from the menu bar. During the convert process, just follow the instructions. Be sure to open the NAI in the folder of the current corrupted MSI. Be careful, as always, about where you save the conversion. The converted MSI should be identical to the old one.*

Editing the MSI

The next phase is using the Software Console. Let's take a look at the MSI we just built. Go to wherever you installed the Software Console (I put mine on the Server 2003.) Open the Software Console by going to the Start menu. If you have never used the Software Console before, it should look like Figure 12.70 (if you have used it before, it will open with the last MSI you were looking at still available).

FIGURE 12.70

Newly opened Software Console

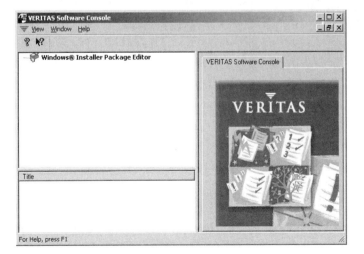

WARNING *If you have an existing MSI open in the Software Console, be careful. If you accidentally choose New instead of Open from the File menu, a new package will be created that will overwrite the currently open existing package. Yeah, the interface is a little quirky.*

As you can see, there are three sections to the Software Console window: tree view at the top left, list view on the bottom left, and data view, which is the largest section, on the right. The first time you use the Software Console, there is no obvious way to open a file. At first, there is no File on the menu bar. There's no Open icon on the toolbar, either. Here's the trick: click the Windows Installer Package Editor icon in tree view (top left). Then and only then will the menu bar change and File will appear. (You can also right-click the Windows Installer Package Editor and get basically the same result.)

NOTE *There still is no Open icon on the toolbar of the Software Console, nor is there any Save As option on the File menu.*

From either the File menu or the context menu, choose Open. Browse to where you have saved your new MSI (in the `WinZip` folder under `Packages`, in the example). Open it.

You will see the new MSI package listed in tree view. There is a plus sign beside it, indicating that there are items under it that haven't been displayed. Those items are separate features and components that help make up the whole package. Each item (from package to component) has properties and objects (such as shortcuts or files) associated with it. If you select the package and look at the list view on the bottom left (see Figure 12.71), you'll see icons representing the different associated properties and objects, such as Registry, Services, and INI edits. These help identify the changes that were recorded as part of the MSI.

FIGURE 12.71

The new MSI package in the Software Console

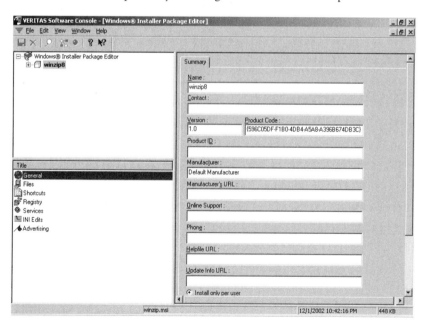

From list view, select General, and on the right side of the window in the data view section, you will see a summary of the properties of the MSI package. The name, version, product ID, even online support and phone number are available to be added. If you scroll down the summary, you will see that you can specify three ways that the package can be installed: per user; per computer; or per machine, or if that fails, per user. Choosing between installing per user or computer has a pretty big effect on how the MSI handles its Registry entries, so it is worth checking out.

If you click the plus sign next to the package in tree view, icons will appear beneath it—some will look like flowcharts with green and yellow shapes and some will look like green balls (as shown in Figure 12.72). The green and yellow icons indicate features, and the balls indicate components. If you click on a feature, note that in data view the summary (assuming you are still looking at General in list view) is different. A feature can be affected by how the MSI handles it, and this summary reflects that. Here is a brief list of the check boxes and what they mean:

Favor advertising   Advertise when possible.

Favor source   Run program from source rather than locally.

Favor parent   It is grayed out if there is no parent; feature inherits parent's properties.

Do not allow advertising   This one's self explanatory.

Do not display option to be Absent   Always install the selected feature (this one could've been more intuitively named).

Advertise only if the OS understands MSI Files   Feature will only install if the target machine has Windows Installer.

FIGURE 12.72

Feature data view summary

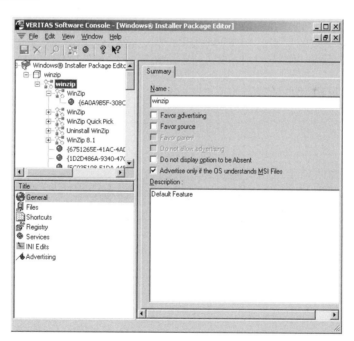

NOTE   *Sometimes WinINSTALL LE might get overzealous about advertising, installing itself every time it is opened. If you are having a reinstall problem, you might want to turn off advertising altogether. If the MSI cannot advertise, it has no choice but to do a full install. In doing so, however, the install will be unable to self-repair, because it will have severed ties with the MSI after installing.*

There is a description field at the bottom of the summary for adding notes or explanations about the feature and its settings. If you clicked on each feature for WinZip, there would be a different description for each, but most would have the same settings.

TIP *The interesting thing about features in WinINSTALL LE is that during the discovery process all shortcuts are identified in the final MSI as features. Strange but true. If you click the plus sign next to one of these shortcuts/features, you will see that there is one component associated with it. If you take a look at the general summary for that component, you will find the executable for that shortcut. That comes in handy when you have to manually change each shortcut's target from feature to executable file.*

If you click on a component in tree view (see Figure 12.73), you'll see that, once again, the summary is different. You could choose to run the component from Local (which is the default and means that it will run from the installed copy), from Source (CD or network share), or Optional (run from source or local, whichever works). If you think that the component will be sharing DLLs, you can do a Reference Count: Shared DLLs to keep track. Also, you can decide whether or not that particular component will be set as Permanent (never uninstall), Never Overwrite, or Transitive (can be overwritten/upgraded).

FIGURE 12.73

Component data view summary

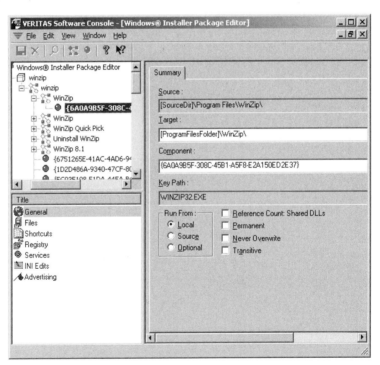

You might think most of the summary information is not that important because I keep everything at its default, but it does give you an idea of some of the changes you can make to an MSI. Also, the summary information does come in handy when troubleshooting the MSI.

Speaking of behavior, it's time to use the Software Console for the task at hand: finding out if DiscoZ has recorded any unnecessary information in the MSI. Remember, the MSI should only contain things that refer to the install of the software directly (in this case, WinZip). You need to go through the different files, shortcuts, Registry entries, and such and ferret out all the unnecessary stuff. This requires a lot of guesswork, especially if it involves Registry entries. When in doubt, keep the entry. Because WinINSTALL LE does not have a Save As option on the File menu, there is no safe way to make a change and then undo it, so I usually make a copy of the MSI's folder and all of its contents. If I mess it up, I can replace it with my backup copy and go back to a cleaner version.

Keep in mind that the package represents all of its features and components, so if you have the package selected in tree view and you remove a file from the list of files added during install, it will remove it from the list of files for any feature or component that uses it. That is true overall, so it is easier to search through the different items while looking at the package and then browse all of the components and features later just to be sure.

As you can see in Figure 12.74, the files added for the WinZip MSI seem in order—license, order, readme, vendor, and whatsnew are all standard files for any software. The files that have WZ in their name are obviously the WinZip files that were added during install. You can tell this because they are under the Add tab in the data view. There are also files that can be removed (especially if this is an upgrade) during install, and fonts that can be added (although WinZip doesn't have any). At the top of each tab is an Add button, a Properties button, and a Delete button. If you find any extraneous files that were added, say wmplayer.exe for example, delete it because it obviously does not refer to the installation (in this example, WinZip). At this time, though, WinINSTALL LE seems to have done a good job recording the correct files to add during install.

FIGURE 12.74

Files to be added by the MSI package

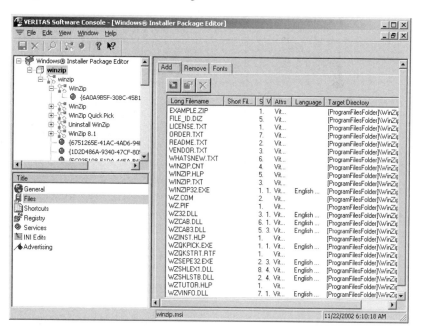

Check the executable file associated with each feature. The executable and its path can be used to redirect the feature's shortcut to point to its executable and avoid any shortcut errors upon install.

Speaking of shortcuts, let's take a closer look at them. While the package is selected in tree view, select Shortcuts from list view. Notice in data view (shown in Figure 12.75) that each shortcut for WinZip was recorded, along with its Description and Target. Note that the targets are all features; there are no actual executable files listed.

FIGURE 12.75

Shortcuts to be created by the MSI package

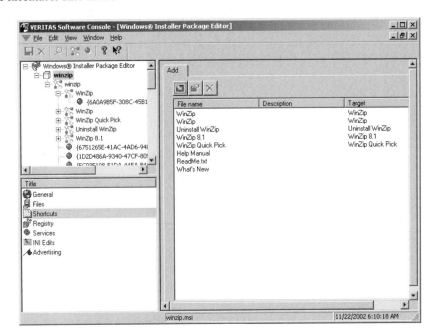

To fix that, you need to edit the properties of each misdirected shortcut. Start by selecting a shortcut (WinZip, for example) and clicking the Properties button (it's the hand holding an envelope) above the shortcut list in data view. In the Shortcut properties dialog box (see Figure 12.76), the target of the shortcut can be a feature or a file. Select the File radio button. In the field that becomes available beneath it, enter the correct executable filename and its path.

Because an MSI was meant to be installed on many different workstations, it uses the Windows variables for standard Windows objects, like the Start menu, or the System folder. For pointing at an executable, the default path would probably start in the Program Files folder. WinZip does create a folder called, appropriately enough, winzip, in the Program Files folder, and it puts its executables (and other files) there. Thus, your path in the File field would be

```
[ProgramFilesFolder]\winzip\winzip32.exe
```

TIP   If you can't remember what the exact name and syntax is for a Windows variable (specifically, those that pertain to locations of files and shortcuts), here's a tip. Above the Target information in the shortcut's properties page is a Create In field. Just to the right of it is a little Build button (it has three dots on it). Click it, and you'll see a list of standard locations that can have a shortcut in it. Beware, though: the variable names cannot have spaces in them, they must be between square brackets, and capitalization counts. For that matter, try to be sure that the entire path that you enter in the File field exactly matches the way the real folders are capitalized.

FIGURE 12.76

Pointing shortcuts at files instead of features

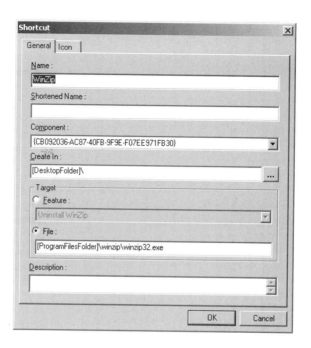

I just noticed the `Readme.txt` shortcut on the Start menu. That document is not generally something users need to see, so I am going to delete it. To delete a shortcut, select it in data view (see Figure 12.77) and click the Delete button (the one with the red X that's to the right of the Properties button).

FIGURE 12.77

Deleting the `Readme.txt` shortcut

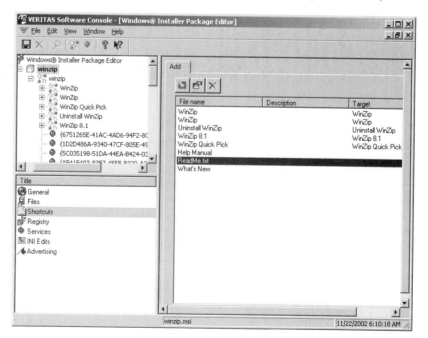

Next on the list of things to check are Registry entries. Be sure that the package is selected in tree view. Click on the Registry icon in list view.

On the right side of the window in data view, there will be two tabs, Add and Remove (see Figure 12.78). On the Add tab is an innocent-looking My Computer icon with a plus sign next to it. If you click the plus sign, you will see the HKEY folders. It's a good idea to avoid playing with the Registry. Too many programs do too many important things in it to be guessing, but you can look for obvious things, like Internet Explorer cache files or Windows cryptography settings. Such things are obviously not related to WinZip. You can also check and see if there are any machine-specific entries under the LOCAL_MACHINE key.

FIGURE 12.78

Registry changes that have been recorded in the MSI package

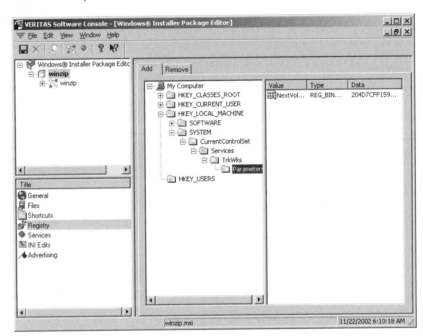

Click the plus sign next to the HKEY_LOCAL_MACHINE (if there is one for you; otherwise just take a look at Figure 12.78 and follow along). In this example, there is data beneath both the SOFTWARE and the SYSTEM subkeys. When I click the plus sign next to SYSTEM and follow the folders down, I discover that a service called TrkWks has been recorded. Hmmm. WinZip doesn't call on any services directly, and I don't believe that it requires the distributed link-tracking client to install (that's what TrkWks is). I can safely get rid of that.

Something to remember when removing an entry, though: be sure to prune as far up the keys as possible. Don't just remove the data and then leave all those empty folders sitting there pointing at nothing. It's bad form. To delete a Registry entry, select the folder containing the bad branch (in this case, SYSTEM has nothing in it but the TrkWks entry, so I'll delete the SYSTEM subkey and all below it), right-click the folder, and choose Delete (see Figure 12.79). Now the SYSTEM folder on the client installs will not be unnecessarily modified by this MSI.

FIGURE 12.79

Deleting SYSTEM
subkey and all its
contents

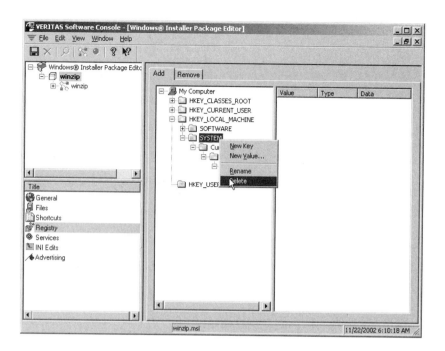

Also under HKEY_LOCAL_MACHINE is a SOFTWARE subkey that looks interesting. If you click the plus sign next to it, you'll discover that there are two subkeys, Microsoft and Nico Mak Computing. Nico Mak, what's that? I don't really know, but it is affiliated with WinZip, so it's okay. If you look under the Microsoft folder, you'll notice that there are two folders: Cryptography and Windows. In my case, the Windows folder (as you can see in Figure 12.80) has only WinZip-related info in it (except, maybe, the BitBucket), but the Cryptography folder, alas, is irrelevant. Delete that subkey, too.

By this point, you're probably getting the hang of this Software Console thing. Just remember, everything in the MSI should relate to the software you are installing. Anything you find that definitely isn't relevant should go. When in doubt, especially in the Registry, leave it alone.

Before you finish with the Software Console and start testing your MSI, let's take a quick look at the Advertising item in list view. Since WinZip does nothing with Services and INI files, they are empty (I checked), but Advertising, well, that's a different story.

As you well know, advertising an MSI involves being able to invoke the installation of a package by activating the correct file extension(s). Thus, you should check out extensions that WinINSTALL LE thinks will invoke (in this example) WinZip. Don't get me wrong—I've never had a problem with a misplaced extension, but it is always a good idea to check. Make sure that the package is selected in tree view and that Advertising is selected in list view, then click the Extensions tab in data view. Yup, there are all of the extensions. If there were any that were missing, you could add one by clicking the Add button. Mine, however (as you can see in Figure 12.81), look fine.

FIGURE 12.80

Perusing the HKEY_
LOCAL_MACHINE
subkeys in search of
irrelevant entries

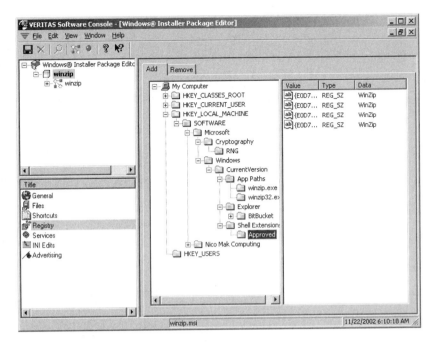

FIGURE 12.81

Extensions
associated with
the MSI package

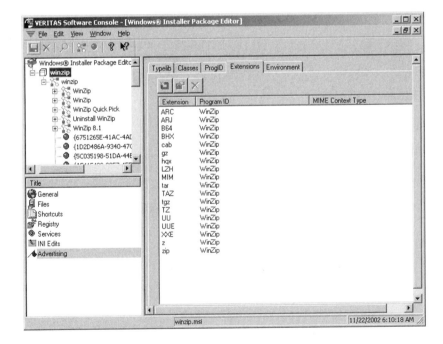

Testing the MSI

Now it is time to take the MSI for a spin around the block. I generally do at least one test run of any MSI I build. There is always a chance that you missed something that might cause a problem later.

TIP   Here's a trick. If you feel that there is a problem with the MSI, particularly on install, install it using MSIEXEC at the command line. Use log switch and record everything the install does. With WinZip, for example, at the command prompt, use the syntax: `msiexec /i \\testsvr1.testlab.local\packages\winzip.msi /L* c:\log_file.txt`*. The* `/L` *switch indicates that a log file should be kept, the asterisk indicates that all flags (such as errors or warnings) will be logged, and then the text file that will be created is specified. This should install the MSI on the workstation. Once it is done, open the log file in Notepad and see what happened. If there was an error, you can often see it there, even if all you actually see is a quick dialog box during install. It is also interesting to see what Registry entries get written when.*

Because I do so much testing, I have an OU called "test" that has two user accounts in it to log in to my test workstations. To do a trial run on my brand new MSI, I create a Group Policy Object called `winzipMSI` for the test OU. I then edit the new GPO and, as you can see in Figure 12.82, assign the `winzip.MSI` to the users.

FIGURE 12.82

Doing a test run assignment of new package

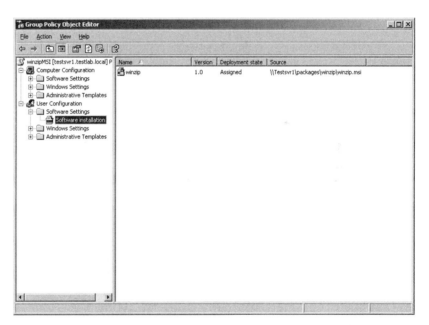

Then I log in at a clean workstation with one of the test OU user accounts and see if the install works. It does, right down to the Make EXE icon on the toolbar.

Once I try out the MSI on a few more machines and am certain that it will work in production, I create a GPO for the domain and assign the new WinZip MSI to the users. That's it. The users get their WinZip and we're done with the scenario—all items on the list have been accounted for. Congratulations.

NOTE *I used a simple, tried and true piece of software to demonstrate creating an MSI. Because of that, I really didn't have any problems. However, it is not uncommon to do several snapshots and numerous MSI edits, a test deployment, make some more changes, and then redeploy it, before the MSI is acceptable. Don't despair, and remember that OnDemand Software does support WinINSTALL LE by both e-mail and a Knowledge Base of known issues. Bear in mind that the software you are making into an MSI might have installation problems (even WinZip can), so check the software's Web site, too.*

Software deployment has come a long way. Gone are the days when you had to spend hours watching progress bars as you installed software at the users' computers. I certainly hope that the information in this chapter will help you get started with your company's software deployment methods. To recap, let's run down a list of what we have covered:

- Publishing software
- Assigning software to users and computers
- Uninstalling software because the client fell out of the scope of management
- Removing software
- Redeploying software
- Using Software Deployment to update computer operating systems
- Creating an administrative install to deploy Office XP
- Updating administrative installs
- Upgrading software
- Resolving some possible issues concerning synchronization
- Creating and deploying ZAP files
- Creating and deploying MSI files

Hmmmmm, not bad for a day's work. Thanks for stopping by.

Chapter 13

Configuring and Troubleshooting Network Print Services

"PAPERLESS OFFICE," MY SORE head. Even after years of interoffice e-mail and online documents, in many offices it's not official until you hold the printed evidence in your hand. Printing isn't sexy, but it's an inescapable—and vital—part of life in the networked office.

It's simply not practical—or necessary—to provide everyone in the office with a personal printer. Instead, you connect a printer to a print server and share the printer from there so that dozens or hundreds of people can use one printer. Of course, once dozens or hundreds of people depend on a single piece of equipment, that piece of equipment becomes pretty crucial. It needs to be up and running, dependable, and accessible to those who need it but off-limits to those who don't.

Hence this chapter. In the following pages, I'll talk about how to use Windows Server 2003 to complete the following tasks:

◆ Create a new local printer or connect to one already set up on the network or Internet.

◆ Secure the printer so that only those people who should be using it have access to it.

◆ Configure printer settings to help people find and troubleshoot print jobs.

◆ Speed up printing by making multiple printers look like one.

◆ Connect to a printer from a variety of different platforms.

◆ Troubleshoot the printing problems that will inevitably occur.

In the course of this chapter, I'll use the Microsoft terminology for referring to printers and printing functions. If you're not familiar with this vocabulary, read on before jumping in.

Print Services Terminology

Contrary to what you might have believed, a *printer* is, in fact, not that putty-colored box that you put paper into and printed documents come out of. In the Microsoft world, a printer is a logical device that's an intermediary between user applications and the *print device* (the thing that actually does the printing). All configuration settings apply to printers, not to print devices. The ratio of printers to print devices is not necessarily 1:1. You can have one printer and one print device, two printers for a single print device, or one printer and several print devices. I'll talk about *why* you might want to do any of these in the course of this chapter.

When you send documents to a printer, they become part of the printer's *queue*, the group of documents waiting to be printed. Although in other operating systems, such as OS/2, the queue was important as a primary interface between the application and printing devices, in all other forms of Windows NT (including NT, Win2K, and Server 2003), the printer plays this role. Even if they're pointing to the same print device, these printers work independently, so you can set up different printing options and permissions for each one and then set up the appropriate printer for people on the network.

Most people on your network won't have their own print device on their desk. Instead, to print they'll connect to a network-accessible printer via its connection to a *print server*, the computer on which printer drivers are stored. Most of this chapter will operate under the assumption that your network's printers are connected to a print server running Windows Server 2003. A *network-interface printer* is a printer directly connected to the network via a built-in network card.

NOTE *Even if the rest of your network is running Server 2003 or XP, your print server doesn't have to—and vice versa. A print server can run Windows for Workgroups, Windows 9x, any version of NT Workstation or Server, LAN Manager, or even (if you installed MS-Net) Windows 3.x or DOS. The options available to you will depend on the operating system; if your print server runs an operating system other than Server 2003, then some of the information in this chapter may not apply to you.*

GETTING ACQUAINTED WITH THE SERVER 2003 PRINTING INTERFACE

As with much of Server 2003, the first step in learning how to administer printers is to find out where all the printer management tools *are*. I won't get into the details of how to use these tools just yet, but when you're looking for the right tool for the job, this sidebar should help you find it.

To set up the printer for using forms, to configure printer ports, to add or update printer drivers, or to set spooling or error management options, you'll need to configure the printer server, not the printer or print device. Printer server properties are available from the Properties option in the File menu of the Printers and Faxes window. The Printers and Faxes window is accessible from the Control Panel, or from the Start menu.

Individual printer properties, such as the printer's description, sharing options, port used, spooling options, and device settings, are set from printer-specific properties pages. You can get to them either by right-clicking a printer's icon in the Printers and Faxes menu and choosing Properties from the context menu or by choosing Properties from the File menu of a particular printer's queue window. Because all printers are independent entities—even if pointing to the same print device—editing one printer's properties pages has no effect on any other printer.

The Server 2003 Printing Model

The process of printing is a bit more complex than it (hopefully) looks from the outside. The NT printing model uses several components to render application data for graphical output, get the data to a printer, and then help the printer manage multiple print jobs. Some of the following information on *how* printing works is background, but it's also helpful when it comes to troubleshooting, so wade through it if you can.

The main chunks of NT-based printing are the Graphics Device Interface (GDI), the printer driver, and the print spooler.

NOTE *The explanations here apply to all NT-based server operating systems: NT, Windows 2000, and Server 2003.*

The Graphics Device Interface

The Graphics Device Interface (GDI) is the portion of the operating system that begins the process of producing visual output, whether that output is to the screen or to the printer. Without the GDI, WYSIWYG output would be impossible. To produce screen output, the GDI calls the video driver; to produce printed output, the GDI calls the printer driver, providing information about the print device needed and the type of data used.

The Printer Driver

Printer drivers are the software that enable the operating system to communicate with a printer. They're incompatible across operating systems, so although any Win32 operating system can print to a print server without first installing a local printer driver—they'll just download it from the print server—you'll have to make sure the drivers are available for the clients that will be using the printer. That means that even though you've attached the printer to a print server, you'll need to install the Windows 98 printer drivers on that server if any network client computers are running Windows 98.

These printer drivers are composed of three subdrivers that work together as a unit:

◆ Printer graphics driver
◆ Printer interface driver
◆ Characterization data file

The printer graphics driver renders the GDI commands into Device Driver Interface (DDI) commands that can be sent to the printer.

You need some means of interacting with and configuring the printer. The role of the printer interface driver is to provide that means. The printer interface driver is your intermediary to the characterization data file, providing the information you see in a printer's properties pages.

The characterization data file provides information about the make and model of a specific type of print device, including what it can do: print on both sides of a piece of paper, print at various resolutions, and accept certain paper sizes.

The Print Spooler

The print spooler (SPOOLSS.DLL, in %systemroot%\system32) is a collection of dynamic link libraries (DLLs) and device drivers that receive, process, schedule, and distribute print jobs. It's implemented with the Spooler service, which is required for printing, and has the following components:

◆ Print router
◆ Local print provider
◆ Remote print provider

◆ Print processors

◆ Print monitor

THE PRINT ROUTER

When a client computer connects to a print server, communication takes place in the form of remote procedure calls from the client's print router (`WINSPOOL.DRV`) to the server's print router (`SPOOLSS.DLL`). At this point, the server's print router passes the print request to the appropriate print provider: the local print provider if it's a local job, and either the Windows or NetWare print provider if sent over the network.

THE PRINT PROVIDER

To find the right print provider, the print router polls the Windows print provider. This provider then finds the connection that recognizes the printer name and sends a remote procedure call to the print router on the print server. That local print provider then writes the contents of the print job to a spool file (which will have the extension `.spl`) and tracks administration information for that print job.

TIP   *By default, all spool files are stored in the* `%systemroot%\system32\spool\printers` *directory. If you like (perhaps if you've installed a faster hard drive that you'd prefer to spool from, or you're trying to avoid a fragmented hard disk), you can change that location by adjusting the value of the print server settings on the Advanced tab. To get there, open the Printers and Faxes folder and choose Server Properties from the File menu. Move to the Advanced tab, and you'll see the spooler settings, including the location of the spool file.*

The print server normally deletes spool files after the print job they apply to is completed, because they only exist to keep the print job from getting lost in case of a power failure to the print server. If you want to keep track of such data as the amount of disk space required by spool files and what printer traffic is like, you can enable spooler event logging.

THE PRINT PROCESSOR

A print processor works with the printer driver to "de-spool" spool files during playback, making any necessary changes to the spool file based on its data type.

Er—*data type?*

The data type for a print job tells the print spooler whether and how to modify the print job to print properly. This is necessary because methods of print job creation aren't standardized; for example, a Win2K client won't create a job the same way a Linux client does. Therefore, a variety of print server services exist to receive print jobs and prepare them for printing. Some of these print services assign no data type (in which case Server 2003 uses the default data type in the Print Processor dialog box), and some assign a data type.

The spool file can accept data from the print provider in one of two forms: Enhanced Metafile (EMF) or RAW. EMF spool files are device-independent files used to reduce the amount of time spent processing a print job; all GDI calls needed to produce the print job are included in the file. Once the EMF file is rendered, you can continue using the application from which you were printing. All the rest of the print processing will take place in the background. Unlike EMF spool files, which still require some rendering once it's determined which printer they'll be spooled to, RAW spool files are fully rendered when created. All else being equal, EMF spool files are normally smaller than RAW spool files because they're generic instructions for rendering, not complete renderings.

WinPrint, the NT operating systems print processor, understands four versions of EMF data files (1.003–1.008), three kinds of RAW data files, and TEXT files, which have the characteristics shown in Table 13.1.

TABLE 13.1: WHICH DATA TYPE DO I NEED?

DATA TYPE	DESCRIPTION	SUPPORTED BY
EMF	Tells WinPrint that the job was created in Windows and is already partially rendered. WinPrint works with the GDI and printer driver to complete the rendering, then returns the job to the local print provider.	Print clients with NT-based operating systems
RAW	Tells WinPrint not to modify the print job at all, but to return it to the local print provider.	All printer clients
RAW [FF Auto]	Tells WinPrint to check for a form-feed command at the end of the print job. If one isn't there, WinPrint adds it and then returns the job to the local print provider.	All printer clients
RAW [FF Appended]	WinPrint adds a form-feed command to the print job and then returns the job to the local print provider.	All printer clients
TEXT	Tells WinPrint that the print job is ASCII text to be printed as hard copy and as is. WinPrint uses the GDI and the printer driver to produce this output, then sends the new job to the local print provider.	All printer clients

The default data type is RAW, supported by all Windows clients. To select a different data type, open a printer's properties pages and turn to the Advanced tab. Click the Print Processor button to display a list of possible print processor types. Select a different data type from the list and click OK. The new data type will be used for all print jobs that don't specify that another data type should be used.

That said, don't change the data type unless you're *sure* it's a good idea. It isn't often. If a print client can use EMF files, it will do so even if the default data type is RAW, so you're not losing anything by making RAW the default. In contrast, if you make EMF the default data type, then Windows $9x$ clients won't be able to print. No error messages will appear on the client that initiated the print job, and no errors will show up on the print server's console, but the print jobs they send along will disappear into the ether.

THE PRINT MONITOR

The print monitor is the final link in the chain getting the print job from the client application to the print device. It's actually two monitors: a language monitor and a port monitor.

The *language monitor*, created when you install a printer driver if a language monitor is associated with the driver, comes into play only if the print device is bidirectional. A bidirectional print device can send meaningful messages about print job status to the computer. In this case, the language monitor sets up the communication with the printer and then passes control to the port monitor. The language monitor supplied with Server 2003 uses the Printer Job Language. If a manufacturer created a printer that spoke a different language, it would need to create another language monitor, as the computer and print device must speak the same language for the communication to work.

The *port monitor's* job is to transmit the print job either to the print device or to another server. It controls the flow of information to the I/O port to which the print device is connected (a serial, parallel, network, or SCSI port). The local port monitor supplied with Server 2003 controls parallel and serial ports; if you want to connect a print device to a SCSI port or network port, you must use a port monitor supplied by the vendor. Regardless of type, however, port monitors interface with ports, not printers, and are in fact unaware of the type of print device to which they're connected. The print job was already configured by the print processor.

By default, only the locally required print monitor is installed. To use another monitor, you'll have to create a new port in the printer configuration settings.

The Printing Process

Those are the parts of the printing process. Here's how they fit together when printing from an NT-based client operating system:

1. The user chooses to print from an application, causing the application to call the GDI. The GDI, in its turn, calls the printer driver associated with the target print device. Using the document information from the application and the printer information from the printer driver, the GDI renders the print job.

2. The print job is next passed to the spooler. The client side of the spooler makes a remote procedure call to the server side, which then calls the print router component of the server.

3. The print router passes the job to the local print provider, which spools the job to disk.

4. The local print provider polls the print processors, passing the print job to the one that recognizes the selected printer. Based on the data type (EMF or RAW) used in the spool file, any necessary changes are made to the spool file in order to make it printable on the selected print device.

5. If desired, the separator page processor adds a separator page to the print job.

6. The print job is de-spooled to the print monitor. If the printer device is bidirectional, then the language monitor sets up communications. If not, or once the language monitor is done, the job is passed to the port monitor, which handles the task of getting the print job to the port the print device is connected to.

7. The print job arrives at the print device and prints.

That's how print servers see printing. Good stuff to know when it comes time to troubleshoot printing problems. For the rest of the chapter, however, we'll concentrate on how *you* see printing.

Setting Up a Printer Connection

The day hasn't yet come when you can always plug a printer into a server and expect the server to find it without you telling it that there's a printer there. Until it does, you'll need to either create the printer locally or connect to a printer on the network. You will need to set up support for a printer to use it from a computer if any of the following conditions apply:

♦ You're installing support for a printer connected directly to one of the parallel or USB ports of the local machine.

♦ You're installing support for a network-interface printer.

♦ You're defining a printer that sends information to a file (as opposed to a print device).

♦ You're making a second printer for a print device.

I'll describe first how to set up a new printer and then how to connect to a printer already installed on the network.

Installing a Printer on a Print Server

All printer management begins in the Printers and Faxes window, available either from its shortcut in the Control Panel or from the Start menu. There's an Add Printer Wizard in the `Printers and Faxes` folder that you must run to set up a printer on the local computer.

To create a new printer connected to the local machine, follow these steps:

1. Open the Printers menu and click the Add Printer icon you'll see there. Click Next in the opening screen of the Add Printer Wizard (the opening window isn't important; it tells you only that you're using the Add Printer Wizard in case you hadn't figured that out) to get to the screen shown in Figure 13.1. For this example, choose the default option, Local Printer, and click Next.

FIGURE 13.1

Specify first whether the printer is connected to the local computer or on the network.

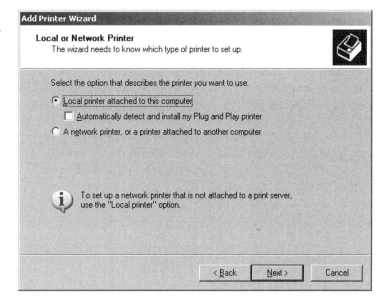

2. If you're setting up a Plug-and-Play printer attached to the printer server, you can tell the server to detect it by clicking the check box visible in Figure 13.1. If not, or if you're creating a printer to send output to a file, you will have to tell the Add Printer Wizard which port the printer is connected to from the drop-down list (see Figure 13.2). When connecting to a locally attached printer, this is simple—just make sure you've selected the port the printer is plugged into. To create a printer that stores print information in a file, choose the FILE option near the bottom of the list. Click Next.

FIGURE 13.2

Choose the printer's port from the list.

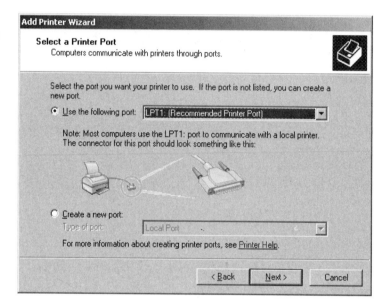

NOTE *Any TS ports (e.g., TS0001) near the bottom of the list represent printers connected to a computer currently connected to the server via RDP connection. There will be one port for each network or locally attached printer on the client computer. Don't connect a printer to them unless you're manually redirecting a printer to a terminal client session—something you'll rarely need to do. (See Chapter 16, "Terminal Services," to find out why.)*

3. Next, you'll choose the driver needed for your particular printer. From the list presented, choose the printer's manufacturer from the left and the printer model from the right. By default, the server will use its own printer driver. If you've got a newer one from the manufacturer or from the manufacturer's Web site, click the Have Disk button and provide the path to the driver. If the Windows Server 2003 is connected to the Internet, you can alternatively click the Windows Update button to automatically download a newer driver from the Microsoft Web site, if one is available. Click Next.

TIP *If the driver you need is already installed on the system—perhaps for a different printer that you already created—the Add Printer wizard will ask if you want to use the existing driver or replace it with the new one. Generally speaking, newer is better. Just make sure that you test printer drivers before putting them into production, as a buggy printer driver can cause a server to crash.*

4. After you've chosen a driver to use, the Add Printer Wizard asks you to name the printer using, by default, the printer's model name (see Figure 13.3). The name cannot contain a comma, backward slash, or exclamation point, but it has few other restrictions. The name you choose can be quite long—up to 220 characters—but I don't recommend making the name any longer than is strictly necessary to be descriptive, and if you plan to do any command-line management your life will be simpler if the printer name has no spaces in it. (Names with spaces must be enclosed in quotes when you address them in batch files.) Click Next to move on.

FIGURE 13.3

Choose a local name for the printer.

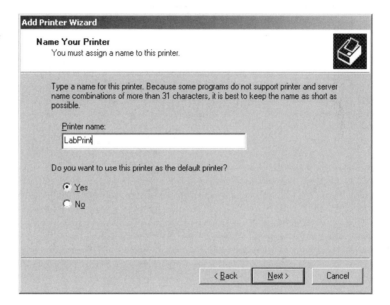

TIP *Keep printer names short and don't put spaces in them. First, if you're ever connecting to or managing the printer from the command line, do you really want to have to type* "This is the printer by the coffee machine; it's got a single paper tray and faces west" *when prompted for the name of the printer? Even identifying the printer in the Printers dialog box is harder if all the printers have overly long names because the names get cut off in the display. Second, some applications can't work with a name longer than 31 characters. If you can't fully identify a printer without creating a long name, you can always add a location and printer description, as I'll describe in a moment.*

5. Next, if you're sharing the printer, choose a share name for it. If the name you've given the printer has more than one word or a forward slash, the wizard will delete the spaces and combine the words until it has a single word up to eight characters long (see Figure 13.4). The reason for this is backward compatibility: DOS clients won't be able to connect to printers with names more than eight characters long or with spaces.

If you don't have DOS clients to worry about, you can make a new share name for the printer. Once again, the name may be up to 220 characters long and include spaces, but it can't contain commas, backward slashes, or exclamation points.

FIGURE 13.4

By default, the Add Printer Wizard will make a DOS-compatible name for the printer.

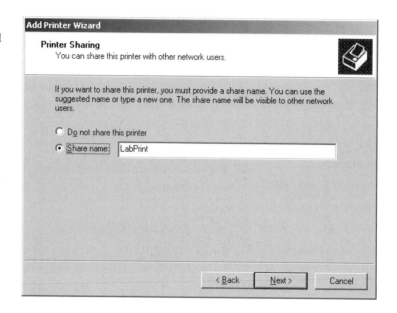

6. In the next stage of the installation, you'll have a chance to describe the printer and location (see Figure 13.5). The usefulness of these descriptions varies. Older clients (DOS, NT 4, Windows 9x, etc.) will display the information you enter into the Comment text box, but they won't be able to display what you enter into the Location box. Win2K and XP (and other Server 2003 servers) clients will be able to display both the Location and the Comments. Therefore, unless your network is composed entirely of Win2K or later computers, all important information should go into the Comment box. Click Next to move to the next screen.

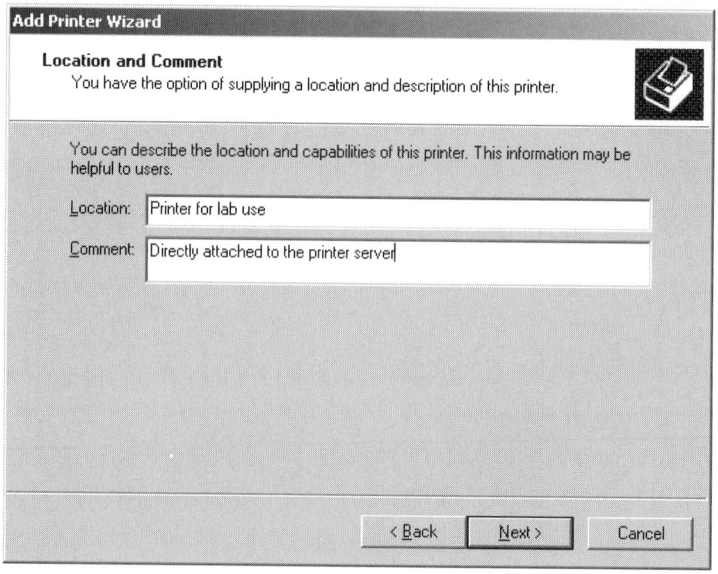

FIGURE 13.5

Only Win2K and later clients will be able to see the information you enter in the Location box.

7. The next screen asks whether you'll want to print a test page when you're done. Choose the Yes or No radio button and click Next. Can't hurt—it's a good way of seeing whether you set up the printer properly *before* you try to use it.

8. The final screen in the information-gathering part of the Add Printer Wizard (see Figure 13.6) shows the options that you entered at each stage so you can go back and change options if necessary. Review your choices and click the Finish button if you want to keep the settings. The computer will copy the drivers needed and, if you told it to do so, print the test page.

FIGURE 13.6

Review your choices before committing yourself with the Finish button.

Connecting to a Network-Enabled Printer

Network-enabled printers work similarly to locally attached printers, but with a couple of important differences. You'll need to be careful to set up the print device only on a single print server, and you'll need to set up a port to connect the printer to.

The reason for the first consideration may not be obvious. The thing is, that independent air the print device has as it sits off in the corner, separate from the printers on the network, is deceptive. That network-connected print device still needs a print server to spool documents to it, to manage its print queue, and so forth. It's just communicating with this print server through the network instead of through a parallel port. If a print device has two print servers pointing to it, it can get confused about which printer servers are sending which jobs to it, which can lead to garbled output as it tries to read two spooled files at once. (The busier the print device is, the more likely it is to get confused.) So don't confuse it. Although any server—or even workstation—could set up a printer for that print device locally, only give it one printer server.

The good news is that you're not likely to be overrun with people setting up rogue print servers. First, to set up a locally attached printer, you need Administrator or Account Operator privileges for the computer. Second, you'll need to create a special TCP/IP port for that printer's use. Since anyone doing so will need to know the name of the port and have the permission to create it on their computer, that should limit the number of people setting up rogue print servers.

Setting up a printer for a networked print device is much like setting up a printer for a locally attached printer, with a few exceptions. First, there's the matter of telling the Add Printer Wizard where the printer is. *Do* tell it that the printer is local. *Don't* check the box telling the wizard to automatically detect Plug-and-Play printers. It won't find it and you'll waste time searching for it.

Second, if you're creating the first printer for this network print device on the print server, you'll need to create the port for the printer to connect to. In the page prompting you to select a printer port, select Create a New Port and choose Standard TCP/IP port from the drop-down list. Click Next to begin the Add Standard TCP/IP Printer Port Wizard, and click Next to move through its opening screen.

1. Type the name of the port that the new print device uses. You can't make up a name here but must supply the name unique to this print device on the network, as shown in Figure 13.7. The port name must also be unique on the print server—you can't create the same port twice.

NOTE *If a printer for the networked print device is already set up somewhere on the network, you can find the port name by opening the printer's properties.*

FIGURE 13.7

Type the print device's port name.

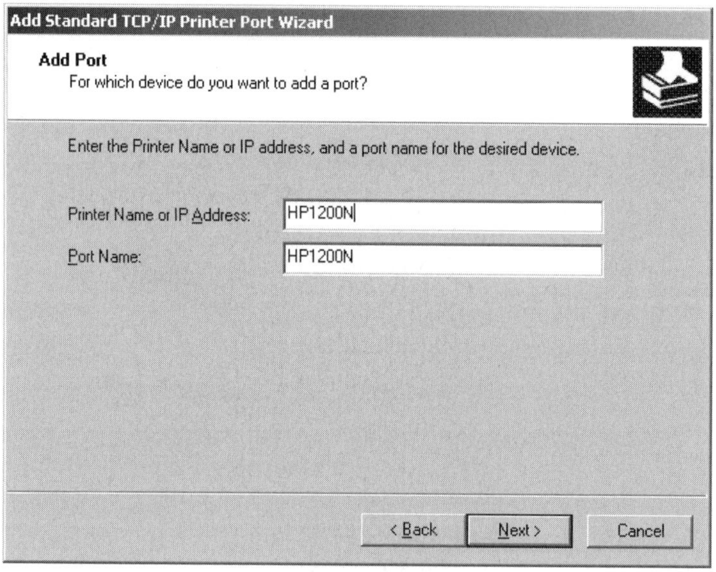

2. The wizard will look for a device using that name on the network. When it finds it, it may ask you for more information about the printer device's type, as in Figure 13.8. This isn't a fatal error—just find the printer in the drop-down list (in this example, HP Jet Direct) and click Next.

FIGURE 13.8

You may need to provide more information about the type of print device.

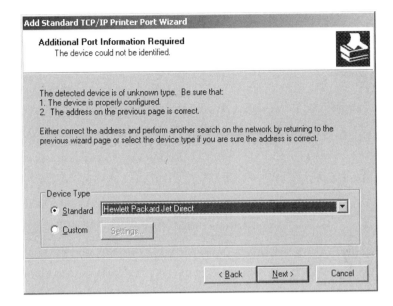

3. If the wizard can't find the print device at *all*, make sure that you've entered the port name correctly, that the print device is on, and that the network is set up correctly. Don't try to continue if the wizard simply cannot find the device (it's okay if it's unsure that the device is configured correctly), as doing so will just set up a useless port. When you've told the wizard about the kind of device it's looking for (or when it's found it on its own), click Next to review your choices in the box shown in Figure 13.9.

FIGURE 13.9

Review the port settings and click Finish to continue setting up the printer.

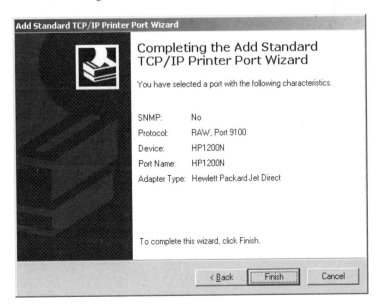

That's it. You've now created a TCP/IP port, and the Add Printer Wizard will continue as it did for creating a locally attached printer.

Connecting to a Shared Printer

Some servers—such as the terminal servers discussed in Chapter 16—may need to connect to printers already set up on other print servers. To do so, start the Add Printer Wizard in Printers and Faxes and click the Add a Printer button on the left side of the folder. Click Next to move past the opening page. On the Local or Network page, choose A Network Printer, or a Printer Attached to Another Computer. (This option is terribly misleading, since the *only* printer you can connect to here is one previously set up on another computer, but we'll let that go for now.) Click Next to move to the Specify a Printer page in Figure 13.10.

FIGURE 13.10

You have several options for specifying a printer path.

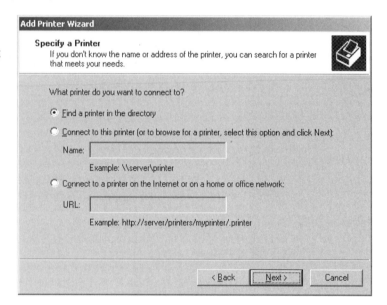

What you do from here depends how you're connecting to the printer:

◆ If you know the name of the share name of the printer, type it in the space provided. (Of course, if you know the printer's share name, you might as well type **net use *servername*** ***printername*/persistent:yes** from the command line and save yourself the trouble of running the wizard.)

◆ If you need to browse for the printer, choose the second option and click Next.

NOTE *If you're still using an NT 4 domain controller, the first option in the list will be Browse for Printer, not Find a Printer in the Directory, and browsing using the first two options will show the same dialog boxes.*

◆ If someone's configured the print server to share its printers through a browser window, type the URL for the printer and click Next.

BROWSING FOR PRINTERS

Since I'll cover Internet printing a little later in this chapter, for now let's assume that you're browsing for the printer. When you choose this option and click Next, you'll see a dialog box like the one in Figure 13.11, prompting you to pick a domain, look for a server, then find the appropriate printer.

FIGURE 13.11

Browsing for a shared printer

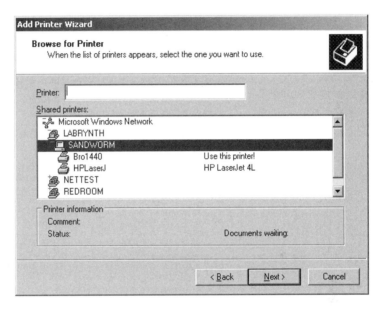

That's it. The next screen will show you the printer you chose. When you click Finish, the computer you're configuring will be set up to use that printer.

If you provided a path to the printer, it's even easier. When you click Next you'll see the Finish screen showing the name of the printer you connected to. Frankly, it's not worth running the wizard if you know the server and printer name—just use **net use** to connect from the command line.

FINDING A PRINTER IN THE DIRECTORY

Browsing is fine for a small network, but if you don't know which server a printer is connected to or even what domain it's in, it's easier to search the Active Directory for a printer matching the features that you need, or that's in a particular location. To do so, choose the first option in the Specify a Printer page and click Next to open the dialog box in Figure 13.12.

You can search for a printer based on just about any characteristic—or combination of characteristics—that you like. Searching for a printer by name doesn't seem very likely, since if you knew that much you'd probably know its domain and its server as well. And you almost certainly don't know the model precisely enough to type it exactly, not with printer model names having a length reminiscent of the names of minor royalty. However, you might know the printer's location, so you can enter that in the appropriate box.

FIGURE 13.12

Searching the
Active Directory
for a printer

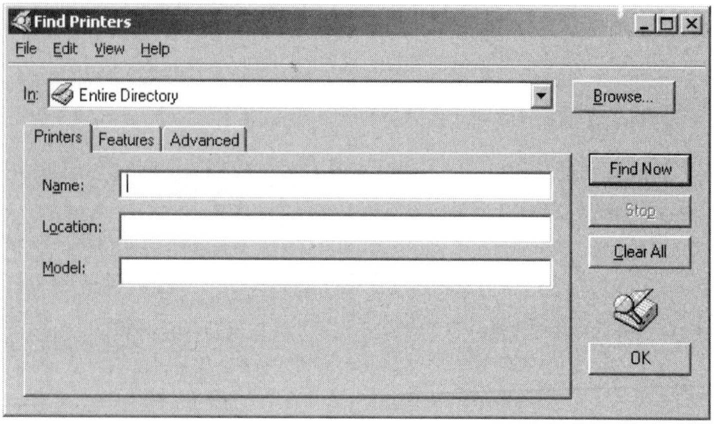

TIP *Since people may be using a printer's location to search the Active Directory for that printer, keep printer locations short and consistent (e.g., "Lab" or "Reception").*

In addition to knowing where the printer you want is, you probably know enough to know that you're looking for a color printer, or one that can staple. Therefore, in addition to the location on the Printers tab you can turn to the Features tab and check the box for the appropriate feature. When you click Find Now, the wizard will query the Active Directory, looking for a match for all the criteria you specified, and return the results as shown in Figure 13.13. I've listed the standard search criteria in Table 13.2.

The contents of the Advanced tab will be most suited to people who *really* know their printers, since the search criteria there get more granular than most people will need. Whereas the first two tabs allow you to describe a printer in terms of where it is, what it's called, and/or what you want it to be able to do, the Advanced tab allows you to describe the printer exactly. When you click the Field button, you can choose from any of the characteristics visible in Figure 13.14.

Performing a search using these advanced criteria works like the search you performed already. Choose the features you want to search for and click the Find Now button. The screen will display the results as it does in Figure 13.13.

Once you've found the printer you want, the rest is easy. Choose the printer you want and click OK. If this is not the first printer installed for the computer, the wizard will ask if you want this to be the default printer. After you've chosen, you'll see the familiar dialog box prompting you to review your choices and click Finish to set up the printer connection.

FIGURE 13.13

Results of searching for a printer by feature and location

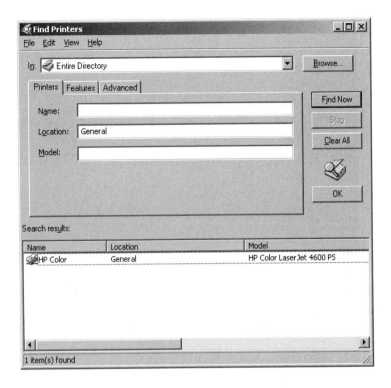

TABLE 13.2: STANDARD SEARCH CRITERIA FOR FINDING PRINTERS IN THE ACTIVE DIRECTORY

PRINTER CHARACTERISTIC	LOCATION
Color support	Features
Double-sided printing support	Features
Location	Printers
Minimum resolution	Features
Minimum speed	Features
Model	Printers
Name	Printers
Paper size	Features
Stapling support	Features

FIGURE 13.14

Advanced search criteria for finding printers in the Active Directory

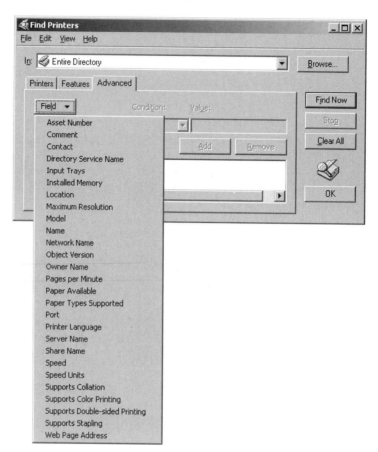

Creating a Second Printer for One Print Device

At this point, you have one printer for one print device. If you'd like to create a second printer—perhaps to configure a different set of permissions for it—you can do so in the same way you created the first printer. Follow the procedure to create a local printer, making sure you do two things:

- ◆ Give the new printer a different local name and share name.
- ◆ Choose the exact same settings (port, printer manufacturer and model, and so on) you chose for the first printer.

Sending documents to the new printer will cause them to print on the same print device. The only difference will lie in the configuration options you set for the new printer.

NOTE   *Not all options set in a printer's properties pages are printer specific. Port time-outs, for example, apply to any parallel port on the print server. One printer's time-outs will apply to all printers for that print device.*

Deleting a Printer

Sometimes, you'll need to delete a printer from a print server. Most of the time, this process is extremely simple: you open the Printers and Faxes section of the Control Panel, right-click the printer about to be sent to that big network in the sky, and choose Delete from the context menu. The printer should disappear immediately. If the printer you deleted was the default, another printer on that computer will become the new default.

If the printer you deleted *doesn't* disappear immediately, make sure that it's not in the middle of trying to print a document. Even if a printer never worked—for example, you were trying to set up a network-attached printer and specified the wrong port name—it can still have waiting print jobs. (Actually, this is *especially* likely if the printer never worked but you insisted on setting it up, damn the errors and full speed ahead.) Check the print queue of the printer you're trying to delete. If it has waiting print jobs, choose Cancel All Print Jobs from the Printer menu and then try to delete the printer again. Rebooting the print server will not clear the list of spooled print jobs—you must explicitly cancel them.

Preparing for Web Printing

Web-based printing allows users to print or manage documents from their Web browsers with very minimal setup. It takes a little more prep work than sharing a printer with the local network, but it's easier for inexperienced users to set up their own computers. As you saw earlier, to connect to a networked printer, you need to know something about that printer so you can either name it explicitly, browse for it, or find it in the Active Directory. With Web printing, you just have to click the right link—or the only link, if a particular person only has access to one printer—and the printer installs itself.

What Can (and Can't) Web Printing Accomplish?

Your first thought might be that Web printing will be a good way to add remote printer access so that people who don't work in your office can send print jobs to your printers. For example, I recently had to FedEx 50 pages of a presentation to another office, which meant that I had to print out the presentation, put it in an envelope, fill out the slip, and call FedEx to pick up the package. If the recipient had set up their printer for Internet printing, then I could have just sent the print job to their printer directly and skipped the FedExing part, right?

Well, maybe not. First, the flow of information in Web-based printing is no different from that of an ordinary print job, except that you've added a Web server into the mix. Print jobs are *big*, bigger than the files they're printing, because formatting a print job requires extra information. If you try to send a big print job across a slow link, it may take a while to get there.

What about printing shorter documents? It would be possible to use Internet printing just as you would a fax. So long as you only used the printer like you would a fax—you don't often fax 50-page PowerPoint presentations, do you?—then you'd be okay. But doing that requires setting up a printer explicitly for this purpose, and it opens up a security hole because you're allowing people to log in to the domain from the Internet. If I were doing this, I'd set up a network printer just for anonymous users to connect to, and explicitly deny those anonymous users from doing anything else on the network. I'd also set up the print server for this printer outside the network's DMZ, so that access to the printer server didn't give people access to other network computers.

Frankly, the best use I've seen for Web printing is that it really streamlines the printer setup process for the client. As you'll see in the "Internet Printing" section (on setting up client access to the printer via the Web), this process is much simpler than using the Add Printer Wizard: You tell the user to run Internet Explorer 4 or later, connect to the print server by typing **http://*printservername*/ printers** in the Address section of the browser, then click the printer they see there—since you will have used security permissions to make sure that they can only see the printer they're supposed to connect to. The user clicks the link for that server, then clicks the Connect link to automagically download the driver to their computer. That's it—the printer is installed and available to any application.

SETTING UP A WEB PRINT SERVER

The protocol used in Web printing depends on whether the printer is available on the LAN or on a WAN. Web printing uses the Internet Printing Protocol (IPP), encapsulated within the HyperText Transfer Protocol (HTTP) used for browsing the Web. Printers on the local LAN will use the faster remote procedure calls (RPCs) to send jobs to the printer, just as they do for traditional print jobs. Because an Internet print server must be able to accept incoming HTTP traffic to communicate with print clients not on the LAN, the print server must also be a Web server. This means that you'll need to install the Internet Information Services (IIS) on the print server and run the service. You can install IIS from the Add/Remove Windows Components tool in the Add/Remove Programs applet in the Control Panel—it's one of the components of the Web Application Server service.

If you look at IIS's details, you'll notice that Internet Printing is one of its components and selected for installation by default. This means that Internet printing is enabled, right? Well—not exactly. For security reasons, Internet Printing is prohibited *even if you install it along with IIS*. To enable it, open Internet Information Services from Administrative Tools after you've installed the core service. One folder there is labeled "Web Services Extensions." Open this folder, and you'll see a list of services and three buttons: Allow, Prohibit, and Properties. Select Internet Printing and click the Allow button.

SECURING A WEB PRINT SERVER

Once you've got IIS installed and have allowed the Internet Printing Web extension, the print server can accept clients connecting to it by typing its URL into IE. However, as it stands, the printer is open to everyone who can type its URL, and you do *not* want just anyone connecting to network computers—or even just anyone printing large print jobs. You should do some security tweaking before making this printer available. Open the Internet Information Services tool in the Administrative Tools program group. (If it's not there, make sure that you installed IIS. Unlike in Windows 2000, in Server 2003 IIS is not installed by default.) All the Web servers in the domain will be listed below the `Internet Information Services` folder. Find the Web print server in this list. Within its `Default Web Site` folder, look for the `Printers` folder. At this point, your management console should look something like the one in Figure 13.15.

Now, right-click the `Printers` folder and choose Properties from the context menu that appears. You'll see a tabbed properties page like the one in Figure 13.16.

On the Virtual Directory tab shown here, make sure the entry points to the right information for printing. If you're setting up Internet printing on the print server, this should be the selected option— a directory on this computer. To configure Internet printing for another computer, provide the network path to that print server. If you do provide a connection to another print server here, the printer will only be available so long as the printer is online and has a live connection to the Web server.

FIGURE 13.15

Find the **Printers** folder for your Web printer.

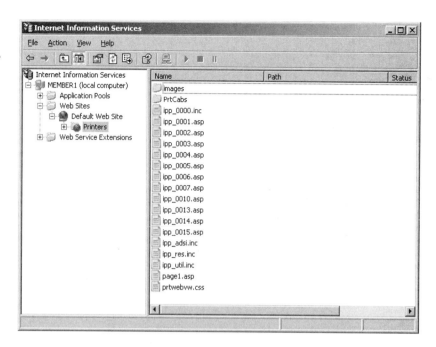

FIGURE 13.16

The properties page for the **Printers** folder

TIP   If creating a connection to a shared printer on another computer, you have the option of either letting people use their own credentials to access that computer or supplying other credentials, if people accessing the Web page would not normally have access to the remote print server. Click the Connect As button (visible when you choose to connect to a remote resource) to provide the alternate credentials.

Secure access to the printer from the Directory Security tab (see Figure 13.17).

FIGURE 13.17

Printer security settings

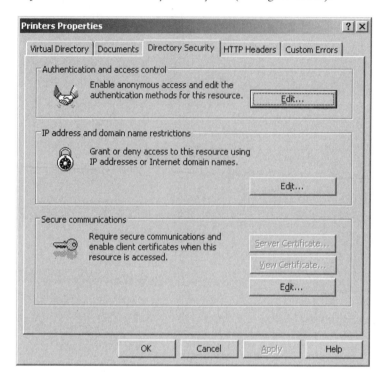

User authentication is set from the Authentication Methods dialog box (see Figure 13.18), accessible from the Directory Security tab when you click the Edit button for Authentication and Access Control. You can enable anonymous access with the privileges assigned to IUSR_MEMBER1, or you can choose another account for people to use for anonymous access—even creating a Printer User account so you can track what people using the printer are doing. Edit the authentication settings by clicking the Edit button (see Figure 13.19).

Alternatively, you can require that anyone connecting to the printer via the Web get authenticated on the network first. Set up the Printers virtual folder for basic authentication if you want people to be able to manage printers from any browser. IIS will fuss at you for choosing this option because it sends passwords in clear (unencrypted) text, but if you choose Kerberos (Integrated Windows authentication) or challenge/response (Digest authentication) for greater security, you'll limit yourself to managing printers from Internet Explorer 4 or later. Server 2003 Passport authentication is (obviously) limited to those with a Server 2003 Passport account. By default, authentication will be based on the domain that the Web printer is part of; to choose a different domain, click the Edit button and browse for the domain you want to use. If the box in the Browse dialog box is blank, the local domain will be used for authentication.

FIGURE 13.18

Choose an authentication method for Web print management.

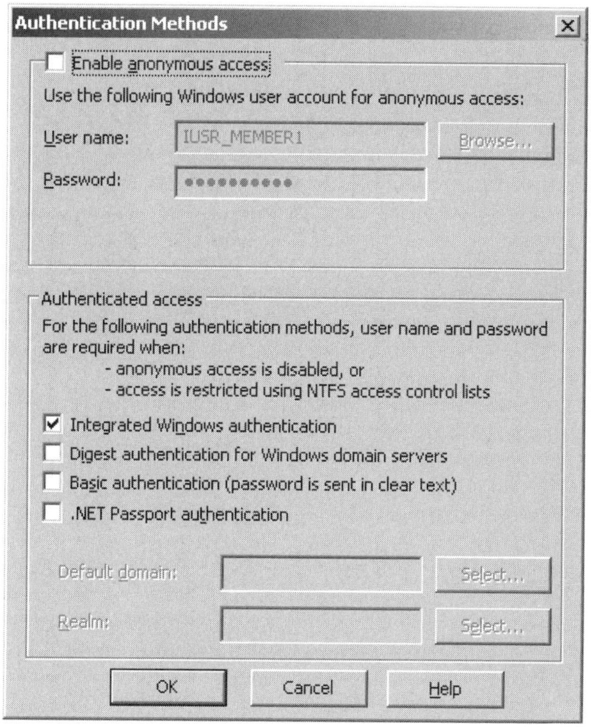

FIGURE 13.19

You can edit the authentication settings for people accessing the Printers folder.

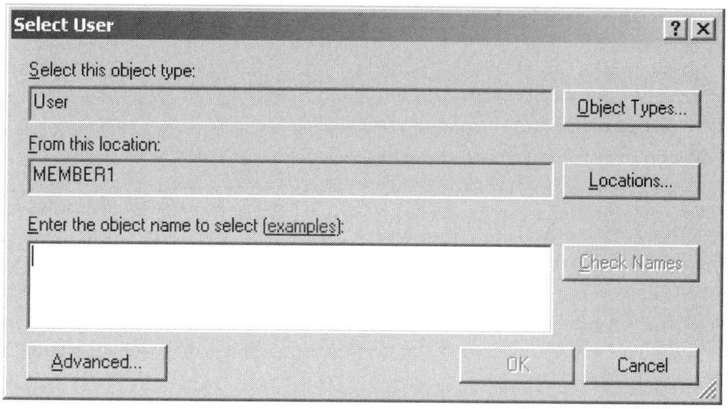

Another method you can use to restrict access to a Web printer is to permit only members of a particular domain or only those with a specific IP address. To do so, go back to the Directory Security tab and click the Edit button for IP Address and Domain Name Restrictions. You'll see a dialog box like the one in Figure 13.20.

When you first open this dialog box, no one will be specifically denied or granted access. (Note that you can use this dialog box to either explicitly permit or deny access.) To add an entry to the list, first click the appropriate radio button to indicate whether you're adding a "denied" entry (the Denied Access radio button) or a "permitted" entry (the Granted Access radio button). When you've made your choice, click the Add button to open the dialog box in Figure 13.21. You must *deny* someone print access to keep them off the printer. Even if you delete the Everyone group and remove the explicitly given permission, people will still be able to print unless denied print access.

FIGURE 13.20

A list of permitted or forbidden domains and networks

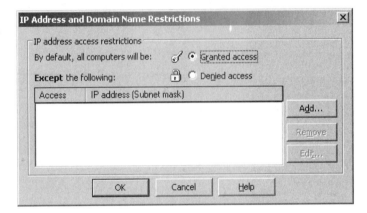

FIGURE 13.21

Choose the domain name, IP address, or network to which you want to permit or deny access to the Web printer.

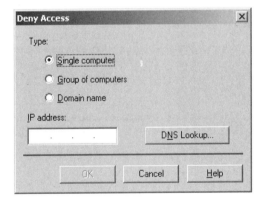

TIP   *Be sure to pick the right radio button (Granted Access or Denied Access) before you define the IP address/ domain/group of computers to which you're permitting or denying access. Otherwise, you'll have to re-create the entry.*

To permit or deny a single IP address, use the Single Computer option. Of course, if that single computer is getting its IP address from a Dynamic Host Configuration Protocol (DHCP) server, this option won't always apply to the same computer. A more effective method of restricting printer access is to define access for a group of computers, using the network IP address and the subnet mask (when you click each option, the boxes to fill in change accordingly). You *can* also permit or deny access to the computer based on domain membership, but this is an expensive operation. If you identify a domain by name, the name must be resolved on both ends of the connection before the Web server can identify the domain, and this will slow down print jobs considerably.

Once you've identified the computer(s) for which you want to permit or deny access to the Web printers folder, they'll appear in the list in the IP Address and Domain Name Restrictions dialog box. Permitted addresses will have a key icon; denied addresses will have a lock icon. The print server is now ready to accept print requests from clients.

TIP *Performance will be better if you grant/deny access based on IP address rather than domain name. If you choose to make domain name the criterion, every time the server needs to authenticate someone it will need to look up the domain— a time-consuming operation.*

Getting the Printer to the Clients

The method you use to connect a client workstation to a networked printer depends on the operating system the client is using. DOS clients must connect from the command line and need locally installed drivers, 16-bit Windows clients can connect from the graphical interface and need their own drivers, and 32-bit Windows clients connect from Network Neighborhood or My Network Places and don't even need locally installed printer drivers—they can grab them from the server, so long as you made sure that the appropriate drivers were installed there. (We'll talk about how to install other drivers a little later in this chapter.)

NOTE *As you may recall, 16-bit Windows is not an operating system, it's a graphical operating environment for DOS. All DOS workstations must have locally installed printer drivers. You may need to install the driver more than once or install it to application directories to make sure the applications see the printer. You'll also need to manually update drivers should new versions become available (unlikely as that is).*

CONNECTING FROM DOS

To set up LPT1 from DOS, type **net use lpt1: ***server******printername* at the command prompt, where *server* is the name of the print server and *printername* is the name of the printer. If you want to reconnect to this printer every time you log in to the network, add the **/persistent:yes** switch to the end of the command. Just typing **/persistent** won't do anything, but if you leave off the switch altogether, the connection will default to the persistency settings previously defined.

TIP *Not sure of the name of the print server or the printer? Type* **net view** *at the command prompt to see a list of all servers. Type* **net view ***servername* *to see a list of all resources shared from that server.*

For example, suppose you're setting up network printer support for a DOS workstation that does not have a locally connected printer. Some older DOS applications don't give you a chance to select an output port—it's their way or the highway. Therefore, you'd like to automatically redirect *any* output sent to LPT1 to be intercepted by the network-accessible printer HP5 attached to the print server BIGSERVER. You want to remake this connection every time you log in to the network so that you don't have to worry about printer support.

The command to fulfill this set of conditions would look like this:

```
net use lpt1: \\bigserver\hp5 /persistent:yes
```

This command will work not only from DOS, but from the command line for any Windows operating system.

CONNECTING FROM WINDOWS 3.x OR WINDOWS FOR WORKGROUPS

To connect to a shared printer from network-enabled Windows or from Windows for Workgroups, select the Printers icon in the Control Panel. You should see a dialog box that shows the printer connections you already have, like the one in Figure 13.22.

What you do from here depends on whether you're just reconnecting to a previously established network connection, creating a new network connection to a printer you can support, or starting at the beginning by installing local support for the printer.

FIGURE 13.22

A list of installed printers for Windows for Workgroups

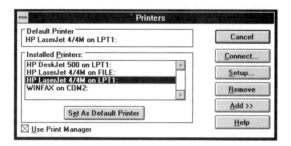

Connecting to an Available Printer

To connect to any of these previously connected printers, you just click the Connect button to open the dialog box shown in Figure 13.23. Click OK, and you're done.

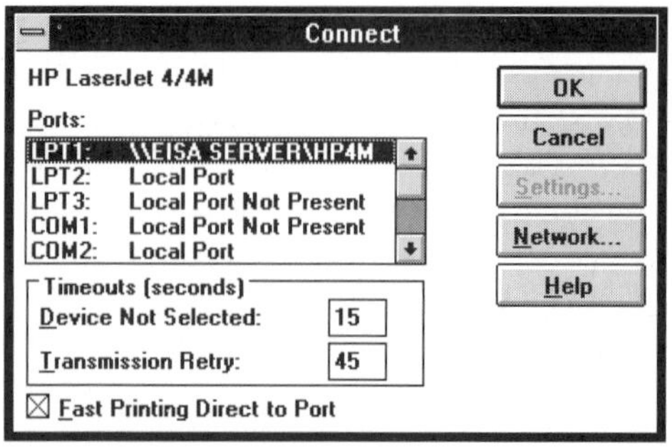

FIGURE 13.23

Connecting a Windows for Workgroups client to a previously installed network printer

Creating a New Network Connection

If you're connecting to a new printer, then instead of clicking Connect, choose the Network button to open the dialog box shown in Figure 13.24. Find the print server and printer you want and click OK.

FIGURE 13.24

Creating a new connection to a networked printer

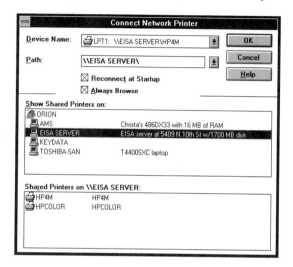

Installing a Printer Driver for Win16 Operating Systems

If you haven't already installed support for the printer, you've got a couple steps ahead of you. Rather than clicking the Connect or Network button, click Add to see a list of installed printers and available printer types (see Figure 13.25).

FIGURE 13.25

A list of available printer types

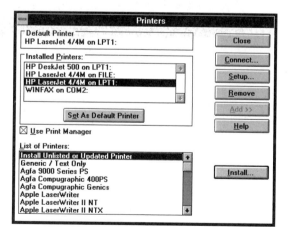

Find the printer you want from the list and click the Install button. The system will prompt you for the location of the printer drivers. Browse for the drivers or insert the requested disk.

Once you've installed the correct driver, you can create the network connection to the printer and connect to it.

CONNECTING FROM WINDOWS 95 OR NT CLIENTS

The first time I connected to an NT printer from an NT Workstation back in 1993 (NTW predated Windows 95, you may recall), I thought that I must have missed a step—it was too easy. You don't have to install local driver support at all; just connect to the printer. 32-bit Windows clients don't use locally stored drivers but instead reference the ones you've installed on the server to support them. This not only saves you a step in the process of installing printer support, it makes it much easier to update printer drivers. When there's a new driver out, you don't have to run around to each client with a floppy disk or set up some kind of remote installation script—you just install it to the server, and when the clients connect, they'll use it automatically.

To install a printer from Windows 9*x* or Windows NT, open the Printers folder, accessible as a shortcut from the Control Panel, and start the Add Printer Wizard. Click the Next button to open the dialog box shown in Figure 13.26.

FIGURE 13.26

Specify that the printer is connected remotely, not locally.

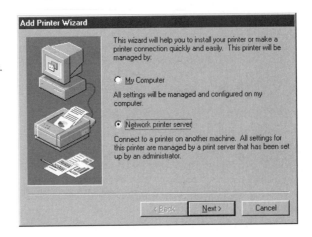

Be sure to say that the printer will be managed by a printer server, not locally. Click Next and choose the printer you want from the list, as shown in Figure 13.27. Click Finish and the printer is locally available.

TIP   *If you want to connect to multiple printers, you must do so one printer at a time.*

You can also connect to network-accessible printers from the NT and Windows 9*x* Network Neighborhood. Open Network Neighborhood and double-click the appropriate print server. As shown in Figure 13.28, Network Neighborhood will then display all resources shared from that server, including printers.

From here, you can right-click the appropriate printer and either capture the printer port (redirecting all output sent to, say, LPT1 to the network printer) or install support for the printer to make it accessible with UNC nomenclature.

FIGURE 13.27

Choose a printer from the list of servers and printers.

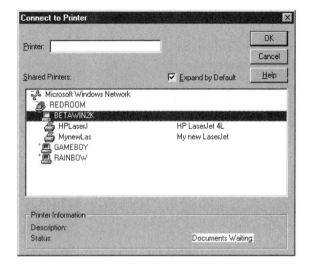

FIGURE 13.28

Installing printer support from Network Neighborhood

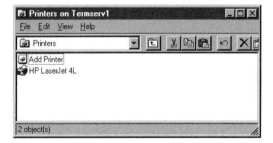

CONNECTING FROM WINDOWS 2000 AND WINDOWS XP

The Add Printer Wizard in Win2K and Windows XP looks a little different from the one in Windows NT or Windows 9*x*, but the basic effect is much the same for all three operating systems:

1. Start the Add Printer Wizard and click through the obligatory Welcome to the Add Printer Wizard opening screen. When asked whether you want to create a local or network connection to a printer, choose the network option, as shown in Figure 13.29.

2. Next, indicate the printer's location. What happens here depends on whether your network is using NT 4 domains or the Active Directory.

   If you're connecting from a Win2K/XP computer that's part of an NT 4 domain, then, as you can see in Figure 13.30, Win2K supports connecting to printers either in terms of the printer's name or by an intranet/Internet address, like this:

   ```
   http://printservername/printers/printername/.printer
   ```

where *printservername* and *printername* are what they sound like: the print server and its share name. If you aren't sure of the printer's name, you can leave that space blank and browse for the print server. The browse function doesn't work for printers with their own name or URL; you must enter a valid name for the printer if you choose that option.

FIGURE 13.29

When connecting to a network printer, be sure to specify the network connection.

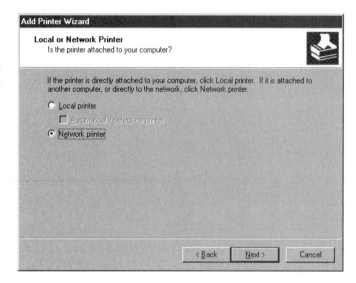

FIGURE 13.30

Type the name of the printer's server or its URL.

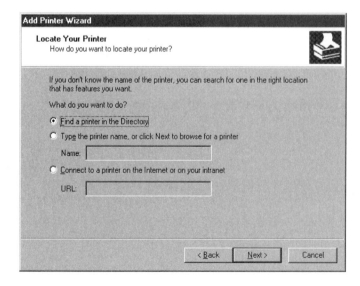

TIP   *Frankly, if you're connecting with a URL, it's a lot easier to do it from a browser so you can click links to printers rather than having to know their share names. One mistyped letter in that URL and you get an error message telling you that the printer setup utility could not connect to the printer. If you're using a browser, all you need to know is the name of the print server.*

3. If you choose to browse for a printer, you'll see a browse list like the one in Figure 13.31, showing the printers on the network and the servers they're connected to. As you can see, any location information or comments attached to a printer will show up when you select a printer, so you can easily find the one you want.

FIGURE 13.31

Scan the list of available printers and choose the one you want to connect to.

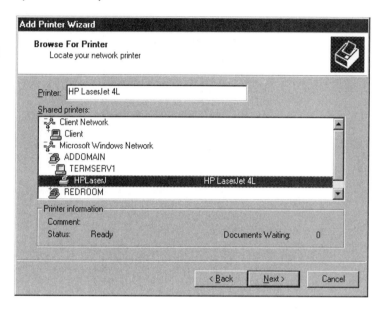

If you're connecting from a computer with an account in the Active Directory, you have another option: searching the Active Directory for the printer you want. Check the box that says Find a Printer in the Directory and click Next, and instead of browsing as described previously, open a dialog box from which you can browse for printers by a collection of different criteria and in different parts of the Active Directory (users, computers, domain controllers, and so forth). You can also search for printers based on their name or on other criteria, such as what features they support. I've explained these settings in detail in "Connecting to a Network-Enabled Printer," earlier in this chapter. Although that section discussed connection from the perspective of a Server 2003 computer, the details are identical.

4. Once you've chosen the printer, the wizard will ask if you want to set up the printer as the preassigned printer for all applications (Figure 13.32). If you've already got a preassigned printer, the default option is No; if this is the first printer connection you're setting up, the printer is set up as the default without any prompting from you.

NOTE   *The default printer will have a check mark on its icon in the* `Printers` *folder.*

5. Finally, the Add Printer Wizard will show you the options you've chosen so far, letting you click either Finish to install support or Back to change an option. If you've already got the drivers installed, that's it—you can use the new printer immediately. Otherwise, you'll have to copy the new drivers from the CD or your installation directory.

FIGURE 13.32

Specify whether the new printer should be the one all applications choose to print to.

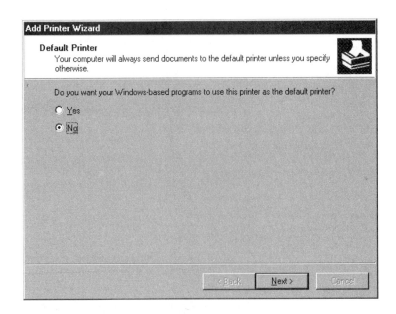

The printer should appear in the Printers dialog box. Its icon will look like that of a locally connected printer, with the addition of a network connection attached to it.

INTERNET PRINTING

If your network clients are running Internet Explorer 4 or later and you're having users connect to their own printers, forget the Add Printer Wizards: There's now a better way. If your print server is running IIS, people can connect to any shared printers from a browser and it's *really easy.*

NOTE *Although the documentation implies that this procedure might work with Netscape, I haven't been able to make it work. I'd stick with Internet Explorer.*

You have a couple of options when it comes to connecting to a printer via a Web browser. If you know the print server's name but not the name of the printer you want to connect to, then in the Address box in IE type **http://***servername***/printers** to open a browser page like the one in Figure 13.33. In this example, the name of the print server is CLONE300 (original, yes). You do need to know the print server's name. There's no "browse the network for printers" option built into this.

NOTE *If you're one of the people who avoids the pesky* http:// *prefix by typing* **www** *instead (I do it so I don't have to squint at the screen to see that I typed both the colon and the two forward slashes), you should know that the* **www** *prefix won't work here. If connecting locally, you can just skip the* http:// *prefix altogether, though, like this:* **//printservername/printers**.

To connect to a particular printer, click its link in the list to open the screen in Figure 13.34. You're not connected yet, you just have the option of connecting.

FIGURE 13.33

List of all available printers on a print server

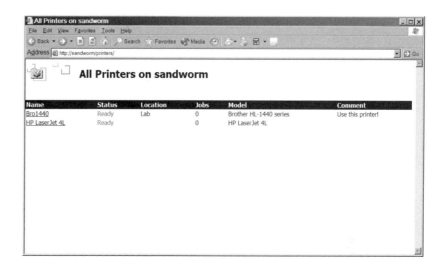

FIGURE 13.34

You must explicitly connect to a printer to use it.

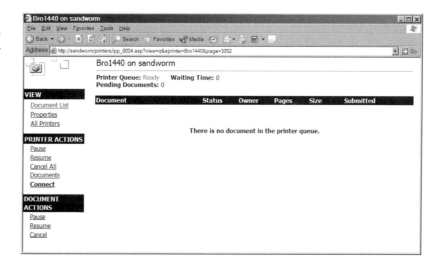

To connect to the printer, click Connect in the list of printer actions. A small status bar will display the progression as the print server sends you the drivers you need, and you'll be connected just as you would had you connected from the Add Printer Wizard. The only difference is that because the installation process is so simplified—you connect to a printer and you click Connect—you never get the option of setting the new printer as the default. If you want to make the new printer the default over an existing printer, you'll need to open the Printers folder, right-click the printer in question, and choose Make Default from the context menu.

TIP *If you know the name of the printer, you can link to it directly like this:* `http://servername/printername`. *If you have permission to access the printer, then that puts you directly into the printer's information screen, from which you can connect to the printer.*

As I said earlier, Internet printing represents an excellent way of simplifying client-side printer setup. If you have a corporate home page, you could put a link on the home page, something along the lines of "click HERE to connect to a printer." The user clicks THERE, they go to the page where the printers are listed (and, by tweaking security settings, you can make sure that they only see the printer they're supposed to connect to), they click the printer, and then click to connect. This works for any client that can run IE4 or later. If you're connecting across the Internet, a dialog box appears asking for the domain name, username, and password; if you're connecting locally, this dialog box does not appear.

Using Client-Side Printers in a Terminal Server Environment

When the Terminal Services Edition of Windows NT was first released, the display protocol—the protocol downloading application output to the client machines and uploading keystrokes and mouse clicks to the server—had some holes in it. Remote and local sessions didn't share a Clipboard, so you couldn't cut and paste between applications running on the client and those running on the server. Remote control of sessions wasn't supported. Session clients couldn't use their locally connected printers without sharing them from the network and then connecting to them from the terminal server session.

Beginning with Win2K, terminal sessions could get local access to client-side ports. Using the new desktop client, clients can access their local printer from a terminal server session without sharing the printer with the network. The only catch is that it's not quite as simple as that for all clients.

Win32 desktop client print requests sent to local printers will be automatically redirected to the local printer so long as you've previously installed the driver needed for the printer on the terminal server (and are using RDP 5 or later, since this feature requires the printer mapping virtual channel to be enabled). You'll have to manually configure Windows terminals and Win16 clients to use locally attached printers.

AUTOMATICALLY REDIRECTING PRINTERS

Other than making sure the driver is installed on the terminal server, you don't have to do anything to set up an automatically redirected printer. When a person with a client-side printer—locally attached or set up on the network—logs onto a terminal server and initiates a session, a fake print job owned by the Administrator is sent to the printer. This isn't a real print job, just a notice to the printer that it's being redirected for use with the terminal server session—you'll probably never notice it if you don't deliberately look at the status box for the printer during the second or two required for the redirection to take place. Behind the scenes, what's happening is that the terminal server checks the name of the printer driver on the client and looks for the same printer driver on the terminal server's NTPRINT.INF file. If the terminal server doesn't find that driver name, then the Event Viewer will log error messages and the redirection won't work.

Assuming the redirection does work, if you look in the Printers folder for the terminal server session, you'll see the redirected printer there identified by its name, the name of the computer it's connected to, and the number of the terminal server session. For example, the printer HPLaser that's connected to the computer MONSTER, using Session ID4, will be identified in the Printers folder as HPLaser\MONSTER\Session 4.

For automatic printer mapping to work, all of the following must be true:

- The name of the printer driver on the client and the server must be identical. It's not enough that they be the drivers for the same printer—the names have to match.
- The client session must have printer redirection enabled.

If the printer *doesn't* automatically redirect, check the System event log in the terminal server to find out why.

MANUALLY REDIRECTING PRINTERS

Win16 clients and those using Windows-based terminals (WBTs) will need to manually redirect printers. This may not always be possible with a WBT because the RDP client for older WBTs may not have been updated to version 5 (version 4 does not support redirection of client-side printers). However, new WBTs generally have the RDP5 or later client, and you should be able to get an updated client for older terminals that don't already include it.

To manually redirect a printer for a terminal services client, follow these steps:

1. Get the name or IP address of the client device. (If your Window's terminals don't use names—not all do—you'll need to use the terminal's IP address.) Start a terminal session from that client machine.

2. Start the process of manually adding a locally connected printer to the terminal server.

3. In the part of the wizard where you're choosing the port the printer is connected to, scroll down in the list until you see the name or IP address of the client computer with the printer attached, like this:

    Ts002 CLIENTPC LPT1

4. Choose that port to attach the printer to, and install the printer normally.

When a client disconnects or logs off a session, the printer queue is deleted and any incomplete or waiting print jobs are deleted. Once you have manually redirected a printer for a terminal session, that redirection will take place automatically thereafter, and the print queue will be automatically created from the information stored on the client.

PREVENTING PRINTERS FROM BEING REDIRECTED

But what if you don't want clients to use their local printers during terminal server sessions? You may not, especially if the client is connecting to a printer across a dial-up connection. Sending a print job from terminal server to client-side printer may be acceptable at LAN speeds but unwise over a 56Kbps modem connection since sending the print job back to the client for printing can make the connection slow to a crawl. Or you may want people to use a networked printer for their terminal server sessions for auditing purposes. Whatever the reason, you may want to disable printer redirection.

To prevent printer redirection on a per-user basis, open the user account's properties pages and turn to the Environment tab. On that tab is a section called Client Devices, underneath which are three check boxes that control whether that person has access to client-side drives and client-side printers and whether that client should automatically print to the client-side default printer. By default, all three boxes are checked, enabling all client-side printers and drivers. To keep the client's printer from being redirected to the terminal session, uncheck the box that says Connect Client Printers at Logon. To permit the user to redirect client-side printers but to keep the default printer from changing to the client-side default, uncheck the box that says Default to Main Client Printer. Alternatively, turn off printer redirection from the Remote Desktop Connection client on their computer. Turn to the Local Resources tab and make sure that the Printers box is unchecked. (To avoid duplicating effort, you can save settings and distribute them to users.)

If you don't want *anyone* connecting to the terminal server via a given display protocol to use their local printers, you can do this as well. Open the Terminal Services Configuration tool that's in the Administrative Tools section of the terminal server. Click the `Connections` folder in the left pane so that the installed display protocols (only RDP, unless you have MetaFrame installed) appear in the right. Open the properties pages for RDP and turn to the Client Settings tab.

There are two sections on this tab. The Connection section on the top is a duplicate of the Client Devices section of the per-user Environment properties just discussed. By default, the per-user settings control, but if you want to apply the settings discussed previously not just to individual users but to everyone using the display protocol, you can deselect the option that says Use Connection Settings from User Settings and edit the entries accordingly. The section at the bottom of the Client Devices tab controls which client-side resources are disabled. Disable client-side printing as follows:

◆ To prevent users from redirecting any client-side printers, deselect Windows printer mapping.

◆ To prevent terminal users from redirecting client-side printers attached to parallel ports, disable LPT port mapping.

◆ To prevent terminal users from redirecting client-side printers attached to serial ports, disable COM port mapping.

Automatically Installing Printers

You've seen now how to get printers to people by walking through the installation wizards. However, this method requires you either to permit users to create their own printers—which is prone to error—or to install them yourself on each computer. In the interests of saving a little time, let's take a look at some methods of simplified printer deployment.

INTERNET PRINTING

As I mentioned earlier, the best use of Internet printing is not, in fact, allowing people to send print jobs over the Internet—it's a security hole and will require an awful lot of bandwidth. Instead, consider using Internet printing to automatically set up printers. When a person connects to the printer via the Web page (which you have locked down as described earlier so that only their approved printers show), the driver is automatically downloaded to the client computer if it's not already there.

PROGRAMMATICALLY INSTALLING PRINTERS

If you don't mind doing a little scripting, then you can also automatically install printers on the basis of user or computer identity when the user logs on—and then unmap the printer connection when a particular user logs off. As is true of scripting in general, this takes some work up front. However, for any task you'll be repeating on a regular basis, scripting it will save you an awful lot of time and trouble. This will only fully work on NT-based operating systems such as NT, Windows 2000,

Windows XP, and Windows Server 2003, but if you preinstall drivers onto Windows 9*x* computers it will work there as well.

NOTE   *A Resource Kit tool called PrintAdmin enables you to programmatically install and manage printers on the local computer or remote computers running NT operating systems. To use it, you'll need to know how to use VBScript, and, to be perfectly frank, I think the method I'm describing here is easier and completely adequate if installing is your main goal.*

I don't have space for a complete treatise on scripting Windows 2000 here, but the basic idea is this: Win32 operating systems support a scripting environment called Windows Scripting Host (WSH) that enables you to run VBScript and JScript scripts to perform tasks that you'd normally have to perform by hand. In scripting, real objects such as printers are represented by scripting objects, which you manipulate by addressing the *properties* (characteristics) of those objects and exploiting their *methods* (things they can do). Objects are nouns, properties are adjectives, and methods are verbs. WSH is supported on all Win32 operating systems. WSH abstracts the interface to a number of Win32 objects. One of these is `WshNetwork`, a collection of network resources—shared drives and printers. It can also "see" the name of the computer the script is running on and the name of the person currently logged on; the computer name (`.ComputerName`), username (`.UserName`), and computer domain (`.UserDomain`) are all properties of the `WshNetwork` object.

TIP   *For those who've never touched scripting before, create scripts in a text editor such as Notepad and save them with a* `.vbs` *extension. Windows cannot interpret VBScript—this isn't a command-line language like the* **net** *commands.*

For our purposes, we care about only `WshNetwork`'s printing-related methods. To map a printer explicitly to a port as you would with **net use**, use the `.AddPrinterConnection` method. To create a Windows printer connection (and automatically install the driver on NT-based operating systems) use the `.AddWindowsPrinterConnection` method—this is the method I'll use here. To set the default printer for a computer, use the `.SetDefaultPrinter` method.

Creating a Generic Printer Connection

Good so far? Let's take a look at the simplest way of accomplishing this with VBScript:

```
Option Explicit
Dim oNetwork, sPrintPath
Set oNetwork = CreateObject("WScript.Network")
sPrintPath = "\\sandworm\printer"
oNetwork.AddWindowsPrinterConnection sPrintPath
oNetwork.SetDefaultPrinter sPrintPath
Set oNetwork = vbEmpty
Set sPrintPath = vbEmpty
```

In this example, I've defined the variables the script will use (so that if I mistype a variable name then I'll get an error message instead of a new variable), created a connection to the `WshNetwork` object (which we must do to call on its properties and methods), assigned the UNC path to the shared printer path to the *sPrintPath* variable to make the path information easier to deal with, and then called on the appropriate methods to create the printer and make it the default, supplying the variable representing the printer path as an argument. Finally, I've been a good little coder and set the variables I used equal to vbEmpty now that I'm done with them so that the memory required to support those variables may be released. So long as I assign a valid path in line 4, then this script will work on any NT-based computer. To make this script work for yourself, just replace the highlighted path in line 4 with a valid shared printer UNC path.

Incidentally, there's nothing stopping you from using this script to install support for more than one printer but making one of those printers the default. You'll need one variable for each separate UNC path to the printers for which you want to install support.

Creating a Computer- or User-Specific Printer Connection

Thing is, you probably don't want to install the same printer on every computer in the network. Rather, you'd prefer to establish a connection based on user identity or computer name—particularly the latter because it's often more important that the printer you use be close to where you're sitting than that it be assigned to you personally. That script could look something like this:

```
Option Explicit
Dim oNetwork, sPrintPath
Set oNetwork = CreateObject("WScript.Network")
Select Case oNetwork.ComputerName
  Case "Gamma"
      sPrintPath = "\\sandworm\printer1"
  Case "Geektoy"
      sPrintPath = "\\sandworm\printer2"
   Case Else
      sPrintPath = "\\sandworm\printer3"
End Select
oNetwork.AddWindowsPrinterConnection sPrintPath
oNetwork.SetDefaultPrinter sPrintPath
Set oNetwork = vbEmpty
Set sPrintPath = vbEmpty
```

As you can see, this script starts out just like the other one: I've defined the variables I'm using and established a connection to the WshNetwork object. By including the Select Case statement, however, I've allowed the script to read the local computer name and make a decision about what printer to install based on that information. I've included two valid options, but just so I don't have to create options for *every* computer on the network I've also included a Case Else option that says in effect, "If you can't do anything else, do this." The value of the computer name determines the value for *sPrintPath*, which then gets plugged into the .AddWindowsPrinterConnection and .SetDefaultPrinter methods as in the previous example. Again, replace my computer names and printer paths with yours.

I could have done exactly the same thing using the name of the user logged in as the argument for Select Case. Taking only the Select Case snippet, that could have looked like this:

```
Select Case oNetwork.UserName
  Case "Christa"
      sPrintPath = "\\sandworm\printer1"
```

```
      Case "Mark"
          sPrintPath = "\\sandworm\printer2"
      Case Else
          sPrintPath = "\\sandworm\printer3"
  End Select
```

The rest of the script looks just like the previous example. User-specific mappings are not persistent, incidentally. If Christa logs on and gets her printer mapped, then logs off, when Mark logs on and gets his printers mapped he will not see both Christa's printers and his printers—just his. If you want to disable a computer-specific mapping or a mapping not replaced by another mapping, however, you'll need to manually remove the printer or use the `.RemovePrinterConnection` method to `WshNetwork`, supplying the printer path as an argument as you did to add the printer. For example, you could create a script to include in the logoff script for Windows 2000 computers.

Creating a Location-Specific Printer Connection

The previous example allows us to create a default printer based on which computer the script runs on. As you can see, though, you'll need to either create options for each computer on the network, or make up more than one version of the script to distribute according to computer location. In a large network, either option could get cumbersome. There is a third way: you could ask the user to tell you where they are in broad terms (e.g., "library" or "second floor") and then install the appropriate printer based on that information. For example:

```
Option Explicit
Dim oNetwork, sPrintPath, sLocate
Set oNetwork = CreateObject("WScript.Network")
sLocate =_
    InputBox("Where are you? Type 'Lab', 'Library', or 'Reception'.")
Select Case sLocate
  Case "Lab"
      sPrintPath = "\\sandworm\printer1"
  Case "Library"
      sPrintPath = "\\sandworm\printer2"
  Case "Reception"
      sPrintPath = "\\sandworm\printer3"
  Case Else
      Wscript.Echo "That is not a valid choice." :Wscript.Quit
End Select
oNetwork.AddWindowsPrinterConnection sPrintPath
oNetwork.SetDefaultPrinter sPrintPath
Set oNetwork = vbEmpty
Set sPrintPath = vbEmpty
```

What I've done here is create an input box prompting the person running the script to tell me where they are. Based on that input, the script will assign a printer to their computer. If they type an invalid choice, then the script nags at them and ends—that's what the `Wscript.Quit` method does. Alternatively, you could assign a generic printer if the person running the script didn't choose one of the three valid options. This script does require user input, but so long as you trust your user base to know what part of the building they're in, it should work.

TIP   Use the location-specific printer installation script as a template for creating default printers based on user location. If you use group policies to disable the Add Printers applet in the Control Panel and hide shared printers by ending their names in a dollar sign ($), then people will be able to connect to only the printers programmatically assigned to their username, computer name, or location—and you can set the default. This will keep the people in Lab A from mistakenly sending their print jobs to Lab Z, three buildings away.

`WshNetwork` methods are not the only ways to manage printers through VBScript, but without getting into Windows Management Instrumentation (WMI) and the Active Directory Services Interface (ADSI), they are the simplest. For much more information about scripting Windows 2000 administration, check out *Windows 2000 Automated Deployment and Remote Management* (Sybex, 2001), a guide to using VBScript for Windows 2000 management for anyone who's used to working from the GUI. I've also written several "Scripting Solutions" columns for Windows and .NET Magazine, available from www.winnetmag.com, which go into some more detailed scripted printer installations using WMI and ADSI to work with computer IP addresses and group memberships.

Securing Printers

Just because you've networked a printer doesn't mean you want everyone with a domain account to be able to use it. Maybe you'd like to reserve the color printer for people who need to use the more expensive ink, or you want to keep people from printing their résumés after hours. Perhaps it's something as simple as wanting to make sure people connect to the right printer so you're not plagued with people complaining that their job didn't print when they've actually sent five copies to the wrong printer. In this section, let's talk about what you can do to make printers available only to the people you say at the times you say.

TIP   Printer security doesn't always give you the degree of granularity you need to give everyone the permissions they need and no more. Consider setting up multiple printers for each print device, setting different permissions for each, and only giving people access to the printer tuned for their needs.

Tuning Printer Permissions

You can make printers available all the time to everybody, or you can pick and choose the times and circumstances under which the printer will be available. Here's how.

SETTING AVAILABLE HOURS

By default, a printer will always accept print jobs. You can determine the hours during which a printer will send jobs to the print device. If a print job is sent to a printer after hours, the job will be queued but not printed until the printer is again available.

To edit a printer's hours of availability, turn to the Advanced tab of its properties pages (see Figure 13.35) and set new times. This tells the print server to hold print jobs in the spooler until the printer is again available. The new settings won't affect any jobs that have already been sent to the printer.

FIGURE 13.35
Define times for
the printer to be
available.

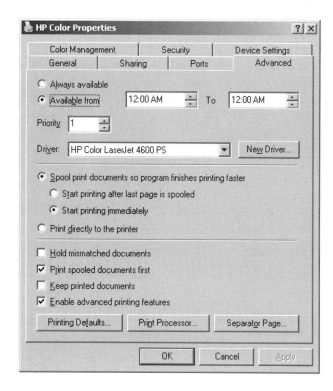

If you want a print device to be always available to some users and only available during certain hours to others, you'll need to create multiple printers for the single print device, as explained earlier in this chapter. Once you've done so, you can configure the printing hours separately for each printer.

SETTING PRINTER PERMISSIONS

Those familiar with the NT/Win2K argot will remember that you secure an NT-based network by defining user rights for what people can *do* on the network and setting permissions for the resources that people can *use*. Printer security is controlled with permissions on a per-group or per-user basis. Permissions generally stack—that is, the most permissive set of permissions available to you applies—unless you're talking about denied access. Denied access overrides permissions.

To set or edit the permissions assigned to a printer, log in with an account that has Administrator permissions, open the printer's properties pages, and turn to the Security tab. You'll see a dialog box like the one in Figure 13.36.

TIP *If you turn to a printer's Security tab and see a list of Security IDs (SIDs) instead of user or group names, and the cursor changes to an hourglass when over the dialog box, don't panic. The print server is retrieving the names from the domain controller and will show the user and group names after a few seconds. If this doesn't happen—if the SIDs never resolve to user and group names—then there's something wrong with either the domain controller or the connection between the two servers.*

FIGURE 13.36

Default printer
permissions

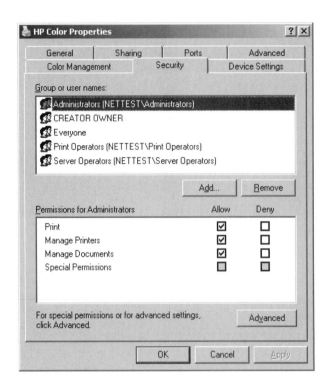

From here, you can edit the basic permission sets of the groups for whom some kind of printer access has been defined, denying or granting explicit access in three areas: printing (the ability to send print jobs to the printer), managing print jobs (the ability to control whether a print job is printed or the order in which it's printed relative to other jobs), or managing the printer (controlling *all* printing activity on a printer).

NOTE   *Table 13.3 includes a complete list of all permissions and how they apply to printers.*

Not sure how to interpret the check boxes? If a permission is checked, then it's either explicitly enabled or disabled, depending on which box is checked. If a permission is clear on both sides, then it's implicitly enabled. Shaded permission boxes imply that a permission is granted or denied through inheritance. You can explicitly enable or disable the permission by checking the appropriate box.

Fine-Tuning Printer Access

The Security page only shows the default groups and the basic permissions they've been assigned. For more control over the permission process, click the Advanced button to open the dialog box seen in Figure 13.37.

From here, you can see the state of the defined permissions and whether they're allowed or disallowed. To begin with, all defined permissions are allowed. The comment below the list of users and groups notes whether the highlighted permission applies to the basic membership of that group only or also to subgroups within that group. You can adjust these permissions either by adding new users or groups to the list (getting them from the domain controller) or by editing the permissions of the groups already there.

FIGURE 13.37

Setting advanced printer permissions

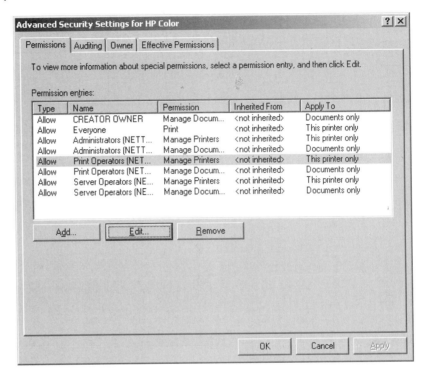

To define permissions for a new user or group, click the Add button to open the dialog box in Figure 13.38. If you know the name of the user or group account you want to set printer permissions for, then you can type it here, clicking the Check Names button to confirm that the user or group account exists. If a user or group account beginning with the string you typed exists, then the name will be underlined in the text box in this dialog box.

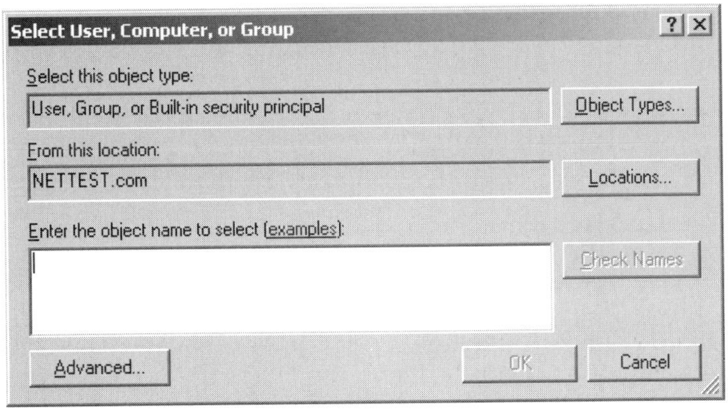

FIGURE 13.38

Choosing a user or group account for which to configure printer permissions

If there's more than one match (for example, I have one account that I use for administrative purposes and another that I use in Ordinary User mode, but both have my name in them), then a dialog box like the one in Figure 13.39 will prompt you to choose the one you mean. If there are *no* matches for the string you typed, then clicking Check Names will display a message box telling you so and nagging you to try again.

FIGURE 13.39

There may be more than one match for the string you're checking

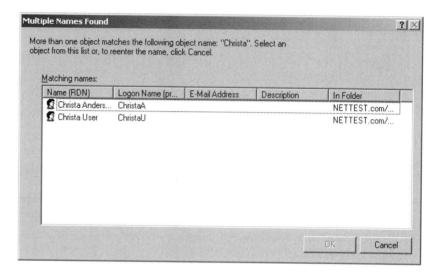

Theoretically, if you're not sure of the name, you can search for it by clicking the Advanced button to open the dialog box in Figure 13.40. You can even edit the columns setting to include more information in the results of the query, to make sure that you've got the right person. However, if you click the Name drop-down list, you'll see that you can search for either the exact name or the name that the account you need begins with. In other words, you can perform the exact same search that you can perform from the standard search tool shown in Figure 13.38. The moral of the story is that you need to know at least the beginning—at least the beginning *letter*—of any account for which you want to configure printer permissions.

Anyway, let's get back to configuring printer permissions for the account we've found. Once you've clicked OK in the dialog box in Figure 13.38, you'll open a dialog box like the one in Figure 13.41. The permissions listed here have the characteristics outlined in Table 13.3.

TIP *If the user or group you want isn't displayed in the list, type it into the Name box. If you've already created an account for this user or group, you'll be able to edit its permissions.*

You can customize user permissions by explicitly permitting some actions and denying others. For example, permission to manage printers normally implies permission to change permissions for that printer. However, you can get around this by allowing printer management while denying the ability to change permissions. This doesn't always work—you can't permit people to print yet deny them the ability to read permissions—but it's worth experimenting to see whether you can get the degree of granularity you want in access permissions.

FIGURE 13.40

Performing an advanced search for an account name

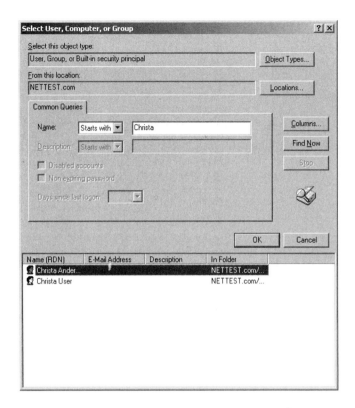

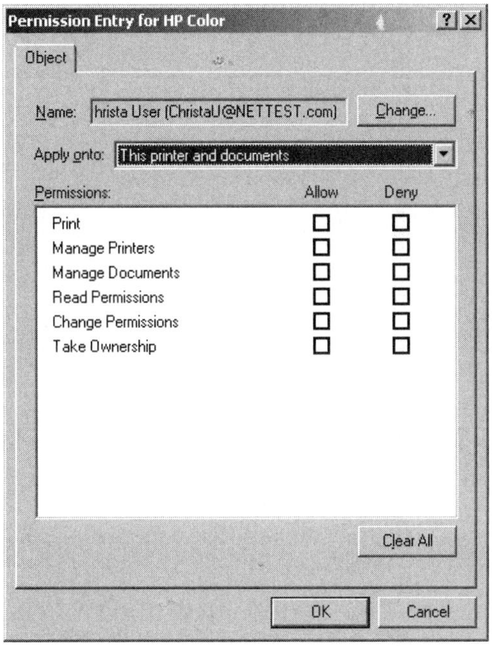

FIGURE 13.41

Defining the permissions of a new user

TABLE 13.3: PRINTER PERMISSIONS AND THEIR IMPLICATIONS

ACCESS TYPE	EFFECT	TIED TO
Print	User can send jobs to the printer.	Read permissions
Manage Printers	User can change printer properties and permissions.	Print, read permissions, change permissions, and take ownership of the printer
Manage Documents	User can control document-specific settings and pause, resume, restart, and delete spooled print jobs.	Read permissions, change permissions, and take ownership of the printer
Read Permissions	User can see the permissions all users and groups have for that printer.	N/A
Change Permissions	User can change the permissions all users and groups have for that printer.	Read permissions (although this won't be checked)
Take Ownership	User can take ownership of the printer.	Any permissions assigned to the creator/ owner of the printer

NOTE *Printer permissions can apply to the printer only, to documents only, or to both the printer and the documents printed on it.*

Changing permissions for an existing user or group works in much the same way: Select a name, click the View/Edit button, and you'll see the same set of options to explicitly grant or deny permissions.

Since a user account may belong to more than one group, and those groups may have different permissions, it can sometimes be hard to sort out what permissions an individual has. The Effective Permissions tab in Server 2003 should theoretically make it easier to sort this out, but doesn't do a very good job of it, since edited permissions are checked but look identical whether they're allowed or denied (see Figure 13.42).

Auditing Printer Access

Curious to know who's doing what to the printers under your care? Turn to the Auditing tab shown in Figure 13.43 (accessible from the Advanced button of the Security section of a printer's properties) to set up auditing to list events in the event log. Unlike Windows 2000, in Server 2003 you don't need to turn on auditing—it's on by default.

Although Server 2003 has security auditing enabled, it's not set up for printer auditing. By default, the print server doesn't log printer use or security events, so the list on the Auditing tab of a printer's properties pages will be empty when you originally turn to it. To add events to audit, click the Add button to move to a dialog box like the one you used to edit printer permissions (see Figure 13.44). Again, you can enter either the exact name of the user or group account to audit, or you can enter the beginning of the account name. Just make sure that you check the names for validity before continuing, or your audit won't do much good—monitoring a nonexisting account and all.

FIGURE 13.42

Sadly, the Effective Permissions tab doesn't tell you much.

FIGURE 13.43

Print servers don't initially audit any events.

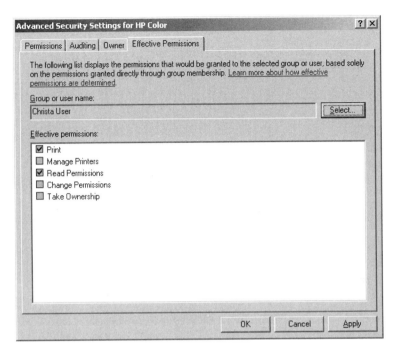

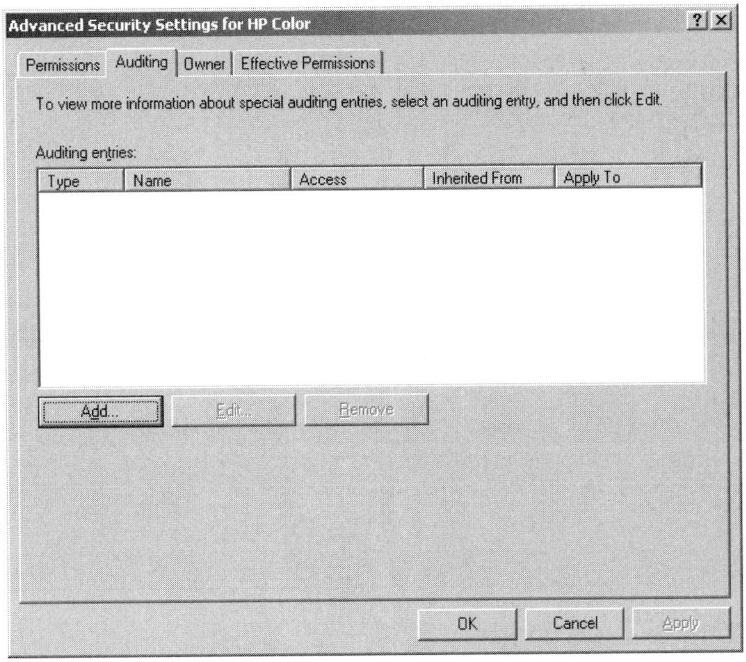

FIGURE 13.44

Choose a group
or user to audit.

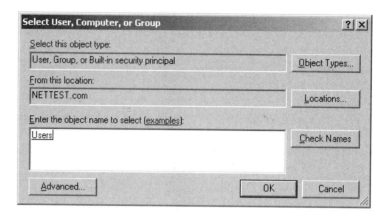

As when setting printer permissions, you'll first choose a group or user to audit from the list, then you'll choose events to audit. After you've chosen a group or user to audit and clicked OK, you'll move to a dialog box like the one in Figure 13.45.

FIGURE 13.45

Choose the events
to audit.

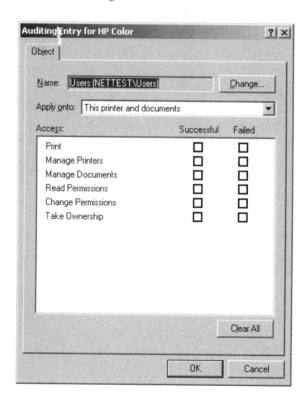

The dependencies shown here work the same way as the ones described in Table 13.3. The main difference is that here you're monitoring the attempts to *do* these things, not granting or denying permission to do them. Also, the Successful and Failed columns aren't mutually exclusive like the Allow and Deny ones are—you can monitor both failed and successful attempts to take ownership of a printer, for example. When you've finished tweaking the auditing options, click OK to return to the main Auditing tab, which will now look something like the one shown in Figure 13.46. Entries for these audits will now appear in the Security portion of the Event log.

FIGURE 13.46

A list of users and events to audit

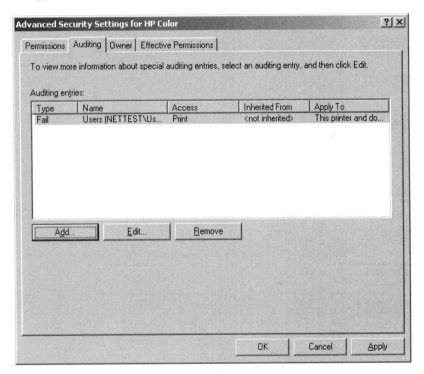

Assigning an Owner to a Printer

Even if a printer's owner is a user (and thus has minimal control over a printer), that owner has permission to manage documents—a permission ordinary users do not normally have. Administrators can give the printer to a new owner from the Owner tab of the Access Control Settings dialog box accessible from the advanced security options. The options are the person who made the printer in the first place and an administrator of the domain, as you can see from Figure 13.47.

To make a new owner, just double-click the appropriate entry. You'll open the by-now familiar dialog box from which you can choose user accounts. Find the person you want to be an owner of that computer, and click OK. That person's name will be listed alongside the other printer owners.

FIGURE 13.47

A list of possible owners for the printer

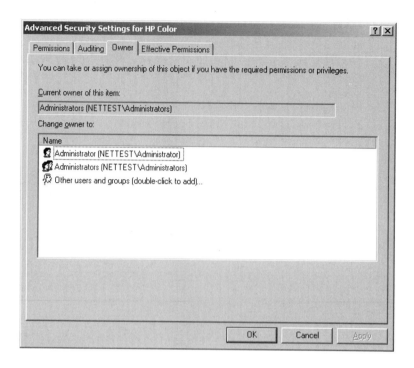

Group Policy Settings for Printers

Server 2003 has some group policies that you can edit to configure how much control users have over adding and removing printers and over how those printers appear in the Active Directory.

PRINTER-SPECIFIC GROUP POLICY SETTINGS

The Group Policy settings in the Microsoft Management Console include some policies you can tweak to configure how the printer appears in the Active Directory or in the domain (see Figure 13.48). To get to these settings, open the Group Policy snap-in and move to the Administrative Templates section of the Computer Configuration settings. As you can see from Table 13.4, some of these settings apply only to Active Directory–aware clients, but others apply to any client because they're actually settings to the print server or the way the printer is published in Active Directory.

When you first install the operating system, none of these settings will be configured. To enable or disable a policy, right-click that policy and choose Properties from the pop-up list that appears. You'll see a dialog box that looks like the one in Figure 13.49.

Click appropriate radio buttons to enable or disable the policy, and enter a value as needed. If you need more information about what a policy actually does if enabled, turn to the Explain tab, but this information also appears in the left margin of the policy pane when you've selected a policy, as shown in Figure 13.49. Once you've chosen to actively clear or check a box, the policy's entry will change from Not Configured to Enabled or Disabled.

FIGURE 13.48

Group policies
controlling printer
publishing

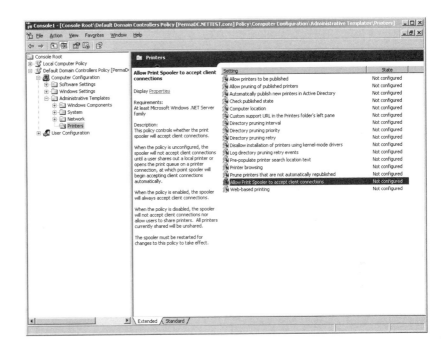

TABLE 13.4: PRINTER PUBLICATION POLICIES

POLICY	DEFAULT VALUE (WHEN UNCONFIGURED)	DESCRIPTION
Allow Printers to be Published	On (permits publishing)	Toggles to allow printers to be published. If a printer isn't published, clients can't find it in the Active Directory using the procedure described earlier. When configured, overrides Automatically Publish New Printers in Active Directory policy.
Allow Pruning of Published Printers	On (will prune)	Controls whether the pruning service may remove printers that it can't find when browsing for them. If you enable this option, you can tune it with the pruning interval, retry, and priority policies.
Automatically Publish New Printers in Active Directory	On (will publish)	Controls whether newly shared printers are added to the Active Directory. Allow Printers to be Published overrides this policy, so if that policy is disabled, printers will not be published even if this policy is enabled.
Check Published State	Only at startup	Verifies that published printers are indeed in the Active Directory. You can set this value to Never (the default) or at varying intervals ranging from 30 minutes to 1 day.

Continued on next page

TABLE 13.4: PRINTER PUBLICATION POLICIES *(continued)*

POLICY	DEFAULT VALUE (WHEN UNCONFIGURED)	DESCRIPTION
Computer Location	None	Identifies the location of the printer server. Use this setting in combination with Prepopulate Printer Search Location Text to make people choose a particular location for their printer, avoiding the possibility of choosing the wrong printer and sending print jobs three states away.
Custom Support URL in the Printer Window's Left Pane	Off	Ordinarily, the left window of the `Printers` folder displays the Microsoft URL and (if available) the URL for the printer's maker. If you enable this policy and type in a URL, you can point people to a different location— perhaps a customized troubleshooting guide on the company Web site.
Directory Pruning Interval	8 hours	Determines the interval at which printers that haven't announced themselves recently are removed from the directory of published printers. The pruner reads this value every hour, so changes will not take effect immediately. This policy applies only to domain controllers.
Directory Pruning Priority	Normal	Tunes the priority of the pruning thread, responsible for deleting outdated printer entries in the Active Directory. The higher the priority of the pruner thread (or any thread), the more often it will get CPU cycles and thus the more often the Active Directory will be updated— but the fewer CPU cycles the other threads will get. You can set this value to Lowest, Below Normal, Normal, Above Normal, or Highest. This policy applies only to domain controllers.
Directory Pruning Retry	2 tries	Determines how many times the pruning thread will attempt to contact a print server before giving up and deleting that printer's entry from the Active Directory. This policy applies only to domain controllers.
Prepopulate Printer Search Location Text	On	Enables location tracking (based on the subnet of the printer server and the client) and a browse feature. Use this feature to point people to a certain location for their printers.
Printer Browsing	Off in domains using the Active Directory; on in NT 4 domains dependent on browsing to publish resources	Controls whether the print subsystem can add printers to the browse list. In a domain that uses the Active Directory, the print subsystem does not announce printers to the master browsers in the domain. If you disable printer browsing, you prevent the print subsystem from announcing the printers even in an NT 4 domain.

Continued on next page

TABLE 13.4: PRINTER PUBLICATION POLICIES *(continued)*

POLICY	DEFAULT VALUE (WHEN UNCONFIGURED)	DESCRIPTION
Prune Printers That Are Not Automatically Republished	Never	Controls the circumstances under which a printer connected to a computer running an operating system not using the Active Directory or a printer published outside its own domain—and thus not controlled by the domain-level pruning rules earlier in this table—may be pruned. Choosing Never means that the printer will never be pruned. Choosing Only When the Print Server Is Found means that the printer will be pruned if the print server is found but the printer isn't available. Choosing Only When the Printer Isn't Found prunes printers that are not automatically republished. This setting applies only to printers published from Active Directory Users and Computers, not from the Printers section of the Control Panel.
Allow Print Spooler to Accept Client Connections	No, until a client shares a printer with the network or views the print queue on a shared printer	Server 2003 only
Web-Based Printing	Web-based printing allowed	When disabled, won't accept print requests sent via HTTP, or publish printers to the Web. You'll still need to enable the Internet Printing Web extension, though.

FIGURE 13.49

Configuring print server policies

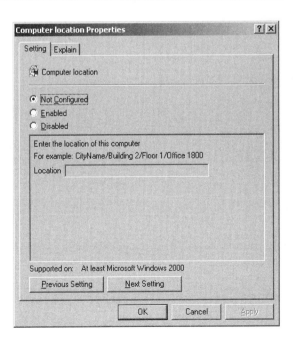

TIP *You can run through the list of policies with the Previous Setting and Next Setting buttons without exiting and reentering the policy properties box. The only catch is that if you click Cancel, you'll cancel every policy change you made while the window was open.*

USER-SPECIFIC PRINTER SETTINGS

To edit user settings for adding and removing printers, click Start/Programs/Administrative Tools/ Active Directory Users and Computers. Click the Active Directory container of the domain you want to manage (an organizational unit or a domain). Right-click that container, and then click Properties. On the Group Policy tab, click New to create a new group policy, then Edit to open the Group Policy Editor. The settings you're looking for are in User Configuration/Administrative Templates/ Control Panel/Printers and are described in Table 13.5.

WARNING *These settings generally apply to the Add Printer Wizard. If someone uses the Add Hardware tool to add a printer, for example, then they can circumvent Disable Addition of Printers.*

TABLE 13.5: GROUP POLICIES FOR USER CONTROL OVER PRINTERS

POLICY	DESCRIPTION
Browse a Common Web Site to Find Printers	Adds the path to an Internet or intranet Web page to the Add Printer Wizard. You can use this policy to direct users to a Web page from which they can install printers, making it easy for users to find the printers you want them to add. Without this policy, users must know the exact URL of the print server configured for Internet printing. When users click Browse, Windows opens an Internet browser and navigates to the specified address to display the available printers.
Browse the Network to Find Printers	Permits users to browse the network for shared printers from the Add Printer Wizard. If you disable this policy, users will need to know the exact name of a printer to connect to it from the Add Printer Wizard.
Default Active Directory Path When Searching for Printers	Specifies the Active Directory location in which searches for printers begin. If you enable this policy, these searches begin at the location you specify in the Default Active Directory Path box. Otherwise, searches begin at the root of Active Directory. However, this policy does not restrict searches to that point.
Point and Print Restrictions	When enabled, restricts users either to the printers named here (identified by fully qualified domain names) or to the printers in their forest, depending on which setting you pick. (XP SP1 and Server 2003 only)
Prevent Addition of Printers	Removes the Add Printer Wizard from the Start menu and from the Printers folder in Control Panel. This policy does not prevent users from accessing Add/Remove Hardware or running a program (such as an administrative script) to add a printer. Nor does it delete printers already added—it just prevents them from using the Add Printer Wizard to add more of them.

Continued on next page

TABLE 13.5: GROUP POLICIES FOR USER CONTROL OVER PRINTERS *(continued)*

POLICY	DESCRIPTION
Prevent Deletion of Printers	Prevents users from deleting local and network printers. If a user tries to delete a printer, such as by using the Delete command in the Printers tool in the Control Panel, Windows displays a message explaining that the action is prevented by a policy. This policy does not prevent users from running programs to delete a printer.

Configuring Printer Settings

Sharing a printer with the network and securing it isn't generally the end of the story. You haven't yet added support for separator pages used to help dozens of printer users avoid picking up each other's documents, and you haven't configured messaging so the right people get printer messages. And what about setting up printer priorities so that the print server will print user documents on the right printer, without user intervention?

NOTE   *The options described in this section apply to both network and locally connected printers.*

To configure a printer's settings, right-click its icon in the printer's properties pages and choose Properties from the pop-up menu that appears (see Figure 13.50).

FIGURE 13.50

Use this dialog box to fine-tune a printer's settings.

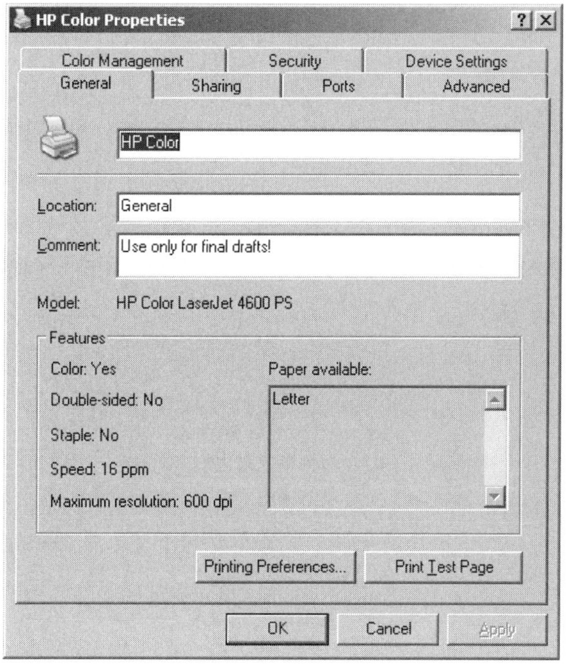

Most of the basic configuration options, such as name changes and sharing, are pretty self-explanatory once you look at the screen. I'll go over the more complex options, but if you're trying to figure out where an option is configured, refer to Table 13.6 for a quick guide to what's where.

TABLE 13.6: PRINTER OPTIONS AND LOCATIONS IN THE PROPERTIES PAGE

OPTION TO CHANGE	LOCATION	REASON TO EDIT
Add more client drivers	Additional Drivers dialog box, available from the Sharing tab	Load drivers for printer clients so they can be automatically downloaded to the client (available for 32-bit Windows and Itanium only).
Add more ports	Ports tab	Restore ports that you've deleted or add support for direct network connections to the printer.
Change port time-outs	Ports tab when you click the Configure Port button	Increase port time-out settings to make ports wait longer to receive printer data. Helps if the print job isn't getting to the printer quickly enough.
Edit printer configuration settings	Device Settings tab	Edit the printer settings, including the amount of memory installed, fonts installed on the printer, page protection, and the like.
Edit user or group permissions to the printer	Security tab	Edit the list of users or groups with access to the printer or change the permissions they have.
Set the hours printer will accept print jobs	Advanced tab	Edit to shut off a printer after certain hours, perhaps when the workday is over.
Change local printer name	General tab	Use for local printer identification.
Change network printer name	Sharing tab	Use for printer identification on the network.
Set the page order	Layout tab of Printing Preferences dialog box, available from the Printing Preferences button on the General tab or the Printing Defaults button on the Advanced tab	Toggle between printing pages in normal or reverse order.
Set paper orientation	Layout tab of Printing Preferences dialog box, available from the Printing Preferences button on the General tab or the Printing Defaults button on the Advanced tab	Toggle between portrait and landscape orientation of printer output.

Continued on next page

TABLE 13.6: PRINTER OPTIONS AND LOCATIONS IN THE PROPERTIES PAGE *(continued)*

OPTION TO CHANGE	LOCATION	REASON TO EDIT
Identify the paper source	Paper/Quality tab of Printing Preferences dialog box, available from the Printing Preferences button on the General tab or the Printing Defaults button on the Advanced tab	Choose a different paper tray to print from, perhaps for higher-quality paper or printing from transparencies.
Set the print processor	Print Processor button on the Advanced tab	Toggle between default print formats (EMF, TEXT, or RAW).
Set the printer spooling	Advanced tab	Toggle between using printer spooling and sending documents directly to the printer.
Edit separator pages	Separator button on the Advanced tab	Specify a new separator page for print jobs.
Enable printer pooling	Ports tab	Use to connect two or more print devices to a single printer.

Defining Port Settings

Port settings control how the print server sends print jobs to its ports. You can't do too much to configure ports other than define which port a printer sends print jobs to and, in the case of parallel ports, how long the printer is willing to wait for an expected print job before reporting an error condition. Unless I say otherwise, you'll be controlling most port settings from the Ports tab (see Figure 13.51).

ASSIGNING A PRINTER TO A NEW PORT

If you move a print device from one port to another, you'll need to edit the device's port settings. Open the printer properties pages, turn to the Ports tab, and check the box next to the correct port. Notice that you can select multiple ports only if printer pooling is enabled.

Not sure what all those ports are? TS ports are printer ports of terminal server sessions. LPT ports are parallel (8-bit) ports. COM ports are serial (1-bit) ports. Finally, any port prefaced with a server name indicates a network connection. The terminal server session ports show the ports attached to currently connected terminal server clients and can be used to manually redirect ports, as described in "Manually Redirecting Printers." Any TCP/IP ports you've installed for network-connected printers will also appear in this list.

CREATING A PRINTER POOL

As I mentioned in the beginning of this chapter, the ratio of printers to print devices isn't always 1:1. You've already seen how you can create multiple printers for a single print device. I'm talking here about how to make a single printer support multiple print devices.

Why would you want to do this? It's mostly a matter of efficiency. Even with the fast print devices available today, busy offices may have more print jobs coming through than one printer can handle.

To keep things running smoother and reduce delays, you can distribute print jobs among multiple printers. Print clients will all send their print jobs to the same printer, but the jobs will go to the printer that's least busy at any given time. This is called *printer pooling*.

FIGURE 13.51

The Ports tab for a printer

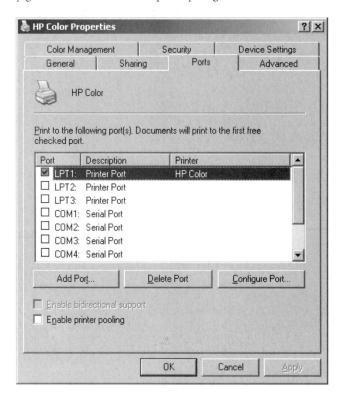

To set up a printer pool, turn to the Ports tab for the printer. Make sure the box enabling printer pooling is checked, then select all the ports to which printers in the printer pool are attached. These ports can be local ports, ports connected to terminal server clients, or network ports.

There are a couple catches to printer pooling. First, the printers in the pool must be identical to each other—same make, model, and amount of installed memory. Second, I highly recommend putting the pooled printers in the same physical location. It's not going to endear you to your user base if they have to wander from place to place looking for their print jobs.

TIP   Consider using separator pages with usernames in printer pools since users will not necessarily know which printer their job went to.

SENDING DOCUMENTS DIRECTLY TO THE PRINTER

As I explained in the description of the printing model at the beginning of this chapter, the print server normally creates a spool file that's sent to the printer for printing rather than sending documents directly to the printer port. Spooling documents means the application you're printing from is only tied up for the time it takes to create the spool file, not to print the entire document. This is called *printing in the background*.

If you can't use print spooling for some reason—perhaps if the print server's hard disk is so full that it can't create the spool file—then you can send documents directly to the printer port, without creating a spool file or using print server resources. Turn to the Advanced tab of the printer's properties pages and select Print Directly to the Printer, as shown in Figure 13.52.

FIGURE 13.52

Disabling print spooling

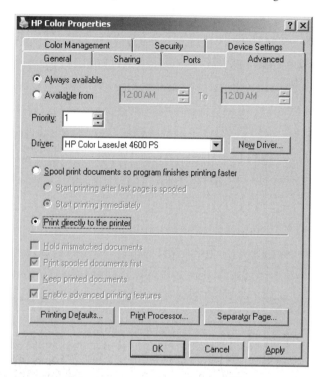

This is not something you'll often want to do. Spool files allow you to print large and complex documents without running out of printer memory. They also allow users to regain control of their applications quicker. Only disable print spooling if you can't print otherwise—it's something to mess around with if images aren't coming out properly.

Using Separator Pages

When a lot of people are using the same printer, keeping print jobs organized can get complicated. To help you minimize the number of people who wander off with each other's print jobs, the operating system supports separator pages. These extra pages are printed at the beginning of documents to identify the person doing the printing, the time, the job number, or whatever other information is defined in the page. (I'll explain how you can tell what information a page will print, and how you can create your own custom separator pages, in a minute.)

TIP *Like other printer options, separator pages are assigned to printers, not to print devices, so you can use a different separator page for each printer.*

Choosing a Separator Page

By default, printers don't use separator pages. To use one of the default separator pages provided with Server 2003, move to the Advanced tab of a printer's properties pages and click the Separator Page button. You'll see a dialog box like the one in Figure 13.53.

Figure 13.53

Choose a separator page.

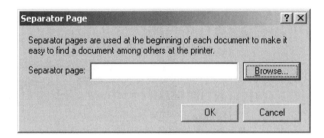

Type the name of the separator page or click the Browse button to open the %*systemroot*%\system32 folder (where the pages are stored) and find the one you want. Table 13.7 describes the four built-in separator pages.

Table 13.7: Default Separator Pages

Page Name	Description	Compatibility
SYSPRINT.SEP	Prints a blank page before print jobs	PostScript
PCL.SEP	Switches a dual-language printer to PCL mode	PCL
PSCRIPT.SEP	Switches a dual-language printer to PostScript mode	PostScript
SYSPRTJ.SEP	Prints a blank page before print jobs sent to a PostScript printer	PostScript

There's one catch to choosing a separator page: The page must be available locally. Although you can choose an SEP file stored in a network-accessible folder, a separator page that's in a networked location will not print. The system won't fuss at you either when you choose the SEP file or when you send a print job to a printer, but print jobs will have no separator page.

Creating a New Separator Page

Given that the built-in separator pages are mostly necessary in specific instances, you'll probably want to create your own separator pages if you use them at all. Separator page files are just text files, so you can create the file in Notepad.

On the first line of the new file, type a single character—any character will do—and press Enter. This character will now be the *escape character* that alerts the print server that you're performing a function, not entering text, so make it one that you won't need for anything else. Dollar signs ($) and pound signs (#) are both good escape characters, but the only rule is that you can't use the character as text.

Once you've picked an escape code, customize the separator page with any of the variables shown in Table 13.8. Be sure to include the escape character before each function, as I've shown in this table with a dollar sign.

TABLE 13.8: SEPARATOR PAGE FUNCTIONS

VARIABLE	FUNCTION
BS	Prints text in block characters created with pound signs (#) until you insert a $U. Be warned—printing text like this takes up a lot of room. You probably don't want to use this option.
$D	Prints the date the job was printed, using the format defined on the Date tab of the Regional Options applet in the Control Panel.
$E	Equivalent to the Page Break function in Word; all further functions will be executed on a new page. If you get an extra blank separator page when you print, remove this function from the SEP file.
$F*pathname\filename*	Prints the contents of the specified file to the separator page, starting on a blank line. As separator pages are strictly text-only, only the text will be printed—no formatting.
$H*nn*	Sets a printer-specific control sequence, where *nn* is a hex ASCII code that goes directly to the printer. Look in your printer manual for any codes that you might set this way and for instructions on how and when to use them.
$I	Prints the job number. Each print job has a job number associated with it.
$L*xxx*	Prints all the characters following (represented here with *xxx*) until it comes to another escape code. Use this function to print any customized text you like.
$N	Prints the login name of the person who submitted the print job.
$*n*	Skips *n* lines (where *n* is a number from 0 to 9). Skipping 0 lines just moves printing to the next line, so you could use that function to define where line breaks should occur.
$T	Prints the time the job was printed, using the format defined on the Time tab of the Regional Options applet in the Control Panel.
$U	Turns off block character printing.
$W*nn*	Sets the line width, where *nn* is a number of characters. Any characters in excess of this line width are truncated. The default (which you don't have to define) is 80 characters.

For example, the following SEP file

```
$
$N
$0
$D
```

```
$L This is a separator page. Only use these pages to organize
$L print jobs because they're otherwise a waste of paper.
$1
$T
```

produces this output:

> Christa
>
> 10/31/02 This is a separator page. Only use these pages to organize print jobs because they're otherwise a waste of paper.
>
> 3:49:11 P.M.

Notice that there are only line breaks if you specifically include them. Without the $n codes, all output will be on a single line.

When you're done, save the separator page file with an .sep extension to the %*systemroot*%\system32 folder if you want to store it with other separator pages. Otherwise, you can store the page anywhere on the print server. To use the new page, just load it as you would one of the defaults.

Adjusting Print Server Settings

To edit server-wide printer settings, open the Printers folder, make sure that no installed printers are highlighted, and choose File/Server Properties. You'll see a tabbed dialog box like the one in Figure 13.54.

FIGURE 13.54

Edit server properties to change settings that apply to all printers.

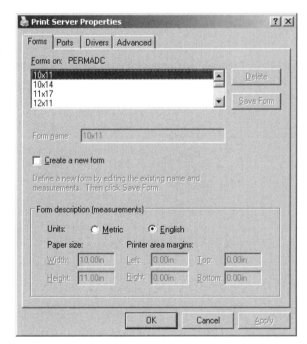

TIP *To make sure you're editing server-wide settings, highlight the Add Printer icon in the* `Printers` *folder before choosing Server Properties from the File menu.*

Choosing Form Settings

A Server 2003 arranges its print jobs on the paper based on forms, which define a template for where text should appear. Print servers come with a long list of predefined forms you can choose from, but they also allows you to define your own form settings for customized needs such as printing to company letterhead.

Print servers are set up to print on blank 8.5 × 11 paper (the standard size). To choose a new form, find it in the list. To create a new form, edit the settings in the dialog box, choose a new name for the form, and then click the Save Form button.

NOTE *You must choose a new name for the form. You can't overwrite or delete the built-in forms on the print server.*

Configuring Server Port Settings

Although you can configure the following settings from any printer's properties pages, I think it's less confusing to edit them in the server properties. That way, you're reminded that the settings you make here apply not just to a single printer but to all affected printers.

ADDING AND DELETING PORTS

We've already discussed how to create a TCP/IP port for a network-connected printer. Most people won't need to add or delete other kinds of ports, but here's how you do it if you need to:

1. Open the print server's properties pages and turn to the Ports tab. You'll see a list of the currently installed ports.
2. Click the Add Port button to open the Printer Ports dialog box.
3. Click the New Port button and provide a name for the port in the text box that appears, then click OK.
4. Back in the Printer Ports box, click Close to return to the Ports tab.

The new port should appear in the list of installed ports.

NOTE *Add COM ports if you have a multiport serial adapter and will support more than four serial printing connections. Add network ports if you're supporting a printer connected directly to the network.*

This will add a new port listing to `HKLM\Software\Microsoft\Windows NT\CurrentVersion\Ports`—no reboot required.

To delete a port, just select it in the list and click the Delete Port button. You'll be prompted to confirm that you really want to delete the port. When you do so, the port listing will immediately disappear from the Registry.

OOPS! I DELETED A PORT I WAS USING!

It is easy to replace accidentally deleted parallel ports. Click the Add Port button and choose to add a local port. Give the port the appropriate name (such as LPT1) and you're done.

It is *not* so easy to replace an accidentally deleted serial port. In that case, you'll need to add the port, then edit the Registry to define it as a serial port. Add the port as described earlier, then open REGEDT32 and move to HKLM\Software\Microsoft\Windows NT\Current Version\Ports. Find the value for the port you deleted, then double-click it to edit its value to 9600,n,8,1. Unless you deleted every COM port, you'll have other COM port values there for reference.

Parallel, file, terminal client, and network connections have no values in the Registry—just entries.

EDITING PORT TIME-OUTS

A print device connected to a parallel port (identified as LPT*x*) will wait a certain interval from the time it expects to receive a print job to the time it gets it. If the print device doesn't get the job within that time, it will notify the person sending the print job that there's an error. Technically speaking, it's not the printer that's complaining, but the parallel port.

You can adjust the interval of time that a parallel port will wait before complaining that it hasn't yet received an expected print job. Turn to any printer's Ports tab, select a port, and click the Configure Port button. You'll see a dialog box like the one in Figure 13.55.

FIGURE 13.55

Edit the value to increase or decrease the transmission time-out.

The normal time-out period is 90 seconds. Raise or lower this value by typing in a new number. The lower the value, the more sensitive the port will be to delays. Higher values may make the printer more forgiving of transmission delays, but if you do have a real problem printing, it will take longer for you to discover this. As noted earlier, port settings apply to all printers using that port.

Adding or Updating the Printer Driver on a Print Server

One of the cool things about using Win32 clients for network printing is that you don't have to install local driver support anymore. This really speeds up the client installation process and makes it easier to update drivers since you no longer have to run from workstation to workstation with the new driver media.

For this to work, however, you *do* need to install support for those clients on the server end so that the client can access them as necessary. Drivers are added on a server-wide basis—if you have more than one printer of the same type connected to your print server, you'll update all drivers at once, not just the ones that printer is using.

To add a driver:

1. Turn to the Drivers tab of the printer server's properties pages. You should see a list of installed drivers that looks like the one in Figure 13.56.

FIGURE 13.56

Drivers previously installed on the server

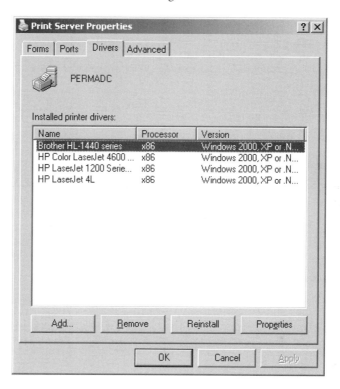

2. Click the Add button on this screen to start the Add Printer Driver Wizard. Click through the opening screen to the point where you can choose the manufacturer and printer model for which you're adding support.

TIP *The list of available printer drivers includes only those that come on the installation CD. If you've got an updated driver, click the Have Disk button and provide the path to the driver file.*

3. From the list that appears, choose all the Win32 clients that will be connecting to this printer from the network. Server 2003 supports drivers for all Win32 platforms on Intel and Server 2003 and XP on Itanium.

NOTE *Remember, the fact that DOS and Windows 3.x drivers aren't listed doesn't mean that you can't print from those clients. It just means that those drivers are not included with the operating system, and you'll need to install them on the clients.*

4. When you click Next, you'll see the wizard's final screen, telling you what driver support you have added.

Updating a driver is simpler:

1. From the Drivers tab of the server's properties pages, highlight the driver you want to update and click the Update button. The print server will ask you whether you're sure you want to update the driver.

2. You'll be prompted for the location of the driver files—either the installation CD or a floppy or network connection.

That's it—the driver's updated.

TIP   *Not sure where to get driver updates? Forget any floppy disks that came with your hardware—those drivers are apt to be very out of date. Instead, go to the printer manufacturer's Web site and look for a Downloads section. The most recent drivers should be available there.*

Keeping Track of Your Printing

Server 2003 offers some messaging and logging capabilities that you can use to monitor the printing process or refer to for troubleshooting when something's not going right. To configure these capabilities, turn to the Advanced tab of the server's properties pages (see Figure 13.57).

FIGURE 13.57

Set logging and messaging options for your print server.

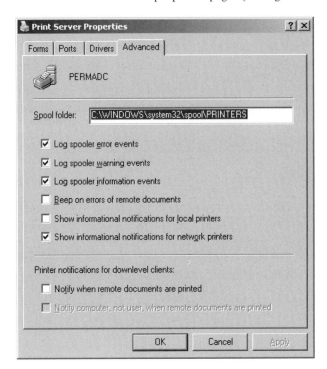

Most of these options are fairly self-explanatory. The spooler error, warning, and information events go into the logs visible from the Event Viewer. They don't record every print job sent to the printer (thank goodness, or you'd end up with a huge event log), only spool events.

Messaging is configured from the same tab. By default, the person originating a print job gets a message when the print job is completed or if there's a problem with it. You can disable messaging here, send the error message to the *computer* originating the job, or set up the print server to beep when there's a printing error. Most of the time, the default options will work fine.

Managing Print Jobs

Managing print jobs is pretty straightforward whether you're doing it from the Printers folder or from the Web.

Managing Printers and Documents from the *Printers* Folder

If you double-click a printer's entry in the Printers folder, you'll see a list of all print jobs currently waiting to be printed and the following information:

◆ The filename of the document being printed

◆ The job's status (printing, spooling, or paused)

◆ Who sent the job to the printer

◆ How many pages are in the job and how many remain to be printed

◆ The file size of the print job

◆ The time and date the user submitted the job

When you select a job in the list, you can use the tools in the Document menu to pause a job, resume a paused job, restart a print job from the beginning, or delete a print job. The only catch is that you have to do all this while the job is still spooling to the print device. You can't control the parts of the job that have already spooled to the physical printer's memory from this console.

If you pause a print job, you can edit its priority or printing times in the middle of printing. From the Document menu, choose Properties to open the dialog box in Figure 13.58.

From here, you can view many properties inherited from the printer and passed to the job, and you can raise or lower the job's priority. The higher a job's priority, the higher its place in line, so you can use this feature to manipulate the order in which jobs print even if one job got to the printer before another did. This can be very useful on those occasions when the person printing the 200-page manual sends their job to the printer before the person creating a cover sheet for the FedEx package that has to be ready by 3:30.

FIGURE 13.58

Properties of a print job

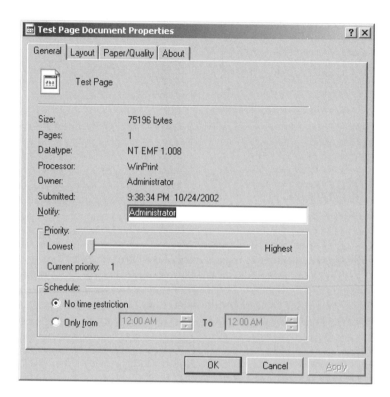

Managing Printers and Documents from a Browser

You can't completely manage a printer from a browser—you can't adjust printer settings, paper sizes, and the like—but you can do Basic Printer and Document Management Stuff.

You can pause, resume, or cancel all print jobs for a particular printer. From the printer's page, click the link naming what you want to do to the printer.

You can pause, resume, or cancel individual print jobs from the Web browser. When print jobs are active, they're displayed on the printer's Documents page, visible when you click the Documents link under Printer Actions. Each print job has a radio button next to it; to select a print job, click it so that it's highlighted. When you've selected the print job, you can pause, resume, or delete it using the links provided there.

Troubleshooting Printer Problems

Printing under Server 2003 is usually pretty trouble-free—in the software, at any rate—but every once in a while you may run into problems. The remainder of this chapter describes some of the more common printing problems and tells you how to solve them.

Basic Troubleshooting: Identifying the Situation

First, try to figure out *where* the problem lies. Is it the printer? The application? The network? If you can tell where the problem lies, you'll simplify the troubleshooting process.

TIP   The printing problem that frustrates me most is paper jams. Getting that last shred of jammed paper out of the printer can drive you to madness. To minimize paper jams, store paper somewhere with low humidity (curled paper jams easier), don't overfill the paper tray, and keep paper neat before it goes in the tray.

Printer troubles can happen due to any combination of three different causes:

◆ Hardware errors

◆ Software errors

◆ User errors

TIP   One basic part of printer troubleshooting is to make sure the person is connected to the right printer and knows which print device is associated with that printer. Some troubleshooting jobs end with the task of finding the printer with five unclaimed print jobs on top of it.

NO ONE CAN PRINT

If no one can print, check the print device and network connection. Check the easy stuff first: Is the printer on and online? Does the cartridge have ink? Is the printer server up and running? Did the printer *ever* work, or is this its maiden voyage? If it never worked, make sure you've got the right driver installed, or try downloading a newer one from the manufacturer's Web site.

From the console, check the port settings. Is the printer sending data to the port the print device is connected to? Make sure to set up the TCP/IP port for a network-connected printer properly.

Also, see if you can print from the print server's console. There could be a network problem preventing people from reaching the print server.

Make sure there's enough space on the print server's hard disk to store spool files. If the print server can't create spool files, it can't print from a spool.

Make sure the printer is set up to use the proper print processor.

If using Internet Printing, make sure that this service is enabled.

SOME PEOPLE CAN'T PRINT

What do those people have in common? Are they all in a single subnet? In the same user group? Using the same application? Printing to the same printer? Find the element they have in common, and that's probably the element that's causing the printing problem. For example, if everyone who's printing from NT clients can print and everyone printing from Windows 9x clients can't, then check the data type (on the Advanced tag of a printer's properties—click the Print Processor button to see what the currently selected default data type is). Unless the data type is RAW, then print jobs that people create from Windows 9x clients will disappear—you won't see any error messages, they just won't print.

ONE PERSON CAN'T PRINT

If only one person can't print, try to narrow down the source of the problem. Can the person print from another application? Can the person print from another computer? If this person can't print at all, see if someone else can print from their computer. If so, check the permissions attached to the person who can't print. They may be denied access to the printer altogether.

TIP   *If only one person is having printing problems, try rebooting the computer and retrying the print job. Some applications (such as Netscape Navigator 4.51) have a problem if they crash in the middle of creating a print file—they won't accept another one because they think the previous job is still being created. Sometimes, this problem will prevent any application from printing from that computer. In such a case, the only thing to do is reboot and try again. Logging out and in again won't do it.*

Using Online Resources

If you get completely stuck, try the links included in the left pane of the Printers folder. (Note that these links will be visible only if you've got Web content enabled. If you disabled Web content to clean up the desktop, you can reenable it for this folder only by opening Tools/Folder Options and, on the General tab of the Folder Options dialog box, choosing Enable Web Content on My Desktop.)

The More Info link leads to a printer page on the Microsoft Web site at www.microsoft.com, the manufacturer's link leads to their printing page (if they have one), and the Microsoft Support link leads to the printing home page in the Microsoft support area of its Web site. (I'd provide the link, but given how often Microsoft rearranges its Web site, by the time you read this it wouldn't be accurate.) If your print server has an Internet connection, you can connect directly from the Printers folder, but if not, you can still plug the URLs into a browser to see if the online resources can help you with your question.

TIP   *Considering how often Microsoft reorganizes its Web site, you might be better off using the URL policy I described earlier to link to a custom home page with a troubleshooting guide and perhaps the latest drivers. Nothing is more frustrating than being desperate enough to try the Web tool but then discovering the link is dead.*

Unglamorous as printing is, it's an essential service for just about any organization. In the previous pages I've talked about how to set up printers for local use or for your network, how to get those printers to the people who need them, how to automatically deploy printers through Internet printing and simple administrative scripts, and how to keep those printers from those who haven't any reason to be using them. After reading this chapter, you should feel ready to do your part to help keep those recycling bins full.

Chapter 14

Connecting Microsoft Clients to the Server

YOU'VE BUILT YOUR SERVER, created users, and shared network resources. Now you need to configure your client systems to use those resources. In this chapter, I'll show you how to set up various client systems with networking components, how to log on to the network, how to find and connect to shared resources, how to manage your passwords, and, when applicable, how to find and connect to the Active Directory.

Throughout this chapter, I'll connect to the same server, on the same domain, and with the same user account.

- My username is phewson.
- My domain name is REDHILLTOWN.COM.
- The domain controller is ZOOROPA.
- Other servers on the network are OCTOBER and SALOME.

What You Should Know Before Setting Up Network Clients

Before you jump into configuring workstations, there are a few things you should know about clients and the network environment. If you are new to Microsoft networks and have just picked up this book and opened it to this page, you might want to look over some of the previous chapters before attempting to configure clients:

- Chapter 2 covers the basics of networking software and security.
- Chapters 6 and 7 deal with TCP/IP protocol and infrastructure; TCP/IP is likely to be the only protocol used on your network these days.
- Chapter 9 shows you how to set up user accounts and computer accounts, for systems that can participate in domain-level security.

If you've read these chapters, or are generally familiar with the concepts, you can safely skip to the section on configuring your type of workstation. Otherwise, I'd like to point out some general issues that form the background for this chapter. If you need more detail than I can provide in an overview, please review the chapters just listed.

Client Software

For each client you configure, you'll be loading three basic software components: a *driver* for the network interface card (NIC), a *network protocol*, and a *network client*.

The NIC driver is vendor and hardware specific. Before loading any network protocol or client software, the operating system must recognize the network card and load the appropriate driver. Fortunately, due to the advancement of Plug and Play, most of the client systems in this chapter can automatically detect the NIC and load a driver included with the OS. If the driver is not included with the OS, or if your client system fails to detect the network card, you must use the driver and installation instructions for your operating system that are provided by the manufacturer. However, I recommend that you always use the vendor-supplied driver if it is more recent than the one supplied with the OS. The network card's OEM disk or CD usually includes release notes, installation instructions, and any available diagnostic software. If it's feasible, use the same type of network card throughout your network; you will become familiar with any idiosyncrasies of the hardware, and you can use the same installation procedures, drivers, and diagnostic software on all of your workstations.

The network protocol software is usually included with the operating system and sets message packaging and routing standards for network communications. Client and server systems must use a common protocol to communicate. For the vast majority of Microsoft networks these days, TCP/IP is the standard. Windows Server 2003 Enterprise Edition and Active Directory require TCP/IP to function properly. This server release also includes NWLink, an IPX/SPX-compatible protocol for connectivity to Netware servers, and AppleTalk for Macintosh clients, but the legacy (and nonroutable) protocol NetBEUI is no longer an option. If you have worked with several different releases of Microsoft operating systems, you'll have noticed that the default protocols and client components have changed with every release. To keep things simple, and to reflect current networking practices, all of the network clients in this chapter will use TCP/IP to communicate with the server. For convenience (mine and yours), the clients in the examples will obtain a unique IP address and other necessary protocol configuration information from a DHCP server on the network. Why? In the real world, you will have a static IP address for 99 percent of your servers 99 percent of the time. For workstations, however, it is much more convenient to assign addresses dynamically. A DHCP server not only assigns IP addresses to clients, it can also supply all of the other values required in your particular TCP/IP environment. DHCP also keeps track of IP assignments and updates clients dynamically when you want to make configuration changes. Refer to Chapter 6 for more information on TCP/IP addressing and Chapter 7 for more details on DHCP.

The network client is the software component that locates network resources and connects to them. On older client systems, the network client may also need to conceal the network from legacy applications, making network resources appear to be local when an application is not network-aware. For any given flavor of file-mounting, printer-sharing software that runs on a server, there is a client counterpart. To connect to Netware servers, for example, clients need a Netware-compatible client. The Microsoft network client component is usually called the Client for Microsoft Networks. On NT 3.*x* and 4, however, it is called the Workstation Service.

Domains, Workgroups, and Active Directory

The client systems discussed in this chapter may participate in workgroups and/or domains (I purposely use the term "and/or" because membership in these isn't mutually exclusive). Additionally, some clients can access directory services to locate network resources. To optimize your client configurations, you'll need to understand these three levels of association.

Workgroups are simply logical groups of clients and servers. They populate the browse list you see in Network Neighborhood or My Network Places. Workgroups make it easier for clients to find and attach to network resources. Servers that belong only to workgroups, however, lack centralized security. Each server maintains separate security information.

Domains provide centralized security, along with the resource grouping function of workgroups. Domain user accounts exist to permit people to use a single login name to log on to any workstation and access resources on any server that belongs to the domain. Only systems based on the NT operating system, however, can be domain members. NT-based systems include NT 4, Windows 2000 Server and Professional, Windows XP, and Windows Server 2003 . Domain member systems have a computer account in the security database; this account is very similar to a user account. If a Windows 2000 Professional system, for example, is only in a workgroup, domain users cannot log on to the workstation with a domain account. If you want your users to log on to one of the systems just listed and access resources on a domain, you must join the workstation to the domain.

Systems not based on NT (this includes Windows 9*x*, Windows for Workgroups, and DOS clients) cannot be domain members. These systems can only participate in workgroups. No real security database exists on the workstation; users can log on without a domain account, or even a local account. To enable users access to domain servers and resources, however, the network client software on these systems can be configured to log users on to a domain.

Active Directory (AD) adds a layer of functionality to the workgroup and domain model; the AD is a database of domains, user and computer accounts, resources and services, and even trust relationships. AD does use domain security, but it has been designed to manage bigger and more complex networks than domains and workgroups can handle. For a full rundown of Active Directory, check out Chapter 8. The thing to remember here is that only Windows 2000 and XP include fully functional AD client software. However, Active Directory client extension packages are available for Windows 9*x* and NT 4. The AD Client extensions for 9*x* and NT 4 include support for newer authentication methods and directory searches.

NOTE   *The Active Directory Client Extension (commonly called DS Client) for Windows 95 and Windows 98 is included on the Windows 2000 CD-ROM in* `\CLIENTS\WIN9X\DSCLIENT.EXE`. *The client for NT 4 is available for download from Microsoft at:* `http://www.microsoft.com/windows2000/server/evaluation/news/bulletins/adextension.asp`.

Table 14.1 summarizes the network association capabilities of the clients you'll be configuring in this chapter:

TABLE 14.1: NETWORK CAPABILITIES OF CLIENT OPERATING SYSTEMS

CLIENT OPERATING SYSTEM	WORKGROUP MEMBER	DOMAIN MEMBER	ACTIVE DIRECTORY CLIENT
Windows XP Professional	✓	✓	✓
Windows 2000 Professional	✓	✓	✓

Continued on next page

TABLE 14.1: NETWORK CAPABILITIES OF CLIENT OPERATING SYSTEMS *(continued)*

CLIENT OPERATING SYSTEM	WORKGROUP MEMBER	DOMAIN MEMBER	ACTIVE DIRECTORY CLIENT
Windows NT 4	✓	✓	Add-on
Windows 98	✓		Add-on
Windows 95	✓		Add-on
Windows for Workgroups	✓		
DOS	✓		

A final word: systems based on the NT operating system maintain local security databases. The configuration changes you are about to perform require administrative privileges. When configuring Windows NT, Windows 2000, or Windows XP clients, you must first log on as Administrator or use an equivalent account.

Now you are ready to begin connecting client systems to the Windows Server 2003 network.

Connecting Windows XP Professional Workstations

Windows XP Professional is the ideal client for Windows Server 2003. The client and server operating system and user interface are the same, and XP supports all of the great Server 2003 features, including remote administration, remote installation services, and group policies. Universal Plug and Play makes installation of your supported network card driver virtually automatic. If your network card is present and detected when the OS is being installed, XP automatically loads the driver. If you accept the typical network settings during the installation of XP, setup will go ahead and install TCP/IP Protocol and the Client for Microsoft Networks. If you install the NIC later, XP automatically detects the new hardware and loads a driver, or prompts the user for the location of the correct driver. Either way, once the driver for the NIC is loaded, you're home free. If you only need the TCP/IP protocol and the Client for Microsoft Networks, there's not much for the admin to do except join a domain or specify a workgroup.

Verify Your Network Configuration

First, log on to the system as a user with administrative rights. Before trying to join the domain, you should at least take a look at the Network Connections applet in the Control Panel to ensure that the network card was detected and the appropriate software has been loaded. As shown in Figure 14.1, if the network software has loaded properly, you will see an icon named Local Area Connection (if you have more than one NIC installed, you will see more than one Local Area Connection icon). You should see that the connection is enabled, and if you highlight the connection and expand the details (as in Figure 14.1), you should also see the IP address that was assigned by DHCP. If you do not see a Local Area Connection icon, your NIC may not have been properly detected. Use the Device Manager to isolate the problem, or try to add the network adapter manually using the Add New Hardware Wizard in the Control Panel and your OEM-provided disk or CD-ROM.

FIGURE 14.1

The Local Area
Connection Icon
in Network
Connections

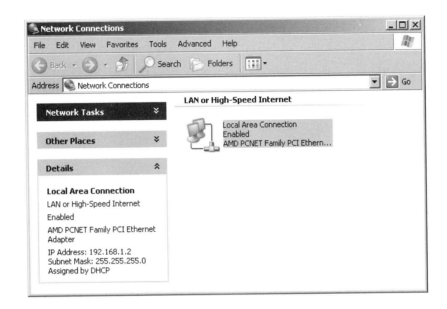

If everything looks rosy, right-click the Local Area Connection icon and click Properties to view your network configuration information. The properties page, shown in Figure 14.2, lists installed components: network card type, protocol, and the client software. TCP/IP is automatically configured to use DHCP; to statically assign IP information, select TCP/IP and click Properties. Figure 14.3 shows the Internet Protocol (TCP/IP) properties page.

FIGURE 14.2

Local Area
Connection
properties page

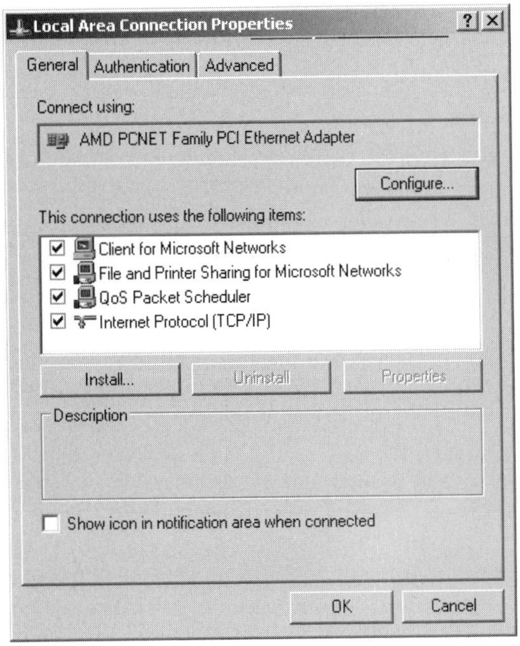

FIGURE 14.3

Internet Protocol
properties page

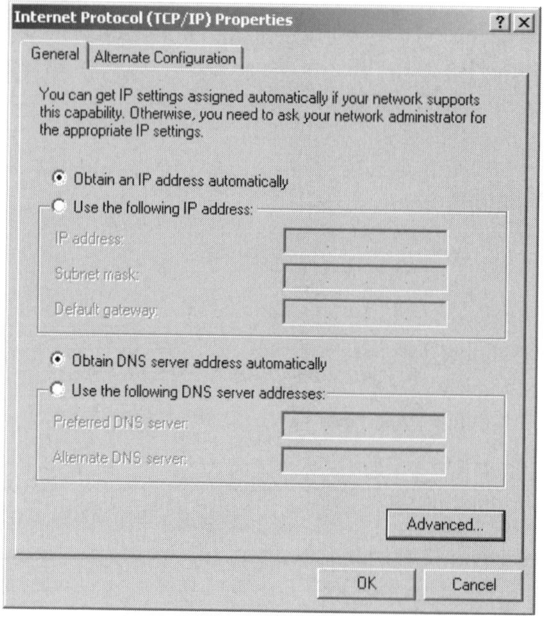

NOTE   *To be absolutely certain that your network card and TCP/IP are working properly, open a command prompt, use IPCONFIG to verify your DHCP addressing, and then use Ping to test network connectivity. Ping your IP address, the IP of the router, and the IP of the server or another node on your network. While you are at it, ping a couple of systems by name to test your DNS resolution. See Chapter 6 for more information on troubleshooting network problems with TCP/IP. This applies to all of the workstations you'll configure in this chapter, although the syntax and supported arguments of IPCONFIG and Ping will change with the operating system.*

Joining a Domain

Now that you know your network card is working properly and you have successfully obtained configuration information from DHCP, it's time to join the domain. If your Windows XP Professional client will exist in an Active Directory environment, you need to create a machine account for it in the target domain. Members of the Administrators and Account Operators group on the domain can use the Active Directory Users and Computers tool to do this beforehand, and that is the recommended course of action. However, you can also create a machine account from the workstation during the network part of the setup program, or you can use the System Control Panel, if you know the username and password of an account with the ability to create machine accounts in the domain. Since this chapter deals with client-side configuration, I'll give you the steps to create the machine account from the workstation as you join the machine to the domain.

To join a domain, open the System applet. The System applet is in the Control Panel, or you right-click My Computer from the Start menu and click Properties. I prefer this to wrangling with the XP Control Panel's Category View. Navigate to the Computer Name tab (see Figure 14.4). The XP Professional System, ANGEL, currently belongs to a workgroup named WORKGROUP. Click Change to join a domain. As shown in Figure 14.5, change the radio selection to Domain and type in your domain name, **REDHILLTOWN.COM** in this case. Notice that you use the full Active

Directory domain name here, not the NetBIOS name REDHILLTOWN. Click OK. If an account for the system does not already exist on the domain, XP prompts you to supply a domain username and password with permission to create the account (see Figure 14.6). If all goes well, you'll see a message welcoming you to the domain.

FIGURE 14.4

Computer Name tab in System Properties

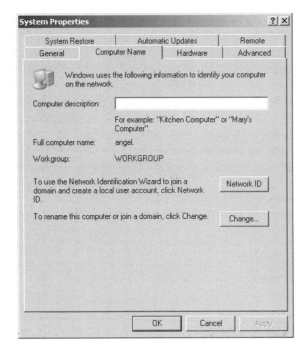

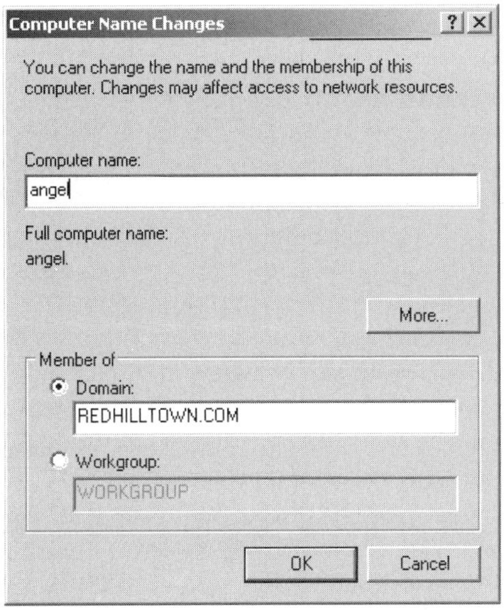

FIGURE 14.5

The Computer Name Changes dialog box

FIGURE 14.6

Supply a username and password to join the domain.

Restart the system for the changes to take effect. When the system restarts, you'll have the option to log on using a local account or using a domain user account. To access resources on the domain, users need to log on with a domain user account. Activate the drop-down list for Log On To and choose your domain name. From now on, the default choice will be to log on to the domain, not the local machine. When XP is finished logging you on and loading your personal settings, it's time to connect to network resources.

NOTE *How is it possible to join the workstation to the domain and then log on using a domain account? How does the workstation identify you and assign you rights and permissions? Actually, when the workstation joins the domain, the domain's Domain Users group is added to the workstation's local Users group membership. In addition, the Domain Admins group is added to the Administrators group on the local workstation. By default, then, if a domain controller authenticates you as a member of the Domain Users group, the workstation will accept you as a local user. And if the domain controller recognizes you as a Domain Admin, the workstation will grant you local admin rights as well. This is the default behavior for all NT-based client operating systems: Windows XP, Windows 2000, and Windows NT.*

Connecting to Network Resources

In Windows XP, My Network Places is not shown on the Desktop by default; the easiest way to open it is from My Computer. Open My Computer from the Start menu and choose My Network Places from the list of Other Places (see Figure 14.7).

As you can see in Figure 14.8, My Network Places offers three different options for finding and connecting to network resources:

◆ Use the Add Network Place Wizard to create a shortcut to a network resource. The wizard can locate the resource using a UNC name (**\\SERVER\SHARE**), which you provide, or you can open a browse list from within the wizard.

◆ Use Search Active Directory for shared folders or printers. This only works for shares and printers that have actually been published in the Active Directory, though.

◆ Browse the network by choosing Entire Network from Other Places. This is the Network Neighborhood–style browse list that you've been familiar with since Windows 95.

FIGURE 14.7

Open My Network Places from My Computer.

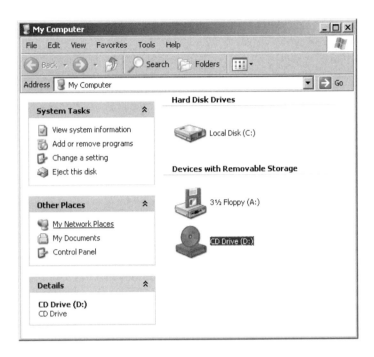

FIGURE 14.8

Finding resources from My Network Places

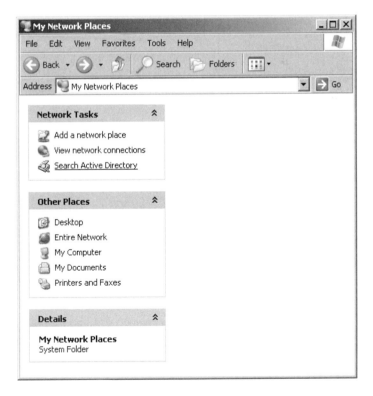

The Add Network Place Wizard is fairly straightforward, so let's skip to the Search Active Directory option. Select it from the list of Network Tasks with a single click (remember, it's a link), and a dialog box called Find Users, Contacts, and Groups will open (see Figure 14.9). This powerful little applet gives you access to a searchable directory of computers, shared folders, and printers, as well as users, groups, and contacts. From the Find drop-down list, choose Shared Folders. If there are multiple domains on the network, you can make the search more specific by choosing your domain name from the In drop-down list. If the list of shared folders is likely to be long, you can search by name or keyword or use the Advanced tab to search by other properties. Once you've set your search criteria, click Find Now to locate the shared folders. Figure 14.10 shows the results of a search for shares on the REDHILLTOWN domain.

FIGURE 14.9

The Find Users, Contacts, and Groups dialog box

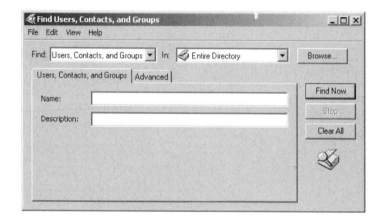

FIGURE 14.10

Active Directory search results

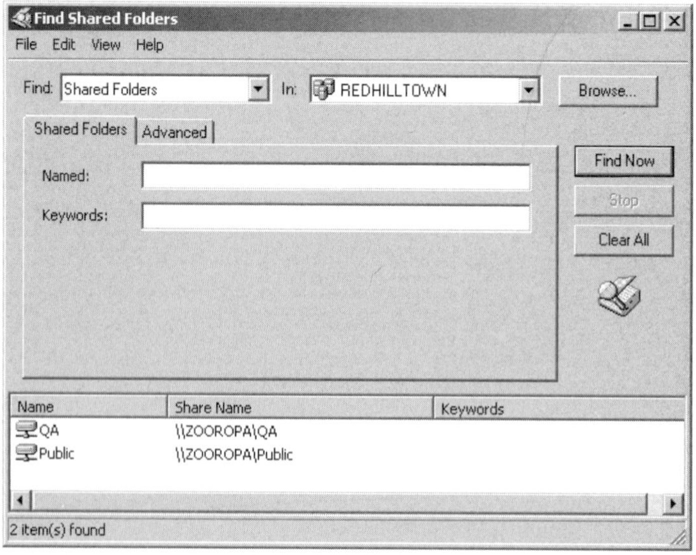

To connect to a shared folder found by the Active Directory search engine, double-click your selection in the results window to open the folder in Explorer, or right-click the folder and choose Map Network Drive. As shown in Figure 14.11, the Map Network Drive dialog box will automatically fill in the server and share information. Mapped drives will be persistent unless you deselect the check box labeled Reconnect at Logon. By default, the current username and password will be used; click Connect Using a Different Username to specify a different account to use for the connection. If you want to create a shortcut to this resource instead of mapping a drive letter to it, the link named Sign Up for Online Storage or Connect to a Network Server invokes the Add Network Place Wizard.

FIGURE 14.11

Mapping a network drive to a shared resource

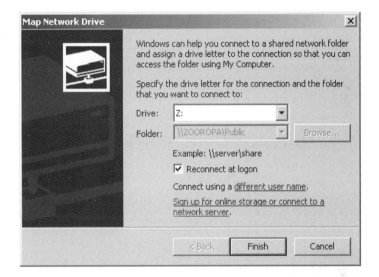

If you prefer browsing the network to searching the Active Directory, use the Entire Network link in My Network Places. This is the same type of browse list found in Windows 2000, NT 4, and Windows 9x. One advantage to using the browse list is that all shares and printers will be listed, not just AD-published resources. If administrators forget, or don't bother, to publish share and printer information to the directory, shared resources will still appear on the browse list.

Once you've located and selected the resource on the browse list, double-click to open it, or right-click to see a list of options. As you see in Figure 14.12, right-click options include Map Network Drive and Create Shortcut. If you choose the latter, Windows will offer to put the shortcut on your Desktop. Although you cannot choose a different location for the shortcut, it's a simple matter to copy or move the shortcut after creating it.

FIGURE 14.12

Options for
connecting to a
shared folder

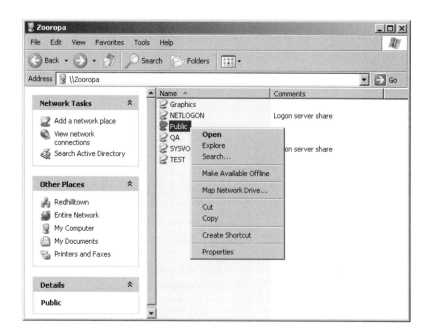

Changing Domain Passwords

It's good security practice for a new user to change their password the first time they log on to the network. It's also a default parameter set when the admin first creates a new user account. So if a user is logging on to the network for the first time, they will see a message informing them that they must change their password. The Change Password dialog box then opens and the user types the old password and the new one (twice for confirmation). If the old password is correct and the new password meets the password criteria (these are discussed in Chapter 9) and both entries match each other, the user sees a confirmation of the password change and the logon process continues.

After the initial logon and password change, administrators can use Active Directory Users and Computers to reset a user's password or to expire a password so that the user must change it the next time they log on. See Chapter 9 for the procedures to reset and expire domain account passwords. Users can change their own domain passwords after logging on by using Ctrl+Alt+Del and the Change Password button. The Ctrl+Alt+Del sequence is the same one used to lock the computer or shut it down, so it's important that users know about it.

Connecting Windows 2000 Professional Workstations

Windows 2000 Professional and Windows XP share many of the same features, so the steps to configure Windows 2000 Professional are virtually the same as the ones for Windows XP Professional. Sure, some of the names for things have changed, or the applets been have moved around, but don't let that throw you. In case you skipped right to this section, I'll go through the steps again. Before proceeding, log on to the workstation as a user with administrative rights.

Verify Your Network Configuration

To verify your network configuration, open Network and Dialup Connections (Start/Settings/ Network and Dialup Connections). Check to make sure that the Local Area Connection is enabled. Double-click the icon to see the status of the connection. If you do not see a Local Area Connection icon, the card may not have been detected. In that case, try to use the Device Manager or the Add New Hardware Wizard (both of these are found in the Hardware tab of the System Applet in the Control Panel) and your OEM-provided disk or CD-ROM to install the driver. If the icon is present but grayed out, the connection may be disabled for some reason. Right-click the icon and choose Enable if you see the choice. If there is a red X on the icon, the NIC is not receiving a signal from the cable. It may be unplugged or defective. If the icon has no red X and is not grayed out, verify that the network software components have loaded properly. Right-click the Local Area Connection icon and choose Properties, or click the Properties button from the Status dialog box. Open the TCP/IP properties page and verify that DHCP is enabled. If you are still not convinced, open a command prompt (Start/Run/cmd.exe) and type `ipconfig /all` to see the dynamic IP configuration, then try pinging some other nodes on the network. When you are satisfied that everything is working, close your open windows and join the workstation to the domain.

Joining a Domain

To join your Windows 2000 Professional system to the domain, open the System applet (right-click My Computer on the Desktop and choose Properties, or open Start/Settings/Control Panel/System). Go to the Network Identification tab (it's called Computer Name in Windows XP). Click the Properties button to open the same dialog box you encountered back in Figure 14.5. Click the Member of Domain radio button information and type in the domain name. Click OK. If you have not already created the machine account on the domain, the system will prompt you for the username and password of an account authorized to create the machine account in the domain. Type in the username and password and click OK. If all goes well, you'll see a dialog box welcoming you to the domain.

When prompted, restart the system for the changes to take effect. When the system restarts, you'll have the option to log on using a local account or using a domain user account. To access resources on the domain, you need to log on using a domain user account. Activate the drop-down list for Log On To and select your domain name. From now on, the default choice will be to log on to the domain, not the local machine.

Connecting to Network Resources

To connect to network resources from a Windows 2000 Professional workstation, open My Network Places on the Desktop (see Figure 14.13) and you'll see two choices: Add Network Place or Entire Network.

Choose Add Network Place if you want to create a shortcut to a network resource. Figure 14.14 shows the Add Network Place Wizard. Type the name of the resource or select a share from a list using the Browse button. Click OK. Provide a user-friendly name for the connection in the next window and click Finish. The wizard will automatically open the folder for viewing, and a shortcut will appear in the list of My Network Places. This shortcut can be moved or copied to a different location, such as the user's Desktop.

FIGURE 14.13

My Network Places

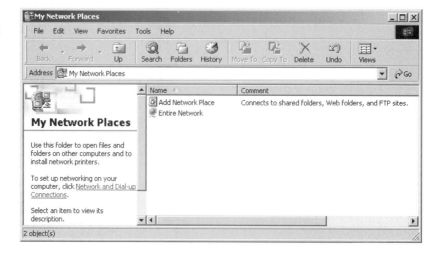

FIGURE 14.14

The Add Network Place Wizard

To access resources using a browse list or by searching the Active Directory, choose the Entire Network option in My Network Places. You'll see a list of links to search for different types of objects and a link to view the entire contents of the network. Click the link to view the entire contents of the network and you'll have two more choices (see Figure 14.15). Choose Microsoft Windows Network, not Active Directory (you will not find a list of shares by opening Active Directory). Finally, a list of domains and workgroups appears. Click your domain name and select a server from the list to see its shared folders. Figure 14.16 shows a list of shares on the server ZOOROPA. Double-click to open the shared folder, or right-click to see a list of options as shown in Figure 14.16.

Available options include Map Network Drive or Create Shortcut. The latter choice will create a shortcut on your Desktop.

FIGURE 14.15

Browsing the entire network

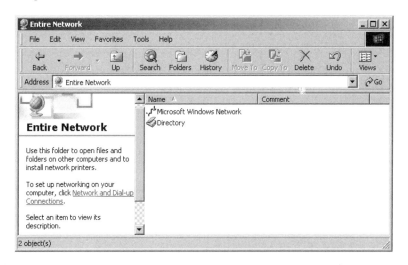

FIGURE 14.16

Connecting to a shared folder from the browse list

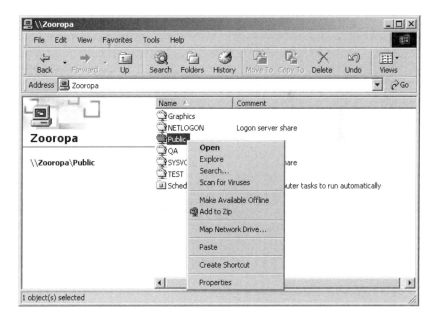

NOTE *You cannot search for a list of shared folders using the Search for Files and Folders link found in My Network Places/Entire Network, but you can search for computers. Once a list of computers is found, double-clicking a computer on the list will present a list of shares. However, this process is not as intuitive as the Active Directory search function you saw back in Windows XP.*

Changing Domain Passwords

The steps for changing a user's password on the domain are the same in Windows 2000 Professional as they are in Windows XP Professional. After logging on successfully, press Ctrl+Alt+Del on the keyboard and click the Change Password button to change your domain password.

Connecting Windows NT Workstations

Because it is still so frequently used on corporate networks, Windows NT 4 is next on our list of clients. Microsoft designed NT and its descendants to be more secure (and therefore more suitable for corporate networks) than Windows 9x or Me. Like Windows 2000 and XP, Windows NT can participate in domain security. Businesses with security concerns are more likely to use NT systems on their corporate offices; Windows 9x/Me is often used only for laptops with special hardware requirements.

If you've installed Windows NT 4 on your system already, chances are you've already installed all of the required networking components. However, NT doesn't have the broad hardware support and the advanced Plug-and-Play features of Windows 2000 and XP. So, to be on the safe side, I'll walk you through all of the configuration steps. This section, like previous ones, assumes that you already have a fully functioning operating system.

Configuring the Workstation

Windows NT will detect your network card during setup and install most or all of your required networking components by default. However, unlike Windows XP and 2000, if you install a network card after the operating system is configured, you may have to manually install the driver because NT does not support Plug and Play. In any case, you will probably want to verify your configuration to make sure you are set up for your particular network. To do this, log on to the system as Administrator, or use a local account that is a member of the local Administrators group. Now fire up the Network Control Panel and select the Adapters tab. If you need to install a network card, click Add to see a list of supported network cards (shown in Figure 14.17).

FIGURE 14.17

Selecting a network adapter

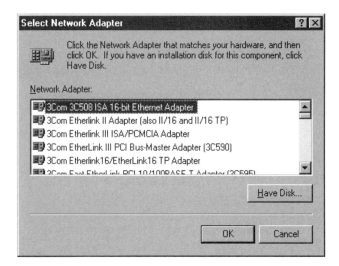

Scroll down the list to find your network adapter, or click Have Disk to install an unlisted—but supported—network adapter. The system will prompt you for the location of the driver files. If you want setup to get the driver from the NT CD-ROM, most of them are in the \i386 directory. However, additional network card drivers are located on the CD-ROM under \drvlib\netcard\X86. Type in the path for the files and click Continue to load the adapter.

Now you need to select a network protocol. Move to the Protocols tab. Default protocols are TCP/IP, NWLink IPX/SPX Compatible Transport, and NWLink NetBIOS. If you don't need the NWLink components, remove them now. If the protocol you need is not listed, click Add to see a list of supported protocols. Select your protocol from the list and click OK. If you select the TCP/IP protocol, setup will offer to use DHCP protocol to dynamically provide an IP address. Choose Yes if you want the workstation to use DHCP. Now setup will ask for the location of the protocol files. Type in the path, or if the default path in the dialog box is correct, click Continue to copy files from the \i386 directory on the NT CD-ROM. To configure a static address or other TCP/IP parameter, highlight the protocol and click Properties. The TCP/IP properties page is shown in Figure 14.18.

FIGURE 14.18

TCP/IP properties

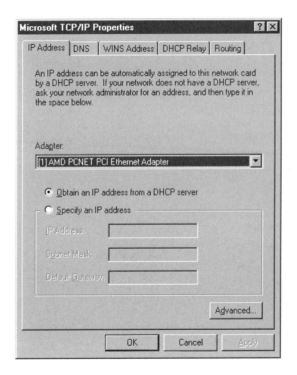

NOTE *If you enable DHCP but configure any other parameters in the TCP/IP properties pages, the parameters you supply—such as DNS servers, WINS servers, default gateways, or domain names—will override any setting that the DHCP server gives the client. This is true for all clients discussed in this chapter.*

Now let's look at the Services tab in the Network Control Panel (shown in Figure 14.19). You may already be familiar with the terms *Client for Microsoft Networks* and *File and printer sharing for*

Microsoft Networks. These names for Microsoft networking components are replaced by the terms *Workstation* and *Server* in Windows NT. The Workstation service, called Client for Microsoft Networks in every Windows OS except NT, is the network client component. The Server service (usually called File and printer sharing for Microsoft Networks) allows resource sharing to the network. These components require little or no configuration to operate effectively as a network client.

FIGURE 14.19

Network services

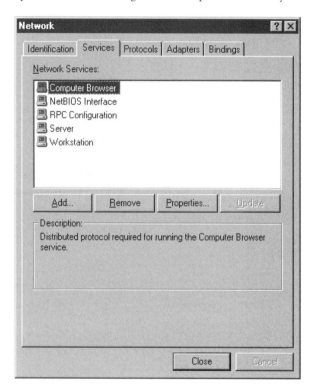

If you've added an adapter or modified a protocol in the Network Control Panel, click Close, and NT will ask you to restart the system. After rebooting, note whether there are any errors at startup and check the Event log for more information if necessary. It's not a bad idea to verify your network connectivity at this point by opening a command prompt. IPCONFIG will verify that your PC has acquired an IP address from a DHCP server. IPCONFIG /ALL will show you more details. Use the Ping command to test connectivity to other nodes on the network. When you are satisfied that everything is working properly, it's time to join the domain.

Joining a Domain

Open the Network Control Panel again and select the Identification tab. You will see your computer name and domain or workgroup membership configuration. Like Windows XP and 2000, a Windows NT system needs a computer account in the domain. If the account has not already been created, you'll need to use an account with Account Operator or Administrator privileges to join the domain. You do not need to hold any special domain privileges to assign the system to a workgroup, however.

To join a domain, click the Change button from the Identification tab. You will see your current domain and workgroup membership, along with your current computer name. In the Identification Changes dialog box, change the selection from Workgroup to Domain and type your domain name in the text box (shown in Figure 14.20). If a computer account has already been created for this system, click OK. Otherwise, check the check box labeled Create a Computer Account in the Domain and type in a username and password to create the computer account. This username and password must have either Account Operator or Administrator rights on the domain you are joining. To be on the safe side, enter the full domain name in the Username text box. Instead of typing **Administrator**, for example, type **REDHILLTOWN\Administrator**. This ensures that you use the Administrator account from the REDHILLTOWN domain. Click OK and wait for the pop-up dialog box welcoming you to the domain.

FIGURE 14.20

Changing the domain name

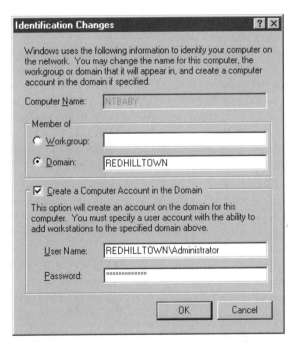

After completing the domain membership change, you are prompted to reboot the server for the changes to take effect. When the logon dialog box appears after rebooting, pull down the Domain list and select your domain name. This also changes the default domain for future logons. Type a valid domain user account and password in the space provided. Click OK to log on with your domain user account. From now on, the default choice in the logon dialog box will be to log on to that domain instead of the local machine.

TIP *By the way, if there are multiple domains on your network, you can choose one of the trusted domains from the list in the logon dialog box. It depends on the security configuration of your network, but domain member workstations can accept logons for users from their domain and from trusted domains. This makes it much easier for staff visiting from other offices to use local workstations.*

Connecting to Network Resources

To connect to a network resource with a Windows NT client, open Network Neighborhood to see a list of systems with shared resources in your local domain or workgroup. To view resources in other domains and workgroups, click Entire Network, and then choose Microsoft Windows network. Once you've found the server and shared folder you are looking for, select it in the window and double-click to open the folder, or right-click and choose from a list of options. Like your previous clients, the options include Map Network Drive and Create Shortcut.

NOTE You may have noticed that you have to choose Microsoft Windows Network to access the browse list. Clicking Microsoft Windows Network tells your software that you want to use the Client for Microsoft Networks, instead of some other installed client, to find servers. For instance, if the Netware client were installed, you would select Netware Network from the browse list to search for Netware servers. If a Unix client were present (there are a number of these on the market), an option that probably includes the term NFS would show up on the list. You would select it to look for servers running the NFS file server software.

If you want to map one or more logical drives to network resources, try a more direct approach than the Entire Network/Microsoft Windows Network browse list. Simply right-click Network Neighborhood and choose Map Network Drive. A dialog box similar to the one shown in Figure 14.21 will appear.

FIGURE 14.21

Mapping a network drive

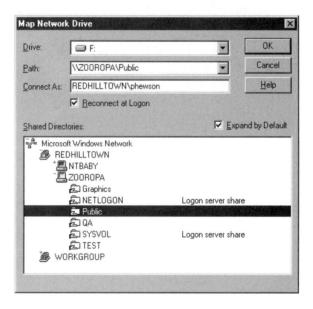

Drill down the list to your target server and share, and change the default drive assignment if necessary. If you know the server name and share name, however, you don't need to browse for it. Just type it in to the Path text box. Notice the option Connect As. If you don't specify another user account, Windows NT will use the credentials of the logged-in user to establish the network connection. The Connect As option allows you to connect to a network share with a different set of credentials. To do so, type the username in the Connect As box or, as shown in Figure 14.21, type in the full **DOMAINNAME*username*** to designate a domain account to use. If you want to specify a local account on the target server, use the **MACHINENAME*username*** convention. If prompted, supply the password for the account you are using to connect and click OK. Keep in mind when using this option that Windows NT can only map to a given server with one set of credentials. If I have already connected to a server, I can't specify a different username for a new connection, even if I'm connecting to a different share.

There are times, though, that you may get an error message saying that your credentials conflict, indicating that you are already connected under a different username. This can occur even if you don't have any drive connections to that server. If this happens, open a command prompt (open Start/Run and type **cmd** in the Run box) and type **net use** to see your open connections. You will probably see a connection to that machine's IPC$ share without a drive letter specified. This happens when you do things like open an administrative tool and point it to another machine. You don't realize that you have connected to that server already, but you have. First, make sure all programs using that connection are closed, then drop the connection by typing **net use \\server\share /d**. For example, if I had previously connected to ZOOROPA with the Event Viewer and saw a connection to \\ZOOROPA\IPC$, I would type **net use \\ZOOROPA\ipc$ /d**. Now go back to the Map Network Drive dialog box and give it another try.

Changing Domain Passwords

The steps for changing a password on the domain are the same in Windows NT as they are in Windows XP and Windows 2000. After logging on successfully, press Ctrl+Alt+Del on the keyboard and click the Change Password button to change your domain password.

Accessing the Active Directory

The DS Client for NT 4 is available for download from Microsoft's Web site—just open the Windows 2000 Server home page and search for "Active Directory Client Extensions". The client requires Service Pack 6a and Internet Explorer 4.01 or higher. DSCLIENT.EXE is a self-extracting executable with a straightforward wizard installation. It also supports quiet mode with the /q switch for deploying to multiple workstations. The client replaces many DLL files for changes "under the hood." Some of these files will not be removed if the DS Client is uninstalled. From the user's point of view, the DS Client adds the capability to search for people and printers published in Active Directory and replaces the Windows Address Book with an updated, AD-aware version.

NOTE   *Files that cannot be removed by uninstalling the DS Client are:* Netlogon.dll, Netapi32.dll, Mup.sys, Wkssvc.dll, *and* Wldap32.dll. *These files upgrade NT 4's basic logon and networking behavior for compatibility with Active Directory networks.*

Connecting Windows 9x and Windows Me Workstations

Connecting a Windows 9x or Windows Me workstation to the network is almost as simple as connecting Windows XP and Windows 2000. You have Plug and Play on your side, which usually takes the guesswork out of installing the network card. Once the card is installed, a default set of network components loads automatically. Unlike Windows XP, 2000, and NT 4, Windows 9x cannot join the domain and does not require a machine account. You'll still need to tell the workstation about the user's logon domain, however.

Configuring the Workstation

Let's assume that your workstation is up and running with Windows 9x and has no networking components installed. Open the Network Control Panel (select Start/Settings/Control Panel, then open up the Network applet). You should see an empty network configuration dialog box like the one shown in Figure 14.22.

FIGURE 14.22

The Configuration tab of the Network Control Panel for Windows 9x

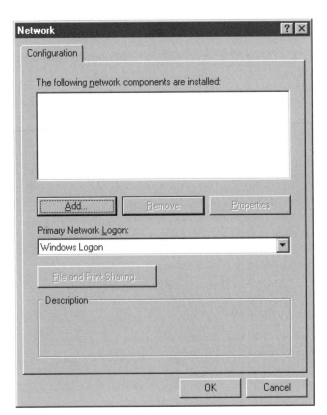

You need to install a network adapter, at least one protocol, and at least one type of networking *client*. Additionally, you can add a *service*, such as file and print sharing. I am assuming that your system has none of these, so click the Add button. As shown in Figure 14.23, you are asked which type of networking component to add.

As always, you'll start off by adding an adapter. From the list of component types, select Adapter and then click Add once again to open up the dialog box shown in Figure 14.24.

FIGURE 14.23

The Select Network Component Type dialog box

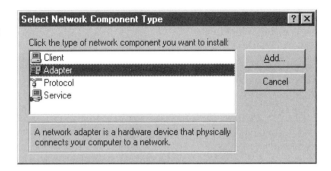

FIGURE 14.24

The Select Network Adapters dialog box

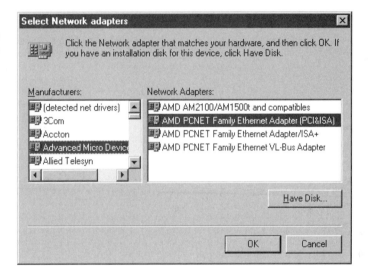

In the Select Network Adapters dialog box, you'll see a list of adapter manufacturers on the left and corresponding adapters on the right. Choose your adapter from the list, or if your adapter is not on the list and you have the OEM disk, click Have Disk and then click OK. Setup will try to copy the files needed from the Windows CD-ROM or the manufacturer's disk.

Once the adapter is installed, an interesting thing happens. Windows knows that adapters need protocols and network clients, so it installs a set of default components to make your life easier. In Windows 95, IPX/SPX and NetBEUI are the default protocols. Two clients are loaded as well: the Client for Microsoft Networks and the Client for Netware Networks. In Windows 98, as you can see in Figure 14.25, only the Client for Microsoft Networks and TCP/IP are installed by default. If your system is Windows 95, you may need to add TCP/IP Protocol and then remove the Netware Components and NetBEUI protocol. If you add TCP/IP, Windows will need to copy files from the CD-ROM. For convenience, TCP/IP is already configured to use DHCP automatically. To statically assign an IP address or other configuration information, highlight TCP/IP and click Properties.

FIGURE 14.25

A full complement
of networking
components is
installed by default.

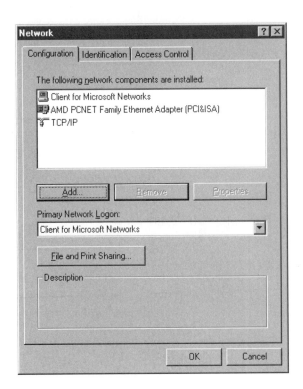

After adding the adapter and configuring the other network components, but before designating a workgroup and logon domain, I suggest that you close the Network Control Panel, let Windows copy the files it needs from the CD-ROM, and restart when prompted. Look for any errors at startup. If you don't see any, log on and use `WINIPCFG.EXE` and the command prompt to verify TCP/IP connectivity.

Designating a Workgroup and a Logon Domain

Unlike a Windows NT or Windows 2000 machine, and more like a Windows for Workgroups machine, a Windows 9*x* machine cannot be a domain member. However, it does not have to *belong* to a specific domain in order for a user to log on to that domain.

Before you configure Windows to log users on to a domain, you should also change the workgroup name to be the same as the domain name. Why? To make browsing for resources easier, the members of a domain also form a workgroup of the same name (remember, workgroups are for browsing and domains are for security). When you open up Network Neighborhood, your workgroup is the starting point. You see the servers in your workgroup first. By putting your machine into the same workgroup as your domain, your domain resources will be more accessible. Also, if your Windows 9*x* workstation is running the server component (File and Printer Sharing for Microsoft Networks), it registers itself with the other servers in the workgroup.

In the example that follows, assume that the domain where user accounts live is also a resource domain. That is, the same domain holds all the user accounts and all the computer accounts.

NOTE *It is not a foregone conclusion that all the user accounts and all the computer accounts exist in the same domain; on some networks, the domain that contains user accounts (the user domain) is separate from the domain with the machine accounts and shared resources (the resource domain). In this case, your Windows 9x machine should join a workgroup with the same name as the resource domain, and you should configure Windows to log folks on to the user domain.*

To specify a workgroup for your Windows 9*x* system, open the Identification tab in the Network Control Panel (see Figure 14.26) and type the name of the workgroup in the space provided. This system's unique computer name is JOSHUATREE. My workgroup name is REDHILLTOWN.

FIGURE 14.26

The Network Control Panel's Identification tab

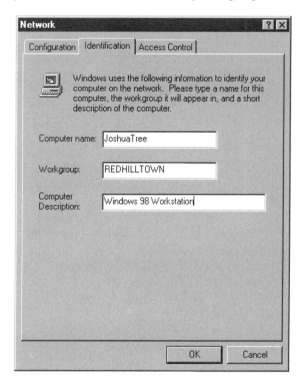

To specify a logon domain for users, go back to the Configuration tab of the Network Control Panel. Select the Client for Microsoft Networks and click Properties to open the dialog box shown in Figure 14.27. Check the box labeled Log On to Windows NT Domain and type the NetBIOS name of the domain where the user accounts live. Click OK and close the Network Control Panel. Now restart your system.

After rebooting, users will be prompted to supply a network password for Microsoft networking. The default domain name in the Domain text box is the one you specified in the Network Control Panel. However, unlike our NT-based cousins, you can type any domain name in the Domain text box. Windows 9*x* does not require that you log on to the domain specified in the Network Control Panel.

FIGURE 14.27
Client for Micro-
soft Networks
properties page

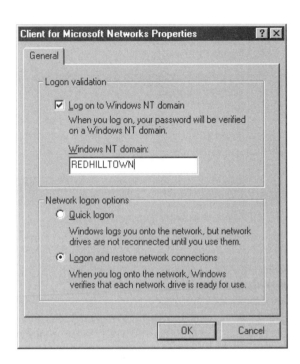

NOTE *Unlike Windows XP, 2000, and NT, Windows 9x will not require users to log on to any domain at all. You can simply click Cancel at the logon prompt and you're in—to the workstation, but not the domain. This is good to know if you are having a problem with the configuration after you specify a logon domain. After all, you may need access to the system to solve the problem.*

Connecting to Network Resources

Now it's time to find and connect to some network stuff. Double-click the Network Neighborhood icon on the Desktop (my Network Neighborhood is shown in Figure 14.28).

FIGURE 14.28
Network
Neighborhood

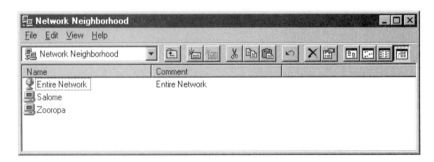

If you are following along on your own system, what you see in your Network Neighborhood is the browse list for your workgroup—or domain, if the name is the same. In my domain,

REDHILLTOWN, there are currently two servers on the browse list, Zooropa and Salome. Double-click a server on the list to see a list of its shares, as shown in Figure 14.29.

FIGURE 14.29

Shared resources on Salome

In Figure 14.29, Salome has several shares. Double-click to open a share in a window and browse files and folders, or right-click and choose Map Network Drive to map a logical drive to a share.

By the way, Network Neighborhood will show printer shares as well as directory shares. To attach to a network printer, click Start/Settings and then Printers. Choose the option to create a new printer. A wizard starts and asks you if you are installing a locally attached printer or a network printer. Choose network printer and click Next. The wizard asks you where to find the printer. Type in a UNC name (**\\SERVERNAME\PRINTERSHARENAME**) or click the Browse button to find your printer on the browse list. Next, tell the wizard where to find the printer driver (the Windows installation CD-ROM or a vendor-supplied floppy, perhaps). When prompted, have Windows print a test page to verify the connection.

Changing Passwords

If your password has expired, or it is your first logon since the account was created, a handy little message and a Change Password dialog box appears, complete with fields to type in the old password and the new password (twice for confirmation, of course). To change the domain password before it expires, however, open the Passwords applet in the Control Panel. As you can see in Figure 14.30, there are two options for changing passwords: Change Windows Password and Change Other Passwords. If you choose the option to Change Other Passwords, you can change your domain password but your local password will not be changed. It's important to keep your Windows password synchronized with your domain password, or chaos will ensue. To change your local Windows password and the domain password at the same time, click the Change Windows Password button and select the check box to change your Microsoft Networking password (see Figure 14.31).

It's important to keep your Windows password and your domain password synchronized because Windows keeps a separate password for each person who logs on to the workstation. This password allows Windows to distinguish between users and their individual settings and to access users' individual password files. The password file may contain a number of other passwords, including the domain password. When the Windows password and domain password are the same, users can log on to Windows and to the domain simultaneously. If they are different, however, domain servers may deny access to resources because Windows is offering up the wrong password.

FIGURE 14.30

The Passwords properties page

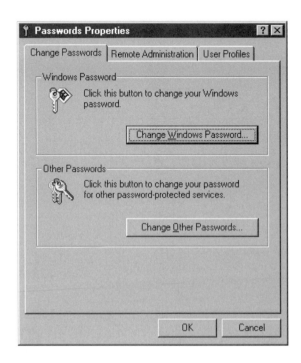

FIGURE 14.31

The Change Windows Password dialog box

Accessing the Active Directory

Earlier in this chapter I mentioned that Directory Services Clients are available for Windows 9*x* clients. To install them, get your hands on a Windows 2000 Server CD. At this time the DS client is not included on the Server 2003 CD. DSCLIENT.EXE is in \CLIENTS\WIN9X on the Windows 2000 CD. It's an auto-extracting 3MB CAB file. The installation is a straightforward click-Next-to-continue and reboot process.

Once the Active Directory client is installed, what exactly has changed? You won't see a new program or anything because most of the changes are under the hood. There are a couple of new options and capabilities under the Find menu within Windows Explorer, though. Now you can search the Active Directory for printers. The DS Client also installs a new version of the Windows Address Book, which can find people published in the Active Directory. Clearly, this little client doesn't give you a direct tap into the heart of the Active Directory, but it does provide some essential functionality required to make Active Directory published resources visible to Windows 9x clients.

ARE YOU HAVING PROBLEMS LOGGING ON TO AN ACTIVE DIRECTORY DOMAIN FROM WINDOWS 9X?

Here's a short list of possible problem areas to check:

◆ First, make sure you have installed all the recommended patches and security fixes on the client systems.

◆ Install the DS Client from the Windows 2000 CD-ROM (\CLIENTS|WIN9X\DSCLIENT.EXE). It upgrades several libraries that affect logon and authentication. The DS Client for Windows 9x requires Internet Explorer 4.01 or later.

◆ Windows 95/98 doesn't register with Active DNS, so try putting a WINS server on the network. Your Windows clients and your domain controllers should be configured to use it.

◆ Active Directory domain controllers use DNS for name resolution. Create static entries in DNS for your Win 9x clients. This also means that the Windows 9x systems will need to keep the same addresses all the time, so consider static addressing or DCHP reservations for these clients.

◆ Make sure you specify the NetBIOS domain name in the Network Control Panel. Use REDHILLTOWN instead of REDHILLTOWN.COM, for example.

Connecting Windows for Workgroups Workstations

Windows for Workgroups computers are becoming more and more and rare on today's corporate networks, but occasionally a business relies on an application or system that's stuck in the Windows 3.11 environment, so it might not hurt to be prepared. It's probably safe to say that we have all gotten too used to the Windows 9x, Windows NT, and Windows 2000 interfaces to be very efficient when sitting in front of an old Windows for Workgroups machine. Everything is in a different place. There's no Start menu! How embarrassing would it be to sit down at a workstation—you being the senior administrator—and not have the slightest clue how to connect to your servers? Well, relax. I'll walk you through the basic networking configuration of Windows for Workgroups and discuss how to connect to network resources.

Before trying to use a Windows for Workgroups client in a Windows Server 2003 environment, you need to be aware of two important issues. First, the Active Directory—and all the benefits that come with it—is not available. You are pretty much limited to basic network share access. Second, before WFW (or DOS) clients can log on successfully to an Active Directory domain at all, a domain controller security setting which requires digitally signed communications must be disabled. I'll discuss this second issue in more detail a bit later.

Configuring the Workstation

All of the examples in this chapter use TCP/IP as the default protocol. However, WFW (also called Windows 3.11) does not ship with the TCP/IP protocol. If you want Windows 3.11 to use TCP/IP, you'll need to put it on a floppy or make it otherwise accessible during the installation. The 32-bit TCP/IP stack is available on the Windows NT Server 4 CD-ROM, under \CLIENTS\TCP32WFW\ DISKS\DISK1. You can also download the latest version of the 32-bit TCP/IP stack from Microsoft's FTP site.

As you did with Windows 9x, start from the very beginning: assume that an NIC has been installed on the system but has not yet been configured and that no other networking components are installed. In the Program Manager window, find and open the Network program group. Now double-click Network Setup to launch the setup process. A dialog box like the one shown in Figure 14.32 will appear.

FIGURE 14.32

The Network Setup dialog box

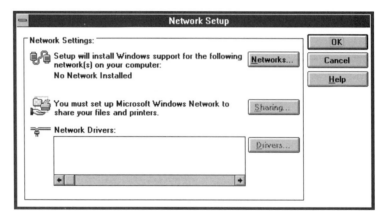

The Network Setup dialog box reports that no network support is installed. Click the Networks button. In the Networks dialog box, choose Install Microsoft Windows Network (see Figure 14.33) and click OK. This tells Windows that you want to install the Client for Microsoft Networks.

FIGURE 14.33

Selecting a network client

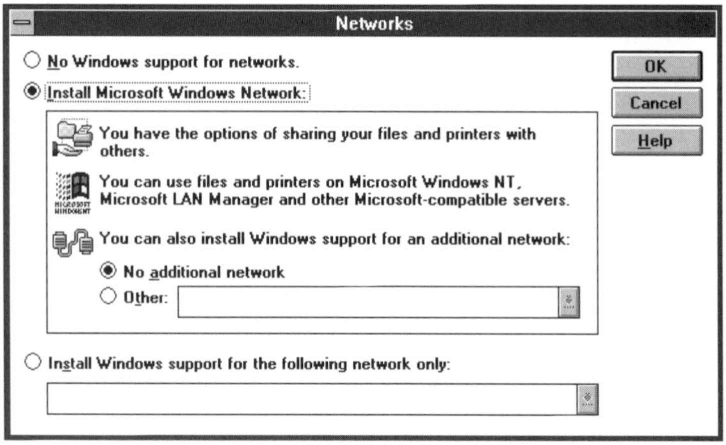

Back in the Network Setup dialog box, it's time to install an adapter. Click the Drivers button. Although no components are present yet, the Network Drivers dialog box will be used to add both network adapters and protocols. To see how the Network Drivers dialog box will look after adding these components, look ahead to Figure 14.35. Click Add Adapter to see a list of supported network cards (see Figure 14.34). Locate and select your adapter in the list, or if you're feeling brave, click the Detect button to have setup attempt to detect your card. If you have a card that is not on the list, and you have the OEM disk with Windows 3.11 drivers, highlight Unlisted or Updated Network Adapter and click OK. Setup will ask you where to find the driver files. Type in the path for the files and click OK.

FIGURE 14.34

Selecting an adapter

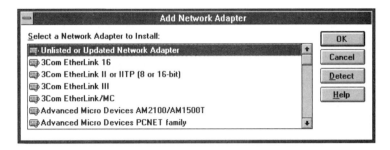

I say you have to be brave to use the Detect button because the Windows for Workgroups programming predates Plug and Play by quite some time. The risk of system lockup during this detection phase is substantial. Nevertheless, on my system with a 3Com EtherLink III ISA card, setup was able to detect the adapter.

After installing your adapter, setup will return you to the Network Drivers dialog box. As shown in Figure 14.35, a set of default protocols has been installed as well.

FIGURE 14.35

Default protocols

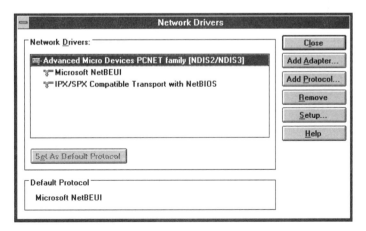

Remove the components you don't need by highlighting them and clicking Remove. Answer Yes to the confirmation dialog box that will pop up. But wait. If you remove the last protocol, the setup program will also remove the adapter (Windows will tell you this if you try it). So you should add the protocol you want to use as the default (TCP/IP in our case) before you remove the last unwanted protocol.

To add TCP/IP and set it to be the default protocol, click the Add Protocol button. If TCP/IP has not yet been installed on the system, choose Unlisted or Updated Protocol. When prompted, put your TCP/IP floppy in the drive, tell setup where to find the TCP/IP protocol files, and click OK. Setup should report that it has found driver files for Microsoft TCP/IP-32 3.11b. Click OK to copy the files to your system. Now setup kicks you back to the Network Setup dialog box. Highlight Microsoft TCP/IP on the list of installed drivers and click the Set as Default Protocol button. Now you can remove the last unneeded protocol.

By default, the TCP/IP stack for Windows 3.11 does not use DHCP. If you wish to enable DHCP, highlight TCP/IP and click the Setup button. Check the box labeled Enable Automatic DHCP Configuration and click Yes when asked to confirm your choice. Now click OK to commit your changes and return to the Network Drivers dialog box. Close the Network Drivers dialog box and then click OK to close Network Setup. The system will inform you that it has modified some of your setup files and will ask you to restart.

When Windows restarts, verify your network connectivity. Open the MS-DOS prompt in the Main Program group and use the IPCONFIG and Ping commands as described in the previous sections.

Now we'll move on to configuring your workgroup and logon settings. Once you've set up a network, there is a new applet in the Main Program Group Control Panel. Find and open the Network applet in the Control Panel to see the Microsoft Windows Network configuration dialog box (shown in Figure 14.36). Type in a unique computer name for the system and provide the workgroup name. These settings determine how your system will register itself on the network and how it will browse lists of servers.

FIGURE 14.36

The Network Control Panel in Windows for Workgroups

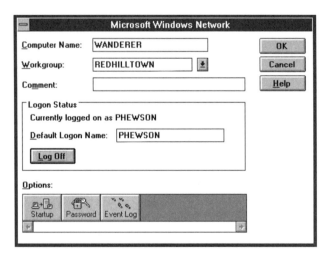

In Figure 14.36, the logon status section of the Network applet displays the currently logged on username and a Log Off button. Logging in to Windows for Workgroups is more simplistic than even Windows 95. Windows for Workgroups does not support user-specific settings at all. Every user receives the same program groups, Desktop, and program settings. User profiles do not exist. Since there is no need to keep up with user-specific information, you can log in and out using the Network Control Panel.

To configure the system for domain logins, click the Startup button in the Network applet. Figure 14.37 shows the default startup parameters for Windows networking. Log On at Startup, which is checked by default, tells Windows for Workgroups to present you with a logon dialog box before the Program Manager loads your Desktop. Check the box labeled Log On to Windows NT or LAN Manager Domain and supply a domain name to specify a user login domain. Use the NetBIOS name of the domain—REDHILLTOWN, in my case—and not the fully qualified domain name REDHILLTOWN.COM.

FIGURE 14.37

Startup settings

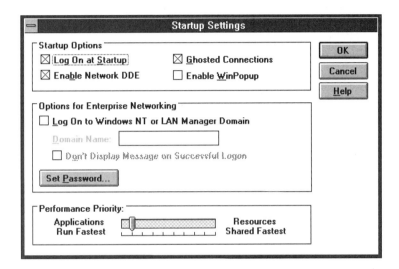

If you want your Windows 3.11 system to log on to a Windows Server 2003 domain, there's an important issue to consider: Server 2003 domain controllers will not communicate with WFW or DOS systems by default. This is due to a domain controller security policy setting that requires all clients to digitally sign SMB protocol packets. WFW and DOS clients can't do packet signing at all. When the client attempts to log the user on and does not agree to do SMB packet signing, the domain controller refuses the request. Users will see a message saying that the account is invalid or the password has expired.

Only domain controllers require client-side SMB packet signing by default. This behavior is controlled by the Default Domain Controller group policy. To disable this setting and permit domain logons for WFW (and DOS) clients, open the Domain Controller Security Policy tool in the Administrative Tools program group on a domain controller. Expand the Computer Configuration and open Windows Settings/Security Settings/Local Policy/Security Options. Locate and disable the policy called Windows Network Server: digitally sign communications (always). There is another setting called Windows Network Server: digitally sign communications (if client agrees). Leave this setting enabled; it tells the domain controller to negotiate for SMB packet signing whenever possible.

As you can see, the requirement for client-side SMB packet signing is easily disabled; however, you should fully understand the security implications of such a move before proceeding. SMB packet signing is designed to prevent "man-in-the-middle" attacks. In case you aren't familiar with this term already, a man-in-the-middle attack occurs when a third system is able to monitor, capture, and modify communications between two other computers. Among other things, this type of attack can be used to capture authentication packets and decrypt them. If you don't require SMB packet signing between a domain controller and a client, you are downgrading the default security and leaving not only your system but also your entire domain open to a potential security breach.

If you want to have your WFW systems connect to shared resources without downgrading domain controller security, there is a workaround using pass-through authentication. For details, check out the sidebar "How Can My WFW System Connect to Shares and Printers without Downgrading Security on Domain Controllers?" in the next section.

Connecting to Network Resources

Now that Windows for Workgroups is configured for networking, it's time to connect to some resources. If you checked the Log On at Startup option in the Network Control Panel, when Windows restarts you'll see a logon box with fields for your username, password, and domain, if configured.

Log in and open the File Manager (remember? It's the little yellow file cabinet in the Main program group). You will discover, as shown in Figure 14.38, that there are two new commands in your Disk menu: Connect Network Drive and Disconnect Network Drive. Select Connect Network Drive to open the Connect Network Drive dialog box (see Figure 14.39). From here you can browse the network for available shares. If you are the impatient sort, type in the UNC name of the server and share in the Path text box. Change the logical drive letter assignment if you wish, and click OK to connect. Now the drive will be listed along with your physical drives in File Manager.

FIGURE 14.38

File Manager
network commands

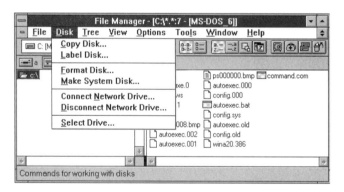

When I say that Windows for Workgroups doesn't distinguish between users and their settings, it applies to drive mappings as well. They are persistent by default. Occasionally you may need to disconnect a drive mapped by another user and recreate a mapping you need. To disconnect from a network drive, choose Disconnect Network Drive from the Disk menu, choose from the list of mapped drives, and click OK.

NOTE   *Sorry, but you can't view or access Active Directory information with a Windows for Workgroups client.*

FIGURE 14.39

The Connect
Network Drive
dialog box

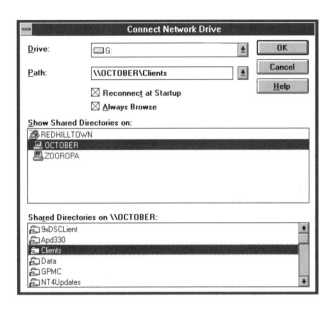

TIP *One of the limitations of Windows for Workgroups systems is that they do not recognize UNC names as valid pathnames. For example, if I have a share on ZOOROPA named WFWUPDATE, which contains a batch file named* UPDATE.BAT, *I can't simply open File/Run in File Manager and run the command* \\ZOOROPA\WFWUPDATE\ UPDATE.BAT. *Instead, I have to map a drive—let's call it Z: — to* \\ZOOROPA\WFWUPDATE *and then run* Z:\UPDATE.BAT.

HOW CAN MY WFW SYSTEM CONNECT TO SHARES AND PRINTERS WITHOUT DOWNGRADING SECURITY ON DOMAIN CONTROLLERS?

In the previous section I broke the bad news that Windows Server 2003 Enterprise Edition does not support domain logons from Windows for Workgroups (or DOS) clients without disabling the SMB packet signing requirement on domain controllers. You can't fix this problem without compromising security. However, there is an unofficial workaround that allows a DOS or Windows 3.11 client to access shared folders on domain member servers.

To use the workaround, do not configure the workstation to log on to a domain at all. Instead, log on to the workstation with a username and password that matches a username and password on the domain. If you try connecting to shared resources on a domain controller server, access will be denied; however, you can connect to a member server on the domain. When your local workstation makes a connection request, the member server will take the username and password that Windows 3.11 supplies and check with the domain controller to see if that information is valid for a user on the domain. If your user ID matches up with a domain account ID and password, the DC gives the member server a "thumbs up" and the member server lets you connect. Pretty slick, eh? If you happen to have any workgroup servers on your network, Windows 3.11 and DOS clients can also connect to Server 2003 that do not belong to a domain, using a Windows username and password that matches a local account on the workgroup server.

Changing Passwords

Unlike Windows 9x, Windows for Workgroups doesn't make it convenient to synchronize passwords. To change your Windows password, open the Network Control Panel in the Main Program Group. Click the Password button (shown back in Figure 14.36) to open the Change Logon Password dialog box. If you want to change a domain password, however, click the Startup button in the Network Control Panel. In the Options for Enterprise Networking section (shown back in Figure 14.37), click Set Password to open the Change Domain Password dialog box. In either case, (and like all change password boxes throughout history), type in your old password, then your new password twice, and click OK to finish.

Connecting DOS Workstations

Now we enter into the realm of the forgotten GUI-less operating system: DOS. If you've perused the preceding section, you already know that Windows Server 2003 domain controllers will not authenticate users from a Windows 3.11 or DOS system. If this is new information to you, check out the sidebar at the end of the preceding section on Windows for Workgroups clients to learn how to work around this limitation.

I won't ask why the heck you still have DOS clients hanging around on your network. I myself used to work for a small technology company whose Customer Support department relied heavily on a DOS-based protocol analyzer. Any suggestions from IT people about replacing or upgrading the software or the system provoked loudly pronounced phrases like "over my dead body." Not all business decisions are rational. Once in a while you get stuck with supporting a dinosaur (um, I mean legacy operating system). And sometimes that legacy operating system needs access to the network. So here we go.

If you were working with Microsoft networks in the days of Windows NT 3.x and 4, you'll recall that NT had this Network Client Administrator utility in the Administrative Tools program group. The Network Client Administrator could make a bootable network startup disk to connect DOS clients to an installation source. It could also make a two-disk set of a DOS networking client stack called MSCLIENT 3.0.

Both of those little tools disappeared with Windows 2000 and are completely off the radar with Server 2003. This is probably due to the fact that DOS is no longer a supported operating system. Calling Microsoft with a DOS networking problem is likely to result in the sound of muffled laughter and faint snickers drifting over the phone line. Even in the days of NT 3.x and 4, the inclusion of DOS tools on the CD was mainly for the purpose of launching an install.

The emergence of new and improved installation methods makes DOS-based network startup disks largely unnecessary today. Instead of booting from a DOS diskette with CD or network drivers to connect to your install source, you can boot from the installation CD-ROM. Setup programs, particularly upgrades, are also smarter; it's usually unnecessary to wipe a machine clean before an installation.

Nevertheless, if you do find that you have a need to connect DOS clients to Windows Server 2003, Server 2003 doesn't come with any handy utilities to create network startup disks or MS Client disks. So you need to be resourceful. In the next section, I'll step you through the process of making MS Client disks and loading the network software on a DOS system.

NOTE   You may search the Internet and find instructions for installing the Network Client Administrator (NCA) from the NT 4 Server CD. However, I recommend against using it to make a network startup disk, for a couple of reasons. The most important reason is limited support for network cards. NCA only includes drivers for a very short list of network cards; if your adapter isn't on the list, well, you're in that proverbial state of SOL. To add support for your card, you need to manually add the DOS driver to the disk and manually edit a couple of INI files. NCA also does not give you the opportunity to specify an I/O address or IRQ settings for the network card. In short, unless you will use the same floppy for a whole bunch of machines with the same adapter and network card settings, it's not worth the extra effort to configure a working startup boot disk.

Making the MS Client Disk Set

Follow these steps to make a network client disk set for DOS:

1. Make a bootable floppy to use as Disk 1 of the set. Use another DOS-based system, or Windows 9x. In case this is before your time, the command to format a floppy and make it bootable is `format a: /s`. It's not necessary to make the first client disk bootable if the system can already boot to DOS (or if you want to carry around a separate boot disk).

2. Format a second floppy to use as Disk 2 of the set. It doesn't need to be bootable.

3. Go exploring on the Windows NT 4 Server CD-ROM. Find the DOS client files under `\CLIENTS\MSCLIENT\DISKS`. Copy the contents of the `DISK1` directory to the first floppy. Copy the contents of the `DISK2` directory to the second floppy. The second diskette has all the TCP/IP protocol files, so you definitely need it. Label the disks appropriately. I'll refer to them as Disk 1 and Disk 2.

4. If you don't have access to the NT Server 4 CD, download the MS Client disk files from Microsoft's FTP site: `ftp://ftp.microsoft.com/bussys/Clients/MSCLIENT/`. There are two self-extracting executable files: `DSK3-1.EXE` and `DSK3-2.EXE`. Download these two files and put them into separate directories. Double-click to extract the files into their current directories. Now copy the contents of the directories (minus the original executables!) to the two floppies as described in the previous step.

5. If you like, create an `autoexec.bat` file on the first floppy that includes the command `setup .exe`. If you do this, the MS Client setup program will launch automatically.

Installing and Configuring MS Client

Now that you have made the MS Client disk set, take those two floppies and the OEM disk for the workstation's network card in hand and proceed to your workstation. Before running the MS Client installation program, I highly recommend that you use the OEM disk for your network card to make sure the card has no resource conflicts. The setup program usually cannot correct these. 3Com cards, which are very popular and well supported, usually have a diagnostics program and can automatically configure the card's settings.

Now boot your workstation with MS Client Disk 1. If you didn't put the setup command in an `autoexec.bat file`, type **setup.exe** at the command prompt. When you see the Welcome screen for the MS Network Client, press Enter to continue. Setup asks you where to put the network files. The default path is `C:\NET`. Actually, if you booted from the floppy, it's `A:\NET` and you don't want that, so type in the path you want to use and press Enter. Now setup asks you to select a network adapter from a list (see Figure 14.40). Select an adapter from the list, or choose Network Adapter Not Shown on List to type in the path for the OEM driver you want to use.

FIGURE 14.40

Select a network adapter.

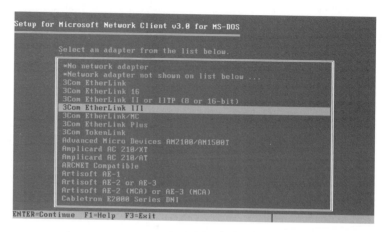

```
Setup for Microsoft Network Client v3.0 for MS-DOS

              Select an adapter from the list below.

        *No network adapter
        *Network adapter not shown on list below ...
        3Com EtherLink
        3Com EtherLink 16
        3Com EtherLink II or IITP (8 or 16-bit)
        3Com EtherLink III
        3Com EtherLink/MC
        3Com EtherLink Plus
        3Com TokenLink
        Advanced Micro Devices AM2100/AM1500T
        Amplicard AC 210/XT
        Amplicard AC 210/AT
        ARCNET Compatible
        Artisoft AE-1
        Artisoft AE-2 or AE-3
        Artisoft AE-2 (MCA) or AE-3 (MCA)
        Cabletron E2000 Series DNI

ENTER=Continue  F1=Help  F3=Exit
```

TIP   DOS network card drivers are usually labeled NDIS 3.0 or NDIS 3 or Windows 3.11 drivers on the OEM disk. They don't call them DOS drivers or MS Client 3 drivers.

Now the setup program offers to use more memory for greater performance. You can give this a try, but the TCP/IP stack uses a lot of memory (relatively speaking) so I usually press C to skip the extra buffers. In the next screen, type in a username for use on the network.

Setup presents a configuration screen labeled Setup for Microsoft Network Client v3.0 for MS-DOS (shown in Figure 14.41). There are three separate configuration sections: Names, Setup Options, and Network Configuration. You'll configure each of these in turn.

FIGURE 14.41

The main configuration screen

```
Setup for Microsoft Network Client v3.0 for MS-DOS

        Names:
              Your User Name is phewson

        Setup Options:
              Use the Full Redirector.
              Run Network Client.

        Network Configuration:
              Modify your adapter and protocols with this option.

        ┌─────────────────────────────────────────────────┐
        │ Change Names                                     │
        │ Change Setup Options                             │
        │ Change Network Configuration                     │
        ├─────────────────────────────────────────────────┤
        │ The listed options are correct.                  │
        └─────────────────────────────────────────────────┘

ENTER=Continue  F1=Help  F3=Exit
```

Use the up arrow to highlight Names and press Enter. You've already supplied your username, so go ahead and enter a unique computer name, your workgroup name, and a domain name if desired. Don't worry, you'll configure the option to log on to a domain in the next section. This tells setup what domain that will be if you enable the option. For each option, use the up and down arrows on the keyboard to highlight the desired item, and press Enter. In Figure 14.42, I have configured the system to log me on as PHEWSON with the computer name WANDERER, and REDHILLTOWN is the name of both my workgroup and my domain. When all the names are configured to your liking, highlight The Listed Names Are Correct and press Enter to return to the main configuration screen.

FIGURE 14.42

Configuring network names

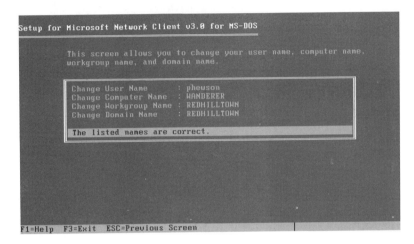

Now go to the setup options. Figure 14.43 shows the default options. Do Not Logon to Domain is the default; to tell the software to log on to a domain, highlight the selection, press Enter, and change the option to Log On to Domain. Accept these options and go back to the main configuration screen. Choose Change Network Configuration to configure your network adapter and protocols. From this screen (shown in Figure 14.44) you can add or remove an adapter or modify the adapter's settings. The available adapter settings are often vendor and card-specific. The default protocol is NWLink IPX Compatible Transport. If your network is like mine, TCP/IP is the only protocol in use. To remove NWLink, use the Tab and arrow keys to highlight it, and then hop back down to the second box and click Remove. Setup will remove the protocol and ask you which protocol you want to use. If you choose TCP/IP, setup will automatically use DHCP for addressing. To configure static addressing information, highlight TCP/IP and choose Settings. To disable DHCP, change the values of the parameter named Disable Automatic Configuration from zero to one (see Figure 14.45). Notice also that the IP addressing syntax uses spaces instead of a decimal point to indicate octets; type in **192 168 1 1**, for example, instead of **192.168.1.1**.

FIGURE 14.43

MS Client setup
options

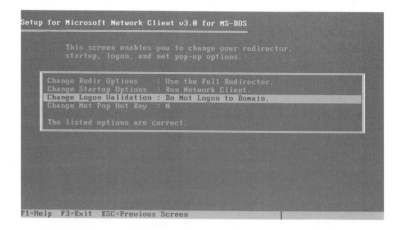

FIGURE 14.44

Installed adapters
and protocols

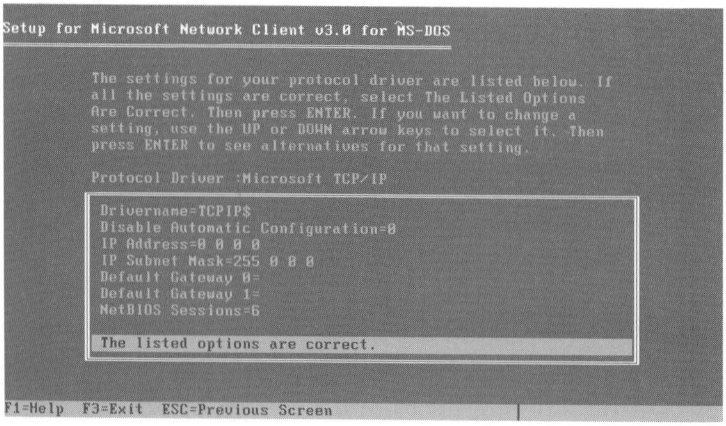

FIGURE 14.45

Modify TCP/IP
protocol settings.

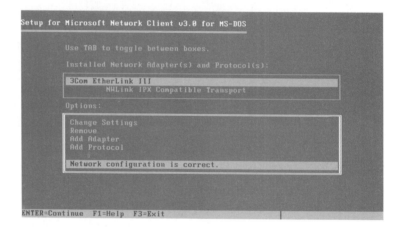

When you are finished configuring TCP/IP parameters, indicate that the listed options are correct and press Enter. Back at the network configuration screen (Figure 14.44 again), highlight Network Configuration Is Correct and press Enter to return to the main configuration screen (shown in Figure 14.41). If you are finished configuring the client, highlight The Listed Options Are Correct and press Enter. Now setup begins to copy files. Keep the OEM setup disk handy if the driver is not included with MS Client. Insert the second MS Client disk when you are prompted. Next, the program will modify startup files (`AUTOEXEC.BAT` and `CONFIG.SYS`) and prompt you to reboot. From now on, if you need to modify any of these settings, run **setup.exe** from the `\NET` directory.

When the system restarts, watch the networking programs initialize. You might see something similar to Figure 14.46. If your network adapter fails to load (perhaps due to an unresolved resource conflict), it will be very obvious, and all of the dependent processes will fail. If everything initializes properly, log in and supply a Windows password. Now you are ready to connect to the network.

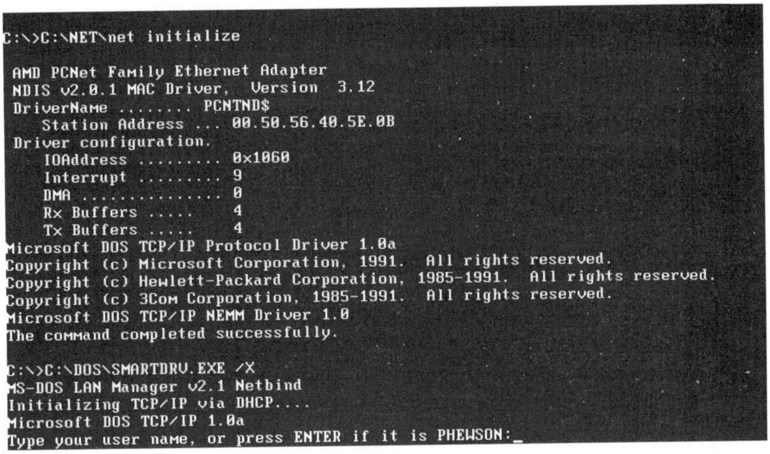

FIGURE 14.46

The MS Client software initializes.

```
C:\>C:\NET\net initialize

AMD PCNet Family Ethernet Adapter
NDIS v2.0.1 MAC Driver,  Version  3.12
DriverName ........ PCNTND$
    Station Address ... 00.50.56.40.5E.0B
Driver configuration.
    IOAddress ........ 0x1060
    Interrupt ........ 9
    DMA ............. 0
    Rx Buffers ..... 4
    Tx Buffers ..... 4
Microsoft DOS TCP/IP Protocol Driver 1.0a
Copyright (c) Microsoft Corporation, 1991.  All rights reserved.
Copyright (c) Hewlett-Packard Corporation, 1985-1991.  All rights reserved.
Copyright (c) 3Com Corporation, 1985-1991.  All rights reserved.
Microsoft DOS TCP/IP NEMM Driver 1.0
The command completed successfully.

C:\>C:\DOS\SMARTDRV.EXE /X
MS-DOS LAN Manager v2.1 Netbind
Initializing TCP/IP via DHCP....
Microsoft DOS TCP/IP 1.0a
Type your user name, or press ENTER if it is PHEWSON:_
```

Be aware that DOS clients cannot do SMB packet signing, which is required by default on domain controllers. This will prevent the DOS client from authenticating a user on the domain, unless the policy requiring SMB packet signing is disabled. Disabling the policy downgrades default security settings and opens up domain controllers to man-in-the-middle attacks, but if you decide to do it anyway, the procedure is outlined in the previous section on configuring WFW clients. There is also a sidebar in the previous section with a workaround to permit DOS and WFW clients to access shares on nondomain controller servers in the domain.

Connecting to Network Resources

With the Windows and NT-based clients, you used the graphical interface to browse the network and connect to shared folders and printers. Now you will use `NET.EXE` commands to accomplish these things.

TIP   NET.EXE is a self-standing utility. Typing **net** *calls up your network program; the next parameter, like* **use,** *is the function you want to perform. Additional parameters or arguments tell the function how or on what to perform the function. Understand that* **net** *is a simple command-line utility, and everything else is a little less confusing. To learn about all of the possible net commands, type* **NET HELP** *at any DOS, Windows 3.11, Windows NT, Windows 2000, or Windows XP command prompt.*

Net logon is the command that logs you on to the network, or domain, as the case may be. The MSClient setup program will insert this command into the AUTOEXEC.BAT file to initiate the logon sequence at startup. To log on manually, type **net logon** *username*. Logon also accepts the parameter /domain:*domainname* for logging on to a Windows NT domain. The counterpart to net logon is net logoff.

To browse the network, use net view. The net view statement by itself will return a list of servers in your workgroup:

```
Servers available in workgroup REDHILLTOWN.
Server Name      Remark
_____

\\ZOOROPA
\\OCTOBER
\\SALOME
The command completed successfully.
```

To see a list of shares on one of these servers, type **net view ***SERVERNAME*.
A response to the command net view \\OCTOBER would return something like this:

```
Shared resources at \\OCTOBER
Sharename      Type      Comment
Clients      Disk      Client Updates
Data      Disk      Database Directory
WFW311      Disk      WFW Source Files
HP4M      Print      Printer on 15th Floor
```

Once you've located your share, connect using the net use command:

```
net use E: \\OCTOBER\WFW311
```

TIP   DOS only allows five drive letters to be mapped by default. To allow more drive letters, add a LASTDRIVE statement to CONFIG.SYS. For instance, to permit mappings up to J:, add LASTDRIVE=J to CONFIG.SYS.

To see the full syntax of net use (or any other net command, for that matter), type the command followed by **/?** or type **NET HELP USE**. The basic syntax of net use is net use DRIVE: *SERVERNAME*\ *SHARENAME*.

This syntax can also be used for connecting to printers: **net use PORT: ***SERVERNAME******PRINTSHARENAME*.

For the port, use a local port, such as LPT1 or LPT2. This tells the network software to redirect any print requests addressed to the local port to the network share.

By default, network connections are persistent. To make a connection that is not persistent, add the /PERSISTENT:NO argument to the net use command. To delete existing connections, use the /DELETE argument: **net use E: /DELETE**. Or to delete all connections, type **net use * /DELETE**.

Changing Passwords

To change your password on a DOS client machine, type **net password** *USERNAME OLDPASSWORD*
NEWPASSWORD. For example, if the user Paul Hewson wanted to change his password from bonovoxx
to macphisto, he would type:

```
net password phewson bonovoxx macphisto
```

To change a password on the domain, just add the /DOMAIN:*DOMAINNAME* argument with net
password:

```
net password phewson /DOMAIN:REDHILLTOWN
```

DOS network clients are a bit more work than Windows clients, but look on the bright side.
You'll be an expert at using the NET commands. With only minor syntax variations, NET commands
work on every Microsoft Network client and server system, even Windows XP and Windows
Server 2003.

Chapter 15

Macintosh and Windows Server Integration

THIS CHAPTER MAKES A couple of assumptions. One, that the reader is (or wants to be) primarily a PC/Windows professional (otherwise, why read this book?). Two, that you, the reader, need some information concerning integrating Apple Macintoshes into your Windows Server network (and on Macintoshes in general). In other words, you have inherited a graphics department that needs to have access to public data, printers, Internet, etc. Three, said graphics department has no intention of switching to PCs for your administrative convenience.

It is possible that you feel that you're better off leaving well enough alone and keeping the graphics department isolated from the rest of the network. That integration is a big hassle, nigh to impossible, and not worth the effort. Well, let's admit that some effort will have to be made. But not as much as you might think.

Over the course of this chapter, I will be giving you some ideas (and step-by-step instructions) about how and why you might want to give the Macs access to Windows resources, and vice versa. These are suggestions and they reflect my personal opinion and experience. Generally, I have a limited amount of time to do administrative tasks so I tend to want to do only quick and easy things that still get the implementation and maintenance effectively done. I figure you might only want to do those kinds of things too. Minimal effort, maximum results. That doesn't mean there will be no work up front, but certainly no more work than is necessary.

This chapter was created to give you insights as to what might be happening with the Macintoshes on your network right now and how to effectively integrate them with your Windows Server network with the minimum amount of stress for everyone involved.

Macintosh Hardware and Operating System Inventory

In order to really get an idea of what kind of integration you can actually do with the Macs you have, you'll need to go look at them. Yes, I know that you want a fix that you can push over the network and without ever having to touch the workstations. For the most part, you will only have to touch them once or twice, but a brief "hello, Mac" can't be avoided. Here are some quick tips to give you some frame of reference when doing your inventory.

Hardware

If you have any Macintoshes that were purchased before 1998, chances are they will not be able to do what you need them to do as well as you need them to. Think about trying to run Windows XP on a 486 and you'll get the picture.

Here is a good rule of thumb concerning Macintoshes: Try to avoid any Macintosh model prior to the Power Macintosh series. That means avoid LC ("low cost," Celeron type of processor), Quadra, most Performas, Centris, Classic, or II. Any Power Macintosh or newer Performa will have the model number/processor speed right on the case, such as Power Macintosh 7600/200.

IN CASE YOUR PREDECESSOR DID NOT LEAVE YOU A NICE, DETAILED INVENTORY OF THE MACS

To get a rundown of which Macintoshes are on your network, what they're capable of, and what they're currently running without visiting every machine, just have your users print out the Apple System Profiler.

The Apple System Profiler is a program that has come with essentially every Macintosh OS since 7.6.1. It should be right on the Apple menu. If not, use Find to locate it because the users may have moved it. Then tell the users to follow these steps from the Apple menu:

1. Click Apple System Profile.

2. Click File\New Report.

3. Keep all default settings, then click OK.

4. Select Text Document at the top of the page.

5. Save the report with their machine name as the filename.

Then have them e-mail the document to you.

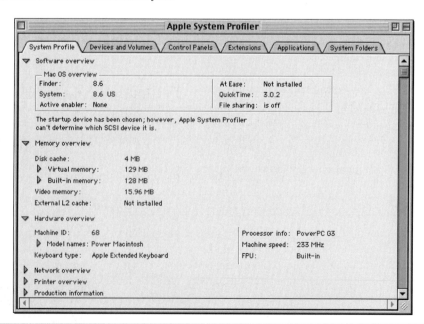

To run OS 8.6 (the lowest operating system version I suggest you use to integrate with Windows Server—more on that in a moment), you will need to have a processor that runs at 180MHz or faster and have at least 64MB RAM. (I know, technically you can run OS 8.6 on 32MB of RAM, but would you want to run even Windows 98 on 32MB? I rest my case.) These requirements, enough hard drive space to install the operating system, and an Ethernet network card are basically all you need to do file sharing smoothly and easily with the Server 2003 network users.

Here is a short list of acceptable Mac models for integration with Server 2003:

◆ Power Macintoshes that have processors of over 180MHz

◆ Power Macintosh G3 (they're sort of the PIII of Mac processors)

◆ Power Macintosh G4 (P4)

◆ iMac (all-in-one models are G3s, the flat-screen "swivelheads" are G4s)

◆ eMac (G4s, so far)

◆ Powerbook G3 and G4 (laptop)

◆ iBook (G3)

All of these Macs are capable of having 64MB RAM installed, and many of them come with at least that much.

Macintosh Operating Systems

Now you've checked out what machines you have. Chances are they're all capable of running OS 8.6 or higher. (I assume that because these days, graphics departments generally can't support Photoshop, Quark Express, and other high-end graphics and publishing software on older, low-end workstations.)

In January 2003, Apple started selling machines that only work with OS X or higher (It's a ROM thing). OS 9 came out in October 1999. Chances are good that you will have no Macs that have anything less than OS 9.1 on them. But, having said that, Macintoshes are hardy and seem to run forever. I'll be cautious and won't rule out entirely the fact that you could have some older machines on your network.

Still, you should only be working with hardware that can run OS 8.6 or better. Why? Well, previous versions may be able to do what you want, but it'll involve more work. In other words, previous versions of the Mac OS will require you to download several patches. If you don't want to have to download and patch anything, OS 8.6 is as old-fashioned as you should get, and from this point I'll assume that all your Macs are running OS 8.6 or higher. This means they can all do TCP/IP natively and they all have Ethernet network cards.

The newer and more likely OS versions you will be seeing are as follows:

◆ OS 9.1

◆ OS 9.2.2

◆ OS X 10.1.5

◆ OS X 10.2.x

You may note a bit of discrepancy in this list in so far as the versions are concerned. Well, there are many, many Mac OS versions. There was a time at Apple when an OS would be sent out that ended up needing enough patches that the patched version would be a slightly different version than what it originally was, much like Windows 95a versus Windows 95b. So, you'd have 9.0 and 9.0.1 and then 9.1 and 9.1.1, and so on. To keep things simple, I am going to focus on the OSes that don't necessarily need any patches to function well—because if your users are using Macs without mishap, their OS version is probably one of the versions I just listed.

TO GET TECHNICAL FOR A MOMENT

To do file sharing between Macintosh systems and Windows, you need AppleShare Client and something called Open Transport.

AppleShare Client is the equivalent of Windows Client for Networking. You need to have AppleShare Client version 3.8.x (preferably at least 3.8.3, which comes with OS 8.6) to work properly with Server 2003.

Open Transport is the networking service that manages TCP/IP (and AppleTalk) and handles Apple File Protocol (AFP, Apple's file sharing protocol) over TCP/IP or AppleTalk. Open Transport must be at least version 1.1.2. I much prefer version 2.0.3 or higher (OS 8.6 has 2.0.3). Open Transport goes hand in hand with AppleShare Client; you shouldn't have one without the other.

Note also that Windows Server has authentication modules that are based on AppleShare. The module that works with Apple File Protocol over TCP/IP is 5.0. It works only with AppleShare 3.8.x and higher (if you try it with a lower version, you get module 1.0, which may crash when trying to use TCP/IP). There also is an authentication module available for OS X. For more information, hit the Apple Web site. You'll have to troll the archives for some of this information, but it is there in abundance.

At this point, I'd like to comment on the fact that many network administrators feel that there are two main drawbacks to networking Macintoshes with a Windows network:

◆ Security
◆ AppleTalk

DEBUNKING A SECURITY MYTH

Due to the fact that Active Directory saves Macintosh passwords in clear text (yes, I know, you'd think Microsoft could figure out how to not do that by now), some people may hesitate to integrate the Macs into their Windows network. If that's so, then don't worry about it. Macs can use Microsoft authentication to access Windows network resources, eliminating that concern. Instead, Macintosh users can log in with an account that you create and control. If you want to control their use of the printer, share the printer out to the Mac users with a specific logon account that you specify.

THE TRUTH ABOUT APPLETALK

Macs don't need it. They can easily use TCP/IP to access resources just like any other workstation. AppleTalk is a convenience because it broadcasts information rather than you having to go get it. Just like NetBEUI makes browsing network places easy by propagating the network window with icons, AppleTalk lets Mac users look in the Chooser window and see if there are any printers or file shares out there. Just like NetBEUI, AppleTalk can be chatty. It can be a problem for some networks, and therefore should be avoided. I repeat: AppleTalk is not a necessity. That is, not unless you are using Print Server for Macintosh Service, but more on that later. Also, be aware that Macs primarily use

AppleTalk these days to find resources; once they've found the resource, they prefer to connect via TCP/IP. You actually have to do some tweaking to get Macs to use AppleTalk if TCP/IP is available.

A BRIEF LOOK AT APPLETALK AND ITS PARTICULARS

When Apple wanted to network their Macintosh workstations, they were basically on their own in creating a standard. It was during the infancy of peer-to-peer or small-business networking that Apple came up with the easy-to-use and ingenious LocalTalk/AppleTalk network. They wanted something that was as simple and unbreakable as two cups on a string, with a media that was cheap and readily available.

LocalTalk, in addition to having its own access protocol (like Ethernet), defined the physical media. It had a connector on the printer port that used common everyday phone cord (RJ-11) to daisy chain the machines together. Pretty convenient. It was as slow as molasses, running at a blazing 230Kbps. Furthermore, although it was a great idea, it could only handle about 32 devices per network. Needless to say, it's highly unlikely that today your network is running over LocalTalk.

AppleTalk, like NetBEUI, is the stack of simple little protocols that make it possible for the machines to use the LocalTalk media (or Ethernet, or even Token Ring) to broadcast their unique existence to all others on the network, as well as receive broadcasts.

Because Apple tends to think ahead, despite LocalTalk's limitations, they assumed that their users would want to be able to browse for their network resources easily. You may have heard of AppleTalk zones? These zones were created to help organize how devices show up in the Chooser. It is purely a logical process and is not dependent on subnets, routers, domains, or workgroups. Anyone who is sitting at a computer that happens to be in one zone is not going to be cut off from anything in another zone. Zones were created for convenience, so resources would be listed in a logical fashion. Think of them as something like a Windows workgroup.

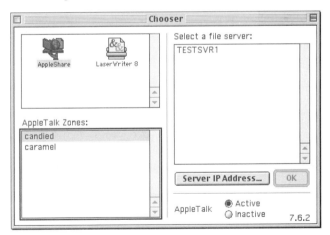

And finally, if you thought that AppleTalk, being so similar to NetBEUI, couldn't be routed, you're wrong. It can be. AppleTalk routers come in two flavors: seed routers (sort of the master browser of AppleTalk routers) and nonseed routers. A seed router keeps a kind of master list of all nearby networks (each identified with a number) and which zones those networks have in them. The AppleTalk routers on those networks get the overall view of the network from the seed router and use it to help them forward packets to the correct place. It's also at the seed routers that zones are created.

Continued on next page

A BRIEF LOOK AT APPLETALK AND ITS PARTICULARS *(continued)*

Server 2003 can not only be an AppleTalk router, but it can also be a seed router (just in case you don't have one and you have several subnets of Macintoshes on your network). To enable seeding and/or create some zones, right-click the AppleTalk routing connection in the RRAS console, and select Properties. To add a zone (such as "candied"), just click the New button.

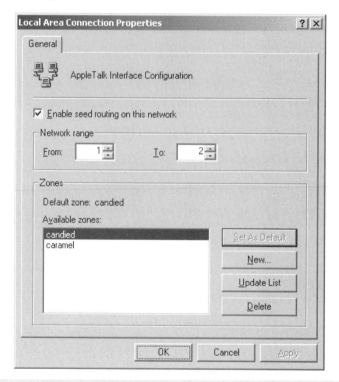

Integration Objectives

Now that you know which Macs you have and what they are capable of, what do you want them to actually do? In answer to that, I am going to go by the following list of objectives:

- ◆ Internet access using DHCP and DNS
- ◆ File sharing
- ◆ Printing to network printers

Essentially, the way you fulfill those objectives depends on which operating system you have, so I've divided the chapter into three subsets—the two major sections will deal with Mac classic OS clients (8.6 to 9.2.2) and OS X, respectively. In addition, at the end of the chapter I'll include a section about how to integrate Mac servers, for those lucky few of you who have them.

Classic OS Client Integration

Chances are your Mac users are using the network gateway to get to the Internet. People are pretty stubborn and ingenious about getting their mail, sports scores and, ahem, other Internet-based info. But, just to be clear, I'll spend a moment explaining a few basics about this topic.

USING DHCP AND DNS FOR INTERNET ACCESS

The Mac OS uses TCP/IP. DHCP and DNS are TCP/IP features. Because of that, the workstations absolutely do not need to have static IP addresses. If they have been an administrative pain because you have been changing their IPs manually whenever there have been changes on the network, stop that. They can communicate with the DHCP server. They understand DNS. They can see the gateway from here.

To configure DHCP on a classic Mac, follow these steps:

1. From the Apple desktop, go to the Apple menu.

2. Go to Control Panels and select TCP/IP (see Figure 15.1).

FIGURE 15.1

Opening the TCP/IP Control Panel

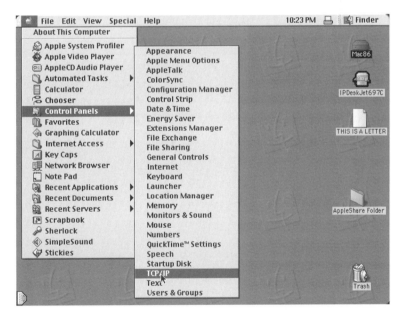

3. In the TCP/IP window (shown in Figure 15.2), you can configure the Mac to use a static IP, use a DHCP server, use a BootP server, or a RARP (Reverse Address Resolution Protocol) server to pull IP information. Choose Using DHCP Server.

As soon as you close the TCP/IP window, the Mac will attempt to get an IP address via DHCP. No rebooting necessary. It will add the name server information to the bottom of the TCP/IP window to indicate the DNS server. If the DHCP server has an address for an Internet gateway, it will show up in the Router Address field.

FIGURE 15.2

Setting up DHCP in the Macintosh TCP/IP Control Panel

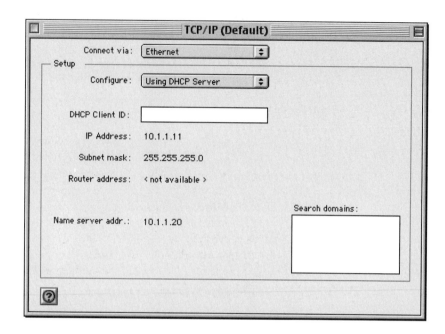

That's all she wrote. The Mac will now use the DHCP server to get its IP information. No more static addressing. Note, as shown in Figure 15.3, that the Server 2003 DHCP has assigned the Macintoshes Mac86 and Esher IP addresses as if they were Windows workstations.

FIGURE 15.3

Server 2003 DHCP assigning IP addresses to Macintoshes

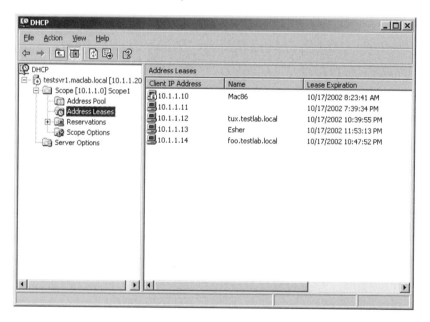

FILE SHARING

Until now, your Mac users may have thought the only way they could share a file with a coworker who uses a PC was to e-mail it. Well, that's not true. You can use a server as a drop-off point between the two types of workstations.

NOTE *If you are running IIS on your server, you can make files available to the Macintoshes through FTP. It's not the most convenient way of sharing files, but it works.*

Classic Macintosh OSes use a filesystem called Apple File Protocol (AFP) to share files. Microsoft uses Small Machine Block (SMB) protocol to share files. These two things are not at all the same. Since our network is a Windows network, and we have files we'd like to share with the Macs, it stands to reason that we should use the File Server for Macintosh (FSM) service.

This service will do a few things:

◆ Teach the Server 2003 how to speak AppleTalk, how to understand Apple File Protocol, and how to accept Apple authentication.

◆ Create a Microsoft User Authentication Module Volume (volume is Macintosh-speak for sharepoint).

◆ Add the capacity to create, monitor, and manage shares that can be accessed by Macintosh users.

Setting it up is easy. Just remember to create user accounts on the Server 2003 for the Macintosh users (so you can control their permissions). FSM has a few issues, but it works like a champ.

There are two parts to making it possible for Macintosh users to access a sharepoint on the Server 2003. The first part is preparing the Server 2003 to host the Macintosh volumes. The second part is getting the Macintosh workstations to find shared volumes and authenticate themselves to Server 2003 to access those shares.

Now, for all practical purposes, the whole file sharing process (after AppleTalk and Apple File Protocol are installed) hinges on one thing: authentication. The Server 2003 does not store Apple passwords in anything but clear text, which discourages anyone from allowing Macintoshes to use Apple authentication. Furthermore, allowing Microsoft authentication only is set as a default. But, to make it possible for the Macs to use Microsoft's authentication, Server 2003 creates a Macintosh shared folder on its hard drive with a Microsoft User Authentication Module in it. Are you sensing a problem here?

Have you ever seen that old western where the hero is unfairly locked in jail, while his jailer, asleep a few feet away, has the key dangling out of his pocket? He can see it, but he can't reach it. Tantalizingly close, but oh so far away. Well, that sums up the "I need to authenticate to get the authentication module, but I can't authenticate until I have the authentication module" process quite nicely. That is one of the issues I mentioned earlier. You can't just turn it on and go. You have to play with authentication first.

Now that I have mentioned that, the process of installing and setting up the File Server for Macintosh service will make a little more sense.

Installing FSM on Server 2003

You would think since FSM is a service, you could just add it to the network card properties, like file and print sharing, but no. You have to go to Add/Remove Programs and add File Server for Macintosh as a Windows component:

1. Go to Add/Remove Programs.
2. Scroll to Other Network File and Print Services.
3. Select Other Network File and Print Services (do not just put a check mark in the check box), and click the Details button.
4. There are three services listed in this dialog box (see Figure 15.4); put a check in the File Services for Macintosh check box only at this point (it's never good to have services running that you don't need. It wastes resources) and click OK, then click Next. Click Finish and you're done.

FIGURE 15.4

Adding File Services for Macintosh Windows Component

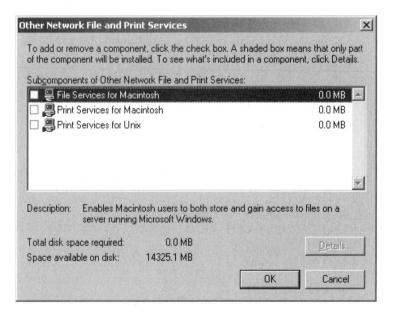

Now, let's check four things to be sure that File Server for Macintosh installed correctly.

1. Go to the Local Area Connections properties and see if AppleTalk Protocol is running. If it is, it will have a check mark next to it (see Figure 15.5).
2. Open the Services Console under Administrative Tools, and check to see if the File Server for Macintosh service is installed and started (see Figure 15.6).

FIGURE 15.5

Confirming that
AppleTalk is
installed and enabled

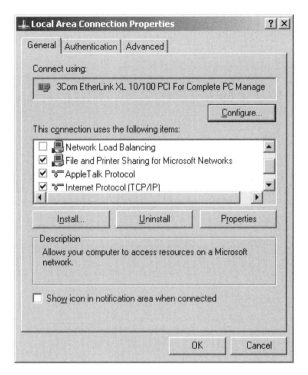

FIGURE 15.6

Confirming that File
Server for Macintosh
service is installed
and started

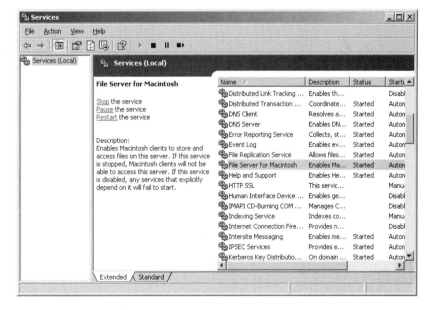

3. Go to the C: drive of the server and see if there is a new folder called `Microsoft UAM Volume` (see Figure 15.7). It will not look as if it has been set up as a sharepoint. That is because it has not been shared to Microsoft machines.

FIGURE 15.7

Confirming the Microsoft UAM volume has been created

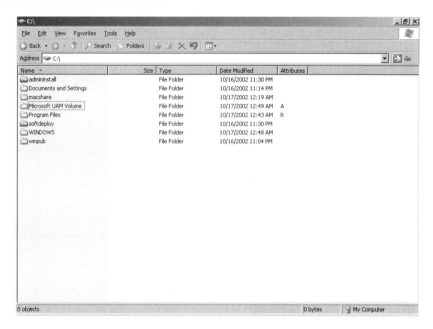

4. And finally, open the Computer Management Console under Administrative Tools. It is from here that you will manage your Macintosh file shares (see Figure 15.8), and you should see the new Microsoft UAM Volume share for Macintoshes.

FIGURE 15.8

Confirming the creation of a Macintosh share of the Microsoft UAM Volume

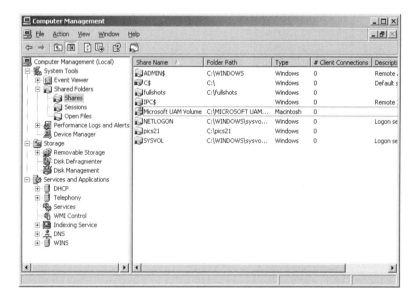

Now that you are sure that FSM is functioning, it's time to configure it. In the Computer Management window (see Figure 15.9), right-click Shared Folders and from the context menu, select Configure File Server for Macintosh.

FIGURE 15.9

Configuring File Server for Macintosh

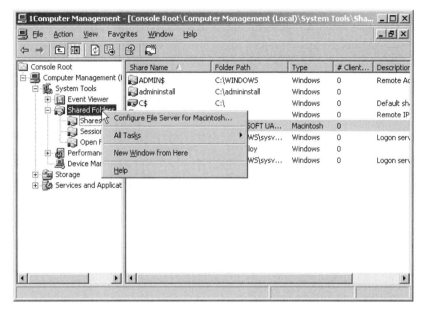

This will take you to the Configuration tab of the File Server for Macintosh Properties dialog box (see Figure 15.10). Let's look over this dialog box before we proceed. At the Configuration tab are the following options:

Server Name for AppleTalk Workstations   This is what will show up in the Chooser window on the Macintoshes.

Logon Message   Anything you type in here will show up in a pop-up dialog box announcing that the Macs have successfully logged in and accessed a sharepoint (which mounts on the desktop as a volume). This message can get annoying after a couple of days, so don't be too verbose. The example is a little congratulatory message.

Security   In this area you can have the user save their password locally to make it easier to log in, but this is not a secure idea.

Enable Authentication   What you choose here is really important if you want to overcome the "can't authenticate to get the authentication module" problem. There are several choices:

Microsoft Only   The default.

Apple Clear Text   Unencrypted Apple authentication only (which means, somewhat ironically, that a Mac that has the Microsoft UAM installed will not be able to authenticate).

Apple Encrypted   Encrypted at the Apple end, but stored as clear text at the Microsoft end. Again, Apple only; the UAM would fail to authenticate for this one too.

Apple Clear Text or Microsoft, or Apple Encrypted or Microsoft   Either of these choices allows Microsoft or Apple authentication, making it possible for the Macs that have installed the Microsoft UAM to log in, and for Macs that haven't to log in to get it. In my world, it doesn't matter which I choose, but having the passwords encrypted at least until they reach the Server 2003 isn't a bad thing.

Enable Authentication helps you jump the first hurdle in the race to get Server 2003 to share nicely with the Macs. You may prefer the encrypted Apple password, but I like to set this to Apple Clear Text or Microsoft. I prefer to allow Apple authentication *only* until all of the Macs have installed the Microsoft UAM. Once I am sure that everyone has installed the Microsoft UAM, then I set authentication back to Microsoft Only.

FIGURE 15.10

Configuration tab of the FSM properties page

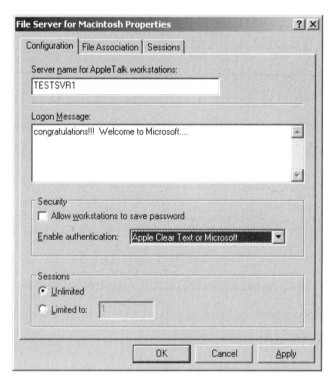

NOTE   *There is another way to allow Mac users to access the Microsoft UAM Volume if your company insists on not allowing Apple authentication: you can enable the guest account. If a Macintosh cannot use Apple authentication, and the FSM has been configured for Microsoft only, it can authenticate as a guest. Not my favorite option, but it is there.*

Sessions   Below the security area of the dialog box is the Sessions section, where you can set how many sessions can be running simultaneously. I tend to leave it at Unlimited.

The next two tabs in the FSM properties page are File Association and Sessions. File Associations are used to specify what extensions link to what program so the Macintoshes can understand flat file extensions and open the correct application with a double-click. Sessions displays the Usage Summary (see Figure 15.11), which displays how many sessions are running and includes a text area to send a message to all Mac users of this system. That comes in handy when you need to warn the users that the server is going to go offline.

FIGURE 15.11

Sessions tab

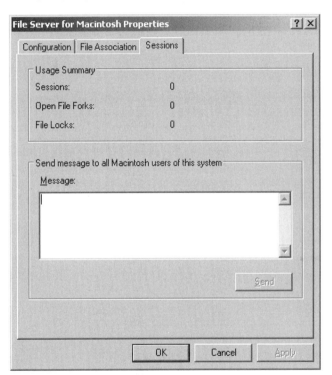

Once you have configured your FSM to your liking, click OK. The changes will be applied and the dialog box will close.

RESOURCE FORKS, FILE EXTENSIONS, AND WHY OS X DOESN'T CARE

The Microsoft filesystem is a flat database. It lists all files with two parts: data and extension. The extension part of the file does two things: it defines the file type and it defines what application opens the file. Those extensions are listed in a File Associations database kept in Windows so extensions can be associated with the application that opens them. This database can be edited anytime. Of course, you already know that.

Continued on next page

RESOURCE FORKS, FILE EXTENSIONS, AND WHY OS X DOESN'T CARE *(continued)*

The Macintosh filesystem is not flat, it's layered. In this two-dimensional, two-prong (so to speak) file structure, all files have two parts, data and resource. The resource "fork" of the file does two things: it defines the file type and defines the file Creator (that is, which application opens the file). Although they do similar things, Macs have a problem understanding Windows file extensions, and Windows systems have a problem understanding resource forks. If you move a file from a Macintosh to a PC and then back again, the Mac will have no idea what kind of file it is because the PC stripped it of its resource fork. Also, those pesky Macs leave resource fork files all over the place when they browse Windows resources. It's how you can know they've been there...

With the File Server for Macintosh service for Windows Server installed, Windows Server knows what resource forks are and will try to help map extensions to resource fork "creators" so Mac users can use the Windows files. And, on the Macintosh end, PC Exchange maps extensions to resource fork information for Windows users.

Despite the assistance FSM and PC Exchange give, it is best to teach your Mac users to go ahead and add extensions to the end of all of the files they intend to share with PC users. Also, remind them of the characters that are not allowed to be used in Windows filenames. It is just good network etiquette.

Finally, after all these years of covert file interpreting, OS X uses a flat file structure like Windows, extensions and all. It still supports the Macintosh layered filesystem for backward compatibility, but otherwise, it's just like any other Windows filesystem. It's a shame really—that two-layered file structure was pretty clever.

Now that File Server for Macintosh is running and AppleTalk is installed, you need to think about how you are going to handle sharing folders.

Right now there is only one Macintosh share on the server, the Microsoft UAM Volume. Macintosh users on the network can see the fileserver in the Chooser because AppleTalk is doing its job and broadcasting it. It's a good idea not to build any more shares right now. Why? Because if there were other Macintosh shares on the server, and Apple authentication is turned on, Mac users will be able to easily access the other folders without getting the Microsoft UAM.

While you wait for your Macintosh users to actually install the Microsoft UAM, let's go over some ground rules about making Mac shares on a Server 2003:

- Macintoshes prefer share names that are 31 characters or less.
- The Finder (the Mac's equivalent of Windows Explorer) can only handle 50 volumes with 27-character length names. That means, in total, you can have only 1350 characters for all the mounted volumes on the desktop. So, just in case, keep your names short. It is possible to have more than 50 shared volumes; you just have to have really short share names of only several characters each. Windows will compensate for illegal characters in Mac filenames and will keep track of short filenames for DOS-level work, but Windows won't worry about the exact length of long filenames. You are going to have to keep that in mind on your own.
- Macintoshes can't handle directory paths that are more than 260 characters, so be careful about nesting folders.
- If you have a shared volume, don't bother trying to create a shared volume within it. If a folder is a shared Macintosh volume, then all nested folders within it are shared by default.

♦ By the same token, you cannot decide to share a volume that already has a shared volume nested in it. Basically a folder cannot be shared twice. Either it is in a shared folder or it is the shared folder.

It's important to note that, by default, all Macintosh shared volumes created on the Server 2003 are set to read-only (another FSM quirk). No matter what permissions you give the Macintosh user accounts concerning the volumes, you will have to manually turn off the read-only setting in the individual share properties. This is great for the Microsoft UAM volume, because it is meant to be used only to install the authentication module, nothing else. Later though, when you want to allow the Mac users to add things to the shares and make changes to documents stored there, the read-only setting will become a problem. To see what I am talking about, right-click the Microsoft UAM Volume in the Computer Management window and select Properties. As you can see in Figure 15.12, the This Volume is Read-Only check box is on by default.

FIGURE 15.12

Read-only default permission on Macintosh shares

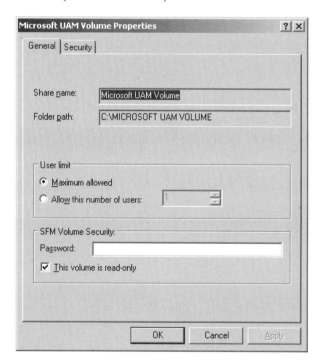

THE CHOOSER

Going to the Chooser to find a printer is as natural to a Mac user as breathing oxygen, but it may seem like breathing water to a Windows person.

The Chooser is an archaic application that came out with Macintosh OS1 (back when it was known as System 1). It was originally intended to let the user choose which serial port they were going to use for what device. That led to choosing a printer, which led to using AppleTalk to choose a network resource, which led to the Chooser becoming a network browser. Now the Chooser, no longer aptly named, is used to connect to file servers and printers, as well as locally-attached devices.

Continued on next page

THE CHOOSER *(continued)*

The Chooser started out listing the different drivers you might have installed, like a serial printer or modem, on the left side of the window. Upon clicking the driver, the right side of the window shows you the ports (and the device attached to that port) that driver can use. You choose a port, then the job is sent to that port packaged in the way the driver likes it.

Now you can see the drivers on the left side of the Chooser window, such as AppleShare for file servers or LaserWriter8 for printers, or a fax driver for the modem. If you click one of the drivers, whatever device (network or local) that uses that driver will display on the right.

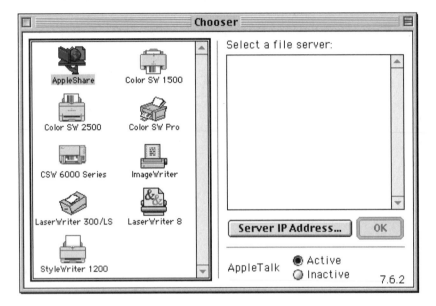

After choosing AppleShare (which is poorly named—it's really Apple File Protocol), you can click the Server IP Address button on the right side of the window and type in the IP address of the server you want to access. This is especially useful, since most file servers are not AppleTalk enabled these days.

Also on the right side of the Chooser window, you can set AppleTalk to Active or Inactive.

You might be wondering why there isn't a TCP/IP or IPShare or some such icon on the left side of the Chooser so you can click it and use it to display a list of all of the IP file servers on the network. Funny, that. It seems that Chooser, being an old-timer, generally only lists things that have been broadcast to it through AppleTalk. AppleTalk is nearly as old as the Chooser—it's very chatty and easily announces all of its available resources any time the Chooser asks. IP, on the other hand, doesn't broadcast nearly as much (or as continuously) and therefore the Chooser doesn't list it automatically. With an IP resource, you are just going to have to type it in.

Connecting a Macintosh to the Server 2003 Share and Installing UAM

The hard stuff is already finished. Now you just have to install the Microsoft UAM onto the Macintosh (or have the Mac users do it).

1. Go to the Apple menu on the Macintosh desktop.
2. Select Chooser.
3. In the left side of the Chooser window, click AppleShare.
4. As you can see in Figure 15.13, on the right side of the window is listed all resources that can be accessed using AppleShare. The only resource that should be listed is the Server 2003 running AppleTalk and FSM (my server is TESTSVR1), since no other shares have been created. If the server name does not display after you select AppleShare, check to see if AppleTalk is active.

FIGURE 15.13

AppleTalk Active in the Chooser window

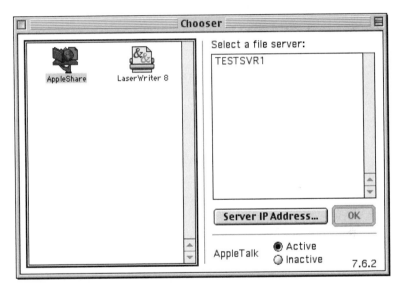

5. Click the server name and then click the Server IP Address button, which makes it possible to access the server without AppleTalk. Type in the IP address of the server to access the share that way (thus eliminating the need for AppleTalk on your network).
6. Click the OK button.
7. This will bring up a dialog box prompting the user to enter a username and password (see Figure 15.14). The username will default to the owner name of the system (so wouldn't it be clever if you created user accounts that matched? Less typing, fewer calls to the help desk). Below the password field is a note that indicates how the data will be sent (mine is in clear text). After typing in the username (if necessary) and password (which you can change...don't know why you'd want to, though), click Connect.

FIGURE 15.14

Authenticating to
Microsoft UAM
Volume

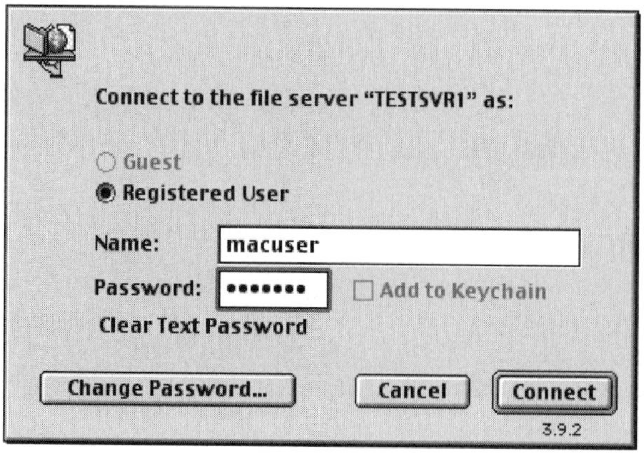

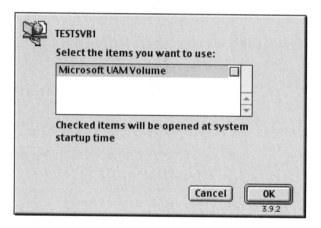

8. The next dialog box displays the Macintosh volumes available on the server (see Figure 15.15). The only volume there at the moment is the Microsoft UAM volume. Select it and click OK.

FIGURE 15.15

Displaying the
available Macintosh
volumes

NOTE *Note the little gray box to the right of the volume in the list. Do not check that box. It allows Apple authenticated shares to be mounted on the desktop at startup. If you later change authentication to Microsoft only, you will get authentication errors upon startup. In OS 9, you would have to remove any reference to the share from the servers folder under the System folder. In OS 8.6, you would have to re-enable Apple authentication on the Server 2003, let the Mac log in, and uncheck any volumes to ensure that they will not open at startup. Then you would again be able to set authentication back to Microsoft on the Server 2003.*

The next dialog box should have the congratulatory logon message and a notice that you reached the server via TCP/IP (see Figure 15.16). Note that, although AppleTalk was used to display the server name in the Chooser, the Mac actually connected using TCP/IP. It's faster that way.

FIGURE 15.16

Connection
confirmation and
welcome message

> "TESTSVR1 (10.1.1.20) via TCP/IP"
>
> congratulations!!! Welcome to Microsoft....
>
> [OK]

Now, as you can see in Figure 15.17, the Microsoft volume will show up on the right side of the desktop in whatever free space is available. It looks like a network drive icon with a Microsoft flying window over it.

FIGURE 15.17

Microsoft UAM
Volume on the
desktop

9. Close out of the Chooser (click the box on the left side of the title bar); you're done with it for now. Double-click the new Microsoft UAM Volume icon, which will open to a window like the one in Figure 15.18.

   In the open window there will be several items. The important one is the MS UAM Installer. Double-click the installer. A dialog box will come up confirming the installation (see Figure 15.19).

10. Click Continue. You'll soon see a dialog box announcing the successful install (see Figure 15.20). If you don't see a dialog box like this, don't assume it installed.

FIGURE 15.18

Opening Microsoft
UAM Volume

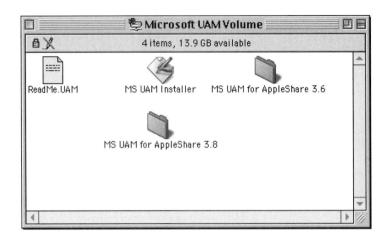

FIGURE 15.19

Installing the
Microsoft UAM

FIGURE 15.20

Confirmation
of installation of
MS UAM

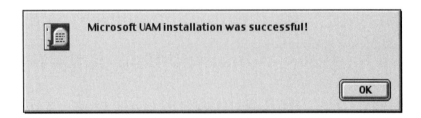

To see if the Microsoft User Authentication Module works, you'll need to close the existing connection with the server. Currently the mounted volume is authenticated via Apple authentication. Closing the connection is simple: just drag the volume icon into the trash. No, seriously, it's what you're supposed to do. (You can make CDs eject by dragging their icons to the trash, too.)

Creating Mac Shares on the Server 2003

Let's assume that all of your users have installed the MS UAM. Now it is time to reset authentication to Microsoft only. To do this, open the Computer Management Console, right-click the shared folder, configure File Server for Macintosh and change the Enable Authentication field to Microsoft Only.

FIGURE 15.21

Returning
Macintosh share
authentication to
Microsoft Only

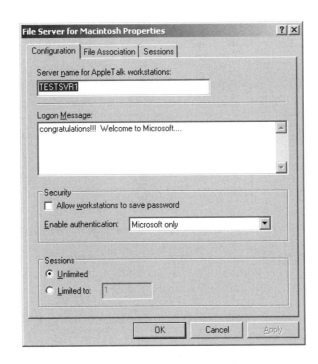

Now you can create all of those shares that you've been looking forward to:

1. To create a share, right-click Shares in the Computer Management Console. From the context menu, select New Share (see Figure 15.22).

FIGURE 15.22

Creating a new share

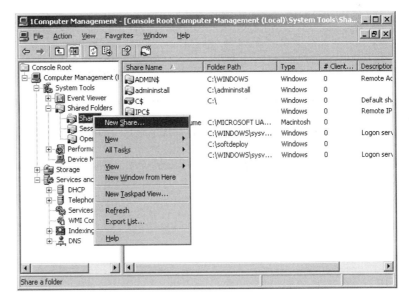

2. The Share a Folder Wizard starts (see Figure 15.23). You need to indicate what folder you are going to share with the Macintoshes. Make sure the folder path is not too long. I am going to create a folder called **macshare** on the C: drive.

FIGURE 15.23

Share a Folder Wizard, Folder Path screen

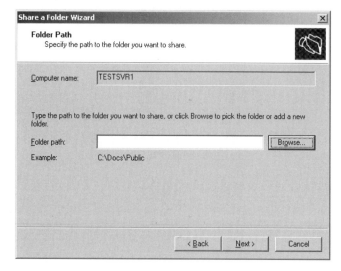

3. You need to indicate if it is going to be shared by Windows users and/or Macintosh users. The macshare folder I created is going to be available to both sets of users as a common sharepoint to exchange files. Note the length of my share names. If I were planning to have more than 50 Macintosh shares on the server, I would seriously consider using a very short Macintosh volume name. However, I don't plan to have more than 12 shared Mac volumes, so macshare is fine for a Macintosh share name.

FIGURE 15.24

Making the share accessible to both Windows and Macintosh clients

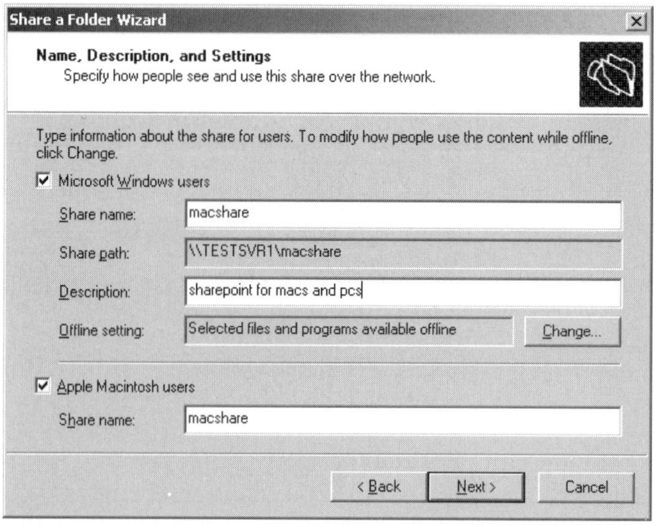

4. Set permissions on the share. These permissions are primarily for the Microsoft users at this point because no matter what you set here, the folder will still be read-only for Mac users until

you explicitly set it otherwise in the share properties. For all users to be able to read and write to the share, select the third option, as shown in Figure 15.25.

FIGURE 15.25

Setting access permissions

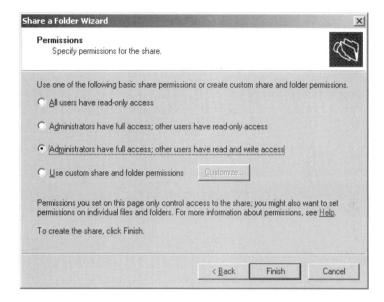

5. The summary page of the wizard confirms your decisions concerning the new share (see Figure 15.26).

FIGURE 15.26

Confirmation of the new share

6. In the Computer Management Console (see Figure 15.27), you'll see the new share. It will show up twice because there are two different kinds of shares applied to it. The one with the tiny Mac Classic computer on the top right corner of the folder is the Macintosh share. (Pretty clever, actually. The icon is pretty small, but kudos for trying.)

Figure 15.27

macshare folder
in the Computer
Management
Console

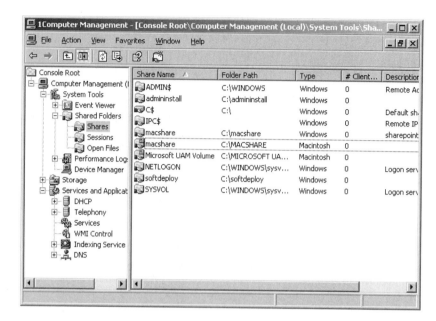

7. To make sure that the new Macintosh share is not read-only (despite whatever permissions you may have set for the users), right-click it, select Properties, and remove the check from the This Volume is Read-Only check box (see Figure 15.28). Remember, this overrides any permissions you may have given the Mac user accounts for this folder.

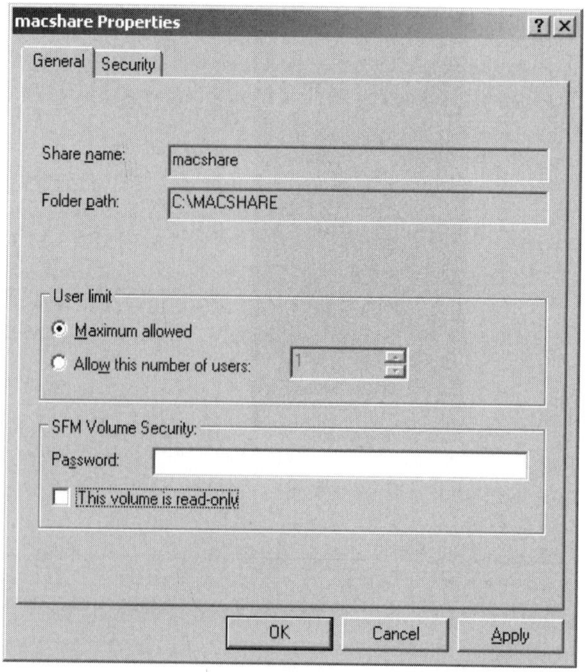

Figure 15.28

Turning off the
read-only default
on the macshare
folder

macshare Properties   ? X

General | Security

Share name: macshare

Folder path: C:\MACSHARE

┌─ User limit ───┐
│ ● Maximum allowed   │
│ ○ Allow this number of users: 1   │
└──┘

┌─ SFM Volume Security: ───────────────────────────────┐
│ Password: [   ]   │
│ ☐ This volume is read-only   │
└──┘

                            OK   Cancel   Apply

Connecting the Mac to a Shared Volume using the UAM

All right then, back to the Macintosh. It's time to see if the Microsoft User Authentication Module works:

1. Open the Chooser. Select AppleShare. Select the server (TESTSVR1, in the example). Click Connect.

2. In the Authentication dialog box, enter the appropriate username and password and click Connect (see Figure 15.29). Notice that it no longer says Clear Text under the password and that TCP/IP is indicated in the lower-left corner of the box.

FIGURE 15.29

Authenticating from a Macintosh using the Microsoft Authentication Module

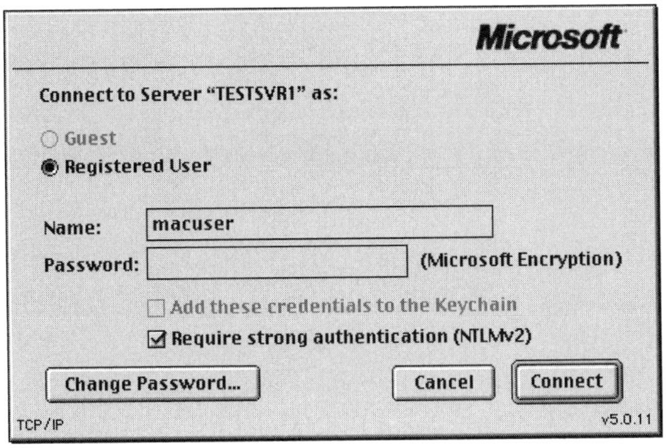

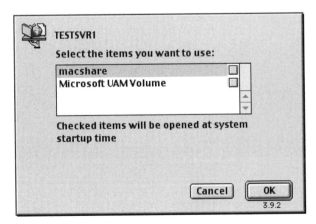

3. In the next dialog box (see Figure 15.30), select the new share (which is macshare, in the example). Click OK.

FIGURE 15.30

Selecting the macshare volume

4. A message dialog box will display to indicate a successful login and connection to the share.

The share will show up on the desktop as shown in Figure 15.31.

FIGURE 15.31

The macshare volume on the desktop

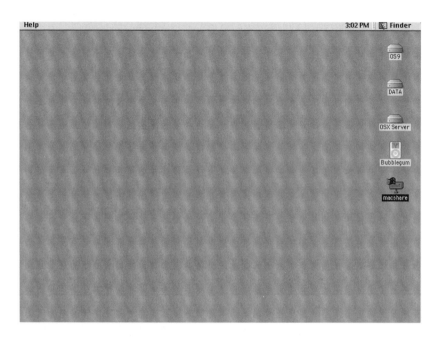

The final test, of course, is to add a file to the macshare volume. I saved a big important contract on a Macintosh to macshare (I made sure that I added the .doc extension). It shows up fine in Figure 15.32, which is on Server 2003.

FIGURE 15.32

Copying a file to the new macshare volume on Server 2003

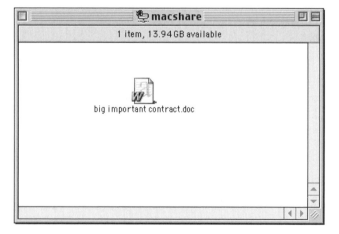

One final note about file sharing: let's take a quick look at how to do it without AppleTalk.

1. Disable AppleTalk on the server by going into the Local Area Connection properties and removing the check mark in the AppleTalk check box (see Figure 15.33). Be patient: when you click OK, it might take a moment to think about it.

FIGURE 15.33

Disabling
AppleTalk
Protocol

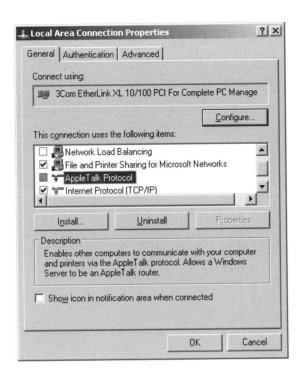

2. Go to a Macintosh workstation that can do Microsoft authentication. Go to the Chooser, select AppleShare, and you will see that the server does not show up in the resource list on the right. As you can see in Figure 15.34, the OK button is grayed out.

FIGURE 15.34

File sharing in
Chooser when
Server 2003 is not
using AppleTalk
to broadcast its
resources

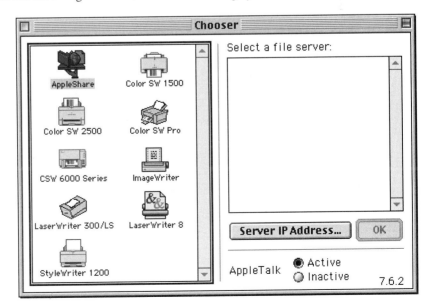

3. You still can access the shares; you just have to use the Server IP Address button. Click it and type in the IP address of the Server 2003 in the dialog that comes up (see Figure 15.35). The authentication and connection process will proceed as usual.

FIGURE 15.35

Using TCP/IP to access Server 2003 Macintosh shared volumes

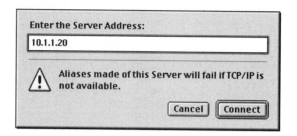

Enter the Server Address:

10.1.1.20

⚠ Aliases made of this Server will fail if TCP/IP is not available.

[Cancel] [Connect]

Although disabling AppleTalk does mean that users will need to learn the Server 2003's IP address or DNS name, you can file share on just TCP/IP.

CLASSIC OS PRINTING TO THE NETWORK PRINTER

Chances are good that, just as they are already using the Internet, Mac users are already printing to the network printer. You just may not know it.

Macintoshes print using Adobe Postscript Printer Language. Luckily, most network printers, such as HP LaserJets for example, can support both Postscript and PCL (printer control language, which is what PCs use). However, you may want to check and see which of your printers support Postscript (or just find out what printers your Mac users can print to).

Most network-caliber printers can support Postscript and even speak AppleTalk. By default, AppleTalk usually is on, and you have to manually turn it off.

If a Printer Is AppleTalk Enabled

To see if a network is AppleTalk enabled, at a Mac workstation, go to the Chooser. Click the Laser-Writer 8 driver icon (which can be used as the default driver for any Postscript printer). The network printer(s) should show up in the box on the right (see Figure 15.36). If it doesn't show up, it either can't use AppleTalk or AppleTalk is not enabled (if you didn't set AppleTalk as active in the Chooser of that machine, click the Active button, which is on the bottom right of the window). Using AppleTalk for printing is pretty standard because it's so easy to use and hard to break.

If the printer can do Postscript, then it might have a driver file, a PPD (Postscript printer definition) file, or both, which the Mac can use to really get the most out of the printer's features. But if you think that not having those printer-specific file(s) is going to stop the Mac users from printing, you are wrong. If the printer is out there and it's AppleTalk ready, then the user can use their default Postscript driver (that non-intuitively named LaserWriter 8 icon), to print standard Postscript documents. It's that easy. And remember, there are no securities being applied to these users—they are using AppleTalk to get to the printer and bypassing any domain restrictions. That may be why all those pretty pictures keep printing out on the printer in the accounting department.

Even if the printer can't do AppleTalk, as long as it can do Postscript, the Macs can still get to it. They just have to use the Desktop Printer Utility, which comes with the Mac OS. It's not rocket science, and Mac users are usually "if there's a will, there's a way" kind of people. They've grown used to having to take care of themselves. Half of them are probably using it right now.

FIGURE 15.36

Chooser window displaying AppleTalk-enabled printers

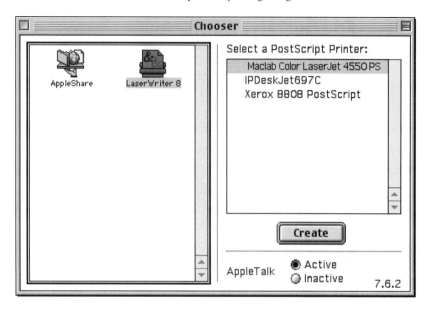

USING DESKTOP PRINTER UTILITY TO DO TCP/IP PRINTING

To use TCP/IP to connect to a printer, a Macintosh user does not go to the Chooser. The Chooser only shows printers that are AppleTalk enabled or printers that are being shared by a Server 2003 using AppleTalk. If the Postscript printer in question is on the network and has an IP address, a Macintosh user can just run the Desktop Printer Utility. It comes with the OS and is usually located in a folder called Apple LaserWriter Software (as shown in Figure 15.37), in the Apple Extras folder on the hard drive. It is really easy to get to.

FIGURE 15.37

Desktop Printer Utility in the Apple LaserWriter Software folder

To run the utility:

1. Just double-click the Desktop Printer Utility. It will open into a list of ways to access the printer (see Figure 15.38). LPR (Line Printer Remote, a common Unix printer protocol using TCP/IP) is the choice for TCP/IP printing. Choose that. Click OK.

FIGURE 15.38

List of available printer connection types

2. The next dialog box that opens has two parts, as you can see in Figure 15.39. The top part is where you choose the correct PPD for the network printer you want to use. Using the correct PPD is always the best option, but if you don't have it, the generic one (the default) will work.

FIGURE 15.39

Creating a desktop printer

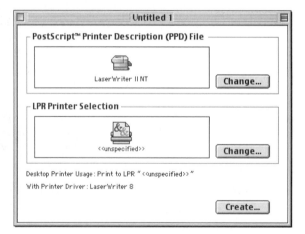

3. The bottom part is for specifying the IP address of the printer. Click the Change button (I know, you haven't added anything so how can you change it? They're just thinking ahead, that's all).

4. It will give you a dialog box to add the IP address of the printer (see Figure 15.40). If it is attached to a print server that is serving several printers, you can specify which queue as well as the IP. Be sure to click the Verify button so the utility can check to see if there is a printer at the IP/queue you've specified. Once the address has been verified, click OK.

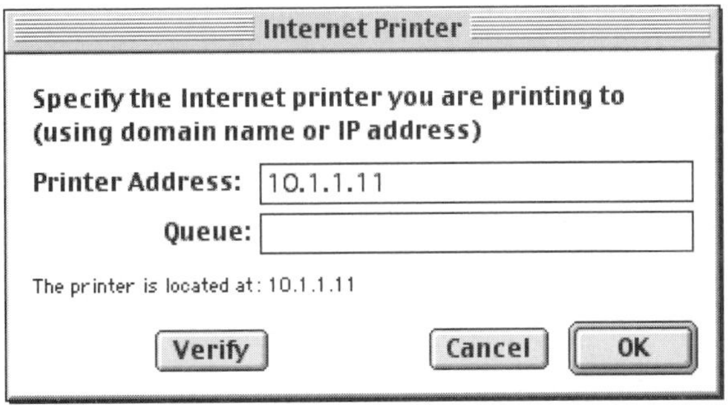

FIGURE 15.40

Specifying the
printer IP address

> ┌───┐
> │ ▓▓▓▓▓▓▓▓ **Internet Printer** ▓▓▓▓▓▓▓▓ │
> ├───┤
> │ **Specify the Internet printer you are printing to** │
> │ **(using domain name or IP address)** │
> │   │
> │ **Printer Address:** ┌─────────────────────┐ │
> │   │ 10.1.1.11   │ │
> │   └─────────────────────┘ │
> │   **Queue:** ┌─────────────────────┐   │
> │   │   │   │
> │   └─────────────────────┘   │
> │ The printer is located at: 10.1.1.11   │
> │   │
> │   (Verify)   (Cancel) ((OK))   │
> └───┘

5. Back at the main dialog box, click Create. You'll be prompted to pick a location to save the printer icon. The desktop works for me. I named my printer Business Laser (as you can see in Figure 15.41) and put it on the desktop. Now I can print to it from any application or I can just drag and drop documents onto the printer icon.

FIGURE 15.41

IP printer icon on
the desktop

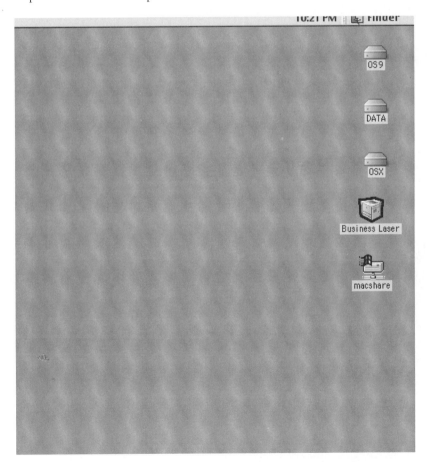

Classic Mac Printing to a Non-Postscript Printer

What if you find a printer that does *not* support Postscript? Well, as long as you don't want the Mac print job to be in color or to use any of the specific printer's fancy features, you can have the server intercept the print job and convert it to PCL.

Yes, you heard me right, the Mac can print to non-Postscript printers on a Windows Server network.

By using the Print Server for Macintosh service, you can share out a local or network printer through the Server 2003 to make it possible to print Mac print jobs on a non-Postscript printer. This does work, but what it does is take a snapshot of the Macintosh print job (as if it were a fax machine) and send it "as is" to the printer. At this point, that means it doesn't do color. Also, it is not always effective with special feed print jobs, such as envelopes. But, when a Mac absolutely, positively, must print on a non-Postscript printer, it can be done.

Installing Print Server for Macintosh on Server 2003

1. Installing the Print Server for Macintosh service is exactly like installing the File Server for Macintosh. You go to Add/Remove Programs\Add Windows Components.

2. Scroll to Other Network File and Print Services and select it. Click Details. In the dialog box that appears, click the check box next to Print Services for Macintosh (see Figure 15.42). Click OK and click OK again.

FIGURE 15.42

Installing Print Services for Macintosh

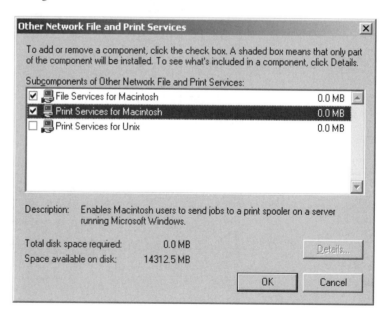

That's it. Print Server for Macintosh service is installed. You can make sure it's in the Services console if you'd like.

Even if you disabled AppleTalk while working with File Server for Macintosh, it will be enabled for the Print Server for Macintosh service. You see, Server 2003 can't run the service without it. Due to the fact that it is going to be doing Macintosh Postscript to PCL print job translation on the fly, I'm not really going to argue. If it wants to make it easy for the Mac to see the printer in the Chooser window, that's fine with me. But seriously, the Print Server for Macintosh service will not work without AppleTalk.

If you want to, you can have the Print Server for Macintosh service log on to the printer share as something other than the usual local system. If you are particularly concerned about security and want to track print jobs, just go to the Print Server for Macintosh service in the Service console (or under Services in the Computer Management Console), open its properties, click the Log On tab, and change the default logon to the account of your choice. I myself am not that worried about it. But the option is there if you need it, as shown in Figure 15.43.

FIGURE 15.43

Changing the Print Server for Macintosh logon account

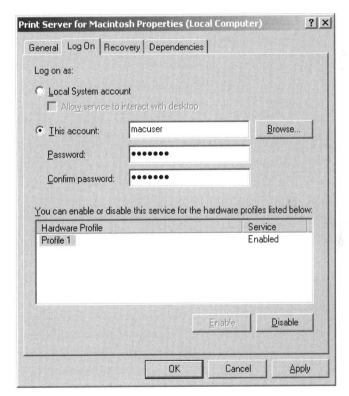

Now any printer that uses the Server 2003 as its print server can take print jobs from the Mac, even if it does not support Postscript.

To prove it, I had the Server 2003 be the print server for my HP DeskJet697c (see Figure 15.44). The DeskJet definitely does not use Postscript.

FIGURE 15.44

Shared printer on Server 2003

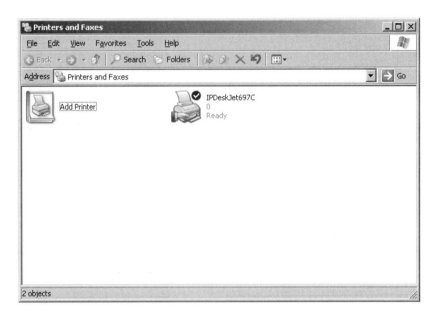

The second half of this Print sharing equation is, of course, the Macintosh.

1. At the Mac, go to the Chooser. Select LaserWriter 8 from the drivers list (be it short or long). Select the printer from the resource list (mine will be the trusty DeskJet), as shown in Figure 15.45. Click Create.

FIGURE 15.45

Listing of shared Server 2003 printer in Chooser

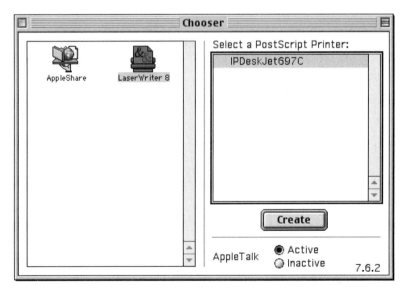

2. It will try to auto-detect the PPD for the printer (see Figure 15.46). If it can't, it will prompt you to choose the PPD. In this case, click the Generic button.

FIGURE 15.46

Suggested drivers for
the shared printer

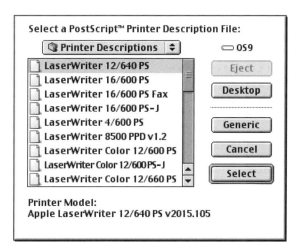

That's it. A desktop printer icon will be built that sends print jobs to the Server 2003 (see
Figure 15.47). It may only be in black and white, but it will let the Macintosh print where it may
never have printed before.

FIGURE 15.47

Shared printer icon
being created on the
desktop

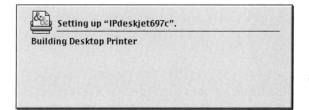

OS X Client Integration

To start, make sure that you avoid using any OS X version before 10.1.2; previous versions needed
a lot of patches.

An important concept to understand is that OS X is not just an upgrade of OS 9. It is fundamentally different. Its core is now Unix. It has a command line and practically everything has either
gotten a new name, gotten a new look, been put in a different place, or all three. On the Windows
side, the service File Server for Macintosh will still work with it. OS X can run in Classic mode.
If you dual boot between OS 9 and OS X, OS X will run an emulator called Classic during OS X
to let you work with pre-OS X applications. OS X is a pretty grand departure from all that came
before it.

Obviously OS X can do everything that OS 9 and earlier can do, so I am primarily going to cover
the interface differences and some significant upgrades. There are basically three main flavors of OS X
so far: OS X 10.0 to 10.0.4 (not a spectacular OS version and not something I am going to go into),
OS X 10.1 to 10.1.5, and OS X 10.2 to 10.2.3.

The biggest difference between OS X 10.1 and 10.2 is that 10.2 can support SMB natively (that is, it can recognize the file sharing protocol that Windows uses). 10.1 can support SMB, but you have to download a free SMB client for Unix, such as Samba. Oh, and OS X 10.2 doesn't need a server to intervene on its behalf to authenticate to an AD server that has an OS X-ready schema. More on that later.

OS X will be the only OS available on machines purchased as of January 2003. As of this writing, Macintoshes are being sold with both OS 9 and OS X installed.

CONFIGURING DHCP

So let's get to it. To begin with, an OS X workstation can be a DHCP client just like OS 9, but the interface is a bit different.

The TCP/IP settings are no longer in the Control Panel. The Control Panel has become the System Preferences. To access System Preferences, you can:

1. Go to the Apple menu and select System Preferences. Alternatively, you can go to the Dock. (The Dock is rather like the quick launch area on the taskbar in Windows 98. Like the taskbar, it normally is at the bottom of the desktop.) Click the System Preferences icon, which looks like a light switch with an Apple logo on it.

2. In the System Preferences window, click the Network button. In the Network window, make sure you are on the TCP/IP tab (note that there are several tabs, including one for AppleTalk).

3. Beneath the TCP/IP tab are all of the familiar settings. Choose Using DHCP from the Configure list box (see Figure 15.48), just as you would in OS 9.

FIGURE 15.48

Configuring TCP/IP on an OS X workstation

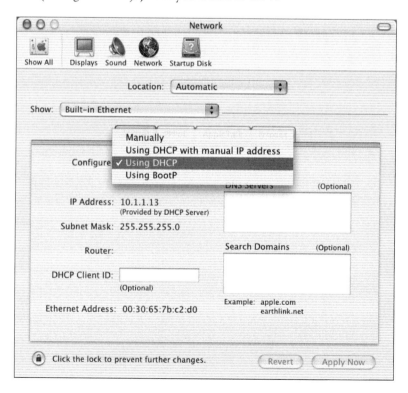

NOTE *Macintoshes don't see domains, they only see "workgroups". That means that they also don't see normal workgroup/ domain boundaries. They may well be able to see servers they shouldn't. They don't log in to a domain, they just consider themselves as part of a workgroup as a sort of network courtesy. This may seem strange, but domains are a Microsoft thing. Many network operating systems don't have them. Instead, they rely on directory services.*

FILE SHARING

In a departure from tradition that is sure to break Mac users' hearts, OS X no longer has a Chooser. To access printers and file shares, you will have to get used to both a different interface and a few new features. In addition, there is a new Microsoft UAM for OS X at the Microsoft Mactopia Web site. If you're going to do any file sharing with Windows machines, be sure to download the new UAM and make it available to the OS X systems. Also, several updates have already been made available to make OS X better at file sharing with Windows.

XP DESKTOP ON THE MAC

With Terminal Services enabled on the Server 2003, Macintosh users can be treated like any other Terminal Services Client. Just install Microsoft's remote desktop client for OS X, and the Mac becomes able to run Windows applications as if it were an XP workstation. Very useful for those users who need to use a PC-only application on a Macintosh. This is frequently an issue for graphics departments who have Mac-only drawing software but must use a PC-only product, such as a time-tracking package for billing purposes. Although the OS X remote desktop client is a free download from Microsoft, you must have a legal Terminal Services client license for it. (Don't think of me as a member of the Microsoft police, I'm more like a crossing guard. Just looking out for your safety.)

If you have pre-OS X Macintoshes, you can use Citrix to do Terminal Services (it is sort of a rider package). Citrix enhances Microsoft Terminal Services in many ways, one of which is providing additional non-standard clients, such as Macintosh classic OSes, with access to the terminal server.

Be warned: Citrix is not cheap. You need a Citrix Client license and a Terminal Services Client license for each user. But if you have a few but crucial OS 9.2 Macintoshes, and you are already running Terminal Services, it might be worth looking into.

Accessing the Server 2003

OS X can access file shares on a Server 2003 just as any classic OS could (with the correct Microsoft UAM). But, instead of going to the Chooser, you go to the Go menu at the top of the desktop, as shown in Figure 15.49. From the Go menu, select Connect to Server.

As soon as the window opens, OS X 10.1 scans the local network for all AppleTalk zones and AFP (Apple File Protocol) accessible servers. My Server 2003 TESTSVR1 for example, would show up next to the candied AppleTalk zone as well as next to the local network, because the workstation found it by using both AppleTalk and TCP/IP.

OS X 10.2 goes one step further and can recognize SMB, or Windows resources, as well as AFP. This is why TESTSVR1 also appears in Maclab (the NetBIOS name for the Server 2003 domain)— OS X 10.2 will display resources in Windows Workgroups or Domains. As of this writing, however, SMB tends to like to authenticate locally, which can be a problem at the server level. For shares on the server, I suggest using AFP for the time being. Using OS X 10.2 workstations to do SMB is still new to Apple and may have some growing pains, but it is a great convenience.

FIGURE 15.49

Connecting to a
file share with the
Go menu

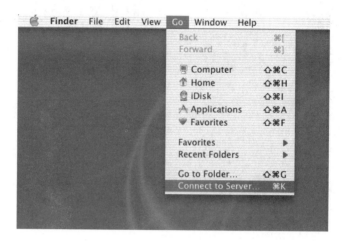

You can select the resource you wish to access in the Connect to Server window, or type in an
address in the Address box below the resource list.

By the way, OS X requires URL syntax for these addresses. For example, to connect to a server
with a Macintosh shared volume through AppleTalk, you would type: **AFP:/at/machine:zone** (as
shown in Figure 15.50).

FIGURE 15.50

Connecting to a
server using Apple
File Protocol

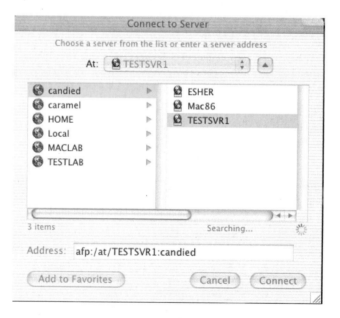

To connect to an AFP server through TCP/IP, you would type: **AFP://IPADDRESS** or **AFP:
//SERVERNAME.DOMAINNAME**.

For OS X 10.2 and higher, to connect to a Windows server that has a shared folder on it, you can
choose not to use AppleTalk or AFP, and just use SMB by typing: **SMB://IPADDRESS** or **SMB://
SERVER.DOMAINNAME** (see Figure 15.51).

FIGURE 15.51

Connecting to a
network share
using SMB

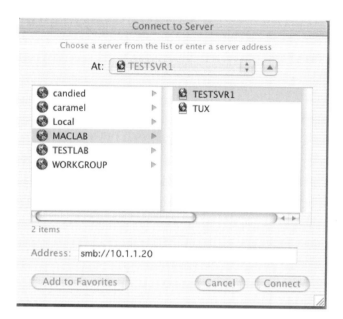

Remember, the Macintosh user does need a user account to authenticate to the Server 2003. Once authenticated, the shared volume will show up on the desktop, as usual (see Figure 15.52).

FIGURE 15.52

Shared volume on
the desktop

TIP *Are your OS 9 workstations authenticating to a Server 2003 share, but your OS X workstations aren't? Check the authentication setting under Configure File Server for Macintosh. Make certain that you don't have Apple Encrypted set as your authentication type. OS X has a problem with Apple Encrypted authentication because Windows does Apple Encryption in a random, one-way exchange, and OS X wants a two-way exchange. To fix it, either use Apple Clear Text Authentication, or Microsoft Authentication Only if they have the new UAM.*

OS X PRINTING

To access printers on the network in OS X, the Macintosh user will have to go to the Applications folder on the hard drive and look in Utilities. This process is somewhat reminiscent of using the Desktop Printer Utility.

Within the Utilities folder is the Print Center (see Figure 15.53). For some reason, when you open the Print Center, the title bar of the window says Print List. Don't let that put you off, it is the Print Center, but the window does list Printers, so I guess they opted for a task-oriented title. This is the window within which almost every printer activity occurs. From this window, by clicking the Add icon, a Macintosh user can connect to a AppleTalk, TCP/IP, or even a shared printer on a Server 2003 that is running Print Server for Macintosh service.

FIGURE 15.53

Print Center window

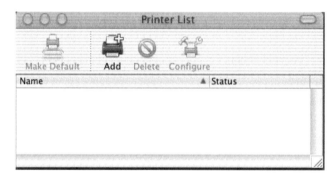

In the Add window, you can choose the kind of connection you'll be using to get to the printer, as shown in Figure 15.54.

FIGURE 15.54

Choosing a connection type

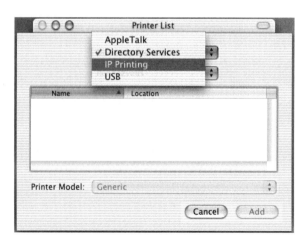

If you chose AppleTalk, you will once again see the list of AppleTalk network printers, as shown in Figure 15.55.

FIGURE 15.55
List of AppleTalk printers in the Print Center

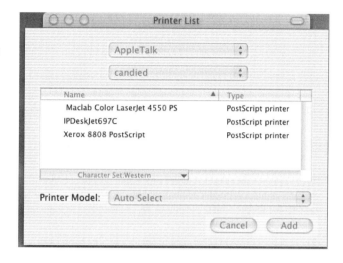

That would normally be it for new printer activities—except for the introduction of CUPS in OS X 10.2.1.

CUPS Printing

CUPS stands for Common Unix Printing System. It is a Web browser–based printer administration environment. With this system, an OS X 10.2 workstation can print to a non-Postscript printer (a DeskJet697c, for example) *in color* without the assistance of Server 2003's Print Server for Macintosh. It's extremely convenient to set up, and it has a surprising number of non-Postscript print drivers organized by manufacturer. The drivers are made to apply by model series, taking advantage of the fact that there are few differences between printers in a single model line.

1. To use CUPS, open a Web browser.
2. In the address field, type **http://127.0.0.1:631** (127.0.0.1 being the machine's loopback address, and 631 being the port that CUPS uses).
3. As you can see in Figure 15.56, CUPS will take you to a page with text links concerning managing printers. To add a printer, click Printers from the bar along the top of the page.
4. At this point, there are no printers in the Print Center, so this page doesn't list any (as you can see in Figure 15.57). If you had any printers already added in the Print Center, they'd show up here. To add a printer, just click the Add Printer button.
5. The next screen (see Figure 15.58) asks you to enter the name, location, and description of the printer you are adding.
6. Next, you will get a chance to select the type of connection you will use to access the printer (see Figure 15.59). I chose LPR since my printer is connected to an external TCP/IP print server (Jet Direct). Different connection types will require different connection information later.

FIGURE 15.56

CUPS printer administration page in browser

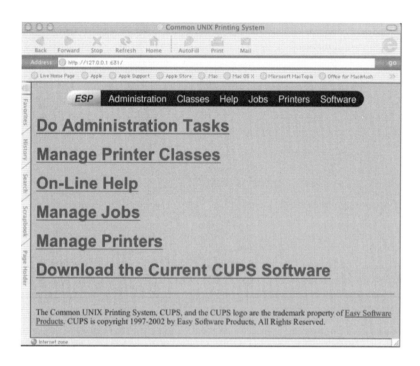

FIGURE 15.57

Adding printers

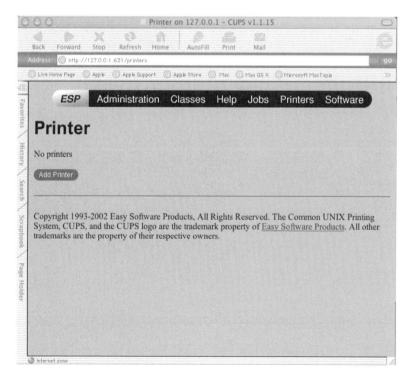

FIGURE 15.58

Naming the added printer

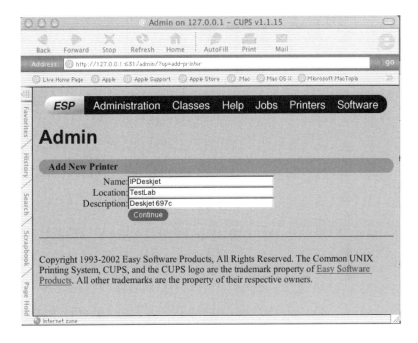

FIGURE 15.59

Choosing the printer connection type

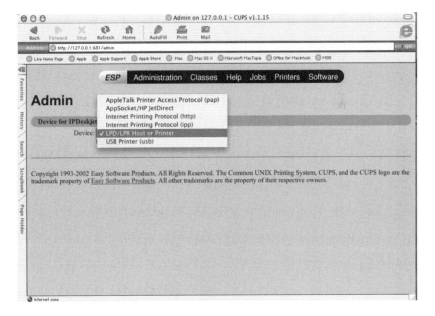

7. The next screen (see Figure 15.60) prompts you for the address of the printer. In addition to the IP address, I also specified /p1, because my printer is on the first port on the Jet Direct print server.

FIGURE 15.60

Entering the
IP address of
the printer

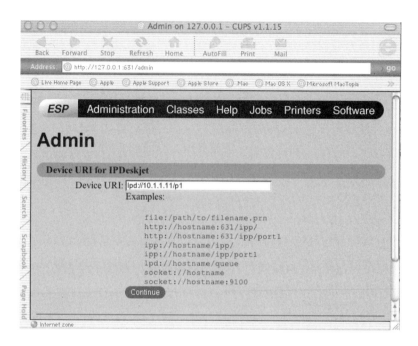

8. The next screen lets you choose the manufacturer of the printer, and the following screen (see Figure 15.61) lets you choose from a series of driver types from that manufacturer. Since I have an HP printer, I chose that manufacturer, then HP DeskJet series.

FIGURE 15.61

Choosing a driver
for a particular
manufacturer's
printer series

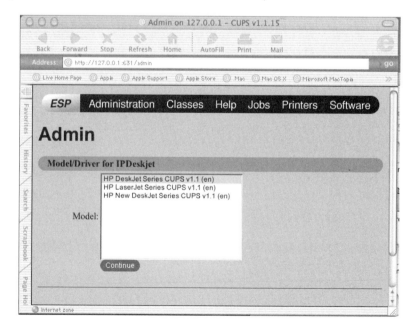

That's it; the printer has been successfully set up. If you look in the Print Center window (see Figure 15.62), you'll see the printer ready for action. When I sent a print job from the OS X 10.2 workstation to the DeskJet printer, it printed out in full color.

FIGURE 15.62

New printer added with CUPS in Print Center window

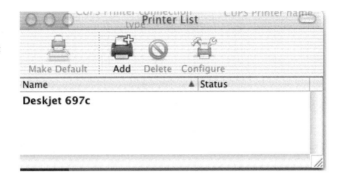

With OS X 10.2, you, as an administrator, can now tell your users that they can print in color to printers they never could print to before. Being able to say yes always makes you look good.

Integrating with a Macintosh Server

Now it's time to go full circle. You know that if you have the File Server for Macintosh service running on Server 2003, Macintoshes can access file shares. Well, if you have a Macintosh server, it can be configured to support Windows file shares too. This is convenient if you don't want the Mac users in the graphics department to be copying several gigabytes of pictures on to Server 2003 when they could just leave it on their Mac server and have the Windows users go get them.

It may not be easily apparent to you which Mac is a server since prior to OS X, there was no specific Mac Server OS. To turn a workstation into a server before OS X, you just had to load AppleShare IP (ASIP), preferably 6.1 or higher, onto a workstation, and voila, you've got a server.

The coolest thing about ASIP is that now the Macintosh server can be indistinguishable from a Windows server, as far as Windows clients are concerned. By clicking a check box in ASIP, you can teach the Mac server to speak SMB. Windows users can see the files on the ASIP server and save to it. The Mac users can use it natively, of course. The only additional work to be done is to be sure that the Windows users have an account to log in with, since the Mac server will want to do some sort of authentication.

ENABLING SMB FILE SHARING ON A CLASSIC OS SERVER

1. Go to the Apple menu.
2. Select AppleShare IP Admin.
3. Select Mac OS Server Admin.
4. Enter the administrator's username and password.

5. When a bar of server tools (otherwise known as a control strip) comes up (see Figure 15.63), select the File Server icon (a document in an open folder). From the pop-up menu, select Configure File Server.

FIGURE 15.63

Mac OS Server admin tools

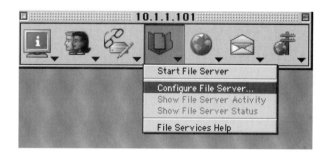

6. In the System Settings panel, click the Windows tab.
7. Click the Enable Windows File Sharing check box.
8. In the General section (see Figure 15.64), you can enter the server name, the workgroup, and a description. In the WINS Registration section, choose whether or not this server will register itself to an existing WINS server for the Windows users' convenience.

FIGURE 15.64

Server settings for Windows file sharing

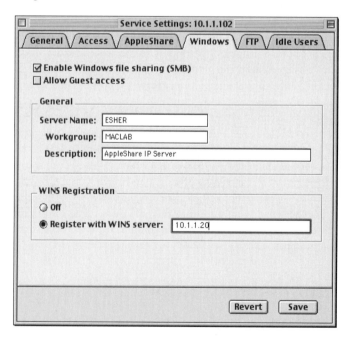

Then, whenever a shared volume is created it can be accessed by Windows users. The Mac server treats the Windows users (at that point) exactly as if they were Mac users. If the Windows user has a valid account on the server, they will be given access to the folders they have permission to.

NOTE   *There can be a certain amount of redundancy with the accounts on both the Apple and Windows side of the network. To use the Mac and Windows servers together most effectively, it helps to have identical accounts on both servers for each user. That way, the users can securely access resources anywhere on the network without worrying about being unnecessarily restricted or confused as to which username or password should be used when.*

ENABLING WINDOWS FILE SHARING ON AN OS X SERVER

To file share with an OS X server, the same rules apply: you just have to enable Windows file sharing in the server service and Windows users will be able to use the shares (with the proper authentication, of course).

NOTE   *In addition to file sharing, the OS X server is a full-featured network server with the capability to do DNS, DHCP, SLP, Web services, e-mail services, and print services to a number of different clients, including Windows.*

1. Go to the Server Settings Utility, which is located either on the Dock (that quick launch-type bar, usually located at the bottom of the desktop) or in the Utilities folder under Applications.

2. At the prompt, authenticate with the administrative username and password.

3. When the Server Settings control strip appears (see Figure 15.65), click the Windows button.

FIGURE 15.65

Server Settings
control strip

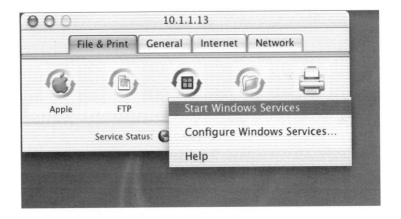

4. The pop-up menu will contain Start Windows Services and Configure Windows Services (does all of this sound familiar?). When you configure Windows Services (see Figure 15.66), you can set the server name, workgroup, and description under the General tab; guest access and simultaneous SMB connections under the Access tab; and logging under the Logging tab.

5. The last tab, Neighborhood (see Figure 15.67), is where you can specify whether or not the server will register with a WINS server and (not to be out done by ASIP) whether or not it should be a master browser for the Windows clients, either locally or for the whole domain (oh, how thoughtful—scary, but thoughtful).

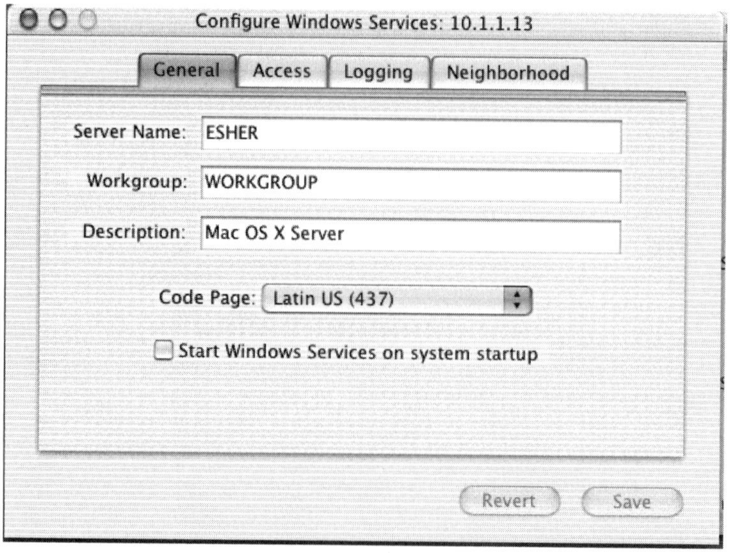

FIGURE 15.66

Configuring
Windows Services

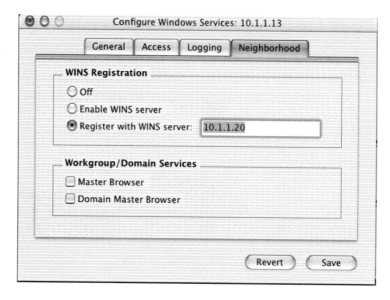

FIGURE 15.67

Configuring WINS
and Master Browser
settings

With Windows Services configured, a user can browse from an XP workstation to the OS X server in Network Places (see Figure 15.68) as if it were any other Windows computer.

NOTE   *If you experience any problems authenticating to the OS X server from an XP workstation or Server 2003, check to see if Password Server is enabled on OS X. Earlier versions of Windows, such as 2000 or 98, can authenticate to an OS X server shared volume without any problems. The issue arises due to the increased security on later versions of Windows.*

FIGURE 15.68

Browsing for the OS X server on an XP workstation

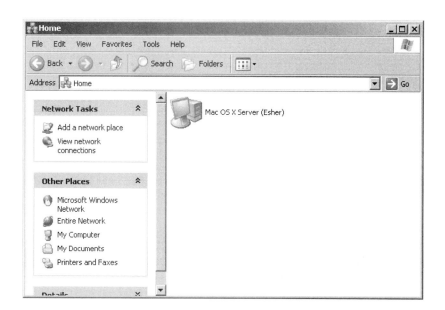

From there, the user can double-click the OS X server icon, be authenticated with an OS X server account name and password, and access whatever shares are permissible to them (see Figure 15.69).

FIGURE 15.69

Opening the shared folder to access resources

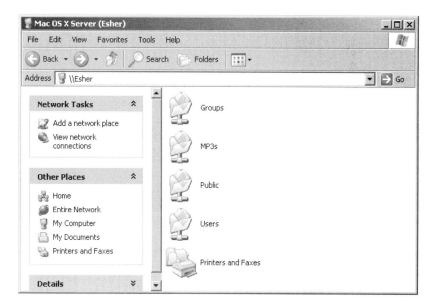

THE COUP DE GRACE: AUTHENTICATION

It used to be that when sharing Windows resources with Macintosh clients, there were some authentication obstacles that made things awkward. When sharing resources through a pre-OS X server, both Windows and Macintosh clients got access to additional resources, but still, no matter what, there was that dual platform, dual login issue. Well, with some work, the dual login problem can be resolved.

Currently, integrating OS X's authentication through its directory service (Net Info) with Microsoft's Active Directory involves mapping Net Info fields to Active Directory's Schema objects. It is a painstaking task (not to mention something that should be done only in a test lab first). However, if you set up Net Info properly, do a little file copying of some Kerberos files, and follow some step-by-step instructions on how to modify the Net Info directory domain and the Windows AD (scary, yes, but when this puppy works, it really works), then you can have a seamless integration between the Apple OS X server's user database and the Windows user database. This will create one single directory structure that encompasses both OS X and AD servers. No dual user accounts, no security issues.

This solution is still in its infancy, and I predict that any information I might give you now (particularly in meticulous, step-by-step instructions) would be obsolete by the time you read this, as Apple is sure to release patches and upgrades to make integrated authentication easier. Furthermore, there will probably soon be a snap-in of some sort from Apple that will make the Net Info/AD schema changes for you, wizard style. If it doesn't come to pass, or you just can't wait, then you don't have to do this work alone—there are many hands to hold. On the www.apple.com Web site, there are links to excellent PDFs concerning Net Info and step-by-step instructions on how to do the directory integration. Another great site to help you with Mac/Windows integration is, of course, www.macwindows.com. This is the site for up-to-date information on current integration issues and other important insider information about how to make integration tools really work. Apple also has discussion groups that can help you with any problem you might be having with your Macs.

I hope this chapter has solved some Macintosh mysteries and has been able to give you some insights as to how easy it is to share resources between Macs and Windows computers. With any luck, this information will free you from the drudgery of manually changing IP settings and the frustrated complaints of Mac users who can't access Server 2003 resources.

Chapter 16

Supporting Clients with Windows Terminal Services

MULTIUSER WINDOWS, SERVER-BASED computing, thin client computing—whatever you call it, it's part of the core Windows Server OS. Multiuser Windows has been around for quite a while. Citrix created MultiWin, the set of extensions to Windows NT that enables it to run multiple user sessions from the same machine. The first MultiWin product was multiuser NT 3.51, Citrix's WinFrame. Starting in July 1998, Microsoft began shipping its Terminal Server Edition of NT 4 (TSE). Terminal Services first became part of the core OS with Windows 2000, and in Server 2003 is installed (if not enabled, for security reasons) by default. There's even a very limited version of Terminal Services in Windows XP, making Remote Desktop Connection possible. And in Server 2003, Terminal Services has gained a number of new client- and server-side features that make the service attractive even without using the once unavoidable MetaFrame.

Installing Terminal Services is easy. Creating a working terminal server capable of supporting multiple users, all running different applications and wanting to use their client-side resources, may not be. You'll need to do a fair amount of tweaking once you get past the basic step of running Notepad from the terminal server. If you're serious about administering a terminal server, I *highly* recommend you make the Terminal Services section of the Microsoft Knowledge Base your favorite pleasure reading because this is relatively new territory to Microsoft and it's still working the bugs out. This chapter will do the basic legwork for you, however.

NOTE *To help you keep up with the Knowledge Base updates, I've restarted the free thin client newsletter that (among other things) summarizes recent Terminal Services–related updates. You can sign up at* www.isinglassconsulting.com.

Why Care about Terminal Services?

Terminal Services gives you secure remote access to a computer and requires little enough bandwidth that you can use it over low-speed connections. So?

The first reason to care about Terminal Services applies to anyone using Windows Servers, not just people wanting to support an application server. Terminal Services has two modes: Remote Administration (the default, discussed at the end of this chapter) and Application Server (which I'll concentrate on in this chapter). Remote Administration enables you to manage Windows Server computers from across a network, without limiting your access to tools within the

Microsoft Management Console (MMC) or even requiring you to use Windows Server 2003 or 2000 as the managing operating system. If you don't use Terminal Services for anything else, use it for managing servers without having to physically move from console to console. Turn to the section "Using Remote Administration Mode" to read more about the requirements for remote management access, how to enable it, how to connect, and what you should know about it.

In this chapter, however, I'll focus on how you can use Application Server mode—the "terminal server" part of Terminal Services—to support clients. If any of the following are important to you, then seriously consider how you could use Application Server mode:

◆ Simplifying application deployment and management

◆ Reducing the impact of hardware failures or misconfigured computers that keep people from working

◆ Getting out of the hardware rat race that constantly requires more updates to support the latest and greatest software

◆ Using computers in environments that are not compatible with desktop computers

◆ Simplified help desk and training support

Centralized Deployment of Applications

One great benefit to Terminal Services is how it simplifies application deployment to the clients. Windows Server 2003 has some application deployment tools in the form of group policy objects (GPOs), and Chapter 9 discusses those tools in detail. If you use GPOs to deploy applications to the Desktop you can create packages that enable you to run applications on the client computer while making those applications "maintainable" from a central point. GPOs have their failings, however. First, you can't use GPOs with just any Win32 operating system; instead you must use Windows 2000 Professional or Windows XP clients—and you will need to check the version information for the GPOs, as some require Windows XP clients. Second, setting up GPOs effectively is not necessarily a simple matter. Third, you can't always use GPOs to deploy applications across a low-bandwidth network connection well—the application packages may not be small. Finally, all these factors make GPOs a questionable method of application deployment for any applications that need to be updated frequently (as some database clients do). The more often you need to deploy an application across the network, the greater the chance something weird will happen along the way. (The technical term for the time between unexpected and inexplicable failures is *Mean Time Between Weirdness*—MTBW—and the concept is probably familiar to you.)

Using Terminal Services to deploy applications has its own difficulties—namely, getting all the applications and all the users to play nicely in the same space and keeping users connected to the server—but it avoids the problems and limitations associated with GPOs. For example, when you update an application installed on a terminal server, it's instantly updated for everyone using that server. Any operating system that has a Remote Desktop Protocol (RDP) client (and, these days, that can include Macintosh and Linux clients as well as Win32) can use the terminal server, so you're not limited to deploying applications to the higher-end clients. A Terminal Services connection requires little bandwidth, so you can use it on busy or slow network connections. And, because you're not actually sending applications or data across the network or installing applications on the clients, the MTBW rating for clients using Terminal Services is low—so long as nothing changes and it's working right in the first place.

Running applications on a terminal server is not a trouble-free process; getting things set up properly and keeping people from fiddling with the terminal server can be tricky. Some applications won't work at all in a multiuser environment. And in case you thought installing applications on a terminal server meant you could support many users with a single license, think again—you'll still need to pay for application licensing for each user or computer connecting to the applications published on the terminal server. However, this basic fact remains true: Set a compatible application up once on the terminal server, and its updates are available to everyone who has access to the terminal server, without the need for any changes to the client.

Supporting PC-Unfriendly Environments

The dream of "a PC on every desktop" will remain a dream, if for no other reason than in some environments the conditions are bad for the PC or the PC is bad for the conditions. In other words, you can't run a PC everywhere.

First, there are environments that are bad for PCs. PCs do not like dust, excessive heat, or vibration, and *you* will not like maintaining the PCs if you try to use them in an environment that has any of these characteristics. PCs are also a commodity item; if you leave them unattended and unguarded where just anyone can get to them, they will disappear. For these reasons, Windows terminals are becoming a popular choice in environments that are PC-unfriendly but still need access to Windows applications. Warehouses and unattended trucker kiosks (where the truckers can log in to display and print their shipping orders from a terminal) are two good examples of how to use Windows terminals in PC-unfriendly environments. I've also seen terminals in health club cafés and coffeehouses set up so that only the monitor is visible, thus reducing the chances of someone dropping a strawberry-banana low-fat smoothie with a shot of wheatgrass juice down the vents. For that matter, if someone does drop said smoothie down the terminal's vents, then, because the applications are installed on and running from the terminal server, replacing the device to provide an identical environment is as simple as unplugging the sticky terminal and plugging in a new one. If you drop the smoothie down a computer's vents, then restoring an identical working environment is significantly more complicated.

What about PCs being bad for the conditions? Clean rooms where chips and boards are made are good candidates for Windows terminals. You can't have dust in a clean room, and the fans in a PC kick up dust. Additionally, becoming sanitized to enter a clean room is neither simple nor inexpensive; you don't want to put devices that need care and feeding from the IT staff in there. Another factor applies to many situations, not just clean rooms: Anyplace where space is at a premium is a good candidate for Windows terminals.

This section isn't to sell you on the idea of Windows terminals but to point out that sometimes they're useful, even required—and you can't use them without a terminal server.

POWER STRUGGLES

Another aspect of the environment-unfriendly PC applies to the power a desktop PC uses. Inspired by the California energy crises of 2000 and 2001, my cohort Steve Greenberg and I did a couple of lab and real-world studies to see how desktop-centric computing and server-based computing compared in terms of power usage. What we found was sobering: A server-based computing network required less power to provide application support than did a desktop-centric environment, even when the client computers for accessing the terminal server were desktop computers instead of terminals. In fact, the Windows terminals used so little power that the use of terminals increased the difference dramatically.

Continued on next page

POWER STRUGGLES *(continued)*

If you're interested in the results of our research, you can download the main study at www.thinclient.net (look in the "What's New" section for the link), but here are the highlights: The desktop PCs we tested had a constant power draw of about 85 watts when running applications locally (excluding a 15" CRT monitor, which drew an additional 85 watts). Running applications from a terminal server, the desktop PC power usage dropped to 69 watts—not a big difference on a small scale, but this difference increases as the network grows. The terminals we tested drew less than 10 watts, or 24 watts with a built-in LCD display. If you're assuming (as many did) that the power use of the terminal server was great enough to offset the gains realized by using server-based computing, think again. Although a terminal server used an average of 141 watts in our testing (the power draw fluctuated depending on how many people were using it), a terminal server can support many clients, so its greater power draw is offset by the number of people it's supporting.

The power savings realized become more dramatic as the network gets larger—and as power gets more expensive. If you'd like to figure out how much you're spending on power, then calculate the result of $n*p*h*52$ to get the number of kilowatts (kW) your client computers use each year, where n is the number of desktop devices, p is the power (in kW) used by each device, h is the number of hours each week that the devices are turned on, and 52 is the number of weeks in a year. For example, say your network has 5,000 client computers, each powered on 50 hours a week. If the 5,000 clients are PCs with CRT displays running applications locally (.17kW), then they'll use $5000*1.7kW*50*52$, or 2,210,000 kW each year. If the 5,000 clients are thin clients with integrated LCD panels (.024kW), they'll use $5000*.024kW*50*52$, or 31,200kW each year. Say those 5000 thin clients need 200 servers (.141kW) to support them, and those servers are on 24/7. In that case, the calculation is $200*.141kW*168*52$, or 246,355.2, giving you a total of 277,555.2kW.

Based on these calculations, at 0.20 per kW, serving applications with the PC network costs $442,000 to run each year. Serving applications via a thin client network—with servers on all the time—costs $55,511.04. And we haven't even begun to talk about other aspects of Total Cost of Ownership or the investment required to keep IT hardware up and running. Nor have we talked about how reducing power usage reduces power costs because dissipating two units of heat (generated by power-sucking devices—put your hand on a CRT lately?) requires one unit of energy.

Saving on power costs is not the only reason to use Windows terminals, but, if you're tossing around the idea of replacing PCs with terminals, it's a compelling argument in favor of it.

Less Processing Power Required on the Client

First, about those ever-more-powerful computers: Does it take a 2GHz Pentium 4 with 256MB of RAM installed to check e-mail, do accounting, and poke around on the Web a bit? Of course it doesn't, but, as of late 2002, that's not an unusual hardware profile for a desktop computer. Not that these computers are too expensive in absolute terms; I'm wryly amused that every time I buy a new computer, I pay less for a system more powerful than the last one I bought. But although they're not too expensive in absolute terms, the new computers aren't always worth it because what you're doing doesn't demand all that much from your hardware. Ironically, unless your job is something demanding such as computer-assisted design, you're often more likely to need a powerful computer at home than at work because game hardware requirements are so high. It takes more computing power to play a few swift rounds of WarCraft III than it does to write this chapter. (Fighting orcs is hard work!)

The trouble is, sometimes you do need those more powerful computers if you're planning to keep up with existing software technology. True—you don't need the world's fastest computer to do word processing. You may, however, need a computer faster than the one you have if you're going to keep up with the latest and greatest word processing package that everyone's using. If you want to be able to read all those charts and graphs, you can't always do it when the word processor you're using is six years old, even if it still suits your in-house needs. Trouble is, if your computer is also six years old, it may not be able to run the newest word processor, or the latest OS, since (for example) Microsoft announced in October 2002 that it would support the next version of Office only on Windows 2000 SP3 and Windows XP. If you're using Terminal Services to support applications, the client only displays applications running on the terminal server, rather than running them locally—you don't have to concern yourself with whether the applications will run on the client computer, just the server. If the application will run on the terminal server, then it will display on the client. As I'll discuss in this chapter, you may need to tweak an application to make it run *well* on the terminal server and some applications won't run well at all, but you can use Terminal Services to get an application to a computer that would not normally support it, thus lengthening your client upgrade cycle.

Simplifying the User Interface

Another potential benefit to Terminal Services is it can simplify the user interface (UI). I'm not sure why Microsoft keeps talking about how using a computer is getting easier and easier. Speaking as the favorite source of free tech support for my parents (and some of my friends and *their* parents), I, for one, am not buying this idea. Experienced users may find it easier to customize their interface, but those who are less experienced find all sorts of pitfalls when it comes to using their computers: so many options that they get confused, and too many ways to break something. Colorful icons with rounded corners do not a simple UI make.

Terminal Services does not automatically make the UI simpler. In fact, to use Terminal Services effectively, you'll need to make sure you've locked down the user environment pretty securely because many people will be using the same computer, and one deleted file can screw up a lot of people. But, as I'll explain later in this chapter, it's possible to run either a complete desktop from a terminal server or a single application. If the people you're supporting only need a single application, then you can save yourself and them a lot of grief by providing a connection that runs it and nothing else. This is particularly true with Windows-based terminals, which are little more than a monitor, a box, a keyboard, and mouse.

Providing Help Desk Support

Finally, Terminal Services can make application support easier, not just in terms of installing new applications and applying fixes but in helping people learn to use those applications. Remote Control lets administrators connect to another person's terminal session either to watch what they're doing or to interact with the session. (This isn't the security hole it may seem—you must have permission to do this, and by default the person to whom you're connecting has to permit the connection before you can see their screen.) When you have remote control of another user's session, you can either watch what they're doing and coach them (perhaps over the telephone) or actually interact with the session so that you can demonstrate a process. This beats standing over someone's shoulder saying, "Click the File button at the top left. No, *File*. The FILE button..." or trying to figure out what they're doing when your only information comes from their description of the screen. I'll talk more about how to use Remote Control later in this chapter.

The Terminal Server Processing Model

I mentioned the many versions of Terminal Services earlier in this chapter. Regardless of which one you're using, in a broad sense they all work pretty much the same way. *Thin client networking* or *server-based computing* (same thing, different emphasis) refers to any computing environment in which most application processing takes place on a server enabled for multiuser access, instead of a client. The terms refer to a network by definition, so it leaves out stand-alone small computing devices such as personal digital assistants (PDAs) or handheld PCs, although you can add thin client support to some of these devices. What makes thin client networking and computing "thin" is neither the size of the operating system nor the complexity of the apps run on the client, but how processing is distributed. In a thin client network, all processing takes place on the server, instructions for creating video output travel from server to client, and all video output is rendered on the client.

Son of Mainframe?

You may have heard thin client networking described as *a return to the mainframe paradigm*. (I have heard this less politely phrased as "You just reinvented the mainframe, stupid!" Sheesh. You kiss your mother with that mouth?) This comparison is partly apt and partly misleading. It's true that applications are stored and run on a central server, with only output shown at the client. However, the applications being run in the thin client environment are different from those run in a mainframe environment; mainframes didn't support word processing or slideshow packages, and the video demands on the graphical Windows client are necessarily greater than they were with a text-based green-screen terminal. Yet the degree of control that thin client networking offers is mainframe-like, and I've heard one person happily describe thin client networking and the command it gave him over his user base as "a return to the good old mainframe days."

Why the move from centralized computing to personal computers and back again? Business applications drove the development of PCs—the new applications simply couldn't work in a mainframe environment. Not all mainframes were scrapped, by any means, but the newer application designs were too hardware-intensive to work well in a shared computing environment. But those applications came back to a centralized model when it became clear that the mainframe model had some things to offer that a PC-based LAN did not:

- Grouping of computing resources to make sure none are wasted
- Centralized distribution and maintenance of applications
- Clients that don't have to be running the latest and greatest operating system with the latest and greatest hardware to support it
- Client machines that don't require power protection because they're not running any applications locally

All in all, reinventing the mainframe has its advantages. Just as PCs didn't replace mainframes, server-based computing isn't replacing PCs, but it's nice to have more options that allow you to tune your computing model to meet your environmental and administrative needs.

Anatomy of a Thin Client Session

A thin client networking session has three parts:

- The *terminal server,* running a multiuser operating system
- The *display protocol,* which is a data link layer protocol that creates a virtual channel between server and client through which user input and graphical output can flow
- The *client,* which can be running any kind of operating system that supports the terminal client

THE TERMINAL SERVER

Terminal Services is one of the optional components you can choose to install during Setup, similar to Transaction Services or Internet Information Services. If you've enabled Terminal Services, when the server boots up and loads the core operating system, the terminal service begins listening at TCP port 3389 for incoming client connection requests.

TIP   Because Terminal Services is essential to the operation of a terminal server, you can't shut this service down. If you try it from the command line with the net stop termserv *command, you'll get an error. Click the service in the Services section of the Computer Management tool, and you'll see that the options to pause or stop the service are grayed out in the context menu. If you want to keep people from logging onto the terminal server for a while (perhaps while you're doing maintenance on it), then open the Terminal Services Configuration tool and disable RDP. This will end any current connections and prevent anyone else from logging on until you enable the display protocol again.*

Understanding Sessions

When a client requests a connection to the server and the server accepts the request, the client's unique view of the terminal server is called its *session.* In order to start these sessions as quickly as possible, the terminal server creates two dormant sessions. When clients connect to the dormant sessions, Terminal Services will create more dormant sessions so that it's always got two ready to go. In addition to the remote sessions, a special client session for the console (that is, the interface available from the terminal server itself) is created.

NOTE   Some have asked if there's any way to make Windows 2000 Professional multiuser. Nope—no Microsoft desktop operating system includes full-fledged Terminal Services, and there is no way to add it. Even Windows XP, which has the Remote Desktop feature that allows someone to connect to the computer via the RDP display protocol, can only support one connection at a time—console or terminal session. The Terminal Services I discuss in this chapter is solely a server-class feature.

All sessions have unique Session IDs that the server uses to distinguish the processes (processes are roughly equivalent to executable files) running within different terminal sessions on the same computer. The console session is assigned Session ID 0. When a client connects to the terminal server, the Virtual Memory Manager generates a new Session ID for the session and passes it to the Session Manager once the SessionSpace for that session has been created.

Every session, whether displaying an entire Desktop or a single application, runs the processes shown in Table 16.1.

NOTE *In NT-based operating systems, an executable file is internally known as an* image. *This is because, technically speaking, an application isn't the piece getting processor cycles but instead is a collection of commands called* threads *that get processor time to do whatever they need to do. The threads have an executing environment called the* process *that tells them where to store and retrieve their data. You don't really have to worry about these details except to understand what these processes and images the administration tool refers to are. Technically speaking, a process is an environment for the parts of an application that run, not an executable component itself. The EXE is the executable image of this process— the part that includes the code that needs processor cycles. For the sake of consistency with the interface, I'll refer to programs running on the terminal server as* processes.

TABLE 16.1: PROCESSES COMMON TO TERMINAL SERVICES SESSIONS

COMPONENT	FUNCTION
Win32 Subsystem	Win32 subsystem required for running Win32 applications (including the Win2K GUI).
User Authentication Module	Logon process responsible for capturing username and password information and passing it to the security subsystem for authentication.
Executable Environment for Applications	All Win32 user applications and virtual DOS machines run in the context of the user shell.

The other processes in the session will depend on the applications the user is running. The crucial points to be learned from this are that every session has its own copy of the Win32 subsystem (so it has a unique Desktop and unique instances of the processes that support the Desktop) and its own copy of the WinLogon application that authenticates user identity. In practical terms, what this means is that every separate session a single person runs on the terminal server is using memory to support these basic files. I said earlier that you could set up terminal sessions that display only single applications—no Desktop. The flip side of this convenience is that supplying a full suite of applications connected separately requires a lot more memory on the terminal server than supplying all those applications from a single Desktop in a terminal session. That is, if you create one session to use Microsoft Word, one session to use Outlook, one session to use AutoCAD, and one session to use Solitaire, this will place a heavier strain on the server than running all those applications from a single Desktop session.

NOTE *With each generation, Terminal Services has become more parsimonious with memory allocation. The amount of memory reserved for the SessionSpace has been reduced from 80MB to 60MB, and the per-session mapped views was reduced from 48MB in TSE to 20MB in Win2K. Server 2003 has changed the way that it reads user Registry information into memory, reducing one serious crunch on another area of memory outside SessionSpace. Being more frugal with memory is a Good Thing—greater efficiency in memory allocation means support for more users, all else being equal.*

The terminal session keeps per-session processes from corrupting each other or viewing each other's data. However, although the sessions are allowed to ignore each other, they still have to coexist. All sessions use the same resources—processor time, memory, operating system functions—so the operating system must divide the use of these resources among all of the sessions while keeping them separate. To do so, the terminal server identifies the processes initiated in each session not only by their Process ID but by their Session ID as well. Each session has a high-priority thread reserved for keyboard and mouse input and display output, but ordinary applications run at the priority they'd have in a single-user environment. Because all session threads have the same priority, the scheduler processes user input in round-robin format, with each session's input thread having a certain amount of time to process data before control of the processor passes to another user thread. The more active sessions, the greater the competition for processor time.

The number of sessions a terminal server can support depends on how many sessions the hardware (generally memory but also processor time, network bandwidth, and disk access) can support and how many licenses are available. When a client logs out of his session, the virtual channels to that client machine close and the resources allocated to that session are released.

Memory Sharing on a Terminal Server

The terminal server does not necessarily have to run a separate copy of each application used in each session—in fact, ideally it does not. When you start an application, you're loading certain data into memory. For example, say that running WordMangler loads files A–E into memory. If you start a second instance of WordMangler, is it really necessary to load a second instance of all those files into memory? You could do this, but as more and more sessions started up on the terminal server the duplicated DLLs and EXEs would cause the server to quickly run out of memory. But if you let all instances of WordMangler use the same copies of A–E, then if one instance needs to change a file that's in use, all other instances will be affected by that change. To get around the wasted-space/data-corruption dilemma, the server uses *copy-on-write* data sharing. "Helper files" are available on a read-only basis to as many applications that need them and are able to reference them. Let an application *write* to that data, however, and the memory manager will copy the edited data to a new location for that application's exclusive use. Copy-on-write works on any NT-based operating system, not just a terminal server, but because terminal servers are likely to be running multiple copies of the same application simultaneously, they greatly benefit from this memory-sharing technique.

The catch to copy-on-write is that only 32-bit applications really benefit from it. The reason for this has to do with how 16-bit applications run in a 32-bit operating system. Namely, they don't: To run a 16-bit application, NT-based operating systems have to create a 32-bit operating environment called a *NT virtual DOS machine* (NTVDM) that contains the 16-bit application. The NTVDMs can do copy-on-write data sharing, but the 16-bit applications they're hosting cannot. Therefore, all else being equal, Win16 and DOS applications will use more memory than Win32 applications.

With the advent of 64-bit Windows on the horizon, it's reasonable to ask how a larger memory space will affect terminal servers. Right now, it's a little hard to say. Having a larger memory space to work with should reduce the memory bottleneck on the servers. However, the overhead required to chunk 32-bit applications into a 64-bit operating system—much like that required to make those 16-bit applications run on a 32-bit operating system—may reduce some of the benefit. 64-bit Windows on Itanium is showing some pretty serious overhead in this regard; it's hoped that it will perform better on AMD's 64-bit chip. The bottom line is that 64-bit Windows should help alleviate the memory bottleneck, but the full benefits of the new architecture may not really materialize until we've got 64-bit applications to run on the terminal servers. Incidentally, 16-bit applications won't work at all on 64-bit Windows, since Microsoft has not included a 64-bit NTVDM for them to execute in.

THE REMOTE DESKTOP PROTOCOL

You can run all the sessions you like on the terminal server, but that won't do you any good unless you can view the session output from a remote computer and upload your input to the terminal server for processing. The mechanism that allows you to do both is the *display protocol*.

How RDP Works

A display protocol downloads instructions for rendering graphical images from the terminal server to the client and uploads keyboard and mouse input from the client to the server. Terminal Services natively supports the Remote Desktop Protocol (RDP), and with Citrix's MetaFrame add-on to Terminal Services, it supports the Independent Computing Architecture (ICA) protocol. RDP is based on the T.120 protocol originally developed for NetMeeting, and as such has some theoretical capabilities that aren't realized in the release product. The way it's implemented now, RDP provides a point-to-point connection dependent on TCP/IP that displays either the Desktop or a single application on the Desktop of a client running RDP.

NOTE *Yes, you can run multiple sessions from a single client and even multiple sessions for a single user (although for reasons of profile maintenance and memory usage, this may not be the best plan—I'll get into this later). However, each session is still a point-to-point connection rather than a one-to-many connection such as that possible with Citrix MetaFrame's Seamless Windows connection.*

The processing demands placed on the client are reduced by a feature called *client-side caching* that allows the client to "remember" images that have already been downloaded during the session. With caching, only the changed parts of the screen are downloaded to the client during each refresh. For example, if the Microsoft Word icon has already been downloaded to the client, there's no need for it to be downloaded again as the image of the Desktop is updated. The hard disk's cache stores data for a limited amount of time and then eventually discards data using the Least Recently Used (LRU) algorithm. When the cache gets full, it discards the data that has been unused the longest in favor of new data.

NOTE *The image on the screen is updated about 20 times per second when the session is active. If the person logged in to the session stops sending mouse clicks and keystrokes to the server, then the terminal server notes the inactivity and reduces the refresh rate to 10 times per second until client activity picks up again.*

Note that in addition to each client session, there's also a session for the server's use. All locally run services and executables run within the context of this server session.

Understanding RDP Channels

The way that the Desktop or single application in a terminal session look and interact with the client's computer depends on the *channels* used in the display protocol. Channels work like roads between two locations in that they must be open on *both sides* to work. For example, Route 29 in Virginia presents a straight shot between two cities: Charlottesville and Gainesville. If either Gainesville or Charlottesville shut down their end of the road—in other words, if the road became unavailable on either side— then traffic could no longer travel along that road. It doesn't matter that Gainesville's end is open if Charlottesville is closed. Channels work the same way: They're like roads between the terminal server and the client. If the road is not available on one side, it's closed—it does not matter if it's available on the other.

The capabilities of any one version of RDP are entirely dependent on what channels that version exploits. RDP has room for lots of channels for doing different things, and each version of RDP enables more of them. However, channels must be enabled on both the client and on the server to be useable, as shown in Figure 16.1. That's why, even though the Remote Desktop Connection tool downloadable from Microsoft's Web site can map client-side drives to terminal sessions, this feature does not work when you use this client to connect to a Windows 2000 terminal server. The virtual channel required to support this feature is not enabled on Windows 2000 Server.

NOTE *Although you can update the RDP client component by downloading the latest client from the Microsoft Web site or getting it from the Setup CD for Windows XP, you cannot update the RDP server component that goes on the terminal server. There is no way to make a TSE terminal server or a Windows 2000 terminal server as capable as a Server 2003 terminal server.*

FIGURE 16.1

RDP is a collection of channels conveying data between the terminal server and terminal client.

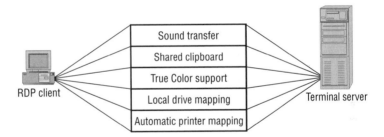

Notice something about channels: The more capable the RDP version—that is, the more channels it uses—the more bandwidth is required to support those channels. Because each version of RDP is written more efficiently than its predecessors, this doesn't mean TSE connections are more responsive than sessions using Windows XP's Remote Desktop. In fact, quite the opposite is true—the most recent version of RDP is pretty snappy even when connecting to an older terminal server. However, the more channels your RDP connection is using, the more bandwidth they'll need. Therefore, you will not always want to enable all these channels. I'll show you how to selectively enable and disable them in the course of this chapter.

THE CLIENT

So you've got a terminal server running sessions and a display protocol to pass information to and from the sessions. All you're missing now is someone to use the sessions.

A client session is *connected* when a client computer chooses a terminal server from the RDP interface and gets far enough to see the login screen. The session becomes *active* when the user successfully logs onto the domain or onto the terminal server's local account. During this session, client input in the form of mouse clicks and keystrokes is uploaded to the server via a virtual channel. The commands to render bitmaps showing the interface are downloaded to the client via another virtual channel. If client-printer mapping is enabled for the connection, the communication between terminal server application and client-printer takes places along yet another channel. A buffer supports the shared Clipboard data for local and remote sessions, too.

NOTE *Session 0—the console session—does not use the same keyboard and video drivers that client sessions use. Whereas Session 0 uses the normal video and keyboard drivers, the client sessions use drivers based in the RDP.*

Once the graphics-rendering instructions download to the client, the client resources create the images for display. During the course of the session, the user can work on the terminal server as though he or she were physically at the terminal server, using the client machine's keyboard and mouse. As the client runs applications, loads data into memory, and accesses shared resources on the network as though logged on directly (clients are not restricted to accessing the terminal server, but can access any available network resources), the client uses the hardware on the server. The only restrictions on the client are those defined by security settings.

What's New in Server 2003?

Although the model in general applies to any version of Terminal Services, some virtual channels are version-dependent and only available in Server 2003. Additionally, some features of Server 2003 don't have anything immediately to do with the client experience but will make your life as an administrator a lot easier.

On the user side, the client experience is a lot richer. The maximum color depth is greater, RDP now supports sound, and drive mapping is an option. You can also limit users to a single session if you like.

Client enhancements are good, but as administrator types we're probably more worried about the server component. As you'll see in the course of this chapter, most of the tools in Server 2003 work very much like their counterparts in Windows 2000. The biggest difference for anyone running Server 2003 is the new support for group policies, which greatly simplifies server management. Those using Enterprise Server will have another option: a simple form of clustering. Using Network Load Balancing or another third-party load-balancing tool, you can arrange multiple servers into a cluster with a single IP address, so that users are always connected to the least-stressed server in the cluster. If a user disconnects from a session, the Session Server Database maintained for the cluster tells the session manager which session the disconnected user was using, so that they're able to reconnect to their old session.

It's now also possible to use group policy objects to create licensing security zones defining which servers are allowed to draw licenses from the license pool. This reduces the possible damage introduced by rogue application servers in the domain taking licenses from a pool planned for a certain number of users.

DO I NEED THIRD-PARTY TOOLS?

That's a look at Server 2003 Terminal Services in a nutshell. But you can't talk about Windows Terminal Services and ignore MetaFrame.

Microsoft didn't invent multiuser Windows—a company called Citrix did. Citrix still makes its multiuser Windows product, now called MetaFrame—MetaFrame XP in its latest version. Although MetaFrame is dependent on the presence of Windows terminal services, it adds a lot to it. With the advent of Microsoft's Remote Desktop version of the RDP client, the RDP client has just about caught up with ICA, MetaFrame's display protocol. But for some purposes you may still need MetaFrame even after Server 2003 and its updated RDP server component are available.

NOTE   *Incidentally, MetaFrame XP's name has no relation to Windows XP.*

I don't have room here to discuss MetaFrame in real detail, but let's take a look at some features that might make MetaFrame XP a valuable addition to your Windows terminal servers. As you'll see, most of these features have to do with the servers, not the clients. These aren't *all* the features that MetaFrame adds to Terminal Services, but it's a good sample.

Multiprotocol Support   Terminal Services uses RDP to pass user input and terminal output between client and server. RDP depends on TCP/IP, which means that both the client and the server must be running it. This isn't all that big a deal because the Win32 clients that Terminal Services supports all come with TCP/IP. The ubiquity of the Internet makes TCP/IP the transport protocol of choice on most networks anyway, but Terminal Services does lock you into one protocol. The ICA protocol used with Citrix's MetaFrame, in contrast, supports IPX/SPX and NetBEUI.

Application Publishing   Terminal Services can create client connections that supply only applications, but the user must know which server is running the application and make an explicit connection to it. With MetaFrame, you can create general client connections to a set of servers running a certain application without the client having to know or care which server is providing the application. These connections may be displayed on the user Desktop (for Win32 clients) or in a folder called `Program Neighborhood` or in a browser using MetaFrame's NFuse Web-based application publishing. NFuse is not the same as the TSAC, which is an RDP client in the form of an ActiveX control. All TSAC does is build the RDP client into a Web page so that people can connect to the terminal server through Internet Explorer. TSAC doesn't have any application-publishing features at all.

Seamless Windows   Seamless Windows—the display of applications or a Desktop that fits perfectly into the local environment—is important for a couple of reasons. From the client perspective, Seamless Windows means you can see the entire Desktop or entire published application without having to scroll or display the session in full-screen mode. From the server perspective, all sessions displayed using Seamless Windows and running on the same MetaFrame server are actually running from the same session, and are thus using up less memory than connecting to each application individually.

Load Balancing   Load balancing is not unique to multiuser Windows; it's the ability of multiple servers to work in tandem so that the least-busy server processes client requests. Windows 2000 Server does not support load balancing. Server 2003 supports Network Load Balancing for user logons, but it's restricted to load balancing according to client IP address. To get application load balancing for Win2K Server, you'll need the load-balancing version of MetaFrame XP: XPa or XPe.

MetaFrame XP's load balancing allows you to allocate work among servers according to processor load, memory load, the client's IP address, the applications being run, and other rules. (Windows Server 2003, Enterprise Edition supports load balancing, but only in a limited sense.)

And that's just the core product of MetaFrame XP. Citrix also releases Feature Releases (FR), which are like service packs (they have those, too) for features. FR1, for example, adds a sort of generic printer driver to MetaFrame so that you don't have to worry about supporting user printers. (It's a limited printer driver in that it supports only 300 dpi and black and white printing, but it works.) As of late 2002, Feature Release 3 is in the works.

All that said, Terminal Services is a perfectly serviceable tool for implementing server-based computing in your network, particularly for smaller environments. And Server 2003 has one *great* advantage over third-party products: price. Although Terminal Services Client Access Licenses (TSCALs) aren't free for most client platforms, if you install MetaFrame you'll have to purchase both the TSCALs and *additional* licenses for the MetaFrame access. And MetaFrame isn't cheap. If you only need a small set of MetaFrame's capabilities, then I'd recommend checking out some of the other third-party solutions out there. I like MetaFrame, but not everyone needs it and it's not the only game in town.

Server and Client Requirements

The computing model for thin client networking means that the horsepower is typically concentrated on the server end, not the client end. Because the server will be supporting a couple of dozen people—maybe more—this is not the time to skimp on power.

Server Hardware

The notion of using a bigger server so that you can skimp on client-side hardware isn't new. That's all a file server is: a computer running a big, fast hard disk so that you don't have to buy big, fast hard disks for everyone in the office. Terminal servers are designed on a similar principle: If most of the processing takes place in a single location, you can concentrate the hardware resources needed to support that processing in a single location and worry less about power on the client end.

CORE HARDWARE RECOMMENDATIONS

For the purposes of running an efficient terminal server, the bare minimum required to run Server 2003 won't cut it. It was technically possible to run a TSE session from a terminal server with a Pentium 133 and 32MB of RAM—I've done it. It worked fine…so long as only one person wanted to use the terminal server. Although there are no hard and fast specifications for a terminal server, some general guidelines for server sizing follow.

Processor   Faster is better…to a point. More important than a fast processor is one with enough cache so that it doesn't have to reach out to the (slower) system memory for code and data. Faced with a choice between more cache and more speed, go with more cache. It's a good idea to at least *plan* for a multiprocessor computer. Although only multithreaded applications will actually use more than one processor, if there are two processors, then threads needing execution can line up at both. At this point, however, I'd stick with two processors. Processor time is not the only bottleneck in a terminal server and using more servers instead of fewer removes some of the other bottlenecks.

Memory   Terminal servers tend to be memory bound, not processor bound. Get high-speed, error-correcting memory, get plenty of it, and be prepared to add more as you add more users or applications to the terminal server. The amount of memory you'll need depends on the applications that people use, the number of concurrent sessions, and the memory demands of the files opened in those sessions—CAD programs will stress the system more than, say, Notepad. Because memory is relatively inexpensive these days, most terminal servers I've seen use at least 1GB of RAM.

Disk   Use SCSI disks on a terminal server if at all possible. A SCSI disk controller can multitask among all the devices in the SCSI chain, unlike an EIDE disk controller that can only work with one device at a time. This is an important capability in any server, and especially so in a terminal server.

Network   Even if it were easy to get ISA network cards these days, you'd want to use PCI and its higher data-transfer speeds instead. On a busy terminal server, consider load-balancing network cards, which can assign multiple NICs to the same IP address and thus split the load of network traffic. Another alternative is a multihomed server with one NIC dedicated to terminal session traffic. So far as network *speed* goes, sending application output and client-side input back and forth requires little bandwidth, but client-print jobs sent to mapped printers can take quite a bit. Mapped drives may also increase the load by making it possible to copy files back and forth across the RDP connection. Be sure to only support client-mapped printers and other bandwidth-intensive features over networks that can handle it, or get helper software to compress print jobs sent to mapped printers.

USING THE SYSTEM MONITOR

The System Monitor discussed in Chapter 18 can help you get an idea of how test terminal sessions are stressing the server. Server load will scale linearly with the number of people using the server, so as long as you pick a representative group of around five people, you should be able to extrapolate your needs for larger groups. The key objects and counters for measuring general server stress introduced in that chapter will help you size terminal servers, too. But, a couple of Terminal Services-specific System Monitor objects are worth examining.

First, the Terminal Services object has counters representing the number of active sessions (sessions where the user has connected to the terminal server and successfully logged on), inactive sessions (where the user is still logged onto the terminal server but has stopped using the session), and the total combined. Mostly, this object is useful for keeping track of how many sessions a terminal server has to support. Chapter 18 discusses performance logging and alerts; if you find that a terminal server functions best below a certain number of connections, you could set up an alert log with that threshold and then, if the server breaches that tolerance, use the `change logon /disable` command to disable the server for new connections and send you a message to alert you. (Do disable connections at the upper limit, or else you'll go mad intercepting the alert messages telling you that the threshold has been breached.)

Although you can get some session-level information from the Terminal Services Manager, a performance object called Terminal Services Session provides quite a bit more. Use the Terminal

Services Manager to find the session you want to monitor (because they're identified to System Monitor by their session numbers, not user login name) and then add counters to monitor that session. Each session object has processor and memory counters that should look familiar to anyone who's used System Monitor, but it's also got session-specific counters such as the ones in Table 16.2. I haven't included all the counters here, just the ones to show you the kind of information that will be useful when you're calculating the load on the server and looking at the kind of performance the sessions are getting.

NOTE   *If you click the Explain button in System Monitor when adding counters, you'll see a description of these counters, but the explanations for counters similar to those found in other performance monitoring objects may have been copied straight from there. Don't worry about this—just substitute* session *for* process.

TABLE 16.2: KEY TERMINAL SERVICES SESSION SYSTEM MONITOR COUNTERS

COUNTER	DESCRIPTION	SEE ALSO
% Processor Time	Percentage of time that all of the threads in the session used the processor to execute instructions. On multiprocessor machines the maximum value of the counter is 100 percent times the number of processors.	
Total Bytes	Total number of bytes sent to and from this session, including all protocol overhead.	Input Bytes, Output Bytes
Total Compressed Bytes	Total number of bytes after compression. Total Compressed Bytes compared with Total Bytes is the compression ratio.	Total Compression Ratio
Total Protocol Cache Hit Ratio	Total hits in all protocol caches holding Windows objects likely to be reused. Hits in the cache represent objects that did not need to be re-sent, so a higher hit ratio implies more cache reuse and possibly a more responsive session.	Protocol Save Screen Bitmap Cache Hit Ratio, Protocol Glyph Cache Hit Ratio, Protocol Brush Cache Hit Ratio
Working Set	Current number of bytes in the Working Set of this session.	Virtual Bytes, Page Faults/Sec

WARNING   *When experimenting with terminal sessions to find out how many users you'll be able to support for each session, do* not *set up a license server; let the terminal server issue its temporary 120-day licenses for this purpose. Although this sounds counterintuitive, using the temporary licenses prevents you from unwittingly assigning per-seat licenses to test equipment. See the "Terminal Services Licensing" section for an explanation of how licensing and license allocation works.*

Client Hardware

When connecting to a terminal server via a native RDP client, you'll use a PC with a Win32 operating system loaded, a Windows terminal, or a handheld PC using Windows CE.

NOTE *In this context, a native RDP client means one available from Microsoft and thus implies Win32 or (rarely) Win16. Although Microsoft does not support other platforms (except for their OS X Macintosh client, available for download from the Web site), Hoblink sells a cross-platform (Windows, Mac, Linux, DOS) Java client at* `www.hob.de/www_us/produkte/connect/jwt.htm`*, and there is a free Linux RDP client available at* `www.rdesktop.org`*.*

WINDOWS TERMINALS

In its narrowest definition, a Windows terminal is a network-dependent device running Windows CE that supports one or more display protocols such as RDP or ICA, the display protocol used to connect to MetaFrame servers. Many Windows terminals also support some form of terminal emulation.

NOTE *In this section, a* Windows terminal *is any terminal device designed to connect to a Windows terminal server; it can run any operating system that's got an RDP client. A Windows-based terminal (WBT) is such a device that's running a Windows operating system locally—CE or (more rarely) Embedded NT—and follows the Microsoft system design requirements for WBTs.*

The main thing defining a Windows terminal is its thin hardware profile: Because the main job of most Windows terminals is to run a display protocol, they don't need much memory or processing power, and they don't use any storage. A Windows terminal includes a processor, some amount of memory, network and video support, and input devices: a keyboard (or equivalent) and mouse (or equivalent). The terminals don't generally have hard disks, CD-ROMs, or DVD players. The operating system (these days, PocketPC, one version or another of NT or XP Embedded, or Linux) is stored in local memory. Beyond those similarities, Windows terminals range physically from a "toaster" form factor to a pad to a small box that can attach to the back of a monitor—or even be part of the monitor itself. Some new models of Windows terminals are wireless tablets, intended for people (such as doctors and nurses) who would ordinarily use clipboards and folders to store information.

Although most Windows terminals are entirely dependent on their terminal server, a small set of them can run applications locally. The devices still don't have hard disks; the applications are stored in ROM like the operating system. The types of applications available depend on the terminal's operating system since locally stored applications must run locally instead of just being displayed. Generally speaking, however, it's more common for Windows terminals to depend on a terminal server for applications.

Windows terminals are most popular in environments where people are using a single application, where supporting PCs would be logistically difficult, or anywhere else that PCs aren't a good fit. However, PCs still outnumber Windows terminals as thin clients, if for no other reasons than that companies already have PCs, and taking away a powerful PC to replace it with a less-powerful PC can be a difficult political decision—even for people who don't need a whole PC.

PC CLIENTS

At this point, people are using more than twice as many PCs as Windows terminals for terminal server client machines. This isn't surprising. First, unless they're starting afresh, people already have the PCs. Even though WBTs are a little less expensive than low-end PCs—not much, though—they're still an added cost. Second, not all applications work well in a terminal server environment. It's often best to run some applications from the terminal server and some locally. Unless you're buying new hardware and don't anticipate any need to run applications locally, you're likely to have to work with PCs for at least some of your terminal clients.

To work with Terminal Services, the PCs must be running a Win32 operating system, have the RDP display protocol installed, and have a live network connection using TCP/IP and a valid IP address.

HANDHELD PCs

I'm surprised that handheld PCs (H/PCs) aren't more popular than they are, given how handy they are and how much time I spend explaining to curious people what mine is. They're a terrific substitute for a laptop—inexpensive, lightweight, and thrifty with their power so that you can actually use them during the entire flight instead of having to give up two hours after takeoff. (You can also use one on a plane without worrying that the person in front of you will suddenly recline their seat and crack your laptop's display.) Usually, they run PocketPC and, thus, only compatible applications such as Pocket Office. But by downloading and installing the Terminal Services client for handheld PCs and getting network support if it isn't already built in, you can use wired, wireless LAN, or dial-up connections to connect to a terminal server.

NOTE *Because Microsoft rearranges its Web site regularly, there's no use providing a link to the RDP client—it'll be outdated by the time you read this. Look in the Downloads section of the WinCE area on* www.microsoft.com; *you should be able to find it there.*

What a H/PC looks like depends on who makes it. Some (mine among them) look like a laptop's baby brother. Others fold into a little portfolio shape or are a flat tablet. Some devices known as H/PCs are small pocket-sized deals that are, in my personal opinion, too small to really work on. Some—the ones I prefer—have keyboards; others have only pointers. What all this comes down to is that a H/PC isn't really in a position to replace a desktop PC. Instead, it's usually used in cooperation with a desktop machine with which it's partnered.

Installing (or Removing) Support for Terminal Services

Terminal Services is preinstalled on Server 2003, but you still need to set it up to be an application server. The easiest way to do that is by assigning the appropriate role to the server, using the Manage Your Server tool. Doing so will permit the server to accept incoming connections and tweak the server to make it perform well as a terminal server.

Assigning the Application Server role is dead simple. From the Manage Your Server tool, click the Add or Remove a Role button near the top. You'll see a short checklist of things to make sure of before adding a role (network's connected, path to installation media in case you need it, Internet connection if it will be necessary—by this point in this book, you've probably seen this screen a few times). Click Next to open the dialog box displaying the available roles (see Figure 16.2). Select that role, and click Next.

FIGURE 16.2

List of available
roles for the server

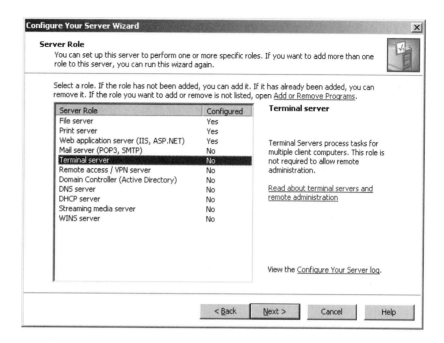

Confirm that you want to assign the selected role to the server, as in Figure 16.3.

FIGURE 16.3

List of available
roles to add

When you click Next, you'll see the status bar begin chugging away and a dialog box warning you that the Configure Your Server Wizard will restart the computer. Click OK and close any open dialog boxes. In a minute or two, the server will automatically restart. After it's rebooted, it's ready to be an application server.

To remove the role and make the server function like an ordinary server, run the wizard again and select the enabled role. When confirming that you want to remove the role, you'll need to check a box confirming its removal. When you do so, the wizard will remove that role and restore the normal Server 2003 performance.

NOTE *Every time you add or remove a server role, when you reboot the final page of the Configure Your Server Wizard, it will display the changes you made and offer a link to the change log (stored in* \%systemroot%\debug.configure your server.log) *that records all such changes and the time and date you made them. The System log will also record Event ID 7036 when the Terminal Service starts.*

Creating a New Terminal Server Client

The procedure for connecting a client to the terminal server varies slightly depending on whether you're talking about PC clients, handheld PCs, or WBTs.

PC-Based RDP Clients

To connect a PC-based client to Terminal Services, you have to run a short installation program on the PC to install client support for RDP. This process is quite simple and (wonder of wonders in the Windows world) does not require that you reboot the computer afterward to use the client. The only catch is that you have to *get* those installation files to the client.

If that client is a Windows XP or Server 2003 computer, then you're done—the client is preinstalled on both operating systems. Other Win32 clients that can use the Remote Desktop Connection (which I strongly recommend, as it is not only required for the richest client environment but is also noticeably faster than the older versions of the RDP client) will need it installed. The client files are no longer installed with Terminal Services, but you can get them off the Server 2003 installation CD. Better yet, download msrdpcli.exe, currently available from the Microsoft Web site (look in the Downloads section) and run the executable to install Remote Desktop Connection on any Win32 computer.

Once you run the EXE and start the installation wizard, follow these steps:

1. Agree to the terms of the EULA.
2. Enter your name and company if Setup does not populate these fields for you and indicate whether you want the Remote Desktop available to anyone who uses the computer or just you.
3. Click Install to let the Setup Wizard copy the files, and the Remote Desktop icon will be added to Programs/Accessories/Communications.

You don't need to reboot when you're finished.

Setting Up and Connecting a Windows-Based Terminal

Setting up a WBT for the first time is pretty simple. It's largely a matter of plugging everything in (power supply, monitor, network connection, mouse, and keyboard) and supplying the information the WBT needs to interact with the terminal server. For this example, I'll set up a Windows CE–based Windows terminal on a LAN. Although some Windows have different options from others, the basic setup information required is the same on all CE-based Windows terminals.

NOTE *Setting up Linux-based Windows terminals gets a bit more complicated because the UI is not necessarily consistent across terminal manufacturers. Sadly, there is no standardized way of doing this, so you'll need to peruse your Linux terminal's documentation for instructions. You'll be providing much the same information to the Linux-based terminal that you're providing to the Windows-based terminal. In some newer Linux-based terminals, the setup is similar to the CE-based setup I'm describing here, using the same tabbed configuration tools.*

SETTING UP THE TERMINAL

Once everything is plugged in and you've powered on the unit, choose to begin creating a new connection. The Setup Wizard walks you through the following steps:

1. First off, you're faced with the EULA, which states that use of the unit with Terminal Services is predicated upon your having a valid Terminal Services user license and that you must follow the licensing for any applications run from the terminal server. You must click Accept to continue with the wizard.

2. Indicate whether the WBT is connecting to the terminal server via a LAN (the default) or a dial-up connection.

3. Choose the display protocol that should be used to make connections. You have the option of the Microsoft Terminal Server Client (the default, which I'll use here) or the Citrix ICA client, which you'd choose if connecting to a terminal server running WinFrame or MetaFrame. Most modern Windows terminals also offer some kind of terminal emulation support, but you will not use this to connect to a Windows terminal server.

4. The Setup Wizard will attempt to locate a DHCP server on your network. If it can't find one, the wizard will tell you so. You'll have the option of telling the wizard to use the IP information supplied by DHCP or supplying a static IP address.

TIP *If you have a DHCP server and the wizard doesn't detect it, make sure the DHCP service on the server is up and running properly and that the server is connected to the network. If they are, then restart the wizard to see whether it finds the DHCP server. Don't tell the wizard to use DHCP information if it's not able to find it, or you may run into problems in getting an IP address assigned to the terminal. No IP address, no connection to the terminal server.*

5. If you choose to supply a static IP address, you'll be prompted for it, the subnet mask, and (if applicable) the default gateway. The IP address, recall, is the identifier for the network node, and the subnet mask identifies the network segment that the node is on. The default gateway is only necessary if the network is subnetted and the terminal will need to connect to another subnet.

6. Next, you'll be prompted to supply the servers used for name resolution: WINS, DNS, or both. You'll need to know the IP addresses of the servers, as there is no browse function. If you're using one of the name resolution services, be sure to check the box that enables that service. Otherwise, the connection won't work, and you'll have to edit it to use the IP address instead of the NetBIOS name. To establish support for WINS, you'll need to reenter the unit's network setup.

7. Choose a video resolution. One possible option is Best Available Using DDC. DDC, which stands for Display Data Channel, is a VESA standard for communication between a monitor and a video card. If it supports DDC, a monitor can inform the video card about its capabilities, including maximum color depth and resolution.

When you click the Finish button in the final screen, you'll be prompted to restart the terminal to make the settings take effect. After restarting the system, you'll begin the second half of the terminal setup: the connection.

TIP   To manually restart a WBT, turn the unit off and back on again. If you're one of those people (like myself) who normally leave a PC on, don't worry. Turning off a WBT is equivalent in seriousness to turning off a printer. Doing so will disconnect any current sessions you have open, but it's not like rebooting a computer.

CREATING A NEW CONNECTION

To create a new connection, follow these steps:

1. Choose a name for the new connection and the name of the terminal server to which you're connecting. If you're using a dial-up connection instead of a LAN, be sure to check the Low-Speed Connection box so that RDP will compress the data a little further.

2. To configure the terminal for automatic logon to the terminal server session, fill in the name, password, and domain of the person using the terminal. If you leave this section blank, you'll have to explicitly log in each time you connect to the terminal server. For tighter security, leave it blank; if it doesn't matter whether someone can log in to the terminal server, you can set it up for automatic login.

3. Choose whether you want the terminal server session to display a Desktop or run a single application. Once again, there's no browse function, so you need to know the name and path (from the server's perspective) of any application you choose. If you don't provide correct path information, the connection will fail.

At this point, the connection is set up and you're ready to go. The Connection Manager displays a list of the available connections. To use one, select it and click the Connect button. You'll see a logon screen (assuming you didn't set up the connection for an automatic login). Type your name and password, and you're in.

Setting Up a Handheld PC

To use a handheld PC (H/PC) to connect to a terminal server, you must install the RDP client on the H/PC and then create a session on the client.

First, you must get the RDP client. Go to the Microsoft Web site and navigate to the Downloads section of the WinCE section. You'll have to go through some screens where you agree that you understand that having the RDP client installed does not imply that you're licensed to access a terminal server. (There's also a link to a place where you can buy more licenses if needed.) Download the 1MB-client setup program (`hpcrdp.exe`) to the desktop partner of the H/PC.

NOTE   *As of this writing, the Windows CE RDP client is located at* www.microsoft.com/mobile/downloads/ ts.asp, *but it may have been moved by the time you read this.*

To install the RDP client on the H/PC, follow these steps.

1. Turn on the H/PC and connect it to the desktop partner. Make sure that they're connected.
2. Run hpcrdp.exe to start the installation wizard.
3. Click Yes to agree to the EULA.
4. Choose an installation folder for the client on the desktop partner. The default location is a subfolder of the Windows CE Services folder, which you'll have installed in the course of partnering the desktop machine and the H/PC.
5. The installation program will start copying the files to the H/PC. This may take a few minutes if you're using the sync cable instead of a network connection—a sync cable is a serial connection.
6. Once the files have been copied, click Finish on the desktop side to end the Setup program.

To set up a connection, go to the H/PC and look in Start/Programs/Terminal Server Client. There are two options here: the Client Connection Wizard and the Terminal Server Client.

To use the default connection settings, click the Terminal Server Client and type in the name or IP address of the terminal server to which you want to connect. Click the Connect button, and the client will search for that terminal server. You'll need to log in as if you were logging into the server or domain.

For a little more control over the connection settings, run the Client Connection Wizard. You don't have as many options as you do when running the similar wizard for the PC client, but you can specify a connection name, provide your username and password for automatic logon, and choose whether to run an application or display the entire Desktop. Click the Finish button, and the wizard will put a shortcut to that connection on your H/PC's Desktop.

Creating, Deleting, and Modifying Connections

Now that the client is installed, you're ready to connect to the terminal server. Let's take a look at how to do this from a PC.

To set up a connection on the Remote Desktop client, open it (Programs/Accessories/ Communications/Remote Desktop). When you first run the tool, no servers will be selected, but you can either type a server's name or browse for them by clicking the down-arrow button in the Computer box and choosing Browse for More to open the dialog box shown in Figure 16.4.

When you've found the terminal server to connect to, double-click it or click it OK to return to the main login window, which should now have a server selected, as shown in Figure 16.5. To connect to this server with the default settings, just click the Connect button. This will connect you to the selected terminal server and prompt you to log in. When you have successfully logged in, by default the session will run in full-screen mode with a sizing bar at the top so that you can easily minimize or resize the window to show the local Desktop.

FIGURE 16.4

Browsing for terminal servers from the Remote Desktop

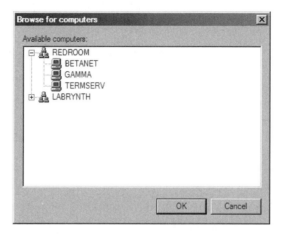

FIGURE 16.5

To use the selected terminal server with the default settings, click the Connect button.

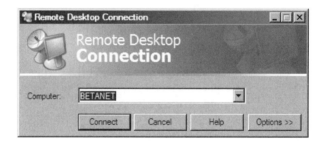

Notice that I didn't touch the Options button in Figure 16.5. If you're using the default settings, you'll never need to touch it. Let's take a look at what those settings involve.

When you first click the Options button, you'll see the General tab, as shown in Figure 16.6. From here, you can choose user credentials to log in with, to save or open shared connection settings, and, if you like, pick another server to log into. The only part that might cause confusion (and with reason) is the box prompting you for your user password. Even if you supply this information, you'll still be prompted for your password when you connect to the terminal server.

The Display tab controls all session settings relating to display. The default settings shown in Figure 16.7 may not apply to the terminal session, since the maximum color depth on the terminal server will override the color depth you specify on this tab), but the full-screen mode will. The connection bar at the top of the terminal session window is useful for full-screen sessions, as it offers an easy way to minimize the session and reach the local Desktop. The resolution for the setting will depend on the local client settings—the settings for Remote Desktop size apply only to the window's size.

FIGURE 16.6

Use the General tab to supply user credentials and save connection settings to a file.

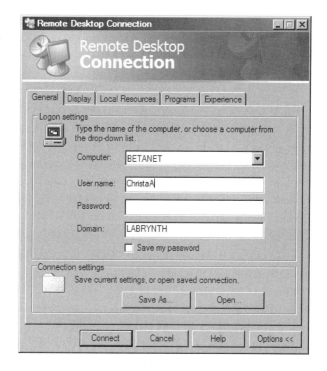

FIGURE 16.7

The Remote Desktop display settings are intended to mimic a user's local Desktop.

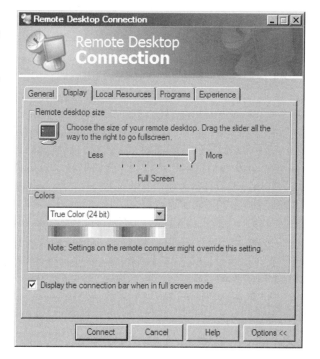

The Local Resources tab shown in Figure 16.8 is a little more in-depth containing some options that have not been previously available to people using RDP. Most of the settings are fairly self-explanatory, however. RDP's sound channel is enabled in Server 2003, so you can control where sound initiated in terminal sessions (perhaps from a training video) is played: on the user's computer, on the terminal server, or not played at all. In a terminal server environment, the two options that make sense are playing the sound on the client computer and not playing it; the option to play the sounds on the remote computer would really only apply to a Windows XP computer whose Desktop you were connecting to, and even then it seems like a bit of a stretch.

The key combinations settings specify whether standard Windows key combinations should apply to the remote session only in full-screen mode, all the time, or if they should always apply to the local session. This is something new, and I really like it. Previously, to use key combinations to navigate around the Desktop of a terminal session, you had to memorize a new set of key combinations—e.g., rather than pressing Ctrl+Esc to open the Start menu, you had to press Alt+Home. Now you have the option of using the standard key combinations in terminal sessions. I like the default option of sending the key combinations to the Desktop when it's in full-screen mode, as that way the key combinations always go to the most prominent work area. You can still use the nonstandard key combinations listed in Table 16.3 when a session is running in a window.

FIGURE 16.8

Edit local resource settings to determine how the local and remote sessions will work together.

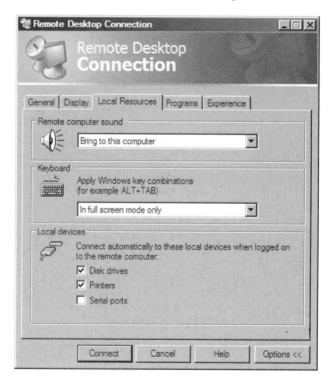

NOTE   *One nonstandard keyboard combination still applies even if the session is in full-screen mode and you've chosen to send key combinations to the terminal session. To bring up the Task Manager in a terminal session, you must press Ctrl+Alt+End. Pressing Ctrl+Alt+Del still opens the Task Manager on the local computer.*

TABLE 16.3: KEYBOARD SHORTCUTS IN TERMINAL SERVICES CLIENT SESSIONS

FUNCTION	LOCALLY USED COMBINATION	SESSION-SPECIFIC COMBINATION
Brings up application selector and moves selection to the right	Alt+Tab	Alt+PgUp
Brings up application selector and moves selection to the left	Alt+Shift+Tab	Alt+PgDn
Swaps between running applications	Alt+Esc	Alt+Insert
Opens the Start menu	Ctrl+Esc	Alt+Home
Right-clicks the active application's icon button in the upper left of the application window	Alt+spacebar	Alt+Del
Brings up the Windows NT Security window	Ctrl+Alt+Del	Ctrl+Alt+Esc

The Programs tab displayed in Figure 16.9 is pretty self-explanatory if you've used Terminal Services before. If you choose a program to run here, then that program will be the only one available—if the user closes it, then they'll end their session. The starting folder settings supply a working directory for the program if you don't want to use the default (often My Documents), but this is an optional setting.

FIGURE 16.9

Choose a single program for terminal sessions.

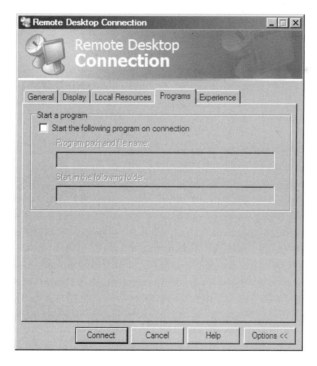

Finally, the Experience tab determines some features to enable based on Microsoft's guesses about what will work best on the selected connection speed (see Figure 16.10). Although you can

manually check or uncheck boxes to enable and disable features, for each network speed offered Remote Desktop will have some default settings.

TIP   *Although you can't control printer mapping from here, when creating a connection to work over a slow network, seriously consider disabling printer mapping.*

FIGURE 16.10
Enable or disable session features depending on the network speed the connection will be using.

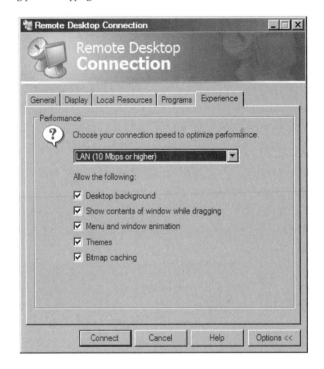

Troubleshooting Connection Problems

When you set up a connection properly, it should work—but *should* is a nice word that doesn't always apply to reality. Table 16.4 lists a few error messages that users might encounter when trying to access a terminal server, either in Application Server mode or in Remote Administration mode.

TABLE 16.4: CONNECTION ERROR MESSAGES

ERROR MESSAGE	PROBABLE MEANING
The local policy of this system does not allow you to log in interactively.	The user attempting to log in does not have the "logon locally" permission available under Security Settings\Local Policies\User Rights Assignment\Log On Locally. Modify the appropriate GPO to grant the user or group this permission. This right is granted to ordinary users when you add the Application Server role, but normally only administrators are allowed to connect to a server via RDP when that server is not using that role.

Continued on next page

TABLE 16.4: CONNECTION ERROR MESSAGES *(continued)*

ERROR MESSAGE	PROBABLE MEANING
You do not have access to this session.	The user attempting to log in does not have sufficient permissions on the RDP-TCP connection. Modify the RDP-TCP permissions by using Terminal Services Configuration to grant the user or group the logon permission.
Your interactive logon privilege has been disabled. Please contact your system administrator.	The user attempting to log in does not have the Allow Logon to Terminal Server check box selected on the Terminal Services Profile tab of their account. Use Active Directory Users and Computers to modify this setting.
The terminal server has exceeded the maximum number of allowed connections. The system cannot log you on. Please try again or consult your system administrator.	The user is attempting to log in to a terminal server in Remote Administration mode, but the server has reached its connection limit. Terminal servers in Remote Administration mode allow a maximum of two concurrent administrative sessions, active or disconnected.
Terminal server sessions disabled. Remote logins are currently disabled.	The user is attempting to log in to a terminal server where an administrator has disabled additional logons by issuing the CHANGE LOGON /DISABLE command. To enable logon, issue the CHANGE LOGON /ENABLE command.
Because of a network error, the session will be disconnected. Please try to reconnect.	The user is attempting to log in to a terminal server where an administrator has specified a maximum connection limit, and the limit has been reached. To change this value, open the Terminal Services Configuration MMC snap-in, click Connections, double-click a connection—i.e., RDP-TCP—then select the Network Adapter tab. At the bottom of this tab are two options, Unlimited Connections and Maximum Connections.
The client could not connect to the terminal server. The server may be too busy. Please try connecting later.	The user is attempting to log in to a terminal server where an administrator has disabled one or more connections. To check this, open the Terminal Services Configuration MMC snap-in, click Connections, right-click a connection—i.e., RDP-TCP—and select All Tasks. If Enable Connection is an option, the connection is currently disabled. There will also be a red *X* over the icon for the specified connection when disabled.
	This is also known as the World's Most Unhelpful Error Message because it may appear for any number of problems that don't have anything to do with the server being busy. For example, if your client can't find the subnet where your terminal server is, you'll see this error message. If the connection is enabled, start looking for network glitches.

Editing Client Account Settings

Everything's ready to go on the client side, but you may still have some work to do to get the server side configured. The following are optional—but useful—settings that allow you to define how long a session may last, whether someone can take remote control of a user's terminal session, how the RDP protocol is configured, and client path and profile information. The location of these settings depends on whether you've set up the member accounts on the terminal server itself (as a member server) or are editing the main user database on a domain controller for the Active Directory—Windows 2000 or Server 2003. If the accounts are local to the server, the settings will be in the Local Users and Groups section of the Computer Management tool in the `Administrative Tools` folder. If the accounts are in the domain, the settings will be in the Active Directory Users and Computers tool in the `Administrative Tools` folder.

In this example, I'll use the Active Directory Users and Groups tool, shown in Figure 16.11. The settings for user accounts in the Local Users and Groups option are the same as the ones in the user accounts stored in the Active Directory, the only difference being that the Active Directory account properties have tabs related to user contact information.

FIGURE 16.11

Edit account properties from the Users folder in Active Directory Users and Computers.

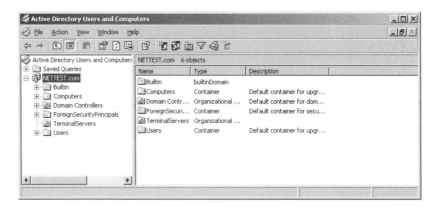

Open the Users folder, find the user you want, then right-click it and choose the Properties item. This properties page controls all user settings, so I'll concentrate on the settings that apply to Terminal Services.

NOTE   *In previous versions of Windows, you had to edit all user (and server settings) on an individual basis, or apply settings to everyone using a protocol on a particular server. Not to mince words (or to mince them only a little) this was a pain in the tuchis for anyone with more than two servers or user accounts to edit. One excellent new feature of Server 2003 is its support for user and server management through group policies. To avoid rehashing the discussion of group policies that's in Chapter 9, I'll point out the relevant group policies where applicable and let that chapter show you how to apply them. I've noted each case where a GPO may be set for either user accounts or computer accounts. Although per-user accounts normally control if you configure settings from the user account properties, computer-based GPOs control if a policy may be set for both users and computers and is set for both.*

Remote Control

The ability to take remote control of a user's session comes in handy when troubleshooting time comes. Rather than trying to blindly talk someone through a series of commands ("Okay, find the `Programs` folder. Got it? Now look for the icon that says 'Microsoft Word'"), you can take over the session, manipulating it from your session while displaying it also for the user. The person whose session you're controlling will be able to see exactly how to complete the task and will have it done for them.

The settings for the kind of remote control that you can take are defined on the Remote Control tab of each user's properties pages, shown in Figure 16.12.

FIGURE 16.12

Setting remote control options for taking over user sessions

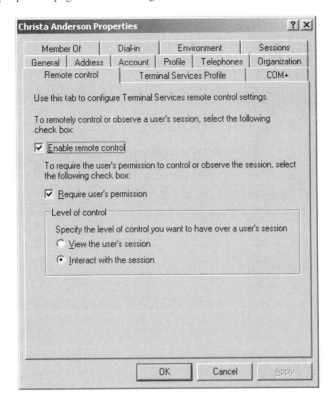

First, you must specify whether remote control is even permitted for the session (by default, you can take control of any session, no matter what rights the owner of the session has). Specify also whether the user whose session is being shadowed must permit the action before the remote control can begin. If you choose this option, the person who originated the session will see a message box telling them that such and such person of such and such domain is attempting to control their session, offering the chance to accept or refuse the control.

NOTE *If permission is required, and a user refuses the remote control connection (or doesn't agree to it within the timeout period of about a minute), you can't control or view the session even from an account with Administrator privileges.*

The final option on this tab determines what kind of control you can have over this user's session. For troubleshooting purposes, you'll find it most useful to be able to interact with the session, so you can actually show the user how to do something (or just do it for them). Choosing this option means that both the original user and the person with remote control over the session can send mouse clicks and keystrokes to the terminal server for interpretation. Graphical output is displayed on both the original session and the remote control view of the session.

If you're choosing the option to view the user's session, the person remotely controlling the session isn't really controlling it, but is only able to watch and see what the original user is doing. The person who set up remote control can't use the mouse or keyboard with the remotely controlled session. This could potentially be a troubleshooting tool if you're trying to find out exactly what someone's doing wrong and help them correct it, while making sure that you can't interfere. Most often, however, I find the option to take control of the session more useful than the ability to watch.

To control remote control settings via GPOs, turn to User Configuration\Administrative Templates\Windows Components\Terminal Services and enable Set Rules for Remote Control of Terminal Services User Sessions. When you do, you'll be able to choose options from the drop-down menu visible in Figure 16.13.

FIGURE 16.13

Remote control settings

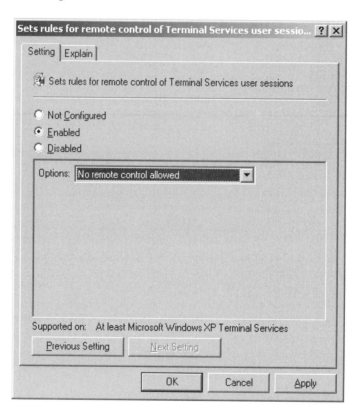

Once you've permitted administrators to use remote control, the options here are divided into two main groups: full control, which lets the administrator interact with the user's session, and View Session, which lets the administrator only watch what the user is doing. Within those two main groups, you can specify whether the user must explicitly permit the administrator to take remote control of his session. All five options are listed in this drop-down list.

NOTE   *These settings are also available from the same path in the Computer Configuration section of the Group Policy Editor. If you set policies in both places, then the computer policies apply.*

Session Time-Outs

The status of a client session isn't a binary proposition. Rather than on/off, the state of a client session may be active, disconnected, or reset. An *active* session is what it sounds like: a session that's actively in use. In a *disconnected* session, the client has shut off the client interface to the session, but the session—and all its applications—is still running on the server. When a client *resets* or *terminates* a session with the Logoff command, the session ends and all applications in the session are shut down. Although the distinction may not sound significant at first, it's important. When clients disconnect from their sessions, all their data is still loaded into memory and their applications are running, exactly as they left them. This means that a client can disconnect while going to lunch, and thus secure the session without having to start over. The only catch to a disconnected session is that it still uses up processor cycles and some memory because the session thread still gets its crack at the processor and because all the user data is still active. However, as the data stops being accessed, the server will swap it out to the paging file on the hard disk and replace it in physical memory with more recent data; when the client reconnects to the session and tries to use the data, the data will be paged back in. The still-running client session also won't impact available network bandwidth much because the terminal server will detect that the session is idle and stop sending video updates to the client machine. You'll need to train users to make sure that they don't just close session windows and inadvertently disconnect when they mean to log off. If a user attempts to reconnect to the terminal server with more than one disconnected session running, a dialog box will display the disconnected sessions, their resolution, and the time that they've been disconnected. The user can then pick the session to reconnect. If the user doesn't pick a session in a minute or so, the highlighted session will be reestablished. The other session will remain on the terminal server, still in its inactive state.

You can control how long a session may stay active, how long it may stay disconnected without being terminated, how long active but idle sessions may stay active before they're disconnected—and even whether a particular user may connect to the server at all. These settings are controlled from the Sessions tab, shown in Figure 16.14.

You can control how long the setting may remain active before being disconnected or terminated. If you want to prevent people from forgetting to log out from their terminal session at the end of the day or at lunch, use this setting.

As I already discussed, a disconnected session is still using up terminal server resources—in the page file if nowhere else. This is by design, so that users can reconnect to a session and have all their applications and data still loaded, but if a session is permanently abandoned, there's no point in leaving it up. Choose a time-out period that reflects the amount of time you're willing to give a user to get back and use their connection before their applications are all closed.

You can also determine how long a session can be idle before being disconnected or terminated. This isn't quite the same setting as the first one, which limits connection time whether or not the session is still getting input. Rather, this setting limits the amount of time that a session can be idle before being shut down. This setting is a little more useful in most cases, given that the session must be unused for a certain period before it is shut down.

The default for all three settings is Never, meaning there's no restriction on how long a session may be running, disconnected, or idle. The maximum time-out period is two days.

TIP   If you want to gather some statistics about how long people are staying logged in, or how long disconnected sessions are remaining idle on the server, you can get this information from the Terminal Services Manager. System Monitor can tell you how many active or inactive sessions are currently running on a given terminal server.

FIGURE 16.14

Configuring session
connection settings

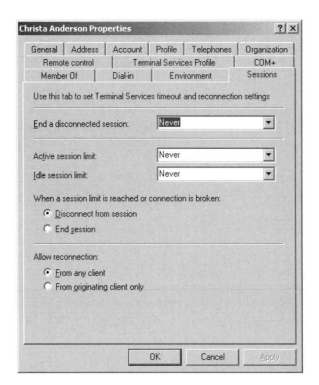

The settings on the bottom of the tab determine how disconnected and reestablished connections should be handled. You may have noticed that two of the time-out options give you the choice of disconnecting or terminating the session at the end of the time-out session, but no option for specifying which it should be—disconnection or resetting the connection. The answer depends on whether you pick Disconnect from Session (the default) or End Session (which resets the connection) for broken or timed-out connections. The other option controls how users may reconnect to disconnected sessions. RDP sessions can reconnect to their client session from any client machine. Only ICA sessions can be forced to reestablish the connection from the same machine from which they started, and then only if you set up the ICA client to identify the computer it's running on. If a user has more than one disconnected session running on the same terminal server, when they reconnect they'll have a choice of which session they want to use. The session(s) not chosen will continue to run on the terminal server.

To configure these settings with GPOs, turn to User Configuration\Administrative Templates\ Windows Components\Terminal Services\Sessions. You'll see the available policies in Figure 16.15.

The editing for each policy works the same way in all cases: enable a policy, and then pick the timeout period that you want, exactly as you would if configuring the setting on a per-user basis as described already in this section. The only policy in this area that might cause you difficulty is the one about only permitting people to reconnect from the same computer. Again, this setting is only available to those using properly configured ICA clients, but this isn't obvious unless you scroll down to the very bottom of the explanation.

NOTE *These settings are also available from the same path in the Computer Configuration section of the Group Policy Editor. If you set policies in both places, then the computer policies apply.*

FIGURE 16.15

Session timeout GPOs for user accounts

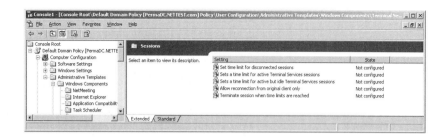

Setting Client Path Information

Unless you specify otherwise, user home directories are in subfolders of the terminal server's `Profiles` folder and are identified by username. Their temporary directories are subfolders of the terminal server's temporary directory and identified by Session ID. To keep all per-user information in a single place, you may want to specify a new home directory. This will give you a fighting chance of applying per-user system quotas and keeping all files in one place for easier recovery—not to mention keeping the home directories off the terminal server, which could ultimately take up a lot of room.

PROFILE PATHS AND HOME DIRECTORIES

Roaming profiles are stored on a profile server instead of a local machine, so the user can log in with the same settings wherever she connects to the network. The other option is locally stored profiles, stored on the computer where they're displayed. When a profile is applied, it makes per-user changes to the Registry of the computer the person is logged in to that apply only to that user. So far, this is just like NT profiles have been for years.

Terminal Services still works more or less the same way. The profiles may still be stored either locally or on a profile server—but in this case *locally* means on the terminal server. As you probably know, you can't *not* use a profile—if you don't specify one, then you'll get the Default User profile.

You have a couple of options when it comes to profiles and Terminal Services. If you only provide a path for the user profile, then that path applies to both "normal" user settings and settings for terminal sessions that the user starts up. Filling in only the information the Profile tab in a user's profile will have this effect—the person will have the same profile path and home directory for terminal sessions as they do normally.

This may sound like a good plan, but in most cases it's not. First off, what works well for local use may not work well when logging onto a terminal session. For one example, the screensaver you might use on a Desktop without a second thought is a resource-draining vanity in a terminal session. For another, using the same profile for both ordinary sessions and terminal sessions leaves you exposed to lost profile changes. Consider how profiles work. When you open a profile and make changes to it, those changes are stored locally and don't get written back to the profile server until you log out. So what happens if you have two copies open, make a change in one and then log out, then make a change in the other copy and then log out? Right—you lose all the changes made to the first one because the copy you saved last to the profile server overwrote the copy you saved first. This can happen any time you open a profile more than once—it's not just a problem with Terminal Services—but you're not likely to log in two or more times when you're logging in to the domain from a fat client. Log in to both the fat client (since you needed to log in to the domain to get to a computer from which you could run the terminal session) and to the terminal server, and you immediately have two copies open. For these reasons, it's probably best to use different profiles for terminal sessions and fat client sessions.

How about roaming profiles for terminal sessions, if those profiles are different from the ordinary user profiles? This is still not a good idea because of the possibility that you'll have multiple copies of your profile open at once. Particularly if your terminal session is set up to only serve applications and you use more than one application, you're likely to open multiple copies of your profile at the same time.

So does this mean that local profiles are the way to go? Nope—not if you have many users to support and those users won't always log in to the same server. When you use local profiles, they're stored on the terminal server. If you have 60 users, each with his or her own profile, and you can't predict which of four servers those 60 users will connect to, then that means that you've got to store those 60 profiles on each server. That's a lot of room to munch up on the terminal server's system drive. It can also lead to inconsistency in the user environment if a user changes his profile on one server and not on another. It's especially important to not keep user profiles locally if you're using load balancing of any kind because doing so would mean that people would never know which profile they'd get.

For this reason, the best plan might be to use mandatory profiles, which are just ordinary profiles with a .man extension. Users can edit mandatory profiles to the degree their system policies allow them to, but those changes don't get saved to the server. Limiting to the user experience, perhaps, but if you use mandatory profiles with terminal sessions, then you avoid the problems of lost profile edits from multiple copies of the profile being opened. To specify a profile location, set the path location for the Terminal Services profile from each user's properties pages, as shown in Figure 16.16.

The Allow Logon to Terminal Server check box controls whether the person is permitted to log in to the terminal server at all. By default, anyone with an account on the domain or server may do so.

FIGURE 16.16

Specify the path to the user profile and home directory in the Terminal Services Profile tab.

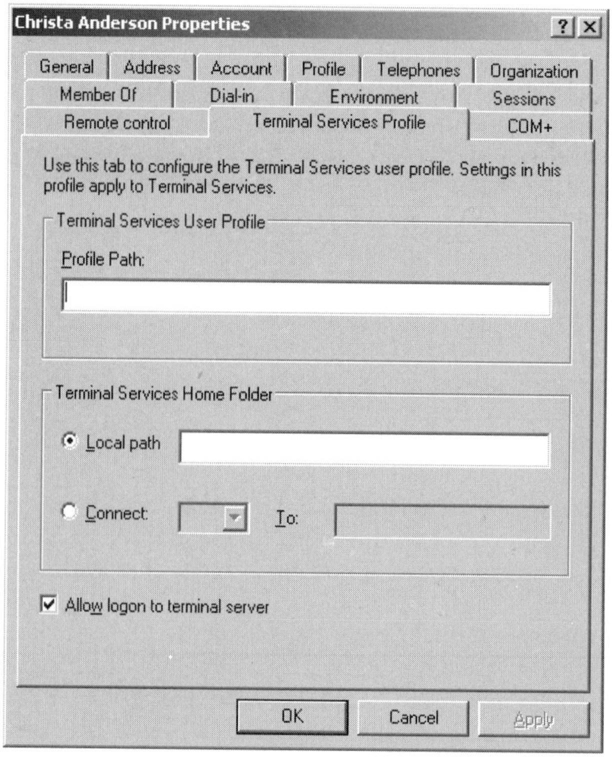

User profile and home directory information are configured in computer group policies located in Computer Configuration\Administrative Templates\Windows Components\Terminal Services. The policies you're looking for are Set Path for TS Roaming Profiles and TS User Home Directory. Just include the computer name and path to the profile directory; the policy will fill in the username automatically. If the path you provide does not exist (or the server can't reach it) then it will use local profiles.

The same goes for setting up the home directory—type the UNC name for the network share, and assign a local drive letter if necessary (for applications that demand a drive letter), as I've done in Figure 16.17. I do not recommend putting the user home directory on the local terminal server unless you really have no other options, as doing so will give users separate home directories depending on which server they're connected to.

FIGURE 16.17

You can set home directory paths through group policies.

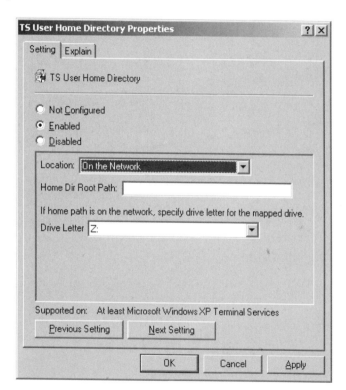

PROGRAMMATIC UPDATES TO PROFILE INFORMATION

To change or set user profile information for one user account is no big deal: Open Active Directory Users and Computers, open the user account's properties sheet, turn to the Terminal Services Profile tab, and make the change. Multiply this procedure by 50, 500, or 5000 users, however, and it gets less easy. However, all is not lost: You can make these edits through ADSI (the profile path is now exposed as a property of the object representing the terminal server—this wasn't an option in previous versions of Terminal Services) or, if you're VBScript-challenged, with the `tsprof` command-line tool.

Continued on next page

PROGRAMMATIC UPDATES TO PROFILE INFORMATION *(continued)*

Tsprof supports three actions: You can update account profile information, you can copy it to another user account, or you can query a user account to make sure your changes took or see what the current profile settings are. The basic syntax for these commands looks like this:

```
TSPROF /UPDATE [/DOMAIN:domainname|/LOCAL] /PROFILE:<path> username
TSPROF /COPY   [/DOMAIN:domainname|/LOCAL] [/PROFILE:<path>] sourceuser
   destinationuser
TSPROF /Q      [/DOMAIN:domainname|/LOCAL] username
```

Make sure you don't include extra spaces in the command, or you could accidentally query the domain name as though it were a username.

For example, say that my Terminal Services users don't have session-explicit user accounts; they're using the same accounts they typically use to log on to the domain. The profile settings that work well for a full-color session on a single-user computer might not translate well to a terminal session, so I want to edit that account information to C:\profiles. I can do so from the command line, like this:

```
tsprof /update /domain:redroom /profile:c:\profiles\profile.man christa
```

In this example, the user account is in the REDROOM domain, the profile path is C:\profiles, and the user account I'm editing is named Christa. This command will spit back the following information:

```
Terminal Services Profile Path for redroom\christa is { c:\profiles\profile.man }
```

If the curly brackets don't contain any information, you haven't set a Terminal Services profile for that user account. The /update argument doesn't tell you what the profile path information was *before* you changed it, so if you want to ensure that it needs to be updated, query the account. To perform the query, use the /q argument, like this:

```
tsprof /q /domain:labrynth christa
```

If you used tsprof with TSE, notice that the command now is /q, not /query. The command changed in Windows 2000 and retains that change in Server 2003.

Finally, you can copy profile-path information from one account to another. The /copy command works similar to /update, except you must provide the source and destination account names, in this case, Christa and Vera, respectively:

```
Tsprof /copy /domain:redroom christa vera
```

The system will now copy Christa's profile account information to Vera's user account; if I query Vera's account, the profile information will be there.

Be careful when you use these tools. Tsprof can't tell whether a profile path is valid any more than the graphical user account management tools can; tsprof will enter whatever information you give it. If the account name is invalid, tsprof will generate an error when it attempts to update the information—Failed Setting User Configuration, Error = 1332 (0x534)—but won't show any problems when you perform a query.

DEFINING THE SESSION ENVIRONMENT AND MAPPING CLIENT RESOURCES

The Environment tab in the properties pages (see Figure 16.18) sets the Terminal Services environment for the user, replacing any related settings (such as an application to run at logon) that might already appear in a user's client logon settings. If you want to automatically run an application at logon, type its path in the Program File Name box (sadly, there's no browse function). The working directory goes in the Start In box. Notice that supplying the name of an application does not limit the terminal server session to only running that application and then ending when the application is terminated. All this does is run the application when the session starts—the main Desktop still remains available. If you want to provide a terminal session running only a single application, and then closing when that application closes, you'll need to set that up when configuring the client connections, as described earlier in this chapter.

FIGURE 16.18

Tuning the user environment and mapping client resources

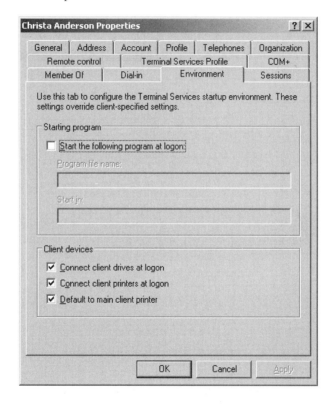

The settings in the Client Devices section at the bottom of this tab apply to clients using Remote Desktop Connection. The first one, Connect Client Drives at Logon, applies only to sessions where remapping client drives for use in terminal server sessions is enabled (and it may confuse users as to whether they're saving files to their local drives or to the terminal server, so this may be an option to give only to experienced users). Mapped drives will show up as "Other" drives in My Computer, retaining their original drive letters but without colons (that is, drive C: on your local computer will be drive C when mapped to a terminal session). The printing options, however, do apply to RDP clients. Checking Connect Client Printers at Logon specifies that any printers mapped from the terminal server session should be reconnected. Default to Main Client Printer specifies that the client should use its own default printer, not the one defined for the terminal server.

To specify a program to run in the terminal session via group policies, go to Computer Configuration\Administrative Templates\Windows Components\Terminal Services and enable Start a Program on Connection. (You can also edit this setting in user GPOs, but if the policies conflict then the per-computer settings take control.) As when editing the setting for individual users, you'll need to know the path and working directory—you can't browse for it here.

All decisions about client resource mapping are set with policies in Computer Configuration\ Administrative Templates\Windows Components\Terminal Services\Client/Server Data Redirection (see Figure 16.19).

FIGURE 16.19

Many policies control client resource mapping.

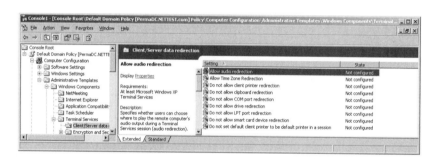

Most of these settings are easy to associate with their counterparts in the user account properties. One that you might not recognize (both because it's not on the Environment tab—it's a protocol configuration setting, not a user setting—and because it's new to Terminal Services in Server 2003) is Allow Time Zone Redirection. This policy pertains to how time zones work in terminal sessions. Prior to this, terminal sessions displayed the time zone of the terminal server, and if this time zone was different from that of the person connected to the terminal session it confused things like e-mail arrival times, that was just too darn bad. (Some third-party utilities fixed this problem, but Microsoft had no built-in fix for it.) Server 2003 allows time zone redirection, which is on by default. You must enable this setting to turn it off.

Configuring Terminal Services for All Connections

You can configure general settings for all Terminal Services connections from the Terminal Services Configuration tool in the `Administrative Tools` folder. If you're running Terminal Services alone, you'll have only the RDP connection in this folder; if you have other multiuser Windows components added (like MetaFrame's ICA protocol or direct video support), they'll be in the folder as well.

What can you do here? The `Server Settings` folder contains settings that apply to all connections made to the server. The `Connections` folder shows all installed display protocols.

NOTE   *Server 2003 only supports one RDP connection per network adapter. If your terminal server has more than one NIC installed and you're using RDP with both of them, you can configure the RDP protocol for each adapter separately.*

THE *SERVER SETTINGS* FOLDER

The Server Settings folder (see Figure 16.20) contains options that control the creation and deletion of per-session temporary files and the types of access permitted to the terminal server. The options here are identical whether the server is set up to be an ordinary server with remote administration capabilities or an application server.

FIGURE 16.20

Server Settings folder for a terminal server in Application Server mode

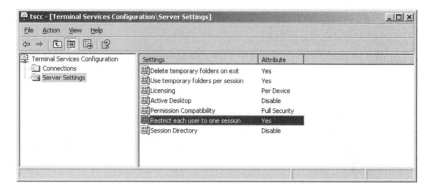

Licensing

On an application server, the licensing may be either Per Seat (the default) or Per Session. (On a server using RDP only for remote administration, the licensing information here will read Remote Administration.) Per Seat licensing is new in Server 2003.

Temporary Folder Settings

Ordinarily, a terminal server stores temporary files for each session as a subfolder to each user's profile in %userprofile%\Local Settings\Temp\sessionID (the SessionID folders are necessary in case a user has more than one session open at a time). For applications that can't deal with per-user settings, you can force all temporary files to be written to the same folder on the server: %userprofile%\Local Settings\Temp on the server.

Deleting the temporary folders on exit means that when a user logs out of a terminal server session, the temporary folder they used—and all the TMP files in it—is deleted. This setting, set to Yes by default, keeps the terminal server from getting cluttered with TMP files, but ensures that those files are only deleted when they're no longer needed.

You can also apply these settings to temporary directories using GPOs, using the policies in Computer Configuration\Administrative Templates\Windows Components\Terminal Services\Temporary Folders. There are two policies here. Do Not Use Temp Folders Per Session and Do Not Delete Temp Folder Upon Exit, which you can enable or disable as appropriate. If you leave them unconfigured, then the default settings (to use temporary folders per session and delete those folders when the session ends) apply.

Active Desktop Use

Another option lets you turn off the Active Desktop on the terminal server sessions. Unless you really need it for some reason, I'd turn it off and save the resources.

User Connection Restrictions

This is something new to Windows Terminal Services—the ability to allow each person connecting to a particular server only one connection. If you have only one terminal server, then using this setting prevents the I-have-three-copies-of-my-profile-open problem. On multiple servers, this setting makes it easier for users to reconnect to disconnected sessions by giving them only one possible choice. The default setting limits users to one session per server.

To configure this setting using GPOs, you'll need the Restrict Terminal Services Users to a Single Remote Session setting, found in Computer Configuration\Administrative Templates\Windows Components\Terminal Services.

Security Settings

Finally, you can choose the type of permissions you want to apply to this terminal server. Relaxed Security file access is compatible with all applications (but may leave some system folders vulnerable to changes from user applications) or Full Security file access may not work with all applications (because it denies permissions to some system folders) but does not allow applications to tamper with system folders. Always start out using Full Security, and only use Relaxed Security if a vital application simply won't run without it. Newer applications should work with Full Security.

THE *CONNECTIONS* FOLDER

Use the Connections folder to configure protocol-wide settings. First, you can disable RDP so that no one can connect to the server, something you might want to do if you know you're going to be taking the server down for maintenance and don't want to have to bother with kicking new people off. Since you can't turn off the terminal server service, this is the easiest way to keep people off the server while still keeping it running. To do so, just right-click the protocol and choose Disable Connection from the All Tasks part of the pop-up menu. The command to re-enable the connection is in the same All Tasks section.

NOTE   *This setting does not end existing sessions. To end all sessions—ungracefully and at once—you can reset a RDP listening session from Terminal Services Manager.*

For more detailed control of RDP, choose the Properties option from the pop-up menu. Most settings in the RDP-Tcp dialog box work the same way as their counterparts in the per-user connection settings, which normally take precedence. For a more uniform set of protocol configurations, you may edit the settings here and check the boxes that tell the protocol properties not to inherit their settings according to the user. The two settings that aren't configurable on a per-user basis control security are found on the General and Permissions tabs.

THE GENERAL TAB

The General tab shown in Figure 16.21 controls the degree of encryption used with RDP. The encryption can protect both logins and the stream of text, but at a minimum protects the information passed during the login process.

By default, the client's level of encryption determines the level of encryption between client and server, which means that all communications between client and server are encrypted with the standard 40-bit algorithm (56-bit if the client is running Win2K Professional or XP Pro). High encryption forces 128-bit encryption, which means that clients incapable of supporting this encryption level won't be able to connect to the terminal server.

FIGURE 16.21

Configuring RDP
access security

You don't have to worry about the Use Standard Windows Authentication check box unless you've installed a third-party authentication package on the server. In that case, checking this box tells the terminal server to use its native authentication scheme to validate terminal session user logons, rather than using the third-party package.

PERMISSIONS

Those familiar with the NT security model will remember that you secure a network by defining user rights for what people can *do* on the network and setting permissions for the resources that people can *use*. Terminal Services security is controlled with permissions, on a per-group or per-user basis.

To set or edit the permissions assigned to terminal server sessions, turn to the Permissions tab. You'll see a dialog box like the one in Figure 16.22. From here, you can edit the basic permission sets of the groups for whom some kind of access to terminal server functions has been defined.

TIP   If you turn to the Permissions tab and see a list of security IDs instead of user or group names, and the cursor changes to an hourglass when over the dialog box, don't panic. The terminal server is retrieving the names from the domain controller and will show the user and group names after a few seconds. If this doesn't happen—if the SIDs never resolve to user and group names—then there's something wrong with either the domain controller or the connection between the two servers.

FIGURE 16.22

Default terminal
server permissions

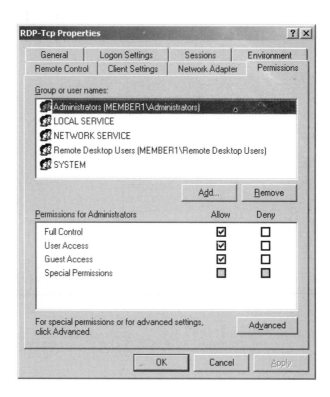

Not sure how to interpret the check boxes? If a permission is checked, then it's explicitly enabled or disabled, depending on which box is checked. If a permission is clear on both sides, then it's implicitly enabled. You can explicitly enable or disable the permission by checking the appropriate box.

Fine-Tuning Access to Terminal Server Functions

The first page shows only the default groups and the basic permissions they've been assigned. For more control over the permission process, click the Advanced button to open the dialog box shown in Figure 16.23.

From here, you can see the state of the defined permissions. The Inherited From field indicates the level at which the permissions were set—here, or at a higher level.

You can adjust these permissions either by adding new users or groups to the list (getting them from the domain controller) or by editing the permissions of the groups already there. To define permissions for a new user or group, click the Add button. You'll open a dialog box where you can choose the name of the account to edit. Type the name of a user or group, then click the Check Names button to confirm that you got it right. When you've got the right user or group account name, click OK to open the dialog box in Figure 16.24.

FIGURE 16.23

Setting advanced permissions

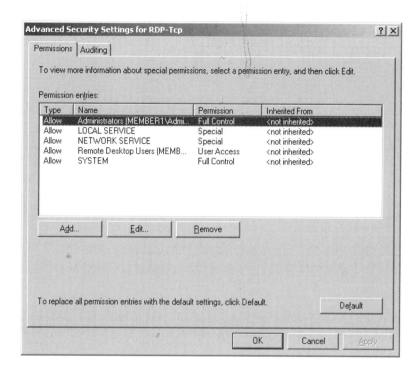

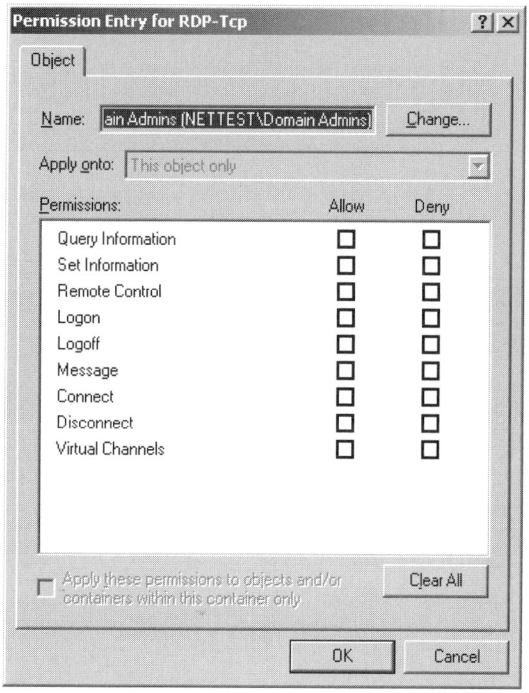

FIGURE 16.24

Defining the permissions for a new user

By default, new users and groups (even domain administrators) have no permissions at all. You will need to specify the access you'd like to grant or deny to the groups and users you're adding to the list.

The permissions listed here have the characteristics outlined in Table 16.5. I'll talk more about how to *use* these functions in the later section "Managing Terminal Sessions."

TABLE 16.5: TERMINAL SERVICES PERMISSIONS

ACCESS TYPE	EFFECT	INCLUDED IN
Query Information	Allows users to gather information about people using the terminal server, processes running on the server, sessions, and so forth	Full Control, Service Permissions
Set Information	Allows users to set the level of control other users have over the session	Full Control
Reset	Allows users to reset other connections, ending them and logging the other user off the computer	Full Control
Remote Control	Allows users to take control of or view other user sessions	Full Control
Logon	Allows users to log on to the terminal server	Full Control, User Access, Guest
Logoff	Allows users to log off from the terminal server	Full Control, User Access, Guest
Message	Allows users to send messages to other terminal server clients	Full Control, Service Permissions, User Access
Connect	Allows users to connect to other terminal servers	Full Control, User Access
Disconnect	Allows users to disconnect from other terminal servers	Full Control
Virtual Channels	Enables virtual channels for that group	Full Control

NOTE   *Service Permissions are identified also as "Special". Same thing.*

Changing permissions for an existing user or group works in much the same way as adding permissions for a newly defined group: Select a name, click the Edit button, and you'll see the same set of options to explicitly grant or deny permissions.

TIP   *If you want to cancel all permission changes for a user or group and start over, click the Cancel button. If you want to remove every granted or denied permission associated with a user or group, click Clear All, or just select them in the list on the Permissions tab of the RDP Properties sheet and click the Remove button—this will have the same effect.*

Terminal Services Licensing

Licensing single-user computers is complicated enough. Bring terminal servers into the equation, and the complications increases. Do you have to pay for only the operating system? Only the client sessions active at any given time? Only some client sessions? What about applications—an application is only loaded on one machine, so you should only have to pay for one license, right? And who's in charge of keeping track of all these licenses, anyway?

Licensing is never fun and it's not glamorous, but it's part of the cost of doing business. Read on to make some sense of the Terminal Services licensing model.

The Terminal Services Licensing Model

First, let's take a look at how the licensing model works in Win2K. In TSE, licensing was handled by a license manager service that came with TSE. You told the license manager how many Terminal Services licenses you had, and it kept track of how they were used. Windows 2000 added a license server, which might or might not be the terminal server—depended on the security model you were using. Beginning with Windows 2000, you also had to activate the licenses through Microsoft. You can't just tell the license server how many TS licenses you have, you must get official licenses from Microsoft and activate them.

As shown in Figure 16.25, several players cooperate to make Terminal Services licensing work in Server 2003:

- The terminal servers
- The license servers
- The Microsoft clearinghouse that enables the license servers and the access licenses

FIGURE 16.25

The Terminal Services licensing model

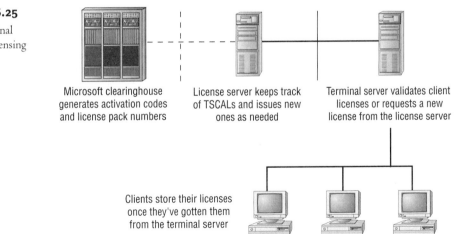

Microsoft clearinghouse generates activation codes and license pack numbers

License server keeps track of TSCALs and issues new ones as needed

Terminal server validates client licenses or requests a new license from the license server

Clients store their licenses once they've gotten them from the terminal server

The first time a client connects to a terminal server, one of two things happens. When the user logs in, the terminal server will take the license the client proffers—I'll get to the question of just how a client would *have* such a license in a minute—or, if the client doesn't have a license, the terminal server will find the license server by discovery (broadcasts in workgroups and NT 4 domains or by polling the domain controllers in Active Directory domains) and request a license from the license server. If the license server has a license to issue, it will give it to the terminal server, who will issue it to the client *computer* that's attempting to make the terminal connection. The client can then present its license to the terminal server. If the license server does not have an available license—even a temporary license—then the client cannot complete the connection and will be rejected. If the terminal server can't connect to the license server for some reason, then the terminal server will accept pre-existing licenses, but clients without valid temporary or permanent licenses will not be able to log in to the terminal server.

When a client disconnects from the terminal server, it retains its license—the license does not go back to a pool. Therefore, if I log in to the terminal server once from my office desk and once from my home office, I'll use up two separate licenses. You cannot give these licenses back to the license server; they're marked in the license server's database as given to a particular machine, identified by GUID.

Understanding Session Licensing

When Microsoft first released Windows NT, Terminal Server Edition, it made a terrible marketing decision. Any client connecting to the terminal had to have a valid NT Workstation license. At $400 a pop, NTW licenses weren't cheap, so a lot of people looked at TSE and said, "Nice, but not worth the money." This didn't do much to promote the use of Terminal Services by anyone not already using NTW. In an effort to win those people back, in February 1999 Microsoft revamped their licensing structure, giving NT Workstation clients a built-in license to access the terminal server but requiring you to purchase terminal server licenses (which cost approximately $150 per seat instead of $400) for computers running any other operating system. However, by default access to the server running Terminal Services is licensed on a per-seat basis, not per user—computers are licensed, not people.

The licensing structure includes four license types:

◆ Terminal Server Client Access Licenses (TSCALs)
◆ Built-in licenses
◆ Temporary licenses

NOTE *Not all Terminal Services functions use licenses. When you're running Terminal Services capabilities in Remote Administration mode you don't need TSCALs because Remote Administration mode comes with two administrator's licenses. You cannot use this licensing mode on a server configured with the Application Server role.*

TERMINAL SERVER CLIENT ACCESS LICENSES

Terminal Server Client Access Licenses (TSCALs) are for named user accounts in the domain and issued on a per-seat basis. Anyone in a company who's using the terminal server must have a TSCAL, regardless of whether they're connecting to the terminal server via Microsoft's RDP display protocol or Citrix's ICA display protocol (which they will if you install MetaFrame). To access a terminal server at all, of course, a client also needs a Client Access License (CAL).

License Packaging

The way you buy TSCALs determines how you pay for them and how much flexibility you have in the purchase. Most people who buy small volumes of Microsoft products will buy their TSCALs as part of a 5-CAL or 20-CAL Microsoft License Pak (MLP). Physically, an MLP is a thin cardboard envelope that contains the EULA denoting the number of CALs purchased. The MLP for TSCALs also includes a license code, a 25-character alphanumeric code that indicates what the license is for and how many TSCALs it purchases (so that you can't fudge the entries and say that you bought 20 TSCALs when you really only bought 5). You can only install an MLP once. Small to medium customers will get their licenses through a program called Microsoft Open License, which allows you to purchase a user-specified quantity of licenses, after which Microsoft issues you an Open License Authorization and license numbers for the licenses, which you can install as many times as you need to. Select and Enterprise Agreements for large customers work like open licenses, except that the customer provides their Enrollment Agreement number instead of the Open License numbers.

Reclaiming TSCALs

Once allocated to a computer, a TSCAL belongs to that computer and is identified as such in the license server's database. You cannot manually reclaim TSCALs from a computer, so the visiting consultant who logs in to the terminal server once leaves with a TSCAL. Not only that, but if you wipe a computer's hard disk and reinstall, then there's no record of that TSCAL on the computer and it will have to request a second one. Unused TSCALs will eventually revert to the license pool on their own, but the process takes a while.

Rather than permanently assigning TSCALs to clients, the license server will give first-time requesters a TSCAL with a time-out period (a randomly assigned interval between 52 and 89 days). When the user logs onto the terminal server, the terminal server tells the license server that the license has been validated (used by someone with permission to log onto the terminal server). The TSCAL is then assigned to that machine. Every time someone connects to the terminal server from that machine, the terminal server will check the expiration date on the TSCAL. When the expiration date is less than 7 days, the terminal server renews the TSCAL assignment to that machine for another 52 to 89 days. Should the client machine not log into the terminal server before its TSCAL expires, its TSCAL will return to the pool of available licenses.

UNLIMITED AND TEMPORARY LICENSES

Win2K and XP Professional computers can draw from the license server's pool of unlimited licenses, which effectively gives them a built-in license. Finally, the license server issues temporary licenses when a terminal server requests a license and the license server has none to give (perhaps because you haven't installed a license pack yet). The license server then tracks the issuance and expiration of the temporary licenses.

NOTE *Although the Unlimited license pool existed in RC1 of Server 2003, it will not exist in the final release of Server 2003. Windows XP OSes bought before April 2003 are grandfathered in, but all other OSes—and copies of Windows XP purchased after April—will need a TSCAL.*

Byzantine enough for you? Table 16.6 is a cheat sheet.

TABLE 16.6: TERMINAL SERVICES CLIENT ACCESS LICENSE TYPES

SITUATION	TERMINAL SERVICES LICENSE TYPE REQUIRED
Users connecting from Win2K Professional and XP Pro Desktops	Unlimited pool
Users connecting from any desktop not using Win2K or XP Professional	Terminal Server Client Access License (TSCAL)
Anonymous users connecting to the terminal server via the Internet	Terminal Services Internet Connector License (TSICL)

Server 2003 may offer Per Session licensing. Per session licensing allocates licenses to sessions, not to machines, so that the licenses are reclaimed when the session ends.

The Terminal Server Licensing Tool

The Terminal Server Licensing tool, found in the Administrative Tools program group of any Server with the Terminal Server Licensing service running on it, helps you keep track of license usage.

TIP   To add Terminal Services Licensing, open the Add/Remove Programs applet in the Control Panel and click the Add Windows Components icon. Follow the Windows Components Wizard and just pick the component from the list of available options. In a purely Active Directory domain, this license server must be on a domain controller. In a Mixed domain, the license server may be on a member server.

When you first start the licensing tool, it will browse for license servers on the network and then report back with the ones it found, as shown in Figure 16.26.

FIGURE 16.26

Use the Terminal Server Licensing tool to manage license usage.

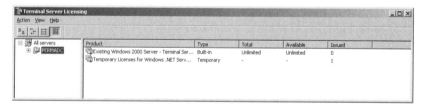

Creating a license server is a two-step process: you need to install the service, and you need to activate the license server. Although the temporary licenses will function for a limited time (120 days), to fully enable the terminal server licenses, you'll need to activate the server and download the license key.

Activation is essentially a way of making sure you've really paid for the licenses you're using. (According to Citrix, it also helps technical support keep track of you for better customer support, but I have a sneaking suspicion that the "let's make sure people are paying for what they use" issue is a little more important—not that it wouldn't be important to me, of course.) When you activate a license, you're providing your product number to Microsoft. Microsoft then runs an encryption algorithm on it and sends you back the results as your activation code. You then give Microsoft back the activation code, they run another encrypting algorithm on it, and they send you a license code that corresponds to that activation code. This is an extra step, and that's annoying, but the procedure itself really isn't too arduous.

When you first open the Terminal Services Licensing tool, it looks like Figure 16.26. As you can see, the licensing server is present but not yet activated, as indicated by the red dot. To make the license server ready to monitor license usage and to issue TSCALs, you'll need to activate the server and install the license pack assigned to that server. To do so, connect the server to the Internet (easiest, as otherwise you'll need to recite license numbers and activation codes over the telephone) and follow these steps:

1. Right-click the server and choose Activate Server from the context menu. Click through the opening screen.

2. Choose a method of contacting Microsoft to get a license. You have three options for contacting Microsoft to give them your product number. Automatic Connection, the default option, gives you a direct connection to Microsoft but requires that the license server have an Internet connection. Other options include the Web (whether from the license server or another computer with an Internet connection) or telephone. For this example, choose the Automatic Connection (see Figure 16.27) and click Next to display the screen shown in Figure 16.28.

FIGURE 16.27

Choose a way of contacting the Microsoft clearing-house to get an activation code and valid license packs.

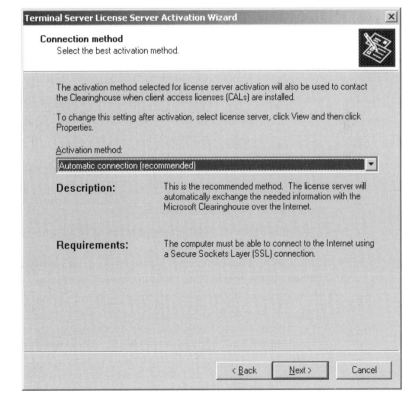

NOTE   *If you choose to contact the licensing people via telephone, the next screen of the wizard will display a list of countries to choose from so that you've got a shot at making a toll-free call.*

3. Next, fill out the form identifying yourself.

FIGURE 16.28

Fill in your name and company.

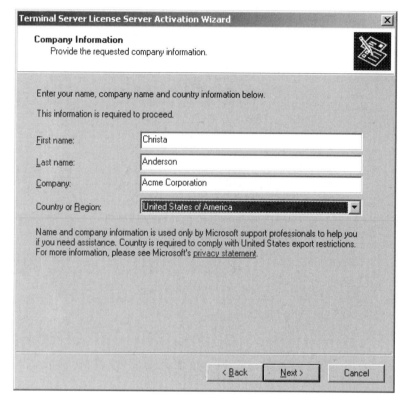

4. Next, the wizard will prompt you for some further contact information (see Figure 16.29).
5. The wizard will contact the Microsoft licensing clearinghouse and activate the server, then show you the confirmation screen in Figure 16.30.
6. You'll need client licenses, so you might as well continue. Click Next to move to the next screen of the licensing tool (see Figure 16.31), where you'll need to fill in the codes of all the license packs you have (the MLP number, or your Open License or Enrollment Agreement number, depending on what kind of customer you are). Again, confirm the information that you've entered and click Next to submit it.
7. In the next page of the wizard, you'll need to provide the license pack numbers. You can add more than one at a time—just click the Add button to add them to the list.

FIGURE 16.29

Other contact information is optional.

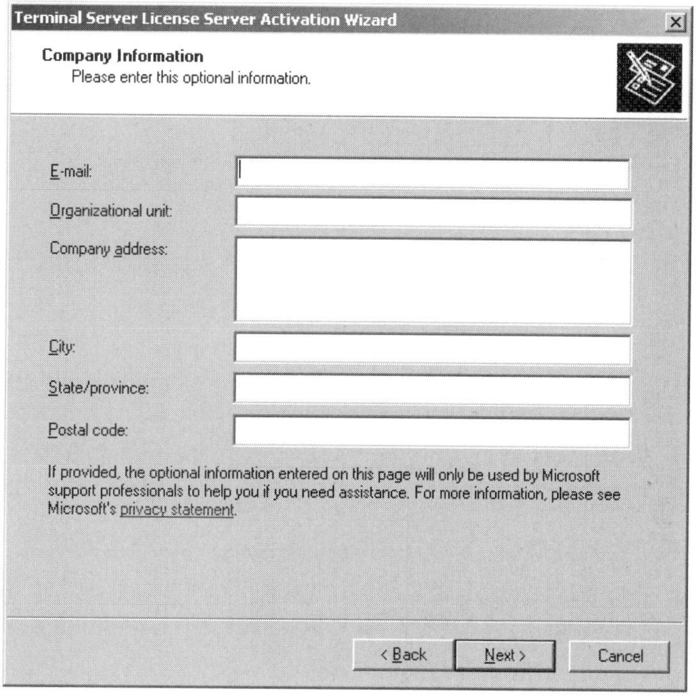

FIGURE 16.30

Completed license server activation

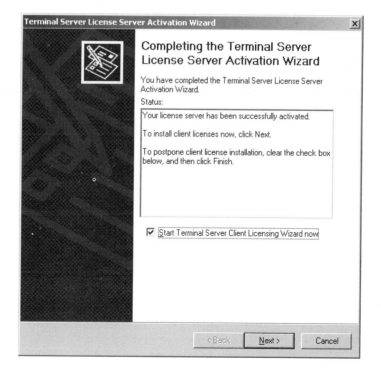

FIGURE 16.31

Installing a
license pack

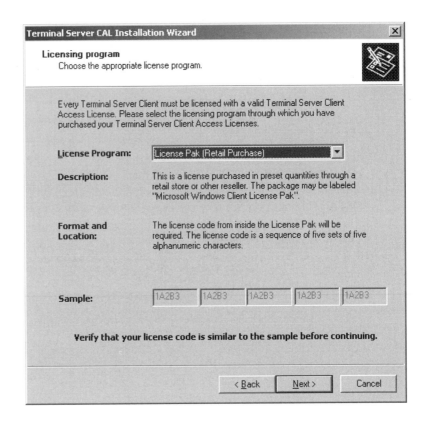

Once you install the license pack, the license server is ready to go.

TIP   If the license server won't accept a license pack and you're sure you typed it correctly, the database might be damaged. If it is, you can rebuild by uninstalling the licensing service, reinstalling it, and then reactivating the server.

All that said, here's a warning: You have 120 days to activate a TSCAL license server. Use those 120 days to make sure you're running the licensing service on the computer that you want to take the job. The client licenses you create will only work on the server you've activated, and the activation code is based on the product ID.

Application Licensing

Application licensing in a terminal server environment is simpler than you might think: Whatever licensing is applied to a product in a single-user environment applies to the terminal server environment. For example, Microsoft Office 2000 is licensed on a per-seat basis. If you install Microsoft Office onto the terminal server, then every computer that will ever run a Microsoft Office application will need to have an Office license, even if the application only runs once a year, because the application is *apparently* running on the client workstation. However, because Office is licensed on a per-seat basis, if you already have a licensed copy of Office installed on a PC client running terminal services, that client may use Office in the terminal session (perhaps when dialing into the terminal server from home) without purchasing an additional Office license because that computer is already licensed to run the application suite. Be sure to get familiar with the licensing a given application requires so you can see how it will work in the multiuser environment.

Configuring Applications for a Multiuser Environment

Not all applications work well in a thin client environment. Some use up too many processor cycles or too much memory; some can't tell the difference between a user and a computer; some store information in locations inappropriate to a multiuser operating system. Sometimes you're stuck with these problems, and if you really need to run those applications, you'll need to do it from the client Desktop. However, some problems are fixable, if you take a little time.

Choosing Applications

First, which applications should you be trying to run at all? An application suitable for a terminal server environment fits the following profile:

- Undemanding of processor cycles and memory
- Modular in video output for better caching
- Stores user data in per-user spaces, not in per-machine spaces
- Identifies users by username, not computer name
- Stores global data in global locations, not local ones

WARNING *Poorly designed applications that can function in a single-user environment will bring a terminal server to a screeching halt. For example, the effect of memory leaks in an application is exponentially increased because multiple instances of the application—all leaking—may be running.*

In addition to these traits, consider the operating system for which the application was originally designed. Although some Win16 and DOS applications can work in a multiuser environment, Terminal Services works best for Win32 applications. The reason for this has to do with how the terminal server runs Win32 and Win16 applications. As a Win32 operating system, Windows 2000 can't run Win16 applications on its own. Instead, it creates a Virtual DOS Machine (VDM), which is a 32-bit application, and runs the Win16 application within the context of that VDM. Whereas Win32 applications running normally on the server can share files and structures among themselves, so long as they're not changing those files or structures, applications running within VDMs can't "see" each other to share files. The practical upshot of this, combined with the fact that translating 16-bit calls to the operating system into 32-bit calls takes some overhead, means that Win16 applications perform less well in this environment than Win32 applications. They'll work—a good thing because you may not have a choice about running them if that's what you're using—but they'll use more memory than Win32 apps.

DOS applications present another kind of problem. Actually, they present two other kinds of problems. First, DOS applications were written for a single-user, single-tasking environment. To be as responsive as possible, some DOS applications constantly poll the keyboard buffer, looking for input that's meant for them. This means that a DOS application in the foreground, even when not doing anything, is using up an astounding amount of processor time. This is acceptable in a single-user environment, but won't work when that processor time has to be shared with a dozen people.

TAMING DOS APPLICATIONS

Windows NT, Terminal Server Edition (TSE), included a utility called DOSKBD that modifies a program's keyboard polling to improve system performance when you run DOS-based programs. Essentially, DOSKBD puts a program to sleep when it polls the keyboard buffer too often and negatively affects server performance. Server 2003 doesn't include a copy of DOSKBD, and the TSE version doesn't work with later versions of Terminal Services. However, there's another option. Go to `http://www.tamedos.com` and check out Tame, a tool for tuning DOS applications in an NT environment. That's the advice you'll get from Microsoft Support if you ask about tuning DOS applications.

Also, DOS applications with a graphical UI don't use Windows graphics rendering instructions, but bitmaps. Bitmaps take much longer to download to the client than GDI rendering instructions, so session responsiveness will suffer. Bitmap-displaying applications are jerky at best in a terminal server environment and more often are completely unusable, particularly on slower connections. Another problem with DOS applications in a multiuser environment is that you can't run them in full-screen mode. Because full-screen mode requires loading a different font set from the Windows one used for DOS applications running in a window (and thus increased memory overhead), Microsoft decided not to permit this.

You *can* run DOS and Win16 applications in a terminal server environment. They just won't cooperate with other applications as well as Win32 applications will. DOS applications in particular probably won't look as good as they would running locally.

However, you can often tweak an application to make it work better in a multiuser environment than it would if left to its own fell devices. Installing applications in a multiuser environment takes a little more care than does installing them for a single-user environment, but that's part of the price of thin client networking.

Making Your Applications Play Well with Others

Even if an application doesn't need any massaging to make it work right when shared among multiple people, you can't install it in the same way you would if installing it for a single person's use.

To work properly in a multiuser environment, applications should edit the HKCU branch of the Registry to add user-specific information, rather than HKLM. Otherwise, those settings apply to the machine, not to the user. This means that not only are per-user settings available to everyone using that particular machine, but the settings will only be available at that machine—if the user logs in to another machine, the settings won't be available. If you've only got one terminal server in your network, it won't matter for this reason if application settings are machine specific, but a single terminal server will generally only serve a couple of dozen people, tops, and maybe fewer than that if client demands are high. Even if you do only have one terminal server, you've still got the problem of trying to keep user-specific information limited to the people who set it up. For example, say that Web browser bookmarks are stored in a machine-specific area. In a terminal server environment, that means everyone will have the same bookmarks—and will overwrite each other's settings at will.

Point being: User-specific settings should go into HKCU, not HKLM. However, you can't *install* applications into HKCU. HKCU applies only to the current user, not all users, and the identity of the current user will change depending on who's logged in—the contents of HKCU are different for each terminal server session. To get around this dilemma you need some user-specific settings, but you need to keep them someplace all users can get to, at least at first. The terminal server manages this by providing a global installation mode that exploits the machine-wide settings of HKLM.

INSTALLING APPLICATIONS FOR MULTIPLE USERS

Each Terminal Services session has two operating modes: Execute and Install. The names are descriptive of what the modes are for: Execute mode is for running applications or installing for single users, and Install mode is for installing applications to be available to multiple users. The mechanics of installing an application depend on which mode you're in when running the application's Setup program.

If you install an application while in Execute mode, it installs and edits the Registry as it would if you installed it for use on a single-user computer. When a session is in Install mode, all Registry entries created during that session are shadowed under HKLM\Software\Microsoft\Windows NT\ CurrentVersion\Terminal Server\Install. Any edits that an application makes to HKCU or HKLM are copied to HKLM\Software\Microsoft\Windows NT\CurrentVersion\Terminal Server\Install\Machine. You don't have to know all this to install applications. What you *do* have to know is that when the session is in Execute mode, if an application attempts to read an HKCU Registry entry that doesn't exist, Terminal Services will look in HKLM\Software\Microsoft\Windows NT\CurrentVersion\Terminal Server\Install for the missing key. If the key is there, Terminal Services will copy it and its subkeys to the appropriate location under HKCU and copy any INI files or user-specific DLLs to the user's home directory. For users without home directories, the files go to their profile folder. In short, the server makes the basic settings for each application machine specific, then copies these base settings into the user Registry entries so that the user can customize the application. Notice that this doesn't mean the application keeps returning to its pristine state every time the user runs it—the keys are only copied from their Install mode location to their user location if the keys don't already exist under HKCU.

NOTE   Unfortunately, there's no way to spoof a user's identity to install an application for an individual while logged in with another account (if you logged in as Administrator and wanted to install an application for a particular user, for example). Nor can you specify a subset of users who should have access to a particular application. If you only want some people to use an application stored on a terminal server, the easiest way to manage that is to limit the people allowed to use that server.

So how do you put the server into Install mode? On a terminal server, it's easy: If you attempt to install an application from its Setup program (named `Setup.exe`) without using the Add/Remove Programs applet, the installation will fail, and the server will nag you to run the Add/Remove Programs applet to install applications on a terminal server. You cannot install an application for a single user if you've set up the server to be an application server.

NOTE   Some applications allow you to bypass Add/Remove Programs because the Setup program isn't named `Setup.exe`. For these applications, you'll need to make sure that you put the server into Install Mode manually, either by running Add/Remove Programs or by using the change user command (discussed below).

When the application's Setup program finishes running, you'll go back to the wizard, which will prompt you to click the Next button. Finally, you'll see a dire-looking dialog box (see Figure 16.32) telling you to click the Finish or Cancel buttons when the installation process is complete, but warning you in capital letters not to do so *until* the installation is complete. Clicking Finish or Cancel returns the session to Execute mode.

FIGURE 16.32

Don't click the Finish button until the application is completely installed, or all the settings won't get copied.

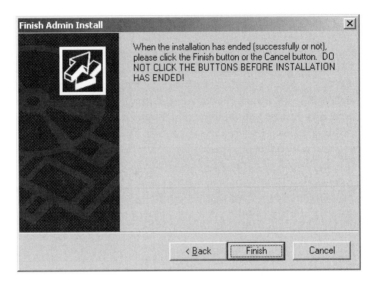

Install mode's usefulness isn't limited to the installation process. Using application compatibility scripts or hand tuning, you can use Install mode to configure an application with general settings to apply to all users. Outside of Add/Remove Programs, you can put a session into Install mode with the change user command-line utility. change user has three options:

◆ /execute, the default, in which applications install in single-user mode

◆ /install, used to put the session into Install mode so that applications will be available to all users

◆ /query, which reports the mode that the session is in, like this:

```
Application EXECUTE mode is enabled.
```

So, before running a setup program, open a command prompt and type **change user /install**. This will cause the server to shadow new Registry entries, as I described earlier, so that they'll be copied to each user's personal Registry settings as the user runs the application for the first time. Just bear in mind that *any* changes you make to an application while in Install mode will be copied to that Registry key and therefore apply to all users using the application for the first time.

USING APPLICATION COMPATIBILITY SCRIPTS

Given that just about all of the applications the terminal server users will be running were originally designed for a single-user environment, many applications require a little manipulation to get them optimized for a multiuser system. Server 2003 includes application compatibility scripts for some applications. You can find the scripts for the applications in `%systemroot%\Application Compatibility Scripts\Install`. Server 2003 comes with three of them: one for Eudora 4, one for Outlook 98, and one for Visual Studio 6.

These scripts are designed to customize the application's setup to be appropriate for terminal server users, first setting up the command environment, then making sure that the session is in Install mode, checking the Registry for evidence of the application to be configured, and finally editing the Registry as needed. The contents of the scripts vary based on the application, but generally speaking, they do things like turn off processor-intensive features, add multiuser support to the application, or set user-specific application directories for applications that need them.

To use the scripts, just run them right after you install the application they customize, before anyone has had a chance to use the application. For example, when you run the script for Outlook 98, Notepad will open and display the `RootDrv2.cmd` file, prompting you to pick a drive letter for the customized installation to use. Provide a drive letter, save the file, and close Notepad, and the script will run. Log out and log back in, and the new settings will be applied.

TIP   To make sure that no one tries to use the application before you've run the compatibility script, disable the RDP connection while finalizing the application setup.

You're not limited to using the default settings included in these scripts. To edit one of them, right-click the script's icon and choose Edit from the context menu to open the file in Notepad. You'll need to be familiar with the NT command-line tools to do this.

What if your application doesn't have a script made for it? The `Templates` folder in the `Install` directory includes KEY files (you can open these in Notepad as well) that show you where each Registry entry for application settings is located and what the values should be. Based on this information and using an existing CMD file for a template, you can use the Windows scripting language to create a new script. Alternatively, you can manually edit the user settings from the application interface while the session is in Install mode, as described in the later section "Hand-Tuning Applications."

INSTALLING MULTIUSER-ENABLED APPLICATIONS

As Terminal Services becomes more widespread, it's probable that more applications will come with multiuser installation packages. Microsoft Office 2000 is one that presently does. If you try to run the normal installation program on a terminal server, you'll see a nag screen telling you that you can't do that and prompting you to use the installation files provided with the Office 2000 Resource Kit:

1. First, get the terminal server transform file, `TermSrvr.mst`, and place it in an accessible location for the installation. You can obtain the transform file from the `\ORK\PFiles\ORKTools\Toolbox\Tools\TermSrvr` folder of the Office 2000 Resource Kit CD, or in `\Program Files\ORKtools\Toolbox\Terminal Server Tools` if you installed the Resource Kit.

2. Install Office Disc 1 on the Terminal Server computer.

3. In the Control Panel, double-click Add/Remove Programs, click Add New Programs, and then click CD or Floppy. Click Next, then click Browse, and then move to the root folder of the installation CD and select `Setup.exe`. Click Open to add `Setup.exe` to the Run Installation Program box.

4. Don't run it yet. On the command line, append the following command after `Setup.exe`, separated by a space: `TRANSFORMS=path\TermSrvr.mst`, where *path* is the location where you copied `TermSrvr.mst`.

5. From here, all goes as expected. In successive windows of the installation wizard, provide your customer information and accept the EULA, then choose Install Now. When you see a message telling you that the installation completed successfully, click OK, click Next, and then click Finish.

HAND-TUNING APPLICATIONS

If you don't need to edit many per-application settings, it might be simpler to make the changes from the user interface while in Install mode, rather than trying to create a new compatibility script. You can also manually edit applications that *have* compatibility scripts but don't include some settings that you need to configure.

Turn Off Processor- and Bandwidth-Stressing Features

Terminal servers are designed to squeeze every last bit of juice out of system resources so that nothing is wasted. Therefore, they're often stressed—they're *supposed* to be stressed. Given that, don't waste processor cycles on producing effects that don't necessarily add any real content to the end product, and don't waste network bandwidth on sending those useless effects to the client.

Provide Path Information

Many applications have settings for file locations—places to save files to, places to open files from, template locations, and so forth. However, those locations will often be different for different users. To make sure that file locations for each user are correct, enter a drive letter—and then map that drive letter to different locations for each user. For example, the Save As location for all Word users could be H:, but H: would direct each user to their private home directory.

USING THE REGISTRY TO TUNE APPLICATIONS

Of course, if an application doesn't have a setting in its interface, you can't use Install mode to tune that setting. However, all is not necessarily lost. You can edit some application settings directly within the Registry, in `HKLM\Software\Microsoft\Windows NT\CurrentVersion\Terminal Server\ Compatibility\Applications`. (Obligatory warning follows.)

WARNING *Be careful when editing the Registry. The Registry Editor has no Undo feature, and will not tell you if you give a meaningless value to an entry. Back up the Registry before you edit it, and remember that a mistyped entry in the wrong place can wipe out needed information or render the server unbootable.*

More specifically, keep the following in mind:

◆ When editing value data, notice whether the values are shown in hex, decimal, or binary. When you're editing string values, you can choose to display them in any of those formats. Just be sure that you're entering the data in the chosen format. 15 decimal is F hex, but 15 hex is 21 decimal. You can guess how mixing up hex and decimal could get very ugly very quickly.

◆ If you're replacing a key (and, if you try out these hacks, you will be), be sure that the key that's selected is the one you want to replace. Restoring a key deletes all the present information in the key and replaces it with what's in the restored key. For example, say that you want to replace the contents of the `MSOFFICE` key that's a subkey of `Applications`. If you have `Applications` selected when you restore the saved REG file, you will wipe out every subkey of `Applications` and replace it with the information that should have gone into `MSOFFICE`.

◆ Never run a REG file unless you know exactly what it contains and what it will do. Executing a REG file imports the contents of that file into the Registry—permanently. There is no Undo feature.

Now that you're thoroughly intimidated, read on to see how to make your applications play well with others and call you by your name.

Bad! Bad Application! Go to Sleep! Reducing Demands of Windows Applications

Even if you turn off processor-hogging effects, some applications are just more cycle-hungry than others. In a terminal server environment, this is a Bad Thing. Not only do processor-sucking applications themselves under perform in a multiuser environment because they're contending with other applications, but they hurt other applications' performance by denying them cycles. You can edit the Registry to make the server keep a closer eye on Windows application management, denying processor cycles to applications that use too many, known internally as Bad Applications. Doing so will give more cycles to the other applications that the processor-sucker was starving, but will also make the errant application less responsive itself.

To make the edit, open the Registry Editor and turn to the key `HKLM\Software\Microsoft\ Windows NT\CurrentVersion\Terminal Server\Compatibility\Applications`. As you can see in Figure 16.33, within the `Applications` key, you'll see a long list of keys for available applications.

FIGURE 16.33

The contents of the **Applications** subkey

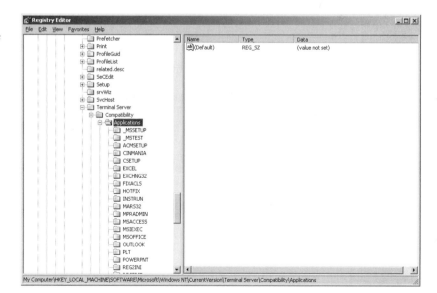

First, check to see whether the application you want to configure is already listed; if it is, then a key with the name of the application will be present. If the key exists, then open it and look at the values within it, which are described in Table 16.7.

TABLE 16.7: BAD APPLICATION REGISTRY VALUES

VALUE NAME	DESCRIPTION	DEFAULT VALUE
FirstCountMsgQPeeks-SleepBadApp	Number of times that the application will query the message queue before the server decides the application is a Bad Application. The lower this value, the sooner the server will decide that the application is bad, and the more quickly the other two values will apply.	0xf (15 decimal)
MsgQBadAppSleepTime-InMillisec	The number of milliseconds that a suspended application will be denied processor cycles. The higher this value is, the longer the application will sleep.	0
NthCountMsgQPeeks-SleepBadApp	The number of times that a Bad Application can query the message queue before the server will put it to sleep again. The lower this number, the more often the misbehaving application will go to sleep.	0x5 (5 decimal)
Flags	Describes the type of application to which these settings apply. Your options are 0x4 for Win16 applications, 0x8 for Win32 applications, or 0xc for both types.	0x8 (Win32 only)

To make your edits in the dialog box shown in Figure 16.34, double-click the value data to edit the values, bearing in mind the information I gave you about what those edits will do. Make sure you've set the flags properly according to whether the application you're editing is a 16-bit or 32-bit application, and don't forget to notice whether you're making changes in hex or decimal.

FIGURE 16.34

Edit string values to set the Bad Application parameters you want.

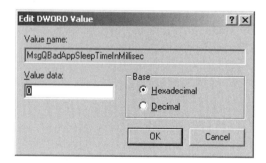

The settings will take effect when you next open the application. Because you edited a key in HKLM, the changes will apply to all instances of the application running on this terminal server.

Making Applications Reference Usernames

Windows Terminal Server, and terminal sessions running on early betas of Win2K Server, had a little problem when it came to running WinChat, the graphical chat application that comes with Windows. Because WinChat referenced computers, not users, you couldn't use it from a terminal server session to talk to someone running another terminal session. Try to connect to someone, and you'd see a list of computers to choose from. Chat sessions with yourself get dull, so that made WinChat pretty well useless from terminal sessions.

The intrepid user of Terminal Services is not foiled by such petty machinations, however. You could use to make the application reference usernames instead of computer names. In `HKLM\Software\Microsoft\Windows NT\CurrentVersion\Terminal Server\Compatibility\Applications`, where you just edited the Bad Application settings, there's a value for Flags, which in the previous section was 8 or c, signifying that the settings applied either to a Win32 application or to both Win16 and Win32 applications.

TIP *To apply more than one flag to an application, add together the value of all the flags you want to use and make that the value of the Flags entry.*

You can apply several other compatibility flags to Flags with varying results. One flag tells the server to make the application return the version number; another tells it to make the application use the system root directory instead of the user's system directory. For our purposes, the important value is 0x10 (that is, 10 hex), which tells an application to look for users by their usernames, not their computer names. So, you could edit the value of Flags for the `WINCHAT` key to 18, telling the server, "Not only is this a Win32 application, but it should reference usernames, not computer names." No reboot is necessary; just restart WinChat. It wouldn't display usernames—that would have been handy, but no dice—but if you plug a username into the browse function, it would find that user and place the call.

You're probably thinking that I'm going to tell you that Microsoft fixed this problem. In a way, you would be correct: You will no longer have problems running WinChat in a terminal server session and only being able to reference computers. This is because Microsoft decided there was no point in having a messaging application that "didn't work" from terminal server sessions available to those sessions. Now, if you attempt to run WinChat from a terminal session on a server running Windows 2000 or Server 2003, you get an error message telling you that that application can't be used from a terminal server remote session. Well, that's *one* way to cut down on support calls, I suppose.

The good news is that this hack will still work if you have any other applications that reference computer names instead of usernames—just edit that application's key as I described here. You just can't use it any longer to fix WinChat.

Managing Terminal Sessions

Thus far, you've configured client settings and set up applications. Everyone's happily typing away in their sessions. But what if they're not so happy? Terminal Services management capabilities allow you to keep tabs on what's happening on the terminal server. These capabilities work both from the GUI and from the command line.

Introducing Command-Line Tools

Terminal Services has some excellent GUI tools that make it easy to quickly get used to working with the service. That GUI can't do everything, however, and what it can do it can't always do *quickly*. Thus, the command-line tools that allow you to manage terminal sessions come in handy when it's time to make batch files—or just to do something quickly without taking the time to hunt down the right tool or part of the MMC.

There are far too many options to go into complete detail about every one of the command-line tools listed in Table 16.8, but the following sections should help you get an idea of how you can manipulate Terminal Services from the command line and the graphical administration tool. I already discussed some of these—flattemp and tsprof, for two—earlier in this chapter.

TIP To see a complete list of all options for a command, type its name and /? at the command line.

TABLE 16.8: SUPPORTED TERMINAL SERVICES UTILITIES

COMMAND	FUNCTION
change logon	Temporarily disables logons to a terminal server.
change port	Changes or displays COM port mappings for MS-DOS program compatibility. For example, you could use this utility to map one port to another one so that data sent to the first would actually go to the second.
change user	Flips between Execute mode and Install mode.
cprofile	Removes unnecessary files from a user profile. You can only run this tool on profiles not currently being used.
dbgtrace	Enables or disables debug tracing.
flattemp	Enables or disables redirected temporary directories, which you can use to send TMP files to a location other than the default.
logoff	Ends a client session specified by session name or Session ID, either on the local terminal server or on one specified.
msg	Sends a message to one or more clients.
query process	Displays information about processes.
query session	Displays information about a terminal server session.
query termserver	Lists the available application terminal servers on the network.
query user	Displays information about users logged on to the system.
register	Registers applications to execute in a system or user global context on the computer.
reset	Resets (ends) the specified terminal session.

Continued on next page

TABLE 16.8: SUPPORTED TERMINAL SERVICES UTILITIES *(continued)*

COMMAND	FUNCTION
shadow	Monitors another user's session. Cannot be executed from the console and cannot shadow the console. Equivalent to the graphical remote control tools.
tscon	Connects to another existing terminal server session.
tsdiscon	Disconnects from a terminal server session.
tskill	Terminates a process, identified by name or by Process ID.
tsprof	Copies the user configuration and changes the profile path.
tsshutdn	Shuts down a terminal server.

Those who went straight from TSE to Server 2003 will notice that their tools are here, but many of the command names have changed. The utilities still provide the same functions as the commands in TSE, but you'll have to learn new names for most of them.

Using the Terminal Services Manager

To help you keep track of who's using the terminal server, what processes they're running, and the status of their connections, you'll use the Terminal Services Manager, found in the Administrative Tools program group and shown in Figure 16.35.

FIGURE 16.35

The Terminal Services Manager tool

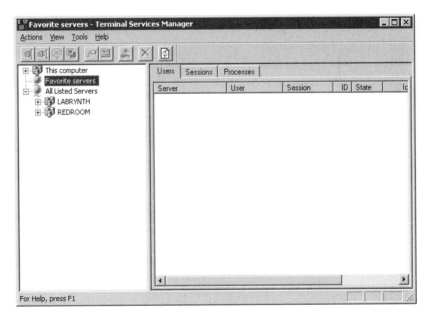

The left pane shows all domains in the network and all terminal servers within those domains. (You can use this tool to manage any terminal server that's listed; you don't need to be physically at that console.) The right pane's content depends on what's selected: If it's the domain or the entire network, then all current connections to that server (active or disconnected) and the name of the server hosting them are displayed; if it's a terminal server, then all current connections to that server are displayed; if it's a username, then all the processes running in that user's context, or information about the user session, are displayed. Notice also that the right pane is tabbed, with the contents of the tabs depending on whether you've got a domain, server, or user selected on the left. Broadly speaking, you use the administration tool to get information about:

- Users, including what their Session IDs are, what applications they're running, and what server they're using

- Sessions, including what the ID of that session is, what's running in that session, what the status of the session is, how long the client has been logged in, and information about the computer the client is logged in from (IP address, RDP version, and so forth)

- Processes, including the Process IDs and the executable files (*images*) with which these processes are associated

NOTE   *It's not hard to figure out what information you're looking at—a short period of poking around will teach you where everything is. More important is the question of what you can do with this tool. In the following example, I'll show you how to use the management tools to see what's running on the server, send messages to people on the server, terminate remote processes, and close user sessions. For this example, I'll refer to a fictional game called TSQUAKE, a Terminal Services–compliant version of Quake.*

GATHERING INFORMATION

Who's playing TSQUAKE again?

To find out, you'll need to know who's logged in to the server or servers and what processes are running in their sessions. You can use both the Terminal Services Manager and the command line to get this data.

From the GUI, select the terminal server or domain for which you want information. In the right pane, three tabs will become visible: one listing users currently logged in to the terminal server, one showing the current active and disconnected sessions, and one showing the processes currently running on the terminal server.

Flip to the Processes tab associated with the domain (see Figure 16.36) to see a complete list of all processes running in the domain, the server they're running on, the session they're in, and the name of the user who owns that session. This screen will also show the Process ID (PID), which will come in handy when it comes time to terminate processes.

You can get more than just process information from this screen. Select a terminal server in the left pane. From the tabs that appear on the right, you can find the information described in Table 16.9.

FIGURE 16.36

Viewing processes
running on a
terminal server

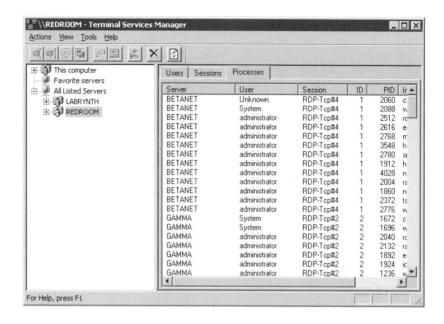

TABLE 16.9: FINDING INFORMATION IN THE TERMINAL SERVICES MANAGER

DATA TYPE	TAB
Client computer name or IP address	Sessions
Image names for processes	Processes
Process IDs	Processes
Protocol used for each session	Sessions
Session idle time	Users
Session IDs associated with processes	Processes
Session status	Users, Sessions
User logon time	Users, Sessions
Username associated with processes	Processes
User Session IDs	Users, Sessions

Everything you need to find out—which user and which PID is associated with which session, and
how busy that session is—is here. If you use the command-line `query` utility, you can get much the
same information that you can from the Terminal Services Manager tool, but you have to do it a piece

at a time. From the command line, there's no way to retrieve a list of all processes running in a domain or across all domains, so first you'll have to isolate the terminal server. For example, to see a complete list of all terminal servers in the current domain, type **query termserv**. The server will return a complete list of all terminal servers in the domain, like this:

```
Known Terminal servers
-----------
BETANET
GAMMA
TERMSERV
-----------
```

Need the list from another domain? Add the domain name you're retrieving the list from to the command, like this:

```
query termserv /domain:domainname
```

You'll get the same output, customized for the domain you specified.

Once you've got the name of the server you need to check out, look for TSQUAKE by querying for processes, like this:

```
query process
```

The server will return a list of all user-launched processes running in the current session (even if that session is the console), as shown:

```
   USERNAME        SESSIONNAME  ID    PID IMAGE
>administrator     console       0   1152 explorer.exe
>administrator     console       0   1348 osa.exe
>administrator     console       0   1360 findfast.exe
>administrator     console       0    532 infoview.exe
>administrator     console       0   2052 depends.exe
>administrator     console       0   2172 cmd.exe
>administrator     console       0    764 taskmgr.exe
>administrator     console       0   1256 tsadmin.exe
>administrator     console       0   1636 mmc.exe
>administrator     console       0   1500 winword.exe
>administrator     console       0   2092 regedit.exe
>administrator     console       0   1776 query.exe
>administrator     console       0   1652 qprocess.exe
```

To query the process list for a different user, add that person's username to the command, like this:

```
query process gertrude
```

TIP *You can also list processes associated with a particular session name or Session ID, although for most purposes I find it easier to reference usernames. You'll use the Session ID to determine if a user has more than one session open.*

Okay, but what you really want is a list of everyone who's goofing off and using up processor cycles. Although you can't get a list of all processes running in a single domain or across domains, you can retrieve a list of all users with a particular process running in their sessions, like this:

```
C:\>query process winword.exe
 USERNAME        SESSIONNAME    ID   PID IMAGE
>administrator   console         0  1500 winword.exe
 christa         rdp-tcp#1       1  1400 winword.exe
```

Use this command to track down those TSQUAKE users.

SENDING MESSAGES

Once you've got your list of people running TSQUAKE, you can let them know that they're caught. From both the GUI and the command line, you can send messages to a single person, to multiple people, and even across domains.

From the left pane of the Terminal Services Manager tool, select the terminal server the people are using. In the right, select the people to whom you want to send a message (Ctrl+click to select multiple usernames). From the Actions menu, choose Send Message to open the dialog box shown in Figure 16.37. Click OK, and the message will instantly pop up on the screen of everyone you included on the recipient list.

FIGURE 16.37

Sending a message to users

You can also send messages from the command line with the msg utility. This works much like msg did in single-user Windows, with one exception: messages sent to a username will be sent to all instances of that name, not just one. This is so that a person running multiple sessions will be sure to get their message.

msg has lots of options. Its basic syntax looks like this:

```
msg {identifier}[/SERVER:servername] [/TIME:sec] [/v] [/w] [message]
```

The *identifier* can be a username, Session ID, session name, or a filename containing an ASCII list of all users to whom the message should go. The /TIME parameter doesn't delay the message; rather, it's a time-out period that cooperates with the /w switch that waits for user response before giving control of the command prompt back to the message's sender.

NOTE *Like the other command-line utilities,* msg *operates on the server you're connected to unless you specify otherwise.*

To send a message to a single user, run `msg` like this:

```
msg gertrude Gertrude, please close TSQUAKE. You're wasting processor time.
```

If you want some kind of record that Gertrude saw the message—or at least clicked OK—use the /v (for "verbose") switch as follows:

```
msg gertrude /v Gertrude, I mean it. Close the game.
```

You'll see output like the following:

```
Sending message to session RDP-Tcp#1, display time 60
Timeout on message to session RDP-Tcp#1 before user response
```

To send a message to everyone logged in to that terminal server, use an asterisk, like so:

```
msg * Hey, everyone–Gertrude's got enough free time to play TSQUAKE. Anyone got
   anything for her to do?
```

Alternatively, send a message to a preset group by typing all recipient names into a Notepad file and saving it, then referencing the file like this:

```
msg @users Hey, everyone–Gertrude has enough free time to play TSQUAKE. Anyone got
   anything for her to do?
```

The only catch to sending messages to multiple users is that if you add the /w option, `msg` works sequentially. That is, it will send the message to the first person in the list (going in order of Session ID) and wait for either a response or a time-out before sending the message to the second person in the list.

TERMINATING APPLICATIONS

Gertrude and the other TSQUAKE players aren't paying attention to your pleas. Time to get tough and terminate the application. Every instance of TSQUAKE that you close will exit immediately, with no warning to the user and no chance to save data.

NOTE *Before I get into this, let me distinguish again between terminating and resetting. Both options close applications with no warning, but single processes are terminated and entire sessions are reset.*

To kill a single application from the GUI, select the server or domain in the left pane and turn to the Processes tab in the right. All running processes will appear here, identified by the name of the server they're running on, who's got them open, the PIDs of the processes, and other relevant information. As elsewhere, you can Ctrl+click to select multiple processes. When every process to be terminated is selected, right-click and choose End Process from the context menu (it's the only option). The selected applications will close instantly.

You can also terminate applications from the command line. Just be careful. This procedure is open to error, and you will not make people happy if you accidentally close the wrong process and lose all their data.

The command to kill terminal server applications is `tskill`, related to the `kill` command that appeared for the first time in NT 3.5's Resource Kit and which stops an application by killing its process. Like the Terminate menu command, `tskill` will stop an application as soon as it's executed, with no time allowed for saving data or other tasks. It's very intrusive, so you should only use it when there's simply no other way of getting an application to stop.

The syntax of `tskill` is as follows:

```
tskill processid | processname [/SERVER:servername] [/ID:sessionid | /a] [/v]
```

Notice that you can reference a process either by its name or its Process ID. The former is easier and necessary if you're using the `/a` switch to close all instances of an application on the terminal server. The latter is necessary if you're only trying to close specific instances of the application, perhaps leaving untouched the instance of TSQUAKE that your boss has open.

So, to kill all instances of TSQUAKE running on the currently selected server, you type:

`tskill tsquake.exe /a`

To kill only selected instances, get the PID by running `query process` or `query user` and plug it in, like this:

`tskill 1875`

Sadly, you can't list several PIDs at once to kill, so if you need to pick and choose processes without killing all instances, you'll need to terminate instances of a process one at a time.

TIP   Although you need to supply the executable extension with `query process`, *the command won't work if you supply the extension with* `tskill`. *So, it's* **`query process tsquake.exe`**, *but* **`tskill tsquake`**.

TAKING CONTROL OF USER SESSIONS

Sometimes, the best plan isn't to just shut down applications from the terminal server. Instead, you can take control of a user session and see what they're doing (as opposed to listing processes, which just tells you what processes are active in the context of a given session). This can be especially helpful for troubleshooting purposes, such as if Gertrude says she didn't mean to run TSQUAKE but couldn't figure out how to shut it down once she had it running. Taking remote control of the session gives you the same degree of control that you'd have if logged on as that user.

You can remotely control a user's session in one of two ways: from the Terminal Services Manager or from the command line.

TIP   You can only take remote control of a terminal server session from another terminal server session, not from the console. The remote control option in the Terminal Services Manager and the `shadow` *command-line utility won't work from the console.*

To use the GUI, start a terminal server session, logging in with an account with Administrator privileges. From within the session, start the Terminal Services Manager. Select a terminal server in the left pane and switch to the Users tab so that user sessions are showing. Find the session you want to shadow, and choose Remote Control from the Actions menu. A dialog box like the one shown in Figure 16.38 will prompt you for the hotkey combination you want to use to end remote control of your own session (so you can get back to the original session).

If the user session is configured to require user permission for control, then a dialog box will appear on the screen, letting the user know that someone has requested permission to control their session. If they permit the control, then you're in charge of their session without further ado. If they don't permit the control, then you'll see an error message telling you that you couldn't get permission to control the session.

FIGURE 16.38

Choose a hot key combination to toggle back to your original session.

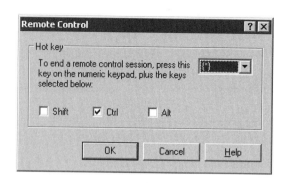

NOTE *The degree of control you have over a user's session that you're remotely controlling depends on the settings in the user's account settings.*

The command-line utility for taking remote control of a user session is called `shadow`, after the WinFrame and MetaFrame name for remote control. Its syntax is as follows:

```
shadow {sessionname | sessionid} [/SERVER:servername] [/v]
```

To use it, start a terminal services session with administrative privileges. Open the command prompt and run **query user *username*** or **query session *username*** to find the Session ID or session name of the user whose session you want to shadow. You can't shadow based on *username*, so you'll need this information even if you know the account name of the person whose session you're shadowing.

If shadowing a session on the same terminal server that you're logged in to, the command syntax for shadowing Session ID 1 is as follows:

```
shadow 1
```

If that session requires user permission to be remotely controlled, then you'll see the following message while your session waits for permission to take over the remote one:

```
Your session may appear frozen while the remote control approval is being negotiated.
Please wait...
```

Once you have permission, you're in, just as you would be when using the GUI remote control option. The session must have someone logged in at the time—you cannot shadow a disconnected session.

The only tricky part to shadowing from the command prompt is that you had best do it at least once from the GUI before trying the command-line utility. The `shadow` command does not prompt you for a hotkey combination to end remote control and return to your session. It will use the one defined for the GUI, so if you know what that hotkey combination is, you can use it. Just make sure you know how to return to your own session from the remote control.

ENDING—OR PREVENTING—USER SESSIONS

That's it—Gertrude's kicked off the server until she can learn to stop using it incorrectly.

If you want to stop an entire terminal session, not just a single process within it, you can either disconnect or reset the connection. Disconnecting, you recall, cuts the user off from the session (although there's normally nothing to keep a user from reconnecting), but leaves all applications running and data in memory. When the user reconnects to a session they were disconnected from, then they're right back where they left off. A reset connection, in contrast, closes all applications the person had open and ends the session without saving any changes to the user profile. Disconnected sessions still use some system resources, albeit not much because their data will eventually be paged to disk and they won't have new user input to process. Reset sessions use no resources.

To disconnect or reset a session from the Terminal Services Manager tool, select it in the left pane and choose Reset or Disconnect from the Action menu. You'll see a dialog box warning you that the session will be disconnected or reset; click OK, and the selected session or sessions will be ended.

You can also end user sessions from the command line with the `tsdiscon` and `reset session` commands. The syntax for `tsdiscon` is as follows:

```
tsdiscon [sessionid | sessionname] [/SERVER:servername] [/v]
```

Once again, you can choose to identify sessions to close by session name or Session ID. To find out both, run `query session` to get output like the following:

```
SESSIONNAME   USERNAME       ID  STATE   TYPE   DEVICE
>console      Administrator  0   active  wdcon
 rdp-tcp      65537              listen  rdpwd
 rdp-tcp#2    Christa        2   active  rdpwd
                             1   idle
                             3   idle
```

Find the session name or ID you want, and plug it into the `tsdiscon` command like this: **tsdiscon 2**. Once you've pressed the Enter key, the user of the selected session sees a message, "Terminal Server has ended the connection," and is given a Close button to push.

TIP   *I find it easiest to reference Session IDs. You always have to use a number—you can't choose to disconnect a session attached to a particular username—so you might as well choose the shortest identifier you can get away with.*

The syntax for resetting a session is similar to that used for disconnecting it:

```
reset session {sessionname | sessionid} [/SERVER:servername] [/v]
```

Once again, the user will see a dialog box telling them that Terminal Server ended the connection and prompting them to close.

What if you'd like to keep people off the terminal server altogether, perhaps while you're installing new applications on it? If no one's yet connected, you can disable the RDP protocol from the Terminal Services Configuration tool located in the Administrative Tools program group. Right-click the RDP protocol, and from the pop-up menu that appears, choose All Tasks/Disable Connection.

WARNING   *If you disable the connection from the Terminal Services Configuration tool, you'll reset any existing sessions.*

If you've reset all connections in preparation for shutting down the server, you can also shut down the server without going to the console. tsshutdn's syntax is as follows:

```
tsshutdn [wait_time] [/SERVER:servername] [/REBOOT] [/POWERDOWN]
    [/DELAY:logoffdelay] [/v]
```

Most of these options are what they appear to be. *wait_time* specifies the amount of time (in seconds) until the server is shut down, and *servername* specifies a server if you don't want to shut down the one you're currently logged in to. /REBOOT reboots the server, and /POWERDOWN shuts it down if the server has Advanced Power Management drivers (if not, the server shuts down all server processes and displays the Click to Restart message).

TIP *Use* tsshutdn *to circumvent the nag screen asking you why you want to shut down a perfectly good server. This works on any Server 2003, not just terminal servers.*

So, for example, you could combine tsshutdn and msg to tell everyone that the server's going to be rebooted in five minutes. First, send the following message:

Msg * The server will go down in 5 minutes for maintenance. Please log out.

Second, run the tshutdn command with the following parameters:

```
tshutdn 300 /reboot
```

NOTE *Any dialog boxes that require user response (for example, one asking you if you want to save changes to a MMC snap-in that you edited) will want your response—they won't just go away without a response. Therefore, if using* tsshutdn *you must respond to those dialog boxes before the* tshutdn *timeout period. Otherwise,* tsshutdn *will respond that the shutdown operation completed successfully, but the server will still be running.*

Say, however, that you don't want to shut down the server. You just want to keep any new sessions from starting. To disable the protocol for new sessions without disturbing the ones already in place, you'll need to use the change logon command utility. Its syntax is as follows:

```
change logon {/QUERY | /ENABLE | /DISABLE}
    /QUERY    Query current terminal session login mode.
    /ENABLE   Enable user login from terminal sessions.
    /DISABLE  Disable user login from terminal sessions.
```

Typing **change logon /disable** prevents any further connections from being made until you reenable the protocol. Anyone who tries to connect will see an error message telling them that remote logins are currently disabled. Disabling RDP does not, obviously, affect the console session as it's not dependent on RDP. As I mentioned earlier, you'll need to disable logins if you want to keep people off the terminal server, as the service itself does not shut off.

Using Remote Administration Mode

This chapter is generally about how to use Terminal Services to create application servers, but as I've said, Terminal Services gives you a handy way of accessing *any* server that can accept incoming RDP connections. If you've never used Terminal Services for remote management and you've just read this chapter about how to set up an application server, you may have some questions about how Remote Administration mode works and what you can do with it, so let's address those now.

Enabling Remote Administration

Although Terminal Services is installed by default, for security reasons the server will not accept incoming connections by default. To enable them, open the Control Panel and turn to the Remote tab of the System applet (see Figure 16.39).

FIGURE 16.39

You must enable Remote Desktop to permit incoming connections.

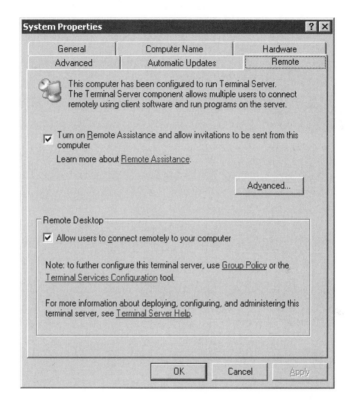

NOTE *If using a firewall to secure servers, you'll need to open port 3389. If you're using Server 2003's Internet Connection Firewall, this means opening the Remote Connection port (available from the Settings button on the Advanced tab of the connection's properties sheet).*

Once you've done that and ensured that the RDP port is open for the network connection, the server can accept incoming connections.

Connecting to Remote Servers Using the Remote Desktops Tool

The Remote Desktop Connection client comes preinstalled on Server 2003, but this isn't the best tool for server administration unless you normally only interact with one server at a time. Instead, try the Remote Desktops tool in the Administrative Tools section of the Start menu. Using this tool, you can connect to multiple servers and flip back and forth between them without having to maximize and minimize session windows. This tool works for both Windows 2000 and Server 2003 servers—the servers just have to have Terminal Services installed and be accepting incoming connections.

When you first open Remote Desktops, it won't have any servers in it—just a Remote Desktops icon. To create a connection, right-click this icon and choose Add New Connection from the context menu. You'll open the dialog box in Figure 16.40.

FIGURE 16.40

Adding a new
Remote Desktops
connection

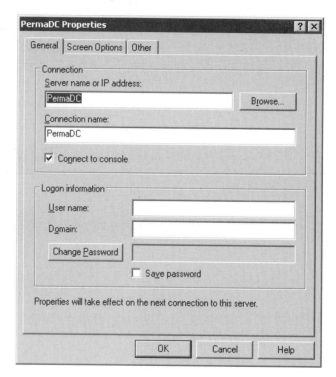

There's an annoying bug here (or feature—I suppose it depends on your outlook). See that Browse button in Figure 16.40? It looks like you can browse for servers to connect to, doesn't it? Well, you can... but the only servers that it will return are application servers (and Windows 2000 servers in remote administration mode, if you have any). Server 2003 computers using Remote Administration will not appear. However, you can connect to them by typing their names or IP addresses—you just can't browse for them.

Notice that you can connect to the console of the server, both for Server 2003 computers and Windows 2000 computers. This is helpful if you're doing something that requires interacting with the console directly—for example, running software that sends messages to the console, not to sessions. If you connect to a server's console session, you'll lock the local console session so that two people aren't interacting with it at once.

Finally, notice that you can provide a name and password to use when connecting to the remote computer. When you're finished setting up the connection, click OK to save the connection. The new connection will appear in Remote Desktops as in Figure 16.41. (I've added a couple of additional connections to show you what they look like.) To launch the connection, right-click a server's icon in the left pane and choose Connect. To toggle between multiple open sessions, just click the appropriate server's icon in the left pane.

FIGURE 16.41

You can manage several servers at once using the Remote Desktops tool.

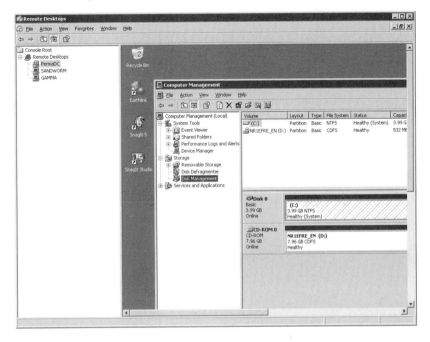

TIP   The display for Remote Desktops is currently a little buggy and does not resize the terminal session window when you resize the display pane or adjust its resolution to fit the display window. I find that I get the best display if I maximize the Remote Desktops tool and the right display pane before launching a connection.

To end a session, either disconnect or log out as you would if using Remote Desktop Connection, or right-click a server's icon and choose Disconnect. Disconnecting, once again, does not completely close a terminal session. Disconnected sessions count toward the two concurrent administrative logins permitted.

Questions about Using Remote Administration

You've connected... but how does this work? Read on.

HOW MUCH WILL REMOTE ADMINISTRATION MODE AFFECT SERVER PERFORMANCE?

You're probably aware that a terminal server requires a lot of horsepower to support all those clients and may be wondering whether Remote Administration mode is going to require you to seriously beef up your ordinary servers. Nope. Application servers require so much memory because many people are using them at once, not because the service itself is particularly power-hungry. The total memory requirements for running Terminal Services in Remote Administration mode are a little less than 2.5MB of RAM. In other words, if the server can do what it's supposed to do, unless it's very stressed, remote administration shouldn't faze it.

HOW MANY PEOPLE CAN LOG IN TO THE SERVER?

When you install Terminal Services into this mode, you're permitting up to two simultaneous administrative connections to the terminal server. (Anyone whose account does not have administrative privileges on the domain will be denied access to the server, so you don't have to worry about Joe User logging into the Web server if he doesn't have an administrative account.) The licenses for these connections are built in, so you don't need additional licenses for server management—or a Terminal Services license manager—if you're only using Terminal Services for this purpose.

CAN I RUN ANY MANAGEMENT TOOL FROM A TERMINAL SESSION?

Sort of Microsoft notes several tools that won't work in a terminal session and that you must operate from the console. Microsoft SQL Server 6.5 and 7 PerfMon counters cannot be accessed from a remote session (this is fine; you really don't want to be running System Monitor from an RDP session anyway—too many graphical updates) and must be viewed from the console. Also, Pervasive SQL v7 has a namespace problem that prevents the tool from installing properly from a terminal session. Otherwise, though, most tools will work in a remote session. With the faster RDP connections available today, even fairly graphically intense management tools are working pretty well.

Chapter 17

TCP/IP Server Services (IIS, NNTP, Telnet, SMTP, POP3, and FTP)

UNLESS YOU'VE BEEN LIVING in a cave somewhere for the past five years, you're undoubtedly aware that the Internet is becoming a major part of the way that the world works. Notice I said world, not just companies. With each passing day, the Internet is having more and more of an impact on the daily lives of countless people. The amount of information available to anyone, anywhere, at any time is simply mind boggling, and this trend is only going to continue to grow in the future.

Not one to miss out on such a significant part of people's lives, Microsoft is doing everything that they can to be a part of this revolution. While some of their tactics might be questionable—such as tying their Internet Explorer browser directly in with their most recent operating systems—other approaches are quite beneficial. The most significant benefit is the inclusion of the latest version of Internet Information Services (IIS) with the base Windows Server 2003 operating system.

Internet Information Services is a full-featured platform capable of servicing HTTP (Web), FTP (file transfers), NNTP (news), and SMTP (e-mail) tasks for an organization. Due to its integration with the Windows operating system, it is relatively easy to set up, configure, and manage. IIS is capable of scaling to meet even the most demanding of environments—Microsoft runs their own Web site on IIS, and their site receives millions of hits per day. Currently, Internet Information Services is enjoying second-place title as the most widely implemented Web server around, according to Web server statistics available at Netcraft (www.netcraft.com/survey/). According to the December 2002 statistics, Internet Information Services (in its various versions) accounted for 27.58 percent of 35,543,105 Web sites that were queried. So what was the first-place Web server? A package known as Apache, an open-source version of the original NCSA HTTP Web server. In the same survey, Apache (and its different versions, including some commercial implementations) accounted for 62.02 percent of the servers sampled and was still increasing in market share.

Despite its second-place title (or perhaps because of it) IIS 5 was plagued with security holes and exploits. IIS administrators spent the last three years patching software, disabling the very open default configuration, and biting their nails while scanning the latest security bulletins. However, Microsoft has really stepped up to the plate with IIS 6, implementing a complete reversal of attitude about security and default configurations. In keeping with their new "locked down" philosophy for the Windows Server 2003 operating system, IIS 6 is not installed with the operating system, and a default installation of IIS 6 is so locked down that it will only serve static content. If that were the only change in IIS, it would be a great improvement, but the fun doesn't stop there. The biggest changes are "under the hood" and a full explanation would require quite a long discussion, but here's a short list of new features and improvements:

◆ The code for IIS has been completely revamped to achieve greater stability and performance. The new processing model, called *worker process isolation mode*, permits one or more sites or applications to run in designated application pools. Since sites and applications can run on separate worker processes, a bug or security exploit that brings down one site doesn't have to affect any other sites on the system. For backward compatibility with IIS 5–dependent applications, IIS 6 also supports *IIS 5 isolation mode.*

◆ A set of command-line administration scripts are now included in the \Windows\system32 directory. These VBScripts can perform most common administration tasks.

◆ Configuration information is now stored in two XML files instead of a binary file. These XML files can be viewed and modified with a common text editor like Notepad. Administrators can now read and edit the IIS configuration directly (and while IIS is running!) instead of using scripts or code.

◆ IIS 6 supports importing and exporting configuration information at any level (site, server, or directory). This makes it easy to duplicate settings across servers.

◆ IIS 6 permits server-independent backups. You can now back up a configuration and restore it to another system, using an encrypted password.

◆ If an IPv6 protocol stack is installed on the IIS Server, IIS 6 will support HTTP requests over IPv6.

◆ An improved method of response compression permits dynamic content to be compressed on-the-fly while static content is stored in a disk cache.

◆ FTP now supports *user isolation*, which means that individual FTP clients can be restricted to their own home directories without the ability to view or modify content in other users' directories.

◆ Technically it's not part of IIS, but the inclusion of a POP3 Server in Windows Server 2003 means that the system can act as a real mail server, not just a mail forwarder, without installing any third-party software.

Overview of IIS and Other Web Server Applications

Internet Information Services (IIS) is really a suite of TCP/IP-based services all running on the same system. Although some of the services rely on shared components, they are functionally independent from one another. Just as an electrician has different tools for different jobs, IIS has different Internet capabilities to help meet different needs. With the release of Windows Server 2003, Microsoft has reached version 6 for Internet Information Services. The following sections will briefly discuss some of the web application server functionality included with IIS 6.

World Wide Web (HTTP) Server

If you're reading this book, and this chapter specifically, I'll assume that the World Wide Web is nothing new to you. IIS includes an HTTP server so that you can publish data to the World Wide Web quickly and easily. IIS's Web service is easily configurable and reliable, and it supports security and encryption to protect sensitive data.

You can use IIS's Web service to host a Web site for your own domain or multiple domains, an intranet, and the Internet, and even allow users to pass through your IIS Web server to access HTML documents on machines within your organization.

If you worked with Windows 2000 Server and IIS 5, you know that the default Windows 2000 Server installation also installed IIS 5 automatically, including almost any optional component you could conceivably need. Windows Server 2003, however, emphasizes security over convenience. IIS 6 is not installed on Windows Server 2003 by default; furthermore, a default installation of IIS 6 will only serve static content, meaning that the default service configuration will not process any scripts or code embedded in the Web pages. Components that support Active Server Pages, Server Side Includes, and FrontPage server extensions (which allow clients to publish and manage Web sites using Microsoft FrontPage), are not installed by default. Basically, everything that could be considered a security issue must be specifically installed or enabled.

File Transfer (FTP) Server

Although the use of File Transfer Protocol is not the only way to send a file from one location to another, it is by far the most widely supported as far as the Internet is concerned. FTP was one of the original means of copying files from one location to another on the Internet, long before the days of graphical browsers, HTTP, and Web sites. Since the protocol has been around for so long, support is available on almost any platform, including midrange and mainframe systems that might not typically support HTTP.

In IIS 6, the FTP service now includes support for individual user directories. This feature can be used to permit access to private directories while preventing users from seeing or writing to directories other than their own.

Network News (NNTP) Server

Sometimes referred to as Usenet, Network News Transport Protocol (NNTP) is something that I hope to see start taking off in the near future, simply due to the great functionality it provides. By using Internet standards (RFC 977), the NNTP service can be used as a means of maintaining a threaded conversation database on an IIS server, just like in Usenet groups on the Internet. Users with properly configured newsreader programs can navigate through and participate in these conversation databases.

Although services like Google Groups (`http://groups.google.com`) have made Usenet better known, it still isn't as widely used as something like HTTP. That's unfortunate; NNTP represents a great cross-platform protocol for managing threaded conversation databases. Let's hope the inclusion of NNTP with IIS will increase the use of this capability.

E-Mail Services

Microsoft included an SMTP service with IIS version 5; however, it was not sufficient to act as a full-blown e-mail server for an organization. The SMTP service included with IIS 5 was only meant to support the other services within IIS—namely HTTP and NNTP. You see, the SMTP service included with IIS 5 was missing an important component—a POP3 or IMAP service. POP3 or IMAP is the means by which clients retrieve their specific messages from their mailbox on a mail server. SMTP provides a "store-and-forward" service for mail but does not support individual user mailboxes or a method to retrieve mail. If you wanted a Windows 2000–based mail server, you had to use a commercial product that included POP3 or IMAP, or use the free EMWACS SMTP/POP3 server product.

Windows Server 2003 now includes a POP3 service that can work with the SMTP service to provide a very simple but functional mail server platform. Although it's not technically part of the IIS services and must be installed separately, it does offer a more simple (and cheaper) alternative to Exchange or other expensive commercial products for organizations with simple e-mail requirements.

Installing Internet Information Services

The only real requirement to install IIS is that the TCP/IP protocol be installed on the system. The system should also have a static IP address (instead of a DHCP-assigned address), although this is not required for IIS services to run on the server. If you want clients to be able to use friendly names instead of IP addresses to connect to the server, you'll also need some method of name resolution. If you are deploying an intranet Web server, you'll want to have a DNS server running on your network, although it's also possible to use HOSTS files on individual systems. The dynamic DNS that runs on Windows 2000 and Windows Server 2003 makes it possible to have an intranet server with a dynamically assigned IP address (although personally, I would not use that strategy on my intranet). If the server will be accessible from the Internet, you must register your domain name for your site and either maintain two DNS servers on the Internet or work with an ISP to maintain your DNS records. Finally, for maximum security configuration capabilities on an Internet-accessible IIS server, format your drives with the NTFS file system.

It is possible to use the Manage Your Server application to install IIS; however, I recommend using the Add/Remove Programs applet in the Control Panel for finer control of installed components.

To install Internet Information Services, open the Control Panel and launch Add/Remove Programs, then click the Add/Remove Windows Components button. This will launch the Windows Components Wizard, from which you can add or remove any parts of the operating system. In the list of components, check the option for Web Application Server, as shown in Figure 17.1.

FIGURE 17.1

Installing Web Application Services

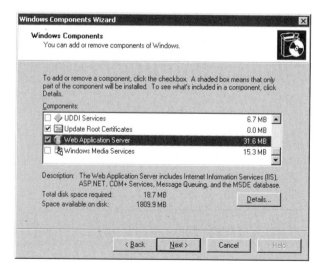

Selecting this option will install several Web application components on your system, including IIS, which is installed in "locked down" mode by default; only HTTP, NNTP, and SMTP are enabled. To install FTP and FrontPage server extensions, click the Details button for Web Application Server and highlight Internet Information Services (IIS) from the list of subcomponents. Click the Details button for IIS to see a list of components that includes FTP and FrontPage 2002 server extensions (shown in Figure 17.2). Select the options that you want to install.

FIGURE 17.2

Subcomponents of Internet Information Services

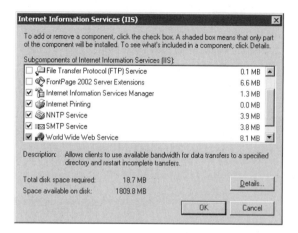

To enable active content and install HTML-based remote administration, highlight World Wide Web Service from the list of IIS components and click the Details button for that selection. From the list of WWW service subcomponents shown in Figure 17.3, check the corresponding option boxes to enable active content or install Remote Administration support. It's not strictly necessary to enable the active content options at this point, though. You can enable them later, using the Internet Information Services console. However, FrontPage extensions, FTP, and the Web interface for Remote Administration cannot be enabled from the management console; you must install them using the Windows Components Wizard.

FIGURE 17.3

Subcomponents of the World Wide Web Service

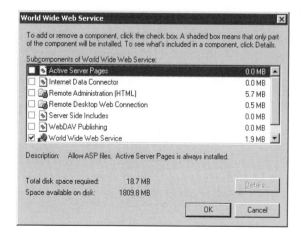

TIP   You can also install the Remote Administration Tool (HTML) by running `sasetup.msi` *from the Run dialog box.*

When you've selected the options you want to install, click OK to close all the open details windows and return to the Windows Components Wizard. Click Next and Setup will begin installing the selected components. You may also be prompted to insert the Windows Server 2003 CD-ROM at this point. Once the components are successfully installed, click Finish to close the wizard.

Default Configuration

If you accept the defaults and do not choose to install any optional components, you should end up with a default configuration similar to the following:

◆ Default (empty) Web site without FrontPage extensions, responding on TCP/IP port 80 on all configured IP addresses. The home directory for the default Web site is c:\inetpub\wwwroot

◆ Default SMTP virtual server, responding on TCP/IP port 25 on all configured IP addresses

◆ Default NNTP virtual server, responding on TCP/IP port 119 on all configured IP addresses

Looking at these services through the Internet Information Services console (`iis.msc`), you should see a screen similar to the one in Figure 17.4.

FIGURE 17.4

IIS.MSC with default settings

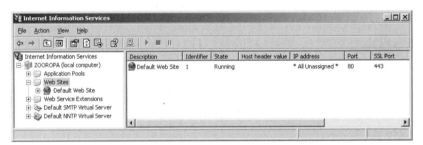

If you install FrontPage server extension, FTP, or Remote Administration (HTML) components, additional sites will be created as follows:

◆ If you install the FTP server, Setup will create a default FTP site responding on TCP/IP port 21 on all configured IP addresses.

◆ Installation of the Web Interface for Remote Administration will create an Administrative Web site, responding on TCP/IP port number 8098 using SSL on all configured IP addresses.

◆ Installation of FrontPage server extensions will create a Web site named Microsoft SharePoint Administration, responding on a randomly assigned TCP/IP port on all configured IP addresses.

The `iis.msc` tool shown in Figure 17.4 is a bit different from the administration tool for IIS 5. Sites are listed by category now, and there are two new nodes in the console tree: Application Pools and Web Service Extensions. The Application Pools node is only available when running IIS in worker process isolation mode (which is the default mode). This new feature of IIS 6 allows individual applications or sites to be isolated from other sites or applications by assigning them to run on separate processes. You'll use the Web Service Extensions node to enable and disable handlers for dynamic content, including Active Server pages and Server Side Includes.

Global IIS Configuration Options

IIS is a suite of services with a diverse set of configuration parameters, but there are a few settings that are common to all IIS services. To see these, select your server name at the top of the console tree in `iis.msc`, right-click and choose Properties (shown in Figure 17.5). From here you can enable Direct Metabase Edits while IIS is running, use UTF-8 encoding in log files to support international and non-ASCII characters, or configure MIME types.

FIGURE 17.5

Configuring global server properties for IIS

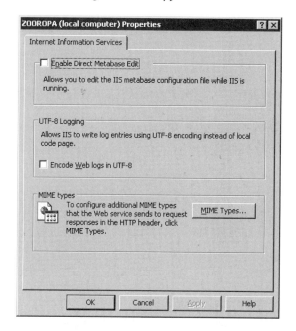

The third option you can set globally for IIS services is the MIME (Multipurpose Internet Mail Extensions) mappings that the IIS Web service will send to client browsers when a file is requested. Web servers use MIME mappings to send file type information to browsers or mail applications. The browser or mail application needs to know whether the information it is receiving is text, graphics, an audio file, executable code, or an embedded file that requires another application for viewing, such as an Excel spreadsheet.

MIME type settings specified here in the master properties will be used by all sites on the system. Mappings may also be customized at the All Web Sites level or for individual sites. However, if you change a MIME type in the master properties after modifying the same MIME type at a lower level, the master properties configuration will override the modified mapping at the site or directory level. To avoid confusion, you may want to leave the default MIME mappings untouched at the global level and modify them only for individual sites as necessary. The default mappings should be sufficient for most situations anyway. The exception would be if you wish to remove certain mappings at the global level to prevent the system from serving certain types of content completely. IIS will only serve files that have defined MIME types unless you create a wildcard entry for undefined files in the mappings.

If you need to add, remove, or change MIME mappings on your system, click the Mime Types button in the global server properties page to open the dialog box shown in Figure 17.6. From here you can view, add, remove, or edit file extension mappings for all Web sites and directories.

FIGURE 17.6

Configuring MIME types for all IIS services and sites

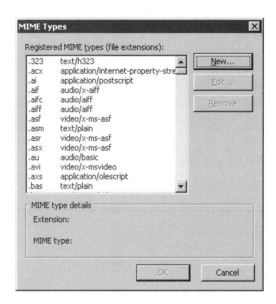

Configuring Web Services

Once you have the global settings configured correctly on your server, it's time to start publishing content. In the following sections, I will discuss setting up Web and FTP sites on your system and the configuration items associated with each. For the purposes of our discussions throughout the remainder of this chapter, I'll assume that you are configuring new sites or virtual servers in each case.

Master Properties for Web Sites

To set defaults and parameters for all Web sites on your system, select your IIS server in the console of iis.msc, expand the list of nodes, select Web Sites, and then choose Properties from the Action menu. You should see a property page with a set of tabs similar to those shown in Figure 17.7. Properties that are unique to individual sites, such as the Web site identification information shown in Figure 17.7, are grayed out in the master properties page.

The Service tab shown in Figure 17.8 is not available in the property page for individual Web sites. This tab presents options for two new features of the Web server. By default, the Web service runs in *worker process isolation mode*, which is a new process model for IIS 6. In worker process isolation mode, applications can be assigned to individual worker processes, offering enhanced security and reliability over the IIS 5 process model. However, you can choose to run the Web service in IIS 5 isolation mode if you have applications that rely on the IIS 5 process model and encounter compatibility issues. Choosing this option will require IIS to restart.

FIGURE 17.7

Configuring
properties for all
Web sites on a server

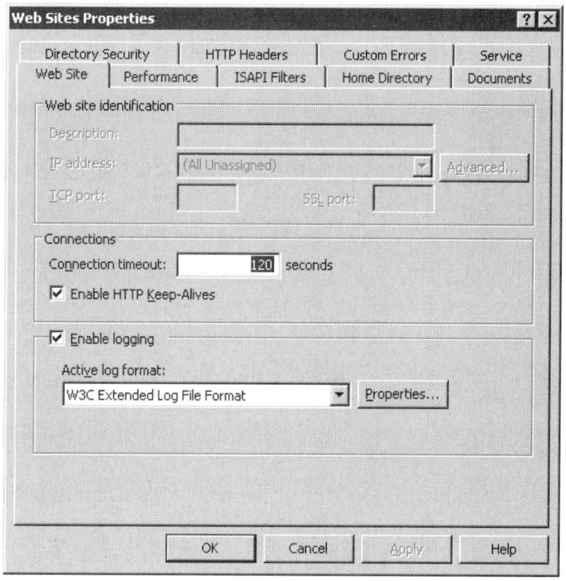

FIGURE 17.8

The Service tab
in the Web Sites
properties page

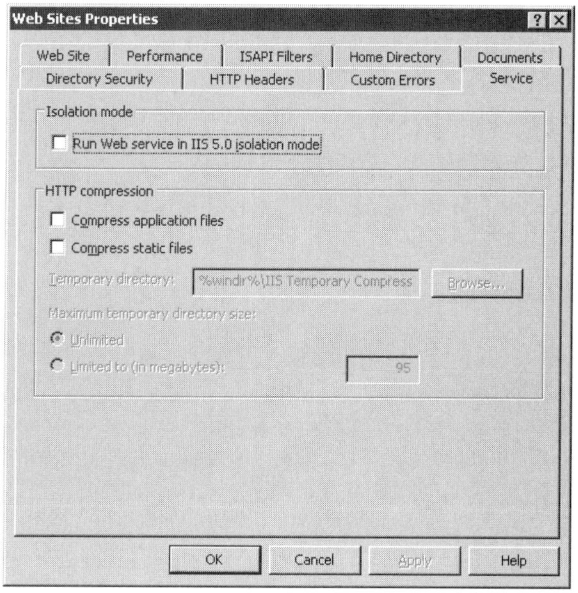

The ability to compress responses to HTTP requests isn't entirely new, but under IIS 5 it was implemented as an ISAPI filter. In IIS 6, compression is implemented as a feature of the service and can be enabled separately for static files or dynamically created content (application files). If compression is enabled for static content, compressed files are stored in a temporary file directory, found in `\Windows\IIS Temporary Compressed Files` by default. Compressed application files are not stored in the temporary directory; they are compressed as they are created. You can use the HTTP Compression options in the Service tab to specify a different temporary directory and to set a size limit on the directory.

In general, you will use the other master property page tabs to configure settings that apply to all of your Web sites. Individual sites inherit these master configuration settings, but configuration settings at the site level can override those specified at the higher level. For example, if you choose to limit the total network bandwidth available for all sites on the server to 64KB per second, and then limit bandwidth for an individual Web site to 16KB per second, the individual Web site throttles according to its own settings and the IIS service throttles connections to all other unthrottled sites as a whole (more on throttling in a moment). Similarly, anonymous access is enabled globally, but specifically disabled for the Administration site. With this configuration in place, anonymous access is automatically permitted for any new sites that are created, but individual sites can be configured to require one of the other modes of authentication.

The other settings in the Web Sites property pages are covered in the "Modifying Web Site Properties" section later in this chapter. If you already have sites running and configured on your system and change the master parameters for the Web sites, IIS will also give you the option to apply these changes to the individual Web or FTP sites on that system. For example, in Figure 17.9, I have specified that Web site content should expire immediately for each Web site on my server. IIS is indicating that this conflicts with settings for two of the Web sites on the system.

FIGURE 17.9

Setting global properties that override individual site properties

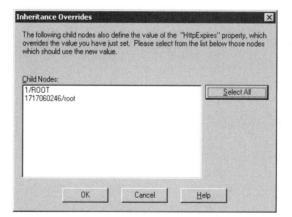

Two existing Web sites already have different content expiration policies in place, so the system is asking if I would like to apply the new global default to the individual Web sites in question. The child node reference numbers shown in the figure correspond to the identifier field for the Web sites. The identifier field is shown in the details pane of the console when the Web sites are listed. I guess it was too hard to use the human-friendly description of the Web site, eh? By selecting the site(s) to change and then clicking OK, the operating system will apply the global defaults to the individual site(s). If you plan on hosting multiple Web sites on your server, this is a great way to make across-the-board changes to your system.

In addition to setting defaults for all Web sites, you can also use a feature called bandwidth throttling to control how much bandwidth IIS uses on your network. This option is a great feature for several reasons. First, if you have other Internet-based services on your network that require a set amount of bandwidth, setting this parameter will ensure that IIS doesn't consume all of your available bandwidth. This is good for making sure that there is enough bandwidth left on your Internet connection for e-mail and other services.

For example, let's say that you have a T1 connected to your organization's network, but you don't want the IIS process to ever consume more than one-quarter of the bandwidth on this connection. By using the figures in Table 17.1, you can see that a full T1 (1,544,000 bits per second) represents approximately 193KBps, so to limit IIS to one-quarter of your T1, you would enter a value of 48 here.

TABLE 17.1: COMMON BANDWIDTH CONVERSIONS

CONNECTION TYPE	BANDWIDTH, IN BITS/SEC	BANDWIDTH, IN KILOBYTES/SEC
56K	56,000	7
64K	64,000	8
128K	128,000	16
256K	256,000	32
512K	512,000	64
T1	1,544,000	193
10Base-T	10,000,000	1250
T3	44,736,000	5592
100Base-T	100,000,000	12,500

Bandwidth throttling is also a great feature for testing how well a Web site will perform over a slow link. Want to see how a Web site is going to look and perform for someone dialing in over a 56K connection? Try setting the bandwidth throttle down to 7 or 6KBps. It is also useful in benchmarking and scaling systems.

Setting Up a New Web Site

When you are ready to start building a Web site, the steps you must follow are quite easy. First, you will need to have the following information available:

♦ What IP address you want this Web server to live on (or if it should respond on all available IP addresses).

♦ What TCP/IP port number this Web server should listen to on the previously specified IP address(es). Typically, this is port 80.

♦ What TCP/IP port number this Web server should listen to for secure communications on the previously specified IP address(es). Typically, this is port 443.

♦ What *host header name* your Web site will respond to if you will be configuring multiple Web sites on a single IP address. Host header names are common Web site names, such as `www.microsoft.com`. (I'll explain host header records soon.)

♦ What directory on your system will house your Web site content (HTML, scripts, etc.)?

Begin creating your Web site by highlighting the Web Sites node in `iis.msc` and then choosing New/Web Site from the Action pull-down menu. This will launch the Web Site Creation Wizard, which will walk you through the process to create a Web site. The first question the wizard will ask is for a descriptive name for your site. Enter an appropriate name, and then click Next to proceed to the step shown in Figure 17.10.

FIGURE 17.10

Web Site Creation Wizard, IP Address and Port Settings section

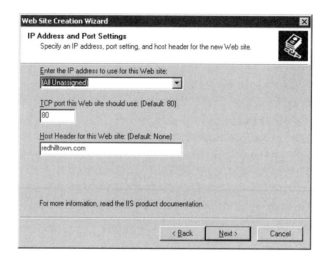

In this second step of the Web Site Creation Wizard, you will need to enter information about how your Web site can be reached. This is defined by three items: the IP address used, the port used, and any host header strings sent to your server. IIS will use any and/or all of these items to determine which Web site on your system to direct users to. If you are only hosting one Web site, the defaults should be acceptable. However, if you will be hosting multiple Web sites (for example, a private, internal Web site and a public, external Web site), the correct configuration here is important.

SERVER IP ADDRESS

The first piece of information the Web Site Creation Wizard wants to know about is which IP address to use for this Web site. This is primarily for servers with more than one network adapter or with multiple IP addresses assigned to a single network adapter. For systems with more than one network adapter, you can host a different site on each adapter by choosing the appropriate IP address in this field. If you have a network adapter with multiple IP addresses assigned to it (see Chapter 6), you can assign a different Web site to each address. Although the latter configuration is primarily seen in larger Web-hosting type arrangements, it can still be useful. If you'd prefer to have IIS simply display the same site to any IP address configured on the server, leave the default All Unassigned value in place; otherwise, select the appropriate IP address from the pull-down list.

TIP   *If you are going to have an internal, private Web site published on your internal network adapter and an external, public Web site published on your external Internet network adapter, make sure that the IP address for your internal adapter is unreachable from the outside world. You can test this by trying to ping—from the public Internet—your internal IP address, or by trying to connect to it via a browser.*

HTTP Port for Web Site

The second thing the Web Site Creation Wizard needs to know is which port to use for your Web site. By default, port 80 is the standard port assigned to the HTTP protocol. If you will be hosting a public Web site, accessible to anyone, leave the selection at port 80. Browsers will try to connect to Web sites on this port when a user types in a URL. However, if you have custom needs or want to secure your Web site a bit, you can change this port to any number from 1 to 65535. To connect to your Web server with a customized port, users will need to know the port number and append it to the URL string as follows: `http://www.redhilltown.com:9000/`. This would direct a user's browser to attempt to open up an HTTP session on port 9000 instead of the default port 80. So, for example, you could access my Web site as `http://www.minasi.com/` or `http://www.minasi.com:80/` and either would work.

Host Header Records

Unique IP addresses were once the way that multiple Web sites were hosted on the same physical box. However, since IP addresses are becoming more and more of a commodity, there is a means of assigning multiple Web sites to the same IP address and port number through the use of something called host header names. A host header name is a way to include the host name a browser is requesting (e.g., `www.microsoft.com`) into the HTTP header transmitted to the HTTP server. Modern (post-1997) browsers not only say to Web sites, "Please give me your Web pages," they also say, "Please give me your Web pages—and by the way, *I* think I'm talking to `www.bigfirm.biz`." That's important because just one Web site can have several names; for example, if you type `www.minasi.com`, `www.learnwindows.biz`, or `www.windowsnetworking.info`, you'll still end up at my Web site. It doesn't matter which URL you use to get to my site in this case. But that same Web server also runs a completely different site, `www.softwareconspiracy.com`. The IP addresses and port numbers are the same for the two Web sites, so how does IIS know which site you want? It listens to that host header record that your Web browser sent along with its HTTP request.

More specifically, when a client browser begins to open a Web site, it will (by default) look up the IP address for the host name in the URL and open a TCP connection on port number 80. Once that connection is established, it will transmit its request for a page to the server and include the host header name information in with the request. IIS will look at the host header name information, compare the name to those in its list of servers, and then respond accordingly by returning the correct pages for the corresponding site. This is a quick and easy way to host multiple sites on a single server, but clients must be using at least Microsoft Internet Explorer 3 or Netscape Navigator 2 for this to work correctly. Anyone using an earlier browser will be directed to the default Web site instead.

SSL and Host Header Conflicts

SSL is the means by which Web servers and browsers can maintain secure communications between each other. You have probably used SSL if you have ever purchased anything over the Internet.

SSL and host header names don't mix. If you are planning on using SSL, you can only assign one host header name to your site, since the domain name is encoded in the certificate. If you need to host multiple SSL sites on the same box, use multiple IP addresses.

Once you have all the information entered correctly, click Next to move on to the next step of the wizard, shown in Figure 17.11.

FIGURE 17.11

Specifying
anonymous access
and the path to files
for a site

FIGURE 17.11

Specifying
anonymous access
and the path to files
for a site

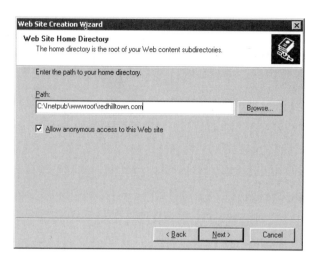

Now you will define a location for your files for this Web site, and whether to allow anonymous access to the site. The path is pretty much straightforward: enter the local path that IIS should use for files when someone connects to this site. Or, if you intend on hosting your content on another machine within your organization, you can enter a UNC path in the form of \\servername\sharename. If you choose the UNC option, the wizard will prompt you for an appropriate username and password combination to use when retrieving content from the target system.

If you will be making this a publicly accessible Web site, leave the Allow Anonymous Access to This Web Site box checked. This will allow any user to connect to the Web site without providing any form of authentication. However, if you want this to be a private, secured site, uncheck the box to remove anonymous access. Specific security settings that you can apply are discussed in the "Modifying Web Site Properties" section later in this chapter. Click Next to move on to the final step in the wizard, shown in Figure 17.12.

FIGURE 17.12

Setting Web site
access permissions

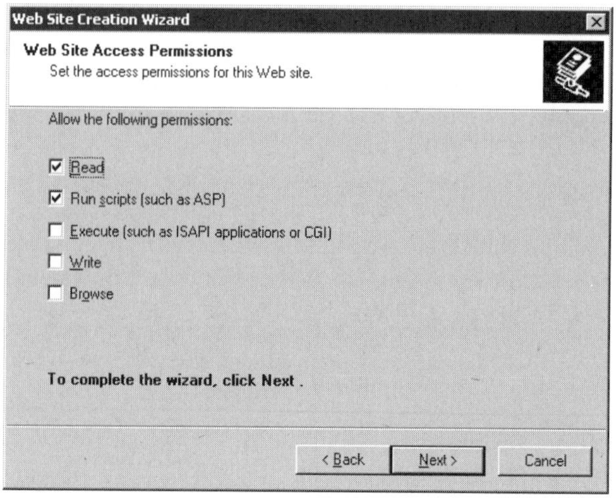

The last step in the Web Site Creation Wizard is to define access permissions to be used for this site. The permissions applied here will start at the root of the site and automatically be applied to any subdirectories below this site. Of course, you can always change the site settings later, or implement custom settings for any subdirectories below the site. Briefly, each of these access settings controls the following:

Read   Allows users to read files from your Web server. In most instances, you will want this option set for the root of a new site. The primary reason for disabling this option is for directories that contain CGI (Common Gateway Interface) or ISAPI (Internet Server Application Program Interface) applications, which will usually be set on a subdirectory level.

Run Scripts (Such as ASP)   If you need to allow the execution of Active Server Pages (ASP) scripts on your site, enable this option.

Execute (Such as ISAPI Applications or CGI)   If you need to allow the execution of ISAPI or CGI applications on your site, enable this option. When you enable this option, it is inclusive of the Run Scripts option as well.

Write   If client browsers either will need to upload files on your Web server or will be writing data to a file (maybe filling out a registration form or something like that), you will need to have write permissions enabled. Personally, I prefer to only enable write permissions in subdirectories of a Web site, not the main directory itself.

Browse   If a user does not send a request for a specific file on your Web server (for example, `default.html`) and there is no default document defined on your system, IIS will return an HTML representation of the files and subdirectories in the root of your site. Except in special circumstances, this option should be left disabled.

Once you have defined the necessary security for your site, click Next to finish the wizard, and your Web site will be created. If you have HTML content to publish, you can start by putting the necessary files in the directory you defined for this site. By default, all new Web sites (unless you changed the master properties for this option) will look for a file named `default.htm`, `default.asp`, `index.htm`, or `Default.aspx` (in that order) to use as the default home page, so make sure that the file you want presented to users when they first connect to your site is named appropriately. Using a client workstation with a browser, test your site to make sure that it is operating correctly.

And don't forget the NTFS permissions! When an anonymous Web user tries to access content such as an HTML file, a JPEG, or the like, NTFS thinks that person is the user named IUSR_*computername*. If you have denied that user access, then people on the Internet won't be able to get to your Web site—IIS will pop up a box requiring them to log in.

TIP   You can also use the command-line script `iisWeb.vbs` to create or delete Web sites and to stop, start, or pause individual sites. To create a site called Web Pizza, for example, with a home directory at `F:\PizzaSite` and a host header name `www.Webpizza.com`, you would use the following syntax: `iisWeb /create F:\PizzaSite "Web Pizza" /d www.Webpizza.com`. If you don't want IIS to start the site right away, add the switch `/dontstart` to the end of the line.

SETTING UP MULTIPLE VIRTUAL WEB SITES

With that background out of the way, let's look at how to set up more than one separate and distinct Web site on an IIS server.

In early versions of IIS, hosting multiple Web sites (sometimes referred to as "virtual sites") on the same physical system was often a tricky operation, sometimes requiring modifications to the system Registry. Fortunately, this process has been made much easier in IIS 5 and 6. To host two different Web sites on your server, one for `www.redhilltown.com` and one for `www.hawkmoon.org`, you'd follow these steps:

1. Create DNS records for each of your Web sites, each pointing to the same IP address or to unique IP addresses. (For more information on creating DNS records, please see Chapter 7).

2. Choose how you want to determine which site on your server visitors are trying to reach, via one of the following options:

   Host header records   The easiest of all three choices, host header records allow you to specifically enter the site name—for example, `redhilltown.com`—in your definition of a Web site. As you've just read, modern browsers (IE 3 or Netscape 2 or later) will transmit the name of the site to the server, and the server will return the pages for the appropriate sites.

   Multiple IP addresses   Whether you have multiple NIC cards installed in your server or you have programmed multiple IP addresses for a single NIC card, assigning a unique IP address to each unique Web site is one of the more common ways to host multiple Web sites on the same system. In the IP address, enter an appropriate, unique IP address for each site that matches the DNS records you defined.

   Unique port numbers   Although less common than the other two methods of hosting multiple sites, using a unique TCP port number for each site can also allow you to host multiple sites on the same system. This is more commonly seen with sites that don't need to be publicly accessible, since browsers will use port 80 by default. You can enter a custom port number in the TCP port field; however, client browsers will have to append the port number to their URL to be able to access the site (e.g., `http://www.redhilltown.com:200` for accessing port 200).

3. Using the Web Site Creation Wizard, create the new Web sites on your system. Define each site with a unique host header name, IP address, or TCP port—depending on how you want to control virtual sites on your system. If you accidentally create a conflict with a Web site using the same IP address and TCP/IP port, or if DNS can't resolve the specified host header name, you'll see an error message and the site will not start. Once you correct the problem, start the Web site by right-clicking it and choosing Start from the Context menu.

4. Place the necessary Web content for each site in the directory defined for the site. Now go test it with a browser, or select the site in the IIS MMC, right-click and choose Browse from the context menu to open the home page in the results pane of the console.

A MULTISITE EXAMPLE, STEP-BY-STEP

Let's wrap up this section with an example of how you'd put a site named `www.joeslabs.com` and another named `www.janesmarket.com` on a single server—say, on a machine named `spider.acme.com` at 210.10.20.40:

1. Create a folder for the Joeslabs content on the `spider.acme.com` machine; for example's sake, let's say that you put it on `E:\joeslabs`. Put the files relevant to the Joeslabs site—`default.htm`, the JPEGs, any other HTML or script files—in `E:\joeslabs`.

2. Similarly, create a folder for the `www.janesmarket.com` content, perhaps on `E:\janesmarket`. Put the Janesmarket content in `E:\janesmarket`.

3. Ensure that DNS points to 210.10.20.40 for both `www.janesmarket.com` and `www.joeslabs.com`. In each zone, you'd probably just create a CNAME record pointing to `spider.acme.com`.

4. Install IIS on `spider.acme.com`.

5. Create the Joeslabs site: From the `iis.msc`, right-click the icon representing `spider.acme.com` and choose New/Web Site, which starts up the Web Site Creation Wizard. Click Next to get past the opening screen, then type in some descriptive text for the Joeslabs Web site: **Joeslabs Web site** will do fine, although the actual text is pretty irrelevant; it's mainly to remind you as the Web administrator which of your sites does what. Then click Next to get to the IP Address and Port Settings page.

6. In the IP Address and Port Settings page (see Figure 17.10 earlier in this chapter), you'll see the three alternative methods that you can use to distinguish this site from others running on this server: you can use a different IP address, a different port, or a different host header record. Of the three, the third option—different host header record—is by far the easiest and least costly. (Who wants to burn up an IP address for each Web site? Well, you'd have to if you were still using IIS 4!) In the field labeled Host Header for This Web Site (Default: None), fill in the URL that you want people to use when referring to this site—**www.joeslabs.com**.

7. Click Next and then fill in the home directory for this site, which means point the server to the folder with the content. Fill in **E:\joeslabs** and click Next.

8. Set the access permissions on this directory. In most cases, you can just take the defaults and only allow users to read files and run scripts. Click Next and then Finish, and `www.joeslabs.com` is done.

9. Repeat Steps 5 through 8 to create the janesmarket.com site, but choose a different IP address, port, or host header name to distinguish this Web site from the Joeslabs Web site.

Modifying Web Site Properties

Once you are sure that your site is functioning correctly, you might find a need to fine-tune some of the parameters of the site. To change any of the settings for your site, return to `iis.msc` and select your site in the scope pane. From the Action pull-down menu, select Properties to edit the properties pages for this site.

WEB SITE PROPERTIES

The Web Site properties tab shown in Figure 17.13 contains some general parameters for your Web site:

Web Site Identification   Here, you can change the description, IP address, TCP port number, or SSL port number assigned to your Web site. Obviously, changing any of these options will change the way clients access your site, so plan your changes accordingly. If you want to change the host header record for your Web site, click the Advanced button to get to the advanced identification properties for this site. As you can see from the example in Figure 17.14, it's possible to have the same Web site associated with several different identities (defined by different IP addresses, TCP/IP port numbers, or host headers). For example, if you want clients to see the same Web site whether they point their browsers to www.salome.com or to www.hawkmoon.org, add an additional identity for the Web site by clicking the Add button and specifying a different IP address or host header name to associate with this site. From the dialog box that appears (see Figure 17.15), you can change the host header name for this Web site either by adding a new identity (IP address, port, or host header name) or by modifying the existing record.

FIGURE 17.13

Web site properties for an IIS Web site

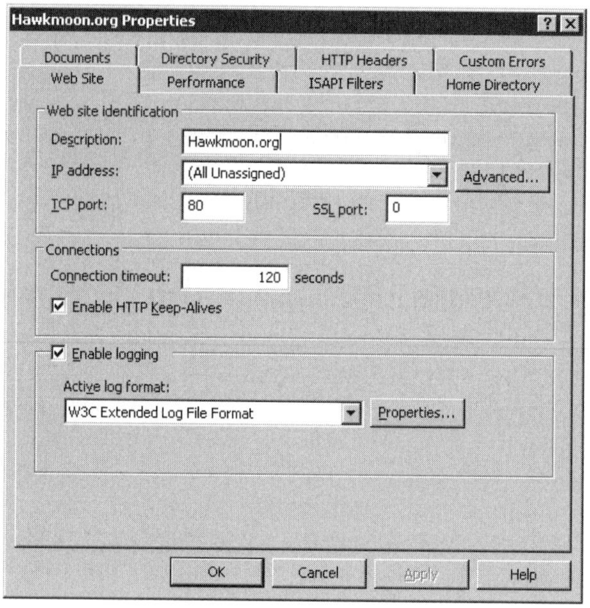

FIGURE 17.14

Advanced Web Site configuration properties

FIGURE 17.15

Advanced Web site identification properties

Connections Returning to the properties page shown in Figure 17.13, the next group of options you can modify is how IIS will manage incoming connections. You can enter a time-out value for IIS to close out idle connections, and you can enable HTTP keep-alives. Enabling HTTP keep-alives allows client browsers to maintain an open connection in between individual requests to a Web server. Since Web pages are often made up of several elements (text, graphics, etc.) that must be opened individually, this option increases performance on servers. Disabling this option could cause browsers to open a separate connection for each Web page element.

Enable Logging You can enable or disable logging for this Web site by checking or unchecking the Enable Logging box. Since log files take up space on your system, you might consider disabling this option for an internal Web site. If you enable logging, you have format options to choose from in the Active Log Format pull-down box, including W3C Extended Log File Format, ODBC Logging, NCSA Common Log File Format, and Microsoft IIS Log File Format. Depending on which option you choose, you can edit properties for that format by clicking the Properties button. For example, choosing the ODBC Logging option and clicking Properties will take you to a dialog box where you can define the ODBC data source name, table, etc. The W3C Extended Log File Format properties will allow you to define how often new logs are created, where they are stored, and which data items to log.

PERFORMANCE PROPERTIES

The next options you can configure for your Web site are performance related, and can be found under the Performance properties page shown in Figure 17.16.

Depending on the size of your Web site and the amount of traffic you expect you will be handling, you can modify these parameters to adjust the behavior of your site:

Enable bandwidth throttling As I discussed back in the "Master Properties for Web Sites" section, you can control the amount of bandwidth that the overall server or an individual site can consume. Settings defined here will override the master settings. Refer back to Table 17.1 for a listing of common bandwidth sizes and their translations into kilobytes/second.

Limit Web site connections You can limit the number of simultaneous client connections to your Web site, or use the master properties pages to limit the total number of simultaneous client connections to all sites. This is useful if your server is a busy Web server but also runs a mail server or performs other important tasks. Setting a limit can ensure that the system has enough memory and CPU resources to spare for its other tasks. The default setting for unlimited connections will permit as many connections as the system and network bandwidth can handle. Limiting the number of simultaneous connections can also protect your system against attacks aimed at overloading the server with thousands of client requests.

FIGURE 17.16

Performance properties for an IIS Web site

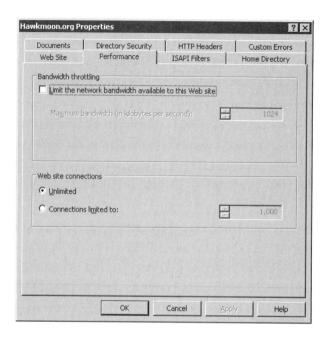

ISAPI FILTERS

The next properties page—ISAPI Filters (shown in Figure 17.17)—lets you set options for which ISAPI filters are installed for a specific Web site and the order they execute in.

FIGURE 17.17

ISAPI filters properties for an IIS Web site

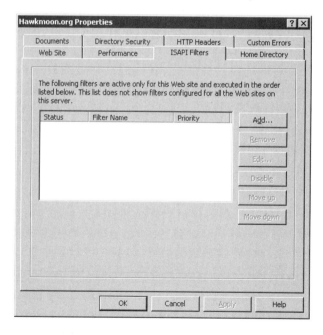

ISAPI filters are programs that respond to events that occur on the server during the processing of an HTTP request. The ISAPI filters displayed in this property page are active for this Web site only, although filters may also be defined globally for the Web server. In that case, both sets of filters apply for the Web site. If two or more filters are registered for the same event, filters with a higher priority are executed first. Filters can be added, removed, modified, or disabled from this list by using the buttons on the right side of this properties page. To change the order of execution for filters, adjust them with the Move Up and Move Down buttons.

HOME DIRECTORY PROPERTIES

The next tab in the Web Site properties pages is the Home Directory page, shown in Figure 17.18. This group of settings lets you control where IIS will look for Web content, and what security permissions to use while handling it.

FIGURE 17.18

Home directory properties for an IIS Web site

By selecting the appropriate radio button on the top of this properties page, you can control where IIS will go to look for the content for this site, or if it will send users to another Web site. Based on the selection you make, the lower portion of this properties page will change accordingly. If you select the option for a directory located on this computer, you will need to enter the local path in the middle section (as in Figure 17.18) of the dialog box.

If you select the option for a share located on another computer, the Local Path field will change to a Network Directory field, where you will need to enter the correct \\servername\sharename UNC path. When you choose to use a share located on another computer for your files, you might need to use the Connect As button that appears to enter logon credentials for the IIS service to use when it is accessing the other system. The IIS service will actually log in to the other system, retrieve the files, and present them to the user just as if the files were local. This is a great way to distribute an entire Web site throughout an organization. If individual departments are responsible for maintaining different sections of a site, you can use this feature to direct requests for their content to their servers, instead of requiring all your departments to publish their data to one system.

Lastly, if you choose to redirect users to another URL, IIS will create an HTML redirection page pointing users to the URL you specify. The Local Path field will change to a Redirect To field, where you can enter a full URL to send users to. Redirecting users to a URL can be configured through three different options: redirect users to an exact URL, redirect users to a lower subdirectory, or permanently redirect users to an exact URL. Redirecting users to an exact URL is pretty straightforward; users are sent to the exact URL you enter, just as if you typed it into their browser for them. Redirecting users to a lower subdirectory will let you create an alternate directory in your Web site structure. The last option, for permanently redirecting users to a URL, is very similar to the first option, with the exception that a permanent redirection will send a "301 Permanent Redirect" message to the browser, instead of the usual "302 Temporary Redirect." The net result of this is that some browsers will modify any bookmarks or favorites on file if they receive a permanent redirection.

If you chose either of the first two options for your content location—a directory on your IIS computer or a share on another server—several security settings will be displayed under the Local Path field. These settings can be used to control what can and can't be done on your site:

Script Source Access   This option is only available when read or write access is enabled. This option allows access to source code, including scripts in ASP applications.

Read   Allows users to read files from your Web server. In most instances, you will want this option set for the root of a new site. The primary reason for disabling this option is for directories that contain CGI or ISAPI applications, which will usually be set on a subdirectory level.

Write   If client browsers either will need to upload files on your Web server or will be writing data to a file (filling out a registration form, etc.), you will need to have write permissions enabled. It's safer to enable write permissions only in subdirectories of a Web site and not in the main directory itself.

Directory Browsing   If a user does not send a request for a specific file on your Web server (for example, default.html), and there is no default document defined on your system (see the next section), IIS will return an HTML representation of the files and subdirectories in the root of your site. Except in special circumstances, this option should be left disabled.

Log Visits   Depending on whether or not you want logging information stored about visitors to your site, check or uncheck this box. Logs will be stored in the format defined in the Web Site properties page described earlier in this section.

Index This Resource   To speed searching for text data, select Index This Resource, which will cause the Indexing Service to index all the content of this site.

Application Name   If your site is going to be the starting point for an application, this is where to enter the name of the application.

Execute Permissions   This pull-down box will let you define whether or not to allow the execution of scripts, the execution of scripts and executable files (.exe and .dll), or nothing at all.

Application Pool   To prevent errant applications from taking out other processes on your system, you can assign applications to be run by one or more dedicated worker processes. The set of one or more applications and one or more dedicated worker processes is called an application pool. Applications can run alone, in a dedicated application pool, or together in a pool with other applications. This feature is only available when the server is running in worker process isolation mode. If you must run the Web server in IIS 5 isolation mode for compatibility with applications designed for IIS 5, this option will be named Application Protection and you can choose between Low, Medium, or High protection levels. Low protection will allow applications to execute in the same memory space as the IIS process itself; medium protection will pool applications for this site together; and high protection will isolate each application from any others.

DOCUMENTS PROPERTIES

Continuing with our Web site configuration, the next settings tab in the Web Site properties pages is the Documents tab, shown in Figure 17.19

FIGURE 17.19

Documents properties for an IIS Web site

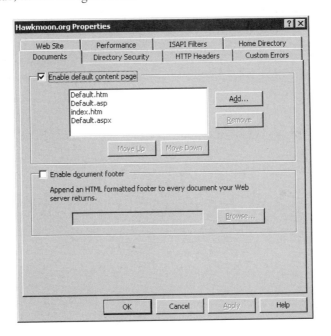

Unless a visitor has clicked a link to a specific page on a Web site, it's much more likely that they will try to connect to a Web site using the name http://www.redhilltown.com, for instance, than with the address http://zooropa.redhilltown.com/default.htm. When users attempt to connect to your Web server without specifying a specific document to retrieve, IIS will look through the list of default documents (if enabled) to return to the user. By default, the IIS installation process will add default.htm, default.asp, index.htm, and default.aspx to this setting in the master properties, which are then inherited by each Web site. If for some reason you would prefer to use another name, you can add the name to the list of default documents by clicking the Add button. IIS will look through this list, in order, and return the first matching document it finds. If you would prefer to adjust the order, use the arrows to the left of the document list to place the documents you want to look for first at the top of the list.

If you want to have every Web page within your site sent out with a common footer (for example, copyright and disclaimer information), you can have IIS do this by selecting the Enable Document Footer option. The document footer is an HTML file that IIS will merge in at the bottom of each page it displays. The footer file should not be a complete HTML file in and of itself (with <HTML> </HTML> tags, for example). Instead, it should just contain the basic HTML code you want displayed, for example:

```
<h2>This is a footer</h2>
```

This is all that would be necessary for a footer file to display the text shown as a heading type 2.

DIRECTORY SECURITY PROPERTIES

The next section of the Web Site properties pages—Directory Security—allows you to control access to your Web site based on authentication, client IP addresses, or ACL settings on files, and gives you the ability to secure communications when clients connect to this Web site. The Directory Security properties page is shown in Figure 17.20.

FIGURE 17.20

Directory security properties for an IIS Web site

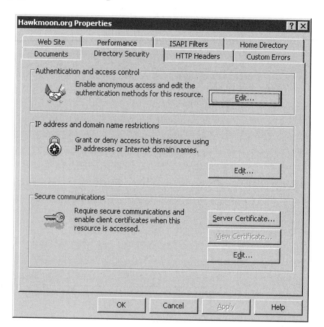

One method for securing a Web site is to define an authentication method to validate users. Since browsers—by default—will try to access a site anonymously, one option available is to remove anonymous access from your site. Click the Edit button in the Authentication and Access Control box to edit the authentication properties of your system. The Authentication Methods dialog box is shown in Figure 17.21.

By default, IIS will allow anonymous access for Web sites and directories, unless you have overridden this option in the master settings. There are two primary means of securing your Web site—or certain areas of your Web site. The first is to remove the check mark from the Enable Anonymous Access box. This will effectively make your entire site a secured site and require an authentication before a user is allowed to connect at all, even to the default home page. If you choose this option, then the Authenticated Access area in the lower half of the figure becomes important in determining just how clients will authenticate themselves. If you remove anonymous access from your site, you must have some authentication option selected, or else you will effectively disable all access to your site.

FIGURE 17.21

The Authentication
Methods dialog box

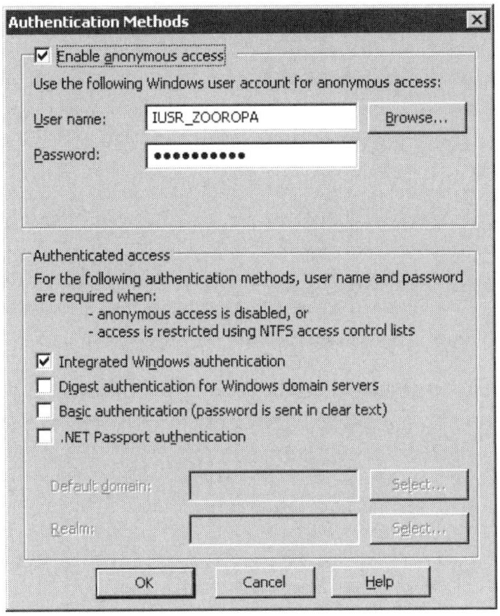

The options under Authenticated Access control what level of authentication users must negotiate to get connected to your protected site. The details of each type are as follows:

Integrated Windows Authentication   If both the client and server are using Active Directory Services, Kerberos 5 authentication will be used. Otherwise, the method used will be NT Challenge/ Response Authentication (also known as NTLM). In this process, the user is not initially prompted for a password. The browser passes the current username and password information to the server transparently. If the transparent authentication attempt fails, the browser will prompt the user for a Windows username and password. You guessed it; integrated Windows authentication requires users to use Internet Explorer for their Web browser. Instead of the actual passwords, Internet Explorer sends a password hash. User accounts are checked against the accounts in the domain of the IIS server. Any version of Internet Explorer after version 2 can support this method of authentication. Since this type of authentication does not work with HTTP proxies or with firewalls that use HTTP proxies, it's best suited for use on intranets. Windows authentication, like anonymous authentication, is enabled by default.

Digest Authentication   Digest authentication securely transmits an MD5 hash value over the Internet instead of a password, thus keeping system passwords confidential. There are a few requirements for using this type of authentication, however. Namely, client workstations must be using Internet Explorer version 5 or later, users must have a valid account in the Active Directory, and user passwords in the Active Directory must also be stored as cleartext.

TIP *If the IIS server is a Windows Server 2003 domain controller, you can edit a metabase key called UseDigestSSP to enable Advanced Digest Authentication, which will store the MD5 hash for passwords in the Active Directory instead of cleartext passwords.*

Basic Authentication This is the most basic level of authentication (and therefore the most widely supported) for validating a user accessing a Web resource. Practically all Web browsers, including Microsoft's and Netscape's, support this type of authentication. Using this authentication method, usernames and passwords are transmitted in cleartext and checked against the accounts in the domain of the IIS server (if you would like to use accounts on another domain for validation, click the Select button next to Default Domain). If you expect to be running a public Web site, accessed by users on various platforms and browsers, this is probably the best option for requiring authentication on your site; however, it is the least secure of all the authentication types unless you use it in combination with SSL. Not only are passwords transmitted in an unencrypted form, but the user accounts also need the Log On Locally right. If your IIS server is a Windows Server 2003 domain controller (and this is not necessarily recommended), you will have to explicitly grant user accounts on the server the right to log on locally.

.NET Passport Authentication The Windows .NET Passport online authentication system is designed to benefit e-commerce Web sites by making it easier and faster to sign in and to make online purchases. Selecting this authentication method tells your server to validate accounts with a .NET Passport Server instead of using a local accounts database or the Active Directory. Since .NET Passport uses standard Web technologies like cookies, SSL, and JavaScript, it is compatible with Internet Explorer 4 and later, Netscape Navigator 4 and later, and even some Unix browsers. On the down side, though, the licensing fees to use .NET Passport can be steep. For more information, check out the .NET Services information at Microsoft's Web site.

USING NTFS PERMISSIONS TO CONTROL ACCESS TO WEB SITES

If you want to make some areas in your Web site open to the public while leaving other areas protected, permit anonymous authentication but also set permissions on the specific files and directories you want to protect. This will only work on NTFS volumes (you can't define permissions on FAT volumes).

When anonymous authentication is enabled, IIS will use the anonymous user account first to try to read a file and pass it back to the user requesting it. For publicly accessible Web content, without any permission settings restricting access, the IIS process should be able to access that content via the anonymous user account (IUSR_*servername*). However, if IIS fails in accessing that file due to a security restriction, it will look to the authentication options defined previously to determine whether it should request an authentication from the user. If an authentication option is set, IIS will prompt the user for a username and password combination (or retrieve that information transparently, depending on the authentication method), and then attempt access using those credentials. Therefore, if you want to restrict access to specific files or directories to certain users, simply add the users or groups to the permissions applied to those files or directories, and exclude or deny access for the anonymous user account. (For more information on placing security rights on files in NTFS, see Chapter 10.)

Another means of securing a Web site is to restrict who can access the site based on an IP address, a range of IP addresses, or a domain name. This requires knowing in advance who should be connecting to your site and from where, but it is particularly useful when setting up Web sites designed to interface with clients or suppliers. Click the Edit button in the IP Address and Domain Name Restrictions area shown in Figure 17.20 to see a screen similar to the one in Figure 17.22.

FIGURE 17.22

The IP Address and Domain Name Restrictions dialog box

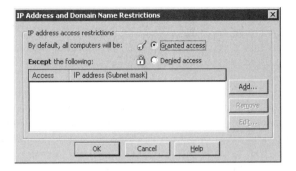

Select the appropriate radio button option to either grant access or deny access to everyone, and then enter the exception list by selecting Add. Exception list entries can be defined by individual IP addresses, network addresses, or by domain name. Individual IP address restrictions can be useful for home users, provided that they have a static IP address assigned by their service provider. However, it is more common for home PCs and laptops on the road to use dynamically assigned IP addresses. Sometimes a business will use a firewall or proxy server that hides all internal IP addresses and uses a single address as the source for all internally generated requests. In that case, you could permit connections from that business and refuse all other connections by entering the IP address of the firewall or proxy server. Groups of computers with static addresses or with dynamic addresses that will always fall within certain network numbers can be defined by entering a network address and subnet mask. Domain name restrictions are only useful as a last resort when you don't know the IP addresses of client systems that will be accessing your Web server. Since IIS only identifies connections by a source IP address, the server must do a reverse-DNS lookup, which can slow down server response time significantly. Unless your situation requires using domain names, it's probably worthwhile to find out the exact IP address ranges to allow into your site and configure them accordingly.

NOTE *Many hosts out on the Internet don't actually have reverse-DNS records assigned to them, and some hosts have incorrect reverse-DNS records assigned to them. Therefore, if you were to put in a restriction based on a host/domain name, it might not work quite as well as you expect.*

Although source IP addresses can be faked, and should not be used as the sole means of protecting sensitive content, IP address restrictions can be combined with authentication restrictions, allowing for some very secure Web site access. For example, if you have users who frequently work from home—on a computer with a fixed IP address—you could secure your site (or a portion of it) by allowing connections only from specific IP addresses, and also require a secure user authentication before allowing access.

The last option for securing a Web site is to require encrypted communications between the client browser and the server, preventing anyone from intercepting data as it travels across the Internet. This is done with SSL (Secure Sockets Layer) encryption, discussed later in this chapter in the "Communicating Securely with SSL" section.

HTTP HEADER PROPERTIES

The next group of settings you can control for your IIS Web site are what headers the IIS service should include with HTTP pages it transmits. These parameters are adjusted under the HTTP Headers tab, pictured in Figure 17.23.

FIGURE 17.23

HTTP header properties for an IIS Web site

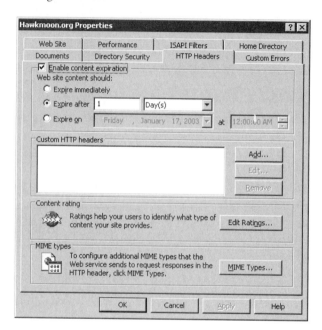

HTTP headers let you control several things that your Web server will transmit to Web browsers along with the HTML pages on your site. The primary things most administrators want to control are content expiration, content ratings, and MIME file types. However, custom headers can be added as necessary for new HTML standards that haven't been implemented in IIS yet.

By checking the Enable Content Expiration box, you can effectively control how browsers will handle their cached pages when communicating with your site. If a user has visited your site before, the pages may still be in the cache of their machine; however, you may only want pages to be valid for a day or two, depending on the type of material being presented. By selecting an expiration option (to expire immediately, expire after a certain number of days, or expire on a set date) you can force browsers to request a new page from your server after the expiration interval has been reached.

If your Web site will be hosting material that contains content some people might find objectionable, you can enable content ratings for your site or for areas of your site as needed. In the Content Rating area, click the Edit Ratings button to open the Content Ratings properties page. From there, you can learn about the Platform for Internet Content Selection (PICS) system that was developed by the Recreational Software Advisory Council (RSAC) and is used to determine a "rating" for a Web site's content. There is also a questionnaire that you can walk through to determine an appropriate rating for your Web site. Once you have a set of ratings you want to apply to your site, click the Ratings tab in the Content Ratings properties page to begin entering those ratings (see Figure 17.24).

FIGURE 17.24

Implementing content ratings

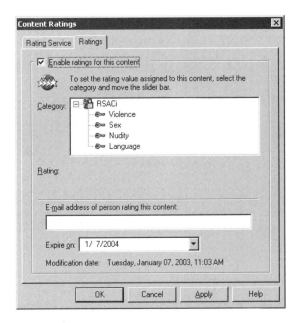

As you can see from the screen, there are four primary categories for rating a Web site—violence, sex, nudity, and language. For each of these categories, there are five levels—0 through 4—that dictate how strongly offensive the content of your site is in each category. For example, level 0 for language is defined as "inoffensive slang," while level 4 is defined as "explicit or crude language." The settings you apply here will have a direct correlation to the content settings available in Internet Explorer or Netscape Navigator, and will effectively block visitors from reaching your site if your content ratings exceed their browser settings. Set your ratings accordingly and enter an e-mail address and an expiration date for your content settings. Once the content ratings are set, IIS will transmit them out with every page on the corresponding Web site or subdirectories of the site.

If you have a need to add or remove MIME types for this site, go back to the HTTP Headers tab and click the MIME Types button. Use the MIME Types dialog box to add additional MIME file types by clicking the New button and entering the appropriate associated extension and content type as prompted. The content type should be in the format of *MIME type/filename extension*. To remove a MIME file type, highlight the file, type in the list of registered file types, and then click the Remove button. The file extensions defined in the properties pages of an individual site will apply only to that site. The master properties pages for the Web server (accessed by right-clicking Web Sites in the iis.msc console) define mappings for all Web sites.

If there are custom HTTP headers you would like transmitted to browsers along with each page, enter them in the Custom HTTP Headers box by clicking the Add button. One thing custom headers are useful for is for HTML standards that have been developed but have not made their way into IIS yet.

CUSTOM ERRORS PROPERTIES

When building your Web server and Web sites, there may be occasions when you want to control how and what is displayed to users who receive an error. For example, you might want to have a custom HTML page displayed when a user reaches a 404 error (file not found). To customize the error messages on your site, click the Custom Errors tab on the Web site properties pages. The page for custom errors is shown in Figure 17.25.

FIGURE 17.25

The Custom Errors properties page

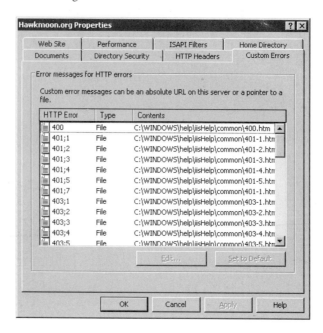

Through this dialog box, you can choose from having a default error message, file, or URL displayed for any type of HTTP 1.1 error. The HTTP error types (along with their subtypes) are listed in the left column, the types of response are in the middle column, and the details of those responses are in the right column. In a default installation of IIS, some messages will contain default responses (just one line of text), and other errors will be defined by HTML files. Windows Server 2003 stores its default IIS error message files in the `%systemroot%\help\iisHelp\common` directory; you can use these as templates to define your own error messages. To change an error message on your system, find the HTTP error number you want to change in the list (along with the subtype if necessary) and click the Edit button to modify the properties of that error message. From the Error Mapping Properties dialog box, you can change the message type and the location of the file or URL to display (if you've chosen that type of response).

FRONTPAGE SERVER EXTENSIONS

Microsoft FrontPage server extensions are server-side components that permit Web developers to open and author a Web site using the FrontPage client. Before this is possible, FrontPage server extensions must be installed on the server (they are not installed by default), a virtual server must be created for each Web site that will be available to FrontPage, and the Web site must be *extended*, which is just a fancy way of saying that server extensions must be explicitly enabled for the site.

Once you install FrontPage server extensions using the Windows Component Wizard in Add/ Remove Programs, each Web site's properties pages will include a tab called Server Extensions 2002. If you've just created a new site, you won't see anything under this tab (except for instructions on how to enable the extensions) until you extend the Web site. By the way, don't think that you must enable FrontPage extensions at all—unless your organization has standardized on FrontPage Web development, there are easier ways to manage content and content development. Simple FTP or Web Distributed Authoring and Versioning (WebDAV) are two alternatives that come to mind.

Installing FrontPage extensions on the server creates a Web site named Microsoft SharePoint Administration. This is the administrative Web site for FrontPage server extensions and replaces the wizard and property pages used to configure FrontPage extensions in IIS 5.

Enabling FrontPage Server Extensions

To enable server extensions to a site, highlight the site in iis.msc, and select the Configure Server Extensions 2002 option from the All Tasks item in the Action pull-down menu. Or right-click your site and select the same option, as shown in Figure 17.26.

FIGURE 17.26

Adding server extensions to a site

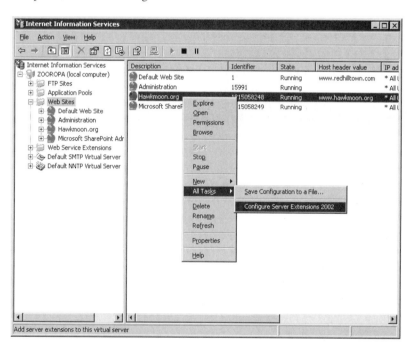

This will open an HTML-based form (shown in Figure 17.27) for extending the site. The form confirms the name of the Web site to extend and asks you to confirm the administrator account for this virtual server. If the default information is correct, you need only to click the Submit button to enable the server extensions.

Once you've enabled server extensions for the Web site, the Server Extensions 2002 tab in the site's properties pages will contain a Settings button, which takes you to the general server extensions configuration pages. Use the Microsoft SharePoint Administrator Web pages to manage server extensions. When you install FrontPage server extensions on the system, a link to the Microsoft SharePoint Administrator is created in the Administrative Tools group.

FIGURE 17.27

Extend a virtual
server with
FrontPage
extensions

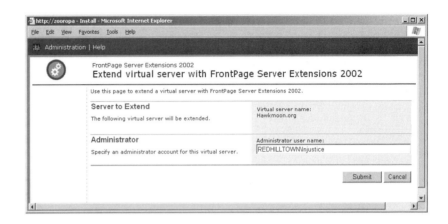

FIGURE 17.27

Extend a virtual
server with
FrontPage
extensions

Virtual Directories

As I discussed in the previous section, a Web site's content is stored initially in a home directory. This home directory is considered the root directory (/) for the Web site and may point to a directory on the local system or a share on another system, or it can be a redirection to another URL. A bare-bones Web site may store all of its files together in the root directory. But as Web sites begin to grow there is often a need to organize levels of content into subdirectories off of the main root of the site. There are two ways to do this for a Web site. The first is to actually create a subdirectory in the root directory and place content into that directory. For example, let's say you have a site that is stored in C:\Inetpub\wwwroot and is accessed by a URL of www.companyname.com. If you decide you want to move all of your graphics files to a separate subdirectory, you could create a subdirectory called C:\Inetpub\wwwroot\images and then move all of your graphical content into that directory. To access files in that directory, client browsers would access the URL www.companyname.com/images.

However, what if you want to have content available as a subdirectory in your site, but you don't want to move the content to a normal subdirectory within your site's structure? Virtual directories are a means of adding a subdirectory off of the root of your site (or even a lower level of your site) and then creating an alias, or a pointer to a directory somewhere else on your system or on another computer on your network. By using virtual directories, you are not forced to move all of your Web content to one system and then place it in an orderly structure for visiting users. Instead, you can have content stored anywhere on your machine or on any system within your network, and users can access it through a simple directory structure.

For example, imagine that you want to visit a Web site named www.redhilltown.com. You click a link you found in a search engine, or type the address www.redhilltown.com into your browser. The IIS 6 server that answers to www.redhilltown.com receives the request, checks its configuration, and sees that the home directory for that Web site is c:\inetpub\wwwroot\redhilltown. Since you haven't requested a particular page, it returns the file default.htm from that directory. Now you are looking at the home page for the redhilltown.com site. You find several interesting links on the page; one is to a selection of images you might like to download (www.redhilltown.com/images/default.htm), another is to a "members only" private area (www.redhilltown.com/private/login.asp). You click the Images link. Although it's transparent to you the user, the Images directory is actually an alias to the directory `d:\webdirs\redhilltown\newimages` on the IIS 6 server, and the private directory is an alias for a shared folder on another system completely. These three different directories could be stored on different machines and different physical hard drives, yet to the browsing user they all seem to be in one logical structure.

Virtual directories are useful for several reasons:

◆ They simplify the Web site structure from the user's point of view. A virtual directory can appear to be right off of the root of the Web server, whether it refers to a location that is ten levels deep in the directory structure or is stored on a separate physical drive or a separate system completely.

◆ They permit greater flexibility in organizing content. A corporate intranet may include virtual directories for several different departments that are actually stored and maintained on departmental servers instead of on the IIS server. If an administrator needs to move directories around, she only needs to modify the alias mapping instead of fixing every link on every darn Web page.

◆ They can provide another layer of security because a) users can't tell where the content is actually stored, and b) even if the root directory of a site is on a FAT partition and accessible to any anonymous user, you can still create a virtual directory pointing to a folder on an NTFS partition and limit access to authenticated users with file and directory permissions.

CREATING A VIRTUAL DIRECTORY

To launch the Virtual Directory Creation Wizard, return to the Internet Information Services tool and highlight the Web site you want to work with in the Scope pane of the window. Select New/Virtual Directory from the Action pull-down menu, and the wizard will start walking you through the configuration process. The first step of the wizard is shown in Figure 17.28.

FIGURE 17.28

Defining an alias for a virtual directory

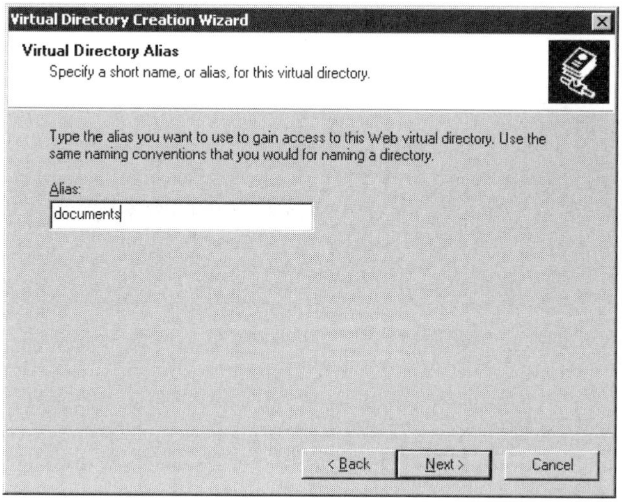

The first thing you will need to specify for your virtual directory is the alias that refers to it. The alias is the directory name that client browsers will need to use to access the directory. For example, if a user were accessing the URL www.companyname.com/documents on your Web server, documents would be the alias. The alias does not need to match the name of the directory where the files are actually coming from, so you can use whatever name works best in this field. Click Next to proceed to the next step of the wizard, shown in Figure 17.29.

FIGURE 17.29

Defining a content directory for a virtual directory

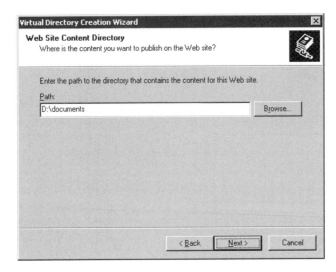

If you want to define a virtual directory that points to another directory on the same computer, enter the path name here (such as D:\documents). IIS will define the virtual directory as pointing to another directory on the same server. However, if you want this virtual directory to point to data located on a share on another server, enter the UNC path to that system here. When you click Next, the Virtual Directory Creation Wizard will take you to another dialog box, shown in Figure 17.30, for entering user credentials.

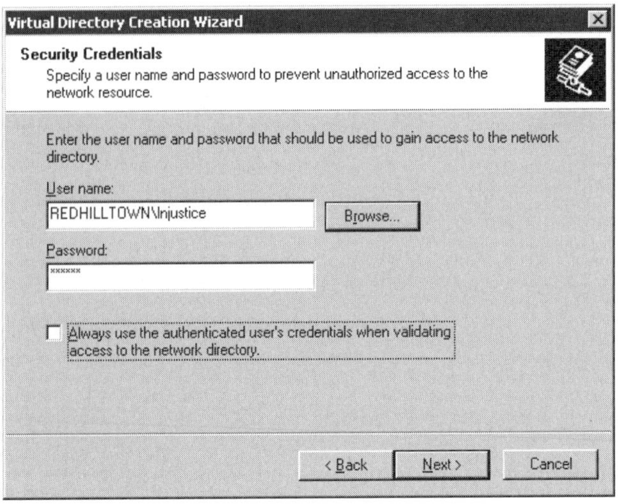

FIGURE 17.30

Entering a username and password to access shared content via a virtual directory

When IIS needs to contact another server for Web content, it will need to do so with a specific username and password combination. Enter an appropriate set of credentials here, one that would have appropriate access rights to the content you are trying to reach. Click Next to move to the last step of the wizard—defining access permissions—shown in Figure 17.31.

FIGURE 17.31

Defining access permissions for a virtual directory

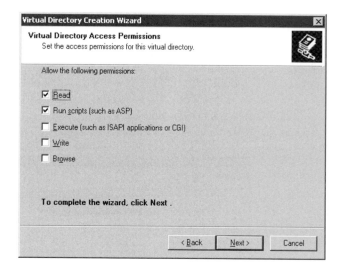

This step in the wizard is identical to the one mentioned earlier in this chapter and shown in Figure 17.12. Return to "Setting Up a New Web Site" for a description of these permissions.

Once you have entered all of the required information, you should have a new virtual directory item listed below your Web site. A virtual directory appears with a gear icon in the IIS Manager tool. You can make sure that the virtual directory is configured properly by launching a browser and then navigating to your virtual directory. To verify your virtual directory from the IIS Manager, just highlight the virtual directory, right-click, and choose Browse from the context menu. If everything has gone according to plan, IIS should return content from the appropriate location.

You can modify properties for a virtual directory in exactly the same manner that you would for a Web site—by editing the properties pages for the directory itself. You can edit the following properties pages for a virtual directory: Virtual Directory (equivalent to Home Directory for a site), Documents, Directory Security, HTTP Headers, and Custom Errors. These pages are functionally identical to the pages defined earlier in this section for modifying the properties for an entire site.

NOTE   *The* iisvdir.vbs *script can create and delete Web virtual directories from a command line. As an example, to create a virtual directory called* Pizzaingredients *for the Web Pizza Site at* f:\ingredients, *use the following syntax:* **iisvdir /create "Web Pizza" pizzaingredients f:\ingredients**. *If the physical path to the virtual directory doesn't exist,* iisvdir *will create it.*

Enabling Dynamic Content

A default installation of IIS 6 will only serve static Web pages. ISAPI and CGI extensions, Active Server Pages, Server Side Includes, and all of the handlers that generate dynamic context are disabled.

In other words, the Web server will not run the required DLL (or sometimes EXE) files required to support that type of dynamic content. If you need to host applications or just permit Indexing Service queries on your Web site, use the Web Service Extensions node in the IIS Management console to enable specific request handlers. From the IIS console, select the Web Service Extensions node. A custom taskpad will be displayed in the results pane, as shown in Figure 17.32. All Web Service extensions are prohibited by default. These extensions are simply one or more DLL files grouped together under a user-friendly name. For example, FrontPage server extensions use about six different DLL files. These library files may also be enabled or disabled individually to prohibit certain operations. To enable a specific extension such as the Indexing Service, highlight it in the results pane and click the Allow button. To disable all extension in one move, click the Prohibit All Extensions link. If you need to permit extensions that are not listed in the console, you may create and permit new extensions by clicking the Add a New Web Service Extension link. You will need to supply a friendly name for the new extension and a list of files that are required by the extension.

FIGURE 17.32

The Web Service
Extensions taskpad

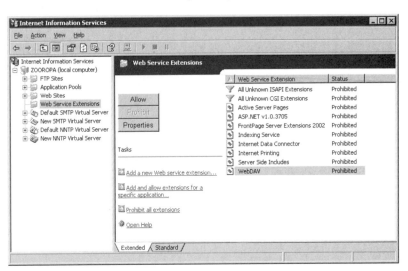

NOTE *You may also use the* iiscnfg.vbs *script to enable or disable Web service extensions. To enable the extensions for WebDAV, for example, type the following single line at a command prompt:* iiscnfg /enapp webdav.

Using WebDAV

Web Distributed Authoring and Versioning (WebDAV) is a great way to manage Web site content; it's more user-friendly to Windows users than FTP file transfers and much simpler to use than FrontPage and its associated server extensions. You set up a WebDAV directory as a virtual directory on a Web site. Users with permission to access it can then use an integrated Web client component on Windows 2000 and XP Professional client systems to access the folder using Windows Explorer. In fact, the remote folder looks very much like a shared folder to the client, although the HTTP protocol is actually being used instead of the Windows file mounting service. WebDAV is particularly useful when an author needs to connect to a Web server through a firewall and upload content (it's not safe to permit file server connections through a firewall). Since WebDAV is designed particularly for managing Web content, only one user can modify a file at a time. Authorized users can also move and copy files, search the directory structure, and modify attributes.

Before you can set up WebDAV publishing on your IIS server, enable the Web service extension for WebDAV, using the IIS MMC or `iiscnfg.vbs`. The procedure to enable a Web service extension is described in the previous section.

First, create a publishing directory anywhere on your Web server and set appropriate permissions on the resource. For convenience, this directory may be the same directory as the root of the Web site, or it may be the same path as another virtual directory in the Web site. If you must put the directory under `\wwwroot`, you'll need to change the default permissions, which only permit read access.

Next, create a virtual directory on your Web site and give it the alias WebDAV. Specify the path to the publishing directory and grant Read, Write, and Browse permission to the virtual directory. Once the virtual directory is created, open the Virtual Directory properties pages in the IIS MMC and go to the Directory Security tab. Edit the Authentication and Access Control settings to disable anonymous access and require integrated Windows authentication (this process has been described previously in the section on configuring virtual directories). You must use Windows integrated authentication and put your publishing directory on an NTFS partition, or user-level security cannot be enforced.

Now you are ready to have users connect to the WebDAV publishing directory. The simplest way for clients to do this is using the Add Network Place wizard on a Windows 2000 or XP Professional client system. You can access WebDAV folders with Internet Explorer version 5 or later. In our first example, we'll use the Add Network Place wizard.

From a Windows 2000 or XP Professional system, open My Network Places and click Add a Network Place. When the wizard asks you for an address or location, type the full URL of the publishing folder, including the virtual directory (`http://www.redhilltown.com/WebDAV`, for example). Give that sucker a friendly name, and you're done. A shortcut to the publishing folder will appear in the list of network places. If you specified that users must do Windows integrated authentication and you set appropriate NTFS permissions on the directory structure, users should not even be prompted for a username or password. The existing user context will be used to access the publishing folders.

To access the publishing directory from Internet Explorer, choose File/Open and type in the full URL including the WebDAV virtual directory, as you did in the Add a Network Place Wizard. Before you click OK, though, select the check box labeled Open as Web Folder. This tells IE that you want to be able to make changes in the folder; otherwise IE will just serve up the content like any other Web page. Since users will have Browse permission, they may see a list of files and folders, but access will be read-only.

Working with Application Pools

IIS 6 has redesigned its Web service to support separate processes and memory space for Web sites, virtual directories, and applications. Because each site or application on the Web server can be assigned to one or more dedicated processes, problems, bugs, and failed processes are isolated and won't bring down the entire Web server or affect other sites. There are also a whole slew of configuration options that allow the Web service to monitor itself and implement safeguards against failures.

Application pools are only available when the HTTP service is running in the default mode, worker process isolation mode. If the Web server is running in IIS 5 isolation mode, the Application Pools node in the IIS MMC is not visible.

CONFIGURING APPLICATION POOL PROPERTIES

Before you create any new application pools, let's take a look at the default settings. Select the Application Pools node in the IIS MMC, right-click and choose Properties from the context menu to view and modify the master properties for all application pools (shown in Figure 17.33). Like the master properties for Web sites, any new pools will inherit these global settings that you create, and properties set for individual pools will override the global settings. These properties pages are identical to the properties pages for new pools and for the existing default pool (DefaultAppPool).

FIGURE 17.33

Recycling settings for application pools

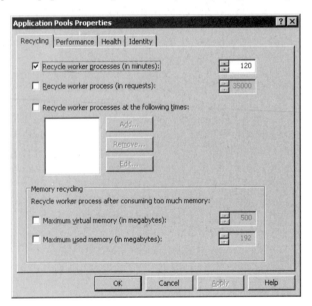

The Recycling tab specifies parameters for process and memory recycling. Process recycling occurs when new worker processes (instances of w3wp.exe) start up periodically and old ones are killed off as they take care of any pending requests. This can be configured to happen at certain intervals, after a certain number of requests are processed, or at a particular time during a 24-hour period. If an application is suffering from a memory leak of some sort, you can also configure the worker process recycling options based on memory usage thresholds.

The Performance tab, shown in Figure 17.34, displays options to protect the server from becoming overloaded. The idle timeout interval permits a worker process to be killed after standing idle for 20 minutes. The request queue limit prevents overloading by monitoring the number of queued requests to the pool. When the number of requests exceeds the limit, new requests are rejected and a 503: Service Unavailable error is returned to the client. Enable CPU monitoring to prevent an application pool from consuming too much of the processor's resources. And finally, a Web garden is a fancy name for an application pool that can run more than one worker process. If you plan to take a lot of hits on a particular application, increase the maximum number of worker processes to distribute the workload.

FIGURE 17.34

Performance
Settings for
Application Pools

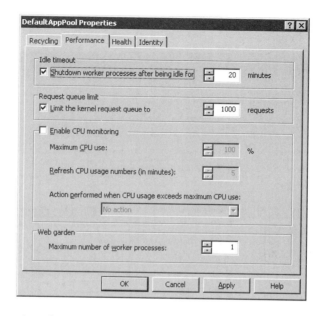

The Health tab settings shown in Figure 17.35 can be used to monitor the, well, the health of your worker processes. By default, a worker process will be pinged every 30 seconds to confirm that it's still running. If the worker process does not respond in a timely fashion, the monitoring process (called the Web Administration Server, or WAS) will terminate the worker process and start another one.

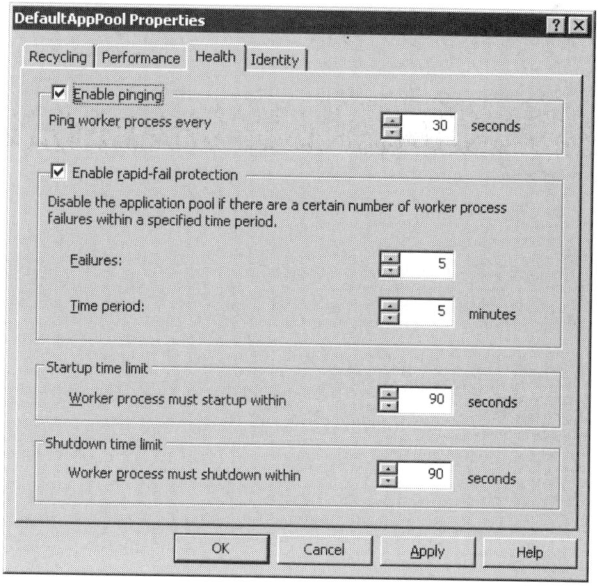

FIGURE 17.35

Health settings for
application pools

By default, if the WAS detects a worker process failure (because of a failed ping or a dropped connection to the WAS control process), it restarts the worker process and sends a message to the

Event log. The rapid-fail protection function tells WAS that if it detects 5 failures within 5 minutes from the same worker process, it should immediately take the pool offline. If this happens, the Web server will start returning 503 messages to requests for the application.

The startup and shutdown time limits ensure that worker processes don't hang while starting up or shutting down. If they do hang, WAS orphans or kills them.

Use the Identity tab (shown in Figure 17.36) to specify a security account for the application pool. By default, application pools run as the Network Service account, which is a pretty powerless account. However, if you want to use another account, perhaps even a more powerless one, it needs to be a member of the IIS_WPG group on the server. This group (IIS_WPG is short for IIS Worker Process Group) already has the rights and permissions needed to run a worker process. The IWAM_*computername* account is already a member of the IIS_WPG group.

FIGURE 17.36

Identity configuration for application pools

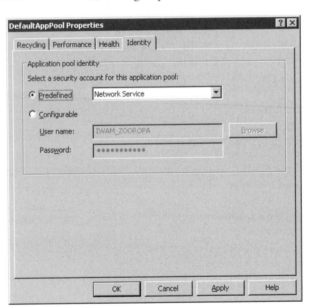

If you aren't grappling with a buggy application, there's probably no need to modify any of these defaults. Still, when problems arise, it's nice to know they are available.

CREATING NEW APPLICATION POOLS

By default, all Web sites and applications run in the DefaultAppPool. That is, they all share the same worker process. If you host multiple Web sites on the same system, or have a test version of a site running alongside a production version (not that I'm recommending this!), you may want to configure a separate application pool for each Web site. In the example that follows, we'll create two application pools, one for our www.redhilltown.com site and another for the www.hawkmoon.org site. Then we will modify the properties for each site to associate it with the new application pool.

To create a new application pool, highlight the Application Pools node in the IIS MMC, right-click, and choose New/Application Pool from either the context menu or the Action menu. The Add New Application Pool dialog box, shown in Figure 17.37, prompts you for a pool ID and asks whether to use the default properties (Performance, Health, Recycling, and Identity settings) for application pools or to use the settings from an existing pool as a template. Type in a pool ID name or accept the default settings, select an option for configuration defaults, and choose OK. Now repeat the process to create a second application pool for the second Web site. I named the two new pools AppPool #1 and AppPool #2 after the defaults, but you can give them friendlier names if you prefer. Now assign the `www.redhilltown.com` site to run in AppPool #1 and the `www.hawkmoon.org` site to run in AppPool #2.

FIGURE 17.37

Adding a new application pool to IIS

Now that the pools are created, let's assign our Web sites to run in their own memory space on dedicated worker processes. In the IIS MMC, select the first site to be reassigned (`www.redhilltown.com`), right-click, and open the properties pages. Select the Home Directory tab and pull down the Application Pool list box to see a list of pools (shown in Figure 17.38). Select the appropriate pool (AppPool #1) from the list and click OK. There's no need to stop and start the site; IIS will handle the transition to a separate application pool automatically. Now repeat the process for `www.hawkmoon.org` and assign it to AppPool #2.

FIGURE 17.38

Assigning a Web site to an application pool

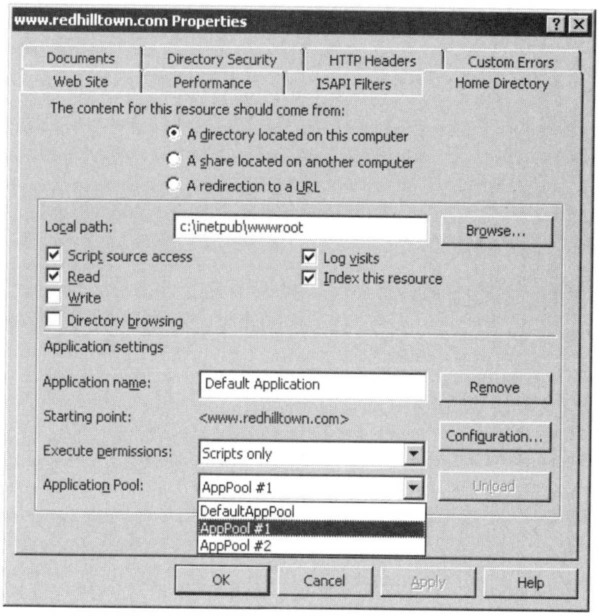

That's it! Now our two Web sites are completely isolated from each other, running in separate memory spaces on separate worker processes. To see this in action, open a couple of browser windows to your Web sites and then open the Windows Task Manager on the server. You should see multiple instances of w3wp.exe running in the list of processes, one for each Web site. Which brings me to a final point: when I checked, each instance of w3wp.exe on my system was using about 4MB of RAM. So application pools are pretty neat, but if you have a bunch of them on the Web server, they are going to increase your memory and CPU overhead.

By the way, you can use the iisapp.vbs script to see what process IDs (PIDs) are assigned to what Application Pool ID. Just type **iisapp** from a command prompt without switches to see output similar to this:

```
W3WP.exe PID: 3420    AppPoolId: AppPool #1
W3WP.exe PID: 2264    AppPoolId: AppPool #2
```

This information tells you that the www.redhilltown.com Web site is assigned to the instance of w3wp.exe running on PID 3420 and the www.hawkmoon.org worker process is PID 2264. It might not sound very exciting at first, but consider this: if a worker process starts eating up all your CPU or memory resources and you configure Task Manager to display a PID column in the Process tab (doesn't every Admin do this?), you can find out what site is having a problem or bogging down the system just by opening the Task Manager and running this single command. It would be even easier if you assigned recognizable application pool ID descriptions—you wouldn't even have to remember which site is running in AppPool #1 and which in AppPool #2.

Setting Up an FTP Site and Configuring FTP Services

Although many file transfers on the Internet today take place via HTTP, FTP is still an important protocol to support if you will be running a public Web site, simply due to its broad range of client support. FTP client software has been developed for almost every computing platform imaginable—including mainframe and midrange systems. Clients who might not be able to retrieve files from your system via HTTP will most likely be able to do so via FTP.

Again, FTP is not installed with IIS 6 by default. You must specifically add it using the Windows Components Wizard. Refer to the earlier section on installing IIS for more information. The FTP service bundled with IIS 6 now includes one big new feature: *user isolation mode* limits user access to designated home directories. This was designed for use by Internet Service Providers to allow clients to upload files and Web content. However, it might also be useful to permit, for instance, a Macintosh or Unix client user to access their home directory on the file server via FTP. In the following examples, first we'll set up an FTP site without user isolation mode, and then we'll set one up with user isolation mode. As we'll discuss in a moment, FTP supports virtual directories, but not host header names, so multiple FTP sites on the same server can only be configured using different IP addresses or other TCP/IP ports.

Setting the Master Properties for FTP Sites

Like the Web (HTTP) service, IIS provides a set of master properties pages to allow administrators to specify default settings for all FTP sites. To set master properties for all FTP sites, right-click the FTP Sites folder in the scope pane of iis.msc. With one exception (the Service tab, which is not available at the FTP site level), the master properties pages are identical to the property pages for individual sites. Information that applies only in the context of individual sites (such as site identification and home directory settings) is grayed out and unavailable in the master properties pages. Settings defined in the master FTP properties will be inherited by all new sites and by existing sites if the properties have not already been defined with a different value. For example, if you deny anonymous access at the FTP Sites level, any new sites you create will not permit anonymous access by default. However, if you explicitly permit anonymous access for your public FTP site, that value will override the setting at the higher level. Later, if you decide to reset the master properties to permit anonymous access by default, IIS will ask you if you wish to reset the Allow Anonymous property on any of the individual sites that do not currently permit anonymous access.

There is one master properties page that is unavailable for individual sites. The Service tab, shown in Figure 17.39, permits you to enable bandwidth throttling for all FTP sites. It is not possible to set specific throttling parameters on individual FTP sites as you can for individual Web sites. For more information on bandwidth throttling, review the earlier section "Master Properties for Web Sites."

FIGURE 17.39

The Service tab of the FTP Sites properties pages

Creating a New FTP Site

To set up FTP services on Internet Information Services, have the following information ready in advance:

◆ Which IP address you want this FTP server to listen on (or if it should respond on all available IP addresses).

◆ Which TCP/IP port number this FTP server should listen to on the previously specified IP address(es). Typically, this is port 21.

- ◆ Whether to allow read access, write access, or both to your FTP site.
- ◆ Which directory on your system will house your FTP files.

The creation of a new FTP site begins with a wizard—in this case, the FTP Site Creation Wizard. To start the wizard, select the FTP Sites folder for your IIS server in the scope pane of the Internet Information Services tool. Select the New/FTP Site command from the Action pull-down menu, and the wizard will walk you through the necessary configuration process.

The first step in the wizard, shown in Figure 17.40, will prompt you for a friendly name to use when referencing your FTP site.

FIGURE 17.40

Entering an FTP site description in the FTP Site Creation Wizard

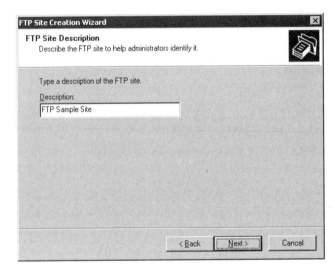

Choose a meaningful name for your site, and click Next to proceed to the next step of the wizard, shown in Figure 17.41.

FIGURE 17.41

Assigning IP addresses and ports in the FTP Site Creation Wizard

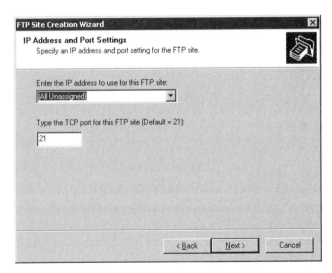

For users to be able to reach your FTP server, you need to assign an IP address and TCP port number for the service to listen to for incoming connections. Host header names are not supported for FTP. By default, the wizard will want to assign your FTP server to listen to TCP port 21 on all available IP addresses on the system. If you have multiple IP addresses assigned to your server (for example, for an internal interface and an external interface), you might want to select the specific address for your system in the IP Address pull-down box. Or if you will be making your FTP site available to the Internet but don't want to have it readily accessible on the default port of 21, you can assign it to any other port number from 1 to 65535.

TIP *Changing the port number for your FTP site is often a good idea if you will only be using it to publish or receive files for a few selected clients, suppliers, etc. One of my own clients recently had their FTP server discovered (presumably by scanning for devices responding to TCP port 21) and used by hackers as a repository for pirated software.*

If the defaults are acceptable, click Next to move on to the next step of the FTP Site Creation Wizard, shown in Figure 17.42.

FIGURE 17.42

Setting user isolation options for a new FTP site

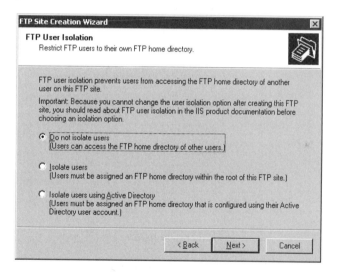

This version of FTP is capable of directing users to a specific home directory and limiting access to that directory. In this first example, choose not to isolate users (which is the default selection). I'll discuss the features of user isolation mode and how to configure it later in this section. Click Next to proceed to the next step, shown in Figure 17.43.

When FTP clients initially connect to your server, they will be placed in the home directory of your system and won't be able to proceed any higher on your system than the home directory. For them, the home directory that you specify will be their "root" directory. Their root directory can be either a directory on your IIS server or a share on another system on the same network. From the root directory, you can create subdirectories below your home directory in order to organize the files available for download or the files you expect to be receiving. Enter the appropriate directory name or UNC path here and click Next to proceed. If you enter a UNC path for your root directory, the next step of the wizard will prompt you for a username and password for IIS to use when accessing that share. Otherwise, if you enter a local path, the next step is the final step of the wizard, shown in Figure 17.44.

FIGURE 17.43

Setting the FTP
site home directory
in the FTP Site
Creation Wizard

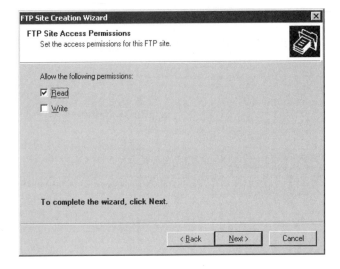

Once you have defined how your site is reachable and what directory on your system should service
the site, the last thing IIS needs to know is whether or not to allow read access, write access, or both
read and write access to your site. The choices here are rather self-explanatory: if you're using your
FTP server simply to provide downloadable files for users or clients, then read access only would
be your best choice; if you want to receive files, then select write access; if necessary, you can also select
both. Click Next to finish your site, and the FTP Site Creation Wizard will build your site and start
it up for you immediately. If the wizard reports a problem, you've most likely created a site using the
same IP address or port number assignments as another pre-existing site. The site will still be created
but will not start up until you correct the problem and manually start the site using the Action menu
or the context menu for that site.

Once your site is created, all you need to do is place the content in the home directory that you
would like visitors to be able to access. This might be anywhere from a few files to a few thousand

files. If you have more than a handful of files, you will probably want to organize them into some logical directory structure to make things easy to find. Whatever the case may be, make the files on your system easy to find and your users will be appreciative.

Also, it is common for FTP sites with more than just a handful of files to put index.txt and/or readme.txt files in directories throughout the site to help users understand what type of content is available in each directory. After all, nobody likes trying to guess what directory names or 8.3 filenames actually mean.

TIP *You can create a new FTP site from a command prompt using the* iisftp.vbs *script. For example, to create a new FTP site called Pizza Recipes with a home directory at* f:\pizzarecipes *listening only on IP address 204.177.51.199, use the following syntax (all on one line):* **iisftp /create f:\pizzarecipes "Pizza Recipes" /i 204.177.51.199**. *You can specify a port other than port 21 with the /b port number switch and add* /dontstart *to keep the site from starting upon creation. The switches* /isolation Local *or* /isolation AD *tell FTP to create the site in one of the isolation modes.*

Modifying FTP Site Properties

Although the FTP Site Creation Wizard does an excellent job of configuring a functional FTP site for you, there are some additional parameters that you might want to adjust for your system. For example, you might want to have a logon message displayed to users connecting to your system, or you may want to limit the number of simultaneous users on your system. In any case, to adjust the parameters for this FTP site after the wizard has created it, you will use the FTP site properties pages. Remember, if you want to set these values for all FTP sites, use the FTP Sites master properties pages.

FTP SITE PROPERTIES

To open the properties pages for your new FTP site, highlight the icon for your new site in the scope pane of iis.msc and then select Properties from the Action menu. This should bring you to a dialog box similar to the one shown in Figure 17.45.

FIGURE 17.45

Editing FTP site properties

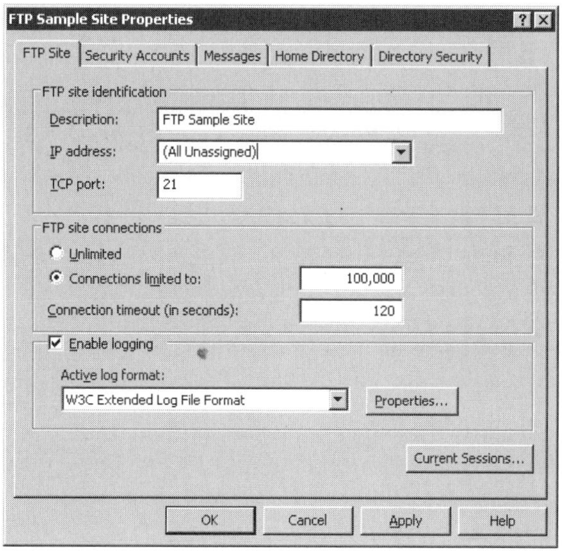

From this page of FTP site properties, you can change parameters about your site, defined as follows:

Identification   This group of controls allows you to change the "friendly name" for your site, the IP address your site listens to, and the TCP port number that it listens to. By default, the IP address for your site to listen to (unless you chose something else in the wizard) will be set to All Unassigned, causing your new site to listen for FTP users on any IP address that isn't already in use by another site on your system. To host multiple FTP sites on your system, assign each site a separate address in this field or adjust the port number.

You can change this port number as a means of securing your site (people won't know to look for an FTP server on port 28,324, for example) or so that you can host multiple FTP sites on the same IP address. You can enter a value from 1 to 65535 in the TCP Port field. However, once you change the port number, users will need to know which port number to use, since FTP client software uses port 21 by default.

Connections   Depending on the capacity and bandwidth available for your system, you may want to limit the number of simultaneous connections to your server to maintain adequate performance. If you are planning on running a large site and handling lots of traffic, the Unlimited option might be the best choice. If you choose to limit the connections, users who attempt to log in after the connection limit has been reached will receive a message (which you may define in the Message Properties page, described later in this section).

A "connection"—as far as IIS is concerned—is not necessarily defined as all activity from a single user. For example, a user connecting to your FTP site through a browser could launch multiple simultaneous downloads from your site. Each download session in that case would be considered a connection. Therefore, limiting your server to five connections doesn't necessarily guarantee that five users will be able to access your site at any time; one user could take up all five connection spots.

TIP   If you plan on allowing write access to your FTP site, and you know that you'll never have more than a few users connected to your FTP server at a time, you might consider limiting your system to one or two connections. If someone on the Internet were to find your server and start using it as a repository for pirated files or pornography, they'll probably start advertising its accessibility. Limiting connections is a way to at least minimize potential abuse of your system.

To make sure that users don't stay connected to your server indefinitely, enter a time-out value in seconds in the Connection Timeout field. The default timeout value is 900 seconds, or 15 minutes. If for some reason an FTP session fails to close its connection appropriately, this will ensure that phantom open connections won't eventually fill up your server.

Enable Logging   One of the best ways to keep track of what's happening on your system is to log the activity. Checking the Enable Logging option (enabled by default) will allow you to log activity on your site in three formats: Microsoft IIS Log Format, W3C Extended Log File Format, or ODBC Logging. Depending on which logging option you choose, clicking the Properties button will yield a specific set of parameters you can adjust for each type of log.

Current Sessions   Although this technically isn't a parameter to be adjusted, at times you may need to monitor who is connected to your FTP server and disconnect some or all of the users connected to your site. Clicking the Current Sessions button will take you to the FTP User Sessions dialog box shown in Figure 17.46.

Monitoring current
FTP user sessions

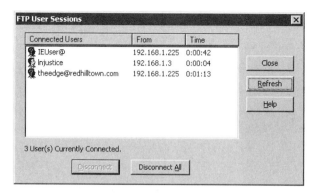

All users connected to your FTP server will be listed in this dialog box, along with their associated IP address and the amount of time they've been connected. Users who are connected to your system anonymously—logging in via the username "anonymous" (more on this subject in the next section)—will have a question mark located in the user icon and will be listed by the e-mail address they supplied to the password prompt from the FTP server. If the visitor used Internet Explorer to log on anonymously, the e-mail address may be shown as IEUser@ or IE40user@, depending on the version of Explorer being used. The icon will have a small question mark over a face. Users who have logged in with an actual Windows Server 2003 user account will have a normal user icon next to their username. To disconnect any users from your system, highlight their record and click the Disconnect button. To disconnect all users from your system (for example, if you're preparing to shut the system down for maintenance), click the Disconnect All button.

SECURITY ACCOUNT PROPERTIES

On an FTP server, there are generally two types of connection that users typically make: anonymous logins or user logins. Anonymous logins are overwhelmingly common on the Internet, and this is how most publicly accessible FTP servers run.

In an anonymous login, users connect to an FTP server with the username "anonymous" and an e-mail address for a password. No checking is done on this password; it is simply recorded for informational purposes. By configuring a server in this manner, any user can gain access and get files as necessary. If you plan on running a publicly accessible FTP site, it is customary to allow anonymous logins.

The opposite of an anonymous login is a user login, which requires a valid username and password combination before logging in. User logins allow you to control user access to a greater level—you can assign security to directories on an FTP server and restrict access to certain directories based on username.

NOTE   *FTP passwords are transmitted over the Internet in cleartext. If you have users who will be logging into your FTP server with their Active Directory user accounts, their passwords will be in plain view of anyone who might intercept their traffic.*

Once you have decided which type of logins you want to allow, you can enforce these settings via the Security Accounts properties page, shown in Figure 17.47.

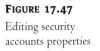

FIGURE 17.47

Editing security
accounts properties

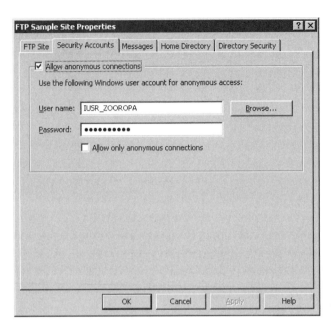

This properties page controls what type of logins to allow on your server. If you don't want to allow any anonymous connections at all, uncheck the Allow Anonymous Connections box; this will disable the remaining options on the top half of the properties page. Otherwise, when anonymous users connect to your system, they will end up inheriting the security rights of the account defined in the Username field.

NOTE   Disabling anonymous logins will force everyone to connect to your FTP server via a username and a password. Since FTP sessions are transmitted over the Internet in cleartext, this could potentially expose user passwords defined on your system to anyone who might be looking for them.

Checking the Allow Only Anonymous Connections check box will effectively restrict any users from accessing your FTP server via a normal user login. This is particularly useful in case any user or administrative passwords within your organization are discovered—FTP cannot be used as a means to gain access through those accounts if this option is checked.

TIP   By default, most Web browsers will attempt to do an anonymous login when connecting to an FTP site. If the anonymous login fails, the user will be prompted for a valid username and password. To override this behavior, you can place the username and password the browser should use in the URL string. The correct URL format for a user login via a browser is `ftp://username:password@sitename.com`.

MESSAGE PROPERTIES

Although the FTP client interface is often cold and impersonal, you can add your own messages to your FTP server. Whether you need to inform users about new files that were recently added, tell them what site they are connected to, display a legal warning message, or just send a friendly message, you can do this through the Messages page, shown in Figure 17.48.

FIGURE 17.48

Editing message properties

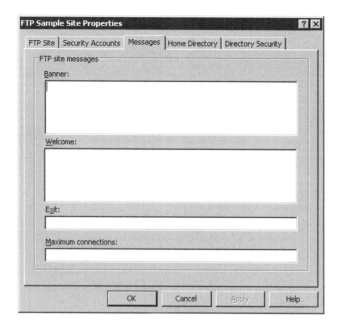

The messages properties are rather self-explanatory. The Banner message is displayed when a user first connects to the FTP site, before logging on. The Welcome message is displayed to users after they log in. If your server has reached the maximum number of allowable connections (set in the FTP site properties discussed earlier in this section), then the Maximum Connections message will be sent to the user and their session will immediately be disconnected.

Speaking of disconnection, if a user (using something other than a browser for FTP access) disconnects properly from your FTP server, they will see the message you have defined in the Exit field. Browsers don't typically display exit messages, so if you have something important to pass along to users, it's better to put it in the welcome message than in the exit message.

HOME DIRECTORY PROPERTIES

If you read through the previous section on setting up Web sites, the properties page for Home Directory (shown in Figure 17.49) should look somewhat familiar to you. Although some of the settings and options are different for FTP sites, the general concept is the same.

This group of settings lets you control where IIS will look for FTP files and what security permissions to use for this location:

Content location By selecting the appropriate radio button on the top of this properties page, you can control whether the content for this site will be stored on the local system, or on a different server's shared folder. Based on the selection you make, the path information box below the radio button options will change. If you select the option for a directory located on this computer, you will need to enter the local path in the lower portion of the properties page.

If you select the option for a share located on another computer, the Local Path field will change to a Network Share field, where you will need to enter the correct \\servername\sharename

UNC path. When you choose to use a share located on another computer for your files, you might need to enter login credentials for the IIS service to use when it is accessing the other system. The IIS service will actually log in to the other system, retrieve the files, and present them to the user just as if the files were local. This allows you to build a distributed FTP site throughout your organization, even though all the files are presented to the user just as if they were all on one machine.

FIGURE 17.49

Editing home directory properties

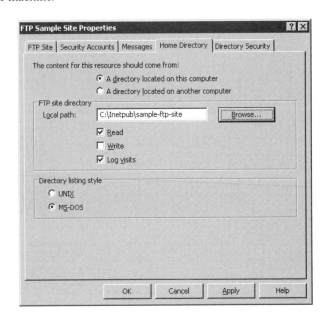

Security settings   Regardless of the location you choose for your content, you can control whether users are allowed read and/or write access to your files as needed. The FTP service will apply these settings for how it handles the directory overall, and these settings can be complemented by additional security permissions applied to files and directories on files stored on an NTFS partition.

Log Visits   Depending on whether or not you want logging information stored about visitors to your site, check or uncheck this box. Logs will be stored in the format defined in the FTP site properties dialog box, covered earlier in this section.

Directory Listing Style   This setting will control how IIS will return directory-listing information to users in response to the `dir` command from an FTP client—in either an MS-DOS-style listing or a Unix-style listing. This setting has no bearing on how IIS will return information in response to the `ls` command from an FTP client.

DIRECTORY SECURITY PROPERTIES

The last section of the FTP site properties pages, Directory Security (Figure 17.50), allows you to control who accesses your Web site based on client IP addresses.

FIGURE 17.50

Editing directory
security properties

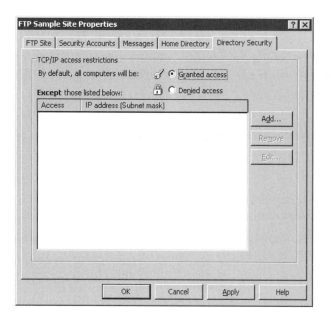

Through this page, you can secure your FTP site somewhat by restricting who can access the site based on an IP address or a range of IP addresses. This requires knowing in advance who should be connecting to your site and from where, but it is particularly useful when setting up FTP sites designed to interface with business partners. Select the appropriate radio button to allow access from all IP addresses by default (Granted Access) or to restrict access from all IP addresses by default (Denied Access). Create exceptions to this rule by clicking the Add button and adding an IP address or a range of IP addresses (by using a network mask). IIS will enforce these restrictions with all visitors to your site.

As with IP address restrictions for Web sites, you can set up some highly secure FTP sites by restricting access based on IP address, and then requiring authentication (i.e., denying anonymous connections) to access your site.

Virtual FTP Directories

If your FTP site begins to grow over time, you might find that you will need to add additional resources to your system as subdirectories off of the main root of the site. Just as with a hard drive on a computer, in time there are often too many files to manage in one directory, so subdirectories become necessary. There are two main ways to do this for an FTP site. The first is to actually create a subdirectory in the site's content directory and place content into that directory. For example, let's say you have a site that is stored in C:\Inetpub\ftproot and is accessed on an FTP server at ftp.companyname.com. If you decide you want to move all of your executable files to a separate subdirectory, you could create a subdirectory called C:\Inetpub\FTProot\bin and then move all of your executable content into that directory. To access files in that directory, FTP clients would access the ftp.companyname.com/bin directory.

However, what if you want to have content available as a subdirectory in your site, but you can't move the content to a normal subdirectory within your site's structure? Virtual directories are a means of defining a subdirectory off of the root of your site (or even a lower level of your site) and then creating an alias or a pointer to a directory somewhere else on your system or on another computer on your network. By using virtual directories, you are not forced to move all of your FTP content to one system and then place it in an orderly structure for visiting users. Instead, you can have content stored anywhere on your machine or on any system within your network, and users can access it through a simple directory structure.

Virtual directories can also be used to grant different security permissions to the same set of files, based on which directory the user is in. For example, you might have an alias called source, which points to a directory called C:\source on your local system. The alias is defined only with read access. You could add a second alias to your system, called source-RW for example, which could point to the exact same directory on your system but allow full read/write access.

DEFINING A VIRTUAL DIRECTORY

To launch the Virtual Directory Creation Wizard, return to the Internet Information Services tool and highlight the FTP site you want to work with in the scope pane of the window. Select New/Virtual Directory from the Action menu and the wizard will start walking you through the configuration process. The first step of the wizard is shown in Figure 17.51.

FIGURE 17.51

Defining an alias for a virtual directory

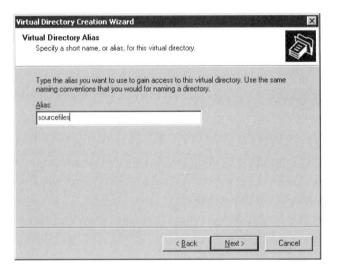

The first thing you will need to specify for your virtual directory is the alias that refers to it. The alias is the directory name that FTP clients will use to access the directory. For example, if you want to have a directory called sourcefiles available off the root of your site when users first connect, then sourcefiles would need to be the alias. The alias does not need to match the name of the directory from where the files are actually coming, so you can use whatever name works best in this field. Click Next to proceed to the next step of the wizard, shown in Figure 17.52.

FIGURE 17.52

Defining a content directory for a virtual directory

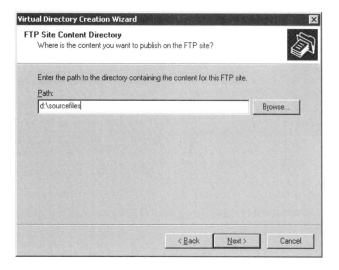

If you want to define a virtual directory that points to another directory on the same computer, enter the path name here (such as **D:\sourcefiles**). IIS will define the virtual directory as pointing to another directory on the same server. However, if you want this virtual directory to point to data located on a share on another server, enter the UNC path to that system here. When you click Next, the Virtual Directory Creation Wizard will take you to another dialog box for entering user credentials, shown in Figure 17.53. Otherwise, you will skip ahead to the dialog box shown in Figure 17.54.

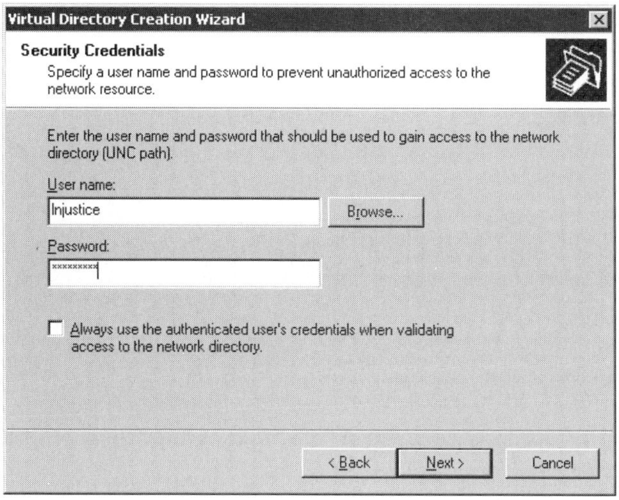

FIGURE 17.53

Entering a username and password to access shared content via a virtual directory

When IIS needs to contact another server for FTP files, it will have to do so with a specific username and password combination. Enter an appropriate set of credentials here, one that would have appropriate access rights to the content you are trying to reach. Notice in Figure 17.53 that instead of entering a user account and password to be used for all connections to the virtual directory, you may alternately use the authenticated user's credentials for access. Click Next to move to the last step of the wizard—defining access permissions—shown in Figure 17.54.

FIGURE 17.54

Defining access permissions for a virtual directory

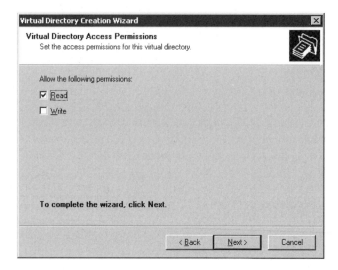

This step in the wizard is identical to the one in the FTP Site Creation Wizard mentioned earlier and shown in Figure 17.44. Decide whether you want to allow read or write access to your system, or both, and check the appropriate boxes.

Once you have entered all of the required information, you should have a new virtual directory item listed below your FTP site. You can test this to make sure that the virtual directory responds appropriately by launching an FTP client and then navigating to your virtual directory. If everything has gone according to plan, IIS should return content from the appropriate location.

In case you aren't already familiar with the concept of virtual directories in FTP, here's an interesting note: virtual directories are not included in the listing returned by a `dir` or `ls` command. These commands query the file system, and virtual directories are not part of the file system. A user has to know the name of the virtual directory in order to navigate to it. For instance, to access the virtual directory we just created named `sourcefiles`, you would have to log on to the FTP server and type **cd sourcefiles** before you could see the contents of that directory. The same is true of virtual directories for Web sites; even if browsing is enabled, the virtual directory can only be accessed by typing in the name of the directory as part of the URL or by using a link created on another Web page. So users can't get to virtual directories if they don't know about them, or if they can't guess their names. Of course, it's not a foolproof security measure, but it's something to consider if you want to create a few directories that are hidden from casually nosy users.

You can modify properties for a virtual directory in exactly the same manner that you do for an FTP site—by editing the properties pages for the directory itself. You can edit the following properties pages for a virtual directory: Virtual Directory and Directory Security. These pages are functionally identical to the pages, defined earlier in this section, for modifying the properties for an entire FTP site.

TIP   *You can use the command-line script* `iisftpdr.vbs` *to create FTP virtual directories. To add a virtual directory called* `VeggieRecipes` *to the Pizza Recipes FTP site at* `f:\vegarchive`, *type the following command (all on one line):* `iisftpdr /create "Pizza Recipes" VeggieRecipes f:\vegarchive`. *One limitation of using the VBScript to create FTP virtual directories is that UNC paths are not supported.*

Using FTP User Isolation

Before the release of IIS 6, there was no clean way to restrict users to particular directories on a given FTP site. You could use NTFS permissions (and still can) to prevent users from making changes or viewing the contents of subdirectories, but they would still see the entire list of directories at the root when they logged in. You could use virtual directories (and still can) to create hidden directories and use NTFS permissions to control access. But this solution is too much work, and it's too complex to deploy for a site that needs to support dozens or hundreds of users. An Internet Service Provider that hosts Web sites for a fee will often provide an FTP account to a site's Webmaster for uploading content. This FTP home directory is often mapped directly to the home directory for the Web site, although in some cases it is only replicated to the actual Web site directory. The Web site creator connects to the designated FTP site and uploads his pages to update the Web site being hosted with the ISP. So it's really important to make this process as easy and as simple as possible for the ISP's clients, while at the same time providing a measure of security. For obvious reasons, they don't want their users to be able to view or modify content from other clients' directories.

User isolation is a new feature of the FTP service bundled with IIS 6. Sites that are configured with user isolation will log users on and shoot them directly into a home directory that appears to be the root directory of the FTP server. Users cannot view or modify files or directories outside of their assigned directory structure. Here's how to set this up:

1. Before you run the FTP Site Creation Wizard, decide where the root of the user isolation site will be. The home directory may be on your local system running IIS or on another server's shared folder on the network. For instance, you may decide to create the site with a home directory located at `d:\ftp-upload`. If you wish to use a shared folder on the network, share the folder on the remote server and set share-level permissions that grant access to your FTP users.

2. Create a subdirectory called `LocalUser` in `d:\ftp-upload`. Yes, it must be named LocalUser because this tells FTP where to look for the home directories.

3. Within `d:\ftp-upload\LocalUser`, create subdirectories for each user who will log on to the site. The directory name and the username for the client must be identical and must also correspond to valid user accounts on the local FTP server or the domain. Remember to set appropriate NTFS permissions on these subdirectories so that your users will have the access they need. Now you are ready to run the FTP Site Creation Wizard.

4. When you get to the User Isolation options step, choose the radio button for Isolate Users (we'll get to the Active Directory option in a moment).

5. In the next step of the wizard, specify the path to the home directory (`d:\ftp-upload` in this case). If you do specify a UNC path for the home directory, you may notice that the wizard does not prompt you for Connect As information. This is because FTP will automatically use the authenticated user's credentials to access the share. So make sure that your users will have permission to access the shared directory on the network server.

6. In the last step of the wizard you may still choose whether to grant read-only permission, write-only permission, or both read and write for the FTP site. In this case, since the user will only be able to access their assigned directory, granting read and write permission to the site does not grant the user permission to read or write to any of the other users' directories.

7. You're done! Use an FTP client to test your configuration by logging on as one of the FTP users.

If you want to make use of the user isolation feature but still want to support anonymous logins, create a subdirectory under the LocalUser directory called Public. If a Public directory exists, and anonymous access is granted to the site, anonymous users will start out in the Public directory and will not be able to navigate above that level. If you've enabled read and write permissions for the entire FTP site, you can still use NTFS permissions on the Public directory to restrict access. Anonymous connections use the IUSR_computername account; simply add an entry to the access list explicitly denying write permission to that account. Now you have a single site that permits read-only access to a Public directory structure for anonymous users and directs authenticated users to their own home directories with read and write access.

Using FTP User Isolation with Active Directory

In the previous example, you set up user isolation for FTP users by creating a root directory and then creating a subdirectory for every permitted user. A disadvantage of this method is that all of the home directories must be physically located in the root directory of the site, under the LocalUser subdirectory. There's no way to distribute home directories across disks or servers.

Another option for FTP user isolation uses account properties set in the Active Directory to determine the location of a user's FTP home directory. This simplifies administration of the FTP site and permits home directories to exist in multiple locations. In fact, if you wish to grant a set of users FTP-based access to their regular file server–based home directories, this is a much better option than the standard form of FTP user isolation.

Although a user's FTP directory may point to the same location as the home directory set with group policies or DSA.MSC, these are separate attributes in the Active Directory. When a user logs on to a site configured to use AD for user isolation, IIS asks the Active Directory for the values of two new properties, FTPRoot and FTPDir. As far as I know, the only easy way to set these properties is by using a VB script, iisftp.vbs.

To use this feature, the IIS 6 server must be a member of a Windows Server 2003 Active Directory domain. Only Windows Server 2003 AD supports the FTPRoot and FTPDir attributes.

The steps to set up an AD-based user isolation site are simple:

1. If you have not already done so, set up home directories for your users. As always, NTFS and (if applicable) share-level permissions should be set appropriately. Because these directories may be spread across multiple servers and disks on your network, keep track of their locations. You'll need this information later when you set the FTPRoot and FTPDir attributes for the accounts.

2. Start the FTP Site Creation Wizard, specify the unique IP address and/or port settings, and choose the Isolate Users Using Active Directory option (shown in Figure 17.55).

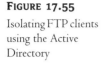

FIGURE 17.55

Isolating FTP clients
using the Active
Directory

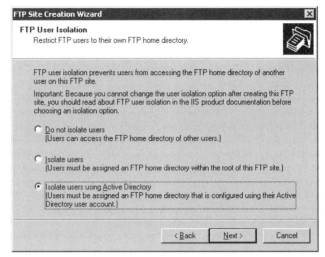

3. Click Next and supply a username and password to be used to gain access to the AD domain, as shown in Figure 17.56. The account you specify in this step does not have to be an administrator account, but it must be a valid user account in the Active Directory domain. If anonymous access is permitted to the site, these credentials will be used to access the AD. Enter the name of the default AD domain (REDHILLTOWN.COM, in the example) to be used when logging on. This default domain name will be assigned to any users who do not specify a domain name at login. For example, if Dave Evans logs in as devans, the FTP service will assume that he's REDHILLTOWN\devans. If you don't set a default value in the wizard, users must specify a domain name at login or access will be denied. Click Next, and the wizard will ask you to retype the user password for confirmation.

FIGURE 17.56

Specifying an AD
account for FTP
user isolation

4. In the final step of the wizard, specify whether users will have read, write, or read and write access to the site. Finish the wizard and IIS creates the site and starts it up for you.

5. Use the VB script `C:\windows\system32\iisftp.vbs` to set FTP home directory information. It doesn't matter whether you perform this step before or after you create the FTP site. In fact, you may set the account attributes as needed to permit new users to access their FTP home directory.

Like other FTP sites, you may specify the home directory path as a local path on the IIS server or as a UNC path. The FTPRoot value sets the root directory; this is either a UNC name (such as `\\zooropa\users`) or it may be a local path on the IIS Server (such as `f:\webdirectories\ftpusers`). The FTPDir value is either the name of the user's directory or a relative path to the directory.

The syntax for this operation is

```
iisftp /SetADProp username FTPRoot path
issftp /SetADProp username FTPDir path
```

For example, if you wanted to use a local path on the IIS server for user Paul, and the path is `F:\ ftpusers\paul`, you'd type in the following two commands (for some reason you can't set both properties at the same time):

```
iisftp /SetADProp paul FTPRoot F:\ftpusers
iisftp /SetADProp paul FTPDir paul
```

If you wanted the FTP root directory to be the shared `Users` folder on the server ZOOROPA, you'd set the FTPRoot and FTPDir attributes like this:

```
iisftp /SetADProp paul FTPRoot \\zooropa\users iisftp /SetADProp paul FTPDir paul
```

In the first case, when Paul logs on to the FTP site, his root directory will correspond to `F:\ftpusers\paul` on the IIS server. In the second scenario, his root directory is `\\zooropa\users\paul`. Like the first method of user isolation, Paul cannot see or navigate to any directories above his starting directory. His ability to read and make changes is determined by the read/write settings on the FTP site, permissions on the shared folder (if applicable), and NTFS ACL entries.

These options for user isolation are pretty neat, but there are a couple of gotchas. My primary complaint is that setting the FTP directory attributes in AD could be a little easier. The `/SetADProp` switch in the `iisftp.vbs` script is not well documented, and you may have to fiddle around with using it until you get the hang of it. Furthermore, IIS doesn't always know right away when the AD attributes for an account have been changed. This is probably due to a replication delay; restarting the site solves the problem. Also, once you create a site with user isolation, you cannot modify that particular attribute. You can't change a regular user isolation site to an AD isolation site, for example.

Finally, although a non-AD user isolation site can be modified and configured in the same way and with the same options as a standard FTP site, the Security Accounts and Home Directory property pages are unavailable for AD isolation sites. After you run the wizard to create the site, you cannot modify read or write permissions on the site, change the directory listing style, or change your mind about anonymous access. In fact, the wizard never asks you whether you want to permit anonymous access on the AD site. In this case, the new site just inherits the global setting for all FTP sites.

This brings us to an interesting question: what if anonymous access is enabled on a user isolation site that uses AD? Well, if no FTP home directory attribute is defined for anonymous users in the Active Directory, then anonymous users cannot log on. But if you do wish to direct anonymous users to a particular directory, define the `FTPRoot` and `FTPDir` attributes for the user account that runs the IIS server (`IUSR_computername`).

Why would you want to enable anonymous access for a site that authenticates users with the Active Directory and then points them to a private home directory? All FTP client software uses port 21 by default and host header names are not supported. You can't tell the FTP server, "By the way, I think I'm connecting to bigserver.redhilltown.com." If you want to host a public site and a separate users-only site on the same box, you either have to configure the server with multiple IP addresses corresponding to different user-friendly names (`bigserver.redhilltown.com` and `intranet.redhilltown.com` and `archives.redhilltown.com`, for example), or have clients connect to the server on nonstandard ports. It's definitely a plus to be able to set up one FTP site that can serve both anonymous and authenticated users.

Using FTP for File Transfer

That's FTP from the server perspective, but what about connecting to an FTP server?

If you have a PC or Macintosh on your desk, think for a moment about how you use that computer in a network situation. You may have a computer elsewhere in your building that acts as a file server, a computer that holds the files shared in your facility or your department. How do you ask that server to transfer a file from itself to your computer? You may say, "I don't do that"—but you do. Whenever you attach to a shared network resource, you are asking that system to provide your computer with shared files. Now, how you actually ask for them is very simple: You just connect to a server, which looks like an extra folder on your desktop if you're a Mac user or an extra drive letter, like X: or E:, if you are a PC user. The intranet world has a facility like that, a facility that lets you attach distant computers to your computer as if that distant computer were a local drive: It is called NFS, the Network File System. But NFS is relatively recent in the TCP/IP world. It's much more common to attach to a host, browse the files that it contains, and selectively transfer them to your local host. You guessed it: the means to do that is FTP.

There are three essentials of using an FTP client: how to start it up, how to navigate around the directories of the FTP server, and how to actually get a file from an FTP server. I'll explain these and, after that, I'll look at a special kind of FTP called anonymous FTP. So let's get started by looking at how the files on an FTP server are organized.

FTP ORGANIZATION

The first time that you get on an FTP server, you'll probably want to get right off. FTP, like much of the TCP/IP world, was built from the perspective that software must be functional and not necessarily user-friendly. If you're a PC user, the Unix file structure will be somewhat familiar, as the DOS file structure was stolen—uh, I mean, borrowed—from Unix. Mac users will need to find an FTP client, of which there are many.

Now, I just referred to the Unix file structure. That's because FTP servers usually use Unix. But some don't (after all, I just spent several pages talking about how to set up FTP sites on a Windows Server 2003), so you may come across FTP servers that don't seem to make any sense. For the purposes of this discussion, I'll assume that the FTP servers here are Unix, but again, be aware that you may run into non-Unix FTP servers. FTP uses a tree-structured directory represented in the Unix fashion. Figure 17.57 shows a sample layout for an FTP site. The top of the directory is called `ourfiles`, and it has two directories below it—subdirectories—called `ourfiles/bin` and `ourfiles/text`. In the Unix world, `.bin` refers to executable files, files we might call program files in other operating systems, or more specifically, EXE or COM files in the PC world. The `text` directory contains two directories below it; one's called `contracts` and one's called `announcements`.

FIGURE 17.57

An example of how files on an FTP server are organized

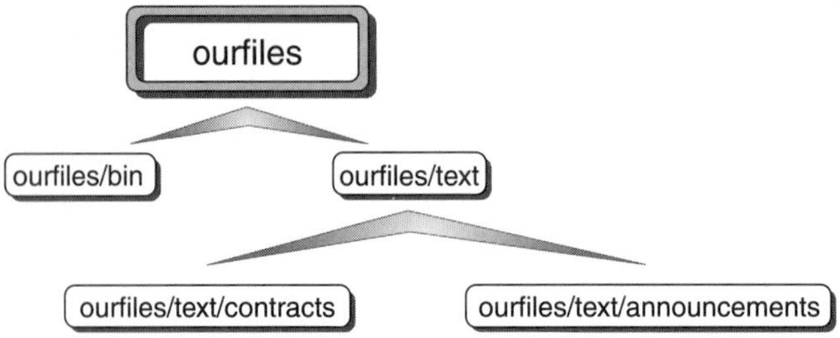

A couple of notes here. PC users may think that things look a bit familiar, but there are some differences. First, notice the subdirectory named `announcements`. That name is more than eight characters long—that's quite acceptable, even though it isn't acceptable in the PC world. Unix accepts filenames of hundreds of characters. Second, notice that there are not backslashes between the different levels, but instead forward slashes; that's also a Unix feature. Now, what complicates matters for users of non-Unix systems is that FTP pretty much assumes that your system uses the Unix file system as well. That means that you have to be comfortable with traversing two directory structures— the one on the remote FTP server and the one on your local hard disk.

FTP CLIENT TYPES

How FTP looks to you from this point depends on what kind of client software you use to access an FTP server. With today's Windows clients (Windows 2000 and XP or Windows 9*x*), you have three choices: a standard command-line interface, Internet Explorer, or My Network Places. First, let's look at the command-line interface.

FILE NAVIGATION WITH COMMAND-LINE FTP CLIENTS

You get an FTP command line—I'll demonstrate it in a minute—that expects you to tell it where to get files from, and where to send files to, using these two commands:

♦ remote: `cd`
♦ local: `lcd`

That's because there's a tree structure on both the remote system—the one that you're getting the files from—and the local system. Let's look at a few examples to nail down exactly how all this cd-ing works.

Moving Around in FTP

When I enter an FTP site, I start out at the top of the directory structure. This top is called the root of the directory. In my example, the root is called `ourfiles`. To move down one level, to `ourfiles/text`,

I could type **cd text**. That says to FTP, "Move down one level relative to the current location." Alternatively, you could skip the relative reference and say absolutely, "Go to `ourfiles/text`"—the way you do that is by typing **cd /ourfiles/text**. The fact that the entry starts with a slash tells `cd` that your command is not a relative one, but an absolute one.

Now let's try moving back up a level. At any point, you can back up one level either by typing the command **cdup** or by typing **cd ..**. The two periods (`..`) mean "one level upward" to both DOS and Unix. Or you can do an absolute reference, as in **cd /ourfiles**.

Now suppose I'm all the way at the bottom of this structure. It's a simple three-level directory, and you often see directory structures that are a good bit more complex than this one. To move back up from `ourfiles/text/announcements` to `ourfiles/text`, you can do as before and either type **cdup** or **cd ..**. Or you could do an absolute reference, as in **cd /ourfiles/text**. To go back two levels, you can either issue two separate **cdup** or **cd ..** commands or use an absolute reference, as in **cd /ourfiles**. To type two **cdup** or **cd ..** commands, you type the command, then press Enter, then type the second command. Do not try to issue two commands on the same line.

AN FTP EXAMPLE OF NAVIGATION: GET A SCANDAL

There's a really neat project run by a group of volunteers called The Gutenberg Project. They take text whose copyright has expired and type it into text files. They then put these text files on both FTP and Web sites for anyone to download and read.

For example, one of my favorites of Arthur Conan Doyle's Sherlock Holmes stories is "A Scandal in Bohemia," which Gutenberg has at `ftp://sailor.gutenberg.org/pub/gutenberg/etext99/advsh10.txt`. (Their general Web home page is at `http://promo.net/pg/`.) Let's go fetch the scandal.

First, I'll FTP to `ftp.gutenberg.org`. From a command prompt, I type **ftp ftp.gutenberg.org**, and then I get a `User:` prompt. This site doesn't know me, so I can't log in with a local name and password. That's where the idea of anonymous FTP becomes useful. You can often log in to an FTP site and download data that's been put there specifically for public use. Anonymous FTP is just the same as regular FTP except that you log in with the name "anonymous." It responds that a guest login is okay but wants my e-mail address for a password. I put in my e-mail address, and I'm in. Now, it might be that there are places on this server that I cannot get to because I signed on as anonymous, but that doesn't matter—Sherlock is in the public area. Next, I can do a `dir` command and see what's on this directory:

```
ftp>dir
200 PORT command successful.
150 Opening ASCII mode data connection for /bin/ls.
total 20
d--x--x--x   2 0        0          4096 Jul 6 2001 bin
d--x--x--x   2 0        0          4096 Jun 28 2001 etc
d--x--x--x   20 0       0          4096 Jun 28 2001 lib
dr-xr-xr-x   20 0       0          4096 Jun 26 2002 pub
226 Transfer complete.
ftp: 321 bytes received in 0.11Seconds 2.94Kbytes/sec.
ftp>
```

It's not a very pretty sight, but let's see what we can see. Notice the letters r, x, and d to the left of each entry? They represent the privilege levels of access to this file. One of the important things is whether or not the leftmost letter is d—if it is, then that's not a file, it's a directory. Notice the pub entry; that's commonly where generally available files are stored—pub is short for public.

Typing **cd pub** takes me a level down. Another `dir` shows a directory named `gutenberg`—a likely candidate—and I could keep searching around, but I know from Gutenberg's Web site that the file I'm looking for is at `ftp://sailor.gutenberg.org/pub/gutenberg/etext99/advsh10.txt`. I can navigate there by typing **cd gutenberg/etext99**.

Notice that there are no spaces except between the `cd` and the directory name, and notice also that, in general, you must be careful about capitalization—if the directory's name is `Literature` with a capital L, then trying to change to a directory whose name is `literature` with a lowercase l will probably fail. Why "probably"? It's another Unix thing; the Unix file system is case sensitive. In contrast, if you found yourself talking to an NT-based TCP/IP host, then case would be irrelevant. How do you know what your host runs? Well, it is sometimes announced in the sign-on message, but not always. The best bet is to always assume that case is important.

Anyway, once I get to the directory, I can do a `dir` command to see if `advsh10.txt` is there. `dir advsh10.txt` confirms that the file is there.

Before I get the file, there's one more thing that I should point out. Years ago, most files that were transferred were simple plain-text ASCII files. Nowadays, many files are not ASCII—even data files created by spreadsheets and word processors contain data other than simple text. Such files are, as you probably know, called binary files. FTP must be alerted that it will transfer binary files. You do that by typing **binary** at the `ftp>` prompt. FTP responds by saying, "Type set to I." That is FTP's inimitable way of saying that it's now ready to do a binary file transfer or, as FTP calls it, an image file transfer.

TRANSFERRING A FILE

Now I'll get the file. Because it's a text file, I just type **get advsh10.txt**, press Enter, and wait. Once the transfer's done, I get some throughput statistics.

Now, when I get the file, it'll take some time to transfer. There's no nice bar graphic or anything like that to say how far the transfer has proceeded. There is a command, however, that will give me some idea about how the transfer is progressing—hash. I type **hash**, and from that point on, the system prints an octothorp (#) for each 2K of file transferred. For example, say I'm on a Gutenberg system and I want to download the Bible, `bible10.zip`. (Is it sacrilegious to compress the Bible? Interesting theological question.) The file is about 1600K in size, so I'll see 800 octothorps.

Each line shows me 80 characters, so each line of # characters means 160K of file were transferred. It'll take 10 lines of # characters (10 lines!) before the file is completely transferred.

Remember that Gutenberg location. If you're ever stuck for something to read, they've got hundreds of books online. Even better, as they are just simple ASCII, there are programs that will transfer the files to a small computer such as a Palm handheld or a Windows CE palmtop—the easily portable, electronic book is almost here!

Downloading to the Screen

Before leaving the command-line FTP client, there's one more tip that I'd like to share with you: how to download directly to your computer screen.

Sometimes you'll come across a short file, like the READMEs that are so common around the computer world. Such a file may describe what's in an FTP directory. You'd like to examine it but the whole idea of first downloading it and then bringing up the file in Notepad seems a lot of work. In that case, download it instead to the screen.

You do that by typing **get** *filename* **-**.

Of course, this depends on the system that you're working with, but it may only be possible to do this "get" if your FTP session is set for ASCII transfers rather than binary transfers. You can change that by just typing **ascii** at the command line. You'll see the response "Type set to A."

GRAPHICAL FTP CLIENTS

In one example of how the world keeps getting better, you can often avoid command-line FTP. In many cases, all you need do is to point your browser to an FTP site by typing **ftp://***address*, like **ftp://ftp.3com.com**, in the Address field.

TIP   You need the ftp:// prefix on the address on some browsers because when you just type in an address, like ignatz.mouse.com, then the browser assumes that you want it to connect to a Web server rather than an FTP, telnet, or other server, and so it interprets the address as `http://ignatz.mouse.com`. *What's the difference between* `ftp://ignatz.mouse.com` *and* `http://ignatz.mouse.com`? *It's a matter of addresses. It's possible to have many kinds of servers running on the same system. They're distinguished by their port numbers. Just as your dentist's office might be at 210 Main Street and your dermatologist's office might also be at 210 Main Street, they probably don't share an office. The dentist's full address isn't 210 Main Street; it's more like Suite 118, 210 Main Street, and perhaps the dermatologist is at Suite 305, 210 Main Street. Different ports on a server are like different rooms in a building. Web servers are by default at port 80—but http:// is easier to remember than "connect me to port 80." FTP works on another port, actually two ports—20 and 21; telnet uses 23; and so on.*

In any case, most Web browsers can double as a graphical FTP client. You can navigate a directory structure by just clicking a directory to enter it or pressing the Backspace key to back up a level. The trouble with most Web browsers as FTP clients, however, is that they only work when you're logging in to the FTP site as anonymous; they don't give you a chance to specify a user ID and password. Thus, if the site requires an account to access it, your browser is just booted off the site.

A feature available on Windows 2000 and later clients, called FTP folders, solves that problem. Just open My Network Places and double-click Add Network Place. You'll be prompted to type either a UNC, like *someserver**somevolume*, or a URL, like `http://www.someplace.com` or `ftp://ftp.someplace.com`. What's particularly nice about this is that the wizard creating the new Network Place entry asks you if you need to specify a user ID and password to access the new Network Place. The FTP site then shows up in My Network Places as if it were a local set of folders, combining the simplicity of a GUI front end for FTP with the flexibility of being able to control how you log on.

That's about all that I'll say here about FTP. There is lots more that FTP can do, but I've given you the basics that you can use to get started and get some work done in the TCP/IP world. If this all looks ugly, user-unfriendly, and hard to remember, then, well, it is—at least to someone used to a Macintosh or Windows. If you're not comfortable working from the command line, you may be better off with one of the graphical FTP programs available, which can make uploading and downloading files a drag-and-drop procedure more like using Windows Explorer than like using the command prompt. FTP is two things—the FTP protocol, which is the set of rules that the computers on an intranet use to communicate, and the program called FTP that you start up in order to do file transfers. The FTP protocol doesn't change and probably won't change. But the FTP program, which is usually known as the FTP client, can be as easy to use as its designer can make it. So go on out, learn to spell anonymous, and have some fun on those FTP sites!

Setting Up an NNTP News Server and Configuring NNTP Services

Newsgroups are one of the Internet's older technologies, but they're not as well known as some of the Internet's more visible counterparts—namely Web browsing and e-mail. Newsgroups are a way of collecting and threading messages posted by users together to form a sort of "conversation" database between the participants of a newsgroup.

These conversation databases can be used to discuss almost anything you can think of—questions about company benefits, organizational news releases, politics, society, technology, etc. This concept was once referred to as collaboration or groupware, in which companies within an organization could collaborate and share ideas electronically on a set of "bulletin boards" focusing on a specific topic. While some organizations have been able to implement this and make their organizations more productive, this capability still hasn't caught on as much as it should have.

The Internet is filled with literally tens of thousands of these groups, covering every imaginable topic under the sun. You name it, and there has probably been a newsgroup defined somewhere to discuss it. Thanks to IIS 6, you can easily set up and administer your own NNTP server for internal users to read, post, and reply to messages related to topics important for your organization.

When you install NNTP, a default virtual server is created. By default, newsgroup messages are stored in `c:\inetpub\nntpfile`.

Creating a New NNTP Server

Even though IIS installs and configures a default newsgroup server when you set it up, you might need to have another server on your system. For example, you might need to have a public newsgroup server available to anyone on the Internet, and then a private newsgroup server available to internal staff.

To get started with setting up a newsgroup server, you'll need to know the following:

◆ Which IP address you want this NNTP server to listen on (or if it should respond on all available IP addresses).

◆ Which TCP/IP port number this NNTP server should listen to on the previously specified IP address(es). Typically, this is port 119.

◆ Whether to allow anonymous access to your site or to require user authentication.

◆ Which directories your system will use to store and manage your NNTP database files.

To start installing your server, begin by making sure that you have all of the bullet items listed above ready, and then select your IIS server in the Internet Information Services Management tool. Selecting the New/NNTP Virtual Server option from the Action pull-down menu will launch the New NNTP Virtual Server Wizard. In the first step of the New NNTP Virtual Server Wizard, specify a friendly name to use when referencing your new NNTP virtual server. This name is simply for administration purposes; your users won't see it, so choose a name that's appropriate, and then click Next to proceed to the next step of the wizard, shown in Figure 17.58.

In order to access your NNTP server, users will need to establish a TCP/IP connection to your server on a specific IP address and TCP port number. By default, NNTP servers typically communicate on port number 119. Unless you have special circumstances, you will probably want to use this as the default port number for your system.

FIGURE 17.58

Defining IP
addresses and TCP
ports for an NNTP
virtual server

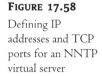

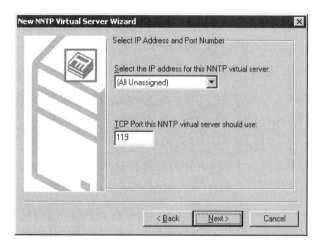

If you are going to be running only one newsgroup server on your system, these settings might be just fine, depending on the content on your newsgroups and the configuration of your system. For example, if you were going to run an internal confidential database for the discussion of sales and marketing strategies, you probably wouldn't want to make that database available on a publicly accessible IP address. Users from the outside world could potentially connect to your system and read all of your confidential information stored in the newsgroup, so make sure you correctly determine which IP address(es) to use for your site.

Newsgroup readers—by default—will look on port 119 for a newsgroup server, so enter 119 here in the port field. If you would prefer to change the TCP port that your server responds on (necessary if you only have one IP address and you want to run multiple newsgroup servers), you can do so here. Keep in mind that all the clients connecting to this system will probably have to manually change their configurations accordingly.

Click Next when you've completed the IP configuration, and you'll move to the next step of the wizard, shown in Figure 17.59.

FIGURE 17.59

Defining directories
for an NNTP
virtual server

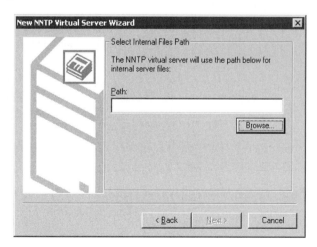

IIS requires two separate directories on your system to maintain an NNTP virtual server: one in which to store internal files for its own processing, and one to store the actual newsgroup content. In this first screen, you need to supply the directory that IIS should use for its own internal files. When you've entered this, click Next to continue to the next step, shown in Figure 17.60.

FIGURE 17.60

Defining a storage area for NNTP content files

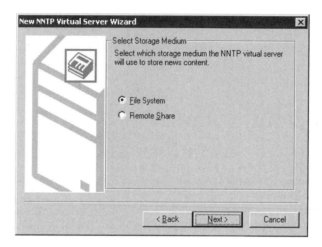

In this step of the wizard, you will be defining a "storage medium" for IIS to use when storing news content. This storage medium can be either on the IIS server itself or on another server. If you will be storing the news content directly on your IIS server, select the radio button for File System and then click Next to proceed to the next step of the New NNTP Virtual Server Wizard, shown in Figure 17.61.

FIGURE 17.61

Defining a path to store newsgroup messages

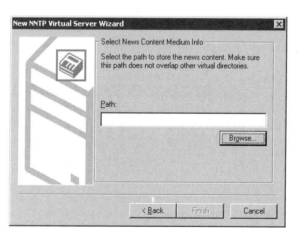

If you decide to store news content on another system, select the radio button for Remote Share. Doing so will change the next step of the wizard to prompt you for a share name and username/password combination to use to access the news content stored on another system. For the sake of brevity, I'll assume you chose the File System option and proceed directly to the next step of the wizard.

NOTE   *IIS will require approximately 548 bytes of storage in its internal working directory for each newsgroup message that will be stored on your system, in addition to the space required for the articles themselves.*

Click Finish after this step, and you will have a functional NNTP virtual server running on your IIS server.

Modifying NNTP Virtual Server Properties

Since the New NNTP Virtual Server Wizard only has a few steps to it, there are settings and parameters that you will probably need to set for your site. For example, you might want to define newsgroup names, control security, limit the size of postings, etc. To adjust the parameters for your NNTP site after the wizard has created it, you will use the NNTP virtual server properties pages.

GENERAL PROPERTIES

To reach the NNTP virtual server properties pages, highlight your new NNTP virtual server in the scope pane of the Internet Information Services tool and then select Properties from the Action pull-down menu. This should bring you to a dialog box similar to the one shown in Figure 17.62.

FIGURE 17.62

Configuring general settings for an NNTP virtual server

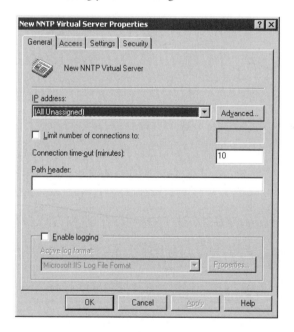

Through this page, you can change the following items to fit your needs:

IP Address   Select the IP address for your site to use here. If you intend to have multiple IP addresses servicing the same site or you want to change the ports this site uses, click the Advanced button.

Advanced TCP Port and SSL Port   By default, NNTP sites typically use TCP port number 119 for standard connections and port 563 for secure connections. Changing these values will usually require changing the configuration of newsreader software on client computers as well.

Connection Time-out   Depending on the capacity of your server and the other jobs it's responsible for, you might want to limit the number of connections you allow into your NNTP server. A timeout interval of 10 minutes for idle connections is defined by default.

Path Header   Path headers refer to a string that is used for the "path" line in each newsgroup posting. Path lines are used to determine how a newsgroup posting will reach its destination. For more information on path lines and having newsgroup servers pass messages to each other, see RFC 1036.

Enable Logging   If you are running an anonymous NNTP server, you might want to enable logging for your system in case you ever need to trace where a specific posting came from.

NNTP SETTINGS

For settings specific to newsgroups and postings themselves, go to the Settings properties page, shown in Figure 17.63.

FIGURE 17.63

Configuring settings for an NNTP virtual server

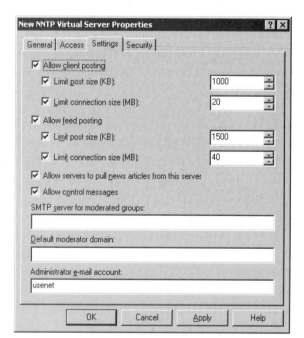

From this page, you can edit the following options:

Allow Client Posting   To disallow client posting on this system, uncheck this box. Obviously, on most systems, you will want to leave this checked.

Limit Post Size   For publicly accessible NNTP servers, you might find a need to limit the size of any one message that can be sent to your system. Otherwise, individuals might overload the server by loading huge binary files to the system, quickly filling up all the available disk space. Enter a reasonable limit here, or accept the default values of 1 megabyte (1000 kilobytes) for clients or 1.5 megabytes (1500 kilobytes) for newsfeed posts.

Limit Connection Size   Much like the Limit Post Size setting, another way that individuals could potentially overload your system is by flooding it with numerous smaller messages that fit within the Limit Post Size restriction. In order to compensate for this, you can set a maximum limit, in megabytes, that an NNTP user can post during a single session to your server.

Allow Feed Posting   When an NNTP server is configured to receive newsgroup data from another server instead of from individual users, or when an NNTP server replicates its own newsgroup data to another server, that flow of information is called a newsfeed. Unfortunately, IIS 6 (like IIS 5) doesn't support newsfeeds at this time. Perhaps this is because Exchange does support newsfeeds? Like the SMTP/POP3 service issue, Microsoft might be reluctant to provide a free service or feature when they have a perfectly good one for sale.

Allow Servers to Pull News Articles from This Server   This option would theoretically permit the server to participate in a newsfeed configuration. Like the Allow Feed Posting option, it's apparently a placeholder for a future implementation of NNTP. Newsfeeds are not supported in IIS 6.

Allow Control Messages   Control messages are specially formatted newsgroup messages designed to control the configuration of an NNTP server; for example, to create a new newsgroup across a collection of NNTP servers, a control message can be sent out instructing all servers to create the new group. Or a control message might instruct all other participating news servers to cancel (delete) a specific message from all systems.

SMTP Server for Moderated Groups   Moderated groups (discussed a bit later in this section) are newsgroups that have their postings approved by a moderator before they are publicly posted. This is done via e-mail, so the NNTP process needs to have an accessible SMTP server to use for sending messages. If you will be configuring the SMTP service on your IIS server (discussed later in this chapter), you can use your own system as the SMTP server.

Default Moderator Domain   When moderated e-mail messages are sent from your IIS system, they will be sent with a To: address of `newsgroup_name@default_moderator_domain` unless a specific moderator is specified for a group. Enter the domain portion of the address to use in this field.

SECURITY ACCOUNT PROPERTIES

In order to define operator permissions for specific user accounts on your NNTP server, click the Security tab to get to the Security properties page (shown in Figure 17.64). Here, you can define operators capable of accessing and making configuration changes to a virtual NNTP server.

Add the Windows user accounts that should have operator privileges to this window by clicking the Add button and selecting the appropriate accounts.

ACCESS PROPERTIES

Through the Access properties page, you can make changes to how your NNTP server is to be accessed. For example, you can allow for anonymous access (this is typically enabled by default), which means that any user who can successfully connect to the IP address of your NT server can access the newsgroups contained on it. Or you can require authenticated access. You can also define SSL encryption certificates (discussed later in this chapter) to use when communicating with your server, and grant or deny connections based on IP addresses. The Access properties page is shown in Figure 17.65.

FIGURE 17.64

Editing security
properties

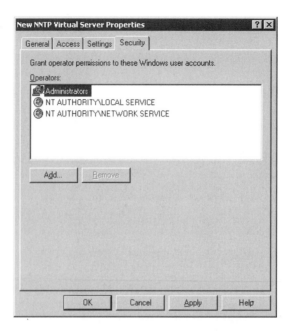

FIGURE 17.65

Editing access
properties

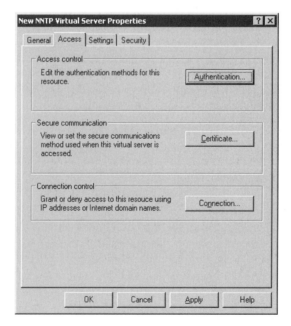

Access Control

Clicking the Authentication button in the Access Control area will take you to another dialog box,
shown in Figure 17.66, for editing what type of authentication users should use when connecting to
your system.

FIGURE 17.66

Editing authentication methods

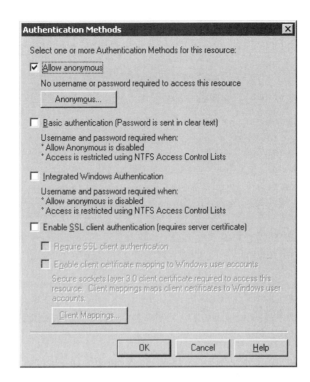

As you can see in Figure 17.66, anonymous access is permitted by default. Anonymous access is rather straightforward; no username or password is required to connect, and all requests for content will be directed through the anonymous account defined on the Security Accounts properties page.

Basic authentication utilizes an authentication protocol built into NNTP called AUTHINFO. This protocol negotiates a username and password authentication over the Internet in cleartext. This authentication method will have the widest means of support but at the risk of transmitting passwords from your system in plain view of anyone who might be looking for them.

Integrated Windows authentication is another way of saying Windows challenge/response authentication. This typically limits client support to Windows platforms only, but it provides a secure means of authenticating users without passing cleartext passwords over the Internet.

If you would prefer to encrypt the authentication process between the client and your NNTP server, you can select the Enable SSL Client Authentication check box. This will allow your server to authenticate the client connecting to it in order to set up a secure, encrypted SSL tunnel. However, the client connecting to your server must have an SSL certificate installed for this to work. If you've enabled SSL client authentication, you can require this type of authentication for all users by checking the Require SSL Client Authentication check box. Based on the certificates that your users have installed, you can have those certificates map directly to a Windows user account by checking the Enable Client Certificate Mapping to Windows User Accounts box and then entering appropriate mappings by clicking the Client Mappings button. Doing this will basically tell IIS, "If someone hands you this certificate, assume that it is Windows user XYZ." The user does not need to actually provide a username and password; simply having the certificate is enough identification.

Secure Communication

If you would like to protect your NNTP data as it travels from your server to the client (and vice versa), you can set up SSL communications properties through the Secure Communication area. This requires having an SSL certificate installed on your system and is discussed in greater detail in the "Communicating Securely with SSL" section later in this chapter.

Connection Control

Another means of securing your NNTP server is to restrict who can access the site based on IP address, a range of IP addresses, or a domain name. This requires knowing in advance who should be connecting to your site and from where. By clicking the Connection button in the Connection Control section of the Access properties page (shown in Figure 17.65), you will see a screen similar to the one back in Figure 17.22, in which you can enter any restrictions you'd like.

DIRECTORY PROPERTIES

Since all newsgroup content must be stored in files, you will need to define where those files are to be stored. Initially, you did that in the wizard when you provided the system with directories to use for the NNTP content. However, since the wizard assumes several defaults for you, you might want to edit the directory properties yourself.

To edit the directory properties, go back to the Internet Information Services console and expand the NNTP server item that you created. Select the Virtual Directories item in the scope pane, and you should see the directories you originally specified for newsgroup content in the results pane. Highlight the appropriate directory to modify, and then either select Action/Properties from the pull-down menu or right-click the directory and select Properties. You should see a properties page similar to the one shown in Figure 17.67.

FIGURE 17.67

Directory properties page

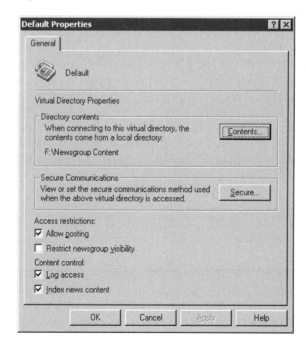

You can store content in a directory on the IIS server itself or on a share on another server by clicking the Contents button in the Directory Contents portion of this properties page. If you decide to use a network share for storing your content, you will need to define an account that IIS uses to connect to the share.

Based on the newsgroups stored in this directory, you can control some specific parameters:

Allow Posting   To disallow posting to newsgroups—that is, to the newsgroups stored in this directory—uncheck this box.

Restrict Newsgroup Visibility   If you will be using access controls on your system to define who can access which newsgroups, you can control what newsgroups those users will even see by selecting this option. Choosing this option can add a significant amount of processing overhead to your system if you have a large number of groups, so you might want to leave this option disabled.

Log Access   This setting works in conjunction with the Enable Logging check box on the General properties page for the NNTP site. If you want to log access to your system, you must have both check boxes checked. This allows you to log access to some directories as needed, without necessarily logging all access to all directories.

Index News Content   Checking this box will instruct the Microsoft Indexing Service to index the content of this site, allowing users to search for text in postings.

The Secure Communications section of this properties page is used to require SSL communication sessions for newsgroups stored in this directory. SSL is discussed in greater detail later in this chapter in the "Communicating Securely with SSL" section.

DEFINING GROUPS

Messages on an NNTP server are typically stored in different hierarchical groups based on their content. Levels of hierarchy are delineated by a dot between each word. For example, on the Internet, common newsgroup names such as `rec.pets.dogs` (for dog lovers) are part of the overall recreation hierarchy (`rec`), then the `pets` subhierarchy. This type of organization gives users an easy way to find the information they are looking for. Additional groups could include `rec.pets.cats` and `rec.pets.ferrets`, thus keeping the messages for each topic isolated from other messages.

Within your organization, you can also use a similar structure for newsgroups. For example, you might choose to define groups along divisional, departmental, and then topical lines. For example, a group called `accounting.payroll.withholding` could be used to handle discussion messages and questions from employees regarding their withholding from their paychecks, whereas `sales.advertising.radio` could be used to discuss the effectiveness of radio advertisements and to brainstorm for new topics.

For each level of hierarchy in the name of the newsgroup, IIS will create a separate directory in the content directory defined for your site (discussed earlier in this chapter). For example, if you create a group called `accounting.payroll.withholding`, IIS will create three subdirectories in your content directory. The first subdirectory will be called `accounting`. Within the `accounting` subdirectory, there will be another subdirectory called `payroll`, and within the `payroll` subdirectory, there will be another subdirectory called `withholding`. If these directories are created on an NTFS volume, you can control which users can access which groups (assuming you've required authenticated access) by applying appropriate permissions to each directory. Therefore, you can restrict confidential information to only the individuals who should receive it and leave everything else open to the public.

As you can see, there are many possible uses for newsgroups. Since the default configuration of a newsgroup server doesn't typically include any groups (other than control groups, if needed), you will most likely want to add some groups to your system.

Define newsgroups from the main Internet Information Services screen by expanding your NNTP server item in the scope pane, and then highlighting the Newsgroups option below it. Once you have the Newsgroups item highlighted, you can select the New/Newsgroup option either from the Action pull-down menu or by right-clicking the Newsgroups option. Selecting New/Newsgroup launches the New Newsgroup Wizard, which will walk you through the process to define a new newsgroup. The first step of the wizard, shown in Figure 17.68, will prompt you for an appropriate name for your newsgroup. As previously discussed, enter the name for your desired newsgroup here and then click Next to proceed to the next step of the wizard, shown in Figure 17.69.

FIGURE 17.68

Defining a new newsgroup name

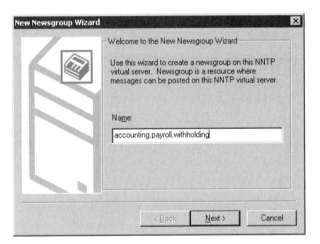

FIGURE 17.69

Defining a news-group description and pretty name

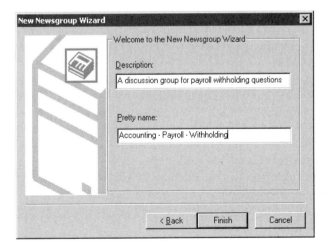

To enter descriptive information about this group above and beyond the information that the name of the group gives, use the Description field. You can also enter a "pretty name" for this newsgroup that will be returned to NNTP clients that issue a LIST PRETTYNAMES command.

Once you have entered this information, click the Finish button and your new newsgroup will be created. However, as is true with most of these wizards, a few assumptions are made for this group and automatically saved as defaults. If you would like to change the properties of the group you've just created, highlight it in the results pane of the MMC and then select the Properties option either from the Action pull-down menu or by right-clicking the group. That should bring you to a group properties page similar to the one shown in Figure 17.70. In this screen, you can edit the properties you just defined for this group, plus enable some additional options, as defined next:

Read Only　If only the moderator should be allowed to post to this group, check this box. No other users will be allowed to make postings to this group.

Moderated　The default setting for new newsgroups is to leave them unmoderated—meaning that all postings are publicly available immediately; there is no "checking" process that occurs. If you prefer to have a moderator manage the messages on your system, click the Moderated option. Enter an appropriate e-mail address for the moderator in the Moderator field, or click the Set Default button if you prefer to use the moderator defined in the NNTP settings (discussed earlier in this section). Newsgroup messages will be e-mailed to the Moderator for approval before being published.

FIGURE 17.70

Editing newsgroup properties

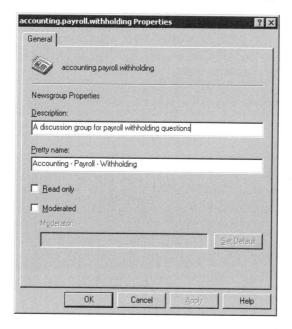

Defining NNTP Server Expiration Policies

In a perfect world, disk space would be amazingly dirt cheap, and installing terabytes worth of storage would simply be a Plug-and-Play operation. This would allow you to keep all news articles posted on your server forever and ever (amen).

Welcome to reality. If you're running an NNTP server that will be handling a fair amount of traffic, it will eventually consume all available disk space on your system, unless you expire old articles. To add an expiration policy to your system, select your NNTP server in the scope pane of the Internet Information Services tool and expand it. Select Expiration Policies, then select New/Expiration Policy from the Action pull-down menu.

This will start you through a wizard in which you define which newsgroups to expire and when. The first step of the wizard will prompt you for a friendly name for your expiration policy. Enter whatever you feel is appropriate in this box and then click Next to move on to the next step of the wizard, shown in Figure 17.71.

FIGURE 17.71

Choosing all groups or selected groups

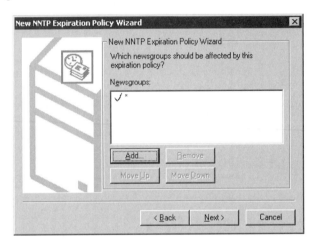

The asterisk and check mark shown in the Newsgroups list box in Figure 17.71 indicate that all groups are included in this policy. If you want to have IIS simply expire all newsgroup articles on your system after a set number of hours or days, accept the default setting and click Next. Otherwise, if you want to have custom expiration policies for certain groups (for example, you might want some groups to never expire), select the Add button. You will be taken to an Add Newsgroup dialog box where you will enter a group name to include or exclude from this policy. Excluded groups appear in a list of newsgroups with an X instead of a check mark. Use the Move Up and Move Down buttons to set the order for application of the policy. For instance, to have the policy apply to all groups on the server except for alt.payroll.accounting, put the wildcard include entry first on the list and the exclude entry for alt.payroll.accounting last. Once you've configured the list of newsgroups and included or excluded them from the policy in the desired order, click Next to move on to the next step of the wizard (shown in Figure 17.72). Now you will enter the number of hours that IIS should wait before purging a newsgroup article. The default value is 168 hours, or 7 days. If you have a low-traffic site and want to keep articles around longer, then increase this value accordingly.

Click Finish when you are done, and you should see your new expiration policy appear in the details pane of the console. To go back and make changes to the policy, simply edit the properties for the policy item.

FIGURE 17.72

Setting an expiration
interval, in hours

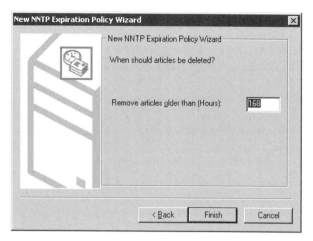

Virtual NNTP Server Directories

Virtual NNTP server directories have a bit of a different function than virtual directories defined for Web and FTP sites. On Web and FTP sites, users can navigate through different directories on your system, but on a newsgroup server the only thing users can navigate to are newsgroups. So what's an NNTP virtual directory designed to do?

NNTP virtual directories are designed primarily as a means to spread newsgroup content out across systems. Content is spread across systems based on hierarchy names. For example, you might have the content for the entire accounting.* hierarchy stored on one server and have the content for the sales.* hierarchy stored on another server.

The primary benefits of doing this are increased speed and performance (you don't have one server doing all the work), and if you suddenly run out of disk space on one system, you can start spreading the content around. To create an NNTP virtual directory, begin by selecting your NNTP virtual server in the scope pane of the Internet Information Services console and highlighting the Virtual Directories option below it. Select the New/Virtual Directory option from the Action pull-down menu to launch the New Virtual Directory Wizard, shown in Figure 17.73.

FIGURE 17.73

Defining a subtree
for an NNTP server
virtual directory

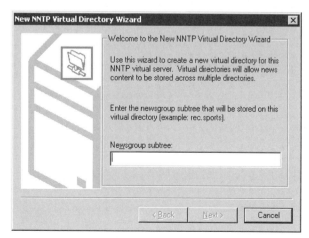

To carve off an entire section of your hierarchy structure and store it in a virtual directory, enter the left-most portion of the group name you want to store. For example, if you entered `rec.pets` in this field, you would end up storing the groups `rec.pets.dogs`, `rec.pets.cats`, and `rec.pets.ferrets` in this virtual directory, but `rec.games.chess` would still be stored in the primary directory defined for this NNTP server. Enter the appropriate hierarchy name and then click Next to proceed to the next step of the wizard.

The next step of the wizard will ask you for a "storage medium" for this content—this is exactly the same as what you saw back in Figure 17.60. The wizard will also prompt you for either a directory or a remote share and username/password combination based on your answer. The location you provide the wizard with is where all of the content for the hierarchy you specified will be stored. By clicking Finish, you will have created a virtual directory on your server for your NNTP content. Once created, you can modify the properties of a virtual directory by right-clicking the item and choosing Properties from the context menu. Refer back to the section "Directory Properties" for more details.

Setting Up an SMTP Server and Configuring SMTP Services

As you've seen throughout this chapter so far, there will probably come a time when your IIS server will need to send e-mail to someone. Whether it is for support of FrontPage extensions or to forward a newsgroup posting to a moderator for approval, your server will need to communicate with another host for the transfer of e-mail. The protocol you'll use to perform this communication is called the Simple Mail Transfer Protocol—SMTP for short.

Microsoft has included a basic SMTP server with IIS 6 for exactly this reason—so that services on your server can send e-mail out to other hosts as needed. Without the optional POP3 component, however, it is *not* a complete mail server, as you'll see, but it can be useful for other things.

Internet E-Mail Protocols

There are two main Internet e-mail protocols that most of us care about: The Simple Mail Transfer Protocol (SMTP) and the Post Office Protocol (POP3).

SMTP is the "mail" Internet e-mail protocol. SMTP grew up at a time when most users on the Internet were running Unix machines, each with its own IP address. Each Unix machine ran two mail programs. The first was a program that could package up a mail message and send it to its destination; the most common one was one named Sendmail. The second program was a so-called daemon, a program that always runs in the background, kind of like a DOS Terminate and Stay Resident (TSR) program. The daemon would constantly listen for incoming mail in the form of TCP/IP packets sent from another system running Sendmail.

The SMTP/Sendmail approach worked fine as long as every system on the Internet could run some kind of mail daemon, and so long as every system was up and running 24 hours a day, seven days a week. But primitive PC operating systems don't handle daemons well, and most people don't leave their workstations up and running all of the time, even if they are running an operating system that handles daemons well. Additionally, while many systems may run all of the time and while they may have an operating system that likes daemons just fine, they aren't connected to the Internet all of the time.

In any case, it'd be nice to enhance SMTP with some kind of mail storage system, allowing one computer to act as a kind of "post office." Suppose you have 500 people on your network with varying operating systems and uptimes. So you set up one computer that is up 24 hours a day, 7 days a week. This computer runs the mail daemon, the program that listens. You tell that computer, "Accept mail for everyone in the company, and hold onto it." That's the computer I'll call a post office. Then, when a user wants her mail, she just connects to that post office and pulls down her mail. In the Internet world, we let a client computer like the one on her desktop communicate with a post office computer with a protocol called POP3, the Post Office Protocol. Such a program is a small application referred to as a POP3 client. Actually, every POP3 client that I know of might be better referred to as a POP3 Message Receiver/SMTP Message Sender. The program only uses POP3 to get your mail; when you create a new message, it just sends it to a computer running the SMTP receiver service (the daemon), which then hands it to the SMTP delivery service (Sendmail or one of Sendmail's cousins).

In order for your office to send and receive Internet mail, you'll need a computer to act as a post office. The computer uses SMTP to talk to other post offices, and those post offices may choose to communicate with you at any hour of the day, so the computer must be attached to the Internet 24 hours a day, 7 days a week. So that your users can retrieve their mail, they'll need programs that act as POP3 clients. Finally, that post office computer will need to run a POP3 server so that it can respond to mail requests.

In the past, if you wanted a POP3 Server for Windows NT or 2000, you had to buy Exchange, some other commercial mail software package, or use the free EMWACS Internet Mail Service software. Now Windows Server 2003 includes a very simple POP3 Server component that you can install from the Control Panel. This is a great option for organizations that don't want all the bells and whistles of Exchange or some other big software package but still need an Internet e-mail solution. We'll talk about the POP3 Server component a bit later.

Where can you find a POP3 client? Right in Windows—the program attached to the Inbox tool (on 95) or Outlook Express (on 98, Me, 2000, XP, or NT 4 with IE 4) can act as a POP3 client. Or, if you find the Microsoft tool not to your liking, surf on over to `www.eudora.com`, where you'll find Eudora Light, an excellent mail client written by the Qualcomm people. They write terrific software, and even better, they have a 32-bit version of their Eudora mail client that they give away absolutely free. You can even get the full version of the software for free if you're willing to put up the displayed ads. I'll talk about how to configure these clients a little later.

Creating a New SMTP Server

As I stated in the earlier section, a default virtual SMTP server is created during the IIS 6 installation. The SMTP server is configured to listen on TCP/IP port 25 for all configured IP addresses. The mail directory for the default virtual server is `\inetpub\mailroot`. Since the virtual server can accept and deliver mail for multiple domain names, it may never be necessary to create another SMTP virtual server on the same system. However, if you find you do need to set up a new SMTP server on IIS, you will need to know the following information in advance:

◆ Which IP address you want this SMTP server to listen to for inbound connections (or if it should respond on all available IP addresses).

◆ Which TCP/IP port number this SMTP server should listen to on the previously specified IP address(es). Typically, this is port 25.

◆ A "default domain" name to use for the sending of messages.

◆ Which directory on your system to use for incoming and outgoing e-mail files.

Once again, Microsoft has included a wizard to make the creation of a new SMTP server relatively straightforward.

To begin the creation of a new SMTP server, start by selecting your IIS server in the scope pane of the Internet Information Services tool, then select the New/SMTP Virtual Server option from the Action pull-down menu. This should bring you to the first step of the New SMTP Virtual Server Wizard, shown in Figure 17.74.

FIGURE 17.74

Defining a friendly name for an SMTP virtual server

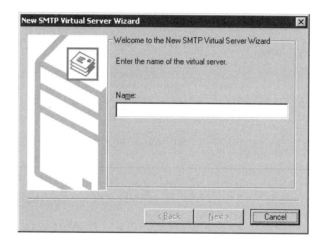

This step of the wizard wants you to specify a friendly name to use when referencing your new SMTP virtual server. This name is simply for administration purposes; your users won't see it, so choose a name that's appropriate and then click Next to proceed to the next step of the wizard, shown in Figure 17.75.

FIGURE 17.75

Defining IP addresses for an SMTP virtual server

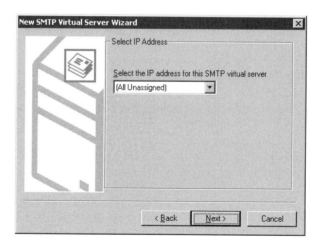

In order to access your SMTP server, other SMTP servers will need to establish a TCP/IP connection to your system on a specific IP address and TCP port number. By default, the New

SMTP Virtual Server Wizard will want to have your site listen on all available IP addresses for incoming connections. If you are going to be running only one SMTP server on your system, these settings should be fine. However, if you intend to run multiple SMTP servers on your system (for example, if you plan on hosting several virtual domains on your IIS server), you might want to specify a specific IP address for this server to use.

Click Next when you've completed the IP configuration, and you'll move to the next step of the wizard, shown in Figure 17.76.

FIGURE 17.76

Defining a directory for an SMTP virtual server

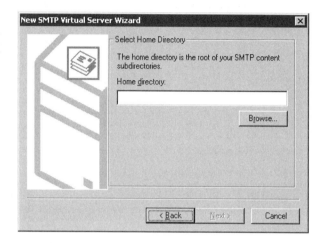

Since IIS will need a location to store incoming and outgoing e-mail messages, you must create a directory on your server to store this information. Unlike other services within IIS, in this service, you cannot define a share on another computer as the target location for your files. Instead, you must define a local path to be used for storing your SMTP content. Enter the appropriate directory to use, and then click Next to proceed to the final step of the wizard, shown in Figure 17.77.

FIGURE 17.77

Defining a default domain

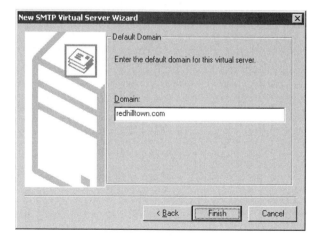

The last step of the wizard will ask you to enter the default domain that this virtual server should serve, such as `redhilltown.com` (you don't need to use the @ sign). Enter the appropriate domain to use, click the Finish button, and your new SMTP virtual server should be created. If you receive an error message at this point, check back in the Internet Information Services tool to see if the default SMTP server installed with IIS is running on the same IP address and TCP port of the system you've just defined. If it is, stop that virtual server and then start your new server again.

Modifying SMTP Virtual Server Properties

Because the New SMTP Virtual Server Wizard only asks you for a few configuration items, there are settings that you will probably want to adjust for your system. To adjust the parameters for your SMTP virtual server after the wizard has created it, you will use the SMTP virtual server properties pages.

GENERAL PROPERTIES

To reach the SMTP virtual server properties pages, highlight your new SMTP virtual server in the scope pane of the Internet Information Services tool and then select Properties from the Action pull-down menu. This will bring you to a dialog box similar to the one shown in Figure 17.78.

FIGURE 17.78

Configuring general settings for an SMTP virtual server

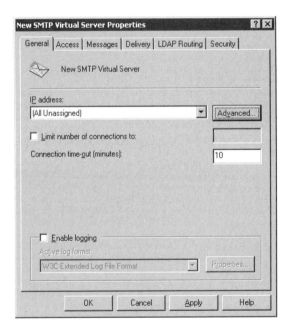

From this page, you can edit options for your server, including the following:

IP Address   Enter the IP address for your SMTP server to use here. You can assign your server to a specific IP address or have it respond on any free IP addresses on the system by selecting the All Unassigned option. To edit the TCP port number for this SMTP server, click the Advanced button.

Concurrent connections and idle timeout   Enable the Limit Number of Connections To option and supply a value in the corresponding field to control the number of concurrent connections. Idle connections will timeout after 10 minutes by default unless you modify this value.

Enable Logging   To keep track of what e-mails your server has sent and received, turn on logging by checking the Enable Logging box. Logging choices include W3C Extended Log Format, IIS Log File Format, NCSA Common Log File Format, and ODBC Logging.

SECURITY PROPERTIES

To delegate administrative controls for this server to specific users, click the Security tab to get to the Operators properties page, shown in Figure 17.79.

FIGURE 17.79

Configuring
operators for an
SMTP virtual
server

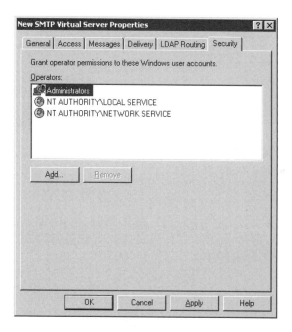

This dialog box is really quite self-explanatory. Simply click Add to add Windows server accounts or groups to the list of administrators for this SMTP server. Users listed here will be able to change parameters for this specific SMTP server via the Internet Information Services tool.

MESSAGES PROPERTIES

Abuse via SMTP—such as someone e-mailing you a 1GB file and consuming too much disk space, or the unauthorized relaying of messages—is not uncommon. To protect your system, you can set parameters regarding the delivery of messages on your system. To fine-tune the default message properties, select the Messages tab, shown in Figure 17.80.

FIGURE 17.80

Configuring message
properties for an
SMTP virtual server

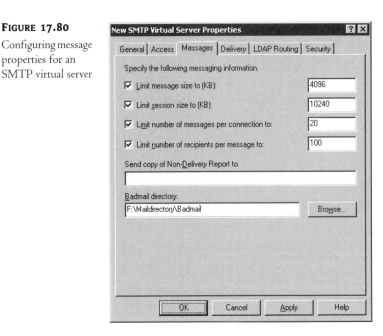

You can change a few properties here that handle how both inbound and outbound messages are
controlled. They are as follows:

Limit Message Size To (Kilobytes)   To limit how large a message a mail client can send to your
server, enter an appropriate value in this field. This limit will be applied after a message has been
received in its entirety. The minimum for this value is 1KB.

Limit Session Size To (Kilobytes)   Instead of waiting around to receive the end of a message
that has already exceeded the maximum message size, you can enter a value in this field; when a
session reaches this point, IIS will close off the connection. The minimum value for this field must
be equal to or greater than the previously defined maximum message size value.

Limit Number of Outbound Messages per Connection To   During a connection to an SMTP
server, a client may send several messages to the system for delivery. Unfortunately, some
SMTP servers are unknowingly used for the unauthorized relay of junk e-mail (often referred to
as spamming), delivering hundreds of thousands of messages. By forcing a client to establish a
new connection every *x* number of messages, an SMTP server becomes less desirable to a spammer
for use as a relay point. I would recommend leaving the default value in this field.

Limit Number of Recipients per Message To   Although this setting would seem to limit the
number of people you can send a single message to, it is really included for compliance with RFC
821, which defines SMTP. RFC 821 states that the maximum number of recipients per e-mail
message is 100. But what if you have a message destined for 150 recipients? The message will be
sent in one session to the first 100 recipients, and then a second session will be opened for the
remaining 50 recipients.

Send Copy of Nondelivery Report To   Nondelivery of a message, for whatever reason (invalid e-mail address, etc.), will typically cause the SMTP server to generate a nondelivery report (NDR) e-mail message for the sender. If you would like to have a copy of the NDRs also e-mailed to a specific mailbox, enter the appropriate e-mail address here.

Badmail Directory   When the SMTP service sends a nondelivery report (as mentioned above), it will go through the typical delivery routine for an e-mail message. However, under certain circumstances, the nondelivery report might be undeliverable. In such cases, the SMTP service will automatically place the message in this directory and consider the message permanently undeliverable. It's a good idea to check this directory every now and then to see if anything is piling up in there.

ACCESS PROPERTIES

Although most SMTP communications across the Internet occur anonymously, you can require authenticated access to your system if you desire. If you choose to require authenticated access to your SMTP server, the Access properties page is where you will make these changes. You can also control what IP addresses and domain names can attach to your system, define secure communications, and set relay restrictions here. The Access properties page is shown in Figure 17.81.

FIGURE 17.81

Configuring access properties for an SMTP server

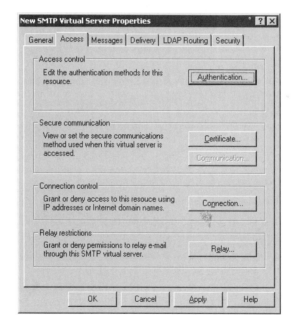

From this dialog box, you can control authentication, secure communications, address restrictions, and relay restrictions on your SMTP server by clicking the appropriate button.

Access Control

By default, SMTP connections are anonymous in nature: no authentication is required from a client accessing your SMTP server in order to send messages through it. If you want to change this behavior, click the Authentication button in this box to go to the Authentication dialog box, shown in Figure 17.82.

FIGURE 17.82

Configuring authentication properties for an SMTP server

Anonymous Access By default, all three authentication options are initially selected. If you don't want clients to be able to send messages anonymously through your SMTP server, uncheck this first option.

Basic Authentication If you choose to disable anonymous access, this is the first option that you can choose for client authentication. Basic authentication works via AUTH and USER/PASS commands sent between systems in cleartext. User accounts are verified against the accounts database local to the IIS machine. If a valid account is found, message processing can proceed. Otherwise, the SMTP session is never completed. Although this isn't necessarily a secure means of authentication, it will have a wider base of support than the next authentication option.

Integrated Windows Authentication Another name for the Microsoft challenge/response authentication, this option requires that both the SMTP server and SMTP client be running a Windows platform. User accounts are verified against the accounts database local to the IIS machine. If a valid account is found, message processing can proceed. Otherwise, the SMTP session is never completed.

Connection Control

If you prefer to control who accesses your SMTP server via IP addresses or domain names instead of authentications, click the Connection button in this area to edit the connection properties, shown in Figure 17.83.

Select the radio button option to either allow only the addresses and domain names you specify or allow everyone except the addresses and domains you specify. Enter the exception list by clicking Add. From the dialog box that follows, you can either grant or deny access to a single computer (via an IP address), a group of computers (via an IP address and a subnet mask), or an entire domain (via a domain name). IP addresses are usually the best option if you know which addresses to allow or deny. Since IIS only knows who is connected to it by an IP number, the server must do a reverse-DNS lookup if you select the domain name option, which adds quite a bit of processing for the server to do just to determine if it's okay to let the user in. Unless your situation requires using domain names, it's probably worthwhile to find out the exact IP address ranges to allow into your site and configure them accordingly.

FIGURE 17.83

Configuring IP address and domain name restrictions for an SMTP server

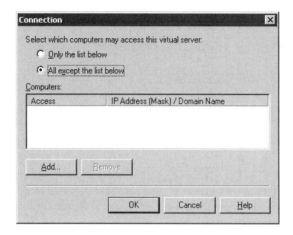

NOTE *Many hosts out on the Internet don't actually have reverse-DNS records assigned to them, and some hosts have incorrect reverse-DNS records assigned to them. Therefore, even if you were to put in a restriction based on a host/domain name, it might not work quite as well as you want it to.*

Relay Restrictions: Stopping Spammers

Because an SMTP server will typically deliver any message sent to it, abuse can become a problem if someone decides to park tens of thousands of messages on your system for delivery. Spammers will often find misconfigured third-party SMTP servers to relay their junk mail, park a few thousand messages on the system, and then move on to another server. This behavior is known as relaying a message, and it is an inherent part of the SMTP protocol—a protocol that was designed when the Internet was a more trusting, friendly place.

To defeat this behavior, many SMTP servers (including Microsoft Exchange) now include powerful relay controls that will allow you to determine whether or not the SMTP server should receive any messages for domains other than the ones that it hosts. For example, if your system lives in a domain called mycompany.com, then your SMTP server will—by default—only accept incoming messages destined to e-mail addresses ending in @mycompany.com. Any other messages will be denied, unless you specifically allow relaying by clicking the Relay button in the Relay Restrictions area and adjusting the properties page shown in Figure 17.84.

The format of this dialog box is similar to that for allowing and denying IP address restrictions to the SMTP service as a whole. By default, all hosts are denied relay access, unless you enter specific hosts in the list box. You can either grant or deny access to a single computer (via an IP address), a group of computers (via an IP address and a subnet mask), or an entire domain (via a domain name). IP addresses are usually the best option if you know which addresses to allow or deny.

FIGURE 17.84

Configuring relay controls on an SMTP server

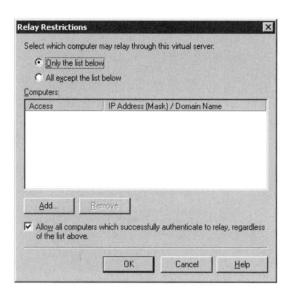

If you have enabled authentication options on your system, you can check the Allow All Computers Which Successfully Authenticate to Relay box at the bottom of this dialog box, giving anyone with an appropriate user authentication the rights to relay.

DELIVERY PROPERTIES

Click the Delivery tab (Figure 17.85) to define parameters about how messages are delivered into and out of your SMTP server.

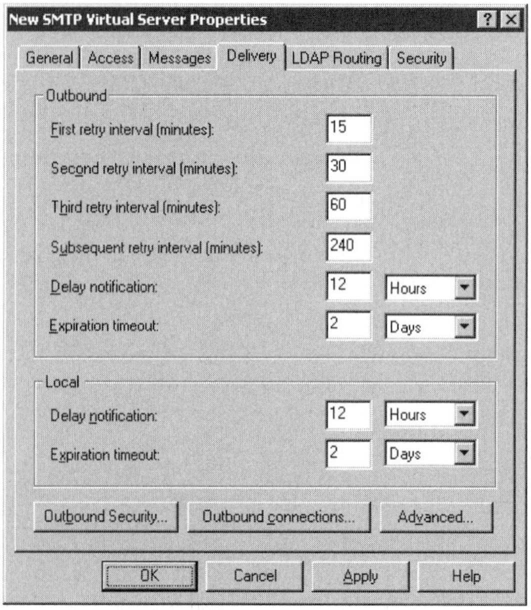

FIGURE 17.85

Configuring delivery properties on an SMTP server

This page is divided up into multiple options, both inbound and outbound, for controlling the delivery of messages.

Outbound

When an SMTP server receives a message, it will attempt to deliver it almost immediately. For various reasons, it is possible that the SMTP server will fail to deliver the message—the receiving host might be too busy, the receiving host might be down, or Internet connectivity might not be available. For whatever reason, the SMTP service will continue to try to deliver the message for the intervals specified in this section.

If the SMTP server fails at delivering the message after the first attempt, it will try again three times at the minute values specified in the First Retry Interval, Second Retry Interval, and Third Retry Interval fields. After the third retry value, if the message still hasn't been delivered, the SMTP service will attempt to deliver the message at the interval defined in the Subsequent Retry Interval field.

Eventually, if the message has failed enough times, the SMTP service will send a notification e-mail message to the user listed in the From: field of the e-mail message, letting him or her know that the message is still "in the queue" but hasn't been delivered to its destination yet. This interval is defined in the Delay Notification field. If the message eventually hits the value defined in the Expiration Timeout field, the message will be aborted and sent back to the user who sent it, along with a notification of the failure. These same values can be set for local delivery as well at the bottom of this screen.

Outbound Security

Inbound authentication controls can be set for the IIS SMTP service using the Access Properties page discussed earlier in this section. However, SMTP servers must connect to other SMTP servers to deliver messages. If the SMTP server that your system will be communicating with requires a similar means of authorization, you will need to define these options in the Outbound Security settings area. Click the Outbound Security button to edit the Outbound Security properties page, shown in Figure 17.86.

FIGURE 17.86

Configuring outbound authentication for an SMTP server

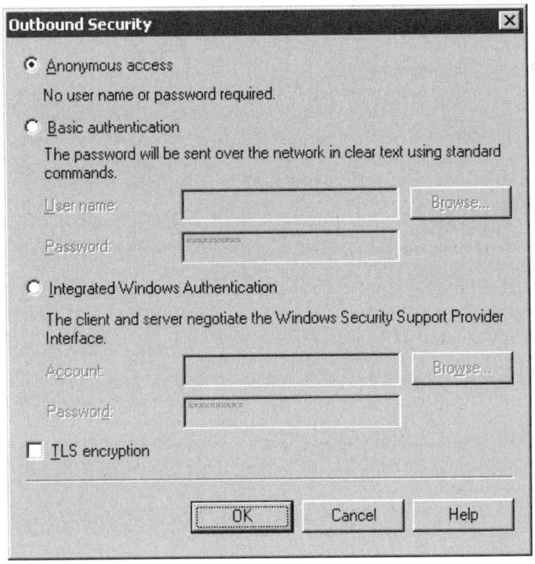

For more detailed information on the types of outbound authentication available, the "Access Control" discussion earlier in this section contains working definitions of anonymous access, basic authentication, and integrated Windows authentication. Whatever authentication your receiving systems will require, select a radio button to enable that type of security and supply the appropriate account information. For basic authentication or integrated Windows authentication, you can click the Browse button to select a username and password to use.

Outbound Connections

To modify the default settings that control outbound connections, click the Outbound Connections button to open the Outbound Connections properties page (shown in Figure 17.87). From here, you can specify a limit for concurrent outbound connections and a timeout value in case a connection becomes idle after communication is established with another STMP (for example, the remote server might stop responding for some reason). You may also specify a limit for the number of simultaneous connections to a given domain or modify the default connection port. TCP/IP port 25 is the standard port used for SMTP communications between servers; if you change the port setting for outbound connections, any remote servers must also be configured to accept incoming STMP connections on the same nonstandard port.

FIGURE 17.87

Configuring out-bound connection parameters

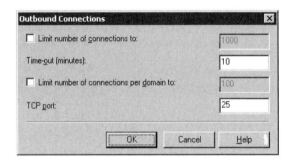

Advanced Delivery Options

The following options are advanced parameters for controlling the outbound delivery of messages. Clicking the Advanced button on the Delivery page will take you to a screen similar to the one in Figure 17.88.

Maximum Hop Count   When an SMTP server receives a message, it may be sent through other servers before reaching its final destination (a mailbox). However, a pair of misconfigured SMTP servers might bounce a message back and forth between themselves indefinitely (known as ping-ponging), with the message getting larger at each step of the way and never reaching its destination. To prevent this, the SMTP service can perform a "hop count" on a message—basically, counting the number of Received headers present in a message—and reject the message if there are too many hops in the message path. By default, this is set to 15, which should be acceptable for most circumstances. If a message exceeds its maximum hop count, then the message fails and the sender gets an error message telling them that the message couldn't be delivered.

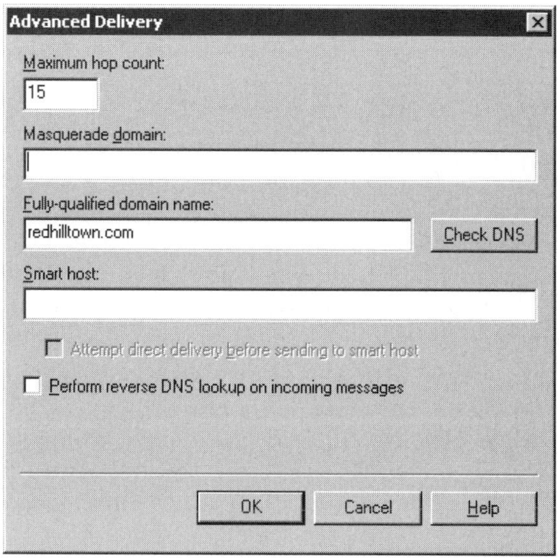

FIGURE 17.88

Configuring
Advanced Delivery
properties

Masquerade Domain   To override the domain name in an outgoing message with a specific domain name, enter the domain name here. The domain name entered in this field—if any—will replace the existing domain name listing in the From: field of the outgoing message.

Fully Qualified Domain Name   Enter the fully qualified domain name (FQDN) of your SMTP server in this field. An FQDN typically has at least three segments to it: host.domain.tld (tld is for top-level domain). When the SMTP service is installed and the default STMP virtual server is created, IIS automatically takes the fully qualified domain name from the full computer name specified in the System properties. So, for example, my SMTP server name is zooropa.redhilltown.com. This is the format for the name that normally appears in the FQDN field for the default SMTP virtual server. Usually, though, people send mail to addresses that read like *username@domainname.tld* instead of addresses like *username@STMPservername.domainname.tld*. So you can specify your fully qualified domain name in this field as redhilltown.com (for example) instead of zooropa.redhilltown.com, as long as you create the appropriate DNS mail exchange (MX) records that point to the SMTP server. Use the Check DNS button to query DNS for an MX record using the FQDN you typed in to verify that a valid record exists and that users can send mail to the server using this name.

Smart Host   One common mail server configuration involves having one SMTP server running on an Internet-accessible network segment, and another running behind a firewall or other gateway device on an internal, protected network. In this case, the external SMTP server handles all of the incoming and outgoing Internet mail while the internal server hosts user mailboxes. Incoming mail is relayed through the external server (called a relay server or a smart host) to the internal mail server, and outgoing mail is relayed from the protected server to the smart host for delivery on the Internet. This configuration protects the internal mail server from direct attack and eases the burden of servicing POP3 clients and delivering messages to other SMTP servers simultaneously.

If you would prefer to have another SMTP server handle all of the outgoing messages, enter a domain name or host address of the smart host here. If you enter an IP address, Microsoft suggests entering it in brackets [ ] so that the SMTP service will immediately know that it should try to connect to the smart host via IP address and skip name resolution.

Attempt Direct Delivery Before Sending to Smart Host   If you have defined a smart host in the previous field, you can tell SMTP that it should try to deliver messages on its own first. If it cannot deliver the messages on its own, it will immediately send them on to the smart host for delivery.

Perform Reverse DNS Lookup on Incoming Messages   When incoming messages are received by SMTP, IIS can perform a reverse-DNS lookup on the IP address noted in the header of the message and insert the fully qualified domain name of the IP address into the Received header. If the reverse-DNS lookup fails, no FQDN is put into the Received header. Reverse-DNS lookups can slow message processing, so depending on the volume of messages that you're receiving, you might want to leave this option unchecked unless necessary.

ADDING ADDITIONAL DOMAINS

By default, your SMTP server will only process messages destined for the domain you specified during the New SMTP Virtual Server Wizard. All other domain names will be considered by IIS to be "nonlocal" and therefore need to be relayed.

However, if you want to host multiple domain names on your system for e-mail or allow relaying for specific domains, you can do so by adding additional domain names through the Internet Information Services tool. Select your SMTP virtual server from the scope pane of the console and expand it. Below the SMTP server, you should see an item for Domains. Select that item, and you will see your currently defined domain in the results pane on the right side of the console. With the Domains option highlighted, select New/Domain from the Action pull-down menu, or simply right-click Domains and choose New/Domain.

Selecting the New/Domain option brings you to a two-step wizard, the first step of which is shown in Figure 17.89.

FIGURE 17.89

Adding a domain to an SMTP server

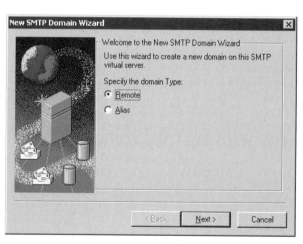

The first step of the wizard wants to know whether to add a local (alias) or remote domain. This will define whether the SMTP service should immediately store the message in the Drop directory once it receives it (local/alias), or if it should try to pass it on to another mail system (remote). Make the appropriate selection and then click Next to proceed to the last step of the wizard, entering the actual domain name. Once you enter a new domain for your system, the SMTP server will begin receiving/accepting traffic for e-mail addresses within that domain.

Local, or Alias, domains are pretty easy to understand. It's not uncommon for a company to have several different domain names and corresponding Web sites. If a company undergoes a name change, or if it operates with several identities, alias domain listings simply tell the SMTP server that mail destined for a user in the alias domain (1njustice@hawkmoon.org, for example) is to be handled as if it were addressed to a user on the default domain (1njustice@redhilltown.com). Since the alias domain is identical to the default domain, there are no separate properties pages for alias domains.

Remote domains are a little different. These may be other domains that you specifically want to relay mail for (recall that relaying mail to other domains is not allowed by default), or you may need a subset of your incoming mail to be relayed to or retrieved by another SMTP server. Accordingly, you may need to set a couple of configuration options in the properties pages for remote domains. Right-click the remote domain name in the Details pane of the console, and choose Properties from the context menu (or choose Properties from the Action pull-down menu) to access the General properties page (shown in Figure 17.90).

FIGURE 17.90

Configuring mail relay for remote domains

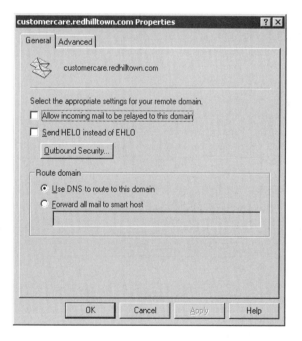

If you want mail for this domain to be relayed to another SMTP server, check the box labeled Allow Incoming Mail to Be Relayed to This Domain. It's worth noting that this option is not checked by default. So if you create a remote domain and don't enable some sort of relay, incoming mail for that remote domain will just sit on the server. Use the checkbox labeled Send HELO instead of EHLO to prevent error messages if you know that the remote server doesn't support ESMTP. The

Outbound Security button allows you to set authentication options and is identical to the settings shown back in Figure 17.86.

Use the radio buttons to choose whether to locate a mail server for the domain using DNS, or to simply forward all mail destined for the remote domain to a smart host. If you want to use a smart host, type in the name of the host in the space provided.

The Advanced properties page shown in Figure 17.91 permits you to configure the remote domain for ATRN. ATRN is an acronym for TURN with Authentication. TURN (also known as Mail Turn; TURN is not an acronym) is a protocol that permits one SMTP server to connect to another one and, instead of delivering mail, become a client and retrieve or "dequeue" mail destined for its own domain. ATRN is simply an implementation of TURN that requires the SMTP server to authenticate before retrieving mail. As far as I know, IIS 6 mail servers can't do this, but if you have servers that are capable of retrieving mail in this way, you may choose to enable queued messages and specify the accounts that are authorized to retrieve messages in this manner.

FIGURE 17.91

Configuring the server for ATRN retrieval

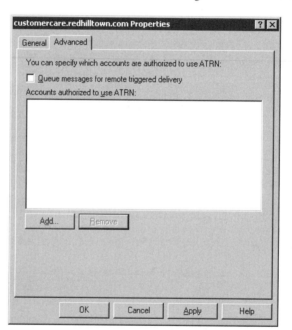

Maintaining Your SMTP Server

After you've gone through all of these configuration items, you should have a fully functional SMTP server on your system servicing the domain you defined in the New SMTP Virtual Server Wizard. As with any process on your system, it will require a bit of maintaining and fine-tuning from time to time.

SMTP DIRECTORIES

If you look at the directory you defined during the setup of your site, you should see four subdirectories, titled Badmail, Drop, Pickup, and Queue.

These are the directories that the SMTP service will use when processing incoming or outgoing messages. Incoming messages for your default domain or any alias domain will end up in the Drop directory, so it is worth looking in there every once in a while to see if mail has been sent to your system.

TIP *You can specify another location for the default drop directory as long as it is a local directory and it's not the designated pickup directory. Right-click the default domain name in the Details pane of the IIS management tool (*`iis.msc`*) to access the General properties page for the domain. Type a local path in the Drop Directory dialog box or use the Browse button to locate the target directory.*

Incoming e-mail messages will be stored in .eml files and will look somewhat like this:

```
Received: from october.redhilltown.com ([192.168.1.3]) by
zooropa.redhilltown.com with Microsoft SMTPSVC(6.0.3663.0);
Sat, 11 Jan 2003 13:32:09 -0500
From: lnjustice@adelphia.net
Bcc:
Return-Path: lnjustice@adelphia.net
Message-ID: <ZOOROPAUimGFX8nwn4000000002@redhilltown.com>
X-OriginalArrivalTime: 11 Jan 2003 18:32:17.0011 (UTC)
FILETIME=[C4A87C30:01C2B99F]
Date: 11 Jan 2003 13:32:17 -0500
Hello. This is a test message.
```

Outgoing messages from your system will be placed in the Pickup directory, either by the FrontPage extensions or the NNTP service as needed. However, you can also use the Pickup directory for your own administrative uses by placing properly formatted messages in there for delivery. For example, if you have a service process that generates a status report every night (perhaps a backup log) and want to have it automatically e-mailed, you can simply have a process create a properly formatted text file and place it in the Pickup directory. The SMTP service will see the file there and attempt to deliver it. A properly formatted outgoing SMTP message would look similar to the following:

```
x-sender: lnjustice@redhilltown.com
x-receiver: lnjustice@adelphia.net
From: lnjustice@redhilltown.com
To: lnjustice@adelphia.net
Subject: Hello from REDHILLTOWN

Hello Lisa. Hope that everything is going well with you.
```

If you intend to use the Pickup directory for your own messages, I'd recommend that you compose your text file in another directory first before placing it in the Pickup directory. If you begin to compose a message directly in the Pickup directory, the SMTP service will attempt to pick it up while you are working on it.

If the SMTP service runs into a message that it can't deliver to its intended recipient, and for which a nondelivery notification can't be returned to the sender, it will drop the message in the Badmail directory and leave it there. Every now and then it is probably worthwhile to check the Badmail directory and see if any messages have piled up.

Lastly, the `Queue` directory is where the SMTP service holds messages that it has pulled out of the `Pickup` or `Drop` directory. It will try sending a message immediately upon taking the message out of the `Pickup` or `Drop` directory, but if for some reason it can't deliver the message, it will hold it in the `Queue` directory until such time that it can be successfully delivered. If you want to make sure that incoming and outgoing messages aren't backing up on the server, a quick and dirty script to check the queue directory would be a very useful thing to run at regular intervals.

SENDING E-MAIL FROM ACTIVE SERVER PAGES

If you're building a Web site that uses IIS's built-in SMTP server and want to mail more sophisticated things—even HTML pages—then you can do that with some built-in capabilities of IIS's Active Server pages. While this isn't a book on Web site construction, I've found this useful.

The key is an object called CDONTS, the Collaboration Data Objects for NT tool. I don't propose to explain it in detail, but I've cooked up a simple example. It sends two pieces of mail: first, a simple one-liner, and second, an HTML file.

To see this work, create the following file (see Listing 17.1). Call it `mailex.asp` and store it in your `wwwroot` directory:

LISTING 17.1: THE *MAILEX.ASP* FILE

```
<html>
<head>
<title>Mail Example</title>
</head>
<body>
<%
dim fso
htmlfile = ENTER THE NAME OF YOUR HTML FILE IN QUOTES
fromaddr = ENTER A "FROM" ADDRESS IN QUOTES
toaddr = ENTER A "TO" ADDRESS IN QUOTES
'Copy HTML file to a string variable
set fso=createobject("Scripting.FileSystemObject")
Set MyFile = fso.OpenTextFile(htmlfile,1) '1=read
HTML=""
while not myfile.atendofstream
    HTML=HTML+myfile.readline
wend
myfile.close
set fso=nothing
set myfile=nothing
'
' First mail:  create and send a simple message
'
  'Create mail object
  Set objNewMail = Server.CreateObject("CDONTS.NewMail")
  objNewMail.From = fromaddr
  objNewMail.To = toaddr
  objNewMail.Subject = "Simple mail test"
```

```
    objNewMail.Body = "Hi there; this is a test from the Web server."
    objNewMail.BodyFormat = 1  '1=text, 0=HTML
    objNewMail.MailFormat = 0
    objNewMail.Importance = 1
    objNewMail.Send
      if Err <> 0 Then  Response.write "<p>CDONTS reported
↳an error:"  & Err.Description & ".</p>"


  ' Second mail:  A piece of HTML mail


    Set objNewMail = Server.CreateObject("CDONTS.NewMail")
    objNewMail.From = fromaddr
    objNewMail.To = toaddr
    objNewMail.Subject = "Simple HTML mail test"
    objNewMail.Body = HTML
    objNewMail.BodyFormat = 0   '1=text, 0=HTML
    objNewMail.MailFormat = 0
    objNewMail.Importance = 1
    objNewMail.Send
      if Err <> 0 Then  Response.write "<p>CDONTS reported
↳an error:"  & Err.Description & ".</p>"
    set objNewMail=nothing
%>
</body>
</html>
```

Create a simple HTML file and put it somewhere on your Web server that the IUSR user account has read access to. For example, you might call the file `test.html` and put it in `C:\JUNK`. Then fill in values for the *htmlfile*, *toaddr*, and *fromaddr* variables. For example, if your e-mail is `wally@acme.com`, you might send this mail to yourself with these three lines:

```
htmlfile="c:\junk\test.html"
toaddr="wally@acme.com"
fromaddr="wally@acme.com"
```

Then run the page by opening your Web browser and calling the `mailex.asp` file. For example, if your Web server is on 192.168.0.2, then you could type into the address bar **http://192.168.0.2/mailex.asp**. Unless you haven't permitted Active Server Pages, or you have mistyped the text or IUSR is denied permission to `test.html`, you won't see anything in your browser. But open up your mail client and you should have two pieces of mail.

A POP3 Server for Windows 2003

Computers all by themselves are of little value for anything more than acting as a glorified calculator or typewriter. Hooking up computers via networks has been what has really made computers useful, and of course networks are a big part of communications. But networks are of no value unless people use them—and people won't use them without a reason. This brings me to electronic mail. E-mail is often the "gateway" application for people, the application that is the first network application that they'll use; for some people, it's the only application that they'll ever use. And e-mail is probably the most important thing running on the Internet.

I just talked about setting up SMTP on your IIS server so that it could send e-mail to other hosts. However, although SMTP is the protocol used to send e-mail, setting up SMTP support does not make your IIS server an e-mail server. You see, SMTP doesn't sort the mail into individual user mailboxes, and there's no method for individual users to retrieve mail. For that, you need the POP3 protocol. Windows 2000 didn't include a POP3 server; if you wanted your Windows 2000 system to be an e-mail server you had to rely on a separate product. These ranged from huge packages like Microsoft Exchange to bare-bones free software like the Internet Mail Service (IMS), which was developed by the European Microsoft Windows Academic Centre (EMWACS). At long last, Windows Server 2003 comes with an optional POP3 service. Although it's not a component of IIS, it can work with the IIS SMTP service and Active Directory to provide full-fledged e-mail services at no additional cost.

Setting Up the POP3 Server

Use Add/Remove Programs in the Control Panel to install the POP3 service, which you'll find listed as E-Mail Services in the Windows Components Wizard. Once you've completed the installation, which is similar to every procedure to install optional Windows components, a new tool called POP3 Service (`p3server.msc`) is available in the Administrative Tools group. Open `p3server.msc` (shown in Figure 17.92) to begin configuring your POP3 server.

FIGURE 17.92

The POP3 Service MMC

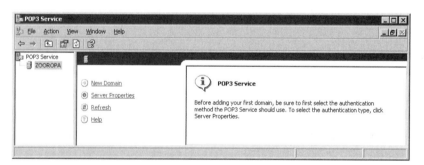

As you can see in Figure 17.92, the POP3 Service console uses extended views and MMC taskpads to help you accomplish your tasks. Before adding a mail domain, you need to configure the POP3 server properties and, in particular, select an authentication method. This authentication method is not configurable on a per-domain basis. If you want to change the authentication method later, you'll need to delete all of the existing e-mail domains first. Changing the authentication method, or any of the other server properties (like the TCP/IP port or the root mail directory location), also requires you to restart the POP3 service. You can stop, start, pause, or restart the POP3 service from the POP3 Service MMC or from the Services tool.

To configure POP3 Server properties, highlight the POP3 server name in the console, right-click, and choose Properties from the context menu. The server properties page is shown in Figure 17.93. The Windows POP3 server supports three different authentication options: Active Directory Integrated, Local Windows Accounts, or Encrypted Password File.

FIGURE 17.93

Configuring server
properties for the
POP3 Server

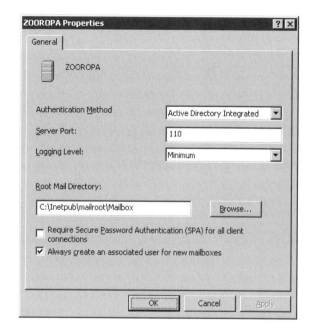

Active Directory Integrated authentication   The Active Directory Integrated option tells
POP3 to authenticate users using an AD domain controller. Use this option if the mail server
is a member of an Active Directory domain, or if it is an AD domain controller. Mailboxes
must correspond to an existing account in the AD, or you can create a new account at the same
time as you create the mailbox. The AD integration option supports multiple domains, and
users can access mailboxes in separate mail domains with the same username and password
(1njustice@redhilltown.com and 1njustice@hawkmoon.org, for example).

Local Windows Accounts authentication   Use Local Windows Accounts authentication if the
server is not a member of an AD domain, or if you just prefer to use local accounts instead of AD
accounts. Mailboxes must correspond to accounts on the local system and be authenticated against
the server's security accounts database (SAM). This option supports multiple e-mail domains, but
mailboxes must correspond to local user accounts and local usernames must be unique. Therefore,
this option does not support using the same username across multiple domains.

Encrypted Password File authentication   If you don't want to create and maintain user accounts
on the POP3 Server at all, choose this authentication type. Hey, if you are going to be hosting
thousands of mailboxes, and especially if those mailbox users are not actually users on your corporate radar, there is no way you want to manage all of those local or AD accounts. Usernames
must be unique to the e-mail domain, but identical usernames can exist across domains. For example,
you can have mailboxes for 1njustice@myisp.net and 1njustice@bignetwork.com, but you cannot have two mailboxes for 1njustice@myisp.net. When a mailbox is created, the administrator
also supplies a password for the user. This password is encrypted and stored in a file in the user's
mailbox directory.

POP3 Server Port   To modify the TCP/IP Port that POP3 uses, type in a port number in the Server Port field. Port 110 is the standard port for POP3. If the server is modified to listen and respond on a nonstandard port, the POP3 client software must also be modified to use the same port number.

Logging Level   The POP3 server sends logging information to the Event log service. Events are written to the Application log and viewable from Event Viewer. To configure the level of event logging for the POP3 server, choose an option from the Logging Level pull-down box.

Root Mail Directory   The default root mail directory, or mail store directory, is `c:\Inetpub\mailroot\Mailbox`. For each domain created on the mail server, a subdirectory with the same name will be created in the `Mailbox` directory. Within the domain subdirectory, mailbox users will have their own directories. For example, I have a user named paulhewson in the redhilltown.com mail domain. If I keep the default mail store location, the path to Paul's mailbox will be `c:\Inetpub\mailroot\Mailbox\redhilltown.com\P3_paulhewson.mbx`. Individual message files in the `.mbx` directory will carry the `.eml` extension. These files are viewable with a text editor like Notepad, but Windows recognizes them as Internet E-mail messages and opens them in an e-mail message window. When you configure the mail directory, NTFS file and directory permissions are set to permit access only to administrators, the System account, and the Network Service account, which runs the Microsoft POP3 service.

Other Server Options   The last two options shown in Figure 17.93 are to require Secure Password Authentication and to automatically create user accounts for new mailboxes. If Active Directory integration or local Windows account authentication is selected, the SPA option requires clients to use SPA-encrypted passwords instead of cleartext. For encrypted password file authentication, POP3 supports the APOP protocol. Both SPA and APOP encrypt the username and password.

Only the Local Windows Account and AD integrated authentication methods use real user accounts, so the option to automatically create user accounts is not available when encrypted password file authentication is chosen. User accounts will be automatically created on the local system or on the AD directory, depending on the logon method in use. Since you will probably create some mailboxes for pre-existing accounts, you can always deselect this option when you are actually creating the mailbox.

CREATE AN E-MAIL DOMAIN AND MAILBOXES

Now that you've configured the server properties for your POP3 Server, it's time to create one or more e-mail domains. You should note that, in this context, the e-mail domain is not the same entity as the AD domain. Sure, you may have an AD domain named, for instance, redhilltown.com, and you may want to configure your server to handle mail addressed to *someuser*@redhilltown.com, but the POP3 and SMTP servers don't care whether there is a corresponding AD domain. The SMTP server component must be configured to accept mail for a given domain name, and the POP3 server must have a corresponding directory for that domain as well, but the only other limitation is name resolution. If you want the same server (zooropa.redhilltown.com, for instance) to accept mail for redhilltown.com, hawkmoon.org, and reallybigISP.net, then you also need mail exchange (MX) records in DNS to point to that server.

   To create an e-mail domain on the POP3 server, select the server in the Scope pane of the console and click on the New Domain link, or right-click and choose New/Domain from the context menu. A simple dialog box appears prompting you for a domain name; type in the name of the domain and click OK. A subdirectory in the mail store will be created for that domain. There are no options to configure on a per-domain basis; the POP3 server handles e-mail for all domains equally. Now it's time to add a few mailboxes. Highlight the domain name in the scope pane of the console, right-click, and choose New/Mailbox from the context menu (or use the Add Mailbox link in the details pane, or choose New/Mailbox from the Action pull-down menu.) You should see a dialog box like the one shown in Figure 17.94.

FIGURE 17.94

Adding a mailbox to the POP3 server

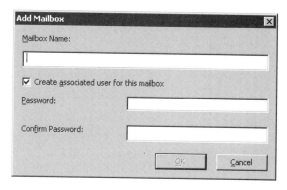

Type in the name of the mailbox. If you want the mailbox to belong to a pre-existing user account on the local system or in the AD, type in the exact name of the user account and deselect the option to create an associated user account. To create a new user account on the server or AD, supply the account name and an initial password. If you are using encrypted password file authentication, the dialog box is identical except that the option to create a new user account is not available. Repeat this procedure as necessary to create additional mailboxes, or use the nifty little command-line tool, `winpop.exe`, located in the `\Windows\system32\pop3server` directory:

```
winpop add phewson@redhilltown.com
```

Or, to create a new user account at the same time:

```
winpop add devans@redhilltown.com /createuser password
```

Figure 17.95 shows six newly created mailboxes in the redhilltown.com domain. Again, the POP3 server treats all mailboxes equally, so there are no configuration options to set. As you can see from Figure 17.96, the only options available for existing mailboxes are to delete the mailbox or to lock the mailbox. When a mailbox is locked, incoming mail for the user is still accepted, but the user cannot connect to the server and retrieve mail. You may also lock or unlock an entire domain, which prevents any users on the domain from retrieving mail.

FIGURE 17.95

A list of mailboxes in the POP3 mail domain

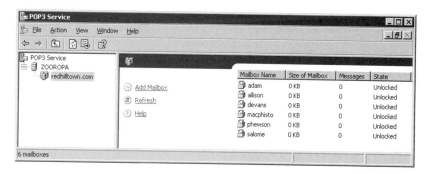

FIGURE 17.96

Mailbox options in the POP3 Service MMC

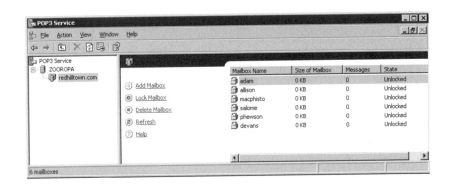

A FEW CLOSING THOUGHTS ON POP3 SERVER

As you can see, administration of the Microsoft POP3 Server is not complicated. However, you should do some planning to ensure that you allocate sufficient disk space for the mail store, based on the numbers of domains and mailboxes you will be hosting and the volume of e-mail that users will receive. It's not a bad idea to enable disk quotas on the partition where the mail store is located. Quotas can be used to set a per-mailbox limit or a domain-wide limit on the disk space used by the mail store. And it goes without saying that your mail store should be located on an NTFS partition both for security purposes and because quotas are only supported on NTFS.

Setting Up Your E-mail Client

A server's no good without clients. In the case of a mail server, the accompanying clients are of course called e-mail clients.

To connect to your mail server, you'll need an Internet mail client of some kind. Examples include Outlook (which can act as an Exchange client, an Internet mail client, or both), Outlook Express, Eudora (the free version or the professional version; it's a great program, and you can find it at www.eudora.com), Pegasus (free, www.pmail.com), or the mail client built into Netscape Navigator. Technically, they are all POP3/SMTP clients. Some support a third protocol, IMAP4, but that doesn't matter to us, as our POP3 and SMTP components don't support IMAP4.

To tell your e-mail client to look to your POP3 server for mail, you've got to configure it to look for your mail account. Exactly how you do that varies from client software to client software, but in every case the e-mail software will probably need to know a few things:

Do you use POP3 or IMAP4?   POP3; again, IIS and the POP3 server don't support IMAP4.

The name of your SMTP server   Fill in the name of the server running the SMTP service.

The name of your POP3 server   Usually your SMTP server is also your POP3 Server.

Your e-mail address   Your e-mail address is *name@servername*, where *name* is your Windows user account name. For example, if your mail server is on the domain FLOWERS.COM and you log in to the FLOWERS.COM domain as JaneD, then your username and the name portion of your address is janed. The *servername* will either be the fully qualified domain name of the machine running SMTP/POP3, such as violets.flowers.com, or just the name of the domain, if you've directed people to the server with an MX record. If an MX record for FLOWERS.COM in

DNS says that mail for FLOWERS.COM should go to violets.flowers.com, then your e-mail address is `janed@flowers.com`. Without an MX record, e-mail addresses must specify the particular server, so in that case the address would be `janed@violets.flowers.com`.

Your account name and password   Fill in the username and password. Although not all types of mail servers require it, you should include the domain prefix if you are connecting to a Windows Server 2003 SMTP/POP3 Server. Enter a username like **mark@redhilltown.com** rather than just **mark**.

From there, any other configuration options will be matters of taste—how often to check for mail and the like. Once your client's set up, send yourself a piece of mail and your mail server will be officially operational!

E-mail Security Concerns

As the Internet grows, more and more gateways will be built to other e-mail systems. You can't get everywhere, but in time, you'll be able to reach anyone from the Internet. Now, that's a good thing, but as e-mail becomes more important, it's also essential to keep your mind on the fact that e-mail is not secure. Your mail packets get bounced all around the Internet, as you know—but think about what that means. Suppose you send a message to someone on the Internet, and my computer is part of the Internet—a piece, as it happens, that sits between you and the person to whom you're sending mail. Mail can sit in intermediate computers like mine, on the hard disk, for seconds, minutes, or hours at a time. It's a simple matter to use any number of utility programs to peek into the mail queue on the mail that's "just passing through." Never say anything on mail that you wouldn't want as public knowledge. Even if someone doesn't peek at your mail, that someone probably backs up his or her disk regularly, meaning that the message may sit on magnetic media for years in some archive. I sometimes imagine that in the middle of the twenty-first century, we'll see "the unpublished letters of Douglas Adams"—e-mail notes that someone stumbled across while picking through some 70-year-old backups; you know, it'll be the latter-day equivalent of going through some dead celebrity's trash. Anyway, the bottom line is this: Don't write anything that you wouldn't want your boss, your spouse, your parents, or your kids to read.

Using Telnet for Remote Login

Back in the mid-Triassic period of computing, around 1973, you wouldn't sit at a computer; you'd sit at a terminal that was connected in some way to a computer. If a computer at the National Institutes of Health contained some database that I wanted to do analysis on, I'd put a modem on my terminal, get an account at NIH, find out the phone numbers of their dial-in modems, and then I'd dial one of those numbers. Once the modem was done squawking and I was connected at the princely speed of 300bps, I'd interact with NIH. But I'd interact solely with characters—25 lines of 80 columns of characters.

From the '60s on, the government has maintained a lot of mainframes with some very useful data on them. Before the growth of the Internet, anyone doing research could get an account and dial in to those mainframes to use the government's data—but the long-distance bills could bankrupt you.

Early Telnet Uses

But then the Internet appeared.

For the early Internet—ARPAnet, actually—programmers built a set of programs, a server program and a terminal program, that would let a mainframe accept incoming connections over the Internet, much like modem dial-ins, and let someone sitting at a Unix terminal somewhere attach to that mainframe as if dialing in. The early (mid-Cretaceous, actually) programmers called the pair of programs *telnet*.

For years, telnet was a great way for groups to offer information over the Internet. Some people adapted programs used to host dial-in PC-based bulletin board systems to telnet. Others put data of general interest on telnet—for example, the University of Michigan once had census data available over telnet, and a travel agency let you book tickets on telnet. Network Solutions, the people who run DNS, had a search engine built into telnet that would let you look up a domain name to see if it was taken. Most of those are gone now, replaced with Web sites.

Modern Uses for Telnet

But telnet's still quite useful for network administrators, so it's great that Windows Server 2003 includes a telnet server. Think of telnet on Windows 2003 as being sort of a low-bandwidth form of Windows Terminal Server. You can't run any graphical applications over it; you just get a C:\> style command line, but you can get an awful lot done with just that.

Before you can telnet into your machine, though, you must start up the server part of telnet. That part's easy, but you have to then configure it to accept regular telnet connections.

Setting Up the Telnet Server

Telnet is built as a service under Windows Server 2003. You can start it by just opening up a command line, typing **net start tlntsvr**, and pressing Enter. Alternatively, you can tell your system to always have the telnet server available by setting up the telnet service to start automatically.

Here's what you need to do to set up the telnet service to start automatically:

1. Right-click the My Computer icon, and select Manage.
2. Under Computer Management, you'll see Services and Applications; open it by clicking the plus sign next to it.
3. Inside Services and Applications, you'll see Services; click that and the list of services in the system will appear in the right pane of the window.
4. The service you're looking for is named just telnet; right-click it and choose Properties.
5. You'll see a single-selection drop-down list box labeled Startup; choose Automatic, then click OK to close the window. Close the Computer Management window.

The telnet server supports two simultaneous connections by default, although you can use the command line administration tool tlntadm to modify this parameter. Because of potential security issues (telnet is a powerful tool), users must also be members of the Administrators group to log in. To grant additional uses permission to telnet to the server, create a local users group called Telnet-Clients and grant membership only to the users who need telnet access. Presumably, any users added to this special group will inherit the right to log on locally, which is also required for telnet access to the server.

While telnet is often a potential security risk because it passes passwords in cleartext over the network, Microsoft has reduced that risk by modifying the way that the telnet server behaves. The Windows Server 2003 telnet server does accept cleartext password authentication by default, but it also uses an NT-style authentication approach called NTLM. The telnet server negotiates the authentication method with connecting clients, and NTLM is the preferred method. It requires not only a modified telnet server but a modified telnet client as well—but Windows 2000 and XP come with a client like that. If the client supports NTLM authentication, not only are passwords encrypted, but the client automatically handles the authentication using the existing security context. With NTLM authentication, users will not be prompted for a username and password. By default, if the client does not support NTLM authentication, cleartext password authentication is used. For maximum security, you can disable cleartext authentication and only permit connections from clients that are capable of NTLM authentication. I'll explain how to do that in a moment.

The command-line tool that you use to configure the telnet server is `tlntadmn.exe`. Among other things, you can use `tlntadmn.exe` to start and stop the server, configure authentication settings, and increase the number of simultaneous connections that are permitted. To see the current settings for the telnet server, type **tlntadmn config** at a command prompt to view a list of settings similar to this:

```
C:\ > tlntadmn config
The following are the settings on localhost

Alt Key Mapped to 'CTRL+A'  :   YES
Idle session timeout        :   1 hours
Max connections             :   2
Telnet port                 :   23
Max failed login attempts   :   3
End tasks on disconnect     :   YES
Mode of Operation           :   Console
Authentication Mechanism    :   NTLM, Password
Default Domain              :   REDHILLTOWN
State                       :   Running
```

To tell a server's telnet server software not to accept cleartext logins, type the following command:

```
tlntadmn config sec -passwd.
```

If you want to disable NTLM authentication and permit only cleartext authentication, use the `config sec` option like this:

```
tlntadmn config sec -NTLM +passwd.
```

To increase the maximum number of concurrent connections to, say 10 connections, type the following:

```
tlntadmin config maxconn = 10
```

To see the full syntax and options for the `tlntadmn` command, type

```
tlntadmn /?
```

Now that you've configured the telnet server to start up and set other options using the `tlntadmn` tool, let's connect to the server using a telnet client. Assuming that you're already logged onto the domain, you can just start a session from a command line by typing **telnet** *servername*, where *servername* is the name of the server that you want to establish the telnet session on. From there, you can do anything that you can do from the command line: run batch files, run scripts, or use command-line versions of utilities.

There are a couple of limitations when using the Windows Server 2003 telnet server. First, and this is nothing new to telnet, applications that use a graphical interface are not available. You must use command-line tools or scripts that run from a command line. Second, and this is not so obvious, you cannot use any existing drive mappings or other connections to network resources. Because those connections were established using a different security context, they are not available to telnet clients. You can, however, create new connections. For example, when I telnet to my server Zooropa and run the **net use** command, I can see that there are already two drives mapped to folders on another server. However, these are listed as unavailable. I have to type **net use * \\servername\sharename** to create a new drive mapping. Because of a limitation of the NTML authentication method, I also have to enter my username and password again to map the drive to make this new network connection available for my use over the telnet connection.

A final word on using telnet: even when NTLM authentication is used to encrypt the sign-in process, the actual data that passes between the client and the server is not encrypted and is visible to anyone who might be capturing packets on the network. Therefore, administrators should not use telnet to perform functions that expose sensitive information to eavesdroppers. This is not specific to Microsoft's implementation of telnet; rather, it's a limitation of telnet in general. In the Unix world, many administrators are disabling telnet access to systems in favor of an encrypted remote shell program called **ssh** (short for secure shell). Maybe Microsoft will include an **ssh** program with a future version of Windows Server.

Communicating Securely with SSL

We all know that the Web is a great place to find information, but I have a feeling that we've only seen the tip of the iceberg as far as the Internet is concerned. The force that is truly driving the Internet into the future is commerce. The Internet lends itself to transactional chores very well, just due to its nature and makeup. However, most commercial transactions contain some form of proprietary or confidential data, whether it's bank account numbers or corporate plans for a new product launch. All sorts of information that is confidential in nature is being transmitted across the Internet, and that trend will continue in the future.

To meet the challenge of securing confidential data, Netscape developed a protocol called Secure Sockets Layer (SSL) to be used in conjunction with HTTP as a means of providing secure communication channels between clients and servers. Through the use of certificates—encryption keys handed out by a trusted third-party organization—Web servers and Web browsers will negotiate an encrypted connection between themselves, preventing any data from being intercepted during transmission.

Some reasons to implement SSL are obvious—for example, if you intend to accept credit card numbers on your Web site from clients who are ordering products. Obviously, your clients might be concerned about their confidential information (their credit card number) crossing the Internet in the clear, so you can encrypt the ordering process to ensure that even if someone does intercept the transmission, it will be in a useless form. However, some reasons for implementing SSL are less obvious but equally as important—for example, confidential information such as brokerage statements, corporate financial statements, tax returns, medical records, etc. All are equally private as far as most individuals are concerned, and will be transmitted over the Internet more and more frequently as time goes on.

Fortunately, Microsoft has made the process of obtaining a security certificate easy in IIS 6 through the inclusion of the IIS Certificate Wizard, an administrative wizard that will create a certificate request for your system. You will, in turn, submit that request to a certificate authority—commonly referred to as a CA—which is the trusted third party. The CA will then send you a certificate that the wizard will help you install on your server. Before getting this process started, you will need to have the following ready:

A functional IIS server Although this seems obvious, there's more to it than simply having an IIS server that runs. Since certificates are highly specialized encryption keys—they even have the name of your server embedded in them—it's best to have your site working exactly how you want it first, and then add the security certificate and turn on encryption as one of the last items to do.

Organizational details Details that a CA will require from your organization include name, organizational unit, country, state, locality, and a name, e-mail address, and phone number for the contact individual requesting the certificate.

Server details Certificates are based on the server that they were requested for and will have that server name (either an internal NetBIOS-style name or an FQDN) embedded within the key. Therefore, once you enable encryption, it's important that you don't change the name of your server—otherwise you will need to request a new certificate.

Requesting a Certificate

To begin the process of requesting a certificate, start the Internet Information Services MMC and select your Web site in the scope pane. Then, select the Properties option from the Action pull-down menu. This will get you into the properties pages for this Web site, as discussed earlier in this chapter. Click the Directory Security tab to get to the security properties pages, shown earlier in Figure 17.20. Click the Server Certificate button to launch the Web Server Certificate Wizard. The first screen of the wizard (after the welcome screen) is shown in Figure 17.97.

FIGURE 17.97

Starting the IIS Certificate Wizard

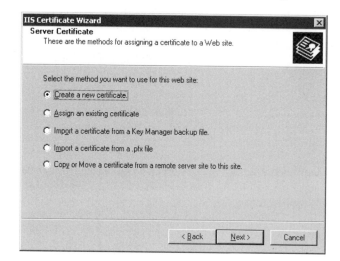

Assuming that you are requesting a new certificate for your site, select the Create a New Certificate option. Clicking Next will take you through roughly six steps required to collect the necessary information about your organization: organization name, organizational unit, server name, contact information, etc. Enter the information requested at each step and click Next to move through the wizard. One of the final steps of the wizard will ask you where you want to store your request (assuming you selected the Prepare the Request Now, but Send It Later option in the second step of the wizard); the default is C:\certreq.txt. If this name is acceptable, click Next to proceed to the final step of the wizard.

After you have entered all of the necessary organizational and server information for your certificate request, the wizard should show you the information it has collected in a step similar to the one shown in Figure 17.98.

FIGURE 17.98

Certificate request confirmation step

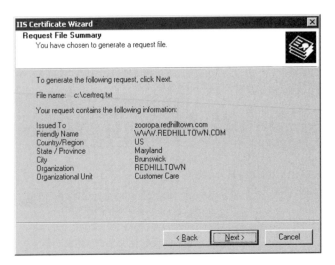

Assuming your information is correct, click Next, and the wizard will create the appropriate certificate request and place it in the file you specified. This file is simply a text file containing all of the information you entered through the wizard, encoded in a certificate request. A sample certificate request is shown here:

```
-----BEGIN NEW CERtifICATE REQUEST-----
MIIDYDCCAskCAQAwgYQxIDAeBgNVBAMTF3pvb3JvcGEucmVkaGlsbHRvd24uY29t
MRYwFAYDVQQLEw1DdXN0b21lciBDYXJlMRQwEgYDVQQKEwtSRURISUxMVE9XTjES
MBAGA1UEBxMJQnJ1bnN3aWNrMREwDwYDVQQIEwhNYXJ5bGFuZDELMAkGA1UEBhMC
VVMwgZ8wDQYJKoZIhvcNAQEBBQADgY0AMIGJAoGBAOWDp90mPf2aMmmPuvUbqm/b
naQ8AWIHZEwJGAJwiR1YJI8kosxeMJalZOtVrQy6chtEfeIBxxyZUupOWcPHwlrs
poZZuBOTqrtJnLC8AiUAmRWw5lrbfOcfmHnI9AHzuutas2dxBx7/fYkQZW4uaB+i
YmNjxqV8V6Aj55ILr9dtAgMBAAGgggGZMBoGCisGAQQBgjcNAgMxDBYKNS4yLjM2
NjMuMjB7BgorBgEEAYI3AgEOMWOwazAOBgNVHQ8BAf8EBAMCBPAwRAYJKoZIhvcN
AQkPBDcwNTAOBggqhkiG9w0DAgICAIAwDgYIKoZIhvcNAwQCAgCAMAcGBSsOAwIH
MAoGCCqGSIb3DQMHMBMGA1UdJQQMMAoGCCsGAQUFBwMBMIH9BgorBgEEAYI3DQIC
MYHuMIHrAgEBHloATQBpAGMAcgBvAHMAbwBmAHQAIABSAFMAQQAgAFMAQwBoAGEA
bgBuAGUAbAAgAEMAcgB5AHAAdABvAGcAcgBhAHAAaABpAGMAIABQAHIAbwB2AGkA
```

```
ZAB1AHIDgYkAAAAAAAAAAAAAAAAAAAAAAAAAAAAAAAAAAAAAAAAAAAAAAAAAAAA
AAAAAAAAAAAAAAAAAAAAAAAAAAAAAAAAAAAAAAAAAAAAAAAAAAAAAAAAAAAAAAAA
AAAAAAAAAAAAAAAAAAAAAAAAAAAAAAAAAAAAAAAAAAAAAAAAAAAAAAAAAAAAAAAA
ADANBgkqhkiG9w0BAQUFAAOBgQAfCaFAmO3Q8Yuteob+ONWWtl/3EwmagshLr1oE
4102G4WeNyL6wZBbwmGLnZhxfBuSpzQ7VCVa4E4CLh22WP72KGQtpxA7TpcF8kbJ
h+wiX1aS7jfcNt9d4PXdgapwODj5/ijyFIv7SrSWUE4f/I1GSL3bs3b1zO9o4iJs
nezonQ==
-----END NEW CERtifICATE REQUEST-----
```

Once you have your request file, you need to submit that file to a CA so that they can issue a certificate to you. For my testing purposes, I chose to use VeriSign over at www.verisign.com. In any case, choose a CA that you would like to use and then submit your request file through whatever mechanism they provide.

Depending on the CA you are working with and the level of trust you want for your certificate, your request might take anywhere from a few minutes to a few days or weeks to process. Once your request has been approved, you will receive a certificate for installation on your server (a sample certificate basically looks exactly like the encryption key in the certificate request). To install the certificate, return to the Directory Security tab in the properties of your Web site (you need to install your certificate to the same site you requested it from) and click the Server Certificate button again.

This time when you launch the IIS Certificate Wizard, it will realize that you have previously requested a certificate for this Web server and it will ask you if you would like to import that certificate now (see Figure 17.99).

FIGURE 17.99

Importing a certificate with the IIS Certificate Wizard

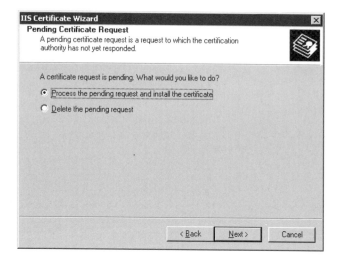

Import the certificate by entering the path to the certificate in the next step of the wizard. If everything goes as it should, you should see a summary of your certificate, similar to the one shown in Figure 17.100.

If this certificate is acceptable, click Next, and the certificate will be installed into your Web server.

FIGURE 17.100

Summary of an
imported certificate

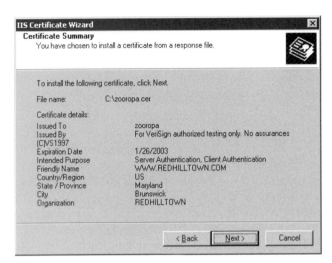

Securing a Site or Directory

Once your certificate is installed, the Edit button should light up in the Directory Security properties page for your Web site. You can require SSL security for your entire site or in directories (real or virtual) within your site. In either case, the settings are mostly the same.

To enable encryption on a specific directory or site, go to the Directory Security properties page for that directory or site. Click the Edit button to enable security, and you will go to a Secure Communications properties page similar to the one shown in Figure 17.101.

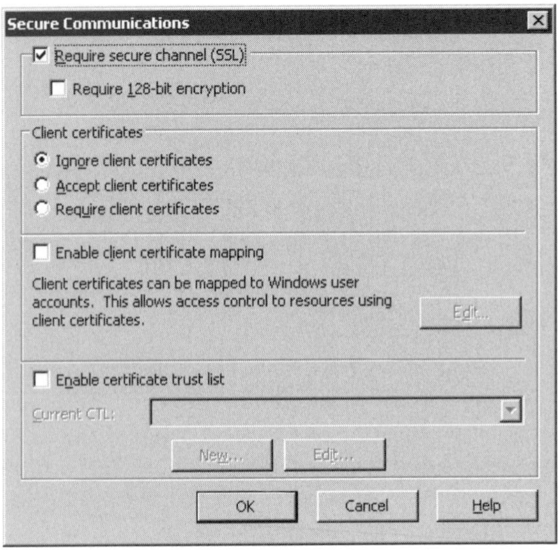

FIGURE 17.101

Implementing secure
communications

In this page, the most important setting to enable is Require Secure Channel (SSL). This will enforce secure communications for anyone trying to reach this resource (directory or site). Anyone attempting to access this resource over a standard HTTP connection will be instructed that they cannot reach the content unsecured and that they must use HTTPS to access the desired content. If you have a domestic-only build of Windows Server 2003, you will also have the option to enable strong (128-bit) encryption, instead of relying on standard 40-bit encryption (sometimes referred to as weak encryption).

As clients access your system, you can also accept or require client certificates as a means of authenticating who can access your system. If you want to require that only users with certificates access your system, select the Require Client Certificates radio button, and any users who do not have a client certificate installed in their system will not be able to access the secure content of your site.

Since it is possible for clients to provide certificates to your server (in addition to your server presenting a certificate to your clients), you can use this as a means of authenticating users and knowing exactly who is accessing your Web site. By checking the Enable Client Certificate Mapping check box, and then clicking the Edit button, you can "map" specific certificates to specific Windows user accounts. In effect, you are telling your IIS server, "If you receive this particular certificate, then assume that this is user John Doe accessing the Web server." If IIS knows who the exact user is, it can take advantage of permissions placed on files and directories for controlling who can access what content.

Finally, you can also create and enable a Certificate Trust List (CTL). This is a signed list of root certificates issued by various certificate authorities. A CTL allows administrators to specify which certificate authorities will be trusted by this Web site.

Once you've installed the certificate and enabled SSL for the Web site, use a browser to test for secure access to the Web site. Unless you've specified a nonstandard port for SSL to use, simply access the site using `https://` and the URL instead of `http://` and the URL. For instance, `http://www.redhilltown.com` will now be accessible at `https://www.redhilltown.com`.

Configuring and Troubleshooting Indexing Service and Building Web-Based Query Pages

Next, let's take up an IIS-related topic: Indexing Service. Index Server has surely gotten a fair amount of press attention because it contained the security hole that the Code Red weasels used to attack Web servers around the world. But it's harder to find useful information on making Indexing Service *work*, and that's a shame, as it can be a useful tool. This section describes how it works and offers some very simple Web pages that will let you exploit the service's power.

What Indexing Service Does

First of all, note that its name is Indexing *Service* rather than Index Server, as 2000 and later OSes include it "in the box." Many people (myself included) tend to erroneously call it Index Server because it was originally a separate add-on program that shipped for NT 4 called Index Server. Windows 2000 Server and Windows Server 2003 include it as a basic system service named Indexing Service. What it *does* is make searching today's huge hard disks a tractable affair.

Working in the background, Indexing Service examines and analyzes the files on your system, building and maintaining an index of the words that it finds there. At first blush, that'd make Indexing Service sound like something that just keeps track of every word, where "word" is just defined as a bunch of letters surrounded by spaces or punctuation. But think a bit more about it, and you'll see that Indexing Service has a harder job than that. Extracting words is simple if your document is plain ASCII text. But if it's an HTML file, how would Indexing Service know whether "
," the HTML command for "break the line here," is or isn't a word? How would it understand words in a Microsoft Word document? The answer is that Indexing Service includes a bunch of *filters*, programs that understand particular file formats. Indexing Service comes with filters that let it understand ASCII files, HTML files, Microsoft Office files, and what Help calls "Internet mail and news documents." There's no PDF filter included; you can download it, I'm told, from Adobe's Web site at `www.adobe.com/support/downloads/`. Do a search for the product name, PDF filter.

The Annoying Thing about Indexing Service: Little Documentation

The fact that Microsoft first documented it when it was Index Server means that, unfortunately, most of the Index-related documentation that you'll find on Microsoft's Web site and in books refers to the Index Server, which sort of works like Indexing Service, but not quite. To make things worse, the old Index Server documentation explained how to build HTML pages to query a cataloged directory, and for some reason Microsoft chose not to do that in the Indexing Service documentation. You're just supposed to know that things "kind of" work the same with Indexing Service as they did with Index Server, so I guess you're supposed to try the old code and hope it works. It does, sometimes; but I'll give you some basic HTML pages that you can use to create a Web page that will let you search any catalog from a Web browser. As always, once you know the magic words, then you can extract the information that you need from Microsoft's Web site.

What documentation there *is* about Indexing Service is in the Windows Server 2003 Server Help and Support Center files and in old-fashioned Windows Help files. Open the Help and Support Center from the Start menu and search for Indexing Service. One of the sublinks that you'll see is called Indexing Service. Or check out the Windows Help file found at `\Windows\help\is.chm`.

How You'll Use It (Why You Care)

I've found Indexing Service a great tool for building a fast, flexible Web-based search engine. But you can also use it within your network or just on your computer without any Web interface at all. For example, if you had a huge directory of ASCII, Office, and HTML documents, then you could catalog that and search for particular files extremely quickly.

How It Works

You tell Indexing Service that you want to create a catalog of a particular directory by telling Indexing Service two things: what directory you want to index (catalog) and where to put that catalog—after all, the catalog files must reside somewhere. Indexing Service creates a folder named `catalog.wci` in the directory that you've told it to store the catalog in. That leads to the following *very* important performance concerns—ones that I learned the hard way.

- Do *not* put the catalog in the directory that you're cataloging. If you want to catalog `C:\MYSTUFF`, then nothing at all will stop you from *storing* its catalog in that same directory. But it's a bad idea, and here's why. Let's say that you put a new file into `C:\MYSTUFF`, and so Indexing Service notices the new file and indexes it. That indexed information goes into the `CATALOG.WCI` directory, which is *inside* C:\MYSTUFF. This causes Indexing Service to notice that—aha!—there is some new data in C:\MYSTUFF and... oh, no, that's just the catalog, I'll ignore it. I know this sounds insignificant, but it isn't; I created a small directory with just a couple dozen files and put the index inside the directory; Indexing Service took about 10 minutes to index it. When I put those files into a different directory and cataloged that new directory—but put the catalog in still another directory—then Indexing Service cataloged the new directory almost instantaneously.

◆ IIS *really* doesn't like catalogs anywhere in the wwwroot directory or in the directories under it. It seems to slow down both IIS *and* Indexing Service.

MANAGING IT

Indexing Service is a service that you handle much like other services—you can start it, stop it, or restart it. A standard Windows Server 2003 install sets it up as an automatic service that runs as the local System account. You can start or stop the service using the Services applet, from the Indexing Services node in Computer Management, or with the stand-alone Indexing Service tool (ciadv.msc), which is also available as an MMC snap-in. The Indexing Service console looks like Figure 17.102.

FIGURE 17.102

Initial Indexing Service, showing System and Web catalogs

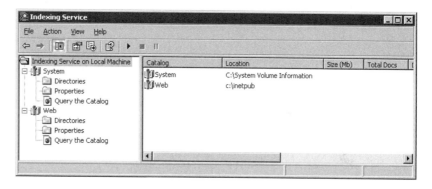

Like DNS and IIS, the Indexing Service's snap-in is incorporated in Computer Management under Services and Applications. Open it and you'll see one or more icons that look sort of like a stack of pages with a wrench paperweight on top—those are the catalogs, and we'll get to them in a minute. First, though, right-click the Indexing Service icon and choose Properties. As you see in Figure 17.103, you'll see two tabs on the page—Generation and Tracking.

Generation controls how Indexing Service creates indexes. One check box says Index Files with Unknown Extensions; it's not checked here, but if you check it, then Indexing Service just says, "Damn the torpedoes," and indexes *everything*, even if it doesn't have a filter for it. I don't use it, but I'm sure that *someone* thought it was a good idea. The other check box, Generate Abstracts, is also unchecked by default, but might be worth checking. When checked, Indexing Service tries to create an abstract of each file that it indexes. It's a nice feature but isn't always that smart; for example, it seems to create abstracts of HTML files by displaying the <h1> and <h2> elements of the document, which may not correctly characterize that document. Click the other tab, Tracking, and you'll see a page like the one in Figure 17.104.

FIGURE 17.103

Indexing Service
properties

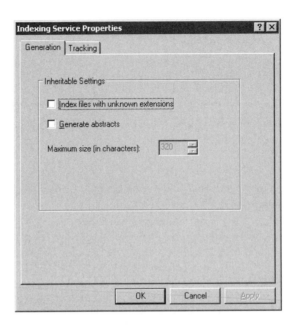

FIGURE 17.104

Tracking tab in
Indexing Service
properties

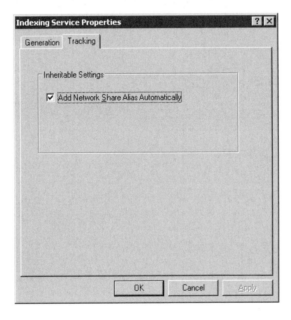

The Tracking tab just includes one check box, Add Network Share Alias Automatically, and it's
checked by default. This ensures that if Indexing Service indexes a drive that it sees as a mapped drive
letter, it remembers not only the drive letter, but the entire UNC. For example, if you've mapped
\\server01\data to X: and indexed X:, then Indexing Service would remember that those files are

available at \\server01\data even *if* you don't have that UNC mapped back to X: when you try to retrieve the indexed documents.

STANDARD CATALOGS

Even if you've never used Indexing Service before, you're likely to already see two catalogs: one called System and, if you're running a Web server on the computer, another catalog called Web. As their names suggest, they index system information and whatever content there is on your Web server.

Personally, the first thing I do is to delete both of them. Having my entire Web site as well as every hard disk on my server indexed gives me the heebie-jeebies. I mean, why *not* just make it easy for crackers to spy on my system once they've cracked Indexing Service? My feeling is that *I'll* decide what gets indexed on my system, thanks very much.

To delete a catalog, you must stop the Indexing Service. Then just left-click the catalog and press the Delete key, or right-click the catalog and choose the Delete option from the context menu.

CREATING A CATALOG

You create a catalog in Indexing Service by right-clicking the Indexing Service icon and choosing New and then Catalog to raise a dialog like the one in Figure 17.105.

FIGURE 17.105

Creating a new catalog

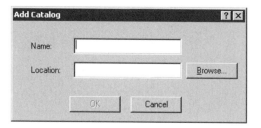

This dialog box, labeled Add Catalog, contains just two text fields: Name and Location. In Name, just fill in the descriptive name of your catalog—no spaces allowed! This name doesn't have to relate in any way to the name of the directory that you're going to index. For example, I named the catalog for my online newsletters "Newsletters" even though they don't reside in a directory named `Newsletters`. Location is the location of the *catalog files*, not the files to be cataloged. This was what I was talking about a while back: specify a location for your catalog that is different from the location *to be* cataloged. For example, if I were indexing newsletters in a directory named `C:\Newsletters`, I might put the catalog's location in, say, `C:\Newsletter Index`. But no matter where you put the catalog, remember not to put it in `wwwroot` or anywhere under that directory.

If Indexing Service is off when you create the catalog, you'll get a dialog to that effect: "Catalog will remain offline until Indexing Service is restarted." No surprise there.

TELL IT WHAT TO CATALOG, AND WHAT NOT TO

Now Indexing Service knows that you want to catalog *something*, but it doesn't know what. So add one or more directories to its list of things to index. Right-click the catalog's icon and choose New/Directory and you'll see a dialog box like the one in Figure 17.106.

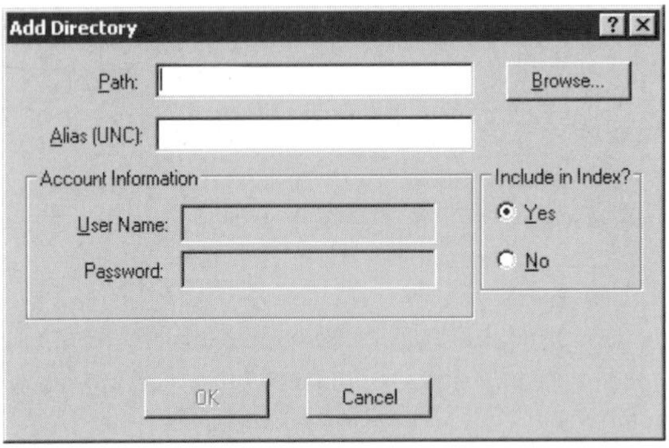

FIGURE 17.106

Adding a directory to the catalog

That dialog asks you to fill in the path and, if relevant, the UNC of the directory to catalog. If the directory points to a network resource, type in a username and password to be used to access the directory. Next to that is an odd-looking set of radio buttons asking, "Include in Index?"

Is this about the dumbest question you can imagine, or what? Here you are, adding a directory to a catalog—whose sole function in life is to *index* data, and this dialog asks if you want to index the data. What were they thinking? Well, Indexing Service not only indexes the top level of the directory that you specify, but any *subdirectories* as well. So suppose I've decided to index C:\Newsletters, as it contains my old newsletters. But suppose that *inside* the C:\Newsletters directory is a C:\Newsletters\In-Progress directory, where I keep my newsletters that I'm still working on. Well, by default, Indexing Service would catalog *that* directory as well—so a well-placed query would let you see my newsletters before I'm even finished writing them! That's not what I want, so I might add C:\Newsletters, as I've described, and then add C:\Newsletters\In-Progress—and then tell Indexing Service *not* to include C:\Newsletters\In-Progress in the catalog. The net effect would be to defeat Indexing Service's natural inclination to index everything in C:\Newsletters, even my work-in-progress directory.

You can also block Indexing Service from cataloging a file or directory by using that file or directory's advanced attributes. Locate the file or directory in Windows Explorer or My Computer, right-click the file or directory, choose Properties, and then click the Advanced button in the General tab to open the Advanced Attributes dialog box (shown in Figure 17.107).

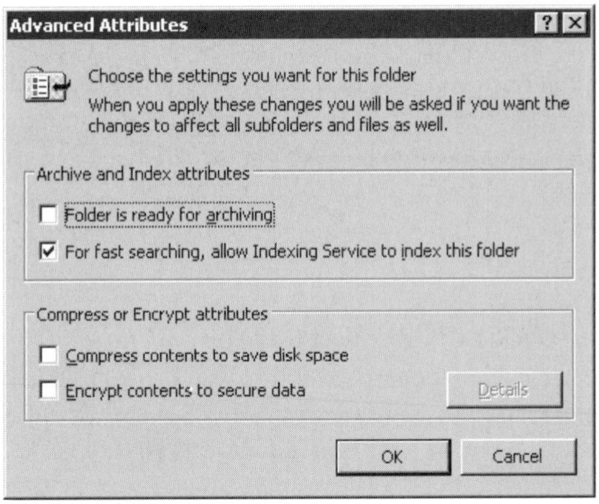

FIGURE 17.107

A folder's advanced attributes

Uncheck the option labeled For Fast Searching, and the folder will be essentially invisible to Indexing Service.

CONSIDER FILE PERMISSIONS, OR YOUR CATALOG WON'T WORK

Sometimes security gets in the way of Indexing Service. So take a minute and consider the file and directory permissions on the things that you want to index.

When I first used Indexing Service, it drove me absolutely crazy. It could index many files, but not the ones that I wanted—not the ones on my Web server. I set up a pristine new computer, built a catalog on it with copies of the exact same data files that I wanted to index, and it worked…but not on my Web server. Then it dawned on me: I'd monkeyed with the directory permissions on my server.

My original plan had been to adjust the permissions so that the IUSR account didn't have access to parts of the disk that it had no need to have. But in the process of disconnecting some directory permissions from inheriting permissions from their parent directory, I cleared all previous permissions. Including the System account.

But, as you've already learned, the Indexing Service runs *under* the System account. And therein lay the problem. I'd set up the catalog right; I'd just denied Indexing Service the ability to actually read the files that I wanted it to index. Now, in my defense, let me just squawk a bit that it'd have been nice if Microsoft offered a verbose logging feature of Indexing Service, where I'd have gotten a clue a bit earlier…but it was still dumb on my part. So let's stop for a minute and consider permissions.

- Indexing Service needs to be able to read whatever you want cataloged, so make sure that System can read whatever you're cataloging.
- Indexing Service needs to be able to write and modify its catalog, so be sure that System can write, read, and modify whatever directory you've put the catalog in.

But we're not done yet. Eventually you will want to query that catalog, using either the query tool built into the snap-in, which I'll show you in a minute, or perhaps through a Web interface. Before releasing the answers to a query, Indexing Service checks that the asker has the permissions to see the answer. So let's see what that means for my example of a Web-based search engine for my online newsletters.

Suppose the newsletter directory gave System Full Control permissions, but denied the IUSR account all access. What would happen? Well, Indexing Service would build the catalog for the newsletter directory just fine. And if I logged onto the server as an administrator and queried that catalog with some command-line tool or the built-in one that I'll show you in a minute, then perhaps the query would work fine. But from the Web-based interface, the query failed—why? Indexing Service sees that the IUSR account isn't allowed to see that data.

In my experience, security is a major cause of failed queries, so keep it in mind when using Indexing Service–based tools.

Using the Catalog: Querying Indexing Service from Computer Management

Once you've created that catalog, how do you try it out? You use a tool built into the Computer Management tool, under the Indexing Service icon, called Query the Catalog, as you see in Figure 17.108.

FIGURE 17.108

Sample Indexing
Service query

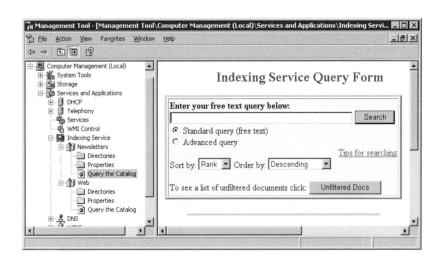

As you see in that figure, you'll see a field where you can type in your query words next to a button labeled Search. The query tool will show you all of your hits and provide hyperlinks that you can click to view the files that matched your query.

This isn't really an all-purpose tool, as it's cumbersome to search a catalog unless you're physically seated at the server whose Indexing Service hosts that catalog. But it's a great debugging tool because it's a quick-and-dirty way to find out if your catalog is working. And because you're usually running it while logged in as an administrator, you typically do that test query with maximum permissions. *Then*, if you try the same query from a Web page and it fails while the Query the Catalog tool succeeds, you can be pretty sure that the problem lies with permissions rather than with something else.

USING THE CATALOG: THE QUERY LANGUAGE

But how do you address queries? Indexing Service has its own built-in query language that's pretty extensive but also pretty ugly. You can get the whole scoop in the Indexing Service help file, \Windows\help\is.chm. Open the top-level booklet icon, Indexing Service, and inside that you'll see another booklet, Concepts. Inside there you'll find another booklet entitled Using Indexing Service, and finally, below that, is a topic called Making Queries. In this section, I'll just offer a short summary of the Indexing Service's query language and provide a few examples.

Simple Words

Of course, you can type just one word and Indexing Service will look for that. Searching for "Kerberos" will turn up any document with the word "Kerberos" in it. Indexing Service seems not to care about case—"kerberos" would turn up the same hits as "Kerberos."

Word Variations Work, Too

Indexing Service understands variations on words. For example, if you search for "patches," then you'll not only get hits that match "patches," you'll also get hits that match simply "patch" or "patching."

To do an exact search, surround the search with double quotes. Thus, if you type **patches**, you'll get patch, patches, patching, and the like, but typing **patches** will match only that exact phrase.

Wildcards Are Harder

But recall that Indexing Service tries to understand text not merely as a sequence of characters, but instead as a series of *words*, so searching for "Kerb" would not yield any hits that matched "Kerberos." How, then, to do wildcards? By giving Indexing Service what Microsoft calls a phrase, wherein you surround your query with {phrase} and {/phrase}; it's sort of HTML-ish. The asterisk is the generic wildcard, as always, so to search for any line that contains "Kerb," type

```
{phrase}Kerb*{/phrase}
```

In theory, you can make Unix-style regular expressions work by surrounding them with {regex} and {/regex}, but I've not been successful making them work.

Logical Operators

Indexing Service also understands AND, OR, NOT, and parentheses. You could search for:

```
"domain controller" and (kerberos or "LAN Manager")
```

It also understands NEAR, but only in a very lame way—NEAR is defined as "within 50 words" and, no matter what the docs say, it's not possible to redefine. So this works:

```
"domain controller" near Kerberos
```

It's a pretty powerful language—it's just a little cryptic.

Filtering "Noise" Words Via noise.enu—And, Or, Numerals, Etc.

A large number of the words in English text are simple words that you probably would never search on: and, or, also, have, could, and the like. You don't want your catalog to track every single use of *those* words. So Indexing Service includes a file called noise.enu in \winnt\system32. It's a simple ASCII file listing "noise" words—words not to index. You can change it to include (or exclude) any word, as you like. It's called noise.enu because it lists the *English* noise words. Look in \winnt\system32 and you'll also see noise.esn (Spanish), noise.deu (German), and noise.ita (Italian), among others.

Using the Catalog: Querying Indexing Service from the Web

Now that you have a working catalog and can query it from the Query the Catalog option in the Indexing Service node of Computer Management, how do you let the rest of the world (or maybe just the rest of your intranet) query the catalog? With a Web-based query client. While this isn't a programming text—nor am I an expert programmer—here's a very bare-bones, stripped-down set of Web pages that you can modify and put up to let people query some catalog.

GETTING READY

For this example, let me assume that you're going to index files in a directory called Newsletters, which sits in your wwwroot directory. (Yes, you can do this for files that *aren't* in wwwroot, but this is simplest.) You have already:

- ◆ Set up IIS on a computer (with all the current security patches, please!)
- ◆ Created a directory named Newsletters inside \Inetpub\wwwroot
- ◆ Placed a few text, HTML, or Office documents in \Inetpub\wwwroot\Newsletters

- Started Indexing Service on that computer
- Created a catalog called Newsletters, which indexes the Newsletters directory inside wwwroot
- Tested that queries to it work with Query the Catalog

CREATING THE HTML

You'll need two files: ask.htm, which contains a form that lets people type in their queries, and find.asp, which takes the information collected in ask.htm, executes the query, and returns the answers. Ask.htm is pretty short, as you can see in Listing 17.2.

LISTING 17.2: THE *ASK.HTM* FILE

```
<HTML>
<HEAD>
<TITLE>Search Newsletter Archive</TITLE>
</HEAD>
<BODY>
<Form ACTION="find.asp" METHOD=POST>
Type in your query<br>
<INPUT TYPE=TEXT NAME="SearchString" SIZE="94" MAXLENGTH="100" VALUE=""><br>
<BUTTON TYPE=SUBMIT>Submit</BUTTON>
<BUTTON TYPE=RESET>Clear Form</BUTTON>
</FORM>
</BODY>
</HTML>
```

This just prompts you to "Type in your query," then packages your query in a variable called SearchString, and then calls another HTML page called find.asp. (Both ask.htm and find.asp should be in your wwwroot directory.)

Find.asp is a bit more complex (see Listing 17.3), as it must first perform the query and then format it nicely for the user.

LISTING 17.3: THE *FIND.ASP* FILE

```
<HTML>
<HEAD>
<TITLE>Search Results</TITLE>
</HEAD>
<BODY>
<%

'Set the search parameters

'The following line is a comment; it shows how you'd restrict the search
'To just a directory "folderinnews" inside Newsletters.
'FormScope = "/folderinnews"
```

```
'These lines set the search parameters

FormScope = "/"PageSize = 1000
MaxRecords=1000
SearchString = Request.Form("SearchString")
CatalogToSearch = "Newsletters"
SearchRankOrder="rank[d]"
OrigSearch=SearchString

'
' Create query object

set Q = Server.CreateObject("ixsso.Query")
set util = Server.CreateObject("ixsso.Util")
Q.Query = SearchString
Q.Catalog = CatalogToSearch
Q.SortBy = SearchRankOrder
Q.Columns = "DocTitle, vpath, filename, size, write,
characterization, rank, directory, path"
Q.MaxRecords = MaxRecords
'util.AddScopeToQuery Q, FormScope, "deep"

'
' Do query
'

set RS = Q.CreateRecordSet("nonsequential")
RS.PageSize = PageSize
response.write "<p>Your search for <b>" & OrigSearch & "</b> yielded "

If RS.RecordCount=0 then response.write "no results."
If RS.RecordCount=1 then response.write "1 result:"
If RS.RecordCount>1 then response.write RS.RecordCount & " results:"

response.write "<table
border=1><tr><td>Doctitle</td><td>Vpath</td><td>Filename</td>"
response.write "<td>Size</td><td>Write</td><td>Characterization</td><td>Rank</td>"
response.write "<td>Directory</td><td>Path</td></tr>"

'Display the results

Do While Not RS.EOF
' loop through the results.
' Build a hyperlink to the document
hlink = "<a href=""/newsletters/" & RS("filename")
& """>" & RS("doctitle") & "</a>"
' Display attributesresponse.write "<tr><td>" &
hlink & "</td><td>" & RS("Vpath") & "</td><td>"
```

```
response.write RS("filename") & "</td><td>" & RS("size")
↳& "</td><td>" & RS("write")
response.write "</td><td>" & RS("characterization") & "</td><td>" & RS("rank")
response.write "</td><td>" & RS("directory") & "</td><td>"
↳& RS("path") & "</td><tr>"
'Get the next result
RS.MoveNext
Loop 'end of DO WHILE loop

response.write "</table>"
set rs=nothing
set q=nothing
set util=nothing
%>

</BODY>
</HTML>
```

If you just want to try these out, then type the lines into Notepad and copy the files to your wwwroot directory. While still sitting at that computer, open up Internet Explorer, type **http://localhost/ask.htm**, press Enter, and you'll see your form come up.

HOW THE QUERY CODE WORKS

To understand `find.asp`—which, again, is a very stripped-down query page—let's take it in pieces. The first part, through the <BODY> command, is just HTML. After that, you see this:

```
<%
'Set the search parameters
'The following line is a comment; it shows how you'd restrict the search to
'just a directory "folderinnews" inside Newsletters.
'FormScope = "/folderinnews"
'These lines set the search parameters
FormScope = "/"
PageSize = 1000
MaxRecords=1000
SearchString = Request.Form("SearchString")
CatalogToSearch = "Newsletters"
SearchRankOrder="rank[d]"
OrigSearch=SearchString
```

That line with just the <% tells the IIS server that a program is starting. Lines that begin with a single quote are just ignored by the server; they're comments. The next bunch of lines sets the parameters for the search. FormScope lets you tell Indexing Service that you don't want to search an entire directory, just a subdirectory. If, for example, you had a directory called \inetpub\wwwroot\newsletters\goodstuff and you wanted the search to *only* look in the \goodstuff directory, then you'd change the line to

```
Formscope = "/goodstuff"
```

PageSize and MaxRecords restrict the search, limiting the number of hits that Indexing Service reports. SearchString just retrieves the search text. CatalogToSearch, of course, says to search "Newsletters." If there were other catalogs on this server, then you'd change this variable to point the search elsewhere. SearchRankOrder just says to report them from the best to the worst match. OrigSearch is just for programming convenience.

The next set of lines forms and executes the query:

```
' Create query object

set Q = Server.CreateObject("ixsso.Query")
set util = Server.CreateObject("ixsso.Util")
Q.Query = SearchString
Q.Catalog = CatalogToSearch
Q.SortBy = SearchRankOrder
Q.Columns = "DocTitle, vpath, filename, size, write,
⮑characterization, rank, directory, path"
Q.MaxRecords = MaxRecords
' util.AddScopeToQuery Q, FormScope, "deep"


' Do query


set RS = Q.CreateRecordSet("nonsequential")
RS.PageSize = PageSize
```

The piece toward the top is just "boilerplate," the particular magic words that you must say to ask Indexing Service a question. Note, however, types of "objects"—that's the programmer word for them—in the ServerCreateObject commands. The first in particular, ixsso.Query, is the built-in set of routines that controls queries. To find all of the developer documentation about it, search msdn.microsoft.com for "ixsso.query."

CONTROLLING A QUERY: WHAT TO RETRIEVE

If you did that search, you'd see that the "query" method of the "ixsso" object—I'm so glad the developers kept it simple for us—has attributes with names like Query, Catalog, SortBy, and so on. You needn't look that stuff up unless you want to extend this example; I've already done most of the work. But you *do* have to fill those attributes with values, and that's what the Q.Query=, Q.Catalog=, and nearby lines do—they just transfer the values that we set up top into a place where Indexing Service can find it.

A couple of the lines need a bit more explaining. First, notice the Q.Columns= line; that tells Indexing Service exactly which data to retrieve.

- DocTitle is the title, if the file has one. HTML files have titles; ASCII files don't; Office files can have titles.

- Vpath is the relative path from the top of the catalog. In other words, you're looking in a directory called \Inetpub\wwwroot\newsletters for files, but what if the files are in a directory *inside* that directory? Vpath would show that. If it turns up a file named \Inetpub\wwwroot\newsletters\ goodfiles\hints.txt, then the Vpath would be goodfiles, as it's the subdirectory inside the catalog.

◆ Filename is, logically, the filename—`hints.txt` in the previous example.

◆ Size is the size in bytes.

◆ Write is the date the file was last written to.

◆ Characterization is the "abstract" that Indexing Service can optionally create.

◆ Rank is a numeric score that Indexing Service uses to rate how well something matches a query.

◆ Directory is the complete directory path of the file `d:\inetpub\wwwroot\Newsletters\goodfiles` in the example.

◆ Path is the combination of the filename and the directory; in the example, it'd be `d:\inetpub\wwwroot\Newsletters\goodfiles\hints.txt`.

You can see the entire list of columns in a catalog in the Indexing Service snap-in in Computer Management. Under the icon for the catalog itself there is a folder named `Properties`. Look in there and you'll see the entire list of a catalog's properties or, as the query calls it, columns. (Most of them are of no value—the preceding list is about all you'd probably want.)

CONTROLLING A QUERY: WHERE TO LOOK

Second, note the comment that starts util.AddScope. This tells Indexing Service two things about the search: first, which directory in the catalog should it search and, second, should it search at that directory level, or search that directory and the directories *inside* of it? Recall that Indexing Service automatically *catalogs* as far down as the directory structure goes; this command doesn't affect that. Instead, it reflects the fact that Indexing Service doesn't automatically show all of its cards when you make a query—it only reveals what the query asks for.

Suppose you've got that directory structure that I mentioned before, `\Inetpub\wwwroot\Newsletters\goodfiles\hints.txt`. Suppose also that you chose this time to index the *whole* wwwroot directory. What would that mean for the scope of the search? Without an AddScopeToQuery command, Indexing Service will only show results that it found in the top-level directory of the catalog, `\Inetpub\wwwroot`. To search the *whole* directory and the directories inside it, including `\Inetpub\wwwroot\Newsletters`, `\Inetpub\wwwroot\Newsletters\goodfiles`, and whatever else is in there, you'd use this command:

```
util.AddScopeToQuery Q, "/", "deep"
```

That says that the query defined by the object *Q* should start at the top—"/"—and should search all directories. The "deep" keyword is the part that says to search the directories inside the directories.

But what if you only wanted to search `\Inetpub\wwwroot\Newsletters`? Then you'd use a scope of /Newsletters—note that this uses the forward slash rather than backslash. The command would look like this:

```
util.AddScopeToQuery Q, "/Newsletters", "shallow"
```

Finally, what if you wanted to restrict the search to keep it out of the `\Inetpub\wwwroot` directory and start searching at `\Inetpub\wwwroot\Newsletters`, but also search directories below `Newsletters`? Then you'd do this:

```
util.AddScopeToQuery Q, "/Newsletters", "deep"
```

It's a *really* good idea to restrict your query scopes—you'll be surprised what Indexing Service turns up! For example, if you *did* index your entire Web site, then you'd probably be exposing things like code in progress, old code, or notes to yourself, much of which you might not want publicly visible.

To finish examining `find.asp`, the set RS= line tells IIS where to put the output of the query: into an object called a "record set" that I've unimaginatively called "RS." And finally, the rest of the program just loops through the returned values and creates a table that reports what it found. The three commands that say "set *something*=nothing" recover memory on the IIS server.

Troubleshooting Failed Queries

When you first get started with building your search pages and catalogs, you'll probably turn up a lot of failed queries. They can be frustrating; here's what to check:

Permissions   SYSTEM must have read access to the data to be cataloged, full control of the directory where the catalog is stored, and, Microsoft adds (although I've not checked it), that SYSTEM must also have full control to the root of the drive where the catalog is stored. But the querying person must also have the permissions to see the documents, or Indexing Service won't even display it. So, for example, if your query fails from your Web browser, try logging onto the server as an administrator and try the query tool in Computer Management. If *that* works and the Web browser doesn't, chances are good that IUSR doesn't have the permissions necessary to see the data. And when you're testing your Web-based app, make sure that you're not logged on as an administrator of the domain. Depending on how you have IIS set up, it may try to get you the catalog info as IUSR and, when that fails, it may automatically try again using your currently logged-on credentials as an administrator, and succeed. But non-admins won't be able to access the data.

Check the query syntax   It's a bizarre language. Make sure you have a few simple queries whose syntax you *know* works.

Be patient   Indexing Service is built to run in the background, which means that when you're fussing with it, the indexing part of Indexing Service goes to sleep, waiting for the server to quiet down before it does its work. Get a cup of coffee or check your e-mail, give it a few minutes, and then try again.

Dump the catalog and start over   Stop the Indexing Service, then right-click the icon for the catalog, and choose All Tasks/Empty Catalog. Then restart the Indexing Service. You start out with a fresh catalog this way, and you know that no old junk's sitting around in it.

Go to the directories and files that you want to catalog, right-click them and choose Properties, then click the Advanced button   There's a check box on the resulting dialog box labeled For Fast Searching, Allow Indexing Service to Index This Folder. It's checked by default, but if someone's unchecked it, then Indexing Service will skip it altogether.

By now, you should not only have a working catalog, but also a nifty Web-based front end for it. Indexing Service is pretty cool once you get it set up, but, as always with complex tools, it's the initial setup that's the pain.

Windows Server 2003 Internet Security: Some Thoughts

A security engineer at a major tier-one ISP recently told me his opinion of Windows NT in regard to security. "It's an exploit in a box," he told me, very matter of factly, and you know what? Even though he's a "Unix guy," he was absolutely right. Windows NT was extremely permissive in its default configurations. However, Windows 2000 Server made a bunch of improvements in the security arena, and Windows Server 2003 is the most secure operating system that they've ever published. But does that mean that you should simply accept it with its default configuration? In the pages that follow, I'll walk through some items that you should be certain to secure on your Windows Server in order to protect it even more.

Although the security suggestions that follow will help secure your system, it is important to realize that there is no quick fix for Internet security. Entire volumes are published on the subject, much more than I could possibly cover in the pages of this book.

There are, however, several types of actions you can take to detect and/or deter an outside attack. In this section, I'll talk about deterring and detecting attacks and cover security recommendations for three primary areas: accounts, file and print sharing, and network services.

Whether "security" is officially part of your job description or not, the twenty-first century seems to have a few new truths about it. First, we seem to be running a lot more Web servers than before. Even simple network-attached appliances like JetDirect modules or 3Com's Lanmodem make you control them via a Web interface, which means that—you guessed it—they've all got a Web server built into them. But what's the second truth of the twenty-first century? Virus- and worm-writing jerks the world over have targeted IIS. So anyone running an IIS-based Web server should understand that it is *very* likely that his or her system will be attacked by a worm; such an attack is a near certainty. But there's a third and final truth here: If you put an insecure Web server on a network, then you aren't merely a neutral party in the ongoing war between the worm-writing weasels and systems administrators; rather, you are helping the weasels.

To see what I mean by that, let's look at who would get hurt if I set up a Web server but didn't protect it from a worm. Worms like Code Red, Code Blue, Nimda, and their successors do several things. First, they usually rewrite and damage Web pages. That means that if I don't do anything to protect my Web server from infection, then I may be hurt, in that I must restore my Web pages to their predefacement state. But what if I've put a system on the Internet that runs a Web server, but only because I installed with the defaults? In that case, I shouldn't care whether a worm attacks the Web server, should I?

Of course I should, because of the *second* effect of a worm. Once planted in a Web server, worms seek out other Web servers to infect. That means that my unwitting Web server might end up as the vehicle that some weasel uses to infect an important Web server. At minimum, that's certainly not nice and I would prefer *not* to be a vector of e-infection; at worst, I might even be sued over it.

Even worse, a worm has a third effect: it chomps bandwidth. There have been days when so many copies of a given worm are busy scanning IP addresses trying to find potential victim servers that they have significantly slowed down the Internet.

The bottom line is this: If I've put an unsecured computer on the Internet, then I've put a loaded weapon into the hands of a network criminal. I've aided and abetted one of the bad guys. I worry that as more and more home users get high-speed DSL and cable-modem connections, and as those home users' operating systems get more and more sophisticated, that it will be possible for one cleverly written worm to simply shut the Internet down. Edmund Burke is credited with saying that all that is required for evil to triumph is for a "few good men to do nothing." Let's update that to say that all that is required for the weasels to destroy or severely damage an important artery of communication— the Internet—is for a few otherwise-good people to get lazy about securing their operating system's Web servers.

The most important point here, however, is that you can do some very simple, basic things to secure your IIS servers; let's see how.

Disable IIS If You Aren't Using It

Probably the most effective and simplest way to secure your server is to disable unnecessary services. You can test if a computer is running a Web server in a few simple ways. First, check its services in Computer Management: right-click My Computer, choose Manage, then locate the object labeled Services and Applications and click the plus sign next to it. That should reveal, among other things, an object named Services; click it and the right panel will show the services that your computer is running. You'll see that there isn't a service called IIS or Internet Information Service or anything like that; it's called World Wide Web Publishing Service. Right-click it, choose Properties, and you'll get a property page that lets you stop the service. But that only stops the Web server for now—reboot, and it'll probably start up all by itself. You can change that by clicking a drop-down list box labeled Startup Type, which offers you three choices: Automatic (which starts the service up at boot time), Manual (which does not start the service at boot time but lets you turn it on when you feel like it), or Disabled (which doesn't start the service and doesn't give you the option to start it). Just choose Disabled if you don't want this server to be a Web server, and then click OK.

Windows Server 2003 makes this less of a problem, as it discontinues Microsoft's practice of automatically installing a Web server on every system. Additionally, IIS 6 first comes up in a very "locked-down" mode, making it harder to attack an IIS 6 server whose administrator has chosen all of the defaults for it.

Get and Apply the Latest Service Packs and Hotfixes

Whenever a new worm appears, people castigate Microsoft for being "unprepared" for this latest attack, and administrators everywhere bemoan Windows' "terrible security."

Just about anyone who's ever been hit by an IIS-based worm could have avoided the infection had he just kept up-to-date with Microsoft's patches. (Up-to-date Web servers were safe from Code Red, Blue, and Nimda, for example.) The problem is that most of us are a bit sloppy about getting around to downloading and applying the latest patches, and for years that wasn't really a problem. Unfortunately, our modern-day "world of worms" has made staying on top of patches mandatory.

Windows Server 2003 makes it easier than ever to stay up to date on service packs, patches, and hotfixes. The Autoupdate feature, available in the System applet, lets you configure a server to automatically check for updates and download them when they are released. Or you can use the Windows Update Web site (`http://windowsupdate.microsoft.com`) to scan your system, review and then install updates.

But service packs aren't the end of your update task. Stay up to date on the latest developments by checking out the security bulletins that you can find at `www.microsoft.com/technet/treeview/default.asp?url=/technet/security/current.asp`. This site gets rearranged on a regular basis, so if that doesn't work, just search for "security bulletin" on the `microsoft.com` site. The Security Bulletins site offers a notification service when new bulletins are issued, and access to the Microsoft

Baseline Security Analyzer (MBSA) tool, which scans a system for vulnerabilities and missing hotfixes. The patches released from the bulletin site are EXE files with names like `Q329390_WXP_SP2_X86_ENU.exe`. The first part refers to the Knowledge Base article that explains what the patch does, `WXP` clearly says that it's a Windows XP patch, and `SP2` means that it is a *post*–Service Pack 2 fix and that this patch will eventually be part of Service Pack 3.

NOTE *Microsoft is retiring the "Q" naming scheme for Knowledge Base articles. Articles previously named "QXXXXX" will retain the same number, but without the "Q" prefix.*

Simplifying Hotfix Application

If you've ever downloaded and applied a hotfix, then you're probably shaking your head and thinking, "Has this guy ever actually *done* this?" But, wait, give me a chance.

Hotfixes are a pain for two reasons. First, there are a *lot* of them. It's not unusual to see a couple or three dozen hotfixes that you need to apply *even if you have the most recent service pack*. Second, try applying one and you'll see that most of them force you to reboot after you apply them. So let's see, first I download the 18 relevant hotfixes. Then I apply the first one and wait for my system to reboot, then I do the second, and... wait a minute, you mean that I've got to do that for *all* of my computers? And then how do I check which computers have and don't have a given set of hotfixes?

Thankfully, Microsoft has offered a couple of programs to simplify the process, `qchain.exe` and `hfnetchk.exe`. You can find the link for `qchain.exe` at Knowledge Base article 296861, or if that article's gone by the time that you read this, then search for "qchain.exe." You can find `hfnetchk.exe` at article Q303215, or, again, if that doesn't exist when you look for it, search on the program's name.

qchain lets you apply a whole bunch of hotfixes all at once. You invoke the hotfixes—each with the options -m, -z, unattended, and don't force reboot—and then qchain rearranges them on disk and in the Registry so that they don't conflict with one another. Then you can reboot. For example, suppose you had some hotfixes with the names q335825_w2k_sp3.exe, qf843615_w2k_sp3.exe, and q745622_w2k_sp3.exe (all imaginary hotfix names, by the way). You could put them on a server named srv1 on a share called patches, and then put the hotfixes, `qchain.exe`, and a batch file to install the patches in that share. The batch file could look something like this:

```
set lc=\\srv1\patches\
%lc%q335825_w2k_sp3.exe -z -m
%lc%qf843615_w2k_sp3.exe -z -m
%lc%q745622_w2k_sp3.exe -z -m
%lc%qchain mylog.txt
```

Create the batch file by opening up Notepad and typing those lines into Notepad, but don't type the names of the imaginary hotfixes; instead, type one line for each of the hotfixes that you've got in that directory, prefixing them with "%lc%" and adding "-z -m" to the end. Then save them as `applypatches.bat`, again in that share. Now you can, from any machine on the network, just type

```
\\svr1\patches\applypatches.bat
```

and it'll apply all of the patches. You can then reboot the system, and it'll be up-to-date. But how do you check later to see what hotfixes have been applied to a given system and if it's still up-to-date? That's where `hfnetchk.exe` helps out. In its simplest form, you just run `hfnetchk.exe` on a system without any options. It then contacts the Microsoft site, downloads information about the latest hotfixes, and checks that your system has those hotfixes. It'll then report about hotfixes that Microsoft thinks that you should have but that you don't.

You can run it with the -v, verbose, switch to find out why hfnetchk thinks that you don't have a given hotfix. There are a few that apparently don't leave enough of a fingerprint behind for hfnetchk to be able to verify whether or not you actually have the hotfix installed, like one that appeared in 2001 named MS01-022. Apparently you could apply it all that you wanted, but hfnetchk couldn't find it. But running hfnetchk -v could allay your fears:

```
WARNING          MS01-022        Q296441
The XML file does not contain any file or registry details
  ⮦for this patch.  As a result, this tool is unable to
  ⮦confirm that this patch has been applied.  Please
  ⮦verify patch installation or refer to Q303215 for
  ⮦more information.
```

In other words, hfnetchk is saying, "Well, I can't *prove* that this is here, so I won't say that it's there...but I couldn't prove it in either case."

Use IIS and NTFS Permissions

When the bad guys get control of your IIS server, the system sees them as one of two user accounts— either the IUSR account or the System account. If they're running a script or a Web page, then they're the IUSR account. Intruders can only act as the System account in those cases where IIS has some pretty egregious bug and the intruder exploits that bug.

Let me underscore that point: visitors to your Web site are actually logged into your Web server's security system, whether it's a local SAM or a domain-based Active Directory. Such so-called "anonymous" Web visitors are logged in as the IUSR account. Armed with that knowledge, you can recruit NTFS to help you secure your system.

Unlike Windows 2000 and earlier systems, which set all of their NTFS permissions to Everyone/Full Control (of course IUSR is a member of Everyone), Windows Server 2003 sets more restrictive permissions on disk resources:

1. The wwwroot directory only grants the IUSR account NTFS permissions to read and list folder contents. This will work fine unless there is a script in wwwroot, in which case you need to grant execute permissions as well. You'll only need to give IUSR write permissions on any directories that Web-based scripts use to write files to.

2. In the Windows directory, IUSR has the same permissions as Authenticated Users: read, execute, and list folder contents.

3. Throughout the rest of the server's hard disk, IUSR has no access permissions.

TIP Your system might need somewhat different permissions. Microsoft has a pretty nitty-gritty Knowledge Base article about required IIS 5 permissions at 271071. As far as I know, they haven't updated it for IIS 6 yet.

Now, you might be running some set of programs or scripts that require different permissions than the defaults; work with the content folks to find out what permissions you need for each directory but, again, in my experience IIS works very well with extremely minimal permissions for IUSR.

But IIS itself also has a set of permissions that you can use to secure your Web site. They work in tandem with NTFS permissions in the same way that file-sharing permissions work with NTFS permissions: both apply and the most restrictive ones win. IIS permissions are simpler and less flexible than NTFS permissions, as they apply to everyone accessing a site—there's no way, for example, to say that the IIS read permission (which is different from the familiar NTFS read permission) should be granted to Administrators and denied to everyone else. Instead, you just check the Read box and every visitor gets it.

Although the default IIS permissions are more restrictive in IIS 6 than they were in IIS 5, you should still check out the Execute Permissions box for every directory in your Web site. My site was once composed of a basic wwwroot directory that contained a bunch of directories, most of which contained only static HTML pages and images. I was surprised to find that the IIS permission on all of those directories was scripts and executables!

To view a given directory's IIS permissions, just open up the site in the IIS administration snap-in, and you'll see a folder icon for each directory. Right-click the folder and choose Properties, and you'll see the IIS permissions for that directory in the Directory, Home Directory, or Virtual Directory tab, depending on the context.

Disable Indexing

The Indexing Service is not installed by default in Windows Server 2003, but if you do install it, delete the two default catalogs named Web and System to prevent automatic indexing of all your hard drives and Web sites. Only create catalogs for folders you explicitly want indexed, and keep in mind that all files and subfolders will be indexed from that point in the directory structure. Be sure to disable indexing for any subfolders with content you don't want to include in the catalog. Consider taking the extra precaution of explicitly disabling indexing for all other files and directories on your hard disks. I know this seems like overkill, but there are some directories that you don't ever want to be indexed, even if some bright-eyed administrator later decides that it would be a good idea to index all the hard drives on the server. Mail directories would fall into this category. Imagine doing an innocent search and having the query return a confidential e-mail from the accounting department on salary reviews!

Disable All Nonessential Ports

In Chapter 6, you learned how to enable TCP/IP filtering to close particular ports on the server. Consider doing this for your Web servers. But remember, if you close all incoming ports except for 80 and 443, then you won't be able to do remote administration of your computer. You can close ports from the GUI in the Advanced properties of the TCP/IP protocol, or use IPSec, as you saw in Chapter 6.

Move *wwwroot*

By default, IIS puts its wwwroot directory on the same drive as the operating system, in the \Inetpub directory. Some particularly badly written worms can't even *find* your Web site to attack it unless the site is in Inetpub. So moving the root of your document directories will provide some small protection.

Get Rid of the IIS Admin, Documentation, Web-Based Printing, Extra Directories, and Samples

IIS ships with a whole bunch of sample files and extra doodads. Many are useful, but they're also potential security holes.

For example, there is a Web-based administration tool for IIS. If someone cracks that, they *own* your Web site. Don't install it. It's not installed by default with the rest of IIS. If it is installed, get rid of it from the Control Panel in Add/Remove Programs/Windows Components. Highlight the Web Application Server option and click the Details button. From here, choose Internet Information Services (IIS) and then the Details button again. Uncheck Remote Administration (HTML), which you'll find among the list of World Wide Web server components. And while you're at it, if you don't use FrontPage-based Webs, then uncheck the box next to FrontPage Server 2002 Extensions. Personally, I find the FrontPage bots to be fragile, so I avoid them altogether. I would also take this opportunity to remove anything else I don't need. Then click Next, OK, and Finish until you're out of Add/Remove Programs. Back in the IIS snap-in, go ahead and also delete the Microsoft SharePoint Administration site, as well as the Printers folder (in the default Web site) to get rid of Web-based printing. In fact, before I start using a newly built IIS system, I just delete everything in `wwwroot`.

Disable Unnecessary Services on Your Servers

You can safely shut down unused services on Web servers or, for that matter, shut them down on *any* server—it saves CPU power and RAM, and closes any potential security holes that those services might contain. Here are some other services that you might disable or remove using Add/Remove Programs in the Control Panel:

Server service This isn't a generic service required by all server services; instead, it's just the file and print server service. And while it's true that Web servers are a kind of file server, they do *not* necessarily need a working file server service.

FTP service If you need this to let Web authors upload content changes, then enable it. But be careful about running anonymous FTP sites; you'd hate to find out that you accidentally let the bad guys store their stuff on your FTP site. Consider using WebDAV instead of FTP for uploading content.

Simple Mail Transport Protocol If your Web site doesn't do automated mail-outs, stop this service; SMTP holes have been giving Unix administrators fits for years.

Routing and Remote Access Service

WebDAV A sort of twenty-first-century upgrade to FTP server, it lets you do what basically looks like normal file sharing over HTTP. It's far better than FTP, but you have to wonder if it's secure. If you're not using it, get rid of it. (It's off by default.) One way to make sure that it stays off is to deny the Everyone group access to `winnt\system32\inetsrv\httpext.dll`.

But you know which service I'd *really* like to kill? The GUI. It sucks up all kinds of CPU and RAM, and what do I need it for when my Web server is just sitting in the corner waiting for requests? Maybe in Windows 2015, I guess. Here the Linux guys have the right idea.

Consider Disabling Microsoft File and Print Sharing

The same file and print sharing protocols that let you build file/print servers in your organization let you share files and printers over the Internet as well. You might want to disable that service—the Server service. Here's why.

First of all, what is it that you want to secure? I'll assume it is your data. Because you don't want an outside intruder to be able to destroy data on your servers or lock you out of your own network, let's consider this question: How could someone get access to your data?

Assume that you weren't even running a Web or FTP server; consider what an attacker could do just to a simple file/print server that's exposed to the Internet. Attacks could come in the following forms:

◆ Someone with read access to your files could steal company information.

◆ Someone with write access to your files could modify or delete them.

◆ Someone with write access could use your file servers to store their own personal data—data they might not want to keep on their own computers, perhaps because the data is unlawful to have, like someone else's credit card numbers.

◆ Someone with write access could cripple your servers by filling up their free space with nonsense files, crashing the servers.

◆ Presumably someone could crash your mail servers by sending thousands of automatically generated pieces of mail to the servers. Enough mail messages will fill the hard disks of those servers as well.

◆ Access to your print servers could, again, let intruders fill up the print servers' hard disks with spooled files, as well as cause your printers to run out of paper.

Eliminate Nonessential ISAPI

ISAPI filters are an IIS-specific alternative to scripts and CGI programs. They were introduced back in IIS 2 and allow IIS to support some very fast extensions to basic Web functionality, like Active Server Pages.

You can see your site's ISAPI filters from the ISAPI Filters tab of the properties pages. Take a look at the file extensions associated with various ISAPI filters. Unless you or another admin added some ISAPI filters at some point, the only one you are likely to see is the ASP.NET filter, which is defined in the master properties for all Web sites. If there are others, though, and you don't see any files with that given extension in your Web site pages, then just delete the reference to that ISAPI filter. Code Red looked for an extension .IDA; had the ISAPI filter for IDA not been in place, then the virus would have gotten a Page Not Found, and wouldn't have infected that server.

Detecting Outside Attacks

Windows Server 2003 comes with some built-in tools to make detecting attacks easier. You can do the following:

◆ Audit failed logons.

◆ Use the Performance Monitor to alert you when logon failures exceed some reasonable value.

◆ Periodically log network activity levels. If all of a sudden your network gets really busy at 3 A.M. for no good reason, then look closely into exactly what's going on at 3 A.M.

In addition to these, consider reviewing your IIS log files (found in `\Windows\system32\logfiles`) periodically. If you've been getting 100 hits a day and suddenly it's 10,000 hits a day, something is up. These logs also record source IP addresses for hits; you may be able to identify vulnerability scanning patterns by frequency and by the pages requested, and then notify the ISP or organization that administers the source addresses of any suspicious activity. There are some very good log analyzer tools available for Web servers; some are even free.

Deterring Attacks

The main steps to take to deter attacks include the following:

1. Don't use obvious passwords.
2. Don't enable Guest accounts on Internet-connected machines.
3. Rename the built-in Administrator account.
4. Don't let the built-in Administrator account access the servers over the network.
5. Lock out users after a certain number of failed attempts.
6. Make passwords expire after a certain length of time.
7. Install a firewall to filter out UDP ports 136 and 137, used for Microsoft networking commands such as `net use`.
8. Install Web, news, and FTP servers on a separate machine in their own domains, with no trust links to other domains. Even better, install each Internet-accessible box as a stand-alone system with no ties to any internal domain. Sure, it's a pain to administer local accounts for FTP users and such, but the system can be locked down more radically since there's no need to communicate with domain controllers. This way, a compromised Web server doesn't have to mean a compromised Active Directory domain.
9. Don't put any services on your DNS servers except for DNS.

It seems to me that only by directly accessing your file servers through the normal `net use` interface, via an NFS interface, or through an FTP service would someone be able to read or write data on your computers over the Internet. I'll assume that you're not going to run NFS, that you'll put the FTP server where compromising it won't matter, and that you'll focus on the file server interface.

In a nutshell, here's the scenario that you should worry about. Suppose I know that you have a server named S01 whose IP address is 253.12.12.9 and that it has a share on it named SECRET. I just create an LMHOSTS file with one line in it, like so:

```
253.12.12.9 S01
```

Now I can type **net use X: \\s01\secret**, and my Internet-connected PC sends a request to 253.12.12.9 for access to the share. Assuming the Guest account isn't enabled on S01, then S01 will first ask my PC, "Who are you?" I'll see that as a request for a username and password. When I respond with a valid username and password from the server's domain, I'm in. Actually, this is how I access my network's resources from across the Internet when I'm on a client site—two seconds' work with an LMHOSTS file, a `net use`, and I'm accessing my home directory from thousands of miles away.

To do that, I needed to know:

◆ A valid username on my network

◆ The password for that account

◆ The IP address of a server on the domain

◆ The name of a share on the domain

All right, suppose I want to hack some company with the name `bigfirm.com`. Where do I start? Step one is to find out what its range of IP addresses is. That's easy. Just telnet to `internic.net`, type **`whois bigfirm.com`**, and you'll get the network number and responsible person for that network. (You can alternatively run a Web-based search page with your Web browser; point it to `www.internic.net`.) You'll also get the IP address of their DNS name servers. The other way to find this information would be to type:

```
nslookup
set type=all
bigfirm.com
```

Bigfirm will dump the names and addresses of their DNS servers and their mail servers. Because there has to be a secondary DNS server to make the InterNIC happy, there will be at least two name servers. Now, bigfirm is probably thinking—the way most of us do—"It doesn't take much CPU power to run a DNS server. Let's put some shared directories there, too."

As Jane Slimeball Hacker, I'm thinking, "Cool—fresh meat."

You see, you've got no choice but to publish two of your IP addresses, the addresses of your DNS server and its backup. So don't put anything else on it. Once, I would suggest to firms that they just run DNS on old, slow machines. That's not an option anymore, as we now need dynamic DNS, which means you're running Windows 2000 on a system and DNS on that system. It's a shame to make a server solely a DNS server, but it might not be a bad idea from a security point of view.

Now suppose you're smart and there's nothing else on the DNS servers. So I have to fish a bit, but that's not hard, as `whois` told me your range of IP addresses. I'm a slimeball, but I'm a thorough slimeball (after all, I don't have a life, so I've got lots of time), and I'm willing to try all of your IP addresses to find out which ones have servers. There are even, believe it or not, freeware programs for Windows systems that will scan a range of IP addresses looking for machines attached to those addresses.

Alternatively, it's a simple matter to create an LMHOSTS file that includes a NetBIOS name for every possible IP address. For example, if I know that you have class C network 200.200.200.0, then I can create an LMHOSTS file with NetBIOS named N1, which equals 200.200.200.1; N2 equals 200.200.200.2, and so on. Then I need only do a `net view \\servername` for each name from N1 through N254. The IP addresses that have a computer attached to them running the server service will be the ones that challenge me for a name and password. The ones that don't won't respond at all.

What can you do? Not terribly much, except to be sure that the default Administrator accounts on those systems aren't blank—no sense in making things too easy. And it sure offers some incentive for getting rid of your old machines and applications and getting your enterprise off NetBIOS, doesn't it?

Next, I'm looking for a user account name or two. How can I get this? I don't think you can do a `net user` remotely without contacting the domain controller, which means you'll have to have a domain ID and password to get `net user` to work from the outside—whew, that's one less thing to worry about!

But there is a way to find at least some usernames. When a user logs in to a Windows system, the machine registers not only its own machine name on the network, but the user's name as well. It does that so alerts with that name on them can get to the proper user. For example, suppose you've asked the Performance Monitor to alert you in your username of JILL02 if a server gets low on free space. How does the network know where you are?

It's quite simple. When you log in, the Messenger Service—assuming that it's running—registers your username as one of the NetBIOS names attached to your workstation. Assuming you are logged on to a server whose IP address is 200.200.200.200, anyone doing an `nbtstat -A 200.200.200.200` would not only see the computer's name, they'd see your name as well.

So, supposing that someone named paulad was logged in at the 200.200.200.200 machine (that's physically logged in, not connected over the network), a look at the NBTSTAT output would show me that there's a user named paulad who's logged in.

So now I have a username—and probably the username of an administrative account, since paulad is logged in to a server; good news for Joe Hacker. What can you do about that? Disable the Messenger Service, and the name never gets registered. And, by the way, speaking of NBTSTAT, if you run an `nbtstat -A` and the name MSBROWSE shows up, you've found a browse master. There's a good chance that a browse master is a domain controller, right? So maybe it's a good idea to set Maintain-ServerList=No for the domain controllers; you make that change in `HKLM\System\CurrentControlSet\Services\Browser\Parameters`. Just let the other servers handle the browse master part; you'll remove a clue that a hacker could use. Unfortunately, however, all domain controllers have other names registered to them that pretty much identify them as domain controllers.

Now that I have a username, I need a password. Now that's a problem. Even if I could physically attach my computer to your network, I wouldn't get a password with a network sniffer—NT uses a challenge/response approach to password verification. When you try to log in to an NT domain, the domain controller sends your workstation a random number that your workstation then applies to your password using some kind of hashing function, a mathematical function that produces a number when supplied with two inputs. The result is what gets sent over the network, not the password. (As I said earlier, there is one exception to this rule; when you change your password, the new password does go over the network to the server, but that's pretty rare.)

Where do I get the password? I can do one of two things. First, taking what I know about the user, I can try to guess a password. Second, I can run a program that tries to log in repeatedly, using as passwords every word in the dictionary—this is sometimes known as a dictionary hack.

The defense against this should be obvious. First, don't use easy-to-guess passwords. Use more than one word with a character between it, like fungus#polygon. Second, don't make it easy for people to try a lot of random passwords: Lock them out after five bad tries.

That leads me to a note about the Administrator account. Windows Server 2003 extends the lockout policy to include the Administrator account. After five bad login attempts, by default, the Administrator account can only be used to log in locally at the domain controllers, not remotely or over the network. If the lockout policy didn't apply to the Administrator account (and it didn't in Windows 2000, not without a Resource Kit utility called `passprop.exe`), then no matter how many times you tried to log on with a bad password, the Administrator account wouldn't lock. The slimeballs on the Internet could spend all of their free time trying to figure out your Administrator password. To protect the Administrator password further, rename the account. Don't leave it as Administrator. Second, limit its powers. You cannot delete the Administrator account, nor can you disable it. But you can remove its right to access the server over the network. By removing this right, you force someone with the Administrator password to physically sit down at the server in order to control that server. Unfortunately, that won't be easy, because the ability to log in to a server locally is granted to the Administrators group, and the Administrator account is a member of that group. You aren't allowed to remove the Administrator account from the Administrators group, so all you can do, I suppose, is to remove the entire Administrators group's right. Then just grant the individual administrative accounts the Log On over the Network right. Now, these measures—disabling Guest, renaming Administrator, removing Administrator's right to log in over the network, locking out repeated penetration attempts, setting Performance Monitor to alert you to excessive failed logon attempts, using well-chosen passwords—may be sufficient, and you've no doubt noticed that they're all options that don't cost a dime. But if you want greater security, then look into a firewall. The firewall doesn't have to do much, but it has one really important job: to filter out two ports on UDP.

UDP (User Datagram Protocol) is the sister protocol to TCP; just as there is a TCP/IP, there is also a UDP/IP. TCP is connection oriented, whereas UDP is connection oriented; it just drops messages on the network like messages in a bottle, hoping that they'll get where they should go. Whenever you execute a Microsoft networking command, such as `net use` or `net view`, you are running an application that sends commands to a server using UDP and UDP port numbers 136 and 137. Ports are software interfaces that are used to identify particular servers; for example, when you send mail from your desktop, you usually use TCP port number 25, and when you receive mail from your desktop, you usually do it on TCP port 110. Web browsers listen on TCP port 80, in another example.

Firewalls are powerful and sometimes complex devices. Once you install them, they have a million setup options and you're likely to wonder if you've caught all the ones you need. Running NetBIOS over IP services happens on UDP ports 136 and 137; tell your firewall to filter those and it's impossible for someone to access normal file server services.

SECURING ACCOUNTS

Since an account is required to perform most actions on a Windows Server 2003, it would make sense that the accounts database should be the first line of security for any publicly connected server. Try starting with the following suggestions to harden your accounts database a bit more:

♦   Set a minimum password length of 8 characters. This one should be pretty straightforward: short passwords = easy to guess, long passwords = harder to guess. On any publicly connected system, a minimum password length of no less than 8 characters should be enforced.

♦   Set a minimum password age of 2 days. Microsoft's secure Web server recommendations call for setting a minimum password age of 2 days. This means that if someone—authorized or not—changes a password, that password cannot be changed again until 48 hours have passed. This is designed to catch situations where an attacker might know a user's password and attempt to change it temporarily for a specific purpose, with the intention of changing it back immediately afterward, going unnoticed.

◆ Set a maximum password age of 42 days. Again, common sense security practices dictate that no password should be kept forever. Therefore, setting a maximum password age of no more than 42 days is a good security precaution. Depending on your specific needs, you could set this to an even shorter interval if necessary.

◆ Keep the last 24 passwords. When used in combination with the maximum and minimum password ages, this prevents anyone from reusing any of the last 24 passwords used for an account. This is designed to defeat a common habit by some administrators of simply flipping back and forth between a few different passwords each time a change is required.

◆ Set an account lockout policy. If I could only make one recommendation for securing a publicly connected system, it would be that there must be an account lockout policy in place. In other words, if x number of invalid login attempts occur within y minutes, then the account should be locked out for a duration of z minutes/hours/days. You can use your own values for x, y, and z, but this is one of the most valuable security precautions you can take!

◆ Require complex passwords. You read how to do this in Chapter 9.

◆ Assign the Deny Access to This Computer from the Network right to the Administrator account. Windows servers know whether an account is logging in from over the network or from the keyboard or mouse (or through a Terminal Services session). If you have physical access to your IIS server whenever you need it, you should strongly consider removing this right from your Administrator account. By default, most any hacker is going to know that Administrator is the default account to go after on any system, so removing this right will make it impossible to connect to the server over the network as the Administrator. This will restrict you to managing your system at the console only (or through a Terminal Server session), but it's a small price to pay for making sure that no one connects to your server over the Internet as Administrator. For more information on granting/revoking user rights, please see Chapter 9.

◆ Rename the Administrator account. As I mentioned in the last paragraph, everyone knows that the Administrator account is the default account on any Windows Server 2003 with the most privileges. Hackers want to "get Admin," so make it more difficult by renaming your Administrator account to something else—maybe something like "God," "root," "ToothFairy," or something equally obscure. Some people have commented to me that this is not useful advice because it's relatively simple to actually find out the default administrator's name, and I'd have to agree that it's easy for a determined hacker to get that information. But there are many attacks that rely on very simply built scripts or programs, and many of those programs aren't built to be very sophisticated—they assume that your home Web directory is Inetpub\wwwroot, that your administrator is named Administrator, and the like. Renaming the account will slow those guys down.

◆ Create a "bait" Administrator account. If you do decide to rename your Administrator account, an additional step you can take is to create a bait Administrator account on your system. Start by renaming your Administrator account to something else. Then create a new account and call it Administrator. Give it an extremely obscure password, disable the account, and make the account is a member of the Guests group only. That way, hackers can spend (and waste) their time hacking away at an Administrator account that won't yield anything if they do get the password.

◆ Disable the Guest account. By default, Windows Server 2003 will disable the default Guest account that is installed. It's worth double-checking this account to make sure that it is still disabled.

SECURING FILE AND PRINT SHARING

By default, Windows Server 2003 assumes that you'd like to enable file and print sharing on each of the interface cards installed in your server. If you have a server with multiple NICs (one for the public Internet and one for your internal network), you can disable file and print sharing on the public interface very easily.

To disable file and print sharing, start up Control Panel/Network and Dial-Up Connections and find the icon for your public interface. Right-click the public interface, then uncheck the box for File and Print Sharing for Microsoft Networks. You can test to make sure this works by mapping to a share on your server before changing this setting and then mapping to a share on your server after changing this setting. Just for kicks, if you wanted to try to "decoy" someone who might compromise your system, you could put in decoy `winnt` and `inetpub` directories and if anyone hacked into your system, they'd simply be hacking at a dummy installation.

Don't Forget Hazards from Within

Finally, remember that, all too often, the bad guys aren't outside the walls; they're right inside the company with you. Here are a few thoughts to consider about internal attackers.

INTERNAL USERS CAN EASILY GET A LIST OF USER IDS

Earlier in this book, you learned how to configure a set of home directories. First, you create a share called USERS on an NTFS volume, giving the Everyone group or, better, the Domain Users group, full control permissions. Then you set the top-level directory permissions to read and execute, and assign Domain Users no file permissions at all. Users need to read and execute to navigate from the top-level directory to their individual home directories. Then you set the file and directory permissions for each directory to full control for each particular user.

The problem is that there's no way to keep a user from moving up to the top-level directory and seeing the names of all of the users' home directories. Result: Now that user has a list of all of the users' IDs, hacking is made a bit easier.

Additionally, any user on an NT Workstation ,Windows 2000 Professional, or XP Professional machine can type **net user/domain** and get a list of users in the workstation's domain. Again, these are mainly things you're concerned about for internal users, but inside hacking is probably more prevalent than outside hacking.

INTERNAL USERS CAN EASILY CRASH SHARED VOLUMES

If you haven't enabled disk quotas, any user with write access to a volume can, either accidentally or purposefully, write as much data to a shared volume as the volume can hold. The result is that now there's no space left for other users. Worse yet, if that's the volume that holds the pagefile, then the pagefile can't grow in size, which might crash Windows altogether.

It wasn't SMB file and print sharing that built the Internet or that builds e-businesses—it was and is the Web. Almost anyone working with servers will find herself the proud administrator of a Web server or two—whether she wanted to be or not. Just a bit of work can make those servers run well and run safely.

Chapter 18

Tuning and Monitoring Your Windows Server Network

IF A SERVER ISN'T performing well—if it seems unresponsive or if you're getting funny error messages—then you could install more memory or add another processor and hope for the best. Alternatively, you could try to find out what was going on and address that question specifically. Why is the server slow? Is it running short of memory? Has someone tapped into your computer and is running unauthorized processes on it? If you ask the right questions of the tuning and monitoring tools, then you may find out the answers.

Whether you use the graphical tools or write scripts to reach performance or event monitoring data, the trick to using performance monitoring tools effectively is *asking the right questions*. These tools are not omnipotent gods, but more like slightly dim-witted genies. Like such genies, performance monitoring tools are very literal-minded little cusses. They may be able to give you the answers if you ask—depends on what you want to know and whether that information is exposed by the tools—but only if you ask correctly. If you ask the wrong questions you'll drown in a sea of irrelevant data. (Somewhat less metaphorically, if you ask indiscriminate questions you'll slow down your servers and/or clog your network's bandwidth with unimportant queries, not to mention get a bunch of information that you can't use and which can cloud the important stuff.) Thus, in this chapter I'll talk about the genies—er, performance monitoring and event viewing tools— that come with Server 2003 and give you background to help you figure out which questions to ask the oracle. Once that's done, I'll discuss the tuning you can do based on the information you gathered.

NOTE *This chapter will focus on how to gather and evaluate performance information using the graphical and command-line tools built into Server 2003. However, the performance monitoring tools accessible from the MMC are Windows Management Instrumentation (WMI) providers, meaning that it's also possible to gather performance information through one of Server 2003's supported scripting languages—VBScript or JScript.*

Roundup of Tuning Support Tools and What to Do with Them

Before I get into a description of how to use these tools, here's a quick tour of the monitoring tools that come with Server 2003:

◆ System Monitor

◆ Performance Logs and Alerts

◆ Event Viewer

◆ Task Manager

NOTE *Server 2003 also has a Network Monitor tool that's a crippled version of the one included with Microsoft System Management Server. Unfortunately, it can only monitor data traveling between the monitored computer and the rest of the network, not network traffic in general.*

System Monitor

The System Monitor in Server 2003 is very similar to the tool by the same name in Windows 2000. When you open the System Monitor, you'll see that it has two components: a Performance Monitor–like tool called the System Monitor that displays real-time performance statistics and Performance Logs and Alerts, which is the System Monitor's logging function.

TIP *To open the System Monitor quickly, type* **perfmon** *(the executable name of the System Monitor) into Run. Server 2003 will start the Performance tool with the System Monitor screen active.*

With the System Monitor, you can do the following:

◆ Provide a simple, visual view of your servers' vital signs (one that looks great on a PowerPoint presentation of why you need more hardware) in charts or reports

◆ Output real-time system monitoring information to a browser

◆ Keep an eye on how processes are using processor time, memory, disk space, and other server resources

◆ Log network data over time and export that data to a file that you can import into a spreadsheet for further analysis

◆ Open saved logs to review historical data

Performance Logs and Alerts

The other half of the Performance tools is the Performance Logs and Alerts, which takes over the logging functions of NT 4's Performance Monitor. You can do the following using the logging function:

◆ Monitor system stress and performance over a period of time, instead of watching the current output

◆ Automatically keep track of minimum, maximum, average, and current values of critical system values

◆ Send alerts to the Event log, notify someone, or run a program when counters exceed the tolerances you set or when important events occur

Event Viewer

The Event Viewer (located in the Administrative Tools program group) maintains several separate event logs on the server:

- System log
- Security log
- Application log
- DNS Server log
- File Replication Service log
- Directory Service log

NOTE *The Event Viewer for member servers in the domain displays only the Application log, System log, and Security log.*

The System log records the starting and stopping of services and any system-related events. This is where you'll find out that time synching isn't working, that the DHCP server has successfully cleaned up its database, or that a print job was successfully completed. If you see a message box telling you that something didn't work and to check the Event Monitor for more details, the System log is the first place to look. If there are noninformational messages here, don't ignore them!

The Security log records any audited events that relate to security issues, such as users accessing files or changing the Security Accounts Database. In Windows 2000, you had to explicitly turn on security logging. In Server 2003, it's turned on by default.

The Application log records application-specific events that aren't far-reaching enough to make it into the System log. The name of this log might be misleading. It's not about user applications so much as about licensing, the BINL service used to back Remote Installation Services (see Chapter 20, "Installing and Managing Remote Access Service in Windows Server"), backups, the successful (or unsuccessful) application of security policies, performance library issues, and the like.

You'll find the System, Application, and Security logs on any Server 2003 computer. The remaining logs only apply to computers that need them because of their role in the network. The DNS Server log (found, as you'd expect, on the DNS server) records events associated with resolving computer names to or from IP addresses. The File Replication Service log lists events relating to the File Replication Service, and the Directory Service log records events related to domain controllers keeping up with the security database.

Windows Task Manager

The Task Manager gives you a way to monitor the general state of the server without going to the trouble of creating a customized chart with the System Monitor. In Server 2003, the Task Manager has five tabs:

Applications   Displays the applications separate from the core OS that are running on the server and shows whether they're running or not responding.

Processes   Lists the image names of the processes running on the server, including those processes that are part of the core OS, and shows statistics about the resources allocated to those processes.

NOTE *For those not familiar with the distinction between an application, a process, and an image name, allow me to digress for a minute. The executable name of an application (e.g., MYAPP.EXE) is known to Server 2003 as its image name. A process is a collection of resources allocated to some executable portion—a thread—of that image. An image may have one or more processes supporting it, depending on how the developer split the code up.*

Performance   Displays current processor and memory usage.

Networking   Displays the current network utilization for the server's connection to the network.

Users   Lists the current local and remote Desktop sessions connected to the server.

You can use the Task Manager not only to gather information about a server, but to interact with it and resolve some problems. For example, if the server seems sluggish, you can open the Task Manager and turn to the Performance tab to get a real-time view of processor usage. If the chart there indicates that the processor is running full-time, you can turn to the Processes tab to see which process is taking up all the processor time and find out from the Applications tab whether an application has stopped responding and needs to be shut down.

Observing Performance Patterns with the System Monitor

If you can't measure it, you can't tune it.

As noted earlier, the System Monitor is the graphical display tool in Server 2003's collection of monitoring tools. To use it, you'll need to be familiar with objects, instances, and counters.

Object   Any system component that possesses a set of measurable properties. An object can be a physical part of the system (such as the memory or the processor), a logical component (such as a disk volume), or a software element (such as a process or a thread).

Instance   Shows how many occurrences of an object are available in the system.

Counter   Represents one measurable characteristic of an object. For example, the Processor object has several counters, including the percentage of processor time in use and the percentage of time the processor spends in Privileged and User modes.

Written out, the object name comes first, then the counter name. For example, System Monitor opens with a sample chart of three commonly monitored object counters: Memory: Pages/sec, Physical Disk: Avg Disk Queue Length, and Processor: % Processor Time. Server 2003 contains hundreds of counters to track system data, such as the number of network packets transmitted per second, the percentage of time a processor spends in User mode versus Kernel mode, and the number of pages swapped in and out of memory per second.

You'll also need to be familiar with the various types of output that the System Monitor can produce—graphs, histograms, and reports—to know when each would be most useful.

Graph   By default, System Monitor displays its output in a line graph. This way of presenting data makes it easy to identify spikes in the data and show trends over time. Graphs always show current values, whether working from real-time or logged data.

Histogram   Histograms display current values for counters in a bar chart. They're very useful for visually comparing values—say, the percentage of time that the processor on three separate servers is busy. By default, histograms show current values when working from real-time data and average values when working from logged data.

Report   Reports display the objects and counters being monitored and their current value (in text). They're useful for getting an exact value, since you don't need to interpret a graph or histogram to find out what the current value is—you can just read the text on the screen. By default, reports show current values when working from real-time data and average values when working from logged data.

NEW TO SERVER 2003: COMMAND-LINE PERFORMANCE LOGGING TOOLS

Windows 2000 offered only graphical tools for working with performance logs. In Server 2003 (and Windows XP), you also have command-line performance logging tools. Logman lets you create and manage performance logs from the command line, and relog allows you to take existing performance logs and change the sampling rate and file format. You can monitor performance data and create new counter logs with typeperf. And, using tracerpt, you can convert trace logs into a CSV file and/or summary report.

Creating a Chart

Every System Monitor chart is a custom collection of counters to monitor. To add a counter to the chart, open the Add Counters dialog box by clicking the button in the toolbar that has a plus sign (+) on it or right-clicking in the chart display window and choosing Add Counters from the context menu. This will open the dialog box shown in Figure 18.1.

FIGURE 18.1

Add counters to the System Monitor.

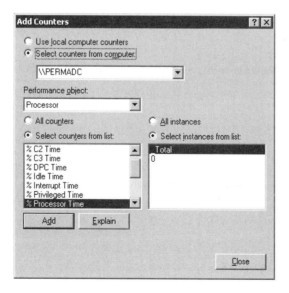

Adding counters to a chart is easy. Choose a performance object, then pick one of its performance counters. If there's more than one instance of the object (for example, if the server has more than one processor), then you'll have the choice of monitoring counters for all objects of that class or only a specific one. Click the Add button, and that counter will be added to the chart and will show up in the System Monitor, as in Figure 18.2.

NOTE *Installing some software on servers may add performance objects and counters to the list. For example, installing MetaFrame (helper software used to enhance the capabilities of a Server 2003 application server) adds objects and counters for monitoring remote sessions using MetaFrame.*

FIGURE 18.2

System Monitor
output

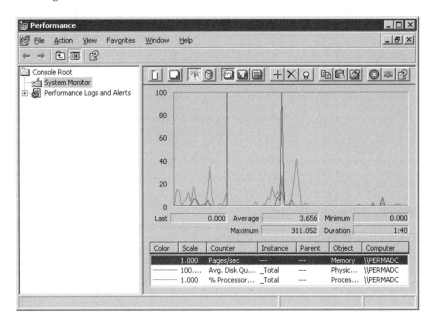

Adding counters may be easy, but *choosing* the counters to add and interpreting what you're seeing requires a bit more work. Let's take a look at how you could pick counters to monitor.

NOTE *The System Monitor's Add Counters dialog box has an Explain button you can click to show more information about the currently highlighted counter. However, the information that's displayed isn't always all that useful—especially for the counters new to Server 2003—and not always strictly accurate. Use the information in the Explain text box as a starting point for further research if you need details about what a counter's monitoring, not as the final word.*

Incidentally, I've described here how to add counters to monitor on the current computer. As I'll explain a little later in this chapter, you can also—and you frequently should—monitor other computers with the System Monitor. The procedure for adding the counters is identical to adding counters to monitor locally, however.

CHOOSING OBJECTS AND COUNTERS TO MONITOR

When you first open the Add Counters dialog box, it's easy to get information overload. I haven't yet been bored enough to count all the counters for all the objects, but there must be thousands. Even if you just look at the objects, how do you tell which of the dozens available is the one you want? It's not easy, and to make the performance monitoring useful at all, you'll need to be selective. Monitoring all the counters would give you more information than you could possibly handle. You need to know what to look for.

Let me set the following scenario: You have a network up and running. But with time, the network seems to be slowing down. People are complaining. The Powers That Be start applying pressure on you to find out what's wrong and to find it out *now*. What can you do? Well, the obvious thing to do is to throw hardware at the problem, right? Go buy more memory, an extra processor if the servers support multiple processors and have slots available; get a faster network card; get a faster disk.

Jacking up, say, the processor speed *may* get you a faster server. But if the problem is lack of memory, getting a faster processor won't really help. You tune a troubled server by locating and removing its bottlenecks as much as you can. Eventually, you will bump into the limits of performance improvements, so the trick is to find the most effective performance improvements and apply them. What I want to do next is to (1) introduce you to the art of tuning, (2) point out the most likely causes of problems for file servers and application servers in particular, and (3) recommend a few objects and counters that you can monitor to keep an eye on your server performance with minimum trouble.

A server's job on the network will influence the counters that are important to it: IIS Servers serving Active Server Pages (ASP) or SMTP servers providing e-mail will call on entire object classes that you can ignore on servers not performing those roles. If a server has no printer directly attached, then you needn't monitor the print queue object counters. However, there are four big sources of performance bottlenecks common to any server:

◆ Memory
◆ Disk subsystem
◆ Network card and software
◆ Processor

Resolving Memory Bottlenecks

The biggest performance drain on a Server 2003 system is memory. Windows applications are memory-hungry, and the operating system itself is memory-hungry—although, thankfully, the jump in resource demands between Windows 2000 and Server 2003 is nowhere near as dramatic as the jump between NT and Windows 2000—in fact, Server 2003 has changed the way it uses memory to make it more efficient. Still, if you install Server 2003 with the bare minimum of memory and then actually try to use it as a server, you're not going to be happy with the result.

When you're monitoring memory, you're actually monitoring both physical memory and hard disk access. The reason has to do with how Windows operating systems eke the most use possible out of physical memory—some of the apparent contents of that physical memory are actually on disk, in what's called *virtual memory*.

Virtual memory is a result of what Dorothy Parker would have said if she had been a network administrator: you can never be too rich, too thin, or have too much RAM installed. No matter how much you have, it seems, physical memory can't keep up with the data storage needs of Server 2003 and any applications it's running. Therefore, Windows operating systems use virtual memory, a kind of memory simulation that allows the server to support more applications and data in memory than it actually has physical memory to support. Regardless of the amount of *physical* memory installed, Win32 operating systems support up to 4GB of virtual memory space—2GB to be shared among all system-level processes and 2GB for the exclusive use of each user process running on the server. The memory manager is responsible for organizing each process's access to virtual memory so that processes don't write on each other's data in *physical* memory.

NOTE *One of the reasons Server 2003 needs so much memory is because it uses a big chunk (25 percent or so) of this memory for cacheing recently used file data. Servers that aren't file servers don't need to do this. In the "Basic Tuning Stuff" section later in this chapter I'll explain how to make a server stop thinking of itself as a file server and start giving you back some memory.*

Virtual memory works like this: When an application is loaded into memory, it stores its data in physical memory to store data it needs to run and present user files. As more and more applications (and the operating system) use RAM to store data, things start getting crowded. To allow applications to keep their important data in physical memory where they can get to it more or less instantly, the memory manager shuffles less important data to a file on disk called the *paging file*. The applications don't care whether data is stored in RAM or the paging file, the applications just keep referring to the data according to the virtual address where it was originally stored. Among the memory manager's many jobs is the task of keeping track of how the virtual memory storage area corresponds to the physical memory storage area, since it is almost inevitable that the physical storage area for memory will change.

What kind of data is stored in memory? Several kinds, actually:

◆ Each application (and the operating system) has a *working set* that is the sum of all the data that application is currently working with. The memory manager can trim working sets if there's a shortage of physical memory. But the smaller an application's working set, the slower the application will run, because it's going to have to keep requesting data back from the paging file, and paging data back into memory takes time.

NOTE *If you're using Terminal Services (see Chapter 16), then there will also be a per-session working set.*

◆ *Page table entries (PTEs)* are structures the memory manager needs to map each user process's virtual address space to an area of physical memory. The memory manager needs this map to see how each process is using its view of the 2GB of user virtual memory addresses and to keep processes from overwriting each other's memory.

◆ Some operating system data must remain in memory all the time and cannot be paged to disk. The range of virtual memory addresses called the *nonpaged pool* stores this data. The *paged pool* stores operating system data that can be paged to disk.

◆ The *system cache* is the data used by the entire operating system kept in RAM for quick access. The System Monitor Help describes the system cache as though it were synonymous with the disk cache, but it's not—the disk cache of recently used on-disk data and disk data structure is one part of the entire system cache.

The Server 2003 memory manager allocates memory to the system and user processes by first *reserving* it for the process that needs it (defining a range of virtual memory addresses for later use) and then *committing* it (ensuring that a place in the paging file is available to store the data the process wants to put in those virtual memory addresses). Processes can reserve all the memory they want, but when it comes time to commit that memory, some on-disk storage *must* be available to back it. Server 2003 has to assume that all user data will move to the paging file at some time. When a process is done with memory, it's supposed to give it back to the system to be marked as available for other processes—*free* it. Some processes do the opposite, taking more and more memory even though they're not using it or just not giving back memory that they're not using anymore until you reboot the machine. This is a result of buggy programming and is called a *memory leak*. Memory leaks are frustrating because they starve other processes without giving you any gain at all. Give them enough time, and memory leaks will shut down your server from lack of resources. The only way to reclaim this memory is by rebooting the computer. Processes can't use data that's stored on disk, so when an application calls on data that the memory manager has paged to disk, the memory manager tracks down the data's current location and executes a *hard page fault* to send that data to RAM where the memory controller can retrieve it for the application. Something similar happens if the memory manager moved data from one location in RAM to another, except that retrieving this data—called a *soft page fault*—takes less time than retrieving data from the hard disk. The end result of a soft or hard page fault is the same, however: even if data has been moved to a location other than the one the application expects, the application gets its data with no more than a little finger drumming at the slight delay. To the process, it looks as though the data was in memory all the time, but it really wasn't.

There is one catch to the paging file: disks are slower than RAM. You measure access times (the time required to read or write data) on RAM in nanoseconds (billionths of a second) and on disk in milliseconds (thousandths of a second). So, although you can't escape paging—Server 2003 is designed to use it, and it will, no matter how much RAM you install—you will improve server performance if you seek to minimize the amount of time your server spends on hard page faults.

That's not everything there is to know about virtual memory, but it's enough to make people avoid you. The important memory counters are described in Table 18.1. You can use this information to help you read other memory counters, too.

TABLE 18.1: IMPORTANT MEMORY COUNTERS

COUNTER	DESCRIPTION	WHAT THIS TELLS YOU
Memory: Available Bytes	Records the memory currently available on the server.	A low value may indicate that your server is low on memory or that one of the programs is experiencing memory leaks (especially if the number keeps decreasing). You should always have 4MB or more available. If you don't, then check for memory leaks or add more memory.
Memory: Commit Limit	Records the amount of memory that can be committed without extending the paging file. You can increase the paging file up to the limit of available space on the volume.	Extending the paging file is an expensive procedure (and requires processor time), so it's a good idea to do this as little as possible. Make the paging file as large as you think you'll need—at least 2.5x the size of RAM you have installed.

Continued on next page

TABLE 18.1: IMPORTANT MEMORY COUNTERS *(continued)*

COUNTER	DESCRIPTION	WHAT THIS TELLS YOU
Memory: Committed Bytes	Records the amount of memory committed to processes running on the server.	Records the amount of used RAM that requires space in the paging file in case the data must be paged to disk. Therefore, this is memory in use and unavailable to other processes, not just reserved in case a process needs it.
Memory: Pages Input/sec	Records the rate at which pages of data are written to RAM from the paging file to resolve page faults.	As this value describes hard page faults (the Page Faults counter includes soft page faults, which pull data from another area of memory and don't incur much of a hit), it's a good measure of how often you're having to pull data back from disk.
Memory: Pages Output/sec	Records the rate at which pages of data are written to the paging file to free RAM.	If the server seems to be running more slowly than it used to, monitor this counter. A high rate may indicate that the server doesn't have enough RAM to support all the data that the running applications need to keep handy.
Memory: Pages/sec	Records the current rate at which pages (4KB chunks of data on an x86 system, 8KB on an Alpha system) are read from disk back into physical memory to satisfy a hard page fault or are written to disk to free RAM.	A value of more than 20 pages per second implies a lot of paging and suggests that your server needs more memory.
Paging File: % Usage	Records the percentage of the paging file currently in use.	If this value approaches 100 percent, then you need to reduce the pressure on the paging file, either by enlarging the file or adding more RAM. Although the memory manager will make the paging file larger if necessary, doing so takes up processor cycles, and the memory manager will only increase the paging file's size as needed immediately. It's better to increase the size of the paging file manually.
Paging File: Usage Peak	Records the peak size of the paging file.	If this value is close to the maximum size of the paging file, you need to either enlarge the paging file or add more RAM. A high value implies that the paging file isn't big enough to hold all the data it must.

Continued on next page

TABLE 18.1: IMPORTANT MEMORY COUNTERS *(continued)*

COUNTER	DESCRIPTION	WHAT THIS TELLS YOU
Physical Disk: % Disk Time	Records the percentage of time the disk spends servicing read or write requests.	Monitor this value for the physical disk that the paging file(s) are located on. If this amount seems to be increasing, check paging file usage and consider adding more memory.
Physical Disk: Avg Disk Queue Length	Records the average number of read and write requests waiting for the disk during the selected interval.	If this number is increasing at the same time the number of Memory: Page Reads/sec is increasing, that indicates that a lot of paging is going on. Monitor this value for the physical disk that the paging file(s) are located on.
Physical Disk: Avg Disk sec/Transfer	Records the length of time it takes the disk to transfer data to or from disk.	Monitor this value for the physical disk that the paging file(s) are located on to find out how responsive those disks are. This information may encourage you to move the paging file to a faster disk.
Process: Private Bytes	Records the virtual memory committed to that process.	This counter shows you how much memory a process (for all practical purposes, an application) is using. Especially if you're monitoring a terminal server, consider moving demanding applications to the client side or to a server dedicated to those applications, to prevent other processes from being starved for memory.
Process: Working Set	Records the amount of RAM that the process is using to store data. The larger the working set, the more memory the process is consuming.	If a process's working set increases over a period when you're not doing anything with it (for example, over a weekend), the process may be experiencing a memory leak.

NOTE   *Notice that not all the counters you'll be monitoring for memory usage are in the Memory object.*

Memory is complicated. Examining other potential server bottlenecks is, thankfully, a bit simpler.

Resolving Processor Bottlenecks

If you look at the counters available for the Processor object, you'll see a lot of counters for DPC and APC objects, some percentages of User and Privileged execution time, and so forth. Most of these won't help you much with server tuning. The DPC counters refer to *deferred procedure calls (DPCs)*, functions that perform a system task that is less essential than the currently executing system task, but which can grab a little processor time while the more important task is waiting for information that isn't yet ready. The APC counters refer to *asynchronous procedure calls (APCs)*, which provide a way for user programs and system code to execute code using the memory allocated to a specific application, and at a low level of priority. Basically, APCs interrupt an application that's using the processor to make it do something else without going through the usually necessary rigamarole of shutting down the application's access to the processor. In a broad sense, the counters for User and Privileged time refer to the percentage of time that the processor is spending executing instructions for user applications and system functions, respectively. Again, this isn't information you can use for a lot of system tuning unless you're interested in the time that Server 2003 spends executing system code in contrast to user code.

The information you *can* use for system tuning lies in the % Processor time and the Interrupts counters. Processor: % Processor Time tells you the percentage of time that the selected processor is doing something other than executing its "marking time" thread, the system Idle thread. Ideally, the processor is supposed to spend most of its time executing the Idle thread, because if that's the case, then the processor is available when it's needed. If Processor: % Processor Time rises above 75 percent on average, then that processor is working pretty hard and the server might benefit from a faster processor or an additional processor—and from you tracking down whatever it is that's using up all those processor cycles.

Interrupts/sec and % Interrupt time tell you how much time the processor is spending interrupting itself to handle requests from its hardware (network cards, video cards, keyboards, and so forth). If the value of Interrupts/sec exceeds 3500, then more than likely something's going wrong, either a buggy program or a board spewing out spurious interrupts. One common cause of excessive interrupts is badly designed device drivers. Are you running any beta device drivers? I've seen beta video drivers that spew out thousands of interrupts per second. You can test this by running the standard VGA driver and comparing the interrupts before and after. Another source of excessive interrupts is timer-driver programs. Some years ago, one network manager I know was seeing 4000 interrupts/second on a fairly quiet 486-based file server. After some playing around with the system, he realized that he was opening Schedule+ in his Startup group. He shut it down, and his interrupts/second dropped to a normal rate.

NOTE *I'd like to tell you that there's a System Monitor counter that lets you track interrupts/second on a program-by-program basis, but there isn't—much of this is just trial and error. Now and then I see a board that sends out a blizzard of interrupts if it's failing or, sometimes, when it's just cold. You might see this when you turn a workstation on Monday morning and it acts strangely for half an hour, then settles down.*

Resolving Disk Bottlenecks

The hard disks on your servers represent another potential sticking point for server production. For file servers, the bottleneck is obvious: the whole point of a file server is to grab data and pass it to the network for distribution. For application servers, the disk problem is more related to paging because of the memory burden that applications incur. If you're running SQL Server or Exchange or supporting terminal server sessions, it's easy to run up against the amount of memory installed in the server— and when that happens, the server goes after your disk drive to support virtual memory.

There are a lot of counters for physical disks, but most of them don't tell you much in diagnostic terms except to help you see whether the disks are living up to their specifications. A couple that *do* are in Table 18.2.

TABLE 18.2: IMPORTANT PHYSICAL DISK COUNTERS

COUNTER	DESCRIPTION	WHAT THIS COUNTER TELLS YOU
Physical Disk: % Disk Time	Reports the percentage of time the physical disk is busy.	If it's busy more than 90 percent of the time, then it's too busy—you'll improve performance if you get another disk or do less with that one.
Physical Disk: Current Disk Queue Length	Reports the current number of data transfer operations waiting for the specified physical disk (or all disks, if you choose) to handle them.	This value should be as small as possible. A high value indicates that disk waits are impacting users.

The counters in Table 18.2 can also apply to logical disks (C: drive, E: drive, and so on, as opposed to Disk 0 or Disk 1, which identify physical disks). However, you may not *need* the logical disk counters for the performance monitoring described in Table 18.2. You've already got counters telling you how many jobs are waiting in the physical disk queue at any given time and how often the disk is busy; monitoring logical disks instead of physical disks won't really tell you anything you didn't already know, since what you're looking at is disk stress. Logical disk counters are more useful when it comes to performance metrics such as Free Megabytes, which shows the amount of free space remaining on the selected disk. Another logical disk counter you might find useful for logical disks is Split IO/Sec, which keeps track of the number of split input/output actions on the disk. This counter is useful because a high number of split writes or reads (meaning that the disk controller is having to read from or write to more than one place on the disk during a single I/O action) can indicate a fragmented disk.

Resolving Network Bottlenecks

Your network's apparent speed (not what it's rated at, but how responsive it is) is a function of how much traffic there is on the network and how quickly the server can process user requests.

First, how busy is the network? You'll need to monitor the transport protocols you're running on the server. Recall that TCP/IP has several different parts—it's a suite of protocols, not a single one like NetBEUI—and the parts do different things. So, for example, a lot of IP datagrams tells you that your network card is getting a lot of regular (that is, data-related) traffic. A suddenly large number of ICMP datagrams could signify problems—or suggest that someone is pinging the heck out of your server. Look for differences in traffic levels, both on the protocol level and for the entire network card (you can monitor both). Are you getting transmission errors for inbound or outbound network traffic? How busy is the local network segment?

Second, how busy is the server? Is it seeing logon errors? How quickly are people logging in at different times of day? How many files are open on the server? If it's a terminal server session, how many users is it supporting? If it's an FTP server, then how many connections are you having to maintain? Is the server experiencing nonpaged pool failures, failing to allocate memory to components that need nonpaged memory because there's too little RAM installed on the system?

NOTE   *You can only get accurate network segment data if you have the Network Monitor for SMS installed. The Network Monitor that comes with Server 2003 only monitors data going to and from the monitored server. Therefore, you can get pretty much the same information from Network Interface that you can from Network Segment.*

Lots of questions. I'd suggest that you poke around the performance objects a bit to look for specific counters you want to monitor for your server, but Table 18.3 includes some of the more common counters you should watch.

TABLE 18.3: IMPORTANT NETWORK-RELATED COUNTERS

COUNTER	DESCRIPTION	WHAT THIS COUNTER TELLS YOU
Server: Bytes Total/sec	Reports the rate at which the server is sending and receiving network data.	The total of bytes going in and out of the server per second gives you a pretty good indication of how busy the server is. If you do something to change the server load, like adding another server of that kind or added load balancing to the network, you can monitor this value to see whether the change actually did any good.
Server: Files Open	Reports the current number of files open at the moment of reporting. This is a current total, not a total of all the files that have been opened during a given time.	This counter indicates the traffic load a file server is experiencing. Sadly, there's no way to monitor file openings on a per-user or per-file basis.
Server: Pool Non-paged Failures	Reports the number of errors the server is reporting as it tries to allocate nonpaged pool.	Nonpaged pool is an area of virtual memory whose contents cannot be paged to disk because they must be ready immediately when called on—no time for page faults. Lots of errors suggests that the server is running low on RAM and you'll need to add more.
Server: Server Sessions	Reports the number of current connections to the server.	This counter may not tell you how *busy* the server is, but it can tell you how popular it is—especially if it's popular at an hour when no one should be accessing the server at all.
Network Interface: Bytes Total/sec	Reports the rate at which the network card is sending and receiving network data.	If this rate is significantly lower than what you'd expect, given the speed of your network and network card, it's time to do a little investigating to see whether something's wrong with the card.

TIP   If your server is an Internet server of some kind (e-mail, FTP, Web, etc.), be sure to monitor the counters appropriate to its function.

Be sure to also monitor installed protocols for error conditions or heavy traffic at odd times.

Remote Performance Monitoring

There's one big problem with running the Performance Monitor on a server: the Performance Monitor *itself* consumes resources, and thus skews the resource-usage reports on a server. Consider monitoring servers remotely. If you do, then you'll use a little network bandwidth but fewer resources on the monitored machine—and you'll get a more accurate reading, because you're not stressing the server by running the monitor on it.

TIP   The only time it's to your benefit to run Performance Monitor locally is when you're monitoring counters related to network traffic. Monitoring remotely will increase network traffic and skew the results.

Setting up remote performance monitoring is quite simple. When you're adding a counter to the monitor, you have a choice between adding the counter for the local machine or another one. You can monitor any generation of NT computer, so if you've got a mixed environment it doesn't matter. When you connect to a remote computer, the counters available to that computer will be visible, so it doesn't matter which counters are available on the computer from which you're running Performance Monitor. You can even use Win2K Professional or Windows XP workstations to do the monitoring, so you don't have to tie up a server for this task.

Make sure you've selected Select Counters from Computer, and type in the name of the computer you want to monitor with two preceding backslashes, like this: **Serpent**. (There's no Browse feature, so you have to know the name of the server you want to monitor. Annoyingly, Performance Monitor doesn't consistently "remember" the names of remote servers that it has monitored previously. Sometimes it does, and sometimes it develops amnesia. However, it is generally able to find servers across trusted domains, even if you can't specify a server's domain.)

WARNING   Type server names carefully. If you mistype, it takes the System Monitor a while to discover that the server you've specified does not exist on the network.

When you're done choosing the counter you want to monitor, add it as you normally would and close the dialog box. The remote computer's counter will be added to the list and identified by the computer name (see Figure 18.3).

One of the cool things about doing remote performance monitoring is that it lets you compare server stress easily. If you select the same performance counter on two servers, you can compare the stress on those two servers.

WARNING   As explained in Chapter 16, Server 2003 supports remote server administration using Terminal Services. Do not try to run the Performance Monitor from a Remote Administration session. You're still running the monitor on the server and consuming server resources—you're just watching from a different computer.

FIGURE 18.3

Performance counters to remote computers will be displayed alongside local ones.

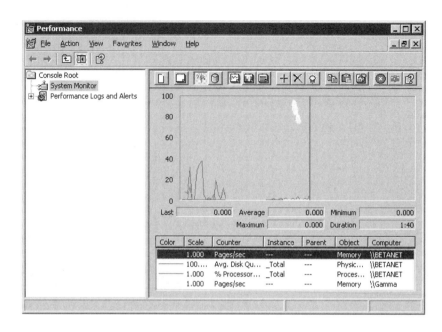

Saving Chart Data

When you've identified the counters you want to monitor, you can save that information and reuse it later, either to monitor again (on the principle that what you need to monitor once, you almost certainly will need to monitor again) or to make them into an HTML file that you can display in a browser. To save chart settings, right-click somewhere in the Performance Monitor's display of current counters. From the context menu that appears, choose Save As to save the data, and you'll be prompted for the name of the HTML file. (This data will always be saved as a hypertext document.) The default folder is the My Documents folder for the person currently logged in, but you can browse for another folder as you would with any Save As operation. Type a name for the file, and it's saved.

If you open the file, it will open in your browser as shown in Figure 18.4.

The cool part about this is that the file you're opening here will continue to display the monitored data. So long as the System Monitor is still running, you can dynamically update the output in this HTML chart. Why do it this way rather than just running the System Monitor? Mostly so you can streamline the UI. As you can see in Figure 18.4, the HTML view shows only the monitor, not the entire System Monitor tool.

To update the view steadily, click the Freeze Display button (the red button with the white X on it) in the browser to disable it. You'll see a warning that all current data will be cleared from the display; click OK. The display will clear and the browser will fill with the updated Performance Monitor data. To manually update the data (perhaps if you're making a presentation and don't want people to be distracted watching the updates to the output), then keep the Freeze Display button activated and click the Update Data button (the camera between the Freeze Display and Help buttons). After the first freeze/unfreeze action, the chart data will remain displayed in the browser.

FIGURE 18.4

A saved Performance Monitor chart opened in Internet Explorer

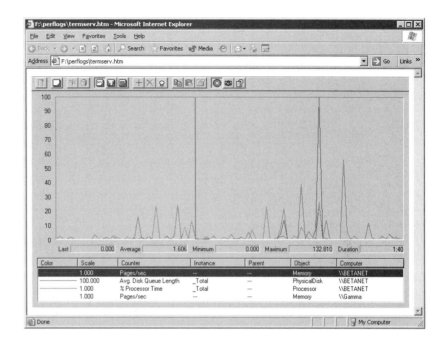

What about reusing this data in a later Performance Monitor session? I'll talk more about how to use this data in the next section, "Logging Performance Data."

Logging Performance Data

Knowing how the server is performing now is useful, but knowing how the server was performing last week or two months ago can also be useful, since previous records can give you a reality check for current performance. The Server 2003 Performance Logs and Alerts section of the System Monitor works much like the tool of the same name in Windows 2000. Using a combination of comma-delimited and tab-delimited files and HTML documents, you can pass information between the Performance Monitor and the Logs and Alerts—or even pass it to another application that can accept comma-delimited or tab-delimited files, such as Excel.

The System Monitor supports three types of logs: counter logs, trace logs, and alert logs. *Counter logs* record data from local or remote computers about hardware usage and system service activity. *Trace logs* are event driven, recording monitored data such as disk I/O or page faults. When a traced event occurs, it's recorded in the log. *Alert logs* take counter and trace logs one step further. They monitor counters that you specify and wait for them to exceed user-defined tolerances. When this happens, the event is logged. You can also set up an alert log to *do* something when the event happens, like send a message alerting someone to the situation, or run an application. You'll often use logs in combination—for example, using a counter log to develop a "normal" baseline for a server and then creating an alert log to notify you when the server's activity falls outside that normal range.

NOTE   *You can either set up perpetual logging or log only for a preset period of time so you aren't overwhelmed with data.*

Creating Logs

To create a log, turn to the Performance Logs and Alerts section of the System Monitor. Open the folder for the type of log you want, so that its contents (or lack thereof) are displayed in the right details window. Right-click empty space in the Details window and choose an option for creating a new log from the shortcut menu that appears. What happens from here depends on the type of log you're creating: a counter log, a trace log, or an alert log.

NOTE *As an administrator, you'll use counter logs and alert logs most often.*

Counter logs record system counters, like static versions of the performance logs we've discussed so far in this chapter. You can save the log data in a binary file that will open in System Monitor (looking like real-time data) or in a text (comma-delimited or tab-delimited) file that you can open in a spreadsheet application.

Trace logs keep track of data according to the part of the operating system that collects it. Unlike counter logs, which just record at regular intervals, trace logs are event-driven. They also provide a more general and less granular view of system activity than counter logs do—for example, rather than monitoring Physical Disk object counters, a trace log will monitor disk input and output. Trace logs can also draw information from nonsystem providers such as the Local Security Authority or the Active Directory Service to get information. To log some information (such as kernel monitoring information), you must either be logged in as the server's local administrator or use RunAs—accessible while setting up the trace log—to do the logging in the appropriate security context. To read a trace log without writing an interpreter or getting the TRACELOG tool from the Windows 2000 Resource Kit, you'll need to process it with the tracerpt tool found in Server 2003 and Windows XP.

Alert logs are like counter logs but taken one step further. Counter logs just collect data. Alert logs monitor performance object data for selected counters, using the same UI used for monitoring performance objects, but they assess those counters against tolerances that you set when creating the log. In other words, with an alert log you don't collect *all* the data for the selected counters; alerts are only logged when the performance data falls outside the acceptable range. Alert logs are kept in the Application log of a server's Event Viewer.

COUNTER LOGS

If you're starting from scratch, choose the New Log Settings option. Provide a unique descriptive name for the log in the box provided. Click OK, and you'll see the General tab of the log property sheet as shown in Figure 18.5.

TIP *It's acceptable to put blanks in the names of performance logs, but if you plan to manage those logs from the command line you'll simplify your life if you don't. Including blanks in the log name means that you'll need to put the filename in quotes.*

You aren't yet monitoring anything. You have two options for adding counters to the log. To add individual counters, click the Add Counters button to open the same window you used to add counters to the System Monitor. To monitor *all* the counters for an object in the log, click the Add Objects button to see a list of all available objects for the selected server (see Figure 18.6). If you choose one of these objects, then you'll record activity for all counters associated with that object.

FIGURE 18.5

When you create a new log, it will contain no counters to monitor.

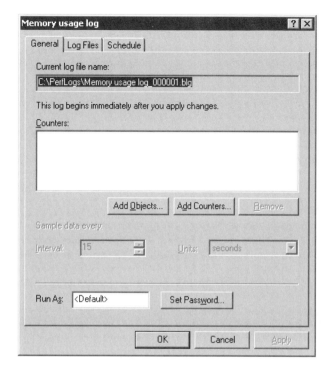

FIGURE 18.6

Adding objects and all their counters to a counter log

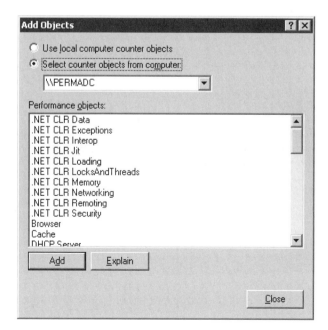

To begin, click the Add button, and you'll open the same Select Counters dialog box you used to add counters to a Performance Monitor chart. Make sure you've selected the computer that you want to log. As with charting, logging takes up resources on a server, so consider running logs remotely. Whichever option you go with—most often, you'll probably want to add individual counters—the counters you selected will now be added to the Counters list on the General tab.

Back in the General tab, you can edit the sampling interval from its default of 15 seconds. The Sample Data Every box will accept an integer between 1 and 10,000, and the drop-down list of time units supports seconds, minutes, hours, or days. Pick an interval based on the duration of your expected logging time—the longer the period you're logging for, the wider you'll probably want the interval to be so you can see trends. The shorter the sampling interval, the more processing time the sampling will take and the more datapoints you'll have.

NOTE *You can reuse Performance Monitor counters that you've previously saved as an HTML file. If you plan to do so, start the creation process by choosing New Log Settings From from the context menu. You'll be prompted to provide the name of the saved file. After that, the process will work exactly as it does for creating a new counter log file from scratch. The General tab will display the counters used in the saved Performance Monitor file.*

Turn to the Log Files tab (see Figure 18.7) to edit file settings for the log.

FIGURE 18.7

Edit file settings to control file type, size, and name.

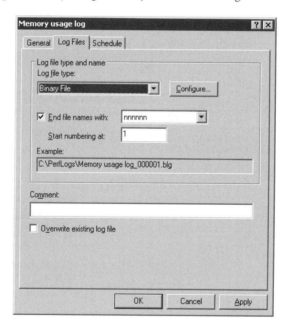

Most of these options are fairly self-explanatory, but let's take a quick tour:

◆ By default, logs are stored in a `Perflogs` folder on the server's boot partition. Unless you regularly back up this location, you might want to put the logs somewhere else for safekeeping.

- The name of the log is the filename. It must conform to the naming convention of the filesystem where you're storing the log.

- The auto filename suffix is an extension to the log filename that allows you to identify logs by their name, if you maintain more than one log with the same filename. The *nnnnnn* naming means that the files will be numbered in order (the first serial number determines the first number that will be used). Other options identify the file by the date it was created, whether by year; month, day, and hour; or some other mechanism. Open the drop-down list to find the naming convention that works best for you.

- The log file comment will appear next to the list of log names in the folder, so add a comment if the log file requires further description.

- Unless you specify otherwise, the file is a binary file that will open in System Monitor, but you can also save the data as a binary circular file, comma-delimited file (CSV), or tab-delimited file (TSV). CSVs and TSVs can both be opened in text editors or spreadsheet applications such as Microsoft Excel for analysis. The only limitation to CSV and TSV logs is that they must log all at once—they can't accommodate logs that start and stop. Binary and binary circular files (both of which have .BLG extensions) are for recording data intermittently, when data collection may stop and then resume while the log is recording data. The binary files create sequential lists of all events, while the binary circular files record data continuously to the same log file so that previously written records are overwritten when new data is available.

- Choose whether to limit the log file size. If you're planning to log for only a certain period of time (specified on the Schedule tab), then you may not want to limit the log's size, so you don't lose any of the data you choose to save. However, if you don't plan to choose an automatic ending time, it might not be a bad idea to limit the log size so you don't get more data than you can usefully examine.

When you've edited all the file settings, turn to the Schedule tab (see Figure 18.8) to finish creating the counter log file.

Normally, the log is set to start as soon as you finish—that is, it's set to start automatically at the time you started creating the log, which means it will begin logging as soon as you finish setting up options. If you're trying to gather information about server information under circumstances that you know will apply at a specific time, you can choose to either manually start the log or specify a specific date and time the log should start.

Unless you specify otherwise, the log will keep collecting data until you shut it off manually. To schedule a stopping time or logging duration, select the After radio button and specify the time or period for which you want to log. In this same dialog box, you can also tell the System Monitor to restart the log when the preset period is ended (as you might do if you wanted to compare data from several different times of day) and provide a command or batch file to run when the log is completed. Click OK, and the new log will appear in the Details side of the Counter Logs folder. Its icon will be red until the log starts collecting data, either at the time you specified on the Schedule tab or when you right-click the log object and choose Start from the context menu.

FIGURE 18.8
Editing scheduling settings for the log file

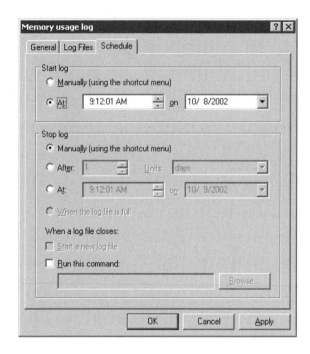

You can also monitor performance data from the command line, using typeperf. In its most basic form, it's another form of System Monitor, spitting out performance data into the command window from which you initiated the logging. For example, typing this on computer BETANET

```
typeperf "\Processor(_Total)\% Processor Time"
```

gives you output like this:

```
"(PDH-CSV 4.0)","\\BETANET\Processor(0)\% Processor Time"
"10/01/2002 17:24:28.272","1.000000"
"10/01/2002 17:24:29.274","9.000000"
"10/01/2002 17:24:30.275","2.000000"
"10/01/2002 17:24:31.277","0.000000"
"10/01/2002 17:24:32.278","0.000000"
"10/01/2002 17:24:33.279","4.000000"
"10/01/2002 17:24:34.281","1.000000"
"10/01/2002 17:24:35.282","0.000000"
"10/01/2002 17:24:36.284","2.000000"
"10/01/2002 17:24:37.285","8.000000"
"10/01/2002 17:24:38.287","0.000000"
"10/01/2002 17:24:39.288","1.000000"
"10/01/2002 17:24:40.289","1.000000"
"10/01/2002 17:24:41.291","0.000000"
"10/01/2002 17:24:42.292","1.000000"
```

WARNING *You must watch the command syntax very carefully. Yes, you really need that underscore before "Total", but if you're specifying a particular processor (0, to monitor the first one) then you should not have the underscore. If you leave out a space—or add an extra one—when naming the counters, you'll see a warning that the counter isn't accessible and there are no valid counters for the monitoring you proposed.*

You can monitor more than one counter by enclosing both counters in quotation marks:

```
typeperf "\Processor(0)\% Processor Time" "\Processor(0)\Interrupts/sec"
```

The counters will be displayed in the order you gave them to typeperf, like this:

```
"(PDH-CSV 4.0)","\\BETANET\Processor(0)\% Processor
    Time","\\BETANET\Processor(0)\Interrupts/sec"
"10/01/2002 17:41:17.594","9.000000","109.830447"
"10/01/2002 17:41:18.595","0.000000","105.844672"
"10/01/2002 17:41:19.596","0.000000","108.843920"
"10/01/2002 17:41:20.598","0.000000","110.840128"
"10/01/2002 17:41:21.599","0.000000","109.838443"
"10/01/2002 17:41:22.601","2.000000","167.760419"
"10/01/2002 17:41:23.602","0.000000","122.818836"
"10/01/2002 17:41:24.604","0.000000","125.822315"
"10/01/2002 17:41:25.605","0.000000","107.850406"
"10/01/2002 17:41:26.606","0.000000","108.841461"
"10/01/2002 17:41:27.608","0.000000","130.810447"
"10/01/2002 17:41:28.609","2.000000","117.829948"
"10/01/2002 17:41:29.611","6.000000","107.844991"
"10/01/2002 17:41:30.612","0.000000","106.846337"
"10/01/2002 17:41:31.614","0.000000","105.847418"
"10/01/2002 17:41:32.615","0.000000","109.840925"
"10/01/2002 17:41:33.617","0.000000","108.844831"
"10/01/2002 17:41:34.618","0.000000","114.838308"
"10/01/2002 17:41:35.619","0.000000","116.827087"
"10/01/2002 17:41:36.621","0.000000","108.842918"
"10/01/2002 17:41:37.622","0.000000","111.839624"
```

You can also monitor a remote computer by including its name in the counter argument. For example

```
typeperf "\\Gamma\Processor(0)\% Processor Time"
```

will monitor Processor: % Processor Time on the server named Gamma—even though Gamma is running Windows 2000 and therefore does not locally support typeperf. To stop monitoring the selected counters, type Ctrl+C. Stopping the monitoring may take a minute, especially if you mistyped the instance identifier and are therefore getting weird output suggesting that the processor is busy −1 percent of the time.

As you are probably beginning to suspect, the real value of typeperf is not in its ability to send performance logging output to a command window. It's much more useful as a shortcut to making counter logs without using the GUI. Table 18.4 lists the switches for this command.

TABLE 18.4: SWITCHES FOR THE TYPEPERF COMMAND-LINE LOGGING TOOL

SWITCH	MEANING
-f <CSV ∣ TSV ∣ BIN ∣ SQL>	Output file format, with the default of CSV (comma-delimited file).
-cf <filename>	The file containing the performance counters to monitor. Each counter must be on its own line.
-si <[[hh:]mm:]ss>	Time between samples, with a default value of one second.
-o <filename>	Path of the output file or SQL database. If you don't specify an output file, the output is displayed in the command window from which you launched typeperf.
-q [object]	List installed counters (no instances). To list counters for one object, include the object name, such as Processor.
-qx [object]	List installed counters with instances. To list counters for one object, include the object name, such as Processor.
-sc <samples>	Number of samples to collect. Unless you specify otherwise, typeperf will keep sampling until you press Ctrl+C.
-config <filename>	Settings file containing command options.
-s <computer_name>	Server to monitor if you don't specify a server in the counter path. You do not need to specify a server if you are monitoring the local computer. To log counters on more than one server, you're best off including the server path with the performance object to monitor.
-y	Answer yes to all questions (such as whether or not to overwrite files) without prompting.

These switches make typeperf much more useful and a lot simpler to work with.

First off, let's skip that pesky parameter bit—it's too hard to type accurately. Rather than type the counters you want to monitor as part of the command, collect them with the -qx switch and write them to a text file with the -o switch. For example, the following will write all instances of the LogicalDisk object into f:\perflogs\diskcount.txt:

```
typeperf -qx LogicalDisk -o f:\perflogs\diskcount.txt
```

The file now contains neatly formatted counters for all instances of the LogicalDisk object, nicely formatted (one per line) in the way that typeperf requires. However, you don't need to monitor *all* these counters, so delete the ones you don't want. You'll need to do that manually, but when you've edited the file and saved it as diskcounted.txt, you can point to that file with the -cf switch and then create a printed log (called output.csv) of the results of monitoring those counters, like this:

```
typeperf -cf f:\perflogs\diskcounted.txt -o f:\perflogs\output.csv
```

NOTE *Writing output to a file not only makes it easier to keep and format the log data, but it makes Server 2003 more responsive when you press Ctrl+C to end the logging. While typeperf is writing to the file, the command window will show a spinning cursor.*

Finally, you can refine this logging a bit further to use a different file format (-f), change the sampling rate (-si), stop monitoring after collecting 50 samples (-sc), and direct typeperf to another server to collect performance data (-s). The following example will save the log as a tab-delimited file, take a sample every 5 seconds, stop logging after 50 samples, and check data for server \\Gamma:

```
typeperf -cf f:\perflogs\diskcounted.txt -si 5 -sc 50 -f tsv -o
    f:\perflogs\Goutput.tsv
```

TRACE LOGS

Trace logs are more of an application or database developer's tool, testing to see how often a selected event occurs and logging the time, the thread ID that initiated the event, and the user data. To create a new trace log, right-click the Trace Logs icon in the right pane to open the context menu. As with counter logs, you can choose to either start from a saved Performance Monitor chart (New Log Settings From) or create a new log from scratch (New Log Settings). Type a unique name for the trace log when prompted (in this case, I've named it NetLogon), and click OK. When you do so, you'll see the General tab in Figure 18.9.

FIGURE 18.9

Choose counters for the TraceNet-Logontrace log.

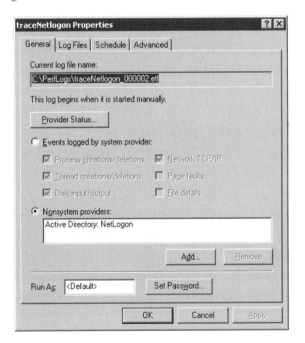

As you can see from this figure, you can collect data from two different types of providers. (A *provider* is just what it sounds like: something that provides information to an external application. In this case, the external application is the trace logging tool.). Services such as Kerberos can also send data to a trace log. The available nonsystem providers are visible when you select nonsystem providers to log and then click the Add button. From the list in the box that appears, you can pick available providers, such as the Active Directory service or Kerberos.

TIP *File I/O and page faults are not normally included in the trace log because of the very high values they're likely to register—a lot of I/O and page faults happen on a server operating normally. Microsoft recommends limiting the log to two hours if you want to include that data in the log.*

The Log Files tab of the trace log creator works the same way the one for counter logs does, except that your options are between a circular trace file (one that starts writing over itself) and a sequential one (where all data is appended to the end of the file). So does the scheduler—pick a time and date for the trace log to begin, or choose to begin it manually.

TIP *If you can't start a trace log, check the Application log of the Event Viewer. Some providers require a local administrator's account name and password to let their data be logged.*

The trace log creator includes one tab not in the counter log creator: Advanced (see Figure 18.10). Trace logs don't log data in real time; they store it in buffers until the buffers are full. Edit the settings here to make the buffers smaller or larger or to force the buffers to write to the logs at a definite interval. (Since trace logs are event driven, buffering the events before putting them into the log shouldn't matter.)

FIGURE 18.10

You can edit the size of the buffers reserved for a trace log.

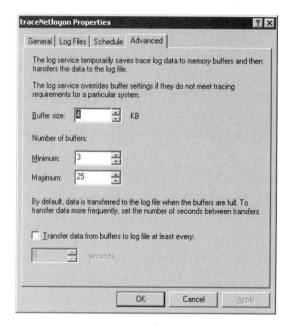

When you've edited all the trace log settings, click OK to return to the System Monitor. The log file will appear in the list. Its icon will be red until the log is running, then it'll turn green when it starts automatically or when you start it by right-clicking it and choosing Start.

ALERT LOGS

Finally, you can use Performance Monitor to keep track of failed logon attempts (Server: Errors Logon), file access attempts, and other types of attempted access that can indicate someone's trying to break into the network. That's what alert logs are for. After all, you don't just want to know about this stuff after the fact, you want to know when it's happening.

The initial stages of creating an alert log are much like those of creating a trace or counter log. Open the `Alert Logs` folder so that its contents are displayed on the right side of the System Monitor tool. Right-click anywhere in the blank area on the right of the display and choose New Alert Settings to define new counters to log or New Alert Settings From to open a saved Performance Monitor file and use its counters. Choose a name for the new alert, then click OK to open the alert log's property sheet (see Figure 18.11).

FIGURE 18.11

General tab of the alert log's property sheet

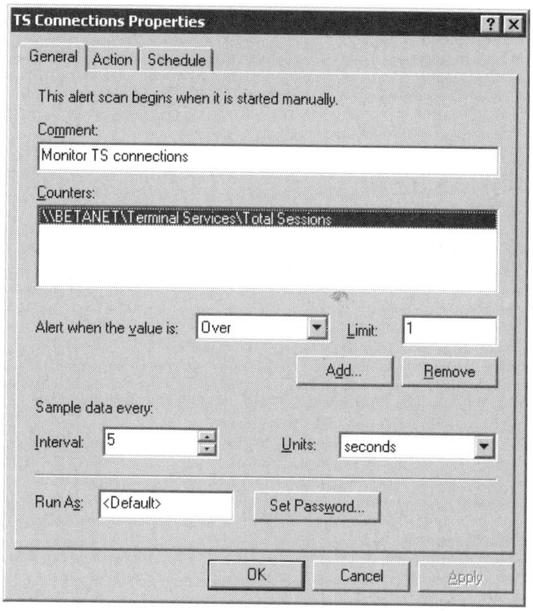

Assuming you're creating this log from new data, you'll need to add counters to the log as you did for a counter log. Click the Add button to open the Add Counters dialog box, and choose the computer and performance counters you want to monitor. When you're done making selections (remember, you can add as many counters as you like by clicking the Add button), click Close to return to the General tab. The counters will show up in the list.

So far, creating an alert log hasn't been any different from creating a counter log, but we haven't yet gotten to the good stuff. Below the list of added counters, you'll need to specify tolerances for each counter you choose. When the counter exceeds those tolerances, Performance Logging will add an entry to the alert log. For example, say that you added Terminal Services: Total Sessions to the log so you know whenever someone logs onto a server via RDP. In that case, you'd set the upper tolerance to 1—or 2, if you want to be able to log into the server yourself.

NOTE *In this example, the System Monitor will keep sending messages and recording events until the number of remote sessions is below the alert threshold. Bear that in mind when setting up alerts.*

Notice that the default sampling interval for alert logs (five seconds) is much shorter than the one for counter logs. This is because of the different nature of the log—it's assumed that you're a little more concerned about the contents of this one. Use the drop-down lists to edit the sampling intervals if you need to. The alert log will only record events where the tolerances were breached, so you don't have to worry about drowning in data, but more frequent monitoring takes a toll on the server.

The scheduling tab for alert logs works just like the one you used to configure counter and trace logs—just pick a date and time to begin and end the log, or choose to start and stop it manually—but the Action tab (see Figure 18.12) is something new. From this tab, you'll need to tell the System Monitor what you want it to *do* when it generates an alert.

FIGURE 18.12

Edit alert log action settings.

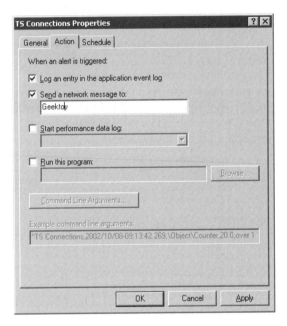

Normally, System Monitor just adds an entry to the Event Viewer's application Event log. If the alert isn't something that you need to know about right away, then you can leave it at that. More important alerts, however, like those generated by unauthorized logins in a pattern that suggests that the network is being hacked, or a severe shortage of memory, may require immediate action. From the Action tab, you can tell System Monitor to send a message to your computer when writing an entry in the alert log or even to have it run a specific application that you can use to resolve the problem. Use this tab to send arguments to the application.

Once again, when you're done editing the alert log's properties, click OK to add it to the Alert Logs folder. When it's running, its icon will be green.

Editing Log Settings

You can edit any log's settings by right-clicking its icon and opening its properties sheet in the same way that you created the log in the first place. However, in Server 2003 you can also edit log properties from the command line, using the new relog tool that allows you to change the sampling rate and file format of existing logs.

Relog allows you to take existing performance logs and change the sampling rate and file format.

Viewing Log Data

Setting up the log data is the easy part, once you know what you want to monitor. Reading and interpreting that data is harder. The method of viewing log output depends on the type of log and its file format.

COUNTER LOGS

Recall that when you're creating counter logs, you have a choice about how to present the data. The default option is to save the data in a binary log file (BLG) that you can examine from System Monitor. To see this data, click the icon on the System Monitor that has the database symbol (a cylinder) on it and browse to the location where you saved the log file when setting it up. This will open the contents of the log like a static performance monitoring chart, so you can see what performance was like at a given time without having to be on the spot at that moment. Charts are nice, but there will also be times when you want to view the information in a spreadsheet so you can manipulate the way it's presented. To do so, save the log data in a tab-delimited (TSV) or comma-delimited file (CSV) that you can open with a spreadsheet application such as Microsoft Excel. To view the data, just open the file with Excel. If the log is still active, you'll see an error message telling you that another user or application is using the data, but you can open it as a read-only document or click the Notify option to open the file—you just can't save it to its current name while the log is still writing to the file. From there, you can use Excel's charting tools to massage the data to make a good presentation.

ALERT LOGS

Alert logs don't go into a regular file but directly to the Event Viewer's Application log (see Figure 18.13). When the counters exceed the tolerances you've set up, Server 2003 will add an Information record to the Application Event log.

FIGURE 18.13

Output of an alert log

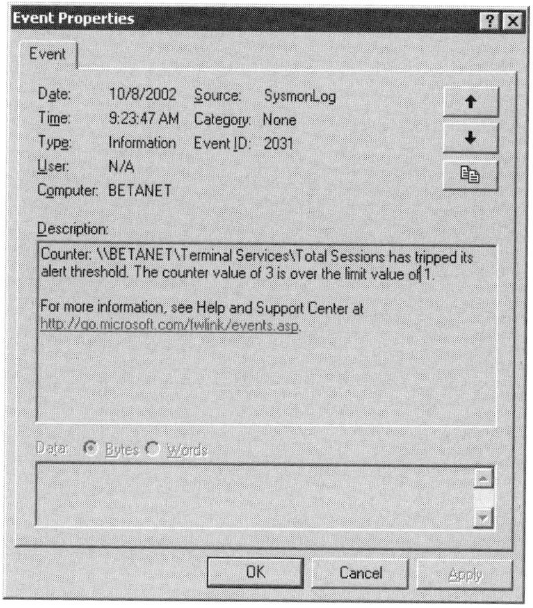

Of course, for more serious alerts, you'll have to set up the alert log to e-mail you or send a message to the location on the network where you're logged in so that you know that the alert occurred.

TRACE LOGS

Server 2003 (and other Windows Server operating systems) doesn't come with any program that can read the ETL files created when you make a trace log. You *can* view the contents of a trace log without writing an interpreter, but to do so you'll need to use tracerpt to convert the output to comma-delimited file (CSV). Luckily, it's a pretty simple tool, with only the switches in Table 18.5.

TABLE 18.5: SWITCHES FOR THE TRACERPT TOOL

-o [filename]	Text (CSV) output file. Default is `dumpfile.csv`.
-summary [filename]	The name of the summary file for the trace log. The default is `summary.txt`.
-report [filename]	Text output report file. Default is `workload.txt`.
-rt <session_name [session_name ...]>	Real-time Event Trace Session data source, used to generate a readable log from real-time data instead of a converted log.
-config <filename>	Settings file containing command options.
-y	Answer yes to all questions (such as whether or not to overwrite files) without prompting.

For example, running

```
tracerpt trace1_000003.etl -o tracelog.csv -summary tracesum.txt
```

yields the following output:

```
Input
----------------
File(s):
     trace1_000003.etl


Output
----------------
Text (CSV):      tracelog.csv
Summary:         tracesum.txt

The command completed successfully.
```

Troubleshooting Performance Monitoring

Performance monitoring doesn't always work as expected. The reasons for this vary with the situation.

The descriptions for the counters can be misleading or inaccurate, so you may not be measuring what you think you're measuring—I've pointed out a couple of instances that I've noticed. Since there are thousands of counters, I'm sure that I haven't caught them all.

Be as specific as possible when monitoring particular instances, and make sure that you know which instance you're monitoring—for example, be sure of physical and logical disk identifiers before you begin monitoring disk activity. Similarly, it is very difficult to get any real process or thread information with the System Monitor, because the tool identifies processes and threads by instance, not by PID or TID. (There are Process: ID Process and Thread: ID Thread counters. They don't work. To get PID and TID information, you need to use the Task Manager.) If a server is running more than one instance of the same image, it is very difficult to tell which one you're collecting the data for. You could collect data for *all* instances of a particular image—say, EXCEL.EXE—but that doesn't help you figure out usage patters for a particular instance.

Since histograms and reports display averages by default when working from logged data, be careful not to let unexpected zeros and spikes skew those averages. A value of zero doesn't necessarily mean that the real value is zero. Rather, it may mean that the service you're monitoring (if applicable) is not running—check the Services tool in Computer Management or the Event Viewer to make sure that a service that should be running but isn't reporting any data hasn't stopped. If you're remotely monitoring a server, make sure that you can get to it—particularly if you're opening a saved console that someone else set up for you; they might have permissions that you do not, and all you'll know is that you can't get any information about the remote server. Similarly, spikes might be part of the normal routine for a server and require investigation, or they might reflect an aberration. For example, say you're trying to find out how stressed a domain controller's processor is during an average hour. If you make that average hour at 8 A.M. when everyone is getting to work and logging in, you'll probably get a result different from the one you see when monitoring at 2–3 P.M. If logged averages are high, check the graph and look for spikes that can throw off the average, and consider lengthening the monitored period to put spikes into perspective.

Whattheheckhappened? Troubleshooting with the Event Viewer

Server 2003 defines an event as any significant occurrence in the system or in an application that users should be aware of and have the chance to log. Critical events—those that can impact server availability—deserve immediate notifications, which is why you'll see "low on virtual memory" announcements on your monitor without asking for them. Less-critical but still important events are recorded in the Event Viewer, a tool in the Administrative Tools program group. You can log just about any kind of event on a server: file and directory access, services starting (or failing to start), unexpected conditions on the server, or, as discussed earlier, alert logs based on System Monitor data. And you'll *need* these logs. Any time that something strange starts happening on a server, those event log entries are your first key to finding out what went wrong and how to fix it.

Understanding Log Types

The Event Viewer can display six types of logs. All servers will accumulate system, security, and application events. System events are generated by system components or related services and drivers.

Security events record changes to any security settings or any audited access such as attempts to open files or folders. You can monitor both successful and failed security events. Application logs contain events generated by applications, installed printers, or (as you've seen) alert logs. The Application log is a good place to look for important events not related to the core functioning of the OS or its services, but important nonetheless. If you set up event logging with administrative scripts, the events you record will also be in the Application log.

Three other logs—Directory Service, DNS Server, and File Replication Service—are for keeping track of AD-related events. The Directory Service log entries record information regarding the NT Directory Service (NTDS), problems connecting to the global catalog, and any issues regarding Active Directory in your network. The DNS Server entries record any events related to running the Directory Name Service in your Active Directory. Finally, the File Replication log entries record any notable events that took place while the domain controller attempted to update other domain controllers.

To view any log, open the Event Viewer. From the left pane showing the log types, click the type you want to view. The display in the right pane will change to show the log's contents.

Viewing Remote Event Log Data

You can connect to any Windows server with an account in your domain (or in another, trusted domain). To do so, right-click the main Event Viewer folder in the left pane of the tool. From the context menu that appears, choose Connect to Another Computer. You'll see a dialog box that looks like the one in Figure 18.14.

FIGURE 18.14

Enter the name of a remote computer to manage.

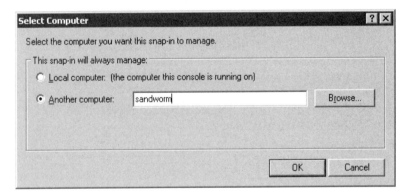

Type the name of the computer you want to monitor (for example, **sandworm**—you don't need backslashes) and then click OK. If the new computer is accessible across a low-speed connection, right-click the log you want to view (not the remote server, the actual log), and then click Properties. Near the bottom of the General tab, check the box for low-speed connection.

If you're not sure of a remote server's name, you can browse for it in an NT or Active Directory domain. Instead of typing a server's name and clicking OK, click the Browse button to open the Select Computer dialog box. If you're unsure of a remote computer's name, the first dialog box is unlikely to help you, so click the Advanced button to open the dialog box in Figure 18.15.

FIGURE 18.15

Browsing a domain for a computer account

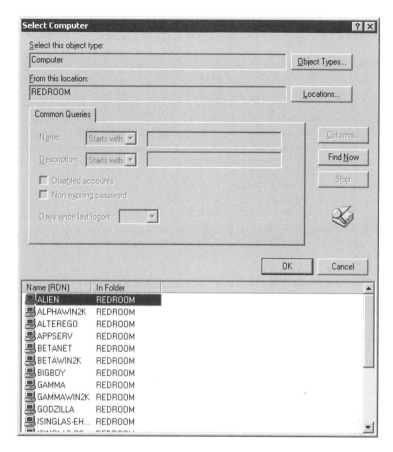

From here, click the Locations button to choose a domain, and then click the Find Now button to list the computer accounts in that domain.

NOTE *You can only connect to the logs of computers that have a computer account in the selected domain and are currently connected to the network. All computer accounts will be listed, even if a particular computer is offline at the moment.*

When you've chosen a computer, click OK, and then click OK again back in the Select Computer dialog box. The Event Viewer information displayed will now be the remote computer's. To reconnect to the local computer, just open the Select Computer dialog box again and pick the option for monitoring the local computer.

Reading Log Entries

There are five categories of log entries, each identifiable by an icon:

◆ Information events describe the successful completion of a task, such as the beginning of a service. If you're using Alert logging, information events in the Application log may also indicate that an alert's been triggered, so don't assume that all information events are benign.

- Warning events aren't necessarily fatal—they describe unexpected behavior that might point to future problems if not corrected.

- Error events describe fatal errors that mean a task failed. Error events may lead to data loss; they always mean that the server wasn't able to do something you asked it to do.

- Success events describe an audited security event completed as requested—for example, a machine account's login.

TIP   *Some third-party services record successful initialization as a success event instead of an information event.*

- Failed events describe an audited security event that the server could not complete as requested. Failed security events can point to attempts to hack the computer, or may signify that a service does not have the permissions it needs to do something that it's supposed to do.

Each entry also includes the following information pertinent to the event:

- Date and time logged
- Object logging the event (such as the service that failed to start)
- Computer name of the server where the event was generated and, if applicable, the name of the person responsible for generating the event
- If applicable, the category of event, which won't tell you much—it's for the internal use of whatever server component logged the event
- Event number describing the event type

TIP   *You can search for event numbers at* www.eventid.net *to find out what a particular event number means, since the descriptions for events aren't always very clear. This Web site doesn't have all event ID information, but it's a good place to start when trying to track down problems.*

Double-click any event in any log to open its property sheet (see Figure 18.16) and see more information about the event. The explanation is sometimes more than a little cryptic or is incomplete, but sometimes—and this gets easier with practice—you can glean useful information from the explanations of the events.

Troubleshooting with the Event Viewer takes a little practice. For best results, you'll need to know what your system looks like when it's running normally so you can more easily identify the events that indicate something is broken. Reading the Event Viewer on a regular basis also lets you find out about problems you may not have known you had, like misconfigured services, undetected because no one's using them much, or a drive running low on disk space. If a server seems to be acting oddly, then check the Event Viewer for warnings or informational messages that may explain what's going on. For example, reading the System log once helped me find a rogue program running on a server that I hadn't properly firewalled. A terminal server refusing connections because of a lack of licenses will also log this information in the System log, as will a service that can't start. (You'll still have to track down *why* the service won't start, but knowing that it didn't will help you figure out why a server isn't acting as expected.) And if a printer isn't appearing in a terminal session, the System log may indicate the reason.

FIGURE 18.16

Event details for a
System log entry

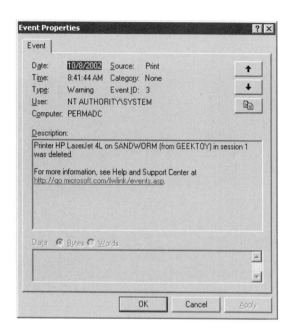

Managing and Archiving Log Contents

That's what you're looking at in the Event Viewer. *Managing* all that data can be a task unto itself.

DISCARDING OLD DATA

The Event Viewer logs will keep filling up according to their settings. After a while (and, if you're recording something that happens a lot, "a while" may not be long), they get full. Unless you specify otherwise, an Event log cannot get any bigger than 16384KB (up from 512KB in Windows 2000).

To keep the data fresh, the Event Viewer normally overwrites events as it needs to keep the log under that size, overwriting the oldest data first. To edit this, open the property sheet for a log by right-clicking its icon and choosing Properties. Turn to the General tab shown in Figure 18.17. Most of these settings are pretty clear—from here, you can edit the maximum size of the log, the way in which old entries are overwritten (or not) and whether to clear an existing log and start over.

WARNING   *If you click the Clear Log button on this tab, you'll delete all the entries in that log (Event Viewer will prompt you to save them). Save logs before clearing them if you think you might need the data again.*

FILTERING DATA

Normally, the Event Viewer will display all records that it's collected, with the most recent entries at the top of the log. You can simplify the view of all this data by applying filters to the logged data. Filters don't affect what information is logged, only how it's displayed.

To filter a log's events, right-click the log's icon in the left pane and choose Filter from the View menu. You'll see the Filter tab shown in Figure 18.18. Choose the filtering options you want, described in Table 18.6. Only event logs with the options you specify (you can apply as many as you like) will appear in the Event log once you've applied the filter.

FIGURE 18.17

Edit the settings governing how data is discarded when the log is full.

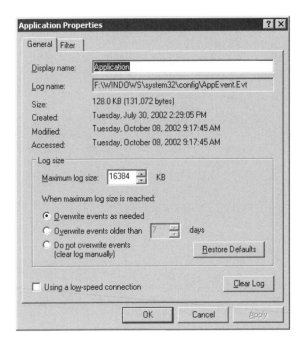

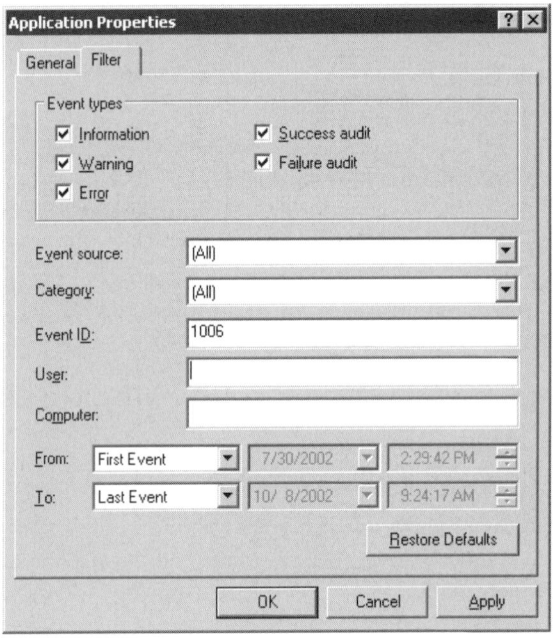

FIGURE 18.18

Filter data to display only pertinent information.

TABLE 18.6: FILTERING OPTIONS FOR EVENT LOGGING

OPTION	DESCRIPTION
Category	Includes all events within a given category. This filter is most useful for security events, as most system events do not belong to any category and the application categories are numbered, with no keys.
Computer	Includes all events on that particular computer. As the computer in question is the one you're monitoring and you can only display one computer's Event log at a time, it's not clear to me why this filter is part of the Event Viewer.
Error	Includes all error events, which are requested tasks that the server was unable to complete for some reason.
Event ID	Includes all events with the event ID you specify. You can only specify one event ID at a time—you can't, for example, filter the Event log to display both event ID 7000 and event ID 4002.
Event Source	Displays events stemming from a source you specify (a driver, system component, or service).
Failure Audit	Displays failed security events such as opening a file or changing a security setting. The events this will include depend on the security and auditing settings for the domain or computer.
Information	Displays information events. Information events typically mean that everything worked as planned, but you can use information events to reassure yourself that yes, that service started as planned, so it couldn't be a problem there.
Success Audit	Displays successful security events such as opening a file or changing a security setting. The events this will include depend on the security and auditing settings for the domain or computer.
User	Displays events that are associated with a particular user, generally the user working at the console when the event was generated. Not all events have a user associated with them—this is mostly a system log thing.
View From and To	Use these boxes to specify a range of events to display. Unless you tell it otherwise, the Event log will display all events in the log from the oldest to the newest, but you can provide starting and finishing dates and times.
Warning	Includes warning events, which tell you that something didn't go as expected (or, for alert logs, that a counter exceeded the tolerance you set up) but that the problem isn't immediately critical.

Filters work like Boolean AND statements, not OR statements. That is, if you specify event ID 7000 and check the Error box, then the log will only display entries that are errors associated with event ID 7000, not all errors and all entries with event ID 7000.

TIP *Want to view all data of a certain type but aren't sure how to filter the Event log? Click the column heading that corresponds to the type of data you want to view, and the log will sort its entries based on that type. For example, if you want to see all the entries associated with the Browser service, click the header for the Source column. All entries related to the Browser service will be grouped together.*

SAVING AND RETRIEVING LOG DATA

Like I said, logs get full. You may want the data in them for future reference, however, so you don't necessarily want to just clear all log file entries. To save a log file, right-click the log's icon in the left pane of the Event Viewer. From the context menu, choose Save Log File As. A dialog box will open; type the name of the log, click Save, and you're done. You can now clear the file to begin logging afresh.

To open a saved log, right-click the Event Viewer icon in the left pane and choose Open Log File. Browse for the EVT file containing the saved log, choose a log type (this isn't an option) and a display name, and click Open. When you've loaded the saved Event log, it will appear alongside the other event logs as shown in Figure 18.19.

FIGURE 18.19

Loaded event logs don't replace existing log files of the same type, they supplement them.

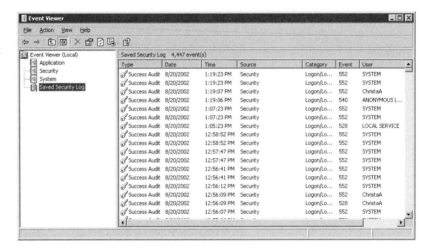

Quick Looks: Using the Task Manager

The tools we've talked about so far are good for gathering information for the long term, but setting them up and finding the relevant data takes a little time. When you want to get a quick view of the State of the Computer, the Task Manager is the way to go. It requires almost no preparation, gives you an easy way to determine which applications are hogging resources—as well as providing a shortcut to shutting down runaways—and generally offers you an instantaneous look at how the server is operating. You can't save or log data with the Task Manager, but you can see how the server is performing without having to set up performance counters. I use the Task Manager frequently on both servers and workstations. Just keep in mind that you cannot use the Task Manager to monitor a remote computer, and this tool uses server resources. I will leave it running on a not-too-stressed workstation, but I won't leave it running on a server.

To get to the Task Manager, press Ctrl+Alt+Del to bring up the Windows Security dialog box, and click the Task Manager button. This tool has five tabs: Performance, Applications, Processes, Networking, and Users.

TIP *If you're remotely administering a server using RDP, press Ctrl+Alt+End to open the Windows Security dialog box.*

Processor and Memory Usage

Graphically, the Performance tab in Figure 18.20 is pretty easy to interpret.

FIGURE 18.20

Get a visual snapshot of the server with the Task Manager's Performance tab.

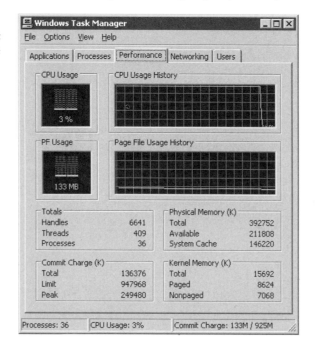

Processor-wise, the server was recently very stressed but is now better, and it's using a moderate amount of memory at the moment—overall, the server's in pretty good shape. This graphical data is collected from the time I open the Task Manager, so it will take a minute or two to get much of a snapshot of current processor and memory usage. The text on the bottom of the page takes a little more interpretation. In the Totals section in the upper left, the Processes count is a rough estimate of the number of executable files (not just user applications, but any executable file, including service images and files supporting the operating system) running on the server. The Threads count represents the number of executable threads that are using those process resources and contending for processor time. The Handles count represents the number of connections that the processes have to system resources such as internal timers. Moving to the right, the Physical Memory section gives you a little more useful information: how much memory is available on the computer and how much of it is currently in use. This memory count includes only the installed RAM in the computer, not the paging file. The Kernel Memory section on the bottom right shows how much memory kernel processes are using, and how much is paged to disk. Finally, the Commit Charge section in the bottom left shows how much memory is committed to particular processes and is not available to other processes.

Application-Specific Information

The Applications tab of the Task Manager shows (some of) the executable files running on the computer, along with the data files they have open (if applicable). As you can see from Figure 18.21, you can use the buttons on this tab to navigate to running applications or end runaway applications—a hung program will show a status of Not Responding. You can also right-click individual applications to change their window state (maximized or minimized), switch to them, close them, or find their process on the Processes tab.

NOTE If an application crashes and is in the middle of being debugged, you can't end it until the debugger is done gathering information, and if closing the application causes the application to open a window prompting you for information (perhaps to save a file) then you'll need to either answer the prompt or choose the End Now option when prompted to override the application's prompt. Generally speaking, you're better off closing the application normally if you can.

FIGURE 18.21

The Applications tab shows running applications and any data files they have open.

Process-Level Information

The Processes tab in the Task Manager (see Figure 18.22) takes the basic information presented with the Applications tab and significantly expands on it. The Image Name column shows the executable files associated with the applications on the Applications tab and displays all the operating system executables—that CSRSS.EXE file is the Win32 subsystem. The PID column shows the process ID for that executable, the identifier for the process created to support the needs of that executable. The OS identifies running processes both by the name of the executable file they're supporting and by their Process ID. The CPU column shows the processor that each executable is using; in a single-processor system this won't tell you anything you don't already know, but in a multiprocessor system could be useful. The CPU Time column, which you can add as described below, on the other hand, shows you useful information—you can tell which executables are using the most CPU time. If all is going well, then the System Idle Process should be at the top of the list when you're sorting for CPU time. The Mem Usage column shows the size of the working set for each executable. However, since this total includes shared pages, you can't add all these numbers up to get a complete count of the RAM installed in a particular computer.

FIGURE 18.22

Use the Processes tab to find out how much memory or processor time an executable file is using.

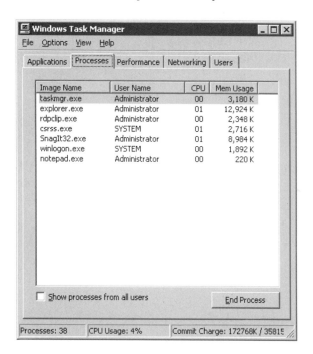

TIP *To sort the data displayed on the Processes tab, click the appropriate column head.*

This is only a small sample of the data available to you when it comes to getting a current snapshot of the computer. When the Processes tab is in the foreground, the View menu in the Task Manager has a Select Columns option. Pick this menu item, and you'll see a dialog box like the one in Figure 18.23. The selected boxes will be listed on the Processes tab.

For example, notice that my Processes tab does not have a Session ID column, whereas yours may. (This option will only be available if you install Terminal Services.) This column is used on servers with Terminal Services enabled, whether in Remote Administration or Application Server mode, to identify the session in which a particular executable file is running.

FIGURE 18.23

You can choose additional per-process information to monitor.

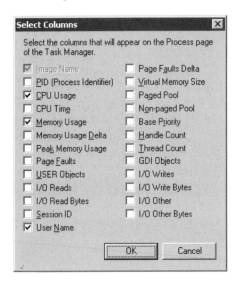

Select Columns

Select the columns that will appear on the Process page of the Task Manager.

☑ Image Name   ☐ Page Faults Delta
☐ PID (Process Identifier)   ☐ Virtual Memory Size
☑ CPU Usage   ☐ Paged Pool
☐ CPU Time   ☐ Non-paged Pool
☑ Memory Usage   ☐ Base Priority
☐ Memory Usage Delta   ☐ Handle Count
☐ Peak Memory Usage   ☐ Thread Count
☐ Page Faults   ☐ GDI Objects
☐ USER Objects   ☐ I/O Writes
☐ I/O Reads   ☐ I/O Write Bytes
☐ I/O Read Bytes   ☐ I/O Other
☐ Session ID   ☐ I/O Other Bytes
☑ User Name

OK   Cancel

NOTE   *By default, the Task Manager will display processes only for the console session (Session 0), but it can display process information for all connections to the server, whether from the console or via RDP. Clear the check box on the Processes tab to get a more streamlined view of the server, or select it if you want to know what executables are running in all sessions, whether visible to you or not.*

I find myself using the Processes tab most often of all the parts of the Task Manager. It's a very easy way to find out what's active on your server quickly, without mucking around with adding counters or checking the Event log. If you see something that looks like an ongoing problem, then you can set up logging in the System Monitor. You can also kill processes from this tab—just right-click the process and choose End Process—or End Process Tree to kill a process and every other process it spawned.

Network Information

The Networking tab in the Task Manager (see Figure 18.24) displays the current state of all virtual network adapters in the server, whether they're responding, and how much of their network capacity is currently in use. This network information applies only to traffic going to and from the currently connected server, so it's not much of a tool for general network diagnostics. It can help you track down server-specific network problems, however.

User Session Information

Because Terminal Services is enabled on all Server 2003 computers, the Task Manager now includes a Users tab that you can use to keep track of those remote sessions. From this tab (see Figure 18.25) you can see the session ID for each session (including the console, which will have Session ID 0), the username for the person who's logged in, the status of that session (Active or Disconnected) and the name of the computer they're running the remote session from.

FIGURE 18.24

The Networking tab displays connection status for all virtual networks on a server.

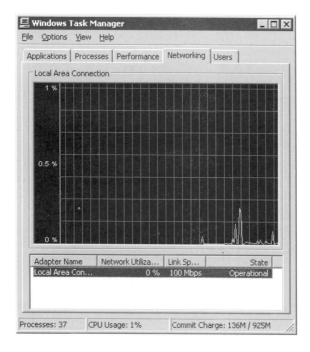

FIGURE 18.25

Use the Users tab to monitor and manage remote connections to the server.

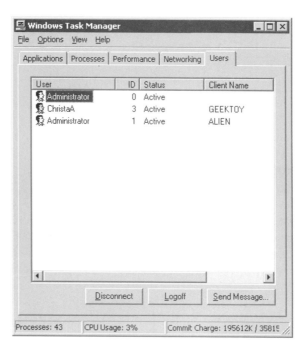

This tab will come in handy in several ways. First of all, a Server 2003 only supports a maximum of one console and two remote administrative sessions—and disconnected sessions count toward that total. This tab can show you how many remote connections are currently running on the server and show you their status, as well as let you communicate with those sessions.

You can send a message to an active session by right-clicking the session and choosing Send Message from the context menu. A dialog box opens, in which you can type a short message—perhaps asking one administrator to log off the console because the server has accepted the maximum number of connections and someone else needs to log on. When you send a message to a session, it will immediately pop up on the screen of that session.

If another administrator is having trouble with the server, you can take over their session from the Task Manager. Right-click their active session, choose Connect from the context menu, and type their password, and you'll take over that session. (Doing this will kick the other user out; to shadow a session, you'll need to use the Remote Control tool in Terminal Services Manager.) Because connecting to a session disconnects your own session, you cannot connect to a session from the console; you must be working from a remote administration session yourself. You can, however, connect to the console session—you'll just lock it.

Finally, if someone has disconnected from their session and you need to reclaim the session, you can log them off their session. Right-click the session and choose Log Off. The Task Manager will ask if you're sure about logging off the selected user. Click Yes, and you'll boot that person off the server.

NOTE   *For more information about working with terminal sessions (including more options for sending messages to remote sessions and connecting to them), see Chapter 16.*

Basic Tuning Stuff

So far, we've talked a lot about how to *collect* information from a server using the System Monitor, the Event Viewer, and the Task Manager, but not so much about how you can exploit this information to make your servers run more efficiently. Let's open the Control Panel and see what settings you can edit now that you know a little better what state of health your servers are in.

Optimizing Server Processing Power

Windows NT Server 4 and NT Workstation had several obvious differences, but one of the major differences wasn't obvious. The core files required to run NT Server and NT Workstation were and are the same, but at boot time the OS looks in the Registry key `HKLM\System\CurrentControlSet\Control\ProductOptions`. Run REGEDT32 and look in that key, and, among other information, you'll see a value for Product Type. That value was (and is—this hasn't changed) since NT 4: WinNT for workstations (e.g., Windows XP), LanmanNT for domain controllers, and ServerNT for server computers.

Why does this value matter? Based on the value of this key, NTLDR makes some decisions about how to configure the system, including runtime policy decisions such as how operating system components and user processes contend for memory and even how the processes contend for CPU time.

The most obvious result of this is that server operating systems give a little more time to the application in the foreground than the ones in the background, but they generally assume that all applications on the server need more or less equal time. But workstation operating systems give a *lot* more time to the application in the foreground, on the premise that the application you're directly interacting with is the one you want to be most responsive. If you ran, say, Microsoft Word from a Server 2003 machine, it would run rather less efficiently than if you ran the application from XP Professional. This is because even when you were typing into Word, the server would be a little distracted, checking with any other running processes to make sure they were happy and getting enough processor time. Windows Server 2003 is meant to be a *server*, not a workstation supporting the needs of one person.

NOTE *You could edit the Performance settings in the System applet of the Control Panel, but I'm talking about the way the operating systems were set to run under normal conditions.*

Ah, but what about Terminal Services? It's a server, but a server of a very special kind, since it's providing computing resources to a bunch of client machines. For that reason, Terminal Services should give more time to foreground applications than to background applications and services, as the foreground applications are the most important to the overall performance of the server. If Terminal Services is running and you've set up the application server role, then the operating system is optimized for running foreground applications. (You've got another option of installing Terminal Services only for remote administration of the server, in which case the server is optimized for fulfilling server functions.)

Under rare circumstances, however, you may want to give equal time to all running applications even when the server is supporting user applications. To do so while still running Terminal Services in Application Server mode, open the System applet in the Control Panel. Turn to the Advanced tab, click the Settings button in the Performance area, and turn to the Advanced tab to open the dialog box you see in Figure 18.26.

In the Application Response section, make sure the Background option is selected. This tells the server to give all running applications equal access to processor cycles. This may make your foreground applications a little more jerky, but other applications will respond to user requests more smoothly.

WARNING *Generally speaking, you should* not *edit the Application Response options setting; this is for the exceptional case. When you use Terminal Services in Remote Administration mode, processor time will remain equally distributed among running applications, so you won't need to edit this setting then.*

FIGURE 18.26

Edit performance
options.

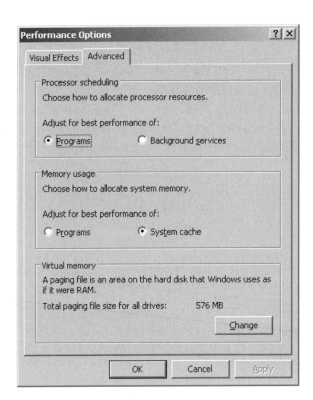

Editing Virtual Memory Settings

While you're in the Performance dialog box of the System applet, click the Change button in the Virtual Memory section to take a look at the paging file settings (see Figure 18.27).

The default location for the paging file is on the root of the same logical drive where you installed Server 2003. This isn't always the best place for it, however. Generally speaking, your server will be happier if its paging file is on a separate disk from the operating system files. Paging files are good candidates for disk fragmentation, and a fragmented disk is not a fast disk—not good when you're trying to use an operating system from that disk.

To move the paging file from its original location, open the dialog box shown in Figure 18.26 and select the local drive where you want the paging file to go. Type in a minimum and maximum size for the paging file in the boxes provided. Also, select the drive where the paging file *was* and zero it out. For what should be obvious reasons, you can't put the paging file on a network-accessible drive. And although removable drives will show up in the list of local drives that you could put a paging file on, they're displayed with a free space of 0MB, so you can't put the drives there.

TIP   *Try to make sure that the paging file is as large as it needs to be from the beginning. Although it will get bigger as needed, the process of making the file get bigger is resource-intensive. You'll get better performance if you make the minimum size of the paging file something resembling its necessary size.*

FIGURE 18.27

Virtual memory settings for Server 2003

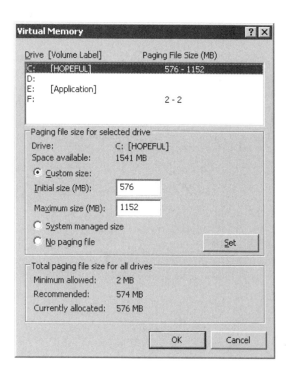

When you finish, the size of the new paging file should be shown in the Paging File Size column next to the right drive, and that space in the original drive should be blank. Click the Set button to establish the paging file. You'll need to restart the server, but once you do, the paging file will be moved to the new location.

What if you zero out the original page file but forget to specify the location of a new one? You'll be prompted to reboot the computer as usual for changing the size of the paging file. However, when you reboot, the server will be extremely unresponsive. You must follow the instructions here (and also provided on the nastygram) for creating a new paging file on the appropriate disk. Your server will work until you do this, but it will start with no virtual memory. The new paging file will grow slowly as needed, probably causing you to run low on virtual memory from time to time, and using a ton of processor cycles to grow the paging file. In other words, don't delete the paging file without creating a new one unless you want to see how the server will operate in low-memory conditions.

Turning Off Silly Visual Effects

Okay, maybe this is just me being a Luddite, but in my view a server needs to be *fast*, not spending cycles on fancy visual effects when opening and closing windows. (Fancy visual effects will also impact performance in remote administration sessions.) Therefore, I keep visual effects to an absolute minimum—even easier, now that Server 2003's picked up better command-line support. By default, Server 2003 is actually pretty smart about visual effects. If you stick with the defaults, it only uses one effect. In case someone turns on more bells and whistles, you can turn this off from the Visual Effects tab, which is available on the same Advanced tab that let you reach Application Response. In the dialog box shown in Figure 18.28, make sure that the server is tuned for Adjust for Best Performance and keep those boxes unchecked.

FIGURE 18.28

Keep visual effects to a minimum on servers.

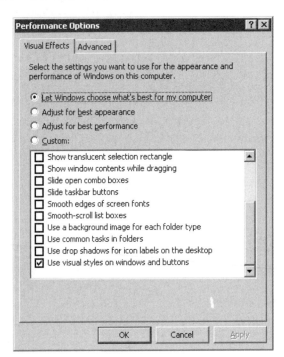

Tuning the System Cache

Server 2003's default memory settings reflect NT's legacy as a file-sharing NOS. By default, it's set up with a large *system cache*, which is a range of virtual memory addresses reserved for holding recently used data related to file sharing, whether from hard disks, CD-ROMs, or network-accessible drives. The cache includes any data related to file reads and writes, including file contents, read and write activity to a file, or the metadata that describes a drive's structure and organization. The system cache has a range of virtual memory addresses dedicated to it, with the exact size of the range depending on the amount of physical memory installed in the server. Just as the size of the paging file increases as you install more physical memory, the system cache does, too.

NOTE   You can see how much physical memory your server's system cache is using by monitoring the value of Memory: System Cache Resident Bytes. Although the System Monitor has a counter called Memory: Cache Bytes, this counter doesn't actually reflect just the System Cache working set. It reflects the entire system working set, including paged pool and any driver code and kernel data that can be paged to disk. System Cache memory usage is also visible from the Performance tab of the Task Manager.

If a server's supporting file sharing, then it needs this big reserved virtual memory space. However, cacheing all that data may cause a lot of disk thrashing as the data goes in and out of physical memory.

If a particular server isn't doing file sharing, you can save yourself some physical memory by changing the memory usage parameters for network use. To do so, open Network Connections from the Control Panel. Right-click Local Area Connection and open its property sheet. Select File and Printer Sharing for Microsoft Networks, and open that service's property sheet as shown in Figure 18.29.

FIGURE 18.29

Server Optimization options

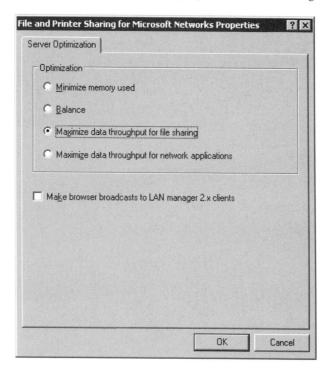

The default setting is Maximize Data Throughput for File Sharing. If you're not using the server to share files, change this setting to Maximize Data Throughput for Network Applications, or to Balance. (The Minimize Memory Used setting is only a good idea for servers serving a very few users, like fewer than 10.) This should reduce the amount of paging to disk that your server's doing.

Chapter 19

Preparing for and Recovering from Server Failures

COINCIDENCE, GREMLINS, OR INCENTIVE from The Powers That Be to do my homework?

The day I planned to start working on this chapter, one server on my network stopped booting. I'd been out of town for a few days and so I'd shut all the computers on the network down (power in Virginia is notoriously chancy during the summer months). Came back, booted up the server, and it worked fine. Added support for an additional transport protocol, and rebooted as required. This time, the system couldn't find a bootable device.

Uh-oh.

Why did this happen? Dead hard disk? Something disconnected? NetBEUI ate my hard disk when I installed it? (Geez—when Microsoft makes TCP/IP the default transport protocol, they're not kidding around, are they?) The initial question, however, wasn't "What happened?" but "How badly is this going to screw me up?" Regardless of the reason *why* the machine didn't boot, the fact remains that it didn't. Had this been a production server instead of a test machine, I would have been in a world of hurt. Or could have been, if I hadn't been prepared for this kind of eventuality.

There's nothing quite like that sinking feeling when a server dies. You can't always prevent this from happening; sometimes, you're just stuck with the whims of the malignant forces in the universe. What you *can* do is either fix the problem or recover from it. That—and how to prevent problems when you can—is what I'll talk about in the course of this chapter. In this chapter, I'll cover the following:

- The importance of redundancy in a fault-resistant server and network
- Some basics of preventing preventable disasters
- How to use the Windows Backup tools to create manual and automatic backups
- How to use the System Information tool to isolate hardware problems
- What's going on when your computer boots
- The use of the recovery tools found in Server 2003
- Disaster recovery tips

Let's start with some ways to avoid some disasters in the first place.

Preventing Stupid Accidents

Deliberate external attacks on your network are frustrating, but at least they allow you to get mad at someone else. It's the *preventable* infiltrations or server crashes that lead to the most gray hair. To keep your servers running and secure, you need to do the following:

◆ Keep multiple copies of important data and important server roles such as domain controllers.

◆ Physically secure your network. If the bad guys (and the careless good guys) or Mother Nature can't get to your network hardware, it's a lot harder for them to damage it. The degree to which you can physically secure your network varies—not all of us have the option of running our fiber cable through concrete pipe—but you can, at least, keep the servers behind a locked door.

◆ Protect your network's user and system data with a good backup strategy.

◆ Prepare for the worst with a point-by-point disaster recovery plan that anyone in your organization can follow. Don't depend on one person knowing how to return the network to working order—that one person may be unavailable when the time comes to restore the network.

◆ Understand how your server works so you can troubleshoot problems and perhaps prevent more problems in the future.

◆ Install the service packs and patches that Microsoft issues. I know this may shock you, but Windows products have flaws. (Other operating systems also have flaws, but we're talking about Windows here.) Microsoft issues patches for these flaws, but if you never install these patches, they're useless.

When something goes wrong with your system, think *noninvasive*. Step 1 is *not* popping the top on the server. Three of your most valuable troubleshooting implements are the OS installation CD, data and system state backups, and your notebook, in which you record every change you make to the network and record resolutions to problems. (The brain is Tool 3A. Sometimes it shuts off in times of stress, so you rely on the notebook.) When the time comes for troubleshooting, that notebook will be an invaluable diagnostic tool and a cheat sheet for "I know I've seen this before. How did I fix it last time?"

A basic concern in any computer security system is the need for physical security, a blanket term for the many ways in which you can protect your server and network from physical harm: stupid accidents, environmental—er—"incidents," and theft. Entire books have been devoted to the question of how to physically secure a network, so I'm not going to cover everything here. What follows is an outline of the kinds of protection you should be looking for, both physical and logical.

NOTE *Protecting your network is a never-ending process; every safeguard has a counter. You can't protect yourself from every possible disaster, so you have to come up with a balance between how much it would cost you to recover from a disaster, how likely it is that you'll be hit by that particular disaster, and how much the protection costs. If protecting your data costs more than the data is worth, then it's time to relax a little.*

Redundancy: The First Line of Defense

This is a theme that has come up several times in the course of this book, but it's worth repeating here: a redundant server—or network—is a fault-resistant server or network. You can be redundant at several layers.

On the server, protect important data with fault-tolerant volumes, whether with software, as discussed in Chapter 10, or in hardware. The pros and cons of the various RAID types supported in Server 2003 are also discussed in Chapter 10. As you'll see there, RAID 5 gives you the most protected storage space for the number of disks involved, but mirroring is less processor-intensive than the RAID 5 protection supported in software. Do *not* put important data on any multidisk volume that is not fault tolerant unless you are backing it up early and often. Although multivolume disks can improve performance and make a larger single volume, if one disk in the volume dies, the entire volume is inaccessible. Since having more disks increases the chance that any one disk will die at any given time, multidisk volumes are more vulnerable to disk failure than single-disk volumes. To protect data from complete server failures, not just disk failures, you can choose to replicate it across the network.

The same principle of redundancy applies to the network. As you'll see in this chapter, having multiple domain controllers can simplify your restore process if you lose a DC. Rather than having to restore the domain structure from backups or completely rebuild it, you can let the usual replication take care of the restoration for you. Of course, if you're restoring a more recent version of the directory structure, you can choose to propagate those changes to the other domain controllers, but the bottom line is that having more than one domain controller allows you to keep the domain working while getting a failed domain controller back on line. The same principle applies to WINS servers (for name resolution) and DHCP servers. You don't want two DHCP servers actually dispensing IP addresses, but you do want a backup of the scope. See Chapter 7 for more about WINS and DHCP.

Finally, if you're using Windows Server 2003, Enterprise Edition (or a third-party clustering solution) you can use clustering to keep vital servers from going down. There are two main types of clustering. Load-balancing clustering distributes requests among clustered servers to keep the—well, to keep the server load balanced so one server isn't hammered while another one is standing idle. Fault-tolerant clustering can actually transfer connections from a failed server to one that's standing ready for new connections.

Power-Protect Servers

Always use a UPS to power-protect servers and network hardware such as hubs and routers. This will protect the backbone of your network from power surges and dirty power. Power protection also will help prevent data loss and will let you shut down the servers in an orderly fashion (or shut down the servers automatically). Personally, I've had very good luck with APC's UPSes (strictly speaking, SPSes) for workstations and test servers, but the Web server that *cannot* go down is protected with a true UPS (a Powerware Prestige XT, if you're interested). For those who don't know, a switched power supply has a very short (under 4ms) break when switching from line power to battery power—not enough to be noticeable for most computers. An uninterrupted power supply cycles all power through the battery even if line power is available, so if the line power fails there is no switching time. Most devices you see sold as UPSes are SPSes.

WARNING *Don't ground only the server room, ground the entire office. Grounding only the server room is equivalent to putting a giant "KICK ME" sign on your servers, as they'll be the easiest path to ground.*

What about client-side power protection? At one time, UPSes were so expensive that it wasn't cost-effective to protect each client station. These days, you can get a low-end UPS for less than

$100, so think about the investment to give user machines power protection and a little bit of time to save documents and shut down. Power strips with surge protectors don't do the trick. Because of their high tolerance for voltage—they'll pass jolts that will damage a PC—power strips are a convenient way of plugging several devices into one outlet, but not a power-protection mechanism.

TIP *Don't plug a printer into a UPS designed for a computer only. First, it won't hurt the printer to lose power suddenly and if the power goes out, printing documents is probably not a vital concern. Second, laser printers draw far more power than a PC and will drain the battery life too quickly. Do plug a monitor into the UPS. Although the monitor draws power, you'll need it to shut down the computer gracefully.*

Speaking of client power protection, one advantage to running Terminal Services instead of a traditional desktop environment is that you don't have to worry about power-protecting a Windows terminal—at least not for reasons of protecting data. If a Terminal Services client computer loses power, the client's session is disconnected, not terminated. That is, all client applications and data remain active and in memory on the terminal server so long as the server is running. When you power the client back up and reconnect the session, it will be exactly as it was when it was disconnected. In other words, a power outage on the client will cause no data loss as long as the terminal server is protected. For more information about Terminal Services in Server 2003, turn to Chapter 16.

For extreme quick-and-dirty power protection for network client machines, tie five knots in each computer's power cord, as close to the wall as you can. If lightning strikes the wiring, the concentration of current within the loop of the knot will kill the cord and thus break the lightning's path to the client machine. I know that this one is hard to believe, but it really works. As Mark tells it:

> *During the summer of 1990, a massive electrical storm hit Washington, D.C. (where Mark lived at the time). I had tied knots in the cords of all of the computers in the house beforehand but hadn't thought to do this to the television. During the storm, one of my neighbor's houses took a direct lightning hit and a huge power surge hit my house's wiring. The cords of all the computers were warmed up a bit, but the power surge never touched the computers themselves. The television was another matter. The surge traveled straight through the cord to the TV's innards and rendered the television DOA. I couldn't have asked for a better test, although at the time I wasn't in a mood to appreciate the benefits of having had a control group.*

Environmental Concerns

Reduce the likelihood of Bad Things happening to your servers by keeping them away from potential problems. Look for evidence of old leaks in the ceiling, and keep equipment away from them—an old leak could become a present leak. Make sure that the server room is climate-controlled. The air conditioning used for the rest of the office might not be sufficient in an enclosed room, given all the heat that computers emit. And don't position *any* computer in direct sunlight.

Finally, avoid introducing new contaminants around the servers. Although it may be impossible to keep people from eating or drinking near their workstations, you can—and should—keep food out of the server room. If your office permits smoking, don't smoke or let other people smoke around the servers or workstations. Smoke particles inside a hard disk can chew up its surface.

Limit Access to Servers

Most people using the network don't have a valid reason to do anything to a server (except a terminal server, of course, and then they're only using it remotely). One way to keep people away from your servers is to lock said servers in a separate room to which only trusted people have access—and you can make that even more secure by using a card-key system that records the identities and in-and-out times of the people entering the locked room, if necessary. If people can't get near the servers, they can't:

♦ Reboot or shut down the server manually.

♦ Steal data-containing hard disks from the server.

♦ Reinstall the OS and thus have the chance to create a new Administrator account with full access to the server.

User permissions that prevent a person from shutting down a server from the console don't prevent that same person from shutting down a server with the Big Switch. Therefore, if locking up the servers isn't an option, you can physically disable the Reset button and/or the A: drive so that people can't just shut down the server unless they have permissions to do so.

NOTE *An OS-dependent protection utility such as* `floplock` *(in the NT 4 Resource Kit) doesn't prevent people from using the floppy drives from another operating system or from booting from a floppy, because the OS isn't yet loaded when you're booting. If you want to disable the floppy drives for all operating systems, edit the BIOS to remove support for floppy drives (this setting is typically in the Standard BIOS setup) and password-protect the machine for booting. Alternatively, use a keyboard-video-mouse switch with long cables so you can keep the monitor isolated from the server to which you're providing access.*

Use Passwords Effectively

Server 2003's security is built on user authentication. When you log in to a domain, your username and password are compared with the information stored in the Active Directory on the domain controller. Once you're authenticated on the network, you're assigned a security token that contains a list of your rights and permissions based on your user identity and group membership. Whenever you try to do something—read a file, install an application, whatever—the security manager compares your rights and permissions with what you want to do, and permits or denies access based on the results of that comparison.

The only thing that keeps people from impersonating each other, therefore, is the password on their accounts. Once someone has an account's password, they can use that account and all the rights and permissions associated with it. Passwords are the biggest port of entry into your network.

WHY PASSWORDS ARE VULNERABLE

Previous editions of this book included some tips on creating hard-to-crack passwords. The widespread availability of password-cracking programs such as L0phtCrack (now more innocuously known as LC3) renders most of these tips semi-obsolete for stopping anyone who *really* wants to break in and who can get physical access to the server because they give anyone with access to the network an extremely powerful tool for cracking passwords. LC3, for example, can retrieve password hashes from the Registry or even from the network. Once the tool has the password file, it extracts the password hashes (encrypted passwords) and performs a series of three attacks to decrypt the hash:

Dictionary attack In a dictionary attack, LC3 tests all the words in a dictionary or word file (the tool itself comes with an optional word file) until it finds a match.

Hybrid attack   If the dictionary attack doesn't produce results, the next step is to see whether the user took a known word and added numbers or other characters to it, so as to foil a dictionary attack.

Brute force attack   The final stage is a brute force attack, in which the password hash is compared against every key combination possible. Brute force attacks take much longer (sometimes days—depends on how fast the computer doing the cracking is) than either of the other two attacks, but they can eventually crack just about any password using characters found only on a standard keyboard.

Just about any password is vulnerable to a brute force attack if given enough time. "Enough time" may mean a couple of days even on a fast computer, but if the cracker has the password hashes, then the delay won't stop the cracker unless people change their passwords during the cracking process.

NOTE   The longer and more complicated a password is, the longer it will take to crack it—and the more likely that your user base will write down passwords. You'll need to balance the need for complex passwords with the reality that if you make them too complex they'll be unusable or compromised by people writing them down.

All that said, passwords are far from useless. You'll notice that using a tool such as LC3 requires physical access to the server or to the network. The answer? *Keep untrusted people off the network.* Protect the Administrators account, only giving Administrator rights to the most trusted people. If your network is connected to the Internet, close TCP/IP ports that you don't need, and audit failed attempts to connect to the gateway from the Internet. For the people on the inside who *do* have access to the network, institute a zero-tolerance policy for password-cracking tools for anyone without a really good reason to have them, and don't set up e-mail to execute attachments automatically, since some malicious software will execute not only with the permissions of the person currently logged in (as software normally does) but can give itself *elevated privileges*, allowing the software to execute as though a member of Administrators or Domain Administrators was logged in—and thus wreak all kinds of havoc.

NOTE   Although servers would seem to be safe from an elevated privileges attack (since users are not likely to be logged in at the console, and administrators won't pick up their e-mail there), terminal servers, in particular, are vulnerable to them because ordinary users do effectively log on locally.

KEEPING OUT THE IDLE CURIOUS

Your network's security is threatened not only by the actively malicious, but also by the idle curious. Password-choosing schemes are best for keeping out those people who aren't interested enough to get serious about breaking into someone's account, but will go poking through Joe Blow's files in his private home directory if Joe makes it easy for them. To keep these people out of other people's accounts, follow the guidelines for choosing passwords below. They won't foil LC3, but they'll foil someone guessing passwords.

Impose Password Policies   Passwords must be of a minimum length, changed regularly (but not too regularly, to avoid people reusing passwords too often), and shouldn't be reused often. Set policies to require passwords to include numerals and other nonletter characters, and take advantage of the fact that passwords are CasEs3nSitiVe (hint, hint).

Don't Let People Use Easy-to-Guess Passwords   No personal names, spouse's names, dog's names, or other easy associations. Ideally, passwords should not reflect that person's job, either. A few years ago, a friend of mine doing network security for one department of the Pentagon told me that he'd had to institute this rule after discovering that the analysts in his division had all chosen passwords based on the names of battleships—words directly related to their division's mission.

Don't Write Down Passwords   The most difficult password in the world will do no good if it's on a sticky note on the base of the monitor or under the keyboard. This is the dilemma inherent to all password protection. If you make passwords easy to remember, they're often easy to guess. Make them too hard to remember or require too many of them, and users will start writing them down.

Delete or Disable Unused Accounts   An unused account is an account that isn't getting its password changed regularly and doesn't have someone using it who might notice something strange going on. If you'll need an account later, but not now, disable it so as to retain its security ID while making it impossible to use at the moment. If you'll never need an account again (perhaps for someone who has left the company), delete it.

NOTE   *If you delete an account and then re-create it, the account will have a new security ID even if it has the same username and password as the original account. You'll have to re-create all user rights and permissions from scratch.*

If passwords don't supply enough security, you can replace or supplement them with other means of validation. Biometric devices can scan retinas or (less intrusively) fingerprints and provide a second layer of security that confirms the person supplying the password is the person authorized to do so. Another alternative is the token-generating tools that create a token (with a smart card or similar device) to be supplied along with the password; the password won't work unless it's the proper token. In short, passwords are a good start, but you needn't rely solely on them.

Backup Programs and Approaches

Security from intrusion is important, but so is security from data loss. Backups are your first line of defense against server failures and your last recourse when all else fails. When it comes right down to it, the data on your servers is the important part. The box is replaceable, and you can reinstall the operating system if you need to. What you can't replace is the data on the drive. And if you lose that data and can't get it back, your company's life is probably over.

To help you protect your company's most important asset, Server 2003 comes with a version of Windows Backup, complete with support for a wider array of backup destinations and an integrated scheduler.

Using this backup program, you can back up either to files or to tapes or create files for system recovery.

Basic Data Backups

Backup is in the System Tools section of the `Accessories` folder. Open the Backup application, and you'll begin the Backup or Restore Wizard. Let's start with a backup.

After the opening screen, you'll see the screen shown in Figure 19.1, asking you whether you'd like to back up or restore files. Choose to back up.

FIGURE 19.1

The simple wizard can accommodate either backups or restorations.

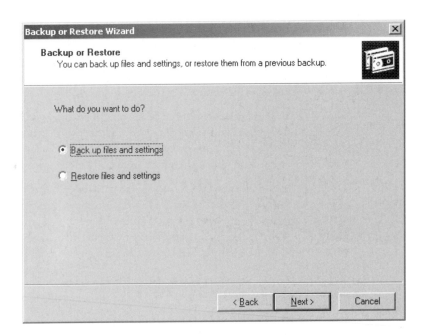

Next, you'll need to choose the range of data to back up. As you can see in Figure 19.2, in Server 2003, you've got two options—to back up everything and make a system recovery disk, or choose the individual files you want to back up. (Domain controllers will have a third option—backing up only the System State data.) For now, pick the option that allows you to choose the files.

FIGURE 19.2

Backing up selected files

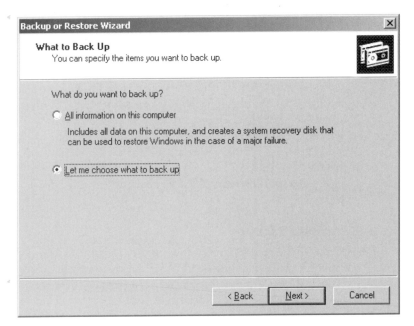

In the next window, you can drill down to find the files and folders you want to back up, whether on the local computer, the network, or even in trusted domains (see Figure 19.3). This is a list of the assigned drive letters of all partitions. The drives listed are *logical* drives, not physical drives. You can sort the available drives by clicking the headings of the Name, Total Size, or Free Space. This list includes all drives on the server, not just fixed or local drives.

FIGURE 19.3

Backing up the contents of the Win2K folder

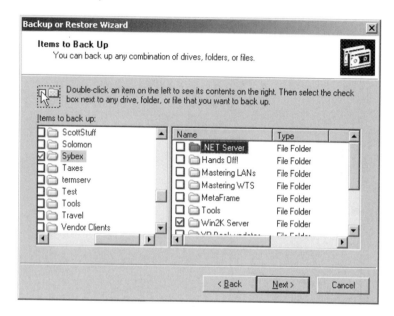

You may have to do a little exploring to find the files you want to back up. Perhaps you *think* that the Applications drive (drive D:) is the one with the data you want to protect, but you're not sure. You can find out for sure by double-clicking the drive to see its folders. If you want to, you can drill down yet further within those folders to expose the subfolders, all the way down to file level. When you find the appropriate folder, you can deselect any object within this folder and prevent it from being backed up. If you do so, the check mark in the folder's box will be gray, instead of the blue that indicates all its contents are selected. Similarly, the box next to the logical drive that a selected folder is stored on will have a gray check mark indicating that part of its contents are selected for backup, but not all.

You can choose as many different files and folders on as many different drives as you like to be part of a backup set. They don't have to be juxtaposed or arranged in any kind of logical form, but they will retain their location on the final backup media. You can't, however, choose to back up all files of a certain type, regardless of location. Backup is organized by location, not by file type. You can't check boxes next to any structures except files or folders—this keeps you from accidentally choosing to back up all the shared files in a domain, for example.

TIP   If you're backing up network drives or backing up to a network location, make sure this network location is available at the time you run the backup. This is really an issue with scheduled backups, but it can be a frustrating one if it catches you off guard.

Next, choose a location for the backup using the dialog box in Figure 19.4. If you've got a tape drive, you'll be able to back up to tape; otherwise, you'll need to choose a location for the backup file (.BKF).

By default, the backup file is named `Backup.bkf` and stored in `My Documents` for whomever is logged in and performing the backup, but you can click the Browse button to choose an alternative backup location. The first time you run Backup, you *will* need to choose a backup location.

FIGURE 19.4

Choosing a backup location

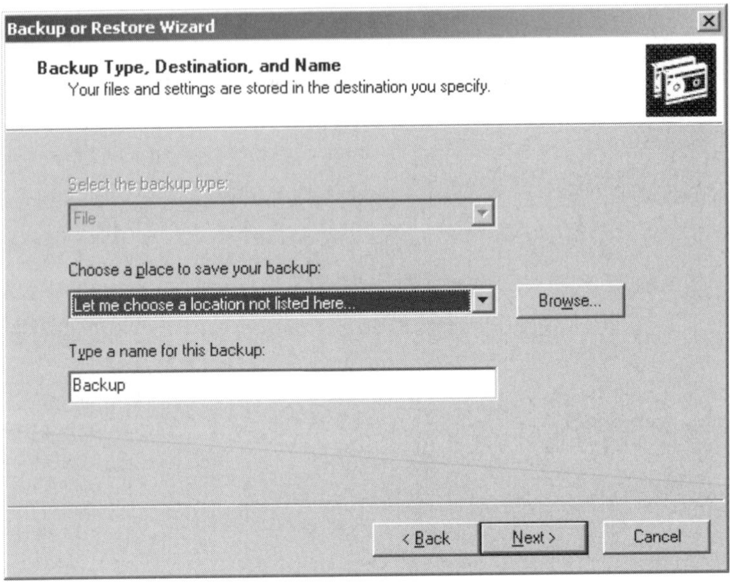

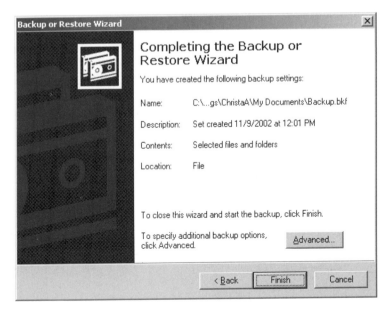

Once you've told Windows Backup where to put the backup file, click Next to display the final screen that displays your backup options (see Figure 19.5). If you click the Finish button, you'll start the backup.

FIGURE 19.5

The final screen of the wizard displays the current backup settings.

That's a basic backup, using all the default options. If you want a little more control over how the backup is performed (that is, the options for How and When), click the Advanced button before clicking Finish to start the second part of the wizard and decide on the options listed in Table 19.1.

TABLE 19.1: ADVANCED BACKUP OPTIONS

OPTION	DEFAULT SETTING	WHAT IT MEANS
What type of backup should be performed?	Normal	You can choose from normal, copy, incremental, differential, or daily backups. These backup types are described later, under "Choosing a Backup Type."
Verify data?	No	Verifying a backup compares the data on the backup media with the source media to make sure that the data was copied correctly. Verifying a backup takes some additional time, but I'd do it anyway—it's a good way of getting a record that the data was written as expected.
Use hardware compression?	No	This option is only available if you're backing up to tape. If you choose it, then the tape will have a higher capacity than it would have had otherwise.
Append or replace existing backup sets?	Append	If the backup media already contains a backup, you have the option of either replacing that backup or adding the present backup to the catalog. The option you choose depends on which is more important to you: keeping the backup media uncluttered so you can easily find the backup set for restoration or maintaining multiple backup sets. I'd suggest replacing full backups (although you should always archive at least one full backup in case something happens to the current one) and appending incremental and differential backups.
Restrict access?	No	If you've chosen to replace any backup sets already on the media, you can choose whether to restrict access to those sets to members of the Administrators group and the person creating the backups.
What is the name of the backup and the media?	Time and date backup was created	Provide a name for the backup set. If you're using new media, or replacing the data on existing media, you can choose a new name for the tape or file.
When should the backup run?	Now	You can choose to run the backup now or pick a time at which it should run. If you're backing up a server, then you'll almost certainly want to schedule it for later, when people aren't using the data.
Back up migrated remote storage data?	No	This option backs up rarely used files that have been automatically archived in remote storage.
Disable volume shadow copy?	No	Volume shadow copying allows files to be backed up while in use.

The only Advanced backup option that might cause you any trouble is the scheduling tool, which I'll cover later in the section "Scheduling Automated Backups." When you've finished choosing options, you'll see the Finish screen again, showing the updated options.

Advanced Backup Options

Let's look at these advanced backup options in some more detail. Open the Backup tool in Advanced mode (this will make it look like the Backup tool in Windows 2000) and choose Tools/Options to open the tabbed Options dialog box.

NOTE   Settings you choose from this tabbed dialog box will apply to all backups. To set advanced options on for individual backups, click the Advanced button on the last page of the Backup or Restore Wizard.

CHOOSING A BACKUP TYPE

The default backup type for Windows Backup is Normal, which is a not-very-descriptive way of saying that Windows Backup performs full backups (copies all files and resets the archive bit on all copied files) unless told otherwise. If you turn to the Backup Type tab shown in Figure 19.6, you can choose one of the options described in Table 19.2.

FIGURE 19.6

Choose a new backup type if you don't want to perform full backups.

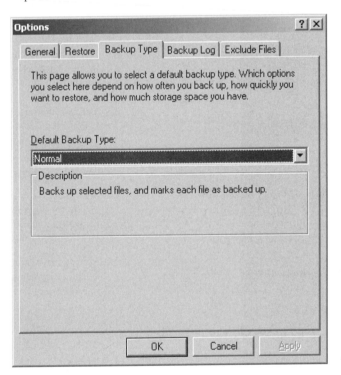

NOTE   The archive bit is a hidden file attribute applied to a file when it's created or edited. It's used to tell a backup or copy utility, "Hey, this file has changed." Resetting the archive bit removes the archive bit from a file; setting the bit adds it.

TABLE 19.2: SUPPORTED BACKUP TYPES

BACKUP TYPE	DESCRIPTION
Normal	Copies all selected files and then resets the archive bit
Incremental	Copies all selected files with the archive bit set and resets the bit
Differential	Copies all selected files with the archive bit set but does not reset the bit
Daily	Copies all selected files that were edited the day the backup was performed
Copy	Copies all selected files but does not reset the archive bit

You can use these backup types in combination to back up files completely and efficiently. The longest interval you'll want to have between backups is probably a day—lose more than a day's worth of work, and you're in big trouble. (Losing a day's worth of work is bad enough, which is why companies with really critical data use RAID to protect their data, as discussed in Chapter 10.) Running a normal backup every day takes up a lot of time and space, so you can run a normal backup at regular intervals, perhaps once a week, but supplement this weekly full backup with a daily differential or incremental backup. Running a daily differential backup gives you a daily copy of all the files that have changed since the last full backup; incremental backups copy all the files that have their archive bit set. Either differential or incremental backups work well as a supplement to a regular normal backup. I find differential backups easier to perform and restore because restoring a server becomes a matter of restoring the most recent normal backup and the last differential one. Restoring incremental backups is a slower process, as you must restore each incremental backup made since the last full backup individually. However, incremental backups take less time to perform than differential backups.

Daily backups aren't really a method of preserving data, but more a way of quickly finding files that you're currently using and transferring them to other media. You might find it useful to run a daily backup on a user's files to copy the ones he needs to a laptop for a business trip, if the client isn't using Win2K Pro or Windows XP (or they're using a common computer) and so doesn't have the option of using Offline Files. *Copying* files is only useful if you want to make a complete copy of all selected files without resetting the archive bit. A copy action like that is a way of copying files to a new location.

CHOOSING A LOGGING TYPE

Backup logs are a useful troubleshooting tool. If something goes wrong with the backup, then you can inspect a text-based log to see *what* went wrong. In fact, it's a good idea to at least scan the backup logs produced after each backup to make sure that the procedure went as expected.

How much information do you log? Normally, Backup logs only errors and important events, but if you turn to the Backup Log tab of the Options dialog box (see Figure 19.7), you can choose not to log (bad idea, as that disables a troubleshooting tool) or to log *everything* (also a bad idea for anything other than a daily or perhaps incremental backup, as it will make your logs so big that it will be hard to find errors). Unless you need a complete record for some reason, the summary log option (the default) is probably your best bet.

FIGURE 19.7

Choose a logging option.

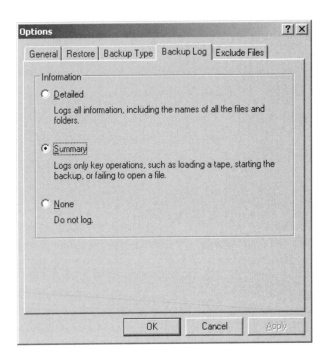

WHICH FILES DO YOU WANT TO BACK UP?

Even if you're running a full backup, you don't necessarily want to save *everything*. For example, do you really need to preserve the contents of the paging file? Probably not. For this reason, Windows Backup does not normally back up any files that don't contain real data—a user cache, a page file, temporary Internet files for the person running the backup, and the like. You can edit this list from the Exclude Files tab of the Options dialog box (see Figure 19.8).

The Add New and Remove buttons on this tab are pretty self-explanatory. Unless you have real reason to remove one of the already excluded files from the list, I suggest that you leave them alone, as the files listed are not really anything you need to back up.

To add files to exclude from the backup, click the upper Add New button to display the dialog box shown in Figure 19.9. The list in the upper half of the dialog box contains all the file types recognized by the server. You have to know the extension for the type of file you want to exclude from the backup, but many of the extensions are labeled so you can be sure that you've got the right one. (If an extension isn't labeled and you don't recognize it as an application file extension, files of that type are probably part of the operating system and can be reinstalled. Just be sure to check before you exclude the files from the backup.) In the Registered File Type list, click the file type that you don't want to back up, Ctrl+clicking to select more than one option at a time. When you click OK, you'll see your selection(s) added to the list of excluded file types. For example, if you don't want to back up any application files (on the principle that you can reinstall the applications if necessary), then you'd find .exe in the list, highlight it, and click OK.

The Custom File Mask text box is for extensions that aren't registered file types (ones you've created yourself for certain files) or for filtering files by name. The syntax for this file mask depends on whether you're filtering by filename or extension. If you want to eliminate all files *named* abc.* from the backup, then type **abc** in the box—no asterisks necessary. To eliminate all files with the *extension* .abc, then type **.abc** (note the period) in the box.

FIGURE 19.8

Change the files to exclude, or edit the settings for excluded files.

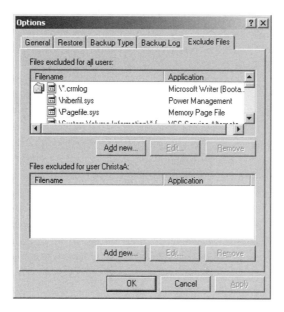

FIGURE 19.9

Choose from registered file types, or type in custom extensions.

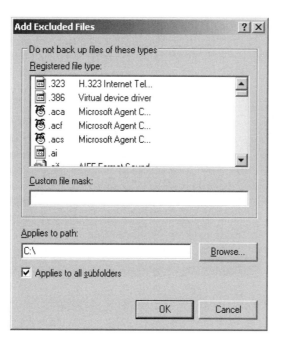

NOTE *You must enter each custom file mask separately. If you enter two at once—say, for* `.abc` *files and* `.def` *files—then you're telling Backup to skip all files with the extension* `.abc.def`. *Using semicolons or other punctuation to separate the entries doesn't work.*

By default, your file mask will apply to the entire C: drive. To edit this to apply to a different drive or only a specific folder, type in a new path or click the Browse button to open a file tree (see Figure 19.10) from which you can choose the path you want the mask to apply to. You can choose drives either on the local machine or on network-accessible drives.

FIGURE 19.10

Browse for the path to apply a file mask to.

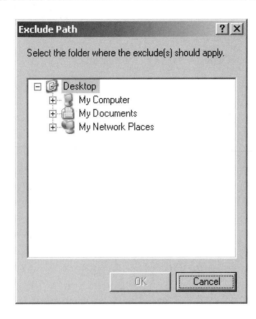

When you click OK to exit the Add Excluded Files dialog box, the path information will be listed with the file types to be excluded on the Exclude Files tab.

The file types you've excluded will apply to all users. If you'd like to exclude file types only for the person currently logged in (there's no way to specify another user or a group), then click the Add New button for the *bottom* window of the Exclude Files tab. You'll enter the same Add Excluded Files box that you saw previously, and it works the same way. The only difference is that the files you exclude will only apply to the ones you own. For example, if I chose to exclude `.doc` files for myself, then everyone else's `.doc` files would be backed up, but mine (the ones I created and own) would not.

TIP *The per-user masking depends on current file ownership, so if a file was created by Joe but Jane took ownership of it, the file would still be backed up if Joe added it to his personal file mask, but not if Jane did. It doesn't matter whether Joe, Jane, or Fred is running the backup: So long as Jane owns that file, then it's excluded from the backup.*

Notice that the exclude tool really only excludes files—you can't use it to include only files with certain extensions in the backup. Sadly, there doesn't seem to be any way to specify that only certain files should be backed up. Even the command-line utility NTBACKUP (which I'll discuss a little later in the "Scheduling Automated Backups" section) doesn't accept wildcards.

GENERAL BACKUP OPTIONS

The General tab of the Options dialog box contains the options explained in Table 19.3. These options control the settings that really don't fit anywhere else in the categories of options.

TABLE 19.3: GENERAL OPTIONS FOR BACKUP AND RESTORE OPERATIONS

OPTION	DEFAULT SETTING	WHAT IT MEANS
Compute selection information before backup and restore operations.	Enabled	This is a confusingly worded way of saying that Backup will count the files and folders to be backed up or restored before actually performing the operation. I'd leave this enabled; it doesn't add much to the time required to run the operation, and this information can save you from backing up or restoring the wrong volume or backing up to media that's too small.
Use the catalogs on the media to speed up building restore catalogs on disk.	Enabled	This is the fastest way for Windows Backup to create a list of all the files and folders in the backup. You should only disable this option if you're restoring data from several tapes and don't have the one with the catalog (the first tape) or if the catalog is damaged. With this option disabled, Windows Backup will scan the entire backup set and attempt to build its own catalog. Since reading tapes is a slow process, this could take a long time for a large backup set—perhaps hours.
Verify data after the backup completes.	Disabled	This compares the data on the disk with the data on the backup media after the backup has been completed and records any differences. Although verifying adds some time to a backup, I'd recommend doing it. It's a good way to be sure that files were written correctly.
Back up the contents of mounted drives.	Enabled	Normally, mounted drives (logical drives mapped to a path on another logical drive—read Chapter 10 to learn more about them) can be backed up like other media. If you check this box, the data won't be backed up—just the path information.
Show alert message when I start Backup and Removable Storage Management is not running.	Enabled	If the Removable Storage Management (RSM) service isn't running, you can start it from the Services object in the System Tools folder of Local Computer Management. This service must be running for you to back up files onto RSM media such as tape drives.
Show alert message when I start Backup and there is compatible Import Media available.	Enabled	If this box is checked and you add new RSM storage media, Backup will display a message on startup saying that it's found more media for the Import pool (to which files can be archived).

Continued on next page

TABLE 19.3: GENERAL OPTIONS FOR BACKUP AND RESTORE OPERATIONS *(continued)*

OPTION	DEFAULT SETTING	WHAT IT MEANS
Show alert message when new media is inserted into Removable Storage.	Enabled	If this box is checked, Backup will display a dialog box when it detects new RSM media.
Always move new import media to the Backup media pool.	Disabled	If this box is checked, Backup will assume that any new media it detects should be added to the Backup media pool, and thus be available for backups.

NOTE *Removable Storage Management is used with tape drives and other archiving media. If you normally back up to a file on any kind of disk (including a removable disk like a Jaz drive) instead of tape, you don't have to worry about the Removable Storage Management settings.*

SAVING BACKUP OPTIONS

You can define settings for a backup job and save them to be used later or reused at your discretion. To do so, make sure that you've chosen the files to back up. Then, in the Advanced view of the Backup utility, choose Job/Save Selections. You'll see a Save Selections dialog box prompting you to save the backup script (normally saved in `%systemroot%\Documents and Settings\%username%\Local Settings\Application Data\Microsoft\Windows NT\NT Backup\data`).

If you load a saved backup script when you have files and folders selected for backup, Backup will ask whether you want to use the currently selected folders or clear them. Clear them to load the backup script, and you'll be ready to run the backup job.

Scheduling Automated Backups

To be safe, you should back up data servers at least once a day. Trouble is, the best time to back up is late at night when everyone's off the network. With NT 4, you could use the AT command or WinAT utility to schedule backups created from the command line. Beginning with Windows 2000, you had the choice of two backup-scheduling methods, one using the GUI, and one using the AT command for running scripted backups created with an updated command-line version of `NTBackup.exe`.

There are a few ways you can schedule jobs from Windows Backup:

◆ In the Backup Wizard one of the Advanced options asks whether you want to run the backup you've created now or schedule it for later. If you choose to schedule it for later, you'll be taken to the Schedule Job dialog box, which I'll discuss in a minute.

◆ In Windows Backup, when you create a backup job from the Backup tab and click the Start Backup button, you'll see a dialog box that prompts you for the name of the backup and allows you to start the backup now or schedule it for later (see Figure 19.11). If you click the Schedule button, you'll be taken to the Schedule Job dialog box. If you're creating a new backup job, you must save the backup and provide the username and password of the account used to run it before you can save the backup settings.

FIGURE 19.11

When creating a backup job, you have the option of running it immediately or running it at a later time.

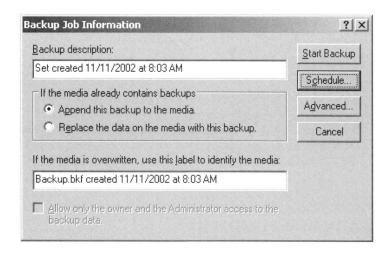

If you're creating a new backup job, you can turn to the Schedule Jobs tab, where you'll see a month calendar like the one shown in Figure 19.12. To create and schedule a backup job from the Schedule Jobs tab, click the Add Job button in the lower-right corner of the screen to start a Backup Wizard similar to the one described earlier under "Basic Backup Procedures"—the only difference between the two wizards is that this one includes the advanced options in the main wizard, rather than through the Advanced button on the wizard's final screen. One of the options you'll be presented with is the choice of running the backup now or later, with the default time for "later" being midnight of the day you set up the backup job. To schedule a job, select Later and click the Set Schedule button to open the scheduler.

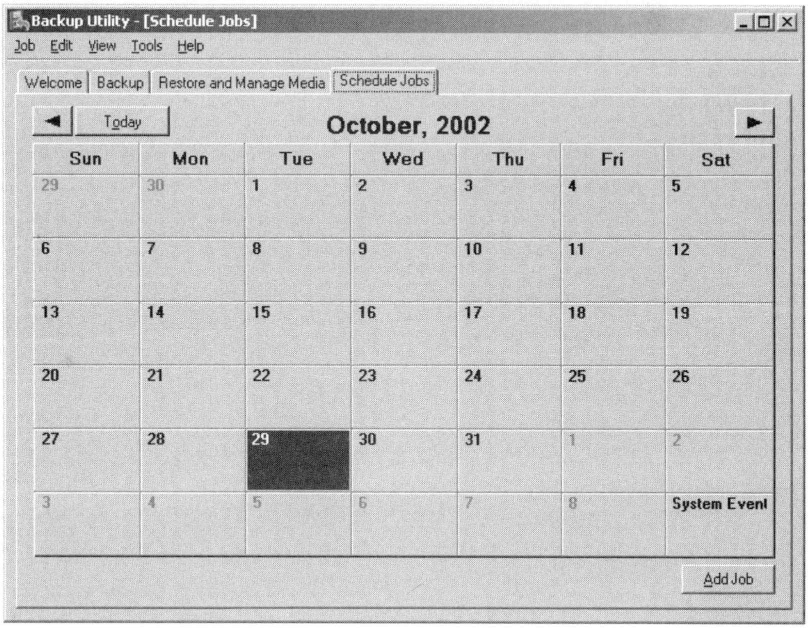

FIGURE 19.12

The Schedule Jobs tab of Windows Backup

No matter how you get to it, the Schedule tab of the Schedule Job dialog box looks like Figure 19.13. The basic options are pretty straightforward. Choose the interval at which you want the backup job to run (once, daily, weekly, monthly, at system startup, at logon, or when the computer is idle) and the starting time and date. If you select the Show Multiple Schedules check box at the bottom of the screen, a new drop-down list will appear at the top of this dialog box, showing the varying intervals and starting times that you've chosen for this job.

FIGURE 19.13

Choose a time and frequency for the backup job.

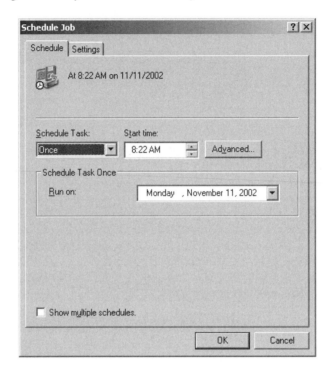

TIP   *If you want to run a backup job biweekly (once every two weeks), show multiple schedules and create two monthly backup jobs that start on different days.*

The Advanced button takes you to the Advanced Schedule Options (see Figure 19.14), which apply only if you want to repeat the backup job, apart from any interval that you set in the main scheduling screen. Most often, you won't need to touch these options. You don't need to use them for scheduling jobs at regular intervals; this set of options would be more useful for a shorter task and one that might actually need to be run every 10 minutes or so. (Frequent backups are a Good Thing, but let's not get carried away.)

More likely, you'll use the Settings tab back in the main Schedule Job dialog box (see Figure 19.15). From here, you can specify how long the job should run (a backup job that lasts more than 72 hours seems suboptimal) and whether the job should be deleted from the list of tasks when it's done unless it's supposed to run again. The Idle Time settings apply to interaction from the console—keyboard or mouse input—so they shouldn't prevent a backup job from running on a server being accessed from the network.

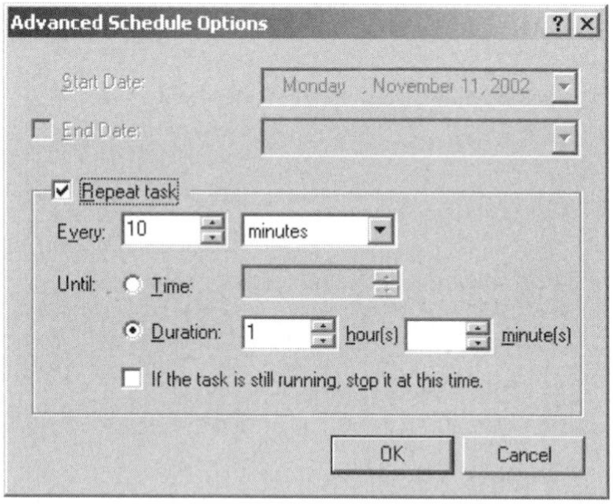

FIGURE 19.14

Advanced backup
scheduling options

FIGURE 19.15

Configure job
settings for the
scheduled backup.

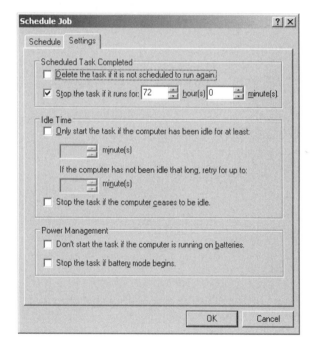

TIP *With the volume shadow copy service, Backup can now back up open files.*

The final options in the Settings tab, on battery use, aren't likely to apply to a server unless you frequently use laptops as servers. These settings help you conserve battery power by not running non-essential tasks when your power supply is limited. Accessing the hard disk takes a lot of power, so backups are an especially draining task when the power is low.

When you've finished adding jobs to the scheduler, they'll appear on the Schedule Jobs tab's calendar, as shown in Figure 19.16.

FIGURE 19.16
Scheduled jobs appear in the calendar.

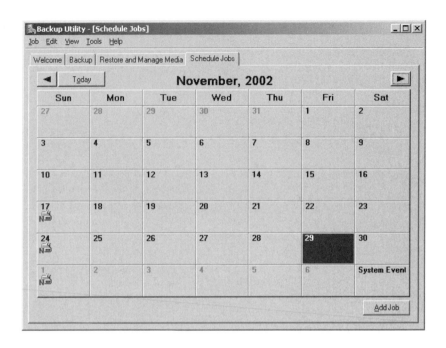

You're not stuck with the options for a scheduled job once it's created. To edit the settings for a scheduled job, just click its icon in the calendar to open the Scheduled Job dialog box shown in Figure 19.17. To delete the job, just click the Delete button.

FIGURE 19.17
You can edit all job settings even after the job is added to the task list.

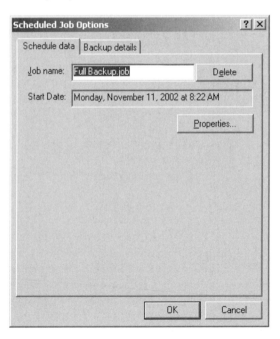

Click the Properties button to edit the timing and settings for the backup job. The Schedule and Settings tabs that appear are the same ones you saw when scheduling the job. The Task tab that also appears, however, is new. Here, you can choose a different job to run at the scheduled time, specify a different user account in whose context the job should run, and create some identifying information for the job.

Backing Up to Tape

Windows 2000 introduced a whole new layer of software called the Removable Storage Manager (RSM). You wouldn't think that you'd need to know anything about RSM to do backups, but RSM is the basis of Windows 2000's and Server 2003's backup and archival capabilities. A backup program needs both drivers for the storage devices it works with and the intelligence to control those devices. NT 4's backup program directly managed the tape drives it worked with (as you may recall, NT 4's backup program only worked with a tape drive—you couldn't even *start* the program unless you had a tape drive installed). So long as you were happy with NT 4's choices, this was fine, but NT 4 was designed in a day when hard disks were a lot smaller than they are now. For example, NT 4's backup program did not support DAT *autoloaders*, systems where there's usually only one tape drive (although there can be more) with a built-in capacity to store and automatically load or unload several other tapes. If you wanted to use a DAT autoloader, you needed a third-party backup program that knew how to handle it.

NOTE   *If it's not clear why you'd want an autoloader, a tape drive that can automatically insert and eject a stack of tapes, then you've never done regular backups on a hard disk (or a group of disks) whose capacity is greater than your tape drive's. For instance, 4-mm DAT drives are pretty good, fairly fast, and reliable…but only store about 8GB. To back up an entire 40GB hard disk using DAT drives, you'll need to baby-sit a backup program that prompts you every now and then to "please insert tape 4. …" I'll pass.*

One way to make NT 4's backup program more flexible about its storage would be to create special tape-emulating drivers that would make *any* storage appear to be a tape drive. That is, even if the storage were, say, a CD-RW drive, then it could accept tape-related commands such as "rewind" and "retension" even though it can't use them. However, to my knowledge no such drivers exist. RSM performs a similar function by abstracting the interface not just to tape drives but to all removable storage. Backup doesn't manage its storage, RSM does.

NOTE   *Even though they're not RSM aware, NT 4–era backup programs will generally run on Windows 2000. However, they won't back up anything that employs the new features of NTFS: encrypted files, Single Instance Store volumes, or sparse files.*

Although it's an intrinsic part of Backup, RSM also supports *any* program that uses removable storage, such as the archiving capabilities that back hard disk space with offline storage. In other words, RSM is not just about making backups work, but that's the part I'll focus on here.

RSM CONCEPTS: PHYSICAL LOCATIONS, LIBRARIES, DRIVES, MEDIA

To use the RSM-enabled features of backup, you'll need to know a physical location from a library from a drive from media. You can see the GUI interface for the Removable Storage Manager in Manage Computer. Right-click My Computer and choose Manage, then open up the icon labeled Storage, and you'll see something like Figure 19.18.

FIGURE 19.18

RSM before any backups

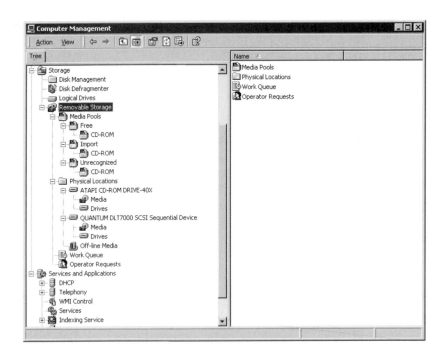

This computer has just two removable storage devices—a standard EIDE-connected CD-ROM drive and a DLT1 tape drive. There are no tapes in the DLT1 drive and NTBACKUP has never run on this system (you'll see why I mention that in a minute). Notice that under the `Removable Storage` level, there are four objects:

◆ `Media Pools`

◆ `Physical Locations`

◆ `Work Queue`

◆ `Operator Requests`

I'm going to skip the last two and just focus on the first two because they apply to backing up.

Physical Locations = Mechanical Drives

Of these two, `Physical Locations` is the easier to understand. In Figure 19.18, I expanded it, so you can see three objects—a drive icon representing the CD-ROM (`ATAPI CD-ROM DRIVE-40X`), one representing the tape drive (`QUANTUM DLT7000 SCSI Sequential Device`), and one labeled `Off-Line Media`. `Physical Locations`, therefore, are the drives that RSM can manage. Not the *media* in those drives, but the drives.

Library = "Autoloader" or "Stand-Alone Drive"

When I right-click either the CD-ROM or the tape and choose Properties, I get a properties page describing not the drive, but the drive's interface. I'll also see a lot of references to the device as a *library.* There is, for example, no button or check box to disable the device; instead, you'd see an Enable Library check box and unchecking it would disable the device. To RSM, a *library* is one or more drives that have an automatic changer for their tapes, cartridges, discs, or whatever. (For shorthand, I'll call them generically *tapes.*)

As you can see, Microsoft has upped the ante on its definition of the "basic removable storage doodad." Where it once was a tape, now it's a *tape library,* one or more tape drives and zero or more *changers,* the little robotic hands. My humble DLT tape drive is, then, a library consisting of *one* tape drive and *zero* changers. (Yeah, it's kind of simple. I couldn't afford that really cool HP autoloader with four drives and capacity to hold 60 tapes—$46,000 was a bit out of my budget—so I'll stick to DLT for the moment.) Microsoft even has a name for a zero-changer, one-tape-drive library: a *stand-alone library.* That's not just a CD-ROM on your system, my friend, it's an optical stand-alone library. Notice also that in addition to my DLT and CD-ROM "libraries," I have a third one called my Off-Line Media library. *Off-line media* is Microsoft's way of describing wherever you store tapes when they're not in your drives. So tapes sitting in a desk drawer or on a shelf are in a library.

This may sound odd, but it kind of makes sense once you adopt the RSM way of thinking. RSM's main job actually seems to be a kind of database that lets you keep track of your tapes. As you'll see, this database keeps track of the following information about tapes:

♦ Where they are physically located—on a shelf, in an autoloader waiting to be inserted into a drive, actually in a drive

♦ What program wrote them

♦ What sort of drive can read and write them

♦ What data is on them

RSM really only *secondarily* concerns itself with the specifics of what sort of drives you have. Calling them all libraries allows you to concern yourself with where your *data* are, not where your tapes or CDs are.

This information is not just available from the GUI; RSM has a command-line tool called RSM.EXE. To get the list of your libraries, just type **rsm view /tlibrary**. That gets a result like this:

```
LIBRARY

Off-line Media
ATAPI CD-ROM DRIVE-40X
QUANTUM DLT7000 SCSI Sequential Device

The command completed successfully.
```

Notice the odd spacing—there is no space between /t and library. We'll use rsm view /t again— the /t means "type of thing to view"—and its odd syntax requires no spaces between /t and the parameter describing what you want to view. As with other things in Server 2003, though, those names are just the human-friendly names. Under the hood, the OS *really* identifies things by globally unique IDs (GUIDs), and sometimes you'll need to know what they are, as you'll see later. You can find that out by adding the /guiddisplay switch, like this:

```
C:\>rsm view /tlibrary /guiddisplay
```

```
LIBRARY

Off-line Media   D49F02AE9CEA46BFB58E51AB6C7FE262
ATAPI CD-ROM DRIVE-40X   6043C178219841208E034076D0566885
QUANTUM DLT7000 SCSI Sequential Device   E30ADF03E8014BA4BB824AD69B39FBE7

The command completed successfully.

C:\>
```

Media = Tapes, Cartridges, CD-ROM Discs, Etc.

Within the CD-ROM and tape drive objects there are then, in turn, two objects, Media and Drives. *Drives* of course refers to the physical drive. But *media* needs some defining. To RSM, media means anything that you put into a drive. Tapes go in tape drives, so tapes are media. CD-ROMs go into CD-ROM drives, so they're media. But media doesn't mean a *type* of media, it means particular *instances* of media. As I suggested before, RSM's job seems to be to maintain a database that keeps track of every single tape that you ever shove into one of your tape drives.

The folder labeled Media under a drive's icon in the Physical Locations object will contain an object representing the particular tape, cartridge, or disc sitting in your drive at that moment. For example, if I insert a CD into my CD-ROM drive and click the Media folder under ATAPI CD-ROM... then I'll see something like Figure 19.19. Notice that under Loaded Media it says STREETS9. That refers to a piece of software, as this is the installation CD for a mapping program.

FIGURE 19.19

CD-ROM as media

NOTE   *In truth, RSM isn't very useful for CD-ROMs; this is just an example of how it works that you can try out on almost any system. As I've said before, NTBACKUP cannot use CD-R, CD-RW, DVD-RW, or DVD+RW drives.*

I can easily use the GUI to see that my CD-ROM drive contains a CD whose label is STREETS9, but I'm going to want to be able to retrieve that kind of information from the command line; for that, I'll use more of RSM.EXE. To get information on a particular tape, I'll use the physical_media option on the rsm view command. But just typing **rsm view /tphysical_media** won't do the job—that will display *every* bit of removable media on the system at the moment. (Admittedly that's not a real problem on *this* computer, as it only contains one bit of removable media, the CD. But let's see how to do it on more real-world systems.)

To narrow the scope of rsm view /tphysical_media, I'll add a parameter, /cg for "container GUID." As I'm trying to find the GUID of the CD-ROM disc sitting in the CD-ROM drive at the moment, the container is the CD-ROM drive. As you saw a moment ago, I get that with the rsm view /tlibrary /guiddisplay command. As you can see here, to find out about the media in the drive, I'll just plug the drive's GUID into the command like this:

```
C:\>rsm view /tphysical_media /cg6043C178219841208E034076D0566885

PHYSICAL_MEDIA

STREETS9

The command completed successfully.
```

> **TIP** *If you're wondering how you can accurately type a GUID, don't worry. To type that command, I highlighted the GUID from the* rsm view /tlibrary /guiddisplay *output and pressed Enter, which puts the highlighted text into the Clipboard. Then I typed* **rsm view /tphysical_media /cg**, *clicked the icon in the upper-left corner of the window to drop the Control Menu for that window, then chose Edit/Paste.*

Note that as with the parameters following /t, I typed the GUID after the /cg command without any spaces after the /cg. Note also that if I needed to retrieve the GUID of the media (which we'll want to do later in with tapes), I could have added the logical_media command.

You can drill down even further than a given tape—physical media contain one or more partitions, and partitions contain one or more logical_media. In each case, you'd just use /guiddisplay to get the GUID of the container and then feed that with /cg as the GUID of the container to view.

MEDIA POOLS: CLASSIFYING TAPES

Thus far, I haven't shown you much of anything that has to do with tapes, so let's pop a tape into the drive and see what happens. Note that this is a *new* tape, fresh out of the box. It's never been introduced to this drive, or to NTBACKUP, before.

After inserting the tape and waiting for the tape drive to settle down, I right-click the QUANTUM DLT7000... drive and choose Refresh to force RSM to reexamine the drive's status. I then click the Media Pools folder under the tape and see a screen like Figure 19.20.

Notice that a few things happened. First, the Free, Import, and Unrecognized media pools (I'll get to what they are in a minute) now have a DLT folder underneath them, where previously they only had a CD-ROM folder there. Second, the Media folder for the tape drive now contains something called "7" that is said to be in Drive 0 in a media pool called Unrecognized\DLT; its state is reported to be Idle, New. And sure enough, clicking the DLT folder under the Unrecognized folder in the Media Pools object shows another item named 7—it's the same tape—in that folder. (If you're not crazy about naming a tape "7," then fear not. The later section "Renaming a Tape" explains how to change a tape's name.)

FIGURE 19.20

Remote Storage
Manager after
inserting new tape

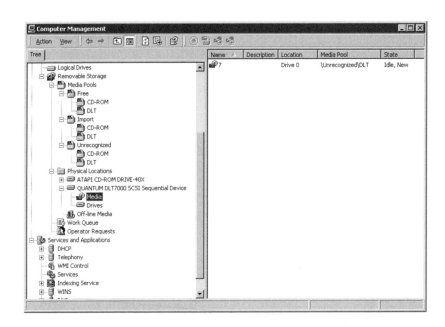

Basically, this is RSM-ese for "this tape is unformatted." That's not exactly right, as DLT tapes ship formatted, but RSM wants to write a bit of identifying data onto the tape. I can do that by right-clicking the tape's icon in the right pane; I'll get a menu that offers Eject, Mount, Prepare, and Dismount. I choose Prepare and see a dialog box that says:

```
This operation will destroy the data on the media and move it to a Free media pool.
     Are you sure you want to write a Free media label on the selected medium?
```

I choose Yes and get *another* confirmation message:

```
Are you sure you want to write a Free media label on 7?
```

What *are* you, hard of hearing, RSM? I click Yes again and the tape's media pool changes to Free\DLT and its state goes to Loaded, Unprepared while the tape spins for a few minutes. It finally finishes whatever it does when "preparing" the tape, and the tape ends up in Free\DLT in a state of Idle, Available.

NOTE *There is not, as far as I can see, a command-line tool in* RSM.EXE *that will prepare never-before-used tapes. But that won't be a problem since NTBACKUP has a* /um *option that automatically erases and prepares tapes before backing up.*

Now I can explain the next RSM concept, *media pools*. Remember that RSM is a database of tapes. Even if you just shove a tape into a drive once, prepare it, remove it, bury it in a mine shaft, and never look at it again, RSM remembers that tape. Remember also that the RSM word for a tape is *media*.

RSM wants to organize the media that it has met into categories and, by default, it categorizes media in one of three ways:

- *Free media* are tapes that RSM has "prepared" but that don't have any data on them. They're waiting to be used by some RSM-aware application such as NTBACKUP.

- *Import media* are tapes that RSM recognizes as having been prepared by RSM on this or some other machine in the past. They're RSM tapes, all right, but they're not blank (so they don't go into Free). They're also not associated with a particular RSM-aware application. As you will soon see, RSM-aware applications create their *own* media pools, and RSM will then be able to categorize some media as neither Free, Import, or Unrecognized—they'll be categorized as Backup tapes, ArcServe tapes, BackupExec tapes, or the like. So Import is a kind of catch-all category meaning, "This tape has been prepared, so it doesn't go into Unrecognized, it's not blank, so it doesn't go into Free, so some application *has* worked with it before, but I don't remember it, so it'll stay here in Import until the user decides to drop it into some application's folder."

- *Unrecognized media* have not been prepared to work with RSM. RSM can't do anything with them until they are.

This will make a lot more sense once we get an RSM-aware application running. When I run NTBACKUP for the first time, that causes it to introduce itself to RSM, and tells RSM to create a new fourth media pool called Backup. Now that I've run Windows 2000's backup program, any tape that NTBACKUP writes to will become essentially the "property" of NTBACKUP. As a matter of fact, if I *had* media sitting in the Import media pool that had been originally created by NTBACKUP on some other system, then the first time that I started up NTBACKUP I'd have gotten the dialog box that you see in Figure 19.21.

FIGURE 19.21

Should Backup be able to claim old backup tapes?

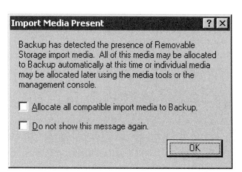

Even if you don't allow NTBACKUP to import the media now, you can do it by hand later; you can just drag any media item out of one media pool and drop it into another. (Of course, if you try to drop it into Free, then you'll get a warning that dropping it into Free will cause RSM to erase it.)

MANAGING MEDIA IN RSM

That's an overview of how RSM works—it tracks particular tapes, giving each one a GUID (which changes whenever you "prepare" a tape) and categorizing it in either an application's media pool

(Backup on most systems, but if you've purchased other RSM-aware apps then you might have more than one application media pool), or one of the "holding tanks": Free, Import, or Unrecognized. Understand also that you can move media between media pools even if the actual physical tape isn't currently in the tape drive; the tape doesn't know and doesn't care which media pool it belongs to. Tapes *do*, however, carry on them the mark of their associated RSM-aware application, which is why you can take a tape created on one system, pop it into another Server 2003 system, and it will immediately be recognized as having already been seen by RSM *and* NTBACKUP will recognize that this tape contains data written by NTBACKUP.

We're just about done with RSM and almost ready to tackle NTBACKUP.

Renaming a Tape

As intuitive names for my first tape go, "7" is not ranking high. So how about I give it a more useful name? I intend to use this tape as one of two tapes that I'll store differential backups on, so I'll rename it "Diff1." To do so, I'll right-click the tape and choose Properties. The General tab has a text field that includes the name of the tape.

For some reason, renaming the tape doesn't seem to be enough to convince NTBACKUP that the tape has a new name. In my experience, you need to then put the tape in the Free media pool so that it is reinitialized.

WARNING *Moving the tape to the Free media pool deletes any data on the tape, so don't do this if there is any data on the tape that you'd miss!*

Moving a Tape to Free

Sometimes you won't be able to move a tape from the Backup media pool to the Free media pool. You must first "deallocate" it. Now, *finding* where to deallocate a tape may be a challenge.

You've already seen that by right-clicking a media object you'll get a drop-down context menu that includes four actions—Eject, Prepare, Mount, and Unmount. Below that is a submenu, All Tasks, which on *most* MMCs would just repeat Eject, Prepare, Mount, Unmount. But *this* one includes a fifth option…Deallocate. So to free an existing tape, first right-click it and choose All Tasks/Deallocate, and then drag it to Free. (And along the way, say "yes" to all of the "are you sure?" messages.)

Ejecting a Tape from the Command Line

We've been going over RSM to get ready to do backups and command-line backups in particular. Over the years I've seen people write batch files for handling backups, and some folks like to end off the backup process with an **eject** command. I guess it makes for a slightly more secure backup because once the tape's ejected, then there's no hacker on earth who can convince the tape drive to reinsert the tape. (That's not true for autoloaders, of course, but it is for stand-alone drives, at least in my experience.) So how do you tell NTBACKUP to eject your tape? With RSM. The command looks like this:

```
rsm eject /pf"name of tape to eject" /ast art
```

Or alternatively:

```
rsm eject /pgGUID /astart
```

In the first case, you fill in the media's name; in the second, you fill in its GUID. Note that if you let NTBACKUP prepare the tape, then it'll have a name like `Media created 1/4/2003 at 5:21 PM - 1`, and for the command to work right, you'll need to type in the media name precisely.

The only real problem with this is that you probably want a fairly generic "eject" batch file, but both versions of `rsm eject` are very tape specific: You've got to either know the name of the particular tape, or know the tape's GUID. Unless you intend to use the very same tape night after night, then this won't be too useful. But consider:

- The GUID of the tape *drive* won't vary from day to day.
- If you have the tape drive's GUID, you can use `rsm view /tphysical_media` to get the GUID of the particular tape in the drive at that moment.

Here's how to put all of that together into a batch file that needs only to know the GUID of the drive in order to eject any tape in that drive. If you don't know how batch files work internally, then don't worry about following this—I'll have a ready-made batch file prepared at the end of this section that you can just type in and use (replacing my GUID with the one for your tape drive, of course).

My plan for the batch file will be that I'll use `rsm view` to retrieve the tape's GUID and put it in a variable *%tguid%*. Then I'll just issue the `rsm eject` command with the `/pg` option, specifying the GUID of the tape. I can do all that with just three lines (the second one is broken but should be all on one line):

```
set drvguid=E30ADF03E8014BA4BB824AD69B39FBE7
FOR /F "usebackq" %%i IN ('rsm view /tphysical_media /cg%drvguid% /b /guiddisplay')
    DO set x=%%i
rsm eject /pg%X% /astart
```

In the first line, I'm just filling up an environment variable named *drvguid*. That long value that I'm stuffing in it, E30ADF03E8014BA4BB824AD69B39FBE7, is the GUID of *my* DLT drive. Yours will be different, so use `rsm view /tlibrary /guiddisplay` to get the particular GUID for your tape drive and replace my drive's GUID with yours in that line.

In the second line, I'm executing the command `rsm view /tphysical_media /cg` to get the GUID of the tape in the drive. But, as you've already seen, you must provide the GUID of a container for that to work—that's what *%drvguid%* does. You filled in your drive's GUID in the line before and that gets inserted before the command executes. The `/guiddisplay /b` says to display the GUID, and the `/b` option says to show *only* the GUID. That makes life easier, as it's only the GUID that I want. The result of that—the GUID—goes into a variable named *%x*. (The two percent signs are required syntax for the `FOR` command.)

Once I've got the GUID for the tape in X, then I can construct the last line, which executes an eject command for the tape whose GUID is in X.

Here are the steps to creating and using this batch file:

1. Get the GUID of your tape drive. From the command line, type **`rsm view /tlibrary /guiddisplay`**. You'll see a line for all of the removable devices on your system, including CD-ROMs. The name of the device should make clear which one is your tape drive. Grab the GUID next to that device's name—again, you can copy this value by selecting it and pressing Enter.

2. Open up Notepad and type in the batch file as you see in the previous text. In the first line, substitute your drive's GUID in place of E30ADF03E8014BA4BB824AD69B39FBE7. Note that the single quotes in the second line are *backquotes*. On many keyboards they are on the same key as the tilde (~).

3. Save the file in the WINNT directory as tapeeject.cmd.

Try it out by opening up a command line and typing **tapeeject**. The tape should eject.

TIP If you want to run tapeeject *from inside a batch file, then don't just put the line* tapeeject *in the batch file; instead, use* call tapeeject, *or the batch file will end when* tapeeject *ends.*

Refreshing a Tape from the Command Line

Sometimes you'll pop a tape into a drive and try to do something with it from the GUI or the command line, and the command fails—the system acts as if there is no tape in the drive. There are two possible reasons for that. First, remember, you're working with tapes here—they're not the fastest things in the world. When you pop a tape in, the drive may take a minute or two to figure the tape out. Second, RSM for some reason doesn't always automatically figure out that you just put a tape in a drive. The *drive* knows that it's there, it's just RSM that doesn't know. So it never hurts to smack RSM upside the head before trying to do something—that's called *refreshing*.

You can refresh just about any object in the RSM by right-clicking it and choosing Refresh. But if you're about to run a batch job to automatically back up a system, then you want a command-line method to do that. RSM lets you do that with an rsm refresh command. It looks like this:

```
rsm refresh /lf"drive name"
```

or

```
rsm refresh /lgdrive-GUID
```

So, for example, my drive could be refreshed either with this:

```
rsm refresh /lf"QUANTUM DLT7000 SCSI Sequential Device"
```

or

```
rsm refresh /lgE30ADF03E8014BA4BB824AD69B39FBE7
```

Notice that the drive name needs quotes and the spelling must be exact; the GUID, on the other hand, must be exact but does not need quotes.

Automating Tape Backups

You've seen that Backup manages tapes through RSM, and you've seen RSM's notions of libraries, physical media, and media pools—and that it assigns GUIDs to everything, and how much it relies upon those GUIDs. That was all necessary preparation for controlling NTBACKUP from the command line.

The basic idea with automating NTBACKUP is simple: Write a batch file that wakes up the NTBACKUP.EXE program and tells it to back up to tape. Then use the Schedule service—the AT.EXE command—to tell the operating system to run that batch file whenever you want it run—daily, every other day, or whatever.

The hardest part is usually writing the batch file. It's typically just one line, a long invocation of the NTBACKUP command. That's what I'm going to focus on here. As you can see in Table 19.4, these options are fairly complex. But I'm going to simplify them as much as possible, starting from a very basic command and then adding things as we go.

TABLE 19.4: NTBACKUP OPTIONS

ARGUMENT	FUNCTION
backup	Tells NTBACKUP that you're running a backup operation. You must include this argument.
systemstate	Specifies that all System State data should be backed up and sets the backup type to normal or copy.
bks file name	This is the name of the selection information file in which the backup will be stored (if you're backing up to a file instead of a tape). More than one backup can go in the same BKS file, if you choose to append backups. You must create this file from the GUI before referencing it from the command line.
/j "job name"	Tells NTBACKUP the name of the backup job.
/p "pool name"	Tells NTBACKUP which media pool (a logical grouping of removable media, such as a tape library) to copy the backup files to. If you're using Backup, this will be the Backup media pool. You won't use this option with /g or /t, as those switches specify that a certain tape should be used; with /f, which specifies the name of a file to back up to; or with /a because you must append backup files to a specific tape, not an entire media pool.
/g "guid name"	Specifies the GUID of the tape that will be overwritten or appended with this backup job. Don't use this switch with /p, as that specifies that NTBACKUP should back up to a media pool instead of a particular tape. The GUID must be in quotes and hyphenated, so that it looks like this: "b471ff3b-101f-43bc-9d15-ffb7176cf2f3"; those demarcations must be respected— 8 characters, hyphen, 4, hyphen, 4, hyphen, 4, hyphen, 12 characters.
/t "tape name"	Specifies the media name of the tape that will be overwritten or appended with this backup job. Don't use this switch with /p, as this specifies that NTBACKUP will use a media pool instead of a particular tape.
/n "new tape name"	Specifies the new tape name of the tape that will be overwritten or appended with this backup job. Use this switch to name a tape, but use it sparingly. Don't use this switch with /p, as this specifies that NTBACKUP will use a media pool instead of a particular tape. You also can't use this switch with /a because you can't append data onto a tape that is new or that you're renaming. Finally, it's best not to use this switch with /um since that switch is for unattended tape backups, and it may work best to let Backup name the tape on its own.
/f "file name"	Specifies the path and name of the file in which the backup will be copied. As this switch directs the backup to a file, not a tape or media pool, you can't use it with any of the switches specific to removable media: /p, /t, or /n.

Continued on next page

TABLE 19.4: NTBACKUP OPTIONS *(continued)*

ARGUMENT	FUNCTION
/d "description"	Specifies the description of the backup set, such as "Full backup of SERPENT on 1/20/03."
/ds "server name"	Backs up the directory service on the specified Microsoft Exchange server.
/is "server name"	Backs up the information store on the specified Microsoft Exchange server.
/a	Appends the backup set to any data on the media. If backing up to a tape, you must use this switch with either /g or /t to specify the tape you want to append to. You can't use this switch with /p, as you must append to a specific tape, not an entire media pool.
/v:yes or no	Specifies whether the backup procedure should be verified or not. Verifying the data (making sure the data in the backup matches the source) takes a little time, but reassures you that the data was written correctly.
/r:yes or no	Specifies whether the tape should be available only to its owner/creator and members of the Administrators group.
/l:f or s or n	Tells NTBACKUP what kind of log file to create: full (logging every copied file), summary (logging only important events and errors), or none (in which case the backup won't be logged).
/m backuptype	Tells NTBACKUP what kind of backup to run: normal, copy, incremental, differential, or daily.
/rs:yes or no	Tells NTBACKUP whether to back up the removable storage database that records the location of archived files. If you're using removable storage, you should back up this database regularly to make sure that you can retrieve archived files.
/hc:on or off	Tells NTBACKUP whether to use hardware compression (available only if you're backing up to a tape drive, and then only if that tape drive supports it—most do). Go ahead and use hardware compression if it's available, as it will allow you to get more use out of your tapes.
/SNAP: on or off	Specifies whether or not the backup should use volume shadow copying to back up open files. By default, it will.

Forget all the options for a minute. The basic NTBACKUP command looks like this:

```
ntbackup backup directory tapedrive
```

directory is, of course, the name of the directory (or UNC) to back up. *tapedrive* is the name of the tape drive to do the backup to. Leave that off, and the command will just not run—and it doesn't even tell you *why* unless you look for and read the log files. You specify a tape drive in one of two ways:

◆ /t "*name*" as in /t "Tape created on Tuesday"
◆ /p "*media-type*" as in /p "DLT"
◆ /g "*guid name*" as in /g "b471ff3b-101f-43bc-9d15-ffb7176cf2f3"

By the way, notice that RSM likes to add - 1 to tape names (apparently assuming that you have more than one tape in a set), but that name won't work with NTBACKUP. If you'd created a tape called mytape, then it'd show up in the GUI as mytape - 1—but when you use the /t option, leave the extra - 1 off. That is, use /t "mytape", not /t "mytape - 1". To identify a tape by its GUID, you must use the GUID of the logical_media *inside* the partition *inside* the physical_media that is *inside* the library.

You'll use /t and /p for different purposes. /t with /a permits you to append new backup sets to an existing tape without deleting the existing ones (which /p doesn't allow) but requires that you know the name of the tape in the drive. /p in combination with /um doesn't need the name of the tape in the drive, as it just tells NTBACKUP, "Whatever's in there, just wipe it clean and start over!"

A COMMAND-LINE BACKUP STRATEGY

For years, I've used a simple backup strategy for servers: Once a week I do a full backup, and every other day I do a differential backup. It's simple to automate with just a little manual work. I keep two tapes: the differential tape, which I leave in the drive for most of the week, and the full backup tape, which I only leave in the drive over Sunday night. (Yes, I rotate tapes, but I'm simplifying this explanation.) Here's how it works: Every Sunday morning, I remove the differential tape from my server's tape drive and put it aside. Then I insert a tape for a full system backup. On Monday morning, I remove that tape, which now has a full system backup on it, and reinsert the differential tape.

Using the Schedule service, I set up three events:

♦ On Sunday night/early Monday morning, I schedule NTBACKUP to back up my server's files (a "normal" backup), but first to wipe clean anything on the hard disk.

♦ On Monday night/Tuesday morning, I schedule NTBACKUP to do a differential backup of my server's files, but first to wipe clean anything on the hard disk. (This reinitializes the differential tape each week.)

♦ On the other evenings, I schedule NTBACKUP to do a differential backup of my server's files, but tell it to *append* the new backup set to the existing ones on the tape. That way, I have backup sets that represent the state of the network for every day of the week.

Furthermore, let's make this example a bit more complicated—and more useful in the real world—by specifying that the only directories that I want to back up are C:\DATA, C:\USERS, and D:\REPORTS.

THE WEEKLY BACKUP

For this backup, I want the drive wiped clean. What command does that? ntbackup backup /p /um. In its simplest form, that would look like this:

```
ntbackup backup directories /p "DLT" /um
```

Remember that your drive may not be a DLT; other possible values might be 4mm DDS, Travan, QIC, or others. Just look in the folder created under your Backup media pool to find out your drive's type.

But we're not out of the woods yet. How do I specify three different directories to back up?

Using a Backup Selection File

You *could* write a batch file that called `ntbackup` three times, but that's too much work. Instead, open up Notepad and type the names of the directories that you want to back up, one to a line:

```
C:\data\
c:\users\
d:\reports\
```

Then click Save As and specify that the file's name is `c:\myfiles.bks`, but don't save yet—in the Save As box, go to the Encoding box and choose Unicode.

WARNING   *This is very important. You don't have to save it in* `C:\`, *you needn't give it the extension* `.bks`—*but you've got to save it in Unicode, or NTBACKUP simply will not read it.*

Now run NTBACKUP as before, but instead of specifying a directory, specify your backup selection filename prefixed by an @ sign. If the directory's name includes spaces, then you'll need to surround the name with quotes. The command looks like this so far:

```
ntbackup backup @c:\myfiles.bks /p "DLT" /UM
```

Choosing Logging Levels

At least until I'm sure that this thing works, I'd be happier with an extensive log. You can set logging levels with the `/l:` option: `/l:s` provides only summaries (and is the default), `/l:f` provides full logs, and `/l:n` produces no logs at all.

Hardware Compression

In theory I can get 80GB of data on this tape if I turn on hardware compression. You control that with the `/hc:` option—it's either `/hc:on` or `/hc:off`.

Verification

In general, I find that I distrust computers when it comes to my data. So I don't mind the extra time required to stop, rewind, and verify backups. You control verification with either `/v:yes` or `/v:no`. (Why `/hc` uses `on` or `off` and `/v` uses `yes` and `no` is known only to the Microsoft developers.)

Append or Replace?

In this particular case, I want to overwrite any existing backup sets, replacing any on the tape. That's the default behavior, so there's nothing to do. If I wanted the system to append its backup set to any existing sets then I'd add `/a`. You can't do `/a` if you've used `/p`, but you can use `/a` in combination with `/t`.

Name the Tape

By default RSM and NTBACKUP name the tape by its date and time of "creation," but you can give it any other name by adding the parameter `/n` followed by a name.

Back Up the Registry?

Adding the parameter `systemstate` will cause NTBACKUP to back up the System State data. The other options can go just about anywhere, but `systemstate` must go after the word `backup` and before the backup selection file's name.

Put it all together and you've got a command like this (all on one line):

```
ntbackup backup systemstate @c:\myfiles.bks /p "DLT" /UM /l:f /hc:on /v:yes
```

Create the Batch File

Finally, let's put the Schedule service to work. Put that line (with your site-specific modifications, of course) into a batch file called `c:\fullback.cmd`. Then open up a command line, type this:

```
at 2:00 /interactive /every:Monday c:\fullback.cmd
```

and press Enter. Now at 2 A.M. every Monday morning, your system will do a normal backup of the directories that you specified in `c:\myfiles.bks`.

How Do I Know It Worked?

NTBACKUP writes ASCII text files called `backup01.txt` through `backup10.txt`, maintaining logs of the last 10 times that NTBACKUP ran. (It starts reusing files once it gets to `backup1.txt`.) You cannot, unfortunately, control either the number of log files that it keeps (it's 10) or where it puts them. NTBACKUP stores the logs in `\Documents and Settings\`*username*`\Local Settings\Application Data\Microsoft\Windows NT\NTbackup\Data`…and it's that *username* thing that'll give you fits.

When you're logged in as you, Joeadmin, then the logs go to `\Documents and Settings\joeadmin\Local Settings\Application Data\Microsoft\Windows NT\NTbackup\Data`. But when the Schedule service starts the process—that is, when you're automatically scheduling a backup—it writes the logs to in `\Documents and Settings\Default User\Local Settings\Application Data\Microsoft\Windows NT\NTbackup\Data`. And don't be surprised if you have more than one of those directories—you might find that you've got a directory named `\Documents and Settings\Default User\Local Settings\Application Data\Microsoft\Windows NT\NTbackup\Data` *and* `\Documents and Settings\Default User.WINNT\Local Settings\Application Data\Microsoft\Windows NT\NTbackup\Data`. Just look in both directories and find the one with the more recent log files—those are the ones you want.

THE DIFFERENTIAL BACKUP

You set up the differential backup basically the same way as the normal backups, but instead of `/p /um` you'll use `/t` and a tape name—we don't want to overwrite the tapes. So you'll need to standardize the name for the tape; I use `diff1`, and append a week's differentials together, so my batch file looks like this:

```
ntbackup backup systemstate @c:\myfiles.bks /t "diff1" /a /l:f /hc:on /v:yes
```

I save that as `c:\diffback.cmd` and tell Schedule to run it every day but Monday morning:

```
at 2:00 /interactive /every:T,W,Th,F,S,Su c:\diffback.cmd
```

And if you wanted to be really snazzy, then you could build a slightly different version that runs only on Tuesday that erases the tape first—use /p /um for that one, if you like.

MAKING RSM AND NTBACKUP SHARE INFORMATION

As I said earlier, RSM and NTBACKUP don't always see eye to eye on how to present data. RSM thinks that all tape sets have more than one tape in them, so it names tapes with a 1 at the end. NTBACKUP won't recognize the name if the 1 is there, so you have to delete the 1 before including the RSM-reported name in a batch file. Similarly, RSM reports GUIDs as unbroken strings. NTBACKUP, on the other hand, is very exacting about the way it wants to see GUIDs: It wants you to type them as 8 characters, hyphen, 4, hyphen, 4, hyphen, 4, hyphen, 12 characters. That is, the GUID RSM reports as b471ff3b101f43bc9d15ffb7176cf2f3 needs to become b471ff3b-101f-43bc-9d15-ffb7176cf2f3 for NTBACKUP to use it. Having tired of counting characters and inserting hyphens at appropriate intervals, I wrote a batch file that will grab GUID data from RSM, format it so that NTBACKUP likes it, then starts a differential backup. Just be sure to supply your own GUIDs when using this batch file!

```
@echo off
set drvguid=E30ADF03E8014BA4BB824AD69B39FBE7
FOR /F "usebackq delims==" %%i IN ('rsm view /tphysical_media /cg%drvguid%
/guiddisplay /b') DO set tapeguid=%%i
FOR /F "usebackq delims==" %%i IN ('rsm view /tpartition /cg%tapeguid%
/guiddisplay /b') DO set partguid=%%i
FOR /F "usebackq delims==" %%i IN ('rsm view /tlogical_media /cg%partguid%
/guiddisplay /b') DO set logguid=%%i
set p1=%logguid:~0,8%
set p2=%logguid:~8,4%
set p3=%logguid:~12,4%
set p4=%logguid:~16,4%
set p5=%logguid:~20,12%
set bkguid=%p1%-%p2%-%p3%-%p4%-%p5%
ntbackup backup @c:\batch\files.bks /g "%bkguid%" /a /v:yes /hc:on /m
differential
```

ADVICE FOR BUILDING YOUR BATCH FILES

Now, you'll probably end up trying different things in your batch files and will have different needs than I do. So you'll have to craft your own solutions, which means trial and error. There is nothing more frustrating than checking your logs in the morning only to find that for some mysterious reason *nothing seems to have happened at all.*

Here's a methodology for making command-line backups tractable.

Try everything out from the command line first   Unless you're *really* good, you'll hit a few syntax snags along the way. Trying your commands out on the command line gives you immediate feedback so that you can work out the bugs quickly.

Build the command line gradually   Start from the most minimal command possible, such as ntbackup backup c:\testfiles /p "dlt" /um or the like. Crawl before you try walking and walk before you try flying.

Keep track of what worked and what didn't   You may have hardware that's cranky about some command and truthfully all tape drives are a bit flaky—something that works today may not work tomorrow unless you clean the tape or restart RSM. When you've got a command that works, make sure you've got its exact syntax saved somewhere. I use Notepad files as my logs when I'm experimenting. I use copy and paste to provide a simple log of the output from my commands.

Once you have the command line perfect, make a batch file   Just copy and paste the command line into Notepad, save it with the `.cmd` extension and you're a batch file builder. Then invoke the batch file by its name—if you called the Notepad file `c:\dotape.cmd`, then open up a command line and type **`c:\dotape.cmd`** and make sure that it still works. If it doesn't, then check that any paths needed in the command are there.

Try the batch file with `at`   Once you've got the batch file running so that it works as expected from the command line, test it with the Schedule service. From a command line, type **`at time /interactive batchfilename`** and press Enter. For *time* just punch in a time a minute or two in the future—you don't want to have to wait forever. (Remember that the Schedule service uses a 24-hour clock, so 3 P.M. should be entered as **15:00**.) If it doesn't work, then make sure that you entered the full path of the batch file.

Once the bugs are out, tell `at` to run the backup regularly   Rerun the `at` command, but add the `/every:` information so that it knows which days to run the command.

Viewing Backup Logs

Unless you specify otherwise, every time you back up, the Backup application creates a backup log. To see the contents of these logs, you can click the Report button in the dialog box that tells you that the backup is complete. Alternatively, to pick any log to view, choose Report from the Tools menu in Backup. You'll see a list of backups, as shown in Figure 19.22.

FIGURE 19.22

Choose a backup log to view.

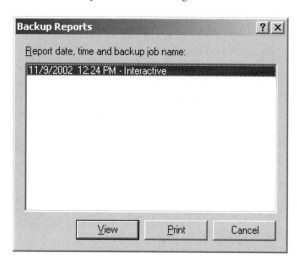

In the Backup Reports dialog box, find the report you want based on its job name or time and date stamp, and click the View button. The log will open in Notepad and provide output something such as this very simple example:

```
Backup Status
Operation: Backup
Active backup destination: File
Media name: "Backup.bkf created 1/11/2003 at 9:37 AM"

Backup (via shadow copy) of "C: "
Backup set #3 on media #1
Backup description: "Set created 1/11/2003 at 9:37 AM"
Media name: "Backup.bkf created 1/9/2003 at 12:24 PM"

Backup Type: Normal

Backup started on 1/11/2003 at 9:37 AM.
Backup completed on 1/11/2003 at 9:37 AM.
Directories: 4
Files: 2
Bytes: 743
Time: 1 second
```

Notice that in this log you can see what folders and directories were backed up, how long it took to run the backup, and whether any errors occurred. Scan these reports after completing backups so you can identify any problems before you need to restore data from those backups. By the way—there's something new here in Server 2003. The backed-up folder contained an open file. In Windows 2000, this would have netted me an error message telling me that a file was skipped because it was in use. In Server 2003, Backup uses the volume shadow copying service (if you've left it enabled), so it will copy even an open file. (Any changes saved after the file was copied didn't make it into the backup, obviously, but at least I've got the core file.)

Restoring Data

Backups don't do you a lot of good unless you can put them back on the server from where they came. To restore files, open Windows Backup again. You can either run the Restore Wizard or turn to the Restore tab.

WARNING   *NTFS 5 uses some file attributes not found in FAT or the Windows NT version of NTFS. You may not be able to restore some data that was originally stored on an NTFS 5 volume to a downlevel volume (FAT, FAT32, or NTFS with NT 4). For example, if you back up encrypted files and then try to restore them to a FAT volume, you'll see an error message telling you that the restore destination doesn't support some system features of the original, so some files (the encrypted ones) won't be restored. What actually happens is that the file's restored, but it no longer has the encryption attribute.*

BASIC RESTORATION TECHNIQUES

To restore files from the Restore Wizard, start Backup and choose to restore files, or (using Advanced View) turn to the Restore and Manage Media tab of Backup. You'll see the usual Welcome screen. Click through it, and you'll be prompted to pick the media you want to restore from (see Figure 19.23). The options available will depend on what kind of media you've backed up to.

FIGURE 19.23

Available media for restoration

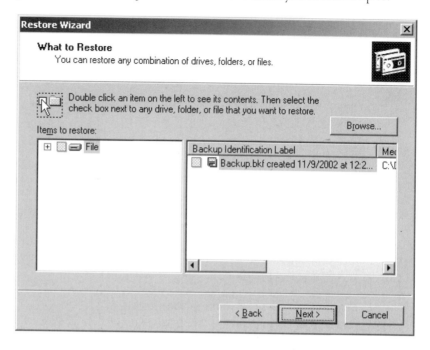

The backup sets on the media will be listed as folders, described according to volume backed up, size, type of backup, and description.

NOTE *If a backup operation was aborted for any reason—by Windows Backup or by the user—you will not be able to restore it. Such backups will still appear in the catalog but will have a question mark where their size should be. This is one more reason to ensure you can restore backups before you need them.*

Double-click a set to catalog it, and you'll be able to browse its contents. Check the boxes next to the files and folders in the backup set that you want to restore. As with selecting files for backup, a checked folder with all contents selected will have a blue check mark; if you've only selected certain files within the folder, its check mark will be gray.

NOTE *If there are any errors within the folders of a backup set, the folder will have a red exclamation point on it and the corrupted file will have another exclamation point. You will not be able to restore any damaged files.*

When you finish picking files to restore, the wizard will display a screen listing the current restore options. Click Back to edit any file or media settings, or click the Advanced button to specify a new restoration location or change the file restoration options for preexisting files and remote storage information.

WARNING *The Advanced options that you choose will apply to all future restoration operations until you change them again. For example, if you edit the options so that the files on the hard disk are always replaced with the files from the backup, that option will remain in place until you manually change it to another one.*

Where Should Files Be Restored?

Unless you tell it otherwise, Windows Backup restores files to their original location. But what if you're restoring data to a new drive with a drive letter that's different from the original? Or you want to put the contents of a daily backup on a Zip disk? From the first screen of the advanced section of the Backup Wizard you can choose from three location options:

◆ Original location

◆ Alternate location (files and folders will be restored, folder structure intact, to the location you specify)

◆ Single folder (files will all be put within a single folder in the folder you specify, and the original folder structure will be lost)

If you tell Windows Backup to restore the files to an alternate location or to a single folder, then the wizard will display a text box where you type (or browse for) the restore path. You can only restore data to an alternate location, not system configuration information such as the Registry. Any system configuration files must go back to their original locations.

TIP   To edit this option without running the Restore Wizard, turn to the Restore and Manage Media tab of Backup. In the lower-left corner of this tab is a drop-down list of the restoration location options. System State data must always be restored to its original location.

What If a File with That Name Already Exists?

The second screen in the advanced section of the Backup Wizard tells Windows Backup what to do if a file with the same name as the file being restored already exists on the volume. Normally, Windows Backup will not replace the file on the existing media, on the principle that if you already have the file, you shouldn't need to replace it. However, sometimes you'll want the file from the backup, not the one on the hard disk. For example, a Word document with a macro virus may be present on the hard disk, but you don't want the infected file. To cope with some of the situations in which you might want to replace the file already on the hard disk, Backup supports three replacement options:

◆ Do not replace the file on the disk (the default).

◆ Replace the file on the disk if it's older than the file on the backup.

◆ Always replace the file on the disk with the one on the backup.

Sadly, Windows Backup does not have an option to prompt you if it discovers a duplicate file on the media that you're restoring data to, or to restore the file but give it a new name on the volume if a file with the same name already exists. That would have been handy for those times when you're restoring corrupted files but don't necessarily want to replace *every* file that already exists on disk.

TIP   To edit this option without running the Restore Wizard, choose Options from the Tools menu in Windows Backup. Turn to the Restore tab and choose the file replacement you want to use.

What Other Data Should Be Restored?

The next screen in the advanced section of the Restore Wizard asks what non-data information you want to replace (see Figure 19.24).

FIGURE 19.24

The non-data information that you can restore depends on the file system the original data was stored in. FAT volumes only let you restore the RSM database.

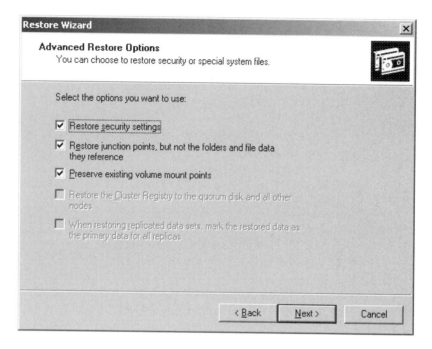

If you're restoring data backed up from an NTFS 5 volume to an NTFS 5 volume, Backup will normally restore all NTFS-related data: security settings, mount points, and junction points pointing to externally stored data. Replicated or clustered data will also normally have their settings preserved.

What happens if you tell Windows Backup to not restore the settings? Depends on whether the file already exists on disk:

◆ If the file exists in the location that you backed it up to, then the security settings attached to the file on disk will be applied, even if you're replacing the file.

◆ If the file does *not* exist on disk (if you're replacing a deleted file, for example) and you choose to not restore security settings, then the restored file will give the administrator of the local server and the system account full control—and wipe out any previous settings.

NOTE *Notice that the way security settings are restored means that if you elect not to restore security settings to a file that Everyone had access to, you'll need to explicitly grant that permission again.*

Junction points are physical locations on a mounted NTFS volume that point to another area of the disk or to another disk. They're used when you choose to mount a new volume to an empty folder on an NTFS volume instead of assigning that folder a drive letter. Normally, Backup will restore both the junction points and the files and folders to which they point. If you check the box that tells it to restore only the points, not the data, you may lose access to the data.

When you've picked all the Advanced settings, click the Finish button on the last page of the wizard. If restoring from a backup file, Windows Backup will prompt you for the name of the file, then complete the restoration. During the process of restoring the files to disk, Windows Backup will display a Restore Progress dialog box.

VIEWING RESTORE LOGS

When a restore operation is over, the Restore Progress dialog box will remain open. Click the Report button to open the restore report in Notepad. Alternatively, you can choose Report from the Tools menu and pick the report you want from the list of available reports. The restoration report will be appended to the backup report originally created for that job, so if you don't see the information you're looking for right away, page down for it.

RESTORING CONFIGURATION SETTINGS

The process of restoring configuration data is much the same as restoring any other data—when prompted to do so, pick the System State folder from the backup set and start the restoration.

However, restoring System State data isn't as simple as restoring user data. If you restore System State data to its original location (that is, you don't specify an alternate location for it), then Windows Backup will replace the System State data currently on your computer with the System State data you're restoring. However, if you restore the System State data to an alternate location, only the Registry files, SYSVOL directory files, and system boot files are restored to the alternate location. You can't restore the Active Directory services database, Certificate Services database, or COM+ Class Registration database to an alternate location.

NOTE *In order to restore the System State data on a domain controller, you must first start your computer in Directory Services Restore mode, available from the Advanced Start menu when you boot the OS. See the next section "Backing Up and Restoring the Active Directory" for details.*

Backing Up and Restoring the Active Directory

As I said earlier in this chapter, when you choose to back up the System State data on a computer, the contents of System State depend on the role of the computer you're backing up. If the computer is a domain controller, then System State includes the Active Directory. Backing up the Active Directory is pretty simple—you choose to back up the System State data on a domain controller. Restoring it, however, is not as simple as restoring user data, especially if you need to restore data from a backup that's older than the current data in the Active Directory. In this section, I'll talk about how to back up the Active Directory, how long you can store it, and how to restore it—or pieces of it.

BACKING UP THE ACTIVE DIRECTORY

You can take a snapshot of the Active Directory at any time by backing up a domain controller's System State data, either from the command line or with the graphical Backup tool. To back up Active Directory, you must be a member of the Backup Operators group, the local Administrators group, or a group that's been given the right to back up the System State data.

RESTORING THE ACTIVE DIRECTORY

To begin restoring Active Directory information, you'll boot the computer into Directory Services Restore Mode (to do so, press F8 while the domain controller is rebooting and choose this option from the Advanced Options menu that appears). You can perform an authoritative restore on either all or part of the Active Directory. I'll discuss the Advanced Options boot menu later in this chapter, but because one of its menu items is crucial to restoring the Active Directory, I'm going to leap ahead a bit, returning to this topic later. When you choose this option, it will kick you back to the main boot menu, showing in text at the bottom of the screen that you're in DSRM. The system will boot in Safe Mode with Networking, run CHKDSK on all the volumes, and then present the logon screen for you to log in as the local machine's administrator.

Once you're in, run the Restore Wizard, choosing the backup set containing the system data. Most of the way, this operation looks like restoring any data. However, when you're clicking through the advanced options, you'll come to the screen in Figure 19.25. Don't just blindly click through this screen, as the options you pick here—specifically, the *last* option you pick here—determine what kind of restoration operation you're performing.

FIGURE 19.25

Advanced options for restoring System State data

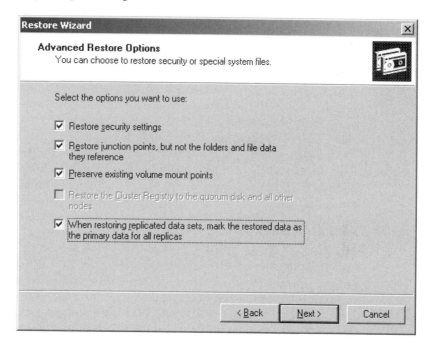

Let me digress for a moment. A normal file restore operation restores all files, including Active Directory objects, with their original update sequence numbers (USNs). The AD replication system uses the USNs to detect and replicate changes to the Active Directory to all of the domain controllers on the network. The Active Directory replication system updates old data with newer data from other domain controllers.

For normal operations, this is fine. It has one sticking point, though: Normally, any Active Directory data that you restore will retain its original USN used by the AD replication system to detect and spread AD changes among the domain controllers in your domain. Because of this, any data restored in nonauthoritative mode (would that be in "peon mode"?) looks like old data and won't get propagated to the other domain controllers. Not only that, but the Active Directory replication system will *replace* that restored data with the "newer" data from the other domain controllers, if any exists. If you're trying to replace bad current data with good old data, this obviously isn't what you want to happen. Authoritative restore solves this problem, forcing the domain to accept the older data and overwrite the new.

Before doing an authoritative restore, consider what effect this will have on the domain. When you restore the Active Directory database, you're restoring the following, among other things (see Chapter 8 for a complete description of what the Active Directory is and what objects it contains):

◆ User and machine accounts

◆ User and machine account passwords

◆ Groups and organizational units

◆ Trust relationships (or lack thereof) with other domains

However, what you're *not* doing is removing any new accounts you created since backing up the Active Directory. The AD isn't a big lump with a single USN, but a directory of objects, each with its own USN. You can pick and choose pieces of the Active Directory to restore. Also, if you perform an authoritative restore to a domain containing other domain controllers, any objects you created in the naming context (in this example, the domain naming context) after making the backup will remain in the Active Directory. Say, for example, that on Monday you create an account for ChristaA (which is then replicated to the other domain controllers in the domain), then back up. On Tuesday you create an account for Christa—also replicated to the rest of the domain. On Wednesday, you delete the ChristaA account. On Thursday, you perform an authoritative restore from the backup you made on Monday. Both the ChristaA and Christa accounts will exist in the domain, not just the ChristaA account you backed up, because the two accounts have unique USNs—they're different objects.

Types of Restoration Actions

The way you should restore Active Directory data depends on what kind of restoration you want to complete. Restoring the entire domain from scratch and must therefore replicate the data across all domain controllers? Restoring a single domain controller and do *not* want that data replicated to any other domain controllers? Restoring particular data in the Active Directory? Each of these actions requires a different kind of restoration process.

To restore the entire domain from scratch—to restore the first copy of all replicated data and use that as the basis for further replication—you'll perform a *primary restore*. From the screen shown in Figure 19.25, choose to mark the restored data as the primary data for all replicas. This will cause all the restored Active Directory data to overwrite any other directory services information in the domain.

To get a domain controller in a working domain back online, restore its System State data, but do *not* check the final box making this domain controller the primary source of replicated data. This is called a *normal restore*. Each object in the Active Directory will keep its original USN number. (In case it's not obvious why you're restoring it at all when some of the data may be overwritten from other domain controllers, consider that it's unlikely that every single object in the Active Directory has changed since you backed up the System State data, and it's a lot quicker to replicate a few changes here and there than it is to replicate the entire Active Directory.)

So far, we've looked at all-or-nothing scenarios: making the entire restored Active Directory the primary source, or none of it. However, you may need to restore part of the Active Directory; for example, if someone accidentally deletes an organizational unit and with it all the computer or user objects within that OU. To selectively restore parts of the Active Directory as primary replication sources, you'll need to perform an *authoritative restore*. This is a two-part process. First, you perform a normal restore. Next—and before you reboot the server—you run NTDSUTIL, a command-line utility that lets you mark selective pieces of the Active Directory for primary restore.

Understanding Tombstone Lifetimes and Backup Lives

Tombstone lifetime sounds like an oxymoron. It's actually a property of the Active Directory Directory Service (NTDS, for NT Directory Service—same thing) object, representing the number of days that a deleted object will exist as a "ghost" in the Active Directory before it's deleted. Tombstoned objects are still replicated but appear in the Active Directory as deleted. A housekeeping process called the *garbage collector* runs every 12 hours on each server to delete objects whose tombstone lifetimes have expired. (Personally, I would have called it the "sexton" to keep the metaphor going—garbage collectors don't normally have much to do with tombstones, or if they do I don't want to know about it.) Left to itself, the default tombstone lifetime is 60 days.

So what does this have to do with the useful lifetime of an Active Directory backup? Simply put, you can't restore data from a backup image older than the tombstone lifetime. If you did, the restored objects would be too old to trigger Active Directory replication and thus never be replicated to other domain controllers, and the restored domain controller would never get the replication data required to delete the objects—the records of those objects being deleted would have been removed by the garbage collector. The result would be an inconsistent Active Directory on the local server, which misses the point of a domainwide database of available resources. In short, don't restore the Active Directory from backups more than 60 days old if you have not explicitly increased the tombstone lifetime.

If you're trying to restore a domain controller and your only backups are older than the 60-day default limit, then you have two choices. If you have at least one domain controller still up and running and its Active Directory information is good, then you have nothing to worry about—just restore the domain controller, and the remaining domain controller with good Active Directory information will replicate its data to the newly restored domain controller. If you're having to rebuild the domain from scratch, then you can pick an outdated backup, restore it to a domain controller, and replicate the other servers from the restored one.

If you *must* restore an older Active Directory backup to a working domain (although I'd hate to think of what could happen to your domain that you had to lose more than 60 days of changes to get it back to working order), then you can force the change by editing the tombstone date. Because .TombstoneLifetime is a property of the NTDS ADSI object, you can modify it with a script or with an AD editor such as ADSIEDIT.MSC or LDP.EXE. If you do, then you can make the tombstone lifetime older than the available backup. At that point, you'll need to perform an *authoritative restore* to force the replication of this old backup to the other domain controllers since this information will be stamped as being too old for replication.

Restoring Part of the Active Directory

As I said earlier, you can use DSRM to restore individual parts of the database, not just the whole thing. For example, you could restore an accidentally deleted machine account for a domain controller. To do so, boot to DSRM and restore the System State data, then run NTDSUTIL for an authoritative restore. This time, though, instead of typing **restore database**, choose to restore part of it, like this (all on one line):

```
restore subtree "cn=domain_controller,ou=Domain Controllers,dc=domain_name,dc=xxx"
```

Here *domain_controller* is the computer name of the domain controller, *domain_name* is the domain name the domain controller resides in, and *xxx* is the top-level domain name of the domain controller, such as com, org, or net. NTDSUTIL will ask you if you're sure you want to perform an authoritative restore. When you click Yes, NTDSUTIL will open the directory information tree (DIT), note the last time it was updated and the number of entries that need updating, then read through the restore subtree command backward to find the domain, the organizational unit, and finally the computer name you want to restore. When you're done with this, type **quit** to exit authoritative restore and then **quit** again to exit NTDSUTIL, then reboot the domain controller.

TIP If you don't know the name of the part of the Active Directory that you want to restore, use ADSIEDIT.MSC *or LDP to find the name. You'll need to enter the name exactly.*

Troubleshooting Hardware with the System Information Tool

If you want current nuts-and-bolts information about the hardware in your servers, you can dig out those PDF files you printed from the Web sites and read all your handwritten notes about configuration changes that you made.

For those less than thrilled about this idea, there's the System Information tool available from the Support section of Help. Using this tool, you can view the following on either the local computer or any Server 2003 or Win2K computer:

◆ A system summary showing you the basic hardware and software configuration of the server

◆ Hardware resources used on the server

◆ Configuration information for the hardware

◆ Information about all parts of the server software environment

TIP Typing **winmsd** *or* **msinfo32** *from Run will start the System Information tool. For those who don't remember, MSD was the original Microsoft Diagnostics tool, which became WinMSD in Windows.*

The System Information tool isn't 100-percent accurate—as I wandered through it, I found a couple of minor pieces of misinformation—but it's close. And it provides a lot more information than WinMSD ever did and in a reasonably organized manner. Read on to learn how to use this tool to inventory and monitor servers.

System Summary

The system summary information is just that—a snapshot of your system, such as the one shown in Figure 19.26. The information is roughly that which used to be on the Version tab of NT 4's WinMSD, with the addition of BIOS version and some memory information. You can't change the data here, just see what the situation is. About the only information you need pay special attention to is the available memory. You can get memory information in *many* places around the operating system (the Task Manager is another tool that you can use for this), but here it is in black and white: how much physical and virtual memory you have available and have remaining.

FIGURE 19.26

System summary information for a Server 2003 computer

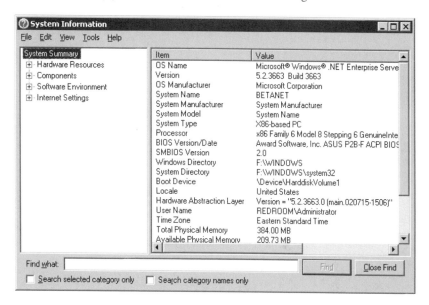

Hardware Resources

The Hardware Resources folder (see Figure 19.27) lists all the resources that might be used by the hardware in your services and shows what hardware actually *is* using those resources, as described in Table 19.5.

Why is this information important? Basically, everything in Table 19.5 represents either a channel for devices to pass information to the processor for processing or a storage place for such data while it's waiting for processor time. Each channel must have its own hotline to the processor so that when the processor responds to a call for processing (an *interrupt*), it knows whose data it's crunching and can pass back the results accordingly. Some devices can share some kinds of channels; IRQs, for example, can be shared by some modern hardware. But memory storage areas cannot be shared, and not all channels can be shared. If you suspect that two or more devices are using the same resources and can't share, then you can use this tool to find out.

FIGURE 19.27

The Hardware
Resources folder
with the contents of
one folder showing

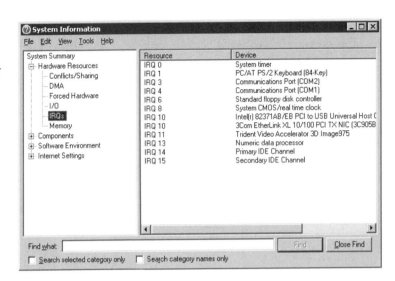

TABLE 19.5: RESOURCES USED BY SERVER HARDWARE

RESOURCE TYPE	DESCRIPTION
Conflicts/Sharing	Lists the components either sharing an IRQ or in conflict over one. Components sharing an IRQ should be working fine (or if they're not, the IRQ in common shouldn't be the problem). If multiple devices are in conflict over an IRQ, however, then one or all won't work.
DMA	Direct Memory Access (DMA) channels are rarely required; most often these days, they're used by audio devices. Basically, the DMA chips on the motherboard can move data from a device to RAM without the CPU having to be involved in the process. Any device that can use DMA needs its own DMA channel as its dedicated path for data moving.
Forced Hardware	Lists older devices not supporting Plug and Play that require specific IRQs.
I/O	Shows what devices are using what parts of virtual memory for storage. The information here is similar to what's in the Memory folder but is taken from the perspective of the memory, not the devices using it.
IRQs	Interrupt request lines, or IRQs, represent each device's hotline to the processor. IRQs are like DMA channels in that they're specific to a given device, but are unlike them in that they don't take care of the process of shoving data to the processor—the processor must still be involved. Some devices can share IRQs.
Memory	Shows the I/O buffer areas that each device is using to store data waiting for processing. Essentially, these buffer areas are mailboxes that the processor can use both to pick up data waiting for it and to drop off instructions for the device to which that I/O area belongs. Each device must have its own I/O area so that the CPU will drop off the appropriate instructions to each device. It's going to cause no end of confusion if the processor asks the network card to play a sound.

Components

The Hardware Resources folder looks at the types of resources available and shows you what devices are using them. The Components folder's approach (Figure 19.28) is the opposite—you look at the devices installed and see what resources they're using. But not only resources. The properties pages for the installed devices provide just about all information relevant to a piece of hardware, including resources used, driver versions, and the type of device it is.

FIGURE 19.28

The contents of the IDE section of the Components folder

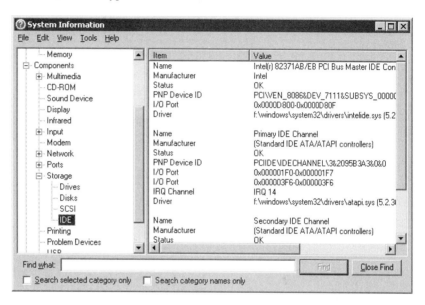

NOTE *The* Components *folder is a list of all* possible *devices, not actual devices. For example, even if your server doesn't have a modem installed, it will still have a* Modem *folder.*

The exact data within a given object in the Components folder depends heavily on what the device it represents does. For example, the data for the display reports information such as the color density, refresh rate and resolution, video adapter's name, and other display-related information. The network's folder has three subfolders: one for the adapter, one for protocols used, and one for Winsock version information. Storage media show their size, media type, compression data, and so forth. There's even a section for problem devices, listing any devices that the OS can tell aren't working as expected. For instance, at one time I had a SCSI removable drive attached to this server. After I removed the drive, the OS still expected to find it, so it's now listed in the Problem Devices folder.

Software Environment

The information in the Software Environment folder (Figure 19.29) describes all of the software running on the system, who's using it, and what files and services are loaded. It includes the components listed in Table 19.6.

FIGURE 19.29

The Software Environment folder with one folder open

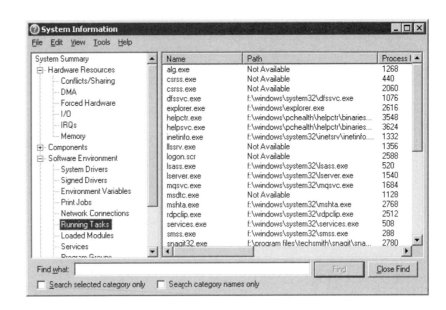

TABLE 19.6: SYSTEM PARTS DESCRIBED IN THE SOFTWARE ENVIRONMENT FOLDER

SYSTEM PART	DESCRIPTION
System Drivers	Lists all the system drivers. Each driver lists a brief description, its type (kernel driver or file system driver), its state (whether stopped or running), its start mode, its status (all drivers are OK) and whether it can be stopped or paused.
Signed Drivers	Lists all the signed drivers installed on the server and information about them, including whether they really are signed (the options are Yes and Not Available), the device class (e.g., NET for network drivers), the driver version (available only for signed drives), the manufacturer, the INF name, and (theoretically) the driver name. "Theoretically" because this information is available for neither signed nor unsigned drivers.
Environment Variables	Lists all the environment variables for the server, including the processor identification, location of all temporary files, path information for system files, and OS version.
Print Jobs	Lists all currently running print jobs.
Network Connections	Lists all current network connections and the drive letters they're mapped to (if applicable).
Running Tasks	Lists all the executable files run by the services running on the server. File path, version, file size, and file date are all listed here. If you want to know what version of a given EXE you've got, this is where to look.

Continued on next page

TABLE 19.6: SYSTEM PARTS DESCRIBED IN THE SOFTWARE ENVIRONMENT FOLDER *(continued)*

SYSTEM PART	DESCRIPTION
Loaded Modules	Like the Running Tasks folder, except that it lists all dynamic link libraries in memory. Version, size, file date, manufacturer, and path information are all displayed. If you want to know what version of a given DLL you've got, this is where to look.
Services	Lists all the (nonboot or system) services available on the server by name. The state of each service, its start mode (manual, automatic, or disabled), and its type are all shown.
Program Groups	Lists all the groups available from the Start menu. The view shows the users for whom the groups are customized (this information is stored as part of each user's profile, so you may have several different listings of the same program group, each associated with a different user). Terminal server profile associations will be displayed here.
Startup Programs	Lists all the programs configured to run at system startup.
OLE Registration	Shows all the object linking and embedding associations used to open data files in the right kind of application.
Windows Error Reporting	Lists some errors appearing in the Event Log, their type (e.g., DHCP errors or hanging applications) and some details for the error.

Internet Settings

As you can see in Figure 19.30 and Table 19.7, all the settings for IE are listed in the Internet Explorer folder within the Internet Settings folder, although (as with the other settings in the System Summary folder) you can't change any of them.

FIGURE 19.30

Contents of the Internet Explorer folder

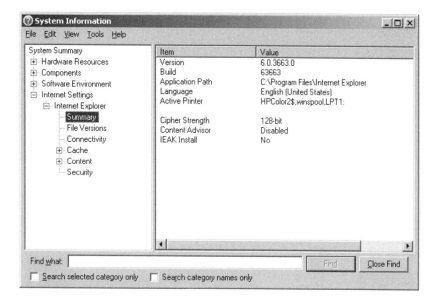

TABLE 19.7: SYSTEM CONFIGURATION SETTINGS IN THE INTERNET EXPLORER FOLDER

SYSTEM PART	DESCRIPTION
Summary	Lists basic version and path information about IE. The most useful information indicates the degree of encryption IE is set up to use, which printers are set up to work with IE, whether the Content Advisor (ratings software) is on, and whether the Internet Explorer Administration Kit is installed.
File Versions	Lists all the files installed that support IE, including their version number, date, size, path, and the company supplying them. If a file is expected but not present, it's still listed, but its version is recorded as "file missing."
Connectivity	Lists the connection settings for the browser. Most of what's here applies to proxy server settings, but also listed is whether the dialer is set up to kick in when you start IE.
Cache	Lists the objects in the IE cache (stored when you view online content so that when you need the images again they can be loaded from the cache). It also lists the size of the cache.
Content	Lists the content controls in place on your IE setup. Again, it's indicating whether the Content Advisor is enabled. Any certificates in place (your own or someone else's) are also listed here.
Security	Lists the security settings you have in place for different site classes: trusted, local intranet, Internet, and restricted.

Saving System Configuration Information

All this information is great, but sometimes it won't help you get the answers you need to resolve problems with the server. That doesn't mean that it can't get someone *else* the answers they need to fix problems. The System Information tool lets you save and load configuration information. Using this capability, you can save your server's configuration to a text file or system information file. You can then e-mail that file to a tech support person who has Server 2003 installed (or not, but if not they'll have to read the text file) and can then load the file and view your computer's information as if they were connected to the server.

TIP *To save only part of the system information, select the part you want to save before starting the save procedure. For example, to save only information related to the network card's configuration, make sure that folder is selected in the left pane.*

SAVING AND OPENING SYSTEM INFORMATION FILES

To save information as a file, open the File menu in the System Information tool and choose Save. In the dialog box that appears, type a name for the file (it will have an .nfo extension, just as these files did in Windows 2000) and click Save. The server will chug away for a minute or two as it inventories your system (so that the saved file reflects the most current information), and then store the file in your My Documents folder unless you specify otherwise. The file isn't too big—mine is 198KB—so you can fit it onto a floppy if necessary. To open a saved file, choose Open from the File menu, browse for the file, and—get this—open it. (I detail this mostly because opening saved files in Windows 2000 was something of a pain. It's much simpler in Server 2003.)

SAVING SYSTEM INFORMATION AS TEXT

Saving system information as a text file works much the same way as saving it as an NFO file. In the System Information tool, choose Export from the File menu. Again, the default location is the My Documents folder. When you click the Save button, the server will inventory itself to make sure that the most current settings are saved, then put them into a TXT file that you can read with an editor such as Notepad. It's a long file; this is a partial dump of the information I collected from one server:

```
Directory                  C:\WINNT
User Name                  REDROOM\ChristaA
Time Zone                  Eastern Standard Time
Daylight Savings Time      Eastern Daylight Time
Total Physical Memory      130612 kbytes
Available Physical Memory  14572 kbytes
Total Virtual Memory       2097024 kbytes
Available Virtual Memory   1988656 kbytes
Page File Space            311252 kbytes
Page File                  C:\pagefile.sys
```

Needless to say, I'd rather analyze the data from an organized system information file than from a 225KB ASCII file, but the fact that you can save the information as text means that you *can* give someone your system configuration for analysis without them being able to read NFO files.

SAVING INFORMATION FROM THE COMMAND LINE

You don't have to open the graphical tool if all you want to do is create a system information log. Msinfo32.exe supports the command-line switches shown in Table 19.8 to generate a local or remote system information file.

TABLE 19.8: WinMSD Command-Line Options

SWITCH	DESCRIPTION
/?	Displays Help
/*msinfo_file*	Opens the specified saved file
/nfo *filename*	Outputs an NFO file with the specified filename and quits
/report *filename*	Outputs a text-format file to the specified filename and quits
/computer *computername*	Connects to the specified computer
/categories *catlist*	Displays or outputs the specified categories
/category *catlist*	Sets the focus to a specific category at startup

So, for example, typing `msinfo32.exe /nfo g:\tools\report.nfo` will generate a complete copy of the local computer's system information and store it as an NFO file in `G:\tools`. (Notice that I must include the file suffix even though I've specified that I want to create an NFO file—`winmsd` isn't smart enough to generate the suffix information on its own.) When I open this file on any computer with the MMC installed, it will show up as the local system information. If I wanted to create a text report (again, I don't recommend doing this unless you simply have no other options— it's too long), then I'd type the command like this: `misinfo32.exe /report g:\tools\report.txt`.

NOTE   *Generating the report takes a few minutes, even on a fast computer.*

Troubleshooting the Boot Process

The operating system includes several tools that can help you recover from problems related to the operating system, but these tools are no good if you can't get to the Advanced Options menu (discussed later) available at boot time for troubleshooting or get the Setup menu to recognize that your server does, in fact, have a hard disk. In this section, I'll describe the steps the server follows to boot, including the outward manifestations of those steps so you can figure out which step went wrong.

Prequel: The Hardware Must Work

Before you can even attack the problem of "What's wrong with the operating system?" you must make sure that it's not a problem of "What's wrong with the server?" You will not be able to boot the server at all if either of the following are true:

◆ The boot drive, the boot drive's disk controller, or the cable connecting the two is malfunctioning or incorrectly set up.

◆ The processor or the motherboard is dead.

Other hardware can give you problems, but these are the two that will really stop you in your tracks. To isolate the problem, watch and see where the problem appears:

◆ A computer that does not boot *at all*, does not make noise, does not do anything at all, probably has a dead (or turned off) power supply or a dead power cord.

◆ A computer that will start its fan but doesn't do anything beyond that probably has a problem with its motherboard.

◆ A computer that will count up memory but isn't displaying anything on the monitor (you can hear it, but you can't see it) and beeps at you probably has a problem with the video card.

◆ A computer that starts to load the operating system (in this example) and then blue-screens before displaying the logon screen may be having memory problems. Bad device drivers are also a possibility.

◆ A computer that will boot and find the CD and floppy but doesn't find the hard disk controller probably has a problem with the hard disk controller.

◆ A computer that will boot and identify the hard disk controller but doesn't find a bootable hard disk probably has a hard disk problem. If you're still not positive and you have a spare system around, swap in an easy part of the computer, such as the hard disk controller, if you're not sure whether the problem lies in the disk or the controller.

TIP   *Keep an eye on the fans in your servers. Those fans are vital to keeping delicate components cool. A cooked computer is a dead computer, sooner or later. A company called PC Power and Cooling (`www.pcpowercooling.com`) makes a temperature sensor, the 110 Alert, that fits inside a PC and squawks when the internal temperature rises above 110 degrees.*

Finally—is the server plugged in? Is its UPS turned on? I know, I know—but check.

Using the Advanced Options Menu

If it's not the hardware, then what if it's the operating system?

No matter how careful you are, mistakes sometimes happen or something just goes wrong. In such a case, you'll need to fix your installation, hopefully without reinstalling the operating system. Sometimes you have to reinstall to make things right again, but it's definitely something to be avoided, since restoring a server back to its original greatness is generally a bit more comprehensive than just running Setup and blasting by all the defaults. When installing isn't the only option, I prefer to spend my time doing something a little more useful.

If you've made some change to your operating system that makes it unusable, all is not lost—so long as the system will boot at all and can recognize the hard disk that the operating system is installed on. The Advanced Options menu gives you several methods for fixing or debugging a broken operating system. You get to this menu by pressing F8 when the boot menu appears, or (if Server 2003 is the only available operating system) by pressing it when the OS is loading—early on, please. Do so, and you'll see a text menu like the following:

```
Windows Advanced Options Menu
Please Select an option:

Safe Mode
Safe Mode with Networking
Safe Mode with Command Prompt

Enable Boot Logging
Enable VGA Mode
Last Known Good Configuration (your most recent settings that worked)
Directory Services Restore Mode (Windows domain controllers Only)
Debugging Mode

Start Windows Normally
Reboot
Return to OS Choices Menu
```

Incidentally, the Advanced Options menu is one more reason why, any time you're running a dual-boot computer supporting two versions of NT (e.g., NT and Server 2003), you *must* install the older one first. If you install the older OS second, then you may not see the prompt to press F8 to open the Windows Advanced Options menu, the "Starting Windows" progress bar at the bottom of the screen, or the proper startup graphic. The problem is that NT 4 overwrites the shared Windows boot files (`Ntldr` and `Ntdetect.com`). To fix this, boot from the installation CD-ROM. At the Windows Setup screen, press R to repair the Windows installation. Then, press C to use Recovery Console. Copy the `Ntldr` and `Ntdetect.com` files from the `I386` folder on the CD-ROM to the root folder of the boot drive.

I discussed Directory Services Restore Mode earlier in "Backing Up and Restoring the Active Directory." Let's take a look at the other modes.

Using Safe Mode Options

The various forms of Safe Mode—with networking, without networking, with command prompt—load a minimal version of the operating system with only the drivers and files needed to support that minimal version (such as NTOSKRNL). These tools can be handy when something is preventing your system from booting and you suspect an errant driver. Whichever mode you choose, during boot, the OS will display a list of all the drivers and services as they're loading. When you log out, the machine will restart as usual.

SAFE MODE

Safe Mode starts the OS with only the drivers and services required to boot the computer. No network drivers are loaded, and network-dependent services are changed to start option 3 (meaning that they're set for manual starting) but can't be started even from the Services section of the MMC or with `net start`. Use this version of Safe Mode to fix problems related to network services that are keeping the computer from working at all.

SAFE MODE WITH NETWORKING

Safe Mode with Networking is what it sounds like—a pared-down version of the OS that includes network support. Use this version when you need network support and you're sure that the network drivers are not causing any problems. When you boot the computer into Directory Services Restore Mode, it's booting into Safe Mode with Networking.

SAFE MODE WITH COMMAND PROMPT

If you're expecting Safe Mode with Command Prompt to be a strictly command-line version of Server 2003, you're mistaken. When you boot to this option, you'll see a list of the files that the OS is loading, and then the graphical interface will appear, running in 640×480. However, rather than loading the Desktop, Server 2003 will use the command prompt for its shell.

Safe Mode with Command Prompt is a network-disabled version of Server 2003 that replaces the `Explorer.exe` shell normally used with `cmd.exe`. You can do anything on the local computer that you can do in the usual shell—you can even run GUI applications, if you don't mind them running with a maximum resolution of 640×480 and 16 colors, with no working network services. But everything you do you must start from the command prompt or from the Task Manager (still available if you press Ctrl+Alt+Delete). Use Safe Mode with Command Prompt to run a stand-alone version of Server 2003 when something is wrong with Explorer that keeps the OS from starting. You can run Explorer from this mode and gain access to the graphical Desktop, if you like, but you're not dependent on it as you are in the other versions of Safe Mode. If you don't open Explorer, you can shut down the server with the `shutdown` command.

*TIP   To get a complete list of all the commands supported from the command prompt, type **help | more**. (You can just type **help**, but there's more commands than will fit on a single screen.) To get help with the syntax of a specific command, type **commandname** /?.*

Please note that Safe Mode with Command Prompt is *not* the same thing as the Recovery Console, which I'll get to shortly. I've seen some confusion about this and want to make sure that the difference is clear. Safe Mode with Command Prompt is a minimal version of the OS that uses `cmd.exe` as the default shell (operating environment) but can run any graphical tool so long as you know the command to invoke it. The Recovery Console is for resolving problems that can keep the computer from booting at all. It supports only a subset of commands and cannot run graphical utilities under any circumstances.

The Last Known Good Configuration

One purpose of the Last Known Good Configuration option is to save you from your better ideas. For example, one time I thought I'd try installing the CD-burning software designed for a Windows 98 computer on a Windows 2000 Professional computer. While installing, I saw an error warning me that the software was not designed for Windows 2000, but I persevered. (Rules? Ha! We spit at rules.) Everything went smoothly, and I finished installing the tool. Feeling a little smug, I rebooted when prompted.

And Windows 2000 refused to start and instead displayed a blue screen. I stopped feeling smug.

Instead, I rebooted again, pressed F8 to display the Advanced Options menu, and chose to boot to the Last Known Good Configuration—the configuration that had been in place the last time I'd been logged into the computer. The computer unloaded the new driver, I booted successfully, and life was good. So long as the change you made produced no system-critical errors (at the time, that is—as you can see, it's okay if the change you made prevents the OS from starting up properly), and you successfully booted and logged in to the server once before you ran into the problem, all is not lost. You can load the Last Known Good Configuration and choose from three different system start-up options:

- Using the current configuration
- Using the Last Known Good Configuration—loaded the last time the server successfully booted and you started a session from the console
- Restarting the computer

UNDERSTANDING HOW LAST KNOWN GOOD WORKS

The Last Known Good Configuration option works because of the way NT-based operating systems maintain configuration information. Every time you boot the computer and log in, the configuration information for the local machine is stored in `HKLM\System\CurrentControlSet`. The OS also stores a backup copy of this information and assigns it a number for organization purposes. This backup is used should the default set of configuration information—the current set—become corrupted and unusable.

Server 2003 stores several copies of the configuration information, numbering them consecutively (see Figure 19.31). Another numbered set is maintained as a Last Known Good Configuration, to be used if the default configuration set becomes unusable.

You can't tell from the numbers which configuration set your server is currently using. To find this information, look in the `\Select` key in `HKLM\System` (see Figure 19.32). There are four values here: Current, Default, Failed, and LastKnownGood. If you restart the machine and boot normally (that is, without using the Advanced Options menu), then the Default control set will be used. The value of Failed is the configuration set that had been the default when you chose to start the machine from the Last Known Good Configuration menu. Because you told the OS to not start with that configuration set, it's now marked as Failed even if nothing is actually wrong with it.

FIGURE 19.31

Contents of HKLM\System

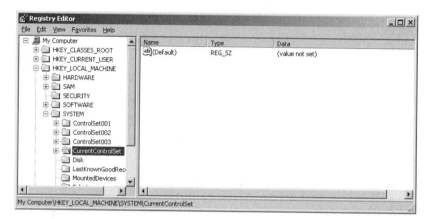

FIGURE 19.32

The \Select key displays all current control sets.

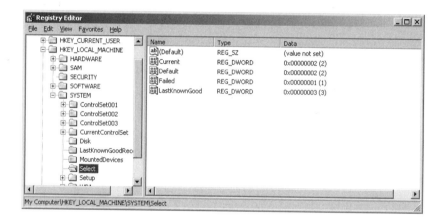

REPAIRING A SERVER WITH THE LAST KNOWN GOOD CONFIGURATION

That's just background so that you know what's happening; you don't have to tweak the Registry to make the Last Known Good option work.

If you do something that keeps the computer from starting normally, do *not* log on and try to fix it right away. Instead, restart the computer and follow these steps:

1. When the system has finished recognizing its hardware (and displays the boot menu if more than one OS is available), press F8 to open the Advanced Options menu.

2. Choose Last Known Good from the boot menu and press Enter. The boot menu will now reappear with the words *Last Known Good Configuration* at the bottom of the screen. This is to

remind you that, by loading that option, you're choosing to reverse all nonsecurity-related changes made to the Registry during the last session. As I mentioned in my earlier example, this includes unloading drivers installed during the previous session.

Server 2003 will start with the settings with which you started your last session. After you log in, you'll see an information message telling you that Server 2003 couldn't start with the current configuration and is starting with a previously saved configuration.

The Last Known Good option can't always help you. It applies only so long as you have never logged in with the new configuration, but *have* logged in at least once, and can boot the computer now. That means that it won't work if any of the following apply:

◆ You have never logged in successfully (that is, if you're just installing the OS).

◆ You edited the server's configuration, rebooted, and logged in successfully, and now want to restore your system to the way it was before the change.

◆ The change that you want to reverse is not related to control set information. You can't remove changes to user profiles or system policies with the Last Known Good menu, for example. Passwords are also unaffected by the Last Known Good option, so you can't use this option to recover from a forgotten Administrator's password.

◆ The system boots, someone logs in (even with automatic logon), and the system hangs or the problem you wanted to avoid still exists.

◆ The system won't boot at all and is unable to get to the boot menu.

Enable VGA Mode

Those familiar with NT Server will remember that in previous versions of the operating system, the boot menu had two entries for each instance of NT installed on the computer: one with whatever graphics settings you'd chosen and one designed to run in vanilla VGA mode. There was a good reason for this. In NT 3.1, there was no VGA mode, and if you set up the wrong driver and logged in (making the Last Known Good option useless), then you had to go through a complicated sequence of keystrokes to navigate blindly to the Display applet in the Control Panel and fix things. This gave you a terrific sense of accomplishment when it actually worked, but it made video problems more than a little painful to resolve.

The VGA option is no longer in the main menu, however. To get to it, you must press F8 at boot time and choose Enable VGA Mode from the Advanced Options menu. Use this option if you've installed a bad video driver and need to correct the problem. Unlike the Last Known Good menu, this option will work at any time, not just before you've successfully logged in.

Enable Boot Logging

Enabling boot logging from the Advanced Options menu starts Windows as usual, except that it creates a file called NTBTlog.txt and stores it in the top of your system root directory. The output will look like this snippet:

```
Microsoft (R) Windows (R) Version 5.2 (Build 3663)
11 11 2002 15:53:05.500
Loaded driver \WINDOWS\system32\ntoskrnl.exe
Loaded driver \WINDOWS\system32\hal.dll
```

```
Loaded driver \WINDOWS\system32\KDCOM.DLL
Loaded driver \WINDOWS\system32\BOOTVID.dll
Loaded driver pci.sys
Loaded driver isapnp.sys
Loaded driver intelide.sys
Loaded driver \WINDOWS\system32\DRIVERS\PCIIDEX.SYS
Loaded driver MountMgr.sys
Loaded driver ftdisk.sys
Loaded driver \WINDOWS\system32\DRIVERS\WMILIB.SYS
Loaded driver dmload.sys
Loaded driver dmio.sys
Loaded driver PartMgr.sys
Loaded driver VolSnap.sys
Loaded driver atapi.sys
Loaded driver disk.sys
Loaded driver \WINDOWS\system32\DRIVERS\CLASSPNP.SYS
Loaded driver Dfs.sys
Loaded driver KSecDD.sys
Loaded driver Ntfs.sys
Loaded driver NDIS.sys
Loaded driver Mup.sys
Loaded driver crcdisk.sys
Did not load driver Audio Codecs
Did not load driver Legacy Audio Drivers
Did not load driver Media Control Devices
Did not load driver Legacy Video Capture Devices
Did not load driver Video Codecs
```

If you're running into problems, then you can check this log to see what drivers did—and did not—load. It's normal for some drivers to not load; they're available, but if you haven't got anything running that requires them, the OS won't start them, so as to save memory. But if your network, for example, isn't working, you can scan the list of drivers to make sure that NDIS.SYS is present.

TIP   At a time when the server is working normally, enable boot logging and save the output under another name, noting the date and any new changes to the server. (You can do this pretty easily—all filesystems in Server 2003 support long filenames.) If something does go wrong with the machine, you can compare the healthy boot record with the sick one to find the discrepancy.

Debugging Mode

This final option in the Advanced Options menu, Debugging Mode, sends debugging information to a computer connected to a Windows 2000 computer you're booting via the serial port. The basic gist of this is that it's a way to monitor the progress of a server's boot from another server.

Preparing for Recovery

If the situation is too dire for any of the Advanced Options menu options to help you, all is not lost. Before it's time to reinstall, it's time to drag out one the recovery tools: the emergency repair disk or the Recovery Console, both of which are available through the Repair option in Setup.

Installing the Recovery Console

How do you get to the recovery tools? You can install the Recovery Console from the Windows 2000 installation CD. Open the Run tool in the Start menu and type **d:\i386\winnt32 /cmdcons** where *d:* is the drive letter of your installation CD. The first time you do this, the setup program will display the message box shown in Figure 19.33.

FIGURE 19.33

Initial screen for installing the Recovery Console

Setup will copy some files from the installation CD (or, if you have a live connection to the Internet, from the Microsoft Web site), then prompt you to restart the computer. The Recovery Console will be in the Startup menu (the text menu you see when you start up the computer) when you reboot, listed as Microsoft Windows Recovery Console. To start it, just choose that option before the 30-second time-out to whatever your default startup option is.

TIP   *If you install the system partition as FAT and then think, "Huh. I have this Recovery Console that I could use to repair the system partition, so I'm going to install the Recovery Console and then convert that partition to NTFS," you aren't going to like the results. The Recovery Console uses different support files for NTFS and FAT partitions, so if you install it and then convert the system partition to NTFS, the computer will hang when you choose that option from the boot menu. Convert first, then install the Recovery Console.*

Incidentally, you can install the Recovery Console onto NT computers as well. If you do so, then you can use NTFS to format the system partition without worrying that you won't be able to reach this partition if you can't boot normally.

Why isn't it a default option to install the Recovery Console when you install the core OS? Good question—it's so useful that you'd think it would be installed by default or that at least you'd have the option of doing so during Setup. The problem is that installing the Recovery Console deletes necessary files from the win_nt.~bt folder and thus prevents the existing Setup process from completing if the Setup process you're using writes that folder to the disk. You *can* install the Recovery Console from within another operating system if you experience a problem that prevents Setup from continuing and that the Recovery Console could fix, such as a damaged master boot record (MBR).

You can also preinstall the Recovery Console by running the winnt32 /cmdcons command from the installation CD-ROM to place the files on the local hard disk. The only catch is that you must do this to a volume contained on a single physical disk, even if you later plan to mirror the system partition for system security. You can't perform a clean installation of Server 2003 onto a currently mirrored partition, and installing the Recovery Console has the same restriction.

Creating the Automated System Recovery Disk

Every time you successfully edit your system's configuration, you should back the configuration up against the time when you unsuccessfully edit the settings. This backup disk is called the *automated system recovery* (ASR) *disk.* (It used to be the "emergency repair disk", but I'm guessing some focus group somewhere decided that that was too scary a name.)

TIP *Re-create the automated system recovery disk after you have successfully booted with the new configuration information. This way, you'll know that the configuration you're backing up works.*

KNOW THY RECOVERY DISK

It's important that you realize that the ASR disk you get with Server 2003 is different from the NT 4 emergency repair disk. The ASR disk does not include Registry data—probably because people could easily have a Security key file too big to fit on a disk.

You can replace parts of the system Registry from the Recovery Console, if you update the information in the RegBack folder on a regular basis. (The original files are in the \Config folder; the backups in \Repair\RegBack.) Just don't expect to have that information anywhere if you don't back it up when creating the ASR.

Curious about what you *do* with the ASR Disk? Turn to the next section.

To create the ASR disk, follow these steps:

1. Run the Backup utility found in Accessories/System Tools. On the initial screen of the utility, you'll find buttons for three wizards: Backup Wizard, Restore Wizard, and Automated System Recovery Wizard. Click the latter button.

2. Choose a backup location for a complete system state backup of your computer. Do not choose the floppy disk—it won't all fit. You'll need a fair chunk of space for all the System State data.

3. After Backup is finished, insert a blank, formatted floppy disk in drive A: and press OK when prompted to let the wizard copy files to the disk.

Backup will copy the System State data, service information, and disk configuration information to the backup location and asr.sif, asrpnp.sif, and setup.log to the disk. The files are not bootable—this isn't a boot disk. Those are system information files, like those used to install the OS. Basically, the SIF files.

Creating a Boot Floppy

The ASR disk is not a bootable disk. If you want to make a floppy that you can use to load the OS when it won't load off the hard disk, you'll have to copy those files to a floppy. That floppy will not be machine-specific so long as all computers have the OS installed in the same directory, so you can keep it in your panic kit, and it's filesystem-independent.

A boot floppy is useful in any of the following situations:

◆ Corrupted boot sector
◆ Corrupted master boot record (MBR)

◆ Boot virus infections that keep the machine from booting

◆ Missing or corrupt NTLDR or `NTDetect.com`

◆ Incorrect `NTBootdd.sys` driver

Oddly enough, although making an NT boot floppy has been common practice for years, there's still no utility in the OS that you can employ to make one. (You can create Setup disks from the `\bootdisk\makeboot` command on the installation CD, but that's not the same thing. Those are Setup disks, this is a boot floppy, like a DOS boot floppy with `autoexec.bat` and `config.sys` on it.) The Windows NT floppy disk must include the files `NTLDR`, `NTDetect.com`, `boot.ini`, and the correct device driver for your hard drive.

CREATING A BOOT FLOPPY FROM THE CD

If you don't have another Server 2003 box around but do have the installation CD, then you can get the files you need. Copy the `NTDetect.com` and `NTLDR` files from the `i386` folder on the CD-ROM to the new disk. Rename the `NTLDR` file to `setupldr.bin`.

The next step is to create the `boot.ini` file that the OS uses to determine which operating system it should load and where that operating system is located. `boot.ini` files are just text files. For example, the following works for a single partition IDE drive with Server 2003 installed under `\winnt`; the exact value in the `[operating systems]` section depends upon the configuration of the Windows NT System you want to boot:

```
[boot loader]
 timeout=30
 Default= multi(0)disk(0)rdisk(0)partition(1)\winnt

[operating systems]
 multi(0)disk(0)rdisk(0)partition(1)\winnt="Server 2003 "
```

WINNT, in this case, is the name of the system root directory.

TIP　*If your computer boots from a SCSI hard drive, replace the* `multi(0)` *with* `scsi(0)`. *If you are using* `scsi(x)` *in the* `boot.ini`, *copy the correct device driver for the SCSI controller in use on the computer, and then rename it on the floppy to* `NTBootdd.sys`. *If you are using* `multi(x)` *in* `boot.ini`, *you do not need to do this.*

CREATING A BOOT FLOPPY FROM ANOTHER COMPUTER

If you have a working copy of Server 2003 around, you can copy the files you need from it. Format a floppy disk using the ORMAT command on the working computer. Do a full format, not a quick format. Next, copy `NTLDR` and `NTDetect.com` from the computer to the floppy. Both `NTLDR` and `NTDetect.com` are in the root directory of the system folder.

Next, create a `boot.ini` file or copy one from a running computer (it's also in the root directory of the system folder) and modify it to match the computer you are trying to access.

TIP　*You'll need to edit the options on the View tab of Folder options (available from the folder's Tools menu) to stop hiding protected operating system files such as* `NTLDR`, `NTDetect.com`, *and* `boot.ini`. *Just choosing to show hidden files and folders won't show this file.*

Repairing—or Recovering—a Damaged Installation

The Last Known Good menu and the Safe Mode boot options aren't always enough to get a wounded installation back on its feet again. You still have some options before reinstalling, though. As I discussed in the previous section, Server 2003 offers two repair tools: the Recovery Console and automated system recovery. Both work on volumes formatted with either FAT or NTFS; one of the cool things about the Recovery Console is that you can format a system partition with NTFS for greater security but still have access to troubleshooting tools.

Understanding Repair Options

The two repair options aren't identical. Automated system recovery is a simple procedure for those times when you don't know precisely what the problem is, but you want to fix it and get on with your life. There's little finesse involved: You start installing the OS; when asked whether you're doing a real installation or a repair, you choose to repair; and then you pop in the ASR disk and let Setup repair files that are different from the ones originally installed. (There's a little more to it than that, but that's the basic story. I'll go through the procedure a bit later in "Using the ASR Disk.") So long as you haven't replaced any drivers or DLLs in your system folders with new ones, you can safely choose to restore all system files to their originals, and you'll still get your installation back as you left it—just fixed.

The Recovery Console is a little more complicated. Rather than a means of restoring damaged files, it's a command-line utility from which you can perform a variety of tasks:

- Copy system files from a floppy disk or CD to a hard disk (although not from a hard disk to a floppy disk)
- Start and stop services
- Read and write data in the system directory on the local hard disk
- Format disks
- Repartition disks

Use the Recovery Console when you know precisely what's wrong and what you want to accomplish. If you don't know what's wrong, this is not an easy way of finding out.

In short, if your installation is dead and you're not sure why, then use the ASR disk to see whether restoring the original installation files will fix the problem. If you know what the problem is—like, for example, a bad or missing SYS file or a runaway service—then you can use the Recovery Console to copy the missing file to its new location without changing any other files.

If you didn't set up the Recovery Console before the OS became unbootable (or you want to run the ASR disk utility), then you'll need to run Setup from the installation CD. After Setup has copied all the files it needs to access the hardware it needs to run Setup, it will ask you whether you want to install the OS, repair it, or exit Setup. Choose R to open the Windows Repair Options menu, from which you can repair an installation either with the Recovery Console (press C) or with the automated system recovery disk (press F2).

Using the Recovery Console

When you choose to run the Recovery Console, it will scan the disk and find any installations of Windows NT-based operating systems on the disk. Pick the one you want to repair. Type the number of the option you want, and supply the password for the Administrator account—*not the* account of someone in the Administrators group, the Administrator account. So long as the SAM database is present and you can be properly authenticated, you're in. (If it's not, then you need to restore the backed-up Registry files you stored in `%systemroot%\repair\regback` before you can use the Recovery Console.)

TIP *On the off chance that you have a dual-boot NT/Server 2003 computer, you can repair Windows NT Server 4 installations on dual-boot computers with the Recovery Console even though NT does not come with the Recovery Console. Start the Repair Console as you normally would. When it returns the list of found NT installations, pick the NT 4 one.*

Although it looks like an ordinary command prompt, the Recovery Console is not the command prompt that you can open from the **Accessories** folder. First, it supports only a few commands and only locally—this is not a network tool, and you can't run just any command-line program or utility on it. Second, those commands are specialized for this interface and only perform a limited set of functions. By default, the wildcard options in the **copy** command don't work in the console; by default, you can only copy files from removable media to the system partition (but not the other way around—you can't use the console to back up files to other media); and although you can move to other logical drives on the hard disk, by default you can't read files on any partition other than the system partition—or even perform a **dir** function on them. If you try, you'll get an Access Denied error. (As you'll see, you can change some of the security settings to make the Recovery Console more useful, but these are the defaults.) The Recovery Console is not a command-line version of Server 2003, cool as that would be.

NOTE *Sadly, the Recovery Console does not include a command-line version of REGEDIT, like Windows 9x does.*

You can't back up files. You can't read the contents of any directory not in the system root. You can't use wildcards. You can't edit security information. What *can* you do with the Recovery Console?

Quite a lot, actually, if recovery is what interests you. As you can see in Table 19.9, the Recovery Console is a set of commands you can use to manipulate the files and structure of the system partition. As you can see, a lot of functions with duplicate commands use the same syntax; unless I specify otherwise, there's no difference between the two commands.

TABLE 19.9: SUPPORTED RECOVERY CONSOLE COMMANDS

COMMAND NAME	FUNCTION
attrib	Changes the attributes of a selected file or folder.
batch	Runs the commands specified in a text file so that you can complete many tasks in a single step.
cd or chdir	Displays the name of the current directory, or changes directories. Typing **cd..** closes the current directory and moves you up one in the tree.
chkdsk	Runs CheckDisk.
cls	Wipes the screen of any previous output.

Continued on next page

TABLE 19.9: SUPPORTED RECOVERY CONSOLE COMMANDS *(continued)*

COMMAND NAME	FUNCTION
copy or extract	Copies files from removable media to the system folders on the hard disk. Does not accept wildcards.
del or delete	Deletes one or more files (does not accept wildcards).
dir	Lists the contents of the current or selected directory.
disable	Disables the named service or driver.
diskpart	Replaces the FDISK tool with which you're probably familiar. Creates or deletes disk partitions. Only use this command on basic disks—it can damage dynamic disks.
enable	Enables the named service or driver.
expand	Expands a compressed installation file (one with a .cab extension) onto the local fixed disk. Only works if you're running the Recovery Console from the installation CD.
fixboot	Writes a new partition boot sector on the system partition.
fixmbr	Writes a new master boot record (MBR) for the partition boot sector.
format	Formats the selected disk.
listsvc	Lists all the services running on the server installation.
logon	If you have multiple Server 2003 installations on the local hard disk, you can use this command to pick the installation you want to repair.
map	Displays the drive letter mappings currently in place. Handy for getting the information you need to use DISKPART. Only lists drives found in the partition table, not volumes listed only in the dynamic disks volume database.
md or mkdir	Creates a directory.
more, type	Displays the contents of the chosen text file.
rd or rmdir	Deletes a directory.
rename or ren	Renames a single file.
set	When enabled, allows you to display or modify four security settings governing file and folder access.
systemroot	Makes the current directory the system root of the drive you're logged in to.
Type	Displays a text file's contents to the screen of the Recovery Console.

WARNING *If you thought the Registry Editor was potentially dangerous, the Recovery Console is just as bad or worse. You can really screw up your system here, to the point that the only thing to do is reinstall and reload your backups. There's no Undo feature, not all the commands ask for confirmation, and there's no Read-Only setting such as the one in REGEDT32. If you're not used to working from the command line, review what you want to do and the tools you need to do it before you open the console, and practice on a test system before attempting any real recovery.*

Some of the commands in Table 19.9 will look familiar to old DOS hands, but many of them work a little differently from the way they did under DOS, using a slightly different syntax or only working under specific circumstances. Let's take a look at how you can use these commands to get things back up and running.

BEFORE YOU BEGIN: FIX THE SECURITY SETTINGS

Did you notice that I said *by default* you can't copy files to external media and *by default* you can't access any partition other than the system partition? The weasel wording wasn't accidental.

Normally, from the Recovery Console you can only use the following folders:

♦ The root folder

♦ The `%SystemRoot%` folder and the subfolders of the Windows installation you are currently logged in to

♦ The `Cmdcons` folder

♦ Removable media drives such as CD-ROM drives

You also can't use wildcards with commands that would normally support them or copy data to disks.

Bah. Let's use the SET command to make the Recovery Console a bit more flexible. This command allows you to display or modify four environment options:

Option	Default Setting	Description
AllowWildCards	FALSE	Controls whether you can use wildcards with some commands (such as `del *.tmp`)
AllowAllPaths	FALSE	Controls whether you can change directories (with the `cd` command) to include all folders on all local drives
AllowRemovableMedia	FALSE	Controls whether you can copy files from the hard disk to a floppy disk or other recognized removable media
NoCopyPrompt	FALSE	Controls whether you can copy files without being prompted to continue when you are overwriting an existing file

Oho—so you run `set AllowAllPaths = TRUE` (don't forget the spaces around the equal sign) and you can navigate anywhere on the local disk, right? Almost right. Before you ever start the Recovery Console, you need to edit some security settings before the SET command will work. Depending on what kind of computer this is—a server or a domain controller—go to the Security Configuration and Analysis snap-in in the MMC, the Domain Controller Security Policy in Administrative Tools, the Domain Security Policy in Administrative Tools, or the Local Security Policy in Administrative Tools. Whichever tool you choose, look under Computer Configuration\Windows Settings\Security Settings\Security Options and locate the two security policies pertaining to Recovery Console: `Recovery Console: Allow Automatic Administrative Logon` and `Recovery Console: Allow floppy copy and access to all drives and all folders`.

The first policy allows you to start Recovery Console without prompting for the administrative password stored in the local computer's account database. (That's kind of handy, but it does represent a security risk and I don't think it's a good idea.) The second policy enables the SET command while you are using Recovery Console. If you enable this policy, you can change any of the four environment variables to TRUE during a Recovery Console session.

After you enable the security policy, it must be applied (possibly across the domain) before becoming the effective policy on the local computer. This is necessary before the SET command is truly enabled and available for use during a Recovery Console session. To make it snappy, you can run `secedit /refreshpolicy machine_policy` to force a refresh of the local computer's policy after performing the policy change described previously.

After the local policy is refreshed and the enabled Recovery Console security policy is in effect, you should be able to start Recovery Console and use the SET command to enable any of the four environment options.

One last thing: You need to run SET every time you run the Recovery Console—it won't remember that you changed any settings from their defaults.

TIP *Put the SET commands you want to apply to your Recovery Console sessions in a batch file so you can run the batch file with the BATCH command when you start the Recovery Console.*

ENABLING AND DISABLING SERVICES

Why would you need to enable or disable services from the command line? Therein lies a tale.

Lo these many years ago, I bought a new PC. Installed Windows NT Server; ran the installation program for the 3Com network card in the server. Life was good.

Until I rebooted the computer.

You see, a diagnostic program was part of the setup for the NIC—an unavoidable part that you could not choose to not install. (Trust me: I tried, on several computers with the same set of hardware.) Whenever I started up NT, this diagnostic program would scan the system and display a message that a newer version of my NIC's driver was available—did I want to use the new driver? Click OK or Cancel, and the message box would close for a second and then reopen, with the same message. Add to this that the searching and displaying was using up 100 percent of CPU time for a 350MHz Pentium II doing *nothing else but running the diagnostic*. Running the Task Manager (when I could get a spare cycle here or there to open it) didn't help because the program wouldn't shut down even when I killed the process.

NOTE *Worried about this happening to you? Although I've run into several people who've had the same problem with one version of the driver for the 3Com 3C905X Ethernet 10Base-T card, this issue seems to be fixed in the driver published in April 1999. Other than this glitch, I've been very happy with these NICs.*

Okay, I figured—the problem is a runaway service, so if I can shut down the service I will resolve the problem. But shutting down the service is hard when you're clicking OK in a repeatedly reappearing dialog box and then frantically grabbing CPU cycles to open the Control Panel and then Services before the dialog box opens and the processor usage starts running at 100 percent again.

In this case, I was finally able to get to the Services applet, find the service (named 3Com Diagnostics or some such, so identifying the problem child wasn't hard), and then stop and disable it.

Problem solved. But it took a lot of time and mouse-clicking to get to that point. A tool that would enable me to boot to the command prompt and disable that service without having to work around the cycle-eating message box would have been nice. And that's where the services-related tools in the Recovery Console come in.

The first step to fixing a problem like this is running the `listsvc` utility. There are no arguments to this—just type **listsvc** from the command prompt, and the Recovery Console will display a list of all the services and drivers currently installed, a short description of what they are, and their start type (boot, automatic, manual, system, or disabled). Seeing all the services will probably take a few pages of screen, but the services are listed alphabetically, so you can find the one you want fairly easily. Write down its name.

TIP   The names of services and drivers are not case sensitive.

Once you've found the suspected problem child, it's time for the `disable` command. The syntax is simple: `disable servicename`. The Recovery Console will then notify you that it found the Registry entry for this service (or tell you that it can't find an entry for this service, in which case you need to check your spelling and try again). It will also display the current start type and new start type for the service. Write down the current start type for the service in case you want to start it again.

To make the change take effect, type **exit** to leave the Recovery Console and restart the computer. See whether disabling that service fixed the problem. If it did, then you're home free. (Not sure how you'd know? Depends on what the problem was. In the case of the runaway 3Com diagnostics, the fix was pretty immediate. As soon as I turned off the service, the problem disappeared.) If it didn't, then you can return to the console, enable that service, and try something else.

You don't have to disable a service to keep it from running when the OS starts, however. Instead, you could change its start type from automatic to manual. To do so, or to reenable a service you disabled, you'll need to use the **enable** command. Like `disable`, `enable`'s syntax is simple: `enable servicename`. If run on a disabled service, using this syntax will enable the service and restore it to whatever its start type was when it was disabled.

To change a service's start type without disabling it, add the new start type to the end of the **enable** command, like this:

```
enable servicename start_type
```

where *start_type* is one of the options in Table 19.10.

TABLE 19.10: START TYPES

START TYPE	MEANING
Service_boot_start	Boot
Service_system_start	System
Service_demand_start	Manual
Service_auto_start	Automatic

So, for example, instead of disabling the 3Com diagnostic service, I could have changed its start type from automatic to manual. That way, I could have started it at any time, but it wouldn't start automatically.

Replacing Damaged Files

Perhaps the problem isn't a runaway driver or service, but a corrupted part of the operating system, as in error messages that say Bad or Missing NTOSKRNL.EXE. In such a case, you may need to replace all or part of your operating system (although, if we're talking about more than a few files here or you aren't sure what's broken, it might be time for an automated system recovery). The tools most likely to apply to this scenario are the ones to create and delete directories, rename files, change attributes, and copy or extract files from other media.

Creating directories is simple. The command syntax is as follows:

```
md [drive:]path
mkdir [drive:]path
```

where *drive:* is the drive letter of the drive on which you want to create the folder, if it's not the current one, and *path* is the name of the directory you want to create. Just make sure that, if you don't spell out the location of the new directory, you're currently in the place where the new directory should be created.

The syntax for the rmdir and rd commands (for deleting directories) is the same as that for md. The only part of directory deletion that you have to watch is that you can't delete directories unless they're empty, with no subdirectories. If you try, you'll get an error message telling you that the directory is not empty, and there's no switch to make rd act like deltree (an old DOS command that would delete subdirectories).

Before you delete a directory, run the dir command to check out its contents and make sure that you really do want to remove it. Conveniently, dir displays all files, hidden or not, and shows their attributes.

Rather than deleting entire directories, however, you're more likely to need to replace individual files. That's where copy and extract come in. The copy command is what it sounds like: a method of copying a file from one location to another, with the caveat I've mentioned before that you can only copy *to* the system directory, not copy files from the system directory to removable media such as a Jaz drive. The syntax for copying files is simple:

```
copy source [destination]
```

where *source* is the name of the original file and *destination* is the directory where you're pasting the original (along with a new name, if you need it). If you don't specify a directory, the file will be copied to the directory from which you're running the command. The extract utility works the same way as copy and uses the same syntax, with one exception: You can only use extract if you started the Recovery Console from the Repair option in Setup. Neither copying utility supports wildcards (so you can't copy the entire contents of a directory very easily), but copy automatically decompresses compressed installation files for you. Both utilities will alert you if a file with the name of the one you're pasting already exists in that location.

If you're not sure that you want to replace an existing file, try renaming it and then copying the new file to the relevant location. The syntax for rename is as follows:

```
rename [drive:][path] filename1 filename2
```

`rename` works only on single files, and the renamed file must be in the same place as the original. That is, you can't use this command to move files. To do that, you'd need to use `copy`.

FIXING BOOT SECTORS AND BOOT RECORDS

Your computer uses a couple of pieces of information to navigate your hard disk. Those two pieces are the boot sector and the master boot record (MBR). Most of the time, these pieces are pretty safe, but some things (such as some viruses) can target and infect them, or they can be lost. In such a case, you'll need a way to restore them.

First, a little background. The partition boot sector contains the information that the file system uses to access the volume. The MBR (discussed next) examines the information in the boot sector to load the boot loader.

The boot sector contains the following information:

◆ A jump instruction

◆ The name and version of the operating system files (such as Server 2003)

◆ A data structure called the BIOS Parameter Block, which describes the physical characteristics of the partition

◆ A data structure called the BIOS Extended Parameter Block, which describes the location of the master file table for NTFS volumes

◆ The bootstrap code

Most of the information in the boot sector describes the physical characteristics of the disk (for example, the number of sectors per track and clusters per sector), in addition to the location of the file allocation table (for FAT volumes) or the master file table (for NTFS volumes). The layout and exact information included in the boot sector depends on the disk format used.

Given that a disk may have more than one partition, how does the hard disk know where to find the different partitions? The first sector on every hard disk (whether the hard disk has an operating system on it or not) contains that disk's MBR. The MBR contains the partition table for that disk and a small amount of code used to read the partition table and find the system partition for that hard disk. Once it finds that partition, the MBR loads a copy of that partition's boot sector into memory. If the disk is not bootable (has no system partition), the code never gets used and the boot sector is not loaded.

In short, a hard disk needs a functioning MBR to boot. The MBR is in the same place on every hard disk, so it's potentially an easy virus target.

Okay—all that said, to write a new boot sector to a drive, type **fixboot**. This will write a new boot sector to the current boot drive. To create a new MBR, type **fixmbr**.

DELETING, CREATING, AND FORMATTING PARTITIONS

The Recovery Console includes tools not only for fixing the OS, but for completely wiping things out and starting over. With these tools you can repartition and reformat your hard disk. *Partitioning* is setting up logical divisions of the disk; *formatting* is placing a file system on those drives so you can store data on them.

WARNING   *You probably already know this, but just in case you've forgotten, repartitioning and formatting are destructive. Any data on the hard disk you've reformatted or repartitioned is history. Keep your backups.*

Before you start formatting or repartitioning, you might want to take a look at what you've already got in place. The Recovery Console's `map` command can help you do that. Type **map** at the command prompt, and you'll see output like the following:

```
?                 0MB       Device\HardDisk0\Partition0
C:      FAT16     1028MB    Device\HardDisk0\Partition1
?                 3310MB    Device\HardDisk0\Partition0
E:      NTFS      1028MB    Device\HardDisk0\Partition2
H:      NTFS      1028MB    Device\HardDisk0\Partition3
G:                1028MB    Device\HardDisk0\Partition4
?                 227MB     Device\HardDisk0\Partition0
A:                          Device\Floppy0
D:                          Device\CDROM0
```

TIP   If you're running MAP on a dynamic disk, only volumes created before you updated the disk (that is, volumes that were originally primary partitions or logical drives) will show up. MAP reads the partition table, and dynamic volumes created on dynamic disks are not in the partition table.

You can see from this that logical drive G: on the hard disk hasn't been formatted because it's not showing any file system. To format it, you would use the following syntax:

```
format g: [/q] [/fs:filesystem]
```

Here, /q tells `format` to do a quick format (not checking for bad sectors), and the /fs switch is for specifying the file system to use. You don't have to specify a file system (your options are NTFS, FAT32, and FAT), but if you don't, Win2K will format it to NTFS. When you run this command, Win2K will tell you that all data on that drive will be lost and ask you to confirm that the format should proceed. Do so, and a few seconds later you will have a newly formatted drive.

TIP   You can convert a FAT partition to NTFS, but you cannot convert an NTFS partition to FAT.

You can format the G: drive safely, or at least without affecting any other logical drives. What you *can't* do, even before formatting, is repartition to make the G: drive bigger, perhaps giving it some of that space that isn't used on the disk. To do that, you need to boot the Disk Administrator and make G: part of a volume and then extend that volume—anyway, it's all in Chapter 10. If you do want to repartition the disk to reorganize its structure, run DISKPART.

WARNING   DISKPART can damage your partition table if you've upgraded the disk to a dynamic disk. Do not modify the structure of dynamic disks unless you are using the Disk Management tool.

When you're done with the Recovery Console, type **exit** and press Enter. The computer will reboot.

Using Automated System Recovery

Those who've read previous versions of this book may recall that the Windows 2000 recovery process using the ERD was fairly involved, requiring you to choose manual or fast repair to restore the system from the Registry backup. Automated System Recovery is more automatic than using the ERD was with NT or Windows 2000. To make it work, you'll need the original installation CD and the ASR disk you created using the process described earlier in the "Creating the Automated System Recovery Disk" section. Start Setup on the damaged computer, then press F2 at the beginning of text-mode Setup when prompted at the bottom of the screen. (You'll see this prompt right after the prompt to press F6 to install third-party disk drivers.)

Setup will start formatting the disk as it would during a typical Setup operation. Next, Setup will copy the files to the Windows installation folders and load the configuration files. The computer will reboot and boot to Server 2003, going through the first stage of graphical Setup.

So far, the process is very similar to a typical Setup and you may find yourself wondering if you picked the right option. Fear not—after completing the first stage of graphical Setup, the recovery process will automatically begin Backup and start a Restore operation from the backup you created when making the ASR disk. This is a nonauthoritative restore of System State data, so if you're restoring a domain controller you'll need to use NTDSUTIL as described previously to make it authoritative for the domain. Also, since this backup only copied System State data, you'll need to restore any of that data separately.

The computer will reboot again, but this time normally. That's it—the computer is restored with all the settings that were in place at the time of your backup, even to the display resolution.

Planning for Disaster Recovery

Sometimes using the Last Known Good Configuration or the Recovery Console doesn't fix your problems. Hard disk failures or natural disasters require a bit more in the way of hard-core disaster recovery.

What does *disaster recovery* mean? Essentially, it's exactly what it sounds like: a way of recovering from disaster—at best, turning a potential disaster into a minor inconvenience. Disaster can mean anything: theft, flood, an earthquake, a virus, or anything else that keeps you from being able to access your data. After all, it's not really the server that's important. Although a server may be expensive, it is replaceable. Your data, on the other hand, is either difficult or impossible to recover. Could you reproduce your client mailing list from memory? What about the corporate accounts?

Creating a Disaster Recovery Plan

The most important part of a disaster recovery plan is identifying what "disaster" means to you and your company. Obviously, permanently losing all of your company's data would be a disaster, but what else would? How about your installation becoming inaccessible for a week or longer? When planning for disaster, think about all the conditions that could render your data or your workplace unreachable and plan accordingly.

Implementing Disaster Recovery

Okay, it's 2:00 P.M. on Thursday, and you get a report that an important server has died. What do you do?

WRITE THINGS DOWN

Immediately write down everything that everyone tells you: what happened, when it happened, who gave you the information, and anything else that happened at the same time that might possibly be related. Do not trust it to memory. First, you're apt to be a bit stressed at this point. Second, if it happened once, it could happen again—and if you write down the results of your interviews, you may not have to start from scratch.

CHECK THE EVENT LOGS

If you can get to them, look at the security and event logs on the server to see if you can tell what happened right before the server crashed. If you're using directory replication to maintain a physically identical file server (also known as a *hot start* server because it's ready to go whenever you need it), the log information may be on the replicated server, even if you can't get to the original.

ASCERTAIN THE CAUSE OF THE FAILURE AND FIX IT

"Easy for you to say," I hear someone muttering. It can be done, however. Once you know what events happened, it becomes easier to find out what they happened to.

Find Out If It's a Software Problem

Is it a software problem? If it is, have you changed the configuration? If you've changed something, rebooted, and been unable to boot, it's time to use the Last Known Good Configuration discussed earlier. If you can boot but the operating system won't function properly, use the automated system recovery disk to restore the hardware configuration.

If you have another server with a Server 2003 installation identical to the server that failed, switch servers and see if the backup server works before you reinstall the operating system. If the hot start server doesn't work, you could be facing a network problem.

Find Out If It's a Hardware Problem

Is it a hardware problem? If you have a hot start server around the office, put it in place of the failed server and see if you can bring the network back up. If so, the problem lies with the dead server, and you can fix or replace it while you have the other one in place. If not, check the network's cabling.

If one drive from a fault tolerant stripe set or mirror set has died, the system should still be fine (if the drive that died is not the one with the system partition on it), but you should still fix the set anyway. Striping and mirroring gives you access to your data while the missing data is being regenerated, but if something else happens to the set before you regenerate the missing data, you're sunk, because the set can only deal with one error at a time.

If necessary, reload the backups.

Make a Recovery "Coloring Book"

No matter how much you know about reformatting SCSI drives or rebuilding boot sectors byte by byte, I guarantee you that the fastest way to recover from a disaster will often turn out to be a three-step process: replacing the bad hard disk and attendant hardware, installing a fresh copy of NT Server on the new hard disk, and restoring the data on the disk.

That sounds simple, but it's amazing how complex it can be in the heat of battle. Let's see, I'm reinstalling Server 2003, but what was the name of the domain? What IP address does the domain controller get? What's the WINS server address? Which services went on this server? What was the administrator's password set to?

At my shop, we decided to sit down and write a step-by-step, click-by-click instruction manual. It tells future network administrators which buttons to click and what text to type in the unlikely event that they ever need to take a new machine and rebuild our domain controller on it.

Just for an example, we have a primary domain controller on one of our domains that (as the logon traffic is relatively light) is also our DHCP, WINS, and DNS server. So, suppose the machine goes up in smoke, leaving us nothing but backup tapes—how do we rebuild that machine? We sat down and wrote out exactly what to do:

- Install Server 2003 on a new machine.
- Restore the SAM and SECURITY databases.
- Install DHCP on the machine.
- Restore the old DHCP database to the machine.
- Install WINS on the machine.
- Restore the WINS database.
- Install the DNS server on the machine.
- Restore our DNS zones and records.
- Restore the user data.

Assume that the person who'll be doing this knows nothing more than how to click a mouse and shove CDs into drives—someone with oatmeal for brains. Sound insulting? It's not; I like to think of myself as of at least basic intelligence, but under pressure I sometimes just don't think as well as I need to—oatmeal's as good as it gets, and if I'm really pressed my brains have the power of unidentified goo. If you're good under pressure, that's great—but making the disaster recovery guide an easy read is also a big help to your coworkers.

TIP *An easier and less error-prone solution is to create unattended installations for key servers, either using answer files or Remote Installation Services. See Chapter 5 for more information about unattended installations.*

Don't underestimate how long this will take: Putting the whole document together took two research assistants a couple of weeks, and it ended up being a 100+ page Word document! (Part of the reason why it was so large is that it made lavish use of screen shots wherever possible, and yours should, too. Just click the window you want to include in your document, press Alt+Prtsc, choose Edit/Paste Special in Word, choose Bitmap, and uncheck Float over Text.)

WARNING *Once you finish the document, be careful where you keep it. The document will contain the keys to your network: usernames of domain administrator accounts, the passwords of those accounts, and the like.*

Making Sure the Plan Works

The first casualty of war isn't always the truth—it's often the battle plan itself.

The most crucial part of any disaster recovery plan is making sure that it works down to the last detail. Don't just check the hardware; check everything. When a server crashes, backups do no good at all if they are locked in a cabinet to which only the business manager has the keys and the business manager is on vacation in Tahiti.

In the interest of having your plan actually work, make sure you know the answers to the following questions.

WHO HAS THE KEYS?

Who has the keys to the backups and/or the file server case? The example mentioned previously of the business manager having the only set of keys is an unacceptable situation, for reasons that should be painfully obvious. At any given time, someone *must* have access to the backups.

You could set up a rotating schedule of duty, where one person who has the keys is always on call, and the keys are passed on to the next person when a shift is up. However, that solution is not foolproof. If there's an emergency, the person on call could forget to hand the keys off to the next person, or the person on call could be rendered inaccessible through a dead beeper battery or downed telephone line. Better to trust two people with the keys to the backups and server so that if the person on call can't be reached, you have a backup key person.

CALLING IN THE MARINES: DISASTER RECOVERY SERVICES

Disaster recovery isn't always fully successful. Perhaps your backups don't work or have themselves been destroyed. One more option remains before you have to tell everyone that everything they were working on for the past month is irretrievably gone: data recovery centers. Data recovery centers are staffed by people who are expert at getting data off media (most often hard disks, but not always) that can't be accessed by normal means.

Not all data recovery centers are the same. Some data recovery centers (in fact, the first data recovery centers) are staffed with people who are really, really good at getting dead hard disks back up and running. Using their skill, they can resuscitate the dead drive, copy its contents to other media, and then return the data—on the new media—to you.

Other data recovery services can retrieve data not recoverable with ordinary methods. These services operate at a binary level, reading the data from the dead media (sometimes even opening the hard disk, if the problem is serious enough) and then copying the data to your preferred media. Turnaround time is typically no more than a day or two, plus the shipping time.

The cost of data recovery depends on the following:

◆ The method of recovery used (the places that just fix hard disks tend to be cheaper but can't always recover the data)

◆ The turnaround time requested

◆ The amount of data recovered

Consider storing irreplaceable data on a different physical drive from data you can easily replace. A data recovery service can't selectively restore data. That is, if the data files and the system files are stored on a single physical disk, you can't save yourself a little money by asking the center only to recover the data files, even if the data is on two different logical partitions.

Until recently, you had to send the hard disk to the data recovery center to have its data retrieved, and this meant not having the data for at least a couple of days. Remote data recovery services can fix some software-related problems without requiring you to ship the drive anywhere or even take it out of the computer case. Using a direct dial-up connection, the data recovery center may be able to fix the problem across the telephone line.

IS SPECIAL SOFTWARE REQUIRED FOR THE BACKUPS?

Must any special software be loaded for the backups to work? I once nearly gave myself heart failure when, after repartitioning a hard disk and reinstalling the operating system, I attempted to restore the backups that I'd made before wiping out all the data on the file server's hard disk. The backups wouldn't work. After much frustration, I figured out that Service Pack 2 had been installed on the server. I reinstalled the service pack from my copy on another computer, and the backups worked. I just wish I had figured that out several hours earlier.

DO THE BACKUPS WORK, AND CAN YOU RESTORE THEM?

Do the backups work, and do you know how to restore them? Verifying backups takes a little longer than just backing them up, but if you verify, you know that what's on the tape matches what's on the drive. So, as far as restoring goes, practice restoring files *before* you have a problem. Learning to do it right is a lot easier if you don't have to learn under pressure, and if you restore files periodically, you know that the files backed up okay.

HAVE USERS BACKED UP THEIR OWN WORK?

In the interest of preventing your operation from coming to a complete halt while you're fixing the downed network, it might not be a bad idea to have people store a copy of whatever they're working on, and the application needed to run it, on their workstation. People who only work on one or two things at a time could still work while you're getting the server back online.

Disasters shouldn't happen, but they sometimes do. With the proper preventive planning beforehand, they can become entertaining war stories, rather than sources of battle fatigue.

Chapter 20

Installing and Managing Remote Access Service in Windows Server 2003

IT SEEMS LIKE IT was only a few years ago that the concept of remote computing or dial-up connectivity was relatively unknown. As far as most of the world was concerned, there was no such thing as the Internet, the idea of telecommuting hadn't been born yet, and e-mail didn't exist. Remote connectivity and dial-up modems were vague, mysterious technologies as far as the average person was concerned. Once considered the tools of businesses and technically oriented individuals to simply get "data" from one location to another, these concepts have now become part of even Grandma's everyday life.

Technology has changed the world in some remarkable ways, but the most amazing way is how "connected" people are these days (or, at least, they can be if they *want* to). Home computers are becoming more and more common, and the average home consumer can buy a dial-up modem just as easily as a toaster or CD player. Employees are being equipped with everything from laptops to palmtops and being sent out on the road, with the expectation that they should be just as connected on the road as they are when they're in the office. For better or for worse, this onslaught of technology has brought with it a demand for easy connectivity—anytime, anywhere.

These demands have put a heavy burden on the backs of system administrators. Not only does the typical administrator have to handle day-to-day support issues *within* the office, but with so much work happening outside the office an already difficult job seems impossible at times. Unfortunately, there isn't a magical solution for everyone yet (I doubt there ever will be), but Microsoft's Remote Access Service (RAS) has been designed and improved over the years to help administrators deal with some of these demands.

Originally developed in the early days of Windows NT, RAS was initially bundled as part of the base operating system. I've always felt the reason for this (at least partially) was to give NT a competitive advantage against other network operating systems out on the market—namely Novell. When remote computing was first starting to take off, Novell was the primary player in the Network Operating System market and they had developed add-on products like NetWare Connect to support dial-up connections to NetWare networks. Products like NetWare Connect worked well and gave users the connectivity they needed, but these products had to be purchased separately and the license costs often increased in direct proportion to the number of simultaneous dial-in connections that needed to be supported.

While I can't be absolutely certain this is the reason Microsoft chose to bundle RAS with the operating system for free, it certainly seems like a reasonable assumption. As many recent court cases have highlighted, "bundling" is a popular Microsoft tactic to gain market share. Personally, I know of at least a few organizations that started deploying NT in its early days simply because of the number of things that were included for free with the operating system—things they would have had to pay extra for with any other network operating system. Whatever the reasons were, NT began to take off, and RAS capabilities grew with each new version of the operating system.

Microsoft has improved RAS with each new version of Windows NT to the point where it has grown into a full-featured remote access platform capable of handling even the most demanding environments. By the time Windows NT 4 was released, RAS was a solid, reliable part of the NT operating system. The Internet was a few years along in its transition from the government and education environment into the commercial world, and it was becoming more common for people to try to leverage their investments in Internet connectivity to meet their remote access needs. With the release of NT 4, Microsoft included support for Point-to-Point Tunneling Protocol as a means of encapsulating RAS packets and sending them over the Internet instead of a modem. The phrase "virtual private networking" started becoming a buzzword in the vocabulary of network administrators, and Microsoft improved on the virtual private networking capabilities of NT 4 by later releasing a routing update called Routing and Remote Access Service (RRAS).

With the advent of Windows Server 2003, Microsoft has put together the most comprehensive set of remote access capabilities to date, consolidating all the previous technologies and capacities in an easy-to-use interface. But with *so* many options available, at times it can be hard to know which solution is your best choice. In the pages that follow, I'll discuss what some of your options are, some common scenarios you will probably run into, and the solutions for those problems.

Common Applications for Remote Access Service

For the purposes of this text, we'll assume that Remote Access Service is divided into two distinct functions: accepting inbound calls and placing outbound calls. Microsoft now commonly refers to the latter as Dial-Up Networking (DUN for short), and receiving inbound calls has pretty much always been referred to as Remote Access Service (or RAS). Even though RAS and DUN share some of the same setup and installation routines, when you see a reference to DUN, you can assume it is for an outbound call.

With that clarification taken care of, let's take a look at some of the tasks you can accomplish with the Remote Access Service in Windows Server 2003.

Connecting Clients to the Internet

One of the more commonly used capabilities of Dial-Up Networking is to allow your computer to dial in to an ISP—usually via Point-to-Point Protocol (PPP)—and communicate with distant servers and hosts across the Internet. Although this might commonly be used for simple browsing and file transfers on a server, it is becoming common for e-mail and proxy servers to function entirely over dial-up connections to the Internet.

Windows 2000 Server included several functional improvements over previous versions of Windows NT for dial-up networking on the client side. Features such as demand dialing, reestablishing failed links, and the ability to repetitively dial unresponsive numbers made Win2K dial-up networking a pretty robust platform for establishing Internet connections and for keeping them online. Windows Server 2003 adds even more new features to the RAS environment. The introduction of Point to Point Protocol over Ethernet (PPPoE) drivers allows you to utilize your broadband connection for demand-dial connections. There are a few other improvements as well, including the ability to make your NAT interfaces work with Basic Firewall, the addition of support for L2TP/IPSec connections which originate from VPN clients located behind a NAT (network address translation) network, support for preshared keys using L2TP/IPSec authentication, and broadcast name resolution by a NetBT proxy located on the VPN server for networks which are operating without WINS or DNS. But first, I'll talk about the basics of RAS and why we need it.

Accepting Incoming Calls from Remote Clients

Traveling workers, telecommuters, and late-night workaholics all share one thing in common: they all eventually need access to corporate resources from remote locations. Remote Access Service can serve as a platform to get these users connected to your internal networks and servers.

Whether you need to allow access to your NT network, Novell servers, Unix hosts, or any other internal devices, RAS can act as a universal gateway for all your inbound communication needs. By accepting inbound connections from several different devices (analog, ISDN, X.25, VPN) and routing the traffic to your internal network, RAS can provide seamless networking for your users. Workstations dialed into a network over RAS will work exactly the same as they would if they were connected directly to the network (albeit a bit slower—more on that later).

Connecting to a Private Network

In addition to connecting a Windows Server 2003 to the Internet, it's often necessary to connect one network to another—perhaps to transfer data to suppliers or clients. In any case, Windows Server 2003 can be connected to another private network just as easily as to the Internet and take advantage of the same link-reliability features.

Acting as an Internet Gateway

In response to popular demand, Microsoft added the capability for a Windows 2000 or Server 2003 to share an Internet connection among clients connected to an internal network. By the addition of NAT capabilities, Windows can act as a sort of proxy for getting internal clients connected to the Internet.

NOTE   *It is worthwhile to note that this "proxy" service for getting internal clients connected to the Internet over a shared connection is completely different from the Microsoft Proxy BackOffice application, or their current version of Proxy, Internet Security and Acceleration (ISA) Server.*

Although this service is primarily of use to small and home offices, it has been a dramatic (and welcome) addition to the suite of services contained in RAS.

Accepting VPN Connections from Remote Clients

Along with the advent of the Internet in the corporate world, the concept of virtual private networking (VPN) has emerged and become one of the hottest areas in networking. Virtual private networking, loosely defined, is a means of running a secure private network over an insecure public network. Or, in plain English, you can have clients get connected (securely) to your office network by simply having an Internet connection and a valid (public) IP address and then establishing a VPN session to your RAS server. The VPN session is secure and encrypted, so your private data is protected as it passes over the public network (i.e., the Internet).

Microsoft leveraged their investments in RAS with the development of virtual private networking and this feature is continued in Server 2003. By incorporating PPTP and L2TP protocols within the operating system, you can effectively set up "virtual" modems that work over IP networks, instead of analog or digital circuits. The methodology and terms used to implement these virtual modems are the same that are used for regular modems, so learning how to implement virtual private networking is made easier.

Microsoft offers two choices for communication using VPNs. You can use the older PPTP and MPPE combination of encryption and authentication protocols, or you can use L2TP and IPSec. In Windows Server 2003, Microsoft has expanded the capabilities of using L2TP and IPSec from behind a network address translation interface, which was impossible previously. We'll talk more about VPNs in the section titled "VPN Overview."

Dialing Up a Remote Network and Routing Traffic

With the addition of the Routing and Remote Access Service Update to Windows NT 4, Microsoft made it easier for a Windows NT Server to act as a router, connecting to remote networks as needed and routing traffic. This type of connection between locations is commonly referred to as wide area networking, or WAN connectivity.

With no more hardware than a dial-up modem at each site, internal clients and workstations can access resources on remote networks through this capability. By simply programming your internal workstations and devices to use your Windows Server 2003 as a "gateway," RAS can accept client traffic destined for a remote network, establish a connection to that network, and then pass the traffic across the connection as necessary. Since most office-to-office connectivity has traditionally been handled via costly dedicated circuits, having this ability is a tremendous benefit.

This capability has helped organizations act in a completely "virtual" capacity—appearing to have a centralized network of resources that are actually individual servers spread across several sites, joined by demand-dial connections.

Bandwidth Planning and Considerations

Before we begin discussing what types of hardware and software you need to start using RAS, it's important to make sure you have an understanding of when RAS would and wouldn't be a good solution. The two most important factors in determining this are speed and reliability.

No discussion of remote access would be complete without defining the two different types of communication that are often referred to when you hear the phrase "remote access." These are sometimes referred to as *remote-node* and *remote-control* technologies. They may sound similar, and as far as end users are concerned they're basically the same, but these two methods of remote access are in fact very different. Unfortunately, many administrators are often left with implementing vague management directives such as "make sure that our employees can work while they're on the road," which are amazing oversimplifications of remote access's complexities. It's important to understand the capabilities and limitations of each type of access so you can make the best decision for your needs.

Remote Node

RAS is a remote-node method of communication and a very flexible and versatile means of getting users or networks connected to one another. Overall, I prefer remote-node solutions over remote control for most applications, but having an understanding of how remote node works will help you recognize the best time to use it.

One of the simplest ways to visualize remote-node communication is to view the phone line connecting a client to a network as a *very* long network cable. Like any normal network cable in your office, this one is plugged into two locations. It starts at the user's workstation or laptop, goes through the phone company, and then ends at a modem in your office. Visualize that entire connection as a network cable. That modem, in turn, is connected to a RAS server (or another similar device), and the RAS server is—presumably—connected to your network. The RAS server accepts the incoming data from that dial-in user and then simply "passes" their data onto a local network segment. The same is true for outgoing data. The RAS server will see any outgoing data destined for that user on the network and transmit it over the phone line. As far as end-user functionality goes, your network should work exactly the same way in the office as it does dialing in, albeit much slower.

Since typical office network connections these days are running at speeds of upwards of 10,000,000 to 100,000,000 bits per second, throughput can be amazingly fast. So fast, that it is easy to overlook the amount of data that is actually traveling across your network. Considering the fact that the best analog modems available today are only reaching speeds of 56,000 bits per second, throughput can be a problem with remote-node solutions. Basic math indicates that there's only about 1/20th of the bandwidth available over a 56K modem in comparison to a 10-megabit Ethernet connection. That simple fact has a direct impact on the speed and performance of applications being used on the network. For example, a 2.5MB Word document might open up in just a few seconds on a 10-megabit Ethernet connection in an office, but on a 56K modem connection, that document could take upwards of a few minutes to open up.

CALCULATING MODEM TRANSMISSION TIMES

Use the following formula to calculate modem transmission times:

$$\frac{\text{File size in "bytes"} \times 8}{\text{Speed of connection in "bits" (i.e., 56k = 56,000)}} = \text{Transmission time in seconds}$$

CASE IN POINT: CHOOSING THE RIGHT REMOTE ACCESS SOLUTION

If you implement a RAS solution without having some of these facts in your arsenal, you could end up with a solution that is effectively useless. Consider, for example, the case of one of my clients— let's call them the XYZ Corporation. The XYZ Corporation was in the process of moving into a new building but had to leave their accounting software and data on the file server in their old building due to several licensing and political issues. The accounting software was an old FoxPro file-based program that had served them well for many years, but it was eventually being replaced when they moved.

Their initial desire was to just have users dial in to the network in the old building and work on the accounting application as they did before. However, since the accounting application was file-based as opposed to being client-server (more on that later), the amount of data going back and forth between their workstations and servers was simply too great to make a remote-node solution work for their application. Simple analysis of their traffic indicated that their primary users of the accounting software were easily transferring 20 to 40 megabytes worth of data across their network in *as little as an hour*. If you've ever downloaded a large application from the Internet over a modem, you know how long it takes to move that much data—you probably start your download overnight and check it again the next morning.

Remembering our calculations from earlier, only about 1/20th of the bandwidth was available to XYZ Corporation over a dial-up remote-node connection. Quite simply, they were not going to be able to move that much data over a modem and maintain usable response times—a remote-node solution was *not* going to work for this client with this specific application.

The key factor that worked against XYZ Corporation was the fact that their critical application was file-based instead of being client-server. I can't emphasize enough how important it is to understand the mechanisms that computers typically use to move data around, so let's walk through some example applications of each of these types, see how they work, and see why some don't work well with remote-node solutions while others do.

FILE-BASED APPS VERSUS CLIENT-SERVER APPS

Consider, if you will, a simple Microsoft Access database of names and phone numbers that you have stored on your computer. For discussion purposes, we'll assume that you have not "indexed" this database (a process which makes searching databases faster) and are trying to look up the phone number for an individual with the last name of Justice. To find this name and number, you'd launch your Microsoft Access application, open your phone number database, and then do a search on the last name. Once you submit your search, your CPU would talk to your hard drive controller, tell it to open the database on your hard drive, and retrieve the first record in the database. When the first record comes back, it turns out that it's for somebody named Anderson. The CPU realizes that Anderson doesn't equal Justice, so it dumps the first record from its memory and then requests the second one. The second record is for Beveridge. Beveridge doesn't equal Justice either, so once again the CPU dumps that record from memory and reads the third one. And so on, and so on, until it finally gets to the record for Justice. Once it successfully finds Justice, it displays the record on the screen.

The important factor to take note of is the repetitive process the CPU had to go through to get the data it needed. It had to keep communicating with the hard drive controller to get the next record, and then receive the response (the actual data) and check it. Given how speedy today's computers are, this all happens in the blink of an eye. But as you can see, there's a lot of communication that has to go on to make that simple operation work.

That communication, however, is all taking place between the internal components of your systems—from the CPU, across the data bus, through the hard drive controller, to the hard drive, and back again. Since these devices are directly connected to each other, they're very fast. However, suppose you move that phone number database off your hard drive and onto a file server so everyone in your office can access it. If you do the same search as before, each time Microsoft Access has to get a new record to check, the CPU will send a request to the network controller instead of the hard drive controller. The network controller will transmit the request to the server for the record and wait for the response from the file server. Once again, the CPU has to request this information over and over again from the network until it finally finds the record for Justice. Since a hard drive on a network file server probably isn't going to respond as fast as the hard drive in your computer, response time suffers.

To put some rough numbers to it, when the database was stored on the computer's internal hard drive, you might have had a maximum of 20 megabits' worth of bandwidth between the components inside your computer (hard drive, controller, bus, and CPU). Let's assume the last-name search took 1 second to complete. Once you move the database on your file server, your maximum bandwidth might have stepped down to only 10 megabits, assuming you're on a 10-megabit network. In theory, a search that took 1 second before could now take 2 seconds. That's still not too bad, and these are rough numbers (don't hold me to them), but they do illustrate the point I'm about to make.

The 1-second query operation became a 2-second query operation when the phone number database was moved off the local hard drive and onto the network file server. Part of the reason for that is the fact that the bandwidth between our CPU and the actual data was cut in half, from 20 megabits to 10. Since the CPU had to keep requesting each record in the file, the bandwidth available between the CPU and the data source plays a key role. Now, what if someone was dialing in to the network and trying to perform the same query? If you recall the 1/20th figure discussed earlier in regards to 56K modems, you can probably see where this is heading. Cutting the bandwidth down from 10 megabits to 56 kilobytes could potentially increase our search time twentyfold. It's entirely possible that our simple query could take upwards of 40 seconds over the 56K dial-up connection.

Now, I'll be the first to admit that I'm oversimplifying things here considerably to make a point. In reality, our example query probably wouldn't take 40 seconds over a dial-up connection, but the response time would be noticeably sluggish. Even if it only took 10 to 15 seconds to retrieve the data, slowdowns like that eventually produce productivity problems. The key to all this is the fact that bandwidth is a huge factor in remote computing if you have any applications that are file-based. So what's the solution? Try to stick with applications that are client-server based.

In keeping with our name-lookup scenario, let's assume that the data is stored in a SQL Server database instead of a standard Microsoft Access file. Using Microsoft Access (the *client* in client-server) as a "front-end" on your workstation, you can submit the same query for the last name Justice as before. However, instead of requesting each record individually this time and checking them one by one, Access will transmit a request to the SQL Server software (the *server* in client-server) for a specific record. Access will transmit a specific request such as "get me the record(s) with a last name of Justice." Small requests like those transmit very quickly, even over a slow connection (like a 56K modem). At that point, the responsibility of retrieving the correct data has shifted from the copy of Microsoft Access running on your CPU and is now in the hands of the SQL Server. Since the SQL Server presumably has high-speed access to the drives that store the data (most likely its own drives), it can find the answer in a few microseconds and then return an appropriate response back to Access.

The key thing to look for in determining whether an application is client-server or not is to see if there are two separate parts to the application. One part will run on your client workstations, and a second part will run on the server that stores your data (or at least on a server nearby with a high-speed connection on it). If there are two parts to your application, it is probably a client-server application and you shouldn't run into too many difficulties with remote-node users using it. However, if there aren't two parts to your application—if the only part is the client software that just uses directories and files on your file servers—you might run into performance problems using remote-node solutions.

Opening Word documents and Excel spreadsheets is, in effect, a file-based application, so it's worthwhile to look at your average document size to see how quickly it might transmit over a slow connection. Refer to the transmission times formula earlier in this section and figure out how long some sample documents would take to transmit over a modem. If most of your documents are simple and text-based, you probably won't run into too many performance issues. However, if your users typically work with large, multimegabyte documents on your server, you might need to consider other options.

Remote Control

If remote-node communications can be viewed as using a phone line as a long network cable, then remote-control communications should be viewed as using a phone line as a long keyboard, mouse, and video cable. Remote-control solutions, by definition, allow you to remotely take control of a workstation on your network over a dial-up connection. Software on a workstation would typically have some sort of remote-control software running on it (such as pcAnywhere or VNC) and a modem attached to it. This is sometimes referred to as the host PC, since it is typically waiting to host an incoming caller. Then, presumably from another location, another workstation with compatible remote-control software would call into the host PC.

Once the two PCs have negotiated a connection, the host would begin sending its screen data to the calling computer, in effect, letting the person at that calling station see everything that is on the remote screen. The calling workstation would then pass any keystrokes or mouse movements to the host PC, which would perform those actions just as if the user were sitting at the host PC doing them herself. In effect, the remote-control software is tapping into the keyboard, mouse, and video input/output of the host PC and making it available to a remote PC over a phone line.

Traditionally, remote-control solutions have been a bit more expensive to develop and scale due to the increased hardware requirements on each side. Whereas one RAS server with an adequate amount of modems would theoretically be able to handle 256 simultaneous inbound modem connections, having that many simultaneous connections using certain remote-control products could require 256 computers—one to receive each of the connections. That can be rather cost prohibitive in most cases, not to mention difficult to manage. However, it is worth mentioning because in some cases it might be the only remote access solution that would work in your environment.

Microsoft began including some remote-control functionality in Win2K with the bundling of Terminal Services with the base operating system (hmmm, there's that "bundling" concept again). If you are using Windows XP, you can use the Remote Desktop Connection software to remotely control your computer. If you are in a position where a remote-node solution won't meet your needs, you might want to take a look at it and see if Terminal Services or Remote Desktop will work for you. Terminal Services can be a worthy option since it doesn't require a separate computer to handle each inbound connection; instead, it requires one huge computer, and everybody runs a Windows session on that device (note: there are some other third-party products that function in a similar manner).

NOTE   For more detailed information on Terminal Services, see Chapter 16.

Since you've gotten this far, I'm assuming that you feel RAS is the right solution for you and you're ready to start working with it and implementing it on your network. If that's the case, keep reading. Let's talk a bit about what type of hardware and circuits you're going to need to have in place to make this all work.

RAS Hardware Requirements

One of the first things to determine in remote networking is where you plan on connecting to and how fast you want to connect. Often, one or both of those criteria will help you determine what your available communications options are. In most instances, that will leave you with one of the following options:

Connection Type	Typical Maximum Speed	Typical Maximum Distance
Analog modem	Asymmetrical: 53Kbps down, 33.6Kbps up	Unlimited, usually domestic
ISDN	BRI—128Kbps, PRI—1.544Mbps	Unlimited, usually domestic
X.25	2400bps—64Kbps	Global
Serial cable	Serial port max—230Kbps in most cases	"Physically near (less than 50 feet)," according to Microsoft
Infrared	Varies	Very close, line-of-sight
Parallel cable	Up to 500Kbps	Very close
Frame relay	1.544Mbps	Global
Cable modem	Asymmetrical: 3–10Mbps down, 256Kbps–2Mbps up	Connect to a local provider
(A)DSL	Asymmetrical: up to 2Mbps down, 256Kbps–1Mbps up	~5 Kilometers (local provider)

Of course, it should go without saying that any devices you are considering purchasing for use with RAS should be checked against Microsoft's Hardware Compatibility List (HCL) to make sure they are compatible with Windows Server 2003. By checking for HCL compatibility, you can be sure your choice of hardware has been specifically tested for compatibility with Server 2003 and has met the standards Microsoft has deemed necessary to be considered "compatible."

Also, if you're purchasing modems from a manufacturer that has several different models to choose from, pick your product carefully. While some modems might cost more than others due to features like voice or fax capability, if you're looking at two different models from the same manufacturer with the same capabilities, I'd suggest buying the more expensive of the two. The reason for this is quite simple: lower-cost modems are often designed by manufacturers primarily for light-duty home use applications. These are usually the modems you will see on the shelves in retail computer outlets. They are marketed to consumers and designed with tolerances and specifications targeted at the average consumer's needs. This doesn't take into consideration the more demanding needs of using modems for routing links, mail servers, etc.

With that out of the way, let's take a closer look at your hardware and circuit options, and then we'll jump into configuring RAS on your Windows Server 2003.

Analog Modems

Analog modems are the most commonly used connection device on RAS servers these days, so a good portion of our examples and configurations throughout this chapter will be using them.

A primer on how modems operate is in order for those of you who are unfamiliar with the technology. Modems are devices that accept binary signals (ones and zeros) from whatever device they are connected to, convert those binary signals into audible tones, and then transmit those tones over a phone line at a prescribed speed. (This process is described as "modulation" and is the derivative of the "mo" part of the word "modem.")

On the other side of the telephone line, another modem receives these audible tones and converts them back into the binary ones and zeros they represent. Once they have been converted back ("demodulated"), they are passed through to the device the modem is connected to as binary data. As you probably guessed, this "demodulation" process represents the "dem" in the word "modem."

Therefore, to complete a remote access or dial-up networking connection via a modem, you will need the following:

♦ Modem on the transmitting computer

♦ Modem on the receiving computer (this may be out of your control, for example, if you are dialing in to an ISP)

♦ Telephone connection between the two modems

In today's world, analog modems can transmit *and* receive data over traditional phone lines at speeds anywhere from 300 to 33,600 bits per second (sometimes referred to as the baud of the modem). As I mentioned earlier, the modems on either end of the connection convert the stream of bits to analog signals and transmit them over the phone line at a prenegotiated speed. But what about those "56K" modems?

WHEN 56K ISN'T QUITE 56K

A lot of hype and marketing has gone into the 56K modems that are currently available on the market. The modem manufacturers would love for you to believe that these modems are running at the full 56,000 bits per second, in both directions, but unfortunately that isn't quite the case. If you're planning on implementing a remote access solution for your organization, it's important to understand exactly how these modems work, what speeds you can hope to get from them, and what you can and can't expect from them.

First, you should realize that 56K modems *cannot* send and receive data at that speed in both directions. At the time of this writing, the maximum bidirectional speed anyone has been able to get out of typical analog connections is 33,600 bits per second. Much of that has to do with analog connections and the signal loss that is inherent as the analog data travels from one location to another. However, modem manufacturers are clever and have found a way to work around that limitation by removing half the analog signaling from the equation. By using a special server-side modem at one of the locations and a digital connection directly to the phone company's central office, data can be sent all the way from the server-side modem to the phone company with zero signal loss. Once the signal is within the phone company's systems, it usually travels through their system completely digital as well. The net result of this is that speeds of up to 56,000 bits per second are possible but only in one direction—the direction going from the server-side modem to the phone company. Communication in the other direction—from the location with the analog modem toward the phone company—is still limited by the inherent signal loss and peaks out at 33,600 bits per second.

Companies like Internet service providers have been the primary beneficiaries of 56K technology, and 56K modems are a great tool for getting a bit more speed when connecting to the Internet. However, it's important to realize that *you cannot purchase two identical 56K modems, plug them into regular analog lines, and expect to get a connection any higher than 33,600 bits per second between them*. Without having a server-side modem at one of your locations and a digital line from that modem to the phone company, you will be bound by the existing 33,600 limitations.

It's also worth mentioning that even when dialing in to a location with a server-side modem that supports 56K, under current FCC regulations in the United States, if you're using an analog line you will *never* get a 56,000 connection. The FCC has placed limits on the amount of voltage *any* device can transmit over a phone line, which currently restricts all modems to a maximum capability of 53,000 bits per second. However, most analyses and studies of 56K modems have revealed that reasonable speeds to expect for your connections are anywhere from 42,000 to 48,000 for data coming from the server-side modem (or "downlink speed") and, of course, 33,600 for data going to the server-side modem (or "uplink speed"). The amount of speed you get will depend on the quality of the equipment at your local phone company, the condition of the lines in your area, and your physical distance from the phone company's central office. One of my own computers was never able to get speeds higher than 42,000–44,000bps when dialing in to a local ISP until I recently moved. Nothing else changed with my computer except the location it was in, but when I dialed in from my new home, I was consistently connecting at 48,000 bits per second.

ISDN

A few years ago, a 56K analog modem would be more than enough bandwidth for most remote data needs. However, as computers have grown in size and complexity, so have the files and data that computers typically need to move around. Downloading multimegabyte items from the Internet, such as Windows 2000 Service Packs, could literally take hours over a standard dial-up connection. Fortunately, Integrated Services Digital Network (ISDN) is an option to get more bandwidth without having to get a dedicated circuit in place.

ISDN typically comes in two different flavors, ISDN Basic Rate Interface (BRI) or ISDN Primary Rate Interface (PRI). The main difference between the two is speed (and therefore, price). BRI can support data speeds of up to 128Kbps over standard copper telephone lines, and PRI supports data speeds of up to 1.544Mbps over T1 cable. Since ISDN BRI can run over the same copper wires that most people have wired in their homes, it's more commonly implemented.

ISDN BRI consists of three separate data channels on one connection. Two of the channels are 64Kbps bearer channels, commonly referred to as B channels. These two channels, when combined, make up the 128Kbps that ISDN can use to move data from one location to another. The third channel (commonly referred to as the D channel) is a special 16Kbps out-of-band channel used for signaling between your equipment and the phone company. Although all three channels add up to 144Kbps, most ISDN implementations will either use one or both B channels, so I'll refer to ISDN as being able to support 64Kbps or 128Kbps.

To use ISDN for remote access, you will need the following:

- An ISDN modem at each location and, optionally, an NT1 network termination device (most ISDN modems come with these built-in today)
- A digital ISDN connection at each location

Digital Subscriber Line (DSL)

DSL (Digital Subscriber Line) has become a more common and affordable high-speed connection method in recent years. Using broadband technology, DSL passes data over your phone line and can reach speeds of approximately 140 times the speed of the fastest analog modems. There are many different implementations of DSL, but the most common form is ADSL, or Asymmetric DSL, which is what I'll be referring to here.

One of the benefits of using DSL as a connection method is its "always on" functionality. Unlike analog modems, DSL doesn't require you to connect and disconnect by dialing up to a receiving modem. Instead, once the DSL modem is installed, the connection is persistent and remains on at all times. Another great benefit of using DSL is that, although it does use your phone line to transmit data, you can still transmit voice data at the same time, which means that you don't have to stop talking on the phone so that you can dial up to the Internet.

While analog modems transmit signals through a public telephone network—the same facility that's used to connect telephone conversations—DSL modems "piggyback" data signals over the voice signal. This means that the data gets sent to two different places—your voice calls are sent to the telephone network and your data signals go to the Internet.

DSL modems are generally equipped with Ethernet ports so that, by adding a router, you can connect many machines to a single DSL connection, thus sharing the connection among all of the computers in a small office.

Cable Modems

Another "always on" technology that is becoming more and more popular is called a cable modem. Cable modems offer high-speed Internet access over a shared cable television line in a geographical area. Like DSL, the connection is persistent, no logging on or off or dealing with busy signals. Unlike DSL though, this technology uses a cable television line rather than a phone line.

While cable modems have greater downstream bandwidth capabilities than DSL, keep in mind that the bandwidth will be shared between all users in the near geographic neighborhood. As a result, the available bandwidth will vary, sometimes dramatically, as more people in that area access the Internet at the same time.

In general, the upstream traffic on a cable modem tends to be slower than that of DSL, sometimes because the individual cable modem equipment is slower and sometimes because there are just too many people in the area are trying to utilize the bandwidth at a time.

Like DSL modems, most cable modems offer an Ethernet connection so that you can tie in the rest of your network and have all your machines use that single access to the Internet. Keep in mind, that although we refer to modems when we talk about both DSL and cable modem technologies, we aren't really talking about modems in the traditional sense. You can't dial up to a RAS server using a telephone number with either of these connection types. What you get is a permanent connection to the Internet, allowing you lots more functionality than the traditional method of using dialup.

Direct Options (Null Modem, Parallel, and Infrared)

Given the affordability and broad universal support for network cards these days, using a null modem or parallel cable to connect two computers has really become more of a niche than a mainstream use of RAS. However, there may be occasions when it is the only option—maybe you have a specialty device that can't support a network card and can only communicate with the outside world via a serial or parallel port. If that's the case, a null modem cable, parallel cable, or infrared connection between your systems can be used for a connection.

Null modem cables are typically available at any computer store or through mail-order catalogs. However, according to Microsoft, standard off-the-shelf null modem cables might not be wired correctly for use with RAS. If possible, have your cabling vendor build a custom cable according to the pin configurations listed in Table 20.1. By connecting the null modem cable to the serial ports on each of your devices, you can connect your two computers together as needed. However, you will be limited to your serial port's speed and distance limitations of roughly 50 feet.

TABLE 20.1: MICROSOFT-SPECIFIED NULL MODEM CABLING REQUIREMENTS FOR RAS

9-PIN TO 9-PIN		9-PIN TO 25-PIN		25-PIN TO 25-PIN		MAC RS422/423 TO 25-PIN	
HOST SYSTEM	CALLING	25-PIN	9-PIN SYSTEM	HOST SYSTEM	CALLING	MAC	SERVER 2003
3	2	2	2	2	3	1	6, 8
2	3	3	3	3	2	2	20
7	8	4	8	4	5	3	3
8	7	5	7	5	4	4, 8	7
6, 1	4	6, 8	4	6, 8	20	5	2
5	5	7	5	7	7	6	—
4	6, 1	20	6, 1	20	6, 8	7	—

Source: Microsoft Corporation

Parallel connections can be made between two computers using the standard or enhanced (ECP) parallel ports of each device. By connecting devices together in this fashion, it is reasonable to expect throughput speeds of up to 500–600Kbps, but the distance between devices is again very limited. Microsoft lists a specific vendor, Parallel Technologies, in their help files included with Windows Server 2003 as a source for compatible parallel cables to use.

NOTE *To contact Parallel Technologies about their DirectParallel line of products, call (800) 789-4784 or visit them on the Web at* www.1pt.com.

Infrared connections were new in Windows 2000 Server and will continue in Server 2003 to serve as a useful option for small offices. Since the connection distance is limited by the strength of the infrared signal *and* a direct line-of-sight requirement, it will be an easy method of connecting (no cables!) but limited in usefulness.

X.25

X.25 is a protocol that coordinates communication between multiple machines, routing information through a packet-switched public data network. Instead of establishing direct connections from one device to another, all devices in an X.25 network simply connect to a "cloud" and pass their data to the cloud. It is up to the company that maintains and manages the cloud to ensure that the data reaches the correct destination point. X.25 is a relatively outdated technology, which is why through-put speeds top out at 56K to 64K.

So, why use X.25? Well, even though it is an extremely slow transport medium, it is also an exceptionally reliable one. There is an extensive amount of error checking and correction that occurs as a part of the X.25 protocol, which makes it a worthwhile consideration in areas with poor telecommunication services. X.25 is available globally and in some cases may be the only reasonable option for connectivity in certain countries.

Frame Relay

Frame relay is quickly becoming a preferred option to X.25 connections, as it functions on roughly the same principle—each system passing data into a data cloud—but at much higher speeds. Frame relay can support connections ranging from 56Kbps all the way up to 1.544Mbps. Since frame relay only requires a single connection from each site into the cloud, it is an excellent choice for global connectivity; otherwise dedicated wide area network links across continents could end up being prohibitively expensive to implement.

RAS Installation and Setup

Now that I've laid the groundwork for you to understand how remote access works, it's time to start working through some of the sample applications discussed earlier.

Installing Devices for Remote Access

Since a modem is one of the most widely used tools for remote access services, I'll start by quickly walking you through installing your modem on a Windows Server 2003, making sure that the correct drivers are installed, ports are selected, etc.

To begin adding modems to your system, click the Start button. Choose the Control Panel option, and then click the Phone and Modem Options icon. If this is your first time using this option, you will be probably be prompted for information about your area code, what type of dialing the system should use (tone or pulse), etc. After you've entered some of that preliminary information, you will be taken to the Phone and Modem Options applet. Click the Modems tab. More than likely, you won't have any modems listed. Click the Add button to launch the Add Hardware Wizard, as seen in Figure 20.1.

Depending on your preferences, you can either have Windows Server 2003 attempt to detect your modem automatically or you can select it manually from a list. If your modem is a bit older (as in, it was on the market before Server 2003 was introduced), you are probably safe letting Server 2003 attempt to find the correct driver for your modem. Leave the Don't Detect My Modem; I Will Select It From a List box unchecked, and click Next to begin the detection process.

If your modem is newer than the release of Windows Server 2003, or if you prefer to configure these options yourself (I prefer setting all these things myself), check the Don't Detect My Modem; I Will Select It From a List box, and click Next. You'll be taken to the screen shown in Figure 20.2.

FIGURE 20.1

Add Hardware
Wizard

FIGURE 20.2

Install New Modem
selection screen

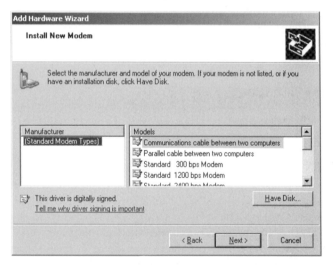

From here, you can choose from a myriad of different modem drivers. Find the driver that matches your modem, select it, and then click Next to install it. If, for some reason, an appropriate driver isn't listed for your modem, you can always use one of the standard modem drivers listed in the Standard Modem Types selection under Manufacturer. The standard modem drivers are reasonably good and are reliable in most circumstances. There are even standard modem drivers for 56K modems supporting the V.90, x2, and k56Flex standards. If your modem manufacturer included a driver disk along with the purchase of your modem, click the Have Disk button and insert your driver disk in the appropriate drive. You will need to tell Windows to look in that location by giving it the appropriate path to check for the driver (usually A:\; consult your modem manufacturer's documentation for further information).

If you are installing your driver by hand, you will need to tell Windows what communications port this modem is connected to, as shown in Figure 20.3.

FIGURE 20.3

Selecting communications ports

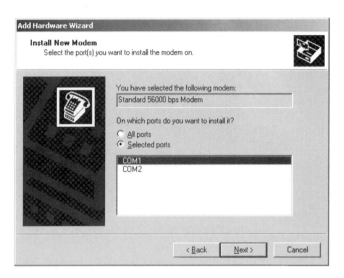

If you have identical modems on all your communications ports, you can select the All Ports radio button. Otherwise, you should select the port your modem is currently attached to. If you have multiple modems on many ports (but not *all* ports), hold down the Ctrl key while selecting each port. When you have selected the correct ports, click Next to complete the installation. You should receive a confirmation dialog box indicating that your modem has been successfully installed.

Now that you have a modem installed, it's time to take it for a test drive. One of the easiest things to do in Windows Server 2003 is to define a dial-up connection to the Internet, so we'll start there first.

Connecting to the Internet

It's no secret that Windows Server 2003 was designed with the Internet in mind. Given that fact, Microsoft has made it easy to get your computer connected to the Internet. If you are running Windows Server 2003 as a proxy server so your internal clients can surf the Web, or if you're running it as an e-mail server, dial-up connections to the Internet are an option worth looking into. Due to some readily available fine-tuning parameters you can set for dial-up connections, you can create a rather reliable link to the Internet with just a modem. Let's get started.

The first thing you'll need to do before connecting to the Internet is set up an account with an Internet service provider (ISP). We won't go through the specifics of how to do that here, but once you have an account you will need a minimum of three things handy to create your dial-up connection to the Internet:

◆ A local access phone number to dial (whether analog or ISDN)

◆ A username and password combination

◆ Optionally, an IP address to assign to your dial-up connection, and DNS addresses to use (most ISPs won't require you to program this information in, but in case yours does, be sure to have this handy in advance)

When you're ready to build your connection to the Internet, choose Start/Control Panel/Network Connections. You should get a window that looks like the screen in Figure 20.4.

FIGURE 20.4

Network Connections window

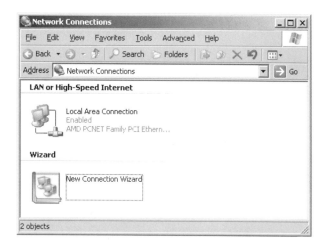

From here, double-click the New Connection Wizard icon to start the wizard. Click Next in the initial screen of the wizard and you will be presented with a list of connection types you can establish. Select the Connect to the Internet option and then click Next. This will walk you through the process of setting up an ISP account. You will be asked whether you want to set up your Internet connection over a modem, a broadband connection such as DSL or cable modem (with or without requiring a password), or a LAN. If you have in-house Internet connectivity that is already running, then a LAN would be the option you would want to choose. However, since we're discussing modems, let's walk through the modem configuration.

After you select the Connect Using a Dial-Up Modem option and click Next, you will be taken through a process to collect the information we discussed earlier, beginning with the name of your ISP. Once you enter the name of your ISP and the phone number to dial, and choose whether to make this connection available to all users on the system or save it in your profile for your exclusive use, you will need to enter the account information used to authenticate to your provider, as shown in Figure 20.5.

FIGURE 20.5

Entering account information

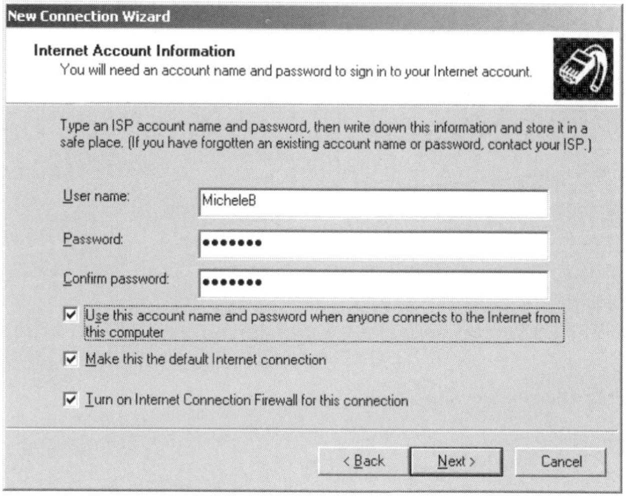

Here you will enter the user credentials (username and password) your ISP has provided you for use with your account. This information will be stored along with all the other information for this dial-up networking entry so Windows Server 2003 doesn't have to prompt you for it every time you want to make a connection. If you don't feel comfortable having this information stored on your machine, leave the password field blank.

The final options on this screen enable you to choose whether to apply the authentication information to all users, decide if you want this to act as the default Internet connection, and decide whether to turn on the built-in firewall software for the local machine. When you click Next, you will be reminded of your choices in the final screen of the New Connection Wizard. Click Finish to end the wizard and you will be presented with a Connect <*YOUR ISP NAME*> dialog box that contains the account information for the ISP you just entered, as shown in Figure 20.6. Click Dial to test your connection.

FIGURE 20.6

Connect to your ISP.

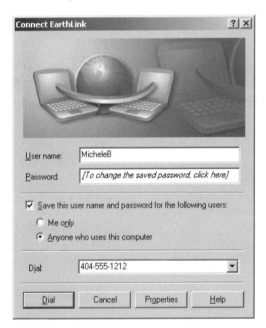

You may have noticed that you weren't required to enter an IP address to use for this connection. That's because, unlike Windows 2000, the New Connection Wizard in Server 2003 now assumes that your IP address for this connection will be issued by your ISP. Of course, you have the option of setting that information manually if you prefer, as well as choosing the settings for your default gateway, DNS servers, and WINS server information. Let's look at the various options that are available for this dial-up connection. Click the Properties button to view the properties for the connection, then choose the Networking tab to view the screen in Figure 20.7. Highlight the TCP/IP protocol option and then click the Properties button to view the TCP/IP properties page.

FIGURE 20.7

Networking
properties

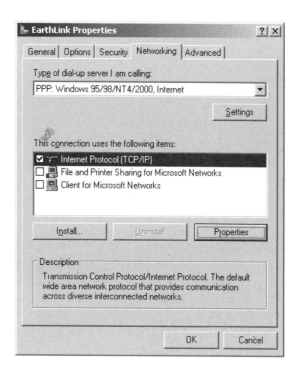

Even though most ISPs automatically assign you an IP address, if your ISP requires you to manually assign yourself an address, click the Use the Following IP Address radio button in the top of the window and enter the appropriate address in the IP Address field. Some ISPs may still require you to enter DNS server information (DNS is how Windows Server 2003 translates names like www.microsoft.com into IP addresses). If so, click the Use the Following DNS Server Addresses radio button in the bottom half of the window, and enter your primary and secondary DNS server IP addresses exactly as your ISP provided them to you.

Clicking the Advanced button in this screen will allow you to configure the additional network settings you see in Figure 20.8. Notice the check box called Use Default Gateway On Remote Network. If your machine is not connected to a LAN, you don't need to worry about this option. If your machine does have a LAN connection, in addition to your dial-up connection, then you'll need to understand something about default gateways.

A default gateway is a network address to which your IP requests are sent when the request is for an IP address that lies outside of the local network that your machine resides on.

The default in Windows Server 2003, as you can see here, is to use the default gateway of your ISP provider when connected using the dial-up connection. This enables you to communicate on the Internet via your ISP. However, since your machine can only have one default gateway at any one time, your ability to communicate on your local LAN is limited, at least outside your local network. So, if your computer resides in a larger network environment, your computer will be unable to make requests that would normally need to be sent to the default gateway on your LAN. You can get more information about default gateways in Chapter 6.

FIGURE 20.8

Advanced TCP/IP
Settings screen

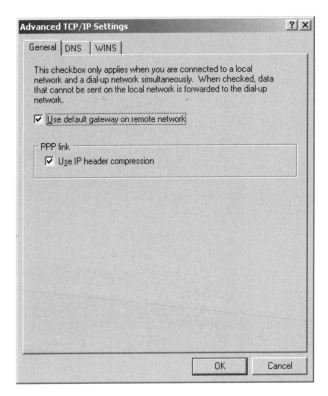

Click OK, and then click OK again to return to the Networking properties sheet for your ISP connection. Now that you have configured your networking properties for the connection, let's look at some additional options for the dial-up connection.

Optional Internet Connection Settings

Since you have verified that your Internet connection is working properly, there are some optional settings you might find useful for controlling the behavior of this dial-up connection. Such items include:

◆ Programming a list of alternate numbers for Windows Server 2003 to attempt when dialing

◆ Disconnecting idle connections (good for per-minute connections such as ISDN)

◆ Automatic redialing of busy or nonresponsive numbers

◆ Automatic reestablishing of connections that have dropped

All these features are useful enough by themselves. However, if you're running a Windows Server 2003 that *depends* on having an Internet connection available, you'll find these extra features useful. It takes much less administration when a server can take care of establishing and reestablishing its own Internet connections without any human intervention.

To get to these options, you can either click the Properties button from the Connect <*YOUR ISP NAME*> dialog box or right-click the connection and choose Properties in the Network Connections dialog box. Open the Network Connections window again and right-click your ISP dial-up entry. Select the Properties option, and you should get to the dialog box shown in Figure 20.9.

FIGURE 20.9

Advanced Properties for the dial-up connection

If your ISP has several local phone numbers available for you to use, you can program Windows Server 2003 to cycle through the entire list until it gets a connection. Click the Alternates button next to the phone number, and you should see a screen like the one in Figure 20.10.

From the Alternate Phone Numbers dialog, you can enter as many numbers as you would like Windows Server 2003 to use to attempt to establish this connection. Click the Add button to add a new number to the list, and then use the arrow buttons on the right side of the dialog box to adjust the order of which number should be dialed first.

As an additional option, Windows Server 2003 can remember which number was successful last time you connected and try that one first if you check the Move Successful Number to Top of List option. This will make sure that if for some reason one of your ISP's local access numbers goes offline for a while, it won't stay in the top of the list and Windows Server 2003 won't keep trying to dial that number first.

When you're finished entering alternate numbers, click the OK button to return to the main properties dialog box for this dial-up connection. To reach the next set of editable items for this connection, click the Options tab. This should bring you to a screen similar to Figure 20.11.

FIGURE 20.10

Entering alternate
dial-up numbers

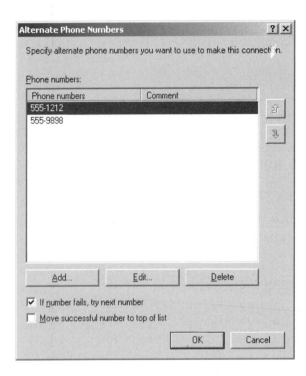

FIGURE 20.11

Editing options for
dial-up entries

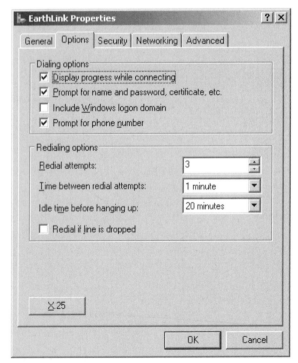

This dialog box has several options available, the most useful of which regard dialing, idle time-outs, and reestablishing broken connections. Let's go through these one by one and show how they can be used.

Prompt for Name and Password, Certificate, etc.   When you first created this dial-up networking entry using the New Connection Wizard, one of the steps you should have gone through was for entering a username and password to use for this connection. If you decided not to enter your password directly into the settings for this dial-up networking entry, you will want to check this option. Otherwise, Windows Server 2003 will simply try to use a blank password when establishing this connection. Checking this option will cause Windows to prompt you for a username and password to use instead of the existing username and password stored with this dial-up networking entry.

Redial Attempts and Time Between Redial Attempts   If your local ISP has a problem with busy signals, you will appreciate these options. By choosing the number of times to attempt to redial and the time to wait between attempts, you can program Server 2003 to keep dialing your ISP until a number becomes available. Personally, I've found this setting to be extremely useful in times of inclement weather when everyone is stuck in their homes and clogging my ISP's lines.

Idle Time Before Hanging Up   If the same phone company that serves my area serves yours, then you are accustomed to paying for your ISDN access by the minute. These per-minute charges can add up to a rather substantial phone bill if your ISDN connection stays up all day. If your server only really needs to have a connection during business hours (for example, for proxy server clients browsing the Internet), set an appropriate idle time-out value here in minutes. Once the specified number of minutes has passed without any activity, Windows Server 2003 will drop the connection.

Redial If Line Is Dropped   It's simply a fact of life—dial-up connections "drop" sometimes. It just happens, but it can cause considerable headaches if people are depending on this connection being up and you happen to be away when it goes down. Checking this option causes Windows Server 2003 to automatically redial and reestablish your connection if it drops. Assuming something hasn't failed on the ISP side of your connection, your link should come back up automatically within about a minute.

For this feature to work, you must have the Remote Access Auto Connection Manager service running. This service doesn't automatically start on Windows Server 2003 by default, so you will need to enable it manually. To do this, enter the Computer Management Console by selecting Start/Programs/Administrative Tools/Computer Management or by right-clicking My Computer and selecting the Manage option. This will bring you into the Microsoft Management Console (MMC) for managing computers on your network. In the left pane of the MMC, you should see an option for Services under the Services and Applications group (you might need to expand Services and Applications to see it). Click the Services icon in the left pane, and you should see a listing of all the services running on your Windows Server 2003 in the result pane. The MMC screen should look like Figure 20.12.

Find the Remote Access Auto Connection Manager service in the listing on the right, and double-click it to edit the properties. From here, you can start the service manually and configure it to start up automatically every time your Windows Server 2003 boots up. The properties page for this service should look like Figure 20.13.

FIGURE 20.12

Computer Management MMC for enabling Remote Access Auto Connection Manager

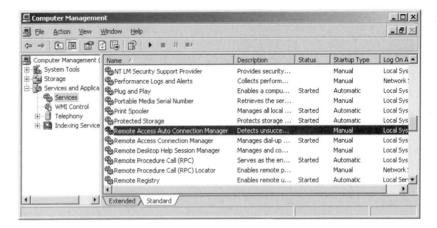

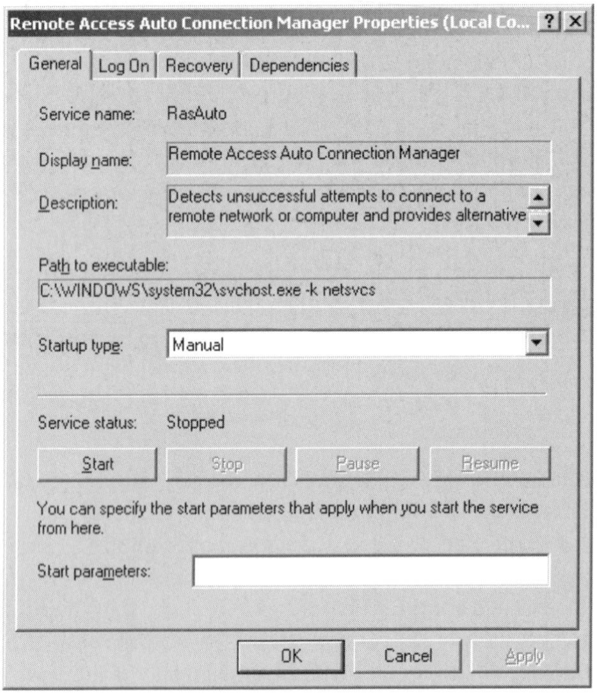

FIGURE 20.13

Service properties for RAS Auto Connection Manager

To start this service manually, click the Start button in the dialog box. If everything goes okay, the status of this service should change to Started. Now, to make sure that this service starts every time your Windows Server 2003 boots, select the Automatic option from the Startup Type pull-down box. Click OK to save your changes and then exit the Computer Management MMC.

To test the redial functionality, try establishing a connection with this ISP dial-up entry and then pull the phone plug out of your modem. Wait a few seconds so that you're sure the carrier has dropped (if you have an icon in your Taskbar indicating that you're connected, it should disappear), and then plug the phone line back in. Within a minute, Windows Server 2003 should attempt to reestablish this connection for you without any intervention whatsoever.

Accepting Incoming Calls from Remote Users

In today's business world, there are several buzzwords that tend to make an administrator's job a bit more challenging. Phrases like telecommuting, mobile computing, and sales force automation are all centered around one common principle—getting corporate data into the hands of people who need it, exactly when they need it, wherever they are located. In terms of systems administration, this typically means accepting inbound connections from remote clients. If you have yet to face this administrative challenge, rest assured that in the near future you most likely will. The tendency toward remote computing simply shows no signs of slowing down anytime soon.

Whatever your dial-in needs are, Windows Server 2003 can act as a universal gateway to get remote clients into your network. Thanks to built-in support for PPP, an RFC-defined dial-up standard, Windows Server 2003 can receive calls from almost any type of device. Windows PCs, Macintosh systems, Unix hosts, and even personal digital assistants (PDAs) can all establish PPP connections to remote networks. Windows Server 2003 can accept traffic from any of these devices and route it to the devices on your internal network, whether they're NT servers, Novell servers, Unix hosts, etc.

To start accepting incoming calls from remote clients, you will need the following:

◆ Windows Server 2003 with remote access software configured to accept incoming calls

◆ Connection device of some sort (modem, ISDN, X.25, etc.) connected to Windows Server 2003 to accept calls from the remote clients

◆ Client computer capable of establishing a PPP session (Windows 9x/Me, NT 4, 2000, and XP; Macintosh; 3Com Palm; etc.)

◆ Connection device of some sort (modem, ISDN, X.25, etc.) connected to the remote client and capable of establishing a connection to the corresponding device on Windows Server 2003

◆ Circuit (phone line, ISDN line, etc.) between the two devices

◆ User account on your Windows Server 2003 (or within your Active Directory) with dial-in rights granted to it

For the sake of brevity, we'll assume that you've gone through the detailed steps earlier in this chapter to add your modems (ISDN devices or whatever you might be using) to your Windows Server 2003 and that they are functioning properly. With that out of the way, let's get started on accepting incoming calls from remote clients.

To be sure we're all working from the same baseline, I'll assume that you do not have the Routing and Remote Access Service installed on your computer. If you do have it installed, going through this procedure will stop your existing services and reinstall them with the answers provided to the configuration wizard.

Remote Access Server Installation and Setup

Start the installation for Routing and Remote Access Service by clicking Start/Administrative Tools/Routing and Remote Access. You will see an MMC window appear, and you should see your server listed somewhere in the left pane. Right-click your server, and select the Configure and Enable Routing and Remote Access option.

This will begin the RRAS installation process. This process is aided by a wizard that will help you configure the necessary services to allow remote clients to dial in. After a welcome dialog box (in which you will click Next), the first dialog box you will see should look similar to the screen shown in Figure 20.14.

FIGURE 20.14

RRAS Setup Wizard: role of server

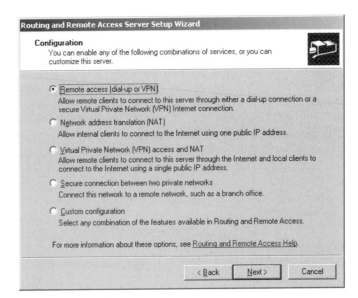

The first step of the configuration wizard is to determine what role your Windows Server 2003 will play. If you are simply looking to accept connections from dial-in clients, click the Remote Access (Dial-Up or VPN) radio button, and then click Next to move on to the next step of the wizard. On the next screen (Figure 20.15) you can decide whether you want to offer a VPN service, dial-up, or both of these types of connections to your clients. Choose Dial-Up and click Next to continue to the next step of the wizard, shown in Figure 20.16.

The next step of the wizard—assuming you have TCP/IP installed on your server—will ask you how to handle assignment of IP addresses to remote dial-in clients. Since every device on the network must have its own IP address, your dial-in workstations need a way to get addresses as well. By default, RRAS will want to assign addresses to your dial-in users automatically from a DHCP server. If you have a DHCP server running, you will probably want to accept the default Automatically option. Whether DHCP and RAS are running on the same server or on separate systems, the RAS service will attempt to obtain a DHCP-assigned address from the internal network and then pass it along to the remote client to use. The key with this option is to make sure you have a working DHCP server somewhere on your network and that it has enough IP addresses that can be used for dial-in connections.

NOTE *For further reading on setting up a DHCP server, see Chapter 7.*

FIGURE 20.15

RRAS Setup Wizard: configuring connection types

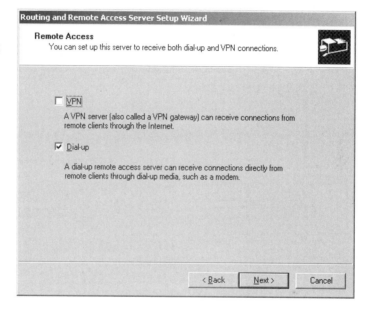

FIGURE 20.16

RRAS Setup Wizard: IP address assignment

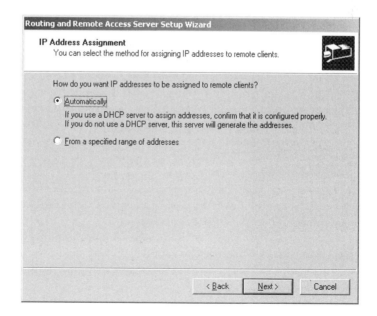

Under some special circumstances, you might want to control which IP addresses RAS hands out to dial-in clients. For example, if you have developed login scripts or other automation routines that depend on IP addresses, having a preset range might be useful. Or you might have security policies in place on your networks that only allow certain IP addresses to connect to certain devices. Either way, if you need to make sure RAS clients always fall within a certain range of IP addresses, select the From a Specified Range of Addresses option and then click Next to proceed to Address Range Assignment, shown in Figure 20.17.

FIGURE 20.17

RRAS Setup
Wizard: address
range assignment

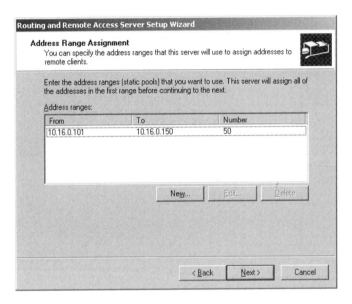

Through address range assignment, you can enter a series of IP address ranges for RRAS to use when clients dial in to your network. You can make these ranges as small or as large as you would like—just so long as you know that they are usable addresses within your network. To add a range (or ranges) to your system, click the New button and enter a start and end range of IP addresses to use. The New Address Range dialog box will automatically calculate how many addresses are in the range you provided. In the example shown in Figure 20.17, I have already entered a range of 10.16.0.101 to 10.16.0.150 for this RRAS server to use. When you have finished entering your addresses, click Next to proceed with the next step in the wizard, shown in Figure 20.18.

Although the next step of the wizard might look like it's simply asking if you have a RADIUS (Remote Authentication Dial-In User Service) server available on your network, it's actually asking far more than that. This step of the wizard is asking how you would like to handle dial-in authentications. Your choices are limited to two simple options.

If you are currently using RADIUS services on your network for authentication and logging of other dial-in access, you can set up your RRAS server to use the existing RADIUS server instead of using its own authentication and logging mechanisms. To specify your own RADIUS information, select the Yes, Set Up This Server to Work with a RADIUS Server option, and then click Next. Since RADIUS is outside the scope of this chapter, we'll assume that you will stick to using

Windows Server 2003's own authentication and logging mechanisms. Therefore, you can leave the default No, Use Routing and Remote Access to Authenticate Connection Requests option, and then click Next to continue.

FIGURE 20.18

RRAS Setup
Wizard: RADIUS
services

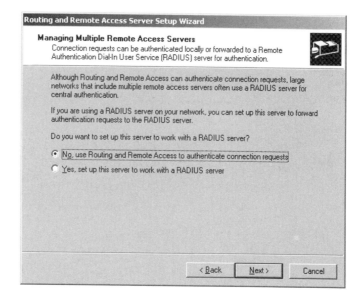

Since the option for RADIUS selection is the final step of the wizard, your server should be configured after you click Finish on the final panel of the wizard.

Granting Dial-In Permissions to User(s)

Once you've successfully installed the Routing and Remote Access Service, the next thing to do is grant dial-in permissions to a user account in your Active Directory tree. (We'll assume you already have an account created for this purpose.)

NOTE   *If you need to add a new account for this exercise, see Chapter 9.*

To grant dial-in permissions to selected users, choose the Active Directory Users and Computers MMC by clicking Start/Administrative Tools/Active Directory Users and Computers. Navigate through the Active Directory tree to the user you want to grant dial-in permissions to, and right-click the corresponding record. By selecting the option to edit the properties for this user, you'll be taken to a dialog box to edit options for this user. Click the Dial-In tab, and you should be left with a screen similar to the one in Figure 20.19.

By default, the user account you've selected will probably have the Deny Access option selected at the top of the dialog box. Click Allow Access to grant dial-in permissions to this user. You also have the option to edit some user-specific settings through this dialog box.

For example, if you'd like to implement an additional measure of security by making sure a certain user's remote access session always comes from a specific phone number, you have a few options available. First, if your modem and phone line supports caller ID service, you can simply select the Verify

Caller-ID option box and enter the phone number this user must call in on. However, if you are using hardware that doesn't support caller ID or that service is unavailable in your area, you can achieve the same type of security by having your RAS server call the user back at a certain phone number. Selecting one of the Callback Options available in the middle of the screen activates this feature.

FIGURE 20.19

Granting dial-in permissions via user properties

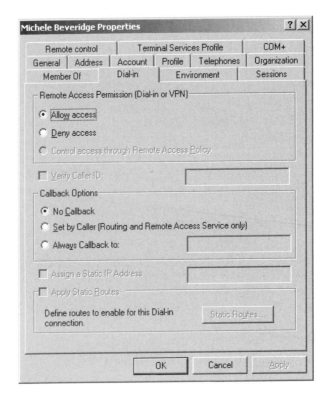

If you have home users who dial in either via long-distance or local long-distance, callback options might also save you some money when it comes to your remote access costs. If the telephone service you have in your office has a better per-minute rate than the rates your users typically have in their homes, you can save money on your remote access connections by having your RAS server call users back at the cheaper rates.

In addition to callback options, you can also specify a fixed IP address for this specific user to receive. This feature first occurred in Windows 2000 and can be exceptionally useful when setting up internal access policies based on IP address (firewall rules, etc.).

Now, take a moment and relax. Your server is set up to receive calls. You should be able to test this by calling the number associated with your RAS server from a standard phone and getting a carrier tone. If you don't hear a carrier tone, double-check your work and make sure everything is connected properly. If, for some reason, you still don't get a carrier tone when you call in, try rebooting the server (oddly enough, this happened to me once, and rebooting it corrected the problem).

WARNING *In Figure 20.19 you can see that some of the options are unavailable. These settings only become available if your domain is running in at least Windows 2000 Native Mode. Why? If your domain is still in Mixed Mode, then you still have NT 4 DCs, which means that you can only edit the user attributes that were available in NT 4. NT 4 does not have the ability to store user attributes that are new to Windows 2000 and Server 2003.*

Changing RAS Server Configurations after Installation

Wizards are both a blessing and a curse for the Windows operating system. Although they make complex tasks easier, they also tend to assume several answers for you with no chance to change those assumptions. The RRAS configuration wizard is guilty of this practice; it will make several assumptions for you as you configure your system. You may want to check these configurations to make sure they are exactly the way you want them to be.

If you need to change any of your configurations at a later time, you can easily do so by right-clicking your server in the Routing and Remote Access MMC and then selecting Properties. Through the RRAS properties dialog boxes, you can add or remove support for certain protocols for dial-up connections, increase authentication security, and fine-tune the PPP controls for establishing connections to client systems. I'll walk you through each of these areas, starting with the controls for security shown in Figure 20.20.

FIGURE 20.20

Editing security properties for RAS service

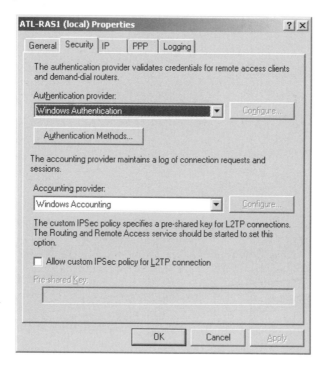

Through this screen, you can control several behaviors for the security and encryption used with your dial-up connections. Although there are pros and cons for using each (with the pros usually being increased security and the cons being limited client support), we'll discuss each option briefly so you can make your own judgments as to which one is best to use.

By default, the authentication provider that should be automatically configured is Windows Authentication. If you have an external RADIUS server, you can change Windows to use the RADIUS server instead by selecting the RADIUS option from the pull-down box and then clicking the Configure button to define the RADIUS servers to use. You can also configure Microsoft's implementation of RADIUS, called IAS, to manage authentication. But again, since RADIUS servers are outside of the scope of this chapter, we'll simply stick to Windows Authentication methods.

By clicking the Authentication Methods button below the Authentication Provider pull-down box, you will be taken to a screen similar to the one shown in Figure 20.21.

FIGURE 20.21

Editing authentication types for RAS service

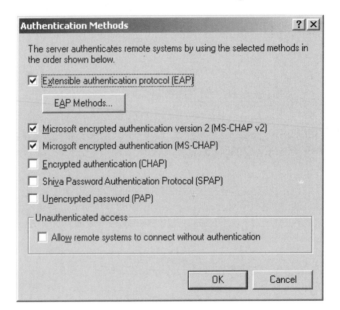

As you can see, there are several authentication options to choose from:

Extensible Authentication Protocol (EAP)   Because security and authentication is a constantly changing field, embedding authentication schemes into an operating system is impractical at times. To solve this problem, Microsoft has included support for EAP, which is simply a means of "plugging in" new authentication schemes as needed. Currently, Windows Server 2003 supports MD-5 Challenge, Smart Card or other Certificate (TLS), Protected EAP (PEAP), and Secured Password (EAP-MSCHAP v2), but this option will allow for future authentication protocols to be plugged into the operating system easily.

Microsoft Encrypted Authentication version 2 (MS-CHAP v2)   Microsoft's derivative of CHAP, or Challenge Handshake Authentication Protocol (see the next entry). Using MS-CHAP allows you to encrypt an entire dial-up session, not just the original authentication, which is especially important when it comes to setting up virtual private networking sessions. MS-CHAP v2 support is included in Windows 2000 and Server 2003 for all types of connections and in Windows NT 4 and Windows 9*x* (with the Dial-Up Networking 1.3 upgrade) for VPN connections.

Encrypted Authentication (CHAP)   Defined in RFC 1334 and later revised in RFC 1994, the Challenge Handshake Authentication Protocol is a means of encrypting authentication sessions between a client and server. Since this protocol is defined by an RFC, it enjoys a broad base of support among many operating systems and other devices.

Shiva Password Authentication Protocol (SPAP)   SPAP, short for Shiva Password Authentication Protocol, is an encrypted password authentication method used by Shiva LAN Rover clients and servers. Windows Server 2003 can act as a server when Shiva LAN Rover clients are dialing in by providing the correct authentication sequence for them.

Unencrypted Password (PAP)   Password Authentication Protocol (PAP) is one of the last two options listed, and it is also one of the least secure. It is no more secure than a simple conversation from your server saying, "What is your name and password?" to the client and the client responding with, "My name is Marty and my password is 'let-me-in'." There is no encryption of authentication credentials whatsoever.

Unauthenticated Access   At first glance, this option wouldn't seem to make much sense—leaving a wide-open access point to your network with no authentication required whatsoever. However, when paired with caller ID verification, this option can make a simple and secure method for getting clients connected to your network.

If a dial-in user provides a username only, that username will be checked against the Active Directory. If there is a caller ID verification set for that user, the caller ID information will be checked and the connection will be accepted or rejected based on whether the information matches. If the user does not send a username at all, the Guest account will be used by default. Therefore, if you intend to use this option, you might want to make sure the Guest account is still disabled on your system (it is disabled by default in Windows Server 2003).

Once you've set your authentication methods, click OK to return to the security properties page. The final option available allows you to direct the client to a custom IPSec policy using a preshared key.

TIP   *To learn more about IPSec, see Chapter 6.*

Although Windows Server 2003 still supports IPX/SPX as a protocol, it is no longer available for use by the RRAS service. And, with the advent of Windows Server 2003, we can formally say so long to our old friend the NetBEUI protocol. It is no longer supported in Windows Server 2003, although it may still be possible to make it work if you add the correct DLLs. Within the properties for the RAS service, you have the ability to fine-tune each protocol accepted by the RAS server and passed on to the internal network. By clicking the appropriate tabs (shown in Figure 20.22) for IP and AppleTalk, you can edit the following options for each protocol:

Enable IP Routing   One way to increase the security of your dial-in system is to only allow dial-in users to access the dial-in server itself. For example, if traveling workers only need to access a set of word-processing documents or spreadsheets, these could be kept on the remote access server.

By unchecking the Enable IP Routing option, clients will only be able to access the RAS server itself.

FIGURE 20.22

Editing protocol security properties for RAS service

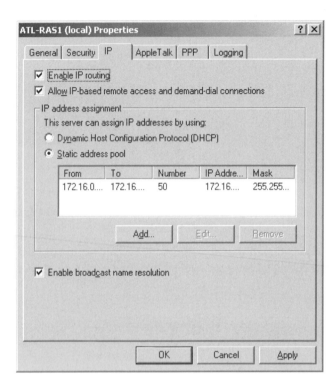

Allow <*Protocol*>-Based Remote Access and Demand-Dial Connections (available for IP and AppleTalk)   To enable or disable support for individual protocols, check the boxes for each protocol to allow and uncheck the boxes for each protocol to reject. If you used the automatic wizard to install Remote Access Service, you might find that Windows Server 2003 enabled support for all the protocols on your system by default. However, good security practices dictate only opening up support for the protocols you need, so it's probably a good idea to remove any protocols you aren't using.

Dynamic Host Configuration Protocol (DHCP) or Static Address Pool (available for IP Only)   As was previously discussed in the configuration of Remote Access Service, here you can select whether your RAS server will use a DHCP server to hand out IP addresses to dial-in clients or if it will manually assign addresses from a static pool. If you choose to assign addresses from a static pool, you will need to provide the correct TCP/IP network address range and subnet mask to use.

NOTE   For more information on calculating address ranges and subnet masks, see Chapter 6.

If you need to fine-tune the parameters for your RAS server to use when establishing PPP sessions with clients, click the PPP tab to edit the properties of these items, as shown in Figure 20.23. The default settings will be acceptable in most instances, but, if needed, you can enable or disable the following options.

FIGURE 20.23

Editing PPP properties for RAS service

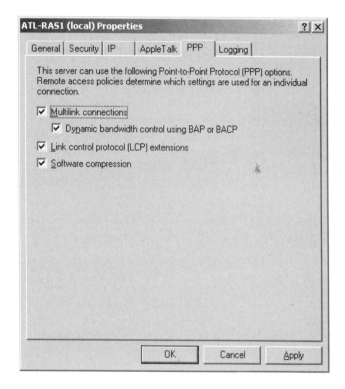

Multilink Connections   Multilink Point-to-Point Protocol (MPPP for short) was defined in RFC 1717 as a means of joining (often referred to as "bonding") two or more PPP sessions together to increase bandwidth. Effectively, you could double or triple your bandwidth between a client and a server if you had two or three modems at each location, two or three phone numbers, etc. This option must be selected if you want to be able to choose the next option.

Dynamic Bandwidth Control Using BAP or BACP   Defined in RFC 2125, Bandwidth Allocation Protocol (BAP), and Bandwidth Allocation Control Protocol (BACP) are similar in nature to Multilink Protocol in that they are both used to bond connections together for increased bandwidth. However, while Multilink Protocol is a "fixed" solution that will automatically join all the channels it can, BAP/BACP will only initiate additional connections as needed due to high bandwidth utilization. This is an excellent option if you have connections that are subject to per-minute charges and don't need to have them online all the time.

Link Control Protocol (LCP) Extensions   Enabling Link Control Protocol (LCP) extensions is a necessary part of supporting callback security on a RAS server. If you are planning on having your system be able to call users back at a specified number, you must have this option enabled.

Software Compression   Never missing an opportunity to define a protocol for something and create another standard, Microsoft has developed the Microsoft Point-to-Point Compression (MPPC) protocol to compress data as it travels across a remote access link. MPPC is defined in RFC 2118.

In addition to configuring protocol and authentication types to use, you may also want to configure what ports on your system are used to accept incoming RRAS calls. For example, you may have some modems that are to be used strictly for dial-in and others strictly for dial-out. The RRAS configuration wizard will simply assume you want to use *all* your modems for dial-in purposes.

To alter the configuration of ports on your system, return to the Routing and Remote Access MMC and expand your server in the left pane of the window. Below your server, you should see an option for Ports. Highlight that option, and then select Properties from the Action pull-down menu (or by right-clicking the item). That should take you to a window similar to the one shown in Figure 20.24.

FIGURE 20.24

Configuring RRAS ports via the Routing and Remote Access Service MMC

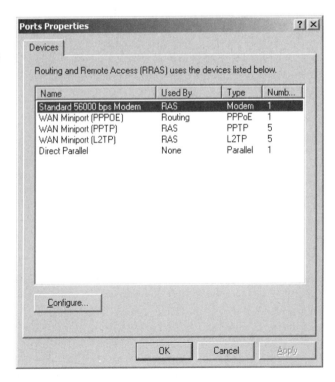

As you can see on this screen, all the interfaces that can support RRAS clients are listed for you to choose from. Highlight the interface(s) that you'd like to accept incoming calls from and then click the Configure button. This will open the individual properties page for this device. Check the box labeled Remote Access Connections (Inbound Only) and—if you can—enter the phone number for the line connected to that device in the Phone Number of This Device field. The phone number will allow you to support BAP for devices to initiate additional connections to your server (although since this requires multiple modems and lines at each location, it might not be an option you need). Repeat this procedure for all the ports on your server.

NOTE *It is important to note that all types of ports are automatically configured for your RRAS server—including the VPN ports for PPTP and L2TP. If this server is accessible over the Internet, these ports will be "openings" that outsiders can use to try to authenticate to your network. I recommend that you change the Maximum Ports value for L2TP to zero and for PPTP to one (the minimum value allowed), unless you specifically intend to implement virtual private networking (discussed later in this chapter).*

Client Configurations

Now that you have a RAS server that's running smoothly, it's time to enable some clients and get connected into the network. While I can't cover every possible platform under the sun when it comes to remote access, we'll look at a few of the more common options, namely Windows NT 4 Workstation, Windows 9x, and Windows XP Professional. Windows 2000 Professional Dial-Up Networking will follow a routine very similar to the Windows Server 2003 Dial-Up Networking steps, outlined in detail in the next section, so I won't cover it here.

All these client configurations assume that you have Dial-Up Networking already installed on your system and correctly configured. Assistance on installing Dial-Up Networking on other platforms is outside the scope of this book.

TIP *I frequently get calls from clients who have configured one of their users' home computers to dial in to the corporate network but are having trouble browsing the Network Neighborhood and seeing any resources. In most cases, this is due to the workgroup and domain settings on the home system not matching the settings for workstations in the office. Make sure you use the same settings in both locations.*

WINDOWS NT 4 WORKSTATION

From the Windows NT 4 Desktop, double-click My Computer and then Dial-Up Networking to bring up the main Dial-Up Networking program. If this is the first time you are using Dial-Up Networking, you might get a message about your phonebook being empty—this is okay because it is simply Windows telling you it doesn't know how to dial anyone yet. If you get that message, click OK to continue, and that should leave you at the main Dial-Up Networking screen as shown in Figure 20.25.

To add a new entry for your Windows Server 2003, click the New button to start defining a new phonebook entry. The initial screen will let you enter information such as a friendly name to use for this phonebook entry, the number to dial, which modem to use, etc. Enter the appropriate information as needed and then click the Server tab to enter information about the server you are calling into. Your phonebook entry screen should look similar to Figure 20.26.

FIGURE 20.25

Dial-Up
Networking in
Windows NT 4
Workstation

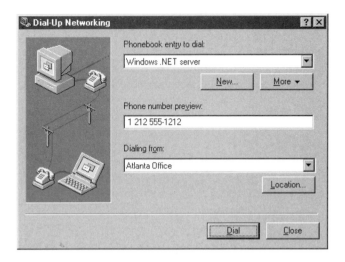

FIGURE 20.26

Selecting server
options for a new
phonebook entry,
Windows NT 4
Workstation

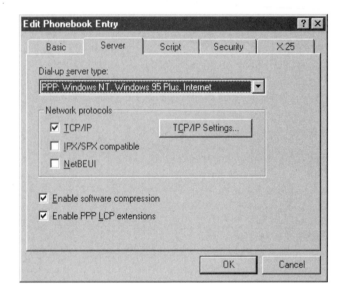

By default, Windows NT 4 Workstation will assume you are going to be dialing in to a PPP-compatible server, so it will use that selection as a default for the Dial-Up Server Type pull-down box. Also, NT Workstation will assume you want to use software compression and PPP LCP extensions (as seen by the check boxes in the bottom of the window). These are also acceptable defaults for most dial-up connections and can be left checked in most cases. These settings directly correspond to the PPP settings defined on the configured RAS server.

By far, the most important settings in this dialog are the network protocol settings. In general, these settings should correspond directly to the protocols configured when installing RAS, as seen back in Figure 20.15. The client workstation obviously cannot connect on certain protocols if they are not installed on your server, so make sure you are using the same protocols in each location. If you plan on using TCP/IP (and I expect most readers will), click the TCP/IP Settings button to define protocol-specific parameters if necessary. The TCP/IP Settings screen should look like the one in Figure 20.27.

FIGURE 20.27

TCP/IP settings on Windows NT 4 Workstation dial-up networking

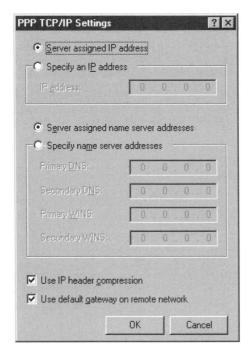

For most installations, the default TCP/IP settings should work fine, but if your situation is a bit more specific, you can enter values for the IP address that the client should use and which DNS servers and WINS servers to use for name resolution. If you don't enter any settings for the DNS and WINS servers to use, the dial-up networking client will inherit the same values the RAS server uses itself. This is an important point, because if you are using DHCP to assign addresses, you might assume that any DHCP scope options you have added to your address space would be automatically passed along to your RAS clients. However, even if your RAS server is consulting your DHCP server for addresses to use, it will not pass DHCP scope options along to RAS clients. Settings for DNS servers and WINS servers to use will come directly from the same settings programmed into your RAS server. So, if you're using DHCP on your network, make sure you hard-code an IP address for your RAS server and program in the correct name server addresses.

Once you have set your server and protocol settings as necessary, click the Security tab to define the appropriate authentication options for your dial-in client. The security settings are shown in Figure 20.28. Just as the correct configuration for the server settings on the dial-up client depends on how your RAS server was configured, the security settings on the client will depend on how the security is configured on the RAS server as well.

FIGURE 20.28

Security settings on Windows NT 4 Workstation dial-up networking

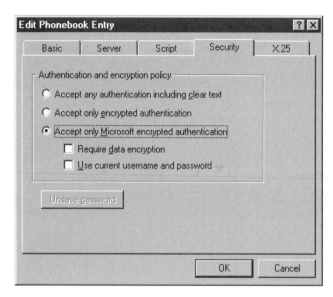

By default, Windows NT 4 Workstation selects the option to Accept Any Authentication Including Clear Text. If the RAS server is configured to only allow MS-CHAP authentication, then the dial-up networking client will submit an MS-CHAP authentication and should be validated without any difficulty. If you run into problems logging in, make sure your authentication settings between your server and your client match on at least some level.

When you have completed making the necessary settings for this dial-up networking entry, click OK and then click Dial to dial in to your Windows Server 2003. You will be prompted for a valid username, password, and domain name to log in with. Use the username(s) you granted dial-in permission to on your servers, click OK, and if everything goes according to plan your Windows NT 4 Workstation should be connected!

WINDOWS 9x

From the Windows 9x Desktop, double-click My Computer and then Dial-Up Networking to bring up the Dial-Up Networking program. If this is the first time you are using dial-up networking, you might be asked to enter information about your local area code, whether to use touch-tone or pulse dialing, and any prefixes you need to dial. Simply fill in the information and click OK to continue. This should bring you to the Make New Connection window shown in Figure 20.29.

FIGURE 20.29

Windows 9x Make
New Connection
window

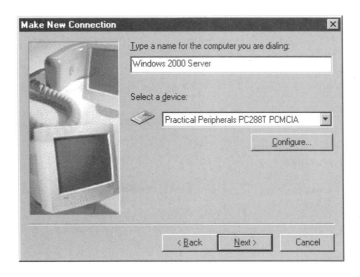

At the first step of the Make New Connection dialog box, you can enter a friendly name for this Dial-Up Networking connection and select which modem device you'd like to use. Enter this information and then click Next to continue to the next step, shown in Figure 20.30.

FIGURE 20.30

Windows 9x Make
New Connection
window, step two

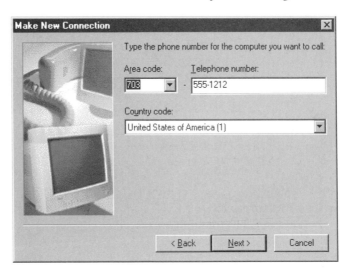

In the second (and final) step, enter the area code and phone number of your RAS server and then click Next to complete the creation of this Dial-Up Networking entry. By default, Windows 9x will assume several things about this Dial-Up Networking entry, including which protocols and security settings you'd like to use. For example, Windows 9x will select all the protocols installed on your system and try to use them over this Dial-Up Networking connection.

If you'd prefer to configure these options yourself instead of having Windows 9*x* assume what you want, go back to the main Dial-Up Networking window (the one with the Make New Connection icon) and you should see an icon for your Dial-Up Networking session. Right-click the icon, and select Properties to edit the configuration. You will see the properties pages for this Dial-Up Networking connection, as shown in Figure 20.31.

FIGURE 20.31

Editing Windows 9*x* Dial-Up Networking entry properties

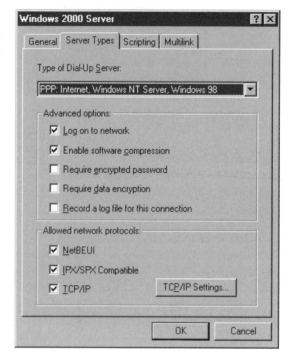

From here, you can (and should) change the security and protocol settings to match those of your RAS server. Configure the settings accordingly, and then launch your session to verify that it works.

WINDOWS XP PROFESSIONAL

Once you have installed your modem, from the Windows XP Desktop, click Start/Control Panel/Network Connections (in category view, click Network and Internet Connections). From here you will need to start the New Connection Wizard to add a new connection to the server you wish to dial. Click Next to get through the initial screen of the wizard and you will see the screen shown in Figure 20.32. To create a connection using dial-up, choose the Connect to the Network at My Workplace option and click Next. Choose the Dial-up Connection option and continue by clicking Next.

Specify a name for the connection and, in the following screen of the wizard, type in the phone number for the connection. Next you will need to decide whether this connection will be used for everyone who uses your computer or whether it should only apply to your account profile. In the final screen of the wizard, you will be shown a summary of the options you selected, and you are given the option of creating a shortcut to the connection on your Desktop. Click Finish to complete the wizard and you will be shown the Connect <*Connection Name*> dialog box, as seen in Figure 20.33.

FIGURE 20.32

Choosing a connection type

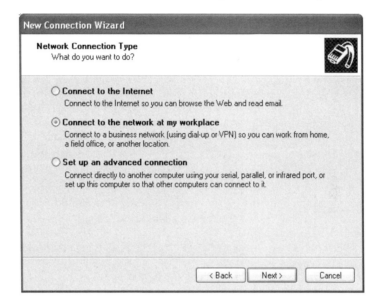

FIGURE 20.33

Connecting to the dial-up server

From here, choose the Dial button to test your connection. Since you already know the basics about adjusting the settings for your dial-up connection, just know that by choosing the Properties button from this screen you can configure the security settings, protocols, and phone options.

Managing Connected Users

If you need to keep tabs on users connected to your network, the Routing and Remote Access MMC can give you an overview of all remote access connections currently connected to your server. Whether connections are coming into your systems from VPN connections, serial connections, analog modems, or ISDN lines, you can get an overview of all your remote connections from one convenient console.

To manage connected users, start by launching the Routing and Remote Access MMC by selecting Start/Administrative Tools/Routing and Remote Access. By expanding the details for your RAS server in the left pane, you should see a subitem for Remote Access Clients listed below your system, along with a number next to it in parentheses. This number indicates the number of dial-in users currently connected to your system. This screen should look similar to the one in Figure 20.34.

FIGURE 20.34

Managing remote access users through RRAS MMC

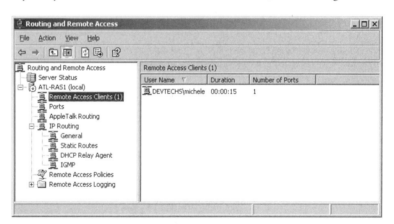

From this screen, you can get an overview of how long users have been connected to your network, who is currently connected, which ports are in use, etc. By double-clicking any of the listed connections on your system, you can get advanced details about that individual connection, such as what IP addresses were assigned to the system, how much data has been transferred, etc. You can disconnect an individual connection from the same properties page by clicking the Disconnect button, or you can disconnect a user by right-clicking that user's connection in the main list of connected users and choosing Disconnect. In addition to being able to disconnect a user from the main listing of connected users, you can also send a message to an individual user or to all connected users by right-clicking a connection and selecting either Send Message or Send to All, respectively.

Connecting to a Private Network

Much like connecting to the Internet, at times you might need to connect your Windows Server 2003 to another private network. Maybe one of your servers needs to collect data from a client's systems or transmit product orders to a supplier. The private network might be a Win2K network, an NT network, a Novell network, or a network that contains a combination of servers and other systems. In any case, dial-up networking can get your Windows Server 2003 connected with a minimal amount of effort.

Before getting started, there are a few things you will need to have to complete making a connection to another network. Namely, you will need to have the following information available in advance:

♦ Access phone number to dial

♦ Username and password combination

♦ Protocols that will be used on the remote network

♦ Authentication the remote network will require

To get started, we'll once again be working through the Network Connection Wizard by clicking Start/Control Panel/Network Connections and then choosing the New Connection Wizard icon. When the wizard starts, you should see the screen shown in Figure 20.35. Click Next to jump to the second screen of the wizard.

FIGURE 20.35

New Connection Wizard: welcome screen

From this point, select the second option, Connect to the Network at My Workplace, and click Next to continue to the next step of the wizard, as seen in Figure 20.36. Here you'll have to choose whether you want to connect to the remote network using dial-up or a VPN. Choose Dial-Up Connection and continue to the next wizard screen. Enter the name that you want to give this connection and click Next.

Enter the phone number as prompted, and then click Next to get to the last step of the wizard, pictured in Figure 20.37.

FIGURE 20.36

New Connection
Wizard: Network
Connection

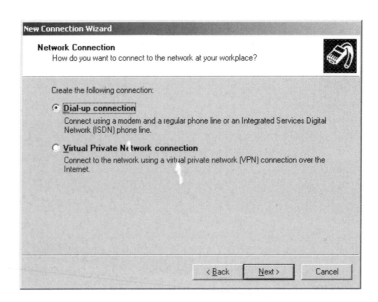

FIGURE 20.37

New Connection
Wizard: Connection
Availability

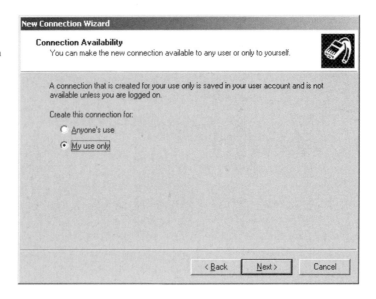

The last step of the Network Connection Wizard will ask if you would like to make this dial-up connection available to all users or to make it available only to the user who is creating this connection. For the purposes of simply connecting Windows Server 2003 to another network, select the My Use Only option here. The other option, Anyone's Use, would end up sharing this connection for other users on the network, a topic discussed in the next section ("Acting as an Internet Gateway"). Click Next when you are finished, click Finish when presented with the summary, and you will have successfully created a Dial-Up Networking entry.

Once the wizard is completed and your connection has been created, you will find that Server 2003 will have assumed several things about your dial-up networking entry that might not work for your specific situation. To double-check everything, edit the properties for this dial-up connection by right-clicking the icon for it in the Network Connections window. Clicking the Networking tab on the properties page should bring you to a page similar to the one shown in Figure 20.38.

FIGURE 20.38

Dial-Up Networking entry properties

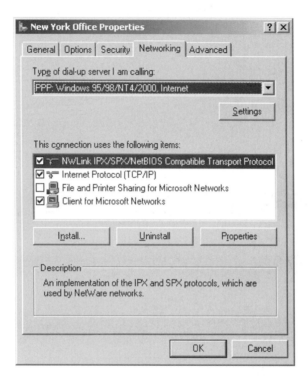

Windows Server 2003 will assume you want to use several defaults when you try to connect to this remote network. For example, it will assume you want to use *all* the protocols loaded on your system for this connection, it will assume it can use unsecured passwords, etc. Some of these options might not make sense in specific situations. For example, if you are connecting to an IP-only network, it doesn't make much sense to try and negotiate an AppleTalk connection. Even though Server 2003 will realize that it can't establish the AppleTalk connection, why even try?

To fine-tune this connection, remove or add specific protocols as needed by checking the boxes next to the protocols listed under the Networking tab of the Dial-Up Networking entry properties pages. If you are connecting to a remote TCP/IP network and the device you are dialing in to does not provide you with an IP address or DNS server addresses automatically, you can program these in by highlighting the TCP/IP protocol and then clicking the Properties button. This will bring you to the specific TCP/IP settings to use for this connection (Figure 20.39).

FIGURE 20.39
Editing TCP/IP
properties for Dial-
Up Networking
entries

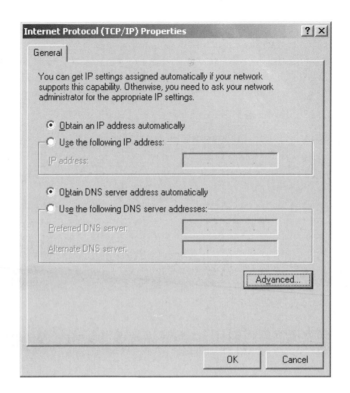

On this screen you can enter the necessary information for your TCP/IP connection. If you are accessing a remote network that uses WINS servers but does not provide those addresses to you, enter them in the advanced TCP/IP settings area by clicking the Advanced button and then clicking the WINS tab.

Once you have your protocols configured correctly, click OK to get back to the main properties page for this dial-up connection. If you need to edit any other properties, such as the type of security or authentication to use, click the appropriate tabs and make those settings as necessary.

If you think this looks similar to the steps to connect to the Internet described earlier in this chapter, you are correct. Basically, all the mechanisms are the same in Dial-Up Networking, but different wizards will take a different approach to the settings that are applied by default. Therefore, some of the same advanced options discussed in the "Connecting to the Internet" section (reestablishing failed links, redialing non-responsive numbers, etc.) are available for regular dial-up connections to private networks.

Acting as an Internet Gateway

One of the hottest little "niche" applications people always seemed to want to do with Windows NT 4 Server was to share an Internet connection with everyone else inside their organization. After all, NT servers were usually set up to share other resources (files, printers, etc.)—so it made sense that NT Server should have been able to share an Internet connection, right? Not exactly.

With enough tweaking and some strict rules to follow, you *could* actually have NT Server dial an Internet connection and route traffic for internal hosts out to the Internet. However, the setup is difficult and cumbersome, and it requires having valid (InterNIC-assigned) IP addresses available for everyone within the organization. Without using a third-party software solution, the act of simply sharing a $20/month unlimited-access Internet account wasn't a viable option.

Now, Microsoft has included a variety of capabilities in Windows Server 2003—actually, this was around in Win2K too—that make this task relatively easy. With the correct information about what type of connectivity you need to the outside world, Windows Server 2003 can act as an Internet gateway for your internal clients, leveraging an existing Internet connection among all the workstations in your organization.

Although Microsoft has included some great tools for sharing connections on your network, it is important to note several subtle hints Microsoft has included in their documentation for this feature of Windows Server 2003. First and foremost, Microsoft often makes several references to small or home office networks, implying that this capability really isn't designed for use in medium-to-large environments. I would have to agree with them on this point; if you have a reasonable number of workstations on your network, you will probably be far better off going with a product such as Microsoft Proxy Server and a dedicated Internet connection.

The second point Microsoft makes repeatedly throughout their documentation is that "you should not use this feature in an existing network with other Windows Server 2003 domain controllers, DNS servers, gateways, DHCP servers, or systems configured for static IP." Since this configuration requires a very specific IP configuration to work correctly, implementing this on a network that doesn't conform to that configuration could cause lots of difficulty. I would agree with Microsoft on this point as well.

Although acting as an Internet router isn't one of the options normally available through the New Connection Wizard used throughout this chapter, fortunately one of the other options will configure most everything necessary. By using the steps detailed in the last section, "Connecting to a Private Network," and connecting to the Internet as the "private" network, you can make Windows Server 2003 act as an Internet gateway, routing traffic from your internal clients out to the Internet and back again.

Configuring Windows Server 2003 to Act as an Internet Gateway

Start with the same steps listed in the section "Connecting to a Private Network" and go all the way up to the point where you enter the phone number, using a local access number for your ISP as the number of the private network to dial.

This time, when the New Connection Wizard (pictured back in Figure 20.37) asks if you would like to make this connection available to all users, select Anyone's Use instead of My Use Only. When you finish the wizard, you will be presented with the Connection dialog box. Here you need to enter a username and password in order to share the connection among all your users. Once you have entered the name and password, you will need to allow the connection to save the credentials by checking the Save This User Name and Password for the Following Users box. Of the two available sets of users, you will need to select the Anyone Who Uses This Computer radio button. Once you have finished, click the Properties button. Although there is no Apply button on the Connect <*Connection Name*> dialog box, the simple act of clicking the Properties button seems to save the username and password combination. From the properties sheet, click the Advanced tab to complete the final step for the process of sharing this connection with your users (see Figure 20.40).

FIGURE 20.40

Defining sharing options

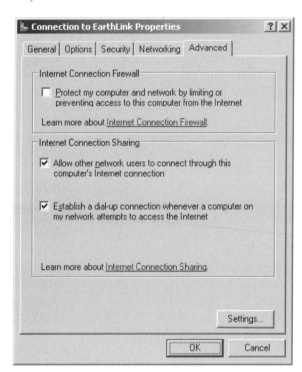

Click the check box entitled Allow Other Network Users to Connect through This Computer's Internet Connection. This will enable the sharing properties for this connection. The other option you can see in the Internet Connection Sharing (ICS) section of this property sheet allows for a dial on-demand feature for the connection. That way, any time a user makes a request for this connection, the computer will know to automatically establish the connection. Since you are implementing a shared Internet connection, you probably want to select this option also. When you check the box for this feature and click OK, you should receive a warning dialog box similar to the one in Figure 20.41.

FIGURE 20.41

Static IP address change warning

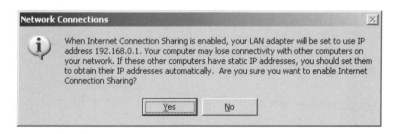

This dialog box lets you know that Windows Server 2003 will need to make several changes to its IP configuration for this functionality to work, including specifying a fixed IP address to use for the server's internal network connection. If anyone is connected to your server at this point, make sure they are disconnected before continuing, otherwise they may lose their connections to the system. Click Yes to continue, and Windows Server 2003 will make the appropriate IP changes to support sharing an Internet connection.

Once you have completed the wizard and made any changes to the settings, you should see an icon for your shared connection in the Network Connections dialog box. Launch the connection to verify that everything is working correctly. Since you have saved the username and password combination for this connection, when it is demand-dialed it will have what it needs. Once you have established that the connection works correctly in and of itself, it's time to define a few rules as to what you want to allow across your Internet connection.

DEFINING SERVICE CONFIGURATIONS

By default, Windows Server 2003 will not automatically route any traffic from the Internet to the machines on your network. You must define specific rules as to what type of traffic (i.e., what TCP/IP packets) can go across your shared connection. To do this, begin by editing the properties for your shared Internet access connection by right-clicking the Shared Internet Connection icon in the Network Connections window and then selecting Properties. Click the Advanced tab, and you should see the same settings for enabling shared access for this connection and on-demand dialing that you saw in Figure 20.40. At the bottom of the window is a button labeled Settings. By clicking the button, you can define settings for which services can go across your shared Internet connection, as shown in Figure 20.42.

FIGURE 20.42

Configuring services settings for Internet Connection Sharing

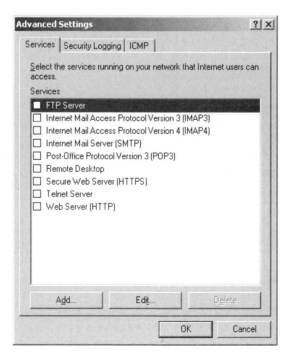

NOTE *The other two tabs you see in Figure 20.42 are only visible if you enable the Internet Connection Firewall (ICF) on the advanced properties sheet for the connection. Here's the short version of what ICF gives you. Basically, even if you don't enable ICF, your shared Internet connection won't allow any incoming traffic by default. Once you enable it, however, you can allow your connection to accept and/or respond to ICMP traffic, like ping (echo requests). You can also set up logging in the connection and record dropped packets and successful connections.*

Sharing an Internet connection allows you to accept traffic from external hosts targeted at systems within your network. For example, maybe you have a small Web server running in your organization that you would like people to be able to access. Using a shared Internet connection not only lets your users share access to the Internet, but it can be programmed to allow Internet access to your internal shared resources as well. This is one of the reasons why it's important to define rules as to what is allowed in to your shared Internet connection.

If you need to have outside clients access services on a computer on your internal network, you will need to enable them from the Services tab in the Advanced Settings dialog box of your connection properties. Unless you want people from the outside world connecting to your internal systems, I recommend leaving this blank. But if you have a Web server or an FTP server that you need to have people connect to, this is the place to do it. Click the check box for the type of service that you want to allow external access to.

To define an internal host that Windows Server 2003 should direct that type of traffic to, click Edit. You should see the dialog box pictured in Figure 20.43.

FIGURE 20.43

Configuring a predefined service for ICS

As you can see in this example, you don't really need to know anything about ports to do this because Windows Server 2003 assumes the standard port settings for these services. However, if you prefer to use different port settings for any of your services, or if you want to add a service that is not in the predefined list, click OK to return to the Advanced Settings property sheet you saw in Figure 20.42. To define your own services, click the Add button and you will see the dialog box shown in Figure 20.44.

FIGURE 20.44

Adding a shared access service

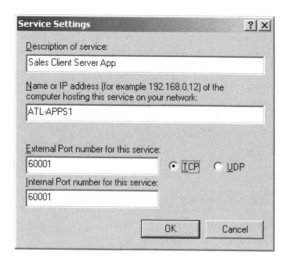

Keep in mind that services that are accessed on your network using ICS by external clients won't connect *directly* to the IP address assigned to your internal workstation that has the destination service (especially since in most cases the internal IP addresses won't be routable addresses on the Internet). Instead, external systems will connect to your Windows Server 2003 on a specific port, and based on what port they connect to, Server 2003 will redirect the request to one of your internal systems.

Start defining your service by giving it a name—for example, the name of your Web server or an application your clients will access, etc. and then list the name of the server that will host the service or application. If you are using DHCP to assign IP addresses to your internal computers, I recommend referencing the system by name in this dialog box, rather than the IP address. In the External Port Number for This Service field , enter the port you will expect incoming connections to come to. If you wanted to allow incoming HTTP traffic, for example, you would enter **80**. The Internal Port field is used to route your traffic to whatever port your service is being hosted on. Some services or applications use both TCP and UDP packets. You can't enable them both here, though. If you define this application to accept TCP packets as shown in Figure 20.44, you'd need to create another service definition with the same configurations to allow UDP packets to access the application across the port.

Once you have completed this definition, click OK and you should see the new service listed in the Services list. If you have a connection that is dialed on demand, though, it's important to note that this won't typically work for incoming connections. That is, your ISP won't know that it should dial *your* server whenever someone on the Internet tries to access a service or application on one of your systems. Therefore, if you are going to accept incoming service connections I'd recommend having your Internet connection online at all times.

Once you have defined the appropriate service settings, it's time to configure your clients to direct their Internet traffic to your Windows Server 2003 for routing.

CONFIGURING CLIENTS

Once your server is ready, you will need to tell your clients to route their Internet traffic to your Windows Server 2003. When Windows Server 2003 receives these packets, it will realize that they are destined for the Internet and route them as necessary (initiating your demand-dialed connection if needed). You can either program each workstation manually or let DHCP do it for you by defining the correct scope and options to use.

NOTE *For more information on configuring DHCP scopes, see Chapter 7.*

The following information will work in your DHCP scope for getting your clients connected to the Internet (other slight variations would work as well; this is merely an example):

◆ Address range: 192.168.0.2 to 192.168.0.254

◆ Address mask: 255.255.255.0

◆ Default gateway: 192.168.0.1

◆ DNS servers to use: enter your ISP's DNS server addresses

To enter these settings manually on a Windows XP, 2000 Professional, NT 4, or 9*x* client, edit the TCP/IP properties of your computer to change the IP address to something in the range just listed. The mask should be 255.255.255.0 as listed, and the default gateway should be 192.168.0.1, the IP address your Windows Server 2003 will give itself once you enable the shared connection. In Windows XP Professional, this would look similar to the dialog box shown in Figure 20.45.

FIGURE 20.45

TCP/IP settings for shared access on Windows XP

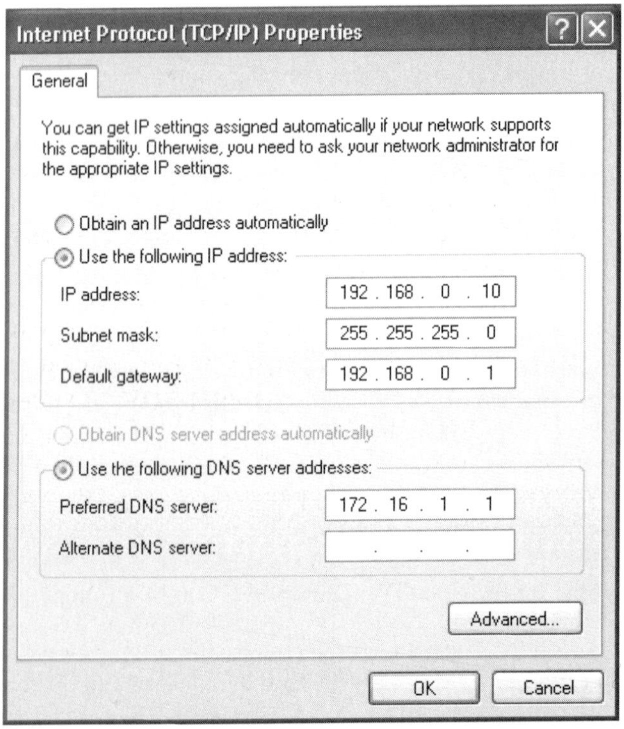

The last setting to make is the DNS server setting. Since your workstation will need to look somewhere to translate host names into IP addresses, you will need to put the DNS server IP addresses for your ISP into your connection settings. If you don't know the IP addresses of your ISP's DNS servers, I recommend contacting them to ask them directly or see if they list the appropriate settings somewhere on their Web site.

Once you have the correct DNS and TCP/IP settings programmed in, you should be able to connect to the Internet using your newly configured ICS. You should see that your Windows Server 2003 automatically initiates the connection as needed whenever one of your client systems tries to access the Internet.

Accepting VPN Connections from Remote Clients

Virtual private networking (VPN) is one of the hottest subjects in networking today. With the widespread presence of the Internet, it only makes sense that corporations and organizations would want to try to leverage existing investments in Internet connections for their corporate networks. But as exciting as VPN can be, it can also be a rather complex subject. Since it is basically a means of layering one logical network over another, the complexities of making a network connection are, in effect, doubled.

VPN Overview

Loosely defined, a VPN allows you to run a secure, private network over an unsecured public network. You can use virtual private networking to get clients connected to your network over the Internet and do it securely, even though the Internet is inherently an unsecured network.

One of the better analogies I've found for explaining the concepts of a virtual private network is to refer to them as "pipes." To conceptualize VPNs, think of two pipes, one large and one small. Now, imagine that the small pipe actually runs *inside* of the large one. It starts and ends at the same places the large pipe does, and it can carry materials on its own, completely independent of whatever is happening in the large pipe. As a matter of fact, the only thing the small pipe depends on the large pipe for is the determination of the start and end points. Beyond that, the small pipe can operate independently of the large pipe in terms of direction of travel, materials it carries, etc.

To add another layer to this analogy, let's assume that the large pipe is made out of a transparent material, and the small pipe is made out of metal. If anyone were to take a look at the pipe-within-a-pipe, they would easily be able to see whatever was moving through the outside (large) pipe. However, whatever was traveling through the inside pipe would remain a mystery.

If this is starting to make sense, you should be thinking to yourself that the large pipe represents the unsecured network (i.e., the Internet) and the small pipe represents the virtual private network. VPN is a way of tunneling data packets through a connection that already exists but that can't be used on its own for privacy reasons. Obviously, the Internet is a perfect example of a network that often can't be used alone for privacy reasons.

So, what benefit does this have for the overworked network administrator? Well, for starters, it could reduce or eliminate your need to maintain a pool of modems at your site for remote dial-in users. Remote users don't need to call directly into your network to get connected; they can simply call in to a local ISP and get a valid Internet (unsecured) connection. Assuming you have a VPN/RAS server running on your network (and it's connected to the Internet), once the remote user has connected to their ISP, the client just has to establish the VPN (secured) session with the RAS server. The cost of maintaining modems and phone lines is shifted to the ISP. As long as your RAS server is connected to the Internet, you can support multiple incoming calls all over that one connection. Also, in keeping with this example, since the VPN session is being established over the Internet, there is no need for any long-distance calls. If your remote user is hundreds of miles away, the cost to connect to your network is the same as if they were local, since the only call they would need to make would be to their ISP. This is a great way to support a geographically dispersed user base.

Microsoft has gone a long way toward making virtual private networking easy to implement since its inception in Windows NT 4. However, if there is one piece of advice I could give everyone trying to implement virtual private networking, it is this: get a good, solid RAS server working and accepting incoming connections *first*. Use standard connections (analog modems, ISDN, etc.) on your RAS server first to make sure everything is functioning correctly. Once you are sure RAS is working correctly for standard connections, only then is it advisable to try implementing VPN connections. Since virtual private networking adds another layer of functionality "on top of" RAS, it is crucial to have a stable foundation to begin with. RAS can be peculiar in its behavior at times, so it is important to have all your configurations working correctly (DHCP address assignment, browsing, etc.). If only I had a nickel for every time I heard someone say "this VPN thing is messed up," only to find out that if they dial in to their network over a modem connection, they experience the exact same problems.

A Brief History of VPN: PPTP, L2F, and L2TP

When virtual private networking was first being developed back in the mid-1990s, two of the largest companies in the computer/networking industry tried to run with implementations of VPNs in the hopes that they would enjoy widespread implementation and therefore become an "industry standard." The two companies were Microsoft and Cisco, and each had its respective VPN technologies. Microsoft was approaching the VPN market from the operating systems point of view and had developed Point-to-Point Tunneling Protocol (PPTP) as a means to securely transmit data across unsecured networks. At the same time, Cisco was taking the lead in VPN from a strictly networking point of view with a protocol called Layer 2 Forwarding, or L2F.

Now, when either of these companies decides to develop an industry standard, they can usually get away with it if one doesn't already exist. No single standard had obtained a large enough share of the VPN market to be considered an industry standard, so the playing field was literally wide open. However, the sheer muscle and momentum that either one of these companies can put behind an initiative wasn't necessarily enough to displace the other. Each protocol had its strengths and weaknesses, and Microsoft's and Cisco's offerings enjoyed moderate successes.

Now, I'm speculating a bit here, but I think that since neither industry giant was going to successfully displace the other in the VPN market, they decided it would be better to cooperate than compete. In any case, Microsoft and Cisco made the decision to collaborate on virtual private networking by merging their protocols, PPTP and L2F, into one hybrid protocol. The final product of that collaboration is Layer 2 Tunneling Protocol, or L2TP for short.

Windows Server 2003 includes L2TP support for establishing virtual private networking connections, but it also includes support for PPTP for backward compatibility with other operating systems. L2TP is supported in Windows 2000 (Server and Professional) and Windows Server 2003. Windows 98, Me, and NT 4 can utilize the functionality of L2TP and IP Security (IPSec) by installing an additional client. Okay, enough said. Let's assume you've got a good solid RAS server running and get on to the fun stuff.

Implementing VPN via PPTP and L2TP

If you went through the section "Accepting Incoming Calls from Remote Users," congratulations—you have 80 percent of what you need to support VPN connections in place already. When you install Remote Access Service, Windows Server 2003 should have added support for five PPTP connections and five L2TP connections by default. If you didn't go through the section to accept incoming calls from remote users, stop reading now and go back to complete the steps listed there. For the remainder of this section, we'll assume you have a functional RAS server in place.

We'll start by verifying that support for PPTP and L2TP is in place through the Routing and Remote Access MMC. Start the RRAS MMC by selecting Start/Administrative Tools/Routing and Remote Access. In the left portion of the MMC window, you should see the name of your RAS server listed; expand the information for that server by double-clicking it or clicking the plus sign next to the server. Right-click the listing for ports, and then select Properties to edit the ports (Figure 20.46).

FIGURE 20.46

Ports Properties screen

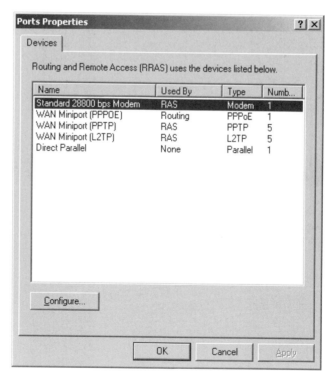

In the Ports Properties screen, you will see all the ports that Server 2003 has recognized and can use for Remote Access Service. Each device has a usage listed, a device name, a type, and a number of ports associated with it. By default, RAS should have PPTP and L2TP devices installed on your system with five ports allocated to each.

Depending on which type of connections you will be allowing and how many you want to allow, you can edit your protocols and ports accordingly from here. For example, you may only need to support L2TP for your VPN, but if you still have clients using PPTP, then you'll need to keep those available. You can also extend the number of L2TP and PPTP ports to 128 each, if required. In any case, to edit the port properties for either type, double-click the item to edit or just highlight it and click the Configure button. This will take you into the port configuration screen shown in Figure 20.47 (the screen looks the same whether you are configuring PPTP, L2TP, or modem ports).

Figure 20.47

Configuring RAS ports (PPTP shown)

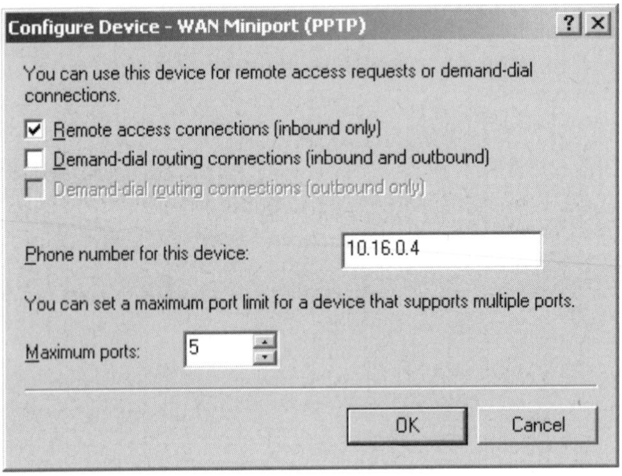

To configure your server to accept VPN connections, make sure the Remote Access Connections (Inbound Only) option is checked in the Configure Device dialog box. Despite the fact that the dialog box has a Phone Number for This Device field, you need to enter the public Internet IP address of your server (assuming the Internet is the public, unsecured network you will be using). This is the IP address that clients will eventually connect to across the Internet for establishing VPN circuits.

TIP   I strongly recommend that you use a fixed IP address and Internet connection for your server. Yes, you can use a dial-up connection from your RAS server to the Internet, and you can even make dynamic IP addresses work for this. But with dynamic IP addresses, your server's IP address will change every time it has to reestablish its link, quickly becoming a management nightmare.

Depending on how many simultaneous virtual private networking connections you plan on supporting, adjust the Maximum Ports value accordingly (up to 128) and then click OK.

TIP   I recommend disabling any and all VPN connections that you don't plan on using. For example, if you are only going to support L2TP connections, disable PPTP by unchecking the Remote Access Connections (Inbound Only) option on the properties page for PPTP. This will prevent anyone from trying to establish a connection to your server via PPTP without your knowing about it.

CLIENT CONFIGURATION

To get a client workstation connected to a Windows Server 2003 running VPN protocols, you will need to have one of the following:

- Windows 95 with the Dial-Up Networking 1.2 upgrade or better (PPTP only)
- Windows 98 (PPTP or L2TP)
- Windows Me (PPTP or L2TP)
- Windows NT 4 Workstation or Server (PPTP or L2TP)
- Windows 2000 Professional or Server (PPTP or L2TP)
- Windows XP Professional (PPTP or L2TP)

Let's go through getting some of these clients connected to a VPN using PPTP. Since older operating systems such as Windows 95 and Windows NT 4 don't install tunneling protocols by default, the first thing to do is add PPTP support to the client system. PPTP is a standard protocol, just like NetBEUI or NWLink, so the procedures for adding this new protocol are roughly the same. In addition, support for L2TP is relatively recent in most of these clients. Microsoft released a VPN client software download recently to upgrade the VPN clients on these older systems so that they could be compatible with the L2TP/IPSec standards.

Windows NT 4 Workstation

Assuming you already have Dial-Up Networking set up on your NT 4 Workstation, the first step to adding VPN support is to add the Point-to-Point Tunneling Protocol in the Control Panel/Network applet. Start by clicking Start/Settings/Control Panel/Network, and then click the Protocols tab. Clicking the Add button from the protocols properties page will bring you to the protocol properties dialog box, as shown in Figure 20.48.

FIGURE 20.48

Protocols properties page in NT 4 Workstation

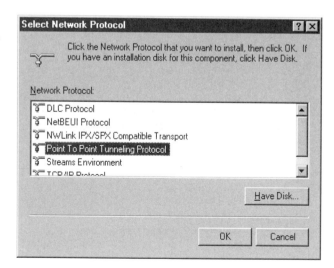

Once you have selected the Point-to-Point Tunneling Protocol and clicked OK, NT 4 Workstation will ask you how many simultaneous virtual circuits you'd like to support in the dialog box in Figure 20.49.

FIGURE 20.49

Configuring the number of virtual circuits to support

The number of circuits you choose here will determine how many virtual ports Windows NT 4 will add to its configuration. Each virtual port will be called VPNx, with x referring to the specific port number. In effect, they function similarly to modems running on COM ports (COMx), so think of these VPN devices as virtual modems. If you will only be connecting to one virtual private network at a time, choose 1 and click OK.

Once you have completed selecting the number of virtual circuits to support, NT 4 Workstation will invoke RAS setup to allow you to add your new virtual modem(s) to the RAS configuration.

Click the Add button in Remote Access Setup and you should see your VPN device in the Add RAS Device window (see Figure 20.50). If you see a modem or some other device there, try pulling down the list and then selecting your VPN device. Once you have your VPN device selected, click OK and it will be added to your RAS configuration.

FIGURE 20.50

Adding VPN devices to RAS in NT 4 Workstation

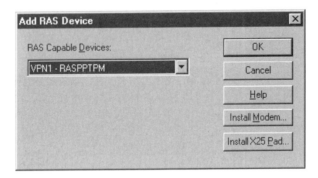

Once you are back to the Remote Access Setup screen, highlight your VPN device and click the Configure button. This device should be configured for Dial-Out Only, as shown in Figure 20.51.

Once everything is set correctly, click OK and RAS will start the installation routine. This will most likely require a reboot of your computer, so go ahead and restart it and get back into Windows. To use your VPN device, the last step you need to perform is creating a Dial-Up Networking entry.

FIGURE 20.51

Configuring VPN devices for dial-out only in NT 4 Workstation

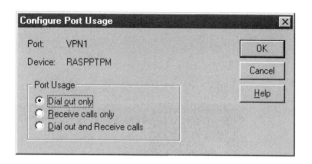

Double-click My Computer and then Dial-Up Networking to begin creating a new Dial-Up Networking entry. Creating a VPN Dial-Up Networking entry is almost identical to creating a regular Dial-Up Networking entry for a phone line, except that you will use an IP address instead of a phone number to dial and the VPN*x* device instead of a modem. This is shown in Figure 20.52.

FIGURE 20.52

Creating a VPN Dial-Up Networking entry in Windows NT 4 Workstation

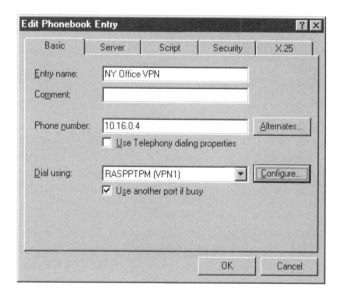

As you can see, this Dial-Up Networking entry will call a VPN server at IP address 10.16.0.4, the same IP address used in the configuration of the RAS/VPN server earlier in this chapter. As long as the VPN device is selected in the Dial Using pull-down box, everything should be set for this connection.

Unlike the newer clients, you may have to perform two steps to initiate a connection to your VPN server. The first step to making this connection is to make sure you have an actual, valid Internet IP address before doing so. If you need to use Dial-Up Networking to connect to an ISP for this, do that first. Once you have a valid IP address available, launch your VPN Dial-Up Networking Connection to get connected to your remote system. Once you provide a set of valid user credentials, you'll be connected to your VPN. To disconnect from the VPN, simply double-click the Dial-Up Networking icon in My Computer, select the phonebook entry for the VPN, and click the Hang Up button, as shown in Figure 20.53. You can also right-click the Dial-Up Networking Monitor icon in the system tray and choose Hang Up.

FIGURE 20.53

Disconnecting a VPN session in NT 4 Workstation

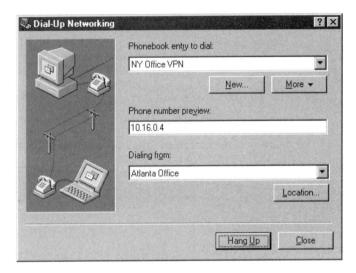

Windows 9x

Windows 9x takes a unique approach to implementing virtual private networking through the use of a Microsoft VPN adapter. Instead of adding support for PPTP or other protocols (like in other Microsoft operating systems), all you need to do is add the VPN adapter to your system to get connected.

NOTE *To add VPN support for Windows 95, you must have the Dial-Up Networking upgrade v1.2 or later installed on your system. Windows 95 only has support for PPTP, remember. VPN support for PPTP is included in Windows 98 right out of the box, and with the addition of the L2TP VPN client, which you can download from the Microsoft Web site, Windows 98 will support L2TP as well as PPTP.*

Start by editing the network properties of Windows 9x by selecting Start/Settings/Control Panel/Network. When the Network properties page comes up, click the Add button, and then select Adapter as the component type you'd like to install. Your screen should look like Figure 20.54.

In the list of adapters supplied, scroll down to Microsoft for the manufacturer, then select the Microsoft Virtual Private Networking Adapter listed on the right side of the screen. Click OK, and Windows 9x will add the VPN adapter to its system. Of course, this will require a reboot for the changes to take effect.

Once your system has rebooted, the next step to getting connected is creating a Dial-Up Networking entry to connect to your VPN server. From the Windows 9x Desktop, double-click My Computer, then Dial-Up Networking, and then Make New Connection to launch the Make New Connection Wizard, shown in Figure 20.55.

FIGURE 20.54

Adding the Microsoft VPN Adapter to Windows 9*x*

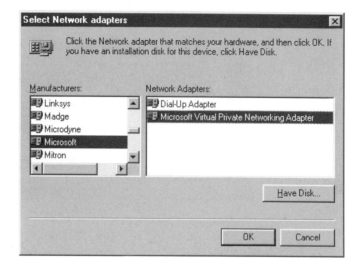

FIGURE 20.55

Windows 9*x* Make New Connection Wizard

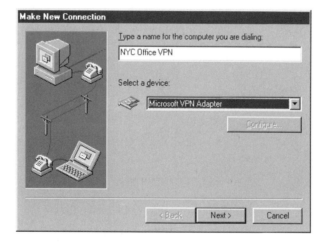

From the Select a Device pull-down box, choose the Microsoft VPN Adapter if it isn't already selected. Click Next to move to the next step of the wizard shown in Figure 20.56.

Enter the IP address or DNS name of your VPN server in the box as needed. In the example in Figure 20.56, we have used an IP address of 10.16.0.4. You may remember that this is the same IP address used in the configuration of the RAS/VPN server earlier in this chapter. After entering the hostname or address, clicking Next will complete the wizard and place a VPN Dial-Up Networking entry on your system.

FIGURE 20.56

Entering the IP address of a VPN server in Windows 9x

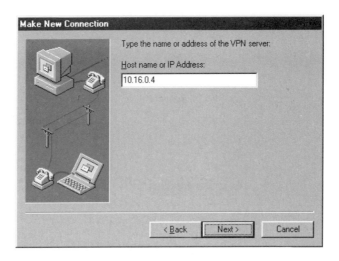

To make the VPN connection, you must make sure you have an actual, valid Internet IP address before doing so. As with NT 4, you may need to connect to the VPN in two steps. If you need to use Dial-Up Networking to connect to an ISP for your IP address, do that first. Once you have a valid IP address available, you can then launch your VPN Dial-Up Networking connection to get connected to your remote system. After providing a valid set of user credentials, you'll be connected to the VPN server. To disconnect the connection, simply double-click Dial-Up Networking from My Computer, double-click the connection to the VPN server, and then click Disconnect, as shown in Figure 20.57. Or you can right-click the connection in the Dial-Up Networking window and click Disconnect.

FIGURE 20.57

Disconnecting the VPN connection in Windows 9x

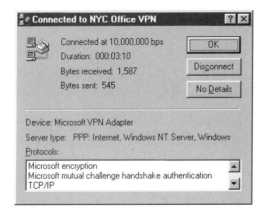

Windows 2000

Windows 2000 added a few nice features to the client side of establishing VPN connections, namely the ability to automatically associate one DUN entry with another. For example, if you need to dial an ISP before you can connect with your virtual private network, Windows 2000 can join these two functions. The end result is that when you (or your users) need to connect to the virtual private network, doing so only requires launching one Dial-Up Networking session, rather than the two steps required with the older clients. Windows 2000 also includes support for L2TP without any additional add-on software components.

Like most of the remote access functionality in Win2K, to define a VPN connection, you will begin with Start/Settings/Network and Dial-Up Connections, and then the Make New Connection Wizard. Remember, you may have to add your phone information here if this is the first time you've initiated this. After clicking Next in the initial screen of the wizard, select the option Connect to a Private Network Through the Internet, as shown in Figure 20.58.

FIGURE 20.58

Creating a VPN connection on Windows 2000

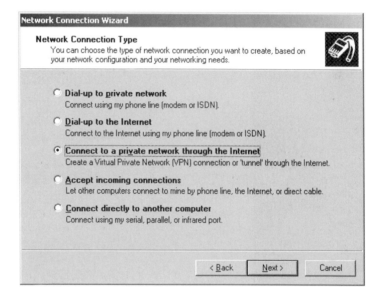

Click Next to continue. If you have already created a dial-up connection on your system, Win2K will then ask if you need to establish a public network (Internet) connection first before establishing the VPN connection, as shown in Figure 20.59.

TIP   *If you have not yet created a dial-up connection, Win2K will not give you the option to decide whether or not to dial it during the wizard. However, if you create a dial-up connection after you create the VPN connection, you can make sure that Win2K knows to use the dial-up connection first by changing the setting in the VPN connection properties sheet. To set this, simply right-click the VPN Connection icon from the Network and Dial-Up Connections window and click Properties. Then check the Dial Another Connection First check box.*

If the Win2K device you will be connecting already has a valid, public Internet IP address, answer Do Not Dial the Initial Connection to this question. Otherwise, if you need to obtain an IP address first from an ISP, select Automatically Dial This Initial Connection and choose the connection that will get you connected to the Internet. Doing so will cause your VPN Dial-Up Networking connection to initiate an ISP connection first. Click Next to continue on to entering the IP address or hostname of the target server, as shown in Figure 20.60.

FIGURE 20.59

Creating a public
connection before a
VPN connection

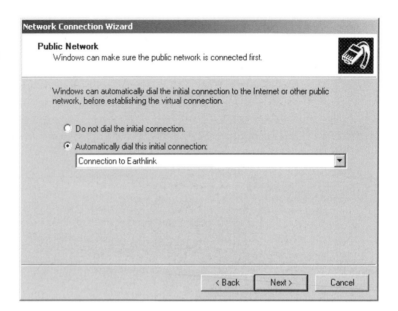

FIGURE 20.60

Entering the
IP address of the
VPN server

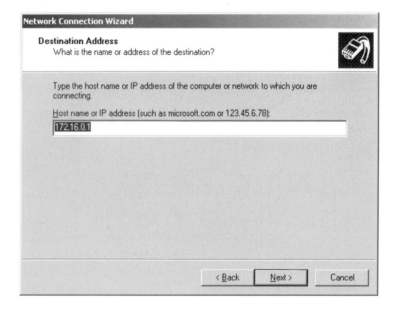

Much like many of the other client platforms we've already discussed, you will need to enter
the IP address of your target system or a DNS-resolvable hostname. As you can see, this Dial-Up
Networking entry will call a VPN server at IP address 172.16.0.1. Click Next to continue, and the
final step of the wizard will ask you whether you want to make this VPN connection available to

all users or just yourself. For the purposes of this section, I'll assume that you just want to use the VPN connection for yourself, so click the Only for Myself radio button and click Next to finish creating the Dial-Up Networking entry. Select a name for the connection and click Next to finish the wizard. You also have the opportunity here to have Win2K create a shortcut on the Desktop for this connection, a handy feature if the connection will be used often.

Once you have completed the wizard, you will have an opportunity to test the connection. When it comes time to actually establish this connection, if you selected the option to have Win2K dial an initial connection, you will see a dialog box like the one in Figure 20.61 asking you if the public network connection should be initiated first.

FIGURE 20.61

Windows 2000 asking if an initial public network connection should be established first

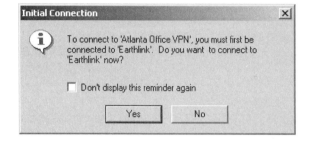

Windows XP

To create a virtual private network connection in Windows XP, open Control Panel from the Start menu and double-click the Network Connections icon. Start the New Connection Wizard by double-clicking that icon and click Next in the initial screen of the wizard. Click the Connect to the Network at My Workplace radio button (Figure 20.62) and then click Next.

FIGURE 20.62

Setting up a VPN connection in Windows XP

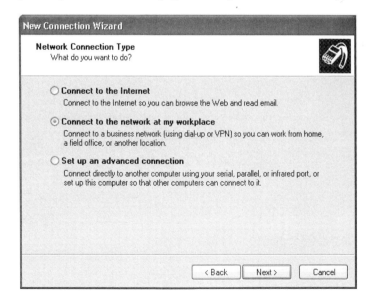

In the next screen, choose the Virtual Private Network Connection option and click Next. Type in the name you want to use for this connection and click Next. If you have previously set up a dial-up connection on your XP client, you will now receive the option of whether to dial that first, before connecting to the VPN. If, for instance, you need to connect to an ISP to receive a valid IP address, which is required before you can utilize the VPN, choose the Automatically Dial This Initial Connection option as seen in Figure 20.63.

FIGURE 20.63

Windows XP asking if an initial dial-up connection should be established before connecting to the VPN

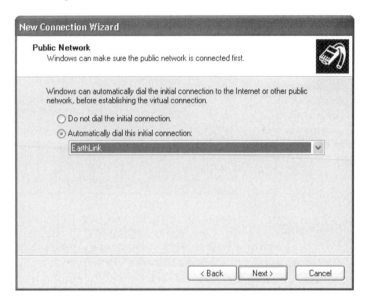

NOTE *When I say that your VPN client needs a valid IP address, realize that if your client machine is on a network which uses NAT or private IP addresses routed through a centralized device like a router, a demand-dial server, or your cable modem at home—as long as that device supports VPN traffic—you will be able to connect to the VPN just as you would to the Internet from that machine, no matter what kind of IP address you have.*

In the next screen of the wizard, type in the IP address or hostname of the VPN server (172.16.0.1 in the example) and click Next. The next screen asks you to decide who will use this VPN connection that you are creating (see Figure 20.64). If you want to share the connection among several users on the machine, choose the Anyone's Use option and the connection will be copied to the All Users profile on the machine. For now, choose the My Use Only radio button to reserve the use of this connection and user credentials to one user.

The final screen of the wizard allows you to view the options you have selected and enables you to create a shortcut to this VPN connection on your Desktop, which can be handy if you will be using it often. When you have completed the wizard, if you have opted to dial another connection first, you will be asked if you would like to dial that initial connection at this time. If you do not have another connection that you need to dial before connecting to the VPN, you will be taken to the Connect *<Connection Name>* dialog box, where you can click the Connect button to test your connection (Figure 20.65).

FIGURE 20.64

Decide who will be allowed to use the VPN connection on this machine.

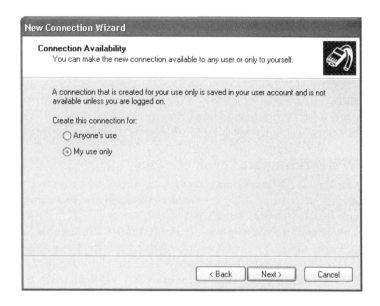

FIGURE 20.65

Test your connection.

Once you are connected and your credentials are verified, you can use the VPN connection to access resources on the remote network, use drive mappings and even browse the remote network using Network Places. You can copy this VPN connection in the Network Connections folder and rename it if you need to create multiple VPN connections on this machine. Just change the connection and security settings for each connection to accommodate the various VPN servers you need to connect to.

To disconnect the VPN connection in Windows XP, right-click the connection and choose Disconnect. You can also, of course, double-click the connection and do the same thing or right-click the network icon in the notification area of the system tray and choose Disconnect. There are always at least three ways to do anything in a Windows environment, remember?

NOTE *Keep in mind that a firewall can keep you from being able to connect using your new VPN. If you are having trouble connecting, consider any firewalls that may exist, whether it is on a home pc or in the corporate environment in the course of your troubleshooting.*

VPN Performance Considerations

Our section on virtual private networking wouldn't be complete without taking a bit of time to discuss performance issues to consider. Although virtual private networking is a neat technology, unfortunately there are some times when it just might not make sense to use it. Careful planning and consideration should help you determine if it is a solution that can add value to your organization.

In the right set of circumstances, virtual private networking can provide fast, reliable, and secure connections to remote networks across the Internet (or another unsecured network). However, in the wrong set of circumstances, a VPN can make an already slow dial-up connection seem even slower.

So what are the right circumstances? In my professional opinion, the right circumstances are when you have high-speed connectivity on your RAS server at the very least and preferably when you have high-speed connectivity on both your RAS server and your DUN client. On occasions when I have been able to implement VPN circuits at locations with a T1 or better available at both the server and client ends, performance has been wonderful and the connections reliable. However, due to the protocol overhead involved with PPTP and L2TP and the inherent latency of the Internet, if you are planning on implementing a VPN with dial-up modems on each side of your connection, I urge you to think twice.

I wish I could say that Microsoft's VPN implementations were going to give you the performance you might expect over modem connections, but they just won't. Simply due to the additional complexities of encrypting the data, bundling the payload data inside a TCP/IP packet, and the latency of communications across the Internet, you can expect a decrease in your performance ranging anywhere from 10 to 50 percent. Now, without getting into all the technical details, it is worthwhile to note that this isn't entirely Microsoft's fault; after all, they can't be blamed for the fact that the Internet can be inherently slow at times (or can they?). However, even with the worst-case scenario of a 50 percent reduction in performance, if there is a T1 on each side of the virtual private network, the effective speeds of the network are still roughly in the 760Kbps range. However, if you're using a 56K modem on each side of the virtual private network, which probably won't connect much faster than 48Kbps, you can easily see how a 50 percent performance penalty can make a connection go from "slow" to "unusable."

Simply put, if you are using a modem on your RAS server and a modem on your DUN client, you will get your best possible speeds by having one dial directly in to the other. And without a VPN, there is no protocol overhead getting in the way, nor is there the need for your data to travel across dozens of routers as it works its way to its destination. By creating a direct connection, data packets go directly from the DUN client to the target network.

However, everything in life is a trade-off, and it will be up to you to decide whether this will work adequately enough for your needs. After all, what is adequate to one person might be great to another and unacceptable to yet another. In either case, expect a performance penalty when implementing virtual private networking and plan your bandwidth accordingly.

Dialing Up a Remote Network and Routing Traffic

With the release of the Routing and Remote Access Service update to Windows NT 4 Server, Microsoft was able to improve on the routing capabilities that already existed in Windows NT. Although Windows NT 4 shipped with routing capabilities right out of the box, they were limited and cumbersome, to say the least. Microsoft then included all the capabilities of the Routing and Remote Access Service update in Windows 2000 Server, making that operating system a platform capable of solving several common routing scenarios right out of the box. Microsoft has added a few more features to Server 2003, including support for preshared keys in L2TP/IPSec authentication, the ability for NAT interfaces to work with Basic Firewall, support for L2TP/IPSec connections originating from VPN clients behind a network using NAT, and broadcast name resolution by a NetBT proxy on the VPN server for networks operating without WINS or DNS. All in all, Windows Server 2003 offers a fairly comprehensive package in its RRAS implementation.

Let's take an example of routing traffic from a central office to a remote office over an analog connection. Many organizations are often faced with a connectivity dilemma when opening remote offices, especially if there are only a small number of computers at the remote site. Installing dedicated links between locations can be cost-prohibitive depending on the number of people at the remote site, but having a group of individuals completely isolated from the organizational network usually isn't an acceptable alternative either. Windows Server 2003 is a perfect solution for this scenario, as it can establish demand-dialed links between locations whenever traffic needs to pass from one site to another. By using simple modems and ordinary phone lines, Windows Server 2003 can be a low-cost alternative to installing dedicated WAN links. To get started, let's walk through the details of a sample scenario.

Sample Network

Our sample network consists of the following:

♦ Number of sites: two (New York and Atlanta)

♦ TCP/IP subnet for New York: 10.16.0.x with a subnet mask of 255.255.255.0

♦ TCP/IP subnet for Atlanta: 172.16.0.x with a subnet mask of 255.255.255.0

♦ Windows Server 2003 RRAS server in New York: NYC-RAS1 with an IP address of 10.16.0.4

♦ Windows Server 2003 RRAS server in Atlanta: ATL-RAS1 with an IP address of 172.16.0.1

♦ Phone number for analog line connected to New York Windows Server 2003 RRAS server: (212) 555-1212

♦ Phone number for analog line connected to Atlanta Windows Server 2003 RRAS server: (404) 555-1212

♦ User account created in the New York Active Directory and granted dial-in permissions: ATLANTA-ROUTER, password: atlanta

♦ User account created in the Atlanta Active Directory and granted dial-in permissions: NEWYORK-ROUTER, password: newyork

In effect, our network looks similar to the diagram shown in Figure 20.66.

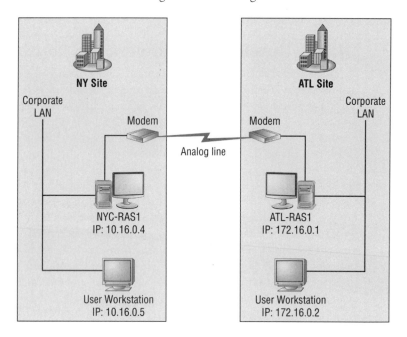

Setting Up the First Server

To start building a demand-dialed analog connection between these two locations, you will need to
have your Windows Server 2003 able to function as a router. If you've worked through any of the
configurations previously discussed in this chapter, your system is probably configured to simply
act as a Remote Access Server. Changing roles for the server is as simple as editing the properties
for the Remote Access Service.

*NOTE   For the purposes of walking through the first server configuration, I will be configuring the necessary components
on our New York router first, using the details just defined.*

To change roles for your server, open the Routing and Remote Access MMC by selecting Start/
Administrative Tools/Routing and Remote Access. Edit the properties for Remote Access Service
on your server by right-clicking your server name and then selecting Properties. You should see
a dialog box similar to the one pictured in Figure 20.67.

To add routing services to your system, put a check in the box labeled Router and then select one
of the two radio buttons below that option. If you will only be using LAN-based interfaces (Ethernet
adapters, etc.) as your routing devices on your system, you can leave the Local Area Network (LAN)
Routing Only option selected. However, if you intend to use dial-up connections (as we will in this
example), demand-dialed links, or VPN connections, select the LAN and Demand-Dial Routing
option. Click OK to apply the changes, and Windows Server 2003 should stop and restart the
Routing and Remote Access Service to implement the changes.

FIGURE 20.67

Editing RAS server properties to add routing capabilities

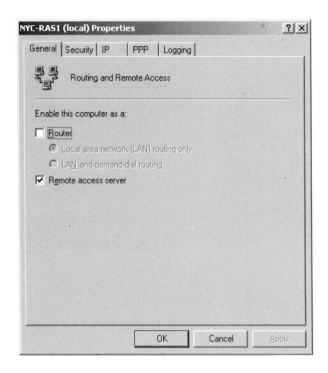

When you return to the Routing and Remote Access MMC, the next step will be to enable routing support for one of the ports on your system. In the Routing and Remote Access MMC, make sure you have expanded the RAS server by clicking the plus symbol next to it, then right-click the option for Ports and select Properties to get to the ports properties pages. Once you have the ports properties pages available, double-click the device you intend to use as your demand-dialed connection (if the device you want to use isn't listed, go back to the section on adding RAS devices earlier in this chapter). The configuration page for that device should look similar to the dialog box in Figure 20.68.

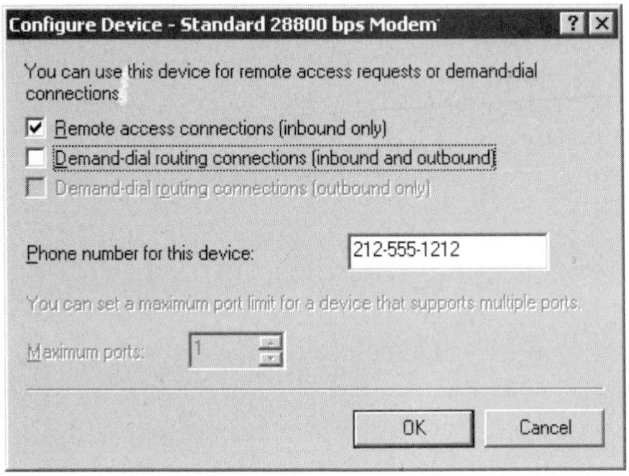

FIGURE 20.68

Editing properties for the demand-dial port

Configure this device by checking the Demand-Dial Routing Connections (Inbound and Outbound) option and clicking OK. If you would eventually like to use Bandwidth Allocation Protocol with this configuration—to increase bandwidth by adding more dial-up connections as needed—enter the phone number for your connection and click OK to accept the changes.

When you return to the Routing and Remote Access MMC, you might have noticed a new item called Network Interfaces in the results pane of the window when you look at your Windows Server 2003, as shown in Figure 20.69. This option was added when routing services were added to the server, and it is where you will begin to add your demand-dialed interface.

FIGURE 20.69

Adding a demand-dial interface to the RRAS MMC via Network Interfaces

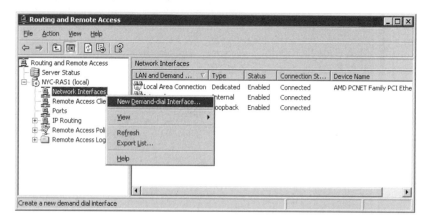

To start creating a demand-dial interface, right-click the Network Interfaces selection, and then choose the option to add a new demand-dial interface. This will launch the Demand-Dial Interface Wizard, which will walk you through steps to create the interface. Once you click Next to get through the initial wizard screen, the first step of the wizard appears, as shown in Figure 20.70.

FIGURE 20.70

Defining a name for a demand-dial interface

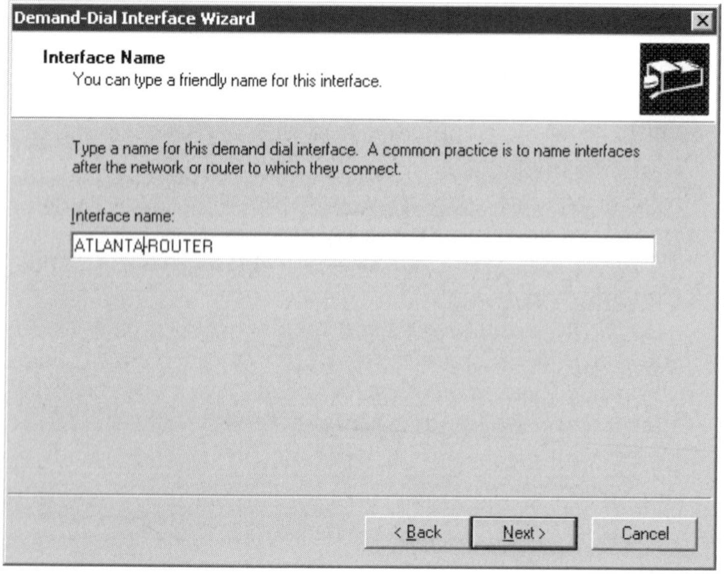

In most cases of assigning a friendly name to a RAS or other type of connection, any name will do. However, in creating demand-dial routing connections, the name assigned to a demand-dial interface is important. The name assigned to a demand-dial connection *must* match the name of the user account entered into the Active Directory at the *same* site. The same must be true on both sides of the wide area network. To quote Microsoft directly: "The username in the authentication credentials sent by the calling router must exactly match the name of a demand-dial interface on the answering router." If the username does not match a demand-dial interface name, the answering router will assume that the incoming call is a RAS *user*, not a remote router. Therefore, whatever name is entered here must also be used as a username on the same system's Active Directory. Since we're walking through setting up our New York remote office in our example that will dial out to the Atlanta office, I've decided to call this interface ATLANTA-ROUTER. When you have entered the appropriate name, click Next to continue to the next stage of the wizard, shown in Figure 20.71.

FIGURE 20.71

Selecting the connection type for the demand-dial interface

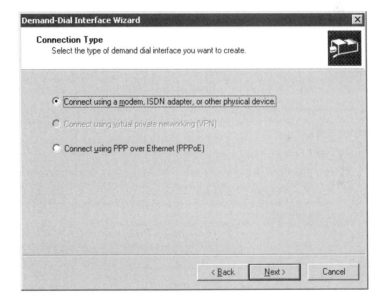

Here you will need to choose the option to Connect Using a Modem, ISDN Adapter or Other Physical Device or you can choose to use Point to Point Protocol over Ethernet (PPPoE), which allows you to utilize your broadband connection to pass packets from one LAN to another. Choose the first option and click Next. In the screen that follows, select the modem or adapter that you want to use. This step of the wizard should be relatively self-explanatory. The wizard needs to know what phone number Windows Server 2003 should dial when it is attempting to connect to Atlanta. Enter the number exactly as your system should dial it, including any prefixes, area codes, etc. If you have a list of alternate numbers that Windows Server 2003 can use to establish this demand-dial connection, click the Alternates button and enter the information there. When you click Next to move to the next step in the Demand-Dial Interface Wizard, you should see a dialog box similar to the one pictured in Figure 20.72.

FIGURE 20.72

Selecting protocol and security options for a demand-dial interface

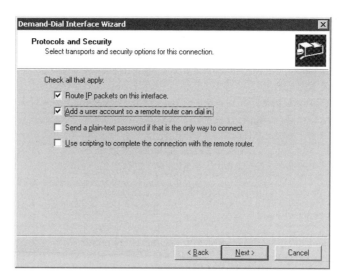

Depending on the network you are connecting to, here you can select which protocols Windows Server 2003 should route, although since Microsoft has dropped IPX/SPX from its list of RRAS protocols, this list is becoming pretty slim. In addition to selecting the appropriate protocols for the remote network, you can also choose to have Windows Server 2003 create a user account so that the remote network's router can dial in to your system. Lastly, you can choose custom connection options such as sending a plain-text password if that is the only way the remote router will let you connect, or any advanced scripting options you might need. Depending on the options you select from this screen, the remainder of the Demand-Dial Interface Wizard will vary, but for the purposes of our example we'll assume you've selected IP and decided to create a user account for a remote router as seen in this figure. Click Next to continue to the next step of the wizard, shown in Figure 20.73.

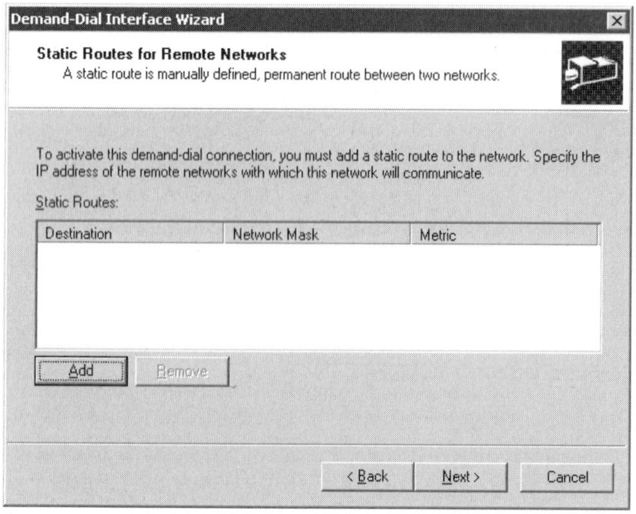

FIGURE 20.73

Adding static routes for the remote network

Here you will need to define a static route entry for the remote IP network. In effect, you will need to tell your Windows Server 2003 "whenever you need to contact these IP addresses, use this demand-dial interface to get there." By entering a static routing entry for the remote network's IP address range in the Atlanta office and then defining the demand-dial interface as the connection to use, Windows Server 2003 will know to route any packets for that network by dialing in to the remote router.

To add a static route, click Add and you should end up with a dialog box similar to the one in Figure 20.74.

FIGURE 20.74

Defining a static route to a remote network

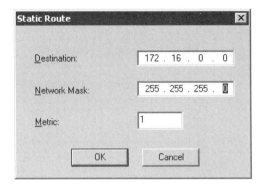

Here you can define the network address and mask for the remote network, which this interface will use to get the packets to their destination. Windows Server 2003 will use this information to determine if packets—when it receives them—match the IP address range of the remote network. If the packets match the range defined, Windows Server 2003 will route them. Lastly, you can leave the metric at 1. Once you have all this information entered, click OK and you should see your static route appear in the list of Static Routes. Click Next to move to the Dial-In Credentials pane of the wizard, as seen in Figure 20.75.

FIGURE 20.75

Configuring router dial-in credentials

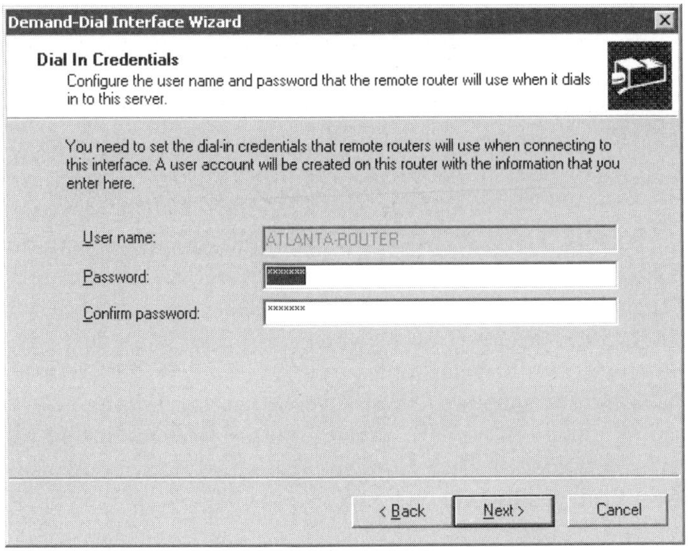

Remember that, although we are creating this interface to route our New York users to Atlanta by using the demand-dial connection, when users in Atlanta are routed to the New York office, the RAS server in Atlanta (ATL-RAS1) will need to access this interface we are creating in New York. When ATL-RAS1 attempts to connect to this interface, it will need to have credentials that are valid in New York. As previously stated, the friendly or descriptive name you use for a demand-dial interface needs to be the same as the credentials for that connection, otherwise the answering router (NYC-RAS1) will assume the incoming caller (ATL-RAS1) is simply a RAS connection, not a router. Since we are defining a demand-dial interface to also allow calls *into* the ATLANTA-ROUTER device we are creating here in New York, if ATL-RAS1 were to call the NYC-RAS1 system we're now configuring, it would need to identify itself as ATLANTA-ROUTER. Therefore, the username field is grayed out by default, preventing you from changing it. This is an important point, because if you decide to change the user accounts used by RRAS at a later date, but you don't change the interface names accordingly, you could end up with a broken routing system. Enter a password for this account to use, and make a note of it. Click Next to continue to the next screen in the wizard, as seen in Figure 20.76.

FIGURE 20.76

Configuring router dial-out credentials

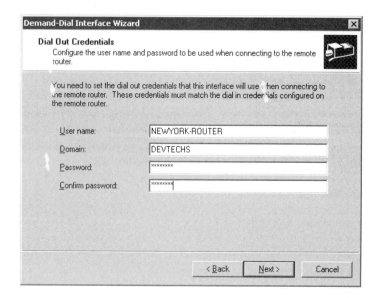

Now we'll look at how we dial out to the Atlanta office from the interface we are creating here in New York. You will need to define the user credentials that NYC-RAS1 will use when calling the Atlanta office and dialing in to ATL-RAS1. The username entered here must match the name of the demand-dial interface configured on the remote system (ATL-RAS1) exactly or else the remote system in Atlanta will simply assume your Server 2003 is a standard RAS user. Remember the network configuration I showed you earlier for our scenario? We called the interface in Atlanta NEWYORK-ROUTER, so that is the user account that we will need to use when we connect to Atlanta from New York. Enter the appropriate domain, username, and password combination for your configuration and then click Next.

At this point, you have completed exactly half the work required to have your systems routing data over analog links. The other half of the job, of course, is to go through the exact same steps on the other system by configuring a demand-dial interface in the same manner we just described. In our case that other system would be the Atlanta system, called ATL-RAS1. On that system we will create a demand-dial interface called NEWYORK-ROUTER, which will be used both to route Atlanta network traffic destined for the New York office to NYC-RAS1 and to receive incoming calls from our NYC-RAS1 system.

Once you have both systems configured correctly, you should be able to test your connection to see if it works by doing a ping from one system to another.

NOTE   *For more information about Ping, see Chapter 6.*

WARNING   *This may just be a bug that hasn't been ironed out, but despite the fact that the Demand-Dial Interface Wizard told me that it would create a user account for me, it didn't, at least not in the Active Directory. When I initially tested my new connection to the Atlanta office, I found that I couldn't authenticate. What happened? In Figure 20.75, you can see that I have no choice in the username that will need to authenticate in New York since it has to be the same as the interface name. Note that it doesn't specify any domain information. On the following screen (Figure 20.76), I configured the dial-out credentials to use the interface name of the RAS server in Atlanta (NEWYORK-ROUTER). Note also that I was given the opportunity to add the domain name for those dial-out credentials in the wizard. I assumed that a domain account would be created. So, in New York, I told the interface to use the domain account DEVTECHS\ NEWYORK-ROUTER for the outbound connection to Atlanta. In Atlanta, however, the user account created in the wizard for the dial-in credentials, although it was called NEWYORK-ROUTER, was not actually created in the DEVTECHS domain. Upon closer inspection, I found that when I created the interfaces, both in New York and in Atlanta, an account was indeed created, but it was a local account. So, in the same wizard in which you can specify a domain account for the dial-out credentials, you get no opportunity to add the domain information to the dial-in account, leaving you with two different sets of credentials on each interface.*

Start at one of your Windows Server 2003 boxes configured with a demand-dial interface, go to a command prompt, and ping one of the IP addresses on the distant network. You should see your demand-dial connection come online and start passing traffic. However, it is important to realize that for the type of communication you are attempting, your call setup times might take too long. For example, the `ping` command typically sends four ICMP echo requests, and then waits 1.5 seconds after each one for a response. All total, a test of four pings should take no longer than 6 seconds. However, if you are using analog connections, your call setup times are most likely going to be in the range of 20–30 seconds. Therefore, your connection won't come online in time to satisfy the request. For testing purposes, I would recommend using an indefinite ping by using the `-t` option on the command line, such as `ping -t 172.16.0.2`, which is an address in the Atlanta office in our scenario.

To solve problems like these and others, you can use some fine-tuning controls for your demand-dial connection. For example, if you are using analog lines to connect sites and the analog lines aren't billed per-minute, it might make sense to have your demand-dial connection online all the time. This is called making a *persistent* connection. From the Routing and Remote Access MMC, click the selection for Routing Interfaces in the left pane of the window. In the results pane, you should see your demand-dialed interface listed. Right-click the demand-dialed interface and select Properties to edit the properties page for this connection. You should see a four-tabbed dialog box similar to the one in Figure 20.77 (shown with the Options tab selected).

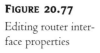

Figure 20.77

Editing router inter-
face properties

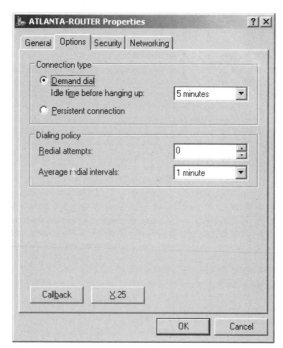

There are several settings you can control through this dialog box, but some of the most useful are listed under the Options tab shown in Figure 20.77. For example, if you are using an ISDN connection to reach your distant network and your ISDN is billed per minute, you can enter an idle time-out value in the Connection Type area of the window so your connections don't stay on any longer than necessary. Or, if the opposite is true, and you aren't billed per minute for your connections, you can select the persistent connection option to have the link stay online all the time. If, for some reason, the link fails, Windows Server 2003 will bring it right back online again. Set the options you would like to use for this interface. Now click the Security tab to view your authentication protocol and encryption options, as shown in Figure 20.78.

If you leave the default option checked for Typical (Recommended Settings) in the Security Options section of this dialog box, you are telling the RAS server to require a secured password for the connection, but you are given the opportunity to allow unsecured passwords here as well by clicking the drop-down box. The check box labeled Require Data Encryption is not a default setting, but if you want to make sure that the data that passes in and out of this interface is encrypted, select Require Data Encryption (Disconnect if None) to force the system to disallow any unencrypted communication. Otherwise, by default, the server will request encryption, but will allow nonencrypted clients to connect anyway. Dial-up connections in RAS use Microsoft Point-to-Point Encryption (MPPE). VPNs have two options for encryption. You can specify either MPPE and Point-to-Point Tunneling Protocol (PPTP), or IP Security (IPSec) encryption along with Layer 2 Tunneling Protocol (L2TP). Remote Access Policies are used to specify encryption levels, which can be set to Basic (40-bit), Strong (56-bit), or Strongest (128-bit). MPPE requires the use of the MS-CHAP (v1 or v2) or EAP-TLS authentication protocols. To set your authentication protocols for this interface, check the box labeled Advanced (Custom Settings) and click the now-highlighted Settings button. You should see the screen shown in Figure 20.79.

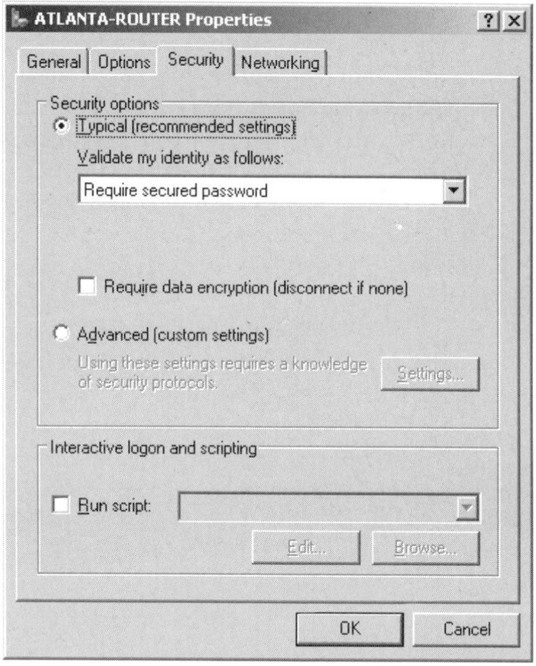

FIGURE 20.78

Security settings for the RAS interface

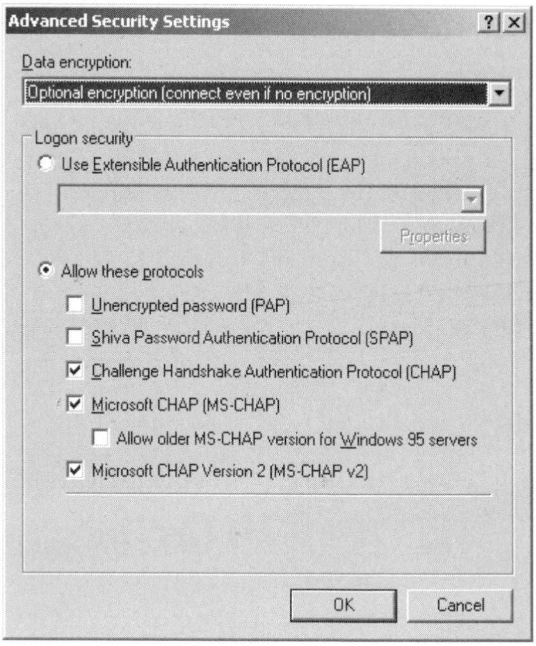

FIGURE 20.79

Authentication protocols for the RAS interface

Use this properties page to decide which authentication protocols to allow on the interface. You can also customize in more detail how the interface handles encryption. Rather than simply requiring encryption or asking for it and then allowing the connection anyway, you can also choose to disallow all encryption. This will disconnect any connection that tries to send encrypted data; you even have the ability to require strongest encryption without having to set this in your Remote Access Policies. If you need to create anything more customized than these settings allow, you will have to learn all about Remote Access Policies, which allow you to fine-tune exactly what your clients can do with the connection based on various attributes—for instance, the phone number that they dial in from, the type of OS they are using, group membership, or perhaps the time of day that they are calling. By using these attributes, you can create policies that will affect the way a user can connect, how long they can use the connection, IP addressing, idle times, and more. Don't forget to make sure to give the users the ability to connect by checking the Allow Access setting in their user properties. Also, remember that this interface is set up to dial another network, as well as to receive inbound calls from clients. It is, then, a client itself at times. The Networking tab allows you to adjust the client settings for this interface for the times that it is dialing in to another network, in this case, Atlanta. Click OK to save your settings and return to the RRAS MMC.

Take a look at Figure 20.80. When you right-click the demand-dial routing interface in the Routing and Remote Access MMC, there are some additional options you could set, in addition to editing the property sheets of the item itself. For instance, you can reset the credentials that this interface uses when it dials another network, in this case, our Atlanta office. Remember, though, that if you reset the username here for the dial-out credentials, you will also have to change it in the Active Directory of the remote network (it could be that both of these offices are in the *same* AD, of course) or on the local server, if the remote RAS server is not a member of a domain.

FIGURE 20.80

Additional interface settings

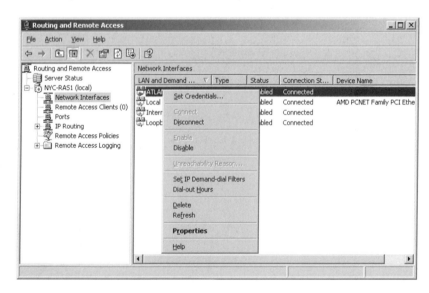

You can also manually connect or disconnect from here, which can be very useful for testing or troubleshooting. One of the more useful items listed is the ability to create IP filters for the connection. With this option, you can discriminate against certain types of traffic and allow or prohibit the traffic through the interface. You can even specify whether the connection should be initiated at all, based on the type of traffic. If you click the Dial-Out Hours menu option, you can set the hours in which this connection can be established. If you would like to restrict the times when your demand-dial connections can be brought online, select the Dialing Hours option when you right-click the routing interface. You should end up with an hourly grid dialog box, like the one in Figure 20.81, in which you can select the hours to allow and disallow connections. By default, users can access the connection at any time of day or night.

FIGURE 20.81

Defining dialing
hours for demand-
dial connections

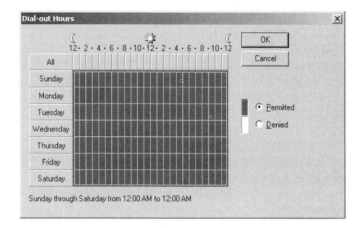

Once you have completed everything, you should have a functional wide area network running between locations and passing data as necessary. Through the use of this functionality, I have seen organizations that have set up completely "virtual" WANs consisting of multiple sites that all look as if they're operating as one large network, but in reality they are each small sites which are connected to a master network over analog links. Although Windows Server 2003 isn't designed to displace high-end routers in complex routing scenarios, it is a good solution for a lot of networking problems—some of which you may face.

The Most Common (and Poorly Documented) RAS Problems

Microsoft's RAS service is a great feature in Windows Server 2003—and even though they've made it simple to set up, under the hood a complex communication mechanism is working away to get packets from one system to another. Often, the Microsoft wizards will help you with setting up most of the settings necessary for RAS itself, but RAS depends on some other specific settings within Windows Server 2003 to function properly. In this section, we'll take a look at some common (and poorly documented) problems that users run into when they're trying to set up RAS.

"I've connected to a RAS server from my home PC, but I can't browse anything on the network!"

Okay, technically this doesn't fall under a RAS problem per se—but browsing remote networks is a problem most commonly found on RAS connections. Actually, it's the number one problem that I see posted on Usenet when people are trying to get RAS configured and running on their network.

Let's say that you gave the phone number for the RAS server to Jane in Accounting so that she can work at home. After giving her a quick lesson on how to create a dial-up networking connection, you're hoping that Jane will be able to connect to the network from her Windows 98 PC, and then navigate through the network to get to the resources that she needs.

So Jane successfully dials in over the weekend but she can't see anything in her Network Neighborhood. If she knew how to map a drive, she'd be able to do it—but she's accustomed to double-clicking things in the NetHood to find her files. So, she can't work. On Monday, she calls for help—frustrated that she's now behind in her work.

That leaves you with the unpleasant task of remotely troubleshooting a home user's PC. Who knows, maybe her 14-year-old kid messed up the TCP/IP stack? Or maybe there's some odd problem with her modem? In any case, it might seem like it's going to be a painful issue to troubleshoot since you can't easily get your hands on the PC.

Well, here's a quick tip that could save you a lot of headaches: More often than not, when a user experiences this type of problem, it's due to a misconfigured workgroup configuration on their computer.

For example, let's say that your network domain is called COMPANY (we'll stick with down-level NetBIOS names here to make it easier). Now, most retail PCs that a user might buy for their home are configured out-of-the-box with something like Workgroup for their workgroup setting. Odds are good that the company that your user bought her PC from didn't give it the same workgroup setting as the name of your domain. And that's what you need so Microsoft browsing will work properly.

The solution is to configure the workgroup name on the client's workstation to be the same as the Windows NT/2000/Server 2003 domain or workgroup to which your users are connecting. If you've run into this problem, give it a shot and see if it works.

"How can I keep RAS connections alive when a user logs off of their workstation?"

By default, RAS connections (on Windows NT and 2000 clients) are automatically disconnected whenever a user logs out of their workstation. If you have a workstation setup at a remote site that multiple people use, you might not want this to be the case. In order to change this default behavior, you'll need to modify the registry on the RAS *client*—the system that is dialing in.

Look in the following key in the Registry:

```
HKEY_Local_Machine\Software\Microsoft\Windows NT\Current Version\Winlogon
```

You may see a value in that key called KeepRasConnections, but most likely you won't. It's not there by default. Add this value to your system as a type REG_SZ, and give it a value of 1 (the default behavior is indicated by a 0). This will instruct the client workstation to keep the RAS connection open, even when the user at the workstation logs out.

"No matter what I try, I can't seem to get a modem connection from a workstation to my RAS server."

If you're in this boat, you have two places to start diagnosing the problem: the server or the client. Fortunately, you might get lucky with the server diagnosis—if other users or workstations can successfully dial in to the RAS server, then it's probably not a server problem. So, the next course of action is to start troubleshooting the workstation.

The great advantage—and disadvantage—of the Windows operating system is that it hides the complexity of operating the underlying components of a system. For example, instead of knowing that to dial a modem you need to issue the command ATDT5551212 and wait for the response, you simply need to know how to enter a phone number in the appropriate dialog box within Windows. But, what if you want to troubleshoot the dialing function? It would be helpful to see those commands as they are passed back and forth to your modem. Windows Server 2003 makes it an easy process to view the modem commands that RAS clients or RAS servers send.

By default, Windows Server 2003 will automatically log the commands that it sends to any modem. To view the log files for a particular modem, start out by selecting the Phone and Modem Options icon from the Control Panel. Click the Modems tab and then select the modem whose log file you want to view. Edit the properties for the modem, and then select the Diagnostics tab on the modem properties. You should see a View Log button on the diagnostics page—click it, and it will bring up a file named %systemroot%\ModemLog_modemname.txt. This file contains the history of all the commands passed back and forth between Windows Server 2003 and your modem.

Got a problem with a modem on a RAS server that never wants to answer calls? Try checking the log files to see if they're arguing over something. Got a RAS client that just can't seem to dial in, even though everything is configured correctly? Check the log and see if there's a problem with the initialization strings that Windows Server 2003 is sending. These log files can help you go far in your troubleshooting endeavors.

"Can I make a RAS client automatically dial in to a RAS server at a specified time?"

Absolutely!

For example, let's say that you wanted to have an automatic routine set up for each office to call into the home server (called HOMEBASE) every night and transmit its sales figures, back up a few key data files, etc. You'll need to create the following:

- ◆ A dial-up networking connection with the properties for the remote server (we'll call it HOMEOFFICE in our example)
- ◆ A batch file to dial the dial-up networking connection and transfer the files
- ◆ A job in Scheduled Tasks to trigger the batch file to run nightly

Now, the creation of the dial-up networking entry is pretty straightforward. We've covered that at length earlier in this chapter. The batch file that you create might look similar to the following (the important line to note is the RASDIAL command):

```
@ECHO OFF
CLS
ECHO Transmitting updates to HOMEBASE server
RASDIAL HOMEOFFICE
NET USE X: \\HOMEBASE\sharename
XCOPY C:\TRANSFER\*.* X: /S /E /Y
ECHO Updates to HOMEBASE server completed—hanging up
RASDIAL HOMEOFFICE /DISCONNECT
```

TIP   *If you receive an error telling you that RASDIAL can't find the phonebook entry HOMEOFFICE, you might have to specify the path to the phonebook file (.pbk) in the batch file.*

Now, the commands here are pretty straightforward, but the key is the RASDIAL command. This is a command-line utility that will automatically dial a dial-up networking entry. For this to work you will need to have cached the username and password credentials on the dial-up networking entry that is named (HOMEOFFICE in this case). After that, the batch file runs some standard commands to connect to a share on a server, and then copy files up to the server. After the commands are completed, the RASDIAL command will hang up the connection.

Test the command out to make sure that it works properly interactively—running it from the keyboard. Once you're sure that all the timing and sequence is correct for your needs, it's time to schedule the batch file to run nightly.

By default, the scheduler service is automatically installed in Windows Server 2003, so setting up a job is as simple as a few point and clicks. To create a schedule, start out by launching the Scheduled Tasks icon from the Programs/Accessories/System Tools menu. Click Add Scheduled Task to add a new task to your system, and then proceed through the wizard panels as prompted. Schedule the batch job to execute on a nightly basis, and then leave it alone as the system obeys and runs your batch file every night.

You could even get fancy with your batch file by trapping certain error levels—sending alert messages if there are errors, etc.

"My dial-up users aren't getting the WINS and DNS addresses that are defined on our network."

Due to the nature of the communications protocols used for dial-up connections versus local network connections, the rules are a little bit different when it comes to how clients get their WINS and DNS configurations.

For LAN connections, it's a pretty straightforward process: the workstations will use WINS and DNS settings that are either hard-coded into the TCP/IP stack, or whatever they receive from a DHCP server's scope properties.

So, it should work the same for dial-up connections, right? The workstation should either use its own hard-coded settings or the settings defined on a DHCP server, right? *Wrong!*

Once, this little quirk had me stumped for the better part of a day at a client's site. Here's what happens—by default, Windows Server 2003 RAS servers will offer WINS and DNS addresses to clients based not on what the DHCP scope says, but whatever is configured for the RAS server *itself.* So, if you have your network's DHCP configuration setup perfectly, but you forgot to hard-code the correct WINS or DNS configuration in the RAS server, your RAS clients will be misconfigured when they dial in.

"I don't want my dial-up users to get the WINS and DNS addresses that are defined on our network."

Okay, so let's say that you want to override the default behavior of RAS to offer its WINS and/or DNS addresses to clients that are dialing in, without removing the WINS and DNS configuration from the RAS server itself. In that circumstance, you'll need to dive into the Registry to tweak Windows Server 2003 a bit.

To prevent your RAS server from offering a WINS address to dial-in clients, look in the following key in the Registry:

```
HKEY_Local_Machine\System\CurrentControlSet\Services\
RemoteAccess\Parameters\IP
```

You may see a value in that key called SuppressWINSNameServers. If you do, set the value to 1. If you don't see the value in there, add it and set it to a value of 1.

To prevent your RAS server from offering a DNS address to dial-in clients, look for a value called SuppressDNSNameServers. If you see that value there, set it to a 1. If you don't see the value in there, add it and set it to a value of 1.

Chapter 21

Novell NetWare and Windows Server

THIS CHAPTER WAS INTENDED for those of you who are working on a network that has both Server 2003 servers and NetWare. Although it is always possible to migrate all of your servers over to Windows Server, there may be some compelling reasons not to—the best reason being that Novell NetWare will run (and run well) on computers that cannot run Server 2003. To migrate, you'd have to buy new equipment. Frankly, if the NetWare servers are working, why get rid of them? Integration may be the cheapest, most convenient, and most efficient way to make the best of the resources you have. That is why this chapter will cover what is left of Windows' integration components with NetWare—and what Novell has done to compensate for Microsoft's lack of NetWare support.

In order to be sure that we're all on the same page, I am going to cover some NetWare terminology and basic concepts before actually going into integration. It helps to know what I'm talking about before I start telling you what to do. My apologies to those of you who are CNEs. I'll try to be brief.

Ever try to buy the workstation version of NetWare? You know, call your local software vendor and ask them to quote you a price on NetWare 6 workstation. You are not going to be asked if you would like the professional or home edition, that's for certain.

NetWare has always been a server product only. From the beginning, Novell was wise to keep it simple. NetWare is simply a network operating system that services clients with files, printers, and the like. A true server. No solitaire, no word processor. Heck, until relatively recently, it was menu driven. No wasted processor effort drawing windows.

And that is both its strength and its weakness. You see, NetWare is a server that services clients. Any client. DOS, Unix, Macintosh, Windows of any flavor. It was built that way, already supporting diversity out of the box. Integration is NetWare's game by definition. But the craving to just buy the workstation operating system that was designed to be a particular server's client is pretty overwhelming. Thus, Windows dominates in the networking world.

In order to get a Unix, Mac, DOS, or Windows 95 through XP workstation to access a NetWare server, you need to make them a NetWare client. To do that, you just install the appropriate client software on the workstation of your choice. Once the software is installed, you can log in to the NetWare server and access the resources that are located there. It's the software that is the client. NetWare makes the client software available from their Web site. (It may take some searching if you actually want to use a DOS client. There is a client available from the cool solutions/cool tools page.)

Now then, why would Microsoft want to make its own NetWare integration tools? If Novell's already got it covered, then what's the point, right? Well, two things: One, Novell's client software for Windows was not necessarily without flaws. Two, Microsoft, saw an opportunity to service its customers and corner a little bit more of the market. Because of that, Microsoft added the Client for NetWare component to its operating systems (both server and workstation).

That is why Windows supports their version of Novell's IPX/SPX networking protocol, which they called NWLink. That, along with their own design of the Novell Client, made it possible for the Windows machines to access NetWare files without resorting to using anything but Microsoft products to get there.

There is one small inconvenience, of course, and that is having to install the client software (or add the Windows component) on all of the machines that will need it. You can use the Novell client, you can use the Windows client, but however you cut, client software must be on each workstation.

Thus, Gateway service for NetWare was created. This service is available on NT and 2000 but *not* Server 2003. The Gateway service made it possible for machines that do not have the NetWare client software installed to access files on the NetWare server. The Gateway service used the Windows server to handle NetWare share points as if they were located on the Windows server itself. Completely transparent to the workstations, it removed the necessity of loading the client software.

Unfortunately, Server 2003 does not have Gateway service for NetWare. Strangely enough, it can still be a NetWare client. I'm sure we all find that comforting.

Also, an interesting fact. Let's say that you want to migrate away from your NetWare servers to Windows Server. I would think that Microsoft would love the idea and would definitely have software at the ready for you to do just that. Free on the CD, and an easy download away.

I would be wrong.

Originally, Windows NT had migration software available on the Server CD. The beta version of Windows 2000 had it on the CD. But by the time Windows 2000 went retail, Directory Service Migration Tool (DSMT) and File Migration Utility (FMU) were pulled from the CD, bundled together with a few other tools for about $200 (give or take, check with your vendor) and called "Services for NetWare." Thus, quite possibly making migrating to Windows not entirely cost effective.

If you are turned off by the idea of having to install Client for NetWare on all of your workstations and servers to access the NetWare files, don't be. Novell has come up with a way to centrally manage client access from the NetWare server, avoiding client software altogether. They created Native File Access (NFA), so Windows clients can access the servers as if they were Server 2003 servers. And, being as broad minded as they are, Novell also has native file access for Unix and Macintosh too. (Not that we are going to need them here, I just thought I'd mention it.) Make note, NFA is relatively new, and because of that it works only with NetWare 5.1 (with Service Pack 3 and higher) and 6 (straight out of the box). I think it goes without saying that it will probably be available on all new versions of the NOS as well.

NetWare 101: The Basics

Although I don't intend to use this chapter to prepare you for Novell certification, I am going to briefly explain two concepts that I think will help you understand why NetWare uses the terminology it does, when it does. These two concepts are NetWare's Directory Service and the way it handles its filesystem.

Directory Service

In 2000, Microsoft came out with its own directory service, Active Directory. NetWare has had had its own Novell Directory Service (NDS) for quite a while. It has been upgraded with newer versions of NetWare and is now called eDirectory but, for our purposes, any version does what we need it to do, so I will refer to Novell's Directory Services, new or old, as NDS. This directory service is suspiciously similar to Active Directory but has been around much longer (you can make your own assumptions). There are trees, containers such as organizations and organizational units (OUs), users, computers, and other objects.

As in AD, designing the NetWare tree takes some planning. It is a bit different though. With an NDS tree, you define the tree name, and then you choose the container that the server or servers will reside in. These large containers can be called country, organization, or domain. There are several large container types to choose from because some businesses are structured geographically while others are structured organizationally. Recently, Novell added the domain type of container for administrators who are partial to domain models. All the containers function in basically the same way: they organize groups of servers, user accounts, and other resources for management and logical convenience. And, just like domains in a tree in AD, there can be more than one of these large containers in a NetWare tree, any of which can contain any number of organizational units and other objects.

NDS tends to think of users as an object essentially equal to servers and not "contained" in them per se. They can be in the same organization as the server, or they can be located in an OU within that organization (and they are generally organized by OU, just as they are in AD). Because of this, NetWare users may need to specify the "context" or container their account is in explicitly, not just their tree and organization. Generally, when you log in to a NetWare server, you are really logging in to the container where your user account resides. You will typically be using a login dialog box that has a field in which to specify the tree, a field for the big container, and a field for the username. To further specify where the user account really is, you will need to add the context of the exact container in which the user account is located by adding it to the username itself. The syntax for entering a username with context on one line is *username.container*. Just like a domain name, there has to be a period between the username and the container name. If the container (probably an OU) is nested within another container, the context will be nested as well, from small to big: for example, *username.subOU.OU*.

In your network environment, your NetWare administrators may have set up their Novell servers and clients to allow for Contextless Login. This can require NetWare to scan the NDS tree for all users regardless of what OU they are in (especially if the NetWare admin has not set up a catalog on the server of containers for the users). If there are several John Smiths and one of them is trying to log in, a list will pop up to allow him to choose the right one (you hope), then enter his password.

Filesystem

Because NetWare likes to keep it simple, doesn't fix what isn't broken, and has been around for a long time, it uses DOS. DR DOS to be precise, but DOS nonetheless. As a matter of fact, the boot partition of the NetWare server's hard drive is a DOS partition. That also brings us to another NetWare naming convention. The NetWare partitions are not given a new drive letter and a name, as they are in Windows. They are volumes, so they are given volume names. In NetWare, the first partition is usually called SYS, and additional volumes are inevitably named, vol1, vol2, vol3, and so on. Not particularly creative or intuitive, I know. This is probably because, being rooted in DOS, the administrators instinctively keep names short (especially since many patches and support packs are DOS based). Mind you, this does not mean that NetWare cannot handle long filenames.

In order to access files on a Server 2003 server, the user must have a valid account and password. That account must have the right to access the folders and use files. That helps secure the resources on the network. I guess it comes as no surprise that NetWare also requires any user accessing its filesystem to have a valid user account and password. Although it is redundant (and therefore must be managed at both servers), it is logical.

I can almost hear you groaning about the extra work necessary to create and manage dual user accounts. Chances are that the NetWare server already has user accounts for all users who access files there, but even if they haven't been created already, there are several handy tools that the NetWare administrator can use to import users into NetWare from AD. All you need is a valid username and password. There is no need, on the NetWare side, to do anything else but give the users rights to folders, so no fussing with home directories or login scripts unless you want to.

TIP   *Native File Access (NFA) has a User Import Utility that will pull user account names and passwords from the authenticating domain controller and create simple NetWare accounts with them. Just make sure NFA is set to Domain Mode so it can find the correct Domain Controller to pull from.*

Now that I've covered the particulars of NetWare, specifying a user context during login and browsing through volumes on the server should make more sense. That said, it's time to delve into the mysteries of the NetWare client.

CSNW (Client Service for NetWare)

Client Service for NetWare (CSNW) hasn't changed much over the years. It requires NWLink IPX/SPX and NetBIOS over IPX/SPX to communicate with the NetWare servers, so it installs these protocols during its install process. It uses the username and password that is being utilized to log in to the workstation to authenticate to the NetWare server. Obviously that inhibits logging in to the Server 2003 network as one person and logging in to the NetWare network as another. It's important to make sure the NetWare user account matches the user account on the Server 2003 domain controller for everyone who will be using CSNW. Once CSNW is installed, it runs pretty much invisibly.

To add the CSNW to the Server 2003 server (or to an XP workstation, for that matter), you will need to access the Local Area Connection properties page. On an XP Workstation, right-click Network Places on the Start menu and choose Properties. Alternatively, go to the Control Panel and select Internet and Network Connections, choose Network Connections, right-click the Local Area Connection icon, and select Properties from the drop-down menu. On a Server 2003 server, choose Control Panel from the Start menu, go to Network Connections, and select Local Area Connection (see Figure 21.1).

FIGURE 21.1

Local Area
Connection
properties page

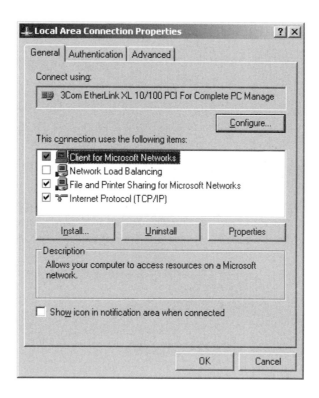

Click Install. It will bring up a dialog box that will list the type of component you could install. Select Client and click Add. In the Select Network Client dialog box (see Figure 21.2), choose Client Service for NetWare (it may be your only choice) and click OK.

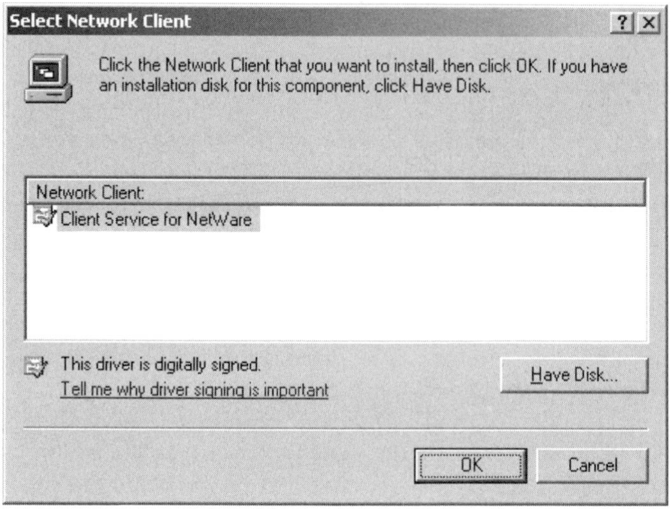

FIGURE 21.2

Installing Client
Service for NetWare

In a moment or two, you will be prompted to reboot the computer. Because, by definition, the Client Service for NetWare is intended for clients, it does require a reboot. This, of course, is not generally something that an administrator wants to do with a Server 2003 server during business hours—unless they actually enjoy talking to a large number of irate users.

Once the computer has rebooted and you log back in, you will be prompted to enter either the name of the NetWare server you prefer to use, or the tree and context (container) in which your NetWare account is located (see Figure 21.3). This second option is useful if there is more than one server in the organization (or country or domain) your account belongs to.

FIGURE 21.3

Logging in to
NetWare Network

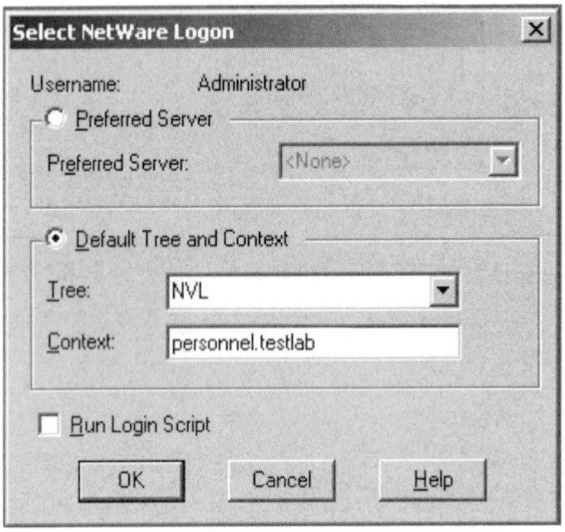

TIP *The choices you make in the Select NetWare Logon dialog box will be saved to the local drive and used when you log in again. If you want to change your preferred server or context, you will need to go to the Control Panel, change to Classic View, and double-click the CSNW icon.*

Once the Desktop comes up, it will appear as if nothing has changed. To see if CSNW did in fact install NWLink IPX/SPX–compatible protocol and NWLink NetBIOS, go to the Local Area Connection properties page (see Figure 21.4). They should be listed.

NOTE *If you are having a problem getting CSNW to work, remember that it uses IPX/SPX. Early versions of NetWare used the nonstandard Ethernet frame type 802.3; all newer NetWare servers use 802.2. It is possible for the auto-detect feature of NWLink to choose the wrong one. Pretty unlikely, but possible. You can fix this problem by selecting the NWLink IPX/SPX/NetBIOS Compatible Transport Protocol, then clicking the Properties button. In the properties page, you can choose to manually add the appropriate frame type.*

To access the newly available NetWare servers, simply browse to your network though My Network Places (or whatever way suits your fancy). You will notice that there is a new NetWare or Compatible Network icon (see Figure 21.5).

If you double-click the NetWare network icon (or select it in the Folders list, as I did in Figure 21.6), you will be presented with the icons for the tree and/or server(s) that fit your context (if you've ever played with Windows' pre-existing icons and wondered what the tree was for, now you know).

FIGURE 21.4

Making sure
NetWare-
compatible
protocols are
installed

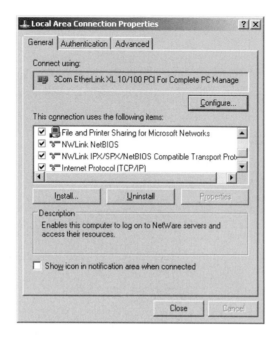

FIGURE 21.5

New NetWare
Network icon

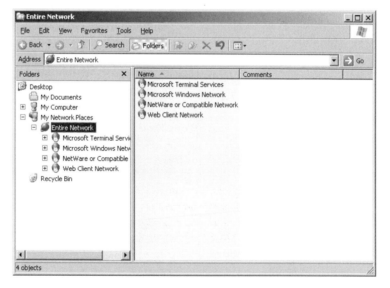

If you double-click a server, it will display the volumes available (see Figure 21.7). You may not have the right to access them all, but they are there. You can map a drive letter to a volume or directory just like any other network drive.

If you were to open up one of those volumes (assuming you have the rights to), you would see that the filesystem (as shown in Figure 21.8), complete with long names, is just like that of Windows.

FIGURE 21.6

NetWare resource
icons

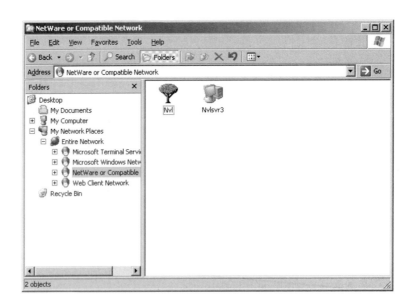

FIGURE 21.7

NetWare volumes

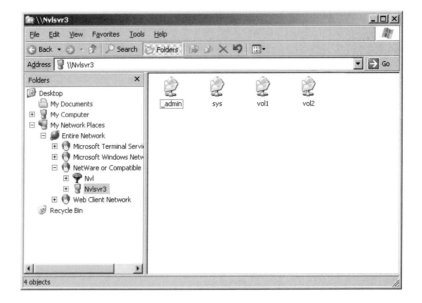

Windows' Client Service for NetWare is pretty straightforward. It integrates well with Windows software (for obvious reasons). Also, since it is not a separate software package, you don't have to worry about installing upgrades, patches, or service packs.

CSNW does have some limitations, one of which is the fact that your Windows login has to match your NetWare login. If this is a problem and you would like to monitor your connections or have additional functionality other than logging in and that's it, installing Novell's Client may be the right thing for you. Be aware that this product is not supported by Microsoft (since it's made by Novell), so it may not play nice with some software packages, and it may be difficult to uninstall. I suggest you test it before you install it on a production machine. And, just to be safe, never load it on a Server 2003 server that's in production (to avoid any software fighting on the server during work).

FIGURE 21.8

List of folders on the NetWare server

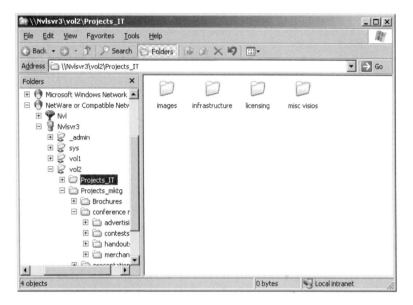

On the other hand, the Novell Client is really convenient to use. Once you've had it installed for a while, you'll wonder how you got along without it. It is especially useful for and designed to support administering NetWare servers and services from the client (by someone with the correct rights of course).

Novell's Client for Windows (Client32)

To install the Novell Client for Windows, affectionately known as Client32, you first need to download it from Novell's Web site. It will be easy to find, even if Novell makes changes to their site.

Once you have downloaded the client software, unzip it to a location of your choice (preferably a network share, if you are going to be using it elsewhere in the future). In that location, it will unzip to a folder called `WINNT`.

Open `WINNT`, open the subfolder called `i386`, and scroll to the `setupnw` file. Double-click `setupnw` to launch the Novell Client Installation program (see Figure 21.9). For a typical client, perform the typical install. If you are going to be administering any NetWare servers, you may want to do a custom install and add additional components.

WARNING *If you have Microsoft's Client Services for NetWare running, it will be uninstalled during the Novell Client installation process, otherwise it will cause conflicts as to which software package controls NetWare server access. You will be prompted to allow the installer to remove CSNW. You really don't have any choice; the install will abort if you don't allow the removal of CSNW to happen.*

FIGURE 21.9

NetWare Client
Installation program

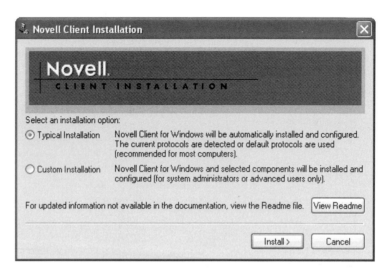

After the installation is complete, you'll be prompted to reboot. The first thing you'll notice after rebooting is that the Windows Welcome screen has been replaced by a Novell Client box with a picture of three big Ctrl, Alt, and Del buttons on it (and the words "to login" next to them). If you press Ctrl+Alt+Del, the Novell Login dialog box displays (see Figure 21.10).

FIGURE 21.10

Novell Login
dialog box

This dialog box obviously has more going on than CSNW did. It can have separate tabs (if you click the Advanced button during login, as shown in Figure 21.10) for things like logging in with different NetWare and Windows accounts and displaying login scripts. If the NetWare server needs to be accessed via dial-up, dial-up settings can be managed here. At the very least, the Novell Client gives the user the opportunity to log in to Windows as one user and NetWare as another if they need to. This can be very useful if you need to log in using an administrative account on the Windows machine, and you need to log in as an administrator on the NetWare server. These two accounts will usually be different, if only for the sake of security. There are separate tabs for NetWare and Windows.

Once you've logged in, you may notice that there is a red *N* next to the clock in the system tray on the taskbar. Right-click the *N* and you will get a menu with a plethora of extra options for managing your client connection, mapping network drives, and configuring your client login (see Figure 21.11).

FIGURE 21.11

Novell Client menu

TO WHOM IT MAY CONCERN: CONTEXTLESS LOGINS

To save time, especially if there is no one else on the NetWare server with your username, the Novell Client can be set up to do contextless logins. (The NetWare server(s) may need to be first prepped by your NetWare admin to handle logins without context, depending on which version they are running, so check first.) Select Novell Client Properties from the red N pop-up menu and go to the Contextless Login tab to enable a contextless login (see Figure 21.12). Be sure to specify the user's tree and, if there is one, the catalog of OUs to search for users in this dialog box. If you don't do this, NetWare will browse every container in the tree looking for any account that matches your username. That will slow down the login process and possibly bring up that list of matching names (like John Smith) to choose from.

Continued on next page

TO WHOM IT MAY CONCERN: CONTEXTLESS LOGINS *(continued)*

FIGURE 21.12

Novell Client
Configuration,
Contextless Login

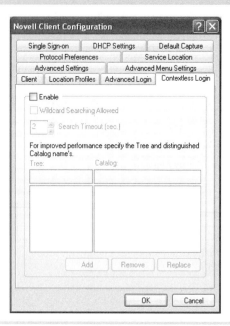

As far as file access is concerned, that has also changed a bit with the installation of the Novell Client. In My Network Places, there is now an icon consisting of a circle of red Ns that denotes a NetWare client's Novell NetWare connection (see Figure 21.13) and there is a new NetWare Services icon under Entire Network.

FIGURE 21.13

New Novell
Connections icon

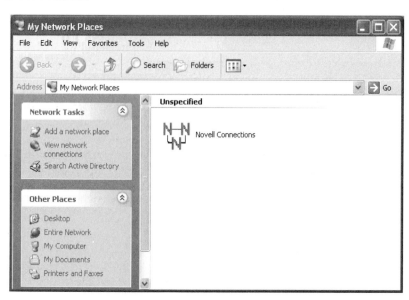

Double-click the red Ns to access the NetWare resources (see Figure 21.14).

FIGURE 21.14

NetWare resources

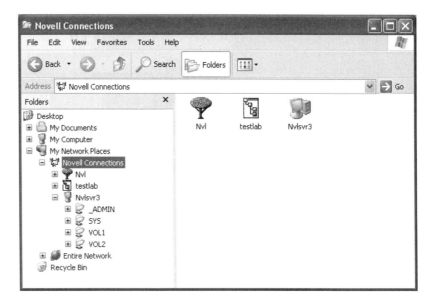

Up until this point, I have focused on managing the client's access to the NetWare network from the workstation point of view. If you do not want to install and support client software on every client machine just to access files on the NetWare servers, then you are in luck. Novell has created Native File Access (NFA) for Windows just for you… Well, maybe not you exactly, but people just like you.

Native File Access for Windows

Available as part of the Native File Access Pack (NFAP) from Novell, NFA for Windows is a NetWare server–based software package that makes client-side opening, saving, and working with Net-Ware stored files possible, without installing any NetWare client software. In many cases you can take a new Windows workstation, configure TCP/IP and, as long as there is a valid NetWare user account (and license), immediately start using it to access files on the NetWare servers.

NFA for Windows uses CIFS (Common Internet File System) over TCP/IP to give Windows clients the impression that they are browsing a Windows server. Like SMB (Small Machine Block) protocol, it is easily recognized by Windows clients as a filesystem it can use to share files.

CIFS file shares, and the display name for the server to the Windows clients, can be set in the CIFS properties page during install or under the properties of the NetWare server. If no file shares are specified, CIFS should display all volumes. (This is another good reason for the NetWare administrator to take user rights to files and folders seriously.)

To use CIFS, the Windows clients need to authenticate somewhere to be given access to the volumes on the NetWare servers. To this end, Novell offers two different authentication methods: Local and Domain.

Local authentication means that the Windows user has a user account on the NetWare server that has a simple password. The name is misleading though. It doesn't mean the password is insecure or needs to be short and easy to crack. Novell's eDirectory Service password uses a one-way hashed algorithm. Microsoft clients cannot do one-way hash. Thus, the simple password was created as a work-around. It allows Windows clients to have NetWare passwords that they can understand, while allowing the password to be encrypted enough to be secure. This means, however, that either the user updates their NetWare password every time they change their Windows password (which means administrators have to make sure that every NetWare user account has a simple password that matches their Windows account), or they end up with two passwords. Although inconvenient, using simple passwords with local authentication is the method preferred by Novell and is extremely stable and easy to use.

NOTE   *An NDS password and a simple password are not the same thing. They can and should match, but a NetWare account can have both.*

Domain authentication means that the users utilize their Windows username and password to get to the files on the NetWare servers. The NetWare server gets the user information and passes it on to the domain controller, which accepts it if it's valid and passes the acceptance back to the NetWare server, which then lets the user access whatever files they have rights to. Mind you, there still needs to be a user account on the NetWare server that matches the Windows account because it is something to apply rights and restrictions to. Using Domain authentication allows Windows clients to only have one password. If their Windows password changes, that's okay because they don't have a simple password on the NetWare server to update.

Domain authentication is more complicated to implement and, if something goes wrong, it's harder to troubleshoot. However, it is a great way to limit the administrative load while giving users NetWare file access.

NOTE   *NetWare 6 installs NFAP during its setup. The administrator can choose at that time to initiate the Local or Domain login method. They can change the method after installation, but they may have to stop and start CIFS in order for it to take hold properly.*

TIP   *NetWare 5.1 does not set up NFAP during installation (since it was released to CD before NFAP came out), but it can be added after the fact. The administrator needs to be sure that Service Pack 3 and any necessary patches have been installed before installing NFAP.*

NetWare does not use fully qualified domain names to find Windows servers. Because of that, a WINS server needs to be up and accessible to the NetWare server if it is supposed to handle Domain logins. NetWare communicates with the Server 2003 server by way of NetBIOS over TCP/IP (NBT), especially while negotiating Domain authentication, so the Server 2003 server needs to be sure that it is accepting NBT over TCP/IP at all times. By default, Server 2003 enables NBT if the address from which it is receiving NetBIOS broadcasts is a static address, but it is best to manually set the Server 2003 server to explicitly accept NetBIOS over TCP/IP.

To check if NBT is enabled, go to the Local Area Connection properties page. Select Internet Protocol (TCP/IP) and click Properties. Click Advanced and turn to the WINS tab (see Figure 21.15). Make certain that Enable NetBIOS over TCP/IP is selected.

There are a few other preparations you can make on the Server 2003 server to prepare it to perform domain logins with NetWare. The NetWare server will need to have a computer account in the Server 2003 domain. When creating the computer account, make sure that you check the Assign This Computer Account as a Pre-Windows 2000 Computer. This will help Server 2003 realize that it uses NetBIOS.

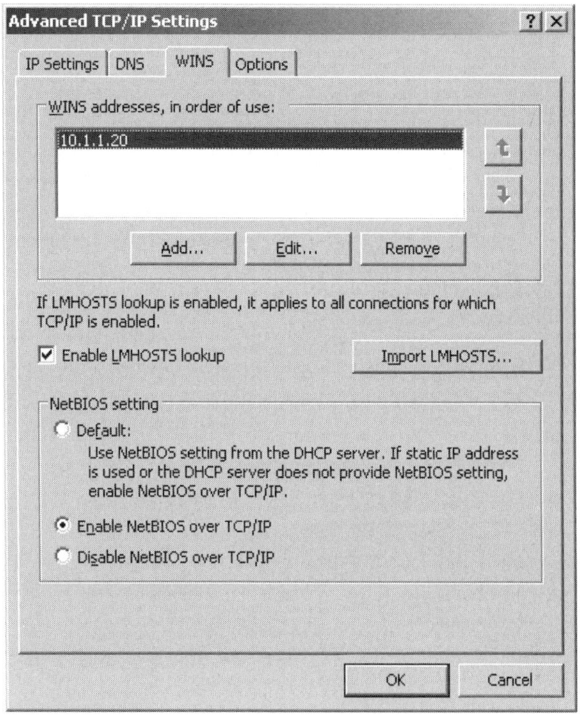

FIGURE 21.15

Enabling NetBIOS over TCP/IP

TIP *If authentication is set to Local, once there are user accounts in the NetWare tree, the NetWare administrator can use NFAP Security in the Remote Manager to generate simple passwords for every user it finds.*

To use files stored on a NetWare server from the Windows client side, just browse to it in My Network Places (or however you generally like to get to network resources). Once you select the server you would like to access, a dialog box will pop up requiring a username and password (see Figure 21.16).

FIGURE 21.16

Connecting to a NetWare server with NFA

NOTE *Remember that you may need to use the syntax* `username.context` *in the Username field if CIFS is set for Local authentication.*

Authentication will take place (it may take a few moments), and then the contents available for CIFS sharing will appear in the window (see Figure 21.17). It's that easy. Notice that the Net-Ware server (I gave mine the name "netshare," otherwise known as nvlsvr3w) shows up under Microsoft Networks looking just like a Windows server.

FIGURE 21.17

Native file access to NetWare resources

Integration seems to be a word that many network administrators avoid. I'll admit that it may be easier to handle a homogenous environment, where every server is just like every other one, and workstations are identical. But in the real world, operating systems (and hardware) can vary greatly. Things come and go over time, directions change. And, just like the people who use them, these different networks can work together. It may take some effort, but it's worth it. Or maybe, just maybe, you might not have any choice. Sometimes you just have to make it work.

I hope that, instead of giving up on your NetWare resources, you have learned from this chapter how easy it is to give Server 2003 network users access to the NetWare servers, despite their differences.

Index

Note to the Reader: Throughout this index **boldfaced** page numbers indicate primary discussions of a topic. *Italicized* page numbers indicate illustrations.

The PC Problem-Solving Wonder!

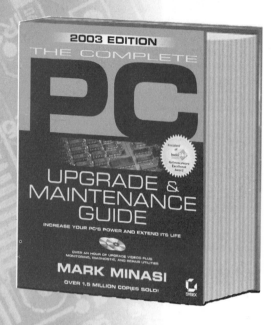

Using easy-to-follow language, this book shows you how to prevent disasters, fix the ones that occur, and maximize your PC's power and longevity. Based on author Mark Minasi's popular $800 seminars, it is an unbelievable value.

ISBN: 0-7821-4075-0
$59.99 US

Updated to Cover Recent PC Advances

Over 1.5 Million copies sold!

Major Coverage of the 2003 Edition includes:

- QuickSteps Section
- Distinct Troubleshooting Sections
- Exclusive Mark Minasi Video
- Visual Guides to Nine Essential Upgrades
- New Section on Scanners

- Building the Ultimate Computer
- Rejuvenating Your Old Computer
- Buyers Guide
- Notebook Computers
- Flash Memory Cards

www.sybex.com   SYBEX®

The Mark Minasi Windows® Administrator Series

The Essential Resource for Windows Administrators

- Written by leading authorities and reviewed by series editor **Mark Minasi,** author of the best-selling *Mastering Windows 2000 Server*

- Concise, focused material based upon real-world implementation of Windows

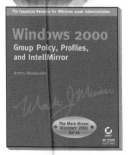

Windows 2000 Group Policy, Profiles, and IntelliMirror

Windows 2000 Group Policy has one goal: to make your administrative life easier. This book will help you understand what Group Policies are, and how they're created, applied, and modified.

By Jeremy Moskowitz
0-7821-2881-5 • $49.99

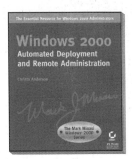

Windows 2000 Automated Deployment and Remote Administration

If you're frustrated with the time required to perform simple tasks in Windows, then this book is for you. It is for experienced administrators who want to learn how to automate tasks they've been doing by hand.

By Christa Anderson
0-7821-2885-8 • $49.99

Windows 2000 Enterprise Storage Solutions

This book offers real-world coverage and examples of Windows 2000 storage enhancements, Storage Area Networks (SANs), cluster technology, file system backup/recovery, and SCSI (Small Computer Systems Integration) solutions.

By J. Peter Bruzzese and Chris Wolf
0-7821-2883-1 • $49.99

Windows Terminal Services

If you're a Windows administrator needing to provide remote employees and local clients access to applications installed on the server, then this is the book you can't afford to be without. It addresses every issue Windows administrators need to know about how to install, configure, and maintain Terminal Services from the ground up.

By Christa Anderson
0-7821-2895-5 • $49.99

Linux for Windows Administrators

For Windows administrators or consultants who recognize the growing need for Linux skills, this book provides practical information on integrating Linux and Windows. Using familiar Windows terminology, the authors explain all of Linux's essentials, dispel its myths, and show how to use Linux in enterprise networks alongside Windows.

By Mark Minasi and Dan York
0-7821-4119-6 • $49.99

SYBEX®

www.sybex.com

CENTRAL

_Masteri

DUE

Mastering™ Active Directory for
Windows® Server 2003
by Robert R. King
ISBN 0-7821-4079-3
US $49.99

Coverage Includes:

- Understanding the concept of a network directory service
- Understanding benefits specific to Microsoft's Active Directory
- Designing your Active Directory environment
- Developing and executing a roll-out plan
- Securing the Active Directory database
- Installing and configuring DNS under AD
- Creating users, groups, and objects
- Implementing group policies
- Controlling Active Directory sites
- Managing replication
- Performing backups and recoveries
- Migrating from both Windows NT and Novell environments
- Integrating Active Directory and Novell Directory Services

Master the Technology Behind Network Managment

Active Directory represents an enormous advance in network administration. It provides a ast set of powerful tools and technologies for maaging a network within a native Windows envirome nt. *Mastering Active Directory for Windows Se rver 2003* is the resource you need to take ull advantage of all it has to offer. You get a sound introduction to network directory servics, then detailed, practical instruction in the wok of implementing Active Directory and using all of its tools. This edition addresses features new to Active Directory for Windows Server 2003.

SYBEX®

www.sybex.com